Psychology

From Inquiry to Understanding

Scott O. Lilienfeld
Emory University

Steven Jay Lynn
Binghamton University

Laura L. Namy
Emory University

Nancy J. Woolf
University of California at Los Angeles

PEARSON

Boston • New York • San Francisco
Mexico City • Montreal • Toronto • London • Madrid • Munich • Paris
Hong Kong • Singapore • Tokyo • Cape Town • Sydney

Editor in Chief: Susan Hartman
Series Editorial Assistant: Courtney Mullen
Director of Development: Sharon Geary
Senior Development Editor: Julie Swasey
Associate Editor: Angela Pickard
Media Producer: Jill Gorman
Executive Marketing Manager: Karen Natale
Market Development Manager: Tara Kelly
Director, Market Research and Development: Laura Coaty
Advertising Senior Graphic Designer/Copyeditor: Monica Chas
Production Supervisor: Karen Mason

Production Assistants: Maggie Brobeck and Sarah O'Connor
Editorial Production Service: Nesbitt Graphics
Composition Buyer: Linda Cox
Manufacturing Buyer: JoAnne Sweeney
Electronic Composition: Nesbitt Graphics
Illustrator: Imagineering Media Services Inc.
Interior Design: Stuart Jackman, Joyce Weston, Nesbitt Graphics
Photo Research: Katharine S. Cebik, with the assistance of Annie Pickert
Cover Designer: Kristina Mose-Libon

For related titles and support materials, visit our online catalog at www.ablongman.com.

Between the time website information is gathered and then published, it is not unusual for some sites to have closed. Also, the transcription of URLs can result in typographical errors. The publisher would appreciate notification where these errors occur so that they may be corrected in subsequent editions.

While the author and Publisher of this publication have made every attempt to locate the copyright owners of material that appeared on the World Wide Web, they were not always successful. The Publisher welcomes information about copyright owners for uncredited text and photos included in this book. It may be sent to the Permissions Department at the address shown on this page.

Library of Congress Cataloging-in-Publication Data
Psychology : from inquiry to understanding / Scott O. Lilienfeld . . . [et al.].
    p. cm.
    Includes bibliographical references and indexes.
        ISBN-13: 978-0-205-41243-4 (casebound)
        ISBN-10: 0-205-41243-3 (casebound)
        ISBN-13: 0-205-60890-4 (paperback)
        ISBN-10: 0-205-60890-6 (paperback)
  1.   Psychology.   I. Lilienfeld, Scott O., 1960–

BF121.P7625 2009
150--dc22   2007049151
Printed in the United States of America

10 9 8 7 6 5 4 3 2 1 [Q-WC-V] 11 10 09 08 07

We dedicate this book to Barry Lane Beyerstein
(1947–2007), great scholar and valued friend.

My deepest gratitude to David Lykken, Paul Meehl,
Tom Bouchard, Auke Tellegen, and my other graduate mentors
for an invaluable gift that I will always cherish:
scientific thinking.

—Scott Lilienfeld

To Fern Pritikin Lynn, my heart and my soul.

—Steven Jay Lynn

Dedicated to the "Divas" of my past and present who have
helped me to think critically—about my science and my life.

—Laura Namy

To Larry, Lawson, and Ashley.

—Nancy Woolf

Brief Contents

Contents

5. Consciousness: Expanding the Boundaries of Psychological Inquiry • 195

6. Learning: How Nurture Changes Us • 231

7. Memory: Constructing and Reconstructing Our Pasts • 273

8. Language, Thinking, and Reasoning: Getting Inside Our Talking Heads • 317

9. Intelligence and IQ Testing: Controversy and Consensus • 353

10. Human Development: How and Why We Change • 397

11. Emotion and Motivation: What Moves Us • 445

12. Stress, Coping, and Health: The Mind–Body Interconnection • 493

13. Social Psychology: How Others Affect Us • 533

14. Personality: Who We Are • 577

15. Psychological Disorders: When Adaptation Breaks Down • 623

16. Psychological and Biological Treatments: Helping People Change • 671

Preface

"What did that frightening dream I had last night mean?" "Why do I often forget where I parked my car?" "Why do I sometimes become angry at the people I love?" "How can I better manage my stress levels?" "Why do I find some people attractive?" "Why do I sometimes feel depressed for no apparent reason?" "Why am I so similar to my parents in some ways yet so different in others?" "Why do I sometimes go along with the group even when I don't agree with them?"

Every day, each of us encounters a host of questions that challenge our understanding of ourselves and others. In many ways, these are the same fascinating questions about the mind and brain that psychologists confront in their research, teaching, and practice.

Approach

We're All Psychologists

As we begin our study of psychology, it's crucial to understand that we're *all* psychologists. We need to be. We're incessantly bombarded with a bewildering variety of claims from the vast world of popular psychology. Whether it's from the Internet, television programs, radio call-in shows, movies, self-help books, or advice from friends, our daily lives are a continual stream of information—and often misinformation—about intelligence testing, parenting, romantic relationships, mental illness, drug abuse, psychotherapy, and a host of other topics.

Although often relevant to our everyday lives, a great deal of this psychological information comes across as conflicting or confusing. It's no surprise that we find claims regarding memory- and mood-enhancing drugs, the over prescription of stimulants, the effectiveness of Prozac, and the genetic bases of psychiatric disorders, to name a few examples, to be difficult to evaluate. Much of this information is intriguing—indeed, we're all captivated by extraordinary psychological claims that lie on the fringes of scientific knowledge: extrasensory perception, subliminal persuasion, astrology, alien abductions, lie-detector testing, hypnosis, handwriting analysis, and inkblot tests, to name only a few.

Because information about all of these topics is so readily available in the media and on the Internet, it shapes our understanding of psychology far more than do most traditional psychological topics. Why is that a problem? Because popular psychology is a confusing mix of accurate and inaccurate information. Consider these recent news headlines:

As a result of the media's often misleading coverage, most of us hold misconceptions regarding many everyday psychological claims, often making it difficult for us to evaluate genuine psychological knowledge. For example, because many of us mistakenly believe that memory operates like a tape or video recorder, we may find it difficult to accept findings that some recovered memories of child abuse are false. What's more, because the popular psychology industry rarely provides us with the tools for evaluating both ordinary and extraordinary claims about everyday life, most us are left to our own devices to sort out what's true from what's not. Throughout this text, in our end-of-chapter review sections (called Think Again . . .) and in our online MyPsychLab tool, we strive to teach students to think in a way that reflects how psychologists use science to test popular assumptions.

Goals of the Text

A Focus on How to Think, Not Merely What to Think

1 *Psychologists have found that the best safeguard against human error is scientific thinking—thinking that helps protect us against our tendencies to make mistakes.* By applying scientific thinking, we can better evaluate claims about both laboratory research and everyday life. In turn, that knowledge can often allow us to make better real-world decisions. Thus, the core goal of this text is to empower students to apply scientific thinking to the psychology of everyday life. In this way, readers can come to see that scientific *inquiry* enhances their *understanding* of their psychological worlds.

2 *Our text uses psychological misconceptions as a starting point to help readers learn to analyze information, consider alternative hypotheses, and generate their own conclusions.* Distinguishing pseudoscientific claims from scientific claims arms the reader with the necessary skills for sorting through the often bewildering maze of popular psychology. By encouraging students to evaluate the bases for claims, we show them *how* to think rather than merely *what* to think. This approach gives the readers the thinking skills needed to become their own teachers, ultimately allowing them to emerge as educated consumers of psychological claims in both scientific research and daily life.

"A down-to-earth, practical application of psychological concepts and their relation to students and their world. Instructors spend most of their time making psychology relevant to students—this text starts with relevance and moves forward. An enjoyable read."

— Dale V. Doty, Monroe Community College

3 *Readers need to explore not only what's true, but what's false or questionable.* In this way, they can gain experience with the complex task of distinguishing among confusing and often conflicting sources of information. As psychologist George Kelly observed, a full appreciation of most real-world phenomena comes only with an understanding of their opposites. For example, the concept of "cold" means nothing until we've gained experience with the concept of "hot." Similarly, we can't fully grasp psychological science without knowing something about psychological pseudoscience and fringe science.

4 *In our text, we've worked hard to place the field of psychology within the broader context of both natural and physical sciences.* This emphasis should enable readers to see psychology as a science—a science like all others—that relies on basic safeguards against error.

To highlight the link between scientific thinking and scientific methodology, our text integrates this material into all chapters—in addition to showcasing research design in Chapter 2. We've complemented this coverage by stressing basic issues in the philosophy of science: the importance of falsifiability as a criterion for scientific status, the distinction between scientific and metaphysical questions, and the dangers of overusing ad hoc hypotheses to protect our cherished ideas from refutation. This strategy, we believe, will afford students the necessary tools to assess scientific research with a more critical eye.

"This text is a refreshing variation to the cookie cutter introductory psychology text."

— Yousef A. Fahoum, University of Arkansas, Little Rock

5 *As instructors, we find that students new to psychology are most successful when information is presented within a clear, effective, and meaningful framework—one that encourages inquiry along the path to understanding.* As part of the inquiry to understanding framework, our pedagogical features and assessment tools work to empower students to develop a more critical eye in understanding the psychological world and their place in it.

From Inquiry to Understanding: The Framework in Action

6 Flags of Scientific Thinking

Correlation vs. Causation

Falsifiability

Extraordinary Claims

Occam's Razor

Replicability

Ruling Out Rival Hypotheses

"I want my students to not only learn the basic studies, findings, vocabulary and ways of thinking that is psychology, but I want them to understand themselves and their world more accurately. I want them to have greater compassion for others (and for themselves) by better comprehending their behaviors, thoughts and perceptions . . . This book goes further in this direction that other books I have reviewed."

— Michael Hillard, University of New Mexico and Albuquerque TVI Community College

• **Thinking Scientifically**

In Chapter 1, we introduce readers to six key scientific thinking principles that we bring up repeatedly in later chapters. We denote each principle in the margin with a colored "flag" whenever this principle appears in the text. In this way, we reinforce these scientific thinking principles in readers' minds as key skills for evaluating claims in scientific research and in life.

• **Focus on Popular Psychology**

Throughout the text, we intersperse examples from popular ("pop") psychology, such as claims from self-help books and popular television psychologists, so that students can acquire experience in distinguishing the wheat from the chaff in the news and entertainment media, on the Internet, in popular books and magazines, and in conversations with their friends. We also provide students with scientific thinking tools for evaluating a variety of pop psychology claims. Throughout the book, we highlight examples of both accurate and inaccurate pop psychology.

• **Emphasis on Misconceptions**

More broadly, throughout the text we sprinkle a variety of misconceptions often held by introductory psychology students. Equally important, we use many of these misconceptions as starting points for discussions of legitimate scientific knowledge. We also present pieces of psychological knowledge that violate common sense, but that are true. In keeping with the text's theme on how we can be fooled from time to time, each chapter opens with a piece of artwork depicting an illusion, reminding readers that their minds sometimes deceive them.

• **Cultural Emphasis**

Wherever possible, we highlight noteworthy research findings bearing on cultural and racial differences. By doing so, students will come to understand that many psychological principles have boundary conditions, and that much of contemporary psychology focuses on differences as much as commonalities.

• **Focus on Everyday Life**

In keeping with the text's scientific thinking theme, we emphasize the application of critical thinking skills to everyday life claims, especially claims students are likely to encounter on television, in films, in popular portrayals, and in conversations outside of class.

In the end, we hope that readers of our text emerge with the "psychological smarts," or open-minded skepticism, needed to distinguish psychological misinformation from psychological information in the media, self-help books, popular magazines, Internet sources, and other coursework. We'll consistently urge readers to keep an open mind to new claims but to *insist on evidence*. Indeed, our overarching motto is that of space scientist James Oberg (sometimes referred to as "Oberg's dictum"): Keeping an open mind is a virtue, just so long as it is not so open that our brains fall out.

Yet our text was developed to do far more than debunk false or questionable psychological claims. It attempts to expose readers to the excitement and mystery of the still evolving field of psychology in an engaging and entertaining way. We'll consider our text successful if our readers come away from this experience with a heightened appreciation of both the scientific rigor of contemporary psychology and of the fascinating unanswered questions that lie ahead.

Features

A Focus on Meaningful Pedagogy

Our goal of applying scientific thinking to the psychology of everyday life is reflected in the text's pedagogical plan. Each aspect of this plan was developed organically within the context of the text, the end-of-chapter review, our online MyPsychLab resource, and the print and media supplements to ensure its effectiveness, value, and conceptual application. And, most importantly, these features were designed to help students meet their goal of masering psychological understanding. Among the highlights of this plan are the following features:

• Chapter Learning Objectives

The chapter outline contains several learning objectives tied to each major topic section to help students get a sense of the chapter's contents and enable them to pre-test their current knowledge.

> **What Is Social Psychology?**   534
> Humans as a Social Species • The Great Lesson of Social Psychology • Social Comparison: Person See, Person Do
>
> **LEARNING OBJECTIVES:**
> - Identify the ways in which social situations influence the behavior of individuals
> - Explain how and why our attributions about the causes of others' behavior are accurate in some cases but biased in others
> - Explain the power of our observations of others to influence our thoughts, beliefs, and decisions

• Preview "Think" questions

Each chapter begins with a set of questions designed to tap students' intuitive conceptions—and misconceptions—regarding the subject matter.

> **PREVIEW**
> ## Think
> First, think about these questions. Then, as you read, think again. . . .
> ▶ How good are we at judging the causes of others' behavior?
> ▶ What causes mass hysteria over rumors about things like Martian landings?
> ▶ Were the Nazis particularly evil, or would we have done the same thing in their boots?
> ▶ How do cults persuade people to become fanatics?
> ▶ How can a woman be stabbed to death in

• Apply Your Thinking questions

Throughout each section of the chapter, we have included several critical thinking questions contained in the "Apply Your Thinking" boxes, which are designed to enhance students' processing of the text material and to facilitate class discussion.

> **APPLY YOUR THINKING**
> In what ways were the thinking processes of the Seekers and other cult members similar to those of many proponents of pseudoscience?

> **ASSESS YOUR KNOWLEDGE: FACT OR FICTION?**
> (1) The neocortex is divided into the frontal, parietal, temporal, and hippocampal lobes. (True/False)
> (2) The basal ganglia control sensation. (True/False)
> (3) Drugs that treat ADHD may work by decreasing the signal-to-noise ratio in the prefrontal cortex. (True/False)
> (4) The cerebellum regulates only our sense of balance. (True/False)
> (5) Muscles come in opposing pairs. (True/False)
>
> **Answers:** (1) F (p. 110); (2) F (p. 113); (3) F (p. 115); (4) F (p. 115); (5) T (p. 116)

• Assess Your Knowledge: Fact or Fiction?

At the end of each major topic heading, students are provided with a helpful True or False review of selected material to further reinforce concept comprehension and advance their ability to distinguish psychological fact from fiction.

• Factoids and Fictoids

Sprinkled throughout the margins of each chapter we offer several "factoids," which present interesting and surprising facts, and "fictoids," which present widely held beliefs that are false or unsupported. In both cases, students will find their conceptions and misconceptions of psychology challenged and their perspectives of psychology broadened. These features also underscore a crucial point: Psychology can be fun!

> **fact**oid
> In one of the most creative demonstrations of cognitive dissonance theory, four researchers asked subjects to taste fried grasshoppers (Zimbardo, Weisenberg, Firest & Levy, 1965). They randoml assigned some subjects to this bizarre request from a person, and others to re from an unfriendly p

> **fict**oid
> **Myth:** Poverty and poor education are key causes of terrorism, including suicide bombings.
> **Reality:** Most suicide bombers in the Middle East, including the September 11 hijackers and many Al Qaida members, are relatively well off and well educated (Sageman, 2004).

Think again...

The Complete Review System
THINK / ASSESS / STUDY / SUCCEED

What Is Social Psychology? (pp. 534–539)

STUDY the Learning Objectives

► Identify the ways in which social situations influence the behaviors of individuals
- The need to belong theory proposes that humans have a biological need for interpersonal connections.
- Social facilitation refers to the presence of others enhancing our performance in certain situations.

► Explain how and why our attributions about the causes of others' behavior are accurate in some cases but biased in others
- Attributions refer to our efforts to explain behavior; some attributions are internal, others external.
- The great lesson of social psychology is the fundamental attribution error—the tendency to overestimate the impact of dispositions on others' behavior.

► Explain the power of our observations of others to influence our thoughts, beliefs, and decisions
- According to social comparison theory, we're motivated to evaluate our beliefs, attitudes, and reactions by comparing them with the beliefs, attitudes, and reactions of others.
- Mass hysteria is an outbreak of irrational behavior spread by social contagion.

DO YOU KNOW THESE TERMS?
- ☐ social psychology (p. 534)
- ☐ social facilitation (p. 536)
- ☐ attribution (p. 536)
- ☐ fundamental attribution error (p. 537)
- ☐ social comparison theory (p. 538)
- ☐ mass hysteria (p. 538)

 You are standing in a crowded elevator when suddenly all of the other riders turn to the right. How likely would you be to follow suit? (p. 537)

While still alive, Walt Disney arranged to have his body frozen after his death so that it could be unfrozen at a future date when advanced technology will permit him to live again.

What factors contribute to the rise and spread of urban legends? (p. 539)

what You would do... How important to you are your social bonds? How would you feel if isolated from human contact for an extended period of time? (p. 535)

mypsychlab Internal and External Attributions Find out how accurate (or inaccurate) the attributions you assign to people can be. (p. 536)

ASSESS your knowledge

1. Social psychologists study how people influence others' _____, and _____, for both good and bad. (p. 534)
2. The size of our neocortex relative to the rest of our brain (limits/doesn't limit) the number of people we can closely associate with. (p. 535)
3. The idea that we have a biologically based need for interpersonal connections is known as the _____ theory. (p. 535)
4. An improved performance in the presence of others is explained by _____. (p. 536)
5. A worsened performance in the presence of others is explained by _____. (p. 536)
6. Researchers have found that our performance in front of others is determined by our level of _____ in that particular performance area. (p. 536)
7. We tend to form _____ in our desire to assign causes to other people's behavior. (p. 536)
8. The tendency to overestimate the impact of _____ on others' behavior is called the fundamental attribution error. (p. 537)
9. According to Festinger's _____ theory, when a situation is unclear, we look to others for guidance about what to believe and how to act. (p. 538)
10. Stories of people waking up after partying in a bathtub full of ice with their kidneys removed are examples of _____. (p. 539)

Social Influence: Conformity and Obedience (pp. 539–551)

STUDY the Learning Objectives
► Determine the factors that influence when we conform to the behaviors and beliefs of others
- Conformity refers to the tendency of people

what You would do... Leaving a championship basketball game, you witness a violent riot that begins to spread through the stadium.

• Think Again . . . The Complete Review System
This review system appears at the end of each chapter and provides students with a quick, effective, and interactive visual review of the chapter. Organized by sections, each review includes a bulleted chapter summary with learning objectives, review questions, activities, application questions, and a MyPsychLab question related to an online activity—all designed to help students assess their comprehension of the chapter concepts. Page references are provided to assist students who may want to review their answers or revisit a particular concept.

PsychoMythology
Is Brainstorming in Groups a Good Way to Generate Ideas?

Imagine that you've been hired by an advertising firm to cook up a new marketing campaign for Mrs. Yummy's Chicken Noodle Soup. The soup hasn't been selling well of late and your job is to come up with an advertising jingle that will instill in every American an uncontrollable urge to reach for the nearest cup of chicken noodle soup.

Although you initially plan to come up with possible slogans on your own, your boss walks into your cubicle and informs you that you'll be participating in a "group brainstorming" meeting later that afternoon in the executive suite. There, you and twelve other firm members will let your imaginations run wild, saying whatever comes to mind in the hopes of hitting on a winning chicken noodle soup advertising formula. Indeed, companies across the world regularly use group brainstorming as a means of generating novel ideas. They assume that several heads that generate a flurry of ideas are better than one. In a book titled *Applied Imagination*, which influenced many companies to adopt brainstorming, Osborn (1957) argued that "the

• PsychoMythology Boxes
Each chapter contains one "PsychoMythology" box focusing in depth on a widespread psychology misconception. In this way, students will come to recognize that their common-sense intuitions about the psychological world are not always correct, and that scientific methods are needed to separate accurate from inaccurate claims.

NEW FRONTIERS
Jesse's Story: The Million Dollar Man

What would it be like if your mind could no longer control your body? How much would you want that ability restored if you lost it? High-power lineman Jesse Sullivan knows the answers to these questions. One day in May 2001, he received an electric shock so powerful that his arms were burned beyond repair (Oppenheim, 2006). His arms needed to be amputated and were replaced with prosthetic, or artificial, limbs.

What happened next is extraordinary. Jesse was chosen to trade one of his ordinary prosthetic arms for the first "thought-controlled" bionic arm, a limb that was literally hardwired to his nervous system. In so doing, he became a unique example of how intricately brain, body, and behavior interact.

To make Jesse's million-dollar arm function, surgeons grafted nerves, which had once controlled his natural arm, from his shoulder to his chest muscle. They then placed sensors over his chest muscle and connected them to tiny wires that control the bionic limb. Jesse controls the arm by simply *thinking* about what he wants to do with it. When Jesse thinks about closing his hand, neurons in his basal ganglia and cerebral cortex release chemicals signaling his intention to use his bionic arm. Next, neurons in the motor cortex carry this message to the spinal cord and motor neurons then carry the message to the muscles in his chest. From there, the tiny wires control Jesse's bionic arm, enabling him to grasp nearly anything from a paintbrush to a garden tool.

 With practice, Jesse has become so adept at using his new arm and hand that he can paint his house, take care of

• New Frontiers Boxes
To highlight the point that psychological science is a thriving, evolving, and self-correcting discipline, each chapter contains one "New Frontiers" box that focuses on a recent and exciting scientific innovation or new direction in the field.

• Art as an Integrative Learning Tool
Each of the figures and illustrations in the text were developed and designed to enhance student understanding and promote learning. Our anatomical art pieces were drawn to maintain accuracy and consistency throughout the text. For example, each component has been color-coded across each brain image when possible to help orient students at both the micro- and macro-level as they move throughout the text and begin to make connections among concepts.

Supplements

Putting It All Together: Innovative and Integrated Supplements

We have assembled a team of talented instructors who share our belief in the importance of critical thinking and a scientific approach to psychology to develop a unique and comprehensive supplements package.

Amy Hackney-Hansen, Georgia Southern University, Managing Editor
Kimberley Duff, Cerritos College, Managing Editor for MyPsychLab

Lisa Farwell, Santa Monica College, Instructor's Manual co-author
Scott Lilienfeld, Emory University, Instructor's Manual co-author
Heidi Shaw, Yakima Valley Community College, Instructor's Manual co-author
James Stringham, University of Georgia, Instructor's Manual co-author

David Alfano, Community College of Rhode Island, Test Bank co-author
Mei Jiang, Texas A&M University, Commerce, Test Bank co-author
Brian Johnson, University of Tennessee at Martin, Test Bank co-author
Valerie Smith, Collin County Community College, Test Bank co-author
Keith Williams, Richard Stockton College of New Jersey, Test Bank co-author
Adena Young, Texas A&M University, Commerce, Test Bank co-author

Jennifer Sage, University of California at San Diego, PowerPoint author

Patricia Kowalski, University of San Diego, Grade Aid Study Guide co-author
Annette Taylor, University of San Diego, Grade Aid Study Guide co-author

This was truly a team effort, with all of the instructors meeting on a weekly basis and working closely with the main author team over the course of the text's development. Each of the authors brought his or her own unique teaching experiences to the project. Amy Hackney-Hansen, acting as managing editor for the project, read and offered feedback on every aspect of the supplements to ensure quality and accuracy. The result is a supplements package of teaching and study materials that reinforce the critical thinking skills of the text, provide instructors with a wealth of teaching and lecture materials, and offer detailed student assessment of the text and specific learning objectives.

Instructor Supplements

Instructor supplements are available to qualified instructors. Please contact your local Pearson representative for details.

MyPsychLab . . . where learning comes to life!

MyPsychLab is a state-of-the-art interactive and instructive solution, designed to be used as a supplement to a traditional lecture course, or to completely administer an online course. MyPsychLab gives you and your students access to a wealth of resources all geared to meet the individual teaching and learning needs of every instructor and every student.

Kimberley Duff, the MyPsychLab managing editor for this text, emphasizes scientific thinking in her own classroom at Cerritos College. Through teaching online and hybrid courses, Kimberley knows the benefits and the challenges instructors face when having to deliver courses online. Kimberley has helped make MyPsychLab an easy-to-use solution for teaching students how to develop and apply scientific thinking in their lives.

"What makes an introductory psychology text perfect? In my mind it is one that provides a reasonably comprehensive and objective review of major theoretical constructs and empirical findings in both basic and applied psychology, is highly engaging and readable, rich with case examples, parsimonious, and encourages critical thinking. And to my way of thinking, that is an incredibly tall order for any author to fill. In my opinion, these authors have taken on the challenge, stepped up to the plate, and hit the proverbial home run . . . my students will love this text."

— Susan Lonberg, Central Washington University

MyPsychLab Features

- **A variety of hands-on activities and videos** lets students experience significant psychological phenomena firsthand, through visual illusions, cognitive maps, memory retrieval exercises, and more, to help them understand and learn key concepts. Students can simulate experiments, take practice tests, watch videos, listen to Podcasts, and more!

- **A customized study plan,** generated from chapter pre-tests and post-tests, identifies areas of weakness and strength to help students focus their attention and efforts where they're needed the most.

- **Think Again,** the complete end-of-chapter review system, comes alive in the interactive e-book where students can complete the activities online to sharpen their comprehension of important psychological concepts. Students can evaluate their own assumptions through the "Think" questions at the beginning and end of each chapter.

- **In the News,** a regularly updated blog, keeps students current with links to recent research and psychology in the media. Each article is followed by a series of critical thinking questions to encourage students to be critical consumers of information.

- **Unlimited use of Pearson's Research Navigator™** is the easiest way for students to start a research assignment. Complete with extensive help on the research process and four exclusive databases of credible and reliable source material including the EBSCO Academic Journal and Abstract Database, the *New York Times* Search by Subject Archive, "Best of the Web" Link Library, and Financial Times Article Archive and Company Financial, Research Navigator helps students quickly and efficiently make the most of their research time.

- **A wealth of instructor support material** simplifies and enriches the teaching experience. MyPsychLab gives you access to text-specific materials, including the Classroom Kit, Computerized Test Bank, and PowerPoint presentations. Having all of these resources in one place makes preparing for class quick and easy.

- **Research Evidence!** MyPsychLab's white paper details the results of several studies on the effectiveness of MyPsychLab in the classroom. The results suggest that students assigned to use MyPsychLab obtain higher final course grades than control students who aren't assigned to use MyPsychLab.

Instructor's Classroom Kit: Volumes I and II and CD-ROM

Our unparalleled Classroom Kit includes every instructional aid an introductory psychology professor needs to manage the classroom. We have made our resources even easier to use by placing all of our print supplements in two convenient volumes. Organized by chapter, each volume contains the Instructor's Manual, Test Bank, and Power-Point lecture presentations. A CD-ROM, which comes packaged with the Classroom Kit, gives instructors access to electronic versions of all of the supplements.

Instructor's Manual: A Teaching Resources Grid appears at the start of each chapter, allowing instructors to see how resources from the Instructor's Manual, Test Bank, Grade Aid Study Guide, PowerPoints, and MyPsychLab correspond to each of the chapter's sections. Each chapter begins with a "From Your Author . . . " section written by Scott Lilienfeld, in which he offers advice on how to approach the chapter and coach students on specific critical thinking skills. Each chapter also includes a brief prose overview of the chapter, a detailed chapter outline with boldface key terms, lecture ideas, in-class activities and discussion topics, out-of-class activities, handouts, and a list of media resources. A special section on integrating MyPsychLab into the course also appears in every chapter.

"[This text] tackles the myths and misperceptions head on and, in teaching students to be good critical thinkers of psychological theories and concepts, the text should eliminate the misgivings of even the most hesitant student. In short, [it] can be a powerful tool to help us teach more effectively."

— Tammy D. Barry, U of Southern Mississippi

"I appreciate the author's focus on critical thinking to help students become better consumers of information, as well as to evaluate claims related to psychology and human behavior that they are likely to encounter on a daily basis. This approach stands out among many currently available Introductory Psychology textbooks and will be among its strengths. I would recommend that my colleagues take a close look at this textbook."

— Dawn Delaney, Madison Area Technical College

Test Bank: The Test Bank contains for each chapter, 100 multiple-choice questions, some of which address myths or factoids addressed in the text and others from the MyPsychLab pre-tests, along with 25 fill-in-the-blank questions. Each of these questions has an answer justification with page reference, a difficulty rating (easy/medium/difficult), topic, and skill type (conceptual/factual/analytical). In addition, these questions have all been correlated to both the text's learning objectives and the APA learning outcomes, enabling instructors to assess students' knowledge of specific skill types. Essay questions and short-answer questions, which deal specifically with critical thinking skills, have also been included along with sample answers for each. A Midterm and a Final Exam offer instructors a way to test students on their cumulative knowledge of the text. There is also a selection of validated questions that have been tested on over 100 students. In addition to the print version, the complete Computerized Test Bank is also available in TestGen for use in creating personalized tests for the classroom.

PowerPoint Presentations: We are pleased to offer a unique collection of PowerPoint presentations for use in your classroom. A complete lecture presentation highlights major topics from the chapter, pairing them with select art images. To assist in delivering the lectures, additional examples and explanations from the Instructor's Manual appear in the "notes" section. A condensed version of the lecture presentation, with briefer outlines, which could serve as handouts to students, is available as well. Finally, we offer a PowerPoint collection of the complete art files from the text to allow customized lectures with any of the figures from the text. The PowerPoint presentations are included on the Instructor's Classroom Kit CD-ROM, and can be downloaded from our Instructor Resource Center.

Lecture Questions for Clickers

For instructors using clickers in their classroom, we offer a collection of text-specific lecture questions for each chapter of the book. These questions can be used to evaluate students' knowledge of material or to enhance classroom discussions. Many of the clicker questions address specific critical thinking skills from the textbook.

APA Correlation Guide

This detailed correlation guide, which appears in the Instructor's Manual, shows how the learning outcomes in the text correspond to the APA learning goals and assessment guidelines.

Allyn and Bacon Transparencies for Introductory Psychology

This set of approximately 200 revised, full-color acetates will enhance classroom lecture and discussion. It includes images from Allyn and Bacon's major introductory psychology texts.

Insights into Psychology, I, II, and III

These video programs include 2–3 short clips per topic, covering such topics as animal research, parapsychology, health and stress, Alzheimer's disease, bilingual education, genetics and IQ, and much more. A Video Guide containing critical thinking questions accompanies each video—also available on DVD.

Allyn and Bacon Digital Media Archive for Psychology

This comprehensive source includes still images, audio clips, web links, animation and video clips. Highlights include classic psychology experimental footage, biology animations, and more—with coverage of such topics as eating disorders, aggression, therapy, intelligence, and sensation and perception.

CourseCompass

Powered by Blackboard, this course management system uses a powerful suite of tools that allow instructors to create an online presence for any course.

Student Supplements

Grade Aid Study Guide

This comprehensive study guide is filled with review material, in-depth activities, and self-assessments. Special sections devoted to study skills, concept mapping, and the evaluation of websites appear at the start of the guide. Each chapter of the Grade Aid is organized into three main sections: "Before You Read," "As You Read," and "After You Read."

The "Before You Read" section includes a brief chapter overview, a list of learning objectives, and a list of the key terms (with page references) in the chapter.

The "As You Read" section features a variety of hands-on activities for students to complete while working through the chapter. Practice Activities, including short-answer, matching, fill-in-the-blank, and other questions, are included for every section of the chapter and are tied to the text learning objectives; Concept Map Activities require students to complete missing portions of concept maps for key topics in the chapter; Myth or Reality sections provide examples of common myths and realities and ask students to evaluate them using the skills learned in the chapter; and Putting Your Critical Thinking Skills to the Test sections teach students how to apply their critical thinking skills to real-world problems. Finally, the MyPsychLab Connection activities teach students how to incorporate the MyPsychLab resources into their study plan for each chapter.

The "After You Read" section, which offers students a chance to assess their understanding of the chapter, includes two chapter practice tests, each with 20 multiple-choice questions. Students are encouraged to predict what percentage of questions they will answer correctly before they take the test and then compare this number with their actual results. A complete answer key with page references is also provided.

MyPsychLab . . . where learning comes to life!

MyPsychLab is a state-of-the-art interactive and instructive solution designed to help you master introductory psychology. MyPsychLab provides access to a wealth of resources all geared to meet your learning needs.

Features

- **A wealth of hands-on activities and videos** lets you experience significant psychological phenomena firsthand, through visual illusions, cognitive maps, memory retrieval exercises, and more, to help you understand and master key concepts. Simulate experiments, take practice tests, watch videos, listen to Podcasts, and more!

- **A customized study plan,** generated from chapter pre-tests and post-tests, identifies areas of weakness and strength to help focus your attention and efforts where they're needed the most.

- **Think Again . . . The Complete Review System,** the end-of-chapter review system comes alive in the interactive e-book where you can complete the activities online to sharpen your comprehension of important psychological concepts. Evaluate your own assumptions about psychological principles using the "Think" questions at the beginning of each chapter.

- **In the News,** a regularly updated blog, keeps you updated with links to recent research and psychology in the media. Each article is followed by a series of critical thinking questions to hone your skills in becoming a critical consumer of information.

- **Unlimited use of Pearson's Research Navigator™** is the easiest way for you to start a research assignment. Complete with extensive help on the research process and four exclusive databases of credible and reliable source material including the EBSCO Academic Journal and Abstract Database, the *New York Times* Search by Subject Archive, "Best of the Web" Link Library, and Financial Times Article Archive and Company Financials. Research Navigator helps you quickly and efficiently make the most of your research time.

Introductory Psychology Study Site accessed at http://www.abintropsychology.com. This website features psychology study material for students, including flashcards and a complete set of practice tests. Also included are web links to valuable sites for further exploration of major topics.

A Final Word

From the Authors

For the four authors, writing this book has been a momentous undertaking, but it's also been a labor of love. All of us share a passionate commitment to teaching students to think critically and clearly about psychology, and for that matter, the world. As idealists at heart, we believe that students who learn to think scientifically will become not merely more knowledgeable about psychology, but more discerning consumers of claims regarding medicine, politics, economics, friendships, relationships, and myriad domains of life. In short, they will become better scholars and better citizens.

Our book is an effort to realize this ambitious vision by crafting a text that seamlessly integrates scientific thinking throughout all of its chapters. In this way, we believe that students will emerge from their introductory psychology course better prepared to evaluate claims in psychological studies, in the media, on the Internet, and in daily life. Indeed, we view this text not merely as a book about psychology, but a book about how to *think about* psychology.

& Thanks

Acknowledging Our Amazing Psychology Community

When we began this undertaking—about 5 years ago—we as authors could never have imagined the number of committed, selfless, and enthusiastic colleagues in the psychology community who would join us on this path to making our textbook a reality. During the long months of writing and revising, the feedback and support from fellow instructors, researchers, and students helped keep our energy high and our minds sharp. We stand in awe of their love of the discipline and the enthusiasm and imagination each of these individuals brings to the psychology classroom every day. This text is the culmination of their ongoing support from first to final draft and we are forever grateful to them.

In addition, the authors would like to extend our heartfelt gratitude and sincere thanks to a host of people on the Allyn & Bacon team. We consider ourselves remarkably fortunate to have worked with such an uncommonly dedicated, talented, and genuinely kind group of people. Needless to say, this project was a monumental team effort, and every member of the team played an invaluable role in its inception. Particular thanks go to our Editor-in-Chief Susan Hartman for her exceptional professionalism, generosity, support, and grace under pressure, not to mention her undying commitment to the project. We also owe special thanks to Karen Mason, our truly exceptional production manager, for her astonishingly high-quality work and wonderful attitude; Sharon Geary, director of development, and Cheryl deJong-Lambert, developmental editor, for their invaluable assistance in polishing our prose and sharpening our ideas; and to Karen Natale, executive marketing manager, for her energy, creativity, and contagious enthusiasm.

Warm thanks also go to many, many others, especially Mark Mykytiuk, art coordination; Kate Cebik, photo research; Annie Pickert, assistance with photo research and shoots; Renee Nicholls, Sherry Hoesley, Maggie Brobeck, Sarah Bylund, and Jenelle Forschler, permissions research; Joyce Weston, design of the review sections; Gail Wagner and Jerilyn Bockorick, page design; Courtney Mullen, assistance on all matters editorial; Stuart Jackman at DK for design concept; Susan McIntyre, copyediting; Julie Swasey, supplements managing and hiring; Angela Pickard, supplements assistance; Jill Gorman, coordination of MyPsychLab; Tara Kelly, market development; Kristina Mose-Libon, cover design; Savino Longo, market research support; and Deb Hanlon, Leah Strauss, Jen DeMambro, and Peg Markow, additional support.

Thanks also go to Barry Beyerstein, whose early efforts were invaluable; Kelly May, for encouraging us to undertake this project and providing us with early support for it; Judy Hauck, for developmental editing guidance in the early phases of the project; Tunisa Williams at Kinkos and Jack Murray at Emory for technical support; Robyn Fivush, chair of psychology at Emory, for encouragement and assistance; and Susan Himes for helpful advice. Last but by no means least, we thank the countless others who helped in small but significant ways in bringing this text to fruition.

Review Panel
Our Review Panel evaluated every chapter of the text from first page manuscript to the text's publication, spanning a nine-month period. Their input proved invaluable to us, and we thank them for it.

John Bickford, University of Massachusetts–Amherst; **Tracie Blumentritt,** University of Wisconsin–LaCrosse; **Mary Coplen,** Hutchinson Community College; **Linda Fayard,** Mississippi Gulf Coast Community College; **Robert Hensley,** Mansfield University; **Caleb W. Lack,** Arkansas Tech University; **Angelina MacKewn,** University of Tennessee at Martin; **James Stringham,** University of Georgia; **John W. Wright,** Washington State University

Reviewers
The following professors and experts reviewed individual chapters of the text. The many diverse backgrounds, areas of expertise and styles of instruction of these reviewers added to the text's universal perspective and evolution.

Gina Andrews, Volunteer State Community College; **Pamela Ansburg,** Metropolitan State College of Denver; **Louis E. Banderet,** Northeastern University; **Jack Barnhardt,** Wesley College; **Tammy D. Barry,** University of Southern Mississippi; **David Baskind,** Delta College; **Scott C. Bates,** Utah State University; **Stefanie M. Bell,** Pikes Peak Community College; **Jennifer Bellingtier,** University of Northern Iowa; **Sylvia Beyer,** University of Wisconsin-Parkside; **John Bickford,** University of Massachusetts–Amherst; **Joseph Bilotta,** Western Kentucky University; **Tracie Blumentritt,** University of Wisconsin–La Crosse; **Michael C. Boyle,** Sam Houston State University; **Michele Y. Breault,** Truman State University; **Nathan Brody,** Wesleyan University; **Gayle L Brosnan-Watters,** Slippery Rock University; **Thomas Brothen,** University of Minnesota; **Jay Brown,** Southwest Missouri State University; **Veda Brown,** Prairie View A&M University; **Eric L. Bruns,** Campbellsville University; **Susan R. Burns,** Morningside College; **David E. Campbell,** Humboldt State University; **Thomas Capo,** University of Maryland; **Etzel Cardena,** University of Lund; **Lorelei A. Carvajal,** Triton Community College; **Michael Clayton,** Jacksonville State University; **Andrea D. Clements,** East Tennessee State University; **Lorry Cology,** Owens Community College; **Mary Coplen,** Hutchinson Community College; **Luis A. Cordon,** Eastern Connecticut State University; **Gregory M. Corso,** Georgia Institute of Technology; **Layton Seth Curl,** Metropolitan State College of Denver; **Dawn Delaney,** Madison Area Technical College; **Bruce J. Diamond,** William Paterson University; **Anastasia Dimitropoulos White,** Case Western Reserve University; **G. William Domhoff,** University of California-Santa Cruz; **Dale Doty,** Monroe Community College; **Perri B. Druen,** York College; **Michael G. Dudley,** Southern Illinois

University–Edwardsville; **Kimberley Duff,** Cerritos College; **David Echevarria,** University of Southern Mississippi; **Carla Edwards,** Northwest Missouri State University; **David R. Entwistle,** Malone College; **Audrey M. Ervin,** Delaware County Community College; **Yousef Fahoum,** University of Arkansas-Little Rock; **Matthew Fanetti,** Missouri State University; **Linda Fayard,** Mississippi Gulf Coast Community College; **Joseph R. Ferrari,** DePaul University; **Joseph M. Fitzgerald,** Wayne State University; **Christine Floether,** Centenary College; **William F. Ford,** Bucks County Community College; **Daniel J. Fox,** Sam Houston State University; **Marjorie A. Getz,** Bradley University; **Vicki Gier,** University of South Florida; **Debra L. Golden,** Grossmont College; **Richard M. Gorman,** Central New Mexico Community College; **Joseph P. Green,** Ohio State University–Lima; **Jeff D. Green,** Virginia Commonwealth University; **Gary J. Greguras,** Louisiana State University; **R. J. Grisham,** Indian River Community College; **Jennifer Grossheim,** University of Northern Iowa; **Laura Gruntmeir,** Redlands Community College; **Amy Hackney-Hansen,** Georgia Southern University; **Erin Hardin,** Texas Tech University; **Bert Hayslip, Jr.,** University of North Texas; **Rebecca Hendrix,** Northwest Missouri State University; **Jeffrey B. Henriques,** University of Wisconsin–Madison; **Robert Hensley,** Mansfield University; **Rebecca Hester,** Western Carolina University; **Michael Hillard,** Albuquerque Tech Vocational Institute; **Tammy Hutcheson,** Garden City Community College; **Matthew I. Isaak,** University of Louisiana–Lafayette; **Linda A. Jackson,** Michigan State University; **James Jakubow,** Florida Atlantic University; **Brian Johnson,** University of Tennessee at Martin; **James R. Johnson,** Central New Mexico Community College; **Lance Jones,** Bowling Green State University; **Deana Julka,** University of Portland; **Michael J. Kane,** University of North Carolina-Greensboro; **Paul M. Kasenow,** Henderson Community College; **Natalie Lawrence,** James Madison University; **Melvyn King,** State University of New York–Cortland; **Katherine Kipp,** Gainesville State College; **Brenda E. Koneczny,** Lake Superior College; **Caleb W. Lack,** Arkansas Tech University; **Travis Langley,** Henderson State University; **Cynthia Lausberg,** University of Pittsburgh; **Tera Letzring,** Idaho State University; **Mary B. Lewis,** Oakland University; **Robin Lightner,** University of Cincinnati; **Linda Lockwood,** Metropolitan State College of Denver; **Susan D. Lonborg,** Central Washington University; **Don Lucas,** Northwest Vista College; **Angelina MacKewn,** University of Tennessee at Martin; **Jean Mandernach,** University of Nebraska at Kearney; **Howard Markowitz,** Hawaii Pacific University; **Tammy McClain,** West Liberty State College; **Steven E. Meier,** University of Idaho; **Thomas J. Mount,** Yakima Valley Community College; **Glenn Musgrove,** Broward Community College-Central; **Margaret Nauta,** Illinois State University; **Cindy Nordstrom,** Southern Illinois University-Edwardsville; **Peggy Norwood,** Red Rocks Community College; **Mark O'DeKirk,** Meredith College; **Cynthia O'Dell,** Indiana University Northwest; **Elaine Olaoye,** Brookdale Community College; **Wendy Ann Olson,** Texas A&M University; **David Payne,** Wallace Community College; **Brady J. Phelps,** South Dakota State University; **Lloyd R. Pilkington,** Midlands Technical College; **Celia Reaves,** Monroe Community College; **Dennis T. Regan,** Cornell University; **Tanya Renner,** Kapi'olani Community College; **Michelle Rivera,** University of Maine; **Christopher Robinson,** University of Alabama-Birmingham; **Scott Roesch,** San Diego State University; **Wade C. Rowatt,** Baylor University; **Linda Ruehlman,** Arizona State University; **John Ruscio,** The College of New Jersey; **Catherine Sandhofer,** University of California-Los Angeles; **David A. Schroeder,** University of Arkansas; **Heidi Shaw,** Yakima Valley Community College; **Wayne Shebilske,** Wright State University; **Valerie T. Smith,** Collin County Community College; **Carrie Veronica Smith,** University of Delaware; **Jakob Steinberg,** Fairleigh Dickinson University; **Robert Barry Stennett,** Gainesville State College; **James Stringham,** University of Georgia; **Richard W. Townsend,** Miami-Dade College-Kendall; **Barbara VanHorn,** Indian River Community College; **Jeffrey Wagman,** Illinois State University; **Colin William,** Columbus State Community College; **Keith Williams,** Richard Stockton College of New Jersey; **Thomas W. Williams,** Western Kentucky University; **Kevin M.P. Woller,** Rogers State University; **John W. Wright,** Washington State University; **Michael Zvolensky,** University of Vermont

Advisory Council

We would like to thank our faculty advisors for providing us with ongoing feedback at critical strategies of development. Their insights were extremely valuable in helping to shape the project and achieve our goal of encouraging students to think about psychology in an accessible and engaging way.

David Alfano, Community College of Rhode Island; **Renee Babcock,** Central Michigan University; **Scott C. Bates,** Utah State University; **Stefanie M. Bell,** Pikes Peak Community College; **Jennifer Bellingtier,** University of Northern Iowa; **Tracie Blumentritt,** University of Wisconsin–La Crosse; **Fred Bonato,** St. Peter's College; **Vicki Dretchen,** Volunteer State Community College; **David Echevarria,** University of Southern Mississippi; **Rebecca Hester,** Western Carolina University; **Linda A. Jackson,** Michigan State University; **James Johnson,** Central New Mexico Community College; **Brenda E. Koneczny,** Lake Superior College; **Elissa Koplik,** Bloomfield College; **Tera Letzring,** Idaho State University; **Mary B. Lewis,** Oakland University; **Robin Lightner,** University of Cincinnati; **Linda Lockwood,** Metropolitan State College of Denver; **William McIntosh,** Georgia Southern University; **Jason Moses,** El Paso Community College; **Cynthia O'Dell,** Indiana University-Northwest; **Eileen Olaoye,** Brookdale Community College; **Frank Provenzano,** Greenville Technical College; **Christopher Robinson,** University of Alabama–Birmingham; **James Rodgers,** Hawkeye Community College; **Laura Sherrick,** Front Range Community College–Westminster; **Randy Simonson,** College of Southern Idaho; **Paul Vonnahme,** New Mexico State University; **Dean Yoshizumi,** Sierra College

Focus Groups

We would like to thank our faculty focus group participants who helped at every stage of development from early drafts through final manuscript. Their advice and creative problem solving helped to further develop and polish the text's content, tone, design, art, and supplements.

Pamela Ansburg, Metropolitan State College of Denver; **Mark Basham,** Regis University; **Robert Brill,** Moravian College; **Richard Catrambone,** Georgia Institute of Technology; **Jennifer Cina,** Barnard College; **Dale Doty,** Monroe Community College; **Kimberley Duff,** Cerritos College; **Donald Fischer,** Missouri State University; **Stephen Flora,** Youngstown State University; **Doug Gentile,** Iowa State University; **Rebecca Hendrix,** Northwest Missouri State University; **Joseph Horvat,** Weber State University; **Joanne Hsu,** Houston Community College–Town and Country; **Natalie Lawrence,** James Madison University; **Shirin Khosropour,** Austin Community College; **Angelina MacKewn,** University of Tennessee at Martin; **David Marcus,** University of Southern Mississippi; **Ann McKim,** Goucher College; **Carlotta Ocampo,** Trinity College; **Jack Palmer,** University of Louisiana at Monroe; **Alan Pope,** University of West Georgia; **Jermaine Robertson,** Florida A&M University; **Melinda Russell-Stamp,** Northwest Missouri State University; **Mary Ann Schmitt,** North Virginia Community College–Manassas; **Valerie T. Smith,** Collin County Community College; **Jeanne Spaulding,** Houston Community College–Town and Country; **Jennifer Yanowitz,** Utica College; **Karen Yanowitz,** Arkansas State University

Student Focus Groups and Class-Testing

Thousands of students participated in the development of this project through student focus groups, usability testing research, and in-class testing of sample materials.

Student Focus Groups

We would like to thank **David Alfano,** Community College of Rhode Island and **Margaret Lynch,** San Francisco State University, as well as their students for participating in student focus groups on the manuscript and design at critical stages in development.

Usability Testing

We learned a great deal from scientific usability tests conducted by Dr. Tharon Howard, Director of Clemson University's Usability Testing Facility. His work with introductory psychology students from Clemson University and TriCounty Technical College helped to test the text's unique design and integrated learning system.

Class-Testing

We'd also like to acknowledge several of the instructors who class-tested the project with their students and played a pivotal role in helping us gather feedback from thousands of students nationwide.

David Baskind, Delta College; **James Becker,** Pulaski Technical College; **Jennifer Bellingtier,** University of Northern Iowa; **Dale Doty,** Monroe Community College; **Celeste Favela,** El Paso Community College; **Debra Golden,** Grossmont College; **Mark Griffin,** Georgia Perimeter College–Dunwoody; **James Johnson,** Illinois State University; **Caleb W. Lack,** Arkansas Tech University; **Angelina MacKewn,** University of Tennessee at Martin; **James Rodgers,** Hawkeye Community College; **John Skowronski,** Northern Illinois University; **Robert Barry Stennett,** Gainesville State College

Faculty Forum

We appreciate the wonderful faculty who met with our editorial team to share their insights into the common challenges they face in teaching the introductory psychology course. Their experiences and feedback helped put the finishing touches on the text, supplements, and media.

Marlene Adelman, Norwalk Community College; **Mark Akiyama,** Diablo Valley College; **Charles Brown,** University of South Alabama; **Brad Brubaker,** Indiana State University; **Job Clement,** Daytona Beach Community College; **Mark Cloud,** Lock Haven University; **Kathryn Demitrakis,** Central New Mexico Community College; **Kimberley Duff,** Cerritos College; **Robert Dushay,** Morrisville State College; **Janet Frick,** University of Georgia; **Randy Gordon,** University of Minnesota–Duluth; **Traci Haynes,** Columbus State Community College; **Samuel Jones,** Jefferson State Community College; **Mike Majors,** Delgado Community College; **Joe Melcher,** St. Cloud State University; **Tibor Palfai,** Syracuse University; **Barbara Radigan,** Community College of Allegheny County; **Celia Reaves,** Monroe Community College; **Amira Rezec,** Saddleback College; **Ron Salazar,** San Juan College; **David Schroeder,** University of Arkansas; **Amy Shapiro,** University of Massachusetts, Dartmouth; **Vivian Smith,** Lakeland Community College; **Susan Spooner,** McLennan Community College; **Amy Van Buren,** Sacred Heart University; **Jeffrey Wagman,** Illinois State University; **Kathy Weatherford,** Trident Technical College; **Jeff Weatherly,** University of North Dakota; **Sharon Wiederstein,** Blinn College, Bryan

Meet the Authors . . .

Scott O. Lilienfeld received his B.A. in Psychology from Cornell University in 1982 and his Ph.D. in Clinical Psychology from the University of Minnesota in 1990. He completed his clinical internship at Western Psychiatric Institute and Clinic in Pittsburgh, Pennsylvania from 1986-1987. He was assistant professor in the Department of Psychology at SUNY Albany from 1990-1994, and now is Professor of Psychology at Emory University. He recently was appointed a Fellow of the Association of Psychological Science, and was the recipient of the 1998 David Shakow Award from Division 12 (Clinical Psychology) of the American Psychological Association for Early Career Contributions to Clinical Psychology. Dr. Lilienfeld is a past president of the Society for a Science of Clinical Psychology within Division 12. He is the founder and editor of the Scientific Review of Mental Health Practice, Associate Editor of Applied and Preventive Psychology, and a regular columnist for Scientific American Mind magazine. He has authored or co-authored six books and over 160 journal articles and chapters. Dr. Lilienfeld has also been a participant in Emory University's "Great Teachers" lecturer series, as well as the Distinguished Speaker for the Psi Chi Honor Society at the American Psychological Association and Midwestern Psychological Association conventions.

Steven Jay Lynn received his B.A. in Psychology from the University of Michigan, and his Ph.D. in Clinical Psychology from Indiana University. He completed an NIMH Postdoctoral Fellowship at Lafayette Clinic, Detroit Michigan in 1976, and is now Professor of Psychology at Binghamton University (SUNY), where he is the director of the Psychological Clinic. Dr. Lynn is a Fellow of numerous professional organizations, including the American Psychological Association and the American Psychological Society, and he was the recipient of the Chancellor's Award of the State University of New York for Scholarship and Creative Activities. Dr. Lynn has authored or edited 17 books, and authored more than 230 journal articles and chapters. Dr. Lynn has served as the editor of a book series for the American Psychological Association, and he has served on 11 editorial boards, including the Journal of Abnormal Psychology. Dr. Lynn's research has been supported by the National Institute of Mental Health and the Ohio Department of Mental Health.

Laura L. Namy received her B.A. in Philosophy and Psychology from Indiana University in 1993 and her doctorate in Cognitive Psychology at Northwestern University in 1998. She is now Associate Professor of Psychology at Emory University. Dr. Namy was recently appointed editor of the Journal of Cognition and Development and serves as the Treasurer of the Cognitive Development Society. She is also coordinator of the joint major in Psychology and Linguistics, and the director of the graduate program in Cognition and Development at Emory. Her research focuses on the origins and development of verbal and non-verbal symbol use in young children, and the role of comparison in conceptual development.

Nancy J. Woolf received her B.S. in Psychobiology at UCLA in 1978 and her Ph.D. in Neuroscience at UCLA School of Medicine in 1983. She is Adjunct Professor in the Department of Psychology at UCLA. Her specialization is behavioral neuroscience and her research spans the organization of acetylcholine systems, neural plasticity, memory, neural degeneration, Alzheimer's disease, and consciousness. In 1990 she won the Colby Prize from the Sigma Kappa Foundation, awarded for her achievements in scientific research in Alzheimer's disease. In 2002 she received the Academic Advancement Program Faculty Recognition Award. Dr. Woolf is currently on the editorial board of Science and Consciousness Review and Nanoneuroscience.

Using this Text to Succeed in Psychology: A Reader's Guide

Step 1
Begin each chapter by reading through the **Contents** and focusing on the **Learning Objectives.** Can you answer them?

LEARNING OBJECTIVES:
- Identify the ways in which social situations influence the behavior of individuals
- Explain how and why our attributions about the causes of others' behavior are accurate in some cases but biased in others
- Explain the power of our observations of others to influence our thoughts, beliefs, and decisions

---

PREVIEW
Think

First, think about these questions. Then, as you read, think again. . . .

▶ How good are we at judging the causes of others' behavior?

▶ What causes mass hysteria over rumors about things like Martian landings?

▶ Were the Nazis particularly evil, or would we have done the same thing in their boots?

▶ How do cults persuade people to become fanatics?

▶ How can a woman be stabbed to death in plain view of many people without anyone coming to her aid?

▶ Does how we act reflect what we believe, or

Step 2
Before you begin reading the chapter, take a moment to think about the Preview questions. How would you answer these based on what you currently know about psychology?

Step 3
As you read each section, take special note of the critical terms bolded within the text and defined again in the margins. To ensure you understand the material as you read, there are two helpful stopping points along the way **Apply Your Thinking** and **Assess Your Knowledge: Fact or Fiction?** "Apply Your Thinking" questions help you begin to synthesize the concepts of the section and provide thought-provoking questions for discussion. "Assess Your Knowledge" allows you to quickly test your understanding of the section's concepts and will alert you if more review is needed.

Correlation vs. Causation

Falsifiability

ASSESS YOUR KNOWLEDGE: FACT OR FICTION?
(1) The neocortex is divided into the frontal, parietal, temporal, and hippocampal lobes. (True/False)
(2) The basal ganglia control sensation. (True/False)
(3) Drugs that treat ADHD may work by decreasing the signal-to-noise ratio in the prefrontal cortex. (True/False)
(4) The cerebellum regulates only our sense of balance. (True/False)
(5) Muscles come in opposing pairs. (True/False)

Answers: (1) F (p. 110); (2) F (p. 113); (3) F (p. 115); (4) F (p. 115); (5) T (p. 116)

Extraordinary Claims

Occam's Razor

APPLY YOUR THINKING
In what ways were the thinking processes of the Seekers and other cult members similar to those of many proponents of pseudoscience?

Replicability

Step 4
As you read the chapter, you will see the **Six Flags of Scientific Thinking** in the margin. These flags, as you will read about in Chapter 1, represent the six key scientific thinking principles in the text. Each time a flag appears you should take a moment to evaluate the scientific claim being made and how it does or doesn't hold up.

Ruling Out Rival Hypotheses

Step 5

Along the way, you'll notice some interesting and informative boxes that will help you gain a broader understanding of the field of psychology. These features are called **PsychoMythology,** which provides in-depth discussions of popular ideas and issues that we all may not understand enough, and **New Frontiers,** which focuses on cutting-edge research that is changing people's lives.

Step 6

Think Again . . . Your Complete Review System. Once you finish reading the chapter, it's time to review what you've learned. The end of chapter review provides a section-by-section inter-active study site to review key concepts and test your understanding of the chapter material in a variety of ways.

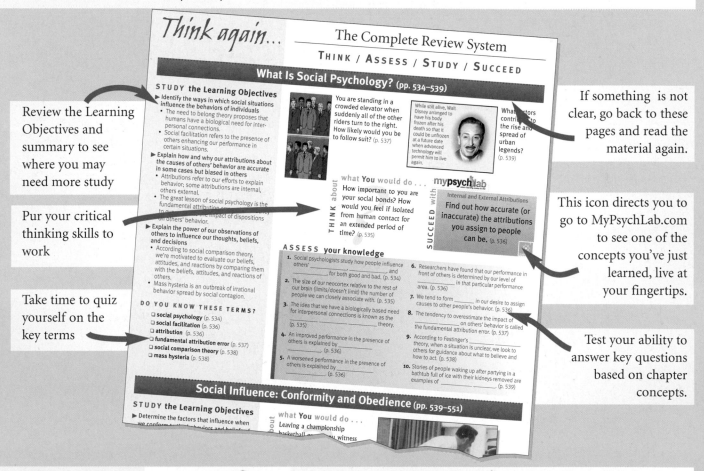

Review the Learning Objectives and summary to see where you may need more study

Pur your critical thinking skills to work

Take time to quiz yourself on the key terms

If something is not clear, go back to these pages and read the material again.

This icon directs you to go to MyPsychLab.com to see one of the concepts you've just learned, live at your fingertips.

Test your ability to answer key questions based on chapter concepts.

Step 7

mypsychlab *where learning comes to life!* . . . where your textbook and learning come to life! MyPsychLab is a state of the art interactive and instructional solution, designed to help you master the material. MyPsychLab gives you access to a wealth of resources all geared to meet your learning needs.

Go to www.mypsychlab.com to register. You'll find the interactive activities icons on this site, as well as answers to the "Think" questions from the beginning of the chapter.

Prologue
How Psychology Became a Science

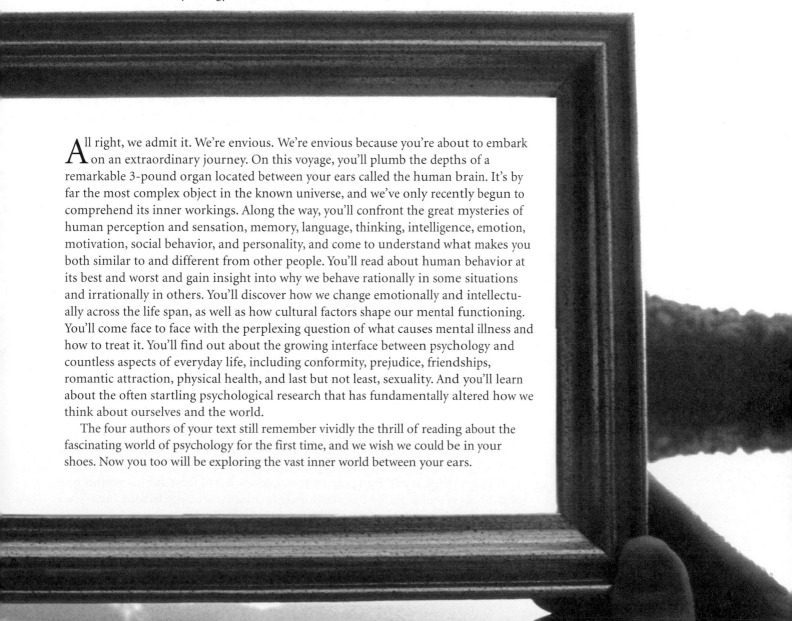

All right, we admit it. We're envious. We're envious because you're about to embark on an extraordinary journey. On this voyage, you'll plumb the depths of a remarkable 3-pound organ located between your ears called the human brain. It's by far the most complex object in the known universe, and we've only recently begun to comprehend its inner workings. Along the way, you'll confront the great mysteries of human perception and sensation, memory, language, thinking, intelligence, emotion, motivation, social behavior, and personality, and come to understand what makes you both similar to and different from other people. You'll read about human behavior at its best and worst and gain insight into why we behave rationally in some situations and irrationally in others. You'll discover how we change emotionally and intellectually across the life span, as well as how cultural factors shape our mental functioning. You'll come face to face with the perplexing question of what causes mental illness and how to treat it. You'll find out about the growing interface between psychology and countless aspects of everyday life, including conformity, prejudice, friendships, romantic attraction, physical health, and last but not least, sexuality. And you'll learn about the often startling psychological research that has fundamentally altered how we think about ourselves and the world.

The four authors of your text still remember vividly the thrill of reading about the fascinating world of psychology for the first time, and we wish we could be in your shoes. Now you too will be exploring the vast inner world between your ears.

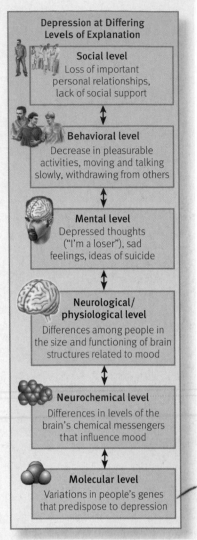

Depression at Differing Levels of Explanation

Social level
Loss of important personal relationships, lack of social support

Behavioral level
Decrease in pleasurable activities, moving and talking slowly, withdrawing from others

Mental level
Depressed thoughts ("I'm a loser"), sad feelings, ideas of suicide

Neurological/ physiological level
Differences among people in the size and functioning of brain structures related to mood

Neurochemical level
Differences in levels of the brain's chemical messengers that influence mood

Molecular level
Variations in people's genes that predispose to depression

Figure P.1 Disorder of Depression.
We can view psychological phenomena, in this case the disorder of depression, at multiple levels of explanation, with lower levels being more biological and higher levels being more social. Each level provides us with unique information and offers us a distinctive view of the phenomenon at hand. (*Source:* Adapted from Ilardi, Rand, & Karwoski, 2007)

psychology
the study of the mind and brain

levels of explanation
rungs on a ladder of explanation, with lower levels tied most closely to biological influences and higher levels tied most closely to social influences

What Is Psychology?
Basic Questions and Key Challenges

The first question often posed in introductory psychology textbooks could hardly seem simpler: "What is psychology?" Although psychologists disagree about many things, they agree on one thing: psychology isn't easy to define (Henriques, 2004). Psychologist George Miller (1966) related the following story:

> Several years ago a professor who teaches psychology at a large university had to ask his assistant . . . to take over the introductory psychology course for a short time. The assistant was challenged by the opportunity and planned an ambitious series of lectures. But he made a mistake. He decided to open with a short definition of his subject. When the professor got back to his classroom two weeks later he found his conscientious assistant still struggling to define psychology. (p. 15)

Unlike the professor's assistant, we're not going to worry about how to define psychology, because in our view no one's been able to come up with an airtight definition. In fact, such a definition may ultimately be impossible, because psychology is a huge, sprawling enterprise with fuzzy boundaries (Lilienfeld, 2004). So for the purposes of this text, we'll simply refer to **psychology** as what scientific psychologists do, namely, study the mind and brain.

PSYCHOLOGY AND LEVELS OF EXPLANATION

The key point for our purposes is that psychology is a discipline that spans many **levels of explanation.** We can think of levels of explanation as rungs on a ladder, with the lower rungs tied most closely to biological influences and the higher rungs tied most closely to social influences (Ilardi & Feldman, 2001). The levels of explanation in psychology stretch all the way from molecules to brain structures to thoughts, feelings, and emotions, and to social and cultural influences, with many levels in between (Cacioppo, Berntson, Sheridan, & McClintock, 2000) (see **Figure P.1**).

We'll traverse all of these levels of explanation in coming chapters. When doing so, we'll keep one crucial guideline in mind: *We can't understand psychology by focusing on only one level of explanation.* That's because each level tells us something different, and we gain new knowledge from each vantage point. Some psychologists think of themselves as *biotropes,* who believe that biological factors—like the actions of the brain and its billions of nerve cells—are most critical for understanding the causes of behavior. Others think of themselves as *sociotropes,* who believe that social factors—like parenting practices, peer influences, and culture—are most critical for understanding the causes of behavior (Meehl, 1972). In this text, we'll be steering away from these two extremes, because both biological and social factors are essential for a complete science of psychology (Kendler, 2005).

PSYCHOLOGY: A NASTY LITTLE SUBJECT

William James (1842–1910), often regarded as the founder of American psychology, once described psychology as a "nasty little subject." As James pointed out, many of the everyday questions that most intrigue us don't lend themselves to simple answers: *Why do I act in one way with my friends and in another way with my boyfriend or girlfriend? Why can't I speak up in class even when I want to? Why do I sometimes forget the names of people I know well? Why do I sometimes become angry with people I love?*

If you enrolled in this course expecting simple answers to these and many other questions about everyday psychology, you're likely to come away empty-handed. But if you enrolled in the hopes of acquiring more insight into the hows and whys of human behavior, stay tuned, because a host of delightful surprises are in store. Prepare to find many of your preconceptions about psychology challenged; to learn new ways of thinking about the causes of your everyday thoughts, feelings, and actions; and to apply these ways of thinking to evaluating psychological claims in your daily life.

In addition to everyday questions about the causes of our behaviors, psychology poses a number of Great Questions, such as the question of *consciousness*—that is, how we become aware of our own existence—and the question of whether all human behavior derives from the activity of the nervous system. Some psychologists and philosophers contend that many of these Great Questions are unanswerable. These thinkers, called **mysterians,** believe that certain deep questions regarding human nature are so difficult that they lie beyond our capacity to solve them (McGinn, 2002). The human brain, they suggest, just isn't smart enough to comprehend itself fully. We won't take a stand on whether the mysterians are right, because we don't know. But the mysterians remind us that many of the central questions of psychology are just as difficult as those of physics, chemistry, and other "hard" sciences, if not more so. Indeed, evolutionary biologist E. O. Wilson (1998) suggested that psychology and other social sciences, sometimes collectively called the "soft" sciences, are the *true* hard sciences, because their central questions are exceptionally challenging.

WHAT MAKES PSYCHOLOGY CHALLENGING—AND FASCINATING

A variety of challenges make psychology complicated. It's precisely these challenges that make psychology so fascinating, because they remind us of the almost unimaginable complexity of human behavior. Each challenge points us toward one more mystery to be solved.

So for starters, here's our list (in no particular order) of Ten Things That Make Psychology Challenging (Meehl, 1978). We should bear them in mind throughout the book, because they'll reappear in numerous contexts.

Ten Things That Make Psychology Challenging.

(1) Behavior Is Difficult to Predict. Probably the best guideline for predicting behavior is **Meehl's maxim,** named after brilliant American psychologist Paul Meehl: The best predictor of future behavior is past behavior (Garb, 1998; Meehl, 1954). If we want to know whether someone will be a good employee, we should look at her performance in previous jobs; if we want to know whether someone will be a dependable relationship partner, we should look at his history of prior romantic involvements. Yet past behavior isn't necessarily a *good* predictor of future behavior. It's just the best we have. As a result, the best we can usually do is to make *probabilistic* predictions of behavior—that is, forecasts that are uncertain.

(2) Behavior Is Multiply Determined. One reason that behavior is so difficult to predict is that almost all actions are **multiply determined,** that is, produced by many factors. As a consequence, we should be profoundly skeptical of **single-variable explanations** of behavior, which are the stock-in-trade of pop psychology. These explanations try to pin down the causes of complex human behaviors, like violence, anxiety, or depression, to a single cause, like child abuse, poverty, or divorce. Single-variable explanations are misleading not because they're entirely wrong—some of them are partly right—but because they're incomplete. They rarely, if ever, tell the whole story.

(3) Psychological Influences Are Rarely Independent of One Another. One problem that often makes psychological researchers pull out their hair is **multicollinearity:** the overlap among different causes of behavior. Because of multicollinearity, it's often difficult to pinpoint which cause or causes are operating.

Imagine we're scientists attempting to explain why some women develop *anorexia nervosa,* a severe eating disorder we'll encounter in Chapters 11 and 15. We could start by identifying several factors that may contribute to anorexia nervosa, like anxiety-proneness, compulsive exercise, perfectionism, excessive concern with body image, and exposure to television programs that feature thin models. Let's say that we now want to focus on just one of these possible influences, say, perfectionism. Here's the problem: Women who are perfectionistic also tend to be anxious, to exercise a lot, to be overconcerned with their body image, to watch television programs that feature thin models, and

(1)

(2)

(3)

Each of these panels from everyday life poses a different psychological question: (1) Why do we fall in love? (2) Why do some of us become depressed for no apparent reason? (3) What makes us angry? Although the science of psychology doesn't provide easy answers to any of these questions, it does offer valuable insights into them.

mysterians
people who believe that certain questions regarding human nature are unanswerable

Meehl's maxim
guideline that the best predictor of future behavior is past behavior

multiply determined
caused by many factors

single-variable explanations
explanations that try to account for complex behaviors in terms of only a single cause

multicollinearity
overlap among different causes of behavior, often making it difficult to identify which cause or causes are operating

Psychology may not be one of the traditional "hard sciences," like chemistry, but many of its fundamental questions are even harder to answer.

In the museum of everyday life, causation isn't a one-way street. In conversations, one person influences a second person, who in turn influences the first person, who in turn influences the second person, and so on. This principle, called *reciprocal determinism,* makes it challenging to pinpoint the causes of behavior.

reciprocal determinism
tendency for people to mutually influence each other's behavior

jangle fallacy
error of assuming that measures that carry the same label necessarily assess the same thing

reflexivity
paradox referring to the fact that the human brain is trying to understand itself

so on. The fact that all of these factors are interrelated makes it tricky to put our finger on which of them actually contributes to anorexia nervosa. They could all be playing a role, but it's hard to know for sure.

(4) Psychological Influences Are Often Unknown. Much of the time, we simply aren't aware of the key causes of people's behavior (Meehl, 1978). As a result, it may never have crossed our minds to study them; in other cases, they may be virtually impossible to study.

Let's imagine we're trying to understand how two identical twins (who share all of their genetic material; see Chapter 3) ended up so different. Joe is a healthy, popular, and well-adjusted 21-year-old who's a star forward on his college basketball team. His identical twin, Bill, is shy and tense, and never made it to college because of disabling problems with anxiety. What caused the difference? Perhaps Bill experienced a head injury during his birth that went unnoticed. Or perhaps Bill was bitten several times by dogs when he was a young child (which he's since forgotten about), which set him on a downward spiral toward avoiding most things that scared him. One or both of these explanations could be right, or they could both be wrong. Still other influences that we never measured might have caused the difference.

(5) People Affect Each Other. In the secluded confines of the psychological laboratory, it's often easy to isolate influences on people's behavior, because experimenters typically treat all subjects identically. In other words, in psychological research the behavior of experimenters is usually *standardized,* or maintained the same across all subjects. As a consequence, it's difficult for subjects to influence experimenters' actions (Wachtel, 1973). In contrast, in the real world people almost always influence each other.

For example, if you're an extraverted person, you're likely to make people around you more outgoing. In turn, their outgoing behavior will tend to "feed back" to make you even more extraverted, and so on. This is an example of what Albert Bandura (1983) called **reciprocal determinism:** people mutually influence each other's behavior. Reciprocal determinism makes it difficult for us to determine what's causing what.

(6) Many Psychological Concepts Are Difficult to Define. As we'll discover in later chapters, psychologists often can't agree on the definitions of important psychological concepts, like intelligence or mental illness (we've already seen that they can't even agree on how to define psychology!). This problem makes these concepts challenging to study, because different psychologists measure them in different ways. One of the most frequent errors in psychology is the **jangle fallacy** (Block, 1995; Thorndike, 1903): the mistake of assuming that measures that carry the same label, like "IQ test" or "hostility survey," necessarily assess the same thing. They often don't. As a result, it's not always clear how well we can generalize from one researcher's findings to another's.

For example, some investigators, including the first author of your textbook, study a puzzling condition called *psychopathic personality.* As we'll learn in Chapters 6 and 15, people with this condition, known as psychopaths or sociopaths, tend to be charming, dishonest, guiltless, callous, and manipulative. Until fairly recently, most measures of psychopathic personality assessed very different things, probably because investigators in various laboratories defined this condition in different ways (Hare, 1985; Lilienfeld, 1994). As a result, many of the research findings concerning psychopathic personality were confusing and contradictory.

(7) The Human Brain Didn't Evolve to Understand Itself. Many psychologists agree that our brains evolved for one reason: to maximize the chances that our genes are passed on to later generations. There's no reason to believe that the brain evolved to understand itself, any more than it evolved to understand the innermost workings of the heart, liver, or gallbladder. Do you really know how your pancreas works, for example? Probably not, and you don't need to.

As science writer Jacob Bronowski (1966) observed, psychologists are trapped in the paradox of **reflexivity:** They're trying to use the human brain to understand itself. This monumental task may never be fully achievable. In fact, some evolutionary theorists, like Robert Trivers (2000), believe that the human mind evolved to deceive itself. By fooling ourselves about our true motives, he maintained, we can more easily fool others. We don't need to accept Trivers's intriguing speculation to accept the possibility that there are limits to how well we can understand the reasons for our behavior.

Complicating matters, we humans are veritable experts in cooking up plausible and sincerely held reasons for why we do things, even when those reasons are entirely false (Fine, 2006; Nisbett & Wilson, 1977; see Chapter 14). We may be supremely confident that we voted against a political candidate because of her views on capital punishment and abortion, when in fact we voted against her because she reminds us of our annoying second-grade teacher. We can't always rely on people's self-reports to infer why they did what they did (Bruce & Desmond, 1997; Fowler & Lilienfeld, 2006).

(8) People in Psychological Research Usually Know They're Being Studied. Most natural sciences, such as astronomy, geology, and chemistry, study inanimate objects, such as planets, rocks, and compounds. Although these disciplines are exceedingly complicated, there's one crucial way in which studying them is simpler than psychology: Inanimate objects don't know they're being studied. When an astronomer points her telescope toward Saturn, Saturn doesn't look back. Nor does it alter its orbit or become worried about what we think of it. Moreover, most animals, even the most intelligent ones like chimpanzees and dolphins, probably don't realize they're being studied either.

In contrast, except for infants, most humans who are the subjects of behavioral research are well aware that psychologists are studying them. This fact often results in the problem of **reactivity:** the tendency for people to act differently when they know they're the subjects of research. For example, subjects who know that psychologists are interested in finding out whether they'll conform to group opinion may conform less than they would ordinarily. As we'll learn in Chapter 2, psychologists have developed various methods to get around the problem of reactivity, but few offer perfect solutions (Shadish, Cook, & Campbell, 2002; Webb, Campbell, Schwartz, & Sechrest, 1966).

(9) People Differ from Each Other. One thing that makes psychology both so fascinating and so complicated is the existence of **individual differences:** variations among people in their thinking, emotion, and behavior (Harkness & Lilienfeld, 1997; Willerman, 1979). Individual differences in response to the same situation are often remarkable. For example, when confronted with a white-coated authority figure who commands them to deliver painful electric shocks to another subject, some people boldly defy the experimenter whereas others comply submissively with his every order (Milgram, 1974; see Chapter 13). Entire fields of psychology, such as the study of intelligence, interests, personality, and mental illness, focus on individual differences (Lubinski, 2000). Individual differences make psychology challenging, because they make it difficult to come up with sweeping conclusions that apply to everyone.

(10) Culture Influences People's Behavior. Over the past few decades, psychologists have increasingly come to appreciate the need to take not only individual differences, but cultural differences into account when explaining behavior. Culture often shapes how we interpret the world.

To take one example, Richard Nisbett and his colleagues found that European American and Chinese subjects often attend to strikingly different things in pictures (Chua, Boland, & Nisbett, 2005). In one case, they showed subjects a photograph of a tiger walking on rocks next to a river. Using eye-tracking technology, which allows researchers to determine where subjects are moving their eyes, they found that European Americans tended to look mostly at the tiger, whereas Chinese tended to look mostly at the plants and rocks surrounding it. This finding dovetails with evidence that European Americans tend to focus on central details, whereas Asian Americans tend to focus on peripheral or incidental details (Nisbett, 2003; Nisbett, Peng, Choi, & Norenzayan, 2001). Cultural differences place further limits on the broad generalizations about human nature that psychologists can draw.

Social scientists sometimes distinguish between emic and etic approaches to cross-cultural psychology. In an **emic** approach, investigators study the behavior of a culture

Charming mass murderer Ted Bundy (seen here acting as his own attorney at his criminal trial) was a well-documented psychopath. Progress in understanding psychopathy has been slow, in part because until fairly recently researchers often defined this condition in markedly different ways.

In the Chua, Boland, and Nisbett (2003) study, European Americans tend to focus more on the central details of photographs, like the tiger itself (top), whereas Asian Americans tend to focus more on the peripheral details, like the rocks and leaves surrounding the tiger (bottom).

reactivity
tendency for people to behave differently when they know they're being studied

individual differences
variations among people in their thinking, emotion, and behavior

emic
approach of studying a culture's behavior from the perspective of an insider

from the perspective of a native, or insider, whereas in an **etic** approach, they study the behavior of a culture from the perspective of an outsider (Harris, 1976; Sabbagh, 2005). A researcher using an emic approach who's studying the personality of individuals on an isolated Pacific Island would probably rely on personality terms used by members of that culture. In contrast, a researcher using an etic approach would probably adapt and translate personality terms used by Western culture, like *shyness, extraversion*, and *anxiety,* to that culture. Each approach has its pluses and minuses. Investigators who adopt an emic approach may better understand the unique characteristics of a culture, but they may overlook characteristics that this culture shares with others. In contrast, investigators who adopt an etic approach may be better able to view this culture within the broader perspective of other cultures, but they may unintentionally impose perspectives from their own culture onto others.

Psychology in Historical Perspective: What a Long, Strange Trip It's Been

As we've seen, psychology hasn't yet solved many of the Great Questions of human nature. When asked to explain why, psychologists sometimes respond, "Well, psychology is a young science, so we haven't had much time to investigate these questions." Even some classic psychology textbooks excuse psychology's slow progress by appealing to its tender age (Heidbronner, 1933). In many respects, this familiar answer is a cop-out, because psychology as the study of behavior has been around since at least the time of the ancient Greeks (Loevinger, 1987). Psychology is by no means young, although it's been a truly experimental science for only about 130 years. In the words of the late nineteenth-century psychologist Hermann Ebbinghaus (whose classic work we'll read about in Chapter 7), "Psychology has a long past, but only a short history."

Beginning students often expect the history of psychology to be deadly dull. In fact, one of the first and still best-known books on the history of psychology was authored by a psychologist with the unfortunate name of E. G. Boring (1923), which may have gotten things off on the wrong foot. In reality, the history of psychology is anything but boring, because it tells the fascinating, vibrant, and still-evolving story of how we've come to understand ourselves.

PSYCHOLOGY: FROM SÉANCE TO SCIENCE

We'll start our journey with a capsule summary of psychology's bumpy road from non-science to a science (a timeline of significant events in the evolution of scientific psychology can be seen in **Figure P.2**). In the words of psychology historians Ludy Benjamin and David Baker (2004), we can view much of psychology's history as the slow but steady voyage from "séance to science."

Psychology's Liberation from Philosophy. For many centuries, the field of psychology was difficult to distinguish from philosophy. Most academic psychologists held positions in departments of philosophy (psychology departments didn't even exist back then) and didn't conduct research. Instead, they mostly sat around and tried to comprehend the human mind from the armchair. In fact, some prominent philosophers, such as Immanuel Kant (1724–1804), argued that psychology shouldn't even bother to become a science. They maintained that mental experiences could never be quantified (measured using numbers) or subjected to experimentation. As a result, they insisted, psychology couldn't and shouldn't aspire to be anything remotely like biology, chemistry, or physics (Fuchs & Milar, 2004).

Yet beginning in the late 1800s, the landscape of psychology changed dramatically. In 1879, Wilhelm Wundt (1832–1920) developed the first full-fledged psychological laboratory in Leipzig, Germany, 4 years after William James had founded a less formal laboratory at Harvard University. Psychology was thereby launched as an experimental science.

Wilhelm Wundt *(right)* in the world's first psychology laboratory. Wundt is generally credited with launching psychology as a laboratory science in 1879.

etic
approach of studying a culture's behavior from the perspective of an outsider

Late 1700s: Frans Anton Mesmer discovers principles of hypnosis

1850: Gustav Fechner experiences crucial insight linking physical changes in the external world to subjective changes in perception; leads to establishment of psychophysics

1875: William James creates small psychological laboratory at Harvard University

1881: Wundt establishes first psychology journal

1888: James McKeen Cattell becomes first professor of psychology in United States

1890: William James writes *Principles of Psychology*

1896: Lightmer Witmer creates first psychological clinic at the University of Pennsylvania, launching field of clinical psychology

1904: Mary Calkins is first woman elected president of the American Psychological Association

1905: Alfred Binet and Henri Simon develop first intelligence test

1910: Ivan Pavlov discovers classical conditioning

1911: E. L. Thorndike discovers instrumental (later called operant) conditioning

1920s: Gordon Allport helps to initiate field of personality trait psychology

1935: Kurt Koffka writes *Principles of Gestalt Psychology*

1949: Conference held at University of Colorado at Boulder to outline principles of scientific clinical psychology; founding of the "Boulder" (scientist-practitioner) model of clinical training

1953: Francis Crick and James Watson discover structure of DNA, launching genetic revolution

1953: Rapid eye movement (REM) sleep discovered

1963: Stanley Milgram publishes classic laboratory studies of obedience

1974: Positron emission tomography (PET) scanning introduced, launching field of functional brain imaging

1976: Founding of Committee for the Scientific Investigation of Claims of the Paranormal, first major organization to apply scientific skepticism to paranormal claims

1980: *Diagnostic and Statistical Manual of Mental Disorders, Third Edition (DSM-III)* published; helps standardize the diagnosis of major mental disorders

1990: Thomas Bouchard and colleagues publish major results of Minnesota Study of Twins Reared Apart, demonstrating substantial genetic bases for intelligence, personality, interests, and other important individual differences

1995: Task force of Division 12 (Society of Clinical Psychology) of American Psychological Association publishes list of, and criteria for, empirically supported psychotherapies

2004: APS members vote to change name to Association for Psychological Science

1600
1700
1800
1850
1900
1950
2000

1649: René Descartes writes about the mind–body problem

Early 1800s: Due to efforts of Franz Joseph Gall and Joseph Spurzheim, phrenology becomes immensely popular in Europe and United States

1849: Charles Darwin writes *Origin of Species*

1879: Wilhelm Wundt creates world's first formal psychological laboratory, launching psychology as an experimental science

1883: J. Stanley Hall, one of Wundt's students, opens first major psychology laboratory in the United States, at the Johns Hopkins University

1889: Sir Francis Galton introduces concept of correlation, allowing psychologists to quantify associations among variables

1892: American Psychological Association (APA) founded

1900: Sigmund Freud writes *The Interpretation of Dreams*, landmark book in the history of psychoanalysis

1907: Oscar Pfungst demonstrates that the amazing counting horse, Clever Hans, responds to cues from observers; demonstrates power of expectancies

1913: John B. Watson writes *Psychology as Behavior*, launching field of behaviorism

1920: Jean Piaget writes *The Child's Conception of the World*

1938: B. F. Skinner writes *The Behavior of Organisms*

1952: Antipsychotic drug Thorazine tested in France, launching modern era of psychopharmacology

1954: Paul Meehl writes *Clinical versus Statistical Prediction*, first major book to describe both the strengths and weaknesses of clinical judgment

1958: Joseph Wolpe writes *Psychotherapy by Reciprocal Inhibition*, helping to launch field of behavioral therapy

1967: Ulric Neisser writes *Cognitive Psychology*; helps to launch field of cognitive psychology

1974: Elizabeth Loftus and Robert Palmer publish classic paper on the malleability of human memory, showing that memory is more reconstructive than previously believed

1977: First use of statistical technique of meta-analysis, which allows researchers to systematically combine results of multiple studies; demonstrated that psychotherapy is effective

1980s: Recovered memory craze sweeps across America; pits academic researchers against many clinicians

1988: Many scientifically oriented psychologists break off from American Psychological Association to found American Psychological Society (APS)

2000: Human genome sequenced

2002: Daniel Kahneman becomes first Ph.D. psychologist to win Nobel Prize; honored for his pioneering work (with the late Amos Tversky) on biases and heuristics

Figure P.2 Timeline of Major Events in Scientific Psychology.

In séances, which were popular in the nineteenth century, the spirit of a deceased person supposedly occupies a room. Much of psychology's early history was closely tied to séances and other forms of spiritualism.

The Fox sisters (Margaret, Kate, and Leah) were supposedly the source of haunted spirits at their farmhouse.

introspection
method by which trained observers carefully reflect and report on their mental experiences

paranormal
events, like extrasensory perception, that fall outside the boundaries of traditional science

Most of Wundt's investigations and those of his students focused on basic questions concerning our mental experiences: How different must two colors be for us to tell them apart? How long does it take us to react to a sound? What thoughts come to mind when we solve a math problem? Wundt used a combination of experimental methods, including reaction time equipment, and a technique called **introspection,** which required trained observers to carefully reflect and report on their mental experiences. The field founded by Wundt and his followers came to be known as *New Psychology,* because it broke loose from the chains of philosophy and tried to emulate the methods of traditional sciences, like physics (Coon, 1992). In many respects, the pioneering work of Wundt marked the beginnings of psychology as a science, because he demonstrated that Kant and other doubters were wrong: Mental events *could* be quantified. Soon, psychologists elsewhere around the world followed Wundt's bold lead and opened laboratories in departments of psychology.

Psychology's Liberation from Spiritualism. To become a full-fledged and independent discipline, psychology needed to break free not only from philosophy but from another influence: spiritualism. Indeed, the term *psychology* literally means the study of the *psyche,* that is, the spirit or soul. In the mid- and late 1800s, Americans became fascinated with *spirit mediums,* people who claimed to contact the dead, often during séances (Blum, 2006). Séances were group sessions that took place in darkened rooms, in which mediums attempted to "channel" the spirits of deceased individuals. Americans of that time were equally enchanted with psychics, individuals who claimed to possess powers of mind reading and other extrasensory capacities (see Chapter 4).

For example, two young sisters from a small town near Rochester, New York, Kate and Margaret Fox, created a sensation in the mid-1800s by claiming to hear spooky rapping and knocking sounds emanating from the basement of their farmhouse (Coon, 1992; Hines, 2003). These sounds supposedly originated from a man who'd been murdered and buried there. The two Fox sisters eventually confessed to fraud; under the direction of a third sister, Leah, they were creating the knocking sounds themselves using simple parlor tricks, like cracking their toes. Still, their admission barely made a dent in the public's preoccupation with the **paranormal,** the term used to describe events, like extrasensory perception (ESP), that fall outside the boundaries of traditional science.

In the eyes of the general public of the nineteenth century, psychology and spiritualism were inextricably linked. In fact, popular and scientific writers used the word *psychological* interchangeably with *psychical* (Coon, 1992). Moreover, Harvard University's William James spent much of his spare time investigating self-professed spirit mediums and psychics. In so doing, he hoped to uncover definitive scientific evidence for their paranormal powers (Benjamin & Baker, 2004). Many of James's scientific contemporaries looked down on his research adventures and went out of their way to try to debunk these and other paranormal claims.

Despite their concerted efforts, James and his fellow psychic inquirers failed (Blum, 2006). They never obtained compelling evidence for paranormal phenomena, and psychology eventually developed a respectful distance from spiritualism. It did so largely by forging a new field: the psychology of human error and self-deception. Rather than focusing on whether extrasensory powers exist, a growing number of psychologists in the late 1800s began asking an equally interesting question: *How can people fool themselves into believing things for which there isn't solid evidence?*

The leader of this field, a University of Wisconsin researcher named Joseph Jastrow (1863–1944), has never received the credit he richly deserves as a pioneer of psychological science (Kimble, Wertheimer, & While, 1991). Jastrow and his colleagues argued that the human psychological apparatus is vulnerable to a host of errors of thinking and emotion that can lead people to accept uncritically the existence of the paranormal (Coon, 1992). Learning about these errors, and learning how to avoid them, is a major theme of this textbook. In later chapters, we'll learn how we can all be fooled into accepting psychological claims that seem true, but aren't.

To this day, the flames of psychology's on-and-off love affair with the paranormal have never burned out entirely, and the existence of ESP remains controversial in some scientific quarters (Bem & Honorton, 1994; Hyman, 1996; see Chapter 4). But by and large, the general public today views *parapsychology*, the study of extrasensory capacities, as only one tiny branch of psychology rather than as synonymous with it.

PSYCHOLOGY TODAY: REASONS FOR BOTH OPTIMISM AND CONCERN

In the early twenty-first century, the field of psychology is an active, growing, and rapidly changing discipline. As we'll discover, the present state of psychology gives us cause for both optimism and concern.

Psychology and Psychologists in the Early Twenty-First Century. Today, there are about 500,000 psychologists worldwide (Kassin, 2004), with more than 40,000 in the United States alone (Bailey, 2004). The American Psychological Association (APA), founded in 1892 and now the world's largest association of psychologists, consists of more than 150,000 members. (To give us a sense of how much the field has grown, there were only 150 APA members in 1900.) These members are spread across fifty-four divisions spanning such topics as addiction, art psychology, clinical psychology, hypnosis, law and psychology, media psychology, mental retardation, neuroscience, peace psychology, psychology and religion, sports psychology, the psychology of women, and gay, lesbian, bisexual, and transgendered issues. Moreover, people with degrees in psychology work in a remarkably diverse array of settings. Psychology is alive and well.

Psychology and Controversy. With so many specialties, it stands to reason that psychologists sometimes disagree in their approach to the subject matter and interpretation of evidence. The central flashpoint of controversy in modern psychology lies in the domain of clinical practice, particularly psychotherapy. The principal fault line is between psychologists who believe that clinical practice should primarily reflect scientific findings and those who believe that clinical practice should primarily reflect subjective clinical experience and intuition (Dawes, 1994; Lilienfeld, Lynn, & Lohr, 2003; McFall, 1991). For the first group, many of whom hold positions in colleges and universities, psychotherapy should be based as much as possible on evidence derived from carefully controlled studies. These psychologists bemoan the nonscientific aspects of their discipline and challenge the increasing popularity of many questionable, even downright bizarre, therapeutic techniques.

For the second group, some of whom are in private practice, psychotherapy is more of an art than a science—and should remain that way (although many psychologists in full-time practice fall into the former group). The sharp cleft between these two groups of psychologists is sometimes called the **scientist–practitioner gap** (Fox, 1993), although it's probably closer to a "canyon" than a gap (Tavris, 2003).

The scientist–practitioner gap widened in the 1980s and early 1990s when thousands of individuals claimed to recover long-forgotten early memories of child sexual abuse during or following psychotherapy. The lion's share of scientifically oriented psychologists concluded that many or even most of these *recovered memories*, as they came to be known, were false, and had been induced inadvertently by well-meaning but careless therapists. In contrast, many clinicians believed that recovered memories were typically genuine (see Chapter 7). The recovered memory controversy became intense and bitter, culminating in personal attacks at scientific conferences (Loftus & Ketcham, 1994).

The scientist–practitioner battle came to a head in 1988, when a renegade band of psychologists—most of them academics—split off from the APA to form a smaller organization, then called the American Psychological Society (APS). The founders of the APS felt that the APA had largely forsaken the scientific foundations of the discipline. Both organizations now elect their own officers, publish their own journals, and pursue different agendas, the APA primarily clinically related and the APS primarily science related.

Joseph Jastrow, an unsung pioneer of early scientific psychology, was among the first psychologists to emphasize how human fallibility can lead people to accept paranormal claims uncritically.

factoid

The first female president of the APA was Mary Whiton Calkins (1863–1930), who served in 1905. Despite being an outstanding student at Harvard University, the faculty denied her tenure because of her gender. Calkins made significant contributions to the study of memory, sensation, and self-concept.

scientist–practitioner gap
divide between psychologists who believe that clinical practice should primarily be a science versus those who believe that clinical practice should primarily be an art

Some therapeutic techniques are premised on dubious scientific principles. For example, proponents of hypnotic age regression claim to be able to "return" individuals psychologically to an earlier age using hypnosis; here, a therapist regresses a hypnotic subject to age 3. Yet research suggests that age-regressed subjects are merely behaving in accord with their expectations of how a child of that age should act (Nash, 1987; see Chapter 5).

Although some APS members have remained in the APA, the tensions between these organizations persist, as does the gulf between psychological science and clinical practice. In 2005, the members of APS voted to change its name to the Association for Psychological Science, largely to affirm their commitment to the scientific bases of the discipline. Although APS has only about 18,000 members, about a tenth that of APA, its influence on scientific psychology is substantial.

The Great Theoretical Frameworks of Psychology

In its continued struggle to become a full-fledged science, psychology has suffered from an unresolved identity crisis. Almost since its inception, psychological science has confronted a thorny question: What unifying theoretical perspective best explains behavior?

Five major theoretical perspectives—structuralism, functionalism, behaviorism, psychoanalysis, and cognitivism—have played pivotal roles in shaping contemporary psychological thought. Many beginning psychology students understandably ask, "Which of these perspectives is the right one?" As it turns out, the answer isn't entirely clear. Each theoretical viewpoint has something valuable to contribute to scientific psychology, but each has its limitations. As we wend our way through these five frameworks, we'll discover that psychology's view of what constitutes a scientific approach to behavior has changed over time. Indeed, it continues to change even today.

STRUCTURALISM: THE ELEMENTS OF THE MIND

Edward Bradford Titchener (1867–1927), a British student of Wundt who emigrated to the United States to teach at Cornell University, founded the field of structuralism (because Titchener donated his brain to science, you can find his preserved brain in a jar in Cornell's psychology department). **Structuralism** aimed to identify the basic elements, or "structures," of psychological experience. Adopting Wundt's method of introspection, structuralists dreamed of creating a comprehensive "map" of the elements of consciousness—which they believed consisted of sensations, images, and feelings—much like the periodic table of the elements we can find in every chemistry classroom (Evans, 1972). Using painstaking methods of introspection, Titchener and his students claimed to identify over 44,400 sensations, including 32,800 pertaining to vision, 11,600 pertaining to hearing, and 4 pertaining to taste (Loevinger, 1987).

Nevertheless, structuralism eventually ran out of steam. At least two major problems eventually did it in. First, even highly trained introspectionists often disagreed on their subjective reports. Because science depends on the ability to duplicate findings across different laboratories (see Chapter 1), this lack of consensus proved to be an embarrassment. Second, German psychologist Oswald Kulpe (1862–1915) showed that subjects asked to solve certain mental problems engage in *imageless thought:* thinking unaccompanied by conscious experience. If we ask an introspecting subject to add 10 and 5, she'll quickly respond "15," but she'll usually be unable to report what came to her mind when performing this calculation (Hergenhahn, 2000). The phenomenon of imageless thought dealt a serious body blow to structuralism, because it demonstrated that some important aspects of human psychology lie outside of conscious awareness.

Structuralism's Contribution to Scientific Psychology. Although structuralism no longer exists as a formal school of psychological thought, it underscored the importance of *systematic observation* to the study of conscious experience. That is, structuralists emphasized that to become a science, psychology must rely on rigorous and carefully standardized reports, not on casual or informal impressions. Nevertheless, structuralists went astray by assuming that a single, imperfect method—introspection—could provide all of the information needed for a complete science of psychology.

structuralism
school of psychology that aimed to identify the basic elements of psychological experience

FUNCTIONALISM: PSYCHOLOGY MEETS DARWIN

Proponents of **functionalism** hoped to understand the adaptive purposes, or functions, of psychological characteristics, such as thoughts, feelings, and behaviors (Hunt, 1993). Whereas structuralists asked "what" questions, like "What is conscious thought like?" functionalists asked "why" questions, like, "Why do we sometimes forget things?" The founder of functionalism, William James, rejected structuralists' approach and methods, arguing that careful introspection yields not a fixed number of static elements of consciousness, but rather an ever-changing "stream of consciousness," a famous phrase he coined. Consciousness, functionalists argued, is more akin to a flowing river than a dried-out riverbed.

The functionalists of the late 1800s were influenced substantially by biologist Charles Darwin's (1809–1882) still-young theory of natural selection, which emphasized that many physical characteristics evolved because they were useful for organisms. The functionalists believed that Darwin's theory applied to psychological characteristics too. Just as the trunk of an elephant serves useful functions for survival, such as snaring distant water and food, the human memory system, for example, must similarly serve a purpose. It's the job of psychologists, functionalists maintained, to act as "detectives," figuring out the evolved functions that psychological characteristics serve for organisms.

Functionalism's Contribution to Scientific Psychology. Like structuralism, functionalism doesn't exist in its original form today. Instead, functionalism was gradually absorbed into mainstream scientific psychology and continues to influence it indirectly in many ways. As we'll soon discover, an increasing number of psychologists are attempting to use evolutionary theory to understand the nature of romantic attraction; the functions of jealousy, anger, and other emotions; the origins of human personality; and even the causes of mental illness. These psychologists owe a great debt of gratitude to William James and his fellow functionalists.

BEHAVIORISM: THE LAWS OF LEARNING

In the early twentieth century, many American psychologists were growing impatient with the touchy-feely nature of their discipline. In particular, they believed that Titchener and other introspectionists were leading psychology down a misguided path. For these critics, the study of consciousness was a waste of time, because researchers could never verify conclusively the existence of the basic elements of psychological experience. Psychological science, they contended, must be objective, not subjective.

Foremost among these critics was a flamboyant American psychologist, John B. Watson (1878–1958). Watson founded the still-influential school of **behaviorism,** which focuses on uncovering the general principles of learning underlying human and animal behavior. For Watson (1913), the proper subject matter of psychology was observable behavior, plain and simple. Subjective reports of conscious experience should play no part in psychology. If it followed his brave lead, Watson proclaimed, psychology could become just as scientific as physics, chemistry, and other "hard" sciences.

Watson further insisted that psychology should aspire to uncover the general laws of learning that explain all behaviors, whether they be riding a bicycle, eating a sandwich, or becoming depressed. All of these behaviors, Watson proposed, were products of a handful of basic learning principles (see Chapter 6). Moreover, according to Watson, we don't need to peer "inside" the organism to grasp these principles. We can comprehend human behavior exclusively by looking *outside* the organism, to rewards and punishments delivered by the environment. For traditional behaviorists, the human mind is a **black box:** We know what goes into it and what comes out of it, but we needn't worry about what happens between the inputs and the outputs. For this reason, psychologists sometimes call behaviorism "black box psychology."

Some of Watson's followers, especially the Harvard psychologist Burrhus Frederick (B. F.) Skinner (1904–1990), agreed that psychology should focus on basic laws of

Charles Darwin's theory of evolution by natural selection was a significant influence on functionalism, which strove to understand the adaptive purposes of psychological characteristics.

John B. Watson, the founder of behaviorism. Watson's stubborn insistence on scientific rigor made him a hero to some and an enemy to others.

functionalism
school of psychology that aimed to understand the adaptive purposes of psychological characteristics

behaviorism
school of psychology that focuses on uncovering the general laws of learning by looking outside the organism

black box
term sometimes used to describe behaviorists' view of the mind, namely, an unknown entity that we don't need to understand to explain behavior

For B. F. Skinner and his behaviorist followers, emotions are no different in their origins from other behaviors: they're shaped by rewards and punishments.

learning, but disagreed with Watson that psychology should focus exclusively on observable behaviors. For Skinner (1953), thoughts, feelings, and observable behaviors all fall within the province of scientific psychology. According to Skinner, thoughts and feelings *are* behaviors; they just happen to be unobservable. Moreover, according to Skinner, the causes of our thoughts and feelings are no different from the causes of our observable behaviors. They too are the products of rewards and punishments originating in the environment.

Behaviorism's Contribution to Scientific Psychology. Behaviorism has left an indelible stamp on scientific psychology that continues to be felt today. By identifying the fundamental laws of learning that help to explain human and animal behavior, behaviorists placed psychology on firmer scientific footing. Although early behaviorists' deep mistrust of subjective observations of conscious experience probably went too far, these psychologists properly warned us of the hazards of relying too heavily on reports that we can't verify objectively.

COGNITIVISM: OPENING THE BLACK BOX

Beginning in the 1950s and 1960s, growing numbers of psychologists grew disillusioned with behaviorists' neglect of **cognition,** the fancy term psychologists use to describe the mental processes involved in different aspects of thinking. Although Skinner and his followers acknowledged that humans and even many intelligent animals do think, they viewed thinking as merely another form of behavior. The cognitivists, in contrast, argued that our thinking affects our behavior in powerful ways. For example, Swiss psychologist Jean Piaget (1896–1980) argued compellingly that children conceptualize the world in markedly different ways than do adults (see Chapter 10). Later, led by Ulric Neisser (1928–), cognitivists argued that thinking is so central to psychology that it merits a separate discipline in its own right (Neisser, 1967; see Chapter 8).

According to cognitivists, a psychology based solely on rewards and punishments from the environment will never be adequate, because our *interpretation* of rewards and punishments is a crucial determinant of our behavior. Take a student who receives a B+ on his first psychology exam. A student accustomed to getting Fs on his tests might regard this grade as a reward, whereas a student accustomed to As might view it as a punishment. Without understanding how people evaluate information, cognitivists maintain, we'll never fully grasp the causes of their behavior. Moreover, according to cognitivists, we often learn not merely by rewards and punishments but by *insight,* that is, by grasping the underlying nature of problems (see Chapter 6).

Cognitivism's Contribution to Scientific Psychology. Cognitive psychology remains enormously influential today, and its tentacles have spread to such diverse domains as language, problem solving, concept formation, intelligence, memory, and psychotherapy. By focusing not merely on rewards and punishments but on organisms' interpretation of them, cognitivism has encouraged psychologists to peek inside the black box to examine the connections between inputs and outputs. Moreover, cognitivism has increasingly established strong linkages to the study of brain functioning, allowing psychologists to better understand the physiological bases of thinking, memory, and other key mental functions (Ilardi & Feldman, 2001).

PSYCHOANALYSIS: THE DEPTHS OF THE UNCONSCIOUS

Around the time that behaviorism was becoming dominant in the United States, a parallel movement was gathering momentum in Europe. This field, psychoanalysis, was founded by the Viennese neurologist Sigmund Freud (1856–1939). In sharp contrast to behaviorism, **psychoanalysis** focused on internal psychological processes, especially impulses, thoughts, and memories of which we're unaware. According to Freud (1900) and other psychoanalysts, the primary influences on behavior aren't forces outside the organism, like rewards and punishments, but rather unconscious drives, especially sexuality and aggression.

cognition
mental processes involved in different aspects of thinking

psychoanalysis
school of psychology, founded by Sigmund Freud, that focuses on internal psychological processes of which we're unaware

Psychoanalysts maintain that much of our everyday psychological lives is filled with symbols—things that represent other things (Loevinger, 1987; Moore & Fine, 1995). For example, if you refer accidentally to one of your female professors as "Mommy," Freudians would be unlikely to treat this embarrassing blooper as an isolated mistake. Instead, they'd quickly suggest that your professor probably reminds you of your mother, which may be a good reason to transfer to a different course. The goal of the psychoanalyst, therefore, is to decode the symbolic meaning of our slips of the tongue (or *Freudian slips*, as they're often called), dreams, and psychological symptoms. By doing so, psychoanalysts contend, they can get to the roots of our deep-seated psychological conflicts. Psychoanalysts also place considerably more emphasis than do other schools of thought on the role of early experience. For Freud and others, the core of the personality is molded in the first few years of life.

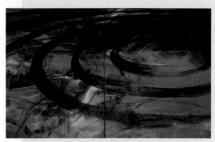

Psychoanalysts argue that "decoding" the symbolic meaning of dream images can bring us closer to the unconscious roots of our psychological conflicts. Many modern scientific thinkers disagree.

Psychoanalysis's Contribution to Scientific Psychology. The influence of Freud and psychoanalysis on scientific psychology is controversial. On the one hand, some critics insist that psychoanalysis retarded the progress of scientific psychology, because it focused heavily on unconscious processes that are difficult or impossible to verify. As we'll learn in Chapter 14, these critics probably have a point (Crews, 2005; Esterson, 1993). On the other hand, at least some psychoanalytic claims, such as the assertion that a great deal of important mental processing goes on outside of conscious awareness, have held up well in scientific research (Westen, 1998; Wilson, 2002). It's not clear, however, whether the Freudian view of the unconscious bears anything more than a superficial resemblance to more contemporary views of unconscious processing (Kihlstroma, 1987; see Chapter 14).

The Multifaceted World of Modern Psychology

As is probably evident from what we've presented thus far, psychology isn't just one discipline, but rather a motley assortment of many subdisciplines. In most major psychology departments, we can find researchers examining areas as varied as the brain bases of visual perception, the mechanisms of memory, the causes of prejudice, and the treatment of depression.

CRITICAL MULTIPLISM: PSYCHOLOGY'S INTELLECTUAL DIVERSITY

Modern psychologists have adopted an enormous variety of methods, such as questionnaires, interviews, laboratory studies, and observation of real-world events, to help them understand behavior. No one method is necessarily better than any other. By using many different methods in concert—an approach termed **critical multiplism** (Cook, 1985)—psychologists have arrived slowly but surely at a more complete picture of human nature. They still have a long way to go, which is what helps to make psychology so exciting: countless fascinating mysteries lie ahead.

The couch that Sigmund Freud used to psychoanalyze his patients, now located in the Freud museum in London, England. Contrary to popular conception, most psychologists aren't psychotherapists, and most psychotherapists aren't even psychoanalysts. Nor do most modern therapists ask patients to recline on couches.

The great diversity of psychology is both a disadvantage and an advantage. It's a disadvantage because it's proven difficult to come up with a grand theory that unifies all subdisciplines of psychology (Cronbach, 1975; Kimble, 1989; Meehl, 1978; Staats, 1991). Some psychologists doubt we'll ever achieve such an overarching theory (Green, 1992). But psychology's diversity is also an advantage, because psychologists have so many approaches at their disposal to address questions regarding human nature.

Because psychology is so broad in scope, it's not surprising that modern psychologists work in a bewildering array of settings. For much of the general public, psychologists are pretty much all alike: They are therapists who use a couch to psychoanalyze people. In fact, most psychotherapists nowadays don't even use a couch (Kernick, 1997). If you tell a person you've just met at a party that you're taking an introductory psychology course, don't

critical multiplism
approach of using many different methods in concert

be surprised if he asks, "So, are you analyzing me right now?" Yet only about 45 percent of psychologists are psychotherapists, and less than 20 percent of psychotherapists are psychoanalysts (Milan, Montgomery, & Rogers, 1994), that is, therapists who embrace the theories and techniques of Sigmund Freud and his followers.

APPLICATIONS OF PSYCHOLOGICAL SCIENCE TO EVERYDAY LIFE

One piece of evidence for the slow but steady progress of psychology comes from the growing applications of psychological science to myriad domains of everyday life. Psychological science has found its way into far more aspects of contemporary society than most of us realize (Salzinger, 2002; Zimbardo, 2004).

Basic versus Applied Research. Psychological scientists often distinguish basic from applied research. **Basic research** examines how the mind works, whereas **applied research** examines how we can use basic research to solve real-world problems. Within most large psychology departments, we'll find a healthy mix of people conducting mostly basic research, such as investigators who study the workings of the human brain or the laws of learning, and mostly applied research, such as investigators who study how to select effective airport security screeners or help people cope with the psychological burden of cancer.

Still, the boundaries between basic and applied psychological research are blurry and getting blurrier all the time. That's probably a good thing, because it suggests that more and more researchers are "translating" basic psychological findings into beneficial real-world uses.

Giving Psychology Away. In his presidential address to the American Psychological Association about four decades ago, George Miller (1969) urged his academic colleagues to spend less of their time holed up in their dark and dingy offices and more of their time "giving psychology away" to the general public. By that, he meant furnishing the average person with the fruits of psychological knowledge.

Because they're so busy doing research, applying for grants, and teaching, many scientific psychologists haven't done a great job of spreading their knowledge to the public. Nor have they devoted as much time as they should to popularizing their discipline (Benjamin, 2003; Lilienfeld, 1998). If we were to ask most Americans to name a psychologist, they'd probably say Sigmund Freud or B. F. Skinner (Duncan, 1976; Stanovich, 2006). Many would also name Dr. Phil, Dr. Laura, and perhaps one or two others. Yet as we've already learned, Sigmund Freud wasn't even a psychologist. Neither is Dr. Laura; her doctoral degree is in physiology, although she obtained a master's degree in marriage, family, and child counseling. Regrettably, precious few Americans have heard of the names Roy Baumeister, Paul Ekman, Leon Festinger, Daniel Kahneman, Elizabeth Loftus, Paul Meehl, Stanley Milgram, Ulric Neisser, Robert Rescorla, Robert Rosenthal, Stanley Schachter, Martin Seligman, Amos Tversky, Endel Tulving, Shelley Taylor, Timothy Wilson, or Philip Zimbardo. Nevertheless, these psychologists and scores of others we'll meet in this book have forever changed how we think about ourselves and the world.

How Psychology Affects Us: Applications to Everyday Life. Examples of how psychological research has affected our everyday lives abound. Many of us have encountered these applications in our lives, although we may not realize that they emanated from psychological research. Let's look at a sampling of them; we can discover more about these and other examples on a website maintained by the American Psychological Association: www.Psychologymatters.org.

- If you live in or near a big city, you've probably noticed a gradual change in the color of fire engines. Although old fire engines were bright red, most new ones are lime-yellow. That's because psychological researchers who study perception found that lime-yellow objects are easier to detect in the dark. Indeed, lime-yellow fire trucks are only about half as likely to be involved in traffic accidents as red fire trucks (American Psychological Association, 2000; Solomon & King, 1995).

- As a car driver, have you ever had to slam on your brakes to avoid hitting a driver directly in front of you who stopped short suddenly? If so, and if you managed to avoid a bad accident,

(1)

(2)

(3)

(4)

Psychologists Elizabeth Loftus (1) and Paul Meehl (2) are far less well known to the general public than psychologists Dr. Phil (3) and John Gray (4), but they've had a much greater impact on how we think about ourselves and the world.

Increasingly, today's fire trucks are lime-yellow rather than red. That's because psychological research has demonstrated that lime-yellow objects are easier to spot in the dark than red objects.

basic research
research examining how the mind works

applied research
research examining how we can use basic research to solve real-world problems

you may have John Voevodsky to thank. For decades, cars had only two brake lights. In the early 1970s, Voevodsky hit on the bright (pun intended) idea of placing a third brake light at the base of cars' back windshields. He reasoned that this additional visual information would decrease the risk of rear-end collisions. He conducted a 10-month study of taxis with and without the new brake lights and found a 61 percent lower rate of rear-end accidents in the first group (Voevodsky, 1974). As a result of his research, all new American cars have three brake lights (http://www.psychologymatters.org/voevodsky.html).

• To get into college, you probably had to take one or more tests, like the Scholastic Assessment Test (SAT) or American College Test (ACT). If so, you can thank—or blame—psychologists with expertise in measuring academic achievement and knowledge, who were primarily responsible for developing these measures (Zimbardo, 2004). Although these tests are far from perfect predictors of academic performance, they do significantly better than chance in forecasting how students perform in college (Geiser & Studley, 2002).

• If you're anything like the average American, you see more than 100 commercial messages every day. The chances are high that psychologists had a hand in crafting many of them. The founder of behaviorism, John B. Watson, pioneered the application of psychology to advertising in the 1920s and 1930s. He introduced the now familiar concept of the "blind taste test," in which volunteers try out two products without knowing which is which, and he helped Maxwell House to make the coffee break a familiar tradition in many American workplaces (Buckley, 1982; Hunt, 1993; Kreshel, 1990). Today, psychological researchers still contribute to the marketing success of companies. For example, psychologists who study magazine advertisements have discovered that human faces better capture readers' attention on the left rather than right side of pages. Written text, in contrast, better captures readers' attention on the right rather than left side of pages (Clay, 2000).

• Hopefully, you won't be a victim of a violent crime, although odds are high that you know someone who has. Police officers often ask victims of such crimes to select a suspect from a lineup. When doing so, they've traditionally used *simultaneous lineups,* in which one or more suspects and several decoys (people who aren't really suspects) are lined up in a row, often of five to eight individuals (see Chapter 7). These are the kinds of lineups we've most often seen on television crime shows. Yet psychological research generally shows that *sequential lineups*—those in which victims view each person individually and then decide whether he or she was the perpetrator of the crime—are more accurate than simultaneous lineups (Steblay, Dysart, Fulero, & Lindsay, 2003; Wells, Memon, & Penrod, 2006; Wells & Olson, 2003). As a result of this research, police departments around the United States are increasingly using sequential rather than simultaneous lineups.

• For many years, many American public schools were legally required to be racially segregated. Before 1954, the law of the land in the United States was that "separate but equal" facilities were sufficient to guarantee racial equality. But based in part on the pioneering research of psychologists Kenneth and Mamie Clark (1950), who demonstrated that African American children preferred White to African American dolls, the U.S. Supreme Court decided—in the landmark 1954 case of *Brown v. Board of Education of Topeka, Kansas*—that school segregation exerted a negative impact on the self-esteem of African American children. The Clarks' research had its shortcomings (for example, the evidence that we can use doll choices to infer children's racial preferences isn't as clear-cut as they believed), and it didn't prove that racial segregation produced African American children's doll preferences, but it was consistent with that possibility (Bersoff, 1986). Citing the Clarks' research, the high court ordered American classrooms to be racially integrated (Benjamin & Crouse, 2000).

• The odds are also high that you at least know someone who's in psychotherapy. Perhaps you've received psychotherapy at some point in your life. If so, you're far from alone. About one in five adult Americans has sought treatment for an emotional problem over the past year (Kessler et al., 2005). Psychologists have played a pivotal role in developing and testing most forms of psychotherapy (Chapter 16). Moreover, well-conducted studies consistently demonstrate that psychotherapy can be effective for treating a wide range of psychological difficulties, including depression, anxiety, eating problems, insomnia, and sexual disturbances (Chambless & Ollendick, 2001).

A classic simultaneous eyewitness lineup. Although police commonly use such lineups, most research suggests that they're more prone to error than sequential lineups.

The classic doll studies of Kenneth and Mamie Clark paved the way for the 1954 Supreme Court decision of *Brown v. Board of Education,* which mandated racial integration of public schools.

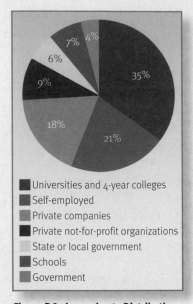

Figure P.3 Approximate Distribution of Psychologists in Different Settings. Psychologists are employed in a diverse array of settings. (*Source:* Data from NSF, 2003)

Universities and 4-year colleges
Self-employed
Private companies
Private not-for-profit organizations
State or local government
Schools
Government

The popular media and much of the general public often use the terms *psychiatrist* and *psychologist* interchangeably. But only psychiatrists are doctors, and with the exception of a few states, only they can prescribe medication.

So, far more than most of us realize, the fruits of psychological research are all around us. Psychology has dramatically altered the landscape of everyday life.

Types of Psychologists: Fact and Fiction. In this section, we'll describe a few of the most important types of psychologists whose work we'll encounter in this book. Along the way, we'll dispel common misconceptions about what each psychologist does (see **Figure P.3**).

(1) **Clinical psychologists,** who include the first two authors of this text, focus on the assessment, diagnosis, causes, and treatment of mental disorders, like schizophrenia, depression, and obsessive-compulsive disorder. Clinical psychology is the most populous sub-specialty of psychology. Some clinical psychologists conduct research on people with mental disorders, whereas others primarily assess, diagnose, and treat individuals with these disorders. Some work in colleges and universities, others in hospitals, others in mental health centers, and still others in private practice (but for those of you who want to become therapists, be aware that it takes an enormous amount of money to open a private practice). In most U.S. states—the only exceptions as of 2008 being New Mexico and Louisiana—clinical psychologists can't prescribe medication. That's a major difference between clinical psychologists and psychiatrists; psychiatrists are M.D.s just like other physicians and can dispense drugs for mental disorders.

Most frequent misconception: If you want to become a therapist, you need to earn a Ph.D. in clinical psychology. In fact, most clinical psychology Ph.D. programs are highly research oriented. They're designed primarily to train researchers in academic settings and medical schools, although they also train students in the techniques of psychotherapy. If your principal career goal is to become a therapist only, there are other options, such as the Psy.D. (doctor of psychology) degree, a doctoral degree that focuses on training therapists rather than clinical researchers, and the M.S.W. (social work) degree, a master's degree that also focuses on training therapists.

(2) **Counseling psychologists** tend to work with relatively normal people who are experiencing temporary or relatively self-contained life problems, like marital conflict, sexual difficulties, occupational stressors, or uncertainty about their careers (psychologists who specialize in the last problem area perform what's called vocational counseling). Most counseling psychologists work in counseling centers, hospitals, or private practice, although some work in academic and research settings. The chances are good that your college or university has a counseling center and that one or more of the therapists who work there are counseling psychologists, although some may be clinical psychologists.

Most frequent misconception: Counseling psychology is pretty much the same thing as clinical psychology. Whereas most clinical psychologists work with people with serious mental disorders, like severe depression, most counseling psychologists don't. Moreover, you'll often find clinical and counseling psychology graduate programs in entirely different departments. If you're interested in pursuing counseling psychology in graduate school, be sure to check out departments of education as well as departments of psychology, because many counseling psychology programs are located in education departments.

(3) **School psychologists** work with teachers, parents, and children to remedy students' behavioral, emotional, and learning difficulties. They typically assess schoolchildren's psychological problems and develop intervention programs to eliminate or minimize the impact of these problems.

Most frequent misconception: School psychology is just another term for educational psychology. Educational psychology is a substantially different discipline that focuses on helping instructors identify better methods for teaching and presenting course material, as well as for evaluating student learning.

(4) **Developmental psychologists** study why and how people change over time. Most conduct research on infants' and children's emotional, social, physiological, and cognitive (thinking) processes, and how these processes change with age. A growing minority of

developmental psychologists study these processes in elderly individuals. Most developmental psychologists work in research settings, although some consult with schools and community agencies to help them evaluate the effectiveness of intervention programs, like Head Start (see Chapter 9).

Most frequent misconception: Developmental psychologists spend most of their time on their hands and knees playing with children. In fact, developmental psychologists spend most of their time locked away in the laboratory, collecting and analyzing data on children's behavior.

(5) Experimental psychologists use sophisticated research methods, like reaction time equipment and high-powered computers, to study the memory, language, and thinking of humans. They work primarily in research settings, although some consult for businesses.

Most frequent misconception: Experimental psychologists do all of their work in psychological laboratories. Many experimental psychologists conduct research in real-world settings, examining how people acquire language, remember events, apply mental concepts, and so on, in everyday life. Moreover, even experimental psychologists who spend most of their time in laboratories are interested in how well their findings generalize to the real world.

(6) Biopsychologists, sometimes also called psychobiologists or physiological psychologists, examine the physiological bases of behavior in animals and humans. They may be interested in the functioning of different brain areas, the effects of hormones on behavior, or the relation of neurotransmitters (chemical messengers in the nervous system; see Chapter 3) to behavior. Most biopsychologists work in research settings.

Most frequent misconception: All biopsychologists use invasive methods in their research (by *invasive methods,* psychologists mean techniques that damage animals' nervous systems). Although many biopsychologists create brain lesions to examine their effects on animals' behavior, others, especially those who work with humans, use brain imaging methods (see Chapter 3), which don't require investigators to damage organisms' nervous systems.

(7) Forensic psychologists work in prisons, jails, and other settings to assess and diagnose inmates and assist with their rehabilitation and treatment. Still others conduct research on eyewitness testimony or jury decision making. Many forensic psychologists hold degrees in clinical or counseling psychology.

Most frequent misconception: Most forensic psychologists are criminal profilers, like those employed by the FBI. Criminal profiling is only a tiny subspecialty within forensic psychology. Moreover, as we'll learn in Chapter 14, criminal profiling is controversial from a scientific perspective, because there's relatively feeble evidence that it's an effective method for solving crimes (Scott, Lambie, Henwood, & Lamb, 2003).

(8) Industrial–organizational psychologists work in companies and businesses to help select productive employees, evaluate employee performance, examine the effects of different working or living conditions on people's behavior (they're called *environmental psychologists*), or design equipment to maximize employee performance and minimize employee accidents (they're called *human factors* or *engineering psychologists*). Others have academic positions or work for governmental organizations.

Most frequent misconception: Most industrial–organizational psychologists work on a one-to-one basis with employees to increase their motivation and productivity. Most industrial–organizational psychologists spend the lion's share of their time constructing tests and selection procedures or implementing organizational changes to improve worker productivity and satisfaction. If you want to pursue industrial–organizational psychology as a graduate degree, be aware that this field requires extensive training in statistical and mathematical methods.

Believe it or not, we're not quite done yet. There are a few other types of psychologists we'd like you to know about, including social psychologists (see Chapter 13); personality psychologists (see Chapter 14); quantitative psychologists; cross-cultural psychologists; and sports psychologists. To learn more about these and other fields of psychology, as well as other career options for psychology majors (see **Figure P.4** on page 18), visit http://psychcareers.apa.org.

fictoid

Myth: If you want to become a psychotherapist, you don't need to learn about research.
Reality: The "scientist–practitioner model" of training—often called the "Boulder model" because it was formulated over a half century ago at a conference in Boulder, Colorado—is the predominant model for educating clinical psychology Ph.D. students. This model requires all graduate students, even those who intend to become therapists, to receive extensive training in how to interpret psychological research.

Most developmental psychologists are researchers who study the cognitions (thinking) and emotions of children using carefully controlled tasks.

Sports psychologist *(right)* discussing techniques for improving performance with an athlete. Sports psychologists apply well-documented psychological learning principles to diminish athletes' anxiety and enhance their success.

**Figure P.4 Some Famous and
Infamous Psychology Majors.** As we
can see from this figure, many famous—
and infamous—people have graduated
from college with majors in psychology.

"The title of my science project is
'My Little Brother: Nature or Nurture.'"

(© The New Yorker Collection 2003
Michael Shaw from cartoonbank.com.
All Rights Reserved)

By now, we hope we've persuaded you that the field of psychology is remarkably diverse. Moreover, the face of psychology is changing, with more women and minorities entering many of its subfields (see **Figure P.5** on page 19). Despite their differences in content, all of these areas of psychology have one thing in common: Most of the psychologists who specialize in them rely on scientific methods. Specifically, they use scientific methods to generate new findings about human or animal behavior—basic research—or use existing findings to enhance human welfare—applied research. Yet some psychologists don't adopt a scientific approach even though they claim to, a topic we'll delve into more in Chapter 1.

The Great Debates of Psychology

Before embarking on our journey through psychology, we need to set the stage for things to come. To do so, we'll introduce three Great Debates that have shaped the field of psychology since its inception. Because these debates are alive and well, we'll find traces of them in virtually all of the chapters of this book.

THE NATURE–NURTURE DEBATE

The nature–nurture debate poses the following question: *Are our behaviors attributable mostly to our genes (nature) or to our rearing environments (nurture)?*

Early Assumptions. As we'll discover later in this text, this debate has proven especially controversial in the domains of intelligence, personality, and psychopathology (mental illness). Like most major debates in psychology, this one has a lengthy history. Many early thinkers, such as British philosopher John Locke (1632–1704), likened the human mind at birth to white paper that hadn't been written on. Others after him referred to the mind as a *tabula rasa* ("blank slate"). For Locke and his followers, we enter the world with no genetic preconceptions or preconceived ideas: We're shaped exclusively by our environments (Pinker, 2002).

The Turning Tide. For much of the twentieth century, most psychologists assumed that virtually all human behavior was exclusively a product of learning. Nevertheless, the tide is now turning. Research conducted by *behavior geneticists,* who use sophisticated designs, like twin and adoption studies (see Chapter 3), shows that most important psychological traits, including intelligence, interests, personality, and many mental illnesses, are influenced substantially by genes. Increasingly, modern psychologists have come to recognize that human behavior is attributable not only to our environments but to our genes (Bouchard, 2004; Harris, 2002; Pinker, 2002).

One word of warning: The nature–nurture debate can be confusing because psychologists sometimes use this term to refer to two entirely different questions: (1) Which is more influential in the causes of a single person's behavior, genes or environment? (2) Which is more influential in the causes of the *differences among people,* genes or environment? These two questions often yield quite different answers. As we might guess, genes and environment both play important roles in any given person's behavior, and both often contribute to differences among people in their behaviors. But the relative balance differs depending on the psychological characteristics we're measuring. To take just one example, investigators have shown that genes account for more than half (and perhaps as much as 80 percent) of the differences among children in their risk for attention-deficit/hyperactivity disorder (ADHD), once known as childhood hyperactivity (Levy, Hay, McStephen, Wood, & Waldman, 1997). In contrast, differences among people in their religious affiliations are due almost entirely to their environments (Harris, 2002).

Current Status of the Nature–Nurture Debate. Some people have declared the nature–nurture debate dead (Ferris, 1996), because just about everyone now agrees that both genes and environment play crucial roles in most human behaviors. Yet this debate is far from dead, because we still have a great deal to learn about how much nature or nurture contribute to different behaviors, and how nature and nurture work together. Indeed, we'll discover in later chapters that the old dichotomy between nature and nurture is far less clear-cut—and far more interesting—than once believed. Nature and nurture sometimes interact in complex ways; for example, people with a certain genetic makeup who also experience life stressors are especially prone to clinical depression (Caspi et al., 2003; see Chapter 15). Nature and nurture, although separable, frequently cross paths in a variety of ways, many of them still poorly understood (see Chapter 10).

Evolutionary Psychology.   One domain of psychology that's shed light on the nature–nurture debate is **evolutionary psychology,** sometimes also called *sociobiology:* a discipline that applies Darwin's theory of natural selection to human and animal behavior (Barkow et al., 1992; Dennett, 1995; Tooby & Cosmides, 1989). It begins with the assumption, shared by William James and other functionalists, that many human psychological systems, like memory, emotion, and personality, serve key adaptive functions: They help organisms survive and reproduce. Darwin and his followers suggested that natural selection favored certain kinds of mental traits, just as it did physical ones, like our hands, livers, and hearts.

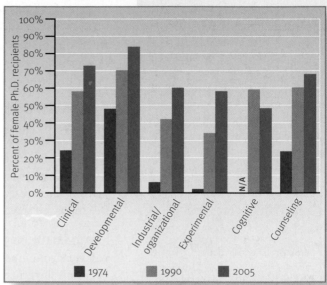

Figure P.5 **The Face of Psychology Has Changed Dramatically over the Past Three Decades.** Across most areas, the percentage of women earning doctoral degrees has increased. In clinical and developmental psychology, women comprise three-fourths to four-fifths of those attaining Ph.D.s. (*Source:* www.apa.org/monitor/jun07/changing .html)

Biologists refer to *fitness* as the extent to which a trait increases the chances that organisms that possess this trait will survive and reproduce at a higher rate than competitors who lack it (see Chapter 3). Fitness has nothing to do, by the way, with how strong or powerful an organism is. By surviving and reproducing at higher rates than other organisms, more fit organisms pass on their genes more successfully to later generations. For example, humans who have at least some degree of anxiety probably survived at higher rates than humans who lacked it, because anxiety serves an essential function: It warns us of impending danger (Barlow, 2001). Remember this point the next time you're crossing the street and become alarmed by a reckless driver whizzing past you. If you didn't experience anxiety, you might not have jumped out of the way.

Still, evolutionary psychology has received more than its share of criticism (de Waal, 2002; Kitcher, 1985; Panksepp & Panksepp, 2000); we'll consider two criticisms here. First, many of its predictions are extremely difficult to test. In part, that's because behavior, unlike the bones of dinosaurs, early humans, and other animals, doesn't leave fossils. As a consequence, it's far more challenging to determine the evolutionary functions of anxiety or depression than the functions of birds' wings.

Second, critics have argued that many evolutionary psychology hypotheses are **just-so stories** (Gould & Lewontin, 1979), that is, superficial explanations made up after the fact. This phrase derives from the title of a children's book by Rudyard Kipling, which featured fanciful stories of how leopards got their spots and camels got their humps. Indeed, some evolutionary hypotheses seem dubious at best. For example, two researchers speculated that male baldness serves an evolutionary function, because women supposedly perceive a receding hairline as a sign of maturity (Muscarella & Cunningham, 1996). This conjecture seems difficult to square with the fact that male hair replacement is a multibillion dollar a year industry in the United States alone (de Waal, 2002). Moreover, if it turned out that women preferred men with lots of hair to bald men, it would be just as easy to cook up an after-the-fact explanation for that finding ("Women perceive men with a full head of hair as stronger and more athletic"). Evolutionary psychology may one day prove to be an important unifying framework for psychology (Buss, 1995), but we should beware of evolutionary explanations that can fit almost any piece of evidence after the fact.

THE FREE WILL–DETERMINISM DEBATE

The free will–determinism debate poses the following question: *To what extent are our behaviors freely selected rather than caused by factors outside of our control?*

Free Will: Our Subjective Experience.   Most of us like to believe that we're free to select any course of events we wish. Fewer truths seem more self-evident than the fact that we're free to do what we want whenever we want. For example, you may believe that at this very moment you can decide to either continue reading to the end of the Prologue or take a

The fact that American men spend billions of dollars per year on hair replacement treatments is difficult to square with evolutionary hypotheses suggesting that women prefer bald men. The bottom line: Beware of evolutionary just-so stories.

evolutionary psychology
discipline that applies Darwin's theory of natural selection to human and animal behavior

just-so stories
superficial explanations made up after the fact; a term sometimes applied by critics to some evolutionary psychology hypotheses

Pioneering behaviorist B. F. Skinner, seen here with one of his rat "subjects," argued that free will is an illusion. According to Skinner, we believe we're free only because we're blissfully unaware of all of the environmental influences on our behaviors.

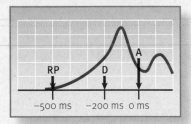

Figure P.6 Is Free Will Imaginary? The work of Benjamin Libet shows that our brain begins to ready itself to perform a movement about a third of a second—note the difference between 500 and 200 milliseconds (ms)—before we're even aware of our intention to do so. "RP" stands for readiness potential; "D" for the conscious decision to perform an action, in this case, lifting our finger; and "A" for the action itself. (*Source:* Adapted from Libet, 1985)

compatibilism
compromise between free will and determinism that says the two can coexist

well-deserved break to watch TV. Indeed, our legal system is premised on the concept of free will. We punish criminals because they're supposedly free to abide by the law, but choose otherwise. One major exception, of course, is the insanity defense (see Chapter 15), in which the legal system assumes that severe mental illness can interfere with people's free will (Hoffman & Morse, 2006; Stone, 1982).

Free Will: An Illusion? Many psychologists maintain that free will is actually an illusion (Wegner, 2002). It's such a powerful illusion, they insist, that we have a hard time imagining it could be an illusion. Some psychologists, like behaviorist B. F. Skinner, argue that our sense of free will stems from the fact that we aren't consciously aware of the thousands of subtle environmental influences impinging on our behavior at any given moment. Much like puppets in a play who don't realize that actors are pulling their strings, we conclude mistakenly that we're free simply because we don't realize all of the influences acting on our behavior.

Automatic Behaviors. If these psychologists are right, why does the illusion of free will seem so compelling to us? Some psychologists argue that most or even all of our behaviors are generated *automatically*—that is, without conscious awareness—even though we perceive them as under our control (Kirsch & Lynn, 1999; Wegner, 2002).

In an astonishing demonstration of this possibility, neuroscientist Benjamin Libet (1985) asked subjects to lift a finger whenever they wished. He also asked them to let him know as soon as they became consciously aware of their intention to perform this act. At the same time, Libet used electrodes (small devices that can be attached to the surface of the scalp, about which we'll learn in Chapter 3) to measure a brain wave known as the *readiness potential,* which is most prominent at the top of the head. This brain wave measures our preparedness for bodily action. Remarkably, Libet found that the readiness potential starts up about 300 milliseconds (that's about a third of a second) prior to our conscious awareness of the intention to move our finger. If you move the index finger of your right hand right now (go ahead, try it), you'll almost certainly perceive that movement as under your control. Yet Libet's work suggests that this sense of control is imaginary (see **Figure P.6**).

Lack of Access to the Causes of Our Behavior. Research on automatic behaviors suggests that we often perceive our behaviors as freely controlled even when they're determined. As Richard Nisbett and Timothy Wilson (1977) pointed out, we probably lack direct access to the causes of most of our behaviors. Nevertheless, when asked, we'll happily oblige by offering a reason for why we did something, even though this reason may be wildly off base. If we ask a friend, "Why did you just twirl your hair?" our friend may respond, "Oh, I was thinking about my upcoming psychology exam and was nervous. I always find that twirling my hair relieves tension." This plausible-sounding response implies that the hair twirling was under your friend's conscious control. But this response may simply be a plausible after-the-fact explanation for a behavior that your friend didn't perform freely. Nisbett and Wilson's arguments, by the way, provide another strike against the structuralists' exclusive reliance on introspection.

A Compromise? Some psychologists have proposed a compromise between free will and determinism called **compatibilism.** According to compatibilists, free will and determinism aren't mutually exclusive; our genes and environments greatly limit our behavioral choices, but we retain the freedom to select certain options and reject others (Dennett, 1984; Sappington, 1990). Nevertheless, most scholars discount compatibilism as illogical. For them, it makes no more sense to say that we can be "partly free" than to say a woman can be "partly pregnant." We're either free or we're not.

THE MIND–BODY DEBATE

The mind–body debate poses the following question: *Are our behaviors due entirely to the action of the brain and nervous system or are they also due to the action of a nonmaterial entity, like a soul?*

The "Duel" between Monism and Dualism.   There are two opposing camps here. **Mind–body monists,** who include most scientific psychologists, believe that the "mind" is just the brain and nervous system in action (Crick, 1995; Pinker, 1997). According to them, the mind is the product of the actions of billions of nerve cells working in tandem. In contrast, **mind–body dualists,** who go back at least to the French philosopher René Descartes (pronounced day-cart) (1596–1650), believe that the mind is more than the brain and nervous system. Although not denying that our behaviors are due partly to the actions of the brain and nervous system, dualists maintain that the brain and nervous system will never be sufficient to explain behavior. According to dualists, that's because at least some behavior is produced by a mysterious nonmaterial entity that can't be measured, like the soul.

A Debate That Science Can't Resolve.   The mind–body debate—which should probably be called the mind–brain debate—is probably impossible to resolve scientifically. We can't test the claim that a soul or other nonmaterial essence exists, so we'll probably never know for sure. Still, regardless of their beliefs about this question, most psychologists operate as mind–body monists when they conduct their research. They adopt monism as a working scientific assumption, while recognizing that, as Hamlet told Horatio in Shakespeare's great play, there might always be "more things in Heaven and earth than are dreamt of in [their] philosophy."

   Press Coverage of the Mind–Body Debate.   The mind–body debate runs through a great deal of popular psychology. As we'll learn in Chapter 15, modern brain imaging studies are demonstrating consistent links between specific psychological disorders and activations in specific brain areas. For example, schizophrenia is characterized by abnormally low levels of activity in certain parts of the brain's frontal lobes. Such findings would seem to be a point in favor of mind–body monism.

Yet when reporting such findings, the popular press typically behaves as though they were mind–body dualists (Bloom, 2004). For example, after the publication of a brain imaging study linking schizophrenia to certain brain areas, we'll frequently see headlines like "Schizophrenia Shown to Be Brain Disease." If we think about this headline for a moment, we'll realize that it actually presumes a mind–body dualist position. The headline suggests that before the results of the study were published, the newspaper editor who penned the headline presumably thought that schizophrenia *wasn't* necessarily a disorder of the brain. If the editor were truly a mind–body monist, she would have taken the assertion that "schizophrenia is a brain disease" as a given regardless of the study's results.

The Psychology Journey

In this prologue, we hope we've given you a taste of the fascinating subject matter of psychology, as well as a bird's-eye view of how the modern science of psychology came to be. As we've discovered, psychologists have made substantial strides in understanding human behavior and applying this knowledge to everyday life. They've also learned that the human mind can be fooled—and can even fool itself. As a result, understanding human nature is fraught with challenges, and sorting out fact from fiction in psychology is rarely easy. As we'll soon learn, the world of popular psychology, including the media and Internet, has often made this difficult task even more challenging. In coming chapters, we'll be providing you with a user's guide for distinguishing what's true from what's not in the vast field of psychology. You'll come to better appreciate what we know, how we know it, and what we believe to be true that isn't. Now that we've whetted your appetite, we invite you to join us on the journey and enjoy the rest of the book.

---

factoid

Descartes believed that the mind and brain made contact in a pea-sized area of the brain called the *pineal gland,* which he believed housed the soul. He held this belief because, in contrast to almost all other parts of the brain, there's only one pineal gland—it's not present on both the left and right sides of the brain.

mind–body monists
scientists who believe that the mind is the brain and nervous system in action

mind–body dualists
scientists who believe that the mind is more than the brain and nervous system

---

DO YOU KNOW THESE TERMS?

1
Science and Pseudoscience in Psychology
Skills for Thinking Scientifically in Everyday Life

For most of you reading this book, this is your first psychology course; for others, it may be your second or third. But it's a safe bet you believe you've learned an awful lot about psychology already. Pause for a moment and ask yourself: "Where have I learned what I know about psychology?"

Science versus Popular Psychology: Common versus Uncommon Sense

If you're like most beginning psychology students, you've gleaned much of what you know about psychology from watching television programs and movies, listening to radio call-in shows, reading self-help books and popular magazines, surfing the Internet, and talking to friends. In short, most of your psychology knowledge probably derives from the **popular psychology industry:** a sprawling network of everyday sources of information about human behavior.

Just how trustworthy is the information generated by this industry? To find out, let's consider the following fifteen notions that many of us take for granted, and that are deeply ingrained in the popular psychology of our culture. Take no more than 60 seconds total to read these statements and decide whether each is correct. Then, using your pen, pencil, or highlighter, circle *True* or *False*. Ready? Okay, begin.

The image of the hypnotist and swinging watch is among the most familiar in all of popular psychology. But how much of hypnosis is scientific?

Test of Popular Psychology Knowledge

TRUE	FALSE	(1)	Most people use only about 10 percent of their brain capacity.
TRUE	FALSE	(2)	Drinking coffee is a good way to sober up after heavy drinking.
TRUE	FALSE	(3)	Newborn babies are virtually blind and deaf.
TRUE	FALSE	(4)	The memory of everything we've experienced is stored permanently in our brains, even if we can't access all of it.
TRUE	FALSE	(5)	Hypnosis can help us to recall things we've forgotten.
TRUE	FALSE	(6)	If you're unsure of your answer while taking a test, it's best to stick with your initial answer.
TRUE	FALSE	(7)	All people with dyslexia see words backward (like *tac* instead of *cat*)
TRUE	FALSE	(8)	Psychologists have shown that dreams consist of symbolic representations of unconscious processes.
TRUE	FALSE	(9)	In general, it's better to express anger than to hold it in.
TRUE	FALSE	(10)	The lie-detector (polygraph) test is 90 to 95 percent accurate at detecting falsehoods.
TRUE	FALSE	(11)	People tend to be romantically attracted to individuals who are opposite to them in personality and attitudes.
TRUE	FALSE	(12)	The more people present at an emergency, the more likely it is that at least one of them will help.
TRUE	FALSE	(13)	High self-esteem is crucial for good psychological adjustment.
TRUE	FALSE	(14)	Schizophrenics have more than one personality.
TRUE	FALSE	(15)	All effective psychotherapies require clients to get to the root of their problems in childhood.

If you're like most students taking their first psychology course, you'll probably assume that most or even all of these statements are true. That's hardly surprising, as they've become part of popular psychology lore. Moreover, most of them strike us as resonating

popular psychology industry
sprawling network of everyday sources of information about human behavior

with our common sense. So you may be surprised to learn that *all* of these fifteen statements are false!

COMMON AND UNCOMMON SENSE

This little exercise illustrates a take-home message we'll emphasize throughout the text: *Although common sense can be enormously useful for some purposes, it's sometimes completely wrong.* As the French writer Voltaire noted, "Common sense is not especially common." Or putting it somewhat differently, our intuitive understanding of ourselves and the world is frequently mistaken (Cacioppo, 2004; van Hecke, 2007). In fact, at times our commonsensical understanding of psychology isn't merely incorrect, but entirely backward. For example, although many people believe the old adage "There's safety in numbers" (statement #12), psychological research actually shows that the more people present at an emergency, the *less* likely it is that at least one of them will help (Darley & Latané, 1968; Latané & Nida, 1981; see Chapter 13).

If you assumed that many of the fifteen statements were true, you shouldn't feel bad, because you're in good company. Surveys show that many introductory psychology students believe these statements are correct, even though research contradicts them (Lamal, 1979; McCutcheon, 1991; Taylor & Kowalski, 2004; Vaughan, 1977).

Throughout this text, we'll learn about research that debunks widespread misconceptions about psychology, including the fifteen we've presented. If you're like most readers, you may initially resist some of what we have to say. That's entirely to be expected, because few of us enjoy discovering that our cherished beliefs are mistaken. We'll ask you only to keep an open mind when reading about research findings that challenge your preconceptions.

Here's another illustration of why we can't always trust our common sense. Read the following well-known proverbs, most of which deal with human behavior, and ask yourself whether you agree with them.

Marriages like that of Mary Matalin, a prominent conservative political strategist, and James Carville, a prominent liberal political strategist, may contribute to the common sense belief that opposites attract. Yet psychological research shows that such marriages are marked exceptions: People are generally drawn to others who are similar to them in beliefs and values.

(1) Look before you leap.

(2) Birds of a feather flock together.

(3) Absence makes the heart grow fonder.

(4) Better safe than sorry.

(5) Two heads are better than one.

(6) The bigger, the better.

(7) Actions speak louder than words.

(8) Clothes make the man.

(9) The more the merrier.

(10) You can't teach an old dog new tricks.

Most or all of these proverbs are hard to quarrel with, right? Now read these ten familiar proverbs.

(1) He who hesitates is lost.

(2) Opposites attract.

(3) Out of sight, out of mind.

(4) Nothing ventured, nothing gained.

(5) Too many cooks spoil the broth.

(6) Good things come in small packages.

(7) The pen is mightier than the sword.

(8) Don't judge a book by its cover.

(9) Two's company, three's a crowd.

(10) You're never too old to learn.

These proverbs similarly ring true, don't they? Yet each of these proverbs contradicts the same-numbered proverb from the first list! So our common sense can lead us to believe two things that can't both be true simultaneously, or at least that are largely at odds with each other. Strangely enough, in most cases we never notice the contradictions until other people, like the authors of an introductory psychology textbook, point them out to us.

NAIVE REALISM: SEEING IS BELIEVING, OR IS IT?

As psychologist Lee Ross noted, we trust our common sense largely because we're prone to **naive realism**: the belief that we see the world precisely as it is (Ross & Ward, 1996). We assume that "seeing is believing" and trust our intuitive perceptions of the world and ourselves. In daily life, naive realism often serves us well. If we're driving down a one-lane

naive realism
belief that we see the world precisely as it is

Figure 1.1 Naive Realism Can Fool Us.
Even though our perceptions are often accurate, we can't always trust them to provide us with an error-free picture of the world. In this case, take a look at *Shepard's tables*, courtesy of psychologist Roger Shepard. Believe it or not, the tops of these tables are identical in size: one can be directly superimposed on top of the other (get out a ruler if you don't believe us!). (*Source:* Shepard, 1990)

Here's another case in which our naive realism can trick us. Take a look at these two upside-down photos of George W. Bush. They look quite similar, if not identical. Now turn your book upside-down. (*Source:* Based on Thompson, 1980)

road and see a tractor trailer barreling toward us at 85 miles per hour, it's a wise idea to get out of the way. Much of the time, we *should* trust our perceptions.

Yet appearances can sometimes be deceiving. The earth *seems* flat. The sun *seems* to revolve around the earth, as we watch the sun paint a large semicircle across the sky each day as our feet remain planted firmly on the ground. We *seem* to be standing—or sitting—entirely still. Yet we now know that the earth is round, that the earth revolves around the sun, and that at this very moment we're all hurtling through space at a breathtaking 18.5 miles per second (see **Figure 1.1**).

Similarly, naive realism can trip us up when it comes to evaluating ourselves and others. Our common sense tells us that our memories accurately capture virtually everything we've seen, although scientific research demonstrates otherwise (Loftus, 1997; see Chapter 7). Our common sense also assures us that people who don't share our political views are biased, but that we're objective. Yet psychological research demonstrates that we're all susceptible to evaluating political issues in a biased fashion (Pronin, Gilovich, & Ross, 2004). So our tendencies toward naive realism can lead us to draw erroneous conclusions about human nature. In many cases, "believing is seeing" rather than the reverse: Our beliefs shape our perceptions of the world (Gilovich, 1991).

WHEN OUR COMMON SENSE IS RIGHT

That's not to say that our common sense is always wrong. Our intuition comes in handy in many situations and sometimes guides us to the truth (Gigerenzer, 2007; Gladwell, 2005; Myers, 2002). For example, our snap (5-second) judgments about whether someone we've just watched on a videotape is trustworthy or untrustworthy tend to be right more often than would be expected by chance (Fowler, Lilienfeld, & Patrick, 2007). Common sense can also be a helpful guide for generating hypotheses that scientists can later test in rigorous investigations (Redding, 1998). Moreover, some everyday psychological notions are indeed correct. For example, most people believe that happy employees tend to be more productive on the job than unhappy employees, and research indicates that they're right (Kluger & Tikochinsky, 2001).

But to think like scientific psychologists, we must learn when to trust our common sense and when not to. Doing so will help us become more informed consumers of popular psychology and make better real-world decisions. One of our major goals in this text is to provide you with thinking tools for making this crucial distinction. These thinking tools should help you to better evaluate psychological claims in everyday life.

TRUTH IS OFTEN STRANGER THAN FICTION

Yet psychology is about far more than challenging our common sense and debunking false claims. In this text, we'll learn a great deal not only about what isn't true about the mind, but also about what *is* true. For example, we'll learn about remarkable psychological findings, like the following:

- Patients whose corpus callosum (a large band of fibers connecting the brain's left and right hemispheres) has been surgically removed show many unusual behaviors. For example, when researchers flash a photograph of a naked person to the right side of their brains, they may laugh. Yet when asked why they laughed, they can't offer any good reason.

- Pigeons can distinguish paintings by Monet from paintings by Picasso and music by Bach from music by Stravinsky.

- Some people, especially children, possess true "photographic memories": When shown a painting for a few seconds they're later able to recall astonishing details, such as the number of bands on a cat's tail, with minimal effort.

- People with extreme forms of anterograde amnesia, a severe memory disorder, can't consciously recall any new information they've learned, and may repeatedly (even over many years) express catastrophic shock when told of the death of the same family member.

- People exposed repeatedly to certain nonsense syllables—like *zab* or *gar*—beneath the level of consciousness later prefer these syllables to other nonsense syllables, even though they're unaware of having ever seen any of them.

- People who watch cartoons while holding a pen between their teeth tend to find these cartoons funnier than do people who watch these cartoons with a pen between their lips.

- A man who meets a woman on a swaying bridge will typically find her more attractive than a man who meets her on a steady bridge.

- Many complex human behaviors and preferences, including divorce, religiosity, and television viewing, are influenced substantially by genetic factors.

- Some people suffer from a bizarre condition called apotemnophilia, which is marked by an overpowering desire to have one's limbs amputated.

As many of these findings demonstrate, psychological truth is often far more remarkable—and even more fascinating—than psychological fiction. A good deal of what we'll learn in this text is difficult to believe, but it's been well supported by research.

THE AMAZING GROWTH OF POPULAR PSYCHOLOGY

The popular psychology industry is expanding rapidly. On the positive side, this fact means that the American public has unprecedented access to psychological knowledge. On the negative side, the remarkable growth of popular psychology has led not only to an information explosion but to a *misinformation explosion,* because there's scant quality control over what this industry produces.

In most major bookstores, the self-help section is larger than the psychology section. Although studies show that many self-help books can be helpful, only a small fraction of them have ever been tested in scientific studies.

Self-Help and the Media. To take just one example, about 3,500 self-help books are published every year (Arkowitz & Lilienfeld, 2006), although only a handful are written or even screened by scientific experts. Investigators have found some of these books to be effective for treating depression, anxiety, and other psychological problems, but about 95 percent of them remain untested (Gould & Clum, 1993; Gregory, Canning, Lee, & Wise, 2004; Rosen, 1993). Still other self-help books may actually make certain psychological conditions worse (Rosen, Glasgow, & Moore, 2003). And although some self-help books contain high-quality and scientifically supported information, others are misleading, even dangerous. For example, some of these books encourage readers who suspect they might have been sexually abused in childhood to try hard to "remember" the abuse. Yet this procedure may increase many readers' risk for false memories of abuse (Lindsay & Read, 1994).

The Internet is doubling in size about every 6 months (Levine, Young, & Baroudi, 2003). When Bill Clinton became president of the United States in 1992, there were about fifty sites on the Internet; today, there are more than 135 million and still counting. Yet when it comes to the tens of thousands of Internet sites concerning psychology, it's anyone's guess as to how many contain scientifically accurate information. In fact, a substantial proportion of Internet sites dealing with mental or medical health contain either incorrect or incomplete information (Lissman & Boehnlein, 2001; Matthews, Camacho, Mills, & Dimsdale, 2003). Perhaps it's not surprising that the general public is often misinformed about mental illness and its treatment. For example, most laypersons believe that diets and vitamins are more effective for depression than are antidepressant medications, even though research suggests otherwise (Jorm et al., 1997).

Scores of television programs regularly feature self-proclaimed psychics, who claim to read others' minds or foretell the future, or "channelers," who claim to communicate with the spirits of deceased loved ones (Mooney, 2003). Yet when psychics have been put to the test in tightly controlled scientific studies, they've almost always flopped (Hines, 2003).

Quick Fixes. Coinciding with the rapid expansion of the popular psychology industry is the enormous growth of treatments and products that purport to cure almost every

fict**oid**

Myth: Physicists and other "hard" scientists are more skeptical about most extraordinary claims, like extrasensory perception, than psychologists are.

Reality: Academic psychologists are more skeptical of many controversial claims than their colleagues in more traditional sciences are. For example, psychologists are considerably less likely to believe that extrasensory perception is an established scientific fact than physicists, chemists, and biologists are (Wagner & Monnet, 1979).

Table 1.1 Some Trustworthy Websites for Scientific Psychology.

Organization / URL
American Psychological Association *www.apa.org*
Association for Psychological Science *www.psychologicalscience.org*
Canadian Psychological Association *www.cpa.ca*
American Psychiatric Association *www.psych.org*
Society for General Psychology *www.apa.org/divisions/div1/ div1homepage.html*
Association for Behavioral and Cognitive Therapies *www.aabt.org*
Psychonomic Society *www.psychonomic.org*
Association for Behavior Analysis *www.abainternational.org*
Society for Research in Child Development *www.srcd.org*
Society for Personality and Social Psychology *www.spsp.org*
Society for Research in Psychopathology *www.psychopathology.org*
Society for a Science of Clinical Psychology *http://pantheon.yale.edu/~tat22*
Scientific Review of Mental Health Practice *www.srmhp.org*
Center for Evidence-Based Mental Health *http://cebmh.warne.ox.ac.uk/ cebmh*
Empirically Supported Treatments for Psychological Disorders *www.apa.org/divisions/div12/ rev_est*
***Skeptical Inquirer* magazine** *www.csicop.org/si*
***Skeptic* magazine** *www.skeptic.com*

imaginable psychological ailment. There are well over 500 "brands" of psychotherapy (Eisner, 2000), with new ones being added every year. Fortunately, as we'll learn in Chapter 16, research shows that some of these treatments are clearly helpful for depression, anxiety disorders, eating disorders, sleep difficulties, and a host of other psychological problems. Yet the substantial majority of psychotherapies remain untested, so we don't know whether they help. Some may even be harmful (Lilienfeld, 2007).

Proponents of certain psychotherapies even promise virtual "miracle cures." For example, many advocates of "Thought Field Therapy," a treatment that claims to alleviate severe anxiety by tapping on body areas that supposedly radiate important psychological "energies," report cure rates of 98 percent (Lohr, Hooke, Gist, & Tolin, 2003). Researchers have never verified this 98 percent figure. By the way, we should be skeptical anytime we hear claims of "cures" rather than "treatments" for psychological disorders, because even the best psychological treatments aren't magic wands that make people's problems disappear. More and more companies are marketing herbal remedies for improving our memories, increasing our intelligence, combating our depression, or enhancing our sex lives. Yet most of these remedies are either untested or ineffective (Gold, Cahill, & Wenk, 2003; McDaniel, Maier, & Einstein, 2002; Walach & Kirsch, 2003; also see Chapter 7).

Popular Psychology as Information. Certainly, a good deal of popular psychology wisdom is useful. Radio and television talk show psychologists are right to remind us that we should take responsibility for our mistakes, parents need to provide appropriate discipline for their children, and early sexual intercourse and drug use are dangerous.

The popular psychology industry also contains plenty of accurate information about human behavior, although we need to know where to find it. Some self-help books base their recommendations on solid research about psychological problems and their treatment. We can often find excellent articles in the *New York Times, Scientific American Mind,* and *Discover* magazines and other media outlets that present high-quality information regarding the science of psychology. In addition, hundreds of websites provide remarkably helpful information and advice concerning a host of psychological topics, like memory, personality testing, and psychological disorders and their treatment (see **Table 1.1**). The average American of the early twenty-first century knows far more about the workings of the brain or the symptoms of infantile autism, for example, than did the average American of only 20 or 30 years ago.

Popular Psychology as Misinformation. The central problem is that it's often difficult to tell the difference between popular psychology information and misinformation, because they can look surprisingly similar on the surface. Without clear guidance, we can be fooled. Read on.

When we examine the image at the top of page 29, we'll see what at first looks to be an advertisement for a legitimate product. It's an ad for a set of recordings that supposedly allow us to listen to *subliminal messages,* that is, messages that aren't consciously perceived but that supposedly affect behavior (see Chapter 4). According to the ad, these messages will cause us to lose weight. Yet the ad conveniently leaves out one key piece of information: The developer of this program has never demonstrated that it works. In fact, as we'll learn in Chapter 4, there's no solid research evidence that subliminal messages exert long-term effects on our actions or attitudes, let alone our weight. Still, subliminal self-help tapes continue to be a multimillion-dollar-a-year industry in North America alone (Moore, 1992; Rosen, Glasgow, & Moore, 2003).

The bottom line is clear. Be open to claims about psychological products in ads, but don't believe everything you read. *Insist on evidence.*

Distinguishing Psychological Information from Misinformation: Navigating the Maze. Although we defined the popular psychology industry as a "sprawling network of everyday sources of information about human behavior," we've already seen that the true story is more complicated. This industry is a bewildering mix of both accurate and inaccurate information. Many popular psychology sources, including some newspapers and television documentaries, do a superb job of presenting psychological knowledge. But others are more concerned about telling a good story than conveying scientifically accurate information. In their understandable desire to stimulate readers' interest or distill complicated findings into a few paragraphs, they may cut corners or present an incomplete picture of psychological knowledge.

So, let's take stock of what we've learned. We've discovered that the popular psychology industry is a confusing landscape of accurate and inaccurate information. It's a remarkably valuable resource, but we need a road map to make effective use of it. That's a challenging task, because this industry offers us minimal guidance for finding our way through the minefield of often contradictory claims. Fortunately, there's a reasonably dependable, although not perfect, means of sorting the wheat from the chaff in popular psychology. It's called science.

PSYCHOLOGY AS A SCIENCE

A few years ago, one of our academic colleagues was advising a psychology major about his career plans. Out of curiosity, he asked him, "So why did you decide to go into psychology?" He responded, "Well, I took a lot of science courses and realized I didn't like science, so I picked psychology instead."

We're going to try to persuade you that the student was wrong—not about selecting a psychology major, that is, but about psychology not being a science. A central theme of this text is that modern psychology, or at least hefty chunks of it, are scientific. But what does the word *science* really mean, anyway?

What's Science, Anyway? Most students think that *science* is just a word for all of that really complicated stuff they learn in their biology, chemistry, and physics classes. But science isn't a body of knowledge. Instead, it's an *approach* to evidence (Bunge, 1998). Specifically, science is a toolbox of skills designed to prevent us from fooling ourselves. As Nobel Prize–winning physicist Richard Feynman (1985) pointed out, science is a means of bending over backward to prove ourselves wrong.

Scientific Attitudes: Approaches to Knowledge. Science carries with it a set of attitudes about knowledge. Foremost among them is what sociologist Robert Merton (1942) called **communalism,** meaning a willingness to share our findings with others. Merton called this willingness *communalism* because it underscores the point that scientists are part of a *community* of scholars who work together. Without communalism, the scientific enterprise grinds to a screeching halt, because research progress hinges on the ability to evaluate other investigators' findings objectively.

Another crucial scientific attitude is what Merton called **disinterestedness,** meaning that scientists should try their best to be objective when evaluating evidence (it doesn't mean, by the way, that scientists aren't interested in what they do!). That is, scientists should try not to be influenced by personal or financial investments in their research. Disinterestedness is easier said than done, because scientists are human and therefore almost inevitably biased to some degree. So what distinguishes good scientists from bad ones?

Science as a Safeguard against Bias: Protecting Us from Ourselves. One critical distinction is that the best scientists are aware of their biases, or at least aware they have them. In particular, the best scientists realize that they *want* their pet theories to turn out to be correct. After all, they've invested months or even years in designing and running a study to test a theory, sometimes a theory they've developed. If the results of the study are negative, they'll often be bitterly disappointed. They also know that because of this deep personal investment, they may bias the results unintentionally to make them turn out the way they want. We say "unintentionally," because as we'll learn in Chapter 2 there are numerous ways in which researchers can distort the design and execution of studies, and the interpretation of results, without even realizing it. Scientists are prone to self-deception, just like the rest of us mere mortals.

Confirmation Bias. To protect themselves against bias, good scientists adopt procedural safeguards against errors, especially errors that could work in their favor (see Chapter 2).

Subliminal self-help tapes supposedly influence behavior by means of messages delivered to the unconscious. But do they really work?

Arthur Darbishire (1879–1915), a British geneticist and mathematician. Darbishire's favorite saying was that the attitude of the scientist should be "one of continual, unceasing, and active distrust of oneself."

communalism
willingness to share our findings with others

disinterestedness
attempt to be objective when evaluating the evidence

In other words, science is a set of tools for overcoming **confirmation bias:** the tendency to seek out evidence that supports our hypotheses and neglect or distort evidence that contradicts them (Nickerson, 1998; Risen & Gilovich, 2007). We can sum up confirmation bias in five words: *Seek and ye shall find.*

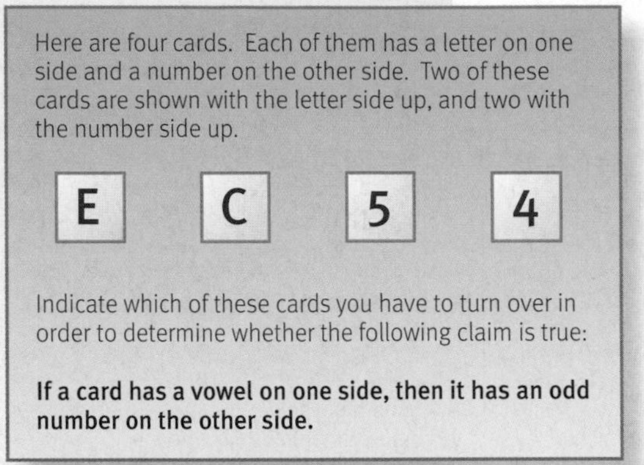

Here are four cards. Each of them has a letter on one side and a number on the other side. Two of these cards are shown with the letter side up, and two with the number side up.

E	C	5	4

Indicate which of these cards you have to turn over in order to determine whether the following claim is true:

If a card has a vowel on one side, then it has an odd number on the other side.

Figure 1.2 Diagram of Wason Selection Task. In the Wason selection task, you must pick two cards to test the hypothesis that all cards that have a vowel on one side have an odd number on the other. Which two will you select?

Because of confirmation bias, our preconceptions often lead us to focus on evidence that supports our beliefs, resulting in psychological tunnel vision. One of the simplest demonstrations of confirmation bias comes from research on the *Wason selection task* (Wason, 1966), an example of which we can find in **Figure 1.2.** There we'll see four cards, each of which has a number on one side, and a letter on the other. Your task is to determine whether the following hypothesis is correct: *All cards that have a vowel on one side have an odd number on the other.* To test this hypothesis, you need to select *two* cards to turn over. Which two will you pick? Decide on your two cards before reading further.

Most people pick the cards showing E and 5. If you selected E, you were right, so give yourself one point there. But if you selected 5, you've fallen prey to confirmation bias, although you'd be in good company because most people make this mistake. Although 5 *seems* to be a correct choice, it can only confirm the hypothesis, not disconfirm it. Think of it this way: If there's a vowel on the other side of the 5 card, that doesn't rule out the possibility that the 4 card has a vowel on the other side, which would disconfirm the hypothesis. So the 4 card is actually the other card to turn over, as that's the only other card that could disconfirm the hypothesis.

Confirmation bias wouldn't be especially interesting if it were limited to cards with numbers and letters. What makes confirmation bias so important is that it extends to myriad domains of our daily lives (Nickerson, 1998). For example, Mark Snyder and William Swann asked subjects to find out whether another person was an extravert or an introvert, and they gave these subjects numerous questions from which to choose in making this determination. In testing the hypothesis that the person was extraverted, subjects frequently picked the question, "What would you do if you wanted to liven things up at a party?" (Snyder & Swann, 1978). Yet this question is virtually useless in this context, because it's a recipe for confirmation bias. That's because even extreme introverts can easily come up with a good answer to this question ("Well, I guess I'd go up to some people I don't know and crack some jokes").

Interestingly, tape recordings of the conversations, coded by independent observers, revealed that when Snyder and Swann instructed subjects to find out whether the person was extraverted, that person actually behaved in a more extraverted fashion than when they instructed subjects to find out whether the person was introverted—and vice versa when they instructed subjects to find out whether the person was introverted. Confirmation bias can create a self-fulfilling prophecy, lending credence to the very hypothesis we have in mind. Beliefs can create reality.

APPLY YOUR THINKING

If you wanted to find out whether a person is extraverted, what kinds of questions could help you to avoid confirmation bias?

As anyone who's followed a political campaign knows, confirmation bias also affects how we evaluate candidates for political office (Tavris & Aronson, 2007). Of course, it's only people on the *other* side of the political spectrum who fall prey to confirmation bias, not us. At least that's how it seems.

Drew Westen and his colleagues discovered this double standard in a study of political partisans during the 2004 U.S. presidential election between George W. Bush and John Kerry (Westen, Kilts, Blagov, Harenski, & Hamann, 2006). They recruited a group of subjects who were extremely pro-Bush and another group who were extremely pro-Kerry. Then they presented all subjects with one statement from each candidate, say, one indicating

confirmation bias
tendency to seek out evidence that supports our hypotheses and neglect or distort evidence that contradicts them

that he strongly supported funding the war in Iraq, followed by a second statement from that candidate that contradicted it, say, one indicating that he later opposed funding the war in Iraq. Bush supporters perceived little, if any, contradiction in the statements of their man, whereas they perceived Kerry's statements as proof positive of flip-flopping. Kerry supporters displayed precisely the opposite pattern. So all subjects forgave their favored candidate for contradicting himself while faulting the opposing candidate for doing the same. Furthermore, brain imaging (see Chapter 3) showed that all subjects exhibited activity in their orbitofrontal cortex (a part of the brain immediately behind our eyes) while evaluating their candidate's contradictions, suggesting emotional processing. Like Westen's subjects, most of us become defensive when confronted with contradictions in our points of view or those of people on our "home team." But we quickly find ways of minimizing these contradictions or explaining them away.

Most of us believe that we evaluate political information objectively. Yet psychological research suggests that when our favorite presidential candidates contradict themselves, we quickly forgive them and explain away the inconsistency. But when candidates we don't like contradict themselves, we criticize them as hypocritical.

Although we'll be encountering a variety of biases in this text, we can think of confirmation bias as the "mother of all biases." That's because it's the bias that can most easily fool us into seeing what we want to see. For that reason, it's also the most crucial bias that scientists need to counteract. Incidentally, scientists are probably just as prone to confirmation bias as everyone else (Meehl, 1993). For example, research shows that academic psychologists are more likely to recommend an article for publication if the findings are consistent with their favorite theory of behavior than if they aren't (Mahoney, 1977). What distinguishes scientists from nonscientists is that the former adopt systematic safeguards to protect against confirmation bias, whereas the latter don't. We'll learn about these safeguards in Chapter 2.

Scientists must be especially wary of confirmation bias when they're deeply invested in a theory personally. Being overly ego-involved in one's cherished ideas is dangerous, as it can lead researchers to wear blinders, screening out or misinterpreting evidence that runs counter to their theories (Greenwald, Pratkanis, Leippe, & Baumgardner, 1986). As psychologist Edwin Boring (1964) noted, "A theory which has built up its author's image of himself has become part of him. To abandon it would be suicidal or at least an act of self-mutilation" (p. 682).

Confirmation bias can also lead psychologists to design studies to confirm their theories rather than disconfirm them, which is a poor way of doing science. Ideally, psychologists should be constructing their studies to maximize the odds that their findings will *disprove* their theories. This doesn't always happen, especially when they're married to their theories. As the great psychologist Edward Bradford Titchener advised wisely, all psychological scientists—and psychology students, we might add—should "know all theories, love a few, but wed none."

Belief Perseverance: It's My Story and I'm Sticking to It. Confirmation bias can predispose us to another shortcoming to which we're all prone: **belief perseverance.** Belief perseverance refers to the tendency to stick to our initial beliefs even when evidence contradicts them. In everyday parlance, belief perseverance is the "don't confuse me with the facts" effect. Because none of us wants to believe we're wrong, we're usually reluctant to give up our cherished notions. Indeed, as evidence against our deep-seated beliefs mounts, we often search desperately for evidence that confirms them. More often than not, we'll manage to find it.

In a striking demonstration of belief perseverance, Lee Ross and his colleagues asked students to inspect fifty suicide notes and determine which were genuine and which were fake (in reality, half were genuine, half fake). They then gave the students feedback on how well they did. Unbeknownst to students, this feedback bore no relation to their actual performance. Instead, the researchers randomly told some students they were good at detecting real suicide notes and others they were bad at it. *Even after investigators told the students that their feedback was completely bogus*—which it was—the students based their estimates of ability on the feedback they'd received. That is, students told they were good

belief perseverance
tendency to stick to our initial beliefs even when evidence contradicts them

at detecting real suicide notes were convinced they were better at it than students told they were bad at it. In contrast to the second group of students, the first group of students even predicted they'd do well on a similar task in the future (Ross, Lepper, & Hubbard, 1975).

Beliefs endure. Even when informed we're wrong, we don't completely wipe our mental slates clean and start from scratch.

Frequently, newspapers present headlines of medical and psychological findings, only to retract them weeks or months later. How can we know how much trust to place in them?

Recognizing That We Might Be Wrong. Good scientists are keenly aware that they might be mistaken (Sagan, 1995). They try to avoid belief perseverance, even though they know that surrendering their favorite hypotheses can be painful. In fact, initial scientific conclusions are often wrong, or at least partly off base. Medical findings are prime examples. Breast self-exams reduce the risk of breast cancer; oops, no, they don't. Drinking a little red wine now and then is good for you; no, actually, it's bad for you. Estrogen reduces the risk of heart attacks; oh, sorry about that, it increases the risk of heart attacks. And on and on it goes. It's no wonder that many people just throw up their hands and give up reading medical reports altogether. A recent study (Ioannidis, 2005) showed that nearly one-third of findings from published medical studies don't hold up in later studies (of course, we have to wonder: Do we know for sure that the results of *this* study will hold up?). Scientific knowledge is almost always tentative and potentially open to revision.

The news media frequently compound this confusion by reporting scientific findings, including psychological findings, as though they were etched in stone (Taubes, 2007). For example, we might read the headline, "Researchers prove that drinking too much coffee makes people more likely to develop depression." Yet rarely do the news media report findings with all of the necessary qualifiers. For example, they might not mention that the coffee and depression study was conducted only on people receiving psychotherapy, who are more prone to depression to begin with. Nor do the news media typically convey the crucial point that we shouldn't place too much trust in any one finding.

The fact that science is a process of perpetually revising and updating findings lends it strength as a method of inquiry. But it means that we usually acquire knowledge slowly and in small bits and pieces.

Science and Humility. One way of characterizing this process is to describe science as a *prescription for humility* (McFall, 1996). Good scientists never claim to "prove" anything and try to avoid committing to definitive conclusions unless the evidence clearly supports them. Such phrases as "suggests," "appears," and "raises the possibility that" are widespread in scientific writing and allow scientists to remain tentative in their interpretations of findings. Many beginning students understandably find this hemming and hawing frustrating and difficult to understand.

Yet as Carl Sagan (1995) observed, the best scientists hear a little voice in their heads that keeps repeating the same words: "But I might be wrong." Or as psychologists Carol Tavris and Elliot Aronson (2007) reminded us, science is a remedy for "arrogance control." It forces us to question our findings and conclusions, and encourages us to seek out mistakes in our belief systems (O'Donohue, Lilienfeld, & Fowler, 2007). Science also forces us to attend to data that aren't to our liking, whether or not we want to. In this respect, good scientists differ from politicians, who rarely admit when they've made a mistake and are often punished when they do.

Science and Opinion. You may have heard the humorous saying "Everyone is entitled to my opinion." In science, this saying doesn't pass muster. Many people believe that they don't need science to help get them closer to the truth, because they assume psychology is just a matter of opinion. "If it seems true to me," many of us assume, "it probably is." Yet adopting a scientific mind-set requires us to abandon this comforting way of thinking. That's because psychology is more than a matter of opinion: It's a matter of finding out which explanations best fit the data about how our minds work. Hard-nosed as it may sound, some psychological explanations are just plain better than others—because they're better supported by evidence.

Scientific Thinking and Everyday Life. Of course, you might have enrolled in this course to understand yourself, your friends, or a boyfriend or girlfriend. If so, you might well be thinking, "But I don't want to become a scientist. In fact, I'm not even interested in research. I just want to understand people."

Actually, we're not trying to persuade you to become a scientist. Instead, our goal is to persuade you to *think scientifically:* to become aware of your biases and to avail yourself of the tools of the scientific method to try to overcome them. In this way, you'll become better at making educated choices in your everyday life, like what weight loss plan to choose, what psychotherapy to recommend to a friend, or even what potential romantic partner is a better long-term bet. Not everyone can become a scientist, but just about everyone can learn to think like one. Moreover, learning to think scientifically is nothing more than learning to think in ways that minimize errors.

Scientific thinking can help us to make better everyday decisions, like choosing among a bewildering variety of diet plans.

PsychoMythology
What a Scientific Theory Is and What It Isn't

Few terms in science have generated more confusion than the deceptively simple term *theory.* Some of this confusion has contributed to serious misunderstandings about how science works. We'll first examine what a scientific theory is, and then address two widespread misconceptions about what a scientific theory *isn't.*

A **scientific theory** is an explanation for a large number of findings in the natural world, including the psychological world. That is, a scientific theory accounts for diverse observations by proposing a model that ties all of them together into one pretty package. For example, the big bang theory in astronomy, which proposes that the universe began in a gigantic explosion about 14 billion years ago, helps scientists to explain a diverse array of observations. They include the findings that (a) galaxies are rushing away from each other at remarkable speeds, (b) the universe exhibits a background radiation suggestive of the remnants of a tremendous explosion, and (c) powerful telescopes reveal that the oldest galaxies originated about 14 billion years ago, right around the same time predicted by the big bang theory. Like all scientific theories, the big bang theory can never be "proved," because it's always conceivable that a better explanation might come along one day. Nevertheless, because this theory is consistent with many differing lines of evidence, the overwhelming majority of scientists accept it as a good explanation.

Scientific theories do more than account for existing data. They generate predictions regarding new data we haven't observed. For a theory to be scientific, it must be capable of generating novel predictions that researchers can test. Scientists call a testable prediction a **hypothesis.** In other words, theories are general explanations, whereas hypotheses are specific predictions derived from these explanations (Bolles, 1962; Meehl, 1967).

Misconception 1: *A theory explains one specific event.* The first misunderstanding is that a theory is a specific explanation for an event. The popular media get this distinction wrong much of the time. For example, we'll often hear television reporters say something like, "The most likely theory for the robbery at the downtown bank is that it was committed by two former bank employees who dressed up as armed guards." But this isn't a "theory" of the robbery. For one thing, it attempts to explain only one event rather than a variety of diverse observations. In addition, it doesn't generate testable predictions. In contrast, *forensic psychologists*—those who study the causes and treatment of criminal behavior—have constructed theories about robberies that attempt to explain why certain people steal and to forecast when people are most likely to steal (Katz, 1988).

scientific theory
explanation for a large number of findings in the natural world

hypothesis
testable prediction derived from a theory

This textbook contains material on evolution. Evolution is a theory, not a fact, regarding the origin of living things. This material should be approached with an open mind, studied carefully, and critically considered.

Approved by
Cobb County Board of Education
Thursday, March 28, 2002

Evolution "sticker" required for several years in biology textbooks in Cobb County, Georgia.

" …and, as you go out into the world, I predict that you will, gradually and imperceptibly, forget all you ever learned at this university."

You'll probably forget many of the things you'll learn in college. But you'll be able to use the approach of scientific skepticism throughout your life to evaluate claims. (© Science CartoonsPlus.com)

scientific skepticism
approach of evaluating all claims with an open mind, but insisting on persuasive evidence before accepting them

Misconception 2: *A theory is just an educated guess.* A second myth is that a scientific theory is merely a guess about how the world works. Some creationists who've demanded that creationism be granted equal time with evolutionary theory in biology classes argue that evolution is "just a theory." In fact, until recently some counties, like Cobb County, Georgia, have periodically required high school biology textbooks to carry stickers featuring the disclaimer that Darwinian evolution is "only" a theory (Pinker, 2002).

The creationists are both right and wrong. They're right that Darwinian evolution is indeed a theory, because it's an explanation for a host of phenomena regarding living and extinct species. But they're wrong, because Darwinian evolution isn't "just" a theory. This phrase mistakenly implies that some explanations about the natural world are "more than theories." In fact, *all* general scientific explanations about how the world works are theories. A few theories are extremely well supported by multiple lines of evidence, and Darwinian evolution is one of them. Darwinian evolution has been overwhelmingly supported by studies of fossil evidence, genetic similarities among species, physical similarities among species, and even studies of how species change over brief time periods in response to environmental conditions. Darwinian evolution and other well-established theories aren't guesses about how the world works, because they've been substantiated over and over again by independent investigators. In contrast, many other scientific theories are only moderately well supported, and still others are questionable or entirely discredited. Not all theories are created equal.

So, when we hear that a scientific explanation is "just a theory," we should remember that not all theories are guesses. Some theories have survived repeated efforts to refute them and are well-confirmed models of how the world works.

ASSESS YOUR KNOWLEDGE: FACT OR FICTION?
(1) Science is a body of knowledge consisting of all of the findings that scientists have discovered. (True/False)
(2) Science at its best works by trying to confirm researchers' hypotheses. (True/False)
(3) In general, scientists are just as prone to confirmation bias as nonscientists. (True/False)
(4) A scientific hypothesis is essentially the same thing as a scientific theory, only more specific in its predictions. (True/False)

Answers: (1) F (p. 29); (2) F (p. 31); (3) T (p. 31); (4) F (p. 33)

Critical Thinking: Sorting the Wheat from the Chaff

Given that the world of popular psychology is chock-full of remarkable claims, how can we distinguish psychological fact from psychological fiction? How can we critically evaluate psychological claims without dismissing all of them off the bat?

SCIENTIFIC SKEPTICISM

The approach we'll emphasize throughout this text is **scientific skepticism.** To many people, the term *skepticism* implies closed-mindedness, but nothing could be further from the truth. The term *skepticism* actually derives from the Greek word *skeptikos*, which means "to consider carefully" (Shermer, 2002). The scientific skeptic evaluates all claims with an open mind, but insists on persuasive evidence before accepting them.

Attitudes of Scientific Skepticism.
As astronomer Carl Sagan (1995) noted, to be a scientific skeptic, we must adopt two attitudes that may seem contradictory but aren't: *first,* a willingness to keep an open mind to all claims and, *second,* a willingness to accept these claims only after researchers have subjected them to careful scientific tests. Scientific skeptics are willing to change their minds when confronted with evidence that challenges their preconceptions. At the same time, they change their minds only when this evidence is persuasive. The motto of the scientific skeptic is the Missouri principle, which we'll find on many Missouri state license plates: "Show me" (Dawes, 1994). Scientific skeptics require proponents of claims to provide evidence for these claims, and they're willing to revise their beliefs if this evidence is sufficiently convincing. A closed-minded scientist isn't a good scientist.

The license plate of the state of Missouri captures the central motto of scientific skepticism.

Hazards of Excessive Skepticism.
It's crucial to distinguish scientific skepticism from **pathological skepticism** (Beyerstein, 1995). Pathological skepticism, which is synonymous with cynicism or closed-mindedness, is marked by a tendency to dismiss any claims that contradict our beliefs. The pathological skeptic (or "scoffer") is just as problematic as the gullible individual who accepts all claims at face value. Both are equally guilty of belief perseverence.

Moreover, just as we can fall prey to confirmation bias, we can just as easily fall prey to *disconfirmation bias:* the tendency to seek out evidence inconsistent with a hypothesis we don't believe and neglect evidence consistent with it (Ditto & Lopez, 1992; Edwards & Smith, 1996). A scientist strongly predisposed to doubt the existence of extrasensory perception (ESP) may reflexively dismiss all evidence favoring ESP just because it doesn't fit his worldview. Or he may carefully scrutinize every miniscule piece of data confirming ESP while giving all data disconfirming ESP a free pass (Risen & Gilovich, 2006). If so, he's not behaving scientifically, because he's allowing his motives and emotions to guide his evaluation of the evidence.

Oberg's Dictum: A Delicate Balance.
Open-mindedness is a hallmark of the good scientist. Yet, like all good things in life, we can take it too far. **Oberg's dictum,** named after space engineer James Oberg who first uttered it, tells us that keeping an open mind is a virtue, just so long as it's not so open that our brains fall out (Sagan, 1995). Oberg's dictum warns us to avoid the perils of gullibility on one extreme and pathological skepticism on the other. We should initially remain open to all new claims. But once scientists have refuted these claims soundly, it's time to give them a proper burial and move on.

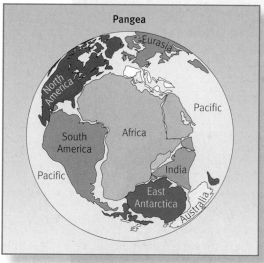

Figure 1.3 Drawing of Alfred Wegener's Pangea. Alfred Wegener conjectured that all of the major continents were once "stuck together" in a gigantic continent he called Pangea. Although Wegener was ridiculed mercilessly during his lifetime, he turned out to be essentially correct.

Scientists have sometimes been guilty of dismissing the claims of their colleagues out of hand merely because they seemed downright silly. In 1912, a young German scientist named Alfred Wegener proposed what seemed to be a blatantly preposterous idea to account for the fact that scientists were unearthing similar fossils on different continents. He proposed that these continents were once stuck together in one gigantic land mass (he called it *Pangea*) and are now moving apart. Indeed, if we look at a globe, we'll notice that some of the continents fit together snugly like pieces in a jigsaw puzzle. Critics dismissed Wegener's theory of "continental drift" as utterly ridiculous during his lifetime, largely because Wegener couldn't explain how the continents moved (see **Figure 1.3**). One American scientist mockingly said, "If we are to believe [this] hypothesis, we must forget everything we have learned in the last seventy years and start all over again." It was only several decades after Wegener's death that scientists showed him to be right. Today, we understand that the theory of continental drift explains a host of scientific phenomena, including the evolution of species and the causes of earthquakes. Wegener's story reminds us that we shouldn't automatically discount new ideas merely because they seem implausible (see **Table 1.2** on the next page).

At the same time, scientists have every right to stop paying attention to ideas that have repeatedly failed well-conducted scientific tests. For example, the ever-popular pseudoscience of **astrology** asserts that we can predict individuals' personalities and futures from knowledge of the precise date and time of their birth. According to astrologers, the planets

pathological skepticism
tendency to dismiss any claims that contradict our beliefs

Oberg's dictum
premise that we should keep our minds open, but not so open that we believe virtually everything

astrology
pseudoscience that claims to predict people's personalities and futures from the precise date and time of their birth

Table 1.2 The Dangers of Discounting New Ideas. Many scientific and technological developments that are now widely accepted were once viewed as implausible, even preposterous. These quotations—all from highly intelligent people—remind us that we should keep an open mind to novel ideas, even if they seem bizarre.

Quotation	Source
I would more easily believe that two Yankee professors would lie than that stones would fall from heaven.	—Thomas Jefferson, U.S. President (1807), commenting on the scientific likelihood of meteorites
What can be more palpably absurd than the prospect held out of locomotives traveling twice as fast as stagecoaches?	—The Quarterly Review (1825)
Well informed people know it is impossible to transmit the voice over wires and that were it possible to do so, the thing would be of no practical value.	—Boston Post editorial (1865)
Heavier-than-air flying machines are impossible.	—Lord Kelvin (1895), British physicist
That the automobile has practically reached the limit of its development is suggested by the fact that during the past year no improvements of a radical nature have been introduced.	—Scientific American (1909)
The foolish idea of shooting at the moon is an example of the absurd length to which vicious specialization will carry scientists working in thought-tight compartments.	—A. W. Bickerton (1926), Professor of Physics and Chemistry, Canterbury College
There is not the slightest indication that [nuclear energy] will ever be obtainable. It would mean that the atom would have to be shattered at will.	—Albert Einstein, Nobel Prize–winning physicist (1932)
I think there is a world market for maybe five computers.	—Thomas Watson, Chairman of IBM (1943)

and stars exert a remarkably powerful but still unexplained influence on the fetus as it emerges from the birth canal. Yet, investigators have found that individuals' astrological signs are unrelated to their personality traits (Hines, 2003; Wiseman, 2007). Scientists have given astrology a fair hearing, and they've repeatedly found it doesn't predict people's behavior at all. There's no longer any need to continue to study astrology or other thoroughly discredited belief systems, as scientists have more pressing matters to investigate.

Incidentally, we shouldn't fall into the trap of assuming there must be something to a strange-sounding hypothesis merely because the scientific community has rejected it wholeheartedly. Many fringe researchers who promote weird ideas dismissed by the scientific community like to compare themselves to great thinkers, like Alfred Wegener, whose ideas were once considered radical but were later confirmed (Gardner, 1957). But genuine Wegeners come along only a few times a century at most. Most scientific ideas that seem silly probably *are* silly. As Carl Sagan (1993) reminded us, they laughed at Galileo, they laughed at Einstein, and they laughed at Wegener. But they also laughed at Bozo the Clown. The bottom line: When we evaluate a psychological claim, we should ask ourselves whether we're being open to this claim while insisting on strong scientific evidence for it.

The Role of Authority. Another key feature of scientific skepticism is an unwillingness to accept claims on the basis of authority alone. Scientific skeptics evaluate claims on their own merits, and refuse to accept them until they meet a high standard of evidence. The oldest scientific society still in existence, the Royal Society of London (founded in 1660), features a Latin inscription on its coat of arms that read, "Nullius in Verba," meaning "On the Word of No One." For members of the Royal Society of London, as for all scientific skeptics, truth emerges not from blindly accepting the word of an established authority figure, but from the fruits of independent research.

Most of us place a good deal of weight on what authority figures tell us. If we're not careful, we can end up accepting some pretty strange claims as a result. For example, people are more likely to believe that food stays fresher if placed in a pyramid-shaped container if they hear it from a high-status person than from a low-status person (Markovsky & Thye, 2001). There's not a shred of evidence for this belief, but if we hear it from an authority figure we may accept it blindly. Moreover, in other cases the power of authority can overrule our ability to evaluate arguments objectively. In one study, Geoffrey Cohen (2003) presented college students (some of them Democrats, others Republicans) with a proposed governmental welfare policy. In some cases, Cohen led them to believe Democrats overwhelmingly endorsed the policy; in other cases, he led them to believe Republi-

The motto of the Royal Society of London translates into "On the Word of No One." Science is premised on the notion that we acquire truth through evidence, not through the word of a trusted authority.

cans overwhelmingly endorsed it. The results were striking: Even though students were convinced they were evaluating the policy on its own merits, the best predictor of whether they agreed with the policy was whether they thought their preferred party endorsed it.

Of course, in everyday life we're often forced to accept the word of authorities simply because we don't possess the expertise, time, or resources to evaluate every claim on our own. Most of us are willing to accept the claim that our local governments keep our drinking water safe without conducting our own chemical tests. While reading this chapter, you're also placing trust in us—the authors, that is—to provide you with accurate information about psychology. Still, this doesn't mean you should blindly accept everything we've written hook, line, and sinker. Consider what we've written with an open mind, but evaluate it skeptically. If you disagree with something we've written, be sure to get a second opinion by asking your instructor.

Throughout this text, we'll be encouraging you to think skeptically about psychology. This won't always be easy, because it will require you to cast aside familiar and comfortable ways of thinking. Most, if not all, of us have come to trust our gut instincts to guide us toward right answers. We've also come to trust what others have told us. Learning to think skeptically requires us to rely less on what intuitively seems to be right and on what we've learned elsewhere and more on objective evidence. That is, scientific skepticism involves at least as much *unlearning* of old habits of thinking as learning new ones. Thinking scientifically doesn't come naturally to any of us. Or put a bit differently, science is "uncommon sense" (Wolpert, 2000).

BASIC PRINCIPLES OF CRITICAL THINKING

The hallmark of scientific skepticism is characterized by **critical thinking.** Many students misunderstand the word *critical* in *critical thinking,* assuming incorrectly that it entails a tendency to attack all claims. In fact, critical thinking is a set of skills for evaluating all claims in an open-minded and careful fashion. We can also think of critical thinking in psychology as *scientific thinking,* as it's the form of thinking that allows us to evaluate scientific claims, not only in the laboratory but in everyday life as well (Willingham, 2007).

Just as important, critical thinking is a set of skills for overcoming our own biases, especially confirmation bias, which as we've learned can blind us to evidence we'd prefer to ignore (Alcock, 1995). Throughout this text, we'll be teaching you specific critical thinking skills to distinguish fact from fiction in both popular and scientific psychology.

In particular, in this text we'll be emphasizing *six* principles of critical thinking (Bartz, 2002; Lett, 1990). We should bear these six principles in mind when evaluating all psychological claims, including claims in the media, self-help books, the Internet, your introductory psychology course, and, yes, even this textbook.

These six critical thinking principles are so crucial that we'll indicate each of them with a different-colored *icon,* or flag, that you'll see throughout the text. Whenever one of these critical thinking principles arises in our discussion, we'll display that icon in the margin to remind you of the principle that goes along with it. So you'll be coming to know and love (we hope) these six icons (see **Figure 1.4** on the next page).

Critical Thinking Principle #1: *Extraordinary Claims Require Extraordinary Evidence.* (Throughout the book, we'll be abbreviating this principle as "Extraordinary Claims.") This principle was proposed in slightly different terms by eighteenth-century Scottish philosopher David Hume (Sagan, 1995; Truzzi, 1978). According to Hume, the more a claim contradicts what we already know, the more persuasive the evidence for this claim must be before we should accept it.

For example, a handful of researchers believe that every night hundreds or even thousands of Americans are being magically lifted out of their beds, brought aboard flying saucers, and experimented on by aliens, only to be returned safely to their beds hours later (Clancy, 2005; see Chapter 5). As Carl Sagan (1995) commented, it's a wonder the neighbors haven't noticed. Psychiatrist John Mack of Harvard University was foremost among alien abduction proponents. Based largely on the reports of individuals who've been hypnotized, Mack concluded that the claims of alien abductees (he called them "experiencers")

According to a few researchers, tens of thousands of Americans have been abducted by aliens and brought aboard spaceships to be experimented on. Could it really be happening, and how would we know?

critical thinking
set of skills for evaluating all claims in an open-minded and careful fashion

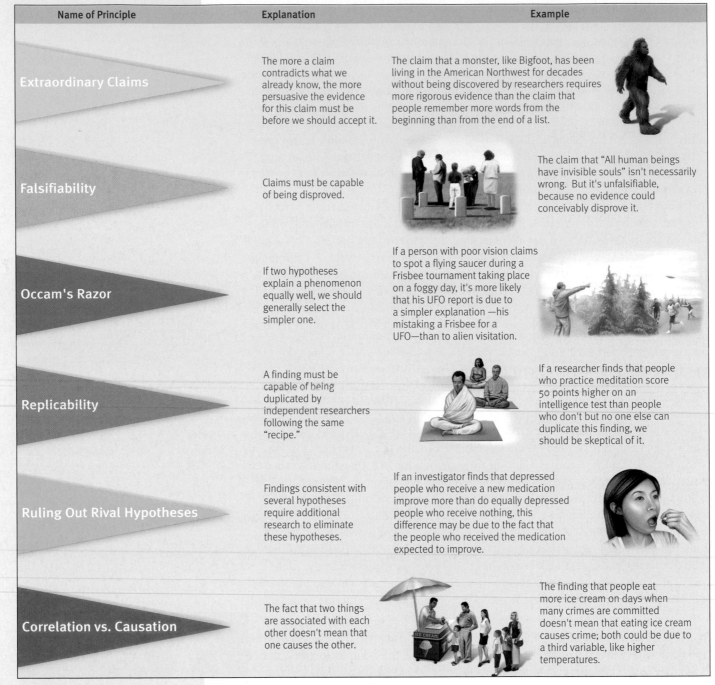

Name of Principle	Explanation	Example
Extraordinary Claims	The more a claim contradicts what we already know, the more persuasive the evidence for this claim must be before we should accept it.	The claim that a monster, like Bigfoot, has been living in the American Northwest for decades without being discovered by researchers requires more rigorous evidence than the claim that people remember more words from the beginning than from the end of a list.
Falsifiability	Claims must be capable of being disproved.	The claim that "All human beings have invisible souls" isn't necessarily wrong. But it's unfalsifiable, because no evidence could conceivably disprove it.
Occam's Razor	If two hypotheses explain a phenomenon equally well, we should generally select the simpler one.	If a person with poor vision claims to spot a flying saucer during a Frisbee tournament taking place on a foggy day, it's more likely that his UFO report is due to a simpler explanation —his mistaking a Frisbee for a UFO—than to alien visitation.
Replicability	A finding must be capable of being duplicated by independent researchers following the same "recipe."	If a researcher finds that people who practice meditation score 50 points higher on an intelligence test than people who don't but no one else can duplicate this finding, we should be skeptical of it.
Ruling Out Rival Hypotheses	Findings consistent with several hypotheses require additional research to eliminate these hypotheses.	If an investigator finds that depressed people who receive a new medication improve more than do equally depressed people who receive nothing, this difference may be due to the fact that the people who received the medication expected to improve.
Correlation vs. Causation	The fact that two things are associated with each other doesn't mean that one causes the other.	The finding that people eat more ice cream on days when many crimes are committed doesn't mean that eating ice cream causes crime; both could be due to a third variable, like higher temperatures.

Figure 1.4 The Six Flags of Scientific Thinking That Are Used Throughout This Textbook.

are genuine (Mack, 2000). According to alien abduction advocates, aliens are extracting semen from human males to impregnate female aliens in an effort to create a race of alien–human hybrids.

Of course, alien abduction proponents *might* be right, and we shouldn't dismiss their claims out of hand. But their claims are pretty darned extraordinary, especially because they imply that tens of thousands of invading flying saucers from other solar systems have inexplicably managed to escape detection by astronomers, not to mention air traffic controllers and radar operators. Scientific skeptics, who point out that hypnosis can sometimes create vivid memories of bizarre events that never occurred (Blackmore, 1998; Lynn, Lock, Myers, & Payne, 1997; see Chapters 5 and 7), have challenged alien abduction proponents to provide even a shred of concrete evidence that supposed abductees have actually encountered extraterrestrials—say, a convincing photograph of an alien, a tiny piece of a metal probe inserted by an alien, or even a strand of hair or shred of skin from an authentic alien. Thus far, all that alien abduction proponents have to show for their claims are the self-reports of supposed abductees, most of which have been contaminated by hypnosis. Extraordinary claims, decidedly ordinary evidence.

The bottom line: Whenever we evaluate a psychological claim, we should ask ourselves whether this claim runs counter to many things we know already and, if it does, whether the evidence is as extraordinary as the claim.

Critical Thinking Principle #2: *Falsifiability.* Philosopher of science Sir Karl Popper (1959) observed that for a claim to be meaningful, it must be **falsifiable,** that is, capable of being disproved. Some students misunderstand this point, confusing the question of whether a theory is *falsifiable* with whether it's *false.* The principle of falsifiability doesn't mean that a theory must be false to be meaningful. Instead, it means that for a theory to be meaningful, it *could* be proved wrong if there were certain types of evidence against it. For a claim to be falsifiable, its proponent must state clearly *in advance*, not after the fact, which findings would count as evidence for and against the claim.

A key implication of the falsifiability principle is that a theory that explains everything—that is, a theory that can account for every conceivable outcome—in effect explains nothing. That's because a good scientific theory must predict only certain outcomes, but not others. If a friend told you he was a master "psychic sports forecaster" and predicted with great confidence, "Tomorrow, all of the major league baseball teams that are playing a game will either win or lose," you'd probably start laughing. By predicting every potential outcome, your friend hasn't really predicted anything.

According to Popper, good scientific theories take risks. By a **risky prediction,** Popper meant a forecast that stands a decent chance of being wrong. The best theories make risky predictions and emerge unscathed. Most bad theories don't take such risks. If as a psychic sports forecaster, your friend instead predicted, "The New York Yankees and New York Mets will both win tomorrow, but the Boston Red Sox and Los Angeles Dodgers will lose," and this prediction came true, you might say to yourself, "Well, that's sort of interesting, but it still could be due to chance." But if he predicted, "Tomorrow, the Yankees will win by seven runs and Mets will win by only one run, but the Red Sox and Dodgers will both lose by nine runs," and this prediction came true, you'd be mightily impressed (Meehl, 1978). Only the last of these predictions was especially risky—it stood an excellent chance of being wrong—and it survived this risk with flying colors. Thus, your friend's theory of baseball is in good shape, although it still hasn't been "proved," because it's always possible that some other theory we hadn't considered could account for our baseball findings.

Some television shows, like *Medium* (featuring actress Patricia Arquette as Allison Dubois), feature "psychic detectives"; people with supposed extrasensory powers who can help police to locate missing people. Yet psychic detectives' predictions are typically so vague—"I see a body near water," "The body is near a wooded area"—that they're virtually impossible to falsify.

As we'll discover in Chapter 14, one major criticism of Sigmund Freud's theory of psychoanalysis is that many of its predictions are difficult to falsify (Cioffi, 1998). For example, Freudians believe that all young boys pass through a phase, the Oedipus complex, during which they're sexually attracted to their mothers. How could we try to falsify this claim? Let's imagine we asked 100 men on the street whether they recall ever being sexually attracted to their mothers. Let's further imagine that most of them answered, "Well, now that you mention it, I do remember a time when I was attracted to my mom." A committed Freudian could proclaim triumphantly, "Aha! Freud's theory of the Oedipus complex has been confirmed." But if these 100 men instead responded, "Hmmm . . . no, I really don't ever recall being attracted to my mom in that way," the same Freudian could reply, "Aha! This finding is also consistent with Freud's theory of the Oedipus complex, because these men's memories of being attracted to their mothers were so emotionally painful that they repressed them" (according to Freudians, repression is the unconscious forgetting of painful emotional experiences or impulses). So Freud's theory of the Oedipus complex is hard to disprove, because it's potentially consistent with many different lines of evidence.

The bottom line: Whenever we evaluate a psychological claim, we should ask ourselves whether one could in principle disprove it or whether it's consistent with any conceivable body of evidence.

falsifiable
capable of being disproved

risky prediction
forecast that stands a good chance of being wrong

Extraordinary Claims

Falsifiability

APPLY YOUR THINKING

Which of the following claims are falsifiable, and why? (1) Republicans are better people than Democrats. (2) Psychotherapy is effective. (3) All people are surrounded by invisible auras that scientists can't measure. (4) The four authors of this text were all famous people (Julius Caesar, Napoleon Bonaparte, Cleopatra, and Marilyn Monroe) in their previous lives. (5) On average, men are more physically aggressive than women.

Critical Thinking Principle #3: *Occam's Razor.* Occam's razor, named after fourteenth-century British philosopher and monk Sir William of Occam, is also called the "principle of parsimony" (*parsimony* is a synonym for logical simplicity). According to Occam's razor, if two explanations account equally well for a phenomenon, we should generally select the more parsimonious one. Good researchers use Occam's razor to "shave off" needlessly complicated explanations to arrive at the simplest explanation that does a good job of accounting for the evidence. Scientists of a romantic persuasion refer to Occam's razor as the principle of KISS: Keep it simple, Stupid. Occam's razor is only a guideline, not a hard-and-fast rule (Uttal, 2003). Every once in a while the best explanation for a phenomenon is the most complex, not the simplest. But Occam's razor is a helpful rule of thumb, as it's right far more often than wrong.

During the late 1970s and 1980s, hundreds of mysterious designs, called crop circles, began appearing in wheat fields in England. Most of these designs were remarkably intricate, even beautiful. How on earth (pun intended) can we explain these designs? Many believers in the paranormal concluded that these designs originated not on Earth, but on distant worlds. The crop circles, they concluded, are proof positive of alien visitations to our world. One crop circle even featured the message, "We are not alone" (which would have been more convincing had it read "You are not alone"; Sagan, 1995). In response to the growing excitement, believers launched an entire journal devoted to the study of crop circles called the *Journal of Cereology* (the name derives from the same word root as *cereal,* which is made from wheat).

The crop circle hysteria came crashing down in 1991, when two British men, David Bower and Doug Chorley, confessed to creating the crop circles as a barroom prank intended to poke fun at uncritical believers in extraterrestrials. They even demonstrated on camera how they used wooden planks and rope to stomp through tall fields of wheat and craft the complex designs. Many of these designs, incidentally, had been signed with two Ds (for David and Doug), which true believers in crop circles had interpreted as an encoded message from aliens.

Following David and Doug's 1991 confession, a few committed cereologists (crop circle experts) still weren't convinced. After all, David and Doug couldn't demonstrate that they'd created every crop circle. Moreover, after David and Doug revealed their hoax on television, additional crop circles began to materialize, some in England and others in the United States. How can we know for sure that *these* crop circles weren't the products of extraterrestrial intelligence or perhaps of a bored extraterrestrial artist? We can't. But Occam's razor reminds us that when confronted with two explanations that fit the evidence equally well, we should generally select the simpler one. In this way, Occam's razor helps us to sort out the wheat (we couldn't resist the pun) from the chaff. Which explanation is more plausible, that crop circles are the products of (a) hoaxers who've demonstrated beyond a shadow of a doubt that they possess the means to create such designs or (b) undetected extraterrestrials who've traveled trillions of miles through space to inscribe hidden messages to earthlings in wheat fields? You decide.

The bottom line: Whenever we evaluate a psychological claim, we should ask ourselves whether it's the simplest explanation that accounts for the data, or whether simpler explanations can account for the data equally well.

Critical Thinking Principle #4: *Replicability.* Barely a week goes by that we don't hear about another stunning psychological finding on the evening news: "Researchers at Cupcake State University detect a new gene linked to excessive shopping"; "Investigators at the

There are two explanations for crop circles, one supernatural and the other natural. Which should we believe?

Occam's razor implies that we should generally select the simplest of two explanations when both account equally well for the data. Is the object in this photograph more likely to be a cloud or a flying saucer? In fact, it's what meteorologists call a lenticular cloud formation, a common source of mistaken flying saucer sightings.

Occam's Razor

University of Antarctica at Igloo report that alcoholism is associated with a heightened risk of murdering one's spouse"; "Nobel Prize–winning professor at Cucumber State College isolates brain area responsible for the enjoyment of popcorn." One major problem with these conclusions, in addition to the fact that the news media often tell us nothing about the design of the studies on which they're based, is that the findings often haven't yet been replicated. **Replicability** means that a study's findings can be duplicated consistently. If they can't be duplicated, it's possible that the original findings were due to chance. *We shouldn't place too much stock in a psychological finding until it's been replicated.*

We should bear in mind that the media are far more likely to report initial positive findings than failures to replicate. The initial findings may be especially fascinating or sensational, whereas replication failures are often disappointing. They rarely make for thrilling news headlines. As a consequence, we may never hear about them. As we'll learn in Chapter 10, the news media allotted a great deal of coverage to preliminary findings that playing Mozart's music to students enhances their intelligence, but barely mentioned a slew of failures to replicate them.

It's especially important that investigators other than the original researchers replicate the results, because this increases our confidence in them. If I tell you that I've created a recipe for the world's most delicious veal parmigiana, but it turns out that every chef who follows my recipe ends up with a meal that tastes like an old piece of cardboard smothered in a putrid mixture of rotten cheese and 6-month-old tomato sauce, you'd be justifiably skeptical of my claim. Maybe I flat out lied about my recipe. Or perhaps I wasn't actually following the recipe very closely, and was instead tossing in ingredients that weren't even in the recipe. Or perhaps I'm such an extraordinary Italian chef that nobody else can come close to duplicating my miraculous culinary feats. In any case, you'd have every right to doubt my recipe until someone else replicated it. The same goes for psychological research.

The literature on ESP offers an excellent example of why replicability is so essential (see Chapter 4). Every once in a blue moon, a researcher reports a striking new finding that seemingly confirms the existence of ESP. This finding often garners media publicity. Yet time and again, independent researchers haven't been able to replicate these tantalizing results (Gilovich, 1991; Hyman, 1989; Lilienfeld, 1999). This lack of replicability doesn't mean that ESP isn't real. Still, the absence of a reproducible "experimental recipe" for ESP has left most psychological scientists doubtful of its existence.

In ESP research, researchers often ask subjects to predict the outcomes of random events. Yet ESP findings have proven difficult to replicate.

APPLY YOUR THINKING

Some proponents of ESP acknowledge that the research evidence for it is weak, but they claim that only certain people possess ESP. As a consequence, they maintain, research studies of ESP usually yield negative results because most participants don't possess ESP. Is this claim scientifically justifiable? Why or why not?

Not all replications are created equal. Just because a finding has been replicated doesn't necessarily mean it's believable, because we still need to make sure that the studies are well conducted. If an investigator performs a flawed study and a second investigator replicates her findings while repeating the same mistakes, we should disregard this replication. Similarly, not all replication failures are created equal. A second investigator could fail to replicate a previous investigator's findings because she didn't conduct the study properly. So before deciding how much weight to place on either a replication or replication failure, we must first evaluate the study's quality.

The bottom line: Whenever we evaluate a psychological claim, we should ask ourselves whether independent investigators have replicated the findings that support this claim; otherwise, the findings might be a one-time-only fluke.

Critical Thinking Principle #5: *Ruling Out Rival Hypotheses.* Most psychological findings we'll hear about on television or read about on the Internet lend themselves to multiple explanations. Yet, more often than not, the media report only one explanation. We

Replicability

replicability
demand that a study's findings be duplicated, ideally by independent investigators

shouldn't automatically assume it's the correct one. Instead, we should ask ourselves: Is this the only good explanation for this finding? Have we ruled out all important competing explanations (Platt, 1964)?

Let's take a popular treatment for anxiety disorders, eye movement desensitization and reprocessing (EMDR; see also Chapter 16). Introduced in the late 1980s by Francine Shapiro (1989), EMDR asks clients to track the therapist's back-and-forth finger movements with their eyes while imagining distressing memories that are the source of their anxiety, such as the memory of seeing someone being killed.

More than 60,000 therapists have received formal training in EMDR. Proponents of EMDR have consistently maintained that it's far more effective and efficient than other treatments for anxiety disorders. Many have even hailed it as a "breakthrough" (Shapiro & Forrest, 1997) or "miracle cure." In addition, they've claimed that the eye movements of EMDR are a uniquely effective feature of the treatment. For example, some have suggested that these eye movements somehow synchronize the brain's two hemispheres—although why that would reduce anxiety isn't exactly clear—or stimulate brain mechanisms that speed up the processing of emotional memories.

Yet there's a problem. A slew of well-controlled studies show that the eye movements of EMDR don't contribute to its effectiveness. EMDR works just as well when people stare straight ahead at an immobile dot as when they move their eyes back and forth (Davidson & Parker, 2001; Lohr, Tolin, & Lilienfeld, 1998). Moreover, most EMDR advocates neglected to consider a rival explanation for EMDR's success: Like a wide variety of other effective treatments, EMDR asks patients to expose themselves to anxiety-provoking imagery. Researchers and therapists alike have long known that prolonged exposure itself can be therapeutic (Lohr, Hooke, Gist, & Tolin, 2003; see Chapter 16). By not excluding the rival hypothesis that EMDR's effectiveness stemmed from exposure rather than eye movements, EMDR advocates made claims that ran well ahead of the data.

The bottom line: Whenever we evaluate a psychological claim, we should ask ourselves whether we've excluded other plausible explanations for it.

Ruling Out Rival Hypotheses

Critical Thinking Principle #6: *Correlation Isn't Causation*. Perhaps the most common mistake beginning psychology students make when interpreting studies is to conclude that when two things that are associated with each other—or what psychologists call "correlated" with each other—one thing must cause the other. This point leads us to one of the most crucial principles in this book (get your highlighters out for this one): *Correlations don't permit causal inferences*, or, putting it less formally, *correlation isn't causation*. When we mistakenly conclude that a correlation means causation, we've committed the **correlation–causation fallacy.** This conclusion is a fallacy because the fact that two variables are correlated doesn't necessarily mean that one causes the other (also see Chapter 2). Incidentally, a **variable** is anything that can *vary*, like height, IQ, or extraversion. Let's see why correlation isn't causation.

If we start with two variables, A and B, that are correlated, there are three major explanations for this correlation.

(1) A → B. First, it's possible that variable A causes variable B.
(2) B → A. Second, it's possible that variable B causes variable A. Here the "causal arrow" (the arrow is reversed between A and B) connects the variables in the opposite order, with B coming before A.

So far, so good. But many people forget about a third possibility, namely, that:

(3) C ↗ A
      ↘ B

correlation–causation fallacy
error of assuming that because one thing is associated with another, it must cause the other

variable
anything that can vary

third variable problem
case in which a third variable causes the correlation between two other variables

In this third scenario, there's a third variable, C, that causes *both* A and B. This scenario is known as the **third variable problem.** The reason it's a "problem" is it can lead us to conclude mistakenly that A and B are causally related to each other when they're not.

Making matters worse, we may never have thought to measure third variable C in our study. Indeed, we might not even know that this variable exists. As a consequence, we can fool ourselves into concluding that a causal relationship between A and B exists when it doesn't. *Correlation isn't causation.*

This point is so crucial that we'll come back to it and discuss it in more depth in Chapter 2. For now, we'll give you just one example of how we can confuse correlation with causation. In one recent study, researchers found that teenagers who listened to music with lots of sexual lyrics had sexual intercourse considerably more often than teenagers who listened to music with far tamer lyrics (Martino et al., 2006). Putting it a bit differently, they found that listening to sexual lyrics is *correlated* with sexual behavior. One newspaper summarized the findings with an attention-grabbing headline: "Sexual lyrics prompt teens to have sex" (Tanner, 2006). But like many headlines, this one went well beyond the data. It's indeed possible that music with sexual lyrics (A) causes sexual behavior (B). But it's also possible that sexual behavior (B) causes teens to listen to music with sexual lyrics (A), or that a third variable, like impulsivity (C), both causes teens to listen to music with sexual lyrics *and* to engage in sexual behavior. Given the data reported by the authors, there's no way to know.

The bottom line: We should remember that a correlation between two things doesn't demonstrate a causal connection between them.

THE FAMILY CIRCUS.   By Bil Keane

"I wish they didn't turn on that seatbelt sign so much! Every time they do, it gets bumpy."

Correlation isn't always causation. (© Bil Keane, Inc. King Features Syndicate)

Correlation vs. Causation

ASSESS YOUR KNOWLEDGE: FACT OR FICTION?

(1) As scientists, we should dismiss all popular psychology claims unless there's a very good reason to consider them. (True/False)

(2) Cynicism is just an extreme form of skepticism. (True/False)

(3) Oberg's dictum implies that we can sometimes take scientific open-mindedness too far. (True/False)

(4) A risky prediction is one that stands a good chance of being wrong if the theory generating it is also wrong. (True/False)

(5) When psychological findings are replicated, it's especially important that the replications be conducted by the same team of investigators. (True/False)

Answers: (1) F (p. 35); (2) F (p. 35); (3) T (p. 35); (4) T (p. 39); (5) F (p. 41)

Psychological Pseudoscience: Imposters of Science

Imagine that you're smack in the middle of the semester, just a few days before midterms, and you're running hopelessly behind on all of the reading for your courses. So many textbooks, so little time! Worst of all, you've got eight chapters of your darned introductory psychology textbook to plow through.

Late one night, after a grueling day of studying in the library, you see a commercial on television that piques your interest. It's for a speed-reading course, called The Speed of Light, being offered by a private firm in town. According to the commercial, after taking The Speed of Light course, you'll boost your reading speed from a measly 200 words per minute to a lightning-fast 2,000–3,000 words per minute. "Our remarkable course materials are scientifically proven to work," says a bearded man in a white lab coat, speaking in a deep, authoritative voice. He introduces himself as Professor Krak-Pott, M.A., P.D.Q., X.Y.Z. (the multiple initials look awfully impressive) of the Hyperscientific Polytechnical Institute. "We've conducted hundreds of studies proving that The Speed of Light is amazingly effective," Professor Krak-Pott intones. By now he's really grabbed your attention. "By simultaneously activating millions of specialized cells in your outermost retinal layers, The Speed of Light course allows your eyeballs to process sensory information at astonishing speeds. And you can do so while increasing your reading comprehension." Wow. That sounds really scientific, even if you have no earthly idea what a "specialized cell in your outermost retinal layer" is.

"HOWEVER, IT'S EXCELLENT PSEUDOSCIENCE."

(© ScienceCartoonsPlus.com)

Then the camera pans to the right of the screen. There we see a woman in her early twenties, seated at a desk, who's paging quickly through a thick textbook. She looks up at the camera and smiles. "Before I took The Speed of Light course, I was a solid C− student in college," she says. "Now I'm in my final year of college, and I'm getting straight As. Books that would have taken me weeks to read I can now polish off in an hour or less. I'm headed straight for Harvard Medical School!"

It all sounds too good to be true. Is it? How could we know?

WHAT IS PSEUDOSCIENCE?

The answers to the two questions at the end of the last section can help us distinguish claims that are genuinely scientific from those that are merely imposters of science. An imposter of science is a **pseudoscience**: a set of claims that *seems* scientific but isn't. In particular, *pseudoscience lacks the safeguards against confirmation bias and belief perseverance that characterize science.*

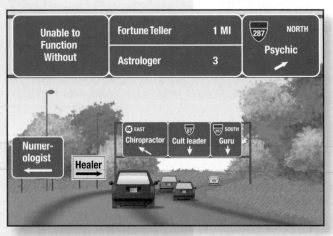

Pseudoscientific and otherwise questionable claims have increasingly altered the landscape of modern life.

As we've discovered, popular psychology is a mix of high-quality science and pseudoscience. The problem is that unless we're careful, we can be easily duped into confusing these two sorts of evidence and accepting impressive-sounding claims that are devoid of scientific substance.

As we'll discover throughout this text, some popular psychology claims are largely or entirely pseudoscientific. These include many assertions regarding astrology, extrasensory perception, out-of-body experiences, polygraph ("lie-detector") testing, recovered memories of child abuse, the analysis of handwriting to infer people's personality traits, multiple personality disorder, and some questionable psychotherapies. That's not to say that all of these claims are entirely false. In fact, at least a few of them possess a core of truth. Still others might be shown to be true in future research. Yet, as we'll soon see, the proponents of these claims don't typically "play by the rules" of the game of science.

The difference between science and pseudoscience isn't always clear-cut. Some psychological products and treatments are based mostly on science but partly on pseudoscience, and vice versa. Still, as we'll soon learn, we can pinpoint a number of helpful distinctions between science and pseudoscience, even if the boundaries between them become fuzzy around the edges (Leahy & Leahy, 1982; Lindeman, 1998).

METAPHYSICAL CLAIMS: THE BOUNDARIES OF SCIENCE

It's essential to distinguish pseudoscientific claims from **metaphysical claims**: assertions about the world that are *unfalsifiable* (Popper, 1959). Metaphysical claims include assertions about the existence of God, the soul, and the afterlife. These claims differ from pseudoscientific claims in that we could never falsify them using scientific methods. (How could we design a scientific test to conclusively refute the existence of God?) They therefore fall outside the boundaries of science (Gould, 1997) because, as we've learned, falsifiability is a cornerstone of a scientific theory.

This point doesn't mean that metaphysical claims are wrong, let alone unimportant. To the contrary, many thoughtful scholars would contend that questions concerning the existence of God are even more significant and profound than scientific questions. Moreover, regardless of our beliefs about religion, we all need to treat these questions with the profound respect they deserve.

But it's crucial to understand that there are certain questions about the world that science can—and can't—answer. Science has its limits. So it needs to respect the boundaries of religion and other metaphysical domains. Falsifiable claims fall within the province of science; unfalsifiable claims don't (see **Figure 1.5**).

Falsifiability

pseudoscience
set of claims that seems scientific but isn't

metaphysical claims
assertions about the world that are unfalsifiable

THE PREVALENCE OF PSEUDOSCIENTIFIC BELIEFS

Pseudoscientific and other questionable beliefs are widespread. Let's look at **Table 1.3**, which displays findings from a large recent survey of the American public (Musella, 2005). As we can see, between one-third and one-half believe in extrasensory perception, one-third or more in haunted houses and ghosts, about one-quarter in astrology and extraterrestrial visitations, and about one-fifth in communication with the dead.

The fact that many Americans *entertain* the possibility of such beliefs isn't by itself worrisome, because a certain amount of open-mindedness is essential for scientific thinking. Instead, what's troubling is that many Americans appear convinced that such claims are correct even though the scientific evidence for them is either weak, as in the case of ESP, or essentially nonexistent, as in the case of astrology. It's also troubling that far more Americans seem interested in pseudoscience than in science. For example, there are about twenty times more astrologers than astronomers in the United States (Gilovich, 1991), and in most major bookstores, the New Age and occult sections are substantially larger than the psychology sections (Lilienfeld, 1999).

THE SEVEN DEADLY SINS OF PSEUDOSCIENCE: USEFUL WARNING SIGNS

To help us distinguish science from pseudoscience, we'll present seven warning signs that set pseudosciences apart from sciences. We can think of these warning signs as the Seven Deadly Sins of Pseudoscience. They're extremely useful rules of thumb, so useful in fact that we'll draw on many of them in later chapters to help us become more informed consumers of psychological claims. We can—and should—also use them in everyday life.

None of these deadly sins is by itself proof positive that a set of claims is pseudoscientific. Nevertheless, the more deadly sins a set of claims displays, the more skeptical of these claims we should become. Using each of these seven deadly sins, let's evaluate whether the speed-reading course we saw advertised is scientific or pseudoscientific.

Deadly Sin #1: *Overuse of ad hoc immunizing hypotheses.* Yes, we know this one is a mouthful. But it's actually not as complicated as it appears, because an **ad hoc immunizing hypothesis** is just an escape hatch that defenders of a theory use to protect their theory from being falsified. When proponents of a theory come across negative evidence, they often try to explain it away by invoking loopholes. Sometimes these loopholes are justified, but in other cases they amount to nothing more than excuses for negative findings.

As we'll discuss in greater detail in Chapter 8, a number of well-conducted studies show that speed-reading courses don't work. Specifically, they demonstrate that we can't easily increase reading speed without decreasing our comprehension (Carver, 1987; Graf, 1973). Once we teach people to read more quickly, they end up absorbing and understanding less material. These findings would seem to falsify the claims of speed-reading advocates like Professor Krak-Pott. But these advocates often invoke ad hoc immunizing hypotheses to explain away the contrary evidence: "Well, maybe our speed-reading courses increased a different kind of comprehension than the kind the investigators measured." Or how about this one: "Maybe the subjects in these studies were really nervous about being tested, so they did poorly on the comprehension tests. Their comprehension only *seemed* to become worse after taking the speed-reading course."

Of course, it's *possible* that these ad hoc hypotheses are right. But it's up to the advocates of speed-reading courses, not their critics, to design studies to demonstrate that they are. If they don't, and if they keep on offering excuse after excuse for negative findings, they're behaving pseudoscientifically, not scientifically.

Deadly Sin #2: *Lack of self-correction.* As we've learned, many scientific claims turn out to be wrong. In science, incorrect claims tend to be weeded out eventually, even though it often takes a while. In contrast, in pseudosciences, incorrect claims never seem to go away, because their proponents cling to them stubbornly despite contrary evidence. In the case

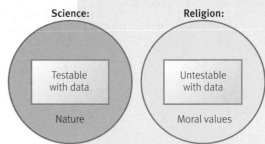

Figure 1.5 Nonoverlapping Realms. Scientist Stephen Jay Gould (1997) argued that science and religion are entirely different and nonoverlapping realms of understanding the world. Science deals with testable claims about the natural world that can be answered with data, whereas religion deals with untestable claims about moral values that can't be answered with data. Although not all scientists and theologians accept Gould's model, we adopt it for the purposes of this textbook. (*Source:* Gould, 1997)

Table 1.3 Survey of Selected Beliefs of Average Americans (as of 2005).

Belief	Percentage Who Believe In
Extrasensory perception	41%
Haunted houses	37%
Ghosts	32%
Telepathy (mind-reading)	37%
Astrology	25%
Visits to earth by aliens	24%
Communication with the dead	21%
Witches	21%
(*Source:* Musella, 2005)	

Falsifiability

ad hoc immunizing hypothesis escape hatch or loophole that defenders of a theory use to protect their theory from falsification

of speed-reading courses, the claims of most advocates haven't been changed one bit by the overwhelmingly negative findings.

Deadly Sin #3: *Exaggerated claims.* Not all amazing claims are false. But remember that extraordinary claims require extraordinary evidence. Pseudosciences tend to promise remarkable or dramatic cures but rarely deliver the goods.

Recall that the advertisement for The Speed of Light course claimed that people could increase their reading speeds by a factor of 10 or even 15. Other speed-reading courses have made even more miraculous claims; some purport to teach people to read at speeds of up to 25,000 words a minute (Carroll, 2003). That's about eighty to ninety pages a minute, or a page in less than a second. At that rate, you could polish off this entire text-book in 6 to 7 minutes. So, if you've already spent more than 6 or 7 minutes on this chap-ter, you'd better pick up your pace (of course, if you've only spent 5 minutes so far, don't worry, as you still have a minute or two left).

Also, recall that the commercial claimed that The Speed of Light course was "proven" to work. As we've already cautioned, we should be skeptical of products or treatments that have been "proven" effective, because scientific knowledge is rarely, if ever, conclusive. Even well-established scientific findings are occasionally overturned by new evidence.

Deadly Sin #4: *Overreliance on anecdotes.* There's an old saying that the "plural of anecdote is not data." A mountain of numerous anecdotes may seem impressive, but it shouldn't persuade us to put much stock in others' claims. Anecdotes are *I know a person who* assertions (Nisbett & Ross, 1980; Stanovich, 2004). This kind of secondhand evidence—"I know a person who says his self-esteem skyrocketed after receiving hypno-sis"; "I know a person who tried to commit suicide after taking an antidepressant"—is commonplace in everyday life.

Pseudosciences tend to rely heavily on anecdotal evidence. In many cases, they base claims on the dramatic reports of one or two people: "I lost 85 pounds in 3 weeks on the Matzo Ball Soup Weight Loss Program." "I know three people whose IQs went up by 45 points after enrolling in the Albert Einstein Memory Improvement Program." "My brother was clinically depressed until he took vitamin D for 5 days, and immediately after that his depression lifted completely."

As compelling as these anecdotes seem, they don't constitute good scientific evidence. That's because anecdotes are severely limited in three major ways (Lazarus & Davison, 2007; Loftus & Guyer, 2002).

(1) *Anecdotes don't tell us anything about cause and effect.* It's possible that the Matzo Ball Soup Weight Loss program was responsible for the person's loss of 85 pounds, but other factors may have been responsible. Maybe the person went on an additional diet or started to exercise frantically during that time. Or maybe he underwent drastic weight loss surgery during this time, but didn't mention it.

(2) *Anecdotes don't tell us anything about how representative the cases are.* Even if one person's IQ went up 45 points after enrolling in the Albert Einstein Memory Improvement Program, we don't know anything about the thousands of other people who enrolled in this program. Maybe their IQs stayed the same or even went down. Without access to all of the data (or least most of it) from people who underwent a treatment, we can't evaluate how well it worked.

(3) *Anecdotes are difficult to verify.* How do we know that the person's brother was actually clinically depressed? Or that he really took vitamin D? Or that his depression lifted immediately after taking it? We don't know any of these things for certain, so we're forced to accept his testimonial on the basis of faith alone. Faith plays an extremely valuable role in many people's lives, but it has no place in science.

In the case of the speed-reading course, the commercial presented a striking anecdote of a former C− student who's now headed for Harvard Medical School. Yet we don't know whether the speed-reading course contributed to her admission to Harvard Medical School; perhaps her father is the president of Harvard Medical School, and she would have been admitted even with an F average. Nor do we know how representative her story is; hundreds of people not pictured in the commercial might have found the speed-reading course worthless. For that matter, we don't even know whether she's telling the

factoid

Astrology, which has been around for almost 5,000 years, provides a striking example of the absence of self-correction found in many pseudosciences. Some of the star charts used by modern astrologers are virtually identical to those used thousands of years ago (Hines, 2003). This is in spite of a phenomenon known as *precession,* a gradual shift in the earth's axis, rendering the appearance of the stars in the night sky substantially different from what it was thousands of years ago.

Anecdotal evidence can seem convincing. Nevertheless, the claim that a given person has lost weight as a result of a treatment is open to multiple interpretations.

truth about attending Harvard Medical School, or whether she could be exaggerating; perhaps she was hired to work at the school, not accepted as a medical student.

Simply put, the central problem with anecdotes is that they're difficult to interpret as evidence. As psychologist Paul Meehl (1995) put it, "The clear message of history is that the anecdotal method delivers both wheat and chaff, but it does not enable us to tell which is which" (p. 1019).

Deadly Sin #5: *Evasion of peer review.* The scientific community relies on a procedure called **peer review:** a mechanism whereby experts in the field carefully screen the work of their fellow scientists. When scientists submit a report of their research to a journal, it's almost always sent to a panel of researchers from other colleges and universities, who must decide whether the report is worthy of publication. In many cases, the report is rejected outright; in still others, it's rejected in its current form, with the authors being asked to undertake substantial revisions before the work is reconsidered for publication. In still other cases, the report is accepted for publication, but almost always with the requirement that revisions be made. The peer review process isn't for the thin-skinned or faint of heart: The authors of your text have all received more than a few brutally negative, even vicious, reviews over the years.

Most scientists regarded the new streamlined peer-review process as 'quite an improvement.'

Scientists who make it through the peer review process sometimes take quite a beating. (Cartoon by Nick Kim, nearingzero.net)

The peer review process isn't perfect, because reviewers aren't immune from biases, including confirmation bias (Mahoney, 1977; Peters & Ceci, 1982). Valuable research that challenges the status quo is sometimes rejected; poor-quality research that affirms the status quo is sometimes accepted. Still, as Winston Churchill said of democracy, the peer review process is the worst system in the world—except for every other system (McCarty, 1999). It's the best mechanism we have for weeding out problematic research.

Most pseudosciences bypass the peer review process, preferring instead to rely on anecdotes or conduct informal research that's never submitted to scientific journals. Note that the speed-reading course advertised in the commercial referred to hundreds of studies attesting to its astonishing effectiveness. It's likely that these studies were done "in-house," that is, by proponents of speed-reading courses themselves. In-house studies are next to worthless, because there's usually no means of evaluating whether researchers conducted them properly.

Like all sciences, psychology has a hierarchy—or pecking order—of journals. There are more than 2,000 journals in psychology and similar fields, but not all are equally rigorous. Some journals are exceedingly selective; for example, *Psychological Bulletin, Psychological Review, Psychological Science,* and the *Journal of Personality and Social Psychology* routinely reject 80 to 90 percent of the manuscripts they receive. In contrast, some other journals accept the substantial majority of manuscripts they receive. All else being equal, research reports published in journals with higher rejection rates tend to be more credible, because they've withstood a higher level of critical scrutiny. *Don't assume that all findings published in a peer-reviewed journal are accurate.* Still, peer review provides at least a minimal quality-control safeguard against bad research. Without it, it's sometimes anybody's guess whether we can trust a researcher's conclusions.

The three journals shown here are among the most prestigious in the field of psychology. A major reason for their reputation is their rigorous system of peer review, which enhances the likelihood that only high-quality manuscripts will be published.

Deadly Sin #6: *Absence of connectivity.* **Connectivity** refers to the extent to which a researcher's findings build on, or "connect up with," previous scientific findings (Stanovich, 2004). Most sciences are cumulative: New findings typically extend earlier ones. In contrast, most pseudosciences neglect previous research and purport to create grand new ideas out of whole cloth.

Speed-reading courses lack connectivity with research findings on the physical capacity of the human eye. Carefully conducted studies demonstrate that the human eyeball can process a maximum of about 300 words per minute (Carroll, 2004). Thus, the reading speeds advertised by most speed-reading courses greatly exceed the scanning capacity of the human eyeball! This fact tells us that speed "readers" aren't reading at all. They're skimming.

Deadly Sin #7: *Psychobabble.* Be skeptical of claims accompanied by oodles of psychological or neurological language that sounds highly scientific (van Rillaer, 1991). Sometimes such language is genuinely scientific, but much of the time it's designed to

peer review
mechanism whereby experts in a field carefully screen the work of their colleagues

connectivity
extent to which a researcher's findings build on previous findings

Psychobabble is a hallmark of many pseudoscientific researchers and therapists. (© ScienceCartoonsPlus.com)

impress gullible people who lack extensive psychological or neurological training. Many pseudosciences attempt to lure consumers into accepting their claims by peppering their advertising with technical terms that are devoid of meaning. In the commercial for the speed-reading course, Professor Krak-Pott spoke of specialized cells in "your outermost retinal layers," but the good professor conveniently neglected to mention that the cells in your outermost retina have nothing whatsoever to do with your reading speed.

The bottom line: Some claims mimic the *style* of scientific claims but possess little of their substance. By remembering the Seven Deadly Sins of Pseudoscience, we can more easily spot scientific imposters and distinguish pseudoscience from science.

ASSESS YOUR KNOWLEDGE: FACT OR FICTION?

(1) Metaphysical claims can never be proved incorrect. (True/False)
(2) In general, the more anecdotal evidence there is for a scientific claim, the more persuasive that claim becomes. (True/False)
(3) The peer review system works because reviewers of articles are immune from confirmation bias. (True/False)
(4) Most important scientific discoveries build on and extend previous knowledge. (True/False)

Answers: (1) T (p. 44); (2) F (p. 46); (3) F (p. 47); (4) T (p. 47)

Pseudoscientific Beliefs: Origins and Dangers

Why are pseudoscientific beliefs so popular? To answer this question, it's critical to understand a point we'll emphasize throughout this text: *We're all prone to pseudoscientific beliefs.* The psychological influences that give rise to pseudoscientific beliefs operate in every one of us. So, as we discuss the principal sources of pseudoscientific thinking in this section, we should bear in mind that they apply not just to other people, but to you and, yes, even to the authors of this text. We must all remain on guard against the seductive charms of pseudoscience.

WHY ARE WE DRAWN TO PSEUDOSCIENCE?

There are a host of reasons why we're drawn to pseudoscientific beliefs. One clue comes from the work of Seymour Epstein (1990; Epstein, Lipson, Holstein, & Huh, 1992), who proposed that our brains operate in two very different modes of thinking: *rational* and *experiential*. Loosely speaking, we can think of these two modes as thinking from the "brain" versus the "heart" (Lindemann, 1998).

Rational thinking, according to Epstein, relies on careful reasoning and an objective analysis of the evidence at hand. This mode of thinking is slow and effortful, because in this mode we take our time to evaluate evidence.

Experiential thinking, in contrast, depends on intuitive judgments and emotional reactions ("vibes"). This mode of thinking is fast and effortless, because we use it to make snap judgments of situations (Gladwell, 2005; Kahneman, 2003). According to Epstein, experiential thinking is our "default mode" of operating. We generally fall back on it unless forced to do otherwise (Beike & Sherman, 1994).

Both modes of thinking are invaluable in everyday life, and we need both to function successfully (Kahneman, 2003; Risen & Gilovich, 2006; Stanovich & West, 2000). Rational thinking comes in handy for evaluating our psychology textbook, whereas experiential thinking comes in handy for judging whether we enjoyed a first date. Nevertheless, if we rely too heavily on our experiential mode of thinking—and we all do at times—we can find ourselves vulnerable to pseudoscientific beliefs. That's because we can reach

The ever-present threat of terrorist attacks leaves us with a sense of vulnerability. It's therefore not surprising that the levels of certain supernatural beliefs appear to have increased following the terrorist attacks of September 11, 2001.

rational thinking
thinking that relies on careful reasoning and objective analysis

experiential thinking
thinking that depends on intuitive judgments and emotional reactions

decisions based not on a reasoned evaluation of the data, but on gut-level inferences ("I know the scientific evidence doesn't support astrology, but the idea of astrology 'feels right' to me"). So although experiential thinking is immensely useful in "sizing up" people and situations quickly, it can mislead us when evaluating scientific questions.

To understand why we're all prone to pseudoscientific thinking from time to time, we need to understand three sources of erroneous beliefs: motivational factors, scientific illiteracy, and cognitive (thinking) factors. We'll examine each in turn.

Motivational Factors. One key reason we find pseudoscientific beliefs so appealing is that they serve a powerful motivational function. More than anything else, they give us hope. As we're all too well aware, the world is frightening. We know that we'll die one day, and none of us knows precisely when that fateful day will come. Our friendships and love relationships are fraught with uncertainty and with the ever-present possibility of rejection from those about whom we care most deeply. As we head out of our homes every morning, we know that we risk failure at school or work. We have plenty of reason to feel anxious.

These fears leave us vulnerable to what philosopher Paul Kurtz (1991) termed the **transcendental temptation:** the desire to alleviate our anxiety by embracing the lofty promises of the supernatural. Although many of us find the possibility of ghosts frightening at one level, we may find this possibility reassuring at another level, as it implies that our souls can survive after our deaths. Similarly, many of us find astrology to be anxiety reducing, as it implies that we can predict scary events that would otherwise be unknowable. The transcendental temptation is perfectly fine just so long as it remains within the realm of metaphysical claims, such as the existence of God or the soul. But when it leads us to embrace testable claims that are questionable or false, it may put us on the slippery slope toward pseudoscience.

Pseudoscientific beliefs also fulfill our deep-seated need for wonder (Beyerstein, 1999; Sagan, 1995). Many of us find the great mysteries of nature and the universe to be intrinsically fascinating. It's therefore no surprise that we avidly gobble up media reports of flying saucers, alien abductions, extrasensory perception, ghosts, near-death experiences, and astrology, as these paranormal phenomena feed our insatiable hunger for mystery. The problem is that our powerful desire for wonder can easily override our critical thinking skills, leading us to accept claims for which there's minimal evidence. We believe because we want to believe.

Television programs on the paranormal, such as *Lost*, are extremely popular, suggesting that these shows fill a deep-seated psychological need.

Scientific Illiteracy. Another reason for the popularity of pseudoscience is our society's overall lack of knowledge of science. As a result, many of us are ill-equipped to critically evaluate scientific claims about the world that sound authentic but that are bogus (Eve, 2007).

Even in the United States, the most scientifically and technologically advanced country in world history, most citizens are shockingly unaware of elementary scientific findings. Only about 28 percent of Americans are "scientifically literate," meaning sufficiently knowledgeable to properly evaluate scientific findings in the everyday media (Culliton, 1989; Lederman, 1996; *Science Daily,* 2007). About half of Americans don't know that the earth takes a year to revolve around the sun or that electrons are smaller than atoms. Almost two-thirds of Americans believe that humans and dinosaurs coexisted (Sagan, 1995). Devastating as this news may be to those of us who are lovers of old Saturday morning cartoons, the Flintstones aren't a dependable source of paleontological knowledge.

Surveys demonstrate that almost two-thirds of Americans believe that humans and dinosaurs coexisted. Our low levels of scientific literacy may be a major contributor to our acceptance of certain pseudoscientific beliefs.

Cognitive Factors: Making Sense out of Nonsense. But perhaps the central reason for the popularity of pseudoscience stems from the way our brains work. Our brains are constantly on the lookout for patterns, helping us to detect meaning in our complex and confusing environments. *Our brains are predisposed to make order out of disorder and find sense in nonsense.* This tendency is generally adaptive, as it helps us to simplify the often bewildering world in which we live (Alcock, 1995; Pinker, 1997). Without it, we'd be constantly overwhelmed by endless streams of information that we don't have the time or ability to process. Yet this adaptive tendency can sometimes lead us astray, because it can lead us to perceive meaningful patterns even when they're not there (Schneider, 2007).

transcendental temptation
desire to alleviate our anxiety by embracing the supernatural

NEW FRONTIERS

Terror Management Theory and Its Implications for Pseudoscientific Beliefs

Paul Kurtz's writings on the transcendental temptation remind us that our fears of death render us vulnerable to accepting paranormal claims, even if they're based on weak scientific evidence. A related perspective comes from recent research on **terror management theory** (Solomon, Greenberg, & Pyszczynski, 2000). According to terror management theory, our awareness of our own inevitable death leaves many of us with an underlying sense of terror (by the way, despite its name this theory has little to do with the causes of terrorism). We cope with these feelings of terror, advocates of this theory propose, by adopting cultural worldviews that reassure us that our lives possess a broader meaning and purpose—one that extends well beyond our vanishingly brief existence on this planet.

Terror management researchers typically test this model by manipulating *mortality salience:* the extent to which thoughts of death are foremost in our minds. They may ask participants to think about the emotions they experience when contemplating their deaths or to imagine themselves dying (Friedman & Arndt, 2005). Numerous studies demonstrate that manipulating mortality salience makes many subjects more likely to adopt certain reassuring cultural perspectives (Pyszczynski, Solomon, & Greenberg, 2003).

In one study, investigators reminded some subjects, but not others, of their own inevitable death, and then asked all of them to select one of three hypothetical political candidates. One candidate was highly task oriented, with a primary emphasis on achieving goals; a second was highly relationship oriented, with a primary emphasis on making all of his constituents feel valued; and a third was charismatic, with a primary emphasis on national greatness. Subjects who didn't receive the mortality salience manipulation overwhelmingly preferred either the task-focused or relationship-focused candidate, with only 4 percent preferring the charismatic candidate. In contrast, more than 30 percent of subjects who received the mortality salience manipulation preferred the charismatic candidate, reflecting a nearly 800 percent increase relative to the other condition. In comparison with other subjects, their preference for the task-oriented leader was about the same, whereas their preference for the relationship-oriented candidate was lower (Cohen, Solomon, Maxfield, Pyszzynksi, & Greenberg, 2004). By making subjects more keenly aware of their mortality, researchers may have bolstered their desire for a powerful leader who could protect them against threats.

According to terror management theory, reminders of our death can lead us to adopt comforting worldviews—perhaps, in some cases, beliefs in the paranormal.

Can terror management theory help to explain the popularity of certain paranormal beliefs, such as astrology, extrasensory perception, and communication with the dead? Perhaps. Our society's widespread beliefs in life after death and reincarnation may stem in part from the terror that results from knowing we'll eventually die (Lindeman, 1998). Two researchers (Morier & Podlipentseva, 1997) found that compared with other subjects, subjects who underwent a mortality salience manipulation reported higher levels of beliefs in the paranormal, such as ESP, ghosts, reincarnation, and astrology than subjects who didn't. It seems likely that such beliefs are comforting to many of us, especially when confronted with reminders of our demise, because they suggest that there's another dimension beyond our own.

Of course, terror management theory doesn't demonstrate that paranormal claims are false; we still need to evaluate these claims on their own merits. Instead, this theory suggests that we're likely to hold many paranormal beliefs regardless of whether they're correct.

terror management theory
theory proposing that our awareness of our death leaves us with an underlying sense of terror with which we cope by adopting reassuring cultural worldviews

Our tendency to perceive meaning and purpose in the world may trace its origins to childhood. As early as 4 years of age, children see most objects, events, and animals as having a purpose. When adults ask them why mountains exist, they may say "for people to climb on"; when adults ask them why zebras exist, they may say "so they can go to the zoo" (Kelemen, 1999). This deep-seated tendency to find purposes for things persists into adulthood and may help to explain certain pseudoscientific beliefs (Bloom & Weisberg, 2007). When we hear a mysterious noise at night we can't explain, we might assume it's produced by a ghost trying to communicate with us; when we see a strange object in the sky that we don't recognize, we might assume it's produced by an alien civilization hoping to pay us a visit.

The Interpreter: Making Sense of the World. Michael Gazzaniga (2002) contended that the human brain, especially our left hemisphere, functions as an *interpreter,* a system that seeks meaning in random data. By interpreting the millions of inputs it receives at every moment, our brain helps us to make sense of the world. It weaves these diverse inputs into a coherent story that our brains can comprehend. But in doing so, our brain almost always goes well beyond the information it receives, sometimes detecting nonexistent patterns (Bruner, 1957; Hines, 2003).

Imagine for a moment that you're a participant in a study by George Wolford and his collaborators. They've programmed the computer to make a dot appear at either the top or the bottom of the screen. Your task couldn't be simpler; all you need to do is guess whether the next dot will appear at the top or bottom. If you think the dot will appear at the top of the screen, press the button at the top; if you think the dot will appear at the bottom of the screen, press the button at the bottom. Unbeknownst to you, Wolford and his colleagues designed the task so that the dot appears at the top of the screen 80 percent of the time. But the dot appears at the top in an entirely random sequence: You can't predict when it will appear there (Wolford et al., 2000).

If you're like most participants, you struggle desperately to figure out in what sequence the lights are appearing. Yet you're wasting your time, because there *is* no sequence, just random dots that happen to flash at the top of the screen four out of five times. Because most people think they've detected a consistent pattern in the dots, they make many errors. In fact, the average human participant in this study is correct only 68 percent of the time (Gazzaniga, 2002). Remarkably, rats outperform humans on this task, guessing correctly that the dot will appear at the top of the screen 80 percent of the time. The rats don't generate hypotheses about patterns; they base their predictions only on what they've seen. Unlike humans, they don't go beyond the data given to them. We humans are sometimes too smart for our own good.

> ### APPLY YOUR THINKING
> How might our tendency to perceive patterns even when they don't exist lead us to accept certain superstitions, like believing that we'll experience bad luck whenever we walk under a ladder?

Pareidolia: I'll See It When I Believe It. How can our tendency to detect patterns in data predispose us to accept pseudoscientific claims? We can find one example in the striking phenomenon of **pareidolia:** the tendency to perceive meaningful images in meaningless visual stimuli. Any of us who's looked at a cloud and perceived the vague shape of an animal has experienced pareidolia, as have any of us who's seen the oddly misshapen face of a "man" in the moon.

Here's an even more stunning example. In 1976, the *Mars Viking Orbiter* snapped a remarkable photograph of a set of features on the Martian surface. As we can see from the middle photo in the margin, these features bear an eerie resemblance to a human face. Indeed, the resemblance was so striking that some individuals maintained that the "Face on Mars" offers conclusive proof of intelligent life on the Red Planet (Hoagland, 1987). A few went even further, claiming that this face was surrounded by pyramids and the remains of a huge city. This is an extraordinary claim; is the evidence equally extraordinary?

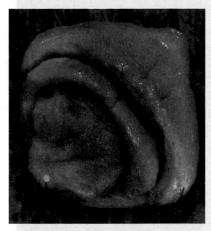

Pareidolia can lead us to perceive meaningful people or objects in largely random stimuli. The "nun bun," a cinnamon roll resembling the face of nun Mother Teresa, was discovered in 1996 in a Nashville, Tennessee, coffee shop.

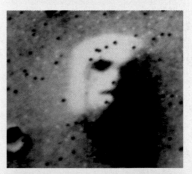

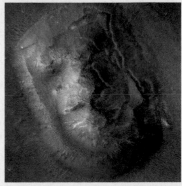

At top is the remarkable "Face on Mars" photo taken by the *Mars Viking Orbiter* in 1976. Some argued that this face provides conclusive proof of intelligent life off of the Earth. Below is a more detailed photograph of the Face on Mars taken in 2001, which revealed that this "face" was just an illusion.

pareidolia
tendency to perceive meaningful images in meaningless visual stimuli

Extraordinary Claims

In 2001, during a mission of a different spacecraft, the *Mars Global Surveyor*, the National Aeronautics and Space Administration (NASA) decided to adopt a scientific approach to the Face on Mars. They were open-minded but demanded evidence. So this time, they swooped down much closer to the face, and pointed the *Surveyor's* cameras directly at it. If we look at the third photo in the margin on page 51, we'll see what they found: absolutely nothing. The Face on Mars was indeed a striking phenomenon, but it was a psychological reality, not an extraterrestrial one. The pareidolia in this instance was a consequence of a peculiar configuration of rocks and shadows present at the angle at which the photographs were taken in 1976, combined with our innate tendency to perceive meaningful faces in what are essentially random visual stimuli (see Chapter 4). Not surprisingly, shortly after NASA released the better and far less interesting photographs of the Face on Mars, some believers in the paranormal insisted that these photographs merely provided proof that NASA was hiding evidence of extraterrestrial life. Nevertheless, this ad hoc immunizing hypothesis doesn't do much other than offer an excuse—in this case, a not especially convincing one—for negative findings.

Apophenia: What a Coincidence! We can see a second example of our tendency to perceive order in disorder in the phenomenon of **apophenia:** the tendency to perceive meaningful connections among unrelated phenomena (Carroll, 2003). We all fall victim to apophenia from time to time. If we think of a friend with whom we haven't spoken in a few months and then immediately afterward receive a phone call from her, we may jump to the conclusion that this striking co-occurrence of events stems from ESP. It's of course *possible* that it does, although we'll learn in Chapter 4 that the scientific evidence for ESP is weak. Our error in this instance is to draw a definitive connection between events where none may exist.

After all, it's entirely possible, if not likely, that these two events happened at about the same time by chance alone. For a moment, think of the number of times one of your old friends comes to mind, and then think of the number of phone calls you receive each month. You'll realize that the laws of probability make it likely that at least once over the next few years, you'll be thinking of an old friend at about the same time she calls. As Greek philosopher Aristotle said, time converts the improbable into the inevitable. We'll learn in Chapter 2 that one reason for apophenia in this instance is that we don't bother to keep track of all of the times we think of old friends when they *don't* call, and of all of the times we don't think of old friends when they *do* call.

Another manifestation of apophenia is our tendency to detect eerie coincidences between persons or events. To take one example, consider the uncanny similarities between Abraham Lincoln and John F. Kennedy, the two most prominent American presidents who were the victims of assassination:

- Abraham Lincoln was elected to Congress in 1846;
  John F. Kennedy was elected to Congress in 1946.
- Abraham Lincoln was elected president in 1860; John F. Kennedy was elected president in 1960.
- The names Lincoln and Kennedy both contain seven letters.
- Both Lincoln and Kennedy were assassinated on a Friday.
- Kennedy was shot in a Lincoln brand convertible.
- When they were assassinated, Kennedy's and Lincoln's wives were sitting next to them.
- Lincoln's secretary, named Kennedy, warned him not to go to the theater; Kennedy's secretary, named Lincoln, warned him not to go to Dallas.
- Both men were assassinated and succeeded by Southerners.
- Both presidents who succeeded them were named Johnson.
- Andrew Johnson, who succeeded Lincoln, was born in 1808; Lyndon Johnson, who succeeded Kennedy, was born in 1908.
- John Wilkes Booth (Lincoln's assassin) was born in 1839; Lee Harvey Oswald (Kennedy's assassin) was born in 1939.
- Both assassins' names consist of fifteen letters.
- Booth fled from the theater and was found in a warehouse; Oswald fled from a warehouse and was found in a theater.
- Both assassins were shot before their trials.

Our minds work in such a way that we often detect patterns in unrelated events, such as thinking of an old friend and then receiving a telephone call from that friend.

factoid

Nobel Prize–winning physicist Luis Alvarez once had an eerie experience: While reading the newspaper, he came across a phrase that reminded him of an old childhood friend he hadn't thought about for decades. A few pages later, he came upon his friend's obituary! Initially stunned, Alvarez (1965) performed some calculations and determined that given the number of people on Earth and the number of people who die every day, this kind of strange coincidence probably occurs about 3,000 times across the world each year.

apophenia
tendency to perceive meaningful connections among unrelated phenomena

Pretty amazing stuff, isn't it? So extraordinary, in fact, that some writers have argued that Lincoln and Kennedy are somehow linked by supernatural forces (Leavy, 1992).

Just how improbable are the Lincoln–Kennedy coincidences? To find out, the magazine *Skeptical Inquirer*, which is a wonderful resource for pseudoscience in psychology, invited its readers to participate in a "Spooky Presidential Coincidences Contest." Sure enough, many readers identified coincidences between other pairs of presidents that were almost as striking as those between Lincoln and Kennedy. Consider the following coincidences between two other presidents, William McKinley and James Garfield (Leavy, 1992; Schick & Vaughn, 2004):

Some people have noted eerie similarities between presidents Abraham Lincoln and John Fitzgerald Kennedy. But are these coincidences as improbable as they seem?

- McKinley and Garfield were both Republicans.
- Both were born and raised in Ohio.
- Both were Civil War veterans.
- Both served in the House of Representatives before becoming president.
- Both supported the gold standard and taxes for protecting U.S. industries.
- Both of their names consist of eight letters.
- After being assassinated, both were replaced by vice presidents from New York.
- Both vice presidents had mustaches.
- Both were assassinated in September during the first year of their current terms.
- The names of their vice presidents (Chester Alan Arthur and Theodore Roosevelt) both consist of seventeen letters.
- Both of their assassins, Charles Guiteau and Leon Czolgosz, had foreign names.

The point here is that coincidences are everywhere: They're surprisingly easy to detect if we just make the effort to look for them. Because of apophenia, we may attribute paranormal significance to coincidences that are probably due to chance. Without convincing evidence to the contrary, it's usually more parsimonious to conclude that coincidences are attributable to chance rather than to supernatural influences.

Occam's Razor

As in the example of our old friend phoning us immediately after she came to mind, one reason we may leap to the conclusion that such presidential coincidences are meaningful is that we fall prey to confirmation bias: We neglect to consider the evidence that *doesn't* support our hypothesis. Because we typically find coincidences to be far more interesting than noncoincidences, we tend to forget that Lincoln was a Republican whereas Kennedy was a Democrat, that Lincoln was assassinated in a theater whereas Kennedy was assassinated in a limousine, that Lincoln was shot in Washington, DC whereas Kennedy was shot in Dallas, that Lincoln had a beard but Kennedy didn't, that Kennedy's wife was glamorous but Lincoln's wife wasn't, and so on. Recall that scientific thinking is designed to counteract confirmation bias. To do so, we must seek out evidence that contradicts our ideas rather than merely confirms them.

The Hot Hand: Reality or Illusion? Because we're meaning-seeking organisms, we find it almost impossible *not* to detect patterns in random data. If we flip a coin four times and it comes up heads all four times, we may begin to think we're on a streak. Instead, we're probably just being fooled by randomness. The same phenomenon extends to sports.

Basketball players, coaches, and fans are fond of talking about the "hot hand." Once a player has made three or four shots in a row, he's "hot," "he's in the zone," and "he's on a roll." One television basketball announcer, former star center Bill Walton, once criticized a team's players for not getting the ball to a fellow player who'd just made several consecutive baskets ("He's got the hot hand—get him the ball!"). It certainly *seems* as though basketball players go on streaks. Do they?

To find out, Thomas Gilovich and his colleagues got hold of the shooting records of the 1980–1981 Philadelphia 76ers, then the only basketball team to keep precise records of which player made which shot in which order (Gilovich, Vallone, & Tversky, 1985). Let's

Table 1.4 Is the Hot Hand a Reality or an Illusion? Let's look at the data from these two players on the Philadelphia 76ers to help us find out.

	Erving	Toney
P(h/mmm)	0.52	0.52
P(h/mm)	0.51	0.53
P(h/m)	0.51	0.51
P(h/h)	0.53	0.43
P(h/hh)	0.52	0.40
P(h/hhh)	0.48	0.32

(*Source:* Gilovich, 1991)

Ruling Out Rival Hypotheses

Replicability

fictoid

Myth: "Streaks" of several consecutive heads (H) or tails (T) in a row when flipping a coin, like HTTTHTTTHTTHHHTHHTTHH, are proof of a nonrandom sequence.

Reality: Streaks like this are not only widespread, but inevitable, in lengthy random sequences. Indeed, the sequence HTTTHTTTHTTHHHTHHTTHH is almost perfectly random (Gilovich, 1991). Because we usually underestimate the likelihood of consecutive sequences, we may be prone to attributing more significance ("Wow . . . I must be on a winning streak!") to these sequences than they deserve.

logical fallacies
traps in thinking that can lead to mistaken conclusions

emotional reasoning fallacy
error of using our emotions as guides for evaluating the validity of a claim

look at **Table 1.4,** which displays the results of two representative players on the 76ers (you basketball fans out there may recognize "Erving" as the famous "Dr. J," widely regarded as one of the greatest players of all time). There we can see six rows, with *h* standing for a hit, that is, a successful shot, and *m* standing for a miss, that is, an unsuccessful shot. As we go from top to bottom, we see six different probabilities (abbreviated with *P*), starting with the probability of a successful shot (a hit) following three misses, then the probability of a successful shot following two misses, all the way (in the sixth and final row) to the probability of a successful shot following three successful shots.

If the hot hand is real, we should see the probabilities of a successful shot increasing from top to bottom. Once a player has made a few shots in a row, he should be more likely to make another shot. But as we can see from the data on these two players, *there's no evidence for the hot hand.* The proportions don't go up and, in fact, go down slightly (perhaps we should call this the "cool hand"?). Gilovich and his colleagues found the same pattern for all the other 76ers' players.

Perhaps the absence of a hot hand is due to the fact that once a player has made several shots in a row, the defensive team makes adjustments, making it tougher for him to make another shot. To rule out this possibility, Gilovich and his colleagues examined foul shots, which are immune from this problem because players attempt these shots without any interference from the defensive team. Once again, they found no hint of "streaky" shooting.

Later researchers have not only replicated these findings for other basketball players, but have found little or no evidence for "streaky performance" in other sports, including golf and baseball (Bar-Eli, Avugos, & Raab, 2006; Clark, 2006). Still, belief perseverance makes it unlikely that these findings will shake the convictions of dyed-in-the-wool hot hand believers. When told about the results of the Gilovich hot hand study, Hall of Fame basketball coach Red Auerbach replied, "Who is this guy? So he makes a study. I couldn't care less." The hot hand may be an illusion, but it's a remarkably stubborn one.

LOGICAL FALLACIES IN PSYCHOLOGICAL THINKING

To avoid being seduced by the charms of pseudoscience, we must learn to avoid commonplace pitfalls in reasoning. Students new to psychology commonly fall prey to **logical fallacies:** traps in thinking that can lead to mistaken conclusions. It's easy for all of us to make these errors, because they seem to make intuitive sense. Politicians, radio talk show hosts, and news reporters make these errors routinely, although few people call them on it. We should remember that scientific thinking often requires us to cast aside our beloved intuitions, although doing so can be extremely difficult at first.

Here we'll introduce four widespread fallacies that are especially relevant to psychology (Gray, 1991; Gula, 2006; Schick & Vaughn, 2004). We should keep these fallacies in mind throughout the book, because they can sometimes give rise to pseudoscientific beliefs. After presenting the name of each fallacy, we'll provide an example of it. Then, we'll define the fallacy and explain why the reasoning in the example is illogical.

Emotional Reasoning Fallacy. "The idea that day care might have negative emotional effects on children gets me really upset, so I refuse to believe it."

The **emotional reasoning fallacy** is the error of using our emotions as guides for evaluating the validity of a claim (some psychologists also refer to this tendency as the *affect heuristic;* Slovic & Peters, 2006). If we're honest with ourselves, we'll realize that findings that challenge our preexisting beliefs often make us angry, whereas findings that confirm these beliefs often make us happy or at least relieved. We shouldn't make the mistake of assuming that because a scientific claim makes us feel uncomfortable or indignant, it's necessarily wrong. For example, in the case of scientific questions concerning the effects of day care on children's emotional and intellectual development, which are scientifically controversial and politically loaded (Belsky, 1988; Hunt, 1999), we need to keep an open mind to the data, regardless of whether they confirm or disconfirm our preconceptions.

When we rely on emotional reasoning, we're falling into the trap of using our experiential mode of thinking to evaluate scientific issues. For such issues, we should instead be relying on our rational mode.

APPLY YOUR THINKING

How can politicians exploit the emotional reasoning fallacy to rally support for certain politically popular positions?

Bandwagon Fallacy. "Lots of people I know believe in astrology, so there's got to be something to it."

The **bandwagon fallacy** is the error of assuming that a claim is correct just because many people believe it. It's an error because popular opinion isn't a dependable guide to the accuracy of an assertion. Prior to 1500, almost everyone believed the sun revolved around the earth, rather than vice versa, but they were woefully mistaken. Similarly, the fact that many people today accept the validity of astrology says nothing about whether astrology is accurate.

Either–Or Fallacy. "I just read in my psychology textbook that some people with schizophrenia were treated extremely well by their parents when they were growing up. This means that schizophrenia can't be due to environmental factors and therefore must be completely genetic."

The **either–or fallacy** is the error of framing a question as though we can only answer it in one of two extreme ways (that's why this fallacy is sometimes also called the *black-or-white fallacy*). Few psychological questions lend themselves to only two completely distinct alternatives. The fact that some people with schizophrenia were raised in a supportive fashion by their parents could imply that the causes of schizophrenia aren't attributable entirely to the psychosocial environment. Yet it doesn't imply that the causes of schizophrenia are entirely genetic, because parenting could in principle play a role in some cases of schizophrenia (although as we'll learn in Chapter 15, there isn't much evidence for this possibility). Or perhaps environmental influences other than parenting, such as life stress, criticism from others, or exposure to viruses while in the womb, could contribute to schizophrenia.

Not Me Fallacy. "My psychology professor keeps talking about how the scientific method is important for overcoming biases. But these biases don't apply to me, because *I'm* objective."

The **not me fallacy** may be the most widespread and dangerous of all logical fallacies. It's the error of believing we're immune from errors in thinking that afflict other people. This fallacy can get us into deep trouble, because it can lead us to conclude mistakenly that we don't require the safeguards of the scientific method. Many pseudoscientists fall into this trap: They're so certain their claims are right—and uncontaminated by mistakes in their thinking—that they don't bother to conduct scientific studies to back up these claims.

Social psychologists have recently uncovered a fascinating phenomenon called **bias blind spot,** which means that most people are unaware of their biases but keenly aware of them in others (Pronin et al., 2004; van Hecke, 2007). None of us believes we have an accent because we live with our accents all of the time. Similarly, few of us believe we have biases, because we've grown accustomed to seeing the world through our own psychological lenses. To see the not me fallacy at work, watch a debate between two intelligent people who hold extremely polarized views on a political issue. More likely than not, you'll see that the debate participants are quite adept at pointing out biases in their opponents, but are often oblivious of their own equally glaring biases.

The bandwagon fallacy reminds us that the number of people who hold a belief isn't a dependable barometer of its accuracy.

When driving, we have blind spots, but our side view mirror helps us to compensate for them. Similarly, in everyday life, we all have our psychological blind spots. Scientific methods can help us compensate for our blind spots and avoid confirming mistaken beliefs.

bandwagon fallacy
error of assuming that a claim is correct just because many people believe it

either–or fallacy
error of framing a question as though we can answer it in only one of two extreme ways

not me fallacy
error of believing we're immune from thinking errors that afflict others

bias blind spot
lack of awareness of our biases, coupled with an awareness of others' biases

APPLY YOUR THINKING

What does the existence of bias blind spot imply about relying on questionnaires (self-report measures) to detect people's personality weaknesses, like self-centeredness or insensitivity to others?

Learning to avoid these and other logical fallacies, some of which we'll encounter in later chapters (see **Table 1.5**), takes considerable time and effort. To do so, we must unlearn deeply entrenched habits of thinking. Nevertheless, if we bear these fallacies in mind when evaluating scientific evidence, we'll find ourselves becoming better critical thinkers in everyday life.

Table 1.5 Other Logical Fallacies to Remember When Evaluating Psychological Claims.

Name	Definition	Example of the Fallacy
Appeal to authority fallacy	Error of accepting a claim merely because an authority figure endorses it	"My professor says that psychotherapy is worthless; because I trust my professor, she must be right."
Genetic fallacy	Error of confusing the correctness of a belief with its origins (genesis)	"Freud's views about personality development can't be right, because Freud's thinking was shaped by sexist views popular at the time."
Argument from antiquity fallacy	Error of assuming that a belief must be valid just because it's been around a long time	"There must be something to the Rorschach Inkblot Test, because psychologists have been using it for decades."
Argument from adverse consequences fallacy	Error of confusing the validity of an idea with its potential real-world consequences	"IQ can't be influenced by genetic factors, because if that were true it would give the government an excuse to prevent low-IQ individuals from reproducing."
Appeal to ignorance fallacy	Error of assuming that a claim must be true because no one has shown it to be false	"No scientist has been able to explain away every reported case of ESP, so ESP probably exists."
Naturalistic fallacy	Error of inferring a moral judgment from a scientific fact	"Evolutionary psychologists say that sexual infidelity is a product of natural selection. Therefore, sexual infidelity is ethically justifiable."
Hasty generalization fallacy	Error of drawing a conclusion on the basis of insufficient evidence	"All three people I know who are severely depressed had strict fathers, so severe depression is clearly associated with having a strict father."
Circular reasoning fallacy	Error of basing a claim on the same claim reworded in slightly different terms	"Dr. Smith's theory of personality is the best, because it seems to have the most evidence supporting it."

THE DANGERS OF PSEUDOSCIENCE: WHY SHOULD WE CARE?

Up to this point, we've been making a big deal about pseudoscience. But why should we care about it? After all, isn't a great deal of pseudoscience, like astrology, pretty harmless? In fact, pseudoscience can be dangerous, even deadly. There are four major reasons why we should all be concerned about pseudoscience.

Opportunity Cost: What We Give Up. Pseudoscientific treatments for mental disorders can lead people to forgo effective treatments. As a consequence, even treatments that are themselves harmless can cause harm indirectly. This phenomenon is called **opportunity cost:** people who invest time, effort, and energy in obtaining a questionable treatment may forfeit the chance to obtain a treatment that works. For example, a major community survey (Kessler et al., 2001) revealed that Americans with histories of severe depression or anxiety attacks more often received scientifically unsupported treatments than scientifically supported treatments, like cognitive-behavioral therapy (see Chapter 16). The unsupported treatments included acupuncture, which has never been shown to work for depression despite a few scattered positive findings; laughter therapy, which is based on the untested notion that laughing can cure depression; and energy therapy, which is based on the unfalsifiable notion that all people possess invisible energy fields that influence their moods (see Chapter 16). Although some of these treatments could prove helpful in future studies, consumers who seek them out are rolling the dice with their mental health.

Animal Deaths and Extinctions: An Unappreciated Cost. Pseudoscientific medical treatments have resulted in the deaths of untold numbers of animals, and even brought certain species to the brink of extinction (Gilovich, 1991). For example, hunters have vir-

opportunity cost
investment of time, energy, and effort in a questionable treatment that can lead people to forfeit the chance to obtain an effective treatment

tually eliminated the black rhinoceros from Africa because its horns fetch a pretty penny in the Far East. There, natives grind up its horns into powder to supposedly cure fevers, headaches, and sexual dysfunction, even though there's not a shred of scientific evidence that they're useful for these purposes. The Chinese green-haired turtle has similarly been nearly extinguished because many residents of Taiwan believe—again, without any scientific evidence—that ingesting it can cure cancer. And tens of thousands of seals have been slaughtered on the West Coast of the United States because some people believe that seal penises can be used as aphrodisiacs.

Direct Harm. Pseudoscientific treatments occasionally do dreadful harm to those who receive them. Take the tragic case of Candace Newmaker, a 10-year-old North Carolina girl brought to Evergreen, Colorado, by her mother in 2000 for treatment of her behavioral problems (Mercer, Sarner, & Rosa, 2003). There, Candace received a treatment called *rebirthing therapy,* which is premised on the scientifically doubtful notion that children's behavioral problems are attributable to difficulties in forming attachments to their parents stemming from birth—in some cases, even before birth (see Prologue and Chapter 16). During rebirthing, children or adolescents reenact the trauma of birth with the "assistance" of one or more therapists. Hundreds of therapists practice this treatment even though there's no evidence that it works (Mercer, 2002). During Candace's rebirthing session, two therapists wrapped her in a flannel blanket, sat on her, and squeezed her repeatedly in an effort to simulate birth contractions. During the 40-minute session, Candace vomited several times and begged the therapists for air, complaining desperately that she couldn't breathe and felt as though she were going to die. When Candace was unwrapped from her symbolic "birth canal," she was dead (Mercer et al., 2003).

An Inability to Think Critically as Citizens. We may be tempted to pass off beliefs in astrology, unidentified flying saucers, crystal healing, and energy fields as innocuous. But in our increasingly complex scientific and technological society, we all need critical thinking skills to reach educated decisions about global warming, toxic waste dumps, cloning, genetic engineering, stem cell research, novel medical treatments, and parenting and teaching practices. Some of these decisions will take place in the voting booth, and others will take place in our communities, homes, and schools. If we're not careful, an inability to think critically about a seemingly unimportant domain, like astrology, can easily spill over to an inability to think critically about issues that can crucially affect our planet's future, not to mention our own futures and those of our children.

The take-home message is clear: Pseudoscience matters. That's what makes scientific thinking so critical: Although far from foolproof, it's our best safeguard against human error.

The magnificent black rhinoceros has been hunted to near extinction because of pseudoscientific medical beliefs.

Candace Newmaker was a tragic victim of what science writer Michael Shermer (2004) aptly called "death by theory." The rebirthing therapists who smothered her to death were convinced that she needed to reenact the birth trauma to eliminate her psychological problems.

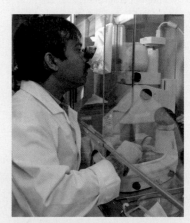

Stem cell research is controversial on both scientific and ethical grounds. To evaluate this and other controversies properly, we need to be able to think critically about the potential costs and benefits of such research.

ASSESS YOUR KNOWLEDGE: FACT OR FICTION?

(1) Both our rational and experiential modes of thinking are useful in certain circumstances. (True/False)

(2) According to terror management theory, our fears of death are an important reason for pseudoscientific beliefs. (True/False)

(3) Humans' tendency to see patterns in random data is entirely maladaptive. (True/False)

(4) Once a basketball player has made several shots in a row, he's more likely to make another shot. (True/False)

(5) Research on bias blind spot implies that we often don't perceive biases in people to whom we're emotionally close. (True/False)

Answers: (1) T (p. 48); (2) T (p. 50); (3) F (p. 51); (4) F (p. 53); (5) F (p. 55)

Think again...

Science vs. Popular Psychology: Common vs. Uncommon Sense (pp. 24–34)

STUDY the Learning Objectives

▶ Distinguish common from uncommon sense
- Psychological research shows that many widely agreed-on "truisms" about human nature aren't true. Much of psychology is uncommon sense.

▶ Describe naive realism and its perils
- Naive realism is the error of believing that we see the world precisely as it is. It can lead us to false beliefs about ourselves and our world, such as believing that our perceptions and memories are always accurate.

▶ Differentiate popular psychology information from misinformation
- Some of popular psychology is accurate, but some of it isn't. For example, although some self-help books are helpful, most have never been tested. When inaccurate, popular psychology often oversimplifies scientific findings.

▶ Describe the importance of science as a set of safeguards against biases
- Confirmation bias is the tendency to seek out evidence that supports our hypotheses and disregard or distort evidence that doesn't. Belief perseverance is the tendency to cling to our beliefs despite contrary evidence. The scientific method is a set of safeguards against these two errors.

DO YOU KNOW THESE TERMS?
- ❏ popular psychology industry (p. 24)
- ❏ naive realism (p. 25)
- ❏ communalism (p. 29)
- ❏ disinterestedness (p. 29)
- ❏ confirmation bias (p. 30)
- ❏ belief perseverance (p. 31)
- ❏ scientific theory (p. 33)
- ❏ hypothesis (p. 33)

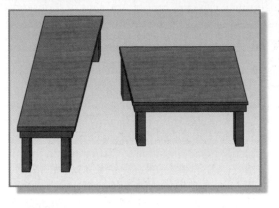

Which table seems bigger and what does this tell us about our ability to trust our own intuitions and experiences? (p. 26)

THINK about what You would do . . .
One of your roommates has been experiencing panic attacks. Keeping in mind the popular psychology industry, how would you begin to find information on panic attacks that you could be reasonably sure was accurate? (p. 28)

Review each of these statements below and identify whether each is a theory (T) or hypothesis (H). (pp. 33–34)

_____ Sarah's motivation for cheating on the test was fear of failure.

_____ Darwin's evolutionary explanation regarding living and extinct species.

_____ The world began in a gigantic explosion about 14 billion years ago.

_____ Our motivation to help a stranger in need is influenced by the number of people present.

_____ Crime rates in Nashville increase as the temperature rises.

ASSESS your knowledge

1. Television, radio, and the Internet, likely the sources of most people's knowledge of human behavior, all fall under the category of the _____ _____. (p. 24)

2. Our intuitive understanding of ourselves and the world (is/isn't) always accurate. (p. 25)

3. The phenomenon, as discussed by psychologist Lee Ross, in which individuals believe the world is precisely as he/she sees it is known as _____ _____. (p. 25)

4. The majority of medical and health information available on the Internet (is/isn't) rigorously reviewed for accuracy to ensure the public's safety. (p. 27)

5. Efforts by research scientists to share their findings with others for objective evaluation is called _____. (p. 29)

6. Maintaining a level of _____ is a crucial component in scientific endeavors to maintain objectivity. (p. 29)

7. When presented with both contradictory and supportive evidence regarding a hypothesis we are researching, our tendency to disregard the contradictory evidence is our _____ _____. (p. 30)

8. Our _____ _____ kicks in when we refuse to admit our beliefs are incorrect in the face of evidence that contradicts them. (p. 31)

9. A scientific model like the Big Bang theory that provides an explanation for a large number of findings in the natural world, is known as a _____ _____. (p. 33)

10. In scientific research, _____ are general explanations, whereas _____ are specific predictions derived from these explanations. (p. 33)

Critical Thinking: Sorting the Wheat from the Chaff (pp. 34–43)

How would you use Occam's Razor to explain crop circles such as this? (p. 40)

Match the Critical Thinking Principle (left) with the accurate description (right). (p. 38)

Name of Critical Thinking Principle	Explanation of Critical Thinking Principle
___ Extraordinary Claims Require Extraordinary Evidence (abbreviated as "Extraordinary Claims")	1. Claims must be capable of being disproved.
___ Falsifiability	2. If two hypothoses explain a phenomenon equally well, we should generally select the simpler one.
___ Occam's Razor	3. The fact that two things are associated with each other doesn't mean that one causes the other.
___ Replicability	4. The more a claim contradicts what we already know, the more persuasive the evidence for this claim must be before we should accept it.
___ Ruling Out Rival Hypotheses	5. A finding must be capable of being duplicated by independent researchers following the same "recipe."
___ Correlation vs. Causation	6. Findings consistent with several hypotheses require additional research to eliminate these hypotheses.

THINK about what **You** would do . . .

A friend swears by her new diet plan, which involves eating only hard-boiled eggs and steak for a month. She's lost 15 lbs since the semester began. You've wanted to lose 15 lbs yourself. How would you investigate and ultimately decide (or not) to try your friend's diet plan? (p. 37)

mypsychlab
where learning comes to life!

SUCCEED with

How to Be a Critical Thinker
Six easy-to-follow steps to improve critical thinking.
(p. 37)

EXPLORE

ASSESS your knowledge

1. Insistence on obtaining persuasive evidence, while evaluating all claims with an open mind, is known as _____ _____. (p. 34)

2. _____ _____ is the phenomenon of being entrenched in our beliefs to the point of dismissing any claims that contradict these beliefs. (p. 35)

3. The flip side of confirmation bias—the disconfirmation bias—is the tendency to _____ evidence inconsistent with a hypothesis we don't believe and _____ evidence consistent with it. (p. 35)

4. The premise that maintaining a balance in scientific work between keeping an open mind and being stridently skeptical is known as _____ _____. (p. 35)

5. Astrology, personality predictions based on the date and time of one's birth, (is/isn't) considered pseudoscience. (pp. 35–36)

6. The skill set for evaluating all claims in an open-minded and careful manner, both inside and outside the classroom or laboratory, is called _____ _____. (p. 37)

7. Scientific thinking (can/can't) be applied to claims in the media, Internet, self-help books, and any other information outlet outside the psychology laboratory. (p. 37)

8. A claim is considered _____, if it could in principle be disproved. (p. 39)

9. The ability of others to consistently duplicate a study's findings is called _____. (p. 41)

10. The assumption that because one thing is associated with another, it must cause the other is the definition of the _____ _____. (p. 42)

STUDY the Learning Objectives

▶ Identify the key features of scientific skepticism and distinguish it from pathological skepticism
  • Scientific skepticism requires us to evaluate all claims with an open mind but to insist on compelling evidence before accepting them. Pathological skepticism, in contrast, implies close-mindedness.

▶ Identify and explain six key principles of critical thinking that will be used throughout the text
  • Six key thinking principles are Extraordinary Claims Require Extraordinary Evidence, Falsifiability, Occam's Razor, Replicability, Ruling Out Rival Hypotheses, and the distinction between Correlation and Causation.

DO YOU KNOW THESE TERMS?

- ☐ **scientific skepticism** (p. 34)
- ☐ **pathological skepticism** (p. 35)
- ☐ **Oberg's dictum** (p. 35)
- ☐ **astrology** (p. 35)
- ☐ **critical thinking** (p. 37)
- ☐ **falsifiable** (p. 39)
- ☐ **risky prediction** (p. 39)
- ☐ **replicability** (p. 41)
- ☐ **correlation–causation fallacy** (p. 42)
- ☐ **variable** (p. 42)
- ☐ **third variable problem** (p. 42)

Psychological Pseudoscience: Impostors of Science (pp. 43–48)

STUDY the Learning Objectives

▶ Describe pseudoscience and its differences from science and metaphysics
- Pseudoscientific claims appear scientific, but don't play by the rules of science. In particular, pseudoscience lacks the safeguards against confirmation bias and belief perseverance that characterize science. Metaphysical claims, in contrast, aren't falsifiable and therefore lie outside the boundaries of science.

▶ Describe the prevalence of pseudoscientific beliefs
- Pseudoscientific and otherwise questionable beliefs are widespread in American culture. Large numbers of Americans accept the existence of extrasensory perception and astrology despite compelling evidence.

▶ Identify seven key warning signs of pseudoscience
- Seven key warning signs of pseudoscience are overuse of ad hoc immunizing hypotheses, lack of self-correction, exaggerated claims, overreliance on anecdotes, evasion of peer review, absence of connectivity, and psychobabble.

DO YOU KNOW THESE TERMS?

- ❑ **pseudoscience** (p. 44)
- ❑ **metaphysical claims** (p. 44)
- ❑ **ad hoc immunizing hypothesis** (p. 45)
- ❑ **peer review** (p. 47)
- ❑ **connectivity** (p. 47)

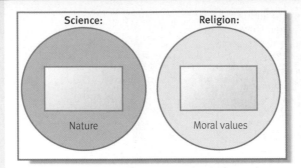

Complete the diagram using Gould's argument of non-overlapping realms of understanding the world. Which scenario is "testable" and which is "untestable"? (p. 45)

SUCCEED with

mypsychlab where learning comes to life!

Astrology
What is your sign: Should we believe our daily horoscope? (p. 44)

EXPLORE

Describe each of the Seven Deadly Sins of Pseudoscience in the space provided (pp. 45–48)

Seven Deadly Sins of Pseudoscience

Overuse of ad hoc immunizing hypotheses _____

Lack of self-correction _____

Exaggerated claims _____

Overreliance on anecdotes _____

Evasion of peer review _____

Absence of connectivity _____

Psychobabble _____

ASSESS your knowledge

1. _____ is a set of claims that may seem scientific, but in fact (is not/is). (p. 44)

2. Science and pseudoscience (are/aren't) distinct entities; if something is considered science, it (can/can't) be considered pseudoscience. (p. 44)

3. Metaphysical claims, such as the existence of God, the soul, or the afterlife, differ from pseudoscience in that they are _____. (p. 44)

4. When a proponent of a theory faces negative evidence, his attempts to explain away the negative evidence to protect his theory are known as ____ ____ ____. (p. 45)

5. Pseudosciences tend to promise remarkable or dramatic cures. This is an example of _____ _____. (p. 46)

6. (Scientific/Pseudoscientific) evidence relies heavily on anecdotal testimony to validate claims. (p. 46)

7. The filter mechanism experts in a field use to carefully screen the work of their colleagues is known as _____. (p. 47)

8. Psychological journals use a selection process that results in (acceptance/rejection) of most manuscripts they receive after peer reviewing. (p. 47)

9. Most scientific findings are cumulative—that is they show _____ with previous scientific work. (p. 47)

10. _____ is language (scientific or otherwise) intended to support pseudoscientific claims and lure in customers. (p. 47)

Pseudoscientific Beliefs: Origins and Dangers (pp. 48–57)

List 4 similarities between Lincoln and Kennedy and explain some possible reasons for these commonalities. (pp. 52–53)

1. _____

2. _____

3. _____

4. _____

SUCCEED with

mypsychlab *where learning comes to life!*

Coin Toss

Heads or tails, can you predict the outcome of a coin toss? (p. 53)

EXPLORE

THINK about

what You would do . . .
An old boyfriend or girlfriend you haven't thought about in years suddenly enters your mind. The same day, he/she calls you. What would you have to do to disconfirm your feelings of apophenia? (pp. 52–53)

How has pseudoscience influenced your ability to identify what is wrong with this photo? (p. 49)

ASSESS your knowledge

1. An objective analysis and careful reasoning of the facts at hand is the hallmark of _____ _____. (p. 48)

2. _____ thinking is used in evaluating your new cell phone while _____ thinking is used in judging whether your best friend is upset with you. (p. 48)

3. Our attraction to the supernatural—with its exciting and reassuring promises—and its ability to alleviate our anxiety over death or spirits is called _____ _____. (p. 49)

4. Human's fear of death, and our awareness of that fear, leads us to adopt reassuring cultural world-views and is known as _____ _____ _____. (p. 50)

5. Our brains (are/aren't) predisposed to make order out of disorder which is why we (adapt/don't adapt) well to pseudoscientific claims. (p. 51)

6. Within the human brain, the _____ hemisphere, known as the interpreter, seeks meaning in random data. (p. 51)

7. Our tendency to see meaningful images in uncommon places or random visual stimuli (such as faces in cloud formations or in food) is a phenomenon called _____. (p. 51)

8. Apophenia is the tendency for us to make meaningful connections among (related/unrelated) phenomena. (p. 52)

9. Scientific thinking often requires us to avoid traps in thinking that can lead to mistaken conclusions, otherwise known as _____. (p. 54)

10. The _____ _____ fallacy is the belief that one is immune to biases and thinking errors that afflict others. (p. 55)

STUDY the Learning Objectives

▶ Describe the motivational factors that predispose us to pseudoscientific beliefs
  • Many pseudoscientific beliefs offer comfort to us, especially in the face of our own inevitable deaths.

▶ Describe the role that scientific illiteracy may play in the public's acceptance of pseudoscience
  • Only a small minority of the American public have the scientific literacy to distinguish scientific from pseudoscientific claims.

▶ Explain the importance of cognitive factors as contributors to pseudoscientific thinking
  • The human mind tends to perceive sense in nonsense and order in disorder. Although generally adaptive, this tendency can lead us to see patterns when they don't exist.

▶ Identify key logical fallacies in psychological thinking that can predispose us to pseudoscientific beliefs
  • Four key logical fallacies to beware of when evaluating psychological claims are the emotional reasoning fallacy, the bandwagon fallacy, the either–or fallacy, and the not me fallacy.

▶ Describe the dangers of pseudoscience
  • Pseudoscientific claims can result in opportunity costs and direct harm due to dangerous treatments. They may also result in a slippery slope, leading us to think less critically about other important domains of modern life.

DO YOU KNOW THESE TERMS?

☐ **rational thinking** (p. 48)
☐ **experiential thinking** (p. 48)
☐ **transcendental temptation** (p. 49)
☐ **terror management theory** (p. 50)
☐ **pareidolia** (p. 51)
☐ **apophenia** (p. 52)
☐ **logical fallacies** (p. 54)
☐ **emotional reasoning fallacy** (p. 54)
☐ **bandwagon fallacy** (p. 55)
☐ **either–or fallacy** (p. 55)
☐ **not me fallacy** (p. 55)
☐ **bias blind spot** (p. 55)
☐ **opportunity cost** (p. 56)

Remember these questions from the beginning of the chapter? Think again and ask yourself if you would answer them differently based on what you now know about science and pseudoscience in psychology. (For more detailed explanations, see MyPsychLab.com)

▶ Is psychology mostly just common sense? (p. 25)
▶ Should we trust most self-help books? (p. 27)
▶ Is psychology really a science? (p. 29)
▶ Are we good at evaluating evidence that contradicts our views? (p. 29–31)
▶ Are claims that can't be proven wrong scientific? (p. 39)
▶ Is anecdotal evidence that a treatment works good evidence for its effectiveness? (p. 46)
▶ Do basketball players shoot in "streaks"? (pp. 53–54)
▶ Is the number of people who share a belief a dependable guide to its accuracy? (p. 55)

THINKING Scientifically

Correlation vs. Causation p. 43

Falsifiability pp. 39, 44, 45

Extraordinary Claims pp. 39, 46, 51

Occam's Razor pp. 40, 53

Replicability pp. 41, 54

Ruling Out Rival Hypotheses pp. 42, 46, 54

2
Research Methods
Safeguards against Error

PREVIEW

Think

First, think about these questions. Then, as you read, think again. . . .

▶ Do we really need research designs to figure out the answers to psychological questions?

▶ Can studying one person in depth yield valuable information?

▶ How do our intuitions sometimes deceive us?

▶ Can we perceive statistical associations even when they don't exist?

▶ What's an "experiment," and is it just like any other psychological study?

▶ What are the major pitfalls to watch out for when evaluating experiments?

▶ What are the pluses and minuses of asking people to describe themselves?

▶ How can we be fooled by statistics?

Facilitated communication in action. The rationale is that, because of a severe motor impairment, some autistic children are unable to speak or type on their own. Therefore, with the help of a facilitator, they can supposedly type out complete sentences on a keyboard or letter pad. Is it too good to be true?

Jenny Storch was 14 years old, but she was no ordinary 14-year-old. She was mute. Like all people with infantile autism, a severe psychological disorder that begins in early childhood (see Chapter 15), Jenny's language and ability to bond with others were severely impaired. Like three-fourths of individuals with infantile autism (American Psychiatric Association, 2000), Jenny was mentally retarded. And, like all parents of children with infantile autism, Mark and Laura Storch were desperate to find some means of connecting emotionally with their child.

Then one day something remarkable happened. In the fall of 1991, Mark and Laura Storch had enrolled Jenny in the Devereux School in Red Hook, a peaceful town nestled in the foothills of the Adirondack Mountains in upstate New York. The timing seemed remarkably fortunate. Only the year before, Douglas Biklen, a professor of education at Syracuse University, had published an article in the *Harvard Educational Review* announcing the development of a technique called *facilitated communication*. Developed in Australia, facilitated communication was a stunning breakthrough in the treatment of infantile autism—or so it seemed. Biklen, like so many others in the autism field, had witnessed numerous "overnight successes" and "miracle cures" for infantile autism come and go over the years. Almost all of them seemed too good to be true, and they were. But facilitated communication was different. It bore every hallmark of being the real thing.

Indeed, facilitated communication possessed a charming simplicity that somehow rang true. Here's how it works. A "facilitator" sits next to the autistic child, who in turn sits in front of a computer keyboard or letter pad. According to Biklen, the facilitator is required to be present because infantile autism is actually a motor (movement) disorder, not a mental disorder as scientists had long assumed. Boldly challenging conventional wisdom, Biklen (1990) proclaimed that autistic children are just as intelligent as other children. But they suffer from a severe motor disorder that prevents them from talking or typing on their own. By guiding the child's hands ever so gently across the letters, the facilitator permits the autistic child to communicate by typing out words. Not just isolated words, like *Mommy,* but complete sentences like, *Mommy, I want you to know that I love you even though I can't speak.* Using facilitated communication, one autistic child even asked his mother to change his medication after reading an article in a medical journal (Mann, 2005). Facilitated communication was the long-sought-after bridge between the hopelessly isolated world of the autistic child and the adult world of social interaction.

The psychiatric aides at Devereux had heard about facilitated communication, which was beginning to spread like wildfire throughout the autism treatment community. Thousands of mental health and education professionals across America were using it, most with apparently astonishing effects. Almost immediately after trying facilitated communication with Jenny, the Devereux aides similarly reported amazing results. For the first time, Jenny produced eloquent statements describing her innermost thoughts and feelings, including her deep love for her parents. The emotional bond with Jenny that Mark and Laura Storch had dreamt of for 14 years was at last a reality.

Yet the Storchs' joy proved to be short-lived. In November 1991, Mark Storch received a startling piece of news that was to forever change his life. With the aid of a facilitator, Jenny had begun to type out allegations of brutal sexual abuse against him. When all was said and done, Jenny had typed out 200 gruesome accusations of rape, all supposedly perpetrated by her father. A second facilitator, who'd heard about these accusations, reported similar findings while assisting Jenny at the keyboard.

Although there was no physical evidence against Mark Storch, the Department of Social Services in Ulster County, New York, promptly restricted contact between Jenny and her parents. They later removed Jenny from the Storch home. Jenny was eventually returned to her parents following a legal challenge, but not before Mark Storch's reputation had been forever stained.

The claims of facilitated communication proponents seemed extraordinary. Was the evidence for these claims equally extraordinary?

Since Douglas Biklen introduced facilitated communication to thousands of eager mental health professionals in the United States, dozens of investigators have examined this procedure under tightly controlled experimental conditions. In a typical study, the facilitator and autistic child are seated in adjoining cubicles. A wall separates them, but an opening between them permits hand-to-hand contact on a keyboard (see **Figure 2.1**). Then, researchers flash two different pictures on adjacent screens, one of which is seen only by the facilitator and the other of which is seen only by the child. For example, the facilitator might view a photograph of a dog, the child a cat. The crucial question is this: Will the word typed out by the child be the picture shown to the facilitator—*dog*—or the picture shown to the child—*cat*?

The results of these studies were as stunning as they were unanimous. In virtually 100 percent of trials, the typed word corresponded to the picture flashed to the facilitator, not the child (Jacobson, Mulick, & Schwartz, 1995; Romancyzk, Arnstein, Soorya, & Gillis, 2003). Unbelievable as it seems, facilitated communication originates entirely from the minds of facilitators. *Unbeknownst to facilitators, their hands are effortlessly guiding the fingers of the autistic child toward the keyboard, and the resulting words are coming from their minds, not the child's.* Scientists, who'd known about a similar phenomenon for decades before facilitated communication appeared on the scene, term it the *ideomotor effect*, because facilitators' ideas are unknowingly influencing their movements (Wegner, 2002). The facilitated communication keyboard turns out to be nothing more than a modern version of the Ouija board, a popular device used by spiritualists to communicate with the dead. Regrettably, proponents of facilitated communication neglected to consider rival hypotheses for its apparent effects.

One would have thought that the facilitated communication story would have ended there. After all, when claims are demolished by a deluge of overwhelmingly negative findings, it's surely time to call it quits and go back to the drawing board. Yet facilitated communication, although shown by psychological research to be ineffective, lives on. Most clinicians have given up on it, but some still use it as a treatment for autistic children's language deficits. There are even indications that it's mounting a comeback in certain quarters.

Figure 2.1 How Facilitated Communication Works. By placing an autistic child and the facilitator in nearby cubicles and flashing different pictures to each of them on some trials, researchers demonstrated that the "facilitated communications" emanated from the mind of the facilitator, not the child.

The facilitated communication keyboard appears to be little more than a modern version of the Ouija board, which is used widely in spiritual circles to supposedly "contact" the dead. Both rely on the ideomotor effect.

The Beauty and Necessity of Good Research Design

The facilitated communication story imparts an invaluable lesson that we'll highlight throughout this book: *Research design matters*. This story is also a powerful illustration of the triumph of good science over pseudoscience.

WHY WE NEED RESEARCH DESIGNS

Many beginning psychology students understandably wonder why they need to learn about research design. Indeed, some of you may be puzzling over the same thing: I took this course to learn about people, not about numbers. Why do I need to learn how to design research studies?

The facilitated communication story tells us the answer. Without research designs, even intelligent and well-educated people can be fooled. Had the proponents of other facilitated communication made use of some of the research designs we'll discuss in this chapter, they wouldn't have been fooled either. As we learned in Chapter 1, the scientific method is a set of tools that helps us to avoid being tricked by our own biases. In this chapter, we'll learn what these tools are and how we can use them to evaluate psychological claims, not only in psychology courses but in everyday life.

"But I Know It Works!" If we're really persistent, we might ask, Do I really need to use research methods to avoid being fooled? Can't I just rely on my experience and common sense? Yet experience and common sense, although enormously helpful in generating hypotheses, are extremely limited for the purposes of testing hypotheses (see Chapter 1). After all, the Devereux aides who worked with Jenny Storch "knew" that facilitated communication worked: They saw Jenny's abuse allegations with their own eyes. But like so many advocates of pseudoscientific techniques, they were the victims of an illusion. Their confirmation bias led them to see what they hoped to see. By relying on naive realism, the faulty assumption that "seeing is always believing" (Chapter 1), these aides were fooled.

If the history of psychology teaches us anything, it's that we should be deeply skeptical of the "Trust me; I know it works" claim. We need rigorous research methods to find out whether a technique really works. Firsthand experience can be helpful in this regard as a starting point, but it's never sufficient, because it's not an adequate safeguard against confirmation bias (see Chapter 1) and other sources of human error.

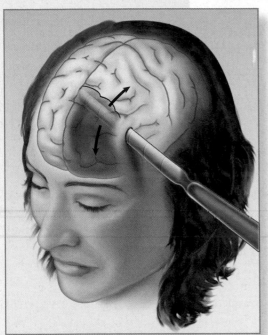

Figure 2.2 The Prefrontal Lobotomy. In a prefrontal lobotomy, the surgeon severs the fibers connecting the brain's frontal lobes from the underlying thalamus.

Prefrontal Lobotomy: What Happens When We Rely on Our Subjective Impressions. Let's take another tragic example. For several decades of the early twentieth century, mental health professionals were convinced that the surgical technique known as **prefrontal lobotomy** (referred to in popular lingo as a "lobotomy") was an effective treatment for schizophrenia and other severe mental disorders (see also Chapter 16). Surgeons who used this technique—which was featured in the Academy Award–winning film *One Flew Over the Cuckoo's Nest* (1975)—severed the neural fibers that connect the brain's frontal lobes to the underlying thalamus (**Figure 2.2**).

The scientific world was so certain that prefrontal lobotomy was a remarkable breakthrough that they awarded the developer of this treatment, Portuguese neurosurgeon Egas Moniz, the Nobel Prize in 1948. As in the case of facilitated communication, stunning reports of the effectiveness of prefrontal lobotomy were based almost exclusively on subjective clinical reports. One physician who performed lobotomies proclaimed, "I am a sensitive observer, and my conclusion is that a vast majority of my patients get better as opposed to worse after my treatment" (see Dawes, 1994, p. 48).

Like proponents of facilitated communication, proponents of prefrontal lobotomy didn't conduct systematic research. They simply assumed that their clinical observations—"I can see that it works"—were sufficient evidence for this treatment's effectiveness. They were wrong; when scientists finally performed carefully controlled studies on the effectiveness of prefrontal lobotomy, they found it to be virtually useless. The operation certainly produced radical changes in behavior, but it didn't target the specific behaviors associated with severe mental illness. Moreover, it created a host of other problems, including extreme apathy (Valenstein, 1986). Nowadays, prefrontal lobotomy is little more than a relic of an earlier pseudoscientific era of mental health treatment. Research design matters.

A Portuguese postage stamp honoring Egas Moniz, who won the Nobel Prize for inventing the prefrontal lobotomy. Moniz made the disastrous error of basing his conclusions regarding the effectiveness of lobotomy entirely on subjective observations.

prefrontal lobotomy
surgical procedure that severs fibers connecting the frontal lobes of the brain from the underlying thalamus

HEURISTICS AND BIASES: HOW WE CAN BE FOOLED

At this point, some of you may be feeling a bit defensive. At first glance, the authors of your text may seem to be implying that many people, perhaps you included, are foolish. But we shouldn't take any of this personally, because one of this text's central themes is that we're *all* capable of being fooled, and that includes your text's authors. That doesn't make you—or us—foolish. It merely makes us human.

How can we all be fooled so easily? A key finding emerging from the past few decades of research is that *the same psychological processes that serve us well in most situations also predispose us to errors in thinking.* Putting it differently, most mistaken thinking is cut from the same cloth as our most useful thinking (Pinker, 1997).

Heuristics: Double-Edged Swords. Psychologists have identified several **heuristics**—mental shortcuts or rules of thumb—that help us to streamline our thinking and make sense of our world. These heuristics probably have evolutionary survival value, because without them we'd quickly become overwhelmed by the tens of thousands of pieces of information with which we're bombarded every day. According to cognitive psychologists (psychologists who study thought; see Prologue and Chapter 8), we're all *cognitive misers* (Taylor & Fiske, 1991). That is, we're mentally lazy and try to conserve our mental energies by simplifying the world. Just as a miser doesn't spend much money, a cognitive miser doesn't expend any more effort in thinking than is necessary.

Although our heuristics work well most of the time (Gigerenzer, 2007; Kruger & Funder, 2005; Sheppard & Koch, 2005), they occasionally get us into trouble. Typically, heuristics cause problems when we use them either too often or in inappropriate situations. In these cases, they can lead us to not merely simplify reality, but to *oversimplify* it. Although most heuristics are probably useful overall, the modern world sometimes presents us with complicated information for which these shortcuts were never intended. The good news is that research designs can help us avoid the pitfalls that can result from misapplying heuristics.

To understand the concept of a heuristic, try to answer the following question. *Imagine that you are in Reno, Nevada. If you wanted to get to San Diego, California, what compass direction would you take? Close your eyes for a moment and picture how you'd get there* (Piatelli-Palmarini, 1994).

Well, we'd of course need to go southwest to get to San Diego from Reno, because California is west of Nevada, right? Wrong! Actually, to get from Reno to San Diego, we would go *southeast*, not southwest. If you don't believe us, look at **Figure 2.3** on the next page.

If you got this one wrong (and, if you did, don't feel bad, because your four authors all got it wrong too!), you almost certainly relied on a heuristic. The mental shortcut you probably used was this: *California is west of Nevada, and San Diego is at the bottom of California, whereas Reno has a lot more land south of it before you hit Mexico.* What you either forgot or didn't know is that a large chunk of California (the bottom third or so) is actually *east* of Nevada. Of course, for most geographical questions (such as, "Is St. Louis east or west of Los Angeles?") these kinds of mental shortcuts work just fine. But in this case the heuristic tripped us up.

History of Heuristics. Two Israeli psychologists who later emigrated to the United States, Daniel Kahneman and Amos Tversky, pioneered the study of heuristics. Their research fundamentally changed how psychologists think about thinking. Indeed, in 2002, Kahneman became the first Ph.D. psychologist to be awarded a Nobel Prize. (Tversky would almost surely have shared the Nobel Prize with Kahneman save for the fact that he had died in 1996, and Nobel committees are prohibited from awarding prizes to deceased individuals.) Although Kahneman never took an economics course in his life, his Nobel Prize was in Economics because his research helped to demolish the longstanding assumption that most people make rational choices about their money. As Kahneman showed, most of us behave irrationally in many domains of our lives, including our financial decisions, although we're typically rational enough to get through the day in one piece.

The Representativeness Heuristic: Like Goes with Like. Kahneman and Tversky focused on three heuristics, two of which we'll discuss. They termed the first heuristic *representativeness* (Kahneman, Slovic, & Tversky, 1982; Tversky & Kahneman, 1974). When we use the **representativeness** heuristic, we judge the probability of an event by its superficial similarity to a prototype. According to this heuristic, "Like goes with like." Imagine that on the first day of your introductory psychology class you sit next to Roger

Daniel Kahneman of Princeton University (*left*) was the first Ph.D. psychologist to be awarded a Nobel Prize. The Nobel Committee recognized him for his groundbreaking work on the cognitive sources of human irrationality.

heuristics
mental shortcuts that help us to streamline our thinking and make sense of our world

representativeness
heuristic that involves judging the probability of an event by its superficial similarity to a prototype

Figure 2.3 In Which Compass Direction Would You Travel to Get from Reno, Nevada, to San Diego, California? If you didn't guess southeast (which is the correct answer), you're not alone. By relying on a heuristic—that is, a mental shortcut—we can sometimes be fooled.

Davis, whom you've never met. You have a few minutes before the first class begins, so you try to strike up a conversation with him. Despite your best efforts, Roger says almost nothing. He appears painfully shy, looks away from you when you ask him a question, stammers, and finally manages to blurt out a few awkward words about being a member of the college chess team and treasurer of the local Star Trek fan club.

Based on your brief interaction with him, would you say that Roger is more likely to be a major in communications or a major in computer science? You're more likely to pick the latter than the former, and you'd probably be right. You relied on a representativeness heuristic to answer this question, because Roger matched your stereotype (see Chapter 13) of a computer science major far better than your stereotype of a communications major. According to the representativeness heuristic, we judge the similarity between two things by gauging the extent to which they resemble each other superficially. Putting it in everyday language, when we use this heuristic we're judging a book by its cover. In many cases, this strategy works—or works well enough—in everyday life.

Now consider a slightly different example. Imagine that on the second day of class you sit next to a young woman who introduces herself as Amy Chang. Amy is polite and soft-spoken, but friendly, and describes herself as having grown up in the Chinatown section of San Francisco. In response to a question about her interests, she mentions that she's vice president of the college Chinese Students' Association.

Based on your brief interaction with Amy, would you say that she's more likely to be a psychology major or an Asian American studies major? You'd probably be more likely to pick the latter than the former. Yet in this case, you'd probably be wrong. Why?

Although Amy fits your stereotype of an Asian American studies major better than your stereotype of a psychology major, you probably forgot one crucial fact: There are many more psychology majors in your college than Asian American studies majors. By focusing too heavily on the superficial similarity of Amy to your stereotype of an Asian American studies major—that is, by relying too heavily on the representativeness heuristic—you neglected to consider what psychologists call the extremely low *base rate* of this major.

Base rate is just a fancy term for how common a behavior or characteristic is (Finn & Kamphuis, 1995; Meehl & Rosen, 1955). When we say that alcoholism has a base rate of about 5 percent in the U.S. population (American Psychiatric Association, 2000), we mean that about 1 in 20 Americans is alcoholic at any given time. When evaluating the probability that a person (for example, Amy) belongs to a category (for example, Asian American studies major), we need to consider not only how similar that person is to other members of the category, but also the base rate of this category. We commit the *base rate fallacy* when we neglect to consider base rates, as we'd have done if we'd concluded that Amy was more likely to be an Asian American studies major than a psychology major.

The Availability Heuristic: "Off the Top of My Head . . ." Kahneman and Tversky termed the second heuristic *availability*. Using the **availability** heuristic, we estimate the likelihood of an occurrence based on the ease with which it comes to our minds—that is, on how "available" it is in our memories (Kahneman et al., 1982). Like representativeness, availability often works well. If I ask you whether there's a higher density of trees (a) on your college campus or (b) in the downtown area of the nearest major city, you're likely to answer (a). Odds are you'd be right (unless, of course, your college campus is *in* a downtown area!). When answering this question, it's unlikely you actually calculated the precise proportion of trees you've observed in each place. Instead, you probably called to mind mental images of your campus and of the downtown area of the nearest big city, and you recalled correctly that the former contains a much higher density of trees than the latter.

Now try answering the following question: Are there more words in the English language with the letter *k* as the first letter in the word or the third letter in the word? If you're like most people, you responded that there are more English words beginning with the

base rate
how common a characteristic or behavior is in the general population

availability
heuristic that involves estimating the likelihood of an occurrence based on the ease with which it comes to our minds

letter *k* than with *k* in the third position. In fact, there are more than twice as many words with *k* in the third position as there are words beginning with the letter *k*. Why do most of us get this question wrong? We rely on the availability heuristic: Because of how our brains categorize words, we find it easier to think of words with *k* in the first position (like *kite* and *kill*) than words with *k* in the third position (like *bike* and *cake*).

Here's an even more surprising example that you can try on your friends (Jaffe, 2004). Ask half of your friends to guess the number of murders per year in Michigan, and average the answers. Then ask the other half to guess the number of murders per year in the city of Detroit, Michigan, and again average the answers. (If one or more of your friends are from Michigan, this example might not work, so you may want to try substituting Illinois for Michigan and Chicago for Detroit.) If the results of your informal "poll" are anything like those of Kahneman, you're likely to find that your friends give higher estimates for the number of murders in Detroit, Michigan, than for the entire state of Michigan! Kahneman found that when he asked people about the state of Michigan they estimated about 100 murders per year, whereas when he asked people about the city of Detroit they estimated about 200 murders per year.

This paradoxical result is almost certainly due to our reliance on the availability heuristic. When we imagine the state of Michigan, we conjure up images of sprawling farms and peaceful suburbs. Yet when we imagine the city of Detroit, we conjure up images of bustling inner-city areas and rundown buildings. So thinking of Detroit makes us think of more dangerous areas and therefore more murders.

Our mental images of Michigan (*top*) and Detroit, Michigan (*bottom*), conjure up markedly different estimates of violent crime. In this case, the availability heuristic can lead us to faulty conclusions.

> **APPLY YOUR THINKING**
> How could the availability heuristic lead many of us to be much more fearful of flying in commercial airliners than of driving in automobiles, even though driving is far more dangerous?

We should keep the representativeness and availability heuristics in mind, because we'll soon learn that many research methods help us to avoid the mistakes that arise from applying these heuristics uncritically. As Kahneman and Tversky noted, however, it's not only heuristics that can lead us astray. We can also fall prey to a variety of **cognitive biases**—systematic errors in thinking.

COGNITIVE BIASES

As we'll recall from Chapter 1, *confirmation bias* is our natural tendency to seek out evidence that supports our hypotheses and to ignore, downplay, or distort evidence that doesn't. One crucial function of the scientific method, as we've seen, is to help us compensate for confirmation bias. By forcing us to adopt safeguards against confirming our pet hypotheses, the scientific method makes us less likely to fool ourselves.

Yet confirmation bias is only one bias that can lead us to draw misleading conclusions. Two others are hindsight bias and overconfidence.

Hindsight Bias. **Hindsight bias,** sometimes known also as the "I knew it all along effect," refers to our tendency to overestimate how well we could have successfully forecasted known outcomes (Fischoff, 1975; Kunda, 1999). As the old saying goes, "Hindsight is always 20/20." This is one case in which common wisdom appears to be correct. Following the terrorist attacks of September 11, 2001, many television pundits and politicians engaged in Monday-morning quarterbacking regarding what could or should have been done to prevent these attacks: better airport security, better covert intelligence, better warnings to the American public, better prosecution of known terrorists, and so on. There may well have been some truth to each of these after-the-fact recommendations, but they all miss a crucial point: Once an event has occurred, it's

If a couple of your friends were dating and later became happily married, would you say, "I knew from the start they were made for each other!"? If so, you might be engaging in hindsight bias.

cognitive biases
systematic errors in thinking

hindsight bias
tendency to overestimate how well we could have successfully forecasted known outcomes

awfully easy in retrospect to "predict" it and then suggest ways in which we could have prevented it. As the Nobel Prize–winning physicist Niels Bohr joked, "Prediction is difficult, especially for the future."

Overconfidence. Related to hindsight bias is **overconfidence**: our tendency to overestimate our ability to make correct predictions. Across a wide variety of tasks, most of us are more confident in our predictive abilities than we should be (Hoffrage, 2004; Smith & Dumont, 2002). Try answering the following four questions:

(1) Which city is farther north—Rome, Italy, or New York City?

(2) Is absinthe a precious stone or a liqueur?

(3) How old was Dr. Martin Luther King when he was assassinated, 39 or 49?

(4) How many bones are in the human body, 107 or 206?

Then, using a 0–100 scale, estimate how confident you are regarding whether each answer is correct (with 0 being "I am not confident at all" and 100 being "I am completely confident"). Now, look at the bottom of page 71 to find the correct answers to these questions. Researchers typically find that for the questions we get wrong, we're much more confident than we should have been that we got them right.

We're overconfident in many domains of our lives. A national survey of nearly a million high school seniors revealed that 100 percent (yes, all of them!) believed they were *above* average in their ability to get along with others. Twenty-five percent believed that that they were in the top 1 percent (College Board, 1976–1977). A survey of college professors revealed that 94 percent believed they were better scholars than their colleagues (Cross, 1977). The authors of this book can attest to the fact that few of their professor colleagues suffer from feelings of inadequacy. Obviously, we can't all be above average, but most of us think we are. Some psychologists have referred to this belief as the "Lake Wobegone effect" after the fictional town (in Garrison Keillor's popular radio show, *A Prairie Home Companion*) in which "all the women are strong, all the men are good-looking, and all the children are above average."

It's not only students and professors who are prone to overconfidence. Social psychologist Philip Tetlock (2005) demonstrated that television and radio political pundits—so-called talking heads—are prone to exceedingly confident predictions regarding domestic and foreign policy events ("Will Congress pass the big new spending bill?" "Who will be the next Democratic nominee for president?"), even though they're often wildly wrong. Moreover, Tetlock found that the more extreme pundits were in their political views, whether liberal or conservative, the *less* likely their predictions were to be accurate. Moderates are typically more accurate in their predictions, perhaps because they tend to possess a better appreciation of alternative points of view.

The heuristics and biases we've discussed can make us certain we're right even when we're not. As a consequence, we can not only draw false conclusions, but become convinced of them. Not to worry: The scientific method is here to the rescue.

Television commentators with extreme political views are often popular, because they appeal to strongly partisan supporters. Yet research suggests that these individuals tend to be overconfident—and inaccurate—in their predictions, perhaps because they lack a sufficient appreciation of alternative points of view.

overconfidence
tendency to overestimate our ability to make correct predictions

ASSESS YOUR KNOWLEDGE: FACT OR FICTION?

(1) The psychological processes that give rise to heuristics are generally maladaptive. (True/False)

(2) Psychological research suggests that we're all capable of being fooled by our heuristics. (True/False)

(3) The representativeness heuristic often leads us to attend too closely to base rates. (True/False)

(4) Most of us tend to be less confident than we should be when making predictions about future events. (True/False)

Answers: (1) F (p. 66); (2) T (p. 66); (3) F (p. 68); (4) F (p. 70)

The Scientific Method: Toolbox of Skills

In actuality, the heading of this section is a bit of a fib, because there's no *single* scientific method. "The" scientific method is a myth, because the techniques that psychologists use are very different from those that their colleagues in chemistry, physics, and biology use (Bauer, 1992).

As we discovered in Chapter 1, the scientific method is a toolbox of skills designed to counteract our tendency to fool ourselves. All of the tools we'll describe have one major thing in common: they permit us to test *hypotheses,* which as we learned in Chapter 1 are specific predictions. Psychologists often derive these hypotheses from broader theories. If these hypotheses are confirmed, our confidence in the theory is strengthened, although we should remember that this theory is never truly "proven." If these hypotheses are disconfirmed, scientists often revise this theory or eventually abandon it entirely. Using the toolbox of the scientific method allows us to test hypotheses in a way that minimizes our biases. This toolbox isn't foolproof by any means, but it's the best set of safeguards against bias we have at our disposal. Let's now open up this toolbox and take a peek at what's inside.

NATURALISTIC OBSERVATION: STUDYING HUMANS "IN THE WILD"

Let's say we wanted to conduct a study to find out about laughter. How often do people laugh in the real world, and what kinds of things make them laugh? Do men laugh more often than women? In what settings are people most likely to laugh? We could try to answer these questions by bringing people into our laboratory and observing their laughter across various situations. But it's unlikely we'd be able to re-create the full range of situations that trigger laughter. Moreover, even if we observed participants without their knowing it, their laughter could still have been influenced by the fact that they were in a laboratory. Among other things, they may have been more nervous or less spontaneous than in the real world.

One way of getting around these problems is **naturalistic observation:** watching behavior in real-world settings. We can perform naturalistic observation using a video camera or tape recorder or, if we're willing to go low-tech, only a paper and pencil. Many psychologists who study animals, such as chimpanzees or gorillas, in their natural habitats use naturalistic observation, although psychologists who study humans sometimes use it too. By doing so, we can better understand the range of behaviors displayed by individuals in the "real world," as well as the situations in which they exhibit them.

Robert Provine (1996, 2000) relied on naturalistic observation in an investigation of human laughter. Provine and his research assistants eavesdropped on 1,200 instances of laughter in social situations—shopping malls, restaurants, and street corners—and recorded the gender of participants, the remarks that preceded laughter, and others' reactions to laughter. Provine found that women laugh much more than men in social situations. Surprisingly, he discovered that less than 20 percent of laughing incidents are preceded by statements that could remotely be described as funny. Instead, most cases of laughter are preceded by nonhumorous, often quite ordinary, comments (such as, "It was nice meeting you, too"). Provine also found that speakers laugh considerably more than listeners, a finding painfully familiar to any of us who've had the experience of laughing out loud at one of our jokes while our friends looked back at us with a blank stare. Provine's work, which would have been difficult to pull off in a laboratory, sheds new light on the interpersonal triggers and consequences of laughter.

The major advantage of naturalistic designs is that they are often high in **external validity:** the extent to which we can generalize our findings to real-world settings (Neisser

Researcher Jane Goodall has spent much of her career using techniques of naturalistic observation with chimpanzees in Gombe, Kenya. As we'll learn in Chapter 13, her work strongly suggests that warfare is not unique to humans.

naturalistic observation
watching behavior in real-world settings

external validity
extent to which we can generalize findings to real-world settings

72

& Hyman, 1999). Because psychologists apply these designs to organisms as they go about their everyday business, their findings are often directly applicable to the real world. Some psychologists contend that naturalistic designs almost always have higher external validity than laboratory experiments, although actually there's not much research support for this claim (Mook, 1983).

Still, naturalistic designs have a disadvantage. They tend to be low in **internal validity:** the extent to which we can draw cause-and-effect inferences. As we'll soon learn, well-conducted laboratory experiments are high in internal validity, because we can manipulate the key variables ourselves. In contrast, in naturalistic designs we have no control over these variables and need to wait for behavior to unfold before our eyes.

CASE STUDY DESIGNS: GETTING TO KNOW YOU

One of the simplest designs in the psychologist's investigative toolbox is the case study. In a **case study,** researchers examine either one person or a small number of people, often over an extended period of time (Davison & Lazarus, 2007). An investigator could spend 10 or even 20 years studying one man with schizophrenia, carefully documenting his childhood experiences, academic and job performance, family life, friendships, psychological treatment, and the ups and downs of his mental problems. There's no single "recipe" for how to perform a case study. Some researchers might observe a person over time, others might administer questionnaires, and still others might conduct repeated interviews. The richness of detail yielded by case studies often affords researchers a valuable source of fruitful hypotheses. The downside is that we can't generalize these ideas from one person to persons in general, so there's a trade-off between the *depth* of our description and the *breadth* of its applicability to the population.

Advantages of Case Studies. Case studies can be helpful in providing **existence proofs:** demonstrations that a given psychological phenomenon can occur. As we learned in the Prologue (see also Chapter 7), one of the most bitter controversies in psychology surrounds the question of "recovered memories" of child abuse. Can individuals completely forget episodes of childhood sexual abuse for years or even decades, only to remember them, often with the aid of a psychotherapist, in perfectly accurate form in adulthood? To demonstrate the possibility of recovered memories, all we'd need is *one* clear-cut case of a person who'd forgotten an abuse memory for decades and then recalled it suddenly. Although there have been several suggestive existence proofs of recovered memories (Duggal & Sroufe, 1998; Schooler, 1997), none has been entirely convincing (McNally, 2003).

Case studies also provide a valuable opportunity to study rare or unusual phenomena that are difficult or impossible to re-create in the laboratory, such as people with atypical symptoms or rare types of brain damage. Richard McNally and Brian Lukach (1991) reported a case history of a man who exposed himself sexually to large dogs, and who obtained sexual gratification from doing so, a condition known as "zoophilic exhibitionism." To treat this man's condition, they developed a 6-month treatment program that incorporated techniques designed to enhance his sexual arousal in response to women and extinguish his sexual response to dogs. Needless to say, researchers could wait around for decades in the laboratory before accumulating a sample of fifty or even five individuals with this bizarre condition. McNally and Lukach's single case provided helpful insights into the treatment of this condition that laboratory research couldn't.

Case studies can also offer useful insights that researchers can later test in systematic investigations (Davison & Lazarus, 2007). As we'll learn in Chapter 16, one treatment for phobias (severe and irrational fears of objects, places, or situations) that's been demonstrated to be scientifically effective is *systematic desensitization,* a method that combines deep muscle relaxation with a hierarchy (ladder) of anxiety-provoking experiences. The initial ideas underlying systematic desensitization derived from informal observations by therapists who noticed that clients who were extremely relaxed were virtually incapable of experiencing anxiety (Wolpe, 1958). Of course, before therapists could conclude that systematic desensitization was effective, they needed to conduct more elaborate controlled

Case studies can sometimes provide access to the rare or unusual. For example, people with the condition of Capgras' syndrome believe that their relatives or loved ones have been replaced by identical-looking doubles. The study of this condition has shed light on neurological and psychological processes involved in identifying other people.

internal validity
extent to which we can draw cause-and-effect inferences from a study

case study
research design that examines one person or a small number of people in depth, often over an extended time period

existence proofs
demonstrations that a given psychological phenomenon can occur

studies. Yet without their initial informal observations, systematic desensitization might never have seen the light of day.

Disadvantages of Case Studies. Nevertheless, if we're not careful, case studies can lead to misleading, even disastrously wrong, conclusions. As we discovered in Chapter 1, the *plural of anecdote isn't fact.* Hundreds of observations purporting to show that facilitated communication is effective for autism aren't sufficient to conclude that it's effective, because carefully controlled studies have pinpointed alternative explanations for its effects. As a consequence, case studies don't typically lend themselves to systematic tests of hypotheses about *why* a given phenomenon occurred. Nevertheless, they're often an invaluable way to generate hypotheses that psychologists can later test in well-conducted studies.

Because of the limitations of case studies, psychologists are cautious about relying on them too heavily to draw conclusions. As a consequence, they've turned to research designs that are more systematic, that is, that allow more rigorous conclusions.

CORRELATIONAL DESIGNS

The first important systematic research method we'll discuss is the correlational design. When using a **correlational design,** psychologists examine the extent to which two variables are associated. Recall from Chapter 1 that a *variable* is anything that can take on different values across individuals, like impulsivity, creativity, brain size, and religiosity. When we think of the word *correlate,* we should decompose it into its two parts: *co-* and *relate.* If two things are correlated, they relate to each other—not interpersonally, but statistically.

Identifying Correlational Designs. Identifying a correlational design can be tricky at first, because investigators who use this design—and news reporters who describe it—don't always use the word *correlated* in their description of findings. Instead, they'll often use terms like *associated, related, linked,* or *went together.* Anytime researchers conduct a study of the extent to which two variables tend to "travel together," their design is correlational even if they don't describe it that way explicitly.

Correlations: A Beginner's Guide. Before we go any further, let's lay some groundwork by examining three basic facts about correlations:

(1) Correlations can be *positive, zero,* or *negative.* A positive correlation means that as the value of one variable goes up, the other also goes up. If the number of friends children have is positively correlated with how outgoing they are, then more outgoing children have more friends and less outgoing children have fewer friends. A zero correlation means that the variables don't go together. If math ability has a zero correlation with singing ability, then knowing that someone is good at math tells us nothing about whether his singing ability is good, bad, or mediocre. Finally, a negative correlation means that when the value of one variable goes up, the other goes down, and vice versa. If social anxiety is negatively correlated with perceived physical attractiveness, then more socially anxious people would be rated as less attractive, and less socially anxious people as more attractive.

(2) Correlations, at least the ones we'll be discussing in this textbook, range in value from −1.0 to 1.0. A correlation of −1.0 is a perfect negative correlation, whereas a correlation of +1.0 is a perfect positive correlation. We won't talk about how to calculate correlations, because the mathematics of doing so gets pretty technical (those of you who are really ambitious can check out http://www.psychstat.smsu.edu/introbook/sbk17.htm to learn how to calculate a correlation). Values lower than 1.0 (either positive or negative values), such as .23 or .69, indicate a less-than-perfect correlation. To find how strong a correlation is, we should look at its *absolute value,* that is, the size of the correlation without the plus or minus sign in front of it. Thus, the absolute value of a correlation of +.27 is .27, and the absolute value of a correlation of −.27 is also .27. Interestingly, both correlations are equally large in size—and equally informative—but they're going in opposite directions.

(3) To find out how much of one variable is accounted for by another variable, we square the correlation. For example, the correlation between scores on the Scholastic Assessment Test

Ruling Out Rival Hypotheses

correlational design
research design that examines the extent to which two variables are associated

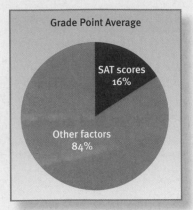

Figure 2.4 Grade Point Average. A correlation of .4 means that only 16 percent of variability in students' grades in college can be predicted by SATs. The other 84 percent is due to other factors, some of which are probably unknown.

scatterplot

grouping of points on a two-dimensional graph in which each dot represents a single person's data

(SAT) and grade point average in college is typically about $r = .4$. (The lowercase r, by the way, is the letter used to indicate a correlation.) This correlation means that SAT scores account for about 16 percent (that's .4 squared) of the differences in people's grades (see **Figure 2.4**). We can also reverse that statement to say that people's grades account for about 16 percent of the differences in people's SAT scores. We can see from this example that there's some good news and some bad news for SAT fans. First, the good news: SATs do considerably better than chance at predicting college grades; if the correlation were $r = 0$ (a chance correlation), then SAT scores would account for 0 percent of the differences in people's grades, because 0 squared is still 0. Now, the bad news: about 84 percent of the differences among people in their college grades is unexplained by their SAT scores; these differences must be due to something else. That "something else" may include motivation, creativity, drive, intellectual curiosity, and perhaps variables that psychologists haven't figured out how to measure.

The Scatterplot. **Figure** 2.5 shows three panels depicting three types of correlations. Each panel shows a **scatterplot:** a grouping of points on a two-dimensional graph. Each dot on the scatterplot represents a person. As we can see, each person differs from other persons in his or her scores on one or both variables displayed on the scatterplot.

In the panel on the left is a fictional scatterplot of a moderate ($r = -.5$) negative correlation; this correlation shows the association between the average number of beers that students drink each night and their scores on their first psychology exam in college. We can tell that this correlation is negative because the clump of dots goes from higher on the left of the graph to lower on the right of the graph. Because this correlation is negative, it means that the more beers students drink, the worse they tend to do on their first psychology exam. Note that this negative correlation isn't perfect (that is, it's not $r = -1.0$). That means that some students drink a lot of beers and still do well on their first psychology exam and that some students drink almost no beer and still do poorly on their first psychology exam.

In the middle panel is a fictional scatterplot of a zero ($r = 0$) correlation; this correlation displays the association between the students' shoe sizes and scores on their first psy-

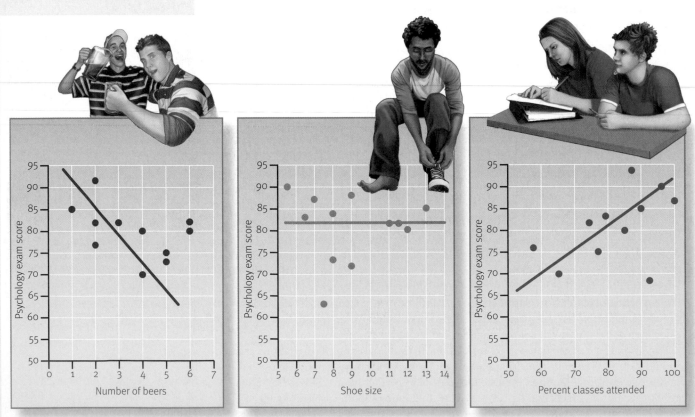

Figure 2.5 Diagram of Three Scatterplots. Scatterplot (*left*) depicts a moderate negative correlation ($r = -.5$); scatterplot (*middle*) depicts a zero correlation; and scatterplot (*right*) depicts a moderate positive correlation ($r = .5$).

chology exam. The easiest way to identify a zero correlation is that the scatterplot looks like a blob of dots that's pointing neither upward nor downward. This zero correlation means there's no association whatsoever between students' shoe sizes and how well they do on their first psychology exam. Knowing one variable tells us absolutely nothing about the other (that's good news for those of us with tiny feet).

The panel on the right shows a fictional scatterplot of a moderate ($r = .5$) positive correlation; this correlation shows the association between students' attendance in their psychology course and their scores on their first psychology exam. Here, the clump of dots goes from lower on the left of the graph to higher on the right of the graph. This positive correlation means that the more psychology classes students attend, the better they tend to do on their first psychology exam. Again, because the correlation isn't perfect (it's not $r = 1.0$), there will always be the inevitable annoying students (yes, psychology professors are irritated by them too) who don't attend any classes yet do well on their exams, and the incredibly frustrated souls who attend all of their classes and still do poorly.

Remember that unless a correlation is perfect, that is, 1.0 or −1.0, there will always be exceptions to the general trend. Because virtually all correlations in psychology have an absolute value of less than 1, *psychology is a science of exceptions*. To argue against the existence of a correlation, it's tempting to resort to "I know a person who . . ." reasoning (see Chapter 1). So if we're trying to refute the overwhelming evidence that cigarette smoking is correlated with lung cancer, we might insist, "But I know a person who smoked five packs of cigarettes a day for 40 years and never got lung cancer." But this anecdote, intriguing as it is, doesn't refute the existence of the correlation, because the correlation between cigarette smoking and lung cancer isn't perfect. Because the correlation is less than 1.0, such exceptions are to be completely expected—in fact, they're mathematically required.

Illusory Correlation. Why do we need to calculate correlations? Can't we just use our eyeballs to estimate how well two variables go together?

No, we can't, because psychological research demonstrates that we're remarkably poor at accurately estimating the sizes of correlations. In fact, we're often prone to an extraordinary phenomenon termed **illusory correlation:** a statistical association between two variables where none exists (Chapman & Chapman, 1967, 1969). An illusory correlation is a statistical mirage. Here are two striking examples:

(1) Many people are convinced of a strong statistical association between the full moon and a variety of strange occurrences, like violent crimes, suicides, psychiatric hospital admissions, and births—the so-called lunar lunacy effect (the word *lunatic* derives from *Luna,* the Roman goddess of the moon). Some police departments even put more cops on the beat on nights when there's a full moon, and many emergency room nurses insist that more babies are born during full moons (Hines, 2003). Yet a mountain of data shows that the full moon isn't correlated with any of these events: that is, the true correlation is almost exactly $r = 0$ (Rotton & Kelly, 1985).

(2) Many individuals with arthritis are convinced that their joint pain increases during rainy weather, yet several carefully conducted studies show no association between joint pain and rainy weather (Quick, 1999).

Illusory Correlation and Superstition. Illusory correlations also form the basis of many superstitions (Vyse, 2000). Take the case of Wade Boggs, Hall of Fame baseball player and one of the game's greatest hitters. For 20 years, Boggs ate chicken before every game, believing this peculiar habit was correlated with successful performance in the batter's box. Boggs eventually became so skilled at cooking chicken that he even wrote a cookbook called *Fowl Tips.* It's unlikely that eating chicken and belting 95 mile an hour fastballs into the outfield have much to do with each other, but Boggs perceived such an association. Countless other superstitions, like keeping a rabbit's foot for good luck and not walking under ladders to avoid bad luck, probably also stem in part from illusory correlation (see Chapter 6).

Just because we know one person who was a lifelong smoker and lived to a ripe old age doesn't mean there's no correlation between smoking and serious illnesses, like lung cancer and heart disease. Exceptions don't invalidate the existence of correlations.

Although legend has it that animals and humans behave strangely during full moons, research evidence demonstrates that this supposed correlation is an illusion.

illusory correlation
perception of a statistical association between two variables where none exists

The Great Fourfold Table of Life. So you may be wondering: How on earth could so many people be so wrong? The first point to understand is that we're all susceptible to illusory correlation. Indeed, illusory correlations are an inescapable fact of everyday life. To understand why, we need to introduce a concept called the *Great Fourfold Table of Life*. We can think of much of everyday life in terms of a table of four probabilities, like that shown in **Table 2.1**. We can use the Great Fourfold Table of Life to describe the correlation between any two occurrences.

Table 2.1 The Great Fourfold Table of Life.

		Did a Crime Occur?	
		Yes	**No**
Did a Full Moon Occur?	**Yes**	(A) Full moon + crime	(B) Full moon + no crime
	No	(C) No full moon + crime	(D) No full moon + no crime

Returning to the lunar lunacy effect, there are four possible relations between the phase of the moon and whether a crime is committed. The upper left-hand (A) cell of the Great Fourfold Table of Life consists of cases in which there was a full moon and a crime occurred. The upper right-hand (B) cell consists of cases in which there was a full moon and no crime occurred. The bottom left-hand (C) cell consists of cases in which there was no full moon and a crime occurred. Finally, the bottom right-hand (D) cell consists of cases in which there was no full moon and no crime.

Decades of psychological research lead to one inescapable conclusion: We tend to pay too much attention to the *upper left-hand (A) cell* (Gilovich, 1991). This cell is especially interesting to us, because it typically confirms our expectations. Our tendency to attend too closely to this cell is called the *fallacy of positive instances,* because we're committing the error of honing in on occurrences that match what we expect to find. In the case of the lunar lunacy effect, instances in which there was both a full moon and a crime are especially interesting and memorable ("See, just like I've always said, weird things happen during full moons"). Moreover, when we think about what tends to occur during a full moon, we rely on the availability heuristic, so we tend to remember the instances that come most easily to mind. In this case, these instances are usually those that grab our attention, namely, those that fall into the (A) cell.

Unfortunately, our minds aren't good at detecting and remembering *nonevents,* that is, things that don't happen. It's unlikely we're going to rush home excitedly to tell our friend, "Wow, you're not going to believe this. There was a full moon tonight, and guess what happened? Nothing!" Our uneven attention to the different cells in the Great Fourfold Table of Life leads us to perceive illusory correlations.

How can we avoid or at least minimize our tendencies toward illusory correlation? Probably the best way is to force ourselves to keep track of disconfirming instances—to give those other three cells a little more of our time and attention. For example, when James Alcock and his students asked a group of participants who claimed they could predict the future from their dreams—so-called prophetic dreamers—to keep careful track of their dreams by using a diary, their beliefs that they were prophetic dreamers vanished (Hines, 2003). By forcing participants to record all of their dreams, Alcock forced them to attend to the (B) cell in the Great Fourfold Table of Life, the cell consisting of cases that disconfirm prophetic dreams.

The phenomenon of illusory correlation explains why we can't rely on our subjective impressions to tell us whether two variables are associated. Our intuitions often mislead us, especially when we've learned to expect two things to go together (Myers, 2002). Indeed, adults may be more prone to illusory correlation than children, because they've built up expectations about whether certain events—like full moons and odd behavior—go together (Kuhn, 2007).

Many superstitions, such as avoiding walking under ladders, probably stem from illusory correlation.

Correlation versus Causation: Jumping the Gun. Correlational designs can be extremely useful for determining whether two (or more) variables are related. Nevertheless, there are important limitations to the conclusions we can draw from them. As we learned in Chapter 1, the most common mistake we make when interpreting correlational designs is to jump the gun and draw *causal* conclusions from them. Correlation doesn't necessarily mean causation. Although a correlation *sometimes* results from a causal relationship, we can't determine from a correlational study alone whether the relationship is causal.

Incidentally, we shouldn't confuse the correlation versus causation fallacy—that is, the error of equating correlation with causation (see Chapter 1)—with illusory correlation. Illusory correlation refers to perceiving a correlation where none exists. In the case of the correlation versus causation fallacy, a correlation exists, but we mistakenly interpret it as implying a causal association. Let's look at two examples of how a correlation between variables *A* and *B* can actually be due to a third variable, *C*, rather than to a direct causal association between variables *A* and *B*.

(1) A statistician with too much time on his hands once uncovered a substantial negative correlation between the number of Ph.D. degrees awarded in a state within the United States and the number of mules in that state (Lilienfeld, 1995). Yes, *mules*. Does this negative correlation imply that the number of Ph.D. degrees (*A*) causes or influences the number of mules (*B*)? It's possible—perhaps people with Ph.D.s have something against mules and campaign vigorously to have them relocated to neighboring states. But this scenario seems rather unlikely. Or does this negative correlation instead imply that mules (*B*) cause people with Ph.D. degrees (*A*) to flee the state? Again, this possibility seems rather unlikely. Before reading the next paragraph, ask yourself whether there's a third explanation.

Indeed there is. Although we don't know for sure, the most likely explanation is that a third variable, *C*, is correlated with both *A* and *B*. In this case, the most probable culprit for this third variable is *rural versus urban status*. States with large rural areas, like Wyoming, contain many mules and few universities. In contrast, states with many urban (big city) areas, like New York, contain few mules and many universities. So in this case, the correlation between variables *A* and *B* is almost certainly due to a third variable, *C*.

(2) There's a substantial positive correlation between the amount of ice cream people eat on a given day and the number of violent crimes committed on that day. It's unlikely that eating ice cream (*A*) causes violent crime (*B*) or that violent crime (*B*) causes people to eat ice cream (*A*). Instead, it's far more likely that a third variable, *C*, accounts for this correlation. What could it be?

The most likely candidate for *C* is temperature. When the temperature is warm, more people consume ice cream; also, when the temperature is warm, more people commit violent crimes (Anderson, Bushman, & Groom, 1997).

Observational and case studies allow us to describe the state of the psychological world, but rarely allow us to make general predictions about the future. In contrast, correlational designs often allow us to make predictions. For example, if SAT scores are correlated with college grades, then knowing people's SAT scores allows us to predict—although by no means perfectly—what their grades will be. Nevertheless, our conclusions from correlational research are always limited because we can't be sure *why* these predicted relationships exist.

There's a positive correlation between the amount of ice cream consumed and the number of violent crimes committed on the same day. But does eating ice cream cause crime?

Correlation vs. Causation

APPLY YOUR THINKING
Some researchers have reported that children whose parents don't supervise them closely tend to have higher rates of sexual activity and drug abuse than do other children. Does this finding demonstrate that close parental supervision reduces sexual activity and drug abuse? Why or why not?

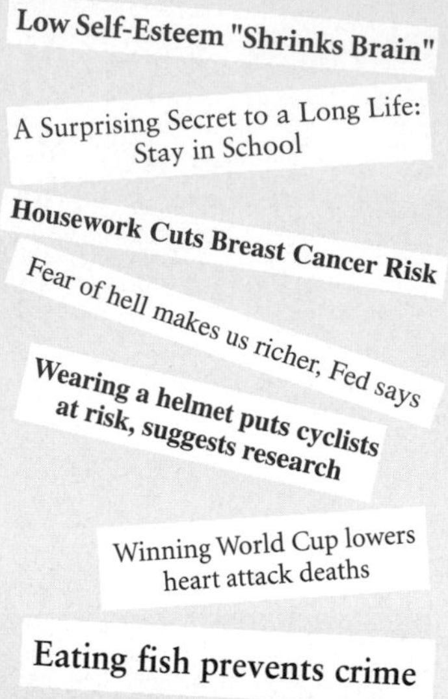

Low Self-Esteem "Shrinks Brain"

A Surprising Secret to a Long Life:
Stay in School

Housework Cuts Breast Cancer Risk

Fear of hell makes us richer, Fed says

Wearing a helmet puts cyclists
at risk, suggests research

Winning World Cup lowers
heart attack deaths

Eating fish prevents crime

Figure 2.6 Examples of Newspaper Headlines That Confuse Correlation with Causation. Here are some actual newspaper headlines that suggest a causal association between two variables. Can you think of alternative explanations for the findings reported in each headline? (See http://jonathan.mueller .faculty.noctrl.edu/100/correlation_or_ causation.htm for a good source of other newspaper headlines incorrectly suggesting causation from correlational findings.)

experiment
research design characterized by random assignment of participants to conditions and manipulation of an independent variable

random assignment
randomly sorting participants into two groups

experimental group
in an experiment, the group of participants that receives the manipulation

control group
in an experiment, the group of participants that doesn't receive the manipulation

independent variable
variable that an experimenter manipulates

dependent variable
variable that an experimenter measures to see whether the manipulation has an effect

We shouldn't rely on the news media to help us distinguish correlation from causation, because they frequently fall prey to the correlation versus causation fallacy (see some examples of misleading headlines in **Figure 2.6**). Take, for example, the headline "Low Self-Esteem Shrinks Brain." The article reports a correlation: Self-esteem is negatively correlated with brain size. Yet the article's title implies a direct causal association between low self-esteem and brain size. Although it's possible that low self-esteem "shrinks" people's brains, it's also possible that shrinking brains lower people's self-esteem. Alternatively, it's possible that an undetected third variable, such as alcohol use, contributes to both low self-esteem and smaller brains (people who drink heavily may both think more poorly of themselves and suffer long-term brain damage). *The bottom line:* Be on the lookout for headlines or news stories that proclaim a causal association between two variables. If the study is based on correlational data alone, we know they're taking their conclusions too far.

EXPERIMENTAL DESIGNS

If correlational designs don't allow us to draw cause-and-effect conclusions, what kinds of designs do? The answer: Experimental designs, often known simply as "experiments." These designs differ from correlational designs in one crucial way: *they permit cause-and-effect inferences.* To see why, it's crucial to understand that in correlational designs researchers are measuring preexisting differences in participants, like age, gender, IQ, and extraversion. In contrast, in experimental designs researchers are *manipulating* variables to see whether these manipulations produce differences in participants' behavior. Putting it another way, in correlational designs the differences among participants are *measured*, whereas in experimental designs they're *created*.

What Makes a Study an Experiment: Two Components. Although news reporters frequently use the term *experiment* rather loosely to refer to any kind of research study, this term actually carries a specific meaning in psychology. To be precise, an **experiment** consists of *two* ingredients:

(1) Random assignment of participants to conditions.
(2) Manipulation of an independent variable.

Both of these ingredients are necessary for the recipe; if a study doesn't contain both of them, it's *not* an experiment. Let's look at each in turn.

Random Assignment. By **random assignment,** we mean that the experimenter randomly sorts participants into one of two groups. One of these groups is called the **experimental group:** This group receives the manipulation. The other is called the **control group:** This group doesn't receive the manipulation. As we learned in Chapter 1, scientific thinking doesn't come naturally to the human species. When viewed through this lens, it's perhaps not surprising that the concept of the control group didn't clearly emerge in psychology until the turn of the twentieth century (Coover & Angell, 1907; Dehue, 1995).

To take an example of random assignment, let's imagine that we wanted to determine whether a new drug, Miraculin, is effective for treating depression. We'd first start with a large sample of individuals with depression. We'd then randomly assign (say, by flipping a coin) half of the participants to an experimental group, which receives Miraculin, and the other half to a control group, which doesn't receive Miraculin. By randomly assigning participants to experimental and control groups, we're helping to cancel out any preexisting differences between these groups.

Manipulation of an Independent Variable. The second ingredient of an experiment is manipulation of an independent variable. An **independent variable** is the variable the experimenter manipulates. The **dependent variable** is the variable that the experimenter measures to see whether this manipulation has had an effect. To remember this distinction, think about the fact that the dependent variable is "dependent on" the level of the independent variable. In the experiment using Miraculin as a treatment for depression, the independent variable is the presence versus absence of Miraculin. The dependent variable is the level of participants' depression following the experimental manipulation.

Confounds: A Source of False Conclusions. For an experiment to be valid, the level of the independent variable must be the *only* difference between the experimental group and the control group. If there's some other difference between groups, there's no way of knowing whether the independent variable really exerted an effect on the dependent variable. Psychologists use the term *confounding variable,* or **confound,** to refer to any difference between the experimental and control groups other than the independent variable. In our depression treatment example, let's imagine that the patients who received Miraculin also received a few sessions of psychotherapy. This additional psychotherapy would be a confound, because it's a variable in addition to the independent variable that differed between the experimental and control groups. This confound makes it impossible for us to determine whether the differences between groups concerning the dependent variable (level of depression) were due to Miraculin, to psychotherapy, or to both.

Cause and Effect: Permission to Infer. The two major features of an experiment—random assignment to conditions and manipulation of an independent variable—permit us to infer cause-and-effect relations if we've conducted the study correctly. To decide whether to infer cause-and-effect relations from the study, here's an easy tip that will work 100 percent of the time. *First,* using the criteria we've outlined, we ask ourselves whether a study is an experiment. *Second,* if it isn't an experiment, we shouldn't draw causal conclusions from that study, no matter how tempting it might be to do so.

Before going further, let's make sure the major points concerning experimental designs are clear. Read this description of a study, and then answer the four questions below it. (You can find the answers upside down on the bottom of page 81.)

Does yoga help people to lower their blood pressure and relieve stress? Only an experiment, with random assignment to conditions and manipulation of an independent variable, gives us permission to infer a cause-and-effect relationship.

Acupuncture Study: Assess Your Knowledge

A researcher hypothesizes that acupuncture, an ancient Chinese medical practice that involves inserting thin needles in specific places on the body (see Chapter 12), can allow stressed-out psychology students to decrease their levels of anxiety. She randomly assigns half of her participants to undergo acupuncture and half to receive no treatment. Two months later, she measures their levels of anxiety and finds that people who received acupuncture are less stressed out than other participants, who received no treatment.

(1) Is this a correlational or an experimental design?

(2) What are the independent and dependent variables?

(3) Is there a confound in this design? If so, what is it?

(4) Can we infer cause and effect from this study? Why or why not?

NEW FRONTIERS
Meta-Analysis: A Safeguard against Confirmation Bias

As we learned in the Prologue and Chapter 1, no single study provides all the answers to any scientific question. As consumers of the psychological literature, we should never hang our hats on the outcome of a single experiment, no matter how well designed it may be. Moreover, interpreting the psychological literature can be

(continued)

confound
any difference between the experimental and control groups other than the independent variable

confusing, because the results of experiments sometimes conflict. One investigator may find that a new psychotherapy is effective, whereas a different investigator may find that it isn't. How should we make sense of these contradictory findings?

To help interpret large bodies of psychological literature, researchers have developed a statistical technique called **meta-analysis,** which literally means an "analysis of analysis." Although meta-analysis is a relatively recent development—the first meta-analysis was conducted in the late 1970s (Smith & Glass, 1977)—it's now a standard methodology in psychology and other social sciences.

We won't bother with the mathematical details of meta-analysis, which can get pretty complicated. What's important to understand is that meta-analysis pools the results of many studies and treats them as though they were one big study (Hunt, 1997; Rosenthal & DiMatteo, 2001). In essence, meta-analysis allows researchers to seek patterns across large numbers of studies and draw general conclusions that hold up across different laboratories. For example, before the mid-1970s, there was considerable controversy regarding whether psychotherapy was effective at all. Some investigators concluded that it was virtually worthless (Eysenck, 1952), whereas others concluded the opposite. It wasn't until a group of researchers performed a meta-analysis of 375 studies of psychotherapy that they settled the issue: psychotherapy works (Smith & Glass, 1977). Later meta-analyses confirmed these overall findings, although they also identified exceptions. For example, as we'll discover in Chapter 16, some psychotherapies may be ineffective, and a few may even make people worse. In recent years, psychologists have used meta-analysis to examine a host of questions: sex differences in empathy, the effects of rehabilitation programs on criminals, and cultural differences in conformity, to name just a few (Hunt, 1997).

Like any statistical technique, meta-analysis can be misused and abused. For example, researchers who perform a meta-analysis sometimes lump together studies that are extremely different from each other, resulting in misleading conclusions (sometimes called the *apples and oranges problem;* Kirsch & Scoboria, 2001). In other cases, we can draw mistaken conclusions from a meta-analysis because of the **file drawer problem:** the tendency for negative findings—those that don't support a researcher's hypothesis—to remain unpublished (Rosenthal, 1979). Because journals are more likely to accept articles reporting positive than negative findings, we can overestimate the effectiveness of a treatment or the evidence for a theory if we rely exclusively on published results.

Still, because we often perceive patterns that aren't there (see Chapter 1), meta-analysis is a helpful tool for sorting through findings. Without it, we can conclude that a large and contradictory mass of studies supports a theory even when it doesn't. Meta-analysis can help us determine which patterns across studies are imaginary and which are real, thereby partly shielding us from confirmation bias.

In psychological research, negative findings may end up in the researcher's "file drawer," leading to skewed overall conclusions.

meta-analysis
investigation of the consistency of patterns of results across large numbers of studies conducted in different laboratories

file drawer problem
tendency for negative findings to remain unpublished

Pitfalls in Experimental Design. Like correlational designs, experimental designs can be tricky to interpret, because there are numerous pitfalls to beware of when evaluating them. We'll focus on the most important of these traps here.

The Placebo Effect. To understand the first major pitfall in experiments, imagine we've developed what we believe to be a new wonder drug that treats hyperactivity (now called attention-deficit/hyperactivity disorder; see Chapter 15) in children. We randomly assign half of our participants with this condition to receive the drug and the other half to receive no treatment. At the conclusion of our study, we find that children who received the drug are much less hyperactive than children who received nothing. That's good news, to be sure, but does it mean we can now break out the champagne and celebrate the news that the drug is effective? Before reading the next paragraph, try to answer this question yourself.

If you answered no, you were right. The reason we can't pop the corks on our champagne bottles is that we haven't controlled for the placebo effect. The term *placebo* is derived from the Latin for "I will please." The **placebo effect** is improvement resulting from the mere expectation of improvement (Kirsch, 1999). Participants who received the drug may have gotten better merely because they knew they were receiving treatment. This knowledge could have instilled confidence or exerted a calming influence. The placebo effect is a powerful reminder that expectations can become reality. In the words of Reverend Jesse Jackson, "What the mind believes and conceives, it can achieve."

In medication research, researchers typically control for the placebo effect by administering a sugar pill (also sometimes referred to as a "dummy pill," although this term isn't meant as an insult to either the researchers or patients), which is itself often called a *placebo*, to the members of the control group. In this way, patients in both the experimental and control groups don't know whether they're taking the actual medication or a placebo, so they're roughly equated in their expectations of improvement.

To avoid placebo effects, it's critical that patients not know whether they're receiving the real medication or a placebo. That is, patients must remain **blind** to the condition to which they've been assigned, namely, experimental or control. If patients aren't blind to this condition, then the experiment is essentially ruined, because the patients differ in their expectations of improvement.

Two different things can happen if the "blind is broken," which is psychological lingo for what happens when patients find out which group (experimental or control) they're in. First, patients in the experimental group (the ones receiving the drug) might improve more than patients in the control group (the ones receiving the placebo) because they know their treatment is real rather than fake. Second, patients in the control group might become resentful that they're receiving a placebo and try to "beat out" the patients in the experimental group ("Hey, we're going to show those experimenters what we're really made of"). Researchers call this phenomenon the *John Henry effect*, after the legendary railroad worker who collapsed from exhaustion after outcompeting a steel drill in a contest of man versus machine. This effect is defined as better-than-expected performance by a control group in response to competition.

Some researchers refer to the placebo effect as though it were purely an uninteresting artifact. Yet placebo effects are just as real as those of actual drugs and are worthy of psychological investigation in their own right (see Chapters 12 and 16). Placebos show many of the same characteristics as do real drugs, such as having a more powerful effect at higher doses (Buckalew & Ross, 1981; Rickels, Hesbacher, Weise, Gray, & Feldman, 1970). Placebos injected through a needle (researchers usually use a salt and water solution for this purpose) tend to show more rapid and powerful effects than placebos that are swallowed (Buckalew & Ross, 1981), probably because people assume that injectable placebos enter the bloodstream more quickly than pill placebos. Some patients even become addicted to placebo pills (Mintz, 1977).

Moreover, some researchers maintain that up to 80 percent of the effectiveness of antidepressants is attributable to placebo effects (Kirsch & Saperstein, 1998, 1999), although some others suspect the true percentage is somewhat lower (Dawes, 1998; Klein, 1998). Placebo effects aren't equally powerful for all conditions. They generally exert their strongest effects on subjective reports of depression and pain, but their effects on objective measures of physical illnesses, such as cancer and heart disease, are weaker (Hrobjartsson & Götzsche, 2001). Also, the effects of placebos tend to be more short-lived than those of actual medications (Rothschild & Quitkin, 1992).

"FIND OUT WHO SET UP THIS EXPERIMENT. IT SEEMS THAT HALF OF THE PATIENTS WERE GIVEN A PLACEBO, AND THE OTHER HALF WERE GIVEN A DIFFERENT PLACEBO."

(© ScienceCartoonsPlus.com)

placebo effect
improvement resulting from the mere expectation of improvement

blind
unaware of whether one is in the experimental or control group

Answers to questions on page 79:
(1) This study is experimental because there's random assignment to groups and the experimenter manipulated whether or not participants received treatment. (2) The independent variable is the presence versus absence of acupuncture treatment. The dependent variable is the anxiety level of participants. (3) There is a potential confound in that those who received acupuncture knew they were receiving treatment. Their lower anxiety may have been the result of expectations that they'd be feeling better following treatment. (4) Yes. Because of the confound, we don't know why the experimental group was less anxious. But we can conclude that something about the treatment reduced anxiety.

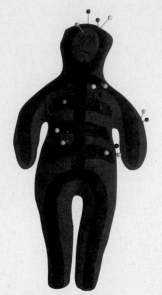

The ancient practice of voodoo illustrates the nocebo effect, the "evil twin" of the placebo effect. People who believe (falsely) that others are sticking them with pins may experience pain.

The Nocebo Effect. The placebo effect has an "evil twin" of sorts: the nocebo effect (Kirsch, 1999). The **nocebo effect** is harm resulting from the mere expectation of harm (*nocebo* comes from the Latin phrase meaning "to harm"). The ancient African, and later Caribbean, practice of voodoo presumably capitalizes on the nocebo effect: People who believe that others are sticking them with pins sometimes experience pain themselves. In one study, individuals who were allergic to roses sneezed when presented with fake roses (Reid, 2002). In another, researchers deceived a group of college students into believing that an electric current being passed into their heads could produce a headache. More than two-thirds of the students reported headaches, even though the current was imaginary (Morse, 1999). Like the placebo effect, the nocebo effect demonstrates that expectations can become reality—except that in this case the expectations and reality are negative.

The Experimenter Expectancy Effect. It's clear that including a control condition that provides a placebo treatment is extremely important, as is keeping participants blind to their condition assignment. Still, there's one more potential concern with experimental designs. In some cases, the subject doesn't know the condition assignment, but the experimenter does.

When this happens, a problem can arise: The **experimenter expectancy effect** or *Rosenthal effect*. It occurs when researchers' hypotheses lead them to unintentionally bias the outcome of a study. You may want to underline the word *unintentionally* in the previous sentence, because this effect doesn't refer to deliberate "fudging" or making up of data, which fortunately happens only rarely in science. Instead, in the experimenter expectancy effect, researchers' biases subtly affect the results. In some cases, researchers may end up confirming their hypotheses even when these hypotheses are wrong.

Because of this effect, it's essential that experiments be conducted whenever possible in a **double-blind** fashion. By double-blind, we mean that neither researchers nor participants know who's in the experimental or control group. By voluntarily shielding themselves from the knowledge of which subjects are in which group, researchers are again guarding themselves against confirmation bias.

One of the oldest and best-known examples of the experimenter expectancy effect is the infamous tale of a man and his horse. The man's name was Wilhem van Osten. He was a German schoolteacher who became convinced he'd hit the big time. In 1900, van Osten had purchased a handsome Arabian stallion, known in the psychological literature as Clever Hans, who seemingly displayed astonishing mathematical abilities. By tapping with his hooves, Clever Hans responded correctly to mathematical questions from van Osten (such as, "How much is 8 plus 3?"). He even calculated square roots and could tell the time of day. Understandably, van Osten was so proud of Clever Hans that he began showing him off in public. Eventually, Clever Hans's performances drew large throngs of amazed spectators.

You might be wondering whether Clever Hans's feats were the result of trickery. A panel of thirteen psychologists who investigated Clever Hans witnessed no evidence of fraud on van Osten's part, and concluded that Clever Hans possessed the arithmetic abilities of a 14-year-old human. Moreover, Clever Hans seemed to be a true-blue math whiz, because he could add and subtract even when van Osten wasn't posing the questions.

Nevertheless, psychologist Oscar Pfungst was skeptical of just how clever Clever Hans really was, and in 1904 he launched a series of careful observations. In this case, Pfungst did something that previous psychologists didn't think to do: He focused not on the horse, but on the people asking him questions. When he did, he found that van Osten and others were *unintentionally cuing* the horse to produce correct answers. Specifically, Pfungst found that Clever Hans's questioners almost invariably tightened their muscles immediately before the correct answer. When Pfungst prevented Clever Hans from seeing

"IT WAS MORE OF A 'TRIPLE-BLIND' TEST. THE PATIENTS DIDN'T KNOW WHICH ONES WERE GETTING THE REAL DRUG, THE DOCTORS DIDN'T KNOW, AND, I'M AFRAID, NOBODY KNEW."

(© ScienceCartoonsPlus.com)

nocebo effect
harm resulting from the mere expectation of harm

experimenter expectancy effect
phenomenon in which researchers' hypotheses lead them to unintentionally bias the outcome of a study

double-blind
when neither researchers nor participants are aware of who's in the experimental or control group

the questioner or anyone else who knew the correct answer, the horse did no better than chance. The puzzle was solved: Clever Hans was cleverly detecting subtle physical cues emitted by questioners.

The Clever Hans story was one of the first demonstrations of the experimenter expectancy effect. It showed that people can—even without their knowledge—give off cues that affect a subject's behavior, even when that subject is a horse. This story also reminds us that an extraordinary claim, in this case that a horse can perform arithmetic, requires extraordinary evidence. Van Osten's claims were extraordinary, but his evidence wasn't. Interestingly, some authors have referred to facilitated communication, which we encountered at the beginning of this chapter, as the "phenomenon of Clever Hands" (Wegner, Fuller, & Sparrow, 2003), because it too appeared to be the result of an experimenter expectancy effect.

We mentioned that the experimenter expectancy effect is also called the Rosenthal effect. That's because in the 1960s psychologist Robert Rosenthal conducted an elegant series of experiments that persuaded the psychological community that experimenter expectancy effects were genuine. Rosenthal and his colleagues were so adept at identifying experimental artifacts that they became known as "artifactologists."

In one of these experiments, Rosenthal and Fode (1963) randomly assigned some psychology students a group of five so-called maze bright rats—rats bred over many generations to run mazes quickly—and other students a group of five so-called maze dull rats—rats bred over many generations to run mazes slowly. Note that this is an experiment, because Rosenthal and Fode randomly assigned students to groups and manipulated which type of rat the students supposedly received. They then asked the students to run the rats in mazes and to record each rat's completion time. But there was a catch: Rosenthal and Fode had told a fib. They had randomly assigned rats to the students rather than the other way around. The story about the "maze bright" and "maze dull" rats was all cooked up. Yet when Rosenthal and Fode tabulated their results, they found that students assigned the "maze bright" rats reported 29 percent faster maze running times than did students assigned the "maze dull" rats. In some unknown fashion, the students had influenced their rats' running times.

APPLY YOUR THINKING

In sporting events evaluated by a panel of judges, such as figure skating, judges know the identities of all athletes, as well as their countries of origin. This arrangement has invited charges of bias, with judges being accused of favoring athletes from their home countries. If someone put you in charge of creating a judging system for figure skating that was less vulnerable to bias, what changes would you suggest?

Hawthorne Effect. A final potential pitfall of psychological research can be difficult or even impossible to eliminate. In most cases, we can only do our best to minimize it. To understand this pitfall, let's revisit the classic study that uncovered it.

In the 1920s and early 1930s, a group of industrial–organizational psychologists from Harvard University conducted a study of worker productivity in the Western Electric Hawthorne works plant in Cicero, Illinois (Mayo, 1933; Roethlisberger & Dickson, 1939). As one facet of their study, they wanted to determine the effects of different lighting conditions on employee performance. The researchers varied the amount of light in the factory over time, sometimes increasing it, sometimes decreasing it. To their bewilderment, they found that worker productivity almost always either stayed the same or increased regardless of lighting conditions. In one condition, productivity continued to improve even though the researchers lowered the illumination to the level of moonlight (Rosenberg & Daly, 1993)! What was going on? Before reading the next paragraph, see if you can figure it out.

Extraordinary Claims

Clever Hans performing in public. If one can observe powerful experimenter (in this case, owner) expectancy effects even in animals, how powerful might such effects be in humans?

factoid

Clever Hans wasn't the only horse to fool dozens of people. In the 1920s, Lady Wonder, a horse in Richmond, Virginia, amazed observers by what appeared to be psychic abilities. She answered her trainer's questions by arranging alphabet blocks with her mouth, including questions that only her trainer knew. A magician, Milbourne Christopher, later determined that when the trainer didn't know the right answer to the question, Lady Wonder didn't perform any better than chance.

The Hawthorne effect suggests that workers' levels of productivity can be affected, perhaps dramatically, by their knowledge of whether they're being studied.

After scratching their heads a bit, the researchers realized that the workers had increased their productivity because they knew they were being studied. Simply put, they'd wanted to impress the investigators. These researchers had hit on what came to be known as the **Hawthorne effect:** participants' knowledge that they're being studied can affect their behavior. Admittedly, a number of later investigators pointed out flaws in the original Hawthorne studies. For example, the investigators didn't include a control group of workers for whom lighting wasn't manipulated, nor did they consider the fact that bosses at the plant disciplined, and in two cases even fired, workers whose productivity decreased (Bramel & Friend, 1981; Rice, 1982). Still, the researchers' central point stands: The mere act of observing participants can influence their behavior.

An especially widespread type of Hawthorne effect is **demand characteristics.** Demand characteristics are cues that participants pick up from an experiment that allow them to generate guesses regarding the experimenter's hypotheses (Orne, 1962; Rosnow, 2002). In some cases, participants' guesses about what the experimenter is up to may be correct; in other cases, they may not. The problem is that when participants think they know how the experimenter wants them to act, they may alter their behavior accordingly. As we'll recall from the Prologue, psychologists call this nasty little problem *reactivity:* people who know they're being studied may act differently than they would otherwise.

There are two major ways of minimizing Hawthorne effects, including demand characteristics. Using the first method, *covert observation,* researchers conceal themselves. As a result, participants don't even know they're being watched. Many modern psychological laboratories contain one-way mirrors to permit investigators to observe participants without their knowledge.

Other investigators have adopted more offbeat approaches to covert observation. In one experiment famous—or perhaps we should say *infamous*—for its unconventional methodology, researchers examined the effects of interpersonal distance on the onset of urination in males (Middlemist, Knowles, & Matter, 1976). To conduct the study, they set up shop in a men's bathroom. Whenever a male subject approached a urinal, they randomly placed another man, actually a research assistant, at one of three urinals that differed in their distance from the subject. Meanwhile, a second research assistant sat on the toilet seat in a nearby stall and (using a stopwatch) timed the onset of urination by means of a periscope pressed up against a peep hole in the stall wall. Middlemist and colleagues found that men took longer to begin urinating when another man was closer to them than when another man was farther away. Needless to say, this study might have been difficult to pull off without covert observation, as we have a sneaking suspicion that most men entering bathrooms might not appreciate having an audience.

Many psychology laboratories are equipped with one-way mirrors so that researchers can watch subjects without their knowledge.

The second method of minimizing Hawthorne effects is virtually opposite to the first. In this method, *participant observation,* investigators become members of a group and then observe the behavior of other group members. In contrast to covert observation, in which researchers hide, participant observation requires researchers to make their presence known—in fact, well known—to other participants. By becoming a group member and earning other members' trust, researchers can observe group members' behavior without being overly concerned that their presence will affect others' behavior.

In a classic use of participant observation in the 1950s, three social psychologists infiltrated a cult group known as Mrs. Keech and the Seekers (Festinger, Riecken, & Schacter,

Hawthorne effect
phenomenon in which participants' knowledge that they're being studied can affect their behavior

demand characteristics
cues that participants pick up from a study that allow them to generate guesses regarding the researcher's hypotheses

1956). While pretending to be cult members, the investigators carefully observed others' behaviors. The cult was led by Mrs. Keech, a middle-aged woman in Illinois who claimed to communicate with aliens on a distant planet. Based on secret messages from the aliens, Mrs. Keech had learned that on December 21, the Earth would be destroyed in a cataclysmic flood. Moreover, the aliens were conveniently scheduled to arrive that very day and carry the devoted band of Seekers to the aliens' home planet in a comfortably equipped flying saucer. The cult members were convinced that Mrs. Keech was right and made travel arrangements to depart planet Earth a few days before Christmas. The social psychologists wanted to find out what would happen when December 21 came and went without incident. Would the Seekers' belief in Mrs. Keech be destroyed? We'll find out in Chapter 13.

ASKING PEOPLE ABOUT THEMSELVES AND OTHERS

Imagine being hired by a research firm to estimate people's attitudes toward a newly released brand of toothpaste, Brightooth, which supposedly prevents 99.99 percent of cavities. How will we do it? We could flag people off the street, pay them money to brush their teeth with Brightooth, and measure their reactions to Brightooth on a survey. Is this a good approach?

No, because the people on your neighborhood street probably aren't typical of people in general. Moreover, some people will almost surely refuse to participate, and they may differ from those who agreed to participate. For example, people with especially bad teeth might refuse to try Brightooth, and they may be the very people to whom Brightooth executives would most want to market their product.

Random Selection: The Key to Generalizability. A better approach would be to identify a representative sample of the population, and then administer our survey to people drawn from that sample. For example, we could look at U.S. population census data and try to contact every 10,000th person listed. This approach, often used in survey research, is called **random selection.** In random selection, every person in the population has an equal chance of being chosen to participate. Random selection is crucial if we want our results to generalize to the broader population. Political pollsters keep themselves awake at night worrying about random selection. If their selection of survey respondents from the population is nonrandom (that is, biased), their election forecasts will be hopelessly skewed.

Incidentally, we shouldn't confuse random selection with *random assignment,* which, as we discussed earlier, is one of the two ingredients of an experiment. Here's how to remember the difference: Random selection deals with how we initially choose our participants, whereas random assignment deals with how we assign our participants *after we've already chosen them.*

An example of how nonrandom selection can lead to disastrously misleading conclusions comes from the infamous *Hite Report* (1987). In the mid-1980s, sex researcher Sheri Hite sent out 100,000 surveys to American women inquiring about their relationships with men. She'd identified potential survey respondents from lists of subscribers to women's magazines. Hite's findings were so startling that *Time* magazine and other prominent publications featured them as their cover story. Here's a sampling of Hite's findings:

- 70 percent of women married 5 or more years say they've had extramarital affairs.
- 87 percent of married women say their closest emotional relationship is with someone other than their husband.
- 95 percent of women say they're "emotionally and psychologically harassed" by their love partner.
- 98 percent of women say they're generally unsatisfied with their present love relationship.

Democrat Harry Truman at his presidential victory rally (*top*), famously holding up an early edition of the *Chicago Daily Tribune* incorrectly proclaiming Republican Thomas Dewey the winner of the 1948 presidential election. In fact, Truman won by nearly 5 percentage points. The pollsters got it wrong largely because they based their survey results on people with telephones. Back in 1948, considerably more Republicans (who tended to be richer) owned telephones than Democrats, resulting in a skewed preelection prediction.

random selection
procedure that ensures every person in a population has an equal chance of being chosen to participate

That's pretty depressing news, to put it mildly. Yet lost in the furor over Hite's findings was one crucial point: Only 4.5 percent of her sample had responded to her survey. What's more, Hite had no way of knowing whether this 4.5 percent was representative of her full sample. Interestingly, a poll conducted by the Harris organization at around the same time used random selection and reported results virtually opposite to Hite's. In their better-conducted survey, 89 percent of women said they were generally satisfied with their current relationship, and only a small minority reported extramarital affairs. More likely than not, Hite's high percentages were a result of nonrandom selection: the 4.5 percent of participants who responded to her survey were probably the very women experiencing the most relationship problems to begin with and therefore the most motivated to participate.

Evaluating Measures. When evaluating the results from any dependent variable or measure, we need to ask two critical questions: Is the measure reliable? Is it valid?

Reliability. **Reliability** refers to consistency of measurement. For example, a reliable questionnaire yields similar scores over time; this type of reliability is called *test-retest reliability*. To assess test-retest reliability, we could administer a personality questionnaire to a large group of people today and readminister it in 2 months. If the measure is reasonably reliable, the correlation between these scores should be at least $r = .80$, which is a high level of association. Reliability also applies to interviews and observational data. *Interrater reliability* is the extent to which different people who conduct an interview, or make behavioral observations, agree on the characteristics, like depression, they're measuring.

Validity. **Validity** is the extent to which a measure assesses what it purports (claims) to measure. We can think of validity as "truth in advertising." If we went to the grocery store, purchased a can labeled "Aunt Barbara's Baked Beans," and on opening the can discovered a bunch of artichokes, we'd demand our money back (unless we really like artichokes). Similarly, if a questionnaire we're administering purports to be a valid measure of introversion, but studies show it's really measuring anxiety, then this measure isn't valid. As users of the test, we should similarly demand our money back.

Reliability and Validity: The Differences. Reliability and validity are different concepts, although people routinely confuse them. In courts of law, we'll frequently hear debates about whether the polygraph (or so-called lie-detector) test is scientifically "reliable." But as we'll learn in Chapter 11, the central question concerning the polygraph isn't its reliability, because it typically yields fairly consistent scores over time. Instead, the central question is its validity, because many critics maintain that the polygraph isn't a detector of lies at all. Instead, they maintain that the polygraph detects emotional arousal, which can be produced not only by lies but by anxiety, anger, surprise, and other emotions (Lykken, 1998).

Reliability is necessary for validity. In other words, we need to measure something consistently before we can measure it well. Imagine trying to measure the floors and walls of our apartment or house using a ruler made of Silly Putty, that is, a ruler whose length changes every time we pick it up. Our efforts at accurate measurement would be doomed. The same goes for personality questionnaires, because we can't expect a measure that yields very different scores each time we administer it to measure anything well.

Nevertheless, reliability isn't sufficient for validity. Although a test must be reliable to be valid, a reliable test can still be completely invalid. Imagine we've developed a new measure of intelligence, the "Distance Index-Middle Width Intelligence Test" (DIMWIT), which computes the average width of our middle finger and the average width of our index finger, and then subtracts the lesser of these from the greater one. The DIMWIT would be a highly reliable measure of intelligence, because the widths of our middle and index fingers are unlikely to change much over time. But the DIMWIT would be a completely invalid measure of intelligence, because finger width has nothing to do with intelligence.

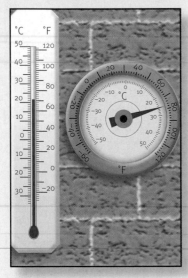

These two thermometers are providing different readings for temperature in almost the identical location. Psychologists might say that these thermometers display less-than-perfect interrater reliability.

reliability
consistency of measurement

validity
extent to which a measure assesses what it purports to measure

Self-Report Measures and Surveys. Psychologists frequently use *self-report measures,* often called questionnaires, to assess a variety of characteristics, such as personality traits, mental illnesses, and interests. Closely related to self-report measures are *surveys,* which psychologists typically use to measure people's opinions and attitudes (say, their reactions to Brightooth and other toothpastes). Yet not all self-report measures and surveys are created equal; some have high levels of reliability and validity, but others don't.

When interpreting the results of self-report measures and surveys, we should bear in mind that we can obtain quite different answers depending on how we phrase the questions (Schwarz, 1999). One researcher administered surveys to 300 women homemakers. In some surveys, women answered a question that asked, "Would you like to have a job, if this were possible?" whereas others answered a question that asked, "Would you prefer to have a job, or do you prefer to do just your housework?" These two questions seem remarkably similar. Yet although 81 percent answered yes to the first question, only 32 percent answered yes to the second (Noelle-Neumann, 1970; Walonick, 1994). The reason for this whopping difference isn't clear, although the use of the words "if this were possible" in the first question might have encouraged respondents to think about employment options that wouldn't ordinarily have occurred to them. Moreover, we shouldn't assume that people who respond to survey questions even understand the answers they're giving. In one survey study, researchers asked subjects their opinions about the "Agricultural Trade Act of 1978." About 30 percent of subjects expressed an opinion about this act, even though no such act exists (Bishop, Oldendick, & Tuchfarber, 1986; Schwarz, 1999).

Advantages of Self-Report Measures. Self-report measures have an important advantage: they're easy to administer. All we need are a pencil, paper, and a willing participant, and we're ready to go. Moreover, if we have a question about someone, it's usually a good idea to first ask that person directly. Often that person will have access to subtle information regarding his or her emotional states, like anxiety or guilt, about which outside observers aren't aware (Grove & Tellegen, 1991).

Self-report measures of personality traits and behaviors often work reasonably well (see Chapter 14). For example, people's reports of how outgoing or shy they are tend to be moderately correlated (often about $r = .5$) with the reports of people who know them well. The correlations tend to be somewhat higher for more observable traits, like extraversion, than for less observable traits, like anxiety (Kendrick & Funder, 1988).

Disadvantages of Self-Report Measures. Yet self-report measures have their disadvantages too. First, they typically assume that respondents possess enough insight into their own personality characteristics to report on them accurately. This assumption is questionable for certain groups of people. For example, people with high levels of narcissistic personality traits, like self-centeredness and excessive self-confidence (the word *narcissistic* derives from the Greek mythological character Narcissus, who fell in love with his reflection in the water), tend to view themselves more positively than others do (John & Robins, 1994). It's likely that narcissistic people tend to perceive themselves through rose-colored glasses.

Second, self-report questionnaires typically assume that participants are honest in their responses. Imagine you applied for a job that you really wanted and the company required you to take a personality test as part of this application. Would you be completely frank in your evaluation of yourself, or would you minimize your personality quirks? Not surprisingly, some questionnaire respondents engage in **response sets**—tendencies to distort their answers to items.

A widely publicized 1992 poll by the Roper organization asked Americans the following confusing question, which contained two negatives: "Does it seem possible or does it seem impossible to you that the Nazi extermination of the Jews never happened?" A shocking 22 percent of respondents replied that the Holocaust may not have happened. Yet when a later poll asked the question more clearly, this number dropped to only 1 percent. Survey wording counts.

Like the Greek mythological character Narcissus, who fell in love with his own reflection, narcissistic people tend to have an excessively high opinion of themselves.

response sets
tendencies of research participants to distort their responses to questionnaire items

Two especially problematic response sets are positive impression management and malingering. *Positive impression management* is the tendency to make ourselves look better than we actually are (Paulhus, 1991). We're especially likely to engage in this response set if we've applied for an important job. Positive impression management can make it difficult to trust people's reports of their abilities and achievements. For example, college students overstate their SAT scores by an average of 17 points (Hagen, 2001). Some self-report questionnaires contain items designed to detect positive impression management (see Chapter 14). Most of these items assess an unwillingness to admit to trivial flaws. For example, an answer of "True" to the item "I never become more upset over things than I should," suggests positive impression management.

A nearly opposite response set is *malingering,* the tendency to make ourselves appear psychologically disturbed with the aim of achieving a clear-cut personal goal (Rogers, 1997). We're especially likely to observe this response set among people who are trying to obtain financial compensation for an injury or mistreatment on the job, or among people trying to escape military duty or imprisonment—in the last case, often by faking insanity (see Chapter 15). Most malingering scales contain items that many laypeople might assume are actual symptoms of mental disorders, but that are symptoms of fictional disorders (such as "I often hear voices in my head whenever I look at large clouds").

Rating Data: How Do They Rate?   An alternative to asking people about themselves is asking people who know them well to provide ratings on them. In job settings, employers frequently rate their employees' work productivity and cooperativeness in regular evaluations. Toward the end of your introductory psychology course, there's a good chance you'll be asked to rate your instructor's teaching effectiveness. Rating data can circumvent some of the problems with self-report data, because observers may not have the same "blind spots" as the people they're rating (who are often called the "targets" of the rating). Imagine asking your introductory psychology instructor, "How good a job do you think you did in teaching this course?" It's unlikely he or she would say "Just awful."

Nevertheless, like self-report measures, rating data have their drawbacks, each of which can limit their validity. We'll discuss three drawbacks here: the halo effect, the leniency effect, and the error of central tendency.

Halo Effect.   The *halo effect* is the tendency of ratings of one positive characteristic to "spill over" to influence the ratings of other positive characteristics (Guilford, 1954). Raters who fall prey to the halo effect seem almost to regard the targets as "angels"—hence the halo—who can do no wrong. If we find an employee physically attractive, we may unknowingly allow this perception to influence our ratings of his or her other features, such as conscientiousness and productivity. Indeed, people perceive physically attractive people as more successful, confident, assertive, and intelligent than other people even though these differences often don't reflect objective reality (Dion, Berscheid, & Walster, 1972; Eagly, Makhijani, Ashmore, & Longo, 1991). There's even a converse effect of the halo effect called the *horns effect*—picture a devil's horns—in which the ratings of one negative trait, such as arrogance, spill over to influence the ratings of other negative traits (Corsini, 1999).

Student course evaluations of teaching are especially vulnerable to halo effects, because if you like a teacher personally you're likely to give him "a break" on the quality of his teaching. In one study, Richard Nisbett and Timothy Wilson (1977) randomly assigned participants to one of two conditions. In one condition, participants watched a videotape of a college professor who was friendly to his students; in the other condition, they watched a videotape of a foreign-born college professor who was unfriendly to his students (Nisbett and Wilson videotaped the same professor in both conditions). Participants watching the videotapes not only liked the friendly professor better, but rated his physical appearance, mannerisms, and accent more positively. Students who like their professors also tend to give them high ratings on characteristics that are largely irrelevant to teaching effectiveness, like the quality of the classroom audiovisual equipment and even the readability of their handwriting (Greenwald & Gilmore, 1997; Williams & Ceci, 1997).

People often perceive highly attractive individuals as possessing many other desirable attributes. This phenomenon is one illustration of the halo effect.

Leniency Effect. A second potential pitfall in rating data is the *leniency effect,* the tendency of raters to provide ratings that are overly generous. Leniency effects frequently arise in job evaluations, because employers who like their employees are reluctant to give them low ratings (Range et al., 1991). The problem is that if employers are too kind to employees in their ratings, these ratings can't distinguish effective from ineffective workers. Leniency effects also limit the usefulness of letters of recommendation for jobs, colleges, and graduate schools. Because many recommenders give high ratings to almost everyone for whom they write letters, recommendation letters aren't especially predictive of later success in jobs or in school (Hunter & Hunter, 1984). Moreover, letters of recommendation are often more a function of letter writers themselves than of the students for whom they're writing letters. In part, this is probably because some letter writers are more prone to leniency effects than others. Indeed, recommendation letters written by the same person about different students are more similar than recommendation letters written by different people about the same student (Baxter, Brock, Hill, & Rozelle, 1981).

Leniency effects often limit the usefulness of ratings for students and employees.

> **APPLY YOUR THINKING**
> If you were a college administrator asked to design recommendation forms for faculty to complete on students, how would you try to minimize leniency effects on recommenders' ratings?

Error of Central Tendency. A third pitfall to beware of when interpreting ratings is the *error of central tendency,* which is an unwillingness to provide extreme (either very low or very high) ratings. Raters who make this error are playing it safe, refusing to "go out on a limb" when evaluating others. There's some evidence that Asians are more likely to pick middle scores than European Americans (Chen, Lee, & Stevenson, 1995), so we need to consider cultural factors when interpreting rating data. One way of minimizing the error of central tendency is to provide raters with an even number—like four or six—of response choices (like False, Somewhat False, Somewhat True, True). In this way, raters are forced to take a stand and can't simply cop out by giving a response that's smack in the middle.

PsychoMythology

Laboratory Research Doesn't Apply to the Real World, Right?

Beginning psychology students often assume that most laboratory research doesn't generalize to the real world. This assumption seems reasonable at first blush, because behavior that emerges in the artificial confines of the laboratory doesn't always mirror behavior in natural settings. Moreover, psychologists conduct a great deal of their research on college students, who tend to be more intelligent, more self-absorbed, less certain of their identities, and more reliant on social approval than noncollege participants. Indeed, about 75 percent of published studies of interpersonal interactions are conducted on undergraduates (Sears, 1986). It's not always clear how generalizable these findings are to the rest of humanity (Peterson, 2000).

But is the "truism" that laboratory research is low in external validity really true? As Douglas Mook (1983) pointed out, high internal validity can often lead to high external validity. That's because carefully controlled experiments generate conclusions

(continued)

Replicability

that are more trustworthy and more likely to apply to the real world than are loosely controlled studies. In addition, the results of carefully controlled experiments are typically more likely to replicate than the results of loosely controlled studies.

Craig Anderson, James Lindsay, and Brad Bushman (1999) decided to take a systematic look at this issue. They examined the correspondence between laboratory studies of various psychological phenomena—including aggression, helping, leadership, interpersonal perception, performance on exams, and the causes of depressed mood—as measured in both the laboratory and real world. Anderson and his colleagues computed how large the effects were in both laboratory and real-world studies and then correlated these effects. For example, in studies of the relation between watching violent television and aggressive behavior, they examined the correspondence between findings from controlled laboratory studies—in which investigators randomly assign participants to watch either violent television or nonviolent television, and then measure their aggression—and real-world studies—in which investigators observe people's television viewing habits and aggression in daily life.

Contrary to what many psychologists have assumed, Anderson and his collaborators found the correlation between the sizes of the effects in laboratory and real-world studies to be $r = .73$, which is a high association (see **Figure 2.7**). Laboratory research often generalizes surprisingly well to the real world.

Even so, we shouldn't simply assume that a laboratory study has high external validity. The best approach is to examine both well-controlled laboratory experiments and studies using naturalistic observation to make sure that the results from both research designs converge. If they do, that should make us even more confident in our conclusions (Shadish, Cook, & Campbell, 2002). If they don't, that should make us scratch our heads and try to figure out what's accounting for the difference.

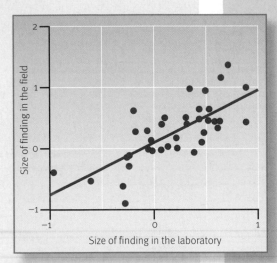

Figure 2.7 Does Laboratory Research Relate to the Real World? This scatterplot displays the data from the findings of studies in the laboratory versus the real world from Anderson, Lindsay, and Bushman (1999).

ASSESS YOUR KNOWLEDGE: FACT OR FICTION?

(1) Case studies can sometimes provide existence proofs of psychological phenomena. (True/False)

(2) A correlation of −.8 is just as large in magnitude as a correlation of +.8. (True/False)

(3) Experiments are characterized by two, and only two, features. (True/False)

(4) To control for experimenter expectancy effects, only participants need to be blind to who's in the experimental and control groups. (True/False)

(5) Self-report measures are more dependent on the honesty of participants than are most other kinds of measures. (True/False)

(6) Rating data can be biased because some respondents allow their ratings of one positive characteristic to spill over to other positive characteristics. (True/False)

Answers: (1) T (p. 72); (2) T (p. 73); (3) T (p. 78); (4) F (p. 82); (5) T (p. 87); (6) T (p. 88)

Ethical Issues in Research Design

When designing and conducting research studies, psychologists need to worry about more than their scientific value. The ethics of these studies also matter. Although psychology adheres to the same basic scientific principles as other sciences, let's just face it: A chemist needn't worry about hurting his mineral's feelings, and a physicist needn't be concerned about the long-term emotional well-being of a neutron. The scientific study of people and their behavior raises unique concerns.

Many philosophers believe—and the authors of this text agree—that science itself is value-neutral. In less technical terms, this means that because science is a search for the truth, it's neither inherently good nor bad. Truth is what it is. This fact doesn't imply, though, that scientific *research,* including psychological research, is value-neutral. There are both ethical and unethical ways of searching for the truth. Moreover, we may not all agree on which ways of searching for the truth are ethical. We'd probably all agree that it's perfectly acceptable to learn about brain damage by studying the behavior of people with brain damage on laboratory tasks of learning, just so long as these tasks don't cause participants much stress. We'd also all agree (we hope!) that it's unacceptable for us to learn about brain damage by hitting people over the head with baseball bats and then testing their motor coordination by measuring how often they fall down a flight of stairs. Nevertheless, we might not all agree on whether it's acceptable to learn about brain damage by creating severe lesions (wounds) in the brains of cats and examining their effects on cats' responses to fear-provoking stimuli (like scary dogs). In many cases, the question of whether research is ethical isn't clear-cut.

TUSKEGEE: A SHAMEFUL MORAL TALE

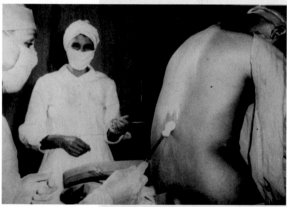

Scientists have learned the hard way that their thirst for knowledge can blind them to crucial ethical considerations. One deeply troubling example comes from the Tuskegee study performed by the United States Public Health Service, an agency of the United States Government, from 1932 to 1972 (Jones, 1993). During this time, a number of researchers wanted to learn more about the natural course of syphilis, a sexually transmitted disease. What happens, they wondered, to syphilis over time if left untreated?

The "subjects" in this study were 399 African American men living in the poorest rural areas of Alabama who'd been diagnosed with syphilis. Remarkably, the researchers never informed these men that they had syphilis, nor that an effective treatment for syphilis, namely, antibiotics, had become available. Indeed, the subjects didn't even know they were subjects, as the researchers hadn't informed them of that crucial piece of information. Instead, the researchers merely tracked subjects' progress over time, withholding all medical information and all available treatments. By the end of the study, twenty-eight of the men had died of syphilis, one hundred had died of syphilis-related complications, forty of the men's wives had been infected with syphilis, and nineteen children had been born with syphilis. In 1997—25 years after the termination of this study—then President Bill Clinton, on behalf of the United States government, offered a formal apology for the Tuskegee study to the study's eight remaining survivors.

In this 1933 photograph, an African American subject undergoes a painful medical procedure (spinal tap) as part of the Tuskegee study. This study demonstrates the tragic consequences of ignoring crucial ethical considerations in research.

ETHICAL GUIDELINES FOR HUMAN RESEARCH

If any good at all came out of the horrific Tuskegee study and other ethical catastrophes in scientific research, it was a heightened appreciation for protecting the rights of human subjects. Fortunately, researchers could never perform the Tuskegee study today, at least not in the United States. That's because every major American research college and university has at least one *institutional review board* (IRB), which reviews all research carefully with an eye toward protecting participants against abuses. IRBs typically consist of faculty members drawn from various departments within a college or university, as well as one or more outside members, such as a person drawn from the community surrounding the college or university.

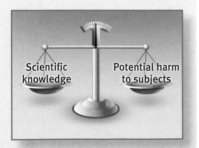

Psychological researchers must often carefully weigh the potential scientific benefits of their research against the potential danger to participants.

informed consent
informing research participants of what is involved in a study before asking them to participate

Informed Consent. IRBs insist on a procedure called **informed consent:** researchers must tell subjects what they're getting into before asking them to participate. During the informed consent process, participants can ask questions about the study and learn more about what will be involved. The Tuskegee subjects never received informed consent, and we can be certain they wouldn't have agreed to participate had they known they wouldn't be receiving treatment for a potentially fatal illness.

Nevertheless, IRBs may sometimes allow researchers to forgo at least some elements of informed consent. In particular, some psychological research entails *deception*. When researchers use deception, they deliberately mislead participants about the study's purpose. In one of the most controversial and best-known studies in the history of psychology (see Chapter 13), Stanley Milgram (1963), then at Yale University, invited volunteers to participate in a study of the "effects of punishment on learning." The experimenter deceived the participants into believing they were administering painful electric shocks of increasing intensity to another participant, who made repeated errors on a learning task. In reality, no shocks were delivered, and the other "participant" was actually a *confederate* (a research assistant who plays the part of a participant) of the experimenter. Moreover, Milgram had no interest in the effects of punishment on learning; he was actually interested in the influence of authority figures on obedience. Many of the actual participants experienced considerable distress during the procedure, and some were understandably distressed by the fact that they delivered what they believed to be extremely painful—even potentially fatal—electric shocks to an innocent person.

Was Milgram's elaborate deception justified? Milgram (1964) argued that the hoax was required to pull off the study, because informing subjects of the true purpose of the study would have generated obvious demand characteristics. He further noted that he went out of his way to later explain the study's true purpose to participants and inform them that their obedience wasn't a sign of cruelty or psychological disturbance. In addition, he sent a questionnaire to all subjects after the studies were completed and found that only 1.3 percent reported any negative emotional aftereffects. In contrast, Diana Baumrind (1964) argued that Milgram's study wasn't worth the knowledge or psychological distress it generated. Milgram's failure to provide subjects with full informed consent, she maintained, was ethically indefensible. Simply put, Milgram's subjects didn't know what they were getting into when they volunteered.

The debate concerning the ethics of Milgram's study continues to this day (Blass, 2004). Although we won't try to resolve this controversy here, we'll say only that the ethical standards of the American Psychological Association (1990) affirm that deception is justified only when (a) researchers couldn't have performed the study without the deception and (b) the scientific knowledge to be gained from the study outweighs its costs. Needless to say, evaluating (b) isn't easy, and it's up to researchers—and ultimately, to the IRB—to decide whether the potential scientific benefits of a study are sufficient to justify deception. Over the years, IRBs—which didn't exist in Milgram's day—have become more stringent about the need for informed consent. Milgram's study almost certainly wouldn't be approved by any college or university IRBs in the United States today.

Debriefing: Educating Participants. IRBs may also request that a full debriefing be performed at the conclusion of the research session. *Debriefing* is a process whereby researchers inform participants what the study was about. In some cases, researchers even use debriefings to explain their hypotheses in nontechnical language. The authors of your text believe that all research participants are entitled to a debriefing. The research study should be a learning experience for not only the investigator, but also the subject.

ETHICAL ISSUES IN ANIMAL RESEARCH

Few topics generate as much anger and discomfort as animal research. This is especially true of *invasive* research, in which investigators cause physical harm to animals. In psychology departments, invasive research most often takes the form of producing lesions in animals' brains, usually by means of surgery, and observing their effects on animals' behavior (see Chapter 3). About 7 to 8 percent of published research in psychology relies on animals (American Psychological Association, 2007) with the overwhelming majority of studies conducted on rodents (especially rats and mice) and birds. The goal of such research is to generate ideas about how the brain relates to behavior in humans without having to inflict harm on people.

Many animal rights protestors have raised useful concerns regarding the ethical treatment of animals and have underscored the need for adequate housing and feeding conditions (Ott, 1995). In contrast, others have gone to extremes that many critics would describe as unethical in themselves. Some have ransacked laboratories and liberated animals. In 1999, the Animal Liberation Front attacked several psychology laboratories at the University of Minnesota, releasing rats and pigeons and inflicting about $2 million worth of damage (Azar, 1999; Hunt 1999). Incidentally, most individuals on both sides of the animal rights debate agree that liberating animals is a dreadful idea, because many or most animals die shortly after being released.

These excessive tactics aside, the ethical issues here aren't easily resolved. Some commentators maintain that the deaths of approximately 20 million laboratory animals every year (Cunningham, 1985) aren't worth the cost. For many critics, the knowledge gleaned from animal research on aggression, fear, learning, memory, and related topics is of such doubtful external validity to humans as to be virtually useless (Ulrich, 1991).

This position has some merit but is probably too extreme. Some animal research has led to direct benefits to humans, as well as immensely useful knowledge in its own right. For example, many psychological treatments, especially those based on principles of learning (see Chapter 6), were derived from animal research. Without animal research, we'd know relatively little about the physiology of the brain (Domjan & Purdy, 1995). Moreover, to answer many critical psychological questions, there are simply no good alternatives to using animals (Gallup & Suarez, 1985). For example, without animals we'd be unable to test the safety and effectiveness of many medications.

None of this tells us when we should and shouldn't use animals in research. Nevertheless, it's clear that animal research has yielded enormously important insights about the brain and behavior and that psychologists are likely to rely on such research for some time to come. It's also clear that animal researchers must weigh carefully the potential scientific gains of their inquiries against the costs in death and suffering they produce. Because reasonable people will inevitably disagree about how to weigh these pros and cons, the intense controversy surrounding animal research is unlikely to subside anytime soon.

A great deal of animal research remains intensely controversial. It will probably always remain this way, given the complex ethical questions involved.

ASSESS YOUR KNOWLEDGE: FACT OR FICTION?

(1) The Tuskegee study violated the principles of informed consent. (True/False)
(2) Milgram's study would be considered unethical today because the shock could have caused injury or death. (True/False)
(3) In debriefing, the researcher informs participants of what will happen in the procedure before asking them to participate. (True/False)
(4) Before conducting invasive research on animals, investigators should weigh carefully the potential scientific benefits of this research against the costs of animal death and suffering. (True/False)

Answers: (1) T (p. 91); (2) F (p. 92); (3) F (p. 92); (4) T (p. 93)

Statistics: The Language of Psychological Research

FORMULA APPRECIATION CLASS AT THE MATH MUSEUM

(© ScienceCartoonsPlus.com)

Up to this point in the chapter, we've mostly spared you the gory mathematical details of psychological research. Aside from correlation coefficients, we haven't said much about how psychologists analyze their findings. Still, to understand psychological research and how to interpret it, we need to know a bit about **statistics:** the application of mathematics to describing and analyzing data. For you math phobics (or "arithmophobics," if you want to impress your friends with a technical term) out there, there's no cause for alarm. We promise to keep things simple.

DESCRIPTIVE STATISTICS: WHAT'S WHAT?

Psychologists use two kinds of statistics. The first are **descriptive statistics.** They do exactly what the name implies: describe data. For example, using descriptive statistics on a sample of one hundred men and one hundred women whose levels of extraversion we assess using a self-report measure, we could ask the following questions:

- What's the average level of extraversion in this sample?
- What's the average level of extraversion among men, and what's the average level of extraversion among women?
- How much do all of our participants, as well as men and women separately, vary in how extraverted they are?

To maintain our promise we'd keep things simple, we'll discuss only two major types of descriptive statistics. The first is the **central tendency,** which gives us a sense of the "central" score in our data set or where the group tends to cluster. In turn, there are three measures of central tendency: mean, median, and mode (known as the "three Ms"). Follow along in **Table 2.2a** (the left half of the table below) as we calculate each.

statistics
application of mathematics to describing and analyzing data

descriptive statistics
numerical characterizations that describe data

central tendency
measure of the "central" scores in a data set, or where the group tends to cluster

mean
average; a measure of central tendency

median
middle score in a data set; a measure of central tendency

mode
most frequent score in a data set; a measure of central tendency

dispersion
measure of how loosely or tightly bunched scores are

range
difference between the highest and lowest scores; a measure of dispersion

standard deviation
measure of dispersion that takes into account how far each data point is from the mean

inferential statistics
mathematical methods that allow us to determine whether we can generalize findings from our sample to the full population

Table 2.2 The Three Ms: Mean, Median, and Mode.

(a)	(b)
Sample IQ scores: 100, 90, 80, 120, 120	**Sample IQ scores:** 80, 85, 95, 95, 220
Mean: (100 + 90 + 80 +120 +120)/5 = 102	**Mean:** (80 + 85 + 95 + 95 + 220)/5 = 116
Median: order scores from lowest to highest: 80, 90, 100, 120, 120; middle score is 100	**Median:** 95
Mode: only 120 appears twice in the data set, so it's the most common score	**Mode:** 95
	Note: Mean is affected by one extreme score, but median and mode aren't

The **mean,** also known as the average, is just the total score divided by the number of people. If our sample consists of five people as shown in the table, the mean IQ is simply the total of the five scores divided by five, which happens to be 102.

The **median,** which we shouldn't confuse with that patch of grass in the middle of a highway, is the middle score in our data set. We obtain the median by lining up our scores in order and then finding the middle one. So in this case, we'd line up the five IQ scores in order from lowest to highest, and then find that 100 is the median because that's the score smack in the middle of the distribution.

The **mode** is the most frequent score in our data set. In this case, the mode is 120, because two people in our sample received scores of 120 on the IQ test and one person each received other scores.

As we can see, the three Ms sometimes give us rather different measures of central tendency. In this case, the mean and median were close to each other, but the mode was much higher than both. The mean is generally the best statistic to report when our data form a bell-shaped or "normal" distribution, as we can see in the left panel of **Figure 2.8.** But what happens when our distribution is "skewed," that is, tilted sharply to one side or the other, as in the right panels of Figure 2.7? Here the mean provides a misleading picture of the central tendency, so it's better to use the median or mode instead.

To hammer this point home, let's now look at **Table 2.2b** (page 94) to see what happens to our measures of central tendency. The mean of this distribution is 116, but four of the scores are much below 116, and the only reason the mean is this high is the presence of one person who scored 220 (who in technical terms we call an *outlier,* because his or her score lies way outside the other scores). In contrast, both the median and mode are 95, which capture the central tendency of the distribution much better.

The second type of descriptive statistic is **dispersion,** which gives us a sense of how loosely or tightly bunched the scores are. Consider the following two sets of IQ scores from five people:

- 80, 85, 85, 90, 95
- 25, 65, 70, 125, 150

In both groups of scores, the mean is 87. But the second set of scores is much more spread out (dispersed) than the first. So we need some means of describing the differences in dispersion in these two data sets.

Although there are several measures of dispersion, the simplest is the **range.** The range is the difference between the highest and lowest scores. In the first set of IQ scores, the range is only 15, whereas in the second set the range is 125. So the range tells us that although the two sets of scores have a similar central tendency, their dispersion is wildly different (as in **Figure 2.9a**). Although the range is the easiest measure of dispersion to calculate, it can be deceptive because, as shown in **Figure 2.9b**, two data sets with the same range can display a very different distribution of scores across that range. To compensate for this fact, psychologists often use another measure called the **standard deviation** to depict dispersion. Without getting into the mathematical details, this measure is less likely to be deceptive than the range because it takes into account how far *each* data point is from the mean, rather than simply looking at how widely scattered the most extreme scores are.

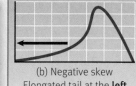

What's wrong with this (fake) newspaper headline?

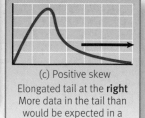

(b) Negative skew
Elongated tail at the **left**
More data in the tail than would be expected in a normal distribution

(c) Positive skew
Elongated tail at the **right**
More data in the tail than would be expected in a normal distribution

68% of data
95% of data
99.7% of data
(a) Normal (bell-shaped) distribution

Figure 2.8 Distribution Curves. (a) a normal (bell-shaped) distribution, (b) a markedly negative skewed distribution, and (c) a markedly positive skewed distribution.

INFERENTIAL STATISTICS: TESTING HYPOTHESES

In addition to descriptive statistics, psychologists use **inferential statistics,** which allow us to determine whether we can generalize findings from our sample to the full population. When we use inferential statistics, we're asking whether we can draw "inferences" (conclusions) regarding whether the differences we've observed in our sample apply to similar samples. Previously, we mentioned a study of one hundred men and one hundred women who took a self-report measure of extraversion. In this study, inferential statistics allow us to answer the following question: Are the differences we've found in extraversion between men and women believable, or are they just a fluke occurrence in our sample? Let's imagine we calculated the means for men and women (we first verified that the

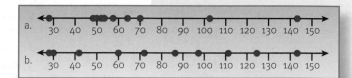

Figure 2.9 The Range versus the Standard Deviation. These two number lines display data sets with the same *range* but different *standard deviations.* The dispersion is more tightly clustered in (a) than in (b), so the standard deviation in (a) will be smaller.

distribution of scores in both men and women approximated a bell curve). After doing so, we found that men scored 10.4 on our extraversion scale (the scores range from 0 to 15) and that women scored 9.9. So, *in our sample*, men are more extraverted, or at least say they are, than women. Can we conclude from this finding that men are more extraverted than women in general? How can we rule out the possibility that this small sex difference in our sample is due to chance? That's where inferential statistics enter the picture.

Statistical Significance. To figure out whether the difference we've observed in our sample is a believable (real) one, we need to conduct statistical tests to determine whether we can generalize our findings to the broader population. To do so, we can use a variety of statistics depending on the research design. But regardless of which test we use, we generally use a .05 level of confidence when deciding whether a finding is believable. This means that we don't typically accept a finding as believable unless it would have occurred by chance less than 1 out of every 20 times (that's .05, which is one divided by 20) we conducted the study. When the finding would have occurred by chance less than 1 in 20 times, we say that the finding is *statistically significant*. A statistically significant result is believable; it's probably a real difference. In psychology journals, we'll often see the expression "$p < .05$," meaning that the probability (the lowercase *p* stands for probability) that our finding would have occurred by chance alone is less than one in 20.

A large sample size can yield a statistically significant result, but this result may have little or no practical significance.

Practical Significance. Writer Gertrude Stein said that "a difference is a difference that makes a difference." Stein's quotation reminds us not to confuse statistical significance with *practical significance*, that is, real-world importance. A finding can be statistically significant yet be of virtually no importance in real-world predictions. To understand this point, we need to understand that a major determinant of statistical significance is sample size. The larger the sample size, the greater the odds (all else being equal) that a result will be statistically significant. With huge sample sizes, virtually all findings—even tiny ones—will be statistically significant.

If we were to find a correlation of $r = .06$ between IQ and nose length in a sample of 500,000 people, this correlation would be statistically significant at the $p < .05$ level. Yet it's so tiny in magnitude that it would be essentially useless for predicting anything. As we'll recall, to find out how much of one variable is accounted for by the other, we square the correlation. Following this rule, we discover that knowing people's nose lengths allows us to account for less than 4/1,000 (.0036) of their IQs.

HOW PEOPLE LIE WITH STATISTICS

American humorist Mark Twain once said there are three kinds of untruths: "lies, damned lies, and statistics." He was right: Because many people's eyes glaze over when they see lots of numbers, it's easy to fool them with statistical sleight of hand. Here, we'll provide three examples of how people can misuse statistics. Our goal, of course, isn't to encourage you to lie with statistics, but to equip you with critical thinking skills for spotting widespread statistical abuses (Huff, 1954).

Example 1

Your Congressional Representative, Ms. Dee Section, is running for reelection. As part of her platform, she's just proposed a new tax plan for everyone in your state. According to the "fine print" in Ms. Section's plan, 99 percent of the people in your state will receive a $100 tax cut this year. The remaining 1 percent, who make over $3 million per year, will receive a tax cut of

"There are lies, damn lies, and statistics. We're looking for someone who can make all three of these work for us."

(© www.CartoonStock.com)

$500,000 (according to Ms. Section, this large tax cut for the people in the uppermost 1 percent of the population is necessary because she gets her biggest campaign contributions from them).

Based on this plan, Ms. Dee Section announces at a press conference, "If I'm elected and my tax plan goes through, the average person in our state will receive a tax cut of $5,099." Watching this press conference on television, you think, "Wow . . . what a deal! I'm definitely going to vote for Dee Section. If she wins, I'll have over 5,000 extra bucks in my bank account."

Question: *Why should you be skeptical of Dee Section's claim?*

Answer: Ms. Dee Section has engaged in a not especially subtle deception, suggesting that she's aptly named. She assures us that under her plan the "average person" in her state will receive a tax cut of $5,099. In one respect she's right, because the *mean* tax cut is indeed $5,099. But in this case, the mean is highly misleading, because under Section's plan virtually everyone in her state will receive only a $100 tax cut. Only the richest of the rich will receive a tax cut of $500,000, making the mean highly unrepresentative of the central tendency. Dee Section should have instead reported the median or mode, which are both only $100, as measures of central tendency.

Example 2

A researcher, Dr. Faulty Conclusion, conducts a study to demonstrate that transcendental meditation (TM), a form of relaxation that originated in East Asian cultures, reduces crime rates. According to Dr. Conclusion, towns whose citizens are taught to practice TM will experience a dramatic drop in numbers of arrests. He finds a small town, Pancake, Iowa (population 300), and teaches all of the citizens of Pancake to practice TM. For his control group, he identifies a small neighboring town in Iowa, called Waffle (population also 300) and doesn't introduce them to TM. According to Dr. Conclusion, Waffle is a good control group for Pancake, because it has the same population, ethnic makeup, income, and initial arrest rates.

Two months after the introduction of TM to Pancake, Dr. Conclusion measures the arrest rates in Pancake and Waffle. At a major conference, he proudly announces that although the arrest rates in Waffle stayed exactly the same, the arrest rates in Pancake experienced a spectacular plunge. To demonstrate this astonishing effect in Pancake, he directs the audience to a graph (see **Figure 2.10** to see this effect). As he does, the audience gasps in astonishment. "As you can see from this graph," Conclusion proclaims, "the arrest rates in Pancake were initially very high. But after I taught Pancake's citizens TM, their arrest rates 2 months later were much, much lower." Dr. Conclusion concludes triumphantly, "Our findings show beyond a shadow of a doubt that TM reduces crime rates."

Question: *What's wrong with Dr. Conclusion's conclusion?*

Answer: Dr. Conclusion's graph in Figure 2.9 sure looks impressive, doesn't it? The arrest rates have indeed gone down from the beginning to the end of the study. But let's take a good close look at the *y* axis (that's the vertical axis) of the graph. Can we see anything suspicious about it?

Dr. Conclusion has tricked us, or perhaps he's tricked himself. The *y* axis starts at 15.5 arrests per month and goes up to 16 arrests per month. In fact, Dr. Conclusion has demonstrated only that the arrest rate in Pancake declined from 15.9 arrests per month to 15.6 arrests per month—a grand total of less than one-third of an arrest per month! That's hardly worth writing home about, let alone mastering transcendental meditation for.

Dr. Conclusion used what's termed a "truncated line graph." That kind of graph is a real "no-no" in statistics, although researchers use it all the time (Huff, 1954; Smith, 2001). In a truncated line graph, the *y* axis starts not at the lowest possible score, where it should start (in this case, it should start at 0, because the lowest possible number of arrests per month is 0), but somewhere close to the highest possible score. By using a truncated line graph, Dr. Conclusion made the apparent effects of TM appear huge. In fact, they were pitifully small.

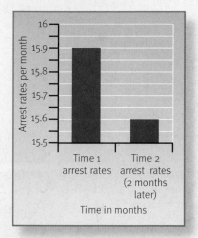

Figure 2.10 Arrest Rates Before and After Transcendental Meditation. Arrest rates per month in Pancake before (left) and (right) introduction of transcendental meditation.

Example 3

Ms. Representation conducts a study to determine the association between nationality and drinking patterns. According to Professor Representation's new "Grand Unified Theory of Drinking Behavior," people of German descent are at higher risk for alcoholism than people of Norwegian descent. To test this hypothesis, she begins with a randomly selected sample of 10,000 people from the city of Inebriated, Indiana. She administers a survey to all participants inquiring about their drinking habits and national background. When she analyzes her data, she finds that 1,200 citizens of Inebriated meet official diagnostic criteria for alcoholism. Of these 1,200 individuals, 450 are of German descent, whereas only 30 are of Norwegian descent—a 15-fold difference! She conducts a statistical test (we won't trouble you with the precise mathematics) and determines that this amazingly large difference is statistically significant at $p < .05$. At the annual convention of the International Society of Really, Really Smart Alcoholism Researchers, Ms. Representation asserts, "My bold hypothesis has been confirmed. Based on my study, I can conclude confidently that Germans are at higher risk for alcoholism than Norwegians."

Question: *Why are Ms. Representation's conclusions about drinking all washed up?*

Answer: Remember the *base rate fallacy* we introduced in this chapter? When interpreting the results of studies, it's easy to forget about base rates. That's because base rates often "lurk in the distance" of our minds and aren't especially vivid. In this case, Ms. Representation forgot to take a crucial fact into account: In Inebriated, Indiana, the base rate of people of German descent is twenty-five times higher than the base rate of people of Norwegian descent. As a result, the fact that there are fifteen times more German than Norwegian alcoholics in Inebriated doesn't support her hypothesis. In fact, given there are twenty-five times more Germans than Norwegians in Inebriated, the data actually run *opposite* to Ms. Representation's hypothesis: The percentage of alcoholic Norwegians is higher than the percentage of alcoholic Germans!

The bottom line: *Don't trust all of the statistics you read in a newspaper.*

But bear in mind that we've focused here on misuses and abuses of statistics. That's because we want to immunize you against statistical errors you're likely to encounter in the newspaper as well as on TV and the Internet. But you shouldn't conclude from our examples that we can *never* trust statistics. As we'll learn throughout this text, statistics are a wonderful set of tools that can help us to better understand behavior. When evaluating statistics, it's best to steer a middle course between dismissing them out of hand and accepting them uncritically. As is so often the case in psychology, Oberg's dictum (see Chapter 1) applies: We should keep our minds open, but not so open that our brains fall out.

To evaluate claims about statistics on the Internet, we must equip ourselves with tools against errors in reasoning.

ASSESS YOUR KNOWLEDGE: FACT OR FICTION?
(1) The mean is not always the best measure of central tendency. (True/False)
(2) The mode and standard deviation are both measures of dispersion. (True/False)
(3) All statistically significant findings are important and large in size. (True/False)
(4) Researchers can easily manipulate statistics to make it appear that their hypotheses are confirmed. (True/False)

Answers: (1) T (p. 94); (2) F (p. 94); (3) F (p. 96); (4) T (p. 96)

Becoming a Peer Reviewer of Psychological Research

As we learned in Chapter 1, almost all psychological journals send submitted articles to outside reviewers, who screen the articles carefully for quality control. As we'll recall, this often ego-bruising process is called *peer review*. One crucial task of peer reviewers is to identify flaws that could undermine a study's findings and conclusions. Now that we've learned the key ingredients of a psychological experiment and the pitfalls that can cause experiments to go wrong, let's try our hands at becoming peer reviewers.

We're going to present descriptions of three studies, each of which contains at least one hidden flaw. Read each study and try to figure out what's wrong with it. Once you've done so, read the paragraph below it to see how close you came.

Ready? Here goes.

"THAT'S IT? THAT'S PEER REVIEW?"

(© ScienceCartoonsPlus.com)

Study 1

An investigator, Dr. Sudo Sigh-Ents, sets out to test the hypothesis that subliminal self-help tapes (see Chapter 4) are effective in increasing self-esteem. She randomly selects fifty college freshmen from the subject pool to receive a commercially available subliminal self-help tape. She asks them to play the tape for 2 months each night for 1 hour before going to sleep (which is consistent with the standard instructions on the tape). Dr. Sigh-Ents measures participants' self-esteem at the start of the study and again after the 2-month period. She finds that their self-esteem has increased significantly over these 2 months. On the basis of this finding, Dr. Sigh-Ents concludes that "subliminal self-help tapes increase self-esteem."

Question: *What's wrong with this experiment?*

Answer: What's wrong with this "experiment" is that it's not even an experiment. There's no random assignment of participants to experimental and control groups; in fact, there's no control group at all. There's also no manipulation of an independent variable. Remember that a variable is something that varies. In this case, there's no independent variable because all participants received the same manipulation, namely, playing the subliminal self-help tape every night. As a result, we can't know whether the increase in self-esteem was really due to the tape. It could have been due to any number of other factors, such as placebo effects or increases in self-esteem that might often occur over the course of one's freshman year.

Study 2

A researcher, Dr. Art E. Fact, is interested in determining whether a new form of therapy, Anger Expression Therapy, is effective in treating anxiety. He randomly assigns one hundred individuals with anxiety disorders to two groups. The experimental group receives Anger Expression Therapy (which is administered by Dr. Fact himself), whereas the control group is placed on a waiting list and receives no treatment. At the conclusion of 6 months, Dr. Fact finds that the rate of anxiety disorders is significantly lower in the experimental group than in the control group. He concludes, "Anger Expression Therapy is helpful in the treatment of anxiety disorders."

Question: *What's wrong with this experiment?*

Answer: On its surface, this experiment looks OK. There's random assignment of participants to experimental and control groups, and manipulation of an independent variable, namely, the presence versus absence of Anger Expression Therapy. But Dr. Fact hasn't controlled for two crucial pitfalls. First, he hasn't controlled for the placebo effect, because

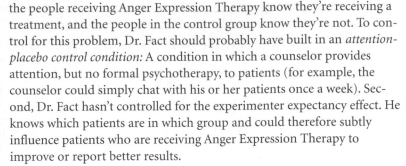

In an attention-placebo control condition, a counselor typically chats with patients but provides no formal treatment.

the people receiving Anger Expression Therapy know they're receiving a treatment, and the people in the control group know they're not. To control for this problem, Dr. Fact should probably have built in an *attention-placebo control condition:* A condition in which a counselor provides attention, but no formal psychotherapy, to patients (for example, the counselor could simply chat with his or her patients once a week). Second, Dr. Fact hasn't controlled for the experimenter expectancy effect. He knows which patients are in which group and could therefore subtly influence patients who are receiving Anger Expression Therapy to improve or report better results.

Study 3

Dr. E. Roney Us wants to find out whether listening to loud rock music impairs college students' performance on psychology tests. She randomly assigns fifty college students in Psychology 101 to listen to loud rock music for 2 hours (from 7 P.M. to 9 P.M.) every day for 1 week. Dr. Us asks her research assistant to randomly assign fifty other college students in Psychology 101 to use these same 2 hours to do whatever they like, except that they can't listen to loud rock music during this time period. She has no contact with the subjects in either group throughout the week and doesn't know who's in which group, although she monitors their music listening by means of a secret recording device hidden in their dorm rooms. At the end of the week, she examines their scores on their first Psychology 101 test (she doesn't know the Psychology 101 instructor and has no contact with him) and finds that students who listen to loud rock music do significantly worse than other students. Dr. Us concludes that "listening to loud rock music impairs students' performance on psychology tests."

Question: *What's wrong with this experiment?*

Answer: Again, this study looks pretty decent at first glance. There's random assignment of participants to conditions, and there's also manipulation of an independent variable—either listening to, or not listening to, loud rock music. In addition, Dr. Us has ensured that she's blind to who's in the experimental and control groups and that she has no contact with either participants or the Psychology 101 instructor during this time. She also uses covert observation (placing a hidden audio recorder in their dorm rooms) to minimize Hawthorne effects. But Dr. Us has forgotten to control for one crucial confound: Subjects in the control group could have used the extra time to study for their exams. Because of this confound, it's impossible to know whether rock music leads to poorer test performance or whether extra study time leads to better test performance. Of course, both could be true, but we don't know for sure.

MOST REPORTERS AREN'T SCIENTISTS: EVALUATING PSYCHOLOGY IN THE MEDIA

News coverage of scientific claims isn't always trustworthy.

Few major American newspapers hire reporters with any formal psychological training—the *New York Times* is a notable exception—so we shouldn't assume that people who write news stories about psychology are trained to distinguish psychological fact from fiction. Most aren't. This means that news stories are prone to faulty conclusions because reporters rely on the same heuristics and biases that we all do.

When evaluating the legitimacy of psychological reports in the media, here are some tips to keep in mind. First, we should *consider the source* (Gilovich, 1991). We should generally place more confidence in a finding reported in a reputable science magazine (like *Scientific American Mind* or *Discover*) than one reported in a supermarket tabloid (like the *National Enquirer*) or a popular magazine (like *People* or *Vogue*). The "consider the source" principle also applies to websites. We should generally place more trust in findings reported on websites of well-established psychological organizations, such as the American Psychological Association (www.apa.org) or Association for Psychological

Science (www.psychologicalscience.org), than on websites that aren't hosted by a formal organization. Moreover, we should place more trust in findings from primary sources, such as the original journal articles themselves (if we can look them up in the library or on the Internet) than from secondary sources, such as newspapers, magazines, or websites that merely report findings from primary sources.

Second, we need to be on the lookout for excessive *sharpening* and *leveling* (Gilovich, 1991). *Sharpening* refers to the tendency to exaggerate the gist, or central message, of a study, whereas *leveling* refers to the tendency to minimize the less central details of a study. Sharpening and leveling often result in a "good story," because they end up bringing the most important facts of a study into sharper focus. Of course, secondary sources in the news media need to engage in a certain amount of sharpening and leveling when reporting studies, because they can't possibly describe every minor detail of an investigation. Still, too much sharpening and leveling can result in a misleading picture. If an investigator discovers that a new medication is effective for 35 percent of people with anxiety disorders, but that a placebo is effective for 33 percent of people with anxiety disorders, the newspaper editor may lead off the story with this eye-popping headline: "Breakthrough: New Medication Outperforms Other Pills in Treating Anxiety." This headline isn't literally wrong, but it oversimplifies greatly what the researcher found.

When it comes to evaluating psychological claims in the news or entertainment media, there's a simple bottom-line message: we should always insist on rigorous research evidence.

Third, we can easily be misled by seemingly "balanced" coverage of a story. There's a crucial difference between genuine scientific controversy and the kind of balanced coverage that news reporters create by ensuring that representatives from both sides of the story receive equal air time. When covering a psychological story, the news media usually try to include comments from "experts" (we place this term in quotation marks, because they're not always genuine experts) on opposing sides of an issue. In this way, the media make their coverage appear more balanced. They also help to generate greater reader interest, because almost everybody enjoys a juicy controversy.

The problem is that "balanced coverage" sometimes creates *pseudosymmetry* (Park, 2002): the appearance of a scientific controversy where none exists. For example, a newspaper might feature a story about a study that provides scientific evidence against extrasensory perception (ESP). They might devote the first four paragraphs to a description of the study but the last four paragraphs to impassioned critiques of the study from advocates of ESP. This coverage may create the impression that the scientific evidence for ESP is split right down the middle, with about half of the research supporting it and about half disputing it. It's easy to overlook the fact that there was no scientific evidence in the last four paragraphs, only criticisms of the evidence against ESP. Moreover, the article might fail to note that the scientific evidence regarding ESP is almost entirely negative (Hines, 2003; see Chapter 4).

One reason why most of us find it difficult to think critically about scientific evidence is that we're constantly bombarded by media reports that (unintentionally) provide us with poor role models for interpreting research (Lilienfeld, Ruscio, & Lynn, in press; Stanovich, 2006). Fortunately, keeping these tips in mind should help us to become better consumers of psychological science in everyday life.

ASSESS YOUR KNOWLEDGE: FACT OR FICTION?

(1) Few psychological journals use a peer-review process. (True/False)

(2) When evaluating the quality of a study, we must be on the lookout for potential confounds, expectancy effects, and nonrandom assignment to experimental and control groups. (True/False)

(3) Most newspaper reporters who write stories about psychology have advanced degrees in psychology. (True/False)

(4) "Balanced" coverage of a psychology story is sometimes inaccurate. (True/False)

Answers: (1) F (p. 98); (2) T (p. 99); (3) F (p. 100); (4) T (p. 101)

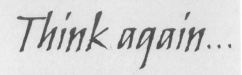

The Complete Review System

THINK / ASSESS / STUDY / SUCCEED

The Beauty and Necessity of Good Research Design (pp. 65–70)

STUDY the Learning Objectives

▶ Explain what research designs accomplish that we can't discover by intuition alone

- Numerous examples from history and recent times demonstrate that our intuitions that a particular phenomenon has occurred can be wrong. Only when there is an objective, consistent, replicable measure can we confirm our subjective hunches.

▶ Identify heuristics and biases that prevent us from thinking clearly about psychology

- Our heuristics are highly useful but can sometimes steer us wrong. Representativeness and availability heuristics can lead us to rely too heavily on inaccurate measures of the probability of events. Biases such as hindsight bias and overconfidence can lead us to overestimate our ability to predict outcomes accurately.

DO YOU KNOW THESE TERMS?

- ❏ **prefrontal lobotomy** (p. 66)
- ❏ **heuristics** (p. 67)
- ❏ **representativeness** (p. 67)
- ❏ **base rate** (p. 68)
- ❏ **availability** (p. 68)
- ❏ **cognitive biases** (p. 69)
- ❏ **hindsight bias** (p. 69)
- ❏ **overconfidence** (p. 70)

Using your knowledge of research design, explain the flaws in Biklen's claims regarding facilitated communication. (p. 65)

SUCCEED with mypsych lab

Anchoring and Adjustment
Bias in the mind of the beholder: Avoiding bias in everyday thinking.
(pp. 66–69)

THINK about what **You** would do . . .
Imagine you were conducting a study to test your belief that women blush more than men. How could you design the study to avoid confirmation bias and maintain objectivity? (pp. 69–70)

How can we explain that most people say they'd have to travel southwest to get from Reno to San Diego? (p. 68)

ASSESS your knowledge

1. Bias can get in the way of our evaluation of claims unless we use dependable _____ _____. (p. 65)

2. Scientists (confirmed/disconfirmed) the effectiveness of prefrontal lobotomy by conducting controlled studies. (p. 66)

3. Kahneman and Tversky pioneered the study of _____; mental shortcuts that help us make sense of the world. (p. 67)

4. When we use a _____ heuristic, we are essentially judging a book by its cover. (p. 67)

5. The _____ heuristic involves estimating the likelihood of an occurrence based on the ease with which it comes to our minds. (p. 68)

6. A _____ _____ is another term for how

common a characteristic or behavior is. (p. 68)

7. In addition to confirmation bias, two other tendencies that can lead us to draw misleading conclusions are _____ _____ and _____. (pp. 69–70)

8. Once an event occurs, if you say, "I knew that was going to happen," you might be engaging in _____ _____. (p. 69)

9. Most of us tend to engage in _____ when we overestimate our ability to make correct predictions. (p. 70)

10. In a 2005 study, Tetlock found that extreme pundits are (more/less) likely than less extreme pundits to be accurate in their predictions. (p. 70)

If you did not receive an access code to MyPsychLab with this text and wish to purchase access online, please visit www.mypsychlab.com.

The Scientific Method: Toolbox of Skills (pp. 71–90)

STUDY the Learning Objectives

▶ Distinguish the types of designs and the conclusions that we can draw from each

- Four key types of research designs are naturalistic observation, case studies, correlational designs, and experimental designs. Naturalistic observation involves recording behaviors in real-world settings but are often not carefully controlled. Case studies involve examining one or a few individuals over long periods of time; these designs are often useful in generating hypotheses but limited in testing them rigorously. Correlational studies allow us to

Using your knowledge of random selection, what did the pollsters do wrong in reporting the 1948 presidential election results? (p. 85)

THINK about

what You would do . . .
How would you convince a friend who believes that strange things seem to happen to her during a full moon that it's an illusory correlation? (p. 75)

mypsychlab
where learning comes to life!

Correlations Do Not Show Causation

SUCCEED with

Challenge your assumptions about explanations of behavior. (p. 77)

EXPLORE

How does the ancient practice of voodoo illustrate the nocebo effect? (p. 82)

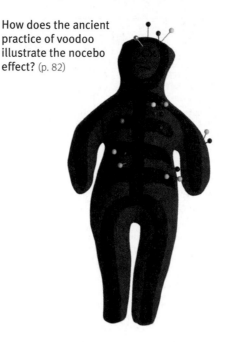

establish the relations among two or more measures, but do not allow causal conclusions. Experimental designs involve random assignment of participants to conditions and manipulation of an independent variable, and they allow us to draw conclusions about the causes of a particular behavior.

▶ Identify the potential pitfalls of each design that can lead to faulty conclusions
  • Placebo effects, experimenter expectancy effects, and response sets are examples of problems in research designs that can lead to faulty conclusions. Other limitations, such as halo effects and errors of central tendency, often arise for rating data.

DO YOU KNOW THESE TERMS?
  ❏ **naturalistic observation** (p. 71)
  ❏ **external validity** (p. 71)
  ❏ **internal validity** (p. 72)
  ❏ **case study** (p. 72)
  ❏ **existence proofs** (p. 72)
  ❏ **correlational design** (p. 73)
  ❏ **scatterplot** (p. 74)
  ❏ **illusory correlation** (p. 75)
  ❏ **experiment** (p. 78)
  ❏ **random assignment** (p. 78)
  ❏ **experimental group** (p. 78)
  ❏ **control group** (p. 78)
  ❏ **independent variable** (p. 78)
  ❏ **dependent variable** (p. 78)
  ❏ **confound** (p. 79)
  ❏ **meta-analysis** (p. 80)
  ❏ **file drawer problem** (p. 80)
  ❏ **placebo effect** (p. 81)
  ❏ **blind** (p. 81)
  ❏ **nocebo effect** (p. 82)
  ❏ **experimenter expectancy effect** (p. 82)
  ❏ **double-blind** (p. 82)
  ❏ **Hawthorne effect** (p. 84)
  ❏ **demand characteristics** (p. 84)
  ❏ **random selection** (p. 85)
  ❏ **reliability** (p. 86)
  ❏ **validity** (p. 86)
  ❏ **response sets** (p. 87)

ASSESS your knowledge

1. A _____ _____ examines one person or a small group of people, and a _____ _____ examines the extent to which two variables are associated. (pp. 72–73)

2. A positive correlation is one in which the value of one variable goes up while the other one goes (up/down). (p. 73)

3. An _____ is a research design that consists of two components: 1) a random assignment of participants to conditions, and 2) manipulation of an independent variable. (p. 78)

4. If a study is an experiment we (can/can't) infer cause and effect, but if the study is correlational we (can/can't). (p. 78)

5. The group of participants in a study that doesn't receive the manipulation is the _____ group. (p. 78)

6. To avoid the _____ effect during medication research, it is crucial that the subject remain _____ to whether he/she has been assigned to the experimental group. (p. 81)

7. To make an experiment safe from the Rosenthal effect, it is best if the experiment is conducted in a _____ fashion. (p. 83)

8. In a classic study that revealed the _____ effect, participants' knowledge that they were being studied increased their productivity. (p. 83)

9. When evaluating results, we need to be able to evaluate the consistency of the measurement, or _____, and the extent to which a measure assesses what it claims to measure, or _____. (p. 86)

10. In using _____ _____, psychologists need to evaluate whether questionnaire respondents engaged in _____ _____. (p. 87)

Ethical Issues in Research Design (pp. 90–93)

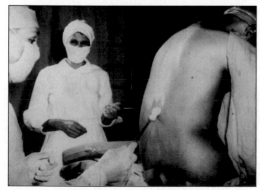

What important changes have been made to research procedures in the United States to ensure that an ethical catastrophe like the Tuskegee study doesn't happen again? (p. 91)

THINK about

what You would do . . .
As a psychology student, you agree to participate in two research studies. You understand the scope of the first study, but you are confused about what is involved in the second study. How would you assert your rights as a subject in the second study to find out more information before consenting? (p. 92)

STUDY the Learning Objectives

▶ Explain the ethical obligations of researchers toward their research participants
  • Concerns about ethical treatment of research participants have led research institutions to establish institutional review boards that review all research and require informed consent by participants. In some cases, they may also require a full debriefing at the conclusion of the research session.

▶ Describe both sides of the debate on the use of animals as research subjects
  • Animal research has led to clear benefits in our understanding of human learning, brain physiology, and psychological treatment, to mention only a few advances. To answer many critical psychological questions, there are simply no good alternatives to using

animals. Those who question the ethics of animal research have raised useful questions about the treatment of these animals and emphasized the need for adequate housing and feeding conditions. Many protest the large number of laboratory animals that are used each year and question whether animal research offers sufficient external validity to justify such uses.

DO YOU KNOW THIS TERM?

❏ **informed consent** (p. 92)

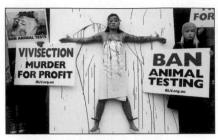

What are some of the arguments for and against the ethics of animal testing? (p. 93)

ASSESS your knowledge

1. Psychologists need to be concerned about the scientific value of their research studies but also the _____ of these studies. (p. 90)

2. A tragic example of a study in which researchers ignored ethical considerations is the _____ study performed by the U.S. Public Health Service. (p. 91)

3. In this U.S. government study started in 1932, the researchers never informed the subjects that they had _____, nor did they inform them that _____ were available to treat the disease. (p. 91)

4. Every major American research college and university now has an _____ _____ _____, which reviews all research and seeks to protect study participants against abuses. (p. 91)

5. The process in which researchers tell participants what's involved in a study is called _____ _____. (p. 92)

6. Milgram's controversial study relied on _____ because he deliberately misled the participants about the study's purpose. (p. 92)

7. Milgram's study likely (would/would not) be approved by a college or university IRB today in the United States. (p. 92)

8. The goal of an _____ research study on animals is to learn how the brain relates to behavior in humans without having to inflict harm on people. (pp. 92–93)

9. About ____ percent of published psychology research relies on animals. (p. 93)

10. Animal researchers must carefully weigh the potential _____ _____ against the costs in death and suffering they produce. (p. 93)

Statistics: The Language of Psychological Research (pp. 94–98)

STUDY the Learning Objectives

▶ Explain how to calculate measures of central tendency
  • Three measures of central tendency are the mean, median, and mode. The mean is the average of all scores. The median is the middle score. The mode is the most frequent score.

▶ Identify uses of various measures of central tendency and dispersion
  • Among the three measures of central tendency, the mean is the most widely used measure and is also the most sensitive to extreme scores. Two measures of dispersion are the range and standard deviation. The range is a more intuitive measure of variability, but can yield a deceptive picture of how spread out or clustered individual scores are. The standard deviation is a better measure of dispersion, although it is more difficult to calculate.

▶ Show how statistics can be misused for purposes of persuasion
  • Reporting measures of central tendency that are nonrepresentative of most participants, creating visual representations that exaggerate effects, and failing to take base rates into account are all frequent methods of manipulating statistics for the purposes of persuasion.

what You would do . . .

A local corporation at which you hope to work after college funds a research study you are conducting to explore the benefits of their product on learning. The research results fail to support the company's claims that the product improves learning. How would you report your findings to the company and how would you characterize the results in your conclusions? (pp. 96–98)

THINK about

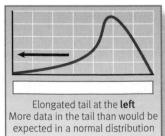

| Elongated tail at the **left** More data in the tail than would be expected in a normal distribution | Elongated tail at the **right** More data in the tail than would be expected in a normal distribution |

Using your knowledge of distribution curves, label these two different types of skews. (p. 95)

Match up the measure to the definition (p. 94)

____ Mode	1. Middle score in a data set
____ Mean	2. Most frequent score in a data set
____ Median	3. Average score in a data set

ASSESS your knowledge

1. The application of mathematics to describing and analyzing data is called _____. (p. 94)

2. Psychologists use two types of statistics: _____ and _____. (pp. 94–95)

3. In _____ statistics, the _____ _____ provides a sense of the "central" score in a data set, or where the group tends to cluster. (p. 94)

4. The three measures of central tendency are _____, _____, and _____. (p. 94)

5. The most frequent score in a data set is the _____. (p. 94)

6. The best measure of central tendency to report when the data form a "bell-shaped" or normal distribution is the _____. (p. 95)

7. The difference between the highest and lowest scores is the _____. (p. 95)

8. Another type of descriptive statistic is _____ which gives a sense of how loosely or tightly bunched the data are. (p. 95)

9. The _____ _____ takes into account how far each data point is from the mean. (p. 95)

10. By using _____ statistics, psychologists can determine whether they can generalize findings from a sample to the full population. (p. 95)

DO YOU KNOW THESE TERMS?

- ☐ **statistics** (p. 94)
- ☐ **descriptive statistics** (p. 94)
- ☐ **central tendency** (p. 94)
- ☐ **mean** (p. 94)
- ☐ **median** (p. 94)
- ☐ **mode** (p. 94)
- ☐ **dispersion** (p. 95)
- ☐ **range** (p. 95)
- ☐ **standard deviation** (p. 95)
- ☐ **inferential statistics** (p. 95)

Becoming a Peer Reviewer of Psychological Research (pp. 99–101)

THINK about what You would do . . .

When researching online articles in support of your upcoming debate, how do you detect sharpening or leveling by the writers to ensure the information is not misleading in any way? (p. 101)

SUCCEED with mypsychlab
where learning comes to life!

Reviewing Reports of Psychology in the News

Impress your friends as you apply your skills to critically evaluating psychological articles in the news. (p. 100)

LISTEN

STUDY the Learning Objectives

▶ Identify flaws in research designs
- Good research design requires not only random assignment and manipulation of an independent variable, but also inclusion of an appropriate control condition to rule out placebo effects. Most important, it requires careful attention to the possibility of alternative explanations of observed effects.

▶ Identify skills for evaluating psychological claims in the popular media
- To evaluate psychological claims in the news and elsewhere in the popular media, we should bear in mind that few psychology reporters have formal psychological training. When considering media claims, we should consider the source, beware of excessive sharpening and leveling, and be on the lookout for pseudosymmetry.

ASSESS your knowledge

1. The crucial task of a ____ _____ is to identify flaws that could undermine a study's findings. (p. 99)

2. By definition, an experiment is flawed if it doesn't include a manipulation of an _____ _____. (p. 99)

3. In Study 1, the researcher puts all the subjects in a single group and is therefore lacking a necessary _____ group. (p. 99)

4. In Study 2, the researcher has not controlled for the _____ effect because the participants are aware of whether they are receiving treatment or not. (p. 99)

5. In Study 2, the researcher knows which participants are in which groups so he has created an opportunity for the _____ _____ effect. (p. 99)

6. In Study 3, the researcher protected her study from the _____ effect by using covert observation of her subjects. (p. 100)

7. News stories about psychology (are/are not) typically written by people who have formal training in psychology. (p. 100)

8. When evaluating the legitimacy of psychological reports in the media, one should consider the _____. (p. 100)

9. Newspapers, magazines, and websites tend to engage in a certain amount of _____ and _____ to make a good story. (p. 101)

10. When a news story mistakenly suggests that experts are equally divided over a topic, it creates _____. (p. 101)

Remember these questions from the beginning of the chapter? Think again and ask yourself if you would answer them differently based on what you now know about research methods. (For more detailed explanations, see MyPsychLab.com)

▶ Do we really need research designs to figure out the answers to psychological questions? (p. 65)
▶ Can studying one person in depth yield valuable information? (p. 72)
▶ Can we perceive statistical associations even when they don't exist? (p. 75)
▶ How do our intuitions sometimes deceive us? (p. 76)
▶ What's an "experiment" and is it just like any other psychological study? (p. 78)
▶ What are the major pitfalls to watch out for when evaluating experiments? (pp. 80–85)
▶ What are the pluses and minuses of asking people to describe themselves? (pp. 85–89)
▶ How can we be fooled by statistics? (pp. 96–98)

THINKING Scientifically

Correlation vs. Causation p. 77

Extraordinary Claims pp. 65, 83

Replicability p. 90

Ruling Out Rival Hypotheses pp. 65, 73

3

Biological Psychology
The Brain–Body Communication Superhighway

PREVIEW
Think

First, think about these questions. Then, as you read, think again. . . .

▶ How far does the longest neuron in the human body reach?

▶ Is the mind different from the brain, or is it just the brain in action?

▶ Do specific regions on the brain's surface correspond to different personality traits?

▶ Do we use only about 10 percent of our brain's capacity?

▶ Can we trace complex psychological functions, like religious belief, to specific brain regions?

▶ Are there left- and right-brained people?

▶ Are humans the largest brained animals?

▶ Is heritability a fixed value, or can it change over time?

▶ Is the adult brain of humans completely hardwired?

Correlation vs. Causation

neurons
nerve cells specialized for communication

central nervous system (CNS)
part of nervous system containing brain and spinal cord that enables mind and behavior

peripheral nervous system (PNS)
nerves in the body that extend outside the central nervous system (CNS)

forebrain
forward part of the brain that allows advanced intellectual abilities; also known as the cerebrum

cerebral cortex
outermost part of forebrain, responsible for analyzing sensory processing and higher brain functions

As you begin reading this chapter, close your eyes and place your hands over your ears. What lies between your hands is the most complicated structure in the known universe—the human brain (see **Figure 3.1**). Your brain has the consistency of gelatin, and it weighs a mere 3 pounds. Despite its humble appearance, the human brain is almost incomprehensibly complex. And it's capable of astonishing feats. As poet Robert Frost wrote, "The brain is a wonderful organ. It starts working the moment you get up in the morning and does not stop until you get into the office."

The workings of the brain depend on cross-talk among **neurons**—that is, nerve cells specialized for communication with each other. Our brains contain about 100 billion neurons. To give you a sense of how large this number is, there are more than fifteen times as many neurons in our brains as there are people on Earth. More graphically, 100 billion neurons lined up side to side would reach back and forth from New York to California five times. In addition, many neurons make tens of thousands of connections with other neurons. In total, there are about 160 trillion—that's a whopping 160,000,000,000,000—connections in the human brain (Tang, Nyengaard, De Groot, & Gunderson, 2001).

The huge number of neurons and connections tells only part of the story. Brain functions capture the imagination like few other topics in psychology. The mysterious relationship between brain and behavior has fascinated people throughout the ages. Is the mind—consisting of our thoughts, memories, and ability to reason—essentially the same as brain function (see Prologue)? This question dates back at least to the time of the ancient Greeks Hippocrates and Aristotle. Equally fascinating is the question of how our brains evolved. What evolutionary changes enabled us to be more intelligent than other animals? We'll address these questions in the coming pages.

Today we know so much about the brain and its functions because scientists have made numerous technological breakthroughs in studying brain function. We call researchers who study the brain and behavior *biological psychologists* or *neuroscientists*. As we discuss what these scientists have discovered about the brain, we'll compare our current state-of-the-art knowledge with misconceptions that have arisen along the way. If you harbor misconceptions about the brain and behavior, you're not alone. Even experts subscribe to certain myths about brain, behavior, and mind. Fortunately, reading popular science magazines and increased education are correlated with an increased rejection of misconceptions (Herculano-Houzel, 2002). Of course, this finding is only correlational and may not reflect a direct causal relationship. But it gives us hope that education about the brain can help us dispel misinformation about it.

The Brain and Behavior: Networked with the Somatic Nervous System

When we behave in a specific manner or ponder a certain thought, our nervous systems become active. Let's say we decide to walk to a vending machine to buy a can of soda. First, we make a conscious decision to do so—or so it would seem. Second, our nervous system, composed of the brain, spinal cord, and nerves, propels our body into action. Then we need to locate and operate the vending machine. We must be able to perceive it, that is, accurately identify it on the basis of how it looks and feels. Next, we need to put in the right amount of money, which requires us to remember how vending machines work and where we need to go to get correct change. Finally, we retrieve our soda and take a well-deserved drink. Without knowing it, we've just put into practice a large number of the psychological principles covered in this textbook. Whew!

The metaphor of the nervous system as a superhighway captures the two-way flow of traffic. Sensory information comes into—and decisions to act go away from—the **central nervous system (CNS),** composed of the brain and spinal cord. Scientists call all the nerves that extend outside of the CNS the **peripheral nervous system (PNS).** As shown in **Figure 3.2,** the peripheral nervous system is further divided into the somatic nervous system, which controls behavior, and the autonomic nervous system, which helps us experience and express emotion (see Chapter 11).

So what do contemporary psychologists know about the brain, and what insights does that knowledge provide? To start with, scientists divide the CNS into the forebrain, brain stem, and spinal cord (see **Table 3.1** on page 110). We'll begin our guided tour of the brain with the forebrain.

THE FOREBRAIN

The forward part of the brain, known as the *cerebrum* or **forebrain,** is the most highly developed area in the human brain. Our forebrains give us our advanced intellectual abilities.

The largest component of the forebrain is the **cerebral cortex,** which contains some 12 to 20 billion neurons. The cortex is the outermost part of the forebrain and is aptly named, because *cortex* means "bark." The cerebral cortex analyzes sensory information and is responsible for our higher brain functions, including our ability to think, talk, and reason.

Forebrain (including cerebral cortex) The site of most of the brain's conscious functions

Corpus callosum Bundle of nerve fibers connecting the cerebrum's two hemispheres

Hypothalamus Controls the body's endocrine, or hormone-producing, system

Thalamus Area that relays nerve signals to the cerebral cortex

Cerebellum Regulates balance and body control

Brain stem Regulates control of involuntary functions such as breathing and heart rate

Figure 3.1 The Human Brain: A Simple Map. (*Source:* Modified from Dorling Kindersley)

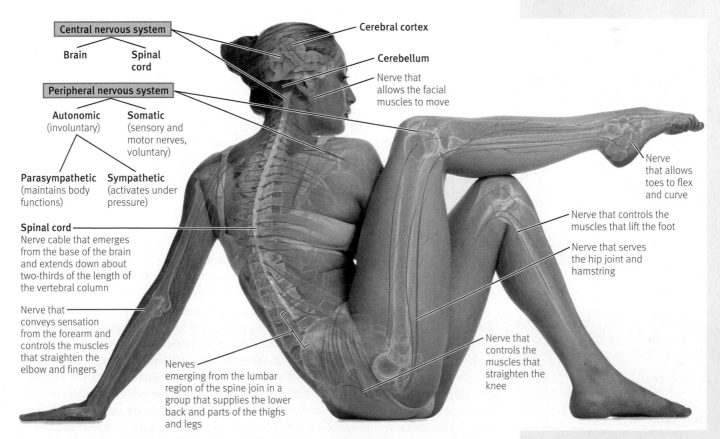

Central nervous system
Brain   Spinal cord

Cerebral cortex

Cerebellum

Nerve that allows the facial muscles to move

Peripheral nervous system

Autonomic (involuntary)   Somatic (sensory and motor nerves, voluntary)

Parasympathetic (maintains body functions)   Sympathetic (activates under pressure)

Nerve that allows toes to flex and curve

Nerve that controls the muscles that lift the foot

Nerve that serves the hip joint and hamstring

Spinal cord—Nerve cable that emerges from the base of the brain and extends down about two-thirds of the length of the vertebral column

Nerve that conveys sensation from the forearm and controls the muscles that straighten the elbow and fingers

Nerves emerging from the lumbar region of the spine join in a group that supplies the lower back and parts of the thighs and legs

Nerve that controls the muscles that straighten the knee

Figure 3.2 The Nervous System Exerts Control over the Body. (*Source:* Modified from Dorling Kindersley)

Table 3.1 Overview of the Central Nervous System (CNS).

Regions of the CNS		Areas with Action and Arousal Functions	Areas with Sensory and Perceptual Functions
Forebrain		*Basal ganglia*—generate motor programs	*Neocortex*—processes sensory information about external stimuli and helps control perception
		Basal forebrain—regulates cortical arousal	*Limbic system (cingulate cortex, hippocampus, and amygdala)*—processes internal sensations and helps produce emotion
		Hypothalamus—controls the autonomic nervous system and endocrine system	*Thalamus*—relays sensory information to the cerebral cortex
Brain Stem	**Midbrain**	*Substantia nigra*—activates the basal ganglia to respond to rewards	*Superior colliculus*—processes information about sight in the context of head and neck reflexes
		Reticular activating system (RAS)—regulates cortical arousal	*Inferior colliculus*—processes information about sound in the context of head and neck reflexes
	Hindbrain	*RAS*—regulates cortical arousal	*Cerebellum (cerebellar cortex)*—controls sense of balance
		Pons—regulates the cerebellum	
		Medulla—regulates breathing and heartbeat	
Spinal Cord		*Motor neurons*—command muscle contraction	*Sensory neurons*—bring sensory information into the CNS

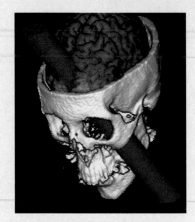

A computer-generated image showing the tamping iron that pierced through the skull and frontal lobes of Phineas Gage.

cerebral hemispheres
two halves of the cerebral cortex, which serve different yet highly integrated cognition functions

corpus callosum
large band of fibers connecting the two cerebral hemispheres

frontal lobe
forward part of cerebral cortex containing the motor cortex and the prefrontal cortex; responsible for motor function, language, and memory

motor cortex
part of frontal lobe responsible for body movement

prefrontal cortex
part of frontal lobe responsible for thinking, planning, and language

Broca's area
language area in the prefrontal cortex that helps to control speech production

The Neocortex: It's What's New in the Cerebral Cortex. In terms of evolutionary development of brain regions, the *neocortex* is a relatively recent addition. That's what we mean by a "new" (the prefix *neo-* means "new") brain area. Our neocortex accounts for the vast majority of our cerebral cortex. It's present in all mammals, yet absent in birds and reptiles. Compared with other mammals, evolution has enabled the human neocortex to attain a larger size in proportion to our bodies. We have more cortical areas and more connections than do other species.

The cerebral cortex is divided into two **cerebral hemispheres** (see **Figure 3.3**). The two cerebral hemispheres look alike, but they serve different yet highly integrated cognitive functions. The large ("colossal") band of fibers connecting the two cerebral hemispheres is called the **corpus callosum** (see **Figure 3.3**). The neocortex contains four lobes, each associated with somewhat different functions (see **Figure 3.4** on page 112).

Frontal Lobe. The **frontal lobe** lies in the forward part of the cerebral cortex, containing the motor cortex and prefrontal cortex. If you touch your forehead right now, your fingers are less than an inch away from your frontal lobe. The frontal lobe is responsible for motor function, language, and memory, as well as overseeing most other mental functions, a process called *executive function*. Just as the U.S. president exerts control over the members of his Cabinet, the brain's executive function provides a kind of top-level governance over simpler cognitive functions.

In most brains a deep groove, called the *central sulcus*, separates the frontal lobe from the rest of the neocortex. The **motor cortex** lies next to the central sulcus. We know a great deal about motor cortex function because of the research of neurosurgeon Wilder Penfield. Penfield (1958) applied mild electrical shocks to the motor cortex of patients who were awake during surgery for epilepsy. He elicited movements ranging from small muscle twitches to large and complex bodily movements. Penfield found that each part of the motor cortex controlled a specific part of the body (see **Figure 3.5** on page 112).

In front of the motor cortex lies a large expanse of the frontal lobe called the **prefrontal cortex,** the part of the frontal lobe responsible for thinking, planning, and language (see **Figure 3.6** on page 113). One region of the prefrontal cortex, **Broca's area,** was named after French surgeon Paul Broca after he discovered that this brain site plays a key role in language production (Broca, 1861). People with damage to Broca's area exhibit a serious speech deficit called **aphasia.** Aphasia, particularly *Broca's aphasia*, is characterized by difficulties in speaking smoothly and an inability to come up with certain words. Broca's first patient was nicknamed "Tan" because of his inability to articulate words other than "tan." Broca soon discovered that this site was damaged in many of his aphasic patients. It didn't take long for Broca and others to notice that brain damage resulting in aphasia was almost always located in the left cerebral hemisphere. Many researchers have since replicated this finding.

The prefrontal cortex serves additional functions, including memory, abstract thinking, and decision making. Part of the reason the prefrontal area assumes an executive role is that it receives information from many other regions of the cerebral cortex (Fuster, 2000). The prefrontal cortex also contributes to mood, personality, and self-awareness (Chayer & Freedman, 2001). The tragic story of Phineas Gage demonstrates how the prefrontal cortex can be crucial to personality.

Phineas Gage was a railroad foreman who experienced a horrific accident in 1848. His job at the time was to build railroad tracks running through rural Vermont. Gage was doing his usual job of filling holes with gunpowder to break up stubborn rock formations. He was pressing gunpowder into one hole with a tamping iron when suddenly an explosion propelled the iron with great thrust through his head. The iron pierced Gage's face under his cheekbone and destroyed much of his prefrontal cortex. Remarkably, Gage survived the accident, but he was never the same. His physician, J. M. Harlow (1848), describes Gage's personality after the accident as

> fitful, irreverent, indulging at times in the grossest profanity (which was not previously his custom) . . . his mind was radically changed, so decidedly that his friends and acquaintances said he was "no longer Gage."

Admittedly, we don't know exactly what Gage was like before the accident, and some scholars have contended that his personality didn't change as much as is often claimed (Macmillan, 2000). We do know more about the exact location of Gage's brain damage, however. Hanna Damasio and colleagues (1994) examined the skull of Phineas Gage with modern brain imaging techniques and confirmed that both the right and left sides of his prefrontal cortex were seriously damaged (see photo on page 110).

Parietal Lobe. The **parietal lobe** is the upper middle part of the cerebral cortex lying behind the frontal lobe (see Figure 3.4). The part of the parietal lobe that lies next to the motor cortex is the *somatosensory cortex,* devoted to touch. It's sensitive to pressure, temperature, and pain. The parietal lobe plays roles in many kinds of perception. Spatial perception, which is the detection of objects in space, is most frequently associated with the upper part of the parietal lobe (Nachev & Husain, 2006; Shomstein & Yantis, 2006). Other parietal lobe functions include the perception of object shape and orientation, the perception of others' actions, and the representation of numbers (Gobel & Rushworth, 2004). The parietal lobe integrates visual and touch inputs with motor outputs every time we reach, grasp, and move our eyes (Culham & Valyear, 2006). Let's examine a visuospatial task to better understand typical parietal lobe function.

As you're rushing to get out the door, you ask your roommate to put a blank CD in your jacket pocket because you're going to copy an assignment for him at school today. You grab your jacket, go to school, and forget about it until you're in the library sitting at the computer terminal and then you reach into your pocket. What do you expect to feel? A hard disk or disk case, or a soft sleeve? You're probably not sure how, or even if, your roommate packaged the blank CD, but you can envision how the possibilities look. So you can translate that information into how it should feel. That's a parietal lobe function.

Damage to different regions of the parietal lobe can cause a host of curious deficits. An injury to certain parts of the left parietal lobe can cause *acalculia:* difficulty with mathematics. (Sorry, that low quiz score in calculus probably isn't due to acalculia unless you've suffered a serious head injury.) Damage to the right parietal lobe can result in *contralateral neglect,* producing a complete lack of attention to the left half of the body. Patients with contralateral neglect may wash or shave only half their faces. When asked about their odd behavior, they're at a loss to understand what they did wrong.

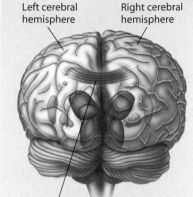

Left cerebral hemisphere

Right cerebral hemisphere

Corpus callosum

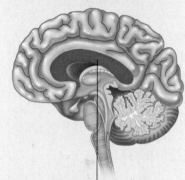

Corpus callosum

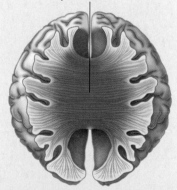

Figure 3.3 The Cerebral Hemispheres and the Corpus Callosum. The corpus callosum connects the two cerebral hemispheres.

aphasia
serious speech deficit that renders a person unable to communicate effectively

parietal lobe
upper middle part of the cerebral cortex lying behind the frontal lobe specialized for touch and perception

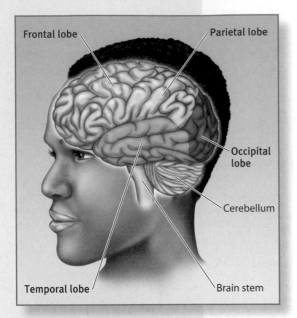

Figure 3.4 The Four Lobes of the Cerebral Cortex. The cerebral cortex consists of four interacting lobes: frontal, parietal, temporal, and occipital.

Ruling Out Rival Hypotheses

Oliver Sacks, a famous neurologist, described this and other fascinating cases in his book *The Man Who Mistook His Wife for a Hat* (1985). Sacks discussed a patient with parietal lobe damage who refused to acknowledge that one of his legs was his own. The patient insisted that someone else's leg was in his bed! As bizarre as this example sounds, a patient's inability to recognize a neurological or psychiatric impairment—called *anosagnosia*—is relatively common.

Temporal Lobe. The **temporal lobe** is the site of hearing, understanding language, and storing autobiographical memories (see Figure 3.4). This lobe is separated from the rest of the neocortex by the *lateral fissure.*

The top of the temporal lobe contains the *auditory cortex,* the part of the neocortex devoted to hearing (see Chapter 4). The language area in the temporal lobe is called **Wernicke's area,** although this area also includes the lower parietal lobe (see Figure 3.6). Damage to Wernicke's area results in difficulties with understanding speech. It leads to a unique kind of aphasia characterized by disorganized speech sometimes called "word salad" because words are haphazardly "tossed" together (see Chapter 15). If we were to listen to an individual with Wernicke's aphasia speaking behind a closed door, the normal pace of speech would give us the impression that the speech was understandable. Nevertheless, Wernicke's aphasics speak mostly nonsense; they make up words, and most problematic, they're unaware of their speech deficits.

The lower part of the temporal lobe contains circuitry critical to storing memories of autobiographical events (see Chapter 7). Penfield (1958) discovered that stimulating this region with electrical probes elicited memories, like vivid recollections of "a certain song" or "the view from a childhood window." Amazing as these descriptions seem, psychologists today aren't certain if stimulating the brain elicits genuine memories of past events or rather altered perceptions, making them closer to hallucinations (Schacter, 1996; see Chapter 7).

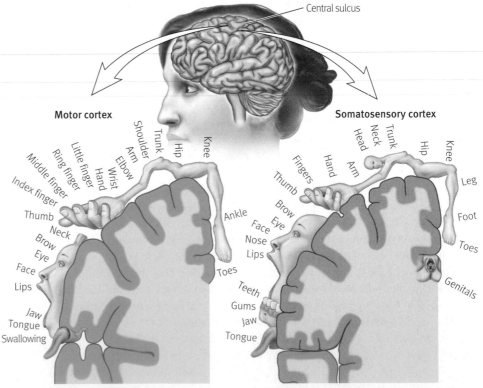

temporal lobe
lower part of cerebral cortex below the temples, which plays roles in hearing, understanding language, and memory

Wernicke's area
part of the temporal lobe involved in understanding speech

Figure 3.5 Representation of the Body Mapped onto the Motor and Sensory Areas of the Cerebral Cortex. The brain networks with the body in a systematic way, with specific regions of both the motor and somatosensory cortex mapping onto specific regions of the body. (*Source:* Adapted from Marieb, 2007)

Occipital Lobe. At the very back of the brain lies the **occipital lobe,** containing the *visual cortex,* dedicated to vision. We human beings are highly dependent on our visual systems, so it stands to reason that we have a lot of visual cortex. Not all animals rely as much on vision as we do, but we're not the only highly visual creatures. For each species, the amount of sensory cortex of each type is proportional to the degree to which it relies on that sense. Ghost bats depend highly on auditory cues and have proportionally more auditory cortex; the platypus relies heavily on touch cues and has proportionally more touch cortex; and squirrels, like humans, rely strongly on visual inputs and have proportionally more visual cortex (Krubitzer & Kaas, 2005).

Cortical Hierarchies. There are different levels of cortical processing. Information from the outside world transmitted by a particular sense (sight, hearing, touch) reaches the **sensory cortex,** which is specific to a particular sense: primary visual cortex is specific to vision, primary auditory cortex to hearing, and primary sensory cortex to touch and body position (see Figure 3.6). Next, sensory information travels to cortical regions that integrate (pull together) simpler functions to perform more complex functions; these areas are called **association cortexes,** and they play key roles in perception, memory, attention, and conscious awareness. The overall organization of the neocortex is functionally "hierarchical" because processing becomes increasingly complex at successively higher levels.

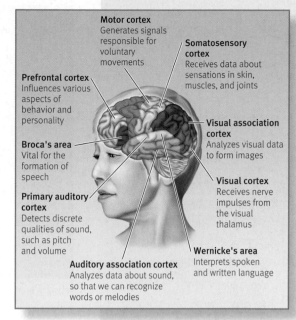

Motor cortex
Generates signals responsible for voluntary movements

Somatosensory cortex
Receives data about sensations in skin, muscles, and joints

Prefrontal cortex
Influences various aspects of behavior and personality

Visual association cortex
Analyzes visual data to form images

Broca's area
Vital for the formation of speech

Visual cortex
Receives nerve impulses from the visual thalamus

Primary auditory cortex
Detects discrete qualities of sound, such as pitch and volume

Wernicke's area
Interprets spoken and written language

Auditory association cortex
Analyzes data about sound, so that we can recognize words or melodies

Figure 3.6 Selected Areas of the Cerebral Cortex. The prefrontal cortex controls various aspects of behavior and personality. Broca's area is vital for the formation of speech, and Wernicke's area interprets spoken and written language. Other cortical areas include the motor cortex, primary sensory areas, and association areas.

> **APPLY YOUR THINKING**
>
> What area of the cerebral cortex would you expect to be most highly correlated with increased intelligence? Why?

The Basal Ganglia. The **basal ganglia** are two sets of structures buried in the forebrain that help to control movement (see **Figure 3.7**). The basal ganglia work with the cerebral cortex. After processing sensory information, the cerebral cortex informs the basal ganglia, which in turn calculate a course of action and transmit that plan to the motor cortex.

The basal ganglia are also responsible for making sure our movements help us obtain rewards, that is, pleasurable activities (Graybiel et al., 1994). When we anticipate rewards, such as a tasty sandwich or hot date, we depend on activity in our basal ganglia. There's even evidence that our basal ganglia increase their level of activity when we work for rewards, but not when we receive rewards for doing nothing (Zink et al., 2004).

Damage to the basal ganglia plays a key role in *Parkinson's disease,* a disorder of movement. In Parkinson's disease, cells degenerate in an area of the midbrain that pumps a special chemical into the basal ganglia. This midbrain area is called the *substantia nigra* and the special chemical is a neurotransmitter called **dopamine.** *Neurotransmitters* are chemical messengers that neurons use to converse with each other. Cells in the substantia nigra release dopamine into the basal ganglia whenever we feel motivated to do something. When these cells degenerate in Parkinson's disease, the link between initiating movement and the reward that follows is broken.

Actor Michael J. Fox and boxer Muhammad Ali are celebrities with Parkinson's disease. Both men have done a great deal to educate the public about the disease and the need for research funds. As Michael J. Fox wrote in his autobiography *Lucky Man: A Memoir:*

> That morning—November 13, 1990—my brain was serving notice; it had initiated a divorce from my mind . . . my brain was demanding, and incrementally seizing, custody of my body, beginning with the baby: the outermost finger of my left hand. (2002, p. 4)

Michael J. Fox refers to his mind as responsible for what he'd like to do, and to his brain as the mechanistic controller of movement. What Fox appears to be experiencing is

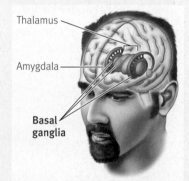

Thalamus

Amygdala

Basal ganglia

Figure 3.7 The Basal Ganglia Play Critical Roles in Voluntary Movement.

occipital lobe
back part of cerebral cortex specialized for vision

sensory cortex
regions of the cerebral cortex devoted to vision, touch, hearing, balance, taste, and smell

association cortex
regions of the cerebral cortex that integrate simpler functions to perform more complex functions

basal ganglia
structures in the forebrain that help to control movement

dopamine
neurotransmitter that plays a key role in movement and reward

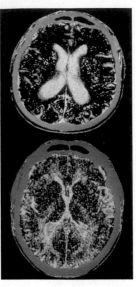

Boxer Muhammad Ali (*left*) and actor Michael J. Fox (*right*) both live with Parkinson's disease. Ali and his wife, Lonnie, founded the Muhammad Ali Parkinson Center and created *Ali Care,* a special fund for people with Parkinson's disease. The photo on the right shows the loss of dopamine neurons, which naturally contain a dark pigment, in a brain affected by Parkinson's disease (*bottom*) compared with a normal brain (*top*).

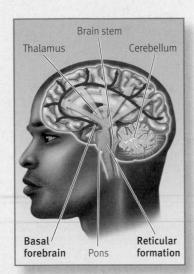

Figure 3.8 The Basal Forebrain and Reticular Formation. The reticular formation (shown in yellow) works with the basal forebrain (shown in red) to regulate cortical arousal.

Correlation vs. Causation

basal forebrain
region in forebrain containing acetylcholine neurons that affect activity of the cortex

acetylcholine
neurotransmitter used to control activity, including movement, memory, attention, and dreaming

thalamus
part of the brain that processes sensory information and serves as a gateway to the cerebral cortex

brain stem
part of the brain between the spinal cord and cerebral cortex that contains the medulla, midbrain, and pons

midbrain
part of the brain stem that lies between the forebrain and hindbrain. It helps to control head and neck reflexes and modulate motor activity

the increasing lack of cooperation among different parts of his brain—those affiliated with mind function and those affiliated with motor commands.

The Basal Forebrain. Whereas the basal ganglia interact with the cortex during movement, the **basal forebrain**—the lower part of the forebrain—interacts with the cortex when it comes to mental activities. The basal forebrain selectively activates different parts of the cortex, allowing us to attend to some things and ignore others (see **Figure 3.8**). Certain cells in the basal forebrain manufacture the neurotransmitter **acetylcholine,** which they then disperse throughout the cerebral cortex to stimulate movement, memory, selective attention, and even dreaming (Sarter & Bruno, 2000; Woolf, 1991). We can think of the basal forebrain as having a spotlight that it can shine onto any part of the cortex it selects.

Acetylcholine-containing neurons in the basal forebrain degenerate in patients with *Alzheimer's disease* (Wenk, 2006). The main symptom of Alzheimer's disease is *dementia,* which is a combination of severe memory loss and intellectual decline (see Chapter 7). Scientists have shown that acetylcholine loss correlates with intellectual decline in Alzheimer's disease, but correlation isn't conclusive evidence of causation, because other kinds of brain damage could be responsible for the symptoms of Alzheimer's disease.

The Thalamus. The term **thalamus** derives from the Greek word for bedroom or chamber. But the thalamus is actually more than one room. It contains many areas, each of which connects to a specific region of the cerebral cortex (see also Chapter 4). We might think of the thalamus as the gateway to the cerebral cortex. The vast majority of sensory information passes through its doors (refer to Figure 3.7).

THE BRAIN STEM

Now that we've learned enough to navigate around the forebrain, we're ready to visit the **brain stem**, which connects with the forebrain and contains the medulla, midbrain, and pons. The best way to appreciate the position of the brain stem is to view it in relation to the rest of the brain (see **Figure 3.9**).

The Midbrain. The **midbrain** lies between the forebrain and hindbrain. The midbrain contains the substantia nigra, superior colliculus, and inferior colliculus (see Table 3.1). We've already discussed the role that the substantia nigra plays in movement. The superior colliculus controls the tracking of visual stimuli and the inferior colliculus controls reflexes triggered by sound.

THE BRAIN AND BEHAVIOR: NETWORKED WITH THE SOMATIC NERVOUS SYSTEM

The Reticular Activating System. The **reticular activating system (RAS)** connects to the basal forebrain and cerebral cortex (refer back to Figure 3.8); the entire system plays a key role in arousal. Turn off a dog's RAS, for example, and it instantly falls asleep. Damage to the RAS can result in a coma. Some scientists even believe that many knockdowns in boxing result from a temporary compression of the RAS following a powerful punch (Weisberg, Garcia, & Strub, 1996).

The pathways emanating from the RAS activate the cortex by increasing the *signal-to-noise ratio* (Gu, 2002). When working well, a cell phone produces sound with a high signal-to-noise ratio so that the person on each end of the conversation can understand the other's message. When there's a great deal of static in the background (a low signal-to-noise ratio), people's messages can be unintelligible even when they shout (see Chapter 4).

A possible example of this problem occurs in attention-deficit/hyperactivity disorder (ADHD), a disorder originating in childhood (see Chapter 15). ADHD is marked by inattention, overactivity, and impulsivity. Stimulant drugs used to treat ADHD, such as methylphenidate (often marketed under the brand name Ritalin), appear to increase the signal-to-noise ratio in the prefrontal cortex (Devilbiss & Berridge, 2006). One hypothesis is that these drugs mimic activity in the RAS and neighboring brain regions, but other explanations are possible. For example, methylphenidate increases levels of the neurotransmitter dopamine, which may be responsible for increases in attention and decreases in impulsivity (Volkow, Wang, Fowler, & Ding, 2005).

The Hindbrain. The **hindbrain** lies below the midbrain; it consists of the **cerebellum, pons,** and **medulla** (the last two being part of the brain stem). *Cerebellum* is the Latin word for "little brain," and in many respects the cerebellum is a miniature version of the cerebral cortex (see **Figure 3.10**). The pons connects the cerebral cortex with the cerebellum. The cerebellum plays a predominant role in our sense of balance and enables us to coordinate movement and learn motor skills. Among other things, it helps us catch ourselves from falling down. Additionally, the cerebellum contributes to executive, visuospatial, and linguistic abilities (Schmahmann, 2004).

Structures in the medulla regulate breathing, heartbeat, and other vital functions. Damage to the medulla can cause *brain death,* which is defined as irreversible coma. We can't revive a person in this condition. People who are brain dead are totally unaware of their surroundings and unresponsive, even to ordinarily very painful stimuli. They show no signs of spontaneous movement, respiration, or reflex activity.

People often confuse a *persistent vegetative state,* or cortical death, with brain death, but the two aren't the same. Terri Schiavo made history as the woman who had lain unconscious in a hospital bed for 15 years. Schiavo collapsed in her Florida home in 1990 following temporary cardiac arrest. Her heart stopped long enough to deprive her brain of vital oxygen, such that when her heart was restarted, the brain damage she suffered left her in a persistent vegetative state. The deep structures in her brain stem that control breathing, heart rate, digestion, and certain reflexive responses were still operating, so Schiavo wasn't brain dead, as much of the news media incorrectly reported. Nevertheless, her higher cerebral structures, necessary for awareness of herself and her environment, were damaged permanently. Her doctors knew that much of her cerebrum had withered away, and an autopsy later showed that she'd lost about half of her brain.

Those who believe that death of the higher brain centers essential for consciousness and behavior is equivalent to actual death felt that Terri had, in fact, died 15 years earlier. Nevertheless, Schiavo's death raises difficult and troubling questions that science can't fully resolve: Should brain death be the true criterion for death, or should this criterion instead be the permanent loss of consciousness?

The Cerebral Ventricles. The **cerebral ventricles** are the waterways of the CNS (**Figure 3.11** on page 116), and extend throughout the entire brain and spinal cord. A clear liquid,

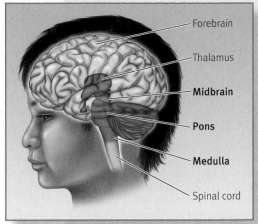

Figure 3.9 The Brain Stem. The brain stem is located at the top of the spinal cord, below the forebrain.

Forebrain
Thalamus
Midbrain
Pons
Medulla
Spinal cord

Ruling Out Rival Hypotheses

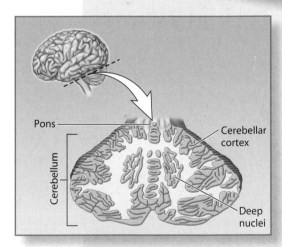

Pons
Cerebellum
Cerebellar cortex
Deep nuclei

Figure 3.10 The Cerebellum and Pons in the Hindbrain. The cerebellum and pons are major components of the hindbrain (see Figure 3.9 for medulla).

reticular activating system (RAS)
group of neurons in the brain stem that plays a key role in arousal

hindbrain
part of the brain between the spinal cord and midbrain, consisting of the pons, cerebellum, and medulla

cerebellum
small cerebrum in hindbrain, responsible for our sense of balance

pons
part of hindbrain that connects the cerebral cortex with cerebellum

medulla
part of brain stem involved in vital functions, such as heartbeat and breathing

cerebral ventricles
internal waterways of the CNS that carry cerebrospinal fluid (CSF), which provides the brain with nutrients and cushioning against injury

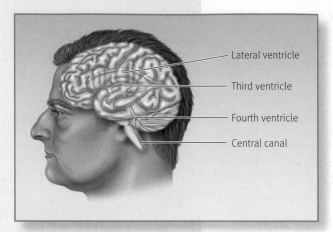

Figure 3.11 The Cerebral Ventricles.
Cerebrospinal fluid (CSF) flows through the cerebral ventricles, providing nutrients and cushioning against injury. (*Source:* Adapted from Marieb, 2007)

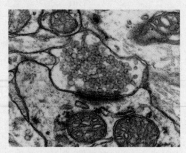

Electron microscopic image of a synapse (shown here in red).

Falsifiability

interneurons
neurons that send messages to other neurons nearby and stimulate neurons

reflex
an automatic motor response to a sensory stimulus like muscle stretch

synapse
space between two connecting neurons through which messages are transmitted

somatic nervous system
part of the peripheral nervous system carrying messages from the CNS through the body to control movement

called *cerebrospinal fluid (CSF)*, runs through the cerebral ventricles and bathes the brain and spinal cord, providing nutrients and cushioning against injury.

THE SPINAL CORD

The spinal cord has a simple organization, yet it contains all the nervous tissue needed for *spinal reflexes. Nerves,* the long extensions arising from neurons, travel in two directions. Sensory information arrives by way of *sensory nerves* and motor commands exit the spinal cord by way of *motor nerves.* Sensory nerves bring information to the spinal cord about the sense of touch and about the stretch and force of muscle fibers. Sensory nerves originate from *sensory neurons,* which lie next to the spinal cord. Within the spinal cord, sensory neurons contact **interneurons,** neurons that send messages to other neurons located nearby. Interneurons then stimulate *motor neurons.* Motor neurons in turn send messages through motor nerves, which cause muscles to contract. We'll discuss nerves and neurons in more detail later in the chapter.

Consider the stretch **reflex,** which relies only on the spinal cord. We're carrying our books in our arms but over time our grasp releases ever so slightly without our even noticing. Our sensory nerves detect the muscle stretch and relay this information to the spinal cord. Interneurons intervene and the motor neurons send messages causing our arm muscles to contract. Without our ever knowing it, a simple reflex causes our arm muscles to tighten, preventing us from dropping our books (see **Figure 3.12**).

Sir Charles Sherrington studied spinal reflexes in the late 1800s. He measured the time it took for muscles to become active following nerve stimulation. From these data, he deduced the existence of microscopic physical spaces between neurons and between neurons and muscle cells (Pearce, 2004). At this time no microscopes were powerful enough to observe these spaces. Consequently, some scientists believed that all neurons melded together into one giant complex, a *reticulum,* much like a fisherman's net. But Sherrington (1906), among others, argued strongly for neurons being separate, individual cells that nonetheless communicated with each other and with muscle cells. What Sherrington hypothesized could have been falsified had he been wrong. Yet Sherrington had the right idea. Later studies with the *electron microscope* confirmed that his hypothesized tiny gaps responsible for transmitting messages between neurons, which we now call **synapses,** indeed exist.

THE SOMATIC NERVOUS SYSTEM

Now that we've completed our tour of the CNS areas involved with sensing and behaving, let's see how the CNS is hooked up to the body through the somatic nervous system. The **somatic nervous system** carries messages from the CNS to muscles throughout the body, controlling movement (see Figure 3.12). Muscle contraction is our only choice—we can't lengthen muscles directly. But we can cause a muscle to lengthen by contracting the opposing muscle. Muscles come in pairs that mobilize a body part around a joint. When we bend our arm at the elbow, we contract the muscles responsible for flexing the arm, while we relax the muscles responsible for extending the arm. When we straighten our arm, we do the opposite (see **Figure 3.13**). Whenever we stabilize or move our many joints, the CNS works with the somatic nervous system to regulate posture and bodily movement.

Let's review what happens when we decide to walk over to the vending machine to purchase a can of soda. Sensory inputs of all types reach the neocortex. Then all parts of the neocortex send information to the basal ganglia. The basal ganglia contribute to our decision about what to do and send that information to the motor cortex. Next the motor cortex sends commands to the spinal cord, activating certain motor neurons. These motor neurons send messages through nerves that reach muscles throughout the body and trigger muscle contractions. We walk, reach, touch, and grasp. Our brain triggers all these movements, but our somatic nervous system executes them. And after we finish our drink, our somatic nervous system keeps on working, enabling us to walk away—hopefully to the nearest recycling container.

ASSESS YOUR KNOWLEDGE: FACT OR FICTION?

(1) The neocortex is divided into the frontal, parietal, temporal, and hippocampal lobes. (True/False)
(2) The basal ganglia control sensation. (True/False)
(3) Drugs that treat ADHD may work by decreasing the signal-to-noise ratio in the prefrontal cortex. (True/False)
(4) The cerebellum regulates only our sense of balance. (True/False)
(5) Muscles come in opposing pairs. (True/False)

Answers: (1) F (p. 110); (2) F (p. 113); (3) F (p. 115); (4) F (p. 115); (5) T (p. 116)

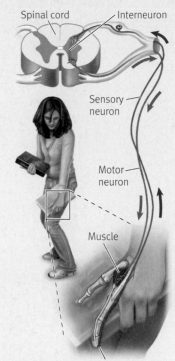

Figure 3.12 The Spinal Reflex. We detect even small amounts of muscle stretch and compensate by contraction. In this way we can maintain balance or keep from losing our grip.

NEW FRONTIERS

Jesse's Story: The Million Dollar Man

What would it be like if your mind could no longer control your body? How much would you want that ability restored if you lost it? High-power lineman Jesse Sullivan knows the answers to these questions. One day in May 2001, he received an electric shock so powerful that his arms were burned beyond repair (Oppenheim, 2006). His arms needed to be amputated and were replaced with prosthetic, or artificial, limbs.

What happened next is extraordinary. Jesse was chosen to trade one of his ordinary prosthetic arms for the first "thought-controlled" bionic arm, a limb that was literally hardwired to his nervous system. In so doing, he became a unique example of how intricately brain, body, and behavior interact.

To make Jesse's million-dollar arm function, surgeons grafted nerves, which had once controlled his natural arm, from his shoulder to his chest muscle. They then placed sensors over his chest muscle and connected them to tiny wires that control the bionic limb. Jesse controls the arm by simply *thinking* about what he wants to do with it. When Jesse thinks about closing his hand, neurons in his basal ganglia and cerebral cortex release chemicals signaling his intention to use his bionic arm. Next, neurons in the motor cortex carry this message to the spinal cord and motor neurons then carry the message to the muscles in his chest. From there, the tiny wires control Jesse's bionic arm, enabling him to grasp nearly anything from a paintbrush to a garden tool.

Jesse Sullivan paints his house with his bionic arm.

With practice, Jesse has become so adept at using his new arm and hand that he can paint his house, take care of his lawn, and do nearly any chore that the rest of us might do.

Jesse's arm is the culmination of more than 20 years of research funded by the U.S.

(continued)

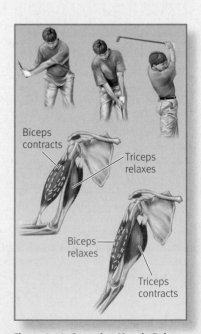

Figure 3.13 Opposing Muscle Pairs. We use opposing muscle pairs in everyday movements.

Biceps contracts
Triceps relaxes
Biceps relaxes
Triceps contracts

Defense Advanced Research Projects Agency (DARPA), whose mission it is to develop new technology. Because of the huge expense and experimental nature of the endeavor, Jesse received only one high-tech limb. But even with just one bionic arm, Jesse can put on his socks, shave, hug his grandchildren, and enjoy the everyday experiences that help to make life fulfilling.

Jesse's story is an excellent real-life example that enables us to distinguish real science from pseudoscience. Early research on "mind-controlled limbs" could have been mistaken as pseudoscience because the concept stretches the imagination and sounds like science fiction. The researchers who pioneered the bionic limb had to believe they were working on real science, and they were right. We know the bionic arm is an example of real science and not pseudoscience for one major reason: Jesse can demonstrate how his bionic arm works and the researchers who developed it can explain why. Moreover, the bionic arm demonstrates the basic principle that the mind controls behavior, whether through nerves or wires. So when it comes to assessing the success of the bionic arm the verdict is: superhuman, no—utterly amazing, yes.

The Brain and Emotion: Networked with the Autonomic Nervous System

You can't put your finger on what you're feeling, let alone why, but your heart is pounding, you're taking short, shallow breaths, and your stomach is tense. You're emotionally aroused. It could be due to many things—an intolerable insult, the most gorgeous creature you've ever set eyes on, your best experience, or your worst. This is the curious nature of emotion. Just as there are specialized parts of the brain devoted to sensing and behaving, there are specialized parts of the brain, specialized nerves, and even specialized blood-borne chemicals devoted to emotion (see also Chapter 11).

The parts of the brain dedicated to emotion are housed within the **limbic system.** This specialized set of brain regions is highly interconnected. Brain circuits dealing with emotion network with a specific part of the peripheral nervous system—the autonomic nervous system. Under the control of the limbic system, the autonomic nervous system communicates with the body's internal organs. In contrast to neocortical systems, which process information about external stimuli, the limbic system processes information about our internal states, such as blood pressure. The limbic system, along with the autonomic nervous system, also controls heart rate, respiration rate, perspiration, and the *endocrine system*, which secretes blood-borne chemical messengers.

THE LIMBIC SYSTEM

We can think of the limbic system as the *emotional center* of the brain (see **Figure 3.14**). Limbic system structures also play roles in smell, motivation, and memory. The limbic system evolved out of the primitive olfactory system (dedicated to smell), and it controlled various survival behaviors in early mammals. As anyone who's walked a dog knows, smell remains vitally important to many animals, and it continues to play key roles in feeding, establishing territories, and mating. Limbic structures aren't as well developed as neocortical systems. As a result, we sometimes find it difficult to put our feelings into words.

We'll next explore the individual areas of the limbic system. Each area has specific roles, although different areas cooperate in many shared functions.

limbic system
emotional center of brain that also plays roles in smell, motivation, and memory

The Hypothalamus. The **hypothalamus** regulates and maintains constant internal bodily states by overseeing the endocrine and autonomic nervous systems. It's located on the floor of the brain above the optic nerves, centered where the optic nerves cross from one side to the other (forming the *optic chiasm*). Separate areas of the hypothalamus play different roles in emotion and motivation. Some parts of the hypothalamus play a role in hunger, others in sexual motivation (see Chapter 11). Even though specific areas of the hypothalamus are linked to certain emotions and motivations, we should avoid thinking of them as existing for that purpose alone. Most areas of the hypothalamus engage in multitasking.

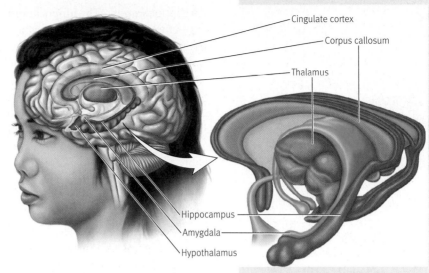

Cingulate cortex
Corpus callosum
Thalamus
Hippocampus
Amygdala
Hypothalamus

Figure 3.14 The Limbic System. The limbic system consists mainly of the hypothalamus, amygdala, cingulate cortex, and hippocampus. (Left brain modified from Dorling Kindersley & right art from Kalat, 2007)

The Amygdala. The **amygdala** is named for its almond shape (*amygdala* is Greek for "almond"). Excitement, arousal, and fear are all part of the amygdala's job description. For example, the amygdala kicks into high gear when teenagers play violent video games (Mathews et al., 2006). The amygdala also plays a role in fear conditioning, a process by which animals learn that something scary is about to happen (LeDoux, 2000). Fear conditioning is easy to demonstrate in rats or mice. Researchers place the animals in a novel training chamber and after a 2- to 3-minute period—just long enough to let them get acquainted with the chamber—they deliver a brief shock via an electrified floor grid. This shock frightens the animal, in much the same way we'd be frightened if the floor we were standing on delivered us a swift shock. In many studies, researchers deliver a signal, such as a tone or light, before the shock. This signal clues the animal in on what's about to happen and enables it to prepare. Researchers can measure these preparatory behaviors to determine if the animal has learned to predict the shock. What behavior do you think rats and mice display following fear conditioning? If you guessed "freeze in place," give yourself a point. The purpose of this behavior may seem perplexing in the laboratory, but in the wild it enables small animals to go undetected by large predators whose visual systems, like ours, are exquisitely sensitive to movement.

The human amygdala also plays a role in fear. Ralph Adolphs and his colleagues studied a 30-year-old woman whose left and right amygdalae were both almost entirely destroyed by disease. Although she had no difficulty identifying faces, she was markedly impaired in detecting fear in these faces (Adolphs, Tranel, Damasio, & Damasio, 1994).

The amygdala receives information from neocortical centers that process cognitive and social information. It deciphers social signals and uses this information to learn that certain emotional states correspond to certain threats or rewards (Hooker et al., 2006). Our amygdala might help us to learn that when our boss is in a good mood, she's more likely to say yes to a raise than when she's in a bad mood.

Snakes evoke fear in many animals, including squirrels, by activating the amygdala.

The Cingulate Cortex. The *cingulate cortex* lies buried between the two cerebral hemispheres. Indeed, this region of the limbic system is visible only when we split these hemispheres down the middle. Broca coined the term "limbic" from limbus (meaning "border") based mainly on the appearance of the cingulate cortex bordering the corpus callosum in each hemisphere.

The cingulate cortex becomes active when we express our emotions, and like the hypothalamus, it regulates the autonomic nervous system (Luu & Posner, 2003). Like the amygdala, the cingulate cortex contributes to social behavior and is necessary for learning how to act in complex social situations, such as how to introduce our friends to each other. One research team showed that monkeys with damage to the cingulate cortex behaved like patients with *acquired sociopathy*—a lack of empathy or concern for others resulting from brain damage (Rudebeck, Buckley, Walton, & Rushworth, 2006).

hypothalamus
part of the brain responsible for maintaining a constant internal state

amygdala
part of limbic system that plays key roles in fear, excitement, and arousal

The Hippocampus. The **hippocampus** is a portion of the association cortex that evolved long before the neocortex, and has since taken over distinct memory functions, particularly spatial memory. When we make a mental map of how to get from one place to another, we're using our hippocampus. Special cells in the hippocampus, known as *place cells*, become active when an animal returns to a specific "place" in a familiar environment (O'Keefe, 1976). These findings probably help to explain why a portion of the hippocampus is larger in London taxi drivers than in non–taxi drivers, and why this portion is especially large in more experienced taxi drivers (Maguire et al., 2000). This correlation could mean either that people with greater amounts of experience navigating complex environments develop larger hippocampi, or that people with larger hippocampi seek out occupations, like taxi driving, that depend on spatial navigation.

Together with the amygdala and the prefrontal cortex, the hippocampus also contributes to fear conditioning (Maren, 2005; Phelps, 2006). When confronted with fear, the hippocampus interacts with these brain regions to integrate the emotional significance of an event with its cognitive interpretation. By interpreting emotionally charged situations as challenges rather than catastrophes, we can rein in our emotions. Cognitive appraisals of crisis situations enable us to think rationally during emergencies and stay calm, thereby increasing our chances of survival (see Chapter 12).

Damage to the hippocampus causes problems with forming new memories, but leaves old memories intact. A favorite hypothesis is that the hippocampus temporarily stores memories and then transfers them to other sites, such as the neocortex, for permanent storage (Sanchez-Andres et al., 1993). The *multiple trace theory* is a rival hypothesis of memory storage in the hippocampus (Moscovitch et al., 2005). According to this theory, memories are initially stored at multiple sites. Over time, storage strengthens at some sites, but weakens at others. The multiple trace theory avoids the need to "transfer" memory from the hippocampus to the neocortex. The memory is already stored in the neocortex and merely strengthens over time.

THE AUTONOMIC NERVOUS SYSTEM

As we discussed earlier, the forebrain, brain stem, and spinal cord interact with the somatic nervous system to bring about sensation and behavior. In much the same manner, the hypothalamus, amygdala, and other limbic regions interact with the **autonomic nervous system** to regulate emotion.

There are two divisions of the autonomic nervous system: the **sympathetic division** and the **parasympathetic division** (see **Figure 3.15**). These two divisions work in opposing directions: when one division is active, the other is passive. The sympathetic nervous system is active during emotional arousal, especially during a crisis, whereas the parasympathetic nervous system is active during rest and digestion. The sympathetic nervous system mobilizes the *fight-or-flight response,* first described by Walton Cannon in 1929 (see also Chapter 12). Cannon noticed that when animals encounter threats, the sympathetic nervous system becomes aroused and prepares animals for fighting or fleeing. Sympathetic activation triggers a variety of physical responses, including increased heart rate, respiration, and perspiration. Autonomic nerves that reach the heart, diaphragm, and sweat glands control these reactions.

THE ENDOCRINE SYSTEM

The limbic system also cooperates with the **endocrine system** to regulate emotion. The endocrine system consists of glands that release **hormones,** blood-borne molecules that influence target tissues, into the bloodstream (see **Figure 3.16** on page 122). The hypothalamus controls the endocrine system and receives feedback from it. The rest of the limbic system exerts control over the hypothalamus, creating a hierarchy of control with multiple feedback loops (see **Figure 3.17** on page 123).

The hippocampi of taxi drivers seem to be especially large, although the causal direction of this finding is unclear.

hippocampus
part of the brain that plays a role in spatial memory

autonomic nervous system
part of the peripheral nervous system controlling the involuntary actions of our internal organs and glands, which (along with the limbic system) participates in emotion

sympathetic division
part of the autonomic nervous system engaged during a crisis, or after actions requiring fight or flight

parasympathetic division
part of autonomic nervous system that controls rest and digestion

endocrine system
system of glands and hormones that controls secretion of blood-borne chemical messengers

hormones
blood-borne chemical that influences target tissues and glands

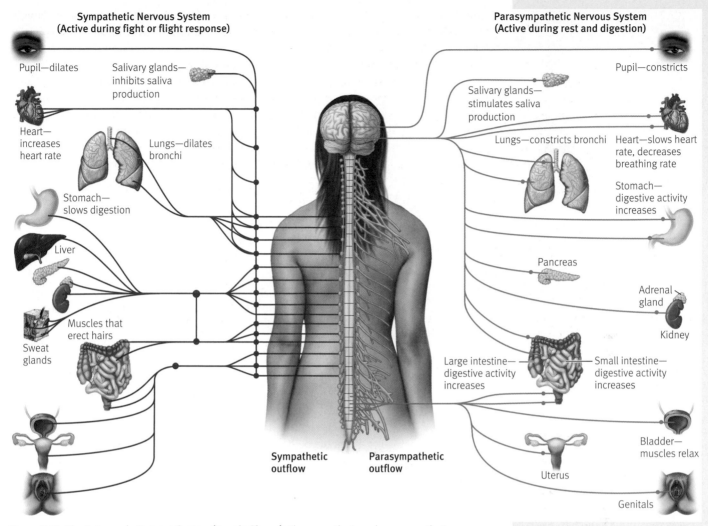

Sympathetic Nervous System
(Active during fight or flight response)

Pupil—dilates

Salivary glands—inhibits saliva production

Heart—increases heart rate

Lungs—dilates bronchi

Stomach—slows digestion

Liver

Muscles that erect hairs

Sweat glands

Sympathetic outflow

Parasympathetic Nervous System
(Active during rest and digestion)

Pupil—constricts

Salivary glands—stimulates saliva production

Lungs—constricts bronchi

Heart—slows heart rate, decreases breathing rate

Stomach—digestive activity increases

Pancreas

Adrenal gland

Kidney

Large intestine—digestive activity increases

Small intestine—digestive activity increases

Bladder—muscles relax

Uterus

Genitals

Parasympathetic outflow

Figure 3.15 The Autonomic Nervous System (Female Shown). The sympathetic and parasympathetic divisions of the autonomic nervous system control the internal organs and glands.

The Pituitary Gland and Pituitary Hormones. The **pituitary gland** controls the other glands in the body; for this reason, it's known as the "master gland." It, in turn, is under the control of the hypothalamus. There are two ways hormones get from the hypothalamus to the pituitary. One is for hypothalamic neurons to release hormones directly into the pituitary. Neurons in the hypothalamus make *vasopressin* and *oxytocin* and secrete them directly into the pituitary. Then the pituitary releases these hormones into the bloodstream. Vasopressin regulates water retention by the kidneys, and oxytocin is responsible for stretching the cervix and vagina during birth and for ejecting milk in nursing mothers. Oxytocin and vasopressin also play roles in maternal and romantic love (Esch & Stefano, 2005). Oxytocin may also be a key player in interpersonal trust. In one study, men exposed to a nasal spray containing oxytocin were more likely than other men to hand over money to their team partners in a risky investment game (Kosfeld et al., 2005).

Hypothalamic hormones control the pituitary gland in another way. Small blood vessels permeate the hypothalamus and carry *hypothalamic hormones* from the hypothalamus to the pituitary. These hormones then cause it to release (or not release) *pituitary hormones* into the general circulatory system. Pituitary hormones in the blood circulation system trigger other glands throughout the body to release their respective hormones (refer again to Figure 3.17).

pituitary gland
master gland, which, under the control of the hypothalamus, directs the other glands of body

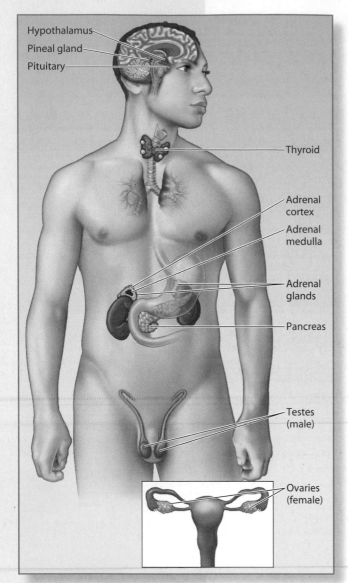

Hypothalamus
Pineal gland
Pituitary

Thyroid

Adrenal cortex

Adrenal medulla

Adrenal glands

Pancreas

Testes (male)

Ovaries (female)

Figure 3.16 The Major Endocrine Glands of the Body. Endocrine glands throughout the body play specialized roles.

Skydiving activates the sympathetic nervous system.

adrenal gland
tissue located on top of the kidneys that releases adrenaline and cortisol during states of emotional arousal

Growth hormone is an exception in that it doesn't act directly on a gland. This hormone, released by the pituitary gland, acts directly on cells throughout the body, causing them to grow. As a result, growth hormone largely determines height. Occasionally, a deficit of growth hormone results in short stature in an otherwise healthy child. Synthetic growth hormone can help a child make up those extra inches, and quickly, too—sometimes 6 or 7 inches in a year. These treatments aren't meant for anyone who merely wishes to be taller; they work only in children who are short because of a lack of growth hormone.

The Adrenal Glands and Adrenaline. Psychologists sometimes call the **adrenal glands** the emergency centers of the body. Located on top of the kidneys, they manufacture *adrenaline* (also called *epinephrine*) and *cortisol*. Adrenaline boosts energy production in muscle cells, thrusting them into action, while conserving as much energy as possible outside of muscle cells. Nerves of the sympathetic nervous system trigger the release of adrenaline by the adrenal gland. Adrenaline triggers many actions, including (1) contraction of the heart muscle and constriction of the blood vessels to provide more blood to the body, (2) opening of the bronchioles (small airways) of the lungs to allow inhalation of more air, (3) breakdown of fat into fatty acids, providing more fuel, (4) break down of glycogen (a carbohydrate) into glucose (a sugar) to energize muscles, and (5) opening the pupils of the eye to enable better sight in low levels of light during emergencies. Adrenaline also inhibits gastrointestinal secretions, illustrating that sympathetic arousal is incompatible with parasympathetic arousal. (Remember that the parasympathetic nervous system is active during digestion.) This last fact helps explain why we often lose our appetites when we feel nervous, as when we're preparing for a big test or anticipating a long-awaited date.

Adrenaline allows people to perform amazing feats in crisis situations, although these acts are constrained by people's physical limits. One desperate mother was energized to lift a heavy automobile to save her trapped infant (Solomon, 2002). Why do threatening or stressful situations activate the sympathetic nervous system? Evolution has probably predisposed this system to detect dangerous stimuli so we can better prepare for counterattack or escape. We're especially likely to interpret sudden and intense stimuli as threatening (Graham et al., 2005). But adrenaline isn't activated only during threatening situations. Pleasurable and exciting activities, like race car driving and skydiving, can produce adrenaline surges.

Like adrenaline, cortisol secretion by the adrenal gland increases in response to physical and psychological stress. Cortisol regulates blood pressure and cardiovascular function, as well as the body's use of proteins, carbohydrates, and fats. The way in which cortisol regulates nutrients has suggested to some researchers that it might regulate body weight, leading to the development of the popular *cortisol diet*. Proponents of this diet claim that elevated levels of cortisol produced by stress cause weight gain (Talbott, 2002). The solution: reduce stress, increase exercise, and monitor nutrition—reasonable advice for those of us who want to lose weight—and it doesn't require us to take supplements. Some people get frustrated or want faster results, however, so health food supplement outlets are happy to oblige by selling cortisol blockers and other dieting supplements. Unfortunately, there's little scientific evidence that these supplements work better than dieting measures that naturally inactivate the body's cortisol.

Sexual Reproductive Glands and Sex Hormones. The sexual reproductive glands are the testes in males and ovaries in females (refer back to Figure 3.16). We think of *sex hormones* as traditionally male or female. After all, the testes make the male sex hormone, called *testosterone*, and the ovaries make the female sex hormones, called *estrogen*. Although males and females do have more of their own type of sex hormone, both sexes manufacture some amount of the sex hormone associated with the opposite sex. For example, women make about one-twentieth the amount of testosterone as males. This is because the ovaries also make testosterone, and the adrenal gland makes low amounts of testosterone in both sexes. Conversely, the testes manufacture low levels of estrogen (Hess, 2003).

Scientists have long debated the relationship between sex hormones and sex drive (Bancroft, 2005). Most scientists believe that testosterone, which increases sex drive in men, also increases sex drive in women, but to a lesser degree. Australian researchers conducted a survey of 18- to 75-year-old women regarding their sexual arousal and frequency of orgasm (Davis et al., 2005). Before they administered the survey, they took blood samples from women and measured their testosterone. At the conclusion of the study, the researchers found no correlation between the levels of male sex hormone in a woman's blood and her sex drive. Possible weaknesses of this study include the fact that the researchers took only one blood sample from each subject, the study relied on self-reports, and there weren't controls for demand characteristics (see Chapter 2). For example, because women knew they were being studied for sexual experiences, they might have altered their reports of them. Most researchers still accept the idea that testosterone influences female sex drive. Nevertheless, given mixed reports, more research from multiple laboratories must be conducted before we can draw firm conclusions.

If the male sex hormone doesn't influence a woman's sex drive, what does? The participants in the Australian study suggested that stress and fatigue decreased their libido (sex drive) and that relationship problems affected their libido more than any other factor (Davis et al., 2005). Curiously, women tend to have sexual intercourse 24 percent more frequently during the six days in the middle of their menstrual cycles leading up to ovulation than during unfertile days (Wilcox et al., 2004). This finding might tie female sex drive to estrogen levels, because circulating estrogen is highest around ovulation. Nonetheless, the complexity of variables involved in such a study—such as potential changes in activity level, mood, or alertness of the subjects—doesn't enable us to determine the precise physiological basis for the increase in sexual activity.

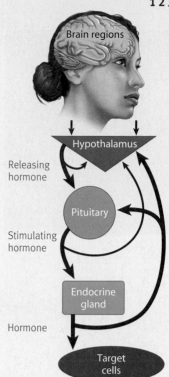

Figure 3.17 The Hierarchy of Control over the Endocrine System. (*Source:* Adapted from Sternberg, 2004)

Replicability

Ruling Out Rival Hypotheses

ASSESS YOUR KNOWLEDGE: FACT OR FICTION?

(1) The hippocampus, amygdala, and cingulate cortex never contribute to the same emotions or learning experiences. (True/False)
(2) The amygdala plays a key role in fear. (True/False)
(3) There are two divisions of the autonomic nervous system. (True/False)
(4) Human beings are capable of incredible feats when energized by adrenaline. (True/False)
(5) Females don't have any male hormones. (True/False)

Answers: (1) F (p. 118); (2) T (p. 119); (3) T (p. 120); (4) T (p. 122); (5) F (p. 123)

factoid

The thrill of watching others win increases testosterone in sports fans. Males watching World Cup soccer matches showed increased testosterone levels in their saliva if their favorite team won, but decreased testosterone levels if their favorite team lost (Bernhardt et al., 1998).

Nerve Cells: Communication Portals

In the preceding sections, we examined the organization of the nervous system and the structure and function of the brain. We'll now take an in-depth look at the substance of the nervous system, down to the cellular level, and then proceed even deeper, down to the level of individual molecules.

NEURONS: THE BRAIN'S COMMUNICATORS

Although many cells have simple and regular shapes, neurons are different. They have long branches or extensions, which help them receive and transmit information. These special features enable neurons to respond to inputs and communicate with each other.

The Cell Body. The *neuronal membrane*, which separates the inside from the outside of the cell, encases the entire neuron. The *cell body* is the central region of the neuron that manu-

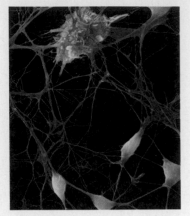

Neurons and their dendrites (shown stained pink) with their nuclei (shown stained blue).

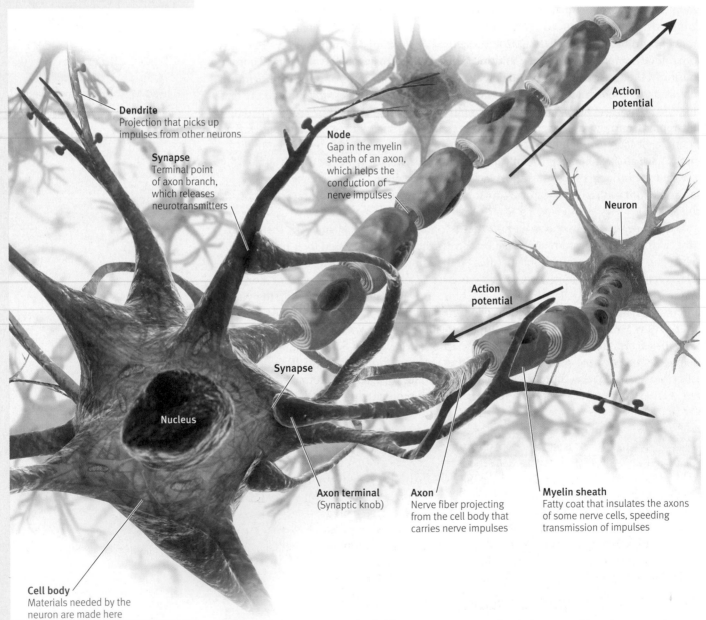

Dendrite
Projection that picks up impulses from other neurons

Synapse
Terminal point of axon branch, which releases neurotransmitters

Node
Gap in the myelin sheath of an axon, which helps the conduction of nerve impulses

Action potential

Neuron

Action potential

Synapse

Nucleus

Cell body
Materials needed by the neuron are made here

Axon terminal
(Synaptic knob)

Axon
Nerve fiber projecting from the cell body that carries nerve impulses

Myelin sheath
Fatty coat that insulates the axons of some nerve cells, speeding transmission of impulses

Figure 3.18 A Neuron with a Myelin Sheath. Neurons receive chemical messages from other neurons by way of synaptic contacts with dendrites and spines. Next, neurons send action potentials down along their axons, some of which are coated with myelin to make the electrical signal travel faster. (*Source:* Modified from Dorling Kindersley)

factures new cell components, consisting of small and large molecules. A neuron won't survive severe damage to the cell body because it's the main site where proteins are synthesized and it provides continuous renewal of cell components.

Dendrites. Neurons differ from other cells in that they have extensions for receiving information from other neurons. These receiving parts are called **dendrites** and gradually taper from the cell body region, much as a branch on a tree narrows as it extends outward (see **Figure 3.18**). Most synaptic contacts between neurons occur directly onto dendrites or onto small appendages on dendrites called *spines*.

Synapses. A synapse is a complex arrangement consisting of a **synaptic cleft,** a gap into which neurotransmitters are released from the axon terminal. On either side of the gap lie specialized patches of membrane called the *presynaptic* and *postsynaptic membranes*, respectively. Different proteins become integrated into each of these opposing membranes, depending on whether the protein plays a role in sending or receiving messages.

Axons and Axon Terminals. **Axons** are long extensions specialized for sending messages from one neuron to another. Unlike dendrites, axons are usually very thin at their site of origin near the cell body. This narrowness creates a *trigger zone*, a site that's easy to activate. The *axon terminal* is a knoblike structure at the end of the axon (see **Figure 3.19**). Axon terminals contain **synaptic vesicles,** spheres that contain **neurotransmitters,** chemical messengers specialized for communication. We might think of the synaptic vesicles as gel capsules filled with cold medicine. When we swallow each capsule, it's carried down our digestive tracts. This is similar to how synaptic vesicles travel to the axon terminal. In our stomachs, the gel capsules dissolve and release the medicine, much like the way the synaptic vesicle releases neurotransmitters into the synaptic cleft. Synaptic vesicles also contain proteins that synthesize neurotransmitters. Synaptic vesicles are constructed in the cell body and travel down along the length of the axon. When synaptic vesicles reach the axon terminal, they manufacture and accumulate high levels of neurotransmitter. Upon activation of axon terminals, synaptic vesicles fuse with the presynaptic membrane and release neurotransmitters into the synaptic cleft.

GLIAL CELLS: SUPPORTING ROLES

Glial cells are the supporting actors in the nervous system; among other things, they protect neurons. Glial cells are about ten times more numerous than neurons; different types play various supporting roles. Certain glial cells respond to injury. Sometimes they release chemicals that promote healing (but other times they interfere with regrowth). Other glial cells form a fatty coating called the **blood–brain barrier** by wrapping around tiny blood vessels. Large molecules, highly charged particles, and molecules that dissolve in water but not fat are blocked from entering the brain. However, glucose enters the brain by a special mechanism. The blood–brain barrier is the brain's way of protecting itself from bacterial infection and from high levels of circulating hormones (see **Figure 3.20**).

Still other glial cells wrap around the sending portion of neurons, which speeds up the passage of electrical messages by insulating the neuronal signal. This wrapper is called the **myelin sheath** (refer again to Figure 3.18). In the autoimmune disease *multiple sclerosis*, the myelin sheaths surrounding neurons are "eaten away," resulting in a progressive loss of insulation of neural messages. As a consequence, these messages become hopelessly scrambled, eventually resulting in a wide variety of physical and emotional symptoms. Other glial cells clear away debris, acting as the brain's cellular garbage disposals.

ELECTRICAL RESPONSES OF NEURONS

Neurons respond to neurotransmitters by generating electrical activity (see **Figure 3.21** on page 126). We know this because scientists have recorded electrical activity from neurons using tiny *electrodes*, small devices made from wire or fine glass tubes. These

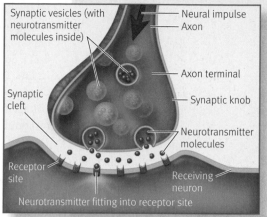

Figure 3.19 The Axon Terminal. The axon terminal contains synaptic vesicles filled with neurotransmitter molecules.

Figure 3.20 The Blood–Brain Barrier. The blood–brain barrier keeps harmful molecules from entering the brain.

dendrites
portions of neurons that receive signals

synaptic cleft
space between two connecting neurons where neurotransmitters are released

axons
portions of neurons that send signals

synaptic vesicles
spherical sacs containing neurotransmitters

neurotransmitters
chemical messengers specialized for communication and released at the synapse

glia (glial) cells
support cells in nervous system that play roles in the formation of myelin and blood–brain barrier, respond to injury, and remove debris

blood–brain barrier
glial cells forming a fatty coating that prevents certain substances from entering the brain

myelin sheath
glial cell-wrappers around axons that act as insulators of the neuron's signal

electrodes allowed them to measure what's called the *potential difference* of electrical charge across the neuronal membrane. The basis of all electrical responses in neurons depends on an uneven distribution of charged particles across the membrane (see **Figure 3.21**). Some particles are positively charged, others negatively charged. When there are no inputs, the membrane is at the **resting potential.** In this resting state, the negative charges inside the neuron remain higher than on the outside. In some large neurons, the voltage of the resting potential can be about one-twentieth that of a flashlight battery, or about −70 millivolts (inside negative with respect to the outside).

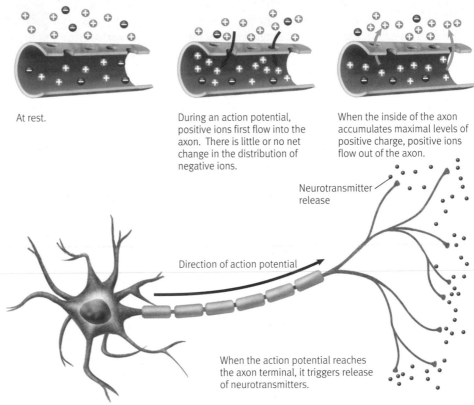

At rest.

During an action potential, positive ions first flow into the axon. There is little or no net change in the distribution of negative ions.

When the inside of the axon accumulates maximal levels of positive charge, positive ions flow out of the axon.

Neurotransmitter release

Direction of action potential

When the action potential reaches the axon terminal, it triggers release of neurotransmitters.

Figure 3.21 The Action Potential. When a neuron is at rest there are positive and negative ions on both sides of the membrane. During an action potential, positive ions rush in and then out of the axon. This process occurs along the axon until the axon terminal releases a neurotransmitter. (*Source:* Adapted from Sternberg, 2004)

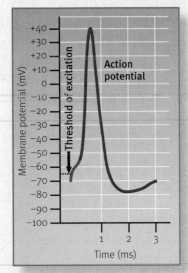

Figure 3.22 Voltage across the Membrane during the Action Potential. The membrane potential needed to trigger an action potential is called the *threshold*. Many neurons have a threshold of −65 mV. That means only 5 mV of current above resting is needed to trigger an action potential. (*Source:* Adapted from Sternberg, 2004)

resting potential
electrical charge difference (−70 millivolts) across the neuronal membrane, when the neuron is not being stimulated or inhibited

threshold
membrane potential necessary to trigger an action potential

action potential
regenerative electrical impulse that travels down the axon and allows neurons to communicate

absolute refractory period
time during which another action potential is impossible; limits maximal firing rate

Graded Potentials. Graded potentials are *postsynaptic potentials* that can be excitatory or inhibitory depending on whether positively or negatively charged particles flow across the neuronal membrane and in which direction they flow (refer again to Figure 3.21). Excitatory inputs and inhibitory inputs add together or cancel out. When excitation prevails and reaches a high enough level, called the **threshold,** an action potential occurs.

Action Potentials. **Action potentials** are abrupt waves of electric discharge that allow neurons to communicate. They're quite a bit different from graded potentials. First, they're all-or-none, meaning that either a full-strength action potential occurs or none occurs at all. All action potentials reach maximal amplitude. We can think of them as similar to the firing of a gun; when we pull the gun's trigger, it either fires with maximum power or it doesn't fire at all. Second, action potentials are *regenerative*, meaning that once started, the process is self-perpetuating; the action potential continues all the way down to the axon terminal. Third, the mechanism of action potentials differs from that of graded potentials. During an action potential, a positive charge flows rapidly into the axon and then rapidly flows out, bringing the membrane potential slightly below its original resting value (see **Figures** 3.21 and **3.22**).

Neurons can fire at rates up to 100–1,000 per second, at speeds of about 220 miles per hour. After each action potential there's an **absolute refractory period,** a brief time during which another action potential can't occur. The absolute refractory period limits the *maximal firing rate*, which is the fastest rate at which a neuron can fire. The rate at which action potentials travel becomes an issue in very long axons, such as the sciatic nerve, which runs from the spinal cord down the leg. Believe it or not, in humans this axon extends an average of 3 feet. To accommodate the need for fast conduction, the myelin sheath covers most long axons, leaving only an occasional myelin-free patch or *node* (refer back to Figure 3.18). Action potentials hop from node to node, resulting in more rapid relay than if the entire axonal membrane participated in perpetuating them.

CHEMICAL NEUROTRANSMISSION

Whereas electrical events transmit information within neurons, neurotransmitters orchestrate intercellular communication among neurons. These small- to medium-sized molecules bind to specific **receptor sites** that uniquely recognize a specific neurotransmitter. Psychologists often use a lock-and-key analogy to describe this binding specificity (see **Figure 3.23**). We can think of each neurotransmitter as a key that fits only its receptor, or lock.

There are three steps in neurotransmission:

(1) release of the neurotransmitter from the axon terminal into the synaptic cleft;

(2) binding of the neurotransmitter to its receptor site; and

(3) halting neurotransmission by either the chemical breakdown of the neurotransmitter or by **reuptake** of the neurotransmitter back into the axon terminal—a process by which the synaptic vesicle engulfs the neurotransmitter. We might think of release and reuptake as similar to squeezing a small amount of mustard out of a plastic container onto a plate and then sucking it back into the container. It's one of nature's recycling mechanisms.

Neurotransmitters. The major neurotransmitters, along with some drugs that act on them, are listed in **Table 3.2**. We can think of different neurotransmitters as messengers with slightly different things to say. In the cerebral cortex, all these messages are integrated into perception and action.

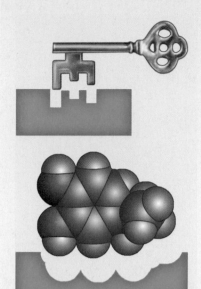

Figure 3.23 The Lock-and-Key Model of Neurotransmitter Binding to Receptor Sites.

> **fict**oid
>
> **Myth:** As adults, we lose about 100,000 neurons each day.
> **Reality:** Although we do lose neurons each day, the actual number is considerably lower, perhaps one tenth of that (Juan, 2006).

Table 3.2 Neurotransmitters and Their Major Functional Roles.

Neurotransmitter	Selected Roles	Drugs That Interact with the Neurotransmitter System
Glutamate	Main excitatory neurotransmitter in the nervous system; participates in relay of sensory information and learning	*Alcohol* and *memory enhancers* interact with N-methyl-D-aspartate (NMDA) receptors, a specific type of glutamate receptor.
Gamma-aminobutyric acid (GABA)	Main inhibitory neurotransmitter in the nervous system	*Alcohol* and *antianxiety drugs* increase GABA activity.
Acetylcholine (ACh)	Muscle contraction (PNS) Cortical arousal (CNS)	*Nicotine* stimulates ACh receptors. *Memory enhancers* increase ACh. *Insecticides* block the breakdown of ACh. *Botox* causes paralysis by blocking ACh.
Norepinephrine (NE)	Cortical arousal	*Amphetamine* and *methamphetamine* increase NE.
Dopamine	Motor function and reward	*L-Dopa,* which increases dopamine, is used to treat Parkinson's disease. *Antipsychotic drugs*, which block dopamine action, are used to treat schizophrenia.
Serotonin	Cortical arousal	*Serotonin-selective reuptake inhibitor (SSRI) antidepressants* are used to treat depression.
Endorphins	Pain reduction	*Narcotic drugs*—codeine, morphine, and heroin—reduce pain and produce euphoria.
Anandamide	Pain reduction, increase in appetite	*Tetrahydrocannabinol (THC)*—found in marijuana—produces euphoria.

(*Source:* Adapted from Carlson & Heth, 2007)

receptor sites
locations that uniquely recognize a neurotransmitter

reuptake
means of recycling neurotransmitters

Glutamate and GABA. *Glutamate* and gamma-aminobutyric acid (*GABA*) are the most common neurotransmitters in the CNS. Neurons in virtually every brain area use these neurotransmitters to communicate with other neurons (Fagg & Foster, 1983). Glutamate rapidly excites the neurons it acts on. GABA, in contrast, inhibits neurons, dampening neural activity. That's why most antianxiety drugs activate GABA receptor sites.

Acetylcholine. Acetylcholine was the first substance shown to act as a neurotransmitter. In 1921, Otto Loewi dreamt the experiment that he later performed. He took two isolated frog hearts and bathed them in saline-filled beakers while they continued to beat. Then he stimulated the nerve that slowed the beating of one frog's heart and transferred some of the saline solution to the other beaker. Amazingly, the second heart slowed as well. There was only one explanation: A chemical in the saline-solution caused the action.

Acetylcholine, which is manufactured in the basal forebrain and released in the cerebral cortex, plays a role in cortical arousal, selective attention, and memory (McKinney & Jacksonville, 2005; Woolf, 1991) (refer back to Figure 3.8). Neurons that synapse onto muscle cells also release acetylcholine, so acetylcholine also plays a key role in movement.

Monoamine Neurotransmitters. *Norepinephrine, dopamine,* and *serotonin* are the monoamine neurotransmitters, so named because of their chemical structure. As we discussed earlier, dopamine, which is synthesized in the substantia nigra and released in the basal ganglia, plays a role in tying reward to movement. Other cells in the brain stem also make norepinephrine and serotonin, which along with acetylcholine and glutamate, activate or deactivate parts of the cerebral cortex (Jones, 2003).

Athletes, like this bicyclist, often rely on their endorphins to push them through intense pain.

Neuropeptides. Neuropeptides are short strings of amino acids in the nervous system. They act somewhat like neurotransmitters, the difference being that their roles are typically specialized. **Endorphins** play a specialized role in pain reduction (Holden, Jeong, & Forrest, 2005). Endorphins are *endogenous opioids,* meaning that they're the brain's natural narcotics. Opiates—the narcotic substances derived from the opium plant—were widely used long before we knew we had our own endorphins. Opiate use may have begun as early as 3400 B.C. in parts of the Middle East. Indeed, many narcotic drugs, such as heroin, act by mimicking the action of endorphins. Our brains contain a host of other neuropeptides; some of them regulate hunger and satiety (fullness).

Anandamide. Just as we knew about opiates long before we knew about the endogenous opioids, we knew about marijuana and its active ingredient, *tetrahydrocannabinol* (THC), long before we knew about anandamide. Cells in our bodies, like neurons, make anandamide, and it binds to the same receptors as THC. *Anandamide* plays a role in eating, motivation, memory, and sleep.

Psychoactive Drugs. Drugs that interact with neurotransmitter systems are called *psychoactive,* meaning they affect mood, arousal, or behavior in some way (see Chapter 5). At high doses virtually any psychoactive drug can be toxic. A few are toxic at very low doses. For example, botulinum toxin, also known as the cosmetic agent *Botox,* causes paralysis by blocking acetylcholine's actions on muscles. This paralysis temporarily decreases small wrinkles, such as those on the forehead and around the eyes, by relaxing those muscles. Whereas it takes 1–2 teaspoons of the poison arsenic to kill a person, a microscopic amount of Botox is lethal (Kamrin, 1988).

Knowing how psychoactive drugs interact with neurotransmitter systems enables us to predict how they affect our mental state, mood, or behavior. Opiate drugs, such as codeine and morphine, function as *agonists,* meaning they enhance receptor site activity. Specifically, they reduce pain and the emotional response to painful stimuli by binding with opioid receptors and mimicking endorphins (Evans, 2004). Tranquilizers, like Xanax, which relax people with high levels of anxiety, stimulate GABA receptor sites, thereby reducing neuronal activity (Roy-Byrne, 2005). Still other drugs block reuptake of neurotransmitters into the axon terminal. Many antidepressants, like Prozac, block the reuptake mechanism that removes serotonin, norepinephrine, or dopamine from the synaptic cleft (Schatzberg,

endorphins
chemicals in the brain that play a specialized role in pain reduction

1998). When these neurotransmitters remain in the synaptic cleft longer than usual, their effects are enhanced.

Some drugs work in the opposite way, functioning as receptor *antagonists*, meaning they decrease receptor site activity. Drugs used to treat schizophrenia—a complex mental disorder we'll describe more fully in Chapter 15—typically block dopamine receptors by binding to them and then blocking the usual effects of dopamine (Bennett, 1998).

ASSESS YOUR KNOWLEDGE: FACT OR FICTION?

(1) Dendrites are the sending portions of neurons. (True/False)
(2) Positive ions flowing into the neuron inhibit its action. (True/False)
(3) Action potentials are all-or-none. (True/False)
(4) Neurotransmitters send messages between neurons. (True/False)
(5) Some antidepressants block the reuptake of serotonin into the axon terminal.
(True/False)

Answers: (1) F (p. 125); (2) F (p. 126); (3) T (p. 126); (4) T (p. 127); (5) T (pp. 128–129)

Mapping the Mind to Understand Our Actions

Now that we've explored the parts of the brain and the ways in which neurons work, we can tackle one of the most elusive topics in psychology—the mind. The human mind is one of the greatest feats of nature. After all, few things in this world can achieve self-understanding, if that's what we do in those exalted, yet fleeting moments of insight.

U.S. Army Specialist Erik Castillo (*left*) lost almost 60 percent of his skull and suffered serious brain damage (technically called "traumatic brain injury") following a bomb blast in Operation Iraqi Freedom. Such brain damage can produce long-term deficits in memory, thinking, perception, and personality. Fortunately, rehabilitation therapy, such as that shown here, can sometimes partly reverse these deficits.

MIND–BRAIN IDENTITY

Modern science points toward one clear-cut conclusion: Mind and brain function are essentially the same thing (Crick, 1994). Put another way, the mind is the brain in action.

We can look to three kinds of evidence for mind–brain identity:

• Brain activity changes with different behaviors and perceptions.
• Brain damage causes deficits in behavior and perception.
• Stimulating the brain activates behavior or perception.

Although different parts of the brain possess specialized functions, many brain areas act in concert during complex mental processes. Does that mean that the complexity of ongoing brain activity accounts entirely for the mind? Scientists can't test this hypothesis because it isn't falsifiable: We could never refute the possibility that the soul or other metaphysical influences (see Chapter 1) account partly for mental activity. Still, scientists have made significant inroads to understanding how our minds work.

As we'll recall from the Prologue, the mind–brain debate has long been one of the most controversial issues in all of psychology. The seventeenth-century philosopher George Berkeley even went so far as to argue that reality, as we know it, exists solely in our minds. Although these kinds of statements provide fuel for interesting debates at coffeehouses or in dorm rooms, Berkeley wasn't an experimentalist. Modern psychology, in contrast, is an empirical science based on experimentation.

Falsifiability

APPLY YOUR THINKING
Why can't we conduct research to falsify the hypothesis that "reality exists only in the mind"?

Although many questions remain unanswered, the mind–brain debate has been responsible for jump-starting a host of startling discoveries. As a result, we know far more about the brain and mind today than we did two hundred, or even twenty, years ago. For this, we can thank psychologists and related scientists who've developed a host of methods to explore the brain and test hypotheses about its functioning.

A TOUR OF BRAIN-MAPPING METHODS

Many advances and major breakthroughs of the last two centuries have enabled scientists to measure brain activity. We know a great many facts about the brain and behavior today because our current methods have been scrutinized and substantiated again and again. Nonetheless, brain research tools weren't always reliable or valid. Some of the earliest methods turned out to be fundamentally flawed, but they paved the way for the sounder methods used today.

Phrenology: A Questionable Map of the Mind. Phrenology was one of the earliest methods that attempted to map mind onto brain. Phrenology was wildly popular in the 1800s, when phrenologists assessed enlargements of the skull—literally bumps on the head—and attributed various personality traits and abilities to those who sought their "expertise." Phrenologists assumed that bumps on the head were intimately related to brain enlargements (for this reason, critics of phrenology sometimes jokingly called it "bumpology"). From the 1820s through the 1840s, thousands of phrenology shops popped up in Europe and North America. Anyone could go to a phrenology parlor to discover his or her psychological makeup. This popular practice was the origin of the familiar expression, "having one's head examined."

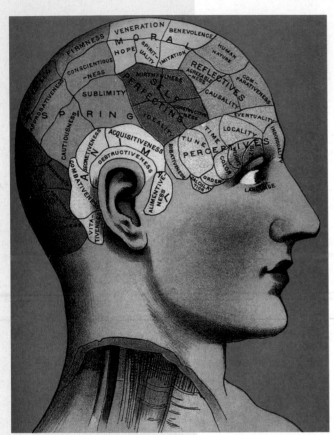

A phrenologist's chart showing where certain psychological traits are supposedly associated with bumps on the skull.

The founder of phrenology, Viennese physician Franz Joseph Gall (1758–1828), began with some valid assumptions about the brain. He correctly predicted a positive relationship between enlargements in specific brain areas and certain traits and abilities, like language. Gall was incorrect, however, in assuming that brain area enlargements created bumps that made impressions on the overlying parts of the skull. Moreover, the thirty-seven different traits that phrenologists described—aggressiveness, vanity, friendliness, and happiness among them—are vastly different from what scientists studying the brain today ascribe to different brain areas.

Phrenology isn't a valid method of assessment. Still, it had one virtue: It was falsifiable. Ironically, this lone asset proved to be its undoing. Eventually, researchers discovered that patients with damage to specific brain areas didn't suffer the kinds of psychological deficits the phrenologists predicted. Phrenologists also committed some embarrassing errors. For example, after examining the skull bumps of Mark Twain, often regarded as American's greatest comedian, one famous phrenologist concluded that he lacked any sense of humor (Lopez, 2002). Even more critically, because the shape of the outer surface of the skull doesn't closely match that of the underlying brain, phrenologists weren't even measuring bumps on the brain, as they'd believed.

Brain Damage: Studying How the Brain Works by Seeing How It Doesn't. New methods quickly arose to fill the void left by phrenology. These included methods of studying brain function following damage. We've already mentioned studies conducted by Broca and others that linked specific areas of the cerebral cortex to precise functions. More recently, scientists have created **lesions;** that is areas of damage, in experimental animals using *stereotaxic methods,* techniques that permitted them to pinpoint the location of specific brain areas using coordinates, much like those that navigators use on a map. Today, *neuropsychologists* (see Prologue) rely on sophisticated psychological tests, like measures of reasoning, attention, and verbal and spatial ability, to infer the location of brain damage in human patients.

lesion
area of damage due to surgery, injury, or disease

Electrical Stimulation and Recording of Nervous System Activity. Although early studies of function following brain damage provided valuable insights into which brain areas are responsible for which behaviors, many questions concerning the workings of neurons remained. Gustav Fritsch and Eduard Hitzig (1870) were the first to show that stimulating the cerebral cortex in an experimental animal caused specific movements. As we'll recall, it was several decades later that Penfield (1958) stimulated selected parts of the human motor cortex and produced specific movements in those patients. These experiments and others like them showed that nerves respond to electrical stimulation, leading to the hypothesis that nerves themselves might use electrical activity to send information. To test that hypothesis, scientists would need to record electrical activity from the nervous system.

To that end, another method arose that enabled scientists to probe the brain's electrical activity. In the late 1920s, Hans Berger (1929) developed the **electroencephalograph (EEG),** a device that measures electrical activity generated by the brain (see **Figure 3.24**). Patterns and sequences in the EEG allow scientists to infer whether a person is awake, asleep, or dreaming, and to tell what parts of the brain are active during specific tasks. To obtain an EEG record, researchers record electrical activity from electrodes placed on the scalp's surface.

Because it's noninvasive, researchers frequently use the EEG in both animal and human experiments. The method has a high *temporal resolution* ("temporal" refers to time and "resolution" to sharpness of image), meaning it can detect very rapid changes in the overall electrical activity of the brain occurring in the range of milliseconds (one-thousandths of seconds). Even though the EEG is an old method, researchers still use it to study brain activity in normal brains and in brains of individuals afflicted with schizophrenia, epilepsy, and other psychiatric and neurological disorders. But EEGs have a few disadvantages. Because they show averaged activity that reaches the surface of the scalp, they tell us little, if anything, about what's happening inside neurons. Furthermore, EEGs have low *spatial resolution*, meaning that they aren't especially good for determining where in the brain the action is occurring.

Brain Scans. Although electrical recording and stimulation provided the initial routes for mapping mind functions onto brain areas, a virtual explosion of brain research occurred with the advent of brain scans, or *neuroimaging*. Researchers developed imaging methods to satisfy clinical and research needs unmet by other techniques. As a group, these imaging methods enable us to peer inside the brain or body. Let's first look at imaging methods that provide a picture of the brain's structure.

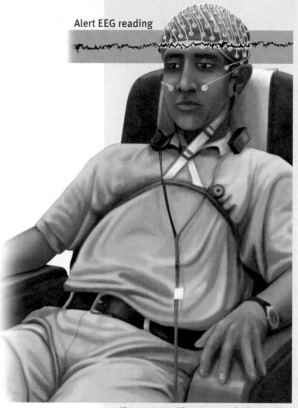

Alert EEG reading

Figure 3.24 Electroencephalograph (EEG). An EEG reading during wakefulness.

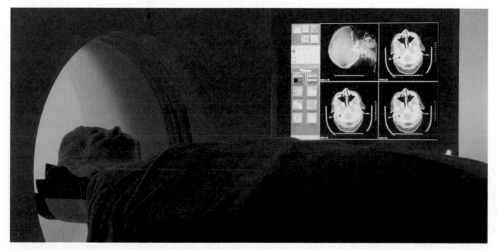

Magnetic resonance imaging (MRI) is a noninvasive procedure that reveals high-resolution images of soft tissue, such as the brain.

fictoid

Myth: Research using brain imaging is more "scientific" than other psychological research.
Reality: Brain imaging research can be extremely useful but, like all research, can be misused and abused. Yet because it seems scientific, we can be more persuaded by brain imaging research than we should be. In fact, studies show that undergraduates are more impressed by claims accompanied by brain imaging findings than research that doesn't, even when the claims are bogus (McCabe & Castel, 2007; Weisberg, Keil, Goodstein, Rawson, & Gray, in press).

electroencephalography (EEG)
recording of brain's electrical activity at the surface of the skull

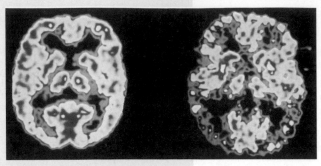

Brain activity decreases with Alzheimer's disease. Positron emission tomography (PET) scans show more regions displaying low activity (blue and black areas) in an Alzheimer's disease brain *(right)* than a control brain *(left)*, whereas the control brain displays more areas showing high activity (red and yellow).

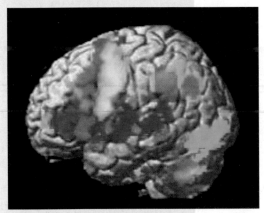

An fMRI of the brain showing areas that were active when subjects remembered something they saw (green), something they heard (red), or both (yellow). *(Source:* M. Kirschen/Stanford University.)

computed tomography (CT)
a scanning technique using multiple x-rays to construct three-dimensional images

magnetic resonance imaging (MRI)
technique that uses magnetic fields to indirectly visualize brain structure

positron emission tomography (PET)
imaging technique that measures uptake of glucoselike molecules, yielding a picture of regional metabolic activity in brain in different regions

functional MRI (fMRI)
technique that uses magnetic fields to visualize brain activity

transcranial magnetic stimulation (TMS)
technique that applies strong and quickly changing magnetic fields to the surface of the skull and that can either enhance or interrupt brain function

magnetoencephalography (MEG)
measure of brain activity using magnotometers that sense tiny magnetic fields generated by the brain

CT Scans and MRI Images. In the mid-1970s, independent teams of researchers developed **computed tomography (CT)** and **magnetic resonance imaging (MRI)** (Hounsfield, 1973; Lauterbur, 1973). The discovery of the CT scan earned its developers the Nobel Prize. It's a three-dimensional reconstruction of many x-rays taken though a part of the body, such as the brain. It shows much more detail than an individual x-ray. The MRI shows structural detail using a totally different principle. The MRI scanner measures the release of energy from water in biological tissues following exposure to a uniform magnetic field. MRI images are superior to CT scans for detecting soft tissues, such as brain tumors. Neuroscientists interested in thought and emotion typically don't use CT or MRI scans, except to localize brain damage. Instead, they typically use the functional imaging techniques we'll discuss next.

PET. Martin Reivich and colleagues (1979) developed **positron emission tomography (PET),** which is a *functional imaging* technique, meaning it measures changes in the brain's activity levels. PET relies on the fact that neurons, like other cells in the body, increase their uptake of glucose when they're active. We can think of glucose as the brain's gasoline. PET is an invasive tool that requires the injection of glucoselike molecules attached to radiotracers into patients. Radiotracers are radioactive, but because they're short-lived, they do little or no harm. The scanner measures where in the brain the most glucoselike molecules are taken up, allowing neuroscientists to figure out which parts of the brain are most active during a psychological task. Clinicians use PET scans to see where brain activity increases when patients, such as those with Parkinson's disease, take a medication. Because PET is invasive, researchers later looked for functional imaging methods that wouldn't require injections of radiotracers.

BOLD Response and fMRI. Seiji Ogawa and his colleagues first reported the *blood oxygenation level dependent* (BOLD) response in 1990. The discovery of the BOLD response enabled the development of the **functional MRI,** known as **fMRI.** As neural activity picks up its pace, there's an increase in oxygenated blood in response to heightened demand. Because fMRI measures the change in blood oxygen level, it's an indirect correlate of neural activity. Neuroscientists frequently use fMRI to image brain activity. The fMRI relies on magnetic fields, as does MRI. Whereas MRI has a high resolution, fMRI operates at a low resolution so that researchers can snap many scans in rapid succession. Individual fMRI images aren't very sharp, but the method shows changes in brain activity level over time because it creates a sequence of images.

Magnetic Stimulation and Recording. To provide access to surface brain structures and improve on the resolution afforded by functional imaging, researchers developed methods that relied on magnetic fields. Anthony Barker and colleagues (1985) were the first to report on a method called **transcranial magnetic stimulation (TMS),** which applies strong and quickly changing magnetic fields to the skull to induce electric fields in the brain (see Chapter 8). Depending on the level of stimulation, TMS can either enhance or interrupt brain function. TMS treatments have apparent clinical applications. Some reports suggest that TMS provides relief for depression and may decrease auditory hallucinations, that is, the hearing of sounds, typically voices (Saba, Schurhoff, & Leboyer, 2006). *Repetitive TMS* (*rTMS*), pulsed at medium to high frequency, additionally shows promise as a treatment for depression (Rachid & Bertschy, 2006).

Whereas TMS applies magnetic fields to the brain, **magnetoencephalography (MEG)** measures tiny magnetic fields, and in this way detects electrical activity in the brain and the rest of the nervous system. This technique involves the use of extremely sensitive magnetometers (devices that detect magnetism) because the magnetic fields generated by the brain are extremely weak. The resulting images produced by MEG reveal patterns of magnetic fields on the surface of the skull. MEG has good spatial resolution and excellent temporal resolution—measuring activity changes millisecond by millisecond—whereas PET and fMRI scans measure activity changes second by second.

HOW MUCH OF OUR BRAIN DO WE USE?

Despite having so much information available today regarding the relationship between brain and behavior, misconceptions about the brain still abound. One widely held myth is that most people use only 10 percent of their brains (Beyerstein, 1999). What could we do if we could access the 90 percent of the brain that's supposedly inactive? Would we find the cure for cancer, acquire wealth beyond belief, or write our own psychology textbook?

The 10 percent myth gained its toehold at around the same time as phrenology, in the late 1800s. William James (1842–1910), one of the fathers of modern psychology (see Prologue), wrote that most people fulfill only a small percent of their intellectual potential. Some people misconstrued this quote as meaning that we only use about 10 percent of our brains. As the 10 percent myth was repeated, it acquired the status of an urban legend (see Chapter 13).

Early difficulties in identifying the functions of the association cortex probably reinforced this misconception. In 1929, Karl Lashley showed that there was no single memory area in the brain (see Chapter 7). He made multiple knife cuts in the brains of rats and tested them on a series of mazes. The result was that no specific cortical area was more critical to maze learning than any other. Unfortunately, Lashley's results were ripe for misinterpretation as evidence for excessive "silent" areas in the cerebral cortex.

Given how appealing the idea of tapping into our full potential is, it's no wonder that scores of pop psychology writers, media figures, and so-called self-improvement experts have assured us they know how to harness our brain's full potential. Some authors of self-help books who were particularly fond of the 10 percent myth liberally misquoted scientists as saying that 90 percent of the brain isn't doing anything. Believers in psychic phenomena have even spun the yarn that because scientists don't know what 90 percent of the brain is doing, it must be serving a psychic purpose, like extrasensory perception (ESP) (Clark, 1997).

We now know enough about all parts of the brain that we can safely conclude that every part of the brain has a function. Specialists in the fields of clinical neurology and neuropsychology, who deal with the effects of brain damage, have shown that losses of small areas of certain parts of the brain can cause devastating, often permanent, losses of function (Sacks, 1985). Even when brain damage doesn't cause severe deficits, it produces some change in behavior, however subtle.

The fatal blow against the 10 percent myth, however, comes from neuroimaging and brain stimulation studies. No one's ever discovered any perpetually silent areas, nor is it the case that 90 percent of the brain produces nothing of psychological interest when stimulated. All brain areas become active on brain scans at one time or another as we think, feel, and perceive (Beyerstein, 1999).

The 10 percent myth may have inspired a few people to strive harder and accomplish more in life. As with many other uplifting fictions, this isn't a bad thing. But as a scientific depiction of how our brains are organized, it could hardly be further from the truth.

WHAT PARTS OF OUR BRAIN DO WE USE?

Scientists refer to *localization of function* when they identify brain areas that are active over and above a baseline rate of activity during a psychological task. We should be careful not to overemphasize localization of function, however, and particularly cautious in our interpretations of neuroimaging results. William Uttal (2001) warned that neuroimaging might be creating a kind of "new phrenology" insofar as researchers are too quick to assign narrowly defined functions to specific brain regions. He argued that we can't always dissect higher cognitive functions into narrower components. Take visual perception, for example:

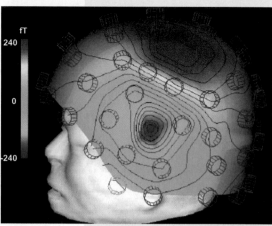

An example of magnetoencephalography (MEG) illustrating the presence of magnetic fields on the surface of the cerebral cortex. (*Source:* Arye Nehori/Washington University, St. Louis)

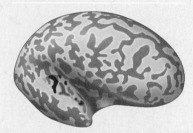

Popular mythology aside, we don't use only 10 percent of our brains.

Can we divide it into subcomponents dealing with color, form, and motion, as cortical localization of functions might imply, or is visual perception an indivisible concept?

Regrettably, much of the popular media hasn't taken Uttal's useful cautions to heart. To take one example, some newspapers announced the discovery of a specific "God spot" in the brain when scientists found that areas of the frontal lobe become active when individuals think of God. Yet later brain imaging research showed that religious experiences activate a wide variety of brain areas, not just one (Beauregard & Paquette, 2006). As Uttal reminds us, few if any complex psychological functions are likely to be confined to a single brain area.

Just as multiple brain regions contribute to each psychological function, individual brain areas contribute to multiple psychological functions. Broca's area, well known to play a role in speech, is also active when we notice that a musical note is off-key (Limb, 2006). There's enhanced activity in such emotional centers as the amygdala and orbitofrontal cortex when we listen to inspiring music, even though these regions aren't traditionally known as "musical areas" (Blood & Zatorre, 2001). The rule of thumb is that each brain region participates in many functions—some expected, some unexpected—leading to a distributed set of brain regions contributing to each function.

We also need to consider the temporal pattern of activity across cortical areas. Activity in different brain regions can be in step, that is, *synchronized,* or not. Cortical synchronization, which involves similar patterns of activity across multiple brain areas, is critical to cognition. We might think of synchronization as what singers do when they sing in unison. When one or two individuals sing badly, their off-key notes are cancelled out, and the ensemble typically sounds much better than the worst voices in the group. EEG studies show that synchronized, fast-paced activity, also called *gamma frequency* activity, occurs during a variety of tasks, including perception, attention, and other higher cognitive functions (Axmacher et al., 2006; Kaiser & Lutzenberger, 2005). An eye-catching stimulus, such as an interesting picture, triggers gamma frequency activity in multiple brain areas simultaneously.

Regarding localization of function, there certainly are areas of functional specialization within the neocortex and hippocampus, but there's a great deal of distributed function too. The timing of activity is also critical. We can think of cortical areas as similar to people, each of whom has different friends he or she sees in different settings. Although there's a great deal of interaction among some people, there's also separation. Not everyone talks to everyone else, at least not at the same time.

WHICH SIDE OF OUR BRAIN DO WE USE?

Just as we can localize certain functions to specific parts of the brain, we can localize certain functions to our right or left hemispheres. Roger Sperry (1974) won the Nobel Prize for his studies revealing that the two cerebral hemispheres possess different functions, in particular different levels of language ability. These studies examined patients who underwent **split-brain surgery** because their doctors couldn't control their epilepsy with medication. In this rare operation, neurosurgeons separate a patient's cerebral hemispheres by severing the corpus callosum. Split-brain surgery typically offers marked relief from seizures, and patients behave normally under most conditions.

Nevertheless, carefully designed experiments have revealed unusual fragmenting of cognitive functions that we normally experience as fused into indivisible wholes. The two hemispheres of split-brain subjects have different abilities and even different "personalities" (Gazzaniga, 2000; Zaidel, 1994). Nonetheless, a split-brain subject usually experiences himself as a single, unified person.

Right and Left Hemispheres: Worlds Apart. Split-brain surgery showed that many cognitive functions rely on one cerebral hemisphere more than the other; scientists call this phenomenon **lateralization.** The left or the right hemisphere demonstrates specialization for various cognitive functions (see **Table 3.3**). Many of the lateralized functions concern specific language and verbal skills.

factoid

Buddhist monks (see photo above) who've been meditating for many years show increased amounts of synchronized high-amplitude gamma activity while they engage in their mental practice (Lutz et al., 2004).

split-brain surgery
procedure that involves severing the corpus callosum to reduce the spread of epileptic seizures

lateralization
cognitive function that relies more on one side of the brain than the other

A classic way to study split-brain subjects is for researchers to present stimuli, such as written words, to either their right or left *visual field*. To understand why researchers do that, we need to know where visual information goes in the brain. In a normal brain, most visual information from either the left or right visual field ends up on the opposite side of the visual cortex. There's also crossing over for motor control. The left hemisphere controls the right hand and the right hemisphere controls the left hand.

The corpus callosum shares information between the two halves of the cerebral cortex. As a result, cutting the corpus callosum prevents most visual information in each visual field from reaching the visual cortex on the opposite side. When the corpus callosum is cut, there's a striking decoupling of functions. In one extreme case, a split-brain subject complained that his left hand wouldn't cooperate with his right hand. His left hand misbehaved frequently; it turned off TV shows while he was in the middle of watching them and frequently struck at family members against his will (Joseph, 1988).

Split-brain subjects often experience difficulties integrating information presented to separate hemispheres, as when "hot" and "dog" are presented to different hemispheres (see **Figure 3.25**). Split-brain patients frequently find a way to rationalize or make sense of their puzzling behaviors. In one experiment, researchers flashed a chicken claw to a split-brain patient's left hemisphere and a snow scene to his right hemisphere. When asked to match what he saw with a set of choices, he pointed to a shovel with his left hand (controlled by his right hemisphere) and a chicken with his right hand (controlled by his left hemisphere). When asked to explain these actions, he said, "I saw a claw and I picked the chicken, and you have to clean out the chicken shed with a shovel." In this case, the patient's left hemisphere, which as we learned in Chapter 1 tries its best to make sense of the world, concocted a plausible-sounding explanation to account for why he pointed to both a shovel and a chicken.

Consciousness and Self-Awareness. The split-brain study also provides a unique framework for understanding human self-awareness. One component of self-awareness is the ability to distinguish ourselves from others. We make this distinction whenever we recognize our face as our own, such as in the mirror when we comb our hair. In a study entitled "Mike or Me," a 48-year-old split-brain subject identified by his initials, J.W., viewed a series of eleven faces ranging from a 100 percent likeness of himself to a 0 percent likeness (Turk et al., 2002). The 100 percent likeness was a photograph of J.W. The 0 percent non-self image was a photograph of the researcher who'd been testing J.W. for many years. These two photographs were combined by 10 percent increments using morphing software to provide an additional nine intermediate images. During the study, researchers presented one of the eleven images to either J.W.'s right or left visual field and asked him whether the image was himself or a familiar other.

The results showed a hemispheric difference in response. Faces that reached J.W.'s right hemisphere produced responses biased toward recognizing morphed faces as non-self, and faces that reached his left hemisphere produced responses biased toward identifying morphed faces as his own. So when it comes to recognizing the self, the left hemisphere seems to have an edge over its right-sided counterpart.

Researchers from Eran Zaidel's laboratory obtained a slightly different result: They found that both hemispheres were equally good at self-recognition, but that only the right hemisphere could detect familiar people (Uddin, Rayman, & Zaidel, 2005). These studies each examined only one split-brain subject, which may have contributed to the subtle differences obtained.

We should guard against placing too much emphasis on lateralization of function and taking it to an extreme. Remarkably, it's possible to live with only half of a brain, that is, only one hemisphere. Indeed, a number of people have survived operations to

Table 3.3 Lateralized Functions.

Left Hemisphere	Right Hemisphere
Fine-tuned language skills • Speech comprehension • Speech production • Phonology • Syntax • Reading • Writing	**Coarse language skills** • Simple speech • Simple writing • Tone of voice
Actions • Making facial expressions • Motion detection	**Visuospatial skills** • Perceptual grouping • Face perception

(*Source:* Adapted from Gazzaniga, 2000)

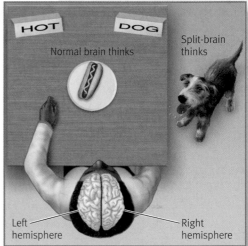

Figure 3.25 Split-Brain Subject. The seated person is looking at the two words "HOT" and "DOG" presented in the left and right visual fields. A normal brain puts the two words together and thinks "hotdog," like the one on the table. The split-brain thinks "a hot dog," like the one on the side.

remove one hemisphere to spare the brain from serious disease. The outlook for such individuals is best when surgeons perform the operation in childhood, which gives the remaining hemisphere a better chance to assume the functions of the missing hemisphere (Kenneally, 2006).

Psycho*Mythology*
Left-Brained versus Right-Brained Persons

Despite the great scientific contribution of split-brain studies, the popular notion that normal people are either "left-brained" or "right-brained" is a myth. According to this myth, left-brained people are scholarly, logical, and analytical, and right-brained people are artistic, creative, and emotional. One Internet blogger tried to explain the differences between people's political beliefs in terms of the left–right brain distinction; conservatives, he claimed, tend to be left-brained and liberals right-brained (Block, 2006). Yet these claims are vast oversimplifications (Hines, 1987). After reviewing numerous studies, Michael Corballis (1999) concluded that we use both sides of our brains in a complementary way. Furthermore, the corpus callosum and other interconnections ensure that both hemispheres are in constant communication. If the left-brained versus right-brained dichotomy were accurate, then people who were artistic would be unlikely to be verbally gifted. In reality, there are scores of multitalented people: Consider actors who are also screenwriters.

"Roger doesn't use the left side of his brain <u>or</u> the right side. He just uses the middle."

(© ScienceCartoonsPlus.com)

We can trace the myth of exaggerated left-brain versus right-brain differences to misinterpretations of what scientists reported. Self-help books incorporating the topic have flourished. Robert E. Ornstein was among those to promote the idea of using different ways to tap into our creative right brains versus our intellectual left brains in his 1997 book *The Right Mind: Making Sense of the Hemispheres.* Right brain–oriented educational programs for children sprang up that deemphasized getting the correct answers on tests in favor of developing creative ability. Such programs as the "Applied Creative Thinking Workshop" trained business managers to use their right brains (Herrmann, 1996). For a mere $195, "whole brain learning" supposedly expanded the mind in new ways using "megasubliminal messages," heard only by the left or the right brain (Corballis, 1999). Although there's nothing wrong with trying to be more creative by using our minds in different ways, using both hemispheres in tandem works far better.

The idea of using left-brain, right-brain differences to treat mood disorders or anger

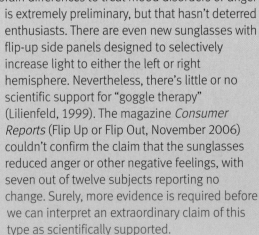

Left-side, right-side flip-up sunglasses designed to improve mental state.

is extremely preliminary, but that hasn't deterred enthusiasts. There are even new sunglasses with flip-up side panels designed to selectively increase light to either the left or right hemisphere. Nevertheless, there's little or no scientific support for "goggle therapy" (Lilienfeld, 1999). The magazine *Consumer Reports* (Flip Up or Flip Out, November 2006) couldn't confirm the claim that the sunglasses reduced anger or other negative feelings, with seven out of twelve subjects reporting no change. Surely, more evidence is required before we can interpret an extraordinary claim of this type as scientifically supported.

Extraordinary Claims

Nature and Nurture: Did Your Genes—Or Parents—Make You Do It?

By this point in the chapter, we've learned a fair amount about the brain and nervous system and how they contribute to behavior. Now we're ready to tackle an equally complex set of questions. How much does what we inherit from our parents—as opposed to the events in our lives—influence our behavior and mental activities?

HOW WE CAME TO BE WHO WE ARE

As little as 150 years ago, even the smartest of scientists knew almost nothing about how we humans came to be. Yet at the turn of the twenty-first century, the average educated person knows more about the origins of human life and the human brain than did Charles Darwin. Today, we're remarkably fortunate to be armed with scientific principles concerning heredity, adaptation, and evolution that enable us to understand the origins of our psychological characteristics.

The Biological Material of Heredity. In 1866 Gregor Mendel published his classic treatise on inheritance based on his research on pea plants. We now know that humans have 46 **chromosomes** (see **Figure 3.26**). Chromosomes are the slender threads inside the cell's nucleus that carry *genes:* genetic material. **Genes** are made of deoxyribonucleic acid (DNA), the material that stores everything cells need to replicate (reproduce) themselves (see **Figure 3.27** on page 138). DNA is structured as a double helix, which unravels to allow messenger ribonucleic acid (mRNA) to make a reverse template. Next, mRNA leaves the cell's nucleus and provides a sequence template for synthesizing proteins needed by the cell.

The genome is a full set of chromosomes and the heritable traits associated with them. The *Human Genome Project,* which characterized all the human genes, was completed in 2001. We're fortunate to live in an age when we know so much about genes, because this information can help us treat and prevent diseases.

Genotype versus Phenotype. People's genetic makeup, or the set of genes transmitted from the parents to offspring, is their **genotype.** Their **phenotype** is their set of observable traits. We can't tell people's genotypes from their phenotypes in part because some genes are **dominant,** meaning they mask other genes' effects, or **recessive,** meaning they're expressed only in the absence of a dominant gene.

Eye color and some racial characteristics are either recessive or dominant. Many physical features of the African American race, for example, are dominant. Two forms of melanin, a darker and lighter type, determine skin color, and African Americans possess dominant genes resulting in darker skin (Bonilla et al., 2005). Because highly pigmented skin is dominant over fairer skin (as dark eyes and dark hair are dominant over lighter

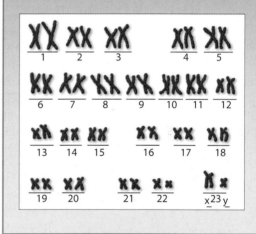

Figure 3.26 Human Chromosomes. Humans have 46 chromosomes. Males have an XY pair and females have an XX pair. The other 22 pairs of chromosomes aren't sex-linked.

chromosomes
slender threads inside a cell's nucleus that carry genes

genes
genetic material, composed of deoxyribonucleic acid (DNA)

genotype
our genetic make-up

phenotype
our observable traits

dominant genes
genes that mask other genes' effects

recessive genes
genes that are expressed only in the absence of a dominant gene

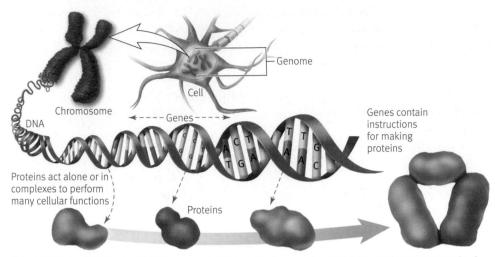

Figure 3.27 Genetic Expression. The nucleus of the neuron houses chromosomes, which contain strands of DNA. They store codes for constructing proteins needed by the cell.

eyes and hair), many African Americans, even those who've inherited considerable numbers of European Caucasian genes, have darker pigmented skin. At least some Caucasian ancestry among African Americans is estimated to be as high as 20%–25% in certain regions of the United States (Chakraborty et al., 1992; Para et al., 1998). As a result, some children of two African American parents are appreciably lighter skinned than their parents because they've inherited recessive genes from both parents.

Although different races possess varying amounts of some genes that influence susceptibility to certain diseases (Hughes et al., 2006), most genes vary so much from one individual to another of the same race that differences *among* races typically pale by comparison to differences *within* each race (see also Chapter 9). But there are exceptions. Sickle cell anemia is a genetic disorder that preferentially afflicts African Americans (Bonds, 2005). In this disorder, red blood cells have an abnormal shape that interferes with their normal function, predisposing people to pain, stroke, and increased infection, among other complications.

Behavioral Adaptation. Charles Darwin's classic book *On the Origin of Species* (1859) introduced the concept of **natural selection** and the broad strokes of his theory of evolution. Darwin hypothesized that populations of organisms, rather than individuals, change by selective breeding with other organisms possessing some apparent advantage. According to these principles, organisms that possess *adaptations* that make them better suited to their environments survive and reproduce at a higher rate than other organisms. Physical adaptations include changes that enable animals to better manipulate their environments. An opposable thumb (one that can be moved away from the other fingers), for example, greatly improved our hand function.

Some adaptations are behavioral. According to most evolutionary psychologists (see Prologue), aggressive behavior is an adaptation because it enables organisms to obtain more resources. (Too much aggression, of course, is usually maladaptive, meaning it often doesn't increase organisms' chances of survival or reproduction.) Organisms with many successful adaptations have high levels of **fitness,** meaning that they have a good chance of getting their genes into later generations.

Brain Evolution. The relationship between the human nervous system and behavior has been finely tuned over millions of years of evolution (Cartwright, 2000). Brain regions with complicated functions, such as the neocortex, have evolved the most (Karlen & Krubitzer, 2006). As a result, our behavioral repertoires are more complex and flexible than those of any other animal, allowing us to respond in many more ways to a given situation.

natural selection
principle that organisms that possess adaptations survive and reproduce at a higher rate than other organisms

fitness
organisms' capacity to pass on their genes

What makes us so distinctive in the animal kingdom? Fossil and genetic evidence suggests that somewhere between 6 and 7 million years ago, humans and apes split off from a shared ancestor. After that critical fork in the evolutionary road, we went our separate ways. The human line eventually resulted in our species, *Homo sapiens*, whereas the ape line resulted in chimpanzees, gorillas, and orangutans (the "great apes"). We often fail to appreciate that *Homo sapiens*—modern humans—have been around for only about 1 percent of the total time period of the human race (Calvin, 2004). We're a mere flash in the pan of human history.

Around the time of our divergence from apes, our brains weren't that much larger than theirs. Then, around 3 to 4 million years ago, something dramatic happened, although we don't why. We do know that within a span of only a few million years—a mere blink of an eye in the earth's 4.5 billion-year history—one tiny area of the human genome responsible for protein synthesis in the cerebral cortex changed about 70 times more rapidly than other areas (Pollard et al., 2006). The human brain mushroomed in size, more than tripling from less than 400 grams—a bit less than a pound—to its present hefty weight of 1,300 grams—about 3 pounds (Holloway, 1983). The brains of modern great apes weigh between 300 and 500 grams, even though their overall body size doesn't differ that much from humans' (Bradbury, 2005).

Relative to our body size, we're proportionally the biggest brained animals (we need to correct for body size, because large animals, like elephants, have huge brains in part because their bodies are also huge). Second in line are dolphins (Marino, McShea, & Uhen, 2004), followed by chimpanzees and other great apes. Research suggests that across species, relative brain size—brain size corrected for body size—is associated with behaviors we typically regard as intelligent (Jerison, 1983). For example, big-brained animals tend to have especially large and complex social networks (Dunbar, 2003; see Chapter 13).

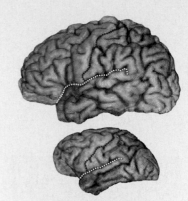

The brain of a human (*above*) and that of a chimpanzee. The human brain is about three times larger, even though humans are only about two times as large overall.

The distinction of the largest brain in the animal kingdom—between 15 and 20 pounds—goes to the sperm whale. Still, this fact doesn't make the sperm whale the "brainiest" creature on the planet, because we must correct for its huge body size when determining its relative brain size.

BEHAVIORAL GENETICS: HOW WE STUDY HERITABILITY

Scientists use *behavioral genetics* to examine the roles of nature and nurture in the origins of traits, such as intelligence (see Chapter 9). In reality, behavioral genetic designs are misnamed, because they permit us to look at the roles of both genetic *and* environmental influences on behavior (Waldman, 2006).

Behavioral genetic designs also allow us to estimate the **heritability** of traits and diseases. By heritability, we mean the extent to which genes contribute to differences in a trait *among individuals*. Typically, we express heritability as a percentage of 100. So, if we say that the heritability of a trait is 60 percent, we mean that more than half of the differences *among individuals* in their levels of that trait are due to differences in their genes. By definition, the other 40 percent is due to differences in their environments. Some traits, like height, are highly heritable; the heritability of height in adults is between 70 and 80 percent (Silventoinen et al., 2003). In contrast, other traits, like the accent in speech, are due almost entirely to environment; the heritability of accent is essentially 0. That's because our accents are almost entirely a product of the dialect spoken by our parents or in the community in which we're raised.

Three Major Misconceptions about Heritability. Heritability isn't as simple a concept as it seems, and it confuses even some psychologists. So before discussing how psychologists use heritability in different kinds of experiments, we'll first address three widespread misunderstandings about it.

The first misconception is that heritability applies to a single individual rather than to differences among individuals. Heritability applies only to groups of people. If someone asks you, "What's the heritability of your IQ?" you should promptly hand him a copy of this chapter. Heritability tells us about the causes of differences among people, not within a person.

heritability
percentage of the variability in a trait across individuals that is due to genes

A second misconception is that heritability tells us whether a trait can be changed. Many laypeople believe that if a trait is highly heritable, then by definition we can't change it. Yet, logically speaking, heritability says little or nothing about how malleable (alterable) a trait is. In fact, a trait can in principle have a heritability of 100 percent, and still be extremely malleable. Here's how.

Imagine 10 plants that differ markedly in height, with some of them only 2 or 3 inches tall and others 5 or 6 inches tall. Imagine they're only a few days old, and that since their germination we've exposed them to *exactly equal* environmental conditions: the same amount of water, and identical soil and lighting conditions. What's the heritability of height in this group of plants? It's 100 percent: The causes of differences in their heights *must be* completely genetic, because we've kept all environmental influences constant.

Now let's find out why 100 percent heritability doesn't mean we can't change a characteristic. Imagine that we suddenly decide to stop watering these plants and providing them with light. We don't need a Ph.D. in botany to figure out what will happen next. All of the plants will soon die, and their heights will all become 0 inches. So, to recap: The heritability of height in these plants was 100 percent, yet we can easily change their heights by changing their environments.

To take an example more relevant to humans, consider *phenylketonuria*, or PKU. PKU is a rare genetic disorder marked by a mutation that prevents its sufferers from metabolizing (breaking down) an amino acid called phenylalanine. As a consequence of this mutation, phenylalanine builds up in the brain, producing severe mental retardation. Even though PKU is almost entirely genetic, there's good news. We can prevent most of the negative mental effects of PKU by placing PKU children on a low phenylalanine diet (which includes avoiding milk, eggs, NutraSweet, and other selected foods). So even though the heritability of PKU is virtually 100 percent, we can alter its effects substantially by a simple environmental manipulation: diet (McLafferty, 2006; Sternberg, Grigorenko, & Kidd, 2005).

A third misconception is that heritability is a fixed number. Actually, heritability can differ dramatically across different time periods and populations. Remember that heritability is the extent to which differences among people in a trait are due to genetic influences. So if we reduce the range of environmental influences on a trait within a population, heritability will increase, because more of the differences in that trait will be due to genetic factors. Conversely, if we increase the range of environmental influences on a trait within a population, heritability will go down, because fewer of the differences in that trait will be due to genetic factors.

Behavioral Genetic Designs. Scientists estimate heritability by means of one of three behavioral genetic designs: *family studies, twin studies,* and *adoption studies.* In such studies, scientists track the presence or absence of a trait among different relatives. These studies help them determine how much both genes and environment contribute to the causes of that trait.

Family Studies. In a **family study,** researchers examine the extent to which a trait "runs" or goes together in intact families, namely, those in which all family members are raised in the same home. In these studies, it's crucial to consider a crucial limitation: Relatives share a similar environment as well as similar genetic material. As a consequence, family studies don't allow us to disentangle the effects of nature from nurture. Investigators have therefore turned to more informative research designs to separate these influences.

Twin Studies. To understand **twin studies,** we first need to say a bit about the birds and the bees. Two different things can happen when a sperm fertilizes an egg. First, a single sperm may fertilize a single egg, producing a *zygote,* or fertilized egg (see Chapter 10). For reasons that scientists still don't fully understand, that zygote occasionally (in about 1 in

Even though differences in height among plants may be largely heritable, watering these plants—an environmental manipulation—can result in substantial increases in their height. Bottom line: High heritability doesn't imply lack of malleability (an inability to change).

factoid
If you have a diet soda can handy that says "sweetened with NutraSweet®," check the back label. You'll notice the warning "PHENYLKETONURICS: CONTAINS PHENYLALANINE." The artificial sweetener NutraSweet® contains phenylalanine, which people with PKU must be careful to avoid.

Ruling Out Rival Hypotheses

family studies
analyses of how traits run in families
twin studies
analyses of how traits differ in identical versus fraternal twins

250 births) splits into two, yielding two identical genetic copies. Researchers refer to these identical twins as *monozygotic* (MZ), because they originate from one zygote. Identical twins are essentially genetic clones of each other, because they share 100 percent of their genes. In other cases, two different sperm may fertilize two different eggs, resulting in two zygotes. These twins are *dizygotic* (DZ), or, more loosely, fraternal. In contrast to identical twins, fraternal twins share only 50 percent of their genes on average and are no more alike genetically than ordinary singlet brothers or sisters. Women who take fertility pills increase their odds of having fraternal twins (and triplets, quadruplets, and so on), but not identical twins, because they're increasing the number of eggs they produce but not affecting whether a single egg will split.

The logic of *twin studies* rests on the fact that identical twins are more similar genetically than are fraternal twins. Consequently, if identical twins are more alike on a psychological characteristic, such as intelligence or extraversion, than are fraternal twins, we can infer that this characteristic is genetically influenced. Nevertheless, twin studies hinge on the "equal environments assumption"—the assumption that the environmental influences on the characteristic we're studying are the same in identical and fraternal twins. If this assumption is violated, we can't be sure that the reason identical twins are more similar in a characteristic than fraternal twins is genetic rather than environmental. Fortunately, most research upholds the equal environments assumption (Kendler et al., 1993), suggesting that we can usually rely on twin studies to draw conclusions about genetic and environmental influences.

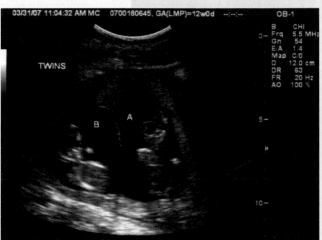

Identical twin fetuses developing in utero. Behavior geneticists compare identical with fraternal twins to estimate genetic and environmental influences on psychological traits.

Adoption Studies. As we've noted, studies of intact family members are limited because they can't disentangle genetic from environmental influences. To address this shortcoming, psychologists have turned to **adoption studies,** which examine the extent to which children adopted into new homes resemble their adoptive as opposed to biological parents. Children adopted into other homes share genes with their biological relatives, but not environment. As a consequence, if adopted children resemble their biological parents on a psychological characteristic, we can typically assume that it's genetically influenced.

One potential confound in adoption studies is *selective placement:* adoption agencies frequently place children in homes similar to those of their biological parents (DeFries & Plomin, 1978). This confound can lead investigators to mistakenly interpret the similarity between adoptive children and their biological parents as a genetic effect. In adoption studies of IQ (see Chapter 9), researchers try to control for selective placement by correcting statistically for the correlation in IQ between biological and adoptive parents.

Genetic Markers of Disease. In addition to PKU, early-onset forms of Alzheimer's disease (Schellenberg, 2006), Huntington's chorea (Frohman & Martin, 1987), and a host of other neurological disorders are strongly genetically influenced. In some cases, researchers can identify the molecular "signature" of these conditions using genetic testing. A *genetic marker* is a known DNA sequence that enables us to forecast the expression of an illness that's at least partly heritable. An example is a mutation in a gene that results in that person making a defective protein. The marker could be the gene for the defective protein or a gene nearby that's inherited along with the mutated gene. Researchers examine whether a genetic marker is associated with a disease by comparing the probabilities that a genetic marker and a phenotype are linked with the probabilities that they aren't.

Sometimes genetic testing enables patients to take health precautions to avoid or lessen the impact of an illness. For other genetic diseases, there's little or nothing we can do. Huntington's chorea is an inherited and untreatable neurological disorder that causes neurons to waste away. Its symptoms include uncontrolled movements, emotional outbursts, and cognitive difficulties. When people have immediate family members with Huntington's chorea, they may choose to undergo genetic screening to learn if they too carry the gene for the illness. Having a single copy of the gene means the person will get

adoption studies
analyses of how traits vary in individuals raised apart from their biological relatives

Folk singer Woody Guthrie (*second from left*), who wrote "This Land Is Your Land," among other classics, receiving an award. His son Arlo, who later became a famous folk singer in his own right, looks on. Woody Guthrie died of Huntington's chorea in 1967; although Arlo, now in his 60s, has a 50 percent chance of developing the disease himself (because it's caused by a dominant gene), he appears to have escaped its clutches.

the disorder sooner or later, because the gene is dominant. Although there's no way to prevent Huntington's chorea, people who know they'll develop the disease sometimes elect to adopt children or use in vitro fertilization methods (after embryos have been prescreened for an absence of the defective gene) so that they can avoid passing the disease on to their children.

NEURAL PLASTICITY: HOW AND WHEN THE BRAIN CHANGES

We'll conclude our examination of nature and nurture by looking at the ability of the nervous system to change. Nature, or our genetic makeup, determines what kind of change is possible and when it will occur during the trajectory that our brain follows from birth to old age. Nurture, consisting of learning, injuries, and illnesses, affects our genetically influenced course. Scientists use the term **plasticity** to describe the nervous system's ability to change. We talk about brain circuits being "hardwired" when they don't change very much, if at all. The nervous system is constantly changing, by leaps and bounds, as in early development, or subtly, as with learning. Unfortunately, the CNS often doesn't change enough following injury, which can lead to permanent paralysis and disability. Researchers are working hard to find ways of getting around the CNS's resistance to healing.

Neural Plasticity during Development and Experience. The nervous system is most capable of changing during early development, the times before birth and after birth until maturation is complete. By 5 weeks after conception, we've developed a rudimentary forebrain, midbrain, and hindbrain (see **Figure 3.28**), but our brains don't mature fully until late adolescence or early adulthood. This means the period of heightened plasticity in the human brain is lengthy. This is particularly true of cortical brain regions. The cerebral cortex takes a long time to mature and different cortical areas reach maturity at different times. Sensory and motor cortexes are the first to mature, the prefrontal association cortex the last (Casey et al., 2005).

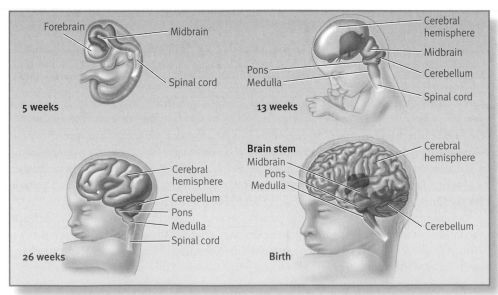

plasticity
ability of the nervous system to change

Figure 3.28 Early Brain Development. The developing nervous system from embryonic week 5 to birth. (*Source:* Adapted from Marieb, 2007)

The first step in neural development is an initial burst of cell division, followed by cell migration and then by the establishment of connections among neurons. The creation and subsequent fine-tuning of connections is perhaps the most complex of the earlier mentioned steps, encompassing these processes:

(1) growth of dendrites and axons;

(2) *synaptogenesis,* or the formation of new synapses;

(3) *pruning,* consisting of the death of certain neurons and the retraction of axons that make connections that aren't useful; and

(4) myelination, or the insulation of axons with a myelin sheath.

In pruning, as many as 70 percent of neurons die off. This process streamlines neural organization, enhancing communication among brain structures (Oppenheim, 1991). One theory of infantile autism (see Chapter 15) suggests that this disorder is caused by inadequate pruning (Hill & Frith, 2003), which may explain why autistic individuals tend to have unusually large brains (Herbert, 2005).

Late maturation of certain cortical areas has fueled interest in the brains of teenagers and how brain maturation status affects their decision making. By age 12, the human brain is adult in size and weight. Nonetheless, adolescent brain activity patterns—such as those shown by PET and fMRI—are still far different from those of adults (see Chapter 10).

Neural Plasticity Related to Learning. Our brains change when we learn; that's no surprise. The simplest kind of change is for synapses to just perform better, that is, to show stronger and more prolonged excitatory responses. Researchers call this phenomenon potentiation, and when it's enduring, *long-term potentiation* (LTP) (see Chapter 7). Many scientists believe that structural plasticity, in the form of altered neuronal shape, is also critical for learning and supports LTP. A number of investigators have demonstrated learning-related structural changes, both in axons and in dendrites. In one study, researchers trained rats to swim to a platform hidden in a tub of milky water. By the time the rats became adept at finding their way to the platform, axons entering a part of the rats' hippocampi had expanded (Holahan et al., 2006). Exposure to enriched environments also results in structural enhancements to dendrites (see **Figure 3.29**). Two studies compared rats exposed to an enriched environment—such as large cages with multiple animals, toys, and running wheels—with rats exposed to a standard environment of a cage with only two animals and no objects (Freire & Cheng, 2004; Leggio et al., 2005). Enriched environments led to more elaborate dendrites with more branches.

Specific proteins determine the shape of neurons, dendrites, and axons; these proteins also enable neurotransmitters to act. When animals are trained to learn certain associations, there's a reorganization of the major proteins in dendrites, particularly those that participate in carrying proteins to synapses enabling neurotransmitters to act (Woolf, 2006). Experimenters have demonstrated this phenomenon in fear-conditioned rats by examining their brains for the chemical breakdown of a protein called MAP2. This protein is broken down in the brain region related specifically to the type of training (Woolf, 1998). Fear conditioning to a place, for example, corresponds to this protein's breakdown in the hippocampus. Fear conditioning to a tone corresponds to this protein's breakdown in the part of the cortex receiving auditory signals. Both types of conditioning correspond to this protein's being altered in the amygdala, the brain's fear center. Studies using genetically altered mice have additionally shown that MAP2 is essential to fear conditioning (Khuchua et al., 2003). Fear learning is impaired when this protein is genetically altered. In yet another study, rats isolated from each other ended up with MAP2 levels lower than rats raised together (Bianchi et al., 2006). The rats raised in social isolation also showed significant memory deficits.

LTP also appears to increase levels of MAP2 and other proteins (Roberts et al., 1998). This result suggests that such potentiation leads to structural rebuilding within neurons.

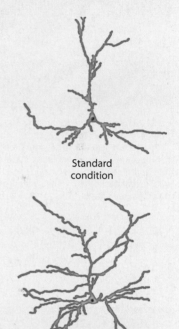

Standard condition

Enriched condition

Figure 3.29 Neurons in Standard and Enriched Conditions. Neurons from rats reared in standard (*top*) or enriched (*bottom*) conditions. Note the increase in branching and extension of dendrites in the enriched condition. (*Source:* Giuseppa Leggio et al., 2005)

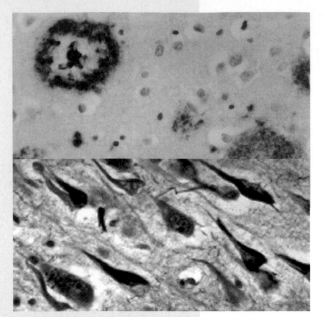

Senile plaques and neurofibrillary tangles in a brain of a patient with Alzheimer's disease. This degeneration in hippocampus and association cortex may contribute to the memory loss and intellectual decline associated with the disorder (see Chapter 7).

In other words, it supports a scenario of the laying down of a new structure following breakdown of the old one.

Neural Plasticity Following Injury and Degeneration. In adults, plasticity within the CNS decreases markedly, occurring only on a small scale, such as with learning. Peripheral nerves are often good at regenerating after injury, but this isn't the case for axons in the CNS of mammals. The human CNS exhibits only a limited degree of regeneration following injury. Spinal cord and head injuries can occur after accidents, such as falls or automobile and motorcycle crashes. Every 15 seconds someone suffers a traumatic brain injury in the United States, and about half of those injuries result in emergency room admissions (Thurman, Alverson, Dunn, Guerrero, & Sniezek, 1999).

Not surprisingly, scientists are focused on finding ways to get around the barriers that prevent brain and spinal cord axons from growing back following injury (Maier & Schwab, 2006). Some patients and experimental animals recover sensory and motor function following certain treatments, but the degree of recovery varies greatly (Bradbury & McMahon, 2006; Jones et al., 2001). Neurons respond to chemicals called *neurotrophic factors* that aid their survival and stimulate growth ("trophic" means "growth"). Just the right amount and right kind of neurotrophic factor can coax an axon into growing. A growing axon can actually follow the trail of a neurotrophic factor, much as a hunting dog tracks a scent. Another way researchers get axons to grow is by using "glial cell bridges"—trails of glial cells that make a path for axon growth. Glial cell bridges provide structural support to guide growing axons and release neurotrophic factors along the way. Other conditions, such as a positive attitude on the part of patients, also enhance nerve regeneration following spinal cord injury (Bradbury & McMahon, 2006). Although scientists don't know the reasons for this effect, chemical factors may play a role, particularly those that reduce the pain of injury. Pain reduction may increase motion and thereby decrease nerve and muscle degeneration that result from a lack of use.

Because degenerative disorders, such as Alzheimer's disease and Parkinson's disease, pose enormous challenges to society, scientists are actively investigating ways of preventing damage or enabling the CNS to heal itself. Deposits, known as *senile plaques* and *neurofibrillary tangles*, accumulate in the hippocampus, amygdala, and association cortex of Alzheimer's disease patients (see Chapter 7). Many scientists agree that by better understanding neural plasticity we may someday be able to partly reverse neural degeneration or at least prevent it from occurring.

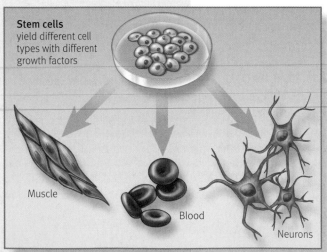

Stem cells yield different cell types with different growth factors

Muscle

Blood

Neurons

Figure 3.30 Stem Cells and Growth Factors. Stem cells have the capacity to become many different cell types depending on the growth factors to which they're exposed.

stem cells
unspecialized cells that retain the ability to become a wide variety of specialized cells

Stem Cells. You've probably heard or read about research on **stem cells** in the news. The reason they've garnered so much attention is that these cells have the potential to become a wide variety of specialized cells (see **Figure 3.30**). This is akin to being a first- or second-year undergraduate who's yet to declare a major: he or she might still become nearly anything. Once the cell makes certain choices, however, the cell type becomes more and more permanently cast. Stem cells offer at least three novel ways of treating neurodegenerative disease (Fukuda & Takahashi, 2005; Miller, 2006; Muller, Snyder, & Loring, 2006). First, researchers can implant stem cells directly into the host's nervous system and induce them to grow and replace damaged cells. Second, researchers can genetically engineer stem cells so that the cells can administer *gene therapy;* that is, provide the patient with replacement genes. Third, stem cells can allow scientists to acquire a better understanding of how neurons age. In addition to neurodegenerative disorders, cancer, diabetes, and heart disease may be aided by stem cell research.

Yet stem cell research is exceedingly controversial for ethical reasons. Its advocates point to its potential for treating serious diseases, but its opponents point out that such research requires investigators to destroy lab-created balls of cells that are four or five days old (which at that stage are smaller than the period at the end of this sentence). For stem cell research opponents, these cells are an early form of human life. As we learned in Chapter 1, certain profoundly important questions lie outside the boundaries of science: Science deals only with testable claims within the realm of the natural world (Gould, 1997). The question of whether stem cell research may one day cure diseases falls within the scope of science, but the question of whether such research is ethical doesn't. Nor, in all likelihood, can science ever resolve definitively the question of when human life begins. As a consequence, people will continue to disagree on whether stem cell research should be performed.

Neurogenesis: Neurons Giving Birth to New Neurons. There's a final way that researchers may be able to get around the problems associated with lack of regeneration following injury and with neural degeneration. **Neurogenesis** is the creation of new neurons in the adult brain. Less than 20 years ago, scientists believed that we're born with all the neurons we'll ever have. Then Fred Gage (ironically, a descendant of Phineas Gage), Elizabeth Gould, and their colleagues discovered that neurogenesis occurs in some brain areas (Gage, 2002; Gould & Gross, 2002). Scientists first observed neurogenesis in the hippocampus and later in the cerebral cortex.

Neurogenesis is exciting because it opens up new possibilities. Why does neurogenesis occur in adults? One possibility is that it plays a role in learning (Aimone et al., 2006; Leuner et al., 2006). Another role may be recovery following brain injury. By manipulating neurogenesis, scientists may be able to induce the adult nervous system to heal itself (Kozorovitskiy & Gould, 2003; Lie et al., 2004).

Today we know more about the brain than ever before. We're on firm ground when it comes to understanding brain regions and their functions, as well as the electrical and chemical processes by which neurons communicate. We've yet to fully understand how to heal the nervous system, but the rapid pace of research in this critical area gives us considerable hope.

ASSESS YOUR KNOWLEDGE: FACT OR FICTION?

(1) Brain evolution is responsible for humans' advanced abilities. (True/False)

(2) Heritability values can't change over time. (True/False)

(3) Identical twins have similar phenotypes (observable traits), but may have different genotypes (sets of genes). (True/False)

(4) Early development is a time of heightened neural plasticity. (True/False)

(5) Adult brains can create new cells. (True/False)

(6) Neurogenesis is the same thing as pruning. (True/False)

Answers: (1) T (p. 138); (2) F (p. 140); (3) F (p. 141); (4) T (p. 142); (5) T (p. 144); (6) F (p. 145)

neurogenesis
creation of new neurons in adult brain

Think again...

The Brain and Behavior: Networked with the Somatic Nervous System (pp. 108–118)

STUDY the Learning Objectives

▶ Identify the parts of the nervous system that play a role in sensation and perception
- The cerebral cortex consists of the frontal, parietal, temporal, and occipital lobes. Cortex involved with vision lies in the occipital lobe, cortex involved with hearing in the temporal lobe, and cortex involved with touch in the parietal lobe. Association areas throughout the cortex analyze and reanalyze sensory inputs to build up our perceptions.

▶ Track the parts of the nervous system that play a role in motor functions
- The motor cortex in the frontal lobe, the basal ganglia, and the spinal cord work together with the somatic nervous system to bring about movement and action. Our decision to choose a particular action relies on the brain, whereas only the spinal cord is necessary to accomplish certain reflexes. The somatic nervous system has a sensory as well as a motor component, which enables touch and feedback from the muscles to guide our actions.

▶ Clarify the relationship between the nervous system and the body
- Interactions between the nervous system and body make psychological functions possible. The nervous system controls the body. The body in turn provides feedback to the nervous system.

DO YOU KNOW THESE TERMS?

- ❑ **neurons** (p. 108)
- ❑ **central nervous system (CNS)** (p. 109)
- ❑ **peripheral nervous system (PNS)** (p. 109)
- ❑ **forebrain** (p. 109)
- ❑ **cerebral cortex** (p. 109)
- ❑ **cerebral hemispheres** (p. 110)
- ❑ **corpus callosum** (p. 110)
- ❑ **frontal lobe** (p. 110)
- ❑ **motor cortex** (p. 110)
- ❑ **prefrontal cortex** (p. 110)
- ❑ **Broca's area** (p. 110)
- ❑ **aphasia** (p. 110)
- ❑ **parietal lobe** (p. 111)
- ❑ **temporal lobe** (p. 112)
- ❑ **Wernicke's area** (p. 112)
- ❑ **occipital lobe** (p. 113)
- ❑ **sensory cortex** (p. 113)

- ❑ **association cortex** (p. 113)
- ❑ **basal ganglia** (p. 113)
- ❑ **dopamine** (p. 113)
- ❑ **basal forebrain** (p. 114)
- ❑ **acetylcholine** (p. 114)
- ❑ **thalamus** (p. 114)
- ❑ **brain stem** (p. 114)
- ❑ **midbrain** (p. 114)
- ❑ **reticular activating system (RAS)** (p. 115)
- ❑ **hindbrain** (p. 115)
- ❑ **cerebellum** (p. 115)
- ❑ **pons** (p. 115)
- ❑ **medulla** (p. 115)
- ❑ **cerebral ventricles** (p. 115)
- ❑ **interneurons** (p. 116)
- ❑ **reflex** (p. 116)
- ❑ **synapse** (p. 116)
- ❑ **somatic nervous system** (p. 116)

Identify each component and describe its role within the human brain. (p. 109)

THINK about

what You would do . . .
The case of Terri Schiavo raised questions scientists can't fully resolve involving comparisons between a persistent vegetative state and brain death. What do you consider to be the true criterion for death? (p. 115)

SUCCEED with

mypsychlab
Physiological Bases of Behavioral Problems
How does your brain work? Explore the brain's components and each one's role in specific body functions. (p. 109)
EXPLORE

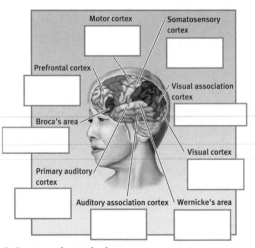

Fill in the function of each brain component identified in this figure. (p. 113)

Motor cortex, Somatosensory cortex, Prefrontal cortex, Visual association cortex, Broca's area, Visual cortex, Primary auditory cortex, Auditory association cortex, Wernicke's area

ASSESS your knowledge

1. The 100 billion nerve cells specialized for communication within the brain are called _____. (p. 108)

2. The brain and spinal cord combine to form the superhighway known as the _____. (p. 109)

3. Outside of the CNS, the _____ _____ system works to help us control behavior and express emotion. (p. 109)

4. Humans' advanced intellectual abilities can be attributed to the _____, the most highly developed area of the brain. (p. 109)

5. The brain component responsible for analyzing sensory information and our ability to think, talk, and reason is called the _____. (p. 109)

6. Broca's area, named after physician Paul Broca, plays a key role in _____ and is located in one region of the _____ _____. (p. 110)

7. Aphasia, a serious _____ deficit, is almost always the result of damage to the _____ cerebral hemisphere. (pp. 110–111)

8. The four lobes of the neocortex are the _____, _____, _____, and _____. (pp. 110–114)

9. Parkinson's disease is the result of damage to the _____ _____, which play a critical role in voluntary movement. (p. 113)

10. Our ability to execute the messages or commands of our central nervous system, through physical action, is dependent on the _____ _____ system. (p. 116)

If you did not receive an access code to MyPsychLab with this text and wish to purchase access online, please visit www.mypsychlab.com.

The Brain and Emotion: Networked with the Autonomic Nervous System (pp. 118–123)

Complete each box to describe the body's internal reaction during the fight-or-flight response. (p. 121)

Sympathetic Nervous System
(Active during fight or flight response)

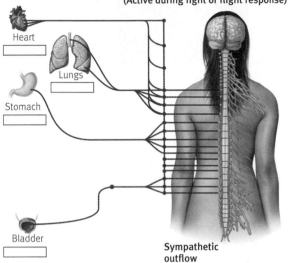

Heart

Lungs

Stomach

Bladder

Sympathetic outflow

THINK about

what You would do . . .
If you wanted to design a study of the role of hormones in interpersonal trust, which hormone would you be most interested in measuring? (p. 121)

my psych lab

SUCCEED with

The Endocrine System

Which organs and glands make up the body's endocrine system?
(pp. 120–123)

EXPLORE

ASSESS your knowledge

1. Considered the emotional center of the brain, the _____ system also plays a role in _____, _____, and _____. (p. 118)

2. The hypothalamus, amygdala, _____, and _____, are the four main components of the _____ system. (pp. 119–120)

3. In complex social situations—such as making introductions at a college or business reception—the _____ and _____ _____ contribute to our ability to act appropriately. (p. 119)

4. Damage to the hippocampus causes problems with (new/old) memories but not (new/old) memories. (p. 120)

5. Our ability to react physically to a perceived threat is dependent on the _____ division of the autonomic system. (p. 120)

6. Our ability to recover from an emotional crisis is dependent upon the _____ division of the autonomic system. (p. 120)

7. The body's "master gland" which, under the control of the hypothalamus, directs all other body glands is known as the _____. (p. 121)

8. During high-risk activities, such as mountain biking or sky diving, people can experience _____ surges from activation of the _____ system. (p. 122)

9. _____ and _____ are chemicals manufactured in the adrenal glands that help boost energy production in muscle cells. (p. 122)

10. Males and females (do/don't) manufacture both estrogen and testosterone. (p. 123)

STUDY the Learning Objectives

▶ Identify the parts of the brain that play a role in emotion
  • The limbic system includes the hypothalamus, amygdala, cingulate cortex, and hippocampus. The hypothalamus maintains constant internal states, the amygdala plays a key role in fear, the cingulate cortex is active during avoidance, and the hippocampus is especially known for its role in spatial memory. These structures additionally participate in other functions related to emotion, memory, and motivation.

▶ Clarify how the autonomic nervous system works in emergency and everyday situations
  • The autonomic nervous system consists of the parasympathetic and sympathetic divisions. Whereas the parasympathetic nervous system is active during rest and digestion, the sympathetic division propels the body into action during an emergency or crisis. Sympathetic arousal also occurs in response to everyday stress.

▶ Describe what hormones are and how they affect behavior
  • Hormones are chemicals released into the bloodstream that trigger specific effects in the body. Activation of the sympathetic nervous system triggers the release of adrenaline and cortisol by the adrenal glands, which energize our bodies. Growth hormone enables our bodies to grow. Sex hormones control sexual responses.

DO YOU KNOW THESE TERMS?

☐ **limbic system** (p. 118)

☐ **hypothalamus** (p. 119)

☐ **amygdala** (p. 119)

☐ **hippocampus** (p. 120)

☐ **autonomic nervous system** (p. 120)

☐ **sympathetic division** (p. 120)

☐ **parasympathetic division** (p. 120)

☐ **endocrine system** (p. 120)

☐ **hormones** (p. 120)

☐ **pituitary gland** (p. 121)

☐ **adrenal gland** (p. 122)

Nerve Cells: Communication Portals (pp. 124–129)

Label the image showing the process of action potential in a neuron. Include (a) neuron, (b) arrow depicting the direction of action potential, and (c) neurotransmitters. (p. 126)

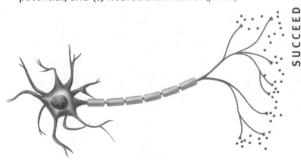

my psych lab

SUCCEED with

Neuronal Transmission

How do neurotransmitters communicate their messages within the body? (p. 125)

EXPLORE

STUDY the Learning Objectives

▶ Distinguish the parts of neurons and what they do
  • The neuron has a cell body, which contains the nucleus filled with deoxyribonucleic acid (DNA), responsible for manufacturing the proteins that make up our cells. Neurons usually have one or more dendrites, long extensions that receive messages from other neurons. There is usually a single axon arising from the cell body of each neuron, which is responsible for sending messages.

▶ Describe electrical responses of neurons and what makes them possible
  • Neurons exhibit excitatory and inhibitory responses to inputs from other neurons.

When excitation is strong enough, the neuron generates an action potential, which travels all the way down the axon to the axon terminal. Charged particles crossing the neuronal membrane are responsible for these events.

▶ Explain how neurons use neurotransmitters to communicate with each other
  • Neurotransmitters are the chemical messengers neurons use to communicate with each other or to cause muscle contraction. When an action potential arrives at the axon terminal, it triggers the release of a neurotransmitter at the synapse. This process then produces excitatory or inhibitory responses in the recipient neuron.

DO YOU KNOW THESE TERMS?

❑ dendrites (p. 125)
❑ synaptic cleft (p. 125)
❑ axons (p. 125)
❑ synaptic vesicles (p. 125)
❑ neurotransmitters (p. 125)
❑ glia (glial) cells (p. 125)
❑ blood–brain barrier (p. 125)
❑ myelin sheath (p. 125)
❑ resting potential (p. 126)
❑ threshold (p. 126)
❑ action potential (p. 126)
❑ absolute refractory period (p. 126)
❑ receptor sites (p. 127)
❑ reuptake (p. 127)
❑ endorphins (p. 128)

THINK about

what You would do . . .
Your mother has been invited to a Botox party. What should she know about how Botox affects neurotransmitters before deciding to attend? (p. 128)

What "natural narcotic" produced by the brain helps athletes endure intense workouts or pain? (p. 128)

ASSESS your knowledge

1. The central region of the neuron which manufactures new cell components is called the _____. (pp. 124–125)

2. A neuron (can/can't) survive severe damage to the cell body. (p. 125)

3. The receiving ends of a neuron, extending from the cell body like a tree branch, are known as the _____. (p. 125)

4. The space between two connecting neurons where neurotransmitters are released is called the _____ _____. (p. 125)

5. _____ are long extensions from the neuron at the cell body that _____ messages from one neuron to another. (p. 125)

6. _____ _____ are the small spheres within the axon terminal that contain chemical messages specialized for communication. (p. 125)

7. The brain's ability to protect itself from infection and high hormone levels is through the _____ _____. (p. 125)

8. The autoimmune disease multiple sclerosis is linked to the destruction of the glial cells wrapped around the axon—called the _____ _____. (p. 125)

9. The electrical charge difference across the membrane of the neuron when it is not being stimulated is called the _____ _____. (p. 126)

10. Action potentials are abrupt waves of ____ ____ that allow neurons to communicate. (p. 126)

Mapping the Mind to Understand Our Actions (pp. 129–137)

STUDY the Learning Objectives

▶ Describe the relationship between mind and brain
  • The brain is responsible for the mind, that is, our perceptions, emotions, thoughts, and decisions. We know this is the case because brain damage disrupts these functions, brain stimulation elicits these functions, and brain activity changes in selected areas during these functions.

▶ Identify the different brain stimulating, recording, and imaging techniques
  • Electrical stimulation of the brain or of nerves can elicit vivid imagery or movement. Methods such as electroencephalography (EEG) and magnetoencephalography (MEG) enable researchers to record brain activity. Imaging techniques provide a way to see the brain. The first imaging techniques included computed tomography (CT) and magnetic resonance imaging (MRI). Brain imaging techniques that allow us to see where activity changes during psychological function include positron emission tomography (PET) and functional MRI (fMRI).

▶ Evaluate results demonstrating the brain's localization of function
  • Stimulating, recording, and imaging techniques have shown that specific brain areas correspond to specific functions. Although these results provide valuable insight into how our brains divide up the many tasks we perform, many parts of the brain contribute to each specific task. Because individual brain areas participate in multiple functions, many cognitive functions cannot be neatly divided into subcomponent tasks.

Based on EEG studies, what brain wave changes occur when Buddhist monks meditate? (p. 134)

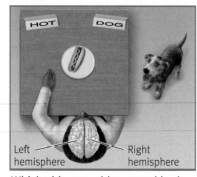

Left hemisphere   Right hemisphere

Which object would a normal brain patient think of when seeing these two words flashed to different hemispheres? Which object would a split brain patient think of? (p. 135)

ASSESS your knowledge

1. According to most neuroscientists, the brain (is/isn't) the mind in action. (p. 129)

2. Franz Joseph Gall made one of the earliest attempts to create a method to connect mind and brain by measuring head bumps, otherwise known as _____. (p. 130)

3. Early efforts by Hans Berger to measure electrical activity in the brain resulted in the development of the _____. (p. 131)

4. Neuroscientists interested in measuring thought and emotion (would/wouldn't) employ an MRI scan. (p. 132)

5. Functional MRI (fMRI) measures the change in _____ _____ to capture brain activity. (p. 132)

6. Neuroscientists have confirmed that there (are/aren't) parts of the brain that remain completely inactive and unutilized. (p. 133)

7. Severing the corpus callosum to reduce the incidence of epileptic seizures is known as the _____ _____ surgery. (p. 134)

8. The phenomenon known as _____ explains how many cognitive functions rely on one cerebral hemisphere over another. (p. 134)

9. The _____ hemisphere of the brain is related to coarse language skills and visuo-spatial skills whereas the _____ hemisphere is related to fine-tuned language skills and actions. (p. 135)

10. Artists and other creative thinkers (are able/aren't able) to make use only of their right hemisphere. (p. 136)

mypsych lab
where learning comes to life!

Split-Brain Experiments

In order to lessen the occurrence of violent epileptic seizures, some patients undergo a split-brain operation. What are the effects of this procedure? (p. 134)

THINK about

what You would do . . .
Your employer asks you to participate in a creativity workshop in which the company will make job assignments based on its determination of left- versus right-brained employees. Is this workshop based on good science? (p. 136)

DO YOU KNOW THESE TERMS?

- ☐ lesion (p. 130)
- ☐ electroencephalography (EEG) (p. 131)
- ☐ computed tomography (CT) (p. 132)
- ☐ magnetic resonance imaging (MRI) (p. 132)
- ☐ positron emission tomography (PET) (p. 132)
- ☐ functional MRI (fMRI) (p. 132)
- ☐ transcranial magnetic stimulation (TMS) (p. 132)
- ☐ magnetoencephalography (MEG) (p. 132)
- ☐ split-brain surgery (p. 134)
- ☐ lateralization (p. 134)

Nature and Nurture: Did Your Genes—Or Parents—Make You Do It? (pp. 137–145)

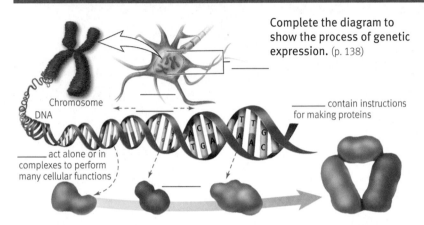

Complete the diagram to show the process of genetic expression. (p. 138)

Chromosome
DNA

_____ contain instructions for making proteins

_____ act alone or in complexes to perform many cellular functions

STUDY the Learning Objectives

▶ **Describe genes and how they influence observable traits**
- Genes are made of deoxyribonucleic acid (DNA). They are arranged on chromosomes. We inherit this genetic material from our parents. Each gene carries a code to manufacture a particular protein. These proteins determine our observable traits.

▶ **Explain the concept of heritability and the misconceptions surrounding it**
- Heritability refers to how differences in a trait across people are influenced by our genes as opposed to environmental factors. Highly heritable traits can sometimes change and the heritability of a trait can also change over time.

▶ **Recognize when the brain changes most and least**
- The brain changes the most before birth and during early development. Throughout the life span the brain demonstrates some degree of plasticity, which plays a role in learning and memory. Later in life, healthy brain plasticity decreases and neurons can show signs of degeneration.

DO YOU KNOW THESE TERMS?

- ☐ chromosomes (p. 137)
- ☐ genes (p. 137)
- ☐ genotype (p. 137)
- ☐ phenotype (p. 137)
- ☐ dominant genes (p. 137)
- ☐ recessive genes (p. 137)
- ☐ natural selection (p. 138)
- ☐ fitness (p. 138)
- ☐ heritability (p. 139)
- ☐ family studies (p. 140)
- ☐ twin studies (p. 140)
- ☐ adoption studies (p. 141)
- ☐ plasticity (p. 142)
- ☐ stem cells (p. 144)
- ☐ neurogenesis (p. 145)

mypsych lab
where learning comes to life!

Dominant and Ressessive Traits

Can you explain the genetic origins of your hair and eye color? (p. 137)

THINK about

what You would do . . .
If you knew someone in your family history had a disease whose genetic marker could now be identified by genetic testing, how would you use that information to inform your personal health decisions? (p. 141)

ASSESS your knowledge

1. _____ are the thin threads within a nucleus that carry genes. (p. 137)

2. _____ are made up of deoxyribonucleic acid (DNA), the material that stores everything cells need to reproduce themselves. (p. 137)

3. Our _____ is the set of our observable traits, and our genetic makeup is our _____. (p. 137)

4. (Recessive/dominant) genes work to mask other genes' effects. (p. 137)

5. The principle that organisms that possess adaptations survive and reproduce at a higher rate than other organisms is known as _____ _____. (p. 138)

6. The three misconceptions regarding heritability are that it can be applied to an _____, cannot be _____, and is not a _____ _____. (pp. 139–140)

7. Following an injury, the nervous system's ability to change—referred to as _____ —may be compromised. (p. 142)

8. _____ are unspecialized cells that retain the ability to become a variety of specialized cells. (p. 144)

9. Three uses for stem cells in treating neurodegenerative disease are _____, _____, and _____. (pp. 144–145)

10. Scientists are working to improve ways to encourage neurogenesis, the adult brain's ability to create _____. (p. 145)

THINKING Scientifically

Correlation vs. Causation pp. 108, 114, 120

Falsifiability pp. 116, 129, 130

Extraordinary Claims pp. 118, 136

Replicability pp. 111, 123

Ruling Out Rival Hypotheses pp. 112, 115, 120, 123, 140

Remember these questions from the beginning of the chapter? Think again and ask yourself if you would answer them differently based on what you now know about biological psychology. (For more detailed explanations, see MyPsychLab.)

▶ How far does the longest neuron in the human body reach? (p. 108)
▶ Is the mind different from the brain, or is it just the brain in action? (p. 129)
▶ Do specific regions on the brain's surface correspond to different personality traits? (p. 130)
▶ Do we use only about 10 percent of our brain's capacity? (p. 133)

▶ Can we trace complex psychological functions, like religious belief, to specific brain regions? (p. 134)
▶ Are there left- and right-brained people? (p. 136)
▶ Are humans the largest brained animals? (p. 139)
▶ Is heritability a fixed value, or can it change over time? (p. 139)
▶ Is the adult brain completely hardwired? (p. 142)

4

Sensation and Perception
How We Sense and Conceptualize the World

PREVIEW

Think

First, think about these questions. Then, as you read, think again....

▶ Can we perceive invisible stimuli?

▶ Can we "read" someone else's thoughts?

▶ Can our eyes detect only a single particle of light?

▶ Can certain blind people still "see" some of their surroundings?

▶ Do some people "taste" shapes or "hear" colors?

▶ Does music activate the same brain areas as food, sex, and drugs?

▶ Why can't we taste food when we have a bad cold?

Before you read any further, try the exercise in **Figure 4.1.** Be sure to do it now, because if you skip it, you'll miss the point of the next paragraph.

Were you surprised that the white "X" disappeared from view? Were you even more surprised that you filled the missing space occupied by the "X" with a mental image exactly matching the fancy background pattern?

Sensation and perception are the underlying processes operating in this visual illusion; it's an illusion because your brain perceived a complete pattern even though some of it was missing. **Sensation** refers to the detection of physical energy by sense organs in the eyes, ears, skin, nose, and tongue, which then send information to the brain (see Chapter 3). **Perception** is the brain's interpretation of these raw sensory inputs. Simplifying things just a bit, sensation allows us to pick up the signals in our environments, and perception allows us to assemble these signals into something meaningful.

We often assume that our sensory systems are infallible and that our perceptions are perfect representations of the world around us. As we learned in the Prologue, we term these beliefs *naive realism.* We'll discover in this chapter that naive realism is wrong; the world isn't precisely as we see it. Somewhere in our brains we reconstructed that fancy pattern in the figure and put it smack in the middle of the empty space; this perceptual process is called *filling-in.* Most of the time, filling-in is adaptive, as it helps us to make sense of our often confusing and chaotic perceptual worlds. But sometimes it can fool us, as in the case of illusions.

Perception researchers have studied filling-in by showing participants incomplete objects on computer screens and determining which *pixels,* or picture elements, subjects rely on to make perceptual judgments (Gold, Murray, Bennett, & Sekuler, 2000). The pixels that participants use to perceive images are often located next to regions where there's no sensory information, leading researchers to conclude that we interpolate—or mix— illusory with sensory-based information to arrive at perceptual decisions. We often blend the real with the imagined, going beyond the information given to us. By doing so, we simplify the world, but make better sense of it in the process.

Research suggests that we often rely on preconceived notions about typical object shapes to help us decide what to fill in (DeWeerd, 2006). Our perceptions are guided by past experience. Now look around the room in which you're sitting. Imagine how many other things you're seeing, or *think* you're seeing, that is, right now that may be altered slightly by illusions similar to the one you've just experienced.

Figure 4.1 Find Your Blind Spot. Hold this page about 10 inches from your face. Close your right eye and keep focusing on the white circle. Can you see the white "X"? Now slowly move the page toward your face and then away from it; at some point the white "X" will disappear and then reappear. The "X" can't be seen when the image is directly on your blind spot. Surprisingly, an illusory background pattern will "fill-in" the white space occupied by the "X" (*Source:* Glynn, 1999).

sensation
detection of physical energy by sense organs, which then send information to the brain

perception
the brain's interpretation of raw sensory inputs

Two Sides of the Coin:
Sensation and Perception

How do signals that impinge on our sense organs—like our eyes, ears, and tongue—become translated into information that our brains can interpret and act on? And how does the raw sensory information delivered to our brains become integrated with what we already know about the world, allowing us to recognize objects, avoid accidents, and (hopefully) find our way out the door each morning?

Here's how. Our brain picks and chooses among the types of sensory information it uses, often relying on expectations and prior experiences to fill in the gaps and simplify processing. The end result is often more than the sum of its parts—and in some cases it's a completely wrong number! Errors in perception, like the illusion in Figure 4.1 and others we'll present in this chapter, are often extremely informative, not to mention fun. They show us which parts of our sensory experiences are accurate and which parts our brains fill in for us.

We'll first review what our sensory systems can accomplish and how they manage to transform physical signals in the outside world into neural activity in the "inside world"—our brains. Then we'll explore how and when our brains flesh out the details, moving beyond the raw sensory information available to us.

(© ScienceCartoonsPlus.com)

SENSATION: OUR SENSES AS DETECTIVES

Our senses enable us to see and hear, to feel a touch, determine body position, maintain balance, and smell and taste. Despite their differences, all of these senses rely on a mere handful of basic principles.

Transduction: Going from the Outside World to Within. The first step in sensation is to convert external energies or substances into a "language" the nervous system understands, such as the action potential (see Chapter 3). The process by which the nervous system converts an external energy or a substance into excitation or inhibition is **transduction.** A particular type of **sense receptor,** or specialized cell, transduces a specific stimulus. As we'll learn, specialized cells at the back of the eye transduce light, cells in a spiral-shaped organ in the ear transduce sound, odd-looking endings attached to axons embedded in deep layers of the skin transduce pressure, receptor cells lining the inside of the nose transduce airborne odorants, and taste buds transduce chemicals containing flavor.

For all of our senses, activation is greatest when we first detect a stimulus. After that, the response declines in strength, a process called *sensory adaptation*. A good example is feeling the seat of a chair when we first sit on it. What happens in a matter of seconds? We no longer feel the chair, unless it's an extremely hard seat, or worse, has a thumbtack on it. The adaptation takes place at the level of the sense receptor. This receptor reacts strongly at first and then turns down its level of responding. Our nervous systems are probably arranged his efforts way to conserve energy and attentional resources. If we didn't engage in sensory adaptation, we'd be attending to just about everything around us, all of the time.

Psychophysics: Measuring the Barely Detectable. Back in the nineteenth century, when psychology was gradually distinguishing itself as a science apart from philosophy (see the Prologue), many researchers focused on sensation and perception. In 1860, German scientist Gustav Fechner published a landmark piece on perception. Out of his efforts grew the field of *psychophysics*, the study of how we perceive sensory stimuli based on their physical characteristics.

Absolute Threshold. Fechner and later psychophysicists studied phenomena like the **absolute threshold** of a stimulus—the lowest level of a stimulus we can detect on 50 percent

transduction
the process of converting an external energy or substance into neural activity

sense receptor
specialized cell responsible for converting external stimuli into neural activity for a specific sensory system

absolute threshold
lowest level of a stimulus needed for the nervous system to detect a change 50 percent of the time

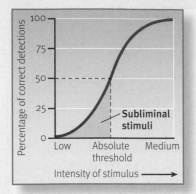

Figure 4.2 Fechner's Concept of Absolute Threshold. As we can see from this graph, the absolute threshold is the lowest level of a stimulus we can detect on 50 percent of the trials.

Table 4.1 Distinguishing Signal from Noise. In signal detection theory there are hits, misses, false alarms, and correct rejections. Subject biases affect the probability of "yes" and "no" responses to the question "Was there a stimulus?"

	Respond "Yes"	Respond "No"
Stimulus present	Hit	Miss
Stimulus absent	False alarm	Correct rejection

just noticeable difference (JND)
the smallest change in the intensity of a stimulus that we can detect

of trials when that stimulus appears by itself, that is, with no other stimuli of that type present. Imagine that a researcher fits us with a pair of headphones and places us in a quiet room. She asks repeatedly if we've heard one of many very faint tones. Detection isn't an all-or-none state of affairs because human error increases as stimuli become weaker (see **Figure 4.2**). Our absolute thresholds demonstrate how remarkably sensitive our sensory systems are. In complete darkness, our visual systems can detect a single photon, that is, one particle of light. We can detect a smell from as few as fifty airborne odorant molecules; salamanders can pull off this feat with only one (Menini, Picco, & Firestein, 1995).

Just Noticeable Difference. The **just noticeable difference (JND)** is the smallest change in the intensity of a stimulus that we can detect. The JND is relevant to our ability to distinguish a stronger from a weaker stimulus, like a soft noise from a slightly louder noise.

Weber's law says that there's a constant proportional relationship between the JND and the original stimulus intensity. In plain language, the stronger the stimulus, the bigger the change needed for a change in stimulus intensity to be noticeable. Think of how much light we'd need to add to a brightly lit kitchen to notice an increase in illumination compared with the amount of light we'd need to add to a dark bedroom to notice a change in illumination. We'd need a lot of light in the first case and only a smidgeon in the second.

Signal Detection Theory. David Green and John Swets (1966) developed *signal detection theory* to help psychologists determine how we detect stimuli under uncertain conditions, as when we're driving on a foggy night and trying to decide whether there's an animal on the road in front of us. Think of how difficult it is to talk on a cell phone when there's static in the connection; that's high background noise. We need to increase the signal by shouting over the static or it will prevent the other party from understanding us. If we have a good connection, however, others can easily understand us without our shouting. This point illustrates the concept of the *signal-to-noise ratio:* It becomes harder to detect a signal as background noise increases.

Green and Swets were also interested in *response biases,* or tendencies to make one type of guess over another when we're in doubt. They developed a clever way to take into account some people's tendency to say "yes" when they're uncertain and other people's tendency to say "no" when they're uncertain. Instead of always delivering a sound stimulus, they sometimes presented a sound, sometimes not. This procedure provides a way to detect and account for subjects' response biases. As we can see in **Table 4.1**, subjects can report that they heard a sound when it was present (a hit), deny hearing a sound when it was present (a miss), report hearing a sound that wasn't there (a false alarm), or deny hearing a sound that wasn't there (a correct rejection). The frequency of false alarms and misses helps us measure how biased subjects are to respond "yes" or "no" in general.

APPLY YOUR THINKING
If you were anticipating a crucial telephone call and were overly responsive to the slightest noise, what kind of response bias would this create?

Sensory Systems Stick to One Sense—Or Do They? Back in 1826, Johannes Müller proposed the doctrine of *specific nerve energies,* which states that even though there are many distinct stimulus energies—like light, sound, or touch—the sensation we experience is determined by the nature of the sense receptor, not the stimulus. We can look to *phosphenes* as an illustration of this principle. Phosphenes are vivid sensations of light caused by pressure on our eye's receptor cells. Most of us have experienced phosphenes after rubbing our eyes shortly after waking up. Many phosphenes look like sparks, and some even look like the multicolored shapes we see in a kaleidoscope. Perhaps not surprisingly, some people have speculated that phosphenes may help to explain certain reports of ghosts and UFOs (Neher, 1990).

Why do phosphenes occur? The answer lies in specific sensory pathways, leading all the way to the cerebral cortex. In the cerebral cortex, different areas are devoted to different senses (see Chapter 3). It doesn't matter to our brain whether light or touch activated the sense receptor: Our brains react the same way in either case.

Specific nerve energies follow specific pathways up to the cerebral cortex, and then specific sensory pathways disperse throughout the cortex. Most areas of the cortex are connected to cortical areas devoted to the same sense: Vision areas tend to be connected to other vision areas, hearing areas to other hearing areas, and so on. Claus Hilgetag and his colleagues (2000) found that most cortical areas connected to each other respond to the same sense, and connections linking different senses are fewer in number. For this reason, we might not expect much in the way of *cross-modal processing,* that is, the mixing of senses across brain areas.

Yet this expectation turns out to be false. Scientists have found many examples of cross-modal processing that produce different perceptual experiences than either modality provides by itself. One striking example is the *McGurk effect* (McGurk & MacDonald, 1976). This effect demonstrates that we integrate visual and auditory information when processing spoken language, and our brains automatically calculate the most probable sound given the information from the two sources. In the McGurk effect, hearing the audio track of one syllable (such as "ba") spoken repeatedly while seeing a video track of a different syllable being spoken (such as "ga") results in the perceptual experience of a different third sound (such as "da"). This third sound is the brain's best "guess" at integrating the two conflicting sources of information.

Another fascinating example is the *rubber hand illusion,* which shows how our senses of touch and sight interact to create a false perceptual experience (Erhsson, Spence, & Passingham, 2004; Knox et al., 2006). This illusion involves placing a rubber hand on top of a table with the precise positioning that a subject's hand would have if she were resting it on the table. The subject's hand is placed under the table, out of her view. An experimenter simultaneously strokes the subject's hidden hand and rubber hand gently with a paintbrush. When the strokes match each other, the subject experiences an eerie illusion: The rubber hand seems to be her own hand.

As we've seen, these cross-modal effects may reflect "cross-talk" among different brain regions. But there's an alternative explanation: In some cases, a single brain region may serve double duty, helping to process multiple senses. For example, neurons in the auditory cortex tuned to sound also respond weakly to touch (Fu et al., 2003). Visual stimuli enhance touch perception in the somatosensory cortex (Taylor-Clarke, Kennett, & Hagard, 2002). The reading of Braille by people blind from birth activates their visual cortex (Gizewski et al., 2003). And monkeys viewing videos with sound experience increased activity in the primary auditory cortex compared with exposure to sound alone (Kayser, Petkov, Augath, & Logothetis, 2007).

Parallel Processing: The Way Our Brain Multitasks. We can attend to many sense modalities simultaneously, a phenomenon called parallel processing (Rumelhart & McClelland, 1987). Two important concepts that go along with parallel processing are *bottom-up* and *top-down processing* (see Chapter 8). In bottom-up processing, we construct a whole stimulus from its parts. An example is perceiving an object on the basis of its edges. This kind of processing is stimulus-driven and results from activity in the primary sensory cortex (see Chapter 3), followed by processing in the secondary sensory cortex, and then in the association cortex. In contrast, top-down processing is conceptually driven and influenced by our beliefs and expectations. Typically, these high-level cognitions correspond to activity in the association cortex and feedback connections to lower-brain areas.

Some perceptions rely more heavily on bottom-up processing (Koch, 1993), others on top-down processing (McClelland & Plaut, 1993). In most cases, though, bottom-up and top-down processing work hand in hand (Patel & Sathian, 2000). We can illustrate this point by how we process ambiguous figures. Depending on our expectations, we typically perceive these figures differently. The top-down influence that we're thinking of a jazz musician biases our bottom-up processing of the shapes in **Figure 4.3** and increases the chances we'll perceive a saxophone player. In contrast, if our top-down expectation were of a woman's face, our sensory-based bottom-up processing would change accordingly. (Can you see both figures?)

Ruling Out Rival Hypotheses

Figure 4.3 What Do You See? Due to the influence of top-down processing, reading the caption "saxophone player" beneath this ambiguous figure tends to produce a different perception than reading the caption "woman."

Subliminal Information Processing. You're home on a Sunday afternoon, curled up on your couch watching a movie on TV. Suddenly, within a span of a few minutes you see three or four quick flashes of light on the screen. Only a few minutes later, you're seized with an uncontrollable desire to eat a hamburger. Did the advertiser fiendishly insert several photographs of a hamburger in the midst of the movie, so quickly you couldn't detect them? If we can detect stimuli without knowing it, does that affect our behavior? We'll find out.

Subliminal Perception. The American public has long been fascinated with the possibility of *subliminal perception*—the processing of sensory information that occurs below the level of conscious awareness (Cheesman & Merikle, 1986; Rogers & Smith, 1993). To study subliminal perception, researchers typically present a word or photograph extremely quickly, say at 50 milliseconds ($\frac{1}{20}$ of a second). They frequently follow this stimulus immediately with a *mask,* another stimulus (like a pattern of dots or lines) that blocks out mental processing of the subliminal stimulus. When subjects can't correctly identify the content of the stimulus at better than chance levels, researchers deem it subliminal.

The claim for subliminal perception is extraordinary, but the evidence supporting it is compelling (Seitzer & Watanabe, 2003). When investigators subliminally trigger emotions by exposing subjects to words related to anger, these subjects are more likely to rate other people as hostile (Bargh & Pietromonaco, 1982). In one study, researchers asked graduate students in psychology to list three ideas for future research projects. Researchers then exposed them subliminally to photographs of either (a) the smiling face of a postdoctoral research assistant in their laboratory or (b) the contemptuous face of their primary professor. Despite being unable to identify what they saw, graduate students who saw their faculty mentor's contemptuous face rated their research ideas less positively than did those who saw the postdoctoral assistant's smiling face (Baldwin, Carrel, & Lopez, 1991).

Subliminal Persuasion. Even though we're subject to subliminal perception, that doesn't mean we numbly succumb to *subliminal persuasion,* that is, subthreshold influences over our product choices, votes in elections, and life decisions. For decades, Americans have envisioned nightmare scenarios in which advertisers flash subliminal messages in movies and television programs, leading them to buy merchandise against their will (Key, 1973). Yet research demonstrates that subliminal persuasion, although not impossible (Epley, Savitsky, & Kachelski, 1999; Weinberger & Hardaway, 1990), is unlikely in most cases. That's because we can't engage in much, if any, in-depth processing of the *meaning* of subliminal stimuli (Rosen, Glasgow, & Moore, 2003). As a result, these stimuli probably can't produce large-scale or enduring changes in our attitudes, let alone our everyday decisions.

Still, subliminal self-help audiotapes and videotapes are a multimillion-dollar-a-year industry in the United States alone. They purportedly contain repeated subliminal messages (such as "Feel better about yourself") designed to influence our behavior or emotions. In stores and on the Internet, we can find subliminal tapes for self-esteem, memory, sexual performance, and weight loss (Rosen et al., 2003).

Yet scores of studies show that subliminal self-help tapes are ineffective (Eich & Hyman, 1991; Moore, 1992). In one investigation, Anthony Greenwald and his colleagues examined the effectiveness of subliminal audiotapes designed to enhance memory or self-esteem. They switched the labels on half of the tapes, so that half of the participants received the tapes they believed they'd received, and half received the other set of tapes. On objective tests of memory and self-esteem, all of the tapes were useless. Yet participants *thought* they'd improved, and their reports corresponded to the tape they *thought* they'd received. So those who thought they'd received self-esteem tapes said their self-esteem improved even when they received memory tapes, and vice versa for those who believed they'd received memory tapes. The authors termed this phenomenon the *illusory placebo effect:* Subjects didn't improve, but they thought they had (Greenwald, Spangenberg, Pratkanis, & Eskenazi, 1991). Phil Merikle (1988) uncovered another reason why subliminal self-help tapes don't work: His auditory analyses revealed that many of these tapes contain no message at all!

Some people even claim that *reversed* subliminal messages can influence behavior. In 1990 the heavy metal rock band Judas Priest was put on trial for the suicide of a teenager and the attempted suicide of another. These boys had listened to a Judas Priest album and

fictoid

Myth: In the late 1950s, advertisers subliminally flashed the words "Eat popcorn" and "Drink Coke" during films in a New Jersey movie theater over the span of several weeks. The rates of popcorn and Coca-Cola consumption in the theater skyrocketed.

Reality: The originator of this claim, advertising expert James Vicary, later admitted that it was a hoax cooked up to generate publicity for his failing business (Pratkanis, 1992).

The rock band Judas Priest was sued in 1990 for supposedly inserting reversed subliminal messages in a song.

supposedly heard the words "Do it" played backward in one of the songs. The prosecution claimed that these reversed messages, which Judas Priest denied having inserted, led the boys to shoot themselves. In the end, the members of Judas Priest were acquitted (Moore, 1996). The court was persuaded by arguments from expert witnesses that because forward subliminal messages can't produce major changes in behavior, it's even less likely that backward messages can do so.

PERCEPTION: WHEN OUR SENSES MEET OUR MINDS

Now that we've encountered the basic principles governing how we process sensory information, we'll embark on an exciting voyage into how our minds organize the little pieces of sensory data into more meaningful concepts. What's so remarkable about our mind's ability to bring together so much data? The answer is that our mind doesn't rely only on what's out there in the sensory field: It pieces together (a) what's in the sensory field, along with (b) what was just there a moment ago, and (c) what we remember from our past. Just as we perceive the broad strokes of a stimulus, we remember the typical characteristics of objects. When we perceive the world, we sacrifice small details in favor of crisp and often more meaningful representations. In most cases, the trade-off is well worth it, because it helps us to make sense of our surroundings.

Perceptual Hypotheses: Guessing What's Out There. Because our brains rely so much on what we know and have experienced, we can usually get away with economizing in our sensory processing and making educated guesses about what sensory information is telling us. Moreover, a pretty decent guess with fewer neurons is more efficient than a more sure answer with a huge number of neurons. As cognitive misers (see Chapter 2), we generally try to get by with as little neural firepower as we can.

Perceptual Sets. The relation between a stimulus and its context is a *perceptual set*. We tend to organize information into perceptual sets: We group things together that go together. We may perceive a misshapen letter as an "H" or as an "A" depending on the surrounding letters and the words that would result (see **Figure 4.4**). We also tend to perceive the world in accord with our preconceptions. An ambiguous cartoon drawn by W. E. Hill raises the question: Is it a young woman or an old witch? Participants placed in the perceptual set of a young woman by viewing a version of the cartoon exaggerating those features (see **Figure 4.5**) reported seeing a young woman. In contrast, participants placed in the perceptual set of an old woman by viewing a version of the cartoon exaggerating those features reported seeing an old woman (Boring, 1930).

Things we take for granted alter our perceptions. In one study, researchers asked subjects to modify the color of fruits on a computer screen until they appeared gray (Hansen, Olkkonen, Walter, & Gegenfurtner, 2006). Subjects found that even when gray, these fruits still "looked" like their natural colors. For example, subjects reported that gray bananas appeared yellowish, because their memory of the yellow color of bananas colored their perceptions—literally.

Perceptual Constancy. The process by which we perceive stimuli consistently across varied conditions is **perceptual constancy.** There are several kinds of perceptual constancy—shape, size, and color constancy. Consider a door we view from differing perspectives (see **Figure 4.6**). Because of *shape constancy*, we still see a door as a door whether it's completely shut, barely open, or more fully open, even though these shapes differ markedly from each other.

Or take *size constancy*, our ability to perceive objects as the same size no matter how near or far away they are from us. When a friend walks away from us, her image becomes smaller. But we almost never realize this is happening, nor do we conclude that our friend is mysteriously shrinking. Outside of our conscious awareness, our brains mentally enlarge figures far away from us so that they appear more like similar objects in the same scene.

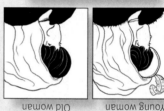

Figure 4.4 Context Influences Perception. Depending on the perceptual set provided by the context of the surrounding letters, the middle letter can appear as an "H" or as an "A." Most of us read this phrase as "THE BAT" because of the context.

Old woman   Young woman

Figure 4.5 An Example of Perceptual Set. Depending on our perspective, the drawing on top can appear to be a young woman or an old one. Which did you perceive first? Look at the biased pictures (turn the page upside down) to alter your perceptual set. (*Source:* Hill, 1915)

Figure 4.6 Shape Constancy. We perceive a door as a door whether it appears as a rectangle or a trapezoid.

perceptual constancy
the process by which we perceive stimuli consistently across varied conditions

Figure 4.7 The Checker-Shadow Illusion. We perceive a checkerboard pattern of black and white alternating squares, and because of color constancy, we ignore the dramatic change due to the shadow cast by the green cylinder. Believe it or not, the A and B squares are identical. Turn to page 160 to see the proof. (*Source:* © 1995 Edward H. Adelson)

Replicability

The man standing toward the back of the bridge looks to be of normal size, but the exact duplicate image appears in the foreground and looks like a toy because of size constancy.

selective attention
process of selecting one sensory channel and ignoring or minimizing others

Color constancy is our ability to perceive color consistently across different levels of illumination. Consider a group of firemen dressed in bright yellow jackets. Their jackets look bright yellow even in very low levels of ambient light. That's because our perceptual apparatus evaluates the color of an object in the context of background light and surrounding colors. Take a moment to examine **Figure 4.7.** The checkerboard appears to contain all black and white squares, but they're actually varying shades of gray. Remarkably, the A and B squares (one from the black set and one from the white set) are exactly the same shade of gray (if you don't believe your eyes, see the proof on page 160). Dale Purves and colleagues (2002) applied the same principle to cubes composed of smaller squares that appear to have different colors, even though some of the smaller squares are actually gray (see **Figure 4.8**). We base our perception of color in these smaller squares on the surrounding context.

Selective Attention: How We Focus on Particular Inputs. Like a TV set with all channels switched on at once, our brains are constantly receiving inputs from all our sensory channels. How do we keep from becoming hopelessly confused? **Selective attention** allows us to select one channel and turn off the others, or at least turn down their volume. The major brain regions that control selective attention are the reticular activating system (RAS) and basal forebrain (see Chapter 3). These brain areas activate regions of the cerebral cortex, such as the frontal cortex, during selective attention.

Donald Broadbent's (1957) *filter theory of attention* views attention as a bottleneck through which information passes. This mental filter enables us to pay attention to important stimuli and ignore others. Broadbent tested his theory using a task called *dichotic listening*—in which subjects hear two different messages, one delivered to the left ear and one to the right ear. When Broadbent asked subjects to ignore the messages delivered to one of the ears, subjects seemed to know little about the ignored message. Anne Treismann (1960) replicated these findings on the dichotic listening task, but elaborated on these results by asking subjects to repeat the messages they heard, a technique called *shadowing*. Although subjects could only repeat the messages to which they'd attended, they'd sometimes mix in some of the information they were supposed to ignore, especially if it made sense to add it. If the attended ear heard, "I saw the girl . . . song was wishing," and the unattended ear heard, "me that bird . . . jumping in the street," then a participant might perceive, "I saw the girl jumping in the street," because the combination forms a meaningful sentence. This finding shows that information we've supposedly filtered out of our attention is still being processed at some level—even when we're not aware of it (Beaman, Bridges, & Scott, 2007).

Figure 4.8 Color Perception Depends on Context. Gray can appear like a color depending on surrounding colors. The blue-colored squares on the top of the cube at the left are actually gray (*see map below the cube*). Similarly, the yellow-colored squares on the top of the cube at the right are actually gray (*see map below the cube*). (*Source:* © Dale Purves and R. Beau Lotto, 2002)

An attention-related phenomenon called the *cocktail party effect* refers to our ability to pick out an important message, like our name, in a conversation that doesn't involve us. We don't typically notice what other people are saying in a noisy restaurant or at a party unless it's relevant to us—and then suddenly, we perk up. This finding tells us that the filter inside our brain, which selects what will and won't receive our attention, is more complex than just an "on" or "off" switch (see **Figure 4.9**).

The Binding Problem: Putting the Pieces Together. The *binding problem* is one of the great mysteries of psychology. It refers to how our brains take multiple pieces of information and combine them to represent something concrete, like an apple. An apple looks red and round, feels smooth, tastes sweet and tart, and smells, well, like an apple. Any one of its characteristics in isolation isn't an apple or even a part of an apple (that would be an apple slice). How do our brains pull off binding? We don't know for sure, but one suggestion is that fast, coordinated activity across multiple cortical areas does the trick (Engel & Singer, 2001). Binding may explain many aspects of perception and attention. When we see the world, we rely on shape, motion, color, and depth cues, each of which requires different amounts of time to detect individually (Bartels & Zeki, 2006). Yet our minds seamlessly combine these visual cues into a single unified perception of a scene. That's binding.

EXTRASENSORY PERCEPTION (ESP): FACT OR FICTION?

As we've seen, scientists have learned a great deal about perception. Yet might some forms of perception remain to be discovered? This question takes us into the mysterious realm of **extrasensory perception (ESP)**. Proponents of ESP argue that we can perceive events outside of the known channels of sensation, like seeing, hearing, and touch.

What's ESP, Anyway? ESP isn't one thing. Instead, *parapsychologists*—investigators who study ESP and related psychic phenomena—have subdivided ESP into three major types (Hines, 2003; Hyman, 1989):

(1) *Precognition:* predicting events before they occur through paranormal means, that is, mechanisms that lie outside of traditional science. (You knew we were going to say that, didn't you?);

(2) *Telepathy:* reading other people's minds; and

(3) *Clairvoyance:* detecting the presence of objects or people that are hidden from view.

Closely related to ESP, although usually distinguished from it, is *psychokinesis*: Moving objects by mental power alone.

Beliefs about ESP. Surveys indicate that 41 percent of American adults believe in ESP (Haraldsson & Houtkooper, 1991; Moore, 2005). Scores of Americans also believe in the power of psychics and spirit mediums, like John Edward and James von Pragh, who claim to be able to forecast events or contact lost or dead relatives. Moreover, two-thirds of Americans say they've had a psychic experience, like a dream foretelling the death of a loved one or a premonition about a car accident that came true (Greeley, 1987).

Believers in ESP aren't limited to the general public. Beginning in 1972, the U.S. government invested $20 million in the *Stargate* program to study the ability of "remote viewers" to acquire militarily useful information in distant places, like the location of nuclear facilities in enemy countries, through clairvoyance. The government discontinued the program in 1995, apparently because the remote viewers provided no useful information. They often claimed to pinpoint secret military sites with great accuracy, but follow-up investigations showed them to be wildly wrong (Hyman, 1996).

Scientific Evidence for ESP. The real-world implications of ESP are mind-boggling. Imagine that we could forecast catastrophic events, like the terrorist attacks of September 11, 2001, or figure out whether a romantic partner is cheating by viewing his actions at a distance or reading his mind. How different our worlds would be! We could prevent mass

Figure 4.9 The Cocktail Party Effect. The cocktail party effect helps explain how we can become aware of stimuli outside of our immediate attention when it's relevant to us—like our names.

Selective attention during a spatial task correlates with certain regions of neural activity (see the red zones) in the prefrontal cortex. The yellow spots depict the placements of recording electrodes on the scalp (from Stern & Mangels, 2006).

extrasensory perception (ESP) perception of events outside the known channels of sensation

The Zener cards, named after a collaborator of Joseph B. Rhine, have been used widely in ESP research.

Replicability

A subject in a Ganzfeld experiment attempting to receive images from a sender. The uniform sensory field he's experiencing is designed to minimize visual and auditory "noise" from the environment, supposedly permitting him to detect otherwise weak ESP signals.

The Checker-Shadow Illusion Decoded. (See Figure 4.7.)

Replicability

disasters and save ourselves from spending months of time in fruitless relationships. However, we might also never enjoy a birthday surprise again.

Zener Card Studies. In the 1930s, Duke University psychologist Joseph B. Rhine, who coined the term *extrasensory perception,* launched the full-scale study of ESP in the United States. Rhine used a set of stimuli called *Zener cards,* which consist of five standard symbols: squiggly lines, star, circle, plus sign, and square. He presented these cards to subjects in random order and asked them to guess which card would appear (precognition), which card another subject had in mind (telepathy), and which card was hidden from view (clairvoyance). Rhine (1933) initially reported positive results, as his subjects averaged about 7 correct Zener card identifications per deck of 25, where 5 would be chance performance.

But there was a problem, one that has dogged ESP research for well over a century: Try as they might, other investigators couldn't replicate Rhine's findings. Moreover, scientists later pointed out serious flaws in Rhine's methods. Some of the Zener cards were so worn down or poorly manufactured that subjects could see the imprint of the symbols through the backs of the cards (Alcock, 1990; Gilovich, 1991). In other cases, scientists found that Rhine and his colleagues hadn't properly randomized the order of the cards, rendering his analyses essentially meaningless. Eventually, enthusiasm for Zener card research dried up.

Ganzfeld Technique. More recently, considerable excitement has been generated by findings using the *Ganzfeld technique* (*Ganzfeld* translates roughly into "whole field" in German)—an experimental setup devised to reduce background noise to increase sensitivity to ESP signals. As a participant in a Ganzfeld study, you enter a chamber and take a seat in a comfortable chair. The experimenter covers your eyes with Ping-Pong ball halves, directs a red floodlight toward your eyes, and pipes white noise into your ears through headphones. According to ESP proponents, the mental information detected by ESP "receivers" is an extremely weak signal that's typically obscured by irrelevant stimuli in the environment. By placing you in a uniform sensory field, the Ganzfeld technique decreases the amount of extraneous noise relative to ESP signal, supposedly permitting researchers to uncover weak ESP effects (Lilienfeld, 1999).

Down the hall, another person sits in a soundproof room with one goal in mind: to mentally transmit a picture to you, perhaps a photograph of a specific building on your campus. Meanwhile, the experimenter asks you to report all mental images that come to mind. Finally, she presents you with four pictures, only one of which the sender down the hall had viewed. Your job is to rate the extent to which each picture matches the mental imagery you experienced. If your performance were at chance levels, you'd score a "hit," or match with the target picture, 25 percent of the time, given that there were four stimuli you could pick. Hit rates much higher than 25 percent would strongly suggest ESP.

In 1994, Daryl Bem and Charles Honorton statistically analyzed multiple studies on the Ganzfeld technique and published their findings in *Psychological Bulletin,* one of psychology's most prestigious journals. Their meta-analysis, or statistical overview (see Chapter 2), included eleven studies and seemingly provided convincing evidence for ESP. Their subjects obtained hit rates of approximately 35 percent, exceeding chance performance. Yet parapsychologists' optimism was again short-lived. In 1999, Julie Milton and Richard Wiseman published an updated meta-analysis of thirty Ganzfeld studies that Bem and Honorton (1994) hadn't reviewed. In contrast to Bem and Honorton, Milton and Wiseman (1999) found that the size of Ganzfeld effects was small and corresponded to chance differences in performance.

Hurdles to Demonstrating ESP. Other ESP paradigms have proven equally disappointing. For example, research conducted over three decades ago suggested that people could mentally transmit images to dreaming subjects (Ullman, Krippner, & Vaughn, 1973). Yet later investigators couldn't replicate these results. All of these findings underscore the absence of a feature that's a hallmark of mature sciences: an "experimental recipe" that yields replicable results across independent laboratories (Hyman, 1999).

Indeed, unlike other areas of psychology, which contain terms for positive findings, parapsychology contains terms for negative findings, that is, effects that explain why researchers *don't* find the results they're seeking. The *experimenter effect* refers to the tendency of skeptical experimenters to inhibit ESP; the *decline effect* refers to the tendency for initial positive ESP results to disappear over time; and *psi missing* refers to significantly *worse* than chance performance on ESP tasks (Gilovich, 1991; Lilienfeld, 1999). Yet these terms appear to be little more than ad hoc hypotheses (see Chapter 1) for explaining away negative findings. Some ESP proponents have even argued that psi missing demonstrates the existence of ESP, because below chance performance indicates that subjects with ESP are deliberately selecting incorrect answers!

Why People Believe in ESP. The negative findings we've reviewed suggest that the extraordinary claim of ESP isn't matched by equally extraordinary evidence. But these findings don't demonstrate that ESP doesn't exist. In science, it's exceedingly difficult to prove a negative. Moreover, it's conceivable that parapsychologists will one day hit on a paradigm for generating replicable ESP effects. But in light of more than 150 years of failed replications, it's reasonable to ask why our beliefs in ESP are so strong given that the research evidence for it is so weak.

The *fallacy of positive instances* (see Chapter 2) offers one likely answer. We attend to and recall events that appear to be striking coincidences, and ignore or forget events that don't. Imagine we're in a new city and thinking of an old friend we haven't seen in years. A few hours later, we run into that friend on the street. "What a coincidence!" we tell ourselves. This remarkable event is evidence of ESP, right? Perhaps. But we're forgetting about the thousands of times we've been in new cities and thought about old friends whom we never encountered (Presley, 1997).

Contributing to the fallacy of positive instances is our tendency to underestimate the frequency of coincidences (see Chapter 1). Most of us don't realize just how probable certain seemingly "improbable" events are. Take a crack at this question: *How large must a group of people be before the probability of two people sharing the same birthday exceeds 50 percent?*

Many subjects respond with answers like 365, 100, or even 1,000. To most people's surprise, the correct answer is 23. That is, in a group of 23 people it's more likely than not that at least two people have the same birthday (see **Figure 4.10**). Once we get up to a group of 60 people, the odds exceed 99 percent. Because we tend to underestimate the likelihood of coincidences, we may be inclined to attribute them incorrectly to psychic phenomena.

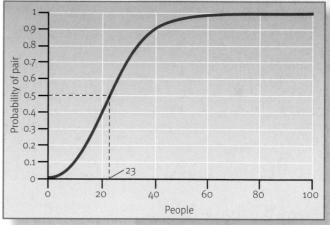

Figure 4.10 The "Birthday Paradox." As we reach a group size of 23 people, the probability that at least two people share the same birthday exceeds 0.5, or 50 percent. Research demonstrates that most people markedly underestimate the likelihood of this and other coincidences, sometimes leading them to attribute these coincidences to paranormal events.

Extraordinary Claims

Tricks of the Psychics. When a psychic forecaster predicts correctly that a major event will happen, people take special notice of it. But people forget about all of the events the psychic predicted that didn't occur, not to mention all of the events that occurred that the forecaster didn't predict. As a consequence, people tend to overestimate the psychic's accuracy.

Failed Psychic Predictions. Science journalist Gene Emery has been tracking failed psychic predictions since 1979. For example, he found that in 2005 psychics predicted that an airplane would crash into the Egyptian pyramids, astronauts would discover a Nazi flag planted on the moon, the earth's magnetic field would reverse, and a participant on a television reality show would cannibalize one of the contestants. Conversely, no psychic predicted any of the significant events that *did* occur in 2005, like Hurricane Katrina, which inflicted terrible loss of life and property damage on New Orleans and neighboring areas (Emery, 2005).

Multiple End Points. Many psychic forecasters make use of *multiple end points,* meaning they keep their predictions so open-ended that they're consistent with almost any conceivable set of outcomes (Gilovich, 1991). For example, a psychic may predict, "A celebrity will get caught in a scandal this year." But aside from being vague, this prediction

Crystal ball readers claim to be able to tell us a great deal about ourselves and our futures. Yet many of them probably rely on cold reading techniques that most of us could duplicate with relatively little training.

is extremely open-ended. What counts as a "celebrity"? Sure, we'd all agree that Paris Hilton and Brad Pitt are celebrities, but does our congressional representative count? What about a local television newscaster? Similarly, what counts as a "scandal"?

Cold Reading. What about psychics, like John Edward or James von Pragh, who claim to tell us things about ourselves or our dead relatives that they couldn't possibly have known? In reality, their feats aren't all that impressive and can be easily duplicated by experienced *mentalists*, that is, magicians who specialize in "psychological magic."

Most of these psychics probably rely on a set of skills known as *cold reading*, the art of persuading people we've just met that we know all about them (Hines, 2003; Hyman, 1977). If you want to impress your friends with a cold reading, **Table 4.2** contains some tips to keep in mind.

Table 4.2 Cold Reading Techniques.

Technique	Example
Let the person know at the outset that you won't be perfect.	"I pick up a lot of different signals. Some will be accurate, but others may not be."
Start off with a *stock spiel*, a list of general statements that apply to just about everyone.	"You've recently been struggling with some tough decisions in life."
Fish for details by peppering your reading with vague probes.	"I'm sensing that someone with the letter *M* or maybe *N* has been important in your life lately."
Use the technique of *sleight of tongue*, meaning that you toss out so many guesses in rapid-fire fashion that at least a few of them are bound to be right.	"Has your father been ill?"; "How about your mother?"; "Hmmm . . . I sense that someone in your family is ill or worried about getting ill."
Use a prop.	A crystal ball, set of tarot cards, or horoscope convey the impression that you're basing your reading on mystical information to which you have special access.
Make use of *population stereotypes*, responses or characteristics reported by many or even most people.	"I believe you have a piece of clothing, like an old dress or blouse, that you haven't worn in years but have kept for sentimental value."
Look for physical cues to the individual's personality or life history.	A traditional manner of dress often suggests a conventional and proper person, a great deal of shiny jewelry often suggests a flamboyant person, and so on.
Remember that "flattery will get you everywhere."	Tell people what they want to hear, like "I see a great romance on the horizon."

(*Source:* Hines, 2003; Hyman, 1977; Rowland, 2001)

Cold reading works for one major reason: As we've learned in earlier chapters, we humans seek meaning in our worlds and often find it even when it's not there. So in many respects we're reading into the cold reading at least as much as the cold reader is reading into us.

factoid

To persuade people you have ESP, try the following demonstration in a large group of friends. Tell them, "I want you to think of an odd two-digit number that's less than fifty, the only catch being that the two digits must be different—because that would make it too easy for me." Give them a few moments, and say, "I get the sense that some of you were thinking of 37." Then pause and say, "I was initially thinking of 35, but changed my mind. Was I close?" Research shows that slightly more than half of people will pick either 37 or 35, which are population stereotypes (see Table 4.2) that can convince many people you possess telepathic powers (French, 1992; Hines, 2003).

ASSESS YOUR KNOWLEDGE: FACT OR FICTION?

(1) Perception is an exact translation of our sensory experiences into neural activity.
(2) In signal detection theory, false alarms and misses help us measure how much someone is paying attention.
(3) Cross-modal activation often helps us process information more accurately.
(4) Subliminal perception typically influences our behavior.
(5) Belief in ESP can be partly explained by our tendency to underestimate the probability of coincidences.

Answers: (1) F (p. 152); (2) F (p. 154); (3) T (p. 155); (4) F (p. 156); (5) T (p. 161)

Seeing: The Visual System

The first thing we see after waking up is typically unbiased by any previous image. If by chance we're on vacation and sleeping somewhere new, what we see on awakening may startle us. We may not recognize our surroundings for a moment or two. Building up an image involves many external elements, such as light, along with biological systems in the eye and brain that process images for us.

LIGHT: THE ENERGY OF LIFE

One of the central players in our perception of the world is light, a form of electromagnetic energy composed of fluctuating electric and magnetic waves. Visible light has a *wavelength* in the hundreds of nanometers (a nanometer is one billionth of a meter).

The Human Visible Spectrum. As we can see in **Figure 4.11,** we respond only to a narrow range of wavelengths of light; this range is the human visible spectrum. Each animal species detects a specific visible range, which can extend slightly above or below the human visible spectrum. Butterflies are sensitive to all of the wavelengths we detect in addition to ultraviolet light, which has a shorter wavelength than violet light. We might assume that the human visible spectrum is fixed, but increasing the amount of vitamin A in our diets can increase our ability to see infrared light, which has a longer wavelength than red light (Rubin & Walls, 1969).

Brightness. When light reaches an object, part of that light gets reflected by the object and part gets absorbed. **Brightness** is the intensity of the reflected light that reaches our eyes. Completely white objects reflect all of the light shone on them and absorb none of it, whereas black objects do the opposite. The brightness of an object depends not only on the amount of reflected light, but on the overall lighting surrounding the object.

Hue. Psychologists call the color of light **hue.** We're sensitive to three primary colors of light: red, green, and blue. The mixing of varying amounts of these three primary colors—called *additive color mixing*—can produce any color (**Figure 4.12**). Mixing equal amounts of red, green, and blue light produces white light. This process is quite different from the mixing of colored pigments in paint or ink, called *subtractive color mixing*. As we can see in most printer color ink cartridges, the primary colors of pigment are yellow, cyan, and magenta, and mixing them produces a dark color (Figure 4.12).

THE EYE: HOW WE REPRESENT THE VISUAL REALM

Without our eyes we couldn't sense or perceive much of anything about light, aside from the heat it generates. Keep an "eye" on **Figure 4.13** as we tour the structures of the eye.

How Light Enters the Eye. Different parts of the eye allow in varying amounts of light. This feature is critical to our ability to see in bright sunshine or in a dark room. Other parts of the eye ensure that what we see stays in focus.

The Sclera, Iris, and Pupil. Although poets have told us that the eyes are windows onto the soul, when we look people squarely in the eye all we can see is their sclera, iris, and pupil (see **Figure 4.14**). The sclera is simply the white of the eye.

The iris is the colored part of the eye, usually blue, brown, green, or hazel. The chemicals responsible for eye color are called *pigments*. Only two pigments—melanin, which is brown, and lipochrome, which is yellowish-brown—account for all of the remarkable variations in eye colors across people. Blue eyes contain a small amount of yellow pigment and little or no brown pigment; green and hazel eyes, an intermediate amount of brown pigment; and brown eyes, a lot of brown pigment. The reason blue eyes appear blue, and not yellow, is that blue light is scattered more by irises containing less pigment. Popular

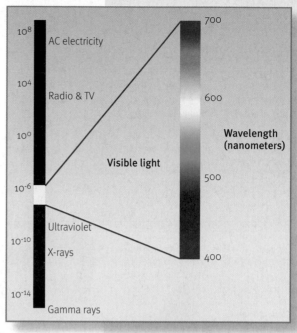

Figure 4.11 The Visible Spectrum Is a Subset of the Electromagnetic Spectrum. Visible light is electromagnetic energy between ultraviolet and infrared. Humans are sensitive to wavelengths ranging from slightly less than 400 nanometers (violet) to slightly more than 700 nanometers (red).

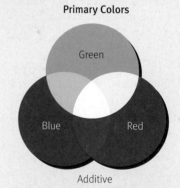

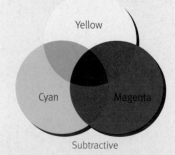

Figure 4.12 Additive and Subtractive Color Mixing. Additive color mixing of light differs from subtractive color mixing of paint.

brightness
intensity of reflected light that reaches our eyes

hue
color of light

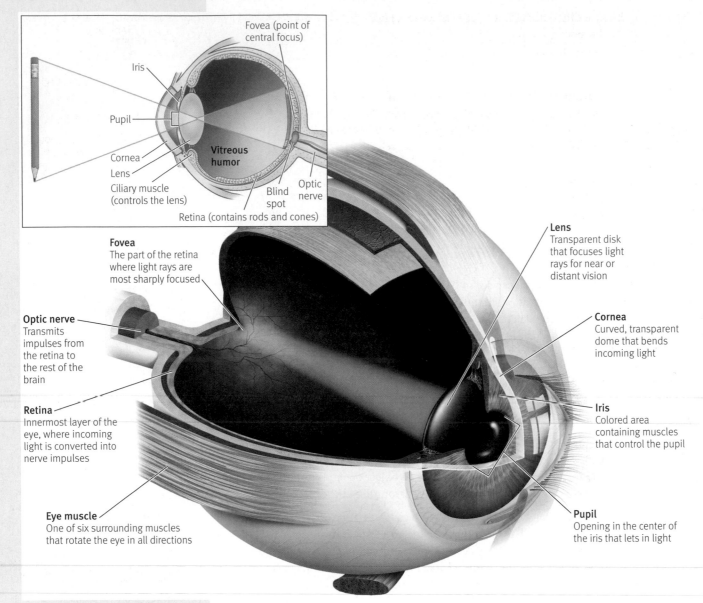

Fovea (point of central focus)

Iris

Pupil

Cornea

Lens

Ciliary muscle (controls the lens)

Vitreous humor

Blind spot

Optic nerve

Retina (contains rods and cones)

Fovea
The part of the retina where light rays are most sharply focused

Optic nerve
Transmits impulses from the retina to the rest of the brain

Retina
Innermost layer of the eye, where incoming light is converted into nerve impulses

Eye muscle
One of six surrounding muscles that rotate the eye in all directions

Lens
Transparent disk that focuses light rays for near or distant vision

Cornea
Curved, transparent dome that bends incoming light

Iris
Colored area containing muscles that control the pupil

Pupil
Opening in the center of the iris that lets in light

Figure 4.13 The Key Parts of the Eye. (*Source:* Adapted from Dorling Kindersley)

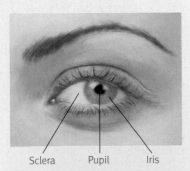

Sclera   Pupil   Iris

Figure 4.14 The Iris, Pupil, and Sclera of the Eye.

belief notwithstanding, our irises don't change color over brief periods of time, although they may seem to do so depending on lighting conditions. Like the shutter of a camera, the iris controls how much light enters our eyes.

The pupil is a circular hole through which light enters the eye. The closing of the pupil is a reflex response to light or objects coming toward us. If we walk out of a building into bright sunshine, our eyes respond with the *pupillary reflex* to decrease the amount of light allowed into them. This reflex occurs simultaneously in both eyes, so shining a flashlight into one eye triggers it in both.

The dilation (expansion) of the pupil also has psychological significance. Our pupils dilate when we're trying to process complex information, like difficult math problems (Beatty, 1982; Karetekin, 2004). They also dilate when we view someone we find physically attractive (Tombs & Silverman, 2004). This finding may help to explain why people find faces with large pupils more attractive than faces with small pupils, even when they're oblivious to this physical difference (Hess, 1965; Tomlinson, Hicks, & Pelligrini, 1978). Indeed, for centuries European women applied a juice from a plant called *Belladonna* (Italian for "beautiful woman") to their eyes to dilate their pupils, and thereby make themselves more attractive to men.

The Cornea, Lens, and Eye Muscles. The **cornea** is a curved, transparent layer covering the iris and pupil. Its curvature is responsible for bending incoming light to focus it on the back of the eye. The **lens** also bends light, but unlike the cornea, the lens changes its curvature. The lens consists of some of the most unusual cells in the body: They're completely transparent, allowing light to pass through them.

In a process called **accommodation,** the lenses change shape to focus light on the back of the eyes; in this way, they adapt to different lighting conditions. So nature has generously supplied us with a pair of "internal" corrective lenses, although they're often far from perfect. Accommodation can either make the lens "flat," enabling us to see distant objects, or "fat," enabling us to focus on nearby objects. For nearby objects, a fat lens works better because it more effectively bends the scattered light and focuses it on a single point at the back of the eye.

The Shape of the Eye. How much our eyes need to bend the path of light to focus properly depends on the curve of our corneas and overall shape of our eyes. Nearsightedness, or *myopia,* results when images are focused in front of the rear of the eye, due to our cornea being too steep or our eyes too long (**Figure 4.15a**). Nearsightedness, as the name implies, is an ability to see close objects well coupled with an inability to see far objects well. Farsightedness, or *hyperopia,* results when our cornea is too flat or our eyes too short (**Figure 4.15b**). Farsightedness, as the name implies, is an ability to see far objects well coupled with an inability to see near objects well. Our vision tends to worsen as we become older. That's because the lens can accommodate and overcome the effects of most mildly misshapen eyeballs until it loses its flexibility due to aging. This explains why only a few first-graders need eyeglasses, whereas most senior citizens do.

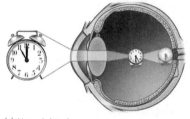

(a) Nearsighted eye

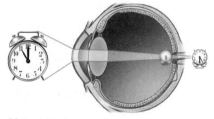

(b) Farsighted eye

Figure 4.15 Nearsighted and Farsighted Eyes. Nearsightedness or farsightedness results when light is focused in front of or behind the rear of the eye, respectively. (*Source:* St. Luke's Cataract & Laser Institute)

The Retina: Changing Light into Neural Activity.

The **retina,** which is technically part of the brain, is a thin membrane at the back of the eye. The **fovea** is the central part of the retina and is responsible for **acuity,** or sharpness of vision. We need a sharp image to read, drive, sew, or do just about anything requiring fine detail. We can think of the retina as a "movie screen" onto which light from the world is projected. It contains a hundred million sense receptor cells for vision, along with cells that process visual information and send it to the brain.

Rods and Cones. Light passes through the retina to sense receptor cells located in its outermost layer. The retina contains two types of receptor cells. The far more plentiful **rods,** which are long and narrow, enable us to see basic shapes and forms. We rely on rods to see in low levels of light. When we enter a dimly lit room, like a movie theater, from a bright environment, *dark adaptation* occurs. Dark adaptation takes about 30 minutes, or

Research demonstrates that men tend to find the faces of women with larger pupils (in this case, the face on the top) more attractive than those with smaller pupils, even when they're unaware of the reason for their preference. (Hess, 1965; Tombs & Silverman, 2004)

cornea
part of the eye containing transparent cells that focus light on the retina

lens
part of the eye that changes curvature to keep images in focus

accommodation
changing the shape of the lens to focus on objects near or far

retina
membrane at the back of the eye responsible for converting light into neural activity

fovea
central portion of the retina

acuity
sharpness of vision

rods
receptor cells in the retina allowing us to see in low levels of light

Figure 4.16 The Negative Afterimage.
Look at the center of this light bulb for at least 30 seconds. Don't take your eyes off of it. Then look at the blank white space above the figure. You should see a glowing light bulb.

Extraordinary Claims

fictoid

Myth: Our eyes emit tiny rays of light, which allow us to perceive our surroundings.

Reality: Many children and about 50 percent of college students (including those who've taken introductory psychology classes) harbor this belief, often called "emission theory" (Winer, Cottrell, Gregg, Fornier, & Bica, 2003). Nevertheless, there's no scientific evidence for this theory, and considerable evidence against it.

cones
receptor cells in the retina allowing us to see in color

blind spot
part of the visual field we can't see because of an absence of rods and cones

about the time it takes rods to regain their maximum sensitivity to light. There are no rods in the fovea, which explains why we should tilt our heads slightly to the side to see a dim star at night. By relying on our peripheral vision, we allow more light to fall on our rods.

The less numerous **cones,** which are shaped like small cones, give us our color vision. We put our cones to work when reading because they're sensitive to detail; however, cones also require more light than do rods. That's why most of us have trouble reading in a dark room.

Different types of receptor cells contain *photopigments,* chemicals that change following exposure to light. The photopigment in rods is *rhodopsin.* Vitamin A, found in abundance in carrots, is needed to make rhodopsin. This fact led to the urban legend that eating carrots is good for our vision. Unfortunately, the only time vitamin A improves vision in the normal visual spectrum is when vision is impaired due to vitamin A deficiency.

When light enters the rods it bleaches rhodopsin, causing a cascade of chemical reactions inside the rods. Rods fatigue when photopigments are depleted. That's why we often see something called a *negative afterimage* if we stare at an image for a long time. Try it for yourself: Stare at the image in **Figure 4.16** for at least half a minute, and then look at the white space above the figure. What do you see? A reverse image appears because our sense receptors become fatigued after too much photopigment is bleached. The brightest parts of an image result in the most fatigue, the darkest parts the least. When we stare at a white space, these differences in response translate into the perception of an image—the reverse image.

Some people occasionally report faint negative afterimages surrounding objects or other individuals. This phenomenon may have given rise to the paranormal idea that we're all encircled by mystical "auras" consisting of psychical energy (Neher, 1990). Nevertheless, because no one's been able to photograph auras under carefully controlled conditions, there's no support for this extraordinary claim (Nickel, 2000).

Ganglion Cells.   Only the last cells in the retinal circuit, the *ganglion cells,* contain axons. Ganglion cells bundle all their axons together and depart the eye to reach the brain.

The Blind Spot.   The **blind spot** is the part of the visual field we can't see. It's a region of the retina containing no rods and totally devoid of sense receptors (refer back to Figure 4.13). The reason we have a blind spot is that the axons of ganglion cells push everything else aside. The exercise we performed at the outset of this chapter made use of the blind spot to generate an illusion (refer back to Figure 4.1). Our blind spot is there all of the time, not only when we're looking at an optical illusion. Yet because our visual system fills in the gaps and because each of our eyes supplies us with a slightly different picture of the world, we don't ordinarily notice it.

The Optic Nerve.   The *optic nerve,* which contains the axons of ganglion cells, travels from the retina to the rest of the brain. After the optic nerves leave both eyes, they come to a fork in the road called the *optic chiasm.* Half the axons cross in the optic chiasm and the other half stay on the same side. Within a short distance, the optic nerves enter the brain, turning into the optic tracts. The optic tracts send most of their axons to the visual thalamus and then to the primary visual cortex—called V1—the primary route for visual perception (see **Figure 4.17**). Some of the axons go instead to the *superior colliculus* in the midbrain (see Chapter 3). These axons play a key role in reflexes, like turning our heads to follow something interesting we've seen.

VISUAL PERCEPTION

Now that we know how our nervous system gathers and transmits visual information, we can examine how we perceive shape, motion, color, and depth, all of which are handled by different parts of the visual cortex (see Figure 4.17). Even though different parts of the brain process different aspects of visual perception, we perceive whole objects and unified scenes, not isolated components. By compensating for missing information, our perceptual systems help us make sense of the world, but they occasionally out-and-out deceive us along the way.

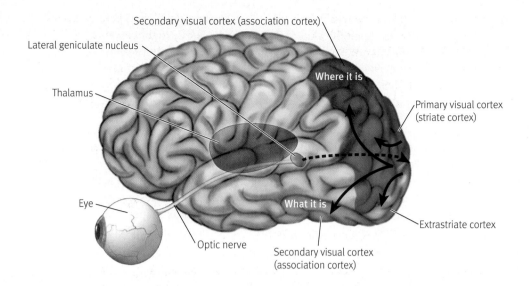

Secondary visual cortex (association cortex)

Lateral geniculate nucleus

Thalamus

Where it is

Primary visual cortex
(striate cortex)

Eye

What it is

Extrastriate cortex

Optic nerve

Secondary visual cortex
(association cortex)

Figure 4.17 Perception and the Visual Cortex. Visual information from the retina travels to the superior colliculus and visual thalamus. Next, the visual thalamus sends inputs to the primary visual cortex (V1), and then to V2, and then along two visual pathways: one going to the parietal lobe, which processes visual form, position, and motion, and one to the temporal lobe, which processes visual form and color.

How We Perceive Shape and Contour. In the 1960s, David Hubel and Torsten Wiesel sought to unlock the secrets of how we perceive shape and form; their work eventually led to a Nobel Prize. They used cats as their subjects because their visual responses are much like ours. Hubel and Wiesel recorded electrical activity in the visual cortexes of cats while presenting them with visual stimuli on a screen (**Figure 4.18**). At first, Hubel and Wiesel were unaware of which stimuli would work best, so they tried many different types, including bright and dark spots. At one point, they put up a different kind of stimulus on the screen, a long slit of light. As the story goes, one of their slides jammed in the slide projector slightly off-center, producing a slit of light (Horgan, 1999). Cells in V1 suddenly went haywire, firing action potentials at an amazingly high rate when the slit moved across the screen. Motivated by this surprising result, Hubel and Wiesel devoted years to figuring out which types of slits elicited such responses.

Here's what they found (Hubel & Wiesel, 1962; 1963). Many cells in V1 respond to slits of light of a specific orientation, for example, vertical, horizontal, or oblique lines or edges (refer again to Figure 4.18). Cells in the visual cortex are of different types. *Simple cells* display distinctive responses to slits of a specific orientation, but these slits need to be in a specific location. *Complex cells* are also orientation-specific, but their responses are less restricted to one location. This feature makes complex cells markedly advanced over simple cells. Here's why.

Let's say we've learned a concept in our psychology class that allows us to give simple yes or no answers to questions. That would be similar to a simple cell responding: Yes, this part of the visual field sees a vertical line, or no, it doesn't. Now let's suppose our professor has a nasty reputation for requiring us to apply a concept rather than merely regurgitate it (don't you hate that?). Applying a concept is analogous to the workings of a complex cell. A complex cell responds to the abstract idea of a line of a specific orientation, and for this reason, it may well represent the first cell in which sensation transitions to perception. The simplest idea in our minds may be a straight line!

Feature Detection. Our ability to use certain minimal patterns to identify objects is called *feature detection*. Although simple and complex cells are *feature detector cells* insofar as they detect lines and edges, there are more complex feature detector cells at higher levels of visual processing, which detect lines of specific lengths, complex shapes, and even moving objects. We use our ability to detect edges and corners to perceive lots of human-made objects, like furniture, toasters, laptops, and even the corners of the page you're reading at this moment.

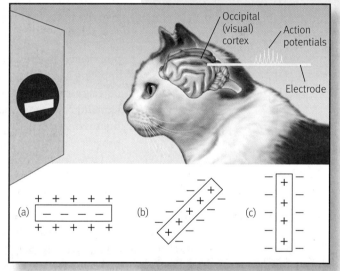

Occipital (visual) cortex

Action potentials

Electrode

(a)   (b)   (c)

Figure 4.18 Cells Respond to Slits of Light of a Particular Orientation. *Top:* Hubel and Wiesel studied activity in the visual cortex of cats viewing slits of light on a screen. *Bottom:* Visual responses were specific to slits of dark on light (minuses on pluses—a) or light on dark (pluses on minuses—b), which were of particular orientations, such as horizontal, oblique, or vertical—(c). Cells in the visual cortex also detected edges.

We're not alone when it comes to detecting edges and corners. In this example, a computer program detects edges (*blue*) and corners (*red*).

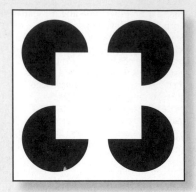

Figure 4.19 Kanizsa Square. This Kanizsa square illustrates subjective contours. The square you perceive in the middle of this figure is imaginary. (*Source:* Herrmann & Friederici, 2001)

APPLY YOUR THINKING
How can we explain why our visual systems are fundamentally sensitive to straight edges resembling human-made objects, when in evolutionary terms, these abilities came before humans?

As we saw in Figure 4.17, visual information travels from V1 to higher visual areas along two major routes, one of which goes to the upper parts of the parietal lobe, and the other of which goes to the lower part of the temporal lobe. Maximilian Riesenhuber and Tomaso Poggio (1999) proposed a hierarchical model of visual processing in which successively higher cortical regions process more and more complex shapes. The many visual processing areas of cortex enable us to move from basic shapes to the complex objects we see in our everyday worlds.

Subjective Contours. Our brains often provide missing information about outlines, a phenomenon called *subjective contours*. Gaetano Kanizsa sparked interest in this phenomenon in 1955. His Kanizsa figures illustrate how a mere hint of three or four corners can give rise to the perception of an imaginary triangle or square (see **Figure 4.19**).

Gestalt Principles. As we learned in our discussion of top-down processing, much of our visual perception involves analyzing an image in the context of its surroundings and applying what we already know. *Gestalt principles* are rules governing how we perceive objects as wholes within their overall context (*Gestalt* is a German word meaning "whole"). Gestalt principles of perception help to explain why we see much of our world as unified figures or forms rather than as a confusing jumble of lines and curves. These principles provide a road map for how we organize and make sense of our perceptual world.

Here are the main Gestalt principles, formulated by Gestalt psychologists Max Wertheimer, Wolfgang Kohler, and Kurt Koffka in the early twentieth century (see **Figure 4.20**):

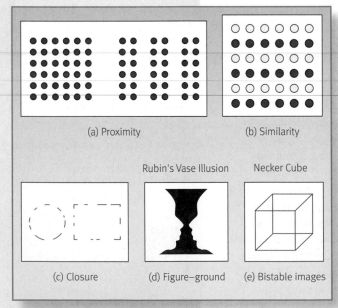

Figure 4.20 Gestalt Principles of Perception. As Gestalt psychologists discovered, we use a variety of principles to help us organize the world.

(1) *Proximity:* Objects physically close to each other tend to be perceived as unified wholes (**Figure 4.20a**).

(2) *Similarity:* All things being equal, we see similar objects as comprising a whole, much more so than dissimilar objects. For example, if patterns of red circles and yellow circles are randomly mixed, we perceive nothing special. But if the red and yellow circles are lined up horizontally, we perceive separate rows of circles (**Figure 4.20b**).

(3) *Good continuation:* We still perceive objects as wholes, even if other objects block part of them.

(4) *Closure:* When partial visual information is present, the mind fills in what's missing. When the missing information is a contour, this principle is essentially the same as subjective contours. This Gestalt principle is the main illusion in the Kanizsa figures (**Figure 4.20c**).

(5) *Symmetry:* We perceive objects that are symmetrically arranged as wholes more often than those that aren't.

(6) *Figure–ground:* Perceptually, we make an instant decision to focus attention on what we believe to be the central figure, and largely ignore what we believe to be the background. We can view some figures, such as Rubin's vase illusion, in two ways (**Figure 4.20d**). The vase can be the figure, in which case we ignore the background. If we look again, we can see an image in the background: two faces looking at each other.

Rubin's vase illusion is also an example of a *bistable* image, an image we can perceive in one of two ways. When we look at bistable images, we can typically perceive them only one way at a time, and there are limits to how quickly we can shift from one view to the other. The Necker cube is another example of a bistable image (**Figure 4.20e**). A concept related to the bistable image is *emergence*—a perceptual gestalt that almost jumps out from the page and hits us all at once. Try to find the Dalmatian dog in the photo on this page. If you have trouble, keep staring at the black-and-white photo until the dog emerges. It's worth the wait.

Face Recognition. Our ability to recognize familiar faces, including our own, lies at the core of our social selves. After all, don't we refer to a friend as "a familiar face"? Even nonhuman primates can recognize faces (Pinsk et al., 2005).

We don't need an exact picture of a face to recognize it. Caricature artists have known this fact for a long time and amused us with their versions of famous faces, usually with some feature exaggerated way out of proportion. Why can we recognize these wacky faces? As we've already learned, our brains get by with only partial information, because we acquire information from the surrounding context and our preconceptions.

Do individual neurons respond specifically to certain faces? Scientists have known for some time that the lower part of the temporal lobe responds to faces (refer back to Figure 4.17). As we'll learn in Chapter 7, researchers have recently identified neurons in the human hippocampus that fire selectively in response to celebrity faces, such as those of Jennifer Aniston and Halle Berry (Quiroga et al., 2005). In the 1960s, Jerry Lettvin half-jokingly proposed that each neuron in the brain might store a single memory, like the recollection of our grandmother sitting in our living room when we were children. Lettvin coined the term "grandmother cell" to represent this straw man argument, assuming it could be easily falsified (Horgan, 2005). Certain neurons, such as those responding to Jennifer Aniston, are suggestive of the grandmother cell idea, but we shouldn't be too quick to accept this possibility. Even though individual cells may respond to Aniston and Berry, many other neurons in other lobes of the brain probably chime in too. Researchers can only make recordings from a small number of neurons at a time, so we don't know what the rest of the brain is doing. At present, the most parsimonious hypothesis is that sprawling networks of neurons, rather than single cells, are responsible for face recognition.

How We Perceive Motion. The brain judges how things in our world are constantly changing by comparing visual frames, like those in a movie. Perceiving the motion of a car coming toward us as we cross the street relies on this kind of motion detection, and we couldn't cross the street, let alone drive a car, without it. We can also be fooled into seeing motion when it's not there. Moving closer to and farther from certain clever designs produces the illusion of motion, as we can see in **Figure 4.21**. The *phi phenomenon*, discovered by Gestalt psychologist Max Wertheimer, is the illusory perception of movement produced by the successive flashing of images, like the flashing lights that seem to circle around a movie marquee. These lights are actually jumping from one spot on the marquee to another, but they appear continuous. The phi phenomenon and other illusions show that our perceptions of what's moving and what's not are based on only partial information, with our brains making their best guesses about what's missing. Luckily, many of these guesses are accurate, or at least accurate enough for us to get along in everyday life.

How We Perceive Color. Color delights our senses and stirs our imagination. Colorization, the process of adding color, breathes new life into old black-and-white movies. When critics bemoaned the colorization of the classic film *Casablanca,* the president of Colorization Incorporated responded, "People don't like black and white. When we color it, they buy it" (Krauthammer, 1987).

We use the lower visual pathway leading to the temporal lobe to process color information (refer back to Figure 4.17), but it hardly starts there. Different theories of color perception explain different aspects of our ability to detect color, enabling us to see the world, watch TV, and enjoy movies, all in vibrant color.

Embedded in this photograph is an image of a Dalmatian dog. Can you find it?

Falsifiability

Occam's Razor

Figure 4.21 Moving Spiral Illusion. Focus on the plus sign in the middle of the figure and move the page closer to your face and then farther away. The two rings should appear to move in opposite directions, and those directions should reverse when you reverse the direction in which you move the page. (*Source:* coolopticalillusions.com)

Trichromatic Theory. **Trichromatic theory** is the idea that we base our color vision on three primary colors—blue, green, and red. Trichromatic theory dovetails with our having three kinds of cones, each maximally sensitive to different wavelengths of light. Given that the three types of cones were discovered in the 1960s (Brown & Wald, 1964), it's perhaps surprising that Thomas Young and Hermann von Helmholtz described trichromatic theory over 100 years earlier. Young's theory (1802) proposed that our vision is sensitive to three primary colors of light. Hermann von Helmholtz (1850) replicated and extended Young's proposal by testing the colors that color-blind subjects could see, and the Young-Helmholtz trichromatic theory of color vision was born. Persons with **color blindness** can't see all colors.

Humans, apes, and some monkeys are *trichromats*, meaning we and our close biological relatives possess three kinds of cones. Most other mammals, including dogs and cats, see the world with only two cones, which is about the same as how people with green-red color blindness (the most frequent form of color blindness) see the world. Color vision evolved about 35 million years ago. Some scientists have proposed that trichromatic color vision evolved because it allowed animals to easily pick ripe fruit out of a green background. Recent fossil evidence suggests an alternative hypothesis, namely, that trichromatic vision may have enabled primates to find young, reddish, tender leaves that were nutritionally superior (Simon-Moffat, 2002). All scientists agree that being able to see more colors gave our ancestors a leg up in foraging for food.

Opponent Process Theory. For many years the trichromatic theory was pitted against a different theory of color vision based on perceiving one of two complementary color pairs, such as red versus green. According to *opponent process* theory, we perceive color as either red or green, or as either blue or yellow. Afterimages, which appear in complementary colors (like red images appearing after exposure to green images), illustrate opponent processing in the visual system. As predicted by opponent process theory, ganglion cells of the retina and cells in the visual thalamus that respond to red spots are inhibited by green spots. Other cells show the opposite responses, and still others distinguish yellow from blue spots. It turns out that our nervous system uses both trichromatic and opponent principles during color vision, but different neurons in our brains rely on one principle more than the other. There's a useful lesson here that applies to many controversies in science: Two ideas that seem to contradict each other are sometimes both partly correct—they're merely describing differing aspects of a phenomenon.

How We Perceive Depth. **Depth perception** is the ability to see spatial relations in three dimensions; it enables us to reach for a glass and grasp it rather than knock it over and spill its contents. We need to have some idea of how close or far we are from objects to navigate around our environments. We use two kinds of cues to gauge depth: **monocular depth cues,** which rely on one eye alone, and **binocular depth cues,** which require both eyes.

Monocular Cues. We can perceive three dimensions using only one eye. We do so by relying on *pictorial cues* to give us a sense of what's located where in stationary scenes. The following pictorial cues help us to perceive depth.

- *Relative size:* More distant objects look smaller than closer objects.
- *Texture gradient:* The texture of objects becomes less apparent as objects move farther away.
- *Interposition:* One object that's closer blocks our view of an object behind it. From this fact, we know which object is closer and which is farther away.
- *Linear perspective:* The outlines of rooms or buildings converge as distance increases. Artists often make use of linear perspective. We can trace most lines in a scene to a point where they meet—the *vanishing point.* In reality, lines in parallel never meet, but they appear to do so at great distances. Some *impossible figures*—figures that break physical laws—have more than one vanishing point. Artist M. C. Escher was fond of violating this rule in his prints.
- *Height in plane:* In a scene, distant objects appear higher, and nearer objects lower.
- *Light and shadow:* Objects cast shadows that give us a sense of their three-dimensional form.

One additional monocular cue that's not pictorial is *motion parallax:* the ability to judge the distance of moving objects from their speed. Nearby objects seem to move faster than those far away traveling at the same speed. Motion parallax also works when we're

---

Replicability

Ruling Out Rival Hypotheses

fact**oid**

There's preliminary evidence that a small proportion of women are *tetrachromats,* meaning their eyes contain four types of cones: the three cone types most of us possess plus an additional cone for a color between red and green (Jameson, Highnote, & Wasserman, 2001).

New evidence suggests that primates evolved trichromatic color vision to detect tender red leaves rich in protein and nutrients.

trichromatic theory
idea that color vision is based on our sensitivity to three different colors

color blindness
inability to see some or all colors

depth perception
ability to judge distance and three-dimensional relations

monocular depth cues
stimuli that enable us to judge depth using only one eye

binocular depth cues
stimuli that enable us to judge depth using both eyes

moving. Stationary objects nearer to us pass us more quickly than objects farther away, a fact we'll discover when looking out of the windows of a moving car. Our brains compute these differences in speed and calculate approximate distances from us.

Binocular Cues. Our visual system is set up so that we view each of our two visual fields with both eyes. We'll recall that half of the axons in the optic nerve cross to the other side and half stay on the same side before entering the brain. Visual information from both sides is sent to neighboring cells in the visual cortex, where our brains can make comparisons. These comparisons form the basis of binocular depth perception.

- *Binocular disparity:* Like the two lenses from a pair of binoculars, our left and right eyes transmit quite different information for near objects but see distant objects similarly. This depth cue is easy to demonstrate. Close one of your eyes and hold a pen up about a foot away from your face, lining the top of it up with a distant point on the wall (like a door knob or corner of a picture frame). Then, hold the pen steady while alternating which of your eyes is open. You'll find that although the pen is lined up with one eye, it's no longer lined up when you switch to the other eye. Each eye sees the world a bit differently, and our brains ingeniously make use of this information to judge depth.
- *Binocular convergence:* When we look at nearby objects, we reflexively focus on them by using our eye muscles to turn our eyes inward, a phenomenon called *convergence*. Our brains are aware of how much our eyes are converging, and they use this information to estimate distance.

Depth Perception Appears in Infancy. We can judge depth as soon as we learn to crawl. Eleanor Gibson established this phenomenon in a classic experimental setup called the *visual cliff* (Gibson, 1991; Gibson & Walk, 1960). The typical visual cliff consists of a table covered with a checkered cloth that drops to the floor, which is covered by the same checkered cloth. A clear glass surface extends from the table out over the floor. Infants between 6 and 14 months of age hesitate to crawl over the glass elevated several feet above the floor, even when their mothers beckon. The visual cliff findings tell us that depth cues are present soon after birth, and are probably largely innate rather than learned.

When Perception Deceives Us. Sometimes the best way to understand how something works is to see how it doesn't work—or works in unusual circumstances. We've already examined a number of illusions that illustrate principles of sensation and perception. Now we'll examine further how optical illusions and other unusual phenomena help us to understand everyday perception.

The Moon Illusion. The *moon illusion* has fascinated laypersons, philosophers, and scientists for centuries (Ross & Plug, 2003). The illusion is that the moon appears larger when it's near the horizon than high in the sky. There are many explanations for this illusion. A common misconception is that the moon appears larger near the horizon due to a magnification effect caused by the Earth's atmosphere. But we can easily refute this hypothesis. Although the Earth's atmosphere does alter the moon's color at the horizon, it doesn't enlarge it. In fact, the angle of the moon relative to Earth at the horizon *decreases* the appearance of the moon's diameter by 1.5 percent.

Let's contrast this common misconception with a few better-supported explanations. The first is that the moon illusion is due to errors in perceived distance. The moon is some 240,000 miles away, a huge distance we've had little experience judging. When the moon is high in the sky, there's nothing else around for comparison. In contrast, when the moon is near the horizon, we may unconsciously perceive it as farther away because we can see it next to things we know to be far away, like buildings, mountains, and trees. Because we know these things are large, we perceive the moon as larger still. Still another explanation is that we're mistaken about the three-dimensional space in which we live, along with the moon. For example, many people have the misperception that the sky is shaped like a flattened dome, leading us to see the moon as farther away on the horizon than at the top of the sky. (Rock & Kaufman, 1962).

This lithograph by M. C. Escher titled *Belvedere* (1958) features two vanishing points, resulting in an impossible structure. Can you locate the vanishing points off the page?

The visual cliff tests infants' ability to judge depth.

Falsifiability

The moon illusion causes us to perceive the moon as larger near the horizon than high in the sky. Here, the moon looks huge at the San Francisco skyline.

The Ames Room. The Ames room is another well-known illusion, designed by Adelbert Ames Jr. (1946). As shown in **Figure 4.22,** this distorted room is actually trapezoidal. The walls are slanted and the ceiling and floor are at an incline. Insert two people of the same size and the Ames room creates the impression of a giant person on the side of the room where the ceiling is lower (but doesn't appear to be) and of a tiny person on the side of the room where the ceiling is higher. This striking illusion is due to the relative size principle. The height of the ceiling is the key to the illusion. The other distortions in the room are only necessary to make the room appear normal to the observer standing in front of it.

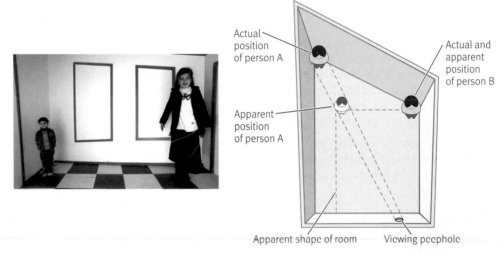

Figure 4.22 The Ames Room. Viewed through a small peephole, the Ames room makes small people look impossibly large and large people look impossibly small. Who is the younger and smaller child in this picture?

More Size-Distorting Illusions. Other illusions give rise to the misperception of size.

- In the *Müller-Lyer illusion,* a line of identical length appears longer when it ends in a set of arrowheads pointing inward than in a set of arrowheads pointing outward (see **Figure 4.23a**). That's because we perceive lines as part of a larger context. Three researchers (Segall, Campbell, & Herskovitz, 1966) found that people from different cultures displayed differing reactions to the Müller-Lyer illusion. The Zulu, who live in round huts and plow their fields in circles rather than rows, are less susceptible to the Müller-Lyer illusion, probably because they have less experience with linear environments.

- In the *Ponzo illusion,* known also as the railroad tracks illusion, converging lines enclose two objects of identical size, leading us to perceive the object closer to the converging lines as larger (see **Figure 4.23b**). Our brain "assumes" that the object closer to the converging lines is farther away, and compensates for this knowledge by making the object look bigger.

- The *horizontal–vertical illusion* causes us to perceive the vertical part of an upside-down "T" as longer than the horizontal part, because the horizontal part is divided in half by the vertical part (see **Figure 4.23c**).

- The *Ebbinghaus–Titchener* illusion causes us to perceive a circle as larger when surrounded by smaller circles and smaller when surrounded by larger circles (see **Figure 4.23d**). Although this illusion fools our eyes, it doesn't fool our hands! Experiments in which subjects have to reach for the center circle indicate that their grasp remains on target (Milner & Goodale, 1995), although some scientists have recently challenged this finding (Franz et al., 2003).

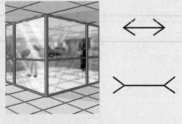

(a) Which horizontal line is longer?

(b) Which line above is longer, and which circle is bigger?

(c) Which line is longer?

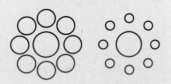

(d) Which center circle is bigger?

Figure 4.23 How Well Can You Judge Relative Size? The Müller-Lyer (a), Ponzo (b), horizontal–vertical (c), and Ebbinghaus–Titchener (d) illusions.

APPLY YOUR THINKING

Auditory stimuli can affect our visual perceptions. In one such illusion, two balls headed toward one another on a computer screen ordinarily appear to cross through each other instead of colliding. When a "pong" sound occurs precisely as they meet, they appear to collide and bounce off each other (Sekuler, Sekuler, & Lau, 1997). What everyday situations does this illusion resemble?

Change Blindness. We're surprisingly poor at detecting obvious changes in complex scenes if those changes occur during eye movements, while lights are flickering, or during frame changes in a video series (Henderson & Hollingworth, 1999; Levin & Simons, 1997; McConkie & Currie, 1996). In an astonishing demonstration of this phenomenon, called *change blindness,* Daniel Simons and Christopher Chabris (1999) asked subjects to watch a videotape of people tossing a basketball, and required them to keep track of the number of passes. Then, smack in the middle of the videotape, a woman dressed in a gorilla suit strolled across the scene for a full 9 seconds. Remarkably, about half the subjects failed to notice the hairy misfit even though she paused to face the camera and thump her chest. This and other findings demonstrate that we often need to pay close attention to pick out even dramatic changes in our environments (Koivisto & Revonsuo, 2007; Rensink, O'Regan, & Clark, 1997). Change blindness is a particular concern for airplane pilots, who may fail to notice another plane taxiing across the runway as they're preparing to land (Podczerwinski, Wickens, & Alexander, 2002). You may be relieved to hear that industrial/organizational psychologists (see the Prologue) are working actively with aviation agencies to reduce the incidence of this problem.

Synesthesia. Sir Francis Galton (1880) was the first to describe *synesthesia,* a condition in which people experience cross-modal sensations, like hearing sounds when they see colors—sometimes called "colored hearing"—or even tasting colors (Cytowic, 1993). Synesthesia may be an extreme version of the cross-modal responses that most of us experience from time to time, as we described earlier (Rader & Tellegen, 1987). The great Finnish composer Jean Sibelius saw notes as colors and even claimed to smell them. In one case, he asked a worker to repaint his kitchen stove in the key of F major. No one knows for sure how widespread synesthesia is, but some estimates put it at no higher than about 1 in 2,500 people (Baron-Cohen, Harrison, Goldstein, & Wyke, 1993).

There are different kinds of synesthesias, including *grapheme-color* synesthesia. In this most common type of synesthesia, a "6" may always seem red and a "5" green. In *music-color* synesthesia, people see a specific color on hearing a specific musical note. In *lexical-taste* synesthesia, words have associated tastes, and in yet other synesthesias, letters take on "personality traits," such as an *A* being perceived as bold and confident.

Some scientists have questioned the authenticity of synesthesia and accused synesthetes of having overly vivid imaginations, seeking attention, or being on hallucinogenic drugs. Yet research clearly demonstrates that the condition is genuine (Ramachandran & Hubbard, 2001). **Figure 4.24** illustrates a clever test that detects grapheme-color synesthesia. Specific parts of the visual cortex become active during colored hearing and during grapheme-color synesthetic experiences, further verifying that these experiences are associated with brain activity (Paulesu et al., 1995; Ramachandran & Hubbard, 2001).

WHEN WE CAN'T SEE OR PERCEIVE VISUALLY

We've learned how we see, and how we don't always see exactly what's there. Yet some 40 million people worldwide can't see at all.

Blindness. Blindness is the inability to see, or more specifically, the presence of vision less than or equal to 20/200 on the Snellen eye test. That's the well-known eye chart in which 20/20 is perfect vision. For people with 20/200 vision, objects at 20 feet appear as they would at 200 feet in a normally sighted person. Many people in underdeveloped countries

In these frames from the videoclip, a woman in a gorilla suit fails to catch the attention of most subjects, who are too busy counting basketball passes.

Figure 4.24 Are You Synesthetic? Although most of us see the top image as a bunch of jumbled numbers, some grapheme-color synesthetes perceive it as looking like the image on the bottom. Synesthesia makes it much easier to find the 2s embedded in a field of 5s. (*Source:* Adapted from Ramachandran & Hubbard, 2001)

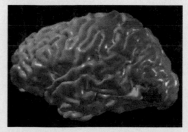

Regions of the brain showing enhanced activity during grapheme-color synesthetic experience. (*Source:* Ramachandran & Hubbard, 2001)

are blind because they lack access to medical care. The major causes of blindness worldwide are listed in **Table 4.3,** and the percentages of blind persons in each part of the world are illustrated in **Figure 4.25.**

The blind cope with their loss of vision in various ways, often relying more on other senses, including touch. This issue has been controversial over the years, with studies both replicating and contradicting a heightened sense of touch in the blind. Recent studies suggest that tactile (touch) sensitivity is indeed heightened in blind adults, giving them the same sensitivity as someone 23 years younger (Goldreich & Kanics, 2003). It's further known that the visual cortex of blind persons undergoes profound changes in function, rendering it sensitive to touch inputs (Sadato, 2005). This means they can devote more cortex—somatosensory cortex and visual cortex—to a touch task, such as reading Braille.

The blind also demonstrate their reliance on tactile cues when they draw pictures. John Kennedy (2006) has been studying Betty, a blind teenager from Canada who lost her sight at age 2. With such early blindness, there's little opportunity to learn visual skills, such as how to draw pictures. Nonetheless, Betty and others with early blindness have amazingly similar drawing abilities as those of sighted persons, just so long as they set up their paper on felt or rubber to feel the indentations made by their pens.

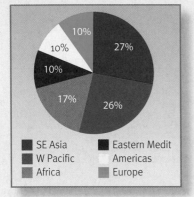

Replicability

Figure 4.25 Percent of Blind Persons in Each Part of the World. (*Source:* WHO, 2002)

Table 4.3 Major Causes of Blindness.

Cause of Blindness	Percent of All Blind Persons Worldwide	Treatable
Cataract	47.8%	Yes
Glaucoma	12.3%	Yes
Macular degeneration	8.7%	No
Diabetic retinopathy	4.8%	No
Childhood blindness	3.9%	Some types are treatable

(*Source:* Data reported by the World Health Organization based on the 2002 population)

Gisela Leibold is unable to detect motion. She's understandably concerned about important information she might miss riding down an escalator in Munich.

Color Blindness. *Color blindness,* the loss of perception for one or more colors, is most often due to the absence or reduced number of one or more types of cones stemming from genetic abnormalities. Still another cause is damage to a brain area related to color vision. Contrary to a popular misconception, *monochromats*—who have only one type of cone and thereby lose all color vision—are extremely rare, making up only about 0.0007 percent of the population. Most color-blind individuals can perceive a good deal of their world in color because they're *dichromats,* meaning they have two cones and are missing only one. Red-green dichromats see considerable color but can't distinguish reds as well as people with normal color vision. We can find a test for red-green color blindness in **Figure 4.26;** many males have this condition but don't even know it because it doesn't interfere much with their everyday functioning.

Motion Blindness. Motion blindness is a serious disorder in which patients can't seamlessly string still images processed by their brains into the perception of ongoing motion. As we noted earlier, motion perception is much like creating a movie in our heads. Actual movies contain twenty-four frames of still photos per second, creating the illusory perception of motion. In patients with motion blindness, many of these "frames" are missing. This disability interferes with many simple tasks, like crossing the street. Imagine a car appearing to be 1,000 feet away and then suddenly jumping to only 10 feet away a second or two later. Needless to say, the experience would be terrifying. Life indoors often isn't much better. Simply pouring a cup of coffee can be enormously challenging, because the person doesn't see the cup fill up. First, it's empty and then suddenly the coffee may be over-flowing onto the table.

Visual Agnosia. *Visual agnosia* is a deficit in perceiving objects. A person with this agnosia can tell us the shape and color of an object, but can't recognize it. Oliver Sacks's 1985 book, *The Man Who Mistook His Wife for a Hat,* includes a case study of a visual agnosic who did exactly as the title suggests; he misperceived his wife as a fashion accessory. David Milner and Melvyn Goodale (1995) described the case of D.F., a woman suffering from visual agnosia resulting from carbon monoxide poisoning. In visual agnosics, there's typically no damage to the optic nerve, retina, or V1—the primary visual cortex. The damage lies in visual areas that piece together visual elements; D.F.'s damage was in her visual association cortex. Curiously, D.F. was impaired at reporting the position of things, such as estimating the position or height of a barrier, but not when stepping over it (Allard, 2001).

Blindsight. *Blindsight* is the remarkable phenomenon in which people with cortical blindness resulting from damage in V1 can make correct guesses about things in their environment, even though they can't see them. Larry Weiskrantz (1986) asked cortically blind subjects whether they saw stimuli consisting of stripes arranged either vertically or horizontally within circles. When these cortically blind subjects answered at better than chance levels—while reporting they *saw nothing*—many scientists were understandably baffled. Because blindsight operates outside the bounds of conscious activity, some nonscientists have suggested that it may be a supernatural phenomenon. Yet there's a parsimonious natural explanation: People with blindsight have suffered damage to V1, so that route of information flow to visual association areas is blocked. Coarser visual information still reaches the visual association cortex without going through V1, so this visual information probably accounts for blindsight (Rodman, 1995; Stoerig & Cowey, 1997; Weiskrantz, 1986).

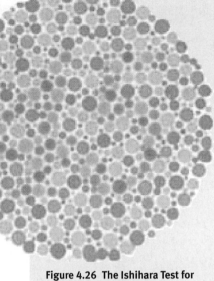

Figure 4.26 The Ishihara Test for Red-Green Color Blindness. If you can't see the two-digit number, you probably have red-green color blindness. This condition is common, especially among males.

Occam's Razor

NEW FRONTIERS
LASIK Surgery: The Pros and Cons

Should you throw away your glasses or contact lenses in favor of eye surgery to correct your vision permanently? Like many things, there are pros and cons.

LASIK is an acronym for *laser-assisted in situ keratomileusis* (*keratomileusis* is a whopper of a word referring to the carving of the cornea to reshape it). In this procedure, which lasts only 60–90 seconds, the outermost flap of the cornea is folded over, while the laser reshapes the exposed inner surface of the cornea according to precise measurements based on a person's corrective lens prescription. After reshaping, the flap readily adheres to the rest of the cornea and requires no stitches. By the next morning, if not sooner, patients begin to experience better vision. Nonetheless, patients receiving LASIK need to be careful not to rub their eyes for a few days.

There are many advantages to undergoing this procedure. People with LASIK-corrected vision need not bother with inserting contact lenses or wearing glasses. They can wake up in the morning able to see well immediately. Currently, LASIK procedures exist for correcting nearsightedness, farsightedness, and *astigmatisms* (impaired vision

(continued)

LASIK surgery reshapes the inner layer of the cornea.

caused by irregularly shaped corneas and lenses). A major disadvantage is that LASIK is expensive compared with eyeglasses or contact lenses.

There are some common misconceptions about LASIK. It's not always the case that people who undergo LASIK will never again need glasses or contact lenses. In some cases of farsightedness, patients still need reading glasses to correct near vision. In rare cases, LASIK has made vision worse or resulted in infections (Schallhorn, Amesbury, & Tanzer, 2006).

Some people are better candidates for LASIK than others. Being over 18 years of age and having a stable eye lens prescription is critical. Having a mild to moderate visual impairment, rather than a severe one, makes us a better candidate. Being in good general health is also important.

Tens of thousands of people have undergone LASIK surgery and many express complete satisfaction. It's largely a matter of personal choice.

ASSESS YOUR KNOWLEDGE: FACT OR FICTION?

(1) The visible spectrum of light differs across species and can differ across individuals.
(2) The lens of the eye changes shape depending on whether lighting conditions are bright or dim.
(3) Although we perceive objects as unified wholes, different parts of our brains process different kinds of visual information, such as shape, color, and motion.
(4) We perceive depth only when we have two slightly different views from our eyes.
(5) Red-green color blindness results when rods are missing but cones are intact.

Answers: (1) T (p. 163); (2) F (p. 165); (3) T (p. 166); (4) F (p. 170); (5) F (p. 174)

Hearing: The Auditory System

If a tree falls in the forest and no one is around to hear it, does it make a sound? Ponder that age-old question while we explore our sense of hearing: **audition.** Next to vision, hearing is probably the sensory modality we rely on most to acquire information about our world.

SOUND: MECHANICAL VIBRATION

Sound is vibration, a kind of mechanical energy traveling through a medium, usually air. The disturbance created by vibration of molecules of air produces sound waves. Sound waves can travel through any gas, liquid, or solid, but we hear them best when they travel through air. In a perfectly empty space (a vacuum), there can't be sound because there aren't any airborne molecules to vibrate. That should help us answer the question about the fallen tree: Are there air molecules in the forest?

Pitch.   Sounds have *pitch*, which corresponds to the frequency of the wave. Higher frequency corresponds to higher pitch, lower frequency to lower pitch. Scientists measure pitch in cycles per second, or hertz (Hz) (see **Figure 4.27**). The human ear is sensitive to frequencies ranging from 20 to 20,000 Hz (see **Figure 4.28**). When it comes to sensitivity to pitch, age matters. Younger people are more sensitive to higher pitch tones than older adults. A new ring tone for cell phones has ingeniously exploited this simple fact of nature, allowing teenagers to hear their cell phones ring while many of their parents or teachers can't (Vitello, 2006).

audition
our sense of hearing

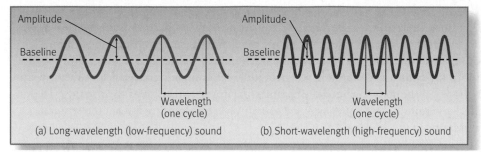

Figure 4.27 Sound Wave Frequency and Amplitude. Sound wave frequency (cycles per second) is the inverse of wavelength (cycle width). Sound wave amplitude is the height of the cycle. The frequency for middle C (a) is lower than that for middle A (b).

Loudness. The amplitude—or height—of the sound wave corresponds to *loudness,* measured in decibels (dB) (refer again to Figure 4.27). Loud noise results in increased wave amplitude because there's more mechanical disturbance, that is, more vibrating airborne molecules. **Table 4.4** lists various common sounds and their typical loudness.

Table 4.4 Common Sounds. This decibel (dB) table compares some common sounds and shows how they rank in potential harm to hearing.

Sound	Noise Level (dB)	Effect
Boom Cars	145	
Jet Engines (near)	140	
Jet Takeoff (100–200 ft.)	130	
Rock Concerts (varies)	110–140	We begin to feel pain at about 125 dB
Thunderclap (near)	120	
Stereos (over 100 watts)	110–125	
Power Saw (chainsaw)	110	Regular exposure to sound over 100 dB of more than one minute risks permanent hearing loss
Jet Flyover (1000 ft.)	103	
Electric Furnace Area Garbage Truck/Cement Mixer	100	No more than 15 minutes of unprotected exposure is recommended for sounds between 90 and 100 dB
Farm Tractor	98	
Subway, Motorcycle (25 ft.)	88	Very annoying
Lawnmower, Food Blender	85–90	85 dB is the level at which hearing damage (after 8 hr.) begins
Recreational Vehicles, TV	70–90	
Average City Traffic	80	Annoying; interferes with conversation; constant exposure may cause damage
Vacuum Cleaner, Hair Dryer	70	Intrusive; interferes with telephone conversation
Normal Conversation	50–65	Comfortable hearing levels are under 60 dB
Refrigerator Humming	40	
Whisper	30	Very quiet
Rustling Leaves	20	Just audible
Normal Breathing	10	

(*Source:* NIDCD)

Timbre. **Timbre** refers to the quality or complexity of the sound. Different musical instruments sound different because they differ in timbre, and human voices sound different for the same reason.

HOW THE EAR WORKS

Just as sense receptors for vision transduce light into neural activity, sense receptors for hearing transduce sound into neural activity.

A high school student responds to the "teenagers only" ringtone.

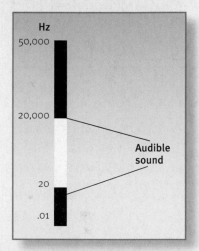

Figure 4.28 The Audible Spectrum (in Hz). The human ear is sensitive to mechanical vibration from about 20 Hz to 20,000 Hz.

timbre
complexity or quality of sound that makes musical instruments, human voices, or other sources sound unique

The Structure of the Ear. The ear has three parts: outer, middle, and inner, each of which performs a different job. The outer ear, consisting of the *pinna* (the part of the ear we see, namely, its skin and cartilage flap) and ear canal, has the simplest function; it funnels sound waves onto the *tympanic membrane*, commonly called the eardrum. On the other side of the tympanic membrane lies the middle ear, containing the *ossicles*—the three tiniest bones in the body—named the hammer, anvil, and stirrup, after their shapes. These ossicles vibrate at the frequency of the sound wave, transmitting it from the tympanic membrane to the inner ear.

The Cochlea and Organ of Corti. The **cochlea** lies in the inner ear and converts vibration into neural activity. The term *cochlea* derives from the Greek word *kokhlias*, meaning "snail" or "screw," and as its name implies, it has a spiral shape (**Figure 4.29**). The outer part of the cochlea is bony, but its inner cavity is filled with a thick fluid. Vibrations from sound waves disturb this fluid, and travel to the base of the cochlea, where pressure is released and transduction occurs.

The **organ of Corti** and **basilar membrane** are critical to hearing because *hair cells* are embedded within them (see Figure 4.29). Hair cells are where transduction of auditory information takes place: They convert acoustic information into action potentials. Here's how. Hair cells contain cilia (hairlike structures) that protrude into the fluid of the cochlea. When sound waves travel through the cochlea, the resulting pressure deflects these cilia, exciting the hair cells (Roberts, Howard, & Hudspeth, 1988). That information feeds into the *auditory nerve,* which travels to the brain.

AUDITORY PERCEPTION

Once the auditory nerve enters the brain, it makes contacts in the brain stem, which sends auditory information higher—all the way up the auditory cortex. At each stage, perception becomes increasingly complex. In this respect, auditory perception is like visual perception.

fictoid

Myth: Some psychics claim to possess clairaudience, or "clear hearing." Clairaudience is hearing voices, music, or other sounds having a supernatural rather than physical source.

Reality: There's no scientific evidence for clairaudience.

cochlea
bony, spiral-shaped sense organ used for hearing

organ of Corti
tissue containing the hair cells necessary for hearing

basilar membrane
membrane supporting the organ of Corti and hair cells in the cochlea

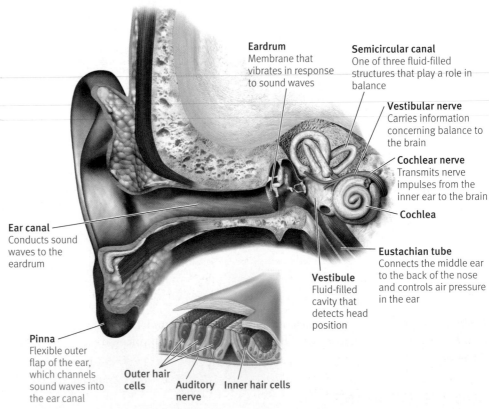

Eardrum
Membrane that vibrates in response to sound waves

Semicircular canal
One of three fluid-filled structures that play a role in balance

Vestibular nerve
Carries information concerning balance to the brain

Cochlear nerve
Transmits nerve impulses from the inner ear to the brain

Cochlea

Eustachian tube
Connects the middle ear to the back of the nose and controls air pressure in the ear

Vestibule
Fluid-filled cavity that detects head position

Ear canal
Conducts sound waves to the eardrum

Pinna
Flexible outer flap of the ear, which channels sound waves into the ear canal

Outer hair cells

Auditory nerve

Inner hair cells

Figure 4.29 The Human Ear and Its Parts. A cutaway section through the human ear, and a close-up diagram of the hair cells. (*Source:* Adapted from Dorling Kindersley)

Pitch Perception. Different tones are represented in different places in the primary auditory cortex (see **Figure 4.30**). This is because each place receives information from a specific place in the basilar membrane. Hair cells located at the base of the basilar membrane are most excited by high-pitched tones, whereas hair cells at the top of the basilar membrane are most excited by low-pitched tones. Scientists call this mode of pitch perception *place theory,* because a specific place along the basilar membrane (and also in the auditory cortex) matches a tone with a specific pitch. Although Helmholtz originally proposed place theory, Georg von Békésy won the Nobel Prize for his research supporting place theory (Békésy, 1949). Place theory accounts only for our perception of high-pitched tones, namely those from 5,000 to 20,000 Hz.

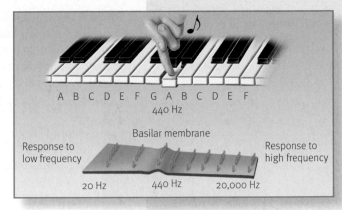

Figure 4.30 The Tone-Based Organization of the Basilar Membrane. Hair cells at the base of the basilar membrane respond to high-pitched tones, whereas hair cells at the apex of the basilar membrane respond to low-pitched tones.

There are two routes to perceiving low-pitched tones. We'll discuss the simpler way first. In *frequency theory,* the rate at which neurons fire action potentials faithfully reproduces the pitch. This method works well up to 100 Hz, because many neurons have maximal firing rates near that limit. *Volley theory* is a variation of frequency theory that works for tones between 100 and 5,000 Hz. According to volley theory, sets of neurons fire at their highest rate, say 100 Hz, slightly out of sync with each other to reach overall rates up to 5,000 Hz.

When it comes to listening to music, we're sensitive not only to different tones, but to the arrangement of tones into melodies (Weinberger, 2006). We react to pleasant melodies differently from unpleasant ones. In one study, powerful music that literally provoked feelings of "chills" or "shivers" boosted activity in the same brain regions corresponding to euphoric responses to sex, food, and drugs (Blood & Zatorre, 2001). So there may be a good reason why the words "sex," "drugs," and "rock-and-roll" seem to go together.

Localization of Sound. We use various brain centers to localize sounds with respect to our bodies. When the auditory nerve enters the brain stem, some of the axons connect with cells on the same side of the brain, whereas others cross over to the other side of the brain. This clever arrangement enables information from both ears to reach the same structures in the brain stem. Because the two sources of information take different routes, they arrive at the brain stem slightly out of sync with each other. Our brains compare this difference to localize sound sources (**Figure 4.31**). The presentation of dissimilar sounds to the two ears is called *binaural cues.* There's also a loudness difference between our ears, because the ear closest to the sound source is in the direct path of the sound wave, whereas the ear farthest away is in a *sound shadow,* created by the head. We rely mostly on binaural cues to detect the source of sounds, but there are other types of localization. *Monaural cues,* heard by one ear only, help us distinguish sounds that are clear from sounds that are muffled due to obstruction by the ear, head, and shoulders, allowing us to figure out where sounds are coming from.

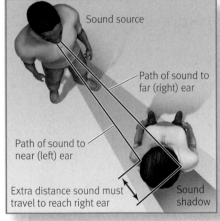

Figure 4.31 How We Locate Sounds. When someone standing to our left speaks to us, the sound reaches our left ear slightly earlier than it reaches our right. Also, the intensity detected by the left ear is greater than the intensity detected by the right ear, because the right ear lies in a sound shadow produced by the head and shoulders.

Echolocation. Certain animals, such as bats, dolphins, and many whales, emit sounds and listen to the echoes to determine their distance from a wall or barrier, a phenomenon called *echolocation.* Small bats emit high-pitched sounds ranging from 14,000 to 100,000 Hz, most of which we can't hear.

Remarkably, there's evidence that humans are capable of a crude form of echolocation. Near-sighted people display greater sensitivity to echoes and superior echolocation skills compared with normal-sighted individuals (Despres, Candas, & Dufour, 2005). This correlation suggests that people hone echolocation skills if they need them, but scientists haven't experimentally verified direct causation. Human echolocation may account for the fact that blind persons can sometimes detect objects a few feet away. This seems likely in the case of Ben Underwood, who was blinded at age 3 by retinal cancer. Ben learned to

Correlation vs. Causation

Ruling Out Rival Hypotheses

make clicking noises that bounced off surfaces and clued him in to his surroundings. He rides his skateboard and plays basketball and video games. Ben is a rare example of what's possible; however, his doctors point out that Ben was sighted for his first few years, long enough for him to acquire a perspective of the world.

Ben Underwood has developed an amazing ability to use human echolocation to overcome many of the limitations of his blindness. Humans don't usually rely much on echolocation, although many whales do.

WHEN WE CAN'T HEAR

About 1 in 1,000 people are deaf: They suffer from a profound loss of hearing. Many others have hearing deficits, called being "hard of hearing." There are several causes of deafness, some largely genetic, others deriving from disease, injury, or exposure to loud noise (Willems, 2000). *Conductive deafness* is due to a malfunctioning of the ear, especially a failure of the eardrum or the ossicles of the inner ear. In contrast, *nerve deafness* occurs after damage to the auditory nerve. We all tend to lose some hearing ability as we age, especially for high-frequency sounds.

ASSESS YOUR KNOWLEDGE: FACT OR FICTION?

(1) Sound waves are converted to neural impulses by creating vibrations of the fluid inside the cochlea.

(2) We can determine the location of a sound because the pitch seems higher in the closer ear.

(3) Place theory states that each hair cell in the inner ear has a particular pitch or frequency to which it's most responsive.

(4) As we age, we tend to lose hearing for low-pitched sounds more than high-pitched sounds.

Answers: (1) T (p. 178); (2) F (p. 179); (3) T (p. 179); (4) F (p. 180)

Smell and Taste: The Sensual Senses

The star-nosed mole exhales air bubbles underwater only to reinhale them and smell the contents (Catania, 2006).

Without smell and taste many of our everyday experiences would be bland. Cuisines of the world feature characteristic spices that enliven their dishes. Similarly, smell and taste stimulate our senses and elevate our spirits. The term "comfort food" refers to familiar dishes that we seek because of the warm memories they evoke.

Smell is also called **olfaction,** and taste **gustation.** These senses work hand-in-hand, enhancing our liking of some foods and our disliking of others. Smell and taste are the chemical senses because we derive these sensory experiences from chemicals in substances.

Nobel Prize winners Richard Axel and Linda Buck work on isolating olfactory receptors.

Animals use their sense of smell for many purposes—tracking prey, establishing territories, and recognizing the opposite sex, to name but a few. We humans aren't the most smell-oriented of creatures. The average dog is at least 100,000 times more sensitive to smell than we are, which explains why police use trained dogs rather than nosy people to sniff for bombs and banned substances.

The most critical function of our chemical senses is to sample our food before swallowing it. The smell and taste of sour milk are powerful stimuli that few of us can ignore even if we want to. An unfamiliar bitter taste may signal dangerous bacteria or poison in our food. We develop food preferences for "safe" foods and base them on a combination of smell and taste. One study of young French women found that only those who already liked red meat—its smell and its taste—responded favorably to pictures of it (Audebert, Deiss, & Rousset, 2006). We like what smells and tastes good to us.

WHAT ARE ODORS AND FLAVORS?

olfaction
our sense of smell

gustation
our sense of taste

Odors are airborne chemicals that interact with receptors in the lining of our nasal passages. Estimates suggest that our noses are veritable smell connoisseurs, capable of detecting between 2,000 and 4,000 different odors. Not everything, though, has an odor. (We bet you're pleased to hear that!) Clean water, for example, has no odor or taste. Not all animals smell airborne molecules. The star-nosed mole, named for its peculiarly shaped snout, can detect odors underwater (Catania, 2006). The animal blows out air bubbles and "sniffs" them back in to find food underwater and underground.

In contrast to our sense of smell, we can detect only a few tastes. We're sensitive to five basic tastes—sweet, salty, sour, bitter, and umami, the last of which is a recently uncovered "meaty" or "savory" taste. There's preliminary evidence for a sixth taste, one for fatty foods (Gilbertson et al., 1997).

APPLY YOUR THINKING

Why don't we have a more elaborate set of taste receptors?

SENSE RECEPTORS FOR SMELL AND TASTE

In 2004, Linda Buck and Richard Axel won the Nobel Prize for discovering over 1,000 human olfactory genes. Of these, 347 code for olfactory receptors (Buck & Axel, 1991). Each olfactory neuron contains a single type of olfactory receptor, which "recognizes" an odorant on the basis of its shape. This lock-and-key concept is similar to the one we encountered in Chapter 3 for neurotransmitters recognizing receptor sites. When olfactory receptors come into contact with odor molecules, action potentials in olfactory neurons are triggered.

We detect taste with **taste buds** on our tongues. Bumps on the tongue called *papillae* contain numerous taste buds (**Figure 4.32**). There are separate taste buds for sweet, salty, sour, bitter, and the "meaty flavor" umami (Chandrashekar, Hoon, Ryba, & Zuker, 2006).

It's a myth, however, that a "taste map" describes the tongue's sensitivity to different flavors, even though some books still contain this map (see **Figure 4.33**). In reality, there's only a weak tendency for individual taste receptors to concentrate at certain locations on the tongue. Try this exercise: Place a bit of salt on the tip of your tongue. Can you taste it? Now try placing a small amount of sugar on the back of your tongue. Chances are good you'll taste both the salt and the sugar, even though you placed them outside the mythical taste map. This is because receptors that detect sweet tastes are often located on the tip of the tongue and receptors that detect salt are often on the sides, but there's a good mix of receptors everywhere on the tongue.

Umami taste receptors were controversial until physiological studies replicated earlier results and showed that these receptors were present on taste buds (Chandrashekar, Hoon, Ryba, & Zuker, 2006). That was nearly a century after 1908, when Kikunae Ikeda isolated the molecules responsible for the savory flavor found in many Japanese foods, such as broth or dried seaweed (Yamaguchi & Ninomiya, 2000). These molecules producing a savory or meaty flavor all had one thing in common: They contained a lot of the neurotransmitter glutamate (see Chapter 3). Monosodium glutamate (MSG), a derivative of glutamate, is a well-known flavor enhancer (the commercial flavor enhancer *Accent* consists almost entirely of MSG). Today, most scientists consider umami the fifth taste.

A similar controversy swirls around taste receptors for fat. It's clear that fat does something to our tongues. Richard Mattes (2005) and his associates found that merely putting fat on people's tongues alters their blood levels of fat. This means that as soon as fat enters our mouths it starts to affect our bodies' metabolism of fat. At first, researchers thought the responses were triggered by an olfactory receptor for fat. This hypothesis was ruled out when they showed that smelling fat didn't alter blood levels of fat; the fat had to make contact with the tongue.

With only five or six taste receptors, how can we taste so many flavors? The secret lies in the fact that our taste perception is biased strongly by our sense of smell, which explains why we find food much less tasty when our noses are stuffed. Far more than we realize, we find certain foods "delicious" because of their smell. Indeed, we perceive a

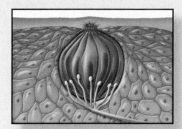

Figure 4.32 How We Detect Taste.
The tongue contains many taste buds, as shown in this close-up.

Figure 4.33 The "Tongue Map" Myth.
Although diagrams of the tongue, like this one, appear in many popular sources, they're more fiction than fact.

Replicability

Ruling Out Rival Hypotheses

taste buds
sense receptors in the tongue that respond to sweet, salty, sour, bitter, umami, and perhaps fat

combination of taste and smell. If you're not persuaded, try this exercise. Buy some multiflavored jellybeans, open the bag, and close your eyes so you can't see which color you're picking. Then pinch your nose with one hand and pop a jellybean in your mouth. At first you won't be able to identify the flavor. Then gradually release your fingers from your nose and you'll soon be able to perceive the jellybean's taste.

Our tongues differ in their number of taste receptors. Linda Bartoshuk (2004) calls those of us with a marked overabundance of taste buds—about 25 percent of people—"supertasters." If you find broccoli and coffee to be unbearably bitter, and sugary foods to be unbearably sweet, the odds are high you're a supertaster. Supertasters, who are overrepresented among women and people of African or Asian descent, are also especially sensitive to oral pain, and tend to avoid bitter tastes as a result. They also tend to avoid bitter tastes in alcohol and smoking tobacco, which may make them healthier than the rest of us.

OLFACTORY AND GUSTATORY PERCEPTION

Our perceptions of smell and taste are often remarkably sensitive—and more informative than we consciously realize. Studies show that babies can identify their mothers' odor and siblings can recognize each other on the basis of odor. Research suggests that women can even tell whether people just watched a happy or a sad movie from samples of their armpit odor (Wysocki & Preti, 2004); should we perhaps call sad movies sweat-jerkers rather than tear-jerkers?

How do odors and tastes excite our receptors for smell and taste? After odors interact with sense receptors in the nasal passages, the resulting information enters the brain, reaching the olfactory cortex and parts of the limbic system (see **Figure 4.34**). Similarly, after taste information interacts with taste buds, it enters the brain, reaching the gustatory cortex, somatosensory cortex (because food also has texture), and parts of the limbic system. The orbitofrontal cortex (see Chapter 3) is a site of convergence for smell and taste (Rolls, 2004).

We analyze the intensity of smell and determine whether it's pleasing. Parts of the limbic system, such as the amygdala and the orbitofrontal cortex, help us to distinguish pleasant from disgusting smells (Anderson et al., 2003). Taste can also be pleasant or disgusting; "disgust," not surprisingly, means "bad taste." Both tasting disgusting food and viewing facial expressions of disgust (see Chapter 11) activate the gustatory cortex (Wicker et al., 2003). Moreover, persons who suffer damage to the gustatory cortex don't experience disgust (Calder et al., 2000). These results underscore the powerful links among smell, taste, and emotion.

Emotional disorders, like anxiety and depression, can distort taste perception (Heath, Melichar, Nutt, & Donaldson, 2006). Certain neurotransmitters, such as serotonin and norepinephrine—the same neurotransmitters whose activity is enhanced by antidepressants (see Chapters 3 and 16)—make us more sensitive to tastes. Tom Heath and colleagues (2006) found that antidepressant drugs rendered subjects more sensitive to various combinations of sweet, sour, and bitter tastes. Their research may shed light on a frequent symptom of depression, namely, loss of appetite.

Smell plays a particularly strong role in sexual behavior. Mice with a genetic defect in smell don't even bother to mate (Mandiyan, Coats, & Shah, 2005). Is smell central to human sexuality too? Many perfume and cologne manufacturers sure seem to think so. Curiously, though, it may not be fragrant odors, but **pheromones**—odorless chemicals that serve as social signals to members of one's species—that alter our sexual behavior. There's evidence that rodents respond to pheromones during mating and social behavior (Biasi, Silvotti, & Tirindelli, 2001). So do most other mammals, including whales and

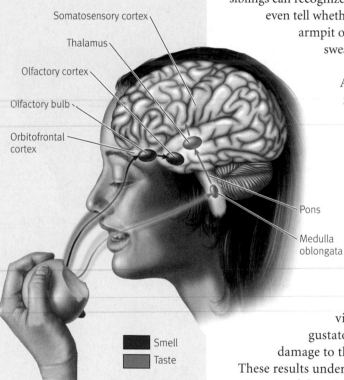

Somatosensory cortex

Thalamus

Olfactory cortex

Olfactory bulb

Orbitofrontal cortex

Pons

Medulla oblongata

■ Smell
■ Taste

Figure 4.34 Smell and Taste. Our senses of smell and taste enter the brain by different routes but converge on the orbitofrontal cortex.

pheromones
odorless chemicals that serve as social signals to members of one's species

horses (Fields, 2007). Most mammals use the *vomeronasal organ,* located in the bone between the nose and the mouth, to detect pheromones. The vomeronasal organ doesn't develop in humans (Witt & Wozniak, 2006), causing some to suggest that humans are insensitive to pheromones. An alternative hypothesis is that humans detect pheromones via a different route. This idea is supported by the discovery of human pheromones (Pearson, 2006). A nerve that's only recently received attention, called "nerve zero," may step in to enable pheromones to trigger responses in the "hot-button sex regions of the brain" (Fields, 2007).

Ruling Out Rival Hypotheses

Still, we should be cautious about shelling out sizeable chunks of our salaries on pheromone-based products that promise to stir up romance. Scientific evidence suggests they probably won't work. Pheromones are large molecules, so although it's easy to transfer a pheromone from one person to another during a passionate kiss, sending them across a restaurant table is definitely a stretch. Moreover, there's far more to human romance than physical chemistry; psychological chemistry matters too (see Chapter 11).

Smells other than pheromones may contribute to human sexual behavior. Remarkably, human sperm cells may contain smell receptors that help them to find their way to female eggs (Spehr et al., 2003). Sometimes truth *is* stranger than fiction.

WHEN WE CAN'T SMELL OR TASTE

About 2 million Americans suffer from disorders of taste, smell, or both. Gradual loss of taste and smell can be a part of normal aging, but it can also result from diseases, such as diabetes and high blood pressure.

There are many disorders of olfaction (Hirsch, 2003). Although these disorders aren't as serious as blindness, deafness, or pain insensitivity, they can pose several dangers, such as an inability to detect gas leaks and smell rotten food. (We can smell spoiled food before it enters our mouth.) Damage to the olfactory nerve, along with brain damage caused by disorders such as Parkinson's and Alzheimer's disease (Chapter 3), can damage our sense of smell (Doty, Deems, & Stellar, 1988; Murphy, 1999).

There are also many disorders of taste. In addition to robbing us of quality of life, losing our sense of taste, alone or along with our sense of smell, can produce negative health consequences. Researchers at Duke University showed that cancer patients who lose their sense of taste have a worse prognosis, because they eat less and die sooner (Schiffman & Graham, 2000). This effect isn't due merely to a lack of nutrition. Adding flavor enhancers to the diet appears to appreciably improve patients' health status. This finding led the researchers to conclude that taste adds an essential "zest" to life, a psychological flavoring that can help to ward off disease by boosting appetite.

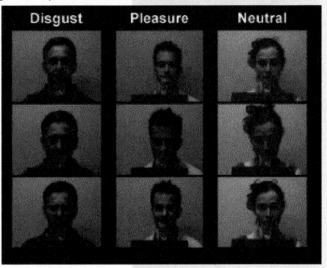

Subjects lean forward to sniff at the content of a glass and show facial expressions of disgust *(left),* pleasure *(center),* or neutrality *(right). (Source:* Wicker et al., 2003)

Perfume manufacturers have long advertised fragrances as increasing attraction and romance. But at least in nonhuman animals, the chemicals that produce the most potent effects on sexual behaviors are actually odorless pheromones.

ASSESS YOUR KNOWLEDGE: FACT OR FICTION?

(1) Humans can detect only a small number of odors, but thousands of tastes.
(2) There's a "tongue map," with specific taste receptors located on specific parts of the tongue.
(3) The limbic system plays a key role in smell and taste perception.
(4) The vomeronasal organ helps to detect pheromones in many mammals but doesn't develop in humans.

Answers: (1) F (pp. 180–181); (2) F (p. 181); (3) T (p. 182); (4) T (p. 183)

Our Body Senses: Touch, Body Position, and Balance

It was the summer of 1974 and all eyes were focused on daredevil Philippe Petit, who navigated ever so skillfully across a tightrope of steel cable that stretched from one of the Twin Towers of New York City's World Trade Center to the other. Each time he lowered his foot onto the cable he relied on his sense of touch. Each time he moved forward he relied on his senses of body position and balance. One miscalculation and he would have plummeted nearly a quarter of a mile to the ground.

Fortunately, Petit, like the rest of us, has three body senses. The system we use for touch and pain is the **somatosensory** (*somato-,* for "body," and sensory) system. We also have a body position sense, called **proprioception,** or kinesthetic sense, and a sense of equilibrium or balance, called the **vestibular sense.** We'll address these systems separately, but bear in mind that they work together.

THE SOMATOSENSORY SYSTEM: TOUCH AND PAIN

The stimuli that activate the somatosensory system come in a variety of types. In this respect, this sense differs from vision and audition, each of which is devoted mainly to a single stimulus type.

Pressure, Temperature, and Injury. Our somatosensory system responds to stimuli applied to the skin, such as light touch or deep pressure, hot or cold temperature, or chemical or mechanical (touch-related) injury that produces pain. Somatosensory stimuli can be very specific, such as the embossed patterns of a letter written in Braille, or generalized to a large area of the body. Damage to internal organs sometimes causes "referred pain"—pain in a different location—such as an ache or numbness felt throughout the left arm and shoulder during a heart attack.

Specialized and Free Nerve Endings in the Skin. We sense light touch and deep pressure with *mechanoreceptors* located on the ends of sensory nerves in the skin. These mechanoreceptors are specialized nerve endings (see **Figure 4.35**). One example is the Pacinian corpuscle named after anatomist Filippo Pacini, who discovered them in 1831.

Bystanders looked on as tightrope artist Philippe Petit made his way across the chasm between the Twin Towers of the World Trade Center on August 7, 1974.

somatosensory
our sense of touch, temperature, and pain

proprioception
our sense of body position

vestibular sense
our sense of equilibrium or balance

fictoid

Myth: Consuming ice cream or other cold substances too quickly causes pain in our brains.

Reality: "Brain freeze," as it's sometimes called, doesn't affect the brain at all. It's produced by a constriction of blood vessels in the roof of our mouths in response to intense cold temperatures, followed by an expansion of these blood vessels, producing pain.

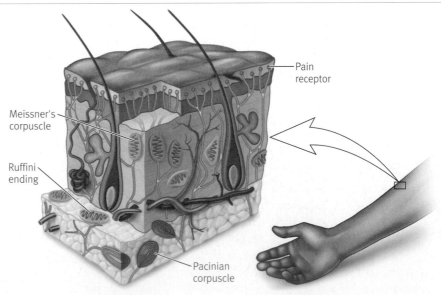

Figure 4.35 The Sense of Touch. The skin contains many specialized and free nerve endings that detect mechanical pressure, temperature, and pain.

We have other specialized nerve endings, many of which are sensitive to temperature (refer again to Figure 4.35).

We sense touch, temperature, and especially pain with *free nerve endings* (refer once more to Figure 4.35). There are many more free nerve endings than specialized endings. Nerve endings of all types are distributed unevenly across our body surface. Most of our nerve endings are in our fingertips (which explains why it really hurts when we cut our finger, say, in a paper cut), followed by our lips, face, hands, and feet. We have the fewest in the middle of our backs, perhaps explaining why even a strenuous deep back massage rarely makes us scream out in agony.

How We Perceive Touch and Pain. Information about body touch, temperature, and painful stimuli travels in the somatic nerves before entering the spinal cord. Touch information travels more quickly than information about pain stimuli. Many of us have discovered this fact when stubbing our toes on a piece of furniture: We first feel our toes hitting the furniture, but don't experience the stinging pain (ouch!) until a second or two later. That's because touch and pain have different functions. Touch informs us of our immediate surroundings, which is often an urgent matter, whereas pain alerts us to take care of that part of our bodies.

Often touch and pain information activates local spinal reflexes (see Chapter 3) before traveling to brain sites dedicated to perception. In some cases, painful stimuli trigger the *withdrawal reflex*. When we touch a fire or hot stove, we pull away immediately to avoid getting burned.

After activating spinal reflexes, touch and pain information travels upward through parts of the brain stem and thalamus to reach the somatosensory cortex (Bushnell et al., 1999). Additional cortical areas are active during the localization of touch information, such as certain association areas of the parietal lobe.

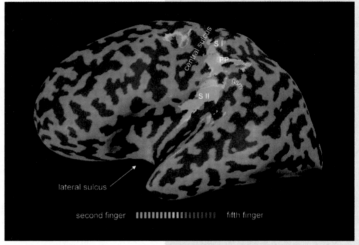

Touch to our fingers, in this case the second and fifth digits, activates many cortical areas, as shown in this fMRI scan. (*Source:* Ruben et al., 2001)

We can't localize pain as precisely as touch. Moreover, pain has a large emotional component. That's because pain information goes partly to the somatosensory cortex and partly to limbic centers in the brain stem and forebrain. Scientists believe we can control pain in part by controlling our emotional reaction to painful stimuli. This belief has been bolstered by stories of people withstanding excruciating pain during combat, natural childbirth, or right-of-passage ceremonies. Patrick Wall (2000) showed that the brain controls activity in the spinal cord, enabling us to amplify, diminish, or in some cases ignore pain. The body also manufactures its own natural painkillers: endorphins (see Chapter 3).

As we've all discovered, there are different kinds of pain: sharp, stabbing, throbbing, burning, and aching. Many of the types of pain perception relate to the pain-causing stimulus—thermal (heat-related), chemical, or mechanical. Pain can also be acute, that is, short-lived, or chronic, that is, enduring, perhaps even lasting years. Each kind of pain-producing stimulus has a *threshold,* or point at which we perceive it as painful. People differ in their pain thresholds. Surprisingly, one study showed that people with naturally red hair require more anesthetic than do people with other hair colors (Liem et al., 2004). Of course, this correlational finding doesn't mean that red hair causes lower pain thresholds. Instead, it suggests that some of the differences in people's thresholds are due to genetic factors that happen to be associated with hair color.

Correlation vs. Causation

For many years the scientific consensus has been that we can ignore pain, or at least withstand it, with a stoic mind-set. There's evidence that people of certain cultural backgrounds, such as American Indians, Cambodians, Chinese, and Germans, are more reserved and less likely to communicate openly about pain, whereas South and Central Americans consider it more acceptable to moan and cry out when in pain (Ondeck, 2003). Although these descriptions of average behavior may help physicians deal with diverse populations, the premise that pain perception varies with ethnicity isn't universally accepted. An alternative hypothesis is that health care professionals treat certain ethnic

Ruling Out Rival Hypotheses

groups differently. Blacks and Hispanics are less likely than Caucasians to receive analgesic (antipain) medication during emergency room visits (Bonham, 2001), which could account for some of the differences in reports of pain.

Are there any unusual activities for which a stoic mind-set may come in handy? Some popular psychology gurus certainly think so. Firewalkers, popular in India, Japan, North Africa, and the Polynesian islands, have walked 20- to 40-foot-long beds of burning embers. The practice has been around since as early as 1200 B.C. But there's recently been a glut of "Firewalking Seminars" in California, New York, and other states. These motivational seminars promise ordinary people everything from heightened self-confidence to spiritual enlightenment—all by walking down an 8- to 12-foot-long path of burning embers. Contrary to what we might learn at these seminars, success in firewalking has nothing to do with our mind-set and everything to do with physics. The type of coal or wood used in firewalking has a low rate of heat exchange, such that it burns red hot in the center while remaining less hot on the outside (Kurtus, 2000). So any of us can firewalk successfully just so long as we walk over the burning embers quickly enough. Still, serious accidents can occur if the fire isn't prepared properly or if the firewalker walks too slowly.

APPLY YOUR THINKING
Why did evolution result in our having pain sensitivity at all? Why do we have a slowly acting pain system?

Phantom Limb Illusion. Persons with amputated limbs often experience the eerie phenomenon of **phantom pain,** pain or discomfort felt in the missing limb. About 50 to 80 percent of amputees have phantom limb sensations (Sherman, Sherman, & Parker 1984). The missing limb often feels as if it's in an uncomfortably distorted position.

Vilayanur Ramachandran and colleagues developed a creative treatment for phantom limb pain called the mirror box (Ramachandran & Rogers-Ramachandran, 1996). Phantom limb patients position their other limb so that it's reflected in exactly the position that the amputated limb would assume. Then the patient performs the "mirror equivalent" of the exercise the amputated limb needs to relieve a cramp or otherwise get comfortable. For the mirror box to relieve pain or discomfort in the amputated limb, the illusion must be completely realistic. Some subjects report pain relief the first time the illusion works, but not thereafter. In other cases, the mirror box causes the phantom limb pain to disappear permanently.

Dermo-Optical Perception (DOP). Can our body senses produce visual sensations? *Dermo-optical perception* (DOP) is the supposed ability to "see" without using the eyes, typically by running the fingers across a page of written text. There's reason to be skeptical of DOP, because the history of "seeing" while blindfolded is laced with anecdotes of magicians finding clever ways to peek through their blindfolds (Bernski, 1998). Nonetheless, this phenomenon, once considered an open-and-shut case of pseudoscience, is being reexamined in double-blind studies (see Chapter 2), in which neither research assistants nor subjects know what subjects are reading. An ophthalmologist, neurologist, and radiologist working in France claim to have found MRI and EEG evidence of activity in the visual cortex during DOP (Bernski, 1998). Strangely, these scientists requested anonymity. By failing to stand up for their data, they're preventing others from asking them necessary questions needed to replicate their results.

Pain Insensitivity. Just as some people are blind or deaf, some people experience disorders that impair their ability to sense pain. Pain insensitivity present from birth is an extremely rare condition that in some cases is inherited (Victor & Ropper, 2001). Children with inherited pain insensitivity usually have a normal ability to discriminate touch, although not necessarily temperature. For the most part, they're completely unable to detect painful stimuli. In some cases, they chew off parts of their bodies, like their fingertips or the ends of their tongues, or suffer bone fractures without even realizing it. Needless to say, this condition can be exceedingly dangerous. Other individuals show an indifference to painful stimuli: They can identify the type of pain, but experience no significant discomfort from it.

The mirror box consists of a two-chamber box with a mirror in the center. When the subject looks at her right hand in the box, it creates the illusion that the mirror image of her right hand is her left hand. This box can sometimes alleviate the discomfort of phantom limb pain by positioning the intact limb as the phantom limb appears to be positioned, and then moving it to a more comfortable position. (*Source:* Ramachandran & Rogers-Ramachandran, 1996)

Replicability

phantom pain
pain or discomfort felt in an amputated limb

PsychoMythology
Psychic Healing of Chronic Pain

Many people believe in the power of mind over pain, but some individuals claim to possess supernatural psychic abilities or "gifts" that enable them to reduce others' pain. Is this fact or fiction? In the summer of 2003, the Australian television show *A Current Affair* approached psychologists at the University of Bond to conduct a double-blind, randomized, controlled test of psychic healing powers.

Volunteers suffering from pain caused by cancer, chronic back conditions, and fibromyalgia (a chronic condition of muscle, joint, and bone pain and fatigue) were located by a newspaper advertisement (Lyvers, Barling, & Harding-Clark, 2006). The researchers assigned half of the chronic pain subjects to a group that received psychic healing and the other half to a control condition that didn't. Neither the subjects nor those interacting with them knew who was assigned to which group. In the healing condition, the psychic healer viewed and touched photographs of the chronic pain subjects in another room. The healer was given all the time deemed necessary.

The researchers used the McGill Pain Questionnaire (Melzak, 1975) to test chronic pain subjects' level of discomfort before and after the trial. Then, researchers compared their before and after scores. On average the scores showed no change before and after treatment, with half the subjects reporting more pain and half reporting less pain regardless of whether psychic healing occurred.

These results agreed with earlier results obtained by British researchers on spiritual healing (Abbot et al., 2001). In a large study of 120 chronic pain sufferers, they similarly used the McGill Pain Questionnaire. These researchers compared pain reports before and after face-to-face versus distant spiritual healing compared with no spiritual healing. The results of this study suggested that despite the popularity of spiritual healing in England, this method lacked scientific support. A different research team, however, reported an improvement in neck pain following spiritual healing (Gerald, Smith, & Simpson, 2003). But because their study lacked a placebo treatment or blinding of the therapist, these authors couldn't rule out a placebo effect (see Chapter 2).

Lyvers and colleagues (2006) addressed the placebo effect with a double-blind design, and rated their chronic pain subjects on a five-point scale that assessed the degree to which subjects believed in psychic phenomena. They found no correlation between psychic healing and decreased pain; however, they did find that decreases in reported pain correlated with increased belief in psychic phenomena. So beliefs in the paranormal may create reality, at least psychological reality.

Ashlyn Blocker has congenital insensitivity to pain with anhidrosis. *Congenital* means "present at birth," and *anhidrosis* means "inability to sweat." CIPA is a rare disorder that renders people unable to detect pain or temperature; those affected also can't regulate body temperature well because of an inability to sweat. Her parents and teachers need to monitor her constantly because she's prone to eating scalding hot food without the slightest hesitation. She may badly injure herself on the playground and continue to play.

Ruling Out Rival Hypotheses

PROPRIOCEPTION AND VESTIBULAR SENSE: BODY POSITION AND BALANCE

Right at this moment you're probably sitting somewhere. You may not be thinking about body control or keeping your head and shoulders up, because your brain is kindly taking care of all that for you. If you decided to stand up and grab a snack, you'd need to maintain posture and balance, as well as navigate bodily motion. *Proprioception,* also called our kinesthetic sense, helps us keep track of where we are and move efficiently. The *vestibular sense,* also called our sense of equilibrium, enables us to sense and maintain our balance as we move about. Our senses of body position and balance work together.

Proprioceptors: Telling the Inside Story. We use *proprioceptors* to sense muscle stretch and force. From these two sources of information we can tell what our bodies are doing, even with our eyes closed. There are two kinds of proprioceptors: stretch receptors embedded in our muscles, and force detectors embedded in our muscle tendons.

Proprioceptive information enters the spinal cord and travels upward through the brain stem and thalamus to reach the somatosensory and motor cortexes (Naito, 2004). Here our brains combine information from our muscles and tendons, along with a sense of our intentions (which is computed in other brain areas), to obtain a perception of our body's location (Proske, 2006).

The Semicircular Canals and Otoliths: A Balancing Act. In addition to the cochlea, the inner ear contains three **semicircular canals** and *otoliths* (**Figure 4.36**). The semicircular canals, which are filled with fluid and half-circular canals, sense equilibrium and help us maintain our balance. The otoliths, which are tiny crystals, sense linear movement and gravity. Hair cells line the inside of the semicircular canals and otoliths, and feed into the vestibular nerve. Linear movement, gravity, and acceleration disturb the fluid in the semicircular canals and otoliths and activate the hair cells. Sound familiar? These sense receptors use the same principles as the cochlea uses for hearing.

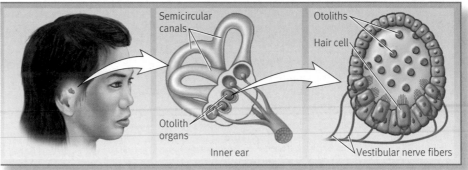

semicircular canals
three fluid-filled canals in the inner ear responsible for our sense of balance

Figure 4.36 How We Sense Motion. The semicircular canals and otoliths of the inner ear detect acceleration and linear movement.

Vestibular information reaches parts of the brain stem that control eye muscles and triggers reflexes that coordinate eye and head movements (Highstein, Fay, & Popper, 2004). Vestibular information also travels to the cerebellum, which controls bodily responses that enable us to catch our balance when we're falling.

The vestibular sense isn't heavily represented in our cerebral cortex, so our awareness of this sense is limited. We typically become aware of this sense only when we lose our sense of balance or experience dramatic mismatches between our vestibular and visual inputs, which result when our vestibular system and our eyes tell us different things. We commonly experience dizziness and nausea following these mismatches, such as when we're moving quickly in a car while not being able to look outside at the road whizzing past us.

Body Sense Illusions. Have you ever worn a baseball cap all day and still felt it on your head after you took it off? Or placed your left hand in hot water and your right hand in cold water and then placed both hands in lukewarm water, only to find them feeling different from how they just felt (and from each other)? If so, you know what a body sense illusion is like.

This room is designed to rotate around subjects seated at the table. Illusory movement and scene distortions often result. (*Source:* Palmisano et al., 2006)

Rotation Illusions. We've all experienced dizziness or other strange perceptions after spinning around. One such illusion is the misperception that stationary objects are still moving after we stop rotating. When rotation of the body stops, fluid in the semicircular canal and otoliths decelerates more slowly than the canals themselves, resulting in the continued bending of hair cells. As a result, our brains tell us we're still moving even after we've stopped.

Experimenters have demonstrated other rotation illusions when a furnished room circles around a stationary observer or when a person rotates in a stationary room (Palmisano, Allison, & Howard, 2006). These situations distort the usual relationships between near and distant parts of the scene.

Ergonomics: Human Engineering. How do our bodies interact with new technologies? A field of psychology called *human factors* (see the Prologue) optimizes technology to better suit our sensory and perceptual capabilities. We can use what we know about human sensory systems—ranging from our body position sense to vision—to build more *ergonomic*, or worker-friendly, gadgets and tools of the trade.

Psychologist Donald Norman, posing in his office behind a teapot. Can you figure out why this teapot is poorly designed?

As psychologist Donald Norman (1998) pointed out, many everyday objects are designed without the perceptual experiences of users in mind. As a result, they can be extremely difficult to figure out how to operate, as anyone who's tried to program a new VCR knows. Have you ever tried to repeatedly push open a door that needed to be pulled open, or spent several minutes trying to figure out how to turn on a shower in an apartment or hotel room? Poor design helped to keep the United States in limbo for 5 weeks following the 2000 presidential election between George W. Bush and Al Gore, when a confusing election ballot in some Florida counties left state officials unable to figure out which candidate voters picked.

Fortunately, human factors psychologists have been able to apply their extensive knowledge of sensation and perception to improve the design of many everyday devices. To take just one example, many people hold jobs that require them to sit at a computer terminal most of the day. This means that a new design for a computer screen, keyboard, or mouse that enables them to better reach for their computers or see their screens can increase their efficiency. Human factors psychologists design not only computer components, but devices like control panels on aircraft carriers, to make them safer and easier to use. Human factors reminds us that much of what we know about sensation and perception has useful applications to many domains of everyday life.

The cockpit of an airplane contains many controls that human factors psychologists can make safer and more user-friendly.

ASSESS YOUR KNOWLEDGE: FACT OR FICTION?

(1) Pain information travels more quickly to the spinal cord than does touch information.

(2) Pain thresholds vary depending on the person and type of pain (stabbing, burning, or aching, for example).

(3) Firewalking requires both an insensitivity to pain and extremely high levels of motivation.

(4) Proprioception enables us to coordinate our movements without having to look at our bodies.

(5) The inner ear plays a key role in our ability to keep our balance.

Answers: (1) F (p. 185); (2) T (p. 185); (3) F (p. 186); (4) T (p. 187); (5) T (p. 188)

Think again... The Complete Review System

THINK / ASSESS / STUDY / SUCCEED

Two Sides of the Coin: Sensation and Perception (pp. 153–162)

STUDY the Learning Objectives

▶ Identify the basic principles that apply to all senses
  • Transduction is the process of converting an external energy, such as light or sound vibration, into activity in the nervous system. The doctrine of specific nerve energies refers to how each of the sensory modalities (vision, hearing, touch, and so on) is handled by specific regions of the brain, especially specific regions of the cerebral cortex (visual cortex, auditory cortex, and so on). Evidence suggests that even though most connections in the brain are faithful to one sense modality, brain regions often respond to information from a different sense. For example, what we see affects what we hear when watching video with sound.

▶ Track how our minds build up perceptions
  • Information travels from primary sensory to secondary sensory cortex and then on to association cortex. Along the way, perception becomes increasingly complex. We also process many different inputs simultaneously, a phenomenon called parallel processing. All the processing comes together to generate an integrated perceptual experience referred to as binding.

▶ Analyze the scientific support for and against ESP
  • Most people accept the existence of ESP without the need for scientific evidence in part because we greatly underestimate how likely it is that coincidence, like two people at a gathering having the same birthday, occur by chance.

DO YOU KNOW THESE TERMS?

  ❑ **sensation** (p. 152)
  ❑ **perception** (p. 152)
  ❑ **transduction** (p. 153)
  ❑ **sense receptor** (p. 153)
  ❑ **absolute threshold** (p. 153)
  ❑ **just noticeable difference (JND)** (p. 154)
  ❑ **perceptual constancy** (p. 157)
  ❑ **selective attention** (p. 158)
  ❑ **extrasensory perception (ESP)** (p. 159)

Name the processing model taking place when you look at this image with a caption of "woman" versus a caption of "saxophone player." (p. 155)

THINK about what You would do . . .
Your friends plan to spend an afternoon trying to expose the subliminal messages they believe are hidden on a CD of your favorite band? What would you do to help them understand how subliminal messaging works (or doesn't work)? (p. 156)

SUCCEED with

mypsych lab
where learning comes to life!

Subliminal Messages and Persuasion
Are you worried you can be unknowingly influenced to do something? (p. 156)
🎧 LISTEN

What concept is being tested by this ambiguous figure? Does your perspective change when looking at it as an "old woman" or "young woman"? (p. 157)

ASSESS your knowledge

1. The detection of physical energy by means of the activation of sense organs, followed by transmission of this activation to higher brain areas, is called _____. (p. 152)

2. _____ is the interpretation of raw sensory inputs. (p. 152)

3. The process of converting external stimulus energy into neural activity is called _____. (p. 153)

4. A _____ _____ is a specialized cell that transduces a specific stimulus. (p. 153)

5. The _____ is the lowest level of a stimulus needed for the nervous system to detect a change 50 percent of the time. (p. 153)

6. The _____ _____ _____ tells us how easily we can detect changes in stimulus intensity. (p. 154)

7. Research demonstrates that subliminal persuasion is (likely/unlikely) in most cases. (p. 156)

8. The process by which we perceive stimuli consistently across varied conditions is _____ _____. (p. 157)

9. We are able to focus on one object or idea while ignoring others thanks to _____. (p. 158)

10. Proponents of _____ _____ argue that we can perceive events outside of the known channels of sensation. (p. 159)

Seeing: The Visual System (pp. 163–176)

STUDY the Learning Objectives

▶ Explain how the eye starts the visual process
  • The lens in the eye accommodates to focus on images both near and far by changing from "fat" to "flat." The lens optimally focuses light on the retina, which lies at the

If you did not receive an access code to MyPsychLab with this text and wish to purchase access online, please visit www.mypsychlab.com.

THINK about what You would do . . .
A neighbor claims to have trained her dog to find and retrieve a ball in the yard based on its red color. What would you do to convince her that the trick can't be based on the ball's color? (p. 170)

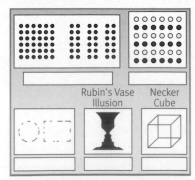

Rubin's Vase Illusion   Necker Cube

Apply what you have learned about the Gestalt principles of visual perception by identifying each rule as shown. (p. 168)

THINK / ASSESS / STUDY/ SUCCEED

191

Identify each eye component and its function. (p. 164)

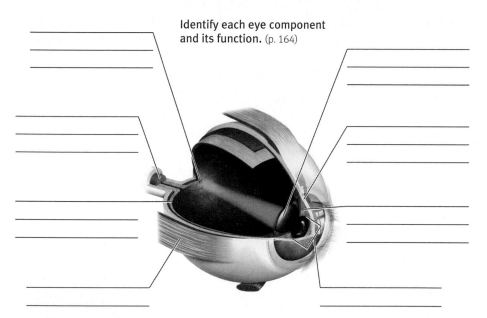

rear of the eye. The retina contains rods and cones filled with pigments. Additional cells in the retina transmit information about light to the ganglion cells, and the axons of these cells form the optic nerve.

▶ **Identify the different kinds of visual perception**
• Our visual system is sensitive to shape, color, and motion. We use different parts of the visual cortex to process these different aspects of visual perception. Cells in the primary visual cortex, called V1, are sensitive to lines of a particular orientation, like a horizontal line or a vertical line. Color perception involves comparing the reflectance from an object with the reflectance of surrounding elements in the scene. Our visual system detects motion by comparing individual "still frames" of visual content.

▶ **Describe different visual problems**
• Blindness is a worldwide problem in underdeveloped countries. Curable causes of blindness, like cataracts and glaucoma, often go untreated. Other forms of blindness such as diabetic retinopathy are incurable. There are several types of color blindness; red-green color blindness is the most common type, and it affects mostly males.

DO YOU KNOW THESE TERMS?
- ❑ **brightness** (p. 163)
- ❑ **hue** (p. 163)
- ❑ **cornea** (p. 165)
- ❑ **lens** (p. 165)
- ❑ **accommodation** (p. 165)
- ❑ **retina** (p. 165)
- ❑ **fovea** (p. 165)
- ❑ **acuity** (p. 165)
- ❑ **rods** (p. 165)
- ❑ **cones** (p. 166)
- ❑ **blind spot** (p. 166)
- ❑ **trichromatic theory** (p. 170)
- ❑ **color blindness** (p. 170)
- ❑ **depth perception** (p. 170)
- ❑ **monocular depth cues** (p. 170)
- ❑ **binocular depth cues** (p. 170)

A S S E S S your knowledge

1. The _____ _____ spectrum refers to the range of wavelengths of light that humans can see. (p. 163)

2. The intensity of reflected light that reaches our eyes is called _____. (p. 163)

3. Consisting of cells that are completely transparent, the _____ changes its curvature to keep images in focus. (p. 165)

4. We can think of the _____ as a "movie screen" onto which light from the world is projected. (p. 165)

5. _____ are receptor cells that allow us to see in low light, and _____ are receptor cells that allow us to see in color. (pp. 165–166)

6. Different parts of our _____ _____ help us to perceive shape, motion, color, and depth. (p. 166)

7. _____ principles are rules governing how we perceive objects as wholes within their overall context. (p. 168)

8. The idea that color vision is based on our sensitivity to three different colors is called the _____ theory. (p. 170)

9. Our ability to see spatial relations in three dimensions is called _____ _____. (p. 170)

10. The percentage of people with blindness in underdeveloped countries (would/wouldn't) decrease with improved access to medical care. (pp. 173–174)

mypsychlab

SUCCEED with

Distinguishing Figure–Ground Relationships

Is it possible to not see an object, even when it is right in front of us? (p. 168)

Hearing: The Auditory System (pp. 176–180)

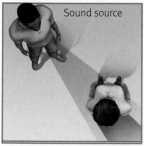

Map out, showing direction lines and steps, how we locate sound starting from the "sound source." (p. 179)

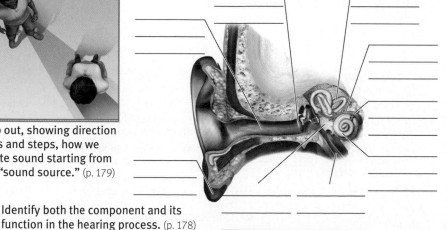

Identify both the component and its function in the hearing process. (p. 178)

S T U D Y the Learning Objectives

▶ Explain how the ear starts the auditory process
• Sound waves created by vibration of air molecules are funneled into the outer ear. These vibrations perturb the eardrum, causing the three small bones in the middle ear to vibrate. This process creates pressure in the cochlea containing the basilar membrane and organ of Corti, in which hair cells are embedded. The hair cells then bend, thereby exciting them. The message is relayed through the auditory nerve.

▶ Identify the different kinds of auditory perception
• We accomplish pitch perception in three ways. Place theory is pitch perception based on where along the basilar membrane hair cells were maximally excited. Frequency

theory is based on the hair cells reproducing the frequency of the pitch in their firing rates. In Volley theory, groups of neurons stagger their responses to follow a pitch. We also perceive where a sound is coming from, a phenomenon called "sound localization."

DO YOU KNOW THESE TERMS?
- ❏ **audition** (p. 176)
- ❏ **timbre** (p. 177)
- ❏ **cochlea** (p. 178)
- ❏ **organ of Corti** (p. 178)
- ❏ **basilar membrane** (p. 178)

ASSESS your knowledge

1. _____ refers to the frequency of the sound wave, and is measured in hertz (Hz). (p. 176)

2. The height of the sound wave corresponds to _____ and is measured in decibels (dB). (p. 177)

3. We refer to _____ to describe the complexity or quality of a sound. (p. 177)

4. The ear _____ funnels sounds waves onto the eardrum. (p. 178)

5. The _____ lies in the inner ear and converts vibration into neural activity. (p. 178)

6. The organ of Corti and basilar membrane are especially critical to hearing because _____ _____ are embedded within them. (p. 178)

7. The perception of high-pitched tones by the basilar membrane can be explained by the _____ theory. (p. 179)

8. We use various brain centers to _____ sounds with respect to our bodies. (p. 179)

9. Certain animals emit sounds and listen to their echoes to determine their distance from a barrier in a phenomenon called _____. (p. 179)

10. We all tend to lose some hearing ability as we age, especially for (high/low) frequency sounds. (p. 180)

THINK about what You would do . . .
If you didn't want your elderly parents to be able to hear your phone's ringtone, what would you look for in selecting a ringtone? (p. 176)

mypsychlab
where learning comes to life!

Listening to Blues Test
Listening skills may predict reaction to antidepressants.
(p. 179)

SUCCEED with

Smell and Taste: The Sensual Senses (pp. 180–183)

STUDY the Learning Objectives

▶ Identify how we sense and perceive tastes and odors
- Gustation (taste) and olfaction (smell) are chemical senses because our sense receptors interact with molecules containing flavor and odor. The tongue contains taste receptors for sweet, sour, salty, umami (a "meaty" or "savory" flavor), and perhaps fat. Our ability to taste different food also relies largely on smell. Olfactory receptors in our noses are sensitive to hundreds of different airborne molecules. We use our senses of taste and smell to sample our food. We react to extremely sour tastes, which may be due to food spoilage, with disgust. We also appear sensitive to pheromones, odorless molecules that can affect sexual response.

DO YOU KNOW THESE TERMS?
- ❏ **olfaction** (p. 180)
- ❏ **gustation** (p. 180)
- ❏ **taste buds** (p. 181)
- ❏ **pheromones** (p. 182)

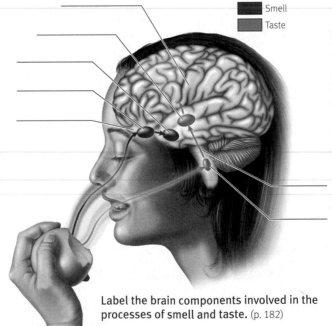
Smell
Taste

Label the brain components involved in the processes of smell and taste. (p. 182)

What chemicals do some perfume advertisers inaccurately claim are contained in their products which, when worn, alleged-ly trigger a physical response from others? (p. 183)

ASSESS your knowledge

1. Our sense of smell is called _____, and our sense of taste is called _____. (p. 180)

2. Smell and taste are the _____ senses because we derive these sensory experiences from chemicals in substances. (p. 180)

3. Airborne chemicals that interact with receptors in the lining of our nasal passages are called _____. (p. 180)

4. We detect taste with _____ _____ that are on our tongue. (p. 181)

5. We're sensitive to _____ basic tastes, the last of which, _____, was recently discovered. (p. 181)

6. Recent research has shown that when _____ is put on our tongue, it starts to affect our body's metabolism of fat. (p. 181)

7. Our taste perception (is/isn't) dependent on our sense of smell. (p. 181)

8. A part of the limbic system, the _____ _____, is a site of convergence for smell and taste. (p. 182)

9. Both tasting disgusting food and viewing facial expressions of disgust activate the _____ _____ (p. 182)

10. _____ are odorless chemicals that serve as social signals to one's species and alter animals' sexual behavior. (p. 182)

THINK about — what **You** would do . . .
As a realtor, what "tricks" could you play with smells to entice potential homebuyers when showing a house or apartment? (p. 180)

SUCCEED with — mypsychlab *where learning comes to life!*
Alzheimer's Smell Test
Can a scratch and sniff test assess our memory ability? (p. 183)

Our Body Senses: Touch, Body Position, and Balance (pp. 184–189)

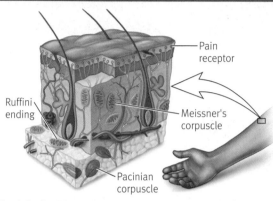

Ruffini ending

Pain receptor

Meissner's corpuscle

Pacinian corpuscle

Explain the process by which humans detect physical pressure, temperature, and pain. (p. 184)

Describe the phenomenon of the "mirror box" and identify its role in helping people who have lost limbs. (p. 186)

SUCCEED with — mypsychlab *where learning comes to life!*
Brain Pain
Imagine if virtual reality games could ease pain. (p. 185)

THINK about — what **You** would do . . .
If you were an admitting clerk at a local health clinic serving a diverse population, what what factors would you consider when gauging the level of pain your patients report? (p. 185)

STUDY the Learning Objectives

▶ Describe the three different body senses
- We process information about touch to the skin, muscle activity, and acceleration. These are called "somatosensory" for body sensation, "proprioception" for muscle position sense, and "vestibular sense" for the sense of balance and equilibrium. The somatosensory system responds to light touch, deep pressure, hot and cold temperature, and tissue damage. Our muscles contain sense receptors that detect stretch and others that detect force. We calculate where our bodies are located from this information. We're typically unaware of our sense of equilibrium.

▶ Explain how pain perception differs from touch perception
- The perception of pain differs from the perception of touch because there's a large emotional component to pain not present with touch. This is because pain information activates parts of the limbic system in addition to the somatosensory cortex. There's evidence that pain perception can be reduced by a "stoic" mind-set as well as cultural and genetic factors. Disorders of pain perception, called pain insensitivities, are associated with an increased risk of injury. As unpleasant as pain may be, it's essential to our survival.

DO YOU KNOW THESE TERMS?
- ❑ **somatosensory** (p. 184)
- ❑ **proprioception** (p. 184)
- ❑ **vestibular sense** (p. 184)
- ❑ **phantom pain** (p. 186)
- ❑ **semicircular canals** (p. 188)

ASSESS your knowledge

1. The body's system for touch and pain is the _____ system. (p. 184)

2. We sense touch, temperature, and especially pain, with _____ _____ _____. (p. 184)

3. Our fingertips have the (least/most) nerve endings. (p. 185)

4. Information about body touch, temperature, and painful stimuli travels in the _____ nerves before entering the spinal cord. (p. 185)

5. Touch information travels more (slowly/quickly) than pain stimuli information. (p. 185)

6. Persons with amputated limbs often experience the eerie phenomenon of pain or discomfort in the missing limb, known as _____ _____. (p. 186)

7. Our sense of body position is called _____. (p. 187)

8. The _____ _____, also called the sense of equilibrium, enables us to sense and maintain our balance. (p. 187)

9. The three fluid-filled _____ _____ in the inner ear maintain our sense of balance. (p. 188)

10. Tiny crystals called _____ sense linear movement and gravity. (p. 188)

Remember these questions from the beginning of the chapter? Think again and ask yourself if you would answer them differently based on what you now know about sensation and perception. (For more detailed explanations, see MyPsychLab.)

▶ Can we perceive invisible stimuli? (p. 152)
▶ Can we "read" someone else's thoughts? (p. 159)
▶ Can our eyes detect only a single particle of light? (p. 163)
▶ Can certain blind people still "see" some of their surroundings? (p. 173)
▶ Do some people "taste" shapes or "hear" colors? (p. 173)
▶ Does music activate the same brain areas as food, sex, and drugs? (p. 179)
▶ Why can't we taste food when we have a bad cold? (pp. 181–182)

THINKING Scientifically

Correlation vs. Causation pp. 179, 185

Falsifiability pp. 169, 171

Extraordinary Claims pp. 156, 161, 166

Occam's Razor pp. 169, 175

Replicability pp. 158, 160, 170, 174, 181, 186

Ruling Out Rival Hypotheses
pp. 155, 170, 180, 181, 183, 185, 187

5
Consciousness
Expanding the Boundaries of Psychological Inquiry

Sleep paralysis has been reported in many cultures, with the terrifying night-time visitors ranging from an "Old Hag" to demonlike entities, as depicted in this painting, *The Nightmare*, by Henry Fuseli.

sleep paralysis
state of being unable to move just after falling asleep or right before waking up

Consider this fascinating story related by a subject in Susan Clancy's (2006) landmark research on people who come to believe they were kidnapped by aliens.

"I had this terrible nightmare—at least I think it was a nightmare. Something was on top of me. It wasn't human. It was pushing into me, I couldn't move, I couldn't scream, I was being suffocated. It was the worst dream I ever had. When I told my therapist about it she basically asked me if anything had happened to me as a kid. . . . I don't think I got abused . . . but she made me think. Had something happened to me? Maybe something did happen? . . . Well, for some reason, I started to have images of aliens pop into my head. Did you see that movie *Signs*—the one with Mel Gibson? The aliens looked more like those, not the more typical ones. I'd be walking to school and then—POP— an alien head would be in my head. Sometimes I'd hit my fist against a wall because then the pain would help me think of something else. I really thought I was going crazy. . . . Once I started thinking maybe I was abducted I couldn't stop. Finally I told my therapist about what was going on and she said she couldn't help me with this, but she referred me to a psychologist in Somerville, someone who worked with people who believed this. The first time, when he asked me why I was there I opened my mouth to talk but I started crying and I couldn't stop. . . . He said that I shouldn't be afraid, that this was very common, that it was the first stage of coming to realize what happened to me, that in some people the memories only get partially erased and that those people can access them if they are willing to do the work, to undergo hypnosis and allow yourself to find out." (Clancy, 2006, pp. 30–31)

This subject isn't alone. Tens of thousands of Americans believe they've had at least some contact with aliens (Jacobs, 1992). But were they *really* abducted by aliens? Clancy and her Harvard University colleagues (Clancy, McNally, Schachter, Lenzenweger, & Pitman, 2002; McNally & Clancy, 2005) say there's a slim chance at best. But they happened on a startling discovery that might explain the abduction reports.

Hailing from all walks of life, many of their subjects shared a history of **sleep paralysis.** The term may not be familiar to most of us, but many of us are acquainted with a strange feeling of being unable to move just after falling asleep or immediately upon awakening. This puzzling experience is surprisingly common. One-third to one-half of college students report having experienced at least one episode of sleep paralysis, which typically is no cause for concern (Fukuda, Ogilvie, Chilcott, Venditelli, & Takeuchi, 1998). Sleep paralysis is caused by a disruption in the sleep cycle and is often associated with anxiety or even terror, feelings of vibrations, humming noises, and the eerie sense of menacing figures perceived to be close to or even on top of the immobile person.

Explanations for sleep paralysis vary across cultures. In Thailand, people attribute this strange experience to a ghost, in Korea to being squeezed by scissors, and in the Caribbean island of St. Lucia to an attack by babies who haven't been baptized (Blackmore, 2004). People in Newfoundland associate the graphic image of an "old hag" (an elderly witch) sitting on the chest with sleep paralysis. In medieval times, the myths of the incubus (male demon) and succubus (female demon)— evil spirits that descend on vulnerable sleepers and engage in sexual relations with them— probably arose from sleep paralysis experiences (Sagan, 1995). According to Susan Blackmore (2004), the "latest sleep paralysis myth may be alien abduction" (p. 315).

Unfortunately, the therapist that Clancy's subject consulted wasn't aware of sleep paralysis. Nor did he know that hypnosis isn't a trustworthy means of unearthing accurate memories. In fact, we'll soon learn that hypnosis can help to create false memories in many people. In many of the cases Clancy reported, it's not a big leap for people who suspect they were abducted to elaborate on their story during hypnosis and to imagine that aliens performed medical experiments on them. After all, that's what the media often lead people to believe happens when the aliens come calling.

Sleep paralysis is only one of many remarkable sleep-related experiences we'll encounter in this chapter, along with other fascinating examples of profound alterations in **consciousness**—our subjective experience of the world, our bodies, and our mental perspectives. To study consciousness is to grapple with the full range of human experience, including the mysteries of sleeping and dreaming; hallucinations; near-death, out-of-body, mystical, and déjà vu experiences; hypnosis; meditation; and the mind-bending effects of consciousness-altering drugs. These mysterious phenomena, once at the outermost fringes of scientific psychology, are now receiving increasing attention as leading-edge scientists strive to comprehend the intricate links between our brains and our perceptions of the world and ourselves (Cardeña, Lynn, & Krippner, 2000).

It's easy to see why many scientists describe sleep, hypnosis, and other phenomena we'll explore as radical departures from our ordinary state of consciousness. Yet our sleeping and waking experiences shade subtly into one another; for example, research shows that our waking thoughts are sometimes bizarre and fragmented, much as sleep thoughts are (Klinger, 1990, 1999; Klinger & Cox, 1987/1988). Indeed, across a typical day, we experience many altered states in our stream of consciousness, ranging from subtle to profound (Neher, 1990). Throughout the day and night, the spotlight of awareness and our level of alertness change constantly in response to external (sights, sounds) and internal (bodily processes) stimuli to meet the shifting demands of daily living. Honed by hundreds of thousands of years of natural selection, our fine-tuned mental apparatus is prepared to respond to virtually any situation or threat efficiently, seamlessly, and often unconsciously, allowing us to do many things, such as walking and talking, simultaneously (Kirsch & Lynn, 1998; Wegner, 2004).

In this chapter, we'll encounter numerous examples of how consciousness is remarkably attuned to changes in our brain chemistry, expectations, culture, and the biological rhythms that govern the ebb and flow of our awareness. We'll also examine how the unity of consciousness can break down in unusual ways, such as during sleepwalking, when we're unconscious yet move about as if awake, and déjà vu, when we feel as though we're reliving an event we've never experienced. As in many cases in psychology (see also Chapter 15), abnormalities in functioning can often shed light on normal functioning (Cooper, 2003; Harkness, 2007). Such is the case in consciousness, in which altered states of awareness can reveal how our minds operate under typical circumstances.

The Biology of Sleep

We spend as much as one-third or more of our lives in one specific state of consciousness. No, we don't mean zoning out when listening to an incredibly boring lecture. We're referring to sleep. Have you ever wondered why you dream and what your dreams mean? If these questions have piqued your curiosity, you're in the company of scientists who've devoted many hours of their lives (and pulled many an all-nighter) studying thousands of subjects in sleep laboratories around the world (Dement, 1974). We'll next address these questions and learn about breakthroughs in our understanding of the mysteries of sleep.

THE CIRCADIAN RHYTHM: THE CYCLE OF EVERYDAY LIFE

Long before scientists began to probe the secrets of sleep in the laboratory, primitive hunters were keenly aware of daily cycles of sleep and wakefulness. The circadian rhythm controls our feelings of sleepiness and drowsiness. **Circadian rhythm** is a fancy term (it's Latin for "around a day") for changes that occur on a roughly 24-hour basis in many of our biological processes, including hormone release, brain waves, body temperature, and drowsiness. Popularly known as the brain's **biological clock,** the meager 20,000 neurons located in the *suprachiasmatic nucleus* (SCN) in the hypothalamus (see Chapter 3) make us feel drowsy at different times of the day and night. Many of us have noticed that we feel like taking a nap at around 3 or 4 in the afternoon. Indeed, in many European and Latin American countries, a midafternoon nap (a "siesta" in Spanish) is part of the daily ritual.

Circadian rhythms drive our bodies to wake up and fall asleep.

Sleep deprivation can lead to extreme fatigue the next day.

consciousness
our subjective experience of the world, our bodies, and our mental perspectives

circadian rhythm
cyclical changes that occur on a roughly 24-hour basis in many biological processes

biological clock
term for the suprachiasmatic nucleus (SCN) in the hypothalamus that's responsible for controlling our levels of alertness

Jet lag, which can create sleep problems, occurs when travelers cross time zones.

Sleep deprivation in night-shift workers may have been responsible for the Three Mile Island nuclear reactor plant accident in Pennsylvania in 1979 and the Exxon Valdez shipwreck that caused a massive oil spill in Alaska in 1989 (Coren, 1996).

rapid eye movements (REM)
darting of the eyes underneath the closed eyelids during sleep

This sense of fatigue is triggered by our biological clocks. The urge to snooze comes over us at night as well because levels of the hormone *melatonin,* which triggers feelings of sleepiness, increase after dark.

How much sleep do we need? Some lucky people function reasonably well on only 4–6 hours of sleep, but most of us require 7–10 hours of sleep to feel rested the next day. The average adult gets about 7 hours of sleep, but as many as 60 percent don't get this much on a regular basis. Newborns are gluttons for sleep and need about 16 hours over the course of a day. Most college students need 9 hours of sleep a night to be fully alert the next day. They like to sleep until later in the morning, because that's how their biological clocks are set. Unfortunately, most college students sleep no more than 6 hours a night (Maas, 1999), creating a powerful urge to nap the next day (Rock, 2004).

Ordinarily, there don't seem to be many negative consequences of losing one night's sleep other than feeling edgy, irritable, and unable to concentrate well the next day. Yet after a few nights of sleep deprivation, we feel more "out of it" and begin to accumulate a balance of "sleep debt." If we don't settle that balance, sleep deprivation will catch up with us. People deprived of multiple nights of sleep often experience depression and difficulties in acquiring new information. After more than 4 days of severe sleep deprivation, we may even experience brief hallucinations, such as hearing voices or seeing things (Wolfe & Pruitt, 2003). Sleep deprivation is associated with a variety of adverse health outcomes: weight gain (we burn off a lot of calories just by sleeping); increased risk for high blood pressure, diabetes, and heart problems; and a less vigorous immune response to viral infections (Dement & Vaughan, 1999). Some researchers even believe that the massive increase in obesity in the United States over the past few decades (see Chapter 11) is due largely to Americans' chronic sleep deprivation (Hasler et al., 2004), although this claim is scientifically controversial.

If you've ever taken a long flight across time zones, you'll be no stranger to *jet lag,* the result of a disruption of our body's circadian rhythms. Imagine traveling cross-country and "losing" 3 hours in the flight from California to Florida. When we wake up at 8 A.M. the next morning, we probably won't feel rested because our bodies' clocks are set for 5 A.M., the time it would be in California. The more time zones we pass through, the longer it takes our bodies' clocks to reset.

Our biological clocks can also be disrupted when we work late shifts, which can result in sleeping problems, including drowsiness during work and insomnia when we try to fall asleep. Numerous famous catastrophes, including airplane crashes, have probably resulted largely from sleep deprivation.

STAGES OF SLEEP AND DREAMING

Sixty years ago, most people believed there was something like a switch in our brains that turned consciousness on when we were awake and off when we were asleep. If we were to ask scientists of the time what our brains do while we snooze, most would have answered "not much." But that's not the reply we'd get today. To understand why, consider what happened one night in 1951 in Nathaniel Kleitman's sleep laboratory at the University of Chicago. Eugene Aserinsky, Kleitman's graduate student, monitored his son Armond's eye movements and brain waves while he slept. Aserinsky was astonished to observe that Armond's eyes danced periodically back and forth under his closed lids, like the eyes of the sleeping babies Aserinsky had observed on other occasions. Whenever the eye movements occurred, Armond's brain pulsed with electrical activity, as measured by an electroencephalogram (EEG; see Chapter 3), much as it did when Armond was awake (Aserinsky, 1996).

The fledgling scientist had the good sense to know that he was onto something of immense importance. The slumbering brain wasn't an inert tangle of neurons; rather, it was abuzz with activity, at least at various intervals. Aserinsky further suspected that Armond's eye movements signaled episodes of dreaming. Aserinsky and Kleitman (1953) confirmed this hunch when they awakened subjects while they were displaying **rapid eye movements (REM).** In almost all cases, these subjects reported vivid dreams. In contrast, subjects were much less likely to report experiencing vivid dreams when researchers awakened them from

non-REM (NREM) sleep, although later research showed that vivid dreams sometimes happened during NREM sleep too.

Following close on the heels of Aserinsky and Kleitman's (1953) pioneering research, Kleitman and William Dement (Dement & Kleitman, 1957) went on to discover that during sleep we pass through five distinct stages. Using all-night recording devices, including an *electrooculogram* (EOG) to measure eye movements, an EEG to measure brain waves, and an *electromyogram* (EMG) to measure muscular activity, they found that we travel through repeated cycles of these five stages every night. Each cycle lasts about 90 minutes, and each stage of sleep is clearly distinguishable from awake states, as shown in **Figure 5.1.**

Stage 1 Sleep. Has someone ever nudged you to wake up, and you weren't even sure whether you were awake or asleep? Perhaps you even replied, "No, I wasn't really sleeping," but your friend insisted, "Yes you were. You were starting to snore." If so, you were probably in stage 1 sleep. In this light stage of sleep, which lasts for 5–10 minutes, our brain activity powers down by 50 percent or more, producing waves of 4–7 times per second known as *theta* waves. These waves are slower than the *beta* waves of 13 or more times per second produced during active alert states, and the *alpha* waves of 8–12 times per second when we're quiet and relaxed. As we drift off to deeper sleep, we become more relaxed, and we may experience *hypnagogic imagery*—scrambled, bizarre, and dreamlike images that flit in and out of consciousness. In this state of sleep, we're typically quite confused. Some scientists have speculated that many reports of ghosts stem from hypnagogic imagery that sleepers have misinterpreted as human figures (Hines, 2003). If you've ever experienced sudden jerks of your limbs in a light sleep, and felt like you were startled or falling, it's perfectly normal for stage 1 sleep. The technical name for these sudden muscle contractions is *hypnic myoclonia*.

Stage 2 Sleep. In stage 2 sleep, our brain waves slow down even more. Sudden intense bursts of electrical activity called *sleep spindles* of about 12–14 cycles a second, and occasional sudden sharply rising and falling waves known as *K-complexes,* first appear in the EEG (Aldritch, 1999). K-complexes appear only when we're asleep. As our brain activity decelerates, our heart rate slows, our body temperature decreases, our muscles relax even more, and our eye movements cease. We spend as much as 65 percent of our sleep in stage 2.

Stages 3 and 4 Sleep. After about 10–30 minutes, light sleep gives way to much deeper slow-wave sleep, in which we can observe *delta waves,* which are as slow as 1 or 2 cycles a second, in the EEG. In stage 3, delta waves appear 20 to 50 percent of the time, and in stage 4, they appear more than half the time. To feel fully rested in the morning, we need to experience these deeper stages of sleep throughout the night. Children are famously good sleepers because they spend as much as 40 percent of their sleep time in deep sleep, when they may appear "dead to the world" and are difficult to awaken. Just try it sometime! In contrast, adults spend only about one-quarter of their sleep "sleeping like a baby," in deep sleep.

Stage 5: Paradoxical or REM Sleep. After 15–30 minutes, we return to stage 2 before our brains shift dramatically into high gear, with wakelike high-frequency, low-amplitude waves. We've entered stage 5, known commonly as *paradoxical* or **REM sleep.** It's called paradoxical sleep because the brain is active at the same time that the body is inactive. As we've seen, it's during this stage that most vivid dreaming occurs.

The Physiology of REM Sleep. Our hyped brain waves are accompanied by increased heart rate and blood pressure and rapid and irregular breathing, a state that

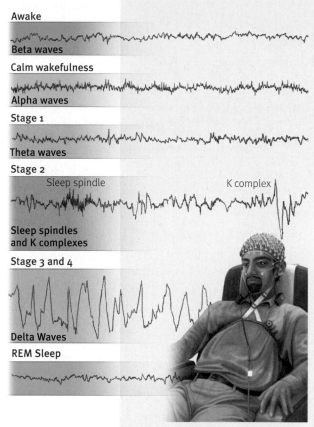

Awake
Beta waves

Calm wakefulness
Alpha waves

Stage 1
Theta waves

Stage 2
Sleep spindle | K complex
Sleep spindles and K complexes

Stage 3 and 4
Delta Waves

REM Sleep

Figure 5.1 The Stages of Sleep. The EEG allows scientists to distinguish among the major stages of sleep, along with two levels of wakefulness. As we can see, brain activity during REM sleep is similar to that when we're awake and alert, because our brains during REM are typically engaged in vivid dreaming.

Electrical recording devices make it possible to study the relations among brain activity, eye movements, and physical relaxation.

non-REM (NREM) sleep
Stages 1 through 4 of the sleep cycle, during which eye movements do not occur and dreaming is less frequent and vivid

REM sleep
stage of sleep during which the brain is most active and during which vivid dreaming most often occurs

occupies about 20 to 25 percent of our night's sleep. After 10–20 minutes of REM sleep, the cycle starts up again, as we glide back to the early stages of sleep and then back into deeper sleep. The amount of time spent in REM sleep increases with each cycle. By the morning, we may spend as much as an hour in REM sleep, compared with the 10–20 minutes we spend in REM after falling asleep. Each night, we circle back to REM sleep five or six times.

REM sleep is biologically important, probably even essential. Depriving rats of REM sleep typically leads to their death within a few weeks (National Institute on Alcohol Use and Alcoholism, 1998), although rats die even sooner from total sleep deprivation (Rechtschaffen, 1998). When we humans are deprived of REM for a few nights, we experience a phenomenon known as *REM rebound:* The amount and intensity of REM sleep increases, suggesting that REM serves a critical biological function (Ocampo-Garces, Molina, Rodriguez, & Vivaldi, 2000). Many of us have observed REM rebound in our night lives when we haven't slept much for a few nights in a row. When we finally get a good night's sleep, we often experience much more intense dreams, even nightmares, reflecting a powerful bounce-back of REM sleep. Yet scientists are still debating the biological functions of REM sleep.

REM sleep, as we've seen, is accompanied by rapidly darting eye movements. The function of these movements is unknown (Rechtschaffen, 1998; Siegel, 2005); some researchers once believed they served to scan the images of dreams (Dement, 1974). For example, William Dement once observed a subject during REM engaging in a striking pattern of back-and-forth horizontal eye movements. When Dement awakened him, he reported dreaming of a Ping-Pong match. Nevertheless, the evidence for this "scanning hypothesis" of REM is mixed, and evidence that subjects blind from birth engage in REM seems to call it into question (Gross, 1965). Also occurring during REM is a phenomenon called *middle ear muscle activity* (MEMA), in which the muscles of our middle ears become active, almost as though they're assisting us to hear sounds in the dream (Pessah & Roffwarg, 1972; Slegel, Benson, Zarcone, & Schubert, 1991).

During REM sleep, our supercharged brains are creating dreams, but our bodies are relaxed and, for all practical purposes, paralyzed. If we weren't paralyzed by REM, we'd act out our dreams. In fact, people with the strange condition called *REM behavior disorder* (RBD) do just that. In one case, for 20 years a 77-year-old minister acted out violent dreams in his sleep and occasionally injured his wife (Mahowald & Schenck, 2000). Fortunately, only about 1 person in 200 has symptoms of RBD, which occurs most frequently in men over the age of 50. In this condition, the brain stem structures (see Chapter 3) that ordinarily prevent us from moving during REM sleep don't function properly. Classic work by Michel Jouvet (1962) showed that lesioning a brain stem region called the locus coeruleus, which is responsible for keeping us paralyzed during REM, leads cats to act out their dreams. If Jouvet gave cats a ball of yarn to play with during the day, they'd often reenact this play behavior in their dreams.

The physiology of REM sleep helps us to understand why Susan Clancy's (2006) subjects thought they'd been abducted by aliens. For reasons that are poorly understood, many or most alien abductees appear to experience short-term intrusions of REM sleep into wakefulness (Blackmore, 1998). Most also report a consistent set of symptoms: paralysis, seeing visions, and hearing buzzing sounds. We can now recognize these symptoms as the penetration of REM phenomena into waking life: sleep paralysis, vivid dreams, and MEMA, respectively.

REM Sleep and Dreaming. Early sleep researchers (Dement & Kleitman,1957) believed that dreams were confined to REM sleep. But it soon became apparent that we don't dream *only* during REM sleep, although we dream *more* in REM (Domhoff, 1996, 1999). Across many studies, 82 percent of REM periods are associated with dream reports, whereas only 43 percent of non-REM periods (time spent in stages 1 through 4 sleep) are associated with dream reports (Nielson, 1999). Although some people insist they never dream, research shows that this phenomenon is usually due to a failure to recall their dreams rather than a failure to experience them. When brought into a sleep laboratory, virtually everyone reports vivid dreaming when awakened during a REM period

(Dement, 1974; Domhoff & Schneider, 2004), although a few people don't (Butler, 1985; Pagel, 2003).

Moreover, REM and non-REM dreams tend to differ. Many REM dreams are emotional, illogical, and prone to sudden shifts in "plot" (Foulkes, 1962; Hobson, Pace-Schott, & Stickgold, 2000). In contrast, non-REM dreams often are shorter (Antrobus, 1983; Foulkes & Rechtschaffen, 1964), are more thoughtlike and repetitive, and deal with topics that are of current concern to us, like homework, shopping lists, or taxes (Hobson, 2002; Rechtschaffen, Verdone, & Wheaton, 1963).

Nevertheless, as the night wears on, dream reports from NREM sleep (starting with Stage 2) resemble REM dream reports, leading some researchers to suggest that REM and NREM dreams aren't as distinct as once believed (Antrobus, 1983; Foulkes & Schmidt, 1983; McNamara, McLaren, Smith, Brown, & Stickgold, 2005). Thus, consciousness during sleep may vary with our level of brain activity and sleep stage (Siegel, 2005; Wamsley, Hirota, Tucker, Smith, Doan, & Antrobus, 2007).

Whether we're researchers in Timbuktu or New York City, we'll find cross-culturally consistent patterns in dreaming. Virtually all of us experience dreams that contain more aggression than friendliness, more negative than positive emotions, and more misfortune than good fortune. The dreams of older adults resemble those of college students, but with age, negative emotions and physical aggression may decrease (Hall & Domhoff, 1963; Lortie-Lussier, Cote, & Vachon, 2000). Women's dreams are likely to contain more emotion than men's dreams, and their dream characters are about evenly divided between men and women. In contrast, men are more likely to dream about men by a 2:1 ratio (Hall, 1984). At least a few differences in dreams depend on cultural factors. For example, the dreams of people in more technologically advanced societies feature fewer animals than those in small, traditional societies (Domhoff, 1996, 2001).

Even blind people dream. But whether their dreams contain visual imagery depends on when their blindness occurred. People blinded before age 4 don't experience visual dream imagery, whereas those blinded after age 7 do so, suggesting that ages 4 to 6 are a window within which the ability to generate visual imagery develops (Kerr, 1993; Kerr & Domhoff, 2004). Blind persons who can "see" in their dreams often delight in this ability. One blind man reported that he could "describe in detail the gold braid on his postmaster father's hat, which he could see when he visited his father during his dreams" (Hobson, 2002, p. 118).

Whether blind people have visual images in their dreams depends on whether they were blind from age 7 onward. What might the dreams of someone who's never seen anything be like?

LUCID DREAMING

Although we've been talking about sleeping and waking as distinct stages, they may shade gradually into one another (Antrobus, Antrobus, & Fischer, 1965). Consider a phenomenon that challenges the idea that we're either totally asleep or totally awake: lucid dreaming. If you've ever dreamed and known you were dreaming, you've experienced **lucid dreaming** (Blackmore, 1991; LaBerge, 1980, 2000; Van Eeden, 1913).

Most of us dream in color. But most of us don't realize we do so because we have poor recall of our dreams (Hobson, 2002). One of the authors of your text first realized he dreamt in color during a lucid dream. In the dream, he gazed at a lake, painted in vibrant, magnificent colors as he'd never seen before. He looked up and saw a purple bird with a human face silhouetted against a maroon and gold sky. Awed by these sights, he told himself, "This can't be happening, I must be dreaming." Sure enough, he was asleep.

Most of us have experienced at least one lucid dream, and about one-fifth of Americans report dreaming lucidly on a monthly basis (Snyder & Gackenbach, 1988). Like one of the authors of your text, many lucid dreamers become aware they're dreaming when they see something so bizarre or improbable that they conclude (correctly) that they're having a dream. Dream lucidity is also associated with anxiety dreams. Still, researchers haven't resolved the question of whether lucid dreamers are asleep when

Lucid dreams often contain bizarre combinations of images that alert dreamers to the fact that they're dreaming.

lucid dreaming
experience of becoming aware that one is dreaming

they're aware of their dream content or whether some merely report that their dreams have a lucid quality after they awaken (LaBerge, Nagel, Dement, & Zarcone, 1981).

Lucid dreaming opens up the possibility of controlling our dreams. The ability to become lucid during a nightmare usually improves the dream's outcome (Levitan & LeBerge, 1990; Spoormaker & van den Bout, 2006). When lucid dreamers adopt a conciliatory approach toward hostile characters in their dreams, the characters become less frightening and often act in a friendlier manner (Tholey, 1988). Nevertheless, there's no good evidence that changing our lucid dreams can help us to overcome depression, anxiety, or other adjustment problems, despite the claims of some popular psychology books (Mindell, 1990).

DISORDERS OF SLEEP

Nearly all of us have trouble falling asleep or staying asleep from time to time. When sleep problems recur, interfere with our ability to function at work or school, or affect our health, they can exact a dear price. The cost of sleep disorders in terms of health and lost work productivity amounts to as much as $35 billion per year (Althius, Fredman, Langenberg, & Magaziner, 1998). We can also gauge the cost in human lives, with an estimated 1500 Americans who fall asleep at the wheel killed each year (Fenton, 2007). These grim statistics are understandable given that 30 to 50 percent of people report some sort of sleep problem (Althius et al., 1998).

Insomnia. The most common sleep disturbance is **insomnia.** Insomnia can take the following forms: (a) having trouble falling asleep (regularly taking more than 30 minutes to doze off), (b) waking too early in the morning, and (c) waking up during the night and having trouble returning to sleep. An estimated 15 percent of people report severe or longstanding problems with insomnia (Ancoli-Israel & Roth, 1999; Hauri, 1998).

Insomnia is the most common sleep-related problem.

People who suffer from depression, pain, or a variety of medical conditions report especially high rates of insomnia (Ford & Kamerow, 1989; Katz & McHorney, 2002; Smith & Haythornwaite, 2004). Brief bouts of insomnia are often due to stress and relationship problems, medications and illness, working late or variable shifts, jet lag, drinking caffeine, and napping during the day. Insomnia can become recurrent if we become frustrated and anxious when we can't fall asleep right away. Many people don't know that even most "good sleepers" take 15–20 minutes to fall asleep. James Maas (1999) recommends hiding clocks to avoid becoming preoccupied with the inability to fall asleep quickly.

Short-term psychotherapy can effectively treat most cases of general insomnia (Morin et al., 1999). Here are some tips, based on the research literature, that can help us get a good night's sleep:

(1) Don't do anything stressful and relax as much as possible before bedtime.

(2) Sleep and wake up at regular times.

(3) Sleep in a cool room.

(4) Avoid consuming caffeine (especially after 2 P.M.), taking naps longer than 20 minutes, or watching television and surfing the web right before bedtime.

(5) Try to sleep only when you're tired.

(6) Get out of bed if you're having a hard time sleeping and go back to bed when you're tired so that your bed becomes a classically conditioned stimulus (see Chapter 6) for sleep.

Another common approach to treating insomnia is sleeping pills. Although sleeping pills can be effective, researchers have discovered that brief psychotherapy is more effective than Ambien, a popular sleeping pill (Jacobs, Pace-Schott, Stickgold, & Otto, 2004). Moreover, longstanding use of many sleeping pills can make it more difficult to sleep once people stop taking them, a phenomenon called *rebound insomnia*. So, in an ironic twist, sleeping pills can actually cause insomnia (Bellon, 2006).

When people try sleeping pills, they should use them for short periods of time and with caution, as there's a risk of dependency. Recently, it's come to light that in rare instances, people who use Ambien engage in eating, walking, and even driving while asleep (Schenck, 2006). When people take sleep medications, it's crucial that they mon-

insomnia
difficulty falling and staying asleep

itor their reactions carefully and ensure they have plenty of time to sleep before needing to be active again.

Some people have problems with drifting off to sleep or awakening during sleep because of **restless legs syndrome,** an unsettling urge to shake or move their legs and sometimes other parts of the body. Restless legs affect as many as 15 percent of people (Trenkwalder, Walters, & Hening, 1996) and become more common and uncomfortable with age. People with restless legs can often find some relief by taking one of the many medications available, exercising moderately, massaging their legs, and reducing their caffeine, alcohol, and tobacco intake.

Narcolepsy. **Narcolepsy** is the virtual mirror image of insomnia. In narcolepsy, the most prominent symptom is the rapid and often unexpected onset of sleep. Consider the case of Mr. Norton. Being unable to fall asleep certainly wasn't his problem. He fell asleep at his favorite movies and at the wheel of his car. Once he was jarred from his slumber while driving when he careened down a hill. He even fell asleep while standing in the shower. He was a prison guard, and he couldn't stay awake on the job. Occasionally, he'd be completely overcome by the urge to sleep. Sometimes he experienced vivid, dreamlike hallucinations and a brief paralysis of his muscles. He feared his boss would fire him, and stifled many a yawn in his presence. He asked himself, "Who would want a person like me guarding violent men?"

This dog with narcolepsy has a genetic defect in orexin that causes the dog to collapse after playful fighting. People and animals with narcolepsy can experience cataplexy when they become excited.

People with narcolepsy can experience episodes of sudden sleep lasting anywhere from a few seconds to several minutes and, less frequently, as long as an hour. The overwhelming urge to sleep can strike at any moment. Surprise, elation, or other strong emotions—even those associated with laughing at a joke or engaging in sexual intercourse—can lead people with narcolepsy to experience *cataplexy,* a complete loss of muscle tone. During cataplexy, people can fall because their muscles become limp as a rag doll. Cataplexy occurs in healthy people during REM sleep. But in narcolepsy, people experiencing cataplexy remain alert the whole time, even though they can't move. Ordinarily, sleepers don't enter REM sleep for more than an hour after they fall asleep. But when people who experience an episode of narcolepsy doze off, they plummet into REM sleep immediately, suggesting that it results from a sleep–wake cycle that's badly off-kilter. Vivid hypnagogic hallucinations often accompany the onset of narcoleptic episodes, raising the possibility that REM intrusions are one cause of brief waking hallucinations.

The hormone *orexin* appears to play a key role in triggering sudden attacks of sleepiness (Mieda et al., 2004). People with narcolepsy have fewer brain cells that produce orexin. One hypothesis is that these cells are destroyed by an overaggressive immune response. There's hope that scientists will develop medications that will either replace orexin or mimic its effects in the brain and thereby cure narcolepsy. Fortunately, people with narcolepsy can be helped by taking short naps, taking antidepressant and stimulant medication, and avoiding alcohol and caffeine.

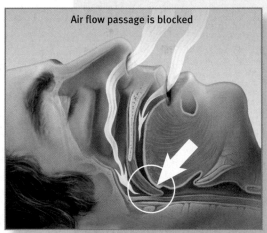

Air flow passage is blocked

Figure 5.2 Flow of Air and Quality of Sleep. When the flow of air is blocked, as in sleep apnea, the quality of sleep can be seriously disrupted.

Sleep Apnea. Being tired during the day and falling asleep during class or on the job is rarely due to narcolepsy. Many more people with these problems suffer from **sleep apnea,** which afflicts between 2 and 20 percent of the general population, depending on how broadly or narrowly it's defined (Shamsuzzaman, Gersta, & Somers, 2003; Strohl & Redline, 1996). Apnea is caused by a blockage of the airway during sleep, as shown in **Figure 5.2.** This problem causes people with apnea to snore loudly, gasp, and sometimes stop breathing for more than 20 seconds. Struggling to breathe rouses the person many times—often several hundred times—during the night and interferes with sleep, causing fatigue the next day. Yet most people with sleep apnea have no awareness of these multiple awakenings. A lack of oxygen and the buildup of carbon dioxide can lead to many problems, including night sweats, weight gain, fatigue, and an irregular heartbeat. Because apnea is associated with being overweight, doctors typically recommend weight loss as a first option. When enlarged tonsils cause apnea in children, doctors can remove them surgically. But in adults, surgical procedures often don't work very well. Many people benefit

restless legs syndrome
urge to move our legs or other body parts, often while attempting to sleep

narcolepsy
disorder characterized by the rapid and often unexpected onset of sleep

sleep apnea
disorder caused by a blockage of the airway during sleep, resulting in daytime fatigue

Person using a device to combat sleep apnea at home.

from wearing a face mask attached to a machine that blows air into their nasal passages, forcing the airway to remain open. Nevertheless, adjusting to this machine can be challenging (Wolfe & Pruitt, 2003).

Night Terrors. Night terrors are often more disturbing to onlookers than to sleepers. Parents who witness a child's night terrors can hardly believe that the child has no recollection of what occurred. Screaming, perspiring, confused, and wide-eyed, the child may even thrash about before falling back into a deep sleep. Such episodes usually last for only a few minutes, although they may seem like an eternity to a distraught parent.

Despite their dramatic nature, **night terrors** are typically harmless events that take place during deep non-REM sleep (stages 3 and 4). They occur almost exclusively in children, who spend more time than adults in deep stages of sleep (Wolfe & Pruit, 2003). Night terrors are often confused with nightmares, which typically occur only during REM sleep (American Psychiatric Association, 2000). Parents often learn not to overreact and even to ignore the episodes if the child isn't in physical danger. Night terrors occasionally occur in adults, especially when they're under intense stress.

Sleepwalking. Picture a sleepwalking person. For many of us, the image that comes to mind is a person with eyes closed, arms outstretched, and both hands at shoulder height, walking like a zombie. That's the popular image of a "somnambulist," or sleepwalker. In actuality, a sleepwalking person often acts like any fully awake person, although a sleepwalker may be somewhat clumsier. **Sleepwalking** (walking while fully asleep) often involves relatively little activity, but sleepwalkers have been known to drive cars, turn on computers, or fire guns. In a closely related condition (sometimes called "sexsomnia"), people may have sexual intercourse while asleep. One husband even snored while having sex with his wife (Underwood, 2007). In fact, a few people who committed murder have used sleepwalking as a legal defense. In one controversial case, tried before the Canadian Supreme Court, a young man who drove almost 20 miles, removed a tire iron from a car, and killed his mother-in-law and seriously injured his father-in-law with a knife, was declared innocent because he maintained (and the judges agreed) that he slept through the whole event and wasn't responsible for his behavior (McCall, Smith, & Shapiro, 1997).

For most people, sleepwalking is harmless, and sleepwalkers rarely remember their actions on awakening. But for children and adults who engage in potentially dangerous activities (such as climbing out an open window) while sleepwalking, doors and windows can be wired with alarms to alert others to direct them back to bed. If someone is sleepwalking, it's perfectly safe to wake him or her up, despite what we may have seen in movies (Wolfe & Pruitt, 2003).

Chances are you walked in your sleep at least once as a child. That's because sleepwalking is most frequent in childhood. Rest assured that, contrary to a popular myth, sleepwalking isn't associated with deep-seated psychological problems, although episodes of sleepwalking can be triggered by stress. And, contrary to another common myth, most sleepwalkers aren't dreaming, because sleepwalking almost always occurs during non-REM (especially stage 3 or 4) sleep.

ASSESS YOUR KNOWLEDGE: FACT OR FICTION?

(1) The average adult needs about 6 hours of sleep a night. (True/False)
(2) People move slowly through the first four stages of sleep but then spend the rest of the night in REM sleep. (True/False)
(3) When we dream, our brains are much less active than when awake. (True/False)
(4) People who are blind from birth dream, but not in visual images. (True/False)
(5) Night terrors are unrelated to nightmares. (True/False)

Answers: (1) F (p. 198); (2) F (p. 199); (3) F (p. 200); (4) T (p. 201); (5) T (p. 204)

night terrors
sudden waking episodes characterized by screaming, perspiring, and confusion followed by a return to a deep sleep

sleepwalking
walking while fully asleep

Theories and Psychology of Dreams

We can trace the quest to decipher the meaning of dreams to thousands of years before Aserinsky and Kleitman began to comprehend the complicated doings of our brains during sleep. By the seventh century B.C., accounts of dreams related to the story of the epic hero Gilgamesh were transcribed onto tablets in Mesopotamia. In one instance, Gilgamesh allegedly dreamt of a mountain falling on him, which some interpreted to mean he would defeat his enemy. The Babylonians believed that dreams were sent by the gods, the Assyrians thought that dreams contained signs or omens, the Greeks built dream temples in which visitors awaited prophecies sent by the gods during dreams, and North American Indians believed that dreams revealed hidden wishes and desires (Van de Castle, 1994).

One of the oldest written records in civilization includes accounts of dream experiences, in this case of the hero Gilgamesh.

FREUD AND WISH FULFILLMENT: THE DREAM PROTECTION THEORY

Sigmund Freud sided with the Native Americans. His landmark book, *The Interpretation of Dreams* (1900), shaped how people thought of dreams for decades before rigorous laboratory research. According to Freud, dreams are the guardians or protectors of sleep. During sleep, the ego (see Chapter 14), which acts as a sort of mental censor, is less able than when awake to keep sexual and aggressive instincts at bay by repressing them. If not for dreams, these instincts would bubble up, disturbing sleep. The *dream-work* disguises and contains the pesky sexual and aggressive impulses by transforming them into symbols that represent *wish fulfillment*—how we wish things could be (see also Chapter 14).

According to Freud, dreams don't give up their secrets easily—they require interpretation to reverse the dream-work and reveal their true meaning. He distinguished between the details of the dream itself, which he called the *manifest content,* and the true, hidden meaning, which he called the *latent content.* For example, a dream about getting a flat tire (manifest content) might signify anxiety about the loss of status at your job (latent content).

Challenges to Wish Fulfillment Theory: Dream Content and Nightmares. Most scientists have rejected the dream protection and wish fulfillment theories of dreams (Domhoff, 2001). Contrary to Freud's dream protection theory, some patients with brain injuries don't report they dream, yet sleep soundly (Jus et al., 1973). If, as Freud claimed, "wish fulfillment is the meaning of each and every dream" (Freud, 1900, p. 106), we'd expect dream content to be mostly positive. Yet although most of us have occasional dreams of flying, winning the lottery, or being with the object of our wildest fantasies, these themes are less frequent than dreams of misfortune. Freud believed that many dreams are sexual in nature. But sexual themes account for as little as 10 percent of the dreams we remember (see **Table 5.1**) (Domhoff, 2003).

In addition, many dreams don't appear to be disguised, as Freud contended. As many as 90 percent of dream reports are straightforward descriptions of everyday activities and problems (Domhoff, 2003; Dorus, Dorus, & Rechtschaffen, 1971). A further challenge to wish fulfillment theory is that people who've experienced highly traumatic events often have repetitive nightmares (Barratt, 1996). But nightmares clearly aren't wish fulfillments, and they aren't at all uncommon in either adults or children. So, if you have an occasional nightmare, rest assured: It's perfectly normal.

ACTIVATION–SYNTHESIS THEORY

Starting in the 1960s and 1970s, Alan Hobson and Robert McCarley developed a theory that links dreams to brain activity. According to their **activation–synthesis theory** (Hobson & McCarley, 1977; Hobson, Pace-Schott, & Stickgold, 2000), dreams reflect brain activation

Table 5.1 Most Frequent Dream Themes.

(1) Being chased or pursued
(2) Being lost, late, or trapped
(3) Falling
(4) Flying
(5) Losing valuable possessions
(6) Sexual dreams
(7) Experiencing great natural beauty
(8) Being naked or dressed oddly
(9) Injury or illness
(*Source:* Domhoff, 2003)

Falsifiability

Nightmares are most frequent in children, but are also common in adults.

activation–synthesis theory
theory that dreams reflect inputs from brain activation originating in the pons, which the forebrain then attempts to weave into a story

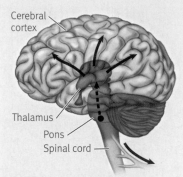

Figure 5.3 Activation–Synthesis Theory. According to activation–synthesis theory, the pons transmits random signals to the thalamus, which relays information to the forebrain of the cerebral cortex. The forebrain in turn attempts to create a story from the incomplete information it receives.

in sleep, rather than a repressed unconscious wish, as Freud claimed. Far from having deep, universal meaning, Hobson and McCarley maintained dreams reflect the activated brain's attempt to make sense of random and internally generated neural signals during REM sleep.

Throughout the day and night, the balance of neurotransmitters in the brain shifts continually, affecting our consciousness. REM is turned on by surges of the neurotransmitter acetylcholine, as serotonin and norepinephrine are shut down. Acetylcholine activates nerve cells in the pons, located at the base of the brain (see Chapter 3), while dwindling levels of serotonin and norepinephrine decrease reflective thought, reasoning, attention, and memory. The activated pons sends incomplete signals to the lateral geniculate nucleus of the thalamus, a relay for sensory information to the language and visual areas of the forebrain, as shown in **Figure 5.3** (see Chapter 3). The forebrain does its best to piece together the signals it receives into a meaningful story. Nevertheless, the bits of information it receives are random and chaotic, so the narrative is rarely coherent or logical. The amygdala is also ramped up, adding the emotional colors of fear, anxiety, anger, sadness, and elation to the mix (see Chapters 3 and 11). According to activation-synthesis theory, the net result of these complex brain changes is what we experience as a dream.

DREAMING AND THE FOREBRAIN

Scientists have used positron emission tomography (PET) scans to reveal remarkable changes in brain activity in areas essential to REM sleep and dreaming (Braun et al., 1997, 1998; Maquet et al., 1996). They've discovered that the prefrontal cortex, the area of the forebrain responsible for logical thinking, problem solving, and planning while we're awake (see Chapter 3), plunges in activity as we descend into deep sleep. When a complex mix of neurotransmitters, including acetylcholine, triggers REM sleep, the pons and brain areas associated with emotion and creating hallucinatory mental images spring into action. In contrast, areas of the forebrain responsible for reasoning and integrating neural information remain much less active than during waking. These dramatic shifts in brain activity may explain why many of our dreams are vivid, bizarre, and intensely emotional.

Although the forebrain "powers down" during dreaming, it's clear that it plays a critical role in the experience of dreams. As we learned in Chapter 3, brain injuries are "experiments of nature," which have taught students of biopsychology a great deal about the brain's functioning. Studies of dreaming are no exception. Psychiatrist Mark Solms (1977; Solms & Turnbull, 2002) surveyed 332 cases of patients with brain damage from stroke, tumors, and injury. From this gold mine of data, he determined that damage to (a) the deep frontal white matter, which connects different parts of the cortex to the lower parts of the brain, and (b) the parietal lobes can lead to a complete loss of dreaming. It's likely that the damaged brain areas are pathways that allow brain centers involved in dreaming to communicate. When they're disconnected, dreaming stops.

Thus, damage to the forebrain can eliminate dreams entirely, even when the brain stem is working properly. This finding gives us reason to doubt the brain stem's role in producing dreams and underscores the role the forebrain plays in dreaming. According to Solms, dreams are driven largely by the motivational and emotional control centers of the forebrain while the logical "executive" parts of the brain snooze.

NEUROCOGNITIVE PERSPECTIVES ON DREAMING: INFORMATION PROCESSING AND DEVELOPMENT

Do Androids Dream of Electric Sheep? is the intriguing title of a novel by Philip K. Dick that conveys the idea that who we are determines, at least in part, what we dream about. Just as androids (robots that appear human) possess different abilities from humans, children and adults differ in significant ways, including their information-processing abilities.

Scientists who've advanced a *neurocognitive* view of dreaming argue that explaining dreams only in terms of neurotransmitters and random neural impulses doesn't tell the full story. Instead, they contend, we must also consider our cognitive capacities, which shape what we dream about. For example, children under the age of 7 or 8 recall dreaming on only 20 to 30 percent of occasions when awakened from REM sleep compared with 80 to 90 percent of adults (Foulkes, 1982, 1999). Until they reach the age of 9 or 10, children's dreams tend to be simple, lacking in movement, and less emotional and bizarre than adult dreams (Domhoff, 1996). A typical 5-year-old's dream may be of a pet or animal in a zoo. Apart from an occasional nightmare, children's dreams feature little aggression or negative emotion (Domhoff, 2003; Foulkes, 1999). According to the neurocognitive perspective, complex dreams are "cognitive achievements" that parallel the gradual development of visual imagination and other advanced cognitive abilities. We begin to dream like adults when our brains develop the "wiring" to do so (Domhoff, 2001).

Content analyses of tens of thousands of dreams (Hall & Van de Castle, 1966) reveal that many are associated with emotional concerns and everyday preoccupations, and that dream content is surprisingly stable over long time periods (Domhoff, 1996; Hall & Nordby, 1972; Smith & Hall, 1964). In a journal containing details about 904 dreams that a person kept for more than five decades, six themes (eating or thinking of food, the loss of an object, going to the toilet, being in a small or messy room, missing a bus or train, doing something with her mother) accounted for more than three-fourths of the contents of her dreams (Domhoff, 1993). Additionally, 50 to 80 percent of people report recurrent dreams over many years (Cartwright & Romanek, 1978; Zadra, 1996). The bottom line? Although dreams are sometimes bizarre, they're more consistent over time than we'd expect if they reflected only random neural impulses generated by the brain stem (Domhoff, 2001b; Foulkes, 1985; Revonsuo, 2000; Strauch & Meier, 1996).

As we've seen, there are sharp disagreements among scientists about the role of the brain stem and REM sleep, and the role that development plays in dreaming. Nevertheless, scientists generally agree that (1) acetylcholine turns on REM sleep and (2) the forebrain plays an important role in dreams.

Children under the age of 9 or 10 generally have static, uncomplicated dreams involving very little action or "plot."

WHAT'S THE FUNCTION OF DREAMS?

Scientists still don't know for sure why we dream. But evidence from a variety of sources suggests that dreams are involved in (a) processing emotional memories (Marquet & Franck, 1997); (b) integrating new experiences with established memories to make sense of the world (Stickgold, James, & Hobson, 2002); (c) learning new strategies and ways of doing things, like swinging a golf club (Walker, Brakefield, Morgan, Hobson, & Stickgold, 2002); (d) simulating threatening events so we can better cope with them in everyday life (Revonsuo, 2000); and (e) reorganizing and consolidating memories (Crick & Mitchison, 1983, 1986). Still, the function of dreams remains a puzzle because research evidence concerning the role of learning and memory in dreams is controversial and mixed.

ASSESS YOUR KNOWLEDGE: FACT OR FICTION?
(1) Dreams often reflect unfulfilled wishes, as Freud suggested. (True/False)
(2) Activation–synthesis theory proposes that dreams result from incomplete neural signals being generated by the pons. (True/False)
(3) REM sleep is triggered by the neurotransmitter acetylcholine. (True/False)
(4) The prefrontal cortex shows a dramatic reduction in activity during deep sleep. (True/False)
(5) Recurrent dreams are extremely rare. (True/False)

Answers: (1) F (p. 205); (2) T (p. 205); (3) T (p. 206); (4) T (p. 206); (5) F (p. 207)

Other Alterations of Consciousness and Unusual Experiences

As the stages of sleep demonstrate, consciousness is far more complicated than just "conscious" versus "unconscious." Moreover, there are other variations on the theme of consciousness besides sleep and waking. Some of the more radical alterations in consciousness include hallucinations, as well as out-of-body, near-death, and déjà vu experiences.

HALLUCINATIONS: EXPERIENCING WHAT ISN'T THERE

We have a remarkable ability to create realistic perceptual experiences in the absence of any external stimuli. We call these profound changes in consciousness hallucinations. Hallucinations can occur in any sensory modality, including auditory (such as voices), olfactory (such as the smell of gasoline), gustatory (such as the taste of lemonade), or tactile (such as sensations of bugs crawling on the skin). Brain scans reveal that when people report visual hallucinations, their visual cortex becomes active, just as it does when they see a real object (Bentall, 2000). The same correspondence is true for other senses modalities, underscoring the link between our perceptual experiences and brain activity.

A frequent misconception is that hallucinations occur only in psychologically disturbed individuals. As we'll learn in Chapter 16, most people with schizophrenia hallucinate (American Psychiatric Association, 2000; Sartorius, Shapiro, & Jablensky, 1974). But hallucinations are far more common than many people realize. Surveys reveal that between 10 and 14 percent (Sidgewick, 1894; Tien, 1991; West, 1948) to as many as 39 percent (Ohayon, 2000; Posey & Losch, 1983) of college students and people in the general population report having hallucinated during the day at least once, even when not taking drugs or experiencing psychological problems (Chayon, 2000).

Hallucinations vary a great deal across people and occasions. Although patients with schizophrenia often experience frightening and disturbing hallucinations, they occasionally report pleasant and even comforting hallucinations. Richard Bentall (2000) described a patient who heard reassuring voices that came from a point in space somewhere to her left and offered "encouraging messages about her likelihood of succeeding in her career" (Bentall, 2000, p. 89).

The meaning and type of hallucinations vary across cultures. Some non-Western cultures, including some in Africa, believe that hallucinations impart wisdom. Some of these cultures value hallucinations as gifts from the gods and incorporate them into their religious rituals. People in these societies may even go out of their way to induce hallucinations by means of prayer, sensory deprivation, fasting, and hallucinogenic drugs (Al-Issa, 1995; Bourguignon, 1970). Moreover, visual hallucinations are more frequent in developing cultures than in technologically advanced ones (Al-Issa, 1977).

Hallucinations, like most other alterations in consciousness, have multiple causes. As we'll learn in Chapter 15, auditory hallucinations can occur when patients mistakenly attribute their thoughts, or inner speech, to an external source (Bentall, 1990, 2000; Frith, 1992). Healthy people can also confuse their imaginings with reality. Adults and college students who report having engaged in a great deal of fantasizing and imaginative activities since childhood—so-called fantasy-prone persons—report having problems distinguishing fantasy from reality, and hallucinate persons and objects on occasion (Barber & Wilson, 1981, 1983; Lynn & Rhue, 1988).

OUT-OF-BODY EXPERIENCES

Carlos Alvarado (2000) described a 36-year-old police officer's account of an **out-of-body experience (OBE),** an extraordinary sense of her consciousness leaving her body, when she pursued an armed suspect on her first night on patrol. "When I and three other officers stopped the vehicle and started getting (to) the suspect . . . I was afraid. I promptly

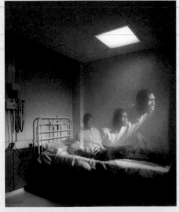

As real as an out-of-body experience seems to the person having it, research has found no evidence that consciousness exists outside the body.

out-of-body experience (OBE)
sense of our consciousness leaving our body

near-death experiences (NDE)
out-of-body experiences reported by people who've nearly died or thought they were going to die

went out of my body and up into the air maybe 20 feet above the scene. I remained there, extremely calm, while I watched the entire procedure—including myself do exactly what I had been trained to do." Alvarado reported that "[s]uddenly, she found herself back in her body after the suspect had been subdued" (p. 183).

OBEs represent profound changes in perceptions of the self. They're surprisingly common: About 25 percent of college students and 10 percent of the general population report having experienced one or more OBEs (Alvarado, 2000). Some people claim to be able to create OBEs at will and mentally visit distant places during their out-of-body journeys (a phenomenon called *astral projection*). In many cases, they describe themselves as floating above their bodies, calmly observing themselves from high above.

Are people really outside of their bodies during an OBE? Laboratory studies have permitted scientists to check what's reported during an OBE against sights and sounds known to be present in a given location. Interestingly, even though participants report they can see or hear what's occurring at a faraway place, their reports are generally inaccurate or, at best, a "good guess" when they are accurate. When researchers have reported positive results, these results have rarely been replicated (Alvarado, 2000). So there's no good evidence that people are truly floating above their bodies during an OBE, although it certainly seems that way to them (Ehrsson, 2007; Lenggenhager, Todi, Metzinger & Blanke, 2007).

In some cases, scientists can't rule out alternative explanations for accurate reports during an OBE. In one study, Charles Tart (1968) tested a woman's ability to read a five-digit number on a shelf above her bed during an OBE that occurred after she'd just awakened from sleep. Although she was able to "read" the number, the glass surface of a clock mounted on a wall above the shelf may have permitted her to see the reflected number.

(© www.CartoonStock.com)

Replicability

Ruling Out Rival Hypotheses

APPLY YOUR THINKING
What would be another way to test the hypothesis that a person's consciousness actually leaves the body during an OBE that addresses the criticism of Tart's study?

Most scientists don't believe that a person's consciousness actually exits the body during an OBE. Instead, OBEs are related to people's ability to fantasize (Wilson & Barber, 1983) and to become absorbed in experiences to the extent that they lose an awareness of their bodies (Irwin, 1985). OBEs occur fairly frequently in people who report other unusual experiences in everyday life, including hallucinations, perceptual distortions, and strange body sensations (Blackmore, 1984, 1986). Some people also experience OBEs when they're either extremely relaxed or under extreme stress, as was the case with the police officer who subdued a suspect. In the next section, we examine **near-death experiences (NDEs),** OBEs reported by people who've nearly died or thought they were going to die.

NEAR-DEATH EXPERIENCES

Soldiers in war, mountain climbers who've fallen in the Alps, individuals who undergo triple bypass surgery, and people who've nearly drowned or suffered serious automobile accidents have all reported NDEs. Estimates vary, but roughly 12 to 33 percent of people who've been close to death report NDEs (Greyson, 2000; Ring, 1984; Sabom, 1982; van Lommel, van Wees, Meyers, & Elfferich, 2001). Ever since Raymond Moody (1975) cataloged them some 30 years ago, Americans have become familiar with the "classical" elements of the NDE, widely circulated in books and movies—passing through a dark tunnel, experiencing a bright light as a "being of light," the *life review* (seeing our lives pass before our eyes), and meeting spiritual beings or long-dead relatives, all before "coming back into the body."

The features of NDEs listed in **Table 5.2** are present in many, but by no means all, accounts. In fact, NDEs vary greatly from person to person. As many as 15 percent are described as "hellish" (Blackmore, 2004) and can include scenes of being tortured by

Although there are many variations of a "near-death experience," most people in our culture believe it involves moving through a tunnel and toward a white light.

Table 5.2 Common Elements in Adult Near-Death Experiences.

- Difficulty describing the experience in words
- Hearing ourselves pronounced dead
- Feelings of peace and quiet
- Hearing unusual noises
- Meeting "spiritual beings"
- Experiencing a bright light as a "being of light"
- Panoramic "life review," that is, seeing our entire life pass before our eyes
- Experiencing a realm in which all knowledge exists
- Experiencing cities of light
- Experiencing a realm of ghosts and spirits
- Sensing a border or limit
- Coming back "into the body"

(*Source:* Moody, 1975, 1977; adapted from Greyson, 2000)

demons, giants, and elves. NDEs differ across cultures, suggesting they don't provide a genuine glimpse of the afterlife, but are constructed from prevalent beliefs about the hereafter in response to the threat of death (Ehrenwald, 1974; Noyes & Kletti, 1976). People from Christian and Buddhist cultures frequently report the sensation of moving through a tunnel, but native people in North America, the Pacific Islands, and Australia rarely do (Kellehear, 1993).

It's tempting to believe that NDEs prove that when we die we'll all be ushered into the afterlife by friends or loved ones. Nevertheless, many scientists argue that the evidence is insufficient to support this extraordinary claim. After all, a person who experiences an NDE lives to tell about it and doesn't "return from death," which is (we can all agree) a permanent condition. Accordingly, scientists have offered explanations based on changes in the chemistry of the brain associated with cardiac arrest, anesthesia, and other physical traumas (Blackmore, 1993). For example, a feeling of complete peace that can accompany an NDE may result from the massive release of *endorphins* (endogenous opiates in the brain; see Chapter 3) in a dying brain, and buzzing, ringing, or other unusual sounds may be the rumblings of an oxygen-starved brain (Blackmore, 1993). Many, if not all, of the experiences associated with NDEs occur in circumstances in which people don't face imminent death. For example, NDE-like experiences can be triggered by (a) electrical stimulation of the brain's temporal lobes (Persinger, 1994); (b) lack of oxygen to the brain in rapid acceleration during fighter pilot training (Whinnery, 1997); and (c) psychedelic (such as LSD and mescaline) and anesthetic (such as ketamine) drugs (Jansen, 1991).

Believers in NDEs contend that none of these means of creating NDE-like experiences captures all features of the phenomenon. However, there's also substantial variability in reports of NDEs themselves, and many people who come close to dying don't experience NDEs at all. Until more definitive evidence is marshaled to demonstrate that NDEs reflect anything more than changes in physiology in the dying brain, there seems to be no reason to discard this more parsimonious explanation for NDEs.

Many people who've experienced pleasant NDEs report afterward that they're less afraid of death. They have a greater appreciation for life as well as heightened religious feelings and belief in the afterlife (Grayson, 2000; Noyes, 1980; Ring, 1984). Nevertheless, people who participate in NDE studies may differ from people who don't. That is, people who've experienced frightening NDEs or who are less convinced that their NDEs were a glimpse of the afterlife may be less likely to volunteer for studies and share their disturbing experiences with researchers.

DÉJÀ VU EXPERIENCES

Have you ever had the mind-boggling sense that you've "been there" or "done that" before? Or have you ever felt you were reliving something, scene by scene, even though you knew that the situation was new or unfamiliar? Maybe you even had the spooky feeling you could predict what would happen next. In 1977, when your text's first author first visited his undergraduate alma mater, Cornell University in Ithaca, New York, he had the unmistakable feeling of having seen the campus even though he'd never been there before.

If you've had one or more of these eerie flashes of familiarity, then you've experienced **déjà vu,** which is French for "already seen." More than two-thirds of us have experienced at least one episode of déjà vu. For reasons that aren't well understood, these 10- to 30-second illusions are more likely to be reported by people who remember their dreams, travel frequently, are young, and have liberal political and religious beliefs, a college education, and a high income (Brown, 2003, 2004).

Scientists don't fully understand these fascinating changes in consciousness. Some propose that the déjà vu experience is a memory from a past life. Although not impossible, this explanation is unfalsifiable and therefore outside the boundaries of science (Stevenson, 1960).

So we'll instead turn to testable explanations. One hypothesis is that déjà vu is triggered by small seizures in the right temporal lobe, which is largely responsible for feelings of

Extraordinary Claims

déjà vu
feeling of reliving an experience that's new

Occam's Razor

Ruling Out Rival Hypotheses

(© Chris Slane)

Falsifiability

familiarity (Bancaud, Brunet-Bourgin, Chauvel, & Halgren, 1994). This explanation is consistent with the finding that people with temporal lobe epilepsy often report déjà vu just before a seizure. An excess of the neurotransmitter dopamine in the temporal lobes may also play a role in déjà vu (Taiminen & Jääskeläinen, 2001).

As we've seen (see Chapter 4), one of the great achievements of the human brain is its ability to integrate sensory information from different pathways into a unified experience. According to *dual processing theory,* déjà vu arises when input from separate neural pathways that process sensory information is slightly out of sync. This can occur because a glitch in neurotransmitters in one pathway delays the signal, perhaps by only a few milliseconds. This short delay tricks the brain into interpreting the data as separate copies of the same experience, leading to the experience that "what's happening now has happened before" (Brown, 2003). In a sense, it *has* happened before, although only on the scale of a few thousandths of a second.

Another possibility is that déjà vu is related to situations in which we're mentally or physically distracted and don't consciously register something we're seeing. For example, imagine we visit a park we know we've never seen, but we experience déjà vu. Perhaps we've driven by this park many times without ever noticing it, but our minds processed the information unconsciously (Strayer, Drews, & Johnston, 2003).

A final possibility is that déjà vu is triggered by a present experience that resembles, in whole or in part, an earlier experience. The familiar feeling arises because we don't consciously recall the previous experience, which may have originated in childhood or earlier in life. This account implies that the situation feels familiar because it is, in some unrecognized sense, familiar. To better understand déjà vu, scientists will need to conduct further studies of people with epilepsy and record the brain activity of people with repeated déjà vu episodes who don't have epilepsy.

factoid

Some people experience a phenomenon called "jamais vu," French for "never seen," which is essentially the opposite of déjà vu. In jamais vu, the person reports feeling as though a previously familiar experience suddenly seems unfamiliar. Jamais vu is sometimes seen in neurological disorders, such as amnesia (see Chapter 7) and epilepsy (Brown, 2004).

NEW FRONTIERS
Demystifying Mystical Experiences

Although mystical experiences can last for only a few moments or minutes, they can sometimes leave a lifelong impression. **Mystical experiences** involve a common core of features that include a sense of unity or oneness with the world, transcendence of time and space, and a feeling of wonder and awe. These psychological phenomena often have strong religious overtones and may have played a role in the formation of many world religions. Yet they differ across religious faiths. For instance, Christians often describe mystical experiences in terms of an awe-inspiring merging with God's presence. In contrast, Buddhists, whose spiritual practices focus more on achieving personal enlightenment than worship of a deity, often describe mystical incidents in terms of bliss and selfless peace. Although shaped by learning and culture, each person's mystical experience is probably unique. As many as 35 percent of Americans say they've felt very close to a powerful, uplifting spiritual force at least once (Greeley, 1975).

Because intense mystical experiences are rare, unpredictable, difficult to put into words, and often fleeting, they're difficult to study in the laboratory (Wulff, 2000). Nevertheless, scientists have recently begun to probe the mysteries of these events. One approach they've adopted is to study people who report a history of mystical experiences; another is to induce mystical experiences and examine their consequences.

Adopting the first approach, two researchers (Beauregard & Paquette, 2006) used fMRI to scan the brains of fifteen Roman Catholic nuns after asking them to close their eyes and relive the most intense mystical occurrence they'd ever experienced. They also instructed them to relive the most intense state of union with another human they'd felt as a nun. Compared with a condition in which the nuns sat quietly with eyes closed and the condition in which the nuns relived the interpersonal

(continued)

mystical experience
feelings of unity or oneness with the world

experience, the "mystical experiences" condition produced distinctive patterns of brain activation. In fact, at least twelve areas of the brain associated with emotion, perception, and cognition were activated when the nuns relived mystical experiences.

Still, we can question whether the researchers actually captured mystical experiences. Several, but not all, of the nuns said they actually felt in the presence of God, and the nuns rated the intensity of their experience in the mystical and interpersonal conditions equally. Thus, reliving an experience in the laboratory may differ from more spontaneous mystical events produced by fasting, prayer, fevers, seizures in the temporal lobes, or meditation (Geschwind, 1983; Persinger, 1987). However, the research suggests that brain scanning techniques hold promise in studying mystical states of consciousness and in revealing links between these states and biological mechanisms.

Adopting the second approach, neuroscientists (Griffiths, Richards, McCann, & Jesse, 2006) asked participants to ingest psilocybin. Psilocybin is a substance that, like other hallucinogenic drugs, affects serotonin receptors and is the active ingredient in the "sacred mushroom," used for centuries in religious ceremonies. The investigators screened thirty-six participants for psychological problems and a family history of mental illness. They prepared participants with information about the drug, monitored them throughout the research, and provided them with support when needed. Participants in a control condition received Ritalin, a medication used in the treatment of attention-deficit/hyperactivity disorder (see Chapter 16). The rationale for administering Ritalin is that it alters consciousness but has no known ability to produce mystical experiences. Neither participants nor monitors knew which medication was which, making the experiment double-blind (see Chapter 2).

A number of key findings emerged. First, 61 percent of participants who ingested psilocybin reported a mystical experience. Second, 47 percent felt that the mystical experience was either the most meaningful experience of their lives or one of their top five most meaningful experiences. Third, 79 percent of participants reported increases in life satisfaction 2 months after ingesting psilocybin. The percentages of mystical and positive experiences were much lower among participants who ingested Ritalin.

However, even with carefully selected participants studied under conditions designed to decrease the likelihood of negative reactions, 31 percent of participants who ingested psilocybin reported extreme fears and paranoia during the session. In the Ritalin condition, none reported such fears. Although the authors noted there were no indications of long-term psychological harm to any participants, their research adds to serious concerns about the widespread recreational use of hallucinogenic drugs. The primary significance of this research is that it offers us a glimpse of the promise of studying mystical experiences in the laboratory. At the same time, it reminds us that caution is warranted in studying hallucinogenic drugs that have the potential to induce negative as well as positive feelings.

MEDITATION

Unlike the unexpected and unintentional alterations in consciousness we've examined, some other ways of changing consciousness, including meditation, hypnosis, and consuming drugs, are under our direct control. **Meditation** refers to a variety of practices that train attention and awareness (Shapiro & Walsh, 2003).

Types of Meditation. Meditative practices are embedded in many world religions and are integrated into the lives of people of all races and creeds. In Western countries, people typically practice meditation to achieve stress reduction, whereas in non-Western countries people typically practice meditation to achieve insight and spiritual growth. Contrary

These meditators are focusing on their breathing.

meditation
set of ritualized practices that train attention and awareness

to stereotypes, there's no one "right" way to meditate, nor is there a single "altered state" of consciousness associated with meditation. What people experience depends very much on their goals. In *concentrative meditation,* the goal is to focus attention on a single thing, such as one's breath, the flame of a candle, or a *mantra* (an internal sound). In *awareness meditation,* attention flows freely and examines whatever comes to mind.

Evaluating the Benefits of Meditation.   For centuries, meditation fell well outside the scientific mainstream. Yet in the 1960s, scientists began to take a serious look at its possible benefits. Since then, they've identified a wide range of positive effects. These effects include heightened creativity, empathy, alertness, and self-esteem (Haimerl & Valentine, 2001; So & Orme-Johnson, 2001), along with decreases in anxiety, interpersonal problems (Tlocczynski & Tantriella, 1998), and recurrences of depression (Segal, Williams, & Teasdale, 2001). Clinicians have added meditative techniques to a variety of psychotherapies and used them with some success in treating pain and numerous medical conditions (Baer, 2003; Kabatt-Zinn, 2003). Meditative practices can affect brain waves while we're awake (Alexander, Rainforth, & Gelderloos, 1991; Travis, 2001) or asleep (Lazar et al., 2000; Mason et al., 1997). In particular, meditation tends to be associated with increases in alpha waves, a brain wave frequently associated with relaxation (Cahn & Polich, 2006). Meditation can also enhance blood flow in the brain (Newberg et al., 2001) and immune function (Davidson, Kabatt-Zinn et al, 2003).

    Many people seem to benefit from meditation, although it's not clear why: Its positive effects may derive from a greater acceptance of our troubling thoughts and feelings (Kabatt-Zinn, 2003; Lynn, Surya Das Hallquist, & Williams, 2006). They may also derive not from meditation itself, but from sitting quietly, resting, and relaxing with eyes closed (Farthing, 1992; Holmes, 1987). People's positive attitudes, beliefs, and expectancies about meditation may also account for why it's beneficial. Few studies have followed meditators for long periods of time, so we don't know whether positive effects persist, generalize to different situations, or apply to large numbers of meditators. When researchers find differences between experienced meditators and nonmeditators, they need to be careful about how they interpret the results. Meditation might create specific changes in brain wave activity, but people who show certain brain wave patterns may be especially attracted to meditation in the first place (Lutz, Greischar, Rawlings, Matthieu, & Davidson, 2004). Therefore, the direction of the causal arrow is difficult to determine. Apart from occasional reports of people experiencing anxiety during meditation (Shapiro, 1992), it appears to be a largely harmless technique that holds potential for helping some people.

HYPNOSIS

The hypnotist drones, "Your hand is getting lighter, lighter, it is rising, rising by itself, lifting off the resting surface." Slowly, slowly, Jessica's hand lifts in herky-jerky movements, in sync with the suggestions. After hypnosis, she insists that her hand moved by itself, without her doing anything to lift it. The hypnotist suggests that Jessica will remember many events from her past that she's long forgotten. When she hears the words, "Now you can remember everything," she experiences a flood of memories from her early childhood. Two more suggestions follow: one for numbness in her hand, after which she appears insensitive to her hand being pricked lightly with a needle, and another for her to hallucinate a dog sitting in the corner. With little prompting, she walks over to the imaginary dog and pets him (Lynn & Rhue, 1991). At the end of the session, after Jessica opens her eyes, she still appears a bit sleepy.

Myths and Misconceptions about Hypnosis: What Hypnosis Is and Isn't.   This example illustrates that hypnotic suggestions can produce profound changes in consciousness and behavior (Cardena, 2005; Nash & Barnier, in press). Jessica's thoughts, feelings, and reactions to hypnosis seem so out of the ordinary that they imply that she experienced something extraordinary. Was Jessica in a trance or sleeplike state? Might it be possible to exploit Jessica's suggestibility for therapeutic purposes—say, for pain relief?

    These sorts of questions stoked the curiosity of laypersons, scientists, and therapists for more than 200 years and stimulated scientific studies of hypnosis around the world. **Hypnosis** is a set of techniques that provides people with suggestions for alterations in

Ruling Out Rival Hypotheses

Correlation vs. Causation

Hypnosis has fascinated scientists and clinical practitioners for more than two centuries, yet the basic methods for inducing hypnosis have changed little over the years.

hypnosis
set of techniques that provides people with suggestions for alterations in their perceptions, thoughts, feelings, and behaviors

fictoid

Myth: Most hypnotists use a swinging watch to lull subjects into a state of relaxation.

Reality: Few hypnotists today use a watch; any procedure that effectively induces expectancies of hypnosis can boost suggestibility in most people (Kirsch, 1991).

People who perform in stage hypnosis shows are carefully selected before the performance for high suggestibility.

This classic picture of a person suspended between two chairs illustrates the "human plank phenomenon," often demonstrated at stage hypnosis shows as "proof" of the special powers of hypnosis. In actuality, people who stiffen their bodies can do this without hypnosis; however, we don't recommend you try it. If the chairs aren't placed properly, the person can be injured.

their perceptions, thoughts, feelings, and behaviors (Kirsch & Lynn, 1998). To increase people's suggestibility, most hypnotists use an induction method, which often includes suggestions for relaxation and calmness (Kirsch, 1994). Today, we have a much better understanding of hypnotic phenomena than when such renowned late nineteenth- and early twentieth-century scholars as Sigmund Freud, Alfred Binet, and William James addressed the thorny questions posed in the previous paragraph. It's safe to say that hypnosis has since moved into the mainstream of science and clinical practice. Still, public knowledge about hypnosis hasn't kept pace with scientific developments. We'll first examine six misconceptions about hypnosis before evaluating two prominent theories of how it works.

Myth 1: Hypnosis Produces a Trance State in Which "Amazing" Things Happen. Consider a sampling of movies that portray the hypnotic trance state as so overpowering that otherwise normal people will: (a) commit suicide (*The Garden Murders*); (b) disfigure themselves with scalding water (*The Hypnotic Eye*); (c) assist in blackmail (*On Her Majesty's Secret Service*); (d) perceive only a person's internal beauty (*Shallow Hal*); (e) steal (*Curse of the Jade Scorpion*); and our personal favorite, (f) fall victim to brainwashing by alien preachers using messages in sermons (*Invasion of the Space Preachers*).

Other popular stereotypes of hypnosis derive from *stage hypnosis* shows, in which hypnotists seemingly program people to enact commands ranging from quacking like a duck to playing a wicked air guitar to the music of U2 (MacKillop, Lynn, & Meyer, 2004). But the wacky actions of people in movies and onstage have nothing to do with a trance state. In stage shows, the hypnotist carefully selects potential performers by observing how they respond to waking suggestions. For example, those whose outstretched hands drop or sag when asked to imagine holding a heavy dictionary are likely to be invited onstage because they're probably highly suggestible to begin with. Moreover, hypnotized volunteers often feel compelled to do outlandish things because they're under intense pressure to entertain the audience. Many stage hypnotists also use the *stage whispers* technique, in which they whisper instructions ("When I snap my fingers, bark like a dog") into volunteers' ears (Meeker & Barber, 1971).

Actually, hypnosis doesn't have a great impact on suggestibility, nor does it turn people into mindless robots. A person who responds to six out of twelve suggestions (for example, "your hands are moving together because of a magnetic force") without being hypnotized might respond to seven or eight after hypnosis (Kirsch & Lynn, 1995). In one study, 44 percent of college students agreed that "A deeply hypnotized person is robot-like and goes along automatically with whatever the hypnotist suggests" (Green, Page, Rasekhy, Johnson, & Bernhardt, 2006). Nevertheless, people can resist and even oppose hypnotic suggestions at will (Lynn, Rhue, & Weekes, 1990). So, Hollywood thrillers aside, hypnosis can't turn a mild-mannered person into a cold-blooded murderer.

Myth 2: Hypnotic Phenomena Are Unique. Contrary to popular belief, subjects can experience many hypnotic phenomena, such as hallucinations and pain insensitivity, when they receive suggestions alone, even without hypnosis (Barber, 1969; Sarbin & Coe, 1979; Spanos, 1986, 1991). What's more, some of the tricks we see in stage hypnosis shows, like suspending volunteers between the tops of two chairs, are easily duplicated in highly motivated participants without hypnosis.

Scientists haven't yet identified any unique physiological states or markers of hypnosis (Dixon & Laurence, 1993; Hasegawa & Jamieson, 2002; Sarbin & Slagle, 1979; Wagstaff, 1998). So there's no clear biological distinction between hypnosis and wakefulness. Moreover, people's brain activity during hypnosis depends very much on the suggestions they receive. People who receive suggestions for deep relaxation show different patterns of brain activity from those who receive suggestions to listen to an imaginary CD with the song "Jingle Bells."

Myth 3: Hypnosis Is a Sleeplike State. James Braid (1843), a Scottish physician, claimed that the hypnotized brain produces a condition akin to sleep. Braid labeled the phenomenon *neurohypnosis* (from the Greek word *hypno,* meaning "sleep"), and the shortened term "hypnosis" eventually stuck. Yet although we've all seen films in which therapists induce a hypnotic state by saying, "You're getting sleepy. . . . ," we now know that hypnosis isn't related to sleep. People who are hypnotized don't show brain waves similar to those of sleep. One study showed that people are just as responsive to hypnotic suggestions administered while exercising on a stationary bicycle as they are following hypnotic suggestions for sleep and relaxation (Bányai & Hilgard, 1976; Wark, 2006).

Myth 4: Hypnotized People Are Unaware of Their Surroundings.   Another popular idea is that hypnotized people are so "entranced" that they lose touch with their surroundings. In actuality, most hypnotized people are fully aware of their immediate surroundings, and can even recall the details of an overheard telephone conversation that took place during hypnosis (Lynn, Weekes, & Milano,1989).

Myth 5: Hypnotized People Forget What Happened during Hypnosis.   In the popular 1962 film *The Manchurian Candidate,* remade in 2004, a person is programmed by hypnosis to commit an assassination and has no memory of what transpired during hypnosis. In real life, *spontaneous amnesia* for what happens during hypnosis is rare and mostly limited to people who expect to be amnesic following hypnosis (Salzberg & Simon, 1985; Young & Cooper, 1972).

Myth 6: Hypnosis Improves Memory.   In 1976 in Chowchilla, California, three young men intent on committing the "perfect crime" kidnapped twenty-six children and their bus driver (see Chapter 7). The blundering criminals didn't anticipate that their captives would escape after being hidden underground for 6 hours. After police apprehended the criminals, the bus driver was hypnotized and correctly provided numbers from the license plate of the kidnappers' car. The media capitalized on this now famous case to publicize the power of hypnosis to enhance recall. The problem is that the anecdote doesn't tell us whether hypnosis was responsible for what the driver remembered. Perhaps the driver recalled the event because people often can remember additional details when they try to recall an event a second time, regardless of whether they're hypnotized.

Moreover, the media tend not to report the scores of cases in which hypnosis fails to enhance memory, such as a Brinks armored car robbery that took place in Boston (Kihlstrom, 1987). In this case, the witness was hypnotized and confidently recalled the license plate of the car of the president of Harvard University, where the witness was employed. Apparently, he confused a car he'd seen multiple times with the car involved in the robbery.

Scientific studies generally reveal that hypnosis (a) doesn't improve memory (Erdelyi, 1994; Scoboria, Mazzoni, Kirsch, & Milling, 2002); (b) leads to an increase in recalling information, both accurate and inaccurate (Erdelyi, 1994; Steblay & Bothwell, 1994); and (c) produces more inaccurate memories than do nonhypnotic instructions to remember (Orne, 1979; Steblay & Bothwell, 1994). Indeed, a number of Susan Clancy's (2006) alien abduction subjects had been hypnotized before "recalling" their otherworldly experiences, raising the possibility that hypnosis contributed to their weaving REM sleep phenomena, like sleep paralysis, into a seemingly real but false abduction story.

To make matters worse, hypnosis tends to increase eyewitnesses' confidence in inaccurate, as well as accurate, memories (Green & Lynn, 2005). Courts in most U.S. states have banned the testimony of hypnotized witnesses out of concerns that their inaccurate statements will sway a jury and lead to wrongful convictions. Additionally, therapists are increasingly aware of the pitfalls of using hypnosis to assist their patients with recovering memories, because at least some of these memories are false (Lynn & Kirsch, in press; see Chapter 7).

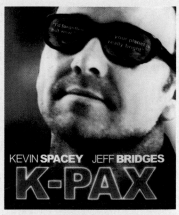

The 2001 movie *K-Pax,* starring Kevin Spacey and Jeff Bridges, reinforces popular stereotypes about hypnosis, including the ideas that hypnosis produces a sleeplike state and hypnosis is a "truth serum."

Ruling Out Rival Hypotheses

Hypnotists frequently present subjects with the suggestion that one of their arms is lifting involuntarily.

PsychoMythology

Age Regression and Past Lives

One of the most popular myths of hypnosis is that it can help people to retrieve memories of events as far back in time as birth. A televised documentary (Bikel, 1995) showed a group therapy session in which a woman was age-regressed through childhood, to the womb, and eventually to being trapped in her mother's

(continued)

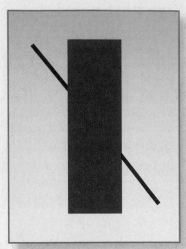

Researchers have used the Poggendorf illusion, shown above, to study the effects of hypnotic age regression. Adults tend to see the two segments of the black line as misaligned (in reality, they're perfectly aligned), whereas children don't. When adult subjects are age-regressed to childhood, they still see the two segments of the black line as misaligned, suggesting that hypnotic age regression doesn't make adults' perceptions more childlike (Asher, Barber, & Spanos, 1972; Nash, 1987).

Fallopian tube. The woman provided a highly emotional demonstration of the discomfort that one would experience if one were indeed stuck in such an uncomfortable position. Although the woman may have believed in the reality of her experience, we can be quite certain that it wasn't memory based. Instead, age-regressed subjects behave in accord with their knowledge, beliefs, and assumptions about age-relevant behaviors. Age-regressed adults don't show the expected patterns on many indices of development. For example, when regressed to childhood, they exhibit the brain waves (EEGs) typical of adults rather than of children. No matter how compelling, age-regressed experiences aren't exact mental replicas of childhood experiences (Nash, 1987).

Some therapists claim to be able to trace current problems to previous lives and practice **past life regression therapy** (Weiss, 1988). Typically, they hypnotize and age-regress patients to "go back to" the source of their present-day psychological and physical problems. For example, some practitioners of past life regression therapy claim that neck and shoulder pains may be a sign of having been executed by hanging or by a guillotine in a previous life.

With some rare exceptions (Stevenson, 1974), scientists agree that reports of a past life are the products of imagination and what's known about a given time period. When checked against known facts (such as whether the country was at war or peace, the face on the coin of the realm), subjects' descriptions of the historical circumstances of their past lives are rarely accurate. When they are, we can often explain this accuracy by "educated guesses" and knowledge about history (Spanos, Menary, Gabora, DuBeruil, & Dewhirst, 1991). One participant regressed to ancient times claimed to be Julius Caesar, emperor of Rome, in 50 B.C., even though the designations of B.C. and A.D. weren't adopted until centuries later and even though Julius Caesar died decades before the first Roman emperor came to power. Moreover, one of the best predictors of whether people will experience a past life memory while regressed is whether they accept the existence of reincarnation (Baker, 1992), bolstering the claim that past life memories are a product of people's beliefs and expectancies.

Theories of Hypnosis. Researchers have argued that hypnosis can be explained by a host of factors, including (a) unconscious drives and motivations (Baker, 1986; Fromm & Nash, 1997); (b) people's willingness to overlook logical inconsistencies (Orne, 1959); (c) receptivity to suggestion (McConkey, 1991; Sheehan, 1991); and (d) inhibition of activation of the frontal lobes (Farvolden & Woody, 2004; Woody & Bowers, 1994; Woody & Farvolden, 1998). Each of these theories has contributed valuable insights into hypnotic phenomena and generated useful research (Kihlstrom, 2003; Nash & Barnier, in press). Nevertheless, the sociocognitive theory and the dissociation theory have received the lion's share of attention.

Sociocognitive Theory. Sociocognitive theorists (Barber, 1969; Lynn, Kirsch, & Hallquist, in press; Coe & Sarbin, 1991; Spanos, 1986) reject the idea that hypnosis is a trance state or unique state of consciousness. Instead, they explain hypnosis in the same way they explain everyday social behaviors. According to **sociocognitive theory,** people's attitudes, beliefs, and expectations about hypnosis shape their responses to hypnosis.

past life regression therapy
therapeutic approach that hypnotizes and supposedly age-regresses patients back to a previous life to identify the source of a present-day problem

sociocognitive theory
approach to hypnosis based on people's attitudes, beliefs, and expectations

Theories of hypnosis, including sociocognitive theory, must address why some people are highly responsive to hypnotic suggestions while others aren't. Approximately 15 to 20 percent of people pass very few suggestions (low suggestibles), for example, 0–3 on a 12-suggestion test of hypnotic responsiveness; another 15 to 20 percent pass 9–12 of the suggestions (high suggestibles); and the remaining 60 to 70 percent pass 5–8 suggestions (medium suggestibles) (Spanos, 1986). High suggestibles are much more likely to respond to suggestions during hypnosis than are low suggestibles (Braffman & Kirsch, 1999).

Peoples' expectations of whether they'll respond to hypnotic suggestions are also correlated with how they respond (Kirsch & Council, 1992). Still, this correlation doesn't necessarily mean that people's expectations cause them to be susceptible to hypnosis. Studies in which participants' responses vary as a function of what they're told about hypnosis provide more convincing evidence of causality. Participants told that hypnotized people can resist sugges-

Correlation vs. Causation

tions find themselves able to resist, whereas those told that hypnotized people can't resist suggestions often fail to resist (Lynn, Nash, Rhue, Frauman, & Sweeney, 1984; Spanos, Cobb, & Gorassini, 1985). Because sociocognitive theory says that attitudes, beliefs, and motivations influence suggestibility, it predicts that we can alter individuals' level of suggestibility by changing their attitudes and beliefs about hypnosis. Many studies show that a training program that increases people's positive feelings and expectancies about hypnosis and their willingness to imagine along with suggestions increases their ability to respond to hypnosis (Gorassini & Spanos, 1986). About half of subjects who initially score at the lowest range of suggestibility test at the top range of suggestibility after training. The results persist for months, and the learning generalizes to new test suggestions. These findings challenge the idea that hypnotic suggestibility is an entirely stable trait (Piccione, Hilgard, & Zimbardo, 1989) and provide support for sociocognitive theory.

APPLY YOUR THINKING

Could some personal characteristics associated with suggestibility be difficult to modify? If so, what might they be?

Dissociation Theory. Ernest Hilgard's (1977, 1986, 1994) **dissociation theory** is an influential alternative to sociocognitive theories of hypnosis (Kihlstrom, 1992, 1998). Hilgard (1977) defined *dissociation* as a division of consciousness, in which attention, effort, and planning are carried out without awareness. He hypothesized that hypnotic suggestions result in a separation between personality functions that are normally well integrated.

Hilgard (1977) happened on a discovery that played a key role in the development of his theory. During a demonstration of hypnotically suggested deafness, a student asked whether some part of the person could hear. Hilgard then told the subject that when he touched the subject's arm he'd be able to talk to the part that could hear, if such a part existed. When Hilgard placed his hand on the subject's arm, the subject described what people in the room said. However, when Hilgard removed his hand, the subject was again "deaf." Hilgard invented the metaphor of the *hidden observer* to describe the dissociated, unhypnotized "part" of the mind that he could access on cue. Much of the support for dissociation theory comes from hidden observer studies of hypnotic blindness, pain, and hallucinations. For example, in studies of hypnotic analgesia (inability to experience pain), experimenters bring forth hidden observers, which report pain even though the "hypnotized part" reports little or no pain (Hilgard, 1977).

More recently, researchers have suggested an alternative explanation for the hidden observer phenomenon (Kirsch & Lynn, 1998; Spanos, 1986, 1991). Nicholas Spanos (1991) believed that the hidden observer comes about because the hypnotist suggests it directly or indirectly. That is, subjects pick up on the fact that the instructions used to bring forth the hidden observer imply they should act as though a separate, nonhypnotized "part" of the person can communicate with the hypnotist. Spanos hypothesized that changing the instructions should change what the hidden observer reports.

Ruling Out Rival Hypotheses

That's exactly what he found. Changing the instructions led hidden observers to experience more pain or less pain, or to perceive a number normally or in reverse (Spanos & Hewitt, 1980), leading Irving Kirsch and Steven Jay Lynn (1998) to dub the phenomenon the *flexible observer.* From their perspective, the hidden observer is no different from any other suggested hypnotic response: It's shaped by what subjects expect and believe.

According to a revision of Hilgard's dissociation theory (Woody & Bowers, 1984), hypnosis bypasses the ordinary sense of control we exert over our behaviors. Thus, suggestions directly bring about responses with little or no sense of effort or conscious control (Jamieson & Sheehan, 2004; Sadler & Woody, in press). This theory does a good job of describing what people experience during hypnosis. Nevertheless, contrary to popular belief, people never completely "give up control" during hypnosis to the point that they'd do something objectionable.

Hypnosis in Clinical Practice. Whatever their differences, hypnosis theorists agree that hypnosis has a wide range of clinical applications. Meta-analyses (see Chapter 2) show that

dissociation theory
approach to explaining hypnosis based on a separation between personality functions that are normally well integrated

Stop Smoking Forever with Hypnosis.

Figure 5.4 Ad for Stop Smoking. Many advertisements for the effectiveness of hypnosis in treating smoking are misleading and exaggerated. Still, hypnosis can sometimes be combined with well-established treatment approaches as a cost-effective means of helping some people quit smoking.

Table 5.3 Major Drug Types and Their Effects on Our Bodies and Consciousness.

Stimulants:
Increased activity of the central nervous system. Examples are tobacco, cocaine, amphetamines, methamphetamine

Depressants:
Decreased activity of the central nervous system. Examples are alcohol, barbiturates, quaaludes, valium

Opiates:
Sense of euphoria, decreased pain, sleep. Examples are heroin, morphine, codeine

Psychedelic:
Dramatically altered perception, mood, and thoughts; hallucinations. Examples are marijuana, LSD, Ecstasy

psychoactive drugs
chemicals similar to those found naturally in our brains that alter consciousness by changing chemical processes in neurons

sedative
drug that exerts a calming effect

hypnotic
drug that exerts a sleep-inducing effect

hypnosis enhances the effectiveness of psychodynamic and cognitive-behavioral psychotherapies (Kirsch, 1990; Kirsch, Montgomery, & Sapirstein, 1995), which we'll discuss in Chapter 16. Hypnosis is also useful for treating pain, medical conditions, and habit disorders (such as smoking addiction) (see **Figure 5.4**), and it boosts the effectiveness of therapies for anxiety, obesity, and other conditions (Lynn & Kirsch, 2006). Nevertheless, the extent to which hypnosis provides benefits beyond relaxation in such cases remains unclear. Moreover, there's no scientific evidence that hypnosis is an effective treatment by itself, so we should be skeptical of professional "hypnotherapists" (many of whom we can find in our local Yellow Pages) who use nothing but hypnosis to treat serious psychological problems.

ASSESS YOUR KNOWLEDGE: FACT OR FICTION?
(1) OBEs are related to the ability to fantasize. (True/False)
(2) Many of the experiences associated with an NDE can be created in circumstances that have nothing to do with being "near death." (True/False)
(3) Déjà vu experiences often last for as long as an hour. (True/False)
(4) Meditation is a more effective self-improvement technique than sitting quietly and relaxing. (True/False)
(5) A hypnosis induction greatly increases suggestibility beyond waking suggestibility. (True/False)

Answers: (1) T (p. 208); (2) T (p. 209); (3) F (p. 210); (4) F (p. 212); (5) F (p. 213)

Drugs and Consciousness

Virtually every culture has discovered that certain plant substances can alter consciousness, often dramatically. Knowledge of the mind-bending qualities of fermented fruits and grains, the juice of the poppy, boiled coffee beans and tea leaves, the burning tobacco or marijuana leaf, certain molds that grow on crops, and the granulated extract of the coca leaf has been handed down from ancient times. We now know that these **psychoactive drugs** contain chemicals similar to those found naturally in our brains and that their molecules alter consciousness by changing chemical processes in neurons. The precise psychological and physical effects depend on the type of drug and dosage, as we've summarized in **Table 5.3**.

But we'll see that the effects of drugs depend on far more than their chemical properties or dosages. *Mental set*—beliefs and expectancies about the effects of drugs—and the setting in which people take these drugs also account for people's responses to them. People's reactions to drugs are also rooted in their cultural heritage and genetic endowment.

THE DEPRESSANT DRUGS: ALCOHOL AND THE SEDATIVE-HYPNOTICS

Alcohol and sedative-hypnotics (barbiturates and benzodiazepines) are depressant drugs, so-called because they depress the effects of the central nervous system. In contrast, stimulant drugs, like nicotine and cocaine, which we'll review in the next section, rev up our central nervous system. We'll learn that the effects of alcohol are remarkably wide-ranging, varying from stimulation at low doses to sedation at higher doses. By the way, **sedative** means "calming," and **hypnotic** means "sleep-inducing" (despite its name, it doesn't mean "hypnosis-inducing").

Alcohol.   Humanity has long had an intimate relationship with alcohol. Some scientists speculate that a long-forgotten person from the late Stone Age, perhaps 10,000 years ago, accidentally partook of a jar of honey that had been left out too long (Vallee, 1988). He or she became the first human to drink alcohol, and the human race has never been quite the same since. From the time that fermented honey was made into the drink of mead more than 8,000 years ago, alcohol has played an important role in social, religious, and medical contexts. Throughout much of early Western civilization, including ancient Rome, alcohol use was so widespread that some historians believe that most citizens went through their average day slightly tipsy. Even Christopher Columbus brought along plenty of wine during his famous voyage to America, and the Pilgrims apparently made landfall on Plymouth Rock only because they'd run out of their supply of beer (Vallee, 1988).

Yet throughout history, people have recognized that misuse of alcohol contributes to human misery. Almost 2,000 years ago, Roman philosopher Seneca commented, "Drunkenness is nothing but a condition of insanity purposely assumed." Today, alcohol is the most widely used and abused drug. Approximately 90 percent of adults in our society have used alcohol, and in 2003, 45 percent of ninth through twelfth graders reported consuming alcohol within the previous month (CDC, 2005).

Subjective, Behavioral, and Physiological Effects of Alcohol. We must look to the effects of alcohol to understand its powerful appeal. These effects are incredibly wide-ranging, varying from stimulation to sedation. Although many people believe that alcohol is a stimulant, physiologically it's primarily a depressant. Alcohol is an emotional and physiological stimulant only at relatively low doses, when it depresses areas of the brain that inhibit emotion and behavior (Pohorecky, 1977; Tucker, Vucinich, & Sobell, 1981). Small amounts of alcohol can promote feelings of relaxation, elevate mood, increase talkativeness and activity, and lower inhibitions and impair judgment. At higher doses, when the blood alcohol content (BAC)—the concentration of alcohol in the blood—reaches .05 to .10, the sedating and depressant effects of alcohol generally become more apparent. Brain centers become depressed, slowing thinking and impairing concentration, walking, and muscular coordination (Erblich, Earleywine, Erblich, & Bovbjerg, 2003). At higher doses, users sometimes experience a mixture of stimulating and sedating effects (King, Houle, de Wit, Holdstock, & Schuser, 2002).

The short-term effects of intoxication are directly related to the BAC. The feeling of intoxication depends on the rate of absorption of alcohol by the bloodstream, mostly through the stomach and intestines. The more food in our stomach, the less quickly alcohol is absorbed. This explains why we feel more of an effect of alcohol on an empty stomach. Compared with men, women have more body fat (alcohol isn't fat-soluble) and less water in which to dilute alcohol. So a woman whose weight equals that of a man, and who's consumed the same amount of alcohol, will have a higher BAC than he will (Kinney & Leaton, 1995). **Figure 5.5** shows the relationship between the amounts of beverage consumed and alcohol concentration in the blood. Because absorption varies depending on factors like stomach contents and body weight, these effects vary across persons and occasions.

In addition to gender differences, there are pronounced ethnic differences in the subjective effects of alcohol. When people consume alcohol, a mutation in the aldehyde 2 (ALDH2) gene causes a distinctly unpleasant response marked by facial flushing, heart palpitations (a strong sense of the heart beating), and nausea (Higuchi, Matsushita, Murayama, Takagi, & Hayashida, 1995). This gene is present in about 40 percent of people of Asian descent, who drink less alcohol than people in most other ethnic groups and are at low risk for alcoholism (Cook & Wall, 2005). Genetic variations in the reactions to drugs may affect the use and abuse of a wide variety of substances. However, as we'll learn in Chapter 16, sociocultural influences, such as whether a particular ethnic group or culture approves or disapproves of drug use, also play an important role.

In most states, a BAC of .08 is the cutoff for legal intoxication while operating a vehicle; at this point the operation of an automobile is clearly hazardous. In the BAC range of .20 to .30, impairment increases to the point at which strong sedation occurs; at .40 to .50, unconsciousness may set in. Blood alcohol levels of .50 to .60 may prove fatal. The body metabolizes alcohol at the rate of about one-half ounce per hour (the equivalent of about an ounce of whiskey).

Although drug effects are influenced by the dose of the drug, the user's expectancies also play a substantial role. The *balanced placebo design* is a four-group design (see **Figure 5.6**) in which researchers tell participants they either are, or are not, receiving an active drug and, in fact, either do or don't receive it (Kirsch, 2003). This design allows researchers to tease apart the relative influence of expectancies (placebo effects) and the physiological effects of alcohol.

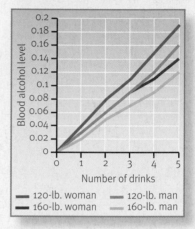

Figure 5.5 Influences on BAC. A person's blood alcohol content (BAC) depends on a variety of factors beyond the number of drinks consumed. The person's weight, gender, and stomach contents all play a role. This graph shows how body weight and gender influence BAC. For both men and women, heavier people have a lower BAC, but at both 120 pounds and 160 pounds, women have a higher BAC than men.

	Received	
	Alcohol	**Placebo**
Told **Alcohol**	(a) Alcohol effect + Placebo effect	(b) Placebo effect
Placebo	(c) Alcohol effect	(d) Baseline

Figure 5.6 The Four Groups of the Balanced Placebo Design. The balanced-placebo design includes four groups in which participants (a) are told they're receiving alcohol and in fact receive alcohol, (b) are told they're receiving alcohol but actually receive a placebo, (c) are told they're receiving a placebo but actually receive alcohol, and (d) are told they're receiving a placebo and in fact receive a placebo.

Research shows that when driving down a highway, our hands are almost constantly performing minor adjustments to the steering wheel of which we're not consciously aware. Excessive alcohol can inhibit these adjustments, causing us to weave or swerve into other lanes without realizing it (Brookhuis, 1998).

tolerance
reduction in the effect of a drug as a result of repeated use, requiring users to consume greater quantities to achieve the same effect

withdrawal
unpleasant effects of reducing or stopping consumption of a drug that users had consumed habitually

The results of balanced placebo studies show that at low alcohol dose levels, culturally learned expectancies influence mood and complex social behaviors. Remarkably, participants who ingest a placebo drink mixed to taste like alcohol display many of the same subjective effects of drunkenness as participants who ingest an actual alcoholic drink. Expectancies are often more important than the physiological effects of alcohol in influencing social behaviors, such as aggression (Lang, Goeckner, Adesso, & Marlatt, 1975). Alcohol may provide some people with an excuse to engage in actions that are socially prohibited or discouraged, like flirting (Hull & Bond, 1986). In males, expectancies may override the pharmacological effects of alcohol in enhancing humor, anxiety reduction, and sexual responsivity. In contrast, nonsocial behaviors, such as reaction time and motor coordination, are more influenced by alcohol itself than by expectancies (Marlatt & Rosenow, 1980). Expectancies that drinking will produce positive outcomes predict who'll drink and how much they'll drink, and expectancies that drinking will produce negative outcomes predict who'll abstain (Goldman, Darkes, & Del Boca, 1999; Leigh & Stacy, 2004).

The *setting*, or social context, in which people consume alcohol also influences its effects. For example, subjects tested in a barlike situation with drinking companions feel more friendly and elated when they drink, and consume nearly twice as much alcohol as subjects who drink by themselves (Lindman, 1982; Sher, Wood, Richardson, & Jackson, 2005; see **Table 5.4**).

Alcohol Tolerance and Withdrawal. **Tolerance** occurs when people need to consume an increased amount of a drug to achieve intoxication. Alternatively, people who develop tolerance might not get the same reaction or "kick" from a drug after they've used it for some time. Tolerance is often associated with increases in the amount of drugs people consume.

When people drink large quantities of alcohol for long periods of time and then stop using it or reduce the amount they drink, they're likely to experience uncomfortable symptoms of **withdrawal.** Exactly which symptoms people experience depends on which drug they use. Alcohol use is associated with a number of serious withdrawal syndromes (collections of symptoms), whereas LSD and other psychedelic drugs we'll consider don't produce clear-cut withdrawal symptoms. The discomfort of withdrawal symptoms can motivate users to avoid or relieve unpleasant symptoms by using more of the drug.

Delirium tremens, commonly known as "the DTs," is the most severe alcohol withdrawal phenomenon. Before proper medical treatment was available, as many as 35 percent

Table 5.4 Ten Other Alcohol Myths. Although we've addressed some popular misconceptions about alcohol in the text, there are scores of others. How many of these have you heard?

Misconception	Truth
(1) Every time we drink, we destroy about 10,000 brain cells.	Scientists haven't precisely determined the effect of a single drink on brain cell loss. Heavy drinking over time is associated with brain damage and memory problems.
(2) It's OK to drive a few hours after drinking.	Coordination can be affected as much as 10–12 hours after drinking, so it's not safe to drink and drive.
(3) To avoid a hangover, take two or three acetaminophen tablets, a common alternative to aspirin.	Taking acetaminophen tablets can increase the toxicity of alcohol to the liver.
(4) Drinking coffee is a good way to sober up an intoxicated person.	Although drinking coffee will help us to wake up, it doesn't reverse intoxication. Neither does a cold shower.
(5) We can always detect alcohol on people's breath.	In some cases, we can't detect alcohol on people's breath.
(6) It's safe to leave people who are very drunk until they sober up.	People who are very drunk may become sick and choke, or have drunk so much that they require immediate medical attention.
(7) Drinking alcohol is a good way to help us sleep.	Although drinking often puts us to sleep more quickly, it disrupts the second half of our sleep.
(8) Our judgment isn't impaired until we're extremely drunk.	Impaired judgment can occur well before obvious signs of intoxication appear.
(9) One can't become alcoholic by drinking only beer.	Some alcoholics drink only beer.
(10) A "blackout" is passing out from drinking.	A "blackout" is a loss of memory for a period of time while drunk, and has nothing to do with passing out.

of people with the DTs died from it (Hamilton, 1998). DTs are much less common than other, less severe types of alcohol withdrawal. DTs can be recognized by the presence of **delirium**—disorientation, confusion, terrifying visual hallucinations (like seeing tiny people—so-called Lilliputian hallucinations), and memory problems. Agitation, sleep problems, tremor, and hyperactivity almost always accompany the delirium. The symptoms usually begin within 2 or 3 days after a drinker stops consuming alcohol and subside within a week.

Alcohol hallucinosis is another rare withdrawal disorder that occurs most frequently about 24 to 48 hours after an extended period of intoxication in persons who are physically dependent on alcohol. The hallmarks of alcohol hallucinosis are auditory hallucinations, sometimes accompanied by paranoid beliefs (such as that the government is implanting electrodes in one's brain).

The Sedative-Hypnotics. When people have problems falling asleep or are excessively anxious, they may consult a physician to obtain sedative-hypnotic drugs. Because these drugs produce depressant effects, they are dangerous at high dosages and can produce unconsciousness, coma, and even death.

Researchers usually group sedative-hypnotics into three categories: *barbiturates* (for example, Seconal, Nembutal, and Tuinal); *nonbarbiturates* (for example, Sopor and Methaqualone, better known as Quaalude); and *benzodiazepines*. Benzodiazepines, including Valium, were extremely popular in the 1960s and 1970s and are still widely used today to relieve anxiety. Barbiturates have the greatest abuse potential, which is troubling because the consequences of overdose are often fatal. Barbiturates produce a state of intoxication very similar to that of alcohol.

THE STIMULANT DRUGS: TOBACCO, COCAINE, AND AMPHETAMINES

Tobacco, cocaine, and amphetamines are **stimulants** because they rev up our central nervous system. In contrast to depressants, they increase heart rate, respiration, and blood pressure. Yet each of these drugs produces distinctive physiological and subjective effects.

Tobacco. Over the course of human history, people have consumed tobacco in various ways: smoking, chewing, dipping, licking, and even drinking (Gritz, 1980). As cigarette companies have long known but were reluctant to admit, the nicotine in tobacco is a potent and addictive drug. It reaches the brain about 10 seconds after it's inhaled, and its effects register at the spinal cord, peripheral nervous system, heart, and other bodily organs shortly thereafter. Nicotine activates receptors sensitive to the neurotransmitter acetylcholine, and smokers often report feelings of stimulation as well as relaxation and alertness.

Smoking serves important psychological needs, such as reducing tension or anxiety, enhancing self-esteem, and providing pleasure in a variety of situations. Like many other drugs taken for nonmedical purposes, it has *adjustive value,* meaning it can enhance positive emotional reactions and minimize negative emotional reactions, including the distress experienced when the nicotine level drops (Leventhal & Cleary, 1988). For many young people, positive images associated with smoking enhance its appeal. In Chapter 12, we'll examine the many negative health consequences of tobacco use.

Cocaine. Cocaine is the most powerful natural stimulant. Cocaine users commonly report euphoria, enhanced mental and physical capacity, stimulation, a decrease in hunger, indifference to pain, and a sense of well-being accompanied by diminished fatigue. These effects peak quickly and usually fade within a half hour.

Cocaine grows in abundance in the mountainous region of South America, where it's obtained from the leaves of a shrub, *Erythoxylin cocoa.* Cocaine has a long and checkered history. Its anesthetic properties were discovered about 30 years after it was extracted from coca leaves. By the late 1800s, doctors hailed cocaine as a cure-all and prescribed it for a wide range of illnesses. Around the turn of the century, medicines, wines, and alcoholic tonics containing cocaine and coca extracts were popular. Until 1903, Coca-Cola contained small amounts of cocaine, and was advertised to "cure your headache and relieve fatigue for only 5 cents."

For years, cigarette companies published advertisements claiming that smoking is good for people's health, as in this 1946 ad boasting of Camel's popularity among physicians.

delirium
disorientation, confusion, visual hallucinations, and memory problems, sometimes resulting from alcohol withdrawal

alcohol hallucinosis
auditory hallucinations, sometimes accompanied by paranoid beliefs, resulting from alcohol withdrawal

stimulants
drugs that increase activity in the central nervous system, including heart rate, respiration, and blood pressure

At the turn of the twentieth century, many nonprescription products, such as the then-new soft drink Coca-Cola, contained tiny amounts of cocaine.

Smoking crack, a highly concentrated form of cocaine, is more dangerous than snorting regular cocaine.

Even Sigmund Freud advocated the use of cocaine to treat morphine addiction and used cocaine to improve his mood. However, he came out against its use after dependence problems surfaced shortly after the drug became popular. Cocaine came under strict government control in the United States in 1906.

Eight percent of college students (Johnston, O'Malley, & Bachman, 2002), and nearly 14 percent of people aged 12 and older report having used cocaine at least once (Office of Applied Studies, 2004). Cocaine is a powerful reinforcer. When conditioned to self-inject cocaine, rhesus monkeys remain intoxicated for long periods of time. They may even "dose themselves to death" when unlimited quantities of cocaine are available (Johanson, Balster, & Bonese, 1976). Heavy intake of cocaine by humans also produces an intense drive to use it (Spotts & Shontz, 1976, 1983). Cocaine increases the activity of dopamine and perhaps serotonin, which contribute to its reinforcing effects.

Cocaine users can inject it intravenously. But they more commonly inhale or "snort" it through the nose, where the nasal mucus membranes absorb it. *Crack cocaine* is a highly concentrated dose of cocaine produced by dissolving cocaine in an alkaline (basic) solution and boiling it until a whitish lump, or "rock," remains that can be smoked. There's been a sharp increase in crack's popularity that's attributable to the intense euphoria it generates and its relative affordability. But the "high" is short-lived and followed by unpleasant feelings, which can lead to consuming cocaine whenever available to regain the high (Gottheil & Weinstein, 1983).

Amphetamines. Amphetamines are among the most commonly abused of all drugs, with 49 percent of Americans trying them at least once by age 40 (Johnston et al., 2003). Amphetamines illustrate how different patterns of use can produce different subjective effects. The first pattern involves occasional use of small doses of oral amphetamines to postpone fatigue, elevate mood while performing an unpleasant task, cram for a test, or experience well-being. In this case, intake of amphetamines doesn't become a routine part of the users' lifestyle.

In the second pattern, users obtain amphetamines from a doctor, but use them on a regular basis for euphoria-producing effects rather than for the prescribed purpose. In these cases, a potent psychological dependence on the drug may occur, followed by depression if regular use is interrupted.

The third pattern is associated with street users—"speed freaks"—who inject large doses of amphetamines intravenously to achieve the "rush" of pleasure immediately following the injection. These users are likely to be restless, talkative, and excited, and to inject amphetamines repeatedly to prolong euphoria. Inability to sleep and loss of appetite are also hallmarks of the so-called speed binge. Users may become increasingly suspicious and hostile and develop paranoid delusions (believing that others are out to get them) as amphetamines accumulate in their bodies.

Amphetamine users may experience exhaustion and sleep continuously for up to two days after their ability to inject amphetamines is interrupted. Following exhaustion, severe depressive symptoms may set in, lasting as long as several weeks. Paranoid symptoms usually disappear within a few days or weeks after drug use stops. But in some cases, symptoms of depression, hallucinations, anxiety, and paranoia persist for long periods after people stop using the drug.

In recent years, *methamphetamine,* a drug closely related chemically to amphetamines, has emerged as a widely used drug of abuse. As many as 1 in 20 high school students report using methamphetamine (Johnston et al., 2003). In its crystalline and highly addictive form, it's known as crystal meth or simply "meth." Users experience intense exhilaration when they smoke it, followed by a feeling of euphoria that can last 12 to 16 hours. Crystal meth is stronger than amphetamines, generally has a higher purity level, and carries a high risk of overdose and dependence. As we can see from the photograph of Theresa Baxter on the next page, meth can destroy tissues and blood vessels and cause acne. It can also lead to weight loss, tremors, and dental problems.

THE OPIATE NARCOTIC DRUGS: HEROIN, MORPHINE, AND CODEINE

The opiate drugs heroin, morphine, and codeine are derived from the opium poppy, a plant found in abundance in Asia. Morphine is the major ingredient in opium. The action of heroin is virtually identical to that of morphine, but heroin is about three times as powerful and now accounts for 90 percent of opiate abuse. The opiates often are called **narcotics** because they relieve pain and induce sleep.

At first glance, heroin's psychological effects might appear mostly pleasurable: "Heroin is the king of drugs. . . . It leaves you floating on a calm sea where nothing seems to matter and everything is okay. . . . Suddenly the emptiness disappears. . . . the terrible growing inadequacy has vanished. And in its place is the power and comfort that's called confidence. No one can get to you when you keep nodding" (Rosenberg, 1973, pp. 25–26).

This description conveys a sense of the euphoria that opiate users may experience. But the pleasurable effects of heroin are limited to the 3 or 4 hours that the usual dose lasts. If people addicted to heroin don't take another dose within 4 to 6 hours, they experience *heroin withdrawal syndrome*, with symptoms like abdominal cramps, vomiting, craving for the drug, yawning, runny nose, sweating, and chills. There's considerable variation in users' withdrawal reactions. Some users' symptoms resemble a bad case of the flu. But for those who develop high levels of tolerance, symptoms can be much more severe. With continued heroin use, the drug's euphoric effect gradually diminishes. The addict may continue using heroin as much to avoid withdrawal symptoms as to experience the intense high of the first few injections (Hutcheson, Everitt, Robbins, & Dickinson, 2001; Julien, 2004).

About 1 to 2 percent of young adults have tried heroin (Johnston et al., 2003). The sleep-inducing properties of heroin derive largely from its depressant effects on the central nervous system: Drowsiness follows injection, breathing and pulse rate slow, and pupils constrict. At higher doses, coma and death may follow.

Even infrequent users risk becoming addicted to heroin. But as we'll discover in Chapter 6, contrary to popular conception, heroin addiction isn't inevitable (Sullum, 2003). For example, people who use opiates for medical purposes don't necessarily become addicted. Postsurgical patients allowed to inject morphine through an intravenous pump inject it only in sufficient amounts to keep the pain bearable and happily give up injections once they no longer need painkillers (Melzack, 1990).

Since the introduction of the powerful opiate pain reliever OxyContin in the mid-1990s, drug abusers have turned to it increasingly for "highs." Unfortunately, injecting or taking Oxy-Contin in pill form in combination with alcohol and other depressant drugs can be lethal.

THE PSYCHEDELIC DRUGS: MARIJUANA, LSD, AND ECSTASY

Scientists describe such drugs as LSD, mescaline, PCP, and ecstasy as **hallucinogenic** or *psychedelic* because their primary effects are dramatic alterations in perception, mood, and thought. Because the effects of marijuana aren't as "mind bending" as those of LSD, some researchers don't classify marijuana as a hallucinogen. In contrast, other researchers describe it as a "mild hallucinogen." Interestingly, marijuana may also have sedative or hypnotic qualities.

Marijuana. Marijuana is the most frequently used illegal drug in the United States. Fifty-four percent of young adults report they've used it at least once (NIDA, 2002). Known in popular culture as pot, grass, herb, and weed, marijuana comes from the leaves and flowering part of the hemp plant (*Cannabis sativa*). The subjective effects of marijuana are produced by its primary ingredient, THC (delta-9-tetrahydrocannabinol). People experience a "high" feeling within a few minutes, which peaks within a half hour. Hashish, manufactured from the buds and flowers of female plants, contains much greater concentrations of THC than does marijuana and is more potent.

Whether marijuana is smoked or, less frequently, eaten or consumed in tea, users report short-term effects, including a sense of time slowing down, enhanced sensations of touch, increased appreciation for sounds, hunger ("the munchies"), feelings of well-being,

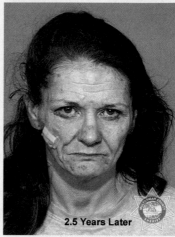

The photo of 42-year-old Theresa Baxter on the top was taken before she became a methamphetamine addict. The photo on the bottom was taken $2\frac{1}{2}$ years later, after she was arrested for fraud and identity theft to support her addiction.

narcotics
drugs that relieve pain and induce sleep

hallucinogenic
causing dramatic alterations of perception, mood, and thought

The ground-up leaves of the hemp plant are the source of marijuana.

and a tendency to giggle and laugh. Later, they may become quiet, introspective, and sleepy. At higher doses, users may experience disturbances in short-term memory, exaggerated emotions, and an altered sense of self. Some reactions are more unpleasant, including difficulty concentrating, slowed thought, depersonalization (a sense of being "out of touch" or disconnected from the self; see Chapter 15), and, more rarely, extreme anxiety, panic, and psychotic episodes (Earleywine, 2005).

The intoxicating effects of marijuana can last for 2 or 3 hours, but begin when THC courses through the bloodstream and travels to the brain, where it stimulates cannabinoid receptors. These specialized receptors are concentrated in areas of the brain that control pleasure, perception, memory, and coordinated body movements. The most prominent physiological changes are increases in heart rate, reddening of the eyes, and dryness of the mouth.

Learning and expectancies play significant roles in marijuana intoxication (Kirk, Doty, & de Wit, 1998). People frequently feel little or nothing the first time they try marijuana. To label their experience as a "high," most users must expect that the drug will produce a "new experience," and learn to recognize the drug's effects (Becker, 1953).

In 1974, U.S. Senator James Eastland cautioned that "if the cannabis epidemic continues . . . we may find ourselves saddled with a large population of semi-zombies—of young people acutely afflicted by the amotivational syndrome" (Ray & Ksir, 1998). These concerns are reminiscent of earlier claims, popularized in the 1936 film *Reefer Madness*, that marijuana leads to personality destruction and degeneration.

Correlation vs. Causation

Does regular use of marijuana lead to passivity, decreased productivity, and a loss of motivation—the so-called amotivational syndrome to which Eastland referred? There's certainly evidence that low achievement is related to marijuana use. High school students who use marijuana earn lower grades and are more likely to get in trouble with the law than other students (Kleinman, Wish, Deron, Rainone, & Morehouse, 1988; Substance Abuse and Mental Health Services Administration, 2001). But as we've learned, an association between two or more variables doesn't necessarily imply a cause–effect relationship. High school students who use marijuana might do so because they have troubled home lives or psychological problems and do poorly in school *before* using marijuana (Shedler & Block, 1990). Poor motivation may be responsible for drug use, rather than the other way around. The causal direction of the link between marijuana and low motivation hasn't been firmly established.

Ruling Out Rival Hypotheses

Still, legitimate concerns about the long-term hazards of marijuana remain. Mounting evidence suggests that marijuana use may trigger schizophrenia, a serious disorder of thinking we'll encounter in Chapter 15, among young adults who have either a personal or family history of the disorder (Dengelhardt & Hall, 2006). In addition, some researchers have argued that marijuana is a "gateway" drug that predisposes users to try more serious drugs, like heroin and cocaine (Kandel, Yamaguchi, & Chen, 1992). In a study of identical twin pairs (see Chapter 3) in which one twin tried marijuana in adolescence but the other didn't, the twin who tried marijuana was later at heightened risk for abusing alcohol and other drugs (Lynskey et al., 2003). Nevertheless, evaluating whether marijuana is a gateway drug isn't easy. Merely because one event precedes another doesn't mean it causes it (see Chapter 10). For example, eating baby foods in infancy doesn't cause us to eat "grown-up" foods later in life. Baby foods just happen to come earlier. Similarly, teens may tend to use marijuana before other drugs because it's less threatening, more readily available, or both. The scientific debate continues.

LSD and Other Hallucinogens.   On Friday, April 16, 1943, an odd thing happened to Swiss chemist Albert Hofman. In 1938, Hofman synthesized a chemical compound, d-lysergic acid diethylamide-25 (LSD), from chemicals found in a fungus that grows on rye. Five years later, when Hofman again decided to work on the compound, he absorbed some of it unknowingly through his skin. When he went home, he felt restless, dizzy, and "perceived an uninterrupted stream of fantastic pictures, extraordinary shapes with intense, kaleidoscopic play of colors. After some two hours this condition faded away" (1980, p. 5).

Hoffman was the first of millions of people to experience the mind-altering effects of LSD. By the age of 40, about 20 percent of Americans have tried LSD (Johnston et al., 2002). The psychedelic effects of LSD may stem from its interference with the action of the neurotransmitter serotonin (see Chapter 3) at the synapse. The effects of LSD are also associated with areas of the brain rich in receptors for the neurotransmitter dopamine. As Hoffman discovered, even tiny amounts of LSD can produce dramatic shifts in our perceptions and consciousness. Pills about the size of two aspirins can provide more than 6,000 "highs." Some users report astonishingly clear thoughts and fascinating changes in sensations and perceptions, including synesthesia (the blending of senses—for example, the "smelling of noises"; see Chapter 4). Some users also report mystical experiences (Pahnke, Kurland, Unger, Savage, & Grof, 1970).

LSD was discovered by sheer accident in a laboratory in the 1940s. It often causes marked distortions in perception.

But LSD and other hallucinogens can also produce panic, paranoid delusions, confusion, depression, and bodily discomfort. Occasionally, psychotic reactions persist long after a psychedelic experience, most often in people with a history of psychological problems (Abraham & Aldridge, 1993). People who are suspicious and insecure before ingesting LSD are most anxious during an LSD session (Linton & Langs, 1964). *Flashbacks*—recurrences of a psychedelic experience—occur occasionally. Curiously, there's no known pharmacological basis for their occurrence. One explanation is that they're triggered by something in the environment or an emotional state associated with a past psychedelic experience.

LSD's subjective effects proved so fascinating to the Central Intelligence Agency (CIA) that in 1953 it launched a research program called MKULTRA to explore LSD's potential as a mind-control drug. This secret program involved administering LSD to unsuspecting individuals, including a group of army scientists. After one of the scientists experienced a psychotic reaction and jumped to his death from a hotel window, the CIA turned to testing the effects of LSD on drug-dependent persons and prostitutes. The full scope of this secret operation came to light and received media exposure after the program was discontinued in 1972. The researchers didn't find LSD to be a promising mind-control agent because its subjective effects were so unpredictable.

All-night dance parties termed "raves," in which ecstasy and other psychedelic drugs are widely available, became popular in the mid-1990s in the United States.

Unlike LSD, ecstasy has both stimulant and hallucinogenic properties. It produces cascades of the neurotransmitter serotonin in the brain, which increases self-confidence and well-being, and produces powerful feelings of empathy for others. But its use has a serious downside: Its side effects can include high blood pressure, depression, nausea, blurred vision, liver problems, and possibly memory loss and damage to neurons that use serotonin (Kish, 2002; Soar, Parrott, & Fox, 2004).

Drugs, like other means of altering consciousness, remind us that the "brain" and the "mind" are merely different ways of looking at the same phenomenon (see Prologue and Chapter 3). They also illustrate the fluid way we experience ourselves and the world. Although a precise grasp of consciousness eludes us, appreciating the nuances of consciousness and their neurological correlates bring us closer to understanding the biological and psychological underpinnings of our waking and sleeping lives.

ASSESS YOUR KNOWLEDGE: FACT OR FICTION?

(1) The effects of many drugs depend on the expectations of the user. (True/False)

(2) Alcohol is a central nervous system depressant. (True/False)

(3) Tobacco is the most potent natural stimulant drug. (True/False)

(4) A causal link between marijuana and the "amotivational syndrome" has been well established. (True/False)

(5) Drug flashbacks are common among people who use LSD. (True/False)

Answers: (1) T (p. 218); (2) T (p. 218); (3) F (p. 221); (4) F (p. 224); (5) F (p. 225)

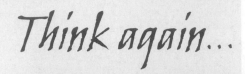
The Biology of Sleep (pp. 197–204)

STUDY the Learning Objectives

▶ Identify the different stages of sleep and the neural activity and dreaming behaviors that occur in each

- Sleep and wakefulness vary in response to a circadian rhythm that regulates many bodily processes over a 24-hour period. The "biological clock" is located in the suprachiasmatic nucleus in the hypothalamus. In the 1950s, researchers identified five stages of sleep that include periods of dreaming in which subjects' eyes move rapidly back and forth (rapid eye movement, or REM, sleep). Although vivid, bizarre, and emotional dreams are most likely to occur in REM sleep, dreams occur in non-REM sleep as well. In stage 1 sleep, we feel drowsy and quickly transition to stage 2 sleep in which our brain waves slow down, heart rate slows, body temperature decreases, and muscles relax. In stages 3 and 4 ("deep") sleep, large amplitude delta waves (1 or 2 cycles/second) become more frequent. In stage 5, REM sleep, the brain is activated much as it is during everyday life.

▶ Identify the features and causes of sleep disorders

- Insomnia (problems falling asleep, waking in the night, or waking early) is the most common sleep disorder and is costly to society in terms of fatigue, missed work, and accidents. Restless legs can also cause insomnia. Episodes of narcolepsy, which can last as long as an hour, are marked by the rapid onset of sleep." Sleep apnea is also related to daytime fatigue and is caused by a blockage of the airways during sleep. Night terrors and sleepwalking, both associated with deep sleep, are typically harmless, and in both conditions the person doesn't remember their occurrence the next day.

DO YOU KNOW THESE TERMS?

- ❑ **sleep paralysis** (p. 196)
- ❑ **consciousness** (p. 197)
- ❑ **circadian rhythm** (p. 197)
- ❑ **biological clock** (p. 197)
- ❑ **rapid eye movements (REM)** (p. 198)
- ❑ **non-REM (NREM) sleep** (p. 199)
- ❑ **REM sleep** (p. 199)
- ❑ **lucid dreaming** (p. 201)
- ❑ **insomnia** (p. 202)
- ❑ **restless legs syndrome** (p. 203)
- ❑ **narcolepsy** (p. 203)
- ❑ **sleep apnea** (p. 203)
- ❑ **night terrors** (p. 204)
- ❑ **sleepwalking** (p. 204)

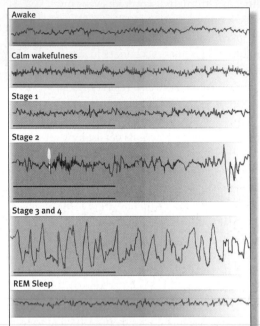

Awake

Calm wakefulness

Stage 1

Stage 2

Stage 3 and 4

REM Sleep

Complete the diagram showing an EEG reading of brain activity at each sleep stage. (p. 199)

THINK about

what **You** would do . . .
Your thesis defense is in three days but you are battling insomnia. What research-supported steps can you take to ensure you are well rested for your important presentation? (p. 202)

SUCCEED with

mypsychlab *where learning comes to life!*

Lucid Dreaming
If I know that I am dreaming, am I really asleep? (p. 201)

▶ WATCH

What factors can contribute to cataplexy in people or animals with narcolepsy? (p. 203)

ASSESS your knowledge

1. A strange feeling of being unable to move right after falling asleep is a disruption in the sleep cycle called _____ _____. (p. 196)

2. Our subjective experience of the world, our bodies, and our mental perspectives is called _____. (p. 197)

3. The changes that occur in many of our biological processes during a 24-hour period are referred to as the _____ _____. (p. 197)

4. As a college student you may like to sleep late in the morning because your _____ _____ is set that way. (p. 198)

5. During the _____ stage of sleep, also called the _____ stage, the activity in our brains is similar to when we are awake because we are typically engaged in vivid dreaming. (p. 199)

6. There are _____ stages in the sleep cycle, and each night we typically circle back to the REM stage (5/10/20) times. (pp. 199–200)

7. If you realize you're having a dream while it's happening, you are experiencing _____ _____. (p. 201)

8. There are several types of sleep disorders, but the most common is _____. (p. 202)

9. People who have _____ fall asleep suddenly and at inopportune times, like while driving a car. (p. 203)

10. During a _____ _____, a child can experience a dramatic episode of crying or thrashing during non-REM sleep, and won't remember it in the morning. (p. 204)

Theories and Psychology of Dreams (pp. 205–207)

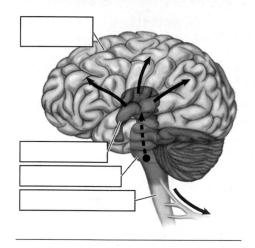

Label the brain components that the activation-synthesis theory suggests are involved in dreaming (a), and describe below the function of each component in reconstructing dreams (b). (p. 206)

mypsychlab *where learning comes to life!*

SUCCEED with

Theories of Dreaming
Does dreaming serve a purpose? Find out what theorists have proposed about dreaming.
(p. 207)

EXPLORE

STUDY the Learning Objectives

▶ Determine how Freud's theory of dreams relates to research evidence on dreaming
• Freud theorized that dreams represent disguised wishes. However, many dreams involve unpleasant or undesirable experiences, and many involve uninteresting reviews of routine daily events. Thus, Freud's dream theory hasn't received much empirical support.

▶ Explain how theories of brain activation attempt to account for dreaming
• According to activation synthesis theory, the forebrain attempts to interpret nonsensical signals from the brain stem (specifically, the pons). Another theory of dreaming suggests that reduction of activity in the prefrontal cortex results in vivid, and emotional, but logically disjointed, dreams. Neurocognitive theories hold that our dreams depend in large part on who we are, so that dreams vary depending on our cognitive and visuospatial abilities.

DO YOU KNOW THIS TERM?
☐ **activation–synthesis theory** (p. 205)

THINK about

what You would do . . .
Given what you have learned about scientists' current understanding of dream function, would you choose to dream like an adult or like a child? (p. 207)

Nightmares, which are common in both children and adults, challenge which of Freud's theories about dreams? (p. 205)

ASSESS your knowledge

1. In the era before rigorous laboratory research, *The Interpretation of Dreams* by _____ _____ played an influential role in how people thought about dreams. (p. 205)

2. According to Freud's _____ _____ theory, our dreams represent how we wish things would be. (p. 205)

3. Studies done on people with brain injuries who don't report dreams yet sleep soundly disconfirm Freud's _____ _____ theory. (p. 205)

4. According to Hobson's and McCarley's _____ theory, dreams reflect brain activation that originates in the _____ at the base of the brain. (pp. 205–206)

5. REM sleep is activated by surges of the neurotransmitter _____, which activates nerve cells in the pons. (p.206)

6. The brain's attempt to create a story from incomplete dream information it receives involves the pons transmitting signals to the _____, which relays information to the forebrain. (p. 206)

7. People who have an injury to the _____, as researched by Solms, do not dream. (p. 206)

8. Scientists who take a _____ view of dreaming contend that we must consider our cognitive capacities, which shape the content of our dreams. (p. 207)

9. Children's dreams tend to be (less/more) emotional and bizarre than adult dreams. (p. 207)

10. Scientists agree that there (is/isn't) a close connection between brain activity and dreaming. (p. 207)

Other Alterations of Consciousness and Unusual Experiences (pp. 208–218)

STUDY the Learning Objectives

▶ **Determine how scientists explain seemingly "mystical" alterations in consciousness**
- Hallucinations and mystical experiences are associated with fasting, sensory deprivation, hallucinogenic drugs, prayer, and like near death experiences, vary considerably in content across cultures. During out of body experiences, people's consciousness don't actually exit their bodies, and some NDEs are experienced by people who aren't near death. Déjà vu experiences don't represent a memory from a past life, but may be triggered by small seizures in the temporal lobe or unconscious information processing.

▶ **Evaluate the benefits of meditation**
- Although proponents have attributed many positive effects to meditation, it is unclear whether meditation yields benefits above and beyond relaxation and whether expectancies can account for its effects.

▶ **Distinguish myths from realities concerning hypnosis**
- Contrary to popular belief, hypnosis is not a sleeplike state, subjects generally do not report having been in a "trance," people are aware of their surroundings and don't forget what happened during hypnosis, the type of induction has little impact, and hypnosis doesn't improve memory. In fact, hypnosis can lead to more false memories and inflated confidence in memories, regardless of their accuracy. According to the socio-cognitive model of hypnosis, the often dramatic effects associated with hypnosis may be attributable largely to preexisting expectations and beliefs about hypnosis. The dissociation model (Hilgard, 1986) is another influential model of hypnosis. This model emphasizes divisions of consciousness during hypnosis.

DO YOU KNOW THESE TERMS?
- ☐ **out-of-body exerience (OBE)** (p. 208)
- ☐ **near-death experiences (NDE)** (p. 209)
- ☐ **déjà vu** (p. 210)
- ☐ **mystical experience** (p. 211)
- ☐ **meditation** (p. 212)
- ☐ **hypnosis** (p. 213)
- ☐ **past life regression therapy** (p. 216)
- ☐ **sociocognitive theory** (p. 216)
- ☐ **dissociation theory** (p. 217)

Would the person shown in this drawing have to be in an altered state of consciousness to achieve this position? (p. 214)

THINK about what You would do . . .
Your new part-time job as a theatre stage director Involves selecting audience members to participate in a hypnotist's show. What characteristics would you look for as you screen potential audience participants? (p. 214)

List some of the positive effects of meditation and possible explanations for each. (pp. 212–213)

ASSESS your knowledge

1. During a state of high stress or extreme relaxation, if you feel like your consciousness has left your body, you may be having an _____ experience. (pp. 208–209)

2. Although there are many variations depending on one's religion and culture, many people in our culture associate a _____ experience with approaching a white light. (pp. 209–210)

3. One of the most common alterations in consciousness, _____ is the sensation that you're reliving something even though you know the situation is new, or that you've been somewhere even though you've never been there before. (p. 210)

4. _____ is a practice that trains attention and awareness, and can have positive effects on some people. (p. 212)

5. In _____ meditation, you maintain focus on a single thing, such as the breath; in _____ meditation, you examine whatever comes to mind. (p. 213)

6. People who perform in stage _____ shows are specifically selected for high suggestibility. (p. 214)

7. One of the most popular myths about hypnosis is that it can make people remember a past life using a therapy called _____ _____ _____. (pp. 215–216)

8. For _____ theorists, people's expectations about hypnosis, including the cues they receive from hypnotists, shape their responses. (p. 216)

9. Hilgard's _____ theory explained hypnosis based on a separation of the part of the personality responsible for planning from the part of the personality that controls memories. (p. 217)

10. Hypnosis in clinical practice (has/has not) demonstrated positive effects in treating pain or habit disorders, such as smoking. (pp. 217–218)

Drugs and Consciousness (pp. 218–225)

	Received	
	Alcohol	**Placebo**
Alcohol (Told)		
Placebo		

To show the balanced placebo design, insert the proper alcohol conditions in each of the four boxes. (p. 219)

THINK about ... what You would do ...
Imagine that you're a dorm counselor to a group of college students who are engaging in heavy drinking. What information could you provide to alter their mental set about using alcohol? (p. 218)

SUCCEED with mypsychlab
Behavioral Effects Associated with Blood Alcohol Levels
I've only had one drink: the real effects of alcohol on behavior. (p. 219)
EXPLORE

Complete the table by adding the effects and examples for each drug type listed. (p. 218)

Drug Type	Effects	Examples
Stimulants		
Depressants		
Opiates		
Psychedelics		

ASSESS your knowledge

1. Psychoactive drugs are chemicals that (are/are not) similar to those found in our brains that alter consciousness by changing chemical processes in _____. (p. 218)

2. Depressant drugs, like alcohol, (increase/decrease) activity of the central nervous system. (p. 218)

3. At high doses, when the _____ _____ reaches 0.05 to 0.10, the sedating and depressant effects of alcohol become apparent. (p. 219)

4. When people drink large amounts of alcohol over a long period of time, and then stop using it, they are likely experiencing symptoms of _____, the most severe type being _____ _____. (p. 220)

5. Examples of stimulant drugs are _____, _____, and _____. (pp. 221–222)

6. The most powerful natural stimulant is _____. (p. 221)

7. Some people abuse _____ to postpone fatigue or elevate their mood while performing an unpleasant task (p. 222).

8. In recent years, as many as 1 in 20 high school students report using methamphetamine, which in its crystalline form is known as _____. (p. 222)

9. Opiate drugs—heroin, morphine, and codeine—are often called _____ because they relieve pain and induce sleep. (p. 223)

10. Hoffman created the mind-altering hallucinogenic drug _____ by accident while creating a compound from chemicals in a fungus. (pp. 224–225)

STUDY the Learning Objective
▶ Distinguish different types of drugs and their effects on consciousness
- The effects of drugs are associated with the dose of the drug, as well as with users' expectancies, personality, and culture. Nicotine, a powerful stimulant drug, is responsible for the effects of tobacco on consciousness. Smokers often report feeling stimulated as well as tranquil, relaxed, and alert. Cocaine is the most powerful natural stimulant drug, with effects similar to those of amphetamine. Cocaine is highly addictive. Alcohol is a central nervous system depressant, like the sedative-hypnotic drugs such as Valium. Sedative-hypnotic drugs reduce anxiety at low doses and induce sleep at moderate doses. Expectancies play a key role in determining how people react to alcohol. Heroin and other opiates are highly addictive. Heroin withdrawal symptoms range from mild to severe. The effects of marijuana, sometimes classified as a mild hallucinogen, include mood changes, alterations in perception, and disturbances in short-term memory. LSD is an incredibly potent hallucinogen. Although flashbacks are rare, LSD can elicit a wide range of positive and negative reactions.

DO YOU KNOW THESE TERMS?
- psychoactive drugs (p. 218)
- sedative (p. 218)
- hypnotic (p. 218)
- tolerance (p. 220)
- withdrawal (p. 220)
- delirium (p. 221)
- alcohol hallucinosis (p. 221)
- stimulants (p. 221)
- narcotics (p. 223)
- hallucinogenic (p. 223)

Remember these questions from the beginning of the chapter? Think again and ask yourself if you would answer them differently based on what you now know about consciousness. (For more detailed explanations, see MyPsychLab.com.)

▶ Can we trust people's reports that they've been abducted by aliens? (p. 196)
▶ Do the blind see in their dreams? (p. 201)
▶ Does a person's consciousness leave the body during an out-of-body experience? (pp. 208–209)
▶ Do people who have a near-death experience truly catch a glimpse of the afterlife? (pp. 209–210)
▶ Are déjà vu experiences memories of a past life? (pp. 210–211)
▶ Is meditation different in its effects from relaxation? (pp. 212–213)
▶ Does hypnosis produce a trance state? (p. 214)
▶ Does hypnosis improve memory? (p. 215)
▶ Is alcohol a stimulant drug? (p. 218)

THINKING Scientifically
Correlation vs. Causation pp. 213, 216, 224
Falsifiability pp. 205, 210
Extraordinary Claims p. 210
Occam's Razor p. 210
Replicability p. 209
Ruling Out Rival Hypotheses pp. 202, 209, 210, 213, 215, 217, 224

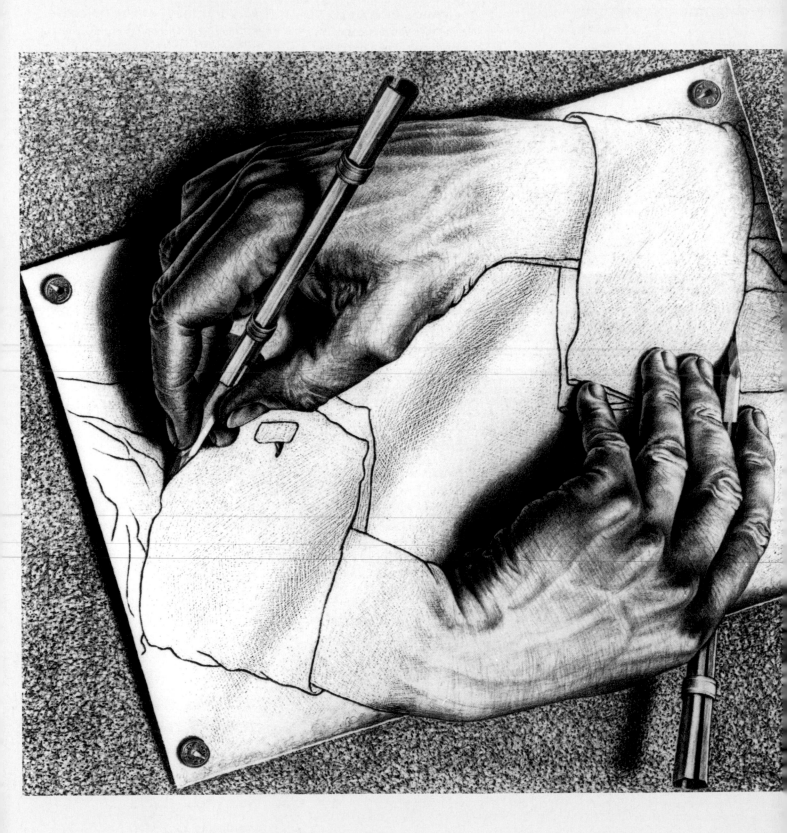

6

Learning
How Nurture Changes Us

PREVIEW

Think

First, think about these questions. Then, as you read, think again....

▶ Does conditioned learning have an impact on our everyday lives?

▶ How do phobias and fetishes develop?

▶ Does human learning differ from animal learning?

▶ How do trainers get animals to do cute tricks, like dancing or water skiing?

▶ Can we learn simply by observing others?

▶ Does watching violence on TV really teach children to become violent?

▶ Is all learning gradual, or do we sometimes learn through sudden flashes of insight?

▶ Can we avoid a delicious food for decades after only one negative experience with it?

▶ Can we learn in our sleep?

▶ Do different people have different learning styles that work best for them?

Before reading further, try your hand at the following four items.

(1) Ivan Pavlov, the discoverer of classical conditioning, was well known as a
    (a) slow eater
    (b) fast walker
    (c) terrible cook
    (d) I have no idea

(2) John B. Watson, the founder of behaviorism, was tossed out of Johns Hopkins University for
    (a) plagiarizing a journal article
    (b) stabbing one of his faculty colleagues
    (c) having an affair with his graduate student
    (d) I have no idea

(3) Watson believed that parents should do which of the following to their children before bedtime?
    (a) spank them
    (b) kiss them on the cheek
    (c) shake their hands
    (d) I have no idea

(4) As a college student, B. F. Skinner, the founder of radical behaviorism, once spread a false rumor that which of the following individuals was coming to campus?
    (a) silent movie comedian Charlie Chaplin
    (b) psychoanalyst Sigmund Freud
    (c) President Theodore Roosevelt
    (d) I have no idea

Now, read the following paragraph.

The three most famous figures in the psychology of learning were each colorful characters in their own way. The discoverer of classical conditioning, Ivan Pavlov, was a notoriously compulsive fellow. He ate lunch every day at precisely 12 noon, went to bed at exactly the same time every night, and departed St. Petersburg, Russia, for vacation the same day every year. Pavlov was also such a rapid walker that his wife frequently had to run frantically to keep up with him. The life of the founder of behaviorism, John B. Watson, was rocked with scandal. Despite becoming one of the world's most famous psychologists, he was unceremoniously booted out of Johns Hopkins University for having an affair with his graduate student, Rosalie Rayner. Watson also had rather unusual ideas about parenting; for example, he believed that all parents should shake hands with their children before bedtime. B. F. Skinner, the founder of radical behaviorism, was something of a prankster in his undergraduate years at Hamilton College in New York. He and a friend once spread a false rumor that comedian Charlie Chaplin was coming to campus. This rumor nearly provoked a riot when Chaplin didn't materialize as expected.

Now go back and try again to answer the four questions at the beginning of this chapter.

Learning the information in this textbook is altering your brain in ways that psychologists are increasingly coming to understand.

If you got more questions right the second time than the first—and odds are you did—then you've experienced something we all take for granted: learning. (The answers, by the way, are b, c, c, and a.) By **learning,** we mean a change in an organism's behavior or thought as a result of experience. As we discovered in Chapter 3, when we learn our brains change along with our behaviors. Remarkably, your brain is physically different now than it was just a few minutes ago, because it underwent chemical changes that allowed you to learn novel facts.

    Learning lies at the heart of just about every domain of psychology. As we discovered in the Prologue, virtually all behaviors are a complex stew of genetic predispositions and learning.

learning
change in an organism's behavior or thought as a result of experience

Without learning, we'd be unable to do much; we couldn't walk, talk, or read an introductory psychology textbook chapter about learning.

Psychologists have long debated how many distinct types of learning there are. We're not going to try to settle this controversy here. Instead, we'll review several types of learning that psychologists have studied in depth, starting with the most basic.

Before we do, place your brain on pause, put down your pen or highlighter, close your eyes, and attend to several things that you almost never notice: the soft buzzing of the lights in the room, the feel of your clothing against your skin, the sensation of your tongue on your teeth or lips. Unless someone draws our attention to these stimuli, we don't even realize they're there, because we've learned to ignore them. **Habituation** is the process by which we respond less strongly over time to repeated stimuli. It helps explain why loud snorers can sleep peacefully through the night while keeping their irritated roommates wide awake. Chronic snorers have become so accustomed to the sound of their own snoring that they no longer notice it.

Habituation is the simplest form of learning. We can find it even in the lowly single-celled amoeba that we see under our microscope. Shine a light on an amoeba and it will contract into a ball. But keep shining the light, and soon it will resume its normal activities, like busily swimming around on our microscope slide. Habituation is probably the earliest form of learning to emerge in humans. Unborn fetuses as young as 32 weeks display habituation when we apply a gentle vibrator to the mother's stomach. At first, the fetus jerks around in response to the stimulus, but after repeated vibrations it stops moving (Morokuma et al., 2004). What was first a shock to the fetus's system later became a mere annoyance that it could safely ignore.

In research that earned him the Nobel Prize in 2000, neurophysiologist Eric Kandel uncovered the biological mechanism of habituation of *Aplysia*, a 5-inch-long sea slug. Prick an *Aplysia* on a certain part of its body, and it retracts its gill in a defensive maneuver. Touch *Aplysia* in the same spot repeatedly, and it begins to ignore the stimulus. This habituation, Kandel found, is accompanied by a progressive decrease in release of the neurotransmitter serotonin (see Chapter 3) at *Aplysia*'s synapses (Siegelbaum, Camardo, & Kandel, 1982). This discovery helped psychologists unravel the neural bases of learning (see **Figure 6.1**).

Figure 6.1 Habituation in a Simple Animal. *Aplysia californicus* is a sea slug about 5 inches long that retracts its gill when pricked, but then habituates (stops retracting its gill) if pricked repeatedly.

Habituation makes good adaptive sense. We wouldn't want to attend to every tiny sensation that comes across our mental radar screens, because most pose no threat. Yet we wouldn't want to habituate to stimuli that might be dangerous. Fortunately, not all repeated stimuli lead to habituation, only those that we deem safe or worth ignoring do. We typically don't habituate to powerful stimuli, like extremely loud tones or painful electric shocks.

Psychologists have studied habituation using the skin conductance response, a measure of the electrical conductivity of the fingertips. As our fingertips moisten with sweat, they become better conductors of electricity. Scientists measure this moistening with electrodes placed on the fingertips. Because sweating generally indicates anxiety (Fowles, 1981), researchers often use the skin conductance response in studies of habituation. Most research shows that we stop sweating sooner for weak than for strong stimuli, meaning that weak stimuli stop producing anxiety fairly quickly. In the case of very strong stimuli, like painful electric shocks, we often see no habituation at all—which means that people continue to sweat anxiously at the same high levels—even across many trials (Lykken, Iacono, Haroian, McGue, & Bouchard, 1988).

Habituating to background noise while studying can be difficult, especially if the noise is loud.

Indeed, some cases of repeated exposure to stimuli lead to *sensitization*—that is, responding more strongly over time—rather than habituation. Sensitization is most likely when a stimulus is dangerous, irritating, or both. *Aplysia* show sensitization as well as habituation. Have you ever tried to study when the person next to you was whispering, and the whispering kept getting more annoying to the point that you couldn't concentrate? If so, you've experienced sensitization.

habituation
process of responding less strongly over time to repeated stimuli

Classical Conditioning

The story of habituation could hardly be more straightforward. We experience a stimulus, respond to it, and then stop responding after repeated exposure. We've learned something significant, but we haven't learned to forge connections between two stimuli. Yet a great deal of learning depends on associating one thing with another. If we never learned to connect one stimulus, like the appearance of an apple, with another stimulus, like its taste, our world would remain what William James (1891) called a "blooming, buzzing confusion"—a world of disconnected sensory experiences.

BRITISH ASSOCIATIONISM

Several centuries ago, a school of thinkers called the *British Associationists* believed that we acquire virtually all of our knowledge by connecting one stimulus with another: the sound of our mother's voice with her face, for example. Once we form these associations, we need only recall one element of the pair to retrieve the other. Even thinking about a sensation often triggers it. For example, as you read about your mother's face, you might have pictured her in your mind. The British Associationists, who included David Hartley (1707–1757) and John Stuart Mill (1806–1873), believed that simple associations provided the mental building blocks for more complex ideas. Your understanding of this paragraph, they surely would have suggested, stems from thousands of linkages you've formed between the words in it—like *sound* and *voice*—and other words, which are in turn linked to simple concepts, which are in turn linked to more complex concepts . . . and, well, you get the picture.

PAVLOV'S DISCOVERIES

The history of science teaches us that many discoveries arise from *serendipity,* or accident. Yet it takes a great scientist to capitalize on serendipitous observations that others regard as meaningless flukes. As French microbiologist Louis Pasteur, who discovered the process of pasteurizing milk, observed, "Chance favors the prepared mind." So it was with the discoveries of Russian scientist Ivan Pavlov. His landmark understanding of classical conditioning emerged from a set of unforeseen observations that were unrelated to his main research interests.

Pavlov's primary research was digestion in dogs—in fact, his discoveries concerning digestion, not classical conditioning, earned him the Nobel Prize in 1904. Pavlov placed dogs in a harness and inserted a *cannula,* or collection tube, into their salivary glands to study their salivary responses to meat powder. In doing so, he observed something unexpected: He found that dogs began salivating not only to the meat powder itself, but to previously neutral stimuli that had become associated with it, such as research assistants who brought in the powder. Indeed, the dogs even salivated to the sound of these assistants' footsteps as they approached the laboratory. The dogs seemed to be anticipating the meat powder and responding to stimuli that signaled its arrival.

We call this process of association **classical conditioning** (or **Pavlovian or respondent conditioning**): a form of learning in which animals come to respond to a previously neutral stimulus that had been paired with another stimulus that elicits an automatic response. Yet Pavlov's initial observations were merely anecdotal, so like any good scientist he put his informal observations to a more rigorous test.

THE CLASSICAL CONDITIONING PHENOMENON

Here's how Pavlov first demonstrated classical conditioning systematically (see **Figure 6.2**).

(1) He started with an initially neutral stimulus, called the **conditioned stimulus (CS).** In this case, Pavlov used a metronome, a clicking pendulum that keeps time (in other studies, Pavlov used a tuning fork or whistle; contrary to urban legend, Pavlov didn't use a bell). This stimulus doesn't elicit much, if any, response from the dogs. Interestingly, the term

The Rolling Stones may be the only major rock band to accurately describe the process of classical conditioning. One of their well-known songs refers to a man salivating like one of Pavlov's dogs whenever the object of his affection calls his name. Not bad for a group of non-psychologists!

classical (Pavlovian or respondent) conditioning
form of learning in which animals come to respond to a previously neutral stimulus that had been paired with another stimulus that elicits an automatic response

conditioned stimulus (CS)
initially neutral stimulus

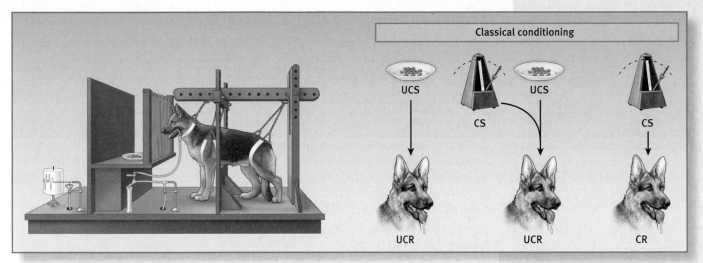

Figure 6.2 Pavlov's Classical Conditioning Model. UCS (meat powder) is paired with CS (metronome clicking) and produces UCR (salivation). Then CS is presented alone, and CR (salivation) occurs.

conditioned stimulus is apparently a mistranslation from the original Russian. Pavlov actually referred to it as the *conditional* stimulus, because the animal's response to it is conditional—that is, dependent—on learning.

(2) He then paired the CS again and again with an **unconditioned stimulus (UCS).** (This term was *unconditional stimulus* in the original Russian, because the animal responds to it unconditionally, that is, all of the time or automatically.) In the case of Pavlov's dogs, the UCS was the meat powder. The UCS elicits an automatic, reflexive response called the **unconditioned response (UCR),** in this case salivation. The key point is that the animal doesn't need to learn to respond to the UCS with the UCR. It produces the UCR without any training at all, because the response is a product of nature, not nurture.

(3) Pavlov repeatedly paired the CS and UCS—and observed something remarkable. If he now presented the CS (the metronome) alone, it elicited a response, namely, salivation. This new response is the **conditioned response (CR):** a response previously associated with a nonneutral stimulus that comes to be elicited by a neutral stimulus. Lo and behold, learning has occurred. The dog, which previously did nothing when it heard the metronome except perhaps turn its head toward it, now salivates when it hears the metronome. The CR, in contrast to the UCR, is a product of nurture, not nature.

In most cases, the CR is similar to the UCR but it's rarely identical to it. For example, Pavlov found that dogs salivated less in response to the metronome (the CS) than to the meat powder (the UCS).

Few findings in psychology are as replicable as classical conditioning. We can apply the classical conditioning paradigm to just about any animal with an intact nervous system, and demonstrate it repeatedly without fail. If only all psychological findings were so dependable!

AVERSIVE CONDITIONING

We can classically condition organisms not only to positive UCSs, like food, but to negative UCSs, like stimuli inducing pain or nausea. If you were allergic to daisies and sneezed uncontrollably whenever you were near them—whether you saw them or not—you'd probably develop an automatic avoidance response, like shying away from a bouquet even before you realized why you were doing it. This type of avoidance response reflects *aversive conditioning:* classical conditioning to an unpleasant UCS (Emmelkamp & Kamphuis, 2005). Stanley Kubrick's 1971 film *A Clockwork Orange* provides an unforgettable example of aversive conditioning involving the main character, Alexander de Large, portrayed by actor Malcolm McDowell. De Large's prison captors, who hoped to eradicate his bloodthirsty lust for violence, forced him to watch film clips of aggressive individuals, like the members of Hitler's army marching in unison, while experiencing nausea induced by injections of a serum. The aversive conditioning worked—but only for a while.

factoid

Classical conditioning may occur not only in animals but in plants. One researcher found that a *Mimosa* plant that folds its leaves (UCR) when touched (UCS) can be conditioned to fold its leaves (CR) in response to a change in lighting condition (CS) that has been repeatedly paired with a touch (Haney, 1969). Nevertheless, this finding is scientifically controversial.

Replicability

unconditioned stimulus (UCS)
stimulus that elicits an automatic response

unconditioned response (UCR)
automatic response to a nonneutral stimulus that does not need to be learned

conditioned response (CR)
response previously associated with a nonneutral stimulus that is elicited by a neutral stimulus through conditioning

Psychopaths don't develop conditioned fear of punishment, so they'll react nonchalantly to the thought of being pulled over by police.

factoid

Backward conditioning—in which the UCS is presented *before* the CS—is extremely difficult to achieve. Because the CS fails to predict the UCS and the UCR often begins before the CS has even occurred, organisms have difficulty using the CS to anticipate the UCS.

acquisition
learning phase during which a conditioned response is established

extinction
gradual reduction and eventual elimination of the conditioned response after the conditioned stimulus is presented repeatedly without the unconditioned stimulus

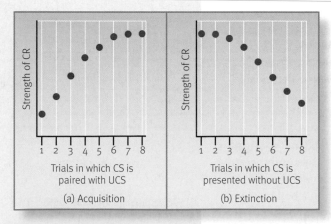

Figure 6.3 Acquisition and Extinction. Acquisition is the repeated pairing of UCS and CS, increasing the CR's strength (a). In extinction, the CS is presented again and again without the UCS, resulting in the gradual disappearance of the CR (b).

ADAPTIVE VALUE OF CLASSICAL CONDITIONING

Without classical conditioning, we couldn't develop physiological associations to stimuli that signal biologically important events, like things we want to eat—or that want to eat us. Many of the physiological responses we display in classical conditioning contribute to our survival. Salivation, for instance, helps us to digest food. Although skin conductance responses aren't especially important for us today, they probably were to our primate ancestors (Stern, Ray, & Davis, 1980), who found that moist fingers and toes came in handy for grasping tree limbs while fleeing from predators. Slightly wet fingertips help us adhere to things, as you'll discover if you moisten the tip of your index finger while turning to the next page of this book.

Moreover, without classical conditioning, we couldn't learn many important associations. People with psychopathic personalities (see Prologue and Chapter 15) are guiltless, callous, and dishonest, and they often commit impulsive crimes. Half a century ago, David Lykken (1957) found that psychopaths tend to show weak classical conditioning to painful electric shocks. He presented psychopaths and nonpsychopaths with repeated tones (CSs), followed almost immediately by electric shocks (UCSs) to the fingertips. Unsurprisingly, both psychopaths and nonpsychopaths showed a whopping skin conductance response (UCR) to the shocks themselves, meaning the shocks made them sweat. Lykken repeated this process over and over: tone–shock, tone–shock, tone–shock. Then, he presented participants with the tones (CSs) alone and measured their skin conductance responses, which were now the CRs. At the mere sound of the tones (CSs), nonpsychopaths began to sweat, having been conditioned to respond to them. Yet psychopaths exhibited weak skin conductance responses, that is, little or no sweating at all.

Lykken's finding probably helps to explain why psychopaths don't learn from punishment and often find themselves in trouble with the law (Hare, 2003; Newman & Kosson, 1986): They don't develop conditioned fear to signals of punishment. Most of us shudder at the mere sight of a police car appearing in our rearview mirrors, but psychopaths typically shrug off this stimulus with nonchalance. As a result of their indifference to signals of threat, psychopaths don't inhibit irresponsible and even criminal behaviors that the rest of us do (Fowles, 1987; Lykken, 1995).

ACQUISITION, EXTINCTION, AND SPONTANEOUS RECOVERY

Pavlov noted, and many others have confirmed, that classical conditioning occurs in three phases—acquisition, extinction, and spontaneous recovery.

Acquisition. In **acquisition,** we gradually learn—or acquire—the CR. If we look at **Figure 6.3a,** we'll see that as the CS and UCS are paired over and over again, the CR increases progressively in strength. The steepness of this curve varies somewhat depending on how close together in time the CS and UCS are presented. In general, the closer in time the pairing of CS and UCS, the faster learning occurs, with about a half second delay typically being the optimal pairing for learning. Longer delays usually decrease the speed and strength of the organism's response.

Extinction. In a process called **extinction,** the CR decreases in magnitude and eventually disappears when the CS is repeatedly presented alone, that is, without the UCS (see **Figure 6.3b**). After numerous presentations of the metronome without meat power, Pavlov's dogs eventually stopped salivating. Most psychologists once believed that extinction was similar to forgetting: The CR fades away over repeated trials, just as many memories gradually decay (see Chapter 7). Yet the truth is more complicated and interesting than that. Extinction is an active, rather than passive, process. During extinction a new response, which in the case of Pavlov's dogs was the *absence* of salivation, gradually "writes over" or inhibits the CR, namely, salivation. The extinguished CR doesn't vanish completely; it's merely overshadowed by the new behavior. This contrasts with most forms of traditional forgetting, in which the memory itself disappears. Interestingly, Pavlov had proposed this hypothesis in his writings, although few people believed him at the time. How do we know he was right? Read on.

Spontaneous Recovery. In a phenomenon called **spontaneous recovery,** a seemingly extinct CR reappears (often in somewhat weaker form) if the CS is presented again. It's as though the CR were lurking in the background, waiting to appear following another presentation of the CS. In a classic study, Pavlov (1927) presented the CS (tone from a metronome) alone again and again and extinguished the CR (salivation) because there was no UCS (mouth-watering meat powder) following it. Two hours later, he presented the CS again and the CR returned. The animal hadn't really forgotten the CR, just suppressed it.

Closely related to spontaneous recovery is the **renewal effect,** which occurs when we extinguish a response in a setting different from the one in which the animal acquired it. When we restore the animal to the original setting, the extinguished response reappears (Bouton, 1994). The renewal effect may help to explain why people with *phobias*—intense, irrational fears (see Chapter 15)—who've overcome their phobias often experience a reappearance of their symptoms when they return to the environment in which they acquired their fears (Denniston, Chang, & Miller, 2003). Even though it may sometimes lead to a return of phobias, the renewal effect is often adaptive. If we've been bitten by a snake in one part of a forest, it makes sense to experience fear when we find ourselves there again, even years later. That same snake or his slithery descendants may still be lying in wait in the same spot.

A person hiking through the woods may experience fear when she approaches an area if she's previously spotted a dangerous animal there.

APPLY YOUR THINKING

Following the first Gulf War in 1992, in which America attacked Iraq following Saddam Hussein's invasion of Kuwait, many veterans who suffered emotional trauma after fighting in the Vietnam War reported that their previously extinguished anxiety symptoms reappeared. How could spontaneous recovery help explain the return of their symptoms?

STIMULUS GENERALIZATION AND DISCRIMINATION

As much as classical conditioning helps us adapt to and learn new things, it would be virtually useless if we couldn't apply it to new stimuli. As Greek philosopher Heraclitus observed, "We never step into the same river twice." No two stimuli are identical; even our friends look a tiny bit different every time we see them. We need to learn to respond to stimuli that differ somewhat from those we originally encountered during conditioning.

Stimulus Generalization. Pavlov found that following classical conditioning, his dogs salivated not merely to the original metronome sound, but to sounds similar to it. This phenomenon is **stimulus generalization:** the process by which CSs that are similar, but not identical, to the original CS elicit a CR. Stimulus generalization occurs along a *generalization gradient:* The more similar to the original CS the new CS is, the stronger the CR will be (see **Figure 6.4**). Pavlov found that his dogs showed their largest amount of salivation to the original sound, with progressively less salivation to sounds that were less and less similar to it in pitch. Stimulus generalization allows us to transfer what we've learned to new things. Yet, like all good things, we can take it too far. People with phobias are often afraid not merely of the original stimulus that triggered their fear, but of stimuli only remotely resembling it.

Stimulus Discrimination. **Stimulus discrimination** is the flip side of the coin to stimulus generalization; it occurs when we exhibit a less pronounced CR to CSs that differ from the original CS. Stimulus discrimination helps us understand why we can enjoy scary movies. Although we may hyperventilate a bit while watching sharks circle the divers in the movie *Open Water,* we'd respond much more strongly if a shark chased us around in a tank at the aquarium. We've learned to discriminate between a motion picture stimulus and the real-world version of it.

spontaneous recovery
sudden reemergence of an extinct conditioned response after a delay in exposure to the conditioned stimulus

renewal effect
sudden reemergence of a conditioned response following extinction when an animal is returned to the environment in which the conditioned response was acquired

stimulus generalization
process by which conditioned stimuli similar, but not identical to, the original conditioned stimulus elicit a conditioned response

stimulus discrimination
displaying a less pronounced conditioned response to conditioned stimuli that differ from the original conditioned stimulus

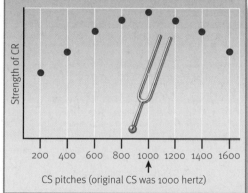

Figure 6.4 Generalization Gradient. The more similar to the original CS the new CS is (for example, Pavlov using a tone pitched close to the original tone's pitch), the stronger the CR will be.

Higher-order conditioning helps explain the seemingly mysterious "power of suggestion." Merely hearing "Want a Coke?" can make us feel thirsty on a hot summer day.

HIGHER-ORDER CONDITIONING

Taking conditioning a step further, organisms learn to develop conditioned associations to CSs that are associated with the original CS. If following Pavlov's original conditioning procedure, we pair a picture of a circle with the original CS (the tone), a dog eventually salivates to the circle as well as to the tone. This finding demonstrates **higher-order conditioning:** the process by which organisms develop classically conditioned responses to CSs associated with the original CS (Gewirtz & Davis, 2000). As we might expect, second-order conditioning—in which a new CS is paired with the original CS—tends to be weaker than garden-variety classical conditioning, and third-order conditioning—in which a third CS is paired with the second-order CS—is even weaker. Fourth-order conditioning and beyond is typically difficult or impossible.

Higher-order conditioning allows us to extend classical conditioning to a host of new stimuli. It helps explain why we feel thirsty after someone merely says "Coke" on a sweltering summer day. We've already come to associate the sight, sound, and smell of a Coca-Cola with quenching our thirst, and we eventually came to associate the word *Coke* with these CSs.

Higher-order conditioning also helps to explain some surprising findings concerning addictions to cigarettes, heroin, and other drugs. Many addictions are shaped in part by higher-order conditioning, with the context in which people take the drugs serving as a higher-order CS. People who don't generally smoke cigarettes may find themselves craving one at a party because they've smoked occasionally at previous parties with their friends who smoke. Behaviorists refer to these higher-order CSs as *occasion setters,* because they refer to the setting in which the CS occurs.

Although public perception has it that "breaking the grip" of heroin addiction is essentially impossible, research suggests that this is true only for some addicts (Sullum, 2003). Lee Robins and her colleagues (Robins, Helzer, & Davis, 1975) examined 451 Vietnam veterans who returned to the United States with cases of serious heroin addiction. Although many mental health experts confidently predicted an epidemic of heroin addiction upon the veterans' return to America, the problem was much less serious than expected. In Robins's sample, 86 percent of heroin-addicted Vietnam veterans lost their addiction shortly after returning to the United States. What happened? Because the occasion setters had changed from Vietnam to the United States, the veterans' classically conditioned responses to heroin extinguished. Of course, this fact doesn't take away from the seriousness of the addiction for the 14 percent of Robins's sample who remained addicted and often went on to abuse other drugs.

APPLICATIONS OF CLASSICAL CONDITIONING TO DAILY LIFE

Classical conditioning applies to myriad domains of everyday life. We'll consider five here: advertising, the acquisition of fears and phobias, the acquisition of fetishes, and disgust reactions.

Classical Conditioning and Advertising. Few people grasp the principles of classical conditioning, especially higher-order conditioning, better than advertisers. By repeatedly pairing the sights and sounds of products with photographs of handsome hunks and scantily clad beauties, marketing whizzes try to establish classically conditioned connections between their brands and positive emotions. They do so for a good reason: It works.

One researcher (Gorn, 1982) paired slides of either blue or beige pens (the CSs) with music that participants had rated as either enjoyable or not enjoyable (the UCSs). Then he gave participants the opportunity to select a pen upon departing the lab. Whereas 79 percent of participants who heard music they liked picked the pen that had been paired with music, only 30 percent of those who heard music they disliked picked the pen that had been paired with music.

Nevertheless, not all researchers who've paired products with pleasurable stimuli have succeeded in demonstrating classical conditioning effects (Smith, 2002). Two researchers (Gresham & Shimp, 1985) paired various products, like Coke, Colgate toothpaste, and Grape Nuts cereal, with television commercials that previous subjects had rated as generating pleasant, unpleasant, or neutral emotions. They found little evidence that these pairings affected participants' preferences for the ads. Nevertheless, their negative findings are

Advertisers use higher-order classical conditioning to get customers to associate their products with an inherently enjoyable stimulus.

higher-order conditioning
developing a conditioned response to a conditioned stimulus by virtue of its association with another conditioned stimulus

open to a rival explanation: latent inhibition. **Latent inhibition** refers to the fact that when we've experienced a CS alone many times, it's difficult to classically condition it to another stimulus (Vaitl & Lipp, 1997). Because the investigators relied on brands with which participants were already familiar, their negative findings may be attributable to latent inhibition. Indeed, when researchers have used novel brands, they've generally been able to show classical conditioning effects (Stuart, Shimp, & Engle, 1987).

Ruling Out Rival Hypotheses

The Acquisition of Fears: The Strange Tale of Little Albert. Can classical conditioning help explain how we come to fear or avoid stimuli? John B. Watson, the founder of behaviorism (see Prologue), answered this question in 1920 when he and his graduate student, Rosalie Rayner, performed what must be regarded as one of the most ethically questionable studies in the history of psychology. Here's what they did.

Watson and Rayner (1920) set out in part to show that the Freudian view (see Prologue and Chapter 14) of phobias, which proposed that phobias stem from deep-seated conflicts buried in the unconscious, was wrong. To do so, they recruited a 9-month-old infant who'll be forever known in the psychological literature as Little Albert. Little Albert was fond of furry little creatures, like white rats. But Watson and Rayner were about to change that.

Watson and Raynor first allowed Little Albert to play with a rat. But only seconds afterward, Watson snuck up behind Little Albert and struck a gong with a steel hammer, creating an earsplitting noise and startling him out of his wits. After seven such pairings of CS (rat) and UCS (loud sound from gong), Little Albert displayed a CR (fear) to the rat alone. This fear was still present when Watson and Rayner exposed Little Albert to the rat 5 days later. Moreover, Watson and Rayner observed that Little Albert had become a victim of stimulus generalization, coming to fear not merely rats, but also a rabbit, a dog, a furry coat, and, to a lesser extent, a Santa Claus mask and John B. Watson's hair. Fortunately, Little Albert also demonstrated at least some stimulus discrimination, as he didn't display much fear toward cotton balls or the hair of Dr. Watson's research assistants.

Classic study in which a 9-month-old boy was conditioned to fear white furry objects. Here, Little Albert, with John B. Watson and Rosalie Rayner, is crying in response to a Santa Claus mask.

Watson and Rayner's demonstration is only a case study. As we saw in Chapter 2, case studies are limited in the conclusions they allow; for example, we can't generalize from Little Albert's case to the development of phobias in other children. But the Little Albert case provides an *existence proof* (see Chapter 2) that classical conditioning can produce phobia-like states in humans. Although not everyone has successfully replicated Watson and Rayner's findings (Harris, 1979; Jones, 1930), Watson and Rayner were probably right that Little Albert's fears arose in part from classical conditioning. Nevertheless, these replication failures may imply that there's more to developing phobias than classical conditioning alone; we'll come back to this point later in the chapter.

Replicability

Incidentally, no one knows what became of poor Little Albert. His mother withdrew him from the study about a month after it began, never to be heard from again. Needless to say, because inducing a phobia-like condition in an infant raises a host of serious ethical questions, Watson and Rayner's Little Albert study would never get past a modern-day college or university IRB (see Chapter 2).

Phobias. Do you suffer from *paraskavedekatriaphobia*? If so, don't be concerned, because you aren't the only person who's afraid of Friday the 13th.

Higher-order conditioning allows our learning to be remarkably flexible. We can develop fears of many stimuli, although certain phobias, such as those of snakes, spiders, heights, water, and blood, are considerably more widespread than others (American Psychiatric Association, 2000). Other, more exotic phobias, like fear of being tickled by feathers (*pteronophobia*), fear of clowns (*coulrophobia*), fear of flutes (*aulophobia*), and fear of bald people (*peladophobia*), are exceedingly rare. See **Table 6.1** on page 240 for a sampling of phobias.

The good news is that if classical conditioning can contribute to our acquiring phobias, it can also contribute to our conquering them. Mary Cover Jones, a student of Watson, treated a 3-year-old named Little Peter, who had a phobia of rabbits. Jones (1924) treated Peter's fear successfully by gradually introducing him to a white rabbit while giving him a piece of his favorite candy. As she moved the rabbit increasingly close to him, the sight of

latent inhibition
difficulty in establishing classical conditioning to a conditioned stimulus we've repeatedly experienced alone, that is, without the unconditioned stimulus

Table 6.1 Phobias Galore. This sampling of phobias—some common, some exceedingly rare—illustrates just how enormously varied people's fears can be. Many of these phobias can be acquired at least partly by classical conditioning.

Alliumphobia: Fear of garlic	*Melissophobia:* Fear of bees
Arachibutyrophobia: Fear of peanut butter sticking to the roof of your mouth	*Ophidiophobia:* Fear of snakes
Brontophobia: Fear of thunderstorms	*Peladophobia:* Fear of bald people
Bufonaophobia: Fear of toads	*Pentheraphobia:* Fear of one's mother-in-law
Catoptrophobia: Fear of mirrors	*Pogonophobia:* Fear of beards
Elurophobia: Fear of cats	*Rhytiphobia:* Fear of getting wrinkles
Epistaxiaophobia: Fear of nosebleeds	*Samhainophobia:* Fear of Halloween
Latrophobia: Fear of doctors	*Taphephobia:* Fear of being buried alive
Lachanophobia: Fear of vegetables	*Xyrophobia:* Fear of razors

Michael Domjan and his colleagues used classical conditioning to instill a fetish in male quails.

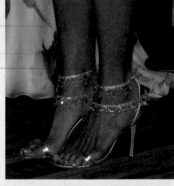

Some researchers have suggested that classical conditioning may similarly help to explain some human fetishes.

fetishism
sexual attraction to nonliving things

the rabbit eventually came to elicit a new CR: pleasure rather than fear. Modern-day psychotherapists, although rarely feeding their clients candy, use similar practices to eliminate phobias. They may pair feared stimuli with relaxation or other pleasurable stimuli (Wolpe, 1990; see Chapter 16).

Fetishes. There's also good reason to believe that **fetishism**—sexual attraction to nonliving things—often arises in part from classical conditioning (Akins, 2004). Like phobias, fetishes come in a bewildering variety of forms: they can become attached to shoes, stockings, and just about anything else.

Although the origins of human fetishes are controversial, Michael Domjan and his colleagues were successful in classically conditioning fetishes in male Japanese quails. In one study, they presented male quails with a cylindrical object made of terrycloth, followed by a female quail with which they happily mated. After thirty such pairings, about half of the male quails attempted to mate with the cylindrical object when it appeared alone (Koksal et al., 2004). Although the generalizability of these findings to humans is unclear, there's good evidence that at least some people develop fetishes by the repeated pairing of neutral objects with sexual activity (Rachman & Hodgson, 1968; Weinberg, Williams, & Calhan, 1995).

Disgust Reactions. Imagine that a researcher asked you to try on a perfectly preserved 70-year-old sweater. No problem, right? Well, let's instead imagine that this researcher asked you to try on this sweater, but informed you that Adolph Hitler had once worn it. If you're like most subjects in the studies of Paul Rozin and his colleagues, you'd hesitate (D'Amato, 1998).

Rozin (who's earned the nickname "Dr. Disgust") and his colleagues have found that we acquire disgust reactions with surprising ease. In most cases, these reactions are probably the product of classical conditioning, because CSs associated with disgusting UCSs come to elicit disgust themselves. In many cases, disgust reactions are tied to stimuli that are biologically important to us, such as animals or objects that are dirty or potentially poisonous (Rozin & Fallon, 1987). Rozin and his colleagues found that subjects who happily gobble up a piece of fudge suddenly express a decided reluctance to do so when the fudge is shaped like dog feces (Rozin, Millman, & Nemeroff, 1986).

In another study, Rozin and his collaborators asked participants to drink from two glasses of water, both of which contained sugar (sucrose). In one case, the sucrose came from a bottle labeled "sucrose"; in another, it came from a bottle labeled "Sodium Cyanide, Poison." The investigators told subjects that both bottles were completely safe. They even asked subjects to select which label went with which glass, proving the labels were meaningless. Even so, subjects were hesitant to drink from the glass that contained the sucrose labeled as poisonous (Rozin, Markwith, & Ross, 1990). Participants' responses in this study were irrational, but perhaps understandable: They were probably relying on the heuristic "better safe than sorry." Classical conditioning helps keep us safe, even if it goes too far on occasion.

PsychoMythology
Are We What We Eat?

Many of us have heard that "we are what we eat," but in the 1950s the flamboyant psychologist James McConnell took this proverb quite literally. McConnell became convinced he'd discovered a means of chemically transferring learning from one animal to another. Indeed, for many years psychology textbooks informed undergraduates that scientists could chemically transfer learning across animals.

McConnell's animal of choice was the *planaria*, a flatworm that's typically no more than a few inches long. Using classical conditioning, McConnell and his colleagues exposed planaria to a light, which served as the CS, while pairing it with a 1-second electric shock, which served as the UCS. When planaria receive an electric shock, they contract reflexively. After numerous pairings between light and shock, the light itself causes planaria to contract (Thompson & McConnell, 1955).

McConnell wanted to find out whether he could chemically transfer the memory of this classical conditioning experience to another planaria. His approach was brutally simple. Relying on the fact that many planaria are miniature cannibals, he chopped up the trained planaria and fed them to their fellow worms. Remarkably, McConnell (1962) reported that planaria who'd gobbled up classically conditioned planaria acquired classically conditioned reactions to the light more quickly than planaria who hadn't.

Understandably, McConnell's memory transfer studies generated enormous excitement. Imagine if McConnell were right! You could sign up for your introductory psychology class, swallow a pill containing all of the psychological knowledge you'd need to get an A, and . . . voila, you're now an expert psychologist. Indeed, McConnell went directly to the general public with his findings, proclaiming in *Time, Newsweek,* and other popular magazines that scientists were on the verge of developing a "memory pill" (Rilling, 1996).

Yet it wasn't long before the wind went out of McConnell's scientific sails: Scientists couldn't replicate his findings. Adding insult to injury, researchers brought up a host of alternative explanations for his results. For one, McConnell hadn't ruled out the possibility that his findings were attributable to **pseudoconditioning,** which occurs when the CS by itself triggers the UCR. That is, he hadn't excluded the possibility that the light itself caused the planaria to contract (Collins & Pinch, 1993), perhaps leading him to the false conclusion that the cannibalistic planaria had acquired a classically conditioned reaction to the light. Eventually, after years of intense debate and failed replications, the scientific community concluded that McConnell had fooled himself into seeing something that was never there. His planaria lab closed its doors in 1971.

Strange as it was, McConnell's story had an even stranger twist. On November 15, 1985, he went to his mailbox to open an innocent-looking package. When he did, it exploded. Fortunately, McConnell wasn't seriously injured, although he suffered permanent hearing loss. The package had been mailed by a man named Theodore Kaczynski, better known as the "Unabomber." Kaczynski, a former mathematics professor later diagnosed with paranoid schizophrenia, had sent bombs to several individuals around the country who were ardent proponents of technological innovation. Apparently Kaczynski had read McConnell's popular articles about the possibility of using memory pills and other revolutionary behavior change techniques for transforming society and identified him as a target (Rilling, 1996).

James McConnell and his colleagues paired a light with an electric shock, which caused the *planaria* worm to contract reflexively.

Replicability
Ruling Out Rival Hypotheses

pseudoconditioning
an apparent conditioned response that actually turns out to be an unconditioned response to the conditioned stimulus

Through operant conditioning, researchers taught pigeons to distinguish paintings by Monet (*top*) from those of Picasso (*bottom*).

Operant Conditioning

What do the following four examples have in common?

- Using bird feed as a reward, a behavioral psychologist teaches a pigeon to distinguish paintings by Monet from paintings by Picasso. By the end of the training, the pigeon is a veritable art aficionado.

- Using fish as a treat, a trainer teaches a dolphin to jump out of the water, spin three times, splash in the water, and propel itself through a hoop.

- In his initial attempt at playing tennis, a frustrated 12-year-old hits his opponent's serve into the net the first fifteen times. After 2 hours of practice, he returns his opponent's serve successfully more than half the time.

- A hospitalized patient with dissociative identity disorder (formerly known as multiple personality disorder), displays features of an "alter" personality whenever staff members pay attention to him. When they ignore him, his alter personality seemingly vanishes.

The answer: All are examples of operant conditioning. The first, incidentally, comes from an actual study (Watanabe, Sakamoto, & Wakita, 1995). **Operant conditioning** is learning controlled by the consequences of the organism's behavior. In each of these examples, superficially different as they are, the organism's behavior is shaped by what comes after it, namely, reward. Psychologists also refer to operant conditioning as *instrumental conditioning*, because the organism's response serves an instrumental function. That is, the organism "gets something" out of the response, like food, sex, attention, or avoiding something unpleasant.

Behaviorists refer to the behaviors emitted by the animal to receive a reward as *operants,* because the animal "operates" on its environment to get what it wants. Dropping 75 cents into a soda machine is an operant, as is asking out an appealing classmate. In the first case, our reward is a refreshing drink and in the second, a hot date if we're lucky.

How could operant conditioning principles explain this boy's ability to improve his tennis game with practice?

OPERANT CONDITIONING: WHAT IT IS AND HOW IT DIFFERS FROM CLASSICAL CONDITIONING

Operant conditioning differs from classical conditioning in three important ways, which we've highlighted in **Table 6.2.**

operant conditioning
learning controlled by the consequences of the organism's behavior

Table 6.2 Key Differences between Operant and Classical Conditioning.

	Classical Conditioning	Operant Conditioning
Target behavior is . . .	Elicited automatically	Emitted voluntarily
Reward is . . .	Provided unconditionally	Contingent on behavior
Behavior depends primarily on . . .	Autonomic nervous system	Skeletal muscles

(1) In classical conditioning, the organism's response is *elicited,* that is, "pulled out" of the organism by the UCS, and later the CS. Remember that in classical conditioning the UCR is a reflexive and automatic response that doesn't require training. In operant conditioning, the organism's response is *emitted,* that is, generated by the organism in a seemingly voluntary fashion.

(2) In classical conditioning, the animal's reward is independent of what it does. Pavlov gave his dogs meat powder regardless of whether, or how much, they salivated. In operant conditioning, the animal's reward is contingent—that is, dependent—on what it does. If the animal doesn't emit a response in an operant conditioning paradigm, it comes out empty-handed (or in the case of a dog, empty-pawed).

(3) In classical conditioning, the organism's responses depend primarily on the autonomic nervous system (see Chapter 3). In operant conditioning, the organism's responses depend primarily on the skeletal muscles. That is, in contrast to classical conditioning, in which learning involves changes in heart rate, breathing, perspiration, and other bodily systems, in operant conditioning learning involves changes in voluntary motor behavior.

THE LAW OF EFFECT

Generations of introductory psychology students have learned to recite the famous **law of effect,** put forth by psychologist E. L. Thorndike. The law of effect is the first and most important commandment of operant conditioning: *If a response, in the presence of a stimulus, is followed by a satisfying state of affairs, the bond between stimulus and response will be strengthened.*

This statement means simply that if an event that precedes something we do is followed by a reward, we're more like to repeat it. Psychologists sometimes refer to early forms of behaviorism as S-R psychology (*S* stands for *stimulus, R* for *response*). According to S-R theorists, most of our complex behaviors reflect the accumulation of associations between stimuli and responses: the sight of a close friend and saying hello, or the smell of a delicious hamburger and reaching for it on our plate. S-R theorists maintain that almost everything we do voluntarily—driving a car, eating a sandwich, or planting a kiss on someone's lips—results from the gradual buildup of S-R bonds due to the law of effect. Thorndike (1898) discovered the law of effect in a classic study of cats and puzzle boxes. Here's what he did.

Thorndike placed a hungry cat in a box and put a tantalizing piece of fish just outside. To escape from the box, the cat needed to hit upon (literally) the right solution, which was pressing on a lever or pulling on a string inside the box (see **Figure 6.5**).

When Thorndike first placed the cat in the puzzle box, it typically flailed around aimlessly in a frantic effort to escape. Then, by sheer accident, the cat eventually found the correct solution, scurried out of the box, and gobbled up its delectable treat. Thorndike wanted to find out what would happen to the cat's behavior over time. Once it figured out the solution to the puzzle, would it then get it right every time?

Thorndike found that the cat's time to escape from the puzzle box decreased *gradually* over sixty trials. There was no point at which the cat abruptly realized what it needed to do to escape. According to Thorndike, his cats were learning by trial and error through the steady buildup of associations. Indeed, Thorndike and many other S-R theorists went so far as to conclude that all learning, including all human learning, occurs by trial and error. For them, S-R bonds are gradually "stamped into" the organism by reward.

These findings, Thorndike concluded, provide a crushing blow to the hypothesis that cats learn by **insight,** that is, by grasping the nature of the problem. Had his cats possessed insight into the nature of the problem, the results presumably would have looked like what we see in **Figure 6.6**. This figure illustrates what psychologists term the *aha reaction:* "Aha—I got it!" Once the animal solves the problem, it gets it correct just about every time after that. Yet Thorndike never found an Aha! moment: The time to a correct solution decreased only gradually.

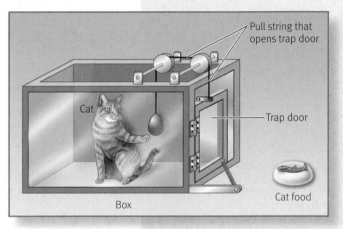

Figure 6.5 Thorndike's Puzzle Box. Thorndike's classic puzzle box research seemed to suggest that cats solve problems solely through trial and error.

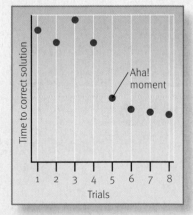

Figure 6.6 "Aha!" Reaction. Insight learning: Once the animal solves the problem, it gets the answer right almost every time after that.

law of effect
principle asserting if a stimulus followed by a behavior results in a reward, the stimulus is more likely to elicit the behavior in the future

insight
grasping the nature of a problem

Skinner box
small animal chamber constructed by Skinner to allow sustained periods of conditioning to be administered and behaviors to be recorded unsupervised

reinforcement
outcome or consequence of a behavior that strengthens the probability of the behavior

positive reinforcement
positive outcome or consequence of a behavior that strengthens the probability of the behavior

negative reinforcement
removal of a negative outcome or consequence of a behavior that strengthens the probability of the behavior

Positive reinforcement in action: Smiling at your professor when he or she performs a target behavior—like moving away from the podium—can increase the likelihood of that target behavior.

B. F. SKINNER AND REINFORCEMENT

Thorndike's pioneering discoveries laid the groundwork for research on operant conditioning. B. F. Skinner then kicked it up a notch using electronic technology.

Skinner found Thorndike's experimental setup unwieldy because the researcher had to stick around to place the unhappy cat back into the puzzle box following each trial. This limitation made it difficult to study the buildup of associations in ongoing operant behavior over hours, days, or weeks. So he developed what came to be known as a **Skinner box** (more formally, an operant chamber), which electronically records an animal's responses and prints out a *cumulative record,* or graph, of the animal's activity. A Skinner box typically contains a bar that delivers food when pressed, a food dispenser, and often a light that signals when reward is forthcoming (see **Figure 6.7**). With this setup, Skinner studied the operant behavior of rats, pigeons, and other animals and mapped out their responses to reward. By allowing a device to record behavior without any direct human observation, Skinner ran the risk of missing some important behaviors that the box wasn't designed to record. Nonetheless, his discoveries forever altered the landscape of psychology.

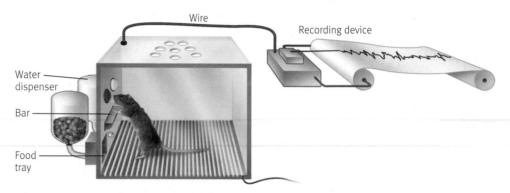

Figure 6.7 Rat in Skinner Box and Electronic Device for Recording the Rat's Behavior. B. F. Skinner devised a small chamber (the Skinner box) containing a bar that the rat presses to obtain food, a food dispenser, and often a light that signals when reward is forthcoming. An electronic device graphs the rat's responses in the researcher's absence.

TERMINOLOGY OF OPERANT CONDITIONING

To understand Skinner's research, you need to learn a bit of psychological jargon. There are three key concepts in Skinnerian psychology: reinforcement, punishment, and discriminant stimulus.

Reinforcement. Up to this point, we've used the term *reward* to refer to any pleasant consequence that makes a behavior more likely to occur. But Skinner found this term imprecise. He preferred the term **reinforcement,** meaning any outcome that strengthens the probability of a response (Skinner, 1953, 1971).

Skinner distinguished **positive reinforcement,** when we administer something pleasant, from **negative reinforcement,** when we take away something unpleasant. Positive reinforcement could be giving a child a Hershey's Kiss when he picks up his toys; negative reinforcement could be ending a child's time-out for bad behavior once she's stopped whining. In both cases, the outcome for the organism is satisfying.

Hundreds of psychology students over the years have demonstrated the power of reinforcement using an unconventional participant: their professor. In the game Condition Your Professor (Vyse, 1997), a class of introductory psychology students agrees to provide positive reinforcement—like smiling or nodding their heads—to their professor whenever he or she moves in a particular direction, such as to the far left side of the room. Your authors know of one famous introductory psychology teacher who spent almost all of his time lecturing from behind his podium. During one class, his students smiled profusely and nodded their heads whenever he ventured out from behind the podium. Sure enough, by the end of class the professor was spending most of his time away from the podium. You and your classmates might want to attempt a similar stunt with your introductory psychology professor: Just don't mention we suggested it.

Punishment. We shouldn't confuse negative reinforcement with **punishment,** which is any outcome that weakens the probability of a response. Punishment typically involves administering an unpleasant stimulus, such as a physical shock or a spanking, or an unpleasant social outcome, like laughing at someone. It can also involve the removal of a positive stimulus, such as a favorite toy or article of clothing.

We also shouldn't confuse punishment with the disciplinary practices often associated with it. Skinner, who insisted on precision in language, argued that certain actions that might superficially appear to be punishments are actually reinforcements. He defined reinforcements and punishments solely in terms of their consequences. Consider this scenario: A mother rushes into her 3-year-old son's bedroom and yells "Stop that!" each time she hears him kicking the wall. Is she punishing the child's demanding behavior? There's no way to tell without knowing the consequences. If the bad behavior increases following the scolding, then perhaps the child is kicking the wall to get attention. If so, the mother is reinforcing, rather than punishing, his angry demands. Negative reinforcement, like all kinds of reinforcement, strengthens the probability of a response. In contrast, punishment weakens it (see **Table 6.3**).

"Oh, not bad. The light comes on, I press the bar, they write me a check. How about you?"

Table 6.3 Distinguishing Reinforcement from Punishment.

	Procedure	Effect on Behavior	Typical Example
Positive Reinforcement	Presenting a desirable stimulus	Increases target behavior	Gold star on homework
Negative Reinforcement	Removing an undesirable stimulus	Increases target behavior	Static on phone that subsides when you move to a different spot in your room
Punishment	Presenting an undesirable stimulus	Decreases target behavior	Scolding by parents

Try labeling each of the following examples as an instance of either negative reinforcement or punishment and explain why (you can find the answers written upside-down in the margin at the bottom of this page):

(1) A boy keeps making noise in the back of a classroom despite a teacher's repeated warnings. The teacher finally sends him to the principal's office. When he returns 2 hours later, he's much quieter.

(2) A woman with diabetes works hard to control her blood sugar through diet and exercise. As a result, her doctor allows her to discontinue administering her unpleasant daily insulin shots, which increases her attempts to eat healthily and exercise.

(3) A parole board releases a previously aggressive criminal from prison early for being a "model citizen" within the institution over the past 5 years. On his release, he continues to behave in a law-abiding manner.

(4) A woman yells at her roommate for leaving dirty clothing scattered all around her apartment. Her roommate apologizes and never makes a mess again.

Does punishment work in the long run? Popular wisdom tells us that it usually does: "Spare the rod, spoil the child." Yet Skinner (1953) and most of his followers argued against the routine use of punishment to change behavior. They believed that reinforcement alone could shape most human behaviors for the better.

punishment
outcome or consequence of a behavior that weakens the probability of the behavior

Answers: (1) punishment; because the boy's teacher reduced his rate of noise-making. (2) negative reinforcement; because her doctor increased the woman's rates of eating well and exercising. (3) negative reinforcement; because the parole board increased the prisoner's rate of law-abiding behavior. (4) punishment; because the woman decreased her roommate's rate of messy behavior.

Forcing a student to see the principal is typically a form of punishment; nevertheless, it can instead serve as a negative reinforcement if it allows the student to escape from an unpleasant class.

Skinner and his followers believed that reinforcement was generally much more effective in shaping children's behavior than punishment.

Correlation vs. Causation

According to Skinner and others (Azrin & Holz, 1966), punishment has several disadvantages:

(1) Punishment tells the organism only what not to do, not *what* to do. A child who's punished for throwing a tantrum won't learn how to deal with frustration more constructively.

(2) Punishment often creates anxiety, which in turn interferes with future learning.

(3) Punishment may encourage subversive behavior, prompting people to become sneakier about the situations in which they can and can't display forbidden behavior. A child who's punished for grabbing his brother's toys may learn to grab his brother's toys only when his parents aren't looking.

(4) Punishment from parents may provide a model for children's aggressive behavior (Straus, Sugarman, & Giles-Sims, 1997). A child whose parents slap him when he misbehaves may "get the message" that slapping is acceptable.

Numerous researchers have reported that the use of physical punishment by parents is positively correlated with aggressive behavior in children (Fang & Corso, 2007; Gershoff, 2002). Across many studies, Murray Strauss (1996) and his colleagues found that physical punishment is associated with more behavioral problems in children. In a study of 1,575 subjects drawn from the general population, Cathy Widom and her colleagues further found that physically abused children are at heightened risk for aggressiveness in adulthood (Widom, 1989a, 1989b). Many researchers interpreted this finding as implying that early physical abuse causes aggression.

Widom (1989a) concluded that her findings reveal the operation of a "cycle of violence," whereby parental aggression begets childhood aggression. When these children become parents, many become abusers themselves. Similarly, Elizabeth Gershoff (2002) conducted a meta-analysis (see Chapter 2) of eighty-eight studies of corporal punishment based on a whopping 39,309 participants. Although she found some evidence that corporal punishment is associated with short-term improvements in children's behavior, she also found that a history of such punishment in childhood is associated with an increased probability of becoming an abuser in adulthood.

Yet we must remember that these studies are correlational and don't demonstrate causality. Other interpretations are possible. For example, because children share half of their genes with each parent, and because aggression is partly heritable (Krueger, Hicks, & McGue, 2001), the correlation between parents' physical aggression and their children's aggression may be due to the fact that parents who are physically aggressive pass on this genetic predisposition to their children (DiLalla & Gottesman, 1991). It's also conceivable that the causal arrow is reversed: Children who are aggressive may be difficult to control and therefore elicit physical abuse from their parents. This hypothesis doesn't in any way excuse physical abuse or imply that it's acceptable, but it may help to explain why it occurs. In addition, it's possible that mild levels of punishment are effective, but that severe forms of punishment, including abuse, aren't (Baumrind, Larazelere, & Cowan, 1992).

The association between physical punishment and childhood behavior problems may depend on race and culture. Spanking and other forms of physical discipline are correlated positively with childhood behavior problems in Caucasian families, but correlated negatively in African American families (Lansford, Deater-Deckard, Dodge, Bates, & Petit, 2004). Apparently, physical discipline means something different—perhaps a deep commitment to rearing children properly—in African American than in Caucasian families. Moreover, spanking tends to be more predictive of higher levels of childhood aggression and anxiety in countries in which spanking is rare, like China or Thailand, than in countries in which it's common, like Kenya or India (Lansford et al., 2005). The reasons for this difference aren't clear, although children who are spanked in countries in which spanking is more culturally accepted may feel less stigmatized than children in countries in which it's culturally condemned.

Still, that's not to say that we should never use punishment, only that we should use it sparingly. Most research suggests that punishment works best when it's delivered consis-

In some countries, such as China and Thailand, spanking is uncommon.

tently and follows the undesired behavior promptly (Brennan & Mednick, 1994). In particular, immediate punishment sometimes tends to be effective, whereas delayed punishment is often useless (Church, 1969; McCord, 2006; Moffitt, 1983). Punishment of an undesired behavior also works best when we simultaneously reinforce a desired behavior (Azrin & Holz, 1966).

> ### APPLY YOUR THINKING
> How would you attempt to test the hypothesis that parents' spanking actually *causes* greater aggression in their children?

Discriminant Stimulus. The final critical term in operant conditioning lingo is **discriminant stimulus,** typically abbreviated simply as S_d. A discriminant stimulus is any stimulus that signals the presence of reinforcement. When we snap our fingers at a dog in the hopes of having it come over to us, the dog may approach us to get a much-appreciated petting. For the dog, our finger snapping is an S_d: It's a signal that if it comes near us, it will receive reinforcement. According to behaviorists, we're responding to S_ds virtually all the time, even if we're not consciously aware of it. When a friend waves at us, and we walk over to her to say hi in return, we're responding to an S_d.

Acquisition, Extinction, Spontaneous Recovery, and Stimulus Generalization and Discrimination. If you feel you're experiencing a case of déjà vu upon reading these bolded terms, don't be concerned, because you've indeed seen all of them before. *Acquisition, extinction, spontaneous recovery, stimulus generalization,* and *stimulus discrimination* apply just as much to operant conditioning as to classical conditioning. We can find the definitions in **Table 6.4.** Below, we'll examine how three of these concepts apply to operant conditioning.

Table 6.4 Definition Reminders of Important Concepts in Both Classical and Operant Conditioning.

Term	Definition
Acquisition	Learning phase during which a response is established
Extinction	Gradual reduction and eventual elimination of the response after a stimulus is presented repeatedly
Spontaneous Recovery	Sudden reemergence of an extinguished response after a delay
Stimulus Generalization	Eliciting a response to stimuli similar to but not identical to the original stimulus
Stimulus Discrimination	Displaying a less pronounced response to stimuli that differs from the original stimulus

Extinction. In operant conditioning, extinction occurs when we stop delivering reinforcement to a previously reinforced behavior. Gradually, this behavior declines in frequency and disappears. If parents give a screaming child a toy to quiet her, they may be inadvertently reinforcing her behavior, because she's learning to scream to get something. If parents buy earplugs and stop placating the child by giving toys, the screaming behavior gradually extinguishes. In such cases we often see an *extinction burst*. That is, shortly after withdrawing reinforcement the undesired behavior initially increases in intensity, probably because the child is trying harder to get reinforcement. So there's some truth to the old saying that things sometimes need to get worse before they get better.

When parents stop giving this boy his favorite toy when he screams, he'll initially scream harder to get what he wants. Eventually he'll realize it won't work and give up the screaming behavior.

discriminant stimulus (S_d)
stimulus associated with the presence of reinforcement

Stimulus Discrimination. As we mentioned earlier, one group of investigators used food reinforcement to train pigeons to distinguish paintings by Monet from those of Picasso (Watanabe et al., 1995). That's stimulus discrimination, because the pigeons are learning to tell the difference between two different types of stimuli.

Stimulus Generalization. Interestingly, these investigators also found that their pigeons displayed stimulus generalization. Following operant conditioning, they distinguished paintings by impressionist artists whose styles were similar to Monet's, such as Renoir, from paintings by cubist artists similar to Picasso, such as Braque.

PRINCIPLES OF REINFORCEMENT

Before we tackle a new principle of behavior, try answering this question: If we want to train a dog to perform a trick, like catching a Frisbee, should we reinforce it for (a) each successful catch or (b) only some of its successful catches? If you're like most people, you'd answer (a), which seems to match our commonsense notions regarding the effects of reinforcement. It seems logical to assume that the more consistent the reinforcement, the more consistent will be the resulting behavior.

Partial Reinforcement. Nevertheless, Skinner's principle of **partial reinforcement,** sometimes called *Humphrey's paradox* after psychologist Lloyd Humphreys (1938) who first described it, shows that our intuitions about reinforcement are backward. According to the principle of partial reinforcement, behaviors we reinforce only occasionally are slower to extinguish than those we reinforce continuously, that is, every time. Although this point may seem counterintuitive, consider that an animal that expects to be rewarded every time it performs the target behavior may become reluctant to continue performing the behavior if the reinforcement becomes undependable. However, if an animal has learned that the behavior will be rewarded only occasionally, it's more likely to continue the behavior in the hopes of getting reinforcement.

So if we want an animal to maintain a trick for a long time, we should actually reinforce it for correct responses only occasionally. Skinner (1968) noted that continuous reinforcement allows animals to learn new behaviors more quickly, but that partial reinforcement leads to a greater resistance to extinction. This principle may help to explain why some people remain trapped for years in terribly dysfunctional, even abusive, relationships. Some relationship partners provide intermittent reinforcement to their significant others, treating them miserably most of the time but treating them well on rare occasions. This pattern of partial reinforcement may keep individuals "hooked" in relationships that aren't working.

Schedules of Reinforcement. Skinner (1938) found that animals' behaviors differ depending on the **schedule of reinforcement,** that is, the pattern of delivering reinforcement. Remarkably, the effects of these reinforcement schedules are consistent across species as diverse as cockroaches, pigeons, rats, and humans. Although there are numerous schedules of reinforcement, we'll discuss the four major ones here. The principal reinforcement schedules vary along two dimensions:

(1) *The consistency of administering reinforcement.* Some reinforcement contingencies are *fixed,* whereas others are *variable.* That is, in some cases experimenters provide reinforcement on a regular (fixed) basis, whereas in others they provide reinforcement on an irregular (variable) basis.

(2) *The basis of administering reinforcement.* Some reinforcement schedules operate on *ratio* schedules, whereas others operate on *interval* schedules. In ratio schedules, the experimenter reinforces the animal based on the *number of responses* it's emitted. In interval schedules, the experimenter reinforces the animal based on the *amount of time* elapsed since the last reinforcement.

We can cross these two dimensions to arrive at four schedules of reinforcement (see **Figure 6.8**):

(1) In a **fixed ratio (FR) schedule,** we provide reinforcement after a regular number of responses. For example, we could give a rat a pellet after it presses the lever in a Skinner box fifteen times.

(2) In a **fixed interval (FI) schedule,** we provide reinforcement for producing the response at least once after a specified amount of time has passed. For example, a worker in a clock

Behaviors that we reinforce only occasionally (partial reinforcement) are slowest to extinguish. So to train a dog to catch a Frisbee, we should reinforce it only intermittently.

partial reinforcement
only occasional reinforcement of a behavior, resulting in slower extinction than if the behavior had been reinforced continually

schedule of reinforcement
pattern of reinforcing a behavior

fixed ratio (FR) schedule
pattern in which we provide reinforcement following a regular number of responses

fixed interval (FI) schedule
pattern in which we provide reinforcement for producing the response at least once following a specified time interval

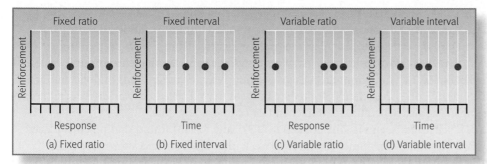

Figure 6.8 Four Major Reinforcement Schedules. The four major reinforcement schedules are (a) fixed ratio, (b) fixed interval, (c) variable ratio, and (d) variable interval.

factory might get paid every Friday for the work she's done, as long as she's generated at least one clock during that 1-week interval.

(3) In a **variable ratio (VR) schedule**, we provide reinforcement after a specific number of responses on average, but the precise number of responses required during any given period varies randomly. A pigeon on a variable ratio schedule with an average ratio of ten might receive a piece of bird feed after six pecks, then after twelve pecks, then after one peck, then after twenty-one pecks, with the average of these ratios being ten.

(4) In a **variable interval (VI) schedule**, we provide reinforcement for producing the response after an average time interval, with the actual interval varying randomly. For example, we could give a dog a treat for performing a trick on a variable interval schedule with an average interval of 8 minutes. This dog may have to perform the trick sometime during a 7-minute interval the first time, then a 1-minute interval the second time, then a 20-minute interval, and then a 4-minute interval, with the average of these intervals being 8 minutes.

Skinner discovered that different reinforcement schedules yield distinctive patterns of responding (see **Figure 6.9**). Ratio schedules tend to yield higher rates of responding than do interval schedules. This finding makes intuitive sense. If a dog gets a treat every five times he rolls over, he's going to roll over more often than if he gets a treat every 5 minutes, regardless of whether he rolls over once or twenty times during that interval. In addition, variable schedules tend to yield more consistent rates of responding than do fixed schedules. This finding also makes intuitive sense. If we never know when our next treat is coming, it's in our best interests to keep emitting the response to ensure we've emitted it enough times to earn the reward.

Two other features of reinforcement schedules are worth noting. First, fixed interval schedules are associated with a "scalloped" pattern of responding. This *FI scallop* reflects the fact that the animal "waits" for a time after it receives reinforcement, and then increases its rate of responding just before the interval is up as it begins to anticipate reinforcement.

Second, variable ratio (VR) schedules usually yield the highest rates of responding of all. It's for this reason that there's one place where we can be guaranteed to find a VR

Gambling is a prime example of a behavior reinforced by a variable ratio reinforcement schedule. The big pay-off may come at any time, so people keep rolling the dice.

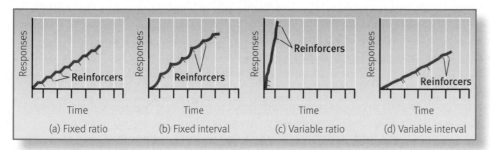

Figure 6.9 Typical Response Patterns for the Four Reinforcement Schedules. Note the "scalloped" pattern in (b), the fixed interval response pattern. The subject decreases the reinforced behavior immediately after receiving reinforcement, then increases the behavior in anticipation of reinforcement as the time for reinforcement approaches.

variable ratio (VR) schedule
pattern in which we provide reinforcement after a specific number of responses on average, with the number varying randomly

variable interval (VI) schedule
pattern in which we provide reinforcement for producing the response following an average time interval, with the interval varying randomly

schedule: A casino. Roulette wheels, slot machines, and the like, deliver cash rewards on an irregular basis, and they do so based on the gambler's responses. Sometimes the gambler has to pull the arm of the slot machine (the "one-armed bandit") hundreds of times before receiving any money at all. At other times, the gambler pulls the arm only once and makes out like a bandit himself, perhaps walking away with thousands of dollars for a few seconds of work. The extreme unpredictability of the VR schedule is precisely what keeps gamblers addicted, because reinforcement can come at any time.

VR schedules keep pigeons hooked too. Skinner (1953) found that pigeons placed on VR schedules sometimes continue to peck on a disk for food after more than 150,000 nonreinforced responses. In some cases, they literally ground down their beaks in the process. Like desperate gamblers in a Las Vegas casino hoping for a huge payoff, they don't give up despite repeated disappointments. For Skinner, much of what he called "persistence"—or what we might call determination or perseverance—is merely a consequence of being on a reinforcement schedule that's difficult to extinguish, especially a VR schedule.

Skinner's shaping principles are used today to train service animals.

> **APPLY YOUR THINKING**
> How might the effect of VR schedules help to explain why some people continue to believe in psychic experiences despite the absence of strong evidence for their existence?

APPLICATIONS OF OPERANT CONDITIONING

There's an old joke that just as magicians pull rabbits out of hats, behaviorists pull habits out of rats. There's a grain of truth to this one. Through operant conditioning, behaviorists train rats and other organisms to develop learned habits. They typically do so by means of a procedure called **shaping by successive approximations,** or *shaping* for short. Using shaping, we reinforce behaviors that aren't exactly the target behavior but that are progressively closer versions of it. Typically, we shape an organism's response by initially reinforcing most or all responses that are close to the desired behavior, and then gradually *fading* (that is, decreasing the frequency of) our reinforcement for the not-exactly-right behaviors over time.

Animal trainers often combine shaping with a technique called *chaining,* in which they link a number of interrelated behaviors to form a longer series. Each behavior in the chain becomes a cue for the next behavior in the chain. When our parents teach us to recite the alphabet, they may first reinforce us for saying *A*, and then for saying *B* and *C*, and then for saying *D* and *E* . . . until eventually we master the whole chain all the way to *Z*.

Although B. F. Skinner's technique of training dolphins to steer torpedoes in World War II was never implemented, today's military has used trained dolphins to detect mines in harbors.

By means of shaping and chaining, Skinner taught pigeons to play Ping-Pong, although they weren't exactly Olympic-caliber table tennis players. During World War II, he also taught dolphins to steer torpedoes toward enemy ships by pecking a target whenever the torpedo got closer to the bull's-eye, although the U.S. military never adopted his innovative approach to naval warfare. In both cases, Skinner began by reinforcing initial approximations to the desired response. When teaching pigeons to play Ping-Pong, he first reinforced them for turning toward the paddles, then approaching the paddles, then placing the paddles in their beaks, then picking up the paddles with their beaks, and so on. Then, he chained later behaviors, like swinging the paddle and then hitting the ball, to the earlier behaviors. As we might imagine, shaping and chaining complex animal behaviors requires patience, as the process can take days or weeks. Still, the payoff can be substantial, because we can train animals to engage in numerous behaviors that lie well outside their normal repertoires. Indeed, all contemporary animal trainers rely on Skinnerian principles.

shaping by successive approximations
conditioning a target behavior by progressively reinforcing behaviors that come closer and closer to the target

Behaviorists do more than pull habits out of rats; they pull habits out of humans too. One of the great triumphs of modern psychology has been the application of operant conditioning to myriad domains of modern life. We'll look at four here: the Premack principle, superstitious behavior, token economies, and applied behavior analysis.

Premack Principle. Be honest: Did you put off reading this chapter until the last moment? If so, don't feel ashamed, because procrastination is one of the most frequent study problems that college students report. Although widespread, procrastination may not be harmless. The stress it causes may be bad for our physical and psychological health. Moreover, procrastinators tend to perform more poorly in their classes than do early birds (Tice & Baumeister, 1997). Although these findings are correlational and don't establish that procrastination is bad for us, they certainly suggest that putting things off isn't likely to be good for us.

How can we overcome procrastination? Hopefully, you won't put off reading the next two paragraphs, because we have a possible remedy for dillydallying. Although there are several potential solutions for procrastination, among the best is probably the one discovered by David Premack (1965) in his research on monkeys. The **Premack principle** states that we can positively reinforce a less frequently performed behavior with a more frequently performed behavior (Danaher, 1974). Although not a foolproof rule (Knapp, 1976), this guideline typically works surprisingly well. The Premack principle is also called "grandma's rule," because our grandmother reminded us to finish our vegetables before moving on to dessert. If we give children the opportunity to choose between spinach and chocolate ice cream, they'll vote with their mouths and choose to eat chocolate ice cream at a much higher frequency than they eat spinach. In this way, we can get children to eat spinach by reinforcing them with chocolate ice cream if, but only if, they've finished their much-dreaded spinach.

Similarly, the Premack principle can help us overcome our schoolwork procrastination. So, if you find yourself putting off a reading or writing task, think of behaviors you'd typically perform if given the chance—perhaps hanging out with a few close friends, watching a favorite TV program, or treating yourself to an ice cream cone. Then, reinforce yourself with these higher frequency behaviors *only* after you've completed your homework. Research suggests this approach may help people to stop putting off things they've long avoided, like going to the dentist (Ramer, 1980). So if you're procrastinating in your schoolwork and are contemplating using the Premack principle to help you get over it, don't put off trying it.

> ### APPLY YOUR THINKING
> What third variables might account for the correlation between procrastination and bad grades?

Superstitious Behavior. How many of the following behaviors do you perform?

- Never opening an umbrella indoors
- Not walking under a ladder
- Crossing the street whenever you see a black cat
- Carrying a lucky charm or necklace
- Going out of your way not to step on cracks in the sidewalk
- Knocking on wood
- Crossing your fingers
- Avoiding the number 13 (like not stopping on the thirteenth floor of a building)

If you've engaged in several of these actions, you're at least somewhat superstitious. So are many Americans. Twelve percent of Americans are afraid of walking under a ladder, while 14 percent are afraid of crossing paths with a black cat (Vyse, 1997). So many people are afraid of the number 13 (*triskaidekaphobia*) that the floor designations in many tall buildings skip directly from 12 to 14 (Hock, 2002). This phobia isn't limited to North America; in Paris, triskaidekaphobics who are going out to dinner with 12 other people can hire a *quatorzieme,* a person paid to serve as a fourteenth guest.

How do superstitions relate to operant conditioning? In a classic study, Skinner (1948) placed eight food-deprived pigeons in a Skinner box while delivering reinforcement (bird

---

Correlation vs. Causation

fictoid

Myth: Few educated people are superstitious.

Reality: People are prone to certain superstitious behaviors regardless of educational level. As many as 90 percent of college students engage in one or more superstitious rituals before taking an exam (Vyse, 1997). More than half use a "lucky" pen or wear a "lucky" piece of jewelry or clothing. Others recite particular words, eat a special food, or skip showering or shaving.

So many people are afraid of the number 13 that many buildings do not have a thirteenth floor.

Premack principle
principle that a less frequently performed behavior can be increased in frequency by reinforcing it with a more frequent behavior

feed) every 15 seconds *independent of their behavior.* That is, the birds received reinforcement regardless of what they did. After a few days, Skinner found that six of the eight pigeons had acquired remarkably strange behaviors. In the words of Skinner:

> One bird was conditioned to turn counterclockwise about the cage, making two or three turns between reinforcements. Another repeatedly thrust its head into one of the upper corners of the cage. A third developed a tossing response as if placing its head beneath an invisible bar and lifting it repeatedly. Two birds developed a pendulum motion of the head and body in which the head was extended forward and swung from right to left. (p. 168)

When Skinner extended the reinforcement interval to a few minutes, one of the pigeons even performed a miniature "ballet dance" of sorts while awaiting food. You may have observed similarly odd behaviors in large groups of birds that people are feeding in city parks; for example, some pigeons may prance around or walk rapidly in circles in anticipation of reinforcement.

According to Skinner, his pigeons had developed *superstitious behavior:* Actions linked to reinforcement by sheer coincidence (Morse & Skinner, 1957). There's no actual association between superstitious behavior and reinforcement, although the animal acts as though there is. The behavior that the pigeon just happened to be performing immediately prior to reinforcement was strengthened—remember that reinforcement increases the probability of a response—so the pigeon kept on doing it (this kind of accidental operant conditioning is sometimes called *superstitious conditioning*). Not all studies have been able to replicate these findings in pigeons (Staddon & Simmelhag, 1971), although it's likely that at least some animal superstitions develop in the fashion Skinner described.

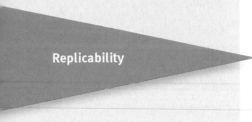
Replicability

Skinner argued that operant conditioning accounts for many human superstitions. He noted that bowlers often angle and twist their bodies in peculiar ways as the ball rolls down the alley (Skinner, 1948). In some cases, they tilt their heads in the direction they want the bowling ball to go. They seem to be trying to "coax" the ball into the pins, although this behavior of course has no effect whatsoever on where the ball ends up.

Studies show that operant conditioning can produce superstitious behaviors in children. Two investigators (Wagner & Morris, 1987) placed children in a room with a mechanical clown, who periodically (either every 15 or every 30 seconds) dispensed marbles that the children later cashed in for an attractive toy. The researchers used covert observation (Chapter 2) by watching the children through a one-way mirror. They found that about three-fourths of the children developed superstitious behaviors; some touched the clown's face, others made faces at him, and another kissed him.

Few people are more prone to superstitions than athletes. That's probably because the outcome of so many sporting events, even those requiring a great deal of skill, depends heavily on chance. As we learned in Chapter 2, baseball Hall of Famer Wade Boggs became famous for eating chicken before each game; he also performed practice runs in the outfield at precisely 7:17 P.M. Hall of Fame football player Jim Kelly forced himself to vomit before every game, and basketball player Chuck Person ate exactly two candy bars (always Snickers or Kit Kats) before every game (Vyse, 1997). Superstar golfer Tiger Woods always wears a red shirt when playing on Sundays.

Interestingly, the prevalence of superstitions in sports depends on the extent to which the outcomes are due to chance. That's what Skinner would have predicted, because, as we've already discovered, partial reinforcement schedules are more likely to produce enduring behaviors than are continuous reinforcement schedules. In baseball, hitting is much less under players' control than is fielding: Even the best hitters succeed only about 3 out of 10 times, whereas the best fielders succeed 9.8 or even 9.9 out of 10 times. So hitting is controlled by a partial reinforcement schedule, whereas fielding is controlled by something close to a continuous reinforcement schedule. As we might expect, baseball players have far more hitting-related superstitions—like drawing a favorite symbol in the sand in the batter's box—than fielding-related superstitions (Gmelch, 1974; Vyse, 1997).

Of course, human superstitions aren't due entirely to operant conditioning. Many superstitions are spread partly by word-of-mouth (Herrnstein, 1966). If our mother tells

Athletes may engage in superstitious behaviors, such as Tiger Woods' "red shirt on Sundays" superstition, because the outcome of many athletic events depends heavily on chance.

us over and over again that black cats bring bad luck, we may become wary of them. Still, word-of-mouth explanations for beliefs don't tell us how these beliefs originated. For many superstitions, operant conditioning may offer the answer.

secondary reinforcers
neutral objects that people can trade in for reinforcers themselves

primary reinforcers
items or outcomes that are naturally pleasurable

APPLY YOUR THINKING

How might superstitious conditioning help to explain why some people continue to read their horoscopes or consult with crystal ball readers despite the absence of evidence that these practices are effective?

Token Economies. One of the most successful applications of operant conditioning has been the *token economy*. Token economies are systems, often set up in psychiatric hospitals, for reinforcing appropriate behaviors and extinguishing inappropriate ones (Carr, Fraizier, & Roland, 2005; Kazdin, 1982). In token economies, staff members reinforce patients who behave in a desired fashion using tokens, chips, points, or other **secondary reinforcers.** Secondary reinforcers are neutral objects that patients can trade in for **primary reinforcers**—things that are naturally pleasurable, like a favorite food or drink.

Typically, psychologists who construct token economies begin by identifying *target behaviors,* that is, actions they hope to make more frequent. One psychiatric hospital unit in which one of the authors of your textbook worked consisted of children with serious behavior problems, including yelling and cursing. In this unit, one target behavior was being polite to staff members. So whenever a child was especially polite to a staff member, he was rewarded with points, which he could trade in for something he wanted, like ice cream or attending a movie with staff members. Whenever a child was rude to a staff member, he was punished with a loss of points.

Research suggests that token economies are often effective in improving behavior in hospitals, group homes, and juvenile detention units (Allyon & Milan, 2002; Paul & Lentz, 1977). Nevertheless, token economies remain controversial, because the behaviors learned in institutions don't always transfer to the outside world (Carr et al., 2005; Wakefield, 2006). That's especially likely if the patients return to settings, like deviant peer groups, in which they're reinforced for socially inappropriate behaviors.

Applied Behavior Analysis. As we learned in Chapter 2, infantile autism is a severe condition marked by shortcomings in social attachment, capacity for imagination, and language. *Applied behavior analysis* (ABA) can be helpful in remedying the language deficits of individuals with autism and other developmental disabilities. ABA is a set of techniques, based on operant conditioning principles, that relies on the careful measurement of behavior before and after implementing interventions (Romanczyk et al., 2003). ABA for autism makes extensive use of shaping techniques; mental health professionals reinforce autistic individuals with food and other primary reinforcers as they reach progressively closer approximations to certain words and, eventually, complete sentences.

Ivar Lovaas and his colleagues have pioneered the best-known ABA program for autism (Lovaas, 1987; McEachlin, Smith, & Lovaas, 1993). The results of Lovaas's work have been promising. Children with autism who undergo ABA training emerge with better language and intellectual skills than do control groups of children with autism who don't undergo such training (Green, 1996; Matson, Benavidez, Compton, Paclawaskyj, & Baglio, 1996; Romanczyk, Arnstein, Soorya, & Gillis, 2003).

Nevertheless, ABA researchers haven't been immune from making exaggerated claims. For example, although Lovaas (1987) asserted that many of the children he treated "recovered" from autism, this conclusion is questionable because Lovaas didn't randomly assign children with autism to experimental and control groups. Thus, his findings are vulnerable to a rival explanation: Perhaps the children in the experimental group had higher levels of functioning to begin with. Indeed, there's evidence this was the case (Schopler, Short, & Mesibov, 1989).

The token economy is one of the most successful applications of operant conditioning.

Applied behavior analysis has yielded some success in treating the deficits of children with autism. Here a teacher uses operant conditioning techniques to help a child with autism name the objects and animals shown in a set of photographs.

Ruling Out Rival Hypotheses

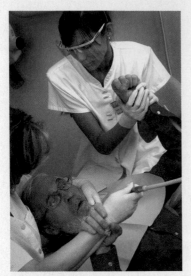

Fears of dental procedures are often reinforced by avoidance behavior over many years, such as a refusal to go to the dentist until it's absolutely necessary.

The current consensus is that ABA isn't a miracle cure for the language deficits of autism, but that it can be extremely helpful in many cases (Herbert, Sharp, & Gaudiano, 2002).

TWO-PROCESS THEORY: PUTTING CLASSICAL AND OPERANT CONDITIONING TOGETHER

Up to this point, we've discussed classical and operant conditioning as though they were two entirely independent processes. Yet the truth is more complicated. The similarities between classical and operant conditioning, including the fact that we find acquisition, extinction, stimulus generalization, and so on, in both, have led some theorists to argue that these two forms of learning aren't as different as some psychologists believe (Brown & Jenkins, 1968; Staddon, 2003).

Although there are certainly important similarities between classical and operant conditioning, brain imaging studies demonstrate that these two forms of learning are associated with activations in different brain regions. Classically conditioned fear reactions are based largely in the amygdala (LeDoux, 1996; Veit, Flor, Erb, Lotze, Grodd, & Birbaumer, 2002), whereas operantly conditioned responses are based largely in the nucleus accumbens and related limbic systems linked to reward (Robbins & Everitt, 1998; see Chapter 3).

These two types of conditioning often interact. To see how, let's revisit the question of how people develop phobias. We've seen that certain phobias arise in part by classical conditioning: A previously neutral stimulus (the CS)—say, a dog—is paired with an unpleasant stimulus (the UCS)—a dog bite—resulting in the CR of fear. So far, so good.

But this tidy scheme doesn't answer an important question: Why doesn't the CR of fear eventually extinguish? Given what we've learned about classical conditioning, we might expect the CR of fear to fade away over time with repeated exposure to the CS of dogs. Yet this often doesn't happen (Rachman, 1977). Many people with phobias remain deathly afraid of their feared stimulus for years, even decades. Indeed, only about 20 percent of untreated adults with phobias ever get over their fears (American Psychiatric Association, 2000). Why?

Enter *two-process theory* to the rescue as an explanation (Mowrer, 1947). According to two-process theory, we need both classical and operant conditioning to explain the persistence of anxiety disorders. Here's how: People acquire phobias by means of classical conditioning. Then, once they're phobic, they start to avoid their feared stimulus whenever they see it. If they have a dog phobia, they may cross the street whenever they see someone walking toward them with a large German shepherd. When they do, they experience a reduction in anxiety—a surge of relief—which *negatively reinforces* their fear. Recall that negative reinforcement, which is one type of operant conditioning, is the removal of an unpleasant stimulus, in this case anxiety. So, by avoiding dogs whenever they see them, dog phobics are negatively reinforcing their fear. Ironically, they're operantly conditioning themselves to make their fears more likely to persist. In essence, they're exchanging short-term gain for long-term pain.

ASSESS YOUR KNOWLEDGE: FACT OR FICTION?

(1) In classical conditioning, responses are emitted; in operant conditioning, they're elicited. (True/False)

(2) Negative reinforcement and punishment are superficially different, but they produce the same short-term effects on behavior. (True/False)

(3) The correlation between spanking and children's behavioral problems appears to be positive in Caucasians but negative in African Americans. (True/False)

(4) The principle of partial reinforcement states that behaviors reinforced only some of the time extinguish more rapidly than behaviors reinforced continuously. (True/False)

(5) According to the Premack principle, we can reinforce less frequent behaviors with more frequent behaviors. (True/False)

Answers: (1) F (p. 242); (2) F (p. 245); (3) T (p. 246); (4) F (p. 248); (5) T (p. 251)

Cognitive Models of Learning

Thus far, we've omitted one word when discussing how we learn: *thinking*. That's not accidental, because early behaviorists didn't believe that thought played much of a causal role in learning.

WATSON, SKINNER, AND THINKING

Watson and Skinner held different views on this matter. Watson (1913) was an advocate of *methodological behaviorism*. According to this school of thought, psychology should focus exclusively on overt (that is, observable) behaviors. From Watson's perspective, thinking and emotion lay outside the domain of scientific psychology. Methodological behaviorists studied only what they could observe: What you see is what you get.

In contrast, Skinner (1953) was an advocate of *radical behaviorism*. For radical behaviorists, observable behavior, thinking, and emotion are all governed by the same laws of learning, namely, classical and operant conditioning. For Skinnerians (the term often used for radical behaviorists), thinking and emotion *are* behaviors, they're just covert—that is, unobservable—behaviors. One frequent misconception about Skinner is that he didn't believe in thinking. On this and a host of other issues, Skinner isn't merely one of the most famous of all psychologists; he's also one of the most misunderstood (DeBell & Harless, 1992; Wyatt, 2001; see **Table 6.5**).

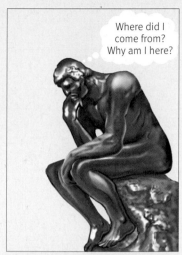

Where did I come from? Why am I here?

Methodological behaviorists, like Watson, held a different view of thinking than did radical behaviorists, like Skinner. Whereas Watson believed that thinking lies outside the boundaries of scientific psychology, Skinner didn't. He regarded thinking as a behavior, just one that happens to be unobservable.

Table 6.5 Widespread Myths about the Psychology of B. F. Skinner.

Fiction	Fact
Skinner believed that genes played no role in human behavior	Skinner acknowledged that genes affected the ease with which people learn habits, although he believed the study of genes was of little relevance to psychology
Skinner didn't believe in thinking or emotion	Skinner believed that humans and other intelligent animals think and experience emotions, although he regarded thinking and feeling merely as covert (unobservable) behaviors
Skinner favored the use of punishment as a behavioral technique	Skinner opposed the use of punishment for shaping human behaviors, and believed that reinforcement should be used whenever possible
Skinner believed that any human behavior could be conditioned	Skinner never argued this, although his predecessor John Watson came close to doing so
Skinner denied the uniqueness of individuals	Skinner openly acknowledged that all individuals are unique, as they are the product of unique genetic predispositions and unique learning histories
Skinner's vision of society was devoid of morality	Skinner advocated a society in which people would be reinforced for ethical and cooperative behavior

(*Sources:* DeBell & Harless, 1992; Wyatt 2001)

On the contrary, Skinner clearly thought—he wouldn't have objected to our use of that word here—that humans and other intelligent animals think, but he insisted that thinking is no different in principle from any other behavior. For Skinner, this view is far more parsimonious than invoking different laws of learning for thinking than for other behaviors. At times, Skinner went even further. In a talk to the American Psychological Association delivered a mere 8 days before his death, Skinner (1990) likened proponents of cognitive psychology, who believe that thinking plays a central role in causing behavior (see Prologue), to pseudoscientists. Cognitive psychology, he argued, invokes unobservable and ultimately meaningless concepts—like "mind"—to explain behavior. Skinner claimed that doing so doesn't bring us any closer to the true causes of behavior.

Occam's Razor

S-O-R PSYCHOLOGY: THROWING THINKING BACK INTO THE MIX

Few psychologists today share Skinner's harsh assessment of cognitive psychology. In fact, the vast majority of psychologists now agree that the story of learning in humans is incomplete without at least some role for cognition, that is, thinking (Bolles, 1979; Kirsch, Lynn, Vigorito, & Miller, 2004; Pinker, 1997).

Over the last 30 or 40 years, psychology has moved increasingly away from a simple S-R (stimulus-response) psychology to a more complex S-O-R psychology, with *O* being the organism that interprets the stimulus before producing a response (Mischel, 1973; Woodworth, 1929). For S-O-R psychologists, the link between S and R isn't mindless or automatic. Instead, the organism's response to a stimulus depends on what this stimulus *means* to it. The S-O-R principle helps to explain a phenomenon we've probably all encountered. You've probably had the experience of giving two friends the same mild criticism (like, "It bothers me a little when you show up late") and found that they reacted quite differently: One was apologetic, the other defensive.

To explain these differing reactions, Skinnerians would probably invoke your friends' differing *learning histories,* in essence how each friend had been trained to react to criticism. In contrast, S-O-R theorists, who believe that cognition is central to explaining learning, would contend that the differences in your friends' reactions stem from how they *interpreted* your criticism. Your first friend may have viewed your criticism as constructive feedback, your second friend as a personal attack.

Although S-O-R theorists attempted to integrate classical and operant conditioning with a more thought-based account, the Gestalt psychologists, about whom we learned in Chapter 4, had long argued for a critical role for the organism. As we'll recall, Gestalt psychologists noted that what we perceive is different from and greater than the sum of the stimuli our sense organs receive. This fact implies that as organisms we're performing mental operations, or transformations, on our experience of stimuli.

S-O-R theorists don't deny that classical and operant conditioning occur, but they believe that these forms of learning usually depend on thinking. Take a person who's been classically conditioned by tones and shock to sweat in response to the tones. Her skin conductance response will extinguish suddenly if she's told that no more shocks are on the way (Grings, 1973). This phenomenon of *cognitive conditioning,* whereby our interpretation of the situation affects conditioning, suggests that conditioning is more than an automatic, mindless process (Brewer, 1974; Kirsch et al., 2004).

To explain psychology's gradual transition from behaviorism to cognitivism, we need to tell the story of a pioneering psychologist and his rats.

Although few of us enjoy criticism, some of us react to it well, whereas others of us don't. According to S-O-R psychologists, this difference hinges on our interpretation of what the criticism means.

LATENT LEARNING

One of the first serious challenges to the radical behaviorist account of learning was mounted by Edward Chase Tolman (1886–1959), who is one of the unsung giants of modern psychology. Although few undergraduates aside from those at the University of California at Berkeley, where the psychology building bears his name, have heard of Tolman, his contribution to the psychology of learning is difficult to overestimate.

Tolman suspected that, contrary to Watson, Thorndike, and others, reinforcement wasn't the be-all and end-all of learning. To understand why, answer this question: "After what psychologist is the University of California at Berkeley psychology building named?" If you've been paying attention, you hopefully answered "Tolman." Yet immediately before we asked that question, you knew the answer, even though you had no opportunity to demonstrate it. According to Tolman (1932), you engaged in **latent learning:** learning that isn't directly observable (Blodgett, 1929). We learn many things without showing them. Putting it a bit differently, there's a crucial difference between *competence*—what we know—and *performance*—showing what we know (Bradbard, Martin, Endsley, & Halverson, 1986).

Why is this distinction important? Because it implies that *reinforcement isn't necessary for learning.* Here's how Tolman and C. H. Honzik (1930) demonstrated this point systematically.

latent learning
learning that's not directly observable

They randomly assigned three groups of rats to go through a maze over a 3-week period (see **Figure 6.10**). One group always received reinforcement in the form of cheese when it got to the end of the maze. A second group never received reinforcement when it got to the end of the maze. The first group made far fewer errors; that's no great surprise. The third group of rats received no reinforcement for the first 10 days, and then started receiving reinforcement on the eleventh day.

As we can see in Figure 6.10, the rats in the third group showed a large and abrupt drop in their number of errors on receiving their very first reinforcement. In fact, within only a few days their number of errors didn't differ significantly from the number of errors among the rats who were always reinforced.

According to Tolman, this finding means that the rats in the third group had been learning all along. They just hadn't bothered to show it because they had nothing to gain. Once there was a payoff for learning, namely, a tasty morsel of cheese, they promptly became miniature maze masters.

According to Tolman (1948), the rats had developed **cognitive maps**—that is, spatial representations—of the maze. If you're like most college students, you were hopelessly confused the first day you arrived on campus. Over time, however, you probably developed a mental sense of the layout of the campus, so that you now hardly ever become lost. That internal spatial blueprint, according to Tolman, is a cognitive map.

In a clever demonstration of cognitive maps, three investigators (McNamara, Long, & Wilke, 1956) had one set of rats run repeatedly through a maze to receive reinforcement. They put another set of rats in little moving "trolley cars," in which the rats could observe the layout of the maze but not obtain the experience of running through it. When the researchers gave the second group of rats the chance to run through the maze, they did just as well as the rats in the first group. As rodent tourists in trolley cars, they'd acquired cognitive maps of the maze.

The latent learning research of Tolman and others challenged strict behavioral models of learning, because their work suggested that learning could occur without reinforcement. To many psychologists, this research falsified the claim that reinforcement is necessary for all forms of learning. It also suggested that thinking, in the form of cognitive maps, plays a central role in at least some forms of learning.

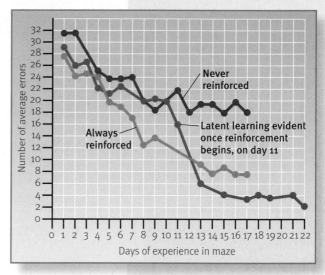

Figure 6.10 Tolman and Honzik's Maze Trials. Graphs from Tolman and Honzik's classic study of latent learning in rats. Pay particular attention to the blue line. The rats in this group weren't reinforced until day 11; note the sudden drop in the number of their errors on receiving reinforcement. The rats were learning all along, even though they weren't showing it. (*Source:* Tolman & Honzik, 1930)

Falsifiability

OBSERVATIONAL LEARNING

According to some psychologists, one important variant of latent learning is **observational learning:** learning by watching others (Bandura, 1965). In many cases, we learn by watching *models:* parents, teachers, and others who are influential to us. Many psychologists regard observational learning as a form of latent learning because it allows us to learn without reinforcement. We can merely watch someone else being reinforced for doing something and take our cues from them.

Observational learning spares us the expense of having to learn everything firsthand (Bandura, 1977). The authors of your book aren't experts in skydiving, but from our observations of people who've gone skydiving we have the distinct impression that it's generally a good idea to have a parachute on before you jump out of a plane. Note that we didn't need to learn this useful tidbit of advice by trial and error. If we had made such an error, we wouldn't be here to tell you about it. As a result, observational learning can spare us from serious, even life-threatening, mistakes. But it can also contribute to our learning of maladaptive habits.

Observational Learning of Aggression. In classic research in the 1960s, Albert Bandura and his colleagues demonstrated that children can learn to act aggressively by watching aggressive role models (Bandura, Ross, & Ross, 1963).

Bandura and his colleagues asked preschool boys and girls to watch an adult (the model) interact with a large Bobo doll, a doll that bounces back to its original upright

Cats have cognitive maps, too. (© Hilary B. Price. King Features Syndicate)

cognitive maps
mental representations of how a physical space is organized

observational learning
learning by watching others

258

CHAPTER 6 LEARNING

Children acquire a great deal of their behavior by observational learning of adults, especially their parents.

Correlation vs. Causation

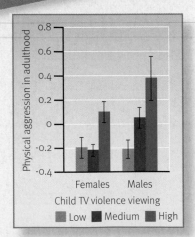

Figure 6.11 Longitudinal Study of Individuals Who Watched Violent TV as Children. In both females and males, there's a positive correlation between viewing violent television in childhood and violent behavior in adulthood. But this correlation doesn't demonstrate causality. Why? (*Source:* Huesmann, Moise-Titus, Podolski, & Eron, 2003)

position after being hit (Bandura, Ross, & Ross, 1961). The experimenters randomly assigned some children to watch the adult model playing quietly and ignoring the Bobo doll, and others to watch the adult model punching the Bobo doll in the nose, hitting it with a mallet, sitting on it, and kicking it around the room. As though that weren't enough, the model in the latter condition shouted out insults and vivid descriptions of his actions while inflicting violence: "Sock him in the nose," "Kick him," "Pow."

Bandura and his coworkers then brought the children into a room with an array of appealing toys, including a miniature fire engine, a jet fighter, and a large doll set. Just as children began playing with these toys, the experimenter interrupted them, informing them that they needed to move to a different room. This interruption was intentional, as the investigators wanted to frustrate the children to make them more likely to behave aggressively. Then the experimenter brought them into a second room, which contained a Bobo doll identical to the one they'd seen.

On a variety of dependent measures, Bandura and his colleagues found that previous exposure to the aggressive model triggered significantly more aggression against the Bobo doll than did exposure to the nonaggressive model. The children who'd watched the aggressive model yelled at the doll much as the model had done, and they even imitated many of his verbal insults. In a later study, Bandura and his colleagues (Bandura, Ross, & Ross, 1963) found essentially the same results when they displayed the aggressive models to children on film rather than in person.

Media Violence and Real-World Aggression. The Bandura studies and scores of later studies of observational learning led psychologists to examine a theoretically and socially important question: Does exposure to media violence, such as in films or movies, contribute to real-world violence—or what Bushman and Anderson (2001) called violence in the "reel world"? The research literature addressing this question is as vast as it is confusing, and could easily occupy an entire book by itself. So we'll only briefly touch on some of the research highlights here.

Hundreds of investigators using correlational designs have reported that children who watch many violent television programs are more aggressive than other children (Wilson & Herrnstein, 1985). These findings, though, don't demonstrate that media violence causes real-world violence (Freedman, 1984). They could simply indicate that highly aggressive children are more likely than other children to tune in to aggressive television programs. Alternatively, these findings could be due to a third variable, such as children's initial levels of aggressiveness. That is, highly aggressive children may be more likely than other children to both watch violent television programs and to act aggressively.

Investigators have tried to get around this problem by using longitudinal designs (see Chapter 10), which track individuals' behavior over time. Longitudinal studies show that children who watch many violent television shows commit more aggressive acts years later than do children who watch fewer violent television shows, even when researchers have equated children in their initial levels of aggression (Huessman, Moise, Podolski, & Eron, 2003; see **Figure 6.11**). These studies offer somewhat more compelling evidence for a causal link between media violence and aggression than do correlational studies, but even they don't demonstrate the existence of this link. For example, an unmeasured personality variable, like impulsivity, or a social variable, like weak parental supervision, might account for these findings. Moreover, just because variable *A* precedes variable *B* doesn't mean that variable *A causes* variable *B* (see Chapter 10). For example, if we found that most common colds start with a scratchy throat and a runny nose, we shouldn't conclude that scratchy throats and runny noses cause colds, only that they're early signs of a cold.

Still other investigators have examined whether the link between media models and later aggression holds up under strictly controlled conditions within the confines of the laboratory. In most of these studies, researchers have exposed subjects to either violent or nonviolent media presentations and seen whether subjects in the former groups behaved more aggressively, such as by yelling at the experimenter or delivering electric shocks to another subject when provoked. In general, meta-analyses (see Chapter 2) of these studies strongly suggest a causal association between media violence and laboratory aggression (Wood, Wong, & Chachere, 1991; see also Chapter 13).

Finally, some investigators have conducted *field studies* of the link between media violence and aggression (Anderson & Bushman, 2002). In field studies, researchers examine the relation between naturally occurring events and aggression in the real world. For example, sociologist David Phillips (1983) found that the number of homicides increased by approximately one-eighth following widely publicized boxing matches. Moreover, when a Caucasian boxer defeated an African American, the victim of the murder was more likely to be an African American, whereas the converse was true when an African American boxer defeated a Caucasian. Nevertheless, some researchers have questioned these findings because the spike in homicides was evident only on the third day after these fights, but not on other days (Baron & Reiss, 1985). Thus, these results may have been due to chance.

Another investigator (Mitchell, 1986) conducted a field study of a small, isolated mountain town in Canada that had no television before 1973. She called it "Notel," short for "*no tele*vision." Compared with school-age children in two other Canadian towns that already had television, children in Notel showed a marked increase in physical and verbal aggression 2 years later. Nevertheless, these findings are difficult to interpret in light of a potential confound: At around the same time that Notel received television, the Canadian government constructed a large highway that connected Notel to nearby towns. This highway might have introduced the children in Notel to negative outside influences, including crime from other cities.

> **Ruling Out Rival Hypotheses**

So what can we make of the literature on media violence and aggressive behaviors? We're confronted with four lines of evidence—correlational studies, longitudinal studies, laboratory studies, and field studies—each with its own strengths and weaknesses. Correlational, longitudinal, and field studies tend to be strong in *external validity,* that is, generalizability to the real world, but weak in *internal validity,* that is, the extent to which they permit cause-and-effect inferences (see Chapter 2). Laboratory studies, in contrast, tend to be weak in external validity but strong in internal validity. Yet despite their shortcomings, all four types of studies point in the direction of at least some causal relation between media violence and aggression (Anderson et al., 2003; Carnagay, Anderson, & Barthololow, 2007). Scientific conclusions are usually the most convincing when we base them on findings from different research designs, each with a slightly different set of imperfections (Shadish, Cook, & Campbell, 2002). As a result, most psychological scientists today agree that media violence contributes to aggression in at least some circumstances (Anderson & Bushman, 2002; Bushman & Anderson, 2001).

Nevertheless, it's equally clear that media violence is only one small piece of a multifaceted puzzle. We can't explain aggression by means of media violence alone because the substantial majority of individuals exposed to high levels of such violence don't become aggressive (Freedman, 2002; Herrnstein & Wilson, 1985). We'll examine other causal factors in aggression in Chapter 13.

NEW FRONTIERS
Mirror Neurons and Observational Learning

You find yourself alone in a new city, standing in line behind someone using an automated teller machine. Like so many other cash machines, this one is slightly—and annoyingly—different from all the other ones you've seen. You watch as the person in front of you inserts her card, pushes a few buttons, and grabs her money from the slot at the bottom of the machine. Now it's your turn, and you know exactly what to do. You learned by watching. But how? Although the question of how our brains engage in observational learning is still shrouded in mystery, neuroscientists have recently begun to pinpoint a potential physiological basis for it.

(continued)

Mirror neurons become active when we watch someone similar to us performing a behavior.

Köhler found that Sultan, his "star" chimpanzee, discovered how to insert one bamboo stick inside another to create an extra-long stick, thereby allowing him to obtain food.

Correlation vs. Causation

Köhler's apes also figured out how to get to a banana suspended well above their heads: Stack a bunch of boxes atop each other, and climb to the top box.

mirror neurons
cells in the prefrontal cortex that become activated by specific motions when an animal both performs and observes that action

When a monkey watches another monkey perform an action, such as reaching for an object, a group of neurons in its prefrontal cortex, near its motor cortex (see Chapter 3), becomes active (Rizzolatti, Fadiga, Gallese, & Fogassi, 1996). These cells are called **mirror neurons** because they're the same cells that would have become active had the monkey performed the same movement. It's as though these neurons are "imagining" what it would be like to perform the behavior.

Mirror neurons appear to be remarkably selective. They don't become active when a monkey sees another monkey that remains stationary or sees a piece of food that another monkey grabbed. Instead, they become active only when a monkey sees another monkey engaging in an action, like grabbing. Moreover, these neurons seem tuned to extremely specific behaviors. Investigators have found one mirror neuron in monkeys that fires only when the monkey himself or a person he's observing grabs a peanut, and a different mirror neuron that fires only when the monkey himself or a person he's observing eats a peanut (Winerman, 2005).

Using PET scanning, researchers have identified a similar mirror neuron system in humans (Gallese & Goldman, 1998), but they've yet to identify individual mirror neurons, as they have in monkeys. No one knows for sure what mirror neurons do or why they're in our brains. But some neuroscientists have conjectured that such neurons play a central role in empathy (Azar, 2005; Ramachandran, 2000). When we see an athlete suffer an injury during a sporting event, like a baseball player grimacing in agony after a bruising slide into home plate, we wince in pain along with him. In some sense, we may be "feeling his pain," because the mirror neurons that correspond to the neurons in his motor areas are becoming activated.

Some authors have gone further to speculate that mirror neuron abnormalities play a key role in infantile autism (see Chapter 2), which is often associated with difficulties in adopting the perspectives of others (Dingelfelder, 2005). Interestingly, one group of investigators found that the mirror neuron areas of autistic individuals become less active than those of nonautistic individuals when observing people's hand movements (Theoret et al., 2005). Still, such findings are only correlational. They don't necessarily show that mirror neuron deficits cause or contribute to autism; perhaps they're merely a consequence of the fact that autistic individuals are less interested in others' actions than are nonautistic individuals.

Even so, the discovery of mirror neurons may ultimately provide valuable insights into how we learn from others. This discovery also helps us appreciate that even when we're alone, we're often not really alone. Even when we're sitting by ourselves watching television, our brain and the brain of that baseball player sliding into home plate may be in sync, our mirror neurons and his lighting up in unison.

INSIGHT LEARNING

Latent learning and observational learning were by no means the only holes poked in behaviorist theory. Another serious challenge came from a German psychologist during World War I: Wolfgang Köhler.

Around the same time that psychologists were conducting the first latent learning studies, Köhler (1925), a founder of Gestalt psychology (see Chapter 4), was posing various problems to four chimpanzees in the Canary Islands off the coast of Africa. His favorite of the four was a genius of an ape named Sultan, who was especially adept at solving puzzles. In one case Köhler placed a tempting bunch of bananas outside of the cage, well out of Sultan's reach, along with two bamboo sticks inside the cage. Neither stick was long enough to reach the bananas. After what appeared to be some heavy-duty pondering, Sultan suddenly hit on the solution: Stick one bamboo stick inside the other, creating one extra-long bamboo stick.

What was notable, according to Köhler, was that his chimpanzees appeared to experience the "aha reaction" we discussed earlier. Their solutions to his problems didn't appear to reflect trial and error, as it did with Thorndike's cats, but rather insight. That is, their solutions resembled what we saw back in Figure 6.6. The chimps seemed to suddenly "get" the solution to the problem, and from then on they got it right just about every time.

Still, Köhler's findings and conclusions weren't without their shortcomings. His observations were anecdotal, and he didn't measure them systematically. Because Köhler videotaped only some of his chimpanzees' problem solving, it's difficult to rule out the possibility that at least some of his chimps had engaged in trial and error before figuring out each problem (Gould & Gould, 1994). Moreover, because the chimps were often in the same cage, they might have engaged in observational learning. Still, Köhler's work suggests that at least some smart animals can learn through insight rather than trial and error.

There's also good evidence that humans solve many problems through insight (Dawes, 1994). Many researchers didn't initially recognize this phenomenon, because they were fooled by their own graphs. If we look at **Figure 6.12,** we'll see the results of a typical investigation of problem solving. In this kind of study, researchers ask human participants to sort various cards that differ in shape (round, triangular, square, and so on), color (green, blue, red, and so on), and number (1, 2, 3, and so on) into piles. Participants need to figure out which of these three categories the experimenter has in mind. On each trial, participants receive feedback from the experimenter about whether they're right or wrong. The dotted line in Figure 6.12 shows the results averaged across many participants. This line seems to provide evidence of gradual, trial-and-error learning, doesn't it?

Don't be fooled, because appearances can be deceiving. If we look at the pattern of learning *within each subject* in Figure 6.12, we can see that individuals are actually learning by insight. They figure out the answer suddenly, and then almost always get it right after that. By lumping together the results across all subjects, the dotted line in the graph misleadingly suggests a gradual rather than sudden decline (Restle, 1962; Trabasso & Bower, 1963). So people often do learn through insight; they just do so at different rates.

Ruling Out Rival Hypotheses

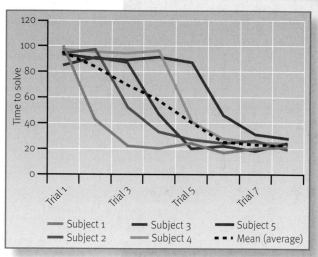

Figure 6.12 Averaged Measures of Learning Can Be Misleading. The results of the study by Trabasso and Bower (1963) show that averaged graphs of learning can be misleading. As we can see from the colored lines, subjects were learning to solve the problem by insight, not trial and error, but they were learning at different rates. By lumping together the results of all subjects, as shown by the dotted line, we can mistakenly conclude that subjects learn by trial and error. (*Source:* Trabasso & Bower, 1963)

ASSESS YOUR KNOWLEDGE: FACT OR FICTION?

(1) According to Skinner, animals don't think or experience emotions. (True/False)
(2) Proponents of latent learning argue that reinforcement isn't necessary for learning. (True/False)
(3) Research on observational learning demonstrates that children can learn aggression by watching aggressive role models. (True/False)
(4) There's no good evidence for insight learning. (True/False)

Answers: (1) F (p. 255); (2) T (p. 256); (3) T (p. 257); (4) F (p. 260)

Biological Influences on Learning

For many decades, most behaviorists regarded learning as entirely distinct from biology. The animal's learning history and genetic makeup were like two ships passing in the night. Yet we now recognize this view as naive, because our biology influences the speed and nature of our learning in complex and fascinating ways. Here are three powerful examples.

CONDITIONED TASTE AVERSIONS

One day in the 1970s, psychologist Martin Seligman went out to dinner with his wife. He ordered a filet mignon steak flavored with sauce béarnaise, his favorite topping.

Psychological science has helped many cancer patients undergoing chemotherapy to minimize conditioned taste aversions to their favorite foods.

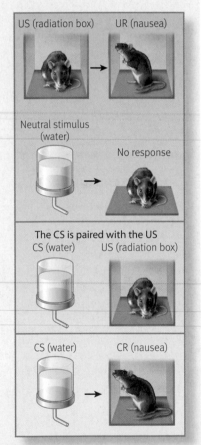

US (radiation box)   UR (nausea)

Neutral stimulus
(water)

No response

The CS is paired with the US
CS (water)   US (radiation box)

CS (water)   CR (nausea)

Figure 6.13 Conditioned Taste Aversion. The work of John Garcia and his colleagues demonstrated that animals tend to develop conditioned taste aversions only to certain stimuli, namely, those that trigger nausea in the real world.

equipotentiality
assumption that any conditioned stimulus can be associated equally well with any unconditioned stimulus

Approximately 6 hours later, while at the opera, Seligman felt nauseated and became violently ill. He and his stomach recovered, but his love of sauce béarnaise didn't. From then on, Seligman couldn't even think of, let alone taste, sauce béarnaise without feeling like vomiting (Seligman & Hager, 1972).

The *sauce béarnaise syndrome,* also known as *conditioned taste aversion,* refers to the fact that classical conditioning can lead us to develop avoidance reactions to the taste of food. Before reading on, ask yourself a question: Does Seligman's story contradict the other examples of classical conditioning we've discussed, like that of Pavlov and his dogs?

In fact, it does in at least three ways (Garcia & Hankins, 1977):

(1) In contrast to most classically conditioned reactions, which require repeated pairings between CS and UCS, conditioned taste aversions typically require *only one trial* to develop. This difference makes good sense. We wouldn't want to have to experience horrific food poisoning again and again to learn a conditioned association between taste and illness. Not only would doing so be incredibly unpleasant, but in some cases, we'd be dead after the first trial.

(2) The delay between CS and UCS in conditioned taste aversions can be as long as 6 or even 8 hours (Rachlin, 1991). Again, this fact makes good sense, because food poisoning often sets in many hours after eating toxic food, even though traditional conditioned learning works best when the CS and UCS are presented close together in time.

(3) Conditioned taste aversions tend to be remarkably specific and display little evidence of stimulus generalization. One of the earliest childhood memories of one of your text's authors is that of eating a delicious piece of lasagna and then becoming violently ill several hours later. For more than 20 years, he avoided lasagna at all costs while thoroughly enjoying spaghetti, manicotti, veal parmigiana, and virtually every other Italian dish despite its similarity to lasagna. He finally forced himself to get over his lasagna phobia, but not without a momentous struggle.

Conditioned taste aversions are a particular problem among cancer patients undergoing chemotherapy, which frequently induces nausea and vomiting. As a result, they frequently begin to avoid any food that preceded chemotherapy, even though they realize it bears no logical connection to the treatment. Fortunately, health psychologists (see Chapter 12) have developed a clever way around this problem. Capitalizing on the specificity of conditioned taste aversions, they ask cancer patients to eat an unfamiliar *scapegoat food*— a novel food of which they aren't fond—prior to chemotherapy. In general, the taste aversion becomes conditioned to the scapegoat food rather than to patients' preferred foods (Andresen, Birch, & Johnson, 1990).

John Garcia and one of his colleagues helped to demonstrate biological influences on conditioned taste aversions (Garcia & Koelling, 1966). They found that rats exposed to X-rays, which make them nauseated, developed conditioned aversions to a specific taste but not to a specific visual or auditory stimulus presented after the X-rays (Garcia & Koelling, 1966). In other words, the rats more readily associated nausea with taste than with other sensory stimuli after a single exposure. Conditioned taste aversions aren't much fun, but they're often adaptive. In the real world, poisoned drinks and foods, not sights and sounds, make animals feel sick. As a consequence, animals more easily develop conditioned aversions to stimuli that tend to trigger nausea in the real world (see **Figure 6.13**).

This finding contradicts the assumption of **equipotentiality**—the claim that we can pair all CSs equally well with all UCSs—a belief held by many traditional behaviorists (Plotkin, 2004). Garcia and others had found that certain CSs, such as those associated with taste, are easily conditioned to certain UCSs, such as those associated with nausea. Psychologists call this phenomenon *belongingness,* because certain stimuli are more likely than others to go together with certain responses (Rachman, 1977; Thorndike, 1911). Recall that following his night out with his wife, Martin Seligman felt nauseated at the thought of sauce béarnaise, but not at the thought of the opera or—thankfully, for his marriage—his wife.

PREPAREDNESS AND PHOBIAS

A second challenge to the equipotentiality assumption comes from research on phobias. If we look at the distribution of phobias in the general population, we'll find something curious: People aren't always afraid of things with which they've had the most frequent unpleasant experiences. Phobias of the dark, heights, snakes, spiders, deep water, and blood are commonplace, even though many people who fear these stimuli have never had a frightening encounter with them. In contrast, phobias of razors, knives, the edges of furniture, ovens, and electrical outlets are extremely rare, although many of us have been cut, bruised, burned, or otherwise hurt by them.

Seligman (1971) proposed that we can explain the distribution of phobias in the population by means of **preparedness:** we're evolutionarily predisposed to fear certain stimuli more than others. According to Seligman, that's because certain stimuli, like steep cliffs and poisonous animals, posed a threat to our early human ancestors (Ohman & Mineka, 2001). In contrast, household items and appliances didn't, because they weren't around back then. In the words of Susan Mineka (1993), prepared fears are "evolutionary memories": Emotional legacies of natural selection.

Mineka and Michael Cook (1993) showed lab-reared rhesus monkeys, who had no previous exposure to snakes, a videotape of fellow monkeys reacting in horror to snakes. Within less than half an hour, the monkeys acquired a fear of snakes by observational learning (surprisingly, rhesus monkeys who've never been exposed to snakes show no fear of them). The researchers then edited the videotape to show the same monkeys reacting in horror, but this time in response to flowers, a toy rabbit, a toy snake, or a toy crocodile. They then showed these doctored videotapes to different groups of monkeys who had no experience with flowers, rabbits, snakes, or crocodiles. The monkeys who observed these altered videotapes acquired fears of the toy snake and toy crocodile, but not the flowers or toy rabbit. From the standpoint of preparedness, this finding is understandable. Snakes and crocodiles were dangerous to our primate ancestors, but flowers and rabbits weren't (Ohman & Mineka, 2003).

This coyote, eating from a sheep carcass that's been tainted with a mild poison, will become sick several hours later. The coyote will avoid sheep from then on. Ranchers have made use of this technique to keep coyotes from attacking their livestock.

Preparedness may render us likely to develop *illusory correlations* between fear-provoking stimuli and negative consequences (Tomarken, Mineka, & Cook, 1989). Recall from Chapter 2 that an illusory correlation is a statistical mirage; it's the perception of a nonexistent association between two variables. One team of investigators administered intermittent electrical shocks to subjects—some of whom feared snakes and some of whom didn't—while they watched slides of snakes and damaged electrical outlets. The pairings of the slide stimuli with the shocks were random, so that the actual correlation between them was zero. Yet subjects with high levels of snake fear perceived a marked correlation between the occurrence of the snake slides, but not the electrical outlets, with the electric shocks. Subjects with low levels of snake fear didn't fall prey to this illusory correlation (Tomarken, Sutton, & Mineka, 1995).

Snake-fearful people were on the lookout for any threatening stimuli that might signal snakes, so they overestimated how often snake slides co-occurred with electric shock. Interestingly, they showed no such overestimation for electrical outlets, even though they're more closely linked in our minds than are snakes to electric shock. This finding suggests that preparedness may be at work, because snakes, but not electrical outlets, posed threats to our primate ancestors (Tomarken, Sutton, & Mineka, 1995).

Mineka and Cook (1993) showed that monkeys can acquire fears of snakes by means of observational learning. Nevertheless, these monkeys didn't acquire fears of nondangerous stimuli, like flowers, suggesting a role for evolutionary predispositions in the development of fears.

APPLY YOUR THINKING
Could the tendency of fearful people to develop illusory correlations between their feared stimuli and unpleasant outcomes be adaptive in certain circumstances? If so, how?

preparedness
evolutionary predisposition to learn some pairings of feared stimuli over others owing to their survival value

Still, the laboratory evidence for preparedness isn't completely consistent. When researchers have paired either prepared stimuli—like snakes or spiders—or unprepared stimuli—like flowers or mushrooms—with electric shocks, they haven't invariably found that subjects more rapidly acquire fears to prepared than unprepared stimuli (Davey, 1995; McNally, 1987). Moreover, some authors have proposed that preparedness findings may be due to an alternative explanation that isn't evolutionary in nature: latent inhibition. As we'll recall from earlier in the chapter, latent inhibition refers to the fact that CSs that have appeared alone (that is, without a UCS) many times are especially difficult to classically condition to a stimulus. Because we routinely encounter electric sockets, stoves, knives, and the like, without experiencing any negative consequences, these stimuli may be resistant to classical conditioning. In contrast, because few of us have regular encounters with snakes, cliffs, deep water, and so on, these stimuli may be more easily classically conditioned to aversive outcomes (Bond & Siddle, 1996).

Aside from preparedness, genetic influences probably play a role in the acquisition of certain phobias. Dog phobics and non-dog phobics don't differ in their number of negative experiences with dogs, such as bites (DiNardo et al., 1988). Moreover, only about half of dog phobics have ever had a scary encounter with a dog; the same holds for people with many other phobias. These results make it unlikely that classical conditioning alone can explain all cases of phobia. Instead, some people appear predisposed genetically to develop phobias *given* a history of certain classical conditioning experiences (Kendler, Neale, Kessler, Heath, & Eaves, 1992).

APPLY YOUR THINKING

How could we test the hypothesis that *both* a genetic predisposition toward phobias *and* a traumatic classical conditioning experience—but neither alone—are required for the development of phobias?

INSTINCTIVE DRIFT

Animal trainers Marian and Keller Breland taught pigeons, chickens, raccoons, pigs, and a host of other creatures to perform a variety of tricks—much like those we might see on David Letterman's Stupid Pet Tricks segment—for circuses and television advertisers. As students of B. F. Skinner at Harvard, they relied on traditional methods of operant conditioning to shape their animals' behavior.

In the process of their animal training adventures, the Brelands discovered that their little charges didn't always behave as anticipated. In one case they tried to train raccoons to drop tokens into a piggy bank. Although they successfully trained the raccoons to pick up the coins using food reinforcement, they soon ran headfirst into a surprising problem. Despite repeated reinforcement to drop the coins into the piggy bank, the raccoons began rubbing the coins together, dropping them, and rubbing them together again.

Instinctive drift is the tendency to return to an evolutionarily selected behavior.

instinctive drift
tendency for animals to return to innate behaviors following repeated reinforcement

The raccoons had reverted to an innate behavior, namely, rinsing. They were treating the tokens like pieces of food, like the small hard shells they extract from the beds of ponds and streams (Timberlake, 2006). Breland and Breland (1961) referred to this phenomenon as **instinctive drift**: the tendency for animals to return to innate behaviors following repeated reinforcement. Researchers have observed instinctive drift in other animals, including rats (Powell & Curley, 1984). Psychologists don't fully understand the reasons for such drift. Nevertheless, instinctive drift suggests that we can't fully understand learning without taking into account innate biological influences, because these influences place limits on contingencies of reinforcement.

Learning Fads: Do They Work?

Although the prospect of learning new languages while sleeping is immensely appealing, psychological research offers no support for it.

If you've made it all the way to this point in the chapter (congratulations!), you know that learning new information is hard work. To have followed the material we've presented took an enormous amount of mental energy and concentration on your part.

Perhaps because learning new things requires so much time and effort on our part, many mental health professionals have marketed a motley assortment of techniques that supposedly help us to learn more quickly, or more easily, than we currently do. Do these newfangled methods work? We'll find out by examining four popular techniques.

SLEEP-ASSISTED LEARNING

Imagine that you could master all of the information in this book while getting a few nights of sound sleep. You could pay someone to audiotape the entire book, play the recording over the span of several weeknights, and you'd be all done. You could say good-bye to those late nights in the library or dorm room reading about psychology.

As in many areas of psychology, hope springs eternal. Many proponents of *sleep-assisted learning*—learning new material while asleep—have made some extraordinary claims regarding this technique's potential. One website (http://www.sleeplearning.com/) informs visitors:

> Sleep learning is a way to harness the power of your subconscious while you sleep, enabling you to learn foreign languages, pass exams, undertake professional studies and implement self-growth by using techniques based on research conducted all over the world with great success. . . . It's the most incredible learning aid for years.

The website offers a variety of CDs that can purportedly help us to learn languages, stop smoking, lose weight, reduce stress, or become a better lover, all while we're comfortably catching up on our *zzzz*s. The site even goes so far as to say that the CDs work better when people are asleep than awake.

These assertions are certainly quite remarkable. Does the scientific evidence for sleep-assisted learning stack up to its proponents' impressive claims?

As is so often the case in life, things that sound too good to be true often are. Admittedly, the early findings on sleep-assisted learning were encouraging. One group of investigators exposed sailors to Morse code (a shorthand form of communication that radio operators sometimes use) while asleep. These sailors mastered Morse code 3 weeks faster than did other sailors (Simon & Emmons, 1955). Other studies from the former Soviet Union seemingly provided support for the claim that people could learn new material, such as tape-recorded words or sentences, while asleep (Aarons, 1976).

Nevertheless, these early positive reports neglected to rule out a crucial alternative explanation: The tape recordings may have awakened the subjects. The problem is that almost all of the studies showing positive effects didn't monitor subjects' electroencephalograms (EEGs; see Chapter 3) to ensure they were asleep while listening to the tapes

Extraordinary Claims

Extraordinary Claims

Ruling Out Rival Hypotheses

(Druckman & Swets, 1988, 1994). Better-controlled studies that monitored subjects' EEGs to make sure they were asleep offered little evidence for sleep-assisted learning. So to the extent that sleep-learning tapes "work," it's because subjects hear snatches of them while drifting in and out of sleep. As for that quick fix for reducing stress, we'd recommend skipping the tapes and just getting a good night's rest.

ACCELERATED LEARNING

Still other companies promise consumers ultrafast techniques for learning. These methods, known as Superlearning or Suggestive Accelerative Learning and Teaching Techniques (SALTT), supposedly allow people to pick up new information at anywhere from twenty-five to several hundred times their normal learning speeds (Wenger, 1983). SALTT relies on a mixture of several techniques, such as generating expectations for enhanced learning (telling students they'll learn more quickly), getting students to visualize information they're learning, playing classical music during learning, and breathing in a regular rhythm while learning (Lozanov, 1978). When combined, these techniques supposedly allow learners to gain access to intuitive aspects of their minds that otherwise remain inaccessible.

Extraordinary Claims

Again, however, the evidence for the effectiveness of SALTT and similar methods doesn't come close to matching the extraordinary claims (Della Salla, 2006). Almost all studies show that SALTT doesn't produce enhanced learning (Dipamo & Job, 1990; Druckman & Swets, 1988). Even when researchers have reported positive results for SALTT, these findings have been open to rival explanations. That's because many of the studies conducted on

Ruling Out Rival Hypotheses

SALTT compared this method with a control condition in which students did little or nothing. As a result, the few positive results reported for SALTT could be attributable to placebo effects (see Chapter 2), especially because one of the major components of SALTT is raising learners' expectations. These scattered positive results could also be due to the *Hawthorne effect* (again, see Chapter 2), because all of the students exposed to SALTT knew they were being studied and knew the experimenter expected them to learn faster (Druckman & Swets, 1998).

APPLY YOUR THINKING
If you were studying the effects of accelerated learning methods, like SALTT, how would you try to rule out the possibility of the Hawthorne effect?

DISCOVERY LEARNING

Ruling Out Rival Hypotheses

As we've discovered throughout this text, learning how to *rule out rival explanations* for findings is a key ingredient of critical thinking. But science educators haven't always agreed on how to teach this crucial skill.

One increasingly popular way of imparting this knowledge is *discovery learning*: giving students experimental materials and asking them to figure out the scientific principles on their own (Klahr & Nigram, 2004). For example, a psychology professor who's teaching operant conditioning might set her students up with a friendly rat, a maze, and a bountiful supply of cheese and ask them to determine which variables affect the rat's learning. For instance, does the rat learn the maze most quickly when we reinforce it continuously or only occasionally?

Nevertheless, as David Klahr and his colleagues have shown, the old-fashioned method of *direct instruction,* in which we simply tell students how to solve problems, is often more effective and efficient than discovery learning. In one study, they examined third- and fourth-graders' ability to isolate the variables that influence how quickly a ball rolls down a ramp, such as the ramp's steepness or length. Only 23 percent of students assigned to a discovery learning condition later solved a slightly different problem on their own, whereas 77 percent of students assigned to a direct instruction condition did (Klahr & Nigram, 2004).

That's not to say that discovery learning has no role in education, as in the long-term it may encourage students to learn how to pose scientific questions on their own (Alferink, in press; Kuhn & Dean, 2005). But because many students may never figure out how to solve certain scientific problems independently, it's ill-advised as a stand-alone approach (Kirschner, Sweller, & Clark, 2006).

LEARNING STYLES

Few claims about learning are as widespread as the belief that all individuals have their own distinctive **learning styles**—their preferred means of acquiring information. According to proponents of this view, some students are "analytical" learners who excel at breaking down problems into different components, whereas others are "holistic" learners who excel at viewing problems as a whole. Still others are "verbal" learners who prefer to talk through problems, whereas others are "spatial" learners who prefer to visualize problems in their heads (Cassidy, 2004; Desmedt & Valcke, 2004). Some educational psychologists have claimed to boost learning dramatically by matching people's learning styles to different methods of instruction. According to them, children who are verbal learners should learn much faster and better with written material, children who are spatial learners should learn much faster and better with visual material, and so on.

The view that students with certain learning styles benefit from specific types of instructional materials is popular in educational psychology. Yet scientific research provides little evidence for this belief.

Appealing as these assertions are, they haven't stood the test of careful research. For one thing, it's difficult to assess learning style reliably (Snider, 1992; Stahl, 1999). As we'll recall from Chapter 2, *reliability* refers to consistency in measurement. In this case, researchers have found that different measures designed to assess people's learning styles often yield very different answers about their preferred mode of learning. In part, that's probably because few of us are purely analytical or holistic learners, verbal or spatial learners, and so on; most of us are a blend of both styles. Moreover, studies have generally revealed that tailoring different methods to people's learning styles doesn't result in enhanced learning (Kavale & Forness, 1987; Kratzig & Arbuthnott, 2006; Tarver & Dawson, 1978). Like a number of other fads in popular psychology, the idea of learning styles seems to be more fiction than fact (Alferink, in press; Stahl, 1999).

ASSESS YOUR KNOWLEDGE: FACT OR FICTION?

(1) Sleep-assisted learning techniques only work if subjects stay completely asleep during learning. (True/False)

(2) The Hawthorne effect may explain accelerated learning in the SALTT program. (True/False)

(3) Discovery learning tends to be more efficient than direct instruction for solving most scientific problems. (True/False)

(4) There's little evidence that matching teaching methods to people's learning styles enhances learning. (True/False)

Answers: (1) F (p. 265); (2) T (p. 266); (3) F (p. 266); (4) T (p. 267)

learning styles
individuals' preferred or optimal method of acquiring new information

Classical Conditioning (pp. 234–242)

STUDY the Learning Objectives

▶ Describe examples of classical conditioning and discriminate conditioned stimuli and responses from unconditioned stimuli and responses
  • In classical conditioning, animals come to respond to a previously neutral stimulus that had been paired with another stimulus (the CS) that elicits an automatic response. After repeated pairings with the UCS, which elicits an automatic, reflexive response (the UCR) from the organism, the CS comes to elicit a conditioned response (CR).

▶ Explain how conditioned responses are acquired, maintained, and extinguished
  • Acquisition is the process by which we gradually learn the CR. Extinction is the process whereby following repeated presentation of the CS alone, the CR decreases in magnitude and eventually disappears. Extinction appears to involve an "overwriting" of the CR by new information.

▶ Explain how complex behaviors can result from classical conditioning and how they emerge in our daily lives
  • Higher-order conditioning occurs when organisms develop classically conditioned responses to other CSs associated with the original CS.

DO YOU KNOW THESE TERMS?

- ❏ **learning** (p. 232)
- ❏ **habituation** (p. 233)
- ❏ **classical conditioning** (p. 234)
- ❏ **conditioned stimulus (CS)** (p. 234)
- ❏ **unconditioned stimulus (UCS)** (p. 235)
- ❏ **unconditioned response (UCR)** (p. 235)
- ❏ **conditioned response (CR)** (p. 235)
- ❏ **acquisition** (p. 236)
- ❏ **extinction** (p. 236)
- ❏ **spontaneous recovery** (p. 237)
- ❏ **renewal effect** (p. 237)
- ❏ **stimulus generalization** (p. 237)
- ❏ **stimulus discrimination** (p. 237)
- ❏ **higher-order conditioning** (p. 238)
- ❏ **latent inhibition** (p. 239)
- ❏ **fetishism** (p. 240)
- ❏ **pseudoconditioning** (p. 241)

SUCCEED with

mypsych lab *where learning comes to life!*

The Three Stages of Classical Conditioning

Can an old dog learn new tricks?

(pp. 234–235)

EXPLORE

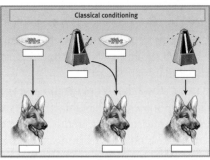

Classical conditioning

Identify the steps of the classical conditioning model used in Pavlov's dog research. (p. 235)

Describe the methods used by Watson and Rayner to condition fear in Little Albert and explain why their work would be considered too unethical to replicate today. (p. 239)

_____
_____
_____
_____

THINK about

what You would do . . .
For years, every time you've gone to the movies you've bought a large buttered popcorn and candy-covered chocolate. Now that you are dieting you want to break that habit. What would you do, using your knowledge of classical conditioning, to change your behavior? (p. 236)

ASSESS your knowledge

1. A change of an organism's behavior or thought as a result of experience is called _____. (p. 232)

2. The process of _____ occurs when we respond less strongly over time to repeated stimuli. (p. 233)

3. Classical conditioning, also known as _____ conditioning, is a form of learning in which animals come to respond to a previously neutral stimulus that had been paired with another stimulus that elicits an automatic response. (p. 234)

4. In Pavlov's experiment, the metronome is the _____ _____, and the meat powder is the _____ _____, which makes the dog salivate, eliciting an _____ _____. (pp. 234–235)

5. If the dog continues to salivate at the sound of the metronome when the meat powder is absent, this is called _____ _____. (p. 235)

6. The learning phase during which a conditioned response is established is called _____. (p.236)

7. After numerous presentations of the metronome without meat powder, Pavlov's dogs eventually stopped salivating; this is the process of _____. (p. 236)

8. A sudden reemergence of an extinguished conditioned response after a delay in exposure to the conditioned stimulus is called _____ _____. (p. 237)

9. Being able to enjoy a scary movie is an example of stimulus (generalization/discrimination). (p. 237)

10. _____ conditioning occurs when we develop a conditioned response to a conditioned stimulus by virtue of its association with another conditioned stimulus. (p. 238)

Operant Conditioning (pp. 242–254)

STUDY the Learning Objectives

▶ Describe how behaviors are acquired through operant conditioning
  • Operant conditioning is learning that is controlled by its consequences.

▶ Identify the similarities and differences between operant and classical conditioning
  • Both forms of conditioning involve many of the

If you did not receive an access code to MyPsychLab with this text and wish to purchase access online, please visit www.mypsychlab.com.

Complete the table to show the differences between classical and operant conditioning. (p. 242)

	Classical Conditioning	Operant Conditioning
Target behavior is . . .	_____	_____
Reward is . . .	_____	_____
Behavior depends primarily on . . .	_____	_____

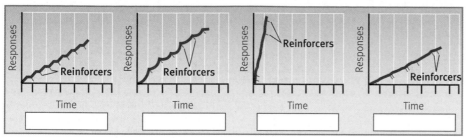

Identify the typical response patterns for the four reinforcement schedule types. (p. 249)

same processes, including acquisition and extinction. Nevertheless, in operant conditioning, responses are emitted rather than elicited, the reward is contingent on behavior, and responses mostly involve skeletal muscles rather than the autonomic nervous system.

▶ **Describe reinforcement and its effects on behavior**
• Thorndike's law of effect tells us that if a response, in the presence of a stimulus, is followed by a reward, it is likely to be repeated resulting in the gradual "stamping in" of S-R connections. Reinforcement can be either positive (pleasant outcome) or negative (withdrawal of a negative outcome).

▶ **Distinguish negative reinforcement from punishment as influences on behavior**
• Negative reinforcement increases a behavior, whereas punishment weakens a response. One disadvantage of punishment is that it tells the organism only what not to do, not what to do.

THINK about

what You would do . . .
As a new Sea World intern, you will be assisting trainers working to teach their youngest dolphin to jump from the water and hit a ball with its snout. What would you do to prepare a plan for achieving this trick using what you know about operant conditioning? (p. 250)

mypsychlab
where learning comes to life!

SUCCEED with

Shaping
Can you learn faster than a chimpanzee can? (p. 250)

DO YOU KNOW THESE TERMS?
☐ **operant conditioning** (p. 242)
☐ **law of effect** (p. 243)
☐ **insight** (p. 243)
☐ **Skinner box** (p. 244)
☐ **reinforcement** (p. 244)
☐ **positive reinforcement** (p. 244)
☐ **negative reinforcement** (p. 244)
☐ **punishment** (p. 245)
☐ **discriminant stimulus (Sd)** (p. 247)
☐ **partial reinforcement** (p. 248)
☐ **schedule of reinforcement** (p. 248)
☐ **fixed ratio (FR) schedule** (p. 248)
☐ **fixed interval (FI) schedule** (p. 248)
☐ **variable ratio (VR) schedule** (p. 249)
☐ **variable interval (VI) schedule** (p. 249)
☐ **shaping by successive approximations** (p. 250)
☐ **Premack principle** (p. 251)
☐ **secondary reinforcers** (p. 253)
☐ **primary reinforcers** (p. 253)

ASSESS your knowledge

1. Acquiring behaviors as a result of the outcome or consequence of these behaviors is called _____ _____. (p. 242)

2. In (classical/operant) conditioning, the reward is contingent on behavior. (pp. 242–243)

3. According to Thorndike's principle, the _____ _____ _____, if a stimulus followed by a behavior results in a reward, the stimulus is more likely to elicit the behavior in the future. (p. 243)

4. A _____ box is a small chamber that allows sustained periods of conditioning to be observed and the animal's behaviors to be electronically recorded. (p. 244)

5. Three key concepts in Skinner's research are _____, _____, and _____ _____. (p. 244)

6. Whereas _____ _____ is the removal of a negative outcome or consequence of a behavior that strengthens the probability of the behavior, _____ is the outcome or consequence of a behavior that weakens the probability of the behavior. (pp. 244–245)

7. According to Skinner, one of the (disadvantages/ advantages) of punishment is that it tells the organism what not to do. (p. 246)

8. A _____ stimulus is any stimulus that signals the presence of reinforcement. (p. 247)

9. Skinner discovered that different _____ _____ yield distinctive patterns of responding. (p. 249)

10. Casino gambling is a prime example of a _____ _____ _____. (pp. 249–250)

Cognitive Models of Learning (pp. 255–261)

mypsychlab
where learning comes to life!

SUCCEED with

Bandura's Bobo Doll
What does the research say on the effects of modeling and aggression?
(pp. 257–258)

What type of learning is taking place in this photo and what is the basis of the learning process shown? (p. 258)

THINK about

what You would do . . .
As the new media director for student affairs, your job is to select movies for the weekly movie night on campus. Due to an incident last semester, there is concern that showing violent movies will provoke violent behavior from students. How would you design a study that would help administrators determine whether there is a cause and effect relation between movie viewing and campus violence? (p. 258)

STUDY the Learning Objectives

▶ Outline the evidence that supports learning in the absence of conditioning
• S-O-R psychologists believe that the organism's interpretation of stimuli plays a central role in learning. Tolman's work on latent learning, which showed that animals can learn without reinforcement, challenged the radical behavioral view of learning.

▶ Explain how learning can occur through observation
• Research suggests that individuals can acquire aggressive behavior by observational learning. Correlational studies, longitudinal studies, laboratory studies, and field studies suggest that media violence contributes to aggression.

▶ Identify evidence of insight learning
• Kohler's work suggested that apes can learn through insight, and later work with humans suggests the same conclusion. This research

calls into question Thorndike's conclusion that all learning occurs through trial and error.

DO YOU KNOW THESE TERMS?
- ❑ **latent learning** (p. 256)
- ❑ **cognitive maps** (p. 257)
- ❑ **observational learning** (p. 257)
- ❑ **mirror neurons** (p. 260)

ASSESS your knowledge

1. Early behaviorists (believed/didn't believe) that thought played an important causal role in learning. (p. 255)

2. An advocate of _____ behaviorism, Watson believed psychologists should focus only on overt, observable behaviors. (p. 255)

3. Skinner was an advocate of _____ behaviorism, in which observable behavior, thinking, and emotion are all governed by the laws of learning. (p. 255)

4. In the past few decades, psychology has increasingly moved away from a simple S-R psychology to a more complex _____ psychology, where the link between S and R isn't automatic. (p. 256)

5. With his classic study of _____ learning in rats, Tolman suggested that learning could occur without reinforcement. (pp. 256–257)

6. According to Tolman, the rats in his study had developed spatial representations of the maze that he called _____ _____. (p. 257)

7. According to some psychologists, an important variant of latent learning is _____ learning, in which one learns by watching others without instruction or reinforcement. (p. 257)

8. Longitudinal studies that correlate the amount of violent TV watched in childhood with the amount of aggressive acts committed in adulthood (have/have not) demonstrated causality. (p. 258)

9. Cells in the prefrontal cortex that become activated by specific motions when an animal performs or observes that an action are called _____ _____. (p. 260)

10. Kohler's work with chimpanzees suggested that at least some smart animals can learn through _____ rather than trial and error. (p. 261)

Biological Influences on Learning (pp. 261–265)

STUDY the Learning Objectives

▶ **Explain how biological predispositions can facilitate learning of some associations**

- Most psychologists have increasingly recognized that our genetic endowment influences learning. Conditioned taste aversions refer to the phenomenon whereby classical conditioning can lead us to develop avoidance reactions to the taste of food. John Garcia and his colleagues showed that conditioned taste aversions violate the principle of equipotentiality, because they demonstrated that certain CSs are more easily conditioned to certain UCSs. Research on preparedness suggests that we are evolutionarily predisposed to learn to fear some stimuli more easily than others.

DO YOU KNOW THESE TERMS?
- ❑ **equipotentiality** (p. 262)
- ❑ **preparedness** (p. 263)
- ❑ **instinctive drift** (p. 264)

Explain how conditioned taste aversions can actually help cancer patients undergoing chemotherapy. (p. 262)

THINK about what You would do . . .

After a bout of food poisoning from undercooked chicken at a wedding last year, you have been unable to even look at chicken without getting queasy. However, you love chicken— what would you do to re-condition yourself to enjoy eating chicken again? (p. 262)

Describe the phenomenon whereby animals return to evolutionarily selected behavior, and how that behavior has affected researchers' understanding of learning. (p. 264)

mypsych lab
where learning comes to life!

SUCCEED with

Taste Aversion
How are scapegoat foods used with cancer patients? (p. 262)

EXPLORE

ASSESS your knowledge

1. Classical conditioning can lead us to develop an avoidance reaction to the taste of food known as _____ _____ _____. (p. 262)

2. Capitalizing on the specificity of conditioned taste aversion, researchers have helped chemotherapy patients to continue to enjoy their favorite foods by giving them a _____ _____ prior to chemotherapy. (p. 262)

3. Through his research with rats, Garcia helped to demonstrate the _____ influences on conditioned taste aversions. (p. 262)

4. The rats in Garcia's study more readily associated nausea with _____ than with any other sensory stimuli. (p. 262)

5. Garcia and others challenged the assumption of _____, the belief of many behaviorists that we can pair all CSs equally well with all UCSs. (p. 262)

6. Pairing a taste with a negative outcome— nausea—that occurred immediately after the taste was (more/less) effective in creating taste aversion than negative outcome that occurred after a delay. (p. 262)

7. When certain stimuli are more likely than others to go together with certain responses, it's called _____. (p. 262)

8. According to Seligman, we're evolutionarily predisposed to fear certain stimuli more than others by means of _____. (p. 263)

9. In Mineka's and Cook's study, the monkeys (acquired/didn't acquire) fears of nondangerous stimuli, such as flowers. (p. 263)

10. The tendency for animals to return to evolutionarily selected behaviors following repeated reinforcement is called _____ _____. (p. 264)

Learning Fads: Do They Work? (pp. 265–267)

Explain the extraordinary claims about how sleep-assisted learning works and identify shortcomings in researchers' attempts to validate those claims. (p. 265)

THINK about

what You would do . . .
A new student has arrived in your classroom whose parents insist she is a strictly visual learner. How would you help educate these parents about current research on learning styles? (p. 267)

Provide a valid argument against teaching to students' learning styles. (p. 267)

SUCCEED with

mypsychlab
where learning comes to life!

Accelerated Learning

How would you evaluate extraordinary claims about learning techniques? (pp. 265–266)

EXPLORE

ASSESS your knowledge

1. Proponents of _____ _____ claim that just by listening to instructional tapes while you sleep, you can learn any number of new things, such as a foreign language. (p. 265)

2. Controlled studies that monitored subjects' EEGs to make sure the subjects were asleep while listening to the instructional tapes revealed evidence (supporting/refuting) the effectiveness of sleep-assisted learning. (p. 265)

3. Methods of accelerated learning, such as _____ _____ _____ __ _____ _____ supposedly allow people to pick up new information anywhere from twenty-five to several hundred times their normal learning speed. (p. 266)

4. SALTT relies on techniques such as getting students to _____ information they're learning, and playing _____ music while they're learning. (p. 266)

5. The evidence for the effectiveness of SALTT (matches/doesn't match) the extraordinary claims. (p. 266)

6. Any scattered positive results for SALTT could be due in part to _____ effects because one of the components of the program is raising learners' expectations. (p. 266)

7. When you give students experimental materials and ask them to figure out a scientific principle on their own, this is known as _____ _____. (p. 266)

8. Klahr and his colleagues have shown that the old-fashioned method of _____ _____, in which we simply tell students how to solve problems, is often most efficient and effective. (p. 266)

9. Individuals' preferred or optimal method of acquiring new information is referred to as _____ _____. (p. 267)

10. Studies have generally shown that tailoring different methods to people's learning styles (does/doesn't) result in enhanced learning. (p. 267)

STUDY the Learning Objectives

▶ Evaluate popular techniques marketed to enhance learning
  • Proponents of sleep-assisted learning claim that individuals can learn new material while asleep. Nevertheless, well-controlled studies of sleep-assisted learning have yielded negative results. Early reports of successful learning during sleep appear to be attributable to a failure to carefully monitor subjects' EEGs to ensure that they were actually asleep while listening to the tapes. Studies of accelerated learning techniques also show few or no positive effects. Positive reports appear to be attributable to placebo effects, Hawthorne effects, and other artifacts. Although popular in science education, discovery learning approaches often appear to be less effective and efficient than direct instruction.

▶ Determine whether individuals' learning ability depends on how well the instructional style matches their learning styles
  • Some educational psychologists claim to be able to boost learning by matching individuals' learning styles with different teaching methods. Nevertheless, learning styles are difficult to assess reliably; moreover, studies that have matched learning styles with teaching methods have typically yielded negative results.

DO YOU KNOW THESE TERMS?
❏ **learning styles** (p. 267)

Remember these questions from the beginning of the chapter? Think again and ask yourself if you would answer them differently based on what you now know about learning. (For more detailed explanations, see MyPsychLab.com.)

▶ Does conditioned learning have an impact on our everyday lives? (p. 236)
▶ How do phobias and fetishes develop? (pp. 239–240)
▶ Does human learning differ from animal learning? (p. 250)
▶ How do trainers get animals to do cute tricks, like dancing or water skiing? (p. 250)
▶ Can we learn simply by observing others? (p. 257)
▶ Does watching violence on TV really teach children to become violent? (p. 258)
▶ Is all learning gradual, or do we sometimes learn through sudden flashes of insight? (pp. 260–261)
▶ Can we avoid a delicious food for decades after only one negative experience with it? (p. 262)
▶ Can we learn in our sleep? (p. 265)
▶ Do different people have different learning styles that work best for them? (p. 267)

THINKING Scientifically

Correlation vs. Causation
pp. 246, 251, 258, 260

Falsifiability p. 257

Extraordinary Claims pp. 265, 266

Occam's Razor p. 255

Replicability pp. 235, 239, 241, 252

Ruling Out Rival Hypotheses
pp. 239, 241, 253, 259, 261, 264, 265, 266

En 1516 Leonard de Vinci franchit les Alpes à dos de mulet
Il emporte avec lui des tableaux qu'il vend
au roi de France

HOMMAGE A LEONARDO DA VINCI

Leonardo da Vinci

Sandro Del-Prete

7

Memory
Constructing and Reconstructing Our Pasts

PREVIEW

Think

First, think about these questions. Then, as you read, think again. . . .

▶ Do we really remember everything that's ever happened to us?

▶ How long do memories last?

▶ Do some people have "photographic" memories?

▶ Do memory aids like "ROYGBIV" (for the colors of the rainbow) really help us to remember?

▶ What are infants' earliest memories?

▶ Are memories for extremely emotional experiences always more accurate than other memories?

▶ Do witnesses to a crime always remember what they observed accurately?

▶ Can people recover repressed memories of traumatic experiences?

Consider the following memorable two tales of memory, both true.

True Story 1. A woman in her forties, known only by the acronym A.J., has such an astounding memory that she's left even seasoned psychological researchers shaking their heads in bewilderment. Although emotionally quite normal, A.J. is markedly abnormal in one way: She remembers just about everything she's ever experienced. When researchers give her a date, like March 17, 1989, she recalls with uncanny accuracy what she was doing on that day—taking a test, eating dinner with a good friend, or traveling to a new city. Researchers have confirmed that she's almost always right. Moreover, she remembers on what day of the week that date fell. In 2003, a team of investigators asked A.J. to remember all of the dates of Easter over the past 24 years. She got all but two correct and reported accurately what she'd done each day (Parker, Cahill, & McCaugh, 2006).

A.J. "suffers" from an exceedingly rare condition called hyperthymestic syndrome: memory that's too good. Or does she really suffer? It's not entirely clear, because she regards her remarkable memory as both a curse and a blessing. A.J. says that she sometimes remembers painful events that she'd prefer to forget, but also that she'd never want to give up her special memory "gift." As to the causes of hyperthymestic syndrome, scientists are baffled (Foer, 2007).

True Story 2. In 1997, Nadean Cool, a 44-year-old nurse's aide in Wisconsin, won a $2.4 million malpractice settlement against her psychotherapist. Nadean entered treatment with relatively mild emotional problems, such as a depressed mood and binge eating. Yet after five years of treatment, Nadean supposedly "recovered" childhood memories of having been a member of a murderous satanic cult, of being raped, and of witnessing the murder of her 8-year-old childhood friend. Her therapist also persuaded her that she harbored more than 130 personalities, including demons, angels, children, and a duck. (Her therapist even listed her treatment as group therapy on the grounds that he needed to treat numerous different personalities.)

All of these memories surfaced after Nadean participated in repeated sessions involving *guided imagery*—in which therapists ask clients to imagine past events—and *hypnotic age regression*—in which therapists use hypnosis to "return" clients to the psychological state of childhood (see Chapter 5). The therapist also subjected Nadean to an exorcism and 15-hour marathon therapy sessions. As therapy progressed, she became overwhelmed by images of terrifying memories she was convinced were genuine. Eventually, however, Nadean came to doubt the reality of these memories, and she terminated treatment.

In a very real sense, we *are* our memories. Our memories define not only our past, but who we are. For A.J., life is like "a movie in her mind that never stops," as she puts it. Her recollections of her life and interactions with friends are remarkably vivid and emotionally intense. A.J.'s memory has shaped her personality in profound ways.

Moreover, when our memories change, as did Nadean Cool's, so do our identities. Following psychotherapy, Nadean came to believe she was a victim of brutal and repeated child abuse. She even came to believe she suffered from a severe condition, namely, *dissociative identity disorder,* or DID (known formerly as multiple personality disorder; see Chapter 15), which is supposedly characterized by the existence of "alter" personalities, or *alters.* The alters reported by DID patients include lobsters, chickens, gorillas, tigers, unicorns, aliens, the bride of Satan, Mr. Spock from *Star Trek,* and the rock star Madonna (Acocella, 1999; Ganaway, 1989).

How Memory Operates: The Memory Assembly Line

We can define **memory** as the retention of information over time. We have memories for many different kinds of information, ranging from our sixteenth birthday party, to how to ride a bike, to the shape of a pyramid. Our memories work pretty well most of the time. Odds are high that tomorrow you'll find your way into school or work just fine and that, with a little luck, you'll even remember some of what you read in this chapter. Yet in other cases, our memories fail us, often when we least expect it. How many times have you misplaced your keys, perhaps even leaving them in your front door for hours without realizing it? Or how often have you forgotten the names of people you've met over and over again? We call this seeming contradiction the *paradox of memory:* Our memories are surprisingly good in some situations and surprisingly poor in others.

THE PARADOX OF MEMORY

To a large extent, this chapter is the story of this mysterious paradox. As we'll see, the answer to the paradox of memory hinges on a crucial fact: *The same memory mechanisms that serve us well in most circumstances can sometimes cause us problems in others.*

When Our Memories Serve Us Well. Research shows that our memories are often astonishingly accurate. Most of us can recognize our schoolmates decades later and recite the lyrics to dozens, even hundreds, of songs. Consider a study by a group of investigators (Standing, Conezio, & Haber, 1970) who showed college students 2,560 photographs of various objects or scenes for only a few seconds each. Three days later, the researchers showed these students each of the original photographs paired with one new photograph, and asked them to say which was which. Remarkably, the students picked out the original photographs correctly 93 percent of the time. In another case, a researcher contacted subjects 17 years (!) after they'd viewed over one hundred line drawings for 1 to 3 seconds in a laboratory study. Remarkably, they identified these drawings at better than chance rates when compared with a control group of participants who'd never seen the drawings (Mitchell, 2006).

The memories of a small subset of individuals with a condition known as *infantile autism* are even more remarkable. Contrary to popular misconception, most autistic individuals lack specialized memory abilities, but there are impressive exceptions. Take the remarkable case of Kim Peek of Salt Lake City, Utah, who was the inspiration for the 1998 Academy Award–winning film, *Rain Man*, starring Dustin Hoffman. Peek's IQ is 87, noticeably below the average of approximately 100. Yet Peek has memorized about 12,000 books word-for-word, the zip codes of every town in the United States, and the number of every highway connecting every city in the United States (Foer, 2007; Treffert & Christiansen, 2005). He's memorized entire phone books and can name the composers of most major classical music pieces, along with the dates of the composers' births and deaths and the date of each composition. Kim Peek is also a *calendar calculator:* Give him any past or future date, like October 17, 2094, and he'll give you the correct day of the week in a matter of seconds. Not surprisingly, Kim has earned the nickname of "Kim-puter" among researchers who've studied his astonishing memory feats.

Yet as we learned with A.J., some nonautistics also possess remarkable memory capacities. Consider the case of Rajan Mahadevan (better known simply as Rajan), now a lecturer in the psychology department of the University of Tennessee. Rajan's memory feats were so spectacular that they were spoofed on an episode of the cartoon show

Salvador Dali's classic painting, *The Persistence of Memory,* is a powerful reminder that our memories are much more like melting wax than hardened metal. They often change over time, far more than we realize.

Phenomenal memory despite low intelligence. Kim Peek, the real "Rain Man" (*top*); Dustin Hoffman playing the title character in the movie *Rain Man* (*bottom*).

memory
retention of information over time

```
Pi=3.
1415926535 8979323846 2643383279 5028841971 6939937510 (50)
5820974944 5923078164 0628620899 8628034825 3421170679 (100)
8214808651 3282306647 0938446095 5058223172 5359408128 (150)
4811174502 8410270193 8521105559 6446229489 5493038196 (200)
4428810975 6659334461 2847564823 3786783165 2712019091 (250)
4564856692 3460348610 4543266482 1339360726 0249141273 (300)
7245870066 0631558817 4881520920 9628292540 9171536436 (350)
7892590360 0113305305 4882046652 1384146951 9415116094 (400)
3305727036 5759591953 0921861173 8193261179 3105118548 (450)
0744623799 6274956735 1885752724 8912279381 8301194912 (500)
9833673362 4406566430 8602139494 6395224737 1907021798 (550)
6094370277 0539217176 2931767523 8467481846 7669405132 (600)
0005681271 4526356082 7785771342 7577896091 7363717872 (650)
1468440901 2249534301 5654958537 1050792279 6892589235 (700)
4201995611 2129021960 8640344181 5981362977 4771309960 (750)
5187072113 4999999837 2978049951 0597317328 1609631859 (800)
5024459455 3469083026 4252230825 3344685035 2619311881 (850)
7101000313 7838752886 5875332083 8142061717 7669147303 (900)
5982534904 2875546873 1159562863 8823537875 9375195778 (950)
1857780532 ̲ ̲ ̲2968065 ̲ ̲ ̲ ̲787 66111 ̲ ̲ ̲ ̲ ̲ ̲64201089 (1000)
```

Figure 7.1 Rajan's Demonstration Sheet of Digits of Pi. Rajan's feats demonstrate the uppermost end of the capacity of human memory.

suggestive memory techniques
procedures that encourage patients to recall memories that may or may not have taken place

memory illusion
false but subjectively compelling memory

Ruling Out Rival Hypotheses

The story of Dr. Jekyll and Mr. Hyde is a classic tale of dissociative identity disorder. Here, actor John Barrymore portrays the evil Mr. Hyde. Increasing evidence suggests that dissociative identity disorder is often a product of therapist suggestion that creates both alter personalities and false memories.

The Simpsons. Rajan had somehow managed to memorize the number *pi*—the ratio of a circle's diameter to its radius—to 38,811 digits (see **Figure 7.1**). When he recited them, it took him 3 hours at a rate of more than 3 digits per second. In sharp contrast to Kim Peek, Rajan is entirely normal emotionally.

In the mid-1990s, one of the authors of this text had the opportunity to watch Rajan show off his pi memorization talents. And show off he did. Someone would read 10 random, sequential digits of pi, and Rajan was off and running: He effortlessly reeled off the next hundred or so digits of pi. Yet Rajan also provides a wonderful illustration of the paradox of memory. Despite finding pi to be a piece of cake, he kept forgetting the location of the men's restroom at the University of Minnesota psychology department although he'd been tested down the hall from it repeatedly (Biederman, Cooper, Fox, & Mahadevan, 1992).

How did Rajan pull off his amazing pi feat? We'll find out later in the chapter.

THE FALLIBILITY OF MEMORY

In some exceedingly rare cases, as with A.J., memory is virtually perfect. Many others of us have extremely good memories in one or two narrow domains, like art history, baseball batting averages, or Civil War trivia. Yet as the cases of Nadean Cool and others with DID illustrate, memory can be surprisingly malleable and prone to error (see Chapter 15). As we've seen, people with this condition can become persuaded of the reality of entirely false memories and even of nonexistent personalities (Lilienfeld et al., 1999; Spanos, 1996).

Of course, it's possible that Nadean Cool's therapist, and other therapists who encourage alter personalities to emerge, aren't creating these alters but *discovering* them. That is, perhaps Nadean's alters had been there all along, and her therapist had merely unearthed them. Yet, as we'll discover later in the chapter, this alternative explanation is unlikely, because there's increasing evidence that **suggestive memory techniques**—procedures that strongly encourage patients to recall memories—often create recollections that were never present to begin with (Lynn et al., 2003).

DID patients aren't the only people whose memories are faulty. As we'll discover throughout the chapter, most and perhaps all of us are prone to false memories under the right conditions. Here's a simple demonstration that requires only a pen or pencil and a piece of paper (for maximum effect, you may want to try this demonstration along with a group of friends). Read the list of words below, taking about a second per word. Read the left column first, then the middle column, then the right. Ready? OK, begin.

Bed	Cot	Sheets
Pillow	Dream	Rest
Tired	Snore	Yawn
Darkness	Blanket	Couch

Now, put down your textbook, and take a minute or so to jot down as many of these words as you can recall.

Did you remember *couch*? If so, give yourself a point. How about *snore*? If so, good—give yourself another point.

OK, how about *sleep*? If you're like about a third of typical subjects, you "remembered" seeing the word *sleep*. But now take a close look at the list. The word *sleep* isn't there.

If you or your friends remembered seeing this word on the list, you experienced a **memory illusion:** a false but subjectively compelling memory (Deese, 1959; Roediger & McDermott, 1995, 1999). Like optical illusions (see Chapter 4), most memory illusions are by-products of our brain's generally adaptive tendency to go beyond the information it has at its disposal. By doing so, our brains help us to make sense of the world, but they sometimes lead us astray (Gilovich, 1991). In this case, you may have remembered seeing the word *sleep* because it was linked closely in meaning to the other words on the list. Your brain correctly extracted the *gist* or central theme of the list, namely, sleeping, dreaming, and resting. As a consequence, it may have been fooled into remembering that the word *sleep* was there. By relying on the *representativeness heuristic* (Chapter 2)—like goes with like—we simplify things to make them easier to remember. In this case, though, our use of this handy heuristic comes with a modest price: a memory illusion.

> ### APPLY YOUR THINKING
> Could our tendency to extract the gist of complex information, rather than to remember it literally, be adaptive? What advantages could there be to *not* remembering events exactly as they happened?

Moreover, most of us have surprisingly poor memories for everyday objects we've seen hundreds, even thousands, of times. Take a look at **Figure 7.2,** where you'll see an array of six pennies. Which of these pennies is the real one?

If you flunked this miniature test of "common cents," don't feel too bad. When two researchers conducted a similar version of this test about three decades ago, they found that fewer than half of 203 Americans identified the correct penny (Nickerson & Adams, 1979).

THE RECONSTRUCTIVE NATURE OF MEMORY

These demonstrations drive home a crucial point: Our memories frequently fool us and fail us. Indeed, a central theme of this chapter is that our memories are far more reconstructive than reproductive. When we try to recall an event, we *actively reconstruct* our memories using the cues and information available to us. We don't *passively reproduce* our memories, as we would if we were downloading information from a web page on the Internet. Remembering is largely a matter of patching together our often fuzzy recollection with our best hunches about what really happened. When we recall our past experiences, we rarely, if ever, reproduce precise replicas of them (Neisser & Hyman, 1999). We should therefore be skeptical of widespread claims that certain vivid memories or even dreams are exact "photocopies" of past events (van der Kolk, Britz, Burr, Sherry, & Hartmann, 1984).

In fact, it's easy to show that our memories are often reconstructive. After reading this sentence, close your eyes for a few moments and picture your most recent walk along a beach, lake, or pond. Then, after opening your eyes, ask yourself what you "saw."

Did you see yourself as if from a distance? If so, you experienced what cognitive psychologists Georgia Nigro and Ulric Neisser termed an *observer memory*, meaning a memory in which we see ourselves as an outside observer would (Nigro & Neisser, 1983). As Sigmund Freud noted well over a century ago, observer memories provide an existence proof (see Chapter 2) that at least some of our memories are reconstructive (Schacter, 1996). You couldn't possibly have seen yourself from a distance, because you don't see yourself when you look at your surroundings. Incidentally, if you instead pictured the scene as you would have seen it through your own eyes, you experienced what Nigro and Neisser called a *field memory:* seeing the world through your visual field.

The science of memory offers yet another striking example of how research contradicts popular opinion. Surveys indicate that many or most people believe our memories operate like video cameras or tape recorders, replaying events precisely as we saw them. Moreover, about 36 percent of us believe our brains contain perfect records of everything we've ever experienced (Alvarez & Brown, 2002). Even most psychotherapists believe that everything we learn is permanently stored in the mind (Loftus & Loftus, 1980; Yapko, 1994). Yet as we'll discover throughout this chapter, research raises serious questions concerning all of these assumptions.

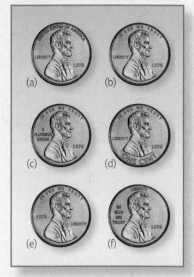

Figure 7.2 Penny Array from Nickerson and Adams (1979). Which of these pennies is the real one? Try to guess before pulling one out of your pocket. (*Source:* Nickerson & Adams, 1979)

The correct answer is b.

When you picture yourself taking a recent walk on the beach, do you see yourself as an outside observer would (an "observer memory")? If so, such a recollection provides compelling evidence that memory can be reconstructive.

How can our memories be both so good in some cases and so bad in others? How can we explain both the astonishing memories of people like A.J. and Rajan and the faulty memories of people like Nadean Cool? To grasp the paradox of memory, we need to figure out how some of our experiences make it into our memories, whereas so many others never do. To do so, let's embark on a guided tour of the factory assembly line inside our heads.

THE THREE SYSTEMS OF MEMORY

Up to this point, we've been talking about memory as though it were a single thing. It isn't. Most psychologists distinguish among three major systems of memory: sensory memory, short-term memory, and long-term memory, as depicted in **Figure 7.3** (Atkinson & Shiffrin, 1968; Waugh & Norman, 1965). These systems serve different purposes and differ along at least two important dimensions: **span**—how much information each system can hold—and **duration**—over how long a period of time that system can hold information.

In reality, the distinctions among these three memory systems aren't always clear-cut. Moreover, many modern researchers suspect that there are more than three memory systems (Baddeley, 1993; Healy & McNamara, 1996). For the sake of simplicity, we'll begin by discussing the three-systems model, although we'll point out some ambiguities along the way.

As we'll soon discover, we can think of these three systems much like different factory workers along an automobile assembly line. The first system, *sensory memory,* is tied closely to the raw materials of our experiences, our perceptions of the world; it holds these perceptions for just a few seconds or less before passing *some* of them on to the second system. This second system, *short-term memory,* works actively with the information handed to it, transforming it into more meaningful material before passing *some* of it on to the third system. Short-term memory holds on to information longer than sensory memory does, but not much longer. The third and final system, *long-term memory,* permits us to retrieve important information minutes, days, weeks, months, or even years later. In some cases, the information in long-term memory lasts for a lifetime. The odds are high, for example, that you'll remember your first kiss and your high school graduation for many decades, perhaps until the last day of your life. As you can tell from our use of the word *some* in the previous sentences, we lose a great deal of information at each stage of the memory assembly line.

Sensory Memory. If you're anywhere near a television set, turn it on for 10 seconds or so. What did you see?

Regardless of what program you were watching, you almost certainly experienced a steady and uninterrupted stream of visual information. In reality, that continuous stream of images was an illusion, because television programs and movies consist of a series of disconnected frames, each separated by an extremely brief interlude of darkness that you can't perceive. Yet your brain sees these frames as blending together into a seamless whole, in part because it continues to detect each frame for an extremely brief period of time after it disappears.

That is, our brains retain each frame in our **sensory memory,** which is the first factory worker in the assembly line of memory. Sensory memory briefly maintains our perceptions in a "buffer" area before passing them on to the next memory system, which is short-term memory. Sensory memory is a helpful system, because it buys our brains a bit of extra time to process incoming sensations. It also allows us to "fill in the blanks" in our perceptions and see the world as an unbroken stream of events.

Psychologists believe each sense, including vision, hearing, touch, taste, and smell, has its own form of sensory memory. In the case of television or movie clips, we experience an **iconic memory,** the type of sensory memory that applies to vision. Iconic memories last for only about a second, and then they're gone forever.

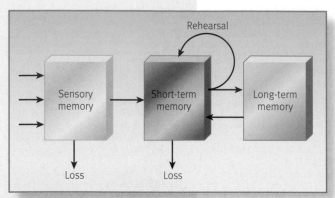

Figure 7.3 The Three-Memory Model. This model subdivides memory into sensory, short-term, and long-term memory. Information flows from left to right, but also from right to left in the case of information retrieved from long-term memory and moved into short-term memory. (*Source:* Atkinson & Shiffrin, 1968)

Iconic memory: After a lightning strike, we retain a visual image of it for about 1 second.

span
how much information a memory system can retain

duration
length of time for which a memory system can retain information

sensory memory
brief storage of perceptual information before it is passed to short-term memory

iconic memory
visual sensory memory

When he was a graduate student, psychologist George Sperling (1960) conducted a pioneering study that demonstrated the existence of iconic memory. He quickly flashed participants a display of twelve letters, with four letters arranged in three rows, as shown in **Figure 7.4.** The display lasted only about one-twentieth of a second. Sperling found that most participants could remember four or five letters. Surprisingly, different participants remembered different letters. This finding suggested to Sperling that all twelve letters had an equal chance of being recalled but that no one person could recall them all. This finding was puzzling. After all, if participants had remembered the whole visual display, why could they recall only a handful of letters and no more?

To find out, Sperling had a "flash" of insight, pun intended. As he flashed the twelve letters, he used a tone (high, medium, or low) to signal participants which of the three rows (top, middle, or bottom) to report. Then he randomly instructed participants to report only one of the three rows. When he used this technique, which he termed the *method of partial report,* he found that virtually all participants now got almost all letters in that row correct. This finding confirmed Sperling's hunch: Participants had access to all twelve letters in their memories. Sperling concluded that our iconic memories fade so quickly that we can't access all the information before it disappears. So Sperling's participants were able to take in all of the information, but retained it in memory only long enough to read off a few letters.

Iconic memory may help to explain the remarkable phenomenon of *eidetic imagery,* popularly called "photographic memory." True photographic memory is exceedingly rare. People with eidetic memory can supposedly hold a visual image in their minds with such clarity that they can describe it perfectly or almost perfectly (see **Figure 7.5**), just as we can describe the details of a painting immediately in front of us with near-perfect accuracy. Some psychologists believe that eidetic memory reflects an unusually long persistence of the iconic image in some lucky people.

Although some psychologists claim that eidetic imagery is especially common among certain mentally retarded individuals or older individuals, the evidence for these claims is spotty. Moreover, recent evidence raises questions about whether any memories are truly photographic (Minsky, 1986). Eidetikers' memories are clearly remarkable, but they're rarely perfect. Their memories often contain minor errors, including information that wasn't present in the original visual stimulus. So even eidetic memory often appears to be reconstructive (Searleman, 2003).

Sensory memory also applies to hearing. Now read that last sentence out loud: "Sensory memory also applies to hearing." If you pause for a few moments after saying it, you'll be able to replay the words precisely as you heard them for a few seconds, much like a soft echo reverberating from a mountaintop. That's why psychologists call this form of sensory memory **echoic memory** (Neisser, 1967). In contrast to iconic memories, echoic memories can last as long as 5 to 10 seconds (Cowan, Lichty, & Grove, 1990), conveniently permitting you to take notes on your psychology professor's most recent sentence even after he or she has finished saying it. Interestingly, there's also some evidence of eidetic memories for hearing, in which a few fortunate individuals report that their echoic memories persist for unusually long periods of time. Now, wouldn't that make taking lecture notes a breeze?

Short-Term Memory.   Once information makes it past our sensory buffers, it passes into our **short-term memory,** a second system for retaining information in our memories for brief periods of time. Short-term memory is the second factory worker in our memory assembly line. Some psychologists also refer to short-term memory as *working memory*— it's the memory store for the information we're currently thinking about, attending to, or processing actively (Baddeley, 1993; Baddeley & Hitch, 1974). If sensory memory is what feeds raw materials into the assembly line, then short-term memory is the workspace where construction happens. After construction takes place, we either move the product into the warehouse for long-term storage or, in some cases, scrap it altogether.

If short-term memory is a short stop on the assembly line, just how brief is it? In the late 1950s, a husband-and-wife psychologist team decided to find out.

Figure 7.4 Display of Twelve Letters as Used in Sperling's 1960 Study. Sperling's partial report method demonstrated that all displayed letters were held in sensory memory, but decayed rapidly before all of them could be transferred to short-term memory. (*Source:* Sperling, 1960)

Figure 7.5 Alice with Cheshire Cat. Memory psychologists have used variations of this drawing from Lewis Carroll's *Alice's Adventures in Wonderland* to test for eidetic imagery. To find out if you have eidetic memory, look for no longer than 30 seconds at the drawing and then cover it with a sheet of paper. Do that now before reading on. Now, can you remember how many stripes were on the cat's tail? Few adults can remember such details (Gray & Gummerman, 1975), although eidetic memory is much more prevalent among elementary school children (Haber, 1979).

echoic memory
auditory sensory memory

short-term memory
memory system that retains information for limited durations

The Duration of Short-Term Memory.   Lloyd and Margaret Peterson (1959) presented participants with lists of three letters each, such as MKP or ASN, and then asked them to recall these three-letter strings. In some cases, they made participants wait only 3 seconds before recalling the letters; in other cases, they made them wait up to 18 seconds. Each time, they told participants to count backward by threes while they were waiting.

Many psychologists were surprised by the Petersons' results, and you may be too. They found that after about 10 or 15 seconds, most participants *did no better than chance.* So the duration of short-term memory is quite brief; it's probably no longer than about 20 seconds. Some researchers believe it's even shorter than that, perhaps even less than 5 seconds, because some subjects in the Peterson and Peterson study may have been able to silently rehearse the letters even when counting backward (Sebrects, Marsh, & Seamon, 1989). Incidentally, many people misuse the term *short-term memory* in everyday language. For example, they may say that their "short-term memory isn't working" because they forgot what they had for dinner yesterday. As we've seen, the duration of short-term memory is far briefer than that.

Memory Loss from Short-Term Memory: Decay versus Interference.   Why did the Petersons' participants lose their short-term memories so quickly, just as we quickly lose our memories of phone numbers we've just heard? The most obvious explanation is that short-term memories **decay,** that is, fade away. The longer we wait, the less is left. Yet there's a competing explanation for the loss of information from short-term memory: **interference.** According to this view, our memories get in the way of each other. That is, our memories are very much like radio signals. They don't change over time, but they're harder to detect if they're jammed by other signals.

As it turns out, there's evidence for both decay and interference. Evidence for decay comes from studies that rely on an intriguing premise: Higher temperatures should produce higher rates of memory decay, because higher temperatures in animals (including humans) are linked to higher levels of metabolism (that is, breakdown) of chemicals in the brain. Indeed, in studies of goldfish and other animals, higher temperatures are related to poorer memories of previously learned tasks (Gleitman, 1971).

Nevertheless, there's even stronger evidence for the role of interference in memory loss. For example, two investigators (Waugh & Norman, 1965) presented subjects with many different lists of sixteen digits, such as 6 2 7 1 8 5 3 4 2 6 9 7 4 5 8 3. Right after subjects saw each list, the researchers gave them one "target" digit to focus on, and then they asked subjects which digit came after this target digit. In all cases, this target digit appeared twice in the list, and subjects had to remember the digit that came after its *first* presentation in the list. In the digit list above, the target item might be "8," so we'd search for the first 8 in the list—and the correct response would be 5.

The experimenters manipulated two variables to figure out which of them influenced forgetting. Specifically, they manipulated both (1) how rapidly they presented digits to subjects—either quickly (one digit every second) or slowly (one digit every four seconds)—and (2) where in the list the target digit appeared (early or late).

Now, if decay were the principal culprit in forgetting, participants' performance should become worse when researchers read the list slowly because more time had passed. In contrast, if interference were the principal culprit, participants' performance should become worse when the target digit appeared later rather than earlier in the list, regardless of speed, because memory for later digits is hampered by memory for earlier digits.

The results showed that interference is the prime culprit in forgetting. Participants' forgetting is due almost entirely to where in the list the target digit appears, rather than to the speed of presentation (Keppel & Underwood, 1962). Still, most researchers believe that both decay and interference play some role in short-term memory loss (Altmann & Schunn, 2002).

We're not quite done with our examination of interference yet, because it turns out that there are two different kinds of interference (Underwood, 1957). One kind,

Ruling Out Rival Hypotheses

decay
fading of information from memory

interference
loss of information from memory because of competition from additional incoming information

retroactive inhibition, or retroactive interference, occurs when learning something new hampers earlier learning (think of the prefix *retro-*, because retroactive inhibition works in a reverse direction). For example, if you've learned one language, say Spanish, and then later learned a somewhat similar language, perhaps Italian, you've probably found that you started making mistakes in Spanish you'd never made before. Specifically, you may have found yourself using Italian words, like *buono*, for Spanish words, like *bueno* (both *buono* and *bueno* mean "good").

In contrast, **proactive inhibition,** or proactive interference, occurs when earlier learning gets in the way of new learning. For example, knowing how to play tennis might interfere with our attempt to learn to play racquetball, which requires a much smaller racquet. Not surprisingly, both retroactive and proactive inhibition are more likely to occur when the old and new stimuli that we've learned are similar. Learning a new language doesn't much affect our ability to master a new spaghetti recipe.

The Capacity of Short-Term Memory: The Magic Number. We've already seen that short-term memory doesn't last very long. Twenty seconds, or even less—and—poof!—the memory is gone, unless we've made an extra-special effort to retain it. But how large is the span of short-term memory?

Try reading each of the following rows of numbers, one row at a time, at a rate of one number per second. Once you're done with each row, close your eyes and try writing down what you remember. Ready? OK, begin.

$$9 - 5 - 2$$
$$2 - 9 - 7 - 3$$
$$5 - 7 - 4 - 9 - 2$$
$$6 - 2 - 7 - 3 - 8 - 4$$
$$2 - 4 - 1 - 8 - 6 - 4 - 7$$
$$3 - 9 - 5 - 7 - 4 - 1 - 8 - 9$$
$$8 - 4 - 6 - 3 - 1 - 7 - 4 - 2 - 5$$
$$5 - 2 - 9 - 3 - 4 - 6 - 1 - 8 - 5 - 7$$

You've just taken a test of "digit span." How did you make out? Odds are that you breezed through three digits, started to find four digits a bit tricky, and maxed out at somewhere between five and nine digits. It's unlikely you got the ten-digit list completely right; if you did, you've earned the right to call yourself a memory superstar.

That's because the digit span of most adults is between five and nine digits, with an average of seven digits. Indeed, this finding is so consistent across people that Princeton University psychologist George Miller (1956) referred to seven plus or minus two pieces of information as the **Magic Number.**

According to Miller, the Magic Number applies to much more than digits. It's the universal limit of short-term memory, and it applies to just about all information we encounter: Numbers, letters, people, vegetables, and cities. Because it's hard to retain much more than seven plus or minus two pieces of information in our short-term memory, it's almost surely not a coincidence that telephone numbers are exactly seven digits long, not counting the area code. When telephone numbers exceed seven digits, we start making mistakes. Some psychologists have since argued that Miller's Magic Number may even overestimate the capacity of short-term memory, and that the true Magic Number may be as low as four (Cowan, 2000). Regardless of who's right, it's clear that the capacity of short-term memory is extremely limited.

Chunking. Multiplying the Magic Number. If our short-term memory capacity is no more than nine digits, and perhaps much less, how do we manage to remember larger amounts of information than this for brief periods of time? For example, read the following sentence, then wait a few seconds and recite it back to yourself: **Harry Potter's white owl Hedwig flew off into the dark and stormy night.** Were you able to remember most or even all of it? The odds are high that you were. Yet this sentence contained thirteen words, which exceeds the Magic Number. How did you accomplish this feat?

This player is actively engaged in a racquetball match. If she was an experienced tennis player before attempting raquetball, the odds are high that her tennis swings would initially get in the way of her learning how to swing a racquetball racquet properly. That is, it will take her a while to "unlearn" her tennis swings. That's a classic case of proactive inhibition.

retroactive inhibition
interference with retention of old information due to acquisition of new information

proactive inhibition
interference with acquisition of new information due to previous learning of information

Magic Number
the span of short-term memory, according to George Miller: seven plus or minus two pieces of information

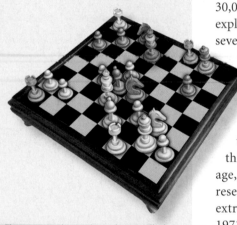

We can expand our ability to remember things in the short term by using a technique called **chunking:** organizing material into meaningful groupings. For example, look at the following string of fifteen letters for a few seconds, and then try to recall them:

G T I Q A K B N R D W E L F O

How'd you do? Odds are you didn't do too well, probably right around the Magic Number, that is, only a subset of the letters listed. Okay, now try this fifteen-letter string instead.

C I A U S A F B I N B C J F K

Did you do any better this time? If so, it's probably because you noticed something different about this group of fifteen letters than the first group: They consisted of meaningful abbreviations. So you probably "chunked" these fifteen letters into five meaningful groups of three letters each: CIA, USA, FBI, NBC, JFK. In this way, you reduced the number of items you needed to remember from fifteen to only five. In fact, you might have even gotten this number down to less than five by combining CIA and FBI (both the initials of U.S. government intelligence agencies) into one chunk.

Earlier, we promised we'd explain how Rajan performed his remarkable pi memorization feats. If you've guessed by now that he relied largely on chunking, you're right. Rajan memorized enormous numbers of area codes, dates of famous historical events, and other meaningful numbers embedded within the list of pi digits to effectively reduce more than 30,000 digits to a much smaller number. Incidentally, the phenomenon of chunking explains why some psychologists believe that the real Magic Number may be lower than seven. According to them, many participants manage to chunk two or more numbers or letters when given lists of seven pieces of information.

Experts rely on chunking to help them process complex information. William Chase and Nobel Prize–winning researcher Herbert Simon showed chess masters and chess novices various sets of *actual* chess positions from a point midway through the game for 5 seconds each. Each position contained up to twenty-six chess pieces (the maximum number of pieces in a chess game is thirty-two). Experts correctly recalled the positions of sixteen chess pieces on average, whereas beginners correctly recalled only four on average. Yet when the researchers showed both groups *random* chess positions—those that would be extremely unlikely to occur in actual games—both did equally poorly (Chase & Simon, 1973). By chunking the chess pieces into patterns they found meaningful, the chess experts easily remembered the complete positions (see **Figure 7.6**). Yet their overall memories were no better than anyone else's when the chess positions were nonsensical. Researchers have reported the same finding when comparing professional basketball players with nonplayers. Players recall actual basketball positions much better than do nonplayers, but do no better when it comes to recalling basketball positions that aren't realistic (Didierjean & Marmèche, 2005).

Figure 7.6 Chess Pieces in a Realistic Position. Experienced chess players recall the positions above much better than chess novices. That's because it's a realistic chess position. Yet experienced players do no better than novices when asked to recall a chess position that wouldn't arise in an actual game.

APPLY YOUR THINKING

Clearly, chunking is a beneficial strategy for increasing our memories. But could chunking actually lead to memory errors in some cases? If so, how?

Rehearsal: Keeping Information Onstage. Whereas chunking increases the span of short-term memory, a strategy called rehearsal extends the duration of information in short-term memory. **Rehearsal** is repeating the information mentally (or even out loud). In that way, we keep the information "alive" in our short-term memories, just as a juggler keeps a bunch of bowling pins "alive" by continuing to catch them and toss them back into the air. Of course, if he pauses for a second to scratch his nose, the bowling pins come crashing to the ground. Similarly, if we stop rehearsing and shift our attention elsewhere, we'll quickly lose material from our short-term memory.

chunking
organizing information into meaningful groupings, allowing us to extend the span of short-term memory

rehearsal
repeating information to extend the duration of retention in short-term memory

There are two major types of rehearsal. The first, **maintenance rehearsal,** simply involves repeating the stimuli in their original form; we don't attempt to change the original stimuli in any way. We engage in maintenance rehearsal whenever we hear a phone number and keep on repeating it—either out loud or in our minds—until we're ready to dial the number. In this way, we keep the information "alive" in our short-term memory. Of course, if someone interrupts us while we're rehearsing, we'll forget the number.

The second type of rehearsal, **elaborative rehearsal,** usually takes more effort. In this type of rehearsal, we "elaborate" on the stimuli we need to remember by linking them in some meaningful way, perhaps by visualizing them or trying to understand their interrelationship (Craik & Lockhart, 1972).

To grasp the difference between maintenance and elaborative rehearsal, let's imagine that a researcher gave us a *paired-associate task,* which is a particular favorite of memory researchers (although not necessarily of subjects in memory experiments). In this task, the investigator first presents us with various pairs of words, such as dog–shoe, tree–pipe, key–monkey, and kite–president. Then, she presents us with the first word in each pair—dog, tree, and so on—and asks us to remember the second word in the pair. If we used maintenance rehearsal, we'd simply repeat the words in each pair over and over again as soon as we heard it—dog–shoe, dog–shoe, dog–shoe, and so on. In contrast, if we used elaborative rehearsal, we'd try to link the words in each pair in a meaningful way. One effective way of accomplishing this goal is to come up with a meaningful, perhaps even absurd, visual image that combines both stimuli (see **Figure 7.7**) (Paivio, 1969). Research shows that we're especially likely to remember the two stimuli if we picture them interacting in some fashion (Wollen, Weber, & Lowry, 1972). That's probably because doing so allows us to chunk them into a single integrated stimulus. So to remember the word pair dog–rocket, for example, we could picture a dog piloting a rocket ship or a rocket ship barking like a dog.

Many studies show that elaborative rehearsal usually works better than maintenance rehearsal (Harris & Qualls, 2000). This finding demolishes a widely held misconception about memory: that rote memorization is typically the best means of retaining information. There's a take-home lesson here when it comes to our study habits. To remember complex information, it's almost always better to connect that information with things we already know than to merely keep repeating it.

Depth of Processing: Everyone into the Deep End! This finding is consistent with a **levels-of-processing** model of memory. According to this model, the more deeply we transform information, the better we tend to remember it. This model identifies three levels of processing of verbal information (Craik & Lockhart, 1972): visual, phonological (sound-related), and semantic (meaning-related). According to this model, visual processing is the most shallow, phonological somewhat less shallow, and semantic the deepest. To understand the differences among these three levels, try to remember the following sentence:

ALL PEOPLE CREATE THEIR OWN MEANING OF LIFE

If you relied on *visual* processing, you'd hone in on how the sentence looks. For example, you might try to focus on the fact that the sentence consists entirely of capital letters. If you relied on *phonological* processing, you'd focus on how the words in the sentence sound. Most likely, you'd repeat the sentence again and again until it began to sound boringly familiar. Finally, if you relied on *semantic* processing, you'd emphasize the sentence's meaning. You might elaborate on how you've tried to create your own meaning of life and how doing so has been beneficial to you. Research shows that deeper levels of processing, especially semantic processing, tend to produce more enduring long-term memories (Craik & Tulving, 1975).

Still, some psychologists have criticized the levels-of-processing model as largely unfalsifiable (Baddeley, 1993). According to them, it's virtually impossible to determine how deeply we've processed a memory in the first place. Moreover, they claim, proponents of the levels-of-processing model are merely equating "depth" with how

Figure 7.7 Word Pairs. Using elaborative rehearsal helps us recall the word pair dog–shoe. (*Source:* Paivio, 1969)

maintenance rehearsal
repeating stimuli in their original form to retain them in short-term memory

elaborative rehearsal
linking stimuli to each other in a meaningful way to improve retention of information in short-term memory

levels of processing
depth of transforming information, which influences how easily we remember it

Falsifiability

well subjects later remember. There may well be some truth to this criticism. Still, it's safe to say that the more meaning we can supply to a stimulus, the more likely we are to recall it in the long term.

Long-Term Memory. Now that the second factory assembly line worker—short-term memory—has finished her construction job, what does she pass on to the third and final worker? And how does what the third worker receives differ from what the second worker started out with? **Long-term memory,** the third worker, is our lasting store of information. It includes the facts, experiences, and skills we've acquired over our life span.

Characteristics of Long-Term Memory and Differences from Short-Term Memory.
Long-term memory differs from short-term memory in several important ways. First, in contrast to short-term memory, which can hold only seven (or maybe even fewer) stimuli in hand at a single time, the capacity of long-term memory is huge. Just how huge? No one knows for sure. Some scientists estimate that a typical person's memory holds about as much information as 500 complete sets of *Encyclopaedia Britannica* (Cardon, 2005). So if someone praises you on your "encyclopedic memory," accept the compliment. They're probably right.

Second, although information in short-term memory vanishes after only about 20 seconds at most, information in long-term memory often endures for years, even decades. Consider the work of psychologist Harry Bahrick, who has studied individuals' memory for languages they learned in school over many decades. In **Figure 7.8,** we can see that people's memory declines markedly about 2 to 3 years after taking a Spanish course. Yet after about 2 years, the decline becomes quite gradual. Indeed, it begins to level out after a while, with almost no additional loss for up to 50 years after they took the course (Bahrick & Phelps, 1987). Bahrick referred to this kind of long-term memory, which remains "frozen" over time, as **permastore,** as an analogy to the permafrost found in the Arctic or Antarctic that never melts, even with dramatic increases in temperature.

Third, the types of mistakes we commit in long-term memory differ from those we make in short-term memory. Long-term memory errors tend to be *semantic,* that is, based on the meaning of the information we've received. So we might misremember a "poodle" as a "terrier." In contrast, short-term memory errors tend to be *acoustic,* that is, based on the sound of the information we've received (Conrad, 1964; Wickelgren, 1965). So, we might misremember hearing "noodle" rather than "poodle."

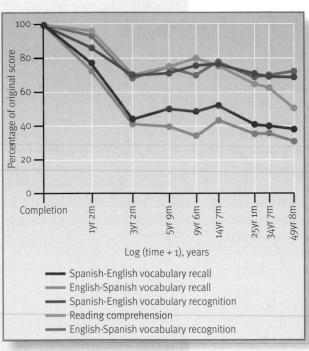

Figure 7.8 The Memory Permastore.
The classic work of Harry Bahrick (1984) shows that retention of a foreign language remains remarkably constant for spans of almost 50 years after an initial drop. (*Source:* Bahrick, 1984)

Primacy and Recency Effects: Forgetting Isn't Random. When we try to remember a large number of items, such as a grocery list or a schedule of events, we often forget some of them. To some extent, psychologists can predict which items we're more likely to forget and which we're more likely to remember.

To demonstrate this point, read the list of twenty words below, either to yourself or out loud. Read the left column first, then the middle column, then the right one. Then, turn away from your book and take a few minutes to try to recall as many of these words as you can in any order you'd like. Psychologists call this a *free recall* task because you're free to recall the words in whatever order they come to mind. Ready? Begin.

long-term memory
sustained (from minutes to years) retention of information stored regarding our facts, experiences, and skills

permastore
type of long-term memory that appears to be permanent

Ball	Sky	Store
Shoe	Desk	Pencil
Tree	Car	Grass
Dog	Rope	Man
Paper	Dress	Cloud
Bird	Xylophone	Hat
House	Knife	Vase

When you're done, check off which words you got right. This demonstration may not work as well as the others in this chapter, because it works best when the results are averaged across a large group of people. Still, let's take a peek at how you did.

If you're like most people, you probably did a bit better with the early words, like *ball*, *shoe*, and *tree*, than with the words in the middle of the list. That's the **primacy effect:** the tendency to remember stimuli, like words, early in a list. Also, you may have done a bit better with the later words, like *cloud*, *hat*, and *vase*. That's the **recency effect:** the tendency to remember stimuli later in a list. As an aside, there's a decent chance you remembered the word *xylophone*, which seems to be something of an oddball in the list. That's the **von Restorff effect:** the tendency to remember stimuli that are distinctive or that stick out like sore thumbs from other stimuli (Neath & Surprenant, 2003).

If we averaged your results along with those of a few hundred other subjects, we'd end up with the graph depicted in **Figure 7.9,** called the **serial position curve.** As we can see from the figure, this curve clearly displays the primacy and recency effects. There's even a serial position curve for U.S. presidents. If given the chance to name as many presidents as they can, most people list early presidents, like Washington, Jefferson, and Adams, and recent presidents, like Reagan, Clinton, and George W. Bush, more than middle presidents with good old Abe Lincoln being a striking exception (Roediger & Crowder, 1976).

What do the primary and recency effects mean? There's still some controversy concerning this question, but most researchers agree that primacy and recency effects reflect the operation of different memory systems. Because the last few words in the list were probably lingering in your short-term memory, you were probably especially likely to recall them. So the recency effect seems to reflect the workings of short-term memory.

What explains the primacy effect? This one is trickier, but there's good evidence that you were more likely to recall the earlier words in the list because you had more opportunity to rehearse them silently. As a consequence, these words were more likely to be transferred from short-term memory into long-term memory. So the primacy effect seems to reflect the operation of long-term memory. In contrast to sensory and short-term memory, long-term memory retains information for substantial durations.

The primacy and recency effects seem to depend on the activity of different brain regions. Memory for early words in a list tends to activate the hippocampus, which, as we learned in Chapter 3, plays a key role in the transfer of information from short-term into long-term memory. In contrast, memory for late words in a list tends to activate the dorsolateral prefrontal cortex, a region of the prefrontal cortex (see Chapter 3) that plays a key role in keeping information "alive" in short-term memory (Talmi, Grady, Goshen-Gottstein, & Moscovitch, 2005).

Types of Long-Term Memory: Different Flavors or Different Meals? As we mentioned earlier, some psychologists argue that there are actually more than three memory systems. In particular, they claim that long-term memory isn't just one system, but many.

To find out why, try your hand at the following four questions.

(1) In what year did the United States become independent from Great Britain?
(2) What Middle-Eastern country did the United States invade in 2003?
(3) How old were you when you first tried to ride a bicycle?
(4) Where did you celebrate your last birthday?

According to Endel Tulving (1972) and many other memory researchers, our answers to the first two questions rely on different memory systems than our answers to the last two. Our answers to the first two questions (1776 and Iraq) depend on

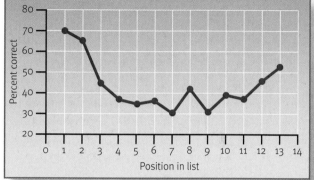

Figure 7.9 The Serial Position Curve. Most psychologists believe that the primacy and recency effects in this curve are the telltale signs of two different memory systems: long-term and short-term memory, respectively.

primacy effect
tendency to remember words at the beginning of a list especially well

recency effect
tendency to remember words at the end of a list especially well

von Restorff effect
tendency to remember distinctive stimuli better than less distinctive stimuli

serial position curve
graph depicting the effect of both primacy and recency on people's ability to recall items on a list

Which key do you use, and which way do you turn it, to lock or unlock your front door? Chances are you'll have trouble "putting your fingers" on this information without performing the action, because it's stored in implicit memory.

Procedural memory is memory for how to do things, even things we do automatically without thinking about how to do them.

semantic memory
our knowledge of facts about the world

episodic memory
recollection of events in our lives

explicit memory
memories we recall intentionally and of which we have conscious awareness

implicit memory
memories we don't deliberately remember or reflect on consciously

procedural memory
memory for how to do things, including motor skills and habits

priming
our ability to identify a stimulus more easily or more quickly after we've encountered similar stimuli

semantic memory, our knowledge of facts about the world. In contrast, our answers to the last two questions, which are unique to us, depend on **episodic memory,** our recollection of events in our lives. A.J., whom we discussed at the beginning of the chapter, experiences remarkably accurate episodic memories. There's good evidence that these two types of memory are housed in different brain regions. Semantic memory tends to activate the left frontal cortex more than the right frontal cortex, and vice versa for episodic memory (Cabeza & Nyberg, 1997). Still, both semantic and episodic memory share one important feature: They require conscious effort and awareness. Whether we're trying to recall the definition of "chunking" from earlier in this chapter or our first kiss, we *know* we're trying to remember. Moreover, when we recall this information, we have a conscious experience of accessing it. That is, both semantic and episodic memory are examples of **explicit memory,** the process of recalling information intentionally. (Some researchers refer to the information recalled by explicit memory as *declarative memory.*)

Explicit memory differs from **implicit memory,** which is the process of recalling information we don't remember deliberately. Implicit memories don't require conscious effort on our part. For example, each of us can go through the steps of unlocking our front doors without consciously recalling the sequence of actions required to do so. In fact, we probably can't tell without reenacting it in our heads or actually standing in front of our doors which way the key turns in the lock and how we'd hold the key in our hands while unlocking the door.

Studies of people with brain damage provide remarkable *existence proofs* (see Chapter 2) for the distinction between implicit and explicit memory. Neurologist Antonio Damasio (2000) has studied a patient named David, whose left and right temporal lobes were largely obliterated by a virus. David has virtually no explicit memory for anyone he's met; when Damasio shows him photographs of people with whom he's recently interacted, he can't recognize any of them. Yet when Damasio asks David which of these people he'd ask for help if he needed it, he points to those who've been kind to him, utterly clueless of who they are. David has no explicit memory for who's helped him, but his implicit memory remains intact.

To make matters still more complicated, there are several subtypes of implicit memory. We'll discuss two of them here: procedural memory and priming. However, according to most psychologists, implicit memory also includes habituation, classical conditioning, and other forms of learning we've encountered in Chapter 6.

One subtype of implicit memory, **procedural memory,** refers to memory for motor skills and habits. Whenever we ride a bicycle or open a soda can, we're relying on procedural memory. In contrast to semantic memory, which is "know what" memory, procedural memory is "know how" memory. Our procedural and semantic memories for the same skills are sometimes surprisingly different. For those of you who are avid typists, find a computer keyboard or typewriter and type the word *the.* That's a breeze, right? Now turn away from the keyboard for a moment, and try to remember where the *t, h,* and *e* are located, but without moving your fingers. If you're like most people, you're hopelessly stymied. You may even find that the only way to remember their location is to use your fingers to type the imaginary letters in mid-air. Although your procedural memory for locating letters on a keyboard is effortless, your semantic memory for locating them is a different story.

A second subtype of implicit memory, **priming,** refers to our ability to identify a stimulus more easily or more quickly when we've previously encountered similar stimuli. Imagine that a researcher flashes the word QUEEN, interspersed with a few hundred other words, very quickly on a computer screen. An hour later, she asks you to perform a *stem completion task,* which requires you to fill in the missing letters of a word. In this case, the stem completion task is K __ __ __. Research shows that having seen the word QUEEN, you're more likely to complete the stem with KING (as opposed to KILL or KNOW, for example) than are subjects who haven't seen QUEEN (Neely, 1976). This is true, incidentally, even for subjects who insist they can't even remember having seen the word QUEEN (Bargh, 1994). This memory is implicit because it doesn't require any deliberate effort on our part.

Priming occurs in everyday life too. During the infamous O.J. Simpson murder trial in 1995, many Americans "suddenly" reported seeing dozens of license plates with the letters "OJ" in them. Almost surely, these license plates had been there all along, but the virtual round-the-clock press coverage of the O.J. trial primed people to see these two letters on the backs of cars. As another example, a few of you may have been hoodwinked by this old prank. Say the word "tin" quickly ten times in a row. OK, what's an aluminum can made out of? If you said "tin," you fell victim to priming (sorry, aluminum cans are made out of aluminum, not tin).

If you're having a hard time keeping all of these subtypes of long-term memory straight, **Figure 7.10** summarizes the major subtypes of explicit and implicit memory.

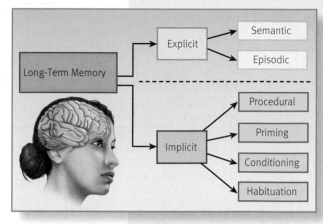

Figure 7.10 The Many Subtypes of Memory. A summary of the subtypes of explicit and implicit memory.

ASSESS YOUR KNOWLEDGE: FACT OR FICTION?

(1) Most of us can accurately recognize thousands of faces we've seen only a few days earlier. (True/False)

(2) Memory is more reconstructive than reproductive. (True/False)

(3) The major reason for forgetting information from long-term memory appears to be the decay of memories. (True/False)

(4) Chunking can permit us to greatly increase the number of digits or letters we hold in our short-term memories. (True/False)

(5) Information in long-term memory often lasts for years or decades. (True/False)

Answers: (1) T (p. 275); (2) T (p. 277); (3) F (p. 280); (4) T (p. 281); (5) T (p. 284).

The Three Stages of Memory

How do we get information into our long-term memories? Memory psychologists agree that there are three major *stages* of memory: *Encoding, storage,* and *retrieval.* By the way, we shouldn't confuse these stages with the three major *systems* of memory we've just discussed (sensory, short-term, and long-term). Instead, these three stages refer to *processes* that explain how information gets into memory and gets back out again when we need it (see **Figure 7.11**).

Stage 1 Encoding: Using a computer, a librarian enters the cataloguing information for a book into the library's database. In the process, the librarian finds out where the book needs to be shelved. The computer prints out a label (what we might think of as an encoding label) that the librarian affixes to the book's spine so that everyone will know where the book should be stored.

Stage 2 Storage: The librarian puts the books in the proper section of the library, according to how they've been catalogued.

Stage 3 Retrieval: When the librarian wants to access the book, he looks up the cataloguing information and then goes to the appropriate shelf with his computer printout or notecard showing the catalogue location of the book to retreive it.

Figure 7.11 Three Stages of Memory. The process of remembering is similar in some ways to the process of filing and fetching a library book.

To understand these three memory stages, picture yourself working as a librarian at your college or university library. When a new book arrives, you first give it a number to identify it; that's encoding. Then you file it away on the bookshelf; that's storage. Then, when you want to find the book a few weeks, months, or even years later, you go to the shelves and fetch it; that's retrieval. Of course, like all metaphors, this one is an oversimplification, because the memories we retrieve are rarely identical to those we initially encoded. To push the metaphor just a bit, it's almost as though our college library were periodically flooded with water, so that the soggy books we've retrieved are rarely, if ever, identical to those we filed away. In some cases, they're barely recognizable. We'll soon discover why.

ENCODING: THE "CALL NUMBERS" OF THE MIND

Encoding refers to the process of getting information into our memory banks. To remember something, we first need to make sure the information is in a format our memories can use. To a far greater extent than we realize, many of our memory failures are actually failures of encoding. Have you ever had the embarrassing experience of going to a party and being introduced to several people at the same time, and then immediately realizing that you'd forgotten all of their names? Odds are high you were so nervous or distracted that you never encoded their names in the first place. Once we lose the chance to encode an event, we'll never remember it. No encoding, no memory. To go back to our library analogy, imagine that the librarian assigns some of the books that come in for processing an identification number but later decides to toss some of them in the trash instead. These books never make it to the shelves.

That principle helps to explain why the popular belief that our brains preserve a record of every event we've ever encountered (Alvarez & Brown, 2002) is almost surely a myth. Most events we've experienced are never encoded, and almost all events we do encode include only some of the details of the experience. Much of our everyday experience never gets into our brains in the first place.

Encoding helps to explain the familiar *next-in-line effect*. You've experienced this phenomenon if you've ever been in a class when the instructor called on several students in a row to answer a question or say their names. You probably found that your memory was especially poor for what the person immediately before you said (Bond, Pitre, & van Leeuwen, 1991). That's because you were so preoccupied with what you were going to say that you weren't paying much attention to what the person right before you was saying.

The next-in-line effect is typically a failure of encoding.

Mnemonics: Valuable Memory Aids.

(1) Please Excuse My Dear Aunt Sally.
(2) Thirty days hath September, April, June, and November. All the rest have 31, except for February, which has twenty-eight, and you probably think it's great. Or maybe it's fine, when on leap year, it has twenty-nine.
(3) Every Good Boy Does Fine.

Music students use the mnemonic "Every good boy does fine" to remember the names of the lines (E, G, B, D, F) in the treble clef.

What do these strange passages have in common? Each is a **mnemonic** (pronounced "nee-mon-ick"): a learning aid, strategy, or device that enhances recall. Mnemonics help us encode memories in a way that makes them easier to recall. From time to time, virtually all of us use recall boosters, like making lists or writing appointments on a calendar or portable computer (Intons-Peterson & Fournier, 1986). Nevertheless, the mnemonics we've presented above differ from these "external" memory aids in that they rely on internal mental strategies, namely, strategies we use during encoding that help us later retrieve useful information. Item 1 specifies the proper order of mathematical operations (parentheses, exponents, multiplication, division, addition, subtraction) by having each word start with the same letter as the mathematical operation. Item 2 is a rhyme that's a handy way of remembering the number of days in each month. Item 3, as everyone who's ever taken music lessons will recall, stands for the note names on the lines of the treble clef in musical notation (E, G, B, D, F).

encoding
process of getting information into our memory banks

mnemonic
a learning aid, strategy, or device that enhances recall

Mnemonic devices share two major features. First, we can apply them to just about anything and everything. We can use them to recall the names of planets, the elements of the periodic table, the bones of the hand, the order of geological time periods, and the colors of the rainbow (the last being ROYGBIV for red, orange, yellow, green, blue, indigo, and violet). Second, most mnemonics depend on having a store of knowledge to begin with. For instance, we need to know something about mathematical operations for the mnemonic about Aunt Sally to make any sense. So mnemonics are mostly useful for encoding information that's already at our disposal. There are many other mnemonic approaches in addition to the examples we've discussed: We'll review three here.

Pegword Method. When we were children, nursery rhymes captivated our attention. By elementary school age, most of us were well acquainted with the exploits of Jack and Jill, Little Bo Peep, and Little Jack Horner. Songs ranging from "Twinkle, Twinkle Little Star" to the rap music of Eminem are easy to remember because they contain rhymes.

Rhyming is a key component of the *pegword method,* often used to recall lists of words. To master this mnemonic, first associate each number in a list with a word that rhymes with each number, such as "One is a bun." The word associated with the number is a "pegword." It's essential to memorize a list like the one that follows, but the fact that the numbers and words rhyme makes it easy to do so: (1) One is a bun, (2) Two is a shoe, (3) Three is a tree, and (4) Four is a door.

Suppose you need to learn four words associated with memory concepts for your psychology class (don't you wish there were only four new terms in this chapter?) and that you need to recall them in the following order: chunking, elaboration, hippocampus, von Restorff. After you've memorized the pegword associated with each number (such as "one is a bun"), create an image that associates the word you want to remember with the pegword (such as *bun*). For the first word, *chunking,* you could imagine a bun (the pegword) with a chunk missing or broken up into chunks. For two—*elaboration*—you might imagine a shoe with elaborate beading, sequins, and bows. For three—*hippocampus*—imagine a tree with a hippo camping under it. Number four, *von Restorff,* might be a bit harder but you could get creative with your imagery, such as picturing the door of a van (for "von") propped open by someone on the seat resting his feet in the doorway (for "Rest-") with his shoes off (for "-orff"). When you need to remember the third thing on your list, for example, you'd say to yourself that three is a tree, which would prompt recall of the hippo camping under it, and you'd know that the third word on the list is hippocampus (see **Figure 7.12**).

Method of Loci. The *method of loci* (pronounced low-sigh) relies on imagery of places, that is, *locations,* hence the name of the mnemonic (Belleza, 1999). This method goes back a long way: Ancient Greek and Roman orators used it to help them recall speeches.

The method is straightforward: Think of a path with which you're familiar and can imagine vividly. Perhaps it's the route from your dorm to the cafeteria, or a stroll through the rooms in your apartment. Think of the path you take and the things that you encounter in a set order. For example, to get to the cafeteria, first you get in the elevator, then you walk under a huge tree before you pass by a fountain, and so on. If you need to remember five words in a particular order, think of five things you'll encounter on your way to the cafeteria; if you need to recall ten words, imagine ten locations along your route. If you were trying to remember the list of memory terms with the method of loci, you might imagine chunks of rock or glass on the floor of the elevator.

Keyword Method. If you've taken a foreign language course, you may be familiar with the *keyword method.* This strategy depends on your ability to think of an English word (the keyword) that reminds you of the word you're trying to remember. Take the Spanish word *casa,* which means "house" in English. Think of an English word that sounds like or brings to mind "casa." Many students come up with "case." Now think of an image that combines "case" (or another word of your choice) and "house." Perhaps you can picture a case of soda on the roof of your house. When you think of this image, it

Figure 7.12 Pegword Method. The pegword method can be a useful mnemonic for helping us recall lists of objects in order. See the text for an explanation of this fanciful illustration.

should help you retrieve the meaning of *casa*. People who learn foreign vocabulary benefit from the keyword strategy compared with more traditional methods (Gruenberg & Sykes, 1991). The keyword method also helps elderly individuals to improve their recall of Spanish words (Gruenberg & Pascoe, 1996).

Generally speaking, mnemonics can be helpful if we're motivated to practice them on a regular basis. Many people seem to prefer external aids, such as making lists (Park, Smith, & Cavanaugh, 1990) to mnemonics, probably because they take less work and effort. Mnemonics require training, patience, and even a dash of creativity.

Ginkgo and other supposed memory-enhancing drugs are a multimillion dollar industry in the United States. These pills are popular, but do they work?

PsychoMythology
Memory Boosters

The next time you're in your local drug store, stop by the aisle containing herbal remedies. There you'll find a virtual museum of so-called "smart pills" designed to enhance memory: ginkgo, vitamin E, and even drugs with unpronounceable, but scientific-sounding names like phosphatidylserine, citicoline, and piracetam. Can any of them help us remember where we mislaid our keys this morning, memorize the names of the ten people we met at last night's party, or recall how to spell "phosphatidylserine"?

You might reasonably assume that you wouldn't find these products lining your drugstore shelves unless researchers had first demonstrated that they work. You'd be wrong. In 1994, the U.S. Congress passed the Dietary Supplement Health and Education Act (DSHEA), which prevented the Food and Drug Administration (FDA) from regulating diet supplements and herbal remedies, including those intended to enhance memory. Before allowing drugs to enter the market, the FDA normally demands controlled experiments to demonstrate their safety and effectiveness. Following the passage of DSHEA, however, there's been no quality control over most diet supplements or herbal remedies. It's anybody's guess whether they work, or even whether any might be harmful.

Probably the best-known herbal remedy for memory is ginkgo (whose scientific name is *Ginkgo biloba*), an ancient Chinese medicine extracted from the leaves of the ginkgo tree. Although it might be tempting to assume that ginkgo is effective because it's been used for many centuries, this would be an example of the *argument from antiquity fallacy* (see Chapter 2), that is, the error of concluding that something must be effective merely because it's been around for a long time. The manufacturers of ginkgo claim that it can markedly improve normal people's memory in as little as 4 weeks. Like many other memory boosters, ginkgo presumably works in part by increasing the amount of acetylcholine in the brain; as we learned in Chapter 3, acetylcholine is a neurotransmitter that plays a key role in memory.

Ginkgo is remarkably popular; Americans spend several hundred million dollars on it per year. Yet controlled studies comparing ginkgo with a placebo show that its effects on memory in normal individuals are minimal, even nonexistent (Gold, Cahill, & Wenk, 2002; Solomon, Adams, Silver, Zimmer, & DeVeaux, 2002). If ginkgo produces any effects on normal memory at all, they appear to be about equal to those of drinking a glass of lemonade or any sugary liquid (as you'll recall from Chapter 3, sugar is the brain's fuel). Ginkgo's effects on memory in people with Alzheimer's disease or other forms of dementia are only slightly more promising (Gold et al., 2002). There's no good evidence that it can reverse severe memory loss. Moreover, like many herbal remedies, ginkgo can be harmful in certain cases. For example, it can interfere with the effects of blood-thinning medicines and thereby cause excessive bleeding.

As for all of the other smart pills with fancy names, the evidence for their effects on memory is too preliminary to draw any strong conclusions (McDaniel, Maier, & Einstein, 2002). As is so often the case in pop psychology, the best advice for those of us hoping to become memory whizzes overnight is *caveat emptor:* Let the buyer beware.

STORAGE: FILING OUR MEMORIES AWAY

Once we've filed away a library book on the shelf, it sits there, often for years at a time, collecting dust and cobwebs. We've stored it, perhaps to be retrieved one day by a student or professor who needs it for a writing project. **Storage** refers to the process of keeping information in memory.

Yet, where in the library we choose to file this book depends on our *interpretation and expectations* regarding the book's content. For example, let's imagine a new book entitled *The Psychology of Dating* has just arrived in the library. Should we file this book in the psychology section, along with books on personality, emotion, and social psychology, or in the relationships section, along with books on dating, attraction, and marriage? The answer depends on what we think the book is about: If we think the book is mostly about psychology, we'll probably file it in the psychology section, but if we think the book is mostly about dating, we'll file it in the relationships section. That judgment call, in turn, hinges on our judgments about the book's content. Similarly, how we store our experiences in memory depends on our interpretations and expectations of these events.

Schemas: The Role Models of Memories for Events. Consider this scenario. You and your friends go to a brand new sit-down restaurant. Although this is your first visit, you've got a pretty good idea of what's in store. That's because you possess a schema for eating at a nice restaurant. A **schema** is an organized knowledge structure or mental model that we've stored in memory. Our schema for restaurants is characterized by a set order of events, sometimes called a *script* (Schank & Abelson, 1977). You're seated at a table, given menus from which you order food, wait while your food is prepared, eat the food, get the check, and pay for the food before leaving. And don't forget the tip! There's even a standard sequence in ordering, at least in U.S. culture. We order drinks first, followed by appetizers, soup or salad, entrees, and finally dessert and coffee.

Schemas also affect how we store memory information (actually, schemas play a role in all three stages of memory—encoding, storage, and retrieval—although we'll just focus on them here in the context of storage). If we interpret an ambiguous experience, like two people on the street engaged in a heated discussion, as negative—say, a bitter argument—we'll file it along with other negative information. In contrast, if we interpret this experience as positive—say, a lively but friendly political discussion—we'll file it along with other positive information.

The Value of Schemas. Schemas serve a valuable function: They equip us with frames of reference for interpreting new situations. Without schemas, we'd find some information almost impossible to comprehend. Read the following paragraph (Bransford & Johnson, 1972, p. 719), to see if you can figure out what it's describing. But be sure not to turn the page upside down before you do.

> If the balloons popped, the sound would not be able to carry since everything would be too far away from the correct floor. A closed window would also prevent the sound from carrying since most buildings tend to be well insulated. Since the whole operation depends on a steady flow of electricity, a break in the middle of the wire would also cause problems. Of course the fellow could shout, but the human voice is not loud enough to carry that far. An additional problem is that a string could break on the instrument. Then there could be no accompaniment to the message. It is clear that the best situation would involve less distance. Then there would be fewer potential problems. With face to face contact, the least number of things could go wrong.

OK, do you have any clue what this is all about? Almost certainly, you were unable to make heads or tails of it. Now turn the page upside-down and look at **Figure 7.13.** Does it make any more sense now? Indeed, when John Bransford and Meriette Johnson (1972) showed a very similar drawing to participants before reading them this passage, participants understood the story better and remembered more of it than did those who hadn't seen this drawing. The drawing enhances memory, because it provides us with a schema for interpreting a story that's otherwise virtually impossible to understand.

Our interpretation of ambiguous events in everyday life, like an animated conversation on the street, depends in part on our schemas.

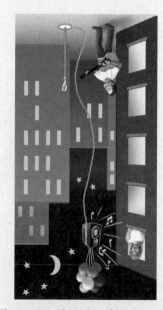

Figure 7.13 The Value of Schemas.
After reading the passage in the text on this page, turn the page upside down, and take a look at the drawing. Now reread the passage. This drawing makes the point that, without schemas, much of what we read is incomprehensible. (*Source:* Adapted from Bransford & Johnson, 1972)

storage
process of keeping information in memory

schema
organized knowledge structure or mental model that we've stored in memory

War of the Ghosts

One night two young men from Egulac went down to the river to hunt seals and while they were there it became foggy and calm. Then they heard war-cries, and they thought: "Maybe this is a war-party." They escaped to the shore, and hid behind a log. Now canoes came up, and they heard the noise of paddles, and saw one canoe coming up to them. There were five men in the canoe, and they said:

"What do you think? We wish to take you along. We are going up the river to make war on the people."

One of the young men said, "I have no arrows."

"Arrows are in the canoe," they said.

"I will not go along. I might be killed. My relatives do not know where I have gone. But you," he said, turning to the other, "may go with them."

So one of the young men went, but the other returned home. And the warriors went on up the river to a town on the other side of Kalama. The people came down to the water and they began to fight, and many were killed. But presently the young man heard one of the warriors say, "Quick, let us go home: that Indian has been hit." Now he thought: "Oh, they are ghosts." He did not feel sick, but they said he had been shot.

So the canoes went back to Egulac and the young man went ashore to his house and made a fire. And he told everybody and said: "Behold I accompanied the ghosts, and we went to fight. Many of our fellows were killed, and many of those who attacked us were killed. They said I was hit, and I did not feel sick."

He told it all, and then he became quiet. When the sun rose he fell down. Something black came out of his mouth. His face became contorted. The people jumped up and cried.

He was dead.

Figure 7.14 War of the Ghosts.
Bartlett's research shows that schemas can lead us to remember events that never happened. (*Source:* Bartlett, 1932)

Figure 7.15 The Danger of Schemas.
Look carefully at this drawing. Allport and Postman (1956) used a similar drawing to show how schemas involving racial prejudice can shape our memories.

retrieval
reactivation or reconstruction of experiences from our memory stores

retrieval cues
hints that make it easier for us to recall information

recall
generating previously remembered information

recognition
selecting previously remembered information from an array of options

relearning
reacquiring knowledge that we'd previously learned but largely forgotten over time

Schemas and Memory Mistakes. Valuable as they are, schemas can sometimes create problems for us, because they can lead us to remember things that never happened. Schemas simplify, which is good because they help to make sense of the world. But schemas sometimes *oversimplify,* which is bad because they can produce memory illusions. Schemas provide one key explanation for the paradox of memory: They enhance memory in some cases, but lead to memory errors in others.

Frederick Bartlett (1932) provided one of the earliest demonstrations of the biasing effects of schemas on recall. He read participants an unusual and unfamiliar text, a Native American folk tale titled "The War of the Ghosts," and asked them to recall the story as accurately as possible (see **Figure 7.14**). As in the popular party game of "telephone," he asked participants to pass the story on to others. Bartlett found that, over time, successive subjects typically distorted the story to fit their expectations. For example, the story says that "something black came out of his mouth" right before the main character died from an arrow wound. However, participants often recalled it as blood coming out of his mouth, an inference more in line with their expectations. Bartlett's work stimulated a great deal of research showing how schemas can distort our memories (Bransford & Franks, 1971; Mandler, 1984; Rummelhart, 1980).

Schemas also help to explain how prejudices distort memory. In a classic study, Gordon Allport and Leo Postman (1956) showed subjects a picture of a scene on a subway. As we can see from a similar drawing in **Figure 7.15,** this picture clearly shows a Caucasian man wielding a razor at a well-dressed African American man as bystanders looked on. Allport and Postman asked Caucasian subjects to recount the scene to others. After repeated tellings, subjects tended to recall the African American man, rather than the Caucasian man, as the person brandishing the razor, presumably because their stereotype of African Americans as violent had biased their memory.

As we'll discover in Chapter 13, we can think of racial stereotypes as schemas gone haywire. It can sometimes be helpful to lump people into categories. For example, it's a safe bet to assume that most masked people walking into banks and holding guns are bank robbers. Nevertheless, it can be dangerous to assume that all people in a category, such as "Muslim," "Jew," or "Woman," behave in the same way. If we're not careful, our schemas can lead us to overgeneralize, painting all people within a category with the same broad brush.

RETRIEVAL: HEADING FOR THE "STACKS"

To remember something, we need to fetch it from our long-term memory banks. This is **retrieval,** the third and final stage of memory. Yet, as we mentioned earlier, this is where our metaphor of a library begins to break down, because what we retrieve from our memory often doesn't match what we put into it. Our memories are reconstructive, often transforming our recollections to fit our beliefs and expectations.

Many types of forgetting result from failures of retrieval: Our memories are still present, but we can't access them. It's pretty easy to demonstrate this point. If a friend is nearby, try the following demonstration, courtesy of psychologist Endel Tulving (even if you don't have a friend handy, you can still follow along). Read each category in **Table 7.1** to your friend, followed by the word that goes along with it. Tell your friend that after you're done reading all of the categories and their corresponding words, you'll ask him or her to recall just the words—in any order—not the categories.

First, read the list to your friend. Now ask him or her to take a few minutes to write down as many words as he or she can remember. Almost certainly, your friend missed some of them. For those missing words, prompt your friend with the category. So if your friend missed *Finger,* ask, "Do you remember the word that went with 'A part of the body'?" You'll probably find that these prompts help your friend to remember some of the forgotten words. In psychological lingo, the category names serve as **retrieval cues:** hints that make it easier for us to recall information. So your friend's long-term memory contained these missing words, but he or she needed the retrieval cues to remember them.

Measuring Memory. Psychologists assess people's memory in three major ways: recall, recognition, and relearning. Think of them as the three Rs (another mnemonic device, by the way).

Recall and Recognition. What kind of exam do you find the toughest: essay or multiple choice? For sure, we've all taken multiple-choice tests that are "killers." Still, all else being equal, essay tests are usually harder than multiple-choice tests. That's because **recall,** that is, generating previously remembered information on our own, tends to be more difficult than **recognition,** selecting previously remembered information from an array of options (Bahrick, Bahrick, & Wittlinger, 1975). To demonstrate what we mean, try recalling the sixth president of the United States. Unless you're an American history buff, you may be stumped. If so, try this question instead.

The sixth president of the United States was:

(a) George Washington   (c) George W. Bush
(b) John Quincy Adams   (d) Arnold Schwarzenegger

With a bit of thought, you probably figured out that (b) was the correct answer. You could safely eliminate (a) because you know George Washington was the first president, (c) because you know George W. Bush is a much more recent president, and (d) because you know Arnold Schwarzenegger hasn't been president. Moreover, you may well have recognized John Quincy Adams as an early U.S. president, even if you didn't know that he was number six.

Why is recall usually harder than recognition? In part, it's because recalling an item requires two steps—generating an answer and then determining whether it seems correct—whereas recognizing an item takes only one step: determining which item from a list seems most correct (Haist, Shimamura, & Squire, 1992).

Some students insist that they do well "only" on essay exams, whereas others insist that they do well "only" on multiple-choice exams. Although it's true that some students do better on one format than the other, the responses to essay and multiple-choice questions within the same test are usually at least moderately correlated (Bridgeman & Morgan, 1996). So students who excel on one test format tend to excel on the other, probably because they possess superior mastery of the subject matter. We're sorry to be the bearer of bad news: Changing the test format isn't a magic bullet for transforming Fs into As.

Relearning. A third way of measuring memory is **relearning:** how much more quickly we learn information when we study something we've already studied relative to when we studied it the first time. For this reason, psychologists often call this approach the method of *savings:* Now that we've studied something, we don't need to take as much time to refresh our memories of it (that is, we've "saved" time by studying it).

The concept of relearning originated with the pioneering work of German researcher Hermann Ebbinghaus (1885) well over a century ago. Ebbinghaus used hundreds of "nonsense syllables," like ZAK and BOL, to test his own recollection across differing time intervals. As we can see in **Figure 7.16,** he found that most of our forgetting occurs almost immediately after learning new material, with less and less forgetting after that. However, he also found that when he attempted to relearn the nonsense syllables he'd forgotten after a delay, he learned them much more quickly the second time around.

Imagine you learned to play the guitar in high school but haven't played it for several years. When you sit down to strum an old song, you're rusty at first. Although you need to go back to your notes to remind yourself the first couple of times you sit down to play, you'll probably find that it doesn't take you nearly as long to get the hang of the song the second time around. That's relearning. Relearning shows that a memory for this skill was still in your brain—somewhere.

Table 7.1 Demonstration of Retrieval Cues. Find a friend and read each category, followed by the word that goes along with it. Then, ask your friend to recall only the words, in any order. As you'll see, this demonstration helps to make a simple point: Many memory failures are actually failures of retrieval.

Category	Word
A metal	Silver
A precious stone	Pearl
A relative	Niece
A bird	Canary
Type of reading material	Journal
A military title	Major
A color	Violet
A four-legged animal	Mouse
A piece of furniture	Dresser
A part of the body	Finger
A fruit	Cherry
A weapon	Cannon
A type of dwelling	Mansion
An alcoholic beverage	Brandy
A crime	Kidnapping
An occupation	Plumber
A sport	Lacrosse
An article of clothing	Sweater
A musical instrument	Saxophone
An insect	Wasp

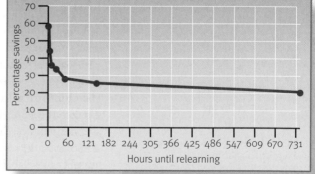

Figure 7.16 Savings and Relearning. This graph shows the percent "savings," or how much faster information is relearned the second time around following various delays.

Relearning is a more sensitive measure of memory than either recall or recognition. That's because relearning allows us to assess memory using a relative amount (how much faster was material learned the second time?) rather than the simple "right" or "wrong" we obtain from recall or recognition (Nelson, 1985). It also allows us to measure memory for procedures like driving a car or playing a piano piece as well as for facts and figures.

When memorizing his nonsense syllables, Ebbinghaus happened on a crucial principle that applies to most forms of learning: the law of **distributed versus massed practice** (Donovan & Radosevich, 1999; Willingham, 2002). Simply put, this law tells us that we tend to remember things better in the long run when we spread our learning over long intervals than when we pack it into short intervals. This principle is probably one of the best-replicated effects in all of psychology (Cepeda, Rashler, Vul, Wixted, & Rohrer, 2006). Even infants show it (Cornell, 1980).

Herein lies another word to the wise. Cramming for an exam helps us remember the information for *that exam*, but it typically produces poor long-term retention. If you want to master the information in your psychology course—or any course, for that matter—you should spread out your review of the material over long intervals. So, when one of your teachers nags you to "start studying at least a week before the exam rather than waiting until the last minute," you have Ebbinghaus to thank—or blame. **Table 7.2** provides a handy list of studying pointers based on several memory concepts introduced in this chapter.

Table 7.2 Helpful Study Hints Derived from Memory Research.

Memory Concept	Pointer
(1) Distributed versus Massed Study	Spread your study time out—review your notes and textbook in increments rather than cramming.
(2) Elaborative Rehearsal	Connect new knowledge with existing knowledge rather than simply memorizing facts or names.
(3) Levels of Processing	Work to process ideas deeply and meaningfully—avoid writing notes down word-for-word from instructors' lectures or slides. Try to capture the information in your own words.
(4) Mnemonic Devices	The more reminders or cues you can connect from your knowledge base to new material, the more likely you are to recall new material when tested.

Tip-of-the-Tongue Phenomenon. We've all experienced retrieval failure in the form of the frustrating **tip-of-the-tongue (TOT) phenomenon,** in which we're sure we know the answer to a question, but can't come up with it (Brown, 1991; Schwartz, 1999). It's surprisingly easy to generate this phenomenon (Baddeley, 1993). Read the names of the ten U.S. states in **Table 7.3,** and try to name their capital cities. Now focus on the states for which you're *unsure* of whether you know the right answer, and keep trying. If you're still stuck, look at the list that follows, which gives you the first letter of the capital of each state: Georgia (A), Wisconsin (M), California (S), Louisiana (B), Florida (T), Colorado (D), New Jersey (T), Arizona (P), Nebraska (L), and Kentucky (F).

Did the first letters help? Research shows when we experience the TOT phenomenon, they often will. The fact that we sometimes experience TOT tells us that there's a difference between something we've forgotten because it didn't get *stored* in memory and something that's in there somewhere that we can't quite retrieve.

Two investigators showed that when people believe that something is on the tip of their tongues, they're frequently right (Brown & McNeill, 1966). They presented subjects with the definitions of relatively rare words (such as "to give up the throne") and asked them to come up with the word (in this case, *abdicate*). About 10 percent of the time, subjects reported a TOT experience; they were pretty sure they "knew" the word, but couldn't generate it. In these cases, the researchers asked participants to guess the first letter of the word or the number of syllables in it. Interestingly, the participants did much better than chance. So subjects *did* know something about the word; they just couldn't spit it out whole.

Encoding Specificity: Finding Things Where We Left Them. Why is it easier to retrieve some things from memory than others? One answer to this mystery lies in the principle of

---

Replicability

factoid

TOT occurs in those who use sign language as well as spoken language; psychologists call this the *tip-of-the-fingers* phenomenon. Deaf signers who are unable to retrieve the names of fairly famous people but feel that they're on the verge of remembering can depict at least some part of the famous person's name with their fingers about 80 percent of the time (Thompson, Emmorey, & Gollan, 2005).

Table 7.3 TOT Phenomenon. First try to come up with the capital of each state. Then, return to the text for some hints.

State	Capital
Georgia	
Wisconsin	
California	
Louisiana	
Florida	
Colorado	
New Jersey	
Arizona	
Nebraska	
Kentucky	

Answers: Atlanta, Madison, Sacramento, Baton Rouge, Tallahassee, Denver, Trenton, Phoenix, Lincoln, Frankfort

distributed versus massed practice studying information in small increments over time (distributed) versus in large increments over a brief amount of time (massed)

tip-of-the-tongue (TOT) phenomenon experience of knowing that we know something but being unable to access it

encoding specificity introduced by Endel Tulving (1982; Tulving & Thompson, 1973). We're more likely to remember something when the conditions present at the time we encoded it are also present at retrieval. We can see this principle at work in several psychological phenomena, two of which we'll examine here: context-dependent learning and state-dependent learning.

Context-Dependent Learning. **Context-dependent learning** refers to superior retrieval when the external context of the original memories matches the retrieval context. Duncan Godden and Alan Baddeley (1975) provided an ingenious example of this effect in a study of scuba divers. They presented divers with forty unrelated words while the divers were either standing on the beach or submerged in about 15 feet of water. Godden and Baddeley then tested the divers in either the same or a different context from which they originally presented the words. The divers' memory was best when the original context matched the retrieval context, regardless of whether they were on land or underwater, as shown in **Figure 7.17.**

There's even evidence for context-dependent learning when undergraduates take exams. Students tend to do slightly better on their exams when tested in the same classroom in which they learned the material (Smith, 1979). You may want to gently remind your introductory psychology instructor of this fact when he or she schedules the room for your next test. Still, this effect isn't all that powerful, and not all researchers have replicated it (Saufley, Otaka, & Bavaresco, 1985). That's probably because you've acquired the information not only in the classroom but in other settings, such as the room in which you're now reading this textbook.

State-Dependent Learning. Despite its name, state-dependent learning doesn't mean that if you learned something while on vacation in Montana, you need to go back to Montana to recall it. Instead, state-dependent learning is similar to context-dependent learning, except that it refers to the internal "state" of the organism rather than the external context. That is, **state-dependent learning** refers to superior retrieval of memories when the organism is in the same physiological or psychological state as it was during encoding.

There's anecdotal evidence for this phenomenon among alcoholics, who often report that they need to get drunk to locate items—including their favorite bottles of liquor—that they'd hidden while drinking (Goodwin, 1995). Of course, we've learned that anecdotes are limited as sources of scientific evidence (see Chapter 2). However, in this case, controlled studies bear out the anecdotes: People who've learned a task while under the influence of alcohol tend to remember it better when under the influence than when sober (Goodwin, Powell, Brenner, Hoine, & Sterne, 1969). Still, researchers haven't always replicated these findings (Lisman, 1974), suggesting that state-dependent effects probably depend in complex ways on the participants tested and stimuli administered.

State-dependent learning sometimes extends to mood, in which case it's termed *mood-dependent learning* (Bower, 1981). Studies show that most people find it easier to recall unpleasant memories than pleasant ones when they're sad, and easier to recall pleasant memories than unpleasant ones when they're happy (Guenther, 1998; Nelson & Craighead, 1977).

Mood-dependent learning can create nasty difficulties for researchers who want to draw conclusions about people's life histories. Specifically, it can result in a *retrospective bias:* Our current psychological state can distort memories of our past (Dawes, 1988). For example, most depressed individuals report having been treated more harshly by their parents in childhood than do nondepressed individuals. One explanation for this finding is that harsh parental treatment predisposes to later depression. But there's another explanation: Perhaps people's bad moods distort their memories of their childhoods.

To evaluate this possibility, researchers asked three groups of participants—(1) people who were clinically depressed, (2) people who had a history of depression but weren't currently depressed, and (3) people who'd never been depressed—about how their parents

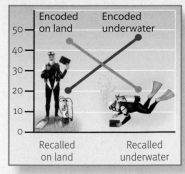

Figure 7.17 Research Shows That the Word Learning of Scuba Divers Depends on Context. If the divers learned words underwater, they recalled them best when underwater again.

Replicability

encoding specificity
phenomenon of remembering something better when the conditions under which we retrieve information are similar to the conditions under which we encoded it

context-dependent learning
superior retrieval of memories when the external context of the original memories matches the retrieval context

state-dependent learning
superior retrieval of memories when the organism is in the same physiological or psychological state as it was during encoding

Replicability

Ruling Out Rival Hypotheses

treated them as children. Currently depressed participants recalled their parents as having been more rejecting and domineering toward them as children than did participants in the other two groups (Lewinsohn & Rosenbaum, 1987). So participants' moods seem to have influenced their evaluations of how their parents had treated them. In this case, we don't know whether the depressed subjects were less *accurate* than the participants in the other groups, only that their memories were different.

APPLY YOUR THINKING

Researchers have found that people with antisocial personality disorder, a condition marked by a history of criminal and irresponsible behavior (see Chapter 15), often report that their parents neglected them in childhood. How might retrospective bias account for these findings, and how could you attempt to minimize its potential effects?

ASSESS YOUR KNOWLEDGE: FACT OR FICTION?

(1) We encode virtually all of our life experiences, even though we can't retrieve more than a tiny proportion of them. (True/False)
(2) We need to practice mnemonics to use them successfully. (True/False)
(3) Schemas only distort memories, but don't enhance them. (True/False)
(4) In general, recall is more difficult than recognition. (True/False)
(5) Cramming for exams, although stressful, is actually a good strategy for enhancing long-term recall of material. (True/False)

Answers: (1) F (p. 288); (2) T (p. 288); (3) F (p. 293); (4) T (p. 291); (5) F (p. 294)

The Biology of Memory

Although few of us think about it, the biology of memory plays a pivotal role in our daily lives, whether it's remembering where we left our keys or the name of that friendly person we met at last night's party. What's more, understanding how our brains store memory may help us find ways of treating devastating diseases that impair our ability to recall everyday events.

THE NEURAL BASIS OF MEMORY STORAGE

Locating where a library book is stored is generally pretty easy. We look it up in our library's computer system or card catalog, write down its number, go to the shelf, and—unless someone's recently plucked it away—find it. If we're lucky, it's right there on the shelf where it's supposed to be. Yet as we'll soon see, memory storage in the brain isn't quite this cut and dry.

The Elusive Engram. Beginning in the 1920s, psychologist Karl Lashley went in search of the *engram:* the physical trace of each memory in the brain. He taught rats how to run mazes, and then lesioned different parts of their brains to see if they forgot how to find their way. By doing so, Lashley hoped to discover where memory is stored in the brain. Yet after years of painstaking work, he came up empty-handed in his quest.

Still, Lashley learned two important things. First, the more brain he removed, the worse the rat performed on the maze: There's no great surprise there. Second, no matter where he removed brain tissue, the rats retained at least some memory of the maze (Lashley, 1929). Even removing up to half of the rat's cortex didn't erase the memory. These findings led Lashley to conclude that we can't simply point to a spot in the brain and say, "There's the memory of my first kiss," because that memory isn't located in a single place. In the words of writer Gertrude Stein, there's "no there there." Lashley's engram doesn't seem to exist, at least in the sense of being in one location, like a library book sitting on a shelf.

long-term potentiation (LTP)
gradual strengthening of the connections among neurons from repetitive stimulation

Over a half century ago, Donald Hebb (1949) suggested that the engram is instead located in *assemblies* (organized groups) of neurons in the brain. According to Hebb, one neuron (A) becomes connected to another neuron (B) when it repeatedly activates that neuron. As we learned in Chapter 3, neurons, fed by a rich blend of neurotransmitters, form circuits, integrate sensory information in meaningful ways, and transform our experience of the world into lifelong memories.

Long-Term Potentiation—A Physiological Basis for Memory. As we learned in Chapter 3, **long-term potentiation (LTP)** refers to a gradual strengthening of the connections among neurons from repetitive stimulation over time (Bliss, Collinridge, & Morris, 2004). Terje Lomo first observed LTP in the hippocampus of rabbits in 1966, and researchers have since identified it in the hippocampus and other brain structures of humans and other mammals. The gist of what neuroscientists have learned since the discovery of LTP is that neurons that "fire together wire together" (Malenka & Nicoll, 1999). To a large extent, Hebb was right.

Today, many researchers believe that our ability to store memories depends on strengthening the connections among neurons arranged in sprawling networks that extend to the far and deep recesses of our brains (Shors & Matzels, 1999). The question of whether LTP is directly responsible for the storage of memories, or whether it affects learning indirectly by increasing arousal and attention, remains unresolved (Shors & Matzel, 1999). Still, most scientists agree that LTP plays a key role in learning, and that the hippocampus plays a key role in forming lasting memories.

LTP and the Hippocampus. To tell what cells are responsible for LTP, many researchers use thin slices of the hippocampus (Kandel, Schwartz, & Jessell, 2000). These slices come from young animals, usually rats or mice, and are bathed in solutions containing nutrients that keep the tissue alive. In a typical LTP experiment, researchers first establish how hippocampal cells respond at baseline. This is much like determining how we respond to someone asking us a question. Researchers then apply a strong stimulus, much like having someone yell at us. After the strong stimulus, hippocampal neurons respond at an enhanced level to ordinary stimuli, much as we might respond to a neutral question with a louder voice than usual after someone yelled at us. That's LTP.

Like the hippocampus, the amygdala and parts of the association cortex exhibit LTP-like activity. Moreover, there's an LTP-like response in the amygdala following the creation of a fear memory (Maren, 2005; Sigurdsson, Doyere, Cain, & LeDoux, 2007). These results establish LTP-like activity as a correlate of memory, but don't demonstrate that LTP serves as the basis of memory.

LTP and Glutamate. LTP tends to occur at synapses where the sending neuron releases the neurotransmitter glutamate into the synaptic cleft—the space between the sending and receiving neuron (see Chapter 3). As shown in **Figure 7.18,** glutamate interacts with receptors for NMDA and another substance (AMPA), both named for drugs to which they bind besides glutamate. LTP enhances the release of glutamate into the synaptic cleft, resulting in enhanced learning (Lisman & Raghavachari, 2007). Joe Tsien and his colleagues were even able to create a "smart mouse" (called the "Doogie mouse" after *Doogie Howser,* a television show based on a brilliant teenage doctor) by manipulating its genes to create extra receptors for NMDA. Compared with everyday mice, the Doogie mouse is an especially quick and effective learner (Tsien, 2000).

WHERE IS MEMORY STORED?

Clearly, the hippocampus is critical to memory. As we saw in Chapter 4, some researchers have even identified neurons in the hippocampus that fire in response only to certain celebrities, such as actress Halle Berry (Quiroga, Reddy, Kreiman, Koch, & Fried, 2005). (See **Figure 7.19** on page 298.)

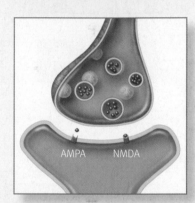

Figure 7.18 Neural Basis of Long-Term Potentiation. LTP enhances the release of glutamate and activates postsynaptic receptors for NMDA and AMPA.

Correlation vs. Causation

The genetically modified Doogie mouse is faster than other mice at recognizing whether an object, shown on the right, is new or old. Scientists can measure this recognition because mice spend more time exploring a new object than an old one.

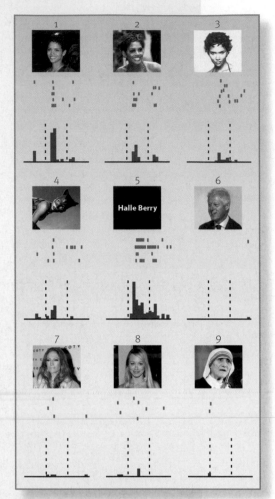

Figure 7.19 Halle Berry Neuron.
Scientists have discovered cells in the human hippocampus that respond preferentially to actress Halle Berry (*see first row*). Indeed, these cells respond to her when she's dressed as Catwoman and even to her name (number 5). The graphs below each figure show the firing rates of the neuron to the picture above it. (*Source:* Quiroga et al., 2005)

The superb 2000 film *Memento* offers a largely accurate portrayal of an individual with virtually complete anterograde amnesia stemming from an accident. The main character in the movie (portrayed by Guy Pearce) tattooed numerous messages on his body in a desperate effort to remind himself of his pre-amnesia life. In reality, such messages rarely help people with anterograde amnesia, because they usually don't remember to look at them.

But is the hippocampus, or any single brain structure, the site of the elusive engram? We can say with some certainty that the answer is no. fMRI studies reveal that learned information isn't stored permanently in the hippocampus itself. Rather, the prefrontal cortex seems to be one of the major "banks" from which we withdraw our memories (Zeinah, Engel, Thompson, & Bookheimer, 2003). But as Lashley discovered, damage to isolated areas of the prefrontal cortex—or other cortical regions, for that matter—doesn't wipe out long-established memories. Much as the smell of a rose diffuses throughout a room, our memories distribute themselves throughout many areas of the cortex.

Amnesia—Biological Bases of Explicit and Implicit Memory. Earlier we learned about explicit and implicit memory. Are these two forms of memory governed by different brain systems? The answer seems to be yes (Squire, 1987). The best evidence comes from individuals with severe amnesia. The two most common types of amnesia are **retrograde amnesia,** in which we lose some memories of our past, and **anterograde amnesia,** in which we lose the capacity to form new memories.

Amnesia Myths. The general public holds a host of misconceptions about amnesia. Perhaps the most prevalent myth is that many amnesics have lost all memories of their previous life, even of who they are. In fact, such *generalized amnesia* is exceedingly rare (American Psychiatric Association [APA], 2000), although it's a favorite plot device of Hollywood moviemakers (Baxendale, 2004). Another myth, also perpetuated by Hollywood, is that memory recovery from amnesia is usually abrupt. Although sudden recoveries from amnesia make for good drama, they don't make for good science. In fact, memory recovery from amnesia tends to occur gradually, if at all (APA, 2000).

Case Studies of Amnesia: H.M. and Clive Wearing. By far the best-known amnesic in the psychological literature is a lonely man living in Connecticut known only by the acronym of H.M., who suffered from severe epileptic seizures that his doctors couldn't control with medication. In March 1953, in a last-ditch attempt to eliminate these seizures, surgeons removed large chunks of H.M.'s temporal lobes, including both his left and right hippocampi, where they had reason to believe the seizures originated (the surgeons of the time didn't anticipate the disastrous impact of this radical operation, which would probably never be performed today). At the time, H.M. was 26 years old. Unless you're experiencing a nasty bout of retrograde amnesia from a few paragraphs ago, you'll recall that the hippocampus plays a key role in long-term memory. Following the operation, H.M. developed virtually complete anterograde amnesia: He can recall almost no new information. Although he also experienced some retrograde amnesia for the eleven years prior to the surgery (Corkin, 1984), his memories from the first fifteen years of his life have remained pretty much intact.

Although H.M.'s surgery took place in 1953, his life today is, for all intents and purposes, frozen in time. H.M. himself put it eloquently: "Every day is alone by itself, whatever enjoyment I have had, whatever sorrow I have had." Despite the fact that H.M.'s IQ is slightly above normal (112) and about equal to his presurgery IQ, he's oblivious to the fact that he underwent surgery. Two years after the operation, in 1955, he reported the current date as March 1953. H.M. read the same magazines and completed the same jigsaw puzzles over and over again without any awareness of having seen them before. He didn't recall having met physicians whom he met just a few minutes earlier, or remember what he ate for lunch 30 minutes ago (Milner, 1972; Scoville & Milner, 1957). Even today, when informed repeatedly of the death of his uncle, he shows the same dramatic grief reaction to this news each time (Shimamura, 1992).

H.M.'s tragic case, like that of Damasio's patient David, illustrates a striking dissociation between explicit and implicit memory. Researchers have asked H.M. to trace simple geometrical shapes from a mirror (**Figure 7.20**), a task that just about all people find infuriatingly difficult when they first try it. Although H.M. had no recollection of ever having performed this task before, his performance improved steadily over time (Milner, 1964, 1965). So although H.M. has no explicit memory for this task, he displays clear-cut implicit—specifically, procedural—memory for it.

When researchers examined H.M.'s brain using imaging techniques, they found that not only his hippocampus but his surrounding cortex and neighboring amygdala (see Chapter 3) were damaged (Corkin, Amaral, Gonzalez, Johnson, & Hyman, 1997). This finding led researchers to hypothesize that large circuits connecting different parts of the limbic system—consisting of the hippocampus, hypothalamus, and amygdala—are critical to memory (see **Figure 7.21**).

Similar evidence for a distinction between explicit and implicit memory comes from the case of Clive Wearing, a former music producer in Great Britain whose hippocampi (along with several other brain structures) were destroyed by a herpes virus in 1985 (D. Wearing, 2005). Like H.M., Clive has virtually complete anterograde amnesia. When his wife leaves the room for a few minutes and returns, he showers her with immense affection, as though he hasn't seen her in years. Yet Clive shows implicit memory in the form of priming effects. When his wife says "St. Mary's," he quickly responds "Paddington," entirely oblivious of why he says that. The name of the hospital to which Clive Wearing was taken after his viral infection was—you guessed it—St. Mary's Paddington (D. Wearing, 2005). The bottom line: Damage to the hippocampus impairs explicit memory, but leaves implicit memory intact.

How well can you draw while looking in a mirror?

Figure 7.20 A Mirror Tracing Task Similar to That Administered to H.M. On this task, used to assess implicit memory, subjects must trace a star while looking only at a mirror.

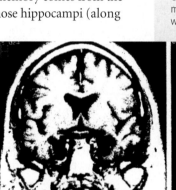
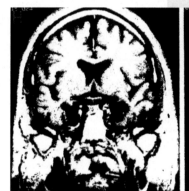

H.M.'s brain damage as imaged in 1997. The scan shows severe damage to his hippocampi and nearby regions. (*Source:* Corkin et al., 1997)

The Amygdala and Emotional Memory. We usually think of memory as our good friend, as a lifelong companion that helps us to store useful information, allowing us to cope with our environment. Yet our memories can also bring us distress, as in the case of a 53-year-old woman who reported olfactory (smell) memories tracking back to a brutal gang rape decades earlier (Vermetten & Bremner, 2003). Olfactory hallucinations of leather, alcohol, and the aftershave "Old Spice"—all of which were present at the rape scene—triggered intense fear responses that led her to retreat to a closet and engage in self-destructive behavior.

The amygdala is where the emotional components of these and other memories, especially those governing fear, are stored. The amygdala interacts with the hippocampus during the formation of memory, but each structure contributes slightly different information (**Figure 7.21**). Researchers uncovered the specific roles of the amygdala and hippocampus in a study of two patients identified by their initials, S.M. and W.S. The first suffered damage to the amygdala, the second to the hippocampus (LeBar & Phelps, 2005). The patient with amygdala damage (S.M.) remembered facts about the fear-producing experience, but not the fear. In contrast, the patient with hippocampal damage (W.S.) remembered the fear, but not the facts surrounding the fear-producing memory. So the amygdala and hippocampus play distinctive roles in memory, with the amygdala helping us to recall the emotions associated with fear-provoking events and the hippocampus helping us to recall the events themselves.

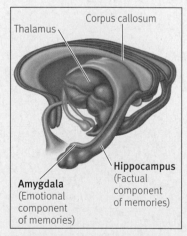

Thalamus

Corpus callosum

Hippocampus (Factual component of memories)

Amygdala (Emotional component of memories)

Figure 7.21 Emotional Memories and the Brain. Research suggests that the amygdala helps us recall the fear associated with scary experiences, and the hippocampus helps us recall the experiences themselves. (*Source:* Adapted from Kalat, 2007)

THE BIOLOGY OF MEMORY DETERIORATION

As we humans pass the ripe old age of 65 years, we usually begin to experience memory problems and some degeneration in the brain. At least some loss of memory and brain tissue is virtually inevitable if we make it to 100 years of age. Yet despite what many people believe, senility isn't an unavoidable part of aging, and some manage to make it past 100

retrograde amnesia
loss of memories from our past

anterograde amnesia
inability to encode new memories from our experiences

with only modest amounts of everyday forgetfulness. But scientists disagree as to how much memory loss is "normal" during the advanced years. Some argue that we needn't accept any memory impairment as normal. Nevertheless, a longitudinal study of subjects aged 59 to 84 years at baseline showed small but consistent reductions in the overall area of the cortex at 2-year and 4-year intervals (Resnick, Pham, Kraut, Zonderman, & Davatzikos, 2003). We might assume that subtle cognitive decline would accompany these tissue losses, but alternative hypotheses are possible. For example, cognition may be fully preserved until a critical amount of tissue loss occurs.

Ruling Out Rival Hypotheses

Many people equate senility with one cause: Alzheimer's disease. Yet Alzheimer's disease is only the most frequent cause of senility, accounting for about 50 to 60 percent of cases of *dementia,* that is, severe memory loss (another common cause of senility is the accumulation of multiple strokes in the brain). Alzheimer's disease occurs at alarming rates as people age. A staggering fact is that one American develops Alzheimer's disease every 72 seconds (Alzheimer's Disease Facts and Fictions, 2007). The risk for Alzheimer's disease is 13 percent for those over 65 years of age, but a whopping 42 percent for those over 85 years of age. The cognitive impairments of Alzheimer's disease are both memory and language related, which corresponds to the patterns of cortical loss in this illness (see **Figure 7.22**). The memory loss begins with recent events, with memories of the distant past being the last to go. Alzheimer's patients forget their grandchildren's names well before forgetting their children's names. Alzheimer's disease patients also experience disorientation and are frequently at a loss as to where they are, what year it is, or who the current president is.

"ON THE CONTRARY, I CAN'T RECALL A THING FROM FIFTY YEARS AGO, BUT I REMEMBER EXACTLY WHAT I HAD FOR LUNCH YESTERDAY."

(© ScienceCartoonsPlus.com)

As we learned in Chapter 3, the Alzheimer's brain contains many senile plaques and neurofibrillary tangles. These abnormalities contribute to the loss of synapses and death of cells in the hippocampus and cerebral cortex. They may also contribute to memory loss and intellectual decline. Loss of synapses is correlated with intellectual status, with greater loss as the disease progresses (Scheff, Price, Schmitt, DeKosky, & Mufson, 2007). But this result doesn't necessarily mean that the reduction in synapses causes the memory decline. Along with loss of synapses comes degeneration and death of acetylcholine neurons in the basal forebrain. Accordingly, the most common treatments for Alzheimer's disease today are drugs that boost the amount of acetylcholine in the brain by inhibiting its breakdown. There are also experimental procedures, such as gene therapies that enhance the production of neurotrophic (growth) factors, which enable acetylcholine neurons to survive and thrive (see Chapter 3). Yet no treatment to date halts or reverses the course of Alzheimer's disease. At best, these treatments only slow its progression.

Correlation vs. Causation

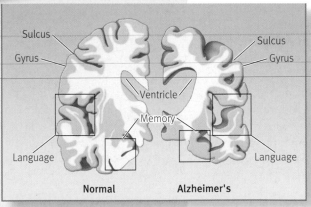

Figure 7.22 Changes in the Brain of Patients with Alzheimer's Disease. Changes include enlargement of the ventricles and severe loss of the cortex in areas involved in language and memory. (*Source:* Courtesy of Alzheimer's Disease Research, a program of the American Health Assistance Foundation)

Correlation vs. Causation

For this reason, researchers have evaluated people's lifestyles to see if anything can be done to reduce the risk of Alzheimer's disease. A massive study assessing over 4,000 people over 65 years of age showed that being physically active reduces the risk of cognitive impairment and Alzheimer's disease (Laurin, Verreault, Landsay, MacPherson, & Rockwood, 2001). This large study dovetails with earlier findings from a small, but telling study of 678 nuns who were hard working, active, and had strong social networks. What's most remarkable about these nuns is their advanced ages—ranging from 87 to over 100 years—along with their low incidence of cognitive impairment, including Alzheimer's disease (Snowdon, 2003). Numerous other studies suggest that people who are highly educated and intellectually active are at decreased risk of Alzheimer's disease (Ngandu et al., 2007). Admittedly, these correlational findings are ambiguous in their causal direction: Perhaps people who are more mentally and physically fit have more brain capacity to begin with. Yet these findings certainly raise the possibility that the old maxim "use it or lose it" may contain more than a grain of truth (Wilson, Scherr, Schneider, Tong, & Bennett, 2007).

The Development of Memory: Acquiring a Personal History

In 2001, the year of the *Time* magazine photoessay on the "Nun Study," Sister Ester was 106, the oldest nun in the order. The results of this study suggest that physical and mental activity may protect against memory loss.

How early can children remember, and what do they remember? The answer depends on what kind of memory we're discussing. In at least one sense, we can remember information even before we're born. That's because fetuses display *habituation*—a decrease in attention to familiar stimuli. As we learned in Chapter 6, fetuses as young as 32 weeks exhibit a decline in their reactions to vibratory stimulators over time. Habituation is a form of implicit memory—to interpret a stimulus as familiar, we need to recall we've experienced it before. It's a far cry from explicitly recalling the words to a song or remembering what we wore to our last birthday party, but it's still a form of remembering.

MEMORY OVER TIME

Memory changes as we age, but there's considerable continuity over the course of development. Infants have worse memories than children, who have worse memories than adults, and young adults have better memories than older adults. But the same basic processes operate across the life span. For example, infants display a serial position curve just as adults do (Cornell & Bergstrom, 1983; Gulya, Galluccio, Wilk, & Rovee-Collier, 2001). Nevertheless, the span of memory and the ability to use strategies increase dramatically across the infant, toddler, preschool, and elementary school years.

Over time, children's memories become increasingly sophisticated. Several factors explain why. First, children's memory spans increase with age (Pascual-Leone, 1989). In fact, their Magic Number doesn't become seven plus or minus two until age 12 or so. If we ask a 3-year-old to remember a string of letters or numbers, she'll remember only about three on average. A 5-year-old will remember about four. By age 9, children are getting close to the adult's Magic Number, remembering six items on average.

Is this increase in span a result of better use of strategies, like rehearsal? That's certainly part of the story (Flavell, Beach, & Chinsky, 1966; McGilly & Siegler, 1989), but there's a large physical maturational component too. So in an odd turn of events, shoe size is actually more highly correlated with memory span in children than with either age or intelligence. Nevertheless, we can assure you that this correlation isn't a causal one! Because different children grow at different rates, this correlation reflects a biological maturity component to memory span, for which variables like shoe size or height are the best predictors.

Correlation vs. Causation

Second, our conceptual understanding increases with age. This fact is important because our ability to chunk related items and store memories in meaningful ways depends on our knowledge of the world. For example, without knowing that "CIA" stands for Central Intelligence Agency, children can't chunk the letters C, I, and A into one unit.

Third, over time children develop enhanced **meta-memory** skills: knowledge about their memory abilities and limitations. These skills help children to identify when they need to use strategies to improve their memories, as well as which strategies work best

meta-memory
knowledge about our own memory abilities and limitations

(Schneider & Bjorkland, 1998; Weinert, 1986; Zabrucky & Ratner, 1986). If we show a 4-year-old ten pictures and ask her how many she thinks she can remember, she'll probably tell you with supreme confidence that she can remember all ten. She can't. Children at this age don't appreciate their own memory limitations and overestimate their capacities as a result. Older children, who actually remember *more* than younger children, estimate they'll remember *less*. As a result, they're more accurate in their ability to gauge their recall (Flavell, Friedrichs, & Hoyt, 1970).

INFANTS' IMPLICIT MEMORY: TALKING WITH THEIR FEET

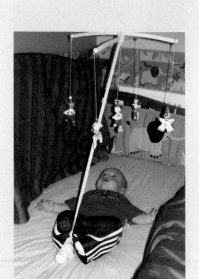

Carolyn Rovee-Collier and other researchers have used mobiles to study infants' implicit memory. Although infants can't tell you they remember the mobiles, their memories "vote with their feet."

Carolyn Rovee-Collier has developed an innovative technique to study infants' implicit memory. Her research capitalizes on the fact that we can operantly condition (see Chapter 6) infants to perform specific behaviors. Rovee-Collier placed infants in a crib with a mobile positioned over their heads. She first watched their behaviors for a few minutes to assess their activity levels in a "baseline" condition. Then, she took a ribbon tied to the mobile and attached it to the infant's ankle. The next time the infant kicked her foot, she was in for a pleasant surprise: The mobile shook and jiggled in response. Infants find the motion of the mobile inherently reinforcing. Because the movement is dependent on infants' behavior, they quickly become conditioned to kick their legs to get the mobile moving.

Once she conditioned infants to kick their legs in response to the mobile, Rovee-Collier sent them home. Then, after a delay—of a day, a week, or even a month—she brought them back to the lab and placed them in the crib again. This time, the mobile wasn't attached to the infant's leg, so there was no reinforcement. The question was: Would infants show an increased kicking rate in response to seeing the mobile? If so, it would imply that they remembered the conditioning experience.

Rovee-Collier (1993) found that children as young as 2 months retained a memory of this experience, although they forgot it after just a few days. Nevertheless, their span of recall increased quickly. Three-month-olds could remember the conditioning for over a week, and 6-month-olds for over 2 weeks. Infants' memories of the experience were surprisingly specific. If researchers modified even a few elements of the mobile or changed the pattern of the crib liner ever so slightly, infants didn't seem to recognize the mobile: Their kicking rate returned to baseline.

INFANTILE AMNESIA

What's your earliest memory? How old were you when the event took place? Research suggests that at least some distinctly recalled early memories, especially those prior to age 3, are either false memories or memories we've dated incorrectly.

infantile amnesia
inability of adults to remember personal experiences that took place before an early age

Take a brief break from reading this chapter, and try to recall your earliest memory. What was it, and how old were you? Most students say their earliest memory falls somewhere between 3 and 5 years of age. **Infantile amnesia** is the inability of adults to retrieve accurate memories before an early age (Malinoski, Lynn, & Sivec, 1998; Wetzler & Sweeney, 1986).

Few, if any, of us correctly recall events before 2 or 3 years of age, the lowest cutoff for infantile amnesia (Nest & Bauer, 1999; Winograd & Killinger, 1983). Memories before that age just aren't trustworthy. So if you have a distinct memory of something that happened at age 1 or before, it's almost certainly either a false memory or a true memory of something that happened later.

Recent research suggests that culture may shape the age and content of our first memories. European Americans report earlier first memories than do people from Taiwan. Moreover, European Americans' earliest memories more often focus on themselves, whereas Taiwanese's earliest memories more often focus on others (Wang, 2006). These findings dovetail with research we'll describe later in the text (see Chapter 10) showing that European American cultures tend to be individually oriented, whereas many Asian cultures tend to be other-oriented (Lehman, Chiu, & Schaller, 2004).

Infantile Amnesia and Pop Psychology. Proponents of some fringe psychological treatments have largely ignored the scientific evidence concerning infantile amnesia. Many advocates of hypnotic age regression, which Nadean Cool's therapist used, claim to be able to retrieve memories from well before age 2, sometimes even before birth (Nash,

1987). At least one therapist even tried to recover his female client's memory of being trapped as an egg in her mother's Fallopian tube prior to fertilization (*Frontline*, 1995). Similarly, proponents of the school of Scientology, popular among many Hollywood celebrities, believe that long-buried memories of negative statements overheard by fetuses, embryos, and even zygotes can be reactivated in adulthood, especially under stress. These memories, Scientologists claim, can trigger low self-esteem and other psychological problems (Carroll, 2003; Gardner, 1958). For example, if a fetus overhears her mother say "I hate you" during a bitter argument with her husband, the grown adult may later misinterpret this statement as referring to herself rather than to her father. Fortunately, for both fetuses and adults, there's no evidence for this extraordinary claim. Fetuses can't accurately make out most sentences they hear from outside the womb (Smith, Gerhardt, Griffiths, Huang, & Abrams, 2003), let alone remember them decades later.

Explanations for Infantile Amnesia. No one knows for sure why the first few years of our lives are lost to us forever, but psychologists have a few promising leads (Bauer, 2006). The hippocampus, which as we've learned plays a key role in long-term memory, especially episodic memory, is only partially developed in infancy (Mishkin, Malamut, & Bachevalier, 1984; Schacter & Moscovitch, 1984). So before age 2 or so, we may not possess the brainpower needed to retain memories of events.

Also, as infants, we possess little or no sense of self (Fivush, 1988; Howe & Courage, 1993). Before about 18 months of age, infants can't recognize themselves in mirrors (Lewis, Brooks-Gunn, & Jaskir, 1985). Without a well-developed sense of self, some psychologists maintain, infants can't encode or store memories of their experiences in a meaningful fashion.

SUGGESTIBILITY AND CHILD TESTIMONY

Probably because they sometimes confuse fantasy with reality, children are especially vulnerable to suggestions to recall events that didn't occur (Ceci & Bruck, 1993). Stephen Ceci and his colleagues (Ceci, Crotteau, Smith, & Loftus, 1994) asked preschool children to imagine real and fictitious events. Once a week, for a total of seven to ten interviews, they instructed children to "think real hard" about whether the events had occurred. For example, they asked the children to try to remember made-up events, like going to the hospital with a mousetrap on their fingers. Fifty-eight percent of children generated stories regarding at least one of these fictitious events. Interestingly, about a quarter of the children continued to insist their memories were real even when their parents and the experimenter assured them the events never happened. The fact that children cling to their false memories even when an authority figure tells them the memories are wrong suggests that such memories can be convincing. These findings are important for another reason: Many social workers and police officers who suspect that a child was abused question the child about this abuse repeatedly. Repeated questioning comes with a risk: Children may give investigators the answers they're seeking, even if these answers are wrong.

Children's memories are also affected by schemas, especially their expectations about how others will act. To demonstrate this point, two researchers (Leichtman & Ceci, 1995) provided 3- to 6-year-old children with information that led them to hold a negative stereotype about a man, "Sam Stone," before he visited the classroom several weeks later. They told the children various stories about Sam, a clumsy character who did things like accidentally break Barbie dolls and rip sweaters. When Sam actually visited, he didn't act clumsily at all, but the next day, the teacher showed the children a soiled teddy bear and a torn book. Afterward, the investigators interviewed some of the children on different occasions about what Sam did during the visit. They asked the children suggestive questions, such as "Did Sam Stone rip the book or did he use scissors?" Then, during the final interview, they asked children to describe Sam's visit. In response to open-ended questions, 46 percent of 3- and 4-year-olds and 30 percent of 5- and 6-year-olds reported that Sam had ripped the book, soiled the teddy bear, or both. With further prompts, 72 percent of the younger preschoolers and 44 percent of the older preschoolers responded to the suggestion. Children in a control condition, who weren't interviewed or provided with negative stereotypes, rarely made these errors.

Extraordinary Claims

Research suggests that other than humans, chimpanzees, gorillas, and dolphins are among the handful of species that exhibit mirror self-recognition—often regarded as one important indicator of the presence of a self-concept (Gallup, 1977; Reiss & Marino, 2001). Here a baby reacts to his mirror image.

fict**oid**

Myth: People who've experienced a traumatic event recall it as equally terrifying no matter how much time passes.

Reality: Some people remember an experience as *more* frightening as time passes. One research team studied a group of women who'd witnessed a school shooting. They first asked the women to describe the shooting 5 months after it happened, and again 12 months later. Some of these women had become more emotionally distressed in the intervening year. They recalled the shooting as having been more terrifying at 17 months than they had at 5 months (Schwarz, Kowalski, & McNally, 1993), probably because their current mood state influenced their memories of the event.

Do you recall precisely where you were and what you were doing on the morning of September 11, 2001? If so, some researchers would claim that you have a flashbulb memory of this event. In reality, however, there's scant evidence that flashbulb memories are either distinctive from other memories or infallible.

flashbulb memories
emotional memories that are extraordinarily vivid and detailed

---

ASSESS YOUR KNOWLEDGE: FACT OR FICTION?

(1) Most young children underestimate their memory abilities. (True/False)
(2) Children as young as 2 months have implicit memories of their experiences. (True/False)
(3) Most adults can accurately recall events that took place before they were 3 years old. (True/False)
(4) Repeatedly asking children if they were abused leads to more accurate answers than asking them only once. (True/False)

Answers: (1) F (p. 301); (2) T (p. 302); (3) F (p. 302); (4) F (p. 303)

When Good Memory Goes Bad: False Memories

We generally trust our memories to provide us with an accurate recounting of our past. In many cases, our memories do the job well enough. Over the past few decades, however, researchers have shown that our memories can be more fallible than any of us could have imagined. Moreover, we're often far more confident of our recollections of events than we should be.

FALSE MEMORIES

At first blush, our everyday experience strongly suggests that we can safely rely on our memories, because many of our recollections seem to be as crisp as scenes from motion pictures we're watching in real time. Do you remember where you were and what you were doing when you heard about the terrorist attacks on September 11, 2001? Most Americans say yes, and many say that, even today, they can "relive" those frightening moments with astonishing clarity. Many older Americans report equally vivid memories of the assassination of President John F. Kennedy on November 22, 1963. Powerful memories of the attempted assassination of President Ronald Reagan (Pillemer, 1984), the explosion of the space shuttle *Challenger* (McCloskey, Wible, & Cohen, 1988), and the death of Princess Diana (Krackow et al., in press) are other examples.

Flashbulb Memories. It's no wonder that Roger Brown and James Kulik (1977) referred to these recollections as **flashbulb memories,** emotional memories that seem so vivid that people seem able to recount them in remarkable, even photographic, detail. They further argued that flashbulb memories don't decay over time like ordinary memories. So flashbulb memories suggest that our memories sometimes operate like video cameras or tape recorders after all, right?

Maybe not. For starters, let's consider the following story from Ulric Neisser (1982), himself a memory researcher. For several decades, Neisser repeatedly related a flashbulb memory of the bombing of Pearl Harbor in 1941. It was right before his thirteenth birthday, he recalled vividly, and he was listening with great interest to a baseball game on the radio. Suddenly, a newsman interrupted the game to announce that the Japanese had attacked the American naval base in Pearl Harbor, Hawaii. Yet there's a problem here. Can you figure it out?

Neisser realized many years later that his flashbulb memory couldn't have been correct, because the bombing of Pearl Harbor occurred in December, and baseball season ends in October. After recovering from the shock of discovering that his memory was wrong, Neisser went back to the drawing board. After a bit of detective work, he discovered that there had been a *football game* broadcast on the radio that day, and that it was between the Giants and the Dodgers, perhaps not coincidentally the names of two baseball teams! Neisser had probably misremembered a football game as a baseball game.

Neisser and Nicole Harsch (1992) decided to find out whether such distortions of vivid memories were common by studying college students' recollection of the explosion of the space shuttle *Challenger* in 1986. For many people, this was a particularly tragic and memorable event because, for the first time, a nonastronaut—a schoolteacher named Christa McAuliffe—was onboard. Neisser and Harsch discovered that $2\frac{1}{2}$ to 3 years after the *Challenger* explosion, 75 percent of college students' reports of the event didn't match their recollections from only a few days following this event. Moreover, about a third of the students' stories changed dramatically over time. Consider this recollection from one of their subjects almost immediately after the *Challenger* explosion.

Initial Recollection (January 1986): "I was in my religion class and some people walked in and started talking about the explosion. I didn't know any details except that it had exploded and the schoolteacher's students had all been watching, which I thought was so sad. Then after class I went to my room and watched the TV program talking about it and I got all the details from that."

Here's the recollection from the *same* student more than $2\frac{1}{2}$ years later:

Later Recollection (September 1988): "When I first heard about the explosion I was sitting in my freshman dorm room with my roommate and we were watching TV. It came on a news flash and we were both totally shocked. I was really upset and went upstairs to talk to a friend of mine and then I called my parents."

When Neisser and Harsch presented students with their written recollections from several years earlier, some insisted that they must have been written by someone else! The authors coined the term *phantom flashbulb memory* to capture the idea that many seeming flashbulb memories are false. This phenomenon has been replicated with a group of students asked to recall their memory of the verdict of the O. J. Simpson trial (Buffalo & Squire, 2000). After 32 months, 40 percent of the memory reports contained "major distortions" relative to their initial recollection only 3 days after the verdict.

This research indicates that flashbulb memories change over time, just like all other memories. They remind us that much as our memories may seem to work like video cameras, they don't. We don't need to invoke an entirely new set of explanations to explain vivid recollections. The most parsimonious hypothesis is that flashbulb memories aren't a separate class of memories; they're much like other memories, just more intense.

Source Monitoring: Who Said That?   Think back to a conversation you had yesterday with a friend. How do you know it really happened? About 25 percent of undergraduates report experiencing a distinct memory of an event but feeling unsure of whether it actually occurred or was part of a dream (Rassin, Merkelbach, & Spann, 2001). This is an example of a *source monitoring confusion,* a lack of clarity about the origin of a memory.

According to a **source monitoring** view of memory (Johnson, Hashtroudi, & Lindsay, 1993; Johnson & Raye, 1981), we try to identify the origins of our memories by seeking cues about how we encoded them. Source monitoring refers to our efforts to identify the origins (sources) of a memory. Whenever we try to figure out whether a memory really reflects something that happened or whether we merely imagined it, we're engaging in source monitoring. For example, we typically rely on cues regarding how vivid and detailed our memories are. All things being equal, memories that are more vivid and detailed are more likely to reflect actual events (Lynn et al., 2003). If our memory of a conversation with a friend on campus is vague and fuzzy, we may begin to wonder whether it really happened or it was merely a product of our overactive imagination.

In many cases, source monitoring works well, by helping us avoid confusing our memories with our fantasies. This ability comes in handy when we're trying to recall whether we actually punched our obnoxious boss in the nose or just fantasized about doing so. Yet because cues regarding the vividness and detail of memories are far from perfect, source monitoring isn't perfect either. We can sometimes be fooled, and false memories can result.

A source monitoring perspective helps us understand why some people are especially receptive to false memories. Remember the memory illusion test with all of the sleepy

Replicability

Occam's Razor

Some dreams are so powerful and vivid that we may confuse them with events in everyday life. This is one example of a source monitoring confusion.

source monitoring
ability to identify the origins of a memory

words earlier in the chapter? (No, it's not a false memory.) Some studies suggest that people who are fantasy-prone are more likely to experience memory illusions on this task (Winograd, Peluso, & Glover, 1998). So are the elderly (Jacoby & Rhodes, 2006). Both groups of people are probably more likely to confuse their imaginations with reality.

Many other memory errors reflect confusions in source monitoring. Take the phenomenon of **cryptomnesia** (literally meaning "hidden memory"), whereby we mistakenly forget that one of "our" ideas originated with someone else. Some cases of plagiarism probably reflect cryptomnesia. When George Harrison, a former member of the Beatles, wrote his hit song, "My Sweet Lord," he apparently forgot that the melody of this song was virtually identical to that of the Chiffons' song, "He's So Fine," which had appeared about 10 years earlier. After the copyright owners of the Chiffons' song sued Harrison, he used cryptomnesia as a legal defense, arguing that he mistakenly believed he'd invented the melody himself. The judge awarded money to the copyright owners of the original song, although he ruled that Harrison probably didn't commit the plagiarism intentionally.

In 2006, Kaavya Viswanathan, a Harvard sophomore and author of the book *How Opal Mehta Got Kissed, Got Wild, and Got a Life,* was accused of plagiarism when reporters revealed that numerous passages in her book were suspiciously similar to those in several other books. Viswanathan's defense was cryptomnesia: She claimed to have read these books and forgotten their source (she also claimed to possess a photographic memory, making it difficult for her to forget the original passages).

APPLY YOUR THINKING

How might source monitoring help to explain the phenomenon of déjà vu, in which people feel as though they've experienced something before?

In the film *Eternal Sunshine of the Spotless Mind,* Joel Barish (portrayed by Jim Carrey) and Clementine Kruczynski (portrayed by Kate Winslet) undergo a medical procedure to erase all memories of an intensely painful romantic relationship. Might researchers one day develop a pill to obliterate traumatic memories? If so, would it be a good idea?

NEW FRONTIERS

Using Medication to Erase Memories

What if it were possible to erase or take the sting out of traumatic or painful memories? The 2004 movie *Eternal Sunshine of the Spotless Mind,* in which two ex-lovers devastated by a failed relationship undergo a medical procedure to erase all memories of each other, envisions just such a possibility.

The movie raises fascinating ethical issues: Is erasing all traces of pain in life always a good thing? Or is emotional suffering instead an essential part of being human? Does psychological pain help us mature? These questions have taken on new urgency with the discovery of a drug that appears to block the formation of traumatic memories.

As we've learned, emotional memories can persist, even if they often become distorted over time. The hormones adrenaline and norepinephrine (see Chapter 3) are released in the face of stress and stimulate protein (beta-adrenergic) receptors on nerve cells, which solidify emotional memories. In the case of posttraumatic stress disorder (PTSD), which we'll discuss in Chapters 12 and 15, unwanted and disturbing memories can cast a dark shadow on virtually every aspect of people's lives.

Lawrence Cahill and James McGaugh (1995) demonstrated the staying power of emotional memories in an elegant study. They created two stories regarding twelve slides they showed to participants. They told half of the participants an emotionally neutral story about a boy's visit to a hospital where his father works. They told the other half a far more disturbing story about the same slides; in the middle of the story, they informed participants that the boy was injured and operated on at a hospital to reattach his severed legs. Participants returned for a memory test 24 hours later, and Cahill and McGaugh asked them what they remembered about the slides. Participants who heard the emotionally arousing story displayed the best recall for the part of the story about the boy's trauma. In contrast, participants who heard the neutral story recalled the same amount of detail for all parts of the story.

Cahill and McGaugh (Cahill, Prins, Weber, & McGaugh, 1994) repeated this experiment with an interesting twist. This time, they gave some participants a drug called *propranolol,* which blocks the effects of adrenaline on beta-adrenergic receptors (doctors also use it to treat high blood pressure). When participants' adrenaline was inhibited by propranolol, they didn't display especially good recall for the emotionally arousing part of the story. In fact, their recall was no different from that of individuals who listened to the emotionally neutral story.

Psychiatrist Roger Pitman was quick to grasp the implications of these findings for PTSD. He reasoned that propranolol might blunt the memories of real-life traumas, such as automobile accidents. Pitman and his colleagues (Pitman et al., 2002) administered propranolol to people for 10 days after they experienced a traumatic event, such as a car accident and, a month later, examined their physical reactions to individually prepared tapes that replayed key aspects of the event. Forty-three percent of participants who received a placebo showed a physical response to the tape that recreated their traumatic experience. Yet none of the people who received the drug did.

Pitman's pill only dampened the effects of traumatic memories; it didn't erase them. Still, his study hasn't laid to rest questions about whether such procedures are ethical, much less desirable. Scientists and ethicists will long debate the personal and societal implications of treatments that alter memory. After all, if we could choose to forget every negative experience, could we learn and grow from our mistakes? Then again, why shouldn't people who suffer from PTSD take a medicine that alleviates their distress, just as people with depression take antidepressant medication? The issues here are complex and not easily resolved.

Implanting False Memories in the Lab. Three decades ago, psychologist Elizabeth Loftus (Loftus, 1979; Loftus, Miller, & Burns, 1978; Wells & Loftus, 1984) opened researchers' eyes to the dramatic effects of misleading suggestions on both everyday memories and eyewitness reports. Her pioneering work demonstrated that our memories are far more malleable than most psychologists had assumed.

Misinformation Effect. In a classic study, Loftus and John Palmer (1974) took advantage of a finding (Marshall, 1969) that people's estimates of the speed of a car traveling at 12 miles per hour varied between 10 and 50 miles per hour. That is, people aren't especially good at estimating the speed of moving vehicles, and can be influenced by subtle suggestions. Loftus and Palmer showed participants brief clips of traffic accidents and asked them to estimate the speed of the vehicles involved. They varied the wording of their question, "About how fast were the cars going when they _____ each other?" When participants heard the word *smashed*, they rated the speed as 9 miles per hour faster than when they heard the word *contacted* (40.8 when *smashed* was used versus 31.8 when *contacted* was used).

In a later study, Loftus and her colleagues asked participants to watch a slide sequence of an accident in which a car passed through an intersection and struck a pedestrian. They asked participants questions about the event. Some of the questions contained misleading suggestions. For example, in the actual slide sequence, the sign at the intersection was a yield sign. Yet Loftus and her colleagues phrased one of the questions, "While the car was stopped at the stop sign, did a red Datsun pass by?" A moment's reflection suggests that the question is misleading because it implies that a different sign—a stop sign—was located at the intersection. Afterward, participants who received the misleading questions were more likely to say that the sign was a stop sign than a yield sign. In contrast, most subjects who didn't receive the phony information recalled the yield sign accurately. This phenomenon is the **misinformation effect:** Providing people with misleading information after an event can lead to fictitious memories (Loftus, Miller, & Burns, 1978).

Lost in the Mall and Other Implanted Memories. Loftus's famous "lost in the mall study" demonstrates that we can implant elaborate memories of a made-up event that never happened. Loftus and her colleagues (Loftus, Coan, & Pickrell, 1996; Loftus & Pickrell, 1995) asked the relatives of twenty-four participants to describe events that participants had experienced in childhood. They then presented participants with a booklet that

In the 1978 study by Loftus and her colleagues, subjects saw a car stopped at a yield sign (*top*). Yet when prompted with the information that the car had been stopped at a stop sign (*bottom*), they later "remembered" seeing the stop sign.

cryptomnesia
failure to recognize that our ideas originated with someone else

misinformation effect
creation of fictitious memories by providing misleading information about an event after it takes place

contained the details of three events the relatives reported, along with a fourth event that the relatives verified never occurred: being lost in a shopping mall as a child. Participants wrote about each event they could recall. In follow-up interviews, a quarter of the subjects claimed to distinctly remember being lost in the mall as a child. Some even provided surprisingly detailed accounts of the event.

Replicability

Many investigators followed in the path of Loftus's groundbreaking work. Using suggestive questions and statements, researchers have implanted memories of a wide variety of events, ranging from accidentally spilling a bowl of punch on the parents of the bride at a wedding reception to a serious animal attack to demonic possession, in about 20 to 25 percent of college students (Bernstein, Laney, Morris, & Loftus, 2005; DeBreuil, Garry, & Loftus, 1998; Hyman, Husband, & Billings, 1995; Mazzoni, Loftus, & Kirsch, 2001; Porter, Yuille, & Lehman, 1999). Of course, these percentages imply that many students aren't especially prone to false memories, although some clearly are.

Event Plausibility. As we might imagine, there are limits to how far we can go in implanting false memories. Much of what we recall hinges on our beliefs, hunches, and "best guesses" about what we've experienced (Hirt et al., 1999). Given what we know, it's easier for us to believe some things than others.

Let's say we asked you to imagine vividly and repeatedly that your instructor wore a Mexican sombrero to your last class, and interrupted her lecture to do the Mexican hat dance. We suspect you wouldn't buy the suggestion for two reasons. First, it's easier to implant a memory of something that's plausible than of something that isn't (Pezdek, Finger, & Hodge, 1997). Second, it's easier to implant a fictitious memory of an event from the distant past for which we have hazy or no recall than of an event from the recent past we remember well.

Memories of Impossible Events. Most of the studies we've reviewed so far are open to at least one major criticism. Perhaps participants actually experienced the suggested event, such as being lost in a mall, but forgot about it until the suggestion reminded them of it. Studies of impossible or highly implausible memories rule out this alternative hypothesis. Indeed, researchers have devised clever *existence proofs* (see Chapter 2) demonstrating that it's possible to create elaborate memories of events that never happened. Here are two "memorable" examples.

Ruling Out Rival Hypotheses

One team of researchers (Wade, Garry, Read, & Lindsay, 2002) showed participants a fake photograph of a hot-air balloon, into which they'd pasted photographs of the participant and a relative (ah, the wonders of computers!). Family members had confirmed that the participant had never experienced a hot-air balloon ride. The investigators showed participants the fake photograph and asked them to describe "everything you can remember without leaving anything out, no matter how trivial it may seem." After two further interviews, 50 percent of subjects recalled at least some of the fictitious hot-air balloon ride, and some embellished their reports with sensory details (such as seeing a road from high up in the air).

Research using fake photographs shows that we can "rewrite" parts of people's life histories. In one case, subjects became convinced that they'd experienced a hot-air balloon ride as a child even when they hadn't.

In a second line of research (Braun, Ellis, & Loftus, 2002), investigators showed participants ads for Disneyland that featured Bugs Bunny and asked them about seeing Bugs at Disneyland as a child. Sixteen percent of subjects said they remembered meeting and shaking hands with Bugs Bunny; some even remembered hearing him say, "What's up, doc?" What's so strange about that? Bugs Bunny is a Warner Brothers, not a Disney, cartoon character, so the memories must have been false.

Generalizing from Lab to Real World. Studies like these we've reviewed, and dramatic cases like that of Nadean Cool, provide vivid examples of how suggestive memory recovery techniques can shape our memories and identities. Ethical limitations render it difficult, if not impossible, to determine whether we can implant memories of sexual and physical abuse inside or outside the laboratory. So we should be cautious about generalizing experimental findings to the real world, because these laboratory studies may be low in *external validity* (see Chapter 2). Still, as we've seen, research shows that it's possible to create elaborate and emotionally meaningful memories of nonexistent events (Johnson, 2001).

Ruling Out Rival Hypotheses

Another unresolved issue is the extent to which changes in participants' reports in false memory studies reflect actual changes in their memories. Could these changes reflect attempts to please experimenters or give experimenters the answers they're seeking? Put in more technical terms, could they reflect *demand characteristics* (Chapter 2)? Probably not, because even when researchers have told subjects they implanted the memories, many continue to insist that the memories are genuine (Ceci et al., 1994). Moreover, the fact that many investigators, using different experimental designs, have replicated the finding that memories are malleable provides strong support for the claim that memory is reconstructive.

Replicability

Eyewitness Testimony. As of today, 208 prisoners have been acquitted of a crime and released because their DNA didn't match genetic material left by perpetrators. Since the mid-1980s, when scientists developed techniques to analyze genetic material, the number of prisoners who've been released due to DNA testing has increased each year. Consider Gene Bibbons, "Number 125," sentenced to life imprisonment for the sexual assault of a 16-year-old girl. The victim described the perpetrator as a man with long curly hair, wearing jeans. However, Bibbons had short, cropped hair at the time and was wearing shorts. Still, she identified Bibbons as the assailant. Years later, investigators located a biological specimen, and genetic testing confirmed that Bibbons's DNA didn't match the DNA at the crime scene. After maintaining his innocence for 16 years, Bibbons walked out of prison a free man.

In 1984, Jennifer Thompson, a 22-year-old college student, was raped. Shortly after, she confidently identified Ronald Cotton (*right*) as the man who raped her, and he was imprisoned following a trial. In 1995, a DNA test showed conclusively that Bobby Poole (*left*) was the actual rapist, and Cotton was released after spending 11 years in prison for a crime he didn't commit. Consumed by guilt, Thompson sought out Cotton following his release from prison; they've since become friends.

If there's a thread that ties Bibbons to the 207 other unjustly imprisoned individuals, it's that an eyewitness misidentified him as guilty. Three-quarters or more of prisoners acquitted by DNA testing are mistakenly identified by eyewitnesses (Scheck, Neufeld, & Dwyer, 2000). This fact isn't surprising when we consider that when witnesses seem sure they've identified a culprit, juries tend to believe them (Smith, Lindsay, Pyrke, & Dysart, 2001; Wells & Bradford, 1998). Yet contrary to popular (mis)conception, the correlation between witnesses' confidence in their testimony and the accuracy of this testimony is weak (Bothwell, Deffenbacher, & Brigham, 1987; Kassin, Ellsworth, & Smith, 1989).

Eyewitnesses sometimes provide invaluable evidence, especially when they have ample time to observe the perpetrator under good lighting conditions, when the criminal isn't disguised, and when little time elapses between witnessing the crime and identifying the guilty party (Memon, Hope, & Bull, 2003). But eyewitness testimony is far from accurate when these optimal conditions aren't met. Moreover, eyewitness testimony is less likely to be accurate when people observe individuals of races different from their own (Kassin, Tubb, Hosch, & Memon, 2001; Meissner & Brigham, 2001; Pezdek, Blandon-Gitlin, & Moore, 2003), when they talk to other witnesses (Wells, Memon, & Ray, 2006), or when they view a crime under stressful circumstances, such as when they feel threatened (Deffenbacher, Bornstein, Penrod, & McGorty, 2004). Eyewitness accuracy is also often impaired by the phenomenon of *weapon focus:* When a crime involves a weapon, people understandably tend to focus on the weapon rather than the perpetrator's appearance (Steblay, 1992). Psychologists can play a critical role in educating jurors about the science of eyewitness recall, so that they can better weigh the evidence.

Psychologists also can inform juries about the best way to conduct eyewitness lineups. In a lineup, police instruct the witness to select the culprit from among potential suspects. In a *simultaneous lineup* (see Prologue), the witness can make the selection "live," from among six people standing behind glass, for example, or, more typically, from photographs. The problem is that when the real criminal isn't in the lineup, witnesses are likely to mistakenly identify the person who most closely resembles the real perpetrator relative to other people in the lineup. To circumvent this problem, police sometimes use *sequential lineups,* in which witnesses view one person at a time, typically by means of photographs

(Lindsay & Wells, 1985; see Prologue). The advantage of this procedure is that witnesses don't have an opportunity to compare one person with another. In this way, they're less likely to incorrectly pick out a person who's innocent but who has the misfortune of looking more like the real criminal than the other people in the lineup. Laboratory evidence suggests that identification of suspects is more accurate with sequential than with simultaneous lineups (Steblay, Deisert, Fulero, & Lindsay, 2001), although important questions about the real-world difference between these two types of lineups remain (McQuiston-Surrett, Malpass, & Tredoux, 2007). Another critical consideration is that the person who conducts the lineup shouldn't know who the suspect is, because this knowledge could unintentionally bias the eyewitness.

The False Memory Controversy. One of the most divisive controversies in all of psychology centers on the possibility that memories of child abuse and other traumatic experiences can be shaped by suggestive techniques in psychotherapy (see Prologue and Chapter 16). In fact, debates concerning false memories have become so bitter that some writers have referred to them as the "memory wars" (Crews, 1990).

On one side of the battle are memory recovery therapists, who claim that patients *repress* memories of traumatic events, such as childhood sexual abuse, and then *recover* them years, even decades, later (Brown, Scheflin, & Hammond, 1997). As we'll learn in Chapter 14, most followers of Sigmund Freud believe that repression is a form of forgetting in which people push painful memories into their unconscious. According to recovered memory therapists, these repressed memories are the root cause of current life problems and must be addressed to make progress in psychotherapy (McNally, 2003). Some, like Nadean Cool's therapist, even claim their clients have repressed memories of murderous satanic cults, even though investigations by the FBI have consistently failed to unearth any evidence of these cults (Lanning, 1989). By the mid-1990s, approximately 25 percent of psychotherapists reported in surveys (Polousny & Follette, 1996; Poole, Lindsay, Memon, & Bull, 1995) that they used two or more potentially suggestive procedures, including dream interpretation, guided imagery, and hypnosis, to help patients who had no recollection of sexual abuse to recover memories of it.

Lined up on the opposing side of the false memory debate is a growing chorus of researchers who claim that there's slim evidence that people repress traumatic memories, including childhood sexual abuse. These researchers point to a mounting body of evidence that painful memories are well remembered and, if anything, remembered too well (Loftus, 1993; McNally, 2003; Pope, Poliakoff, Parker, Boynes, & Hudson, 2007; see Chapter 16). According to them, there's serious reason to doubt that many memories can be repressed and then recovered years or decades later. These researchers have also voiced serious concerns about whether suggestive procedures can lead patients to conclude erroneously that family members abused them in childhood. Indeed, hundreds of individuals have been separated from their families, and in some cases even imprisoned, solely on the basis of recovered memory claims of child sexual abuse.

From a scientific and ethical standpoint, this state of affairs is deeply troubling, often tragic. Given what we now know about how fallible human memory is, recovered memories of child abuse shouldn't be trusted completely unless they're accompanied by corroborating evidence. In the past decade, the false memory controversy has cooled somewhat, largely because a consensus has emerged that suggestive procedures can create false memories of childhood events in many, although perhaps not all, psychotherapy clients.

THE SEVEN SINS OF MEMORY

By this point in the chapter, we hope we've persuaded you that although our memories generally work well and are often accurate, they're anything but perfect. Daniel Schacter (2001) elegantly summarized the tricks that memory can play on us by describing the "seven sins of memory." Schacter's analogy to the ancient seven deadly sins (pride, anger, envy, greed, glut-

---

fictoid

Myth: People who think they might have been sexually abused, but aren't sure, can use symptom checklists in self-help books to help them find out.

Reality: Many therapists who treat patients with suspected sexual abuse histories prescribe "survivor books"—self-help books that often contain checklists of supposed telltale symptoms of past sexual abuse, such as fears of sex, low self-esteem, insecurity about one's appearance, or excessive dependency (Lynn et al., 2003). Yet research shows that most of these symptoms are so vague and general that they can apply to virtually everyone (Emery & Lilienfeld, 2004).

Gary Ramona, a successful California wine executive, was accused by his daughter, Holly, of sexually abusing her in childhood. Siding with her daughter, his wife divorced him. Ramona eventually won a half-million-dollar lawsuit against Holly's psychiatrist. The jury agreed with Ramona that the psychiatrist's suggestive techniques had triggered false memories of sexual abuse in Holly.

tony, lust, and sloth) is hardly accidental. Just as these sins can get us into big trouble, the seven sins of memory, which we've listed below, can lead to a host of memory errors.

(1) **Suggestibility.** As we've learned, misleading information following events, leading questions, and explicit information and suggestions can increase the chances of our believing that fictitious events occurred.

(2) **Misattribution.** Suggestions are often effective because they lead us to misattribute memories to incorrect sources, mistaking what's imagined for a real memory. We can also misremember where we've read or heard about an event.

(3) **Bias.** As we've seen, our schemas can bias our memories. For example, information that conveys stereotypes about people can influence our memories of them. If we expect people to act unethically, we may remember them as acting unethically even when they didn't.

(4) **Transience.** One thing is certain: Many of our memories will fade with time. This loss affects both short- and long-term memories. As we age, it's increasingly difficult to access memories. In cases of massive brain injury or dementia, the ability to access memories can be severely impaired.

(5) **Persistence.** The great author William Faulkner once wrote, "The past is never dead; it's not even past." Remember the last time someone "stole your parking space," that is, sneaked in front of you even though you got there first? Or when someone insulted you in front of your friends? These events can linger in our minds for days or weeks and intrude into our thoughts, even disrupting our ability to sleep.

(6) **Blocking.** Most of us have had the experience of starting to say something, and then suddenly and inexplicably losing all memory of what we intended to say. Although this experience can be embarrassing, most of us recover quickly from *blocking,* a temporary inability to access information. The TOT phenomenon is another example of blocking.

(7) **Absentmindedness.** There's the old stereotype of the "absentminded professor," who looks for his glasses when they're on his face. World-famous cellist Yo-Yo Ma once forgot something fairly important after departing a taxi: his multimillion-dollar cello. Yet virtually all of us suffer from occasional absentmindedness when we're tired or distracted. People who get caught up in fantasies or daydream frequently are especially likely to report being absentminded (Lynn & Rhue, 1988; Wilson & Barber, 1981). Absentmindedness can stem from a failure either to encode memories because we're not paying attention or to retrieve memories we've already stored.

Absentmindedness (forgetting to take items we've paid for, or leaving a briefcase in a taxi) happens to everyone occasionally. Cellist Yo-Yo Ma left his $2.5 million Venetian cello made in 1733 in a cab. The taxi driver discovered the rare instrument in his trunk after completing his shift and gave it to the police.

The seven sins of memory needn't lead us to despair. As Schacter (2001) pointed out, if we look at the flip side of each of the seven sins, we'll find an adaptive function. So these seven sins help us resolve the paradox of memory, because most memory errors stem from basic mechanisms of memory that usually serve us well. For instance, the fact that older memories aren't as accessible as new ones is adaptive, because many new memories are relevant to current life tasks and challenges. In this way, we're likely to keep in mind memories that are distinctive, interesting, and emotionally meaningful. Even absentmindedness has its upside, because paying attention to unnecessary details can derail us from pursuing important life goals. In short, the same mechanisms that falter when memory is imperfect help to explain our ability to use memory as a bridge between the past and the present, and as a gateway to the future.

ASSESS YOUR KNOWLEDGE: FACT OR FICTION?
(1) Flashbulb memories almost never change over time. (True/False)
(2) People often find it difficult to tell the difference between a true and a false memory. (True/False)
(3) It's almost impossible to create false memories of complex events, like undergoing a painful medical procedure. (True/False)
(4) One powerful way of creating false memories is to show people fake photographs of events that didn't happen. (True/False)

Answers: (1) F (p. 304); (2) T (p. 305); (3) F (p. 307); (4) T (p. 308)

How Memory Operates: The Memory Assembly Line (pp. 275–287)

STUDY the Learning Objectives

▶ Identify the ways that memories do and do not accurately reflect experiences
- Memories can be surprisingly accurate over very long periods of time but tend to be reconstructive rather than reproductive.

▶ Explain the function, span, and duration of each of the three memory systems
- Sensory memory, short-term memory, and long-term memory are stages of information processing that vary in how much information they hold and for how long they retain it. Short-term memory has a limited span of seven plus or minus two that can be extended by grouping things together into larger, meaningful units called chunks.

▶ Differentiate the subtypes of long-term memory
- Explicit memory subtypes include semantic and episodic memory. Implicit memory types include procedural and priming memory.

DO YOU KNOW THESE TERMS?

- ❏ **memory** (p. 275)
- ❏ **suggestive memory techniques** (p. 276)
- ❏ **memory illusion** (p. 276)
- ❏ **span** (p. 278)
- ❏ **duration** (p. 278)
- ❏ **sensory memory** (p. 278)
- ❏ **iconic memory** (p. 278)
- ❏ **echoic memory** (p. 279)
- ❏ **short-term memory** (p. 279)
- ❏ **decay** (p. 280)
- ❏ **interference** (p. 280)
- ❏ **retroactive inhibition** (p. 281)
- ❏ **proactive inhibition** (p. 281)
- ❏ **Magic Number** (p. 281)
- ❏ **chunking** (p. 282)
- ❏ **rehearsal** (p. 282)
- ❏ **maintenance rehearsal** (p. 283)
- ❏ **elaborative rehearsal** (p. 283)
- ❏ **levels of processing** (p. 283)
- ❏ **long-term memory** (p. 284)
- ❏ **permastore** (p. 284)
- ❏ **primacy effect** (p. 285)
- ❏ **recency effect** (p. 285)
- ❏ **von Restorff effect** (p. 285)
- ❏ **serial position curve** (p. 285)
- ❏ **semantic memory** (p. 286)
- ❏ **episodic memory** (p. 286)
- ❏ **explicit memory** (p. 286)
- ❏ **implicit memory** (p. 286)
- ❏ **procedural memory** (p. 286)
- ❏ **priming** (p. 286)

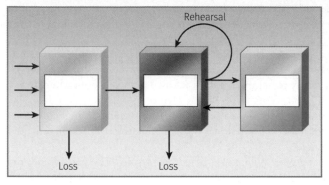

Map out the three memory model process proposed by Atkinson and Shiffrin depicting memory flow. (p. 278)

THINK about what **You** would do . . .

You've just witnessed a hit and run accident in which you were able to see the license plate of the driver who sped away. Using established memory strategies, what could you do to try to recall the license plate long enough to report it to police (assuming you don't have anything to write on or a cell phone with you)? (p. 281)

SUCCEED with

mypsychlab

Digit Span

Can you memorize a phone number? Let's test the Magic Number "7." (p. 281)

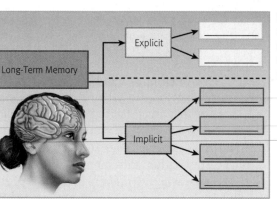

Complete the diagram to show the many subtypes of explicit and implicit memory. (p. 287)

ASSESS your knowledge

1. Procedures that encourage patients to recall memories of events that may or may not have taken place are called _____ _____ _____. (p. 276)

2. A _____ _____ is a false but subjectively compelling memory. (p. 276)

3. Our memories are far more (reproductive/reconstructive) rather than (reproductive/reconstructive). (p. 277)

4. The three major systems of memory are measured by _____, or, how much information each system can hold, and _____, or, how long a period of time the system can hold information. (p. 278)

5. _____ memory is the brief storage of perceptual information before it is passed to _____ memory. (pp. 278–279)

6. The Magic Number for the span of short-term memory is _____ plus or minus _____ pieces of information. (p. 281)

7. To extend the span of short-term memory, we organize information into meaningful groupings using a process called _____. (p. 282)

8. The type of long-term memory that appears to have an infinite duration is called _____. (p. 284)

9. The tendency to remember words at the beginning of a list better than those in the middle is known as the _____ _____. (p. 285)

10. _____ memory is the process of recalling information intentionally, and _____ memory is the process of recalling information we don't remember deliberately. (p. 286)

The Three Stages of Memory (pp. 287–296)

Identify the concepts from memory researchers that can help you in studying for this and other courses. (p. 294)

Memory Concept	Pointer
1. _____	Spread your study time out—review your notes and textbook in increments rather than cramming.
2. _____	Connect new knowledge with existing knowledge rather than simply memorizing facts or names.
3. _____	Work to process ideas deeply and meaningfully—avoid writing notes down word-for-word from instructors' lectures or slides. Try to capture the information in your own words.
4. _____	The more reminders or cues you can connect from your knowledge base to new material, the more likely you are to recall new material when tested.

SUCCEED with

mypsych lab
where learning comes to life!

Encoding, Storage, and Retrieval in Memory

What goes in doesn't always come out. (p. 287)

EXPLORE

THINK about

what You would do . . .

Your final exam in microbiology is scheduled in a different room than where the class was taught, and where you stayed after class each day to study. What information would you use to argue the case for having the exam in the same room as the class? (p. 295)

ASSESS your knowledge

1. The three major stages of memory are _____, _____, and _____. (p. 287)

2. _____ is the process of organizing information in a format that our memories can use. (p. 288)

3. A learning aid, strategy, or device that enhances recall is a _____. (p. 288)

4. _____ refers to the process of keeping information in memory. (p. 291)

5. Organized knowledge structures that we've stored in memory are called _____. (p. 291)

6. _____ is the reactivation or reconstruction of experiences from our memory stores. (p. 292)

7. _____ requires generating previously encountered information on our own, whereas _____ simply requires selecting information from an array of choices. (p. 293)

8. _____ is reacquiring knowledge that we'd previously learned but largely forgotten over time. (p. 293)

9. Research has shown that when people believe that something is on the tip of their tongues, they are frequently (right/wrong). (p. 294)

10. _____ _____ is the phenomenon of remembering something better when the conditions under which we retrieve information are similar to the conditions under which we encoded it. (p. 295)

STUDY the Learning Objectives

▶ **Determine methods for connecting new information to existing knowledge**
- Mnemonics are memory aids that link new information to more familiar knowledge. There are many kinds of mnemonics; they take effort to use but can assist recall.

▶ **Distinguish ways of measuring memory**
- Recall requires generating previously encountered information on our own, whereas recognition simply requires selecting the correct information from an array of choices. How quickly we relearn material previously learned and forgotten is another measure of memory.

▶ **Describe how the relation between encoding and retrieval conditions influences remembering**
- Individuals remember better if they're tested under the same physical and emotional conditions as when they encoded the information.

DO YOU KNOW THESE TERMS?
- ❏ **encoding** (p. 288)
- ❏ **mnemonic** (p. 288)
- ❏ **storage** (p. 291)
- ❏ **schema** (p. 291)
- ❏ **retrieval** (p. 292)
- ❏ **retrieval cues** (p. 292)
- ❏ **recall** (p. 293)
- ❏ **recognition** (p. 293)
- ❏ **relearning** (p. 293)
- ❏ **distributed versus massed practice** (p. 294)
- ❏ **tip-of-the-tongue (TOT) phenomenon** (p. 294)
- ❏ **encoding specificity** (p. 295)
- ❏ **context-dependent learning** (p. 295)
- ❏ **state-dependent learning** (p. 295)

The Biology of Memory (pp. 296–301)

How effective, according to researchers' understanding of anterograde amnesia, would it be for someone with this condition to write notes to (or on) himself in an effort to recall previous experiences? (p. 298)

Label and describe each component of the limbic system and its role in memory. (p. 299)

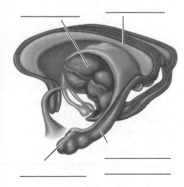

STUDY the Learning Objectives

▶ **Describe the role of long-term potentiation in memory**
- Most scientists believe that long-term potentiation—a gradual strengthening of the connections among neurons from repetitive stimulation—plays a key role in the formation of memories and memory storage.

▶ **Explain how amnesia helps to clarify the distinction between explicit and implicit memory**
- Patients with severe anterograde amnesia, like H.M., often display grossly impaired explicit memory yet intact implicit memory for certain tasks, like tracing shapes from a mirror.

▶ **Distinguish different types of amnesia and the relevance of amnesia to the brain's organization of memory**

- Retrograde amnesia causes forgetting of past experiences, whereas anterograde amnesia prevents us from forming memories of new experiences.
- Evidence from studies of amnesia patients demonstrates that there are distinct memory systems, because people with amnesia for declarative memory can still often form new procedural memories.

▶ **Identify the key impairments of Alzheimer's disease**
- The memory loss of patients with Alzheimer's disease begins with that of recent events, with memories of events of the distant past typically being the last to go. Alzheimer's disease is marked by loss of synapses and acetylcholine neurons.

DO YOU KNOW THESE TERMS?
- ❏ **long-term potentiation (LTP)** (p. 297)
- ❏ **retrograde amnesia** (p. 298)
- ❏ **anterograde amnesia** (p. 298)

THINK about **what You would do . . .**
Your parents are both about to retire. Given what you've learned about memory and the prevention of memory loss in older adults, how could you encourage them to make important lifestyle choices as they get older? (p. 300)

SUCCEED with **mypsychlab**
Alzheimers and Dementia
What causes memory to decline? (p. 300)
▶ WATCH

ASSESS your knowledge

1. Lashley's studies with rats concluded that memory (is/isn't) located in one part of the brain. (p. 296)

2. The gradual strengthening of the connections among neurons from repetitive stimulation is called _____ _____. (p. 297)

3. Today most scientists agree that LTP plays a key role in learning, and that the _____ plays a key role in forming lasting memories. (p. 297)

4. Our _____ are distributed throughout many areas in the brain's prefrontal cortex. (p. 298)

5. A person with _____ amnesia has lost some memories of his/her past. (p. 298)

6. The inability to encode new memories from our experiences is called _____ amnesia. (p. 298)

7. If there is memory recovery from amnesia, it tends to occur (gradually/suddenly). (p. 298)

8. Damage to the hippocampus impairs _____ memory but leaves _____ memory intact. (pp. 298–299)

9. The _____ is where the emotional components of memories, especially fear, are stored. (p. 299)

10. The memory loss of patients with _____ _____ begins with that of recent events, with memories of events of the distant past typically being the last to disappear. (p. 300)

The Development of Memory: Acquiring a Personal History (pp. 301–304)

STUDY the Learning Objectives

▶ **Identify how children's memory abilities change with age**
- Infants display implicit memory for events; both infants' and children's memories are influenced by some of the same factors as adults' memory.
- Children's memory improves in part because of maturational changes in the brain that extend the span of memory.
- Over time, children become better able to use mnemonic and rehearsal strategies and become more aware of their memory limitations.

▶ **Examine why we fail to remember experiences from early childhood**
- The hippocampus, which is critical for the establishment of long-term memory, isn't fully developed in infancy or early childhood.
- Infants have little sense of self, which makes it difficult for them to encode and store experiences in ways that are meaningful.

▶ **Explain how suggestions can shape children's memories**
- Children prompted over repeated trials to remember something that never occurred sometimes report that the event actually took place.
- Children's memories are affected by their expectations about how someone will behave; they're likely to report that an experience consistent with their expectations took place even if they didn't see it happen.

DO YOU KNOW THESE TERMS?
- ❏ **meta-memory** (p. 301)
- ❏ **infantile amnesia** (p. 302)

SUCCEED with **mypsychlab**
Memory: Elizabeth Loftus
How accurate is your memory? (p. 302)
▶ WATCH

How did Carolyn Rovee-Collier and others use infants' kicking behavior to study memory in infants? (p. 302)

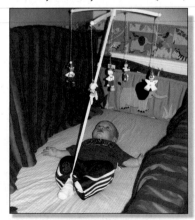

Which important indicator of the presence of a self-concept do humans and chimpanzees exhibit? (p. 303)

ASSESS your knowledge

1. Over time, children develop enhanced _____ skills that provide knowledge about one's own memory ability and limitations. (pp. 301–302)

2. Rovee Collier's experiments utilized operant conditioning to study infants' _____ _____. (p. 302)

3. _____ _____ is the inability to remember personal experiences that took place before the age of three or so. (p. 302)

4. Most people (can/can't) accurately recall events that took place at age 1 or 2. (p. 302)

5. There (is/isn't) evidence that we can remember things that took place at or prior to birth (p. 303)

6. The _____, which is critical for the establishment of long-term memory, isn't fully developed until early adulthood. (p. 303)

7. Infants have little sense of _____, which makes it difficult for them to encode or store experiences in ways that are meaningful. (p. 303)

8. Ceci and his colleagues demonstrated that children can cling to _____ memories. (p. 303)

9. _____ may cause children to provide authority figures with the answers they are seeking, even if those answers are wrong. (p. 303)

10. Children's memories (are/are not) affected by their expectations about how other people will act. (p. 303)

THINK about **what You would do . . .**
In psychology class, a classmate claims to recall memories dating back to her first year of life. How would you explain infant amnesia to her and shed some light on her recall of memories? (p. 302)

When Good Memory Goes Bad: False Memories (pp. 304–311)

Explain Elizabeth Loftus' misinformation effect and its influence on our memory. (p. 307)

Explain how we could have vivid memories of events we never experienced. (p. 308)

mypsych lab
where learning comes to life!

SUCCEED with

Creating False Memories

Can you actually remember events that never happened? (p. 304)

SIMULATION

THINK about

what You would do . . .
In your role as police officer, what would you do to optimize the chance that your eyewitness will correctly identify the guilty party among several suspects? (p. 309)

STUDY the Learning Objectives

▶ Identify factors that influence people's susceptibility to false memories and memory errors

- Flashbulb memories for highly significant events seem more crisp and vivid than other memories but are just as vulnerable to errors as other kinds of memory.
- One source of memory errors is source monitoring difficulty; we can't always remember where or from whom we learned something, or whether it was a figment of our imagination, sometimes resulting in cryptomnesia.
- Our memories for events are easily influenced by suggestions from others that the event happened differently than our observations suggested.
- Researchers have been successful in implanting complex false memories in some people.
- The fact that we're receptive to suggestions about whether and how events took place has important implications for eyewitness testimony.
- Research suggests that some therapists may be unintentionally planting memories of traumatic events, such as child sexual abuse, by means of suggestive procedures.

DO YOU KNOW THESE TERMS?
- ☐ **flashbulb memories** (p. 304)
- ☐ **source monitoring** (p. 305)
- ☐ **cryptomnesia** (p. 306)
- ☐ **misinformation effect** (p. 307)

ASSESS your knowledge

1. _____ _____ are memories that are extremely vivid and detailed, and often highly emotional. (p. 304)

2. Whenever we try to figure out whether a memory reflects something that really happened, we are engaging in _____ _____. (p. 305)

3. The failure to recognize that our ideas come from another source is called _____. (p. 307)

4. In a phenomenon called the _____ _____, Loftus was able to create fictitious memories by providing misleading information to study participants about an event after it took place. (p. 307)

5. Research has shown that it is (impossible/ possible) to implant memories of a made-up event that never happened. (pp. 307–308)

6. The correlation between eyewitnesses' confidence in their testimony and the accuracy of this testimony is (weak/strong). (p. 309)

7. Research suggests that some _____ may be unintentionally planting memories of traumatic events by means of suggestive procedures. (p. 310)

8. In a well-known example of _____, cellist Yo-Yo Ma once left his $2.5 million cello in a cab. (p. 311)

9. Most of us recover quickly from _____, a temporary inability to access information. (p. 311)

10. As we age, it is (typical/atypical) to find it increasingly difficult to access memories. (p. 311)

Remember these questions from the beginning of the chapter? Think again and ask yourself if you would answer them differently based on what you now know about memory. (For more detailed explanations, see MyPsychLab.)

▶ Do we really remember everything that's ever happened to us? (p. 275)
▶ How long do memories last? (p. 278)
▶ Do some people have "photographic" memories? (p. 279)
▶ Do memory aids like "ROYGBIV" (for the colors of the rainbow) really help us to remember? (pp. 288–289)
▶ What are infants' earliest memories? (p. 301)
▶ Are memories for extremely emotional experiences always more accurate than other memories? (p. 309)
▶ Do witnesses to a crime always remember what they observed accurately? (p. 309)
▶ Can people recover repressed memories of traumatic experiences? (p. 310)

THINKING Scientifically

Correlation vs. Causation pp. 297. 300, 301

Falsifiability p. 283

Extraordinary Claims p. 303

Occam's Razor p. 305

Replicability pp. 294, 295, 305, 308, 309

Ruling Out Rival Hypotheses
pp. 276, 280, 295, 300, 308

8
Language, Thinking, and Reasoning
Getting Inside Our Talking Heads

What would you do if you suddenly lost your ability to communicate using language?

One of the most valuable lessons psychology can teach us is to appreciate mental capacities we normally take for granted. Take language and thinking. We rely on them almost every second of our waking hours, but rarely notice the complexity that goes into them until something goes terribly wrong. Psychologist Mark Ashcraft had the unique experience of discovering just how much he took language for granted when he experienced a 45-minute seizure in his office in 1988. This seizure resulted in **anomia,** an inability to name things. He maintained consciousness and recalls being able to think clearly during the seizure, but he couldn't think of or generate names for things.

Sitting at his computer, he recalls, "The message on the screen indicated that I was still logged on to the mainframe computer . . . As I positioned my hands at the keyboard, I could not remember the command to log off—the command, of course is simply *logoff,* a command I issue with great regularity" (Ashcraft, 1993, p. 50). He picked up the phone and called his wife effortlessly, but had enormous difficulty communicating with her. Fortunately, Dr. Ashcraft recovered fully from this brief, but frightening, episode. As soon as the seizure ended, his ability to use language returned, and he was eager (as an experimental psychologist) to share his experience with others—to shed light on how our minds work.

Imagine that one day you, like Ashcraft, suddenly lost the ability to speak. Imagine that no one could understand you. How would it affect you? How would you express thoughts and opinions, tell jokes, swap stories, and enjoy a bit of gossip now and then?

Clearly, language touches and shapes our lives on a personal level. But it also affects our lives on a far grander scale, serving to coordinate complex goals and social organizations. For example, laws are stated in words, and politicians invest an enormous amount of time in shaping the language of legislation to ensure that the law captures what they intend. One reason why attorneys can find loopholes in the law is that our language is an imperfect reflection of our thoughts. In fact, many controversial political issues, such as abortion, capital punishment, and affirmative action, revolve around differing opinions about the interpretation of legal documents, such as the U.S. Constitution.

These disagreements highlight not only the power of language but its ambiguity and subtlety. In fact, most of our ability to communicate about our life experiences derives from mental processes that are *implicit,* that is, not available to conscious awareness (see Chapter 7). We often have a difficult time reconstructing how we know what we know. Anyone who's ever had to diagram a sentence in elementary school can confirm that; we're perfectly capable of distinguishing a grammatical from an ungrammatical sentence but can't always explain how we did it.

Picture this brief conversation between two students:

Male student:	"Just scored us some free tickets to the game!"
Female student:	"Shut up! How?"
Male student:	"I heard this guy at the bank say he had some he couldn't use, did a little back slapping and high-fiving and . . . tah-da!"

Most native speakers of English can follow that conversation with ease. Yet all sorts of complex cognitive processes we take for granted go into comprehending that conversation. Let's look at some of the behind-the-scenes thinking that was probably going on as you read that passage.

(1) You filled in the gaps in grammar. For example, "Just scored us some free tickets" is an incomplete phrase that needs the word "I" at the beginning to make it grammatical, but you realized that the male student was referring to himself.

(2) You figured out that "the game" is either important to the students, about to take place in the near future, or both. You also figured out that the female student knew which game the male was talking about, even though you didn't know which one it was.

anomia
inability to name things

(3) You inferred that "shut up" wasn't a literal command to be quiet, but instead an expression of surprise, even skepticism.

(4) You realized that the male student engaged in a bit of friendly social interaction to persuade the man at the bank to hand over his tickets. This realization goes well beyond the literal action reported in the conversation—he reported only backslapping and high-fiving.

We can probably think of other aspects of the conversation that required us to go beyond the literal information given to us. What enables us to draw these behind-the-scenes inferences? Our implicit ability to access knowledge, draw conclusions, make decisions, and interpret new phrases all contribute to our understanding of this and every other conversation.

We tend to think that words possess fixed meanings, namely, the ones we find in the dictionary. But how we interpret a word depends on its context. Many funny (and sometimes not so funny) misunderstandings can arise when contextual information is missing. **Table 8.1** presents examples of actual newspaper headlines in which interpreting the words literally can result in an unintentionally humorous interpretation.

In this chapter, we'll examine how we communicate and comprehend meaning using words, and the challenges we face when doing so. Then, we'll explore our thinking and reasoning processes in everyday life, and learn to avoid commonplace pitfalls in logic that can lead us to draw mistaken conclusions about the world around us.

More than we typically realize, our ability to follow a conversation depends on a host of sophisticated inferences.

Table 8.1 How's That Again? Ambiguous News Headlines. Language can be ambiguous and even unintentionally humorous when taken out of context. The examples in (A) are ambiguous because they use words that possess multiple meanings. The examples in (B) possess ambiguous grammar, resulting in two possible interpretations.

(A) Ambiguous Word Meaning	(B) Grammatically Ambiguous
Drunk Gets Nine Months in Violin Case	Eye Drops Off Shelf
Iraqi Head Seeks Arms	British Left Waffles on Falkland Islands
Man Struck by Lightning Faces Battery Charge	Killer Sentenced to Die for Second Time in 10 Years
Old School Pillars Are Replaced by Alumni	Ban on Soliciting Dead in Trotwood
Two Convicts Evade Noose, Jury Hung	Include Your Children When Baking Cookies

How Does Language Work?

Language is a system of communication that combines symbols, such as words or gestural signs, in rule-based ways to create meaning. One hallmark of language is that it tends to be arbitrary, meaning that the sounds, words, and sentences bear no clear relation to their meaning. Language serves several functions. The most obvious is the transmission of information. When we tell our roommate "The party starts at 9" or place an order at a coffee shop for a "skim latte," we're communicating information that enables us or someone else to accomplish a goal, like getting to the party on time or making sure our latte is low-fat.

But language serves key social and emotional functions too. It enables us to express our thoughts and views about social interactions, such as conveying, "I thought you were mad at me" or "That guy was hilarious." We spend much of our conversational time using language in ways that help us to establish or maintain relationships with others (Dunbar, 1996).

THE FEATURES OF LANGUAGE

We take language for granted because it's a highly practiced and automatic cognitive process, like driving a car once we've done it for a few months. By *automatic*, we mean that using and interpreting language usually require little attention, enabling us to perform other tasks like walking, cooking, or exercising without speech getting in the way (Posner & Snyder, 1975; see Prologue). We don't realize how complex language is until we try to learn or use a new one. In fact, our ability to use language requires the coordination

language
largely arbitrary system of communication that combines symbols (such as words or gestural signs) in rule-based ways to create meaning

"Sorry, but I'm going to have to issue you a summons for reckless grammar and driving without an apostrophe."

(© The New Yorker Collection 1987 Michael Maslin from cartoonbank.com. All Rights Reserved.)

of an enormous number of cognitive, social, and physical skills. Even the mere ability to produce the sounds of our language requires the delicate coordination of breath control, vocal cords, throat and mouth position, and tongue movement.

We can think about language at four different levels of analysis, all of which we need to coordinate for successful language. These levels are (1) **phonemes,** the sounds of our language; (2) **morphemes,** the smallest units of speech that are meaningful; (3) **syntax,** the grammatical rules that govern how we compose words into meaningful strings; and (4) **extralinguistic information,** elements of communication that aren't part of the content of language but are critical to interpreting its meaning. We can think of each level as similar to the different levels of specificity involved in preparing a meal, ranging from the individual ingredients to the menu items to the meal itself and, last but not least, to the overall dining experience.

Phonemes: The Ingredients. Phonemes are categories of sounds our vocal apparatus produces. The different categories of sound within a language are determined by aspects of the vocal tract, including our lips, teeth, tongue placement, vibration of the vocal cords, opening and closing of our throat, and other physical manipulations of the throat and mouth.

Experts disagree on the total number of phonemes across all of the world's languages—probably around 100 in total—but they agree that each language includes only a subset of them. English contains between 40 and 45 phonemes, depending on how we count them. Some languages have as few as about 15, others more than 60. Although there's some overlap across languages, some languages have sounds that don't occur in other languages. This fact certainly adds to the challenge of learning a second language. **Table 8.2** provides examples of phoneme differences across the world's languages.

Table 8.2 Cross-Linguistic Differences in Phoneme Distinctions. Often, one language perceives speech sounds as belonging to a single phoneme category, whereas another language breaks the category into two or more distinct phonemes. In cases in which English is the language that *doesn't* make a distinction, it's difficult for native English-speakers to imagine that the sounds are distinct.

Phoneme Distinction	Example	Does Have Distinction	Does NOT Have Distinction
R / L	Rid / Lid	ENGLISH	JAPANESE
S / Z	Ice / Eyes	ENGLISH	SPANISH
K / Kh	Keep / Cool	ARABIC	ENGLISH
D / T / TH	Doll/Tall/no example in English; mouth shaped as if pronouncing the letter *d* but with the tongue against back of teeth	HINDI	ENGLISH

Morphemes: The Menu Items. Morphemes are the smallest units of meaning in a language. They're created by stringing phonemes together. Most of our morphemes are words, such as "dog" and "happy." Nevertheless, we also have strings of sounds that aren't words by themselves but modify the meaning of words when they're tacked onto them. For example, the syllable *re-* as in *recall* or *rewrite* carries the meaning "to do again," and the suffix *-ish* as in *warmish* or *pinkish* means "to a moderate degree." These are each morphemes, although they don't stand alone as words.

phonemes
categories of sounds our vocal apparatus produces

morphemes
smallest meaningful units of speech

syntax
grammatical rules that govern how words are composed into meaningful strings

extralinguistic information
elements of communication that aren't part of the content of language but are critical to interpreting its meaning

APPLY YOUR THINKING
How many morphemes are in the word *unfortunately*? (Hint: It's not just the number of syllables, it's the number of different meaningful units. So if you answered "1" or "5," you're off track.)

Syntax: Putting Together a Meal. Syntax is the set of rules of a language by which we construct sentences. Syntax isn't just word order; it also includes *morphological markers* and sentence structure. Morphological markers are grammatical elements that modify words by adding sounds to them that change their meaning. For example, in English, we add *-s* for plural, *-ed* for past tense, and *-ing* for ongoing action.

Although syntactic rules describe how language is organized, real-world language rarely follows them perfectly. If you were to write down word-for-word what your psychology professor says at the beginning of your next class, you'll find that he or she will certainly violate at least one or two syntactic rules. So syntax describes an idealized form of language, much like the formal language we read in written documents, like this textbook.

Syntactic rules differ across languages. Most of us have studied a second language at some point and are familiar with how grammatical rules and markers differ across languages. This principle also applies to **dialects** within a language. Dialects are variations on a language used by a group of people who cluster according to geographic closeness or ethnic background (see **Figure 8.1**). Dialects aren't distinct languages because speakers of two different dialects can (mostly) understand each other. Different dialects may employ slight variations of the standard pronunciations, vocabulary, and syntax of the language. Speakers of dialects that differ from the native language aren't making grammatical errors. So long as they're using constructions systematically, they're using an equally valid form of communication.

Many people assume that speakers of nondominant dialects are trying but failing to speak a majority version of the dialect. This assumption can lead to unwarranted prejudice and perhaps even discrimination. For example, Black Vernacular Englich (sometime known as *Ebonics*) spoken by many African Americans and Appalachian Dialect spoken by many people residing in the Appalachian Mountains share numerous commonalities with the Standard American Dialects spoken by most Americans. But each also differs from mainstream dialects in some aspects of pronunciation, word choice, and syntax. For example, speakers of Black Vernacular English might say "plug it *up*" instead of "plug it *in*." Speakers of Appalachian Dialect might say, "He had *went* to the store" instead of "He had *gone* to the store."

Of course, we all tend to think of our own dialect as the "right" one. But, as we discover when we travel, pronunciation (and sometimes word choice) differs dramatically across different regional dialects within the U.S. and other English-speaking countries. Many people from Boston are known for dropping their *r*'s ("I pahked my cah") and many Texans are known for their "twang." And people from England use many pronunciations, word choices, and sentence structures that differ from American English. Do you drink "soda," "pop," or "Coke"? Do you pronounce "marry," "Mary," and "merry" the same or differently? Does the word "aunt" rhyme with "can't" or "haunt"? Different people answer these questions differently depending on where they grew up. The important point about these dialect variations is that none is inherently right—we speak the dialect we hear. And they all work just fine.

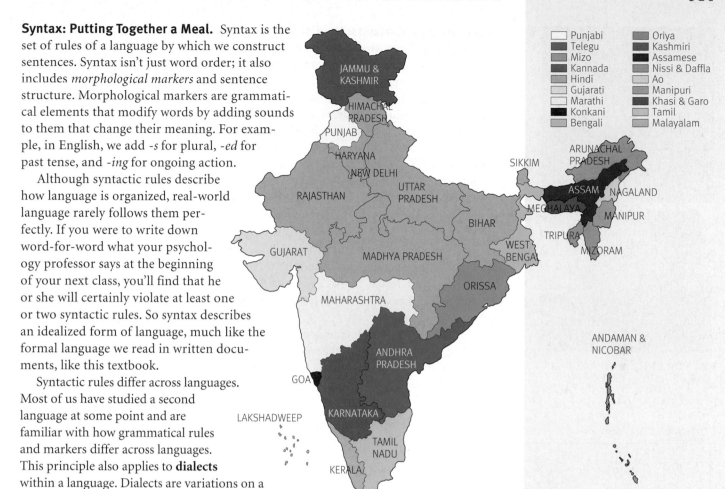

☐ Punjabi	Oriya
☐ Telegu	Kashmiri
☐ Mizo	Assamese
☐ Kannada	Nissi & Daffla
☐ Hindi	Ao
☐ Gujarati	Manipuri
☐ Marathi	Khasi & Garo
☐ Konkani	Tamil
☐ Bengali	Malayalam

Figure 8.1 Hindu Dialect Distinctions across India. Dialects are distinct variations on a shared language that emerge when there's geographic or social separation of populations. Across India, approximately eighteen distinct dialects of Hindi language exist, due to geographic separation of villages or cities.

dialects
language variations used by groups of people who share geographic proximity or ethnic background

How we interpret a sentence depends a great deal on the context. How would your interpretation of the sentence "It's just awful in here!" differ in these two contexts?

(© 1997 Thaves. Reprinted with permission.)

Extralinguistic Information: The Overall Dining Experience. We often think of language as self-explanatory: What we say is what we mean. Yet, we take an awful lot of additional information for granted when understanding language. Extralinguistic information isn't a part of language, but it plays a critical role in interpreting it. Some examples include previous statements by others in the conversation, and the speaker's nonverbal cues—such as his facial expression, posture, gestures, and tone of voice. Misunderstandings can easily arise if people aren't attentive to this information or if some of it's blocked, such as during a phone conversation or in e-mail (see Chapter 11).

Suppose we hear someone say, "It's just awful in here!" This sentence doesn't provide enough information to determine what the speaker means. To understand her, we need to look at her facial expressions and gestures and take into account where she is, what she's doing, and what's going on around her. If she's waving her hand in front of her face and wiping her forehead while standing in a hot kitchen, we'd probably infer that she's referring to the temperature of the room. If she's holding her nose and making a disgusted face while standing in a seafood shop, we'd probably infer she's referring to a really awful smell. And if she has a frustrated look on her face and is trying to make her way through a large throng of people, we'd probably assume she's referring to how crowded the room is.

Clearly, language is more complex than we typically realize. Successful communication depends on (1) the content of the language, (2) the social environment and nonverbal behavior of the speaker, and (3) the knowledge and reasoning ability of the listener to "fill in the gaps" to make sense of the context of the linguistic material.

WHERE DID LANGUAGE ORIGINATE AND WHY?

Imagine our early apelike ancestors beginning to walk upright, use tools, and engage in social activities, like coordinated group hunting. Why would language be useful, and why would a complex communication system be better than a simpler one? Scientists have long debated the question of how language evolved and its possible evolutionary advantages over a simpler system.

There are pros and cons to a complicated communication system. On the plus side, we can communicate extremely complex thoughts. On the minus side, language requires a lengthy learning period and hefty brainpower. Another downside is that the range of sounds we need to produce requires our vocal tract to be configured in a way that increases our chances of choking (Hauser & Fitch, 2003). Because language is so "costly" in terms of brain resources, evolutionary theory would suggest that it must have offered adaptive advantages.

Evolution and Arbitrariness of Language. One challenge to explaining how language evolved is that phonemes, words, and syntax rules are generally arbitrary: They don't resemble the things to which they refer. There's nothing about the word *dog* that resembles a friendly, furry animal that barks, and the word *tarantula* is a lot longer than the word *pig* even though tarantulas are (thankfully) much smaller than pigs. Many scholars argue that language is arbitrary for a good reason. Using arbitrary words allows us more flexibility to express complex ideas that may not contain the sounds that resemble them.

Despite the benefits of arbitrary language, there are intriguing examples of nonarbitrary language in which words *do* resemble their meaning. The most obvious is *onomatopoeia*, or words that resemble the sounds to which they refer, like "buzz," "meow," and "beep." Another example is that across the world's languages, the word for mother nearly always starts with an *m* or *n*, whereas the word for father nearly always starts with a *b*, *p*, or *d*. This fact is probably more than a coincidence, particularly because these phonemes tend to be those that children acquire earliest. Is there something about the

The name *flip-flop* is an example of onomatopoeia. The name is derived from the sound these shoes make while we walk with them on.

concept of a mother that brings an *m* or *n* sound to mind? Perhaps mothers are soothing, so babies tend to produce an "mmm" sound when content. Or perhaps babies tend to produce *m* and *n* sounds while nursing on their mothers' breasts or bottles.

Sharon Hutchins (1999) studied another example of nonarbitrary language called **phonesthemes.** She noted that related words often have similar-sounding initial consonant clusters. For example, the *gl* sound sequence appears in many words related to shininess, such as *glitter, gleam, glisten, glass, glow,* and *glare.* There are exceptions, such as *glad* and *glue,* but it's unlikely that so many related words have these starting sounds by chance. Can you think of other sound sequences that occur in a cluster of related words? One of our favorites is *sn,* which is associated with a large number of nose-related activities including *sneeze, sniff, sneer, snore, snooze, snoop, snort, snicker,* and of course, *snot!* Even a *snob* is someone who "turns up his nose" at others.

HOW DO CHILDREN LEARN LANGUAGE?

Most of us have tried to learn a second language, and some of us are **bilingual,** adept at speaking and comprehending two distinct languages. Given that so many of us have attempted to master a second language, why can so few of us call ourselves bilingual? Part of the answer lies in how we encounter a second language. We usually master a language more easily by living in a foreign country than by learning it in a classroom (Baker & MacIntyre, 2000; Genesee, 1985). Not surprisingly, our motivation to learn a new language also plays a key role (Piske, MacKay, & Flege, 2001). But the best predictor of whether we'll become fluent is the age of acquisition: the earlier, the better (Johnson & Newport, 1989). Language is among the few documented cases in which children are more efficient learners than adults.

The language-learning process starts long before children begin talking. Although children don't begin using words until around their first birthday or later, infants begin learning about their language even before birth. How? Babies begin to hear inside the womb by the fifth month of pregnancy. Although what they hear is a rather muffled version of what we hear (and a lot of what they hear is their mothers' heartbeats and intestinal gurgling), they can make out their mothers' voices, learn to recognize some characteristics of their mothers' native language, and even recognize specific songs or stories they've heard over and over again (DeCasper & Spence, 1988).

We know this to be true because researchers have developed a clever way to test newborn infants' ability to distinguish sounds, namely, a method that capitalizes on operant conditioning (see Chapter 6). The procedure is the *high-amplitude sucking procedure* and takes advantage of one of the few behaviors over which infants have good control at birth—sucking (see **Figure 8.2**). Two-day-old infants suck more on a pacifier when they hear their mothers' native language than when they hear a foreign language, even when total strangers speak both languages. Even at this early age, they display a clear preference for their mothers' native language. This is true of infants of both English-speaking and Spanish-speaking mothers. Infants whose mothers speak English suck harder when they hear English than Spanish, and those whose mothers speak Spanish suck harder when they hear Spanish than English (Moon, Cooper, & Fifer, 1993). The fact that researchers tested babies whose mothers speak multiple languages is an elegant experimental design feature. It allowed them to rule out the possibility that all babies prefer English over another language, regardless of which language their mothers speak.

Fetuses can learn about the melody and rhythm of their native language and learn to recognize their mother's voice before birth. They can even learn to recognize a specific story read to them before birth (DeCasper & Spence, 1988).

Figure 8.2 The High-Amplitude Sucking Procedure. The high-amplitude sucking procedure places a pacifier in an infant's mouth and allows him or her to suck freely. The pacifier is hooked up to a computer that measures the rate and intensity of sucking.

Ruling Out Rival Hypotheses

APPLY YOUR THINKING

What other methods could we use to determine whether a preference for listening to a specific language is acquired through fetal exposure or is innate?

---

phonesthemes
similar-sounding words that have related meanings

bilingual
proficient and fluent at speaking and comprehending two distinct languages

Babies often engage in vocal exchanges such as nonsense "conversations" and turn-taking imitation sequences with others as they approach their first birthdays. Doing so helps cement the social function of language even before they can speak.

Babbling. During the first year or so after birth, infants learn much more about the sounds of their native languages. They begin to figure out the phonemes of their languages and how to use their vocal apparatus to make specific sounds. Although children's babbling seems like nonsense (and it usually is), babbling plays an important role in language development by enabling babies to figure out how to move their vocal tracts to generate specific sounds. **Babbling** refers to any intentional vocalization (other than crying, burping, sighing, and laughing, which are less intentional) that lacks specific meaning. Babbling evolves over the first year of life and follows a progression of stages demonstrating infants' increasing control of their vocal tracts (Kent & Miulo, 1995). By the end of their first year, infants babble using sounds of only their native language. Their babbling takes on a conversational tone that sounds meaningful even though it isn't. We can see the stages of babbling in **Table 8.3.**

Table 8.3 Infant Vocalizations. Babbling becomes gradually more complex over the first year as infants acquire better control over their vocal tracts. Each stage requires better motor control and coordination than the previous stage.

Age	Stage	Description	Examples
2 months	Cooing	Vowel sounds only—simplest to produce because the only motor coordination required is to open the mouth and vibrate the vocal cords	Aaaaaaah Ooooooooh
3–4 months	Syllables	Coordination of consonant and vowel sounds—requires moving the vocal tract during speech	Ga Doh
6 months	Reduplicative (repetitive) babbling	Long strings of repeated syllables in a continuous stream—requires more sustained motor coordination	Badabadabadabada Momomomomo
10 months	Conversational babbling	Mixing syllables in unpredictable order using conversational tone and turn-taking with caretakers	Bagado voodita! Sebowladagee?

Figuring Out the Phonemes. When infants are fine-tuning their vocal tracts, they're also fine-tuning their ears. Remember that different languages have different phoneme categories, so to be successful users of their native languages infants must learn how to classify sounds. Research on infants' acquisition of phonemes has turned up some surprises. The question of how children establish phonemes is an example of the nature–nurture problem (see Prologue), the age-old question of how much of a behavior or ability is innately influenced (nature) or learned through experience (nurture). Like most psychological phenomena, the answer in this case turns out to be "some of both."

One possibility is that when infants are born they don't possess the ability to classify sounds into categories. Actually, this isn't the case, because infants classify some speech sounds into categories as early as 1 month of age (Eimas, Siqueland, Jusczyk, & Vigorito, 1971). All babies initially share the same basic phoneme categories regardless of their parents' native language. The only problem is that some languages don't use the sound categories with which infants are born. Such babies are actually born with the wrong phonemes for their language (Lasky, Suradal-Lasky, & Klein, 1975). For example, all infants distinguish between two sound categories that are relevant for Hindi but not English, regardless of which language they've heard (Werker, Gilbert, Humphrey, & Tees, 1981). Babies who learn English continue to make this distinction even at 7 months of age.

Luckily, babies learning any language can adjust their phonemes rapidly over the course of the first year. By 10 months, infants' phonemes are very much like those of the adult speakers of their native language (Werker & Tees, 1984). The areas of the infant's brain responsible for auditory and language processing identify the sound categories based on regularities in adult language the infant hears.

babbling
intentional vocalization that lacks specific meaning

Learning Words. All of this takes place during the first year of life. How and when do children start to learn to talk? One key principle characterizes early word learning: *comprehension precedes production.* Children are learning to recognize and interpret words well before—sometimes months before—they can produce them (see **Figure 8.3**). This is because they have only a tentative grasp of how to produce sounds. They may be perfectly aware that "elephant" refers to a large gray animal with a long trunk and large ears, but be unable to produce this big word.

One of the first words that children understand is their own name. Although most infants don't clearly start understanding words until 9 or 10 months, they recognize their own names by as early as 6 months (Tincoff & Jucszyk, 1999). They begin to recognize other commonly used and important (to them!) words like "bottle," "mama," and "doggie" by 10 to 12 months.

Children start to *produce* their first words around their first birthdays, although there's considerable variability in this milestone. They acquire their first words slowly. Between 1 and 1½ years of age, they gradually accumulate a vocabulary of between 20 and 100 words. As children become more experienced in learning new words, the rate at which they acquire words increases (Goldfield & Reznick, 1990). By the time they turn 2, most children can produce several hundred words. By kindergarten, their vocabularies have ballooned to several thousand words. Still, children often don't get words quite right at first. They make mistakes in pronunciation and interpretation of words' meaning.

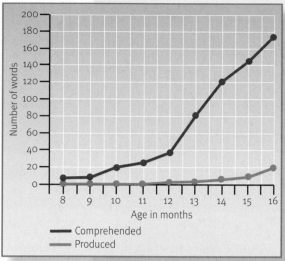

Figure 8.3 Word Comprehension between 8 and 16 Months of Age. In the early stages of word learning, children learn to comprehend new words before they figure out how to say them. This graph depicts the number of words that at least 50 percent of children at each month between 8 and 16 months can comprehend and say. Although not shown on this graph, the discrepancy between the number of words children know and can speak continues to narrow as they approach 24 months. (*Source:* Adapted from Fenson et al., 1994)

APPLY YOUR THINKING

Given that comprehension precedes production, we can't rely on children's talking to provide an accurate measure of the words they know. What other methods could we use to assess what words children understand?

Pronunciation Errors. Mistakes in pronunciation are common in early language learning. Many "mistakes" aren't truly errors that reflect not knowing or forgetting how words sound. Instead, they're a result of *production constraints,* that is, limitations on how easily children can coordinate their vocal apparatus to produce sounds. Children's pronunciation errors tend to occur less often with simpler sounds, which have fewer production constraints, such as *b* and *d,* and more often with complex sounds, which have more constraints, such as *th* (Dobrick & Scarborough, 1992). Because of production constraints, children often use "placeholder" sounds, such as saying "kee-kee" for "kitty" or "ba-ba" for "bottle" (Hura & Echols, 1996). This behavior shows that infants know there are two syllables even though they can't pronounce both properly. Children also delete sounds or even whole syllables if getting the whole word out is too difficult, such as saying "eh-phant" for "elephant" or "poon" for "spoon." Children's pronunciation becomes increasingly clear between ages 1 and 3, but it's not at all uncommon for some production immaturity to persist until school age. Some articulation problems are more serious, though, and may require intervention by a speech therapist. **Table 8.4** on the next page displays some examples of developmental speech disorders.

Errors in Word Meaning. Children typically also make some mistakes in interpreting what words mean and how to use them. In particular, they often make over- and undergeneralizations, applying words in a broader (overgeneralization, like referring to all adult men as "Daddy") or narrower (undergeneralization, like referring to their pet cat as "cat") sense than the word used by adults. Nearly every child gets a word's meaning completely wrong from time to time. One of our favorite examples is of a child who cried out ecstatically, "Downtown!" every time he saw a fountain, because there was a

A common overgeneralization is a child making the mistake of using the word "grandpa" to apply to any gray-haired man. A common undergeneralization would be a child restricting the word "doggie" to her family pet.

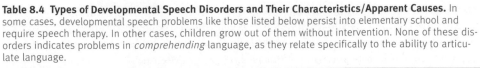

Table 8.4 Types of Developmental Speech Disorders and Their Characteristics/Apparent Causes. In some cases, developmental speech problems like those listed below persist into elementary school and require speech therapy. In other cases, children grow out of them without intervention. None of these disorders indicates problems in *comprehending* language, as they relate specifically to the ability to articulate language.

Speech Disorder	Symptoms	Apparent Cause
Mild articulation disorders	Mispronouncing particular phonemes such as replacing "th" for "s" ("super" becomes "thuper") or "w" for "r" ("ring" becomes "wing")	Incorrect correspondence between the phonemes children hear and the articulation they must engage in to reproduce those sounds
Dyspraxia	Motor planning and coordination difficulties resulting in more pauses, slower speech, more effortful speech, and more variable pronunciation of words	Motor coordination areas of the brain are sending impoverished signals to the vocal tract to move in appropriate ways
Stuttering	Difficulty with smooth, fluid motor coordination of the vocal tract, resulting in repeated articulation of the same sounds, prolonged pronunciation of some sounds, and sudden spurts of speech	The brain appears to be sending appropriate signals to the vocal tract to plan speech production, but the physical coordination of the vocal apparatus is impaired

large fountain located in his city's downtown. He'd noticed that each time his parents said "downtown," he got to see his favorite fountain, so he (quite reasonably, from his standpoint) concluded that this was the word for fountain. Of course, most of the time children manage to get word meanings exactly right, a remarkable achievement.

Syntactic Development: Putting It All Together. The first major milestone in children's syntactic development is combining words into phrases. Initially, children use words as **holophrases,** in which a single word conveys a whole thought. A child may use the word "doggie" to mean "There's a doggie!" "Where's the doggie?" or even "The doggie licked me!" Interpreting what children mean at the holophrase stage can be a monumental challenge. By the time children turn 2, most start to combine words into simple two-word phrases. Although these phrases are still far from complete sentences, they go a long way toward improving comprehensibility. For example, the child can now say "more juice" to request a refill or "uh-oh juice" to notify mom that his juice just spilled. Although these phrases are still simplistic, children at this phase have already grasped something about syntactic rules. They tend to use words in the correct order, even if they're leaving some of them out.

Figure 8.4 Children Display Comprehension of Word Order Prior to Sentence Production. Children can display their grasp of syntax by pointing to a video that matches a sentence they have heard. Here, a 17-month-old child is displaying her comprehension of the sentence "The pig is tickling the dog" by pointing to the video that corresponds to the sentence.

holophrases
single-word phrases used early in language development to convey an entire thought

As is the case with word learning, children understand some basic syntactic rules before they can display them. For example, they understand how word order relates to meaning before they can generate complete sentences. Two researchers showed 17-month-olds two videos side-by-side, one that showed Cookie Monster tickling Big Bird and one that showed Big Bird tickling Cookie Monster. The experimenter asked children, "Show me where Big Bird is tickling Cookie Monster." The children looked and pointed toward the correct video, demonstrating they could determine from word order who was the "tickler" and who was the "ticklee" (Hirsch-Pasek & Golinkoff, 1996) (see **Figure 8.4** for a different example using a pig and a dog).

Several months after they've begun using two-word phrases, children use more complex sentences involving three- or four-word combinations. Around the same time, they begin to produce morphological markers such as *-s* for plural and *-ed* for past tense in English. They acquire most syntactic rules by preschool age, but continue to acquire more complex rules in their early school years (Dennis, Sugar, & Whitaker, 1982).

Development of Extralinguistic Communication. Children acquire extralinguistic knowledge at a much more gradual rate than linguistic information. Children can make use of some basic aspects of extralinguistic communication to help them understand language by the end of their second year. For example, they figure out early on that where speakers are pointing and looking can help them understand what they're talking about (Baldwin, 1993). Children also grasp early on that speakers' emotional expression is related to the content of their speech (Walker-Andrews & Dickson, 1997). Nevertheless, more subtle aspects of extralinguistic knowledge, such as recognizing when someone is being sarcastic, continue to develop well into preschool and elementary school (Demorest, Silberstein, Gardner, & Winner, 1983).

Theoretical Accounts of Language Acquisition. Given we acquire so much of our capacity to learn language at such an early age, how do children solve this challenge? There are several explanations: Some fall more heavily on the nature side of the nature–nurture debate, others on the nurture side. Ultimately, language learning requires nature and nurture. Even the strongest nature account acknowledges that children aren't born knowing their specific language; they learn what they hear. Similarly, the strongest nurture account acknowledges that children's brains are set up in a way that's receptive to learning and organizing language input.

 The Imitation Account. The simplest explanation of children's language learning is that they learn through imitation. Babies hear language used in systematic ways and learn to use language as adults use it. This is certainly true in one sense, because babies learn the language they hear. Behaviorists (see Prologue and Chapter 6) took this account one step further by arguing that babies don't just imitate what they hear, but imitate what they're reinforced for saying (Skinner, 1953). But a purely imitation-based explanation can't be completely right for one reason: Language is **generative.** *Generativity* means that language isn't just a set of predefined sentences that we can pull out and apply in appropriate contexts. Instead, it's a system that allows us to create an infinite number of sentences, producing new statements, thoughts, and ideas never previously uttered. The fact that even very young children use language in generative ways—producing sentences or combinations of words they've never heard—means they're producing things for which they were never directly reinforced, refuting a purely behavioral view.

 The Nativist Account. The strongest nature view is the **nativist** account, which says that children come into the world knowing how language works. Nativists propose that children are born with syntactic rules that determine how sentences are constructed (Chomsky, 1972). Noam Chomsky, who essentially invented the field of contemporary linguistics, even hypothesized that humans possess a specific language "organ" in the brain that houses these rules. He called it the **language acquisition device,** and argued that it comes preprogrammed to enable children to use language.

 A key weakness of the nativist view is that many of its claims are unfalsifiable. Critics have pointed out that children learn syntax gradually and that even adults use grammatically incorrect sentences. The nativist could reply that different aspects of grammar take more or less time to "set," and that ungrammatical sentences don't imply lack of knowledge of grammar. These are certainly reasonable explanations, but the theory's weakness is that it's hard to think of an outcome that nativists couldn't explain. As we've noted in earlier chapters, a theory that can explain every conceivable outcome in essence explains nothing.

 The Social Pragmatics Account. The **social pragmatics** account suggests that particular aspects of the social environment help structure language learning. According to this account, children use the context of a conversation to infer its topic from the actions, expressions, gestures, and other behaviors of speakers. Children can figure out word meaning in this type of situation as early as 24 months of age (Tomasello, Strosberg, & Akhtar, 1996). Still, this account has its weaknesses. Explaining child language on the basis of social understanding requires us to assume that infants understand an awful

Language clearly has an important learned component, because children adopted from a different country learn to speak the language of their adopted rather than biological parents.

Falsifiability

Falsifiability

generative
allowing an infinite number of unique sentences to be created by combining words in novel ways

nativist
account of language acquisition that suggests children are born knowing how language works

language acquisition device
hypothetical organ in the brain in which nativists believe knowledge of syntax resides

social pragmatics
account of language acquisition that proposes children infer what words and sentences mean from context and social interactions

lot about how other people are thinking. In addition, we can explain most social pragmatic abilities without requiring as much insight on the part of the child (Samuelson & Smith, 1998). For example, social pragmatic theorists might say that children learn to infer meaning from pointing by inferring the speaker's intentions. Alternatively, children might use a simpler process; they might notice that every time their caretakers point to a specific object, they utter the same word. In this way, children may infer that where someone is pointing is correlated with word meaning. This deduction doesn't require children to take into account the social context or communicative intentions of others.

The General Cognitive Processing Account. Another explanation for how children learn language is the *general cognitive processing* account. It proposes that children's ability to learn language is a result of general skills that children apply across a variety of activities. For example, children's ability to perceive, learn, and recognize patterns may be all they need to learn language. If so, there'd be no need to propose a language acquisition device as Chomsky did.

Still, there are challenges to the general cognitive processing account. One is that children are better at learning languages than adults, whereas adults are better at learning things in general. Another is that specific areas of the brain (see Chapter 3), especially the left temporal lobe (see **Figure 8.5**), are more active in language processing than in other types of learning, memory, and pattern recognition activities (Gazzaniga, Ivry, & Mangun, 2002). This finding implies that at least some distinct cognitive processes occur during language, but not during other cognitive activities.

When children learn words through pointing, are they exercising social insight or merely associating the object pointed to with the sound uttered by the adult?

Critically Evaluating the Theories. As we've seen, the imitation account can't explain the complexity of language. Nevertheless, each of the other three theoretical views has its strengths, and there's some evidence consistent with each. Yet only the social pragmatics theory and the general cognitive processing theory are clearly falsifiable. Researchers are making important strides in generating experiments that pit these two accounts against each other (Namy & Waxman, 2000; Samuelson & Smith, 1998). Nativism may ultimately be correct about some aspects of language processing. But because scientists can't easily test all of its claims, they'll need to rule out competing accounts before accepting it as a viable explanation for language learning.

NONHUMAN ANIMAL COMMUNICATION

The communication systems of different animal species differ in type and complexity. Some species use scent marking as their primary form of communication. Others rely on visual displays, such as baring their teeth or flapping their wings. Still others, like humans, use vocal communication.

In most nonhuman animals, aggression and mating are the two circumstances in which communication most often takes place. For example, male songbirds, such as canaries and finches, produce a specific song to convey the message, "This is my territory, back off," and another song to attract mates (Kendeigh, 1941). Chimpanzees use a combination of vocalizations and visual displays, such as facial expressions and slapping the ground, to convey aggression (de Waal, 1989). When it comes to mating rituals, male chimpanzees squat with their knees spread to display their penises as an invitation to mate. Of course, we humans have our ways of attracting mates, although we usually call this something more polite like "flirting" when it comes to our own species.

Yet in contrast to most species, we've developed ways of communicating that move substantially beyond aggression and mating to allow for other kinds of information exchange. Precious few nonhuman animal communication systems accomplish this feat.

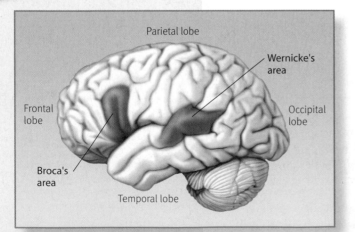

Figure 8.5 Language Processing Areas of the Brain. Two areas of the brain that play key roles in language processing are Broca's area, involved in speech production, and Wernicke's area, involved in speech comprehension (see Chapter 3).

A fascinating example of a nonhuman animal communication system that provides information exchange beyond aggression and mating is the waggle dance of honeybees. Bees use this dance to communicate with their fellow bees about the location of a food source (see **Figure 8.6**). Bees that locate a food source fly back to their hive and perform an intricate series of figure-eight movements, moving the hind segment of their bodies back and forth rapidly (waggling) as they walk. The direction the bee faces indicates which direction to fly, and the duration and intensity of the waggle indicate how far and how plentiful the food supply is (von Frisch, 1967). Inside the hive, where bees are crowded close together and light is dim, bees appear to pick up this information through the vibrations of the dancing bee transmitted through the floor of the honeycomb (Tautz, Rohrseitz, & Sandeman, 1996). The waggle dance is a successful form of communication because bees who observe the dance, but haven't visited the food source, leave the hive and fly directly to that source (von Frisch, 1967). The waggle dance is one of the few nonhuman examples of communication about something beyond the here and now.

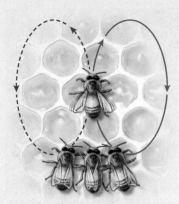

Figure 8.6 Communication among Honeybees. Honeybees use the waggle dance to communicate to other bees the location of a food source: in which direction it lies, how far away it is, and how plentiful it is.

Another example comes from the vervet monkey. A number of bird and mammal species let out a specific vocalization when a predator is nearby. What's distinctive about vervet monkeys is their use of different alarm calls for different predators (Seyfarth & Cheney, 1997). They produce one type of call when they see a leopard, a second when they see a snake, and a third when they see a hawk or other flying predator. These alarm calls are the closest thing to words that scientists have observed outside of human language, because specific sounds correspond to specific meanings. Moreover, all vervets use the same "words" to communicate the same meanings.

Teaching Human Language to Nonhuman Animals. Concerted efforts to teach animals to use human language have been largely unsuccessful. The earliest attempts to teach chimpanzees, one of our nearest living genetic relatives, fell flat. What went wrong? The researchers assumed incorrectly that chimpanzees possess a vocal apparatus similar to ours. But, unlike our vocal apparatus, theirs doesn't permit the same range and coordination of sounds (Lieberman, Crelin, & Klatt, 1972). Later researchers tried to teach chimpanzees to use either sign language or a lexigram board, which allows them to point to printed visual symbols that stand for specific words (see **Figure 8.7**).

These attempts were more successful, but there were still crucial limits:

(1) Chimpanzee word learning doesn't resemble that of human infants. Babies get better and faster at word learning as they acquire more words. In contrast, chimpanzees find it just as hard to learn their sixty-seventh word as their first.

(2) Chimpanzees, unlike human infants, require thousands of trials to learn to associate signs or lexigrams with their meanings.

(3) The vast majority of chimpanzees' attempts to communicate seem to be requests for food or other pleasurable activities, like being tickled or chased.

(4) Chimpanzees combine words into more complex utterances, but they never master syntactic rules.

Two animal species may do better than chimpanzees at learning language. One is the bonobo, once thought to be a type of chimpanzee but now recognized as a distinct species that's genetically even more closely related to humans. The few studies conducted on bonobos suggest a different learning pathway, which more closely resembles human learning (Savage-Rumbaugh, 1986). Bonobos (1) learn better as young animals than as adults, (2) tend to learn through observation rather than reinforcement, and (3) use symbols to comment on or engage in social interactions, rather than simply for food treats. Yet bonobos seem to get stuck when learning syntax. Even the most proficient of the bonobos trained with human language, Kanzi, can't master syntactic rules beyond the level of

Figure 8.7 A Chimpanzee Uses Lexigrams to Communicate with Caretakers. This ape has been trained to associate colored shapes with meanings such as "juice," "fruit," and "tickle" (a favorite pastime for chimpanzees raised in captivity).

Figure 8.8 Two Nonhuman Animals That Have Learned Language. Kanzi (a bonobo) and Alex (an African gray parrot) have both been famous for their impressive language skills. The challenge for researchers is to explain why these species have more potential to learn human language than other animals. Other important questions include whether these species are learning in the same way humans do and, if so, why their language doesn't become more advanced.

fictoid

Myth: Some people engage in *glossolalia,* that is, speaking in tongues or in *xenoglossia,* that is, speaking in a language they've never encountered.

Reality: Scientific research can't resolve the question of whether glossolalia or xenoglossia is of supernatural origin. Nevertheless, careful analyses indicate that glossalalia doesn't exhibit the features of an actual language (Nickell, 1993), and that there are no documented cases of people suddenly acquiring a language they've never spoken (Malony & Lovekin, 1985).

sign language
language developed by members of deaf communities that uses visual rather than auditory communication

about a 2½-year-old human child (see **Figure 8.8,** top). His typical sentences are two or three lexigram combinations such as "Keep-away balloon" and "Sue chase Rose" (Greenfield & Savage-Rumbaugh, 1991). However, as in human children, Kanzi's comprehension outstripped his production.

One other species that seems able to use spoken language much as we do is the African gray parrot. An Einstein of a parrot named Alex, who died in 2007 at the age of 31, was particularly well known for his ability to speak and to solve cognitive tasks (see **Figure 8.8,** bottom). Parrots are, of course, famous, and sometimes infamous, for their ability to mimic sounds. They can reproduce human speech, barking dogs, vacuum cleaners, and locomotive whistles. But their ability to mimic doesn't equate to understanding language. A parrot may say "Hello" when someone walks into the room, but he probably doesn't realize that "Hello" is a form of greeting. He's simply learned that this is what people say when they walk into rooms and is imitating what he's observed.

Furthermore, parrot language typically isn't generative. Like politicians giving stump speeches, parrots usually have a stock set of phrases that they use over and over again in specific contexts. Alex was a striking exception. He generated new and meaningful combinations of words (Pepperberg, 1999). Alex and other African gray parrots appear to use language in a more humanlike manner and even master many syntactic rules. Yet their learning process is more similar to that of chimpanzees than bonobos and humans. It's a result of many repetitions rather than of observing and interacting with the world.

We humans are indeed unique in our ability to use language in such sophisticated ways. Of course, complexity in and of itself doesn't make us better, although it may make us "smarter" in some crucial ways. Squirrels and cockroaches do a pretty decent job of keeping themselves going with whatever communication systems they have to work with. For their purposes, they're every bit as effective in their communication as we are.

SPECIAL CASES OF LANGUAGE LEARNING

Children learning language sometimes confront special challenges. These challenges may prevent, slow down, or complicate acquiring a language. In this section, we review two of them: Sign language learning in deaf children and bilingual language acquisition.

Sign Language. **Sign language** is a type of language developed by members of deaf communities that allows them to use visual rather than auditory communication. It involves using the hands, face, body, and "sign space"—the space in front of the signer—to communicate. Just as there are many spoken languages, there are many sign languages spoken in different countries and deaf communities.

The Linguistic Structure of Sign Languages. Many people think of sign language as an elaborate form of gesturing, a charades-type attempt to act out silently what people would otherwise speak. This couldn't be further from the truth. Sign language is called "language" for a reason. It's a linguistic system of communication with its own phonemes, words, syntax, and extralinguistic information (Newport & Meier, 1985; Poizner, Klima, & Bellugi, 1987; Stokoe, Casterline, & Croneberg, 1976). Linguists who've analyzed the structure and organization of various sign languages (American Sign Language, French Sign Language, even Nicaraguan Sign Language) have confirmed that sign languages exhibit all of the same features as spoken languages, including generativity and a complex set of syntactic rules that determine when a string of signs is a grammatical sentence. Although many signs are *iconic*—they resemble the things to which they refer—many others don't, just as in spoken language (Frishberg, 1975; see **Figure 8.9**).

Further evidence that sign language works just like any other language comes from two sources. First, the same brain areas involved in processing spoken languages are activated in sign languages (Petitto, Zatorre, Gauna, Nikelski, Dostie, & Evans, 2000; Poizner et al., 1987). In fact, native signers' brains involve both traditional "language areas" and other brain areas that play roles in visual or spatial processing (Newman, Bavelier, Corina, Jezzard, & Neville, 2002). Second, babies who learn sign languages pass through the same developmental stages at about the same ages as babies who learn spoken languages.

Sign Language Acquisition. It's harder to study how infants learn sign language than we might think, because comparing language acquisition in babies learning sign versus spoken language requires the learning conditions to be similar. Nevertheless, we learn the substantial majority of deaf babies (more than 90 percent) are actually born to hearing parents who don't know how to sign before their babies are born. This means that most deaf babies are trying to learn their language from a nonnative "speaker" of their language. It would be like an English-speaking mother talking to her baby only in Portuguese, even though she didn't start trying to learn Portuguese until after her baby was born. Imagine how distorted her modeling of the language would be: Her phonemes would be incorrectly pronounced, her syntax would be garbled, and she couldn't communicate many things.

When researchers tracked down families with parents who were fluent signers, they discovered that deaf babies pass through the same stages as hearing babies. They babble with their hands (Petitto & Marentette, 1991), acquire their first "words" (signs) at around the same time as hearing babies (Orlanksy & Bonvillian, 1984), and pass through the same stages of syntactic development at the same ages as hearing babies (Newport & Meier, 1985). Each of these similarities confirms that sign languages work the same way that spoken languages do.

Myths about Sign Language. We should be aware of a few popular misconceptions about deafness and sign language:

Myth #1. Deaf people don't need sign language because they can lip-read. The vocal tract is an enormously complex structure, and only a small part of a phoneme's sound is determined by our lips. Most of the work is done behind the scenes by the throat, tongue, and teeth, which typically aren't visible during speech. Words like *nice* and *dice* look virtually identical when we speak them, and even words as distinct as *queen* and *white* look the same to a lip-reader. As a result, even the most skilled lip-readers can pick up only about 30 to 35 percent of what's being said.

Myth #2. Learning to sign slows down deaf children's ability to learn to speak. Historically, deaf education programs tried to prevent deaf children from learning to sign because they believed that once children learned sign language, they'd never learn to communicate with the hearing world. It's now clear that learning a sign language doesn't interfere with learning spoken language. In fact, those who've learned a sign language make faster progress in speaking (Strong & Prinz, 1997).

Myth #3. American Sign Language is English translated word-for-word into signs. American Sign Language (ASL) was developed by a community of deaf people who lived in the United States but hadn't learned English particularly well because of difficulties with learning a language from lip-reading. So ASL bears no resemblance to English; the syntax in particular differs completely from English syntax. Some deaf communities use what's called Signed English instead of ASL. Signed English translates English sentences word-for-word into signs from ASL. This translation works well for signers who also know English, but can be quite confusing for people fluent in ASL.

Bilingualism. How do individuals who are bilingual manage to learn two languages and become fluent in both? In most bilingual persons, one language is dominant. It's typically the first language learned, the one they heard most often as a child, and the one they use most often. Children exposed to two languages may learn one language at home with

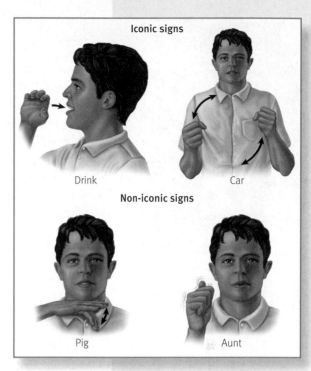

Iconic signs

Drink   Car

Non-iconic signs

Pig   Aunt

Figure 8.9 Iconic and Non-Iconic Sign Language. Some signs, such as the signs for "drink" and "car" (*top*), are iconic—they resemble the things they represent. Others, such as the signs for "pig" and "aunt" (*bottom*), are non-iconic—they are more like spoken words for which there's no clear relation between form and meaning. (*Source:* Adapted from http://lifeprint.com/as1101/pages-signs with permission from William Vicars)

Unlike this deaf child, whose parent is a fluent signer, most deaf babies are born to hearing parents who don't begin learning sign language until after their babies are born (or sometimes even later).

A growing number of children hear one language spoken at home and another at school. Although bilingualism may slow the learning of some aspects of both languages, it may promote metalinguistic insight in the long run.

Ruling Out Rival Hypotheses

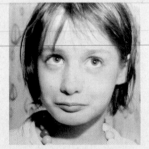

A young girl named Genie was deprived of language until adolescence. Genie's failure to learn to use language fluently is

Ruling Out Rival Hypotheses

consistent with the idea that there exists a critical period for language learning, although the severe abuse and emotional deprivation she experienced make it difficult to draw firm conclusions.

metalinguistic
awareness of how language is structured and used

their parents but hear a different language when they attend school. In this case, the home language is probably dominant. Or a student who speaks one language may spend a year abroad and learn a second language through immersion in this different-language community. The first language the student learned as a child would probably be dominant as well. However, there are cases in which the child is introduced to two languages from the outset, as when her parents speak two different languages or she has a full-time caretaker who speaks a different language from her parents. How do bilingual persons fluent in two languages keep them straight, and how are these languages organized in their brain?

Acquiring Two Languages.   Children learning two languages seem to go about it the same way that monolingual children—those learning a single language—do. They follow the same stages in the same order for each language as do monolingual children. There's some evidence that bilingual children experience some delay in each of their languages relative to their monolingual counterparts (Gathercole, 2002a, b). However, this delay depends on what aspects of language researchers measure. Vocabulary development is relatively unimpaired (Pearson & Fernández, 1994; Pearson, Fernández, & Oller, 1993), whereas syntax is more affected (Gathercole, 2002a, b). Moreover, despite popular claims that children are slowed down in their overall cognitive development, the delays that occur early in the acquisition process are offset by a variety of long-term benefits (Sorace, 2007). Not only can bilingual individuals converse with two language communities rather than one, but the process of figuring out how two languages work gives them heightened **metalinguistic** insight—the awareness of how language is structured and used. As a result, they tend to perform better on language tasks (Bialystok, 1988; Galambos & Hakuta, 1988; Ricciardelli, 1992).

Studies of brain activation during language processing demonstrate that bilingual persons who learned a second language early in development process the two languages using similar brain areas (Fabbro, 1999). In contrast, those who learned their second language later in development use different brain areas (Kim, Relkin, Lee, & Hirsch, 1997), suggesting to some researchers that the brain segregates different, later-learned languages into different regions. An alternative hypothesis is that the distinct brain areas observed for later-age exposure to second language are due to the fact that people acquire later-learned languages less proficiently (Illes et al., 1999).

Second Language Learning and Critical Periods.   As we mentioned earlier, younger children are better at learning language than are older children and adults. How do we know this? The ideal way to examine this phenomenon experimentally would be to deprive children of language entirely during early childhood and then test their ability to acquire their first language across development. Of course, this "thought experiment," as psychologists call it, would be unethical to carry out in real life.

Nevertheless, several tragic cases have served as natural experiments in this regard. Genie was a girl chained to a potty seat in an attic for much of the first 13 years of her life and deprived almost entirely of any social interaction or language input (Curtiss, 1977). The cases of Genie and others are consistent with the hypothesis that earlier exposure to language results in greater fluency, because they failed to become fluent language users. However, there are alternative explanations for impairment in these cases, such as the severe emotional and physical neglect these children experienced. As we learned in Chapter 2, case studies like Genie's tend to be limited in their ability to exclude rival explanations.

Because there's only so much we can conclude from language-deprived children, our main source of insight into age differences in language learning potential comes from research on second language acquisition. Investigators have used second language acquisition to determine whether there's a *critical period* for language (see also Chapter 10). Critical periods are windows of time in development during which an organism must learn an ability if it's going to learn it at all. Although young children are more receptive to learning a new language than older children and adults, language learning doesn't appear to have such a rigid window of opportunity.

In a classic study, researchers examined the critical period for language by testing the English grammar skills of adults who'd immigrated to the United States from China and

Korea at various ages. The test required participants to detect grammatical errors such as "The man climbed the ladder up carefully" and "The little boy is speak to a policeman." The researchers found that overall language proficiency was near native levels for adults first exposed to English between 1 and 7 years of age. However, skills dropped off gradually for adults exposed to English after age 7 (Johnson & Newport, 1989; see **Figure 8.10**). Syntax and pronunciation are more vulnerable to effects of the age of exposure than is vocabulary (Johnson & Newport, 1989; Piske, MacKay, & Flege, 2001). The fact that this drop-off is gradual rather than abrupt suggests that humans aren't subject to a strict critical period, at least when it comes to language.

We don't fully understand why older children and adults are less capable of learning new languages than younger children. The most promising account is Elissa Newport's (1990) "less is more" hypothesis (Newport, Bavelier, & Neville, 2001). According to this hypothesis, children have more limited information-processing abilities, fewer analytic skills, and less specific knowledge about how language works than do adults. As a result, they learn a second language in the same way they learned their first, more naturalistically and gradually from the ground up. In contrast, adults try to impose more organization and structure on their learning, making learning a language more challenging.

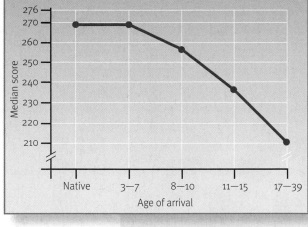

Figure 8.10 Proficiency in Second Language Depends on the Age of Exposure. Adults first exposed to English before age 7 displayed proficiency comparable to that of native English speakers, whereas those who learned English after age 7 were significantly less proficient. (*Source:* Johnson & Newport, 1989)

ASSESS YOUR KNOWLEDGE: FACT OR FICTION?

(1) Nonstandard dialects of English follow syntactic rules that differ from but are just as valid as the rules in standard American English. (True/False)

(2) Children's pronunciation errors are random and unpredictable. (True/False)

(3) Holophrases are a type of overgeneralization. (True/False)

(4) Few nonhuman animal communication systems involve exchanges of information beyond the here and now. (True/False)

(5) Bilingual individuals usually have one preferred language, which they learned earlier in development. (True/False)

Answers: (1) T (p. 321); (2) F (p. 325); (3) F (p. 326); (4) T (p. 329); (5) T (p. 331)

PsychoMythology
Do Twins Have Their Own Language?

The idea of being a twin has a certain appeal and allure. If you're an identical twin, you have a genetic clone! Even if you're a fraternal twin, you know another person who's at exactly the same stage as you are at every step of your development. Twins share their mother's womb, potty train together, and go through school at the same time. It's only natural to expect there to be a special bond between twins not shared by nontwin siblings. One commonly held belief is that this special bond enables twins to invent their own secret language, one only they can understand. This phenomenon is known as **cryptophasia.**

As fascinating as this notion is, the truth is less exotic, but no less interesting. Cases of apparent cryptophasia among twins turn out to be a result of phonological impairment and other types of language delay (Bishop & Bishop, 1998; Dodd & McEvoy, 1994) that are more prevalent among twins than among

(continued)

Popular psychology tells us that twins sometimes develop their own language. Is this fact or fiction?

cryptophasia
secret language developed and understood only by a small number of people, typically twins.

singletons (children born one at a time). Twin pairs who've supposedly developed a secret language are simply attempting to use their native language, but with poor articulation and significant pronunciation errors. These difficulties are serious enough to render their speech largely incomprehensible. This problem sometimes results in longer-term language impairment well into elementary school. Because twin pairs tend to make similar kinds of phonological errors, their speech is more understandable to each other than it is to their parents or nonrelated children (Dodd & McEvoy, 1994; Thorpe, Greenwood, Eivers, & Rutter, 2001).

There *are* interesting, but rare, cases of children inventing their own communication systems. One example is deaf children of hearing parents who sometimes invent their own signs when not being instructed in sign language. This phenomenon is called **homesign** and shows impressive ingenuity (and motivation to communicate) on the part of children, because they're inventing these signs without guidance from adults (Goldin-Meadow & Mylander, 1998). Another example occurred when a group of deaf children in Nicaragua met at a newly opened deaf school, where teachers were instructing them in spoken, but not sign, language. Because they couldn't communicate effectively with each other vocally, they invented a way to communicate through made-up signs (Senghas & Coppola, 2001).

Still, in the cases of homesign and Nicaraguan Sign Language, children didn't invent a full-blown secret language. Homesigners generate some basic sign combinations, but not a full syntax. Nicaraguan Sign Language has been exciting to observe, because its structure has evolved as new generations of students have come to the school and added complexity to the previous generation's language. The first wave of children at the school produced some initial signs and simple rules for combining them, and later waves of students have adopted and refined them. This is probably how most or all spoken languages evolve: gradually across large groups of people, not privately within a pair.

Over the course of several generations, children attending the Nicaraguan School for the Deaf have developed their own sign language. This communication system has become increasingly language-like with each new group of children entering the school.

The Inuit live in Arctic climates in Siberia, Alaska, northern Canada, and Greenland. It's common lore that the Inuit have a thousand words to refer to different types of snow, and as a result, they make finer distinctions among types of snow than do people who speak English. In fact, this claim is a myth: Inuit languages have about the same number of words for snow as does English.

homesign
system of signs invented by deaf children of hearing parents who receive no language input

covert speech
subvocal talking

linguistic determinism
view that all thought is represented verbally and that, as a result, our language defines our thinking

Do We Think in Words? The Relation between Language and Thought

We've all had times when we realized we were conversing with ourselves; we may have even started talking out loud to ourselves. Clearly, we sometimes think in words. What about the rest of the time? Do we usually think in a nonlinguistic fashion or just not notice our internal conversation? One early hypothesis was that thinking is a form of internal speech or what John B. Watson, the founder of behaviorism (see Prologue), called **covert speech.** For Watson, there's no thinking without language, and all thoughts—memories, decisions, emotional reactions, fantasies—are merely verbal descriptions in our minds. Watson believed that thinking is simply subvocal talking, moving the vocal tract as if talking, but below hearing level.

If all thought is represented verbally, this hypothesis implies that (1) children don't think at all until they've mastered language, (2) the complexity of our thinking is limited by the complexity of our language, and (3) the language we speak shapes how we perceive and interact with the world.

LINGUISTIC DETERMINISM: WE SPEAK, THEREFORE WE THINK

The view that all thinking is represented linguistically is called **linguistic determinism.** One of the best-known examples of how language can influence thought is the belief that

Inuits (formerly called Eskimos) have about a thousand words for snow. Linguistic determinists argue that having so many words for snow enables Inuits to perceive incredibly subtle distinctions among types of snow. It's a good story. But there are several reasons to believe it's all a myth:

(1) Analysis of Inuit languages reveals that although Inuits make several fine distinctions among types of snow, a thousand is a substantial exaggeration of these types.

(2) English speakers actually use many different terms to describe snow, such as "slush," "powder," or even "crud." In fact, we have about as many terms as do the Inuits.

(3) Even assuming that the Inuits have more terms for snow than we do, we can't infer that the greater number of terms *caused* the Inuit to make finer distinctions. It is just as likely, and perhaps more, that Inuits and other people who work in snowy conditions, like skiers and hikers, find it helpful to draw fine distinctions among types of snow. If so, language may reflect people's thinking about snow rather than the other way around. The correlation between the number of words and the number of distinctions doesn't mean that the words produced distinctions that wouldn't otherwise have been there.

It's challenging to think of ways to test linguistic determinism. One strong test would be to compare the thought processes of people who can use language versus those who can't to see if their thinking is similar. Of course, nearly everyone learns language, and those few who don't are either severely cognitively impaired or have suffered such serious abuse and neglect that they're deeply disturbed emotionally. So we need to look to other evidence to see whether normal thinking can exist without language.

Helen Keller offers a fascinating case example. She lost her hearing and her sight at 19 months due to illness. Although she was exposed to spoken language during the first year and a half of her life, the combination of blindness and deafness left her unable to communicate either vocally or gesturally. When she was 7, she discovered with the help of her teacher, Annie Sullivan, that signs performed against the palm of her hand were a form of communication. She eventually learned to use language (she actually mastered several languages) and went on to write multiple books about her experiences. In her writing, Keller revealed herself to be a believer in linguistic determinism. She wrote that before learning language, "I did not know that I am. I lived in a world that was a no-world. . . . I did not know that I knew aught [anything] or that I lived or acted or desired. I had neither will nor intellect" (Keller, 1910, pp. 113–114). Of course, this is merely one anecdote, not systematic scientific evidence. Most of us have poor memories of our childhood mental states, thoughts, and perspectives. So there are alternative explanations for Keller's recalling a lack of thought. Still, her perspective provides a tantalizing suggestion that people without language lack thought.

Nevertheless, there are reasons to doubt linguistic determinism. One of the earliest tests of linguistic determinism is one you won't want to try at home; it prevented someone from engaging in covert speech by paralyzing him temporarily. In 1947, a team of researchers wanted to test Watson's claim that all thought is subvocal speech (Smith, Brown, Toman, & Goodman, 1947). They used a drug called *curare,* which paralyzes the muscles and skeleton but leaves the patient conscious. The brave test subject for this experiment was an anesthesiologist himself (scientists and physicians have a long history of attempting experiments on themselves before trying anything dangerous on others). After his vocal tract was completely immobilized, but before the drug had taken complete effect, the subject could wrinkle his forehead in response to questions, confirming his ability to understand spoken speech. After the drug had worn off, he accurately reported events he'd observed, and could report thoughts and sensations he experienced while paralyzed. Clearly, thought isn't completely dependent on subvocalizing. This finding soundly falsified Watson's hypothesis that thought is subvocal language. Yet it didn't entirely rule out linguistic determinism. Among other things, we may think by simulating speech in our minds without moving our facial muscles to produce the sounds.

Later evidence was more conclusive. First, contrary to the predictions of linguistic determinism, children can perform many complex cognitive tasks long before they can

Correlation vs. Causation

Helen Keller, who was blind and deaf from the age of 19 months, learned to communicate through signing and to read using Braille. Her writings suggest she recalled not experiencing much in the way of a mental life before learning to communicate.

Ruling Out Rival Hypotheses

Falsifiability

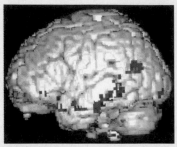

Figure 8.11 Brain Activation during Language Tasks. This PET scan shows the areas in the left temporal lobe that become activated when people are trying to figure out the meanings of words.

fictoid

Myth: Language impairment as a result of stroke or other brain injury occurs only following left hemisphere damage.

Reality: Although more obvious language deficits tend to occur in left-hemisphere-damaged patients, damage to the right temporal and frontal lobes can also disrupt the ability to interpret or use nonliteral speech, such as sarcasm.

Correlation vs. Causation

transcranial magnetic stimulation (TMS)
technique involving a coil that generates a magnetic field that can temporarily block or stimulate neural transmissions within a small brain area

talk about them. For that reason, psychologists have developed cognitive performance tests for infants and children that minimize testers' reliance on verbal instructions and verbal responses.

A second compelling argument against linguistic determinism comes from recent neuroimaging studies of problem solving, thinking, remembering, and reading (see **Figure 8.11**). These studies show that although language areas often become activated when people engage in certain cognitive tasks, such as reading, they aren't activated during others, such as spatial tasks or visual imagery (Gazzaniga, Ivry, & Mangun, 2002). These studies suggest that thought can occur without language.

NEW FRONTIERS
Putting the Brain on "Pause"

Technological advances over the past decade or so have dramatically improved scientists' ability to observe how our brain processes information. **Transcranial magnetic stimulation (TMS)** is perhaps the most bizarre of these techniques, resembling something out of a sci-fi movie. TMS temporarily turns off a small area of our brains. The device is a coil that generates a small but powerful magnetic field, much like the area around a simple refrigerator magnet that draws metal pins toward it. This magnetic field floods the electrical activity of the brain area in its path, temporarily knocking out transmission of information to and from that area. Scientists can also use TMS to activate a brain area, rather than block it, by using a different level of intensity.

Scientists can use this stimulation to knock out only areas of the brain near the surface, which is good news, as breathing and other vital functions are controlled by areas deeper down in the brain stem (see Chapter 3). They can use TMS to investigate questions about brain areas in the outer layer of the cortex. The effects of TMS are brief, lasting only seconds after a pulse of magnetic energy. Fortunately, TMS is also quite safe. The first few times researchers tried it, subjects sometimes experienced seizures, but researchers fortunately solved this problem! They can achieve longer effects by releasing repeated pulses of magnetic energy at several-second intervals. Although scientists first used TMS as a research tool, they're now assessing its potential for treating epilepsy, depression, and the hallucinations associated with schizophrenia (Verdon, Saba, & Januel, 2004).

The most exciting aspect of TMS is that, unlike other neuroimaging techniques that only correlate brain activity with behavior, TMS enables us to draw causal conclusions. Because it's an experimental intervention, we can draw stronger conclusions about the roles that specific brain areas play in behavior, including language. For example, TMS pulses to Broca's area, the region responsible for speech production (Chapter 3; see also Figure 8.5), result in temporary disruptions in speech (Verdon et al., 2004).

More recently, researchers investigated the impact of TMS on people's ability to engage in covert speech (Aziz-Zadeh, Cattaneo, Rochat, & Rizzolatti, 2005). They asked people to count silently the number of syllables in a word they heard. When researchers administered TMS over left hemisphere areas associated with language, participants experienced significant delays in completing the task compared with when researchers administered it over the right hemisphere. This finding suggests that covert speech is controlled, at least in part, by areas of the brain responsible for spoken language production and comprehension. Interestingly, TMS impulses to language areas didn't disrupt overall cognitive processing, indicating that TMS wasn't merely distracting participants or temporarily impairing their intellect.

LINGUISTIC RELATIVITY: LANGUAGE GIVES THOUGHT A GENTLE NUDGE

Clearly, linguistic determinism doesn't have a less radical lot going for it. Nevertheless, there's some promise for **linguistic relativity,** which is a less radical perspective on how language relates to thought. Proponents of linguistic relativity maintain that characteristics of language shape our thought processes. This idea is also known as the Sapir-Whorf hypothesis, named after the two scholars who proposed it (Sapir, 1929; Whorf, 1956). There's evidence both for and against linguistic relativity. Sapir and Whorf might have argued that this mixed evidence is to be expected, because some aspects of thinking are more vulnerable to language influence than others.

Several studies suggest that language can affect thinking. One study examined the memories of Russians who moved to the United States and achieved fluency in Russian and English. These participants recalled events that happened in Russia more accurately when speaking Russian, and recalled events that happened in the United States more accurately when speaking English (Marian & Neisser, 2000). There are other interesting cross-language differences in how people's descriptions of their world influence their perceptions. Korean contains two different words for events that English speakers would describe using the word *in*. The Korean language distinguishes linguistically between tight fit (such as a drawer's fit in a dresser) and loose fit (such as an apple resting in a bowl). The evidence suggests that our classification of spatial events, such as putting things inside other things, is shaped by our native language (see **Figure 8.12**). Nine- and 14-month-old infants learning English or Korean distinguish tight-fitting from loose-fitting events (McDonough, Choi, & Mandler, 2003). Nevertheless, as early as 18 months, children learning English cease to discriminate between tight- and loose-fitting events, whereas Korean children continue to do so (Choi, McDonough, Bowerman, & Mandler, 1999). The linguistic distinction between these two types of events may encourage Korean children to attend to it.

Yet in other cases, researchers have been surprised to discover that language doesn't influence thought. One example is color categorization (Lenneberg, 1967). Different languages contain different numbers of basic color terms. In English, we generally use a set of eleven basic color terms: red, blue, green, yellow, white, black, purple, orange, pink, brown, and gray. However, some languages contain fewer basic color terms. A language community may use a single word to refer to all things that are either blue or green. When it becomes important to distinguish blue from green things, speakers may say "blue/green like the sky" versus "blue/green like the leaves." In a small number of non-Westernized cultures such as the Dani of New Guinea, there are no true color terms at all, only "dark" and "bright."

The fact that there are different numbers of color terms in different languages affords a test case for the Sapir-Whorf hypothesis. If language influences thought, someone from the Dani, whose language contains only two color terms, should have a harder time distinguishing blue from green than those of us whose language contains separate terms for these two colors. Nevertheless, Eleanor Rosch (1973) demonstrated that the Dani perceive colors as dividing up into roughly the same color categories as do English speakers.

So does this mean that speakers of all languages end up thinking in precisely the same ways? No. The evidence suggests that language shapes some, but not all, aspects of perception, memory, and thought. Nevertheless, when researchers identify language-related differences in thought, it's not easy to disentangle the influences of language from culture. In the case of the two Korean terms for *in*, the distinction between tight and loose fit may be especially relevant for Koreans, which could have led them to make this distinction in the first place. In this scenario, the culture creates a difference that language merely reflects. In essence, nearly all cross-linguistic comparisons are correlational rather than experimental because we can't randomly assign people to learn different languages. As a result, language and culture are nearly always confounded. We therefore must be careful when drawing causal conclusions about the impact of language on thinking.

Figure 8.12 Language Influences How Children Perceive Relations. In Korean, the word *nehta* refers to objects that fit loosely inside other objects (*see example, top image*). The word *kkita* refers to objects that fit tightly inside of other objects (*see example, bottom image*). English speakers use the word *in* to describe both images.

The Dani language has only words for "dark" and "bright," not individual colors, but Dani people can distinguish colors, just as we do.

linguistic relativity
view that characteristics of language shape our thought processes

Correlation vs. Causation

ASSESS YOUR KNOWLEDGE: FACT OR FICTION?

(1) We can't determine whether the fine distinctions Inuits make among different kinds of snow are a cause or a consequence of the many terms for *snow* in their language. (True/False)
(2) The curare experiment falsified linguistic determinism. (True/False)
(3) According to the Sapir-Whorf hypothesis, all aspects of thinking are slightly, but not strongly, influenced by language. (True/False)
(4) Language seems to influence how we classify spatial relations more than how we classify colors. (True/False)
(5) People who speak languages that lack terms for distinguishing colors can't tell these colors apart. (True/False)

Answers: (1) T (pp. 334–335); (2) F (p. 335); (3) F (p. 337); (4) T (p. 337); (5) F (p. 337)

Reading: Recognizing the Written Word

Control Condition	Stroop Interference Condition
Rabblt	Red
House	Blue
Blanket	Green
Dance	Yellow
Flower	Purple
Key	Orange
Seven	Black
Dance	Yellow
House	Blue
Key	Orange
Seven	Purple
Flower	Black
Rabbit	Red
Blanket	Green

Figure 8.13 The Stroop Effect. The Stroop task demonstrates that reading is automatic. Go down each column and say aloud the color of ink in which each word is printed. Try the control list first—you'll find that it's relatively straightforward task. Next, try the Stroop interference list. You'll probably find the task considerably more difficult.

Reading, like spoken language, becomes an automatic process, one that doesn't consume our attentional resources, except when we're reading something particularly challenging or engaging. In fact, reading becomes so automatic by the time we reach college-age that we can't turn it off even when we want to. Usually, this is a good thing because it means we can read street signs while driving even when the person sitting next to us distracts us. But the automatic nature of reading can be less than ideal when we accidentally glimpse someone's open diary or credit card bill. In these cases, we almost can't help but violate others' privacy, because we can't put the brakes on our brains to process written language.

A compelling demonstration of the automaticity of language—for better or for worse—is the Stroop color-naming task, named after the researcher who invented it, J. Ridley Stroop (1935). This task requires participants to suppress their attention to printed words to identify the color of the ink. The catch is that the printed words are color names that contradict the ink color (see **Figure 8.13**). Most people experience enormous difficulty ignoring the printed words, even though the task doesn't require them to read. The Stroop task shows that reading is automatic and not easy to inhibit (MacLeod, 1991). Interestingly, children who are still getting the hang of reading don't experience interference in the Stroop task (Schadler & Thissen, 1981). Because their reading is effortful, they can turn off their attention to the words and pay attention only to ink color. As children become more practiced readers, they actually do worse on the Stroop.

HOW DOES READING WORK?

We must master two skills to become experts at reading. The first is learning to recognize how whole printed words look on the page. Without this skill, reading isn't easy or automatic. We need to recognize common words without having to sound out each word as if it were the first time we've seen it. The average reader uses **whole word recognition** to read the vast majority of printed words (LaBerge & Samuels, 1974). Still, this obviously can't be the whole story because we need to develop strategies for reading new words. For these words, we use a second strategy, called **phonetic decomposition** (National Research Council, 1998). This strategy involves sounding out words by figuring out the correspondences between printed letters and sounds. For words like *livid,* this task is simple because each printed consonant (*l, v,* and *d*) corresponds to a single phoneme in English and the vowel (*i*) has the same sound in both instances. However, not all sounds in the English language are linked to a unique letter (or even combination of letters) corresponding to them.

whole word recognition
reading strategy that involves identifying common words without having to sound them out based on their appearance

phonetic decomposition
reading strategy that involves sounding out words by drawing correspondences between printed letters and sounds

For example, sounding out the word *pleasure* based on letter-to-phoneme correspondences won't get us far; we'll end up with something way off base, like "plee-ah-sir-eh." In these cases, we must memorize how the word's spelling translates to the spoken word. In some cases, we can memorize general rules about how specific letter combinations relate to specific pronunciations. For example, we can memorize that *-ight* is used to spell words like *light, might, tight, right, night,* and *sight.* But in the case of *pleasure*, there are no simple rules. *Pleasure* and *measure* are spelled and pronounced the same way, but *-sure* doesn't always take the same pronunciation. For example, in the word *insure*, the *-sure* conveys a different sound sequence.

As we can see, translating from English spelling to spoken English isn't easy. For many of the words that children are learning to spell and read in elementary school, teaching them to assume that each letter has a sound associated with it is a useful starting point. As children become more advanced readers, however, they need to incorporate whole word recognition into their reading strategy and begin reasoning from similar-looking words. If a child has learned the spelling of *sight*, she may be able to use that knowledge to infer how to pronounce a new word, such as *blight*.

APPLY YOUR THINKING

There's a trade-off between speed and accuracy in most types of cognitive processing, including reading. Which of the two reading approaches, whole word recognition or phonetic decomposition, is likely to be quicker? Which is likely to be more accurate?

PREREADING

Before children learn to read, they must realize several things. Some seem self-evident to us, but they aren't always obvious to young children, particularly those whose caretakers don't often read to them. To be reading ready:

(1) Children must realize that writing is meaningful. Young children looking at books and signs may not realize that the seeming gobbledy-gook printed below pictures or on street signs is something more than scribbles (Stanovich & West, 1989).

(2) Children must understand that writing moves in a particular direction (see **Figure 8.14**). Children learning English must learn that writing moves from left to right, children learning Hebrew must figure out that writing moves from right to left, and children learning Japanese must understand that writing moves from top to bottom. Children must also realize that breaks in the print separate distinct words. These aspects of writing are basic starting points for young prereaders (Clay, 1975).

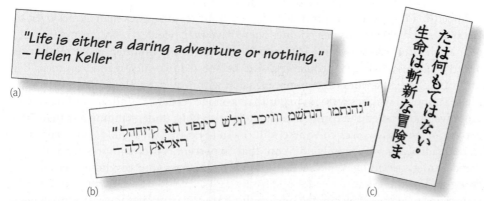

(a) "Life is either a daring adventure or nothing." — Helen Keller

(b) (Hebrew text)

(c) (Japanese text)

Figure 8.14 Learning How Writing Moves. Before learning to read, children must learn which direction is correct for their language. English is written from left to right (a); Hebrew from right to left (b), and Japanese from top to bottom (c).

(3) Children must learn to recognize *graphemes,* the letters of the alphabet. This task is harder than it seems because children must figure out what basic features distinguish an *N* from an *M*, for example, despite the fact that they'll see both *N*s and *M*s printed in a variety of confusingly different sizes and styles (Chall, 1983).

(4) Children must learn that printed letters correspond to specific sounds. As we discussed earlier, the relation between sounds and letters isn't anywhere near perfect, but figuring out what sounds an *F, B,* and *L* make is a crucial starting point. Experiments have shown that training children to be aware of sound–letter correspondences enhances reading (Bradley & Bryant, 1983; Gibb & Randall, 1988; Lunberg, Frost, & Persen, 1988).

There's been heated debate about whether awareness of sound–letter correspondences, known as phonics, is the best strategy for teaching children to read. For a long time, educators believed that teaching children to recognize whole words was the best way to get them started as proficient readers. As a consequence, a great deal of U.S. educational policy was based on whole word learning. Although these educators were right that mature readers rely mostly on whole word recognition, they mistook the correlation between reading proficiency and the whole word recognition strategy as causal. They concluded incorrectly that whole word recognition leads to better reading. In fact, learning to analyze and recognize sound–letter correspondences, even though they're not perfect, is a much more effective way to get children reading and keep them reading (Rayner, Foorman, Perfetti, Pesetsky, & Seidenberg, 2002).

Correlation vs. Causation

fictoid

Myth: *Dyslexia* is defined as a tendency to transpose letters in words (like spelling the word *read* as "raed") or to perceive letters or numbers backward (like seeing a *b* as a *d*).

Reality: Only some people with dyslexia (which means "reading difficulty") display these reversal problems; moreover, many children display these problems at a young age but don't develop dyslexia. Nor do people with dyslexia perceive words backward.

SPEED-READING—A HOAX IN SHEEP'S CLOTHING?

As we learned in Chapter 1, one of the biggest hoaxes perpetuated on educated people is that speed-reading courses are effective. We can find training programs in speed-reading, also known as photoreading, mega speed-reading, and alphanetics, almost everywhere. Some universities even offer sponsored courses to boost students' reading rates. Here's a hot tip: Save your money! Speed-reading "works" in the sense that it speeds up our reading rate. So what's the catch? Our comprehension suffers enormously (Graf, 1973). The same speed–accuracy trade-off that operates in normal reading applies here: The faster we read, the more we miss. The average college student reads about 200–300 words per minute (Carver, 1990). Controlled studies indicate that reading faster than 400 words per minute results in comprehension rates below 50 percent (Cunningham, Stanovich, & Wilson, 1990).

Correlation vs. Causation

So why have speed-reading programs become so popular? Because they're based on a genuine finding, namely, that reading speed is correlated with comprehension. Nevertheless, this correlation doesn't imply that if we start reading faster, we'll comprehend more. Proficient readers tend to be both faster at reading and better at comprehending than poorer readers, but reading speed doesn't cause comprehension.

Extraordinary Claims

Speed-reading programs promise to increase our reading rates many times over, to 1,000 or even 2,000 words per minute. There have even been extraordinary claims of people who can read between 15,000 and 30,000 words per minute. Yet the truth turns out to be far less than extraordinary. Researchers tested two such readers on their identification of specific words and comprehension within a written text (Homa, 1983). These supposed whizzes were no better than average readers at finding specific words. Moreover, both failed the comprehension test miserably, understanding less than 50 percent of what they read. Of course, failure's in the eye of the beholder, and speed-reading advocates will happily point out that 50 percent is pretty impressive at the rate speed-readers are going. Will speed-reading help you pass your psychology exam, though? Don't bet on it.

Is there any hope of improving our reading speed? Fortunately, several approaches are effective. A 1940 experiment demonstrated that the slowest 10 percent of readers in the Harvard freshman class improved their reading speed from an average of 215 words per minute to 335 words per minute after 10 weeks of tutoring for their reading skills (Bond, 1941). Even more important, these students' comprehension improved too. Why did speeding up their reading boost their comprehension? Because their reading rate was still below 400 words per minute, their comprehension didn't suffer. At the same time, they covered more material, so they weren't running out of time by the end of the exam.

ASSESS YOUR KNOWLEDGE: FACT OR FICTION?

(1) The Stroop color-naming task demonstrates that reading is automatic. (True/False)

(2) Whole word recognition is the most efficient reading strategy for fluent readers and the best way to teach children to read. (True/False)

(3) Phonetic decomposition is a straightforward linking of printed letters to phonemes. (True/False)

(4) Learning sound–letter correspondences is causally related to learning to read. (True/False)

(5) Increasing our reading speed can increase our comprehension as long as we stay under 400 words per minute. (True/False)

Answers: (1) T (p. 338); (2) F (p. 338); (3) F (p. 338); (4) T (pp. 338–339); (5) T (p. 341)

We can often spot posters and fliers like this one on college campuses, in coffee shops, and in our spam e-mail. Such speed-reading programs claim to increase our reading rate from 2 to 100 times over the average reading rate (which is 200 to 300 words per minute). Should we trust these claims?

Thinking and Reasoning

Nearly all of the chapters of this book thus far, and more still to come, describe aspects of thinking. Generally speaking, we can define **thinking** as any mental activity or processing of information. It includes learning, remembering, perceiving, believing, and deciding.

As we discovered in Chapter 6, behaviorists attempted to explain thinking in terms of stimulus and response, reinforcement and punishment. Yet psychologists have long known that our minds often go beyond the available information, making leaps of insight and drawing inferences. Our minds fill in the gaps to create information that isn't present in its environmental inputs (see the Prologue and Chapters 2 and 4). Behaviorism's "black box psychology" (see Chapter 6) can't easily account for this phenomenon.

IS THE MIND A LIVING COMPUTER?

In the 1980s, many psychologists adopted a novel analogy for the mind's tendency to process information, fill in gaps, and draw inferences. As the prominence of the computer increased, they began to think about thinking as akin to running data through a computer program. From this perspective, the brain contains preprogrammed abilities; it runs data through its "software program" and spits out an answer.

Although some modern psychologists still rely on the computer model, most believe that thinking is far more complex than expressed by this model. Interestingly, the tasks that best distinguish humans from computers are often those we find the simplest. The field of **artificial intelligence (AI)** investigates how people can design computers to simulate human abilities (Boden, 1989; Newell & Simon, 1972). AI has generated computers that can outstrip humans on tasks like calculating complex numbers, scanning databases for specific information, and even playing chess. In each case, humans are slower and

fictoid

Myth: Subvocalizing (silently pronouncing words in our heads) increases reading comprehension.

Reality: Subvocalizing slows down our reading because we speak much slower than we can read. As a result, people who subvocalize tend to complete less of a text within a given time period, resulting in lower comprehension.

thinking
any mental activity or processing of information, including learning, remembering, perceiving, believing, and deciding

artificial intelligence (AI)
study and design of computer systems created to mimic human cognitive abilities

In 1997, the computer program Deep Blue (from the United States) stunned the world by defeating world chess champion Garry Kasparov (from Russia) in a 6-game match. Yet despite computers' remarkable capacity for certain types of information processing, like chess-playing, they remain well behind humans at tasks we find easy, like voice recognition.

more prone to errors than computers are. Yet some of the biggest challenges for AI have been creating machines that can recognize letters written in different people's handwriting or short words spoken by different people, tasks we generally find effortless. Basic object recognition, such as identifying a rabbit, has also proved a huge challenge for AI.

Why do computers find these tasks so difficult? Part of the answer seems to be that computers, unlike humans, don't have a chance to explore and interact with the world. So their knowledge is fed to them rather than acquired by experience. Recent studies using robots rather than stationary computers have yielded somewhat better success at basic tasks (Cangelosi & Riga, 2006; Prince & Berthouze, 2004). By interacting physically with their world, scanning their environment, and moving around to observe the consequences of their actions, robots can learn in ways that are more similar to humans.

Neuroimaging studies of brain activation during tasks demonstrate that even if computers can solve some of the same problems we can, they don't solve them the same *way* we do. Our brains don't contain fixed programs, like Microsoft Word (Dietrich & Markman, 2000; Gazzaniga, 1973; Posner & Levitin, 2002). Although different brain regions tend to be associated with different kinds of tasks, cognitive processing is flexible, meaning there are few or no set programs run over and over again. Instead, our brains enable us to (1) switch gears, (2) attend to different aspects of a situation on different occasions, and (3) generate creative solutions. Experts are developing computer systems that are less program-based and more flexible, but we're still far from creating the androids of sci-fi books and movies. The incredible complexity and flexibility of human thought remains unparalleled.

COGNITIVE ECONOMY—IMPOSING ORDER ON OUR WORLD

Given the complexity of the cognitive tasks we must perform, our brains have adapted by finding ways to streamline the process. This is where cognitive economy enters the picture. As we learned in Chapter 2, we're *cognitive misers*. Our minds use a variety of *heuristics,* or shortcuts, to increase our thinking efficiency. From an evolutionary perspective, heuristics may have enhanced our survival. However, as we've seen, these shortcuts can backfire if we're not careful (see Chapter 2). Let's first ask ourselves why we've developed these shortcuts and how they're useful in everyday life (Gilovich, Griffin, & Kahneman, 2002).

We process an enormous amount of information every minute of every day. From the moment we wake up, we must take into account what time it is, notice if there are any obstacles on the floor (like a roommate's shoes) between us and the shower, plan what time we need to get to class or work, and collect everything we need to bring with us. Of course, that's all before we've even gone out the door. If we were to attend to and draw conclusions about every aspect of our experience all of the time, we'd be so overwhelmed that we'd be paralyzed psychologically.

As you're reading this paragraph, take a moment to put down your book and focus on all the information that you usually tune out. Notice any background noise: people talking, cars whizzing by outside, a bird singing, and even subtle sounds like air moving through heating vents or the electronic hum of your computer. Think about the visual information you'd normally ignore, such as the shade of grass outside your window, irregularities in the carpet texture, or scratch marks on your desk or chair. Notice the physical sensation of your body, the texture of the surface on which you're sitting, where the weight of your body presses down most firmly on the chair, and your breathing rate. Now imagine if you needed to monitor all that information all the time. You'd never get anything done! In fact, one old but still influential theory (Mathalon, Heinks, & Ford, 2004) of the cause of schizophrenia is that people with this disorder lack the ability to filter their attention (Bleuler, 1908; Shakow, 1962). Cognitive economy allows us to simplify what we attend to and keep the information we need for decision making to a manageable minimum.

Top-Down Processing. One way our minds streamline their processing is by filling in the gaps. Our brains often recruit information from related experiences and use it to organize information. As we learned in Chapter 4, psychologists call this phenomenon *top-down processing*. We can contrast top-down processing with bottom-up processing, in which our brains process only the information they receive and construct meaning from it slowly and surely by building up knowledge through experience. In Chapter 4, we also saw how perception is distinct from sensation because our perceptual experiences rely not only on raw sensory input but on stored knowledge that our brains call up to help us interpret it (see **Figure 8.15**). In Chapter 7, we encountered chunking, another form of top-down processing. Chunking is a memory aid that relies on our ability to organize information into larger units, expanding the span and detail of our memories. The Stroop effect and automaticity of reading, which we've discussed in this chapter, are also examples of top-down knowledge, because we access the knowledge of printed words we've stored instead of analyzing the printed word forms as we read (refer back to Figure 8.13). Each of these examples highlights our brains' tendency to simplify our cognitive functioning by using preexisting knowledge to spare us from reinventing the wheel.

Categories and Schemas. **Categories** and *schemas* help us to achieve cognitive economy. Categories are collections of real or imagined objects, actions, and characteristics that share core properties, such as *motorcycles, fruit, dancing,* and *purple*. As we learned in Chapter 7, schemas are categories we've stored in memory that organize relations among actions, objects, and ideas. Schemas help us to mentally organize events that share core features, say, going to a restaurant, cleaning the house, and visiting the zoo. As we acquire knowledge, we create stored categories and schemas that enable us to draw on knowledge when we experience something new. For example, when encountering an animal we've never seen, we use our knowledge of an animal's characteristics to recognize whether it's a mammal or a reptile, harmless or dangerous.

Categorizing allows us to have all of our general knowledge about dogs at our disposal when dealing with Rover. We don't need to discover from scratch that Rover barks, pants when he's hot, and has a stomach. These things all come "for free" once we recognize Rover as a dog. Similarly, when we go to a new doctor's office, no one has to tell us to sit in the waiting room and that someone will call us when an examining room is ready, because our schema for doctors' visits tells us this is the standard script. Of course, our categories and schemas don't apply to all real-world situations. Rover may be unable to bark because of a throat disorder. Yet most of the time, our categories and schemas safely allow us to exert less cognitive effort over basic knowledge, freeing us up to engage in more complex reasoning and emotional processing.

Allan Collins and M. Ross Quillian demonstrated that we import knowledge of a category in a top-down manner (Collins & Quillian, 1969). They were particularly interested in how we infer information about categories that are part of a *taxonomic hierarchy*. Collins and Quillian borrowed this term from biology, in which categories at one level include a variety of subcategories that all share certain properties (see **Figure 8.16**). For example, the class of mammals contains a variety of orders, including dogs, cats, whales, and primates (of which we humans are a member) that possess some mammalian properties (such as breathing air and bearing live young) but possess distinct properties from each other. Given the knowledge base in Figure 8.16, if we learned that an egret is a bird, we could import all of our knowledge about birds and animals into our knowledge about egrets without having to learn this information anew for egrets.

We organize mental categories so that they're optimally useful to us. For example, we code the degree to which members of a category are typical or atypical, and we use this information as a basis for building categories. In the case of the bird category, we know that ostriches are a type of bird, but we also know that ostriches are atypical because they're much larger than the average bird and don't fly. When constructing categories, we rely more heavily on our knowledge of typical birds, such as robins and sparrows, than on atypical birds, such as ostriches or penguins (Smith, Shoben, & Rips, 1974). However, what we consider to be typical depends on our cultural and social experience (Bailenson, Shum, Atran, Medin, & Coley, 2002). Someone from Brazil or Mexico may have a different notion than a

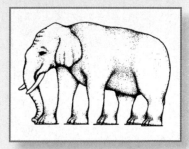

Figure 8.15 Top-Down Processing. Our brains engage in perceptual completion, the use of top-down processing to perceive something that isn't there. Most people see this drawing as a perfectly fine drawing of an elephant, but look closely at its legs. (*Source:* Shepard, 1990)

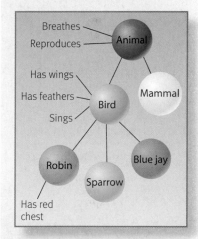

Figure 8.16 A Taxonomic Hierarchy. The category "bird" is part of a broader category, "animal." Members of the bird category share the properties that all animals have, but also possess some distinctive characteristics. Similarly, the category "robin" is part of the broader category "bird." Robins share the properties that birds and animals have, but also possess some distinctive characteristics. Once we learn that a robin is a bird, we can assume all of the knowledge we possess about birds and animals without needing to learn it specifically about robins.

categories
collections of real or imagined objects, actions, and characteristics that share core properties

What's considered a typical member of the fruit category differs for people from the tropics compared with North Americans.

North American of a typical fruit, because the kinds of fruit people encounter in tropical climates differ from those people encounter in the Northern Hemisphere (Pinto, 1992). Lawrence Barsalou (1983) further demonstrated that we can create new categories on the spur of the moment, or *ad hoc categories*. For example, we can easily create categories such as "things on my desk I can use to pound a nail" or "foods to avoid on a diet."

Playing the Odds—An Adaptive Approach.   We often must make snap decisions with incomplete or even misleading information. When that happens, we try to calculate which of a variety of possible solutions is our best bet and then hazard an educated guess. We engage in these calculations all the time. We may decide that the week-old milk in our refrigerator has gone bad based on its smell without tasting it, let alone conducting a microscopic bacterial analysis of it. We may decide that the stressed-out looking woman with an unfriendly expression on her face isn't a good choice to approach for a donation to our local charity. These guesses may not always be right, but they're probably good bets.

Gerd Gigerenzer (2001, 2007; Gigerenzer & Goldstein, 1996) referred to this type of cognitive economy as "fast and frugal" thinking. He argued that it serves us well most of the time. In fact, in many cases, the heuristics we use are more valid than an exhaustive (and exhausting!) analysis of all potential factors.

Natalie Ambady and Robert Rosenthal (1993) provided a remarkable example of how cognitive economy serves us well (also see Prologue). They showed participants 30-second silent clips of instructors teaching and asked them to evaluate their nonverbal behaviors. Participants' ratings on the basis of only 30 seconds of exposure were correlated significantly with the teachers' end-of-course evaluations by their students; in fact, their ratings were still predictive of course evaluations even when the clips were only 6 seconds long! Ambady and Rosenthal referred to our ability to extract useful information from small bits of behavior as "thin slicing." John Gottman and his colleagues also showed that they could predict with more than 90 percent accuracy which couples will divorce within the next 15 years after observing just 15 minutes of a couple's videotaped interaction (Carrère & Gottman, 1999; see also Chapter 11).

Other studies have demonstrated that untrained observers can make surprisingly accurate judgments about people on the basis of limited information. Samuel Gosling and his colleagues asked a group of untrained observers to make personality judgments about students by viewing their dorm rooms or bedrooms for a few minutes. They gave observers no instructions about what features of the room to focus on, and covered all photos in the rooms so that observers couldn't determine the sex, race, or age of the rooms' occupants. Yet observers were surprisingly accurate at judging aspects of the occupants' personalities, such as their emotional stability, openness to new experiences, and conscientiousness (Gosling, Ko, Mannarelli, & Morris, 2002). Presumably, observers were using mental shortcuts to draw conclusions about occupants' personalities because they had no firsthand experience with them. Yet these shortcuts worked: Observers' fast and frugal processing steered them right.

Research by Samuel Gosling and his collaborators suggests that observers can often infer people's personality traits at better than chance levels merely by inspecting their rooms. What might you guess about the level of conscientiousness of this room's occupant?

These studies all highlight the upsides of cognitive economy. Intuition, snap judgments, and heuristics make us quick, efficient, and often accurate processors of information (Gladwell, 2005). This processing affords us some mental legroom, allowing us to engage in more complex mental tasks.

THE RISKS OF ECONOMIZING: YOU GET WHAT YOU PAY FOR

But there are also significant downsides to cognitive economy (Myers, 2002). As we've noted in earlier chapters, we need to guard against cognitive errors when drawing conclusions about behavior. In Chapters 1 and 2, we encountered several biases and heuristics that can lead us to draw faulty conclusions about scientific evidence (see **Table 8.5**).

For many decisions, heuristic-based errors aren't the end of the world. An error in judgment about who might donate to our charity isn't catastrophic, because we can easily find other potential donors. Nevertheless, some cognitive mistakes are expensive financially,

Table 8.5 A Review of Key Heuristics and Biases. People fall prey to each of these heuristics and biases, resulting in poor decisions and incorrect conclusions (see Chapters 1 and 2).

Heuristic and Bias	Description
Availability heuristic	Mis-estimation of how probable an event is based on the ease of generating an example
Confirmation bias	Seeking evidence consistent with our views while ignoring or distorting contrary evidence
Correlation = causation fallacy	Concluding that if two behaviors are related, one caused the other
Hindsight bias	Believing in retrospect that an outcome was much more likely than it was
Ignoring base rates	Failing to take into account the overall likelihood of an event when estimating its likelihood in a specific instance

socially, and even physically. Tens of thousands of people stopped flying during the several months following the terrorist attacks of September 11, 2001. This response was probably a consequence of a heightened sense of fear and vulnerability stemming from the *availability heuristic* (see Chapter 2), that is, the prominence of these attacks in people's memories. Ironically, during the three months following September 11, more Americans who opted to travel by car instead of plane died in traffic fatalities than in the four hijacked planes combined (Gigerenzer, 2004).

Faulty conclusions based on cognitive economy can lead us to draw wrong-headed theories about the causes of people's behaviors and mistaken judgments about their personalities. For example, our snap judgments of people, although usually more accurate than chance, can occasionally be wildly wrong. This fact probably helps to explain why brief open-ended interviews of people, such as college students, job applicants, and psychiatric patients, often yield inaccurate judgments of their personalities (Garb, 1998; see Chapter 14). We should listen to our first impressions but not be imprisoned by them.

Cognitive economy saves us a lot of work, but we need the scientific method to make sure that our drive to economize doesn't mislead us. That's why the scientific method calls for such valuable safeguards as (1) falsifiability, (2) studies that seek to *disconfirm* rather than confirm our hypotheses, (3) generalizability across many participants rather than (or in addition to) case studies, (4) representative and ideally randomly selected participants, and (5) random assignment of participants into groups. These basic elements of the scientific method protect us from the consequences of heuristics and biases, such as confirmation bias, representativeness, availability, and ignoring base rates.

Thousands of people refused to fly in the months following the terrorist attacks on September 11, 2001. The availability heuristic led people to overestimate the probability of dying onboard a hijacked airplane. Ironically, more people died in car accidents as a result.

PROBLEM SOLVING: MORE THINKING HURDLES

Keeping track of when heuristics are and aren't useful is challenging enough. But still other aspects of our cognitive functioning put us at a disadvantage when making decisions and solving complicated problems. **Problem solving** is generating a cognitive strategy to accomplish a goal. We often encounter four hurdles when solving problems: salience of surface similarities, mental sets, functional fixedness, and context and consequence effects.

Salience of Surface Similarities. Salience refers to how attention-grabbing something is. We tend to focus our attention on the surface-level (superficial) properties of a problem, such as the topic of an algebra word problem, and to try to solve problems in the same way we solved problems that exhibited similar surface characteristics. When one algebra word problem calls for subtraction and another calls for division, the fact that they both deal with trains isn't going to help us. Ignoring the surface features of a problem and focusing on the underlying reasoning needed to solve it can be challenging.

problem solving
generating a cognitive strategy to accomplish a goal

The two problems in **Table 8.6** involve the same reasoning processes, so learning how to solve one problem provides us with the solution to the other. Yet in one study, only 20 percent of students who saw the fortress problem figured out how to solve the tumor problem (Gick & Holyoak, 1983). When researchers told students that the fortress problem could help them solve the tumor problem, their success shot up to 92 percent. The students hadn't noticed that the fortress solution was relevant. One way to combat this tendency is to practice solving multiple problems that require the same reasoning (so they should be solved the same way) but possess different surface features. Comparison of the commonalities across these different problems can help us focus on the problem's structure (Loewenstein, Thompson, & Gentner, 1999; Markman & Gentner, 1993).

Table 8.6 Fortress and Tumor Problems. Students who read the first problem rarely used it to solve the second problem because the surface features (a general and a fortress versus radiation and a tumor) were too different. But when researchers encouraged students to use the fortress problem as a basis for solving the tumor problem, they usually generated the correct solution.

Problem	Description
The Fortress Problem	A small country was ruled from a strong fortress by a dictator. The fortress was situated in the middle of the country, surrounded by farms and villages. Many roads led to the fortress through the countryside. A rebel general vowed to capture the fortress. The general knew that an attack by his entire army would capture the fortress. He gathered his army at the head of one of the roads, ready to launch a full-scale direct attack. However, the general then learned that the dictator had planted mines on each of the roads. The mines were set so that small bodies of men could pass over them safely, since the dictator needed to move his troops and workers to and from the fortress. However, any large force would detonate the mines. Not only would this blow up the road, but it would also destroy many neighboring villages. It therefore seemed impossible to capture the fortress. However, the general devised a simple plan. He divided his army into small groups and dispatched each group to the head of a different road. When all was ready he gave the signal and each group marched down a different road. Each group continued down its road to the fortress so that the entire army arrived together at the fortress at the same time. In this way, the general captured the fortress and overthrew the dictator.
The Tumor Problem	Suppose you are a doctor faced with a patient who has a malignant tumor in his stomach. It is impossible to operate on the patient, but unless the tumor is destroyed, the patient will die. There is a kind of ray that can be used to destroy the tumor. If the rays reach the tumor all at once at sufficiently high intensity, the tumor will be destroyed. Unfortunately, at this intensity, the healthy tissue that the rays pass through on the way to the tumor will also be destroyed. At a lower intensity the rays are harmless to healthy tissue but they will not affect the tumor either. What type of procedure might be used to destroy the tumor with the rays and at the same time avoid destroying the healthy tissue?

(*Source:* Gick & Holyoak, 1983)

mental set
phenomenon of becoming stuck in a specific problem-solving strategy, inhibiting our ability to generate alternatives

functional fixedness
difficulty conceptualizing that an object typically used for one purpose can be used for another

Figure 8.17 Mental Set Problems.
Solve these problems by figuring out how to add and remove precise amounts of water using the jars provided. The first two problems using the same formula: Add the amount in the first jug (A), subtract the amount from the second jug (B), and then subtract the amount from the third jug (C) twice (A – B – C – C = Target amount). The third problem requires a different solution. Can you figure it out? If you're stuck, you may be experiencing a "mental set."

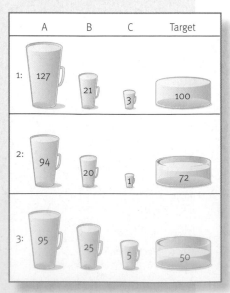

	A	B	C	Target
1:	127	21	3	100
2:	94	20	1	72
3:	95	25	5	50

Mental Sets. Once we find a workable solution that's dependable, we often get stuck in that solution mode; we have trouble generating alternatives. Psychologists term this phenomenon a **mental set.** In a classic study, participants had to solve a series of problems that required measuring out a precise amount of water by adding and subtracting water, given only three odd measuring jars (such as filling a jug with precisely 100 quarts using only a 21-quart jar, a 127-quart jar, and a 3-quart jar; see **Figure 8.17**). Participants either solved eight problems that used the same formula (A – B – C – C = Target amount) before working on a problem that used a different formula, or they solved the ninth problem without working on the first eight. Only 36 percent of participants who solved the first eight problems the same way generated the correct solution on the ninth one. In contrast, participants who solved the ninth problem first generated a correct solution 95 percent of the time (Luchins, 1946). Solving the first eight problems actually made solving the ninth more difficult, because the eight problems created a mental set from which subjects had a hard time breaking free.

Functional Fixedness. **Functional fixedness** occurs when we experience difficulty conceptualizing that an object typically used for one purpose can be used for another (German & Defeyter, 2000). That is, we become "fixated" on one conventional use for an object. One famous demonstration asked participants to figure out a way to mount a candle on a wall given only a candle, book of matches, and box of tacks, as shown in **Figure 8.18** (Duncker, 1945). Can you think of how to do it? Most of us find this problem difficult because it forces us to use conventional objects in unconventional ways. In one study, two investigators tested individuals from a rural area of Ecuador who live in a traditional nontechnological society and consequently have few expectations about the functional roles of objects. Even they displayed functional fixedness (German & Barrett, 2005).

Context and Consequence Effects.   A problem's context often influences our problem-solving approach. Our goals, the setting, and the consequences of getting the problem right or wrong can all influence what approach we take, for better or for worse. For example, whether children and adults adopt a confirming or a disconfirming strategy when testing a hypothesis—recall from Chapter 2 that a disconfirming strategy is better—depends on the consequences. If people hold a hypothesis about what made a cake taste terrible, they'll test that hypothesis by removing the offending ingredient, a disconfirming strategy. In contrast, if they hold a hypothesis about what made a cake taste delicious, they'll test the hypothesis by keeping the ingredient in, a confirming strategy (Tschirgi, 1980).

THE SCIENTIFIC METHOD DOESN'T COME NATURALLY

The song, "Doin' What Comes Natur'lly," in Irving Berlin's musical "Annie Get Your Gun" starts out, "Folks are dumb where I come from; they ain't had any learnin'. Still they're happy as can be, doin' what comes naturally." Although this song isn't exactly about the scientific method, it makes a good point. Most of the time, we're happy as clams doing what comes naturally. The scientific method isn't it (Cromer, 1992; Wolpert, 1993). The moral of the story isn't that we should change our ways entirely, because our fast and frugal thinking often serves us well.

Nevertheless, one of our major goals in this textbook is to raise awareness about how our cognitive systems can lead us astray and how we can guard against it. Such awareness can help us recognize situations in which we're vulnerable to faulty reasoning and think twice about our intuitions. When we hear on the news that vaccines cause autism or that watching violent TV turns entirely normal kids into violent monsters, we should stop to think about the information on which the media based these conclusions. When evaluating political candidates' extravagant promises ("If I'm elected, you'll all have another $5,000 in your pocketbooks by the end of the year!") or deciding whether that incredible deal on laptops ("Laptops for only $200 a piece, and they're five times faster than your home computer!") is too good to be true, we should consider whether the information was sufficient to warrant the extreme claims. When deciding whether the car we're thinking of buying is safe or the diet plan we're considering is effective, we should stop to think about the base rates instead of concentrating on anecdotes from friends. Cognitive economy has a lot going for it, but being aware of its pitfalls will make us more informed consumers of information in our everyday lives.

Figure 8.18 Functional Fixedness. A classic demonstration of functional fixedness requires participants to figure out how to mount a candle on a wall given only a candle, book of matches, and box of tacks (Duncker, 1945). To see the solution, see the upside-down figure toward the bottom of the page.

Extraordinary Claims

Answer to Figure 8.18

ASSESS YOUR KNOWLEDGE: FACT OR FICTION?

(1) Top-down processing involves drawing inferences from previous experience and applying them to current situations. (True/False)
(2) What's considered a typical member of a category varies depending on context and experience. (True/False)
(3) "Thin slicing" almost always leads to false conclusions. (True/False)
(4) Comparing problems that require similar reasoning processes but different surface characteristics can help us overcome deceptive surface similarities. (True/False)
(5) Functional fixedness is a product of Western technology-dependent society. (True/False)

Answers: (1) T (p. 343); (2) T (p. 343); (3) F (p. 344); (4) T (p. 346); (5) F (p. 346)

Think again...

How Does Language Work? (pp. 319–334)

STUDY the Learning Objectives

▶ Describe the four levels of analysis that comprise language
- To fully understand the complexity of language, we must analyze phonemes, morphemes, syntax, and extralinguistic information. These four levels work together to create meaning and transmit information effectively. Morphemes are the smallest units of meaning in language. Extralinguistic information such as tone of voice, facial expression, gestures, contextual cues, and cultural conventions all enter into how we interpret language.

▶ Discover the developmental trajectory of language acquisition in children
- Infants' babbling becomes more sophisticated over the course of their first year, as control over their vocal tracts increases. They also fine-tune their perception of phonemes over the course of the first year of listening to their native language. Children's word and syntax comprehension precedes their production of language.

▶ Compare human and nonhuman animal communication
- Most nonhuman animal communication systems involve aggression and mating displays, but little else. Attempts to teach language to nonhuman animals have been only modestly successful. Chimpanzees and African gray parrots can learn the basics of linguistic communication but learn very differently from humans. Bonobos seem to learn more like humans do but fail to exceed the proficiency level of about a 2½-year-old human.

▶ Determine how sign language in deaf individuals relates to spoken language acquisition in hearing people
- Sign languages possess the same linguistic features and complexity as spoken languages. Learning a sign language first actually facilitates acquisition of a spoken language.

▶ Identify the pros and cons of bilingualism
- Bilingual individuals typically have one dominant language. Learning two languages slows some aspects of the acquisition process but ultimately results in stronger metalinguistic skills. Children learn a second language faster and more fluently than adults. However, there's no specific critical period during which language learning must take place.

DO YOU KNOW THESE TERMS?

- ❑ anomia (p. 318)
- ❑ language (p. 319)
- ❑ phonemes (p. 320)
- ❑ morphemes (p. 320)
- ❑ syntax (p. 320)
- ❑ extralinguistic information (p. 320)
- ❑ dialects (p. 321)
- ❑ phonesthemes (p. 323)
- ❑ bilingual (p. 323)
- ❑ babbling (p.324)
- ❑ holophrases (p. 326)
- ❑ generative (p. 327)
- ❑ nativist (p. 327)
- ❑ language acquisition device (p. 327)
- ❑ social pragmatics (p. 327)
- ❑ sign language (p. 330)
- ❑ metalinguistic (p. 332)
- ❑ cryptophasia (p. 333)
- ❑ homesign (p. 334)

If you did not receive an access code to MyPsychLab with this text and wish to purchase access online, please visit www.mypsychlab.com.

By what month of pregnancy are fetuses' ears developed enough for them to detect sounds and how much do they learn about their mothers' languages and voices in utero? (p. 323)

List the four levels we use to analyze language. (p. 320)

1. _____
2. _____
3. _____
4. _____

THINK about what **You** would do . . .

A colleague is upset over an email he interpreted as sarcastic in response to a sincere email he sent to a friend. How would you explain to him which critical components are missing from email? (p. 322)

SUCCEED with **mypsychlab**

Language Learning

How do we assess infants' understanding of language? (p. 323)

WATCH

ASSESS your knowledge

1. A system of communication that combines symbols in rule-based ways to create meaning is a _____. (p. 319)

2. English contains between 40 and 45 categories of sounds, or _____. (p. 320)

3. _____ is the set of rules of a language by which we construct sentences. (p. 321)

4. A language variation used by a group of people who share geographic proximity or ethnic background is a _____. (p. 321)

5. _____ information, such as facial expressions or social context, plays a critical role in interpreting language. (p. 322).

6. Children (can/can't) learn to recognize and interpret words before they can pronounce them. (p. 325)

7. Even very young children use language in _____ ways, producing sentences or combinations of words they've never heard before. (p. 327)

8. Noam Chomsky theorized that humans possess a specific language "organ" in the brain called the _____ _____. (p. 327)

9. Unlike chimpanzees, _____ have a learning pathway that more closely resembles human learning. (p. 329)

10. Sign languages (exhibit/do not exhibit) the same features as spoken languages, such as generativity and a complex set of syntactic rules. (p. 330)

Do We Think in Words? Relation between Language and Thought (pp. 334–338)

THINK about

what You would do . . .
Why would it be important to keep in mind which country a bilingual eyewitness was in when an event took place and which language she is using to testify? (p. 337)

SUCCEED with

mypsychlab
where learning comes to life!

The Power of Words
Can our words have multiple meanings?
(p. 337)

EXPLORE

The fact that the Dani of New Guinea can perceive different color categories, despite not having terms for colors in their language, presents a challenge to what hypothesis? (p. 337)

Does Helen Keller's view of thought without language correspond more closely to the idea of linguistic determinism or linguistic relativity, and why? (p. 335)

STUDY the Learning Objectives

▶ Identify the ways in which our language may influence our thinking
• The notion that language completely determines our thinking (linguistic determinism) has little or no scientific support. However, evidence supports the idea that language can influence some aspects of our thinking (linguistic relativity).

DO YOU KNOW THESE TERMS?
❑ **covert speech** (p. 334)
❑ **linguistic determinism** (p. 334)
❑ **transcranial magnetic stimulation** (p. 336)
❑ **linguistic relativity** (p. 337)

ASSESS your knowledge

1. Watson, the founder of behaviorism, believed that thinking is simply subvocal talking, also called _____ _____. (p. 334)

2. The view that all thought is represented linguistically is called _____ _____. (p. 334)

3. Recent neuroimaging studies suggest that thought (can/can't) occur without language. (p. 336)

4. _____ _____ _____ is a neuroscience technique that can temporarily block or stimulate neural transmissions within a small area of the brain. (p. 336)

5. The most exciting thing about TMS is that it enables researchers to draw _____ conclusions. (p. 336)

6. Compared with linguistic determinism _____ _____ is a less radical perspective on how language relates to thought. (p. 337)

7. According to the Sapir-Whorf hypothesis, characteristics of _____ shape our thought process. (p. 337)

8. One case in which researchers found that language doesn't influence thought is _____ categorization. (p. 337)

9. The Dani language has words for _____ and _____ but does not have words for individual colors. (p. 337)

10. When researchers identify language-related differences in thought, it (is/isn't) easy to disentangle the influences of language from culture. (p. 337)

Reading: Recognizing the Written Word (pp. 338–341)

STUDY the Learning Objectives

▶ Describe the challenges associated with reading and reading strategies
- We generally use two reading strategies, including whole word recognition and phonetic decomposition. Whole word recognition is more efficient when reading familiar words, but phonetic decomposition is critical for less familiar words. There is no perfect one-to-one correspondence between printed letters and spoken sounds, making sounding out printed words challenging.

▶ Identify the skills required to learn to read
- Before children can begin to read, they must realize that writing is meaningful. They must also learn to recognize individual letters and figure out which printed letters tend to correspond to which sounds.

▶ Analyze the relationship between reading speed and reading comprehension
- Speed-reading courses are ineffective. Although we can learn to increase our speed as readers, reading faster than 400 words per minute seriously impairs text comprehension.

DO YOU KNOW THESE TERMS?
- ❑ **whole word recognition** (p. 338)
- ❑ **phonetic decomposition** (p. 338)

Match up the language with the direction in which it should read. (p. 339)

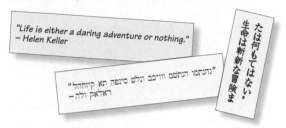

"Life is either a daring adventure or nothing." – Helen Keller

"כהתהמו הנהתשמו ווייכב ונלש סינפה תא קיזחהל" – ראלאק ולה

生命は何もてはない。 たは何もてはない。 生命は斬新的な冒険ま

English is read from ____
Hebrew is read from ____
Japanese is read from ____

a. top to bottom
b. left to right
c. right to left

mypsych lab *where learning comes to life!*

SUCCEED with

Stroop Effect
Can the automaticity of reading cause us to confuse animals with animal names? (p. 338)

Control Condition	Stroop Interference Condition
Rabbit	Red
House	Blue
Blanket	Green
Dance	Yellow
Flower	Purple
Key	Orange
Seven	Black
Dance	Yellow
House	Blue
Key	Orange
Seven	Purple
Flower	Black
Rabbit	Red
Blanket	Green

How did you perform when reading the Stroop Interference list relative to this control list? Did it convince you that reading is automatic? (p. 338)

THINK about

what You would do . . .
What would you do to assure parents worried about their youngest child being taught reading using whole word recognition when their older child was taught to read using phonetic decomposition? (p. 338)

ASSESS your knowledge

1. The Stroop task shows that reading is _____. (p. 338)

2. The average reader uses _____ to read the vast majority of printed words. (p. 338)

3. With a reading strategy called _____ _____, we sound out words by drawing correspondences between printed letters and sounds. (p. 338)

4. Children who frequently hear and recite nursery rhymes (do/don't) tend to be earlier readers. (p. 339)

5. Children must learn which _____ is right for their language. (p. 339)

6. In learning to read, children must recognize the letters of the alphabet, or _____. (p. 340)

7. Children must learn that printed letters correspond to specific _____. (p. 340)

8. There's been heated debate about whether awareness of sound-letter correspondences, known as _____, is the best strategy for teaching children to read. (p. 340)

9. Controlled studies indicate that reading faster than _____ words per minute results in comprehension rates below 50 percent. (p. 340)

10. Subvocalizing (increases/decreases) reading comprehension. (p. 341)

Thinking and Reasoning (pp. 341–347)

STUDY the Learning Objectives

▶ Identify types of cognitive economy and the pros and cons of economizing
- Cognitive economy is a necessary and valuable aspect of our cognitive functioning. We would be unable to function effectively without some way of streamlining our information-processing. Top-down processing, categorization, and

mypsych lab *where learning comes to life!*

SUCCEED with

Saving Mental Energy with a Schema
Can the brain's shortcuts make us misrepresent what we see? (p. 343)

THINK about

what You would do . . .
In a debate about whether computers should replace humans in many industries, what arguments would support the claim that humans possess critical capacities that computers lack? (pp. 341–342)

Which bias or heuristic led people to opt for traveling by car rather than by airplane in the months following the terrorist attacks on 9/11? (p. 345)

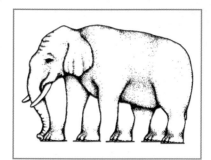

What phenomenon does this drawing of an elephant help to demonstrate? When you first looked at it, did you perceive something different from what was actually there? (p. 343)

estimating probabilities are all examples of cognitive economy. There are downsides to cognitive economy, including the reasoning errors that were outlined in Chapters 1 and 2 as obstacles to critical thinking. Heuristics and biases are often useful, but can lead us to make costly mistakes. The scientific method is designed to guard against biased thinking.

▶ Describe the challenges that humans face when attempting to solve problems or make decisions
  • Three hurdles to effective problem solving are the salience of surface similarities, mental set/functional fixedness, and context effects. The scientific method doesn't come naturally to us. Keeping in mind the principles of critical thinking outlined in this text and our vulnerability to biased reasoning can help make us better consumers of information in everyday life.

DO YOU KNOW THESE TERMS?
  ❏ **thinking** (p. 341)
  ❏ **artificial intelligence (AI)** (p. 341)
  ❏ **categories** (p. 343)
  ❏ **problem solving** (p. 345)
  ❏ **mental set** (p. 346)
  ❏ **functional fixedness** (p. 346)

ASSESS your knowledge

1. We define _____ as any mental activity or processing of information. (p. 341)

2. The field of _____ _____ investigates how people can design computers to simulate human abilities. (p. 341)

3. Our brains (contain/don't contain) fixed programs, like a computer software program. (p. 342)

4. _____ economy allows us to simplify what we need to attend to and keep the information we need to make decisions to a manageable minimum. (p. 342)

5. The way our brains often recruit information from related experiences and use it to organize information is called _____ processing. (p. 343)

6. Collections of objects, actions, characteristics, and other entities that share core properties are called _____. (p. 343)

7. A mental representation of an event that shares core features, such as eating at a restaurant, is an example of a _____. (p. 343)

8. When we generate a cognitive strategy to accomplish a specific goal, we are engaging in _____ _____. (p. 345)

9. The phenomenon of becoming entrenched in a particular problem-solving strategy that inhibits generating alternative strategies is called a _____ _____. (p. 346)

10. _____ _____ occurs when we experience difficulty conceptualizing that an object typically used for one purpose can be used for another. (p. 346)

Remember these questions from the beginning of the chapter? Think again and ask yourself if you would answer them differently based on what you now know about language, thinking, and reasoning. (For more detailed explanations, see MyPsychLab.)

▶ How much does nonverbal information, such as facial expressions, matter for communication? (p. 322)
▶ Is language an "instinct" that we're born knowing how to use? (p. 323)
▶ Is the babbling of babies meaningful? (p. 324)
▶ Do nonhuman animals have language? (p. 328)
▶ Do most deaf people learn language by lip reading? (p. 331)
▶ Are children who learn two languages at a disadvantage? (p. 332)
▶ Does speed-reading work? (p. 340)
▶ Does the mind work like a computer? (p. 341)
▶ Which are more accurate, first impressions or in-depth analyses? (p. 345)

THINKING Scientifically

Correlation vs. Causation
pp. 335, 336, 337, 340

Falsifiability pp. 327, 328, 335

Extraordinary Claims pp. 340, 347

Occam's Razor p. 328

Ruling Out Rival Hypotheses
pp. 323, 328, 332, 335

9

Intelligence and IQ Testing

Controversy and Consensus

PREVIEW

Think

First, think about these questions. Then, as you read, think again. . . .

▶ Is intelligence one ability or many?

▶ Is human intelligence related to brain size?

▶ How do psychologists measure intelligence?

▶ Are IQ scores stable over time?

▶ Do IQ tests predict anything useful?

▶ Is IQ genetically influenced?

▶ What environmental factors contribute to IQ?

▶ Are there sex and race differences in mental abilities?

▶ Are IQ tests biased against certain minority groups?

▶ Does behaving intelligently involve more than IQ?

▶ Are all intelligent people creative, and are all creative people intelligent?

What would it take to get your face on a piece of German currency? Being a brilliant mathematician would probably help. At least it did the trick for Karl Friedrich Gauss (1777–1855).

Gauss, a great German mathematician, bears two intriguing connections to the concept of intelligence. First, he was the first to come up with the concept of the "bell curve," or normal distribution. Today, we sometimes refer to the bell curve as the "Gaussian distribution" in honor of his mathematical insights. As we'll discover, this statistical concept has played an important—and immensely controversial—role in the history of intelligence and intelligence testing. This simple curve does a surprisingly good job of describing how people differ in their scores on intelligence tests. Yet it's also triggered a bitter debate about the place of intelligence in modern life.

Second, Gauss was an undisputed genius. Historians have estimated his **intelligence quotient**—or IQ—at an astonishing 180, perhaps even higher. As we'll soon discover, the IQ is a systematic means of quantifying differences among people in their intelligence, with the average person's IQ typically falling somewhere around 100. Gauss's extraordinary accomplishments underscore the soaring heights that human intelligence can reach. Yet they also raise fascinating and mysterious questions about the origins of intelligence, and even about what intelligence is.

Like many other geniuses, Gauss was a *child prodigy:* an individual who displays astounding intellectual achievements at an early age (Morelock & Feldman, 1993). By the time he was about 2 years old, he had taught himself reading and basic arithmetic. At age 3, he caught a calculation error that his father had made when adding up his family's finances. At age 10, his schoolteacher asked his class to add up all of the numbers from 1 to 100. While his classmates were kept busy for half an hour, Gauss stunned his teacher by coming up with the correct answer within a matter of seconds (Hayes, 2006). Gauss immediately recognized a shortcut around this laborious problem: He combined pairs of numbers at both "ends" from 1 to 100: 1+100, 2+99, 3+98, 4+97, and on and on. He noticed that each pair summed to 101 and that there were 50 of these pairs, so the answer was 101 multiplied by 50, which is 5050. By age 18, Gauss was already discovering complex mathematical proofs that have stood the test of time. Later in life, he made profoundly important and enduring contributions to electricity, physics, astronomy, and mathematics—including the discovery of his famed bell curve (Dunnington, 1955).

How did Gauss become a genius? We don't know. Both of his parents were poor and uneducated, and neither was distinguished in terms of exceptional intellect. Gauss was also an intensely private individual whom others viewed as cold, even arrogant (Hall, 1970). But we don't know how or even if his personality molded his intellectual accomplishments. Nor do we know what mental raw ingredients set Gauss apart from the rest of us mere mortals. Was it his astonishing speed of processing, his ability to think abstractly, his capacity to catch on quickly to new concepts, his intense intellectual drive, or a combination of all four? Or was it something else? These unresolved questions strike to the heart of what we don't know about intelligence.

Genius Karl Friedrich Gauss, who originated the bell curve, was featured on German currency (prior to Germany's adoption of the Euro as its currency). Note the bell curve to the left of his portrait.

What Is Intelligence? Definitional Confusion

As we learned in the Prologue, one of the problems that renders psychology so challenging—and at times exasperating—is the lack of clear-cut definitions for many of its concepts. No area of psychology illustrates this ongoing challenge better than the field of

intelligence quotient (IQ)
systematic means of quantifying differences among people in their intelligence

intelligence. Even today, psychologists can't agree on the precise definition of intelligence (Sternberg, 2003; Sternberg & Detterman, 1986).

SPECIAL CONSIDERATIONS IN INTERPRETING INTELLIGENCE RESEARCH

Before proceeding, a word of warning: Many people experience strong negative emotional reactions to certain aspects of intelligence research. That's understandable. For example, the idea that genes play a substantial role in intelligence makes some of us feel uncomfortable. The idea that genes could play a role in differences in intelligence between sexes or across ethnic groups makes many of us feel even more uncomfortable.

When discussing the intense scientific and ethical controversies surrounding intelligence, we must try to avoid *emotional reasoning,* or the affect heuristic (see Chapter 1), the tendency to judge the validity of an idea by our emotional reactions to it. Just because some of the ideas we'll encounter regarding intelligence may make us feel uneasy or even angry doesn't mean we should dismiss them out of hand. Difficult as it may be, we must try to evaluate these issues objectively and with an open mind to scientific evidence.

Even though not all psychologists agree about what intelligence is, one thing is clear: The way we *think* about intelligence matters. Carol Dweck (2002, 2006) showed that people who believe that intelligence is a fixed entity that doesn't change tend to take fewer academic risks, such as enrolling in challenging classes. According to Dweck, they think, "If I do really poorly in a class, it probably means I'm stupid, and I can't do anything about that." After failing on a problem, they tend to become discouraged and give up, probably because they assume they can't boost their intelligence. In contrast, people who believe that intelligence is a flexible process that can increase over time tend to take more academic risks; they think, "If I do really poorly in a class, I can still do better next time." They tend to persist after failing on a problem, probably because they believe that effort can pay off. Beliefs matter.

Edwin Boring (1923), whom we met in the Prologue, discovered an easy away around the nagging question of what intelligence is. According to *Boring's dictum,* intelligence is whatever intelligence tests measure. Yes, it's that simple. Some modern psychologists have embraced this definition, which lets us off the hook from having to figure out what intelligence is. Yet because this definition sidesteps the central question of what makes some people smarter than others—or whether some people are really smarter than others across the board—it doesn't really get us all that far. The definition of intelligence must go beyond Boring's dictum. With that point in mind, let's examine the most influential attempts to define and understand intelligence.

The work of Carol Dweck suggests that our conceptions of intelligence predict our performance on academic tasks— and our reactions to academic failure.

INTELLIGENCE AS SENSORY CAPACITY: OUT OF SIGHT, OUT OF MIND

Sir Francis Galton (1822–1911) was a cousin of the great biologist Charles Darwin, codeveloper of the theory of evolution by natural selection. Galton was himself something of a genius in many ways. Like Gauss, he was a child prodigy; he also learned to read by about age 2. Galton invented a host of techniques that are still in widespread use today: the method of studying twins to determine the genetic bases of traits, the correlation as a measure of statistical association (see Chapter 2), and criminal fingerprinting. Perhaps as a consequence of his accomplishments, he was fascinated by the question of what makes some people especially smart.

Galton proposed a radical hypothesis: Intelligence is the by-product of sensory capacity. He reasoned that most knowledge first comes through the senses, especially vision and hearing. Therefore, he assumed, people with superior sensory capacities, like better eyesight, should acquire more knowledge than other people.

For a 6-year period beginning in 1884, Galton set up a laboratory at a museum in London, England. There, he administered a battery of seventeen sensory tests to more than 9,000 visitors (Gillham, 2001). He measured just about everything under the sun

Galton's laboratory on display at the International Health Exhibition in London in 1884. The exhibit later moved to the South Kensington Museum where, between 1886 and 1890, thousands of visitors took a battery of seventeen sensory tests.

relating to sensory ability: the highest and lowest pitch of sounds that individuals could detect; their reaction times to various stimuli; their ability to discriminate the weights of similar objects; and their capacity to differentiate the smells of various roses. Galton's student James McKeen Cattell shortly thereafter imported Galton's tests to America, administering them to thousands of college students in an effort to find out what they were measuring. Like his teacher, Cattell assumed that intelligence was a matter of raw sensory ability.

Yet later research showed that different measures of sensory capacities, like the ability to distinguish similar sounds from one another or similar colors from one another, are only weakly correlated (Acton & Schroeder, 2001): That is, one exceptional sense, like heightened hearing, doesn't bear much of a relation to other exceptional senses, like heightened vision. Nor are measures of sensory ability highly correlated with assessments of overall intelligence (Li, Jordanova, & Lindenberger, 1998). These findings falsify Galton's and Cattell's claim that intelligence equals sensory ability. Whatever intelligence is, it's more than just good eyesight, hearing, smell, and taste. A moment's reflection reveals that this must be the case: According to Galton, Helen Keller, the blind and deaf woman who became a brilliant author and social critic (see Chapter 8), would almost by definition have been mentally retarded. Galton's definition can't be right.

Still, as we'll learn later, Galton may have been onto something. Recent research suggests that some forms of sensory ability relate modestly to intelligence, although these two concepts clearly aren't identical.

INTELLIGENCE AS ABSTRACT THINKING

Early in the last century, the French government wanted to find a way to identify children in need of special educational assistance. In 1904, the Minister of Public Instruction in Paris tapped two individuals, Alfred Binet (pronounced "Bee-NAY") and Henri Simon (pronounced "See-MOAN"), to develop an objective psychological test that would separate "slower" learners from other children without having to rely on the subjective judgments of teachers.

Binet and Simon experimented with many different items designed to distinguish students whom teachers perceived as plodding learners from other students. In 1905, they developed what most psychologists today regard as the first **intelligence test,** a diagnostic tool designed to measure overall thinking ability.

Binet and Simon's items were remarkably diverse in content. They involved naming objects, generating the meanings of words, drawing pictures from memory, completing incomplete sentences ("The man wrote a letter using his ___"), determining the similarities between two objects ("In what way are a dog and a rose alike?"), and constructing a sentence from three words ("woman," "house," and "walked"). Despite the superficial differences among these items, they had one thing in common that Binet and Simon (1905) recognized: *higher mental processes.* These processes included reasoning, understanding, and judgment (Siegler, 1992). In this respect, their items differed sharply from those of Galton, which had relied solely on sensation. Virtually all items on modern intelligence tests have followed in Binet and Simon's footsteps.

Intelligence theorists later built on Binet and Simon's notions. Indeed, most experts agree that whatever intelligence is, it has something to do with **abstract thinking:** the capacity to understand hypothetical concepts, rather than concepts in the here-and-now (Gottfredson, 1997; Sternberg, 2003). In 1921, a panel of fourteen American experts generated a list of definitions of intelligence. They didn't succeed in hammering out a single definition, but they mostly agreed that intelligence consists of the abilities to:

- reason abstractly
- learn to adapt to novel environmental circumstances
- acquire knowledge
- benefit from experience

Interestingly, research on how laypeople view intelligence yields similar conclusions, at least in the United States. Most Americans view intelligence as consisting of the capacity to reason well and reason quickly ("to think on one's feet"), as well as to amass large

Falsifiability

Ken Jennings *(top),* who broke the record for winnings on the game show *Jeopardy!,* would be regarded as especially intelligent by most individuals in Western culture. In contrast, a village elder *(bottom)* who can impart wisdom would be regarded as especially intelligent by many individuals in Chinese culture.

intelligence test
diagnostic tool designed to measure overall thinking ability

abstract thinking
capacity to understand hypothetical concepts

amounts of knowledge in brief periods of time (Sternberg, Conway, Ketron, & Bernstein, 1981). In contrast, in some non-Western countries, laypersons view intelligence as reflecting people's wisdom and judgment more than their intellectual brilliance (Baral & Das, 2003). For example, in China people tend to view intelligent individuals as those who perform actions for the greater good of the society and are humble (Yang & Sternberg, 1997). Geniuses who toot their own horns might be showered with fame and fortune in the United States, but they might be viewed as hopeless braggarts in the eyes of many Chinese.

THAT CONTROVERSIAL LITTLE LETTER: *g*

There was one other crucial way that Binet and Simon's items differed from Galton's. When researchers looked at the correlations among these items, they were in for a surprise. Even though Binet and Simon's items differed enormously in content, the correlations among them were all positive: People who got one item correct were more likely than chance to get the others correct. Admittedly, most of these correlations were fairly low, say .2 or .3 (as we learned in Chapter 2, correlations have a maximum of 1.0), but they were almost never zero or negative. Interestingly, this finding has held up with items on modern IQ tests (Alliger, 1988; Carroll, 1993). Given that some of Binet and Simon's items assessed vocabulary, others assessed spatial ability, and still others assessed verbal reasoning, this finding was puzzling.

The phenomenon of positive correlations among intelligence test items caught the attention of psychologist Charles Spearman (1927). To account for these correlations, Spearman hypothesized the existence of a single common factor across all these aspects—**g**, or **general intelligence**—that accounted for the overall differences in intellect among people. All intelligence test items are positively correlated, he thought, because they reflect the influence of overall intelligence.

Spearman wasn't sure what produces individual differences in *g*, although he speculated that it has something to do with "mental energy" (Sternberg, 2003). For Spearman, *g* corresponds to the strength of our mental engines. Just as some cars possess more powerful engines than others, he thought, some people have more "powerful"—more effective and efficient—brains than others. They have more *g*.

The meaning of *g* remains exceedingly controversial (Gould, 1981; Herrnstein & Murray, 1994; Jensen, 1998). All because of this little letter, some intelligence researchers are barely on speaking terms. Why? Because *g* implies that some people are just plain smarter than others. Many people find this view distasteful, because it smacks of elitism. Later in the chapter, we'll revisit the controversies swirling around *g* in the context of possible sex and race differences in intelligence.

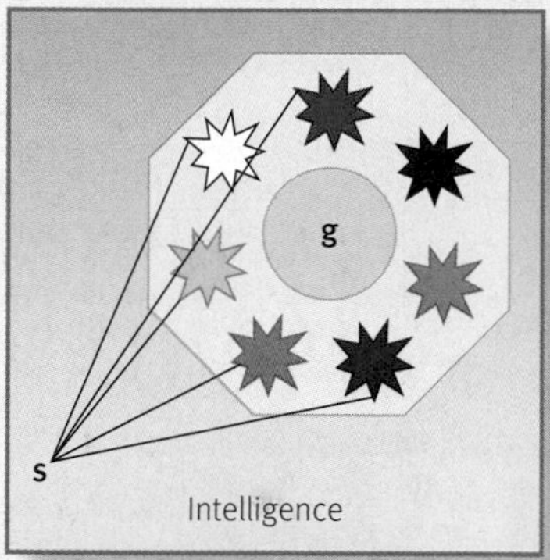

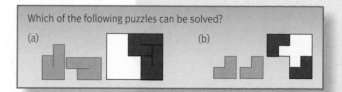

Figure 9.1 shows an octagon-shaped schematic.

Figure 9.1 Schematic of Spearman's Model of *g*. Spearman's model of intelligence posits the existence of *g* (general intelligence) along with specific factors (*s*).

g (general intelligence)
hypothetical factor that accounts for overall differences in intellect among people

s (specific abilities)
particular ability level in a narrow domain

APPLY YOUR THINKING

Spearman explained the presence of positive correlations among all IQ test items by hypothesizing the existence of *g*. What are some other explanations for this finding?

Spearman didn't believe that *g* tells the whole story about intelligence. For every intelligence test item, Spearman (1927) also proposed the existence of a factor called *s* or **specific abilities** that are unique to each item, as shown in **Figure 9.1**. That is, according to Spearman, how well we perform on a given mental task depends not only on our general smarts (*g*), but also on our particular skills in narrow domains (*s*). For example, our ability to solve the spatial problem in **Figure 9.2** is due not only to our general problem-solving ability but to our specific talents with spatial tests, tasks examining the location of objects in physical space. Even if we're really smart—high in overall *g*—we might flunk this item because we have a specific deficiency when it comes to spatial problems. That deficiency may mean

Which of the following puzzles can be solved?
(a)   (b)

Figure 9.2 Spatial Task. Try it! For each of the two puzzles shown, try to fit the yellow shapes into the white space to complete the red figure (*Source:* Smith, 2001).

that we're inherently not adept at spatial tasks or that we haven't had much experience with them.

FLUID AND CRYSTALLIZED INTELLIGENCE

Later researchers found that Spearman's *g* wasn't as uniform as he'd believed (Carroll, 1993; Vernon, 1971). They discovered that some intelligence test items relate more highly to each other than do other items: These items form clumps. Among these investigators were Raymond Cattell (no relation to James McKeen Cattell) and John Horn, both of whom distinguished fluid from crystallized intelligence.

Fluid intelligence refers to the capacity to learn new ways of solving problems. We rely on our fluid intelligence the first time we try to solve a puzzle we've never seen or the first time we try to operate a type of vehicle, like a motorcycle, we've never driven. In contrast, **crystallized intelligence** refers to the accumulated knowledge of the world we acquire over time (Cattell, 1971; Horn, 1994). We rely on our crystallized intelligence to answer questions such as "What's the capital of Italy?" or "How many justices sit on the U.S. Supreme Court?" According to Cattell and Horn, knowledge from newly learned tasks "flows" into our long-term memories, "crystallizing" into lasting knowledge (**Figure 9.3**). Most modern researchers don't believe that the existence of fluid and crystallized intelligence undermines the existence of *g*. They view them as "facets" or more specific aspects of *g* (Messick, 1992).

There's some evidence for the fluid–crystallized distinction. Fluid abilities are more likely to decline with age than are crystallized abilities (see Chapter 10). In fact, some researchers have found that crystallized abilities increase with age, including old age (Salthouse, 1996; Schaie, 1996). In addition, fluid abilities are more highly related to *g* than crystallized abilities (Blair, 2006; Gustafsson, 1988). This finding suggests that of the two abilities, fluid intelligence may better capture the power of the "mental engine" to which Spearman referred.

MULTIPLE INTELLIGENCES: DIFFERENT WAYS OF BEING SMART

Up to this point, we've been talking about "intelligence" as though it were one and only one overarching intellectual ability. But since at least the 1930s, some psychologists have argued for the existence of **multiple intelligences:** different domains of intellectual skill (Thurstone, 1938). According to them, the concept of *g* is wrong, or at least incomplete. These psychologists maintain that we can't simply say that Sally is smarter than Bill, because there are many ways of being smart (Guilford, 1967).

Frames of Mind. Howard Gardner's (1983, 1999) theory of multiple intelligences has been enormously influential in educational practice and theory over the past two decades. According to Gardner, there are numerous "frames of mind," or different ways of thinking about the world. Each frame of mind is a different and fully independent intelligence in its own right.

Gardner (1983) outlined a number of criteria for determining whether a mental ability is a separate intelligence. Among other things, he maintained researchers must demonstrate that different intelligences can be isolated from one another in studies of people with brain damage; people with damage to a specific brain region must show deficits in one intelligence, but not others. In addition, Gardner argued that different intelligences should be especially pronounced in people with exceptional talents. For example, Gardner believed that the presence of *autistic savants*, about whom we learned in Chapter 7, provides support for the existence of multiple intelligences. These individuals show remarkable abilities in one or two narrow domains, such as knowing the precise batting averages of all active baseball players, but not in most other domains. Gardner also suggested that different intelligences should make sense from an evolutionary standpoint: They should help organisms survive or make it easier for them to meet future mates.

Fluid IQ

Crystallized IQ

Figure 9.3 Knowledge "Flowing" into a Flask. According to Cattell and Horn's model, there are two kinds of intelligence, fluid and crystallized. Fluid intelligence "flows" into crystallized intelligence over time.

(a)

(b)

(c)

According to Gardner, individuals vary in the types of intelligence at which they excel. (a) Martin Luther King Jr. was a great orator with high linguistic (and probably interpersonal) intelligence; (b) Sarah McLachlan is a musician with renowned musical intelligence; and (c) professional tennis player Serena Williams has impressive bodily-kinesthetic intelligence.

fluid intelligence
capacity to learn new ways of solving problems

crystallized intelligence
accumulated knowledge of the world acquired over time

multiple intelligences
idea that people vary in their ability levels across different domains of intellectual skill

Gardner (1999) proposed eight different intelligences ranging from linguistic and spatial to musical and interpersonal, as described in **Table 9.1.** He's also tentatively proposed the existence of a ninth intelligence, called *existential* intelligence: the ability to grasp deep philosophical ideas, like the meaning of life.

Table 9.1 Howard Gardner's Multiple Intelligences.

Intelligence Type	Characteristics of High Scorers
Linguistic	Speak and write well
Logico-mathematical	Use logic and mathematical skills to solve problems, such as scientific questions
Spatial	Think and reason about objects in three-dimensional space
Musical	Perform, understand, and enjoy music
Bodily-kinesthetic	Manipulate the body in sports, dance, or other physical endeavors
Interpersonal	Understand and interact effectively with others
Intrapersonal	Understand and possess insight into self
Naturalistic	Recognize, identify, and understand animals, plants, and other living things

Gardner's model has inspired thousands of teachers to tailor their lesson plans around children's individual profiles of multiple intelligences, an effort with which Gardner has said he isn't entirely comfortable (Willingham, 2004). For example, in a class of students with high levels of bodily-kinesthetic intelligence, but low levels of logico-mathematical intelligence, a teacher might encourage students to learn arithmetic problems, like $3 + 4 = 7$, by dividing them into groups of 3 and 4, having them stand up in front of the class, and all join hands to form a bigger group of 7.

Yet this approach may not be a good idea. After all, if a child has a weakness in a specific skill domain, like vocabulary or mathematics, it may make more sense to try to teach "to" that domain rather than "away" from it. Otherwise, we may allow his already poor skills to decay, much like a weak muscle we elect not to exercise.

The scientific reaction to Gardner's model has been mixed. All researchers agree with Gardner that we vary in our intellectual strengths and weaknesses. Gardner also deserves credit for highlighting the point that intelligent people aren't all smart in the same way. But much of Gardner's model is vague and difficult to test. In particular, it's not clear why certain mental abilities, but not others, qualify as multiple intelligences. According to Gardner's criteria, there should probably also be "humor" and "memory" intelligences (Willingham, 2004). Or, given Gardner's emphasis on evolutionary adaptiveness, why not "romantic" intelligence, the ability to attract sexual partners? It's also not clear that all of Gardner's "intelligences" are genuinely related to intelligence. Some, such as bodily-kinesthetic intelligence, seem much closer to talents that depend heavily on nonmental abilities, like athletic skills (Scarr, 1985; Sternberg, 1988).

Moreover, because Gardner hasn't developed formal tests to measure his intelligences, his model is virtually impossible to falsify (Klein, 1998). In particular, there's no good evidence that his multiple intelligences are truly independent, as he claims (Lubinski & Benbow, 1995). If measures of these intelligences were all positively correlated, that could suggest that they're all manifestations of *g*, just as Spearman argued. Even research on autistic savants doesn't clearly support Gardner's model, because autistic savants tend to score higher on measures of general intelligence than do other autistic individuals (Miller, 1999). This finding suggests that their highly specialized abilities are due at least partly to *g*.

The Triarchic Model. Like Gardner, Robert Sternberg has argued that there's more to intelligence than *g*. Sternberg's (1983, 1988) **triarchic model** posits the existence of three largely distinct intelligences (see **Figure 9.4**).

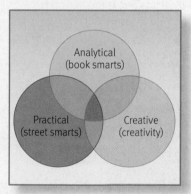

Figure 9.4 Sternberg's Triarchic Model of Intelligence. Sternberg's model proposes three kinds of intelligence: analytical, practical, and creative.

Falsifiability

triarchic model
model of intelligence proposed by Robert Sternberg positing three distinct types of intelligence: analytical, practical, and creative

It's your second year as a manager in a company in the communications industry. You head a department of about 30 people. The evaluation of your first year on the job has been generally favorable. Performance ratings for your department are at least as good as they were before you took over, and perhaps even a little better. You have two assistants. One is quite capable. The other just seems to go through the motions and has been of little real help. You believe that although you are well-liked, there is little that would distinguish you in the eyes of your superiors from the nine other managers at the same level in your company.

Your goal is quick promotion to the top of the company. The following is a list of things you are considering doing in the next 2 months. You can't do them all. Rate the importance of each activity (from 1 being the highest, 5 being the lowest) as a means of attaining your goal.

____ (a) Find a way to get rid of the "dead wood" in your company; that is, the unhelpful assistant and a few others.

____ (b) Participate in a series of panel discussions to be shown on local public television.

____ (c) Find ways to make sure your superiors are aware of your accomplishments.

____ (d) Try to better match the work that needs to be done with the strengths and weaknesses of your employees.

____ (e) Write an article on productivity for your company newsletter.

Figure 9.5 Sample Item from Test of Practical Intelligence (Item for Business Managers). According to Robert Sternberg, items assessing practical intelligence, like this one, predict real-world behaviors that standard IQ items don't. (*Source:* Adapted from Wagner & Sternberg, 1986)

Correlation vs. Causation

Being a successful politician probably requires a certain degree of practical intelligence, as Illinois Democratic Senator Barak Obama (here chatting pleasantly with Republican Karl Rove) demonstrates.

(1) *Analytical intelligence:* the ability to reason logically. In essence, analytical intelligence is "book smarts." It's the kind of intelligence we need to do well on traditional intelligence tests and standardized exams. According to Sternberg, this form of intelligence is closely related to *g*. But it's only one component of intelligence, and not necessarily the most crucial. Indeed, Sternberg has long complained about a "*g*-ocentric" view of intelligence, one in which school-related smarts is the only kind of intelligence that psychologists value (Sternberg & Wagner, 1993).

(2) *Practical intelligence:* also called "tacit intelligence"; the ability to solve real-world problems, especially those involving other people. In contrast to analytical intelligence, this form of intelligence is akin to "street smarts." It's the kind of smarts we need to "size up" people we've just met or figure out how to get ahead on the job. Practical intelligence also relates to what some researchers call *social intelligence,* or the capacity to understand others (Guilford, 1967). Sternberg and his colleagues have developed measures of practical intelligence to assess how well employees and bosses perform in business settings, how well soldiers perform in military settings, and so on (see **Figure 9.5**).

(3) *Creative intelligence:* also called "creativity"; our ability to come up with novel and effective answers to questions. It's the kind of intelligence we need to find new and effective solutions to problems, like composing an emotionally moving poem or exquisite piece of music. Sternberg argues that practical and creative intelligences predict outcomes, like job performance, that analytical intelligence doesn't (Sternberg & Wagner, 1993; Sternberg, Wagner, Williams, & Horvath, 1995).

Our intuitions tell us that these three types of intellect don't always go hand-in-hand. We can all think of people who are extremely book smart but who possess all of the social skills of a block of concrete. Similarly, we can think of people who have high levels of street smarts but who do poorly on school-related tests.

Yet, such anecdotal examples have their limitations. Indeed, many scientists have questioned the bases of Sternberg's claims. In particular, Sternberg hasn't demonstrated convincingly that practical intelligence is independent of *g* (Gottfredson, 2003; Jensen, 1993). Like crystallized intelligence, it may merely be one specialized subtype of *g*. Furthermore, Sternberg's work-related measures of practical intelligence may actually be measures of job knowledge. Not surprisingly, people who know the most about a job tend to perform it the best (Schmidt & Hunter, 1993). Moreover, the causal direction of this correlation isn't clear. Although more practical knowledge may lead to better job performance, better job performance may lead to more practical knowledge (Brody, 1992).

Thus, the concept of multiple intelligences remains controversial. Unquestionably, we all possess different intellectual strengths and weaknesses, but it's not clear that they're as independent of each other as Gardner and Sternberg assert. So there may still be a general intelligence dimension after all.

Revisiting Karl Friedrich Gauss, whom we met at the beginning of this chapter, we can see how Spearman, on the one hand, and Gardner and Sternberg, on the other, would conceptualize his genius. Spearman would have viewed Gauss as possessing extremely high *g*. Even though Gauss excelled at math, physics, and other "hard" sciences, Spearman would probably have guessed that Gauss was above average in language and other skills. In contrast, Gardner and Sternberg, while acknowledging that Gauss had remarkable analytical powers, might emphasize that he appeared to possess poor social skills and to be below average in interpersonal (Gardner) or practical (Sternberg) intelligence.

> **APPLY YOUR THINKING**
> Is Spearman's concept of *g* incompatible with the theory of multiple intelligences?
> Why or why not?

NEW FRONTIERS

How Aware Are We of Our Intellectual Limitations?

Effective functioning in everyday life hinges crucially on our ability to gauge our intellectual limitations. If we enroll in an advanced physics course for which we have little background knowledge or aptitude, the results could be disastrous. If we're an inexperienced pilot and overestimate our capacity to navigate a plane in hazardous weather, the results could be fatal. Knowing what we are—and aren't—good at is terribly important for our effective functioning, even our survival.

Yet there's good reason to believe that most of us don't know much about our intellectual capacities: Self-estimates of IQ correlate only .2 to .3 with objective measures of intelligence (Hansford & Hattie, 1982). Making matters more complicated, recent evidence suggests that people with poor cognitive skills are especially likely to overestimate their intellectual abilities, a phenomenon called the *double curse of incompetence* (Dunning, Heath, & Suls, 2004; Kruger & Dunning, 1999). This curse may explain why some people perform poorly in school and on the job, even though they're convinced they're performing well. It may also explain the embarrassing behavior of our Uncle Ernie, who keeps telling jokes that aren't funny—and keeps laughing at them (Goode, 1999).

Although it's probably going too far to proclaim that "ignorance is bliss," there may be a kernel of truth to the notion that knowing our intellectual limitations makes us more keenly aware of what we don't know. Conversely, not knowing our intellectual limitations may render us overconfident (see Chapter 2) in our knowledge (Kruger & Dunning, 1999). For example, undergraduates who scored in the bottom 25 percent on a psychology exam walked out of the exam certain they'd done better than their average classmates (Dunning, Johnson, Ehrlinger, & Kruger, 2003). Similarly, members of debate teams who scored in the bottom 25 percent of a tournament thought they were better than most other teams (Ehrlinger, Johnson, Banner, Dunning, & Kruger, 2004). The message is clear: We shouldn't necessarily trust our intuitions about how well we've performed. If our abilities in a domain are weak, we're often the last to know about it.

Researchers are still debating how to interpret these findings (Krueger & Mueller, 2002). One possibility is that *metacognitive skills* play a key role in the double curse of incompetence (Koriat & Bjork, 2005). Metacognition refers to knowledge of our own knowledge (see Chapters 8 and 9). People with poor metacognitive skills in a given domain may overestimate their performance, because they don't know what they don't know (Sinkavich, 1995). Ironically, the best means of improving these students' performance may be to help them become *less* confident of their knowledge, in part by providing them with crystal-clear feedback about what they do and don't know (Dunning et al., 2004). Such feedback may allow them to adjust their perceived knowledge to their actual knowledge.

The layperson's stereotype of the alien consistently features a large head and large eyes, presumably indicators of advanced intelligence. Why?

fictoid

Myth: Albert Einstein had dyslexia.

Reality: Scores of popular psychology sources, including many organizations for dyslexia, claim that Albert Einstein suffered from this learning disability, which is marked by difficulties with word recognition and reading in the absence of other intellectual deficits. Although there's some anecdotal but inconsistent evidence that Einstein was an abnormally late talker, there's no good evidence that he had dyslexia or any other learning disability (Thomas, 2004).

BIOLOGICAL BASES OF INTELLIGENCE

One popular notion about intelligence is that it's related positively to brain size. We speak of smart people as "brainy" or having "lots of marbles upstairs." When researchers have asked people to draw pictures of aliens—who supposedly have high levels of extraterrestrial "intelligence"—they've found that depictions of these otherworldly creatures share surprisingly similar features, like big heads, big eyes, and tiny bodies (Blackmore, 1998).

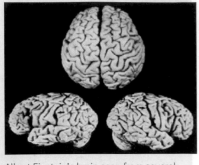

Albert Einstein's brain seen from several angles. His brain was no larger than average, although it differed in interesting ways from normal brains.

Correlation vs. Causation

Replicability

Replicability

It's almost as though large heads—and large brains—are central to our stereotype of intelligent creatures, whether they inhabit Earth or some faraway planet. Galton, who equated sensory perception with intelligence, would surely have been delighted that we perceive intelligent aliens as possessing big eyes! But to what extent is intelligence related to the brain's size and efficiency?

Brain Size and Intelligence in Humans. For years, almost all psychology textbooks informed students that although brain size correlates with intelligence *across* species, it's uncorrelated with intelligence *within* species, including humans. But several studies demonstrate that brain volume, as measured by structural MRI scans (see Chapter 3), correlates positively—between .3 and .4—with measured intelligence (McDaniel, 2005; Willerman, Schultz, Rutlege, & Bigler, 1991). So when we refer to the super smart kid in class who gets 100s on all of his exams without studying as a "brain," we aren't entirely off base.

Still, we don't know whether these findings reflect a direct causal association. Perhaps bigger brains lead to higher intelligence. Or perhaps some third variable, like better nutrition before or shortly after birth, leads to both. Moreover, a correlation of less than .4 tells us that the association between brain size and intelligence is far less than perfect. For example, Albert Einstein's brain actually weighed about 1,230 grams, slightly less than the average brain. Interestingly, though, the lower part of Einstein's parietal cortex, an area that becomes active during mathematical reasoning tasks, was 15 percent wider than normal (Witelson, Kigar, & Harvey, 1999). Further complicating matters, Karl Friedrich Gauss's brain appears to have been completely normal in size and shape (Wittman, Frahm, & Haenicke, 1999).

Recent studies on brain development suggest that there may be more to the story. A study using structural MRI revealed that highly intelligent (IQs in the top 10 percent) 7-year-olds have a *thinner* cerebral cortex than other children. The cortexes of these children then thicken rapidly, peaking at about age 12 (Shaw et al., 2006). We don't yet know what these findings mean, and independent investigators haven't replicated them. But they may indicate that, like fine wines, intelligent brains take longer to mature than others.

Intelligence and the Brain in Action. Functional brain imaging studies and laboratory studies of information processing offer intriguing clues regarding what intelligence is and where in the brain it resides. Over the span of about a month, Richard Haier and his colleagues (Haier, Siegel, MacLachlan, Soderling, Lottenberg, & Buchsbaum, 1992) taught a group of eight undergraduates to play the computer video game Tetris. All subjects improved over time, and those with the highest scores on a measure of intelligence improved the most. Surprisingly, subjects with higher levels of intelligence exhibited *less* brain activity in many areas than subjects with lower levels of intelligence (Haier et al., 2005). Haier's explanation? The brains of the more intelligent students were especially efficient. Much like well-conditioned athletes who barely break a sweat while running a 5-mile race, they could afford to slack off a bit while learning the task. Admittedly, not all researchers have replicated Haier's findings (Fidelman, 1993), but they raise the possibility that intelligence in part reflects efficiency of mental processing.

Intelligence and the Brain in Reaction. When speaking loosely, we sometimes refer to people who don't seem as intelligent as other people as "slow." Psychologists have brought this folk belief to the laboratory by studying the relation of intelligence to *reaction time,* or the speed of responding to a stimulus (Jensen, 2006). Imagine being seated in front of the reaction time box shown in **Figure 9.6** (Hick, 1952), which features a semicircle of eight buttons, with lights alongside of them. On each trial, anywhere from one to eight of the lights turn on, and then one of them suddenly turns off. Your job is to hit the button next to the light that turned off, and to do so as quickly as possible. The results of numerous studies indicate that measured intelligence correlates negatively (about −.3 to −.4) with reaction time on this task (Deary, Der, & Ford, 2001; Detterman, 1987): People with higher intelligence react more quickly than other people when the light turns off. There's also evidence that this gap widens as the number of lights that turn on increases, although this finding hasn't been entirely consistent (Brody, 1992). So Galton may not have been completely wrong in believing that speed of sensory processing contributes to intelligence, although these two concepts clearly aren't identical.

Intelligence and Memory. Intelligence also bears an intimate connection to memory capacity. Many researchers have examined the relation of tasks that assess "working memory" to intelligence. As we learned in Chapter 7, this type of memory is closely related to short-term memory. A typical working memory task might require that subjects perform a test of digit span (see Chapter 7) while trying to figure out the meaning of a proverb (such as "What does the saying 'A bird in the hand is worth two in the bush mean'?"). Scores on working memory tasks are moderately correlated (about .5) with scores on intelligence tests (Ackerman, Beier, & Boyle, 2005; Engle, 2002; Kane, Honbrick, & Conway, 2005).

The Location of Intelligence. Where in the brain is intelligence located? This may seem like a silly question, as it's unlikely that a neurosurgeon can point to a specific region of the brain and say "Right there . . . that's what makes us smart." Yet intelligence is more localized to certain areas of the cortex than others. One group of investigators administered a number of reasoning tasks that are highly "*g*-loaded," meaning they're substantially related to general intelligence (see **Figure 9.7**). They found that these tasks all activated the same area: the prefrontal cortex (Duncan et al., 2000). As we saw in Chapter 3, the prefrontal cortex is intimately involved in planning and impulse control, as well as in short-term memory.

Pulling It All Together. How can we make sense of all of these findings? If there's one central theme, it's that intelligence is related to efficiency or speed of information processing (Vernon, 1987). So common sense may be partly correct: People who are quick thinkers tend to be especially intelligent. Still, the associations are far less than a perfect correlation of 1.0, which tells us that intelligence is more than quickness of thinking. These results also suggest that the capacity to recall short-term information is related to intelligence, although the causal direction of this association isn't clear.

Figure 9.6 Reaction-Time Apparatus. Psychologists have used a reaction-time box to study the relation between intelligence and response to simple stimuli. Typically, the red lights light up and then, as soon as one goes out, the participant tries as quickly as possible to press the blue button next to the unlit light.

Correlation vs. Causation

Intelligence Testing:
The Good, the Bad, and the Ugly

When Binet and Simon created the first intelligence test more than a century ago, they had no inkling that they'd alter the landscape of psychology. Yet their invention has changed how we select people for schools, jobs, and the military; it's changed schooling and social policies; and it's changed how we think about ourselves. The history of intelligence testing begins where Binet and Simon left off.

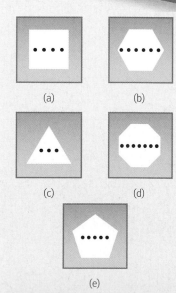

(a)   (b)

(c)   (d)

(e)

Figure 9.7 Sample Task (a Highly *g*-Loaded Item). This sample item is similar to items that researchers have identified as highly "*g*-loaded," meaning that it's a good predictor of general intelligence. In this item, one of the five choices differs from the others. Can you figure out which one it is? (Turn your page upside down to find out.)

Answer to Figure 9.7: d

Addie Lee Anderson, 87, shown August 8, 2006, at her home in Fayetteville, North Carolina, was involuntarily sterilized in 1950 by the Eugenics Board of North Carolina after the birth of her last child.

fact**oid**

The popularity of the eugenics movement of the early twentieth century led the name "Eugene" to become one of the most frequently used boys' names in the United States.

mental age
age corresponding to the average individual's performance on an intelligence test

deviation IQ
expression of a person's IQ relative to his or her same-aged peers

eugenics
movement in the early twentieth century to improve a population's genetic stock by encouraging those with good genes to reproduce, preventing those with bad genes from reproducing, or both

TWO MORE CONTROVERSIAL LETTERS: *IQ*

Shortly before World War I, German psychologist Wilhelm Stern (1912) invented the formula for the intelligence quotient, which will forever be known by two letters: *IQ*. Stern's formula for computing IQ was simple: Divide *mental age* by *chronological age* and multiply the resulting number by 100. **Mental age** is the age corresponding to the average person's performance on an intelligence test. A girl who takes an IQ test and does as well as the average 6-year-old has a mental age of 6, regardless of her actual age. Her chronological age is nothing more than her actual age. So, if a 10-year-old child does as well on an IQ test as the average 8-year-old, his IQ according to Stern's formula would be 80 (a mental age of 8 divided by a chronological age of 10, multiplied by 100). Conversely, if an 8-year-old child does as well on an IQ test as the average 10-year-old, his IQ according to Stern's formula would be 125 (a mental age of 10 divided by a chronological age of 8 multiplied by 100).

Deviation IQ: Rescuing Adults from Declining Intelligence. Some popular sources still refer to Stern's formula for computing IQ. For children and early adolescents, this formula does a respectable job of estimating intelligence. But it soon became evident that Stern's formula contains a critical flaw. Mental age scores increase progressively in childhood, but start to level out at around age 16 (Eysenck, 1994). Once we hit 16 or so, our performance on IQ test items doesn't increase by much. Because our mental age levels off but our chronological age increases with time, Stern's formula would result in everyone's IQ getting lower and lower as they get older.

That's why almost all modern intelligence researchers rely on a statistic called **deviation IQ** when computing IQ for adults (Wechsler, 1939). Basically, the deviation IQ expresses each person's IQ relative to his or her same-aged peers. An IQ of 100, which is average, means that a person's IQ is exactly typical of people of his age. An IQ of 80 is a standard amount below average for any age group, and an IQ of 120 is a standard amount above. In this way, the deviation IQ gets rid of the problem posed by Stern's formula, because it doesn't result in IQ decreasing after age 16.

THE EUGENICS MOVEMENT: MISUSES AND ABUSES OF IQ TESTING

Soon after French psychologists Binet and Simon had developed their test, researchers in other countries began translating it into various languages. Among the first was American psychologist Henry Goddard, who translated it into English in 1908. In only a matter of years, IQ testing became a booming business in the United States. It was no longer merely a vehicle for targeting schoolchildren in need of special help, however, but a means of identifying adults deemed intellectually inferior.

The IQ testing movement quickly spiraled out of control. Examiners frequently administered these tests in English to new American immigrants who barely knew the language. It's hardly surprising, then, that about 40 percent of new immigrants to the United States received IQ scores placing them in the mentally retarded—or what was then called "feebleminded"—range. Moreover, Goddard and others adapted childhood tests for use in testing adults, without fully understanding how the IQ scores applied to adults (Kevles, 1985). As a consequence, legions of adults given his tests, including prison inmates and delinquents, scored in the mentally retarded range. In one especially embarrassing episode, a psychologist administered Goddard's IQ test to the mayor of Chicago, as well as to his running mates and opponents. Almost all scored in the mentally retarded range, creating a public relations disaster for Goddard when the newspapers found out about it (Wood, Garb, & Nezworski, 2006).

Eventually, concern with the low IQs of many immigrants and even many Americans led to a social movement called **eugenics** (meaning "good genes"), a term coined by none other than Sir Francis Galton (Gillham, 2001). Eugenics was the effort to improve a population's "genetic stock" by encouraging people with "good genes" to reproduce (*positive eugenics*), by discouraging people with "bad genes" from reproducing (*negative eugenics*), or both. Galton had been a proponent of only positive eugenics, but many later psychologists advocated negative eugenics.

Although eugenics was by no means unique to America, it became immensely popular there in the early twentieth century, especially from 1910 to 1930. Dozens of universities, among them Harvard, Cornell, Columbia, and Brown, offered courses in eugenics to approximately 20,000 undergraduates (Selden, 1999). Most high school and college biology texts presented eugenics as a scientific enterprise.

Eugenics came to be associated with at least two disturbing practices. First, beginning in the 1920s, the U.S. Congress passed laws designed to restrict immigration from other countries supposedly marked by low intelligence, especially those in eastern and southern Europe (Gould, 1981).

Second, beginning in 1907, thirty-three U.S. states passed laws requiring the sterilization of low-IQ individuals (see **Figure 9.8**). Some of the surgeons who performed these sterilizations tricked their patients into believing they were undergoing emergency appendectomies (removal of their appendices) (Leslie, 2000). The assumption behind mandatory sterilization was that IQ was genetically influenced, so preventing low-IQ individuals from reproducing would halt the supposed deterioration of the population's intelligence. When all was said and done, about 66,000 North Americans, many of them African Americans and other poor minorities, underwent forced sterilizations (Reynolds, 2003). Disturbingly, the U.S. Supreme Court upheld these sterilization practices in 1927 in a famous case called *Buck v. Bell*. Ruling to uphold the sterilization of 18-year-old Carrie Buck, who'd come from two generations of purportedly "feeble-minded" ancestors, Justice Oliver Wendell Holmes wrote that "three generations of imbeciles are enough." Fortunately, the practice of sterilization slowed in the 1940s and had subsided almost completely by the early 1960s, although involuntary sterilization laws remained on the books in America for years. Virginia became the last state to repeal them in 1974.

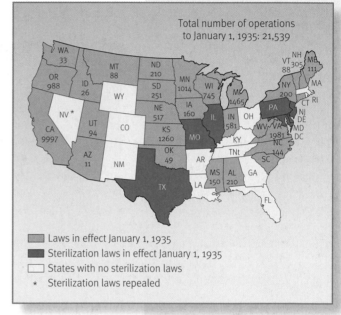

Figure 9.8 **A Sterilization Map of the United States in 1935.** As of 1935, most U.S. states had mandatory sterilization laws, a legacy of the eugenics movement, either on the books or pending. (*Source:* Dolan DNA Learning Center)

A variety of other troubling practices were perpetuated on individuals in the United States and Europe as a result of early IQ testing. In 1917, psychologist Robert Yerkes joined forces with the U.S. Army to launch an IQ testing program that helped determine who'd serve as officers and who'd serve on the front lines in battle during World War I. Not surprisingly, recent immigrants and underprivileged minorities were the most frequently relegated to hazardous duty.

We can still feel the impact of the eugenics movement today. Many people are understandably suspicious of claims regarding IQ and its genetic bases, as these claims remind them of the unethical efforts by eugenics advocates to "purge" low-IQ individuals from the gene pool. Still, we must be careful to avoid the **association fallacy** (Harris, 2000): the error of confusing a claim's validity with the people who advocate it (otherwise known as the error of "guilt by association"). It's true that many eugenics supporters were strong proponents of IQ testing and research on the genetic bases of IQ. But this fact doesn't, by itself, imply that we should dismiss the science of IQ testing or research on genetic bases of IQ. Although it's entirely appropriate to be dismayed by the tragic history of the eugenics movement in America, the two issues are logically separable.

APPLY YOUR THINKING

Is there an ethical difference between positive and negative eugenics? If so, why?

---

association fallacy
error of confusing a claim's validity with the people who advocate it

We can find dozens of informal "Test Yourself" IQ tests on the Internet, in magazines, or in self-help books. Most of these tests haven't been validated, so we shouldn't put much stock in the IQ scores they yield.

IQ TESTING TODAY

Today, the IQ test stands as one of psychology's best-known, yet most controversial, accomplishments. In 1989, the American Academy for the Advancement of Science listed the IQ test as one of the twenty greatest scientific achievements of the twentieth century (Henshaw, 2006). Whether or not we agree with this assessment, there's no question that IQ testing has been remarkably influential. Although psychologists have developed dozens of IQ tests, a mere handful have come to dominate the modern testing scene. We'll discuss these tests next, along with standardized tests like the SAT and measures of infant intelligence.

Commonly Used Adult IQ Tests. The IQ test administered most widely to assess intelligence in adults is the **Wechsler Adult Intelligence Scale,** or **WAIS** (see **Figure 9.9** as an

Wechsler Adult Intelligence Scale (WAIS) Sample Items*		
Test	**Description**	**Example**
Verbal Scale		
Information	Taps general range of information	On which continent is France?
Comprehension	Tests understanding of social conventions and ability to evaluate past experience	Why do people need birth certificates?
Arithmetic	Tests arithmetic reasoning through verbal problems	How many hours will it take to drive 150 miles at 50 miles per hour?
Similarities	Asks in what way certain objects or concepts are similar; measures abstract thinking	How are a calculator and a typewriter alike?
Digit span	Tests attention and rote memory by orally presenting series of digits to be repeated forward or backward	Repeat the following numbers backward: 2 4 3 5 1 8 6
Vocabulary	Tests ability to define increasingly difficult words	What does repudiate mean?
Performance scale		
Digit symbol	Tests speed of learning through timed coding tasks in which numbers must be associated with marks of various shapes	Shown: 1 2 3 4 Fill in: 4 2 1 3 (symbols)
Picture completion	Tests visual alertness and visual memory through presentation of an incompletely drawn figure; the missing part must be discovered and named	Tell me what is missing:
Block design	Tests ability to perceive and analyze patterns presenting designs that must be copied with blocks	Assemble blocks to match this design:
Picture arrangement	Tests understanding of social situations through a series of comic-strip-type pictures that must be arranged in the right sequence to tell a story	Put this picture in the right order: 1 2 3
Object assembly	Tests ability to deal with part/whole relationships by presenting puzzle pieces that must be assembled to form a complete object	Assemble the pieces into a complete object:

Figure 9.9 Sample Items from WAIS. Eleven of fourteen subtests of the WAIS-III, along with items similar to those on the test.
Note: For copyright reasons, we can't present the items on the actual test. (*Source:* Harcourt Assessment, Inc.)

Wechsler Adult Intelligence Scale (WAIS)
most widely used intelligence test for adults today, consisting of fourteen subtests to assess different types of mental abilities

example) (Watkins, Campbell, Nieberding, & Hallmark, 1995), now in its third version (the WAIS-III; Wechsler, 1997). Ironically, David Wechsler, a psychologist who developed this test, was a Romanian immigrant to the United States who was among those classified as feebleminded by early, flawed IQ tests. The WAIS-III consists of fourteen "subtests," or specific tasks, designed to assess mental abilities such as vocabulary, arithmetic, spatial ability, reasoning about proverbs, and general knowledge about the world. We can find sample items from eleven of the fourteen subtests in **Figure 9.9.** The WAIS-III yields three major scores: (1) an overall IQ score, (2) a verbal IQ score, and (3) a performance (non-verbal) IQ score. Verbal IQ relates primarily to crystallized intelligence, and performance IQ relates primarily to fluid intelligence.

Commonly Used Childhood IQ Tests. Two widely used IQ tests for children are the Wechsler Intelligence Scale for Children (WISC) and the Wechsler Primary and Preschool Scale of Intelligence (WPPSI; pronounced "WHIP-see"), both also in their third editions. Both measures are versions of the WAIS adapted for older children and adolescents (the WISC-III) or younger children aged $2\frac{1}{2}$ to 7 years old (the WPPSI-III) (Kaplan & Sacuzzo, 2005).

Shortly after Binet and Simon introduced their test to France, Lewis Terman of Stanford University developed a modified and translated version called the **Stanford-Binet IQ test,** which psychologists still use today. The Stanford-Binet consists of a wide variety of tasks like those Binet and Simon used, such as tests of vocabulary, memory for pictures, naming of familiar objects, repeating sentences, and following commands.

Culture-Fair IQ Tests. One major criticism of IQ tests is that they rely heavily on language. Test takers who aren't fluent in the native language may do poorly on IQ tests largely because they don't comprehend the test instructions or the questions themselves. Moreover, cultural factors can affect people's familiarity with test materials, and in turn their performance on intellectual tasks (Neisser et al., 1996). In one study, a researcher asked schoolchildren in England and Zambia (a country in southern Africa) to reproduce a series of visual patterns using both paper and pencil—a medium with which British children tend to be familiar—and wire—a medium with which Zambian children tend to be familiar. The British children did better than the Zambian children when using paper and pencil, but the Zambian children did better than the British children when using wire (Serpell, 1979).

As a consequence of these problems, psychologists have developed a variety of **culture-fair IQ tests,** which consist of abstract-reasoning items that don't depend on language (Cattell, 1949). Presumably, these tests are less influenced by cultural differences than standard IQ tests are.

Perhaps the best-known culture-fair test is Raven's Progressive Matrices, used widely in Great Britain as a measure of intelligence (Raven, Raven, & Court, 1998). As **Figure 9.10** shows, this test requires examinees to pick out the final geometrical pattern in a sequence (the matrices are "progressive" because they start off easy and become increasingly difficult). Raven's Progressive Matrices is an excellent measure of g (Neisser et al., 1996).

STANDARDIZED TESTS: WHAT DO THEY MEASURE?

The odds are high you've taken at least one, and perhaps many, standardized tests in your life. In fact, to get into college you may have endured the misery of either the Scholastic Assessment Test (SAT), once known as the Scholastic Aptitude Test, or the American College Test (ACT). The SAT now consists of three sections—Mathematics, Reading, and Writing—with the score on each ranging from 200 to 800.

Standardized Tests and IQ. Standardized tests are designed either to test overall competence in a specific domain or to predict academic success. For many years, the Educational Testing Service apparently collected data on the correlation between the SAT and IQ, but didn't release them until recently (Seligman, 2004). Until that time, we knew little or nothing about the SAT–IQ relationship. Murphy Frey and Douglas Detterman (2004) found that the SAT correlated highly (between about .7 and .8) with two standard measures of intelligence, including the Raven's Progressive Matrices. So the SAT is clearly linked to measured intelligence.

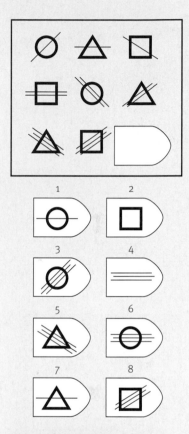

Figure 9.10 Item Similar to That on Raven's Progressive Matrices. An item similar to those in the *Raven's Progressive Matrices—Advanced Progressive Matrices.* The answer is positioned upside down at the bottom of the page. (*Source:* Harcourt Assessment, Inc., 1998)

Stanford-Binet IQ test
intelligence test based on the measure developed by Binet and Simon, adapted by Lewis Terman of Stanford University

culture-fair IQ tests
abstract reasoning items that don't depend on language and are often believed to be less influenced by cultural factors than other IQ tests

Coaching on Standardized Tests. You've probably heard of companies, such as Princeton Review or Kaplan, that prepare students for the SAT and other standardized tests. These companies charge sizable chunks of money and make some pretty lavish claims. For example, Princeton Review has guaranteed 100 point increases on the SAT, and Kaplan has asserted that more than a quarter of students improve by 170 points or more when taking the SAT a second time (Powers & Rock, 1999).

Do these courses really work? The answer isn't clear (DerSimonian & Laird, 1983), which is surprising given how long these programs have been around. Still, the evidence suggests that commercial coaching improves SAT scores only slightly, probably by 10 to 15 points on average per section (Kulik, Bangert-Drowns, & Kulik, 1984; Powers, 1993).

Are the companies deliberately exaggerating? Not necessarily. It's true that some people improve by 100 points or more after taking SAT preparation courses. But the companies are probably neglecting to consider an alternative explanation for these increases: practice effects (Shadish, Cook, & Campbell, 2002). By *practice effects,* we mean that people frequently improve on tests as a result of practice alone. So the companies may be concluding mistakenly that people who take their courses are improving *because* of these courses rather than merely *after* them. When researchers have controlled for practice effects by including a control group of people who take the SAT a second time but haven't taken an SAT preparation course, the improvements resulting from these courses has been much smaller than claimed by the companies (Powers & Rock, 1999). So if you want to gain a slight edge on the SAT or similar standardized tests, by all means consider enrolling in one of these courses, or buy some practice tests of your own. But if you're looking for a 200- or 300-point increase, you'd do best to hold onto your money.

Ruling Out Rival Hypotheses

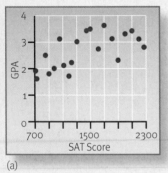

(a)

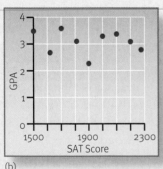

(b)

Figure 9.11 Scatterplot of Correlation between SAT Scores and College GPA. In the graph depicted in (a), SAT scores are clearly correlated with GPA. We can see an upward slant to the data points as we move from lower to higher scores. In the graph depicted in (b), the same data are depicted but only for the narrow range of higher SAT scores (1,500–2,300). As we can see, there is no clear correlation between SAT scores and GPA in this range.

PsychoMythology

Do Standardized Tests Predict Grades?

Psychologists designed the SAT, ACT, Graduate Record Exam (GRE), and other standardized tests to forecast performance in college courses. Yet the correlations between these tests and college grades are often below .5 and in a few cases close to zero (Morrison & Morrison, 1995). Moreover, although SATs and GREs tend to predict first-year grades at reasonable levels, they generally do a worse job of predicting performance in later years of college (Kuncel & Hezlett, 2007).

These low correlations have prompted many critics to conclude that the SAT and GRE aren't helpful for making predictions about grades (Oldfield, 1998; Sternberg & Williams, 1997). More than one-fourth of major liberal arts colleges in the United States no longer require the SAT, and these numbers are growing (Lewin, 2006). Ralph Nader, a consumer advocate and former presidential candidate, argued that the SAT is so invalid that it should be banned (Kaplan, 1982; Nairn, 1980).

Is Nader right? Yes and no. He's right that the SAT and GRE are highly imperfect predictors and that they don't correlate highly with future grades. But he's wrong that this fact renders the tests useless. To understand why, let's look at the graph in **Figure 9.11a.** We call this graph a *scatterplot* (see Chapter 2), because it's a plot of the correlation between two variables, in this case between SAT scores and grade point average (GPA) in college. As we can see, the SAT scores (combined across all three subtests) range from 700 to 2,300, and GPA ranges from 1.5 to almost 4.0. The correlation in this scatterplot is .65, which is fairly high. Recall from Chapter 2 that high positive correlations display a pronounced upward tilt.

But let's now look at **Figure 9.11b,** which is a close-up of the dots that are 1500 or higher on the x (horizontal) axis. As we can see, the range of SAT scores is now only between 1,500 and 2,300 combined. This range is typical of what we find at many highly competitive colleges. That's because few people with SAT scores much below 1500 combined get into these colleges. What does the correlation look like now? As we can see, it's much lower than that in Figure 9.11a; in fact, the correlation is close to zero (it's even slightly negative). The upward tilt of this correlation has clearly disappeared.

These two scatterplots illustrate a crucial phenomenon overlooked by many critics of the SAT and GRE (for example, Sternberg & Williams, 1997): restriction of range. *Restriction of range* refers to the fact that correlations tend to go down when we limit the range of scores on one or both variables (Alexander, Carson, Alliger, & Carr, 1987). To understand restriction of range, think of the relation of height to basketball playing ability. In a group of ordinary people playing a pickup basketball game on a Saturday afternoon, height will correlate highly with who scores more points. But in a game of professional basketball players, height barely matters, because almost everyone who makes it to a professional basketball team is tall.

Restriction of range helps to explain why the SAT and GRE aren't highly predictive of scores in college and graduate school: Colleges and graduate schools rarely admit low scorers. Indeed, when two researchers examined the validity of the GRE in a graduate department that admitted applicants regardless of their GRE scores, the GRE correlated highly (between .55 and .70) with measures of graduate GPA (Huitema & Stein, 1993). So when we remove restriction of range, the GRE becomes highly predictive of later grades. Restriction of range also probably accounts for why SATs and GREs are less predictive of later grades than of first-year grades. When students get to pick the classes in which they do well, they tend to obtain higher grades, thereby limiting the range of GPAs.

To return to the question we posed at the outset—Do standardized tests predict grades?—the answer is, "When we measure the full range of scores, yes, although by no means perfectly."

RELIABILITY OF IQ SCORES: IS IQ FOREVER?

We often think of people's IQ scores in much the same way we think of their social security numbers: as sticking with them for life. Joe's a 116, Maria a 130, and Bill a 97. Yet IQ scores aren't fixed. They almost never remain exactly the same over time; in fact, they occasionally shift within the same person by as much as 10 points or more over a matter of months.

Stability of IQ in Adulthood. IQ scores usually remain reasonably stable in adulthood. As we learned in Chapter 2, *reliability* refers to consistency of measurement. As we also learned, one important type of reliability is *test-retest reliability,* which refers to the extent to which scores on a measure remain stable over time. For adult IQ tests like the WAIS-III, test-retest reliabilities tend to be about .95 over a several week interval (Weschler, 1997). As you'll recall, .95 is an extremely high correlation, nearly but not quite perfect. Even across long stretches of time, IQ scores tend to be reasonably stable. In one study of 101 Scottish schoolchildren followed up over time, IQ scores obtained at age 11 correlated .73 with their IQ scores at age 77 (Deary, Whalley, Lemmon, Crawford, & Starr, 2000).

Stability of IQ in Infancy and Childhood. There's a key exception to the rule regarding the high test-retest reliability of IQ tests. Prior to age 2 or 3, IQ tests aren't stable over time. In fact, IQ measured in the first 6 months of life correlates just about zero with adult IQ (Brody, 1992). Nor do IQ scores obtained in the first few years of life do a good job of forecasting outcomes, unless they're extremely low, such as under 50; such scores tend to be predictive of later mental retardation. That's probably because IQ tests designed for very young children assess the sensory abilities that Galton and Cattell emphasized, which bear little association with intelligence. In contrast, IQ tests designed for older children and beyond assess the abstract reasoning emphasized by Binet, Simon, and others. This reasoning, as we've seen, lies at the heart of what we call intelligence.

Among professional basketball players, height isn't an especially good predictor of who scores the most points, because the range of heights is dramatically restricted.

Some measures of infant intelligence are slightly more promising when it comes to predicting later IQ. One is speed of habituation. As we discovered in Chapter 6, habituation refers to the tendency to stop responding to repeated presentations of the same stimulus. Infants who habituate to a visual stimulus (like a red circle) more quickly—as measured by how long they stare at it—turn out to have higher IQs in later childhood and adolescence, with correlations typically in the .3 to .5 range (McCall & Ganringer, 1993; Slater, 1997).

It's not entirely clear why this is so. Perhaps this correlation reflects a direct causal association between intelligence and habituation: Infants who are smart "take in" information from novel stimuli quickly, so they're ready to move on to new things. Alternatively, this correlation may reflect the influence of a third variable, like interest in new stimuli (Colombo, 1993). Perhaps infants who are more interested in new things both habituate more quickly *and* learn more things, resulting in higher intelligence later on.

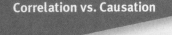

A related approach presents babies with pairs of pictures, like photos of faces. For many trials, the two faces are the same. Then suddenly, a novel face appears along with the familiar face. Infants who attend more to the new face later tend to have higher IQs in childhood and adolescence than other infants (DiLalla et al., 1990; Smith, Fagan, & Ulvund, 2002). Still, this measure has its problems. In particular, its test-retest reliability is fairly low (Benasich & Bejar, 1992).

It remains to be seen whether researchers will develop even better measures of infant intelligence. Ultimately, these measures may yield clues regarding how intelligence develops and perhaps even what intelligence is.

Seated comfortably on mom's lap, a baby takes an experimental measure of infant intelligence that assesses response to novelty. The baby had previously viewed a number of identical pairs of photos of two people playing with toys, is now viewing two different photos (containing different toys). The extent to which infants look at the novel photo modestly predicts their adult intelligence.

VALIDITY OF IQ SCORES: PREDICTING LIFE OUTCOMES

Whatever we think of IQ tests, there's little question that they're valid for at least some purposes. As we learned in Chapter 2, *validity* refers to the extent to which a test measures what it purports to measure. One important indicator of a test's validity is its capacity to forecast future outcomes (or what psychologists call "predictive" validity).

IQ scores do a good job of predicting academic success; they correlate about .5 with grades in high school and college (Neisser et al., 1996). Still, because this correlation is considerably lower than 1.0, it tells us there's more to school success than IQ. Motivation, intellectual curiosity, and effort also play crucial roles.

IQ scores also predict performance across a wide variety of occupations, with the average correlation again being about .5 (Ones, Viswesveran, & Dilchert, 2005). By comparison, the correlation between ratings of how well people do in job interviews and job performance is only about .15, which is ironic given that many employers place heavier weight on interviews than on IQ when selecting job applicants (Hunter & Hunter, 1984). The correlation between IQ and job performance is higher in more mentally demanding occupations, such as physician or lawyer, than in less mentally demanding occupations, like clerk or newspaper delivery person (Salgado et al., 2003). Using estimates from biographers and historians (see **Table 9.2**), one researcher even found that presidents' estimated IQ predicted the quality of leadership among U.S. presidents, with correlations in the .3 to .4 range (Simonton, 2006).

APPLY YOUR THINKING
Why do you think IQ predicts performance better in more mentally demanding jobs than in less mentally demanding ones? How could you test your hypothesis?

Table 9.2 Estimated IQ of Selected U.S. Presidents. Based on biographical and historical information, Dean Keith Simonton (2006) derived estimates of all U.S. presidents' IQs. This table presents the estimated IQ range for each president, meaning his true IQ probably falls somewhere between the two numbers.

President	Estimated IQ	President	Estimated IQ
George Washington	125–140	Harry Truman	116–140
Thomas Jefferson	145–160	John F. Kennedy	139–160
John Quincy Adams	165–175	Richard M. Nixon	119–143
Millard Fillmore	121–149	Jimmy Carter	130–157
Abraham Lincoln	125–150	Ronald Reagan	118–142
Ulysses S. Grant	110–130	Bill Clinton	136–159
Warren Harding	108–140	George W. Bush	111–139
Franklin Delano Roosevelt	127–151		
(*Source:* Simonton, 2006)			

Reading Confusion Into Drug Warnings
When researchers asked consumers to interpret prescription warning stickers, these are among the responses they gave:

DO NOT CHEW OR CRUSH. **SWALLOW WHOLE.**

"Chew pill and crush before swallowing."
"Chew it up so it will dissolve, don't swallow whole or you might choke."

FOR EXTERNAL USE **ONLY**

"Use extreme caution in how you take it."
"Medicine will make you feel dizzy."
"Take only if you need it."

YOU SHOULD **AVOID** PROLONGED OR EXCESSIVE EXPOSURE TO DIRECT AND/OR ARTIFICIAL **SUNLIGHT** WHILE TAKING THIS MEDICATION.

"Don't take medicine if you've been in the sunlight too long."
"Don't leave medicine in the sun."

Low levels of health literacy, which are associated with IQ, can lead to dangerous misunderstandings of medication instructions. On the top are actual warning labels attached to certain medications; underneath each warning label are actual interpretations of these warnings by some subjects in a published study (Davis et al., 2006). (*Source:* Franklin, 2005)

IQ also predicts a variety of important real-world behaviors outside the classroom and workplace. For example, IQ is associated with health-related outcomes, including sickness and car accidents (Gottfredson, 2004; Lubinski & Humphreys, 1992). At least some of the negative correlation between IQ and illness may be attributable to *health literacy*, the ability to understand health-related information, such as instructions from doctors or on drug labels. People with low health literacy may have difficulty maintaining good health behaviors, such as getting enough exercise, eating the right foods, or taking the right dosage of their medications. IQ is also associated with criminal tendencies: The IQs of delinquent adolescents are about 7 points lower than those of other adolescents (Wilson & Herrnstein, 1985).

But there's a potential confound here (see Chapter 2). IQ is negatively associated with social class, as poorer people tend to have lower IQs. So poverty, rather than IQ, may explain at least some of the associations we've discussed. Researchers have tried to address this rival hypothesis by determining whether the correlations hold up even when accounting for social class. In most cases, including health outcomes and crime, they do (Herrnstein & Murray, 1994; Neisser et al., 1997).

bell curve
distribution of scores in which the bulk of the scores fall toward the middle, with progressively fewer scores toward the "tails" or extremes

Ruling Out Rival Hypotheses

A TALE OF TWO TAILS: FROM MENTAL RETARDATION TO GENIUS

As we promised at the chapter's outset, we'll now revisit the **bell curve** discovered by Gauss. In a bell curve distribution, the bulk of the scores fall toward the middle, with progressively fewer scores toward the "tails" or extremes, forming the shape of a bell.

Figure 9.12 shows that the bell curve fits the distribution of IQ scores in the population fairly well, with one minor exception. The bulk of scores fall in the broad middle of the distribution; about 95 percent of people have IQs between 70 and 130. The curve contains a small bump on the left, indicating that there are more very low IQ scores than we'd expect from a perfect bell curve. These extreme scores are probably the result of *assortative mating* (Mackintosh, 1998): the tendency of individuals with similar genes to have children. In this case, individuals with mental retardation are especially likely to parent a child with other individuals with mental retardation, probably because they frequent the same locations (such as special schools), then develop a relationship, and have children.

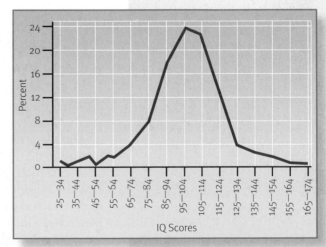

Figure 9.12 Distribution of IQ Scores in General Population. The bell curve roughly approximates the distribution of IQ scores in the general population.

Let's now look at what we know about the two tails of the IQ score distribution: mental retardation and genius.

Mental Retardation. Psychologists define **mental retardation** by three criteria, all of which must be present: (1) onset prior to adulthood, (2) IQ below approximately 70, and (3) inadequate adaptive functioning, as assessed by difficulties with dressing and feeding oneself, communicating with others, and other basic life skills (Greenspan & Switzky, 2003). The adaptive functioning criterion largely explains why about two-thirds of children with mental retardation lose this diagnosis in adulthood (Grossman, 1983); as individuals acquire life-functioning skills, they no longer qualify for this diagnosis. Some experts have also recently placed heightened emphasis on *gullibility* (the susceptibility to being duped by others) as a criterion for mental retardation, in part for social policy reasons. A diagnosis of mental retardation qualifies individuals for additional government services. For this reason, the inability to protect oneself from being taken advantage of by others should be weighted heavily in determining whether a person is mentally retarded (Greenspan, Loughlin, & Black, 2001).

About 1 percent of persons in the United States, most of them males, fulfill the criteria for mental retardation (American Psychiatric Association, 2000). The current system of psychiatric diagnosis classifies mental retardation into four categories: mild (once called "educable"), moderate (once called "trainable"), severe, and profound. Contrary to popular conception, most mentally retarded individuals—at least 85 percent—fall into the "mild" category. In most cases, mildly retarded children can be integrated or *mainstreamed* into classrooms along with nonretarded individuals. Still, the term "mild mental retardation" is misleading, because individuals in this category still have significant deficits in adaptive functioning.

Contrary to what we might expect, the more severe the mental retardation, the *less* likely it is to run in families (Reed & Reed, 1965). Mild forms of mental retardation are typically due to a mix of genetic and environmental influences that parents pass on to their children. In contrast, severe forms of mental retardation are more often the result of rare genetic mutations or accidents during birth, neither of which tend to be transmitted within families.

There are at least 200 different causes of mental retardation. Two of the most common genetic conditions associated with mental retardation are fragile X syndrome, which is produced by a mutation on the X chromosome (females have two copies of this chromosome, males only one), and Down syndrome, which is the result of an extra copy of chromosome 21. Most children with Down syndrome are either mildly or moderately retarded. Nevertheless, a subset of individuals with Down syndrome known as *mosaics* (so called because only some of their cells contain an extra chromosome 21) have relatively normal IQs. People with Down syndrome typically exhibit a distinctive pattern of physical features, including a flat nose, upwardly slanted eyes, a protruding tongue, and a short neck. The prevalence of Down syndrome rises sharply with the birth mother's age; at age 30, it's less than 1 in 1,000, but by age 49, it's about 1 in 12 (Hook & Lindjso, 1978).

Societal attitudes toward individuals with mental retardation have improved dramatically over the past century. Today, if we want to insult someone's intelligence, we might refer to him as a "moron," "idiot," or "imbecile." Yet few of us realize that these terms originally described different classes of individuals with mental retardation: "moron" referred to the mildly retarded, "idiot" to the moderately and severely retarded, and "imbecile" to the profoundly retarded (Scheerenberger, 1983). Thankfully, our views are far more enlightened today. The Americans with Disabilities Act (ADA), passed in 1990, outlawed job and educational discrimination on the basis of mental and physical disabilities, and the Individuals with Disabilities Education Act (IDEA), passed in 1996, provided federal aid to states and local educational districts for accommodations to mentally and physically disabled youth. Both ADA and IDEA have helped bring the mentally retarded out of institutions and into our workplaces and schools. As we increase our regular contact with the mentally retarded, such laws may further erode the lingering stigma that some Americans feel toward these members of society.

Most individuals with Down syndrome are mildly or moderately mentally retarded. Nevertheless, many have been successfully mainstreamed into traditional classrooms.

mental retardation
condition characterized by an onset prior to adulthood, an IQ below about 70, and an inability to engage in adequate daily functioning

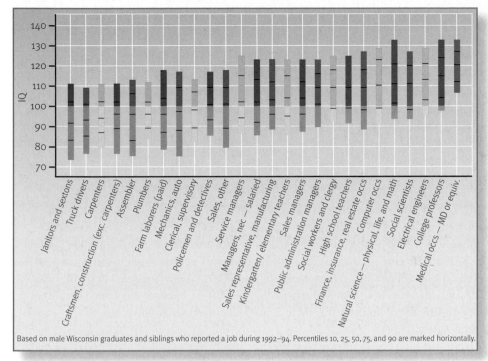

Based on male Wisconsin graduates and siblings who reported a job during 1992–94. Percentiles 10, 25, 50, 75, and 90 are marked horizontally.

Figure 9.13 IQ Scores among Select Professions. A study of IQ scores reveals that among a range of professions, college-level teaching, law, engineering, and medicine attract those with the highest average IQs. However, at least 25 percent of those in every profession score above 90 on IQ tests. There are intelligent people in every profession. (*Source:* Adapted from Hauser, 2002)

Genius and Exceptional Intelligence. Let's now turn to the opposite tail of the bell curve. If you're fortunate enough to score in the top 2 percent of the IQ range, you'll qualify for membership in an organization called Mensa. A large proportion of individuals with IQs at or near this range populate certain occupations, such as doctors, lawyers, engineers, and college professors (Herrnstein & Murray, 1994) (see **Figure 9.13**). Yet we know relatively little about the psychological characteristics of individuals with high IQs or their academic, occupational, and social performance over time. Several research studies offer tantalizing clues.

In the 1920s, Lewis Terman and his colleagues (Terman & Oden, 1959) initiated one of the classic studies of intellectually gifted individuals. From some 250,000 junior high school students in California, Terman selected about 1,500 who scored in the top 1 percent on the Stanford-Binet and similar IQ tests, that is, who had IQs of about 135 or higher. He tracked these individuals, known affectionately as Terman's "Termites," for several decades (some are still alive today). Although Terman's study was flawed, in part because he didn't recruit a control group of individuals with average or low IQs, it refuted three common misconceptions regarding people with high IQs.

First, his study refuted the popular stereotype of the "nerd" or "98-pound weakling"— the highly intelligent individual who is physically frail and nonathletic. We all remember the skinny kid in high school with a calculator in his belt who was always the last guy to be picked for the sports team. Yet Terman found that his Termites were above average in physical health and were taller and heavier than individuals in the general population.

Second, Terman's study raised doubts about the common claim that almost all child prodigies "burn out" in adulthood ("early ripe, early rot," so the saying goes). Terman's subjects became a highly distinguished group: ninety-seven earned doctoral degrees, fifty-seven medical degrees, and ninety-two law degrees (Leslie, 2000). An additional seventy-four became college professors, and collectively they published nearly 100 books and about 2,000 journal articles. These numbers are all considerably higher than what we'd expect from the general population. A later study of an even more select group—young adolescents who scored in the top .001 percent (that's 1 in 10,000) on tests of verbal or mathematical ability—generated similar results. By their early twenties,

The popular stereotype of highly intelligent people as weak and physically uncoordinated doesn't hold true. (© Kevin Menzie)

these individuals were attending graduate school at a rate more than fifty times higher than that in the general population, and many had already published scientific or literary articles (Lubinski, Benbow, Webb, & Bleske-Rechek, 2006).

Third, Terman's results disputed the popular notion that there's an intimate link between genius and insanity. Although the absence of a control group makes it difficult to know for certain, his findings pointed to slightly lower rates of mental illness and suicide among his adult Termites compared with the general population. Later researchers have generally found similar results, although some have reported that exceedingly intelligent children, such as those with IQs over 180, may be at heightened risk for selected mental health problems, especially loneliness and depression (Janos & Robinson, 1985; Winner, 1999). These negative outcomes may be a consequence of the greater ridicule and isolation that these children experience. Still, there's scant evidence that high intelligence is associated with high levels of severe mental illness.

What's the recipe for creating a genius, like Karl Friedrich Gauss? We don't know, although as we'll soon discover, genetic factors probably play a significant role. Still, as the brilliant inventor Thomas Edison said famously, "genius is 1% inspiration, 99% perspiration." Becoming a genius in one's chosen field takes many years of hard work. Gauss was no exception; his biographers describe him as intensely dedicated to mathematics, routinely toiling away for many hours in complete isolation when solving proofs (Dunnington, 1955).

Here common wisdom is correct: Practice makes perfect, or at least pretty darned good. The best predictor of exceptional career success in violin, piano, ballet, chess, and sports is the sheer amount of time we spend in practice. The most talented musicians practice twice as much as the less talented ones (Ericsson, Krampe, & Tesch-Romer, 1993). Of course, the causal arrow here isn't clear. Greater amounts of practice could be causing greater success, or greater levels of initial talent could be causing greater amounts of practice. We won't spend ten hours a day perfecting our guitar playing unless we're decent at it to begin with. In addition, research shows that across many domains, such as science, art, and music, individuals almost never attain remarkable intellectual accomplishments until they've dedicated themselves intensely for at least 10 years in that domain (Simonton, 1997). So the familiar Hollywood stereotype of the teenager or young adult who achieves astonishing intellectual brilliance with virtually no effort is exceedingly unrealistic.

Many Hollywood movies, like the 1997 movie *Good Will Hunting* (starring Matt Damon, shown here, as Will Hunting), portray childhood or adolescent geniuses as requiring minimal effort to make astonishing intellectual discoveries. Yet research shows that such discoveries almost always require a decade or more of hard, concentrated work in a specific area.

Replicability

Correlation vs. Causation

ASSESS YOUR KNOWLEDGE: FACT OR FICTION?

(1) Today, IQ is measured as mental age divided by chronological age, multiplied by 100. (True/False)

(2) Standard IQ tests administered in infancy tend not to be highly predictive of later IQ scores. (True/False)

(3) Although IQ scores predict school achievement, they are almost useless for predicting occupational success. (True/False)

(4) The most prevalent form of mental retardation is mild retardation. (True/False)

(5) Most highly intelligent people tend to be physically weak and underdeveloped. (True/False)

Answers: (1) F (p. 364); (2) T (p. 369); (3) F (p. 370); (4) T (p. 372); (5) F (p. 373)

Genetic and Environmental Influences on IQ

Up to this point, we've talked at length about what intelligence is and how we measure it. But we've said little about its causes, or about the relative roles of nature and nurture in its development. Fortunately, over the past few decades, psychologists have obtained a much better handle on the genetic and environmental contributors to IQ. As we'll discover, however, significant flash points of controversy remain.

EXPLORING GENETIC INFLUENCES ON IQ

As we learned in Chapter 3, scientists can study genetic influences on psychological characteristics in three major ways: family studies, twin studies, and adoption studies. They've done so for intelligence, with surprisingly consistent results.

Family Studies. As we saw in Chapter 3, *family studies* allow us to examine the extent to which a trait "runs" or goes together in intact families, those in which all family members live together in the same home. Sir Francis Galton, who coined the phrase "nature and nurture" (Galton, 1876), conducted one of the first family studies of intelligence. Intrigued by the possibility that intellectual brilliance runs in families, Galton (1869) gathered data on the extent to which persons renowned for their intellectual accomplishments—as gauged by their obituaries in newspapers—had biological relatives who were also renowned for their intellectual accomplishments. He found that the proportion of relatives who'd achieved intellectual greatness declined steadily with increasing biological distance. Intellectually brilliant individuals had many first-degree relatives (parents, siblings, and children) who were also brilliant, but fewer second-degree relatives (such as cousins), and still fewer third-degree relatives (such as second cousins) who were brilliant. Later studies have confirmed that IQ runs in families: The correlation of IQ for brothers and sisters raised in the same family is about .5, whereas for cousins it's about .15 (Bouchard & McGue, 1981). Galton concluded that these findings demonstrated a genetic basis to intellectual greatness, but he overlooked two alternative explanations.

First, he neglected to consider a potential confound: wealth. People who come from rich families are more likely to acquire fame and to be memorialized in newspaper obituaries. And of course, the closer the relatives biologically, the more likely they are to have a similar income level.

Second, Galton largely ignored a crucial limitation that applies to all family studies: *Studies of intact families don't allow us to distinguish the effects of genes from those of the environment.* That's because individuals in these families share both genes and environment. As a consequence, when a trait runs in families, we don't know whether it's for genetic reasons, environmental reasons, or both (see Chapter 3).

Ruling Out Rival Hypotheses

Twin Studies. Because family studies don't permit investigators to disentangle the effects of nature from those of nurture, they've turned to more informative research designs. These include *twin studies,* which as we've seen (Chapter 3) compare correlations in a trait in two types of twins: identical (monozygotic) and fraternal (dizygotic).

The logic of the twin design is straightforward. Because identical twins share twice as many of their genes on average as fraternal twins, we can compare the correlations in IQ in these two different twin types. Given a handful of assumptions, higher identical than fraternal twin correlations strongly suggest genetic influence. In almost all cases, studies of twins reared together have offered evidence of considerably higher identical than fraternal twin correlations for IQ (Bouchard & McGue, 1981; Loehlin, Willerman, & Horn, 1988). In typical studies of IQ, identical twin correlations have been in the .7 to .8 range, whereas fraternal twin correlations have been in the .3 to .4 range. Nevertheless, in all studies of twins raised together, identical twin correlations have been lower than 1.0.

These findings tell us two things. First, the higher identical than fraternal twin correlations tell us that IQ is influenced by genetic factors. The best estimate for the heritability of IQ lies somewhere between 40 and 70 percent (Brody, 1992; Devlin, Daniels, & Roeder, 1997). Interestingly, the heritability of IQ seems to increase from childhood to adulthood (McClearn et al., 1997), perhaps because people become less influenced by their environments, especially their parents, as they move away from home. Although the twin findings don't tell us which genes are relevant to intelligence, the past decade has witnessed progress in identifying specific genes for intelligence. These genes appear to cut across

Twin studies of intelligence compare the mental performance of identical (*top*) versus fraternal (*bottom*) twins raised together.

multiple domains of mental ability, including attention, working memory, and perhaps even risk for Alzheimer's disease (Plomin & Kovas, 2005; Posthuma & de Gues, 2006).

Second, these twin findings provide convincing evidence for environmental influences on IQ. Why? Because the identical twin correlations for IQ are less than perfect. Given that identical twins share 100 percent of their genes, they would correlate 1.0 if genetic influences alone were operative (assuming the IQ tests are reliable). The fact that they correlate less than 1.0 tells us that environmental influences also play a role, although the studies don't tell us what these influences are.

Ruling Out Rival Hypotheses

Note that up to this point, we've discussed only studies of twins raised together. These studies are vulnerable to a rival hypothesis; perhaps identical twins are more similar than fraternal twins because they spend more time together. To exclude this possibility, investigators have conducted studies of identical and fraternal twins reared apart since birth or shortly after birth. Thomas Bouchard and his colleagues at the University of Minnesota conducted the landmark study of twins reared apart in the 1980s and 1990s. Remarkably, the results of this study revealed that a sample of over forty identical twin pairs reared apart were just as similar on three measures of IQ (including the WAIS and Raven's Progressive Matrices) as identical twins reared together (Bouchard, Lykken, McGue, Segal, & Tellegen, 1990). Other investigators have replicated these findings (Pederson, Plomin, Nesselroade, & McClearn, 1992), although because twins reared apart are extremely rare, the sample sizes of these studies are relatively low.

Replicability

Adoption Studies. Studies of intact family members are limited because they can't disentangle genetic from environmental influences. To address this shortcoming, psychologists have turned to *adoption studies* (Chapter 3), which examine the extent to which children adopted into new homes resemble their adoptive versus biological parents. Adoption studies allow us to separate environmental from genetic effects on IQ, because adoptees are raised by parents with whom they share an environment, but not genes. One potential confound in adoption studies is *selective placement:* Adoption agencies frequently place children in homes similar to those of the biological parents (DeFries & Plomin, 1978). This confound can lead investigators to mistakenly interpret the similarity between adoptive children and adoptive parents as an environmental effect. In adoption studies of IQ, researchers often try to control for selective placement by correcting statistically for the correlation in IQ between biological and adoptive parents.

Ruling Out Rival Hypotheses

Adoption studies have established a clear contribution of the environment in IQ. For example, adopted children who come from extremely deprived environments show an increase in IQ when adopted into homes that provide more enriched environments (Capron & Duyme, 1989). In one study of French children raised in an extremely deprived environment, children who were adopted showed an average 16-point IQ edge over children who weren't (Schiff et al., 1982).

But do adopted children's IQs resemble their biological parents' IQs? The results of adoption studies indicate that the IQs of adopted children tend to be similar to the IQs of their biological parents offering evidence of genetic influence. As young children, adoptees tend to resemble the adoptive parents in IQ, but this resemblance dissipates once these children become older and approach adolescence (Loehlin, Horn, & Willerman, 1989; Phillips & Fulker, 1989; Plomin, Fulker, Corley, & Defries, 1997).

Many children adopted from environments of severe deprivation, such as this orphanage in Romania, show increases in IQ after immersion in a healthier and more attentive adoptive environment (see also Chapter 10).

EXPLORING ENVIRONMENTAL INFLUENCES ON IQ

As we've learned, twin and adoption studies paint a consistent picture: Both genes and environment affect IQ scores. But these studies leave a mysterious question unanswered: What environmental factors influence IQ? Psychologists don't know for sure, although they've made significant inroads toward identifying promising candidates. As we'll see, environmental influences can include not only the *social* environment, such as school and parents, but also the *biological* environment, such as the availability of nutrients and exposure to toxic substances, such as lead. We'll also see that the evidence for some of these environmental influences is more convincing than for others.

Birth Order: Are Older Siblings Wiser? In the 1970s, Robert Zajonc (whose name, oddly enough, rhymes with "science"), created a stir by arguing that later-born children tend to be less intelligent than earlier-born children (Zajonc, 1976). According to Zajonc, IQ declines steadily with increasing numbers of children in a family. He even authored an article in the popular magazine *Psychology Today* entitled "Dumber by the Dozen" (Zajonc, 1975).

In one respect, Zajonc was right: later-born children tend to have slightly lower IQs (on the order of a few points) than earlier-born children (Kristensen & Bjerkedal, 2007). But it's not clear that he interpreted this correlation correctly. Here's the problem. Parents with lower IQs are slightly more likely to have many children than are parents with higher IQs. As a consequence, when we look across families, birth order is associated with IQ, but only because low-IQ families have a larger number of later-born children than do high-IQ families. In contrast, when we look *within* families, the relationship between birth order and IQ becomes smaller and may even vanish (Michalski & Shackelford, 2001; Rodgers et al., 2000). So a more accurate way to state the correlation is that children who come from larger families have slightly lower IQs than do children who come from smaller families.

Correlation vs. Causation

Does Schooling Make Us Smarter? Number of years in school correlates between .5 and .6 with IQ scores (Neisser et al., 1995). Although some authors have interpreted this correlation as meaning that schooling leads to higher IQ, it's equally possible that the causal arrow is reversed. Indeed, there's evidence that individuals with high IQ scores enjoy taking classes more than individuals with low IQ scores (Rehberg & Rosenthal, 1978). As a consequence, they may be more likely to stay in school and go on to college and beyond. This wouldn't be terribly surprising given that individuals with high IQ scores tend to do better in their classes.

Correlation vs. Causation

Still, several lines of evidence suggest that schooling exerts a causal influence on IQ (Ceci, 1991; Ceci & Williams, 1997):

(1) Researchers have examined pairs of children who are almost exactly the same age, but in which one child attended an extra year of school because he was born just a few days earlier (say, August 31 as opposed to September 2). This can occur because public schools often have hard-and-fast cutoff dates for how old children must be to begin school. In such cases, children who've attended an extra year of school tend to have higher IQs, despite being nearly identical in chronological age.
(2) Children's IQs tend to drop significantly during summer vacations.
(3) Students who drop out of school end up with lower IQs than students who stay in school, even when they start out with the same IQ.

Boosting IQ by Early Intervention. In a controversial article in the late 1960s, Arthur Jensen contended that IQ was highly heritable and therefore difficult to modify by means of environmental intervention (Jensen, 1969). In making this argument, Jensen fell prey to a logical error we debunked earlier in this book (Chapter 3): namely, that heritability implies that a trait can't be changed. Yet he raised an important question: Can we boost IQ with early educational interventions?

Some of the best evidence comes from studies of *Head Start,* a preschool program launched in the 1960s to give disadvantaged children a "jump start" by offering them an enriched educational experience. The hope was that this program would allow them to catch up intellectually to other children. Dozens of studies of Head Start programs have yielded consistent results, and they've been largely disappointing. Although these programs produce short-term increases in IQ, these increases don't typically persist after the programs end (Caruso, Taylor, & Detterman, 1982; Royce, Darlington, & Murray, 1983). Similar results emerge from studies of other early-intervention programs (Brody, 1992; Herrnstein & Murray, 1994). At the same time, these programs may not be entirely worthless. Several studies indicate that Head Start and other early-intervention programs result in lower rates of high school dropout and of being held back a grade compared with control conditions (Campbell & Raney, 1995; Darlington, 1986; Neisser et al., 1995).

A Self-Fulfilling Prophecy: Expectancy Effects on IQ. In the 1960s, Robert Rosenthal and Lenore Jacobson wanted to examine the effects of teacher expectancies on IQ. As we saw in

Children's IQs tend to drop significantly during summer vacations, suggesting an environmental influence on IQ.

The federal Head Start program was launched in the 1960s to give disadvantaged preschoolers a jump-start on their education. Studies show that Head Start programs typically produce short-term increases in IQ, but that these increases fade with time.

Chapter 2, the *experimenter expectancy effect* refers to the tendency of researchers to unintentionally influence the outcome of studies. In this case, Rosenthal and Jacobson (1966) looked at the expectancies of teachers rather than researchers. They administered an IQ test to students in the first through sixth grades, disguising it with a fake name ("The Harvard Test of Inflected Acquisition"). Then they gave teachers the results, which indicated that 20 percent of their students would show remarkable gains in intelligence during the subsequent 8 months: These students were "bloomers" who'd soon reach their full intellectual potential. But Rosenthal and Jacobson misled the teachers. They had *randomly* selected these 20 percent of students to be classified as bloomers, and these students' initial scores didn't differ from those of other students. Yet when Rosenthal and Jacobson retested all students a year later with the same IQ test, the 20 percent labeled as bloomers scored about 4 IQ points higher than the other students. Expectations had become reality.

This effect has now been replicated in a number of studies, although the size of the effect isn't large (Rosenthal, 1994; Smith, 1980). We don't know how this effect occurs, although there's evidence that teachers more often smile at, make eye contact with, and nod their heads toward students they incorrectly believe are smart compared with other students (Chaiken, Sigler, & Derlega, 1974). As a consequence, they may positively reinforce (see Chapter 6) these students' learning. Nevertheless, the effects of expectancy on IQ have their limits. These effects are substantial only when teachers don't know their students well; when teachers have worked with students for at least a few weeks, the effects often disappear (Raudenbush, 1984). Once teachers form definite impressions of how smart their students are, it's hard to persuade them their impressions are off base.

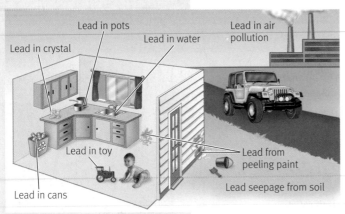

Lead exposure can arise from many sources in everyday life and may contribute to decreased IQ. Nevertheless, the causal association between lead intake and IQ remains controversial.

Poverty and IQ: Socioeconomic and Nutritional Deprivation. It's difficult to put a firm number on the effects of poverty, but there's reason to believe that social and economic deprivation can adversely affect IQ. Arthur Jensen (1977) studied a group of families in an extremely poor area of rural Georgia. For African American (but not Caucasian) children, he found evidence for a *cumulative deficit,* a difference that grows over time. Older siblings consistently had lower IQs than younger siblings, with a steady decrease of about 1.5 IQ points per year. Jensen's explanation was that siblings in this impoverished region experienced progressively more intellectual deprivation as they aged, leading them to fall further behind other children (Willerman, 1979).

Along with poverty often comes inadequate diet. Studies from poor areas in Central America suggest that malnutrition in childhood, especially if prolonged, can lower IQ (Eysenck & Schoenthaler, 1997). In one investigation, researchers gave nutritional (protein) supplements to preschool children from an impoverished region of Guatemala. These children's school-related test scores were significantly higher than those of similar children who didn't receive supplements (Pollitt, German, Engle, Martorell, & Rivera, 1993).

Poor children are also especially likely to be exposed to lead as a result of drinking lead-contaminated water, breathing lead-contaminated dust, or eating lead paint chips. Such exposure is also associated with intellectual deficits (Bellinger & Needleman, 2003; Canfield et al., 2003; Ris, Dietrich, Succop, Berger, & Bornschein, 2004). Nevertheless, it's unclear how much of this correlation is due to the direct effects of lead itself as opposed to poverty or other factors, like malnutrition.

Scientific controversy has swirled around another potential nutritional influence: breast-feeding. On the one side are researchers who claim that infants who are breast-fed end up with higher IQs—perhaps on the order of a few points—than children who are bottle-fed (Mortonsen, Michaelson, Sanders, & Reinisch, 2002; Quinn et al., 2001). Indeed, mothers' milk contains about 100 ingredients absent from milk formula, including several that speed up the myelinization of neurons (see Chapter 3). On the other side are researchers who contend that this IQ difference is due to one or more confounds: For

Replicability

Correlation vs. Causation

example, mothers who breast-feed their babies tend to be somewhat higher in social class and IQ than mothers who bottle-feed their babies (Der, Batty, & Deary, 2006; Jacobson, Chiodo, & Jacobson, 1999). These confounds could account for the seeming effect of breast-feeding on IQ. The debate rages on. (Caspi et al., 2007).

Getting Smarter All the Time: The Mysterious Flynn Effect. In the 1980s, while looking at changes in IQ scores over time in the United States and Europe, political scientist James Flynn noticed something very odd (Dickens & Flynn, 2001; Flynn, 1981, 1987). Mysteriously, IQ scores were rising at a rate of about 3 points per decade, a phenomenon later dubbed the **Flynn effect** (Herrnstein & Murray, 1994). The magnitude of the Flynn effect is mindboggling. It suggests that, on average, our IQs are a full 15 points higher than those of our grandparents who lived 50 years ago (see **Figure 9.14**). With a few exceptions (Mingronin, 2007; Rushton, 1999), most researchers agree that the Flynn effect is a result of unidentified environmental influences on IQ, because it's unlikely that genetic changes could account for such rapid rises in IQ over brief time periods.

What could these environmental influences be? Psychologists have proposed at least four explanations:

(1) *Increased test sophistication.* According to this explanation, the rise in IQ scores results from people becoming more experienced at taking tests. This hypothesis implies that the Flynn effect reflects an increase in IQ scores but not in underlying intelligence (Flynn, 1998). There may be some truth to the test sophistication hypothesis, but there's a fly in the ointment. The Flynn effect is most pronounced on "culture-fair" tests, such as Raven's Progressive Matrices, to which people have had the least exposure (Neisser, 1998).

(2) *Increased complexity of the modern world.* With television, e-mail, the Internet, fax machines, cell phones, and the like, we're forced to process far more information far more quickly than our parents and grandparents ever did. So the modern information explosion may be putting pressure on us to become more intelligent (Greenfield, 1998; Schooler, 1998).

(3) *Better nutrition.* Most evidence suggests that the Flynn effect is affecting primarily the lower, but not the upper, tail of the bell curve. One potential explanation for this finding is diet. People are better fed than ever before, and the rates of severe malnutrition in many (although not all) parts of the world are declining (Lynn, 1998; Sigman & Whaley, 1998). As we've already learned, there's good evidence that nutrition can affect IQ.

(4) *Changes at home and school.* Over the past several decades in the United States, families have become smaller, allowing parents to devote more time to their children. Parents also have more access to intellectual resources than ever. In addition, children and adolescents spend more years in school than in previous generations (Bronfenbrenner, McClelland, Wethington, Moen, & Ceci, 1996).

We don't fully understand the causes of the Flynn effect, and there may be some truth to several of these explanations. But the mystery doesn't end here. Recent data suggest that the Flynn effect may be subsiding or even reversing, at least in Europe (Sundet, Barlaug, & Torjussen, 2004). Some investigators have suggested that children's decreasing amounts of play with other children, perhaps resulting from greater computer and video game use, may be the culprit (Schneider, 2006), but no one knows for sure. The causes of the apparent end to the Flynn effect are as puzzling as the causes of its beginning. Yet it's a safe bet that the rise and fall of the Flynn effect holds the key to unlocking much of the mystery of environmental influences on IQ.

APPLY YOUR THINKING

Let's imagine that psychologists discover the Flynn effect is due primarily to increasing test sophistication. What would that tell us about the validity of IQ tests as measures of intelligence?

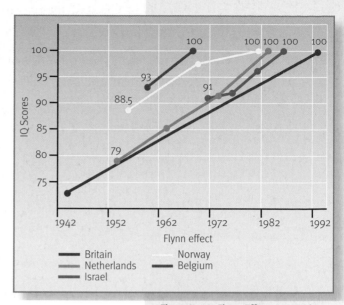

Figure 9.14 Flynn Effect. Research on the Flynn effect demonstrates that IQ scores have been increasing in many countries across several decades. The causes of this effect remain unclear. (*Source:* Flynn, 1999)

One American differs from his Civil War ancestor.

Typical Civil War soldier
(5 feet, 6 inches, 145 pounds)

Typical modern American
(5 feet, 11 inches, 235 pounds)

As can be seen in the sizes of these men and their uniforms, most people are considerably larger today than they were in the era of the U.S. Civil War (1861–1865). That difference reflects dramatic differences in nutrition over the past 150 years. Some psychologists propose that enhanced nutrition may account for the Flynn effect.

Flynn effect
finding that average IQ scores have been rising at a rate of approximately 3 points per decade

Group Differences in IQ: The Science and the Politics

Thus far, we've focused almost entirely on the thorny question of *individual differences* (see Prologue) in IQ: Why does measured intelligence differ among people within a population? If you think that what we've discussed so far is controversial, fasten your seat belts. The topic of *group differences* in IQ is perhaps the most bitterly disputed in all of psychology. Here we'll look at what the research says about two group differences in IQ: (1) differences between men and women and (2) differences among races.

As we'll discover, the issues are as emotionally charged as they are scientifically complex. They've also become deeply entangled with politics (Hunt, 1998), with people on differing sides of these debates accusing each other of biases and bad intentions. When evaluating these issues, it's crucial that we try our best to be as objective as possible. That's not always easy, as it requires us to put aside our understandable emotional reactions to examine the scientific evidence.

SEX DIFFERENCES IN IQ AND MENTAL ABILITIES

In January 2005, then Harvard University President Lawrence Summers created a furor. Speaking at an informal meeting of university faculty from around the country, Summers wondered aloud why there were so few women in the "hard" sciences, like physics, chemistry, and biology (see **Figure 9.15**). He tentatively proposed a few reasons, one involving discrimination against women and a second involving women's preference for raising families rather than for competing in grueling, cutthroat occupations. But it was Summers's third reason that really got people going. Summers conjectured that perhaps women enter the world with a genetic disadvantage in science and mathematics. Many people were appalled. One prominent woman biologist from the Massachusetts Institute of Technology stormed out of Summers' talk in protest. Within days, hundreds of Harvard faculty members were calling for his head (he resigned shortly thereafter). A firestorm of controversy regarding sex differences in mental abilities followed on the heels of Summers's provocative statements. In this section, we'll do our best to take a scientifically balanced look at the evidence.

Sex Differences in IQ. Do men and women differ in overall IQ? A handful of researchers have recently reported that men have slightly higher IQs than women—perhaps between 3 and 5 points (Jackson & Rushton, 2005; Lynn & Irwing, 2004)—but these claims are

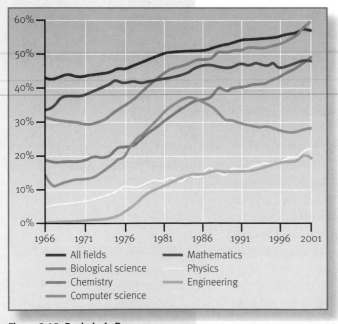

Figure 9.15 Bachelor's Degrees Earned by Women in Selected Fields, 1966–2001. Across a 35-year period, women have been underrepresented in most of the "hard" sciences, comprising only a minority of those graduating with a degree in these areas of study. (*Source:* Ivie & Ray, 2005)

controversial, to put it mildly. Indeed, most researchers have found few or no average sex differences in IQ (Jensen, 1998). The best current scientific bet is that males and females are extremely similar, if not identical, in IQ.

Yet average differences don't tell the whole story. Numerous studies indicate that men are more *variable* in their overall IQ scores than women (Hedges & Nowell, 1995). So although men don't appear to have higher average IQs than women, there are more men at both the low and the high ends of IQ bell curve (see **Figure 9.16**). We don't know the reason for this difference; researchers have, not surprisingly, proposed both genetic and environmental explanations.

Sex Differences in Specific Mental Abilities. Even though there's little, if any, difference in overall IQ between men and women, the picture becomes more interesting—and more complicated—when we get to specific mental abilities. Men and women are quite similar when it comes to most intellectual abilities (Hyde, 2005; Maccoby & Jacklin, 1974), but a closer look reveals some consistent sex differences (Block, 1976; Halpern, 1992; Halpern et al., 2007; Pinker, 2005).

Women tend to do better than men on some verbal tasks, like spelling, writing, and pronouncing words (Feingold, 1988; Halpern et al., 2007; Kimura, 1999). This sex difference may have a hormonal component; even within women, verbal ability seems to ebb and flow along with the level of estrogen, a sex hormone that's more plentiful in women than men (Chapter 3). In one study, women were best at quickly repeating tongue twisters (like "A box of mixed biscuits in a biscuit mixer") when their estrogen levels were at their peak (Hampson & Kimura, 1988). On average, females also do better than males in arithmetic calculation, like adding or subtracting numbers, although this difference is present only in childhood (Hyde, Fennema, & Lamon, 1990). Finally, females tend to be better than males in detecting and recognizing feelings in others, especially when they reach adulthood (Hall, 1978; McClure, 2000). For example, they're usually better than men at distinguishing among faces that display different emotions, such as fear and anger. Incidentally, despite popular stereotypes (Brizendine, 2006), there's no good evidence that women talk more than men. A recent study that tracked six samples of men and women in the United States and Mexico found that both sexes speak about 16,000 words per day (Mehr, Vazire, Ramirez-Esparza, Slatcher, & Pennebaker, 2007).

In contrast, men tend to do better than women on most tasks requiring spatial ability (Halpern et al., 2007). The largest difference emerges on *mental rotation* tasks, like the one shown in **Figure 9.17,** which require subjects to determine which of a series of rotated

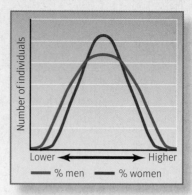

Figure 9.16 Distributions of Men and Women in IQ Tests. The IQ distribution of men is wider than the distribution of women. As a consequence, there are more men than women with both low and high IQ scores and more women with scores in the middle.

fictoid

Myth: Women are worse drivers than men.

Reality: Men's better average spatial ability than women may have contributed to the popular belief that men are better—and safer—drivers than women. In fact, even when controlling for the fact that men drive more miles than women, men get into about 70 percent more car accidents than women (Meyer, 2006), perhaps because they take more risks when driving.

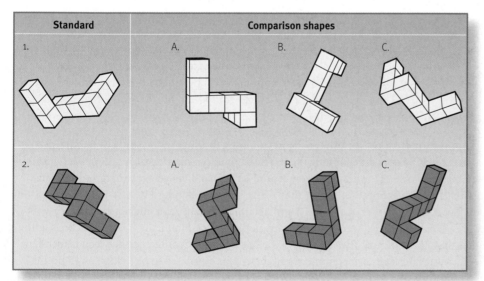

Figure 9.17 Mental Rotation Task. Men tend to do better than women on tests of mental rotation, which require subjects to figure out which "comparison" shape on the right matches the "standard" shape on the left. You may want to try your hand (or your mind, to be more exact) at these two items. Turn the book upside-down and see the bottom of the page for the answers. (*Source:* Metzler & Shepard, 1974)

Answers to Figure 9.17: 1. A, 2. B.

Men and women tend to differ in how they solve spatial problems.

Replicability

Replicability

blocks matches a target group of rotated blocks (Voyer, Voyer, & Bryden, 1995). Interestingly, one of the largest reported psychological sex differences is in geography, an area of study that relies heavily on spatial ability. Among the 5 million children who've participated in the National Geography Bee, 77 percent have been boys (Zernicke, 2000). Males also tend to do better than females on mathematics tasks that involve complicated reasoning, like deriving proofs in geometry (Benbow & Stanley, 1980). This difference doesn't emerge until adolescence (Hyde et al., 1990). At the extreme tails of the bell curve, this difference is magnified. For example, in one study of students who received scores of 700 or above on the SAT math section, males outnumbered females by 13 to 1 (Benbow & Stanley, 1983). But there are more males than females in the low tail of the test too.

So what's the bottom line? On the one hand, it's possible that some sex differences in mental abilities, such as women's higher scores on certain verbal tasks and men's higher scores on spatial and complex math-solving tasks, are rooted in genes. Indeed, despite many changes in men's and women's roles over the past several decades, sex differences in spatial ability haven't decreased over time (Voyer et al., 1995). Moreover, some studies indicate that excess levels of prenatal testosterone, a hormone of which males have more than females, is associated with better spatial ability (Hampson, Rovert, & Altman, 1998), although not all researchers have replicated this finding.

On the other hand, there's ample reason to suspect that some, perhaps even most, of the sex differences in science and math ability are environmental (Levine, Vasilyera, Lourenco, Newcombe, & Huttenlocker, 2006). For one thing, male and female infants show few or no differences in spatial or counting ability (Spelke, 2005). Even when sex differences in these abilities emerge later in life, they may be due more to sex differences in problem-solving strategies than in inherent abilities. For example, when researchers have encouraged both men and women to solve math problems using spatial imagery (which men usually prefer) rather than verbal reasoning (which women usually prefer), the sex difference in math performance becomes noticeably smaller (Geary, 1996). Moreover, if we look back at the graph in Figure 9.15 on page 380, we can see something striking. From 1966 to 2001, the percentage of women entering the "hard" sciences has been increasing steadily. This finding makes us wonder how much of the traditional underrepresentation of women in the "hard" sciences is the result of societal factors, such as discrimination and society's expectations concerning women's intellectual strengths and weaknesses. It also makes us wonder what this graph will look like in 10 years. Stay tuned.

APPLY YOUR THINKING

Earlier in the chapter we learned that heritability doesn't imply that a trait can't be changed. How might this fact bear on Lawrence Summers's comments and on the graph in Figure 9.15?

RACIAL DIFFERENCES IN IQ

Perhaps one of the most controversial and troubling findings in the study of intelligence is that average IQ scores differ among races. The differences vary in size but have been replicated multiple times (Loehlin, Lindzey, & Spuhler, 1977). On average, African Americans and Hispanic Americans score lower than Caucasians on standard IQ tests (Hunt & Carlson, 2007; Lynn, 2006; Neisser et al., 1995), and Asian Americans score higher than Caucasians (Lynn, 1996; Sue, 1993). Among Caucasians in the United States, the IQs of Jews are slightly higher than those of non-Jews (Lynn, 2003). The average IQ difference between Caucasians and African Americans, which some researchers have estimated to be as high as 15 points, has received the most attention. What do these differences tell us about the abilities and potential of individuals from different races, and why these differences exist?

Over the years, some sectors of society have attempted to use these findings in a misguided, and at times even malicious, attempt to argue that some races are innately superior to others. There are several serious problems with this claim. First, claims of inherent racial "superiority" lie outside the boundaries of science and can't be answered by data. Scientists can determine only the origins of racial differences, namely, whether they're genetic, environmental, or both. Second, the IQ differences among races may be narrowing over recent decades (Dickens & Flynn, 2006; Hauser, 1998). Third, the variability *within* any given race tends to be considerably larger than the variability *between* races (Nisbett, 1995). This finding means that the distributions of IQ scores for different races overlap substantially (see **Figure 9.18**). As a result, many African Americans and Hispanic Americans have higher IQs than many Caucasians and Asian Americans. The bottom line is clear: We can't use race as a basis for inferring any given person's IQ.

For Whom the Bell Curve Tolls. In 1994, Richard Herrnstein and Charles Murray touched off a bitter dispute among scientists and politicians alike. In their explosive book, *The Bell Curve*, they argued that IQ plays a much more important role in society than most people are willing to admit. People at the upper tail of the IQ bell curve, they maintained, tend to "rise to the top" of the social ladder, because they possess high levels of cognitive skills. As a consequence, they make more money, assume more positions of leadership, and enter more powerful occupations than people at the lower tail.

Had Herrnstein and Murray (1994) stopped there, their book would probably have attracted scant public attention. But they went further, conjecturing that at least some of the IQ gap between races might be genetic in origin. Herrnstein and Murray were hardly the first to make this suggestion (Jensen, 1973; Rushton & Bogaert, 1987). Nevertheless, their claims received unprecedented press coverage, reawakening a bitter debate that had arisen in the 1960s when Arthur Jensen proposed a genetic basis for racial differences in IQ. Jensen's work aroused widespread suspicions of racism, and was even interpreted by some White supremacists as supporting claims that Caucasians are genetically superior to Blacks. J. Phillippe Rushton (1995) also became a controversial figure in the 1980s and 1990s when he offered an evolutionary explanation for racial differences in IQ. Although some researchers have advanced strong arguments for a genetic basis for racial differences in IQ, we'll soon discover that the preponderance of evidence supports the idea that racial differences in IQ are largely or entirely environmental in origin. Most likely, these differences stem primarily from the different resources and opportunities available to individuals from different races.

Reconciling Racial Differences. To see why racial differences in IQ don't necessarily imply genetic differences in intelligence or learning potential, let's look at the two groups of plants in the upper panel of **Figure 9.19** (Lewontin, 1970). As we can see, in this "thought experiment" the plants within each group differ in height. These differences in height reflect (at least in part) genetic influences on plants' tendencies to grow and flourish. Note, however, that at this point in the growth cycle, the plants in the two groups are, on average, roughly equal in height. Now let's imagine that we provide one of these groups of plants, in this case the one on the left, with plenty of water and light, but provide the other group with minimal water and light. We twiddle our thumbs and wait a few weeks, and then voila: We now find that the plants on the left are, on average, much taller than the plants on the right. Although the two groups each had equal potential to grow and flourish, environmental influences resulted in one group growing taller than the other.

So what's the take-home message? The difference in height between these groups is *entirely environmental*—it's due to watering and light—so we can't explain the difference between the two groups in genetic terms. In other words, the between-group differences aren't at all heritable. If we think of children as little "human plants" (after all, the word

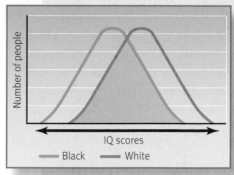

Figure 9.18 Diagram of African American and Caucasian Distributions for IQ. African American and Caucasian IQ distributions differ by an average of 15 IQ points—but they show substantial overlap, as indicated by the shaded area.

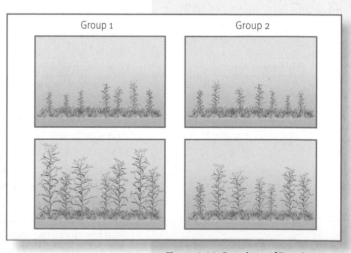

Figure 9.19 Drawings of Two Groups of Plants. These two groups of plants are well matched in height to start, but one outstrips the other over time due to different environmental conditions. This demonstrates how group differences in IQ could be "real" but completely environmentally determined. (*Source:* Based on Lewontin, 1970)

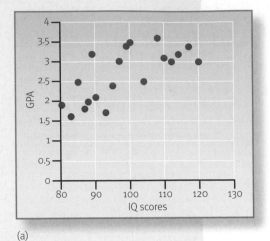

(a)

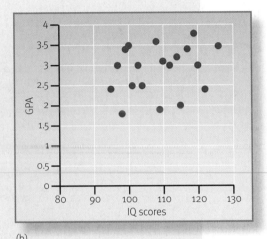

(b)

Figure 9.20 Two Scatterplots Representing Test Bias. These two scatterplots display a made-up example of test bias. In (a) IQ scores correlate highly with GPA for Caucasians (.7 correlation), whereas in (b) correlations between IQ scores and GPA are much lower for Asian Americans (.25). Even though Asian Americans display higher IQs on average in this example, the test is biased against them because it's a weaker predictor of GPA in that group.

test bias
tendency of a test to predict outcomes better in one group than another

"kindergarten" means "child garden" in German), we can easily imagine that different races begin life with no average genetic differences in IQ. But over time, the cumulative effects of factors such as social deprivation and prejudice may produce a notable difference in IQ between racial groups, one that's entirely environmental in origin.

It's also important to point out that although one group of plants in our example grew taller than the other, one or two individual plants in the shorter group actually grew taller than some plants from the taller group. This point highlights the overlapping distributions of heights in the two groups, demonstrating that even within a relatively "deprived" group, some plants exceed the growth of some members of the more "privileged" group. This point reminds us why we can't use group differences in IQ to infer the IQ of any given person. Although this example demonstrates that racial differences in IQ *could* be entirely environmental in nature, it doesn't demonstrate that they *are*. We need to look at the scientific evidence for answers to that question.

Test Bias. One popular explanation for race differences in IQ is that the tests are biased against some groups and in favor of others. *Test bias* has a specific meaning for psychologists, which differs from the popular use of the term. In scientific terms, a test isn't biased merely because some groups perform better on it than others. Psychologists don't regard a tape measure as biased, even though men obtain higher average scores than women when we use it to measure height. When psychologists refer to **test bias,** they mean that a test predicts outcomes—such as grades or occupational success—better in one group than in another (Anastasi & Urbina, 1996). Putting it a bit differently, a biased test means different things in one group than in another. Let's suppose that the correlation between IQ scores and college grade point average (GPA) in Caucasians was .7, as shown in **Figure 9.20a**, but only .25 for Asian Americans, as shown in **Figure 9.20b**. This finding would imply that IQ was a better predictor of GPA in Caucasians than in Asian Americans. In this case, the IQ test would be biased *against* Asian Americans, even though the average IQ scores for that group were higher than those of Caucasians. Thus, average differences between groups *do not* necessarily indicate test bias.

So are IQ tests racially biased? The answer seems to be no (Brody, 1992; Neisser et al., 1995). In almost all studies, researchers have found that the correlations between IQ tests and both academic and occupational achievement are about equal across races (Brody, 1992; Herrnstein & Murray, 1984; Hunter, Schmidt, & Hunter, 1979). This finding leads to the conclusion that IQ differences among races go hand-in-hand with differences in average *achievement* among races. Unfortunately, in U.S. society some races tend to do better in school and have higher-ranking and higher-paying jobs than others. According to some psychologists, the most likely explanation for why both IQ and achievement vary across races is that *society*, not IQ tests themselves, is biased, leading both to differences in IQ test performance and to differences in grades and career achievement among races. For example, African Americans and Hispanic Americans may receive lower scores on IQ tests because of prejudice, inferior schooling, and other environmental disadvantages. These disadvantages, in turn, leave many African and Hispanic Americans less prepared to compete in higher education and the job market. Nevertheless, the finding that IQ tests are also equally correlated with reaction time measures across races suggests that this explanation may not tell the whole story, because these measures are unlikely to be affected by social disadvantage (Jensen, 1980).

Although IQ tests don't appear to be biased in the technical sense, some questions do seem to be biased against people of certain racial or cultural backgrounds. For example, the answer to the question "Who was the prime minister of England during the Second World War?" may be more relevant to some ethnic groups than others, especially those in Europe. But surprisingly, we can't always tell whether a test item is biased just by looking at it (Jensen & McGurk, 1987). For example, a number of years ago, test developers adapting an American IQ test for Canadians removed an item asking them to name four U.S. presidents and replaced it with an item asking them to name four Canadian prime ministers. There was only one problem with this reasonable-sounding idea: Canadians did worse on the new question than the old one (Stanovich, 2006).

Some researchers have tried to develop IQ tests that erase or even reverse the racial IQ gap. For example, African American psychologist Robert Williams (1972) developed the Black Intelligence Test of Cultural Homogeneity (BITCH), a measure designed to assess knowledge specific to African American culture, see **Figure 9.21.** As Williams predicted, African Americans not only did better on the BITCH than on standard IQ tests, but they did better than Caucasians. Although the BITCH received a good deal of attention in the popular press (Williams, 1974), later research showed that it didn't correlate positively with other measures of intelligence (Matarazzo & Weins, 1977).

---

(1) Gospel Bird is a: (a) pheasant, (b) chicken, (c) goose, (d) duck

(2) Alley Apple is: (a) a brick, (b) piece of fruit, (c) dog, (d) horse

(3) Nose Opened means: (a) flirting, (b) teed off, (c) deeply in love, (d) very angry

(4) T.C.B. means: (a) that's cool, baby, (b) taking care of business, (c) they couldn't breathe, (d) took careful behavior

(5) Playing the dozens: (a) playing the numbers, (b) playing baseball, (c) insulting a person's parents, (d) playing with women

---

Figure 9.21 A Few Items from the BITCH Test. Answers are upside-down at the bottom of the page. (*Source:* Williams, 1972)

What Are the Causes of Racial Differences in IQ? The finding that IQ tests aren't biased means we can't blame the tests for the race gap in IQ, but it doesn't address the question of what's producing this gap. Some researchers have pointed out that IQ is heritable and have argued from this finding that racial differences must be due at least partly to genetic influences. However, this is a faulty conclusion based on a misunderstanding of how the heritability of a trait among individuals *within* a group relates to the heritability of this trait *between* groups.

Within-group heritability is the extent to which a trait, like IQ, is heritable within groups, such as Asian Americans or women. **Between-group heritability** is the extent to which the difference in this trait between groups, such as between Asian Americans and Caucasians or between men and women, is heritable. It's critical to keep in mind that *within-group heritability doesn't necessarily imply between-group heritability.* That is, just because IQ is heritable within groups doesn't imply that the difference between these groups has anything to do with their genes. Some researchers have confused within-group and between-group heritability, assuming mistakenly that because IQ is heritable within any group such as a race or gender, racial differences in IQ must themselves be heritable (Lilienfeld & Waldman, 2000; Nisbett, 1995). To return to our plant analogy, we must remember that within each, some plants grew taller than others. These differences were caused by differences in the heartiness of the genetic strain of the individual plants within each group. Nevertheless, the differences between the two groups of plants were due entirely to environmental factors, even though within-group differences were due entirely to genes.

So what's the evidence that racial differences in IQ result from environmental and *not* genetic factors? Most of this research comes from analyses of differences between African Americans and Caucasians, and it largely points away from a genetic explanation of racial IQ gaps.

One study conducted in Germany shortly after World War II compared the IQ scores of children of African American soldiers and Caucasian German mothers with the children of Caucasian American soldiers and Caucasian German mothers. In both groups,

University of California at Berkeley psychologist Frank Worrell (2006) on the controversial topic of race differences in IQ: "Scientists and practitioners must begin to give greater weight to data, even when the data clash with deeply held beliefs. All of us must be willing to have respectful conversations with those who do not agree with us."

within-group heritability
extent to which the variability of a trait within a group is genetically influenced

between-group heritability
extent to which differences in a trait between groups is genetically influenced

Answers: (1) b, (2) a, (3) c, (4) b, (5) c

mothers raised the children, so the societal environment was approximately the same. The IQs of these two groups of children didn't differ (Eyferth, 1961). Thus, the differing race-related genes appeared to have no bearing on children's IQ when environment was roughly equated. Other studies have examined whether African Americans with Caucasian European ancestry obtain a "boost" in IQ relative to those with few European ancestors, which would be expected if racial differences were genetic. The research shows that African Americans with more ancestors of Caucasian descent don't differ significantly in IQ from those with few or no such ancestors (Nisbett, 1995; Scarr, Pakstis, Katz, & Barker, 1977; Witty & Jenkins, 1934). One group of researchers even found a slight tendency in the opposite direction: African Americans with more Caucasian European ancestry had *lower* IQs (Loehlin, Vandenberg, & Osborne, 1973). In any case, these findings provide no evidence for a genetic explanation of the IQ gap between African Americans and Caucasians.

Another study examined the effect of cross-racial adoption on IQ. This study showed that the IQs of African American children adopted by middle-class Caucasian parents were higher at age 7 than those of either the average African American or Caucasian child (Scarr & Weinberg, 1976). This finding suggests that what appears to be a race-related effect may actually be more related to socioeconomic status, because a much higher percentage of African and Hispanic Americans than Caucasians and Asian Americans are living in poverty. A follow-up of these children revealed that their IQs declined over a 10-year period (Weinberg, Scarr, & Waldman, 1992), which may mean that the effects of socioeconomic status are short-lived. Or it may mean that the negative effects (such as discrimination) of being a member of an ethnic minority group in a predominantly Caucasian community gradually counteracts the effects of a changed environment.

Research suggests that stereotype threat can lead African American students to perform worse on tests on which they believe members of their race tend to do poorly.

Stereotype Threat. One environmental factor that may affect how individuals perform and achieve is **stereotype threat.** Stereotype threat refers to the fear that we may confirm a negative group stereotype, such as a stereotype of our group as less intelligent or less athletic than others. Stereotype threat can create a self-fulfilling prophecy, in which those who are anxious about confirming a negative stereotype actually increase their likelihood of doing so. According to Claude Steele, stereotype threat can impair individuals' performance on IQ tests and standardized tests, like the SAT. Here's his reasoning: If we're members of a group that has a reputation for doing poorly on IQ tests, the mere thought that we're taking an IQ test will arouse stereotype threat. We think, "I'm supposed to do really badly on this test." This belief, Steele (1997) contends, can itself influence behavior, leading some people who would otherwise do well to display reduced performance.

Steele has shown that stereotype threat can indeed depress African Americans' IQ scores, at least in the laboratory. When researchers gave African Americans items from an IQ test but told them the items were measuring something other than IQ, like "the ability to solve puzzles," they performed better than when told the items were measuring IQ (Steele & Aronson, 1995). Also, giving African Americans and Caucasians an in-class writing assignment designed to boost their personal identity—by asking them to identify their most important personal value, like friends, family, or expressing themselves through art—reduced the racial gap in academic performance by 40 percent (Cohen, Garcia, Apfel, & Master, 2006). The meaning of these intriguing findings isn't clear. One possibility is that thinking about what's important to us, or focusing on ourselves as individuals rather than as members of a group, renders us less vulnerable to stereotype threat. The extent to which stereotype threat findings extend beyond the laboratory and generalize to the real world remains an active area of investigation and debate (Stricker & Ward, 2004).

Some researchers (McCarty, 2001) and writers in the popular media (Chandler, 1999) have gone so far as to suggest that racial differences between African Americans and Caucasians on IQ tests are due completely to stereotype threat and self-fulfilling prophecies (Brown & Day, 2006). Nevertheless, most studies suggest that the effects of stereotype threat aren't large enough to account fully for this gap (Sackett, Hardison, & Cullen, 2004).

stereotype threat
fear that we may confirm a negative group stereotype

Our discussion leads us to the unsettling conclusion that broader societal differences in resources, opportunities, attitudes, and experiences are probably responsible for much, if not all, of the racial differences in IQ. The encouraging news, however, is that nothing in the research literature implies that racial differences in IQ are unchangeable. If environmental disadvantages can contribute to IQ differences, then eradicating the disadvantages may eliminate these differences.

ASSESS YOUR KNOWLEDGE: FACT OR FICTION?

(1) There are few or no sex differences on spatial tasks, such as mental rotation. (True/False)

(2) The IQ difference between African Americans and Caucasians is smaller than the IQ difference within each group. (True/False)

(3) Average differences between groups on a test don't necessarily indicate that the test is biased. (True/False)

(4) Within-group heritability necessarily implies between-group heritability. (True/False)

(5) Stereotype threat may account for part of the IQ difference between African Americans and Caucasians. (True/False)

Answers: (1) F (p. 381); (2) T (pp. 382–383); (3) T (p. 384); (4) F (p. 385); (5) T (p. 386).

The Rest of the Story: Other Dimensions of Intellect

IQ, IQ, and still more IQ. Pretty much everything we've discussed in this chapter presumes that IQ is a good measure of intelligence. Although there's strong evidence that IQ tests are valid indicators of what psychologists call intelligence, it's clear that there's far more than high IQ to living our lives intelligently. Many people without sky-high IQs are wise and thoughtful citizens of society, and many people with sky-high IQs behave in foolish, even disastrous ways. If you have any doubt about the latter, just look at the string of high-profile corporate scandals over the past 10 years, in which well-educated and highly intelligent CEOs got caught red-handed doing remarkably dumb things. We'll conclude the chapter with a survey of other psychological variables that can make us act intelligently—and not so intelligently.

CREATIVITY

By age 54, German composer Ludwig van Beethoven was almost completely deaf. Yet when he reached that age in 1824, he somehow managed to compose his monumental Ninth Symphony, even though while conducting the orchestra performing its world premiere, he couldn't hear a note of it.

"Beethoven's Ninth," as musicologists call it, was astonishing in its originality and brilliance: It was completely unlike any piece of music ever written. No one had thought of composing a symphony more than an hour long (most symphonies were less than half that long), let alone including singers and a full chorus in a musical form that had always been purely instrumental. Nor had anyone been so daring—or brash—as to switch the long-established order of the symphony's traditional four movements, with the slow movement coming third instead of second. As is often the case in response to works of music, art, and literature that break the mold, some critics condemned Beethoven's Ninth as too abrasive, too reckless, and too "different." One wrote that the piece "sounds to me like the upsetting of a bag of nails, with here and there also a dropped hammer" (Goulding, 1992). Yet today, many experts consider Beethoven's Ninth Symphony the greatest piece of music ever written.

The string of high-profile corporate scandals over the past decade is evidence enough that high IQ doesn't prevent smart and successful people, like the late Enron CEO Ken Lay, from doing foolish and illegal things.

fictoid

Myth: Most creative ideas arrive in sudden flashes of insight.

Reality: Studies of brain activity indicate that well before people report a sudden creative answer to a problem, brain areas involved in problem solving (particularly those in the frontal and temporal lobes) have already been active (Kounios et al., 2006).

Beethoven's music personifies creativity. But like Supreme Court Justice Potter Stewart, who defined obscenity by saying, "I know it when I see it" (*Jacobellis v. Ohio*, 1964), psychologists have found creativity easier to identify than define. Nevertheless, most psychologists agree that creative accomplishments consist of two features: they are *novel* and *successful*. When we hear an exceptionally creative piece of music, like Beethoven's Ninth, or see an exceptionally creative painting, we nod our heads and say "Wow, that's amazing. He—or she—got it exactly right."

Psychologists often measure creativity using tests of **divergent thinking** (Guilford, 1967; Razoumnikova, 2000): the capacity to generate many different solutions to problems. For this reason, psychologists sometimes call it "outside the box" thinking. For example, in the "Uses for Objects" test, subjects must generate as many uses for an ordinary object, like a paper clip or a brick, as they can (Hudson, 1967). It's likely, though, that tests of divergent thinking don't capture everything about creativity. To be creative, we also need to be good at **convergent thinking:** the capacity to find the single best answer to a problem (Bink & Marsh, 2000). As two-time Nobel Prize winner Linus Pauling said, to be creative we need to first come up with lots of ideas, and then toss out all the bad ones.

We shouldn't confuse intelligence with creativity: Measures of these two capacities are only weakly or moderately associated, with correlations often in the .2 or .3 range (Furnham, Zhung, & Chamorro Premuzio, 2006; Willerman, 1979). Many intelligent people aren't especially creative, and vice versa.

Frank Lloyd Wright's architectural masterpiece, "Fallingwater," is a prime example of a remarkable creative achievement. It still stands proudly in rural Pennsylvania.

Highly creative people are an interesting lot. They tend to be emotionally troubled while possessed of high self-esteem. In short, they're not always the easiest folks in the world to get along with (Barron, 1969; Cattell, 1971). Creative individuals also tend to be bold and willing to take intellectual risks (Sternberg & Lubart, 1992). When the Kaufman family asked architect Frank Lloyd Wright to build a house in rural Pennsylvania overlooking a waterfall, they assumed that it would be just another pretty house with a view of flowing water. To their amazement, Wright designed the house not overlooking the waterfall but *over* it, with the water running beneath it! Today, Wright's "Fallingwater," completed in 1937, stands as perhaps the greatest accomplishment in modern American architecture.

There's evidence of a link between creativity and *bipolar disorder*, about which we'll learn more in Chapter 15. People with bipolar disorder (once called manic depression) experience episodes of greatly elevated exuberance, energy, self-esteem, and risk taking. They frequently report that their thoughts race through their heads more quickly than they can speak them, and they can go for days without much sleep. During these dramatic bursts of heightened mood and activity (called manic episodes), individuals with bipolar disorder who have artistic talents may become especially productive. Nevertheless, there's not much evidence that their work increases in quality, only quantity (Weisburg, 1994).

Biographical evidence suggests that many great painters such as Vincent van Gogh, Paul Gauguin, and Jackson Pollack; great writers such as Emily Dickinson, Mark Twain, and Ernest Hemingway; and great composers such as Gustav Mahler, Peter Iylich Tchaikovsky, and Robert Schumann, suffered from bipolar disorder (Jamison, 1993; McDermott, 2001). Moreover, studies show that highly creative individuals in artistic and literary professions have higher than expected levels of bipolar disorder and closely related conditions (Andreasen, 1987; Jamison, 1989). See **Figure 9.22.**

Because they're willing to take intellectual risks, creative people typically fall flat on their faces more often than do uncreative people. Even Beethoven composed a few

divergent thinking
capacity to generate many different solutions to a problem

convergent thinking
capacity to generate the single best solution to a problem

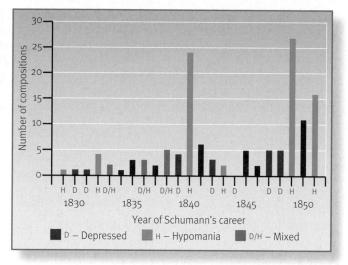

Figure 9.22 Robert Schumann and a Graph of His Productivity. The German composer Robert Schumann almost certainly suffered from bipolar disorder. As we can see, his productivity increased dramatically during "hypomanic" (mild manic) episodes and decreased dramatically during depressive episodes (which most people with bipolar disorder also experience; see Chapter 15). (*Source:* Weisberg, 1994)

notable clunkers. Probably the best predictor of the *quality* of a person's creative accomplishments is the *quantity* of that person's output (Simonton, 1999). Extremely creative artists, musicians, and scientists produce far more stuff than other people. Some of it isn't especially good, but much of it is. And every once in a while, some of it is truly great.

PERSONALITY, INTERESTS, AND INTELLECT

Think of a friend with strong mathematical and engineering skills, perhaps a classmate who's a wizard with computers. Then think of a friend with a strong penchant for literature, perhaps someone who's a poet or even a fiction writer in her spare time. Do they differ in their personalities and interests? Odds are they do. Research shows that people with different intellectual strengths tend to exhibit different personality traits and interest patterns (Ackerman & Beier, 2003).

Although IQ isn't related to most personality traits, it's moderately and positively associated (a correlation of about .3) with one trait we'll encounter in Chapter 14: *openness to experience* (DeYoung, Peterson, & Higgins, 2005; Gignac, Stough, & Lovkonitis, 2004). People high in openness to experience are imaginative, intellectually curious, and excited about exploring new ideas, places, and things (Goldberg, 1993). Nevertheless, the link between IQ and openness is more associated with crystallized than fluid intelligence (Ackerman & Heggestad, 1997). We don't fully understand the causal direction here. Higher crystallized intelligence could give rise to greater openness to experience, as people who know more things to begin with may find learning new things to be easier and therefore more enjoyable. Alternatively, greater openness to experience could give rise to greater crystallized intelligence, as people who are intellectually curious may expose themselves to more knowledge and learn more things.

Correlation vs. Causation

When we get to the level of specific mental abilities, we find that people with different intellectual strengths typically display different intellectual interests. People with high levels of scientific and mathematical ability tend to be especially interested in investigating the workings of nature and often describe themselves as enjoying the practical deeds of everyday life, like balancing checkbooks or fixing things around the house. People with high levels of verbal ability tend to be interested in art and music. And people who are poor at math and spatial ability tend to be especially interested in going into professions that involve helping others (Ackerman & Heggestad, 1997; Ackerman, Kanfer, & Goff, 2005). What we're good at—and not good at—tells us quite a bit about what we like to do.

emotional intelligence
ability to understand our own emotions and those of others, and to apply this information to our daily lives

EMOTIONAL INTELLIGENCE: IS EQ AS IMPORTANT AS IQ?

Emotional intelligence—the ability to understand our emotions and those of others, and to apply this information to our everyday lives (Goleman, 1995; Salovey & Mayer, 1990)—is one of hottest topics in popular psychology today. People with high "EQs" (emotional quotients) know themselves and know others. Most proponents of emotional intelligence maintain that this ability is just as important as traditional intelligence for effective functioning in the world.

Some items on emotional intelligence tests ask subjects to report how good they are at handling their emotions under stress. Others ask subjects to identify which emotion a face is expressing (a skill on which women usually outperform men, as we've already seen). Still others ask subjects to predict what emotion a person will experience in a given situation, like meeting future in-laws for the first time or being asked an embarrassing question during a job interview (**Figure 9.23**). Many American companies now provide their employees and bosses with formal training for boosting their emotional intelligence (Locke, 2005). Among other things, EQ training seminars teach workers to "listen" to their emotions in making decisions, find better means of coping with stressful job situations, and express empathy to coworkers.

> *When Anne's friend Maggie was feeling depressed over a recent break-up with her boyfriend, Anne took several hours off from studying for a big test to drive to Maggie's apartment and comfort her. Two weeks later, Anne was upset over an argument with her sister, and phoned Maggie to talk about it. Maggie told Anne she was busy packing for an upcoming trip and asked if they could put off talking until the following week. Anne felt _____. (Select the best choice.)*

| (a) sad | (b) nervous | (c) embarrassed | (d) resentful | (e) envious |

Figure 9.23 Item Similar to That on a Test of Emotional Intelligence. How would you do on a test of emotional intelligence? Try your hand at this item, modeled after those on actual emotional intelligence measures. The correct answer is upside-down at the bottom of this page.

Few would dispute the claim that these are helpful skills on the job. Still, the emotional intelligence concept has its critics. In particular, it's not clear that this concept offers much beyond personality (Matthews, Zeidner, & Roberts, 2002). Most measures of emotional intelligence assess personality traits, such as extraversion, agreeableness, and openness to experience, at least as much they do intelligence (Conte, 1995). Moreover, although advocates of emotional intelligence claim that this concept predicts job performance beyond general intelligence, research suggests otherwise (Van Rooy & Viswesvaran, 2004). Nor is there much evidence that different measures of emotional intelligence are highly correlated (Conte, 1995). The most parsimonious hypothesis is that emotional intelligence isn't anything new, and that it's instead a mixture of personality traits that psychologists have studied for decades.

Occam's Razor

Even some highly intelligent individuals continue to believe that the Kennedy assassination was the product of an organized conspiracy by the U.S. government despite compelling evidence against this claim.

Answer to Figure 9.23: d

WHY SMART PEOPLE BELIEVE STRANGE THINGS

High levels of intelligence afford no guarantee against beliefs for which there's scant evidence (Hyman, 2002). People with high IQs are at least as prone as other people to beliefs in conspiracy theories, such as the belief that President Kennedy's assassination was the result of a coordinated plot within the U.S. government (Goertzel, 1994) or that the Bush administration orchestrated the September 11 attacks (Molé, 2006). Moreover, the history of science is replete with examples of brilliant individuals holding strange beliefs. Two-time Nobel Prize–winning chemist Linus Pauling, whom we encountered when discussing creativity, insisted that high levels of vitamin C can cure cancer, despite overwhelming evidence to the contrary.

In many cases, smart people embrace odd beliefs because they're adept at finding plausible-sounding reasons to bolster their opinions (Shermer, 2002). IQ is correlated positively with the ability to defend our positions effectively, but correlated negatively with the ability to consider alternative positions (Perkins, 1981). High IQ may be related to the strength of the **ideological immune system:** our defenses against evidence that contradicts our views (Shermer, 2002; Snelson, 1993). We've all felt our ideological immune systems kicking into high gear when a friend challenges our political beliefs (say, about capital punishment) with evidence we'd prefer not to hear. First we first feel defensive, and then we frantically search our mental knowledge banks to find arguments that could refute our friend's irksome evidence. Our knack for defending our positions against competing viewpoints can sometimes lead to confirmation bias, blinding us to information we should take seriously.

Robert Sternberg (2002) suggested that people with high IQs are especially vulnerable to the *sense of omniscience* (knowing everything). Because intelligent people know many things, they frequently make the mistake of thinking they know just about everything. For example, the brilliant writer Sir Arthur Conan Doyle, who invented the character Sherlock Holmes, got taken in by an embarrassingly obvious photographic prank (Hines, 2003). In the 1917 "Cottingley fairies" hoax, two young British girls insisted that they'd photographed themselves along with dancing fairies. Brushing aside the criticisms of doubters, Conan Doyle wrote a book about the Cottingley fairies and defended the girls against accusations of trickery. He'd forgotten the basic principle that extraordinary claims require extraordinary evidence. The girls eventually confessed to doctoring the photographs after someone discovered they'd cut the fairies out of a book (Randi, 1982). Conan Doyle, who had a remarkably sharp mind, may have assumed that he couldn't be duped. Yet, as we've learned throughout this book, none of us is immune from errors in thinking. When intelligent people neglect the safeguards afforded by the scientific method, they'll often be fooled.

One of the photographs from the famous Cottingley fairies hoax that took in writer Arthur Conan Doyle. Even extremely intelligent people can be fooled by fake claims.

Extraordinary Claims

WISDOM

Being intelligent isn't the same as being wise. Indeed, measures of intelligence are only moderately correlated with measures of wisdom (Helson & Srivastava, 2002). Robert Sternberg (2002) defined **wisdom** as the application of intelligence toward a common good. Wise people have learned to achieve a delicate balance among three often-competing interests: (1) concerns about oneself (self-interest), (2) concerns about others, and (3) concerns about the broader society. Wise persons channel their intelligence into avenues that benefit others. To accomplish this end, they come to appreciate alternative points of view, even as they may disagree with them. To a substantial extent, wisdom is marked by an awareness of our biases and cognitive fallibilities (Meacham, 1990). Wisdom sometimes, but by no means always, comes with age (Erikson, 1968).

Abraham Lincoln, although an emotionally troubled man prone to bouts of severe depression (Shenk, 2005), was a wise person who's justifiably regarded as one of America's greatest presidents. He managed to balance his own views about slavery with those of his citizens, rarely making bold political moves until he'd successfully mobilized public opinion in his favor. Lincoln also bent over backward to solicit the views of those who disagreed with him, going so far as to include former opponents in his cabinet (Goodwin, 2005). In all of these cases, Lincoln kept his eye on the ball: the long-term unity of the country. Thanks at least in part to his wisdom, we can today proudly include the word "United" when we say "United States of America."

This stunning stained glass window, *Figure of Wisdom*, created by artist John LaFarge in 1901, stands in the Unity Church in North Easton, Massachusetts. The verse surrounding the window reads in part, "Wisdom is more precious than rubies and all the things that thou canst desire are not to be compared unto her."

ASSESS YOUR KNOWLEDGE: FACT OR FICTION?

(1) Intelligence and creativity are highly correlated. (True/False)
(2) The work of highly creative people is almost always high in quality. (True/False)
(3) Intelligence and personality aren't entirely independent. (True/False)
(4) People with high IQs are almost always better at considering alternative points of view than people with low IQs. (True/False)

Answers: (1) F (p. 388); (2) F (p. 389); (3) T (p. 389); (4) F (p. 390)

ideological immune system
our psychological defenses against evidence that contradicts our views

wisdom
application of intelligence toward a common good

Think again...

What Is Intelligence? Definitional Confusion (pp. 354–363)

STUDY the Learning Objectives

▶ Identify different models and types of intelligence

- Sir Francis Galton proposed that intelligence stems from sensory capacity. Binet and Simon, who developed the first intelligence test, argued that intelligence consists of higher mental processes, such as reasoning, understanding, and judgment. Spearman observed that tests of mental ability tend to be positively correlated. To explain this pattern, he invoked the existence of *g,* or general intelligence, but also posited the existence of *s,* or specific factors unique to particular mental tasks. Some psychologists have argued for the existence of multiple intelligences. According to them, there are many different ways of being smart. However, it's not clear whether these proposed intelligences are independent of each other or of a more general intelligence factor.

▶ Describe the neural correlates of intelligence

- Brain size and intelligence are moderately correlated in humans. Some evidence suggests that people with high levels of intelligence possess especially efficient brains. Intelligence also seems to be related to faster reaction times, as well as working memory capacity, and probably stems in part from the activity of the prefrontal cortex.

DO YOU KNOW THESE TERMS?

- ❑ **intelligence quotient** (p. 354)
- ❑ **intelligence test** (p. 356)
- ❑ **abstract thinking** (p. 356)
- ❑ **g (general intelligence)** (p. 357)
- ❑ **s (specific abilities)** (p. 357)
- ❑ **fluid intelligence** (p. 358)
- ❑ **crystallized intelligence** (p. 358)
- ❑ **multiple intelligences** (p. 358)
- ❑ **triarchic model** (p. 359)

Identify the three kinds of intelligence in Sternberg's Triarchic Model of Intelligence. (p. 359)

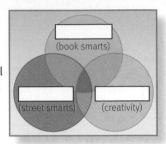
(book smarts)
(street smarts) (creativity)

THINK about what **You** would do . . .

In your introductory psychology class, you are asked to present evidence and arguments in support of the idea that your own gender is LESS intelligent than the other gender. How would you overcome the affect heuristic to fullfill your assignment? (p. 355)

Which of these images displays a different pattern than the others? What underlying abilities might be required to enable someone to answer this *g*-loaded question corrrectly? (p. 363)

 (a)
 (b)
 (c)
 (d)
 (e)

SUCCEED with mypsychlab

Gardner's Theory of Intelligence

What do Multiple Intelligences look like? (p. 358)

ASSESS your knowledge

1. According to Galton's hypothesis about intelligence, someone who has excellent eyesight and hearing would also have (high/low) intelligence. (p. 355)

2. Binet and Simon developed what is considered to be the first _____ _____ , which served as a model for many intelligence researchers who followed in their footsteps. (p. 356)

3. In trying to define intelligence, early 20th century researchers agreed that it was related to _____ _____. (p. 356)

4. The theory of _____ _____, developed by Charles Spearman, that accounted for the believed differences in intellect among people, could be explained by a single common factor. (p. 357)

5. According to Spearman, someone's intelligence is not only dependent on his/her general intelligence, or *g,* but also on his/her _____ or _____ _____. (p. 357)

6. When driving a vehicle you've never driven, you are relying on your capacity for _____ _____, but when you answer a question on a history test, you are relying on your capacity for _____ _____. (p. 358)

7. According to Gardner's influential model of multiple intelligences, there are many different types of intelligence, which he refers to as _____ _____ _____ (p. 358)

8. Sternberg's Triarchic Model argues that there are three types of intelligence: _____, _____, and _____. (pp. 359–360)

9. Albert Einstein's brain weighed (more/less) than the average brain. (p. 362)

10. Haier's study of college students who played the video game Tetris indicated that the brains of the more intelligent students were especially _____ _____ at mental processing. (p. 362)

Intelligence Testing: The Good, the Bad, and the Ugly (pp. 363–374)

STUDY the Learning Objectives

▶ Determine how psychologists calculate IQ

- Stern defined the intelligence quotient (IQ) as mental age divided by chronological age, with the result multiplied by 100. This simple formula becomes problematic in adolescence and adulthood, because mental age tends to level out at around age

Apply your knowledge of the WAIS by viewing each visual example and identifying its corresponding test and description. (p. 366)

Test	Description	Example
_____	_____	Shown: 1 2 3 4 Fill in: 4 2 1 3
_____	_____	Tell me what is missing:
_____	_____	Assemble blocks to match this design:

what **You** would do . . .

THINK about ?

As a student in a diverse urban classroom, you are asked to assess students' "intelligence." How would you try to optimize cultural fairness when doing so? (p. 367)

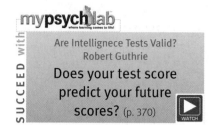

SUCCEED with

mypsych lab
where learning comes to life!

Are Intellignece Tests Valid?
Robert Guthrie

Does your test score predict your future scores? (p. 370)

WATCH

16. As a consequence, most modern intelligence tests define IQ in terms of deviation IQ.

▶ Explain the history of misuse of intelligence tests in the United States
  • Eugenics was the effort to improve a population's "genetic stock" by encouraging people with "good genes" to reproduce, by discouraging people with "bad genes" from reproducing, or both. IQ tests became an important tool of the eugenics movement, because many proponents of eugenics wished to minimize the reproduction of individuals with low IQs. In part because of eugenics, some people today view IQ tests with skepticism.

▶ Distinguish the unique characteristics of mental retardation and genius
  • There are four categories of mental retardation: mild, moderate, severe, and profound. At least 85 percent of mentally retarded individuals fall into the mild category. Terman's study of gifted school children helped to debunk the widespread ideas that highly intelligent individuals are physically frail, that child prodigies "burn out" in adulthood, and that genius often leads to insanity.

Using Wilhelm Stern's IQ formula, complete the equation and calculate IQ for the example provided. Next explain the central flaw in this formula when applying it to two adults with a mental age of 18, the first of whom is 18 years old, and the second of whom is 35 years old. (p. 364)

$$\underset{\text{(mental age)}}{8} \div \underset{\substack{\text{(chronological} \\ \text{age)}}}{10} = \underset{\text{(total)}}{\rule{2cm}{0.4pt}} \times \underset{}{\rule{1.5cm}{0.4pt}} = \underset{\text{(IQ)}}{\rule{2cm}{0.4pt}}$$

A S S E S S your knowledge

1. When computing IQ, modern researchers rely on a statistic called _____ _____. (p. 364)

2. Mandatory sterilization is one of the extremely disturbing practices that came about as a result of the _____ _____. (p. 365)

3. Psychologists have developed many different adult IQ tests, but the most commonly used is the _____ _____ _____ _____. (p. 366)

4. Whereas an IQ test is designed to measure general intelligence, a _____ _____ is designed to measure competence in a particular area or to predict academic success. (p. 367)

5. The test-retest reliability of IQ tests in adults is (high/low), and the test-retest reliability of IQ tests in infancy is (high/low). (p. 369)

6. The _____ of IQ tests indicates whether these tests accurately measure what they purport to measure. (p. 370)

7. There are three criteria that define mental retardation: (1) onset prior to adulthood, (2) IQ below approximately _____, and (3) inadequate adaptive functioning. (p. 372)

8. There are four categories of mental retardation and 85 percent of cases fall into the _____ category. (p. 372)

9. _____ is an organization whose members score in the top _____ percent of the IQ range. (p. 373)

10. Terman's "Termites" refuted common misconceptions about people with (very high/very low) IQs. (p. 373)

DO YOU KNOW THESE TERMS?

- ❏ **mental age** (p. 364)
- ❏ **deviation IQ** (p. 364)
- ❏ **eugenics** (p. 364)
- ❏ **association fallacy** (p. 365)
- ❏ **Wechsler Adult Intelligence Scale (WAIS)** (p. 366)
- ❏ **Stanford-Binet IQ test** (p. 367)
- ❏ **culture-fair IQ tests** (p. 367)
- ❏ **bell curve** (p. 371)
- ❏ **mental retardation** (p. 372)

Genetic and Environmental Influences on IQ (pp. 374–380)

SUCCEED with

mypsych lab
where learning comes to life!

Factors Affecting Intelligence

You be the judge: what contributes to our level of intelligence?

(p. 376)

EXPLORE

Identify four possible environmental influences on IQ as seen in the Flynn effect. (p. 379)

1. _____
2. _____
3. _____
4. _____

What effect, according to Ceci, does summer vacation have on a child's IQ and what does this suggest about the factors contributing to performance on IQ tests? (p. 377)

THINK about ?

what **You** would do . . .

In your prenatal classes the controversy surrounding breast-feeding is raised. Given what we currently know (and don't know) about the breast-feeding–IQ link, would you breast-feed your child? (pp. 378–379)

S T U D Y the Learning Objectives

▶ Explain how genetic influences can be determined from family studies
  • Twin and adoption studies show that at least some of the tendency for IQ to run in families is genetic.

▶ Identify ways in which the environment affects IQ measures
  • Schooling is related to high IQ scores. Research suggests that both poverty and nutrition are causally related to IQ, although disentangling the effects of nutrition from other factors, such as social class, is challenging.

DO YOU KNOW THIS TERM?

- ❏ **Flynn effect** (p. 379)

ASSESS your knowledge

1. Galton conducted one of the first _____ _____ of intelligence to determine whether intellectual brilliance runs in families. (p. 375)

2. Twin studies tell us that IQ is influenced both by _____ and _____ factors. (p. 375)

3. _____ studies are a way for researchers to separate environmental effects from genetic effects. (p. 376)

4. If a child from a deprived environment is adopted into an enriched family environment, we would expect this child's IQ to (increase/decrease/stay the same). (p. 376)

5. Environmental influences on intelligence can be divided into two types: the _____ environment, such as school and parents, and the _____ environment, such as nutrition and exposure to toxins. (p. 376)

6. According to Zajonc, later-born children tend to have a slightly (higher/lower) IQ than earlier-born siblings. (p. 377)

7. If a student drops out of school, it's likely that his/her IQ score will (increase/decrease/stay the same). (p. 377)

8. According to studies like Rosenthal and Jacobson's, if a teacher thinks a student has obtained a high IQ score, that teacher will give (more/less) attention to that student. This is related to the _____ _____ _____ effect. (p. 378)

9. Studies from poor areas in Central America suggest that ____ in childhood can lower IQ. (p. 378)

10. If your IQ is higher than your grandparent's IQ, this may be attributable to the _____ _____. (p. 379)

Group Differences in IQ: The Science and the Politics (pp. 380–387)

STUDY the Learning Objectives

▶ Identify similarities and differences in mental ability between men and women

- Most research suggests little, if any, overall average sex differences in IQ between men and women. Nevertheless, numerous studies indicate that men are more variable in their IQ scores than women. Women tend to do better than men on some verbal tasks, whereas men tend to do better than women on some spatial tasks.

▶ Evaluate the evidence concerning racial differences in IQ

- On average, African Americans score about 15 points lower than Caucasians on standard IQ tests. Asian Americans score about 5 points higher than Caucasians. Nevertheless, there is substantial overlap in the IQ distributions across races. Test bias does not appear to be a viable interpretation of the IQ test gap between African Americans and Caucasians because IQ scores predict the same things in African Americans and Caucasians.

▶ Explain why evidence regarding group differences in IQ does not imply inherent superiority or inferiority of one group relative to another

- Within-group heritability does not imply between-group heritability. Just because IQ scores are heritable within races does not mean that the IQ difference between races is heritable. Most research points toward an environmental explanation for the race IQ gap, with such factors as poverty and societal discrimination playing a role.
- Stereotype threat, which refers to the fear that we may confirm a negative group stereotype, may account for at least some of the IQ difference between Caucasians and African Americans.

DO YOU KNOW THESE TERMS?

- ❏ **test bias** (p. 384)
- ❏ **within-group heritability** (p. 385)
- ❏ **between-group heritability** (p. 385)
- ❏ **stereotype threat** (p. 386)

How can environmental influences explain how two sets of plants that started out at the same height can end up so different? What does this thought experiment tell us about potential environmental effects on IQ? (p. 383)

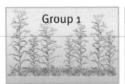
Group 1   Group 2

mypsychlab *where learning comes to life!*

Stereotype Threat

How does stereotype threat affect an individual's performance on an IQ or standardized test? (p. 386)

LISTEN

There is little evidence for sex differences in IQ overall, but research has shown that there are consistent differences between the sexes in some specific skills. Indicate below which sex (M/F) has scored higher on each of the skills listed. (pp. 381–382)

- _____ Spelling
- _____ Arithmetic calculation *(in childhood)*
- _____ Complex mathematical tasks *(in adolescence)*
- _____ Safe driving
- _____ Geography
- _____ Sociability
- _____ Reading facial expression for emotion
- _____ Spatial ability

what You would do . . .

Based on your knowledge of the IQ–gender relationship, how would you work to diffuse a controversy like the one sparked by former president of Harvard University, Lawrence Summers? (p. 380)

ASSESS your knowledge

1. Whereas the topic of individual differences in IQ is controversial, the topic of _____ differences in IQ is even more so. (p. 380)

2. Comments about women in science and mathematics made by a former president of Harvard University sparked a firestorm about _____ differences in IQ. (p. 380)

3. Men and women (are/aren't) similar when it comes to most intellectual abilities. (pp. 380–381)

4. Men tend to do better than women on some tasks requiring _____ ability, and women tend to do better than men on some tasks requiring _____ ability. (p. 381)

5. From 1966–2001, the number of women entering the "hard" sciences (increased/decreased) steadily. (p. 382)

6. Scientists can determine only the origins of racial differences, specifically whether they are genetic,

_____, or both. (p. 383)

7. The authors of *The Bell Curve* revived a bitter public debate when they speculated that the IQ gap between races might be _____ in origin. (p. 383)

8. When a test predicts outcomes better in one group than in another, this is known as _____ _____. (p. 384)

9. In order to demonstate that there is no genetic explanation for the IQ gap between African Americans and Caucasian Americans; one needs to understand the difference between _____ heritability and _____ heritability. (p. 385)

10. If you are a member of a group that has a reputation for doing poorly on standardized tests, you may do poorly when you take one simply because of _____ _____. (p. 386)

The Rest of the Story: Other Dimensions of Intellect (pp. 387–391)

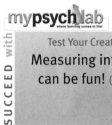

THINK about

what **You** would do . . .

Events like the death of Princess Diana and the 9/11 terrorist attacks often become the basis for conspiracy theories accepted by many people, including those who are highly intelligent. How would you determine whether the supporters of a conspiracy theory have fallen victim to Sternberg's "sense of omniscience"? (pp. 390–391)

SUCCEED with

mypsychlab *where learning comes to life!*

Test Your Creativity

Measuring intellect can be fun! (p. 387)

SIMULATION

What traits do highly creative people—like architect Frank Lloyd Wright—possess that other noncreative people lack? (p. 388)

Identify the three often competing interests that wise people are able to keep in balance: (p. 391)

1. _____

2. _____

3. _____

ASSESS your knowledge

1. Intelligence, as measured by IQ, (is/isn't) the only dimension of intellect. (p. 387)

2. If you are good at thinking "outside the box," you would probably score highly on a test that measures _____ thinking. (p. 388)

3. The ability to find the best single answer to a problem is called _____ _____. (p. 388)

4. Psychologists often measure a person's _____ by using tests of divergent and convergent thinking skills. (p. 388)

5. Correlations between measures of intelligence and creativity tend to be (low/high). (p. 388)

6. Creative people tend to be (willing/not willing) to take intellectual risks. (p. 388)

7. The one personality trait that IQ correlates moderately with is _____ _____ _____. (p. 389)

8. The ability to understand our emotions and those of others is called _____ _____. (p. 390)

9. Nobel-winning chemist Linus Pauling's belief that vitamin C cured cancer, despite overwhelming evidence to the contrary, suggests that he had a strong _____ immune system. (pp. 390–391)

10. Sternberg defines _____ as the application of intelligence toward a common good. (p. 391)

STUDY the Learning Objectives

▶ Show how creativity and personality relate to intelligence

- Creative accomplishments consist of two features: they are novel and successful. Psychologists often measure creativity using tests of divergent thinking, which assess the capacity to generate many different solutions to a problem. Nevertheless, creativity also requires convergent thinking, the capacity to find the single best answer to a problem. IQ isn't related to most personality traits. Nevertheless, IQ is moderately and positively correlated with the personality dimension of openness to experience.

▶ Evaluate scientific research on emotional intelligence and wisdom

- Emotional intelligence refers to the ability to understand our emotions and those of others, and to apply this knowledge to our lives. It's not clear whether the concept of emotional intelligence provides psychological information not provided by personality traits, such as extraversion, or by general intelligence. Wisdom is the application of intelligence toward a common good. Wisdom sometimes, but not always, comes with age.

DO YOU KNOW THESE TERMS?

- ❑ **divergent thinking** (p. 388)
- ❑ **convergent thinking** (p. 388)
- ❑ **emotional intelligence** (p. 390)
- ❑ **ideological immune system** (p. 391)
- ❑ **wisdom** (p. 391)

Remember these questions from the beginning of the chapter? Think again and ask yourself if you would answer them differently based on what you now know about intelligence and IQ testing. (For more detailed explanations, see MyPsychLab.)

▶ Is intelligence one ability or many? (p. 358)
▶ Is human intelligence related to brain size? (p. 362)
▶ How do psychologists measure intelligence? (p. 364)
▶ Are IQ scores stable over time? (p. 369)
▶ Do IQ tests predict anything useful? (p. 370)
▶ Is IQ genetically influenced? (p. 375)
▶ What environmental factors contribute to IQ? (p. 376)
▶ Are there sex and race differences in mental abilities? (pp. 380–382)
▶ Are IQ tests biased against certain minority groups? (p. 384)
▶ Does behaving intelligently involve more than IQ? (p. 387)
▶ Are all intelligent people creative, and are all creative people intelligent? (p. 388)

THINKING Scientifically

Correlation vs. Causation
pp. 360, 362, 363, 370, 374, 377, 378, 389

Falsifiability pp. 356, 359

Extraordinary Claims p. 391

Occam's Razor p. 390

Replicability pp. 362, 374, 376, 378, 382

Ruling Out Rival Hypotheses
pp. 368, 371, 375, 376

10

Human Development
How and Why We Change

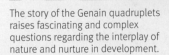

The story of the Genain quadruplets raises fascinating and complex questions regarding the interplay of nature and nurture in development.

Correlation vs. Causation

Nora, Iris, Myra, and Hester Genain grew up together. They're in their 70s now. Yet advancing age isn't the first thing that strikes you when you meet them. After being introduced to them, you soon realize that something is very wrong. All of them are emotionally disturbed in some way that you can't quite put your finger on.

In reality, Nora, Iris, Myra, and Hester aren't their actual names. The first letter of each of their names combine to form an acronym: NIMH. That's because scientists at NIMH—the National Institute of Mental Health, outside of Washington, DC—gave them these false names to safeguard their identities. Scientists at NIMH have been studying them for several decades, measuring their early and later development, personality traits, and even brain activity using functional imaging.

Why have scientists at NIMH been so interested in Nora, Iris, Myra, and Hester? It turns out that these four women have two striking things in common. First, they are identical quadruplets, products of the same **zygote** (fertilized egg; see Chapter 3), and born within 17 minutes of each other. Second, Nora, Iris, Myra, and Hester all have schizophrenia.

The Genain quadruplets, as they're known in the psychological literature, offer a classic illustration of the interplay between nature and nurture over the course of development (Rosenthal, 1963). Both of their parents suffered from serious psychological problems. Given what we know about the genetics of schizophrenia—which as we'll learn in Chapter 15 is a severe disorder of thinking and emotion that usually results in a loss of contact with reality—it's likely that the Genain quadruplets inherited a predisposition toward this condition.

Yet the timing and expression of each quadruplet's disorder differed. This finding, as NIMH researchers recognized, offers powerful evidence for the role of the environment in the manifestation of schizophrenia. That's because identical quadruplets, like identical twins, possess the same DNA; in effect they're genetic clones of one another (see Chapter 3). So any behavioral differences among the Genains must be due to differences in their environments.

Although three of the sisters—Nora, Iris, and Hester—were hospitalized for their disorder, one of them—Myra—wasn't. Indeed, Myra was clearly disturbed but better adjusted than the others. Unlike the other quadruplets, she'd once married and even held a job for many years. In contrast, Hester was the most seriously ill of the sisters; she was disoriented, confused, and almost completely incapable of caring for herself. Nora, although also disturbed, was healthier than Iris, who like Hester was frequently bewildered and out of touch with reality.

What environmental variables might account for these differences? From birth, the four sisters differed in weight. The two severely afflicted sisters—Hester and Iris—weighed less than Myra and Nora (Rosenthal, 1963). Moreover, their mother clearly favored Myra and Nora over Hester and Iris. In particular, she regarded Myra as psychologically healthier and smarter than the other quadruplets. In contrast, their mother frequently punished Hester and Iris for what she perceived as inappropriate sexual behavior (Bernheim & Lewine, 1979; Stierlin, 1972). Yet even today, the role that these environmental factors played in the development of the Genain quadruplets' schizophrenia remains a mystery.

The fascinating story of the Genain quadruplets underscores the enormous challenges that psychologists confront in disentangling nature from nurture throughout development. Was the mother's harsher treatment of Hester and Iris compared with Myra and Nora a *cause* of their more severe schizophrenia? It's certainly possible. Nevertheless, we can't conclude that with certainty, because we know only that unsupportive parental treatment in the Genain family was associated with more severe outcomes in the children. It's equally possible that their mother's harsher treatment of Hester and Iris was a *reaction* to their more severe symptoms in the first place. After all, parents may be less nurturing of their children if their children are difficult to begin with. In these cases, harsher treatment from parents may cause difficult children to become even more disturbed, resulting in even harsher treatment from parents, thereby creating a vicious cycle (Bell, 1968; Rutter et al.,

1997). In the case of the Genain quadruplets, there's no way to distinguish whether chicken or egg came first. Yet, as we'll learn, psychologists have developed methods for figuring out whether environmental factors, like parenting, are causes or effects of children's behavior.

The tale of the Genain quadruplets, like those of other case studies, raises far more questions than answers—in this case, about how the same genes and similar environments can result in different patterns of psychological adjustment. As we discovered in Chapter 2, case studies are almost always better suited for raising questions than for answering them. Yet in the case of the Genain quadruplets, these are the very questions that strike at the heart of how we become who we are.

Special Considerations in Human Development

Developmental psychology is the study of how behavior changes over time. Before we explore issues of how we develop, we need to come to grips with several challenges that often arise when investigating psychological development. Understanding these challenges, along with the critical thinking principles we've relied on throughout this book, will provide us with the equipment we need to evaluate the causes of cognitive and social changes from childhood to old age.

POST HOC FALLACY

One critical consideration to bear in mind is that things that occur first don't necessarily cause things that come later. It's tempting to conclude, for example, that because nearly 100 percent of serial killers drank milk as children, milk drinking creates mass murderers. But of course, drinking milk in infancy has nothing to do with *why* some people became serial (not cereal, that is) killers; it just happens to come beforehand. This logical error is called the **post hoc fallacy** (*post hoc* is Latin for "after this").

> ### APPLY YOUR THINKING
> Imagine that we administer a new-fangled method of teaching mathematics to first-graders. A year later, we find that their math performance has improved. How could the post hoc fallacy lead us to conclude that this method is effective even if it's not?

BIDIRECTIONAL INFLUENCES

Human development is almost always a two-way street. That is, developmental influences are bidirectional. Children's development influences their experiences, but their experiences are also influenced by their development. As we saw with the Genain quintuplets, psychological traffic from parents to children runs in both directions: Parents influence their children's behavior, which in turn feeds back to influence their parents, and so on (Bell, 1968; Collins, Maccoby, Steinberg, Hetherington, & Bornstein, 2000; O'Connor et al., 1998). Children often change their environments by acting in ways that influence their parents, siblings, friends, and teachers to respond differently from how they might have otherwise (Plomin, DeFries, & Loehlin, 1977). Furthermore, as children grow older, they play an increasingly active role in altering and selecting their environments.

It's crucial to keep bidirectional influences in mind, because pop psychology is chock full of *unidirectional* explanations: those that attempt to explain development in terms of a one-headed arrow. Parents fight with each other → their children react negatively. Children witness violence at school → they become more aggressive. There's probably a kernel of truth in each of these explanations. Yet they typically tell only part of the story. That's why so many arrows in psychology contain two heads (↔), not one. In the study of

In some ancient cultures, people believed that solar eclipses were caused by an invisible monster, like a dragon, gobbling up the sun. In response, they yelled at the monster to scare it away. After doing so, the "monster" would soon disappear and the sun would reappear along with it. These ancients fell prey to the post hoc fallacy: They assumed that because their screaming preceded the reappearance of the sun, it must have caused it.

Gangs of delinquent adolescents don't arise by chance. Research suggests that delinquent individuals typically seek out and find each other, in part because of their genetic propensities.

human development, two "heads" are almost always better—or least more accurate—than one, at least as far as arrows are concerned.

KEEPING AN EYE ON COHORT EFFECTS

Imagine we conduct a study designed to examine how people's knowledge of computers changes with age. We enter our study armed with a reasonable hypothesis: People's knowledge of computers should increase steadily from adolescence until early adulthood, after which it should level off at about age 30. After about age 30, we predict, knowledge of computers should remain about the same or increase slightly. To test our hypothesis, we sample 100,000 people in the U.S. population, with a broad age range of 18 to 80. We carefully screen out people with dementias or other forms of brain damage to ensure that we're not accidentally including people with faulty memories. However, contrary to our hypothesis, we find that people's knowledge of computers declines dramatically with age, especially between the ages of 60 and 80. What did we do wrong?

It turns out that we forgot to consider an alternative explanation for our findings. We started out by asking a perfectly sensible question. But in science, we also must make sure that the design we select is the right one for answering it. In this case, it wasn't. We used a **cross-sectional design,** a design in which researchers examine people of different ages at a single point in time (Achenbach, 1982; Raulin & Lilienfeld, in press). In a cross-sectional design, we obtain a "snapshot" of each person at a single age; we assess some people when they're 24, some when they're 47, others when they're 63, and so on.

The major problem with cross-sectional designs is that they don't control for **cohort effects:** effects due to the fact that groups that lived during one time period, called *cohorts,* can differ from other cohorts. In this study, cohort effects are a serious shortcoming, because before the late 1980s, few Americans used computers. So those over 60 years old may not be as computer savvy as younger folks. This has nothing to do with the effects of aging, but everything to do with the effects of the era in which they grew up.

A longitudinal design is the only sure way around this problem. In a **longitudinal design,** psychologists track the development of the same group of subjects over time (Shadish, Cook, & Campbell, 2002). Rather than obtaining a snapshot of each person at only one point in time, we obtain the equivalent of a series of home movies, taken at different ages. This design allows us to examine true *developmental* effects: changes over time as a consequence of growing older. Without longitudinal designs, we can be tricked into concluding that event A comes before result B even when it doesn't. For example, much of the pop psychology literature warns us that divorce leads to *externalizing behaviors*—behaviors such as breaking rules, defying authority figures, and committing crimes—in children (Wallerstein, 1989). Yet a longitudinal study that tracked a sample of boys over several decades revealed otherwise: Boys whose parents divorced exhibited externalizing behaviors *years before* the divorce even occurred (Block & Block, 2006; Block, Block, & Gjerde, 1986).

Although longitudinal designs are ideal for studying change over time, they can be costly and time-consuming. For example, our study of computer literacy would take about six decades to complete. Yet such designs are essential for figuring out what comes before what in development. When longitudinal designs aren't feasible, we should remember to interpret the results of cross-sectional studies with healthy skepticism, bearing in mind that cohort effects may account for any observed changes in behavior at different ages. We should also bear in mind that longitudinal designs aren't experimental designs (see Chapter 2), because we can't randomly assign people to groups in these studies. As a result, we can't use them to infer cause-and-effect relationships.

THE INFLUENCE OF EARLY EXPERIENCE

There's no doubt that early life experiences can sometimes shape later development in powerful ways. Because many diverse influences on behavior operate throughout the life

Ruling Out Rival Hypotheses

The classic "Up Series" directed by Michael Apted traces the lives of fourteen British people over time, from age 7 all the way up through age 49. Here, three "stars" of the documentary, Jackie, Lynn, and Sue, now in their 40s, proudly display photographs of themselves at younger ages. The longitudinal designs used by psychologists work in the same way: They track the lives of the same groups of people over time.

cross-sectional design
research design that examines people of different ages at a single point in time

cohort effects
effects observed in a sample of participants that result from individuals in the sample growing up at the same time

longitudinal design
research design that examines development in the same group of people on multiple occasions over time

span, however, we shouldn't overestimate the impact of experiences in infancy on long-term development (Bruer, 1999; Clarke & Clarke, 1976; Kagan, 1998; Paris, 2000).

In particular, we must be careful to avoid two myths concerning development. The first is the myth of *infant determinism*, the widespread assumption that extremely early experiences—especially in the first three years of life—are almost always more influential than later experiences in shaping us as adults. For example, several popular psychology sources claim that separating an infant from its mother during the first few hours after birth can produce lasting negative consequences for emotional adjustment (Klaus & Kennell, 1976). Yet there's scant evidence for such claims. Neuroscience research shows that the brain changes in important ways in response to experience throughout childhood and well into early adulthood (Greenough, 1997), supporting the notion that later experiences in life can be as influential as those in early childhood.

One striking example comes from the work of Jerome Kagan (1975), who examined Guatemalan infants whose parents had raised them in almost total isolation during their first year of life. These babies lived in small (75 square feet), windowless huts, experienced minimal contact with adults or children, and had few or no toys. The parents did this, incidentally, because of a Guatemalan folk belief in the *ojo* ("evil eye"), namely, the superstition that adults who stare directly into the eyes of infants cause them to become sick and die. These babies were significantly delayed in some developmental milestones; for example, they typically didn't begin to speak until age $2\frac{1}{2}$. Yet by adolescence, they'd caught up with typical American middle-class adolescents in cognitive and social development.

The second myth is that of *childhood fragility*, which holds that children are delicate little creatures who are easily damaged (Paris, 2000). Research shows most children are remarkably *resilient*, or capable of withstanding stress (see Chapter 12), and that most children emerge from potentially traumatic situations, including kidnappings, in surprisingly good shape (Bonanno, 2004; Garmezy, Masten, & Tellegen, 1984; Sommers & Satel, 2005). Remarkably, even many children who experience sexual abuse eventually emerge without severe psychological problems, although some probably experience long-term negative effects (Rind, Tromovitch, & Bauserman, 1998; Skuse, Markey, & Skodnek, 2003).

CLARIFYING THE NATURE–NURTURE DEBATE

As we learned in the Prologue, both *nature*—our genetic endowment—and *nurture*—the environments we encounter—play powerful roles in shaping development. Yet as we'll soon see, disentangling their effects is far from simple, because nature and nurture intersect in a variety of fascinating ways, which we've summarized in **Table 10.1.**

Table 10.1 Intersections of Nature and Nurture. Nature and nurture are hard to disentangle—it's easy to mistake an environmental effect for a genetic effect, and vice versa. Here are some of the ways that genes and environment can intersect, making it difficult to separate out the influence of each.

Nature–Nurture Intersections	Definitions
Gene-Environment Interactions	The impact of genes on behavior depends on the environment in which the behavior develops.
Nature via Nurture	Genetic predispositions can drive us to select and create particular environments, leading to the mistaken appearance of a pure effect of nature.
Gene Expression	Some genes "turn on" only in response to specific environmental events.

Distinguishing Nature from Nurture. In the mid-1990s, Betty Hart and Todd Risley (1995) conducted a 6-month longitudinal investigation that showed that parents who speak a lot to their children produce children with larger vocabularies than parents who don't. Hart and Risley's study provides evidence for a powerful environmental influence on children's vocabulary, right? Well, not so fast. In intact families, parents and children share not only an environment but also genes. To borrow a term we learned in Chapter 2,

Although popular psychology tells us that the period from birth to 3 years of age is much more critical for psychological development than other time periods, research evidence for this claim is relatively weak.

In 1976, twenty-six schoolchildren in Chowchilla, California, were taken hostage on a school bus for 11 hours and then buried underground in a van for 16 hours. Remarkably, they escaped by forcing their way out through a hole in the top of the van. Two years later, although most of the children were haunted by memories of the incident, virtually all were well-adjusted (Terr, 1988; see Chapter 12).

Hart and Risley's study of the relation between parents' talking and children's vocabulary caught the attention of Hillary Clinton, who was then first lady of the United States. She seized on these findings and cited them in her influential 1996 book *It Takes a Village*, arguing on the basis of these findings that parents should spend more time talking to their children.

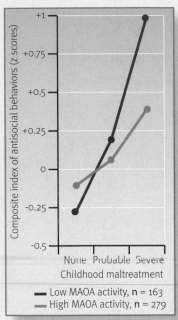

Figure 10.1 Gene-Environment Interactions. Avshalom Caspi and his colleagues demonstrated that genes and environment interact to increase risk for antisocial behavior in adolescents. For adolescents with high MAO activity, maltreatment in childhood made no difference in their risk for later antisocial behavior. But for adolescents with low MAO activity, maltreatment in childhood resulted in increased risk for antisocial behavior. The effects of genes are sometimes dependent on the environment, and vice versa (Caspi et al., 2002).

gene-environment interaction
situation in which the effects of genes depend on the environment in which they are expressed

nature via nurture
tendency of individuals with certain genetic predispositions to seek out and create environments that permit the expression of those predispositions

gene expression
activation or deactivation of genes by environmental experiences throughout development

genes and environment are *confounded*. So there's an alternative explanation for Hart and Risley's findings: Perhaps they reflect the fact that parents who speak a lot to their children have higher vocabularies themselves. It turns out that vocabulary is partly influenced by genetic factors (Stromswald, 2001), so these parents may merely be passing on their genetic predisposition for better vocabularies to their children. Many studies of human development are subject to the same confound.

Gene-Environment Interaction. Nature and nurture often *interact* over the course of development, meaning that the effect of one depends on the contribution of the other. In 2002, Avshalom Caspi and his colleagues conducted a longitudinal study of children who possessed a gene for low levels of an enzyme called *monoamine oxidase* (MAO), which research suggests places them at elevated risk for committing violent crimes later in life (Moore, Scarpa, & Raine, 2002). However, not all children with low MAO activity became violent. Caspi and his colleagues discovered that whether this genetic risk factor is associated with violence depends on a specific environmental factor (see **Figure 10.1**). Specifically, children with *both* the low MAO gene *and* a history of maltreatment (such as physical abuse) were at heightened risk for antisocial behaviors, like stealing, assault, and rape. Children with the low MAO gene alone weren't at heightened risk (Caspi et al., 2002). This finding illustrates the phenomenon of **gene-environment interaction:** In many cases, the effects of genes depend on the environment, and vice versa.

Nature via Nurture. As we learned in the Prologue, nature and nurture are rarely independent. In particular, children with certain genetic predispositions often seek out and create their own environments, a phenomenon psychologists term **nature via nurture** (Lykken, 1995; Ridley, 2003). In this way, nurture affords children the opportunity to express their genetic tendencies (Scarr & McCartney, 1983). For example, as they grow older, highly fearful children tend to seek out environments that protect them from their anxieties (Rose & Ditto, 1983). Because highly fearful children select safer environments, it may appear that safe environments are associated with fear, when the environment is actually a consequence of children's genetic predispositions.

Gene Expression. Strange as it may sound, environmental experiences actually turn genes on and off throughout development. This phenomenon of **gene expression** is one of the most significant discoveries to hit psychology over the past several decades (Plomin & Crabbe, 2000). Every one of the 100 trillion or so (give or take a few trillion) cells in our bodies contains every one of our genes. Yet only some of these genes are active at any given time, and it sometimes takes environmental experiences to flip their switches to "on." For example, children with genes that predispose them to anxiety may never become anxious unless a highly stressful event, like the death of a parent early in development, triggers these genes to become active. Gene expression reminds us that nurture affects nature. In turn, nature affects how we react to nurture, and so on.

ASSESS YOUR KNOWLEDGE: FACT OR FICTION?

(1) Just because one event precedes a second event doesn't necessarily mean that it causes it. (True/False)
(2) Most children exposed to severe stressors, such as a kidnapping, end up with healthy patterns of psychological adjustment. (True/False)
(3) Research shows that most children are passive recipients of their parents' influence. (True/False)
(4) Environmental experiences can turn genes on and off throughout the course of development. (True/False)

Answers: (1) T (p. 339); (2) T (p. 401); (3) F (p. 402); (4) T (p. 402)

The Developing Body before and after Birth: Physical and Motor Development

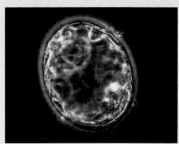

Child development begins long before birth. Learning, memory, and even preferences—for particular sounds or body positions, for example—are already well under way in unborn infants. Nevertheless, most of what develops in the **prenatal** (prior to birth) period is physical, including the form and structure of the body and, most important from a psychological standpoint, the brain.

CONCEPTION AND PRENATAL DEVELOPMENT: FROM ZYGOTE TO BABY

The greatest changes in prenatal development occur in the earliest stages of pregnancy. Following fertilization of an egg by a sperm cell, prenatal physical development unfolds in three basic stages. First, the zygote begins to divide and double, forming a **blastocyst**—a ball of identical cells that haven't yet begun to take on any specific function in a body part. The blastocyst keeps growing as cells continue to divide for the first week and a half or so after fertilization (see **Figure 10.2**). Around the middle of the second week, the cells begin to differentiate, taking on different roles as the organs of the body begin to develop.

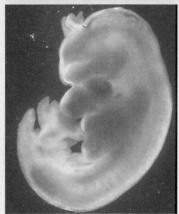

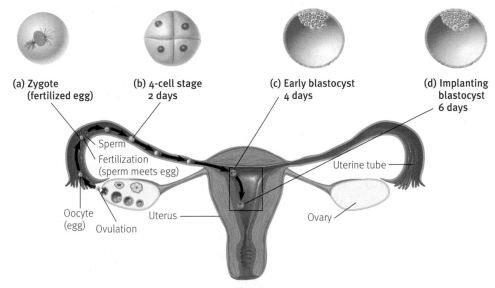

(a) Zygote (fertilized egg) · **(b) 4-cell stage 2 days** · **(c) Early blastocyst 4 days** · **(d) Implanting blastocyst 6 days**

Sperm · Fertilization (sperm meets egg) · Uterine tube · Oocyte (egg) · Ovulation · Uterus · Ovary

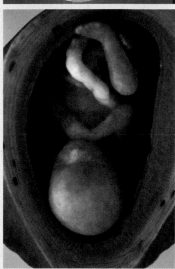

This series of photos depicts the transition from blastocyst (a mass of identical cells) (*top*) to embryo (preliminary development of skeleton, organs, and limbs) (*middle*) to fetus (recognizably human form) (*bottom*) during the first 3 months of pregnancy.

Figure 10.2 The Journey of a Fertilized Egg from Ovary to Uterus. After an egg is fertilized by a sperm cell, it begins traveling through the fallopian tube to the uterus. As it travels, cells begin to divide and duplicate, becoming a blastocyst. The blastocyst implants itself in the uterus by the sixth day. (*Source:* Adapted from Marieb and Hoehn, 2007)

Once different cells start to assume different functions, the blastocyst becomes an **embryo.** The embryonic stage continues from the second to the eighth week of development, during which limbs, facial features, and major organs of the body (including the heart, lungs, and brain) begin to take shape. It's during this stage that many things can go awry in fetal development. Spontaneous miscarriages often occur when the embryo doesn't form properly (Roberts & Lowe, 1975), frequently without the mother ever knowing she was pregnant.

By the ninth week, the major organs are established, and the heart—although it only has two chambers instead of the four we all have—has begun to beat. At this point, the embryo becomes a **fetus.** The fetus's job for the rest of the pregnancy is physical maturation. This phase is more about fleshing out what's already there than establishing new structures.

prenatal
prior to birth

blastocyst
ball of identical cells early in pregnancy that haven't yet begun to take on any specific function in a body part

embryo
second to eighth week of prenatal development, during which limbs, facial features, and major organs of the body take form

fetus
period of prenatal development from ninth week until birth after all major organs are established and physical maturation is the primary change

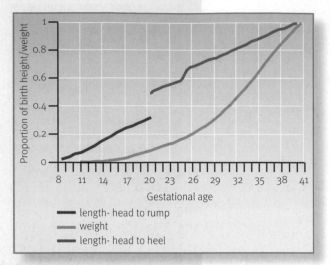

Figure 10.3 Fetal Weight Gain.
Fetuses grow in length continuously over the course of development in a smooth, ever-increasing trajectory. However, they don't begin to bulk up in weight until the last 12 weeks or so, when we see a rapid increase in weight gain from week to week.

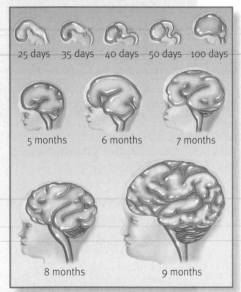

The fetal brain begins as a long tube that develops into a variety of different structures with the brain stem (which controls basic functions like breathing and digestion) developing first, followed by cortical structures later in pregnancy. (*Source:* Restak, 1984).

Ruling Out Rival Hypotheses

teratogens
environmental factors that can exert a negative impact on prenatal development

But the amount of change the basic structures undergo is substantial. The last third of pregnancy in particular is devoted almost entirely to "bulking up" (see **Figure 10.3**).

Brain Development: 18 Days and Beyond. The human brain begins to develop a mere 18 days after fertilization. Unlike most organs, which are completely formed by birth and continue to grow only in size, our brains continue to develop into adolescence and probably even early adulthood (Caviness, Kennedy, Bates, & Makris, 1996).

Between the eighteenth day of pregnancy and the end of the sixth month, neurons begin developing at an astronomical rate, a process called *proliferation*. Some estimates place the rate of neural development as high as an astonishing 250,000 brain cells per minute during peak times. The fetus ends up manufacturing many, many more neurons than it will need as an infant. In addition to producing all of these cells, the brain must organize them to perform coordinated functions. Starting in the fourth month and continuing throughout pregnancy, migration of cells begins to occur. Neurons start to sort themselves out, moving to their final positions in a specific structure of the brain, such as the visual system, cerebellum, and so on.

The final stage of prenatal brain development begins only late in pregnancy but continues well after birth. It includes three additional processes that help the brain work more efficiently—myelinization, synaptogenesis, and pruning (see Chapter 3)—all of which enhance transmission of information within the brain.

Obstacles to Normal Fetal Development. Although most babies are born healthy and fully intact, fetal development can be disrupted in two ways: (1) by exposure to hazardous environmental influences and (2) by biological influences resulting from genetic disorders or errors in cell duplication during cell division.

Teratogens: Hazards to Fetal Health. Most women don't even realize they're pregnant until after the fetus's body and brain development are well under way. Unfortunately, this means that women often engage unknowingly in activities that are potentially harmful to the fetus. **Teratogens** are environmental factors that can exert a negative impact on prenatal development. They run the gamut from drugs and alcohol to chicken pox and X-rays. Even anxiety and depression in the mother are potential teratogens because they alter the fetus's chemical and physiological environment. Depending on the teratogen and when the embryo or fetus is exposed to it, some teratogens influence how specific parts of the brain develop, whereas others exert a more general impact on development. Because the brain has such a long period of maturation relative to most other organs, it's particularly vulnerable to teratogens.

Many researchers have studied how prenatal exposure to various environmental substances impacts brain development. Yet these questions are difficult to answer, in part because brain impairment often doesn't become apparent until children are several years of age or older. As a result, it's difficult to trace problems directly to prenatal conditions, because a host of *post*natal environmental factors may have already contributed adversely to development. Take once widespread claims regarding "crack babies," which appear to have been overblown (Coles, 1993). Some mothers who smoke crack cocaine during pregnancy continue to do so after giving birth, which probably alters their parenting styles relative to mothers who don't smoke crack. Moreover, in many cases, it's challenging to find an appropriate control group. To study the effects of prenatal cocaine exposure on infant development, we'd need to identify a group of pregnant mothers who matched our cocaine-using group in exposure to other teratogens, such as alcohol and amount of prenatal care, but who *didn't* use cocaine during pregnancy. The odds of finding such a perfectly matched group are slim to none, making it difficult to implicate cocaine as a specific cause of birth defects or developmental disorders.

Genetic Disruptions of Fetal Development. Genetic disorders or random errors in cell division are a second adverse influence on prenatal development. Often, a single cell, including the egg or sperm cell prior to fertilization, or a family of cells, is copied with some error or break in the genetic material. Like a page with a smudge that keeps being photocopied with that smudge preserved, these cells go on to replicate with the error retained, resulting in impaired development of organs or organ systems. Any number of irregularities can result, some as minor as a birthmark and others as major as mental retardation, including Down syndrome (see Chapter 9).

Premature and Low-Birth-Weight Babies. A full-term baby is born at 40 weeks. Premature infants ("preemies") are those born at fewer than 36 weeks' gestation. The *viability* point, the point in pregnancy at which infants can typically survive on their own, is around 25 weeks. In rare cases, fetuses as young as 22 weeks have survived, but only with serious physical and cognitive impairments. Preemies have underdeveloped lungs and brains and are often unable to engage in basic physiological functions, such as breathing and maintaining a healthy body temperature. They also often experience serious delays in cognitive and physical development. With each week of pregnancy, the odds of fetal survival increase and the odds of developmental disorders decrease (Hoekstra, Ferrara, Couser, Payne, & Connett, 2004).

Although prematurity may seem to be an obvious risk factor for infant mortality and developmental disorders, a low birth weight, or less than 5.5 pounds (compared with an average birth weight of about 7.5 pounds) for a full-term baby, actually poses a much higher risk of death, infection, and developmental disorders (Copper et al., 1993; Schothorst & van Engeland, 1996). Underweight babies are far more common among low-income families than in middle-class and high-income families, suggesting that malnutrition, poor prenatal care, exposure to teratogens, and stress are partly to blame (Bellamy, 1998). Mothers who smoke during pregnancy are particularly likely to deliver low-birth-weight babies (Friedman, 1996).

Different teratogens adversely affect different systems and may vary in their effects at different stages of pregnancy. For example, high levels of alcohol exposure can result in a collection of symptoms known as *fetal alcohol syndrome*. Fetal alcohol syndrome includes learning disabilities, physical growth retardation, facial malformations, and behavioral disorders (Abel & Sokol, 1986).

GROWTH AND PHYSICAL DEVELOPMENT AFTER INFANCY

Once born, our bodies continue to change dramatically through early childhood, adolescence, and adulthood. A variety of changes in our physical body's proportions take place as we mature. Careful inspection of a young infant reveals that he has no apparent neck, a head almost half the size of his torso, and arms that don't even reach the top of his head. Over the course of childhood, different parts of the body grow at different rates and the ultimate proportions of the body are quite different than they were at birth. For example, the absolute size of the head continues to increase with development, but it grows at a slower pace than the torso or legs. As a result, an adolescent or young adult has a smaller head-size-to-body-size ratio than an infant (**Figure 10.4**).

Throughout this text we've sprinkled numerous examples of popular psychology wisdom that are false. Well, here's some common knowledge that's *true*: Growth spurts are real. No, people don't grow 6 inches overnight, but physical growth happens in a stop–start–stop–start fashion. Michael Hermanussen and his colleagues found what they called "mini growth spurts" occurring every 30 to 55 days in children age 3 to 16, followed by lulls during which growth is much slower (Hermanussen, 1998; Hermanussen, Geiger-Benoit, Burmeister, & Sippell, 1988). One study that measured three infants daily found that infants' growth occurs much more suddenly. The infants in this study showed no growth at all for days at a time, followed by overnight increases of as much as an inch (Lampl, Veldhuis, & Johnson, 1992)! However, other studies have failed to replicate this finding, and Hermanussen proposed that growth is actually more gradual and continuous, with shifts in the *rate* of growth at various points throughout development (Heinrichs et al., 1989; Hermanussen & Geiger-Benoit, 1995). The evidence suggests that there are spurts, but that the periods between aren't characterized by a total absence of growth.

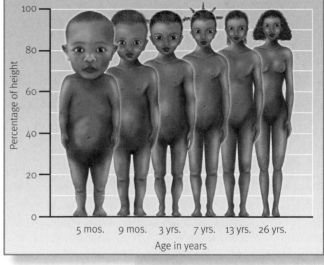

Figure 10.4 Changes in Body Proportions over Development. This figure displays the proportional size of the head, torso, and limbs across the life span when scaled to the same overall height. The size of the head relative to the body decreases dramatically over the course of development, whereas the relative length of the legs increases dramatically.

Replicability

Figure 10.5 The Progression of Motor Development. Different children typically achieve major motor milestones in the same order, although each milestone requires an entirely new set of motor coordination skills. For example, cruising, walking, and running look similar but require very different muscle groups and shifts in weight to accomplish movement.

Sitting without support
6 months

Crawling
9 months

Standing
11 months

Cruising
12 months

Walking without assistance
13 months

Running
18–24 months

Infants are born with the rooting reflex, which causes them to orient their heads and mouths toward anything that brushes up against their cheeks. This reflex helps them to locate and latch on to a potential food source, such as a breast or bottle.

motor behaviors
bodily motions that occur as result of self-initiated force that moves the bones and muscles

cognitive development
study of how children learn, think, reason, communicate, and remember

INFANT MOTOR DEVELOPMENT: HOW BABIES GET GOING

Starting at birth, infants begin to learn how to make use of their bodies through movement and to coordinate interactions with their environment. Some aspects of motor coordination are evident even at birth as a series of reflexes, whereas others develop gradually throughout infancy and early childhood.

Survival Instincts: Two Vital Reflexes. Infants are born with a set of automatic motor behaviors—or *reflexes* (see Chapter 3)—that are triggered by specific types of stimulation and fulfill important survival needs (Swaiman & Ashwal, 1999). The *sucking reflex* is an automatic response to oral stimulation. If we put something in a baby's mouth (including a finger—try it sometime . . . with the parents' permission, of course!), she'll clamp down and begin sucking. A related reflex is the *rooting reflex*, which appears to serve the same survival need: eating. If we softly stroke a hungry infant's cheek, she'll automatically turn her head toward our hand and begin casting about with her mouth, eagerly seeking nipple to suck. These reflexes help keep infants alive because if they needed to learn through association that sucking on an object yields nourishment, they might starve trying to get the hang of it!

Learning to Get Up and Go: Coordinating Movement. These and other reflexes are a critical part of survival, but they get babies only so far. Infants must learn other types of motor behaviors through trial and error. **Motor behaviors** are bodily motions that occur as result of self-initiated force that moves the bones and muscles. The age at which different children reach motor milestones varies enormously, although almost all acquire them in the same order (see **Figure 10.5**).

APPLY YOUR THINKING
There's little overlap in the types of motions involved in reaching and crawling, or crawling and walking. Why do children consistently acquire these milestones in a fixed order?

As expert reachers and expert walkers, we take for granted how easy it is to reach for a cup of coffee sitting on a table. Yet the calculations our body makes—the physical adjustments that control our body's positioning and the direction and speed of our movements—to accomplish that seemingly simple act are incredibly complex and precise. They're also customized to fit each situation, or we'd end up knocking our coffee to the floor (Adolph, 1997). As total novices, babies haven't yet learned to perform the lightning-quick calculations needed for good hand-eye coordination. Moreover, crawling and walking are even more complicated than reaching, because they involve supporting the infant's weight, coordinating all four limbs, and somehow also keeping track of where she's heading.

The Brain, the Body, and the World: Factors Influencing Motor Development. There's a wide range in the rate and manner in which children achieve motor milestones. Some crawl and walk much earlier than others, and a few skip the crawling stage entirely. These findings suggest that these skills don't necessarily build on each other in a causal fashion, as the post hoc fallacy might lead us to believe. What remains to be explained, then, is why all children acquire motor milestones in the same order regardless of when they reach each milestone.

"Nature" Accounts of Motor Development. Physical maturation plays a key role in allowing children to becoming increasingly steady and flexible in their movements. One

explanation for this role is that motor patterns are innately programmed and become activated at specific time points. Some motor achievements, such as crawling and walking, are also dependent on the physical maturation of the body, allowing children to acquire the necessary strength and coordination.

"Nurture" Accounts of Motor Development. There are several reasons to believe that experience plays a crucial role in motor development (Thelen, 1995). First, there's considerable variability across cultures in the timing of developmental milestones. Second, the fact that some children occasionally skip a stage suggests that there isn't an innate and inflexible motor program. Third, even among children who pass through all stages, there are large individual differences (see Prologue) within cultures in the age at which children achieve motor milestones. These findings suggest that over time, children are training their brains and bodies to solve motor-based challenges, building up skills and control with practice (**Figure 10.6**).

The differences among children in the rate at which motor development unfolds are influenced by physical factors. For example, heavier babies tend to achieve milestones more gradually because they need to build up their muscles more before they can support their weight (Thelen & Ulrich, 1982).

Parenting styles and cultural practices also matter. Infants who spend most of their time on Mom's lap or in the crib have fewer opportunities to explore than do infants placed on their bellies on a blanket on the floor. In Peru and China, infants are tightly swaddled in blankets that provide warmth and a sense of security, but that prevent free movement of the limbs (Li et al., 1994). Swaddled babies tend to cry less and sleep more soundly, but prolonged swaddling over the first year of life slows down their motor development. In contrast, many African and West Indian mothers engage in a variety of stretching, massage, and strength-building exercises with their infants. This practice, which can appear harmful to American eyes (how often do we see a mother letting her baby dangle by one arm?), speeds up infants' motor development (Hopkins & Westra, 1988).

Figure 10.6 Reaching Trajectory of the Arm. This figure depicts the reaching trajectory of the arm toward an object at different points in development. Three reach trajectories are depicted at each age. At 5 months, infants' reaches are much more variable and take a much less efficient path than do those of older children and adults. (*Source:* Adapted from Konczak & Dichgans, 1997)

fictoid

Myth: Overweight preschoolers are just carrying "baby fat" that will melt away as they grow older.

Reality: Although it's normal for *infants* to bulk up—and they often look quite chubby during their first year—obesity in preschoolers usually reflects poor diet and insufficient exercise, and is likely to persist throughout the child's lifetime.

ASSESS YOUR KNOWLEDGE: FACT OR FICTION?

(1) Infants' brains produce only as many neurons as they need. (True/False)

(2) Studying the effects of teratogens on infant development is challenging because it's difficult to find a perfect control group. (True/False)

(3) Low-birth-weight full-term infants are at higher risk for physical problems than premature babies. (True/False)

(4) Children tend to achieve motor milestones in the same order even though the age of acquisition varies within and across cultures. (True/False)

Answers: (1) F (p. 404); (2) T (p. 404); (3) T (p. 405); (4) T (p. 406)

Cognitive Development: Children's Learning about the World

Cognitive development—how children learn, think, reason, communicate, and remember—explains the mystery of how we come to understand our worlds. Yet only relatively recently have phychologists constructed systematic theories of cognitive development.

The practices of swaddling and stretching infants can seem extreme to many Americans, but these are our cultural perspectives. Although cultural variability in these practices influences the rate of motor development, none of these early physical experiences result in long-term impairments.

Jean Piaget *(top)* and Lev Vygotsky *(bottom)* were the two most influential scholars to propose theories of cognitive development. Although they were born in the same year, language barriers prevented them from ever interacting during Vygotsky's short lifetime (he died of tuberculosis at age 37).

constructivist theory
Piaget's theoretical perspective that children construct an understanding of their world based on observations of the effects of their behaviors

assimilation
Piagetian process of absorbing new experience into current knowledge structures

accommodation
Piagetian process of altering a belief to make it more compatible with experience

sensorimotor stage
stage in Piaget's theory characterized by a focus on the here and now without the ability to represent experiences mentally

object permanence
the understanding that objects continue to exist even when out of view

preoperational stage
stage in Piaget's theory characterized by the ability to construct mental representations of experience, but not yet perform operations on them

DEVELOPMENTAL PROCESSES: THEORIES AND EVIDENCE

The pioneering Swiss psychologist Jean Piaget (1896–1980) was the first to present a comprehensive account of cognitive development. He attempted to identify the stages that children pass through on their way to adultlike cognitive abilities. Piaget's theory led to the formation of cognitive development as a distinct discipline, and for decades most research in this field focused on substantiating—or in more recent years refuting—his claims.

At around the same time, Russian researcher Lev Vygotsky (1896–1936) was developing a different but equally comprehensive theory of cognitive development. Vygotsky's work has had a substantial impact on European, British, and American researchers and continues to be influential today.

We can distinguish these and more recent cognitive developmental theories on the basis of three core features:

(1) Whether they propose *stagelike* development (sudden spurts in knowledge followed by periods of stability) or more *continuous* (gradual, incremental) changes in understanding.

(2) Whether they adopt a *domain-general* or *domain-specific* account of development. That is, are there cross-cutting changes in children's cognitive skills that affect all areas of cognitive function at once (domain-general), or do children's cognitive skills develop independently and at different rates for different cognitive domains, such as reasoning, language, and counting (domain-specific)?

(3) What they propose as the principal source of learning. Piaget believed that children's active exploration of the physical world is the primary force in cognitive development, whereas Vygotsky believed that social interactions, especially linguistic communication between caretakers and children, are central.

Piaget: How Children Construct Their Worlds. One of Piaget's greatest contributions was his insight that children aren't miniature adults. He showed that children's understanding of the world is fundamentally different from adults', but perfectly rational given the limited experience of children. For example, children often believe that their teachers live at school, a reasonable assumption, given that's the only place they've seen their teachers. Piaget also altered our view of children's learning by demonstrating that children are active learners who seek information and observe the consequences of their actions, rather than passive observers of the world. Piaget's model is a **constructivist theory** because he maintained that children *construct* an understanding of their world based on observations of the results of their behaviors.

Piaget was a *stage theorist*. He believed that children's development is marked by radical reorganizations of thinking at specific points in development—stages—followed by prolonged periods during which their understanding of the world remains stable. Piaget also believed that the end point of cognitive development is achieving the ability to reason logically about hypothetical problems. As we'll soon see, each stage in Piaget's theory is characterized by a certain level of abstract reasoning capacity, with the ability to think beyond the here and now increasing at each stage. Piaget's stages are domain-general, slicing across all areas of cognitive capacity. Thus, a child capable of a certain level of abstract reasoning in mathematics can also achieve this level in a spatial problem-solving task.

Piaget believed that cognitive change is marked by *equilibration:* maintaining a balance between our experience in the world and our thoughts about it. Children, he said, are motivated to match their thinking about the world with their observations. When the child experiences something new, she checks whether that experience fits with what she expected. If the information is inconsistent, as when a child believes that the earth is flat but learns in school that the earth is round, something must give way. Piaget suggested that children use two "adjustment" processes—assimilation and accommodation—to keep their thinking about the world in tune with their experiences.

Assimilation. The process of absorbing new experience into current knowledge structures is **assimilation.** In the case of believing that the earth is flat, a child might assimilate the fact that the earth is round into her knowledge bases by picturing a flat disk, shaped like a coin. This adjustment allows her to absorb this new fact without changing her belief that the earth is flat. Children use assimilation to acquire new knowledge within a stage. During assimilation, the child's underlying cognitive skills and worldviews remain unchanged, so she reinterprets new experiences to fit into what she already knows.

Accommodation. The assimilation process can continue for only so long. Eventually, the child can no longer reconcile what she believes with what she experiences. A child confronted with a globe will have a difficult time assimilating this information into her belief that the earth is flat. When a child can no longer assimilate experiences into her existing knowledge structures, she's compelled to engage in *accommodation.*

Accommodation is the altering of the child's beliefs to make them more compatible with experience. Accommodation drives stage change by forcing children to enter a new way of looking at the world. This process of assimilating and accommodating ensures a state of harmony between the world and mind of the child—equilibrium.

Piaget's Stages of Development. Piaget identified four stages, each marked by a specific way of looking at the world and set of cognitive limitations (see **Table 10.2**).

This child appears to have forgotten the blocks continue to exist after they've been hidden from view. That is, he fails to exhibit object permanence. In contrast, if the child attempted to move the partition or look behind it, this would reveal he understood the blocks continue to exist when out of view.

Table 10.2 Descriptions of the Four Stages of Cognitive Development in Piaget's Theory.

Stage	Typical Ages	Description
Sensorimotor	Birth to 2 years	No thought beyond immediate physical experiences
Preoperational	2 to 7 years	Able to think beyond the here and now, but egocentric and unable to perform mental transformations
Concrete Operations	7 to 11 years	Able to perform mental transformations but only on concrete physical objects
Formal Operations	11 years to adulthood	Able to perform hypothetical and abstract reasoning

(1) *Sensorimotor stage:* From birth to about 2 years, the **sensorimotor stage** is marked by a focus on the here and now. Children's main sources of knowledge, thinking, and experience are their physical interactions with the world. They acquire all information through perceiving sensory information from the world and observing the physical consequences of their actions. The major milestone of this stage, which forces children to accommodate and enter a new stage, is *mental representation*—the ability to think about things that are absent from immediate surroundings, such as remembering previously encountered objects. Children in this stage lack **object permanence,** the understanding that objects continue to exist even when out of view. For them, it's "out of sight, out of mind." *Deferred imitation,* the ability to perform an action that the child observed earlier, is also absent from the sensorimotor stage. Both object permanence and deferred imitation require children to think beyond the here and now.

(2) *Preoperational stage:* From 2 until about 7 years, children go through the **preoperational stage,** which is marked by an ability to construct mental representations of experi-ence. Children in this stage can use such symbols as language, drawings, and objects as representations of ideas. When a child holds a banana and pretends it's a phone, he's displaying symbolic behavior. He has a mental representation that differs from his physical experience. Similarly, playing house in which one child pretends to be the mommy, one pretends to be the daddy, and one pretends to be the baby demonstrates children's ability to assume imaginary roles that differ from their actual roles.

Although the preoperational stage witnesses the emergence of clear advances in thinking, Piaget believed children in this stage were hampered by **egocentrism**—an inability to see the world from others' perspectives (see **Figure 10.7**). The

View 1

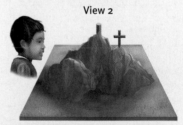

View 2

Figure 10.7 Piaget's Three Mountain Task. Piaget's three mountain task requires children to look at a display from one perspective (View 1) and infer what someone would see if viewing the mountains from a different perspective, such as View 2. Piaget argued that egocentric reasoning in the preoperational stage prevents children from succeeding at this task.

egocentrism
inability to see the world from others' perspectives

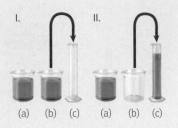

(a) (b) (c)   (a) (b) (c)

Row A
Row B

Which has more, row A or row B, or do they both have the same?

Row A
Row B

Now which has more, row A or row B, or do they both have the same?

Figure 10.8 Piaget's Conservation Tasks. Piaget's conservation tasks ask the child to examine two equal amounts and then watch as the researcher manipulates one of the two amounts in some way. The researcher then asks the child to compare the two quantities. The conservation of liquid task is on the top, the conservation of number task on the bottom. To succeed at the conservation task, children need to say that the amounts remain the same even though they appear unequal. (*Source:* Reprinted with permission from *Human Development*, 7e, by Diane E. Papalia et al. © 1998 The McGraw-Hill Companies, Inc.)

Falsifiability

Replicability

conservation
Piagetian task requiring children to understand that despite a transformation in the physical presentation of an amount, the amount remains the same

concrete operations stage
stage in Piaget's theory characterized by the ability to perform mental operations on physical events only

formal operations stage
stage in Piaget's theory characterized by the ability to perform hypothetical reasoning beyond the here and now

preoperational stage is called "preoperational" because of another limitation, the inability to perform mental operations. Although children in this stage have mental representations, they can't perform mental transformations on them. For example, they can generate a mental image of a vase sitting on a table even if the vase isn't there. But they can't imagine what would happen to the vase if they knocked it off the table. Piaget developed a set of **conservation** tasks like those shown in **Figure 10.8** to test children's ability to perform operations. These tasks ask children whether an amount wil be "conserved" (stay the same) after a physical transformation.

(3) *Concrete operational stage:* Children between 7 and 11 years old enter the **concrete operations stage,** characterized by the long-awaited ability to perform mental operations, but only for actual physical events. Children in this stage can now perform conservation tasks. They can also perform organizational tasks that require mental operations on physical objects, such as sorting coins by size or setting up a battle scene with toy soldiers. But they're still poor at performing mental operations in abstract or hypothetical situations. They need physical experience as an anchor to which they can tether their mental operations.

(4) *Formal operations stage:* Piaget's fourth and final stage, which he believed didn't emerge until adolescence, is the **formal operations stage.** It's then that children can perform what Piaget regarded as the most sophisticated type of thinking: hypothetical reasoning beyond the here and now, such as in the pendulum task in **Figure 10.9**. This task requires children to experiment systematically with hypotheses and explain outcomes. Children at this stage can understand logical concepts, such as if–then statements ("If I'm late for school, then I'll get sent to the principal's office") and either–or statements ("Mom says I can either go to the game tonight or go to the sleepover tomorrow night.").

Pros and Cons of Piaget's Theory. Piaget's theory was a significant landmark in psychology, as it helped us understand how children's thinking evolves into more adultlike thinking. Nevertheless, his theory turned out to be inaccurate in several ways. For example, much of development appears more continuous than stagelike (Flavell, 1992; Klahr & MacWhinney, 1998; Siegler, 1995). Developmental change also appears less general than Piaget proposed. In fact, Piaget used the term *horizontal décalage* to refer to cases in which a child is more advanced in one cognitive domain than another. As some critics have noted (Fischer, 1978), the concept of horizontal décalage renders Piaget's claim that development proceeds in domain-general stages difficult to falsify. Imagine, for example, a child performing at a preoperational level on one task and at a concrete operational level on another, a frequent occurrence. In response, a follower of Piaget could simply invoke horizontal décalage rather than acknowledge that this inconsistency calls into question the idea of domain-general stages.

Many of the phenomena Piaget observed appeared to be at least partly a product of task demands. He often relied on children's ability to reflect and report on their reasoning processes. As a result, he probably underestimated children's underlying competence. Investigators have found it difficult to replicate the developmental progression he observed using less language-dependent tasks.

Piaget's methodologies may have been culturally biased in that they elicited more sophisticated responses from children in Westernized societies with formal education than from those in non-Westernized societies. Yet non-Westernized children often reveal sophisticated insights when interviewed in a more culturally sensitive manner (Cole, 1990; Gellatly, 1987; Luria, 1976; Rogoff & Chavajay, 1995). Meanwhile, even in Western societies, a significant proportion of adolescents fail on some formal operational tasks (Byrnes, 1988; Kuhn, Garcia-Mila, Zohar, & Andersen, 1995), indicating that Piaget may have been overly optimistic about the typical course of cognitive development. Perhaps Piaget based his conclusions on a particularly educated or scientifically sophisticated sample that skewed his estimates of the typical developmental trajectory. Piaget's observations themselves may also have been biased because many were based on tests of his own three children.

Despite these shortcomings, Piaget justifiably remains a towering figure in the field of cognitive development (Lourenco & Machado, 1996). As a result of his legacy, psychologists today have reconceptualized cognitive development by:

(1) viewing children as different in kind rather than degree from adults;

(2) characterizing learning as an active rather than passive process; and

(3) exploring general cognitive processes that may cut across multiple domains of knowledge, thereby accounting for cognitive development in terms of fewer—and more parsimonious—underlying processes.

Vygotsky: Social and Cultural Influences on Learning. Vygotsky adopted a different approach to cognitive development, because he was particularly interested in how social and cultural factors influence learning. He noted that parents and other caretakers tend to structure the learning environment for children in ways that guide them to behave as if they've learned something before they have. Vygostky referred to this process as **scaffolding,** a term he borrowed from building construction. Just as builders provide external scaffolds for support while a building is under construction, parents provide a structure to aid their children. Over time, parents gradually remove structure as children become better able to complete tasks on their own.

One of Vygotsky's most influential notions was the idea of developmental readiness for learning. He identified the **zone of proximal development** as the phase, or learning period, when children are receptive to learning a new skill but aren't yet successful at it. He suggested that for any given skill, children move from a phase when they can't learn a skill, even with assistance, to the zone of proximal development, during which they're ready to make use of scaffolding. In his view, children gradually learn to perform a task independently, but require guidance when getting started. Vygotsky also believed that different children can acquire skills and master tasks at different rates. For him, there were no domain-general stages.

Vygotsky, like Piaget, has had a lasting legacy. His work is particularly influential in educational settings, where guided learning and peer collaboration are common approaches. Vygotsky's influence also lives on in accounts of early learning in infancy and toddlerhood. Whereas Piaget emphasized physical interaction with the world as the primary source of learning, Vygotsky emphasized children's interactions with the social world.

Contemporary Theories of Cognitive Development: Picking Up Where Piaget and Vygotsky Left Off. Theoretical accounts today are much more diverse than when the field of cognitive development got off the ground, and few are strictly Piagetian or Vygotskian. Still, we can trace the roots of each theory to one of these two theorists.

Domain-General Cognitive Accounts. Several influential modern theories resemble Piaget's theories in that they emphasize general cognitive abilities, constructivist learning, and acquired rather than innate knowledge (Elman, 1993; McClelland, 1995; Plunkett, Karmiloff-Smith, Bates, Elman, & Johnson, 1997; Thelen & Smith, 1994). Contemporary theorists share Piaget's commitment to general cognitive processes and experience-based learning. However, they differ from Piaget in that they explain learning as gradual rather than stagelike.

Sociocultural Accounts. These theories emphasize the social context and the ways in which interactions with caretakers and other children guide children's understanding of the world (Rogoff, 1998; Tomasello, 1999). Some sociocultural theorists emphasize experience-based learning, whereas others emphasize innate knowledge. But along with Vygotsky, they share a focus on the child's interaction with the social world as the primary source of development.

Modular Accounts. Like Vygotsky's theory, this class of theories emphasizes the idea of domain-specific learning, that is, separate spheres of knowledge in different learning domains (Carey, 1985; Spelke, 1994; Wellman & Gelman, 1998). For example, the knowledge base for understanding language may be completely independent from the ability to reason about space, with no overlapping cognitive skills between them. Many modularity theorists developed their ideas in reaction to Piaget's constructivist theory and instead argued that children come into the world with innate knowledge.

Occam's Razor

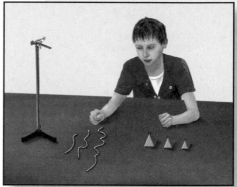

Figure 10.9 Pendulum Task. Piaget's pendulum task requires children to answer the question: "What makes a pendulum swing faster or slower?" Children have the opportunity to construct a pendulum using longer and shorter strings with heavier and lighter weights. Children in the formal operations stage can systematically manipulate various combinations of weights and lengths to observe how they influenced the speed of the swing.

Vygotsky used the term *scaffolding* to refer to the way parents structure the learning environment for children. Here, the father is instructing the child how to fit the shape onto a peg, but allowing the child to insert the shape himself.

scaffolding
Vygotskian learning mechanism in which parents provide initial assistance in children's learning but gradually remove structure as children become more competent

zone of proximal development
phase of learning during which children can benefit from instruction

Claims for the Mozart Effect have contributed to a huge industry of products for babies and young children, yet the scientific evidence for this effect is surprisingly weak.

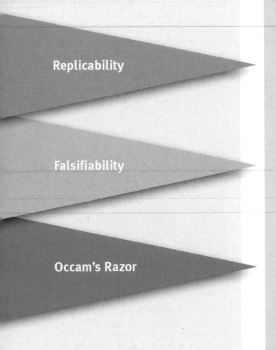

Replicability

Falsifiability

Occam's Razor

PsychoMythology

The Mozart Effect, Baby Einstein, and Creating "Superbabies"

For years, parents have yearned for a quick and easy educational method to boost their infants' intelligence. After all, in today's cutthroat world, what parents wouldn't want to place their child at a competitive advantage? To get a jump-start, of course, parents must begin early, ideally soon after birth. This seemingly far-fetched hope that parents can turn their babies into miniature geniuses turned into apparent reality in 1993 with the publication of an article in the prestigious journal *Nature*. That paper reported that college students who listened to about 10 minutes of a Mozart piano sonata showed a significant improvement on a spatial reasoning task compared with a group of students who listened to a relaxation tape (Shaw & Rauscher, 1993). The *Mozart Effect*—the supposed enhancement in intelligence after listening to classical music (Campbell, 1997)—was born.

The 1993 finding didn't say anything about long-term enhancement of spatial ability, let alone intelligence in general. It applied only to a task administered almost immediately after listening to Mozart's music. And the findings were based entirely on college students. But this didn't stop the popular press or toy companies from taking the Mozart Effect ball and running with it. Companies soon marketed scores of Mozart Effect CDs and cassettes targeted toward babies, featuring claims that listening to the music of Mozart and other composers boosts infant intelligence. In 1998, then Georgia Governor Zell Miller added $105,000 to the state budget to allow each newborn in Georgia to receive a free Mozart CD or cassette.

Miller's decision was premature. In fact, researchers had a devil of a time replicating the Mozart Effect. Many couldn't find the effect at all, and those who did discovered that it was trivial in magnitude (2 IQ points or less) and of short duration (an hour or less; Chabris, 1999; Steele, Bass, & Crook, 1999). Zell Miller (1999) urged advocates of the Mozart Effect to ignore these negative findings, imploring them not "to be misled or discouraged by some academics debunking other academics." But this is precisely how science works at its best: by trying to falsify claims made by other investigators.

Later researchers helped to nail down the source of the Mozart Effect. The results of one study suggested that the effect may be due to the greater emotional arousal produced by listening to Mozart relative to either other composers or silence (Thompson, Schellenberg, & Husain, 2001). Another researcher found that listening to Mozart was no better for improving spatial ability than listening to a passage from a scary story. These findings suggest that a more parsimonious explanation for the Mozart Effect is short-term arousal. Anything that boosts alertness is likely to increase performance on mentally demanding tasks, but it's unlikely to produce long-term effects on spatial ability or, for that matter, overall intelligence. Our advice: It's a wonderful idea to expose infants and children to great music. But don't expect it to turn babies into little geniuses.

The Mozart Effect is only one example of a research finding being overhyped to capitalize on parents' desires to boost their baby's intellect. In the 1980s, thousands of parents bombarded their newborn infants with foreign languages and advanced math in an effort to create "superbabies" (Clarke-Stewart, 1998). Today, alleged intelligence-improving products such as "Baby Einstein" toys and videos are a $100 million a year industry (Minow, 2005; Quart, 2006). Yet there's no evidence that these products work either. In fact, research suggests that babies learn less from videos than from playing actively for the same time period (Anderson & Pempek, 2005; Zimmerman, Christakis, & Metzoff, 2007). Vygotsky wouldn't have been surprised by the ineffectiveness of such products; presenting infants with advanced material well outside their zone of proximal development is likely to be fruitless.

COGNITIVE LANDMARKS OF EARLY DEVELOPMENT

We've already learned about some of the major cognitive accomplishments within the realms of perception (Chapter 4), memory (Chapter 7), and language and reading (Chapter 8). But children must attain a variety of other cognitive skills to make sense of their worlds. Here, we'll review some of the highlights.

Physical Reasoning: Figuring Out Which Way Is Up. To understand their physical worlds, children must learn to reason about them. They need to learn that objects are solid, that they fall when dropped, and that one object can disappear behind another and reappear on the other side. We adults take all of these concepts for granted, but they aren't obvious to novice experiencers of the world.

Piaget proposed that children don't master object permanence until between 8 and 12 months of age, because children younger than 8 months old don't search for an object that an adult has hidden under a cloth. Nevertheless, work by Renee Baillargeon (1987) shows that by 5 months of age and possibly younger, infants display an understanding of object permanence if given a task that doesn't require a physically coordinated search for the object (see **Figure 10.10**). Baillargeon based her conclusions on studies of how long infants looked at displays that were either consistent with or inconsistent with object permanence. Her findings suggest that Piaget underestimated when children achieve object permanence, because Piaget's tasks required not only an understanding of object permanence, but also an ability to plan and perform a physical search for the hidden toy. When Baillargeon eliminated these task demands, an earlier mastery of object permanence appeared.

Ruling Out Rival Hypotheses

Partial rotation

Full rotation

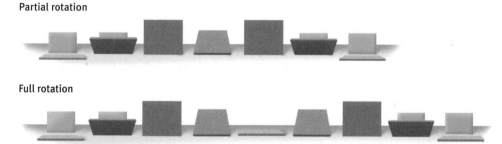

Figure 10.10 Habituation Event. If infants understand that the box continues to exist even when it's out of sight, they should be surprised to see the platform continue to rotate in a way that seems to pass through the box. Contrary to Piaget's claims about the age of object permanence, infants as young as 4 months look longer at the full rotation event, suggesting that they're surprised when the platform appears to rotate through the box. (*Source:* Baillargeon, Spelke, & Wasserman, 1985)

Infants possess a basic understanding of some other aspects of how physical objects behave, a set of beliefs sometimes called *naive physics*. For example, they know that objects that are unsupported should fall (Spelke, 1994). However, this basic knowledge becomes more refined and sophisticated with experience (**Figure 10.11**) (Baillargeon & Hanko-Summers, 1990; Needham & Baillargeon, 1993).

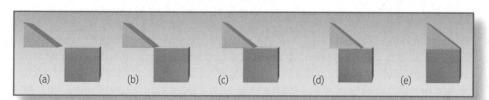

Figure 10.11 Children Learn Gradually That Unsupported Objects Will Fall. As early as $4\frac{1}{2}$ months, infants expect objects that are completely unsupported, as in (a), to fall and objects that are completely supported, as in (e), not to fall. An understanding of how much support must be present to prevent an object from falling develops over time. Early on, infants expect that any contact with a support surface will prevent the object from falling, as in (b), (c), and (d). With experience, infants learn to expect that only those in (d) and (e), in which the majority of the weight is on the support surface, won't fall.

Concepts and Categories: Classifying the World. One of the most basic cognitive accomplishments is learning to categorize objects by kind. Children learn to recognize dogs even though they come in all manner of shapes, sizes, and colors. Categorization is crucial because it frees us from having to explore every object to find out what it is and does (see Chapter 8). Imagine if every time a baby were given a new bottle, she had to discover through trial and error what it was. Kids, not to mention adults, wouldn't get very far without categories.

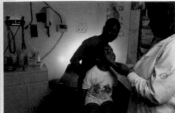

Young children rapidly learn what's likely to occur during routine events such as birthday parties, doctors' office visits, and trips to fast-food restaurants. Children depend so heavily on their expectations of events that they'll sometimes incorrectly recall a typical feature of an event that didn't occur (Fivush & Hammond, 1990; Nelson & Hudson, 1988; see Chapter 7).

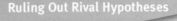
Ruling Out Rival Hypotheses

Even infants can categorize. When shown a series of bird pictures, infants eventually get bored with them and look away, but show fresh interest when they see a picture of a dinosaur. This finding implies that they've categorized the birds as all of the same kind and therefore no longer new, but they regard the dinosaur as belonging to a different category (Quinn & Eimas, 1996).

There are many accounts of how children organize categories. Katherine Nelson (1977) proposed that children's conceptual knowledge is initially organized around thematic relations, such as a dog and its bone. Much early research on this topic suggested that children don't begin to classify objects by kind (dogs, bottles, cars) until elementary school. Nevertheless, more recent research shows that children's apparent difficulty with classifying objects into categories was an artifact of how experimenters were asking the questions (Waxman & Namy, 1997). Depending on the wording, young children may shift their focus to either categories or thematic relations (**Table 10.3**). This finding implies that children are familiar with both kinds of conceptual relations from early in development and can display their knowledge of either, depending on the task. Thus, what appears to be a priority for a particular type of conceptual knowledge is actually a function of question wording.

Table 10.3 Conceptual Organization Depends on the Task. Sandra Waxman and Laura Namy (1997) found that 3- and 4-year-olds who saw a target object (such as a carrot) and were asked to choose between a category match (for example, a tomato) and a thematic match (for example, a bunny) varied their responses depending on how researchers worded the question. Children ranged from predominantly category responses, to no preference for either response, to predominantly thematic responses across the three conditions.

Question Wording	Category	Thematic
"Can you find another one?"	80%	20%
"Which one goes with this?"	46%	54%
"Which goes best with the carrot?"	34%	66%

(*Source:* Waxman & Namy, 1997)

Another area of debate is whether children use perceptual or nonperceptual conceptual features as a basis for categorizing. Some researchers argue that children build up their categories, like birds, from simple perceptual features (such as wings) but eventually figure out that subtler features (such as feathers, a beak, building nests, and laying eggs) are more accurate criteria for membership in the category (Rakison, 2005; Ribar, Oakes, & Spalding, 2004). Others argue that children assume from the start that categories are richer and more complex, including knowledge of whether something is a living thing or an inanimate object (Mandler, 2000), or that all categories contain internal "stuff" (such as DNA or organs) that distinguish them from other categories (Gelman, 2003).

David Rakison's research demonstrates that children's early categorization is based on obvious and noticeable features, such as wheels and legs, rather than a deep understanding of category structure. For example, children might group this strange object with cars and trucks, rather than animals.

Self-Concept and the Concept of "Other": Who We Are, and Who We Aren't. Developing a sense of self, as different from others, is critical for children's development. Their ability to understand themselves as possessing separate and unique identities unfolds gradually during the toddler and preschool years. But even by 3 months of age, infants possess some sense of self as distinct from others. Babies at this age who view videos of themselves side-by-side with another baby prefer to look at the image of the other baby (Bahrick, Moss, & Fadil, 1996; Rochat, 2001). Indeed, infants who see a live-action video of only their legs side-by-side with a recording of another infant's legs still prefer to watch the video of the other baby's legs, even if both sets of legs are dressed identically. This finding reveals that babies aren't just demonstrating a novelty preference for the other baby's face because they've seen their own face before in the mirror or in photographs.

As early as their first birthdays, children can recognize their images in a mirror (Amsterdam, 1972; Priel & deSchonen, 1986; see Chapter 7). By 2 years, they can recognize pictures of themselves and refer to themselves by name (Lewis & Brooks-Gunn, 1979). Well before their first birthdays, they begin to understand that people are a distinct category. They smile more at people than at objects (Ellsworth, Muir, & Hains, 1993) and imitate other people's behaviors more often than the same actions displayed by moving objects (Legerstee, 1991). Imitation implies that children can translate someone else's action into their own and grasp a correspondence between self and other.

A further milestone is children's ability to understand that others' perspectives can differ from their's. An ability called **theory of mind** is a key component of perspective-taking (Premack & Woodruff, 1978). Theory of mind refers to children's ability to reason about what other people know or believe. (Note that according to Chapter 1 this "theory" isn't really a theory!) The big challenge for children on this front is to realize that "other people may not know what I know." In some sense, children know this fact by the time they're 1 or 2 years old, because they ask their parents questions like "Where's Daddy?" and "What's this?" revealing that they expect parents to know things they don't. Yet it's particularly challenging for children to realize that sometimes *they* know things that others don't.

A classic test of theory of mind is the *false-belief task* (Birch & Bloom, 2007; Wimmer & Perner, 1983) (see **Figure 10.12**), which tests children's ability to understand that someone else believes something they know to be wrong. Children typically don't succeed at this task until around age 4 or 5. Yet how early children succeed on false-belief tasks varies enormously depending on the task (Wellman, Cross, & Watson, 2001). If researchers arrange the false-belief task so that it's more of a real-world situation and less of a story, most children can pass it. Also, if researchers tell children the reason for the change was to "trick" someone, they're more successful at an earlier age. Thus, children's failure on the classic false-belief task before age 4 may be due to aspects of the task rather than their inadequate understanding of others' knowledge. Nonetheless, it's clear that the ability to understand others' perspectives increases with age.

Numbers and Mathematics: What Counts. Counting and math are relatively recent cognitive achievements in human history. Humans developed the first counting system only a

Ruling Out Rival Hypotheses

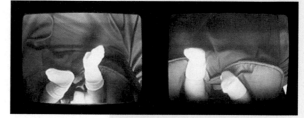

Infants who view a video image of their own legs side by side with a videotape of another infant's legs will look longer at the video of the other baby. This finding suggests infants recognize the correspondence between the video images and their own bodies (Bahrick & Watson, 1985) and find their own actions less interesting to watch.

theory of mind
ability to reason about what other people know or believe

Ruling Out Rival Hypotheses

(a)   (b)   (c)   (d)

Figure 10.12 The False-Belief Task. In the false-belief task, the child participant knows something about which someone else is unaware. In this scenario, the child learns that Joey in the story believes the candy bar is in the cabinet. But because she's heard the whole story, the child knows the candy bar is really in the refrigerator. When asked where Joey thinks the candy is, will the child respond with her own knowledge of the true location, or will she realize that Joey is unaware of this change?

Members of the Pirahã culture don't have a system for calculating precise amounts.

(a)

(b)

Figure 10.13 Children Find It Easier to Match Quantities When the Objects Resemble Each Other. In Mix's studies, children match the display on the top (a) with one of the displays on the bottom (b). Children find this much easier in the top (a) in which the disks resemble the dots, than in the bottom (b), in which the stimuli are different. (*Source:* Mix, 1999)

People have used the abacus for thousands of years and use it today in China and Japan. The beads on each rod enable counting from zero to 10. Each bead on the lower deck stands for 1, and each on the upper deck stands for 5. The farthest rod to the right represents single digits, the next rod to the left represents the 10s place, the next rod to the left is the 100s, and so on. The abacus provides a concrete way of tracking numbers that may help children learn to count.

few thousand years ago. Unlike many cognitive skills that children acquire, counting and mathematics don't always develop. In fact, there are a few remaining nonindustrialized cultures such as the Pirahã, a tribe in Brazil, in which conventional counting and mathematics appear not to exist (Gordon, 2004).

Learning to count is a lot more complex than it seems. Of course, many children learn to "count to ten" at a very early age, reciting "1-2-3-4-5-6-7-8-9-10" in rapid succession and waiting for applause to follow. But there's much more to counting than simply reciting a set of number words in sequence, just as reciting the alphabet doesn't imply that a child can read. Children must learn that (1) numbers are about amount and (2) number words refer to specific quantities (and not just "a bunch" or "a few"). After that, children must grasp many subtle aspects of number concepts before they can count accurately (see **Table 10.4**) (Gelman & Gallistel, 1978). One of the most challenging concepts for children to master is the idea that two elephants is the same number as two grains of rice—that the *size* of entities isn't relevant to quantity. Kelly Mix and her colleagues showed that this insight is extremely difficult for children (Mix, 1999; Mix, Huttenlocher, & Levine, 1996). Children find it easier to match two sets of the same quantity when the objects to be counted closely resemble each other than when they don't (see **Figure 10.13**). When similarity among the objects is high, children master this task at 3 years of age, but when the objects look different, they don't succeed until $3\frac{1}{2}$ years of age. And when they have to match the quantity of a visual set with sets of sounds, they don't succeed until after age 4.

Table 10.4 Children Must Master a Number of Counting Principles before Grasping What Numbers Mean. These principles seem obvious and intuitive to adults who are expert counters, but not to young children. Children typically master these principles during the preschool years.

Principle	Description	Sample Violation of the Principle
One-to-One Correspondence	Assign one number to each object present	Counting some objects twice
Stable Order	Numbers must always occur in the same order	Counting 1-2-3 one time but 1-3-2 another time
Cardinality	The last number counted equals the total amount	Counting the numbers accurately but being unable to report how many
Order Irrelevance	The same amount is there no matter in which order we count them	Counting in one direction and then checking to see if the number changes by counting in a different direction
Ordinality	Numbers have a magnitude associated with them such that some numbers are always larger than others	Understanding that numbers occur in a fixed order but failing to realize that this relates to which is more or less
Abstraction	The same counting process applies regardless of the size or nature of the things to be counted	Believing that the same number of objects possess different quantities because the items in one set are larger

The fact that counting and other mathematical skills in preschool- and school-aged children develop at different rates across cultures challenges the idea that counting is entirely innate. For example, many researchers have examined why children in some Asian countries master mathematics sooner than American children. Cross-cultural differences in how parents and teachers introduce counting to children seem to be part of the explanation. For example, the number terms used in English are more confusing than those in Chinese. In English, the names for teens are related to single-digit numbers in an irregular way. Although some teen numbers involve the single-digit number followed by "teen," such as "sixteen," we say "thirteen" instead of "three-teen" and the number names "eleven" and "twelve" bear no clear relation to "one" and "two." In contrast, the Chinese name for number 13 is literally translated "one-ten, three," which makes the relation to three and the meaning of the number (10 plus 3) transparent. This clear relationship between number terms and their meaning helps Chinese children to get started on the right foot toward mathematical development (Miller, Smith, Zhu, & Zhang, 1995).

NEW FRONTIERS

Gesture as a Window into the Mind

Gestures are a natural part of human interaction. We routinely point, give a thumbs-up, or wave. Gestures supplement our spoken language in ways that enhance our ability to communicate. Nevertheless, gesture also provides a window into our thinking and may reveal knowledge we don't even realize we possess (Goldin-Meadow, 2000). Researchers and educators have begun to study children's gestures as a means of monitoring their comprehension of new material.

Children frequently convey information in their gestures that isn't contained in their verbal explanations and may conflict with their spoken language. A child who attempts to solve the conservation of liquid problem (refer back to Figure 10.8) may explain (incorrectly) that there's more liquid in the tall, thin glass because the liquid is higher. Yet while explaining this point, the child may produce gestures that display a change in *width* rather than height, such as holding the hands side by side and moving them closer together. In this case, the information in the child's gesture reveals that she's aware of the relevance of width to the transformation in height between the short and tall glasses, although she shows no awareness of it in her verbal explanation (Alibali, Bassok, Solomon, Syc, & Goldin-Meadow, 1999; Alibali & Goldin-Meadow, 1993).

Researchers have documented differences between what children say or do and how they gesture while solving math problems (Perry, Church, & Goldin-Meadow, 1988), moral dilemmas (Church, Schonert-Reichl, Goodman, Kelly, & Ayman-Nolley, 1995), and Piagetian tasks (Stone, Webb, & Mahootian, 1991). These differences are valuable indices of transitions in children's thinking. They occur more frequently just before children display a major advance in their mastery of a learning domain (Crowder, 1996). What's more, children who reveal information in their gestures that's not evident in how they solve problems benefit more from instruction than those whose gestures are consistent with their problem-solving strategies (Church & Goldin-Meadow, 1986; Perry et al., 1988). Thus, parents and educators can use children's gestures to gauge their readiness to learn and tailor their instructional strategies to children's conceptual level. Attention to gestures offers greater insight into children's comprehension than their performance on the task could ever reveal on its own (Alibali, Flevares, & Goldin-Meadow, 1997; Goldin-Meadow & Sandhofer, 1999).

fact**oid**

Not all cultures count to 10 on their fingers; many have much more elaborate systems of tracking amounts on their fingers, hands, arms, heads, and other body parts. Some systems have specific body locations assigned for numbers from 1 to as high as 74!

ASSESS YOUR KNOWLEDGE: FACT OR FICTION?

(1) Piaget argued that development was domain-general and continuous. (True/False)
(2) Vygotsky's theory proposes that individual children vary in the age at which they achieve developmental readiness for particular cognitive abilities. (True/False)
(3) Infants display a basic understanding of "naive physics," such as gravity. (True/False)
(4) Children fail to display evidence of theory of mind before age 4. (True/False)
(5) The ability to count precise quantities is absent in some cultures. (True/False)

Answers: (1) F (p. 408); (2) T (p. 411); (3) T (p. 413); (4) F (p. 415); (5) T (p. 416)

Social and Moral Development: Children's Relations with Others

Although infants are largely in their own little worlds almost immediately after birth, they soon begin to take a keen interest in social cues. It's only a matter of time—a few days to be exact—before they start to look to the primary source of social cues in their environment. Infants prefer faces over just about all other visual information. As early as 4 days after birth, infants show a marked preference for Mommy's face compared with that of other women (Pascalis et al., 1995).

These findings point to the emergence of a key attribute in infancy: interest in others. That's because the face communicates most of the social information infants need to know—whether Mommy and Daddy are happy with me, bored with me, or just plain fed with up with me. Moreover, as anyone who's interacted with an infant knows, babies are absolute suckers (forgive the pun) for social contact. Any adult who's willing to get down on his hands and knees and make an utter fool of himself can get a 6-month-old infant to smile, giggle, and open his eyes wide with amusement. Infants soak up social contact. This puts them in an ideal position to establish bonds with caretakers and learn from social interactions.

STRANGER ANXIETY: THE SUDDEN CHANGE AT 8 MONTHS

As sociable as infants can be at 6 months, something changes dramatically over the course of only a few months. The same infant who was giggling on the floor with a perfect stranger at 6 months will probably scream in terror if approached by that same stranger only a few months later. This phenomenon is known as **stranger anxiety.** Known also as *8 months anxiety,* this behavior manifests itself in a fear of strangers beginning at about 8 or 9 months of age (Greenberg, Hillman, & Grice, 1973; Konner, 1990). It generally increases up until about 12 to 15 months of age, and then declines steadily. Interestingly, the onset of stranger anxiety appears to be virtually identical in all cultures (Kagan, 1976) (**Figure 10.14**). Eight months anxiety makes good evolutionary sense, because it's at about this age that most infants begin to crawl around on their own. As a result, it's the age at which infants can—and usually do—find a way to get themselves into trouble. So this anxiety may be an adaptive mechanism for keeping infants away from unknown adults who could pose a danger to them.

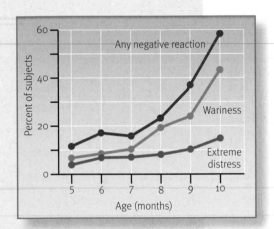

Figure 10.14 Stranger Anxiety.
As we can see in this graph from one published study, infants' anxiety and negative reactions when confronted with a stranger first begin at around 8 or 9 months and continue to increase. Typically, they won't begin to decline until about 12 or 15 months. (*Source:* Waters, Matas, & Sroufe, 1975)

stranger anxiety
a fear of strangers developing at 8 or 9 months of age

attachment
the strong emotional connection we share with those to whom we feel closest

imprinting
phenomenon observed in which baby birds begin to follow around and attach themselves to any large moving object they see in the hours immediately after hatching

ATTACHMENT: ESTABLISHING BONDS

Stranger anxiety is merely one manifestation of a broader phenomenon of **attachment,** the emotional connection we share with those to whom we feel closest. With rare exceptions, such as infantile autism (see Chapters 2 and 15), all infants forge close emotional bonds with important adults, usually their parents. Again, there may be a good evolutionary reason for the attachment bond. It ensures that infants and children don't stray too far from the powerful others who feed and protect them (Bowlby, 1973). To understand the origins of attachment, we need to begin with the story of an Austrian zoologist and his birds.

Imprinting. In the 1930s, Konrad Lorenz—who went on to win a Nobel Prize for the work we're about to describe—was observing the behaviors of geese. By sheer accident, he discovered that goslings (young geese) displayed a remarkable behavior shortly following birth. Specifically, goslings seemed to follow around the first large, moving object they saw after hatching. Although Lorenz (1937) referred to this phenomenon as "stamping in" in German, it's come to be known in English as **imprinting.**

Of course, 99 percent or more of the time, the first large, moving object that a gosling sees after emerging from the egg is none other than Mother Goose. But Lorenz showed that goslings will cheerfully imprint onto whatever large, moving object they see following birth—including Lorenz himself. Newborn goslings will even imprint onto moving objects, such as large white bouncing balls and boxes on wheels if they have nothing better to choose from (Johnson, 2002).

We humans don't imprint onto our mothers in the way that geese do: We don't bond automatically to the first moving thing we see. Still, human infants and most mammalian infants exhibit a "softer" form of imprinting, in which they forge strong bonds with those who tend to them shortly after birth.

Critical Periods. Lorenz discovered that imprinting occurs only during a *critical period* (Almli & Finger, 1987): a specific window of time during which an event must occur (see Chapter 7). In the case of Lorenz's goslings, this critical period was about 36 hours. If the goslings didn't see their mothers until after that window closed, they never imprinted to her, or to anything else for that matter. Once the critical period passes, it's difficult for goslings to establish bonds with their mother or other attachment figures.

In reality, most critical periods don't end as abruptly as Lorenz believed (Bruer, 1999). That's especially true of intelligent mammals, like cats, dogs, and humans, whose behaviors are more flexible than those of geese. That's why most psychologists now use the term *sensitive period* to refer to developmental windows in creatures with more malleable ranges of behaviors.

Do humans also have sensitive periods for social bonding? This question is controversial. As we'll recall from Chapter 8, there's some evidence for a sensitive period for human language. When it comes to attachment, there's some indication that early separation from attachment figures can produce detrimental effects. Some of the best evidence comes from a longitudinal study of Romanian infants in orphanages. In the 1970s and 1980s, President Nicolae Ceausescu attempted to increase Romania's population by banning all forms of birth control. The catastrophic consequence was that many babies were born to parents who couldn't support them, and they became wards of the state. Following the downfall of the Ceausescu regime in the late 1980s, families in the United States and England adopted thousands of these children. Sir Michael Rutter and his colleagues found that although infants adopted before 6 months of age fared well later, those older than 6 months of age when adopted often exhibited what appeared to be negative effects of their early environment, including low IQs and serious emotional problems, such as inattention and hyperactivity (Kreppner, O'Connor, & Rutter, 2001; O'Connor & Rutter, 2000). Nevertheless, there may be another explanation for these findings: The children who were adopted later may have had more emotional difficulties to begin with. As a consequence, they may have been more difficult to place in adoptive families. Still, the unique historical situation with thousands of children being placed, often sight unseen, into adoptive families renders this selection bias less likely. Moreover, the finding that early institutionalization is associated with later emotional problems has been replicated in numerous studies using different methodologies (Ames, 1977; Kreppner et al., 2001).

Contact Comfort: The Healing Touch. Given that human infants don't imprint onto attachment figures, on what basis do they bond to their parents? For decades, psychologists assumed that the primary basis for the attachment bond is the nourishment supplied by mothers. Children bond to those who provide them with milk and food, and in most cases this happens to be Mommy. This view dovetailed with the assumptions of behaviorism (see Chapter 6), which posited that reinforcement is the primary shaping influence on our preferences.

Harry Harlow overturned this assumption in the 1950s with his research on infant rhesus monkeys, which are close genetic relatives of humans (Blum, 2002). Harlow (1958) separated baby monkeys from their mothers only a few hours after birth. He then placed them in a cage with two "surrogate" mothers, both inanimate. One—the "wire mother"— consisted of a round face and a cold, mangled mesh of uncomfortable metal wires. This wire mother did have one thing going for her, though: nourishment. She sported a little bottle of milk from which the baby monkey could drink. In sharp contrast, the second mother, the "terry cloth mother," was made of foam rubber, overlaid with a comfortable

As Nobel Prize–winning biologist Konrad Lorenz goes for a swim, he's followed by three geese who imprinted on him almost immediately after they hatched.

If you've ever tried to befriend a feral cat (one that wasn't raised with humans), you probably found the experience to be frustrating: The cat was probably less than friendly to you. Cats appear to have a sensitive period after which bonding to humans is difficult, but not impossible. Bonding following the sensitive period is occasionally successful, but it requires a great deal of patience.

Ruling Out Rival Hypotheses

Replicability

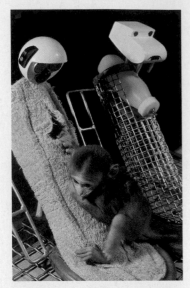

When frightened by a novel object, Harlow's infant monkeys almost always preferred the terry cloth mother over the wire mother. Contact comfort prevails over nourishment.

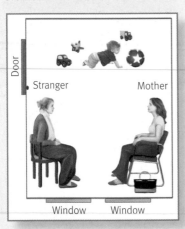

Figure 10.15 Physical Setup of the Strange Situation. In the Strange Situation, both the mother and a stranger are present before the mother leaves the child with the stranger. (*Source:* Ainsworth et al., 1978)

layer of terry cloth, and heated with a light bulb. Harlow found that although baby monkeys routinely went to wire mothers for milk, they actually spent much more of their time with terry cloth mothers. In addition, when Harlow exposed monkeys to a scary stimulus, like a toy robot playing a drum, they were much more likely to run to the terry cloth mother and cling to her for reassurance. Harlow termed this phenomenon **contact comfort:** the positive emotions afforded by touch. Contact comfort may help us to understand why we human primates find simple touch, like holding the hand of a romantic partner, so reassuring. Indeed, Tiffany Field (2003) and her colleagues showed that gentle massage helps premature babies to gain weight, sleep better, and bond more closely with their parents than attention alone.

Some parents are surely better at providing such comfort than others. After Harlow gave a lecture on contact comfort to a public audience, a woman approached him. "Now I know what's wrong with me," she said in an apparent flash of insight. "I'm just a wire mother" (Harlow, 1958, p. 677).

Attachment Styles: The Strange Situation. As every professional baby sitter or day care worker knows, infants attach to their parents in radically different ways. Some are cuddly and affectionate, whereas others are distant and standoffish. Some are calm, whereas others are jittery.

Although these anecdotal observations offer useful insights, it wasn't until Mary Ainsworth and her colleagues developed the *Strange Situation* that psychologists settled on a systematic way of quantifying infants' attachment styles (Ainsworth, Blehar, Waters, & Wall, 1978). The Strange Situation is a laboratory procedure for examining 1-year-olds' reactions to separation from their mothers. Here's how it works. First, researchers place the infant in an unfamiliar room with his or her mother. The room is loaded with all kinds of interesting toys, and the mother gives the infant the chance to play with them. Then, a stranger enters. On two different occasions, the mother exits the room, leaving the infant alone with the stranger before reuniting with her infant. The Strange Situation takes advantage of infants' stranger anxiety, which as we've learned tends to peak at about 1 year. Today, most attachment researchers rely on the Strange Situation to measure infants' attachment styles (**Figure 10.15**).

During the Strange Situation, trained research assistants code the infant's emotional and physical reactions to the mother's departure and return. Most researchers find that infants' behaviors fall into one of four categories:

(1) *Secure attachment* (about 60% of U.S. infants). The infant reacts to mom's departure by becoming upset, but greets her return with joy. In essence, the infant uses mom as a *secure base:* a rock-solid source of support to which to turn in times of trouble (Bowlby, 1990).

(2) *Insecure-avoidant attachment* (about 15%–20% of U.S. infants). The infant reacts to mom's departure with indifference and shows little reaction on her return.

(3) *Insecure-anxious attachment* (about 15%–20% of U.S. infants). The infant reacts to mom's departure with panic. He then shows a mixed emotional reaction on her return, simultaneously reaching for her yet squirming to get away after she picks him up (for this reason, some psychologists refer to this style as "anxious-ambivalent").

(4) *Disorganized attachment* (about 5%–10% of U.S infants). This rarest of attachment styles wasn't included in the original classification, but was added later by Mary Main and her colleagues (Main & Cassidy, 1988). Children with this pattern react to mom's departure and return with an inconsistent and confused set of responses. They may appear dazed when reunited with her.

Note that we wrote "U.S. infants" in parentheses following each classification. That's because there are cultural differences in attachment style. For example, more infants in Japan than in the United States fall into the insecure-anxious category, whereas more infants in the United States than in Japan fall into the insecure-avoidant category (Rothbaum, Weisz, Pott, Miyake, & Morelli, 2000). The reasons for these differences aren't

contact comfort
positive emotions afforded by touch

known, but they may stem in part from the fact that Japanese babies tend to experience fewer separations from mom in everyday life than American babies do. As a consequence, Japanese babies may find the Strange Situation to be even "stranger"—and more stressful—than do American babies (van Ijzendoorn & Sagi, 1999).

The attachment styles derived from the Strange Situation predict children's later behavior. Infants with a secure attachment style tend to grow up to be more well adjusted, helpful, and empathic than infants with other attachment styles (LaFreniere & Sroufe, 1985; Sroufe, 1983). In contrast, infants with an anxious attachment style are more likely to be disliked and mistreated by their peers later in childhood than infants with other attachment styles (Renken, Egeland, Marvinney, Mangeldorf, & Sroufe, 1989).

Still, the Strange Situation has its shortcomings. Researchers must be careful to avoid **mono-operation bias** (Shadish, Cook, & Campbell, 2002): the mistake of relying on only a single measure to draw conclusions. The Strange Situation is, after all, merely one indicator of attachment. To *equate* it with attachment, as some psychologists have done, is a serious error. Indeed, some researchers have begun to develop alternative indicators of attachment, such as interviews in adulthood designed to assess bonding to one's parents (Hesse, 1999).

The Strange Situation also isn't especially *reliable*. As we learned in Chapter 2, reliability refers to the consistency of a measuring instrument. If the Strange Situation were a highly reliable measure of attachment, babies who are securely attached at age 1 should tend to remain that way for a short time afterward, as should babies who are insecurely-avoidantly attached, and so on. Yet research shows that many infants switch their attachment classifications over brief time periods (Lamb, Thompson, Gardner, Charnov, & Estes, 1984; Paris, 2000). In general, attachment styles remain consistent only when parents' living circumstances stay the same. If parents undergo a change in their job status, their children's attachment style often changes along with it (Bruer, 1999; Thompson, 1998). Moreover, almost 40 percent of children display a different attachment style with their mother than with their father (van Ijzendorn & De Wolff, 1997), suggesting that many children can't simply be pigeonholed into a single attachment classification.

Most attachment theorists begin with a central assumption: Infants' attachment styles are attributable largely to their parents' responsiveness to them. For example, infants whose parents respond to their signals of distress by comforting them are supposedly more likely to develop a secure attachment style than other infants (Ainsworth, Blehar, Waters, & Wall, 1978). For most attachment theorists, the cause → effect arrow runs from parent to child.

TEMPERAMENT AND SOCIAL DEVELOPMENT: A MISSING PIECE OF THE PUZZLE?

As we learned at the outset of this chapter, psychological causes can run both ways, so there may be other explanations for the association between attachment style and later emotional adjustment. We must beware of unidirectional thinking concerning human development. A critical third variable that we need to consider when evaluating children's social and emotional development is **temperament.** Psychologists define temperament as comprising differences in people's basic emotional styles (Mervielde, De Clercq, De Fruyt, & Van Leeuwen, 2005). They distinguish temperament from other general personality characteristics by two key features: Temperament is *early appearing* and *largely genetic* in origin.

Types of Temperaments. The idea of temperaments originated with the ancient Greeks and Romans, who described differences among people in terms of four temperaments: sanguine (optimistic), phlegmatic (mellow), choleric (hot-tempered), and melancholic (sad). This early analysis persisted for many centuries and was especially popular in the Middle Ages. Nevertheless, modern psychologists largely ignored the idea of temperament until recent decades when the field gave the concept a second look.

In their studies of 141 American children, Alexander Thomas and Stella Chess (1977) identified three major temperamental styles. *Easy* infants (about 40% of babies) are adaptable and relaxed; *difficult* infants (about 10% of babies) are fussy and easily frustrated; and *slow-to-warm-up* infants (about 15% of babies) are disturbed by new stimuli

Ruling Out Rival Hypotheses

mono-operation bias
drawing conclusions on the basis of only a single measure

temperament
basic emotional style that appears early in development and is largely genetic in origin

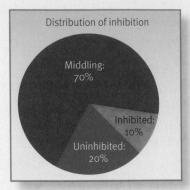

Figure 10.16 Behaviorally Inhibited Children. About 10 percent of children are behaviorally inhibited, with the majority either uninhibited or somewhere in between. (*Source:* Kagan, Reznick, & Snidman, 1988)

Distribution of inhibition

Middling: 70%

Inhibited: 10%

Uninhibited: 20%

Correlation vs. Causation

at first but gradually adjust to them. The remaining 35% of children, Thomas and Chess found, don't fit neatly into any of these three categories.

Based initially on research with cats, Jerome Kagan identified another temperament that he termed *behavioral inhibition* (Kagan, Kahn, Snidman & Towsley, 2007). Like "scaredy cats," who crawl under the nearest bed at the sight of a new moving toy, behaviorally inhibited human infants become frightened at the sight of novel or unexpected stimuli, like unfamiliar faces, loud tones, or little moving robots (Kagan, Reznick, & Snidman, 1988). Their hearts pound, their bodies tense up, and their amygdalae become active (Schwartz, Wright, Shin, Kagan, & Rauch, 2003). This last finding makes sense, because we'll recall from Chapter 3 that the amygdala plays a key role in processing fear. According to Kagan and his colleagues, we find this temperamental style in about 15% of cats and in about 10% or slightly more of human children (see **Figure 10.16**). Infants with high levels of behavioral inhibition are also at heightened risk for shyness and anxiety disorders in childhood or adolescence (Biederman et al., 2001; Turner, Beidel, & Wolff, 1996). Still, behavioral inhibition isn't all bad. Infants with extremely *low* levels of behavioral inhibition may be at increased risk for impulsive behaviors in later childhood (Burgess, Marshall, Rubin, & Fox, 2003), so a certain amount of behavioral inhibition may be healthy.

There are also cultural differences in temperament (Freedman & DeBoer, 1979). Daniel Freedman (1978; Freedman & Freedman, 1969) compared how Chinese American and European American 4-day-old infants reacted when researchers placed a cloth over their faces. Chinese American infants were considerably calmer than European American infants, many of whom struggled mightily to remove the offending cloths. These and other findings (Kagan et al., 1994) don't demonstrate that these cultural differences in temperament are genetic, as they may be a consequence of different intrauterine (within the womb) hormonal environments across cultures. Still, they indicate that differences in infants' basic personality styles appear almost immediately after birth.

Temperament and Attachment Styles. How is all of this relevant to attachment styles? Some psychologists have argued that temperament may act as a third variable that confounds the correlation between parenting behavior and attachment styles. That is, infants with certain temperaments may *elicit* certain attachment behaviors from their parents (Paris, 2000; Rutter, 1995). For example, irritable infants may provoke frustration in their parents, which in turn makes these infants still more irritable, and so on. This bidirectional influence may result in an insecure attachment style. So temperament may predispose to both certain parenting practices and certain attachment styles.

APPLY YOUR THINKING

One team of investigators (Fonagy, Steele, & Steele, 1991) successfully predicted infants' attachment styles in the Strange Situation by interviewing their mothers about their relationship history and views of other people *while they were still pregnant* with these (soon-to-be) infants. How might you explain this finding?

PARENTING: WHAT'S RIGHT AND WHAT'S WRONG?

If you've ever observed a mother dog raising her puppies or a mother cat raising her kittens, the whole process seems utterly effortless. Animal parents seem to know exactly what to do, even though they've never purchased a parenting advice book from their local bookstore (or pet store). Yet when it comes to us human animals, popular psychology lore tells us that things are unimaginably more complicated. If we don't do just about everything right, we're told, our children are supposedly in for big trouble later on.

Parenting Advice: The Elusive Search for the "Right" Parenting Style. Over the past century, self-proclaimed parenting experts have bombarded nervous mothers and fathers with contradictory advice about how to raise their children (Hulbert, 2001; Rankin, 2005). In the 1950s and 1960s, pediatrician Dr. Benjamin Spock became a major proponent of a *child-*

Infant attachment is more complex than researchers once thought. For example, babies may exhibit a different attachment style to their father than to their mother.

centered or "soft" approach to parenting, in which parents should be highly responsive to their children's needs (Hulbert, 2001). According to Spock, healthy parents react to their infant's cries with reassurance and to their infant's pleas for affection with warm hugs. Other experts have instead called for a *parent-centered* or "hard" approach to parenting, in which parents don't reinforce children's calls for excessive attention. Pediatrician John Rosemond, for example, urges parents to instill independence in their children and to resort to tough discipline when necessary.

Making matters more confusing, some parenting advice seems to be at odds with psychological research. For example, parenting expert Dr. James Dobson advocates spanking children as a disciplinary technique (Dobson, 1992), even though there's not much evidence that physical punishment is effective for promoting long-term behavioral change (see Chapter 6).

With all of this confusing and at times inconsistent advice, what are human parents to do aside from shrugging their shoulders? We can find some helpful hints in the work of Diana Baumrind (1971, 1991). Based on her observations of Caucasian middle-class families, Baumrind concluded that parenting styles fall into three major categories:

A host of newsstand magazines provide parents with advice about different parenting behaviors and styles. Psychological science can help them evaluate the validity of this advice.

- *Permissive.* Permissive parents tend to be lenient with their children, allowing them considerable freedom inside and outside the household. They use discipline sparingly, if at all, and often shower their children with affection.

- *Authoritarian.* Authoritarian parents tend to be strict with their children, punishing them when they don't respond appropriately to their demands. They show little affection toward their children.

- *Authoritative.* Authoritative parents combine the best features of both permissive and authoritarian worlds. They're supportive of their children but set clear and firm limits with them.

Some authors refer to these three styles as "too soft," "too hard," and "just right," respectively. Since Baumrind developed her initial threefold classification, some authors (Maccoby & Martin, 1983) identified a fourth style of parenting:

- *Uninvolved.* Neglectful parents tend to ignore their children, paying little attention to either their positive or negative behaviors.

Parenting Styles and Later Adjustment. Baumrind (1991) and other investigators (Weiss & Schwartz, 1996) found that children with *authoritative* parents tend to exhibit the best social and emotional adjustment and the lowest levels of behavior problems, at least among Caucasian middle-class American families. Children with uninvolved parents tend to fare the worst, and children with either permissive or authoritarian parents fall in between.

In collectivist cultures, where obedience to authority is highly valued, authoritarian parenting may be associated with better outcomes than authoritative parenting.

Correlation vs. Causation

Superficially, these findings appear to suggest that parents should raise their children authoritatively. Yet Baumrind's findings are only correlational and therefore don't permit us to draw cause-and-effect inferences. In fact, the correlations that Baumrind reported could be largely or entirely genetic in origin. For example, permissive parents may tend to be impulsive and pass on genes predisposing to impulsivity to their children.

There's one more limitation to Baumrind's conclusions. Some researchers have found that her findings don't hold up as well in *collectivist* cultures, like China, as they do in *individualistic* cultures, like the United States. Collectivist cultures place a high premium on group harmony, whereas individualist cultures place a high premium on achievement and independence (Triandis & Suh, 2002). In particular, some data suggest that authoritarian parenting is associated with better outcomes in collectivist than in individualist societies (Sorkhabi, 2005; Steinberg, 2001). This finding makes sense given that collectivist cultures are more likely than individualistic cultures to value obedience to authority figures.

So what's the bottom line on parenting styles? Disappointingly, after decades of advice from parenting experts, it's hard to say all that much for sure. Still, the bulk of the research suggests that specific parenting styles may not matter as much as experts had once thought. By and large, if parents provide their children with what Heinz Hartmann (1939) termed the **average expectable environment**—that is, an environment that provides children with

average expectable environment
environment that provides children with basic needs for affection and discipline

basic needs for affection and appropriate discipline—most of their children will probably turn out just fine. Or, as David Winnicott (1958) argued, parenting need only be *good enough*, not necessarily excellent or even especially good (Paris, 2000). So contrary to what they may hear from parenting gurus on *Oprah*, parents needn't lose sleep about everything they do or every word they say.

This doesn't let parents entirely off the hook, however. If parenting falls well below the range of the average expectable environment—that is, if it's especially poor—children's social development can suffer. For example, there's good reason to believe that many children raised by extremely abusive (so-called "toxic") parents often experience ill effects later on (Downey & Coyne, 1990; Lykken, 2000). Second, parenting quality matters when children enter the world with a strong genetic predisposition toward psychological disturbance or criminal behavior. For example, when children are genetically prone to high levels of impulsivity and aggressiveness, parents probably need to exert especially firm and consistent discipline (Collins et al., 2000; Lykken, 1995). As we noted earlier, the effects of genes sometimes interact with those of the environment (Caspi et al., 2002; Kagan, 1994; Suomi, 1997).

Peers versus Parents. In 1995, a controversy erupted when Judith Rich Harris published a paper in one of psychology's premier journals, *Psychological Review*, claiming that peers play an even more important role than parents in children's social development. Part of the controversy stemmed from the fact that Ms. Harris wasn't a professor and didn't hold a Ph.D., but published a rigorously reviewed article in a prestigious journal. However, much of the furor focused on Harris's claims that parents play less of a role than previously believed. According to Harris's (1995, 1998) **group socialization theory** of development, most environmental transmission is "horizontal"—from children to other children—rather than "vertical"—from parents to children. Nevertheless, at least one researcher has found that twins who share many of the same peers are only slightly more similar in personality than are twins who share only a few of the same peers (Loehlin, 1997). Furthermore, the causal direction of this association isn't clear: Do similar peers lead twins to develop similar personalities, or do twins with similar personalities seek out similar peers? So it remains to be seen whether Harris's bold claims regarding the power of peers in shaping development hold up in research.

The Role of the Father: The Neglected Parent. Few investigators have examined the role that fathers play in children's social adjustment (Lamb, 1975). Two researchers found that of 577 articles on the role of parents in children's emotional problems, only 26 percent included fathers at all, and a grand total of 1 percent examined fathers only (Phares & Compas, 1992). The existing research shows that fathers differ from mothers in several ways in their interactions with children. First, fathers tend to be less attentive and affectionate than mothers toward their babies. Second, they spend less time with their babies than mothers, even in households in which both mothers and fathers are at home (Golombok, 2000). Third, when fathers interact with their children, they spend more of their time than do mothers in physical play (Parke, 1996). Fourth, both boys and girls tend to choose their fathers over their mothers as playmates (Clarke-Stewart, 1980). Despite these differences, children raised by single fathers do just as well on average as children raised by single mothers (Golombok, 2000; Hetherington & Stanley-Hagan, 1995).

Single-Parent Families: Science and Politics. Back in 1992, a television sitcom called *Murphy Brown* sparked controversy when then U.S. Vice President Dan Quayle suggested in a speech that the lead character was creating a poor role model for American parents by becoming a single mother. According to Quayle, portraying single-motherhood on television as "just another lifestyle choice" is misleading, because all things being equal, some lifestyle choices are just plain better than others. As psychologists, it's tempting to sidestep political topics or respond to them on an emotional level. But we need to do our best to avoid emotional reasoning (see Chapter 1) and evaluate the research evidence bearing on Dan Quayle's assertion.

In fact, the impact of single-parenthood on children is unclear. On the one hand, there's evidence that children from single-parent families have more behavior

Correlation vs. Causation

Fathers tend to be less affectionate with their children than mothers, but both girls and boys tend to prefer their father over their mother as a playmate.

group socialization theory
theory that peers play a more important role than parents in children's social development

problems, such as aggression and impulsivity, than do children from two-parent families (Golombok, 2000). Moreover, their risk for crime is about seven times higher than for children in two-parent families (Lykken, 1993, 2000). Some researchers even argue that the higher proportion of single-parent families today is a key reason for the higher rates of violent crime in the United States today compared with the 1960s (Wilson & Herrnstein, 1985).

On the other hand, data comparing single-parent with two-parent families are only correlational, so we can't draw causal inferences from them. Single mothers differ from married mothers in many ways; they tend to be poorer, less well educated, and marked by higher levels of life stress (Aber & Rappaport, 1994). They also move around much more often than married moms, making it difficult for their children to form stable social bonds with other children (Harris, 1998). Any or all of these factors—or factors researchers haven't considered—could account for the differences between these two groups of women in their children's adjustment.

Moreover, children raised by single mothers whose husbands died—rather than by divorced or separated mothers—generally exhibit no higher rates of emotional or behavioral problems than do children from two-parent households (Felner, Ginter, Boike, & Cowen, 1982; McLeod, 1991). This finding suggests that the apparent effects of single-mother parenting could actually be attributable to characteristics of the *father* or to maternal distress associated with having no second parent in the home.

So we can safely conclude that many single mothers do a fine job of raising their children, and that being raised by a single mom doesn't necessarily doom children to later behavior problems. Although some single mothers have children with more behavioral problems than do other mothers, the causes of this difference remain unclear.

Correlation vs. Causation

Ruling Out Rival Hypotheses

APPLY YOUR THINKING

How would you test the hypothesis that the seeming negative effects of being raised by a single mother are actually due to the father's characteristics?

Effects of Divorce on Children.   Much of the popular psychology literature informs us that divorce often exacts a serious emotional toll on children. On September 25, 2000, *Time* magazine featured a cover story entitled "What Divorce Does to Kids," accompanied by the ominous warning that "New research says the long-term damage is worse than you thought." This story was sparked by a 25-year study by Judith Wallerstein (1989), who tracked a group of sixty families in California in which the parents had divorced. Wallerstein reported that the negative effects of divorce were subtle and enduring: Many years later, the children of divorced parents had difficulties with forming stable romantic relationships and establishing career goals. Yet Wallerstein's study contained a flaw that most of the news media missed: She didn't include a control group of families in which one or both parents had been separated from their children for reasons other than divorce, such as accidental death. As a result, we can't tell whether her findings reflect the effects of divorce itself rather than the effects of any kind of stressful disruption in the family.

Ruling Out Rival Hypotheses

In fact, better-designed studies show that the substantial majority of children survive their parents' divorce without long-term emotional damage (Cherlin et al., 1991; Hetherington, Cox, & Cox, 1985). In addition, the apparent effects of divorce depend on the severity of conflict between parents before the divorce. When parents experience only mild conflict before the divorce, the seeming effects of divorce are actually *more* severe than when parents experience intense conflict before the divorce (Amato & Booth, 1997; Rutter, 1972). In the latter case, divorce typically produces no ill effects on children, probably because they find the divorce to be a welcome relief from their parents' incessant arguing.

Still, divorce can surely produce negative effects on some children. One group of investigators compared the children of identical twins, only one of whom had been divorced.

The design provides an elegant control for genetic effects, because these twins are genetically identical. The researchers found that the children of identical twins who'd divorced had higher levels of depression and substance abuse, as well as poorer school performance, than the children of identical twins who hadn't divorced (D'Onofrio et al., 2006). These findings suggest that divorce can exert negative effects on some children, although they don't rule out the possibility that parental conflict, rather than divorce itself, accounts for the differences.

SELF-CONTROL: LEARNING TO INHIBIT IMPULSES

A crucial ingredient of social development, and one that parents begin wishing for long before it emerges, is **self-control**: the ability to inhibit our impulses (Eigsti et al., 2006). We may be tempted to snag that unclaimed coffee at the Starbucks counter or tell our unbearably arrogant boss what we really think of him, but we usually—and thankfully—restrain our desires to do so. Other times, we must put our desires on the back burner until we fulfill our obligations. Waiting until payday to try that fancy new restaurant or delaying a movie outing with friends until the weekend because we need to study for an exam are examples of delaying gratification to achieve a long-term goal.

As we all know, children are notoriously bad at delaying gratification. They want what they want and they want it *now*. And as we also all know, some children are better at it than others. As Walter Mischel and his colleagues further discovered, our capacity to delay gratification is a good predictor of later social adjustment. They found this out with the help of a simple, yet elegant paradigm. To study delay of gratification, they leave a child all alone in a room with a small reward, like one cookie, and a little bell. Next, they tell the child that if she can wait 15 minutes, she can get an even bigger reward, like two cookies. If she can't wait that long, she can ring the bell to summon the experimenter. Children in this task have several options: wait patiently, ring the bell and sacrifice the big reward, or throw caution to the wind and stuff the cookie in their mouths while no one's looking.

Children's ability to wait for the bigger reward at the age of 4 years forecasts superior ability to cope with stress and frustration in adolescence, probably because handling difficult situations hinges on their ability to inhibit immediate distress. It even predicts teenagers' SAT scores (Mischel, Shoda, & Peake, 1988; Mischel, Shoda, & Rodriguez, 1989). Of course, these findings don't prove that early self-control *causes* these later outcomes. But they suggest that the capacity to delay gratification in childhood is an early indicator of the capacity to restrain impulses, which in turn seems to be rooted in frontal lobe functioning (Eigsti et al., 2006; Mischel & Ayduk, 2004).

MORAL DEVELOPMENT: KNOWING RIGHT FROM WRONG

Children begin to develop ideas of right and wrong as toddlers and preschoolers. But *moral dilemmas*—situations in which there are no clear right or wrong answers—arise much more frequently in the teen and young adult years. Should I lie to my parents about where I've been so they don't worry about me? Should I avoid my nice but dorky friend so that my popular friends will like me better? The approach we adopt to these and other moral problems changes over the course of development.

Origins of Conscience. There's good reason to believe that we can trace the roots of our conscience—that little voice inside our heads that tells us what is and isn't morally appropriate—to *fear*. We initially fear the punishment of our parents—and later our teachers—for misbehavior, so we learn not to do bad things to avoid their wrath. Over time, our fears become internalized. We come to fear not merely the recriminations of our parents and teachers, but the recriminations of our own moral sensibilities (Lykken, 1995). As Freud (1932) observed, we become afraid of ourselves (Freud called guilt "moral anxiety"). Indeed, research indicates that one of the best predictors of the

Children in Mischel's delay-of-gratification task must inhibit their desire to eat a cookie if they want to receive a bigger reward—eating both cookies—later.

Correlation vs. Causation

self-control
ability to inhibit an impulse to act

strength of children's conscience is their level of fear years earlier (Frick & Marsee, 2006; Kochanska, Gross, Lin, & Nichols, 2002).

Piaget and Morality. Piaget believed that children's moral development is constrained by their stage of cognitive development (Loevinger, 1987). For example, he suggested that children in the concrete operational stage tend to evaluate people in terms of *objective responsibility*—how much harm they've done. As they approach formal operations, how-ever, they tend to evaluate people in terms of *subjective responsibility*—their intentions to produce harm (Piaget, 1932).

If we ask a 6- or 7-year-old who's more to blame, (a) a child who accidentally knocks over 20 kitchen plates in his parents' cabinet or (b) a child who purposefully knocks over 10 kitchen plates because he was hopping mad at his parents, she's more likely to say (a), because it produced more damage. In contrast, a 12- or 13-year-old is more likely to say (b), because it was intentional. With age, children become better able to understand that there's more to personal responsibility than the sheer amount of damage one has wrought. Whether they mean to inflict damage also counts.

Kohlberg and Morality: Finding the Moral High Ground. Lawrence Kohlberg extended Piaget's thinking to identify how morality unfolds over time. He studied how morality changes with development by exploring how participants wrestle with moral dilemmas. Because Kohlberg's moral dilemmas don't have clear right or wrong answers, he didn't score the answers that participants provided; he scored only the *reasoning processes* they used. For Kohlberg, what's crucial are the underlying principles that people invoke to solve moral problems.

We'll explain this point using one famous moral dilemma that Kohlberg used. Con-sider Heinz's dilemma and think about how you'd handle it.

Another moral dilemma, in this case adapted slightly from one of Kohlberg's: Imagine you've just learned that one of your next-door neighbors, whom you've known for many years as an extremely kind and caring person, is wanted for an attempted murder she committed as a young woman three decades ago (this scenario describes Sara Jane Olson, ex-member of a violent revolutionary organization, shown here with her daughter). Would you turn her in to the police?

Heinz and the Drug

In Europe, a woman was near death from a special kind of cancer. There was one drug that the doctors thought might save her. It was a form of radium that a druggist in the same town had recently discovered. The drug was expensive to make, but the druggist was charging ten times what the drug cost him to make. He paid $400 for the radium and charged $4,000 for a small dose of the drug. The sick woman's husband, Heinz, went to everyone he knew to borrow the money and tried every legal means, but he could only get together about $2,000, which is half of what it cost. He told the druggist that his wife was dying, and asked him to sell it cheaper or let him pay later. But the druggist said, "No, I discovered the drug and I'm going to make money from it." So, having tried every legal means, Heinz gets desperate and considers breaking into the man's store to steal the drug.

Question: Should Heinz steal the drug? Why or why not?

After testing many children, adolescents, and adults, Kohlberg (1976, 1981) concluded that the development of morality occurs in three major stages, each containing two sub-stages. We can see these stages, along with sample answers to the Heinz dilemma that go along with them, in **Table 10.5.** The first level, *preconventional morality,* is marked by a

Table 10.5 Kohlberg's Scheme of Moral Development and Sample Explanations. Kohlberg scored the reasoning processes underlying the answer to the Heinz dilemma, not the answers themselves.

Level	Heinz should steal the drug because . . .	Heinz should *not* steal the drug because . . .
Preconventional Morality	He can get away with it	He might get caught
Conventional Morality	Others will look down on him if he lets his wife die	It's against the law
Postconventional Morality	The protection of human life is a higher moral principle that can overrule laws against stealing	Doing so violates a basic social contract needed to preserve civilization: Thou shalt not steal

focus on punishment and reward. What's right is what we're rewarded for; what's wrong is what we're punished for. The second level, *conventional morality*, is marked by a focus on societal values. What's right is what society approves of; what's wrong is what society disapproves of. The third level, *postconventional morality*, is marked by a focus on internal moral principles that transcend society. What's right is what is what accords with fundamental human rights and values; what's wrong is what contradicts these rights and values. Like Piaget and other stage theorists, Kohlberg believed the sequence of these levels was invariant, although he acknowledged that different people pass through them at different rates. In fact, Kohlberg's research indicated that most adults never get past conventional morality to achieve postconventional morality.

Criticisms of Kohlberg's Work. Kohlberg's work has been enormously influential; his research has shed light on the development of morality, and it's informed educational efforts to enhance people's moral reasoning (Kohlberg & Turiel, 1971; Loevinger, 1987). Still, Kohlberg's findings have met with more than their share of criticism; we'll examine five criticisms here.

(1) *Cultural Bias.* By and large, studies have confirmed Kohlberg's claim that people pass through his levels in the same order, regardless of their country or culture of origin (Snarey, 1982). So far, so good. But some critics have charged Kohlberg with cultural bias, because people from different cultures tend to achieve different scores on his moral development scheme. For example, people from individualistic societies often score somewhat higher than do those in collectivist societies (Shweder, Mahapatra, & Miller, 1990). Still, as we learned in Chapter 9, group differences don't always indicate bias, so the meaning of this finding is unclear.

(2) *Sex Bias.* Kohlberg's student Carol Gilligan (1982) broke from her mentor to argue that his system was biased against women. For Gilligan, Kohlberg's scheme unfairly favors males, who are more likely than women to adopt a "justice" orientation based on abstract principles of fairness, whereas women are more likely than men to adopt a "caring" orientation based on concrete principles of nurturance. Yet despite gender differences in strategies toward moral problems, there's little evidence that men score higher than women on Kohlberg's scheme (Moon, 1986; Sunar, 2002).

(3) *Low Correlation with Moral Behavior.* Scores on Kohlberg's scheme are only modestly related to real-world moral behavior (Krebs & Denton, 2005). For example, the correlation between Kohlberg's levels and moral behavior, such as honest and altruistic actions, tends to be only about .3 (Blasi, 1980). Kohlberg argued that his moral development system *shouldn't* correlate highly with real-world actions, because it's a measure of how people reason about moral problems, not what behaviors they display. People may perform the same behaviors for very different reasons: A person may steal a coat from a store because he wants to add it to his fashion collection or because he wants to keep his freezing children warm in the winter. Still, this kind of reasoning raises problems for the falsifiability of Kohlberg's system. If the scores in this system correlate with behavior, they provide evidence for it; if they don't correlate with behavior, they don't necessarily provide evidence against it.

(4) *Confound with Verbal Intelligence.* Understanding and responding effectively to Kohlberg's moral dilemmas require some basic smarts. But that fact should make us a bit uneasy, because Kohlberg's scheme may be measuring people's ability to understand and talk about problems in general rather than moral problems specifically (Blasi, 1980). There's only one way to rule out this alternative possibility: measure verbal intelligence in the same study as we measure moral development, and see whether it washes out the findings. Some studies have found that intelligence may explain Kohlberg's findings (Sanders, Lubinski, & Benbow, 1995), but others have found strong relations between scores on Kohlberg's scheme and moral behavior even after taking intelligence into account (Gibbs, 2006). The issue remains unresolved.

(5) *Causal Direction.* Kohlberg's model assumes that our moral reasoning precedes our emotional reactions to moral issues. Yet in some cases, our emotional reactions to morally laden stimuli, like photographs of assaults on innocent people, occur

According to Carol Gilligan, women's preference for a caring orientation affects their responses to moral dilemmas. Even so, women score just as highly as men on Kohlberg's moral development scheme, suggesting that their thinking about moral problems is equally sophisticated.

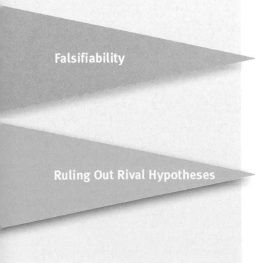

Falsifiability

Ruling Out Rival Hypotheses

almost instantaneously (Lou, Nakic, Wheatley, Richel, Martin, & Blair, 2006). Moreover, we can know something is wrong without being able to explain why; for example, many people "know" intuitively that incest is immoral but can't offer a reason (Haidt, 2007). These findings suggest that moral reasoning may sometimes come after, rather than before, our emotional reactions.

Correlation vs. Causation

GENDER IDENTITY

Gender concepts are crucial to children's understanding of themselves as social beings. Before addressing how we develop a sense of ourselves as boys or girls, men or women, we need to sort through a bit of confusing terminology. Most psychologists distinguish sex from gender, with *sex* referring to individuals' biological status as male or female and *gender* referring to the psychological characteristics—behaviors, thoughts, and emotions—that tend to be associated with being male or female. But we're not done yet. **Gender identity** refers to people's sense of being male or female. Some people with *gender identity disorder,* sometimes called *transsexualism* in adulthood, report feeling "trapped" in the body of the opposite sex. They may be biologically male, yet feel like a woman, or vice versa. In contrast, **gender role** refers to the behaviors that tend to accompany being male or female. Gender identity and gender role don't always go together. An adolescent may see herself as female, yet engage in "stereotypically" masculine behaviors, like playing football and playing the role of class clown. How do gender identity and gender role arise?

Biological Influences on Gender. A popular misconception is that gender differences don't emerge until socializing influences, like parenting practices, have had the opportunity to act on children. Yet some gender differences are evident in early infancy, making this explanation unlikely.

As early as 1 year of age or less, boys and girls prefer to play with different types of toys. Boys generally like balls, guns, and fire trucks; girls like dolls, stuffed animals, and cookware (Caldera, Huston, & O'Brien, 1989; Smith & Daglish, 1977). Remarkably, investigators have observed these preferences in nonhuman primates, including vervet monkeys. When placed in cages with toys, boy monkeys tend to choose trucks and balls, whereas girl monkeys tend to choose dolls and pots (Alexander & Hines, 2002). This finding suggests that toy preferences may reflect differences in biological predispositions, such as aggressiveness and nurturance, shared by many primates. Indeed, in humans, monkeys, and even mice, adult females exposed to excess levels of testosterone (see Chapter 3) during birth tend to engage in more rough-and-tumble play than other females (Berenbaum & Hines, 1992; Edwards, 1970; Young, Goy, & Phoenix, 1964).

As early as age 3, boys prefer to hang out with other boys, and girls with other girls (LaFreniere, Strayer, & Gauthier, 1984; Whiting & Edwards, 1988). This phenomenon of *sex segregation* may be due to biological factors, social factors, or both. Research indicates that sex segregation emerges in rhesus monkeys between 6 and 12 months of age (Rupp, 2003), raising the possibility that this phenomenon has deep-seated biological roots.

Researchers have observed that when monkeys are given a choice of toys to play with, female monkeys *(left)* tend to prefer dolls, whereas male monkeys *(right)* tend to prefer trucks.

Social Influences on Gender. As we've discovered throughout this chapter, nature rarely if ever operates in a vacuum. Indeed, nature is almost always amplified by nurture, such as the reinforcing influences of parents, teachers, and other adults. Research shows that parents tend to encourage children to engage in gender-stereotyped behaviors, such as achievement and independence among boys and dependence and nurturance among girls. Fathers are even more likely than mothers to enforce these stereotypes (Lytton & Romney, 1991).

gender identity
individuals' sense of being male or female
gender roles
behaviors that tend to be associated with being male or female

Research suggests that parents tend to be more accepting of "tomboyish" behaviors among girls than "sissyish" behavior among boys.

Expectations also matter. In one study, two researchers (Condry & Condry, 1976) showed adults videos of an infant reacting to several emotionally arousing stimuli, like a jack-in-the-box toy popping open suddenly. They told some adults that the infant was a boy ("David") and other adults that the infant was a girl ("Dana"). The investigators randomly assigned the adults to these two conditions, making the study a true experiment (see Chapter 2). They found that observers' beliefs about the infant's gender colored their interpretations of the infant's behavior. Adults who thought the infant was named David rated "his" startled reaction to the jack-in-the-box as reflecting anger, whereas adults who thought the infant was named Dana rated "her" startled reaction to the jack-in-the-box as reflecting fear.

Teachers also tend to respond to boys and girls in accord with prevailing gender stereotypes. They give boys more attention when they exhibit aggression and girls more attention when they exhibit dependent or "needy" behaviors (Serbin & O'Leary, 1975). Even when boys and girls are equally assertive and equally verbal, teachers tend to lavish assertive boys and verbal girls with greater amounts of attention (Fagot, Hagan, Leinbach, & Kronsberg, 1985). In modern-day America, gender-role socialization tends to be stricter for boys than for girls. Parents tolerate cross-sex "tomboy" behavior in girls, like playing with both trucks and dolls, more than in boys, who tend to be stereotyped as "sissies" if they play with dolls (Langlois & Downs, 1980; Lytton & Romney, 1991).

ASSESS YOUR KNOWLEDGE: FACT OR FICTION?

(1) There's strong evidence for abruptly ending critical periods in humans. (True/False)

(2) Studies of contact comfort suggest that nourishment isn't the principal basis for attachment in primates. (True/False)

(3) Children's attachment styles almost never change over time. (True/False)

(4) Studies suggest that within the broad range of the average expectable environment, parenting style may not be a crucial determinant of children's development. (True/False)

(5) When evaluating Kohlberg's moral dilemmas, the answers people give are more important than the reasoning processes they used to arrive at these answers. (True/False)

(6) Gender differences don't emerge until parenting practices have the opportunity to influence children's behavior. (True/False)

Answers: (1) F (p. 419); (2) T (p. 419); (3) F (p. 420); (4) T (p. 423); (5) F (p. 427); (6) F (p. 429)

Development Doesn't Stop: Changes in Adolescence and Adulthood

Although people tend to think of developmental psychology as focusing only on children, we don't emerge from elementary school as fully formed individuals. Substantial physical, cognitive, and social changes take place throughout adolescence, adulthood, and even old age.

ADOLESCENCE: A TIME OF DRAMATIC CHANGE

Common wisdom regards **adolescence**—the transition between childhood and adulthood commonly associated with the teenage years—as one of the most traumatic times in development, and it's certainly a time of dramatic changes in body, brain, and social activities. Yet the teenage years can also be a wonderful time of discovery, of opportunity to participate in adultlike activities, and of deep friendships. We might characterize adolescence in the words

adolescence
the transition between childhood and adulthood commonly associated with the teenage years

of Charles Dickens: "It was the best of times, it was the worst of times." There's plenty of turmoil, such as increased conflicts with parents (Laursen, Coy, & Collins, 1998), increased risk-taking (Arnett, 1995), and heightened negative emotions (Larson & Richards, 1994) relative to younger children and adults. Yet most evidence suggests that the idea of adolescence as an intense roller coaster ride is a misconception (Arnett, 1999; Epstein, 2007). On balance, stress and unhappiness aren't that much more pronounced during adolescence than during other times of life. But perhaps because teenagers are less inhibited than adults, they're more likely to talk and complain about their ups and downs. When they're upset, we hear about it.

Physical Maturation: The Power of Puberty. Many of the physical changes that adolescents undergo are hormonal. The pituitary gland stimulates physical growth and the reproductive system releases the sex hormones estrogens and androgens (see Chapters 3 and 11)into the bloodstream, resulting in physical changes in addition to growth. Many people think of androgens, such as testosterone, as male hormones and estrogens as female hormones. In fact, both types of hormones are present in both sexes in varying proportions. In boys, testosterone promotes increases in muscle tissue, growth of facial and body hair, and broadening of the shoulders. In girls, estrogens promote breast growth, uterus and vaginal maturation, hip broadening, and the onset of menstruation. Androgens in girls also induce physical growth and the growth of pubic hair (see **Figure 10.17**). Boys' muscle strength begins to exceed girls' in adolescence, and boys undergo a variety of changes in lung function and blood circulation. These changes result in greater average physical strength and endurance in boys than in girls, explaining the divergence between boys' and girls' athletic ability that emerges in adolescence (Beunen & Malina, 1996; Malina & Bouchard, 1991). Some unpleasant effects of these hormonal changes are increases in body odor, sweat, and oily skin, often leading to acne.

A crucial part of hormonal changes in adolescence is *sexual maturation*—the attainment of physical potential for reproduction. Maturation includes changes in **primary sex characteristics,** which include the reproductive organs and genitals. It also

In 2005, professional golfer Michelle Wie, who is 6 feet, 1 inch tall, became the first ever female golfer to qualify to play in a *men's* United States Golf Association tournament. Men's greater strength, on average, makes it challenging for women to compete at men's level in athletics.

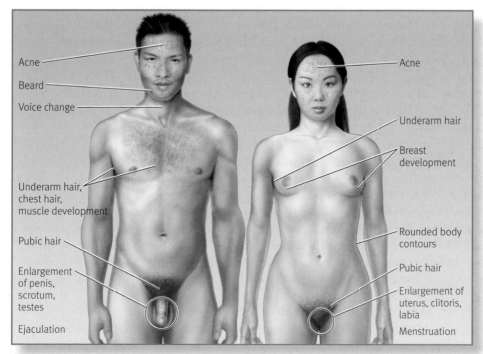

Acne
Beard
Voice change
Underarm hair, chest hair, muscle development
Pubic hair
Enlargement of penis, scrotum, testes
Ejaculation

Acne
Underarm hair
Breast development
Rounded body contours
Pubic hair
Enlargement of uterus, clitoris, labia
Menstruation

Figure 10.17 Physical and Sexual Maturation during the Preteen and Teenage Years. Physical and sexual maturation during the preteen and teenage years. Hormones result in rapid growth to full adult height. They also trigger changes in the reproductive system and in secondary sex characteristics, such as increased breast size, broader hips in girls, and broader shoulders in boys.

factoid

The age of menarche has decreased over the past 100 years, moving from around 15 to around 13 years of age on average. This change is probably due primarily to better nutrition and health care (Tanner, 1998).

primary sex characteristics
the reproductive organs and genitals that distinguish the sexes

includes changes in **secondary sex characteristics,** which include sex-differentiating characteristics that don't relate directly to reproduction, such as breast enlargement in girls, deepening voices in boys, and pubic hair in both genders. In girls, **menarche**— the onset of menstruation—tends not to begin until they've achieved full physical growth. Menarche is the body's insurance plan against allowing girls to become pregnant before their bodies can carry an infant to term and give birth safely (Tanner, 1990). There's variability in when menstruation begins because girls reach full physical maturity at different ages.

Spermarche, the first ejaculation, is the comparable milestone in boys. This event occurs on average at around 13 years of age, but it's also variable. Because boys need not be fully physically mature to bear children, spermarche isn't as closely linked to physical maturity as is menarche. In fact, boys often take a much longer time to mature fully than girls, which is why we'll often see sixth- and seventh-grade girls towering above their male counterparts. The first signs of sexual maturation in boys are enlargement of the testicles and penis, and growth of pubic hair (Graber, Petersen, & Brooks-Gunn, 1996). After these changes, boys begin to see signs of facial and body hair, and their voices deepen.

These seventh-grade students vary in physical height, but the girl (on the right) is the tallest of the bunch. Girls tend to mature earlier and more rapidly than boys. The girl is probably close to reaching her adult height, whereas the boys still have lots of growing to do.

secondary sex characteristics
sex-differentiating characteristics that don't relate directly to reproduction, such as breast enlargement in women and deepening voices in men

menarche
start of menstruation

spermarche
boys' first ejaculation

Ruling Out Rival Hypotheses

The timing of puberty in boys and girls is genetically influenced; identical twins tend to begin menstruating within a month of each other, whereas fraternal twins average about a year's difference in onset (Tanner, 1990). However, a variety of environmental factors, some relating to physical health, affect when adolescents reach puberty. Adolescents from higher socioeconomic status households tend to have better nutrition and health care, and reach puberty earlier as a result (Eveleth & Tanner, 1976). Girls from wealthier countries tend to begin menstruating earlier than those from poorer countries. Girls in Japan and the United States usually start menstruating between $12\frac{1}{2}$ and $13\frac{1}{2}$ years of age, whereas girls in the poorest parts of Africa don't usually start menstruating until between 14 and 17 years of age (Eveleth & Tanner, 1990).

Cognitive Changes in Adolescence: The Teen Brain. Although most brain maturation occurs prenatally and in the first few years of life, the frontal lobes don't mature fully until late adolescence or early adulthood (Casey et al., 2000; Johnson, 1998). As we discovered in Chapter 3, the frontal lobes are responsible primarily for reasoning, planning, decision making, and impulse control. The fact that the frontal lobes are still maturing during adolescence may explain some of the impulsive behaviors, like skateboarding down a steep incline for which teens are notorious (Weinberger, Elvevag, & Giedd, 2005). Even on the simplest of tasks, such as inhibiting the impulse to look at a flashing light, teens have a more difficult time and require more brain processing than do adults (Luna & Sweeney, 2004).

Adolescents routinely encounter new adultlike opportunities to engage in potentially harmful activities, but their brains aren't ready to make mature, well-reasoned decisions. For example, teens are often faced with making decisions such as whether to have sex, to engage in vandalism, or drive drunk. Adolescents must negotiate these choices without a "full deck" of decision-making cards. However, there's debate over whether we can blame teen behavioral problems entirely on the "teen brain." Some researchers have argued that these behaviors don't appear in non-Westernized cultures, suggesting that the causes of this phenomenon may be at least as cultural as biological (Epstein, 2007; Schlegel & Barry, 1991).

According to David Elkind (1967), adolescent behavioral problems stem in part from a sense of invincibility he termed the *personal fable.* However, recent evidence indicates that most adolescents actually don't underestimate the risks of behaviors such as driving fast, taking drugs, or having early sex; they're often aware they're taking chances, but don't care (Reyna & Farley, 2006). Moreover, not all adolescents who see themselves as invulnerable take foolish chances, probably because they can inhibit their impulses (Vartanian, 2000).

Attitudes toward Knowledge in Adolescents and Young Adults: How College Students View "The Truth." One critical transition during the late high school and college years is in adolescents' and young adults' perspectives toward knowledge. Students starting college are often frustrated to find few black-and-white answers to questions. One of the hardest things for undergraduates to appreciate is that the answer to questions like "Which theory is better?" is often "It depends" or "There are multiple views on this issue." William Perry (1970) cataloged the transitions that students undergo during the college years as they discover that their professors have few absolute answers to offer. He noted that over the course of their college years, students pass through a variety of "positions," or perspectives, on knowledge.

Students who expect clear right or wrong answers to all questions may initially resist changing their views and instead try to reconcile their expectations with what they're learning in the classroom (recall Piaget's assimilation process). They may understand that the "it depends" perspective is the one their professors want them to embrace. So they'll often say the "right things" on exams to get good grades, but still believe deep down that there's a right and a wrong answer to most questions. With time and experience, students relax their expectations for absolute answers and construe knowledge as relative.

Over time, though, students typically come to realize that they can't abandon the idea of "truth" or "reality" completely, but that different people hold different and equally valid interpretations of reality. Eventually emerging from this realization is the mature understanding that students can and should hold their own point of view, even as they can respect differing points of view (but recall the pitfalls discussed in Chapter 1 of dismissing evidence on the grounds that "everyone is entitled to my opinion"). Although the past three decades have witnessed minor modifications to Perry's stages, his overall theory has withstood the test of time (Cano, 2005; Cano & Cardelle-Elawar, 2004; Yang, 2005).

Building an Identity in Adolescence. Our personalities, priorities, interests, and most important, self-perceptions all exert an important impact on our decisions. We've all asked ourselves "Who am I?" at some point. Indeed, one of the central challenges of adolescence is to get a firm handle on our **identity,** our sense of who we are, as well as our life goals and priorities. Most teenagers struggle mightily with this problem, "trying on different hats" in an effort to see which one fits best; psychologists call this process *role experimentation.* Even in college, we may juggle "nerdy," "cool," and "jock" friends at varying times, scope out different potential majors, and even explore alternative religious and philosophical beliefs. Our identities undergo a variety of changes over the course of adolescence and early adulthood as we fine-tune the fit between who we are and who we want to be. Erik Erikson (1902–1994) developed the most comprehensive theory of how identity develops.

Erikson's Model of Identity: The Identity Crisis. As an adolescent, Erikson wrestled with more than his fair share of identity issues. Although of Danish descent and unmistakably Scandinavian in his appearance (he was tall, with blue eyes and blonde hair), Erikson was raised Jewish. Largely as a consequence, he felt like an outsider at both his synagogue, where he was teased for being Scandinavian, and at his school, where he was teased for being Jewish (Hunt, 1993; Kushner, 1993). It's probably not merely coincidental that Erikson (1963, 1970) coined the term *identity crisis* to describe the confusion that most adolescents experience regarding their sense of self.

Erikson's theoretical work went well beyond the topic of adolescence. In contrast to Sigmund Freud, who as we'll learn in Chapter 14 believed that personality development stopped largely in late childhood, Erikson believed that personality growth continues throughout the life span. Erikson formulated an eight-stage model of human development from "womb to tomb," as psychologists like to say. In each of his "Eight Ages," we confront a different **psychosocial crisis:** a dilemma concerning our relations to other people, whether they be parents, friends, teachers, or the larger society.

Lee Boyd Malvo participated in the Washington, DC, sniper killings in October 2002. He was 17 years old at the time of the crimes. Some researchers argue that adolescents who commit crimes should be considered "less guilty by reason of adolescence" because their frontal lobes aren't fully mature, preventing them from making mature decisions regarding the consequences of their actions (Steinberg & Scott, 2003). Others disagree, noting that the overwhelming majority of adolescents don't commit violent crimes. What do you think?

Replicability

identity
our sense of who we are, and our life goals and priorities

psychosocial crisis
dilemma concerning an individual's relations to other people

As we can see in **Figure 10.18**, the fifth stage, "Identity versus Role Confusion," is the period during which adolescents grapple with the fundamental question of who they are. In most cases, they emerge from this crisis relatively unscathed. But if they don't, they may be at risk for later psychological conditions marked by confusion regarding identity (such as borderline personality disorder, which we'll encounter in Chapter 15). Indeed, for Erikson the successful resolution of each stage holds crucial implications later on down the line. If we don't solve the challenges posed by earlier stages, we'll experience difficulty solving the challenges posed by later stages.

Erikson's theorizing has been influential, but the research basis for many of his claims is slim. There's not much research on whether there are exactly eight stages, or on whether we pass through them in the same order. There's evidence that individuals who don't successfully negotiate the early stages of development, like identity versus role confusion, experience more difficulty with the later stages than do other individuals (Valliant & Milosky, 1980). Although consistent with Erikson's model, these findings are only correlational. As a consequence, they don't demonstrate that problems with early stages *produce* problems in later stages.

Correlation vs. Causation

1. Infancy
Trust versus mistrust

Developing general security, optimism, and trust in others

2. Toddlerhood
Autonomy versus shame and doubt

Developing a sense of independence and confident self-reliance, taking setbacks in stride

3. Early childhood
Initiative versus guilt

Developing initiative in exploring and manipulating the environment

4. Middle childhood
Industry versus inferiority

Enjoyment and mastery of the developmental tasks of childhood, in and out of school

5. Adolescence
Identity versus identity confusion

Achievement of a stable and satisfying sense of identity and direction

6. Young adulthood
Intimacy versus isolation

Development of the ability to maintain intimate personal relationships

7. Adulthood
Generativity versus stagnation

Satisfaction of personal and familial needs supplemented by development of interest in the welfare of others and the world in general

8. Aging
Ego integrity versus despair

Recognizing and adjusting to aging and the prospect of death with a sense of satisfaction about the future

Figure 10.18 Erikson's Eight Ages of Human Development. (*Source:* Good and Brophy, 1995)

ADULTHOOD AND AGING: THE UPS AND DOWNS OF GETTING OLDER

As we transition from adolescence to adulthood, many aspects of our lives begin to stabilize, but others begin to change even more dramatically. After reaching full physical and sexual maturation during puberty, most of us reach our physical peak in our early twenties (Larsson, Grimby, & Karlsson, 1979; Lindle et al., 1997). Strength, coordination, speed of cognitive processing, and physical and mental flexibility are at their zenith in early adulthood. And some of the most crucial milestones in social development typically occur in early to middle adulthood.

Life Transitions in Adulthood. Adults, like children, undergo a variety of changes. These changes tend to be associated with major transitions in lifestyle or societal status, such as shifting from student to wage earner, entering a serious relationship, or becoming a parent. Many of these transitions are wonderful experiences, but they can be stressful. We tend to think of adults as following a predictable life trajectory: attending college in the late teens and early twenties, getting that first job after graduation, falling in love with someone of the opposite sex, getting married, having two or more children, watching them grow up, and growing old gracefully while rocking on the front porch. In reality, we vastly overestimate the number of individuals who adhere to this tidy stereotype of the road of life (Coontz, 1992). Many college students are in their late twenties, thirties, or forties, attending school while maintaining a job, and have families who are financially dependent on them. Many family units consist of single parents, same-sex parents, unmarried parents, second families following a divorce, and childless couples. Recent census reports (U.S. Census Bureau, 2005) indicate that fewer than 25 percent of adults live in conventional nuclear families (mom, dad, and children). Clearly, the life stages we experience as adults unfold differently for different people.

Although the popular stereotype of a family includes a husband, wife, and several children, a surprisingly small number of families fit this mold. Single-parent families, same-sex parents, blended families following a second marriage, and childless couples are far more common than most people think.

Careers. One of the biggest sources of anxiety for young adults graduating from college—particularly those who haven't served in the workforce—is what they're going to do for a living. Some opt to go on to do graduate work, which is a necessity for such careers as law, medicine, or clinical psychology. Others choose careers related directly to their course of study in college, such as business majors who join consulting firms or English majors who become editors. Yet recent graduates commonly cast around a bit for a career path that matches their qualifications and interests. For some, this can be a beneficial strategy, because they end up discovering unexpected careers that are good fits for their skills and passions. Although it was once the norm for people to work for one company or in one career for their entire lives, this is no longer the case. A longitudinal study conducted by the Bureau of Labor Statistics (2006) revealed that the average American worker changed jobs 10.5 times between the ages of 18 and 40. Although changes were more frequent in the teens and early twenties, people between 36 and 40 changed jobs at least once on average. Each job change, even a promotion, is accompanied by its own stress, no matter how welcome the new position.

Although we usually think of college students as being in their late teens or early twenties and financially dependent on their parents, many "nontraditional" students enroll in college while working full-time and supporting families.

Love and Commitment. One of the most momentous adult transitions is finding a life mate. Falling in love and making a serious commitment to sharing a life with someone can be exciting, romantic, and fulfilling. Yet romantic relationships often call for a major shift in lifestyle. Even something as simple as integrating our music collections with our partners' can be an exceptionally stressful experience. Nevertheless, there may be benefits to sharing life with a significant other. Physical and emotional intimacy is associated with greater physical health and lower stress (Coombs, 1991). Overall, those in serious long-term relationships—both homosexual and heterosexual—report higher overall levels of happiness than those who are single (Gove, Hughes, & Briggs Style, 1983; Wayment & Peplau, 1995). Nevertheless, this finding is only correlational and could reflect a tendency for happier people to enter into stable relationships (see Chapter 11).

Although the average age of marriage in the United States is increasing, from 20 for women and 22 for men in 1960 to about 25 for women and 27 for men today, more than 50 percent of adults in the United States are married, and about 5 percent are cohabitating but unmarried. Approximately 11 percent of unmarried couples today are same-sex couples, almost evenly divided between male and female partner relationships (U.S. Census Bureau, 2000). The vast majority of people become part of a serious, long-term committed relationship at some point during adulthood.

Parenthood.   Becoming a parent is probably the biggest transition that adults can undergo. Having a child involves a fundamental shift in lifestyle because, suddenly, adults are completely responsible for the well-being of someone other than themselves—someone who can't survive on his or her own. Although this experience is incredibly rewarding for most parents, it's also anxiety provoking, particularly because few first-time parents have spent much time caring for newborn babies. Becoming a parent requires a huge change in schedule, a reduction in sleep, and challenges associated with balancing competing demands of work and family. New parents are often unprepared for these changes, imagining that they'll just stick to their routine and bring baby along with them wherever they go—which almost never works the way they envision it. Some new parents may even need to engage in a bit of self-deception about the amount of change required, or they might never go through with it. Nevertheless, research indicates that new parents who have the hardest time adjusting to parenthood are those whose expectations about the amount of change involved are the most unrealistic (Belsky & Kelly, 1994).

Having a baby is a significant and wonderful life event, but becoming a new parent is also a significant source of stress.

Most parents make the adjustment, although each year—and sometimes even each month—can bring new challenges as children develop. Although most adults adjust to parenthood, research suggests that among married couples, marital satisfaction plummets during the first several years of parenthood. Longitudinal studies of couples' marital satisfaction reveals that satisfaction drops for both parents during the year following the birth of a child and remains low throughout the first several years of their child's life (Cowan & Cowan, 1995; Shapiro, Gottman, & Carrere, 2000). Couples matched on initial level of marital satisfaction but who didn't have a child displayed no such decline (Schultz, Cowan, & Cowan, 2006). The good news is that parents' overall level of satisfaction with *life* doesn't decline after the birth of a child. The decline in marital satisfaction seems to be specifically a marriage-related phenomenon, perhaps stemming from parents paying less attention to each other or conflicts over approaches to child rearing. Marital satisfaction typically rebounds once children reach school age.

Midlife Transitions.   Although becoming a parent tends to be the highest-impact life transition in adulthood, major adjustments also take place as adults reach middle age and begin to see the first signs of gray hairs and wrinkles. As adults begin to feel their age, they often confront new challenges, such as having their children leave home or caring for aging parents whose health is declining. The "sandwich generation" refers to adults (typically in their 30s and 40s) who are caring for *both* growing children and aging parents, a particularly difficult situation given the multiple competing demands.

midlife crisis
supposed phase of adulthood characterized by emotional distress about the aging process and an attempt to regain youth

empty-nest syndrome
alleged period of depression in mothers following the departure of their grown children from the home

One popular conception about middle age is that most men, and some women, undergo a **midlife crisis,** marked by emotional distress about the aging process and an attempt to regain their youth. The stereotype is of a man in his 40s or 50s impulsively buying a motorcycle or leaving his wife for a 25-year-old woman. Although psychologists once viewed this period of transition as a normal part of adult development (Gould, 1978), recent work has failed to replicate findings of an increase in emotional distress during middle age (Eisler & Ragsdale, 1992; Rosenberg, Rosenberg, & Farrell, 1999). The midlife crisis seems to be more myth than reality.

The parallel female version of the midlife crisis in popular psychology is the **empty-nest syndrome,** a supposed period of depression in mothers following the "flight" of their children from the house as they reach adulthood. The idea of the empty-nest syndrome, like the midlife crisis, seems to be overstated. In fact, most research suggests that there are cohort effects on the incidence of empty-nest syndrome. Women whose children left the "nest" during or just after World War II seem to have been less affected by the change in role than those whose children moved out of the home in the 1960s and 1970s. This cohort effect appears to relate to the extent to which women were likely to have joined the workforce or were primarily homemakers, because a large percentage of women were employed outside the home during and just after World War II to aid in war efforts, followed by a decline in outside employment during the 1960s and 1970s (Borland, 1982).

Women who define themselves less exclusively in terms of their roles as parents, even those who aren't employed outside the home, are less vulnerable to empty-nest syndrome than those who have more traditional attitudes toward women's roles in society and the family (Harkins, 1978). Some researchers have even speculated that empty-nest syndrome is specific to Caucasian women who don't work outside the home. The social norms, lifestyles, and extended family demands of African American and Mexican American women, and of women of lower socioeconomic status who more commonly work outside the home, seem to buffer them against the feeling of being at loose ends once their children leave the nest (Borland, 1982; Woehrer, 1982). Fortunately, and contrary to popular belief, most empty nesters experience an *increase* in life satisfaction following their newfound flexibility and freedom (Black & Hill, 1984). Nonetheless, the shift in role, not to mention the sudden increase in free time, takes some adjustment (Walsh, 1999).

Who Is Old? Differing Concepts of Age. In the early twenty-first century, people are living longer than ever. The life expectancy of the average American man is 75; for the American woman it's 80. Contrast those numbers with those only a century ago, when the average life span was 48 for men and 51 for women (National Center for Health Statistics, 2005). The elderly are our fastest-growing population, accounting for the increasing "graying" of America. Over the last 100 years, the total population of the United States has more than tripled to over 300 million today. But the number of people over 65 has increased more than seven times as the "baby boomers," the huge population of babies born during the decades after World War II, begin to reach retirement age. The latest census estimates indicate that there are more than 70,000 people in the United States over the age of 100, some born in the nineteenth (!) century. The organization AARP, once known as the American Association of Retired People (they changed their name after discovering that huge numbers of nonretired adults over 50 were joining), is the largest association in the United States, with 35 *million* members! Clearly, aging Americans are a force to be reckoned with.

But how should we define "old age"? Chronological age conveys a variety of expectations. We generally don't expect someone who's 21 to do, know, or be interested in, the same things as someone who's 57. But chronological age doesn't necessarily predict or explain the behavioral or biological changes that accompany aging (Birren & Renner, 1977). An analogy may help: An iron railing on a house porch doesn't rust because it's grown old, but because it's become oxidized over time. How rapidly the railing rusts depends on many factors, so two railings of the same age may contain very different amounts of rust.

Other ways of measuring age may do a better job of describing the impact of changes in later life. Let's consider four indices other than chronological age (Birren & Renner, 1997).

(1) *Biological age:* the estimate of a person's age in terms of biological functioning. How efficiently are the person's organ systems, such as the heart and lungs, functioning? When a 65-year-old brags, "My doctor says I have the body of a 40-year-old," this is what his doctor is talking about.

(2) *Psychological age:* a person's mental attitudes and agility, and the capacity to deal with the stresses of an ever-changing environment. Some people display little change in their memory, ability to learn, and personality from adolescence to old age, whereas others deteriorate substantially.

For women who have worked throughout the years spent raising their children, the "empty-nest" transition tends to be easier than for stay-at-home mothers.

Every day, 95-year-old Mitchell Namy (the great-uncle of one of your book's authors) sends e-mails, web surfs, and trades stocks online. He drives himself to his weekly bridge games. Although his hearing and his knees have declined, his "functional age" is well below his chronological age.

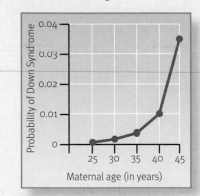

Figure 10.19 Fertility Peaks in the Twenties and Declines Thereafter.
Women reach peak fertility between the ages of 20 and 25. The likelihood of a woman becoming pregnant drops dramatically between 30 to 50. This figure shows how the success of women in becoming pregnant during one year's time declines with age.

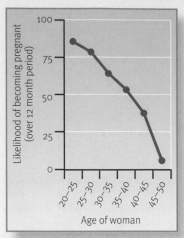

Figure 10.20 Risks of Birth Defects Increase Noticeably in Women Who Become Pregnant in Their 30s and 40s.
The likelihood of a woman bearing a baby with Down syndrome is less than one-tenth of a percent for women at age 25 or 30, but jumps to 1 percent at age 40 and more than 3 percent at age 45.

Thousands of products, programs, and procedures are marketed each year to help reduce the signs of aging. Pills, creams, surgeries, light therapies, exercise programs, and mental exercises all claim to cause dramatic changes in aging adults' appearance, health, or life span. Although staying mentally and physically active can minimize the effects of aging, researchers have found that few of these products slow the aging process. Some may even be harmful.

(3) *Functional age:* a person's ability to function in given roles in society. Functional age may be a more appropriate basis for judging readiness to retire, replacing the arbitrary criterion of chronological age (for example, that people should retire at the age of 65 or 70).

(4) *Social age:* whether people behave in accord with the social behaviors appropriate for their age. When people judge a woman as "dressing too young for her age" or roll their eyes at an 80-year-old man cruising around downtown in a sports car looking for young women, they're invoking expectations about social age.

Physical Decline and Aging. Americans spend millions of dollars each year on products, techniques, and gimmicks marketed to make them look and feel younger as they attempt to stave off the inevitable ravages of aging. However, some of the effects of age on physical appearance and physical functioning are inescapable facts of life.

One of the major milestones of physical aging in women is **menopause**—the termination of menstruation, signaling the end of a woman's reproductive potential. Fertility in women declines sharply during their 30s and 40s (**Figure 10.19**), which has become a challenge for many women in contemporary society who opt to delay childbearing until they achieve career success. As a result, fertility treatments have been on the rise. Unfortunately, the risks of serious birth defects in babies increase substantially among women who become pregnant in their 30s and 40s (**Figure 10.20**).

As women approach 50, their menstrual cycles may become increasingly irregular; ultimately, they stop. Some women find this time difficult because they're faced with evidence of their physical decline, with their youthful, reproductive years behind them. What's more, menopause is often accompanied by unpleasant side effects. Menopause is caused by a reduction in estrogen, which can result in sudden "hot flashes" marked by becoming incredibly hot, sweaty, and dry-mouthed. Many women report mood swings, sleep disruption, and temporary loss of sexual drive or pleasure. Interestingly, the prevalence of these effects varies across cultures. Although about 50 percent of American and Canadian women report hot flashes, less than 15 percent of Japanese women do (Goode, 1999; Lock, 1998). Perhaps because of these changes, a common misconception is that menopause is a period of increased depression. In fact, research suggests that women in menopause are no more prone to depression than other women (Busch, Zonderman, & Costa, 1994; Dennerstein, Lehert, & Guthrie, 2002).

Men experience nothing equivalent to menopause; they can continue to reproduce well into old age. Still, there's a gradual decline in sperm production and testosterone levels with age, and maintaining an erection and achieving ejaculation can become a challenge. Like older women, older men are at heightened risk for having children with developmental disorders. Despite changes in the reproductive equipment of aging adults, most senior citizens—both men and women—experience healthy sex drives (see Chapter 11).

Changes in Agility and Physical Coordination with Age. There are individual and task-specific differences in the effects of aging on motor coordination. Complex tasks show greater effects of age than simpler ones (Luchies et al., 2002; Welford, 1977); simple motor tasks, such as tapping a finger to a beat, show relatively small age-related declines (Ruff & Parker, 1993). This finding suggests that some aspects of decline may be related to either decreasing sensory capacities, such as poor vision or hearing, or to attentional strategies used by older versus younger adults (Botwinick, 1966; Redfern, Muller, Jennings, & Furman, 2002). Elderly adults also become less flexible in their ability to learn new motor skills (Wade, 2000). This change creates a special challenge when vision and other senses decline and individuals must depend more on other senses, such as proprioception (the sense of how parts of the body are oriented in space relative to each other) and vestibular cues (balance information derived from the inner ear) to compensate (Chapter 4).

There are large individual differences in age-related decline. Moreover, strength training and increased physical activity may minimize some of these declines and increase life span (Fiatarone et al., 1990; Frontera, Meredith, O'Reilly, Knuttgen, &

Evans, 1988). Many of the changes we typically associate with aging are actually due to diseases that are correlated with age, like high blood pressure, heart disease, and arthritis. Although chronological age and physical health are correlated, the great variability in how people age refutes the popular notion that old age invariably produces physical decline.

Correlation vs. Causation

Aging and Cognitive Decline. There are minuses and pluses to getting older. On the downside, many aging adults complain they just can't remember things they used to. They're right: Many aspects of cognitive function *do* decline as people get older. In fact, people's ability to recall information begins to decrease sharply after age 30. However, there's considerable variability in how much memory declines, with most people experiencing only modest decreases with age (Shimamura, Berry, Mangels, Rusting, & Jurica, 1995). Basic sensory processing such as vision, hearing, and even smell start to decline when people reach their 60s or 70s (Doty et al., 1984). People's overall speed of processing also declines, which is why teenagers can regularly beat older adults at video games and other speed-sensitive tasks (Cerella, 1985; Salthouse, 2004).

On the upside, some aspects of cognitive function are spared from age-related decline, and others actually improve with age:

(1) Although free recall (being asked to generate items from memory; see Chapter 6) declines with age, cued recall or recognition remain intact (Schonfield & Robertson, 1966).

(2) Aging adults show relatively little decline when asked to remember material that's meaningful or pertinent to their everyday lives as opposed to the random lists of words that some memory researchers prefer (Graf, 1990; Perlmutter, 1983).

(3) A key aspect of cognitive functioning—that which relies heavily on knowledge and experience—stays sharp or even increases with age. Older adults perform better on analogy tests and vocabulary tests than do younger adults (Cattell, 1963). Crystallized intelligence (see Chapter 9), our accumulated knowledge and experience, gives older adults a greater database of information on which to draw when solving problems or interpreting new information (Baltes, Saudinger, & Lindenberger, 1999; Beier & Ackerman, 2001; Horn & Hofer, 1992). Here's a case in which common sense is true: Older *is* wiser!

Research suggests that physical activity and strength training are valuable in minimizing age-related declines.

> ### APPLY YOUR THINKING
> What does the lack of aging effects on recognition memory tell us about which stage of memory (encoding, storage, or retrieval—see Chapter 6) is most adversely affected by aging?

When we consider that older adults have decades of accumulated knowledge and crystallized intelligence outstripping that of younger adults, we can see why many of the world's cultures honor and revere the elderly.

> ### ASSESS YOUR KNOWLEDGE: FACT OR FICTION?
> (1) Androgens cause changes in boys at puberty, whereas estrogens cause changes in girls. (True/False)
> (2) Adolescents may not always make mature decisions about engaging in risky behaviors because their frontal lobes aren't fully mature. (True/False)
> (3) Marriage and becoming a parent both exert an overall positive impact on adults' stress levels. (True/False)
> (4) Elderly people's hearing, sight, and other senses decline, but their reaction times are the same as those of younger adults. (True/False)
> (5) Older adults perform worse on tests that require memory for random lists of words but perform better on tests of analogy and vocabulary. (True/False)
>
> **Answers:** (1) F (p. 431); (2) T (p. 432); (3) F (p. 436); (4) F (p. 438); (5) T (p. 439)

menopause
the termination of menstruation, marking the end of a woman's reproductive potential

Think again...

Special Considerations in Human Development (pp. 399–402)

STUDY the Learning Objectives

▶ Identify ways to think critically about developmental findings
- In evaluating how and why children change, we must resist the temptation to assume that things that happened prior necessarily cause things that happen later, and keep in mind that cause and effect is often a two-way street.

▶ Clarify how nature and nurture can contribute to development
- Genes and environment intersect in complex ways, so we can't always conclude that one or the other is driving behavior. For example, as children develop, how their genes are expressed often depends on their experiences.

DO YOU KNOW THESE TERMS?
- ❏ zygote (p. 398)
- ❏ developmental psychology (p. 399)
- ❏ post hoc fallacy (p. 399)
- ❏ cross-sectional design (p. 400)
- ❏ cohort effects (p. 400)
- ❏ longitudinal design (p. 400)
- ❏ gene-environment interaction (p. 402)
- ❏ nature via nurture (p. 402)
- ❏ gene expression (p. 402)

THINK about

what You would do . . .
As a social worker dealing with young children who have undergone extreme trauma, what would you do to educate others about the realities of childhood fragility and resilience? (p. 401)

How was the classic "Up Series" documentary set up similar to longitudinal designs in psychology? Can you identify two positive and two negative aspects of utilizing longitudinal designs? (p. 400)

Apply what you've learned about the nature–nurture debate by matching each nature-nurture intersection with the appropriate description. (p. 401)

___ Gene Expression   **1.** The impact of genes on behavior depends on the environment in which the behavior develops.

___ Gene-Environment Interactions   **2.** Genetic predispositions can drive us to select and create particular environments, leading to the mistaken appearance of a pure effect of nature.

___ Nature via Nurture   **3.** Some genes "turn on" only in response to specific environmental events.

SUCCEED with

mypsychlab

Cross-Sectional and Longitudinal Research Designs

Should we study you now or later, and does that decision impact what conclusions we draw?

(p. 400)

EXPLORE

ASSESS your knowledge

1. The study of how behavior changes over time is called _____ _____. (p. 399)

2. The _____ _____ fallacy is the assumption that because one event happened before another event, the two events are causally related. (p. 399)

3. In a _____ design, researchers obtain a "snapshot" of people of different ages at a single point in time. (p. 400)

4. _____ can be observed when a sample of participants grew up in the same time period. (p. 400)

5. The best way to examine developmental effects is to use a _____ design, in which subjects can be tracked over time. (p. 400)

6. Research shows that most children (are/aren't)

remarkably resilient and capable of withstanding stress. (p. 401)

7. Both _____, our genetic endowment, and _____, the environments we encounter, play powerful roles in shaping our development. (p. 401)

8. Caspi and colleagues' longitudinal study of children with low levels of MAO illustrates the phenomenon of _____ _____, in which the effect of genes depends on environment, and vice versa. (p. 402)

9. When a highly fearful child selects environments that protect him from his anxieties, it illustrates _____ _____ _____. (p. 402)

10. Genes turning off or on when they are triggered by environmental experiences is called _____ _____. (p. 402)

The Developing Body before & after Birth: Physical & Motor Development (pp. 403–407)

STUDY the Learning Objectives

▶ Track the trajectory of prenatal development and identify barriers to normal development
- Many important aspects of fetal development occur early in pregnancy. The brain begins to develop 18 days after conception and continues to mature into adolescence. Teratogens such as drugs, alcohol, and

If you did not receive an access code to MyPsychLab with this text and wish to purchase access online, please visit www.mypsychlab.com.

How do child-rearing practices in other cultures (such as swaddling in Peru), compared with those in the U.S., effect children's short- and long-term motor development? (p. 407)

Plot the progression of development in the figure by listing the age and major motor milestone depicted by each child. (p. 406)

a)_____
b)_____
c)_____
d)_____
e)_____
f)_____

THINK about

what You would do . . .
Given your knowledge of weight influences in childhood, what would you do if a college friend who works in a child-care center commented that children naturally carry "baby fat" well into their teens and can therefore eat pretty much anything without lasting effects on their adult weight? (p. 407)

mypsychlab
where learning comes to life!

SUCCEED with

Dendritic Spreading: Forming Interconnections in the Brain
What a difference a few months can make (to your brain). (p. 404)

EXPLORE

even maternal stress can damage or slow fetal development. Although premature infants often experience developmental delays, low-birth-weight babies tend to have less positive outcomes than "preemies".

▶ **Describe how infants learn to coordinate motion and achieve major motor milestones**
 • Children tend to achieve motor milestones such as crawling and walking in roughly the same order, although the ages when they accomplish these milestones vary. Infants are born with reflexes that help them get started, but experience plays a critical role in building up children's muscles and motor coordination.

ASSESS your knowledge

1. Early in pregnancy, a ball of identical cells that hasn't yet taken on any specific function is called the _____. (p. 403)

2. The embryonic stage of prenatal development occurs from the _____ to the _____ week of pregnancy. (p. 403)

3. The embryo becomes a _____ once the major organs are established and the heart has begun to beat. (p. 403)

4. The _____ begins to develop 18 days after fertilization and unlike most other organs keeps developing through adolescence and sometimes into early adulthood. (p. 404)

5. Environmental factors that can have a negative effect on prenatal development are called _____. (p. 404)

6. The _____ point at which infants can typically survive on their own is 25 weeks, but a full-term baby is born at _____ weeks. (p. 405)

7. Full-term babies who have a ____ _____ _____ face a higher risk of death, infection, and developmental disorders than premature babies. (p. 405)

8. The concept of growth spurts (has/hasn't) been scientifically demonstrated. (p. 405)

9. Infants are born with certain _____ that are triggered by specific types of stimulation and help them know how to survive in the world. (p. 406)

10. Children rely on _____ _____ as they learn how to coordinate their movements in order to reach or crawl. (p. 406)

DO YOU KNOW THESE TERMS?
☐ **prenatal** (p. 403)
☐ **blastocyst** (p. 403)
☐ **embryo** (p. 403)
☐ **fetus** (p. 403)
☐ **teratogens** (p. 404)
☐ **reflexes** (p. 406)
☐ **motor behaviors** (p. 406)

Cognitive Development: Children's Learning about the World (pp. 407–417)

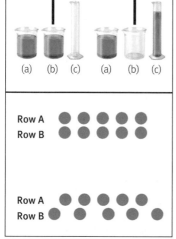

In order for a child to succeed at the conservation tasks shown, how would he need to respond to (a) which container has more liquid in it (top) and (b) which row of numbers contains more circles (bottom)? (p. 410)

THINK about

what You would do . . .
Using Vygotsky's theory of scaffolding, what would you do to create an effective program to teach a young child to brush her teeth by herself? (p. 411)

mypsychlab
where learning comes to life!

SUCCEED with

Piaget's Stages of Cognitive Development
A Swiss man changes the way we view children.
(p. 409)

EXPLORE

STUDY the Learning Objectives

▶ **Understand major theories of the mechanisms by which children learn**
 • Piaget believed that development happens in four stages that influence all aspects of cognitive development. Vygotsky believed that different children develop skills in different domains at different rates, and that social structuring on the part of the parent drives children's learning and development. Researchers continue to debate whether learning happens in more general or domain-specific ways, whether learning is gradual or stage-like, and how much innate cognitive knowledge children possess.

▶ **Explain the processes by which children acquire knowledge in important cognitive domains**
 • Physical reasoning in infants involves both basic, apparently innate knowledge, and refinement of knowledge based on experience. Conceptual development requires children to acquire knowledge of how things look, how they are used, and in what contexts they appear. Self-recognition becomes increasingly sophisticated as children move from understanding they are physically distinct entities to understanding that others have minds distinct from their own. Numerical development requires a complex understanding of counting rules and the nature of precise quantities. This ability develops slowly and is easily disrupted. The ability to count doesn't appear in all cultures.

Using the descriptions provided, complete the table to show Piaget's four stages of cognitive development. (pp. 409–410)

Stage	Typical Ages	Description
_____	_____	No thought beyond immediate physical experiences
_____	_____	Able to think beyond the here and now, but egocentric and unable to perform mental transformations
_____	_____	Able to perform mental transformations but only on concrete physical objects
_____	_____	Able to perform hypothetical and abstract reasoning

DO YOU KNOW THESE TERMS?

- ❑ **cognitive development** (p. 407)
- ❑ **constructivist theory** (p. 408)
- ❑ **assimilation** (p. 409)
- ❑ **accommodation** (p. 409)
- ❑ **sensorimotor stage** (p. 409)
- ❑ **object permanence** (p. 409)
- ❑ **preoperational stage** (p. 409)
- ❑ **egocentrism** (p. 409)
- ❑ **conservation** (p. 410)
- ❑ **concrete operations stage** (p. 410)
- ❑ **formal operations stage** (p. 410)
- ❑ **scaffolding** (p. 411)
- ❑ **zone of proximal development** (p. 411)
- ❑ **theory of mind** (p. 415)

ASSESS your knowledge

1. Piaget's _____ theory maintained that children construct an understanding of the world based on observations of the results of their actions. (p. 408)

2. According to Piaget, when children can no longer use _____ to absorb a new experience into their current knowledge structures, they will engage in _____ by altering an existing belief to make it more compatible with the new experience. (p. 409)

3. In the first of Piaget's four stages of development, the _____ stage (birth to 2 years), children focus on the here and now, and lack an understanding of object _____. (p. 409)

4. Children in Piaget's second stage, called the _____ stage, can't perform _____ tasks. (pp. 409–410)

5. Modern research suggests that cognitive development is (less/more) continuous and (less/more)

6. general than Piaget theorized. (p. 410)

6. Whereas Piaget emphasized children's exploration of the physical world, Vygotsky believed that children's interaction with the _____ world was their primary source of learning. (p. 411)

7. Vygotsky identified the zone of _____ _____ as the phase when a child is receptive to learning a new skill and can make use of _____, the structure provided by parents to aid the child's learning. (p. 411)

8. Infants (do/don't) have a basic understanding of the physics of an object's behavior. (p. 413)

9. A classic test of _____ _____ _____ is the false-belief task which examines children's ability to reason about what other people know or believe. (p. 415)

10. If a child has trouble understanding that two cars are the same number as two apples, that child is struggling with the principle of _____. (p. 416)

Social and Moral Development: Children's Relations with Others (pp. 418–430)

STUDY the Learning Objectives

▶ **Describe how and when children establish emotional bonds with their caregivers**

- Although infants may recognize and react positively to their caregivers, they don't develop a specific attachment until around 8 months of age. The type of attachment that infants form with their caregivers varies depending on both parental style and the infant's temperament.

▶ **Explain the environmental and genetic influences on social behavior and social style in children**

- Parenting style (permissive, authoritative, authoritarian, or uninvolved), family structure, and peers may all influence children's behaviors and emotional adjustment, although their precise causal role is controversial. Aspects of children, such as temperament and self-control, also affect their long term social development.

▶ **Determine how children's understanding of morality and important social concepts like gender develop**

- Children's initial concepts of morality are based largely on fear of punishment, but over time become more sophisticated and based on intentions rather than consequences. Children's understanding of gender develops gradually over the first several years, but gender differences in behavior emerge early on and can't be accounted for entirely by gender socialization. Differences in how parents and teachers interact with boys and girls also play important roles in children's gender-typed behavior.

DO YOU KNOW THESE TERMS?

- ❑ **stranger anxiety** (p. 418)
- ❑ **attachment** (p. 418)
- ❑ **imprinting** (p. 418)
- ❑ **contact comfort** (p. 420)
- ❑ **mono-operation bias** (p. 421)
- ❑ **temperament** (p. 421)

mypsych lab where learning comes to life!

SUCCEED with

Attachment Classifications in the Strange Situation

Why is this baby crying? (p. 420)

THINK about

what You would do . . .
Looking back at your own upbringing, how would you describe the parenting style used by your mother/father /caregiver? What would you do differently, if anything, when raising your own children? (p. 423)

Define Harlow's notion of contact comfort and describe the role each "mother" played in helping meet the monkey's needs. (p. 420)

ASSESS your knowledge

1. Usually starting at 8 or 9 months, babies can develop _____ _____, which may be an adaptive mechanism for keeping infants away from danger. (p. 418)

2. The strong emotional connection we share with those to whom we feel closest is called _____. (p. 418)

3. Lorenz showed that newborn goslings bonded to the first moving thing they see, a phenomenon called _____. (p. 418)

4. Harlow's experiment with rhesus monkeys demonstrated the phenomenon of _____ _____. (p. 420)

5. Ainsworth's _____ _____ provided a systematic way to classify infants' attachment styles into four categories. (p. 420)

6. A person's basic emotional style that appears early in development and is largely genetic is called _____. (p. 421)

7. Most attachment theorists accept the central assumption that infants' attachment styles (are/aren't) attributable largely to their parents' responsiveness to them. (p. 422)

8. Research suggests that specific parenting styles may not matter so much as whether the parent can provide the _____ _____ environment. (pp. 423–424)

9. Kohlberg studied the development of _____ by scoring the _____ people used as they wrestled with a moral dilemma. (p. 427)

10. An individual's sense of being male or female is called gender _____, and the behaviors that tend to accompany being male or female is called gender _____. (p. 429)

Complete the table by describing the four attachment styles identified in Ainsworth's Strange Situation research. (p. 420)

Attachment Style	Description/Child's reaction
1. Secure attachment	_____
2. Insecure-avoidant attachment	_____
3. Insecure-anxious attachment	_____
4. Disorganized attachment	_____

- average expectable environment (p. 423)
- group socialization theory (p. 424)
- self-control (p. 426)
- gender identity (p. 429)
- gender roles (p. 429)

Development Doesn't Stop: Changes in Adolescence & Adulthood (pp. 430–439)

As the profiles of the traditional college student continue to evolve, so do changes in our beliefs about careers and job changes. According to the Bureau of Labor Statistics, how many job changes can the average American expect to make between the ages of 18 and 40? (p. 435)

mypsychlab
where learning comes to life!

SUCCEED with

Major Changes in Important Domains of Adult Functioning

Look into the crystal ball of aging.
(p. 438)

EXPLORE

THINK about

what **You** would do . . .
During college, how would you best prepare yourself for the often ambiguous information you will be learning in your classes? (p. 435)

Describe how different cultures approach aging, and identify some of the myths surrounding physical and cognitive declines in later years. (p. 439)

STUDY the Learning Objectives

▶ Determine the physical, emotional, and cognitive changes that take place during the transition from childhood to adulthood
  - Adolescence is marked by sexual maturation and significant physical changes. Adolescents are also confronted with more adult-like opportunities and decisions that their brain's immature frontal lobes are not always prepared to handle.

▶ Identify developmental changes during major life transitions in adults
  - Major life transitions including career changes, finding a romantic partner, and having children can be stressful for adults. However, midlife crises are infrequent.

▶ Summarize the nature of age-related decline in physical, social, and cognitive domains
  - Chronological age isn't a perfect predictor of physical, social, or cognitive ability in the elderly. Some aspects of cognitive and physical functions begin to decline as early as age 30. However, other cognitive abilities increase with age; how much we slow down depends on a variety of factors, including our activity levels.

DO YOU KNOW THESE TERMS?
- adolescence (p. 430)
- primary sex characteristics (p. 431)
- secondary sex characteristics (p. 432)
- menarche (p. 432)
- spermarche (p. 432)
- identity (p. 433)
- psychosocial crisis (p. 433)
- midlife crisis (p. 436)
- empty-nest syndrome (p. 436)
- menopause (p. 438)

ASSESS your knowledge

1. The transition between childhood and adulthood commonly associated with the teenage years is called _____. (p. 430)

2. Sexual maturation includes changes in _____ ___ _____, such as the reproductive organs and genitals, and _____ ___ _____, such as breast enlargement in girls and deepening voices in boys. (pp. 431–432)

3. One of the challenges during adolescence is to get a handle on our _____, our sense of who we are and how we fit in the world. (p. 433)

4. Erikson coined the term _____ to describe the confusion that most adolescents experience regarding their sense of self. (p. 433)

5. According to Erikson's theory of human development, we travel through _____ stages and we face a different _____ crisis at each stage. (pp. 433–434)

6. One of the biggest transitions an adult can go through is becoming a _____. (p. 436)

7. A 65-year-old person who is in excellent heath and top physical condition may have a _____ _____ of 45 years old. (p. 437)

8. A major physical milestone of aging in women is _____. (p. 438)

9. Some aspects of physical decline may be related to decreasing _____ capacities. (p. 438)

10. (All/Not all) aspects of cognitive function decline as we age. (p. 439)

Remember these questions from the beginning of the chapter? Think again and ask yourself if you would answer them differently based on what you now know about human development. (For more detailed explanations, see MyPsychLab.com.)

▶ Do emotionally traumatic experiences in infancy typically scar children for life? (p. 401)
▶ Are anxious or belligerent children just born that way? (p. 402)
▶ What's the earliest age at which premature babies can survive? (p. 405)
▶ Do infants have survival instincts? (p. 406)
▶ Do American parenting and schooling techniques give children a developmental advantage relative to approaches in other countries? (p. 410)

▶ What parenting styles help or hinder children's development? (pp. 422–423)
▶ Does divorce always produce negative effects on children? (p. 425)
▶ Are there gender differences in moral reasoning? (p. 429)
▶ Can adolescents make mature decisions? (p. 432)
▶ How does becoming a parent affect people's quality of life? (p. 436)
▶ Is the aging process all downhill? (p. 439)

THINKING Scientifically

Correlation vs. Causation pp. 398, 422, 423, 424, 425, 426, 429, 434, 436, 439

Falsifiability pp. 410, 412, 428

Occam's Razor pp. 411, 412

Replicability pp. 405, 410, 412, 419, 433, 436

Ruling Out Rival Hypotheses pp. 400, 402, 404, 413, 414, 415, 419, 421, 425, 428, 432

LA VIE EN ROSE

11
Emotion and Motivation
What Moves Us

We're often fascinated by fictional characters who lack emotion, such as Mr. Spock from *Star Trek*. Although television and films portray such characters as exceedingly rational, psychological research suggests otherwise.

Pop psychology books often tell us that many emotions, especially in the extreme, are "toxic." Are they right?

Meet Elliott. He's a Caucasian male, 30 years of age. At first blush, Elliott looks and acts pretty much like everyone else. He's well dressed and socially appropriate, and his scores on tests of intelligence, memory, and language are boringly normal. On standard measures of personality, he's entirely unremarkable. Yet Elliott is different—very different—from the average person in two ways.

First, Elliott has recently recovered from brain surgery. Diagnosed with a frontal lobe tumor that had ballooned to the size of a small orange, Elliott underwent a radical operation to remove not only the tumor but also a sizable chunk of surrounding brain tissue. In many respects, Elliott is a contemporary version of Vermont railroad worker Phineas Gage, who, as we'll recall from Chapter 3, lost much of his frontal cortex in a catastrophic accident in 1848 (Damasio, 1994; Eslinger & Damasio, 1985).

Second, like Gage, Elliott is strikingly different from how he was before he lost a goodly portion of his brain. Before the operation, Elliott was a successful businessman with a happy and balanced home life. Yet Elliott is now different in one crucial way: he seems entirely devoid of emotion. As Antonio Damasio (1994), who studied Elliott in depth, remarked: "I never saw a tinge of emotion in my many hours of conversation with him: no sadness, no impatience, no frustration. . . ." (p. 45). When Damasio's colleague Daniel Tranel showed Elliott a series of upsetting photographs, including pictures of gruesome injuries, buildings crumbling during earthquakes, and houses in flames, Elliott displayed virtually no emotional response, as measured by either his subjective report or his physiological reactions. Nor does Elliott express much joy when describing the wonderful moments of his life. As Damasio (1994) put it:

> Try to imagine not feeling pleasure when you contemplate a painting you love or hear a favorite piece of music. Try to imagine yourself forever robbed of that possibility and yet aware of the intellectual contents of the visual or musical stimulus, and also aware that it once did give you pleasure. We might summarize Elliott's predicament as *to know but not to feel*. (p. 45)

What's more, Elliott's life, like that of Phineas Gage, is in utter shambles. Elliott has made foolish decisions in his personal life, investing all of his savings in a risky business venture and going bankrupt. He married a woman who was a poor match for him, resulting in an abrupt divorce. His on-the-job performance is no better.

The tragic case of Elliott imparts a valuable lesson: Emotion and reason aren't necessarily opposites. To the contrary, emotion is often the servant of reason (Levine, 1998). Without feelings, we have scant basis for rational decisions. Recent research suggests that college students made a bit angry (by having been asked to write about past infuriating experiences) are actually better than non-angry students at distinguishing strong from weak scientific arguments in research studies (Moons & Mackie, 2007). Elliott married the wrong woman in part because he'd lost access to his "gut feelings" concerning his attraction to members of the opposite sex. He based his choice of a romantic partner largely on reason alone, which is typically a recipe for disaster (Gigerenzer, 2007). Even though Mr. Spock of *Star Trek* fame is the epitome of pure reason, research suggests that a real-life version of Mr. Spock would actually be far more irrational than rational. His absence of emotional reactions would ultimately do him in as he attempted to generate solutions to everyday problems.

Popular wisdom teaches us that many emotions, especially negative ones, are bad for us. A litany of pop psychology books encourages us not to feel angry, guilty, ashamed, or sad. Such emotions, the books inform us, are unhealthy, even "toxic." Pop psychologists are right to remind us that excessive anger, guilt, and the like can be self-destructive. "Everything in moderation," as our grandmother reminded us. But they're wrong to suggest we'd be better off without these feelings. As we'll discover, at least small doses of negative emotions are essential in certain situations.

Theories of Emotion: What Causes Our Feelings?

Elliott and Mr. Spock aside, virtually all of us experience emotions. Yet psychologists don't agree fully on what causes our emotions, or even on what distinguishes our emotions from our thoughts. As we'll soon discover, however, they've made significant strides toward unraveling these enduring mysteries.

DISCRETE EMOTIONS THEORY: EMOTIONS AS EVOLVED EXPRESSIONS

According to **discrete emotions theory,** humans experience a small number of distinct emotions, even if they combine in complex ways (Ekman & Friesen, 1971; Griffiths, 1997; Izard, 1971, 1994; Tomkins, 1962). Advocates of this theory further propose that emotions have distinct biological roots and serve evolutionary functions. Each emotion, they suggest, is associated with a distinct "motor program": a set of genetically influenced physiological responses that are essentially the same in all people.

Adaptive Value of Emotions. Consider the emotion of *disgust*, which derives from the Latin term for "bad taste." Imagine we asked you to swallow a piece of food that you find repulsive, like a dried-up cockroach (apologies to those of you reading this chapter over lunch or dinner). As you picture putting this less than delicious "delicacy" in your mouth, attend carefully to how you react. The odds are high you wrinkled your nose, contracted your mouth, stuck out your tongue, turned your head slightly to one side, and closed your eyes, at least partly (Phillips et al., 1997).

Why did you do these things? Discrete emotions theorists would say that disgust, like other emotions, is a coordinated set of reactions that are evolutionarily adaptive. In the case of disgust, natural selection has made it less likely that a toxic substance will find its way into your body. When you wrinkle your nose and contract your mouth, you're reducing the chances you'll ingest this substance; by sticking out your tongue, you're increasing the chances you'll expel it; by turning your head, you're doing your best to avoid it; and by closing your eyes, you're limiting the damage that it can do to your visual system.

Other emotions similarly prepare us for biologically important actions (Frijda, 1986). For example, our eyes open wide when we're afraid, allowing us to better spot potential dangers, like predators, lurking in our environment. When we're angry, our teeth and fists often become clenched, readying us to bite and fight.

Emotions in Humans and Animals. Charles Darwin (1872) was among the first to point out that the emotional expressions of humans and nonhuman animals are often similar. For example, he observed that the smile of chimpanzees bears an uncanny resemblance to a human smile. He also noted that the angry snarl of dogs, marked by the baring of their fangs, is reminiscent of the dismissive sneer of humans. Our emotional systems and those of animals, he concluded, share the same evolutionary heritage.

Since Darwin, scores of investigators have noted other fascinating similarities between humans and other animals. One of our favorites is the work of Jaak Panksepp (2005), who discovered that rats emit a high-pitched chirp, perhaps similar to human laughter, when tickled. Because this chirp is beyond the range of human hearing, scientists discovered it only recently. The high-pitched panting of dogs during play also seems similar in many ways to human laughter.

Of course, Darwin and Panksepp might have been wrong. The mere fact that two things are superficially similar doesn't prove that they share evolutionary origins. Birds and bats both have wings, but their wings evolved independently of each other. In the case

People have recognized the facial reaction of disgust for centuries. This is a photograph from Charles Darwin's book on the expression of emotions, published in 1872.

David Matsumoto and Bob Willingham, themselves former national judo competitors, examined the facial expressions of judo competition winners and losers at the 2004 Athens Olympics. They found that competitors in thirty-five countries across six continents displayed extremely similar smiles and other facial reactions after winning a match or receiving a medal (Matsumoto & Willingham, 2006).

discrete emotions theory
theory that humans experience a small number of distinct emotions

of emotions, however, we know that all mammals share an evolutionary ancestor. For example, rats and humans appear to have split off from the same ancestor, a small shrew-like creature, about 75 million years ago. The fact that many mammals display similar emotional reactions during similar social behaviors, such as tickling and play, lends itself to a parsimonious hypothesis: Perhaps these reactions stem from the same evolutionary roots.

Development of Emotions. Some emotional expressions emerge in the first few months of life, presumably before parents have had much of an opportunity to shape them through socialization (Ekman & Oster, 1979). Newborn infants smile spontaneously during REM sleep, the sleep stage during which most vivid dreaming occurs (see Chapter 5). At about 6 weeks, babies start to smile whenever they see a favorite face, and at about 3 months, they may smile when they're learning to do something new, even when no one's around (Plutchik, 2003). Irenäus Eibl-Eibesfeldt (1973) showed that even 3-month-old babies who are blind from birth smile in response to playing and tickling. They also frown and cry when left alone. The fact that some emotional expressions emerge even without direct reinforcement suggests that they're by-products of innate motor programs (Freedman, 1964; Panksepp, 2007).

Culture and Emotion: Recognition of Emotions in Different Societies. One telling piece of evidence for discrete emotions theory derives from research showing that people recognize and generate the same emotional expressions across cultures (Izard, 1971). Nevertheless, this research is vulnerable to a rival explanation: Because these people have all been exposed to Western culture, the similarities may be due to shared experiences rather than a shared evolutionary heritage.

Ruling Out Rival Hypotheses

To rule out this explanation, in the late 1960s American psychologist Paul Ekman traveled to the wilds of southeastern New Guinea to study a group of people who'd been essentially isolated from Western culture and still used Stone Age tools. With the aid of a translator, Ekman read them a brief story (for example, "His mother has died, and he feels very sad"), along with a display of photographs of Americans depicting various emotions, like happiness, sadness, and anger. Then, Ekman asked them to select the photograph that matched the story. He later went further, asking U.S. college students to guess which emotions the New Guineans were displaying (Ekman & Friesen, 1971).

Ekman (1994, 1999) and his colleagues (Ekman & Friesen, 1986) concluded that a small number of **primary emotions**—perhaps seven—are cross-culturally universal. Specifically, they found that the facial expressions associated with these emotions are recognized across most, if not all, cultures. Discrete emotions theorists call these emotions "primary" because they're presumably the biologically based emotions from which other emotions arise:

- Happiness
- Sadness
- Surprise
- Anger
- Disgust
- Fear
- Contempt

Recent research suggests that pride may also be a cross-culturally universal emotion, although the evidence for this claim is preliminary (Tracy & Robins, 2007).

Six of the seven primary emotions identified by Paul Ekman and his colleagues. Can you match each face to the corresponding emotions of anger, disgust, fear, happiness, sadness, and surprise?

primary emotions
small number (perhaps seven) of emotions believed by some theorists to be cross-culturally universal

Ekman and his colleagues found that certain primary emotions are easier to detect than others. Happiness tends to be the most easily recognized emotion (Elfenbein & Ambady, 2002); their New Guinea subjects correctly recognized happiness in Americans more than 90 percent of the time (Ekman, 1994). In contrast, negative emotions tend to be more difficult to recognize; many subjects confuse disgust with anger, anger with fear, and fear with surprise (Elfenbein & Ambady, 2002; Tomkins & McCarter, 1964). Although people across widely different cultures don't always agree on which facial expressions go with which emotions (Russell, 1994), they agree often enough to provide some support for discrete emotions theory.

Occam's Razor

Secondary Emotions. Primary emotions don't tell the whole story of our feelings. Just as talented painters create a magnificently complex palette of secondary paint colors, like various shades of green and purple, from a few primary paint colors, like blue and yellow (see Chapter 4), our brains "create" an enormous array of *secondary emotions* from a small number of primary emotions. For example, the secondary emotion of "alarm" seems to be a mixture of fear and surprise, whereas the secondary emotion of "hatred" seems to be a mixture of anger and disgust (Plutchik, 2000).

Moreover, some of these complex emotion blends possess names in other languages, but have no equivalent in English. Take *schadenfreude*, a German term that refers to the glee we experience at witnessing the misfortune of others, especially those we see as arrogant (Ortony, Clore, & Collins, 1988). It seems to be a hybrid of several emotions, like happiness, anger, and pride. We experience *schadenfreude* when we feel secretly happy when a classmate who brags about getting A+s on his exams unexpectedly gets an F.

Accompaniments of Emotional Expressions. According to discrete emotions theorists, each primary emotion is associated with a distinctive constellation of facial expressions. For example, in anger our lips consistently narrow and our eyebrows move downward. In contempt, we frequently lift and tighten our lips on one side of our face, generating a smirk (Matsumoto & Ekman, 2004), or roll our eyes upward, in effect communicating "I'm above (superior to) you." Interestingly, John Gottman and his colleagues have found that contempt, and the facial expressions that go along with it, are among the best predictors of divorce in married couples (Gladwell, 2005; Gottman & Levenson, 1999).

Emotions and Physiology. We can also differentiate at least some primary emotions by their patterns of physiological responding (Ax, 1953; Rainville, Bechara, Naqvi, & Damasio, 2006). The mere act of making a face associated with a specific emotion alters our bodily reactions in characteristic ways (Ekman, Levenson, & Friesen, 1983). Our heart rates tend to increase more when we make angry and fearful facial expressions than when we make happy or surprised facial expressions (Cacioppo et al., 1997), probably because the first two emotions are more closely linked to the emergency reactions we experience when threatened (see Chapters 3 and 12). The heart kicks into high gear when we're in danger, mobilizing us for action (Frijda, 1986). Yet even fear and anger differ physiologically. When we're afraid, our digestive systems tend to slow down. In contrast, when we're angry, our digestive systems tend to speed up, which explains why our "stomachs churn" when we're furious (Carlson & Hatfield, 1992).

Brain imaging data also provide at least some evidence for discrete emotions. Fear, disgust, and anger tend to show different patterns of brain activation (Murphy, Nimmo-Smith, & Lawrence, 2003). Fear seems to be relatively specific to the amygdala (see Chapter 3), disgust to the *insula*, a region within the limbic system, and anger to a region of the frontal cortex behind our eyes (see **Figure 11.1**).

Yet in many other cases we can't distinguish different emotions by means of their physiology (Cacioppo, Tassinary, & Bernstson, 2000; Feldman Barrett, 2006; Feldman Barrett et al., 2007). Surprisingly, happiness and sadness aren't terribly different in their patterns of brain activation (Murphy et al., 2003). Moreover, there's almost certainly no single "fear processor," "disgust processor," and so on, in the brain, because multiple brain regions participate in all emotions (Schienle et al., 2002).

Real versus Fake Emotions. We can use certain facial expressions to help us distinguish real from fake emotions. In genuine happiness, we see an upward turning of the corners of the mouth, along with a drooping of the eyelids and a crinkling of the corners of the eyes (Ekman, Davidson, & Friesen, 1990). Emotion theorists distinguish this genuine emotional expression, called the *Duchenne smile* after the neurologist who discovered it, from the fake or *Pan Am smile*, which is marked by a movement of the mouth but not the eyes. The term *Pan Am smile* derives from an old television commercial featuring the now defunct airline Pan Am, in which all of the flight attendants flashed obviously fake smiles. If you page through your family albums, you'll probably find an abundance of Pan Am smiles, especially

The facial reaction of contempt is frequently marked by an asymmetrical turning upward of the lips (from Matsumoto & Ekman, 1985).

Pair 1

Pair 2

Figure 11.1 Which Mask Conveys a Threat? In hunter–gatherer societies, people often construct masks to convey threat, especially anger. These two pairs of shapes are based on wooden masks worn in these societies. In both cases, the shape on the left communicates more threat. Even American college students can distinguish the threatening from nonthreatening mask at higher than chance levels. (*Source:* Aronoff, Barclay, & Stevenson, 1988)

The Duchenne (genuine) smile is marked by a turning upward of the corners of the mouth and changes in the eyelids and corners of the eye.

Dog barks conform to motivation-structural rules. Dogs tend to let out high-pitched barks when they're giving chase, begging for food, or preparing to go for a walk. In contrast, they let out low-pitched barks when they're angry or confronting a stranger (Pongracz, Molnar, Miklosi, & Csanyi, 2005).

in posed photographs. Interestingly, among subjects asked to produce facial expressions, only Duchenne smiles are associated with increased activity of the front region of the left hemisphere, which appears specialized for positive emotions (Ekman et al., 1990).

Motivation-Structural Rules. Indirect evidence for discrete emotions theory comes from research on animal communication. According to Eugene Morton's (1977, 1982) **motivation-structural rules,** there are deep-seated similarities in communication across most animal species, especially mammals and birds. These rules suggest that certain crucial aspects of emotional expression are products of natural selection, as discrete emotions theorists claim. For example, across the animal kingdom high-pitched sounds are associated with friendly interactions, and low-pitched sounds with hostile interactions.

APPLY YOUR THINKING
Across the animal kingdom, why might high-pitched sounds be associated with friendly interactions and low-pitched sounds with hostile interactions? (*Hint*: Think of what the pitch of an animal's sounds implies about its size.)

Cultural Differences in Emotional Expression: Display Rules. The finding that certain emotions exist across most or all cultures doesn't mean that cultures are identical in their emotional expressions. In part, that's because cultures differ in **display rules,** their societal guidelines for how and when to express emotions (Ekman & Friesen, 1975; Matsumoto, Yoo, Hirayama, & Petrova, 2005). In Western culture, parents teach most boys not to cry, whereas they typically teach girls that crying is acceptable (Plutchik, 2003). Americans can be taken aback when a visitor from South America, the Middle East, or some European countries, like Russia, greets them by planting a gooey kiss on their cheek.

In a study of display rules, Wallace Friesen (1972) used *covert observation* (see Chapter 2) to videotape Japanese and American college students without their knowledge. He asked both groups of students to watch two film clips, one of a neutral travel scene (the control condition) and one of an incredibly gory film depicting a ritual genital mutilation (the experimental condition). When these students were alone, their facial reactions to the films were similar: both groups showed little emotional reaction to the neutral film but clear signs of fear, disgust, and distress to the gory film. Yet when an older experimenter entered the room, the role of culture became apparent. Although American students' reactions to the films didn't change, Japanese students typically smiled during the gory film, concealing their negative emotional reactions. In Japanese culture, deference to authority figures is the norm, so the students acted as though they were happy to see the films. So, in many cases, culture doesn't influence emotion itself; it influences its overt expression.

In April 2007, American actor Richard Gere scandalized much of India by kissing Indian actress Shilpa Shetty's cheek on stage at an AIDS awareness rally. This action even resulted in a warrant being placed for Gere's arrest in India; it was later dropped. Gere was apparently unaware of display rules in India that strictly forbid kissing in public.

motivation-structural rules
deep-seated similarities in communication across most animal species

display rules
cross-cultural guidelines for how and when to express emotions

cognitive theories of emotion
theory proposing that emotions are products of thinking

COGNITIVE THEORIES OF EMOTION: THINK FIRST, FEEL LATER

As we've seen, discrete emotions theorists emphasize the biological underpinnings of emotion. For them, emotions are largely innate motor programs triggered by certain stimuli. Advocates of **cognitive theories of emotion** disagree. For them, emotions are products of thinking. What we feel in response to a situation is determined by how we interpret it (Scherer, 1988). As we'll learn in Chapter 12, the way we appraise situations influences whether we find them stressful (Lazarus & Folkman, 1984). If we see an upcoming job interview as a potential catastrophe, we'll be hopelessly stressed out; if we see it as a healthy challenge, we'll be appropriately geared up for it. Moreover, for cognitive theorists, there are no discrete emotions, because the boundaries across emotions are fuzzy (Feldman Barrett & Russell, 1999; Ortony & Turner, 1990). They believe that there are as many different kinds of emotions as there are kinds of thoughts.

James-Lange Theory of Emotion. Perhaps the oldest cognitive theory of emotion, and still one of the most influential, owes its origins to American psychologist William James (1890), whom we met in the Prologue. Because Danish researcher Carl Lange (1885) advanced a similar version of this theory around the same time, psychologists refer to it as the **James-Lange theory of emotion**. According to the James-Lange theory, emotions result from our interpretations of our bodily reactions to stimuli.

To take James's famous example, let's imagine that while hiking through the forest, we come upon a bear. What happens next? Common wisdom tells us that we first become scared and then run away. Yet as James recognized, the link between our fear and running away is only a correlation; this link doesn't demonstrate that our fear *causes* us to run away. Indeed, James and Lange argued that the causal arrow is reversed: *we're afraid because we run away.* That is, we observe our physiological and behavioral reactions to a stimulus, in this case our hearts pounding, our palms sweating, and our feet running, and then conclude that we must have been scared (see **Figure 11.2**).

In support of this theory, a researcher examined five groups of patients with injuries in different regions of their spinal cord (Hohmann, 1966). Patients with injuries high in their spinal cord had lost almost all of their bodily sensation, and those with lower injuries had lost only part of their bodily sensation. Just as James and Lange would have predicted, patients with higher spinal cord damage reported less emotion—fear and anger—than those with lower spinal cord damage. Presumably, patients with lower injuries could feel more of their bodies, which allowed them a greater range of emotional reactions. Still, some researchers have criticized these findings because of a possible experimenter expectancy effect (Chapter 2): the researcher knew which spinal cord patients were which when he assessed their emotions, and this knowledge could have biased the results (Prinz, 2004). Moreover, some investigators haven't replicated these findings: one research team found no differences in the happiness of patients with or without spinal cord injuries (Chwalisz, Diener, & Gallagher, 1988).

Somatic Marker Theory. Few scientists today are strict believers in the James-Lange theory, but it continues to influence modern-day thinking about emotion. Antonio Damasio's (1994) **somatic marker theory** (*somatic* means "physical") proposes that we use our "gut reactions"—especially our autonomic responses, like our heart rate and sweating (see Chapter 3)—to gauge how we should act. Damasio contends that this process occurs almost instantaneously, so we're typically unaware of it. According to Damasio, if we feel our hearts pounding during a first date, we use that information as a "marker" or signal to help us decide what to do next, like ask that person out for a second date. Elliott, whom we met in this chapter's opening, may have made irrational decisions because he lost much of his frontal cortex, which is the input station for information from the brain's sensory regions. In turn, he may have lost access to somatic markers of emotion (Damasio, 1994).

Still, it's not clear that we need to use somatic markers as guideposts for all of our decisions. There's evidence that people can make decisions solely on the basis of external knowledge and without any bodily feedback (Maia & McClelland, 2004). One team of investigators examined a group of patients who suffered from a rare condition called *pure autonomic failure* (PAF), which is marked by a deterioration of autonomic nervous system neurons beginning in middle age (Heims, Critchley, Dolan, Mathias, & Cipolotti, 2004). These patients don't experience increases in autonomic activity, such as heart rate or sweating, in response to emotional stimuli. Yet the researchers found that

> **Correlation vs. Causation**

> **James-Lange theory of emotion**
> theory proposing that emotions result from our interpretations of our bodily reactions to stimuli
>
> **somatic marker theory**
> theory proposing that we use our "gut reactions" to help us determine how we should act

> **Replicability**

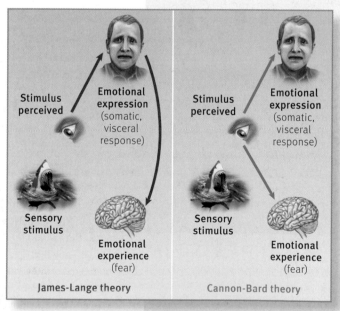

Figure 11.2 What Triggers Emotions?
The James-Lange and Cannon-Bard theories differ in their views of how emotions are generated. (*Source:* Adapted from Cardoso)

these patients had no difficulty on a gambling task that required them to make decisions about monetary risks. These findings don't completely falsify somatic marker theory, as it's possible that somatic markers are helpful to us when making decisions. But they suggest that somatic markers aren't *necessary* for wise choices, even if they sometimes give us a bit of extra guidance.

Cannon-Bard Theory of Emotion. Walter Cannon (1929) and Philip Bard (1942) pointed out several flaws with James's and Lange's reasoning. They noted that most physiological changes occur too slowly—often taking at least a few seconds—to trigger emotional reactions, which happen almost instantaneously. Cannon and Bard also argued that we aren't aware of many of our bodily reactions, like the contractions of our stomach or liver. As a consequence, we can't use them to infer our emotions.

Cannon and Bard proposed a different model for the correlation between emotions and bodily reactions. According to the **Cannon-Bard theory,** an emotion-provoking event leads simultaneously to both an emotion and bodily reactions. To return to James's example, Cannon and Bard would say that when we see a bear while hiking in the forest, the sight of that bear triggers both fear and running at the same time (again refer to Figure 11.2).

Cannon and Bard further proposed that the *thalamus*, which as we learned in Chapter 3 is a relay station for the senses, triggers both an emotion and bodily reactions. Cannon and Bard were probably wrong about this, because later researchers showed that numerous regions of the limbic system, including the hypothalamus and the amygdala (Chapter 3), also play key roles in emotion (Carlson & Hatfield, 1992; Plutchik & Kellerman, 1986). Still, their model of emotion has encouraged investigators to explore the bases of emotion in the brain.

Two-Factor Theory of Emotion. Stanley Schachter and Jerome Singer (1962) argued that both the James-Lange and Cannon-Bard models of emotion were too simple. They agreed with James and Lange that our cognitive interpretations of our bodily reactions play a crucial role in emotions, but they disagreed with James and Lange that these bodily reactions are sufficient for emotion. According to their **two-factor theory** of emotion (Schachter & Singer, 1962), two psychological events are required to produce an emotion:

(1) After encountering an emotion-provoking event, we experience an undifferentiated state of arousal, that is, alertness. By "undifferentiated," Schachter and Singer meant that this arousal is the same across emotions.

(2) We try to explain the source of this autonomic arousal. Once we attribute the arousal to an occurrence, either an occurrence within us or an occurrence in the external environment, we experience an emotion. Once we figure out what's making us aroused, we "label" that arousal with an emotion. This labeling process, Schachter and Singer proposed, typically occurs so rapidly that we're not even aware of it. According to this view, emotions are the explanations we attach to our arousal.

To illustrate, imagine we're hiking in the forest yet again (you'd think we'd have learned by now that we might find a bear there!). Then, sure enough, we come upon a bear. According to Schachter and Singer, we first become physiologically aroused; evolution assures that we do so that we're ready to fight—probably not an especially smart idea in this case—or flee (see Chapter 12). Then, we try to figure out the source of that arousal. One need not have a Ph.D. in psychology to infer that our arousal probably has something to do with the bear. So we label this arousal as fear, and that's the emotion we experience.

It sounds plausible, but do our emotions really work this way? In a classic study, Schachter and Singer (1962) decided to find out. As a "cover story," they informed subjects that they were testing the effectiveness of a new vitamin supplement—"Suproxin"—on vision. But in reality, they were testing the effects of *adrenaline*, a chemical that produces physiological arousal (see Chapter 3). Schachter and Singer randomly assigned some subjects to receive an injection of Suproxin (again, actually adrenaline) and others an injection of placebo. While the adrenaline was entering their systems, Schachter and Singer

According to Schachter and Singer's Two Factor Theory of Emotion, we first experience arousal after an emotion-provoking event, like a car accident, and then seek to interpret the cause of that arousal. The resulting label we attach to our arousal is the emotion.

Cannon-Bard theory
theory proposing that an emotion-provoking event leads simultaneously to an emotion and to bodily reactions

two-factor theory
theory proposing that emotions are produced by an undifferentiated state of arousal along with an attribution (explanation) of that arousal

randomly assigned subjects to two additional conditions: one in which a confederate (an undercover research assistant) acted in a happy fashion while completing questionnaires, and second in which a confederate acted in an angry fashion while completing questionnaires. The confederate was blind as to whether subjects had received an injection of adrenaline or the placebo. Finally, Schachter and Singer asked participants to describe how strongly they were experiencing different emotions.

Schachter and Singer's results dovetailed with two-factor theory. The emotions of the subjects who'd received the placebo weren't influenced by the behavior of the confederate, but the emotions of the subjects who received adrenaline were. Subjects exposed to the happy confederate reported feeling happier, and those exposed to the angry confederate reported feeling angrier—but in both cases only if they'd received adrenaline. Emotion, Schachter and Singer concluded, requires *both* physiological arousal *and* an attribution of that arousal to an emotion-inducing event.

This swaying suspension bridge on the University of British Columbia campus allowed psychologists to test Schachter and Singer's two-factor theory of emotion.

The award for the most creative test of the two-factor theory probably goes to two researchers (Dutton & Aron, 1974), who asked an attractive female confederate to approach male undergraduates on the University of British Columbia campus. She asked them for help with a survey and gave them her phone number in case they had any questions. Half of the time, she approached them on a sturdy bridge that didn't move, and half of the time she approached them on a swaying suspension bridge 200 feet above a river. Although only 30 percent of males in the first condition called her, 60 percent of males in the second condition did. The wobbly bridge in the second condition presumably increased male students' arousal, leading them to feel more intense romantic emotions. In a related study of "love at first fright," investigators approached participants either immediately before or after a roller-coaster ride, and showed them a photograph of an attractive member of the opposite sex. Participants who'd just gotten off the roller coaster rated the person in the photograph as more attractive—and indicated more of an interest in dating him or her—than did participants who were just about to get on the roller coaster (Meston & Frohlich, 2003).

Still, the support for two-factor theory has been mixed. Not all researchers have replicated Schachter and Singer's (1962) results (Marshall & Zimbardo, 1979; Maslach, 1979). Moreover, research suggests that although arousal often intensifies emotions, emotions can occur in the absence of arousal (Reisenzein, 1983). Contrary to what Schachter and Singer claimed, arousal isn't necessary for emotional experience.

Replicability

Putting It All Together. So which of these theories should we believe? As is so often the case in psychology, there's probably a kernel of truth in several explanations. Discrete emotions theory is probably correct that our emotional reactions are shaped in part by natural selection and that these reactions serve crucial adaptive functions. Nevertheless, discrete emotions theory doesn't exclude the possibility that our thinking influences our emotions in significant ways, as cognitive theorists propose. Indeed, the James-Lange and somatic marker theories are probably correct in assuming that our inferences concerning our bodily reactions can influence our emotional states. Finally, two-factor theory may also be right that physiological arousal plays a key role in the intensity of our emotional experiences, although it's unlikely that all emotions require such arousal.

UNCONSCIOUS INFLUENCES ON EMOTION

In recent decades, researchers have become especially interested in *unconscious influences on emotion*: factors outside our awareness that can affect our feelings. One piece of evidence for unconscious influences on emotion comes from research on *automatic behaviors*.

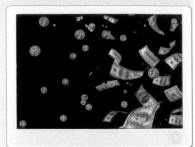

Stimuli can influence our emotional behavior even when we don't recognize them as the culprits. In one study, subjects subtly reminded of money by watching a computer screensaver of floating currency *(above)* later put more physical distance between themselves and a stranger than did subjects who watched a screensaver of floating fish *(below)*, presumably because thinking of money makes people more self-centered (Vohs, Meade, & Goode, 2006).

Correlation vs. Causation

mere exposure effect
phenomenon in which repeated exposure to a stimulus makes us more likely to feel favorably toward it

Replicability

Automatic Generation of Emotion. As we discussed in the Prologue, research suggests that a good deal of our behavior is produced automatically, that is, with no voluntary influence on our part (Bargh & Ferguson, 2000). Yet we often perceive such behavior as intentional (Kirsch & Lynn, 1999; Wegner, 2002). The same may hold for our emotional reactions; many may be generated more or less automatically, like the knee-jerk reflex that our doctor elicits when she taps on our knees with a hammer.

For example, two investigators visually presented some subjects with a set of words describing positive stimuli (like *friends* and *music*) and others describing negative stimuli (like *cancer* and *cockroach*). These stimuli appeared so quickly that they were *subliminal,* that is, below the threshold for awareness (see Chapter 4). Even though subjects couldn't identify what they saw at better than chance levels, those exposed to positive stimuli reported being in a better mood than those exposed to negative stimuli (Bargh & Chartrand, 1999).

Mere Exposure Effect

Psychology: From Inquiry to Understanding

Psychology: From Inquiry to Understanding

Psychology: From Inquiry to Understanding

Psychology: From Inquiry to Understanding

After reading the four lines above, how do you feel about our textbook? Do you like it better than you did before?

Popular wisdom would say no. It tells us that "familiarity breeds contempt": the more often we've seen or heard something, the more we come to dislike it. There's surely some truth to this notion, as most of us have had the experience of hearing a jingle on the radio that grates on our nerves increasingly with each passing repetition. Yet research by Robert Zajonc and others on the **mere exposure effect** suggests that the opposite is actually more common: that is, familiarity breeds *comfort* (Zajonc, 1968). The mere exposure effect refers to the fact that repeated exposure to a stimulus makes us more likely to feel favorably toward it (Bornstein, 1989; Kunst-Wilson & Zajonc, 1980).

Of course, the finding that we like things we've seen many times before isn't itself terribly surprising. This correlation could be due to the fact that we repeatedly seek out things we like. If we love ice cream, we're likely to spend more time seeing ice cream than are people who hate ice cream, assuming such human beings actually exist. So to find out whether mere exposure actually exerts an effect on preferences, we need to turn from correlational studies to experiments. Some of the best evidence for the mere exposure effect derives from experiments using meaningless material, for which individuals are unlikely to have any prior feelings. Experiments show that repeated exposure to various stimuli, such as nonsense syllables (like "zab" and "gar"), Chinese letters (to non-Chinese subjects), and polygons of various shapes, results in greater liking toward these stimuli compared with little or no exposure (see **Figure 11.3**). These effects have been replicated by multiple investigators using quite different stimuli, attesting to their generality. The mere exposure effect even extends to faces. We tend to prefer an image of ourselves as we appear in the mirror to an image of ourselves as we appear in a photograph (Mita, Dermer, & Knight, 1977), probably because we see ourselves in the mirror just about every day. Our friends, in contrast, generally prefer the photographic image. Of course, advertisers are well aware of the mere exposure effect and capitalize on it mercilessly (Baker, 1999; Pechman & Stewart, 1989; Fang, Singh, & AhluWalia, 2007). Repetitions of a commercial tend to increase our liking for the product, especially if we're positively inclined toward it to begin with.

There's evidence that the mere exposure effect can operate unconsciously, because it emerges even when experimenters present meaningless stimuli subliminally (Bornstein, 1992; Zajonc, 2001). Even when people aren't aware of having seen a stimulus, like a specific polygon, they report liking it better than stimuli, like slightly different polygons, they've never seen. Mere exposure effects may be even larger for subliminally than for *supraliminally*

Polygon pairs

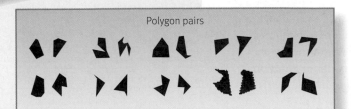

Figure 11.3 Which Polygon Do You Prefer? Pairs of polygons used in the mere exposure research of Robert Zajonc and his colleagues. Subjects exposed repeatedly to only one polygon within the pair prefer that polygon, even if they don't recall having seen it. (*Source:* Epley, 2006)

(consciously) presented stimuli (Bornstein, 1989). The unconscious nature of the mere exposure effect helps to explain a puzzling finding derived from "blind taste tests" of products, including sodas and cigarettes. When product researchers give smokers the opportunity to try several different cigarette brands, smokers do no better than chance when asked to identify which brand they smoke. Yet remarkably, when these researchers ask smokers which brand they prefer, they pick their customary brand, oblivious to the fact that it's the very brand they smoke (Littman & Manning, 1952; Zajonc, 1984). Still, there's controversy about just how enduring the mere exposure effect is. It seems to influence short-term preferences, but not long-term emotions (Lazarus, 1984).

No one knows why mere exposure effects occur. They may be an example of *habituation*, a primitive form of learning we encountered in Chapter 6. The more frequently we encounter a stimulus without anything bad happening, the more comfortable we feel in its presence. Alternatively, we may prefer things we find easier to process (Harmon-Jones & Allen, 2001; Mandler, Nakamura, & Van Zandt, 1987). The more often we experience something, the less effort it typically takes to comprehend it. Recall from Chapter 2 that we're *cognitive misers*: we prefer less mental work to more. So all else being equal, you'll like this paragraph better after having read it a few times than after you read it the first time. That's a not-so-subtle hint to read it again!

Facial Feedback Hypothesis. If no one is near you, and you're not afraid of looking foolish, make a big smile and hold it for a while, maybe for 15 seconds. How do you feel (other than silly)? Next, make a big frown, and again hold it for a while. How do you feel now?

According to the **facial feedback hypothesis,** you're likely to feel emotions that correspond to your facial features—first happy, and then, sad or angry (Adelmann & Zajonc, 1989; Niedenthal, 2007; Zajonc, Murphy, & Inglehart, 1989). This hypothesis originated with none other than Charles Darwin (1872), although Robert Zajonc revived it in the 1980s. Zajonc went beyond Darwin by proposing that changes in the blood vessels of the face "feed back" temperature information to the brain, altering our emotions in predictable ways. Like James and Lange, Zajonc argued that our emotions typically arise from our behaviors and physiological reactions. But unlike James and Lange, Zajonc viewed this process as purely biochemical and noncognitive, that is, as involving no thinking. Moreover, according to Zajonc, it operates outside of our awareness.

There's scientific support for the facial feedback hypothesis. In one study, researchers asked subjects to rate how funny they found various cartoons (Strack, Martin, & Stepper, 1988). They randomly assigned some subjects to watch cartoons while holding a pen with their teeth, and others to watch cartoons while holding a pen with their lips. If you have a pen around, try doing both. You'll discover that when you hold a pen with your teeth, you tend to smile; when you hold a pen with your lips, you tend to frown. Sure enough, the investigators found that subjects who held a pen with their teeth rated the cartoons as funnier than did other subjects.

Still, it's not clear that these effects work by means of facial feedback to the brain, as Zajonc claimed. An alternative hypothesis for these effects is classical conditioning (see Chapter 6). Over the course of our lives, we've experienced countless conditioning "trials" in which we smile while feeling happy and frown while feeling unhappy. Eventually, smiles become conditioned stimuli for happiness, frowns for unhappiness.

Most people prefer their mirror image to their image as taken by a photographer. In this case, this subject is more likely to prefer the photograph on the left, presumably because he is more accustomed to this view of himself.

fact*oid*

The results of a small study suggest that the chemical *Botox*, used to treat wrinkles by paralyzing the skin around them, may be helpful in treating depression (Finzi & Wasserman, 2006). Although this preliminary finding requires replication, it's consistent with the facial feedback hypothesis, because *Botox* may decrease the sad facial expressions of depressed people, in turn dampening their sad emotions.

Ruling Out Rival Hypotheses

APPLY YOUR THINKING

Some individuals are born with an extremely rare condition called *Mobius syndrome*, which is marked by complete facial paralysis. Such individuals can't produce any facial expressions (Calder, Kean, Cole, Campbell, & Young, 2000). What would the facial feedback hypothesis predict about these individuals' ability to experience emotions? What would the James-Lange theory predict?

facial feedback hypothesis
theory that blood vessels in the face feed back temperature information in the brain, altering our experience of emotions

fictoid

Myth: Men and women have distinctly different styles of emotional communication.

Reality: John Gray (1992), author of *Men Are from Mars, Women Are from Venus*, contends that men and women's emotional communications are vastly different. For example, he argues that men are innately programmed to withdraw and not talk to others when upset, whereas women are innately programmed to do the opposite. Yet research offers little support for Gray's claims, because the overlap between men and women's communication styles is substantial (Barnett & Rivers, 2004; Wilson, 2003).

Smile	Surprised	Disappointed
:-) or :)	:-o or :o	:-l or :l

Sad	Confused	Embarrassed
:-(or :(	:-S or :s	:-$ or :$

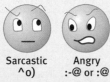

Sarcastic	Angry
^o)	:-@ or :@

Figure 11.4 Emoticons. Because e-mail messages are devoid of nonverbal cues, people have developed a variety of "emoticons" to convey various emotions that might not be obvious over e-mail and instant messaging. (*Source:* Microsoft Corporation)

nonverbal leakage
unconscious spillover of emotions into nonverbal behavior

Nonverbal Expression of Emotion: The Eyes, Bodies, and Cultures Have It

Much of our emotional expression is nonverbal. Not only our facial expressions frequently change when we experience a strong emotion, but so do our gestures and postures. What's more, our nonverbal behaviors are often more valid indicators of our emotions than our words, largely because we're better at disguising our verbal language than our gestures and tone of voice (DePaulo, 1992). So when we ever so subtly roll our eyes while agreeing to our boss's unreasonable request to house-sit her dogs over the weekend ("Sure, I'd be happy to do it"), we can be confident that the "eyes have it."

We often take for granted how important nonverbal behavior is to our everyday communication—until, that is, when we don't have access to it (see Chapter 8). Without nonverbal cues to our emotions, embarrassing miscommunications sometimes arise. Many of us have experienced this effect through e-mail, when a person to whom we send an innocuous or humorous message misinterprets it as hostile. Without being able to hear our vocal inflections or see our facial emotions, recipients of our e-mail messages may misinterpret what we meant to say. This problem is exacerbated by the fact that we overestimate how easily others can figure out the intended meanings of our e-mail messages (Kruger, Epley, Parker, & Ng, 2005). More broadly, psychologists refer to this problem as the *curse of knowledge*: when we know something, in this case what we intend to say, we often make the mistake of thinking others know it too (Birch & Bloom, 2003) (see **Figure 11.4**).

BODY LANGUAGE: LETTING OUR BODIES DO THE TALKING

As baseball Hall of Famer Yogi Berra (known for his funny words of wisdom) said, "You can observe a lot just by watching." **Nonverbal leakage**—an unconscious spillover of emotions into nonverbal behavior—is often a powerful cue that we're trying to hide an emotion. In sharp contrast to our verbal behaviors, we're frequently unaware of our nonverbal behaviors.

GESTURES

Gestures come in a seemingly endless variety of forms. When talking, we often use *illustrators* (Ekman, 2001), gestures that highlight or accentuate speech. For example, while making a particularly important point, we may forcefully move our hands forward. When stressed out, we may engage in *manipulators,* gestures in which one body part strokes, presses, bites, or otherwise touches another body part. For example, while cramming for an exam, we may twirl our hair or bite our fingernails.

We're all familiar with *emblems* (Ekman, 2001), gestures that convey conventional meanings that are recognized by members of a culture, such as the hand wave, the OK sign, and the nodding of the head. Some emblems are surprisingly consistent across cultures, such as crossing one's fingers as a sign of hoping for good luck (Plutchik, 2003). Yet others differ across cultures, which should serve as a word of warning to unwary foreign travelers (Archer, 2004). For example, the "thumbs up" is a sign of approval among Westerners, but an insult in much of the Muslim world. Some surprised American soldiers quickly discovered this awkward fact upon greeting Iraqi civilians following the U.S. invasion in 2003. The familiar American "hello" wave means "go away" in some European countries. Nodding "yes" means "no" in parts of Yugoslavia and Iran, which can cause embarrassing problems if your host asks if you enjoyed the meal he just served (Axtell, 1997).

Differing hand gestures communicate different nuances of emotion. (Sydney Harris, www.CartoonStock.com. Used by permission.)

NEW FRONTIERS
The Emotional Social Intelligence Prosthesis (ESIP)

Have you ever been engaged in a conversation with someone who wouldn't stop talking about himself even though you kept looking at your watch? Or someone who kept interrupting you whenever you tried to make a point? If so, you might have wondered how to give him feedback. Of course, you could always say, "You never seem to shut up!" or "You never let me get a word in edgewise!" but those putdowns might not win you many points in the congeniality department. Researchers at the Massachusetts Institute of Technology have developed a promising new device that might help one day (Kaliouby, Teeters, & Picard, 2006).

They designed this technology, called the Emotional Social Intelligence Prosthesis (ESIP), primarily to help individuals with infantile autism and similar disorders, who frequently have difficulty picking up on social cues, including nonverbal emotional reactions, from others (Nowicki & Duke, 2002). The ESIP uses a fancy camera system that's placed on the head of one person in a two-way conversation. A computer mounted on the speaker then analyzes the camera wearer's facial expressions and head gestures, and tries to "infer" six emotional states that he or she is experiencing in response to what the other person is saying: agreeing, disagreeing, concentrating, thinking, uncertain, and interested (see **Figure 11.5**). Finally, the computer provides feedback to the speaker regarding these emotional states in the listener. For example, head nods and smiling in conjunction with raised eyebrows could signal interest in the listener; conversely, an absence of these nonverbal behaviors could signal boredom (Robinson, 2006). Initial studies suggest that the ESIP accurately identifies about 90 percent of the emotions from actors asked to portray them, although its accuracy rate among non-actors is only about 65 percent. In general, the ESIP seems to do at least as well as the most talented humans when perceiving emotions from nonverbal behaviors.

Still, the ESIP is in its infancy. Investigators haven't yet tried to "feed back" the inferred emotional states to the other participant in the interchange to determine

(continued)

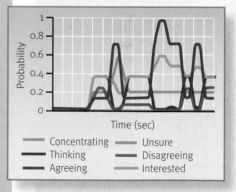

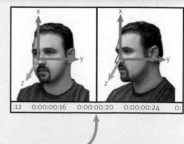

Figure 11.5 The Emotional Social Intelligence Prosthesis. (1) A small camera monitors the person the user is talking to. (2) A computer processes the camera image. (3) A vibrator alerts the user to behavioral cues. (4) A voice for the computer provides feedback to the speaker regarding signs of irritation and other emotions in the listener. (*Source:* New York Times, 2006)

whether it enhances their conversational abilities. Nor do we know whether the ESIP can help to alleviate the emotional deficits of children with autism and similar conditions. So for at least the next few years, you'll need to remain content with looking at your watch when your conversation partner launches into one of those seemingly endless monologues.

PROXEMICS: PERSONAL SPACE

Have you ever walked into a virtually empty movie theater and taken a seat, only to find that someone sits right next to you? Or have you ever approached someone to whom you were attracted, only to find them taking a step away from you? These are among the phenomena addressed by **proxemics**—the study of personal space.

Anthropologist Edward Hall (1966), who coined the term *proxemics*, observed that personal distance is correlated positively with emotional distance. That is, the further we stand from a person, the less emotionally close we usually feel to him or her, and vice versa. But there are exceptions. When we're trying to intimidate people, we typically get closer to them. For example, lawyers tend to stand closer to witnesses they're challenging (Brodsky, Hooper, Tipper, & Yates, 1999).

According to Hall, there are four levels of personal space. Nevertheless, like most distinctions in psychology, the separations between these levels aren't clear-cut:

(1) *Public distance* (12 feet or more): typically used for public speaking, such as lecturing;

(2) *Social distance* (4–12 feet): typically used for conversations among strangers and casual acquaintances;

(3) *Personal distance* (1.5–4 feet): typically used for conversations among close friends or romantic partners;

(4) *Intimate distance* (0–1.5 feet): typically used for kissing, hugging, whispering "sweet nothings," and affectionate touching.

When these implicit rules are violated, we usually feel uncomfortable, as when a stranger gets "in our face" to ask us for a favor.

Hall (1976) argued that cultures differ in personal space. In many Latin and Middle Eastern countries, personal space is relatively close, whereas in many Scandinavian and Asian countries, personal space is more distant. Nevertheless, data suggest that although these cultural differences are real and often important in their implications for everyday interaction, they aren't as large as Hall believed (Hayduk, 1983; Jones, 1979). There are also sex differences in personal space, with women tending to prefer closer space than men (Vrugt & Kerkstra, 1984). Personal space also increases from childhood to early adulthood (Hayduk, 1983), largely because the young haven't yet developed clear interpersonal boundaries.

LYING AND LIE DETECTION

We all lie. That's a scientific fact, and we swear we're telling the truth.

Diary studies suggest that college students tell an average of about two lies per day (DePaulo, Kashy, Kirkendol, Wyer, & Epstein, 1996). Lying is so commonplace that the English language contains 112 different words for lying (Henig, 2006). Psychologists have long been interested in finding a dependable means of detecting lying. How successful have they been? We'll find out.

Humans as Lie Detectors. The world's most widely used lie detector is . . . us. We spend a sizable amount of our everyday lives trying to figure out if others are "being straight" with us or putting us on. To do so, we frequently rely on people's nonverbal behaviors. Illustrators, manipulators, and emblems can be helpful in detecting lies. When researchers ask people to lie about something, like whether they enjoyed watching an unbearably gruesome film,

"BOY, LOOK AT HIS PERSONAL SPACE!"

In the United States, people tend to maintain at least 1.5 feet of space between them. That amount of personal space prevents them from entering the zone of "intimate distance." (Sydney Harris, www.CartoonStock.com. Used by permission.)

fictoid

Myth: "Shifty eyes" are good indicators of lying.

Reality: There's no evidence for this belief, which is held by about 70 percent of people (Bond, 2006). To the contrary, pathological liars and psychopaths, who are notorious liars (see Chapters 6 and 15) tend to stare their victims straight in the eye (Ekman, 2001). Still, because shifty eyes might give away *bad* liars, they may not be useless as emotional cues.

proxemics
study of personal space

their illustrators tend to decrease, whereas their manipulators and emblems tend to increase (Ekman, 2001). Yet none of these gestures are foolproof indicators of dishonesty, so we shouldn't place too much stock in any one of them. Although many of us are confident of our ability to detect lies, research suggests that most of us achieve only about 55 percent accuracy given a 50–50 chance of being right (Ekman, 2001; Zuckerman, DePaulo, & Rosenthal, 1981). Few of us exceed 70 percent. Moreover, occupational groups we might expect to be especially accurate detectors of lies, like people who administer so-called lie detector (polygraph) tests, judges, customs officials, and psychiatrists, usually do no better than the rest of us (Ekman & O'Sullivan, 1991; Kraut & Poe, 1980, DePaulo & Pfeifer, 1986). Researchers have found only three groups to be especially adept at lie detection: secret service agents, law enforcement officials, and clinical psychologists who study deception (Ekman & O'Sullivan, 1991; Ekman, O'Sullivan, & Frank, 1999). These correlational findings may indicate that years of experience in spotting lies make people better at it: Practice makes perfect. Or perhaps the causal arrow is reversed: People who are interpersonally perceptive may pursue professions that allow them to exercise this talent (see **Figure 11.6**).

Another sobering finding is that there's typically little or no correlation between people's confidence in their ability to detect lies and their accuracy (Ekman & O'Sullivan, 1991; Ekman, 2001). So when a juror proclaims with utmost confidence, "I could tell that the witness was lying; I'm positive about it," we should take it with a grain of salt. As in research on eyewitness memory (Chapter 7), we shouldn't confuse confidence with correctness.

The Polygraph Test. The polygraph or "lie detector" test has long been one of the icons of popular psychology. It makes frequent cameo appearances in television courtroom dramas, and features prominently in news stories of criminal suspects, such as former football superstar O. J. Simpson, who reportedly failed a polygraph test prior to his infamous 1996 murder trial. Even popular psychologist Dr. Phil McGraw ("Dr. Phil") has promoted the polygraph test on his television show as a means of finding out which partner in a relationship is lying (Levenson, 2005).

Origins and Rationale of the Polygraph Test. The polygraph test was born in 1915. The psychologist traditionally credited with developing it was William Moulton Marston (1893–1947). The public today remembers Marston not only for the polygraph, but for another invention: the comic-book character Wonder Woman. The connection between Wonder Woman and the polygraph isn't merely coincidental, because Wonder Woman proudly sported a lasso that possessed magical powers. When she corralled a potential criminal, she wrapped the lasso around his waist, compelling him to tell the truth ("Yes, I did rob the bank. . . . I admit it."). For Marston (1938), the polygraph test was the equivalent of Wonder Woman's lasso: It was an infallible detector of lies.

The polygraph test, like most lie-detection techniques, rests on the assumption of the **Pinocchio response**: a perfect physiological or behavioral indicator of lying (Lykken, 1998; Ruscio, 2005). Like Pinocchio's nose, people's bodily reactions supposedly give them away whenever they lie. For example, the largest organization of polygraph examiners in the United States claims the test is 98 percent accurate (Koerner, 2002). Does research support this extraordinary claim?

The Modern Polygraph Test. Like Marston's early apparatus, today's polygraph test measures several physiological signals that often reflect anxiety, most typically blood pressure, respiration, and skin conductance, which is a measure of palm sweating. The assumption is that dishonest suspects experience anxiety—and heightened autonomic activity—when confronted with questions that expose their falsehoods.

The most widely administered version of the polygraph test, the Controlled Question Test (CQT), measures suspects' physiological responses following three major types of yes–no questions listed on the next page (Lykken, 1998).

Correlation vs. Causation

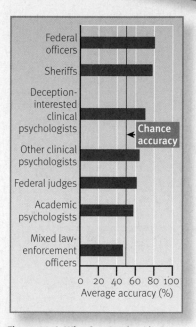

Figure 11.6 Who Can Catch a Liar? Data from Paul Ekman and his colleagues on the accuracy levels of different occupational groups in detecting deception; the chance rate of accuracy in these studies is 50 percent. Several groups do only somewhat better than chance, with law enforcement officers (including police) actually doing slightly worse than chance. (*Source:* Ekman, O'Sullivan, Frank, 1999)

Extraordinary Claims

Pinocchio response
supposedly perfect physiological or behavioral indicator of lying

The comic book character Wonder Woman, portrayed by actress Lynda Carter in a popular television series, sported a magical lasso that would always reveal the truth when wrapped around criminal suspects. What else did the creator of Wonder Woman invent, and how does his other invention relate to her lasso?

The modern polygraph test relies on the assumption of a Pinocchio response, a perfect indicator of lying—much like that of Pinocchio's nose, which became longer whenever he fibbed. Yet psychological research calls the existence of the Pinocchio response into serious question. Some people exhibit physiological arousal when they don't lie, and some people don't exhibit physiological arousal when they do lie.

Falsifiability

(1) *Relevant questions*, or "Did you do it" questions, those bearing on the crime in question ("Did you rob the bank on the afternoon of August 16?");

(2) *Irrelevant questions*, those not bearing on the crime in question or on suspects' lies ("Is your name Sam Jones?");

(3) *Control questions*, those reflecting probable lies. They typically inquire about trivial flaws—misdeeds about which most people will lie, especially under the intense pressure of a polygraph examination ("Have you ever been tempted to steal anything from a store?"). Suspects' physiological activity following these questions supposedly provides a "baseline" for gauging their bodily responses during known lies.

If the suspect's autonomic activity following the relevant questions is higher than that following irrelevant and control questions, polygraph examiners label the CQT results "deceptive." Otherwise, they label them "truthful" (or inconclusive if the responses to irrelevant and control questions are about equal).

Evaluating the Polygraph Test: What's the Truth? There's virtually universal agreement that the polygraph test usually does better than chance for detecting lies (Kircher, Horowitz, & Raskin, 1988). Yet research suggests that this test yields a high rate of *false positives*, that is, innocent individuals whom the test labels incorrectly as guilty (Iacono & Patrick, 2006; Lykken, 1998; National Research Council, 2003). Putting it less technically, *the polygraph test is biased against the innocent.* Field studies of the polygraph test—that is, real-world investigations that compare the results of known criminals with those of known noncriminals—show that the test misclassifies a large proportion of innocent individuals (perhaps 40% or more) as guilty (Patrick & Iacono, 1991). As a consequence, the results of polygraph tests aren't admissible in most U.S. courts (Saxe & Ben-Skakhar, 1999).

The problem is that the polygraph test confuses arousal with evidence of guilt. The polygraph test is misnamed: it's an "arousal detector," not a lie detector (Saxe, 1991). Many people display arousal following relevant questions for reasons other than the anxiety associated with lying, such as the fear of being convicted for a crime they didn't commit. Polygraph enthusiasts' claims to the contrary, there *is* no Pinocchio response, at least none that psychologists have discovered.

These problems plague most other popular lie-detection methods. Some agencies use *voice stress analysis* to detect lies on the basis of findings that people's voices increase in pitch when they lie. Yet because most people's voices also go up in pitch when they're scared or stressed out (Long & Krall, 1990), voice stress analyzers barely do better than chance at detecting lies (Gamer, Rill, Vossel, & Gödart, 2006; Sackett & Decker, 1979).

False positives aren't the only problem for the polygraph test, because this test may also yield a nontrivial number of *false negatives*, that is, guilty individuals whom the test incorrectly labels innocent. Many properly trained subjects can "beat" the test by using *countermeasures*—methods designed to alter their responses to control questions. To pass the polygraph test, as we've seen, we must exhibit a more pronounced physiological response to control questions than to relevant questions. Given less than 30 minutes of preparation, half or more of subjects can accomplish this goal by biting their tongues, curling their toes, or performing difficult mental arithmetic problems (such as counting backward from 1,000 by 17s) during control questions (Honts, Raskin, & Kircher, 1994; Iacono, 2001).

If the polygraph is so flawed, why are polygraph examiners persuaded of its validity? The answer probably lies in the fact that the polygraph is often effective for eliciting confessions, especially when people fail the test (Lykken, 1998; Ruscio, 2005). As a result, polygraph examiners may come to believe the test works, because many people who fail the test later "admit" they were lying. Yet there's good evidence that many criminal confessions are false (Kassin & Gudjonsson, 2004). Moreover, polygraph examiners frequently conclude that suspects who failed the test and who didn't confess to crimes must actually be guilty. But without hard-and-fast criminal evidence against these suspects, this assertion is unfalsifiable.

PsychoMythology

Is "Truth Serum" Really a Truth Serum?

In the 1994 blockbuster movie *True Lies* Arnold Schwarzenegger plays Harry Tasker, a CIA spy. In one scene, terrorists capture Tasker and inject him with "truth serum," forcing him to disclose deep dark secrets of his past. Indeed, scores of Hollywood movies, including the 2004 comedy *Meet the Fockers*, portray truth serum as the chemical version of Wonder Woman's magical lasso. After the suspect receives truth serum, the embarrassing truth supposedly emerges, whether or not we want it to.

Truth serum is a term for a broad class of drugs called *barbiturates*, such as Sodium Pentothal. These drugs typically relax people and, in high doses, make them fall asleep. During the 1930s and 1940s, truth serum was a popular tool in psychotherapy for unearthing supposedly unconscious material (Dysken, Kooser, Harasztzi, & Davis, 1979; Mann, 1969; Winter, 2005). For several decades, the police and military occasionally administered truth serum to suspects in the hopes of dredging up concealed information. In 1963, the U.S. Supreme Court ruled that criminal confessions induced under truth serum were scientifically questionable and unconstitutional, effectively putting a halt to its use for most purposes. Still, fascination with truth serum never died. Following the terrorist attacks of September 11, 2001, some U.S. government organizations displayed a renewed interest in truth serum, largely for the purpose of interrogating suspected terrorists (Brown, 2006).

Yet scientific evidence demonstrates that truth serum is anything but infallible. Studies show that people can lie under the influence of truth serum, falsifying the claim that this chemical invariably produces truthful statements (Piper, 1993). Even more problematic is evidence suggesting that truth serum, like many suggestive memory-recovery techniques (see Chapter 7), doesn't enhance memory: it merely lowers the threshold for reporting all memories, both true and false (Lynn et al., 2003; Piper, 1993). As a consequence, memories retrieved under the influence of truth serum aren't any more trustworthy—and may be less trustworthy—than other memories. Indeed, because the physiological effects of barbiturates are similar to those of alcohol, the effects of truth serum are comparable to those of getting rip-roaring drunk. Our inhibitions are lowered, but what we say can't always be trusted.

Falsifiability

Guilty Knowledge Test. To get around the polygraph test's shortcomings, David Lykken developed the **guilty knowledge test** (GKT), which relies on the premise that criminals harbor concealed knowledge about the crime that innocent people don't (Lykken, 1959, 1960). In contrast to the polygraph test, the GKT doesn't depend on the assumption of a Pinocchio response, because it measures only suspects' recognition of concealed knowledge, not lying.

If we were to administer the GKT to a suspect, we'd concoct a series of multiple-choice questions in which only one of the choices contains the object at the crime scene, such as a red handkerchief, and we'd measure his physiological responses following each choice. If, across many items, the suspect consistently shows pronounced physiological responses to only the objects at the crime scene, we can be reasonably certain that he was present at the crime—and probably committed it.

In contrast to the polygraph, the GKT has a low false-positive rate, that is, it misidentifies few innocent people as guilty. Nevertheless, the GKT has a fairly high false-negative rate, because many criminals may have either not noticed or since forgotten key aspects of the crime scene (Ben-Shakhar & Elaad, 2003; Iacono & Patrick, 2006). Several researchers have attempted to improve on the traditional GKT by measuring suspects' brain waves following each item (Bashore & Rapp, 1993; Farwell & Donchin, 1991), a technique called *brain fingerprinting*. Nevertheless, the scientific support for brain fingerprinting is preliminary (Rosenfeld, 2006).

Aldrich Ames was one of the most notorious spies in American history; while spying for the United States against the then Soviet Union, Ames revealed the names of dozens of American spies to Soviet agents. Yet following these actions, Ames passed two polygraph tests, perhaps because he was largely devoid of anxiety.

guilty knowledge test
alternative to the polygraph test that relies on the premise that criminals harbor concealed knowledge about the crime that innocent people don't

Integrity Tests. The shortcomings of the polygraph test have led many employers to administer paper-and-pencil **integrity tests,** questionnaires that presumably assess workers' tendency to steal or cheat. About 6,000 American companies, including McDonald's, administer these measures to several million people each year (Cullen, 2006). Integrity test questions fall into several categories, including potential employees':

(1) *History of stealing* ("Have you ever stolen anything from your place of work?");

(2) *Attitudes toward stealing* ("Do you think that workers who steal property from a store should always be fired?");

(3) *Perceptions of others' honesty* ("Do you believe that most people steal from their companies every now and then?").

"Yes" responses to questions 1 and 3, and a "no" response to question 2 will put you well on your way to a "dishonest" score on integrity tests.

Although integrity tests predict employee theft and other workplace misbehavior at better than chance levels (Ones, Viswesvaran, & Schmidt, 1993; Sackett & Wanek, 1996), they yield numerous false positives (Lilienfeld, Alliger, & Mitchell, 1995; Office of Technology Assessment, 1990). Ironically, at least some of these false positives may be people who are especially forgiving of others, such as those who believe in giving a second chance to desperate employees who steal a tiny amount of money to feed their families. These people might well answer no to question 2. So integrity tests, like the polygraph test, may be biased against the innocent.

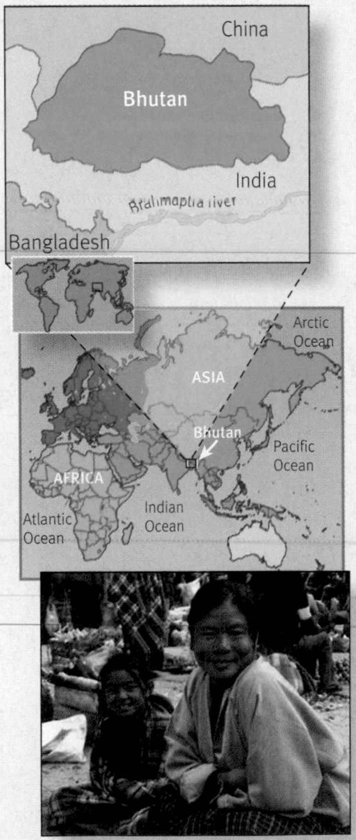

ASSESS YOUR KNOWLEDGE: FACT OR FICTION?

(1) Almost all emblems are cross-culturally universal. (True/False)

(2) Personal distance from others is usually correlated positively with emotional distance. (True/False)

(3) People who've had a great deal of experience with liars are almost always better at detecting them than are other people. (True/False)

(4) The polygraph test tends to have a very low false-positive rate. (True/False)

(5) The effects of "truth serum" are quite similar to those of ingesting several alcoholic drinks. (True/False)

Answers: (1) F (p. 457); (2) T (p. 458); (3) F (p. 459); (4) F (p. 460); (5) T (p. 461)

Figure 11.7 Bhutan, Home of Gross National Happiness. In the Himalayan country of Bhutan, the king has made increasing his country's Gross National Happiness a major domestic policy goal.

Happiness and Self-Esteem: Science Confronts Pop Psychology

The ruler of the tiny country of Bhutan, nestled in the Himalayan mountain range, recently had an unconventional idea (see **Figure 11.7**). Rather than focusing on increasing his nation's gross national product (GNP, a measure of economic success), the king decided to try to improve his nation's gross national happiness (GNH; Nettle, 2005). He hopes to boost Bhutan's GNH, as it's called, by preserving the beauty of its natural environment, promoting positive cultural values, and giving citizens more of a voice in government decisions. Until recently, almost all psychologists would have probably viewed the king as a naive idealist. Not anymore.

POSITIVE PSYCHOLOGY: PSYCHOLOGY'S FUTURE OR PSYCHOLOGY'S FAD?

Since about the turn of the twenty-first century, the emerging discipline of **positive psychology** has sought to emphasize human strengths, such as resilience, coping, life satisfaction, love, and happiness (Myers & Diener, 1996; Seligman, 1998; Seligman & Csikszentmihalyi, 2000). Some authors have argued that much of popular psychology has underestimated peoples' resilience in the face of stressful life events (Bonanno et al., 2002; Garmezy, Masten, & Tellegen, 1984; see also Chapter 12). In this respect, the field of

integrity tests
questionnaires that presumably assess workers' tendency to steal or cheat

positive psychology
discipline that has sought to emphasize human strengths

Table 11.1 The Twenty-Four Character Strengths and Virtues Identified by Positive Psychologists.

Wisdom and Knowledge

- Creativity (originality, ingenuity)
- Curiosity (interest, novelty-seeking, openness to experience)
- Open-mindedness (judgment, critical thinking)
- Love of learning
- Perspective (wisdom)

Courage

- Bravery (valor)
- Persistence (perseverance, industriousness)
- Integrity (authenticity, honesty)
- Vitality (zest, enthusiasm, vigor, energy)

Humanity

- Love
- Kindness (generosity, nurturance, care, compassion, altruistic love, "niceness")
- Social intelligence (emotional intelligence, personal intelligence)

Justice

- Citizenship (social responsibility, loyalty, teamwork)
- Fairness
- Leadership

Temperance

- Forgiveness and mercy
- Humility/modesty
- Prudence
- Self-regulation (self-control)

Transcendence

- Appreciation of beauty and excellence (awe, wonder, elevation)
- Gratitude
- Hope (optimism, future-mindedness, future orientation)
- Humor (playfulness)
- Spirituality (religiousness, faith, purpose)

(*Source:* Park, Peterson, & Seligman, 2004)

positive psychology has considerable potential, as it may help psychologists to pinpoint the traits that allow us to cope with adversity.

Much of contemporary psychology has also focused on minimizing severe distress and on returning disturbed people to adequate levels of functioning. But it's done little to encourage adequately functioning people to achieve their full emotional potential—that is, to become "better than well" (Keyes & Haidt, 2003). To fill this void, Christopher Peterson and Martin Seligman (2004) outlined twenty-four "character strengths and virtues" they view as essential to positive psychology (see **Table 11.1**). Several of these traits, such as curiosity, love, and gratitude, are positively associated with people's long-term life satisfaction (Park, Peterson, & Seligman, 2004). Across the country, positive psychologists have begun to teach students how to incorporate these strengths and virtues into their daily lives with the hope of boosting their happiness (Max, 2007).

WHAT HAPPINESS IS GOOD FOR

For most of the twentieth century, psychologists largely dismissed happiness as a "fluffy" topic better suited to self-help books and motivational seminars than to rigorous research. Yet over the past few decades, a growing body of research has suggested that happiness may produce enduring psychological and physical benefits (see **Figure 11.8**).

Happiness and Longevity. Consider the results of a study that has tracked a group of 180 nuns in Wisconsin for six decades (see Chapter 7). These nuns had kept daily diaries starting in the 1930s, when they were in their early twenties. Nuns whose sentences featured many positive words—such as those dealing with love, joy, and hope—outlived other nuns by an average of almost 10 years (Danner, Snowdon, & Friesen, 2001). Of course, correlation doesn't imply causation, and the nuns who used more happy words may have differed in subtle ways from other nuns, such as in their exercise or health practices. Still, the findings are tantalizing.

Adaptive Value of Happiness. Like all primary emotions, happiness may serve evolutionarily adaptive functions. According to Barbara Fredrickson's (2001, 2003) **broaden and build theory,** happiness predisposes us to think more openly, allowing us to see the "big picture" we might have otherwise overlooked. In turn, this broader thinking often permits

Measure Your Happiness: Take the Satisfaction with Life Scale

Below are five statements that you may agree or disagree with. Using the 1 to 7 scale below, indicate your agreement with each item by placing the appropriate number on the line preceding that item. Please be open and honest in your responding.

1	Strongly disagree	4	Neither agree nor disagree	5	Slightly agree
2	Disagree			6	Agree
3	Slightly disagree			7	Strongly agree

____ In most ways my life is close to my ideal.

____ The conditions of my life are excellent.

____ I am satisfied with my life.

____ So far I have gotten the important things I want in life.

____ If I could live my life over, I would change almost nothing.

Scoring:
- 31–35 Extremely satisfied • 26–30 Satisfied
- 21–25 Slightly satisfied • 20 Neutral • 15–19 Slightly dissatisfied
- 10–14 Dissatisfied • 5–9 Extremely dissatisfied

Figure 11.8 Satisfaction with Life Scale (SWLS). Do you wonder how happy you are? Take this quick test developed by psychologist Ed Diener and his colleagues to help you find out. (*Source:* Diener, Emmons, Larsen, & Griffin, 1985)

Correlation vs. Causation

broaden and build theory
theory proposing that happiness predisposes us to think more openly

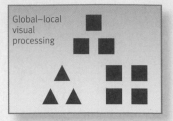

Figure 11.9 Testing Barbara Fredrickson's "Broaden and Build" Theory of Happiness. People put into a good mood are more likely to say that the object on the top resembles a set of triangles *(left)* than a set of squares *(right)*. That's because the triangles on the left resemble the three squares at the top at a "global" (overall) level by forming a triangle rather than a "local" (specific detail) level by being composed of squares. (*Source:* Fredrickson, 2003)

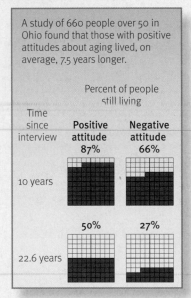

Figure 11.10 Happily Living Longer. Happiness is associated with living longer. Does this finding reflect a direct causal effect? Could we ever know? (*Source:* Duenwald, 2002)

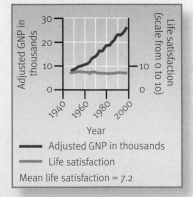

Figure 11.11 Does Wealth Bring Happiness? Over a 60-year span, the U.S. gross national product (a measure of economic prosperity) has increased dramatically. Yet Americans' average level of life satisfaction has stayed remarkably constant over the same time period. (*Source:* Diener & Seligman, 2004.)

us to find novel solutions to life's problems. When we're happy, we see more of the world and seek out more opportunities, like romantic partners we wouldn't have previously considered. Happiness breeds success in our work, family, and love lives, in turn breeding more happiness (Lyubomirsky, King, & Diener, 2005) (see **Figure 11.9**).

As one test of the broaden and build theory, doctors who received a small bag of candy made more accurate diagnoses of liver disease than other doctors, apparently because being in a good mood allowed them to consider alternative diagnostic possibilities (Isen, Rosenzweig, & Young, 1991). So if your doctor is in a bad mood, you might want to first run down the hall to the vending machine and buy her a candy bar.

Moreover, all else being equal, life is easier for those of us who are optimists (see Chapter 12). Optimists tend to be happier in everyday life than pessimists (Seligman & Pawelski, 2003) and find it easier than pessimists to cope with life's rocky road (Watson & Clark, 1984). For example, when given threatening medical information (such as their risk for developing cancer), optimists tend to pay more attention to it and remember it better than pessimists (Aspinwall & Brunhart, 2000). This finding may partly explain why optimists tend to live longer than pessimists (Maruta, Collligan, Malinchoc, & Offord, 2000); they may be less likely to ignore risks to their health (see **Figure 11.10**). Optimism is even a plus in the bruising world of politics. One of the best predictors of who'll win a presidential election is which candidate's speeches contain the more hopeful language (Zullow, Oettingen, Peterson, & Seligman, 1988). When we close the door on the voting booth, we tend to pull the lever for the candidate who promises us a better tomorrow.

WHAT MAKES US HAPPY: THE MYTHS

We all ought to be veritable scientific experts on happiness. After all, we've had thousands of experiences with both joy and sadness. Given that Americans spend about $750 million a year on self-help books designed to make them happy and another $1 billion a year on motivational speakers, we might assume that we have all of the advice about happiness we need. Yet as psychologist Daniel Gilbert observed, "People have a lot of bad theories about happiness" (Martin, 2006). So to understand happiness, we first need to burst some pop psychology bubbles.

(1) **Misconception 1:** *The prime determinant of happiness is what happens to us.* This is arguably the single most widespread myth in all of popular psychology. Ed Diener and Martin Seligman, two scientific experts on happiness, screened more than 200 college students for their levels of happiness, and compared the upper 10 percent with the middle and lowest 10 percent. The happiest students didn't experience any more positive life events than the other groups (Diener & Seligman, 2002). In another study, David Lykken and Auke Tellegen (1996) found that a host of variables, including social class and educational level, accounted for less than 3 percent of the differences among people in happiness. How we react to life events is more critical to our emotional well-being than the events themselves.

(2) **Misconception 2:** *Money makes us happy.* From what psychological research tells us, money can't buy long-term happiness (Wilson, 2002). Admittedly, when we're running short of it, money is a bit related to happiness. Below about $50,000, there's a modest association between how wealthy we are and how happy we are. But above about $50,000, additional money doesn't make us much happier (Helliwell & Putnam, 2004) (see **Figure 11.11**). For example, the average life satisfaction among *Forbes* magazine's 400 richest Americans is 5.8 on a 7-point scale (Diener, Horwitz, & Emmons, 1985). Yet the average life satisfaction of the Pennsylvania Amish, whose average annual income is a few billion (that's right—*billion*) dollars lower, is also 5.8 (Diener & Seligman, 2004). Still, most unhappy people are mistakenly convinced they'd be happier if they could only have more money (Kahneman, Krueger, Schkade, Schwartz, & Stone, 2006).

(3) **Misconception 3:** *Happiness declines in old age.* We're all familiar with the widespread stereotype of the sad old man or woman, sitting all alone in a sparsely decorated room with no one to talk to. Yet this stereotype is misleading, because happiness tends to increase with age, at least through the late sixties and perhaps seventies (Mrozeck &

Kolars, 1998; Nass, 2006). Indeed, surveys suggest that the happiest group of people is men aged 65 and older (Martin, 2006). Only when people become quite old, typically in their eighties, does happiness decrease noticeably. Interestingly, happiness drops dramatically in the last year of life (Mrozeck & Spiro, 2005). Although this correlation may reflect a causal effect of unhappiness on health, it may also reflect a causal effect of poor health on unhappiness.

The increase in happiness with old age appears to be due to the **positivity effect:** the tendency for individuals to remember more positive than negative information with age (Cartensen & Lockenhoff, 2003; Charles, Mather, & Cartensen, 2003). This effect, in turn, is accompanied by diminished activity of the amygdala (Mather et al., 2004), which plays a key role in the processing of negative emotions (see Chapter 3).

(4) **Misconception 4: *Happiness and negative emotions lie on opposite ends of a spectrum.*** It's true that it's hard to be both happy and worried—or otherwise miserable—at exactly the same time. Yet the lasting tendency to experience positive emotions, like happiness, is virtually uncorrelated with the lasting tendency to experience negative emotions, like anxiety, guilt, and mistrust (Tellegen, 1985; Watson & Clark, 1984). We can be prone to both happiness and worry.

(5) **Misconception 5: *People on the West Coast are the happiest.*** Beautiful beaches, sunshine, warm weather, great celebrity watching . . . who could ask for a better recipe for happiness? Maybe some Southern Californians. Research shows that even though non-Californians believe that Southern Californians are especially happy, Southern Californians are no happier than anyone else, including people in the chilly upper Midwest (Schkade & Kahneman, 1998). In this case, non-Californians are probably falling prey to the *availability heuristic* (see Chapter 2). When we think of the West Coast, we think of surfers, glamorous actresses, and millionaires sipping martinis on the beach. We forget about the high cost of living, high crime rates, traffic congestion, and all of the other things that often come with living in popular areas.

WHAT MAKES US HAPPY: THE REALITIES

We've talked about five things that don't make us happy, but we haven't said much about what *does* make us happy. Fortunately, research offers some helpful clues. In particular, psychologists have found that the following variables are correlated with happiness (Martin, 2006; Myers, 1993; Myers & Diener, 1996):

- *Marriage.* Married people tend to be happier than unmarried people (Mastekaasa, 1994). Moreover, among people who are married, happiness is a good predictor of marital satisfaction (Myers, 2000).
- *Friendships.* People with many friends tend to be happier than people with few friends (Diener & Seligman, 2002).
- *College.* People who graduate from college tend to be happier than people who don't (Martin, 2006).
- *Religion.* People who are deeply religious tend to be happier than people who aren't (Myers, 1993).
- *Political affiliation.* Republicans tend to be happier than Democrats, both of whom tend to be happier than Independents (Pew Research Center, 2006).
- *Exercise.* People who exercise regularly tend to be happier and less depressed than people who don't (Babyak et al., 2000; Stathopolou, Powers, Berry, Smits, & Otto, 2006).
- *Gratitude.* Merely asking participants on a daily basis to list reasons why they should be grateful about their lives, like having good friends, intimate romantic partners, and a fulfilling job, can enhance short-term happiness (Emmons & McCullough, 2003; Sheldon & Lyubomirsky, 2006).
- *Flow.* Mihaly Csikszentmihalyi (pronounced "cheeks sent me high") has found that individuals in the midst of *flow,* a mental state in which we're completely immersed in what we are doing, tend to be especially happy (Csikszentmihalyi, 1990, 1997). Some of us experience flow while writing, others while reading, others while performing manual labor, and still others while

Correlation vs. Causation

Contrary to popular conception, older adults are happier, on average, than younger people.

factoid

The world champions of happiness appear to be the Danes. For reasons that are unknown, people in Denmark report the highest level of satisfaction in the world, with Swiss a close second. Americans come in at twenty-third (White, 2006).

Married people are happier, on average, than unmarried people. Whether this correlational finding reflects a causal association is unclear.

positivity effect
tendency for people to remember more positive than negative information with age

playing sports, performing music, or creating works of art. During moments of flow, we're so intensely engaged in a rewarding activity that we screen out unpleasant distractions. We also feel a powerful sense of control over our actions.

We should bear two cautions in mind when interpreting these findings. First, the associations between these variables and happiness are typically modest in magnitude, and there are many exceptions to the trends. For example, although there's a slight tendency for married people to be happier than unmarried people, there are plenty of unhappy married people and happy unmarried people.

Second, most of these findings derive from correlational research alone, so the direction of the causal arrow is unclear. For example, although religious people tend to be happier than nonreligious people, happier people may find it easier than unhappy people to embrace a meaningful religious faith. Moreover, although frequent flow experiences probably contribute to long-term happiness, happy people may be especially prone to flow experiences.

If psychological research tells us anything about how to find happiness, it's that consciously going out of our way to seek it out rarely works. As the concept of flow implies, happiness often emerges from the sheer act of enjoying what we do best, whether it's our work, hobbies, friends, or romantic partners. Happiness lies in the pursuit of the prize, not the prize itself.

FORECASTING HAPPINESS

We're remarkably poor at **affective forecasting:** predicting our own and others' happiness (Gilbert, 2006; Gilbert, Pinel, Wilson, Blumberg, & Wheatley, 1998; Wilson, 2002). We engage in affective forecasting whenever we make a life decision: picking a college, entering into a long-term relationship, or buying a car. We tell ourselves that each of our choices will boost our happiness, but we're typically no more accurate than a meteorologist who tries to forecast next week's weather by poking his head out the window.

Our affective forecasts aren't merely wrong; they're consistently wrong in one direction. Specifically, *we overestimate the long-term impact of events on our moods* (Gilbert, 2006; Sevdalis & Allan, 2007). That is, we suffer from a **durability bias:** We believe that both our good and bad moods will last longer than they do (Frederick & Loewenstein, 1999; Gilbert et al., 1998; Wilson, 2002). Consider the following counterintuitive findings:

- Every month, tens of thousands of Americans wait on hour-long lines in the hopes of winning multimillion dollar lotteries—and guaranteeing a life of never-ending bliss. Sure enough, lottery winners' happiness shoots up sky-high immediately after hitting the big jackpot. Yet by 2 months, their happiness is back to normal—and not much higher than anyone else's (Brickman, Coates, & Janoff-Bulman, 1978).

- Most paraplegics—people paralyzed from the waist down—have returned largely (although not entirely) to their baseline levels of happiness only a few months after their accidents (Brickman et al., 1978). People with other major physical disabilities similarly cope surprisingly well; for example, blind people are on average just as happy as sighted people (Feinman, 1978).

- Before taking an HIV test, people understandably predict that they'd be profoundly distressed were they to turn up HIV-positive. Yet only 5 weeks after discovering they're HIV-positive, people are considerably happier than they expected to be. Moreover, people who discovered they were HIV-negative are considerably less happy than they expected to be (Sieff, Dawes, & Loewenstein, 1999).

What's going on here? We markedly underestimate how rapidly we adjust to our baseline levels of happiness or unhappiness. We forget that we're stuck on what Philip Brickman and Donald Campbell (1971) termed the **hedonic treadmill:** the tendency for our moods to adapt to external circumstances (*hedonic* means "associated with pleasure"). Just as our running speeds quickly adjust to match the speed of a treadmill—or else we'll fall flat on our faces—our levels of happiness quickly adjust to our ongoing life situations.

The state of "flow," in which we're totally absorbed in an activity and don't notice time passing, is associated with high levels of satisfaction and subjective well-being. We can experience flow in many work situations and enjoyable pastimes.

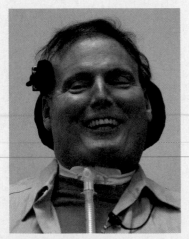

Research shows that following accidents, paraplegics typically regain much of their preaccident levels of happiness. The upbeat attitude of actor Christopher Reeve, who died in 2004, nine years after being paralyzed in a horse-riding accident, was both a surprise and an inspiration to many Americans.

affective forecasting
ability to predict our own and others' happiness

durability bias
belief that both our good and bad moods will last longer than they do

hedonic treadmill
tendency for our moods to adapt to external circumstances

Correlation vs. Causation

When something good happens to us, we feel better in the short term. Yet we soon adapt to our positive life circumstances, bringing us back to emotional square one (Helson, 1948).

The hedonic treadmill hypothesis proposes that we begin life with a genetically influenced happiness "set point" from which we bounce up and down in response to short-term life events (Lykken, 2000). But with few exceptions, we return to that set point after a few days or weeks. We differ from each other in our happiness set points. Studies reveal that most of us are relatively happy most of the time, but others of us are chronically unhappy (Diener, Lucas, & Scollon, 2006) (see **Figure 11.12**). Our happiness set points are quite stable, but they can occasionally shift over time, especially following momentous life events. For example, getting divorced, widowed, or laid off from work often seem to result in lasting increases in unhappiness that don't dissipate completely (Diener et al., 2006).

There's a life lesson lurking in all of this. Here popular wisdom is correct: The grass *is* greener on the other side. It seems greener, that is, until we've been on the other side for a while and realize that the grass is still greener on yet another lawn.

Figure 11.12 How Happy Are Americans? Research shows that most Americans are pretty happy, with about a third describing themselves as "very happy." (*Source:* Pew Research Center Report, 2006)

SELF-ESTEEM: IMPORTANT OR OVERHYPED?

Many pop psychology sources tie virtually all psychological difficulties to one, and only one, core problem: low self-esteem (Branden, 1994; Reasoner, 2000). If you log onto Amazon.com, you'll find over 45 books, tapes, and other products devoted to boosting self-esteem. You can even find a self-esteem cereal bowl emblazoned with positive affirmations, like "I'm talented!" and "I'm good-looking!"

The Great Myths of Self-Esteem. There are two big problems with the widespread claim that low self-esteem is the root of all unhappiness. First, this assertion is a prime example of a *single-variable explanation*, which as we noted in the Prologue reduces complex psychological problems, like depression or aggression, to one cause. Although low self-esteem may play some causal role in these problems, it's unlikely to be the sole culprit.

Second, the evidence linking self-esteem to mental health and life success is feeble (Dawes, 1994; Sommers & Satel, 2004). For example, people with high self-esteem aren't much more likely than people with low self-esteem to have good social skills or to do well in school. They're also just about as likely to abuse alcohol and other drugs (Baumeister, Campbell, Krueger, & Vohs, 2003).

When it comes to aggression, the story becomes more interesting. Most of the popular psychology literature links aggression to low self-esteem. There may be some truth to this view (Donnellen, Trzesniewski, Robins, Moffitt, & Caspi, 2005). Yet most evidence suggests that a subset of *high* self-esteem people is especially prone to aggression, especially when confronted with "ego threats": challenges to their self-worth.

In one study, Brad Bushman and Roy Baumeister asked participants to write essays concerning their attitudes toward abortion, and told them that another participant would be evaluating their essay. In fact, Bushman and Baumeister had randomly assigned the participants to receive either positive evaluations ("No suggestions, great essay!") or negative evaluations ("This is one of the worst essays I have read!"). Then, participants played a game in which they could retaliate against their essay evaluator with a loud blast of noise. High self-esteem subjects who also had high levels of *narcissism*—extreme self-centeredness—responded to negative evaluations by bombarding their opponents with louder noises, but low self-esteem subjects didn't (Bushman & Baumeister, 1998). In addition, in prisons, narcissistic inmates are especially likely to respond with verbal aggression when given orders by guards (Cale & Lilienfeld, 2006).

Happiness is largely a matter of comparison, as this photograph from the 2006 Winter Olympics illustrates. Research shows that second-place finishers (such as Germany's Claudia Kuenzel, *left*) tend to be less happy than third-place finishers (such as Russia's Alena Sidko, *right*), probably because they compare their outcome with what "might have been" (Medvec, Madey, & Gilovich, 1995).

On April 20, 1999, Eric Harris and Dylan Klebold murdered twelve students and a teacher at Columbine High School in Colorado. Although much of the popular press attributed the murders to low self-esteem, Harris and Klebold's diaries (released after their suicides) indicated that they perceived themselves as superior to their classmates.

Correlation vs. Causation

The Realities of Self-Esteem. Still, research suggests that self-esteem affords two apparent benefits (Baumeister et al., 2003). High self-esteem is associated with greater initiative and persistence—that is, a willingness to attempt new challenges and to stick with them even when the going gets rough—and with happiness and resilience in the face of stress. Nevertheless, these findings are correlational and may not be causal.

> **APPLY YOUR THINKING**
> One explanation for the positive correlation between self-esteem and resilience in the face of stress is that high self-esteem gives people the confidence to cope with anxiety-provoking life events. What are some other causal explanations for this correlation?

positive illusions
tendencies to perceive ourselves more positively than others do

defensive pessimism
strategy of anticipating failure and then compensating for this expectation by mentally overpreparing for negative outcomes

fact**oid**

Yes, folks, it's true: Hollywood celebrities *are* self-centered. Dr. Drew Pinsky (better known as "Dr. Drew") and S. Mark Young found that celebrities scored 17 percent higher on a self-report measure of narcissism than did members of the general population. Reality-show contestants scored the highest (Pinsky & Young, 2006).

Self-esteem is also related to **positive illusions,** that is, tendencies to perceive ourselves more positively than others do. Most high self-esteem individuals see themselves as more intelligent, attractive, and likable than do low self-esteem individuals. Yet they don't score any higher than low-self-esteem individuals on objective measures of these characteristics (Baumeister et al., 2003).

The association between positive illusions and psychological adjustment is controversial. Some researchers believe that unrealistically favorable views of ourselves are healthy (Taylor & Brown, 1988, 1994), because they imbue us with self-confidence. Others disagree (Colvin & Block, 1994), contending that positive illusions make it hard for us to see reality clearly. Indeed, people who view themselves much more positively than their peers tend to be self-centered rather than well-adjusted (John & Robins, 1994). Similarly, children who are aggressive and bully other children usually overestimate their popularity (Barry, Frick, & Killian, 2003; Emler, 2001).

There may be some truth to both positions. That is, a slight positive bias may be adaptive, as it may lend us the self-assurance we need to take healthy risks, like asking people out for dates or applying for jobs. Yet when our positive biases become too extreme, they may lead to psychological difficulties, including extreme self-centeredness, because these biases may prevent us from benefiting from constructive feedback (Kistner, David-Ferdon, Repper, & Joiner, 2006).

Criticisms of Positive Psychology. The field of positive psychology has heightened our appreciation for the full range of human experience. Yet some psychologists have condemned positive psychology as a "fad" (Lazarus, 2003) whose claims have outstripped the scientific evidence (Max, 2007).

Many positive psychology proponents have assumed that we'd all be better off if we could just eliminate our strong negative emotions. Yet this "always look on the bright side of life" approach may have its downside. As Julie Norem (2001) observed, **defensive pessimism** probably serves a valuable function for many anxious people. Defensive pessimism is the strategy of anticipating failure and then compensating for this expectation by mentally overpreparing for negative outcomes (see **Table 11.2**). Defensive pessimism helps certain people to improve their performance, probably because it encourages them to work harder (Norem & Cantor, 1986). Robbing defensive pessimists of their pessimism—say, by cheering them up—makes them perform worse (Norem & Chang, 2002).

Moreover, optimists' rose-colored glasses and tendency to gloss over their mistakes may sometimes prevent them from seeing reality clearly. For example, optimists tend to recall

Table 11.2 Defensive Pessimism Questionnaire. Do you use defensive pessimism as a coping strategy? Here are some questions to help you find out.

Think of a situation where you want to do your best. It may be related to work, to your social life, or to any of your goals. When you answer the following questions, please think about how you prepare for that kind of situation. Rate how true each statement is for you.

Not True					True	
1	2	3	4	5	6	7

_____ 1. I often start out expecting the worst, even though I will probably do OK.

_____ 2. I worry about how things will turn out.

_____ 3. I carefully consider all possible outcomes.

_____ 4. I often worry that I won't be able to carry through my intentions.

_____ 5. I spend lots of time imagining what could go wrong.

_____ 6. I imagine how I would feel if things went badly.

_____ 7. I try to picture how I could fix things if something went wrong.

_____ 8. I'm careful not to become overconfident in these situations.

_____ 9. I spend a lot of time planning when one of these situations is coming up.

_____ 10. I imagine how I would feel if things went well.

_____ 11. In these situations, sometimes I worry more about looking like a fool than doing really well.

_____ 12. Considering what can go wrong helps me to prepare.

(*Source:* Norem, 2001)

feedback about their social skills as better than it actually was (Norem, 2001), which could prevent them from learning from their interpersonal errors, like inadvertently offending other people. Moreover, optimists sometimes display greater physiological responses to stressors, like bad health news, than do pessimists, perhaps because they don't spend enough time preparing themselves mentally for the worst (Segerstrom, 2005).

None of this takes away from the value of positive psychology for many people. But the problem of *individual differences* (see Prologue) reminds us to be wary of "one size fits all" solutions to life's multifaceted problems. Positive thinking is a key ingredient in many people's recipe for happiness, but it may not be for everyone.

ASSESS YOUR KNOWLEDGE: FACT OR FICTION?

(1) Good moods often allow us to consider novel alternatives to problems. (True/False)
(2) Money is highly correlated with happiness, especially at high levels of income. (True/False)
(3) Happiness tends to decline sharply after age 50. (True/False)
(4) A few months after hitting it big in a lottery, lottery winners aren't much happier than anyone else. (True/False)
(5) High self-esteem is essential for good mental health. (True/False)
(6) Pessimism is an adaptive strategy for some people. (True/False)

Answers: (1) T (pp. 463–464); (2) F (p. 464); (3) F (pp. 464–465); (4) T (p. 466); (5) F (p. 467); (6) T (p. 468)

Motivation: Our Wants and Needs

Up to this point, we've discussed how and why we experience emotions. Yet to explain why we do things, we also need to understand the psychological forces that pull and push us in various, and sometimes opposing, directions. **Motivation** refers to the drives—especially wants and needs—that propel us in specific directions. When we're motivated to do something, like read an interesting book, talk to a friend, or avoid studying for an exam, we're driven to *move* toward or away from that act—both psychologically and physically. Most of us wish we could be more motivated to perform the tasks of life that we need to do but manage to put off, like pay our bills or begin work on that long-overdue term paper.

So it's no surprise that the world of popular psychology is bursting at the seams with "motivational speakers" who line their pockets with cash from people hoping to receive inspiration in love or work. Although such speakers may get our adrenaline flowing and make us feel good in the short term, there's no evidence that they deliver long-term benefits (Wilson, 2003).

MOTIVATION: A BEGINNER'S GUIDE

As we know, two of the most overpowering motivators in life are food and sex. We'll soon learn about the whys and the hows of these two great "facts of life." Before we do, we first need to learn about a few basic principles of motivation. Does our little teaser motivate you to read on? We hope so.

Drive Reduction Theory. One of the most influential motivational concepts in psychology is **drive reduction theory,** formulated by Clark Hull (1943), Donald Hebb (1949), and others. According to this theory, certain *drives*, like hunger, thirst, and sexual frustration, motivate us to act to minimize aversive states (Dollard & Miller, 1950). Note that all of these drives are unpleasant, but that satisfaction of them is pleasurable.

Some drives are more powerful than others. Thirst is more potent than hunger, and for good reason. Natural selection has probably ensured that our drive to quench our thirst is stronger than our drive to sate our hunger because most of us can survive only a few days without water but over a month without food.

Motivational speakers, like Anthony Robbins, are adept at persuading their audiences that they can accomplish just about anything with enough drive and effort. Nevertheless, there's no solid research evidence that such speakers produce long-term changes in people's behavior.

motivation
psychological drives that propel us in a specific direction

drive reduction theory
theory proposing that certain drives, like hunger, thirst, and sexual frustration motivate us to act in ways that minimize aversive states

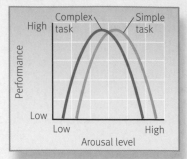

Figure 11.13 Yerkes-Dodson Law.
This law describes an inverted U-shaped relation between arousal on the one hand, and performance or affect, on the other. We tend to do our best—and are most content—when we experience intermediate levels of arousal.

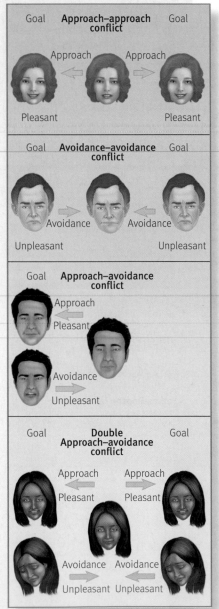

Figure 11.14 When Drives Conflict.
Four types of conflict can arise when approach and avoidance drives clash. (*Source:* Pettijohn, 1998)

Most drive reduction theories propose that we're motivated to maintain a given level of psychological **homeostasis,** that is, equilibrium. To understand homeostasis, think of how a thermostat works to control the temperature in your house or apartment. It's set to a given temperature, say 68 degrees Fahrenheit, and when the room temperature deviates up or down from that set point, the thermostat "tells" your cooling or heating system to restore the equilibrium. Similarly, when we're hungry, we're motivated to satisfy that drive by eating, but ideally not too much. If we eat too much, our brain signals to us that we've overdone things and doesn't allow us to become hungry again for a while.

Drives and Arousal: Not Getting ahead of the Curve. One factor that affects the strength of our drives is arousal. According to the **Yerkes-Dodson law** (Yerkes & Dodson, 1908), formulated about a century ago, there's an inverted U-shaped relation between arousal, on the one hand, and affect and performance, on the other (although its developers actually referred to the strength of stimuli rather than the strength of arousal; Winton, 1987). As we can see in **Figure 11.13,** for each of us there's an optimal point of arousal, typically near the middle of the curve. If we're below that optimal point, we're typically bored and don't perform well. If we're above that optimal point, we're typically stressed out and likewise don't perform well. Moreover, even within each of us, our arousal level often shifts depending on the time of day, substances we've ingested (like caffeine), and complexity of the tasks we're confronting (Revelle, Humphreys, Simon, & Gilliland, 1980).

The Yerkes-Dodson law is popular among sports psychologists. Think of a swimmer who's underaroused before a major meet. She's unlikely to perform as well as she could, because she's not sufficiently motivated to do her best. So her sports psychologist may try to get her into the "psyched up" range of the Yerkes-Dodson curve, where she's feeling just aroused enough to want to do well, but not so aroused she can't concentrate (Anderson, Revelle, & Lynch, 1989).

According to the Yerkes-Dodson law, when we're underaroused we frequently experience "stimulus hunger," that is, a drive for stimulation. We can satisfy this desire in any number of ways: fidgeting, fantasizing, listening to music, socializing with friends, or doing wheelies on a motorcycle. As Daniel Berlyne (1960) noted, underarousal can also heighten our sense of curiosity, motivating us to explore stimuli that are complex or novel, like a challenging book or a piece of abstract art. In classic studies of *sensory deprivation* in the 1950s and 1960s, volunteers who entered isolation tanks for several hours often managed to create their own mental stimulation in this state of extreme underarousal (Jones, 1969; Zuckerman & Hopkins, 1966). Many experienced rich sensory images, and a few began to see or hear things that weren't there. Their brains yanked them out of the low end of the Yerkes-Dodson curve.

When Our Drives Clash: Approach and Avoidance. It's way past midnight. We're incredibly hungry, but too exhausted to get up off the couch to pop a dessert into the microwave. So we sit there frozen pathetically in place, spending several minutes deciding whether to remain on the couch or exert the monumental effort needed to walk the 10 feet over to the kitchen. We're experiencing the often psychologically painful effects of conflicting drives.

Certain drives generate tendencies toward *approach,* that is, a predisposition toward certain stimuli, like food or objects of our sexual desire. In contrast, others generate tendencies toward *avoidance,* that is, a disposition away from certain stimuli, like rude people or frightening animals (Gray, 1982). As Kurt Lewin (1935) observed, approach and avoidance drives often conflict, as when we want to introduce ourselves to an attractive person across the room but are terrified of rejection. In other cases, two approach drives can conflict, as can two avoidance drives (see **Figure 11.14**). As a general rule, the avoidance gradient is steeper than the approach gradient (Bogartz, 1965) (see **Figure 11.15** on the next page). In less technical terms, this means that as we get closer to our goals, our tendencies to avoid increase more rapidly than do our tendencies to approach. This phenomenon helps to explain why we often agree to do things months in advance, only to regret them later. When we volunteer enthusiastically in June to organize our club's holiday party in December, the idea sounds like a lot of fun. But as the date of the party draws near, our sense of enjoyment is swamped by our sense of dread regarding all of the drudge work that lies ahead.

POSITIVE MOTIVATION

Valuable as drive reduction theories have been to psychology, they don't tell the whole story of motivation, because we often engage in behaviors even when our drives are satisfied. For example, drive reduction theories don't do a good job of explaining the creative drives of great writers, artists, and composers. Such theories would predict that once Maya Angelou, Pablo Picasso, or Wolfgang Amadeus Mozart completed a masterpiece, their desire to generate another one would decrease, because they would have quenched their creative thirsts. Yet the opposite often happens; creative success begets still more desire to create.

Incentive Theories. As a consequence, psychologists have come to recognize that drive reduction theories of motivation need to be supplemented by **incentive theories,** which propose that we're often motivated by positive goals, like the pleasure of creating a great painting or the glory of finishing first in a track meet. Many of these theories, in turn, distinguish *intrinsic motivation,* in which people are motivated by internal goals, from *extrinsic motivation,* in which people are motivated by external goals. If we're intrinsically motivated to do well in a psychology class, we're driven primarily by our desire to master the material; if we're extrinsically motivated to do well in this class, we're driven primarily by our desire to get a good grade.

Undermining of Intrinsic Motivation. As we learned in Chapter 6, behaviorists define reinforcement as any outcome that makes the behavior that preceded it more likely. Yet there's evidence that certain reinforcements may *undermine* intrinsic motivation, rendering us less likely to perform behaviors we once enjoyed (Deci, 1971; Deci, Koestner, & Ryan, 1999). In a classic study, Mark Lepper and his colleagues (Lepper, Greene, & Nisbett, 1973) identified preschool children who were especially interested in drawing and randomly assigned them to three conditions: (1) a condition in which children agreed to draw pictures to receive an award (a fancy certificate with a gold seal and red ribbon); (2) a condition in which children drew pictures without knowing they'd receive an award, which they later all received; or (3) a condition in which no children received an award. Two weeks later, the experimenters again gave children the chance to draw pictures and used covert observation (see Chapter 2) to watch them behind a one-way mirror. Interestingly, children in the first condition—who engaged in the activity to achieve a reward—showed significantly less interest in drawing than did children in the other two conditions. Many psychologists and some popular writers have interpreted these findings as implying that when we see ourselves performing a behavior to obtain an external goal, we conclude that we weren't all that interested in that behavior in the first place (Kohn, 1993). "I was only doing it to get the reward," we tell ourselves, "so I guess I wasn't really interested in it for its own sake." As a result, our intrinsic motivation for that behavior decreases.

Not all psychologists accept this interpretation (Carton, 1996; Eisenberger & Cameron, 1996). For one thing, some researchers haven't replicated the undermining effect (Cameron & Pierce, 1994). Still others have offered rival explanations for these findings. One is a *contrast effect:* Once we receive reinforcement for performing a behavior, we anticipate that reinforcement again. If the reinforcement is suddenly withdrawn, we're less likely to perform the behavior. So we're not that different from a rat that's reinforced with a chunk of cheese for completing a maze. When the rat gets to the end of the maze and unexpectedly finds no cheese (the origin of the expression, "Rats!" perhaps?), he's less likely to run the maze quickly the next time (Crespi, 1942; Fagen & Shoemaker, 1984).

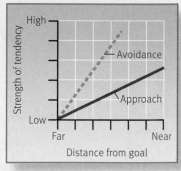

Figure 11.15 Approach and Avoidance over Time. As we get closer to a goal, the avoidance gradient becomes steeper than the approach gradient. Projects that seem desirable a few weeks in the future become more undesirable as the deadline approaches. (*Source:* Dr. Ronald Mayer, www.sfsu.edu)

homeostasis
equilibrium

Yerkes-Dodson law
inverted U-shaped relation between arousal on the one hand, and affect and performance on the other

incentive theories
theories proposing that we're often motivated by positive goals

Replicability

Ruling Out Rival Hypotheses

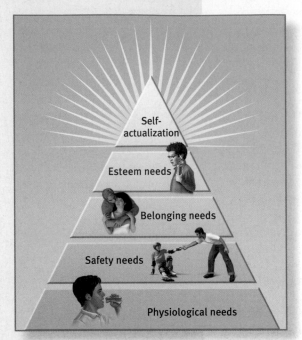

Figure 11.16 Maslow's Hierarchy of Needs. According to Abraham Maslow, our needs are arranged in a hierarchy or pyramid, with the most "basic" needs at the bottom. If our basic needs aren't satisfied, Maslow claimed, we can't progress up the hierarchy. Does research support this assertion?

Falsifiability

hierarchy of needs
model, developed by Abraham Maslow, proposing that we must satisfy physiological needs and needs for safety and security before progressing to more complex needs

Correlation vs. Causation

OUR NEEDS: PHYSICAL AND PSYCHOLOGICAL URGES

We humans have a few basic biological needs; food, drink, and shelter are high on our shopping lists. Yet as Henry Murray (1938) noted, we have a wide variety of other needs. Murray distinguished *primary* from *secondary* needs, with primary needs reflecting biological necessities, like hunger and thirst, and secondary needs reflecting psychological desires. Murray identified more than twenty secondary needs; one such need, the *need for achievement*, has received particular attention from psychologists (McClelland, Atkinson, Clark, & Lowell, 1958). As we'll learn in Chapter 14, researchers have found measures of this need to be useful in predicting individuals' academic performance (Spangler, 1992). David McClelland (1961) even demonstrated that across countries, citizens' need for achievement levels forecast these countries' future economic growth, although this finding hasn't been entirely consistent (Mazur & Rosa, 1977).

Abraham Maslow (1954, 1971) argued that in the grand scheme of life, some needs inevitably take priority over others. According to Maslow's **hierarchy of needs,** we must satisfy physiological needs and needs for safety and security before we can progress to more complex needs. These complex needs include desires for belongingness and love, self-esteem, and finally self-actualization, the drive to realize our full psychological potential (see Chapter 14). As we progress up Maslow's hierarchy, we move away from needs produced by drives, that is, by biological or psychological deficiencies, and toward needs produced by incentives, that is, by positive goals. Maslow's hierarchy reminds us of an often overlooked point: When people are starving or malnourished, they often aren't concerned about abstract principles of psychological growth, such as achieving self-knowledge or obtaining democratic freedoms. First things must come first (see **Figure 11.16**).

Although Maslow's hierarchy is a helpful starting point, we shouldn't take it literally. Some needs are more crucial than others, but there's evidence that people who haven't achieved lower levels of his hierarchy can sometimes attain higher levels (Rowan, 1999; Soper, Milford, & Rosenthal, 1995). The numerous cases of starving artists, who continue to paint masterworks despite being hungry and poor, appear to falsify Maslow's claim of an invariant hierarchy of needs (Zautra, 2003).

HUNGER, EATING, AND EATING DISORDERS

If we're lucky, we don't experience the pangs of hunger very often or for very long, and can refuel with a Big Mac, a veggie sandwich, or whatever satisfies our cravings. But for billions of less privileged people, hunger is a fact of everyday life. As unpleasant as feelings of hunger can be, our very survival depends on it. When we're hungry and thirsty, we're motivated to acquire food and drink, which provide us with nutrients and energy needed to be active and alert, and maintain a properly functioning immune system (Mattes, Hollis, Hayes, & Stunkard, 2005).

Hunger and Eating: Regulatory Processes. If food is available, we eat when we're hungry. And when we feel full (satiated), we stop eating. Simple, right? Not when we consider that inside our bodies, a complex series of events governing hunger and eating unfolds. One early idea, suggested by Alfred Washburn and Walter Cannon (1912), is that stomach contractions, which occur when our stomach is empty, cause hunger. To test this hypothesis, Washburn, Cannon's graduate student, swallowed a balloon (we don't recommend trying this at home) that was inflated inside his stomach by means of a tube. The intrepid student's reports of hunger were associated with muscle contractions, measured by pressure on the balloon. However, as we've learned, we can't presume causation from a correlational finding. Scientists have since observed that people still report hunger pangs when their stomachs are surgically removed, and when surgeons cut the nerve to the stomach responsible for stomach contractions (Bray, 1985). These findings falsify the stomach contraction hypothesis (see **Figure 11.17**).

Children often point to their stomachs when they're hungry, but the brain is far more influential than the stomach as a command and control center for food cravings. Scientists began to get an inkling of this truth more than 50 years ago, when they learned that two areas of the hypothalamus play different roles in eating. Consider two rats in the same cage that couldn't look more different. Rat 1 is very large; some might say humongous. Rat 2 is scrawny to the point of requiring force-feeding to survive. Scientists supersized the first rat by electrically stimulating the lateral (side) parts of its hypothalamus (Delgado & Anand, 1952). The second rat became slimmer than a supermodel rodent when researchers destroyed its lateral hypothalamus by making a small lesion in it (Anand & Brobeck, 1951; Hetherington & Ranson, 1940; Teitelbaum & Epstein, 1962). Based on these findings, scientists concluded that the lateral hypothalamus plays a key role in initiating eating (see photo at right).

Something remarkable happens when researchers stimulate the *ventromedial* or lower middle part of rats' hypothalamus: The furry creatures eat very little or stop eating entirely (Olds, 1959). When researchers lesion the same part of the brain, the rats become so hefty they look like they're about to burst (Anand & Brobeck, 1951; Hetherington & Ranson, 1940; Teitelbaum & Epstein, 1962). The ventromedial hypothalamus seems to let rats know when to stop eating.

Many psychology books have proclaimed that the lateral hypothalamus is a "feeding center" and the ventromedial hypothalamus a "satiety center," but this conclusion is too simple. In reality, a complex sequence of events mediated by different brain areas and body regions choreographs eating (Grill & Kaplan, 2002). A distended or full stomach activates neurons in the hypothalamus, and in response we resist our impulses to reach for that second cookie (Anand & Pillai, 1967; Jordan, 1969; Smith, 1996; Stunkard, 1975). A hormone produced in the stomach called *ghrelin* communicates with the hypothalamus to increase hunger, whereas another hormone, called cholecystokinin (CCK), counteracts the effects of ghrelin and decreases hunger (Badman & Flier, 2005).

Glucose (blood sugar) provides our cells with high-octane energy to score a touchdown or flee from a hungry lion. Our bodies produce glucose from proteins, fats, and carbohydrates in the foods we eat. The hypothalamus is in tune with changing levels of glucose, signaled by receptors for glucose in the liver and hypothalamus (Schwartz, Woods, Porte, Seeley, & Baskin, 2000; Woods, Seeley, Porte, & Schwartz, 1998). According to **glucostatic theory** (Campfield, Smith, Rosenbaum, & Hirsch, 1996; van Litalie, 1990), when our blood glucose levels drop, typically after we haven't eaten for some time, hunger creates a drive to eat to restore the proper level of glucose. In this way, we achieve homeostasis, the balance of energy we take in and expend. People gain weight when there's an imbalance, such that more energy is taken into the body than expended by way of exercise or the body's ability to "burn" excess calories through metabolic processes.

When our glucose levels drop substantially, we generally feel hungry (Levin, Dunn-Meynell, & Routh, 1999). But levels of blood glucose can be quite variable and don't always mirror the amount or types of food we eat. In fact, our self-reported hunger and desire for a meal are better predictors of our energy intake in our meals over a 3-day period than are our glucose levels (Pittas, Hariharan, Stark, Hajduk, Greenberg, & Roberts, 2005). Far more than glucose is involved in regulating eating.

Weight Gain and Obesity: Biological and Psychological Influences. When we go "people watching" in the mall, we can't help but notice that adults and children come in more shapes and sizes than varieties of Campbell's soup. If that mall or supermarket is in the United States, we'll also observe that about two-thirds of the passersby are overweight or obese. We'll explore obesity in Chapter 12, but here we'll examine the physiology and psychology of eating and overeating.

The supersized rat on the left experienced damage to its ventromedial hypothalamus, resulting in massive overeating.

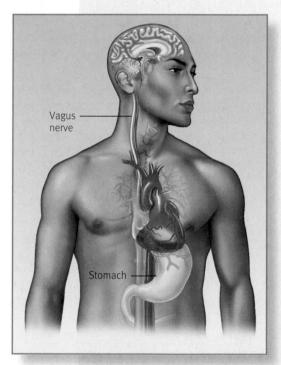

Vagus nerve

Stomach

Figure 11.17 Do Stomach Contractions Cause the Sensation of Hunger? The vagus nerve, responsible for stomach contractions, travels from the brain to the stomach. Yet even when this nerve is cut, people still can experience hunger.

glucostatic theory
theory that when our blood glucose levels drop, hunger creates a drive to eat to restore the proper level of glucose

Chemical Messengers and Eating. When we eat a candy bar, some of the glucose from the treat may get converted into fat, which stores energy for the long term. The more stored energy in fat cells, the more they produce a hormone called **leptin**. Leptin signals the hypothalamus and brain stem to reduce appetite and increase the amount of energy used (Grill et al., 2002). Researchers discovered a clue to the causes of obesity when they found that mice that lacked the gene for leptin become obese at an early age (Hamman & Matthaei, 1996). Interestingly, obese people seem resistant to the effects of leptin.

Obese individuals also find food difficult to resist because they think about food a lot, and find the tasty qualities of food especially rewarding. The mere sight, taste, smell, and thought of plentiful food in our environment can trigger the release of neurotransmitters, including serotonin, that activate the brain's pleasure circuits (Ciarella, Ciarella, Graziani, & Mirante, 1991; Lowe & Levine, 2005). Obese people also may overeat to provide comfort or distraction to counter negative emotions (Hoppa & Hallstrom, 1981; Stice, Presnell, Shaw, & Rhode, 2005).

The Set Point. Another reason why the battle of the bulge isn't easy to win is that each of us may have a genetically programmed **set point,** a value—much like that on our car's fuel gauges—that establishes a range of body fat and muscle mass we tend to maintain (Mrosky & Powley, 1977; Nisbett, 1972). When we eat too little and drop below our set point, regulatory mechanisms kick in to increase our appetite or decrease our metabolism. In this way, our bodies defend against weight loss. When we eat too much, the opposite occurs. Without our ever realizing it, our bodies tune down our appetite and increase our metabolism.

According to the set point hypothesis, an obese person has a biological predisposition toward greater weight than does a thin person. No one knows for sure what "sets" the set point, but obese individuals may be born with more fat cells, with lower metabolic rates at which their bodies burn calories, or with less sensitivity to leptin than thin people. Some people seem to bulk up like Sumo wrestlers no matter how little they eat, whereas others remain thin as a reed no matter how much they eat. Still, we're not fated to remain at a fixed weight; there's a range of weights we "settle into." We can modify our set points, within limits, by staying active and eating a healthy diet.

The Role of Genes in Eating. Genes probably play a major role in our set points. In about 6 percent of cases of severe obesity, a mutation in a major *melanocortin-4 receptor gene* is responsible (Todorovic & Haskell-Leuvano, in press). People born with this mutation never seem to feel full, regardless of whether they've eaten a strawberry or half a strawberry pie. In effect, their brains don't let them know when to stop eating. Scientists have identified other genes, including the leptin gene, but a combination of many genes associated with appetite, amount of fat stored in the body, and metabolism probably work together to increase the likelihood of obesity.

Twin studies point to a genetic predisposition toward obesity. Researchers have found correlations for fat mass in the range of .7–.9 for identical twins, and a range of .35–.45 for fraternal twins (Stunkard, Froch, & Hrubeck, 1986). Because twins are raised in the same family and often share the same general diet and lifestyle, it's especially important for researchers to study identical twins raised in different families. When they've done so, they've found correlations of .4–.7 for body mass (Maes, Neale, & Eaves, 1997). Adoption studies lend further support for the role of genes. People's body mass is correlated with their biological, but not adoptive, parents' body mass (Allison et al., 1996).

Sensitivity to Cues and Expectations. Genes don't completely determine whether a person will be shaped more like a pear than a stick. External cues and expectations also play a prominent role in food consumption.

Stanley Schachter proposed the **internal–external theory,** which holds that obese people are motivated to eat more by such external cues as the taste, smell, and appearance of

People differ in their genetic tendency toward obesity, so differences in food consumption and weight may be apparent at an early age. A mutation in the melanocortin-4 receptor gene may play a role in some early cases of obesity.

leptin
hormone that signals the hypothalamus and brain stem to reduce appetite and increase the amount of energy used

set point
value that establishes a range of body and muscle mass we tend to maintain

internal–external theory
theory holding that obese people are motivated to eat more by external cues than internal cues

Ruling Out Rival Hypotheses

food than by such internal cues as a growling stomach or feelings of fullness (Canetti, Bachar, & Berry 2002; Nisbett, 1968; Schachter, 1968). According to this theory, individuals are at risk for obesity when they continue to eat even after being full, and base their food choices on the appealing qualities of food, time of day, or social circumstances. In the laboratory, obese people are more likely than non-obese people to gorge themselves after researchers manipulate the clocks in the room to fool participants into thinking it's dinner time (Schachter & Gross, 1968). However, another possibility, which research favors, is that the oversensitivity to external cues is a consequence rather than a cause of eating patterns (Nisbett, 1972).

Ruling Out Rival Hypotheses

Unrealistic Expectations and Overeating. According to Richard Nisbett, obese people try to keep their weight below their set point. Consequently, they're hungry much of the time, which increases the appeal of tasty, high-calorie foods and makes dieting difficult (Nisbett, 1972).

Ironically, dieters who establish rigid food rules set themselves up to overeat. If they indulge in an extra helping of ice cream, they may think they've "blown it" and then eat in an unrestrained manner (Herman & Mack, 1975; Herman & Polivy, 1975, 1980). In our food-rich environments, with constant temptations to enjoy the simple pleasures of food, weight gain is inevitable for many of us. Unfortunately, most weight-loss programs aren't effective in helping people shed weight permanently (Mann et al., 2007; Sarwer & Wadden, 1999). Consistent effort is important—virtually all of us can lose weight for a few months, but the trick is to keep the pounds off. To slim down over the long haul, we must eat fewer high-calorie foods, control the size of our portions, and get plenty of exercise. As many of us have found, this is all easier said than done.

Eating Disorders: Bulimia and Anorexia. People who try to lose a lot of weight over a short period of time are especially prone to binge eating (Lowe, Gleaves, Murphy-Eberenz, 1998). Individuals with the eating disorder of *bulimia nervosa,* or bulimia, for short, engage in recurrent binge eating (twice a week or more for 3 months), followed by efforts to minimize weight gain (see Chapter 15). During a binge, some people gorge themselves with food equaling more than 10,000 calories in a 2-hour period and, across a number of studies, average about 3,500 calories per binge. That amounts to about six Big Macs without cheese (Walsh, 1993; Walsh, Hadigan, Kissileff, & LaChaussee, 1992).

Bulimia literally means "ox hunger." Bingeing can be frightening because it's often accompanied by the feeling that it's impossible to stop eating. After a binge, most bulimics feel guilt and anxiety over the loss of control and the prospect of gaining weight. In all likelihood, bulimics' excessive concerns about appearance and weight are in part by-products of societal pressures to be thin (see Chapter 12). Bulimics often see themselves as fat when they're of normal weight. Frequently, their answer to this problem is to *purge,* which typically takes the form of self-induced vomiting, but some abuse laxatives or diet pills or exercise excessively (Williamson et al., 2002).

Bingeing and purging set up a vicious cycle. Purging is rewarding because it relieves anxious feelings after overeating and sidesteps weight gain. But it sets the stage for bouts of overeating. For example, vomiting allows bulimics to "undo" the binge, and to rationalize later bouts of overeating ("I can always get rid of the ice cream"). After bingeing, bulimics may resolve to go on a strict diet. Yet severe dieting leads to hunger and increases preoccupation with food and the temptation to binge. In fact, such dieting, along with vomiting and laxative abuse, boosts the likelihood that people will gain weight (Stice, Cameron, Killen, Hayward, & Taylor, 1999; Stice et al., 2005). As eating spirals out of control, bulimics' self-esteem plummets, increasing their concerns about dieting and the likelihood of a binge. This completes the self-destructive circle (Fairburn, Cooper, & Sharfan, 2003; Lynn & Kirsch, 2006). This binge-purge cycle can be physically hazardous, resulting in heart problems (which can be fatal), tears to the esophagus, and wearing away of tooth enamel (Mehl, 2003).

Bulimia is the most common eating disorder, afflicting 1 to 3 percent of the population (Craighead, 2002). About 95 percent of people with this diagnosis are women. An

The sight of tasty desserts, displayed in an attractive manner, can provide strong "external" cues for eating, even when we aren't particularly hungry. Upscale restaurants have discovered this principle, which is why they bring dessert trays over to our table after our main meal.

fictoid

Myth: People with anorexia (which means "without hunger" in Greek) aren't hungry.

Reality: Anorexics experience hunger, sometimes quite intensely, but rigidly deny themselves food. They feel anxious and guilty when they give in to the urge to eat, and may exercise excessively or abuse laxatives on such occasions to avoid weight gain.

Uncontrolled binge eating, sometimes involving consuming more food in one sitting than people consume in an average day, is a cardinal symptom of bulimia.

Anorexia isn't limited to women, although it's comparatively rare among men. It's associated with body image distortion, which contributes to a fear of being fat despite being severely underweight.

additional 8 percent to 16 percent of young women, including many in college, fall short of a diagnosis of bulimia, but show signs of disordered eating, such as repeated bingeing. Many bulimic women are perfectionists and have an especially strong need for approval from others (Friedman & Wishman, 1998; Joiner, Heatherton, Rudd, & Schmidt, 1997).

Anorexia nervosa, or anorexia, is less common than bulimia, with rates ranging from 0.5 percent to 1 percent of the population (Craighead, 2002). But like bulimia, anorexia usually begins in adolescence, is much more common in girls than boys, and is fueled by sociocultural pressures to be thin (see also Chapter 15). Whereas bulimics tend to be in the normal weight range, anorexics become emaciated in their relentless pursuit of thinness (Golden & Sacker, 1984). Along with a "fear of fatness," anorexics—like bulimics— have a distorted perception of their body size. Even those with bones showing through their skin may describe themselves as fat. Psychologists diagnose anorexia when individuals display a refusal to maintain body weight at or above a minimally normal weight for age and height (specifically, their body weight is less than 85 percent of that expected). Anorexics often lose between 25 percent and 50 percent of their body weight.

Concerns about body shape can become so all-consuming that anorexics stubbornly deny the seriousness of their condition and resist pressure from family and friends to gain weight. Starvation can actually produce symptoms of anorexia. In the "starvation study," thirty-six healthy young men volunteered to severely restrict their food intake for half a year as an alternative to serving in the military (Keys, Brozek, Henschel, Mickelsen, & Taylor, 1950). On average, they lost about 25 percent of their weight. Their preoccupation with food increased dramatically, and some spent a great deal of time planning how, when, and where to eat their daily food portion. Whereas some ate very slowly, others hoarded food or gulped it down as if it were their final meal. Some men broke the eating rules and binged, followed by intense guilt or self-induced vomiting. It's clear that once people severely reduce their food intake, starvation itself can lead to symptoms of anorexia and bulimia (Fairburn et al., 2003; Garner, 1997; Pirke & Ploog, 1987).

With continued low weight, a loss of menstrual periods, hair loss, heart problems, life-threatening electrolyte imbalances, and fragile bones may result (Gottdiener, Gross, Henry, Borer, & Ebert, 1978; Katzmann, 2005). A patient treated by the second author of your text broke her femur (the long bone in the thigh) during an ordinary game of tennis. Some researchers put the mortality rate for anorexia at 5 percent to 10 percent, making it one of the most life-threatening of all psychiatric conditions (Birmingham, Su, Hylnsky, Goldner, & Gao, 2005; Sullivan, 1995).

SEXUAL MOTIVATION

Sexual desire—called *libido*—is a wish or craving for sexual activity and sexual pleasure (Regan & Berscheid, 1999). Sexual desire is deeply rooted in our genes and biology, but as we'll see, it's also influenced by social and cultural factors.

Sexual Desire and Its Determinants. The sex hormone testosterone can enhance sexual interest (see Chapter 3), but other biological influences also are at play. A team of researchers (Houle, Dhingra, Remble, Rokicki, & Penzien, 2006) suggested that the neurotransmitter serotonin is the key to explaining an intriguing link between migraine headaches and increased libido. Based on findings that low sexual desire is associated with high levels of serotonin, and that migraine headaches are associated with low levels of serotonin, the investigators hypothesized that people with migraines would report high levels of sexual desire. The researchers compared participants with migraine headaches with participants matched for age and gender who suffered from tension headaches, which are unrelated to serotonin levels. Sufferers of migraine headaches reported 20% higher levels of sexual desire than did sufferers of tension headaches.

Researchers recently discovered that variations in a gene that produces DRD4, a protein related to dopamine transmission, are correlated with students' reports of sexual desire and arousal (Zion et al., 2006). The scientists estimated that approximately 20 percent of the population possesses the mutation for increased sexual desire, whereas another 70 percent possesses a variant of the gene that depresses sexual desire. These findings dovetail with research showing that dopamine plays a key role in reward (see Chapter 3).

Many people believe that men have a stronger desire for sex than women. This stereotype may hold a kernel of truth. Compared with women, men desire sex more frequently and experience more sexual arousal (Hiller, 2005; Klusman, 2002; Knoth, Boyd, & Singer, 1988), have a greater number and variety of sexual fantasies (Laumann, Gagnon, Michael, & Michaels, 1994; Leitenberg & Henning, 1995), masturbate more frequently (Oliver & Hyde, 1993), want to have more sexual partners (Buss & Schmidt, 1993), and desire sex earlier in a relationship (Sprecher, Barbee, & Schwartz, 1995). Of course, these findings don't necessarily apply to any individual man or woman, and there's tremendous variability in sexual interest among men and women—indeed, at least as much variability as there is between men and women.

Socialization provides another explanation for why men and women appear to differ in sexual desire. Women are socialized to be less assertive and aggressive in many spheres of life, including expressing their sexual desires. So perhaps women and men actually experience comparable sexual drives, but women don't express their desires as much. Although the evidence tilts toward the conclusion that men have an inherently stronger sex drive than women, the evidence isn't definitive.

Ruling Out Rival Hypotheses

The Physiology of the Human Sexual Response. In 1954, the husband and wife team of William Masters and Virginia Johnson launched their pioneering investigations of sexual desire and the human sexual response. Their observations included sexual behaviors under virtually every imaginable condition, and some virtually unimaginable. Masters and Johnson's laboratory wasn't exactly a prescription for romantic intimacy: in addition to a bed, it contained monitoring equipment to measure physiological changes, cameras, and a specially constructed probe that contained a camera to record changes in the vagina during intercourse. Yet most people who volunteered for their studies accommodated to the laboratory with surprising ease.

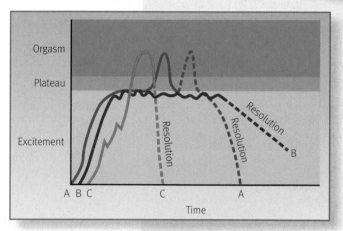

Masters and Johnson (1966) reported that the basic sexual arousal cycle was the same for men and women. Based on their research and other observations (Kaplan, 1977), scientists define the sexual response cycle in terms of four phases: (1) desire, (2) excitement, (3) orgasm, and (4) resolution (see **Figure 11.18**).

The **desire phase** is initiated by whatever prompts sexual interest. People often experience little sexual desire when they're tired, distracted, stressed out, in pain, or ill. Lack of attraction to a partner, depression, anxiety, and resentment can also inhibit sexual desire. In the **excitement phase,** people experience sexual pleasure and start to notice physiological changes, such as penile erection in men and vaginal swelling and lubrication in women. During the **orgasm (climax) phase,** sexual pleasure and physical changes peak, there are involuntary rhythmic contractions in the muscles of the genitals in men and women, and men ejaculate. Brain scans reveal that when individuals achieve orgasm, the areas that control fear in the amygdala become less active than when people aren't sexually aroused (Georgiatis et al., 2006). This finding may explain why in the **resolution phase,** after orgasm, people report relaxation and a sense of well-being as the body returns to its unstimulated state (Belliveau & Richter, 1970).

Masters and Johnson's groundbreaking efforts didn't capture a crucial fact: people's sexuality is deeply embedded in their relationships and feelings for one another. People experience more frequent and consistent orgasms when they love their partner and feel

Figure 11.18 Variations in Female Sexual Response Cycle. This figure depicts the sexual arousal cycle for four different women, each represented by a different color. Three of the four women experienced at least one orgasm. The woman whose response is traced by the red line experienced excitement but no orgasm. (*Source:* Rathus, Nevid, & Fichner-Rathus, 2008)

desire phase
phase in human sexual response triggered by whatever prompts sexual interest

excitement phase
phase in human sexual response in which people experience sexual pleasure and notice physiological changes associated with it

orgasm (climax) phase
phase in human sexual response marked by involuntary rhythmic contractions in the muscles of genitals in both men and women

resolution phase
phase in human sexual response following orgasm, in which people report relaxation and a sense of well-being

Correlation vs. Causation

Ruling Out Rival Hypotheses

loved in return (Birnbaum, Glaubman, & Mikulincer. 2001) and feel satisfied in their relationship (Young, Denny, Young, & Luquis, 2000). But we can question the causal direction between relationship quality and the frequency and consistency of orgasms. Frequent orgasms may not merely reflect healthy relationships but contribute to them too.

Frequency of Sexual Activities and Aging. Early in their marriage, couples have sex on average about twice a week (Laumman et al., 1994). As people age, the frequency of their sexual activities decreases but their sexual satisfaction doesn't. Perhaps people expect their sexual activity to decrease as they age, so they're not disappointed by this change.

Contrary to the myth that sexual activities virtually cease for senior citizens, many people are sexually active well into their seventies and eighties, especially when they're healthy, are in happy marriages, and perceive that their partners desire a sexual relationship (Call, Sprecher, & Schwartz, 1995). Three-fourths of married men and 56 percent of married women are sexually active over age 60, and 30 percent of women 80 to 102 (!) years old and 63 percent of men in that age range are sexually active (Meston, 1999). Women experience complex and sometimes striking changes in hormones during menopause, although there's another explanation for the difference between older men's and women's sexual activities. By the age of 80, women have less opportunity to find male partners; for every 100 women, there are only 39 men (Meston, 1999).

There are at least three problems with much of the research on sex and aging. First, many surveys haven't disentangled age from the length of time people are in relationships (Burgess, 2004). The frequency of sexual activity tends to decrease the longer people are in a relationship. Second, scientists haven't examined the effects of poor health on sexual activity in the elderly. Third, many of the studies on seniors aren't based on random samples, so it's not clear how representative they are of the elderly population (Hayes & Dennerstein, 2005).

Sexuality and Culture. The way people express sexual desires is shaped by social norms and culture. Clellan Ford and Frank Beach's (1951) fascinating observations reveal how cultural norms influence people's ideas of what's sexually appropriate or inappropriate. When members of the Tsonga tribe in Africa first saw Europeans kissing, they laughed and remarked, "Look at them—they eat each other's saliva and dirt" (Ford & Beach, 1951). Admittedly, they have a point. Members of the Apinaly society in Brazil don't kiss, but women of the tribe may bite off their lovers' eyebrows and noisily spit them to one side. Women of the island Turk are even less kind, at least by Western standards: they customarily poke a finger into the man's ear when they're sexually excited.

David Buss (1989) found that residents of non-Western societies, including India, Iran, and China, place a much greater value on chastity in a potential partner than do individuals in Western European countries, including Sweden, the Netherlands, and France. Americans are divided on whether they generally approve (59%) or disapprove (41%) of premarital sex (Widmer, Treas, & Newcomb, 1998). This latter percentage stands at odds with the prevalence of premarital sex in the United States, with men reporting rates of 85 percent and women reporting rates of 80 percent (Laumann et al., 1994).

Sexual Orientation: Science and Politics. Same-sex romantic relationships develop in virtually all cultures and have done so since the dawn of recorded history. Moreover, biologists have documented homosexual behaviors in some 450 species (Bagernihl, 1999). Since pioneering sex researcher Alfred Kinsey reported in the 1940s and 1950s (in what became known as the "Kinsey Report") that homosexuality was far more widespread than believed, scientists have pondered the question of what percentage of people prefer homosexual activities. Perhaps the Kinsey Report's most surprising finding was that 10 percent of the sample was almost exclusively gay for at least 3 years between the ages of 16 and 55 (Kinsey, Pomeroy, & Martin, 1948; Kinsey, Pomeroy, Martin, & Gebhard, 1953). About 4 percent of males reported exclusive homosexuality. More recent research with larger and more representative samples suggests that about 2.8 percent of males and 1.4 percent of females 18 or older identify themselves as gay, lesbian, or bisexual (Laumann et al., 1994; National Opinion Research Center, 2003). Nevertheless, even the

Sales for medications like Viagra and Cialis, used to treat men with difficulties achieving and maintaining an erection (erectile dysfunction), have far exceeded a billion dollars since they were introduced in the late 1990s. These medications have been especially popular with men older than 60 with erectile dysfunction.

The 2004 film Kinsey, in which actor Liam Neeson (left) played Alfred Kinsey, describes the challenges of conducting studies of more than 10,000 men and women in the 1940s and 1950s, when sex research was highly controversial. Here Neeson portrays Kinsey interviewing a woman about her sexual history, a research practice considered scandalous at the time.

best estimates are suspect in representing the general population, because researchers often conduct surveys in prisons, college dorms, military barracks, or under the sponsorship of gay organizations.

> **APPLY YOUR THINKING**
> Kinsey and some other sex researchers relied on people who volunteered to participate in research on human sexuality. What problems could arise when interpreting studies that use this subject recruitment strategy?

Kinsey discovered that people he classified as gay reported widely varying amounts of homosexual experience. Some were exclusively gay, whereas others experienced only a single homosexual contact in early adolescence. People also differ in how they think and feel about their homosexuality. Many people who engage in occasional homosexual activities don't view themselves as gay. Some of the men Kinsey studied were married and identified themselves as heterosexual, even though they reported several homosexual experiences.

Since Kinsey's groundbreaking research, scientists have acquired a better understanding of gay lifestyles and challenged common misconceptions about homosexuality. Contrary to the stereotype that one person in a gay relationship adopts a masculine role, whereas the other adopts a feminine role, less than a fourth of gay men and women fit neatly into these categories (Jay & Young, 1979; Lever, 1995). A good deal of media coverage also implies that gay individuals recruit others to a gay lifestyle, or are especially likely to sexually abuse children and adolescents. Yet scientific evidence supports neither view (Freund, Watson, & Rienzo, 1989; Jenny, Roesler, & Poyer, 1994). Another widespread myth is that gay individuals are unfit to be parents. In fact, gay and heterosexual adults don't differ in their approach to parenting (Bos, van Balen, & van den Boom, 2004, 2007; Patterson, 1992) and are equally likely to provide supportive environments for their children (Patterson & Chan, 1996; Weston, 1991).

Research indicates that gay people are as likely as heterosexual people to provide supportive environments for children.

Can Sexual Orientation Be Changed? Masters and Johnson (1979; Schwartz & Masters, 1984), among others, examined whether it's possible to treat gay men and women who are dissatisfied with their sexual orientation, but their work was methodologically problematic, in part because most of their participants were bisexual rather than homosexual. More recently, Robert Spitzer (2003) evaluated 200 cases of people who underwent sexual reorientation therapy and reported many instances in which people changed from a predominantly homosexual to heterosexual orientation for a 5-year period or longer. Nevertheless, only 11 percent of the men and 37 percent of the women reported a complete change in orientation. Moreover, it's not clear whether these apparently successful individuals were exclusively homosexual before therapy, and whether their sexual orientation changed much beyond their self-reports. Spitzer's sample was also far from a random sample of gay individuals: most were college graduates, 76 percent of the men and 47 percent of the women were married, and less than half of the sample was openly gay at some point prior to the study. Still, Spitzer's research suggests that some degree of sexual reorientation may be possible in certain motivated individuals and that further research is justified.

Critics of sexual reorientation therapies contend that such treatments promote the misconception that homosexuality is a disease that requires a cure (Davison, 1976; Haldeman, 1994). Although gay men and women report relatively high rates of anxiety and depression (Biernbaum & Ruscio, 2005; Ferguson, Horwood, & Beautrais, 1999; Herrell et al., 1999), this fact doesn't indicate that homosexuality itself is a disease, let alone that it requires treatment. Moreover, the higher rates of psychological problems in gay populations holds true only in Caucasians, not Blacks or Latinos (Meyer, Dietrich, & Schwartz, 2007). In many or most cases, gay individuals' psychological problems may reflect their reaction to social oppression and intolerance of their lifestyles rather than preexisting mental disturbance. Accordingly, gay individuals who participate in reorientation therapy and don't achieve the changes they seek may become even more dissatisfied.

Ruling Out Rival Hypotheses

Canadian singers and songwriter twins, Tegan and Sarah Quin, who are openly gay, don't want their music to be defined by their sexual orientation.

Nevertheless, effective programs may one day help many currently distressed people accept and live with their homosexuality.

Genetic and Environmental Influences on Sexual Orientation. Bearing in mind the caveat that heritability doesn't imply that a characteristic can't be changed (Chapter 3), most scientists are skeptical about the ability of gay individuals to change their sexual orientation because there are indications of inborn differences between homosexual and heterosexual individuals. Because many gay men and women report they've felt different from others for as long as they can remember, it's plausible that biological differences are sometimes present even before birth.

Sexual Orientation: Clues from Twin Studies. Indeed, twin studies offer support for a role of genetic influences on homosexuality. Michael Bailey and Richard Pillard (1991) found a concordance rate of 52 percent in identical twins, in contrast with a concordance rate of 22 percent in fraternal twins (*concordance* refers to the proportion of co-twins who exhibit a characteristic, in this case, homosexuality, when the other twin also exhibits this characteristic). Bailey and his colleagues (Bailey, Pillard, Neale, & Agyei, 1993) found roughly similar concordance rates for lesbians (48% in identical twins, 16% in fraternal twins). The fact that a substantial percentage of identical twins aren't concordant tells us that environmental influences play an important role in homosexuality, although it doesn't tell us what these influences are.

Exotic Becomes Erotic. Nestled within Bailey's studies are clues related to the influence of genes and environment on sexual orientation. These studies revealed that men and women inherit a tendency toward childhood gender nonconformity. Gay men reported that they were often feminine boys, and lesbians reported they were often masculine girls.

Daryl Bem (1996) and others (Bailey & Zucker, 1995; Bell et al., 1981; Green, 1987; Zuger, 1988) suggested that childhood gender nonconformity plays a pivotal role in the development of homosexuality. Boys who lack aggressiveness and avoid rough-and-tumble play may prefer the company of girls, and thus be gender-nonconforming. According to Bem's theory, called *exotic becomes erotic,* nonconforming children feel different and estranged from their peers, and perceive their same-sex peers as unfamiliar and exotic (Bem, 2000). Children's sense of being different from their same-sex peers, and possibly being the subject of teasing or ridicule, arouses their autonomic nervous systems. Later in life, this arousal is transformed into attraction for same-sex peers. It's unlikely that Bem's theory accounts for all or even most gay individuals' sexual preferences, because only about half of gay men and lesbian women report having been feminine and masculine, respectively, in childhood (Bell et al., 1981). Still, one strength of Bem's theory is that it acknowledges the interplay of genetic and environmental influences, including play activities and peers' reactions.

Sex Hormones and Sexual Orientation. To trace the biological roots of homosexuality, researchers have turned to a different environment—the womb. When the fetus develops, sex hormones called androgens (see Chapter 3) determine whether the brain sets the child on a path toward more masculine than feminine characteristics, or vice versa. According to one theory, girls exposed to excessive testosterone in the womb develop masculinized brains, and boys exposed to too little testosterone develop feminized brains (Ellis & Amen, 1987). These hormonal influences affect temperament and set the stage for childhood gender nonconformity and a homosexual orientation in later life (Bem, 1996).

Several unusual lines of research—related to fingers and hands—provide support for prenatal influences on sexual orientation. On average, gay individuals have more fingerprint ridges on their left hand than do non-gay individuals (Hall & Kimura, 1994). And on average, lesbian women have a more masculine (lower) ratio of the length of the index finger to the ring finger (Haberman, Breedlove, Breedlove, Jordan, & Breedlove, 2000). Male homosexuals are nearly one and a half times more likely than heterosexuals to be left-handed, while lesbians are almost twice as likely as heterosexual women to be left-handed (Lalumière, Blanchard, & Zucker, 2000). Fingerprints, finger length, and handedness are all determined largely before birth. So there's some justification for pointing the finger (pun intended) at prenatal influences, even though we can't yet specify which influences, such as exposure to sex hormones, are most important.

Sexual Orientation: Brain Differences. In 1981, Simon LeVay created a stir among scientists and laypersons alike by reporting that a small cluster of neurons in the hypothalamus, no larger than a millimeter, was less than half the size in gay men compared with non-gay men. The study is open to several criticisms: LeVay studied gay men's brains at autopsy after they died, and the men died from AIDS-related complications. However, it's unlikely that the differences LeVay uncovered are due entirely to AIDS, because a number of the non-gay men also died of AIDS-related complications. The changes LeVay observed in the hypothalamus might also have been the result rather than the cause of homosexuality and differences in lifestyles between gay and non-gay men. Yet another limitation was that LeVay's sample of gay men with AIDS wasn't necessarily representative of all gay men, so replicating his results is especially important.

> Correlation vs. Causation

> Replicability

Some of the concerns about LeVay's research are tempered by a recent brain imaging study (Savic, Berglund, & Lindstrom, 2005) in which investigators exposed gay men and non-gay men and women to substances believed to be *pheromones* (see Chapter 4). When non-gay men smelled chemicals produced in women's urine, their hypothalamuses became active. When non-gay women smelled a substance derived from testosterone produced in men's sweat, the same thing happened. The most intriguing finding was that gay men's brains responded like women's when they smelled the substance derived from male sweat. These results are consistent with LeVay's finding that the hypothalamus is related to sexual orientation. Once again, though, we must be careful not to assume that the differences in brain activity cause homosexuality, because the pattern of brain activity could be a consequence of sexual orientation.

> Correlation vs. Causation

The findings we've reviewed suggest a crucial role for anatomy in sexual orientation. But anatomy isn't the whole story. To illustrate this point, we'll examine what happens to males born without penises, or with very small ones, who are raised as girls. Not infrequently, close to the time of their birth, these children receive operations to construct female genitals. Because these children are born with normal male hormones, scientists can tease apart the effects of male hormones from those of socializing a child into the male role. William Reiner and John Gearhard followed fourteen children for 5 to 16 years who underwent surgery at birth to create female genitals and were raised as girls (Reiner & Gearhart, 2004). Eight participants categorized themselves as males; most reported interests typical of males and were sexually attracted to females, not males. So in some cases, hormones are apparently more influential than socialization.

Scientists have yet to discover a dependable biological marker of sexual orientation. The great majority of left-handed individuals aren't gay, many non-lesbians have masculine (lower) index finger to ring finger ratios, and the size of the hypothalamus is comparable in most gay and non-gay individuals. Psychologists don't fully grasp how biological and environmental factors figure into the development of sexual orientation. In all likelihood, social and cultural influences that remain to be understood play a substantial role in shaping people's sexual orientation.

ASSESS YOUR KNOWLEDGE: FACT OR FICTION?
(1) According to the Yerkes-Dodson law, we generally do best when we're at our highest levels of arousal. (True/False)
(2) Obese individuals seem resistant to the effects of leptin. (True/False)
(3) Starvation can lead to symptoms of anorexia. (True/False)
(4) Few people are sexually active into their seventies and eighties. (True/False)
(5) Scientists have yet to discover a dependable biological marker of sexual orientation. (True/False)

Answers: (1) F (p. 470); (2) T (p. 474); (3) T (p. 476); (4) F (p. 478); (5) T (p. 481)

Attraction, Love, and Hate:
The Greatest Mysteries of Them All

The origins of love are remarkably old, even ancient. In 2007, archeologists unearthed these skeletons of a male and female couple in Italy (ironically, only 25 miles from Verona, the site of Shakespeare's legendary *Romeo and Juliet*), frozen in an embrace over 5,000 years ago.

In 1975, psychologists Ellen Berscheid and Elaine Hatfield received a dubious distinction (Benson, 2006). They became the first individuals to receive the Golden Fleece Award, an "honor" (actually, a dishonor) bestowed on them by then Wisconsin Senator William Proxmire. Proxmire had cooked up this award as a way of drawing public attention to projects that he regarded as colossal wastes of taxpayer money. Berscheid and Hatfield, it so happens, had won this award for their government-funded research on the psychological determinants of attraction and love (look for their names in the section you're about to read). Proxmire had found the very idea of studying these topics scientifically to be absurd:

"I'm strongly against this," he said, "not only because no one—not even the National Science Foundation—can argue that falling in love is a science; not only because I am sure that even if they spend 84 million or 84 billion they wouldn't get an answer that anyone would believe. I'm also against it because I don't *want* to know the answer!" (Hatfield & Walster, 1978, viii)

Of course, Proxmire was entitled not to know the answer. Yet more than three decades of research have since shown that Proxmire was woefully wrong in one critical respect: Psychologists *can* study love scientifically. None of this takes away from the profound mysteries of falling in love, but it suggests that love may not be quite as unfathomable as we—or the thousands of poets who've written about love across the centuries—might believe.

SOCIAL INFLUENCES ON INTERPERSONAL ATTRACTION

How can two people meet and become lovers in a world teeming with over six and a half billion people? Of course, attraction is only the initial stage in a relationship, but we need to feel a twinkle of chemistry with someone before deciding whether we're compatible enough with them in our core values and attitudes toward relationships before proceeding any further (Murstein, 1977). We might ascribe finding our true love to the fickle finger of destiny, but scientists suggest that friendship, dating, and mate choices aren't random. Three major principles guide attraction and relationship formation: proximity, similarity, and reciprocity (Berscheid & Reis, 1998; Fehr, 1996; Luo & Klohnen, 2005; Sprecher, 1998).

Psychological research shows that physical proximity, such as being seated next to each other in a classroom, can set the stage for later attraction.

proximity
physical nearness, a predictor of attraction

Proximity: When Near Becomes Dear. Common sense tells us that making someone's acquaintance is fundamental to friendships. In this case, common sense is right. A simple truth of human relationships is that our closest friends often live, study, work, or play closest to us. Many years after high school, the second author of your textbook married the woman who sat in front of him in numerous classes. Because their last names started with the letter L, the fact that the seats were arranged alphabetically ensured they'd have an opportunity to become acquainted. After their 30-year high school reunion brought them together again, they fell in love and married.

This example illustrates how physical nearness—or **proximity**—affords the opportunity for relationship formation. Like reunited schoolmates, people in classrooms with alphabetically assigned seats tend to have friends with last names that start with the same letter or a letter close in the alphabet (Segal, 1972). We're most likely to be attracted to and befriend people nearby, whom we see on a regular basis (Nahemow & Lawton, 1975). Leon Festinger, Stanley Schachter, and Kurt Back (1950) asked individuals living in apartments for married students at the Massachusetts Institute of Technology to name three of their closest friends. Of these friends, 65 percent lived in the same building, and 41 percent lived next door.

The effects of mere exposure we encountered earlier in the chapter may explain why seeing someone on a frequent basis, whether in the supermarket or workout room, heightens attraction. In a study conducted in a college classroom, four women with similar appearances posed as students and attended zero, five, ten, or fifteen sessions

(Moreland & Beach, 1992). At the end of the semester, the experimenters showed participants slides of the women and asked them to rate attendees in terms of attractiveness. Although the posers didn't interact with any of the students, participants judged the women who attended more classes as more attractive.

Similarity: Like Attracts Like. Proximity is also critical in establishing relationships because people who frequent the same places may share interests and have a lot to talk about if they meet. This point brings us to our next principle: **similarity,** the extent to which we have things in common with others. Consider this question: Would you rather be stranded on a desert island with someone very much like yourself or very different? Would you prefer a virtual clone of yourself or someone with vastly different tastes in music, books, and food? Perhaps if you like Mozart and your island mate prefers Metallica, you'd have a lot to talk or at least debate about. Yet with little in common, you might find it difficult to establish a personal connection.

Scientists have found that there's much more truth to the adage "Birds of a feather flock together" than the equally well-worn proverb "Opposites attract." Whether it's art, music, food preferences, educational level, physical attractiveness, or values, we're attracted to people who are similar to us (Byrne, 1971; Knox, Zusman, & Nieves, 1997; Newcomb, 1961; Swann & Pelham, 2002). We're also more likely to befriend, date, and marry compatible people (Curran & Lippold, 1972; Knox et al., 1997). There's even evidence that pet owners tend to select dogs who resemble them (Roy & Christenfeld, 2004), although not all researchers are convinced by their findings (Levine, 2005).

Online dating services have caught on to the fact that similarity breeds content (Hill, Rubin, Peplau, 1976). One popular service, eHarmony.com, tries to match prospective partners on the basis of personality similarity, although there's no good evidence that they're especially successful at doing so (Epstein, 2007). Similarity pays off in the long run too. Married couples who share similar traits are more likely to stay together than couples that are dissimilar (Meyer & Pepper, 1977).

APPLY YOUR THINKING

Spouses tend to show interesting similarities in physical appearance, ranging from their height to the length of their earlobes and middle fingers (Hinsz, 1989; Rushton, Russell, & Wells, 1985). One group of scientists (Zajonc, Adelmann, Murphy, & Niedenthal, 1986) found that married couples look more physically similar after 25 years of marriage than at the start of their marriage. Why might this be?

Similarity greases the wheels of social interaction for a few reasons. First, when people's interests and attitudes overlap, the foundation is paved for mutual understanding. Second, we assume we'll be readily accepted and liked by others who see eye-to-eye with us. Third, people who share our likes and dislikes provide validation for our views and help us feel good about ourselves. There may be even considerable truth to the saying "The enemy of my enemy is my friend" (Heider, 1958). Research demonstrates that a glue that binds friendships, especially in the early stages, is sharing negative impressions about others (Bosson, Johnson, Niederhoffer, & Swann, 2006). Negative gossip may permit us to elevate ourselves at the expense of others, thereby enhancing our self-esteem.

We also tend to be attracted to people who share our views of ourselves. **Social identity support** refers to the fact that our friends prop up our sense of self or the social roles we play. When another person validates our concept of who we are or would like to be—for example, "a good athlete" or "smart person"—the conditions are ripe for friendship. Social identity support predicts which new friend will be a best friend 4 years later (Weisz & Wood, 2005).

Reciprocity: All Give and No Take Does Not a Good Relationship Make. For a relationship to move to deeper levels, the third principle of attraction—**reciprocity,** or the rule of give and take—is often crucial. Across cultures, there's a norm of reciprocity (Gouldner, 1960) that begins to kick into motion as early as 11 years of age (Rotenberg & Mann, 1986). That is,

similarity
extent to which we have things in common with others, a predictor of attraction

social identity support
fact that our friends prop up our sense of self or the social roles we play

reciprocity
rule of give and take, a predictor of attraction

we tend to feel obligated to give what we get and maintain equity in a relationship (Walster, Berscheid, & Walster, 1973). Liking begets liking, and revealing personal information begets disclosure. When we believe people like us, we're inclined to feel attracted to them (Brehm, Miller, Perlman, & Campbell, 2002; Carlson & Rose, 2007). When we believe that our partner finds us attractive or likable, we generally act more likable in response to this ego-boosting information (Curtis & Miller, 1986). Talking about meaningful things is a vital element of most friendships. In particular, disclosure about intimate topics often brings about intimacy. When one person talks about superficial topics or discusses intimate topics in a superficial way, low levels of disclosure often result (Lynn, 1978). Although a complete lack of reciprocity can put a relationship into the deep freeze, absolute reciprocity isn't required to make a relationship hum, especially when one partner responds to our disclosures with sympathy and concern (Berg & Archer, 1980).

Physical Attraction: Like It or Not, We Do Judge Books by Their Covers.

As we saw in Chapter 6, some important scientific discoveries arise from *serendipity*, that is, sheer luck. So it was with a study that Elaine Hatfield and her colleagues conducted over 40 years ago (Hatfield, Aronson, Abrahams, & Rottman, 1966). They administered a large battery of personality, attitude, and interest measures to 725 incoming college men and women during freshman "Welcome Week." Hatfield and her coworkers paired these students randomly for a leisurely date and dance lasting two and a half hours, giving them the chance to get acquainted. Which variables, the researchers wondered, would predict whether the partners were interested in a second date? Much to their surprise, the only variable that significantly predicted attraction was one the researchers had included only as an afterthought (Gangestad & Scheyd, 2005): People's level of physical attractiveness as rated by their partners (Hatfield et al., 1966).

If psychologists have learned anything about physical attractiveness, it's that it matters in everyday life. As we learned in Chapter 2, physically attractive people tend to be more popular than physically unattractive people (Bull & Rumsey, 1988; Dion, Berscheid, & Walster, 1972). Yet what makes us find others physically attractive? Is it all merely a matter of "chemistry," an inexplicable process that lies beyond the grasp of science, as Senator Proxmire would have had us believe? Or is there a science to "love at first sight," or at least attraction at first sight?

Sex Differences in What We Find Attractive: Nature or Nurture?

Although physical attractiveness is important to both sexes when it comes to choosing our romantic partners, it's especially important to men (Buss & Schmidt, 1993; Buunk, Dijkstra, Fetchenhauer, & Kenrick, 2002; Feingold, 1992). David Buss (1989) conducted a comprehensive survey of mate preferences in thirty-seven cultures across six continents, with countries as diverse as Canada, Spain, Finland, Greece, Bulgaria, Venezuela, Iran, Japan, and South Africa. Although he found that the importance people attach to physical attractiveness varies across cultures, men consistently place more weight on looks in women than women do in men. Men also prefer women who are somewhat younger than they are. Conversely, Buss found that women tend to place more emphasis than do men on having a partner with a high level of financial resources. In contrast to men, women prefer partners who are somewhat older than they are. Still, men and women value many of the same things. Both sexes put a premium on having a partner who's intelligent, dependable, and a nice person (Buss, 1994).

Although standards of beauty differ somewhat within and across cultures, research suggests that both most African American men and most Caucasian men agree on which African American women (such as Halle Berry, *left*) and Caucasian women (such as Jennifer Anniston, *right*) are physically attractive.

Evolutionary Models of Attraction. Putting aside these commonalities, how can we make sense of sex differences in mate preferences? Evolutionary theorists point out that men, who produce enormous numbers of sperm—an average of about 300 million per ejaculation—typically pursue a mating strategy that maximizes the chances that at least one of these sperm will find a receptive egg at the end of its long journey (Symons, 1979). As a consequence, evolutionary psychologists contend, men are on the lookout for cues of potential fertility, such as physical attractiveness and youth. Women, in contrast, typically produce only one egg per month, so they must be choosy. Therefore, they typically pursue a mating strategy that maximizes the chances that the man with whom they mate will provide well for their offspring; hence women's preference for men who are well off monetarily and a bit more experienced in the ways of life (Buunk et al., 2002).

Social Role Theory. Still, some researchers have offered plausible alternatives to evolutionary models of attraction. According to Alice Eagly and Wendy Wood's (1999) *social role theory*, biological variables play a role in men's and women's preferences but not in the way that evolutionary psychologists contend. Instead, biological factors constrain the roles that men and women adopt (Eagly, Wood, Johannesen-Schmidt, 2004). Because men tend to be bigger and stronger than women, they've more often ended up playing the roles of hunter, food provider, and warrior. Moreover, because men don't bear children, they have considerable opportunities to pursue high-status positions. In contrast, because women bear children, they've more often ended up playing the role of child care provider and have been more limited in pursuing high-status positions.

Some of these differences in traditional roles may help to explain men's and women's differing mate preferences. For example, because women have typically held fewer high-status positions than men, they may have preferred men who are dependable financial providers (Eagly et al., 2004). Consistent with social role theory, men and women have become more similar in their mate preferences over the past half century (Buss, Schackelford, Kirkpatrick, & Larsen, 2001), perhaps reflecting the increasing social opportunities for women across that time period. So although nature may channel men and women into somewhat different roles and therefore different mate preferences, nurture may shape these roles and preferences in significant ways.

Is Beauty in the Eye of the Beholder? Popular wisdom tells us that "beauty is in the eye of the beholder." To some extent that saying is true. Yet it's also an oversimplification. People tend to agree at considerably higher than chance levels about who is, and isn't, physically attractive (Burns & Farina, 1992). This is the case not only within a race but across races; for example, Caucasian and African American men tend to agree on which women are attractive, as do Caucasian and Asian American men (Cunningham, Roberts, Wu, Barbee, & Bruen, 1995). Even across vastly different cultures, both men and women tend to agree on whom they find physically attractive (Langlois et al., 2000).

Furthermore, men and women tend to prefer certain body shapes in members of the opposite sex. Men tend to be especially attracted to women with a waist-to-hip ratio of about .7, that is, with a waist about 70 percent as large as their hips (Singh, 1993), although this ratio is often less important than other variables, like body weight (Tassinary & Hansen, 1998). In contrast, women generally prefer men with a higher waist-to-hip ratio (Singh, 1995). According to evolutionary psychologist Donald Symons (1979), these findings imply that "beauty lies in the adaptations of the beholder." Women's waist-to-hip ratio tends to decline as they become older, so this ratio is a cue—although a highly imperfect one—to fertility.

Still, there are important differences in physical preferences within and across cultures. For example, men from African American and Caribbean cultures often find women with a large body size more physically attractive than do men of European cultures (Rosenblum & Lewis, 1999). Furthermore, preferences toward thinness have frequently shifted over historical time, as even a casual inspection of paintings of nude women over time reveals.

The Cute Response. There are surprising similarities in the facial characteristics of people we find appealing. One striking demonstration of this principle is the virtually universal *cute response:* our positive emotional response to faces that display certain characteristics, especially (a) large eyes; (b) a small, round nose; (c) big round ears; and (d) a large head relative to the body (Lorenz, 1971). These are the very facial features we find in infants, so natural selection may have predisposed us to find these features irresistibly adorable (Angier, 2006). Still, our typical reaction to faces that we find cute is typically closer to affection than to physical attraction. So we must look further to fully explain the causes of physical attraction.

Ruling Out Rival Hypotheses

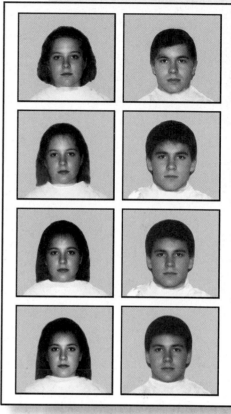

Figure 11.19 Which Face Is Most Attractive? The two columns depict faces that have been averaged with other faces (from top to bottom) 4, 8, 16, and 32 times. Most people find the faces on the bottom, which are the most "average," to be the most attractive (Langlois & Roggman, 1990). Remarkably, Sir Francis Galton (1878), whom we met in Chapter 9, anticipated these findings well over a century ago. (*Source:* Langlois & Roggman, 1990)

Societal standards for women's overall physical size and shape have changed over time, as this 1895 painting of a nude bather by Renoir attests.

When Being "Just Average" Is Just Fine. Which person are we more likely to find attractive: (a) someone who's exotic, unusual, or distinctive in some way or (b) someone who's just plain average? If you're like most people, you'd choose (a). Indeed, men sometimes malign women by calling them "plain Janes," and women sometimes do the same by calling men "average Joes."

Yet as Judith Langlois and Lori Ruggman (1990) showed, being average has its pluses. By using a computer to digitize the faces of students and then combine them progressively, they found that people generally prefer faces that are the most average. In their study, people preferred average faces a whopping 96 percent of the time (see **Figure 11.19;** to try your hand at averaging faces, see a demonstration at http://www.faceresearch.org/tech/demos/average). Although some psychologists found these results difficult to believe, many investigators have since replicated them for European faces as well as Japanese and Chinese faces (Gangestad & Sheyd, 2005; Rhodes, Halberstadt, & Brajkovich, 2001). Averaged faces are also more symmetrical than nonaveraged faces, so our preferences for average faces might be due to their greater symmetry. Yet studies show that even when faces are symmetrical, people still prefer faces that are more average (Valentine, Darling, & Donnelly, 2004).

Evolutionary psychologists have speculated that "averageness" in a face tends to reflect an absence of genetic mutations, serious diseases, and other abnormalities. As a consequence, we could be drawn to people with such faces, as they're often better "genetic catches." Maybe. But there's a fly in the ointment. Studies also show that people prefer not merely averaged faces, but averaged animals, like birds and fish, and even averaged objects, like cars and watches (Halberstadt & Rhodes, 2003). So our preference for averaged faces may be due to an alternative mechanism, namely, a more general preference for anything that's average. Perhaps we find average stimuli to be more familiar and easier to process mentally, because they reflect stimuli we've seen before many times (Gangestad & Sheyd, 2005).

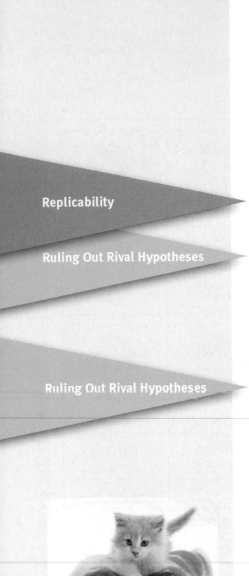

Replicability

Ruling Out Rival Hypotheses

Ruling Out Rival Hypotheses

LOVE: SCIENCE CONFRONTS THE MYSTERIOUS

Elizabeth Barrett Browning wrote famously: "How do I love thee? Let me count the ways." According to some psychologists, we may not need to count all that high. We'll explain.

Love: A Many-Splendored Thing? Psychologists are no different from the rest of us. They've tried to understand the myriad varieties of love, with some concluding that there's only one type of love, and others that love comes in many shapes and sizes. According to Elaine Hatfield and Richard Rapson (1996), there are two major types of love: passionate and companionate. Robert Sternberg, as we'll soon see, puts the number at six.

Hollywood Love. **Passionate love** is marked by a powerful, even overwhelming, longing for one's partner. It's a strange mix of delirious happiness when we're around the object of our desire and utter misery when we're not. It's the stuff of which Hollywood movies are made. As Romeo and Juliet knew all too well, passionate love is fueled when obstacles, such as seemingly insurmountable physical distance or the strenuous objection of parents, are placed in the way of romance (Driscoll, Davis, & Lipetz, 1972). Such obstacles may heighten arousal, thereby intensifying passion, as Schachter and Singer's two-factor theory would predict (Kenrick, Neuberg, & Cialdini, 2005).

Love as Friendship. In contrast, **companionate love** is marked by a sense of deep friendship and fondness for one's partner. Romantic relationships tend to progress over time from passionate to companionate love (Wojciszke, 2002), although most healthy relationships retain at least a spark of passion. In older couples, companionate love may be the overriding emotion in the relationship.

There's growing evidence that companionate and passionate love are psychologically independent. Studies indicate that people can "fall in love" with partners in the sense of caring deeply about them, yet experience little or no sexual desire toward them (Diamond, 2004). In addition, these two forms of love may be associated with differing brain systems (Diamond, 2003; Gonzaga, Turner, Keltner, Campos, & Altemus, 2005). Animal research suggests that emotional attachment to others is influenced largely by hormones such as oxytocin, which as we noted in Chapter 3 plays a key role in pair bonding and

Certain features of the face, like large eyes and a small nose, are nearly universal triggers for the cute response. People not only find kittens that display these features to be irresistibly cute, but cars as well.

passionate love
love marked by powerful, even overwhelming, longing for one's partner

companionate love
love marked by a sense of deep friendship and fondness for one's partner

interpersonal trust. In contrast, sexual desire is influenced by sex hormones, such as testosterone and estrogen.

The Three Sides of Love. Robert Sternberg believes that the "two types of love" model is too simple. In his *triangular theory of love*, Sternberg (1986, 1988) proposes the existence of three major elements of love: (1) intimacy ("I feel really close to this person"); (2) passion ("I'm crazy about this person"); and (3) commitment ("I really want to stay with this person"). These three elements combine to form six varieties of love (see **Figure 11.20**). Sternberg's model is more of a description of love types than an explanation of why people fall in love, but as a road map it's a helpful starting point toward understanding one of life's great mysteries.

Hate: A Neglected Topic. Until recently, psychologists didn't want to have much to do with the topic of hate. Most introductory psychology textbooks don't even list the word *hate* in their indices. Yet with the horrific events of September 11, 2001, and the burgeoning problem of terrorism around the globe, it's clear that psychologists can no longer turn a blind eye to the question of why some people despise others, at times to the point of wanting to destroy them (Sternberg, 2004).

Using his triangular theory of love as a starting point, Robert Sternberg (2004) developed a theory of hate, with hatred consisting of three elements:

(1) negation of intimacy ("I would never want to get close to these people");
(2) passion ("I absolutely and positively despise these people"); and
(3) commitment ("I'm determined to stop or harm these people").

As in his theory of love, differing forms of hate arise from combinations of these three elements, with "burning hate"—the most severe—reflecting high scores on all three. For Sternberg, the key to fueling hate is propaganda. Groups and governments that "teach" hatred of other groups are experts at portraying these groups as evil and worthy of disdain (Keen, 1986; Sternberg, 2003).

As Paul Bloom (2004) noted, the emotion of disgust probably evolved as a means of helping us to avoid dangerous substances, like rotting meats, or repulsive animals, like cockroaches. Yet he observed that we can extend the emotion of disgust to entire groups of people we dislike. In this way, we perceive them as "sub-human" and worthy of extermination, like insects and other pests (Hodson & Costello, 2007; Sternberg, 2003). Not surprisingly, people who detest other groups frequently refer to them with terms that reinforce perceptions of disgust, like *vermin, pigs,* or *scum.* Doing so probably makes it easier for us to hate them.

The good news is that if we can learn hate, we can probably unlearn it. Teaching individuals to overcome their confirmation bias (Chapter 2) toward perceiving only the negative attributes of groups they dislike may be an essential first step (Harrington, 2004). Recognizing that "there's good and bad in everyone," as the saying goes, may help us combat our deep-seated animosity toward our enemies.

Companionate love is often the primary form of love among the elderly. It can be a powerful emotional bond between couples across the life span.

Figure 11.20 What Is Love?
According to Sternberg's triangular theory of love, intimacy, passion, and commitment combine to form six varieties of love, with "consummate love" being the ultimate form of love marked by high levels of all three components.

ASSESS YOUR KNOWLEDGE: FACT OR FICTION?
(1) When it comes to romantic chemistry, opposites attract. (True/False)
(2) In general, people find average faces the most physically attractive. (True/False)
(3) Companionate and passionate love appear to be psychologically and physiologically independent. (True/False)
(4) Passion and commitment play a key role in love, but are irrelevant to hate. (True/False)

Answers: (1) F (p. 483); (2) T (p. 484); (3) T (p. 486); (4) F (p. 487)

Think again...

The Complete Review System

THINK / ASSESS / STUDY / SUCCEED

Theories of Emotion: What Causes Our Feelings? (pp. 447–456)

STUDY the Learning Objectives

▶ Describe the major theories of emotion
- According to discrete emotions theory, people experience a small number (perhaps seven) of distinct biologically determined emotions and combinations of these emotions called secondary emotions. According to cognitive theories, emotions result from our interpretation of situations or our bodily reactions to stimuli. According to the Cannon-Bard theory, emotion-provoking events lead to emotions and bodily reactions. Schachter and Singer's two-factor theory states that emotions are the explanations we attach to our general state of arousal following an emotion-provoking event.

▶ Identify unconscious influences on emotion
- Many emotions are generated automatically and operate unconsciously, as illustrated by the mere exposure effect and the facial feedback hypothesis.

DO YOU KNOW THESE TERMS?
- ❏ discrete emotions theory (p. 447)
- ❏ motivation-structural rules (p. 450)
- ❏ display rules (p. 450)
- ❏ cognitive theories of emotion (p. 450)
- ❏ James-Lange theory of emotion (p. 451)
- ❏ somatic marker theory (p. 451)
- ❏ Cannon-Bard theory (p. 452)
- ❏ two-factor theory (p. 452)
- ❏ mere exposure effect (p. 454)
- ❏ facial feedback hypothesis (p. 455)

According to psychological findings, are people who lack emotions exceedingly rational? (p. 446)

THINK about

what You would do . . .
You are cramming to learn Spanish before your trip to Spain but know you won't have it mastered by the time you leave. Using Ekman's research, what could you do to prepare yourself to better read people's emotions if you can't understand their words? (p. 448)

Using your knowledge of theories of emotion, explain how the James–Lange and Cannon–Bard theories differ in their views of how emotions are generated. (p. 451)

1. _____
2. _____
3. _____
4. _____

mypsychlab

SUCCEED with

Physiological, Evolutionary, and Cognitive Theories of Emotion

Which theory of emotion do you most agree with? (p. 447)

EXPLORE

ASSESS your knowledge

1. According to _____ _____ theory, humans experience a small number of distinct emotions that combine in complex ways. (p. 447)

2. One of the first researchers to study how emotional expressions of humans and nonhumans are similar, _____ observed that the smile of a chimpanzee bears a resemblance to a human smile. (p. 447)

3. Ekman concluded from his studies in New Guinea that there are a small number, perhaps seven, of _____ _____ that are cross-culturally universal. (p. 448)

4. According to Morton's _____ rules, there are deep-seated commonalities across most animal species, especially mammals and birds. (p. 450)

5. Cultures differ in _____ _____, their societal guidelines for how and when to exhibit emotions. (p. 450)

6. According to the _____ theories of emotion, emotions are products of thinking. (p. 450)

7. Emotions result from our interpretations of our bodily reactions to stimuli according to the _____ _____ theory of emotion. (p. 451)

8. According to Damasio's somatic marker theory, we (do/don't) use our "gut reactions" to help us determine how we should act. (p. 451)

9. The _____ theory proposes that emotions are produced by an undifferentiated state of arousal along with an explanation of that arousal. (p. 452)

10. Repeated exposure to a stimulus makes us more likely to feel favorably toward it, a phenomenon called the _____ _____ effect. (p. 454)

Nonverbal Expression of Emotion: The Eyes, Bodies, & Cultures Have It (pp. 456–462)

STUDY the Learning Objectives

▶ Explain the importance of nonverbal expression of emotion
- Much emotional expression is nonverbal; gestures highlight speech (illustrators), involve touches of our bodies (manipulators), or convey specific meanings (emblems). Nonverbal expressions are often more valid indicators of emotions than words.

▶ Describe the four levels of personal space
- The four levels of personal space are public distance (12 ft. or more), social distance (4–12 ft.), personal distance (1.5–4 ft.), and intimate distance (0–1.5 ft.).

▶ Identify major lie detection methods and their pitfalls

If you did not receive an access code to MyPsychLab with this text and wish to purchase access online, please visit www.mypsychlab.com.

THINK about

what You would do . . .
After a friend's counselor provides her with negative feedback on her ability to read others' body language, how could you help her to identify physical cues as she engages in conversation with friends and family? (pp. 456–457)

mypsychlab

SUCCEED with

Why Spy?

Can you tell if people are lying when you look at their eyes? (pp. 458–459)

WATCH

Do you think the polygraph test is biased against the innocent? If so, why? (p. 460)

ASSESS your knowledge

1. The unconscious spillover of emotions into nonverbal behavior is known as _____ _____. (p. 456)

2. When talking, we often use _____, gestures that highlight or accentuate speech. (p. 456)

3. When stressed or nervous, you may engage in _____, such as biting your fingernails or twirling your hair. (p. 456)

4. Gestures that convey specific meanings, such as a hand wave or the OK sign are called _____. (p. 457)

5. Hall coined the term _____ to describe the study of personal space. (p. 458)

6. Typically, the correlation between peoples' confidence in their ability to detect lies and their accuracy in doing so is (low/high). (p. 459)

7. The most widely administered version of the polygraph test, the _____ _____ _____, measures subjects' physiological responses following three major types of yes-no questions. (p. 459)

8. Research shows that the primary problem with the polygraph test is its high rate of (false positives/false negatives). (p. 460)

9. In 1963, the U. S. Supreme Court ruled that criminal confessions induced under _____ _____ were scientifically questionable and unconstitutional. (p. 461)

10. Some employers administer paper-and-pencil _____ tests in an attempt to assess workers' tendency to steal or cheat. (p. 462)

Smile :-) or :)	Surprised :-o or :o
Sad :-(or :(	Confused :-s or :s

How do emoticons help to ensure that an e-mail or text message is interpreted in the manner it was intended? (p. 456)

• The polygraph test measures physiological responses to questions designed to expose falsehoods. The Controlled Question Test (CQT) contains questions relevant and irrelevant to the crime, and control questions that reflect probable lies. Greater physiological reactivity in response to relevant questions suggests deception. The CQT detects general arousal rather than guilt (Othello error) and results in false positives—identifying innocent individuals as guilty. False negatives (guilty are labeled innocent) can result when individuals take countermeasures (bite tongue, curl toes). The Guilty Knowledge Test (GKT) relies on the premise that criminals harbor concealed knowledge about the crime that innocent people don't. The GKT has a low false-positive rate, but a fairly high false-negative rate.

DO YOU KNOW THESE TERMS?
❏ **nonverbal leakage** (p. 456)
❏ **proxemics** (p. 458)
❏ **Pinocchio response** (p. 459)
❏ **guilty knowledge test** (p. 461)
❏ **integrity tests** (p. 462)

Happiness & Self-Esteem: Science Confronts Pop Psychology (pp. 462–469)

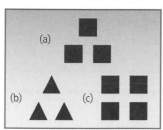

According to Fredrickson's broaden and build theory of happiness, in which mood would a person be likely to interpret the three squares (a) as being more like the four squares (c) than the triangles (b)? (p. 464)

THINK about

what You would do . . .
In order to convince freshmen that the field of psychology deals with more than disorders, what would you do to educate prospective psychology majors about positive psychology's impact on people's lives? (pp. 462–463)

SUCCEED with

mypsychlab
where learning comes to life!

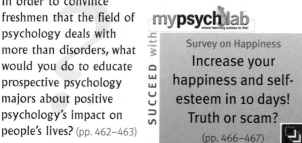

Survey on Happiness

Increase your happiness and self-esteem in 10 days! Truth or scam?

(pp. 466–467)

Explain how the King of Bhutan plans to increase the Gross National Happiness of his country and why this initiative may be beneficial to all. (p.462)

STUDY the Learning Objectives

▶ Describe the emerging discipline of positive psychology
• Positive psychology emphasizes strengths, love, and happiness. Happiness is adaptive; it allows us to build on strengths and opportunities (broaden and build theory).

▶ Identify common myths and realities about happiness and self-esteem
• Myths: The prime determinant of happiness is what happens to us, money makes us happy, happiness declines in old age, happiness and negative emotions are opposites, and people on the West Coast are the happiest. Realities: Happiness is associated with marriage, college education, and religious beliefs; voting Republican; exercise; gratitude; and immersion in what we're doing ("flow"). We tend to overestimate the long-term impact of events on our happiness. Myth: Low self-esteem is the root of all unhappiness. Reality: Self-esteem is associated with greater initiative, persistence, and positive illusions—the tendency to perceive ourselves more positively than others do.

DO YOU KNOW THESE TERMS?
❏ **positive psychology** (p. 462)
❏ **broaden and build theory** (p. 463)
❏ **positivity effect** (p. 465)
❏ **affective forecasting** (p. 466)
❏ **durability bias** (p. 466)
❏ **hedonic treadmill** (p. 466)
❏ **positive illusions** (p. 468)
❏ **defensive pessimism** (p. 468)

ASSESS your knowledge

1. The emerging discipline of _____ _____ seeks to emphasize human strengths, such as resilience, coping, happiness, and life satisfaction. (p. 462)

2. According to Fredrickson's theory, happiness predisposes us to think more openly. (pp. 463–464)

3. According to psychological research, money (can/can't) buy long-term happiness. (p. 464)

4. The increase in happiness with old age appears to be due to the _____ effect. (p. 465)

5. The ability to predict our own and others' happiness is called _____ _____. (p. 466)

6. When we believe that both our good and bad moods will last longer than they do, we are suffering from a _____ _____. (p. 466)

7. The tendency for our moods to adapt to external circumstances is called the _____ (p. 466)

8. The evidence linking self-esteem to mental health and life success is (strong/weak). (p. 467)

9. Most individuals with high self-esteem have _____ _____, in that they see themselves as more intelligent, attractive, and likeable than other individuals. (p. 468)

10. _____ _____ is a strategy of anticipating failures and compensating for this expectation by mentally overpreparing for negative outcomes. (p. 468)

Motivation: Our Wants and Needs (pp. 469–481)

STUDY the Learning Objectives

▶ **Define motivation**
- Motivation refers to the drives—especially our wants and needs—that propel us in a specific direction.

▶ **Explain basic principles and theories of motivation**
- Drive reduction theory states that drives (hunger, thirst) pull us to act in certain ways. According to the Yerkes-Dodson law, there's an inverted U-shaped relation between arousal and affect/performance. Approach and avoidance often drive conflict. According to incentive theories, positive goals are motivators. These motivators include primary (biological) and secondary (psychological desires/achievement, self-actualization) needs.

▶ **Describe the determinants of hunger, weight gain, and obesity**
- The lateral hypothalamus has been called a "feeding center" and the ventromedial hypothalamus a "satiety center." However, hunger is also associated with hormones (ghrelin), low glucose levels, neurotransmitters (leptin, serotonin), a genetically programmed set point for body fat and muscle mass, specific genes (melanocortin-4 receptor gene, leptin gene), and sensitivity to food cues and expectations.

▶ **Identify the symptoms of bulimia and anorexia**
- Bulimia is marked by recurrent binge eating, followed by attempts to minimize weight gain. Anorexia occurs when refusal to eat results in body weight less than 85 percent of that expected for age and height.

▶ **Describe the human sexual response cycle and factors that influence sexual activity**
- Masters and Johnson described four stages: desire, excitement, orgasm, and resolution. Frequency of sexual activity decreases with age, but sexual satisfaction doesn't. Expression of sexual desire is shaped by social norms and culture.

▶ **Identify common misconceptions about sexual orientation**
- Common myths include the notions that gay individuals: (a) typically adopt a masculine or feminine role, (b) are especially likely to sexually abuse children and adolescents, and (c) are inadequate parents.

▶ **Describe potential influences on sexual orientation**
- Potential influences on sexual orientation are an inherited tendency toward childhood gender nonconformity, sex hormones, prenatal influences, and brain differences.

DO YOU KNOW THESE TERMS?

- ❏ **motivation** (p. 469)
- ❏ **drive reduction theory** (p. 469)
- ❏ **homeostasis** (p. 470)
- ❏ **Yerkes-Dodson law** (p. 470)
- ❏ **incentive theories** (p. 471)
- ❏ **hierarchy of needs** (p. 472)
- ❏ **glucostatic theory** (p. 473)
- ❏ **leptin** (p. 474)
- ❏ **set point** (p. 474)
- ❏ **internal–external theory** (p. 474)
- ❏ **desire phase** (p. 477)
- ❏ **excitement phase** (p. 477)
- ❏ **orgasm (climax) phase** (p. 477)
- ❏ **resolution phase** (p. 477))

Using Maslow's Hierarchy of Needs, insert the appropriate need at each level of the pyramid in the path to achieving self-actualization. (p. 472)

What challenges did Kinsey face in his pioneering research, and what factors need to be considered in evaluating his findings? (p. 478)

mypsychlab *where learning comes to life!*

SUCCEED with

The Effects of the Hypothalamus on Eating Behavior

Eat more or less: It really depends more on your hypothalamus than your stomach.

(pp. 472–473)

EXPLORE

THINK about

what You would do . . . According to Maslow's hierarchy of needs, what life changes would you make to achieve self-actualization? (p. 472)

ASSESS your knowledge

1. According to _____ _____ theory, certain drives, like hunger, thirst, and sexual frustration, motivate us to act in ways that minimize aversive reactions. (p. 469)

2. Most drive reduction theories propose that we're motivated to maintain a given level of psychological _____. (p. 470)

3. The _____ law describes an inverted U-shaped relation between arousal on the one hand, and performance and affect, on the other. (p. 470)

4. _____ theories propose that we're often motivated by positive goals. (p. 471)

5. Murray distinguished our _____ needs, or biological needs, from our_____ needs, or psychological desires. (p. 472)

6. According to _____ theory, when our blood glucose levels drop, hunger creates a drive to eat to restore the proper level of glucose. (p. 473)

7. Each of us may have a genetically programmed _____ _____ that establishes a range of body and muscle mass we tend to maintain. (p. 474)

8. _____ is the most common eating disorder, and 95 percent of the people with this diagnosis are women. (p. 475)

9. Masters and Johnson reported in their pioneering investigation that the basic sexual arousal cycle was (the same/different) for men and women. (p. 477)

10. Scientists define the sexual response cycle in terms of four phases: 1) _____, 2) _____, 3) _____, and 4) _____. (p. 477)

Attraction, Love, and Hate: The Greatest Mysteries of Them All (pp. 482–487)

According to Buss, across cultures, which gender attaches more importance to physical attractiveness? (p. 484)

THINK about

what You would do . . .
Imagine you are hired as a consultant to an online dating service. Drawing on the literature on romantic attraction and relationship formation, what advice would you have for matching prospective clients? (p. 482)

Using Sternberg's Triangular theory of love, complete this figure by first identifying the six varieties of love (outside of the triangle) and then inserting the three components which must combine to achieve consummate love. (p. 487)

1. _____
2. _____
3. _____
4. _____
5. _____
6. _____

Intimacy

Passion + Intimacy

Intimacy + Commitment

Consummate love

+   +

Passion   Passion + Commitment   Commitment

STUDY the Learning Objectives

▶ Identify principles and factors that guide attraction and relationship formation
 • Factors guiding attraction and relationship formation are proximity (closeness), similarity (like attracts like), reciprocity (give what we get), physical attractiveness (more important to men than to women), evolutionary influence, social roles, and preference for "average" faces.

▶ Describe the major types of love and the elements of love and hate
 • The major love types are passionate and companionate. The major love elements are intimacy, passion, and commitment. The major hate elements are negation of intimacy, passion, and commitment.

DO YOU KNOW THESE TERMS?
 ❏ **proximity** (p. 482)
 ❏ **similarity** (p. 483)
 ❏ **social identity support** (p. 483)
 ❏ **reciprocity** (p. 483)
 ❏ **passionate love** (p. 486)
 ❏ **companionate love** (p. 486)

SUCCEED with

mypsych lab
where learning comes to life!

Perceptions of Attractiveness

Do we judge a book by its cover? (p. 484)

SIMULATION

ASSESS your knowledge

1. Three major principles that guide attraction and relationship formation are _____, _____, and _____. (p. 482)

2. Physical nearness, or _____, affords the opportunity for relationship formation. (p. 482)

3. We're often attracted to people with whom we have high levels of _____, or things in common. (p. 483)

4. _____ _____ refers to the fact that our friends prop up our sense of self or the social roles we play. (p. 483)

5. In order for a relationship to move to deeper levels, the rule of give and take, or _____ is often crucial. (p. 483)

6. In mate preferences, men consistently place (less/more) emphasis on looks in women than women do in men. (p. 484)

7. _____ _____ is our positive emotional response to faces that share certain features, like large eyes and a small, round nose. (p. 485)

8. _____ love can be a mix of delirious happiness when we're near the object of our desire, and misery when separated from it. (p. 486)

9. A relationship marked by a sense of deep friendship and fondness for our partner is called _____ _____. (p. 486)

10. Sternberg's _____ _____ __ ____ proposes the existence of three major elements in love: intimacy, passion, and commitment. (p. 487)

Remember these questions from the beginning of the chapter? Think again and ask yourself if you would answer them differently based on what you now know about emotion and motivation. (For more detailed explanations, see MyPsychLab.)

▶ Are emotion and reason opposites of each other? (p. 446)
▶ Are emotional expressions unique to different cultures? (p. 448)
▶ Do our emotions influence our actions, or vice versa? (p. 451)
▶ Is the polygraph test really a "lie detector"? (p. 459)
▶ Are people who have good things happen to them happier than other people? (p. 464)
▶ Do genes contribute to obesity? (p. 474)
▶ Does sexual desire disappear in old age? (p. 478)
▶ Can sexual orientation be changed? (p. 479)
▶ Do opposites attract in romantic relationships? (p. 483)

THINKING Scientifically

Correlation vs. Causation pp. 451, 452, 454, 459, 463, 465, 466, 468, 472, 478, 481

Falsifiability pp. 452, 461, 472, 473

Extraordinary Claims p. 459

Occam's Razor p. 448

Replicability pp. 451, 453, 454, 471, 481, 486

Ruling Out Rival Hypotheses pp. 448, 455, 471, 474, 475, 477, 478, 479, 485, 486

12

Stress, Coping, and Health
The Mind–Body Interconnection

PREVIEW

Think

First, think about these questions. Then, as you read, think again. . . .

▶ Can we measure and study stress objectively?

▶ Do all people react to stressful circumstances in the same way?

▶ Do most people who encounter highly aversive events develop posttraumatic stress disorder?

▶ Are some people more prone to heart attacks than others?

▶ Does stress produce ulcers in most people?

▶ Is there one best way to cope with stressful events?

▶ Are some people especially hardy or able to cope with life challenges?

▶ Are crash diets that promise quick and enduring weight loss effective?

▶ Are acupuncture and other alternative medical treatments more effective than traditional medical procedures?

Tuesday, September 11, 2001, is a day that few Americans will forget. Across the country, people glued to their television sets watched in horror as two loaded passenger planes flew into the Twin Towers of the World Trade Center (WTC) in New York City. In the worst terrorist attack in American history, more than 2,700 people were killed at the WTC alone. Hundreds more were killed when terrorists crashed two other planes into the Pentagon and a field in rural Pennsylvania, where passengers attempted to regain control of the plane.

In the aftermath of this tragedy, inspiring stories emerged of courageous first responders—firefighters, paramedics, police, and emergency service workers—who risked their lives to save others. Nearly 400 people who participated in rescue operations died on 9/11. Many others survived to tell their stories. The following accounts by first responders at the WTC (McNally, 2001) are a sample of reactions to some of the most stressful circumstances imaginable— and some unimaginable.

• Juana Lomi, a paramedic, raced to the WTC and survived the collapse of the towers. "It was an overwhelming feeling of fear, horror—and not being able to do more. There were hundreds of people that needed to be treated. I was at risk of losing my life, but I had to stay and help other people."

• Louie Cacchioli, a firefighter, saved the lives of many people. "I stepped outside after bringing about 40 or 50 people down a stairway. I looked around. It was crazy. Somebody yelled, 'Look out! The tower's coming down!' I started running. I tossed my air mask away to make myself lighter. Next thing I know, there's a big black ball of smoke. I threw myself on my knees, and I'm crying. I said to myself, 'Oh, my God, I'm going to die.' I was crawling. Then—the biggest miracle thing in the world. My hands came onto an air mask. It still had air. Another 15 seconds, I wouldn't have made it."

• Mike Hanson, a member of the Emergency Services Unit of the New York Police Department, used a torch to cut through steel to rescue people. "Emotionally, it's taken a toll. Just like I work in small sectors of massive destruction, I have to take it in little pieces mentally. That's the only way I can manage it."

These stories raise fascinating questions that are crucial to the study of stress, coping, and health. What happens after we experience a traumatic event? How do people like Louie Cacchioli fare following a close brush with death? Do the effects reverberate long afterward, producing lasting psychological or physical illnesses? Or can many people instead manage to cope, even thrive, in the aftermath of harrowing circumstances?

In this chapter, we'll explore the myriad ways in which people cope with stressful circumstances, ranging from the annoyance of a computer crash to the terror of surviving a plane crash. We'll also examine the complex interplay between stress and physical health. Ronald Kessler and his colleagues (Kessler, Sonnega, Bromet, Hughes, & Nelson, 1995) studied nearly 6,000 men and women in the general population and found that the majority (60%–90%) had experienced at least one potentially traumatic event, such as a sexual or physical assault or car accident. So it's actually the unusual person who doesn't experience severe stress in his or her lifetime (Ozer, Best, Lipsey, & Weiss, 2003). Groups at especially high risk for experiencing stressful events include young and unmarried people, African Americans, and people of low socioeconomic status (Kessler, Sonnega, Bromet, Hughes, & Nelson, 1994; Miranda & Green, 1999; Turner, Wheaton, & Lloyd, 1995). Many people assume that people who live in rural areas or nonindustrialized countries experience minimal stress compared with residents of urban and more developed areas. Yet scientists have discovered no support for this popular belief: Stress-producing events are universal (Bigbee, 1990).

Firefighters and police officers who merely witness traumatic events often experience high levels of stress.

Fortunately, exposure to events like the 9/11 terrorist attacks, Hurricane Katrina, and frontline combat in Iraq doesn't guarantee that people will be traumatized for life. Herein lies another case in which scientific research contradicts popular psychology. Many self-help books inform us that most people require psychological help in the face of stressful circumstances (Sommers & Satel, 2004). Some companies dispense squadrons of grief counselors to help people cope with the upshot of stressful events; these companies often assume that without psychological help, most witnesses to trauma are doomed to serious psychological problems. In 2007, grief counselors arrived at the scene to help traumatized college students deal with the horrific shootings at Virginia Tech, and in 1998 they even traveled to the Boston Public Library to help librarians deal with their feelings of loss following the destruction of books in a flood.

Yet research shows that even in the face of horrific circumstances, like shootings and natural disasters, most of us are surprisingly resilient (Bonanno, 2004). Even most victims of child sexual abuse turn out to be psychologically healthy adults, although there are certainly exceptions (Rind, Tromovitch, & Bauserman, 1998). Because practicing psychologists tend to see only those people who react emotionally to stress—after all, the healthy people don't come for help—they probably overestimate most people's fragility and underestimate their resilience, an error sometimes called the *clinician's illusion* (Cohen & Cohen, 1984).

Before we discuss why some people thrive and others nosedive when confronted with stressful life events, we'll consider the fundamental question of what stress is. We'll then explore competing views of stress, the mind–body link responsible for stress-related disorders, how people cope with stressful situations, and the rapidly growing fields of health psychology and alternative medicine.

What Is Stress?

Many ways of thinking about stress have evolved over the years (Cooper & Dewe, 2004). Stress and trauma aren't synonymous. **Stress** consists of the tension, discomfort, or physical symptoms that arise when a situation, which we'll refer to as a *stressor,* strains our ability to cope effectively. In contrast, a *traumatic* event is so severe that it has the potential to produce long-term psychological or health consequences.

Before the 1940s, scientists rarely used the term *stress* outside of the engineering profession (Hayward, 1960, p. 185), where it referred to stresses on materials and building structures. A building was said to withstand stress if it didn't collapse under intense pressure. It wasn't until 1944 that the term *stress* found its way into the psychological literature (Jones & Bright, 2001). This engineering analogy highlights the notion that "if the body were like a machine and machines are subject to wear and tear then so too would be the body" (Doublet, 2000, p. 48). But just as two buildings can withstand differing amounts of stress before weakening and collapsing, people differ widely in their personal resources, the meaning and significance they attach to stressful events, and their ability to grapple with them.

STRESS IN THE EYE OF THE BEHOLDER: THREE APPROACHES

Researchers have approached the study of stress in three different, yet interrelated, ways (Kessler, Price, & Wortman, 1985). Each approach has yielded valuable insights, illuminating the big and small events that generate distress and the ways we perceive and respond to stressful situations.

Stressors as Stimuli. When asked to think about stressful life events, some people conjure up catastrophic images of earthquakes, combat, terrorist attacks, and hurricanes. Others think of rape, job loss, physical assault, and car accidents or the typical role alterations that can occur in the unfolding of life: parenthood, retirement, and caring for family members who need special assistance (Pearlin & Lieberman, 1979; see Chapter 10).

Some researchers call the psychological and physical response to a stressor "strain," much as a material can be said to be strained when under stress.

stress
the tension, discomfort, or physical symptoms that arise when a situation strains our ability to cope effectively

The stress of unemployment includes not only the frustration and despair of looking for a new job, but the economic hardship of living on a sharply reduced income.

Hurricane Katrina devastated much of New Orleans in 2005, forcing many displaced residents to relocate as far away as Michigan and California.

Emotion-focused coping may encourage people who've divorced to begin dating again.

primary appraisal
initial decision regarding whether an event is harmful

secondary appraisal
perceptions regarding our ability to cope with an event that follow primary appraisal

problem-focused coping
coping strategy by which we tackle life's challenges head-on

emotion-focused coping
coping strategy that features a positive outlook on feelings or situations accompanied by behaviors that reduce painful emotions

corticosteroids
stress hormones that activate the body and prepare us to respond to stressful circumstances

The stressors as a stimuli approach focuses on identifying different types of stressful events. This approach has succeeded in pinpointing categories of events that most people find dangerous and unpredictable, as well as the people who are most susceptible to stress following different events (Collins, Sorocco, Haala, Miller, & Lovallo, 2003; Costa & McCrae, 1990). For example, college freshmen show a greater response to such negative life events as the breakup of a relationship than do older men or women (Jackson & Finney, 2002). When people are retired, the combination of low income and physical disability can make matters worse, suggesting that stressful situations can produce cumulative effects (Smith, Langa, Kabeto, & Ubel, 2005).

Victims of natural disasters sometimes suffer from collective trauma that damages the bonds among them. Hurricane Katrina in 2005 separated family members for long periods of time and spawned chaos in the streets of New Orleans. But disasters can also unify communities and bring out the best in us, as our examples of first responders powerfully underscored. Christopher Peterson and Martin Seligman (2003) conducted a survey of character strengths (see also Chapter 11) of 4,817 Americans before the 9/11 terrorist attacks, and within 2 months afterward. After the attacks, kindness, teamwork, leadership, gratitude, hope, love, and spirituality increased.

Stress as a Transaction.   Stress is a highly subjective experience. Some people are devastated by the breakup of a meaningful relationship, whereas others are optimistic about the opportunity to start afresh. People's varied reactions to the same event suggest that we can view stress as a transaction between people and their environments (Coyne & Holroyd, 1982; Lazarus, 1999; Lazarus & Folkman, 1984). Researchers who study stress as a transaction examine how people interpret and cope with stressful events. Richard Lazarus and his coworkers contended that a critical factor determining whether we experience an event as stressful is our appraisal, that is, evaluation, of the event. When we encounter a potentially threatening event, we initially engage in **primary appraisal.** That is, we first decide whether the event is harmful and then make a **secondary appraisal** about how well we can cope with it (Lazarus & Folkman, 1984).

When we believe we can't cope, we're more likely to experience a full-blown stress reaction than when we believe we can (Lazarus, 1999). When we're optimistic and think we can achieve our goals, we're more likely to engage in **problem-focused coping,** a coping strategy in which we tackle life's challenges head-on (Carver & Scheier, 1999; Lazarus & Folkman, 1984). When situations arise that we can't avoid or control, we're more likely to adopt **emotion-focused coping,** a coping strategy in which we try to place a positive spin on our feelings or predicaments and engage in behaviors to reduce painful emotions (Carver, Scheier, & Weintraub, 1989; Lazarus & Folkman, 1984). After the breakup of a relationship, we may remind ourselves that we were unhappy months before it occurred and reenter the dating arena.

Stress as a Response.   Stress researchers also study stress as a response—that is, they assess people's psychological and physical reactions to stressful circumstances. Typically, scientists expose subjects to independent variables like stress-producing stimuli; in other cases, they study people who've encountered real-life stressors. Then they measure a host of dependent variables: stress-related feelings such as depression, hopelessness, and hostility, physiological responses such as heart rate, blood pressure, and the release of stress hormones called **corticosteroids.** These hormones activate the body and prepare us for stressful circumstances. But measuring the size and impact of stressors on mental and physical functioning can be challenging.

NO TWO STRESSES ARE CREATED EQUAL: MEASURING STRESS

Measuring stress is a tricky business, largely because what's exceedingly stressful for one person, like an argument with a boss, may be a mere annoyance for another. Two scales—

the Social Readjustment Rating Scale and the Hassles Scale—endeavor to gauge the nature and impact of differing stressful events.

Major Life Events. Adopting the view that stressors are stimuli, David Holmes and his colleagues developed the Social Readjustment Rating Scale (SRRS) based on forty-three life events ranked in terms of how stressful participants rated them (Holmes & Rahe, 1967; Miller & Rahe, 1997). The first of many efforts to measure life events systematically, the SRRS scale is scored by adding the numbers to the right of each item experienced over the preceding 12 months. Before reading further, try your hand at the SRRS in **Figure 12.1**. (Bear in mind that very high scores indicate only a susceptibility to certain emotional problems, not the presence of these problems themselves.)

1. Death of a spouse — 100
2. Divorce — 73
3. Marital separation — 65
4. Jail term — 63
5. Death of a close family member — 63
6. Personal injury or illness — 53
7. Marriage — 50
8. Fired at work — 47
9. Marital reconciliation — 45
10. Retirement — 45
11. Change in health of family member — 44
12. Pregnancy — 40
13. Sex difficulties — 39
14. Gain of a new family member — 39
15. Business readjustments — 39
16. Change in financial state — 38
17. Death of a close friend — 37
18. Change to different line of work — 36
19. Change in number of arguments with spouse — 35
20. Mortgage over $50,000 — 31
21. Foreclosure of mortgage — 30
22. Change in responsibilities at work — 29
23. Son or daughter leaving home — 29
24. Trouble with in-laws — 29
25. Outstanding personal achievements — 28
26. Spouse begins or stops work — 26
27. Begin or end school — 26
28. Change in living conditions — 25
29. Revision of personal habits — 24
30. Trouble with boss — 23
31. Change in work hours or conditions — 20
32. Change in residence — 20
33. Change in school — 20
34. Change in recreation — 19
35. Change in religious activities — 19
36. Change in social activities — 18
37. Loan less than $50,000 — 17
38. Change in sleeping habits — 16
39. Change in number of family get-togethers — 15
40. Change in eating habits — 15
41. Vacation — 13
42. Holidays — 12
43. Minor violation of laws — 11

Figure 12.1 Social Readjustment Rating Scale. (*Source:* Holmes & Rahe, 1967)

Studies using the SRRS and related measures indicate that the number of stressful events people report over the previous year or so is associated with a variety of physical disorders (Dohrenwend & Dohrenwend, 1974; Holmes & Masuda, 1974) and psychological disorders, like depression (Coyne, 1992; Holahan & Moos, 1991; Schmidt, Murphy, Haq, Rubinow, & Danaceau, 2004). Nevertheless, the sheer number of stressful life events is far from a perfect predictor of who'll become physically or psychologically ill (Coyne & Racioppo, 2000). That's because this approach to measuring stressors doesn't take into consideration other crucial factors, including people's interpretation of events, their coping behaviors and resources, and their problems in recalling events accurately (Coyne & Racioppo, 2000; Lazarus, 1999). It also neglects the fact that some stressful life events, like divorce or troubles with bosses, can be *consequences* rather than *causes* of people's psychological problems (Depue & Monroe, 1986).

Correlation vs. Causation

Getting stuck in traffic is one of many "hassles" we encounter in our daily lives. Research suggests that such hassles can be quite stressful over the long haul.

hassles
minor annoyances or nuisances that strain our ability to cope

> ### APPLY YOUR THINKING
> Imagine you're a researcher conducting research on the potential effects of stressful life events, like job-related stress or marital conflict, on people's physical and psychological health. How might you try to figure out whether some of these life events could have been generated by people's own behavior, like their tendency to provoke disagreements with others?

Hassles: Don't Sweat the Small Stuff. We've all had days when just about everything goes wrong and everybody seems to get on our nerves: Our daily lives are often loaded with **hassles,** minor annoyances or nuisances that strain our ability to cope. But can lots of hassles add up to be as taxing as the monumental events that shake the foundations of our world?

Researchers (DeLongis, Folkman, & Lazarus, 1988; Kanner, Coyne, Schaefer, & Lazarus, 1981) developed the Hassles Scale to measure how stressful events, ranging from small annoyances to major daily pressures, impact our adjustment. Both major life events and hassles are associated with poor general health. Nevertheless, the frequency and perceived severity of hassles are better predictors of physical health, depression, and anxiety than are major life events (Fernandez & Sheffield, 1996; Kanner et al., 1981).

Still, it's possible that major stressful events are the real culprits because they set us off when we already feel hassled, or create hassles with which we then need to cope. To test this alternative hypothesis, researchers have used statistical procedures to show that even when the influence of major life events is subtracted from the mix, hassles still predict psychological adjustment (Forshaw, 2002; Kanner et al., 1981).

Ruling Out Rival Hypotheses

Yet questions about the measurement of hassles remain. Some of the items on the scale, such as difficulties with relaxing and insomnia, may reflect symptoms of psychological disorders, such as depression or anxiety, rather than hassles (Monroe, 1983). However, when the scale developers (DeLongis et al., 1988) revised the scale by removing all words related to symptoms, they found that hassles were still associated with health outcomes.

Ruling Out Rival Hypotheses

To recap, it's important to assess not only events that require major life adaptations but everyday hassles as well. Information about how people appraise stressful situations (Peacock & Wong, 1990), their coping abilities and strategies in specific situations (Carver, 1997), and their goals and available social support (Billings & Moos, 1984) can also help us predict who will and won't thrive in the face of potentially stressful circumstances (Brown & Harris, 1978, 1986).

ASSESS YOUR KNOWLEDGE: FACT OR FICTION?

(1) Most people at one time or another will experience an extremely stressful event. (True/False)

(2) The effects of stressors can be cumulative. (True/False)

(3) Natural disasters may sometimes result in stronger community bonds. (True/False)

(4) According to the stress as a transaction viewpoint, almost all people respond to stressful events in the same way. (True/False)

(5) Major life events have a greater effect on adjustment than do everyday hassles. (True/False)

Answers: (1) T (p. 494); (2) T (p. 496); (3) T (p. 496); (4) F (p. 496); (5) F (p. 496)

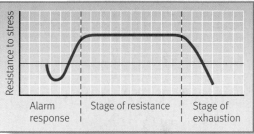

Hans Selye's three-stage account of stress as adaptation shaped most modern-day accounts of the effects of stress on our psychology and physiology.

How We Adapt to Stress: Change and Challenge

As any of us who's had to confront a harrowing event, like a car accident or high-pressure interview for a big job, knows, adapting to stress isn't easy. Yet natural selection has endowed us with a set of responses for coping with anxiety-provoking circumstances.

THE MECHANICS OF STRESS: SELYE'S GENERAL ADAPTATION SYNDROME

In 1956, Canadian physician Hans Selye ignited the field of modern-day stress research by publishing *The Stress of Life*, a landmark book that unveiled his decades of study on the effects of prolonged stress on the body. Selye's search for a new sex hormone in rats led him to discover that animals reacted with similar physical symptoms to a variety of different injections. Ironically, Selye never discovered a new sex hormone. However, his genius was to recognize a connection between his injections and symptoms of stress in the animals, including stomach ulcers and increases in the size of the adrenal gland, which produces stress hormones. Selye further connected this stress response in animals with his observations of ill patients, who showed a consistent pattern of stress-related responses.

Dovetailing with the engineering analogy we've already discussed, Selye believed that too much stress leads to breakdowns. He argued that we're equipped with a sensitive physiology that responds to stressful circumstances by kicking us into high gear. He called the pattern of responding to stress the **general adaptation syndrome (GAS).** According to Selye, all prolonged stressors take us through three stages of adaptation: *alarm, resistance,* and *exhaustion* (see **Figure 12.2**).

To illustrate key aspects of the GAS, and the extent to which our appraisals determine our reactions to stress, let's consider the experience of a participant in one of Barbara Rothbaum's treatment studies of flying phobia (Rothbaum et al., 2006). We'll call the participant Mark and hone in on what he experienced during the sixth treatment session. As Mark feels the plane moving through pockets of turbulence, his cold, clammy hands clutch the shaking seat. His mouth is dry. His heart pounds. His breathing is rapid and shallow. He feels lightheaded and dizzy. Images of plane crashes he's seen on television pop uncontrollably into his mind. On some level he knows he's safe, but that doesn't help.

Mark knows he's safe because he's not actually in a plane; he's in a virtual environment, created by sophisticated, computer-controlled equipment that simulates the experience of being in an airplane making its way through thunderstorms. The head-mounted display

Head-mounted displays provide sights and sounds that create a "virtual environment."

general adaptation syndrome (GAS)
stress-response pattern proposed by Hans Selye that consists of three stages: alarm, resistance, and exhaustion

Figure 12.2 Selye's General Adaptation Syndrome. According to Selye's general adaptation syndrome, our level of resistance to stress drops during the alarm phase, increases during the resistance phase, and drops again during the exhaustion phase. (*Source:* Selye, 1956)

Resistance to stress

Alarm response | Stage of resistance | Stage of exhaustion

that Mark wears provides him with visual and sound cues, and a platform below him that trembles simulates the feeling of turbulence. Altogether, the effect is so convincing that much of the time he forgets he's in a laboratory.

Over the course of ten sessions, Mark successfully confronted and tamed his flying anxiety. Rothbaum and her team first taught Mark anxiety management techniques, including deep breathing and helping him to recognize that his uncomfortable physical reactions are responses to his negative thoughts about flying. Next, they "virtually" exposed him to situations he feared, starting with sitting in the plane with the engines off and progressing all the way to flying in bad weather and landing safely. Rothbaum and her colleagues found that 70 percent of participants who completed virtual exposure therapy could continue to fly in an airplane. In contrast, few participants who didn't complete this therapy could do so. Let's examine Mark's experiences in terms of the GAS.

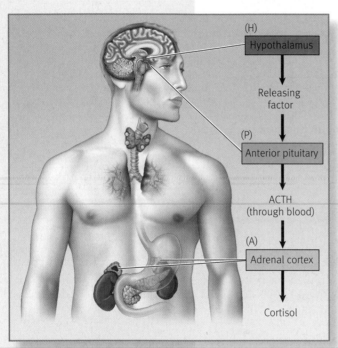

Figure 12.3 The Hypothalamus-Pituitary-Adrenal (HPA) Axis.

The Alarm Reaction. Selye's first stage, the *alarm reaction*, involves excitation of the autonomic nervous system, the discharge of the stress hormone adrenaline, and physical symptoms of anxiety. Joseph LeDoux (1996) and others have identified the seat of anxiety within a region of the midbrain—dubbed the *emotional brain*—that consists of the amygdala, hypothalamus, and hippocampus (see Chapter 3). Mark's swift emotional reaction to his perception of an air pocket bump is tripped largely by the amygdala, where vital emotional memories are stored (see Chapters 7 and 11) and create gut feelings of a possible crash.

The hypothalamus sits atop a mind-body link known as the *hypothalamus-pituitary-adrenal* (HPA) axis, shown in **Figure 12.3**. When the hypothalamus (H) receives signals of fear, it hooks up with the pituitary gland (P), which releases hormones, including adrenaline, that trigger anxiety. Blood pressure rises as adrenaline (A) readies Mark for the **fight-or-flight response** that Walter Cannon first described in 1915. This response is a set of physiological or psychological reactions that mobilize us to either confront or leave a threatening situation. Cannon noted that when people or animals face a threat, they have two options: *fight* (actively attack the threat or cope in the immediate situation) or *flee* (escape). Of course, Mark can't take flight in an actual airplane given that's he's "in flight" and can't physically escape the source of his anxiety. So his fear escalates, with his hippocampus retrieving terrifying images in the news of planes going down in flames.

Resistance. After the initial rush of adrenaline, Mark enters Selye's second stage of the GAS: *resistance*. He adapts to the stressor and finds ways to cope with it. The instant Mark's hippocampus detected danger from the first apparent jolt of rough air, it opened up a gateway to portions of his cerebral cortex, which LeDoux (1996) called the "thinking brain." Confronted with a stressful situation, we examine each new development as it unfolds, consider alternative solutions, and direct our efforts toward constructing a coping plan.

At one point, Mark experienced a sudden impulse to bolt from his seat, but his basal ganglia, linked to the frontal cortex of his thinking brain, wisely led him to think better of it. Mark slowly but surely got a handle on his fears. He reminded himself that flying is statistically much safer than driving and that he's flown through choppy air in the past without being injured. He recalled that most of the passengers looked calm even when the plane flew through a nasty storm.

Mark learned other coping behaviors. He reminded himself to breathe slowly, and with each breath his relaxation replaced tension. He no longer felt lightheaded, and his tingling

fight-or-flight response
physical and psychological reaction that mobilizes people and animals to either defend themselves (fight) or escape (flee) a threatening situation

sensations disappeared. The exercise helps because when we're anxious our breathing is often rapid and shallow. When we don't exhale sufficiently, carbon dioxide accumulates at the bottom of our lungs, and even tiny increases in carbon dioxide level can cause numbness, tingling, and lightheadedness. Excess oxygen that accumulated with each of Mark's shallow, rapid breaths made his heart beat strongly and rapidly.

Exhaustion. Mark calmed down, and when the simulated flight ended he felt more in control of his fear. But what happens when a stressor, such as wartime combat lasting months, is more prolonged and uncontrollable? Here's when the third stage of Selye's GAS—*exhaustion*—sets in. If our personal resources are limited and we lack good coping measures, our resistance may ultimately break down, causing our levels of activation to bottom out. The results can range from damage to an organ system, to depression and anxiety, to a breakdown in the immune system (which we'll discuss later in the chapter).

THE DIVERSITY OF STRESS RESPONSES

Not all of us react to stressors with a fight-or-flight response. Our reactions vary from one stressor to another, and these reactions may be shaped by gender.

Fight or Flight or Tend and Befriend? Shelley Taylor and her colleagues coined the catchy phrase **tend and befriend** to describe a common pattern of reacting to stress among women (Taylor, Klein, Lewis, Gruenwald, Gurung, & Updegraff, 2000), although some men display it too. Taylor observed that in times of stress, women generally rely on their social contacts and nurturing abilities—they *tend* to those around them and to themselves—more than men do. When stressed out, women typically *befriend*, or turn to others for support.

In stressful times, women often rely on friendships for support and comfort, a pattern that psychologist Shelley Taylor called "tend and befriend."

That's not to say that women lack a self-preservation instinct. They don't shirk from defending themselves and their children or from attempting to escape when physically threatened. However, compared with men, women generally have more to lose—especially when they're pregnant, nursing, or caring for children—if they're injured or killed fighting or fleeing. Therefore, over the course of evolutionary history, they've developed a tend-and-befriend rather than a fight-or-flight pattern of reacting to stressful circumstances to boost the odds of their and their offspring's' survival. The hormone *oxytocin* (see Chapter 3) further counters stress and promotes the tend-and-befriend response (Kosfield, Heinrichs, Zaks, Fischbacher, & Fehr, 2005; Taylor et al., 2000).

Still, men and women are more alike than different in how they respond to stressors. Surely many men are invested in close relationships and caring for children, and many women react with a fight-or-flight response when endangered.

The horrific 2007 shooting spree at Virginia Tech left some survivors with symptoms of posttraumatic stress disorder.

Long-Lasting Stress Reactions. Bad things happen to all of us. For most of us, life goes on. But others experience long-lasting psychological repercussions including posttraumatic stress disorder, anxiety, and depression (Meichenbaum, 1994; Yehuda, Resnick, Kahana, & Gilbert, 1993).

When Stress Is Too Much: Posttraumatic Stress Disorder. On April 16, 2007, 23-year-old Cho Seung-Hui, a student at Virginia Tech, went on a shooting rampage, killing thirty-one classmates and professors before taking his own life. When Marjorie Lindholm, 24, heard the news of the massacre, she immediately relived the terror she experienced as a student at Columbine High School on April 20, 1999. On that day, two students, Eric Harris and Dylan Klebold, shot twelve of her classmates and a teacher before turning the guns on themselves. In a television interview she said, "I started crying, then shaking. I remembered everything I saw at Columbine. I got physically ill. There is no way I'm going to forget that day" (Stepp, 2007).

tend and befriend
reaction that mobilizes people to nurture (tend) or seek social support (befriend) under stress

Combat ranks with sexual assault as one of two events producing the highest risk for PTSD.

Marjorie displays some of the hallmark symptoms of *posttraumatic stress disorder* (PTSD), a condition that sometimes follows extremely stressful life events. Its telltale symptoms include vivid memories, feelings, and images of traumatic experiences, known commonly as *flashbacks*. Other symptoms of PTSD, which we'll consider in greater depth in Chapter 15, include efforts to avoid reminders of the trauma, feeling detached or estranged from others, and symptoms of increased arousal, such as difficulty sleeping and startling easily. The lifetime prevalence of PTSD is 5 percent in men and 10 percent in women (Kessler et al., 1995). The severity, duration, and nearness to the stressor all affect people's likelihood of developing PTSD (American Psychiatric Association, 2000).

PsychoMythology

Almost All People Are Traumatized by Highly Aversive Events

A widespread view in popular psychology is that most people exposed to trauma develop PTSD or other serious psychological disorders. Immediately following the 9/11 attacks, for example, many mental health professionals predicted an epidemic of PTSD across the United States (Sommers & Satel, 2004). Were they right?

George Bonanno and his colleagues conducted a study that underscores the remarkable resilience of survivors of extremely aversive events (Bonanno, Galea, Bucciarelli, & Vlahov, 2006). Using a random-digit dialing procedure, researchers sampled 2,752 adults in the New York City area about 6 months after the 9/11 attacks. They conducted their assessments using a computer-assisted telephone interview system. People were judged to be resilient if they reported 0 or 1 PTSD symptoms during the first 6 months after the attack. Bonanno's results offered surprising evidence for psychological adjustment; 65.1 percent of the sample was resilient. A quarter of the people who were in the World Trade Center at the time of the attack had probable PTSD, although more than half of the people in this category were resilient. Other research indicates that although most Americans were profoundly upset for several days following the 9/11 attacks, nearly all quickly regained their equilibrium and returned to their previous level of functioning (McNally, 2002). So when it comes to responses to trauma, resilience is the rule rather than the exception.

People who cope well in the aftermath of a serious stressor tend to display relatively high levels of functioning before the event (Bonanno, Moskowitz, Papa, & Folkman, 2005). Yet resilience isn't limited to a few particularly well-adjusted, brave, or tough-minded people, nor to a single type or class of events. Instead, it's actually the most common response to traumatic events. Most people who take care of a partner dying of AIDS, suffer the death of a spouse, or survive a physical or sexual assault report few long-term psychological symptoms (Bonanno, 2004). **Table 12.1** presents the rates of PTSD and acute stress disorder (a disorder similar to, although briefer in duration than, PTSD) associated with a number of other disturbing events. As we can see, only a minority of people who contend with such events develop PTSD or acute stress disorder.

Table 12.1 Percentages of People Who Develop Posttraumatic Conditions as a Function of the Event.

Percentage of People Who Develop PTSD	
Natural disaster	4%–5%
Bombing	34%
Plane crash into hotel	29%
Mass shooting	28%

Percentage of People Who Develop Acute Stress Disorder	
Typhoon	7%
Industrial accident	6%
Mass shooting	33%
Violent assault	19%
Vehicle accident	14%
Assault, severe burns	13%

(*Source:* Bryant, 2000, National Center for PTSD)

Anxiety and Depression. Anxiety and depression can arise in the wake of stressful events. In dire straits, we're likely to feel overwhelmed by seemingly unresolvable situations and unsolvable problems (Mellinger & Lynn, 2003). When we interpret events as threatening, dangerous, and uncontrollable, we're especially vulnerable to anxiety (Gibb & Coles, 2005).

The longer we feel we lack control over our lives, and the longer we feel helpless or responsible for our failures, the greater the likelihood that our anxiety will morph into depression (Chorpita & Barlow, 1998; see also Chapter 15). People with depression are 2.5 times more likely than nondepressed people to have experienced one or more events that involve loss, like the death of a loved one (Mazure, 1998; Shrout, Link, Dohrenwend, Skodal, Stueve, & Mirotznki, 1989).

ASSESS YOUR KNOWLEDGE: FACT OR FICTION?

(1) People's first reaction to an extreme stressor involves activation of the autonomic nervous system. (True/False)
(2) Physical illness can be a reaction to a prolonged stressor. (True/False)
(3) Men and women are equally likely to exhibit a "tend and befriend" response. (True/False)
(4) The likelihood of developing PTSD is unrelated to the severity or duration of the stressor. (True/False)
(5) Few people are resilient in the face of extreme stress. (True/False)

Answers: (1) T (p. 500); (2) T (p. 501); (3) F (p. 501); (4) F (p. 502); (5) F (p. 502)

The Brain–Body Reaction to Stress

In 1962, two Japanese physicians, Y. Ikemi and S. Nakagawa, conducted a study demonstrating the intimate connection between brain and body. Their study, which researchers today might find difficult to carry out for ethical reasons, showed how hypnotic and direct suggestions from a respected authority figure can produce dramatic skin reactions. The researchers selected thirteen boys who contracted a red, itchy skin reaction when touched with the leaves of a tree similar to poison ivy. Five boys received a hypnotic induction with suggestions for relaxation and drowsiness, and another group of eight boys received no prior hypnotic induction—just suggestions administered while they were awake and alert.

All boys sat with their eyes closed and weren't aware of what types of leaves were touching them. A respected physician told all the boys that he was touching them with the leaves of the poison ivy–type tree, when in fact he was touching them with leaves from a harmless tree. In the second phase, Ikemi and Nakagawa reversed the conditions: they rubbed the boys' arms with the poison–ivy type leaves, but told them the leaves were harmless.

The reactions were remarkable. In the first phase, all hypnotic subjects and all suggestion-alone subjects showed significant skin disturbance as a result of believing they were touched by the poison ivy–type leaves. As is so often the case in psychology, beliefs can create reality, in this case a *nocebo effect* (see Chapter 2). In the second phase, four of five hypnotic subjects and seven of eight suggestion-alone subjects didn't show any skin reactions to the leaves, even though all had developed skin reactions to the leaves prior to the study (Ikemi & Nakagawa, 1962).

This study demonstrates how psychological factors, in this case the stressful idea of contracting an itchy rash, can influence physical processes. Indeed, much of what we call a "psychological" response to events manifests itself in physiological reactions. In this chapter and others, we'll see that stress can spill over into multiple domains of life, creating physical difficulties that disrupt our sleep (Chapter 5) and sexual functioning (Chapter 11). But can stress seep into our cells and weaken our body's defenses against infections? A number of fascinating studies tell us that the answer is yes.

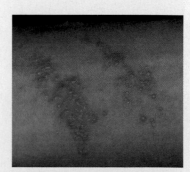

Suggestion alone can produce an uncomfortable rash much like that produced by poison ivy in people who are highly sensitive to poison ivy.

fictoid

Myth: All stress is "bad" and can never be advantageous.

Reality: Selye coined the term *eustress*, based on the Greek word "eu" meaning "good," to distinguish it from *distress*, or "bad" stress. Events that are challenging yet not overwhelming, such as competing in an athletic event or giving a speech, are examples of "positive stress" that provide opportunities for personal growth.

NEW FRONTIERS

Brain Studies Reveal Placebos Are "Strong Medicines"

Placebo effects provide powerful illustrations of the mind—body connection. Remarkably, we can even see them at work in Parkinson's disease, a serious and irreversible illness. It produces slow movements, rigid muscles, and tremors associated with decreased levels of the neurotransmitter dopamine (see Chapter 3). Parkinson's generally afflicts people over 60 years of age, but can occasionally strike people in their 20s and 30s, as in the case of actor Michael J. Fox. The recent discovery of a strong placebo response in Parkinson's disease electrified the scientific community.

In one study (McRae et al., 2004), scientists transplanted dopamine neurons from a fetus into the brains of Parkinson's patients. They hoped this procedure would stimulate dopamine production and improve patients' quality of life. Other patients underwent a sham (fake) operation to persuade them that the cells were actually inserted. (Although it's worth noting that the question of whether such operations are ethical is controversial among scientists; Miller 2003.) A year later, patients who *thought* they underwent the real surgery had a better quality of life—for example, better physical functioning and social support—than those who thought they received the sham surgery, regardless of which procedure surgeons performed.

In another study, researchers injected Parkinson's patients with a placebo saline (salt) solution, leading patients to believe the solution was an anti-Parkinsonian drug. The placebo effect was impressive: the rate of discharge in single nerve cells in the brain slowed and mirrored positive changes in patients' symptoms (Benedetti et al., 2004). Parkinson's patients given placebos and told their movements would improve show not only improved movements, but also increases in brain dopamine (de la Fuente-Fernandez et al., 2001), probably reflecting the role of the dopamine in reward and hope (see Chapter 3).

Physical pain and depression also respond to placebos. Tor Wager and his colleagues told patients that a cream would reduce the pain of heat or electric shock (Wager et al., 2004). After they applied placebo cream to patients' skin, they reported less pain, and brain imaging (fMRI) detected less activity in brain areas that register pain perception.

As we learned in Chapter 2, placebo effects may account for as much as 80 percent of the effects of antidepressant medication (Kirsch, Moore, Scoboria, & Nicholls, 2002). Andrew Leuchter and his associates discovered that placebos produced improvement in 38 percent of depressed patients compared with 52 percent of depressed patients who received antidepressant medication (Leuchter, Cook, Witte, Morgan, & Abrams, 2002). In patients who received placebos, neuronal activity increased in brain structures associated with information processing, memory, and attention. Interestingly, among patients who received the active medication, activity decreased in the same brain region. Depressed people therefore respond to expectations of improvement differently than they do to genuine medication.

Although doctors should certainly prescribe real medications, they may be able to harness the power of placebos—by increasing patients' hope, positive expectancies, and optimism—to alleviate some physical symptoms and enhance the effects of available treatments.

immune system
our body's defense system against invading bacteria, viruses, and other potentially illness-producing organisms and substances

acquired immune deficiency syndrome (AIDS)
a life-threatening, incurable, yet treatable condition in which the human immunodeficiency virus (HIV) attacks and damages the immune system

psychoneuroimmunology
study of the relationship between the immune system and central nervous system

THE IMMUNE SYSTEM

Ordinarily (and thankfully!), we never have to think about the billions of viruses, fungi, protozoa, and bacteria that share our environment or inhabit our body. That's because our **immune system** neutralizes or destroys them. The immune system is our body's defense against invading bacteria, viruses, and other potentially illness-producing organisms and substances. Our first shield from these foreign invaders, called *antigens*, is the skin, which blocks the entry of many disease-producing organisms, called *pathogens*. When we cough or sneeze, the lungs expel harmful bacteria and viruses. Saliva, urine, tears, perspiration, and stomach acid also rid our body of pathogens.

Some viruses or bacteria penetrate these defenses, but the immune system is wily, and has other means of safeguarding us. *Phagocytes* and *lymphocytes* are two types of specialized white blood cells manufactured in the marrow of the bones. One type of phagocyte, called a *neutrophil*, is abundant, and is first at the scene of an infection to engulf an invader. Longer-lived *macrophages* also wander through the body as scavengers, sticking to and destroying remaining antigens and dead tissue. Two types of lymphocytes, *T cells* and *B cells*, are also stalwart soldiers in the night-and-day battle to keep us healthy. Killer T cells, as they're called, move through the body and attach to proteins on the surface of virus- and cancer-infected cells, popping them like balloons. Memory T cells recognize the invading cells after an initial infection and promote an efficient response upon reinfection. B cells produce proteins called *antibodies*, which stick to the surface of the invader, slow its progress, and attract other proteins that destroy the foreign organism.

Because of a rare disorder, severe combined immunodeficiency disease, David Vetter was required to live in a sterile plastic "bubble" from the moment he was born in 1971. Sadly, when David was 12, a procedure intended to let him live outside the bubble resulted in an infection that ended his life.

Under ordinary circumstances, the immune system is remarkably effective. But it's not a perfect barrier against infection. For example, some cancer cells can suppress an effective immune response, multiply, and wreak havoc in the body. Serious disorders of the immune system, such as **acquired immune deficiency syndrome (AIDS),** are life-threatening. AIDS is an incurable yet often treatable condition in which the human immunodeficiency virus (HIV) attacks and damages the immune system. When the immune system is overactive, it can launch an attack on various organs of the body, causing *autoimmune diseases* like arthritis, in which the immune system causes swelling and pain at the joints, and multiple sclerosis, in which the immune system attacks the protective myelin sheath surrounding neurons (see Chapter 3).

People from all walks of life can contract the HIV virus and develop AIDS.

Psychoneuroimmunology: Our Bodies, Our Environments, and Our Health.

The study of the relationship between the immune system and central nervous system—the seat of our emotions and reactions to the environment (Chapter 3)—goes by a mouthful of a name: **psychoneuroimmunology** (Cohen & Herbert, 1996). When evaluating psychoneuroimmunology we must be careful not to fall prey to exaggerated claims. Illnesses aren't the result of negative thinking, nor can positive thinking reverse serious illnesses like cancer (Hines, 2003)—despite assertions by immensely popular alternative medical practitioners like Andrew Weil (2000) and Deepak Chopra (1989). Nor, despite early and widely publicized claims (Fawzy et al., 1993; Spiegel, Bloom, Kramer, & Gottheil, 1989), does psychotherapy appear to prolong the survival of people diagnosed with cancer (Coyne, Stefanek, & Palmer, 2007). Nevertheless, researchers using rigorous designs have discovered at least some fascinating links between our life circumstances and our ability to fend off illnesses.

Dr. Andrew Weil and Dr. Deepak Chopra have popularized the idea that the "mind" can cure serious illnesses. Yet most of their optimistic claims aren't supported by scientific evidence.

Stress and Colds. Many people believe they're more likely to get a cold when they're really stressed out—and they're right. Sheldon Cohen and his associates placed

psychophysiological
illnesses such as asthma and ulcers in which emotions and stress contribute to, maintain, or aggravate the physical condition

biopsychosocial perspective
the view that an illness or medical condition is the product of the interplay of biological, psychological, and social factors

coronary heart disease (CHD)
damage to the heart from the complete or partial blockage of the arteries that provide oxygen to the heart

Type A personality
personality type that describes people who are competitive, driven, hostile, and ambitious

Ruling Out Rival Hypotheses

Caretakers of people with Alzheimer's disease experience high levels of stress, are at heightened risk of developing depression, and even show decreases in their blood's ability to clot (associated with having a stroke) in response to stressful life events (von Kanel, Dimsdale, Patterson, & Grant, 2003). For reasons that are unknown, the negative pyschological effects of such caretaking seem to be lower among African Americans than Caucasians (Janevic & Connell, 2001).

cold viruses into volunteers' nasal passages (Cohen, Tyrell, & Smith, 1991). Other volunteers, in a placebo condition, didn't receive the virus, but instead received nasal drops with a saline solution. Stressful life events in the year preceding the study predicted the number of colds people developed when exposed to the virus. Exposure to the virus was also important. People in the placebo condition didn't develop as many colds, even when they experienced stressful events in the year before the study. The researchers (Cohen, Frank, Doyle, Skoner, Rabin, & Gwaltney, 1998) later discovered that significant stressors, such as unemployment and interpersonal difficulties lasting at least a month, were the best predictors of who developed a cold. But a network of friends and relatives, and close ties to the community, afforded protection against colds (Cohen, Doyle, Skoner, Rabin, & Gwaltney, 1997; Cohen, Doyle, Turner, Alper, & Skoner, 2003).

It's possible that stress affects health-related behaviors but has no direct impact on the immune system. For instance, our susceptibility to a cold may increase because when we're under stress we tend to sleep poorly, eat nonnutritious foods, and smoke and drink alcohol excessively, all of which depress the immune system. Yet Cohen and his colleagues found that even when they controlled for these influences, the relation between stress and colds remained.

Stress and Immune Function: Beyond the Common Cold. Janice Kielcot-Glaser and her associates are pioneers in the study of the connection between stressors and the immune system. Caring for a family member with Alzheimer's disease, a severe form of dementia (see Chapter 3), can be exceedingly stressful and cause long-term deregulation of the immune system. Kiecolt-Glaser demonstrated that a small wound (standardized for size) took 24 percent longer to heal in Alzheimer's caregivers compared with a group of people who weren't taking care of a relative with Alzheimer's (Kiecolt-Glaser, Marucha, Malarkey, Mercado, & Glaser, 1995). All of the following stressors can lead to disruptions in the immune system (Kiecolt-Glaser, McGuire, Robles, & Glaser, 2002):

- taking an important test
- the death of a spouse
- unemployment
- marital conflict
- living near a damaged nuclear reactor
- natural disasters

The good news is that positive emotions and social support, which we'll consider later in the chapter, can fortify our immune systems (Esterling, Kiecolt-Glaser & Glaser, 1996; Kennedy, Kiecolt-Glaser, & Glaser, 1990).

STRESS-RELATED ILLNESSES: A BIOPSYCHOSOCIAL VIEW

We've all heard the expression that an illness is "all in your head." Today that's just a polite way of saying "Quit worrying." But not long ago a common myth of popular psychology was that beliefs and mental states were the root causes of many physical ailments. Certain illnesses or disorders were once called *psychosomatic*, because psychologists believed that psychological conflicts and emotional reactions were the culprits. Today, psychologists use the term **psychophysiological** to describe illnesses like asthma and ulcers in which emotions and stress contribute to, maintain, or aggravate physical conditions.

Today, psychologists widely acknowledge that emotions and stress are associated with physical disorders, including coronary heart disease and AIDS. Most scientists have adopted a **biopsychosocial perspective,** which proposes that most medical conditions are neither all physical nor all psychological. Numerous physical illnesses depend on the interplay of genes, lifestyle, immunity, social support, everyday stressors, and self-perceptions (Markus & Kitayama, 1991; Turk, 1996).

Coronary Heart Disease. Scientists have learned that psychological factors, including stress and personality traits, are key risk factors for **coronary heart disease (CHD).** CHD is the complete or partial blockage of the arteries that provide oxygen to the heart, and is the number one cause of death and disability in the United States (Centers for Disease Control and Prevention, 2004). It accounts for an astonishing 1 in every 2.5 deaths, and almost a million deaths every year (Gatchel & Oordt, 2003). Before age 60, men are more likely than women to die from CHD. But after 60, the statistics even out: 1 in 4 men and women die of CHD. CHD develops when deposits of *cholesterol*—a waxy, fatty substance that travels in the bloodstream—collect in the walls of arteries, narrowing and blocking the coronary arteries, creating a condition called *atherosclerosis*. When atherosclerosis worsens, it can lead to chest pain and the deterioration and death of heart tissue, otherwise known as a heart attack (see **Figure 12.4**).

The Role of Stress in CHD. A host of factors are associated with CHD. Advanced age, diabetes, high blood pressure, and a family history of the disease are high on the list of risk factors. As we mentioned earlier, stress is also associated with CHD risk. Stressful life events predict recurrences of heart attacks, high blood pressure, increased glucose levels, and enlargement of the heart associated with CHD (Repetti, Taylor, & Seeman, 2002; Schnall et al., 1990; Troxel et al., 2003). Although only correlational, these data suggest that stressors may sometimes produce negative physiological effects. Moreover, high levels of stress hormones triggered by extreme stress can lead to disruptions in normal heart rhythm and even sudden death, as well as to atherosclerosis in people who are highly reactive to everyday stressors (Carney, Freedland, & Veith, 2005; Sarafino, 2006). People with CHD also show signs of a hyped-up autonomic nervous system, with elevated heart rates and exaggerated responses to physical stressors (Carney et al., 2005).

The ABCs of Personality in CHD. In addition to stress, researchers have suggested that longstanding behavior patterns or traits contribute to risk for CHD. When we picture someone at risk for a heart attack, certain personality characteristics come to mind: competitive, hard-driving, ambitious, and impatient. The media have widely popularized the so-called **Type A personality** (as opposed to the calmer and mellower *Type B personality*) who fits this description.

Two cardiologists, Meyer Friedman and Ray Rosenman (1959), coined this term to describe a curious behavior pattern they observed among CHD patients. They noticed that the chairs in their hospital waiting room were rapidly becoming worn out around the edges. Many of their CHD patients were literally sitting and bouncing on the edges of their seats because of restlessness. But long before Friedman and Rosenman dubbed some of their patients Type A, in 1892, Canadian physician William Osler described the heart attack–prone person as "a keen and ambitious man, the indicator of whose engines are set a full speed ahead" (Chesney & Rosenman, 1980, p. 1988). Later, Friedman and Rosenman (1974) identified additional characteristics that clustered under the Type A description: perfectionistic, prone to hostility, stubborn, opinionated, cynical, and controlling.

Rosenman and Friedman launched the Western Collaborative Group Study (Rosenman et al., 1975; Rosenman, Friedman, Straus, et al., 1964) of 3,500 males to determine whether Type A personality traits predict CHD risk over an 8 1/2-year period. They found that even when they took other risk factors, like smoking and diet, into account, Type A traits were still associated with later heart disease risk. Although early studies revealed high rates of CHD among extreme Type A individuals, later studies yielded many negative results (Gatchel & Oorts, 2003). Scientists began to question whether the fact that a constellation of traits is associated with increased risk means that each trait is equally important. Is a person who hustles to meet deadlines equally at risk for a heart attack as a person who's cynical and hostile? Scientists soon turned to the question of which Type A traits are most associated with heightened risk.

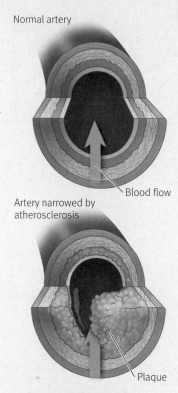

Normal artery

Blood flow

Artery narrowed by atherosclerosis

Plaque

Figure 12.4 Atherosclerosis. Cholesterol deposits in the large arteries form plaque, restricting the flow of blood. This condition, called *atherosclerosis*, can result in stroke, heart attack, and serious chest pain.

"You haven't been taking your cholesterol medication." (Randy Glasbergen, www.glasbergen.com)

The classic Framingham Study, which began in 1948, continues to examine the health of over 5,000 men and women in Framingham, Massachusetts. This longitudinal study has provided a treasure trove of data on risk factors for CHD.

Can chronic anger be bad for our health? Research indicates that the anger component of the Type A personality can be deadly, increasing our risk for coronary heart disease.

Table 12.2 Sample Items from the DS14.

Negative affectivity

- I am often in a bad mood. (T)
- I often find myself worrying about something. (T)
- I am often irritated. (T)

Social inhibition

- I would rather keep people at a distance. (T)
- When socializing, I don't find the right things to talk about. (T)
- I often feel inhibited in social interactions. (T)

(*Source:* Denollet, 2005)

Correlation vs. Causation

Type D personality
personality type that describes people who experience yet inhibit negative emotions

Anger and Hostility. Of all Type A traits, hostility appears to be the most predictive of heart disease (Matthews, Gump, Harris, Haney & Barefoot, 2004; Myrtek, 2001; Smith & Gallo, 2001). In one study, researchers gave medical students a test of hostility and tracked them down 25 years later. Those with high hostility scores were more likely to have suffered and died from CHD than those with low scores (Barefoot, Dahlstrom, & Williams, 1983). In a study of older white men, hostility surpassed traditional risk factors including smoking, weight, and cholesterol in predicting CHD (Niaura, Todaro, Stroud, Spiro, Ward, & Weiss, 2002). But there's a silver lining to this gray cloud: damping down hostility helps. When researchers taught CHD patients techniques to curtail their hostility, they found a 37 percent decrease in deaths from heart attacks compared with other patients (Dusseldorp, van Eldren, Maes, Meulman, & Kraaij, 1999; Friedman et al., 1987).

Type D Personality. A recent addition to the alphabet soup of personality types is the **Type D personality.** The "D" stands for "distressed" and describes people who simultaneously experience strong negative emotions and inhibit expression of these emotions.

John Denollet (2005) developed a test called the DS14 with (not surprisingly) fourteen items that assess "negative affectivity" (worry, irritability, dysphoria, gloom) and "social inhibition" (discomfort in social interactions, reticence, and a lack of social poise). To qualify as a Type D personality, a person must score highly on both negative affectivity and social inhibition (see **Table 12.2**).

Denollet and his associates (Denollet, Sys, & Brutsaert, 1995) followed 105 patients for an average of 3.8 years after they experienced a heart attack. They found that 39 percent of patients with Type D personality died, mostly of a heart attack or stroke, whereas only 5 percent of other patients died. Denollet (2005) reported that 21 percent of people in the general population, 28 percent of patients with CHD, and 53 percent of people with high blood pressure (a risk factor for CHD) had Type D personalities. A key question that remains unanswered is whether relieving distress will help people live longer and better lives and ultimately reduce their risk of CHD.

CHD, Everyday Experiences, and Socioeconomic Factors. Hostility, depression, and hopelessness don't always arise from enduring personality traits. These negative emotions can stem from the many pressures and demands we confront in our fast-paced, competitive society. Let's consider three sources of support for the claim that everyday experiences set the stage for many physical problems, including heart disease. First, people who experience even one significant drop in their income over a 5-year period face a 30 percent increase in their risk of dying from any cause. Two such drops in income jack up the risk to a whopping 70 percent (Duncan, 1996). Second, African American women who experience discrimination and unfair treatment, and who report high stress levels, have more narrowing and blockage of their arteries than other African American women (Troxel, Matthews, Bromberger, & Sutton-Tyrell, 2003). Third, CHD is associated with substantial job stress and dissatisfaction (Quick, Quick, Nelson, & Hurrell, 1997). Although job stress is correlated with CHD, it may not cause it in all circumstances. An interesting possibility that has yet to be fully explored is that the causal arrow is reversed: perhaps CHD causes job stress in some people.

Still, these findings, along with the others we've examined, point to another possibility that's been well supported by research: The burden of most health problems is shared disproportionately by the poor. Researchers have established a strong correlation between poverty and poor health (Antonovsky, 1967; Repetti, Taylor, & Seeman, 2002), but we still need to ask, "What's responsible for this association?"

Linda Gallo and Karen Matthews (2003) addressed this question. They noted that life can prove immensely challenging for people who have little education, struggle in a bad job with a nasty supervisor, and barely make enough money to pay the bills. People from low SES backgrounds who regularly encounter these circumstances experience a powerful drain on their personal and interpersonal resources. This state of affairs decreases their ability to cope with future stressors and with depression, hopelessness, and hostility, which as we've seen, increase the risk of poor health and CHD. To make matters worse, negative thoughts and feelings can promote unhealthy habits like smoking, drinking, and lack of exercise, which further increase the risk of physical problems (Gallo & Matthews, 2003).

APPLY YOUR THINKING

Many people are aware of the risk factors for CHD, yet don't change their behaviors. Why might this be so? Why is providing people with information about the dangers of obesity, for example, not a sufficient motivator for them to exercise more and eat less? We'll address this question later, but think about it now (and don't look ahead!).

Illness Can Create Stress We've seen that stress can contribute to physical disorders, such as CHD. But of course, physical disorders can also create stress. Not surprisingly, being diagnosed with a potentially fatal illness that has an uncertain outcome, like cancer, can be unimaginably stressful and pose innumerable challenges. The specter of death and feelings of hopelessness, along with side effects of treatment, including profound fatigue and embarrassing hair loss, frequently compound the distress of cancer. People who suffer from cancer often endure chronic pain and wonder whether even a slight increase in pain signals a downward, perhaps fatal, turn in the progression of their illness. Irritability, anger, and frustration can also be by-products of prolonged periods of pain-related sleeplessness and the fatigue that results from it (Moffitt, Kalucy, Kalucy, Baum, & Cooke, 1991).

In addition, some people are biased against, or afraid of, others with a potentially fatal disease, like cancer or AIDS. Even though this situation can be stressful for persons with these diseases, successful treatment comes with its own set of challenges. The transition from poor to dramatically improved health can introduce new and difficult decisions, like whether to return to work or to begin or end relationships (Catz & Kelly, 2001).

Asthma: Chronic Illness and Stress. **Asthma** provides another example of how an illness can contribute to stress and hamper people's ability to cope with life's challenges. The 10 to 15 million Americans who suffer from asthma (Gatchel & Oordt, 2003) find it difficult to breathe because the bronchial tubes in their lungs are inflamed, spasm, and become clogged with mucus (see **Figure 12.5** on the next page). People with asthma feel tightness in their chest, cough, and wheeze because of their lung condition. The narrowing of the bronchial tube can become so severe that it's life-threatening (Gatchel & Oordt, 2003).

When asthmatics react to an attack with fear and agitation, their symptoms can intensify to the point of being disabling. Asthma sufferers often must deal with sleep loss, absences from school and work, loss of income, and restriction of everyday activities (Labott, 2004; Mailick, Holden, & Walther, 1994). Understandably, asthma is associated with anxiety (Vila, Nollet-Clemencon, deBlic, Mouren-Simeoni, & Scheinmann, 2000) and depression (Chaney, Mullins, Uretsky, Pace, Werden, & Hartman, 1999). Emotions by themselves don't cause most asthma attacks, but physical responses to stress or emotional responses (such as crying, laughter, and coughing) can trigger attacks in some asthma patients (Purcell, 1963).

Ulcers: Changing Views of Psychophysiological Disorders. In the case of some psychophysiological disorders, such as ulcers, psychologists are still sleuthing the role of stress. Psychologists once believed that psychosomatic disorders were symbolic expressions of underlying emotional conflicts, a view that we can still encounter in popular psychology today. Franz Alexander (1950) argued that psychophysiological disorders occur when conflicts originating in infancy are repressed but triggered again in adulthood by environmental circumstances. According to Alexander, stomach ulcers are linked to infantile cravings to be fed and feelings of dependency. In adulthood, these conflicts become

fictoid

Myth: Sudden stress or trauma can turn one's hair white.

Reality: There's no evidence that intense fear can make one's hair turn white overnight or even over a short period of time. Nor is there any known physical mechanism by which this process could occur (Radford, 2007).

asthma
medical condition in which breathing becomes difficult when the bronchial tubes in the lungs become inflamed, spasm, and are clogged with mucus

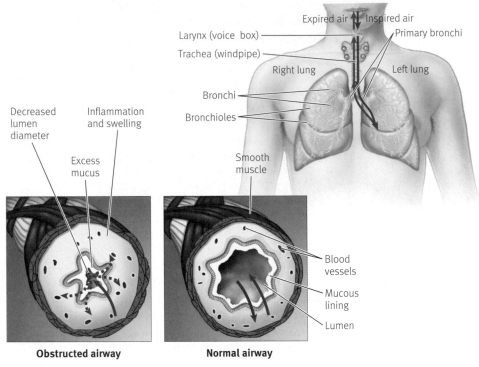

Figure 12.5 **Anatomy of an Asthma Attack.** (*Source:* Encyclopedia Britannica, 2001)

Contrary to popular belief, stress isn't the major cause of ulcers. Instead, the bacterium *Helicobacter pylori* is the prime culprit.

Ruling Out Rival Hypotheses

reawakened and activate the gastrointestinal system (stomach and intestines), which has been associated with feeding. The result, according to Alexander, is a **peptic ulcer**—an inflamed area in the stomach lining that can cause pain, nausea, and loss of appetite.

This *specific emotion hypothesis* regarding ulcers and other psychophysiological disorders has been discredited by research. Yet other ideas about ulcers and their connection with stress have also changed with the times. Here we'll examine two such ideas.

Do hot foods cause ulcers? A popular psychology myth is that ulcers result from overindulging in spicy foods like salsas or flaming hot chicken wings, which create excess stomach acid. Just 30 years ago, many scientists accepted this idea. However, today scientists agree that *Helicobacter pylori* (*H. pylori*)—an unusual bacterium that thrives in stomach acid—is a cause of as many as 90 percent of stomach ulcers. Physicians now treat many ulcers with a combination of powerful antibiotics.

Does stress cause ulcers? The great majority of people infected with *H. pylori* don't develop ulcers. So other influences are clearly at work. Research shows that the widespread belief that stress *by itself* causes ulcers is wrong. Yet stress probably plays some role, because higher rates of ulcers and a poor response to ulcer treatment (Levenstein, Kaplan, & Smith, 1997; Overmier & Murison, 1997) are associated with earthquakes, being a prisoner of war, economic crises, and other anxiety-provoking events (Levenstein, Ackerman, Kiecolt-Glaser, & Dubois, 1999). So stress, together with *H. pylori*, may trigger some cases of ulcers.

ASSESS YOUR KNOWLEDGE: FACT OR FICTION?

(1) Overactivity of the immune system sometimes leads to disease. (True/False)

(2) Psychologists once termed diseases psychophysiological because they believed them to be caused by psychological conflicts and emotional reactions. (True/False)

(3) The number one cause of death and disability in the United States is coronary heart disease. (True/False)

(4) Social economic factors are largely or entirely unrelated to risk for physical diseases. (True/False)

(5) One major cause of ulcers is eating hot, spicy foods late at night. (True/False)

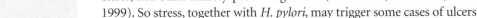

Answers: (1) T (p. 505); (2) F (p. 506); (3) T (p. 507); (4) F (p. 508); (5) F (p. 510)

peptic ulcer
inflamed area in the stomach lining that can cause pain, nausea, and loss of appetite

Coping with Stress

Clearly, some of us adapt better in the face of challenge and change than others. Why is this so, and what can we do to reduce stress, manage our lives, and stay healthy? We'll next take stock of how we can use social support and coping strategies to surmount stressful circumstances.

SOCIAL SUPPORT

Imagine that you survived the 9/11 World Trade Center attack. What would be helpful? When we ask our students this question, many say the support of family, friends, neighbors, teachers, coworkers, and clergy would be invaluable. **Social support** encompasses social relations with people, groups, and the larger community. Social support can provide us with emotional comfort, financial assistance, and information to make decisions, solve problems, and contend with stressful situations (Schaefer, Coyne, & Lazarus, 1981; Stroebe, 2000; Wills & Fegan, 2001).

Lisa Berkman and Leonard Syme (1979) conducted a landmark study of the hypothesis that social support protects against the adverse effects of stress on health. They analyzed data from nearly 5,000 men and women in Alameda County, California, over a 9-year period. They honed in on four kinds of social ties: marriage, contact with friends, church membership, and both formal and informal group associations. They then created a social network index reflecting the number of social connections and social supports available to each person.

Berkman and Syme found a strong relationship between the number of social connections, across every age group, and the probability of dying during the 9-year period. But do these findings mean that isolation increases our chances of dying? A rival hypothesis is that poor health results in few social bonds, rather than the other way around. To rule out this possibility, the researchers surveyed participants when they started the study. People with high and low levels of support reported a comparable illness history, suggesting that poor initial health can't explain why people with the least social support are later more likely to die. Nevertheless, people aren't necessarily accurate when they judge their health.

To address this concern, James House, Cynthia Robbins, and Helen Metzner (1982) ensured that their 2,700 participants received a medical examination *before* their study got under way. This exam provided a more objective assessment of health status. The researchers replicated Berkman and Syme's (1979) findings: even when they took initial health status into account, people with less social support had higher mortality rates.

Fortunately, the positive influence of social support isn't limited to health outcomes. Supportive and caring relationships can help us cope with short-term crises and life transitions. A happy marriage, for example, is protective against depression, even when people encounter major stressors (Alloway & Bebbington, 1987; Gotlib & Hammen, 1992). But the breakup of close relationships through separation, divorce, discrimination, or bereavement ranks among the most stressful events we can experience (Gardner, Gabriel, & Deikman, 2000). Moreover, lonely and socially isolated people have higher mortality rates than other people and are more likely than other people to smoke and drink, get little exercise, and sleep poorly (Cacioppo, Bertson, Sheridan, & McClintock, 2000; Hawkley & Cacioppo, 2007).

Support and comfort from others can buffer the effects of highly aversive situations.

Ruling Out Rival Hypotheses

Replicability

APPLY YOUR THINKING
What rival hypothesis might account for the finding that happy marriages are associated with less depression? What type of study could help determine whether happy marriages reduce depression, or whether happy people create good marriages?

social support
relationships with people and groups that can provide us with emotional comfort and personal and financial resources

STRESS MANAGEMENT TECHNIQUES
1. _____
2. _____
3. _____
4. _____

GLASBERGEN

"Howl at an ambulance or fire siren every chance you get.
Run around the room in circles with a sock in your mouth.
Eat a messy meal without using your hands or utensils.
Ask a friend to scratch your belly..."

(Copyright 2003 by Randy Glasbergen.
www.glasbergen.com)

GRE preparation classes can be one
useful source of informational control.

proactive coping
anticipation of problems and stressful
situations that promotes effective coping

GAINING CONTROL

As mentioned earlier, we can also relieve stress by acquiring control of situations. Next, we'll discuss five types of control we can use in different situations (Bonanno, 2004; Cohen, Evans, Stokols, & Krantz, 1986; Higgins & Endler, 1995; Lazarus & Folkman, 1984; Sarafino, 2006).

Behavioral Control. Behavioral control is the ability to step up and do something to reduce the impact of a stressful situation. As we'll recall, this type of active coping is called *problem-focused* and is generally more effective in relieving stress than *avoidance oriented coping*—that is, avoiding action to solve our problems or giving up hope (Lazarus & Folkman, 1984; Roth & Cohen, 1986). Research in the United States and Iceland shows that the more high school and college students use problem-focused coping techniques, the less likely they are to develop alcohol problems (Rafnsson, Jonsson, & Windle, 2006).

Cognitive Control. Cognitive control is the ability to *cognitively restructure or think differently about* negative emotions that arise in response to stress-provoking events (Higgins & Endler, 1995; Lazarus & Folkman, 1984; Skinner et al., 2003). This type of control includes *emotion-focused coping,* which we introduced earlier, a strategy that comes in handy when we're adjusting to uncertain situations or aversive events we can't control or change. In one study (Strentz & Auerbach, 1988), experimenters exposed subjects to a simulated abduction and 4 days of captivity. During captivity, subjects who received instructions to use emotion-focused coping strategies reported less distress than did those who received instructions to use problem-focused coping.

Decisional Control. Decisional control is the ability to choose among alternative courses of action (Sarafino, 2006). We can consult with trusted friends about which classes to take and which professors to avoid, and make decisions about which surgeon to consult to perform a high-stakes operation.

Informational Control. Informational control is the ability to acquire information about a stressful event. Knowing what types of questions are on the SAT or GRE can help us prepare for them, as can knowing something about the person we're "fixed up with" on an upcoming date. We engage in **proactive coping** when we anticipate stressful situations and take steps to prevent or minimize difficulties before they arise (Greenglass, 2002; Karasek & Theorell, 1990; Schwarzer & Taubert, 2002). People who engage in proactive coping tend to perceive stressful circumstances as opportunities for growth (Greenglass, 2002).

Emotional Control. Emotional control is the ability to suppress and express emotions. Communication can strengthen social bonds, enhance problem solving, and regulate emotions (Bonanno, 2004; Ekman & Davidson, 1993). James Pennebaker (1997) found that "opening up," by talking into a tape recorder or writing about past traumas or daily events, can lead to drops in blood pressure and fewer visits to the student health center over a 6-month period, although these effects aren't especially large in magnitude (Frisina, Borod, & Lepore, 2004).

Still, there are times when it's best to conceal our emotions, such as cloaking our fears when we're giving a speech and suppressing our anger when trying to resolve a problem with a coworker (Bonanno, Papa, Lalande, Westphal, & Coifman, 2004; Gross & Munoz, 1995). As the old saying goes, "There's a time and a place for everything."

Is Catharsis a Good Thing? Contrary to the popular notion that expressing what we feel is always beneficial, disclosing painful feelings, called *catharsis,* is a double-edged sword. When it involves problem solving and constructive efforts to make troubling situations "right," it can be beneficial. But when catharsis reinforces a sense of helplessness, as when we stew endlessly about something we can't or won't change, catharsis can actually be harmful (Littrell, 1998). This finding is worrisome, because a slew of popular psychotherapies rely on catharsis, encouraging clients to "get it out of your system," "get things off your chest," or "let it all hang out." Some of these therapies instruct clients to yell, punch pillows, or throw balls against walls when they become upset (Lewis & Bucher, 1992; Lohr, Olatunji, Baumeister, & Bushman, in press). Yet research shows that these activities rarely reduce our long-term stress, although they may make us feel slightly better for a few moments. In other cases, they actually seem to heighten our anger or anxiety in the long run (Tavris, 1989).

Does Crisis Debriefing Help? Some therapists—especially those employed by fire, police, or other emergency services—administer a popular treatment called *crisis debriefing,* which is designed to ward off PTSD among people exposed to trauma. Several thousand crisis debriefers descended on lower Manhattan in the wake of the 9/11 attacks in a well-meaning effort to help traumatized witnesses of the attacks. Crisis debriefing is a single-session procedure, typically conducted in groups, that usually lasts 3–4 hours. Most often, therapists conduct this procedure within a few days of a traumatic event, such as a terrible accident. It proceeds according to standardized steps, including strongly encouraging group members to discuss and "process" their negative emotions, listing the posttraumatic symptoms that group members are likely to experience, and discouraging group members from discontinuing participation once the session has started.

Recent studies indicate that crisis debriefing isn't effective for trauma reactions. What's worse, several studies suggest that it may actually increase the risk of PTSD among people exposed to trauma, perhaps because it gets in the way of people's natural coping strategies (Litz, Gray, Bryant, & Adler, 2002; Lilienfeld, 2007; McNally, Bryant, & Ehlers, 2003).

Nor is there much evidence that merely talking about our problems when we're upset is helpful. A meta-analysis (see Chapter 2) of sixty-one studies (Meads & Nouwen, 2005) revealed no overall benefits for emotional disclosure (compared with nondisclosure) on a variety of measures of physical and psychological health. None of this implies that we should never discuss our feelings with others when we're upset. But it does mean that doing so is most likely to be beneficial when it allows us to think about and work through our problems in a more constructive light.

The work of James Pennebaker suggests that writing about our stressors can ward off physical illness, although this effect is only modest.

Crisis debriefing sessions, in which people discuss their reactions to a traumatic event in a group, may actually increase PTSD risk.

FLEXIBLE COPING

The ability to adjust coping strategies as the situation demands is critical to contending with many stressful situations (Bonanno & Kaltman, 2001; Cheng, 2001; Westphal & Bonanno, 2004). George Bonanno (Bonanno et al., 2004) and his colleagues studied students who'd just started college in New York City when terrorists destroyed the World Trade Center in 2001. The researchers predicted that students who had difficulties with managing their emotions would find the transition to college life particularly difficult. Participants completed a checklist of psychological symptoms at the start of the study, and then again 2 years later. Participants who were better at flexibly controlling their emotions by suppressing or expressing them on demand on a laboratory task reported less distress 2 years later.

Expending a great deal of effort to suppress and avoid emotions can distract us from problem solving and lead to an unintended consequence: the emotions may return in full or greater force. In fact, the attempt to suppress negative emotions and thoughts associated with aversive events tends to backfire and increase the very negative experiences we're struggling so hard to avoid (Beck, Gudmundsdottir, Palyo, Miller, & Grant, 2006; Richards, Bulter, & Gross, 2003; Wegner, 2005). Accepting circumstances and feelings we can't change, and finding positive ways of thinking about our problems, can be a potent means of contending with stressful situations (Skinner et al., 2003).

Research suggests that instructing someone *not* to think of something, like a white bear, often results in increases in the very thought the person is trying to suppress (Wegner, Schneider, Carter, & White, 1987).

Optimists—who proverbially see the glass as "half full," rather than "half empty"—are more likely than pessimists to view change as a challenge.

Correlation vs. Causation

INDIVIDUAL DIFFERENCES: ATTITUDES, BELIEFS, AND PERSONALITY

Some people survive almost unimaginably horrific circumstances with few or no visible psychological scars, whereas others view the world through the dark lens of pessimism and crumble when the little things in life don't go their way. Our attitudes, personality, and socialization shape our reactions—for better and worse—to potential stressors.

Hardiness: Challenge, Commitment and Control. About three decades ago, Salvatore Maddi and his colleagues (Kobasa, Hiller, & Maddi, 1979) initiated a study of the qualities of stress-resistant people. They determined that resilient people possess a set of attitudes they called **hardiness.** Hardy people view change as a challenge rather than a threat, are committed to their life and work, and believe they can control events. Hardy individuals have the courage and motivation to confront stressors and engage in problem solving to contend with them (Maddi, 2004).

Suzanne Kobasa and Maddi asked 670 managers at a public utility to report their stressful experiences on a checklist. Then they selected executives who scored high on both stress and illness and another group who scored equally high on stress, but reported below-average levels of illness. Managers who showed high stress but low levels of illness were more oriented to challenge and higher in their sense of control over events, and felt a deep sense of involvement in their work and social lives.

When we're physically ill, we don't usually feel especially hardy. So we can appreciate the fact that another explanation for Kobasa and Maddi's findings is that illness creates negative attitudes, rather than the other way around. To address the question of causal direction, Kobasa and Maddi (1984) conducted a longitudinal study (see Chapter 10) that examined changes in health and attitudes over time. At the end of 2 years, people whose attitudes toward life reflected high levels of control, commitment, and challenge remained healthier than those whose attitudes didn't. Hardiness also can boost stress resistance among nurses in hospice settings, immigrants adjusting to life in the United States, and military personnel who survive life-threatening stressors (Bartone, 1999; Maddi, 2002). In short, hardiness can transform stressors from potential disasters into valuable growth opportunities.

Optimism. We know them when we meet them. Optimistic people have a rosy outlook and don't dwell on the dark side of life. Even on a cloudy day, we can bask in their sunshine. As we learned in Chapter 11, there are some distinct advantages to being optimistic. Optimistic people are more productive, focused, persistent, and better at handling frustration than pessimists (Peterson, 2000; Seligman, 1990). Optimism is also associated with a lower mortality rate (Stern, Dhanda, & Hazunda, 2001), a more vigorous immune response (Segerstrom, Taylor, Kemeney, & Fahey, 1998), lower distress in infertile women trying to have a child (Abbey, Halman, & Andrews, 1992), better surgical outcomes (Scheier, Matthews, Owens, et al., 1989), and fewer physical complaints (Scheier & Carver, 1992).

Stress and Self-Enhancement. People who are self-centered and who think highly of themselves also cope successfully under stress. Such people are called *self-enhancers* and adjust remarkably well to the premature death of a spouse and combat exposure (Bonanno, Field, Kovacevic, & Kaltman, 2002). In a study of social adjustment a year and a half after 9/11, self-enhancers' friends and relatives rated them as less socially adjusted, yet their inflated self-esteem allowed them to shrug off many of the ill effects of stress.

Spirituality and Religious Involvement. **Spirituality** is a search for the sacred, which may or may not extend to belief in God. Spiritual and religious beliefs play vital roles in many of our lives. According to a Harris Poll (Taylor, 2003), 79 percent of Americans believe in God. Compared with nonreligious people, religious people have lower mortality rates, improved immune system functioning, lower blood pressure, and a greater ability to

hardiness
set of attitudes marked by a sense of control over events, commitment to life and work, and courage and motivation to confront stressful events

spirituality
search for the sacred, which may or may not extend to belief in God

recover from illnesses (Koenig, McCullough, & Larson, 2001; Levin, 2001; Matthews, Larson, & Barry, 1993). One explanation for these findings is that religious involvements activate a healing energy that scientists can't measure (Ellison & Levin, 1998). This is an intriguing hypothesis. Nevertheless, as we'll see in our discussion of energy medicines, explanations that depend on an undetectable force or energy can't be falsified and therefore lie outside the boundaries of science.

The correlation between religiosity and physical health isn't easy to interpret. Some authors have measured religiosity by counting how often people attend church or other religious services and found that such attendance is associated with better physical health. But this correlation is potentially attributable to a confound: People who are sick are less likely to attend religious services, so the causal arrow may be reversed (Sloan, 1999).

Research on the links between spirituality and religious involvement, on the one hand, and health, on the other, is limited. But until more definitive evidence is available, let's consider several potential reasons why spirituality and religious involvements may be a boon to many people.

(1) Many religions prohibit health risk behaviors, including alcohol, drugs, and unsafe sexual practices.

(2) Religious engagement, such as attendance at services, often boosts social support.

(3) A sense of meaning and purpose, control over life, positive emotions, and positive appraisals of stressful situations associated with prayer and religious activities may enhance coping (Potts, 2004).

Rumination: Recycling the Mental Garbage. So far we've considered adaptive ways of coping with taxing circumstances without becoming unhinged. But some ways of reacting to stressful situations are clearly counterproductive. Susan Nolen-Hoeksema (1987) suggested that recycling negative events in our minds can lead us to become depressed. More specifically, some of us spend a great deal of time *ruminating*—focusing on how bad we feel and endlessly analyzing the causes and consequences of our problems.

Nolen-Hoeksema (2000, 2003) contended that women have much higher rates and more frequent bouts of depression than men (see Chapter 15) because they tend to ruminate more than men. In contrast, when stressed out, men are more likely to focus on pleasurable or distracting activities such as work, watching football games, or drinking copious amounts of alcohol (which we don't recommend). They also adopt a more direct approach to solving their problems than do women (Nolen-Hoeksema, 2002, 2003). Early socialization may in part pave the way for these differing reactions (Nolen-Hoeksema & Girgus, 1994). Although parents encourage girls to analyze and talk about their problems, they often actively discourage boys from expressing their feelings and instead encourage them to take action or tough it out. Still, men and women alike can benefit from cutting down on rumination and confronting their problems head-on.

Falsifiability

Correlation vs. Causation

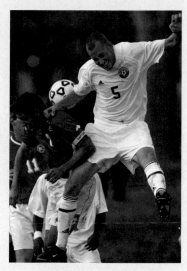

Men may be more likely than women to play sports, which often decreases the tendency to ruminate when stressed out.

ASSESS YOUR KNOWLEDGE: FACT OR FICTION?

(1) Researchers have found a strong connection between social support and people's chance of dying over a 9-year period. (True/False)

(2) One general coping strategy tends to work for all situations. (True/False)

(3) Optimistic people are especially skilled at tolerating frustration. (True/False)

(4) People who overestimate their positive qualities are most likely to break down in the face of stress. (True/False)

(5) Rumination is usually an adaptive strategy for dealing with anxiety and depression. (True/False)

Answers: (1) T (p. 511); (2) F (p. 511); (3) T (p. 514); (4) F (p. 514); (5) F (p. 515)

"I'm learning how to relax, doctor —
but I want to relax *better* and *faster!*
I want to be on the cutting edge of relaxation!"

Health psychologists use a variety of educational and behavioral interventions to promote and maintain health, and assist people in coping with serious illnesses.

Ruling Out Rival Hypotheses

Biofeedback of forehead muscle tension can provide substantial control of this tension, thereby offering relief from muscle contraction headaches. But biofeedback may often be no more effective than relaxation.

health psychology
field of psychology that integrates the behavioral sciences with the practice of medicine

Promoting Good Health— and Less Stress!

If we could all reduce or eliminate stress in our lives, the public health consequences would be enormous. Stress is a risk factor for many behaviors, such as smoking and alcohol, which are themselves risk factors for many illnesses. What can we do to decrease stress-related diseases? How can we modify health-destructive habits and help people stricken with a serious illness?

HEALTH PSYCHOLOGY AND BEHAVIORAL MEDICINE

Health psychology, also called *behavioral medicine,* is a rapidly growing field that has contributed to our understanding of the influences of stress and biological, social, and behavioral factors on physical disorders and their treatment. Health psychologists integrate behavioral sciences with the practice of medicine (Gatchel & Baum, 1983). They also combine educational, research, and psychological interventions to promote and maintain health and prevent and treat illness (Matarazzo, 1980).

Health psychologists are employed in hospitals, rehabilitation centers, medical schools, industry, government agencies, and academic and research settings. Interventions developed within health psychology include teaching patients stress management skills and pain reduction techniques and helping people to mobilize social support, comply with medical regimens, and pursue healthy lifestyles. With the number of elderly citizens increasing each year, we can anticipate that the need for health psychologists who treat chronic conditions such as arthritis, CHD, cancer, and Alzheimer's disease will increase by the time the next edition of this textbook appears.

Health psychologists place a premium on evaluating the outcomes of their interventions. A prime example is *biofeedback,* a technique designed to control physiological responses associated with specific disorders. Biofeedback is feedback by a device that provides almost an immediate output of a biological function, such as heart rate or skin temperature (Miller, 1978). Over time, some patients can learn to use this feedback to modify physiological responses associated with stress or illness. However, health psychologists have raised questions about whether biofeedback yields specific beneficial effects beyond the relaxation associated with sitting quietly. In fact, relaxation training and biofeedback are about equally effective in reducing stress and treating anxiety, headaches, insomnia, and the side effects associated with cancer chemotherapy (Gatchel, 2001).

TOWARD A HEALTHY LIFESTYLE

Health psychologists help patients break the grip of unhealthy habits. Smoking, excessive drinking, and overeating can be triggered by stress, and can be maintained when these activities reduce stress (Polivy, Schueneman, & Carlson, 1976; Young, Oei, & Knight, 1990). Among women who are sexual assault survivors, drinking to reduce distress places them at risk for problem drinking (Ullman, Filipas, Townsend, & Starzynski, 2005). Smokers are four times more likely to suffer from clinical depression as nonsmokers and may smoke in part to relieve distress (Breslau, Kilby, & Andreski, 1993). Moreover, people who report being concerned about stress are more likely to be smokers. According to a survey of more than 2,000 adults (American Psychological Association, 2006), one in four Americans uses food to relieve stress and cope with problems. Unfortunately, when we engage in unhealthy behaviors that reduce stress in the short run, we place ourselves at risk for health and stress-related problems in the long run. We'll next examine five behaviors that can promote health.

Healthy Behavior #1: Stop Smoking. Smoking ranks close to the top of the list of unhealthy habits. About 22 percent of American men and 19 percent of women smoke cigarettes (Centers for Disease Control and Prevention, 2005), with the rates increasing markedly in recent years for young women, including those in college (King, Grizeau, Bendel, Dressen, & Delaronde, 1998). These statistics are alarming given that 1 of 4 regular smokers dies of a smoking-related disease (Woloshin, Schwartz, & Welch, 2002). A 30- to 40-year-old male cigarette smoker with a two pack a day habit loses about 8 years of his life on average (Green, 2000). Smoking doubles our chances of dying from either CHD or stroke (McBride, 1992) and is responsible for one third of all cancer deaths (Haxby, 1995). Smoking is also the primary cause of lung disease among men and women (U.S. Department of Health and Human Services, 1990; Woloshin et al., 2002).

Although as many as 80 percent of smokers want to stop smoking, only about 5 percent of the approximately 40 percent of U.S. smokers who try to stop each year on their own succeed (American Psychiatric Association, 1994; Schoenborn, Adams, Barnes, Vickerie, & Schiller, 2004). Mark Twain captured the challenges that smokers face in his famous quote: "Giving up smoking is the easiest thing in the world. I know because I've done it thousands of times."

Health psychologists make smoking treatment and prevention a high priority. Stop-smoking approaches typically educate people about the health consequences of smoking and teach smokers to manage stress. They also help smokers to pinpoint and avoid high-risk situations associated with past smoking, such as parties and bars (Marlatt & Gordon, 1985; Miller & Rollnick, 2002). These strategies are effective with 25 to 35 percent of long-term smokers and are also helpful for people who tend to eat or drink excessively.

Each time people try to stop smoking, their chances of their succeeding improve (Lynn & Kirsch, 2006). People who stop smoking live longer than those who don't, and women who stop smoking during the first few months of pregnancy reduce their risk of problem pregnancies (such as low-birth-weight babies) to that of women who've never smoked. After 10 to 15 years of nonsmoking, an ex-smoker's risk of premature death approaches that of someone who's never smoked (National Cancer Institute, 2000). So, if you're a smoker, don't quit your attempts to quit!

Healthy Behavior #2: Curb Alcohol Consumption. According to a recent survey, more than 60 percent of adults reported having drunk alcohol in the past year (National Center for Health Statistics, 2003). Repeated bouts of heavy drinking, especially *binge drinking*—defined as drinking five or more drinks on one occasion for men and four or more drinks on one occasion for women—is associated with increases in many different types of cancer, serious and sometimes fatal liver problems, pregnancy complications, and brain shrinkage and other neurological problems (Bagnardi, Blangiardo, LaVecchia, & Corrado, 2001).

Several controversial studies (Mukamal et al., 2005; Mukamal et al., 2003) suggest that light to moderate drinking—defined as two drinks per day for men and one drink per day for women—lessen the risk of heart disease and stroke. However, a rival explanation for these findings is that people who drink only moderate amounts of alcohol, such as wine, may have higher incomes and healthier lifestyles than people who either abstain from drinking or drink more than two drinks at a sitting (Lieber, 2003).

Another hypothesis is that people who abstain are in poorer health to begin with than are light or moderate drinkers. Nevertheless, meta-analyses (Chapter 2) comparing drinkers with nondrinkers who abstained because they chose to do so (not because of poor health, disability, or weakness) found no health differences between drinkers and abstainers (Filmore, Kerr, Stockwell, Chikritzhs, & Bostrom, 2006).

At this time, we can't be sure that any amount of alcohol is safe, much less good for our health. One thing's reasonably certain, however: drinking heavily is associated with a greater risk of cardiovascular disease (Bagnardi et al., 2001). Fortunately, many of the negative effects of alcohol, including changes in the brain, can be reversed or minimized when we abstain from drinking (Tyas, 2001).

Smoking, which is becoming more common among young women in the United States, ranks near the top of the list of unhealthy habits.

Evidence is clear that heavy drinking can produce long-term physical problems.

Ruling Out Rival Hypotheses

Calculate BMI by dividing weight in pounds (lbs) by height in inches (in) squared and multiplying by a conversion factor of 703.

Example: Weight = 155 lbs, height = 5'9" (69")
Calculation: [155 ÷ (69)²] × 703 = 22.89

BMI	Weight Status
Below 18.5	Underweight
18.5 - 24.9	Normal
25.0 - 29.9	Overweight
30.0 and above	Obese

Height	Weight Range	BMI	Weight Status
	124 lbs or less	Below 18.5	Underweight
5'9"	125 lbs to 168 lbs	18.5 to 24.9	Normal
	169 lbs to 202 lbs	25.0 to 29.9	Overweight
	203 lbs or more	30 or higher	Obese

Figure 12.6 Body Mass Index (BMI) and Weight Status. (*Source*: Centers for Disease Control and Prevention, Division of Nutrition and Physical Activity National Center for Chronic Disease Prevention and Health Promotion, ckc.gov/nccdphp/dnpa/bmi/adult_BMI.)

Being overweight or obese increases the risk of various physical health problems, and is also associated with depression and other adjustment difficulties.

Correlation vs. Causation

Healthy Behavior #3: Achieve a Healthy Weight. The statistics tell the grim story. As of 2004, two thirds of Americans are overweight, and in turn about a third (32%) of these Americans are obese, as indicated by a statistic known as the *body mass index (BMI)* (see **Figure 12.6**) (Centers for Disease Control, 2006). The number of obese children and adolescents has tripled over the past decade or so, signaling an ominous trend (Ogden et al., 2006). According to some researchers, our society faces an "obesity epidemic" of enormous proportions, due in large measure to decreases in our physical activity (Heini & Weinsier, 1997; Wing & Polley, 2001).

The supersizing of portions—called *portion distortion*—has probably also contributed to the supersizing of Americans (Geier, Rozin, & Doris, 2006). In the United States, from 1977 to 1996, portion sizes of food served on dinner plates in restaurants increased by 25 percent (Young & Nestle, 2002).

Many of us who don't think twice about the amount of fat we consume are concerned about the number of portions we eat. Think of how we'd feel asking for a third serving of dessert! We may hesitate to go back to the all-you-can eat buffet line for that third portion of food, but not to eat all of the tasty food placed in front of us. When people are served M & Ms with a large spoon, they eat substantially more of them than when they're served in a small spoon (Geier et al., 2006). Because we think in terms of "units" of things as the optimal amount—a heuristic called *unit bias* (Geier et al., 2006)—controlling portions of food consumed is a good way to control our weight. A nifty trick to keep in mind is to eat food on a smaller plate: doing so will make portions appear bigger and help control the amount we eat.

Societal Expectations and Weight. In modern society, the media equate beauty with a slender female figure and a muscular male physique. Movies, sitcoms, and magazines feature extremely underweight females, typically 15 percent below women's average weight (Johnson, Tobin, & Steinberg, 1989). Indeed, about a quarter of professional models meet the official weight criteria for anorexia nervosa, a severe eating disorder marked by weight loss (Leo, 2006; see Chapters 11 and 15). One in four television commercials portrays the importance of beauty or features "beautiful people" to sell products that supposedly improve our appearance or help us to lose weight (Downs & Harrison, 1985; Thompson & Heimberg, 1999).

As the cultural ideal has become thinner, women have become larger (Garner, Garfinkel, Schwartz, & Thompson, 1980; Wiseman, Gray, Mosimann, & Ahrens, 1992). As a result, many obese children are subject to teasing (Thompson, Herbozo, Himes, & Yamamiya, 2005). When they become adolescents and adults, others may stereotype them as lazy, sloppy, or lacking in willpower. They also experience discrimination in the social arena and workplace (Crandall, 1994; Schwartz, Vartanian, Nosek, & Brownell, 2006). In one study of 9,125 adults, obese people were 25 percent more likely to suffer from a mood disorder, including depression and anxiety, compared with people of normal weight (Simon et al., 2006). It's not clear whether depression triggers obesity, or whether obesity sets the stage for depression. Yet the positive association between obesity and depression counters the popular stereotype of the obese person as cheerful or "jolly" (Roberts, Strawbridge, Deleger, & Kaplan, 2002). Our negative attitudes toward obesity run so deep that 46 percent of people say they'd rather give up at least a year of their lives than be obese, and 30 percent would rather be divorced than obese (Schwartz et al., 2006).

Clearly, overweight people suffer in many respects. Researchers followed a group of people age 16 to 24 for 7 years (Gortmaker, Must, Perrin, Sobol, & Dietz, 1993). At the end of the study, individuals who were overweight were less wealthy, didn't progress as far in school, and were less likely to be married. The changes observed over time occurred independently of intelligence and financial status at the start of the study, bolstering the claim that prejudice and discrimination account for the plight of overweight people (see **Table 12.3**).

> **Ruling Out Rival Hypotheses**

Table 12.3 Reasons for Obesity in America Aside from Diet and Lack of Exercise.

(1) Lack of adequate sleep, which directly causes weight gain.

(2) Endocrine disruptors in foods that modify fats in the body.

(3) Comfortable temperatures as a result of heating/air conditioning that decrease calories burned from sweating and shivering.

(4) Use of medicines that contribute to weight gain.

(5) Increases in certain segments of the population, including Hispanics and middle-age people, who have higher rates of obesity.

(6) Increase in mothers who give birth at older ages, which is associated with heavier children.

(7) Genetic influences during pregnancy.

(8) Moderately overweight people may have an evolutionary advantage over very thin people and be more likely to survive: Darwinian natural selection.

(9) People tend to marry people with a similar body type, a phenomenon called *assortative mating*. When heavy people reproduce, they're likely to give birth to relatively heavy children.

Supersized portions, common in the United States but rarer in Europe, make weight control very difficult for many of us.

The Effects of Weight on Health. The obese are at greater risk of heart disease, stroke, high blood pressure, arthritis, some types of cancer, respiratory problems, and diabetes (Klein et al., 2004; Kurth et al., 2003). Those of us who carry our weight around our abdomens (so-called spare tires) are at even greater risk for health problems, including CHD (Yusuf et al., 2004). Exercise is one of the best means of shedding that annoying fat around the belly and of losing weight over the long haul (Pronk & Wing, 1994). The more inactive we are, and the more time we spend watching television, the more likely we are to be obese (Ching, Willett, Rimm, Colditz, & Gortmaker, & Stampfer, 1996; Gortmaker et al., 1996). Of course, these findings are only correlational; it's also possible that people who are obese are weaker and less energetic, and become couch potatoes as a result. Indeed, there's considerable controversy over how much of the negative association between obesity and physical health is due to obesity itself as opposed to the behaviors that often go along with it, such as inactivity and poor nutrition (Campos, 2004; Johnson, 2005). Actually, there's evidence for both causal explanations.

> **Correlation vs. Causation**

If an obese person, say a 300-pound man, sheds even 10 percent of his weight, his health will improve (Wing & Polley, 2001). Losing weight reduces blood pressure, cholesterol, and the risk of diabetes (Kanders & Blackburn, 1992), and often has the added benefit of reducing anxiety and improving mood (Wadden & Stunkard, 1993).

Diets, Genes, and Everyday Habits. Given the many social and medical reasons for losing weight, it's no wonder that people have tried all manner of products touted as effective for weight loss. These fad treatments include appetite-suppressing eyeglasses, magic weight-loss earrings, electrical muscle stimulators, and "magnet diet pills" to flush fat out of the body. Contrary to the advertisements for these products we can see on late-night television, they're entirely devoid of scientific support (Corbett, 2006).

Bookstores are crammed with books on the latest diet crazes that promise to help us lose weight effortlessly and in remarkably short periods of time. Many of them offer conflicting and confusing recommendations based on little more than someone's pet theory,

Diet crazes, like the "grapefruit diet," come into and go out of fashion. Because the reported "success" of most fad diets comes from personal anecdotes rather than from scientific research, we should be skeptical of them.

Replicability

rather than careful research. Some of our favorite fad diets include the "cabbage soup" diet, in which you feast on little more than—guess what?—cabbage soup (sounds yummy, doesn't it?), the popcorn diet (ideal for compulsive movie-goers), and the grapefruit diet (Danbrot, 2004; Herskowitz, 1987; Thompson & Arens, 2004). Some people on these diets may experience dramatic short-term weight loss, but this loss is almost always followed by a gradual return of the initial weight (Brownell & Rodin, 1994), resulting in the well-known "yo-yo effect" that often accompanies dieting. *Crash diets*—those in which people severely restrict calories (often down to 1,000 calories per day for several weeks)—aren't likely to result in long-term weight loss and are unhealthy (Shade et al., 2004). One key tip-off that a diet is based on fad rather than fact is that it promises a quick fix, that is, a way to lose large amounts of weight in short periods of time ("Lose 50 pounds in 2 weeks on the Miracle Weight Loss Plan!"), often without even exercising.

Recently, researchers found that overweight people on the popular Atkins high-fat, low-carbohydrate diet lost more weight than their counterparts on other diets, including a low-fat, high-carbohydrate diet with plenty of fruits, vegetables, and pasta (Gardner et al., 2007). However, after 6 months, people on most or all diets begin to regain their weight and to stray from their diet plans. The bottom line? It's difficult to lose weight, on a long-term basis, on any diet (Mann et al., 2007).

With so much bewildering information presented in the media, how can we make wise health and diet decisions? We should consider whether independent researchers have replicated the findings and the quality of the evidence. Moreover, we should question findings that not only cut against the grain of our beliefs, but that seem to support our preconceived notions.

Diet, portion control, and exercise take us only so far in controlling our weight. Genes play a vital role in determining who'll never have to think twice about ordering a hot fudge sundae and who'll face a mighty struggle with the "battle of the bulge" (Bouchard, 1995). Perhaps as much as half of the differences in people's tendency to become overweight is genetic (Wing & Polley, 2001). Researchers have identified genes associated with obesity, which appear related to appetite and energy use (Bouchard et al., 2004; Campfield, Smith, & Burn, 1996). These discoveries suggest that it might one day be possible to develop drugs that switch genes on and off to control weight.

But while we're waiting, there's still much we can do to achieve a stable, healthy weight, regardless of our genetic heritage. Here's some basic advice to follow for controlling our weight and eating a healthy diet:

(1) Exercise regularly.

(2) Monitor total calories and body weight (Wing & Hill, 2001).

(3) Eat foods with "good fats," such as olive oil and fish oil, which exert protective effects on health.

(4) Get lots of help from our social network to support our efforts to lose weight (Wing & Jeffrey, 1999).

(5) Control portion size. By all means, don't make a habit of "supersizing" your cheeseburgers and fries. At least not just yet. . . .

Healthy Behavior #4: Exercise. Help for some psychological ailments may be as close as our running shoes. Research suggests that such activities as regular jogging, weight lifting, and yoga for 8 weeks or longer, can relieve depression (Mutrie, 1988; Palmer, 1995; Stathopoulou, Powers, Berry, Smits, & Otto, 2006), and running at a fast pace and engaging in other exercise on a regular basis can relieve anxiety (Landers, 1998; Phillips, Kiernan, & King, 2001).

Contrary to the popular "no pain, no gain" belief that exercise must be vigorous and sustained to do any good, 30 minutes of activity on most days of the week, including gardening and cleaning our rooms, can lead to improved fitness and health (Blair, Kohl, Gordon, & Paffenberger, 1992; Pate et al., 1995; see **Table 12.4**).

Aerobic exercise including rowing, swimming, and biking is an excellent way to lose weight, stay fit, and maintain or even improve cardiovascular health.

Table 12.4 Burned Calories Associated with Everyday Activities and Regular Exercise Activities.

10 Minutes of Activity	125 - 174 pounds	175 - 250 pounds	250 + pounds
Everyday Activities			
Sitting and Watching Television	10	14	18
Dressing	26	37	53
Exercise			
Walking Upstairs	146	202	288
Walking at 2 miles per hour	29	40	58
Running at 7 miles per hour	118	164	232
Cycling at 5.5 miles per hour	42	58	83
Housework			
Shoveling Snow	65	89	130
Weeding Garden	49	68	98
Sedentary Activities			
Typing on Computer	19	27	39
Light Physical Labor			
House Painting	29	40	58
Sports			
Basketball	58	82	117
Swimming (Backstroke)	32	45	64
Swimming (Crawl)	40	56	80
Volleyball	43	65	94

factoid
About 20 percent of people can lose at least 10 percent of their body weight and keep it off for at least a year (Wing & Hill, 2001).

Correlation vs. Causation

In a study conducted in Finland (Paffenbarger, Hyde, Wing, & Hsieh, 1986), middle-aged men who didn't get much physical activity on the job but who burned off 2,000 calories (the equivalent of about four Big Macs) a week in their spare time lived 2 1/2 years longer on average than men who were less active in their leisure hours. Of course, people who are less active may be less physically fit to begin with. Still, it's likely that the extra years of life are attributable at least in part to the fact that regular physical exercise can lower blood pressure and risk for CHD, improve lung function, relieve the symptoms of arthritis, decrease diabetes risk, and even cut the risk of breast and colon cancer (Barbour, Houle, & Dubbert, 2003; Wei et al., 1999). Although even moderate exercise—at about the level of a brisk walk—can reap health benefits, more sustained and vigorous exercise is needed to reach our fitness potential.

Healthy Behavior #5: Follow Medical Advice. Unfortunately, 30 to 70 percent of patients don't take their physician's medical advice (National Heart, Lung, and Blood Institute, 1998), and as many as 80 percent don't follow their physician's recommendations to get exercise, stop smoking, change their diet, or take prescribed medications (Berlant & Pruitt, 2003). The extent of some medical noncompliance is truly staggering. Paula Vincent (1971) found that 58 percent of patients with glaucoma, a serious eye disease, didn't take their prescribed eye drops, even though they knew that their failure to do so could make them go blind! It goes without saying that the failure to comply with medical recommendations is a serious health problem. Health psychologists strive to enhance patient compliance by encouraging them to adopt a healthy lifestyle (Meichenbaum & Turk, 1987).

Although heart disease kills many more women than cancer does, breast cancer receives much more media attention. As a result, many women think that breast cancer poses a greater threat to their health.

But, Changing Lifestyles Is Easier Said than Done. Why do we have difficulty changing our lifestyles, even when we know that bad habits can endanger our health?

Personal Inertia. One reason is that it's difficult to overcome personal inertia—to try something new. Many self-destructive habits relieve stress and don't create an imminent health threat, so it's easy for us to "let things be." Eating a heaping portion of ice cream doesn't seem terribly dangerous when we view heart disease as a distant and uncertain catastrophe. John Norcross and his colleagues found that only 19 percent of those who made a New Year's resolution to change a problem behavior, including changing their diet or exercising more, maintained the change when followed up 2 years later (Norcross, Ratzin, & Payne, 1988; Norcross & Vangerelli, 1989).

Misestimating Risk. Another reason we maintain the status quo is that we underestimate certain risks to our health and overestimate others. To illustrate this point, try answering the following three questions:

In the United States, which causes more deaths?

(1) All types of accidents combined or strokes?

(2) All motor vehicle (car, truck, bus, and motorcycle) accidents combined or digestive cancer?

(3) Diabetes or homicide?

The answers are (1) strokes (by about twofold), (2) digestive cancer (by about three-fold), and (3) diabetes (about fourfold). If you got one or more of these questions wrong, the odds are you relied on the *availability heuristic* (see Chapter 2)—the mental shortcut by which we judge the likelihood of an event by the ease with which it comes to mind (Hertwig, Pachur, & Kurzenhauser, 2005; Tversky & Kahneman, 1974). Because the news media provide far more coverage of dramatic accidents and homicides than strokes, digestive cancer, or diabetes, we overestimate the probability of accidents and homicides and underestimate the probability of many diseases. And because the media feature so many emotional and memorable stories of famous women—like rock stars Sheryl Crow and Melissa Etheridge; former first lady Nancy Reagan; actress Suzanne Somers; and Sandra Day O'Connor, the first female U.S. Supreme Court Justice—who've developed breast cancer, we're likely to think of breast cancer as a more frequent and deadly illness than heart disease (Ruscio, 2000). Heart disease is less newsworthy precisely because it's more commonplace, and perhaps less terrifying, than cancer with its troubling treatment-related side effects, including very obvious hair loss.

In general, we underestimate the frequency of the most common causes of death, and overestimate the occurrence of the least common causes of death (Lichtenstein, Slovic, Fischhoff, Layman, & Combs 1978). These errors in judgment can be costly: if women believe heart disease isn't a threat, they may not change their lifestyle.

If we told you that four fully loaded jumbo jets were crashing every day in the United States, you'd be horrified and probably outraged. "Why aren't they doing something to stop this?" you might justifiably ask. Yet the equivalent of that number—about 1,200 people— die each day in America from smoking-related causes (Centers for Disease Control and Prevention, 2005). How likely is it we'll actually die in a plane crash? Not likely at all, even if we spend years racking up our frequent flyer miles. We'd need to fly in commercial airliners for about 10,000 years straight—that is, around the clock without any breaks— before the odds of our dying in a plane crash exceed 50 percent. But because plane crashes make big news, we overestimate their frequency.

Many of us are well aware of health risks, but don't take them to "heart," pun intended. Smokers greatly overestimate their chances of living to the age of 75 (Schoenbaum, 1997). Others of us rationalize our lifestyle choices by telling ourselves, "Something's going to kill me anyway, so I might as well enjoy my life and do whatever I want."

Feeling Powerless. Still others of us feel powerless to change, perhaps because our habits are so deeply ingrained. Consider a person who smokes a pack of cigarettes a day.

Let's calculate the number of times she's inhaled cigarette smoke. There are 20 cigarettes in a pack; the average number of inhalations per cigarette is 10; the number of inhalations per day is 200, and there are 365 days per year. Let's assume she's smoked for 15 years. We arrive at the total number of inhalations by multiplying 365 days/year × 200 (inhalations/day) × 15 (number of years she has smoked). Doing the math, the grand total is more than a million inhalations (1,095,000). Now that's quite an impressive habit!

Prevention Programs. Because modifying such well-ingrained behaviors can be so difficult, we're best off not developing them in the first place. Prevention efforts should begin by adolescence, if not earlier, because the earlier in life we develop unhealthy habits, the more likely they'll create problems, like alcohol abuse, for us later in life (Hingson, Heeren, & Winter, 2006). Health psychologists have developed prevention programs that contain the following elements:

- educating young people about the risks and negative consequences of obesity, smoking, and excessive drinking;
- educating young people about positive health behaviors, such as good nutrition and the importance of exercise;
- teaching young people to recognize and resist peer pressure to engage in unhealthy behaviors;
- exposing young people to positive role models who don't drink or smoke;
- teaching effective coping skills for daily living and dealing with stressful life events.

But not all prevention efforts are successful. The Drug Abuse Resistance Education, or DARE, program is used in schools nationwide to teach students how to avoid getting into drugs, gangs, and violent activities (Ringwalt & Greene, 1993). The program uses police officers and targets fifth and sixth graders. It emphasizes the negative aspects of excessive drinking and substance abuse, and the positive aspects of self-esteem and healthy life choices. The program is popular with school administrators and parents; there's a good chance you've seen DARE bumper stickers on cars in your neighborhood. However, researchers have repeatedly found that the program doesn't produce positive long-term effects on substance abuse or boost self-esteem (Lynam et al., 1999). Some researchers have even found that it may occasionally backfire to produce increases in substance abuse (Werch & Owen, 2002). Programs that focus on coping skills and managing stress generally show better treatment and prevention outcomes (MacKillop, Lisman, Weinstein, & Rosenbaum, 2003). These findings remind us that we need to evaluate programs carefully before they're widely promoted based on their intuitive appeal alone.

Despite its popularity, the DARE program isn't effective for preventing substance abuse or enhancing self-esteem.

ALTERNATIVE AND COMPLEMENTARY MEDICINE

What do the following three practices have in common?

(1) Drinking a solution of snake venom that's diluted to the point that it's not harmful.
(2) Placing thin needles in the external ear to relieve nausea following an operation.
(3) Manipulating the spine to treat pain and prevent disease.

The answer: each is an alternative or nonstandard treatment that falls outside the mainstream of modern medicine. **Alternative medicine** refers to health care practices and products used *in place of* conventional medicine. **Complementary medicine,** in contrast, refers to products and practices that are used *along with* conventional medicine (National Center for Complementary and Alternative Medicine, 2002).

alternative medicine
health care practices and products used in place of conventional medicine

complementary medicine
health care practices and products used along with conventional medicine

The Scope of Alternative Health Care. Of the billions of dollars Americans spend each year on medical services, we fork out about half to practitioners of alternative medicine (Center for Medicare and Medicaid Services, 1997). In the National Health Interview Survey of 31,044 adults, 36 percent of Americans reported using one or more alternative medical treatments (not including prayer) over the preceding year (Barnes, Powell-Griner, McFann, & Nahin, 2004). We can find some of the reasons people opt for alternative medical procedures in **Table 12.5**.

Table 12.5 Reasons Why People Use Complementary and Alternative Medical (CAM) Procedures.

Reason	Percentage
1. Believe that CAM combined with standard medical treatments will help	54%
2. Initially used CAM because they thought it would be interesting to try	50%
3. Believe conventional medicine would not help	28%
4. A medical professional suggested they try it	26%
5. Believe that conventional medical treatment is too expensive	13%

Source: Barnes, Powell-Griner, McFann, & Nahin, 2004.

Biologically Based Therapies: Vitamins, Herbs, and Food Supplements. Americans shell out more than $22 billion each year for herbal treatments of uncertain effectiveness (Gupta, 2007; Walach & Kirsch, 2003). Yet many herbal and natural preparations that some once viewed as promising have generally proved to be no more effective than a placebo (see Chapter 2). For example, negative findings have challenged still-popular beliefs that:

- the herb Saint John's Wort can alleviate the symptoms of moderate to severe depression (Davidson et al., 2002);
- an extract from the saw palmetto plant can relieve prostate problems (Kane et al., 2006);
- shark cartilage can cure some cancers (Loprinzi et al., 2005); and
- the widely used supplements glucosamine and chondroitin, found naturally in the body but extracted from animal tissue, relieve mild arthritis pain (Reichenbach et al., 2007)

Many vitamins and dietary supplements haven't fared well either. Dietary supplementation with calcium doesn't prevent much bone loss in women (Jackson et al., 2006); Vitamin C doesn't markedly decrease the severity or duration of colds (Douglas, Hemila, D'Souza, Chalker, & Treacy, 2004); and high doses of Vitamin E may actually increase the risk of death from many causes (Miller et al., 2005). Vitamin deficiencies can cause serious health problems, but there isn't much benefit in taking "mega doses" of vitamins or minerals far in excess of recommended amounts. Even two-time Nobel Prize winner Linus Pauling was convinced that taking huge doses of Vitamin C—up to 10 grams, well over 100 times the recommended daily allowance—could ward off cancer and other diseases. Yet research suggests that these and similar practices may be bad for our health (Bjelakovic, Nikoluva, Gluud, Simonetti, & Gluud, 2007; Lawson et al., 2007).

APPLY YOUR THINKING
A friend tells you he's been taking huge doses of Vitamin C for the past year and that he hasn't caught a single cold. He suggests you should purchase large quantities of Vitamin C to prevent catching a cold. Should his statement persuade you take the vitamin on a regular basis? Why or why not?

The U.S. Food and Drug Administration (FDA) carefully regulates most medicines. But because of congressional legislation passed in 1999, it doesn't monitor the safety, purity, or effectiveness of herbs, vitamins, or dietary supplements. So if we go to our local drugstore and purchase a bottle of Saint John's Wort or gingko (see Chapter 7), we're gambling with our safety. Some impure herbal preparations contain dangerous amounts of lead and even the poison arsenic (Ernst, 2002). Still other supplements, such as kava (extracted from a shrub, and used for anxiety and insomnia), prompted the FDA to issue a warning about liver damage (Saper et al., 2004). Finally, some natural products can interfere with the actions of conventional medicines. For example, Saint John's Wort can block the effectiveness of drugs used to combat AIDS and blood clots (Gupta, 2007). Just because something is natural doesn't mean that it's necessarily safe or healthy for us (as we note in Chapter 13, Table 13.3, this false belief is called the *natural commonplace*).

Manipulative and Body-Based Methods: The Example of Chiropractic Medicine. Chief among body-based methods is *chiropractic manipulation*, which is, not surprisingly, practiced by chiropractors. Chiropractors are health professionals who manipulate the spine to treat a wide range of pain-related conditions and injuries and often provide nutritional and lifestyle counseling. Nearly 20 percent of Americans reported having visited a chiropractor (Barnes et al., 2004). Unlike medical doctors, chiropractors can't perform surgeries or prescribe medications.

Historically, the practice of chiropractic medicine was based on the idea that irregularities in the alignment of the spine, known as *subluxations*, prevent the nervous and immune systems from functioning properly. The subluxation theory has no scientific support, and even some chiropractors don't subscribe to it. Moreover, although chiropractic procedures may sometimes be helpful, they're no better than standard approaches, including exercise, general practitioner care, pain relievers, and physical therapy (Assendelft, Morton, Yu, Suttorp, & Shekelle, 2003; Astin & Ernst, 2002). More important, there's no evidence that these procedures can cure cancers or other diseases not associated with back problems. Still, some people may benefit from the attention, support, and advice they receive from chiropractors, which may relieve stress and create a strong placebo effect.

Energy Medicine: The Example of Acupuncture. Energy medicines are based on the idea that disruptions in our body's energy field can be mapped and treated. Chinese physicians first developed and practiced **acupuncture** at least 2,000 years ago. In acupuncture, practitioners insert thin needles into specific points in the body. More than 4 percent of Americans (Barnes et al., 2004) have consulted acupuncturists. These practitioners place the needles on specific spots called *meridians*, which they believe channel a subtle energy or life force called *"qi"* (pronounced "chee"). Acupuncturists claim to relieve blockages of qi by applying needles or electrical, laser, or heat stimulation, to one or more of 2,000 points on the body.

Acupuncture by itself can help to relieve nausea following surgical operations and treat pain-related conditions (Berman & Straus, 2004). Still, there's no reason to believe that any of its beneficial effects are due to energy changes (Posner & Sampson, 1999). The acupuncture points were mapped long before the rise of modern science. Even today, scientists haven't been able to measure, much less identify, the energy associated with specific illnesses. We'll recall that if a concept can't be measured and isn't falsifiable—in this case, it's impossible to disprove that "qi" is the effective mechanism—then it's not scientific.

Moreover, patients with low back pain (Brinkhaus et al., 2006) and migraine headaches (Diener, Kronfeld, & Boewing, 2006) benefit from "sham" (fake) acupuncture treatment in which researchers place the needles at locations that don't match the acupuncture points or in which the needles don't actually penetrate the skin. Indeed, most research suggests that sham treatment relieves symptoms as much as standard acupuncture,

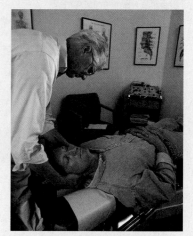

Chiropractors typically manipulate the spine and muscles to treat a variety of health problems. But there's little evidence that their approaches are more effective than those derived from traditional medicine.

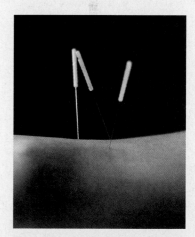

Acupuncture needles are thin and can be inserted virtually any place on the skin of the body.

Falsifiability

acupuncture
ancient Chinese practice of inserting thin needles into more than 2,000 points in the body to alter energy forces believed to run through the body

Occam's Razor

perhaps because of a placebo effect (Hines, 2003). The placebo effect is a simpler explanation that better accounts for the data than the hypothesis that an undetectable energy field is responsible for acupuncture's effects.

Whole Medical Systems: The Example of Homeopathy. Entire medical systems have developed apart from conventional medicine for thousands of years in China and India.

(Nick D. Kim)

A more recent example of an alternative medical system is **homeopathic medicine,** practiced in the United States since the early 1800s. Nearly 4 percent of Americans report having used homeopathic methods (Barnes et al., 2004). Homeopathic remedies are based on the premise that consuming an extremely diluted dose of a substance known to produce an illness in a healthy person will alleviate that illness. To understand how homeopathy supposedly works, we should recall the joke about the patient who forgot to take his homeopathic remedy and died of an underdose. The principle behind homeopathy is that "like cures like." This is a good example of the *representativeness heuristic* (see Chapter 2). When we use this heuristic, we judge the similarity between two things by gauging the extent to which they resemble each other ("like goes with like").

When we rely too heavily on the representativeness heuristic, we can make errors in judgment. In this case, we might assume that the treatment for a disorder must resemble its cause—that is, if a disorder is caused by too much of chemical A, we should treat it by presenting the patient with as little of chemical A as possible. However, homeopaths often dilute remedies to the point that not even a single molecule of the original substance remains. Homeopaths' belief that the "memory" of the substance is enough to stimulate the body's defenses is an extraordinary claim that makes utterly no sense from a scientific perspective: Medicine that contains no medicine isn't medicine.

Extraordinary Claims

Not surprisingly, homeopathic remedies haven't been shown to be effective for any medical condition (Giles, 2007). Nevertheless, some people who try homeopathic remedies, like model Cindy Crawford, claim to reap considerable benefits from them, as well from other medical treatments that have little or no scientific support.

Why is this so? Here are five probable reasons for the apparent effectiveness of homeopathy and other unsupported alternative medical treatments (Beyerstein, 1997):

(1) They produce a placebo effect. They instill hope but not much else.

(2) People may assume that natural products like herbs and megavitamins improve their health because they perceive no adverse effects to counter this belief.

(3) The symptoms of many physical disorders come and go, so consumers may attribute symptom relief to the treatment, rather than to changes in the natural course of the illness.

(4) When alternative treatments accompany conventional treatments, people may attribute their improvement to the alternative treatment rather than to the less dramatic or interesting conventional treatment.

(5) The problem may be misdiagnosed in the first place, so the condition isn't as severe as initially believed.

Alternative Treatments: To Use or Not to Use, That Is the Question. Should we conclude that all alternative treatments are worthless? Not at all. As we'll recall from our discussion of Oberg's dictum (see Chapter 1), it's essential that we keep an open mind and not simply dismiss new and potentially useful treatments out of hand. Many drugs derive from plant and natural products, and many effective medicines surely remain to be discovered. Every year, drug companies screen thousands of natural products for disease-fighting properties, and a few prove worthy of further testing. For example, *taxol,* derived from the Pacific yew tree, has been shown to be effective as an anticancer drug. Although

homeopathic medicine
remedies that feature a small dose of an illness-inducing substance to activate the body's own natural defenses

Saint John's Wort doesn't appear especially effective for severe depression, it may be somewhat helpful for mild depression (Wallach & Kirsch, 2003). These and other herbal medicines may become part of mainstream treatment if they turn out to be safe and effective.

The same is true of psychological practices. Meditation, once regarded as an alternative approach, now appears to be an effective means of reducing stress and has increasingly blended into the spectrum of conventional approaches (see Chapter 5).

Barry Beyerstein (1997) recommended that we ask the following two questions before trying an alternative approach:

(1) Does it lack a scientific rationale, or contradict well-accepted scientific laws or principles?

(2) Do carefully done studies show that the product or treatment is less effective than conventional approaches?

If the answer to both questions is "yes," we should be especially skeptical. When in doubt, it's wise to consult a physician about an alternative or complementary treatment. Doing so will give us confidence that the treatment we select, regardless of whether it's conventional, is genuinely a "good alternative."

Since the late 1700s, physicians have known that digitalis, a drug that comes from the purple foxglove plant (*top*), can control heart rate and treat heart disease. More recently, taxol (*bottom*), which comes from the Pacific yew tree, was identified as an anticancer drug. Some, but by no means all, natural plants are effective medicines.

ASSESS YOUR KNOWLEDGE: FACT OR FICTION?

(1) Scientists haven't established safe amounts of alcohol to consume. (True/False)

(2) Obese people tend to be "jollier" than non-obese people. (True/False)

(3) Women tend to overestimate their risk of dying from breast cancer as opposed to heart disease. (True/False)

(4) The fact that a health product is "natural" means it's likely to be safe. (True/False)

(5) The effects of acupuncture appear to be due to the redistribution of energy in the body. (True/False)

Answers: (1) T (p. 517); (2) F (p. 518); (3) T (p. 522); (4) F (p. 525); (5) F (p. 525)

Think again...

What Is Stress? (pp. 495–499)

STUDY the Learning Objectives

▶ Explain how stress is defined and approached in different ways
- Stress is a part of daily life. Most people experience one or more extremely stressful events in their lifetime. People experience stress when they feel physically threatened, unsafe, or unable to meet the perceived demands of life. Stress can be viewed as a stimulus, a response, or a transaction with the environment. Stressful events and their consequences are important in studying the response aspects of stress, whereas identifying specific categories of stressful events (unemployment, natural disasters) is the focus of stressors as stimuli view of stress. The stress as a transaction view holds that the experience of stress depends on both primary appraisal (the decision regarding whether the event is harmful) and secondary appraisal (perceptions of our ability to cope with the event) of the potentially stressful event.

▶ Identify different approaches to measuring stress
- Psychologists often assess life events that require major adaptations and adjustments, such as illness and unemployment. They also assess hassles—annoying, frustrating daily events, which may be more related to adverse psychological and health outcomes than major stressors.

DO YOU KNOW THESE TERMS?
- ❏ **stress** (p. 495)
- ❏ **primary appraisal** (p. 496)
- ❏ **secondary appraisal** (p. 496)
- ❏ **problem-focused coping** (p. 496)
- ❏ **emotion-focused coping** (p. 496)
- ❏ **corticosteroids** (p. 496)
- ❏ **hassles** (p. 498)

How can daily hassles such as traffic, a difficult relationship with a boss, or getting the wrong order at a drive-through restaurant affect our health? (p. 498)

THINK about **what You would do . . .**
As the college application season approaches, you are asked to help students to identify, appraise, and cope with the stress involved in acceptance and rejection. What coping skills could you teach them? (p. 495)

Survivors of Hurricane Katrina might be of particular interest to researchers who study stress from which viewpoint? (p. 496)

mypsychlab
where learning comes to life!

SUCCEED with

How Stressed Are You?
Exams, papers, and grades. . . Oh my! Find out how daily hassles affect you. (p. 498)

EXPLORE

ASSESS your knowledge

1. The tension, discomfort, or physical symptoms that arise when a situation strains our ability to cope is called _____. (p. 495)

2. The stressors as _____ approach focuses on identifying different types of stressful events. (p. 496)

3. People's varied reactions to the same event suggests that we can view stress as a _____ between people and their environments. (p. 496)

4. When we encounter a potentially threatening event, we initially engage in _____ _____ to decide whether the event is harmful. (p. 496)

5. We make a _____ _____ to determine how well we can cope with a harmful event. (p. 496)

6. _____ _____ is a coping strategy people use to tackle life's challenges head-on. (p. 496)

7. When we try to put a positive spin on our feelings or predicaments and engage in behaviors to reduce painful emotions, we are engaging in _____ _____. (p. 496)

8. _____ are stress hormones that activate the body and prepare us to respond to stressful circumstances. (p. 496)

9. Some researchers study stress as a _____ by trying to assess people's psychological and physical reactions to stressful circumstances. (p. 496)

10. Major life events, as well as daily _____, can impact our adjustment. (p. 498)

How We Adapt to Stress: Change and Challenge (pp. 499–503)

STUDY the Learning Objectives

▶ Describe Selye's general adaptation syndrome (GAS)
- The GAS consists of three stages: (1) Alarm: The autonomic nervous system is activated. (2) Resistance: Adaptation and coping occurs; (3) Exhaustion: When resources and coping abilities are depleted, which can damage organs and engender depression and posttraumatic stress disorder (PTSD).

THINK about **what You would do . . .**
After a school shooting, your younger brother's school has been temporarily closed. How would you and your parents address any symptoms of PTSD he experiences? (p. 501)

What are the similarities and differences between Shelley Taylor's tend and befriend response and the flight-or-fight response? (p. 501)

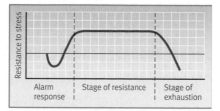

Seyle's General Adaptation Syndrome

SUCCEED with
Explore how our bodies react to stress. (p. 499)

EXPLORE

Identify the brain and body components activated in the alarm reaction depicted here, as proposed by Selye. (pp. 499–500)

Resistance to stress

Alarm response | Stage of resistance | Stage of exhaustion

ASSESS your knowledge

1. According to Hans Selye's _____ _____ _____, we respond to stress in three stages. (p. 499)

2. During the _____ stage, the central nervous system is activated and we experience a rush of adrenalin and physical symptoms of anxiety. (p. 500)

3. The _____ _____ _____ response is a set of physiological or psychological reactions that mobilize us to either confront or escape a threatening situation. (p. 500)

4. During the second stage of the GAS, _____ we adapt to the stressor and try to find a way to cope with it. (p. 500)

5. During the third stage of the GAS, _____, resources and coping abilities are limited, and stress can damage organs and engender depression and posttraumatic stress disorder. (p. 501)

6. Taylor coined the phrase _____ _____ _____ to describe how women typically rely on their social contacts and nurturing abilities during times of stress more than men do. (p. 501)

7. The severity, duration, and nearness to the stressor affect people's likelihood of developing _____ _____ _____. (p. 502)

8. In a survey of NYC area residents after 9/11, researchers found that (one-third/two-thirds) of the sample were resilient. (p. 502)

9. Events that are challenging, yet not overwhelming, such as competing in an athletic event, are examples of a "_____ stress," that provide opportunities for personal growth. (p. 503)

10. People with depression are (more/not more) likely than nondepressed people to have experienced one or more events that involve loss, like the death of a loved one. (p. 503)

▶ **Explain the tend and befriend response to stress**
• The tend and befriend response is more common in women than in men. In times of stress, women often rely more on their social contacts, nurture others, and befriend or turn to others for support.

▶ **Describe diversity of stress responses, including PTSD, anxiety, and depression**
• About 5 percent (men) to 10 percent (women) of people experience PTSD in the face of a potentially traumatic stressor. Yet as many as two-thirds of people are resilient in the face of stressors.

DO YOU KNOW THESE TERMS?
☐ **general adaptation syndrome (GAS)** (p. 499)
☐ **fight-or-flight response** (p. 500)
☐ **tend and befriend** (p. 501)

The Brain–Body Reaction to Stress (pp. 503–510)

What are the characteristics of a Type A personality and what health risks are associated with such a personality? (p. 508)

Stress and Health

SUCCEED with
Go ahead, peek inside. . . The physiology and psychology of the stress response
(p. 503)

SIMULATION

THINK about
what You would do . . .
In your health psychology course, you are asked to make a presentation on the link between stress and the immune system. What would you do to make this link clear using the common cold as an example? (p. 505)

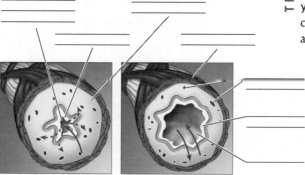

Obstructed airway   Normal airway

Describe the physical and emotional factors related to an asthma attack. (p. 510)

STUDY the Learning Objectives

▶ **Describe how the immune system functions**
• The immune system is the body's defensive barrier against disease. Phagocytes and lymphocytes neutralize antigens, such as viruses and bacteria, and produce proteins called antibodies that fight infection. Diseases of the immune system include AIDS and other autoimmune diseases in which the immune system is overactive.

▶ **Describe the field of psychoneuro-immunology**
• Psychoneuroimmunology explores the link between the immune system and the nervous system. Stress can decrease resistance to illness, delay healing, and impair the immune system.

▶ **Explain the contributions of the bio-psychosocial model to understanding psychophysiological disorders**
• Psychophysiological disorders are influenced by stress and emotional factors. According to the biopsychosocial model, illnesses depend on the interplay of genes, lifestyles, immunity, stress, social support, and self-perceptions.

▶ **Describe the role of personality in everyday experience, and socioeconomic factors in coronary heart disease, and stress in asthma and ulcers**
• For many years, the Type A personality was thought to promote risk of CHD, but more recent work points to chronic hostility as a more central risk factor. Type D or "distressed" persons also are at heightened risk for CHD. Asthma is a

psychophysiological disorder because physical responses to stress or emotional responses can trigger an asthma attack. Ulcers appear to be caused by the Helicobacter pylori bacterium and exacerbated by stress.

DO YOU KNOW THESE TERMS?

❏ **immune system** (p. 505)
❏ **acquired immune deficiency syndrome (AIDS)** (p. 505)
❏ **psychoneuroimmunology** (p. 505)
❏ **psychophysiological** (p. 506)
❏ **biopsychosocial perspective** (p. 506)
❏ **coronary heart disease (CHD)** (p. 507)
❏ **Type A personality** (p. 507)
❏ **Type D personality** (p. 508)
❏ **asthma** (p. 509)
❏ **peptic ulcer** (p. 510)

ASSESS your knowledge

1. The _____ _____ is the body's defense system against invading bacteria, viruses, and other potentially illness-producing organisms and substances. (p. 505)

2. AIDS is a life-threatening, incurable, yet treatable condition in which the _____ _____ _____ attacks and damages the immune system. (p. 505)

3. An example of an autoimmune disease in which the immune system is over-active is (arthritis/alcoholism). (p. 505)

4. Psychoneuroimmunology is the study of the relationship between the immune system and the _____ _____ system. (p. 505)

5. Research has shown that stress (can/can't) decrease resistance to the cold virus. (p. 506)

6. Asthma is an example of a _____ illness in which emotions and stress contribute to, maintain, or aggravate the physical condition. (p. 506)

7. Scientists have learned that psychological factors, including stress and personality traits are key risk factors for _____ _____ _____. (p. 507)

8. Of all Type A personality traits, _____ appears to be the most predictive of heart disease. (p. 508)

9. Type D or "distressed" persons (are/are not) at heightened risk for CHD. (p. 508)

10. Stress itself often (is/isn't) the only cause of a peptic ulcer. (p. 510)

Coping with Stress (pp. 511–515)

STUDY the Learning Objectives

▶ Describe the role of social support and different types of control in coping with stress
  • Social support and the following types of stress control are important: (1) behavioral control (taking action to reduce stress), (2) cognitive control (reappraising stressful events that can't be avoided), (3) decisional control (choosing between alternatives), (4) informational control (acquiring information about a stressor), (5) emotional control (suppressing and expressing emotions at will), and (6) flexible control (adjusting coping strategies to specific situations).

▶ Explain how spirituality, hardiness, self-enhancement, and rumination may influence the responses to stress
  • Hardy people view change as challenge, have a deep sense of commitment to their life and work, and believe they can control events. Flexible coping, trait self-enhancement—a self-serving tendency to overestimate positive personal qualities—boosts stress resistance, as do spirituality and religious involvement, whereas rumination—the tendency to focus on bad feelings and analyze the causes and consequences of problems—can increase vulnerability to stress.

DO YOU KNOW THESE TERMS?

❏ **social support** (p. 511)
❏ **proactive coping** (p. 512)
❏ **hardiness** (p. 514)
❏ **spirituality** (p. 514)

What are the benefits of a strong social network when an individual is undergoing stressful or challenging life events? (p. 511)

What is crisis debriefing and how effective is it for people who have experienced a traumatic event? (p. 513)

mypsych lab
where learning comes to life!

SUCCEED with

Coping Strategies and Their Effects

Are you using effective coping strategies?

(p. 512)

EXPLORE

THINK about what You would do . . .
A close friend is clearly under stress and feels her life is out of control. What are the five types of control you might tell her about to help her cope? (p. 512)

ASSESS your knowledge

1. _____ _____ encompasses our relationships with people and groups that provide emotional and financial assistance as we contend with important decisions or stressful situations. (p. 511)

2. The ability to step up and take action to reduce the impact of a stressful situation is an example of _____ _____. (p. 512)

3. _____ _____ is the ability to think differently about negative emotions that arise in response to stress-provoking events. (p. 512)

4. We engage in _____ _____ when we anticipate stressful situations and take steps to prevent or minimize difficulties before they arise. (p. 512)

5. When you can suppress or express emotions at will, you are exhibiting _____ _____. (p. 512)

6. Recent studies indicate that crisis debriefing (is/isn't) effective for trauma reactions. (p. 513)

7. _____ is a set of attitudes, marked by a sense of control over events, commitment to life and work, and motivation and courage to confront stressful events. (p. 514)

8. Optimistic people are (better/worse) at handling frustration than pessimists. (p. 514)

9. _____ is the search for the sacred, which may or may not extend to belief in God. (p. 514)

10. Spending a good deal of time ruminating is a (productive/counterproductive) way of reacting to a stressful situation. (p. 515)

Promoting Good Health—and Less Stress! (pp. 516–527)

Using what you have learned, identify three to five effective strategies for creating and maintaining healthy habits. (pp. 517–521)

1. _____
2. _____
3. _____
4. _____
5. _____

mypsych lab
where learning comes to life!

SUCCEED with

How Healthy Are You?

What healthy steps are you taking to tackle daily stress? (p. 516)

EXPLORE

THINK about

what **You** would do . . .

As you head home after your freshman year—15 lbs. overweight, having trouble sleeping, and with two semesters of bad eating habits under your belt—what could you do to identify and adopt strategies for more healthy living next semester? (p. 516)

Calculate BMI by dividing weight in pounds (lbs) by height in inches (in) squared and multiplying by a conversion factor of 703.

Example: Weight = 155 lbs, height = 5'9" (69")
Calculation: $[155 \div (69)^2] \times 703 = 22.89$

BMI	Weight Status
Below 18.5	Underweight
18.5 - 24.9	Normal
25.0 - 29.9	Overweight
30.0 and above	Obese

Follow the formula above to calculate your BMI and determine your weight status from the categories listed. (p. 518)

ASSESS your knowledge

1. The field of psychology that integrates the behavioral sciences with the practice of medicine is called _____ medicine. (p. 516)

2. _____ is feedback from a device that provides an almost immediate read-out of a biological function, such as heart rate or skin temperature. (p. 516)

3. When we engage in _____ behaviors that reduce stress in the short run, we put ourselves at risk for health and stress-related problems in the long run. (p. 516)

4. Health psychologists make the treatment and prevention of _____ a high priority. (p. 517)

5. Research has shown that heavy _____ is associated with significant increases in many different types of cancer, serious and sometimes fatal liver problems, and brain shrinkage and other neurological problems. (p. 517)

6. A 2004 study determined that (one-third/two-thirds) of Americans are overweight, gauged by the body mass index (BMI) statistic. (p. 518)

7. Genes (play/do not play) a role in people's tendency to become overweight. (p. 520)

8. _____ _____ refers to health care practices and products that are used in place of conventional medicine. (p. 523)

9. Herbs, vitamins, and dietary supplements (are/are not) regulated by the FDA for safety, purity, and effectiveness. (p. 525)

10. _____ _____ is based on the premise that consuming an extremely diluted dose of an illness-inducing substance will activate the body's own natural defenses against it. (p. 526)

STUDY the Learning Objectives

▶ Identify the goals and practices of behavioral medicine and health psychology

• Behavioral medicine and health psychology study the promotion and maintenance of health, the prevention and treatment of illness, and related dysfunction. In addition to training patients in stress management, health psychologists help them to promote health and minimize risk for smoking, drinking excessive alcohol, and obesity.

▶ Distinguish alternative from complementary medicine

• Alternative medicine refers to health care practices and products used in place of conventional medicine. Complementary medicine refers to products and practices that are used along with conventional medicine.

▶ Describe different alternative medical approaches and compare their effectiveness with placebos

• Alternative medicine approaches include biologically based therapies (vitamins, herbs, food supplements), manipulative and body-based methods (chiropractic medicine), energy medicine (acupuncture), and whole medical systems (homeopathy). Many alternative approaches are no more effective than placebos. Alternative medical products and procedures can become part of conventional medicine when demonstrated to be safe and effective.

DO YOU KNOW THESE TERMS?

❑ **health psychology** (p. 516)
❑ **alternative medicine** (p. 523)
❑ **complementary medicine** (p. 523)
❑ **acupuncture** (p. 525)
❑ **homeopathic medicine** (p. 526)

Remember these questions from the beginning of the chapter? Think again and ask yourself if you would answer them differently based on what you now know about stress, coping, and health. (For more detailed explanations, see MyPsychLab.)

▶ Can we measure and study stress objectively? (p. 496)
▶ Do all people react to stressful circumstances in the same way? (p. 496)
▶ Do most people who encounter highly aversive events develop posttraumatic stress disorder? (p. 502)
▶ Are some people more prone to heart attacks than others? (pp. 507–508)
▶ Does stress produce ulcers in most people? (p. 510)
▶ Is there one best way to cope with stressful events? (p. 511)
▶ Are some people especially hardy or able to cope with life challenges? (p. 514)
▶ Are crash diets that promise quick and enduring weight loss effective? (p. 520)
▶ Are acupuncture and other alternative medical treatments more effective than traditional medical procedures? (pp. 525–526)

THINKING Scientifically

Correlation vs. Causation
pp. 498, 508, 514, 515, 518, 519, 521

Falsifiability pp. 515, 525

Extraordinary Claims p. 526

Occam's Razor p. 526

Replicability pp. 511, 520

Ruling Out Rival Hypotheses
pp. 498, 506, 510, 511, 516, 517, 519

13

Social Psychology
How Others Affect Us

Ruling Out Rival Hypotheses

PREVIEW

Think

First, think about these questions. Then, as you read, think again. . . .

▶ How good are we at judging the causes of others' behavior?

▶ What causes mass hysteria over rumors about things like Martian landings?

▶ How do cults persuade people to become fanatics?

▶ Were the Nazis particularly evil, or would we have done the same thing in their boots?

▶ How can a woman be stabbed to death in plain view of many people without anyone coming to her aid?

▶ Does how we act reflect what we believe, or is it the other way around?

▶ What's the best way to persuade others to do something for us?

▶ Are stereotypes always a bad thing?

On October 30, 1938—a few hours before Halloween—much of the United States temporarily lost its grip on reality. That night, 6 million Americans tuned in to a popular radio show hosted by 23-year-old Hollywood sensation Orson Welles. The program featured an adaptation of H. G. Wells's science fiction classic *The War of the Worlds*, which vividly describes the invasion of Earth by a race of enormous Martians. (In 2005, Steven Spielberg made this book into a movie starring Tom Cruise.) To make *The War of the Worlds* more entertaining—and to play a good-natured pre-Halloween trick on his listeners—Welles presented the story in the form of a phony news broadcast. Anyone listening carefully to the program would have known that it was a clever hoax, as Welles informed his audience no fewer than four times that the show was merely an adaptation of a science fiction story.

As the broadcast unfolded over the next hour, a newscaster periodically interrupted live orchestral music with increasingly alarming news bulletins that first reported a series of explosions on the surface of Mars and later the landing of a mysterious metal capsule on a farm in Grover's Mill, New Jersey, some 50 miles from New York City. Against the backdrop of screaming witnesses, a terrified reporter described a large alien with tentacles emerging from a hatch in the capsule. By the program's end, the newscaster informed listeners that an army of giant Martians was launching a full-scale invasion of New York City.

The War of the Worlds triggered a mass panic (Bartholomew, 1998). Hundreds of frightened listeners fled into the streets, while others hid in their basements. Still others called the police or loaded their guns. Some even wrapped their heads in towels in preparation for a Martian chemical attack (Cantril, 1947). Although most listeners didn't panic, at least tens of thousands did (Brainbridge, 1987). Surprisingly, many listeners apparently never bothered to consider alternative explanations for the program or to seek out evidence that could have falsified claims of a massive alien invasion. Had they tuned their radios to a different station, they would have heard no coverage of this presumably momentous event in human history. That surely would have tipped them off that Welles's program was a huge practical joke. Instead, many listeners fell prey to confirmation bias (see Chapter 1), focusing on only one hypothesis—that the news bulletins were real—at the expense of all others.

In addition to alarming listeners, the show caused many to misinterpret familiar stimuli as unfamiliar. For example, some residents of Grover's Mill panicked at the sight of a tall water tower that they'd surely passed hundreds of times. In their intense fright, they mistook it for a space ship and shot it to smithereens. Our shared beliefs about reality can affect our interpretation of it.

Welles had pulled off the most successful Halloween prank of all time. How did he do it? One thing's for certain: Welles had never taken an introductory psychology course, so he didn't rely on scientific research. Yet he understood the power of social influence, although even he was caught off guard by just how potent it was.

What Is Social Psychology?

Social psychology helps us to understand not only why *The War of the Worlds* hoax succeeded, but why many forms of social influence are so powerful. **Social psychology** is the study of how people influence others' behavior, beliefs, and attitudes—for both good and bad (Lewin, 1951). Social psychology helps us to understand not only why we sometimes act helpfully and even heroically in the presence of others, but also why we occasionally show our worst sides, caving in to group pressure or standing by idly while others suffer. It also helps us to understand why we're prone to blindly accept irrational, even pseudoscientific, beliefs.

social psychology
study of how people influence others' behavior, beliefs, and attitudes

In this chapter, we'll begin by examining the social animals we call human beings (Aronson, 1998) and discuss how and why we often underestimate the impact of social influence on others' behavior. We'll move on to examine two especially potent social influences: conformity and obedience, and then address the question of why we help people at some times and harm them at others. Then, we'll discuss our attitudes and how social pressure shapes them. We'll end by exploring the troubling question of how prejudice toward others arises and, more optimistically, how we can combat it.

HUMANS AS A SOCIAL SPECIES

Social psychology is important for one reason: We humans are a highly social species. Most evidence suggests that as early hominids in Africa hundreds of thousands of years ago, we evolved in relatively small and tight social groups (Barchas, 1986). Even as modern-day humans, most of us naturally gravitate to small groups. In forming cliques, or groups that include some people—in-group members—we by extension exclude others—out-group members.

Gravitating to Each Other—to a Point. Anthropologist Robin Dunbar (1993) has become famous for a number: 150. This number is the approximate size of most human social groups, from the hunter–gatherers of days of yore to today's scientists working a specialized research area (Gladwell, 2002). Research suggests that 150 is also close to the average number of people that each of us knows reasonably well. Dunbar argued that the size of our neocortex (see Chapter 3) relative to the rest of our brain places limits on how many people with whom we can closely associate with. For animals with smaller neocortices relative to the rest of their brains, such as chimpanzees and dolphins, the number of relations may be smaller (Dunbar, 1993; Marino, 2005). Whether or not 150 is the universal "magic number," Dunbar is probably right that our highly social brains are predisposed to forming intimate interpersonal networks that are large—but only so large.

The Need to Belong: Why We Form Groups. When we're deprived of social contact for a considerable length of time, we usually become lonely. According to Roy Baumeister and Mark Leary's (1995) *need to belong theory*, we humans have a biologically based need for interpersonal connections. We seek out social bonds when we can and suffer negative psychological and physical consequences when we can't. Stanley Schacter (1959) discovered the power of this social need in a small pilot study. He asked five male volunteers to live alone in separate rooms for an extended time period. All five were miserable. One bailed out after only 20 minutes, and three lasted only 2 days. The lone holdout, who reported feeling extremely anxious, made it to 8 days.

More systematic research shows that the threat of social isolation can lead us to behave in self-destructive ways and even impair our mental functioning. In a series of experiments, Jean Twenge and her colleagues asked undergraduates to complete a personality measure and gave them bogus feedback based on their test results: They told participants either that "You're the type who will end up alone later in life" or "You're likely to be accident prone later in life." Students who received feedback that they'd be isolated toward the end of their lives were significantly more likely than other students to engage in unhealthy behaviors, like eating a fattening snack or procrastinating on an assignment (Twenge, Catanese, & Baumeister, 2002). The same negative feedback is so upsetting that it even impairs students' performance on IQ tests (Baumeister, Twenge, & Nuss, 2002).

Brain imaging research goes a step further, shedding light on the commonplace observation that being cut off from social contact "hurts," literally and figuratively. Kip Williams and his coworkers placed participants in an fMRI scanner while they played a computerized ball tossing game with other "participants," who didn't actually exist. In a "virtual" version of the popular television show *Survivor*, the researchers rigged the game so that all participants were eventually excluded. Upon experiencing the sting of social rejection, participants displayed pronounced activation in a region of the cingulate cortex (see Chapter 3) that also becomes active during physical pain. So that "ouch" we feel after being thrown out of a group may bear more than a coincidental

Orson Welles created mass panic in 1938 when he persuaded tens of thousands of Americans of the existence of a widespread Martian invasion. Although residents of Grover's Mill, New Jersey, had surely passed by this water tower (top) many times, their panic led them to mistake it for an alien rocket ship (see poster from *The War of the Worlds* on bottom). Social factors can shape how we interpret reality.

In the 2000 film *Cast Away*, actor Tom Hanks (portraying a Federal Express worker stranded on a remote desert island) strikes up an unusual companionship with a volleyball. According to Baumeister and Leary's need to belong theory, our social motives are powerful—so powerful that when deprived of interpersonal contact, we find a way to recreate it.

similarity to the ouch we feel after stubbing our toe (Eisenberger, Lieberman, & Williams, 2003).

How We Came to Be This Way: Evolution and Social Behavior. Because we'll soon be examining many unhealthy forms of social influence, such as how unquestioning acceptance of authority figures can lead us to do foolish things, we might be tempted to conclude that almost all social influence is negative. That would be a serious mistake. Virtually all of the social influence processes we'll discuss are adaptive under most circumstances and help to regulate cultural practices. From the perspective of an evolutionary approach to social behavior, many social influence processes have been naturally selected, because they've generally served us well over the course of evolution (Buss & Kendrick, 1998). Even if we're skeptical of the view that evolution helps to explain much of social behavior, we can still accept a core premise: Social influence processes serve us well most of the time, but they can occasionally backfire on us if we're not careful.

An evolutionary perspective on social behavior leads us to one critical conclusion: *Conformity, obedience, and many other forms of social influence become maladaptive only when they're blind or unquestioning.* From this standpoint, irrational group behavior—like the disastrous obedience of thousands of German citizens during the Nazi regime of the 1930s and 1940s and the massive genocide in Rwanda in the 1990s—are by-products of adaptive processes that have gone wildly wrong. There's nothing wrong with looking to a persuasive leader for guidance, as long as we don't stop asking questions. Once we accept social influence without evaluating it critically, however, we place ourselves at the mercy of powerful others.

Social Facilitation: From Bicyclists to Cockroaches. Because we're social creatures, being surrounded by others can make us perform better. Research shows that the mere presence of others can enhance our performance in certain situations, a phenomenon that Robert Zajonc called **social facilitation.** In the world's first social psychological study, Norman Triplett (1897) found that bicycle racers obtained faster speeds (32.6 miles per hour on average) when racing along with other bicyclists than when racing against only the clock (24 miles per hour on average). Zajonc (1965) found that social facilitation applies to birds, fish, and even insects. In what's surely one of the most creative studies in the history of psychology, Zajonc and two colleagues randomly assigned cockroaches to two conditions: one in which they ran a maze alone and in another in which they ran a maze while being observed by an audience of fellow cockroaches from a "spectator box." Compared with the lone cockroaches, cockroaches in the second condition ran the maze significantly faster and committed fewer errors (Zajonc, Heingartner, & Herman, 1969).

Yet the impact of others on our behavior isn't always positive (Bond & Titus, 1983). Social facilitation occurs only on tasks we find easy, whereas *social disruption*—a worsening of behavior in the presence of others—occurs on tasks we find difficult. You've probably discovered this principle if you've ever "choked" in the company of others while singing a difficult song or telling a lengthy joke with a complicated punch line. One team of five researchers watched people playing pool (Michaels, Blommel, Brocato, Linkous, & Rowe, 1982). The experienced pool players did better in the presence of others, but the inexperienced pool players did worse. The effects of social influence can be either positive or negative depending on the situation.

THE GREAT LESSON OF SOCIAL PSYCHOLOGY

When we try to figure out why other people—or indeed, we ourselves—did something, we're forming **attributions,** or assigning causes to behavior. We make attributions every day. Some attributions are internal (inside the person), such as when we conclude that Joe Smith robbed a bank because he's impulsive. Other attributions are external (outside the person), such as when we conclude that Bill Jones robbed a bank because his family was broke. We can explain a great deal of our everyday behavior by situational factors, like peer pressure, that are external to us.

Group cohesion and at least some degree of conformity are necessary for military units to function effectively.

social facilitation
enhancement of performance brought about by the presence of others

attribution
process of assigning causes to behavior

fundamental attribution error
tendency to overestimate the impact of dispositional influences on *other* people's behavior

The Fundamental Attribution Error. When we read about the frenzied behavior of some Americans during *The War of the Worlds,* we shake our heads in amazement and pat ourselves on the back with the confident reassurance that we'd never have behaved this way. Yet if the field of social psychology imparts one lesson that we should take with us for the rest of our lives (Myers, 1993), it's the **fundamental attribution error.** Coined by Lee Ross (1977), this term refers to the tendency to overestimate the impact of *dispositional influences* on others' behavior. By dispositional influences, we mean enduring characteristics, such as personality traits, attitudes, and intelligence. Because of this error, we attribute too much of people's behavior to who they are.

Because of the fundamental attribution error, we also tend to underestimate the impact of situational influences on others' behavior, so we also attribute too little of their behavior to what's going on around them. We may assume incorrectly that a boss in a failing company who fired several of his loyal employees to save money must be callous, when in fact he was under enormous pressure to rescue his company—and spare the jobs of hundreds of other loyal employees. Similarly, we may assume that we'd never have panicked during *The War of the Worlds* hoax, even though we might well have. Incidentally, the fundamental attribution error applies only to explaining *other* people's behavior; when explaining the causes of our *own* behavior, we typically invoke situational influences (Jones & Nisbett, 1972).

Evidence for the Fundamental Attribution Error. Edward E. Jones and Victor Harris (1967) conducted the first study to demonstrate the fundamental attribution error. They asked undergraduates to serve as "debaters" in a discussion of U.S. attitudes toward Cuba and its controversial leader, Fidel Castro. In full view of the other debaters, they randomly assigned students to read aloud debate speeches that adopted either a pro-Castro or an anti-Castro position.

After hearing these speeches, the researchers asked the other debaters to evaluate each debater's *true* attitudes toward Castro. That is, putting aside the speech he or she read, what do you think each debater *really* believes about Castro? Students fell prey to the fundamental attribution error; they inferred that what debaters said reflected their true position regarding Castro *even though they knew that the assignment to conditions was entirely random* (**Figure 13.1**). They forgot to take the situation—namely, the random assignment of subjects to the experimental condition—into account when evaluating debaters' attitudes (Ross, Anabile, & Steinmetz, 1977).

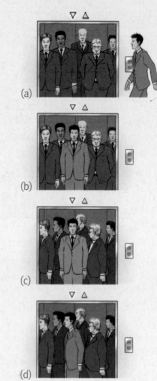

The 1960s television show "Candid Camera," which placed ordinary people in absurd situations, illustrates the *fundamental attribution error* (Maas & Toivanen, 1978). Viewers laugh at people's often silly reactions, underestimating how likely most of us are to fall victim to situational influences—in this case, group pressure. In one classic episode (shown here), an unsuspecting person enters an elevator filled with "Candid Camera" staff (a and b). Suddenly and for no reason, all of the staff turn to the right (c). Sure enough, the bewildered person turns to the right also (d).

APPLY YOUR THINKING

How might the fundamental attribution error lead us to place excessive blame on poor people for their life circumstances?

The Fundamental Attribution Error: Cultural Influences. Interestingly, the fundamental attribution error is associated with cultural factors. Although almost everyone is prone to this error, Japanese and Chinese people seem to be less so (Nisbett, 2003). That may be because they're more likely than those in Western cultures to perceive behaviors in context (see Prologue). As a result, they may be more prone to seeing others' behavior as a complex mix of both dispositional and situational influences.

For example, after reading newspaper descriptions of mass murderers, Chinese subjects are considerably less likely to invoke dispositional explanations for their behavior ("He must be an evil person") and more likely to invoke situational explanations ("He must have been under terrible stress in his life"). In contrast, U.S. subjects tend to show the opposite pattern (Morris & Peng, 1994). This cultural difference even extends to inanimate objects. When shown a circle moving in various directions, Chinese students are more likely to say that the circle's movement is due to situational or external factors ("Something is pushing on the circle") than to dispositional or internal factors ("The circle wants to move to the right"). We again find the opposite pattern among U.S. students (Nisbett, 2003).

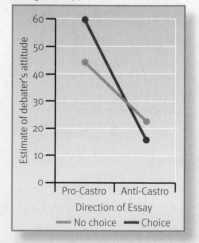

Figure 13.1 Subjects' Performance in Jones & Harris (1967) Castro Study. Subjects inferred that debaters' pro-Castro positions reflected their actual attitudes even though debaters couldn't choose which position to adopt—an example of the fundamental attribution error. (*Source:* Jones & Harris, 1967)

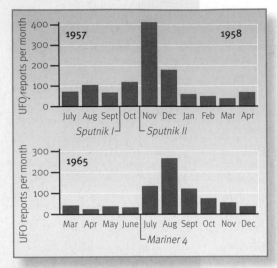

Figure 13.2 Graph of UFO Sightings. In the 1950s and 1960s, the number of UFO sightings shot up dramatically following the launches of *Sputnik I* and *II* (the Russian satellites that were the first objects launched into space) and following the U.S. launch of the space probe *Mariner 4*. Although these data don't permit definite cause-and-effect conclusions, they're consistent with the possibility that UFO sightings are of social origin. (*Source:* Hartmann, 1992)

The flying saucer craze is arguably one of the most widespread cases of collective delusions in world history. Like all photographs of supposed flying saucers, the reality of this one has never been verified (it looks suspiciously like a big hat to us).

social comparison theory
theory that we seek to evaluate our beliefs, attitudes, and abilities by comparing our reactions with others'

Occam's Razor

mass hysteria
outbreak of irrational behavior that is spread by social contagion

Extraordinary Claims

SOCIAL COMPARISON: PERSON SEE, PERSON DO

The War of the Worlds' hoax was successful for one reason: we're inherently social creatures. When a situation is unclear, we look to others for guidance about what to believe and how to act. According to Leon Festinger's (1954) **social comparison theory,** we evaluate our beliefs, abilities, and reactions by comparing them with those of others. Doing so helps us to understand ourselves and our social worlds better. For example, if you want to find out whether you're a good psychology student, it's only natural to compare your exam performance with that of your classmates.

Yet we can take social comparison too far. Although we can often learn valuable information from others' reactions, it's another thing to base our actions solely on their behavior. After all, what if other people are behaving unreasonably? *The War of the Worlds* might seem like an isolated case of human irrationality, but that's far from the truth. *The War of the Worlds* is merely one example of a broad class of events called *mass hysteria.*

Mass Hysteria: Irrationality at a Group Level. **Mass hysteria** is a contagious outbreak of irrational behavior that spreads much like a flu epidemic. Because we tend to engage in social comparison when a situation is ambiguous, most of us are prone to mass hysteria under the right circumstances. In some cases, episodes of mass hysteria can lead to *collective delusions,* in which many people simultaneously come to be convinced of bizarre things that are false. Consider three dramatic examples of mass hysteria and collective delusions (**Figure 13.2**):

- The date of June 24, 1947, probably means nothing to you. Yet this day witnessed the beginning of what's arguably one of the most prolonged collective delusions in world history. On that day, pilot Kenneth Arnold spotted nine mysterious shiny objects while flying over the ocean near Mount Rainier in Washington State. Interestingly, Arnold told reporters that these objects were shaped like *sausages.* Nevertheless, he also made the offhand observation that they'd "skipped over the water like saucers."

  Within days, the phrase "flying saucers" appeared in over 150 newspapers across the United States (Bartholomew & Goode, 2000). Even more interestingly, within only a few years thousands of people were claiming to see saucer-shaped objects in the sky. Had the newspapers been more accurate in their coverage of Arnold's words, we might today be hearing unidentified flying object (UFO) reports of flying sausages rather than flying saucers. But once the media introduced the term "flying saucers," the now familiar circular shape of UFOs took hold in the American consciousness and never let go.

- In the spring of 1954, the city of Seattle, Washington, experienced an epidemic of "windshield pitting." Thousands of residents noticed tiny indentations, or pits, in their car windshields that they suspected were the result of a secret nuclear test performed by the federal government. Their concerns spun so out of control that Seattle's mayor eventually sought emergency help from President Eisenhower (Bartholomew & Goode, 2000). Although the residents of Seattle hadn't realized it, the windshield pits had been there all along, as they are on most cars. The windshield-pitting epidemic offers another illustration of how shared societal beliefs can influence our interpretations of reality, making the familiar seem unfamiliar. When confronted with two explanations for the pitting—a secret nuclear explosion or the impact of dirt particles hitting the windshield—Seattle residents would have been better off picking the simpler one.

- In the 1970s and 1980s, thousands of farmers in the United States and Canada believed that an epidemic of "cattle mutilations" was taking place, as they were coming upon corpses of cows that had been mysteriously picked clean (Stewart, 1977). Many witnesses took these "mutilations" as the work of aliens, but there was a far more mundane explanation. Studies demonstrated that any dead cow left out for a period of days—which can happen when a herd is set to pasture—is soon devoured by carnivores who leave nothing but a bloodless carcass. Cattle mutilation proponents had forgotten a basic principle: Extraordinary claims require extraordinary evidence.

Urban Legends. One of the simplest demonstrations of the power of social influence comes from the study of *urban legends:* false stories repeated so many times that people believe them to be true (Brunvand, 1999). How many of the urban legends in **Figure 13.3** have you heard?

Each of the false stories in Figure 13.3 is too bizarre to be true, yet people consistently believe them, and far more. Urban legends are convincing in part because they fit our preconceptions (Gilovich, 1991). Urban legends also make good stories because they tug on our emotions, especially negative ones (Rosnow, 1980). Research shows that the most popular urban legends contain a heavy dose of material relevant to the emotion of disgust, probably because they arouse our perverse sense of curiosity. As a result, they often spread like wildfire. It's probably not coincidental that many feature rats and other animals that we don't exactly find appealing (Heath, Bell, & Sternberg, 2001).

ASSESS YOUR KNOWLEDGE: FACT OR FICTION?

(1) From the standpoint of an evolutionary approach to social behavior, conformity and obedience are inherently maladaptive. (True/False)
(2) The presence of other people always enhances our performance. (True/False)
(3) The fundamental attribution error reminds us that we tend to attribute others' behavior primarily to their personality traits and attitudes. (True/False)
(4) We're especially likely to engage in social comparison when a situation is clear-cut. (True/False)

Answers: (1) F (p. 536); (2) F (p. 536); (3) T (p. 537); (4) F (p. 538)

Social Influence:
Conformity and Obedience

Think of an organization or group to which you've belonged, like a club, school committee, fraternity, or sorority. Have you ever just gone along with one of the group's ideas even though you knew that it was bad, perhaps even unethical? If you have, don't feel ashamed, because you're in good company. **Conformity** refers to the tendency of people to alter their behavior as a result of group pressure (Kiesler & Kiesler, 1969). We all conform to social pressure from time to time. Yet as we'll see, we occasionally take this tendency too far.

CONFORMITY: THE ASCH PARADIGM

Solomon Asch conducted the classic study of conformity in the 1950s. Asch's (1955) research design was as straightforward as it was elegant. In some social psychological studies, such as Asch's, participants are lured in by a cover story that doesn't reveal the study's true goal. Often, other "participants" in the study are actually *confederates*, or undercover agents of the researcher. But the actual subjects are unaware of that.

In this chapter, we'll ask you to imagine yourself as a subject in several classic social psychological studies. Let's begin with Asch's.

The Setup: Asch invites subjects to participate in a "study of perceptual judgments" that asks eight subjects—including you—to compare a standard line with three comparison lines: 1, 2, and 3. Unbeknownst to you, the other "subjects" are actually Asch's confederates. A researcher explains that your job is to say out loud which of three comparison lines matches the standard line. The researcher starts with a person across the table, so you're always the fifth to be called.

A woman heated her poodle in a microwave oven in a well-meaning attempt to dry it off following a rainstorm. It exploded.

While still alive, Walt Disney arranged to have his body frozen after his death so that it could be unfrozen at a future date when advanced technology will permit him to live again.

Outside her home, a woman found a small stray animal that she identified as a Chihuahua. She cared for the pet for several weeks and eventually brought it to a veterinarian, who informed her that her cute little "dog" was actually a rat.

Many gang members drive around late at night without their car lights on, and then shoot people who flash their lights at them.

A woman on a transAtlantic flight was trapped in the bathroom for over two hours after flushing the toilet created a vacuum, binding her to the seat.

Figure 13.3 Urban Legend? Some popular urban legends: all are widely known, yet all are false. Incidentally, if you ever want to find out whether a remarkable rumor from the Internet or media is true, check the high-quality web site www.snopes.com, which continually tracks the accuracy of urban legends.

conformity
tendency of people to alter their behavior as a result of group pressure

Figure 13.4 Asch's Experiments.
(a) Here we see the lone actual subject (middle), barely believing his eyes, straining to look at the stimulus cards (below) after the confederates gave the wrong answer. This subject was one of only 25 percent of Asch's subjects who stuck to his guns and gave the correct answer in all 12 trials. After the study, he insisted, "I have to call them as I see them."

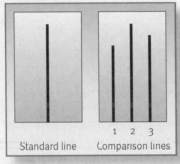

Standard line   Comparison lines

(b) Which of the "comparison lines" is the same length as the "standard line"? If several other participants said it was line #3, would you go along with them?

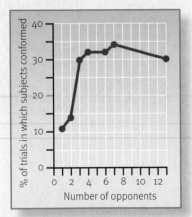

(c) In Asch's studies, conformity increased as the size of the majority increased—but only up to about five or six subjects.
(*Source:* Asch, 1955)

Ruling Out Rival Hypotheses

parametric studies
studies in which an experimenter systematically manipulates the independent variable to observe its effects on the dependent variable

The Study: On the first trial (figure not shown) you listen intently as the first few subjects call out their answers. Subject 1: "1." Subject 2: "1." Subject 3: "1." Subject 4: "1." As Subject 5, you simply follow, and say "1." The three subjects following you give the same answer: 1. "This study is going to be a breeze," you say to yourself.

The second trial displays a similar problem, just as easy to answer, in which the correct answer is clearly "2" (see **Figure 13.4**b). Again, you listen while the subjects call out their answers. Subject 1: "3." Subject 2: "3." Subject 3: "3." Subject 4: "3."

You can hardly believe your eyes. It seems obvious that "2" is the correct answer, but everyone is calling "3." What on earth is going on? Are your eyes deceiving you? Or did you perhaps misunderstand the instructions? What are you going to do?

The Results: If you're like 75 percent of subjects in the original Asch study, you'd conform to the incorrect norm on at least one of twelve trials. Across all twelve trials in the Asch study, subjects conformed to the wrong answer 37 percent of the time. Some subjects conformed even when the comparison line differed from the standard line by more than 6 inches! Understandably, subjects reported being confused and even distressed because they experienced a sharp conflict between their perceptions and what they believed to be others' perceptions.

Parametric Studies: Dissecting Social Influences on Conformity. Using **parametric studies,** Asch (1955) and later researchers pinpointed social factors that influenced the level of conformity. Parametric studies manipulate the *independent variable* in various ways to determine its effects on the *dependent variable*, in this case, conformity. Researchers concluded that conformity was influenced by the following independent variables:

- **Unanimity:** If all confederates gave the wrong answer, the subject was more likely to conform. However, if one confederate gave the correct response, the level of conformity dropped by three-fourths.
- **Difference in the wrong answer:** Knowing that someone else in the group differed from the majority—even if that person held a different view from the subject—the subject is less likely to conform.
- **Size:** The size of the majority made a difference, but only up to about five or six subjects. People were no more likely to conform in a group of ten subjects than in a group of five subjects (see Figure 13.4c).

APPLY YOUR THINKING
In his studies of conformity, Asch found a slight tendency for individuals to conform *less* when the group of confederates was very large (see Figure 13.4c). Why might this effect have occurred?

Asch also tried to rule out alternative hypotheses for his findings. To determine whether group norms affected subjects' *perceptions* of the lines, he replicated his original study but asked subjects to write, rather than call out, their responses. In this condition, subjects' answers were right more than 99 percent of the time.

Imaging Studies: Probing Further Influences. Nevertheless, new brain imaging technology raises the possibility that social pressure can sometimes influence perception. Gregory Berns and his colleagues (Berns et al., 2005) placed subjects in an fMRI scanner (see Chapter 3) and showed them two figures. They asked subjects to determine whether the figures were the same or different. To do so, subjects had to mentally rotate one or both of them. The researchers led the subjects into thinking that four other subjects were making the same judgments along with them; in fact, these judgments were preprogrammed into a computer.

On some trials, the other "participants" gave unanimously correct answers; on others, they gave unanimously incorrect answers. Like Asch, Berns and his collaborators found high levels of conformity; subjects went along with others' wrong answers 41 percent of the time. Their conforming behavior was associated with activity in the amygdala, which triggers anxiety in response to danger cues (see Chapter 3). This finding suggests that conformity may come with a price tag of negative emotions, particularly anxiety. Berns and his colleagues also found that conformity was associated with activity in the parietal and occipital lobes, the areas of the brain responsible for visual perception. This finding suggests that social pressure can sometimes affect how we perceive reality, although activity in these brain areas may have instead reflected the subjects' tendency to doubt and then recheck their initial perceptions.

Ruling Out Rival Hypotheses

Conformity: The Autokinetic Effect. Paralleling Asch's results on conformity are findings demonstrating that group judgments tend to converge gradually around a common norm. We can demonstrate this phenomenon using a curious perceptual illusion called the *autokinetic effect*. Picture yourself a subject seated in a pitch-dark room. You can see nothing, not even your hand a few inches in front of your face. Then, you see a tiny light projected on the wall about 15 feet in front of you. The light is stationary, although you don't realize that. After a few moments, the light seems to dance randomly across the wall.

This autokinetic effect results from tiny movements of the eye muscles that trick your brain into thinking that the dot is in motion. To correct for movements of your eye muscles, your brain constantly alters the perceived position of the external world. Against an entirely dark background, your brain is fooled into perceiving the external world as moving. Incidentally, the autokinetic effect appears to be a frequent cause of UFO reports. In virtually complete darkness, many people mistakenly perceive stars in the sky as moving, and misinterpret them as extraterrestrial vehicles (Hines, 2003).

In your role as a subject, your job is to estimate the amount of movement of the motionless dot by calling out your answer. When Muzafer Sherif (1936) first conducted studies on the autokinetic effect, he found that subjects often gave wildly different responses. Initial estimates of the amount of movement of the dot ranged from 2 inches to 80 feet!

In a second session, Sherif invited two other subjects into the room, and asked them to call out estimates of the light's movement along with the original subject. Across several sessions spread out over a few days, Sherif (1936) found that each subject's estimate converged progressively around a shared norm. This shared norm was influenced substantially by other subjects' answers. So if your initial estimate was 8 inches and other subjects estimated 20 inches, your eventual estimate might be 14 inches; if your initial estimate was 8 inches and other subjects estimated 2 inches, your eventual estimate might be 5 inches. In turn, other subjects' estimates will converge gradually toward yours (Sherif & Sherif, 1969). Even in later sessions with the other subject again absent, subjects clung firmly to the shared norm.

Conformity: Individual, Cultural, and Gender Differences. People's responses to social pressure are associated with individual and cultural differences. People with low self-esteem are especially prone to conformity (Hardy, 1957). Asians are also more likely to conform than Americans (Bond & Smith, 1996), probably because, as discussed in Chapter 10, many Asian cultures are more collectivist than American culture (Oyserman, Coon, & Kemmelmeier, 2002). This greater collectivism probably leads many Asians to be more concerned about group opinion than Americans. In addition, people in individualistic cultures, like the United States, generally prefer to stand out from the crowd, whereas people in collectivist cultures prefer to blend in. In one study, researchers presented American and Asian subjects with a bunch of orange and green pens that had a majority of one color and a minority of the other. Americans tended to pick the minority-colored pens, whereas Asians tended to pick the majority-colored pens (Kim & Markus, 1999).

fictoid

Myth: There's no adequate scientific explanation for most UFO reports.

Reality: Most UFO reports can be accounted for by misinterpretations of ordinary phenomena. Among the most frequent events mistaken for UFOs are lenticular cloud formations (which resemble saucers), the planet Venus (which can be extremely bright on clear nights), bright meteors streaking through Earth's atmosphere, airplanes, satellites, weather balloons, and even swarms of insects. Only about 2 percent of UFOs remain truly unidentified (Carroll, 2003; Hines, 2003).

Many early studies suggested that women are more likely to conform than men (Eagly & Carli, 1981). Nevertheless, this sex difference may have had an alternative explanation: The experimenters were all male. When later studies were conducted by female experimenters, the sex difference in conformity typically vanished (Feldman-Summers, Montano, Kasprzyk, & Wagner, 1980; Javornisky, 1979).

DEINDIVIDUATION: LOSING OUR TYPICAL IDENTITIES

One process that can make us more vulnerable to conformity is **deindividuation:** the tendency of people to engage in atypical behavior when stripped of their usual identities (Festinger, Pepitone, & Newcomb, 1952). Several factors contribute to deindividuation, but the most prominent are a feeling of anonymity and a lack of individual responsibility (Dipboye, 1977; Postmes & Spears, 1998). When we're deindividuated, we become more vulnerable to social influences, including the impact of social roles.

Every day, we play multiple social roles: student or teacher, son or daughter, sister or brother, roommate, athlete, social-club member, and employee, to name but a few. What happens when we temporarily lose our typical social identities and are forced to adopt different identities?

Stanford Prison Study: Chaos in Palo Alto. Philip Zimbardo and his colleagues first approached this question over three decades ago (Haney, Banks, & Zimbardo, 1973). Zimbardo knew about the dehumanizing conditions in many prisons, and he wondered whether they stemmed from peoples' personalities, or from the roles they're required to adopt. The roles of prisoner and guard, which are inherently antagonistic, may carry such powerful expectations that they generate self-fulfilling prophecies. What would happen if ordinary people played the roles of prisoner and guard? Would they begin to assume the identities assigned to them?

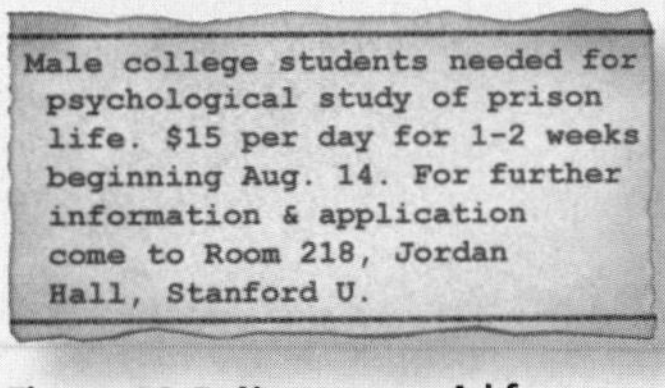

The Setup: Zimbardo and his colleagues advertised for volunteers for a 2-week "psychological study of prison life" (see **Figure 13.5**). Using a coin toss, he randomly assigned twenty-four male undergraduates, prescreened for normal adjustment using personality tests, to be either prisoners or guards.

The Study: Zimbardo transformed the basement of the Stanford psychology department in Palo Alto, California, into a simulated prison, complete with jail cells. To add to the realism, actual Palo Alto police officers arrested the would-be prisoners at their homes and transported them to the simulated prison. The prisoners and guards were forced to dress in clothes befitting their assigned roles. Zimbardo, who acted as the prison "superintendent," instructed guards to refer to prisoners only by numbers, not by names.

The Results: The first day passed without incident, but soon something went horribly wrong. Guards began to treat prisoners cruelly and subject them to harsh punishments. Guards forced prisoners to perform humiliating lineups, do push-ups, sing, strip naked, and clean filthy toilets with their bare hands. In some cases, they even placed bags over prisoners' heads.

By day two, the prisoners mounted a rebellion, which the guards quickly quashed. Things went steadily downhill from there. The guards became increasingly sadistic, using fire extinguishers on the prisoners and forcing them to simulate sodomy. Soon, many prisoners began to display signs of emotional disturbance, including depression, hopelessness, and anger. Zimbardo released two prisoners from the study because they appeared to be on the verge of a psychological breakdown. One prisoner went on a hunger strike in protest.

At day six, Zimbardo—after some prodding from one of his former graduate students, Christina Maslach—ended the study 8 days early. Although the prisoners were relieved at the news, some guards were disappointed (Haney et al., 1973). Perhaps Zimbardo was right; once prisoners and guards had been assigned roles that deemphasized their individuality, they adopted their designated roles more easily than anyone might have imagined.

Nevertheless, Zimbardo's study wasn't carefully controlled: In many respects, it was more of a demonstration than an experiment. In particular, his prisoners and guards may have experienced demand characteristics (Chapter 2) to behave in accord with their

Male college students needed for psychological study of prison life. $15 per day for 1-2 weeks beginning Aug. 14. For further information & application come to Room 218, Jordan Hall, Stanford U.

Figure 13.5 Newspaper Ad for Zimbardo's Prison Study. A facsimile of the newspaper advertisement for Zimbardo's Stanford Prison Study, 1972. (*Source:* Zimbardo, 1972)

deindividuation
tendency of people to engage in uncharacteristic behavior when they are stripped of their usual identities

assigned roles. For example, they may have assumed that the investigators wanted them to play the parts of prisoners and guards, and they obliged. Moreover, at least one attempt to replicate the Stanford prison study was unsuccessful, suggesting that the effects of deindividuation may not be inevitable (Reicher & Haslan, 2006).

Stanford Prison Experiment (1973)

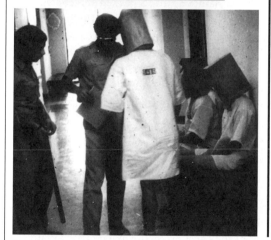

Abu Ghraib (2004)

Psychologist Phil Zimbardo, shown at home with masks on his wall. Zimbardo is fond of masks, as research suggests that they can produce deindividuation.

To some observers, some of the behaviors documented at Abu Ghraib prison in Iraq (photos at right) are eerily similar to those of Zimbardo's prison study (photos at left). Were the same processes of deindividuation at work?

The Real World: Chaos in Abu Ghraib. The Stanford prison study wasn't an isolated event (Zimbardo, 2007). In 2004 the world witnessed disturbingly similar images in the now-infamous Iraqi prison of Abu Ghraib. There, we saw guards—this time, actual U.S. soldiers—placing bags over Iraqi prisoners' heads, leading them around with dog leashes, pointing mockingly at their exposed genitals, and arranging them in human pyramids for their amusement. These similarities weren't lost on Zimbardo (2004, 2007), who maintained that the Abu Ghraib fiasco was a product of situational forces. According to Zimbardo, the dehumanization of prisoners and prison guards made it likely they'd lose themselves in the social roles to which their superiors assigned them.

That said, the overwhelming majority of U.S. prison guards during the Iraqi War didn't engage in abuse, so the reasons for such abuse don't lie entirely in the situation. As research using Asch's paradigm reminds us, individual differences in personality play a key role in conformity. Indeed, several guards who perpetrated the Abu Ghraib abuses had a history of irresponsible behavior (Saletan, 2004).

Furthermore, deindividuation doesn't necessarily make us behave badly; it makes us more likely to conform to whatever norms are present in the situation (Postmes & Spears, 1998). Some researchers have found that a loss of identity actually makes people more likely to engage in prosocial, or helping, behavior when others are helping out (Johnson &

Downing, 1979). For good or bad, deindividuation makes us behave more like a member of the group and less like an individual.

Crowds *sometimes* engage in irrational, even violent, behavior. But research suggests that crowds aren't necessarily more violent than individuals.

Crowds: Mob Psychology in Action. Deindividuation helps explain why crowd behavior is so unpredictable: The actions of people in crowds depend largely on whether others are acting prosocially or antisocially (against others). A myth that's endured for centuries is that crowds are always more aggressive than individuals. In the late nineteenth century, sociologist Gustav Le Bon argued that crowds are a recipe for irrational and even destructive behavior (Le Bon, 1895). According to Le Bon, people in crowds are more anonymous and therefore more likely to act on their impulses than individuals.

In some cases, crowds do become aggressive. On July 1, 2000, eight fans were crushed to death as they attempted to rush the stage during a Pearl Jam concert in Copenhagen, Denmark. The following year, on April 11, forty-three people were killed in Johannesburg, South Africa, as a large group of fans attempted to stampede into a packed soccer stadium.

Yet in other cases, crowds are less aggressive than individuals (de Waal, 1989; de Waal, Aurelli, & Judge, 2000), perhaps because deindividuation can make people either more or less aggressive, depending on prevailing social norms. Moreover, people in crowds typically limit their social interactions to minimize conflict (Baum, 1987). For example, people on crowded buses and elevators generally avoid staring at one another, instead preferring to stare at the road or the floor. This behavior is probably adaptive, because people are less likely to say or do something that could offend others.

GROUPTHINK

Closely related to conformity is a phenomenon that Irving Janis (1972) termed **groupthink:** an emphasis on group unanimity at the expense of critical thinking. Groups sometimes become so intent on ensuring that everyone agrees with everyone else that they give up their capacity to evaluate issues objectively.

Groupthink in action.
(© The New Yorker Collection 1979 Henry Martin from cartoonbank.com. All Rights Reserved.)

Groupthink in the Real World. Janis arrived at the concept of groupthink after studying the reasoning processes that contributed to one of the most notorious fiascos in American history: the 1961 invasion of the Bay of Pigs in Cuba. Following lengthy discussions with cabinet members, President John F. Kennedy recruited 1,400 Cuban immigrants to invade Cuba and overthrow its dictator, Fidel Castro. But Castro found out about the invasion in advance. As a result, the invaders were massively outnumbered and outgunned, and they lacked adequate air backup from American forces. Almost immediately after landing at the Bay of Pigs, nearly all the invaders were captured, and some were killed. It was an enormous humiliation for the United States, and Kennedy apologized for it on national television.

The members of Kennedy's cabinet weren't dumb; to the contrary, they were an uncommonly brilliant group of politicians and diplomats. Yet their actions were astonishingly foolish. After the failed invasion, Kennedy asked, "How could I have been so stupid?" (Dallek, 2003). Janis had a simple answer: Kennedy and his cabinet fell prey to groupthink. They became convinced that their plan was a good one because they all agreed to it and they failed to ask themselves the tough questions that could have averted the disaster.

The Bay of Pigs invasion wasn't the last time that groupthink led intelligent people to make catastrophic decisions. In 1986, the space shuttle *Challenger* exploded, killing the seven astronauts aboard a mere 73 seconds after takeoff. Project managers of the *Chal-*

groupthink
emphasis on group unanimity at the expense of critical thinking and sound decision making

lenger agreed to launch it after a series of bitterly cold days in January, despite warnings from NASA engineers that the shuttle might explode because rubber rings on the rocket booster could fail in freezing temperatures.

Table 13.1 depicts some of the characteristics or "symptoms" identified by Janis (1972) that render groups vulnerable to groupthink. Not all psychologists accept Janis's description of groupthink. For one thing, groupthink doesn't always lead to bad decisions, just overconfident ones (Tyson, 1987). Moreover, seeking group consensus isn't always a bad idea, although doing so before all of the evidence is available is (Longley & Pruitt, 1980).

NASA groupthink may have contributed to the destruction of the space shuttle *Columbia* (crew shown here) in February 2003, which like the 1986 *Challenger* disaster, killed its crew of seven astronauts. As in 1986, project managers ignored warnings about potential dangers—in this case, the hazards posed by debris hitting the tiles on the shuttle's wings during liftoff—resulting in the disintegration of the shuttle upon reentry into the atmosphere (Ferraris & Carveth, 2003).

Table 13.1 Symptoms of Groupthink.

Symptom	Example
An illusion of the group's invulnerability	"We can't possibly fail!"
An illusion of the group's unanimity	"Obviously, we all agree."
An unquestioned belief in the group's moral correctness	"We know we're on the right side."
Conformity pressure—pressure on group members to go along with everyone else	"Don't rock the boat!"
Stereotyping of the out-group—a caricaturing of the enemy	"They're all morons."
Self-censorship—the tendency of group members to keep their mouths shut even when they have doubts (see cartoon on previous page)	"I suspect the group leader's idea is stupid, but I'd better not say anything."
Mindguards—self-appointed individuals whose job it is to stifle disagreement	"Oh, you think you know better than the rest of us?"

Treatments for Groupthink. As a psychological condition, groupthink is often treatable. Janis (1972) noted that the best way to avoid groupthink is to encourage active dissent within an organization. He recommended that all groups appoint a "devil's advocate"—a person whose role is to voice doubts about the wisdom of the group's decisions. In addition, he suggested having independent experts on hand to evaluate whether the group's decisions make sense. Finally, it can be useful to hold a follow-up meeting to evaluate whether the decision reached in the first meeting still seems reasonable.

Group Polarization: Going to Extremes. Related to groupthink is **group polarization,** which occurs when group discussion strengthens the dominant position held by individual group members (Isenberg, 1986; Myers & Lamm, 1976). In one study, a group of students who were slightly unprejudiced became even less prejudiced after discussing racial issues, whereas a group that was slightly prejudiced became *more* prejudiced after discussing racial issues (Myers & Bishop, 1970). Contrary to what our intuitions tell us, talking things over with others isn't always a good idea. Group polarization can be helpful if it leads to efficient decisions when there's no time to waste. Yet in other cases, it can be destructive, as when juries rush to unanimous decisions before they've considered all the evidence (Myers & Kaplan, 1976).

Cult membership involves following the cult's practices without question. Rev. Sun Yung Moon of the Unification Church has united thousands of total strangers in mass wedding ceremonies. The couples are determined by pairing photos of prospective brides and grooms. They meet for the first time during the week leading up to the wedding day, often on the day of the ceremony itself.

group polarization
tendency of group discussion to strengthen the dominant positions held by individual group members

cults
groups of individuals who exhibit intense and unquestioning devotion to a single cause

Cults and Brainwashing. In extreme forms, groupthink can lead to **cults:** groups of individuals who exhibit intense and unquestioning devotion to a single cause. In many cases, they're devoted to one charismatic individual.

Cults can occasionally have disastrous consequences. Consider Heaven's Gate, a southern California–based group founded by Marshall Applewhite, a former psychiatric patient, in 1975. Heaven's Gate members believed that Applewhite was a reincarnated version of Jesus Christ. Applewhite, they were convinced, would take them to a starship in their afterlives. In 1997, a major comet approached Earth, and several false reports circulated in the media that a spaceship was tailing it. The Heaven's Gate members apparently believed this was their calling. Virtually all of the cult members—thirty-nine of them—committed suicide by drinking a poisoned cocktail.

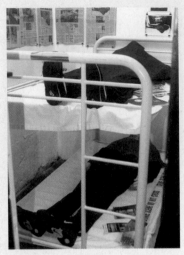

Cult members, as in the case of the Heaven's Gate cult headed by Marshall Applewhite, have been known to commit suicide en masse at the behest of their leader.

fict**oid**

Myth: Poverty and poor education are key causes of terrorism, including suicide bombings.

Reality: Most suicide bombers in the Middle East, including the September 11 hijackers and many Al Qaida members, are relatively well off and well educated (Sageman, 2004).

The 2004 remake of the film *The Manchurian Candidate* portrayed a previously normal individual who was "programmed" to engage in violence by brainwashing. Many Hollywood films present brainwashing in a sensationalized and largely inaccurate fashion.

inoculation effect
approach to convincing people to change their minds about something by first introducing reasons why the perspective might be correct and then debunking it

obedience
adherence to instructions from those of higher authority

Because cults are secretive and difficult to study, psychologists know relatively little about them. But evidence suggests that cults promote groupthink in four major ways (Lalich, 2004): having a persuasive leader who fosters loyalty; disconnecting group members from the outside world; discouraging questioning of the group's or leader's assumptions; and establishing training practices that gradually indoctrinate members (Galanter, 1980).

Cults: Common Misconceptions. Misconceptions about cults abound. One is that cult members are usually emotionally disturbed. Studies show that most cult members are psychologically normal (Aronoff, Lynn, & Malinowski, 2000; Lalich, 2004), although many cult *leaders* probably suffer from serious mental illness. This erroneous belief probably stems from the fundamental attribution error: In trying to explain why people join cults, we overestimate the role of personality traits and underestimate the role of social influences.

Many people hold the same beliefs about suicide bombers, like the September 11 terrorists or those who detonated bus and subway bombs in London on July 7, 2005. Preliminary research on suicide bombers suggests that most are not mentally disordered (Gordon, 2002; Sageman, 2004), although some appear to possess a distinctive profile of traits, such as rigidity of thinking, reluctance to question authority, and a tendency to attribute blame to others (Lester, Yang, & Lindsay, 2004).

A second misconception is that all cult members are *brainwashed,* or transformed by group leaders into unthinking zombies. Journalists introduced the concept of brainwashing during the Korean War in the early 1950s (Hunter, 1951) to describe the influence tactics used by Chinese Communists to persuade American soldiers that communism was superior to democracy. Although some psychologists have argued that many cults use brainwashing techniques (Singer, 1979), there's considerable scientific controversy about the existence of brainwashing. For one thing, there's not much evidence that brainwashing permanently alters victims' beliefs. Most American soldiers supposedly brainwashed by Communists didn't change their minds; they merely spoke and acted as though they'd been converted to communism to avoid punishment (Melton, 1999). Moreover, there's not much evidence that brainwashing is a unique means of changing people's behavior. Instead, the persuasive techniques of brainwashing probably aren't all that different from those used by effective political leaders and salespeople (Zimbardo, 1997). We'll have more to say about these techniques later in the chapter.

Resisting Cult Influence: Inoculation. How can we best resist the indoctrination that leads to cults? Here, the social psychological research is clear, although counterintuitive: first expose people to information consistent with cult beliefs, and then debunk it. In his work on the **inoculation effect,** William McGuire (1964) demonstrated that the best way of immunizing people against an undesirable belief is to gently introduce them to reasons why this belief seems to be correct, and then refute those reasons. This approach works much like a vaccine, which inoculates people against a virus by presenting them with a small dose of it, thereby activating the body's defenses (McGuire, 1964; McGuire & Papageorgis, 1961).

OBEDIENCE: THE PSYCHOLOGY OF FOLLOWING ORDERS

In the case of conformity, we go along to get along. The transmission is "horizontal"— the group influence originates from our peers. In the case of **obedience,** we take our marching orders from people who are above us in the hierarchy of authority, such as a teacher, parent, or boss. Here the transmission is "vertical"—the group influence springs not from our peers, but from our leaders (Loevinger, 1987). Many groups, such as cults, acquire their influence from a potent combination of both conformity and obedience.

Obedience: A Double-Edged Sword. Obedience is a necessary, even essential, ingredient in our daily lives. Without it, society couldn't run smoothly. You're reading this book in part because your professor told you to, and you'll obey the traffic lights and stop signs on your next trip to school or work (we hope!) because you know you're expected to. Yet like conformity, obedience can produce troubling consequences when people stop asking questions about *why* they're behaving as others want them to. As the British writer C. P. Snow wrote, "When you look at the dark and gloomy history of man, you will find that more hideous crimes have been committed in the name of obedience than have ever been committed in the name of rebellion." Let's look at one infamous example.

During the Vietnam War, United States Lieutenant William Calley commanded a platoon of a division named Charlie Company. In March 1968, Calley's platoon had encountered heavy arms fire for several weeks, and many soldiers had been killed or badly wounded. Understandably, the members of Charlie Company were on edge during the morning of March 16, as they entered the village of My Lai (pronounced "Me Lie"), which was suspected of being a hideout for North Vietnamese soldiers. Although the platoon located no enemy soldiers in My Lai, they found hundreds of unarmed civilians. In response to Calley's orders, the soldiers in Charlie Company began firing randomly at the villagers, none of whom had initiated combat. They bludgeoned several old men to death with the butts of their rifles and shot praying children and women in the head. Calley corralled a group of civilians, forced them to walk into a ditch, and mowed them down in a barrage of machine gun fire. When all was said and done, the American platoon had brutally slaughtered about 500 innocent Vietnamese ranging in age from 1 to 82 years.

Two sides of the coin of obedience: Lt. William Calley (left) was charged with murder by the Army for ordering his platoon to massacre unarmed civilians in the My Lai massacre in 1968. Calley was the only one in the platoon to be charged with a crime. Hugh Thompson (right), along with his fellow crew members, landed their helicopter between their fellow Army platoon and the civilians in the My Lai massacre in an effort to save the lives of the unarmed villagers. Thompson and crew were awarded the Soldier's Medal for bravery.

What did Lieutenant Calley have to say about all of this? Read carefully: "I was ordered to go in there and destroy the enemy. That was my job that day. That was the mission I was given. I did not sit down and think in terms of men, women, and children. They were all classified the same" (Calley, 1971). That is, Calley insisted that he was merely taking orders from his superiors and bore no direct responsibility for the massacre. In turn, the soldiers in Calley's platoon claimed they were merely taking orders from Calley. Calley was convicted in 1971 of murder and sentenced to life in military prison, but President Richard Nixon commuted his sentence.

Lost in much of the horror of My Lai was the heroism displayed by several American soldiers. In the midst of the massacre, Officer Hugh Thompson Jr. landed his U.S. Army helicopter between Calley's troops and the innocent villagers. Risking their lives, Thompson and his two crewmen ordered the troops to stop shooting. They evacuated the village, saving scores of innocent lives.

The My Lai massacre may seem inexplicable to us. Yet it's only one instance of the perils of unthinking obedience. How can we make sense of this behavior?

Stanley Milgram: Sources of Destructive Obedience.

Stanley Milgram was a graduate student of Solomon Asch's who wanted to understand the principles underlying irrational group behavior. The child of Jewish parents who grew up during World War II, Milgram became preoccupied with the profoundly troubling question of how the Holocaust could have occurred. The prevailing wisdom in the late 1940s and 1950s was that the Holocaust was primarily the product of twisted minds that had perpetuated dastardly deeds. Yet Milgram suspected that the truth was far subtler. He agreed that the actions of the Germans during the Holocaust were grossly unethical, of course, but he came to believe that the underlying psychological processes that give rise to destructive obedience are surprisingly commonplace. Milgram was fond of the writings of German author Hannah Arendt, who regarded the Holocaust as an example of "the banality of evil." According to Arendt, most of the world's wickedness originates not from a handful of cold-blooded villains, but from large numbers of perfectly normal citizens who follow orders blindly.

The Milgram Paradigm. In the early 1960s, Milgram began to tinker with a laboratory paradigm (a model experiment) that could provide a window into the causes of obedience

Four panels from Milgram's obedience experiment:

The shock generator.

The "learner," Mr. Wallace, being strapped to the shock plate by Mr. Williams and an assistant.

Mr. Williams delivering instructions to the "teacher," the actual subject.

The "teacher" breaking off the experiment after refusing to comply with Mr. Williams' orders.

(Blass, 2004). Although influenced by Asch's work, Milgram was more interested in obedience than in conformity, because he believed that unquestioning acceptance of authority figures is the crucial ingredient in explaining unjustified violence against innocent individuals. Milgram also believed that Asch's paradigm wasn't sufficiently engrossing to simulate the real-life power of dangerous social influence. After a few years of pilot testing, Milgram finally hit on the paradigm he wanted, not knowing that it would become one of the most influential in the history of psychology (Cialdini & Goldstein, 2004; Slater, 2004).

The Setup: You spot an advertisement in a local New Haven, Connecticut, newspaper, asking for volunteers for a study of memory. The ad notes that participants will be paid $4.50, which in the 1960s was a hefty chunk of change. You arrive at the laboratory at Yale University, where a tall and imposing man in a white lab coat, Mr. Williams, greets you. You also meet another friendly, middle-aged subject, Mr. Wallace, who unbeknownst to you is actually a confederate. The cover story is that you and Mr. Wallace will be participating in a study of the effects of "punishment on learning," with one of you being the teacher and the other the learner. You draw lots to see who'll play which role, and get the piece of paper that says "teacher" (the lots are rigged). From here on in, Mr. Williams refers to you as the "teacher" and to Mr. Wallace as the "learner."

As the teacher, Mr. Williams explains, you'll present Mr. Wallace with what psychologists call a *paired-associate task*. In this task, you'll read a long list of word pairs, like strong–arm and black–curtain. Then you'll present the learner with the first word in each pair (such as "strong") and ask him to select the second word ("arm") from a list of four alternative words. Now here's the surprise: To evaluate the effects of punishment on learning, you'll be delivering a series of painful electric shocks to the learner. With each wrong answer, you'll move up one step on a shock generator. The shocks range from 15 volts up to 450 volts and are accompanied by labels ranging from "Slight Shock" and "Moderate Shock," to "Danger: Severe Shock" and finally, and most ominously, "XXX."

The Study: You watch as Mr. Williams brings the learner into a room and straps his arm to a shock plate. The learner, Mr. Williams explains, will push a button corresponding to his answer to the first word in each pair. His answer will light up in an adjoining room where you sit. For a correct answer, you do nothing. But for an incorrect answer, you'll give the learner an electric shock, with the intensity increasing with each mistake. At this point, the learner mentions to Mr. Williams that he has "a slight heart condition" and asks anxiously how powerful the shocks will be. Mr. Williams responds curtly that although the shocks will be painful, they "will cause no permanent tissue damage."

You're led into the adjoining room and seated in front of the shock generator. Following Milgram's plan, the learner makes a few correct responses, but soon begins to make errors. If, at any time, you turn to Mr. Williams to ask if you should continue, he responds with a set of prearranged sentences that urge you to go on ("Please go on," "The experiment requires that you continue," "You have no other choice; you *must* go on"). Milgram standardized the verbal statements of the learner, which also unbeknownst to you, have been prerecorded on audiotape (Milgram, 1974). At 75 volts, the learner grunts "Ugh!" and by 330 volts, he frantically yells "Let me out of here!" repeatedly and complains of chest pain. From 345 volts onward, there's nothing—only silence. The learner stops responding to your items, and Mr. Williams instructs you to treat these nonresponses as incorrect answers and to keep administering increasingly intense shocks.

The Results: When Milgram first designed this study, he asked forty psychiatrists at Yale University to forecast the outcome. Their predictions? According to them, most subjects would break off at 150 volts and only .1 percent (that's 1 in 1,000), representing a "pathological fringe" (Milgram, 1974), would go all the way to 450 volts. Before reading on, you may want to ask yourself what you would have done had you been a subject in Milgram's study. Would you have delivered any shocks? If so, how far would you have gone? Would you have gone all the way to 450 volts?

In fact, in the original Milgram study, all subjects administered at least some shocks. Most went up to at least 150 volts, and a remarkable 62 percent of subjects displayed complete compliance, going all the way up 450 volts. This means that the Yale psychiatrists were off by a factor of several hundred.

These results were, well, shocking. Milgram himself was startled by them (Blass, 2004). Before Milgram's study, most psychologists assumed that the overwhelming majority of normal subjects would disobey what were obviously cruel and outrageous orders. But like the Yale psychiatrists, they committed the fundamental attribution error: they underestimated the impact of the situation on subjects' behaviors.

There were other surprises. Many subjects showed uncontrollable tics and fits of nervous laughter. Yet few appeared to be sadistic. Even those who complied to the bitter end seemed reluctant to deliver shocks, asking or even begging the experimenter to allow them to stop. Yet most subjects still followed Mr. Williams's orders despite these pleas, often assuming no responsibility for their actions. One subject's responses were illustrative; after the study was over he claimed, "I stopped, but he [the experimenter] made me go on" (Milgram, 1974).

The Milgram Paradigm: Themes and Variations. Like his mentor Solomon Asch, Milgram conducted a variety of parametric studies to pinpoint the situational factors that increased or decreased obedience and to rule out alternative explanations for his findings. These parametric studies provide an elegant demonstration of social psychological research at its best. In addition, they afford a powerful test of the replicability of Milgram's paradigm and its generalizability across different situations.

We've summarized the major variations Milgram conducted on his original paradigm in **Table 13.2.** As we can see, the level of subjects' obedience varied substantially depending on the circumstances, including the amount of feedback and proximity from the learner to the teacher and the physical proximity and prestige of the experimenter. Although this table displays numerous variations, two key themes emerge. First, the

Ruling Out Rival Hypotheses

Replicability

Table 13.2 The Milgram Paradigm: Themes and Variations.

Variation/Condition	Description	Percentage Who Complied to 450 Volts
Remote feedback condition (initial study)	No verbal feedback from the learner; teacher hears only the learner pounding the wall in protest after being shocked	65%
Voice feedback condition	Teacher hears the learner's screams of pain and complaints	62%
Proximity condition	Learner is in the same room as the teacher, so that teacher not only hears but observes the learner's agony	40%
Touch proximity condition	Teacher is required to hold the learner's hand on a shock plate; whenever the learner's hand flies off the shock plate, the teacher must jam it back down to ensure electrical contact	30%
Telephone condition	Experimenter gives instructions by telephone from a separate room (*Note:* some subjects "cheated" by giving less intense shocks than what the experimenter directed)	30%
Second experimenter condition	A second experimenter is present and begins disagreeing with the first experimenter about whether to carry on with the session	0%
Less prestigious setting for study	Study is conducted (voice feedback condition is replicated) in a rundown office building in nearby Bridgeport, Connecticut, removing all affiliation with Yale University	48%
Ask teacher to direct a different subject to administer shock	Teacher is asked to give orders to another "subject" (actually a confederate), who then delivers the shocks. In this condition, teachers can reassure themselves, "I'm not actually giving any shocks; I'm just telling him to do it"	93%

In the "touch proximity" condition (see Table 13.2), subjects were forced to hold the "learner's" hand on a shock plate. Here the level of obedience plummeted. This condition illustrates the point that decreasing the psychological distance between teacher and learner leads to decreased obedience.

Rosa Parks (1913–2005) became a role model for "civil disobedience" during the 1950s and 1960s when she refused to give up her seat on a bus to a White man as was required by law. Morality, for her, overrode law.

Replicability

greater the "psychological distance" between teacher (the actual participant) and experimenter, the *less* the obedience. As the experimenter became more psychologically distant, as when he gave instructions by telephone, compliance plummeted. Second, the greater the psychological distance between teacher and learner, the *more* the obedience. Most striking was the level of compliance when Milgram increased the psychological distance between teacher and learner by having the teacher direct someone else to administer the shocks. Here the level of complete compliance shot up to 93 percent. Like Lieutenant Calley, whose defense during the My Lai massacre was that he was "just taking orders," subjects in this condition probably felt relieved of personal responsibility. Many Nazis, like Adolph Eichmann, offered similar excuses for their orders to kill thousands of Jews: They were just following instructions from their superiors (Aronson, 1998). When people do immoral things, they often look to pass the responsibility on to somebody else.

The Milgram Paradigm: Individual, Gender, and Cultural Differences. When evaluating Milgram's findings, it's only natural to focus on the sizable proportion of subjects who followed orders. Yet many of his subjects didn't go along with the experimenter's commands despite intense pressure to do so. Recall that at My Lai, some American soldiers disobeyed Calley's orders by ordering his soldiers to stop firing. Moreover, during the Holocaust thousands of European families risked their lives to offer safe haven to Jewish civilians in clear defiance of Nazi laws (Wilson, 1993). So despite powerful situational pressures, some people disobey authority figures who give unethical orders. Who are they?

Perhaps surprisingly, Milgram (1974) found that obedient and disobedient subjects were similar on most major personality variables. For example, he found no evidence that obedient subjects were more sadistic than disobedient subjects, suggesting that subjects didn't follow orders because they enjoyed doing so (Aronson, 1998).

Nevertheless, researchers have identified a few consistent predictors of obedience in Milgram's paradigm. Lawrence Kohlberg found that the level of moral development using his interview-based scheme (see Chapter 10) was negatively correlated with compliance; more morally advanced subjects were more willing to defy the experimenter (Kohlberg, 1965; Milgram, 1974). This finding suggests that especially moral people may sometimes be more willing to violate rules than less moral people, especially if they view them as unreasonable. Another researcher found that people with high levels of a personality trait called *authoritarianism* are more likely to comply with the experimenters' demands (Alms, 1972). People with high levels of authoritarianism see the world as a big hierarchy of power. For them, authority figures are to be respected, not questioned (Adorno, Frenkel-Brunswick, Levenson, & Sanford, 1950; Dillehay, 1978). It makes sense that authoritarian individuals would exhibit high levels of obedience in Milgram's paradigm, as they presumably viewed Mr. Williams as an authority figure whose orders they shouldn't question.

Milgram found no consistent sex differences in obedience; this finding has held up in later studies using his paradigm (Blass, 1999). Milgram's findings have also been replicated in different countries. The overall rates of obedience among Americans don't differ significantly from those of non-Americans (Blass, 2004), including people in Italy (Ancona & Pareyson, 1968), South Africa (Edwards, Franks, Friedgood, Lobban, & Mackay, 1969), Spain (Miranda, Caballero, Gomez, & Zamorano, 1981), Germany (Mantell, 1971), Australia (Kilham & Mann, 1974), and Jordan (Shanab & Yahya, 1977).

Milgram's Studies: Lessons. Psychologists have learned a great deal from Milgram's work. They've learned that the power of authority figures is greater than almost anyone had imagined. They've learned that obedience doesn't typically result from sadism; most of Milgram's subjects wanted to stop but kept going out of deference to authority. Milgram's research also reminds us of the potency of the fundamental attribution error: Most people, even psychiatrists, underestimate situational influences on behavior (Bierbrauer, 1973).

Psychologists continue to debate whether Milgram's study offers an adequate model of what happened during the Holocaust and at My Lai. Milgram's critics correctly note that, in contrast to Milgram's subjects, some concentration camp guards actively enjoyed torturing innocent people (Cialdini & Goldstein, 2004). These critics further argue that destructive obedience on a grand scale probably requires not only an authority figure bearing an official stamp of approval, but also a core group of genuinely wicked people. They may well be right. These controversies aside, there's no doubt that Stanley Milgram has forever changed how we think about ourselves and others. He's made us more keenly aware of the fact that good people can do bad things and that rational people can behave irrationally (Aronson, 1998). By warning us of these perils, Milgram may have steered us on the path toward guarding against them.

ASSESS YOUR KNOWLEDGE: FACT OR FICTION?

(1) Asch's studies demonstrated that several allies are required to counteract the effects of conformity on an individual. (True/False)

(2) Deindividuation can make people more likely to engage in prosocial, as well as antisocial, behavior. (True/False)

(3) Groups tend to make less extreme decisions than do individuals. (True/False)

(4) Obedience is by itself maladaptive and unhealthy. (True/False)

Answers: (1) F (p. 540); (2) T (p. 542); (3) F (p. 544); (4) F (p. 546)

Helping and Harming Others: Prosocial Behavior and Aggression

For centuries, philosophers have debated the question of whether human nature is good or bad. Yet the either-or fallacy (Chapter 1) reminds us that scientific truth rarely falls neatly into one of two extremes. Indeed, mounting evidence suggests that human nature is an amalgam of both socially constructive and destructive tendencies.

Primate researcher Frans de Waal (1982, 1996) argues that our two closest animal relatives, the bonobo (pygmy chimpanzee; see Chapter 11) and the chimpanzee, display the seeds of both prosocial and anti-social behavior. Because we share more than 98 percent of our DNA with both species, they offer a slightly fuzzy evolutionary window onto our own nature. Although these species overlap in their social behaviors, the bonobo is more of a model for **prosocial behavior**—that is, behavior intended to help others—and the chimpanzee is more of a model for antisocial behavior, including aggressive acts. Bonobos are veritable experts at reconciling after arguments, often making peace by making love—literally. They also engage in helping behaviors that we ordinarily associate with humans. De Waal described a remarkable event at the San Diego Zoo, where bonobo caretakers

This remarkable photo by primate researcher Frans de Waal shows a male chimpanzee (left) extending a hand of appeasement to another chimpanzee after a fight. Many psychologists have argued that our tendency toward prosocial behavior has deep roots in our primate heritage.

were filling up the water moat. The juveniles of the [bonobo] group were playing in the empty moat, and the caretakers had not noticed. When they went to the kitchen to turn on the water, all of a sudden in front of the window they saw Kakowet, the old male of the group, and he was waving and screaming at them to draw their attention. [The care-takers] looked at the moat and saw the juveniles and then got them out of there, before the moat filled up. (p. 4)

Chimpanzees engage in prosocial behavior too, like making up after fights. Yet they're far more prone to aggression than are bonobos. In the 1970s, Jane Goodall (1990) stunned the scientific world by reporting that chimpanzees occasionally wage all-out wars against other chimpanzee groups, replete with brutal murders, infanticide, and cannibalism.

To which species are we more similar, the peace-loving bonobo or the belligerent chimpanzee? In reality, we're a bit of both. De Waal (2006) is fond of calling the human species "the bipolar ape," because our social behavior is a blend of that of our closest ape relatives.

Figure 13.6 The Murder of Kitty Genovese. Place in Kew Gardens, New York, where Kitty Genovese was murdered on March 13, 1964, at 3:20 A.M. She drove into the parking lot at the Kew Gardens train station and parked her car at spot **1**. Noticing a man in the lot, she became nervous and headed toward a police telephone box. The man caught her and attacked her with a knife at spot **2**. She managed to get away, but he attacked her again at spot **3** and again at spot **4**.

Deletha Word was another tragic victim of bystander nonintervention. After her death, loved ones gathered to mourn on the bridge where she was attacked.

pluralistic ignorance
error of assuming that no one in a group perceives things as we do

In this next section, we'll examine the psychological roots of prosocial and antisocial actions, with a particular emphasis on situational factors that contribute to both behaviors. We'll begin by examining why we fail to help in some situations, but why we do help in others. We'll then explore why we occasionally act aggressively toward fellow members of our species. As we've seen, Milgram's obedience research sheds light on the social influences that can lead us to harm others. But we'll soon discover that obedience to authority is only part of the story.

SAFETY IN NUMBERS OR DANGER IN NUMBERS? BYSTANDER NONINTERVENTION

You've probably heard the saying, "There's safety in numbers." Popular wisdom teaches us that when we find ourselves in danger, it's best to be in the company of others. Is that true? Let's look at two real-life examples.

Two Tragic Stories of Bystander Nonintervention.

- On March 13, 1964, at 3 A.M., 28-year-old Catherine (Kitty) Genovese was returning to her apartment in New York City, having just gotten off work. Suddenly, a man appeared and began stabbing her. He came and left no fewer than three times over a 35-minute time span. Kitty repeatedly screamed and pleaded for help as the lights from nearby apartments flipped on. Although the precise facts remain in dispute (Manning, Levine, & Collins, 2007), most of the evidence suggests that at least half a dozen—and perhaps many more—of her 30 or so neighbors heard the events but failed to come to her aid. Most didn't even bother to call the police. By the end of the gruesome attack, Kitty Genovese was dead (see **Figure 13.6**).

- On the morning of August 19, 1995, 33-year-old Deletha Word was driving across a bridge in Detroit, Michigan, when she accidentally hit the fender of a car driven by Martell Welsh. Welsh and the two boys with him jumped out of their car, stripped Deletha down to her underwear and beat her repeatedly with a tire jack. At one point, Welsh even held Deletha up in the air and asked bystanders whether anyone "wanted a piece" of her. About forty people drove by in their cars, but none intervened or even called the police. In a desperate attempt to escape her attackers, Deletha jumped off the bridge into the river below. She drowned.

Causes of Bystander Nonintervention: Why We Don't Help. Like most anecdotes, these real-world stories are useful for illustrating concepts, but they don't allow for scientific generalizations. For years, many psychologists assumed that the nonresponsiveness of bystanders was due simply to a lack of caring. But psychologists John Darley and Bibb Latané suspected that the *bystander effect* was less a consequence of apathy than of "psychological paralysis." According to Darley and Latané (1968), bystanders in emergencies typically want to intervene, but often find themselves frozen, seemingly helpless to help. Darley and Latané also suspected that popular psychology was wrong—that there's actually danger rather than safety in numbers. Bucking conventional wisdom, they hypothesized that the presence of others makes people *less*, not more, likely to help in emergencies. Why?

Pluralistic Ignorance: It Must Just Be Me. Darley and Latané maintained that two major factors explain bystander nonintervention. The first is **pluralistic ignorance**: the error of assuming that no one in the group perceives things as we do. To intervene in an emergency, we first need to recognize that the situation is in fact an emergency. Imagine that on your way to class tomorrow you see a student in dirty clothing slumped across a bench. As you stroll by, thoughts whiz through your mind: Is he asleep? Is he drunk? Could he be seriously ill, even dead? Could my psychology professor be conducting a study to examine my responses to emergencies? Here's where pluralistic ignorance comes into play. We look around, notice that nobody else is responding, and assume—perhaps mistakenly—that the situation isn't an emergency. We assume we're the only one who thinks the situation might be an emergency. Reassured that the coast is clear and that there's nothing to worry about, we continue on our way to class.

So pluralistic ignorance is relevant when we're trying to figure out whether an ambiguous situation is really an emergency. But pluralistic ignorance doesn't fully explain the behavior of bystanders in the Kitty Genovese or Deletha Word tragedies, because those situations were clearly emergencies. Even once we've recognized that the situation is an emergency, the presence of others still tends to inhibit helping.

Diffusion of Responsibility: Passing the Buck. A second step is required for us to intervene in an emergency. We need to feel a burden of responsibility for the consequences of *not* intervening. Here's the rub: The more people present at an emergency, *the less each person feels responsible for the negative consequences of not helping*. Darley and Latané called this phenomenon **diffusion of responsibility:** The presence of others makes each person feel less responsible for the outcome. If you don't assist someone who's having a heart attack and that person later dies, you can always say to yourself, "Well, that's a terrible tragedy, but it wasn't really *my* fault. After all, plenty of other people could have helped too."

So we can experience pluralistic ignorance, which prevents us from interpreting a situation as an emergency, *and* we can experience diffusion of responsibility, which discourages us from offering assistance in an emergency. From this perspective, it's actually surprising that any of us helps in emergencies, because the obstacles to intervening are considerable.

Studies of Bystander Nonintervention. To get at the psychological roots of the bystander effect in tragedies like the Kitty Genovese story, Darley, Latané, and their colleagues tested the effect of bystanders on subjects' willingness to (1) report that smoke was filling a room (Darley & Latané, 1968b); (2) react to what sounded like a woman falling off a ladder and injuring herself (Latané & Rodin, 1969); and (3) respond to what sounded like another student experiencing an epileptic seizure (Darley & Latané, 1968a). In all of these studies, participants were significantly more likely to seek or offer help when they were alone than in a group (see **Figure 13.7**).

Researchers have replicated these kinds of findings many times using slightly different designs. In an analysis of almost 50 studies of bystander intervention involving almost 6,000 participants, Latané and Nida (1981) found that participants were more likely to help when alone than in groups about 90 percent of the time. That's an impressive degree of replicability. Even *thinking* about being in a large group makes us less likely to help in an emergency (Garcia, Weaver, Moskowitz, & Darley, 2002).

APPLY YOUR THINKING
Imagine you found yourself attacked by a mugger in the midst of a crowd of onlookers. Based on Darley and Latané's research on pluralistic ignorance and diffusion of responsibility, how could you maximize the chances you'd receive help?

SOCIAL LOAFING: WITH A LITTLE TOO MUCH HELP FROM MY FRIENDS

Have you ever been a member of a group that got virtually nothing accomplished? (All four authors of your textbook regularly attend meetings of university faculty, so we're particular experts on this topic.) If so, you may have been a victim of **social loafing,** the phenomenon in which people slack off in groups (Latané, Williams, & Harkins, 1979; North, Linley, & Hargreaves, 2000). As a consequence of social loafing, the whole is less than the sum of its parts.

Some psychologists believe that social loafing is a variant of bystander nonintervention. That's because social loafing appears to be due in part to diffusion of responsibility: People working in groups typically feel less personally responsible for the outcome of a project than they do when working alone. As a result, they don't invest as much effort.

Psychologists have demonstrated social loafing in numerous experiments. In one, a researcher placed blindfolds and headphones on six participants and asked them to clap or yell as loudly as possible. When participants thought they were making noises as part of a group, they were less loud than when they thought they were making noises alone

Even when a situation appears to be an emergency, we still may not offer assistance. The social psychological principle of diffusion of responsibility helps to explain why.

Replicability

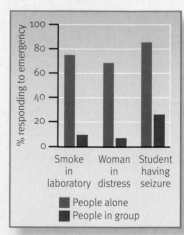

Figure 13.7 Bystander Intervention. Across three classic experiments of bystander intervention, the percentage of people helping when in groups was markedly lower than the percentage of people helping when alone.

diffusion of responsibility
reduction in feelings of personal responsibility in the presence of others

social loafing
phenomenon whereby individuals become less productive in groups

(Harkins, 1981). Cheerleaders also cheer less loudly when they believe they're part of a group than when they believe they're alone (Hardy & Latané, 1986). Investigators have also identified social loafing effects in studies of rope-pulling (the "tug-of-war" game), navigating mazes, identifying radar signals, and evaluating job candidates (Karau & Williams, 1995).

Two researchers even found suggestive evidence for social loafing in Beatles songs cowritten by John Lennon and Paul McCartney as opposed to those written by either singer alone (Jackson & Padgett, 1982). They found that an independent panel of listeners rated the cowritten songs to be lower in quality than the solely authored songs (for example, Paul McCartney himself penned the Beatles' most recorded song, "Yesterday"). Of course, because these data are merely correlational, they don't prove a direct causal connection between social loafing and lower song quality, although they point in this direction. What might be some other possible reasons for this correlation?

One of the best antidotes to social loafing is to ensure that each person in the group is identifiable, for example, by guaranteeing that managers and bosses can evaluate each individual's performance. By doing so, we can help "diffuse" the diffusion of responsibility that often arises in groups.

Correlation vs. Causation

Studies of social loafing demonstrate that in large groups, individuals often work (or in this case, cheer or pull) less hard than they do when alone.

Collaborative efforts are often less fruitful than individual efforts, as songs cowritten by John Lennon and Paul McCartney may demonstrate.

Psycho*Mythology*
Is Brainstorming in Groups a Good Way to Generate Ideas?

Imagine that you've been hired by an advertising firm to cook up a new marketing campaign for Mrs. Yummy's Chicken Noodle Soup. The soup hasn't been selling well of late and your job is to come up with an advertising jingle that will instill in every American an uncontrollable urge to reach for the nearest cup of chicken noodle soup.

Although you initially plan to come up with possible slogans on your own, your boss walks into your cubicle and informs you that you'll be participating in a "group brainstorming" meeting later that afternoon in the executive suite. There, you and twelve other firm members will let your imaginations run wild, saying whatever comes to mind in the hopes of hitting on a winning chicken noodle soup advertising formula. Indeed, companies across the world regularly use group brainstorming as a means of generating novel ideas. They assume that several heads that generate a flurry of ideas are better than one. In a book titled *Applied Imagination*, which influenced many companies to adopt brainstorming, Osborn (1957) argued that "the average person can think up twice as many ideas when working with a group than when working alone" (p. 229).

Although the idea behind group brainstorming is intuitively appealing, it turns out to be wrong. Numerous studies demonstrate that group brainstorming is actually less effective than individual brainstorming (Brown & Paulus, 2002; Diehl & Stroebe, 1987). When brainstorming, groups tend to come up with fewer ideas, and often fewer good ones, than individuals (Paulus, 2004). Group brainstorming generally also results in ideas that are less creative than those generated by individual brainstorming. Making matters worse, groups often overestimate how successful they are at producing new ideas, which may help to explain brainstorming's popularity (Paulus, Larey, & Ortega, 1995).

There are at least two reasons why group brainstorming is less effective than individual brainstorming. One is that group members may be anxious about being evaluated by others, leading them to hold back potentially good ideas. The second is social loafing. When brainstorming in groups, people frequently engage in what's called "free riding": they sit back and let others do the hard work (Diehl & Stroebe, 1987). Whatever the reason, research suggests that when it comes to brainstorming, one brain may be better than two—or many more—at least when the brains can communicate with each other.

PROSOCIAL BEHAVIOR AND ALTRUISM

Even though there's usually danger rather than safety in numbers when it comes to others helping us, many of us do help in emergencies even when others are around (Fischer, Greitneyer, Pollozck, & Frey, 2006). In the Deletha Word tragedy, two men jumped into the water in an unsuccessful attempt to save her from drowning. Indeed, there's good evidence that many of us engage in **altruism,** that is, helping others for unselfish reasons (Batson, 1987; Davidio, Piliavin, Schroeder, & Penner, 2006; Penner, Davidio, Piliavin, & Schroeder, 2005).

Altruism: Helping Selflessly. Over the years, some scientists have argued that we help others entirely for egoistic (self-centered) reasons, like relieving our own distress or experiencing the joy of others we've helped (Hoffman, 1981). From this perspective, we help others only to make ourselves feel better. Yet in a series of experiments, Daniel Batson and his colleagues have shown that we sometimes engage in genuine altruism. That is, in some cases we help others in discomfort primarily because we feel empathic toward them (Batson et al., 1991; Batson & Shaw, 1991; Fischer et al., 2006). In some studies, they exposed participants to a female victim (actually a confederate) who was receiving painful electric shocks and gave them the option of either (a) taking her place and receiving the shocks themselves or (b) turning away and not watching her receive shocks. When participants were made to feel empathic toward the victim (for example, by being informed that their values and interests were similar to hers), they generally offered to take her place and receive shocks rather than turn away (Batson et al., 1981). So in some cases we seem to help not only to relieve our distress but to relieve the distress of others.

Along with empathy, a number of psychological variables increase the odds of helping. Let's look at some of the most crucial ones.

Helping: Situational Influences. People are more likely to help in some situations than in others. They're more likely to help others when they can't easily escape the situation by running away, driving away, or as in the case of the Kitty Genovese murder, turning off their lights and drifting back to sleep. For example, individuals are more likely to help someone who collapses on a crowded subway than on the sidewalk. Characteristics of the victim also affect the likelihood of helping. In one study, bystanders helped a person with a cane 95 percent of the time, but helped an obviously drunk person only 50 percent of the time (Piliavin, Rodin, & Piliavin, 1969). Being in a good mood also makes us more likely to help (Isen, Clark, & Schwartz, 1976). So does exposure to role models who help others (Bryan & Test, 1967; Rushton & Campbell, 1977).

One striking study found that seminary students who were on their way to deliver a sermon on the Biblical story of the Good Samaritan (which describes the moral importance of assisting people who are injured) in another building across campus were significantly less likely to help someone in distress if they were in a rush than if they had time to spare (Darley & Batson, 1973). So much for the Good Samaritan!

There's a silver lining to the gray cloud of bystander nonintervention. Research suggests that exposure to research on bystander effects increases the chances of intervening in emergencies. This is an example of what Kenneth Gergen (1973) called an **enlightenment effect:** Learning about psychological research can change real-world behavior for the better (Katsev & Brownstein, 1989). A group of investigators (Beaman, Barnes, Klentz, & McQuirk, 1978) presented the research literature on bystander intervention effects to one psychology class—containing much of the same information you've just read—but didn't present this literature to a very similar psychology class. Two weeks later, the students, accompanied by a confederate, came upon a person slumped over on a park bench. Compared with 25 percent of students who hadn't received the lecture on bystander intervention, 43 percent of students who'd received the lecture intervened to help. This study worked, probably because it imparted new knowledge about bystander intervention and perhaps also because it made people more aware of the importance of helping. So the very act of reading this chapter may have made you more likely to become a responsive bystander.

Helping: Individual and Gender Differences. Individual differences in personality can also influence the likelihood of helping. Participants who are less concerned about social approval and less traditional are more likely to go against the grain and intervene in

Psychological research suggests that we sometimes engage in genuine altruism, helping largely out of empathy.

altruism
helping others for unselfish reasons

enlightenment effect
learning about psychological research can change real-world behavior for the better

Men are more likely to offer assistance to women, particularly to attractive women. An ulterior motive?

emergencies even when others are present (Latané & Darley, 1970). Extraverted people are also more prone to help others than introverted people (Krueger, Hicks, & McGue, 2001). In addition, people with lifesaving skills, such as trained medical workers, are more likely to offer assistance to others in emergencies than other people are, even when they're off duty (Huston, Ruggiero, Conner, & Geis, 1981). Some people may not help on certain occasions simply because they don't know what to do.

Most researchers have reported a slight tendency for men to help more than women (Eagly & Crowley, 1986). This difference isn't especially consistent across studies (Becker & Eagly, 2004), and it seems to be accounted for by the tendency of men to help more than women in situations involving physical or social risk. Moreover, men are especially likely to help women rather than other men, especially if the women are physically attractive (Eagly & Crowley, 1986). Perhaps men's helping behaviors aren't so altruistic after all!

AGGRESSION: WHY WE HURT OTHERS

Like our primate cousins, the chimpanzees, we occasionally engage in violent behavior toward others. And like them, we're a war-waging species; as we write this chapter, there are at least fifteen full-scale wars raging across the globe. Psychologists define **aggression** as behavior intended to harm others, either verbally or physically. To account for aggressive behavior on both large and small scales, we need to examine the role of situational factors, both short-term and long-term, and dispositional factors.

Aggression: Situational Influences. Using both laboratory and naturalistic designs, psychologists have pinpointed a host of situational influences on human aggression. Next, we'll review some of the best-replicated findings.

Replicability

- **Interpersonal Provocation:** Not surprisingly, we're especially likely to strike out aggressively against those who have provoked us, say, by insulting, threatening, or hitting us (Geen, 2001).
- **Frustration:** We're especially likely to behave aggressively when we're frustrated, that is, thwarted from reaching a goal (Anderson & Bushman, 2002; Berkowitz, 1989). In one study, a research assistant asked participants to perform a difficult paper-folding (origami) task at an unreasonably rapid pace, and either apologized for moving participants along too quickly or told them to pick up the pace ("I would like to hurry and get this over with"). Frustrated participants—those in the first condition—were later more likely to give the research assistant a low job-related evaluation (Dill & Anderson, 1995).
- **Media Influences:** As we learned in Chapter 6, an impressive body of laboratory and naturalistic evidence points to the conclusion that watching media violence increases the odds of violence through observational learning (Anderson et al., 2003; Bandura, 1973). Laboratory experiments show that playing violent video games also boosts the odds of real-world violence (Gentile & Anderson, 2006).
- **Aggressive Cues:** External cues associated with violence, such as guns and knives, can serve as discriminant stimuli (see Chapter 6) for aggression, making us more likely to act violently in response to provocation (Carlson, Marcus-Newhall, & Miller, 1990). Leonard Berkowitz and Anthony LePage (1967) found that the mere presence of a gun—as opposed to a badminton racket—on a table triggered more aggression in subjects who'd been provoked by mild electric shocks for supposed poor performance on a task.
- **Arousal:** When our autonomic nervous systems (see Chapter 3) are hyped up, we may mistakenly attribute this arousal to anger, leading us to act aggressively (Zillman, 1988). Dolf Zillman and his colleagues found that participants who pedaled an exercise bicycle delivered more intense electric shocks to someone who'd annoyed them than did participants who sat still (Zillman, Katcher, & Milavsky, 1972).
- **Alcohol and Other Drugs:** Certain substances can disinhibit our brain's prefrontal cortex (see Chapter 3), lowering our inhibitions toward behaving violently (Kelly, Cherek, Stein-

aggression
behavior intended to harm others, either verbally or physically

berg, & Robinson, 1988). After being provoked with electric shocks by an "opponent" (who was actually fictitious) during a competitive game, participants tended to choose more intense electric shocks after consuming alcohol or benzodiazepines, such as Valium (see Chapter 16), than after consuming a placebo (Taylor, 1993). But alcohol is likely to trigger aggression only when the target of our aggression occupies the focus of our attention, as when someone is threatening us directly (Giancola & Corman, 2007).

- **Temperature:** Rates of violent crime in different regions of the United States mirror the average temperatures in these regions (Anderson, Bushman, & Groom, 1997). Because warm temperatures increase irritability, they may make people more likely to lose their tempers when provoked or frustrated (Anderson & Bushman, 2002). Nevertheless, because extremely warm temperatures are more common in the southern United States, in which violent crime rates are especially high (see the Cultural Differences section on page 558), investigators have had to rule out the rival hypothesis that this "heat effect" is due to geographical region. They've succeeded in doing so by demonstrating that even within the same geographical region, warmer temperatures are associated with higher rates of violence (Anderson & Anderson, 1996). See **Figure 13.8.**

Ruling Out Rival Hypotheses

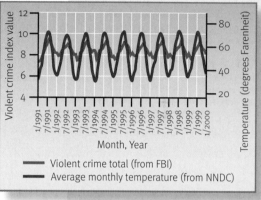

Figure 13.8 Monthly Violent Crime versus Average Temperature, 1991–1999. Research demonstrates that violent crime rates coincide with outdoor temperatures. How might we determine whether this correlation indicates a causal effect? (*Source:* Nienberg)

Aggression: Individual, Gender, and Cultural Differences. On a typical day in the United States, there are between 40 and 45 murders; that's one about every half hour. There are also about 230 reported rapes, or one about every 5 or 6 minutes (Federal Bureau of Investigation, 2005). These statistics paint a grim picture. Yet the substantial majority of people are generally law-abiding citizens, and only a tiny percentage ever engage in serious physical aggression toward others. Across a wide swath of societies that scientists have studied, only a small percentage of people—perhaps 5 or 6 percent—account for more than half of all crimes, including violent crimes (Wilson & Herrnstein, 1985). But why?

Personality Traits. When confronted with the same situation, like an insult, people differ in their tendencies to behave aggressively. Certain personality traits can combine to create a dangerous cocktail of aggression-proneness. People with high levels of negative emotions (such as irritability and mistrust), impulsivity, and a lack of closeness to others are especially prone to violence (Krueger et al., 1994).

Replicability

Sex Differences. One of the best replicated sex differences in humans, and across the animal kingdom for that matter, is the higher level of physical aggressiveness among males than females (Eagly & Steffen, 1986; Maccoby & Jacklin, 1980; Storch, Bagner, Geffken, & Baumeister, 2004). In conjunction with biological sex, age plays a role: The rates of crime, including violent crime, would drop by two-thirds if all males between the ages of 12 and 28 were magically placed into a state of temporary hibernation (Lykken, 1995).

The reasons for the sex difference in aggression are controversial, although some researchers have traced it to the higher levels of the hormone testosterone in males (Dabbs, 2001). One of the precious few exceptions to this sex difference is the spotted hyena (sometimes called the "laughing hyena"), in which females are more aggressive than males. This exception may prove the rule, because there's some evidence that the female spotted hyena has unusually high levels of a hormone closely related to testosterone (Glickman, Frank, Davidson, Smith, & Siiteri, 1987). Social factors almost surely play a role too, at least in humans: Parents and teachers tend to pay more attention to boys when they engage in aggression and to girls when they engage in dependent behaviors, like clinginess (Serbin & O'Leary, 1975).

Yet the well-replicated male predominance in aggression may apply only to physical violence, not indirect aggression. Nicki Crick (1995) discovered that girls tend to be higher than boys in **relational aggression,** a form of indirect aggression marked by spreading rumors, gossiping, social exclusion, and nonverbal putdowns (like giving other girls "the silent treatment") for the purposes of social manipulation. Crick's findings dovetail with other results suggesting that females are more likely than males to

Research suggests although males tend to be more physically aggressive than females, girls are more likely than boys to engage in relational aggression, which includes gossiping and making fun of others behind their backs.

relational aggression
form of indirect aggression, prevalent in girls, involving spreading rumors, gossiping, and nonverbal putdowns for the purpose of social manipulation

In a heated television interview in 2004 with host Chris Matthews (left), former Georgia governor Zell Miller (right) stunned viewers by saying that he wished he could challenge Matthews to a duel. Yet social psychologists familiar with the "culture of honor" could not have been surprised, as Southern gentlemen of days past frequently settled challenges to their reputation in this manner.

express anger in subtle ways (Eagly & Steffen, 1985; Frieze et al., 1978). In contrast, boys tend to have much higher rates of bullying than girls (Olweus, 1993).

Cultural Differences. Culture may also shape aggression. For example, physical aggression and violent crime tend to be less prevalent among Asian individuals, such as Japanese and Chinese, than among Americans or Europeans (Wilson & Herrnstein, 1985; Zhang & Snowdon, 1999). Richard Nisbett, Dov Cohen, and their colleagues have also found that people from the southern regions of the United States are more likely than people from other regions of the country to adhere to a *culture of honor*, that is, a social norm of defending one's reputation in the face of perceived insults (Nisbett & Cohen, 1996). The culture of honor may help to explain why the rates of violence are higher in the South than in other parts of the United States. Interestingly, these rates are higher only for violence that arises in the context of disputes, not in robberies, burglaries, or other crimes (Cohen & Nisbett, 1994). The culture of honor even shows itself in the relatively safe confines of the laboratory. In three experiments, a male confederate bumped into a male college student in a narrow hallway, muttering a profanity about him before walking away. Students from southern states were more likely than students from other states to react with a boost in testosterone and to display aggressive behavior against another confederate (Cohen, Nisbett, Bowdle, & Schwarz, 1996).

ASSESS YOUR KNOWLEDGE: FACT OR FICTION?

(1) Research suggests that the old saying that "there's safety in numbers" is wrong. (True/False)

(2) The primary reason for bystander nonintervention appears to be the apathy of onlookers. (True/False)

(3) Most people tend to work especially hard in groups. (True/False)

(4) People who have life-saving skills are more likely to help than those without. (True/False)

(5) Drinking can calm us down, lowering our risk for aggression. (True/False)

(6) The "culture of honor" may contribute to lower levels of violent crime in the U.S. South. (True/False)

Answers: (1) T (p. 552); (2) F (p. 552); (3) F (p. 553); (4) T (p. 556); (5) F (p. 556); (6) F (p. 558)

Attitudes and Persuasion: Changing Minds

First, answer the following question: Do you think that the death penalty is an effective deterrent against murder? Second, answer this question: How do you feel about the death penalty?

Now that you've gone through this exercise, you can grasp the difference between beliefs and attitudes. The first question assessed your *beliefs* about the death penalty, the second question your *attitudes* toward the death penalty. A **belief** is a conclusion regarding factual evidence; in contrast, an **attitude** is a belief that includes an emotional component. An attitude reflects how you feel about an issue or person. Attitudes are an important part of our social world, because they're shaped in significant ways by the people around us.

belief
conclusion regarding factual evidence

attitude
belief that includes an emotional component

ATTITUDES AND BEHAVIOR

A prevalent misconception is that attitudes are good predictors of behavior. For example, most people believe that how we feel about a political candidate predicts with a high level of certainty whether we'll vote toward or against that candidate. It doesn't (Wicker, 1969). In part, this finding explains why even carefully conducted political polls are rarely fool-proof: we don't always act on our stated preferences.

When Attitudes Don't Predict Behavior. In a study conducted over 70 years ago, Robert LaPiere asked 128 hotel and restaurant owners whether they'd be willing to serve guests who were Chinese, who at the time were widely discriminated against. Perhaps not surprisingly, over 90 percent of LaPiere's subjects said no. Yet when LaPiere had previously toured the country with a Chinese couple, 127 of 128 of the same owners had served them (LaPiere, 1934). Indeed, a meta-analysis (see Chapter 2) of 88 studies revealed that the average correlation between attitudes and behavior is about .38 (Kraus, 1995), which is only a moderate association. So although attitudes forecast behavior at better than chance levels, they're far from guaranteed predictors. This finding probably reflects the fact that our behaviors are the outcome of many factors, only one of which is our attitudes. For example, LaPiere's prejudiced subjects may not have been especially fond of the idea of serving Chinese guests. Yet when they met these guests in person, they may have found them more likable than they expected. Or when push came to shove, they may have been reluctant to pass up the chance for good business.

When Attitudes Do Predict Behavior. Occasionally, though, our attitudes predict our behaviors reasonably well. Attitudes that are highly *accessible*—which come to mind easily—tend to be strongly predictive of our behavior (Fazio, 1995). Imagine that we asked you two questions: (1) How do you feel about the idea of purchasing a new brand of yogurt that's been scientifically demonstrated to produce a 2 percent decrease in the levels of low-density cholesterol over a 5-year period? and (2) How do you feel about the idea of purchasing chocolate ice cream? If you're like most people, you'll find question 2 much easier to answer than question 1, because you've thought more about it. If so, your attitude toward chocolate ice cream is more likely to predict your purchasing behavior than is your attitude toward the new-fangled yogurt.

Attitudes also predict behavior well for a group of people known as low self-monitors (Krause, 1995). **Self-monitoring** is a trait that assesses the extent to which people's behaviors reflect their true feelings and attitudes (Snyder, 1974; Snyder & Gangestad, 1986). Low self-monitors tend to be straight shooters, whereas high self-monitors tend to be social chameleons. Not surprisingly, we can usually trust low self-monitors' actions to mirror their attitudes.

Still, the attitude–behavior correlation is, after all, just a correlation. The fact that attitudes are correlated with behaviors doesn't mean they cause them. Other explanations are possible; for example, our behaviors may sometimes cause our attitudes. Imagine that we start out with a negative attitude toward homeless persons. If a friend persuades us to volunteer to help the homeless for 3 hours a week and we end up enjoying this type of work, our attitudes toward homeless people may improve.

ORIGINS OF ATTITUDES

Our attitudes stem from a variety of sources. Among them are our prior experience, our ability to relate to messengers who provide information, and our personalities.

Recognition. Our experiences shape our attitudes. The *recognition heuristic* makes us more likely to believe something we've heard many times (Arkes, 1993). Like most heuristics (mental shortcuts or rules of thumb; see Chapter 2), the recognition heuristic generally serves us well, because things we hear many times from many different people often *are* true. Moreover, this heuristic can help us to make snap judgments that are surprisingly accurate. To test this possibility, two researchers asked a group of students in Chicago and in Munich, Germany, the following question: *Which city has a larger population: San Diego, California, or San Antonio, Texas?* Unexpectedly, only 62 percent of American students got the correct answer (San Diego), whereas 100 percent of German students did (Goldstein & Gigerenzer, 1999). The German students didn't get it right

People's expressed voting preferences to pollsters don't always predict their actual voting behavior.

Correlation vs. Causation

self-monitoring
personality trait that assesses the extent to which people's behavior reflects their true feelings and attitudes

Endorsements from attractive celebrities, like Hilary Duff, can lead us to prefer some products over others for irrational reasons.

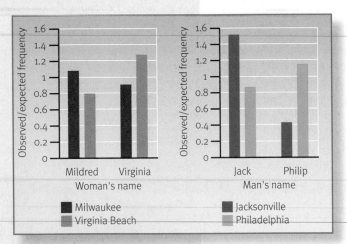

Figure 13.9 Graph Illustrating Implicit Egotism Effect. Research shows a statistical tendency for us to choose to live in cities and other geographical regions with names similar to ours. (*Source:* Pelham, Mirenberg, & Jones, 2002)

Ruling Out Rival Hypotheses

more often than the Americans because they had more knowledge of U.S. cities; in fact, they got it right because they had *less* knowledge of U.S. cities. Most of the German students had never heard of San Antonio, so they simply relied on the recognition heuristic ("The city I've heard of probably has more people in it"). In contrast, the American students had heard of both cities and then tried to guess which one had a larger population. In this case, the recognition heuristic worked.

But when a story is persuasive or interesting, the recognition heuristic can get us into trouble. It can lead us to fall for stories that are too good to be true, like some urban legends, or to buy products that seem familiar just because we've heard their names repeated many times. Indeed, all good advertisers make use of this heuristic by cooking up catchy, easily repeated jingles. If we recall the *bandwagon fallacy* from Chapter 1, we'll remember that we shouldn't believe—or buy—something merely because most people do.

Characteristics of the Messenger. Our attitudes are shaped not only by the message, but by the messenger. Research demonstrates that we're more likely to swallow a persuasive message if famous or attractive people deliver it—whether or not they would logically know something about the product they're hawking. Fortunately, we can safeguard consumers against *maladaptive gullibility*—falling for messages delivered by phony authority figures—by teaching them to distinguish legitimate from illegitimate authorities (Cialdini & Sagarin, 2005).

Messages are also especially persuasive if the messenger seems similar to us. In one study, researchers asked students to read a description of the bizarre and not especially likable Russian mystic, Grigory Rasputin. Some students were randomly assigned a description of Rasputin that featured his birth date (December 16), whereas others were randomly assigned a description of Rasputin that featured the student's birth date. Students who believed they shared a birth date with Rasputin thought more positively of him than students who didn't (Finch & Cialdini, 1989).

Researchers have now reported this *implicit egotism* effect—the finding that we're more positively disposed toward people, places, or things that resemble us—across many domains (Pelham, Carvallo, & Jones, 2005). This effect appears to influence not only our attitudes but our life choices. In matters of love and friendship, we're more likely than chance would predict to select people whose names contain the first letters of our first or last names. All things being equal, Johns tend to be fond of Jessicas, Roberts of Ronalds, and so on. Nevertheless, most people are unaware of this *name-letter effect* (Nuttin, 1985). People even seem to gravitate to places that are similar to their names. One group of researchers found a higher than expected number of Louises living in Louisiana, Virginias in Virginia, Georgias in Georgia, and Florences in Florida (Pelham, Mirenberg, & Jones, 2002; see **Figure 13.9**). Moreover, the investigators ruled out an alternative explanation for this finding, namely, the possibility that parents tended to name their children after the state in which they were born, by determining that adults tend to move into states with names similar to their own.

Attitudes and Personality. Our attitudes are associated in important ways with our personality traits. Although we may persuade ourselves that our political attitudes derive from completely objective analyses of social issues, these attitudes are often affected by our personalities.

In an article that stirred up more than its share of controversy, one team of researchers (Jost, Glaser, & Sulloway, 2003) reported that across many studies, political conservatives tend to be more fearful, more sensitive to threat, and less tolerant of uncertainty than political liberals. They suggested that these personality traits are the "psychological glue" that binds together conservatives' political attitudes toward the death penalty, abortion, gun control, school prayer, national defense, and a host of other seemingly unrelated issues. Nevertheless, some researchers criticized these authors for not considering an alternative hypothesis: namely, that these personality traits predict political extremism in general rather than right-wing conservatism specifically (Greenberg & Jonas, 2003). According to these critics, left-wing extremists are just as likely to be fearful, dogmatic, and the like, as right-wing extremists are. Because there are few studies of left-wing extremists, we don't know who's right.

Our personalities even relate to, and perhaps influence, our attitudes toward religion. The specific religion we adopt is largely a function of our religious exposure while growing up and is mostly independent of our personality traits. Nevertheless, our *religiosity*— that is, the depth of our religious convictions—is linked to certain personality traits. Adolescents with high levels of conscientiousness (see Chapter 14) are especially likely to become deeply religious adults (McCullough, Tsang, & Brion, 2003).

ATTITUDE CHANGE: WAIT, WAIT, I JUST CHANGED MY MIND

Many of us are surprised to discover that our attitudes on many topics, like the death penalty and abortion, change over the years. We tend to perceive ourselves as more consistent over time in our attitudes than we really are (Bem & McConnell, 1970; Goethals & Reckman, 1973; Ross, 1989), perhaps in part because we don't like to think of ourselves as weak-willed flip-floppers. Yet this point raises a question that psychologists have long struggled to answer: What makes us change our attitudes?

Cognitive Dissonance Theory.   In the 1950s, Leon Festinger developed *cognitive dissonance theory,* an influential model of why our attitudes change. According to this theory, we alter our attitudes because we experience an unpleasant state of tension—**cognitive dissonance**—between two or more conflicting thoughts (cognitions). Because we dislike this state of tension, we're motivated to reduce or eliminate it. If we hold an attitude or belief (cognition A) that's inconsistent with another attitude or belief (cognition B), we can reduce the anxiety resulting from this inconsistency in three major ways: change cognition A, change cognition B, or introduce a new cognition, C, that resolves the inconsistency between A and B (see **Figure 13.10**).

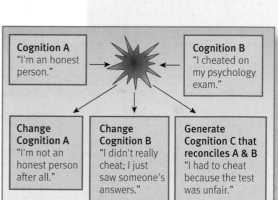

Figure 13.10 Cognitive Dissonance Theory. According to cognitive dissonance theory, we can reduce the conflicts between two cognitions (beliefs) in multiple ways—by changing the first cognition, changing the second cognition, or introducing a third cognition that resolves the conflict.

Let's move from As, Bs, and Cs to a real-world example. Imagine that you believe that your new friend, Sandy, is a nice person. You learn from another friend, Chris, that Sandy recently stole a wallet from a fellow classmate. According to Festinger, this news should produce cognitive dissonance, because it creates a conflict between cognition A (Sandy is a nice person) and cognition B (Sandy stole money from someone and therefore isn't such a nice person after all). To resolve this nagging sense of tension, you can change cognition A and decide that Sandy isn't really a nice person after all. Or you can change cognition B, perhaps by deciding that the news that Sandy stole money must be a false rumor spread by her enemies. Or you can instead introduce a new thought, cognition C, that resolves the discrepancy between cognitions A and B. For example, you could persuade yourself that Sandy is still a nice person but that she took her classmate's wallet because she was starving and in desperate need of a short-term infusion of cash ("I'm sure she'll return the wallet and all of the money in a day or two once she's grabbed something to eat," you reassure yourself).

Festinger and his colleagues (Festinger, Schacter, & Riecken, 1956) took advantage of a unique opportunity to test cognitive dissonance theory (see Chapter 2). They infiltrated a small Illinois cult called the Seekers, led by Mrs. Keech. Inspired by apparent interplanetary communications received by Mrs. Keech, cult members became convinced that the Earth would be annihilated in a gigantic flood on December 21, and that they'd all be rescued and transported by flying saucer to another planet. In anticipation of the

cognitive dissonance
unpleasant mental experience of tension resulting from two conflicting thoughts or beliefs

grand finale to planet Earth, the cult members prayed repeatedly for their salvation. December 21 came, and the cult members waited . . . and waited . . . and waited. Nothing happened.

The researchers wanted to find out how cult members would react to this blatant disconfirmation of their prophecy. Common sense would dictate that this falsification would weaken their convictions. Yet as Festinger recognized, cognitive dissonance theory predicts the opposite. In this case, cognitive dissonance theory won and common sense lost: The failure of their prophecy strengthened cult members' beliefs. They resolved the cognitive dissonance created by the disconfirmation of their prophecy by persuading themselves that their prayers had saved the world. God, they concluded, was so impressed by their loyalty to Mrs. Keech that he'd decided to spare humanity from destruction.

Falsifiability

> ### APPLY YOUR THINKING
> In what ways were the thinking processes of the Seekers and other cult members similar to those of many proponents of pseudoscience?

factoid

In one of the most creative demonstrations of cognitive dissonance theory, four researchers asked subjects to taste fried grasshoppers (Zimbardo, Weisenberg, Firestone, & Levy, 1965). They randomly assigned some subjects to receive this bizarre request from a friendly person, and others to receive it from an unfriendly person. Consistent with cognitive dissonance theory, the latter subjects reported liking the fried grasshoppers more than the former subjects did. Subjects who tasted the grasshoppers at the behest of the friendly person had a good external justification ("I did it to help out a nice person"), but the other subjects didn't. So the latter subjects resolved their dissonance by changing their attitudes—hmmm, those little critters were delicious.

Intriguing as it is, the evidence from Festinger and his cult Seekers is merely anecdotal. So Festinger, along with J. Merrill Carlsmith, conducted the first systematic test of cognitive dissonance theory in the late 1950s (Festinger & Carlsmith, 1959).

The Setup: You sign up for a 2-hour study of "Measures of Performance." At the lab, an experimenter provides you with instructions for some manual tasks—all mind-numbingly boring, like inserting twelve spools into a tray, emptying the tray, refilling the tray, and so on, for half an hour. Now here's the twist: The experimenter explains that a research assistant normally informs the next subject waiting in the hallway about the study and, to help recruit this subject, he says how interesting and enjoyable the study was. Unfortunately, the research assistant couldn't make it into the lab today. So, the experimenter wonders, would you be kind enough to substitute for him?

The Study: Festinger and Carlsmith randomly assigned some subjects to receive $1 to perform this favor and others to receive $20. Afterward, they asked subjects how much they enjoyed performing the tasks. Fom the perspective of learning theory, especially operant conditioning (Chapter 6), we might expect subjects paid $20 to say they enjoyed the task more. Yet cognitive dissonance theory makes a counterintuitive prediction: subjects paid $1 should say they enjoyed the task more. Why? Because all subjects should experience cognitive dissonance: They performed an incredibly boring task but told the next subject it was fun. Yet subjects given $20 had a good *external justification* for telling this little fib, namely, that the experimenter bribed them to do it. In contrast, subjects given $1 had almost no external justification. As a result, the only easy way to resolve their cognitive dissonance was to persuade themselves that they must have enjoyed the task after all. They deceive themselves.

The Results: The results supported this surprising prediction. Subjects given less money reported enjoying the task more, presumably because they needed to justify their lies to themselves. Their behaviors had changed their attitudes. Since Festinger and Carlsmith's study, hundreds of experiments have yielded results consistent with cognitive dissonance theory (Harmon-Jones & Mills, 1999).

Alternatives to Cognitive Dissonance Theory. Cognitive dissonance theory is alive and well, although researchers continue to debate whether alternative processes account for attitude change. Some scholars contend that it's not dissonance itself that's responsible for shifting our attitudes, but rather threats to our self-concepts (Aronson, 1992; Wood, 2000). In Festinger and Carlsmith's (1959) study, perhaps what motivated subjects in the $1 condition to change their attitudes was a discrepancy between who they believed they were (a decent person) and what they did (lie to another subject). From this perspective, only certain conflicts between attitudes produce cognitive dissonance, namely, those that challenge our views of who we are.

Replicability

There are at least two other alternative explanations for cognitive dissonance effects. The first, **self-perception theory,** proposes that we acquire our attitudes by observing our behaviors (Bem, 1967). According to this model, Festinger and Carlsmith's subjects in the $1 condition looked at their behavior and said to themselves, "I told the other subject that I liked the task, and I got paid only one lousy buck to do so. So I guess I must have really liked the task." The second, **impression management theory** (Goffman, 1959), proposes that we don't really change our attitudes in cognitive dissonance studies; we only tell the experimenters we have. We do so because we don't want to appear inconsistent (Tedeschi, Schlenker, & Bonoma, 1971). According to this model, Festinger and Carlsmith's subjects in the $1 condition didn't want to look like hypocrites. So they told the experimenter they enjoyed the task even though they didn't. As is often the case in psychology, there may be some truth to each of these explanations. Some subjects may exhibit attitude change because of cognitive dissonance, others because of self-perception, and still others because of impression management (Bem & Funder, 1978).

PERSUASION: HUMANS AS SALESPEOPLE

Whether or not we realize it, we encounter attempts at persuasion every day. If you're like the average student entering college, you've already watched 360,000 commercials; that number will reach a staggering 2 million by the time you turn 65. Each time you walk into a store or supermarket, you see hundreds of products that marketers have crafted carefully to make you more likely to purchase them.

Routes to Persuasion. According to *dual process models* of persuasion, there are two alternative pathways to persuading others (Petty & Cacioppo, 1986). One, the *central* route, leads us to evaluate the merits of persuasive arguments carefully and thoughtfully. The other, the *peripheral* route, leads us to respond to persuasive arguments on the basis of snap judgments. The danger of persuasive messages that travel through the peripheral route is that we can be easily fooled by superficial factors, such as how physically attractive, famous, or likable the communicator is or how many times we've heard the message (Hemsley & Doob, 1978; Hovland, Janis, & Kelly, 1953; Kenrick, Neuberg, & Cialdini, 2005).

Persuasion Techniques. Drawing on the research literature concerning attitudes and attitude change, psychologists have identified a host of effective techniques for persuading others. Many of these methods operate by means of the peripheral persuasion route, largely bypassing our critical thinking capacities. Interestingly, successful businesspeople have used many of these techniques for decades (Cialdini, 2001). Let's look at three of them.

- **Foot-in-the-door technique:** Following on the heels of cognitive dissonance theory (Freedman & Fraser, 1966; Gorassini & Olson, 1995), the **foot-in-the-door technique** suggests that we start with a small request before making a bigger one. If we want to get our classmate to volunteer 5 hours a week for the "Helping a Starving Psychologist" charity organization, we can first ask her to volunteer 1 hour a week. Once we've gotten her to agree to that request, we have our "foot in the door," because from the perspective of cognitive dissonance theory she'll feel a need to justify her initial commitment. As a consequence, she'll probably end up with a positive attitude toward the organization, making it easier to get her to volunteer even more of her time.

- **Door-in-the-face technique:** Alternatively, we can start with a large request, like asking for a $100 donation to our charity, before asking for a small one, like a $10 donation (Cialdini et al., 1975; O'Keefe & Hale, 2001). One reason the **door-in-the-face technique** works may be that the initial large request often induces guilt in recipients (O'Keefe & Figge, 1997). But if the initial request is so outrageous that it appears insincere or unreasonable, this method often backfires (Cialdini & Goldstein, 2004). Meta-analyses (see Chapter 2) suggest that the foot-in-the-door and door-in-the-face techniques work about equally well (Pascual & Guequen, 2005).

- **Low-ball technique:** In the **low-ball technique,** the seller of a product starts by quoting a price well below the actual sales price (Burger & Petty, 1981; Cialdini, 2001). Once the

Studies of the foot-in-the-door technique suggest that once a person agrees to place a small political sign in her yard, she'll be more likely to later agree to place an even larger sign in her yard.

self-perception theory
theory that we acquire our attitudes by observing our behaviors

impression management theory
theory that we don't really change our attitudes, but report that we have so that our behaviors appear consistent with our attitudes

foot-in-the-door technique
persuasive technique involving making a small request before making a bigger one

door-in-the-face technique
persuasive technique involving making an unreasonably large request before making the small request we're hoping to have granted

low-ball technique
persuasive technique in which the seller of a product starts by quoting a low sales price, and then mentions all of the "add-on" costs once the customer has agreed to purchase the product

In the low-ball technique, a used car salesperson will begin the deal by quoting a low base price and then mention all the extra features that cost more once the person has agreed to purchase the car.

buyer agrees to purchase the product, the seller mentions all of the desirable or necessary "add-ons" that come along with the product. By the time the deal is done, the buyer may end up paying twice as much as he'd initially agreed to pay. We can even use this technique to obtain favors from friends. In one study, a confederate asked strangers to look after his dog while he visited a friend in the hospital. In some cases, he first got the stranger to agree to the request, and only then told him he'd be gone for half an hour; in other cases, he told the stranger up front he'd be gone for half an hour. The first tactic worked better (Gueguen, Pascual, & Dagot, 2002).

The Marketing of Pseudoscience. Many proponents of pseudoscience make good use of persuasion tactics, although they may sometimes do so with the best of intentions. The appeal of these tactics helps to explain why so many intelligent people fall prey to pseudoscientific claims. To resist these tactics, we first must be able to recognize them. Anthony Pratkanis (1995) identified a variety of persuasion tactics to watch out for when evaluating unsubstantiated claims. **Table 13.3** lists eight of them; we should bear in mind that people can use most of these tactics to persuade us of a wide variety of claims of both the pseudoscientific and everyday variety. As we can see, several of these tactics make use of heuristics; that is, mental shortcuts (Chapter 2) that are appealing and seductive, but false. Several also take the peripheral route to persuasion, rendering it less likely that we'll evaluate these claims critically.

Table 13.3 Pseudoscience Marketing Techniques.

Pseudoscience Tactic	Concept	Example	Problem
Creation of a "phantom" goal	Capitalize on desire to accomplish unrealistic objectives	"Master the complete works of Shakespeare while sleeping!"	Extreme claims are usually impossible to achieve
Vivid testimonials	Learning about someone else's personal experience	"Sandra Sadness was severely depressed for 5 years until she underwent rebirthing therapy!"	A single person's perspective is virtually worthless as scientific evidence but can be extremely persuasive (see Chapter 2)
Manufacturing source credibility	We're more likely to believe sources that we judge to be trustworthy or legitimate	"Dr. Jonathan Nobel from Princeton endorses this subliminal tape to build self-esteem."	Advertisers may present source in a deceptive fashion
Scarcity heuristic	Something that's rare must be especially valuable	"Call before midnight to get your copy of Dr. Genius's Improvement Program; it's going to sell out fast!"	Scarcity may be false or a result of low production because of low anticipated demand
Consensus heuristic	If most people believe that something works, it must work	"Thousands of psychologists use the Rorschach Inkblot Test, so it must be valid."	Common "knowledge" is often wrong (see Chapter 1)
The natural commonplace	A widely held belief that things that are natural are good	"Mrs. Candy Cure's new over-the-counter antianxiety medication is made from all-natural ingredients!"	*Natural* doesn't mean healthy—just look at poisonous mushrooms
The goddess-within commonplace	A widely held belief that we all possess a hidden mystical side that traditional Western science neglects or denies	"The Magical Mind ESP Enhancement program allows you to get in touch with your unrecognized psychic potential!"	Carefully controlled tests fail to support supernatural ability or potential (see Chapter 4)

ASSESS YOUR KNOWLEDGE: FACT OR FICTION?
(1) People's attitudes often don't predict their behaviors especially well. (True/False)
(2) We're less likely to believe something we've heard many times. (True/False)
(3) The best way to change people's minds on an issue is to pay them a large sum of money for doing so. (True/False)
(4) Using the door-in-the-face technique, we begin with a small request before making a larger one. (True/False)

Answers: (1) T (p. 559); (2) F (p. 559); (3) F (p. 562); (4) T (p. 563)

Prejudice and Discrimination

The term **prejudice** means to prejudge—to arrive at a conclusion before we've evaluated all of the evidence. If we're prejudiced toward a specific class of persons, whether they be women, African Americans, Norwegians, or hair stylists, it means we've jumped to a premature conclusion about them.

THE NATURE OF PREJUDICE

It's safe to say that we all harbor at least some prejudices against certain groups of people (Aronson, 2000). Some have argued that a tendency toward prejudice is deeply rooted in the human species. From the standpoint of natural selection, organisms benefit from forging close alliances with insiders and mistrusting outsiders (Cottrell & Neuberg, 2005). This is part of a broader evolutionary principle called **adaptive conservatism** (Henderson, 1985; Mineka, 1992): better safe than sorry. Indeed, members of one race are more likely to show pronounced skin conductance responses (see Chapter 6) to fear-relevant stimuli—a snake and a spider—than to fear-irrelevant stimuli—a bird and a butterfly—that have been paired repeatedly with faces of a different race (Olsson, Ebert, Banaji, & Phelps, 2005). We quite easily, and perhaps quite naturally, associate people from other races with scary things.

Still, notice that we used the term "tendency" in the previous paragraph. Even if there's an evolutionary predisposition toward fearing or mistrusting outsiders, that doesn't mean that prejudice is inevitable. Two major biases are associated with our tendency to forge alliances with people like ourselves.

In-group bias, the tendency to favor individuals inside our group relative to members outside our group. If you've ever watched a sporting event, you've observed in-group bias: thousands of red-faced fans (the term "fan," incidentally, is short for "fanatic") cheering their home team wildly and booing the visiting team with equal gusto, even though most of these fans have no financial stake in the game's outcome. Yet the home team is their "tribe," and they'll happily spend several hours out of their day to cheer them on against their mortal enemy.

In-group bias may be reinforced by our tendency to "turn off" our compassion toward out-group members. In one study, researchers using functional magnetic resonance imaging (fMRI) imaged the brains of liberal college students while they pondered the description of someone similar to themselves, a liberal person, and then a person dissimilar from themselves, a Christian conservative. The medial prefrontal cortex, which tends to become active when we feel empathy toward others, became more active when subjects thought about the liberal person. But it became less active when they thought about the Christian conservative (Mitchell, Banaji, & Phelps, 2006).

The second bias is **out-group homogeneity,** the tendency to view all people outside of our group as highly similar (Park & Rothbart, 1982). Out-group homogeneity makes it easy for us to dismiss members of other groups in one fell swoop, because we can simply tell ourselves that they all share at least one undesirable characteristic. In this way, we don't need to bother getting to know them.

DISCRIMINATION

Prejudice can also lead to discrimination, a term with which it's often confused. **Discrimination** is the act of treating members of out-groups differently from members of in-groups. *Whereas prejudice refers to negative attitudes toward others, discrimination refers to negative behaviors toward others.* We can be prejudiced against people without discriminating against them.

Consequences of Discrimination. Discrimination has significant real-world consequences. For example, far fewer women than men are members of major American

Demonizing the enemy is a frequent manifestation of in-group bias.

prejudice
drawing conclusions about a person, group of people, or situation prior to evaluating the evidence

adaptive conservatism
evolutionary principle that creates a predisposition toward distrusting anything or anyone unfamiliar or different

in-group bias
tendency to favor individuals within our group over those from outside our group

out-group homogeneity
tendency to view all individuals outside our group as highly similar

discrimination
negative behavior toward members of out-groups

Most U.S. orchestras now use blind auditions as a safeguard against sex bias and discrimination.

orchestras. To investigate this issue, one research team examined how music judges evaluated female musicians during auditions. In some cases, judges could see the musicians; in others, the musicians played behind a screen. When judges were blind to the musicians' sex, women were 50 percent more likely to pass auditions (Goldin & Rouse, 2000). For this reason, most major American orchestras today use blind auditions (Gladwell, 2004).

In another study, investigators (Word, Zanna, & Cooper, 1974) observed Caucasian undergraduates as they interviewed both Caucasian and African American applicants (who were actually confederates of the experimenters) for a job. When interviewing African American applicants, interviewers sat farther away from the interviewee, made more speech errors, and ended the interview sooner.

These findings, which focused on interviewer behavior, didn't demonstrate whether the different treatment affected the applicants' behavior. So the researchers trained Caucasian interviewers to treat Caucasian job applicants in the same way they'd treated African American applicants. Independent evaluators who were blind to the behavior of the interviewers coded the behavior of applicants from videotaped interviews. The results were striking. The evaluators rated job applicants who received the "African American treatment" as significantly more nervous and less qualified for the job than job applicants who received the "Caucasian treatment." This study shows how subtle discriminatory behaviors can adversely affect the quality of interpersonal interactions. Discrimination can be subtle, yet powerful.

Creating Discrimination: Don't Try This at Home. It's remarkably easy to cook up discrimination. The recipe? Just create two groups that differ on any characteristic, no matter how trivial. Jonathan Swift's classic 1726 novel, *Gulliver's Travels*, featured two groups, the Little Endians and the Big Endians, who found themselves in brutal conflict over whether one should crack open eggs on the little end or the big end.

More than two centuries later, Henry Tajfel (1982) developed the *minimal intergroup paradigm,* a laboratory method for creating groups based on arbitrary differences. In one study, Tajfel and colleagues flashed groups of dots on a screen and asked subjects to estimate how many dots they saw. In reality, the researchers ignored subjects' answers, randomly classifying some as "dot overestimators" and others as "dot underestimators." They then gave subjects the opportunity to distribute money and resources to other subjects. People within each group allotted more goodies to people inside than outside their dot estimator group (Tajfel, Billig, Bundy, & Flament, 1971).

Iowa schoolteacher Jane Elliott created similarly random discrimination in her third-grade classroom in 1969. The day after civil rights leader Reverend Martin Luther King, Jr. was assassinated, she divided her class into favored and disfavored groups based solely on their eye color (Monteith & Winters, 2002). Informing her pupils that brown-eyed children are superior because of excess melanin in their eyes, Elliott deprived blue-eyed children of basic rights, such as second helpings at lunch or drinking from the water fountain. She also insulted blue-eyed children, calling them lazy, dumb, and dishonest. According to Elliott, the results were dramatic; most brown-eyed children quickly become arrogant and condescending, and most blue-eyed children became submissive and insecure.

Jane Elliott's classic blue eyes–brown eyes demonstration highlighted the negative interpersonal effects of discrimination.

Teachers across the United States used the now-famous Blue Eyes–Brown Eyes demonstration in the late 1960s and 1970s to teach students about the dangers of discrimination (the first author of your textbook was a subject in one of these demonstrations as an elementary school student in New York City). One follow-up study investigating the effects of this demonstration suggests that Caucasian students who go through it report less prejudice toward minorities than do Caucasian students in a control group (Stewart, La Duke, Bracht, Sweet, & Gamarel, 2003). Nevertheless, because students who underwent this demonstration may have felt demand characteristics to report less prejudice, additional studies are needed to rule out this alternative explanation.

Ruling Out Rival Hypotheses

STEREOTYPES

Prejudice results in part from stereotyping. A **stereotype** is a belief—positive or negative— about a group's characteristics that we apply to most members of that group. Like many

stereotype
a belief, positive or negative, about the characteristics of members of a group that is applied generally to most members of the group

mental shortcuts, stereotypes typically stem from adaptive psychological processes. As we learned in Chapter 2, we humans are *cognitive misers*—we strive to save mental energy by simplifying reality. By lumping enormous numbers of people who share a single characteristic, like skin color, nationality, or religion, into a single category, stereotypes help us to make sense of our often confusing social worlds (Macrae & Bodenhausen, 2000). In this regard, they're like other schemas (see Chapter 7) in that they help us to process information.

Yet stereotypes can mislead us when we paint them with too broad a brush, as when we assume that *all* members of a group share a given characteristic. They can also mislead us when we cling to them too rigidly and are unwilling to modify them in light of disconfirming evidence.

Once we've learned them, stereotypes come to us naturally. Research suggests that overcoming stereotypes takes hard mental work. The key difference between prejudiced and nonprejudiced people isn't that the former have stereotypes of minority groups and the latter don't, because both groups harbor such stereotypes. Instead, it's that prejudiced

NEW FRONTIERS
Implicit Measures of Prejudice

Surveys demonstrate that interracial prejudice has declined substantially in the United States over the past four to five decades (Schuman, Steeh, Bobo, & Kyrsan, 1997). Nevertheless, some scholars contend that much prejudice, particularly that of Caucasians toward African Americans, has merely "gone underground"—that is, become subtler (Fiske, 2002; Hackney, 2005; Sue et al., 2007). Some researchers refer to this newer form of prejudice as *modern racism,* and they assess it using questions concerning opposition to affirmative action, support for racial profiling, and other controversial political issues (Sears & Henry, 2003). Other researchers maintain that measures of "modern racism" don't necessarily capture racist attitudes, because opponents of affirmative action or proponents of racial profiling may merely be expressing legitimate conservative political values (Redding, 2004).

An alternative approach to studying subtle prejudice is to measure implicit (unconscious) prejudice (Fazio & Olson, 2003; Vanman, Paul, Ito, & Miller, 1997; Vanman, Saltz, Nathan, & Warren, 2004). **Implicit stereotypes** are those of which we're unaware, and **explicit stereotypes** are those of which we're aware. One implicit method is based on the technique of affective priming: quickly presenting subjects with an emotionally charged prime stimulus (typically a word or a face) to see whether it speeds up their response to an emotionally charged word (see Chapter 7). For example, Russell Fazio and his colleagues flashed either Caucasian or African American faces on a computer screen, followed by either positive words (such as "wonderful") or negative words (such as "annoying") words. They asked Caucasian subjects to press a button to indicate whether these words were positive or negative. These subjects responded more quickly to positive words preceded by Caucasian faces and to negative words preceded by African American faces (Fazio, Jackson, Dunton, & Williams, 1995). The researchers reasoned that these findings reflect implicit prejudice, because they demonstrate that many Caucasians associate Caucasian faces with good things and African American faces with bad things.

An implicit prejudice technique that's received even more attention in recent years is the Implicit Association Test (IAT) developed by Anthony Greenwald and Mahzarin Banaji. As shown in **Figure 13.11,** researchers might ask a participant completing the IAT to first press the left key on a computer keyboard if they see a photograph of either an African American *or* a positive word (like "joy") and to press the right key if they see a photograph of a Caucasian *or* a negative word (like "bad"). After performing this task

implicit and explicit stereotypes
beliefs about the characteristics of an out-group about which we're either unaware (implicit) or aware (explicit)

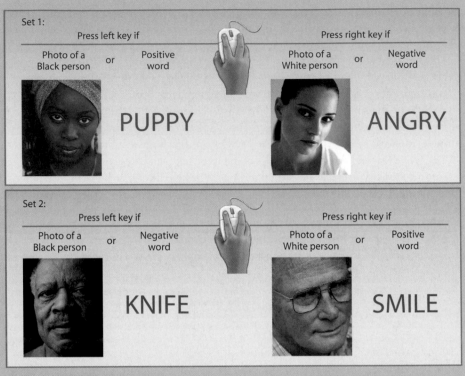

Figure 13.11 The Implicit Association Test. The Implicit Association Test (IAT) is the most widely researched measure of implicit or unconscious prejudice. This is a rendered example: Many people (across races) associate negative words more readily with African American than Causasian faces. But does the test really measure unconscious prejudice, or does it measure something else?

for a number of trials, researchers ask participants to again press the left and right keys, but this time for the reverse pairing (that is, to press the left key for a photograph of either an African American or a negative word, and the right key for a photograph of either a Caucasian or a positive word) (Greenwald, McGhee, & Schwartz, 1998). The results of numerous studies demonstrate that most Caucasian participants respond more quickly to the reverse pairing, that is, when African American faces are paired with negative words and when Caucasian faces are paired with positive words (Banaji, 2001). Investigators have recently expanded the IAT to test a variety of forms of prejudice, including racism, sexism, homophobia, and ageism (prejudice against older individuals). Many authors argue that the results of the IAT reflect unconscious prejudice (Gladwell, 2004; Greenwald & Nosek, 2001). If you want to try out the IAT, check out the website https://implicit.harvard.edu/implicit/demo.

Nevertheless, things may not be quite that simple. For one thing, the IAT rarely correlates significantly with explicit measures of prejudice, such as questionnaire measures of racist attitudes (Arkes & Tetlock, 2004). Proponents of the IAT argue that this absence of a correlation actually supports the IAT's validity, because the IAT supposedly measures unconscious rather than conscious racial attitudes. Yet this reasoning raises questions regarding the falsifiability of the IAT, because IAT proponents could presumably interpret either a positive or a zero correlation as evidence for the IAT's validity. Moreover, it's not clear whether the IAT measures prejudice as much as awareness of stereotypes. That is, unprejudiced persons may correctly perceive that much of mainstream American society links Muslims, for example, with many negative characteristics and Christians with many positive characteristics, yet they may personally reject these associations as biased (Arkes & Tetlock, 2004; Redding, 2004). The true meaning of scores on the IAT and other implicit prejudice measures remains controversial (Gawronski, LeBel, & Peters, 2007).

Falsifiability

people don't try hard to resist their stereotypes, but nonprejudiced people do (Devine, 1989; Devine, Monteith, Zuwerink, & Elliott, 1991).

Stereotypes: Are They Accurate?   Many stereotypes contain a kernel of truth, and still others are largely accurate. Janet Swim (1994) compared laypersons' estimates of the magnitude of sex differences on various psychological traits, such as aggression, helpfulness, talkativeness, and conformity, with the actual magnitude of these differences found by researchers. In most cases, people's estimates of the size of these sex differences corresponded closely to their actual size. For example, most people believe that men are somewhat more likely than women to be physically aggressive, and research shows that they're right.

Nevertheless, some stereotypes are massive overgeneralizations. These stereotypes reflect the presence of *illusory correlation* (Chapter 2), because they indicate the perception of an erroneous association between a minority group and a given characteristic (Hamilton & Rose, 1980). For example, although most people believe that there's a powerful correlation between mental illness and violence, studies indicate that the risk of violence is markedly elevated only among a small subset of mentally ill individuals, particularly those with paranoid beliefs (Faenza, Glover, Hutchings, & Radack, 1999; Monahan, 1984; see Chapter 15). Similarly, surveys demonstrate that most Americans believe that lesbian women are at especially high risk for HIV infection, even though lesbian women actually have lower rates of HIV infection than heterosexuals of both sexes and homosexual men (Aronson, 1992).

Ultimate Attribution Error.   Stereotypes can also result in what Thomas Pettigrew (1979) called the **ultimate attribution error:** the mistake of attributing the behavior of entire groups—like women, Christians, or African Americans—to their dispositions. Like the fundamental attribution error, after which it's named, this error leads us to underestimate the impact of situational factors on people's behavior. For example, Caucasian students are more likely to interpret a shove as intentionally aggressive, as opposed to accidental, when it originates from an African American than from another Caucasian (Duncan, 1976).

ROOTS OF PREJUDICE: A TANGLED WEB

The roots of prejudice are complex and multifaceted. Nevertheless, psychologists have honed in on several crucial factors that contribute to prejudice. We'll examine a few of them: scapegoating, the just-world hypothesis, conformity, and individual differences in psychological traits.

Scapegoat Hypothesis.   According to the **scapegoat hypothesis,** prejudice arises from a need to blame other groups for our misfortunes. Between 1882 and 1930, for instance, the number of lynchings of African Americans in the U.S. South rose when the price of cotton went up (Tolnay & Beck, 1995). This finding suggests that some Caucasians may have blamed African Americans for the bad prices, although we don't know this for certain. For example, it's possible that higher cotton prices were associated with greater violence toward all members of society, not just African Americans. Nevertheless, there's more direct research support for the scapegoat hypothesis. In an experiment disguised as a study of learning, Caucasian students administered more intense electric shocks to an African American student than to a Caucasian student, but only when the African American student was unfriendly (Rogers & Prentice-Dunn, 1981). This finding is consistent with the possibility that frustration can produce aggression, which people then displace onto minority groups.

Just-World Hypothesis.   Melvin Lerner's (1980) **just-world hypothesis** implies that many of us have a deep-seated need to perceive the world as fair—to believe that all things happen for a reason. Ironically, this need for a sense of fair play, especially if powerful, may lead to prejudice. That's because it can lead us to place blame on groups who are already in a one-down position. People with a strong belief in a just world are especially likely to believe that victims of serious illnesses, including cancer and AIDS, are responsible for

factoid

The term *scapegoat* originates from Biblical times, when rabbis engaged in an unusual practice for eliminating sin on the Jewish holy day of Yom Kippur. They brought forth two goats, one of which they sacrificed to God. The other goat lucked out. The rabbis grabbed the lucky goat's head while recounting all of the sins of the people, symbolically transferring these sins onto it. They then released the escaping goat—the *scapegoat*—into the woods, where it carried away the burden of society's moral errors.

Ruling Out Rival Hypotheses

ultimate attribution error
assumption that behaviors among individual members of a group are due to their internal dispositions

scapegoat hypothesis
claim that prejudice arises from a need to blame other groups for our misfortunes

just-world hypothesis
claim that our attributions and behaviors are shaped by a deep-seated assumption that the world is fair and all things happen for a reason

their plights (Hafer & Begue, 2005). Sociologists and psychologists have referred to this phenomenon as "blaming the victim" (Ryan, 1976).

Conformity. Some prejudiced attitudes and behaviors probably stem from conformity to social norms. A study conducted in South Africa half a century ago revealed that Caucasians with a high need for conformity were especially likely to be prejudiced against Blacks (Pettigrew, 1958). Such conformity may originate from a need for social approval. In a study of college fraternities and sororities, researchers found that established members of Greek organizations were about equally likely to express negative views of out-groups (other fraternities and sororities) regardless of whether their opinions were public or private. In contrast, new pledges to these organizations were more likely to express negative views of out-groups when their opinions were public (Noel, Wann, & Branscombe, 1995). Presumably, the pledges wanted to be liked by in-group members and went out of their way to voice their dislike of the "outsiders."

Individual Differences in Prejudice. Some people exhibit high levels of prejudice against a wide variety of out-groups. For example, people with authoritarian personality traits (which we discussed earlier), are prone to high levels of prejudice against many groups, including Native Americans and homosexuals (Altemeyer, 2004; Whitley & Lee, 2000). In addition, people with high levels of *extrinsic religiosity*, who view religion as a means to an end, such as obtaining friends or social support, tend to have high levels of prejudice (Batson & Ventis, 1982). In contrast, people with high levels of *intrinsic religiosity*—for whom religion is a deeply ingrained part of their belief system—tend to have equal or lower levels of prejudice than nonreligious people (Gorsuch, 1988; Pontón & Gorsuch, 1988).

COMBATING PREJUDICE: SOME REMEDIES

Having traversed some depressing ground—blind conformity, destructive obedience, bystander nonintervention, social loafing, and now prejudice—we're pleased to close our chapter with a piece of good news: We can overcome prejudice, at least to some extent. How?

Robbers Cave Study. We can find some clues in a study that Muzafer Sherif and his colleagues conducted in Robbers Cave, Oklahoma (so named because robbers once used these caves to hide from law enforcement authorities). Sherif split twenty-two well-adjusted fifth grade students into two groups, the Eagles and the Rattlers, and sent them packing to summer camp. After giving the boys within each group the chance to form strong bonds, Sherif introduced the groups to each other and engaged them in a 4-day sports and games tournament. When he did, pandemonium ensued. The Eagles and Rattlers displayed intense animosity toward one another, eventually manifesting in name-calling, food throwing, and fistfights.

Sherif next wanted to find out whether he could "cure" the prejudice he'd helped to create. His treatment was simple: engaging the groups in activities that required them to cooperate to achieve an overarching goal. For example, he rigged a series of mishaps, such as a breakdown of a truck carrying food supplies, that forced the Eagles and the Rattlers to work together. Sure enough, such cooperation toward a shared goal produced a dramatic decrease in hostility between the groups (Sherif, Harvey, White, Hood, & Sherif, 1961).

Jigsaw Classrooms. Elliott Aronson (Aronson, Blaney, Stephan, Sikes, & Snapp, 1978) incorporated the lessons of the Robbers Cave research into his educational work on **jigsaw classrooms,** in which teachers assign children separate tasks that all need to be fitted together to complete a project. A teacher might give each student in a class a different piece of history to investigate regarding the U.S. Civil War. One might present on Virginia's role,

In jigsaw classrooms, children cooperate on a multipart project, with each child assuming a small but essential role.

jigsaw classrooms
educational approach designed to minimize prejudice by requiring all children to make independent contributions to a shared project

another on New York's, another on Georgia's, and so on. The students then cooperate to assemble the pieces into an integrated lesson. Numerous studies reveal that jigsaw classrooms result in significant decreases in racial prejudice (Aronson, 2004; Slavin & Cooper, 1999).

The Robbers Cave study and Aronson's work on jigsaw classrooms underscore a lesson confirmed by many other social psychology studies: *increased contact between racial groups is rarely sufficient to reduce prejudice.* Indeed, during the early Civil Rights era in the United States, many attempts to reduce prejudice by means of desegregation backfired, resulting in increases in racial tension (Stephan, 1978). The advocates of these well-intended efforts assumed mistakenly that contact by itself could heal the deep wounds of prejudice. We now know that interventions are most likely to reduce prejudice only if they satisfy several conditions (see **Table 13.4**). These conditions lead to an optimistic conclusion: Prejudice is neither inevitable nor irreversible.

Table 13.4 Ideal Conditions for Reducing Prejudice.

- The groups should cooperate toward shared goals

- The contact between groups should be enjoyable

- The groups should be of roughly equal status

- Group members should disconfirm the other group's negative stereotypes

- Group members should have the potential to become friends

(*Source:* Kenrick et al., 2005; Pettigrew, 1998)

APPLY YOUR THINKING

In 2005, a library in Stockholm, Sweden, launched an innovative "borrow a person" policy in an effort to reduce prejudice. This policy allowed visitors to speak with a member of a stigmatized minority group—such as Muslims, gypsies, and homosexuals—for 45 minutes in the library café. Based on the research we've reviewed, will this program be successful in reducing prejudice? Why or why not?

ASSESS YOUR KNOWLEDGE: FACT OR FICTION?

(1) Prejudice refers to negative behavior against out-group members. (True/False)
(2) By definition, all stereotypes are inaccurate. (True/False)
(3) Research demonstrates that nonprejudiced people lack stereotypes of other groups. (True/False)
(4) Cooperation toward shared goals is a key ingredient in reducing prejudice. (True/False)
(5) Research suggests that increased contact between groups is sufficient to reduce prejudice. (True/False)

Answers: (1) F (p. 565); (2) F (p. 569); (3) F (p. 567); (4) T (p. 570); (5) F (p. 571)

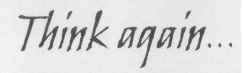

What Is Social Psychology? (pp. 534–539)

STUDY the Learning Objectives

▶ Identify the ways in which social situations influence the behaviors of individuals
  - The need to belong theory proposes that humans have a biological need for interpersonal connections.
  - Social facilitation refers to the presence of others enhancing our performance in certain situations.

▶ Explain how and why our attributions about the causes of others' behavior are accurate in some cases but biased in others
  - Attributions refer to our efforts to explain behavior; some attributions are internal, others external.
  - The great lesson of social psychology is the fundamental attribution error—the tendency to overestimate the impact of dispositions on others' behavior.

▶ Explain the power of our observations of others to influence our thoughts, beliefs, and decisions
  - According to social comparison theory, we're motivated to evaluate our beliefs, attitudes, and reactions by comparing them with the beliefs, attitudes, and reactions of others.
  - Mass hysteria is an outbreak of irrational behavior spread by social contagion.

DO YOU KNOW THESE TERMS?

- ❏ **social psychology** (p. 534)
- ❏ **social facilitation** (p. 536)
- ❏ **attribution** (p. 536)
- ❏ **fundamental attribution error** (p. 537)
- ❏ **social comparison theory** (p. 538)
- ❏ **mass hysteria** (p. 538)

You are standing in a crowded elevator when suddenly all of the other riders turn to the right. How likely would you be to follow suit? (p. 537)

While still alive, Walt Disney arranged to have his body frozen after his death so that it could be unfrozen at a future date when advanced technology will permit him to live again.

What factors contribute to the rise and spread of urban legends? (p. 539)

THINK about

what You would do . . .

How important to you are your social bonds? How would you feel if isolated from human contact for an extended period of time? (p. 535)

SUCCEED with

mypsychlab *where learning comes to life!*

Internal and External Attributions

Find out how accurate (or inaccurate) the attributions you assign to people can be. (p. 536)

 EXPLORE

ASSESS your knowledge

1. Social psychologists study how people influence others' _____, _____, and _____, for both good and bad. (p. 534)

2. The size of our neocortex relative to the rest of our brain (limits/doesn't limit) the number of people we can closely associate with. (p. 535)

3. The idea that we have a biologically based need for interpersonal connections is known as the _____ _____ _____ theory. (p. 535)

4. An improved performance in the presence of others is explained by _____ _____. (p. 536)

5. A worsened performance in the presence of others is explained by _____ _____. (p. 536)

6. Researchers have found that our performance in front of others is determined by our level of _____ in that particular performance area. (p. 536)

7. We tend to form _____ in our desire to assign causes to other people's behavior. (p. 536)

8. The tendency to overestimate the impact of _____ _____ on others' behavior is called the fundamental attribution error. (p. 537)

9. According to Festinger's _____ _____ theory, when a situation is unclear, we look to others for guidance about what to believe and how to act. (p. 538)

10. Stories of people waking up after partying in a bathtub full of ice with their kidneys removed are examples of _____ _____. (p. 539)

Social Influence: Conformity and Obedience (pp. 539–551)

STUDY the Learning Objectives

▶ Determine the factors that influence when we conform to the behaviors and beliefs of others
  - Conformity refers to the tendency of people to change their behavior as a result of group pressure. Asch's conformity studies underscore the power of social pressure, although there are individual and cultural differences in conformity.
  - Deindividuation refers to the tendency of people to engage in atypical behavior when stripped of their usual identities. The Stanford prison study is regarded as a powerful demonstration of the effects of deindividuation on behavior.

If you did not receive an access code to MyPsychLab with this text and wish to purchase access online, please visit www.mypsychlab.com.

THINK about

what You would do . . .

Leaving a championship basketball game, you witness a violent riot that begins to spread through the stadium. How will you react? (p. 544)

At what point in the Milgram study, if any, would you have refused to comply with orders to shock the "learner"? (p. 548)

mypsychlab
where learning comes to life!

SUCCEED with

Stanford Prison Experiment

Experience how easily a person can become over-powering or overpowered when assigned specific social roles.

(p. 542)

WATCH

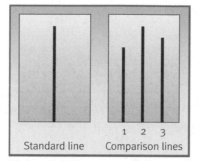

1 2 3

Standard line   Comparison lines

Under what circumstances discussed in the text would you identify line 3 as equal in length to the standard line? (p. 540)

ASSESS your knowledge

1. Changing your personal style, habits, or behavior in order to fit into a social or peer group is an example of _____. (p. 539)

2. Parametric studies manipulate the _____ variable in various ways to determine its effect on the _____ variable. (p. 540)

3. In the Asch experiment, if one confederate gave the correct response, the level of conformity (increased/decreased). (p. 540)

4. Conformity, as found by researcher Berns and his colleagues, is associated with activity in the _____ and _____ lobes of the brain. (pp. 540–541)

5. People's responses to social pressure (are/are not) associated with individual and cultural differences. (pp. 541–542)

6. People with (high/low) self-esteem are especially prone to conformity. (p. 541)

7. Researchers like Phil Zimbardo found that the two prominent factors that contribute to deindividuation are a feeling of _____ and a lack of feeling _____ _____. (p. 542)

8. The _____ study results have been recently compared with the prison guard atrocities at Abu Ghraib in Iraq. (p. 543)

9. NASA's decision to launch the 1986 *Challenger* shuttle despite warnings of potential problems from engineers may have resulted from _____. (p. 544)

10. Milgram's experiment testing the effects of "punishment on learning" was, in reality, an experiment designed to measure _____. (p. 547)

▶ Recognize the dangers of group decision making and identify ways to avoid mistakes common in group decisions
  • Groupthink is a preoccupation with group unanimity that impairs critical thinking. It can be treated by interventions that encourage dissent within the group.
  • Group polarization refers to the tendency of group discussion to strengthen the dominant positions of individual group members.
  • Cults are groups of individuals who exhibit extreme groupthink, marked by intense and unquestioning devotion to a single individual.

▶ Identify the contexts that maximize or minimize obedience to authority
  • Milgram's classic work on authority demonstrates the power of destructive obedience to authority and helps to clarify the situational factors that both foster and impede obedience.

DO YOU KNOW THESE TERMS?

☐ **conformity** (p. 539)
☐ **parametric studies** (p. 540)
☐ **deindividuation** (p. 542)
☐ **groupthink** (p. 544)
☐ **group polarization** (p. 545)
☐ **cults** (p. 545)
☐ **inoculation effect** (p. 546)
☐ **obedience** (p. 546)

Helping & Harming Others: Prosocial Behavior & Aggression (pp. 551–558)

THINK about

what You would do ...

Your professor collapses in front of a packed lecture hall of students. How would you react? (p. 552)

What steps could you take to improve your chances of getting help if you were badly hurt or seriously ill in a public place? (p. 553)

mypsychlab
where learning comes to life!

SUCCEED with

Bystander Effect

Find out how you might react in a bystander intervention situation.

(pp. 552–553)

EXPLORE

What phenomenon did primate researcher Frans de Waal capture in this photo of two chimpanzees? (p. 551)

STUDY the Learning Objectives

▶ Recognize why individuals may not help others in distress in group contexts
  • Although common wisdom suggests that there's "safety in numbers," psychological research suggests otherwise. Bystander nonintervention results from two major factors: pluralistic ignorance and diffusion of responsibility. The first affects whether we recognize ambiguous situations as emergencies, and the second affects how we respond once we've identified situations as emergencies.

▶ Distinguish those aspects of a situation that increase or decrease the likelihood of helping
  • People are more likely to help when they're unable to escape from a situation, have adequate time to intervene, are in a good mood, and have been exposed to research on bystander intervention.

▶ Describe the social and individual difference variables that contribute to human aggression
  • A variety of situational variables, including provocation, frustration, aggressive cues, media influences, arousal, and temperature, increase the likelihood of aggression.
  • Men tend to be more physically aggressive than women, although girls are more relationally aggressive than boys;

the southern "culture of honor" may help to explain why murder rates are higher in the southern United States.

DO YOU KNOW THESE TERMS?

- ❑ **pluralistic ignorance** (p. 552)
- ❑ **diffusion of responsibility** (p. 553)
- ❑ **social loafing** (p. 553)
- ❑ **altruism** (p. 555)
- ❑ **enlightenment effect** (p. 555)
- ❑ **aggression** (p. 556)
- ❑ **relational aggression** (p. 557)

ASSESS your knowledge

1. The presence of others makes people (less/ more) likely to help someone in need. (p. 552)

2. Darley and Latané hypothesized the _____ _____, which explains individual nonintervention in certain situations. (p. 552)

3. The two major factors in bystander non-intervention are _____ _____ and _____ _____ _____. (pp. 552–553)

4. When an individual believes that her perception of a situation is unique among a group of people, that individual could be falling prey to _____ _____. (p. 552)

5. As diffusion of responsibility occurs, each individual feels (more/less) accountable for helping someone in need. (p. 553)

6. The phenomenon in which people exert less effort on a task when in a group than when alone is known as _____ _____. (p. 553)

7. Group brainstorming proves to be (more/less) effective than individual brainstorming. (p. 554)

8. Prior exposure to psychological research (can/can't) change an individual's real-world behavior for the better. (p. 555)

9. Aggressive behavior, both at the individual and group levels, is influenced by _____ and _____ factors. (p. 556)

10. Although males tend to be more physically aggressive than females, girls are more likely than boys to engage in _____ aggression. (p. 557)

Attitudes and Persuasion: Changing Minds (pp. 558–564)

STUDY the Learning Objectives

▶ Describe how attitudes relate to behavior
- Attitudes aren't typically good predictors of behavior, although attitudes predict behavior relatively well when they're highly accessible.

▶ Evaluate theoretical accounts of how and when we alter our attitudes
- According to cognitive dissonance theory, a discrepancy between two beliefs leads to an unpleasant state of tension that we're motivated to reduce. In some cases, we reduce this state by altering our attitudes.

▶ Identify common and effective persuasion techniques and how they're exploited by pseudoscientists
- According to dual process models of persuasion, there are two routes to persuasion: a central route that involves careful evaluation of arguments and a peripheral route that relies on superficial cues.
- Effective persuasion techniques include the foot-in-the-door technique, the door-in-the-face technique, and the low-ball technique.

DO YOU KNOW THESE TERMS?

- ❑ **belief** (p. 558)
- ❑ **attitude** (p. 558)
- ❑ **self-monitoring** (p. 559)
- ❑ **cognitive dissonance** (p. 561)
- ❑ **self-perception theory** (p. 563)
- ❑ **impression management theory** (p. 563)
- ❑ **foot-in-the-door technique** (p. 563)
- ❑ **door-in-the-face technique** (p. 563)
- ❑ **low-ball technique** (p. 563)

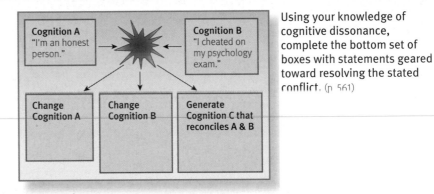

Using your knowledge of cognitive dissonance, complete the bottom set of boxes with statements geared toward resolving the stated conflict. (p. 561)

Match Up the Technique to the Definition (pp. 563–564)

___ **Foot-in-the-door technique**	1. Making an unreasonably large request with the goal of getting someone to agree to a lesser request
___ **Door-in-the-face technique**	2. "Adding on" costs hidden until an agreement to buy the item at lower cost is reached
___ **Low-ball technique**	3. Making a small request of someone followed by a bigger request

mypsychlab
where learning comes to life!

SUCCEED with

Cognitive Dissonance and Attitude Change

Would a monetary reward change your attitude about a situation for the better or worse? (p. 561)

EXPLORE

ASSESS your knowledge

1. The major distinction between a belief and an attitude is that an attitude involves an _____ component. (p. 558)

2. Attitudes are (accurate/inaccurate) predictors of behavior. (pp. 558–559)

3. LaPiere's research showed that people's stated attitudes (did/didn't) accurately predict their situational behavior. (p. 559)

4. Someone who is a (low/high) self-monitor is likely to adapt well to many different social situations. (p. 559)

5. The _____ _____, which makes us more likely to believe something we've heard many times, generally reflects accurate information. (p. 559)

6. Messages are especially persuasive if the messenger seems (similar/different) to us. (p. 560)

7. An unpleasant state of tension between two of more conflicting thoughts is called _____ _____. (p. 561)

8. In Festinger and Carlsmith's test of cognitive dissonance theory, subjects given less money reported enjoying the task (more/less). (p. 563)

9. Once a friend has agreed to help you select paint colors for your dorm room, asking her to help you actually paint the room is an example of the _____ technique. (p. 563)

10. The _____ technique is often practiced by retail stores when they advertise a limited offer price on an item only to exclude mentioning that there are several separately priced items highly desired or essential to making the item purchase complete until you agree to buy the original item. (p. 563)

Prejudice and Discrimination (pp. 565–571)

THINK about what You would do . . .

Imagine that starting today, anyone wearing jeans is considered more important than anyone who wears dress pants. If you were a jeans wearer, how would you react? (p. 566)

How did one school teacher use her pupils' eye color to demonstrate how discrimination occurs? (p. 566)

SUCCEED with mypsychlab

where learning comes to life!

Unconscious Stereotyping

Uncover your unconscious stereotypes about people.

(pp. 566–567)

SIMULATION

List 5 Ideal Conditions for Reducing Prejudice (pp. 570–571)

1 _____
2 _____
3 _____
4 _____
5 _____

STUDY the Learning Objectives

▶ **Distinguish prejudice and stereotypes as beliefs from discrimination as a behavior**
  • Prejudice is coming to a conclusion before we've evaluated all the evidence. Prejudice is accompanied by several other biases, including in-group bias and out-group homogeneity.
  • Discrimination is the act of treating out-group members differently from in-group members.
  • Stereotypes are beliefs about a group's characteristics that we apply to most members of that group. They can be either positive or negative.

▶ **Identify theoretical explanations of the causes of prejudice**
  • There's evidence for various social explanations of prejudice, including scapegoating, belief in a just world, and conformity.

▶ **Identify ways to combat prejudice**
  • Prejudice can be overcome. One of the most effective means of combating prejudice is to make members of different groups work together toward achieving shared overarching goals.

DO YOU KNOW THESE TERMS?

☐ **prejudice** (p. 565)
☐ **adaptive conservatism** (p. 565)
☐ **in-group bias** (p. 565)
☐ **out-group homogeneity** (p. 565)
☐ **discrimination** (p. 565)
☐ **stereotype** (p. 566)
☐ **implicit and explicit stereotypes** (p. 567)
☐ **ultimate attribution error** (p. 569)
☐ **scapegoat hypothesis** (p. 569)
☐ **just-world hypothesis** (p. 569)
☐ **jigsaw classrooms** (p. 570)

ASSESS your knowledge

1. Concluding that all Americans are loud, materialistic, and arrogant without ever having spent time with any of them is an example of _____. (p. 565)

2. The two major biases associated with our tendency to forge alliances with people like ourselves are _____ _____ and _____ _____. (p. 565)

3. Our tendency to view all people outside of our group as highly similar is known as (in-group bias/out-group homogeneity). (p. 565)

4. Believing—without first-hand knowledge—that teens with nose piercings who frequent the local mall are troublemakers is a form of _____, and refusing to serve them in your mall restaurant is a form of _____. (p. 565)

5. A belief that all cheerleaders are ditzy, flirty, and interested only in dating is a _____. (p. 566)

6. The Implicit Association Test (IAT) is a technique to measure _____ _____. (pp. 567–568)

7. The idea that our behaviors and attributions are based on the assumption that all things happen for a reason supports the _____ hypothesis. (p. 569)

8. Sherifs Robber's Cave study, which initially separated two groups of competing 5th graders, used activities requiring _____ across groups to overcome developed prejudices. (p. 570)

9. In Aronson's _____ _____, students are assigned separate tasks that will need to be fitted together with other students' work to complete the project. (p. 570)

10. One condition for reducing prejudice is to (encourage/discourage) group members from becoming friends. (p. 571)

Remember these questions from the beginning of the chapter? Think Again and ask yourself if you would answer them differently based on what you now know about social psychology. (For more detailed explanations, see MyPsychLab.)

▶ How good are we at judging the causes of others' behavior? (p. 536)
▶ What causes mass hysteria over rumors about things like Martian landings? (p. 538)
▶ How do cults persuade people to become fanatics? (pp. 545–546)
▶ Were the Nazis particularly evil, or would we have done the same thing in their boots? (pp. 546–551)
▶ How can a woman be stabbed to death in plain view of many people without anyone coming to her aid? (pp. 552–553)
▶ Does how we act reflect what we believe, or is it the other way around? (pp. 558–559)
▶ What's the best way to persuade others to do something for us? (p. 563)
▶ Are stereotypes always a bad thing? (p. 569)

THINKING Scientifically

Correlation vs. Causation pp. 554, 559

Falsifiability pp. 562, 560

Extraordinary Claims p. 538

Occam's Razor p. 538

Replicability pp. 543, 549, 550, 553, 556, 557, 562

Ruling Out Rival Hypotheses pp. 534, 540, 541, 542, 549, 560, 557, 561, 563, 566, 569

14

Personality: Who We Are

PREVIEW

Think

First, think about these questions. Then, as you read, think again. . . .

▶ Does a similar upbringing lead to similarities in children's personalities?

▶ Did Freud believe that sex is the only important motive in personality?

▶ Would Freud and Skinner have agreed on anything?

▶ How consistent are we in our behavior across situations?

▶ Can we reduce the enormous variation in people's personalities to a mere handful of underlying factors?

▶ Are stereotypes about national character accurate?

▶ Can we use responses to inkblots to infer people's personality traits?

▶ Is criminal profiling scientific?

Oskar Stohr and Jack Yufe, identical twins reared apart, obtained extremely similar scores on personality tests. But the outward expressions of their personality traits were remarkably different. Why?

Born in 1933, Jack and Oskar are alike in two crucial ways. The first is obvious when you meet them: They're identical twins, genetic clones of each other. In contrast to most identical twins, though, they didn't grow up together. Instead, along with several dozen twin pairs studied by Thomas Bouchard and his colleagues at the University of Minnesota during the 1980s and 1990s, Jack and Oskar were separated almost immediately after birth and reunited decades later (Begley & Kasindorf, 1979). There's another similarity: Despite not having known each other for 40 years (they met once only briefly in 1954), Jack and Oskar have nearly identical personalities. Their scores on the Minnesota Multiphasic Personality Inventory, a personality questionnaire we'll discuss later in the chapter, are just about as similar as that of the same person taking the test twice.

That's where the similarities end. Jack was raised by a Jewish family in the Caribbean until age 17, when he moved to Israel and joined a kibbutz. Oskar was raised by his maternal grandmother in a region of the former Czechoslovakia that was under Adolph Hitler's control during World War II. Although Jack's and Oskar's underlying personalities are similar, their political attitudes are as different as night and day. Jack was a deeply religious Jew who enjoyed war movies that portrayed Germans in a bad light. While in Israel, he worked with others to help build the Jewish state. In stark contrast, Oskar was an ardent Nazi and anti-Semite who became a dedicated member of the Hitler Youth movement as World War II drew to a close. So although Jack and Oskar had similar personalities—intense, loyal, and politically engaged—they manifested them in dramatically different ways.

The case of Jack and Oskar is just that—a case. As we learned in Chapter 2, case studies have their limitations. For one thing, it's hard to know how far we can generalize Jack and Oskar's case to other twin pairs, let alone to all other people. Yet like some case studies, Jack and Oskar's story raises a host of fascinating questions that psychologists can examine using rigorous research designs. Why were Jack and Oskar so similar in personality despite having had no contact with each other for decades? What motivated both of them to pursue political causes? How can two people with such similar personalities end up with such dissimilar political attitudes? How did environmental influences shape the expression of their personalities?

The answers to these questions, as we'll soon discover, aren't simple. Although most of us believe we can explain why people act as they do, we're wrong at least as often as we're right (Nisbett & Wilson, 1977).

Few are more confident in their abilities to explain behavior than radio and television "advice experts," many of whom liberally sprinkle their shows with off-the-cuff psychological accounts for people's behavior (Heaton & Wilson, 1995; Williams & Ceci, 1998). Consider the following statements typical of those offered by talk show psychologists: "He murdered all of those people because he had an unhappy childhood." "She overeats because she has low self-esteem." "He cheats on his wife because he's trying to prove his masculinity."

Intuitively appealing as these explanations are, we should treat them with a dose of healthy skepticism, particularly when they lack supporting evidence. As we learned in the Prologue, we must beware of *single-cause explanations* of human behavior. When trying to uncover the root causes of people's actions, we must keep in mind that personality is multiply determined. Indeed, personality is the unimaginably complicated outcome of dozens of causal influences: genetic, intrauterine (within the womb), parenting, peer influences, life stressors, and plain old luck, both good and bad. Tempting as it is to invoke single-cause explanations, we should avoid the errors of radio and television advice experts.

Personality: What Is It and How Can We Study It?

In Chapter 13, we learned how the social context can influence our behavior in profound ways. There, we also met up with the *fundamental attribution error,* the tendency to attribute too much of others' behavior to their personalities and not enough to the situations they confront.

With this critical caution in mind, most psychologists agree that there *is* such a thing as personality; we aren't exclusively a product of the social influences impinging on us at any given moment. Most also agree with the American psychologist Gordon Allport (1966) that personality consists of **traits:** relatively enduring predispositions that influence our behavior across many situations (Funder, 1991; Tellegen, 1991). Personality traits—such as introversion, aggressiveness, and conscientiousness—account in part for consistencies in our behavior, across both time and situations.

How do personality traits originate? We'll first approach this question from the vantage point of behavior-genetic studies of personality and move on to various theories of personality, including Freudian and behavioral models, that offer competing answers to this question. As we'll discover, all of these theories strive to explain *both commonalities and differences* among people in their personality traits. For example, they try to account for not only how we develop a conscience, but also why some of us have a stronger conscience than others.

Radio and talk show personalities, like Dr. Laura Schlessinger ("Dr. Laura"), often provide single-cause explanations for complex, multiply determined psychological problems.

STUDYING PERSONALITY: NOMOTHETIC VERSUS IDIOGRAPHIC APPROACHES

There are two major approaches to studying personality. These approaches differ in emphasis, and each has its strengths and weaknesses. A **nomothetic approach** strives to understand personality by identifying general laws that govern the behavior of all individuals. Most modern personality research, including almost all of the research we'll examine in this chapter, is nomothetic because it attempts to derive principles that explain the thinking, emotions, and behaviors of all people. This approach typically allows for generalization across individuals, but limited insight into the unique patterning of attributes within one person.

In contrast, an **idiographic approach** (think of "idiosyncratic") strives to understand personality by identifying the unique configuration of characteristics and life history experiences within a person. Most case studies are idiographic. Gordon Allport (1965) presented a classic example of the idiographic approach in his book *Letters from Jenny,* which features an analysis of 301 letters written by one woman over 12 years. In these letters Allport uncovered themes that characterized Jenny's attitudes toward her son, Ross. When Jenny wrote about Ross in positive terms, themes of her own early life often emerged; when she wrote about him in negative terms, themes of her unappreciated sacrifices for him often emerged. The idiographic approach reveals the richly detailed tapestry of one person's life but allows limited generalizability to other people. Moreover, it generates hypotheses that are often difficult to falsify, because these hypotheses are frequently post hoc ("after the fact") explanations about events that have already occurred.

traits
relatively enduring predispositions that influence our behavior across many situations

nomothetic approach
approach to personality that focuses on identifying general laws that govern the behavior of all individuals

idiographic approach
approach to personality that focuses on identifying the unique configuration of characteristics and life history experiences within a person

Falsifiability

THE CAUSES OF PERSONALITY DIFFERENCES: HOW WE COME TO BE

Why are some of us flamboyant risk takers and others retiring wallflowers? Psychologists use behavior-genetic methods to disentangle three broad influences on behavior:

- *genetic* factors;
- *shared environmental* factors—experiences that make individuals within the same family more alike. If parents try to make both of their children more outgoing by reinforcing

Bill Gates, a later-born, exhibits many of the features reported by Frank Sulloway to be characteristic of later-borns, including rebelliousness and a willingness to question authority. It's not clear, however, whether Sulloway's findings extend beyond his sample of scientists.

Replicability

factoid

One pair of male identical twins separated at birth in the Minnesota study (both named "Jim" by their adoptive parents) both constructed similar looking tree-houses in their backyards, named their dogs "Toy," and were married twice, both to women named Linda and Betty. Another pair of separated adult male identical twins in that study both flushed toilets before and after using them, and a separated female adult identical twin pair both attempted to conquer their fear of the ocean by entering the water backward up to their ankles and then turning around (Segal, 1999). Yet because these are merely anecdotes and could reflect chance coincidences, we need to turn to systematic studies of reared apart twins, such as those described in the section "Reared-Apart Twins."

them with attention and they succeed in doing so, their parenting in this case is a shared environmental factor; and

- *nonshared environmental* factors—experiences that make individuals within the same family less alike. If a parent treats one child more affectionately than another, and as a consequence this child ends up with higher self-esteem, the parenting in this case is a nonshared environmental factor. For most of the twentieth century, most psychologists put their money on shared environmental influences as causal factors, as they believed that the most important environmental influences are transmitted from parents to all of their children (Harris, 1994; Rowe, 1991).

Researching Personality: Overview of Twin and Adoption Studies. To differentiate among these three influences, behavior geneticists have applied twin studies and adoption studies (see Chapter 3) to the study of personality. Because identical (monozygotic) twins are more similar genetically than fraternal (dizygotic) twins, a higher correlation of a trait among identical than fraternal twins suggests a genetic influence. In contrast, identical twin correlations that are equal to or less than fraternal twin correlations suggest the absence of a genetic component, and instead point to environmental influences.

Reared-Together Twins: Genes or Environment? From the findings of one major twin study of personality, we can see that numerous personality traits—including anxiety proneness, impulse control, and traditionalism—are influenced substantially by genetic factors (see the left side of **Table 14.1**). This study examined identical twin pairs who were raised together and fraternal twins who were either both male or both female (Tellegen et al., 1988). A number of researchers have replicated these findings in other twin samples from intact families (Loehlin, 1992; Plomin, 2004).

Yet the results in Table 14.1 impart another lesson. What do the identical twin correlations have in common? The answer is so self-evident that we can easily overlook it: All of these correlations are substantially less than 1.0. This finding demonstrates that nonshared environment plays an important role in personality (Plomin & Daniels, 1987; Turkheimer, 2000). If heritability were 1.0 (that is, 100%), the identical twin correlations would also be 1.0. Because they're considerably less than 1.0, nonshared environmental influences must play a key role in personality. Regrettably, these twin findings don't tell us what these nonshared environmental influences are.

Birth Order: Does It Matter? As we learned in Chapter 10, some psychologists have hypothesized that peer influences account for much of the nonshared environmental component in personality (Harris, 1995). Birth order is another possible nonshared environmental influence for twins and nontwins alike. Many popular books, such as *The New Birth Order Book* (Leman, 1998), claim that firstborns tend toward achievement, middle-borns toward diplomacy, and later-borns toward risk taking. Yet virtually all of these claims are exaggerated, because most researchers have failed to uncover strong or consistent associations between birth order and personality (Ernst & Angst, 1983; Jefferson, Herbst, & McCrae, 1998).

Nevertheless, popular claims regarding the importance of birth order received a boost from the work of science historian Frank Sulloway (1996). Sulloway examined the association between birth order and attitudes toward revolutionary scientific theories, such as Copernicus' theory of the sun-centered universe and Darwin's theory of natural selection. Sulloway asked panels of historians to evaluate how 4,000 scientists reacted to these and other scientific controversies when their developers initially proposed them between the years 1543 and 1967. He found that later-borns were 3.1 times more likely than firstborns to favor revolutionary ideas; for extremely radical ideas, this ratio increased to 4.7. In contrast, firstborns usually supported the status quo. Sulloway's findings raise the possibility that birth order is an important nonshared environmental influence, but it's not clear how much we can generalize his findings to nonscientific disciplines. Moreover, some scientists have raised ques-

Table 14.1 Comparison of Correlations of Twins Reared Together and Apart for Selected Personality Traits.

	Twins Reared Together		Twins Reared Apart	
	Identical twin correlation	Fraternal twin correlation	Identical twin correlation	Fraternal twin correlation
Anxiety proneness	.52	.24	.61	.27
Aggression	.43	.14	.46	.06
Alienation	.55	.38	.55	.38
Impulse control	.41	.06	.50	.03
Emotional well-being	.58	.23	.48	.18
Traditionalism	.50	.47	.53	.39
Achievement orientation	.36	.07	.36	.07

(*Source:* Tellegen et al., 1988)

tions about Sulloway's methods. For example, when rating whether scientists were revolutionaries, his panel of scientists may not have been blind to their birth order (Harris, 1998).

Reared-Apart Twins: Shining a Spotlight on Genes. Table 14.1 may tempt us to conclude that the similarities between identical twins are primarily a result of their similar upbringing rather than their shared genes. But this explanation is refuted by studies of identical and fraternal twins raised apart.

In an extraordinary investigation, researchers at the University of Minnesota spent more than two decades accumulating the largest sample of identical and fraternal twins—about 130 in total—who were reared apart, sometimes in different countries (Bouchard et al., 1990). Many had been separated almost immediately after birth and reunited for the first time decades later in the Minneapolis–St. Paul airport. Jack and Oskar, whom we met at the outset of this chapter, were among those in the "Minnesota Twins" study, as it came to be known.

Before psychologists conducted these studies, some prominent social scientists predicted confidently that identical twins reared apart would barely resemble one another in personality. Here's one example from a widely used personality textbook:

> Imagine the enormous differences that would be found in the personalities of twins with identical genetic endowments if they were raised apart in two different families or, even more striking, in two totally different cultures. Through social learning, vast differences develop among people in their reactions to most of the stimuli they face in daily life. (Mischel, 1981, p. 311)

Were these social scientists right? The right side of Table 14.1 displays some of the principal findings from the Minnesota twin study. Two findings in the right side of this table cry out loud and clear. First, identical twins reared apart tend to be strikingly similar in their personality traits. They're also far more similar than fraternal twins reared apart (Tellegen et al., 1988). A more convincing case for the role of genetic influences on personality would be hard to come by.

Second, when comparing the results in the left and right sides of Table 14.1, it's evident that identical twins reared apart are about as similar as identical twins reared together! This finding suggests that shared environment plays little or no role in the causes of adult personality. Behavior-genetic researchers have replicated this surprising result in other twin samples (Loehlin, 1992; Pederson, Plomin, & McClearn, 1988).

Ruling Out Rival Hypotheses

Ruling Out Rival Hypotheses

These twin brothers, Gerald Levey and Mark Newman, separated at birth, both became firefighters (one in New Jersey and the other in Queens, New York).

Replicability

This finding is sufficiently remarkable that it bears repeating: *Shared environment plays little or no role in adult personality.* In many respects, this may be the most stunning finding in recent personality psychology, although it's yet to exert a substantial impact on popular psychology (Harris, 2006; Rowe, 1994). Shared environment plays some role in childhood personality, but this role generally dissipates as we grow older. By the time we reach adulthood, the impact of shared environment on our personalities is weak at best (Plomin & McClearn, 1993). This finding suggests that if parents try to make all of their children outgoing, for example, by exposing them to friendly children and encouraging them to attend parties, they're likely to fail in the long run.

Adoption Studies: Further Separating Genes and Environment. *Adoption studies* (see Chapter 3) permit investigators to separate the effects of genes and environment by examining children who were separated at an early age from their biological families. The finding that an adopted child's personality is similar to that of his or her biological parents points to genetic influence; in contrast, the finding that an adopted child's personality is similar to that of his or her adoptive parents points to shared environmental influence.

In one adoption study, Sandra Scarr and her colleagues examined the personality trait of neuroticism (Scarr, Webber, Weinberg, & Wittig, 1981). As we'll discover later in this chapter, people with high levels of neuroticism tend to be tense and high-strung, whereas those with low levels of neuroticism tend to be mellow and calm. In this investigation, children had been separated from their biological parents shortly after birth and adopted into the homes of biologically unrelated individuals.

As we can see in **Table 14.2,** the correlations between biological parents (in this case, mothers) and their adopted-away children are actually slightly higher than the correlations between adoptive parents and their adopted children *even though the biological parents had essentially no environmental contact with their children after birth* (Scarr et al., 1981). These findings have been replicated by other investigators and for other personality traits (Loehlin, 1992). Moreover, Table 14.2 reveals that, unlike biological siblings raised in the same household, adoptive siblings raised in the same household exhibit almost no similarity in personality. This finding further undermines the hypothesis that shared environment is influential in adult personality: Being brought up together doesn't make brothers or sisters more alike.

Table 14.2 Correlations among Various Relatives in an Adoption Study of Neuroticism.

Correlation	
Mother and biological child	.21
Mother and adopted child	.12
Biologically related children	.28
Adoptively related children	.05

(*Source:* Scarr et al., 1981)

Replicability

NEW FRONTIERS
Molecular Genetic Studies of Personality

Twin and adoption studies provide remarkably useful information concerning the heritability of personality traits. Nevertheless, they tell us little about *which* genes are related to personality. Recently, researchers have turned to **molecular genetic studies,** which allow them to pinpoint which genes are associated with specific personality traits (Plomin, DeFries, McClearn, & Rutter, 1997). These studies rest on two premises:

(1) Genes code for proteins that in turn often influence the functioning of neurotransmitters, like dopamine and serotonin (see Chapter 3).

(2) The functioning of many neurotransmitters is associated with certain personality traits (Cloninger, 1987). For example, people with low levels of serotonin activity tend to be more impulsive and aggressive than other persons (Dolan, Anderson, & Deakin, 2001).

Although the methodology of molecular genetic studies is complicated, most of them work by examining the linkage between specific genes and known genetic

molecular genetic studies
investigations that allow researchers to pinpoint genes associated with specific personality traits

markers on each chromosome. At this point, there have been few consistently replicated associations between specific genes and personality traits.

One potential exception is the connection between *novelty seeking*—a trait that refers to the tendency to search out and enjoy new experiences—and genetic markers of the dopamine system, which is intimately involved in reward seeking (see Chapter 3). Several researchers have reported significant associations between measures of novelty seeking and various genes influencing the dopamine receptor. Nevertheless, there have been several failures to replicate these findings (Joensson et al., 1998; Sullivan et al., 1998). In addition, numerous investigators have reported a linkage between symptoms of attention-deficit/hyperactivity disorder, a childhood disorder associated with high novelty seeking (see Chapter 15), and genes influencing the dopamine system. Although many of these findings are promising, they again haven't always been replicated (Waldman & Gizer, 2006). So we should be cautious before accepting claims of linkage between specific genes and personality traits.

Regrettably, the popular press has often rushed to judgment, presenting preliminary findings from molecular genetic studies as conclusive. For example, in 1995 an Associated Press reporter wrote, "Two studies provide the first confirmed association between a particular gene and a normal personality trait—in this case, a characteristic scientists call 'novelty seeking.'" Yet only a year later, scientists found that the gene in question, called DRD4, was no more common in a group of alcoholics who received high scores on tests of risk taking than in a group of cautious comparison participants. Later researchers reported mixed results for the DRD4 gene and novelty seeking (Paterson, Sunohara, & Kennedy, 1999; Sullivan et al., 1998). So despite the promise of molecular genetic studies, we must await replications in independent laboratories before placing too much trust in individual findings.

Replicability

Replicability

Behavior-Genetic Studies: A Note of Caution.

Researchers using twin studies have found that genes influence a variety of behaviors often associated with personality traits. These behaviors include divorce (McGue & Lykken, 1992), religiosity (Waller et al., 1990), and even the tendency to watch television (Plomin et al., 1990). Even many social attitudes, including those concerning the death penalty and nudist colonies, are moderately heritable (Martin et al., 1986). For each of these characteristics, identical twin correlations are considerably higher than fraternal twin correlations.

Do these findings mean, as the popular press often implies, that there are specific genes for divorce, religiosity, death penalty attitudes, and the like? Don't bet on it. Genes code for proteins, not specific behaviors or attitudes. It's far more likely that genes influence behaviors and attitudes in a highly indirect fashion (N. Block, 1995). As we learned from Jack and Oskar, genes probably influence certain personality traits—like deep emotions—but the environment influences how these traits play out in our lives, such as becoming either an observant Jew or a passionate anti-Semite. The pathways from genes to behavior are often lengthy and circuitous. So when we hear media reports of a "gay gene" or a "divorce gene," we should be skeptical. Although there are probably genetic influences on homosexuality (see Chapter 11) and even divorce, it's unlikely that a single gene codes directly for these and other multifaceted behaviors (Nigg & Goldsmith, 1994).

Twin studies demonstrate that religiosity has a substantial genetic component. But does that finding mean there are specific genes for religiosity?

Psychoanalytic Theory:
The Controversial Legacy of
Sigmund Freud and His Followers

Long before researchers stepped in to conduct controlled studies of the causes of personality, psychologists, psychiatrists, and many other thinkers had generated theoretical models that sought to explain the development and workings of personality. These models addressed three key questions:

(1) How do our personalities develop?

(2) What are the core driving forces in our personalities or, more informally, what makes us tick?

(3) What accounts for individual differences in personality?

We'll examine and evaluate four influential models of personality, starting with the granddaddy of them all: Sigmund Freud's psychoanalytic theory.

PSYCHOANALYTIC THEORY: THE FOUNDATION OF FREUD'S THINKING

Sigmund Freud, the founder of psychoanalysis, is simultaneously the most worshipped and most criticized figure in personality psychology.

To most nonpsychologists, psychoanalytic theory is virtually synonymous with the writings of a Viennese physician named Sigmund Freud (1856–1939). American psychology has long had a love–hate relationship with Freud, with his influence waning in recent decades. Nevertheless, even Freud's most vocal detractors acknowledge that he was an ingenious thinker. In fact, one major challenge in evaluating psychoanalytic theory lies in separating the brilliance of Freud the theorist from the scientific soundness of Freud's theory. Freudian theory has been enormously influential in the thinking of psychologists and laypersons, and for that reason alone his ideas merit a careful and balanced look (Kramer, 2007).

Many people don't know that Freud's training wasn't in psychology or psychiatry—specialties that scarcely existed in his day—but in neurology. In his early work, for example, he discovered the testes of the eel (readers of a Freudian orientation may find it difficult to resist speculating on the significance of this fact!).

somatogenic
physiologically caused

catharsis
feeling of relief following a dramatic outpouring of emotion

psychogenic
psychologically caused

psychic determinism
the assumption that all psychological events have a cause

A Clash of Two Paradigms: Mind over Body. Largely as a consequence of his neurological background, Freud thought of mental disorders as **somatogenic,** that is, physiologically caused. Yet his views changed dramatically in 1885, when he spent a year in Paris studying under neurologist Jean Charcot. Charcot had been treating patients, most of them women afflicted with a malady then known as "grande hysteria." Grande hysterics exhibited a motley assortment of spectacular physical symptoms: paralyses of the arms and legs, fainting spells, seizures, and even false pregnancies, a remark-able symptom known as *pseudocyesis*. Careful investigation of these symptoms failed to turn up any physical causes, and some of these symptoms made little or no physiological sense. For exam-ple, some of Charcot's patients exhibited *glove anesthesia*, which is the loss of sensation in the hand alone, with no accompanying loss of sensation in the arm (see **Figure 14.1**). Glove anesthesia defies standard neurological principles because the sensory path-ways extending to the hand run through the arm. If the hand lacks sensation, the arm should too. These observations, among others, shattered Freud's belief in the somatogenic model.

The Happenstance of Hypnosis. Freud and Charcot also hap-pened on what appeared to be a momentous discovery. When they hypnotized their patients, many reported a traumatic experience, such as sexual abuse in childhood, which they'd seemingly forgotten. One of Freud's patients, a young woman named Dora, suffered from myriad physical symptoms, including severe short-ness of breath. In treatment, Freud claimed to trace the origins of this symptom to Dora's repressed childhood memory of her father breathing heavily during sexual intercourse with his wife (Dolnick, 1998). Freud and Charcot further found that patients' recollections of early trauma were often accompanied by a **catharsis**—a feel-ing of relief following a dramatic outpouring of emotion (see Chapter 12). This catharsis was usually followed by a sudden disappearance of these patients' symptoms.

This and related observations led Freud to conclude that many mental disorders weren't somatogenic, but **psychogenic,** that is, caused by psychological factors. This con-troversial conclusion formed the cornerstone on which psychoanalytic theory rests.

A painting of Charcot demonstrating a patient with grande hysteria—who is fainting in response to his suggestions—in front of fellow physicians and staff. Freud was so fond of this painting that he displayed it in his therapy room.

APPLY YOUR THINKING
Do Freud's early observations provide a sturdy cornerstone for psychoanalytic theory or a shaky one? Why?

CORE ASSUMPTIONS OF PSYCHOANALYTIC THEORY

Psychoanalytic theory rests on three core assumptions (Brenner, 1973; Loevinger, 1987). These assumptions, especially the second and third ones, set this theory apart from most other personality theories.

Core Assumption 1: Psychic Determinism. Freudians believe in **psychic determinism:** the assumption that all psychological events have a cause. We aren't free to choose our actions, they claim, because we're at the mercy of powerful forces that lie outside of our awareness. Dreams, neurotic symptoms, and "Freudian slips" of the tongue (see Prologue) are all reflec-tions of deep psychological conflict bubbling up to the surface (**Table 14.3**).

Core Assumption 2: Symbolic Meaning. For Freudians, no action, no matter how seemingly trivial, is meaningless. All are attributable to preceding mental causes, even if we can't always fig-ure out what these causes are. If while teaching a class, your male professor manages to crack a long piece of chalk in two, some might be inclined to disregard this action as uninteresting. Rest assured, however, that most Freudians would find an explanation for it. Specifically, they'd be likely to argue that this piece of chalk is *symbolic* of something else; perhaps something sexual in nature.

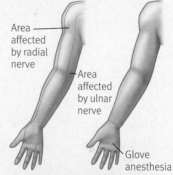
Area affected by radial nerve

Area affected by ulnar nerve

Glove anesthesia

Figure 14.1 "Glove" Anesthesia. Freud noted that some of the symptoms exhibited by patients with hysteria made little or no physiological sense. Patients with glove anesthesia, for example, experience a loss of feeling in the hand alone *(right)*, despite the fact that the nerve pathways extending to the hand traverse the entire arm *(left)*.

Table 14.3 Examples of "Freudian Slips" from Notes by Freud.

"A member of the House of Commons referred to another as the honorable member for Central Hell instead of Central Hull."

"A soldier said to a friend that 'I wish there were a thousand men mortified on that hill' instead of 'fortified on that hill.'"

"A lady, attempting to compliment another, says that 'I am sure that you must have thrown this delightful hat together' instead of 'sewn it together,' thereby betraying her thought that the hat was poorly made."

"A lady states that few gentlemen know how to value the 'ineffectual' qualities in a woman, as opposed to 'intellectual.'"

(*Source:* Freud, 1901)

(© ScienceCartoonsPlus.com)

Yet even strict Freudians agree that not all behaviors are symbolic. In response to a questioner who asked Freud why he enjoyed smoking cigars, Freud supposedly responded that "a cigar is sometimes just a cigar" (some scholars, however, have suggested that this quotation is an urban legend; see Chapter 13). Although the shape of a cigar resembles that of a bodily organ, even most ardent psychoanalysts—indeed, perhaps Freud himself—would acknowledge that symbolic interpretation can go too far.

Core Assumption 3: Unconscious Motivation. Freudians argue for the crucial importance of *unconscious motivation*. According to Freud (1933), we rarely understand why we do what we do, although we quite readily cook up explanations for our actions after the fact. Some authors have likened the Freudian view of the mind (Freud, 1923) to an iceberg, with the unconscious being the vast and largely uncharted area of the psyche submerged entirely underwater (see **Figure 14.2**). The conscious component of the mind is merely the "tip of the iceberg," barely visible above the water's surface. For Freud, the unconscious is of immensely greater importance in the causes of our personality than the conscious.

THE THREE AGENCIES OF THE HUMAN PSYCHE

Freud (1933, 1935) hypothesized that the human psyche consists of three *agencies* or components: id, ego, and superego. For Freud, the interplay among these three agencies gives rise to our personalities, and differences in the strength of these agencies help to account for individual differences in personality.

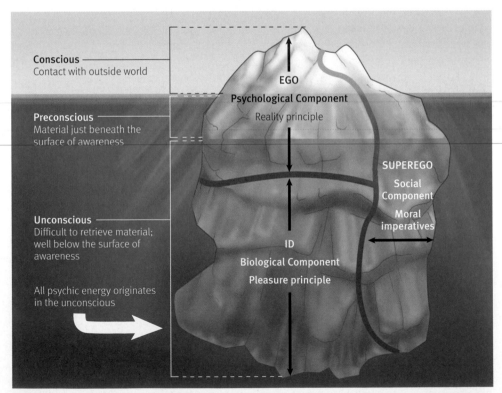

Figure 14.2 Freud's Model of Personality Structure. According to some authors, Freud's conception of personality is analogous to an iceberg, with the conscious mind being the tip barely visible above the surface and the unconscious being the vast submerged area entirely underwater. (Freud also discussed a third area portrayed in this diagram, the preconscious, which lies between the two.) Nevertheless, we shouldn't take the iceberg metaphor too literally (indeed, Freud himself apparently never used it), because according to Freud different aspects of personality are in constant interaction.

The Id: Basic Instincts. The **id,** according to Freud, is the reservoir of our most primitive impulses, a seething cauldron of passions and desires that provides the impetus for much of our behavior. The id is entirely unconscious; it's the part of the iceberg submerged underwater. It contains a variety of drives, particularly the sexual drive or *libido* (see Chapter 11) and the aggressive drive. Although critics have sometimes accused Freud of saying that "everything is sex," this allegation is only partly true. Freud believed the libido to be of crucial importance in the development of personality, but he maintained that other impulses, particularly aggression, play significant shaping roles. According to Freud, the id operates by means of the **pleasure principle.** The pleasure principle strives for immediate gratification: The word *no* isn't in the id's vocabulary.

The Ego: The Boss. The **ego** is the boss of the personality, its principal decision maker. The ego's primary tasks are interacting with the real world and finding ways to resolve the competing demands of the other two psychic agencies. We shouldn't confuse the Freudian ego with the ego, or inflated sense of self-worth, that's crept into everyday language. In fact, Freudians would say that most egotists have poorly developed egos, because people with grossly inflated self-esteem are typically compensating for deep-seated inferiority feelings.

The ego, unlike the id, is governed by the **reality principle.** The reality principle strives to delay gratification until it can find an appropriate outlet. If you find today's introductory psychology lecture to be inordinately frustrating, your id may want to satisfy your aggressive impulses by screaming out loud in class. This is the pleasure principle rearing its ugly head. But the ego's reality principle requires that you delay this gratification until you can find a socially appropriate outlet for your aggression, such as throwing darts at a dartboard—ideally one featuring your professor's face as the bull's-eye—when you get home from class.

The Superego: Moral Standards. The **superego** is our sense of morality. The term literally means "above ego," and Freud conceptualized this agency much like a judgmental parent looking down upon the ego. This psychic agency contains the sense of right and wrong we've internalized from our interactions with society, particularly our parents.

How the Psychic Agencies Interact. According to Freud, the interaction among these psychic agencies is occurring within all of us, all the time. It's almost as though a quiet but continuously running play featuring three characters were being acted out within us (see **Figure 14.3**).

The Three Agencies in Conflict. Freud (1935) hypothesized that psychological distress results from conflict among these three agencies. Much of the time id, ego, and superego interact harmoniously, much like a chamber music trio playing in perfect synchrony. Yet the agendas of these agencies sometimes collide. If you're attracted to your best friend's partner, your id is at odds with your ego and (hopefully!) your superego. You might fantasize about a romantic fling with this person (id), but feel both frightened about what would happen to you (ego) and stricken with pangs of guilt about hurting your friend's feelings (superego) if you were foolish enough to act on your impulses.

The Three Agencies during Sleep. For an intimate view of the three psychic agencies in action, we have only to look to the third of our lives we spend asleep. Dreams, Freud (1900) suggested, are the "royal road to the unconscious mind" (also see Chapter 5) because they reveal the inner workings of our id in action. At the same time, dreams illustrate how ego and superego cooperate to keep the id's wishes in check. According to Freud, all dreams are *wish fulfillments,* that is, expressions of the id's impulses. Because dreams are sometimes bizarre, Freud argued that the wishes in our dreams are disguised with symbols. When the superego perceives the id's desires to be threatening, it "commands" the ego to plaster over these wishes with symbols. We sometimes draw these symbols from our distant past, but in other cases we draw them from what Freud called the "day residue," the

Figure 14.3 Id, Ego, and Superego.
Many works of art portray an individual trying to make a difficult moral decision, with a devil on one shoulder—urging immoral behavior—and an angel—urging moral behavior—on the other. Freudians would say that such artworks capture the distinction among ego (the person trying to make the decision), id (demon), and superego (angel).

id
reservoir of our most primitive impulses, including sex and aggression

pleasure principle
tendency of the id to strive for immediate gratification

ego
psyche's executive and principal decision maker

reality principle
tendency of the ego to postpone gratification until it can find an appropriate outlet

superego
our sense of morality

Most dream dictionaries available in bookstores imply that there are universal meanings for dream symbols. Even most psychoanalysts reject this claim.

accumulation of events we experienced on the day of the dream. So rather than having an explicit dream about a romantic encounter with a classmate, a male might dream of driving a car through a tunnel, a favorite Freudian symbolic representation of sex.

But beware: Popular psychology books notwithstanding, most Freudians don't regard dream symbols as universal. If we were to peruse the section of our local bookstores devoted to dreams, we'd find several dictionaries of dream symbols. One such dictionary (Schoenewolf, 1997) offers the following rules for interpreting dream symbols: a duck, icicle, spear, umbrella, or tie symbolizes the penis; a pocket, tunnel, jug, or gate symbolizes the vagina; and a kangaroo symbolizes sexual vitality (please don't ask us to explain this one). These and other books of dream symbols (Ackroyd, 1993) vastly oversimplify Freudian theory, because Freudians believe that different symbols often mean different things to different dreamers.

ANXIETY AND THE DEFENSE MECHANISMS

A principal function of the ego, according to Freud, is to contend with threats from the outside world. When danger is present, the ego experiences anxiety, signaling it to undertake corrective actions. Sometimes these actions are straightforward, like jumping out of the way of an oncoming car. In other cases, we can't do much to correct the situation, so we must change our *perception* of it.

In these cases, the ego engages in **defense mechanisms:** unconscious maneuvers intended to minimize anxiety. The concept of defense mechanisms has crept into our everyday language ("Stop being so defensive"). Contrary to popular belief, Freud held that defense mechanisms are essential for psychological health. Indeed, the person lacking any defense mechanisms would be at the mercy of uncontrollable anxiety. Nonetheless, an excessive reliance on one or two defense mechanisms, Freud insisted, is pathological. Freud and his daughter, Anna, who became a prominent psychoanalyst in her own right, outlined the principal defense mechanisms (A. Freud, 1937). We'll present a brief tour of them here (see **Table 14.4**).

Table 14.4 Major Freudian Defense Mechanisms and an Example of Each.

Defense Mechanism	Example
Repression	A person who witnesses a traumatic combat scene finds himself unable to remember it
Denial	A mother who loses a child in a car accident insists her child is alive
Regression	A college student starts sucking his thumb during a difficult exam
Reaction-formation	A married woman who's sexually attracted to a coworker experiences hatred and revulsion toward him
Projection	A man with powerful unconscious sexual impulses toward females complains that other women are always "after him"
Displacement	A baseball outfielder throws his glove to the ground in anger after dropping a routine fly ball
Rationalization	A political candidate who loses an election convinces herself that she didn't really want the position after all
Intellectualization	A woman whose husband cheats on her reassures herself that "according to evolutionary psychologists, men are naturally sexually promiscuous, so there's nothing to worry about."
Identification with the aggressor	A college basketball player who initially fears his tyrannical coach comes to like him and adopts his dictatorial qualities
Sublimation	A boy who enjoys beating up on other children grows up to become a professional boxer

defense mechanisms
unconscious maneuvers intended to minimize anxiety

- **Repression** is the most critical defense mechanism in psychoanalytic theory. It's the *motivated forgetting* of emotionally threatening memories or impulses. Unlike the types of forgetting we discussed in Chapter 7, repression is presumably triggered by anxiety: We forget because we want to forget. According to Freud, we repress unhappy childhood memories to avoid the pain they engender. This repression leads all of us to experience *childhood amnesia* (Chapter 7), the inability to remember anything prior to about age three and a half (Fivush & Hudson, 1990). Early childhood, Freud contended, is too anxiety provoking for us to remember fully. We now know this explanation is unlikely, largely because investigators have identified childhood amnesia in other animals, including mice and rats (Berk, Vigorito, & Miller, 1979; Richardson, Riccio, & Axiotis, 1986). A committed Freudian could presumably argue that mice and other rodents also repress traumatic memories of early childhood (perhaps memories of seeing too many cats?), but Occam's razor renders this explanation implausible.

- In contrast to repression, which is the motivated forgetting of distressing internal experiences, **denial** is the motivated forgetting of distressing external experiences. We most often observe denial in people with psychotic disorders, such as schizophrenia (see Chapter 15), although normal individuals undergoing extreme stress may occasionally engage in denial too. It's not uncommon, for example, for the relatives of individuals who have recently died in a tragic accident to insist that their loved ones must somehow, somewhere, be alive.

- **Regression** is the act of returning psychologically to a younger age, typically early childhood, when life was simpler and safer. Older children who've long since stopped sucking their thumbs sometimes suddenly resume thumb sucking under stress.

- **Reaction-formation** is the transformation of an anxiety-provoking emotion into its opposite. The observable emotion we see actually reflects the opposite emotion the person feels unconsciously. Freud contended that we can infer the presence of reaction-formation by the intensity with which the person expresses the emotion, as this emotion displays an exaggerated or "phony" quality. When watching the "play within a play" in Shakespeare's *Hamlet*, the queen observed "The lady doth protest too much," in response to a woman whose expressed love to her husband seemed insincere. The queen was perceptive, as the woman later poisoned her husband.

  In a remarkable study, Henry Adams and his colleagues found that males with high levels of *homophobia*—a dislike (not technically a fear, as the word implies) of homosexuals—showed significantly *greater* increases in penile circumference than males with low levels of homophobia in response to sexually explicit videotapes of homosexual stimuli, such as men engaging in sex with other men (Adams, Wright, & Lohr, 1996). This finding is tantalizingly consistent with the Freudian concept of reaction-formation; some homophobics may harbor unconscious homosexual impulses that they find unacceptable and transform them into a conscious dislike of homosexuals. Still, there's an alternative interpretation for this finding: Research suggests that anxiety can increase sexual arousal and perhaps trigger penile erections (Barlow, Sakheim, & Beck, 1983). Future investigators will need to rule out this rival hypothesis.

- **Projection** is the unconscious attribution of our negative characteristics to others. According to psychoanalysts, people with paranoia are projecting their unconscious hostility onto others. Deep down they wish to harm others, but because they can't accept these impulses they perceive others as wanting to harm them.

- Closely related to projection is **displacement,** in which we direct an impulse from a socially unacceptable target onto a safer and more socially acceptable target. After a frustrating day at work, we may pound our fist against the punching bag at the gym rather than into the faces of our annoying coworkers.

- **Rationalization** provides a reasonable-sounding explanation for our unreasonable behaviors or failures. Some people who receive *posthypnotic suggestions* (see Chapter 5) to perform bizarre actions engage in rationalizations to explain these actions. For example, a subject given a posthypnotic suggestion to bark like a dog after emerging from hypnosis may do so. When the hypnotist asks him why he barked for no apparent reason, he may rationalize his behavior: "Hmmm . . . I was just thinking about how much I missed my dog, so I felt like barking" (see **Figure 14.4**).

repression
motivated forgetting of emotionally threatening memories or impulses

denial
motivated forgetting of distressing external experiences

regression
the act of returning psychologically to a younger, and typically simpler and safer, age

Occam's Razor

Figure 14.4 "Sour Grapes." According to psychoanalysts, rationalization often involves a psychological minimization of previously desired outcomes. This etching from Aesop's fables illustrates one example of rationalization, namely, the famous "sour grapes" phenomenon: The fox, who can't reach the previously desired grapes, tells himself, "These grapes are much too green and sour. Even if I could reach them, I would not eat them."

Ruling Out Rival Hypotheses

reaction-formation
transformation of an anxiety-provoking emotion into its opposite

projection
unconscious attribution of our negative characteristics to others

displacement
directing an impulse from a socially unacceptable target onto a safer and more socially acceptable target

rationalization
providing a reasonable-sounding explanation for unreasonable behaviors or failures

Elizabeth Smart, shown with her mother and father, was abducted in 2002 in Utah at the age of 15 and found alive 9 months later. Some experts suggest that Smart suffered from Stockholm syndrome, which might explain why she elected not to escape from her kidnappers. Yet others have disputed this assertion, arguing that Stockholm syndrome is often applied too loosely.

- By using **intellectualization,** we avoid the emotions associated with anxiety-provoking experiences by focusing on abstract and impersonal thoughts. A husband whose wife leaves him may resort to ruminating about statistics regarding the divorce rate ("Almost 50 percent of marriages in the United States end in divorce"; "Because we'd only been married a few years, we were at high risk for divorce") as a means of buffering himself against emotional pain.

- **Identification with the aggressor** is the process of adopting the characteristics of individuals we find threatening: "If you can't beat 'em, join 'em." Anna Freud (1936) observed identification with the aggressor in concentration camp survivors, some of whom seemed to assume their guards' personality characteristics. Identification with the aggressor may underlie some cases of *Stockholm syndrome*—named after a 1973 hostage crisis in Stockholm, Sweden, in which some hostages developed emotional attachments toward their captors (Kuleshnyk, 1984). Nevertheless, journalists and pop psychologists have often used this term loosely to refer to any friendships that hostages forge with their captors (McKenzie, 2004), which may have little or nothing to do with identification with the aggressor.

- **Sublimation** transforms a socially unacceptable impulse into an admired goal. George Vaillant's (1977) book, *Adaptation to Life,* which is a 40-year longitudinal study of Harvard University graduates, features several examples of sublimation. Among them is the story of a man who set fires in childhood and went on to become chief of his local fire department.

> **APPLY YOUR THINKING**
> Some Freudians contend that psychologists who conduct research on sexuality
> are merely sublimating their unconscious sexual impulses. Is this claim falsifiable?
> Why or why not?

FREUD'S THEORY OF PERSONALITY DEVELOPMENT

No aspect of Freud's theory is more controversial than his model of personality development. Nor has any aspect of his theory been more widely criticized as pseudoscientific (Cioffi, 1998). According to Freud, personality development proceeds through a series of stages. He termed these stages *psychosexual* because each focuses on an **erogenous zone,** or sexually arousing zone of the body. Although we're accustomed to thinking of our genitals as our primary sexual organs, Freud contended that other bodily areas are sources of sexual gratification in early development. Contrary to prevailing wisdom at the time, Freud insisted that sexuality begins in infancy. He further maintained that the extent to which we resolve each stage successfully bears crucial implications for later personality development (see **Table 14.5**). We'll next examine the five psychosexual stages as Freud conceptualized them, bearing in mind that many modern critics don't share his views.

The Oral Stage. The first stage of psychosexual development, the **oral stage,** which generally lasts from birth to 12–18 months, focuses on the mouth. During this stage, infants obtain sexual pleasure primarily by sucking and drinking. If they obtain either too much or too little gratification, they'll become *fixated* or psychologically "stuck" in this stage. According to Freud, we're prone to regressing to these points of fixation under stress. Freud assumed that either too much or too little satisfaction would lead to an insatiable hunger for more oral pleasure. As adults, orally fixated persons tend to react to stress by becoming intensely dependent on others for reassurance (a form of regression, according to Freud), just as infants depend on their mother's breast as a source of satisfaction.

The Anal Stage. At the second stage, the **anal stage,** which lasts from about 18 months to 3 years, children first come face to face with psychological conflict. During this stage,

Table 14.5 Freud's Stages of Psychosexual Development.

Stage	Approximate Age
Oral	Birth to 12–18 months
Anal	18 months to 3 years
Phallic*	3 years to 6 years
Latency	6 years to 12 years
Genital	12 years and beyond

*Oedipus and Electra complexes.

intellectualization
avoiding emotions associated with anxiety-provoking experiences by focusing on abstract and impersonal thoughts

identification with the aggressor
process of adopting the characteristics of individuals we find threatening

sublimation
transforming a socially unacceptable impulse into an admired goal

erogenous zone
sexually arousing zone of the body

oral stage
psychosexual stage that focuses on the mouth

anal stage
psychosexual stage that focuses on toilet training

children want to alleviate tension and experience pleasure by moving their bowels, but soon discover that they can't do so whenever nature calls. Instead, they must learn to inhibit their urges and wait to move their bowels in a socially appropriate place—ideally, the toilet. If children's toilet training is either too harsh or too lenient, they'll become fixated and prone to later regressing to this stage in anxiety-provoking circumstances. Freudians believe that anally fixated individuals—*anal personalities*—are prone to excessive neatness, stinginess, and stubbornness in adulthood. These traits presumably reflect a preoccupation with retaining control over one's bowel movements.

The Phallic Stage. The **phallic stage,** which lasts from approximately age 3 years to 6 years, is of paramount importance to Freudians in explaining personality. During this stage, the penis (for boys) and clitoris (for girls) become the primary erogenous zones for sexual pleasure. Simultaneously, children develop a powerful attraction for the opposite-sex parent, as well as a desire to eliminate the same-sex parent as a rival. Here's where things get complicated, so fasten your seat belts.

In the classic Greek tragedy by Sophocles, Oedipus blinds himself soon after discovering that he'd unknowingly murdered his father and married his mother. Freud was so influenced by this play that he referred to the supposed love of all boys for their mothers as the Oedipus complex.

In boys, the phallic stage is termed the **Oedipus complex** after the Greek character who unknowingly killed his father and married his mother. The boy, who wants Mommy all for himself, wants to kill or at least rid himself of Daddy. The boy comes to believe that his father perceives him as a rival for his mother's affection and fears that his father will castrate him if he doesn't renounce his love for his mother. Ultimately, these castration anxieties and the impossibility of ever attaining mother as a love object lead the boy to abandon this love. He then identifies with the aggressor, in this case his father, and adopts his personality characteristics: Like father, like son. The Oedipus complex is thereby resolved. Nevertheless, if children don't resolve this complex, claimed Freud, the stage is set for psychological problems later in life.

In girls, in contrast, the phallic stage is often termed the **Electra complex** after the Greek character who avenged her father's murder by killing her mother. Girls, like boys, desire the affections of the opposite-sex parent and fantasize about doing away with the same-sex parent. In girls, however, the phallic stage takes the form of **penis envy,** in which the girl desires to possess a penis, just like Daddy has. For reasons that Freud never clearly explained, girls believe themselves inferior to boys because of their "missing" organ. According to Freud, this sense of inferiority persists beyond childhood for years or even decades. Because girls can't experience castration anxiety, their need to renounce their love for the opposite-sex parent isn't as pressing as that of boys. Consequently, they never get over their Electra complex entirely. Remarkably, Freud believed that females can resolve their penis envy only when they give birth to a boy, because a boy has a penis! Penis envy is probably Freud's most ridiculed concept, and with good reason, largely because there's no research support for it.

APPLY YOUR THINKING
In a published study entitled "Penis envy? Or pencil-needing?" Granville B. Johnson (1966) examined 300 introductory psychology students who completed an exam with pencils provided to them by the instructor. At the end of the exam, students deposited their pencils in a box in the classroom. Johnson hypothesized that according to Freud's concept of penis envy, women should keep more pencils than men, because pencils are phallic symbols. As predicted, fewer women returned pencils than men. Do these findings provide support for penis envy? Why or why not?

---

phallic stage
psychosexual stage that focuses on the genitals

Oedipus complex
conflict during phallic stage in which boys supposedly love their mothers romantically and want to eliminate their fathers as rivals

Electra complex
conflict during phallic stage in which girls supposedly love their fathers romantically and want to eliminate their mothers as rivals

penis envy
supposed desire of girls to possess a penis

The Latency Stage.   The fourth psychosexual stage, the **latency stage,** is a period of calm following the stormy phallic stage. In latency, which lasts from about age 6 years to 12 years, sexual impulses are submerged into the unconscious. Most boys and girls during this stage find members of the opposite sex to be "yucky" and utterly unappealing. Try convincing most 8-year-old boys that their feelings toward girls may change dramatically in 4 or 5 years, and you're likely to be spectacularly unsuccessful.

The Genital Stage.   During the fifth and final psychosexual stage, the **genital stage**— which generally begins at around age 12—sexual impulses reawaken. If development up to this point has proceeded without major glitches, this stage witnesses the emergence of mature romantic relationships. In contrast, if serious problems weren't resolved at earlier stages, difficulties with establishing intimate love attachments are likely.

PSYCHOANALYTIC THEORY EVALUATED CRITICALLY

Freud has probably exerted a greater impact on the public's understanding of personality than any other thinker. Nevertheless, an outpouring of recent articles and books has raised troubling questions concerning the scientific status of psychoanalytic theory. Here we'll examine six major criticisms.

Falsifiability

(1) **Unfalsifiability.**   Critics have noted that many features of Freudian theory are unfalsifiable. For example, the concept of reaction-formation offers a convenient escape hatch that allows many psychoanalytic hypotheses to evade falsification. If we were to find evidence that most 5-year-old boys report being sexually repulsed by their mothers, would this observation refute the existence of the Oedipus complex? Superficially, the answer would seem to be yes, but Freudians could maintain that these boys are engaging in reaction-formation and are attracted to their mothers at an unconscious level.

Indeed, Freud often used *ad hoc maneuvers* (see Chapter 1) to protect his pet hypotheses from refutation. One of Freud's patients intensely disliked her mother-in-law and took pains to ensure that she wouldn't spend a summer vacation with her. Yet while in therapy with Freud she dreamt of spending a summer vacation with her mother-in-law. This dream seemingly falsifies Freud's theory that all dreams are wish fulfillments. Yet Freud argued that her dream supported his theory because her underlying wish was to prove Freud incorrect (Dolnick, 1998)! Although we might marvel at Freud's ingenuity, this "heads I win, tails you lose" reasoning renders psychoanalytic theory difficult to falsify.

> **APPLY YOUR THINKING**
> Freud claimed that panic attacks (sudden bursts of intense anxiety; see Chapter 15) in public places are typically reaction-formations against unconscious desires to engage in sexual intercourse with others in public. Panic attacks, he suggested, force people to flee the situation, thereby preventing the sexual behavior from seeing the light of day. Is this hypothesis falsifiable? If not, why?

latency stage
psychosexual stage in which sexual impulses are submerged into the unconscious

genital stage
psychosexual stage in which sexual impulses awaken and typically begin to mature into romantic attraction toward others

(2) **Failed Predictions.**   Although much of Freudian theory is difficult to falsify, those portions of the theory that can be falsified often have been (Grunbaum, 1984). For example, Freud claimed that children exposed to overly harsh toilet training would grow up to be rigid and perfectionistic. Yet most investigators have found no association between toilet training practices and adult personality (Fisher & Greenberg, 1996).

(3) Lack of Evidence for Defense Mechanisms. There's little scientific support for many Freudian defense mechanisms. For example, laboratory studies have failed to yield strong evidence for the existence of repression. In particular, people are no more likely to forget negative life experiences than equally arousing, but positive, life experiences (Holmes, 1974, 1990). Similarly, there's weak support for projection, at least as Freud conceptualized it. Investigators have found that attributing our undesirable traits to others doesn't reduce anxiety or prevent us from consciously recognizing these traits in ourselves (Holmes, 1978). Freud was surely right that we use an array of coping strategies to deal with anxiety, but many of his claims regarding defense mechanisms—such as that they're unconscious—are in doubt.

(4) Questionable Conception of the Unconscious. There's increasing reason to doubt the existence of the unconscious as Freud conceived of it. On the one hand, there's growing research evidence that we're often unaware of why we do things. Richard Nisbett and Timothy Wilson (1977) reviewed a broad range of studies demonstrating that we often convince ourselves that we behave for reasons that are plausible, but incorrect. For example, in the context of a memory study investigators randomly exposed some participants, but not others, to the word pair "ocean–moon" embedded in a list of word pairs. When later asked to name their favorite detergent, the former participants were significantly more likely than the latter to name "Tide." Yet when asked the reasons for their choice, none came up with the correct explanation, namely, that the word "moon" triggered an association to "tide." Instead, they came up with presumably false but plausible explanations (such as, "I recently saw a Tide commercial on television").

Recent evidence suggests that subliminally presented stimuli (see Chapters 4 and 11), that is, stimuli presented below the threshold for awareness, can affect people's behavior. Other evidence comes from priming paradigms, in which researchers observe the effects of subtle stimuli on people's behavior (Chapter 7). In one study, researchers primed some participants, but not others, with words relevant to old age (like "Florida" and "wrinkle") in the context of a language task. Remarkably, after the study was over, primed participants walked down the hallway more slowly than did unprimed participants (Bargh & Chartrand, 1999)!

The findings we've reviewed may seem to support Freudian theory because they suggest that factors of which we're unaware influence our behavior (Westen, 1998). Yet they don't provide evidence for *the* unconscious: a massive reservoir of impulses and memories submerged beneath awareness (Wilson, 2002). Freud viewed the unconscious as a "place" where sexual and aggressive energies, along with repressed memories, are housed. Nevertheless, research doesn't support the existence of this place, let alone tell us where it's located (Kihlstrom, 1987).

(5) Reliance on Unrepresentative Samples. Many critics have charged that Freud based his theories on atypical samples and generalized them to the rest of humanity. Most of Freud's patients were upper-class, neurotic Viennese women, a far cry from the average Nigerian man or Malaysian woman. Freud's theories may therefore possess limited *external validity,* that is, generalizability (see Chapter 2), for people from other cultural backgrounds. Moreover, although Freud's methods of inquiry were idiographic, his theory was nomothetic. That is, he studied a relatively small number of individuals in depth but applied his theories to most or all people.

(6) Flawed Assumption of Shared Environmental Influence. Many Freudian hypotheses presume that shared environment plays a key role in molding personality. For example, Freudians claim that the child emerging from the phallic stage assumes the personality characteristics of the same-sex parent. Nevertheless, as behavior-genetic studies have shown, shared environment plays little or no role in adult personality. These findings contradict a key proposition of Freudian theory.

One of Freud's best-known patients, known as "Anna O.," was Bertha Pappenheim, who later became the founder of social work in Germany (she was even honored with her own postage stamp). Because many of Freud's patients, like Pappenheim, were relatively wealthy Viennese women, critics have questioned the generalizability of his conclusions to other cultures.

Alfred Adler would have argued that German dictator Adolph Hitler's desire to dominate others was due to overcompensation for deep-seated inferiority feelings. Nevertheless, this hypothesis is difficult to falsify.

Summary. Freudian theory has had a profound influence on modern conceptions of the mind, but it's problematic from a scientific standpoint. The one insight of Freud that's best stood the test of time is that we're often unaware of why we do what we do. But this insight wasn't original to Freud (Crews, 1998), and as we'll learn later in the chapter, it's consistent with other models of personality, including behaviorism. Moreover, this insight doesn't hinge on the existence of an unconscious mind, a vast repository of repressed drives and memories that influence behavior outside of our awareness. The Freudian unconscious remains an intriguing hypothesis, but one for which supportive evidence is conspicuously lacking.

FREUD'S FOLLOWERS: THE NEO-FREUDIANS

Largely in reaction to criticisms of Freudian theory, a number of psychiatrists and psychologists—many of them Freud's own students—broke from their mentor to forge their own models of personality. Because these thinkers modified Freud's views in significant ways, their approaches are typically called neo-Freudian theories.

Neo-Freudian Theories: Core Features. Most neo-Freudian theories share with Freudian theory an emphasis on (a) unconscious influences on behavior and (b) the importance of early experience in shaping personality. Nevertheless, **neo-Freudian theories** differ from Freudian theory in two key ways:

(1) Neo-Freudian theories place less emphasis than does Freudian theory on sexuality as a driving force in personality, and more emphasis on social drives, such as the need for approval; and

(2) Most neo-Freudian theories are more optimistic than Freudian theory concerning the prospects for personality growth throughout the life span. Freud was notoriously pessimistic about the possibility of personality change after childhood; he once wrote that the goal of psychoanalysis was to turn neurotic misery into ordinary, everyday unhappiness (Breuer & Freud, 1895).

neo-Freudian theories
theories derived from Freud's model, but that placed less emphasis on sexuality as a driving force in personality and were more optimistic regarding the prospects for long-term personality growth

style of life
according to Adler, each person's distinctive way of achieving superiority

inferiority complex
feelings of low self-esteem that can lead to overcompensation for such feelings

Alfred Adler: The Striving for Superiority. The first major follower of Freud to defect from the fold was Viennese psychiatrist Alfred Adler (1870–1937). According to Adler (1931), the principal motive in human personality is not sex or aggression, but the *striving for superiority*. Our overriding goal in life, said Adler, is to be better than others. We aim to accomplish this goal by crafting our distinctive **style of life,** or longstanding pattern of achieving superiority. People may try to satisfy their superiority strivings by becoming famous entertainers, great athletes, or outstanding parents.

According to Adler (1922), neurotic difficulties stem from early childhood; those who were pampered or neglected by their parents are prone to later developing an **inferiority complex,** a popular term inspired by Adler. People with an inferiority complex are prone to low self-esteem and tend to overcompensate for this feeling. As a result, they often attempt to demonstrate their superiority to others at all costs, even if it means dominating them. According to Adler, most forms of mental illness are unhealthy attempts to overcompensate for the inferiority complex.

Falsifiability

Adler's hypotheses, like Freud's, are difficult to falsify (Popper, 1965). For example, critics once asked Adler to explain how a person's decision to become a homeless alcoholic supported his theory that people always try to attain superiority over others. He responded that a homeless alcoholic has selected a lifestyle that affords a convenient excuse for being unable to achieve greatness. In effect, he can tell himself, "If only I didn't drink, I would have become successful." As we can see, with a little creativity, we can cook up an Adlerian explanation after the fact for almost any behavior.

Carl Jung: The Collective Unconscious. Another pupil of Freud who parted ways with his mentor was Swiss psychiatrist Carl Gustav Jung (1875–1961). Although Freud originally anointed Jung to be the standard-bearer of the next generation of psychoanalysts, Jung became disenchanted with Freud's emphasis on sexuality. Jung's views have become enormously influential in popular psychology, and Jung is something of a cult figure in New Age circles. Jung's theory is extraordinarily complicated—indeed, it may be the only major theory of personality more complex than Freud's—so for our purposes we'll touch on only a few of the highlights here.

Jung (1936) actually believed that Freud didn't take the idea of the unconscious far enough. He argued that in addition to Freud's version of the unconscious—which Jung termed the *personal unconscious*—there's also a **collective unconscious.** For Jung, the collective unconscious comprises all of the memories that ancestors have passed down to us across the generations. It's our shared storehouse of ancestral memories and accounts for cultural similarities in myths and legends. We recognize our mothers immediately after birth, Jung argued, because the memories of thousands of generations of individuals who've seen their mothers after birth have been passed down to us genetically.

The concept of the collective unconscious rests on *Lamarckian evolution*, that is, the inheritance of acquired characteristics (Hogenson, 2001). Lamarckians proposed, for example, that giraffes have long necks because generations of giraffes stretched their necks to reach leaves in tall trees. Their long necks were then passed on to new generations. Nevertheless, scientists have discredited Lamarckian evolution for both physical and psychological traits, because traits acquired in the course of an animal's life can't be transmitted genetically (Gardner, 1958).

Jung believed that the collective unconscious contains numerous **archetypes,** or cross-culturally universal emotional symbols, which explain the similarities across people in their emotional reactions to many features of the world. Archetypes include the mother, the goddess, the hero, and the mandala (circle), which Jung believed symbolized a desire for wholeness or unity (Campbell, 1988; Jung, 1950). Jung (1958) speculated that the modern epidemic of flying saucer reports stems from an unconscious desire to achieve a sense of unity with the universe, because flying saucers are shaped like mandalas. Some psychotherapists even use *Jungian sandplay therapy* (Steinhardt, 1998) to uncover children's deep-seated emotional conflicts. These practitioners try to infer the existence of archetypes on the basis of shapes that children draw in sand, and use them as a springboard for therapy. Nevertheless, there's no evidence that Jungian sandplay therapy is effective (Lilienfeld, 1999), even though it's probably a lot of fun for children, not to mention therapists.

Provocative as it is, Jung's theory suffers from some of the same shortcomings as those of Freud and Adler. It's difficult to falsify, because it generates few clear-cut predictions (Gallo, 1994; Monte, 1995). For example, how could we try to falsify Jung's claim that flying saucer sightings stem from an underlying wish for wholeness with the universe? It's difficult to imagine what evidence could refute this claim. In addition, although Jung hypothesized that archetypes are wired into us by evolution, he may not have sufficiently considered a rival explanation for their origins. Perhaps archetypes are cross-culturally universal because they represent crucial elements of the environment—mothers, wise elders, the sun, and moon (which are, after all, shaped like mandalas)—that people across all cultures experience. Shared experiences rather than shared genes may account for commonalities in archetypes across the world.

Karen Horney: Feminist Psychology. Karen Horney (1885–1952), a German physician, was the first major feminist personality theorist. Although not departing drastically from Freud's core assumptions, Horney (1939) took aim at those aspects of his theory that she saw as gender biased. She viewed Freud's concept of penis envy as especially misguided. Horney maintained that women's sense of inferiority stems not from their anatomy but

Jung believed that the collective unconscious is our shared storehouse of ancestral memories. He even claimed that episodes of synchronicity, which involve the simultaneous occurrence of thoughts and events, reflect the actions of the collective unconscious. Is this claim falsifiable? (© ScienceCartoonPlus.com)

A mandala symbol similar to one drawn by one of Jung's patients. This drawing reminds us that therapists can influence their clients. As a consequence, therapists must be careful not to mistake their clients' drawings or statements as evidence for their preferred theories.

Falsifiability

Ruling Out Rival Hypotheses

collective unconscious
according to Jung, our shared storehouse of memories that ancestors have passed down to us across generations

archetypes
cross-culturally universal emotional symbols

Karen Horney, the first major feminist psychological theorist, believed that Freud greatly underemphasized social factors as causes of inferiority feelings in many women.

Falsifiability

According to object relations theorists, blankets often serve as transitional objects for young children.

Falsifiability

object relations theorists
followers of Freud who emphasized children's mental representations of others

their excessive dependency on men, which parents and society have ingrained in them from an early age. She similarly objected to the Oedipus complex on the grounds that it's neither inevitable nor universal. This complex, she maintained, is a *symptom* rather than a cause of psychological problems, because it arises only when the opposite-sex parent is overly protective and the same-sex parent overly critical.

Erich Fromm: The Escape from Freedom.

A final prominent neo-Freudian was Erich Fromm (1900–1980). Fromm's central thesis is simple. As we humans have acquired increasing independence throughout the ages as a result of our technological advances, we've come to feel increasingly alone. Whether they be high-rise buildings that permit us to wall ourselves off physically from others or iPods that permit us to shut out others' conversations, technology has rendered us more independent from others.

This freedom comes with a price tag, contended Fromm. As modern humans we're continually engaged in frantic efforts to "escape from freedom," that is, to become closer to others (Fromm, 1941). Unless we're careful, such efforts can produce troublesome, even horrific, consequences. According to Fromm, the Nazis under the regime of Hitler attempted to escape from freedom by forging powerful patriotic bonds under the spell of a charismatic leader.

Object Relations Theorists: Mental Representations.

A group of neo-Freudians called **object relations theorists** place particular emphasis on children's mental representations of others, especially their parents. These theorists use the term *object* to refer to anything—typically a person—that's the target of our impulses, such as our sexual desires.

One early object relations theorist was Melanie Klein (1882–1960), who focused on infants' mental representations of their parents. According to Klein (1949), the infant struggles with the fact that her mother is a source of both intense satisfaction and frustration. This is because the mother both gives and takes away. To deal with this ambivalence, the infant "splits" the mother into good and bad mental representations. Klein even believed that infants mentally split the mother's breasts into good and bad breasts. Needless to say, these hypotheses are exceedingly difficult to falsify. As children mature, their extreme representations gradually become integrated. Klein further proposed that some adult mental illnesses are marked by a failure to merge good with bad object representations.

Later object relations theorists explored in greater detail the attachments that infants and children form with their parents. Donald Winnicott (1953) coined the term *transitional objects* to describe objects, like blankets and stuffed animals, that children use to comfort themselves emotionally when they loosen their ties to their caregivers. Heinz Kohut (1971) contended that parents must provide their children with a firm sense of self-esteem. They do so by "mirroring," that is, providing children with empathy and admiration for their accomplishments. If mirroring is insufficient in quantity, children will become egocentric in adulthood to compensate for low self-esteem.

Freud's Followers Evaluated Critically.

Many neo-Freudian theorists tempered some of the excesses of Freudian theory. They pointed out that anatomy isn't always destiny when it comes to the psychological differences between the sexes, and argued that social influences must be reckoned with in the development of personality. Nevertheless, as we've seen, falsifiability remains a serious concern for neo-Freudian theories, especially those of Adler and Jung.

Object relations theorists went beyond other neo-Freudians in emphasizing how children represent others mentally. Yet these theorists frequently neglected research on children's cognitive development, such as that of Piaget (see Chapter 10). As a consequence, many overestimated the extent to which infants and young children can engage in complex cognitive operations, such as splitting.

Behavioral and Social Learning Theories of Personality

We've already encountered behavioral models, including radical behaviorism, in Chapter 5. So why are we again crossing paths with behaviorism? After all, behaviorism is a theory of learning rather than a theory of personality, isn't it?

Actually, behaviorism is both. Radical behaviorists, like B. F. Skinner (see Chapter 6), believe that differences in our personalities stem largely from differences in our learning histories. Unlike Freudians, radical behaviorists reject the notion that the first few years of life are especially critical in personality development. Childhood certainly matters, but learning continues to mold our personalities throughout the life span.

For radical behaviorists, our personalities are bundles of habits acquired by classical and operant conditioning. In contrast to other personality theorists, radical behaviorists don't believe that personality plays a role in *causing* behavior. For them, personality *consists of* behaviors. These behaviors are both overt (observable) and covert (unobservable), such as thoughts and feelings. A radical behaviorist wouldn't have much trouble accepting the idea that some people are extraverted, or that extraverted people tend to have many friends and attend many parties. But tell a radical behaviorist that certain people have many friends and attend many parties *because* they're extraverted, and you're likely to receive a stern lecture on B. F. Skinner's view of personality. We'll beat that behaviorist to the punch and present that lecture here.

BEHAVIORAL VIEWS OF THE CAUSES OF PERSONALITY

Radical behaviorists view personality as under the control of two major influences: (a) genetic factors and (b) *contingencies* in the environment, that is, reinforcers and punishers (see Chapter 6). In tandem, these influences explain why our personalities differ.

Behavioral Views of Determinism. Like psychoanalysts, radical behaviorists are strict determinists: They believe all of our actions are products of preexisting causal influences. This is one of the precious few issues on which Freud and Skinner would probably agree if we could magically bring them back to life for a debate, one that many modern psychologists would probably pay a sizable chunk of their life savings to witness. For radical behaviorists, free will is an illusion (see Prologue). We may believe we're free to either continue reading this sentence or to instead stop to grab a long-awaited bowl of ice cream, but we're fooling ourselves. We're convinced that we're free to select our behaviors only because we're usually oblivious to their short-term triggers.

Although this person may perceive her decision to either eat or not eat a piece of candy as under her control, radical behaviorists would regard her perception as an illusion.

Behavioral Views of Unconscious Processing. The belief in unconscious processing is another point of consensus between Freudians and Skinnerians (Overskeid, 2007), although their views of this processing differ sharply. For Skinner, we're unconscious of many things because we're often unaware of immediate influences on our behavior (Skinner, 1974). We may have had the experience of suddenly humming a song to ourselves and wondering why we were doing so, until we realized that this song had been playing softly on a distant radio. According to Skinner, we were initially unconscious of the reasons for our behavior because we were unaware of the environmental cause of this behavior, in this case, the song in the distant background.

Such unconscious processing is a far cry from the Freudian unconscious, which is a vast storehouse of inaccessible thoughts, memories, and impulses. For radical behaviorists, there's no such storehouse because the unconscious variables that play a role in causing behavior lie outside, not inside, us.

SOCIAL LEARNING THEORIES OF PERSONALITY: THE CAUSAL ROLE OF THINKING RESURRECTED

Although influenced by radical behaviorists, **social learning theorists** believed that Skinner had gone too far in his wholesale rejection of the influence of thoughts on behavior. Spurred on by Edward Chase Tolman and others who believed that learning relies on our plans and goals (see Chapter 6), these theorists emphasized thinking as a cause of personality. How we interpret our environments affects how we react to them; if we perceive others as threatening, we'll typically be hostile and suspicious in return. According to social learning theorists, classical and operant conditioning are cognitively mediated. As we acquire information in classical and operant conditioning, we're actively thinking about and interpreting what it means.

Social Learning Views of Determinism. Most social learning theorists hold a more complex view of determinism than do radical behaviorists. As we learned in the Prologue, Albert Bandura (1986) made a compelling case for *reciprocal determinism*, a form of causation whereby personality and cognitive factors, behavior, and environmental variables mutually influence one another. Our high levels of extraversion may motivate us to introduce ourselves to our introductory psychology classmates and thereby make new friends. In turn, our newly found friends may reinforce our extraversion, leading us to attend parties we'd otherwise skip. Attending these parties may result in our acquiring additional friends who further reinforce our extraversion, and so on.

Observational Learning and Personality. Social learning theorists proposed that much of learning occurs by watching others. As we learned in Chapter 6, *observational learning* appears to be a key form of learning neglected by traditional behaviorists (Bandura, 1965). Observational learning expands greatly the range of stimuli from which we can benefit. It also means that our parents and teachers can play significant roles in shaping our personalities, because we acquire both good and bad habits by watching and, later, emulating them. For example, through observational learning, we can learn to behave altruistically by seeing our parents donate money to charities.

In observational learning, parents, teachers, and other adults play significant roles in shaping children's personalities: Children learn good and bad habits by watching and later emulating adults. This child may learn early that charitable giving is a worthy endeavor.

social learning theorists
theorists who emphasized thinking as a cause of personality

locus of control
extent to which people believe that reinforcers and punishers lie inside or outside of their control

Sense of Perceived Control. Social learning theorists emphasized individuals' sense of control over life events. Julian Rotter (1966) introduced the concept of **locus of control** to describe the extent to which people believe that reinforcers and punishers lie inside or outside of their control. People with an internal locus of control ("internals") believe that life events are due largely to their own efforts and personal characteristics. In contrast, people with an external locus of control ("externals") believe that life events are largely a product of chance and fate, or what Hamlet termed the "slings and arrows of outrageous fortune" (see **Table 14.6**).

Rotter hypothesized that internals are less prone than externals to emotional upset following life stressors, because they're more likely to believe they can remedy problems on

Table 14.6 Sample Items from a Measure of Locus of Control.

	True or False
(1) Many people live miserable lives because of their parents.	True/False
(2) If you set realistic goals, you can succeed no matter what.	True/False
(3) One can climb the professional ladder just by being around at the right time.	True/False
(4) If I study hard enough, I can pass any exam.	True/False

For items 1 and 3, a "True" response is scored in the direction of an external locus of control, and a "False" response is scored in the direction of an internal locus of control. Items 2 and 4 are scored in the opposite fashion. (*Source:* Reprinted with permission of Psychtests.com)

their own. Indeed, almost all forms of psychological distress, including depression and anxiety, are associated with an external locus of control (Benassi, Sweeney, & Dufour, 1988; Carten & Nowicki, 1996). It's not clear, though, whether these correlational findings reflect a causal relationship between external locus of control and mental disorders, as Rotter believed. Perhaps once people develop depression or anxiety, they begin to feel their lives are spiraling out of control. Or perhaps people who doubt their abilities are prone to both an external locus of control, on the one hand, and depression and anxiety, on the other.

Correlation vs. Causation

When people in difficult circumstances obtain a measure of control over their lives, their adjustment improves. Ellen Langer and Judith Rodin (1976) gave residents on one floor of a nursing home control over several aspects of their environment. Residents on that one floor had more freedom in arranging their rooms, lodging complaints, and attending films, whereas residents on a different floor had minimal control over these matters. Langer and Rodin found that residents afforded greater control showed better emotional adjustment than other residents. Remarkably, one year later fewer residents in the former condition had died. Although these results seem to suggest that a heightened sense of control enhances psychological and physical health, they're a bit difficult to interpret. Perhaps residents given greater control actually took advantage of it by sprucing up their rooms or voicing concerns to staff. So it may not be perceived control as much as *actual* control that matters most.

Ruling Out Rival Hypotheses

APPLY YOUR THINKING

How would you design a study of nursing home residents that more directly answers the question of whether perceived control exerts a causal effect on emotional adjustment?

Behavioral and Social Learning Theories Evaluated Critically. B. F. Skinner and his fellow radical behaviorists agreed with Freud that our behavior is determined, but maintained that the primary causes of our behavior—contingencies—lie outside rather than inside of us. Even critics of radical behaviorism acknowledge that Skinner and his followers placed the field of psychology on firmer scientific footing. Many critics charged, however, that radical behaviorists went too far in their exclusion of any causal role for thinking. Indeed, the claim that thoughts play no causal role in behavior strikes most modern thinkers as implausible from an evolutionary perspective. Natural selection has endowed us with an enormous cerebral cortex (see Chapter 3), which is specialized for problem solving, planning, reasoning, and other high-level cognitive processes. It seems difficult to comprehend why our huge cortexes would have evolved if our thoughts were merely by-products of contingencies.

Social learning theorists rekindled psychologists' interests in thinking and argued that observational learning is a crucial form of learning in addition to classical and operant conditioning. Nevertheless, social learning theory isn't immune to criticism. In particular,

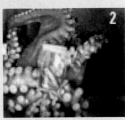

Replicability

Some researchers have claimed to find evidence of observational learning in the octopus, although this evidence is controversial. Billye, a giant Pacific octopus, has a brain the size of a walnut. But she can solve puzzles she'd never encounter in the wild, such as opening a glass jar to remove the fish inside. At top, (1) Billye is offered the jar; (2) she grasps the jar; and in (3) and (4) manipulates it into position and twists; in (5) releases the top.

self-actualization
drive to develop our innate potential to the fullest possible extent

the claim that observational learning exerts a powerful influence over our personalities implies an important causal role of shared environment. After all, if we learn largely by modeling the behaviors of our parents and other relatives, we should become like them. Yet, as we've learned, behavior-genetic studies have shown that the effects of shared environment on adult personality are weak or nonexistent.

Although social learning theorists believe that learning processes depend on cognition (thinking; see Chapter 8), scientists have observed these processes in animals with tiny cerebral cortexes and even with no cortexes at all. For example, they've documented classical conditioning in honeybees (Alcock, 1999) and starfish (McClintock & Lawrence, 1983). There's even evidence that classical conditioning occurs in such microscopic organisms as protozoa (Bergstrom, 1969) and hydra (Tanaka, 1966), although not all researchers have replicated these findings (Applewhite, Gardner, Foley, & Clendenin, 1972). There have also been reports of observational learning in the octopus (Fiorito & Scotto, 1993), although these findings are scientifically controversial.

The fact that learning occurs in relatively simple animals implies any one of three things. First, perhaps social learning theorists are wrong that basic forms of learning depend on cognition. Second, perhaps the thinking processes in these forms of learning are primitive in certain cases, although we might justifiably question whether a starfish, let alone a protozoan, is capable of genuine "thought." Third, the learning processes of simple animals may rely on different mechanisms from those of humans. At this point, the scientific evidence doesn't permit a clear answer.

ASSESS YOUR KNOWLEDGE: FACT OR FICTION?

(1) Radical behaviorists argue that we're sometimes "unconscious" of the true causes of our behavior. (True/False)

(2) Radical behaviorists believe that thoughts and feelings don't exist. (True/False)

(3) Social learning theorists believe that observational learning is a form of learning in addition to classical and operant conditioning. (True/False)

(4) According to social learning theorists, individuals with an internal locus of control—who are more likely to blame themselves for mistakes—are more prone to depression than individuals with an external locus of control. (True/False)

Answers: (1) T (p. 597); (2) F (p. 597); (3) T (p. 598); (4) F (p. 599)

Humanistic Models of Personality: The Third Force

Psychoanalytic theory, along with behavioral and social learning models, dominated personality psychology throughout the first half of the twentieth century. In the 1950s and 1960s, however, *humanistic models* emerged as a powerful "third force" in personality psychology. Humanistic psychologists rejected the determinism of psychoanalysts and behaviorists and embraced the notion of free will. We're perfectly free, they maintained, to choose either socially constructive or destructive paths in life.

Most humanistic psychologists propose that the core motive in personality is **self-actualization:** the drive to develop our innate potential to the fullest possible extent. Freudians would say that self-actualization would be disastrous for society because our innate drives, housed in the id, are selfish and destructive. For Freudians, a society of self-actualized people would probably result in sheer pandemonium, with citizens expressing their sexual and aggressive urges with reckless abandon. Simply put, it wouldn't be pretty. Humanistic theorists, in contrast, view human nature as inherently constructive, so they see self-actualization as a worthy goal.

ROGERS AND MASLOW: SELF-ACTUALIZATION REALIZED AND UNREALIZED

The best-known humanistic theorist was Carl Rogers (1902–1987), who, as we'll learn in Chapter 16, used his personality theory as a point of departure for an influential form of psychotherapy. Ever the optimist, Rogers believed that we could all achieve our full potential for emotional fulfillment if only society allowed it.

Rogers's Model of Personality. According to Rogers (1947), our personalities consist of three major components: organism, self, and conditions of worth.

(1) The *organism* is our innate genetic blueprint. In this regard it's like the Freudian id, except that Rogers viewed the organism as inherently positive and helpful toward others. Rogers wasn't terribly specific, however, about the makeup of the organism.

(2) The *self* is our self-concept, the set of beliefs about who we are.

(3) **Conditions of worth** are the expectations we place on ourselves for appropriate and inappropriate behavior. Like the Freudian superego, they emanate from our parents and society, and eventually we internalize them. Conditions of worth arise when others make their acceptance of us conditional—dependent—only on certain behaviors but not others. As a result, we only accept ourselves if we act in specific ways. A child who enjoys writing poetry may develop conditions of worth if taunted by peers. "When I'm teased for writing poetry, I'm not worthwhile. When I stop, I'm not teased so I become worthwhile." For Rogers, individual differences in personality stem largely from differences in the conditions of worth that others impose on us. Although in his idealistic moments Rogers envisioned a world in which conditions of worth no longer existed, he reluctantly acknowledged that in modern society even the best adjusted among us inevitably harbor certain conditions of worth. Conditions of worth result in **incongruence** between self and organism. Incongruence means that our personalities are inconsistent with our innate dispositions: We're not our true selves.

Carl Rogers, pioneer of humanistic psychology, held an optimistic view of human nature, although some critics have accused him of being naive in minimizing the dark side of human nature.

Maslow: The Characteristics of Self-Actualized People.

Whereas Rogers focused largely on pathological individuals whose tendencies toward self-actualization were thwarted, Abraham Maslow (1908–1970) focused on individuals who were self-actualized, especially historical figures. Among those whom Maslow considered self-actualized were Thomas Jefferson, Abraham Lincoln, Martin Luther King Jr., Helen Keller, and Mahatma Gandhi.

According to Maslow (1970), self-actualized people tend to be creative, spontaneous, and accepting of themselves and others. They're self-confident but not self-centered. They focus on real-world and intellectual problems and have a few deep friendships rather than many superficial ones. Self-actualized individuals typically crave privacy and can come off as introverted, aloof, or even difficult to deal with because they've outgrown the need to be popular. As a consequence, they're not afraid to "rock the boat" when necessary or express unpopular opinions. They're also prone to **peak experiences**—transcendent moments of intense excitement and tranquility marked by a profound sense of connection to the world.

Mahatma Gandhi and Mother Teresa: According to Maslow's theorizing, what do these two people have in common? Can you think of any people in today's society who would be considered self-actualized in Maslow's view?

HUMANISTIC MODELS EVALUATED CRITICALLY

Humanistic models of personality boldly proclaimed the importance of free will and personal choice, and appealed to a generation of young people disenchanted with the determinism of psychoanalysis and behaviorism. Yet investigators in *comparative psychology*, the branch of psychology that compares behavior across species, have challenged Rogers's claim that human nature is entirely positive. Their research suggests that the capacity for aggression is inherent in our closest primate cousins, the chimpanzees (Goodall & van Lawick, 1971; see also Chapter 13). There's also evidence from twin studies that aggression

conditions of worth
according to Rogers, expectations we place on ourselves for appropriate and inappropriate behavior

incongruence
inconsistency between our personalities and innate dispositions

peak experiences
transcendent moments of intense excitement and tranquility marked by a profound sense of connection to the world

is probably part of humans' genetic heritage (Krueger, Hicks, & McGue, 2001). Therefore, actualization of our full genetic potential is unlikely to bring about the state of bliss that Rogers imagined. At the same time, research suggests that the capacity for altruism is intrinsic to both chimpanzees and humans (de Waal, 1990; Wilson, 1995). Human nature, it seems, is a complex mix of selfish and selfless motives.

Rogers's research demonstrated that the discrepancy between people's descriptions of their actual versus ideal selves is greater for emotionally disturbed than for emotionally healthy individuals. This difference decreases over the course of psychotherapy (Rogers & Dymond, 1954). Rogers interpreted this finding as reflecting a lessening of conditions of worth. Yet these results are hard to interpret, because the people who showed decreases in incongruence following therapy weren't the same people who improved (Loevinger, 1987).

Maslow's valuable research on the characteristics of self-actualized individuals provided much of the impetus for today's "positive psychology" movement (see Chapter 11). Indeed, although he rarely receives credit for it, Maslow (1954) was the first person to use this term. Yet, his work is problematic on methodological grounds. In beginning with the assumption that self-actualized individuals tend to be creative and spontaneous, Maslow may have limited his search to historical figures who displayed these traits. As such, Maslow may have fallen prey to confirmation bias: Because he wasn't blind to his hypothesis concerning the personality features of self-actualized individuals, he had no easy way of guarding against this bias.

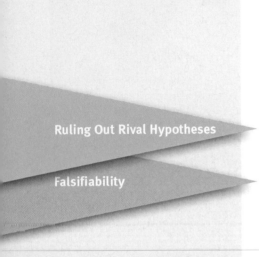

Humanistic models are also difficult to falsify. If a study of the general population showed that many people were self-actualized, humanistic psychologists could interpret this finding as evidence that self-actualization is an important influence on personality. But if this study showed that virtually no one was self-actualized, humanistic psychologists could explain away this finding by saying that most individuals' drives toward self-actualization had been stifled. Although the claim that self-actualization is the central motive in personality is difficult to falsify, the principle that we should develop our potential to the fullest may have considerable value as a philosophy of life.

ASSESS YOUR KNOWLEDGE: FACT OR FICTION?
(1) According to Rogers, human nature is inherently positive. (True/False)
(2) Rogers believed that only severely disturbed individuals acquire conditions of worth. (True/False)
(3) Maslow claimed that almost all self-actualized individuals are sociable and easy to get along with. (True/False)
(4) Many claims of humanistic models are difficult to falsify. (True/False)

Answers: (1) T (p. 600); (2) F (p. 601); (3) F (p. 601); (4) T (p. 602)

Trait Models of Personality: Consistencies in Our Behavior

In contrast to most of the personality theorists we've reviewed, proponents of trait models are interested primarily in describing and understanding the *structure* of personality. Much like early chemists who strove to identify the elements of the periodic table, trait theorists aim to pinpoint the major traits giving rise to differences in our personalities.

TRAIT MODELS: KEY CHALLENGES

Invoking personality traits as causes of behavior has its challenges. To start with, we must avoid the *circular reasoning fallacy* (see Chapter 1). We might conclude that a child who kicks others on the playground is aggressive. But in asking how we know that this child is

Claiming that a child is "aggressive" merely because he engages in aggressive behavior gives us no new information and is an example of circular reasoning. To be meaningful, personality traits must do more than merely describe behaviors we've already observed.

aggressive, we might respond "because he kicks other children on the playground." To avoid this logical trap, we need to demonstrate that personality traits predict behaviors in novel situations or correlate with biological or laboratory measures.

From there, we need to narrow down the pool of possible traits. There are over 17,000 terms in the English language referring to personality traits: shy, stubborn, impulsive, greedy, cheerful, and so on (Allport & Odbert, 1936). To reduce this diversity of traits to perhaps as few as three or five underlying traits, trait theorists use a statistical technique called **factor analysis**. This technique analyzes the correlations among responses on personality inventories and other measures and tries to identify the underlying "factors" that give rise to these correlations.

Table 14.7 presents the correlations among six different variables—sociability, popularity, liveliness, risk-taking, sensation seeking, and impulsivity—in a hypothetical correlation matrix: A table of correlations. As we look over this correlation matrix, we'll notice that only some of the cells contain numbers; that's because correlation matrixes present each correlation only once. (That's why, for example, the matrix displays the correlation between variables 1 and 4 only once.) We can see that variables 1 through 3 are highly correlated, as are variables 4 through 6. But these two sets of variables aren't correlated much with one another, so it suggests the presence of two different factors. The factor comprising variables 1 through 3 (in blue) might be called "extraversion," and the factor comprising variables 4 through 6 (in green) might be called "fearlessness." The formal technique of factor analysis uses much more rigorous statistical criteria to accomplish the same goal as the "eyeball method" we just walked you through.

Table 14.7 An "Eyeball" Factor Analysis of Six Variables. Follow along as we describe this correlation matrix of six personality measures (the 1.00s in the diagonals represent the correlation of each variable with itself, which is a perfect correlation).

	Measures					
	Variable 1 **Sociability**	**Variable 2** **Popularity**	**Variable 3** **Liveliness**	**Variable 4** **Risk Taking**	**Variable 5** **Sensation Seeking**	**Variable 6** **Impulsivity**
Variable 1	1.00	.78	.82	.12	.07	-.03
Variable 2		1.00	.70	.08	.02	.11
Variable 3			1.00	.05	.11	.18
Variable 4				1.00	.69	.85
Variable 5					1.00	.72
Variable 6						1.00

PERSONALITY TRAITS UNDER SIEGE: WALTER MISCHEL'S CRITIQUE

Trait theory was highly influential through the early and mid-twentieth century. Then in a stunning 1968 book, *Personality and Assessment*, Walter Mischel called the very notion of personality traits into question, embroiling the field of trait psychology in heated controversy for over a decade.

Mischel's Argument: Behavioral Inconsistency. As we noted earlier, psychologists had long assumed that traits influence behavior across many situations. But in his review of the literature, Mischel found low correlations among different behaviors believed to reflect the same trait. For example, he cited a study by Hugh Hartschorne and Mark May (1928) that had examined the correlations among various behavioral indicators of honesty among children. Hartschorne and May concocted situations that allowed children to behave either honestly or dishonestly, giving them the opportunity to steal a dime, change answers on an exam, and lie. Surprisingly, the correlations among children's behavior

factor analysis
statistical technique that analyzes the correlations among responses on personality inventories and other measures

Replicability

across these situations were low, with none exceeding .30. So children who steal in one situation, for example, aren't much more likely than other children to cheat in a different situation. Numerous researchers have reported similar findings in adults for such traits as dependency, friendliness, and conscientiousness (Bem & Allen, 1974; Mischel, 1968). People, it seems, aren't nearly as consistent across situations as most of us believe.

Mischel concluded that measures of personality aren't especially helpful for what they were designed to do—forecast behavior. Some psychologists later tried to explain our persistent belief in the predictive power of personality traits in terms of our cognitive biases, especially the fundamental attribution error (see Chapter 13). For them, we "see" people's personalities all around us because we mistake situational influences on their behavior, such as peer pressure, for personality influences (Bem & Allen, 1974; Ross & Nisbett, 1991).

Personality Traits Reborn: Psychologists Respond to Mischel. Were Mischel's criticisms valid? Yes and no. As Seymour Epstein (1979) noted, Mischel was correct that personality traits aren't highly predictive of isolated behaviors, such as lying or cheating in a single situation. Nevertheless, in several studies Epstein showed that personality traits are often highly predictive of *aggregated* behaviors, that is, composites of behavior averaged across many situations. If we use a measure of extraversion to predict whether our friend will attend a party next Saturday night, we'll probably do only slightly better than chance. In contrast, if we use this measure to predict our friend's behavior across an average of many situations—attendance at parties, friendliness in small seminars, and willingness to engage in conversations with strangers—we'll probably do rather well. Contrary to Mischel's conclusions, personality traits can be useful for predicting overall behavioral trends (Rushton, Brainerd, & Presley, 1983). Still, Mischel performed a valuable service by pointing out that traits are rarely useful for predicting people's behavior in a single situation (Kendrick & Funder, 1988).

APPLY YOUR THINKING
A psychologist serving as an expert witness is called by the prosecution to testify about the probability that a defendant murdered his wife 6 months earlier. After reviewing data from several measures of personality traits, he concludes, "In my opinion, the defendant's pattern of personality traits makes him at least 90 to 95 percent likely to be the actual murderer." If you were the defense attorney, what would you say to this expert witness on cross-examination?

Replicability

MODELS OF PERSONALITY STRUCTURE: THE GEOGRAPHY OF THE PSYCHE

Although there's no complete consensus among trait theorists regarding the most scientifically supported model of personality structure, one model has received considerable research support. This model, the **Big Five,** consists of five traits that have surfaced repeatedly in factor analyses of personality measures.

The Big Five. The Big Five were uncovered using a **lexical approach** to personality, which proposes that the most crucial features of human personality are embedded in our language (Goldberg, 1993). The logic here is simple: If a personality trait is important in our daily lives, it's likely that we talk a lot about it. The Big Five emerged from factor analyses of trait terms in dictionaries and works of literature. According to Paul Costa, Robert McCrae, and their collaborators (Costa & McCrae, 1992; Widiger, 2001), these five dimensions are:

- *Extraversion*—extraverted people tend to be social and lively;
- *Neuroticism*—neurotic people tend to be tense and moody;
- *Conscientiousness*—conscientious people tend to be careful and responsible;
- *Agreeableness*—agreeable people tend to be friendly and easy to get along with; and
- *Openness to Experience,* sometimes just called "Openness"—open people tend to be intellectually curious and unconventional.

Big Five
five traits that have surfaced repeatedly in factor analyses of personality measures

lexical approach
approach proposing that the most crucial features of personality are embedded in our language

We can use either of two waterlogged acronyms—OCEAN or CANOE—as a handy mnemonic for remembering the Big Five. According to Big Five advocates, we can use these factors to describe all people, including those with psychological disorders. A severely depressed person, for example, may be low in Extraversion, high in Neuroticism, and about average on the other three dimensions.

The Big Five appear in people's ratings of personality even when researchers ask participants to describe people they've only seen, not met (Passini & Norman, 1966). This finding suggests that we harbor *implicit personality theories,* that is, intuitive ideas concerning personality traits and their associations with behavior. The Big Five, plus a sixth trait of dominance, also emerge in studies of chimpanzee personality (Gosling, 2001; King & Figueredo, 1997), although it's difficult to exclude the possibility that raters in these studies are *anthropomorphizing*—that is, unintentionally imposing their implicit personality theories on chimpanzees.

Ruling Out Rival Hypotheses

The Big Five and Behavior. The Big Five predict many interesting real-world behaviors. For example, high Conscientiousness, low Neuroticism, and perhaps high Agreeableness are correlated with successful job performance (Barrick & Mount, 1991; Tett, Jackson, & Rothstein, 1991). Three researchers (Rubenzer, Fashingbauer, & Ones, 2000) asked presidential biographers to rate the U.S. presidents through Bill Clinton. Scores on Openness to Experience were correlated positively with independently assessed ratings of presidents' historical greatness. Interestingly, Agreeableness was correlated *negatively* with historical greatness, suggesting that the best presidents often aren't always the easiest to get along with.

The Big Five Critically Evaluated. Despite the usefulness of the Big Five, there's reason to question the lexical approach, as people may not be consciously aware of all important features of personality (J. Block, 1995). As a consequence, our language may not adequately reflect these features. In addition, there's no Big Five factor corresponding to morality (Loevinger, 1993), despite the centrality of this variable to many theories of personality, including those of Freud and his followers. Still other psychologists, like Hans Eysenck (1991) and Auke Tellegen (1982), have maintained that three dimensions rather than five offer the most accurate model of personality structure. According to them, the Big Five dimensions of Agreeableness, Conscientiousness, and (low) Openness to Experience combine to form one larger dimension of impulse control along with the dimensions of Extraversion and Neuroticism. The "Big Three" model of personality structure is a worthy alternative to the Big Five (Tellegen & Waller, in press).

Studies show that humans can identify many of the Big Five personality traits in animals, although it's not entirely clear whether this finding reflects anthropomorphism. Which Big Five trait would you say this dog best exemplifies?

CULTURAL INFLUENCES ON PERSONALITY

In seeking to address enduring questions concerning the cross-cultural relevance of personality, researchers have discovered that the Big Five are identifiable in China, Japan, Italy, Hungary, and Turkey (DeRaad, Perugini, Hrebickova, & Szarota, 1998; McCrae & Costa, 1997; Triandis & Suh, 2002). Nevertheless, there may be limits to the Big Five's cross-cultural universality. Openness to experience doesn't emerge clearly in all cultures (DeRaad et al., 2002) and some investigators have found dimensions in addition to the Big Five. For example, personality studies in China have revealed an additional "Chinese tradition" factor that encompasses aspects of personality distinctive to Chinese culture, including an emphasis on group harmony and on saving face to avoid embarrassment (Cheung & Leung, 1998). Moreover, studies in Germany, Finland, and several other countries suggest the presence of a factor comprising honesty and humility in addition to the Big Five (Lee & Ashton, 2004).

His biographers have ranked Harry ("Give 'em hell") Truman (*right*) as low in Big Five Agreeableness, but most presidential historians rank him as among America's best presidents.

Individualism-Collectivism and Personality. Cross-cultural researchers have devoted considerable attention to a key dimension relevant to personality we first encountered in Chapter 10: *Individualism-collectivism.* People from largely individualistic cultures, like the United States, tend to focus on themselves and their personal goals, whereas people from largely collectivist cultures, primarily in Asia, tend to focus on their relations with others (Triandis, 1989). People from individualistic cultures tend to report higher self-esteem than do those from collectivist cultures (Heine, Lehman, Markus, & Kitayama, 1999). In addition, personality traits may be less predictive of behavior in collectivist than individualistic cultures, probably because people's behavior in collectivist cultures is more influenced by social norms (Church & Katigbak, 2002).

Yet we shouldn't oversimplify the distinction between individualistic and collectivist cultures. Only about 60 percent of people in individualist cultures possess individualist personalities, and only about 60 percent of people in collectivist cultures possess collectivist personalities (Triandis & Suh, 2002). Furthermore, Asian countries differ markedly in their levels of collectivism, reminding us of the perils of stereotyping and overgeneralization (see Chapter 13). For example, although Chinese are generally more collectivist than Americans, Japanese and Koreans aren't (Oyserman, Coon, & Kemmelmeier, 2002).

National Character: Myth or Reality? Many of us hold strong preconceptions regarding so-called national character: The French are snobby, Germans rigid, Canadians compliant, and Americans brash. Or at least that's what most people, including citizens of these countries, believe. Yet cross-cultural research using the Big Five suggests that there's little or no truth to these popular stereotypes (McCrae & Terracciano, 2006). Apparently, the notion of national character reflects implicit personality theories more than psychological reality.

BASIC TENDENCIES VERSUS CHARACTERISTIC ADAPTATIONS

Recent personality research suggests that many widespread stereotypes regarding national character are inaccurate. For example, although many Americans believe that Germans tend to be rigid, evidence suggests otherwise—as this photograph of four Germans letting loose illustrates.

Personality traits don't tell us everything about why we differ from each other. The story of Jack and Oskar underscores the distinction between *basic tendencies* and *characteristic adaptations* (Harkness & Lilienfeld, 1997; McCrae & Costa, 1995). Basic tendencies are underlying personality traits, whereas characteristic adaptations are their behavioral manifestations. The key point here is that people can express their personality traits in very different ways. In Jack and Oskar's case, the same basic tendencies—intense loyalty and devotion to social causes—were expressed in two drastically different characteristic adaptations: Jack's Judaism and profound dislike of Germans and Oskar's Nazism and profound dislike of Jews.

Sensation seeking (Zuckerman, 1979), or the tendency to seek out new and exciting stimuli, offers another example of this distinction. High sensation seekers enjoy parachute jumping, sampling spicy foods, and living life in the fast lane. In contrast, low sensation seekers dislike risk, adventure, and novelty; when they go out to eat, they always go to the same restaurant and they always order chicken parmigiana, for example. Interestingly, the average sensation-seeking scores of firefighters and prisoners are essentially identical, but significantly higher than those of average college students (Zuckerman, 1994). Apparently, people can express the same tendencies toward risk taking and danger seeking in either socially constructive (firefighting) or destructive (crime) outlets. Why some sensation seekers end up in firehouses and others in prisons remains mysterious.

Personality research reveals that prisoners and firefighters tend to receive equally high scores on measures of sensation seeking, suggesting that they may have channeled their basic tendencies into dramatically different characteristic adaptations.

CAN PERSONALITY TRAITS CHANGE?

Longitudinal studies (see Chapter 10) show that with a few exceptions (Srivastava, John, Gosling, & Potter, 2003), the levels of most personality traits don't change much after age 30 and change even less after about age 50 (McCrae & Costa, 1994; Roberts & DelVecchio, 2000). We don't know whether psychotherapy can change personality, although many psychologists today are even less optimistic about this prospect than they were in Freud's day.

In the best seller *Listening to Prozac*, Peter Kramer (1993) sparked interest in the possibility that medication can change personality traits. He coined the term *cosmetic psychopharmacology* to describe the use of medications to produce long-term alterations in personality. According to Kramer, there's anecdotal evidence that certain mood-altering medications, like Prozac, Paxil, and Zoloft (see Chapter 16), produce calmness and decreased shyness, even among people without mental illness (Concar, 1994). Kramer argued that these drugs may allow us to become "better than well." Although the evidence is preliminary, the results of one study demonstrated that well-adjusted people who ingested Paxil experienced less hostility and more interest in socializing than those who ingested a placebo (Knutson et al., 1988).

Kramer's arguments raise fascinating scientific and practical questions. On the scientific side, might our personalities, which we think of as being an intrinsic part of ourselves, be more malleable than we supposed? On the practical side, could cosmetic psychopharmacology have any important disadvantages? As we learned in Chapter 11, evolutionary psychologists argue that many negative emotions serve essential adaptive functions. Anxiety, for example, may be a crucial warning signal of potential danger. If we reduced most people's anxiety levels, could we inadvertently produce a civilization of passive citizens blissfully unconcerned about impending disaster? Although this alarmist scenario seems unlikely in anything other than a science fiction thriller, it's clear that cosmetic psychopharmacology poses significant practical challenges that have yet to be resolved.

TRAIT MODELS EVALUATED CRITICALLY

Challenges by Mischel (1968) to the contrary, personality traits can be useful predictors of real-world behaviors, but only when they're aggregated (averaged) across different situations. Trait models have proved helpful to therapists, clinicians in prison settings, and psychologists who hope to predict long-term behavioral trends. In contrast to other personality theories we've reviewed, trait models are primarily efforts to *describe* individual differences in personality rather than to *explain* their causes. This emphasis on description is both a strength and a weakness. On the one hand, these models have advanced our understanding of personality structure and helped psychologists to predict performance in jobs, even the job of leader of the world's largest superpower. On the other hand, some trait models don't provide much insight into the causes of personality. For example, although the Big Five do a decent job of capturing personality differences among people, they don't shed much light on the origins of these differences.

Eysenck's model of personality proposes that introverts tend to be overaroused and extraverts underaroused. As a result, Eysenck argued, introverts try to shut out stimulation, whereas extraverts try to seek it out.

Some researchers, like Hans Eysenck, have tried to remedy this shortcoming. For example, according to Eysenck (1973), the personality dimension of extraversion–introversion is produced by differences in the threshold of arousal of the reticular activating system (RAS). As we learned in Chapter 3, the RAS controls alertness and is responsible for keeping us awake. If your RAS is still functioning at this late point in the chapter, you might be wondering how RAS activity is related to extraversion and introversion. Although the following hypothesis is paradoxical, Eysenck argued that extraverts have an *underactive* RAS: They're habitually underaroused and bored. So they seek out stimulation, including other people, to jack up their arousal (see the Yerkes-Dodson law in Chapter 11). In contrast, introverts tend to have an overactive RAS: They're habitually overaroused and overwhelmed, and try to minimize or shut out stimulation, again including other people. Interestingly, extraverts like loud music more than do introverts (Kageyama, 1999). Although the evidence for Eysenck's hypothesis isn't entirely consistent (Gray, 1981), his theorizing demonstrates that trait theories can generate fruitful hypotheses concerning the relations between personality traits and biological variables.

Personality Assessment: Measuring and Mismeasuring the Psyche

Personality wouldn't be useful to psychologists if they had no way of measuring it. That's where personality assessment enters into the picture: It offers us the promise of detecting individual differences in personality in a rigorous fashion. But developing accurate tools to measure personality is easier said than done.

FAMOUS—AND INFAMOUS—ERRORS IN PERSONALITY ASSESSMENT

Indeed, personality psychology has long been plagued by a parade of dubious assessment methods. Phrenology, which we encountered in Chapter 3, purported to detect people's personality traits by measuring the patterns of bumps on their heads. Related to phrenology was *physiognomy,* popular in the eighteenth and nineteenth centuries, which claimed to detect people's personality traits from their facial characteristics (Collins, 1999). The term "lowbrow," which today refers to someone who's uncultured, derives from the old belief that most nonintellectual people have protruding foreheads and a low brow line. This claim, like virtually all other claims of physiognomy, has been falsified. Still, physiognomy may contain a tiny kernel of truth. Research suggests that women do better than chance at figuring out which men are most interested in children merely by looking at still photographs of their faces (Roney, Hanson, Durante, & Maestripieri, 2006), although it's not clear to which features of men's faces they're attending.

Falsifiability

In the vein of physiognomy, psychologist William Sheldon believed he could draw inferences about people's personalities from their body types (see **Figure 14.5** on the next page). Highly muscular people (mesomorphs), he thought, tend to be assertive and bold, whereas lean and skinny people (ectomorphs) tend to be introverted and intellectual (Sheldon, 1971). Yet Sheldon failed to consider an alternative explanation for his observations: He wasn't blind to people's body types when he judged their personality traits and may have fallen prey to confirmation bias. Perhaps not surprisingly, most well-controlled studies later found the correlations between Sheldon's body types and personality traits to be weak or nonexistent (Deabler, Hartl, & Willis, 1974; Lester, Kaminsky, & McGovern, 1994).

Ruling Out Rival Hypotheses

With these errors of the past in mind, how can we distinguish good from bad personality assessment methods? Two key criteria for evaluating all tests, including personality tests, are reliability and validity (see Chapter 2). *Reliability* refers to consistency of measurement and *validity* to the extent to which a test measures what it

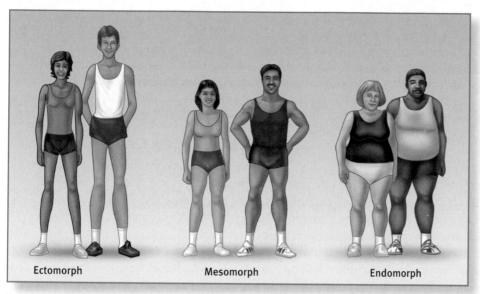

Figure 14.5 Sheldon's Body Types. According to William Sheldon, three major body types are associated with different personality traits. Yet research hasn't borne out most of Sheldon's claims. Because Sheldon wasn't blind to body type when rating people's personality traits, his findings may have been due largely to confirmation bias.

purports to measure. We'll keep these dual criteria in mind as we examine the two major types of personality tests: structured and projective.

STRUCTURED PERSONALITY TESTS

The best-known personality instruments are **structured personality tests.** These are typically paper-and-pencil tests consisting of questions that respondents answer in one of a few fixed ways. By fixed ways, we mean choosing between true and false answers, or by selecting options on a scale with, for example, 1 being "always true," 2 being "somewhat true," and so on, until 5, which is "always false." These numerical scales are called *Likert* formats.

MMPI and MMPI-2: Detecting Abnormal Personality. The **Minnesota Multiphasic Personality Inventory** or **MMPI** (Hathaway & McKinley, 1940) is the most extensively researched of all structured personality tests. Psychologists across the world use the MMPI to detect symptoms of mental disorders. Developed in the early 1940s by psychologist Starke Hathaway and neurologist J. Charnley McKinley of the University of Minnesota, the MMPI was revised in the 1980s by James Butcher and his colleagues (Butcher, Dahlstrom, Graham, Tellegen, & Kaemmer, 1989). This revised test, the MMPI-2, consists of 567 true/false items.

MMPI and MMPI-2: Construction and Content. The MMPI-2, like its predecessor, consists of ten *basic* scales, most of which assess mental disorders, such as paranoia, depression, and schizophrenia (see Chapter 15). Hathaway and McKinley developed these scales by means of an **empirical** (or data-based) **method of test construction.** Using this approach, researchers begin with two or more criterion groups, such as people with and without a specific psychological disorder, and examine which items best distinguish them. For example, the items on the MMPI depression scale are those that best differentiate patients with clinical depression from nondepressed people.

One consequence of the empirical method of test construction is that many MMPI and MMPI-2 items possess low **face validity.** Face validity refers to the extent to which respondents can tell what the items are measuring. In a face valid test, we can take the items on "face value": They assess what they appear to assess. Face validity is actually a misnomer, because it isn't really a form of validity at all. Because Hathaway and McKinley

structured personality tests
paper-and-pencil tests consisting of questions that respondents answer in one of a few fixed ways

Minnesota Multiphasic Personality Inventory (MMPI)
widely used structured test designed to assess symptoms of mental disorders

empirical (or data-based) **method of test construction**
approach to building tests in which researchers begin with two or more criterion groups, and examine which items best distinguish them

face validity
extent to which respondents can tell what the items are measuring

were concerned only with *whether*, but not *why*, the MMPI items differentiated among criterion groups, they ended up with some items that bear little obvious connection with the disorder they supposedly assess. To take an example of an item with low face validity from another structured personality test, can you guess what personality trait the following item assesses: "I think newborn babies look very much like little monkeys"? The answer is nurturance, that is, a tendency to care for others—with a "True" answer reflecting low nurturance and a "False" answer reflecting high nurturance—although few people who take the test can figure that out (Jackson, 1971, p. 238).

Researchers don't agree on whether low face validity is an overall advantage or disadvantage. Some believe that items with low face validity assess key aspects of personality that are subtle or lie outside of respondents' awareness (Meehl, 1945). Moreover, such items have the advantage of being difficult for respondents to fake. In contrast, other researchers believe that these items don't add to the MMPI's diagnostic capacity (Jackson, 1971; Weed, Ben-Porath, & Butcher, 1990).

The MMPI-2 contains 3 major *validity* scales. These scales detect various *response sets*, which are tendencies to distort reponses to items (see Chapter 2). Response sets, which can compromise the validity of psychological tests, include *impression management*—making ourselves look better than we really are—and *malingering*—making ourselves appear psychologically disturbed (see Chapter 2). The MMPI *L* (Lie) Scale consists of items assessing the denial of trivial faults (such as "I occasionally become angry"). If you deny a large number of such faults, it's likely that you're either (a) engaging in impression management or (b) a promising candidate for sainthood. Given that (a) is more likely than (b), psychologists typically use scores on the *L* scale to assess a dishonest approach to test-taking. The *F* (Frequency) Scale consists of items that people in the general population rarely endorse (such as "I have a cough most of the time"). High scores on *F* can indicate malingering, although they can also reflect serious psychological disturbance or carelessness in responding to items. The *K* (correction) Scale consists of items that are similar to, although subtler than, those on the *L* scale; this scale measures defensive or guarded responding.

As we can see in **Figure 14.6** on the next page, psychologists plot the ten basic scales and three validity scales of the MMPI-2 in profile form, which displays the pattern of each person's scale scores. Although many clinicians enjoy interpreting MMPI-2 profiles, research demonstrates that simple statistical formulas that can be programmed into a computer yield interpretations that are equally, if not more, valid than those of experienced clinicians (Garb, 1998; Goldberg, 1969). These findings, however, haven't exerted an appreciable impact on everyday clinical practice (Dawes, Faust, & Meehl, 1989).

The MMPI and MMPI-2 Evaluated Critically. Extensive research supports the reliability of most MMPI-2 scales, as well as their validity for differentiating among mental disorders (Graham, 2006; Greene, 2000). For example, the MMPI-2 schizophrenia scale distinguishes patients with schizophrenia from patients with other severe psychological disorders, like clinical depression (Walters & Greene, 1988).

Nevertheless, the MMPI-2 is problematic in several respects. Because many of its scales are correlated highly, they're largely redundant with each other (Helmes & Reddon, 1993). In addition, psychologists can't use MMPI-2 scales to make formal diagnoses of mental disorders, such as schizophrenia or clinical depression, because high scores on these scales aren't specific to a single disorder. Nevertheless, clinicians sometimes misuse these scales for this purpose (Graham, 2006).

CPI: Descendent of the MMPI. An offspring of the MMPI is the California Psychological Inventory (CPI; Gough, 1957), sometimes called the "common person's MMPI." Like the MMPI, the CPI was constructed empirically. Unlike the MMPI, the CPI is designed primarily for assessing personality traits in the normal range, such as dominance, flexibility, and sociability, making it a popular measure in college counseling centers and industry. Most CPI scales are reasonably reliable over time and are valid for assessing personality traits; for

factoid

There are now more MMPI scales than MMPI items. Researchers have derived hundreds of empirically constructed scales (in addition to the 10 basic scales) from the MMPI and MMPI-2 item pools. Among the strangest of these scales are the "Success in Baseball" scale, constructed by comparing major with minor league baseball players and the "Tired Homemaker" scale, constructed by comparing happy with unhappy homemakers (Dahlstrom, Welsh, & Dahlstrom, 1975; Graham, 2006). Nevertheless, the scientific support for many of these scales is weak.

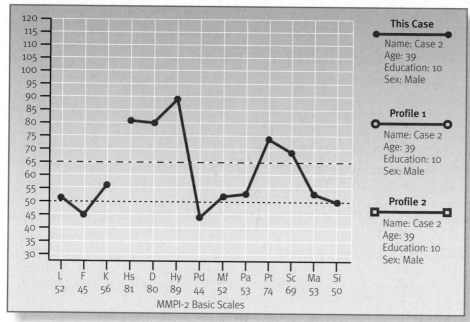

Figure 14.6 An MMPI-2 Profile. MMPI scores of 50 are average, and scores of 65 or above are abnormally high. This individual received elevated scores on several MMPI-2 clinical scales, including Hs (Hypochondriasis), D (Depression), Hy (Hysteria), and Sc (Schizophrenia). (*Source:* University of Minnesota Press)

example, people's CPI scores tend to correlate moderately with how their roommates view them (Ashton & Goldberg, 1973). Nevertheless, the CPI inherited some of its parent's shortcomings. In particular, many of the CPI scales are highly correlated and largely redundant with each other (Megargee, 1972).

Rationally/Theoretically Constructed Tests. Psychologists have also developed many structured personality measures using a **rational/theoretical method of test construction.** In contrast to an empirical approach, this approach requires test developers to begin with a clear-cut conceptualization of a trait and then write items to assess that conceptualization. Auke Tellegen (1982) adopted a rational/theoretical approach in constructing the Multidimensional Personality Questionnaire (MPQ) and later used factor analyses to select the best items for this test. The MPQ assesses three major self-reported personality traits related to (1) positive emotions (such as happiness and social intimacy), (2) negative emotions (such as anxiety and anger), and (3) impulse control (Tellegen et al., 1988). Studies show that the MPQ validly assesses these personality traits; scores on its scales correlate highly with ratings of the same traits by peers (Harkness, Tellegen, & Waller, 1995).

But not all rational/theoretical tests boast a strong track record of validity. The Myers-Briggs Type Indicator (MBTI) is perhaps the most widely administered personality test in the world. Given several million times a year, it's used by thousands of companies in the United States alone, including eighty-nine of the Fortune 100 (Paul, 2004). Even Harry Potter was placed in his mythical school after taking a variant of the MBTI (Rowling & GranPré, 1998). Based loosely on Jung's theory of personality, the MBTI sorts respondents into one of four categories—introversion–extroversion, sensing–intuiting, thinking–feeling, and judging–perceiving—yielding a total of sixteen personality types. Although some claim that the MBTI is helpful for predicting job performance and satisfaction, research raises doubts about its reliability and validity. Most respondents don't obtain the same MBTI personality type on retesting only a few months later, and MBTI scores don't relate in consistent ways to either the Big Five or measures of job preferences (Costa & McCrae, 1998; Hunsley, Lee, & Wood, 2003).

rational/theoretical method of test construction
approach to building tests that requires test developers to begin with a clear-cut conceptualization of a trait and then write items to assess that conceptualization

Another group of popular projective devices are anatomically detailed (also known as "anatomically correct") dolls, which feature representations of the male and female genitals. Many investigators and social workers allow children to play freely with the dolls, and then try to infer whether they've been sexually abused. Nevertheless, these dolls lead to numerous false identifications, because many nonabused children engage in sexualized doll play (Hunsley, Lee, & Wood, 2003).

PROJECTIVE TESTS

Projective tests consist of ambiguous stimuli, such as inkblots, drawings of social situations, or incomplete sentences, that examinees must interpret or make sense of. If you've ever looked for shapes in clouds in the sky, you have a sense of what it's like to take a projective test.

Influenced by psychoanalytic views of personality (Westen, Feit, & Zittel, 1999), especially Freud's notion of projection, these techniques rest on a crucial premise: the **projective hypothesis** (Frank, 1948). This hypothesis assumes that in the process of interpreting ambiguous stimuli, people inevitably project aspects of their personality onto the stimulus. Test interpreters can then work in reverse by examining people's answers for clues concerning their personality traits. In contrast to structured personality measures, projective techniques permit respondents considerable latitude in their answers.

Proponents of projective tests view them as the "stealth weapons" of the psychologist's arsenal. By circumventing respondents' defense mechanisms, they presumably offer valuable information concerning unconscious conflicts (Dosajh, 1966). Projective tests are among the most controversial of all psychological instruments, largely because their reliability and validity remain in dispute (Hunsley & Bailey, 1999; Lilienfeld, 1999; Lilienfeld, Wood, & Garb, 2001).

Rorschach Inkblot Test: What Might This Be? The best-known projective measure is the **Rorschach Inkblot Test,** developed by Swiss psychiatrist Hermann Rorschach in the early 1920s. The Rorschach, as it's commonly known, consists of ten symmetrical inkblots, five in black-and-white and five containing color (**Figure 14.7**). The Rorschach is one of the most commonly used of all personality measures (Watkins, Campbell, Nieberding, & Hallmark, 1995): It's administered about 6 million times every year (Sutherland, 1992; Wood, Nezworski, Lilienfeld, & Garb, 2000).

The Rorschach: Scoring and Interpretation. Rorschach examiners ask respondents to look at each inkblot and say what it resembles. Examiners then score their answers for numerous characteristics supposedly associated with personality traits. For example, people who focus on tiny details in the inkblots presumably have many obsessive-compulsive tendencies, and so on (see **Table 14.8**).

The Rorschach Evaluated Critically. Despite its widespread use, the Rorschach is scientifically controversial. The test-retest reliabilities of many of its scores are unknown, and their interrater reliabilities (see

Figure 14.7 An Inkblot Similar to That on the Rorschach Inkblot Test. Although widely used, the Rorschach appears not to possess the magical powers often attributed to it by its most enthusiastic proponents.

projective tests
tests consisting of ambiguous stimuli that examinees must interpret or make sense of

projective hypothesis
hypothesis that in the process of interpreting ambiguous stimuli, examinees project aspects of their personality onto the stimulus

Rorschach Inkblot Test
projective test consisting of ten symmetrical inkblots

Table 14.8 Widely Used Rorschach Scores and Their Interpretation, and Sample Responses That Reflect Them. These sample responses are based on the Rorschach-like inkblot in Figure 14.7.

Rorschach Score	Sample Response	Typical Interpretation
Pair response	"The top middle part looks like a pair of lungs."	Self-centeredness
Unusual detail response	"I see a tiny spot, like a speck of dust, to the left of the blot."	Obsessive-compulsive tendencies
Space response	"That white area in the lower middle looks like an upside-down bat."	Rebelliousness, anger
Human movement response	"The sides of the blot look like a person raising his hands."	Impulse control, inhibition

Chapter 2) are often problematic (Lilienfeld et al., 2001; Sultan, Andronikof, Reveillere, & Lemmel, 2006; Wood & Lilienfeld, 1999). Moreover, although psychologists commonly use the Rorschach to assist in making psychiatric diagnoses (Weiner, 1997), there's little evidence that it validly detects the features of most mental disorders (Wood, Garb, Nezworski, & Lilienfeld, 2000). Specifically, with the exception of schizophrenia and other conditions marked by abnormal thinking (see Chapter 15), there are few replicated associations between Rorschach scores and mental illnesses. Nor are there consistent associations between Rorschach scores and most personality traits (Wood, Nezworski, & Stejskal, 1996). There's also evidence that respondents can successfully fake schizophrenia, depression, and perhaps other disorders on the Rorschach (Schretlen, 1997). This is a particular problem, because in contrast to the MMPI-2, the Rorschach doesn't contain scales to detect malingering.

Replicability

Perhaps the greatest shortcoming of the Rorschach is the lack of evidence for its incremental validity. **Incremental validity** is the extent to which a test contributes information beyond other, more easily collected, measures (Sechrest, 1963). Given that the Rorschach takes a long time (typically about 45 minutes) to administer and even longer (1.5 to 2 hours) to interpret (Ball, Archer, & Imhoff, 1994), we'd hope that it yields information we couldn't glean from more efficient measures. Yet with only a few exceptions, there's no evidence that the Rorschach exhibits incremental validity beyond more easily collected data, such as life history information or the MMPI (Lilienfeld et al., 2001). In fact, adding the Rorschach to other measures sometimes results in *decreases* in the validity of clinicians' diagnostic judgments (Garb, 1984; Garb, Wood, & Lilienfeld, 2005), probably because clinicians often attend too heavily to invalid Rorschach information at the expense of more valid information.

TAT: Tell a Tale. The second most frequently administered projective test is the **Thematic Apperception Test (TAT),** developed by Henry Murray and his student Christiana Morgan (Morgan & Murray, 1935). The TAT consists of thirty-one cards depicting ambiguous situations, most of them interpersonal in nature (**Figure 14.8**). One of these cards represents the epitome of ambiguity: It's entirely blank. As a mnemonic device, we can think of the TAT as the "Tell a Tale" test, because examinees construct a story based on each card. Most clinicians interpret the TAT on an "impressionistic" basis, meaning that they inspect the content of the examinee's stories and analyze them using clinical intuition alone (Vane, 1981).

Some authors' claims to the contrary (Karon, 2000), there's little evidence that impressionistic TAT interpretations generate scores with adequate reliability or validity (Ryan, 1985). Scores derived from the TAT have often failed to distinguish psychiatric patients, such as people with clinical depression, from nonpatients, or to correlate in predicted directions with personality traits (Lilienfeld, 1999). Nor is there much evidence that TAT scores possess incremental validity beyond other sources of information, such as the MMPI (Garb, 1984; Lilienfeld et al., 2001).

One promising scoring system for the TAT uses cards similar to those on the TAT to assess needs for achievement (McClelland, Atkinson, Clark, & Lowell, 1953; see Chapter 11). Using this system, psychologists score responses to the cards based on the extent to which respondents' stories emphasize achievement-oriented themes, such as academic or career success. In contrast to most TAT scoring schemes, TAT measures of achievement possess at least some validity: They correlate positively with occupational success and income, although these associations are low in magnitude (Spangler, 1992). The TAT is also valid for assessing object relations, such as whether respondents perceive others as helpful or harmful (Westen, 1991).

Human Figure Drawings. Another popular group of projective tests is *human figure drawings*, such as the Draw-A-Person test (DAP; Machover, 1949), which requires respondents to draw a person (or persons) in any way they wish. Many clinicians who administer these measures interpret them on the basis of specific drawing "signs" (Chapman & Chapman, 1967; Smith & Dumont, 1995). For example, large eyes in drawings

Figure 14.8 Thematic Apperception Test (TAT) Sample Item. One of the thirty-one cards of the TAT. Note that the sex of the figure in the foreground is ambiguous (although Murray apparently intended this person to be male), as is the emotional expression of the woman in the background. (Murray, 1971)

incremental validity
extent to which a test contributes information beyond other, more easily collected, measures

Thematic Apperception Test (TAT)
projective test requiring examinees to tell a story in response to ambiguous pictures

Figure 14.9 Handwriting Sample. According to many graphologists, this handwriting sample suggests a person who's confused and scatter-brained. Yet research provides little or no support for graphologists' personality interpretations. In many cases, these interpretations probably stem from a representativeness heuristic—in this case, the (false) assumption that someone with disorganized handwriting has a disorganized personality. (*Source: The Graphology Review*, No. 19)

Ruling Out Rival Hypotheses

One of the most unconventional, yet still popular, projective tests is the Luscher Color Test, which is premised on the notion that respondents' color preferences reveal their personality traits (Luscher & Scott, 1969). For example, people who like blue supposedly harbor needs for tranquility, whereas people who like green supposedly harbor needs to impress others. Research suggests that this test is essentially worthless for assessing personality (Holmes et al., 1984).

graphology
psychological interpretation of handwriting

presumably reflect suspiciousness, while large genitalia in drawings presumably reflect concerns about sexuality.

Nevertheless, the correlations between human figure drawing signs and personality traits are low to nonexistent (Kahill, 1984; Motta, Little, & Tobin, 1993; Swenson, 1968). Moreover, because people often produce markedly different drawing characteristics on different occasions, the test-retest reliabilities of these signs are frequently poor (Kahill, 1984). Perhaps most problematically, scores derived from human figure drawings are confounded with artistic ability: Research suggests that people may be diagnosed as psychologically disturbed merely because they draw poorly (Cressen, 1975; Kahill, 1984).

Graphology. A final widely used projective technique is **graphology:** the psychological interpretation of handwriting (see **Figure 14.9**). Many firms in the United States and abroad use graphology in an effort to detect potential employees who are prone to dishonest behavior (Beyerstein & Beyerstein, 1991). Proponents of "graphotherapeutics" even claim to cure psychological disorders by altering people's handwriting (Beyerstein, 1996).

Many of the handwriting signs used by graphologists rely heavily on the *representativeness heuristic* (Chapter 2): Because certain handwriting features bear a superficial resemblance to certain traits, graphologists assume they go together. For example, some graphologists maintain that individuals who cross their *t*s with lines resembling little whips are sadistic (Carroll, 2000).

Nevertheless, graphological interpretations have low reliability. In one study, Lewis Goldberg (1986) presented professional graphologists with one person's handwriting but told them that it was produced by different people over time. The graphologists' interpretations of the handwriting changed whenever they believed it was generated by a different person. Other carefully conducted studies on graphology have found almost no correlation between handwriting signs and either personality traits or job performance (Ben-Shakhar et al., 1986; Klimoski, 1992). A few investigations (Drory, 1986) suggested that certain handwriting indicators are valid predictors of job success, but these studies were flawed because researchers asked participants to write brief autobiographies. As a consequence, graphologists may have based their interpretations on the *content* of participants' autobiographies rather than their handwriting (Hines, 2003). To exclude this confound, investigators have asked participants to write identical passages. When they've done so, the validities of graphological interpretations have plummeted to about zero.

COMMON PITFALLS IN PERSONALITY ASSESSMENT

Imagine that as part of a research requirement for your introductory psychology class you've just completed a structured personality test, like the MMPI-2. You look on with anxious anticipation as the research assistant inputs your data into a computer, which spits out the following personality description:

> Some of your hopes and dreams are pretty unrealistic. You have a great deal of unused potential that you have not yet turned to your advantage. Although you sometimes enjoy being around others, you value your privacy. You prize your independence and dislike being hemmed in by rules and restrictions. You are an independent thinker and do not accept others' opinions without strong evidence. You sometimes have serious doubts about whether you have made the right decision or done the right thing. Despite these doubts, you are a strong person whom others can count on in times of trouble.

After reading this description, you turn to the research assistant with a mixture of amazement and awe, and exclaim, "This description fits me perfectly. You've hit the nail on the head!"

But there's a catch. This description, the research assistant informs you, wasn't based on your test results at all. Instead, this description is identical to one that all 100 previous participants have received. You've been the victim of a devilish hoax. This example illustrates what Paul Meehl (1956) termed the *P. T. Barnum effect,* after the circus entrepreneur who said, "I try to give a little something to everyone."

The P. T. Barnum Effect: The Perils of Personal Validation. The **P. T. Barnum effect** is the tendency of people to accept high base rate descriptions—descriptions that apply to almost everyone—as accurate. It demonstrates that *personal validation*—the use of subjective judgments of accuracy (Forer, 1949)—is a flawed method of evaluating a test's validity. We may be convinced that the results of a personality test fit us to a T, but that doesn't mean the test is valid.

The P. T. Barnum effect helps to explain the popularity of astrological horoscopes, palmistry, and crystal ball, tea leaf, and tarot card readings. Like the fortunes in fortune cookies, all of these assessment methods generate highly generalized descriptions that apply to just about everyone. Despite their widespread use, there's no evidence for their validity (Hines, 2003; Park, 1982). People are especially likely to accept P. T. Barnum descriptions they believe are tailored specifically to them (Snyder, Shenkel, & Lowery, 1977). This finding probably helps to explain why horoscopes—which specify the precise year, month, day, and occasionally even time of the person's birth—are often so convincing.

In an illustration of the P. T. Barnum effect, Susan Blackmore (1983) found that clients couldn't pick out their own tarot card readings from nine other readings at better than chance levels. Yet when tarot card readers gave their readings to clients on a face-to-face basis, clients found them extremely accurate. Because each reading contained general statements that apply to everyone, clients who heard only one reading found it believable.

The same principle applies to astrology. People can't pick out their horoscope from others at better than chance levels (Dean, 1987). Nevertheless, when people read their horoscope in the newspaper they're often certain it applies to them. One probable reason for this curious discrepancy is that people tend to read only the horoscope for their own sign, but not others. If they bothered to read all twelve horoscopes, they'd probably realize that most or even all of these horoscopes fit them equally well. Although astrology makes extraordinary claims, namely, that it can divine people's personality traits with nearly perfect accuracy, the evidence for these claims is virtually nonexistent.

The P. T. Barnum effect can also fool psychologists into believing that certain traits describe specific groups of people even when they don't. Many pop psychologists claim that adult children of alcoholics (ACOAs), of which recent U.S. President Bill Clinton is an example, display a distinctive constellation of personality traits. ACOAs are supposedly perfectionistic, concerned about others' approval, overly protective of others, and prone to hiding their feelings. But when three researchers (Logue, Sher, & Frensch, 2000) administered a questionnaire consisting of presumed ACOA characteristics (such as, "You sometimes project a front, hiding your own true feelings") to both ACOAs and non-ACOAs, they found no significant differences. Both groups found the supposed ACOA statements to fit them well and about as well as a set of P. T. Barnum statements. Because these traits are so widespread in the general population (who among us doesn't sometimes hide our true feelings?), the commonly accepted personality profile of the ACOA is probably attributable to the P. T. Barnum effect.

The popularity of tarot card reading, crystal ball reading, palmistry, and many similar techniques probably stems largely from the P. T. Barnum effect.

Extraordinary Claims

fact**oid**

The word *disaster*, which means "bad star" in Latin, originates from astrology. Many ancient people believed that catastrophic events often resulted from unfortunate configurations of stars in the night sky.

*Psycho**Mythology***
Criminal Profiling

Another practice whose popularity may derive in part from the P. T. Barnum effect is *criminal profiling,* a technique depicted in the Academy Award–winning 1991 movie *The Silence of the Lambs,* starring Jodie Foster. Criminal profilers at the FBI and other law enforcement agencies claim to draw detailed inferences about perpetrators' personality traits and motives from the pattern of crimes committed.

It's true that we can often guess certain characteristics of criminals at better than chance levels. If we're investigating a homicide, we'll do better than flipping a coin by guessing that the murderer was a male (most murders are committed by men)

(continued)

P. T. Barnum effect
tendency of people to accept high base rate descriptions as accurate

between the ages of 15 and 25 (most murders are committed by adolescents and young adults) who suffers from psychological problems (most murderers suffer from psychological problems). But criminal profilers purport to go considerably beyond such widely available statistics. They typically claim to possess unique expertise and to be able to harness their years of accumulated experience to outperform statistical formulas.

Nevertheless, their assessments sometimes echo P. T. Barnum. In the fall of 2002, when the Washington, DC, area was paralyzed by random sniper shootings at gas stations and in parking lots, one former FBI profiler predicted that the sniper would turn out to be someone who is "self-centered" and "angry" at others (*New York Times,* 2002)—both fairly obvious guesses that most laypeople could make.

Indeed, research demonstrates that police officers can't distinguish genuine criminal profiles from bogus criminal profiles consisting of vague and general personality characteristics (such as "he has deep-seated problems with hostility"). This finding suggests the parsimonious hypothesis that profilers often base their conclusions about criminals on little more than P. T. Barnum statements (Allison, Smith, & Morgan, 2003; Gladwell, 2007). Moreover, although some researchers have found that profilers sometimes perform better than untrained individuals in identifying criminal suspects, others have found that professional profilers are no more accurate in gauging the personality features of murderers than are college students with no training in criminology (Homant & Kennedy, 1998). In one study, chemistry majors actually produced more accurate profiles of a murderer than did experienced homicide detectives and police officers (Kocsis, Hayes, & Irwin, 2002). Perhaps most important, there's no persuasive evidence that criminal profilers outperform statistical formulas that take into account the psychological traits of known murderers.

Criminal profiling may thus be more of an urban legend than a scientifically demonstrated ability. Yet tradition dies hard, and the FBI and other crime organizations remain in the full-time business of training criminal profilers.

Occam's Razor

Hit shows such as *CSI: Crime Scene Investigation* have stimulated Americans' interest in criminal profiling. Nevertheless, research suggests that criminal profiling is more art than science.

Illusory Correlation: Seeing Mirages in Test Results.

Some psychologists and counselors avidly use tests like the Rorschach and TAT in part because they're prone to the same errors in thinking as the rest of us. One such error is *illusory correlation,* which is the perception of nonexistent statistical associations between variables (see Chapter 2). An illusory correlation is a mirage that leads us to see something, namely, a relationship between two variables, that isn't there.

Loren and Jean Chapman (1967) showed college students a series of concocted human figure drawings containing certain physical features (such as large eyes and large genitals) along with a description of the personality traits of the person of who supposedly produced each drawing (such as paranoid and overly concerned about sexuality). They then asked participants to estimate the extent to which these physical features and personality traits co-occurred in the drawings. Unbeknownst to participants, there was *no* correlation between the drawing features and personality traits, because the researchers had paired these two sets of variables randomly.

Yet participants consistently saw certain drawing features as associated with certain personality traits. Interestingly, these were the same drawing features that experienced clinicians tend to believe are associated with these traits—and which research has shown to be invalid (Kahill, 1984; Swenson, 1968). For example, participants incorrectly

Some drivers are convinced that "the lights are always red when I'm in a rush." They're probably falling prey to illusory correlation: They're noticing the red lights much more when they're running late.

reported that people who produced drawings with large eyes tended to be paranoid and that people who produced drawings with large genitals tended to be overly concerned with sexuality.

Like graphologists, students and clinicians probably rely on the representativeness heuristic: Like goes with like. As a result, they can be fooled, because things that seem similar on the surface don't always go together in real life. They may also rely on the availability heuristic (see Chapter 2) recalling the cases in which drawing signs correspond to personality traits and forgetting the cases in which they don't.

APPLY YOUR THINKING

If we were training clinical psychologists, how might we try to reduce the likelihood of illusory correlation?

Personality Assessment Evaluated Critically. Personality assessment has contributed to psychologists' ability to detect personality traits, both normal and abnormal, and has helped them to predict significant real-world behaviors. Moreover, psychologists have succeeded in developing a number of personality measures, especially structured personality tests, with adequate reliability and validity. Given the scientific progress that psychologists have made in assessing personality, it's troubling that many continue to use measures with weak scientific support. In particular, some clinicians still rely on scores derived from the Myers-Briggs and several projective tests, like the Rorschach, TAT, and human figure drawings, that are of questionable reliability and validity.

Still, research indicates that some projective techniques can achieve satisfactory reliability and validity. Certain *sentence completion tests,* which ask respondents to complete a sentence stem (for example, "My father was . . ."), are predictive of delinquency, moral development, and other important characteristics (Loevinger, 1988). Ironically, many of these well-supported projective tests are used less widely than projective tests whose validity is weak (Lilienfeld et al., 2001).

To understand why psychologists continue to use questionable psychological tests, we must remember that they're prone to the same errors in judgment that afflict the rest of us (Lilienfeld, Wood, & Garb, 2007). In particular, the phenomenon of illusory correlation illustrates a theme we've underscored throughout this book: Personal experience, although enormously useful in generating hypotheses, can be misleading when it comes to testing them. Only scientific methods, which are essential safeguards against human error, allow us to determine whether we should trust our personal experience or disregard it in favor of evidence to the contrary.

---

fictoid

Myth: A practitioner's number of years of experience with using a personality test, like the MMPI-2 or Rorschach, is positively correlated with the accuracy of his or her clinical judgments using that test.

Reality: For most personality measures, including the MMPI-2 and Rorschach, there's essentially no correlation between experience with using a test and clinical accuracy (Garb, 1998). Once a person has been thoroughly trained in how to administer and interpret a personality measure, additional years of experience typically makes little or no difference. In one striking illustration of this point, the results of one study showed that a psychologist who'd authored two books on a widely used human figure drawing test did worse than either psychologists or hospital secretaries when using this test to diagnose psychological problems in children (Levenberg, 1975).

ASSESS YOUR KNOWLEDGE: FACT OR FICTION?

(1) Items with low face validity tend to be especially easy for respondents to fake. (True/False)

(2) Simple formulas that can be programmed into computers yield MMPI-2 interpretations equal or superior to those of experienced clinicians. (True/False)

(3) Adding the Rorschach Inkblot Test to other measures in a test battery sometimes produces significant decreases in validity. (True/False)

(4) The more detailed and specific an astrological horoscope is about someone's personality traits, the more likely that person will perceive it as accurate. (True/False)

(5) Research suggests that although students sometimes fall victim to illusory correlation, experienced clinicians do not. (True/False)

Answers: (1) F (p. 610); (2) T (p. 610); (3) T (p. 613); (4) F (p. 615); (5) F (p. 617)

Personality: What Is It and How Can We Study It? (pp. 579–584)

STUDY the Learning Objectives

▶ Distinguish between the two major approaches to studying personality
- There are two key approaches to personality: nomothetic and idiographic. Nomothetic approaches focus on laws that apply to most people; idiographic approaches focus on the unique patterning of characteristics within a person.

▶ Describe how twin and adoption studies shed light on genetic and environmental influences on personality
- Twin and adoption studies suggest that many personality traits are heritable and point to a key role for nonshared environment, but not shared environment.

DO YOU KNOW THESE TERMS?
- ❏ **traits** (p. 579)
- ❏ **nomothetic approach** (p. 579)
- ❏ **idiographic approach** (p. 579)
- ❏ **molecular genetic studies** (p. 582)

How would you challenge the notion that a specific gene exists for divorce, religiosity, or political attitudes? (p. 583)

mypsychlab
where learning comes to life!

SUCCEED with

Genes and Environment on Personality
Do you have the same personality as your siblings? Explore the roles of nature and nurture in the origins of personality. (p. 580)

EXPLORE

THINK about

what You would do . . .
Your mother is an ardent fan of the Dear Abby column, so much so that every piece of advice she gives you is based on Abby's responses to similar situations. How could you help her to evaluate this advice with an appropriately critical eye? (p. 579)

Name the major influences (factors) on personality discussed by behavior geneticists. (pp. 579–580)

1. _____
2. _____
3. _____

ASSESS your knowledge

1. Personality consists of _____, relatively enduring predispositions that influence our behavior across many situations. (p. 579)

2. A _____ approach strives to understand personality by identifying general laws that govern the behavior of all individuals. (p. 579)

3. If you study personality by identifying a person's unique configuration of characteristics and life experiences, you are employing an _____ approach. (p. 579)

4. _____ _____ influences make individuals within the same family less alike. (pp. 579–580)

5. To distinguish the effects of genes from the effects of environment, behavior geneticists have conducted _____ studies and _____ studies of personality. (p. 580)

6. If the heritability of personality were 1.0 (that is,

100%) then correlations of personality traits in identical twins would be _____ (pp. 580–581)

7. The Minnesota Twins study found that identical twins reared apart tend to be strikingly (similar/dissimilar) in their personality traits. (p. 581)

8. According to the Minnesota Twins study, _____ environment plays little to no role in adult personality. (pp. 581–582)

9. In Scarr's adoption study of neuroticism, the correlations between biological parents and their adopted-away children are slightly (lower/higher) than the correlations between adoptive parents and their adopted children. (p. 582)

10. In an attempt to identify which genes are associated with specific personality traits, some researchers have turned to _____ _____ studies, but there have been relatively few replications. (p. 582)

If you did not receive an access code to MyPsychLab with this text and wish to purchase access online, please visit www.mypsychlab.com.

Psychoanalytic Theory: The Controversial Legacy of Sigmund Freud and His Followers (pp. 584–597)

STUDY the Learning Objectives

▶ Describe the core assumptions of psychoanalytic theory
- Freud's psychoanalytic theory rests on three core assumptions: psychic determinism, symbolic meaning, and unconscious motivation.

▶ Distinguish among the three Freudian agencies of the psyche and explain their interactions
- According to Freud, personality results from the interactions among id, ego, and superego. The ego copes with threat by deploying defense mechanisms.

▶ Identify the five psychosexual stages of psychoanalytic theory
- Freud's five psychosexual stages included oral, anal, phallic, latency, and genital.

▶ Describe key criticisms of psychoanalytic theory.

THINK about

what You would do . . .
In a mock courtroom exercise, you must defend a client who murdered her husband in the heat of passion after finding him with another woman. Using Freud's three agencies of personality, how would you attempt to lessen your client's sentence? (pp. 586–588)

Identify and summarize at least four of the six major criticisms of Freud's psychoanalytic theory. (pp. 592–594)

1. _____
2. _____
3. _____
4. _____
5. _____
6. _____

mypsychlab
where learning comes to life!

The Id, Ego, and Superego

Unconscious to Conscious: Exploring the three core constructs of personality according to Freud. (p. 587)

EXPLORE

Describe Jung's theory of archetypes and the collective unconscious, and identify a possible shortcoming in this theory. (p. 595)

ASSESS your knowledge

1. Freud, a neurologist by training, initially thought that mental disorders were _____, physiologically caused, but later converted to the belief that they were _____, psychologically caused. (pp. 584–585)

2. Freud and Charcot found that patients' recollections of early trauma were often accompanied by a _____. (p. 585)

3. Freud's psychoanalytic theory rests on three core assumptions: (1) psychic determinism, (2) symbolic meaning, and (3) _____ _____. (pp. 585–586)

4. Freud hypothesized that the human psyche consists of three agencies: _____, _____, and _____. (pp. 587–588)

5. The reality principle governs the _____, whereas the pleasure principle governs the _____. (p. 587)

6. Freud believed that the ego maintained psychological health by engaging in _____

_____, unconscious maneuvers intended to minimize anxiety. (p. 588)

7. Freud's controversial theory of personality development consisted of five stages: _____, _____ , _____, _____, and _____. (pp. 590–592)

8. Recent research has shown that many aspects of Freud's psychoanalytic theory (are/aren't) supported when scientific standards, such as falsifiability, are applied. (p. 592)

9. Neo-Freudian theories share with Freudian theory an emphasis on unconscious influences on behavior and the importance of early experience in shaping personality, but they differ by placing less emphasis on _____ as a driving force in personality. (p. 594)

10. A pupil of Freud, Jung took the concept of unconscious further and theorized there is a _____ _____ that comprises memories that ancestors have passed down to us across generations. (p. 595)

- Psychoanalytic theory has been criticized for unfalsifiability, failed predictions, lack of evidence, and flawed assumption.

▶ Identify the central features of neo-Freudian theories
- Neo-Freudians shared with Freud an emphasis on unconscious influences and the importance of early experience, but emphasized less sexuality as a driving force in personality.

DO YOU KNOW THESE TERMS?
- ❑ **somatogenic** (p. 584)
- ❑ **catharsis** (p. 585)
- ❑ **psychogenic** (p. 585)
- ❑ **psychic determinism** (p. 585)
- ❑ **id, pleasure principle, ego** (p. 587)
- ❑ **reality principle, superego** (p. 587)
- ❑ **defense mechanisms** (p. 588)
- ❑ **repression, denial, regression** (p. 589)
- ❑ **reaction-formation, projection** (p. 589)
- ❑ **displacement** (p. 589)
- ❑ **rationalization** (p. 589)
- ❑ **intellectualization** (p. 590)
- ❑ **identification with the aggressor** (p. 590)
- ❑ **sublimation, erogenous zone** (p. 590)
- ❑ **oral stage** (p. 590)
- ❑ **anal stage** (p. 590)
- ❑ **phallic stage** (p. 591)
- ❑ **Oedipus & Electra complexes** (p. 591)
- ❑ **penis envy** (p. 591)
- ❑ **latency stage** (p.592)
- ❑ **genital stage** (p. 592)
- ❑ **neo-Freudian theories** (p. 594)
- ❑ **style of life** (p. 594)
- ❑ **inferiority complex** (p. 594)
- ❑ **collective unconscious** (p. 595)
- ❑ **archetypes** (p. 595)
- ❑ **object relations theorists** (p. 596)

Behavioral and Social Learning Theories of Personality (pp. 597–600)

what You would do . . .
Using Bandura's theory of reciprocal determinism, how would you convince your roommate that being sociable has benefits outside the classroom ? (p. 598)

Summarize the role of observational learning in shaping children's personalities. (p. 598)

mypsychlab
where learning comes to life!

Behavioral versus Social Learning Theories of Personality

Does thinking play a role in personality? Find out what behavior and social learning theorists have to say. (pp. 597–598)

EXPLORE

ASSESS your knowledge

1. Radical behaviorists like Skinner believe that our personalities stem largely from differences in our learning _____. (p. 597)

2. Radical behaviorists believe that personality (causes/consists of) behaviors. (p. 597)

3. For radical behaviorists, personality is under the control of two major influences: (1) genetic factors, and (2) _____ in the environment. (p. 597)

4. One of the few things that Freud and Skinner would have agreed on is the concept of _____, the belief that all our actions are products of preexisting causal influences. (p. 597)

5. According to Skinner, the unconscious variables that play a role in causing behavior lie (outside/inside) us. (p. 598)

6. Unlike Skinner, social learning theorists emphasize _____ as a cause of personality. (p. 598)

7. Social learning theorists propose that much of learning occurs through watching others, or _____ learning. (p. 598)

8. Rotter introduced the concept of _____ _____ to describe the extent to which an individual believes that the reinforcers and punishers lie inside or outside of their control. (p. 598)

9. Someone with an internal locus of control is (more/less) prone than someone with an external locus of control to emotional upset following life stressors. (pp. 598–599)

10. Social learning theorists' claim that observational learning plays a powerful role in personality is subject to criticism because it implies that _____ _____ plays a causal role. (pp. 599–600)

STUDY the Learning Objectives

▶ Identify the core assumptions of behavioral views of personality
- Radical behaviorists view personality as under the control of two major influences: genetic factors and contingencies in the environment. Radical behaviorists, like psychoanalysts, are determinists and believe in unconscious processing, but they deny the existence of "the" unconscious.

▶ Identify the core assumptions of social learning theories of personality and their differences from traditional behavioral views
- In contrast to radical behaviorists, social learning theorists accord a central role to thinking in the causes of personality, and argue that observational learning and a sense of personal control play key roles in personality.

▶ Describe key criticisms of behavioral and social learning approaches
- Critics have accused radical behaviorists of going too far in their exclusion of thinking in the causes of personality.
- The social learning theory claim that observational learning plays a crucial role in personality runs counter to findings that shared environmental influence on adult personality is minimal.

DO YOU KNOW THESE TERMS?
- ❑ **social learning theorists** (p. 598)
- ❑ **locus of control** (p. 598)

Humanistic Models of Personality: The Third Force (pp. 600–602)

STUDY the Learning Objectives

▶ Explain the concept of self-actualization and its role in humanistic models
- Most humanistic psychologists argue that the core motive in personality is self-actualization.
- According to Carl Rogers, unhealthy behavior results from the imposition of conditions of worth, which block drives toward self-actualization.

▶ Identify Maslow's characteristics of self-actualized individuals
- According to Maslow, self-actualized individuals are creative, spontaneous, accepting, and prone to peak experiences.

▶ Describe key criticisms of humanistic approaches
- Critics have attacked humanistic models for being naive about human nature and for advancing theories that are difficult to falsify.

DO YOU KNOW THESE TERMS?
- ❏ **self-actualization** (p. 600)
- ❏ **conditions of worth** (p. 601)
- ❏ **incongruence** (p. 601)
- ❏ **peak experiences** (p. 601)

SUCCEED with mypsych lab *where learning comes to life!*

Psychodynamic, Behavioral, Trait and Type, Humanistic, and Cognitive Approaches to Personality

Compare humanistic theories of personality with other personality theories and decide which theory you find most compelling. (pp. 600–601)

EXPLORE

THINK about what **You** would do . . .
You are assigned a project on Maslow's self-actualization personality theory. How would you go about identifying three self-actualized people alive today? (p. 601)

Followers of Maslow would probably argue that both Mother Teresa and Mahatma Gandhi were self-actualized people. Name three to five traits of self-actualized people. (p. 601)

ASSESS your knowledge

1. Humanistic psychologists rejected the _____ of psychoanalysts and behaviorists and embraced the notion of free will. (p. 600)

2. The core motive in personality, according to humanistic psychology, is _____. (p. 600)

3. Carl Rogers, pioneer of humanistic psychology, held an (optimistic/pessimistic) view of human nature. (p. 601)

4. According to Rogers' model of personality, our personalities consist of three major components: _____, _____, and _____ _____ _____. (p. 601)

5. In Rogers' theory, the _____ is our innate genetic blueprint, and the _____ is our set of beliefs about who we are. (p. 601)

6. According to Rogers, _____ __ _____ are the expectations we place on ourselves for appropriate and inappropriate behavior. (p. 601)

7. _____ occurs when our personalities are inconsistent with our innate dispositions. (p. 601)

8. Maslow studied self-actualized people, and found they were prone to _____ _____, transcendent moments of intense excitement. (p. 601)

9. Critics argue that actualization of our full genetic potential is (likely/unlikely) to bring about the state of bliss that Rogers imagined. (pp. 601–602)

10. Maslow may have fallen prey to _____ _____ because he may have limited his study to individuals who displayed the traits he hypothesized were associated with self-actualized people. (p. 602)

Trait Models of Personality: Consistencies in Our Behavior (pp. 602–608)

STUDY the Learning Objectives

▶ Describe key challenges to trait models of personality
- Two challenges to trait models are the danger of circularity and reducing the large number of trait terms to a small number of primary traits.

▶ Explain what personality traits can and can't predict
- Personality traits rarely predict isolated behaviors, but are helpful for predicting long-term behavioral trends.

▶ Identify models of personality structure and their implications and limitations
- One influential model of personality is the Big Five, which may be limited as people may not have conscious access to all important features of personality.

▶ Identify cultural influences on personality
- There may be significant cultural differences in personality, such as differences in individualism versus collectivism.

▶ Identify key criticisms of trait models
- Some models of personality structure, including the Big Five, are more descriptive than explanatory.

THINK about what **You** would do . . .
In a campus forum involving health care professionals and psychologists, the topic of cosmetic psychopharmacology and its potential effect on personality arises. What position would you take on this issue, and why? (pp. 606–607)

SUCCEED with mypsych lab *where learning comes to life!*

Five Factor Model

Find out the buzz behind the "Big Five" factors of personality.

(pp. 604–605)

EXPLORE

ASSESS your knowledge

1. Trait theorists aim to pinpoint the major _____ that give rise to differences in our personalities. (p. 602)

2. A statistical technique called _____ _____ analyzes the correlations among responses on personality inventories. (p. 603)

3. Mischel's review suggested that people's behaviors (are/aren't) very consistent across different situations. (pp. 603–604)

4. A group of traits that have surfaced repeatedly in factor analyses of personality measures is known as the _____ _____. (p. 604)

5. Using the acronym OCEAN as a mnemonic device, the traits in this group are: _____ __ _____, _____, _____, _____, and _____. (pp. 604–605)

6. The _____ approach assumes that the most crucial features of personality are embedded in our language. (p. 604)

7. Morality (is/isn't) one of the Big Five factors. (p. 604)

8. In studying cultural influences on personality, researchers have found that _____ __ _____, doesn't emerge clearly in all cultures. (p. 605)

9. Longitudinal studies have found that our levels of most traits do not change much after age _____. (p. 606)

10. According to Eysenck, extraverts seek out stimulation because they have an (underactive/overactive) reticular activating system (RAS). (p. 607)

Match the appropriate personality trait and description using the Big Five measure. (p. 604)

___ Extraversion	a. tend to be careful and responsible
___ Neuroticism	b. tend to be intellectually curious and unconventional
___ Conscientiousness	c. tend to be friendly and easy to get along with
___ Agreeableness	d. tend to be social and lively
___ Openness to Experience	e. tend to be tense and moody

DO YOU KNOW THESE TERMS?
❑ factor analysis (p. 603)
❑ Big Five (p. 604)
❑ lexical approach (p. 604)

Personality Assessment: Measuring and Mismeasuring the Psyche (pp. 608–617)

what You would do . . .
THINK about

Working in the human resources department of a major credit card company, you are asked to investigate the possible use of handwriting analysis in creating personality profiles of employees. How would you evaluate the advisability of doing so? (p. 614)

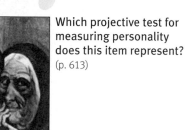

Which projective test for measuring personality does this item represent? (p. 613)

SUCCEED with

 mypsychlab

Personality Assessment
Objective versus subjective measures of personality: Which provide the most accurate results?
(p. 609)

EXPLORE

STUDY the Learning Objectives

▶ Describe structured personality tests, particularly the MMPI-2, and their methods of construction
  • Structured personality tests consist of questions that people can answer in only one of a few fixed ways. Some are developed empirically, others rationally/theoretically.

▶ Describe projective tests, particularly the Rorschach, and their strengths and weaknesses
  • Projective tests consist of ambiguous stimuli that the examinee must interpret. Many of these tests lack reliability, validity, and incremental validity.

▶ Identify common pitfalls in personality assessment
  • Two common pitfalls in personality assessment are the P. T. Barnum Effect and illusory correlation, which highlight the the scientific method as a safeguard against human error.

DO YOU KNOW THESE TERMS?
❑ structured personality tests (p. 609)
❑ Minnesota Multiphasic Personality Inventory (MMPI) (p. 609)
❑ empirical method of test construction (p. 609)
❑ face validity (p. 609)
❑ rational/theoretical method of test construction (p. 611)
❑ projective tests (p. 612)
❑ projective hypothesis (p. 612)
❑ Rorschach Inkblot Test (p. 612)
❑ incremental validity (p. 613)
❑ Thematic Apperception Test (TAT) (p. 613)
❑ graphology (p. 614)
❑ P. T. Barnum effect (p. 615)

ASSESS your knowledge

1. Tests that consist of questions that respondents answer in one of a few fixed ways are called _____ personality tests. (p. 609)

2. The _____ _____ _____ _____ is widely used to assess mental disorders and consists of ten basic scales. (p. 609)

3. Hathaway and McKinley developed these scales using an _____ method of test construction. (p. 609)

4. Many MMPI and MMPI-2 items possess low _____ _____, which refers to the extent to which respondents can tell what the items are measuring. (p. 609)

5. Extensive research (supports/doesn't support) the reliability of most MMPI-2 scales, as well as their validity for differentiating among mental disorders. (p. 610)

6. The _____ method of test construction requires test developers to begin with a clear-cut conceptualization of a trait and then write items to assess that conceptualization. (p. 611)

7. _____ techniques consist of ambiguous stimuli that examinees must interpret or make sense of. (p. 612)

8. The _____ hypothesis assumes that in the process of interpreting ambiguous stimuli, examinees inevitably project aspects of their personality onto the stimulus. (p. 612)

9. The widely used _____ _____ test consists of ten symmetrical inkblots, and remains scientifically controversial. (p. 612)

10. The tendency of people to endorse high base rate descriptions—descriptions that apply to almost everyone—is called the ____ ____ ____. (p.615)

Remember these questions from the beginning of the chapter? Think again and ask yourself if you would answer them differently based on what you now know about personality. (For more detailed explanations, see MyPsychLab.)

▶ Does a similar upbringing lead to similarities in children's personalities? (p. 581)
▶ Did Freud believe that sex is the only important motive in personality? (p. 587)
▶ Would Freud and Skinner have agreed on anything? (p. 597)
▶ How consistent are we in our behavior across situations? (pp. 603–604)
▶ Can we reduce the enormous variation in people's personalities to a mere handful of underlying factors? (pp. 604–605)
▶ Are stereotypes about national character accurate? (p. 606)
▶ Can we use responses to inkblots to infer people's personality traits? (p. 612)
▶ Is criminal profiling scientific? (pp. 615–616)

THINKING Scientifically

Correlation vs. Causation p. 599

Falsifiability
pp. 579, 592, 594, 595, 596, 602, 608

Extraordinary Claims p. 615

Occam's Razor pp. 589, 616

Replicability pp. 580, 581, 582, 583, 600, 604, 613

Ruling Out Rival Hypotheses
pp. 580, 581, 589, 595, 599, 602, 605, 608, 614

15

Psychological Disorders
When Adaptation Breaks Down

PREVIEW

Think

First, think about these questions. Then, as you read, think again. . . .

▶ What is mental illness, and how should we define it?

▶ Are psychiatric diagnoses meaningful, or are they just labels for undesirable behaviors?

▶ Is road rage a valid diagnosis?

▶ Is the insanity defense successful most of the time?

▶ Does everyone who attempts suicide wish to die?

▶ Is it possible for one body to house more than 100 personalities?

▶ Is schizophrenia the same as split personality?

▶ Are all psychopaths violent?

▶ Is there a drug-abusing personality?

Below are descriptions of five actual patients (with their names changed to safeguard their identity) drawn from the clinical experiences of two of your textbook's authors. Read each description, and ask yourself what these five people have in common.

Ida, 43 years old, was strolling around a shopping mall by herself. Suddenly and out of the blue, she experienced a burst of incredibly intense anxiety that left her feeling terrified, faint, and nauseated. She thought she was having a heart attack and took a taxi to the nearest hospital emergency room. The doctors found nothing wrong with her heart and told her the problem was "all in her head." Since then, Ida has refused to leave her house or go anywhere without her husband. She's scared to drive or take buses or trains. Ida's diagnosis: *panic disorder (with agoraphobia)*.

Bill, 45 years old, hasn't shaved or showered in over 10 years. His beard is several feet long. Bill doesn't want to shave or shower because he's terrified that tiny "metal slivers" from the water will find their way into his skin. As much as possible, Bill avoids talking on the telephone or walking through doorways because he's petrified of acquiring germs. Whenever he experiences a thought he feels he shouldn't be having—such as a desire to kiss a married woman—he counts backward from 100 by 7s. Bill recognizes these behaviors as irrational, but hasn't been able to change them despite about 15 years of treatment. Bill's diagnosis: *obsessive-compulsive disorder*.

A few days after having a baby at age 30, Ann became incredibly giddy. She felt on top of the world, barely needed any sleep, and soon began sleeping with men she'd just met. Ann also became convinced she'd turned into a clown—literally. She was even persuaded that she had a bright red round nose, even though her nose was entirely normal. Looking back on this episode a few weeks later, Ann recognizes that her beliefs were out of touch with reality. Ann's diagnosis: *bipolar disorder (manic depression)*.

Terrell, 28 years old, has just been released from the intensive care unit of a city hospital. He had shot himself in the stomach after becoming convinced that fish were swimming there. He suspects these fish are part of a government conspiracy to make him physically ill. Terrell's diagnosis: *schizophrenia*.

Johnny is 13 years old. He's charming, articulate, and fun loving. Yet he's furious that his parents have helped commit him to the inpatient unit of a psychiatric hospital, and he blames them for his problems. Johnny is well aware that his actions, like cursing at teachers, holding live cats under water until they drown, beating up other children, and attempting to blow up his junior high school with stolen dynamite, aren't exactly popular among adults. But he sees nothing especially wrong with these behaviors and admits that he's never felt guilty about anything. Johnny's diagnosis: *conduct disorder (with probable psychopathic personality)*.

Conceptions of Mental Illness: Yesterday and Today

These brief sketches don't do justice to the extraordinarily rich and complex lives of these five people, but they give us some sense of the broad scope of *psychopathology,* or mental illness. In almost all mental disorders, we witness a failure of adaptation to the environment. In one way or another, mentally disturbed people aren't adjusting well to the demands of daily life. Many psychopathology researchers adopt a *failure analysis approach* to understanding mental disorders (Harkness, 2007). Just as engineers use accidents, such as plane crashes, to help them understand how mechanical systems work properly, psychopathology researchers examine breakdowns in adaptation to help them understand healthy functioning.

But what do Ida, Bill, Ann, Terrell, and Johnny have in common? Putting it differently, what distinguishes psychological abnormality from normality?

WHAT IS MENTAL ILLNESS? A DECEPTIVELY COMPLEX QUESTION

The answer to this question isn't as simple as we might assume. Psychologists and psychiatrists have proposed a host of criteria for defining *mental disorder;* we'll review five of them here. Each criterion captures something important about mental disorder, but each has its shortcomings (Gorenstein, 1984; Wakefield, 1992).

Statistical rarity: Many mental disorders, like schizophrenia—Terrell's condition—are uncommon in the population. Yet we can't rely on statistical rarity to define mental disorder, because not all rare conditions—such as extraordinary creativity—are pathological, and many mental illnesses—such as mild depression—are quite common (Kendell, 1975).

Subjective distress: Most mental disorders, including mood and anxiety disorders, produce emotional pain for individuals afflicted with them. But not all psychological disorders generate distress. For example, during the manic phases of bipolar disorder, which Ann experienced, people frequently feel better than normal and perceive nothing wrong with their behaviors. Similarly, many adolescents with conduct disorder, like Johnny, experience less distress than the typical adolescent.

Impairment: Most mental disorders interfere with people's ability to function in everyday life. These disorders may destroy marriages, friendships, and jobs. Yet the presence of impairment by itself can't define mental illness, because some conditions, like laziness, can produce impairment but aren't mental disorders.

Societal disapproval: Nearly 50 years ago, psychiatrist Thomas Szasz (1960) argued famously that "mental illness is a myth" and that "mental disorders" are nothing more than conditions that society dislikes. He even proposed that psychologists and psychiatrists use diagnoses as weapons of control: By attaching negative labels to people whose behaviors they find objectionable, they're putting these people "in their place." Szasz was both right and wrong. He was right that our attitudes toward the seriously mentally ill are often profoundly negative, and that deep-seated social prejudices toward them are widespread. Szasz was also right that societal attitudes shape our views of abnormality. Only a few decades ago, most psychologists regarded homosexuality as a mental illness; the official diagnostic manual listed it as a "sexual deviation." This designation was reversed in 1973 by a vote of the membership of the American Psychiatric Association (Bayer, 1981). As society became more accepting of homosexuality, mental health professionals came to reject the view that such behavior is indicative of psychological disorder.

But Szasz was wrong that society regards all disapproved conditions as mental disorders (Wakefield, 1992). To take just one example, racism is justifiably deplored by society but isn't considered a mental disorder by either lay persons or mental health professionals (Yamey & Shaw, 2002). Neither is messiness or rudeness even though they are both considered undesirable by society.

Biological dysfunction: Many mental disorders probably result from breakdowns or failures of physiological systems. For example, we'll learn that schizophrenia is often marked by an underactivity in the brain's frontal lobes (see also Prologue). In contrast, some mental disorders, like specific *phobias* (intense and irrational fears of objects, places, or situations; see Chapter 6), appear to be acquired largely through learning experiences and may require only a weak genetic predisposition to trigger them.

In fact, it's unlikely that any single criterion distinguishes mental disorders from normality. As a consequence, some authors have argued for a *family resemblance view* of mental disorder (Kirmayer & Young, 1999; Lilienfeld & Marino, 1995; Rosenhan & Seligman, 1989). According to this perspective, mental disorders don't all have one thing in common. Just as brothers and sisters within a family look similar but don't all possess exactly the same eyes, ears, or noses, mental disorders share a loose set of features. These features include those we've described—statistical rarity, subjective distress, impairment, societal disapproval, and biological dysfunction—as well as others, such as a need for treatment,

Brothers and sisters share a family resemblance; they look like each other but don't have any one feature in common. The broad category of "mental disorders" may be similar. Different mental disorders aren't alike in the same exact way, but they share a number of features.

demonic model
view of mental illness in which odd behavior, hearing voices, or talking to oneself was attributed to evil spirits infesting the body

medical model
perception that regarded mental illness as due to a physical disorder requiring medical treatment

asylums
institutions for the mentally ill created in the fifteenth century

The infamous "dunking test" for witches, popular during the witch scares of the sixteenth and seventeenth centuries. According to the dunking test, if a woman drowned, it meant she wasn't a witch. In contrast, if she floated to the top of the water, it meant she was a witch and needed to be executed. Either way, she died.

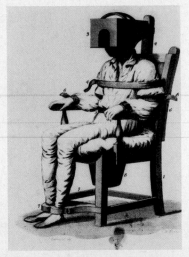

The "tranquilizing chair," designed by psychiatrist Benjamin Rush (1745–1813), founder of American psychiatry and a signer of the Declaration of Independence. By slowing the flow of blood to the brain, this chair was intended to help treat mental disturbances. In fact, this treatment probably accomplished little other than to physically restrain agitated patients.

Ruling Out Rival Hypotheses

irrationality, and loss of control over one's behavior (Bergner, 1997). So Ida, Bill, Ann, Terrell, and Johnny aren't alike in precisely the same way. Yet they overlap enough in their features that we recognize each of them as suffering from a mental disorder.

HISTORICAL CONCEPTIONS OF MENTAL ILLNESS: FROM DEMONS TO ASYLUMS

Throughout history, people have recognized certain behaviors as abnormal. Yet their explanations and treatments for these behaviors have shifted in tune with prevailing cultural conceptions. The history of society's evolving views of mental illness tells the fascinating story of a bumpy road from nonscience to science.

The Demonic Model. During the Middle Ages, many people in Europe and later in America viewed mental illnesses through the lens of a **demonic model.** They attributed hearing voices, talking to oneself, and other odd behaviors to the actions of evil spirits infesting the body (Hunter & Macalpine, 1963). They also viewed at least some, but not all (Schoeneman, 1984), witches as mentally ill. In 1486, two German priests released a detailed manual, the *Malleus Malleficarum* ("The Witches' Hammer"), to assist in identifying witches, whom many religious figures believed were possessed by the devil. For decades, this text was second only to the Bible as the world's best-selling book. According to the *Malleus Malleficarum,* one could detect witches by means of such foolproof indicators as the *Devil's Mark,* a spot on the skin that's insensitive to pain. The *Malleus Malleficarum* played a key role in the witch hunts of the sixteenth and seventeenth centuries, which resulted in the executions of tens of thousands of innocent individuals.

The often bizarre "treatments" of the day, including exorcisms, flowed directly from the demonic model. Yet as the great writer William Faulkner reminded us, "the past is never dead. In fact, it's not even past." The legacy of the demonic model lives on today in the thousands of exorcisms still performed in Italy, Mexico, and other countries (Harrington, 2005).

The Medical Model. As the Middle Ages faded and the Renaissance took hold, views of the mentally ill became more enlightened. Over time, more people came to perceive mental illness primarily as a physical disorder, a view that some scholars refer to as the **medical model.** They also came to see mentally ill individuals as requiring medical treatment. Beginning in the fifteenth century and especially in later centuries, European governments began to house psychologically troubled individuals in **asylums**—institutions for the mentally ill (Gottesman, 1991). Although the term *asylum* means a place of safety, it's acquired a considerably more negative connotation because many institutions were little more than massively overcrowded and understaffed warehouses for mentally disturbed individuals. Indeed, the term *bedlam,* meaning "utter chaos," derives from a shortened version of "Bethlehem," the name of an insane asylum in London established in the Middle Ages (Scull, MacKenzie, & Hervey, 1996).

Moreover, the medical treatments of that era were scarcely more scientific than those of the demonic era, and several were equally barbaric. One gruesome treatment was "bloodletting," which was based on the mistaken notion that excessive blood causes mental illness. In some cases, physicians drained patients of nearly 4 pounds of blood, about 40 percent of the body's total. In still other cases, staff workers tried to frighten patients "out of their diseases" by tossing them into a pit of snakes, hence the term *snake pit* as a synonym for an insane asylum (Szasz, 2006).

Not surprisingly, most patients of this era deteriorated, and in the case of bloodletting, some died. Even those who improved in the short term may have merely been responding to the *placebo effect,* that is, improvement resulting from the expectation of improvement (see Chapter 2). Yet few physicians of the day considered the placebo effect as a rival explanation for these treatments' seeming effectiveness. Although most of these treatments seem preposterous to us today, it's crucial to recognize that psychological and medical treatments are products of the times. Society's beliefs about the causes of mental illness shape its interventions.

Fortunately, reform was on the way. Thanks to the heroic efforts of Phillippe Pinel (1748–1826) in France and Dorothea Dix (1802–1887) in America, an approach called **moral treatment** gained a foothold in Europe and America. Advocates of moral treatment insisted that the mentally ill be treated with dignity, kindness, and respect. Prior to moral treatment, patients in asylums were often bound in chains; following moral treatment, they were free to roam the halls of hospitals, get fresh air, and interact freely with staff and other patients. Still, effective treatments for mental illnesses were virtually nonexistent, so many people continued to suffer for years with no hope of relief.

The Modern Era of Psychiatric Treatment. It wasn't until the early 1950s that a dramatic change in society's treatment of the mentally ill arrived on the scene. It was then that psychiatrists introduced a medication imported from France called *chlorpromazine* (its brand name is Thorazine) into mental hospitals. Chlorpromazine wasn't a miracle cure, but it offered a modestly effective treatment for some symptoms of schizophrenia and other disorders marked by a loss of contact with reality. For the first time, patients with these conditions often became able to function independently, and some returned to their families. Others held jobs for the first time in years, even decades.

By the 1960s and 1970s, the advent of chlorpromazine and similar medications (see also Chapter 16) became the primary impetus for a governmental policy called **deinstitutionalization.** Deinstitutionalization featured two major components: releasing hospitalized psychiatric patients into the community and closing mental hospitals (Torrey, 1997). Following deinstitutionalization, the number of hospitalized psychiatric patients plummeted through the 1990s (see **Figure 15.1**). But deinstitutionalization was a decidedly mixed blessing. Some patients returned to a semblance of a regular life, but tens of thousands of others spilled into cities and rural areas without adequate follow-up care. Many went off their medications and wandered the streets aimlessly. Some of the homeless people we can see today on the streets of major American cities are a tragic legacy of deinstitutionalization (Leeper, 1988). Today, psychologists, social workers, and other mental health professionals are working to improve the quality and availability of community care for severely affected psychiatric patients. Among the consequences of these efforts are *community mental health centers* and *halfway houses,* which are free or low-cost care facilities in which people can obtain treatment.

Thankfully, our understanding of mental illness and its treatment today is considerably more sophisticated than it was centuries ago. Still, few of today's treatments are genuine cures.

PSYCHIATRIC DIAGNOSIS OVER TIME

As with treatment methods, psychiatric diagnoses have mirrored the views of the times. These diagnoses have reflected society's conceptions of undesirable and unhealthy behavior.

For centuries, some psychiatrists invoked the diagnosis of *masturbational insanity* to describe individuals whose compulsive masturbation supposedly drove them mad (Hare, 1962). In the mid-1800s, some psychiatrists used the label *drapetomania* (*drapetes* is Greek for "slave") to describe the "disorder" of slaves who attempted repeatedly to escape from their masters. In a journal article, a physician prescribed whipping and amputation of the toes as effective "treatments" for this condition (Cartwright, 1851; Wakefield, 1992). Today we can see these deeply unfortunate diagnostic labels and practices as by-products of the unscientific prejudices of the day. Yet no historical era is free of biases.

Even modern times have witnessed an explosion of diagnostic labels that are devoid of scientific support (McCann, Shindler, & Hammond, 2003). Although the mental health field doesn't recognize these labels as formal diagnoses, they've become part of the lingo of popular psychology. In some cases, lawyers and expert witnesses have even introduced

Dorothea Dix, a Massachusetts schoolteacher whose lobbying efforts resulted in the establishment of more humane psychiatric facilities in the 1800s.

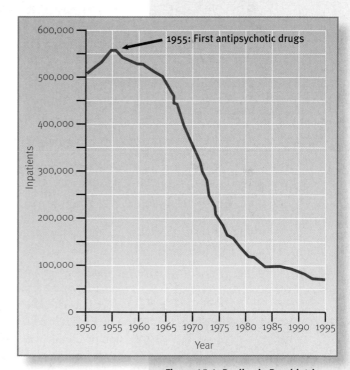

Figure 15.1 Decline in Psychiatric Inpatients. Beginning in the 1950s, the government program of deinstitutionalization resulted in a massive decline in the number of psychiatric inpatients in American hospitals. (*Source:* Torrey, 1997)

moral treatment
approach to mental illness calling for dignity, kindness, and respect for the mentally ill

deinstitutionalization
1960s and 1970s governmental policy that focused on releasing hospitalized psychiatric patients into the community and closing mental hospitals

Clearly, episodes of extreme road rage can be dangerous. But is road rage a valid psychiatric diagnosis, or is it merely a descriptive label for a set of problematic behaviors?

them into courtrooms as legal defenses. You may recognize some of these labels from talk shows, television programs, movies, or self-help books:

- *Codependency:* A condition in which spouses and significant others become excessively dependent on—and overly caring of—loved ones with alcoholism and other substance abuse disorders (Granello & Beamish, 1998).
- *Sexual addiction:* A condition that characterizes people who can't control their sexual impulses (Gold & Hefner, 1998).
- *Road rage disorder:* A condition marked by explosive anger outbursts while driving (Cocarro et al., 2006).
- *Compulsive shopping disorder:* An inability to restrain oneself from purchasing unnecessary items (Koran et al., 2006).

There's a crucial problem with these and a host of other pop psychology terms. Although they describe actions we'd all agree are problematic, they don't tell us anything new. That is, they are *labels* rather than *diagnoses*. A label merely *describes* behaviors; a diagnosis helps to *explain* them (Millon, 1975). That is, a diagnosis gives us novel information, a point to which we'll return shortly.

Does the label of "Internet addiction" tell us anything about diagnosed persons we didn't know before? The answer is unclear (Widyanto & Griffiths, 2005). (Clay Bennett/© 1999 The Christian Science Monitor (www.csmonitor.com.) All rights reserved. Used with permission)

PSYCHIATRIC DIAGNOSIS ACROSS CULTURES: CULTURE-BOUND SYNDROMES

Psychiatric diagnoses are shaped not only by history, but by culture (Chentsova-Dutton & Tsai, 2007). Psychologists have increasingly recognized that certain conditions are *culture-bound*, that is, specific to one or more societies, although many of these conditions remain poorly researched (see **Table 15.1**) (Kleinman, 1988; Simons & Hughes, 1986).

Table 15.1 A Sampling of Common Culture-Bound Syndromes Not Discussed in the Text.

Syndrome	Region/Population Affected	Description
Arctic Hysteria	Alaska Natives	Abrupt episode accompanied by extreme excitement and frequently followed by convulsive seizures and coma.
Ataque de Nervios	Latin America	Symptoms include uncontrollable shouting, attacks of crying, trembling, heat in the chest rising to the head, and verbal or physical aggression.
Brain Fog	West Africa	Symptoms include difficulties in concentrating, remembering, and thinking.
Latah	Malaysia and Southeast Asia	Found mostly among women; marked by an extreme startle reaction, followed by a loss of control, cursing, and mimicking of others' actions and speech.
Mal de Ojo (Evil Eye)	Spain and Latin America	A common term to describe the cause of disease, misfortune, and social disruption.
Windigo	Native Americans Central and N.E. Canada	Morbid state of anxiety with fears of becoming a cannibal.

(*Source:* Data, DSM-IV APA, 2000; Hall, 2001)

"Mal de ojo," or the "evil eye," is a culture-bound syndrome common in many Mediterranean and Latin countries. Believed by its victims to be brought on by the glance of a malicious person, mal de ojo is marked by insomnia, nervousness, crying for no reason, and vomiting. Here, customers in Egypt select pendants for warding off the evil eye.

Diagnoses Unique to Non-Western Cultures. For example, some parts of Malaysia and several other Asian countries, including China and India, have witnessed periodic outbreaks of a strange condition known as *koro*. The victims of koro, most of whom are male, typically believe that their penis and testicles are disappearing and receding into their abdomen (female victims of koro sometimes believe that their breasts are disappearing; American Psychiatric Association, 2000). Koro is spread largely by social contagion. Once one man begins to experience its symptoms, others often follow suit, triggering widespread panics (see also Chapter 13). In one region of India in 1982, the koro epidemic spun so out of control that the local government took to the streets with loudspeakers to reassure terrified civilians that their genitals weren't vanishing. Government officials even measured male residents' penises with rulers in an attempt to prove their fears unfounded (Bartholomew, 1997).

Another disorder specific to Malaysia, the Philippines, and some African countries is called *amok*. This condition is marked by episodes of intense sadness and brooding followed by uncontrolled behavior and unprovoked attacks on people or animals (American Psychiatric Association, 2000). This condition gave rise to the popular phrase "running amok," which is another way of saying "going wild."

Other culture-bound syndromes seem to be variants of conditions in Western culture. In Japan, for example, social anxiety is typically expressed as a fear of offending others (called *taijin kyofushu*), such as by saying something offensive or giving off a terrible body odor (Kleinknecht, Dinnel, Tanouye-Wilson, & Lonner, 1994). But in the United States, social anxiety is more commonly generated by fear of public embarrassment, such as what we might experience when giving a speech. Culture may influence how people express interpersonal anxiety. Because Japanese culture is more collectivistic (see Chapter 10) than Western culture, Japanese tend to be more concerned about their impact on others than are Westerners. In contrast, Western culture is more individualistic, so people tend to worry more about what may happen to them as individuals.

Diagnoses Unique to Western Cultures. The focus on the self in individualistic societies may also contribute to some culture-bound disorders in Western countries. Some eating disorders are largely specific to the United States and Europe, where the media bombard viewers with images of thin models (Keel & Klump, 2003; McCarthy, 1990). **Bulimia nervosa** (better known simply as *bulimia*) is associated with a pattern of *bingeing*—eating large amounts of highly caloric foods in brief periods of time—followed by *purging* (vomiting) or other means of drastic weight loss, like frantic exercise or extreme dieting. Like most eating disorders, bulimia is considerably more common in women than men. As we learned in Chapter 12, only about 5 percent of people with bulimia are male (Craighead, 2002).

There are good reasons to believe that bulimia, although influenced substantially by genetic factors (Bulik, Sullivan, & Kendler, 1998), is triggered by sociocultural expectations concerning the ideal body image. Women with bulimia report high levels of body dissatisfaction (Johnson & Wardel, 2005). Moreover, those who frequently view television programs featuring extremely thin women experience higher levels of body image dissatisfaction than other women (Himes & Thompson, 2007; Thompson, 2004; Tiggerman & Pickering, 1996) (see **Figure 15.2**). Nevertheless, women who are already concerned about their body image may tend to watch television programs featuring idealized images of women, so the causal arrow could run in the opposite direction. Still, there's compelling circumstantial evidence for a causal effect of the media on eating disorders. Following the introduction of American and British television onto the remote Pacific island of Fiji, the symptoms of eating disorders in teenage girls increased fivefold within only 4 years (Becker et al., 2002).

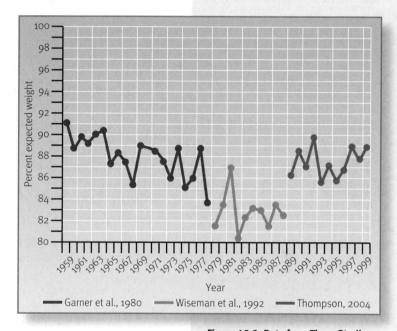

Figure 15.2 Data from Three Studies on the Weights of *Playboy* Centerfolds from 1959 to 1999. *Playboy* centerfold models have consistently been markedly below average in weight, reaching a low point in the mid- to late 1980s and rebounding somewhat in the 1990s. These centerfold models' images may provide women with unrealistic ideals of thinness. (The Y axis shows the percentage of expected weight, with 100 percent being average.) (*Source:* Sypeck et al., 2006)

Correlation vs. Causation

APPLY YOUR THINKING
Does the finding that bulimia nervosa is genetically influenced contradict findings suggesting that media influences contribute to its onset?

bulimia nervosa
eating disorder associated with a pattern of bingeing and purging in an effort to lose or maintain weight

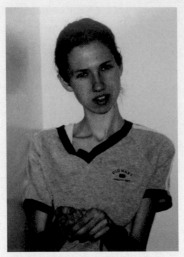

An anorexic woman. In contrast to bulimia, anorexia may be present in many, even most, cultures.

In contrast to bulimia, **anorexia nervosa** (better known simply as *anorexia*) appears to be present not only in Western countries but also in regions that have had little exposure to Western media, including some Middle Eastern nations and parts of India (Keel & Klump, 2003; Lynn et al., 2007). Unlike bulimia, anorexia is marked by excessive weight loss (15 percent or more of one's original body weight) and the irrational perception of being overweight (see Chapter 11). Like bulimia, anorexia is much more common in women than men. Although anorexia appears to be more culturally and historically universal than bulimia, societal *explanations* for its causes have differed across time and place. For example, historical descriptions suggest that some young Catholic nuns in medieval times who starved themselves probably suffered from anorexia. Yet they explained their fasting behaviors as efforts to purify their souls for God (Keel & Klump, 2003; Smith, Spillane, & Annus, 2006).

Cultural Universality. Despite the cultural differences we've noted, we shouldn't exaggerate the cultural relativity of mental disorders. Many mental disorders appear to exist in most, perhaps all, cultures. Jane Murphy (1976) conducted a classic study of two isolated societies— a group of Yorubas in Nigeria and a group of Inuit Eskimos near the Bering Strait—that had experienced essentially no contact with Western culture. These cultures possessed terms for disorders that are strikingly similar to schizophrenia, alcoholism, and *psychopathic personality*, a condition marked by dishonesty, manipulativeness, and an absence of guilt and empathy (see Chapter 6). For example, in Inuit *kunlangeta* describes a person who lies, cheats, steals, is unfaithful to women, and doesn't listen to elders—a description that fits almost perfectly the Western concept of psychopathic personality. When Murphy asked one of the Inuit how they dealt with such individuals, he replied that "somebody would have pushed him off the ice when no one was looking." Apparently, Inuit aren't much fonder of psychopaths than we are.

SPECIAL CONSIDERATIONS IN PSYCHIATRIC CLASSIFICATION AND DIAGNOSIS

Because there are so many ways in which psychological adaptation can go awry, we'd be hopelessly lost without some system of diagnostic classification. Psychiatric diagnoses serve at least two crucial functions. *First,* they help us to pinpoint the psychological problem a person is experiencing. Once we've identified this problem, it's often easier to select a treatment. *Second,* psychiatric diagnoses make it easier for mental health professionals to communicate with each other. When a psychologist diagnoses a patient with schizophrenia, she can be reasonably certain that other psychologists know his or her principal symptoms. So diagnoses operate as forms of mental shorthand, simplifying complex descriptions of problematic behaviors into convenient summary phrases.

Still, there are a host of misconceptions regarding psychiatric diagnosis. Before turning to our present system of psychiatric classification, we'll examine the four most prevalent misconceptions.

Misconception 1. *Psychiatric diagnosis is nothing more than pigeonholing, that is, sorting people into different "boxes."* According to this criticism, when we diagnose people with a mental disorder, we deprive them of their uniqueness: We imply that all people within the same diagnostic category are alike in all important respects. To the contrary, a diagnosis implies only that all people with that diagnosis are alike in at least *one* important respect (Lilienfeld & Landfield, in press). Psychologists recognize that even within a diagnostic category, like schizophrenia or bipolar disorder, people differ dramatically in their race and cultural background, personality traits, interests, cognitive skills, and other psychological difficulties. People are far more than their disorders.

Misconception 2. *Psychiatric diagnoses are unreliable.* As we learned in Chapter 2, *reliability* refers to consistency of measurement. In the case of psychiatric diagnoses, the form of reliability that matters most is *interrater reliability:* the extent to which different raters (such as different psychologists) agree on patients' diagnoses. Many laypersons believe that psychiatric diagnosis is unreliable. This perception is probably fueled by high-profile media cover-

anorexia nervosa

eating disorder associated with excessive weight loss and the irrational perception that one is overweight

age of "dueling expert witnesses" in criminal trials, in which one expert witness diagnoses a defendant as schizophrenic and another diagnoses him as normal.

In fact, for major mental disorders, like schizophrenia, mood disorders, anxiety disorders, and alcoholism, interrater reliabilities are typically about as high—correlations between raters of .8 or above out of a maximum of 1.0—as that for most medical disorders (Matarazzo, 1983). Still, the picture isn't entirely rosy. For many personality disorders, a class of disorders we'll discuss later, interrater reliabilities tend to be considerably lower (Zimmerman, 1994).

Misconception 3. *Psychiatric diagnoses are invalid.* From the standpoint of Thomas Szasz (1960) and other critics, psychiatric diagnoses are largely useless because they don't provide us with much, if any, new information. They're merely descriptive labels for behaviors we don't like.

When it comes to some pop psychology labels, like sexual addiction and road rage disorder, Szasz probably has a point. But there's now considerable evidence that many psychiatric diagnoses *do* tell us something new about the person. In a classic paper, psychiatrists Eli Robins and Samuel Guze (1970) outlined several criteria for determining whether a psychiatric diagnosis is valid. According to Robins and Guze, a valid diagnosis:

Trials involving dueling "expert witnesses" may contribute to the erroneous public perception that psychologists can't agree on the diagnoses of individuals with suspected mental disorders.

(1) distinguishes that diagnosis from other, similar diagnoses;

(2) predicts diagnosed individuals' performance on laboratory tests, including personality measures, neurotransmitter levels, and brain imaging findings (Andreasen, 1995);

(3) predicts diagnosed individuals' family history of psychiatric disorders;

(4) predicts diagnosed individuals' *natural history*—that is, what tends to happen then over time.

In addition, some authors have argued that a valid diagnosis ideally:

(5) predicts diagnosed individuals' response to treatment (Waldman, Lilienfeld, & Lahey, 1996).

There's good evidence that many mental disorders fulfill Robins and Guze's criteria for validity. **Table 15.2** illustrates these criteria using the example of attention-deficit/hyperactivity disorder (ADHD), a condition marked by inattention, impulsivity, and overactivity. ADHD has reasonably good validity, because it's more than a label for behaviors. It tells us something about the diagnosed person we didn't already know (Waldman, Lilienfeld, & Lahey, 1996). Still, like many psychiatric diagnoses, ADHD is controversial. Critics have voiced concerns that ADHD is overdiagnosed and applied indiscriminately to children with mild symptoms of distractibility and restlessness that are normal for their age (Lefever, Arcona, & Antonnucio, 2004).

Many children have problems concentrating. There can be a fine line between children who have trouble paying attention in class and children diagnosed with ADHD.

Table 15.2 Criteria for Validity: The Case of ADHD. Although controversial in many respects, the diagnosis of attention-deficit/hyperactivity disorder (ADHD) largely satisfies the Robins and Guze criteria for validity.

Robins & Guze Criteria	Findings Concerning the ADHD Diagnosis
1. Distinguishes a particular diagnosis from other similar diagnoses	The child's symptoms can't be accounted for by other diagnoses, such as substance abuse and anxiety disorders
2. Predicts performance on laboratory tests (personality measures, neurotransmitter levels, brain imaging findings)	The child is likely to perform poorly on laboratory measures of concentration
3. Predicts family history of psychiatric disorders	The child has a higher probability than the average child of having biological relatives with ADHD
4. Predicts what happens to the individual over time	The child is likely to show continued difficulties with inattention in adulthood, but improvements in impulsivity and overactivity in adulthood
5. Predicts response to treatment	The child has a good chance of responding positively to stimulant medications, like Ritalin (see Chapter 16)

Many parents remain convinced that vaccines trigger autism, despite scientific evidence to the contrary.

Replicability

Diagnostic and Statistical Manual of Mental Disorders (DSM)
diagnostic system containing the American Psychiatric Association (APA) criteria for mental disorders

Ruling Out Rival Hypotheses

PsychoMythology
Is There an Autism Epidemic?

One in 150.

That's the widely proclaimed proportion of autistic individuals in the population that you may have seen on television commercials or read about in magazines. Although this proportion may not seem all that high, it's remarkably high compared with the figure of one in 2,000 to 2,500, which researchers had until recently accepted for many years (Wing & Potter, 1999). Across a mere 10-year period—from 1993 to 2003—statistics from the United States Department of Education revealed a 657 percent increase in the rates of autism (technically called infantile autism) across the country. In Wisconsin, the increase was a staggering 15,117 percent (Rust, 2006). These dramatic upsurges in the prevalence of autism have led many researchers and educators, and even some politicians, to speak of an autism "epidemic" (Kippes & Garrison, 2006). But is the epidemic real?

As we learned in Chapter 2, autistic individuals are marked by severe deficits in language, social bonding, and imagination, usually accompanied by mental retardation (American Psychiatric Association [APA], 2000). The causes of autism remain mysterious, although twin studies suggest that genetic influences play a prominent role (Rutter, 2000). Still, genetic influences alone can't easily account for an astronomical rise in a disorder's prevalence over the span of a decade. It's therefore not surprising that researchers have looked to environmental variables to explain this bewildering increase. In particular, some investigators have pointed their fingers squarely at one potential culprit: vaccines (Rimland, 2004).

Much of the hype surrounding the vaccine–autism link was fueled by a study of only twelve children in the late 1990s (Wakefield et al., 1998) demonstrating an apparent linkage between autistic symptoms and the MMR vaccine, the vaccine for mumps, measles, and rubella (German measles). The symptoms of autism usually become most apparent shortly after the age of 2, not long after infants have received MMR and other vaccinations for a host of diseases. Indeed, tens of thousands of parents have insisted that their children developed autism following the MMR vaccine, or following vaccines containing a preservative known as *thimerosol*, which is present in many mercury-bearing vaccines. Nevertheless, studies failed to replicate the association between the MMR vaccine and autism, strongly suggesting that the seeming correlation between vaccinations and autism was a mirage. For example, the results of several large American, European, and Japanese studies show that even as the rate of MMR vaccinations remained constant or declined, the rate of autism diagnoses continued to soar (Herbert, Sharp, & Gaudiano, 2002; Honda, Shimizu, & Rutter, 2005). Moreover, even after the Danish government stopped administering thimerosol-containing vaccines, the prevalence of autism still skyrocketed (Madsen et al., 2003).

Many parents of autistic children probably fell prey to *illusory correlation* (Chapter 2); they'd "seen" a statistical association that didn't exist. Their error was entirely understandable. Given that their children had received vaccines and developed autistic symptoms at around the same time, it was only natural to perceive an association between the two events.

Making matters more complex, recent research calls into question the very existence of the autism epidemic (Grinker, 2007; Wilson, 2005). Most previous investigators had neglected to take into account an alternative explanation for the reported changes in diagnostic practices. To establish a diagnosis, psychiatrists use the **Diagnostic and Statistical Manual of Mental Disorders (DSM),** a manual we'll soon discuss in more detail. The DSM lists criteria for mental disorders and is updated periodically. Between an earlier version of the diagnostic manual, DSM-III (published in 1980), and the present version, DSM-IV (published in 1994), the criteria for the diagnosis of autism became considerably looser (Gernsbacher, Dawson, & Goldsmith, 2005). Whereas DSM-III required individuals to meet all six of six criteria to satisfy an autism diagnosis (APA, 1980), DSM-IV requires them to meet only any eight of sixteen criteria (APA, 2000). Moreover, whereas DSM-III contained only two diagnoses relevant to autism—autistic disorder and a condition called *Asperger's syndrome*, which appears to be a high-functioning form of autism—DSM-IV contains five such diagnoses, including relatively mild versions of autism. Finally, the Americans with Disabilities Act and Individuals with Disabilities Education Act, both passed in the 1990s, indirectly encouraged school districts to classify more children as having autism and other developmental disabilities, as these children could now receive more extensive educational accommodations.

Most evidence suggests that these changes account for most, if not all, of the reported autism epidemic (Gernsbacher et al., 2005; Lilienfeld & Arkowitz, 2007). Of course, at least a small part of the epidemic might be genuine, and some still unidentified environmental cause could account for the increase. But in evaluating the evidence, we should ask ourselves a critical question. Which is more parsimonious as an explanation of a 657 percent increase within one decade, a vaccine that's yet to be shown to produce any increase in the symptoms of autism or a simple change in diagnostic practices?

Occam's Razor

Misconception 4. *Psychiatric diagnoses stigmatize people.* According to a group of scholars called **labeling theorists,** psychiatric diagnoses exert powerful negative effects on people's perceptions and behaviors (Scheff, 1984; Slater, 2004). Labeling theorists argue that once a psychologist or psychiatrist gives us a diagnosis, others come to perceive us differently. Suddenly, we're "weird," "strange," even "crazy." This diagnosis leads others to treat us differently, perhaps leading us in turn to behave in weird, strange, or even crazy ways. The diagnosis thereby becomes a self-fulfilling prophecy.

In a sensational study, David Rosenhan (1973) got eight normal individuals (himself included) to pose as fake patients in twelve psychiatric hospitals. These "pseudopatients," as Rosenhan called them, presented themselves to the admitting psychiatrists with a single complaint: They were hearing a voice saying "empty, hollow, and thud." In all twelve cases, the psychiatrists admitted these pseudopatients to the hospital, almost always with diagnoses of schizophrenia (one received a diagnosis of manic-depression). Remarkably, they remained there for an average of three weeks despite displaying no further symptoms of mental illness. The diagnosis of schizophrenia, Rosenhan concluded, became a self-fulfilling prophecy, leading doctors and nursing staff to view these normal individuals as disturbed. For example, the nursing staff interpreted one pseudopatient's note taking as "abnormal writing behavior."

It's true that there's still considerable stigma attached to some psychiatric diagnoses. If someone tells us that a normal person has schizophrenia, for instance, we may be wary of him at first or misinterpret his behaviors as consistent with this diagnosis. Yet the negative effects of labels last only so long. Even in Rosenhan's study, all pseudopatients were released from hospitals with diagnoses of either schizophrenia or manic depression "in remission" ("in remission" means without any symptoms) (Spitzer, 1975). These discharge diagnoses tell us that the psychiatrists eventually recognized that these individuals were behaving normally.

Contrary to claims of labeling theorists, there's not much evidence that psychiatric diagnoses themselves generate long-term negative effects (Ruscio, 2004). Indeed, diagnoses may often *improve* people's perceptions of mentally disturbed individuals. For example, school-age children tend to rate disturbed peers more positively after learning that they've been diagnosed with ADHD, probably because the diagnosis provides children with an explanation for their classmates' otherwise difficult-to-understand behaviors (Cornez-Ruiz & Hendricks, 1993). In the long run, valid psychiatric diagnoses are almost certainly more helpful than harmful, because they're frequently the first step toward obtaining treatment.

DSM-IV is the standard manual around the world for diagnosing mental disorders. The "text revision" (DSM-IV-TR), shown here, was published in 2000. DSM-IV-TR is a minor modification of DSM-IV, the most recent version of the manual.

labeling theorists
scholars who argue that psychiatric diagnoses exert powerful negative effects on people's perceptions and behaviors

Table 15.3 The 17 Major Classes of Disorders in DSM-IV.

(1) Disorders Usually First Diagnosed in Infancy, Childhood, or Adolescence—mental retardation, attention deficit and disruptive behavior disorders, tic disorders

(2) Delirium, Dementia, and Amnestic, and Other Cognitive Disorders—Dementia due to Alzheimer's disease and Parkinson's Disease

(3) Mental Disorders due to a General Medical Condition

(4) Substance-Related Disorders

(5) Schizophrenia and Other Psychotic Disorders

(6) Mood Disorders

(7) Anxiety Disorders

(8) Somatoform Disorders

(9) Factitious Disorders

(10) Dissociative Disorders Not Elsewhere Classified

(11) Sexual and Gender Identity Disorders

(12) Eating Disorders

(13) Sleep Disorders

(14) Impulse-Control Disorders Not Elsewhere Classified

(15) Adjustment Disorders

(16) Personality Disorders

(17) Other Conditions That May Be a Focus of Clinical Attention—problems related to abuse or neglect, personality traits that affect coping style, or medical conditions

(*Source:* From *Diagnostic and Statistical Manual of Mental Disorders,* 4th ed., American Psychiatric Association, 2000)

PSYCHIATRIC DIAGNOSIS TODAY: THE DSM-IV

As we've learned, the official system for classifying individuals with mental disorders is the *Diagnostic and Statistical Manual of Mental Disorders,* which originated in 1952 and is now in its fourth edition, called DSM-IV (APA, 2000). The next edition, DSM-V, is due out in about 2012. **Table 15.3** lists the seventeen different classes of disorders in the DSM-IV. We'll be discussing several of these classes in the pages to come.

Diagnostic Criteria and Decision Rules. Psychiatric classification has come a long way since the days of the *Malleus Malleficarum.* The DSM-IV provides psychologists and psychiatrists with a list of diagnostic criteria for each condition, and a set of decision rules for deciding how many of these criteria need to be met. For example, in **Table 15.4,** we'll find the DSM-IV criteria for the diagnosis of *major depression,* a condition we'll encounter later in the chapter. As we can see in Criterion A, to diagnose a person with major depression, DSM-IV requires this person to exhibit at least five of nine symptoms over a 2-week period, with the requirement that at least one of the first two symptoms (depressed mood and diminished interest or pleasure) be present.

Table 15.4 The DSM-IV Criteria for Major Depressive Disorder.

(A) Five (or more) of the following (must include one of the symptoms [1] or [2])

    (1) depressed mood most of the day

    (2) markedly diminished interest or pleasure in all, or almost all, activities

    (3) significant weight loss when not dieting or weight gain (more or less than 5% per month)

    (4) insomnia or hypersomnia (excessive sleep) nearly every day

    (5) psychomotor agitation or retardation (slowing) nearly every day

    (6) fatigue or loss of energy nearly every day

    (7) feelings of worthlessness or excessive or inappropriate guilt nearly every day

    (8) diminished ability to think or concentrate, or indecisiveness, nearly every day

    (9) recurrent thoughts of death (not just fear of dying), recurrent suicidal ideation

(B) Symptoms do not meet criteria for a mixed episode (simultaneous depression and mania)

(C) Symptoms cause clinically significant distress or impairment in social, occupational, or other important areas of functioning.

(D) Symptoms are not due to the physiological effects of a substance or a medical condition

(E) Symptoms are not better accounted for by bereavement (loss of a loved one); that is, after a loss, symptoms persist for longer than 2 months or are characterized by marked functional impairment, morbid preoccupation with worthlessness, suicidal ideation, psychotic symptoms, or psychomotor retardation

(*Source:* From *Diagnostic and Statistical Manual of Mental Disorders,* 4th ed., American Psychiatric Association, 2000)

"Thinking Organic." DSM-IV warns diagnosticians about physical—or "organic," that is, medically induced—conditions that can simulate certain psychological disorders (Morrison, 1997). As we can see in Criterion D in Table 15.4, DSM-IV notes that certain types of substance use or medical disorders can mimic the clinical picture of depression. For example, it informs readers that *hypothyroidism,* a disorder marked by underactivity of the thyroid gland (in our lower necks), can produce depressive symptoms. If a patient's depression appears due to hypothyroidism, the psychologist shouldn't diagnose major depression. It's essential to "think organic," or to first rule out medical causes of a disorder, when diagnosing psychological conditions.

The DSM-IV: Other Features. DSM-IV is more than a tool for diagnosing mental disorders; it's a valuable source of information concerning the characteristics, such as the **prevalence,** of many mental disorders. Prevalence refers to the percentage of people in the population with a disorder. In the case of major depression, the lifetime prevalence is at least 10 percent among women and at least 5 percent among men (some estimates are

prevalence
percentage of people within a population who have a specific mental disorder

even higher). That means that for a woman, the odds are at least 1 in 10 she'll experience an episode of major depression at some point in her life; for a man, the odds are at least 1 in 20 (APA, 2000).

DSM-IV also recognizes that there's more to people than their disorders. Accordingly, it asks psychologists and psychiatrists to assess patients along multiple **axes,** or dimensions of functioning. DSM-IV contains axes not only for mental disorders, but for associated medical conditions, life stressors, and overall level of daily functioning. In this respect, DSM-IV adopts a *biopsychosocial approach* (see Chapter 12), one that acknowledges the interplay of biological (like hormonal abnormalities), psychological (like irrational thoughts), and social (interpersonal interactions) influences. We'll be emphasizing these three factors throughout our discussion of specific disorders.

Finally, DSM-IV acknowledges that we live in a culturally diverse world filled with people from vastly different ethnic, socioeconomic, and cultural backgrounds. Some of them embrace unconventional beliefs, sexual identities, and behaviors that are "abnormal" from the vantage point of our contemporary society. DSM-IV provides information about how differing cultural backgrounds can affect the content and expression of symptoms and how people respond to distress. This information is vital to ensuring that diagnosticians don't "incorrectly judge as psychopathology those normal variations in behavior, belief, or experience that are particular to the individual's culture" (p. xxiv).

The DSM-IV: Criticisms. There's little dispute that DSM-IV is a helpful system for slicing up the enormous pie of psychopathology into more meaningful and manageable pieces. Yet DSM-IV has received more than its share of criticism, and sometimes for good reason (Widiger & Clark, 2000).

There are well over 350 diagnoses in DSM-IV, not all of which meet the Robins and Guze criteria for validity. To take only one example, the DSM-IV diagnosis of "Mathematics Disorder" describes little more than difficulties with performing arithmetic or math reasoning problems. It seems to be more of a label for learning problems than a diagnosis that tells us something new about the person. In addition, although the diagnostic criteria and decision rules for many DSM-IV disorders are based primarily on scientific findings, others are based largely on subjective committee decisions. Another problem with DSM-IV is the high level of **comorbidity** among many of its diagnoses (Angold, 1999; Lilienfeld, Waldman, & Israel, 1994), meaning that individuals with one diagnosis frequently have one or more diagnoses. For example, it's extremely common for people with a major depression diagnosis to meet criteria for one or more anxiety disorders. This extensive comorbidity raises the troubling question of whether DSM-IV is diagnosing genuinely independent conditions as opposed to slightly different variations of a single underlying condition.

Another problem with DSM-IV is its exclusive reliance on a **categorical model** of psychopathology (Trull & Durett, 2005). In a categorical model, a mental disorder—such as depression—is either present or absent, with no in between. Categories differ from each other in kind, not degree. Pregnancy fits a categorical model, because a woman is either pregnant or she's not (see Prologue). Yet scientific evidence suggests that some disorders in DSM-IV better fit a **dimensional model,** meaning they differ from normal functioning in degree, not kind (Krueger & Piasecki, 2002). Height fits a dimensional model, because although people differ in height, these differences aren't all or none. The same may be true of many forms of depression and anxiety, which most recent research suggests lie on a continuum with normality (Kollman, Brown, Liverant, & Hoffman, 2006; Slade & Andrews, 2005). These findings square with our everyday experience, because we all feel at least a bit depressed and anxious from time to time.

Some authors have proposed that the Big Five, a system of personality dimensions we encountered in Chapter 14, may better capture the true "state of nature" than many of the categories in DSM-IV (Widiger & Clark, 2000). For example, depression is typically characterized by high levels of neuroticism and introversion. Yet many psychologists have resisted adopting a dimensional model, perhaps because they, like the rest of us, are *cognitive misers* (see Chapter 2); they strive to simplify the world. Most of us find it easier

Certain practices that strike many Westerners as abnormal are regarded as normal in non-Western cultures. For example, a subgroup of women from the Karen tribe in the countries of Burma (Myanmar) and Thailand wear brass rings around their neck to lend them the appearance of a long neck, which is regarded as a sign of physical beauty and status.

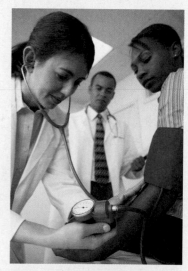

Like some psychological disorders, blood pressure better fits a dimensional than a categorical model, as there's no sharp dividing line between normal and high blood pressure.

axes
dimensions of functioning

comorbidity
co-occurrence of two or more diagnoses within the same person

categorical model
model in which a mental disorder differs from normal functioning in kind rather than degree

dimensional model
model in which a mental disorder differs from normal functioning in degree rather than kind

to think of the world in terms of simple black or white categories than complex shades of gray (Lilienfeld & Waldman, 2004; Macrae & Bondenhausen, 2000).

Like virtually all documents crafted by human beings, DSM-IV is vulnerable to political influences (Kirk & Kutchins, 1992). For example, some researchers have lobbied successfully for the inclusion of their "favorite" disorder or area of specialty. But like all scientific endeavors, the system of psychiatric classification tends to be self-correcting. Just as homosexuality was stricken from the DSM in the 1970s, science will continue to weed out invalid disorders, ensuring that future editions of the DSM will be based on better evidence.

Normality and Abnormality: A Spectrum of Severity. As you read case histories or descriptions in this chapter, you may wonder, "Is my behavior abnormal?" or "Maybe my problems are more serious than I thought." At times like this, it's useful to be aware of the pattern called *medical students' syndrome* (Howes & Salkovskis, 1998). As medical students first become familiar with the symptoms of specific diseases, they often begin to focus on their bodily processes. Soon they find it hard to stop wondering whether a slight twinge in their chest might be an early warning of heart trouble or a headache the first sign of a brain tumor. Similarly, as we learn about psychological disorders in this chapter, it's only natural to "see ourselves" in some patterns of behavior, largely because in meeting the complex demands of daily life we all experience disturbing impulses and thoughts, uncertainties, and fears from time to time. In fact, many high-functioning people struggle with myriad psychological symptoms that don't meet the criteria for a mental illness. So don't become alarmed as you learn about different disorders, as many are probably extremes of psychological difficulties we all experience from time to time.

But at some point in your life, you may experience a psychological problem that's so disturbing and persistent that you'll want to talk with someone about it. If so, you'll probably find it worthwhile to consult with a family member, friend, physician, dormitory counselor, clergy person, or professionally trained counselor such as a social worker, psychologist, or psychiatrist. In Chapter 16, we'll present some tips for what to look for and avoid in a psychotherapist.

Mental Illness and the Law: A Controversial Interface. Psychological problems not only affect our mental functioning; they can place us at risk for legal problems. There are few topics about which the general public is certain it knows more, yet actually knows less, than the interface between mental illness and the law. The issues here are as complex as they are controversial.

Mental Illness and Violence. One of the most pervasive myths in psychology is that mentally ill people are at greatly heightened risk for violence (Link, Phelan, Bresnahan, Stueve, & Pescosolido, 1999). In fact, the overwhelming majority of people with schizophrenia and other psychotic disorders aren't physically aggressive toward others (Friedman, 2006; Steadman et al., 1998; Teplin, 1985). One might have hoped that the seemingly endless parade of "real crime" shows on television would have helped to combat this misconception, but it's probably done the opposite. Although only a few percent of mentally ill people commit aggressive acts, about 75 percent of televised characters with mental illness are violent (Wahl, 1997).

Still, like many misconceptions, this one contains a kernel of truth. Although most mentally ill people aren't at increased risk for violence, a subset—especially those who are convinced they are being persecuted (by the government, for example), and those with substance abuse—are (Monahan, 1992; Steadman et al., 1998).

The Insanity Defense: Free Will versus Determinism. In courts of law, mental illnesses and the law occasionally collide head-on, often with unpredictable consequences. The best-known example of this clash is the **insanity defense,** which is premised on the idea that we shouldn't hold people legally responsible for their crimes if they weren't of "sound mind" when they committed them. The insanity defense comes in many forms, which differ across state and federal courts. Forty-six U.S. states use some version of this defense, with four—Utah, Montana, Idaho, and Kansas—opting out of it.

Most contemporary forms of this defense are based loosely on the *McNaughton rule,* formulated during an 1843 British trial. This rule requires that to be declared insane, persons must either have (1) not known what they were doing at the time of the crime or

---

factoid

People with severe mental illnesses, like schizophrenia, are much more likely to be victims than perpetrators of violence (Teplin, McClelland, Abram, & Weiner, 2005), probably because they often experience difficulty defending themselves against attack or avoiding dangerous situations.

---

insanity defense
legal defense proposing that people shouldn't be held legally responsible for their actions if they weren't of "sound mind" when committing them

(2) not known that what they were doing was wrong (Melton, Petrilla, Poythress, & Slobogin, 1997). A defendant (accused person) who was so disoriented during an epileptic seizure that he didn't even realize he was attacking a police officer might fulfill the first prong of McNaughten; a defendant who believed he was actually murdering Adolph Hitler when he shot his next-door neighbor might fulfill the second. Several other versions of the insanity defense strive to determine whether defendants were incapable of controlling their impulses at the moment of the crime. Because this judgment is exceedingly difficult (how can we know whether a man who murdered his wife in the heat of overwhelming anger *could* have controlled his temper had he really tried?), some courts ignore it.

The insanity defense is controversial, to put it mildly. To its proponents, this defense is necessary for defendants whose mental state is so deranged that it impairs their freedom to decide whether to commit a crime (Sadoff, 1992; Stone, 1982). To its critics, this defense is nothing more than a legal cop-out that excuses criminals of responsibility (Lykken, 1982; Szasz, 1991). These divergent perspectives reflect a more deep-seated disagreement about free will versus determinism (see Prologue). The legal system assumes that our actions are freely chosen, whereas scientific psychology assumes that our actions are completely determined by prior variables, including our genetic makeup and learning history. So lawyers and judges tend to view the insanity defense as a needed exception for the small minority of defendants who lack free will. In contrast, many psychologists view this defense as illogical, because they see all crimes, including those committed by people with severe mental disorders, as equally "determined."

Following an initial conviction and later appeal, Andrea Yates was acquitted on the basis of an insanity verdict in a 2006 trial. Diagnosed with postpartum depression (depression following childbirth), Yates drowned her five young children in the bathtub, apparently convinced that she'd received commands to do so from Satan. The intense publicity surrounding the Yates' trials and several others involving the insanity verdict has probably contributed to public misperceptions regarding this verdict's prevalence.

APPLY YOUR THINKING

If we were to do away with the insanity verdict, how would this change affect our legal system? Would we need to treat all convicted criminals identically, regardless of their psychological status at the time of the crime?

There are numerous misconceptions regarding the insanity verdict (see **Table 15.5**). For example, although most people believe that a sizable proportion, perhaps 15–20 percent, of criminals are acquitted (found innocent) on the basis of the insanity verdict, the actual percentage is less than 1 percent (Silver, Cirincione, & Steadman, 1994). This erroneous belief probably stems from the *availability heuristic* (Chapter 2): Because we hear a great

Table 15.5 Popular Misconceptions Regarding the Insanity Defense.

Myth	Reality
Insanity is a psychological or psychiatric term.	*Insanity* is a purely legal term that refers only to whether the person was responsible for the crime, not to the nature of his or her psychiatric disorder.
The determination of insanity rests on a careful evaluation of the person's current mental state.	The determination of insanity rests on a determination of the person's mental state at the time of the crime.
A large proportion of criminals escape criminal responsibility by using the insanity defense.	The insanity defense is raised in only about 1% of criminal trials and is successful only about one-fourth of the time.
Most people acquitted on the basis of an insanity defense quickly go free.	The average insanity acquittee spends close to 3 years in a psychiatric hospital, often longer than the length of a criminal sentence for the same crime.
Insanity defenses are complicated and frequently fool juries as a result.	Most successful insanity verdicts are delivered by judges, not juries.
Most people who use the insanity defense are faking mental illness.	The rate of faking mental illness among insanity defendants appears to be low.

(*Sources:* Butler, 2006; McCutcheon and McCutcheon, 1994; Pasewark and Pantle, 1979; Phillips, Wolf, and Coons, 1998; Silver, Cirincione, and Steadman, 1994)

John Hinkley, who was declared not guilty by reason of insanity in 1982 for the attempted assassination of then President Ronald Reagan, shown here prior to the shooting. Hinkley's acquittal triggered a major social backlash against the insanity defense.

deal about a few widely publicized cases of defendants acquitted on the grounds of insanity, we overestimate this verdict's prevalence (Butler, 2006).

Many people confuse the insanity verdict with **incompetence to stand trial,** which bears on the question of whether a defendant possesses adequate mental capacity to be tried in a court of law. The answer to this question hinges on two key criteria: (1) Do defendants understand the charges against them? (2) Can defendants assist in their defense, for example, by consulting with their lawyer? (*Dusky v. United States,* 1960; Grisso, 2003). If the answer to *either* question is no, defendants are declared incompetent to stand trial and hospitalized—and typically receive treatment—unless and until they're restored to competence. The most frequent reason for incompetence to stand trial is severe psychosis, with mental retardation coming in second (Murrie & Redding, 2006).

Involuntary Commitment. We're all familiar with *criminal commitment,* which is just a fancy term for putting someone in jail or prison. Yet society possesses another mechanism for committing individuals against their will. Known as **involuntary commitment** or *civil commitment,* it's a procedure for protecting us from certain mentally ill people, and certain mentally ill people from themselves. Most U.S. states specify that mentally ill individuals can be committed against their will only if they (1) pose a clear and present threat to themselves or others or (2) are so psychologically impaired that they can't care for themselves (Appelbaum, 1997; Werth, 2001). Although psychiatrists (but not psychologists) can recommend involuntary commitment to a hospital, only a judge can formally approve it following a hearing. Nevertheless, in most states, two psychiatrists or other physicians can place an emergency "hold" on patients to hospitalize them involuntarily for a brief period of time, typically 3 days. When that period expires, the patient is legally entitled to a judicial hearing.

Involuntary commitment raises difficult ethical questions. Advocates of this procedure contend that the government has the right to assume the role of "parent" over mentally ill individuals who are dangerous and don't possess sufficient insight to appreciate the impact of their actions (Chodoff, 1976; Satel, 1999). In contrast, critics argue that by involuntarily institutionalizing people who haven't committed crimes, the government is depriving them of their civil liberties (Schaler, 2004; Szasz, 1978). Critics of involuntary commitment also point to research demonstrating that mental health professionals typically do a poor job of forecasting violence (Monahan, 1992), often predicting that patients will commit violence when they won't. Research suggests that African American psychiatric patients are especially likely to be misclassified as potentially violent (Garb, 1998). Still, studies show that mental health professionals can predict violence at better than chance levels, especially when patients have very recently engaged in, or are immediately threatening, violence (Kramer & Heilbrun, 2007; Lidz, Mulvey, & Gardner, 1993; Monahan et al., 2000).

incompetence to stand trial
assessment of a defendant's mental capacity to stand trial in a court of law

involuntary commitment
procedure of placing some mentally ill people in a psychiatric hospital or other facility based on their potential danger to themselves or others, or their inability to care for themselves

somatoform disorders
conditions marked by physical symptoms that suggest an underlying medical illness, but that are actually psychological in origin

hypochondriasis
an individual's continual preoccupation with the notion that he is suffering from a serious physical disease

panic attacks
brief, intense episodes of extreme fear characterized by sweating, dizziness, light-headedness, racing heartbeat, and feelings of impending death or going crazy

ASSESS YOUR KNOWLEDGE: FACT OR FICTION?
(1) According to a family resemblance view, no one criterion distinguishes mental disorder from normality. (True/False)
(2) Once the medical model began to take hold in the Renaissance, treatments for mental disorders came to be based on strong scientific evidence. (True/False)
(3) Almost all deinstitutionalized patients returned successfully to their families and communities. (True/False)
(4) Some mental disorders appear to be present in most, if not all, cultures. (True/False)
(5) Virtually all psychiatric diagnoses are unreliable. (True/False)
(6) Most severely mentally ill individuals are not prone to violence. (True/False)

Answers: (1) T (p. 625); (2) F (p. 626); (3) F (p. 627); (4) T (pp. 628–630); (5) F (pp. 630–633); (6) T (p. 636)

Anxiety Disorders: The Many Faces of Worry and Fear

We'll begin our tour of psychological disorders with problems stemming from anxiety. Fortunately, most everyday anxieties generally don't last long or feel especially uncomfortable. Anxiety in small doses can even be adaptive. It can permit a lightning-quick response to danger, steer us away from harmful behaviors, and inspire us to solve festering problems. Yet sometimes anxiety spirals out of control, and it can become excessive and inappropriate. It may even feel life-threatening (Mendelowicz & Stein, 2000).

Anxiety disorders are among the most prevalent of all mental disorders; 29 percent of us will meet the diagnostic criteria for one or more anxiety disorders at some point in our lives (Kessler, Berglund, Denler, Jin, & Walters, 2005). The average age of onset for anxiety disorders (11 years) is much earlier than for most other disorders, including substance use disorders (20 years) and mood disorders (30 years; Kessler et al., 2005). **Table 15.6** displays the lifetime prevalence of anxiety disorders, along with many other disorders we'll consider in this chapter.

Many anxiety disorders, including phobias, frequently have an initial onset in childhood.

Table 15.6 Lifetime Prevalence of DSM-IV Disorders (in percent).

Panic disorder	4.7	Attention-deficit/hyperactivity disorder	8.1
Specific phobia	12.5	Alcohol abuse	13.2
Social phobia	12.1	Alcohol dependence (Alcoholism)	5.4
Generalized anxiety disorder	5.7	Drug abuse	7.9
Obsessive-compulsive disorder	1.6	Drug dependence	3.0
Posttraumatic stress disorder	6.8	Any substance use disorder	14.6
Any anxiety disorder	28.8	Any disorder	46.4
Major depressive disorder	16.6	Two or more disorders	27.7
Dysthymia	2.5	Three or more disorders	17.3
Bipolar I-II disorder	3.9		
Any mood disorder	20.8		

(*Source:* Kessler, et al., 2005)

Yet anxiety isn't limited to anxiety disorders. Anxiety can seep into numerous aspects of our functioning, including our perceived physical health. In a mysterious class of conditions called **somatoform disorders,** people experience physical symptoms that suggest an underlying medical illness, but that are actually of psychological origin (see Table 15.6). *Conversion disorder,* which we encountered in Chapter 14, is one example. High levels of physical anxiety are pervasive in many somatoform disorders; for example, people with **hypochondriasis** are continually preoccupied with the idea that they're suffering from a serious physical disease (Asmundson & Taylor, 2005). Much like radar operators who stay on their toes for signs of incoming enemy planes, they always seem to be on the alert for a new symptom. Despite repeated medical reassurance and physical examinations, hypochondriacs insist that their mild aches, pains, and twinges are signs of serious diseases, like cancer, AIDS, or heart disease (APA, 2000). In this section, however, we'll focus primarily on disorders in which anxiety centers on our thoughts and emotions.

The term *hypochondriasis* literally means "under the chondria," or rib cage, the site of many of the physical symptoms that hypochondriacs report (Vilenski.org).

First Person Account: Panic Disorder

For me, a panic attack is almost a violent experience. I feel disconnected from reality. I feel like I'm losing control in a very extreme way. My heart pounds really hard, I feel like I can't get my breath, and there's an overwhelming feeling that things are crashing in on me. (Dickey, 1994)

PANIC DISORDER: TERROR THAT COMES OUT OF THE BLUE

The Greek god Pan was a mischievous spirit who popped out of the bushes to scare the living daylights out of travelers. Pan lent his name to **panic attacks,** which occur when nervous feelings gather momentum and escalate into intense bouts of fear, even terror. Panic attacks peak in less than 10 minutes and can include sweating, dizziness, faintness, light-headedness, a racing or pounding heart, shortness of breath, feelings of unreality,

The term *panic* stems from the name of Pan, Greek god of shepherds and flocks, who frightened travelers.

Some of the most common fears involve animals, such as spiders and snakes.

fictoid

Myth: Most agoraphobics are housebound.

Reality: Being unable or afraid to leave the house occurs only in severe cases of agoraphobia.

panic disorder
repeated and unexpected panic attacks, along with either persistent concerns about future attacks or a change in personal behavior in an attempt to avoid them

generalized anxiety disorder
continual feelings of worry, anxiety, physical tension, and irritability across many areas of life functioning

phobia
intense fear of an object or situation that's greatly out of proportion to its actual threat

agoraphobia
fear of being in a place or situation from which escape is difficult or embarrassing, or in which help is unavailable in the event of a panic attack

and fears of going crazy or dying. Because many patients experiencing their initial panic attacks believe they're having heart attacks, many first go to emergency rooms, only to be sent home and—like Ida, whom we met at the outset of the chapter—told "it's all in their heads."

Some panic attacks are associated with specific situations, such as riding in elevators or shopping in supermarkets, but others come entirely out of the blue, that is, without warning. Not surprisingly, panic attacks often generate fears of the situations in which they occur. Panic can occur in every anxiety disorder, as well as in mood and eating disorders. Even high-functioning people can experience panic attacks in anticipation of stressful events (Cox & Taylor, 1998): About 20–25 percent of college students report at least one panic attack in a 1-year period, with about half that number reporting unexpected attacks (Lilienfeld, 1997).

Panic attacks can occur only rarely, or on a daily basis, for weeks, months, or even years at a time. People suffer from **panic disorder** when they experience panic attacks that are repeated and unexpected, and when they either experience persistent concerns about panicking or change their behavior (for example, change jobs) as a result of the attacks (APA, 2000).

GENERALIZED ANXIETY DISORDER: PERPETUAL WORRY

We all get caught up with worry from time to time. Yet for people with **generalized anxiety disorder** (GAD), worry is a way of life. They spend an average of 60 percent of each day worrying, compared with 18 percent for the rest of the general population (Craske, Rapee, Jackel, & Barlow, 1989). Many describe themselves as "worry warts." They tend to think anxious thoughts, feel irritable and on edge, have trouble sleeping, and experience a great deal of bodily tension (Barlow, Chorpita, & Turovsky, 1996; Wittchen, 2002). Often they worry too much about the small things in life, like an upcoming meeting at work or a social event (Sanderson & Barlow, 1990). One-third of those with GAD develop it following a major stressful event—like a wedding, illness, or death of a relative—or as the result of lifestyle changes, such as completing school and embarking on a career (Mellinger & Lynn, 2003).

GAD may be the core anxiety disorder out of which all others develop (Barlow, 2002). Indeed, people with GAD often experience other anxiety disorders, including panic disorder and phobias, which we'll consider next.

PHOBIAS: IRRATIONAL FEARS

A **phobia** is an intense fear of an object or situation that's greatly out of proportion to its actual threat (see Chapter 6 for a list of selected phobias). Many of us have mild fears—of things like spiders and snakes—that aren't severe enough to be phobias. For a fear to be diagnosed as a phobia, it must restrict our lives, create considerable distress, or both.

Phobias are the most common of all anxiety disorders. One in nine of us has a phobia of an animal, blood or injury, or a situation like a thunderstorm. Social fears are just as common (Kessler et al., 1994). Agoraphobia, which we'll examine next, is the most debilitating of the phobias, and occurs in about one in twenty of us (Magee, Eaton, Wittchen, McGonagle, & Kessler, 1996).

Agoraphobia. Some 2,700 years ago in the city-states of ancient Greece, agoraphobia acquired its name as a condition in which certain fearful citizens couldn't pass through the central city's open-air markets (*agoras*). A common misconception is that agoraphobia is a fear of crowds or public places. But **agoraphobia** actually refers to a fear of being in a place or situation in which escape is difficult or embarrassing, or in which help is unavailable in the event of a panic attack (APA, 1994).

Most fears originate in childhood, but agoraphobia emerges in the midteens and is typically a direct outgrowth of panic disorder. In fact, most people with panic disorder develop agoraphobia (Cox & Taylor, 1999) and become apprehensive in a host of settings, such as malls, crowded movie theaters, tunnels, bridges, or wide-open spaces. The manifestation of agoraphobia seems to differ across cultures. For example, some Eskimos in

Greenland suffer from a condition called "kayak angst," marked by a pronounced fear of going out to sea by oneself in a kayak (Barlow, 2000; Gusow, 1963).

In rare cases, agoraphobia reaches extreme proportions. Two clinicians saw a 62-year-old woman with agoraphobia who hadn't left her house—even once—for 25 years (Jensvold & Turner, 1988). Having experienced severe panic attacks and terrified by the prospect of still more, she spent almost all of her waking hours locked away in her bedroom, with curtains drawn. The therapists attempted to treat her agoraphobia by encouraging her to take short trips out of her house, but she repeatedly refused to walk even a few steps past her front door. Still, as we'll learn in Chapter 16, many cases of agoraphobia and other anxiety disorders are quite treatable.

Specific Phobia. Phobias of objects, places, or situations—called **specific phobias**—commonly arise in response to animals, insects, thunderstorms, water, elevators, and darkness. Many of these fears, especially of animals, are widespread in childhood but disappear with age (APA, 2000). Blood-injury phobia, a fear of being exposed to blood, injury, pain, needles, or deformity, differs from other phobias (see Prologue). In other phobias, people almost always experience a sharp increase in heart rate and blood pressure when they encounter what they fear. But in blood-injury phobia, people first experience a sudden increase in heart rate and blood pressure, followed by an abrupt drop, which accounts for why they feel dizzy and faint at the prospect of having their blood drawn. Most probably, this parasympathetic reaction (see Chapter 3) is a residue of an evolutionarily adaptive response. When we're losing blood, we want to conserve it, so our body's natural reaction to the idea of blood loss is to restrict blood flow (Lilienfeld & Marino, 1995).

Social Phobia. Surveys show that most people rank public speaking as a greater fear than dying (Wallechinsky, Wallace, & Wallace, 1977). Given that statistic, imagine how people with **social phobia** must feel. People with this condition—a marked fear of public appearances in which embarrassment or humiliation seems likely—experience anxiety well beyond the stage fright that most of us feel occasionally (Heimberg & Juster, 1995). People with social phobia are often deathly afraid of speaking, eating, or performing in public. Singers Barbra Streisand and Carly Simon have both acknowledged having social phobia, which explains why they only rarely go on tour (Heller, 1999). Some people with social phobia even fear using public restrooms. Alert to the slightest hint of disapproval, social phobics may misinterpret ambiguous feedback from others as negative (Coles & Heimberg, 2002; Gray & McNaughton, 2000). In some cases they're so concerned with drawing attention to themselves that they're afraid to sign their names on checks or to swim, breathe, or swallow in public (Lynn & Mellinger, 2003).

POSTTRAUMATIC STRESS DISORDER: THE ENDURING EFFECTS OF EXPERIENCING HORROR

When people experience or witness a traumatic event, such as front-line combat, an earthquake, or sexual assault, they may develop **posttraumatic stress disorder** (**PTSD**; see Chapter 12). To qualify for a diagnosis of PTSD, the event must be physically dangerous or life-threatening, either to oneself or someone else. The person's response must also involve intense fear, helplessness, or horror (APA, 2000).

We learned in Chapter 12 that flashbacks are among the hallmarks of PTSD. The terror of war can return decades after the original trauma and be reactivated by everyday stressful experiences (Foa & Kozak, 1986). In recounting his war experiences, Vietnam veteran Tim O'Brien (1990) commented: "The hardest part, by far, is to make the bad pictures go away. In war time, the world is one big long horror movie, image after image, and if it's anything like Vietnam, I'm in for a lifetime of wee-hour creeps" (p. 56).

Other symptoms include efforts to avoid thoughts, feelings, places, and conversations associated with the trauma; recurrent dreams of the trauma; and increased arousal, such as sleep difficulties and startling easily (APA, 2000). Reminders of the incident can trigger full-blown panic attacks, as in the case of a Vietnam veteran who hid under his bed

Blood-injury phobia, a fear of being exposed to blood, injury, pain, needles, or deformity, is marked by an abrupt decrease in heart rate and blood pressure.

First Person Account: Social Phobia

When I would walk into a room full of people, I'd turn red and it would feel like everybody's eyes were on me. I was embarrassed to stand off in a corner by myself, but I couldn't think of anything to say to anybody. It was humiliating. I felt so clumsy, I couldn't wait to get out. (Dickey, 1994)

Posttraumatic stress disorder involves a constellation of symptoms that can be quite debilitating. Combat veterans are at high risk for developing this disorder.

specific phobias
intense fear of objects, places, or situations that are greatly out of proportion to their actual threat

social phobia
marked fear of public appearances in which embarrassment or humiliation is possible

posttraumatic stress disorder (PTSD)
marked emotional disturbance after experiencing or witnessing a severely stressful event

whenever he heard a city helicopter in the distance—well over 20 years after the war ended (Baum, Cohen, & Hall, 1993; Foa & Rothbaum, 1998; Jones & Barlow, 1990). PTSD isn't easy to diagnose. Some of its symptoms, such as anxiety and difficulty sleeping, may have been present *before* the stressful event. Moreover, some people *malinger* (fake) PTSD to obtain government benefits, so diagnosticians must rule out this possibility (Rosen, 2006).

OBSESSIVE-COMPULSIVE DISORDER: TRAPPED IN ONE'S THOUGHTS

Just about all of us have had a thought or even a silly song jingle that we just couldn't get out of our heads. Patients with **obsessive-compulsive disorder** (**OCD**) know all too well what this experience is like, except that their symptoms are much more severe. Like Bill, whom we'll recall from the opening of the chapter, they typically suffer from **obsessions**: persistent ideas, thoughts, or impulses that are unwanted and inappropriate and cause marked distress. There's a fuzzy line between worry and obsessions. But unlike typical worries, obsessions aren't extreme responses to everyday stressors. They usually center on "unacceptable" thoughts about such topics as contamination, sex, aggression, or religion. For example, OCD sufferers may be consumed with fears of being dirty or thoughts of killing others. Unlike ordinary worriers, people with OCD typically see their disturbing thoughts as irrational or nonsensical, and may label themselves "crazy," evil, or dangerous. Despite their best efforts, people with OCD can't find a way to make these thoughts stop.

Most OCD patients also experience symptoms linked closely to obsessions, namely, **compulsions**: repetitive behaviors or mental acts that they initiate to reduce or prevent distress. In most cases, patients feel driven to perform the action that accompanies an obsession, prevent some dreaded event, or "make things right." A patient treated by one of your book's authors awoke early each morning to wash the hood of his car until it was spotless, and felt compelled to repeat this ritual as soon as he arrived home at the end of the workday. Common OCD-type rituals include:

- repeatedly checking door locks, windows, electronic controls, and ovens
- performing tasks in set ways, like putting on one's shoes in a fixed pattern
- counting the number of dots on a wall or touching or tapping objects
- repeatedly arranging and rearranging objects
- washing and cleaning repeatedly and unnecessarily
- saying a prayer or specific phrase every time an obsession comes to mind
- hoarding newspapers, books, letters, soda cans, or other objects

By definition, people diagnosed with OCD spend at least an hour a day immersed in obsessions, compulsions, or both; one patient spent 15–18 hours per day washing his hands, showering, getting dressed, and cleaning money. Still, many people with OCD lead remarkably successful lives. Charles Darwin, the "father of evolution," and Florence Nightingale, the "mother of nursing," both suffered from OCD (OCD-UK, 2005). More recently, celebrities like Cameron Diaz, Billy Bob Thornton, and David Beckham have spoken publicly about their battles with the disorder. Howard Hughes, the billionaire industrialist, struggled for years with severe, untreated symptoms of OCD. As his disorder progressed, he became so obsessed with possible contamination by germs that he refused to leave the expensive hotel rooms in which he lived. He refused to shake hands with anyone and instructed his servants to engage in elaborate rituals concerning his food and handling objects. For example, he insisted that they wrap the handle of a spoon in tissue paper and seal it with tape. He also installed a huge filtration system in his Chrysler car so that he could breathe only purified air. Although constantly preoccupied with fears of germs, Hughes rarely bathed or brushed his teeth, and cut his hair and fingernails only once a year (Bartlett & Steele, 2004; Brownstein & Solyom, 1986).

Ruling Out Rival Hypotheses

First Person Account: Obsessive-Compulsive Disorder

"I couldn't do anything without rituals. They transcended every aspect of my life. Counting was big for me. When I set my alarm at night, I had to set it to a number that wouldn't add up to a 'bad' number. I would wash my hair three times as opposed to once because three was a good luck number and one wasn't. It took me longer to read because I'd count the lines in a paragraph. If I was writing a term paper, I couldn't have a certain number of words on a line if it added up to a bad number. I was always worried that if I didn't do something, my parents were going to die."
(Dickey, 1994)

factoid

Have you ever been unable to get a tune or a snatch of a tune out of your head? Psychologists have a term for this phenomenon; it's called an "earworm." A recent study revealed that 98 percent of students have experienced earworms. The number 1 earworm as of several years ago? Chili's "Baby Back Ribs" jingle (Kellaris, 2003).

obsessive-compulsive disorder (OCD)
condition marked by repeated and lengthy (at least one hour per day) immersion in obsessions, compulsions, or both

obsessions
persistent ideas, thoughts, or impulses that are unwanted and inappropriate, causing marked distress

compulsions
repetitive behaviors or mental acts performed to reduce or prevent stress

EXPLANATIONS FOR ANXIETY DISORDERS: THE ROOTS OF PATHOLOGICAL WORRY AND FEAR

How do anxiety disorders come about? Differing theories propose explanations focusing on the environment, catastrophic thinking, and biological influences.

Learning Models of Anxiety: Anxious Responses as Acquired Habits. According to learning theories, fears are—you guessed it—learned. Watson and Raynor's (1920) famous demonstration of classical conditioning of the fear of a small furry animal (remember poor little Albert from Chapter 6?) powerfully conveys how people learn fears.

Operant conditioning, which relies on reinforcements and punishments (see Chapter 6), offers another account of how fears are maintained. If a socially awkward girl repeatedly experiences rejection when she asks boys to go to the movies, she may become shy around them. If this pattern of rejection continues, she could develop a full-blown social phobia. Paradoxically, her avoidance of boys provides negative reinforcement, because it allows her to escape the unpleasant consequences of social interaction. This sense of relief perpetuates her avoidance, and ultimately her anxiety.

Learning theorists (Rachman, 1977) believe that fears can arise in two additional ways. First, we can acquire fears by observing others engage in fearful behaviors (Mineka & Cook, 1993). A father's fear of dogs might instill the same in his child. Second, fears can stem from information or misinformation from others. If a mother tells her children that riding in elevators is dangerous, they may end up taking the stairs.

Catastrophizing and Anxiety Sensitivity. People with social phobias predict that many social encounters will be interpersonal disasters, and some people with fears of storms are so fearful that they seek the shelter of a basement when mild thunderstorms are detected on radar 50 miles away (Voncken, Bogels, & deVriees, 2003). As these examples illustrate, *catastrophizing* is a core feature of anxious thinking (Beck, 1976; Ellis, 1962; Ellis & Dryden, 1997). People catastrophize when they predict terrible events—such as contracting a life-threatening illness from turning a doorknob—despite their low probability (A. T. Beck, 1964; J. Beck, 1995).

Anxious people tend to interpret ambiguous situations in a negative light (Matthews & MacLeod, 2005). Many people with anxiety disorders harbor high levels of **anxiety sensitivity,** a fear of anxiety-related sensations (Reiss & McNally, 1985; Stein, Jang, & Livesley, 1999). Think of the times your muscles felt tight, you felt a bit dizzy when you stood up quickly, or your heart raced after climbing a flight of stairs. You may have dismissed these physical symptoms as harmless. Yet people with high anxiety sensitivity tend to misinterpret them as dangerous—perhaps as early signs of a heart attack or stroke—and react with intense worry (Clark, 1986; Lilienfeld, 1993; McNally & Eke, 1996). As a result, their barely noticeable physical sensations or minor anxiety can spiral into full-blown panic attacks.

Anxiety: Genetic and Biological Influences. Numerous twin studies show that many anxiety disorders, including panic disorder and phobias, are genetically influenced (Andrews et al., 1990; Roy, Neale, Pedersen, Mathe, & Kendler, 1995). In particular, genes affect whether we inherit high levels of neuroticism—a tendency to be high strung and irritable (see Chapter 14)—which can set the stage for excessive worry (Anderson, Taylor, & McLean, 1996; Zinbarg & Barlow, 1996). On a genetic basis, people who experience GAD are virtually indistinguishable from those who experience major depression, which also is associated with high levels of neuroticism (Kendler & Karkowski-Shuman, 1997). This finding suggests a shared genetic pathway for these disorders.

Family studies show that people with OCD are twice as likely as people without OCD to inherit a specific overactive gene. This gene is related to the transport of the neurotransmitter serotonin (Goldman et al., 2006). The obsession-compulsive response in the brain is distinctive. It involves a malfunction of the caudate nucleus, a portion of the basal ganglia (see Chapter 3), which initiates and controls body

Howard Hughes, the billionaire industrialist, suffered from debilitating obsessive-compulsive disorder later in his life. His extreme fear of germs and contamination was portrayed in the movie, *The Aviator*, starring Leonardo DiCaprio.

Table 15.7 Anxiety and Interpretation of Ambiguity.

Selected Homophones	
Threatening Meaning/ Spelling	Nonthreatening Meaning/ Spelling
Bury	Berry
Die	Dye
Patients	Patience
Bruise	Brews
Flu	Flew
Sword	Soared
Boar	Bore

Anxiety leads us to interpret ambiguous stimuli negatively. Researchers have asked anxious and nonanxious subjects to listen to *homophones*—words that sound the same but have two different meanings and spellings—and to write down the word they heard. In these studies, they've used homophone pairs in which one meaning (and spelling) is threatening and the other is nonthreatening. Compared with nonanxious subjects, anxious subjects are more likely to write down the version of the homophone that's threatening, such as "bury" as opposed to "berry" (Blanchette & Richards, 2003; Mathews, Richard, & Eysenck, 1989).

anxiety sensitivity
fear of anxiety-related sensations

movement (Hansen, Hasselbach, Low, & Bolwig, 2002; Pigott, Myers, & Williams, 1996). A glitch in the caudate nucleus also seems to create problems in setting aside doubts and misgivings. Much like a car that's stuck in gear, obsessive people experience problems with shifting thoughts and behaviors (Schwartz & Bayette, 1996). Brain scans also reveal increased activity in portions of the frontal lobes where information is filtered, prioritized, and organized. Under these circumstances, people can't seem to get troubling thoughts out of their minds or inhibit repeated rituals.

ASSESS YOUR KNOWLEDGE: FACT OR FICTION?

(1) Panic attacks typically peak in 10 minutes or less. (True/False)

(2) According to some theorists, GAD is the core anxiety disorder out of which others develop. (True/False)

(3) Because PTSD is characterized by dramatic symptoms, it's typically an easy disorder to diagnose. (True/False)

(4) Catastrophizing is a core feature of anxious thinking. (True/False)

(5) Genes exert little influence on obsessive-compulsive disorder. (True/False)

Answers: (1) T (p. 639); (2) T (p. 639); (3) F (p. 641); (4) T (p. 643); (5) F (p. 643)

Mood Disorders and Suicide

Imagine we're interviewing someone who's come to us for help. As the client begins to talk about his life, it becomes clear that even the simplest activities, like dressing or driving to work, have become enormous acts of will. He reports difficulty sleeping and unaccountably wakes up before dawn each day. He refuses to answer the telephone. He lies listlessly for hours staring at the television set. His mood is downcast, and occasionally tears well up in his eyes. He's recently lost a fair amount of weight. His world is gray, a void. Toward the end of the interview, he tells us he's begun to contemplate suicide.

We've just interviewed a person who suffers from a *mood disorder,* so called because his difficulties center on his bleak mood, which colors all aspects of his existence. When we check his symptoms against those in Table 15.4 (refer back to p. 634), we can see that he meets the criteria for a **major depressive episode.** We'll soon encounter another mood disorder, *bipolar disorder,* in which people's mood is often the mirror image of depression. **Table 15.8** outlines the range of mood disorders in DSM-IV.

MAJOR DEPRESSIVE DISORDER: COMMON, BUT NOT THE COMMON COLD

Over the course of a lifetime, more than 20 percent of us will experience a mood disorder. Major depression alone darkens the lives of more than 16 percent of Americans (Kessler et al., 2005). Due to its frequency, some have called depression the "common cold" of psychological disorders (Seligman, 1975). Yet we'll soon see that this description doesn't begin to capture the profound depths of suffering that people with this condition experience. Depressive disorders can begin at any age, but are most likely to strike people in their 30s. Contrary to popular misconception, they're less common in elderly adults (Klerman, 1986).

As we mentioned earlier, women are about twice as likely to be depressed as men. In Chapter 12, we learned that this gender difference may be associated with women's tendency to ruminate more than men (Nolen-Hoeksema, 2002, 2003). Yet it may also be associated with differences between men and women in economic power, sex hormones, social support, and history of physical or sexual abuse (Howland & Thase, 1998). The sex difference in depression is widespread but not universal. In some cultures, such as certain Mediterranean populations, Orthodox Jews, and the Amish, this sex difference is largely absent (Piccinelli & Wilkinson, 2000). But researchers don't know why. One possibility is that the differences in the rates of depression across genders in Western cultures reflect an underdiagnosis of depres-

In most cultures, women are generally at greater risk for developing depression than men. Nevertheless, the reasons for this difference aren't fully understood.

major depressive episode
state in which a person experiences a lingering depressed mood or diminished interest in pleasurable activities, along with symptoms that include weight loss and sleep difficulties

Table 15.8 Mood Disorders and Conditions.

Disorder	Symptoms
Manic Episode	Markedly inflated self-esteem or grandiosity, greatly decreased need for sleep, much more talkative than usual, racing thoughts, distractibility, increased activity level or agitation, and excessive involvement in pleasurable activities that can cause problems (like unprotected sex, excessive spending, reckless driving)
Bipolar Disorder I	Presence of at least one manic episode
Dysthymic Disorder	Low-level depression of at least two years' duration; feelings of inadequacy, sadness, low energy, poor appetite, decreased pleasure and productivity, and hopelessness.
Hypomanic Episode	A less intense and disruptive version of a manic episode. Feelings of elation, grouchiness, or irritability, distractability and talkativeness.
Bipolar Disorder II	Patients must experience at least one episode of major depression and one hypomanic episode.
Cyclothymia	Moods alternate between numerous periods of hypomanic symptoms and numerous periods of depressive symptoms. To remember cyclothymia, think of "cycles" of up and down moods. Cyclothymia increases the risk of developing bipolar disorder.
Postpartum Depression	A depressive episode that occurs within a month after childbirth. As many as 15% of women develop postpartum depression. A much more serious condition, postpartum psychosis, occurs in about 1 or 2 per 1,000 childbirths, with psychotic symptoms, including command hallucinations to kill the infant or delusions that the infant is possessed by an evil spirit (Beck & Gable, 2001).
Seasonal Affective Disorder	Depressive episodes that display a seasonal pattern, most commonly beginning in fall or winter and improving in spring. There must be 2 consecutive years in which the episode appears on a seasonal basis. Symptoms often include weight gain, lack of energy, carbohydrate craving, and excessive sleep.

(*Source:* Data from *DSM-IV*, APA, 2000)

factoid

Following birth, perhaps as many as 2–3% of new mothers experience a condition called postpartum obsessive-compulsive disorder. In some cases, the infant becomes the focus of the mother's bizarre thoughts and compulsive behaviors. These symptoms can include repeatedly checking the child to ensure her safety, hiding knives for fear of stabbing the child, and excessive cleaning. Some mothers become so fearful of what they might do to their children that they're reluctant to take care of them (Arnold, 1999). Fortunately, such women almost never harm their children, and effective treatments are available.

sion in men. In the United States, women are more willing to admit to depression and seek psychological services than men, who are socialized to "act tough" (Kilmartin, 2005).

The symptoms of depression may develop gradually over days or weeks; in other cases, they may surface rather suddenly. Depression, like the common cold, is recurrent. The average person with major depression experiences five or six episodes over the course of a lifetime. Most of these episodes last from 6 months to a year. But in as many as a fifth of cases, depression is *chronic*, that is, present for decades with no relief (Ingram, Scott, & Seigel, 1998). In sharp contrast to the common cold, depression produces severe impairment. In extreme cases, people may fail to feed or clothe themselves or take care of basic health needs, like brushing their teeth or showering.

EXPLANATIONS FOR MAJOR DEPRESSIVE DISORDER: A TANGLED WEB

The multifaceted phenomenon of depression illustrates the biopsychosocial approach, underscoring how different factors can combine to produce psychological symptoms. Let's reconsider the depressed man we imagined interviewing at the beginning of this section. From his depressed father and anxious mother, he may have inherited a tendency to respond to stressful situations with doubt and negative emotions (neuroticism). He felt that a competitive colleague continually tried to undermine his authority as a television producer. In response, he felt insecure, and began to second-guess his every decision. Each day he wasted hours ruminating about losing his job. The quality of his work nose-dived. He withdrew socially and began to refuse invitations to go golfing with his buddies. His friends tried to cheer him up, but the black cloud that hung over his head wouldn't budge. Feeling rebuffed, his friends stopped inviting him to do anything. His once-bright social world became a black void, and he moped around doing virtually nothing. He felt helpless. Eventually, his dark thoughts turned to suicide.

This example highlights a key point. To fully understand depression, we must appreciate the complex interplay of inborn tendencies, stressful events, interpersonal relationships, the loss of reinforcers in everyday life, negative thoughts, and feelings of helplessness (Akiskal & McKinney, 1973; Ilardi & Feldman, 2001).

Depression and Life Events. Sigmund Freud (1917) suggested that early loss can render us vulnerable to depression later in life. He may have been on to something, because the loss of beloved people or even the threat of loss can trigger depression in adulthood. Stressful life events that represent loss or threat of separation are especially tied to depression (Brugha, 1995; Mazure, 1998; Paykel, 2003). But the loss created by a blow to our sense of self-worth can sting every bit as much as the loss of a close relationship (Finlay-Jones & Brown, 1981). A crucial determinant of whether we'll become depressed is whether we've lost or are about to lose something we value dearly, like someone we love, social support, financial support, or self-esteem (Beck, 1983; Blatt, 1974; Prince, Harwood, Blizard, Thomm, & Mann, 1997; Zuroff, Mongrain, & Santor, 2004).

Correlation vs. Causation

Still, as we learned in Chapter 12, pessimism and other symptoms of depression can set the stage for negative life circumstances, like getting fired from a job or losing a close relationship (Hammen, 1991; Harkness & Luther, 2001). The causal arrow of this association thus points in both directions. Negative life events set us up to bring us down, but depression can create problems in living.

Interpersonal Model: Depression as a Social Disorder. James Coyne (1976; Joiner & Coyne, 1999; Rudolf, Hammen, Burge, Lindberg, Herzberg, & Daly, 2006) hypothesized that depression creates interpersonal problems. When people become depressed, he argued, they seek excessive reassurance, which in turn leads others to dislike and reject them. Coyne (1976) asked undergraduates to talk on the telephone for 20 minutes with depressed patients, nondepressed patients, or nonpatient women drawn from the community. He didn't inform students they'd be interacting with depressed patients. Yet following the interaction, students who spoke with depressed patients became more depressed, anxious, and hostile than those who interacted with nondepressed individuals. Moreover, subjects were more rejecting of depressed patients and expressed much less interest in interacting with them in the future. For Coyne, depression is a vicious cycle. Depressed people often elicit hostility and rejection from others, which in turn maintains or worsens their depression.

Replicability

Many, but not all, studies have replicated Coyne's findings that depressed people tend to stir up negative feelings in others (Joiner & Coyne, 1999; McNeil, Arkowitz, & Pritchard, 1987; Sacco & Dunn, 1990). Other research suggests that constant worrying, mistrust, and socially inappropriate behaviors can also be a social turn-off to many people (Zborowski & Garske, 1993).

> **APPLY YOUR THINKING**
>
> Coyne's interpersonal model provides an account of how the depressed state is maintained. But it doesn't explain how the interpersonal cycle of depression gets started. What factors may help to explain how people become depressed in the first place?

According to James Coyne's interpersonal model of depression, depression can trigger rejection from others, in turn contributing to further depression.

Behavioral Model: Depression as a Loss of Reinforcement. Peter Lewinsohn's (1974) *behavioral model* assumes that depression results from a low rate of response-contingent positive reinforcement. Put in simpler terms, when depressed people try different things and receive no payoff for them, they eventually give up. They stop participating in many pleasant activities, leaving them little opportunity to obtain reinforcement from other people. In time, their personal and social worlds shrink, as depression seeps into virtually every nook and cranny of their lives. Lewinsohn later observed that depressed people sometimes lack social skills (Segrin, 2000; Youngren & Lewinsohn, 1980), making it even harder for them to obtain reinforcement from others. To make matters worse, if people respond to depressed individuals with sympathy and concern, they may reinforce and maintain these individuals' withdrawal. This view implies a straightforward recipe for breaking the grip of depression: pushing ourselves to engage in pleasant activities. Sometimes merely getting out of bed can be the first step toward conquering depression (Gorther, Gollan, Dobson, & Jacobson, 1998).

Cognitive Model: Depression as a Disorder of Thinking. In contrast, Aaron Beck's influential **cognitive model of depression** holds that depression is caused by negative beliefs and expectations (Beck, 1967, 1987). Beck focused on the *cognitive triad*, three components of depressed thinking: negative views of oneself, one's experiences, and the future. These habitual thought patterns, called *negative schemas*, presumably originate in early experiences of loss, failure, and rejection. Activated by stressful events in later life, these schemas reinforce depressed people's negative experiences (Scher, Ingram, & Segal, 2005).

Depressed people's view of the world is bleak because they put a decidedly negative mental spin on their experiences. They also suffer from *cognitive distortions,* that is, skewed ways of thinking. Two examples are *overgeneralization* and *selective abstraction.* People engage in overgeneralization when they draw an extremely broad conclusion on the basis of a specific fact or minor event. After receiving a parking ticket, a woman might conclude she's worthless and that nothing will ever go right for her. People engage in selective abstraction when they draw a negative conclusion based on only an isolated aspect of a situation. A man might consistently single out a trivial error he committed in a softball game and blame himself completely for the loss. It's as though depressed people were wearing glasses that filtered out all of life's positive experiences and brought all of life's negative experiences into sharper focus.

There's considerable support for Beck's idea that depressed people hold negative views of themselves, the future, and the world (Haaga, Dyck, & Ernst, 1991; Ingram, 2003). But the evidence for the role of cognitive distortions in nonhospitalized, or not seriously depressed, individuals isn't as strong (Dykman & Abramson, 1996). In fact, some research suggests that compared with nondepressed people, mildly depressed people actually have a *more* accurate view of circumstances, a phenomenon called *depressive realism.* In contrast, people who aren't depressed experience *illusory control* over their environments. This surprising conclusion comes from research in which nondepressed people were more likely than depressed people to believe they controlled a lightbulb when it came on, even though experimenters rigged when it turned on and off (Alloy & Abramson, 1979, 1988). Thus, depressed people were more realistic in their estimates of personal control, because they had no control over the bulb. Researchers (Msefti, Kornbrot, Murphy, & Simpson, 2005) recently replicated this finding, but suggested that depressed individuals experience difficulties attending to and processing information about the light. So rather than being more realistic, depressed people may be less attentive to "reality," a finding consistent with cognitive models.

Not tuning into reality can exact serious costs. Janet Kistner and her colleagues (Kistner, Devid-Ferdon, Repper, & Joiner, 2006) studied 9- and 10-year-old children's perceptions of how their classmates felt about them. The researchers discovered that children with accurate perceptions of their level of social acceptance were less likely to develop depression than those with inaccurate perceptions. Beck's theory implies that negative schemas shape emotional tone rather than the other way around. Nevertheless, Kistner's research suggests that depression itself can create a negative bias. As time went on, children who were depressed at the outset of the study became more negatively biased about how much others liked and perceived them. These findings point to a cycle in which inaccurate perceptions lead to depression, and depression leads to inaccurate perceptions.

Learned Helplessness: Depression as a Consequence of Uncontrollable Events.
Martin Seligman (1975; Seligman & Maier, 1967) accidentally stumbled across some usual findings related to depression in his work with dogs. He was testing dogs in a shuttle box, depicted in **Figure 15.3**; one side of the box was electrified and the other side, separated by a barrier, wasn't. Ordinarily, dogs avoid painful shocks by jumping over the barrier to the

Most people have an illusion of control; for example, they mistakenly believe that they're more likely to win a gamble if they toss the dice than if someone else does. Interestingly, people who are mildly or modestly depressed tend not to fall prey to this thinking error (Golin, Terrell, & Johnson, 1977), suggesting they may actually be more realistic than nondepressed people under certain circumstances.

Replicability

Ruling Out Rival Hypotheses

Correlation vs. Causation

cognitive model of depression
theory that depression is caused by negative beliefs and expectations

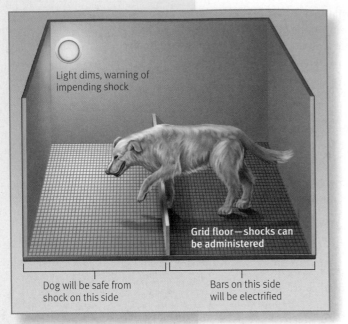

Light dims, warning of impending shock

Grid floor—shocks can be administered

Dog will be safe from shock on this side

Bars on this side will be electrified

Figure 15.3 The Shuttle Box. Using an apparatus like this, Martin Seligman found that dogs gave up trying to escape electric shocks. He called this phenomenon "learned helplessness."

Correlation vs. Causation

nonelectrified side of the box. Yet Seligman found something surprising. Dogs first restrained in a hammock and exposed to shocks they couldn't escape later often made no attempt to escape shocks in the shuttle box, even when they could easily get away from them. Some of the dogs just sat there, whimpering and crying, passively accepting the shocks as though they were inescapable. They'd learned to become helpless.

Bruce Overmier and Seligman (1967) described **learned helplessness** as the tendency to feel helpless in the face of events we can't control and argued that it offers an animal model of depression. He noted striking parallels between the effects of learned helplessness and depressive symptoms: passivity, appetite and weight loss, and difficulty learning that one can change circumstances for the better. But we must be cautious in drawing conclusions from animal studies because many psychological conditions, including depression, may differ in animals and humans (Raulin & Lilienfeld, 1999).

Provocative as it is, Seligman's model can't account for all aspects of depression. It doesn't explain why depressed people make internal attributions (explanations) for failure. In fact, the tendency to assume personal responsibility for failure contradicts the notion that depressed people regard negative events as beyond their control. The original model also doesn't acknowledge that the mere expectation of uncontrollability isn't sufficient to induce depression. After all, people don't become sad when they receive large amounts of money in a lottery, even though they have no control over this event (Abramson, Seligman, & Teasdale, 1978).

When data don't fit a model, good scientists revise it. Seligman and his colleagues (Abramson et al., 1978) altered the learned helplessness model to account for the attributions people make to explain their worlds. They argued that persons prone to depression attribute negative outcomes to *internal* as opposed to external factors, and success to *external* as opposed to internal factors. A depressed person might blame a poor test grade on a lack of ability, an internal factor, and a good score on the ease of the exam, an external factor. The researchers also observed that depression-prone persons make attributions that are *global* and *stable:* They tend to see their failures as general and fixed aspects of their personalities. Still, internal, global, and stable attributions may be more a consequence than a cause of depression (Harvey & Weary, 1984). The state of depression brought on by undesirable life events may skew our thinking, leading us to make negative attributions (Beidel & Turner, 1986; Gibb & Alloy, 2006; Ilardi & Craighead, 1994).

APPLY YOUR THINKING

It's unlikely that most animals, even intelligent ones, can engage in complex attributions about themselves and the world. What does this fact imply about the relevance of the revised model of learned helplessness to animals?

Depression: The Role of Biology. Twin studies indicate that genes exert a moderate effect on the risk of developing major depression (Kendler, Neale, Kessler, Heath, & Eaves, 1993). Depression is often associated with low levels of the neurotransmitter serotonin (Robinson, 2007). Specific variations in the serotonin transporter gene (which affects the rate of reuptake; see Chapter 3) seem to play a role in depression, especially in conjunction with life experiences. People who inherit two copies of this stress-sensitive gene are two and a half times more likely to develop depression following four stressful events than people with another version of the gene that isn't sensitive to stress (Caspi et al., 2003; also see Prologue). The stress-sensitive gene probably affects people's ability to dampen negative emotions in the face of stress (Kendler, Gardner, & Prescott, 2003). It's not clear

learned helplessness
tendency to feel helpless in the face of events we can't control

whether these genetic irregularities are specific to depression; they may be associated with anxiety too (Hariri, Mattay et al., 2002).

People can become sensitized to stressful events, so that it takes only a small amount of stress to bring on the blues (Post, 1984). This phenomenon is called *kindling* after the fact that it requires less heat to set off a large fire once a small one starts. Kindling is supported by findings that later episodes of depression are typically set off by less intense stressful events than earlier episodes (Kendler et al., 2000; Monroe, Slavich, Torres, & Gotlib, 2007). Interestingly, the kindling phenomenon seems to be weakest among those at high genetic risk for depression. When genetic risk is the greatest, the environment exerts less influence (Kendler et al., 2001).

Depression also appears linked to low levels of the neurotransmitter norepinephrine (Leonard, 1997; Robinson, 2007) and to problems in the brain's reward and stress-response systems (Depue & Iacono, 1989). Many depressed patients have decreased levels of dopamine, the neurotransmitter most closely tied to reward (Martinot et al., 2001). This finding may help to explain why depression is often associated with an inability to experience pleasure.

BIPOLAR DISORDER: WHEN MOOD GOES TO EXTREMES

Ann, the giddy bipolar patient we met at the beginning of the chapter, experienced many of the classic symptoms of a **manic episode.** These episodes are typically marked by dramatically elevated mood (feeling "on top of the world"), decreased need for sleep, greatly heightened energy, inflated self-esteem, increased talkativeness, and irresponsible behavior. People in a manic episode often display "pressured speech," as though they can't get their words out quickly enough, and are difficult to interrupt (Goodwin & Jamison, 1990). Their ideas often race through their heads quickly, which may account for the heightened rate of creative accomplishments in some bipolar individuals (see Chapter 9). These and other symptoms, which we can find in Table 15.8 on page 645, typically begin with a rapid increase over only a few days. People usually experience their first manic episode after their early twenties (Kessler et al., 2005).

Bipolar disorder, formerly called manic-depressive disorder, is diagnosed when there's a history of at least one manic episode (APA, 2000). In contrast to major depression, bipolar disorder is equally common in men and women. In the great majority of cases— upward of 90 percent (Alda, 1997)—people who've had one manic episode experience at least one more. Some have episodes separated by many years and then have a series of episodes, one rapidly following the other. More than half the time, a major depressive episode precedes or follows a manic episode (APA, 2000).

Manic episodes often produce serious problems in social and occupational functioning, such as substance abuse and unrestrained sexual behavior. Because their judgment is so impaired, people in the midst of manic episodes may go on wild spending sprees, sleep with many partners in a short period of time, or drive while intoxicated. One of your book's authors treated a manic patient who passed himself off to a financial company as his own father, gained access to his father's savings for retirement, and gambled away his entire family fortune. Another frittered away most of his life's savings by purchasing more than a hundred bowling balls, none of which he needed. The negative effects of a manic episode, including loss of employment, family conflicts, and divorce, can persist for many years (Coryell, Scheftner, Keller, Endicott, Maser, & Klerman, 1993).

Bipolar disorder is among the most genetically influenced of all mental disorders (Miklowitz & Johnson, 2006). Twin studies suggest that its heritability may be as high as 85 percent (Alda, 1997; McGuffin, Rijsdijk, Andrew, Sham, Katz, & Cardno, 2003). Scientists believe that genes that increase the sensitivity of the dopamine receptors (Willner, 1995) and decrease the sensitivity of serotonin receptors may boost the risk of bipolar disorder (Ogden et al., 2004).

Brain imaging studies suggest that people with bipolar disorder experience increased activity in structures related to emotion, including the amygdala (Chang, Adleman, Dienes, Simeonova, Menon, & Riess, 2004; Yergelun-Todd et al., 2000), and decreased activity in structures associated with planning, such as the prefrontal cortex (Kruger, Seminowicz, Goldapple, Kennedy, & Mayberg, 2003). Still, the cause–effect relationship between these

People in the midst of manic episodes frequently go on uncontrolled spending sprees and may "max out" multiple credit cards in the process.

manic episode
experience marked by dramatically elevated mood, decreased need for sleep, increased energy, inflated self-esteem, increased talkativeness, and irresponsible behavior

bipolar disorder
condition marked by a history of at least one manic episode

physiological findings and mood disorders isn't entirely clear. For example, the high levels of norepinephrine and differences in brain activity observed in people with bipolar disorder may be an effect rather than a cause of the disorder (Thase, Jindal, & Howland, 2002).

Most of us can skip a night's sleep and function reasonably well the next day (see Chapter 5). However, after just one night without sleep, about 10 percent of people who've experienced a manic episode display manic symptoms the next day (Barbini et al., 1998). Psychologists believe that sleep deprivation triggers manic symptoms by increasing the sensitivity of dopamine receptors (Ebert, Feistel, Barocks, Kaschka, & Pirner, 1994).

Our discussion might seem to imply that bipolar disorder is determined entirely by biological factors. Not so. Stressful life events are associated with an increased risk of manic episodes, more frequent relapse, and a longer recovery from manic episodes (Johnson & Miller, 1997). Interestingly, some manic episodes appear to be triggered by *positive* life events associated with achieving goals, such as job promotions (Johnson et al., 2000). Once again, we can see that psychological disorders arise from the complex intersection of biological, psychological, and sociocultural forces.

SUICIDE: FACTS AND FICTIONS

Major depression and bipolar disorder are associated with a higher risk of suicide than most other disorders (Miklowitz & Johnson, 2006; Wolfsdorf, Freeman, D'Erano, Overholser, & Spirito, 2003). Estimates suggest that the suicide rate of people with bipolar disorder is about fifteen times higher than that of the general population (Harris & Barraclough, 1997). Some anxiety disorders, like panic disorder and social phobia, and substance abuse are also associated with heightened suicide risk (Spirito & Esposito-Smythers, 2006). But suicide itself isn't a psychological disorder, and its deadly reach extends far beyond any one condition. In 2001, scientists ranked suicide as the eleventh leading cause of death in the United States (NIMH, 2004), and the third leading cause of death for children, adolescents, and young adults (Kochanek et al., 2004).

Typically, more than 30,000 people commit suicide in the United States each year, a number that surely underestimates the problem because relatives report many suicides as accidents. For each completed suicide, there are an estimated 8–25 attempts. Contrary to what many believe, most people are more of a threat to themselves than others. For every two people who are victims of homicide, three take their own lives (NIMH, 2004). In **Table 15.9,** we present a number of other common myths and misconceptions about suicide.

It's essential to try to predict suicide attempts because most people are acutely suicidal for only a brief window of time (Schneidman, Faberow, & Litman, 1970; Simon, 2006), and intervention during that time can be critical. Unfortunately, the prediction of suicide poses serious practical problems. First, we can't easily conduct longitudinal studies (see Chapter 10) to determine which people will attempt suicide. It would be unethical to allow people believed to be at high suicide risk to go through with attempts to allow us to pinpoint pre-

fictoid

Myth: Suicide rates increase around the Christmas holidays, largely because people without close family members feel especially lonely.
Reality: There's little support for this view; in fact, several studies suggest a slight decrease in suicide attempts and completions around Christmas (Ajdacic-Gross et al., 2003; Phillips & Wills, 1987).

Table 15.9 Common Myths and Misconceptions about Suicide.

Myth	Reality
Talking to depressed people about suicide makes them more likely to commit the act.	Talking to depressed persons about suicide often makes them more likely to obtain help.
Suicide is almost always completed with no warning.	Many or most individuals who commit suicide communicate their intent to others.
As a severe depression lifts, people's suicide risk decreases.	As a severe depression lifts, the risk of suicide may actually increase, in part because individuals possess more energy to attempt the act.
Most people who threaten suicide are seeking attention.	Although attention seeking motivates some suicidal behaviors, most suicidal acts stem from severe depression and hopelessness.
People who talk a lot about suicide almost never commit it.	Talking about suicide is associated with a considerably greater risk of suicide.

dictors of suicide. Second, it's difficult to study the psychological states associated with suicide because the period of high risk for a suicide attempt is often very brief. Third, the low prevalence of suicide makes predicting it difficult (Finn & Kamphuis, 1995; Meehl & Rosen, 1955). Most estimates put the rate of completed suicide at 12 or 13 out of 100,000 people in the general population. So if only about one-hundredth of 1 percent of the population completes a suicide, our best guess—with about 99.9 percent accuracy—is that no one will commit suicide. Nevertheless, the social costs of failing to predict a suicide are so great that efforts to accurately predict suicide attempts continue (see **Figure 15.4**).

The good news is that research has taught us a great deal about risk factors for suicide. The single best predictor of suicide is a previous attempt, because 30–40 percent of all people who kill themselves have made at least one prior attempt (Maris, 1992; Pellconen & Marttuneny, 2003). About three times as many men as women commit suicide, but nearly three times as many women try it (NIMH, 2004). Interestingly, hopelessness may be an even better predictor of suicide than depression (Beck, Brown, Berchick, Stewart, & Steer, 1990; Goldston et al., 2001), because people are most likely to try to kill themselves when they see no escape from their pain. Intense agitation is also a powerful predictor of suicide risk (Fawcett, 1997). People who wished they'd died after a suicide attempt are more than twice as likely to later commit suicide as those who are relieved they survived or who were ambivalent about the attempt (Henriques, Wenzel, Brown, & Beck, 2005). A list of risk factors for suicide appears in **Table 15.10**.

Table 15.10 Major Suicide Risk Factors.

(1) Depression
(2) Hopelessness
(3) Substance abuse
(4) Schizophrenia
(5) Homosexuality, probably because of social stigma
(6) Unemployment
(7) Chronic, painful, or disfiguring physical illness
(8) Recent loss of a loved one; being divorced, separated, or widowed
(9) Family history of suicide
(10) Personality disorders, such as borderline personality disorder (see later discussion)
(11) Anxiety disorders, such as panic disorder and social phobia
(12) Old age, especially in men
(13) Recent discharge from a hospital

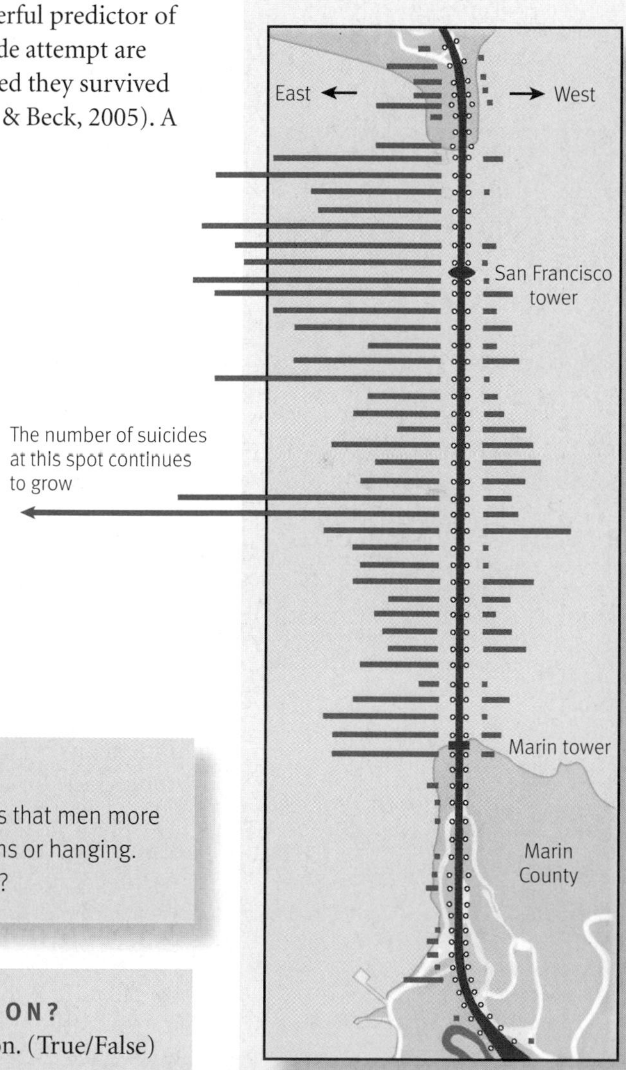

The number of suicides at this spot continues to grow

Figure 15.4 Suicides by Location. The famed Golden Gate Bridge in San Francisco has been the site of well over 1,200 suicides. (*Source:* SFGate.com)

APPLY YOUR THINKING
One reason for the substantial gender difference in completed suicides is that men more often use highly lethal methods of attempting suicides, such as firearms or hanging. What other explanations could account for this difference?

ASSESS YOUR KNOWLEDGE: FACT OR FICTION?
(1) Men and women are equally likely to suffer from major depression. (True/False)
(2) Depression is associated with stressful life events. (True/False)
(3) According to Lewinsohn, depression is caused by a low rate of response-contingent positive reinforcement. (True/False)
(4) According to Seligman, depression-prone people make specific and unstable attributions for negative life events. (True/False)
(5) Most people who have a manic episode never have another. (True/False)
(6) Depression is a better predictor of suicide than hopelessness. (True/False)

Answers: (1) F (p. 644); (2) T (p. 646); (3) T (p. 646); (4) F (pp. 647–648); (5) F (p. 649); (6) F (pp. 650–651)

Dissociative Disorders: The Divided Self

Most of us are accustomed to thinking of ourselves as one unified identity. When speaking about ourselves, we use the words *me* and *I* without giving it a second thought. That's not the case in most **dissociative disorders,** which involve disruptions in consciousness, memory, identity, or perception (APA, 2000). Nadean Cool, whom we met in Chapter 7, was diagnosed with dissociative identity disorder (DID), the best known of dissociative disorders. Before Nadean came to question her diagnosis, she was convinced that her body housed more than 130 distinct personalities. The idea that one person can have more than one identity, let alone more than a hundred, is an extraordinary claim. So it's no wonder that DID is one of the most controversial of all diagnoses. Before we consider the debate that swirls around this condition, we'll consider several other dissociative disorders.

DEPERSONALIZATION DISORDER

If you've ever felt detached from yourself, as though you're living in a movie or dream or observing your body from the perspective of an outsider, then you've experienced *depersonalization*. More than half of all adults have experienced one brief episode of depersonalization, and such experiences are especially common among adolescents and college students (APA, 2000; Simeon et al., 1997). Only if experiences of depersonalization are frequent do people qualify for a diagnosis of **depersonalization disorder.** *Derealization,* the sense that the external world is strange or unreal, often accompanies both depersonalization and panic attacks.

DISSOCIATIVE AMNESIA

In **dissociative amnesia,** people can't recall important personal information—most often following a stressful experience—that isn't due to normal forgetting. Their memory loss is extensive, and can include suicide attempts or violent outbursts (APA, 2000; Sar et al., 2007). More commonly, psychologists diagnose dissociative amnesia when adults report gaps in their memories for child abuse.

This diagnosis has proven controversial for several reasons. First, memory gaps regarding nontraumatic events are common in healthy individuals and aren't necessarily either stress-related or indicative of dissociation (Belli, Winkielman, Read, Schwarz, & Lynn, 1998). Second, most people may not be especially motivated to recall child abuse or other upsetting events. As Richard McNally (2003) pointed out, not thinking about something isn't the same as being *unable* to remember it, which is amnesia. Third, careful studies have turned up no convincing cases of amnesia that can't be explained by other factors, like disease, brain injury, normal forgetting, or an unwillingness to think about disturbing events (Kihlstrom, 2005; Pope, Poliakoff, Parker, Boynes, & Hudson, 2007).

DISSOCIATIVE FUGUE

At times, we've all felt like running away from our troubles. In **dissociative fugue,** people not only forget significant events in their lives, but flee their stressful circumstances (*fugue* is Latin for "flight"). In some cases, they move to another city or even another country, assuming a new identity. Fugues can last for hours or, in unusual cases, years. Dissociative fugue is rare, occurring in about 2 of every 1,000 people (APA, 2000), with more prolonged fugue states even rarer (Karlin & Orne, 1996).

In 2006, a 57-year-old husband, father, and Boy Scout leader from New York was found living under a new name in a homeless shelter in Chicago, after he left his garage near his office and disappeared. When a tip to *America's Most Wanted* uncovered his true identity 6 months later, his family contacted him, but he had no memory of who they were (Brody, 2007).

In this and other fugue cases, it's essential to find out whether the fugue resulted from a head injury, stroke, or other neurological cause. Moreover, some people merely claim

Jeffrey Ingram, age 40, experienced a dissociative fugue in which he claimed for over a month that he couldn't remember anything about his life. He was reunited with his fiancée in 2006 only after he appeared on television shows asking the public to identify him.

dissociative disorders
conditions involving disruptions in consciousness, memory, identity, or perception

depersonalization disorder
condition marked by multiple episodes of depersonalization

dissociative amnesia
inability to recall important personal information—most often related to a stressful experience—that can't be explained by ordinary forgetfulness

dissociative fugue
sudden, unexpected travel away from home or the workplace, accompanied by amnesia for significant life events

amnesia to avoid responsibilities or stressful circumstances, relocate to a different area, and get a fresh start in life. Even when fugues occur shortly after a traumatic event, it's difficult to know whether the trauma caused the amnesia. Scientists don't fully understand the role trauma, psychological factors, and neurological conditions play in fugue states (Kihlstrom, 2005).

Correlation vs. Causation

DISSOCIATIVE IDENTITY DISORDER: MULTIPLE PERSONALITIES: MULTIPLE CONTROVERSIES

According to DSM-IV (APA, 2000), **dissociative identity disorder (DID)** is characterized by the presence of two or more distinct identities or personality states, which are more temporary patterns of behavior (see Chapter 7). The identities or personality states recurrently assume control over the person's behavior. These alternate identities or "alters," as they're called, are often very different from the primary or "host" personality and may be of different names, ages, genders, and even races. In some cases, these features are the opposite of those exhibited by the host personality. For example, if the host personality is shy and retiring, one or more alters may be outgoing or flamboyant. Psychologists have reported the number of alters to range from one (the so-called split personality) to hundreds or even thousands, with one reported case of 4,500 personalities (Acocella, 1999). In general, women are more likely to receive a DID diagnosis and report more alters than men (APA, 2000).

"I HAVE 25 PATIENTS IN MY COUNSELING GROUP--MRS. SHERMAN, MR. MARTIN, AND MR. MARTIN'S 23 OTHER PERSONALITIES."

(*Source:* Dan Rosandich, www.CartoonStock.com)

Researchers have identified intriguing differences among alters in their respiration rates (Bahnson & Smith, 1975), brain wave activity (EEG; Ludwig, Brandsma, Wilbur, Bendefeldt, & Jamson, 1972), eyeglass prescriptions (Miller, 1989), handedness (Savitz, Solms, Pietersen, Ramesar, & Flor-Henry, 2004), skin conductance responses (Brende, 1984), voice patterns, and handwriting (Lilienfeld & Lynn, 2003). Fascinating as these findings are, they don't provide conclusive evidence for the existence of different alters. These differences could arise from changes in mood or thoughts over time or to bodily changes, such as muscle tension, that people can produce on a voluntary basis (Allen & Movius, 2000; Merkelbach, Devilly, & Rassin, 2002). Moreover, scientists have falsified claims that alters are truly distinct. When psychologists have used objective measures of memory, they've typically found that information presented to one alter is available to the other, providing no evidence for amnesia across alters (Allen & Moravius, 2000; Huntjens, Peters, Woertman, Bovenschen, Martin, & Postma, 2006).

Ruling Out Rival Hypotheses

Falsifiability

Controversies and Explanations. The primary controversy surrounding DID revolves around one question: Is DID a response to early trauma, or is it a consequence of social and cultural factors (Merskey, 1992)? According to the *posttraumatic model* (Gleaves, 1996; Gleaves, May, & Cardena, 2001; Ross, 1997), DID arises from a history of severe abuse—physical, sexual, or both—during childhood. This abuse leads individuals to "compartmentalize" their identity into alters as a means of coping with intense emotional pain. In this way, the person can feel as though the abuse happened to someone else.

Advocates of the posttraumatic model claim that 90 percent or more of individuals with DID were severely abused in childhood (Gleaves, 1996). Nevertheless, many of the studies that reported this association didn't check the accuracy of abuse claims against objective information, such as court records of abuse (Coons, Bowman, & Milstein, 1988). Moreover, researchers haven't shown that early abuse is specific to DID, as it's present in many other disorders (Pope & Hudson, 1992). These considerations don't exclude a role for early trauma in DID, but they suggest that researchers must conduct further controlled studies before drawing strong conclusions (Gleaves, 1996; Gleaves et al., 2001).

dissociative identity disorder (DID)
condition characterized by the presence of two or more distinct identities or personality states that recurrently take control of the person's behavior

According to advocates of the competing *sociocognitive model* (see Chapter 5), the claim that some people have hundreds of personalities is extraordinary, and the evidence for it is unconvincing (Lilienfeld, Lynn, et al., 1999; Lynn & Pintar, 1997; McHugh, 1993; Merskey, 1992; Spanos, 1994, 1996). According to this model, people's expectancies and beliefs—shaped by certain psychotherapeutic procedures and cultural influences, rather

Extraordinary Claims

A number of celebrities, including comedian Roseanne Barr, have claimed that they suffer from DID (dissociative identity disorder).

Contrary to popular belief, the symptoms of schizophrenia are not produced by a "split mind" or personality.

British artist Louis Wain (1860–1939), famous for his paintings of cats, developed a severe psychiatric disorder—perhaps schizophrenia—relatively late in life. Some of his paintings, like the two above, seem to capture the profound psychological confusion and fragmentation typical of schizophrenia (although despite widespread claims, there's no good evidence that his paintings became more disturbed as he became increasingly ill).

schizophrenia
severe disorder of thought and emotion associated with a loss of contact with reality

than early traumas—account for the origin and maintenance of DID. Advocates of this model claim that some therapists, like Nadean Cool's, use procedures, like hypnosis and repeated prompting of alters, that suggest to patients that their puzzling symptoms are the products of indwelling identities (Lilienfeld & Lynn, 2003; Lilienfeld et al., 1999). The following observations and findings support this hypothesis:

- Many or most DID patients show few or no clear-cut signs of this condition, such as alters, prior to psychotherapy (Kluft, 1984).
- Mainstream treatment techniques for DID reinforce the idea that the person possesses multiple identities. These techniques include using hypnosis to "bring forth" hidden alters, communicating with alters and giving them different names, and encouraging patients to recover repressed memories supposedly housed in dissociated selves (Spanos, 1994, 1996).
- The number of alters per DID individual tends to increase substantially when therapists use these techniques (Piper, 1997).

As of 1970, there were 79 documented cases of DID in the world literature. As of 1986, the number of DID cases had mushroomed to approximately 6,000 (Lilienfeld et al., 1999), and some estimates in the early twenty-first century are in the hundreds of thousands. The sociocognitive model holds that the popular media have played a pivotal role in the DID epidemic (Elzinga et al., 1998). Indeed, much of the dramatic increase in DID's prevalence followed closely on the release of the best-selling book *Sybil* (Schreiber, 1974) in the mid-1970s, later made into an Emmy Award–winning television movie starring Sally Fields. The book and film told the heartbreaking story of a young woman with sixteen personalities who reported a history of sadistic child abuse. Interestingly, subsequently released audiotapes of Sybil's therapy sessions suggested that she had no alters or memories of child abuse prior to treatment and that her therapist urged her to behave differently on different occasions (Rieber, 1999).

Over the past two decades, media coverage of DID has skyrocketed (Showalter, 1997; Spanos, 1996; Wilson, 2003), with some celebrities, like Roseanne Barr, claiming to suffer from the disorder. DID is now diagnosed with considerable frequency in some countries (such as Holland) in which it's recently received more publicity. In summary, there's considerable support for the sociocognitive model and the claim that therapists, along with the media, are creating alters rather than discovering them. The dissociative disorders provide a powerful, although troubling, example of how social and cultural forces can shape psychological disorders.

ASSESS YOUR KNOWLEDGE: FACT OR FICTION?

(1) Few normal adults ever experience depersonalization. (True/False)
(2) Gaps in memory are common occurrences in healthly people. (True/False)
(3) Child abuse clearly causes DID. (True/False)
(4) Most DID patients show few signs of the disorder before they begin therapy. (True/False)
(5) The media have played little role in the recent increase in DID diagnoses. (True/False)

Answers: (1) F (p. 652); (2) T (p. 652); (3) F (p. 653); (4) T (p. 653); (5) F (p. 654)

The Enigma of Schizophrenia

Psychiatrist Daniel Weinberger has called **schizophrenia** the "cancer" of mental illness: It's perhaps the most severe of all disorders, and the most mysterious (Levy-Reiner, 1996). As we'll discover, it's a devastating disorder of thought and emotion associated with a loss of contact with reality (APA, 2000).

SYMPTOMS OF SCHIZOPHRENIA: THE SHATTERED MIND

Even today, many people confuse schizophrenia with DID (Wahl, 1997). Swiss psychiatrist Eugen Bleuler gave us the modern term *schizophrenia* in 1911. The term literally means "split mind," which no doubt contributed to the popular myth that the symptoms of schizophrenia stem from a split personality. You may have even heard people refer to a "schizophrenic attitude" when explaining that they're "of two minds" regarding an issue. Don't be misled. As Bleuler recognized, the difficulties of individuals with schizophrenia arise from disturbances in thinking, language, emotion, and relationships with others. In contrast to DID, which is supposedly characterized by multiple intact personalities, schizophrenia is characterized by one personality that's shattered.

Schizophrenia causes most of its sufferers' levels of functioning to plunge. More than half suffer from serious disabilities, such as the inability to hold a job and maintain close relationships (Harvey, Reichenberg, & Bowie, 2006). Indeed, a large proportion of homeless people would receive diagnoses of schizophrenia (Cornblatt, Gree, & Walker, 1999). Individuals who experience schizophrenia comprise less than 1 percent of the population, with estimates ranging from .4–.7 percent (Saha, Chant, Welham, & McGrath, 2005). Yet they make up half of the approximately 100,000 patients in state and county mental institutions in the United States (Grob, 1997). But there's some good news. Today, more than ever, people who suffer from schizophrenia can function in society, even though they may need to return periodically to hospitals for treatment (Harding, Zubin, & Strauss, 1992; Lamb & Bachrach, 2001; Mueser & McGurk, 2004).

Researchers have struggled with the problem of describing schizophrenia since the eighteenth century, when Emil Kraepelin first described patients with *dementia praecox,* meaning psychological deterioration in youth. But Kraepelin didn't get it quite right. Even though the typical onset of schizophrenia is in the mid-twenties for men and the late twenties for women, schizophrenia can also strike after age 45 (APA, 2000). Moreover, as many as one-half to two-thirds of people with schizophrenia improve significantly, although not completely, and a small percentage recover completely after a single episode (Robinson, Woerner, McMeniman, Mendelowitz, & Bilder, 2004).

Delusions: Fixed False Beliefs. Among the hallmark symptoms of schizophrenia are **delusions**—strongly held fixed beliefs that have no basis in reality. Delusions are called **psychotic symptoms** because they represent a serious distortion of reality. Terrell, whom we met at the beginning of the chapter, experienced delusions that led to a suicide attempt.

Delusions commonly involve themes of persecution. One of your book's authors treated a man who believed that coworkers tapped his phone and conspired to get him fired. Another was convinced that a helicopter in the distance beamed the Beatles song "All You Need Is Love" into his head to make him feel jealous and inadequate. The authors of your book have also treated patients who reported delusions of grandeur (greatness), including one who believed that she'd discovered the cure for cancer even though she had no medical training. Other delusions center on the body and may include a firm belief that one is infested with brain parasites or even that one is dead (so-called Cotard's syndrome). Still others involve elaborate themes of sexuality or romance. John Hinckley, the man who nearly assassinated then President Ronald Reagan in 1981, was convinced that murdering the president would gain him the affection of actress Jodie Foster.

NEW FRONTIERS

Electrical Brain Stimulation and the "Shadow Man"

Imagine how eerie it would feel to sense that someone is standing behind you when no one's present. Some individuals who develop schizophrenia perceive these sorts of things, but researchers recently created this illusion in a woman with no history of the disorder by electrically stimulating certain areas of her brain as part of an evaluation prior to brain surgery (Arzy, Seeck, Ortigue, Spinelli, & Blanke, 2006). The scientists produced an illusion of the presence of another person in a 22-year-old patient with epilepsy when they stimulated an area of her left hemisphere where the

(continued)

First Person Account: Schizophrenia

The reflection in the store window—it's me, isn't it? I know it is, but it's hard to tell. Glassy shadows, polished pastels, a jigsaw puzzle of my body, face, and clothes, with pieces disappearing whenever I move. . . . Schizophrenia is painful, and it is craziness when I hear voices, when I believe people are following me, wanting to snatch my very soul. I am frightened too when every whisper, every laugh is about me; when newspapers suddenly contain cures, four-letter words shouting at me; when sparkles of light are demon eyes.
(McGrath, 1984)

factoid

One of the more unusual delusions conditions is *folie a deux* (French for the "folly of two"), known more technically as "shared psychotic disorder" in DSM-IV. In *folie a deux,* one person in a close relationship, often a marriage, induces the same delusion in his or her partner. For example, both partners may end up convinced that the government is poisoning their food (Silveira & Seeman, 1995). Rare cases of *folie a deux* in identical twins, *folie a trois* (involving three people) and *folie a famille* (involving an entire family) have also been reported.

delusions
strongly held, fixed beliefs that have no basis in reality

psychotic symptoms
psychological problems reflecting serious distortions in reality

A subject in one of Michael Persinger's studies of the effects of magnetic fields on the subjective experience of a spiritual "presence."

Replicability

temporal and parietal areas of the brain join. When her brain was stimulated as she was lying down, she described the "person" as a "shadow" who didn't speak or move. Curiously, the shadow person was positioned under her back, almost touching her body, mirroring her exact posture. When the researchers next stimulated her, as she sat with her arms wrapped around her knees, she reported that the "man" clasped her in his arms. The next brain stimulation occurred as she used a card in her right hand to perform a language-naming task. This time, she felt the shadow man located behind her on her right, and she reported, "He wants to take the card. . . . he doesn't want me to read" (p. 287). Interestingly, like certain deluded patients with schizophrenia, the woman didn't understand that the person was actually an illusion of her own body (Arzy et al., 2006).

The brain area where the patient was stimulated is related to perception of the self, distinguishing self from others, and combining information about the body from diverse senses. The researchers suggested that the brain stimulation disrupted her ability to integrate sensory information, and produced symptoms much like those experienced by many individuals with schizophrenia.

Years earlier, Michael Persinger (1993, 2002) stimulated nonpatients' temporal lobes with a weak magnetic field and produced reports of a spiritual "presence" in the room. Persinger stimulated not only the brain waves of his participants, but also considerable controversy. Researchers challenged his findings, claiming that participants' suggestibility predicted the sensed presence better than did stimulating the brain with a weak magnetic field. Moreover, researchers couldn't replicate Persinger's findings when they imposed tighter experimental controls for suggestibility effects (Granqvist et al., 2005).

Before they draw firm conclusions about the shadow man, researchers will need to conduct well-controlled studies with nonpatients. Still, brain stimulation research opens new doors to understanding unusual experiences in high-functioning people, as well as individuals with serious psychological disorders.

Hallucinations: False Perceptions. Among the other serious symptoms of schizophrenia are **hallucinations:** sensory perceptions that occur in the absence of an external stimulus. They can be auditory (involving hearing), olfactory (involving smell), gustatory (involving taste), tactile (involving the sense of feeling), or visual. Most hallucinations in schizophrenia are auditory, usually consisting of voices. In some patients, hallucinated voices express disapproval or carry on a running commentary about the person's thoughts or actions. *Command hallucinations,* which tell patients what to do ("Go over to that man and tell him to shut up!") may be associated with a heightened risk of violence toward others (McNiel, Eisner, & Binder, 2000). Incidentally, visual hallucinations in the absence of auditory hallucinations are usually signs of an organic (medical) disorder or substance abuse rather than schizophrenia (Shea, 1998).

Do your thoughts sound like voices in your head? Many people experience their thoughts as inner speech, which is entirely normal. Some researchers suggest that auditory hallucinations occur when people with schizophrenia believe mistakenly that their inner speech arises from a source outside themselves (Bentall, 2000; Frith, 1992; Thomas, 1997). Brain scans reveal that when people experience auditory hallucinations, brain areas associated with speech perception and production become activated (McGuire, Shah, & Murray, 1993).

Disorganized Speech. Consider a 39-year-old schizophrenic patient's reply to the question of whether he felt that people imitated him. "Yes . . . I don't quite gather. I know one right and one left use both hands but I can't follow the system that's working. The idea is meant in a kind way, but it's not the way I understand life. It seems to be people taking sides. If certain people agree with me they speak, and if not, they don't. Everybody seems to be the doctor and Mr. H. [his own name] in turn" (Mayer-Gross, Slater, & Roth, 1969, p. 177).

hallucinations
sensory perceptions that occur in the absence of an external stimulus

We can see that his language skips from topic to topic in a disjointed way. Most researchers believe that this peculiar language results from thought disorder (McGrath, 1991; Meehl, 1962). The usual associations that we forge between two words, such as mother–child, are considerably weakened or highly unusual for schizophrenic individuals (for example, mother–rug). In severe forms, the resulting speech is so jumbled that it's almost impossible to understand, leading psychologists to describe it as *word salad*.

Grossly Disorganized Behavior or Catatonia. When people develop schizophrenia, self-care, personal hygiene, and motivation often deteriorate. These individuals may avoid conversation; laugh, cry, or swear inappropriately; or wear a warm coat on a sweltering summer day.

Catatonic symptoms involve motor (movement) problems, such as extreme resistance to complying with even simple suggestions, holding the body in bizarre or rigid postures, or curling up in a fetal position. Catatonic individuals' withdrawal can be so severe that they refuse to speak and move, or they may pace aimlessly. They may also repeat a phrase in conversation in a parrotlike manner, a symptom called *echolalia*. At the opposite extreme, they may occasionally engage in bouts of frenzied, purposeless motor activity (see **Table 15.11**).

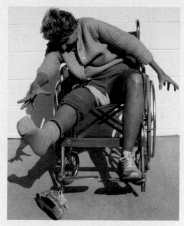

Catatonic individuals, like the one shown here, may permit their limbs to be moved to any position, and maintain this posture for lengthy periods of time, a condition called *waxy flexibility*.

Table 15.11 Main Subtypes of Schizophrenia.

Paranoid Type	Characterized primarily by prominent delusions or auditory hallucinations. Most commonly, the delusions are persecutory or grandiose, but often the two types of delusions are combined, and organized around a consistent theme. Apart from specific delusions, the person's ability to think, reason, and express feelings may not be impaired. Accordingly, paranoid schizophrenics function at a higher level than individuals with other types of schizophrenia.
Disorganized Type	Characterized by disorganized speech and behavior, as well as flat or inappropriate affect, such as unpredictable giggling. Delusions and hallucinations, if present, are not well organized into a single theme and often are short-lived.
Catatonic Type	Characterized by one or more catatonic symptoms. Catatonic patients can harm themselves or others when they are in a stupor and are immobile or when they are extremely excited and agitated. Malnutrition, exhaustion, and self-inflicted injuries are possible.

(*Source:* Data, *DSM-IV*, APA, 2000)

EXPLANATIONS FOR SCHIZOPHRENIA: THE ROOTS OF A SHATTERED MIND

Today, virtually all scientists believe that psychosocial factors play some role in schizophrenia. Nevertheless, they also agree that these factors probably trigger the disorder only in people with a genetic vulnerability.

The Family and Expressed Emotion. Early theories of schizophrenia mistakenly laid the blame for the condition on mothers, with so-called *schizophrenogenic* (schizophrenia-producing) mothers being the culprits. Based on informal observations of families of a schizophrenic child, some authors described such mothers as overprotective, smothering, insensitive, rejecting, and controlling (Arieti, 1959; Lidz, 1973). Other theorists pointed the finger of blame at the interactions among all family members (Dolnick, 1998).

But as important as clinical experience can be in generating hypotheses, it doesn't provide an adequate arena for testing them (see Chapter 2). Indeed, these early studies were severely flawed, largely because they lacked control groups of people without schizophrenia. A now widely accepted rival hypothesis is that family members' responses aren't the cause of schizophrenia, but instead are typically a response to the stressful experience of living with a severely disturbed person.

fictoid

Myth: Many non-Western cultures regard people with schizophrenia and other severe mental illnesses as "shamans," or medicine men, and often worship them as possessing divine powers.
Reality: Jane Murphy's (1976) work suggests that the Yorubas of Nigeria and other cultures distinguish mentally ill people from shamans. The Yorubas, for example, referred to a mentally ill man living on an abandoned anthill as "out of mind and crazy." In contrast, they referred to a shaman during a healing session as "out of mind but not crazy," meaning that he was in a temporary trance state.

catatonic symptoms
motor problems, including extreme resistance to complying with simple suggestions, holding the body in bizarre or rigid postures, or curling up in a fetal position

Ruling Out Rival Hypotheses

It's widely acknowledged that parents and family members don't "cause" schizophrenia (Gottesman, 1991; Walker, Kestler, Bollini, & Hochman, 2004). Still, families may play a role in determining whether schizophrenia patients relapse. After leaving hospitals, patients experience more than twice the likelihood of relapse (50% to 60%) when their relatives display high *expressed emotion* (EE)—that is, criticism, hostility, and overinvolvement (Brown, Monck, Carstairs, & Wing, 1962; Butzlaff & Hooley, 1998). Criticism is especially predictive of relapse (Halweg et al., 1989; McCarty, Lau, Valeri, & Weisz, 2004), and may result in part from relatives' frustrations in living with a person with schizophrenia who displays disruptive behaviors. Indeed, EE may reflect family members' reactions to their loved one's schizophrenia as much as contribute to their loved one's relapse (King, 2000).

The apparent effects of EE vary across ethnic groups. Critical comments from family members may undermine recovering patients' confidence and sense of independence, which are valued in Caucasian American culture (Chentsova-Dutton & Tsai, 2007). In contrast, in Mexican American culture, independence isn't as highly valued, so criticism doesn't predict relapse. Nevertheless, a lack of family warmth, which is prized in Mexican American families, does predict relapse (Lopez et al., 2004). Moreover, in African American families, high levels of EE actually predict *better* outcomes among individuals with schizophrenia, perhaps because family members perceive EE as an expression of openness, honesty, and caring (Rosenfarb, Bellack, & Aziz, 2006). Although EE often predicts relapse, well-controlled studies don't support the hypothesis that child rearing directly *causes* schizophrenia, any more than does extreme poverty, childhood trauma, or parental conflict, all of which are correlated with schizophrenia (Cornblatt, Green, & Walker, 1999; Schofield & Balian, 1959).

Schizophrenia: Brain, Biochemical, and Genetic Findings. Research using a variety of technologies has uncovered intriguing biological clues to the causes of schizophrenia. We'll focus on three such clues: brain abnormalities, neurotransmitter differences, and genetic findings.

Brain Abnormalities. Research indicates that one or more of four fluid-filled structures called *ventricles* (see Chapter 3), which cushion and nourish the brain, are typically enlarged in individuals with schizophrenia. This finding is important for two reasons. First, these brain areas frequently expand when others shrink (Barta, Pearlson, Powers, Richard, & Tune, 1990; Raz & Raz, 1990). Second, deterioration in these areas is associated with thought disorder (Vita et al., 1995).

Other brain abnormalities in schizophrenia include increases in the size of the *sulci,* or spaces between the ridges of the brain (Cannon, Mednick, & Parnas, 1989), and decreases in activation of the amygdala and hippocampus (Hempel, Hempel, Schoenknecht, Stippich, & Schroeder, 2003) and in the symmetry of the brain's hemispheres (Luchins, Weinberger, & Wyatt, 1982; Zivotofsky, Edelman, Green, Fostick, & Strous, 2007). Functional brain imaging studies show that the frontal lobes of people with schizophrenia are less active than those of nonpatients when engaged in demanding mental tasks (Andreasen et al., 1992; Carter et al., 1998), a phenomenon called *hypofrontality* (see Prologue). Still, it's not clear whether these findings are causes or consequences of the disorder. For example, hypofrontality could be due to the tendency of patients with schizophrenia to concentrate less on tasks compared with other individuals. Researchers also need to rule out alternative explanations for brain underactivity that could arise from patients' diet, drinking and smoking habits, and medication use (Hanson & Gottesman, 2005).

Neurotransmitter Differences. The biochemistry of the brain is one of the keys to unlocking the mystery of schizophrenia. One early explanation was the *dopamine hypothesis* (Carlsson, 1995; Keith, Gunderson, Reifman, Buchsbaum, & Mosher, 1976; Nicol & Gottesman, 1983). The evidence for the role of dopamine in schizophrenia is mostly indirect. First, most antischizophrenic drugs block dopamine receptor sites. To put it crudely, they "slow down" nerve impulses by partially blocking the action of dopamine (see Chap-

Correlation vs. Causation

Correlation vs. Causation

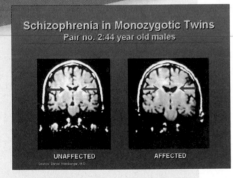

Schizophrenia in Monozygotic Twins
Pair no. 2:44 year old males

UNAFFECTED   AFFECTED

In one identical twin with schizophrenia, the fluid-filled ventricles of the brain (*see red arrows*) are enlarged relative to his or her co-twin without schizophrenia. Such enlargement is typical in schizophrenia and probably reflects a deterioration in brain tissue surrounding the ventricles, which expand to fill the missing space. (Note that "monozygotic" twins are identical and "dizygotic" twins are fraternal.)

Correlation vs. Causation

Ruling Out Rival Hypotheses

ter 16). Second, amphetamine, a stimulant drug (see Chapter 5) that blocks the reuptake of dopamine, tends to make the symptoms of schizophrenia worse (Lieberman & Koreen, 1993; Snyder, 1975).

Nevertheless, the hypothesis that a simple excess of dopamine creates the symptoms of schizophrenia doesn't seem to fit the data. A better-supported rival hypothesis is that abnormalities in dopamine *receptors* produce these symptoms. Receptor sites in the brain appear to be highly specific for dopamine transmission. These sites respond uniquely to drugs designed to reduce psychotic symptoms and are associated with difficulties in attention, memory, and motivation (Busatto, 1995; Keefe & Henry, 1994; Reis, Masson, deOliveira, & Brandano, 2004).

Ruling Out Rival Hypotheses

These findings provide evidence for a direct tie between dopamine pathways and symptoms of schizophrenia, such as paranoia. As we've seen, some of the symptoms of schizophrenia represent distortions or excesses of normal functions and include hallucinations, delusions, and disorganized speech and behavior. We can contrast these so-called *positive symptoms* with *negative symptoms,* which reflect a decrease or loss of normal functions. These symptoms include social withdrawal and diminished motivations, decreased expression of emotions, and brief and limited speech (Andreason, Arndt, Alliger, Miller, & Flaum, 1995). People with schizophrenia are less impaired when their symptoms are predominantly positive rather than negative (Harvey, Reichenberg, & Bowie, 2006). There's evidence that positive symptoms result from dopamine excess in some brain regions and negative symptoms from dopamine deficits in other brain regions (Davis, Kahn, Ko, & Davidson, 1991). However, the cause of negative symptoms can be difficult to pinpoint, because they may arise from prolonged institutionalization and medication side effects (see Chapter 16). Dopamine is probably only one of several neurotransmitters that play a role in schizophrenia; other likely candidates include norepinephrine, glutamate, and serotonin (Cornblatt et al., 1999; Grace, 1991).

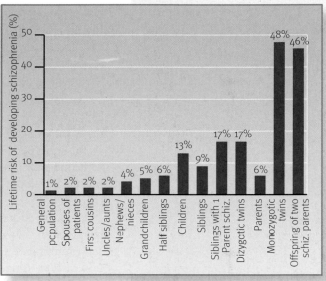

Figure 15.5 Schizophrenia Risk and the Family. The lifetime risk of developing schizophrenia is largely a function of how closely an individual is genetically related to a person with schizophrenia. (*Source:* Feldman, 1991)

Genetic Influences. Still unresolved is the question of which biological deficits are present prior to schizophrenia and which appear after the disorder begins (Seidman et al., 2003). The seeds of schizophrenia are often sown well before birth and lie partly in individuals' genetic endowment. As we can see in **Figure 15.5,** being the offspring of someone diagnosed with schizophrenia greatly increases one's odds of developing the disorder. If we have a sibling with schizophrenia, we have about a one in ten chance of developing the disorder; these odds are about ten times higher than those of the average person. As genetic similarity increases, so does the risk of schizophrenia.

Still, it's possible the environment accounts for these findings because siblings not only share genes but also grow up in the same family. To eliminate this ambiguity, researchers have conducted twin studies (see Chapter 3). These studies provide convincing support for a genetic influence on schizophrenia. If we have an identical twin with schizophrenia, our risk rises to about 50 percent. An identical twin of a person with schizophrenia is about three times as likely as a fraternal twin of a person with schizophrenia to develop the disorder, and about fifty times as likely as an average person (Gottesman & Shields, 1972; Kendler & Diehl, 1993; Meehl, 1962). Adoption data also point to a genetic influence. Even when children who have a biological parent with schizophrenia are adopted by parents with no hint of the disorder, their risk of schizophrenia is greater than that of a person with no biological relative with schizophrenia (Gottesman, 1991).

Ruling Out Rival Hypotheses

Vulnerability to Schizophrenia: Diathesis-Stress Models. **Diathesis-stress models** incorporate much of what we know about schizophrenia. Such models propose that schizophrenia, along with many other mental disorders, is a joint product of a genetic vulnerability, called a *diathesis,* and stressors that trigger this vulnerability (Meehl, 1962; Walker & DiForio, 1997; Zubin & Spring, 1977).

diathesis-stress models
perspective proposing that mental disorders are a joint product of a genetic vulnerability, called a diathesis, and stressors that trigger this vulnerability

Many people with schizotypal personality disorder are prone to "magical thinking"—the belief that their thoughts can influence actions through supernatural or otherwise mysterious processes. For example, they may believe that stepping on a crack in the sidewalk will create misfortune.

Paul Meehl (1990) suggested that approximately 10 percent of the population has a genetic predisposition to schizophrenia. What are people with this predisposition like? During adolescence and adulthood, they may strike us as "odd ducks." They may seem socially uncomfortable, and their speech, thought processes, and perceptions may impress us as unusual. They're likely to endorse items on psychological tests such as "Occasionally, I have felt as though my body did not exist" (Chapman, Chapman, & Raulin, 1978). Such individuals display symptoms of psychosis-proneness or *schizotypal personality disorder* (see **Table 15.12** on page 661). Most people with schizotypal personality disorder don't develop full-blown schizophrenia, perhaps because they have a weaker genetic vulnerability or because they've experienced fewer stressors.

Well before people experience symptoms of schizophrenia, we can identify "early warning signs" or markers of vulnerability to this condition. People with schizotypal personality disorder display some of these markers, which include social withdrawal, thought, and movement abnormalities (Mittal et al., 2007; Walker, Baum, & DiForio, 1998), learning and memory deficits (Volgmaier et al., 2000), temporal lobe abnormalities (Siever & Davis, 2004), impaired attention (Keefe et al., 1997), and eye movement disturbances when tracking moving objects (Iacono, 1985; Lenzenweger, McLachlan, & Rubin, 2007). Their difficulties extend to the social realm and begin early in life. Elaine Walker and Richard Lewine (1990) found that people who viewed home movies of siblings interacting could identify which children later developed schizophrenia at better than chance levels. Even at an early age, vulnerable children's lack of emotions and decreased eye contact and social responsiveness tipped off observers. This design is valuable because it gets around the retrospective bias (see Chapter 7) introduced by asking adults to report on their childhood experiences.

But most people with a vulnerability to schizophrenia don't develop it. Whether someone ends up with the disorder depends on the impact of events that interfere with normal development. Children of women who had the flu during their second trimester of pregnancy (Brown et al., 2004; Mednick, Machon, Huttunen, & Bonett, 1988), suffered starvation early in pregnancy (Susser & Lyn, 1992), or experienced complications during birth (Weinberger, 1987) are at a somewhat heightened risk of schizophrenia. Viral infections in the uterus may also play a key role in triggering certain cases of schizophrenia (Walker & DiForio, 1997). But the great majority of people exposed to infection or trauma before birth never show signs of schizophrenia. So these events probably create problems only for people who are genetically vulnerable to begin with (Cornblatt et al., 1999; Verdoux, 2004).

ASSESS YOUR KNOWLEDGE: FACT OR FICTION?

(1) Delusions are rare in schizophrenia. (True/False)
(2) Most hallucinations in schizophrenia are visual. (True/False)
(3) Schizophrenogenic mothers often cause schizophrenia. (True/False)
(4) The evidence for the dopamine hypothesis is mostly indirect. (True/False)
(5) There's little support for the genetic transmission of schizophrenia. (True/False)

Answers: (1) F (p. 655); (2) F (p. 656); (3) F (p. 657); (4) T (p. 658); (5) F (p. 658)

Personality Disorders and Substance Abuse

---

personality disorder
condition in which personality traits, appearing first in adolescence, are inflexible, stable, expressed in a wide variety of situations, and lead to distress or impairment

Distinguishing normal variations in personality from personality disorders isn't easy, largely because we all have our personality quirks. This fact of life may help to explain why of all psychiatric conditions, personality disorders are historically the least reliably diagnosed (Fowler, Lilienfeld, & O'Donohue, 2007; Perry, 1984; Zimmerman, 1994). DSM-IV states that we should diagnose a **personality disorder** only when personality traits first appear by adolescence; are inflexible, stable, and expressed in a wide variety of situations;

and lead to distress or impairment (APA, 2000, p. 685). But more than most patterns of behavior we've described, whether we perceive someone with a personality disorder as abnormal depends heavily on the context in which their behavior occurs (Price & Bouffard, 1974). The suspiciousness of a person with a paranoid personality disorder may be a liability in a cooperative work group, but an asset in a private investigator.

In Table 15.12 we list the major personality disorders in DSM-IV. DSM-IV groups these disorders into three clusters—odd or eccentric; dramatic, erratic, or emotional; and anxious or fearful. Nevertheless, this framework is based more on these disorders' superficial similarities than on research.

Many personality disorders predispose people to substance abuse, although not all people with personality disorders misuse drugs and alcohol (Serman, Johnson, Geller, Kanost, & Zacharapoulou, 2002). We'll first consider two major and extensively researched personality disorders—borderline personality disorder and psychopathic personality—and then examine the widespread problems of drug and alcohol abuse and dependence that are often associated with personality disorders.

Table 15.12 The DSM-IV Classification of Major Personality Disorders.

Odd, Eccentric Cluster

Paranoid personality disorder	Distrust, suspiciousness, oversensitivity
Schizotypal personality disorder	Intense discomfort in social situations; odd thinking, perception, communication, behaviors
Schizoid personality disorder	Detachment from social relationships, bland or limited expression of emotion

Dramatic, Emotional, Erratic Cluster

Histrionic personality disorder	Attention seeking, overemotional, dramatic, shallow, seductive, suggestible
Narcissistic personality disorder	Grandiose sense of self-importance or uniqueness, need for constant attention and admiration, lacks empathy, preoccupation with fantasies of unlimited success or power
Antisocial personality disorder	Antisocial behavior, violates or disregards rights of others, lying, stealing, irresponsibility, lack of remorse
Borderline personality disorder	Instability in various areas of life, tense and unstable relationships, recurrent suicide attempts, efforts to avoid being abandoned, unstable self-image/identity disturbance

Anxious, Fearful Cluster

Avoidant personality disorder	Unwilling to enter into relationships unless guarantee of uncritical acceptance; social withdrawal; fear of social criticism or rejection; reluctant to take risks or try new things that may bring about embarrassment
Dependent personality disorder	Difficulty making everyday decisions; excessive reliance on and need for reassurance, support, nurturance from others; feels helpless when alone
Obsessive-compulsive personality disorder	Preoccupied with order, organization, rules, small details; perfectionistic; rigid and stubborn; overinvolved in work; inflexible

(*Source*: From *Diagnostic and Statistical Manual of Mental Disorders*, 4th ed., American Psychiatric Association, 2000)

BORDERLINE PERSONALITY DISORDER: STABLE INSTABILITY

About 2 percent of adults, most of them women (Swartz, Blazer, George, & Winfield, 1990), develop **borderline personality disorder,** a condition marked by instability in mood, identity, and impulse control. Individuals with borderline personality tend to be extremely impulsive and unpredictable, although many are married and hold down good jobs. Their relationships frequently alternate from extremes of worshipping partners one

At least in mild doses, features of some personality disorders may be adaptive in certain occupations. For example, the traits of obsessive-compulsive personality disorder, which include attention to detail and perfectionism, may come in handy for accountants.

borderline personality disorder
condition marked by extreme instability in mood, identity, and impulse control

day to hating them the next. Some have aptly described this disorder as a pattern of "stable instability" (Grinker & Werble, 1977). The name *borderline personality* stems from the now outmoded belief that this condition lies on the border between psychotic and "neurotic"—relatively normal, yet mildly disabled—functioning (Stern, 1938).

Borderline Personality: A Volatile Blend of Traits. Borderline persons' impulsivity and rapidly fluctuating emotions often have a self-destructive quality: Many engage in drug abuse, sexual promiscuity, overeating, and even self-mutilation, like cutting themselves when upset. They may threaten suicide to manipulate others, reflecting the chaotic nature of their relationships. Because many of them experience intense feelings of abandonment when alone, they may jump frantically from one unhealthy relationship to another.

Explanations of Borderline Personality Disorder. Object relations theorist (see Chapter 14) Otto Kernberg (1967, 1973) traced the roots of borderline personality to childhood problems with developing a sense of self and bonding emotionally to others. According to Kernberg, borderline individuals can't integrate differing perceptions of people, themselves included. This defect supposedly arises from an inborn tendency to experience intense anger and frustration from living with a cold, unempathic mother. Kernberg argued that borderline individuals experience the world and themselves as unstable because they tend to "split" people and experiences into either all good or all bad. Although influential, Kernberg's model of borderline personality remains inadequately researched.

According to Marsha Linehan's (1993) sociobiological model, individuals with borderline personality disorder inherit a tendency to overreact to stress and experience lifelong difficulties with regulating their emotions. Indeed, twin studies suggest that borderline personality traits are substantially heritable (Torgeson et al., 2000). Difficulties in controlling emotions may be responsible for the rejection many individuals with borderline personality disorder encounter, as well as their concerns about being validated, loved, and accepted. Linehan's clinical work and research suggests the following recipe for creating a borderline personality: Expose a child to a great deal of trauma and stress, don't validate the child's feelings, and don't provide the child with skills to cope with stress. Needless to say, we don't recommend that you follow this prescription with your children.

PSYCHOPATHIC PERSONALITY: DON'T JUDGE A BOOK BY ITS COVER

We don't intend to alarm you. Yet the odds are high that in your life you've met—perhaps even dated—at least one person whom psychologists describe as a **psychopathic personality,** or more informally, a *psychopath* or *sociopath*. Psychopathic personality overlaps with the DSM-IV diagnosis of **antisocial personality disorder** (ASPD), although it's not identical to it. In contrast to ASPD, which is marked by a lengthy history of illegal and irresponsible actions, psychopathic personality is marked by a distinctive set of personality traits (Lilienfeld, 1994). Because most psychological research has concentrated on psychopathic personality rather than ASPD (Hare, 2003)—a strange irony as only the latter diagnosis is in DSM-IV—we'll focus on psychopathy here.

Psychopathic Personality: A Dangerous Mixture of Traits. Psychopaths are guiltless, dishonest, manipulative, callous, and self-centered (Cleckley, 1941/1988; Lykken, 1995). Because of these distinctly unpleasant personality traits, one might assume we'd all go out of our way to avoid psychopaths—and we'd probably be better off if we did. However, many of us seek out psychopaths as friends and even romantic partners because they tend to be charming, personable, and engaging (Hare, 1993). This was certainly the case with Johnny, whom we'll recall from the beginning of the chapter. Like Johnny, many psychopaths have a history of *conduct disorder,* marked by lying, cheating, and stealing in childhood and adolescence.

If the traits we've described fit someone you know to a T, there's no need to panic. Despite popular conception, most psychopaths aren't physically aggressive. Nevertheless, psychopaths are at heightened risk for crime compared with the average person, and a

The homicidal and unstable character in the movie *Fatal Attraction,* played by Glenn Close (opposite Michael Douglas), would probably qualify for a diagnosis of borderline personality disorder, although most people with this diagnosis aren't violent.

psychopathic personality
condition marked by superficial charm, dishonesty, manipulativeness, self-centeredness, and risk-taking

antisocial personality disorder
condition marked by a lengthy history of irresponsible and/or illegal actions

handful—probably a few percent—are habitually violent. Mass murderer Ted Bundy, whom we encountered in the book's Prologue, was almost certainly a psychopath. Psychopaths make up about 25 percent of prison inmates (Hare, 2003). Also, despite scores of movie portrayals of crazed serial killers, psychopaths typically aren't psychotic. To the contrary, most are entirely rational. They know full well that their irresponsible actions are morally wrong; they just don't care.

There's reason to suspect that many psychopaths populate not only much of the criminal justice system, but positions of leadership in corporations and politics (Babiak & Hare, 2006). Many psychopathic traits, such as interpersonal skills, superficial likeability, ruthlessness, and risk taking, may give psychopaths a leg up for getting ahead of the rest of the pack. Still, there's surprisingly little research on "successful psychopaths," people with high levels of psychopathic traits who function well in society (Hall & Benning, 2006; Widom, 1977).

For reasons that are unknown, psychopathic personality is more common in men than women (Vitale & Newman, 2001). Some authors have speculated that *histrionic personality disorder,* a condition marked by vanity, self-centeredness, attention seeking, and dramatic behavior (see Table 15.12) is an analogue of psychopathic personality that's more prevalent in women than men. Interestingly, in several studies researchers have given clinicians a description of a client who's seductive, dishonest, and manipulative and told half of them the client was male, half the client was female. Typically, clinicians diagnose the client as psychopathic if they think he's male, but histrionic if they think she's female (Ford & Widiger, 1989; Hamilton, Rothbart, & Dawes, 1986; Spalt, 1980). Similar sex biases sometimes creep into the diagnosis of other personality disorders, including borderline personality disorder (Becker & Lamb, 1994). Nevertheless, the extent to which psychopathy and histrionic personality disorder reflect the same underlying condition is unclear (Cale & Lilienfeld, 2002).

Causes of Psychopathic Personality. Despite over five decades of research, the causes of psychopathic personality remain mysterious. As we learned in Chapter 6, psychopaths don't show much classical conditioning to unpleasant unconditioned stimuli, like electric shocks. Similarly, when asked to sit patiently in a chair for an impending electric shock or loud blast of noise, psychopaths' levels of skin conductance—an indicator of arousal—increase only about one-fifth as much as that of nonpsychopaths (Hare, 1978; Lorber 2004). These abnormalities probably stem from a deficit in fear, which may give rise to many of the other features of the disorder (Lykken, 1995; Patrick, 2006). Perhaps as a consequence of this dearth of fear, psychopaths aren't motivated to learn from punishment and tend to make the same mistakes in life over and over again (Newman & Kosson, 1986).

An alternative explanation is that psychopaths are underaroused. As we learned in Chapter 11, the *Yerkes-Dodson law* describes a well-established psychological principle: an inverted U-shaped relationship between arousal, on the one hand, and mood and performance, on the other. As this law reminds us, people who are habitually underaroused experience *stimulus hunger:* They're bored and seek out excitement. The underarousal hypothesis may help to explain why psychopaths tend to be risk takers (Zuckerman, 1989). It may also help to explain why they frequently get in trouble with the law and abuse all manner of substances (Taylor & Lang, 2006).

SUBSTANCE ABUSE AND DEPENDENCE

As we learned in Chapter 5, drugs are substances that change the way we think, feel, or act. It's easy to forget that alcohol and the nicotine in tobacco are drugs, because they're commonplace and legal. Still, the misuse of both legal and illegal drugs is a serious societal problem. According to a national survey (Johnston, O'Malley, & Bachman, 2003), 56.7 percent of young people (ages 19–30) reported having tried marijuana, and 32.8 percent report having tried other illegal drugs, like cocaine, heroin, and hallucinogens.

Abuse versus Dependence: A Fine Line. There's often a fine line between drug use and abuse. What starts out as experimentation with drugs to "get high" and be sociable with

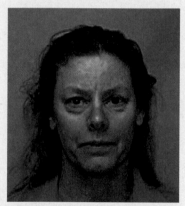

In rare cases, violent psychopaths are women (Arrigo & Griffin, 2004). Aileen Wuomos (pictured above), a serial killer called the Damsel of Death, was executed for the murders of six men she lured to their death by posing as a stranded driver. Charlize Theron won an Academy Award for her portrayal of Wuomos in the movie *Monster.*

fictoid

Myth: All psychopaths are untreatable and can't be rehabilitated.
Reality: Although the view that psychopaths are "hopeless cases" is widely accepted, recent evidence suggests that at least some psychopaths may improve as a consequence of psychotherapy (Salekin, 2002; Skeem, Monahan, & Mulvey, 2002).

friends can become a pattern of intensified use, and lead to substance abuse and dependence. Generally speaking, people qualify for a diagnosis of *substance abuse* when they experience recurrent problems associated with the drug (APA, 2000). Problems often surface in the family, with friends, on the job, in fulfilling life responsibilities, and with the law.

Substance dependence is associated with symptoms of tolerance and withdrawal (see Chapter 5). **Table 15.13** shows the complete set of symptoms required for a diagnosis of substance dependence. According to one survey (Knight et al., 2002), within a 12-month period, 6 percent of college students met the criteria for a diagnosis of alcohol dependence, and 31 percent for the diagnosis of alcohol abuse. Still, most people don't neatly fall into categories of substance abuse versus dependence and vary a good deal in the severity of their symptoms (Harford & Muthen, 2001; Sher, Grekin, & Williams, 2006).

Table 15.13 Symptoms of Substance Dependence. A maladaptive pattern of substance use, leading to clinically significant impairment or distress, as manifested by at least three of the following (in the same 12-month period).

(1) tolerance

(2) withdrawal

(3) the substance is often taken in larger amounts or over a longer period than was intended

(4) persistent desire or unsuccessful efforts to cut down or control substance use

(5) a great deal of time is spent in activities necessary to obtain the substance

(6) important social, occupational, or recreational activities are given up or reduced because of substance use

(7) substance use is continued despite knowledge of having a persistent or recurrent physical or psychological problem related to the substance

(*Source:* From *Diagnostic and Statistical Manual of Mental Disorders,* 4th ed., American Psychiatric Association, 2000)

Explanations for Drug Use and Abuse. People often begin using drugs when they become available; when their family or peers approve of them; and when they don't anticipate serious consequences from their use (Phil, 1999). Illegal drug use typically starts in early adolescence, peaks in early adulthood, and declines sharply thereafter. Young adults may turn to drugs for novel experiences, as a way of rebelling against their parents, and as a means of gaining peer approval (Deater-Deckard, 2001; Fergusson et al., 2002). Fortunately, later in life, pressures to be employed and establish a family often counteract earlier pressures and attitudes associated with drug use (Newcomb & Bentler, 1988). In the sections to come, we'll focus on the causes of alcohol abuse and alcohol dependence (better known as alcoholism) because they're the forms of drug misuse that scientists best understand.

Sociocultural Influences. Cultures or groups in which drinking is strictly prohibited, such as Muslims or Mormons, exhibit low rates of alcoholism (Chentsova-Dutton & Tsai, 2006). In Egypt, the annual rate of alcohol dependence is only .2 percent (World Health Organization, 2004). The situation differs markedly in some so-called vinocultural or "wet" societies, which view drinking as a healthy part of daily life (*vino* refers to wine in many languages). For example, in Poland, a "wet" country, the annual rate of alcohol dependence among adults is 11.2 percent. Some researchers attribute these differences to cultural differences in attitudes toward alcohol and its abuse. Nevertheless, these differences could also be due in part to genetic influences, and the cultural attitudes themselves may reflect these differences.

  Is There an Addictive Personality? Sociocultural factors don't account for individual variations within cultures. We can find alcoholics in societies with strong sanctions against drinking and teetotalers in societies in which drinking is widespread. To explain these facts, popular and scientific psychologists alike have long wondered whether certain people have an "addictive personality" that predisposes them to abuse alcohol and other drugs (Shaffer, 2000). On the one hand, research suggests that common wisdom to the contrary, there's no single addictive personality (Rozin & Stoess, 1993). On the other

In France and other "vinocultural" societies, drinking alcohol is viewed as a healthy part of life.

Correlation vs. Causation

hand, researchers have found that certain personality traits predispose to alcohol and drug abuse. In particular, studies have tied substance abuse to impulsivity (Baker & Yardley, 2002; Kanzler & Rosenthal, 2003; Kollins, 2003), sociability (Wennberg, 2002), and a predisposition toward negative emotions, like anxiety and hostility (Jackson & Sher, 2003). But some of these traits may result from, rather than cause, substance misuse. Also, genetic influences appear to account at least in part for antisocial behavior and alcoholism risk (Slutske, Heath, Dinwiddie, Madden, & Bucholz, 1998).

Correlation vs. Causation

Learning and Expectancies. According to the *tension reduction hypothesis* (Cappell & Herman, 1972; Sayette, 1999; Sher, 1987), people consume alcohol and other drugs to relieve anxiety. Such "self-medication" reinforces drug use and increases the probability of continued use. Alcohol affects brain centers involved in reward (Koob, 2000) as well as dopamine, which plays a crucial role in reward. Nevertheless, people probably drink to relieve anxiety only when they believe alcohol is a stress reducer (Greeley & Oei, 1999). But once individuals become dependent on alcohol, the discomfort of their withdrawal symptoms can motivate drug-seeking behavior and continued use.

Genetic Influences. Alcoholism tends to run in families (Sher, Grekin, & Williams, 2005). But this evidence doesn't tell us whether this finding is due to genes, shared environment, or both. Twin and adoption studies have resolved the issue: They show that genetic factors play a key role in the vulnerability to alcoholism (McGue, 1999). Multiple genes are probably involved (NIAAA, 2000), but what's inherited? No one knows for sure, but researchers have uncovered some promising leads. In Chapter 5, we learned that people who experience an unpleasant physical reaction to alcohol (including facial flushing), including about 40 percent of individuals of Asian descent, are especially unlikely to develop alcoholism. On the flip side of the coin, Marc Schuckit (1988) discovered that nearly 40 percent of people with an alcoholic parent, compared with less than 10 percent of people with nonalcoholic parents, showed few signs of intoxication after drinking, even when they consumed the equivalent of about three alcoholic drinks. For example, after drinking, their bodies didn't sway as much as those of children of nonalcoholic parents. To determine whether reactions to alcohol predict alcohol abuse, Schuckit (1998) followed 435 20-year-olds for ten years. Those with an initial weak response to alcohol displayed a fourfold increase in their risk for alcoholism at age 30. Schuckit (1994) argued that a genetically influenced weak response to alcohol contributes to a later desire to drink heavily to achieve the pleasurable effects of intoxication, although it's unknown whether the initial response to alcohol is due to genes, environment, or both.

Ruling Out Rival Hypotheses

Scientists are hot on the trail of finding other genes associated with alcoholism risk (Sher et al., 2005). Some of these genes may be relevant to alcohol use, whereas others may be relevant to personality traits, like impulsivity or anxiety, that increase people's motivation to drink. In the coming years, scientists may better understand how the genetic predisposition to heavy drinking is activated by environmental factors, such as life stressors, peer pressure, and availability of alcohol.

ASSESS YOUR KNOWLEDGE: FACT OR FICTION?

(1) Personality disorders are almost always reliably diagnosed. (True/False)

(2) Borderline personality is among the most unstable of the personality disorders. (True/False)

(3) Most psychopaths are not habitually violent. (True/False)

(4) There's a clear line or distinction between substance abuse and dependence. (True/False)

(5) Most people of Asian descent are at low risk for alcoholism. (True/False)

Answers: (1) F (p. 661); (2) T (p. 661); (3) T (p. 661); (4) F (pp. 662–663); (5) T (p. 665)

Think again...

The Complete Review System

THINK / ASSESS / STUDY / SUCCEED

Conceptions of Mental Illness: Yesterday and Today (pp. 624–638)

STUDY the Learning Objectives

▶ Identify criteria for defining mental disorders
- Criteria for defining mental disorders include statistical rarity, subjective distress, impairment, societal disapproval, and biological dysfunction.

▶ Describe conceptions of diagnoses across history and cultures
- The demonic model of mental illness was followed by the medical model of the Renaissance. In the early 1950s, medications to treat schizophrenia led to deinstitutionalization. Some psychological conditions are culture-specific. Still, many mental disorders can be found in most cultures.

▶ Identify common misconceptions about psychiatric diagnoses, and the strengths and limitations of the current diagnostic system
- Misconceptions include the ideas that a diagnosis is nothing more than pigeon-holing, and that diagnoses are unreliable, invalid, and stigmatizing. The Diagnostic and Statistical Manual of Mental Disorders (DSM-IV) is a valuable tool that contains separate axes for psychiatric diagnoses, medical conditions, life stressors, and overall life functioning. Its limitations include high levels of comorbidity and an assumption of a categorical model in the absence of compelling evidence.

▶ Identify popular misconceptions about the law and mental illness
- Most mentally ill patients aren't at greatly heightened risk for violence. Well under 1 percent of criminals are acquitted on the basis of the insanity defense, which is not the same as incompetence to stand trial. Civil commitment to a psychiatric facility can occur when patients pose a clear and present threat to themselves and others, or can't care for themselves.

DO YOU KNOW THESE TERMS?

- ❑ demonic model (p. 626)
- ❑ medical model (p. 626)
- ❑ asylums (p. 626)
- ❑ moral treatment (p. 627)
- ❑ deinstitutionalization (p. 627)
- ❑ bulimia nervosa (p. 629)
- ❑ anorexia nervosa (p. 630)
- ❑ *Diagnostic and Statistical Manual of Mental Disorders* (DSM) (p. 632)
- ❑ labeling theorists (p. 633)
- ❑ prevalence (p. 634)
- ❑ axes (p. 635)
- ❑ comorbidity (p. 635)
- ❑ categorical model (p. 635)
- ❑ dimensional model (p. 635)
- ❑ insanity defense (p. 636)
- ❑ incompetence to stand trial (p. 638)
- ❑ involuntary commitment (p. 638)

When was the government program of deinstitutionalization initiated and what were its two goals? (p. 627)

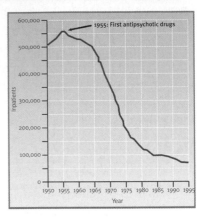

Identify six myths regarding the insanity defense. (p. 637)
1. _____
2. _____
3. _____
4. _____
5. _____
6. _____

mypsychlab
where learning comes to life!

The Axes of the DSM

Classification or labeling? Learn about the five axes of the DSM. (p. 634)

SIMULATION

what You would do...

As you organize an orientation to prepare students to work in a mental health facility, how would you dispel misconceptions they might have about mental illness? (pp. 624–625)

ASSESS your knowledge

1. During the Middle Ages, the _____ model of mental illness was popular, whereas during the Renaissance, the _____ model was popular. (p. 626)

2. In America in the 19th century, Dorothea Dix advocated for _____ _____, an approach calling for dignity, kindness, and respect for the mentally ill. (p. 627)

3. In the early 1950s, medications that treated schizophrenia, like chlorpromazine, led to a government policy called _____. (p. 627)

4. Bulimia is an example of an _____ disorder specific to Western cultures. (p. 629)

5. The diagnostic system containing the APA criteria used to classify individuals with mental disorders is called the _____ _____ _____ _____ _____. (p. 634)

6. The DSM-IV asks psychologists and psychiatrists to assess patients along multiple _____, or dimensions of functioning. (p. 635)

7. One of the problems with the DSM-IV is the high level of _____ among many of its diagnoses. (p. 635)

8. Another problem with the DSM-IV is its reliance on a _____ model without compelling evidence. (p. 635)

9. The legal concept that people should not be held responsible for their actions if they were not in a sound state of mind is called the _____ _____. (p. 636)

10. Assessment of a defendant's mental capacity to stand trial in a court of law is called _____ _____ _____ _____. (p. 638)

Anxiety Disorders: The Many Faces of Worry and Fear (pp. 639–644)

STUDY the Learning Objectives

▶ Describe the many ways people experience anxiety
- Panic involves intense yet brief rushes of fear that are out of proportion to the actual threat. People with generalized anxiety disorder spend much of their day worrying. Fears are highly focused in phobias. In

If you did not receive an access code to MyPsychLab with this text and wish to purchase access online, please visit www.mypsychlab.com.

mypsychlab
where learning comes to life!

The Obsessive-Compulsive Test

When our worries become obsessions.

(p. 642)

SIMULATION

what You would do...

An acquaintance mistakenly uses the phrase "I keep having panic attacks" to describe becoming stressed out over homework and conflicts with friends. What information could you give her to help her become more accurate in her self-descriptions? (pp. 639–640)

Compare the characteristics of blood-injury phobia with those of other phobias. (p. 641)

ASSESS your knowledge

1. An individual's constant preoccupation with the notion that he is suffering from a serious physical disease is called _____. (p. 639)

2. People suffer from _____ _____ when they experience panic attacks that are repeated and unexpected and when they change their behavior in an attempt to avoid panic attacks. (pp. 639–640)

3. People with _____ _____ _____ spend an average of 60 percent of each day worrying. (p. 640)

4. A _____ is an intense fear of an object or a situation that's greatly out of proportion to its actual threat. (pp. 640–641)

5. When people witness or experience a traumatic event, such as front-line combat, or a violent crime, they may develop _____ _____ _____. (pp. 641–642)

6. Persistent ideas, thoughts, or impulses that are unwanted and inappropriate and cause distress are called _____. (p. 642)

7. Repetitive behaviors or mental acts initiated to reduce or prevent stress are called _____. (p. 642)

8. People _____ when they predict terrible events, despite the low probability of their actual occurrence. (p. 643)

9. Anxious people tend to interpret ambiguous situations in a (negative/positive) light. (p. 643)

10. Many people with anxiety disorders harbor high levels of _____ _____, a fear of anxiety-related sensations. (p. 643)

posttraumatic stress disorder, highly aversive events produce enduring anxiety. People with obsessive-compulsive disorder experience intensely disturbing thoughts, senseless or irrational rituals, or both.

▶ Identify explanations of anxiety disorders that center on the environment, catastrophic thinking, and biological causes
• Learning theory proposes that fears can be learned via conditioning and observation. Anxious people tend to catastrophize or exaggerate the likelihood of negative events. Many anxiety disorders are genetically influenced.

DO YOU KNOW THESE TERMS?
❏ **somatoform disorders** (p. 639)
❏ **hypochondriasis** (p. 639)
❏ **panic attacks** (p. 639)
❏ **panic disorder** (p. 640)
❏ **generalized anxiety disorder** (p. 640)
❏ **phobia** (p. 640)
❏ **agoraphobia** (p. 640)
❏ **specific phobias** (p. 641)
❏ **social phobia** (p. 641)
❏ **posttraumatic stress disorder (PTSD)** (p. 641)
❏ **obsessive-compulsive disorder** (p. 642)
❏ **obsessions** (p. 642)
❏ **compulsions** (p. 642)
❏ **anxiety sensitivity** (p. 643)

Mood Disorders and Suicide (pp. 644–651)

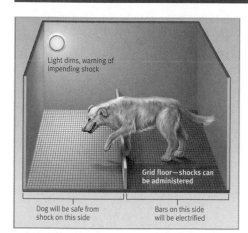

Identify and describe the theory Martin Seligman proposed based on his shuttle box research. (p. 648)

mypsychlab

SUCCEED with
Bipolar Disorder
The roller coaster of psychiatric disorders: Learn more about bipolar disorder. (p. 649)
EXPLORE

THINK about
what **You** would do...
In preparing for a presentation to your psychology class, how would you make the audience aware of the myths about suicide and the realities that rebut each myth? (pp. 650–651)

STUDY the Learning Objectives
▶ Identify the characteristics of different mood disorders
• The sad mood of major depression is the mirror image of the expansive mood associated with a manic episode, seen in bipolar disorder.

▶ Identify risk factors for suicide
• Risk factors include a previous attempt, male gender, family history of suicide, depression, and hopelessness.

▶ Describe the interplay of life events and interpersonal, behavioral, cognitive, and biological factors in producing the symptoms of depression
• Stressful life events are linked to depression. Depressed people may face social rejection, which can amplify depression. According to Lewinsohn's behavioral model, depression results from a low rate of response-contingent positive reinforcement. Aaron Beck's cognitive model holds that negative expectations play an important role in depression, whereas Martin Seligman's model emphasizes learned helplessness. Genes exert a moderate effect on the risk of developing depression.

DO YOU KNOW THESE TERMS?
❏ **major depressive episode** (p. 644)
❏ **cognitive model of depression** (p. 647)
❏ **learned helplessness** (p. 648)
❏ **manic episode** (p. 649)
❏ **bipolar disorder** (p. 649)

ASSESS your knowledge

1. Due to its frequency, some have called _____ the "common cold" of psychological disorders. (p. 644)

2. The state in which a person experiences a lingering depressed mood or diminished interest in pleasurable activities is called a _____ _____. (p. 644)

3. Lewinsohn's behavioral model assumes that depression results from a (low/high) rate of response-contingent positive reinforcement. (p. 646)

4. Aaron Beck's influential _____ _____ holds that depression is caused by negative beliefs and expectations. (p. 647)

5. A tendency to feel helpless in the face of events we can't control is called _____ _____. (pp. 647–648)

6. Seligman's research concluded that people prone to depression attribute negative outcomes to (internal/external) factors. (p. 648)

7. A _____ _____ is typically marked by dramatically elevated mood, decreased need for sleep, increased energy, inflated self-esteem, and irresponsible behavior. (p. 649)

8. Bipolar disorder is (equally common/more common) in women compared with men. (p. 649)

9. Twin studies suggest that the _____ of bipolar disorder may be as high as 85 percent. (p. 649)

10. In 2001, scientists ranked _____ as the eleventh leading cause of death in the United States. (p. 650)

Dissociative Disorders: The Divided Self (pp. 652–654)

STUDY the Learning Objectives

▶ Describe depersonalization, dissociative amnesia, and fugue
- Depersonalization is characterized by feelings of detachment from the self, including the sense of observing the body from the perspective of an outsider or living in a movie or dream. In dissociative amnesia, people are unable to recall important personal information that isn't due to normal forgetting. In dissociative fugue, people forget significant events in their lives and flee their stressful circumstances.

▶ Explain the controversies surrounding dissociative disorders, especially dissociative identity disorder
- The role of severe child abuse in DID is controversial. The sociocognitive model holds that social influences, including the media and suggestive procedures in psychotherapy, shape symptoms of DID.

DO YOU KNOW THESE TERMS?
- ❏ **dissociative disorders** (p. 652)
- ❏ **depersonalization disorder** (p. 652)
- ❏ **dissociative amnesia** (p. 652)
- ❏ **dissociative fugue** (p. 652)
- ❏ **dissociative identity disorder (DID)** (p. 653)

mypsychlab *where learning comes to life!*

SUCCEED with

Dissociative Identity Disorder

DID: The real life Dr. Jekyll and Mr. Hyde of psychiatric disorders.
(pp. 653–654)

EXPLORE

What did this man experience when he disappeared for an extended length of time, only to be found without any memory of his previous life? (p. 652)

THINK about

what You would do . . .
For a journalism class, you are asked to write an article on widely publicized cases of dissociative identity disorder. In your reporting, how would you explain the probable causes of this condition? (pp. 653–654)

ASSESS your knowledge

1. _____ disorders involve disruptions in consciousness, memory, identity, or perception. (p. 652)

2. If you've ever felt detached from yourself, like you're living in a movie, or like you're observing your own body from the perspective of an outsider, then you have experienced _____. (p. 652)

3. It is (common/uncommon) for young adults to experience one brief episode of depersonalization. (p. 652)

4. In _____ _____, people can't recall important personal information and can have extensive memory loss. (p. 652)

5. During a _____ _____, people not only forgets significant events but flee their stressful circumstances. (p. 652)

6. Though rare, a fugue state can cause someone to assume a new _____. (p. 652)

7. _____ _____ _____ is characterized by the presence of two or more distinct identities or personality states which are more temporary patterns of behavior. (p. 653)

8. In DID, the alternate identities are often very (similar to/different from) the primary personality. (p. 653)

9. According to the _____ model, DID arises from a history of severe abuse during childhood. (p. 653)

10. The _____ model argues that certain therapists, along with popular media, fuel the diagnosis of DID by creating alternative personalities rather than discovering them. (pp. 653–654)

The Enigma of Schizophrenia (pp. 654–660)

STUDY the Learning Objectives

▶ Recognize the characteristic symptoms of schizophrenia
- The symptoms of schizophrenia include delusions, hallucinations, disorganized speech, and grossly disorganized behavior or catatonia.

▶ Explain how psychosocial, neural, biochemical, and genetic influences create the vulnerability to schizophrenia
- Schizophrenic patients are prone to relapse when their relatives display high expressed emotion (criticism, hostility, and over-involvement). Scientists have discovered brain abnormalities in patients with schizophrenia, including enlarged ventricles, frontal lobe underactivity, and abnormal dopamine transmission.

From the perspective of what you've learned about schizophrenia, how does this art misrepresent the disorder? (pp. 654–655)

mypsychlab *where learning comes to life!*

SUCCEED with

Schizophrenia

Do patients with schizophrenia possess a split mind?
(pp. 654–655)

SIMULATION

THINK about

what You would do . . .
A friend's brother has been diagnosed with schizophrenia. After helping her set up an appointment with a school counselor, how could you assist her in finding out more information about the disorder? (pp. 658–659)

ASSESS your knowledge

1. _____ is a devastating disorder of thought and emotion associated with a loss of contact with reality. (pp. 654–655)

2. Strongly held, fixed beliefs that have no basis in reality are called _____. (p. 655)

3. _____ symptoms represent serious reality distortions. (p. 655)

4. Most _____ in schizophrenia are auditory, usually consisting of voices. (p. 656)

5. People with schizophrenia can exhibit _____ _____, in which their language skips from topic to topic in a disjointed way. (p. 656)

6. _____ symptoms involve motor problems, extreme resistance to complying with simple suggestions, holding the body in rigid postures,

and refusing to speak or move. (p. 657)

7. Patients with schizophrenia are (prone/not prone) to relapse when their relatives display high expressed emotion, such as criticism and hostility. (p. 658)

8. Scientists (have/haven't) identified brain abnormalities in patients with schizophrenia. (p. 658)

9. Through the study of neurotransmitters, a direct tie between _____ pathways and symptoms of schizophrenia has been identified. (pp. 658–659)

10. A _____ model proposes that schizophrenia, along with many other mental disorders, is a product of genetic vulnerability, and stressors that trigger this vulnerability. (p. 659)

DO YOU KNOW THESE TERMS?

☐ **schizophrenia** (p. 654)
☐ **delusions** (p. 655)
☐ **psychotic symptoms** (p. 655)
☐ **hallucinations** (p. 656)
☐ **catatonic symptoms** (p. 657)
☐ **diathesis-stress models** (p. 659)

Personality Disorders and Substance Abuse (pp. 660–665)

THINK about what You would do . . .

Your roommate has begun to withdraw from your group of friends and seems "out of it" much of the time. You suspect he is using drugs. How can you find out if he is drug dependent? (pp. 663–665)

SUCCEED with mypsychlab *where learning comes to life!*

Personality disorders

How do we distinguish between "normal" and "abnormal" personality traits?

(pp. 660–661)

EXPLORE

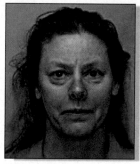

From a psychological perspective, what's rare about the case of serial killer Aileen Wuomos? (p. 663)

STUDY the Learning Objectives

▶ Identify differences between normal variations in personality and personality disorders
  • Personality traits can become abnormal when they are stable and inflexible, and lead to distress and impairment.

▶ Identify the characteristics of borderline and psychopathic personality disorders
  • Borderline personality disorder is marked by instability in mood, identity, and impulse control. Psychopaths are guiltless, dishonest, callous, and self-centered.

▶ Identify differences between substance abuse and dependence
  • Substance abuse is associated with recurrent problems related to the drug. Substance dependence is associated with symptoms of tolerance and withdrawal.

▶ Identify sociocultural, learning, and genetic explanations for drug abuse
  • Cultures that prohibit drinking (Muslims, Mormons) exhibit very low rates of alcoholism. People take drugs and alcohol to reduce tension and anxiety.

ASSESS your knowledge

1. A _____ _____ is diagnosed when stable, inflexible, personality traits first appear in adolescence, and lead to distress or impairment. (p. 660)

2. _____ _____ _____ is a condition marked by instability in mood, identity, and impulse control. (p. 661)

3. Someone who is a _____ personality is dishonest, guiltless, manipulative, and self-centered, but also can be superficially charming. (p. 662)

4. A diagnosis of _____ personality disorder is characterized by a lengthy history of illegal and irresponsible actions. (p. 662)

5. Most psychopaths (are/are not) physically

aggressive. (pp. 662–663)

6. Psychopaths (are/are not) at a heightened risk for crime compared with the average person. (pp. 662–663)

7. People qualify for a diagnosis of _____ _____ when they experience recurrent problems related to the drug. (p. 664)

8. _____ _____ is associated with symptoms of tolerance and withdrawal. (p. 664)

9. Cultures in which drinking is strictly prohibited exhibit (low/high) rates of alcoholism. (p. 664)

10. Children of a parent with alcoholism tend to show a (weaker/stronger) response to alcohol than other children. (p. 665)

DO YOU KNOW THESE TERMS?

☐ **personality disorder** (p. 660)
☐ **borderline personality disorder** (p. 661)
☐ **psychopathic personality** (p. 662)
☐ **antisocial personality disorder** (p. 662)

Remember these questions from the beginning of the chapter? Think again and ask yourself if you would answer them differently based on what you now know about psychological disorders. (For more detailed explanations, see MyPsychLab.)

▶ What is mental illness, and how should we define it? (p. 625)
▶ Are psychiatric diagnoses meaningful, or are they just labels for undesirable behaviors? (p. 627)
▶ Is road rage a valid diagnosis? (p. 628)
▶ Is the insanity defense successful most of the time? (pp. 636–637)
▶ Does everyone who attempts suicide wish to die? (p. 650–651)
▶ Is it possible for one body to house more than 100 personalities? (p. 653)
▶ Is schizophrenia the same as split personality? (pp. 654–655)
▶ Are all psychopaths violent? (pp. 662–663)
▶ Is there a drug-abusing personality? (pp. 664–665)

THINKING Scientifically

Correlation vs. Causation
pp. 829, 848, 847. 848, 850, 633, 838, 664, 663
_____

Falsifiability p. 653
_____

Extraordinary Claims pp. 652, 653
_____

Occam's Razor p. 633
_____

Replicability pp. 632, 646, 647, 656
_____

Ruling Out Rival Hypotheses pp. 626, 631, 632, 642, 647, 652, 653, 657, 658, 659, 665

jos
de mey

16

Psychological and Biological Treatments
Helping People Change

Popular portrayals of psychotherapy have a long history in the media. (*top:* © Cathy Gaines *bottom:* © CartoonBank.com)

Before reading on, try to picture a typical psychotherapy session. What's the patient doing? The therapist? What does the room look like? Perhaps your first thought was of the proverbial patient on a couch, with the therapist sitting behind her, pen and pad in hand, intent on unearthing long-forgotten memories, analyzing dreams, and encouraging the patient to vent painful feelings.

If this scenario came to mind, it's no wonder. From the early days of psychotherapy (often simply called "therapy"), these images have been etched into our cultural consciousness. But we'll discover that this picture doesn't begin to tell the story of the vast array of psychotherapeutic approaches that encompass individual therapy, treatments conducted in groups and with families, and even art, dance, and music therapy. Nor does the scenario capture the powerful biological treatments that have changed the lives of people with serious psychological disorders by targeting the brain's functioning. In this chapter, we'll examine a broad spectrum of therapies, both psychological and biological, that are designed to alleviate emotional suffering. Along the way, we'll offer critical thinking tools for distinguishing scientifically supported from unsupported treatments.

Like some concepts in psychology (see Prologue), *psychotherapy* isn't easy to define. Over a half century ago, one pioneer in psychotherapy wrote, half-jokingly, "Psychotherapy is an undefined technique applied to unspecified problems with unpredictable outcomes. For this technique, we recommend rigorous training" (Raimy, 1950, p. 63). Some might contend that things haven't changed much since then. Still, for the purposes of this text, we can define **psychotherapy** as a psychological intervention designed to help people resolve emotional, behavioral, and interpersonal problems and improve the quality of their lives (Engler & Goleman, 1992, p. 15). Although the popular media often speak of therapy as though it were one thing, there are well over 500 "brands" of psychotherapy (Eisner, 2000). This number is about three times what it was in the 1970s. As we'll learn, research demonstrates that many of these therapies are effective, but many others have never been tested scientifically. Paralleling the remarkable expansion of psychotherapies, scientists have developed biological treatments that include medications, electrical brain stimulation, and even brain surgery. We'll ponder fascinating scientific and ethical questions as we evaluate the application of these treatments.

Psychotherapy: Patients and Practitioners

We'll begin by considering several questions: Who seeks and benefits from psychotherapy? How is psychotherapy practiced? What makes a psychotherapist effective?

WHO SEEKS AND BENEFITS FROM TREATMENT?

A 2006 *Newsweek* poll found that about 20 percent of Americans have received psychological treatment at some point in their lives, and that about 4 percent are currently in psychotherapy. Therapists work with people of all ages and backgrounds as they confront challenges throughout the life cycle, including drug addiction, chronic pain, marital problems, and bouts of depression and anxiety. People grapple with specific problems in psychotherapy, but they also contend frequently with feelings of helplessness, social isolation, and a sense of failure (Garfield, 1978; Lambert, 2003). Still other individuals turn to therapy to expand their self-awareness, learn better ways of relating to others, and consider lifestyle changes.

Entering Treatment: Gender, Ethnicity, and Culture. Some people are more likely to enter treatment than others. Women are more likely to seek treatment than men (Addis & Mahalik, 2003; DuBrin & Zastowny, 1988), although both sexes benefit equally from psychotherapy (Petry, Tennen, & Affleck, 2000). Members of many racial and ethnic minority groups, particularly Asian Americans and Hispanic Americans, are less likely to seek mental health services than Caucasian Americans (Sue & Lam, 2002), perhaps because of the lingering stigma surrounding psychotherapy in these groups. Nevertheless, when individuals hailing from diverse cultural and ethnic backgrounds do obtain psychotherapy, they're likely to benefit from it (Navarro, 1993; Prochaska & Norcross, 2007).

Culturally sensitive psychotherapists tune their interventions to patients' cultural values and the difficulties they encounter in adapting to a dominant culture that at times is vastly different from their own (Sue & Sue, 2003; Whaley & Davis, 2007). Although ethnic minorities prefer therapists with a similar ethnic background (Coleman, Wampold, & Casali, 1995), there's no consistent evidence that therapy outcome is enhanced by patient–therapist ethnic matches (Shin et al., 2005) or gender matches (Bowman, Scogin, Floyd, & McKendree-Smith, 2001). Still, when patients are relative newcomers to a particular culture and not well acquainted with its traditions, therapist–client ethnic match may play a greater role in therapy's effectiveness (Sue, 1998). The good news is that people can probably be helped by therapists who differ from them in significant ways, including ethnicity and gender (Whaley & Davis, 2007).

For many, the decision to enter therapy is difficult. In one study, over half of patients were aware of their problems long before they decided to seek help. Many waited for over 2 years (Strupp, Fox, & Lessler, 1969), a finding replicated by later researchers (DiClemente & Prochaska, 1985; Prochaska & DiClemente, 1984).

Reaping Benefits from Treatment. Regardless of their cultural and socioeconomic backgrounds, patients who experience some anxiety do better in psychotherapy, probably because their distress fuels their motivation to make life changes (Frank, 1974; Miller et al., 1995). Nevertheless, patients with longstanding and severe problems tend to achieve poorer results than those with minor and temporary problems, such as the relationship upheavals we all experience from time to time (Gasperini, Scherillo, Manfredonia, & Franchini, 1993; Steinmetz, Lewinsohn, & Antonuccio, 1983).

Patients who are better adjusted to begin with, aware of their contribution to problems, and willing to work on them are most likely to improve in psychotherapy (Prochaska & DiClemente, 1982; Prochaska & Norcross, 2002). Put more cynically, those who benefit the most from psychotherapy may need it the least.

WHO PRACTICES PSYCHOTHERAPY?

As we learned in the Prologue, clinical psychologists, psychiatrists, mental health counselors, and clinical social workers with professional degrees and licenses are the mainstays of the mental health profession (see **Table 16.1,** on the next page). But unlicensed religious, vocational, and rehabilitation counselors as well as art therapists, some with advanced degrees in fields other than psychology, also provide psychological services.

Contrary to the myth that all psychotherapists have advanced degrees in mental health, volunteers and **paraprofessionals,** helpers who work in the field with no formal professional training, provide psychological services in such settings as crisis intervention centers and other social service agencies. In most states, the term *therapist* isn't legally protected, so virtually anyone can hang up a shingle and offer psychological treatment. Many paraprofessionals obtain agency-specific training and attend workshops that enhance their general education backgrounds. Paraprofessionals may also be taught to recognize situations that require consultation with professionals with greater expertise. Paraprofessionals help to compensate for the sizable gap between the high demand for and meager supply of practitioners (Christensen & Jacobson, 1994).

PROFESSIONALS VERSUS PARAPROFESSIONALS: A DIFFERENCE THAT MAKES A DIFFERENCE?

Again contrary to popular belief, therapists don't need to be professionally trained or have many years of experience to be effective (Berman & Norton, 1985; Blatt, Sanislow, Zuroff,

Replicability

The ideal client? A 1964 study (Schofield, 1964) found that many therapists preferred to treat people who were relatively young, attractive, verbal, intelligent, and successful (YAVIS clients). Nevertheless, therapists have recently become more aware of the importance of assisting a broad clientele of all ages and cultural backgrounds.

psychotherapy
a psychological intervention designed to help people resolve emotional, behavioral, and interpersonal problems and improve the quality of their lives

paraprofessional
person with no professional training who provides mental health services

Table 16.1 Occupations, Degrees, Roles, and Work Settings of Mental Health Professionals. Not all therapists are the same: Mental health consumers are often unaware of the substantial differences in education, training, and roles of different psychotherapists. This table provides some guidance.

Occupation	Degree/License	Role/Settings
Clinical Psychologist	PhD/PsyD, MA	Private practice, hospitals, schools, community agencies, medical settings, academic, other
Psychiatrist	MD or DO	Physicians, private practice, hospitals, medical centers, schools, academic, other
Counseling Psychologist	PhD, EdD, MA, MS, MC	University clinics, mental health centers; treat people with less severe psychological problems
School Psychologist	PhD, PsyD, EdD, EdS, MA, MS, MEd	In school interventions, assessment, prevention programs, work with teachers, students, parents
Clinical Social Worker	Training varies widely; BSW, MSW, DSW, LCSW	Private practice following supervised experience, psychiatric facilities, hospitals/community agencies, schools, case managers; help with social and health problems
Mental Health Counselor	MSW, MS, MC	Private practice, community agencies, hospitals, other; career counseling, marriage issues, substance abuse
Psychiatric Nurse	Training varies widely; associate's degree, BSN, MSN, DNP, PhD	Hospitals, community health centers, primary care facilities, outpatient mental health clinics, manage medications; with advanced degrees can diagnose, treat mental patients
Pastoral Counselor	Training varies; from bachelor's degree to more advanced degrees	Counseling, support in spiritual context, wellness programs; group, family, and couples therapy

Degree Key: BSN, bachelor of science in nursing; BSW, bachelor of social work; DNP, doctorate nurse practitioner; DO, doctor of osteopathy; DSW, doctor of social work; EdD, doctor of education; EdS, specialist in education; LCSW, licensed clinical social worker; MA, master of arts; MC, master of counseling; MD, doctor of medicine; MEd, master of education; MS, master of science; MSN, master of science in nursing; MSW, master of social work; PhD, doctor of philosophy; PsyD, doctor of psychology.

& Pilkonis, 1996; Christensen & Jacobson, 1994). Indeed, many researchers have found few or even no differences in effectiveness between more and less experienced therapists (McFall, 2006; Dawes, 1994). Why is this the case? As Jerome Frank (1961) noted, regardless of level of professional training, people who fulfill the role of therapist may provide patients with hope, empathy, advice, support, and opportunities for new learning experiences (Frank & Frank, 1991; Lambert & Ogles, 2004).

In 1995, *Consumer Reports* magazine surveyed 180,000 subscribers about their experiences with psychotherapy. Fully 90 percent of the 7,000 readers who responded to the mental health questions believed they were helped by psychotherapy. The strongest reported results were for those who consulted with a licensed professional for 6 months or longer (Seligman, 1995). Yet because the *Consumer Reports* study wasn't based on an experimental design (see Chapter 2), with patients randomly assigned to either treatment or no treatment, we need to be cautious in interpreting its results. Perhaps those who stayed in treatment for 6 months or more had already benefited at an earlier point in the process.

Even if there are few or no differences in therapy outcome as a function of professional training, there are certain advantages to consulting with a professional. Professional helpers understand how to operate effectively within the broader mental health system; appreciate complex ethical, professional, and personal issues; and can select treatments of demonstrated effectiveness (Garske & Anderson, 2003). Moreover, trained and experienced therapists may be more confident, less defensive, and better able to appreciate patients' worldview than paraprofessionals and inexperienced therapists (Teyber & McClure, 2000).

Ruling Out Rival Hypotheses

factoid

During the first month of treatment, many patients improve considerably. In fact, 40 to 66 percent of patients report improvement even before attending their first session (Howard, Kopta, Krause, & Orlinsky, 1986). The act of seeking help—doing something about one's problems—apparently inspires hope and breeds confidence (Kirsch, 1990).

WHAT DOES IT TAKE TO BE AN EFFECTIVE PSYCHOTHERAPIST?

Given that years of experience aren't a critical determinant of what makes a good therapist, what is? Researchers are honing in on the answers. Effective therapists (Garske & Anderson, 2003) are likely to be warm and direct (Westerman, Foote, & Winston, 1995), establish a positive working relationship with patients (Kazdin, Marciano, & Whitley, 2005; Luborsky, McLellan, Diguer, Woody, & Seligman, 1997), and tend not to contradict patients (Friedlander, 1984). Effective therapists also select important topics to focus on in sessions (Goldfried, Raue, & Castonguay, 1998), and match their treatments to the needs and characteristics of patients (Beutler & Harwood, 2000). Differences among therapists in their abilities and characteristics may be so great that they overshadow differences in the effectiveness of the treatments they provide (Ahn & Wampold, 2001; Luborsky et al., 1986). That is, when it comes to the success of psychotherapy, the choice of *therapist* may often matter more than the choice of *therapy* (Blow, Sprenkle, & Davis, 2007).

What makes a good therapist from the patient's point of view? Research suggests that the composite view of the "good" therapist is that of an expert who's warm, respectful, caring, and engaged (Littaver, Sexton, & Wyan, 2005; Strupp, Fox, & Lessler, 1969). This description fits exactly the sort of therapist we advise you or your loved ones to seek. In **Table 16.2,** we present some tips for both selecting good therapists and avoiding bad ones.

Ethical behavior is a cornerstone of good psychotherapy. In the enormously popular television series *The Sopranos*, mobster Tony Soprano's therapist (played by Lorraine Bracco) revealed private information about him at a dinner party and then abruptly dismissed him from therapy after becoming convinced he was an untreatable psychopath. Breaking confidentiality and "abandonment" of a patient are serious—and fortunately rare—ethical violations on the part of psychotherapists.

Table 16.2 What Should I Look for in a Therapist, and What Type of Therapist Should I Avoid? Tens of thousands of people call themselves therapists, and it's often hard to know what kind of therapist to seek out or avoid. This checklist may help you, your friends, or your loved ones to select a good therapist—and to steer clear of a bad one.

If your answer is yes to most of the following statements, the therapist should be in a good position to help you:

1. I can talk freely and openly with my therapist.
2. My therapist listens carefully to what I say and understands my feelings.
3. My therapist is warm, direct, and provides useful feedback.
4. My therapist explains up front what he or she will be doing and why, and is willing to answer questions about his or her qualifications and training, my diagnosis, and our treatment plan.
5. My therapist encourages me to confront challenges and solve problems.
6. My therapist uses scientifically based approaches and discusses the pros and cons of other approaches.
7. My therapist regularly monitors how I'm doing and is willing to change course when treatment isn't going well.

If your answer is yes to one or more of the following statements, the therapist may *not* be in a good position to help you, and even may be harmful:

1. My therapist gets defensive and angry when challenged.
2. My therapist has a "one size fits all" approach to all problems.
3. My therapist spends considerable time each session making "small talk," telling me exactly what to do, and sharing personal anecdotes.
4. My therapist isn't clear about what is expected of me in the treatment plan, and our discussions lack any focus and direction.
5. My therapist doesn't seem willing to discuss the scientific support for what he or she is doing.
6. There are no clear professional boundaries in my relationship with my therapist; for example, my therapist talks a lot about his or her personal life or asks me for personal favors.

ASSESS YOUR KNOWLEDGE: FACT OR FICTION?

(1) Asian Americans are more likely to seek psychotherapy than Caucasians. (True/False)
(2) Most people who seek psychotherapy do so two years or more after they first notice they have psychological problems. (True/False)
(3) All people who practice therapy have advanced degrees in mental health. (True/False)
(4) A moderate degree of anxiety in the patient is a predictor of improvement in therapy. (True/False)
(5) Professional training is necessary to produce good therapy outcomes. (True/False)

Answers: (1) F (p. 673); (2) T (p. 673); (3) F (p. 673); (4) T (p. 673); (5) F (pp. 673–674)

Insight Therapies: Acquiring Understanding

In much of the chapter that lies ahead, we'll examine some of the more prominent therapeutic approaches, describe their methods, and evaluate their scientific status. We'll begin with an overview of *psychodynamic therapists*, a term that refers to both Freudian therapists and those influenced by Freud's techniques. After we examine Freud's techniques, we'll consider a group of therapists called *neo-Freudians* (see Chapter 14). These therapists adopted Freud's psychodynamic perspective but modified his therapeutic approach in distinctive ways. Psychodynamic therapies, and the humanistic-existential therapies we'll also discuss, are often called **insight therapies,** as their goal is to cultivate insight, that is, expanded awareness.

PSYCHOANALYTIC AND PSYCHODYNAMIC THERAPIES: FREUD'S LEGACY

To understand what psychodynamic therapists have in common, consider the following five beliefs, which form the core of the psychodynamic approach (see Chapter 14):

(1) Much of human behavior is motivated by unconscious conflicts, wishes, and impulses.

(2) Abnormal behaviors have meaningful causes that therapists can discover.

(3) People's present difficulties are rooted in their childhood experiences.

(4) Emotional expression and the opportunity to reexperience significant past events emotionally are critical aspects of therapy.

(5) When the patient achieves intellectual and emotional insight into previously unconscious material, the causes and the significance of symptoms become evident, often causing the symptoms to disappear.

Psychoanalysis: The First Therapy. Freud's psychoanalysis was the first form of psychotherapy. According to Freud, the goal of psychoanalytic therapy is to *make the unconscious conscious.* By that, he meant making the patient aware of previously repressed impulses, conflicts, and memories that generate psychological distress. Psychoanalytic therapy aims to clear away the emotional distortions bred by past experiences, guilt, and frustrations (Bornstein, 2001; Mellinger & Lynn, 2003). Psychoanalytic therapists attempt to fill this tall order by using six primary approaches.

(1) Free association. As patients lie on the couch in a comfortable, relaxed position, therapists instruct them to say whatever thoughts come to mind, no matter how meaningless or nonsensical they might seem. This process is called **free association,** because patients are permitted to express themselves without censorship of any sort.

(2) Interpretation. From the patient's string of free associations, analysts form hypotheses regarding the origin of the patient's difficulties and share them with him or her as rapport develops. Therapists also formulate *interpretations*—that is, explanations—of the unconscious bases of a patients' dreams, emotions, and behaviors. They point out the supposedly disguised expression of a repressed idea, impulse, or wish, as in the following interpretation of a patient's repeated "accidents" resulting in injury: "Having these accidents perhaps served an unconscious purpose; they assured you of getting the attention you felt you could not get otherwise." As in comedy, timing is everything. If the therapist offers the interpretation before the patient is ready to accept it, psychoanalytics maintain anxiety may derail the flow of new associations.

(3) Dream Analysis. According to Freud, dreams express unconscious themes that influence the patient's conscious life. The therapist's task is to interpret the relation of

The Freudian concept of free association is a bit like a magician pulling kerchiefs out of a hat, with one thought leading to the next, in turn leading to the next, and so on.

insight therapies
psychotherapies, including psychodynamic and humanistic-existential approaches, with the goal of expanding awareness or insight

free association
technique in which patients express themselves without censorship of any sort

the dream to the patient's daytime experience and the dream's symbolic significance. In Chapter 5, we discussed the distinction between a dream's manifest (observable) and latent (hidden) content. Thus, the therapist might interpret the appearance of an ogre in a dream—the manifest content—as representing a hated and feared parent—the latent content.

(4) **Resistance.** As treatment progresses and people become painfully aware of previously unconscious aspects of themselves, they often experience **resistance:** That is, they try to avoid further confrontation. Resistance helps patients sidestep the anxiety brought about by uncovering previously repressed thoughts, emotions, and impulses. Patients express resistance in many ways, including skipping therapy sessions or drawing a blank when the therapist asks a question about painful moments in their past, but all forms of resistance stall their progress. To minimize resistance, psychoanalysts attempt to make patients aware they're unconsciously obstructing therapeutic efforts and make it clear exactly *how* and *what* they're resisting (Anderson & Stewart, 1983; Reich, 1949).

(5) **Transference.** As analysis continues, patients begin to experience **transference:** They project intense, unrealistic feelings and expectations from their past onto the therapist. The ambiguous figure of the analyst supposedly becomes the focus of emotions once directed at significant persons from the patient's childhood. In a classic example, a patient brought a gun into treatment and pointed it at the therapist. The therapist replied: "This is what I meant about your murderous feelings toward your father (Laughs). Do you see it now?" (Monroe, 1955). Freud believed that transference provides a vehicle for patients to understand their irrational expectations and demands of others, including the therapist.

Research suggests that we indeed often react to people in our present lives in ways similar to people in our pasts (Berk & Anderson, 2000; Luborsky et al., 1985). These findings may suggest that Freud was right about the transference; alternatively, they may mean that our stable personality traits (Chapter 14) lead us to react to people in similar ways over time. These lingering questions aside, therapists' interpretations of the transference can be helpful for some patients (Ogrodniczuk & Piper, 1999).

Ruling Out Rival Hypotheses

(6) **Working Through.** In the final stage of psychoanalysis, therapists help patients **work through,** or process, their problems. The insight gained in treatment is a helpful starting point, but it's not sufficient. As a consequence, therapists must repeatedly address conflicts and resistance to achieving healthy behavior patterns and help patients to confront old and ineffective coping responses as they reemerge in everyday life (Menninger, 1958; Wachtel, 1977).

Developments in Psychoanalysis: The Neo-Freudian Tradition. Freud's ideas spawned new schools and therapeutic approaches in the psychodynamic tradition (Baker, 1985). In contrast to Freudian therapists, neo-Freudian therapists are more concerned with conscious aspects of the patient's functioning. They also recognize the impact of cultural and interpersonal influences on behavior across the lifespan (Adler, 1938; Mitchell & Black, 1995). Beyond Freud's emphasis on sexuality and aggression, neo-Freudians acknowledge the impact of other powerful needs, including love, dependence, power, and status. They're also more optimistic than was Freud regarding peoples' prospects for achieving healthy psychological functioning (see Chapter 14).

Jung's Analytic Psychology. Carl Jung's knowledge of mythology and religion imparted depth and color to his thinking. According to Jung, the goal of psychotherapy is *individuation*—the integration of opposing aspects of the patient's personality into a harmonious "whole," namely, the self. Individuation is never complete, because it's a lifelong process. To help patients achieve individuation, Jung considered their aspirations and goals for the future, as well as their past experiences.

resistance
attempts to avoid confrontation and anxiety associated with uncovering previously repressed thoughts, emotions, and impulses

transference
projecting intense, unrealistic feelings and expectations from the past onto the therapist

work through
to confront and resolve problems, conflicts, and ineffective coping responses in everyday life

According to Jung, certain archetypal images and symbols can be appreciated by people across the ages and interpreted in therapy because they tap into the collective unconscious.

Falsifiability
Occam's Razor

To Freud's concept of the personal unconscious, Jung added the *collective unconscious.* As we learned in Chapter 14, this term refers to the memory traces (archetypes or preexistent forms) we inherit from our ancestors that all people supposedly share. Jung believed that drawing, writing and reading poetry, modeling in clay, and discussing fantasies and dreams all allow access to the collective unconscious. Nevertheless, research to date hasn't established the value of these techniques.

As in Freudian therapy, dream analysis is a key technique in Jungian therapy. Jungian dream analysis focuses on the dream material itself rather than relying on free association. In a process called *amplification,* therapists and patients expand on dream associations. Jungian therapists believe that a series of dreams may be one unit with a single message, and they may draw on fairy tales, myths, or legends to enrich their interpretations.

Jungians believe that *prognostic dreams* foretell the future and may warn dreamers of danger. In one account, Jung described how a patient dreamt of stepping off a high mountain into empty space. Jung warned the patient that this dream foreshadowed his death in a mountain accident. In fact, the patient later died when, according to an eyewitness, he "let go" of a rope "while climbing a mountain" (Jung, 1964).

Does this example demonstrate that dreams can reveal the future? In the dream, the man "stepped off the summit," but in reality he let go of a rope, which isn't the same thing. Perhaps Jung fell prey to confirmation bias (see Chapter 2) and selectively ignored facts that didn't fit his hypotheses. As we've learned, it's every bit as important to disconfirm our hunches as to find evidence in support of them. We can also generate more parsimonious hypotheses that don't rely on questionable phenomena, like ESP. The patient may have gotten the idea to jump from Jung's warning, or perhaps he was depressed and acted impulsively despite this warning.

Object Relations Therapists. *Object relations therapists* emphasize patients' mental representations of themselves and others and focus on patients' difficulties with trust, attachment, separation, and identity formation (Fairbairn, 1946; Gill, 1954; Klein, 1948; Sullivan, 1954; Winnicott, 1958). Therapists in this tradition include Otto Kernberg (1975) and Heinz Kohut (1971), who modified and extended psychoanalytic techniques to treat patients with serious personality problems, including borderline personality disorder (see Chapter 15).

The emphasis on interpersonal relationships is the hallmark of Harry Stack Sullivan's *interpersonal psychotherapy.* According to Sullivan (1954), psychotherapy is a collaborative undertaking between patient and therapist. Sullivan contended that the analyst's proper role is that of *participant observer.* Through her ongoing observation of the patient, the analyst discovers and communicates to the patient his unrealistic attitudes and behaviors in social situations and other arenas of everyday life.

Sullivan's work influenced the contemporary approach of **interpersonal therapy** (IPT). Originally a treatment for depression (Klerman, Weissman, Rounsaville, & Chevron, 1984; Santor & Kusumakar, 2001), IPT is a short-term (12–16 sessions) intervention designed to strengthen people's social skills and assist them in coping with interpersonal problems, conflicts (such as disputes with family members), and life transitions (such as childbirth and retirement). In addition to effectively treating depression (Klerman et al., 1984), IPT has demonstrated success in the treatment of substance abuse and eating disorders (Klerman & Weissman, 1993; Weissman, Markowitz, & Klerman, 2000).

Interpersonal therapy aims to resolve interpersonal problems and conflicts and to teach people social skills.

interpersonal therapy
treatment that strengthens social skills and targets interpersonal problems, conflicts, and life transitions

Replicability

Psychodynamic Therapies Evaluated Critically. Valuable as they've been, many psychodynamic therapies are questionable from a scientific standpoint. Freud and Jung based their therapeutic observations largely on small samples of wealthy, intelligent, and successful people, rendering their external validity (see Chapter 2) unclear. Their clinical sessions weren't observed by others or conducted on a systematic basis that permitted examination and replication by others, as would be the case with rigorously controlled research. Moreover, Freud's and Jung's patients relied on memories that stretched to the distant past. As we learned in Chapter 7, many early memories, especially those prompted by suggestive questions, are of questionable validity.

Is Insight Necessary? As we've seen, psychodynamic therapies rely heavily on insight. Many Hollywood films, like the 1997 movie *Good Will Hunting* and the 1999 movie *Analyze This,* reinforce the impression that insight—especially into the childhood origins of one's problems—is always the crucial ingredient in psychotherapeutic change. Yet extensive research demonstrates that understanding our emotional history, however deep and gratifying, isn't required to relieve psychological distress (Weisz, Donenberg, Han, & Weiss, 1995). To improve, patients typically need to practice new and more adaptive behaviors in everyday life—that is, to engage in what Freud called *working through* (Wachtel, 1977).

APPLY YOUR THINKING

In some cases, psychotherapy patients may acquire insights into their past that are convincing but incorrect. For example, they may mistakenly come to believe that their depression resulted from their father's lack of supportiveness of them in childhood. What are the potential dangers of such false insights?

Some psychodynamic concepts, including Freud's and Jung's therapeutic interpretations, are difficult to falsify (see Chapter 15). How can we demonstrate that a person's dream of his father scowling at him, for example, points to repressed memories of child abuse, as a therapist might infer? A patient might respond, "Aha, that's it!" but this reaction could reflect transference or an attempt to please the therapist. If the patient improves, the therapist might conclude that the interpretation is accurate, but the timing could be coincidental rather than causal (Grunbaum, 1984).

Falsifiability

Correlation vs. Causation

Ruling Out Rival Hypotheses

The failure to rule out rival hypotheses may lead both therapist and patient to mistakenly attribute progress to insight and interpretation when other influences are responsible (Meyer, 1981). Research supports this caution. In one long-term study of psychoanalytic treatment (Bachrach, Galatzer-Levy, Skolnikoff, & Waldron, 1991), half of forty-two patients improved but failed to show insight into their "core conflicts." Yet the support the therapist provided was more related to improvement than was insight.

Are Traumatic Memories Repressed? Although many psychodynamic therapists believe that current difficulties often stem from the repression of traumatic events, such as childhood abuse (Frederickson, 1992; Levis, 1995), research doesn't bear out this claim (Lynn, Knox, Fassler, Lilienfeld, & Loftus, 2004). Try this thought experiment. Which event would you be more likely to forget: An instance when your peers ridiculed you and beat you up after school for being the class know-it-all in the third grade, or a time when the teacher praised you in class for your participation? Odds are you thought you'd be better able to recall the unsettling event, and you'd be right. Disturbing or traumatic events are actually *more* memorable and *less* subject to forgetting than everyday occurrences (Loftus, 1993; Lynn et al., 2004; Porter, 2007). After reviewing the accumulated research evidence, Richard McNally (2003) concluded that the scientific support for repressed memories is weak. Nevertheless, the issue remains highly controversial (Anderson & Green, 2001; Bidell, 2006).

Research Evidence. The concerns we've raised aside, research indicates that brief versions of psychodynamic therapy are better than no treatment (Leichsenring, Rabung, & Liebling, 2004). Several meta-analyses (see Chapter 2) suggest that psychoanalytic treatment, though clearly helpful to many patients, may be somewhat less effective than cognitive-behavioral therapies, which don't emphasize insight (Grawe, Donati, & Bernauer, 1998; Shapiro & Shapiro, 1982). Moreover, psychodynamic therapy isn't especially effective for

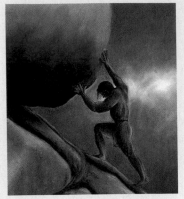

The twentieth-century French writer Albert Camus' classic essay "The Myth of Sisyphus" (based on a Greek myth) captures the essence of existentialism and existential therapy. Sisyphus was a king condemned by the Greek gods to repeatedly roll a huge boulder up a mountain for eternity. As he approached the top of the mountain, the boulder fell to the bottom, forcing Sisyphus to begin the task all over again. In Camus's essay, Sisyphus somehow finds meaning in this absurd process, looking forward to the fresh challenge of ascending the mountain each time.

According to Carl Rogers, when children receive unconditional positive regard from parents, they will develop unconditional self-regard, which promotes self-actualization.

humanistic-existential psychotherapy
therapies that share an emphasis on the development of human potential and the belief that human nature is basically positive

phenomenological approach
perspective in which therapists encounter patients in terms of subjective phenomena (thoughts, feelings) in the present moment

person-centered therapy
therapy centering on the patient's goals and ways of solving problems

Gestalt therapy
therapy that aims to integrate different and sometimes opposing aspects of personality into a unified sense of self

experiential therapies
interventions that recognize the importance of awareness, acceptance, and expression of feelings

logotherapy
therapeutic approach that helps people find meaning in their lives

psychotic disorders, like schizophrenia, even though some practitioners continue to use it for this purpose (Karon, 1994).

HUMANISTIC-EXISTENTIAL PSYCHOTHERAPY: ACHIEVING OUR POTENTIAL

Under the umbrella of **humanistic-existential psychotherapy,** we can find a variety of approaches. We'll look at three such approaches: Carl Rogers's person-centered therapy, Fritz Perls's Gestalt therapy, and Victor Frankl's logotherapy. These therapies are rooted in the humanistic perspective (Chapter 15). In contrast to psychodynamic therapies, therapies within this orientation share an emphasis on the realization of human potential and the belief that human nature is basically positive (Maslow, 1954; Rogers, 1961; Shlien & Levant, 1984).

Humanistic and existential therapists are more alike than different. They share a desire to help people overcome the sense of alienation so prevalent in our culture; to develop their sensory and emotional awareness; and to express their creativity and help them become loving, responsible, and authentic. Humanistic-existential psychotherapists stress the importance of assuming responsibility for decisions, not attributing our problems to the past, and living fully in the present.

Salvatore Maddi (1985) provided a useful distinction between humanistic and existential psychotherapies. He noted that humanistic therapists view self-actualization as a process that unfolds automatically unless roadblocks hamper it. In contrast, existential therapists contend that struggle, pain, and self-discipline inevitably occur along the long path toward personal fulfillment. According to Holocaust survivor Victor Frankl (1965) and other existentialist writers (Maddi, 1985; May, 1969; Schneider, Bugental, & Pierson, 2001), even when no other freedom remains, as when trapped in a concentration camp, we can still choose our own attitudes toward either despair or hope. Irwin Yalom (1980) further argued that confronting thoughts and feelings regarding isolation, meaninglessness, and death can be painful, yet lead to broadened awareness, self-acceptance, and an enhanced sense of control.

Although sharing an emphasis on insight with psychoanalytic therapists, humanistic-existential therapists reject their interpretive techniques. Instead, these therapists strive to understand the inner world of the patient through empathy and intuition. Their approach is a **phenomenological approach,** meaning that therapists encounter patients in terms of the subjective phenomena (thoughts, feelings) they experience in the present moment.

Person-Centered Therapy: Attaining Acceptance. No therapist better exemplifies the practice of humanistic-existential therapy than Carl Rogers (see Chapter 14). His therapy is *nondirective* because therapists don't define or diagnose patients' problems or try to get at the root cause of their difficulties. His approach is also called **person-centered therapy** because therapists don't tell patients how to solve their problems, and patients can use the therapy hour however they choose. Therapists assume that patients will reveal important emotional patterns as the therapist–patient dialogue unfolds (Rogers, 1942). To ensure a positive outcome, the therapist must satisfy three conditions:

(1) The therapist must be an authentic, genuine person who reveals his or her own reactions to what the patient is communicating.

   Patient: I think I'm beyond help.

   Therapist: Huh? Feel as though you're beyond help. I know. You feel just completely hopeless about yourself. I can understand that. I don't feel hopeless, but I realize you do" (Meador & Rogers, 1979, p. 157).

(2) The therapist must express *unconditional positive regard,* that is, a nonjudgmental acceptance of all feelings the patient expresses. Rogers was convinced that unconditional positive regard elicits a more positive self-concept in patients. Over the course of therapy, he maintained, it allows patients to reclaim aspects of their "true selves" that they disowned earlier in life due to others placing conditions of worth (see Chapter 15) on them.

(3) The therapist must relate to patients with empathic understanding. In Rogers's words: "To sense the patient's world as if it were our own, but without ever losing the 'as if' quality. This is empathy" (Rogers, 1957, p. 98).

One way to communicate empathy is by way of *reflection*, that is, mirroring back the patient's feelings—a technique for which Rogers was famous. Here's an example.

> **Patient:** I was small and I envied people who were large. I was—well, I took beatings by boys and I couldn't strike back. . . .
>
> **Therapist:** You've had plenty of experience in being the underdog. (Rogers, 1942, pp. 145–146)

With increased awareness and heightened self-acceptance, people hopefully come to think more realistically, become more tolerant of others, and engage in more adaptive behaviors (Rogers, 1961) (see **Table 16.3**).

Motivational Interviewing. Person-centered interviewing techniques, including warmth and empathy, reflective listening, unconditional acceptance, and avoiding confrontation, lie at the heart of *motivational interviewing* (Miller & Rollnick, 2002). This one- to two-session procedure recognizes that many patients are ambivalent about changing longstanding behaviors and is geared toward clarifying and bringing forth their reasons for changing—and not changing—their lives. Motivational interviewing, initially shown to have promise in treating alcohol-related problems (Project MATCH Research Group, 1997), has been successful in modifying a variety of health-related behaviors, including exercise and diet (Burke, Arkowitz, & Dunn, 2002; Burke, Arkowitz, & Menchola, 2003).

Gestalt Therapy: Becoming Whole. Fritz Perls, the flamboyant founder of **Gestalt therapy,** was trained as a psychodynamic therapist, but borrowed some of the concepts and terminology of his therapy directly from Gestalt psychology, a theory of perception we encountered in Chapter 4. The word *gestalt* (configuration) means an organized whole. Gestalt therapists believe that people with psychological difficulties are "incomplete gestalts" because they've excluded from their awareness experiences and aspects of their personalities that trigger anxiety. As a consequence, Gestalt therapists aim to integrate differing and sometimes opposing aspects of their patients' personalities into a unified sense of self.

For Gestalt therapists, the key to personal growth is accepting responsibility for one's feelings and maintaining contact with the here and now. Gestalt therapy was the first of many **experiential therapies,** so named because they recognize the importance of awareness, acceptance, and expression of feelings.

Gestalt and its therapeutic relatives, like emotion-focused therapy, which combines elements of person-centered, Gestalt, and existential approaches (Greenberg, 2002), are known for innovative techniques that promote self-awareness. In the *two-chair technique,* Gestalt therapists ask patients to move from chair to chair, creating a dialogue with two conflicting aspects of their personalities (see **Figure 16.1**). The "good boy" versus the "spoiled brat" may serve as the focal point for the two-chair technique. Gestalt therapists believe that this procedure allows a synthesis of the two opposing sides to emerge. For example, the good boy, always eager to please others, may learn from an interchange with the spoiled brat that it's acceptable in certain instances to be assertive, even demanding. Thus, the "good brat" may be more effective and authentic than either personality aspect alone.

Logotherapy: The Search for Meaning. Victor Frankl named his therapeutic approach **logotherapy,** meaning "therapy through meaning." Out of the horrific suffering he experienced in Nazi concentration camps, Frankl came to believe that human beings could preserve spiritual freedom and independence of mind even under the worst conditions imaginable (Frankl, 1965). This freedom makes life meaningful in all situations and lends

Table 16.3 Simulated Conversation between Client and Computer Therapist, Eliza. Some researchers have developed computer programs that attempt to simulate Rogers' person-centered therapy, especially Rogers' method of reflection. Here, we can read excerpts from a conversation between a patient and the computer therapist, Eliza, developed by computer scientist Joseph Weizenbaum. Would Eliza make a good therapist?

Client: Men are all alike.

Eliza: IN WHAT WAY?

Client: They're always bugging us about something or other.

Eliza: CAN YOU THINK OF A SPECIFIC EXAMPLE?

Client: Well, my boyfriend made me come here.

Eliza: YOUR BOYFRIEND MADE YOU COME HERE?

Client: He says I'm depressed much of the time.

Eliza: I AM SORRY TO HEAR YOU ARE DEPRESSED.

Client: It's true. I am unhappy.

Eliza: DO YOU THINK COMING HERE WILL HELP YOU NOT TO BE UNHAPPY?

Client: I need some help, that much seems certain.

Eliza: WHAT WOULD IT MEAN TO YOU IF YOU GOT SOME HELP?

Client: Perhaps I could learn to get along with my mother.

Eliza: TELL ME MORE ABOUT YOUR FAMILY.

Client: My mother takes care of me.

Eliza: WHO ELSE IN YOUR FAMILY TAKES CARE OF YOU?

Client: My father.

Eliza: YOUR FATHER?

Client: You are like my father in some ways.

Eliza: WHAT RESEMBLANCE DO YOU SEE?

(*Source:* http://i5.nyu.edu/~mm64/x52.9265/january1966.htm/; Weizenbaum)

Figure 16.1 The Two-Chair Technique. Gestalt therapy's two-chair technique aims to integrate opposing aspects of the client's personality, such as the "good boy" and the "spoiled brat."

significance to our psychological pain and to inevitable confrontation with death. According to Frankl, patients can discover the meaning of their lives in encounters with a therapist who discourages them from blaming past circumstances, other people, and adverse situations for their difficulties.

Humanistic-Existential Therapies Evaluated Critically. The core concepts of humanistic-existential therapy, such as meaning and self-actualization, are difficult to measure and falsify. For example, at exactly what point can we say a person is self-aware and authentic?

Falsifiability

Much to his credit, Rogers specified three key conditions for effective psychotherapy that could be falsified. Research has shown that he was largely on the mark when it comes to the therapeutic relationship. Establishing a strong alliance is extremely helpful to the ultimate success of therapy (Horvath & Bedi, 2002; Wampold, 2001). In fact, the therapeutic relationship is typically a stronger predictor of success in therapy than the use of specific techniques (Bohart, Elliott, Greenberg, & Watson, 2002). But Rogers was wrong in one key respect: The three core conditions he specified aren't "necessary and sufficient" for improvement (Bohart, 2003; Norcross & Beutler, 1997). Although he overstated their impact, empathy (Bohart et al., 2002) and positive regard (Farber & Lane, 2002) are modestly related to therapy outcome (Orlinsky & Howard, 1986). Some studies have revealed a positive relation between genuineness and therapeutic outcome, but others haven't (Klein, Kolden, Michels, & Chisholm-Stockard, 2002; Orlinsky, Grawe, & Parks, 1994). Moreover, we'll learn later in the chapter that some people can derive considerable benefits from self-help programs that don't even involve therapists (Gould & Clum, 1993), so the therapeutic relationship isn't necessary for improvement.

Choruses and orchestras provide illustrations of the Gestalt psychology principle that "the whole is greater than the sum of its parts."

Person-centered therapy is more effective than no treatment (Greenberg, Elliot, & Lietaer, 1994) and is particularly popular in college counseling centers (Champney & Schultz, 1983). But findings concerning the effectiveness of person-centered therapy are inconsistent, with some suggesting it may not help much more than a placebo treatment, such as merely chatting for the same amount of time with a nonprofessional (Smith, Glass, & Miller, 1980). In contrast, other studies suggest that person-centered therapies and experiential approaches often result in substantial gains in many patients and may be comparable in effectiveness to the cognitive-behavioral therapies we'll encounter later (Elliott, 2002; Greenberg & Watson, 1998).

Much of the evidence for existential therapies comes from clinical anecdotes and case studies (Binswanger, 1958; Bugenthal, 1976; May, 1983; Yalom, 1980). Therefore, we can only speculate about their long-term effectiveness and how they compare with other approaches.

Consistent with the assumptions of humanistic-existential therapies, research suggests that by avoiding and suppressing disturbing feelings rather than accepting and coping with them, difficulties can blossom (Amir, Coles, Brigidi, & Foa, 2001; Hayes, Strosahl, & Wilson, 1999; Teasdale, Segal, & Williams, 2003). Perhaps because it helps to reverse these unhealthy tendencies, emotion-focused therapy achieves gains comparable with cognitive-behavioral therapy (Elliott & Greenberg, 2002; Watson, Gordon, Stermac, Steckley, & Kalogerakos, 2003).

ASSESS YOUR KNOWLEDGE: FACT OR FICTION?

(1) Free association is the fundamental rule of Jungian therapy. (True/False)

(2) An important criticism of psychoanalytic therapy is that many of its key concepts aren't falsifiable. (True/False)

(3) Reflection is a central component of Rogers's therapy. (True/False)

(4) According to Gestalt psychotherapy, people can often benefit from avoiding or denying experiences they can't change. (True/False)

(5) Evidence of the effectiveness of existential therapies derives largely from clinical anecdotes and case studies. (True/False)

Answers: (1) F (p. 676); (2) T (p. 678); (3) T (p. 681); (4) F (p. 681); (5) T (p. 682)

Behavioral Approaches: Changing Maladaptive Actions

In sharp contrast to psychotherapists who hold that insight is curative, **behavior therapists** are so named because they focus on the specific behaviors that lead the patient to seek therapy and the current variables that maintain problematic thoughts, feelings, and behaviors (Antony & Roemer, 2003).

The results of behavior therapy are subject to verification, with success defined as measurable improvement in target behaviors, like angry outbursts, checking compulsions (see Chapter 15), or suicidal gestures. Behavior therapists assume that behavior change, whether in the clinic, family, or school, results from the operation of basic principles of learning discovered in the laboratory, especially classical conditioning, operant conditioning, and observational learning (see Chapter 6).

THE PHASES OF BEHAVIOR THERAPY

Assessment is crucial to the scientific enterprise of behavior therapy. Behavior therapists use a wide variety of *behavioral assessment* techniques to pinpoint environmental causes of the person's problem, establish specific and measurable treatment goals, and devise therapeutic procedures. The emphasis is on current, rather than past, behaviors and on specific behaviors, rather than broad traits. Behavior therapists may use verbal descriptions of the nature and dimensions of the problem, scores on paper-and-pencil measures, standardized interviews (First, Spitzer, Gibbon, & Williams, 1996), and measures of physiological processes (Yartz & Hawk, 2001) to plan treatment and monitor its progress. A complete assessment considers patients' gender, race, socioeconomic class, culture, sexual orientation, and ethnic factors (Ivey, Ivey, & Simek-Morgan, 1993), as well as information about their interpersonal relationships and drug use (Lazarus, 2003).

Behavior therapists use the tools of behavioral assessment to perform a *functional analysis.* A functional analysis rests on a core assumption: The patient's problematic behaviors, such as crossing the street whenever he sees a dog in the case of someone with a dog phobia, are maintained by reinforcement (see Chapter 6). That is, these behaviors serve a function for the person in that they help him to obtain reinforcement—in this case, escaping anxiety—although the person is often unaware of this function. When conducting a functional analysis, therapists determine the antecedents of (what came before) the problem, its nature and severity, and its consequences, such as avoidance of distressing situations.

Behavior therapy typically proceeds by first identifying and assessing the problem, establishing behavioral objectives and designing a behavior change strategy, and then implementing the strategy. Evaluation of treatment effectiveness is seamlessly integrated into all phases of behavior therapy. Behavior therapists also encourage patients to apply their newly acquired coping skills to everyday life. Let's now examine the nuts and bolts of several behavioral approaches.

SYSTEMATIC DESENSITIZATION AND EXPOSURE THERAPIES: LEARNING PRINCIPLES IN ACTION

Systematic desensitization is an excellent example of how behavior therapists apply learning principles to treatment. Psychiatrist Joseph Wolpe developed systematic desensitization (SD) in 1958 to help patients manage phobias (see Chapter 2). Systematic desensitization gradually exposes patients to anxiety-producing situations through the use of imagined scenes. Systematic desensitization was the earliest **exposure therapy,** a term that refers to a class of procedures that confronts patients with what they fear with the goal of reducing this fear.

A behavior therapist performing a functional analysis on a bad habit, like nail-biting, would try to determine the situations in which nail-biting occurs, as well as the consequences of nail-biting for the person–such as short-term distraction from anxiety.

behavior therapists
therapist who focuses on specific problem behaviors, and current variables that maintain problematic thoughts, feelings, and behaviors

systematic desensitization
patients are taught to relax as they are gradually exposed to what they fear in a stepwise manner

exposure therapy
therapy that confronts patients with what they fear with the goal of reducing the fear

Table 16.4 A Systematic Desensitization Hierarchy of a Person with a Fear of Heights.

1. You are beginning to climb the ladder leaning against the side of your house. You plan to work on the roof.

2. You are driving with the family on a California coastal highway with a dropoff to the right.

3. You are in a commercial airliner at the time of takeoff.

4. You are in an airliner at an altitude of 30,000 feet experiencing considerable turbulence.

5. You are on a California seaside cliff, approximately two feet (judged to be a safe distance) from the edge and looking down.

6. You are climbing the water tower to assist in painting, about 10 feet from the ground.

7. You are on the catwalk around the water tank, painting the tank.

(*Source:* Rimm & Masters, 1979)

In vivo desensitization: Clients gradually approach and handle any fears, as these clients are doing as they overcome their fear of flying.

Ruling Out Rival Hypotheses

Ruling Out Rival Hypotheses

dismantling
research procedure for examining the effectiveness of isolated components of a larger treatment

How Desensitization Works: One Step at a Time. Systematic desensitization is based on the principle of *reciprocal inhibition,* which says that patients can't experience two conflicting responses simultaneously. We can't be anxious and relaxed at the same time because relaxation inhibits anxiety. Wolpe described his technique as a form of classical conditioning and called it *counterconditioning.* By pairing an incompatible relaxation response with anxiety, we condition a new and more adaptive response to anxiety-arousing stimuli.

A therapist begins systematic desensitization by teaching the patient how to relax. She might imagine pleasant scenes, focus on breathing and maintaining a slow breathing rate, and alternately tense and relax her muscles (Bernstein, Borkovec, & Hazlett-Stevens, 2000; Jacobson, 1938). Next, the therapist helps the patient to construct an *anxiety hierarchy*—a "ladder" of situations or scenes that climb from least to most anxiety provoking. We can find a hierarchy used to treat a person with height phobia in **Table 16.4.** The therapy proceeds in a stepwise manner. The therapist asks the patient to relax and imagine the first scene, and moves to the next, more anxiety-producing scene only after the patient reports feeling relaxed while imagining the first scene.

Consider the following example of how a patient moves stepwise up the anxiety hierarchy, from the least to most anxiety-producing scene.

Therapist: "Soon I shall ask you to imagine a scene. After you hear a description of the situation, please imagine it as vividly as you can, through your own eyes, as if you were actually there. Try to include all the details in the scene. While you're visualizing the situation, you may continue feeling as relaxed as you are now . . . After 5, 10, or 15 seconds, I'll ask you to stop imagining the scene . . . and to just relax. But if you begin to feel even the slightest increase in anxiety or tension, please signal this to me by raising your left forefinger . . . I'll step in and ask you to stop imagining the situation and then will help you get relaxed once more." (Goldfried & Davison, 1976, pp. 124–125)

If the patient reports anxiety at any point, the therapist interrupts the process and helps the patient relax again. Then, the therapist reintroduces the scene that preceded the one that caused anxiety. This process continues until the patient can confront the most frightening scenes without anxiety.

Desensitization can also occur *in vivo,* that is, in "real life." In vivo systematic desensitization involves real-life, gradual exposure to what the patient actually fears, rather than imagining the anxiety-provoking situation. Systematic desensitization is effective for a wide range of phobias, insomnia, speech disorders, asthma attacks, nightmares, and some cases of problem drinking (Spiegler & Guevremont, 2003).

Dismantling Desensitization. Behavior therapists strive to discover not only what works, but why. Researchers can evaluate many therapeutic procedures by isolating the effects of each component and comparing these effects with that of the full treatment package (Wilson & O' Leary, 1980). This approach is called **dismantling,** because it enables researchers to examine the effectiveness of isolated components of a larger treatment. Dismantling helps rule out rival hypotheses about the effective mechanisms of systematic desensitization and other treatments.

Dismantling studies show that no single component of desensitization (relaxation, imagery, an anxiety hierarchy) is essential: Each can be eliminated without affecting treatment outcome. Therefore, the door is open to diverse interpretations for the treatment's success (Kazdin & Wilcoxon, 1976; Lohr, DeMaio, & McGlynn, 2003). One possibility is that the impressive, highly credible treatment creates a strong placebo effect (see Chapter 2; Mineka & Thomas, 1999). Interestingly, desensitization may fare no better than a placebo procedure designed to arouse an equivalent degree of positive expectations (Lick, 1975). Alternatively, when therapists expose patients to what they fear, patients may realize their fears are irrational, or their fear response may extinguish (see Chapter 6) following repeated uneventful contact with the feared stimulus (Casey, Oei, & Newcombe, 2004; Rachman, 1994; Zinbarg, 1993).

Flooding and Virtual Reality Exposure. Flooding therapies provide a vivid contrast to systematic desensitization. Flooding therapists jump right to the top of the anxiety hierarchy and expose patients to images of the stimuli they fear the most for prolonged periods, ranging from 10 minutes to several hours. Flooding therapies are based on the idea that fears are maintained by avoidance. For example, because height phobics continually avoid high places, they never learn that the disastrous consequences they envision won't occur. Ironically, their avoidance only reinforces their fears by means of negative reinforcement (see Chapter 6). The flooding therapist provokes anxiety repeatedly in the absence of actual negative consequences, so that extinction of the fear can proceed.

Implosive therapy is a flooding procedure that borrows concepts from psychodynamic therapy. As such, it's an unusual blend of behavioral and psychoanalytic techniques. Implosive therapists believe that unconscious repressed memories and conflicts contribute to anxiety (Stampfl & Levis, 1967). As such, an implosive therapist might ask patients to imagine scenes containing imagery associated with early conflicts with parents, aggression, sex, and death. The therapist repeatedly recounts anxiety-producing scenes until the patient no longer reports fear.

An implosive therapy patient who's afraid of spiders might imagine herself in a room filled with huge spiders surrounding her on every wall.

Like systematic desensitization, flooding can also be conducted in vivo. To paraphrase the Nike slogan ("Just do it"): "If you're afraid to do it, do it!" (Chambless & Goldstein, 1980). During the very first session, a therapist who practices in vivo flooding might accompany a height phobic to the top of a skyscraper and look down for an hour, or however long it takes for anxiety to dissipate. Remarkably, many people with specific phobias—including those who were in psychodynamic therapy for decades with no relief—have been essentially cured of their fears after only a single session (Antony & Barlow, 2002; Williams, Turner, & Peer, 1985). Therapists have used flooding with success in treating numerous anxiety disorders, including obsessive-compulsive disorder, social phobia, posttraumatic stress disorder, and agoraphobia.

A crucial component of flooding is **response prevention,** in which therapists prevent patients from performing their typical avoidance behaviors (Spiegler, 1983). A therapist may treat a person with a hand-washing compulsion by exposing her to dirt and preventing her from washing her hands (Franklin & Foa, 2002). Some therapists have also applied exposure plus response prevention to patients with bulimia (see Chapter 15) by having them eat large amounts of food, but preventing them from purging, exercising, or otherwise trying to lose weight. Research on the effectiveness of this approach is mixed (Carter, McIntosh, Joyce, Sullivan, & Bulik, 2003).

In Chapter 12, we crossed paths with virtual reality exposure, the new kid on the block of exposure therapies. With high-tech equipment, which provides a "virtually lifelike" experience of fear-provoking situations, therapists can treat many anxiety-related conditions, including height phobia (Emmelkamp, Bruynzeel, Drost, & van der Mast, 2001), storm phobia (Botella et al., 2006), flying phobia (Emmelkamp et al., 2002), and posttraumatic stress disorder (Rothbaum, Hodges, Ready, Graap, & Alarcon, 2001). Virtual reality exposure not only rivals the effectiveness of traditional in vivo exposure, but provides repeated exposure to situations that often aren't feasible in real life, like flying in airplanes.

Exposure: Fringe and Fad Techniques. Traditionally, behavior therapists have been careful not to inflate claims of the effectiveness of exposure therapy and present it to the public as a cure-all. We can contrast this cautious approach with that of recent proponents of fringe therapeutic techniques who've made extraordinary claims that don't stack up well against the evidence.

Roger Callahan, who developed *Thought Field Therapy* (TFT), claimed that his procedure can cure phobias in as little as 5 minutes (Callahan, 1995, 2001) and cure not only human fears, but also fears of horses and dogs. In TFT, the patient thinks of a distressing problem while the therapist taps specific points on her body in a predetermined order. Meanwhile, the patient hums parts of "The Star Spangled Banner," rolls her eyes, or counts (how TFT

Extraordinary Claims

response prevention
technique in which therapists prevent patients from performing their typical avoidance behaviors

therapists accomplish this feat with animals is unknown). These decidedly strange procedures supposedly remove invisible "energy blocks" associated with a specific fear. There's no research evidence for the extraordinary assertion that the technique cures anxiety by manipulating energy fields, which have never been shown to exist, or for the incredible claim of virtually instantaneous cures for the vast majority of phobia sufferers (Lohr, Gist, & Hooke, 2003). Because the "energy blocks" of TFT are not measurable, the theoretical claims of TFT are unfalsifiable.

Some other exposure-based therapies feature numerous "bells and whistles" that provide them with the superficial veneer of science. Take *eye movement desensitization and reprocessing* (EMDR), which has been marketed widely as a "breakthrough" treatment for anxiety disorders (Shapiro, 1995; Shapiro & Forrest, 1997). As of 2007, more than 70,000 therapists have been trained in EMDR. EMDR proponents claim that patients' lateral eye movements, made while they imagine a past traumatic event, enhance their processing of painful memories. Yet dismantling studies and meta-analyses demonstrate that the eye movements of EMDR play no role in this treatment's effectiveness. Moreover, EMDR is no more effective than standard exposure treatments (Davidson & Parker, 2001; Lohr, Tolin, & Lilienfeld, 1998). Accordingly, a parsimonious hypothesis is that the active ingredient of EMDR isn't the eye movements for which it's named, but rather the exposure the technique provides.

Falsifiability

Occam's Razor

MODELING IN THERAPY: LEARNING BY WATCHING

Patients can learn many things by observing therapists model positive behaviors. Modeling is one form of *observational or vicarious learning* (see Chapters 6 and 14). Albert Bandura (1971, 1977) has long advocated **participant modeling,** a technique in which the therapist first models a calm encounter with the patient's feared object or situation, and then guides the patient through the steps of the encounter until she can cope unassisted.

Assertion Training. Modeling is an important component of assertion and social skills training programs designed to help patients with social anxiety. The primary goals of assertion training are to facilitate the expression of thoughts and feelings in a forthright and socially appropriate manner and to ensure that patients aren't taken advantage of, ignored, or denied their legitimate rights (Alberti & Emmons, 2001; Delamater & McNamara, 1986). In assertion training, therapists teach patients to avoid extreme reactions to others' unreasonable demands, such as submissiveness, on the one hand, and aggressiveness, on the other. Assertiveness, the middle ground between these extremes, is the goal.

Behavioral Rehearsal. Behavioral rehearsal is used commonly in assertion training and other participant modeling techniques. In behavioral rehearsal, the patient engages in role-playing with a therapist to learn and practice new skills. The therapist plays the role of a relevant person such as a spouse, parent, or boss. The patient reacts to the character enacted by the therapist, and in return the therapist offers coaching and feedback. To give the patient an opportunity to model assertive behaviors, therapist and patient reverse roles, with the therapist playing the patient's role. In doing so, the therapist models not only what the patient might say, but how the patient might say it.

To transfer what patients learn to everyday life, therapists encourage them to practice their newly found skills outside of therapy sessions. Modeling and social skills training can make valuable contributions to treating (although not curing) schizophrenia, depression, and social anxiety (Antony & Roemer, 2003; Dilk & Bond, 1996). Therapists also use modeling to teach patients communication skills and problem-solving strategies in *behavioral marital therapy,* an approach that's more effective than no treatment (Dunn & Schwebel, 1995; Hahlweg & Markman, 1988; Shadish & Baldwin, 2005).

Thought Field Therapists claim that touching of body parts in a set order can play a role in treating longstanding phobias resistant to treatment by other means.

In EMDR, the patient focuses on the therapist's fingers as they move back and forth. Nevertheless, studies indicate that such eye movements play no useful role in EMDR's effectiveness.

participant modeling
technique in which the therapist first models a problematic situation and then guides the patient through steps to cope with it unassisted

OPERANT PROCEDURES: CONSEQUENCES COUNT

The **token economy** (see Chapter 6) demonstrates how therapists have applied the principles of operant conditioning to treatment programs in institutional and residential settings, as well as the home. As we'll recall, operant procedures modify behaviors based on their consequences. One of the essential features of token economies is that certain behaviors, like helping others, are consistently rewarded with tokens that patients can later exchange for more tangible rewards, whereas other behaviors, like screaming at hospital staff, are ignored or punished. In this way, token economy programs shape, maintain, or alter behaviors by the consistent application of operant conditioning principles (Kazdin, 1978). Token economies have proven successful in the classroom (Bonelsi & Moore, 2003), in treating children with ADHD at home and at school (Mueser & Lieberman, 1995), and in treating patients with schizophrenia in hospitals (Glynn & Mueser, 1992; McMonagle & Sultana, 2000; Paul & Lentz, 1977).

Aversion therapies use punishment to decrease the frequency of undesirable behaviors. Aversion therapies are aptly named. While a person engages in a problem behavior, therapists introduce a wide range of simuli that most people experience as painful, distasteful, unpleasant, or even revolting. For example, therapists have used medications, such as disulfiram—better known as Antabuse—to make people vomit after drinking alcohol (Brewer, 1992), electric shocks to treat psychologically triggered recurrent sneezing (Kushner, 1968), and verbal descriptions of feeling nauseous while people imagine smoking cigarettes (Cautela, 1971).

Research provides at best mixed support for the effectiveness of aversive procedures (Spiegler & Geuvremont, 2003). For example, alcohol abusers often prefer to stop taking Antabuse rather than stop drinking (MacKillop, Lisman, Weinstein, & Rosenbaum, 2003). In general, therapists attempt minimally unpleasant techniques before moving on to more aversive measures. The decision to implement aversion methods should be made only after carefully weighing the costs and benefits of these methods relative to alternative approaches.

COGNITIVE-BEHAVIORAL THERAPIES: LEARNING TO THINK DIFFERENTLY

Advocates of **cognitive-behavioral therapies** hold that beliefs play the central role in our feelings and behaviors. For them, irrational thinking lies at the root of psychopathology. These therapies share the following core assumptions: (1) cognitions can be identified and measured, (2) cognitions are the key players in both healthy and unhealthy psychological functioning, and (3) irrational beliefs, such as "I'm worthless," can be replaced by more rational and adaptive cognitions.

The ABCs of Rational Emotive Behavior Therapy.

Beginning in the mid-1950s, pioneering therapist Albert Ellis (Ellis, 1958, 1962) advocated *rational emotive therapy* (RET), more recently renamed *rational emotive behavior therapy* (REBT). In many respects, REBT is a prime example of a cognitive-behavioral approach. It's cognitive in its emphasis on changing how we think (that's the "cognitive" part), but it also focuses on changing how we act (that's the "behavioral" part).

Ellis argued that we respond to an unpleasant activating (internal or external) event (A) with a range of emotional and behavioral consequences (C). As we all know, people often respond very differently to the same objective events: some students respond to an A— in a course by celebrating, whereas others respond by berating themselves for not getting an A. The crucial differences in how we respond to the same objective events stem largely from differences in (B)—our belief systems. The ABCs Ellis identified lie at the heart of most, if not all, cognitive-behavior therapies.

Some beliefs are rational: They're flexible, logical, and promote self-acceptance. In contrast, irrational beliefs are associated with unrealistic demands about the self ("I must be perfect"), other people ("I must become worried about other people's problems"), and life

---

LOVE ME, LOVE ME, ONLY ME!

Love me, love me, only me
Or I'll die without you!
Make your love a guarantee,
So I can never doubt you!
Love me, love me totally
Really, really try dear.
But if you demand love, too,
I'll hate you till I die, dear!
Love me, love me all the time,
Thoroughly and wholly!
Life turns into slushy slime
Less you love me solely!
Love me with great tenderness,
With no ifs or buts dear.
If you love me somewhat less,
I'll really hate your guts, dear!

Albert Ellis wrote a number of humorous song lyrics to demonstrate REBT principles (Ellis even recorded them commercially, although it's unlikely that he'd make it to the finals of *American Idol*). This song, set to the tune of Yankee Doodle, pokes fun at the widespread but irrational belief that all romantic relationships should be characterized by promises of complete, unconditional, and never-ending love. (Adapted from "Love Me, Love Me, Only Me!" by Albert Ellis. Reprinted with permission of Albert Ellis Institute)

token economy
method in which desirable behaviors are rewarded with tokens that patients can exchange for tangible rewards

aversion therapy
treatment that uses punishment to decrease the frequency of undesirable behaviors

cognitive-behavior therapy
treatment that attempts to replace maladaptive or irrational cognitions with more adaptive, rational cognitions

Table 16.5 Irrational Beliefs: "The Dirty Dozen." Albert Ellis identified twelve irrational ideas ("The Dirty Dozen") that are widespread in our culture. You may find it interesting to see which of these beliefs you've entertained at some point in your life. Because these ideas are so much a part of many people's thinking, don't be surprised if you hold a number of them.

1. The idea that you must have sincere love and approval almost all the time from all the people you find significant.

2. The idea that you must prove yourself thoroughly competent, adequate, and achieving; or that you must at least have real competence or talent at something important.

3. The idea that people who harm you or commit misdeeds rate as generally bad, wicked, or villainous individuals, and that you should severely blame, damn, and punish them for their sins.

4. The idea that life proves awful, terrible, horrible, or catastrophic when things do not go the way you would like them to go.

5. The idea that emotional misery comes from external pressures and that you have little ability to control your feelings or rid yourself of depression and hostility.

6. The idea that if something seems dangerous or fearsome, you must become terribly occupied with and upset about it.

7. The idea that you will find it easier to avoid facing many of life's difficulties and self-responsibilities than to undertake some rewarding forms of self-discipline.

8. The idea that your past remains all-important and that, because something once strongly influenced your life, it has to keep determining your feelings and behavior today.

9. The idea that people and things should turn out better than they do; and that you have to view it as awful and horrible if you do not quickly find good solutions to life's hassles.

10. The idea that you can achieve happiness by inaction or by passively and uncommitedly "enjoying yourself."

11. The idea that you must have a high degree of order or certainty to feel comfortable.

12. The idea that you give yourself a global rating as a human and that your general worth and self-acceptance depends on the goodness of your performance and the degree that people approve of you.

(*Source:* Ellis, 1977)

---

conditions ("I must be worried about things I can't control."). Ellis also maintained that psychologically unhealthy people frequently "awfulize," that is, engage in catastrophic thinking about their problems ("If I don't get this job, it would be the worst thing that ever happened to me"). We can find examples of twelve irrational beliefs outlined by Ellis in **Table 16.5.** According to Ellis, our vulnerability to psychological disturbance is a product of the frequency and strength of our irrational beliefs.

To his ABC scheme, Ellis added a (D) and an (E) component to describe how therapists treat patients. REBT therapists encourage patients to actively dispute (D) their irrational beliefs and adopt more effective (E) and rational beliefs to increase adaptive responses. To modify patients' irrational beliefs, the therapist actively tries to encourage and persuade them to rethink their assumptions and personal philosophy. REBT therapists may assign "homework" designed to falsify clients' maladaptive beliefs. For example, they may give shy patients an assignment to talk to an attractive man or woman in the hopes of falsifying the patient's belief that "If I'm rejected by someone I like, it will be absolutely terrible."

Falsifiability

Other Cognitive-Behavioral Approaches. Cognitive-behavioral therapists differ in the extent to which they incorporate behavioral methods. Aaron Beck's (Beck, Rush, Shaw, & Emery, 1979) enormously popular *cognitive therapy*, which many credit as playing an instrumental role in creating the field of cognitive-behavioral therapy, emphasizes identifying and modifying distorted thoughts and long-held negative core beliefs ("I'm unlovable") (J. Beck, 1995). Nevertheless, cognitive therapy places somewhat greater weight on behavioral procedures than does Ellis's REBT (Stricker & Gold, 2003). Researchers have found Beck's approach helpful for people with depression and perhaps even bipolar disorder and schizophrenia (A. T. Beck, 2005; Hollon, Thase, & Markowitz, 2002).

In Donald Meichenbaum's (1985) *stress inoculation training*, therapists teach patients to prepare for and cope with future stressful life events. In this approach, therapists "inoculate" patients against an upcoming stressor by getting them to anticipate it and develop cognitive skills to minimize its harm, much as we receive a vaccine (inocu-

Two pioneers of cognitive-behavioral therapy, Aaron Beck (*left;* 1921–   ) and Albert Ellis (1913–2007).

lation) containing a small amount of a virus to ward off illness. Therapists modify patients' *self-statements*, that is, their ongoing mental dialogue (Meichenbaum, 1985). For example, patients fearful of giving a speech may learn to say things to themselves like, "Even though it's scary, the outcome probably won't be as bad as I fear." Therapists have successfully applied stress inoculation to children and adults facing medical and surgical procedures, public speaking, and exams (Meichenbaum, 1996), as well as to clients having difficulty controlling their tempers (Cahill, Rauch, Hembree, & Foa, 2003; Novaco, 1995).

The Effectiveness of CBT. Research allows us to draw the following conclusions about the effectiveness of behavioral and cognitive-behavioral therapies: (1) They're more effective than no treatment or placebo treatment (Bowers & Clum, 1988; Smith, Glass, & Miller, 1980); (2) they're at least as effective (Sloane, Staples, Cristal, Yorkston, & Whipple, 1975; Smith & Glass, 1977), and in some cases more effective, than psychodynamic and person-centered therapies (Grawe, Donati, & Bernauer, 1998); (3) therapists can combine them effectively with other forms of treatment, such as drug therapy and marital counseling (Hahlweg & Markman, 1988; MTA Cooperative Group, 1999); and (4) they're at least as effective as drug therapies for depression (Elkin, 1994). In general, CBT and behavioral treatments are about equally effective for most problems (Feske & Chambless, 1995; Jacobson et al., 1996).

THE TREND TOWARD ECLECTICISM AND INTEGRATION

One of the current trends in psychotherapy is for therapists to create individually tailored, *eclectic* approaches—treatments that integrate techniques and theories from many existing therapy approaches (Garske & Anderson, 2003; Lazarus, 2006; Stricker & Gold, 2003). As we can see in **Table 16.6,** the largest percentage of therapists describes their theoretical orientation as eclectic/integrative, with significant percentages describing themselves as behavioral, cognitive, and psychodynamic (Norcross, 2005; Prochaska & Norcross, 2007).

Table 16.6 Primary Theoretical Orientations of Psychotherapists in the United States. As we can see, the largest proportion of therapists calls themselves eclectic/integrative.

Orientation	Clinical Psychologists (%)	Counseling Psychologists (%)	Psychiatrists (%)	Social Workers (%)	Counselors (%)
Behavioral	10	4	1	4	6
Cognitive	28	26	1	4	10
Eclectic/Integrative	29	29	53	34	37
Existential-Humanistic	1	6	1	3	13
Gestalt	1	1	1	1	2
Interpersonal	4	7	3	1	1
Psychoanalytic	3	2	16	11	3
Psychodynamic	12	13	19	22	8
Person-Centered	1	4	0	2	8
Family Systems	3	4	1	13	7
Other	7	5	4	5	5

(*Sources:* Prochaska & Norcross, 2007; derived from Bechtold, Norcross, Wyckoff, Pokrywa, & Campbell, 2001; Norcross, Karpiak, & Santoro, 2005; Norcross, Strausser, & Missar, 1988)

factoid

There's at least some evidence that therapists' theoretical orientation is correlated with their personality traits. Several, although not all, studies suggest that compared with other therapists, psychoanalytic therapists tend to be especially insecure and serious, behavior therapists tend to be especially assertive and self-confident, and cognitive-behavioral therapists tend to be especially rational (Keinan, Almagor, & Ben-Porath, 1989; Walton, 1978).

According to Paul Wachtel's theory of vicious circles, paranoid behavior—like that displayed in this personal ad—can lead other people to become suspicious and wary of the paranoid person, in turn reinforcing the person's paranoid behavior, and so on.

Ruling Out Rival Hypotheses

Paul Wachtel (1977) was among the first to cross-pollinate theories and techniques from diverse approaches. Originally a psychoanalytic therapist, he became convinced that insight alone isn't sufficient for therapeutic change and began to integrate behavioral techniques into his therapy. He maintained that patients' conflicts and anxieties are byproducts of vicious circles that begin early in life but repeat themselves into the present. Consider a man who's shy and displays an undercurrent of hostility in the analyst's office. According to Wachtel (1977), his hostility reflects the fact that his passivity invites others to ignore or discount him. No wonder he's angry! Because his anger creates anxiety and fears of rejection, he covers it up by acting even more passively, completing the vicious cycle. For this reason, Wachtel (1977) called his therapeutic approach *cyclical psychodynamic therapy*. The good news is that therapists can break this cycle by helping the patient acquire social skills and appropriate assertiveness.

Marsha Linehan's (Linehan, 1993; Linehan & Schmidt, 1995) *dialectical behavior therapy*, used frequently in the treatment of borderline personality disordered patients at risk for suicide, and Steven Hayes's (Hayes, Strosahl, & Wilson, 1999) *acceptance and commitment therapy*, incorporate techniques from a wide variety of approaches. Dialectical behavior therapy addresses the *dialectic*—the apparent contradiction between opposing tendencies— of changing problematic behavior and accepting it (Prochaska & Norcross, 2007). Linehan encourages patients to accept their intense emotions while actively attempting to cope with these emotions by making changes in their lives. Similarly, acceptance and commitment therapy assists patients with establishing contact with and accepting thoughts, feelings, memories, and physical sensations that they've avoided or suppressed and in committing to make life changes. In addition to behavioral techniques, these approaches borrow experiential techniques from Gestalt therapy and even meditation techniques from a Buddhist tradition to promote acceptance and the ability to tolerate unsettling feelings.

Although there's growing evidence that integrative approaches are effective (Linehan, Heard, & Armstrong, 1993; Norcross & Goldfried, 2005), psychologists know virtually nothing about the role specific therapeutic components play in accounting for treatment success. The more ingredients tossed into the mix, the more challenging it becomes to dismantle integrative approaches and evaluate rival hypotheses regarding which ingredients matter.

ASSESS YOUR KNOWLEDGE: FACT OR FICTION?

(1) Behavior therapies place a great deal of importance on insight. (True/False)
(2) One commonly used assertion training technique is behavioral rehearsal. (True/False)
(3) Token economy programs are based on operant conditioning principles. (True/False)
(4) According to Albert Ellis, feelings create irrational beliefs. (True/False)
(5) Cyclical psychodynamic therapy focuses almost exclusively on the patient's cognitions. (True/False)

Answers: (1) F (p. 683); (2) T (p. 686); (3) T (p. 687); (4) F (p. 687); (5) F (p. 690)

Group and Family Systems Therapies: The More, the Merrier

Since the early 1920s, when Viennese psychiatrist Jacob Moreno introduced the term **group therapy,** helping professionals have appreciated the value of treating more than one person at a time. Group and family therapies are now well positioned in the mainstream of psychotherapeutic approaches.

group therapy
therapy that treats more than one person at a time

GROUP THERAPIES

The popularity of group approaches has paralleled the increased demand for psychological services in the general population, a trend that became especially apparent in the years following World War II. Group therapies are efficient, time-saving, and less costly than individual treatment methods, and span all major schools of psychotherapy (Levine, 1987). In a safe group environment, participants can provide and receive support, exchange information and feedback, model effective behaviors and practice new skills, and recognize that adjustment problems are shared by many other people (Yalom, 1985).

Today, psychologists conduct group sessions in homes, hospitals, businesses, inpatient and residential settings, weekend retreats, community agencies, and professional offices. They reach people of all races, ages, and economic levels, including people who are blind, divorced, experiencing marital problems, struggling with their gender identity, and suffering from alcoholism and eating disorders (Dies, 2003; Lynn & Frauman, 1985). The most recent trend is for self-help groups to form over the Internet, especially for people with illnesses and problems that may be embarrassing to share in face-to-face encounters (Davison, Pennebaker, & Dickerson, 2000). Research suggests that many group procedures are effective for a wide range of problems and about as helpful as individual treatment methods (Davis, Olmsted, Rockert, Marques, & Dolhanty, 1997; Fuhriman & Burlingame, 1994).

Group therapy procedures are efficient, time-saving, and less costly than many individual treatment methods.

Alcoholics Anonymous. Self-help groups are composed of peers who share a similar problem. Over the past several decades, these groups, of which **Alcoholics Anonymous** (AA) is the best known, have become remarkably popular. Stockbroker Bill Wilson and surgeon Bob Smith (better known as "Bill and Bob"), who were grappling with the demons of alcoholism, founded AA in Akron, Ohio, in 1935. Today, AA is the largest organization for treating alcoholics, with more than 1.7 million members worldwide (Humphreys, 2000). At AA meetings, people share their struggles with alcohol, and new members are "sponsored" or mentored by more senior members, who've often achieved years of sobriety. AA members encourage new participants to attend daily meetings for the first 3 months, and regular meetings thereafter.

The program is organized around the famous "Twelve Steps" toward sobriety and is based on the assumptions that alcohol is a physical disease and "once an alcoholic, always an alcoholic." As a consequence, AA encourages its members to acknowledge their vulnerability to alcohol and never to drink another drop after entering treatment. Several of the Twelve Steps encourage members to entrust their difficulties to a higher power—"God as we understand him"—and to acknowledge powerlessness over their addiction. The Twelve Steps seem to have an interdenominational appeal, and many believe the program helps people renew their self-respect, diminish unproductive guilt feelings, and promote behaviors that substitute for drinking. AA also encourages positive relationships among its members and offers a social support network (Valiant & Milofsky, 1982). Many hospitals and clinics have incorporated AA meetings into their programs. When patients are released, continued care is available through AA meetings in the community. AA has inspired the creation of Al-anon and Alateen, groups that help spouses and children of alcoholics cope with alcohol abuse. Groups based on the Twelve-Step model have been established for drug users (Narcotics Anonymous), gamblers, overeaters, "shopaholics" (compulsive shoppers), sexual addicts, and scores of other people experiencing problems with impulse control. However, there's virtually no research on the effectiveness of these other Twelve Step approaches.

Although AA appears to be helpful for some people, many of the claims regarding its success aren't supported by data. People who attend AA meetings or receive treatment based on the Twelve Steps fare about as well as, but no better than, people who receive other treatments, including cognitive-behavioral therapy (Brandsma, Maultsby, & Welsh, 1980; Ferri, Amoto, & Davoli, 2006; Project Match Research Group, 1997; Walsh et al., 1991). Moreover, people who participate in studies of AA may be atypical in certain respects. AA members who end up in studies are usually the most active participants and have received prior professional help. Also, as many as 68 percent of participants drop out within 3 months of joining AA (Emrick, 1987). Research is needed to clarify which alcoholics AA best serves (MacKillop et al., 2003).

Alcoholics Anonymous has been in existence since the 1930s. Those who attend are known only by their first names, preserving the confidentiality the organization is known for.

Alcoholics Anonymous
Twelve-Step, self-help program that provides social support for achieving sobriety

Controlled Drinking and Relapse Prevention. Contrary to the AA belief that people are powerless to control their drinking and must remain totally abstinent from alcohol, the behavioral view assumes that excessive drinking is a learned behavior that therapists can modify and control without total abstinence (Marlatt, 1983). There's bitter controversy about whether *controlled drinking,* that is, drinking in moderation, is even an appropriate treatment goal. Nevertheless, there's considerable evidence that treatment programs that encourage alcoholics to set limits, drink moderately, and reinforce their progress can be effective for many patients (MacKillop et al., 2003; Miller & Hester, 1980; Sobell & Sobell, 1973, 1976). Programs that teach people skills to cope with stressful life circumstances and tolerate negative emotions (Monti, Gulliver, & Myers, 1994) are at least as effective as Twelve Step programs (Project Match Research Group, 1998).

Bucking the popular belief, sometimes repeated in the AA community, of "one drink, one drunk," *relapse prevention* (RP) treatment assumes that many alcoholics will at some point experience a lapse, or slip, and resume drinking (Larimer, Palmer, & Marlatt, 1999; Marlatt & Gordon, 1985). RP teaches people to not feel ashamed, guilty, or discouraged when they lapse. Negative feelings about a slip can lead to continued drinking, called the **abstinence violation effect** (Marlatt & Gordon, 1985; Polivy & Herman, 2002). That is, once someone slips up, he figures, "Well, I guess I'm back to drinking again," and goes back to drinking at high levels. RP therapists teach people to rebound after a lapse and avoid situations in which they're tempted to drink. Thus, they learn that a *lapse* doesn't mean a *relapse.* Meta-analyses suggest that relapse prevention programs reduce alcohol relapse (Irvin, Bowers, Dunn, & Wang, 1999). Still, total abstinence may be the best goal for people with severe dependence on alcohol or for whom controlled drinking has failed (Rosenberg, 1993).

Figure 16.2 Where's the Problem?
According to the strategic family therapy approach, families often single out one family member as "the problem" when the problem is actually rooted in the interactional patterns of all family members.

abstinence violation effect
lapse in sobriety that can lead to continued drinking if people feel ashamed, guilty, or discouraged when they lapse

strategic family intervention
family therapy approach designed to remove barriers to effective communication

FAMILY THERAPIES: TREATING THE DYSFUNCTIONAL FAMILY SYSTEM

Family therapists see most psychological problems as rooted in a dysfunctional family system. For them, treatment must focus on the family context out of which conflicts presumably arise. In family therapy, the "patient"— the focus of treatment—isn't one person, but rather the family unit itself. Family therapists therefore focus on interactions among family members (see **Figure 16.2**).

Strategic Family Therapy. **Strategic family interventions** are designed to remove barriers to effective communication. According to strategic therapists, including Virginia Satir (1964), Jay Haley (1976), and Paul Watzlawick (Watzlawick, Weakland, & Fisch, 1974), families often scapegoat one family member as the *identified patient* with the problem. But for these therapists, the real source of difficulties lies in the dysfunctional ways in which family members communicate, solve problems, and relate to one another.

Strategic therapists first identify the family's unhealthy communication patterns and its unsuccessful approaches to problem solving. Then, they invite family members to carry out planned tasks known as *directives.* Directives shift how family members solve problems and interact. They often involve *paradoxical requests,* which many of us associate with the popular concept of "reverse psychology." Some researchers (Beutler, Clarkin, & Bongar, 2000) have found that therapists often achieve success when they command their "resistant" or uncooperative patients to intentionally produce the thought, feeling, or behavior that troubled them.

Consider a therapist who "reframed" (cast in a positive light) a couple's arguments by interpreting them as a sign of their emotional closeness. The therapist gave the couple the paradoxical directive to *increase* their arguing to learn more about their love for one another. To show the therapist they were "not in love," they stopped arguing, which was, of course, the therapist's goal in the first place. Once their arguments ceased, their relationship improved (Watzlawick, Beavin, & Jackson, 1967).

Structural Family Therapy. In **structural family therapy** (Minuchin, 1974), the therapist actively immerses herself in the everyday activities of the family to make changes in how they arrange and organize interactions. Salvatore Minuchin and his colleagues' successful treatment of a 14-year-old girl who refused to eat illustrates this treatment. After carefully observing the communication patterns in the family, they noted that the girl, Laura, competed successfully for her father's attention by refusing to eat. By not eating, she exercised considerable power. Eventually, Laura could express in words the message that her refusal to eat conveyed indirectly, and she no longer refused to eat to attain affection (Aponte & Hoffman, 1973). Research indicates that family therapy is more effective than no treatment (Hazelrigg, Cooper, & Borduin, 1987; Vetere, 2001) and at least as effective as individual therapy (Foster & Gurman, 1985; Shadish, 1995).

In structural family therapy, the therapist immerses herself in the family's everyday activities. Having observed what goes on in the family, the therapist can then advocate for changes in how the family arranges and organizes its interactions.

ASSESS YOUR KNOWLEDGE: FACT OR FICTION?

(1) Group psychotherapies are generally as effective as individual psychotherapies. (True/False)

(2) Alcoholics Anonymous is no more effective than many other alcohol abuse treatments. (True/False)

(3) Relapse prevention is based on the goal of complete abstinence from alcohol. (True/False)

(4) Family therapies focus on the one person in the family with the most problems. (True/False)

(5) Strategic family therapists first identify the family's dysfunctional communication patterns. (True/False)

Answers: (1) T (p. 691); (2) T (p. 691); (3) F (p. 692); (4) F (p. 692); (5) T (p. 692)

Is Psychotherapy Effective?

In Lewis Carroll's book *Alice in Wonderland,* the Dodo bird proclaimed after a race that "All have won, and all must have prizes." Seventy years ago, Saul Rosenzweig (1936) delivered the same verdict regarding the effectiveness of different psychotherapies. That is, all appear to be helpful, but are roughly equivalent in terms of their outcomes: "All have won, and all must have prizes" (see **Figure 16.3** on page 694).

THE DODO BIRD VERDICT: ALIVE OR EXTINCT?

Today, some authors have concluded that the "Dodo bird verdict" still holds. Some meta-analyses (see Chapter 2) suggest that a wide range of psychotherapies are about equal in their effects (Anderson & Garske, 2003; Grissom, 1996; Wampold et al., 1997; Wampold, Minami, Baskin, & Tierney, 2002). Studies with experienced therapists who've practiced behavioral, psychodynamic, and person-centered approaches have found that all are more successful in helping patients compared with no treatment but no different from each other in their effects (DiLoretto, 1971; Sloane, Staples, Cristol, Yorkston, & Whipple, 1975).

Other researchers aren't convinced. They contend that the Dodo bird verdict, like the real Dodo bird, is extinct. Although most forms of psychotherapy work well, and many are about

In Lewis Carroll's book *Alice in Wonderland,* the Dodo bird declared, following a race, that "All have won, and all must have prizes." Psychotherapy researchers use the term *dodo bird verdict* to refer to the conclusion that all therapies are equivalent in their effects. Not all investigators accept this verdict.

structural family therapy
treatment in which therapists deeply involve themselves in family activities to change how family members arrange and organize interactions

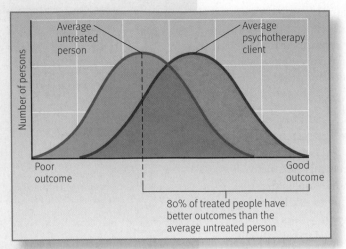

Figure 16.3 The Effectiveness of Psychotherapy. This graph shows two normal distributions (see Chapter 2) derived from nearly 500 studies of psychotherapy outcomes. The distribution on the left shows people who haven't received psychotherapy, and the distribution on the right shows people who've received psychotherapy. As we can see, across a variety of treatments and samples, 80 percent of people who receive therapy do better than people who don't. (*Source:* Sellers, 1988)

equal in their effects, there are notable exceptions (Beutler, 2002; Hunsley & DiGuilio, 2002). For example, behavioral and cognitive-behavioral treatments are clearly more effective than other treatments for children and adolescents with behavior problems (Garske & Anderson, 2003; Weisz, Weiss, Han, Granger, and Morton, 1995). Moreover, behavioral and cognitive-behavioral therapies consistently outperform most other therapies for anxiety disorders, including phobias, panic disorder, and obsessive-compulsive disorder (Addis et al., 2004; Chambless & Ollendick, 2001; Hunsley & DiGuilio, 2002).

Also calling into question the dodo bird verdict are findings that some psychotherapies can make people worse (Lilienfeld, 2007). Although we might assume that doing something is always better than doing nothing for psychological distress, research suggests otherwise. A nontrivial proportion of patients, perhaps 5 to 10 percent, tend to become worse following psychotherapy, and some of them may become worse *because of* psychotherapy (Lilienfeld, 2007; Rhole, 2005; Strupp, Hadley, & Gomez-Schwartz, 1978). For example, several researchers have found that crisis debriefing, a treatment we discussed in Chapter 12, can sometimes increase the risk of posttraumatic stress symptoms in people exposed to trauma. The same may be true for certain grief therapies, especially among people who are experiencing relatively normal grief reactions to the death of loved ones (Neimeyer, 2000). We can see a number of other potentially harmful therapies in **Table 16. 7.**

The bottom line? Many therapies are effective, and many do about equally well. Yet there are clear-cut exceptions to the Dodo bird verdict. Moreover, because at least some therapies appear to be harmful, we shouldn't assume that we'll always be safe picking a random therapist out of the telephone book.

Table 16.7 List of Potentially Harmful Therapies. Research suggests that some psychotherapies are potentially harmful for certain individuals.

Therapy	Intervention	Potential Harm
Facilitated communication	A facilitator holds autistic or developmentally disabled children's hands as they type messages on a keyboard.	False accusations of child abuse against family members
Scared Straight programs	Expose at-risk adolescents to the harsh realities of prison life to frighten them away from a life of future crime.	Worsening of conduct problems
Recovered-memory techniques	Therapists use methods to recover memories, including prompting of memories, leading questions, hypnosis, and guided imagery.	Production of false memories of trauma
Dissociative identity disorder (DID)–oriented psychotherapy	Therapists use techniques that imply to patients that they harbor "alter" personalities. Therapists attempt to summon, and interact with alters.	Production of alters, creation of serious identity problems
Critical incident stress debriefing	Shortly after a traumatic event, therapists urge group members to "process" their negative emotions, describe posttraumatic stress disorder symptoms that members are likely to experience, and discourage members from discontinuing participation.	Heightened risk for posttraumatic stress symptoms
DARE (Drug Abuse and Resistance Education) programs	Police officers teach schoolchildren about the risks of drug use and social skills to resist peer pressure to try drugs.	Increased intake of alcohol and other substances (such as cigarettes)
Coercive restraint therapies	Therapists physically restrain children who have difficulty forming attachments to their parents. These therapies include rebirthing (see Prologue) and holding therapy, in which the therapist holds children down until they stop resisting or begin to show eye contact.	Physical injuries, suffocation, death

(*Source:* Lilienfeld, 2007)

APPLY YOUR THINKING

In struggling with an inability to control your temper, you go to a therapist who describes a treatment called rage reduction therapy (RRT). RRT is premised on the idea that "getting the anger out of your system" by yelling and punching objects (like pillows) will allow you to get your temper under control. What questions would you ask your therapist to determine whether RRT is effective or legitimate?

HOW DIFFERENT GROUPS OF PEOPLE RESPOND TO PSYCHOTHERAPY

A void exists in our knowledge of how certain segments of the population respond to psychotherapy (Brown, 2006; Olkin & Taliaferro, 2005; U.S. Surgeon General, 2001). Research suggests that socioeconomic status (SES), gender, race, ethnicity, and age typically have little or no bearing on the outcome of therapy (Beutler, Machado, & Neufeldt, 1994; Cruz et al., 2007; Petry et al., 2000; Rabinowitz & Renert, 1997; Schmidt & Hancey, 1979). Still, we must be tentative in our conclusions because researchers haven't studied these variables in depth. Many controlled studies of psychotherapy don't report participants' race, ethnicity, disability status, or sexual orientation, nor do they analyze whether the effectiveness of psychotherapy depends on these variables (Sue & Zane, 2006). So we can't be completely confident that therapies that are effective with Caucasians are equally effective in other populations.

COMMON FACTORS

One probable reason why many therapies are comparable in effectiveness is that certain *common factors*—those that cut across many or most therapies—are responsible for improvement across diverse treatments. As Jerome Frank (1961) noted over four decades ago, these common factors include empathic listening, instilling hope, establishing a strong emotional bond with patients, providing a clear theoretical rationale for treatment, and implementing techniques that offer new ways of thinking, feeling, and behaving (Lambert & Ogles, 2004; Miller, Duncan, & Hubbel, 2005; Wampold, 2001).

In contrast, *specific factors* are those that characterize only certain therapies: They include exposure, challenging irrational beliefs, and social skills training. In some instances, specific factors may not enhance treatment effectiveness beyond those held in common with other approaches (Stevens, Hynan, & Allen, 2000). Psychologists are divided about the extent to which common versus specific factors influence the outcome of psychotherapy (Craighead, Sheets, & Bjornsson, 2005; DeRubeis, Brotman, & Gibbons, 2005; Kazdin, 2005), although most agree that both matter.

EMPIRICALLY SUPPORTED TREATMENTS

With 500 or more therapies on the market, how are mental health consumers to tell which ones work better than others? Over the past decade or so, researchers have responded to this question by putting forth lists of **empirically supported therapies (ESTs)**—treatments for specific disorders that are backed by high-quality scientific evidence (Chambless et al., 1996).

Behavior therapy and cognitive-behavioral therapy have emerged as ESTs for depression, anxiety disorders, obesity, marital problems, sexual dysfunction, and alcohol problems. Interpersonal therapy has considerable support for depression and bulimia, as does dialectical behavior therapy for borderline personality disorder. Still, we shouldn't conclude that a treatment that's not on the EST list isn't effective. The fact that a treatment isn't on the list may mean only that investigators haven't yet conducted research to demonstrate its effectiveness (Arkowitz & Lilienfeld, 2006).

Scared Straight programs expose adolescents to prisoners and prison life in an effort to "scare them" away from criminal careers. Despite their popularity, research suggests that such programs are not merely ineffective, but harmful in some cases.

Good psychotherapists keep up with the current state of the research literature, staying informed about which therapies do and don't have strong scientific support.

empirically supported therapies (ESTs)
treatments for specific disorders supported by high-quality scientific evidence

Some therapists claim that contact with dolphins can treat a variety of psychological problems, including autism. However, research does not support the idea that dolphin therapy is effective for any problem or disorder (Marino & Lilienfeld, 1998; 2007).

The movement to develop lists of ESTs is controversial. Critics of this movement contend that the research literature isn't sufficiently well developed to conclude that certain treatments are clearly superior to others for certain disorders (Levant, 2004; Westen, Novotny, & Thompson-Brenner, 2004). In response, proponents of this movement argue that the best scientific evidence available should inform clinical practice. Because current data suggest that at least some treatments are superior to others for some disorders, such as exposure therapy for anxiety disorders, practitioners have an ethical obligation to rely on ESTs unless there's a compelling reason not to (Chambless & Ollendick, 2001; Crits-Christoph, Wilson, & Hollo, 2005; Huasley & DiGuilio, 2002). The authors of your text find the latter argument more compelling, because the burden of proof for selecting and administering a treatment should always fall on therapists. Therefore, if there's reasonable evidence that certain treatments are better than others for certain disorders, therapists should be guided by this evidence. In **Table 16.8,** we list and describe several research-supported treatments.

WHY DO INEFFECTIVE THERAPIES APPEAR TO BE HELPFUL? HOW WE CAN BE FOOLED

Some therapists have successfully marketed a wide variety of interventions that lack research support (Lilienfeld, Lynn, & Lohr, 2003; Norcross, Garofalo, & Koocher, 2006; Singer & Nievod, 2003). They include treatments as seemingly bizarre as dolphin therapy, laughter therapy, treatment for the trauma of abduction by aliens (Appelle, Lynn, & Newman, 2000), and even treatment for resolving problems due to traumas in a past life (Mills & Lynn, 2000).

Many of these treatments rest on questionable premises; for example, advocates of "primal scream therapy" (sometimes called primal therapy) believe that the only way to achieve relief from psychological pain is to release pent up rage in one's nervous system, including rage stemming from the trauma of birth. Thera-

Table 16.8 Empirically Supported Therapies. Selected therapies deemed "empirically supported" by the American Psychological Association Division 12 committee.

Therapy and Problem	Description of Therapy
Behavior therapy for depression	• Monitor and increase positive daily activities • Improve communication skills • Increase assertive behaviors • Increase positive reinforcement for nondepressed behaviors • Decrease life stresses
Cognitive-behavior therapy for depression	• Teach patients to identify, reevaluate, and change negative thinking associated with depressed feelings • Conduct between-session experiments to test thoughts for accuracy • Monitor and increase daily activities
Interpersonal therapy for depression	• Help patients identify and resolve interpersonal difficulties associated with depression
Cognitive-behavior therapy for bulimia	• Teach patients ways to prevent binge eating and create alternative behaviors • Develop a plan for a regular pattern of eating • Support skills to deal with high-risk situations for binge eating and purging • Modify attitudes toward eating and one's physical appearance
Cognitive-behavior therapy for panic disorder	• Produce panic attacks during sessions to help clients perceive them as less "dangerous" (to reassure them that they will not, for example, "go crazy" or die) • Introduce breathing retraining (slow deep breaths) to prevent hyperventilation • Control exposure to situations that trigger panic attacks

(*Source:* Arkowitz & Lilienfeld, 2006)

pists who practice neurolinguistic programming (NLP) claim to treat psychological problems by matching their nonverbal behaviors, like their tone of voice, eye movements, and facial gestures, to those of their patients. In this way, therapists presumably develop a direct communication pathway with patients that permits them to influence patients more easily. Yet there's virtually no research support for either primal scream therapy or NLP (Singer & Lalich, 1996).

How might patients and therapists alike come to believe that treatments that are ineffective are helpful? The following five reasons can help us to understand why bogus therapies can gain a dedicated public following (Arkowitz & Lilienfeld, 2006; Beyerstein, 1996).

(1) **Spontaneous remission.** The patient's recovery may have nothing at all to do with the treatment. All of us have our "ups and downs." Similarly, many psychological problems are self-limiting or cyclical and improve without any intervention. A breakup with our latest "crush" may depress us for a while, but most of us will improve even without professional help. This phenomenon is known as *spontaneous remission*. Even with forms of cancer that are nearly always lethal, tumors occasionally disappear without further treatment, although such events are rare (Silverman, 1987).

Spontaneous remission is surprisingly common in psychotherapy. In the first formal review of psychotherapy outcomes, Hans Eysenck (1952) reported the findings of two uncontrolled studies of neurotic (mildly disturbed) patients who received no formal therapy. The rate of spontaneous remission in these studies was a staggering 72 percent! Admittedly, the studies Eysenck selected may have had unusually high rates of spontaneous remission because the individuals he claimed were "untreated" received reassurance and suggestion. Still, there's no question that many people with psychological problems, like depression, often improve on their own even without treatment. Only if people who are treated improve at a rate that exceeds that of untreated people, or those on a wait list, can we rule out the effects of spontaneous remission.

(2) **The placebo effect.** The pesky placebo effect (see Chapters 2 and 12) can lead to significant symptom relief. By instilling hope and the conviction that we can rise to life's challenges, virtually any credible treatment can be helpful in alleviating our demoralization.

(3) **Self-serving biases.** Even when they don't improve, patients who are strongly invested in psychotherapy and have shelled out a lot of money in the pursuit of well-being can convince themselves they've been helped. Because it would be too troubling to admit to oneself (or others) that it's all been a waste of time, energy, and effort, there's often a strong psychological pull to find value in a treatment (Axsom & Cooper, 1985). Patients may also overestimate their apparent successes while ignoring, downplaying, or explaining away their failures as a means of maintaining their self-esteem (Beyerstein & Hadaway, 1991).

(4) **Regression to the mean.** It's a statistical fact of life that extreme scores tend to become less extreme on re-testing, a phenomenon known as *regression to the mean*. If you receive a zero on your first psychology exam, there's a silver lining to this gray cloud: You'll almost surely do better on your second exam! Conversely, if you receive a 100 on your first exam, odds are also high you won't do as well the second time around. Scores on measures of psychopathology are no different. If a patient comes into treatment extremely depressed, the chances are high she'll be less depressed in a few weeks. Regression to the mean can fool therapists and their patients into believing that a useless treatment is effective. It's an especially tricky problem in evaluating whether psychotherapy is effective, because most patients enter psychotherapy when their symptoms are most extreme.

(5) **Retrospective rewriting of the past.** In some cases, we may believe we've improved even when we haven't because we misremember our initial (pretreatment) level of adjustment as worse than it was. We *expect* to change after treatment, and may adjust our memories to fit this expectation. In one study, investigators randomly assigned college students to either take a study skills course or serve in a wait-list control group. On objective measures of grades, the course proved worthless. Yet students who took the course—but not students in the control group—thought they'd improved. Why? They mistakenly recalled their initial study skills as worse than they actually were (Conway & Ross, 1984; Ross, 1990). The same phenomenon may sometimes occur in psychotherapy.

Positive life events that occur outside of therapy sessions, like major job promotions, can help to explain spontaneous remissions of some psychological problems, such as depression. As neo-Freudian theorist Karen Horney observed, "Life itself still remains a very effective therapist" (Horney, 1945, p. 240; see Chapter 14).

Ruling Out Rival Hypotheses

factoid

Many "jinxes" probably stem from a failure to consider regression to the mean (Kruger, Savitsky, & Gilovich, 1999). If we've been doing far better than we expected in a sports tournament and a friend says "Wow, you're doing great," we may fear that our friend has jinxed us. In fact, we *are* likely to do worse after our friend says that, but because of regression to the mean, not because of a jinx. Recall from the post hoc fallacy (Chapter 10) that because A comes before B doesn't mean that A causes B.

The "secret" to the 2007 best seller *The Secret* by Rhonda Byrne (above) is the so-called *law of attraction*—good thoughts attract good things and bad thoughts attract bad things. Yet there's no evidence that merely wishing for something good to happen without taking concrete steps to accomplish it is effective. We should be skeptical of self-help books that promise simple answers to complex problems.

Psycho*Mythology*
Are Self-Help Books Always Helpful?

Each year Americans can choose from about 3,500 newly published self-help books that promise everything from achieving everlasting bliss and expanded consciousness to freedom from virtually every human failing and foible imaginable. Self-help books are only one piece of the massive quilt of the self-improvement industry that extends to Internet sites, magazines, radio and television shows, CDs, DVDs, lectures, workshops, and advice columns. It's no mystery why self-help books are so popular that Americans spend $650 million a year on them: They're readily available, inexpensive, portable, and contain information that we can digest at our leisure. It's therefore no surprise that at least 80 percent of therapists recommend them to their patients (Arkowitz & Lilienfeld, 2007).

Many researchers have studied the effects of reading self-help books, known in psychology lingo as "bibliotherapy." The relatively small number of studies conducted on self-help books suggests that bibliotherapy and psychotherapy often lead to comparable improvements in depression, anxiety, and other problems (Gould & Clum, 1993).

Still, we should keep three points in mind. First, we can't generalize the limited findings to all of the books on the shelf of our local bookstore, because the overwhelming majority of self-help books remain untested (Rosen, Glasgow, & Moore, 2003). Second, people who volunteer for research on self-help books may be more motivated to read the entire book and benefit from it than the curious person who purchases the book under more casual circumstances. Third, many self-help books address relatively minor problems, like everyday worries and public speaking. When researchers (Menchola, Arkowitz, & Burke, in press) have examined more serious problems, like major depression and panic disorder, psychotherapy has fared better than bibliotherapy, although both do better than no treatment.

Some people don't respond at all to self-help books (Febbraro, Clum, Roodman, & Wright, 1999), and many self-help books promise far more than they can deliver. Readers who fall short of how the promotional materials on the cover assure them they'll respond may feel like failures and be less likely to seek professional help or make changes on their own initiative. Bearing this possibility in mind, Hal Arkowitz and Scott Lilienfeld (2007) offered the following recommendations about selecting self-help books.

- Use books that have research support and are based on valid psychological principles of change (Gambrill, 1992). Make sure the author refers to published research that supports the claims made. Some of the books that have shown positive effects in research studies include *Feeling Good* by David Burns, *Mind over Mood* by Dennis Greenberger and Christine Padesky, and *Coping with Panic* by George Clum.
- Evaluate the author's credentials. Does he or she have the professional training and expertise to write on the topic at hand?
- Be wary of books that make far-fetched promises, such as curing a phobia in 5 minutes. The 2007 blockbuster best seller *The Secret* (Byrne, 2007), popularized by Oprah Winfrey, informs readers that positive thinking alone can cure cancer, help one become a millionaire, or achieve just about any goal one wants. Yet there's not a shred of research evidence that this kind of wishful thinking is helpful (Smythe, 2007).
- Beware of books that rely on a "one size fits all" approach. A book that tells us to always express our anger to our relationship partner fails to take into account the complexity and specifics of the relationship.
- Serious problems like clinical depression, obsessive-compulsive disorder, or schizophrenia warrant professional help rather than self-help alone.

Biological Treatments: Drugs, Physical Stimulation, and Surgery

Biological treatments—including drugs, stimulation techniques, and brain surgery—directly alter the brain's chemistry or physiology. Just as the number of psychotherapy approaches has more than tripled since the 1970s, antidepressant prescriptions have tripled from 1988 to 1994 and from 1990 to 2000 (Smith, 2005). Many people are surprised to learn that about 10 percent of inpatients with major depression still receive electroconvulsive therapy (ECT)—informally called "shock therapy"—which delivers small electric shocks to people's brains to lift their mood (Olfson, Marcus, Sackeim, Thompson, & Pincus, 1998). By the 1950s, as many as 50,000 patients received psychosurgery, in which their frontal lobes or brain regions were damaged or removed in an effort to control serious psychological disorders (Tooth et al., 1961; Valenstein, 1973). Today, surgeons rarely perform such operations, reflecting the controversies surrounding psychosurgery, and the fact that less risky treatments are available to treat many serious psychological conditions. As we consider the pros and cons of various biological treatments, we'll see that each approach has attracted its share of both critics and defenders.

PHARMACOTHERAPY: TARGETING BRAIN CHEMISTRY

We'll begin our tour of biological treatments with **pharmacotherapy**—the use of medications to treat psychological problems. For virtually every psychological disorder treated with psychotherapy, there's an available medication. In 1954, the widespread marketing of the drug Thorazine (chlorpromazine) ushered in the "pharmacological revolution" in the treatment of serious psychological disorders. For the first time, professionals could prescribe powerful medications to ease the symptoms of schizophrenia and related conditions (see Chapter 15). By 1970, it was unusual for any patient with schizophrenia not to be treated with Thorazine or another of the "major tranquilizers," as they came to be known.

Pharmaceutical companies soon sensed the promise of medicines to treat a broad spectrum of patients, and their efforts paid off handsomely. Researchers discovered that the emotional storms that plague people with bipolar disorder could be tamed with Lithium, Tegretol, and a new generation of mood stabilizer drugs. Drug treatments are now available for people who struggle with far more common conditions, ranging from anxiety about public speaking to the harsh realities of stressful circumstances. As of 2004, 10 percent of adult women and 4 percent of adult men were taking antidepressant medications (Smith, 2005). We can attribute the staggering number of prescriptions for depression largely to the phenomenal popularity of the selective serotonin reuptake inhibitor (SSRI) antidepressant drugs, including Prozac, Zoloft, and Paxil, which boost serotonin levels.

In **Table 16.9,** we present commonly used drugs and their presumed mechanisms of action to treat anxiety disorders (anxiolytics or antianxiety drugs), depression (antidepressants), bipolar disorders (mood stabilizers), psychotic conditions (neuroleptics/antipsychotics

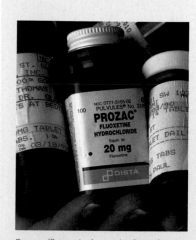

Prozac (fluoxetine) was the first of a new generation of SSRI drugs to treat depression and a variety of other psychological conditions.

pharmacotherapy
use of medications to treat psychological problems

or major tranquilizers), and attention problems (psychostimulants). As we can see from this table, many of these medications ease the symptoms of multiple psychological conditions.

Nevertheless, when evaluating this table, we should bear in mind that we don't know for sure how most of these medications work. Although drug company advertisements, including those we've seen on television, often claim that medications—especially antidepressants—correct a "chemical imbalance" in the brain, this notion is almost surely oversimplified. For one thing, most medications probably work on multiple neurotransmitter systems. Moreover, there's no scientific evidence for an "optimal" level of serotonin or other neurotransmitters in the brain (Lacasse & Leo, 2005). Finally, many medications, including antidepressants, may exert their effects largely by affecting the sensitivity of receptors (see Chapter 3) rather than the levels of neurotransmitters.

Today, psychologists often refer patients to psychiatrists and other professionals who can prescribe medications and consult with prescribers to plan treatment. Until recently, only

Table 16.9 Commonly Used Medications for Psychological Disorders, Mechanisms of Action, and Other Uses.

	Medication	Examples	Action	Other Uses
Antianxiety Medications	Benzodiazepines	Diazepam (Valium), alprazolam (Xanax), clonazepam (Klonopin), lorazepam (Ativan)	Increase efficiency of GABA binding to receptor sites	Use with antipsychotic medications, treat medication side effects, alcohol detox
	Buspirone (Buspar)		Stabilizes serotonin levels	Depressive and anxiety states; sometimes used with antipsychotics; aggression in people with brain injuries and dementia
	Beta blockers	Atenolol (Tenormin), propranolol (Inderal)	Compete with norepinephrine at receptor sites that control heart and muscle function; reduce rapid heartbeat, muscle tension	Control blood pressure, regulate heart beat
Antidepressants	Monoamine oxidase (MAO) inhibitors	Isocarboxazid (Marplan), phenelzine (Nardil), tranylcypromine (Parnate)	Inhibit action of enzymes that metabolize norepinephrine and serotonin; inhibit dopamine	Panic and other anxiety disorders
	Cyclic antidepressants	Amitriptyline (Elavil), imipramine (Tofranil), desipramine (Norpramine), nortriptyline (Pamelor)	Inhibit reuptake of norepinephrine and serotonin	Panic and other anxiety disorders, pain relief
	SSRIs (selective serotonin reuptake inhibitors)	Fluoxetine (Prozac), citalopram (Celexa), sertraline (Zoloft)	Selectively inhibit reuptake of serotonin	Eating disorders (especially bulimia), obsessive-compulsive disorder, social phobia
Mood Stabilizers	Mineral salts	Lithium carbonate (Lithium)	Decrease noradrenaline, increase serotonin	
	Anticonvulsant medications	Carbamazepine (Tegretol), lamotrigine (Lamictal) valproic acid (Depakote)	Increase levels of neurotransmitter GABA, inhibit norepinephrine reuptake (Tegretol)	Bipolar disorder
Antipsychotics	Conventional antipsychotics	Chlorpromazine (Thorazine), haloperidol (Haldol)	Block postsynaptic dopamine receptors	Tourette syndrome (Haldol), bipolar disorder with the exception of Clozaril
	Serotonin-dopamine antagonists (atypical antipsychotics)	Clozapine (Clozaril), risperidone (Risperdal), olanzapine (Zyprexa), ziprasidone (Geodone), quetiapine (Seroquel)	Block activity of both serotonin and/or dopamine; also affect norepinephrine, acetylcholine	
Psychostimulants and Other Medications for Attentional Problems	Methylphenidate (Ritalin, Concerta), amphetamine (Adderall), dexmethylphenidate (Focalin)		Release norepinephrine, dopamine, serotonin in frontal regions of the brain, where attention and behavior are regulated	
	Atomoxetine (Strattera)		Selectively inhibit reuptake of norepinephrine	

psychiatrists and a few other mental health professionals, like psychiatric nurse practitioners, could prescribe medications. But beginning in 1999, psychologists in the U.S. territory of Guam were granted legal permission to prescribe medications followed by two U.S. states (New Mexico in 2002 and Louisiana in 2004). Before being allowed to prescribe, these psychologists must first complete a curriculum of coursework on physiology, anatomy, and psychopharmacology (the study of medications that affect psychological functioning). Nevertheless, the growing movement to allow psychologists to prescribe medications has been exceedingly controversial, in part because many critics charge that psychologists don't possess sufficient knowledge of the anatomy and physiology of the human body to adequately evaluate the intended effects and side effects of medications (Stuart & Heiby, in press).

SEROTONIN

Despite what many drug company ads imply, there's no evidence that SSRIs or other medications work simply by correcting a "chemical imbalance" of serotonin (or other neurotransmitters) in the brain. These medications probably operate by means of more complex mechanisms.

NEW FRONTIERS
Psychotherapy and the Brain

Drug companies promise us better living through chemistry. But scientists are finding that when patients benefit from psychotherapy, this change is reflected in the workings of their brains. In some cases, psychotherapy and medication produce similar brain changes, suggesting that different routes to improvement share similar mechanisms (Kumari, 2006) and reminding us that "mind" and "brain" describe the same phenomena at different levels of explanation (see Prologue and Chapter 3).

Researchers initiated studies of psychotherapy and the brain when neuroimaging techniques came into vogue in the early 1990s. Scientists observed that patients with obsessive-compulsive disorder (OCD; see Chapter 15) who received behavior therapy showed brain changes similar to those who received an SSRI (Prozac; Baxter et al., 1992). Interestingly, researchers detected decreased metabolic activity in the caudate nucleus, a brain region that scientists believe is overactive in OCD. Shortly thereafter, they confirmed these findings with OCD patients who received cognitive-behavioral therapy (CBT) (Schwartz, Stoessel, Baxter, Martin, & Phelps, 1996).

Studies using sophisticated brain imaging equipment reveal that the effects of psychotherapy on the brain extend well beyond OCD. In one study, socially phobic participants received either CBT or treatment with an antianxiety medication (Citalopram). Regardless of whether socially phobic participants were treated with CBT or medication, they showed reduced activity in limbic system structures that house the brain's emotional circuitry and react to threat (Furmark et al., 2002). In studies with spider phobic patients, areas of the brain associated with the processing of fear memories and stimuli were less reactive after CBT (Johanson, Risberg, Tucker, & Gustafson, 2006; Paquette et al., 2003).

As we've learned, most depressed people spend excessive time brooding about negative events. In one study, depressed patients showed decreased activity in the frontal brain structures related to rumination following CBT (Goldapple et al., 2004). Interestingly, in another study, depressed patients treated with interpersonal therapy displayed changes in frontal and other brain areas not only after CBT, but an SSRI (Brody et al., 2001). A third study compared depressed patients treated with CBT with patients treated with an SSRI (Effexor). The researchers found that the treatments produced similar decreases in some frontal brain structures, but differed in their effects on other brain stuctures (Kennedy et al., 2007). These findings support the idea that psychotherapy produces measurable brain changes, but imply that medication and psychotherapy sometimes operate via different brain pathways relevant to depression (Linden, 2006; Martin, Martin, Rai, Richardson, & Royall, 2001).

This research also cautions us against a widespread logical error, namely, inferring a disorder's optimal treatment from its cause (Ross & Pam, 1995). Many people

(continued)

believe mistakenly that a condition that's largely biological in its causes, like schizophrenia, should be treated with medication and that a condition that's largely environmental in its causes, like a specific phobia (see Chapter 15), should be treated with psychotherapy. Yet the research we've reviewed here shows that this logic is erroneous, because psychological treatments affect our biology, just as pharmacological treatments affect our psychology.

It's a logical error to infer a disorder's cause from its treatment, or vice versa. Headaches can be treated with aspirin, but that doesn't imply that headaches are due to a deficiency of aspirin in the body.

Cautions to Consider: Dosage and Side Effects.　Pharmacotherapy isn't a cure-all. Virtually all medications have side effects that practitioners must weigh against their potential benefits. Most adverse reactions, including nausea, drowsiness, weakness, fatigue, and impaired sexual performance, are reversible when medications are discontinued or when their dosage is lowered. Nevertheless, this isn't the case with *tardive dyskinesia* (TD), a serious side effect of some antipsychotic medications, that is, medications used to treat schizophrenia and other psychoses. The symptoms of TD include grotesque involuntary movements of the facial muscles and mouth and twitching of the neck, arms, and legs. Most often, the disorder begins after several years of high-dosage treatment (*tardive*, like *tardy*, means late-appearing), but it occasionally begins after only a few months of therapy at low dosages (Simpson & Kline, 1976). Newer antipsychotic medicines such as Risperdal, which treat the negative, as well as the positive, symptoms of schizophrenia (see Chapter 15), generally produce fewer serious adverse effects, but they're costly.

One Dose Doesn't "Fit All": Differences in Responses to Medication.　Professionals who prescribe drugs must proceed with caution. People don't all respond equally to the same dose of medication. Weight, age, and even racial differences often affect drug response. African Americans tend to require lower doses of certain antianxiety and antidepressant drugs and have a faster response than do Caucasians, and Asians metabolize (break down) these medications more slowly than do Caucasians (Baker & Bell, 1999; Campinah-Bacote, 2002; Strickland, Stein, Lin, Risby, & Fong, 1997). Because some people become physically and psychologically dependent on medications, such as the widely prescribed antianxiety medications Valium and Xanax (benzodiazepines), physicians try to determine the lowest dose possible to achieve positive results and minimize unpleasant side effects (Wigal et al., 2006). Discontinuation of certain drugs, such as those for anxiety and depression, should be performed gradually to minimize withdrawal reactions, including anxiety and agitation (Lejoyeux & Ades, 1997).

Medications on Trial: Harmful and Overprescribed?　Some psychologists have raised serious questions about the effectiveness of the SSRIs, especially among children and adolescents (Kendall, Pilling, & Whittington, 2005). There also are widely publicized indications that SSRIs increase the risk of suicidal thoughts in people younger than 18 years of age, although there's no clear evidence that they increase the risk of completed suicide. For this reason, the U.S. Food and Drug Administration (FDA) now requires drug manufacturers to include warnings of possible suicide risk on the labels of SSRIs. Following these "black box" warnings (so called because they're enclosed in a box with black borders on the medication label), antidepressant prescriptions dropped by nearly 20 percent (Nemeroff et al., 2007).

Scientists don't understand why antidepressants increase suicidal thoughts in some children and adolescents. These drugs sometimes produce agitation, so some researchers have speculated that they can make already depressed people even more distressed and possibly suicidal (Brambilla, Cipriani, Hotopf, & Barbui, 2005). Yet the risk of suicide attempts and completions among people prescribed SSRIs remains very low. Physicians frequently prescribe SSRIs to treat anxiety disorders, including panic disorder and OCD. Fortunately, anxious patients without depression aren't at especially high risk for suicide (Mellinger & Lynn, 2003).

Another area of public concern regarding drug treatments is overprescription. Parents, teachers, and helping professionals have expressed particular alarm that psychostimulants for ADHD such as Ritalin (methylphenidate) are overprescribed and may substitute for effective coping strategies for focusing attention (LeFever, Arcona, & Antonuccio, 2003;

Children with attention-deficit-hyperactivity disorder (ADHD) often benefit from stimulant medication. Nevertheless, critics contend that stimulants are often overprescribed, especially for children who are only slightly overactive, inattentive, or impulsive for their age.

Safer, 2000). Since the early 1990s, the number of prescriptions for ADHD has increased fourfold. Although little is known about the long-term safety of Ritalin with children under 6, the number of prescriptions for children ages 2(!) to 4 nearly tripled between 1991 and 1995 alone (Bentley & Walsh, 2006). Critics of psychostimulants have pointed to their potential for abuse. Moreover, their adverse effects include insomnia, irritability, heart-related complications, and stunted growth.

Children should be diagnosed with ADHD and placed on stimulants only after they've been evaluated with input from parents and teachers. Yet 70 to 80 percent of children with ADHD can be treated effectively with medications (Steele et al., 2006), which can sometimes be combined to good advantage with behavior therapy (Jensen et al., 2005).

A final major area of concern is *polypharmacy:* prescribing many medications—sometimes five or more—at the same time. This practice can be hazardous if not carefully monitored, because certain medications may interfere with the effects of other medications or interact with them in dangerous ways. Polypharmacy is a particular problem among elderly individuals, who tend to be especially susceptible to drug side effects (Fulton & Allen, 2005).

To medicate or not medicate, that is the question. In many instances, psychotherapy, with no added medications, can successfully treat people with many disorders. CBT is at least as effective as antidepressants, even for severe depression, and perhaps more effective than antidepressants in preventing relapse (DeRubeis et al., 2005). Psychotherapy alone is also effective for a variety of anxiety disorders, dysthymia, bulimia, and insomnia (Otto, Smits, & Reese, 2005; Thase, 2000). Critics of pharmacotherapy claim that medications are of little value in helping patients learn social skills, modify self-defeating behaviors, or cope with conflict. Indeed, some patients relapse when they stop taking medications (Hollon, Haman, & Brown, 2002). For example, when patients with anxiety disorders discontinue their medications, half or more may relapse (Marks et. al., 1993). Over the long haul, psychotherapy may be much less expensive than medications, so it often makes sense to try psychotherapy first (Arkowitz & Lilienfeld, 2007).

Still, there are often clear advantages of combining medication with psychotherapy (Thase, 2000). If people's symptoms interfere greatly with their functioning, or if psychotherapy alone hasn't worked for a 2-month period, adding medication is frequently justified. Generally, research suggests that combining medication with psychotherapy is warranted for treating schizophrenia, bipolar disorder, long-term major depression, and major depression with psychotic symptoms (Otto et al., 2005; Thase, 2000).

ELECTRICAL STIMULATION: CONCEPTIONS AND MISCONCEPTIONS

Consider the following account of **electroconvulsive therapy** (**ECT**), which we introduced at the outset of our discussion of biological treatments:

> Strapped to a stretcher, you are wheeled into the ECT room. The electroshock machine is in clear view. The nurse places the electrodes on you. An injection is given. . . . You awaken in your hospital bed. You are confused to find it so difficult to recover memories. Finally you stop struggling in the realization that you have no memory for what has transpired. You were scheduled to have ECT, but something must have happened. Perhaps it was postponed. But the nurse keeps asking, 'How are you feeling?' You think to yourself: 'It must have been given'; but you can't remember. You have forgotten, but something about it remains. (Taylor, 1975, p. 33)

Electroconvulsive Therapy: Fact and Fiction. What exactly happened here? Medical personnel administered brief electrical pulses to the patient's brain to relieve severe depression that hadn't responded to other treatments. Today, patients who undergo ECT first receive an injection of a muscle relaxant. Patients experience a full-blown seizure lasting about a minute, much like that experienced by patients with epilepsy. Physicians typically recommend ECT for individuals with serious depression, bipolar disorder, schizophrenia, and severe catatonia

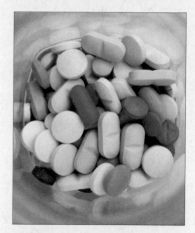

Polypharmacy—the practice of prescribing multiple medications at the same time—is particularly common for elderly individuals with psychological disorders. Nevertheless, it comes with several risks.

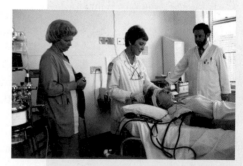

A team of professionals administer electroconvulsive therapy.

electroconvulsive therapy (ECT)
patients receive brief electrical pulses to the brain that produce a seizure to treat serious psychological problems

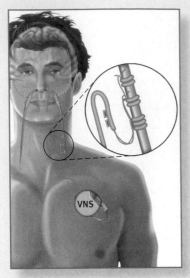

A small vagus nerve stimulator can be implanted under the breastbone in cases of serious treatment-resistant depression.

Ruling Out Rival Hypotheses

fictoid

Myth: Patients who receive ECT display violent convulsions, sometimes leading to serious injuries.

Reality: Although this was true decades ago and is still the case in some developing countries (Giles, 2002), the muscle relaxant and anesthesia now administered along with ECT prevent violent convulsions. In Western countries today, ECT is no more physically dangerous than anesthesia itself.

Ruling Out Rival Hypotheses

psychosurgery
brain surgery to treat psychological problems

(see Chapter 15), and only then as a last resort when psychotherapy and pharmacotherapy have failed. A typical course of ECT is six to ten treatments, given three times a week.

Misconceptions about ECT abound, including the erroneous beliefs that ECT is painful or dangerous and that it invariably produces long-term memory loss, personality changes, and even brain damage (Dowman, Patel, & Rajput, 2005; Malcom, 1989; Santa Maria, Baumeister, & Gouvier, 1999). Media characterizations of ECT, such as in the Academy Award–winning 1975 film *One Flew Over the Cuckoo's Nest*, promote the mistaken idea that ECT is little more than a brutal means of punishment or behavioral control, with no redeeming value. Not surprisingly, most Americans hold negative attitudes about ECT.

Nevertheless, the picture looks quite different when researchers interview individuals who've undergone ECT. In one study of twenty-four patients, 91 percent reported being happy to have received ECT (Goodman, Krahan, Smith, Rummans, & Pileggi, 1999). In another study, 98 percent of patients said they would seek ECT again if their depression returned, and 62 percent said that the treatment was less frightening than a visit to the dentist (Pettinati, Tamburello, Reutsch, & Kaplan, 1994). More important, researchers report improvement rates as high as 80 to 90 percent following ECT for severe depression (APA, 2001), further suggesting that harsh public perceptions about ECT are unwarranted.

Still, we must balance this rosy assessment of ECT against a few cautions. People who experience ECT may be motivated to convince themselves that the treatment helped. Although many patients report feeling better after ECT, they don't always show evidence of parallel changes on objective measures of depression and mental functioning (Scovern & Killman, 1980). ECT may be helpful because it increases the levels of serotonin in the brain (Rasmussen, Sampson, & Rummans, 2002). A rival hypothesis is that ECT induces strong expectations of improvement and serves as an "electrical placebo." But studies showing that ECT works better than "sham" (fake) ECT render this explanation less likely (Carney et al., 2003).

In prescribing ECT, the physician's challenge is to determine whether the therapeutic gains outweigh the potential adverse effects. As the case we read suggested, ECT can create short-term confusion and cloud memory. In most cases, the memory loss is restricted to events that occur right before the treatment and generally subsides within a few weeks (Sackheim, 1988). However, in the first long-term study of patients in the community who received ECT, researchers found that memory and attention problems persist in some patients for 6 months after treatment (Sackheim et al., 2007). When physicians placed electrodes on the right side of the brain (unilateral ECT) rather than on both sides (bilateral ECT) it reduced, but didn't entirely eliminate, these cognitive impairments. When psychiatrists use ECT, it's vitally important that patients and their family members understand the procedure, as well as its potential benefits and risks.

Vagus Nerve Stimulation. In a recent development, surgeons can now implant a small electrical device under the skin near the breastbone to stimulate the *vagus nerve* to treat severe depression. The vagus nerve projects to many brain areas, and researchers believe that electrical pulses to this nerve stimulate serotonin and increase brain blood flow (George et al., 2000). The FDA has approved this procedure for depression that hasn't responded to other treatments, but well-controlled, large-scale studies are lacking. In one study, patients who received devices that weren't turned on performed as well as patients with working devices, suggesting that improvement may be due to placebo effects (Rush et al., 2005). Even if future studies show that vagus nerve stimulation is effective, the decision to try the treatment will need to be weighed against the potential side effects of headache, neck pain, cough, and voice changes.

PSYCHOSURGERY: AN ABSOLUTE LAST RESORT

Psychosurgery, or brain surgery to treat psychological disorders, is the most radical of all biological treatments. So it's no surprise that it's attracted a firestorm of controversy. Critics of psychosurgery have raised questions about the merits of destroying brain tissue to control behavior and emotion, the use of psychosurgery for social control, and the ethical issues surrounding such control.

To understand the controversy that's swirled around psychosurgery, we must understand its history. As is often the case with new treatments, psychosurgery was hailed as a promising innovation not long after it was introduced (see Chapter 2). Walter Freeman and James Watts introduced psychosurgery in the United States and published highly favorable reports about their successful treatment of thousands of patients. As we learned in Chapter 3, most of the early psychosurgical operations were prefrontal lobotomies. Psychosurgery remained popular until the mid-1950s, when the tide of enthusiasm receded in the face of reports of scores of "dehumanized zombies" and the availability of medicines as alternatives to surgery (Mashour, Walker, & Matuza, 2005; Valenstein, 1973). To most critics, the benefits of psychosurgery rarely, if ever, outweighed the costs of impairing memory, diminishing emotion and creativity, and the risks of brain surgery (Neville, 1976).

Critics also noted that the motives for conducting psychosurgery weren't always benign (Valenstein, 1973). Indeed, in the past, surgeons often performed lobotomies on violent sexual criminals and homosexual child abusers and in prisons to control violent inmates (Mashour et al., 2005). Punitive and therapeutic motives were sometimes difficult to separate. Social goals, such as the control of behavior, were occasionally confused with therapeutic goals.

In the 1960s, surgeons ushered new forms of psychosurgery to the forefront. The procedures involved creating small lesions in the amygdala or in other parts of the limbic system, such as the cingulate cortex, which plays a key role in controlling emotions (see Chapter 3). Surgeons replaced primitive procedures with ultrasound, electricity, freezing of tissues, and implants of radioactive materials. Automated surgical devices added precision to delicate brain surgery. With the advent of modern psychosurgical techniques, negative physical side effects became far less frequent.

Today, surgeons sometimes perform psychosurgery as an absolute last resort for patients with a handful of conditions, such as severe obsessive-compulsive disorder, major depression, and bipolar disorder. In a study using strict criteria for improvement, 25 to 30 percent of thirty-three obsessive-compulsive patients who'd failed to respond to all other treatments benefited substantially from psychosurgery (Jenike et al., 1991). Unfortunately, there are few well-controlled long-term studies of psychosurgery and an absence of data about which patients respond best. Even when psychosurgery appears successful, we can generate alternative explanations, including placebo effects and self-serving biases, to account for apparent treatment gains (Dawes, 1994).

Recognizing the need to protect patient interests, institutional review boards (IRBs; see Chapter 2) in hospitals where surgeons perform psychosurgery must approve each operation. IRBs help ensure that (a) there's a clear rationale for the operation, (b) the patient has received an appropriate preoperative and postoperative evaluation, (c) the patient has consented to the operation, and (d) the surgeon is competent to conduct the procedure (Mashour et al., 2005). Scientific research may eventually lead to more effective forms of psychosurgery, but the ethical controversies surrounding such surgery are likely to endure.

Surgeons used tools like these to perform early lobotomies before sophisticated surgical techniques were developed.

Public attitudes and beliefs about psychosurgery may have been influenced by Tennessee Williams's widely acclaimed 1944 play, *The Glass Menagerie*. Its leading character, Laura, is an echo of the playwright's sister Rose, who underwent a botched frontal lobotomy to combat her "madness" several years before Williams wrote the play.

Ruling Out Rival Hypotheses

Psychosurgery has a long history, as this photo of a 2000-plus year old skull from Peru shows. As we can see, this skull contains a huge hole produced by a procedure called "trephining." Scientists believe that trephining may have been performed in an effort to heal mental disorders or to relieve brain diseases, like epilepsy or tumors (Alt, Jeunesse, Buitrago-Tellez, Wichter, & Boes, 1997).

ASSESS YOUR KNOWLEDGE: FACT OR FICTION?
(1) The first major drug for psychological conditions was developed to treat bipolar disorder. (True/False)
(2) One serious side effect of antipsychotic medications is tardive dyskinesia. (True/False)
(3) People of different races and cultures respond similarly to the same dose of medication. (True/False)
(4) Most people experience long-lasting brain damage after a course of ECT. (True/False)
(5) Most early psychosurgery operations were prefrontal lobotomies. (True/False)

Answers: (1) F (p. 699); (2) T (p. 702); (3) F (p. 702); (4) F (p. 704); (5) T (p. 705)

Think again...

Psychotherapy: Patients and Practioners (pp. 672–675)

STUDY the Learning Objectives

▶ Describe who seeks treatment, who benefits from psychotherapy, and who practices psychotherapy
- Therapists treat people of all ages and social, cultural, and ethnic backgrounds.
- Individuals with anxiety, and minor and temporary problems are likely to benefit from therapy. Socioeconomic status, gender, age, and ethnicity do not predict treatment outcome.

▶ Identify the training and effectiveness differences between professionals and paraprofessionals
- Unlicensed paraprofessionals with no formal training, as well as licensed professionals, can be equally effective as therapists.

▶ Describe what it takes to be an effective therapist
- Warmth, selecting important topics to discuss, not contradicting patients, and the ability to establish a positive relationship are more important determinants of a therapist's effectiveness.

DO YOU KNOW THESE TERMS?
- ❏ psychotherapy (p. 672)
- ❏ paraprofessional (p. 673)

If you did not receive an access code to MyPsychLab with this text and wish to purchase access online, please visit www.mypsychlab.com.

How ethical was the client–therapist relationship in the television drama series *The Sopranos*? (p. 675)

THINK about — what You would do . . .
Your parents are divorcing, your father is struggling to adjust, and is resisting your suggestion to speak to a therapist. How could you dispel his preconceived notions about who seeks and benefits from therapy? (pp. 672–673)

SUCCEED with — mypsych lab
Psychotherapy Practitioners and Their Activities
Take a look into the daily work of psychotherapists.
(p. 673)

ASSESS your knowledge

1. _____ can be defined as a psychological intervention designed to help people resolve emotional, behavioral, and interpersonal problems and improve the quality of their lives. (p. 672)

2. In general, (women/men) are more likely to seek psychotherapy. (p. 672)

3. Hispanic Americans are (less/more) likely than non-Hispanic Americans to seek mental health services. (p. 673)

4. Studies have shown that people often (wait/rush) to seek therapy for problems. (p. 673)

5. Individuals who experience some anxiety or minor, temporary problems are (not likely/likely) to benefit from therapy. (p. 673)

6. A person with no professional training who provides mental health services is called a _____. (p. 673)

7. People who fulfill the role of therapist (can/can not) be effective without formal professional training. (p. 673–674)

8. A trained professional understands how to operate within the broader mental health system, which can be an important advantage for the _____. (p. 674)

9. Effective therapists are likely to be warm and direct, establish a positive working relationship with patients, and tend (to/not to) contradict their patients. (pp. 674–675)

10. A therapist who talks a lot about his/her personal life is likely to be (effective/ineffective). (p. 675)

Insight Therapies: Acquiring Understanding (pp. 676–682)

STUDY the Learning Objectives

▶ Describe the core beliefs of psychodynamic therapists
- Their core beliefs are the importance of the unconscious, childhood experiences, expressing emotions and reexperiencing past events, and acquiring insight.

▶ Determine how neo-Freudians, including Jung and Sullivan, departed from traditional psychoanalysis
- They placed less emphasis on the unconscious and greater emphasis on cultural and interpersonal influences on behavior.

▶ Identify criticisms of psychodynamic therapies
- Psychodynamic therapies are based largely on patients' childhood memories, small and highly select patient samples, anecdotal studies, and the questionable curative value of insight.

▶ Identify important aspects of humanistic-existential therapies
- Humanistic-existential therapies hold that self-actualization is a universal human drive, and adopt an experience-based, phenomenological approach.

SUCCEED with — mypsych lab
Key Components to Psychodynamic, Humanistic, Behavior, and Cognitive Therapies
Examine which therapeutic approach you would use with a client (pp. 676–682)

Explain the two-chair technique as used by Gestalt therapists. (p. 681)

According to Jung, what types of images lend themselves to therapeutic interpretation? (p. 678)

THINK about — what You would do . . .
Asked to compare the assertions of Freud's psychoanalytic theories and those of today's neo-Freudians, how would you characterize the differences between Freudian and neo-Freudian theorists in their explanations of individual's needs? (pp. 676–678)

ASSESS your knowledge

1. In _____ the goal is to cultivate insight and expand awareness. (p. 676)

2. The first form of psychotherapy was Freud's _____. (p. 676)

3. Psychodynamic therapists (do not believe/ believe) people's present difficulties are rooted in childhood experiences. (p. 676)

4. In the technique of ____ _____, patients are allowed to express themselves without censorship of any sort. (p. 676)

5. Neo-Freudians place (more/less) emphasis on the unconscious than did Freudians. (p. 677)

6. Jungians believe that _____ _____ foretell the future and may warn of danger. (pp. 677–678)

7. Critics of psychodynamic therapies assert that understanding our emotional history (is/isn't) required to relieve psychological distress. (pp. 678–679)

8. _____ therapies share an emphasis on the development of human potential and the belief that human nature is basically positive. (p. 680)

9. In Roger's _____ therapy, the therapist uses reflection to communicate empathy to the patient. (p. 681)

10. _____ therapy's two-chair technique aims to integrate opposing aspects of the client's personality. (p. 681)

▶ Evaluate the effectiveness of Rogers's person-centered therapy
   • Research suggests that genuineness, unconditional positive regard, and empathic understanding are necessary but not sufficient for improvement.

DO YOU KNOW THESE TERMS?
- ❑ **insight therapies** (p. 676)
- ❑ **free association** (p. 676)
- ❑ **resistance** (p. 677)
- ❑ **transference** (p. 677)
- ❑ **work through** (p. 677)
- ❑ **interpersonal therapy** (p. 678)
- ❑ **humanistic-existential therapy** (p. 680)
- ❑ **phenomenological approach** (p. 680)
- ❑ **person-centered therapy** (p. 680)
- ❑ **Gestalt therapy** (p. 681)
- ❑ **experiential therapy** (p. 681)
- ❑ **logotherapy** (p. 681)

Behavioral Approaches: Changing Maladaptive Actions (pp. 683–690)

THINK about

what You would do ... Using your psychology class as the subject pool, how would you set up a token economy to award extra credit points for class participation? (p. 687)

What is in vivo exposure therapy and how can it help people with a fear of flying? (p. 684)

SUCCEED with

mypsychlab where learning comes to life!

Cognitive Behavioral versus Psychodynamic Theory
Learning not to fear. . . How to change phobias
(pp. 683–684)

What is EMDR therapy, and how effective is it in relieving symptoms of anxiety disorders? (p. 686)

STUDY the Learning Objectives

▶ Describe the characteristics of behavior therapy
   • Behavior therapy is grounded in the scientific method and based on learning principles.

▶ Identify different behavioral approaches
   • Exposure therapies confront people with their fears.
   • Exposure can be gradual and stepwise (systematic desensitization) or start with the most frightening scenes imaginable (flooding). Exposure can occur by imagining scenes in vivo (real life) or by way of virtual reality technology.
   • Modeling techniques, based on observational learning principles, include behavioral rehearsal and role playing to foster assertiveness.
   • Token economies and aversion therapies are based on operant conditioning principles. Token economies shape behaviors using tokens that patients can exchange for tangible rewards. Aversion therapies use unpleasant stimuli to decrease undesirable behaviors.

▶ Describe the features of cognitive-behavioral therapies (CBT)
   • CBT therapists modify irrational beliefs that play a key role in unhealthy feelings and behaviors.
   • Ellis's rational emotive behavior therapy, Beck's cognitive therapy, and Meichenbaum's stress inoculation training are influential variations of CBT.

DO YOU KNOW THESE TERMS?
- ❑ **behavior therapists** (p. 683)
- ❑ **systematic desensitization** (p. 683)
- ❑ **exposure therapy** (p. 683)
- ❑ **dismantling** (p. 684)
- ❑ **response prevention** (p. 685)
- ❑ **participant modeling** (p. 686)
- ❑ **token economy** (p. 687)
- ❑ **aversion therapy** (p. 687)
- ❑ **cognitive-behavior therapy** (p. 687)

ASSESS your knowledge

1. _____ therapists focus on the specific behaviors that led the patient to seek therapy and the current variables that maintain problematic thoughts, feelings, and behaviors. (p. 683)

2. A class of procedures that confronts patients with what they fear with the goal of reducing this fear is called _____ _____. (p. 683)

3. During _____ _____, patients are taught to relax as they are gradually exposed to what they fear in a step-wise manner. (p. 684)

4. Patients are exposed right away to images of stimuli that they fear the most for prolonged periods during _____. (p. 685)

5. A crucial component of flooding is _____ _____, in which the therapist blocks patients from performing their typical avoidance behaviors. (p. 685)

6. During _____ _____, the therapist first models a problematic situation and then guides the patient through steps to cope with it. (p. 686)

7. In _____ _____ programs, desirable behaviors are rewarded through the consistent application of operant conditioning principles. (p. 687)

8. _____ therapy seeks to replace irrational thinking with more adaptive, rational thinking. (p. 687)

9. Ellis's Rational Emotive-Behavior Therapy (REBT) emphasizes that our _____ systems play a key role in how we function psychologically. (p. 687)

10. Nowadays it is (unusual/usual) for therapists to integrate techniques and theories from many existing therapy approaches. (p.689)

Group and Family Systems Therapies: The More, The Merrier (pp. 690–693)

STUDY the Learning Objectives

▶ List the advantages of group methods
- Group methods span all schools of psychotherapy and are cost efficient, time saving, and less costly than individual methods. Participants learn from others' experiences, benefit from feedback and modeling others, and discover that problems and suffering are widespread.

▶ Describe the research evidence concerning the effectiveness of Alcoholics Anonymous
- AA appears to be no more effective than other treatments, including CBT. Research suggests that controlled drinking approaches can be effective with some people.

▶ Identify different approaches to treating the dysfunctional family system
- Family therapies treat problems in the family system. Strategic family therapists remove barriers to effective communication, whereas structural family therapists plan changes in the way family interactions are structured.

DO YOU KNOW THESE TERMS?
- ❏ group therapy (p. 690)
- ❏ Alcoholics Anonymous (p. 691)
- ❏ abstinence violation effect (p. 692)
- ❏ strategic family intervention (p. 692)
- ❏ structural family therapy (p. 693)

mypsych lab

SUCCEED with

Family Therapist

Find out more about the types of cases that a family therapist treats.

(pp. 692–693)

▶ WATCH

THINK about

what You would do . . .
Your mother is recovering from breast cancer surgery and is interested in therapy to help her cope. What would you tell her about the benefits and limitations of individual versus group therapy to help her make a decision? (p. 691)

What are some of the benefits to the individual when participating in group therapy? (p. 691)

ASSESS your knowledge

1. Therapy that treats more than one person at a time is called _____ _____. (p. 690)

2. Group therapies are (more/less) costly than individual treatment methods. (p. 691)

3. It is (rare/common) for self-help groups to form on the Internet. (p. 691)

4. _____ _____ is a well-known self-help program that provides social support for achieving sobriety. (p. 691)

5. People who attend AA meetings and receive treatment based on the "twelve steps" fare (better than/about the same as) people who receive other treatments, including cognitive-behavioral therapy. (p. 691)

6. The behavioral view advocates that total abstinence is (necessary/not necessary) to treat excessive drinking. (p. 692)

7. The relapse prevention approach teaches people to not feel ashamed or discouraged when they lapse, in an effort to avoid the _____ _____ effect. (p. 692)

8. In family therapy, the therapist identifies problems caused by the interactions of (one person/the entire family). (p. 692)

9. _____ _____ _____ is a family therapy approach designed to remove barriers to effective communication. (p. 692)

10. In _____ family therapy, the therapist is actively involved in the everyday activities of the family to change the structure of their interactions. (p. 693)

Is Psychotherapy Effective? (pp. 693–699)

STUDY the Learning Objectives

▶ Evaluate the claim that all psychotherapies are equally effective
- Many therapies are effective. Nevertheless, some therapies, including behavioral and cognitive-behavioral treatments, are more effective than other treatments for specific problems, such as anxiety disorders. Still other treatments appear to be harmful.

▶ Identify common factors in psychotherapy
- Common factors include establishing a strong therapeutic alliance, giving patients hope, and providing a clear treatment rationale.

▶ Explain why ineffective therapies appear to be effective
- Ineffective therapies can appear to be helpful because of spontaneous remission, the placebo effect, self-serving biases, regression to the mean, and retrospective rewriting of the past.

DO YOU KNOW THIS TERM?
- ❏ empirically supported therapies (p. 695)

What does the research suggest about the effectiveness of Scared Straight programs? (p. 695)

THINK about

what You would do . . .
A friends confesses that she buys many self help books but nothing works. What scientifically-based guidelines could you give her to select more effective books? (p. 697)

ASSESS your knowledge

1. The Dodo bird verdict suggests that all types of psychotherapies are equally _____. (p. 693)

2. Among researchers there is (strong consensus/no consensus) that the Dodo bird verdict is correct. (pp. 693–694)

3. Research shows that behavioral and cognitive behavioral therapies are (more/less) effective than other treatments for children and adolescents with behavioral problems. (p. 694)

4. Most studies show that (20 percent/80 percent) of people who receive psychotherapy do better than the average person who does not. (p. 694)

5. Research suggests that some types of therapies, such as Scared Straight programs, (can/can not) harm participants. (p. 694)

6. _____ _____ in psychotherapy include establishing a strong therapeutic bond with patients, giving patients hope, and providing a clear treatment rationale. (p. 695)

7. _____ _____ _____ _____ are treatments for specific disorders that are supported by high-quality scientific evidence. (p. 695)

8. If a treatment is not considered an EST, it (means/doesn't mean) that it is ineffective. (p. 695)

9. Americans spend $650 million a year on _____ _____, also known as bibliotherapy. (p. 697)

10. When a patient recovers without any intervention, or in spite of ineffective treatment, it may be due to _____ _____. (p. 698)

mypsychlab
where learning comes to life!

SUCCEED with

Ineffective Therapies

List five reasons why ineffective therapies seem to work.

(pp. 693–694)

EXPLORE

List three empirically supported therapies. (pp. 695–696)

1. _____

2. _____

3. _____

Biological Treatments: Drugs, Physical Stimulation, and Surgery (pp. 699–705)

THINK about

what **You** would do . . .

Your friend tells you that his anxiety is the result of a chemical imbalance in his brain, for which he received a prescription for an SSRI. How could you make sure he understands that his anxiety is much more complex than a simple chemical imbalance?

(pp. 699–700)

Define psychosurgery and explain the controversy surrounding this treatment, which was famously depicted in the play *The Glass Menagerie*.

(pp. 704–705)

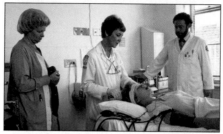

Dispel the myths and describe the facts surrounding the use of ECT as a treatment for severe depression. (p. 703)

_____

_____

_____

mypsychlab
where learning comes to life!

SUCCEED with

Drugs Commonly Used to Treat Psychiatric Disorders

Explore the "Non-talk" versions of psychological therapy. (p. 699)

EXPLORE

STUDY the Learning Objectives

▶ Recognize different types of drugs and cautions associated with drug treatment
  • Medications are available to treat psychotic conditions (neuroleptics/antispsychotics or major tranquilizers), bipolar disorder (mood stabilizers), depression (antidepressants), anxiety (anxiolytics), and attentional problems (psychostimulants).

▶ Outline key considerations in drug treatment
  • People who prescribe drugs must be aware of side effects, not over prescribe medications, and carefully monitor the effects of multiple medications (polypharmacy).

▶ Identify misconceptions about biological treatments
  • Contrary to popular belief, electroconvulsive therapy (ECT) is not painful or dangerous, and doesn't invariably produce memory loss, personality changes, or brain damage. Psychosurgery may be useful as a treatment of absolute last resort.

DO YOU KNOW THESE TERMS?
  ☐ **pharmacotherapy** (p. 699)
  ☐ **electroconvulsive therapy (ECT)** (p. 703)
  ☐ **psychosurgery** (p. 704)

ASSESS your knowledge

1. The use of medications to treat psychological problems is called _____. (p. 699)

2. The first major drug for a psychological disorder, Thorazine, was used to treat _____. (p. 699)

3. Prozac and Zoloft are among the best known _____ _____ _____ _____ inhibitors.(p. 699)

4. Virtually all medications have _____ _____ that practitioners must weigh against their potential benefits. (p. 702)

5. People of different races and cultures (do/do not) respond equally to the same dose of medication. (p. 702)

6. The safety and effectiveness of SSRIs when prescribed to _____ and _____ have been called into question because of increased risk of suicidal thoughts. (p. 702)

7. The drug Ritalin, used to treat ADHD, is an example of a medication that many feel has been _____ and may substitute for effective coping strategies for focusing attention. (p. 702)

8. The practice of _____ must be monitored carefully so the effects of certain medications do not interfere with the effects of other medications or interact in dangerous ways. (p. 703)

9. During _____ _____, patients receive brief electrical pulses to the brain that produce a seizure to treat serious psychological problems. (p. 703)

10. _____, brain surgery to treat psychological disorders, is the most radical of all biological treatments and is rarely performed. (p. 704)

Remember these questions from the beginning of the chapter? Think again and ask yourself if you would answer them differently based on what you now know about psychological and biological treatments.(For more detailed explanations, see MyPsychLab.)

▶ Are more experienced therapists better than inexperienced therapists? (p. 674)
▶ Do all psychotherapies require patients to achieve insight to improve? (p. 679)
▶ Can people overcome their fears by confronting them? (p. 683)
▶ Is Alcoholics Anonymous better than other types of treatment for alcoholism? (p. 691)
▶ Are some therapies harmful? (p. 694)
▶ Does electroconvulsive therapy produce long-term brain damage? (pp. 703–704)
▶ Is psychosurgery, like lobotomy, used primarily to control violent patients? (p. 704)

THINKING Scientifically

Correlation vs. Causation p. 679

Falsifiability pp. 678, 679, 682, 686, 688

Extraordinary Claims p. 685

Occam's Razor pp. 678, 686

Replicability pp. 673, 678

Ruling Out Rival Hypotheses
pp. 674, 677, 679, 684, 690, 697, 704, 705

Glossary

absolute refractory period time during which another action potential is impossible; limits maximal firing rate

absolute threshold lowest level of a stimulus needed for the nervous system to detect a change 50 percent of the time

abstinence violation effect lapse in sobriety that can lead to continued drinking if people feel ashamed, guilty, or discouraged when they lapse

abstract thinking capacity to understand hypothetical concepts

accommodation (Chapter 4) changing the shape of the lens to focus on objects near or far

accommodation (Chapter 10) Piagetian process of altering a belief to make it more compatible with experience

acetylcholine neurotransmitter used to control activity, including movement, memory, attention, and dreaming

acquired immune deficiency syndrome (AIDS) a life-threatening, incurable, yet treatable condition in which the human immunodeficiency virus (HIV) attacks and damages the immune system

acquisition learning phase during which a conditioned response is established

action potential regenerative electrical impulse that travels down the axon and allows neurons to communicate

activation–synthesis theory theory that dreams reflect inputs from brain activation originating in the pons, which the forebrain then attempts to weave into a story

acuity sharpness of vision

acupuncture ancient Chinese practice of inserting thin needles into more than 2,000 points in the body to alter energy forces believed to run through the body

ad hoc immunizing hypothesis escape hatch or loophole that defenders of a theory use to protect their theory from falsification

adaptive conservatism evolutionary principle that creates a predisposition toward distrusting anything or anyone unfamiliar or different

adolescence the transition between childhood and adulthood commonly associated with the teenage years

adoption studies analyses of how traits vary in individuals raised apart from their biological relatives

adrenal gland tissue located on top of the kidneys that releases adrenaline and cortisol during states of emotional arousal

affective forecasting ability to predict our own and others' happiness

aggression behavior intended to harm others, either verbally or physically

agoraphobia fear of being in a place or situation from which escape is difficult or embarrassing, or in which help is unavailable in the event of a panic attack

alcohol hallucinosis auditory hallucinations, sometimes accompanied by paranoid beliefs, resulting from alcohol withdrawal

Alcoholics Anonymous Twelve-Step, self-help program that provides social support for achieving sobriety

alternative medicine health care practices and products used in place of conventional medicine

altruism helping others for unselfish reasons

amygdala part of limbic system that plays key roles in fear, excitement, and arousal

anal stage psychosexual stage that focuses on toilet training

anomia inability to name things

anorexia nervosa eating disorder associated with excessive weight loss and the irrational perception that one is overweight

anterograde amnesia inability to encode new memories from our experiences

antisocial personality disorder condition marked by a lengthy history of irresponsible and/or illegal actions

anxiety sensitivity fear of anxiety-related sensations

aphasia serious speech deficit that renders a person unable to communicate effectively

apophenia tendency to perceive meaningful connections among unrelated phenomena

applied research research examining how we can use basic research to solve real-world problems

archetypes cross-culturally universal emotional symbols

artificial intelligence (AI) study and design of computer systems created to mimic human cognitive abilities

assimilation Piagetian process of absorbing new experience into current knowledge structures

association cortex regions of the cerebral cortex that integrate simpler functions to perform more complex functions

association fallacy error of confusing a claim's validity with the people who advocate it

asthma medical condition in which breathing becomes difficult when the bronchial tubes in the lungs become inflamed, spasm, and are clogged with mucus

astrology pseudoscience that claims to predict people's personalities and futures from the precise date and time of their birth

asylums institutions for the mentally ill created in the fifteenth century

attachment the strong emotional connection we share with those to whom we feel closest

attitude belief that includes an emotional component

attribution process of assigning causes to behavior

audition our sense of hearing

autonomic nervous system part of the peripheral nervous system controlling the involuntary actions of our internal organs and glands, which (along with the limbic system) participates in emotion

availability heuristic that involves estimating the likelihood of an occurrence based on the ease with which it comes to our minds

average expectable environment environment that provides children with basic needs for affection and discipline

aversion therapy treatment that uses punishment to decrease the frequency of undesirable behaviors

axes dimensions of functioning

axons portions of neurons that send signals

babbling intentional vocalization that lacks specific meaning

bandwagon fallacy error of assuming that a claim is correct just because many people believe it

basal forebrain region in forebrain containing acetylcholine neurons that affect activity of the cortex

basal ganglia structures in the forebrain that help to control movement

base rate   how common a characteristic or behavior is in the general population

basic research   research examining how the mind works

basilar membrane   membrane supporting the organ of Corti and hair cells in the cochlea

behavior therapist   therapist who focuses on specific problem behaviors, and current variables that maintain problematic thoughts, feelings, and behaviors

behaviorism   school of psychology that focuses on uncovering the general laws of learning by looking outside the organism

belief   conclusion regarding factual evidence

belief perseverance   tendency to stick to our initial beliefs even when evidence contradicts them

bell curve   distribution of scores in which the bulk of the scores fall toward the middle, with progressively fewer scores toward the "tails" or extremes

between-group heritability   extent to which differences in a trait between groups is genetically influenced

bias blind spot   lack of awareness of our biases, coupled with an awareness of others' biases

Big Five   five traits that have surfaced repeatedly in factor analyses of personality measures

bilingual   proficient and fluent at speaking and comprehending two distinct languages

binocular depth cues   stimuli that enable us to judge depth using both eyes

biological clock   term for the suprachiasmatic nucleus (SCN) in the hypothalamus that's responsible for controlling our levels of alertness

biopsychosocial perspective   the view that an illness or medical condition is the product of the interplay of biological, psychological, and social factors

black box   term sometimes used to describe behaviorists' view of the mind, namely, an unknown entity that we don't need to understand to explain behavior

blastocyst   ball of identical cells early in pregnancy that haven't yet begun to take on any specific function in a body part

blind   unaware of whether one is in the experimental or control group

blind spot   part of the visual field we can't see because of an absence of rods and cones

blood–brain barrier   glial cells forming a fatty coating that prevents certain substances from entering the brain

borderline personality disorder   condition marked by extreme instability in mood, identity, and impulse control

brain stem   part of the brain between the spinal cord and cerebral cortex that contains the medulla, midbrain, and pons

brightness   intensity of reflected light that reaches our eyes

broaden and build theory   theory proposing that happiness predisposes us to think more openly

Broca's area   language area in the prefrontal cortex that helps to control speech production

bulimia nervosa   eating disorder associated with a pattern of bingeing and purging in an effort to lose or maintain weight

Cannon-Bard theory   theory proposing that an emotion-provoking event leads simultaneously to an emotion and to bodily reactions

case study   research design that examines one person or a small number of people in depth, often over an extended time period

catatonic symptoms   motor problems, including extreme resistance to complying with simple suggestions, holding the body in bizarre or rigid postures, or curling up in a fetal position

categorical model   model in which a mental disorder differs from normal functioning in kind rather than degree

categories   collections of real or imagined objects, actions, and characteristics that share core properties

catharsis   feeling of relief following a dramatic outpouring of emotion

central nervous system (CNS)   part of nervous system containing brain and spinal cord that enables mind and behavior

central tendency   measure of the "central" scores in a data set, or where the group tends to cluster

cerebellum   small cerebrum in hindbrain, responsible for our sense of balance

cerebral cortex   outermost part of forebrain, responsible for analyzing sensory processing and higher brain functions

cerebral hemispheres   two halves of the cerebral cortex, which serve different yet highly integrated cognition functions

cerebral ventricles   internal waterways of the CNS that carry cerebrospinal fluid (CSF), which provides the brain with nutrients and cushioning against injury

chromosomes   slender threads inside a cell's nucleus that carry genes

chunking   organizing information into meaningful groupings, allowing us to extend the span of short-term memory

circadian rhythm   cyclical changes that occur on a roughly 24-hour basis in many biological processes

classical (Pavlovian or respondent) conditioning   form of learning in which animals come to respond to a previously neutral stimulus that had been paired with another stimulus that elicits an automatic response

cochlea   bony, spiral-shaped sense organ used for hearing

cognition   mental processes involved in different aspects of thinking

cognitive-behavior therapy   treatment that attempts to replace maladaptive or irrational cognitions with more adaptive, rational cognitions

cognitive biases   systematic errors in thinking

cognitive development   study of how children learn, think, reason, communicate, and remember

cognitive dissonance   unpleasant mental experience of tension resulting from two conflicting thoughts or beliefs

cognitive maps   mental representations of how a physical space is organized

cognitive model of depression   theory that depression is caused by negative beliefs and expectations

cognitive theories of emotion   theory proposing that emotions are products of thinking

cohort effects   effects observed in a sample of participants that result from individuals in the sample growing up at the same time

collective unconscious   according to Jung, our shared storehouse of memories that ancestors have passed down to us across generations

color blindness   inability to see some or all colors

communalism   willingness to share our findings with others

comorbidity   co-occurrence of two or more diagnoses within the same person

companionate love   love marked by a sense of deep friendship and fondness for one's partner

compatibilism   compromise between free will and determinism that says the two can coexist

complementary medicine   health care practices and products used along with conventional medicine

compulsions   repetitive behaviors or mental acts performed to reduce or prevent stress

computed tomography (CT)   a scanning technique using multiple x-rays to construct three-dimensional images

concrete operations stage   stage in Piaget's theory characterized by the ability to perform mental operations on physical events only

conditioned response (CR)   response previously associated with a nonneutral stimulus that is elicited by a neutral stimulus through conditioning

conditioned stimulus (CS)   initially neutral stimulus

conditions of worth   according to Rogers, expectations we place on ourselves for appropriate and inappropriate behavior

cones   receptor cells in the retina allowing us to see in color

confirmation bias   tendency to seek out evidence that supports our hypotheses and neglect or distort evidence that contradicts them

conformity   tendency of people to alter their behavior as a result of group pressure

confound   any difference between the experimental and control groups other than the independent variable

connectivity   extent to which a researcher's findings build on previous findings

consciousness   our subjective experience of the world, our bodies, and our mental perspectives

conservation   Piagetian task requiring children to understand that despite a transformation in the physical presentation of an amount, the amount remains the same

constructivist theory   Piaget's theoretical perspective that children construct an understanding of their world based on observations of the effects of their behaviors

contact comfort   positive emotions afforded by touch

context-dependent learning   superior retrieval of memories when the external context of the original memories matches the retrieval context

control group   in an experiment, the group of participants that doesn't receive the manipulation

convergent thinking   capacity to generate the single best solution to a problem

cornea   part of the eye containing transparent cells that focus light on the retina

coronary heart disease (CHD)   damage to the heart from the complete or partial blockage of the arteries that provide oxygen to the heart

corpus callosum   large band of fibers connecting the two cerebral hemispheres

correlation–causation fallacy   error of assuming that because one thing is associated with another, it must cause the other

correlational design   research design that examines the extent to which two variables are associated

corticosteroids   stress hormones that activate the body and prepare us to respond to stressful circumstances

covert speech   subvocal talking

critical multiplism   approach of using many different methods in concert

critical thinking   set of skills for evaluating all claims in an open-minded and careful fashion

cross-sectional design   research design that examines people of different ages at a single point in time

cryptomnesia   failure to recognize that our ideas originated with someone else

cryptophasia   secret language developed and understood only by a small number of people, typically twins

crystallized intelligence   accumulated knowledge of the world acquired over time

cults   groups of individuals who exhibit intense and unquestioning devotion to a single cause

culture-fair IQ tests   abstract reasoning items that don't depend on language and are often believed to be less influenced by cultural factors than other IQ tests

decay   fading of information from memory

defense mechanisms   unconscious maneuvers intended to minimize anxiety

defensive pessimism   strategy of anticipating failure and then compensating for this expectation by mentally overpreparing for negative outcomes

deindividuation   tendency of people to engage in uncharacteristic behavior when they are stripped of their usual identities

deinstitutionalization   1960s and 1970s governmental policy that focused on releasing hospitalized psychiatric patients into the community and closing mental hospitals

déjà vu   feeling of reliving an experience that's new

delirium   disorientation, confusion, visual hallucinations, and memory problems, sometimes resulting from alcohol withdrawal

delusions   strongly held, fixed beliefs that have no basis in reality

demand characteristics   cues that participants pick up from a study that allow them to generate guesses regarding the researcher's hypotheses

demonic model   view of mental illness in which odd behavior, hearing voices, or talking to oneself was attributed to evil spirits infesting the body

dendrites   portions of neurons that receive signals

denial   motivated forgetting of distressing external experiences

dependent variable   variable that an experimenter measures to see whether the manipulation has an effect

depersonalization disorder   condition marked by multiple episodes of depersonalization

depth perception   ability to judge distance and three-dimensional relations

descriptive statistics   numerical characterizations that describe data

desire phase   phase in human sexual response triggered by whatever prompts sexual interest

developmental psychology   study of how behavior changes over time

deviation IQ   expression of a person's IQ relative to his or her same-aged peers

***Diagnostic and Statistical Manual of Mental Disorders* (DSM)**   diagnostic system containing the American Psychiatric Association (APA) criteria for mental disorders

dialects   language variations used by groups of people who share geographic proximity or ethnic background

diathesis-stress models   perspective proposing that mental disorders are a joint product of a genetic vulnerability, called a diathesis, and stressors that trigger this vulnerability

diffusion of responsibility   reduction in feelings of personal responsibility in the presence of others

dimensional model   model in which a mental disorder differs from normal functioning in degree rather than kind

discrete emotions theory   theory that humans experience a small number of distinct emotions

discriminant stimulus (S_d)   stimulus associated with the presence of reinforcement

discrimination   negative behavior toward members of out-groups

disinterestedness   attempt to be objective when evaluating the evidence

dismantling   research procedure for examining the effectiveness of isolated components of a larger treatment

dispersion   measure of how loosely or tightly bunched scores are

displacement   directing an impulse from a socially unacceptable target onto a safer and more socially acceptable target

display rules   cross-cultural guidelines for how and when to express emotions

dissociation theory   approach to explaining hypnosis based on a separation between personality functions that are normally well integrated

dissociative amnesia   inability to recall important personal information—most often related to a stressful experience—that can't be explained by ordinary forgetfulness

dissociative disorders   conditions involving disruptions in consciousness, memory, identity, or perception

dissociative fugue   sudden, unexpected travel away from home or the workplace, accompanied by amnesia for significant life events

dissociative identity disorder (DID)   condition characterized by the presence of two or more distinct identities or personality states that recurrently take control of the person's behavior

distributed versus massed practice   studying information in small increments over time (distributed) versus in large increments over a brief amount of time (massed)

divergent thinking   capacity to generate many different solutions to a problem

dominant genes   genes that mask other genes' effects

door-in-the-face technique   persuasive technique involving making an unreasonably large request before making the small request we're hoping to have granted

dopamine   neurotransmitter that plays a key role in movement and reward

double-blind   when neither researchers nor participants are aware of who's in the experimental or control group

drive reduction theory   theory proposing that certain drives, like hunger, thirst, and sexual frustration motivate us to act in ways that minimize aversive states

durability bias   belief that both our good and bad moods will last longer than they do

duration   length of time for which a memory system can retain information

echoic memory   auditory sensory memory

egocentrism   inability to see the world from others' perspectives

ego   psyche's executive and principal decision maker

either–or fallacy   error of framing a question as though we can only answer it in one of two extreme ways

elaborative rehearsal   linking stimuli to each other in a meaningful way to improve retention of information in short-term memory

Electra complex   conflict during phallic stage in which girls supposedly love their fathers romantically and want to eliminate their mothers as rivals

electroconvulsive therapy (ECT)   patients receive brief electrical pulses to the brain that produce a seizure to treat serious psychological problems

electroencephalography (EEG)   recording of brain's electrical activity at the surface of the skull

embryo   second to eighth week of prenatal development, during which limbs, facial features, and major organs of the body take form

emic   approach of studying a culture's behavior from the perspective of an insider

emotion-focused coping   coping strategy that features a positive outlook on feelings or situations accompanied by behaviors that reduce painful emotions

emotional intelligence   ability to understand our own emotions and those of others, and to apply this information to our daily lives

emotional reasoning fallacy   error of using our emotions as guides for evaluating the validity of a claim

empirical (or data-based) **method of test construction**   approach to building tests in which researchers begin with two or more criterion groups, and examine which items best distinguish them

empirically supported therapies   treatments for specific disorders supported by high-quality scientific evidence

empty-nest syndrome   alleged period of depression in mothers following the departure of their grown children from the home

encoding   process of getting information into our memory banks

encoding specificity   phenomenon of remembering something better when the conditions under which we retrieve information are similar to the conditions under which we encoded it

endocrine system   system of glands and hormones that controls secretion of blood-borne chemical messengers

endorphins   chemicals in the brain that play a specialized role in pain reduction

enlightenment effect   learning about psychological research can change real-world behavior for the better

episodic memory   recollection of events in our lives

equipotentiality   assumption that any conditioned stimulus can be associated equally well with any unconditioned stimulus

erogenous zone   sexually arousing zone of the body

etic   approach of studying a culture's behavior from the perspective of an outsider

eugenics   movement in the early twentieth century to improve a population's genetic stock by encouraging those with good genes to reproduce, preventing those with bad genes from reproducing, or both

evolutionary psychology   discipline that applies Darwin's theory of natural selection to human and animal behavior

excitement phase   phase in human sexual response in which people experience sexual pleasure and notice physiological changes associated with it

existence proofs   demonstrations that a given psychological phenomenon can occur

experiential therapies   interventions that recognize the importance of awareness, acceptance, and expression of feelings

experiential thinking   thinking that depends on intuitive judgments and emotional reactions

experiment   research design characterized by random assignment of participants to conditions and manipulation of an independent variable

experimental group   in an experiment, the group of participants that receives the manipulation

experimenter expectancy effect   phenomenon in which researchers' hypotheses lead them to unintentionally bias the outcome of a study

explicit memory   memories we recall intentionally and of which we have conscious awareness

exposure therapy   therapy that confronts patients with what they fear with the goal of reducing the fear

external validity   extent to which we can generalize findings to real-world settings

extinction   gradual reduction and eventual elimination of the conditioned response after the conditioned stimulus is presented repeatedly without the unconditioned stimulus

extralinguistic information   elements of communication that aren't part of the content of language but are critical to interpreting its meaning

extrasensory perception (ESP)   perception of events outside the known channels of sensation

face validity   extent to which respondents can tell what the items are measuring

facial feedback hypothesis   theory that blood vessels in the face feed back temperature information in the brain, altering our experience of emotions

factor analysis   statistical technique that analyzes the correlations among responses on personality inventories and other measures

falsifiable   capable of being disproved

family studies   analyses of how traits run in families

fetishism   sexual attraction to nonliving things

fetus   period of prenatal development from ninth week until birth after all major organs are established and physical maturation is the primary change

fight-or-flight response   physical and psychological reaction that mobilizes people and animals to either defend themselves (fight) or escape (flee) a threatening situation

file drawer problem   tendency for negative findings to remain unpublished

fitness   organisms' capacity to pass on their genes

fixed interval (FI) schedule   pattern in which we provide reinforcement for producing the response at least once following a specified time interval

fixed ratio (FR) schedule   pattern in which we provide reinforcement following a regular number of responses

flashbulb memories   emotional memories that are extraordinarily vivid and detailed

fluid intelligence   capacity to learn new ways of solving problems

Flynn effect   finding that average IQ scores have been rising at a rate of approximately 3 points per decade

foot-in-the-door technique   persuasive technique involving making a small request before making a bigger one

forebrain   forward part of the brain that allows advanced intellectual abilities; also known as the cerebrum

formal operations stage   stage in Piaget's theory characterized by the ability to perform hypothetical reasoning beyond the here and now

fovea   central portion of the retina

free association   technique in which patients express themselves without censorship of any sort

frontal lobe   forward part of cerebral cortex containing the motor cortex and the prefrontal cortex; responsible for motor function, language, and memory

functional fixedness   difficulty conceptualizing that an object typically used for one purpose can be used for another

functional MRI (fMRI)   technique that uses magnetic fields to visualize brain activity

functionalism   school of psychology that aimed to understand the adaptive purposes of psychological characteristics

fundamental attribution error   tendency to overestimate the impact of dispositional influences on *other* people's behavior

g (general intelligence)   hypothetical factor that accounts for overall differences in intellect among people

gender identity   individuals' sense of being male or female

gender roles   behaviors that tend to be associated with being male or female

gene-environment interaction   situation in which the effects of genes depend on the environment in which they are expressed

gene expression   activation or deactivation of genes by environmental experiences throughout development

general adaptation syndrome (GAS)   stress-response pattern proposed by Hans Selye that consists of three stages: alarm, resistance, and exhaustion

generalized anxiety disorder   continual feelings of worry, anxiety, physical tension, and irritability across many areas of life functioning

generative   allowing an infinite number of unique sentences to be created by combining words in novel ways

genes   genetic material, composed of deoxyribonucleic acid (DNA)

genital stage   psychosexual stage in which sexual impulses awaken and typically begin to mature into romantic attraction toward others

genotype   our genetic make-up

Gestalt therapy   therapy that aims to integrate different and sometimes opposing aspects of personality into a unified sense of self

glia (glial) cells   support cells in nervous system that play roles in the formation of myelin and blood–brain barrier, respond to injury, and remove debris

glucostatic theory   theory that when our blood glucose levels drop, hunger creates a drive to eat to restore the proper level of glucose

graphology   psychological interpretation of handwriting

group polarization   tendency of group discussion to strengthen the dominant positions held by individual group members

group socialization theory   theory that peers play a more important role than parents in children's social development

group therapy   therapy that treats more than one person at a time

groupthink   emphasis on group unanimity at the expense of critical thinking and sound decision making

guilty knowledge test   alternative to the polygraph test that relies on the premise that criminals harbor concealed knowledge about the crime that innocent people don't

gustation   our sense of taste

habituation   process of responding less strongly over time to repeated stimuli

hallucinations   sensory perceptions that occur in the absence of an external stimulus

hallucinogenic   causing dramatic alterations of perception, mood, and thought

hardiness   set of attitudes marked by a sense of control over events, commitment to life and work, and courage and motivation to confront stressful events

hassles   minor annoyances or nuisances that strain our ability to cope

Hawthorne effect   phenomenon in which participants' knowledge that they're being studied can affect their behavior

health psychology   field of psychology that integrates the behavioral sciences with the practice of medicine

hedonic treadmill   tendency for our moods to adapt to external circumstances

heritability   percentage of the variability in a trait across individuals that is due to genes

heuristics   mental shortcuts that help us to streamline our thinking and make sense of our world

hierarchy of needs   model, developed by Abraham Maslow, proposing that we must satisfy physiological needs and needs for safety and security before progressing to more complex needs

higher-order conditioning   developing a conditioned response to a conditioned stimulus by virtue of its association with another conditioned stimulus

hindbrain   part of the brain between the spinal cord and midbrain, consisting of the pons, cerebellum, and medulla

hindsight bias   tendency to overestimate how well we could have successfully forecasted known outcomes

hippocampus   part of the brain that plays a role in spatial memory

holophrases   single-word phrases used early in language development to convey an entire thought

homeopathic medicine   remedies that feature a small dose of an illness-inducing substance to activate the body's own natural defenses

homeostasis   equilibrium

homesign   system of signs invented by deaf children of hearing parents who receive no language input

hormones   blood-borne chemical that influences target tissues and glands

hue   color of light

humanistic and existential therapy   therapies that share an emphasis on the development of human potential and the belief that human nature is basically positive

hypnosis   set of techniques that provides people with suggestions for alterations in their perceptions, thoughts, feelings, and behaviors

hypnotic   drug that exerts a sleep-inducing effect

hypochondriasis   an individual's continual preoccupation with the notion that he is suffering from a serious physical disease

hypothalamus   part of the brain responsible for maintaining a constant internal state

hypothesis   testable prediction derived from a theory

iconic memory   visual sensory memory

id   reservoir of our most primitive impulses, including sex and aggression

identification with the aggressor   process of adopting the characteristics of individuals we find threatening

identity   our sense of who we are, and our life goals and priorities

ideological immune system   our psychological defenses against evidence that contradicts our views

idiographic approach   approach to personality that focuses on identifying the unique configuration of characteristics and life history experiences within a person

illusory correlation   perception of a statistical association between two variables where none exists

immune system   body's defense system against invading bacteria, viruses, and other potentially illness-producing organisms and substances

implicit and explicit stereotypes   beliefs about the characteristics of an out-group about which we're either unaware (implicit) or aware (explicit)

implicit memory   memories we don't deliberately remember or reflect on consciously

impression management theory   theory that we don't really change our attitudes, but report that we have so that our behaviors appear consistent with our attitudes

imprinting   phenomenon observed in which baby birds begin to follow around and attach themselves to any large moving object they see in the hours immediately after hatching

in-group bias   tendency to favor individuals within our group over those from outside our group

incentive theories   theories proposing that we're often motivated by positive goals

incompetence to stand trial   assessment of a defendant's mental capacity to stand trial in a court of law

incongruence   inconsistency between our personalities and innate dispositions

incremental validity   extent to which a test contributes information beyond other, more easily collected, measures

independent variable   variable that an experimenter manipulates

individual differences   variations among people in their thinking, emotion, and behavior

infantile amnesia   inability of adults to remember personal experiences that took place before an early age

inferential statistics   mathematical methods that allow us to determine whether we can generalize findings from our sample to the full population

inferiority complex   feelings of low self-esteem that can lead to overcompensation for such feelings

informed consent   informing research participants of what is involved in a study before asking them to participate

inoculation effect   approach to convincing people to change their minds about something by first introducing reasons why the perspective might be correct and then debunking it

insanity defense   legal defense proposing that people shouldn't be held legally responsible for their actions if they weren't of "sound mind" when committing them

insight   grasping the nature of a problem

insight therapies   psychotherapies, including psychodynamic and humanistic-existential approaches, with the goal of expanding awareness or insight

insomnia   difficulty falling and staying asleep

instinctive drift   tendency for animals to return to innate behaviors following repeated reinforcement

integrity tests   questionnaires that presumably assess workers' tendency to steal or cheat

intellectualization   avoiding emotions associated with anxiety-provoking experiences by focusing on abstract and impersonal thoughts

intelligence quotient (IQ)   systematic means of quantifying differences among people in their intelligence

intelligence test   diagnostic tool designed to measure overall thinking ability

interference   loss of information from memory because of competition from additional incoming information

internal–external theory   theory holding that obese people are motivated to eat more by external cues than internal cues

internal validity   extent to which we can draw cause-and-effect inferences from a study

interneurons   neurons that send messages to other neurons nearby and stimulate neurons

interpersonal therapy   treatment that strengthens social skills and targets interpersonal problems, conflicts, and life transitions

introspection   method by which trained observers carefully reflect and report on their mental experiences

involuntary commitment   procedure of placing some mentally ill people in a psychiatric hospital or other facility based on their potential danger to themselves or others, or their inability to care for themselves

James-Lange theory of emotion   theory proposing that emotions result from our interpretations of our bodily reactions to stimuli

jangle fallacy   error of assuming that measures that carry the same label necessarily assess the same thing

jigsaw classrooms   educational approach designed to minimize prejudice by requiring all children to make independent contributions to a shared project

just noticeable difference (JND)   the smallest change in the intensity of a stimulus that we can detect

just-so stories   superficial explanations made up after the fact; a term sometimes applied by critics to some evolutionary psychology hypotheses

just-world hypothesis   claim that our attributions and behaviors are shaped by a deep-seated assumption that the world is fair and all things happen for a reason

labeling theorists   scholars who argue that psychiatric diagnoses exert powerful negative effects on people's perceptions and behaviors

language   largely arbitrary system of communication that combines symbols (such as words or gestural signs) in rule-based ways to create meaning

language acquisition device   hypothetical organ in the brain in which nativists believe knowledge of syntax resides

latency stage   psychosexual stage in which sexual impulses are submerged into the unconscious

latent inhibition   difficulty in establishing classical conditioning to a conditioned stimulus we've repeatedly experienced alone, that is, without the unconditioned stimulus

latent learning   learning that's not directly observable

lateralization   cognitive function that relies more on one side of the brain than the other

law of effect   principle asserting if a stimulus followed by a behavior results in a reward, the stimulus is more likely to elicit the behavior in the future

learned helplessness   tendency to feel helpless in the face of events we can't control

learning   change in an organism's behavior or thought as a result of experience

learning styles   individuals' preferred or optimal method of acquiring new information

lens   part of the eye that changes curvature to keep images in focus

leptin   hormone that signals the hypothalamus and brain stem to reduce appetite and increase the amount of energy used

lesion   area of damage due to surgery, injury, or disease

levels of explanation   rungs on a ladder of explanation, with lower levels tied most closely to biological influences and higher levels tied most closely to social influences

levels of processing   depth of transforming information, which influences how easily we remember it

lexical approach   approach proposing that the most crucial features of personality are embedded in our language

limbic system   emotional center of brain that also plays roles in smell, motivation, and memory

linguistic determinism   view that all thought is represented verbally and that, as a result, our language defines our thinking

linguistic relativity   view that characteristics of language shape our thought processes

locus of control   extent to which people believe that reinforcers and punishers lie inside or outside of their control

logical fallacies   traps in thinking that can lead to mistaken conclusions

logotherapy   therapeutic approach that helps people find meaning in their lives

long-term memory   sustained (from minutes to years) retention of information stored regarding our facts, experiences, and skills

long-term potentiation (LTP)   gradual strengthening of the connections among neurons from repetitive stimulation

longitudinal design   research design that examines development in the same group of people on multiple occasions over time

low-ball technique   persuasive technique in which the seller of a product starts by quoting a low sales price, and then mentions all of the "add-on" costs once the customer has agreed to purchase the product

lucid dreaming   experience of becoming aware that one is dreaming

Magic Number   the span of short-term memory, according to George Miller: seven plus or minus two pieces of information

magnetic resonance imaging (MRI)   technique that uses magnetic fields to indirectly visualize brain structure

magnetoencephalography (MEG)   measure of brain activity using magnotometers that sense tiny magnetic fields generated by the brain

maintenance rehearsal   repeating stimuli in their original form to retain them in short-term memory

major depressive episode   state in which a person experiences a lingering depressed mood or diminished interest in pleasurable activities, along with symptoms that include weight loss and sleep difficulties

manic episode   experience marked by dramatically elevated mood, decreased need for sleep, increased energy, inflated self-esteem, increased talkativeness, and irresponsible behavior

mass hysteria   outbreak of irrational behavior that is spread by social contagion

mean   average; a measure of central tendency

median   middle score in a data set; a measure of central tendency

medical model   perception that regarded mental illness as due to a physical disorder requiring medical treatment

meditation   set of ritualized practices that train attention and awareness

medulla   part of brain stem involved in vital functions, such as heartbeat and breathing

Meehl's maxim   guideline that the best predictor of future behavior is past behavior

memory   retention of information over time

memory illusion   false but subjectively compelling memory

menarche   start of menstruation

menopause   the termination of menstruation, marking the end of a woman's reproductive potential

mental age   age corresponding to the average individual's performance on an intelligence test

mental retardation   condition characterized by an onset prior to adulthood, an IQ below about 70, and an inability to engage in adequate daily functioning

mental set   phenomenon of becoming stuck in a specific problem-solving strategy, inhibiting our ability to generate alternatives

mere exposure effect   phenomenon in which repeated exposure to a stimulus makes us more likely to feel favorably toward it

meta-analysis   investigation of the consistency of patterns of results across large numbers of studies conducted in different laboratories

meta-memory   knowledge about our own memory abilities and limitations

metalinguistic   awareness of how language is structured and used

metaphysical claims   assertions about the world that are unfalsifiable

midbrain   part of the brain stem that lies between the forebrain and hindbrain. It helps to control head and neck reflexes and modulate motor activity

midlife crisis   supposed phase of adulthood characterized by emotional distress about the aging process and an attempt to regain youth

mind–body dualists   scientists who believe that the mind is more than the brain and nervous system

mind–body monists   scientists who believe that the mind is the brain and nervous system in action

Minnesota Multiphasic Personality Inventory (MMPI)   widely used structured test designed to assess symptoms of mental disorders

mirror neurons   cells in the prefrontal cortex that become activated by specific motions when an animal both performs and observes that action

misinformation effect   creation of fictitious memories by providing misleading information about an event after it takes place

mnemonic   a learning aid, strategy, or device that enhances recall

mode   most frequent score in a data set; a measure of central tendency

molecular genetic studies   investigations that allow researchers to pinpoint genes associated with specific personality traits

monocular depth cues   stimuli that enable us to judge depth using only one eye

mono-operation bias   drawing conclusions on the basis of only a single measure

moral treatment   approach to mental illness calling for dignity, kindness, and respect for the mentally ill

morphemes   smallest meaningful units of speech

motivation   psychological drives that propel us in a specific direction

motivation-structural rules   deep-seated similarities in communication across most animal species

motor behaviors   bodily motions that occur as result of self-initiated force that moves the bones and muscles

motor cortex   part of frontal lobe responsible for body movement

multicollinearity   overlap among different causes of behavior, often making it difficult to identify which cause or causes are operating

multiple intelligences   idea that people vary in their ability levels across different domains of intellectual skill

multiply determined   caused by many factors

myelin sheath   glial cell-wrappers around axons that act as insulators of the neuron's signal

mysterians   people who believe that certain questions regarding human nature are unanswerable

mystical experience   feelings of unity or oneness with the world

naive realism   belief that we see the world precisely as it is

narcolepsy   disorder characterized by the rapid and often unexpected onset of sleep

narcotics   drugs that relieve pain and induce sleep

nativist   account of language acquisition that suggests children are born knowing how language works

natural selection   principle that organisms that possess adaptations survive and reproduce at a higher rate than other organisms

naturalistic observation   watching behavior in real-world settings

nature via nurture   tendency of individuals with certain genetic predispositions to seek out and create environments that permit the expression of those predispositions

near-death experiences (NDE)   out-of-body experiences reported by people who've nearly died or thought they were going to die

negative reinforcement   removal of a negative outcome or consequence of a behavior that strengthens the probability of the behavior

neo-Freudian theories   theories derived from Freud's model, but that placed less emphasis on sexuality as a driving force in personality and were more optimistic regarding the prospects for long-term personality growth

neurogenesis   creation of new neurons in adult brain

neurons   nerve cells specialized for communication

neurotransmitters   chemical messengers specialized for communication and released at the synapse

night terrors   sudden waking episodes characterized by screaming, perspiring, and confusion followed by a return to a deep sleep

nocebo effect   harm resulting from the mere expectation of harm

nomothetic approach   approach to personality that focuses on identifying general laws that govern the behavior of all individuals

non-REM (NREM) sleep   Stages 1 through 4 of the sleep cycle, during which eye movements do not occur and dreaming is less frequent and vivid

nonverbal leakage   unconscious spillover of emotions into nonverbal behavior

not me fallacy   error of believing we're immune from thinking errors that afflict others

obedience   adherence to instructions from those of higher authority

Oberg's dictum   premise that we should keep our minds open, but not so open that we believe virtually everything

object permanence   the understanding that objects continue to exist even when out of view

object relations theorists   followers of Freud who emphasized children's mental representations of others

observational learning   learning by watching others

obsessions   persistent ideas, thoughts, or impulses that are unwanted and inappropriate, causing marked distress

obsessive-compulsive disorder (OCD)   condition marked by repeated and lengthy (at least one hour per day) immersion in obsessions, compulsions, or both

occipital lobe   back part of cerebral cortex specialized for vision

Oedipus complex   conflict during phallic stage in which boys supposedly love their mothers romantically and want to eliminate their fathers as rivals

olfaction   our sense of smell

operant conditioning   learning controlled by the consequences of the organism's behavior

opportunity cost   investment of time, energy, and effort in a questionable treatment that can lead people to forfeit the chance to obtain an effective treatment

oral stage   psychosexual stage that focuses on the mouth

organ of Corti   tissue containing the hair cells necessary for hearing

orgasm (climax) phase   phase in human sexual response marked by involuntary rhythmic contractions in the muscles of genitals in both men and women

out-group homogeneity   tendency to view all individuals outside our group as highly similar

out-of-body experience (OBE)   sense of our consciousness leaving our body

overconfidence   tendency to overestimate our ability to make correct predictions

panic attacks   brief, intense episodes of extreme fear characterized by sweating, dizziness, light-headedness, racing heartbeat, and feelings of impending death or going crazy

panic disorder   repeated and unexpected panic attacks, along with either persistent concerns about future attacks or a change in personal behavior in an attempt to avoid them

parametric studies   studies in which an experimenter systematically manipulates the independent variable to observe its effects on the dependent variable

paranormal   events, like extrasensory perception, that fall outside the boundaries of traditional science

paraprofessional   person with no professional training who provides mental health services

parasympathetic division   part of autonomic nervous system that controls rest and digestion

pareidolia   tendency to perceive meaningful images in meaningless visual stimuli

parietal lobe   upper middle part of the cerebral cortex lying behind the frontal lobe specialized for touch and perception

partial reinforcement   only occasional reinforcement of a behavior, resulting in slower extinction than if the behavior had been reinforced continually

participant modeling   technique in which the therapist first models a problematic situation and then guides the patient through steps to cope with it unassisted

passionate love   love marked by powerful, even overwhelming, longing for one's partner

past life regression therapy   therapeutic approach that hypnotizes and supposedly age-regresses patients back to a previous life to identify the source of a present-day problem

pathological skepticism   tendency to dismiss any claims that contradict our beliefs

peak experiences   transcendent moments of intense excitement and tranquility marked by a profound sense of connection to the world

peer review   mechanism whereby experts in a field carefully screen the work of their colleagues

penis envy   supposed desire of girls to possess a penis

peptic ulcer   inflamed area in the stomach lining that can cause pain, nausea, and loss of appetite

perception   the brain's interpretation of raw sensory inputs

perceptual constancy   the process by which we perceive stimuli consistently across varied conditions

peripheral nervous system (PNS)   nerves in the body that extend outside the central nervous system (CNS)

permastore   type of long-term memory that appears to be permanent

person-centered therapy   therapy centering on the patient's goals and ways of solving problems

personality disorder   condition in which personality traits, appearing first in adolescence, are inflexible, stable, expressed in a wide variety of situations, and lead to distress or impairment

phallic stage   psychosexual stage that focuses on the genitals

phantom pain   pain or discomfort felt in an amputated limb

pharmacotherapy   use of medications to treat psychological problems

phenomenological approach   perspective in which therapists encounter patients in terms of subjective phenomena (thoughts, feelings) in the present moment

phenotype   our observable traits

pheromones   odorless chemicals that serve as social signals to members of one's species

phobia   intense fear of an object or situation that's greatly out of proportion to its actual threat

phonemes   categories of sounds our vocal apparatus produces

phonesthemes   similar-sounding words that have related meanings

phonetic decomposition   reading strategy that involves sounding out words by drawing correspondences between printed letters and sounds

Pinocchio response   supposedly perfect physiological or behavioral indicator of lying

pituitary gland   master gland, which, under the control of the hypothalamus, directs the other glands of body

placebo effect   improvement resulting from the mere expectation of improvement

plasticity   ability of the nervous system to change

pleasure principle   tendency of the id to strive for immediate gratification

pluralistic ignorance   error of assuming that no one in a group perceives things as we do

pons   part of hindbrain that connects the cerebral cortex with cerebellum

popular psychology industry   sprawling network of everyday sources of information about human behavior

positive illusions   tendencies to perceive ourselves more positively than others do

positive psychology   discipline that has sought to emphasize human strengths

positive reinforcement   positive outcome or consequence of a behavior that strengthens the probability of the behavior

positivity effect   tendency for people to remember more positive than negative information with age

positron emission tomography (PET)   imaging technique that measures uptake of glucoselike molecules, yielding a picture of regional metabolic activity in brain in different regions

post hoc fallacy   false assumption that because one event occurred before another event, it must have caused that event

posttraumatic stress disorder (PTSD)   marked emotional disturbance after experiencing or witnessing a severely stressful events

prefrontal cortex   part of frontal lobe responsible for thinking, planning, and language

prefrontal lobotomy   surgical procedure that severs fibers connecting the frontal lobes of the brain from the underlying thalamus

prejudice   drawing conclusions about a person, group of people, or situation prior to evaluating the evidence

Premack principle   principle that a less frequently performed behavior can be increased in frequency by reinforcing it with a more frequent behavior

prenatal   prior to birth

preoperational stage   stage in Piaget's theory characterized by the ability to construct mental representations of experience, but not yet perform operations on them

preparedness   evolutionary predisposition to learn some pairings of feared stimuli over others owing to their survival value

prevalence   percentage of people within a population who have a specific mental disorder

primacy effect   tendency to remember words at the beginning of a list especially well

primary appraisal   initial decision regarding whether an event is harmful

primary emotions   small number (perhaps seven) of emotions believed by some theorists to be cross-culturally universal

primary reinforcers   items or outcomes that are naturally pleasurable

primary sex characteristics   the reproductive organs and genitals that distinguish the sexes

priming   our ability to identify a stimulus more easily or more quickly when we've previously encountered similar stimuli

proactive coping   anticipation of problems and stressful situations that promotes effective coping

proactive inhibition   interference with acquisition of new information due to previous learning of information

problem solving   generating a cognitive strategy to accomplish a goal

problem-focused coping   coping strategy by which we tackle life's challenges head-on

procedural memory   memory for how to do things, including motor skills and habits

projection   unconscious attribution of our negative characteristics to others

projective hypothesis   hypothesis that in the process of interpreting ambiguous stimuli, examinees project aspects of their personality onto the stimulus

projective tests   tests consisting of ambiguous stimuli that examinees must interpret or make sense of

proprioception   our sense of body position

proxemics   study of personal space

proximity   physical nearness, a predictor of attraction

pseudoconditioning   an apparent conditioned response that actually turns out to be an unconditioned response to the conditioned stimulus

pseudoscience   set of claims that seems scientific but isn't

psychic determinism   the assumption that all psychological events have a cause

psychoactive drugs   chemicals similar to those found naturally in our brains that alter consciousness by changing chemical processes in neurons

psychoanalysis   school of psychology, founded by Sigmund Freud, that focuses on internal psychological processes of which we're unaware

psychogenic   psychologically caused

psychology   the study of the mind and brain

psychoneuroimmunology   study of the relationship between the immune system and central nervous system

psychopathic personality   condition marked by superficial charm, dishonesty, manipulativeness, self-centeredness, and risk-taking

psychophysiological   illnesses such as asthma and ulcers in which emotions and stress contribute to, maintain, or aggravate the physical condition

psychosocial crisis   dilemma concerning an individual's relations to other people

psychosurgery   brain surgery to treat psychological problems

psychotherapy   a psychological intervention designed to help people resolve emotional, behavioral, and interpersonal problems and improve the quality of their lives

psychotic symptoms   psychological problems reflecting serious distortions in reality

P. T. Barnum effect   tendency of people to accept high base rate descriptions as accurate

punishment   outcome or consequence of a behavior that weakens the probability of the behavior

random assignment   randomly sorting participants into two groups

random selection   procedure that ensures every person in a population has an equal chance of being chosen to participate

range   difference between the highest and lowest scores; a measure of dispersion

rapid eye movements (REM)   darting of the eyes underneath the closed eyelids during sleep

rational thinking   thinking that relies on careful reasoning and objective analysis

rational/theoretical method of test construction   approach to building tests that requires test developers to begin with a clear-cut conceptualization of a trait and then write items to assess that conceptualization

rationalization   providing a reasonable-sounding explanation for unreasonable behaviors or failures

reaction-formation   transformation of an anxiety-provoking emotion into its opposite

reactivity   tendency for people to behave differently when they know they're being studied

reality principle   tendency of the ego to postpone gratification until it can find an appropriate outlet

recall   generating previously remembered information

recency effect   tendency to remember words at the end of a list especially well

receptor sites   locations that uniquely recognize a neurotransmitter

recessive genes   genes that are expressed only in the absence of a dominant gene

reciprocal determinism   tendency for people to mutually influence each other's behavior

reciprocity   rule of give and take, a predictor of attraction

recognition   selecting previously remembered information from an array of options

reflexivity   paradox referring to the fact that the human brain is trying to understand itself

reflex   an automatic motor response to a sensory stimulus like muscle stretch

regression   the act of returning psychologically to a younger, and typically simpler and safer, age

rehearsal   repeating information to extend the duration of retention in short-term memory

reinforcement   outcome or consequence of a behavior that strengths the probability of the behavior

relational aggression   form of indirect aggression, prevalent in girls, involving spreading rumors, gossiping, and nonverbal putdowns for the purpose of social manipulation

relearning   reacquiring knowledge that we'd previously learned but largely forgotten over time

reliability   consistency of measurement

REM sleep   stage of sleep during which the brain is most active and during which vivid dreaming most often occurs

renewal effect   sudden reemergence of a conditioned response following extinction when an animal is returned to the environment in which the conditioned response was acquired

replicability   demand that a study's findings be duplicated, ideally by independent investigators

representativeness   heuristic that involves judging the probability of an event by its superficial similarity to a prototype

repression   motivated forgetting of emotionally threatening memories or impulses

resistance   attempts to avoid confrontation and anxiety associated with uncovering previously repressed thoughts, emotions, and impulses

resolution phase   phase in human sexual response following orgasm, in which people report relaxation and a sense of well-being

response prevention   technique in which therapists prevent patients from performing their typical avoidance behaviors

response sets   tendencies of research participants to distort their responses to questionnaire items

resting potential   electrical charge difference (-70 millivolts) across the neuronal membrane, when the neuron is not being stimulated or inhibited

restless legs syndrome   urge to move our legs or other body parts, often while attempting to sleep

reticular activating system (RAS)   group of neurons in the brain stem that plays a key role in arousal

retina   membrane at the back of the eye responsible for converting light into neural activity

retrieval   reactivation or reconstruction of experiences from our memory stores

retrieval cues   hints that make it easier for us to recall information

retroactive inhibition   interference with retention of old information due to acquisition of new information

retrograde amnesia   loss of memories from our past

reuptake   means of recycling neurotransmitters

risky prediction   forecast that stands a good chance of being wrong

rods   receptor cells in the retina allowing us to see in low levels of light

Rorschach Inkblot Test   projective test consisting of ten symmetrical inkblots

s (specific abilities)   particular ability level in a narrow domain

scaffolding   Vygotskian learning mechanism in which parents provide initial assistance in children's learning but gradually remove structure as children become more competent

scapegoat hypothesis   claim that prejudice arises from a need to blame other groups for our misfortunes

scatterplot   grouping of points on a two-dimensional graph in which each dot represents a single person's data

schedule of reinforcement   pattern of reinforcing a behavior

schema   organized knowledge structure or mental model that we've stored in memory

schizophrenia   severe disorder of thought and emotion associated with a loss of contact with reality

scientific skepticism   approach of evaluating all claims with an open mind, but insisting on persuasive evidence before accepting them

scientific theory   explanation for a large number of findings in the natural world

scientist–practitioner gap   divide between psychologists who believe that clinical practice should primarily be a science versus those who believe that clinical practice should primarily be an art

secondary appraisal   perceptions regarding our ability to cope with an event that follow primary appraisal

secondary reinforcers   neutral objects that people can trade in for reinforcers themselves

secondary sex characteristics   sex-differentiating characteristics that don't relate directly to reproduction, such as breast enlargement in women and deepening voices in men

sedative   drug that exerts a calming effect

selective attention   process of selecting one sensory channel and ignoring or minimizing others

self-actualization   drive to develop our innate potential to the fullest possible extent

self-control   ability to inhibit an impulse to act

self-monitoring   personality trait that assesses the extent to which people's behavior reflect their true feelings and attitudes

self-perception theory   theory that we acquire our attitudes by observing our behaviors

semantic memory   our knowledge of facts about the world

semicircular canals   three fluid-filled canals in the inner ear responsible for our sense of balance

sensation   detection of physical energy by sense organs, which then send information to the brain

sense receptor   specialized cell responsible for converting external stimuli into neural activity for a specific sensory system

sensorimotor stage   stage in Piaget's theory characterized by a focus on the here and now without the ability to represent experiences mentally

sensory cortex   regions of the cerebral cortex devoted to vision, touch, hearing, balance, taste, and smell

sensory memory   brief storage of perceptual information before it is passed to short-term memory

serial position curve   graph depicting the effect of both primacy and recency on people's ability to recall items on a list

set point   value that establishes a range of body and muscle mass we tend to maintain

shaping by successive approximations   conditioning a target behavior by progressively reinforcing behaviors that come closer and closer to the target

short-term memory   memory system that retains information for limited durations

sign language   language developed by members of deaf communities that uses visual rather than auditory communication

similarity   extent to which we have things in common with others, a predictor of attraction

single-variable explanations   explanations that try to account for complex behaviors in terms of only a single cause

Skinner box   small animal chamber constructed by Skinner to allow sustained periods of conditioning to be administered and behaviors to be recorded unsupervised

sleep apnea   disorder caused by a blockage of the airway during sleep, resulting in daytime fatigue

sleep paralysis   state of being unable to move just after falling asleep or right before waking up

sleepwalking   walking while fully asleep

social comparison theory   theory that we seek to evaluate our beliefs, attitudes, and abilities by comparing our reactions with others'

social facilitation   enhancement of performance brought about by the presence of others

social identity support   fact that our friends prop up our sense of self or the social roles we play

social learning theorists   theorists who emphasized thinking as a cause of personality

social loafing   phenomenon whereby individuals become less productive in groups

social phobia   marked fear of public appearances in which embarrassment or humiliation is possible

social pragmatics   account of language acquisition that proposes children infer what words and sentences mean from context and social interactions

social psychology   study of how people influence others' behavior, beliefs, and attitudes

social support   relationships with people and groups that can provide us with emotional comfort and personal and financial resources

sociocognitive theory   approach to hypnosis based on people's attitudes, beliefs, and expectations

somatic marker theory   theory proposing that we use our "gut reactions" to help us determine how we should act

somatic nervous system   part of the peripheral nervous system carrying messages from the CNS through the body to control movement

somatoform disorders   conditions marked by physical symptoms that suggest an underlying medical illness, but that are actually psychological in origin

somatogenic   physiologically caused

somatosensory   our sense of touch, temperature, and pain

source monitoring   ability to identify the origins of a memory

span   how much information a memory system can retain

specific phobias   intense fear of objects, places, or situations that are greatly out of proportion to their actual threat

spermarche   boys' first ejaculation

spirituality   search for the sacred, which may or may not extend to belief in God

split-brain surgery   procedure that involves severing the corpus callosum to reduce the spread of epileptic seizures

spontaneous recovery   sudden reemergence of an extinct conditioned response after a delay in exposure to the conditioned stimulus

standard deviation   measure of dispersion that takes into account how far each data point is from the mean

Stanford-Binet IQ test   intelligence test based on the measure developed by Binet and Simon, adapted by Lewis Terman of Stanford University

state-dependent learning   superior retrieval of memories when the organism is in the same physiological or psychological state as it was during encoding

statistics   application of mathematics to describing and analyzing data

stem cells   unspecialized cells that retain the ability to become a wide variety of specialized cells

stereotype   a belief, positive or negative, about the characteristics of members of a group that is applied generally to most members of the group

stereotype threat   fear that we may confirm a negative group stereotype

stimulants   drugs that increase activity in the central nervous system, including heart rate, respiration, and blood pressure

stimulus discrimination   displaying a less pronounced conditioned response to conditioned stimuli that differ from the original conditioned stimulus

stimulus generalization   process by which conditioned stimuli similar, but not identical to, the original conditioned stimulus elicit a conditioned response

storage   process of keeping information in memory

stranger anxiety   a fear of strangers developing at 8 or 9 months of age

strategic family intervention   family therapy approach designed to remove barriers to effective communication

stress   the tension, discomfort, or physical symptoms that arise when a situation strains our ability to cope effectively

structural family therapy   treatment in which therapists deeply involve themselves in family activities to change how family members arrange and organize interactions

structuralism   school of psychology that aimed to identify the basic elements of psychological experience

structured personality tests   paper-and-pencil tests consisting of questions that respondents answer in one of a few fixed ways

style of life   according to Adler, each person's distinctive way of achieving superiority

sublimation   transforming a socially unacceptable impulse into an admired goal

suggestive memory techniques   procedures that encourage patients to recall memories that may or may not have taken place

superego   our sense of morality

sympathetic division   part of the autonomic nervous system engaged during a crisis, or after actions requiring fight or flight

synapse   space between two connecting neurons through which messages are transmitted

synaptic cleft   space between two connecting neurons where neurotransmitters are released

synaptic vesicles   spherical sacs containing neurotransmitters

syntax   grammatical rules that govern how words are composed into meaningful strings

systematic desensitization   patients are taught to relax as they are gradually exposed to what they fear in a stepwise manner

taste buds   sense receptors in the tongue that respond to sweet, salty, sour, bitter, umami, and perhaps fat

temperament   basic emotional style that appears early in development and is largely genetic in origin

temporal lobe   lower part of cerebral cortex below the temples, which plays roles in hearing, understanding language, and memory

tend and befriend   reaction that mobilizes people to nurture (tend) or seek social support (befriend) under stress

teratogens   environmental factors that can exert a negative impact on prenatal development

terror management theory   theory proposing that our awareness of our death leaves us with an underlying sense of terror with which we cope by adopting reassuring cultural worldviews

test bias   tendency of a test to predict outcomes better in one group than another

thalamus   part of the brain that processes sensory information and serves as a gateway to the cerebral cortex

Thematic Apperception Test (TAT)   projective test requiring examinees to tell a story in response to ambiguous pictures

theory of mind   ability to reason about what other people know or believe

thinking   any mental activity or processing of information, including learning, remembering, perceiving, believing, and deciding

third variable problem   case in which a third variable causes the correlation between two other variables

threshold   membrane potential necessary to trigger an action potential

timbre   complexity or quality of sound that makes musical instruments, human voices, or other sources sound unique

tip-of-the-tongue (TOT) phenomenon   experience of knowing that we know something but being unable to access it

token economy   method in which desirable behaviors are rewarded with tokens that patients can exchange for tangible rewards

tolerance   reduction in the effect of a drug as a result of repeated use, requiring users to consume greater quantities to achieve the same effect

traits   relatively enduring predispositions that influence our behavior across many situations

transcendental temptation   desire to alleviate our anxiety by embracing the supernatural

transcranial magnetic stimulation (TMS)   technique that applies strong and quickly changing magnetic fields to the surface of the skull and that can either enhance or interrupt a brain function

transduction   the process of converting an external energy or substance into neural activity

transference   projecting intense, unrealistic feelings and expectations from the past onto the therapist

triarchic model   model of intelligence proposed by Robert Sternberg positing three distinct types of intelligence: analytical, practical, and creative

trichromatic theory   idea that color vision is based on our sensitivity to three different colors

twin studies   analyses of how traits differ in identical versus fraternal twins

two-factor theory   theory proposing that emotions are produced by an undifferentiated state of arousal along with an attribution (explanation) of that arousal

Type A personality   personality type that describes people who are competitive, driven, hostile, and ambitious

Type D personality   personality type that describes people who experience yet inhibit negative emotions

ultimate attribution error   assumption that behaviors among individual members of a group are due to their internal dispositions

unconditioned response (UCR)   automatic response to a nonneutral stimulus that does not need to be learned

unconditioned stimulus (UCS)   stimulus that elicits an automatic response

validity   extent to which a measure assesses what it purports to measure

variable   anything that can vary

variable interval (VI) schedule   pattern in which we provide reinforcement for producing the response following an average time interval, with the interval varying randomly

variable ratio (VR) schedule   pattern in which we provide reinforcement after a specific number of responses on average, with the number varying randomly

vestibular sense   our sense of equilibrium or balance

von Restorff effect   tendency to remember distinctive stimuli better than less distinctive stimuli

Wechler Adult Intelligence Scale (WAIS)   most widely used intelligence test for adults today, consisting of fourteen subtests to assess different types of mental abilities

Wernicke's area   part of the temporal lobe involved in understanding speech

whole word recognition   reading strategy that involves identifying common words without having to sound them out based on their appearance

wisdom   application of intelligence toward a common good

withdrawal   unpleasant effects of reducing or stopping consumption of a drug that users had consumed habitually

within-group heritability   extent to which the variability of a trait within a group is genetically influenced

work through   to confront and resolve problems, conflicts, and ineffective coping responses in everyday life

Yerkes-Dodson law   inverted U-shaped relation between arousal on the one hand, and affect and performance on the other

zone of proximal development   phase of learning during which children can benefit from instruction

zygote   fertilized egg

References

Abbey, A., Halman, L., & Andrews, F. (1992). Psychosocial, treatment and demographic predictors of the stress associated with infertility. *Fertility and Sterility, 57,* 122–127.

Abbot, N. C., Harkness, E. F., Stevinson, C., Marshall, F. P., Conn, D. A., & Ernst, E. (2001). Spiritual healing as a therapy for chronic pain: A randomized, clinical trial. *Pain, 91,* 79–89.

Abel, E. L., & Sokol, R. J. (1986). Fetal alcohol syndrome is now leading cause of mental retardation. *Lancet, 2,* 1222.

Aber, M., & Rappaport, J. (1994). The violence of prediction: The uneasy relationship between social science and social policy. *Applied and Preventive Psychology, 3,* 43–54.

Abraham, H. D., & Aldridge, A. M. (1993). Adverse consequences of lysergic acid diethylamide. *Addiction, 88,* 1327–1334.

Abrahamson, L., Seligman, Y., & Teasdale, M. (1978). Learned helplessness in humans: Critique and reformulation. *Journal of Abnormal Psychology, 87,* 49–74.

Achenbach, T. M. (1982). Research methods in developmental psychopathology. In P. C. Kendall & J. Butcher (Eds.), *Handbook of research methods in clinical psychology* (pp. 127–181). New York: Wiley.

Ackerman, P. L., & Beier, M. E. (2003). Intelligence, personality, and interests in the career choice process. *Journal of Career Assessment, 11,* 205–218.

Ackerman, P. L., Beier, M. E., & Boyle, M. O. (2005). Working memory and intelligence: The same or different constructs? *Psychological Bulletin, 131,* 30–60.

Ackerman, P. L., & Heggestad, E. D. (1997). Intelligence, personality, and interests: Evidence for overlapping traits. *Psychological Bulletin, 121,* 219–245.

Ackerman, P. L., Kanfer, R., & Goff, M. (1995). Cognitive and non-cognitive determinants of complex skill acquisition. *Journal of Experimental Psychology: Applied, 1,* 270–304.

Ackroyd, E. (1993). *A dictionary of dream symbols.* London: Blanford.

Acocella, J. (1998, April 6). The politics of hysteria. *New Yorker,* 64–79.

Acocella, J. (1999). *Creating hysteria: Women and multiple personality disorder.* San Francisco: Jossey-Bass Publishers.

Adair, J. (1973). *The human subject.* Boston: Little, Brown.

Adams, H. E., Wright, L. E., & Lohr, B. A. (1996). Is homophobia associated with homosexual arousal? *Journal of Abnormal Psychology, 105,* 440–445.

Addis, M. E., Hatgis, C., Bourne, L., Krasnow, A. D., Jacob, K., & Mansfield, A. (2004). Effectiveness of cognitive-behavioral treatment for panic disorder versus treatment as usual in a managed care setting. *Journal of Consulting and Clinical Psychology,* 625–635.

Addis, M. E., & Mahalik, J. R. (2003). Men, masculinity, and the contexts of help seeking. *American Psychologist, 58,* 5–14.

Adelmann, P. K., & Zajonc, R. B. (1989). Facial efference and the experience of emotion. *Annual Review of Psychology, 40,* 249–280.

Adelson, E. H. (1993). Perceptual organization and the judgment of brightness. *Science, 262,* 2042–2044.

Adler, A. (1922). *Practice and theory of individual psychology.* London: Routledge and K. Paul.

Adler, A. (1931). *What life should mean to you.* Boston: Little Brown.

Adler, A. (1938). *Social interest: A challenge of mankind.* London: Faber & Faber.

Adolph, K. E. (1997). Learning in the development of infant locomotion. *Monographs of the Society for Research in Child Development, 63,* Serial No. 251.

Adolphs, R., Tranel, D., Damasio, H., & Damasio, A. (1994). Impaired recognition of emotion in facial expressions following bilateral damage to the human amygdala. *Nature, 372,* 669–672.

Adorno, T. W., Frenkel-Brunswik, E., Levinson, D., & Sanford, R. N. (1950). *The authoritarian personality.* New York: Harper & Row.

Ahmed, S. H., & Koob, G. F. (2005). Transition to drug addiction: A negative reinforcement model based on an allostatic decrease in reward function. *Psychopharmacology, 180,* 473–490.

Ahn, H., & Wampold, B. E. (2001). Where oh where are the specific ingredients? A meta-analysis of component studies in counseling and psychotherapy. *Journal of Counseling Psychology, 48,* 251–257.

Aimone, J. B., Wiles, J., & Gage, F. H. (2006). Potential role for adult neurogenesis in the encoding of time in new memories. *Nature Neuroscience, 9,* 723–727.

Ainsworth, M. D. S., Blehar, M. C., Waters, E., & Wall, S. (1978). *Patterns of attachment: A psychological study of the strange situation.* Hillsdale, NJ: Erlbaum.

Ajdacic-Gross, V., Wang, J., Bopp, M., Eich, D., Rossler, W., & Gutzwiller, F. (2003). Are seasonalities in suicide dependent on suicide methods? A reappraisal. *Social Science and Medicine, 57,* 1173–1181.

Akiskal, H. S., & McKinney, W. T. (1973). Depressive disorders: Toward a unified hypothesis. *Science, 182,* 20–29.

Alavarez, C. X., & Brown, S. W. (2002). What people believe about memory despite the research evidence. *The General Psychologist, 37,* 1–6.

Alberti, R. E., & Emmons, M. L. (2001). *Your perfect right: Assertiveness and equality in your life and relationships* (8th ed.). New York: Impact Publishers.

Alcock, J. (1995). The belief engine. *Skeptical Inquirer, 19,* 14–18.

Alcock, J. E. (1990). *Science and supernature: A critical appraisal of parapsychology.* Buffalo, NY: Prometheus Books.

Alcock, J. E. (1995). The belief engine. *Skeptical Inquirer, 19*(3), 14–18.

Alcoholics Anonymous. (1990). *Alcoholics Anonymous 1989 membership survey.* New York: Alcoholics Anonymous World Services.

Aldrich, M. S. (1999). *Sleep medicine.* New York: Oxford University Press.

Alexander, C., Rainforth, M., & Gelderloos, P. (1991). Transcendental meditation, self-actualization and psychological health: A conceptual overview and statistical meta-analysis. *Journal of Social Behavior and Personality, 6,* 189–249.

Alexander, F. (1950). *Psychosomatic medicine: Its principles and applications.* New York: W. W. Norton.

Alexander, G. M., & Hines, M. (2002). Sex differences in response to children's toys in non-human primates (*cercopithecus aethiops sabaeus*). *Evolution and Human Behavior, 23,* 467–479.

Alexander, R. A., Carson, K. P., Alliger, G. M., & Carr, L. (1987). Correcting doubly truncated correlations: An improved approximation for correcting the bivariate normal correlation when truncation has occurred on both variables. *Educational and Psychological Measurement, 47,* 309–315.

Alferink, L. A. (in press). Educational practices, superstitious behavior, and mythed opportunities. *Scientific Review of Mental Health Practice.*

Alibali, M. W., Bassok, M., Solomon, K. O., Syc, S. E., & Goldin-Meadow, S. (1999). Illuminating mental representations through speech and gesture. *Psychological Science, 10,* 327–333.

Alibali, M. W., Flevares, L. M., & Goldin-Meadow, S. (1997). Assessing knowledge conveyed in gesture: Do teachers have the upper hand? *Journal of Educational Psychology, 89,* 183–193.

Alibali, M. W., & Goldin-Meadow, S. (1993). Gesture-speech mismatch and mechanisms of learning: What the hands reveal about a child's state of mind. *Cognitive Psychology, 25,* 468–523.

Alison, L., Smith, M., & Morgan, K. (2003). Interpreting the accuracy of offender profiles. *Psychology, Crime & Law, 9,* 185–195.

Allard, F. (2001). *Information processing in human perceptual motor performance: Kin 356 course notes.* Waterloo, Ontario, Canada: Department of Kinesiology, University of Waterloo.

Allen, J. J. B., & Moravius, H. L. (2000). The objective assessment of amnesia in dissociative identity disorder using event-related potentials. *International Journal of Psychophysiology, 38,* 21–41.

Alliger, G. M. (1988). Do zero correlations really exist among measures of different intellectual abilities? *Educational & Psychological Measurement, 48,* 275–280.

Alliger, G. M., & Dwight, S. A. (2000). A meta-analytic investigation of the susceptibility of integrity tests to response distortion. *Educational and Psychological Measurement, 60,* 59–72.

Alliger, G. M., Lilienfeld, S. O., & Mitchell, K. E. (1996). The susceptibility of overt and covert integrity tests to coaching and faking. *Psychological Science, 7,* 32–39.

Allison, D. B., Kaprio, J., Korkeila, M., Koskenvuo, M., Neale, M. C., & Hayakawa, K. (1996). The heritability of body mass index among an international sample of monozygotic twins reared apart. *International Journal of Obesity and Related Disorders, 20,* 501–506.

Alloway, R., & Bebbington, P. (1987). The buffer theory of social support: A review of the literature. *Psychological Medicine, 17,* 91–108.

Alloy, L. B., & Abramson, L. Y. (1979). Judgment of contingency in depressed and nondepressed students: Sadder but wiser? *Journal of Experimental Psychology: General, 108,* 441–485.

Alloy, L. B., & Abramson, L. Y. (1988). Depressive realism: Four theoretical perspectives. In L. B. Alloy (Ed.), *Cognitive Process in Depression* (pp. 223–265). New York: Guilford.

Allport, G. (1968). *The search for self.* New York: Norton.

Allport, G. W. (1965). *Letters from Jenny.* New York: Harcourt, Brace, & World.

Allport, G. W. (1966). Traits revisited. *American Psychologist, 21,* 1–10.

Allport, G. W., & Odbert, H. S. (1936). Trait names, a psycholexical study. *Psychological Monographs, 47* (1, Whole No. 211).

Allport, G. W., & Postman, L. J. (1956). The basic psychology of rumor. *Journal of Abnormal and Social Psychology, 53,* 27–33.

Almli, C. R., & Finger, S. (1987). Neural insult and critical period concepts. In M. H. Bornstein (Ed.), *Sensitive periods in development: Interdisciplinary perspectives* (pp. 123–143). Hillsdale, NJ: Lawrence Erlbaum.

Alt, K. W., Jeunesse, C., Buitrago-Téllez, C. H., Wächter, R., Boes, E., & Pichler, S. L. (1997). Evidence for Stone Age cranial surgery. *Nature, 387,* 360.

Altemeyer, B. (2004). Highly dominating, highly authoritarian personalities. *Journal of Social Psychology, 14,* 421–27.

Althius, M. D., Fredman, L., Langenberg, P. W., & Magaziner, J. (1998). The relationship between insomnia and mortality among community-dwelling older women. *Journal of the American Geriatric Society, 46,* 1270–1273.

Altmann, E. M., & Schunn, C. D. (2002). Integrating decay and interference: A new look at an old interaction. In the *Proceedings of the 24th Annual Conference of the Cognitive Science Society.* Mahwah, NJ: Erlbaum.

Alvarado, C. S. (2000). Out of body experiences. In E. Cardena, S. J. Lynn, & S. Krippner (Eds.), *The variety of anomalous experiences* (pp. 183–218). Washington, DC: American Psychological Association.

Alzheimer's Disease Facts and Fictions (2007). Alzheimer's disease information: Retrieved from http://www.psychtreatment.com/alzheimer.htm on December 4, 2007.

Amato, P. R., & Booth, A. (1997). *A generation at risk: Growing up in an era of family upheaval.* Cambridge, MA: Harvard University Press.

Ambady, N., & Rosenthal, R. (1993). Half a minute: Predicting teacher evaluations from thin slices of nonverbal behavior and physical attractiveness. *Journal of Personality and Social Psychology, 64,* 431–441.

American Heart Association (2001). *The American Heart Association's complete guide to heart health.* New York: Clarkson Potter/Random House.

American Psychiatric Association. (1980). *Diagnostic and statistical manual of mental disorders* (3rd ed.). Washington, DC: Author.

American Psychiatric Association. (1994). *Diagnostic and statistical manual of mental disorders* (4th ed.). Washington, DC: American Psychiatric Association Author.

American Psychiatric Association. (2000). *Diagnostic and statistical manual of mental disorders* (4th ed.). Washington, DC: Author.

American Psychiatric Association. (2000). *Diagnostic and statistical manual of mental disorders* (text rev.). Washington, DC: Author.

American Psychiatric Association Committee on Electroconvulsive Therapy. (2001). *The practice of electroconvulsive therapy: Recommendations for treatment, training, and privileging* (2nd ed.). Washington, DC: American Psychiatric Association.

American Psychological Association. (1990). *Ethical principles of psychologists* (amended June 2, 1989). *American Psychologist, 45,* 390–395.

American Psychological Association. (2006). Americans engage in unhealthy behaviors to manage stress. *APA Practice Media Room.* Retrieved from http://apahelpcenter.mediaroom.com/index.php?s=press_releases&item=23.

American Psychological Board of Scientific Affairs: Committee on Animal Research and Ethics (2000). *Research with animals in psychology.* Retrieved September 3, 2007, from http://www.apa.org/science/animal2.html.

Ames, E. (1997). *The development of Romanian orphanage children adopted to Canada. Final report to National Welfare Grants Program: Human Resources Development, Canada.* Barnaby, British Columbia, Canada: Simon Fraser University.

Amir, N., Coles, M. E., Brigidi, B., & Foa, E. B. (2001). The effect of practice on recall of emotional information in individuals with generalized social phobia. *Journal of Abnormal Psychology, 110,* 76–78.

Amsterdam, B. (1972). Mirror self-image reactions before the age of two. *Developmental Psychobiology, 5,* 297–305.

Anand, B. K., & Brobeck, J. R. (1951). Hypothalamic control of food intake in rats and cats. *Yale Journal of Biological Medicine, 24,* 123.

Anand, B. K., & Pillai, R. V. (1967). Activity of single neurons in the hypothalamic feeding centres: Effect of gastric distension. *Journal of Physiology, 192,* 63–77.

Anastasi, A., & Urbina, S. (1996). *Psychological testing.* New York: Prentice Hall.

Ancoli-Israel, S., & Roth T. (1999). Characteristics of insomnia in the United States: Results of the 1991 National Sleep Foundation Survey. *Sleep, 22,* 347–353.

Ancona, L., & Pareyson, R. (1968). Contributo allo studio della aggressione: La dinamica della obbedienza distruttiva [Contribution to the study of aggression: The dynamics of destructive obedience]. *Archivio di Psicologia, Neurologia, e Psichiatria, 29,* 340–372.

Anderson, A. K., Christoff, K., Stappen, I., Panitz, D., Ghahremani, D. G., Glover, G., et al. (2003). Dissociated neural representations of intensity and valence in human olfaction. *Nature Neuroscience, 6,* 196–202.

Anderson, C. A., & Anderson, K. B. (1996). Violent crime rate studies in philosophical context: A destructive testing approach to heat and southern culture of violence effects. *Journal of Personality and Social Psychology, 70,* 740–756.

Anderson, C. A., Berkowitz, L., Donnerstein, E., Huesmann, L. R., Johnson, J. D., Linz, D., et al. (2003). The influence of media violence on youth. *Psychological Science in the Public Interest, 4,* 81–110.

Anderson, C. A., & Bushman, B. J. (2002). Human aggression. *Annual Review of Psychology, 53,* 27–51.

Anderson, C. A., & Bushman, B. J. (2002). Media violence and the American public revisited. *American Psychologist, 57,* 448–450.

Anderson, C. A., & Bushman, B. J. (2002). The effects of media violence on society. *Science, 295,* 2377–2378.

Anderson, C. A., Bushman, B. J., & Groom, R. W. (1997). Hot years and serious and deadly assault: Empirical tests of the heat hypothesis. *Journal of Personality and Social Psychology, 73,* 1213–1223.

Anderson, C. A., Lindsay, J. J., & Bushman, B. J. (1999). Research in the psychological laboratory: Truth or triviality? *Current Directions in Psychological Science, 8,* 3–9.

Anderson, C. M., & Stewart, S. (1983). *Mastering resistance.* New York: Guilford Press.

Anderson, D. R., & Pempek, T. A. (2005). Television and very young children. *American Behavioral Scientist, 48,* 505–522.

Anderson, K. J., Revelle, W., & Lynch, M. J. (1989). Caffeine, impulsivity, and memory scanning: A comparison of two explanations for the Yerkes-Dodson effect. *Motivation and Emotion, 13,* 1–20.

Anderson, K. W., Taylor, S., & McLean, P. (1996). Panic disorder associated with blood-injury-reactivity: The necessity of establishing functional relationships among maladaptive behaviors. *Behavior Therapy, 27,* 463–472.

Anderson, M. C., & Green, C. (2001). Suppressing unwanted memories by executive control. *Nature, 410,* 366–369.

Anderson, S. A. (1990). The 1990 Life Sciences Research Office (LSRO) Report on Nutritional Assessment defined terms associated with food access. Core indicators of nutritional state for difficult to sample populations. *Journal of Nutrition, 102,* 1559–1660.

Andreasen, N. C. (1987). Creativity and mental illness: Prevalence rates in writers and their first-degree relatives. *American Journal of Psychiatry, 144,* 1288–1292.

Andreasen, N. C., Arndt, S., Alliger, R., Miller, D., & Flaum, M. (1995). Symptoms of schizophrenia. Methods, meanings, and mechanisms. *Archives of General Psychiatry, 52,* 341–351.

Andreasen, N. C., Rezai, K., Alliger, R., Swayze, V. W. II, Flaum, M., Kirchner, P., et al. (1992). Hypofrontality in neuroleptic-naive patients and in patients with chronic schizophrenia: Assessment with xenon 133 single-photon emission computed tomography and the Tower of London. *Archives of General Psychiatry, 49,* 943–958.

Andrews, G., Stewart, G., Morris-Yates, A., Holt, P., & Henderson, S. (1990). Evidence for a general neurotic syndrome. *The British Journal of Psychiatry, 157,* 6–12.

Angier, N. (2006, January 3). The cute factor. *New York Times.* Retrieved from http://www.nytimes.com/2006/01/03/science/03cute.html?ex=1293944400&en=9942fdaf51f1211c&ei=5090&partner=rssuserland&emc=rss.

Angold, A. (1999). Comorbidity. *Journal of Child Psychology and Psychiatry, 40,* 57–87.

Antonovsky, A. (1967). Social class life expectancy and overall mortality. *Milbank Memorial Fund Quarterly, 45,* 31–73.

Antony, M. A., & Barlow, D. H. (2002). Specific phobia. In D. H. Barlow (Ed.), *Anxiety and its disorders: The nature and treatment of anxiety and panic* (2nd ed., pp. 380–417). New York: Guilford Press.

Antony, M. A., & Roemer, L. (2003). Behavior therapy. In A. S. Gurman & S. B. Messer. *Essential psychotherapies* (2nd ed., pp. 182–223). New York: Guilford Press.

Antrobus, J. S. (1983). REM and NREM sleep reports: Comparison of word frequencies by cognitive classes. *Psychophysiology, 20,* 562–568.

Antrobus, J. S., Antrobus, J. S., & Fisher, C. (1965). Discrimination of dreaming and nondreaming sleep. *Archives of General Psychiatry, 12,* 395–401.

Aponte, H., & Hoffman, L. (1973). The open door: A structural approach to a family with an anorectic child. *Family Process, 12,* 1–44.

Appelbaum, P. S. (1997). Almost a revolution: An international perspective on the law of involuntary commitment. *Journal of the American Academy of Psychiatry and Law, 25*, 135–147.

Appelle, S., Lynn, S. J., & Newman, L. (2000). The alien abduction experience: Theoretical and empirical issues. In E. Cardena, S. J. Lynn, & S. Krippner (Eds.), *The varieties of anomalous experience: Examining the scientific evidence.* Washington, DC: American Psychological Association.

Applewhite, P. B., Gardner, F., Foley, D., & Clendenin, M. (1971). Failure to condition tetrahymena. *Scandinavian Journal of Psychology, 12*, 65–67.

Archer, D. (1997). *A world of differences: Understanding cross-cultural communication* [video]. Berkeley, CA: University of California, Extension Center for Media and Independent Learning.

Arieti, S. (1959). Manic-depressive psychosis. In S. Arieti (Ed.), *American handbook of psychiatry.* New York: Basic Books.

Arkes H. R. (1991). Costs and benefits of judgment errors: Implications for debiasing. *Psychological Review, 110*, 486–498.

Arkes, H. R., & Tetlock, P. E. (2004). Attributions of implicit prejudice or "Would Jesse Jackson 'fail' the Implicit Association Test?" *Psychological Inquiry, 15*, 257–278.

Arkowitz, H., & Lilienfeld, S. O. (2006). Psychotherapy on trial. *Scientific American Mind, 3*, 42–49.

Arkowitz, H., & Lilienfeld, S. O. (2007). A pill to fix your ills? *Scientific American Mind, 18*, 80–81.

Armor, D. J., Polich, J. M., & Stambul, H. B. (1976). *Alcoholism and treatment.* Santa Monica, CA: Rand.

Arnett, J. (1995). The young and the reckless: Adolescent reckless behavior. *Current Directions in Psychological Science, 4*, 67–71.

Arnett, J. J. (1999). Adolescent storm and stress, reconsidered. *American Psychologist, 4*, 317–326.

Arnold L. M. (1999). A case series of women with postpartum-onset obsessive-compulsive disorder. Primary Care Companion. *Journal of Clinical Psychiatry, 1*, 103–108.

Aronoff, J., Lynn, S. J., & Malinowski, P. (2000). Are cultic environments psychologically harmful? *Clinical Psychology Review, 20*, 91–111.

Aronson, E. (1992). *The social animal* (6th ed.). New York: W. H. Freeman.

Aronson, E. (2008). *The social animal* (10th ed.). New York: Worth/Freeman.

Aronson, E., Blaney, N., Stephan, C., Sikes, J., & Snapp, M. (1978). *The jigsaw classroom.* Beverly Hills, CA: Sage.

Arrigo, B., & Griffin, A. (2004). Serial murder and the case of Aileen Wuornos: Attachment theory, psychopathy, and predatory aggression. *Behavioral Sciences and the Law, 22*, 375–393.

Arzy, S., Seeck, M., Ortigue, S., Spinelli, L., & Blanke, O. (2006). Induction of an illusory shadow person. *Nature, 443*, 287.

Asch, S. E. (1955). Opinions and social pressure. *Scientific American, 193*, 31–35.

Aserinsky, E. (1996). Memories of famous neuropsychologists: The discovery of REM sleep. *Journal of the History of the Neurosciences, 5*, 213–227.

Aserinsky, E., & Kleitman, N. (1953). Regularly occurring periods of ocular motility and concomitant phenomena during sleep. *Science, 118*, 361–375.

Ashcraft, M. H. (1993). A personal case history of transient anomia. *Brain and Language, 44*, 47–57.

Asher, R. (1951). Munchausen's syndrome. *Lancet, 1*, 339–341.

Ashton, S. G., & Goldberg, L. W. (1973). In response to Jackson's challenge: The comparative validity of personality scales constructed by the external (empirical) strategy and scales developed intuitively by experts, novices, and laymen. *Journal of Research in Personality, 7*, 1–20.

Asmundson, J. G., & Taylor, S. (2005). *It's not all in your head: How worrying about your health can make you sick—And what you can do about it.* New York: Guilford.

Aspinwall, L., & Brunhart, S. (2000). What I don't know won't hurt me. In J. Gillham (Ed.), *The science of optimism and hope: Research essays in honor of Martin E. P. Seligman* (pp. 163–200). Philadelphia: Templeton Foundation Press.

Assendelft, W. J. J., Morton, S. C., Yu, E. I., Suttorp, M. J., & Shekelle, P. G. (2003). Spinal manipulative therapy for low back pain: A meta-analysis of effectiveness relative to other therapies. *Annals of Internal Medicine, 138*, 871–881.

Astin, J. A., & Ernst, E. (2002). The effectiveness of spinal manipulation for the treatment of headache disorders: A systematic review of randomized clinical trials. *Cephalalgia, 22*, 617–623.

Atkinson, R. C., & Shiffrin, R. M. (1968). Human memory: A proposed system and its control processes. In K. W. Spence and J. T. Spence (Eds.), *The psychology of learning and motivation: Advances in research and theory* (Vol. 2, pp. 89–195). New York: Academic Press.

Audebert, O., Deiss, V., & Rousset, S. (2006). Hedonism as a predictor of attitudes of young French women towards meat. *Appetite, 46*, 239–247.

Ax, A. F. (1953). The physiological differentiation between fear and anger in humans. *Psychosomatic Medicine, 55*, 433–442.

Axmacher, N., Mormann, F., Fernandez, G., Elger, C. E., & Fell, J. (2006). Memory formation by neuronal synchronization. *Brain Research Reviews, 52*, 170–182.

Axsom, D., & Cooper, J. (1985). Cognitive dissonance and psychotherapy: The role of effort justification in inducing weight loss. *Journal of Experimental Social Psychology*, 149–160.

Axtell, R.E. (1997). *Do's and taboos of body language around the world.* New York: Wiley.

Azar, B. (1999, July/August). Destructive lab attack sends a wake-up call. *APA Monitor.* Retrieved October 22, 2007, from www.apa.org/monitor/.

Aziz-Zadeh, L., Cattaneo, L., Rochat, M., & Rizzolatti, G. (2005). Covert speech arrest induced by rTMS over both motor and nonmotor left hemisphere frontal sites. *Journal of Cognitive Neuroscience, 17*, 928–938.

Azrin, N. H. (1960). Effects of punishment intensity during variable-interval reinforcemen-t. *Journal of Experimental Analysis of Behavior, 3*, 123–142.

Azrin, N. H., & Holz, W. C. (1966). Punishment. In W. K. Honig (Ed.), *Operant behavior: Areas of research and application* (pp. 380–447). New York: Appleton-Century-Crofts.

Babiak, P., & Hare, R. D. (2006). *Snakes in suits: When psychopaths go to work.* New York: Regan Books.

Babyak, M. A., Blumenthal, J. A., Herman, S., Khatri, P., Doraiswamy, P. M., Moore, K. A., et al. (2000). Exercise treatment for major depression: Maintenance of therapeutic benefit at 10 months. *Psychosomatic Medicine, 62*, 633–638.

Bachrach, H., Galatzer-Levy, R., Skolnikoff, A., & Waldron, S. (1991). On the efficacy of psychoanalysis. *Journal of the American Psychoanalytic Association, 39*, 871–916.

Baddeley, A. D. (1993). *Your memory: A user's guide* (2nd ed.). London: Lifecycle Publications.

Baddeley, A. D., & Hitch, G. J. (1974). Working memory, In G. A. Bower (Ed.), *Recent advances in learning and motivation, Vol. 8* (pp. 47–90). New York: Academic Press.

Badman, M. K., & Flier, J. S. (2005). The gut and energy balance: Visceral allies in the obesity wars. *Science, 307*, 1909–1914.

Baer, R. A. (2003). Mindfulness training as a clinical intervention: A conceptual and an empirical review. *Clinical Psychology: Science and Practice, 10*, 125–143.

Bagemihl, B. (1999). *Biological exuberance, animal homosexuality and natural diversity.* London: Profile Books.

Bagnardi, V., Blangiardo, M., LaVecchia, C. L., & Corrado, G. (2001). *Alcohol consumption and the risk of cancer: A meta-analysis.* Bethesda, MD: National Institute on Alcohol Abuse and Alcoholism.

Bahnson, C. B., Smith, K. (1975). Autonomic changes in a multiple personality. *Psychosomatic Medicine, 37*, 85–86.

Bahrick, H. P. (1984). Semantic memory content in permastore: Fifty years of memory for Spanish learning in school. *Journal of Experimental Psychology: General, 113*, 1–29.

Bahrick, H. P., Bahrick, P. O., & Wittlinger, R. P. (1975). Fifty years of memory for names and faces: A cross-sectional approach. *Journal of Experimental Psychology: General, 104*, 54–75.

Bahrick, H. P., & Phelps, E. (1987). Retention of Spanish vocabulary over 8 years. *Journal of Experimental Psychology: Learning, Memory, & Cognition, 13*, 344–349.

Bahrick, L. E., Moss, L., & Fadil, C. (1996). The development of self recognition in infancy. *Ecological Psychology, 8*, 189–208.

Bahrick, L. E., & Watson, J. S. (1985). Detection of intermodal proprioceptive visual contingency as a potential basis of self perception in infancy. *Developmental Psychology, 21*, 963–973.

Bailenson, J. N., Shum, M. S., Atran, S., Medin, D. L., & Coley, J. D. (2002). A bird's eye view: Biological categorization and reasoning within and across cultures. *Cognition, 84*, 1–53.

Bailey, J. M., & Zucker, K. J. (1995). Childhood sex-typed behavior and sexual orientation: A conceptual analysis and quantitative review. *Developmental Psychology, 31*, 43–55.

Bailey, J. M., Bobrow, D., Wolfe, M., & Mikach, S. (1995). Sexual orientation of adult sons of gay fathers. *Developmental Psychology, 31*, 124–129.

Bailey, J. M., Pillard, R. C., Neale, M. C., & Agyei, Y. (1993). Heritable factors influence sexual orientation in women. *Archives of General Psychiatry, 50*, 217–223.

Bailey, J. M., & Pillard, R. C. (1991). A genetic study of male sexual orientation. *Archives of General Psychiatry, 48*, 1089–1096.

Baillargeon, R. (1987). Object permanence in $3\frac{1}{2}$- and $4\frac{1}{2}$-month-old infants. *Developmental Psychology, 23*, 655–664.

Baillargeon, R., & Hanko-Summers, S. (1990). Is the top object adequately supported by the bottom object? Young infants' understanding of support relations. *Cognitive Development, 5*, 29–53.

Baillargeon, R., Spelke, E., & Wasserman, S. (1985). Object permanence in five-month-old infants. *Cognition, 20,* 191–208.

Bainbridge, W. S. (1987). Collective behavior and social movements. In R. Stark (Ed.), *Sociology* (pp. 544–576). Belmont, CA: Wadsworth.

Baker, E. (1985). Psychoanalysis and psychoanalytic psychotherapy. In S. J. Lynn & J. P. Garske (Eds.), *Contemporary psychotherapies: Models and methods* (pp. 19–26). Columbus, OH: Merrill.

Baker, F. M., & Bell, C. C. (1999). Issues in the psychiatric treatment of African Americans. *Psychiatry Services, 50,* 362–368.

Baker, J. R., & Yardley, J. K. (2002). Moderating effect of gender on the relationship between sensation-seeking impulsivity and substance use in adolescents. *Journal of Child and Adolescence Substance Abuse, 12,* 27–43.

Baker, R. A. (1992). Hidden memories: Voices and visions from within. Buffalo, NY: Prometheus Books.

Baker, R. A., & Nickell, J. (1992). *Missing pieces: How to investigate ghosts, UFOs, psychics, and other mysteries.* Buffalo, NY: Prometheus Books.

Baker, S. C., & MacIntyre, P. D. (2000). The role of gender and immersion in communication and second language orientations. *Language Learning, 50,* 311–341.

Baker, W. E. (1999). When can affective conditioning and mere exposure directly influence brand choice? *Journal of Advertising, 28,* 31–47.

Baldwin, D. A. (1993). Infant's ability to consult the speaker for clues to word reference. *Journal of Child Language, 20,* 395–418.

Baldwin, M. W., Carell, S. E., & Lopez, D. F. (1991). Priming relationship schemas: My advisor and the pope are watching me from the back of my mind. *Journal of Experimental Social Psychology, 26,* 435–454.

Ball, J. D., Archer, R. P., & Imhoff, E. A. (1994). Time requirements of psychological testing: A survey of practitioners. *Journal of Personality Assessment, 63,* 239–249.

Ballinger, B., & Yalom, I. (1995). Group therapy in practice. In B. Bongar & L. Beutler (Eds.), *Comprehensive textbook of psychotherapy: Theory and practice* (pp. 189–204). New York: Oxford University Press.

Baltes, P. B., Staudinger, U. M., & Lindenberger, U. (1999). Lifespan psychology: Theory and application to intellectual functioning. *Annual Review of Psychology, 50,* 471–507.

Banaji, M. R. (2001). Implicit attitudes can be measured. In H. D. Roediger III, J. S. Naime, I. Neath, & A. Surprenant (Eds.), *The nature of remembering: Essays in honor of Robert G. Crowder* (pp. 117–150). Washington, DC: American Psychological Association.

Banaji, M. R., & Greenwald, A. G. (1995). Implicit gender stereotyping in judgments of fame. *Journal of Personality and Social Psychology, 68,* 181–198.

Bancaud, J., Brunet-Bourgin, F., Chauvel, P., & Halgren, E. (1994). Anatomical origin of déjà vu and vivid "memories" in human temporal lobe epilepsy. *Brain, 117,* 71–90.

Bancroft, J. (2005). The endocrinology of sexual arousal. *Journal of Endocrinology, 186,* 411–427.

Bandura, A. (1965). Vicarious processes: A case of no-trial learning. In L. Berkowitz (Ed.), *Advances in experimental social psychology* (Vol. 2, pp. 3–55). New York: Academic Press.

Bandura, A. (1971). *Psychological modeling.* Chicago: Aldine/Atherton.

Bandura, A. (1977). Self-efficacy: Toward a unifying theory of behavioral change. *Psychological Review, 84,* 191–215.

Bandura, A. (1983). Temporal dynamics and decomposition of reciprocal determinism. *Psychological Review, 90,* 166–170.

Bandura, A. (1986). *Social foundations of thought and action: A social-cognitive theory.* Englewood, Cliffs, NJ: Prentice Hall.

Bandura, A., Ross, D., & Ross, S. A. (1961). Transmission of aggression through imitation of aggressive models. *Journal of Abnormal and Social Psychology, 63,* 575–582.

Bandura, A., Ross, D., & Ross, S. A. (1963). Imitation of film mediated aggressive models. *Journal of Abnormal and Social Psychology, 66,* 3–11.

Banyai, E. (1991). Toward a social-psychobiological model of hypnosis. In S. J. Lynn & J. W. Rhue (Eds.), *Theories of hypnosis: Current models and perspectives* (pp. 564–598). New York: Guilford Press.

Bányai, É. I., & Hilgard, E. R. (1976). A comparison of active-alert hypnotic induction with traditional relaxation induction. *Journal of Abnormal Psychology, 85,* 218–224.

Baral, B. D., & Das, J. P. (2003). Intelligence: What is indigenous to India and what is shared? In R. J. Sternberg (Ed.), *International handbook of intelligence* (pp. 270–301). Cambridge, England: Cambridge University Press.

Barber, T. X. (1969). *Hypnosis: A scientific approach.* New York: Van Nostrand Reinhold.

Barbour, K. A., Houle, T. T., & Dubbert, P. M. (2003). Physical inactivity as a risk factor for chronic disease. In L. M. Cohen, D. E. McCargie, & F. L. Collins (Eds.), *The health psychology handbook* (pp. 146–168). Thousand Oaks, CA: Sage.

Bard, P. (1942). Neural mechanisms in emotional and sexual behavior. *Psychosomatic Medicine, 4,* 171–172.

Barefoot, J. C., Dahlstrom, W. G., & Williams, R. B. (1983). Hostility, CHD incidence, and total mortality. A 25-year follow-up study of 255 physicians. *Psychosomatic Medicine, 45,* 559–563.

Bar-Eli, A., & Raab, M. (2006). Judgment and decision making in sport and exercise: Rediscovery and new visions. *Journal of Sport and Exercise, 7,* 519–524.

Bargh, J. A. (1994). The Four Horsemen of automaticity: Awareness, efficiency, intention, and control in social cognition. In R. S. Wyer Jr. & T. K. Srull (Eds.), *Handbook of social cognition* (2nd ed., pp. 1–40). Hillsdale, NJ: Erlbaum.

Bargh, J. A., & Chartrand, T. L. (1999). The unbearable automaticity of being. *American Psychologist, 54,* 462–479.

Bargh, J. A., & Ferguson, M. L. (2000). Beyond behaviorism: On the automaticity of higher mental processes. *Psychological Bulletin, 126,* 925–945.

Bargh, J. A., & Pietromonaco, P. (1982.) Automatic information processing and social perception: The influence of trait information presented outside of conscious awareness on impression formation. *Journal of Personality and Social Psychology, 43,* 437–449.

Barker, A. T., Jalinous, R., & Freeston, I. L. (1985). Non-invasive magnetic stimulation of human motor cortex. *Lancet, 1,* 1106–1107.

Barlow, D. H. (1988). *Anxiety and its disorders: The nature and treatment of anxiety and panic.* New York: Guilford.

Barlow, D. H. (2000). Unraveling the mysteries of anxiety and its disorders from the perspective of emotion theory. *American Psychologist, 55,* 1247–1263.

Barlow, D. H. (2004). *Anxiety and its disorders: The nature and treatment of anxiety and panic.* New York: Guilford.

Barlow, D. H., Chorpita, B. F., & Turovsky, J. (1996). Fear, panic, anxiety, and disorders of emotion. In D. A. Hope (Ed.), *Perspectives on anxiety, panic, and fear* (The 43rd Annual Nebraska Symposium on Motivation) (pp. 251–328). Lincoln, NE: University of Nebraska Press.

Barlow, D. M., Sakheim, D. K. and Beck, J. G. (1983). Anxiety increases sexual arousal. *Journal of Abnormal Psychology, 92,* 49–54.

Barnes, P. M., Powell-Griner, E., McFann, K., & Nahin, R. L. (2004). *Complementary and alternative medicine use among adults: United States, 2002.* CDC Advance Data Report #343.

Barnett, R. C., & Rivers, C. (2004, October 13). The persistence of gender myths in math. *Education Week, 24*(7), 39.

Barr, C. E., Mednick, S. A., & Munck-Jorgenson, P. (1990). Maternal influenza and schizophrenic births. *Archives of General Psychiatry, 47,* 869–874.

Barratt, D. (1996). *Trauma and dreams.* Cambridge, MA: Harvard University Press.

Barrett, L. F. (2006). Emotions as natural kinds? *Perspectives on Psychological Science, 1,* 28–58.

Barrett, L. F., & Russell, J. A. (1999). Structure of current affect. *Current Directions in Psychological Science, 8,* 10–14.

Barrick, M. R., & Mount, M. K. (1991). The Big Five personality dimensions and job performance: A meta-analysis. *Personnel Psychology, 44,* 1–26.

Barron, F. (1969). *Creative person and creative process.* New York: Holt, Rinehart and Winston.

Barry, C. T., Frick, P. J., & Killian, A. L. (2003). The relation of narcissism and self-esteem to conduct problems in children. *Journal of Clinical Child and Adolescent Psychology, 32,* 139–152.

Barsalou, L. W. (1983). Ad hoc categories. *Memory & Cognition, 11,* 211–227.

Barsky, A. J., & Wyshak, G. (1990). Hypochondriasis and somatosensory amplification. *British Journal of Psychiatry, 36,* 399–403.

Barta, P. E., Pearlson, G. D., Powers, R. E., Richards S. S., & Tune, L. E. (1990). Auditory hallucinations and smaller superior temporal gyral volume in schizophrenia. *American Journal of Psychiatry, 147,* 1457–1462.

Bartels, A., & Zeki, S. (2006). The temporal order of binding visual attributes. *Vision Research, 46,* 2280–2286.

Bartholomew, R. E. (1994). The social psychology of 'epidemic' koro. *International Journal of Social Psychiatry, 40,* 46–60.

Bartholomew, R. E. (1998). The Martian panic sixty years later: What have we learned? *Skeptical Inquirer, 22*(6), 40–43.

Bartlett, D., & Steele, J. L. (2004). *Howard Hughes: His life and madness.* London: Andre Deutsch.

Bartholomew, R. E., & Goode, E. (2000). Mass delusions and hysterias: Highlights from the past millennium. *Skeptical Inquirer, 24,* 20–28.

Bartlett, F. C. (1932). *Remembering: A study in experimental and social psychology.* Cambridge, England: Cambridge University Press.

Bartone, P. T. (1999). Hardiness protects against war-related stress in army reserve forces. *Consulting Psychology Journal, 51,* 72–82.

Bartoshuk, L. M. (2004). Psychophysics: A journey from the laboratory to the clinic. *Appetite, 43,* 15–18.

Bartz, W. R. (2002, September/October). Teaching skepticism via the CRITIC acronym and the *Skeptical Inquirer. Skeptical Inquirer, 17,* 42–44.

Bashore, T. T., & Rapp, P. E. (1993). Are there alternatives to traditional polygraph procedures? *Psychological Bulletin, 113,* 2–22.

Basil, J. A., Kamil, A. C., Balda, R., & Fite, K. V. (1996). Differences in hippocampal volume among food storing corvids. *Brain Behavior and Evolution, 47,* 156–154.

Batson, C. D. (1987). Prosocial motivation: Is it ever truly altruistic? In L. Berkowitz (Ed.), *Advances in experimental social psychology* (Vol. 20, pp. 65–122). New York: Academic Press.

Batson, C. D., Batson, J., Singlsby, J., Harrell, K., Peekna, H., & Todd, R. (1991). Empathic joy and the empathy-altruism hypothesis. *Journal of Personality and Social Psychology, 61,* 413–426.

Batson, C. D., Duncan, B. D., Ackerman, P., Buckley, T., & Birch, K. (1981). Is empathic emotion a source of altruistic motivation? *Journal of Personality and Social Psychology, 40,* 290–302.

Batson, C. D., & Shaw, L. (1991). Evidence for altruism: Toward a pluralism of prosocial motives. *Psychological Inquiry, 2,* 107–122.

Batson, C. D., & Ventis, W. L. (1982). *The religious experience: A social psychological perspective.* New York: Oxford University Press.

Bauer, H. (1992). *Scientific literacy and the myth of the scientific method.* Urbana, IL: University of Illinois Press.

Baum, A., Cohen, L., & Hall, M. (1993). Control and intrusive memories as possible determinants of chronic stress. *Psychosomatic Medicine, 55,* 274–286.

Baum, H. S. (1987). *The invisible bureaucracy.* Oxford, England: Oxford University Press.

Baumeister, R. F. (2000). Gender differences in erotic plasticity: The female sex drive as socially flexible and responsive. *Psychological Bulletin, 126,* 347–374.

Baumeister, R. F., Campbell, J. D., Krueger, J. I., & Vohs, K. D. (2003). Does high self-esteem cause better performance, interpersonal success, happiness, or healthier lifestyles? *Psychological Science in the Public Interest, 4,* 1–44.

Baumeister, R. F., & Leary, M. R. (1995). The need to belong: Desire for interpersonal attachments as a fundamental human motivation. *Psychological Bulletin, 117,* 497–529.

Baumeister, R. F., Twenge, J. M., & Nuss, C. (2002). Effects of social exclusion on cognitive processes: Anticipated aloneness reduces intelligent thought. *Journal of Personality and Social Psychology, 83,* 817–827.

Baumrind, D. (1964). Some thoughts on ethics of research: After reading Milgram's "Behavioral study of obedience." *American Psychologist, 19,* 421–423.

Baumrind, D. (1971). Current patterns of parental authority. *Developmental Psychology Monographs, 4* (Pts. 1 & 2).

Baumrind, D. (1971). Harmonious parents and their preschool children. *Developmental Psychology, 4,* 99–102.

Baumrind, D. (1991). The influence of parenting style on adolescent competence and substance use. *Journal of Early Adolescence, 11,* 56–95.

Baxendale, S. (2004). Memories aren't made of this: Amnesia at the movies. *British Medical Journal, 18,* 1480–1483.

Baxter, J. C., Brock, B., Hill, P. C., & Rozelle, R. M. (1981). Letters of recommendation: A question of value. *Journal of Applied Psychology, 66,* 296–301.

Baxter, L. R., Schwartz, J. M., Bergman, K. S., Szuba, M. P., Guze, B. H., Mazziotta, J. C. et al. (1992). Caudate glucose metabolic rate changes with both drug and behavior therapy for obsessive-compulsive disorder. *Archives of General Psychiatry, 49,* 681–689.

Bayer, R. (1981). *Homosexuality and American psychiatry: The politics of diagnosis.* Princeton, NJ: Princeton University Press.

Beaman, A., Barnes, P., Klentz, B., & McQuirk, B. (1978). Increasing helping rates through information dissemination: Teaching pays. *Personality and Social Psychology Bulletin, 4,* 406–411.

Beaman, C. P., Bridges, A. M., & Scott, S. K. (2007). From dichotic listening to the irrelevant sound effect: A behavioural and neuroimaging analysis of the processing of unattended speech. *Cortex, 43,* 124–134.

Beauregard, M., & Paquette, V. (2006). Neural correlates of a mystical experience in Carmelite nuns. *Neuroscience Letters, 405,* 186–190.

Bechtoldt, H., Norcross, J. C., Wyckoff, L. A., Pokrywa, M. L., & Campbell, L. F. (2001). Theoretical orientations and employment settings of clinical and counseling psychologists: A comparative study. *The Clinical Psychologist, 54,* 3–6.

Beck, A. T. (1963). Thinking and depression. *Archives of General Psychiatry, 9,* 324–333.

Beck, A. T. (1976). *Cognitive therapy and the emotional disorders.* New York: International Universities Press.

Beck, A. T. (2005). The current state of cognitive therapy: A 40-year retrospective. *Archives of General Psychiatry, 62,* 953–959.

Beck, A. T., Brown, G., Berchick, R. J., Stewart, B. L., & Steer, R. A. (1990). Relationship between hopelessness and ultimate suicide: A replication with psychiatric outpatients. *American Journal of Psychiatry, 147,* 190–195.

Beck, A. T., & Emery, G. (1985). *Anxiety disorders and phobias: A cognitive perspective.* New York: Basic Books.

Beck, A. T., Rush, A. J., Shaw, B. F., & Emery, G. (1979). *Cognitive therapy of depression.* New York: Guilford Press.

Beck, C. T., & Gable, R. K. (2001). Comparative analysis of the performance of the Postpartum Depression Screening Scale with two other depression instruments. *Nursing Research, 50,* 242–250.

Beck, J. (1995). *Cognitive therapy: Basics and beyond.* New York: Guilford Press.

Beck, J. G., Gudmundsdottir, B. Palyo, S. A., Miller, L. M., & Grant, D. M. (2006). Rebound effects following deliberate thought suppression: Does PTSD make a difference? *Behavior Therapy, 37,* 170–180.

Becker, A. E., Burwell, R. A., Gilman, S. E., Herzog, D. B., & Hamburg, P. (2002). Eating behaviors and attitudes following prolonged television exposure among ethnic Fijian adolescent girls. *British Journal of Psychiatry, 180,* 509–514.

Becker, D., & Lamb, S. (1994). Sex bias in the diagnosis of borderline personality disorder and posttraumatic stress disorder. *Professional Psychology: Research and Practice, 25,* 55–61.

Becker, H. S. (1953). Becoming a marijuana user. *American Journal of Sociology, 59,* 235–242.

Becker, S. W., & Eagly, A. H. (2004). The heroism of women and men. *American Psychologist, 59,* 163–178.

Begley, S., & Kasindorf, M. (1979, December 3). Twins: Nazi and Jew. *Newsweek,* 139.

Beidel, D. C., & Turner, S. M. (1986). A critique of the theoretical bases of cognitive-behavioral theories and therapy. *Clinical Psychology Review, 6,* 177–197.

Beier, M. E., & Ackerman, P. L. (2001). Current events knowledge in adults: An investigation of age, intelligence and non-ability determinants. *Psychology and Aging, 16,* 615–628.

Beike, D. R., & Sherman, S. J. (1994). Social inference: Inductions, deductions, and analogies. In R. S. Wyer & T. K. Srull (Eds.), *Handbook of social cognition* (2nd ed., Vol. 1, pp. 209–285). Hillsdale, NJ: Erlbaum.

Békésy, G. (1949). On the resonance curve and the decay period at different points along the cochlear partition. *Journal of the Acoustical Society of America, 21,* 245–254.

Bell, A. P., Weinberg, M. S., & Hammersmith, S. K. (1981). *Sexual preference: Its development in men and women.* Bloomington, IN: Indiana University Press.

Bell, R. (1968). A reinterpretation of the direction of effects in studies of socialization. *Psychological Review, 75,* 81–95.

Bellamy, C. (1998). *The state of the world's children 1998.* New York: Oxford University Press.

Bellezza, F. S. (1999). Mnemonic devices. In A. E. Kazdin (Ed.), *Encyclopedia of psychology.* Washington, DC: American Psychological Association.

Belli, R. F., Winkielman, P., Read, J. D., Schwarz, N., & Lynn, S. J. (1998). Recalling more childhood events leads to judgments of poorer memory: Implications for the recovered/false memory debate. *Psychonomic Bulletin & Review, 5,* 318–323.

Bellinger, D. C., & Needleman, H. L. (2003). Intellectual impairment and blood lead levels. *New England Journal of Medicine, 349,* 500–502.

Belliveau, F., & Richter, L. (1970). *Understanding human sexual inadequacy.* New York: Bantam Books.

Bellon, A. (2006). Searching for new options for treating insomnia: Are melatonin and ramelteon beneficial? *Journal of Psychiatric Practice, 12,* 229–243.

Belsky, J. (1988). The "effects" of infant day care reconsidered. *Early Childhood Research Quarterly, 3,* 235–272.

Belsky, J., & Kelly, J. (1994). *The transition to parenthood.* New York: Delacourte.

Bem, D. J. (1967). Self-perception: An alternative interpretation of cognitive dissonance phenomena. *Psychological Review, 74,* 183–200.

Bem, D. J. (1996). Exotic becomes erotic: A developmental theory of sexual orientation. *Psychological Review, 103,* 320–335.

Bem, D. J. (2000). Exotic becomes erotic: Interpreting the biological correlates of sexual orientation. *Archives of Sexual Behavior, 29,* 531–548.

Bem, D. J., & Allen, A. (1974). On predicting some of the people some of the time: The search for cross-situational consistencies in behavior. *Psychological Review, 81,* 506–520.

Bem, D. J., & Funder, D. C. (1978). Predicting more of the people more of the time: Assessing the personality of situations. *Psychological Review, 85,* 485–500.

Bem, D. J., & McConnell, H. K. (1970). Testing the self-perception explanation of dissonance phenomena: On the salience of premanipulation attitudes. *Journal of Personality and Social Psychology, 14,* 23–31.

Benasich, A. A., & Bejar, I. I. (1992). The Fagan Test of Infant Intelligence: A critical review. *Journal of Applied Developmental Psychology, 13,* 153–171.

Benassi, V. A., Sweeney, P. D., & Dufour, C. L. (1988). Is there a relation between locus of control orientation and depression? *Journal of Abnormal Psychology, 8,* 357–367.

Benbow, C. P., & Stanley, J. C. (1980). Sex differences in mathematical ability: Fact or artifact? *Science, 210,* 1262-1264.

Benbow, C. P., & Stanley, J. C. (1983). Sex differences in mathematical reasoning ability: More facts. *Science, 222,* 1029–1031.

Benedetti, F., Colloca, L., Torre, E., Lanotte, M., Melcaarne, A., Pesare, M., et al. (2004). Placebo-responsive Parkinson patients show decreased activity in single neurons of subthalamic nucleus. *Natural Neuroscience, 7,* 587–588.

Benjamin, L. T., & Baker, D. B. (2004). *From séance to science: A history of the profession of psychology in America.* Belmont, CA: Wadsworth.

Benjamin, L. T., Jr., & Crouse, E. M. (2002). The American Psychological Association's response to *Brown v. Board of Education:* The case of Kenneth B. Clark. *American Psychologist, 57,* 38–50.

Bennett, M. R. (1998). Monoaminergic synapses and schizophrenia: 45 years of neuroleptics. *Journal of Psychopharmacology, 12,* 289–304.

Ben-Shakhar, G., & Elaad, E. (2003). The validity of psychophysiological detection of information with the Guilty Knowledge Test: A meta-analytic review. *Journal of Applied Psychology, 88,* 131–151.

Ben-Shakhar, G., Bar-Hillel, M., Bilu, Y., Ben-Abba, E., & Flug, A. (1986). Can graphology predict occupational success? Two empirical studies and some methodological ruminations. *Journal of Applied Psychology, 71,* 645–653.

Benski, C. (1998). Testing new claims of dermo-optical perception. *Skeptical Inquirer, 22*(1), 21–26.

Benson, E. (2006, June). All that's gold doesn't glitter: How the Golden Fleece tarnished psychological science. *APS Observer.* Retrieved from http://www.psychologicalscience.org/observer/getArticle.cfm?id=1998.

Bentall, R. P. (2000). Hallucinatory experiences. In E. Cardena, S. J. Lynn, & S. Krippner (Eds.), *Varieties of anomalous experience: Examining the scientific evidence* (pp. 85–120). Washington, DC: American Psychological Association.

Bentley, K. J., & Walsh, J. (2006). *The social worker and psychotropic medication: Toward effective collaboration with mental health clients, families, and providers* (3rd ed.). Belmont, CA: Thompson.

Beranek, L. L. (1993). *Acoustics.* New York: Acoustical Society of America.

Berenbaum, S. A., & Hines, M. (1992). Early androgens are related to childhood sex-typed toy preference. *Psychological Science, 3,* 203–206.

Berg, J. H., & Archer, R. L. (1980). Disclosure or concern: A second look at liking for the norm breaker. *Journal of Personality, 48,* 245–257.

Berger, H. (1929). Ueber das Elektroenkephalogramm des Menschen. *Archiv für Psychiatrie und Nervenkrankheiten, 87,* 527–570.

Bergner, R. M. (1997). What is psychopathology? And so what? *Clinical Psychology: Science and Practice, 4,* 235–248.

Bergstrom, S. R. (1968). Acquisition of an avoidance reaction to the light in the protozoa tetrahymena. *Scandinavian Journal of Psychology, 9,* 220–224.

Berk, A. M., Vigorito, M., & Miller, R. R. (1979). Retroactive stimulus interference with conditioned emotional response retention in infant and adult rats: Implications for infantile amnesia. *Journal of Experimental Psychology: Animal Behavior Processes, 3,* 284–299.

Berk, M. S., & Andersen, S. M. (2000). The impact of past relationships on interpersonal behavior: Behavioral confirmation in the social-cognitive process of transference. *Journal of Personality and Social Psychology, 79,* 546–562.

Berkman, L. F., & Syme, S. L. (1979). Social networks, host resistance, and mortality: A nine year follow-up study of Alameda County residents. *American Journal of Epidemiology, 109,* 186–204.

Berkowitz, L. (1989). Frustration-aggression hypothesis: Examination and reformulation. *Psychological Bulletin, 106,* 59–73.

Berkowitz, L., & LePage, A. (1967). Weapons as aggression-eliciting stimuli. *Journal of Personality and Social Psychology, 7,* 202–207.

Berlant, N. E., & Pruitt, S. D. (2003). Adherence to medical recommendations. In L. M. Cohen, D. E. McChargue, & F. L. Collins (Eds.), *The health psychology handbook* (pp. 208–224). Thousand Oaks, CA: Sage Publications.

Berlyne, D. E. (1960). *Conflict, arousal, and curiosity.* New York: McGraw-Hill.

Berman, J. D., & Straus, S. E. (2004). Implementing a research agenda for complementary and alternative medicine. *Annual Review of Medicine, 55,* 239–254.

Berman, J. S., & Norton, N. C. (1985). Does professional training make a therapist more effective? *Psychological Bulletin, 98,* 401–406.

Bernhardt, P. C., Dabbs, J. M., Jr., Fielden, J. A., & Lutter, C. D. (1998). Testosterone changes during vicarious experiences of winning and losing among fans at sporting events. *Physiology & Behavior, 65,* 59–62.

Bernheim, K. F., & Lewine, R. R. (1979). *Schizophrenia: symptoms, treatment, causes.* New York: Norton.

Berns, G. S., Chappelow, J., Zink, C. F., Pagnoni, G., Martin-Skurski, M. E., & Richards, J. (2005). Neurobiological correlates of social conformity and independence during mental rotation. *Biological Psychiatry, 58,* 245–253.

Bernstein, D. A., Borkovec, T. D., & Hazlett-Stevens, H. (2000). *New directions in progressive relaxation training: A guidebook for helping professionals.* Westport, CT: Praeger.

Bernstein, D. M., Laney, C., Morris, E. K., & Loftus, E. F. (2005a). False beliefs about fattening foods can have healthy consequences. *Proceedings of the National Academy of Sciences, 102,* 13724–13731.

Bernstein, D. M., Laney, C., Morris, E. K., & Loftus, E. F. (2005b). False memories about food can lead to food avoidance. *Social Cognition, 23,* 11–34.

Berscheid, E., & Reis, H. T. (1998). Attraction and close relationships. In D. Gilbert, S. Fiske, & G. Lindzey (Eds.), *The handbook of social psychology* (Vol. 2, 4th ed., pp. 193–281). New York: McGraw-Hill.

Bersoff, D. N. (1986). Psychologists and the judicial system. *Law and Human Behavior, 10,* 151–165.

Beunen, G., & Malina, R. M. (1996). *The child and adolescent athlete.* Oxford, England: Blackwell.

Beutler, L. E. (2002). The dodo bird is extinct. *Clinical Psychology: Science and Practice, 9,* 30–34.

Beutler, L. E., Clarkin, J. F., & Bongar, B. (2000). *Guidelines for the systematic treatment of the depressed person.* Oxford, England: Oxford University Press.

Beutler, L. E., & Harwood, T. M. (2002). What is and can be attributed to the therapeutic relationship. *Journal of Contemporary Psychotherapy, 32,* 25–33.

Beutler, L. E., Machado, P. P., & Neufeldt, S. A. (1994). Therapist variables. In A. E. Bergin & S. L. Garfield (Eds.), *Handbook of psychotherapy and behavior change* (4th ed.). New York: John Wiley & Sons.

Beyerstein, B. (1996). Graphology. In G. Stein (Ed.), *The encyclopedia of the paranormal* (pp. 309–324). Buffalo, NY: Prometheus Books.

Beyerstein, B. (1997, September/October). Why bogus therapies seem to work. *Skeptical Inquirer, 21,* 29–34.

Beyerstein, B. (1999). Whence cometh the myth that we only use ten percent of our brains? In S. Della Sala (Ed.), *Mind myths: Exploring popular assumptions about the mind and brain.* New York: John Wiley & Sons.

Beyerstein, B. L. (1995). *Distinguishing science from pseudoscience.* Victoria, British Columbia, Canada: The Centre for Curriculum and Professional Development.

Beyerstein, B. L. (1999). Whence cometh the myth that we only use ten percent of our brains? In S. Della Sala (Ed.), *Mind myths: Exploring everyday mysteries of the mind and brain* (pp. 1–24). Chichester, England: John Wiley and Sons.

Beyerstein, B. L., & Beyerstein, D. F. (1992). *The write stuff: Evaluations of graphology—The study of handwriting analysis.* Buffalo, NY: Prometheus.

Beyerstein, B., & Hadaway, P. (1991). On avoiding folly. *Journal of Drug Issues, 20,* 689–700.

Bialystok, E. (1988). Levels of bilingualism and levels of linguistic awareness. *Developmental Psychology, 24,* 560–567.

Bianchi, M., Fone, K. F., Azmi, N., Heidbreder, C. A., Hagan, J. J., & Marsden, C. A. (2006). Isolation rearing induces recognition memory deficits accompanied by cytoskeletal alterations in rat hippocampus. *European Journal of Neuroscience, 24,* 2894–2902.

Biasi, E., Silvotti, L., & Tirindelli, R. (2001). Pheromone detection in rodents. *Neuroreport, 12,* A81–A84.

Biederman, I., Cooper, E. E., Fox, P. W., & Mahadevan, R. S. (1992). Unexceptional spatial memory in an exceptional memorist. *Journal of Experimental Psychology: Learning, Memory, and Cognition, 18,* 654–657.

Biederman, J., Hirshfeld-Becker, D. R., Rosenbaum, J. F., Herot, C., Friedman, D., Snidman, N., et al. (2001). Further evidence of association between behavioral inhibition and social anxiety in children. *American Journal of Psychiatry, 158,* 1673–1679.

Bierbrauer, G. (1973). *Effect of set, perspective, and temporal factors in attribution.* Unpublished doctoral dissertation, Stanford University, Palo Alto, CA.

Biernbaum, M. A., & Ruscio, M. (2004). Differences between matched heterosexual and non-heterosexual college students on measures of defense mechanisms and psychopathological symptoms. *Journal of Homosexuality, 48*(1), 125–141.

Bigbee, J. (1990). Stressful life events and illness occurrence in rural versus urban women. *Journal of Community Health Nursing, 7,* 105–113.

Bikel, Ofra (Producer). (1995, April 11). Frontline [Television broadcast: Divided Memories]. New York: Public Broadcasting Service.

Biklen, D. (1990). Communication unbound: Autism and praxis. *Harvard Educational Review, 60,* 291–314.

Billings, A. G., & Moos, R. H. (1984). Coping, stress and social resources among adults with unipolar depression. *Journal of Personality and Social Psychology, 46*, 877–891.

Binder J. R., Bellgowan, P. S. F., Hammeke, T. A., Possing, E. T., & Frost, J. A. (2005). A comparison of two fMRI protocols for eliciting hippocampal activation. *Epilepsia, 46*, 1061–1070.

Binet, A., & Simon, T. A. (1905). Méthode nouvelle pour le diagnostic du niveau intellectuel des anormaux. *L'Année Psychologique, 11*, 191–244.

Bink, M. L., & Marsh, R. L. (2000). Cognitive regularities in creative activity. *Review of General Psychology, 4*, 59–78.

Binswanger, L. (1958). The existential analysis school of thought. In R. May, E. Angel, & H. F. Ellenberger (Eds.), *Existence: A new dimension in psychiatry and psychology* (pp. 191–214). New York: Basic Books.

Birch, S. A. J., & Bloom, P. (2003). Children are cursed: An asymmetric bias in mental state attribution. *Psychological Science, 14*, 283–286.

Birmingham, C. L., Su, J., Hlynsky, J. A., Goldner, E. M., & Gao, M. (2005). The mortality rate from anorexia nervosa. *International Journal of Eating Disorders, 38*, 143–146.

Birnbaum, G., Glaubman, H., & Mikulincer, M. (2001). Women's experience of heterosexual intercourse—Scale construction, factor structure, and relations to orgasmic disorder. *Journal of Sex Research, 38*, 191–204.

Birren, J. E., & Renner, V. J. (1977). Research on the psychology of aging: Principles and experimentation. In J. E. Birren & K. W. Schaie (Eds.), *Handbook of the psychology of aging* (pp. 3–38). New York: Van Nostrand Reinhold.

Bishop, D. V. M., & Bishop, S. J. (1998). "Twin language": A risk factor for language impairment? *Journal of Speech, Language & Hearing Research, 41*, 150–160.

Bishop, G. F., Tuchfarber, A. J., & Oldendick, R. W. (1986). Opinions on fictitious issues: The pressure to answer survey questions. *Public Opinion Quarterly, 50*, 240–250.

Bixler , E. O., Kales, A., Soldatos, C. R., Kales, J. D., & Healey, S. (1979). Prevalence of sleep disorders in the Los Angeles metropolitan area. *American Journal of Psychiatry, 136*, 1257–1262.

Bjelakovic, G., Nikolova, D., Gluud, L. L., Simonetti, R. G., & Gluud, C. (2007). Mortality in randomized trials of antioxidant supplements for primary and secondary prevention: Systematic review and meta-analysis. *Journal of the American Medical Association, 297*, 842–847.

Black, S. M., & Hill, C. E. (1984). The psychological well-being of women in their middle years. *Psychology of Women Quarterly, 8*, 282–292.

Blackmore, S. (1991). Lucid dreaming: Awake in your sleep? *Skeptical Inquirer, 15*, 362–370.

Blackmore, S. (1993). *Dying to live: Near-death experiences.* Buffalo, NY: Prometheus.

Blackmore, S. (1998). Abduction by aliens or sleep paralysis? *Skeptical Inquirer, 22*, 23–28.

Blackmore, S. (1998). Experiences of anoxia: Do reflex anoxic seizures resemble near-death experiences? *Journal of Near Death Studies, 17*, 111–120.

Blackmore, S. (2004). *Consciousness: An introduction.* New York: Oxford University Press.

Blackmore, S. J. (1983). Divination with tarot cards: An empirical study. *Journal of the Study for Psychical Research, 52*, 97–101.

Blackmore, S. J. (1984). A postal survey of OBEs and other experiences. *Journal of the Society for Psychical Research, 52*, 225–244.

Blackmore, S. J. (1986). Spontaneous and deliberate OBEs: A questionnaire survey. *Journal of the Society for Psychical Research, 53*, 218–224.

Blair, C. (2006). How similar are fluid cognition and general intelligence? A developmental neuroscience perspective on fluid cognition as an aspect of human cognitive ability. *Behavioral and Brain Sciences, 29*, 109–160.

Blair, S. N., Kohl, H. W., Gordon, N. F., & Paffenberger, R. S. (1992). How much physical activity is good for health? *Annual Review of Public Health, 13*, 99–126.

Blanchard, R., & Bogaert, A. F. (1996). Homosexuality in men and number of older brothers. *American Journal of Psychiatry, 153*, 27–31.

Blanchette, I., & Richards, A. (2003). Anxiety and the interpretation of ambiguous stimuli: Beyond the emotion-congruent effect. *Journal of Experimental Psychology: General, 13*, 294–309.

Blasi, A. (1980). Bridging moral cognition and moral action: A critical review of the literature. *Psychological Bulletin, 88*, 593–637.

Blass, T. (1999). The Milgram paradigm after 35 years. *Journal of Applied Social Psychology, 29*, 955–978.

Blass, T. (2004). *The man who shocked the world: The life and legacy of Stanley Milgram.* New York: Perseus.

Blatt, S. J. (1974). Levels of object representation in anaclitic and introjective depression. *Psychoanalytic Studies of the Child, 29*, 107–157.

Blatt, S. J., Sanislow, C. A., Zuroff, D. C., & Pilkonis, P. A. (1996). Characteristics of effective therapists: Further analyses of data from the NIMH. *TDCRP, Journal of Consulting and Clinical Psychology, 64*, 1276–1284.

Bleuler, E. (1950*). Dementia pracox, or the group of schizophrenias.* (J. Zinkin, Trans.). New York: International Universities Press. (Originally published in 1911)

Bliss, T., Collingridge, G., & Morris, R. (2004). *Long-term potentiation: Enhancing neuroscience for 30 years.* Oxford, England: Oxford University Press.

Block, J. (1976). Issues, problems and pitfalls in assessing sex differences: A critical review of "The Psychology of Sex Differences." *Merrill Palmer Quarterly, 22*, 283–340.

Block, J. (1995). A contrarian view of the five-factor approach to personality description. *Psychological Bulletin, 117*, 187–215.

Block, J. H., Block, J., & Gjerde, P. F. (1986). The personality of children prior to divorce: A prospective study. *Child Development, 57*, 827–840.

Block, N. (1995). How heritability misleads about race. *Cognition, 56*, 99–128.

Blodgett, H. C. (1929). The effect of the introduction of reward upon the maze performance of rats. *University of California Publications in Psychology, 4*, 113–134.

Blood, A. J., & Zatorre, R. J. (2001). Intensely pleasurable responses to music correlate with activity in brain regions implicated in reward and emotion. *Proceedings of the National Academy of Sciences, U. S. A., 98*, 11818–11823.

Bloom, P. (2004). *Descartes' baby: How the science of child development explains what makes us human.* New York: Basic Books.

Bloom, P., & Weisberg, D. S. (2007). Childhood origins of adult resistance to science. *Science, 316*, 996–997.

Blow, A. J., Sprenkle, D. H., & Davis, S. D. (2007). Is who delivers the treatment more important than the treatment itself? The role of the therapist in common factors. *Journal of Marital and Family Therapy, 33*, 298–317.

Blum, D. (2002). *Love at Goon Park: Harry Harlow and the science of affection.* Cambridge, MA: Perseus Publishing.

Boden, M. (1989). *Artificial intelligence in psychology.* Cambridge, MA: MIT Press.

Boese, A. (2007, November 3). The whacko files. *New Scientist, 196*, 49–55.

Bogaert, A. F. (2006). Biological versus nonbiological older brothers and men's sexual orientation. *Proceedings of the National Academy of Sciences, 103*, 10771–10774.

Bogartz, R. S. (1965). The criterion method: Some analyses and remarks. *Psychological Bulletin, 64*, 1–14.

Bohannon, J. N., & Simmons, V. L. (1992). Flashbulb memories: Confidence, consistency, & quantity. In E. Winograd & U. Neisser (Eds.), *Affect and accuracy in recall: Studies of flashbulb memories* (pp. 65–91). Cambridge, England: Cambridge University Press.

Bohart, A. C. (2003). Person-centered psychotherapy and related experiential approaches. In A. S. Gurman & S. B. Messer (Eds.), *Essentials of psychotherapy: Theory and practice* (2nd ed., pp. 107–148). New York: Guilford Press.

Bohart, A., Elliott, R., Greenberg, L. S., & Watson, J. C. (2002). Empathy redux. In J. Norcross & M. Lambert (Eds.), *Psychotherapy relationships that work* (pp. 89–109). Oxford, England: Oxford University Press.

Bolles, R. C. (1962). The difference between statistical hypotheses and scientific hypotheses. *Psychological Reports, 11*, 639–645.

Bonanno, G. (2004). Loss, trauma, and human resilience: Have we underestimated the human capacity to thrive after extremely aversive events? *American Psychologist, 59*, 20–28.

Bonanno, G. A., Field, N. P., Kovacevic, A., & Kaltman, S. (2002). Self-enhancement as a buffer against extreme adversity: Civil war in Bosnia and traumatic loss in the United States. *Personality and Social Psychology Bulletin, 28*, 184–196.

Bonanno, G. A., Galea, S., Bucciarelli, A., & Vlahov, D. (2006). Psychological resilience after disaster: New York City in the aftermath of the September 11th terrorist attack. *Psychological Science, 17*, 181–186.

Bonanno, G. A., & Kaltman, S. (2001). The varieties of grief experience. *Clinical Psychology Review, 21*, 705–734.

Bonanno, G. A., Moskowitz, J. T., Papa, A., & Folkman, S. (2005). Resilience to loss in bereaved spouses, bereaved parents, and bereaved gay men. *Journal of Personality and Social Psychology, 88*, 827–843.

Bonanno, G. A., Papa, A., Lalande, K., Westphal, M., & Coifman, K. (2004). The importance of being flexible: The ability to enhance and suppress emotional expression predicts long-term adjustment. *Psychological Science, 157*, 482–487.

Bonanno, G. A., Wortman, C. B., Lehman, D. R., Tweed, R. G., Haring, M., Sonnega, J., et al. (2002). Resilience to loss and chronic grief: A prospective study from pre-loss to 18 months post-loss. *Journal of Personality and Social Psychology, 83*, 1150–1164.

Bond, C. F. (2006). A world of lies. *Journal of Cross-Cultural Psychology, 30*, 60–74.

Bond, C. F., Pitre, U., & Van Leeuwen, M. D. (1991). Encoding operations and the next-in-line effect. *Personality and Social Psychology Bulletin, 17,* 435–441.

Bond, E. A. (1941). The Yale-Harvard freshman speed reading experiment. *School & Society, 54,* 107–111.

Bond, R., & Smith, R. P. (1996). Culture and conformity: A meta-analysis of studies using Asch's line judgment task. *Psychological Bulletin, 119,* 111–137.

Bond, R., & Titus, L. J. (1983). Social facilitation: A meta-analysis of 241 studies. *Psychological Bulletin, 94,* 265–292.

Bonds, D. R. (2005). Three decades of innovation in the management of sickle cell disease: The road to understanding the sickle cell disease clinical phenotype. *Blood Review, 19,* 99–110.

Boneki, K. A., & Moore, S. (2003). Breaking the silence: Using a token economy to reinforce classroom participation. *Teaching of Psychology, 30,* 224–227.

Bonham, V. L. (2001). Race, ethnicity, and pain treatment: Striving to understand the causes and solutions to the disparities in pain treatment. *Journal of Law & Medical Ethics, 29,* 52–68.

Bonilla, C., Boxill, L. A., Donald, S. A., Williams, T., Sylvester, N., Parra, E. J., et al. (2005). The 8818G allele of the agouti signaling protein (ASIP) gene is ancestral and is associated with darker skin color in African Americans. *Human Genetics, 116,* 402–406.

Boring, E. G. (1923). Intelligence as the tests test it. *New Republic, 35,* 35–37.

Boring, E. G. (1929). *A history of experimental psychology.* New York: Century.

Boring, E. G. (1930). A new ambiguous figure. *American Journal of Psychology, 42,* 444.

Boring, E. G. (1964). Cognitive dissonance: Its use in science. *Science, 145,* 680–685.

Borland, D. C. (1982). A cohort analysis approach to the empty nest syndrome among three ethnic groups of women: A theoretical position. *Journal of Marriage and the Family, 44,* 117–129.

Bornstein, R. F. (1989). Exposure and affect: Overview and meta-analysis of research, 1968–1987. *Psychological Bulletin, 106*(2), 265–289.

Bornstein, R. F. (1992). Critical importance of stimulus unawareness for the production of subliminal psychodynamic activation effects: An attributional model. *Journal of Nervous and Mental Disease, 180,* 69–76.

Bornstein, R. F. (2001). The impending death of psychoanalysis. *Psychoanalytic Psychology, 18,* 3–20.

Bos, H. M. W., van Balen, F., & van den Boom, D. C. (2004). Experience of parenthood, couple relationship, social support, and child-rearing goals in planned lesbian mother families. *Journal of Child Psychology and Psychiatry, 45,* 755–764.

Bos, H. M. W., van Balen, F., & van den Boom, D. C. (2007). Child adjustment and parenting in planned lesbian-parent families. *American Journal of Orthopsychiatry, 77,* 38–48.

Bosson, J. K., Johnson, A. B., Niederhoffer, K., & Swann, W. B., Jr. (2006). Interpersonal chemistry through negativity: Bonding by sharing negative attitudes about others. *Personal Relationships, 13,* 135–150.

Botella, C., Banos, R. M., Guerrero, B., Garcia-Palacio, A., Quero, S., & Alcaniz, M. (2006). Using a flexible virtual environment for treating a storm phobia. *PsychNology, 4,* 129–144.

Bothwell, R. K., Deffenbacher, K. A., & Brigham, J. C. (1987). Correlation of eyewitness accuracy and confidence: Optimality hypothesis revisited. *Journal of Applied Psychology, 72,* 691–695.

Botwinick, J. (1966). Cautiousness in advanced age. *Journal of Gerontology, 21,* 347–353.

Bouchard, C. (1995). Genetics and the metabolic syndrome. *International Journal of Obesity, 19,* 552–559.

Bouchard, L., Drapeau, V., Provencher, V., Lemieux, S., Chagnon, Y., Rice, T., et al. (2004). Neuromedin beta: A strong candidate gene linking eating behaviors and susceptibility to obesity. *American Journal of Clinical Nutrition, 80,* 478–486.

Bouchard, T. J., Jr. (2004). Genetic influence on human psychological traits. *Current Directions in Psychological Science, 4,* 148–151.

Bouchard, T. J., Lykken, D. T., McGue, M., Segal, N. L., & Tellegen, A. (1990, October 12). Sources of human psychological differences: The Minnesota study of twins reared apart. *Science, 250,* 223–228.

Bouchard, T. J., & McGue, M. (1981). Familial studies of intelligence: A review. *Science, 212,* 1055–1059.

Bouman, T. K., Eifert, G. H., & Lejuez, C. W. (1999). Somatoform disorders. In T. Millon, H. Blaney, & R. D. Davis (Eds.), *Oxford textbook of psychopathology* (pp. 444–465). Oxford, England: Oxford University Press.

Bouton, M. E. (1994). Context, ambiguity, and classical conditioning. *Current Directions in Psychological Science, 3,* 1–5.

Bower, G. H. (1981). Mood and memory. *American Psychologist, 36,* 129–148.

Bowers, K. S., & Davidson, T. M. (1991). A neodissociative critique of Spanos's social-psychological model of hypnosis. In S. J. Lynn & J. W. Rhue (Eds.),

Theories of hypnosis: Current models and perspectives (pp. 105–143). New York: Guilford.

Bowers, T., & Clum, G. (1988). Specific and nonspecific treatment effects in controlled psychotherapy research. *Psychological Bulletin, 103,* 315–323.

Bowlby, J. (1973). *Attachment and loss. Vol. 2: Separation: Anxiety & anger.* London: Hogarth.

Bowlby, J. (1990). The study and reduction of group tensions in the family. In E. Trist, H. Murray, & B. Trist (Eds.), *The social engagement of social science: A Tavistock anthology, Vol. I: The socio-psychological perspective* (pp. 291–298). Baltimore: University of Pennsylvania Press.

Bowman, D., Scogin, F., Floyd, M., & McKendree-Smith, N. (2001). Psychotherapy length of stay and outcome: A meta-analysis of the effect of therapist sex. *Psychotherapy, 38,* 142–150.

Bradbury, E. J., & McMahon, S. B. (2006). Spinal cord repair strategies: Why do they work? *Nature Reviews Neuroscience, 7,* 644–653.

Bradbury, J. (2005). Molecular insights into human brain evolution. *PLoS Biology 3,* 50.

Bradley, L., & Bryant, P. E. (1983). Categorizing sounds and learning to read: A causal connection. *Nature, 301,* 419–421.

Braffman, W., & Kirsch, I. (1999). Imaginative suggestibility and hypnotizability: An empirical analysis. *Journal of Personality and Social Psychology, 77,* 578–587

Braid, J. (1843). *Neurohypnology, or the rationale of nervous sleep considered in relation with animal magnetism.* London: Churchill.

Brambilla, P., Cipriani, A., Hotopf, M., & Barbui, C. (2005). Side-effect profile of fluoxetine in comparison with other SSRIs, tricyclic, and newer antidepressants: A meta-analysis of clinical trial data. *Pharmacopsychiatry, 38,* 69–77.

Bramel, D., & Friend, R. (1981). Hawthorne, the myth of the docile worker, and class bias in psychology. *American Psychologist, 36,* 867–878.

Branden, N. (1994). *Six pillars of self-esteem.* New York: Bantam Books.

Brandsma, J. M., Maultsby, M. C., & Welsh, R. J. (1980). Alcoholics Anonymous: An empirical outcome study. *Addictive Behaviors, 5,* 359–370.

Brandsma, L., & Herbert, J. D. (1997). The use of creative arts therapies in counseling and psychotherapy. *Counseling and Human Development, 30,* 1–10.

Bransford, J. D., & Franks, F. F. (1971). The abstraction of linguistic ideas. *Cognitive Psychology, 2,* 331–350.

Bransford, J. D., & Johnson, M. K. (1972). Contextual prerequisites for understanding: Some investigations of comprehension and recall. *Journal of Verbal Learning and Verbal Behavior, 11,* 717–726.

Braun, A. R., Balkin, T. J., Wesensten, N. J., Carson, R. E., Varga, M., Baldwin, P., et al. (1997). Regional cerebral blood flow throughout the sleep-wake cycle. *Brain, 120,* 1173–1197.

Braun, A. R., Balkin, T. J., Wesensten, N. J., Gwadry, F., Carson, R. E., Varga, M., et al. (1998). Dissociated pattern of activity in visual cortices and their projections during human rapid eye movement sleep. *Science, 279,* 91–95.

Braun, K. A., Ellis, R., & Loftus, E. F. (2002). Make my memory. *Psychology and Marketing, 19,* 1–23.

Bray G. A. (1985) Complications of obesity. *Journal of the American Medical Association, 240,* 1607–1634.

Brehm, S. S., Miller, R. S., Perlman, D., & Campbell, S. M. (2002). *Intimate relationships* (3rd ed.). New York: McGraw-Hill.

Breland, K., & Breland, M. (1966). The misbehavior of organisms. *American Psychologist, 16,* 681–84.

Brende, J. O. (1984). The psychophysiologic manifestations of dissociation: Electrodermal responses in a multiple personality patient. *Psychiatry Clinics of North America, 7,* 41–50.

Brennan, P. A., & Mednick, S. A. (1994). Learning theory approach to the deterrence of criminal recidivism. *Journal of Abnormal Psychology, 103,* 430–440.

Brenner, C. (1973). *An elementary textbook of psychoanalysis.* New York: International Universities Press.

Breslau, N., Kilbey, K. M., & Andreski, P. (1993). Nicotine dependence and major depression. *Archives of General Psychiatry, 50,* 31–35.

Bresnahan, M., et al. (2004). Serologic evidence for prenatal influenza in the etiology of schizophrenia. *Archives of General Psychiatry, 61,* 774–780.

Breuer, J., & Freud, S. (1895). *Studies on hysteria.* In Strachey, J. et al. (Trans. and ed.), *The standard edition of the Complete Psychological Works of Sigmund Freud (1953–74)* (Vol. 2). London: Hogarth Press and the Institute of Psycho-Analysis.

Brewer, C. (1992). Controlled trials of Antabuse in alcoholism: The importance of supervision and adequate dosage. *Acta Psychiatrica Scandinavica, 86,* 51–58.

Brewer, D. D., Brody, S., Drucker, E., Gisselquist, D., Minkin, S. F., Potterat, J. J., et al. (2003). Mounting anomalies in the epidemiology of HIV in

Africa: Cry the beloved paradigm. *International Journal of STD & AIDS, 14,* 144–147.

Brickman, P., & Campbell, D. T. (1971). Hedonic relativism and planning the good society. In M. H. Appley (Ed.), *Adaptation level theory: A symposium* (pp. 287–302). New York: Academic Press.

Brickman, P., Coates, D., & Janoff-Bulman, R. (1978). Lottery winners and accident victims: Is happiness relative? *Journal of Personality and Social Psychology, 36,* 917–927.

Bridgeman, B., & Morgan, R. (1996). Success in college for students with discrepancies between performance on multiple-choice and essay tests. *Journal of Educational Psychology, 88,* 333–340.

Brier, A., Buchanan, R. W., Ahmed, E., Munson, R. C., Kirkpatrick, B., & Gellad, F. (1992). Brain morphology and schizophrenia: A magnetic resonance imaging study of limbic, prefrontal cortex, and caudate structures. *Archives of General Psychiatry, 49,* 921–927.

Brinkhaus, B., Witt, C. M., Jena, S., Linde, K., Streng, A., Wagenpfeil, S., et al. (2006). Acupuncture in patients with chronic low back pain: A randomized controlled trial. *Archives of Internal Medicine, 166,* 450–457.

Brizendine, L. (2006). *The female brain.* New York: Morgan Road Books.

Broadbent, D. E. (1957). A mechanical model for human attention and immediate memory. *Psychological Review, 54,* 205–215.

Broca, P. P. (1861). Loss of speech, chronic softening and partial destruction of the anterior left lobe of the brain. Bulletin de la Société Anthropologique, 2, 235–238.

Brodsky, S. L., Hooper, N., Tipper, D., and Yates, B. (1999). Attorney invasion of witness space. *Law and Psychology Review, 23,* 49–69.

Brody, A. L., Saxena, S., Stoessel, P., Gillies, L. A., Fairbanks, L. A., Alborzian, S., et al. (2001). Regional brain metabolic changes in patients with major depression treated with either paroxetine or interpersonal therapy. *Archives of General Psychiatry, 58,* 631–640.

Brody, J. (2007, April 17). When a brain forgets where memory is. *New York Times.* Accessed August 2, 2007, from http://www.nytimes.com/2007 /04/17/health/psychology/17brody.html.

Brody, N. (1992). *Intelligence* (2nd ed.). San Diego, CA: Academic Press.

Bronfenbrenner, U., McClelland, P., Wethington, E., Moen, P., & Ceci, S. J. (1996). *The state of Americans: This generation and the next.* New York: Free Press.

Bronowski, J. (1966). The logic of the mind. *American Scientist, 54,* 1–4.

Brookhuis, K. A. (1998). How to measure driving ability under the influence of alcohol and drugs, and why. *Human Psychopharmacology, 13,* 64–69.

Brown, A. S. (1991). A review of the tip of the tongue phenomenon. *Psychological Bulletin, 109,* 204–223.

Brown, A. S. (2003). A review of the déjà vu experience. *Psychological Bulletin, 129,* 394–413.

Brown, A. S. (2004). *The déjà vu experience.* New York: Psychology Press.

Brown, A. S. (2004). The déjà vu illusion. *Current Directions in Psychological Science, 13,* 256–259.

Brown, A. S., Begg, M. D., Gravenstein, S., Schaefer, C. A., Wyatt, W. J., Bresnahan, M., et al. (2004). Serologic evidence for prenatal influenza in the etiology of schizophrenia. *Archives of General Psychiatry, 61,* 774–780.

Brown, D. (2006, November 20). Some believe "truth serums" will come back. *Washington Post,* A08.

Brown D., Scheflin A. W., & Hammond C. (1997). *Trauma, memory, treatment, and the law.* New York: W. W. Norton.

Brown, G. W., & Harris, T. (1978), *Social origins of depression: A study of psychiatric disorder in women.* London: Tavistock Publications.

Brown, G. W., & Harris, T. (1986). Establishing causal links: The Bedford College studies of depression. In H. Katching (Ed.), *Life events and psychiatric disorders* (pp. 87–107). Cambridge, England: Cambridge University Press.

Brown, G. W., Monck, E. M., Carstairs, G. M., & Wing, J. K. (1962). Influence of family life on the course of schizophrenic illness. *British Journal of Preventive and Social Medicine, 16,* 55–68.

Brown, L. S. (2006). The neglect of lesbian, gay, bisexual, and transgendered clients. In J. C. Norcross, L. E. Beutler, & R. F. Levant (Eds.), *Evidence-based practices in mental health* (pp. 346–352). Washington, DC: American Psychological Association.

Brown, P. K., & Wald, G. (1964). Visual pigments in single rods and cones of the human retina. *Science 144,* 45–52.

Brown, R., & Armelagos, G. J. (2001). Apportionment of racial diversity: A review. *Evolutionary Anthropology, 10,* 34–40.

Brown, R., & Kulik, J. (1977). Flashbulb memories. *Cognition, 5,* 73–99.

Brown, R. P., & Day, E. A. (2006). The difference isn't Black and White: Stereotype threat and the race difference on Raven's Progressive Matrices. *Journal of Applied Psychology, 91,* 979–985.

Brown, R. W., & McNeil, D. (1966). The "tip-of-the-tongue" phenomenon. *Journal of Verbal Learning and Verbal Behavior, 5,* 325–337.

Brown, V. R., & Paulus, P. B. (2002). Making group brainstorming more effective: Recommendations from an associative memory perspective. *Current Directions in Psychological Science, 11,* 208–212.

Brownell, K. D., & Rodin, J. (1994). The dieting maelstrom: Is it possible and advisable to lose weight? *American Psychologist, 49,* 781–791.

Brownstein, M., & Solyom, L. (1986). The dilemma of Howard Hughes: Paradoxical behavior in compulsive disorders. *Canadian Journal of Psychiatry, 31,* 238–240.

Bruce, A. S., & Desmond, S. A. (1997). Limitations of self-report delinquency surveys: A "hands-on" approach." *Teaching Sociology, 25,* 315–321.

Bruer, J. T. (1999). *The myth of the first three years: A new understanding of brain development and lifelong learning.* New York: Free Press.

Brugha, T. S. (Ed.). (1995). *Social support and psychiatric disorder research findings and guidelines for clinical practice.* Cambridge, England: Cambridge University Press.

Bruner, J. S. (1957). Going beyond the information given. In J. S. Bruner, E. Brunswik, L. Festinger, F. Heider, K. F. Muenzinger, C. E. Osgood, & D. Rapaport, (Eds.), *Contemporary approaches to cognition* (pp. 41–69). Cambridge, MA: Harvard University Press.

Brunvand, J. H. (1999). *Too good to be true: The colossal book of urban legends.* New York: W. W. Norton.

Bryan, J. H., & Test, M. A. (1967). Models and helping: Naturalistic studies in aiding behavior. *Journal of Personality and Social Psychology, 6,* 400–407.

Bryant, P. E., Bradley, L., MacLean, M., & Crossland, J. (1989). Nursery rhymes, phonological skills, and reading. *Journal of Child Language, 16,* 407–428.

Bryant, R. A. (2000). Cognitive behavioral therapy of violence-related posttraumatic stress disorder. *Aggression and Violent Behavior, 5,* 79-97.

Bryant, R. A., Felmingham, K. L., Kemp, A. H., Barton, M., Peduto, A. S., Rennie, C., et al. (2005). Neural networks of information processing in posttraumatic stress disorder: A functional magnetic resonance imaging study. *Biological Psychology, 58,* 111–118.

Buck, L., & Axel, R. (1991). A novel multigene family may encode odorant receptors: A molecular basis for odor recognition. *Cell, 65,* 175–183.

Buckalew, L. W., & Ross, S (1981). Relationship of perceptual characteristics to. efficacy of placebos. *Psychological Reports, 49,* 955–961.

Buckley, K. W. (1982). The selling of a psychologist: John Broadus Watson and the application of behavioral techniques to advertising. *Journal of the History of the Behavioral Sciences, 18,* 207–221.

Buffalo & Squire, 2000

Bugenthal, J. F. T. (1976). *The search for existential identity.* New York: Jossey-Bass.

Bulik, C. M., Sullivan, P. F., & Kendler, K. S. (1998). Heritability of binge-eating and broadly defined bulimia nervosa. *Biological Psychiatry, 44,* 1210–1218.

Bull, R., & Rumsey, N. (1988). *The social psychology of facial appearance.* New York: Springer-Verlag.

Bunge, M. (1984, Fall). What is pseudoscience? *Skeptical Inquirer, 9,* 36–46.

Bunge, M. (1998). *Philosophy of science: From problem to theory* (Vol. 1). Piscataway, NJ: Transaction Publishers.

Bureau of Labor Statistics. (2006). *Number of jobs held, labor market activity, and earnings growth among the youngest baby boomers: Results from a longitudinal survey.* Retrieved from http://www.bls.gov/news.release /nlsoy.nr0.htm.

Burger, J. M. (1987). Desire for control and conformity to a perceived norm. *Journal of Personality and Social Psychology, 53,* 355–360.

Burger, J. M., & Petty, R. E. (1981). The low-ball compliance technique: Task or person commitment? *Journal of Personality and Social Psychology, 40,* 492–500.

Burgess, E. O. (2004). Sexuality in midlife and later life couples. In J. H. Harvey, A. Wenzel, & S. Sprecher (Eds.), *The handbook of sexuality in close relationships* (pp. 437–454). Mahwah, NJ: Lawrence Erlbaum Associates.

Burgess, K. B., Marshall, P., Rubin K. H., & Fox, N. A. (2003). Infant attachment and temperament as predictors of subsequent behavior problems and psychophysiological functioning. *Journal of Child Psychology and Psychiatry and Allied Disciplines, 44,* 1–13.

Burke, B. L., Arkowitz, H., & Dunn, C. (2002). The efficacy of motivational interviewing. In W. R. Miller & S. Rollnick (Eds.), *Motivational interviewing: Preparing people for change* (2nd ed., pp. 217–250). New York: Guilford Press.

Burke, B. L., Arkowitz, H., & Menchola, M. (2003). The efficacy of motivational interviewing: A meta-analysis of controlled clinical trials. *Journal of Consulting and Clinical Psychology, 71,* 843–861.

Burke, R. S., & Stephens, R. S. (1999). Social anxiety and drinking in college students: A social cognitive theory analysis. *Clinical Psychology Review, 19*(5), 513–530.

Burns, G. L., & Farina, A. (1992). The role of physical attractiveness in adjustment. *Genetic, Social, and General Psychology Monographs, 118,* 157–194.

Busatto, G. F., Pilowsky, L. S., Costa, D. C., Ell, P. J., Lingford-Hughes, A., & Kerwin, R. W. (1995). In vivo imaging of GABAA receptors using sequential whole-volume iodine-123 iomazenil single-photon emission tomography. *European Journal of Nuclear Medicine, 22,* 1–26.

Busch, C. M., Zonderman, A. B., & Costa, P. T. (1994). Menopausal transition and psychological distress in a nationally representative sample: Is menopause associated with psychological distress? *Journal of Aging and Healthy, 6,* 209–228.

Bushman, B. J., & Anderson, C. A. (2001). Media violence and the American public: Scientific facts versus media misinformation. *American Psychologist, 56,* 477–489.

Bushman, B. J., & Baumeister, R. F. (1998). Threatened egotism, narcissism, self-esteem, and direct and displaced aggression: Does self-love or self-hate lead to violence? *Journal of Personality and Social Psychology, 75,* 219–229.

Bushnell, M. C., Duncan, G. H., Hofbauer, R. K., Ha, B., Chen, J. I., & Carrier, B. (1999). Pain perception: Is there a role for primary somatosensory cortex? *Proceedings of the National Academy of Sciences, U.S.A., 96,* 7705–7709.

Buss, D., & Kenrick, D. T. (1998). Evolutionary social psychology. In D. T. Gilbert, S. T. Fiske, & G. Lindzey (Eds.), *The handbook of social psychology* (4th ed., Vol. 1, pp. 982–1026). Boston: McGraw Hill.

Buss, D. M. (1989). Sex differences in human mate preferences: Evolutionary hypotheses tested in 37 cultures. *Behavioral and Brain Sciences, 12,* 1–14.

Buss, D. M. (1994). *The evolution of desire: Strategies of human mating.* New York: Basic Books.

Buss, D. M. (1995). Evolutionary psychology: A new paradigm for psychological science. *Psychological Inquiry, 6,* 1–30.

Buss, D. M., & Schmitt, D. P. (1993). Sexual strategies theory: An evolutionary perspective on human mating. *Psychological Review, 100,* 204–232.

Buss, D. M., Shackelford, T. K., Kirkpatrick, L. A., & Larsen, R. J. (2001). A half-century of mate preferences: The cultural evolution of values. *Journal of Marriage and Families, 63,* 492–503.

Butcher, J. N., Dahlstrom, W. G., Graham, J. R., Tellegen, A., & Kaemmer, B. (1989). *MMPI-2: Manual for administration and scoring.* Minneapolis, MN: University of Minnesota Press.

Butler, B. (2006). NGRI revisited: Venirepersons' attitudes toward the insanity defense. *Journal of Applied Social Psychology, 36,* 1833–1847.

Butler, S., & Watson, R. (1985). Individual differences in memory for dreams: The role of cognitive skills. *Perceptual and Motor Skills, 53,* 841–864.

Butzlaff, R. L., & Hooley, J. M. (1998). Expressed emotion and psychiatric relapse: A meta-analysis. *Archives of General Psychiatry, 55,* 547–552.

Buunk, B. P., Dijkstra, P., Fetchenhauer, D., & Kenrick, D. (2002). Age and gender differences in mate selection criteria for various involvement levels. *Personal Relationships, 9,* 271–278.

Byrne, D. (1971). *The attraction paradigm.* New York: Academic Press.

Byrne, R. (2007). *The secret.* New York: Atria Books.

Byrnes, J. P. (1988). Formal operations: A systematic reformulation. *Developmental Review, 8,* 66–87.

Cabeza, R., & Nyberg, L. (1997). Imaging cognition: An empirical review of PET studies with normal subjects. *Journal of Cognitive Neuroscience, 9,* 1–26.

Cacioppo, J. T. (2004). Common sense, intuition, and theory in personality and social psychology. *Personality and Social Psychology Review, 8,* 114–122.

Cacioppo, J. T., Berntson, G. G., Klein, D. J., & Poehlmann, K. M. (1997). The psychophysiology of emotion across the lifespan. *Annual Review of Gerontology and Geriatrics, 17,* 27–74.

Cacioppo, J. T., Berntson, G. G., Sheridan, J. F., & McClintock, M. K. (2000). Multi-level integrative analyses of human behavior: Social neuroscience and the complementing nature of social and biological approaches. *Psychological Bulletin, 126,* 829–843.

Cacioppo, J. T., Tassinary, L. G., & Bernston, G. G. (2000). *Handbook of psychophysiology.* Cambridge, England: Cambridge University Press.

Cahill, L., & McGaugh, J. L. (1995). A novel demonstration of enhanced memory associated with emotional arousal. *Consciousness and Cognition, 4,* 410–421.

Cahill, L., Prins, B., Weber, M., & McGaugh, J. L. (1994). Beta-adrenergic activation and memory for emotional events. *Nature, 371,* 702–704.

Cahill, S. P., Rauch, S. A. M., Hembree, E. A., & Foa, E. B. (2003). Effectiveness of cognitive behavioral treatments for PTSD on anger. *Journal of Cognitive Psychotherapy, 17*(2), 113–131.

Cahn, B. R., & Polich, J. (2006). Meditation states and traits: EEG, ERP, and neuroimaging studies. *Psychological Bulletin, 132,* 180–211.

Calder, A. J., Keane, J., Cole, J., Campbell, R., & Young, A. W. (2000) Facial expression recognition by people with Möbius syndrome. *Cognitive Neuropsychology. Special Issue: The Cognitive Neuroscience of Face Processing, 17,* 73–87.

Calder, A. J., Keane, J., Manes, F., Antoun, N., & Young, A. W. (2000). Impaired recognition and experience of disgust following brain injury. *Nature Neuroscience, 3,* 1077–1078.

Caldera, Y. M., Huston, A. C., & O'Brien, M. (1989). Social interactions and play patterns of parents and toddlers with feminine, masculine and neutral toys. *Child Development, 60,* 70–76.

Cale, E. M., & Lilienfeld, S. O. (2002). Histrionic personality disorder and antisocial personality disorder: Sex differentiated manifestations of psychopathy? *Journal of Personality Disorders, 16,* 52–72.

Cale, E. M., & Lilienfeld, S. O. (2002). Sex differences in psychopathy and antisocial personality disorder: A review and integration. *Clinical Psychology Review, 22,* 1179–1207.

Cale, E. M., & Lilienfeld, S. O. (2006). Psychopath factors and risk for aggressive behavior: A test of the "threatened egotism" hypothesis. *Law and Human Behavior, 30,* 51–74.

Call, V., Sprecher, S., & Schwartz, P. (1995). The incidence and frequency of marital sex in a national sample. *Journal of Marriage and the Family, 57,* 639–652.

Callahan, R. (1995, August). *A thought field therapy (TFT) algorithm for trauma: A reproducible experiment in psychotherapy.* Paper presented at the 105th Annual Convention of the American Psychological Association, Chicago, IL.

Callahan, R. J. (2001). The impact of thought field therapy on heart rate variability (HRV). *Journal of Clinical Psychology, 57,* 1153–1170.

Calley, W. (1971). From William Calley: Court Martial. Retrieved October 29, 2007, from http://law.jrank.org/pages /3208/William-Calley-Court-Martial-1970.html.

Calvin, W. H. (2004). *A brief history of the mind: From apes to intellect and beyond.* New York: Oxford University Press.

Cameron, J., & Pierce, W. D. (1994). Reinforcement, reward, and intrinsic motivation: A meta-analysis. *Review of Educational Research, 64,* 363–423.

Campbell, D. (1997). *The Mozart effect: Tapping the power of music to heal the body, strengthen the mind, and unlock the creative spirit.* New York: Avon Books.

Campbell, F. A., & Ramey, C. T. (1995). Cognitive and school outcomes for high-risk African-American students at middle adolescence: Positive effects of early intervention. *American Educational Research Journal, 32,* 743–772.

Campbell, J. (1988). *The power of myth.* New York: Doubleday.

Campfield, L. A., Smith, F. J., & Burn, P. (1996). The OB protein (leptin) pathway—A link between adipose tissue mass and central neural networks. *Hormone and Metabolic Research, 28,* 619–632.

Campfield, L. A., Smith, F. J., Rosenbaum, M., & Hirsch, J. (1996). Human eating: Evidence for a physiological basis using a modified paradigm. *Neuroscience Biobehavioral Review, 20,* 133–137.

Campinha-Bacote, J. (2002). *Resources in transcultural care and mental health* (13th ed.). Wyoming, OH: Transcultural Care Associated.

Campos, P. (2004). *The obesity myth: Why America's obsession with weight is hazardous to your health.* New York: Gotham Books.

Canetti, L., Bachar, E., & Berry, E. M. (2002). Food and emotion. *Behavioural Processes, 60,* 157–164.

Canfield, R. L., Henderson, C. R., Jr., Cory-Slechta, D. A., Cox, C., Jusko, T. A., & Lanphear, B. P. (2003). Intellectual impairment in children with blood lead concentrations below 10 microg per deciliter. *New England Journal of Medicine, 348,* 1517–1526.

Cangelosi, A., & Riga, T. (2006). An embodied model for sensorimotor grounding and grounding transfer: Experiments with epigenetic robots. *Cognitive Science, 30,* 673–689.

Cannon, T. D., Mednick, S. A., & Parnas, J. (1989). Genetic and perinatal determinants of structural brain deficits in schizophrenia. *Archives of General Psychiatry, 46,* 883–889.

Cannon, W. B. (1915). *Bodily changes in pain, hunger, fear and rage: An account of recent researches into the functions of emotional excitement.* New York: Appleton.

Cannon, W. B. (1929). *Bodily changes in pain, hunger, fear and rage.* New York: D. Appleton.

Cannon, W. B. (1929). Organization for physiological homoeostasis. *Physiological Review, 9,* 399–431.

Cannon, W. B., & Washburn, A. L. (1912). An explanation of hunger. *American Journal of Physiology, 29,* 441–454.

Cano, F. (2005). Epistemological beliefs and approaches to learning: Their change through secondary school and their influence on academic performance. *British Journal of Educational Psychology, 75,* 203–221.

Cano, F., & Cardelle-Elawar, M. (2004). An integrated analysis of secondary school students' conceptions and beliefs about learning. *European Journal of Psychology of Education, 19,* 167–187.

Cantril, H. (1947). *The invasion from Mars.* Princeton, NJ: Princeton University Press.

Capecchi, M. R. (1989). The new mouse genetics: Altering the genome by gene targeting. *Trends in Genetics, 5,* 70–76.

Cappell, H., & Herman, C. (1972). Alcohol and tension reduction: A review. *Quarterly Journal of Studies in Alcohol, 33,* 33–64.

Capron, C., & Duyme, M. (1989). Assessment of effects of socioeconomic status on IQ in a full cross-fostering study. *Nature, 340,* 552–553.

Cardeña, E. (2005). The phenomenology of deep hypnosis: Quiescent and physically active. *International Journal of Clinical & Experimental Hypnosis, 53,* 37–59.

Cardón, L. A. (2005). *Popular psychology: An encyclopedia.* Westport, CT: Greenwood.

Carey, S. (1985). Conceptual change in childhood. Cambridge, MA: Bradford Books, MIT Press.

Carey, S. (1988). Reorganization of knowledge in the course of acquisition. In S. Strauss (Ed.), *Ontogeny, phylogeny, and historical development* (pp. 1–27). Westport, CT: Ablex Publishing.

Carlson, J. G., & Hatfield, E. (1992). *Psychology of emotion.* New York: Harcourt, Brace, Jovanovich.

Carlson, M., Marcus-Newhall, A., & Miller, N. (1990). The effects of situational aggression cues: A quantitative review. *Journal of Personality and Social Psychology, 58,* 622–633.

Carlson, W., & Rose, A. J. (2007). The role of reciprocity in romantic relationships in middle childhood and early adolescence. *Merrill-Palmer Quarterly, 53,* 262–290.

Carlsson, A. (1995). Towards a new understanding of dopamine receptors. Symposium: Dopamine receptor subtypes in neurological and psychiatric diseases. *Clinical Neuropharmacology, 18*(Suppl.), 65–135.

Carnagey, N. L., Anderson, C. A., & Bartholow, B. D. (2007). Media violence and social neuroscience: New questions and new opportunities. *Current Directions in Psychological Science, 16,* 178–182.

Carney, R. M., Freedland, K. E., & Veith, R. C. (2005). Depression, the autonomic nervous system, and coronary heart disease. *Psychosomatic Medicine, 67,* 29–33.

Carpenter, K. M., Hasin, D. S., Allison, D. B., & Faith, M. S. (2000). Relationships between obesity and DSM-IV major depressive disorder, suicide ideation, and suicide attempts: Results from a general population study. *American Journal of Public Health, 90,* 251–257.

Carrère, S., & Gottman, J. (1999). Predicting divorce among newlyweds from the first three minutes of a marital conflict discussion. *Family Process, 30,* 293 301.

Carroll, J. B. (1993). *Human cognitive abilities: A survey of factor analytic studies.* Cambridge, England: Cambridge University Press.

Carroll, R. T. (2003). *The skeptic's dictionary: A collection of strange beliefs, amusing deceptions, and dangerous delusions.* New York: Wiley.

Carstensen, L. L., & Lockenhoff, C. E. (2003). Aging, emotion, and evolution. *Annals of the New York Academy of Science, 1000,* 152–179.

Carter, C. S., Perlstein, W., Ganguli, R., Brar, J. , Mintun, M., & Cohen, J. D. (1998). Functional hypofrontality and working memory dysfunction in schizophrenia. *American Journal of Psychiatry, 155,* 1285–1287.

Carton, J. S. (1996). The differential effects of tangible rewards and praise on intrinsic motivation: A comparison of cognitive evaluation theory and operant theory. *The Behavior Analyst, 19,* 237–255.

Cartwright, J. (2000). *Evolution and human behaviour.* London: Macmillan.

Cartwright, R., & Romanek, I. (1978). Repetitive dreams of normal subjects. *Sleep Research, 7,* 7–15.

Cartwright, S. A. (1851, May). Report on the diseases and physical peculiarities of the Negro race. *The New Orleans Medical and Surgical Journal,* 691–715.

Caruso, D. R., Taylor, J., & Detterman, D. K. (1982). Intelligence research and intelligent policy. In D. K. Detterman & R. J. Sternberg (Eds.), *How and how much can intelligence be increased?* (pp. 45–65). Norwood, NJ: Ablex Publishing.

Carver, C. S. (1997). You want to measure coping but your protocol's too long: Consider the Brief COPE. *International Journal of Behavioral Medicine, 4,* 92–100.

Carver, C. S., & Scheier, M. F. (1999). Themes and issues in the self-regulation of behavior. In R. S. Wyer Jr. (Ed.), *Advances in social cognition* (Vol. 12). Mahwah, NJ: Erlbaum.

Carver, C. S., Scheier, M. F., & Weintraub, J. K. (1989). Assessing coping strategies: A theoretically based approach. *Journal of Personality and Social Psychology, 56,* 267–283.

Carver, R. P. (1978). The case against statistical significance testing. *Harvard Educational Review, 48,* 378–399

Carver, R. P. (1987). Teaching rapid reading in the intermediate grades: Helpful or harmful? *Reading Research and Instruction, 26,* 65–76.

Carver, R. P. (1990). *Reading rate: A review of research and theory.* San Diego, CA: Academic Press.

Casey, B. J., Galvan, A., & Hare, T. A. (2005). Changes in cerebral functional organization during cognitive development. *Current Opinion in Neurobiology, 15,* 239–244.

Casey, B., Giedd, J. N., & Thomas, K. M. (2000). Structural and functional brain development and its relation to cognitive development. *Biological Psychology, 54,* 241–257.

Casey, L. M., Oei, T. P. S., & Newcombe, P. A. (2004). An integrated cognitive model of panic disorder: The role of positive and negative cognitions. *Clinical Psychology Review, 24,* 529–555.

Caspi, A., Williams, B., Kim-Cohen J., et al. (2007). Moderation of breastfeeding effects on the IQ by genetic variation in fatty acid metabolism. *Proceedings of the National Academy of Sciences, 10,* 1073.

Caspi, A., McClay, J, Moffitt, T. E., Mill, J., Martin, J., Craig, I., et al. (2002). Evidence that the cycle of violence in maltreated children depends on genotype. *Science, 297,* 851–854.

Caspi, A., McClay, J., Moffitt, T., Mill, J., Martin, J., Craig, I. W., et al. (2002). Role of genotype in the cycle of violence in maltreated children. *Science, 297,* 851–854.

Caspi, A., Sugden, K., Moffitt, T. E., Taylor, A., Craig, I., Harrington, H. L., et al. (2003). Influence of life stress on depression: Moderation by a polymorphism in the 5-HTT gene. *Science, 301,* 386–389.

Catania, K. C. (2006). Olfaction: Underwater 'sniffing' by semi-aquatic mammals. *Nature, 444,* 1024–1025.

Cattell, R. B. (1949). *Culture Free Intelligence Test, Scale 1, Handbook.* Champaign, IL: Institute of Personality and Ability.

Cattell, R. B. (1963). Theory of fluid and crystallized intelligence: A critical experiment. *Journal of Educational Psychology, 54,* 1–22.

Cattell, R. B. (1971). *Abilities: Their structure, growth, and action.* Boston: Houghton-Mifflin.

Catz, S. L., & Kelly, J. A. (2001). Living with HIV disease. In A. Baum, T. A. Revenson, & J. E. Singer (Eds.), *Handbook of health psychology* (pp. 841–849). Mahwah, NJ: Lawrence Erlbaum.

Cautela, J. R. (1971). Covert conditioning. In A. Jacobs, & L. B. Sachs (Eds.), *The psychology of private events: Perspectives on covert response systems.* New York: Academic Press.

Caviness, V. S., Jr., Kennedy, D. N., Bates, J. F., & Makris, N. (1996). The developing human brain: A morphometric profile. In R. W. Thatcher, G. R. Lyon, J. Rumsey, & N. Krasnegor (Eds.), *Developmental neuroimaging: Mapping the development of brain and behavior* (pp. 3–14). San Diego, CA: Academic Press.

Ceci, S. J. (1991). How much does schooling Influence general intelligence and its cognitive components? A reassessment of the evidence. *Developmental Psychology, 27,* 703–722.

Ceci, S. J., & Bruck, M. (1993). Suggestibility of the child witness: A historical review and synthesis. *Psychological Bulletin, 113,* 403–439.

Ceci, S. J., Crotteau-Huffman, M., Smith, E., & Loftus, E. W. (1994). Repeatedly thinking about non-events. *Consciousness & Cognition, 3,* 388–407.

Ceci, S. J., & Williams, W. M. (1997). Schooling, intelligence, and income. *American Psychologist, 52,* 1051–1058.

Center for Medicare and Medicaid Services. (1997). National Health Expenditures Survey. Available at: http://www.cms.hhs.gov/statistics/nhe/.

Centers for Disease Control (2005). *Alcohol Use.* National Center for Health Statistics. U.S. Department of Health and Human Sevices. Hyattsville, MD: Centers for Disease Control and Prevention.

Centers for Disease Control and Prevention. (2004). *Surgeon General's 2004 report: The health consequences of smoking.* United States Department of Health and Human Services. Atlanta, GA: Author.

Centers for Disease Control and Prevention (2005). *Cigarette smoking among adults: United States, 2003.* MMWR Highlights, Vol. 54, No. 20. United States Department of Health and Human Services. Atlanta, GA: Author.

Centers for Disease Control and Prevention (2006). National Center for Health Statistics. National Health and Nutrition Examination Survey (2003–2004). United States Department of Health and Human Services, Centers for Disease Control and Prevention. Atlanta, GA: Author.

Cepeda, N. J., Pashler, H., Vul, E., Wixted, J. T., & Rohrer, D. (2006). Distributed practice in verbal recall tasks: A review and quantitative synthesis. *Psychological Bulletin, 132,* 354–380.

Cerella, J. (1985). Information processing rates in the elderly. *Psychological Bulletin, 98,* 67–83.

Chabris, C. F. (1999). Prelude or requiem for the "Mozart effect"? *Nature, 400,* 826–827.

Chaiken, A. L., Sigler, E., & Derlega, V. J. (1974). Nonverbal mediators of supervisor expectancy effects. *Journal of Personality and Social Psychology, 30,* 144–149.

Chakraborty, R., Kamboh, M. I., Nwankwo, M., & Ferrell, R. E. (1992). Caucasian genes in American blacks: new data. *American Journal of Human Genetics, 50,* 145–155.

Chall, J. S. (1983). *Stages of reading development.* New York: McGraw-Hill.

Chambless, D., & Goldstein, A. (1980). The treatment of agoraphobia. In A. Goldstein & E. B. Foz (Eds.), *Handbook of behavioral interventions*. New York: John Wiley & Sons.

Chambless, D. L., & Ollendick, T. H. (2001). Empirically supported psychological interventions: Controversies and evidence. *Annual Review of Psychology, 52,* 685–716.

Chambless, D. L., Sanderson, W. C., Shoham, V., Bennett Johnson, S., Pope, K. S., Crits-Christoph, P., et al. (1996). An update on empirically validated therapies. *The Clinical Psychologist, 49,* 5–18.

Champney, T. F., & Schultz, E. M. (1983). *A reassessment of the effects of psychotherapy.* Paper presented at the 55th annual meeting of the Midwestern Psychological Association, Chicago, IL. (ERIC document ED 237895)

Chandler, M. (Writer & Director). (1999, October 4). "Secrets of the SAT." In M. Sullivan (Executive Producer), *Frontline.* Boston: WGBH.

Chandrashekar, J., Hoon, M. A., Ryba, N. J., & Zuker, C. S. (2006). The receptors and cells for mammalian taste. *Nature, 444,* 288–294.

Chaney, J. M., Mullins, L. L., Uretsky, D. L., Pace, T. M., Werden, D., & Hartman, V. L. (1999). An experimental examination of learned helplessness in older adolescents and young adults with long-standing asthma. *Journal of Pediatric Psychology, 24,* 259–271.

Chaplin, W. F., Phillips, J. B., Brown, J. D., Clanton, N. R., & Stein, J. L. (2000). Handwriting, gender, personality, and first impressions. *Journal of Personality and Social Psychology, 79,* 110–117.

Chapman, J. (1966). The early symptoms of schizophrenia. *British Journal of Psychiatry, 112,* 225–251.

Chapman, L. J., & Chapman, J. P. (1967). Genesis of popular but erroneous diagnostic observations. *Journal of Abnormal Psychology, 72,* 193–204.

Chapman, L. J., & Chapman, J. P. (1967). Genesis of popular but erroneous psychodiagnostic observations. *Journal of Abnormal Psychology, 72,* 193–204.

Chapman, L. J., & Chapman, J. P. (1969). Illusory correlation as an obstacle to the use of valid psychodiagnostic signs. *Journal of Abnormal Psychology, 74,* 271–280.

Chapman, L. J., Chapman J. P., & Raulin M. L. (1978). Body-image aberration in schizophrenia. *Journal of Abnormal Psychology, 87,* 399–407.

Charles, S. T., Mather, M., & Carstensen, L. L. (2003). Aging and emotional memory: The forgettable nature of negative images for older adults. *Journal of Experimental Psychology: General, 132,* 310–324.

Charney, D. S., Nemeroff, C. B., Lewis, L., Laden, S. K., Gorman, J. M., Laska, E. M., et al. (2002). National Depressive and Manic-Depressive Association consensus statement on the use of placebo in clinical trials of mood disorders. *Archives of General Psychiatry, 59,* 262–270.

Chase, W. G., & Simon, H. A. (1973). The mind's eye in chess. In W. G. Chase (Ed.), *Visual information processing* (pp. 215–281). New York: Academic Press.

Chayer, C., & Freedman, M. (2001). Frontal lobe functions. *Current Neurology & Neuroscience Reports, 1,* 547–552.

Cheesman, J., & Merikle, P. M. (1986). Distinguishing conscious from unconscious perceptual processes. *Canadian Journal of Psychology, 40,* 343–367.

Chen, C., Lee, S., & Stevenson, H. W. (1995). Response style and cross-cultural comparisons of rating scales among east Asian and North American students. *Psychological Science, 6,* 170–175.

Cheng, C. (2003). Cognitive and motivational processes underlying coping flexibility: A dual-process model. *Journal of Personality and Social Psychology, 84,* 425–438.

Chentsova-Dutton, Y. E., & Tsai, J. L. (2006). Cultural factors influence the expression of psychopathology. In S. O. Lilienfeld, & W. O'Donoghue (Eds.), *The great ideas of clinical science: The 17 concepts that every mental health practitioner and researcher should understand.* New York: Brunner-Taylor.

Chesney, M. A., & Rosenman, M. D. (1980). Type A behavior in the work setting. In C. L. Cooper & R. Payne (Eds.), *Current concerns in occupational stress* (pp. 187–212). Chichester, England: Wiley.

Cheung, F. M., & Leung, K. (1998). Indigenous personality measures: Chinese examples. *Journal of Cross-Cultural Psychology, 29,* 233–248.

Cheyne, J. A., Rueffer, S. D. and Newby-Clark, I. R. (1999), Hypnagogic anhypnopompic hallucinations during sleep paralysis: Neurological and cultural construction of the nightmare, *Consciousness and Cognition, 8,* 319–37.

Ching, P. I., Willett, W. C., Rimm, E. B., Colditz, G. A., Gortmaker, S. L., & Stampfer, M. J. (1996). Activity level and risk of overweight in male health professionals. *American Journal of Public Health, 86,* 25–30.

Chodoff, P. (1976). The case for involuntary hospitalization of the mentally ill. *American Journal of Psychiatry, 133,* 396–501.

Choi, S., McDonough, L., Bowerman, M., & Mandler, J. M. (1999). Early sensitivity to language-specific spatial categories in English and Korean. *Cognitive Development, 14,* 241–268.

Chomsky, N. (1972). *Language and mind.* New York: Harcourt Brace Jovanovich.

Chopra, D. (1989). *Quantum healing: Exploring the frontiers of mind/body medicine.* New York: Bantam.

Chorpita, B. F., & Barlow, D. H. (1998). The development of anxiety: The role of control in the early environment. *Psychological Bulletin, 124,* 3–21.

Christensen, A., & Jacobson, N. S. (1994). Who (or what) can do psychotherapy: The status and challenge of nonprofessional therapies. *Psychological Science, 5,* 8–14, 156–167.

Christianson, S. (1989). Flashbulb memories: Special, but not so special. *Memory & Cognition, 17,* 435–443·

Chua, H. F., Boland, J. E., & Nisbett, R. E. (2005). Cultural variation in eye movements during scene perception. *Proceedings of the National Academy of Sciences, 102,* 12629–12633.

Church, A. T., & Katigbak, M. S. (2002). The five-factor model in the Philippines: Investigating trait structure and levels across cultures. In R. R. McCrae & J. Allik (Eds.), *The five-factor model across cultures* (pp. 129–154). New York: Kluwer Academic/Plenum Publishers.

Church, R. B., & Goldin-Meadow, S. (1986). The mismatch between gesture and speech as an index of transitional knowledge. *Cognition, 23,* 43–71.

Church, R. B., Schonert-Reichl, K., Goodman, N., Kelly, S. D., & Ayman-Nolley, S. (1995). The role of gesture and speech communication as reflections of cognitive understanding. *Journal of Contemporary Legal Issues, 6,* 123–154.

Church, R. M. (1969). Response suppression. In B. Campbell & R. Church (Eds.), *Punishment and aversive behavior* (pp. 111–156). New York: Appleton-Century-Crofts.

Chwalisz, K., Diener, E., & Gallagher, D. (1988). Autonomic arousal feedback and emotional experience: Evidence from the spinal cord injured. *Journal of Personality and Social Psychology, 54,* 820–828.

Cialdini, R. B. (1975). A reciprocal concessions procedure for inducing compliance: The door-in-the-face technique. *Journal of Personality and Social Psychology, 21,* 206–215.

Cialdini, R. B. (2001). *Influence: Science and practice* (4th ed.). Boston: Allyn & Bacon.

Cialdini, R. B., & Goldstein, N. J. (2004). Social influence: Compliance and conformity. *Annual Review of Psychology, 55,* 591–621.

Cialdini, R. B., & Sagarin, B. J. (2005). Interpersonal influence. In T. Brock & M. Green (Eds.), *Persuasion: Psychological insights and perspectives* (pp. 143–169). Newbury Park, CA: Sage Press.

Ciarella, G., Ciarella, M., Graziani, P., & Mirante, M. (1991). Changes in food consumption of obese patients induced by dietary treatment combined with dexfenfluramine. *International Journal of Obesity, 15,* 69.

Cicogna, P., Natale, V., Occhionero, M., & Bosinelli, M. (1998). A comparison of mental activity during sleep onset and during awakening. *Sleep, 21,* 462–470.

Cioffi, F. (1998). *Freud and the question of pseudoscience.* Chicago: Open Court.

Clancy, S. (2007). *Alien abductions.* Cambridge, MA: Harvard University Press.

Clancy, S. A. (2006). *Abducted: How people come to believe they were kidnapped by aliens.* Cambridge, MA: Harvard University Press.

Clancy, S. A., McNally, R. J., Schachter, D. L., Lenzenweger, M. F., & Pitman, R. K. (2002). Memory distortion in people reporting abduction by aliens. *Journal of Abnormal Psychology, 111,* 455–461.

Clark, D. M. (1986). A cognitive approach to panic. *Behaviour Research and Therapy, 24,* 156–163.

Clark, M. (1997). *Reason to believe.* New York: Avon Books.

Clark, R. D. (2005). Examination of hole-to-hole streakiness on the PGA tour, *Perceptual and Motor Skills, 100,* 806–814.

Clark, R., Hyde, J. S., Essex, M. J., & Klein, M. H. (1997). Length of maternity leave and quality of mother-infant interactions. *Child Development, 68,* 364–383.

Clarke, A. M., & Clarke, A. D. B. (1976). *Early experience: Myth and evidence.* London: Open Books.

Clarke-Stewart, K. A. (1980). The father's contribution to children's cognitive and social development in early childhood. In F. A. Pedersen (Ed.), *The father-infant relationship: Observational studies in the family setting* (pp. 111–146). New York: Praeger.

Clarke-Stewart, K. A. (1998). Historical shifts and underlying themes in ideas about rearing young children in the United States: Where have we been? Where are we going? *Early Development & Parenting, 7,* 101–117.

Clay, M. M. (1975). *What did I write?* Auckland, New Zealand: Heinemann.

Clay, R. A. (2002). Advertising as science. *American Psychological Association Monitor, 33,* 38.

Clearfield, M. W., & Mix, K. S. (1999). Number versus contour length in infants' discrimination of small visual sets. *Psychological Science, 10,* 408–411.

Cleckley, H. (1941/1988). *The mask of sanity.* St. Louis, MO: Mosby.

Cloninger, C. R. (1987). A systematic method for clinical description and classification of personality variants. *Archives of General Psychiatry, 44,* 573–577.

Coan, R. W. (1973). Personality variables associated with cigarette smoking. *Journal of Personality and Social Psychology, 26,* 86–104.

Coe, W. C., & Sarbin, T. R. (1991). Role theory: hypnosis from a dramaturgical and narrational perspective. In S. J. Lynn & J. W. Rhue (Eds.), *Theories of hypnosis: Current models and perspectives* (pp. 303–323). New York: Guilford Press.

Coggins, W. J. (1976). Costa Rica cannabis project: An interim report on the medical aspects. In M. C. Braude & S. Szarn (Eds.), *Pharmacology of marijuana.* New York: Raven Press.

Cohen, D., & Nisbett, R. E. (1994). Self-protection and the culture of honor: Explaining southern violence. *Personality and Social Psychology Bulletin, 20,* 551–567.

Cohen, D., Nisbett, R. E., Bowdle, B. F., & Schwarz, N. (1996). Insult, aggression, and the southern culture of honor: An "experimental ethnography." *Journal of Personality and Social Psychology, 70,* 945–960.

Cohen, F., Solomon, S., Maxfield, M., Pyszczynski, T., & Greenberg, J. (2004). Fatal attraction: The effects of mortality salience on evaluations of charismatic, task-oriented, and relationship-oriented leaders. *Psychological Science, 15,* 846–851.

Cohen, G. L. (2003). Party over policy: The dominating impact of group influence on political beliefs. *Journal of Personality and Social Psychology, 85,* 808–82

Cohen, G. L., Garcia, J., Apfel, N., & Master, A. (2006). Reducing the racial achievement gap: A social-psychological intervention. *Science, 313,* 1307–1310.

Cohen, P., & Cohen, J. (1984). The clinician's illusion. *Archives of General Psychiatry, 41,* 1178-1182.

Cohen, S., Doyle, W. J., Skoner, D. P., Rabin, B. S., & Gwaltney, J. M. (1997). Social ties and susceptibility to the common cold. *Journal of the American Medical Association, 277,* 1940–1944.

Cohen, S., Doyle, W. J., Turner, R. B., Alper, C. M., & Skoner, D. P. (2003). Emotional style and susceptibility to the common cold. *Psychosomatic Medicine, 65,* 652–657.

Cohen, S., Evans, G. W., Stokols, D., & Krantz, D. S. (1986*). Behavior, health, and environmental stress.* New York: Plenum.

Cohen, S., Frank, E., Doyle, B. J., Skoner, D. P., Rabin, B. S. & Gwaltney, J. M. (1998). Types of stressors that increase susceptibility to the common cold. *Health Psychology, 17,* 214–223.

Cohen, S., & Herbert, T. B. (1996). Health psychology: Psychological factors and physical disease from the perspective of human psychoneuroimmunology. *Annual Review of Psychology, 47,* 113–142.

Cohen, S., Tyrell, D. A. J., & Smith, A. P. (1991). Psychological stress and susceptibility to the common cold. *New England Journal of Medicine, 325,* 606–612.

Cole, M. (1990). Cultural psychology: A once and future discipline? In J. J. Berman (Ed.), *Nebraska Symposium on Motivation, 1989: Cross-cultural perspectives* (pp. 279–335). Lincoln, NE: University of Nebraska Press.

Coleman, H. L. K., Wampold, B. E., & Casali, S. L. (1995). Ethnic minorities' ratings of ethnically similar and European American counselors: A meta-analysis. *Journal of Counseling Psychology, 42,* 55–64.

Coles, C. D. (1993). Saying "goodbye" to the "crack baby." *Neurotoxiocology and Teratology, 5,* 290292.

Coles, M. E., & Heimberg, R. G. (2002). Memory biases in the anxiety disorders: Current status. *Clinical Psychology Review, 22,* 587–627.

College Board. (1976–1977). *Student descriptive questionnaire.* Princeton, NJ: Educational Testing Service.

Collins, A. F. (1999). The enduring appeal of physiognomy: Physical appearance as a sign of temperament, character, and intelligence. *History of Psychology, 2,* 251–276.

Collins, A. M., & Quillian, M. R. (1969). Retrieval time from semantic memory. *Journal of Verbal Learning & Verbal Behavior, 8,* 240–247.

Collins, A. W., Maccoby, E. E., Steinberg, L., Hetherington, M. E., & Bornstein, M.H. (2000). Contemporary research on parenting. *American Psychologist, 55,* 218–232.

Collins, F. L., Sorocco, K. H., Haala, K. R., Miller, B. I., & Lovallo, W. R. (2003). Stress and health. In L. M. Cohen, D. E. McChargue, & F. L. Collins (Eds.), *The health psychology handbook: Practical issues for the behavioral medicine specialist* (pp. 169–186). London: Sage Publications.

Colombo J. (1993). *Infant cognition: Predicting later intellectual functioning.* Newbury Park, CA: Sage.

Colvin, C. R., & Block, J. (1994). Do positive illusions foster mental health? An examination of the Taylor and Brown formulation. *Psychological Bulletin, 116,* 3–20.

Concar, D. (1994). Design your own personality. *New Scientist, 141,* 22–26.

Condry, J. C., & Condry, S. (1976). Sex differences: A study in the eye of the beholder. *Child Development, 47,* 812–819.

Conrad, R. (1964). Acoustic confusion and immediate memory. *British Journal of Psychology, 55,* 75–84.

Conte, J. M. (2005). A review and critique of emotional intelligence measures. *Journal of Organizational Behavior, 26,* 433–440.

Conway, M. A., Anderson, S. J., Larsen, S. F., Donnelly, C. M., McDaniel, M. A., McClelland, A. G. R., et al. (1994). The formation of flashbulb memories. *Memory & Cognition, 22,* 326–343.

Conway, M., & Ross, M. (1984). Getting what you want by revising what you had. *Journal of Personality and Social Psychology, 47,* 783–748.

Cook, T. A. R., Luczak, S. E., Shea, S. H., Ehlers, C. L., Carr, L. G., & Wall, T. L. (2005). Associations of ALDH2 and ADH1B genotypes with response to alcohol in Asian Americans. *Journal of Studies on Alcohol, 66,* 196–204.

Cook, T. A. R., & Wall, T. L. (2005). Ethnicity and the subjective effects of alcohol. In M. Earleywine (Ed.), *Mind-altering drugs: The science of subjective experience* (pp. 154–182). Washington, DC: American Psychological Association.

Cook, T. D. (1985). Post-positivist critical multiplism. In R. L. Shotland & M. M. Mark (Eds.), *Social science and social policy* (pp. 21–62). Beverly Hills, CA: Sage.

Coombs, R. H. (1991). Marital status and personal well-being: A literature review. *Family Relations: Journal of Applied Family and Child Studies, 40,* 17–102.

Coon, D. J. (1992). Testing the limits of sense and science: American experimental psychologists combat spiritualism: 1880–1920. *American Psychologist, 47,* 143–151.

Coons, P. M., Bowman, E. S., & Milstein, V. (1988). Multiple personality disorder: A clinical investigation of 50 cases. *Journal of Nervous and Mental Disease, 176,* 519–527.

Coontz, S. (1992). *The way we never were: American families and the nostalgia trap.* New York: Basic Books.

Cooper, C. L., & Dewe, P. (2004). *Stress: A brief history.* Malden, MA: Blackwell Publishing.

Cooper, R. P. (2003). Mechanisms for the generation and regulation of sequential behavior. *Philosophical Psychology, 16,* 389–416.

Coover, J. E. & Angell, F. (1907). General practice effect of special exercise. *American Journal of Psychology, 18,* 328–340.

Copper, R. L., Goldenberg, R. L., Creasy, R. K., DuBard, M. B., Davis, R. O., Entman, S. S., et al. (1993). A multicenter study of preterm, birth weight, and gestational age-specific neonatal mortality. *American Journal of Obstetrics and Gynecology, 168,* 78–84.

Corballis, M. C. (1999). Are we in our right minds? In S. Della Sala (Ed.), *Mind myths* (pp. 26–42). Chichester, England: John Wiley & Sons.

Corballis, M. C. (2002). *From hand to mouth: The origins of language.* Princeton, NJ: Princeton University Press.

Corbett, T. (2006). The facts about weight loss products and programs. Federal Trade Commission, Food and Drug Administration. www.attorneygeneral.gov /uploadedFiles/Consumers/weight_loss. Accessed June 30, 2006.

Coren, S (1996). *Sleep thieves.* New York: Free Press.

Corkin, S. (1984). Lasting consequences of bilateral medial temporal lobectomy: Clinical course and experimental findings in H.M. In S. M. Kosslyn & R. A. Anderson (Eds.), *Frontiers in cognitive neuroscience* (pp. 516–526). London: The MIT Press.

Corkin, S., Amaral, D. G., Gonzales, R. G., Johnson, K. A., & Hyman, B. T. (1997). H.M.'s medial temporal lobe lesion: Findings from magnetic resonance imaging. *Journal of Neuroscience, 17,* 3964–3979.

Cornblatt, B. A., Green, M. F., & Walker, E. F. (1999). Schizophrenia: Etiology and neurocognition. In T. Millon, P. H. Blaney, & R. D. Davis (Eds.), *Oxford textbook of psychopathology* (pp. 227–310). New York: Oxford University Press.

Cornell, E. H. (1980). Distributed study facilitates infants' delayed recognition memory. *Memory and Cognition, 8,* 539–542.

Cornell, E. H., & Bergstrom, L. I. (1983). Serial-position effects in infants' recognition memory. *Memory and Cognition, 11,* 494–499.

Cornez-Ruiz, S., & Hendricks, B. (1993). Effects of labeling and ADHD behaviors on peer and teacher judgments. *Journal of Educational Research, 86,* 349–355.

Corsini, R. J. (Ed.). (1981). *Handbook of innovative psychotherapies.* New York: Wiley.

Corsini, R. J. (1999). *Dictionary of psychology.* Philadelphia: Brunner/Mazel.

Corwin, D. L., & Olafson, E. (1997). Videotaped discovery of a reportedly unrecallable memory of child sexual abuse: Comparison with a childhood interview videotaped 11 years before. *Child Maltreatment, 2,* 91–112.

Coryell, W., Solomon, D., Turvey, C., Keller, M., Leon, A. C., Endicott, J., et al. (2003). The long-term course of rapid-cycling bipolar disorder. *Archives of General Psychiatry, 60,* 914–920.

Costa, P. T., & McCrae, R. R. (1998). Trait theories of personality. In D. F. Barone, M. Hersen, & V. B. Van Hasselt (Eds.), *Advanced Personality* (pp. 103–121). New York: Plenum. Cressen, R. (1975). Artistic quality of drawings and judges' evaluations of the DAP. *Journal of Personality Assessment, 39,* 132–137.

Costa, P. T., Jr., & McCrae, R. R. (1990). Personality disorders and the five-factor model of personality. *Journal of Personality Disorders, 4*, 362–371.

Cotton, N. S. (1979). The familial incidence of alcoholism: A review. *Journal of Studies on Alcohol, 40*, 89–116.

Cottrell, C. A., & Neuberg, S. L. (2005). Different emotional reactions to different groups: A sociofunctional threat-based approach to "prejudice." *Journal of Personality and Social Psychology, 88*, 770–789.

Cowan, C. P., & Cowan, P. A. (1995). Interventions to ease the transition to parenthood: Why they are needed and what they can do. *Family Relations, 44*, 412–423.

Cowan, N. (2001). The magical number 4 in short-term memory: A reconsideration of mental storage capacity. *Behavioral and Brain Sciences, 24*, 87–185.

Cowan, N., Lichty, W., & Grove, T. R. (1990). Properties of memory for unattended spoken syllables. *Journal of Experimental Psychology: Learning, Memory, & Cognition, 16*, 258–269.

Cox, B. J., & Taylor, S. (1999). Anxiety disorders: Panic and phobias. In T. Millon, P. H. Blaney, & R. D. Davis (Eds.), *Oxford textbook of psychopathology* (pp. 81–113). New York: Oxford University Press.

Coyne, J. C. (1976). Depression and the response of others. *Journal of Abnormal Psychology, 85*, 186–193.

Coyne, J. C. (1992). Cognition in depression: A paradigm in crisis. *Psychological Inquiry, 3*, 232–235.

Coyne, J. C., & Holroyd, K. (1982). Stress, coping, and illness: A transactional perspective. In T. Millon, C. Green, & R. Meachem (Eds.), *Handbook of clinical health psychology* (pp. 103–127). New York: Plenum Press.

Coyne, J. C., & Racioppo, M. W. (2000). Never the twain shall meet? Closing the gap between coping research and clinical intervention research. *American Psychologist, 55*, 655–664.

Craighead, E., Sheets, E. S., & Bjornsson, A. S. (2005). Specificity and non-specificity in psychotherapy. *Clinical Psychology: Science and Practice, 12*, 189–193.

Craighead, L. W. (2002). Obesity and eating disorders. In M. M. Antony & D. H. Barlow (Eds.), *A guide to treatments that work* (2nd ed., pp. 245–262). New York: Oxford.

Craik, F. I. M., & Lockhart, R. (1972). Levels of processing: A framework for memory research. *Journal of Verbal Learning & Verbal Behavior, 11*, 671–684.

Craik, F. I. M., & Tulving, E. (1975). Depth of processing and the retention of words in episodic memory. *Journal of Experimental Psychology: General, 104*, 268–294.

Crandall, C. S. (1994). Prejudice against fat people: Ideology and self-interest. *Journal of Personality and Social Psychology, 66*, 882–894.

Craske, M. G. (1999). *Anxiety disorders: Psychological approaches to theory and treatment.* Boulder, CO: Westview Press.

Craske, M. G., Rapee, R. M., Jackel, L., & Barlow, D. H. (1989). Qualitative dimensions of worry in DSM-III-R generalized anxiety disorder subjects and nonanxious controls. *Behaviour Research and Therapy, 27*, 397–402.

Crespi, L. P. (1942). Quantitative variation of incentive and performance in the white rat. *American Journal of Psychology, 55*, 467–517.

Crews, F. (1990). *The memory wars: Freud's legacy in dispute.* New York: New York Times Review of Books.

Crews, F. C. (Ed.). (1998). *Unauthorized Freud: Doubters confront a legend.* New York: Viking Press.

Crick, F. (1995). *The astonishing hypothesis: The scientific search for the soul.* New York: Charles Scribner and Sons.

Crick, F., & Christof, K. (2005). What is the function of the claustrum? *Philosophical Transactions of the Royal Society: Biological Sciences, 360*, 1271–1279.

Crick, F., & Mitchison, G. (1983). The function of dream sleep. *Nature, 304*, 111–114.

Crick, F., & Mitchison, G. (1986). REM sleep and neural nets. *Journal of Mind and Behavior, 7*, 229–250.

Crick, N. (1995). Relational aggression: The role of intent attributions, feelings of distress, and provocation type. *Development and Psychopathology, 7*, 313–322.

Crits-Christoph, P., Wilson, G. T., & Hollon, S. D. (2005). Empirically supported psychotherapies: Comment on Westen, Novotny, and Thompson-Brenner (2004). *Psychological Bulletin, 131*, 412–417.

Cromer, A. (1993). *Uncommon sense: The heretical nature of science.* New York: Oxford University Press.

Cross, P. (1977). Not can but will college teaching be improved? *New Directions for Higher Education, 17*, 1–15.

Crowder, E. M. (1996). Gestures at work in sense-making science talk. *Journal of the Learning Sciences, 5*, 173–208.

Cruz, M., Scott, J., Houck, P., Reynolds, C. F., Frank, E., & Shear, M. K. (2007). Clinical presentation and treatment outcome of African Americans with complicated grief. *Psychiatric Services, 58*, 700–702.

Csikszentmihalyi, M. (1990). *Flow, the psychology of optimal experience.* New York: Harper & Row.

Csikszentmihalyi, M. (1997). *Finding flow: The psychology of engagement with everyday life.* New York: Basic Books.

Culham, J. C., & Valyear, K. F. (2006). Human parietal cortex in action. *Current Opinion in Neurobiology, 16*, 205–212.

Cullen, M. J., & Sackett, P. R. (2004). Integrity testing in the workplace. In J. C. Thomas & M. Hersen (Eds.), *Comprehensive handbook of psychological assessment, Vol. 4: Industrial and organizational psychology* (pp. 149–165). Hoboken, NJ: John Wiley & Sons.

Culliton, B. J. (1989). The dismal state of scientific literacy. *Science, 243*, 600.

Culver, C. A. (1956). *Musical acoustics.* New York: McGraw-Hill.

Cunningham, A. E., Stanovich, K. E., & Wilson, M. R. (1990). Cognitive variation in adult college students differing in reading ability. In Carr, T. H., & Levy, B. A. (Eds.), *Reading and its development: Component skills approaches* (pp. 129–159). San Diego, CA: Academic Press.

Cunningham, M. R., Roberts, A. R., Wu, H., Barbee, A. P., & Bruen, P. B. (1995). Their ideas of beauty are, on the whole, the same as ours: Consistency and variability in the cross-cultural perception of female physical attractiveness. *Journal of Personality and Social Psychology, 68*, 261–279.

Cunningham, P. F. (1993, October). *Can the use of animals in neuropsychological and psychopharmacological experiments continue to be justified?* Paper presented at the New England Psychological Association 33rd Annual Meeting, Goffstown, NH.

Curran, J. P., & Lippold, S. (1975). The effects of physical attraction and attitude similarity on attraction in dating dyads. *Journal of Personality, 43*, 528–539.

Curtis, R. C., & Miller, K. (1986). Believing another likes or dislikes you: Behavior making the beliefs come true. *Journal of Personality and Social Psychology, 51*, 284–290.

Curtiss, S. (1977). *Genie: Psycholinguistic study of a modern-day "wild child."* London: Academic Press.

Dabbs, J. B. (2001). *Heroes, rogues, and lovers: Testosterone and behavior.* New York: McGraw Hill.

Dahlstrom, W. G., Welsh, G. S., & Dahlstrom, L. E. (1975). *An MMPI handbook: A revised edition.* Minneapolis, MN: University of Minnesota Press.

Dallek, R. (2003). *An unfinished life: John F. Kennedy, 1917–1963.* Boston: Little, Brown and Company.

Dalm, R. (2006), Dying to see. *Scientific American, 16*, 12–19.

Damasio, A. (1994). *Descartes' error.* New York: G. P. Putnam's Sons.

Damasio, A. (2000). *The feeling of what happens: Body, emotion and the making of consciousness.* Cambridge, MA: MIT Press.

Damasio, H., Grabowski, T., Frank, R., Galaburda, A. M., & Damasio, A. R. (1994). The return of Phineas Gage: Clues about the brain from the skull of a famous patient. *Science, 264*, 1102–1105.

Danbrot, M. (2004). *The new cabbage soup diet.* New York: St. Martin's Press.

Dane, J. (1984). *An empirical evaluation of two techniques for lucid dream induction.* Unpublished doctoral dissertation, Georgia State University, Atlanta, GA.

Danner, D. D., Snowdon, D. A., & Friesen, W. V. (2001). Positive emotions in early life and longevity: Findings from the nun study. *Journal of Personality and Social Psychology, 80*, 804–813.

Darley, J. M., & Batson, D. (1973). From Jerusalem to Jericho: A study of situational and dispositional variables in helping behavior. *Journal of Personality and Social Psychology, 27*, 100–108.

Darley, J., & Latané, B. (1968a). Bystander intervention in emergencies: Diffusion of responsibility. *Journal of Personality and Social Psychology, 8*, 377–383.

Darley, J. M., & Latane, B. (1968b). When will people help in a crisis? *Psychology Today, 2*, 54–57, 70–71.

Darlington, R. B. (1986). Long-term effects of preschool programs. In U. Neisser (Ed.), *The school achievement of minority children.* Hillsdale, NJ: Erlbaum.

Darwin, C. (1859). *On the origin of species.* London: John Murray.

Darwin, C. R. (1872). *The expression of the emotions in man and animals.* London: John Murray.

Davidson, J. R., Gadde, K. M., Fairbank, J. A., Krishnan, R. R., Califf, R. M., Binanay, C., et al. (2002). Hypericum Depression Trial Study Group. Effect of *Hypericum perforatum* (St. John's wort) in major depressive disorder: A randomized, controlled trial. *Journal of the American Medical Association, 287*, 1807–1814.

Davidson, P. R., & Parker, K. C. (2001). Eye movement desensitization and reprocessing (EMDR): A meta-analysis. *Journal of Consulting and Clinical Psychology, 69*, 305–316.

Davidson, R. J., Kabat-Zinn, J., Schumacher, J., Rosenkranz, M., Muller, D., & Santorelli, S. F. (2003). Alternations in brain and immune function produced by mindfulness meditation. *Psychosomatic Medicine, 65*, 564–570.

Davies, G., Welham, J., Chant, D. Torrey, E. F., & McGrath, J. (2003). A systematic review and meta-analysis of northern hemisphere season of birth in schizophrenia. *Schizophrenia Research, 29*, 587–593.

Davis et al. (2006). Low literacy impairs comprehension of prescription drug warning labels. *Journal of General Internal Medicine, 21*, 847-851.

Davis, K. L., Kahn, R. S., Ko, G., & Davidson, M. (1991). Dopamine in schizophrenia: Review and reconceptualization. *American Journal of Psychiatry, 148*, 1474–1486.

Davis, R., Olmsted, M., Rockert, W., Marques, T., & Dolhanty, J. (1997). Group psychoeducation for bulimia nervosa with and without additional psychotherapy process sessions. *International Journal of Eating Disorders, 22*, 25–35.

Davis, S. R., Davison, S. L., Donath S., & Bell, R. J. (2005). Circulating androgen levels and self-reported sexual function in women. *Journal of the American Medical Association, 294*, 91–96.

Davison, D. C., & Lazarus, A. A. (2007). Case studies are important in the science and practice of psychotherapy. In S. O. Lilienfeld & W. T. O'Donohue (Eds.), *The great ideas of clinical science: 17 principles that every mental health professional should understand* (pp. 149–162). New York: Routledge.

Davison, G. C. (1976). Homosexuality: The ethical challenge. *Journal of Consulting and Clinical Psychology, 44*, 157–162.

Davison, K. P., Pennebaker, J. W., & Dickerson, S. S. (2000). Who talks? The social psychology of illness support groups. *American Psychologist, 55*, 205–217.

Dawes, R. M. (1988). *Rational choice in an uncertain world*. Orlando, FL: Harcourt-Brace Jovanovich.

Dawes, R. M. (1994). *House of cards: Psychology and psychotherapy built on myth*. New York: Free Press.

Dawes, R. M., Faust, D., & Meehl, P. E. (1989). Clinical versus actuarial judgment. *Science, 243*, 1668–1674.

De Groot, A. D. (1965). *Thought and choice in chess*. The Hague, Netherlands: Mouton & Company.

De la Fuente-Fernandez, R., Ruth, T. J., Sossi, V., Schulzer, M., Calne, D. B., & Stoessel, A. J. (2001). Expectation and dopamine release: Mechanism of the placebo effect in Parkinson's disease. *Science, 293*, 1007–1013.

De Raad et al., 2002

De Raad, B., Perugini, M., Hrebickova, M., & Szarota, P. (1998). The lingua franca of personality: Taxonomies and structure. *Journal of Cross Cultural Psychology, 29*, 212–232.

De Renzi, E. (1999). Lazarus' syndrome. In Della Sala, (Ed.). *Mind myths: Exploring popular assumptions about the mind and brain* (pp. 100–109). New York: John Wiley.

de Waal, F. B. M. (1982). *Chimpanzee politics: Power and sex among apes*. Baltimore: Johns Hopkins University Press.

de Waal, F. B. M. (1989). Behavioral contrasts between bonobo and chimpanzee. Heltne, P. G., & Marquardt, L. A. (Eds.), *Understanding chimpanzees* (pp. 154–175). Cambridge, MA: Harvard University Press.

de Waal, F. B. M. (1989). The myth of a simple relation between space and aggression in captive primates. *Zoo Biology, 8*, 141–148.

de Waal, F. B. M. (1990). *Peacemaking among primates*. Cambridge, MA: Harvard University Press.

de Waal, F. B. M. (1996). *Good natured: The origins of right and wrong in humans and other animals*. Cambridge, MA: Harvard University Press.

de Waal, F. B. M. (2002). Evolutionary psychology: The wheat and the chaff. *Current Directions in Psychological Science, 11*, 187–191.

de Waal, F. B. M., Aureli, F., & Judge, P. G. (2000, May). Coping with crowding. *Scientific American, 282*, 76–81.

Deabler, H. L., Hartl, E. M., & Willis, C. A. (1973). Physique and personality: Somatotype and the 16PF. *Perceptual and Motor Skills, 36*, 927–933.

Dean, G. (1987). Does astrology need to be true? Part 2: The answer is no. *Skeptical Inquirer, 11*, 257–273.

Deary, I., Der, G., & Ford, G. (2001). Reaction time and intelligence differences: A population based cohort study. *Intelligence, 29*, 1–11.

Deary, I. J., Whalley, L. J., Lemmon, H., Crawford, J. R., & Starr, J. M. (2000). The stability of individual differences in mental ability from childhood to old age: Follow-up of the 1932 Scottish Mental Survey. *Intelligence, 28*, 49–55.

Deater-Deckard, K. (2001). Annotation: Recent research examining the role of peer relationships in the development of psychopathology. *Journal of Child Psychology and Psychiatry, 42*, 565–579.

DeCasper, A. J., & Spence, M. J. (1988). Prenatal maternal speech influences newborns' perception of speech sounds. In S. Chess, A. Thomas, & M. Hertzig (Eds.), *Annual progress in child psychiatry and child development, 1987* (pp. 5–25). Philadelphia: Brunner/Mazel.

Deci, E. (1971). Effects of externally mediated rewards on intrinsic motivation. *Journal of Personality and Social Psychology, 18*, 105–115.

Deci, E. L., Koestner, R., & Ryan, R. M. (1999). A meta-analytic review of experiments examining the effects of extrinsic rewards on intrinsic motivation. *Psychological Bulletin, 125*, 627–668.

Deese, J. (1959). On the prediction of occurrence of particular verbal intrusions in immediate recall. *Journal of Experimental Psychology, 58*, 17–22.

Deffenbacher, K. A., Bornstein, B. H., Penrod, S. D., & McGorty, E. K. (2004). A meta-analytic review of the effects of high stress on eyewitness memory. *Law and Human Behavior, 28*, 687–706.

DeFries, J. C., & Plomin, R. (1978). Behavioral genetics. *Annual Review of Psychology, 29*, 473–515.

Degenhardt, L., & Hall, W. (2006). Is cannabis a contributory cause of psychosis? *Canadian Journal of Psychiatry, 51*, 556–565.

Dehue, T. (2000). From deception trials to control reagents. The introduction of the control group about a century ago. *American Psychologist, 55*(2), 264–269.

Delamatar, R., & McNamara, J. R. (1986). The social impact of assertiveness. *Behavior Modification, 10*, 139–158.

Delgado, J. M. R., & Anand, B. K. (1952). Increase of food intake induced by electrical stimulation of the lateral hypothalamus. *American Journal of Physiology, 172*, 162–168.

Della Sala, S. (2007). *Tall tales about the mind and brain: Separating fact from fiction*. Oxford, England: Oxford University Press.

DeLongis, A., Folkman, S., & Lazarus, R. (1988). The impact of daily stress on health and mood psychological and social resources as mediators. *Journal of Personality and Social Psychology, 54*, 486–495.

Dement W. (1973). The prevalence of narcolepsy II. *Sleep Research, 2*, 147.

Dement, W. C. (1974). *Some must watch while some must sleep*. San Francisco: W. H. Freeman.

Dement, W., & Kleitman, N. (1957). The relation of eye movements during sleep to dream activity: An objective method for the study of dreaming. *Journal of Experimental Psychology, 53*, 339–346.

Dement, W. C., & Vaughan, C. (1999). *The promise of sleep: A pioneer in sleep medicine explores the vital connection between health, happiness, and a good night's sleep*. New York: Dell Trade Paperbacks.

Demorest, A., Silberstein, L., Gardner, H., & Winner, E. (1983). Telling it as it isn't: Children's understanding of figurative language. *British Journal of Developmental Psychology, 1*, 121–134.

Dennerstein, L., Lehert, P., & Guthrie, J. (2002). The effects of the menopausal transition and biopsychosocial factors on well-being. *Archives of Women's Mental Health, 5*, 15–22.

Dennett, D. (1984). *Elbow room: The varieties of free will worth wanting*. Cambridge, MA: MIT Press.

Dennett, D. C. (1995). *Darwin's dangerous idea: Evolution and the meanings of life*. New York: Simon and Schuster.

Dennis, M., Sugar, J., & Whitaker, H. A. (1982). The acquisition of tag questions. *Child Development, 53*, 1254–1257.

Denniston, J. C., Chang, R., & Miller, R. R. (2003). Massive extinction prevents the renewal effect. *Learning and Motivation, 34*, 68–86.

Denollet, J. (2005). DS14: Standard assessment of negative affectivity, social inhibition, and Type D personality. *Psychosomatic Medicine, 67*, 89–97.

Denollet, J., Sys, S. U., & Brutsaert, D. L. (1995). Personality and mortality after myocardial infarction. *Psychosomatic Medicine, 57*, 582–591.

DeNoon, D. (2005): *Experts: Chelation therapy not worth the risk*. Medscape Psychiatry and Mental Health. Retrieved November 11, 2007, from http://www.medscape.com/viewarticle/511713.

DePaulo, B. M., & Pfeifer, R. L. (1986). On-the-job experience and skill at detecting deception. *Journal of Applied Social Psychology, 16*, 249–267.

DePaulo, B. (1992). Nonverbal behavior and self-presentation. *Psychological Bulletin, 111*, 203–243.

DePaulo, B. M., Kashy, D. A., Kirkendol, S. E., Wyer, M. M., & Epstein, J. A. (1996). Lying in everyday life. *Journal of Personality and Social Psychology, 70*, 979–995.

Depue, R., & Iacono, W. (1989). Neurobehavioral aspects of affective disorders. *Annual Review of Psychology, 40*, 457–492.

Der, G., Batty, G. D., & Deary, I. J. (2006). Effect of breast feeding on intelligence in children: Prospective study, sibling pairs analysis, and meta-analysis. *British Medical Journal, 333*, 945–950.

Deregowski J. B. (1984). *Distortion in art*. London: Routledge & Kegan Paul.

derSimonian, R., & Laird, N. M. (1983). Evaluating the effect of coaching on SAT scores: A meta-analysis. *Harvard Educational Review, 53*, 1–15.

DeRubeis, R. J., Brotman, M. A., & Gibbons, C. J. (2005). A conceptual and methodological analysis of the nonspecifics argument. *Clinical Psychology: Science & Practice, 12*, 174–183.

DeRubeis, R. J., Hollon, S. D., Amsterdam, J. D., Shelton, R. C., Young, P. R., Salomon, R. M., et al. (2005). Cognitive therapy vs medications in the treatment of moderate to severe depression. *Archives of General Psychiatry, 62*, 409–416.

Despres, O., Candas, V., & Dufour, A. (2005). Auditory compensation in myopic humans: Involvement of binaural, monaural, or echo cues? *Brain Research, 1041*, 56–65.

Detterman, D. K. (1987). What does reaction time tell us about intelligence? In P. Vernon (Ed.), *Speed of information-processing and intelligence.* Norwood, NJ: Ablex.

Deutsch, D. (1999). *The psychology of music* (2nd ed.). San Diego, CA: Academic Press.

Devilbiss, D. M., & Berridge, C. W. (2006). Low-dose methylphenidate actions on tonic and phasic locus coeruleus discharge. *Journal of Pharmacology & Experimental Therapeutics, 319*(3), 1327–1335.

Devine, P. G. (1989). Stereotypes and prejudice: Their automatic and controlled components. *Journal of Personality and Social Psychology, 56,* 5–18.

Devine, P. G., Monteith, M. J., Zuwerink, J. R., & Elliot, A. J. (1991). Prejudice with and without compunction. *Journal of Personality and Social Psychology, 60,* 817–830.

Devlin, B., Daniels, M., Roeder, K. (1997). The heritability of IQ. *Nature, 388,* 468–471.

DeYoung, C. G., Peterson, J. B., & Higgins, D. M. (2005). Sources of openness/intellect: Cognitive and neuropsychological correlates of the fifth factor of personality. *Journal of Personality, 73,* 825–858.

Diamond, L. M. (2003). What does sexual orientation orient? A biobehavioral model distinguishing romantic love and sexual desire. *Psychological Review, 110,* 173–192.

Diamond, L. M. (2004). Emerging perspectives on distinctions between romantic love and sexual desire. *Current Directions in Psychological Science, 13,* 116–119.

Dickens, W. T., & Flynn, J. R. (2001). Heritability estimates versus large environmental effects: The IQ paradox resolved. *Psychological Review, 108,* 346–369.

Dickens, W. T., & Flynn, J. R. (2006). Black Americans reduce the racial IQ gap: Evidence from standardization samples. *Psychological Science, 17,* 1101–1107.

Dickey, M. (1994). *Anxiety disorders.* National Institute of Mental Health. Washington, DC: U.S. Government Printing Office

DiClemente, C. C., & Prochaska, J. O. (1985). Coping and competence in smoking behavior change. In S. Shiffman & T. A. Willis (Eds.), *Coping and substance abuse.* New York: Academic Press.

Didierjean, A., & Marmèche, E. (2005). Anticipatory representation of visual basketball scenes by novice and expert players. *Visual Cognition, 12,* 265–283.

Diehl, M., & Strobe, W. (1987). Productivity loss in brainstorming groups: Toward the solution of a riddle. *Journal of Personality and Social Psychology, 53,* 497–509.

Diener, E., & Diener, C. (1996). Most people are happy. *Psychological Science, 3,* 181–85.

Diener, E., Emmons, R. A., Larsen, R. J., & Griffin, S. (1985). The satisfaction with lifescale. *Journal of Personality Assessment, 49,* 71–75.

Diener, E., Horwitz, J., & Emmons, R. A. (1985). Happiness of the very wealthy. *Social Indicators Research, 16,* 263–274.

Diener, E., Lucas, R., & Scollon, C. N. (2006). Beyond the hedonic treadmill: Revising the adaptation theory of well-being. *American Psychologist, 61,* 305–314.

Diener, E., & Seligman, M. E. P. (2002). Very happy people. *Psychological Science, 13,* 81–84.

Diener, E., & Seligman, M. E. P. (2004). Beyond money: Toward an economy of well-being. *Psychological Science in the Public Interest, 5,* 1–31.

Diener, H. C., Kronfeld, K., & Boewing, G. (2006). Efficacy of acupuncture for the prophylaxis of migraine: A multi-center randomized controlled trial. *The Lancet Neurology* Online, March 2.

Dies, R. R. (2003). Group psychotherapies. In A. S. Gurman & S. B. Messer (Eds.), *Essential psychotherapies* (2nd ed., pp. 515–550). New York: Guilford Press.

Dietrich, E., & Markman, A. B. (2000). Cognitive dynamics: Computation and representation regained. In E. Dietrich & A. B. Markman (Eds.), *Cognitive dynamics: Conceptual and representational change in human sand machines* (pp. 5–29). Mahwah, NJ: Lawrence Erlbaum.

DiLalla, L. F., & Gottesman, I. I. (1991). Biological and genetic contributors to violence—Widom's untold tale. *Psychological Bulletin, 109,* 125–129.

DiLalla, L. F., Thompson, L. A., Plomin, R., Phillips, K., Fagan, J. F., Haith, M. M., et al. (1990). Infant predictors of preschool and adult IQ: A study of infant twins and their parents. *Developmental Psychology, 26,* 759–769.

Dilk, M. N., & Bond, G. R. (1996). Meta-analytic evaluation of skills training research for individuals with severe mental illness. *Journal of Consulting and Clinical Psychology, 64,* 1337–1346.

Dill, J. C., & Anderson, C. A. (1995). Effects of frustration justification on hostile aggression. *Aggressive Behavior, 21,* 359–369.

DiLoretto, A. O. (1971). *Comparative psychotherapy: An experimental analysis.* Chicago: Aldine-Atherton.

Dion, K., Berscheid, E., & Walster, E. (1972). What is beautiful is good. *Journal of Personality and Social Psychology, 24,* 285–290.

Dipboye, R. L. (1977). Alternative approaches to deindividuation. *Psychological Bulletin, 85,* 1057–1075.

Ditto, P. H., & Lopez, D. F. (1992). Motivated skepticism: Use of differential decision criteria for preferred and nonpreferred conclusions. *Journal of Personality and Social Psychology, 63,* 568–584.

Dixon, M., & Laurence, J. (1992). Two hundred years of hypnosis research: Questions resolved? Questions unanswered! In E. Fromm and M. Nash (Eds.), *Contemporary hypnosis research* (pp. 34–66). New York: Guilford.

Dobrick, W., & Scarborough, H. S. (1992). Phonological characteristics of words young children try to say. *Journal of Child Language, 19,* 597–616.

Dobson, J. (1992). *The strong-willed child.* Carol Stream, IL: Tyndale.

Dodd, B., & McEvoy, S. (1994). Twin language or phonological disorder? *Journal of Child Language, 21,* 273–289.

Dohrenwend, B. S., & Dohrenwend, B. P. (Eds.), (1974). *Stressful life events: Their nature and effects* (pp. 245–258). New York: Wiley.

Dolan, M., Anderson, I. M., & Deakin, J. F. (2001). Relationship between 5-HT function and impulsivity and aggression in male offenders with personality disorders. *British Journal of Psychiatry, 178,* 352–359.

Dollard, J., & Miller, N. (1950). *Personality and psychotherapy: An analysis in terms of learning, thinking and culture.* New York: McGraw-Hill.

Dolnick, E. (1998). *Madness on the couch: Blaming the victim in the heyday of psychoanalysis.* New York: Simon & Schuster.

Domhoff, G. W. (1993). The repetition of dreams and dream elements: A possible clue to a function of dreams. In A. Moffitt, M. Kramer, & R. Hoffman (Eds.), *The functions of dreams* (pp. 293–320). Albany, NY: SUNY Press.

Domhoff, G. W. (1996). *Finding meaning in dreams: A quantitative approach.* New York: Plenum.

Domhoff, G. W. (1999). *The scientific study of dreams: Neural networks, cognitive development, and content analysis.* Washington, DC: American Psychological Association.

Domhoff, G. W. (2001a). Why did empirical dream researchers reject Freud? A critique of historical claims by Mark Solms. *Dreaming, 14,* 3–17.

Domhoff, G. W. (2001b). A new neurocognitive theory of dreams. *Dreaming, 11,* 13–33.

Domhoff, G. W., & Schneider, A. (2004). Much ado about very little: The small effect size when home and laboratory dreams are compared. *Dreaming, 19,* 139–151.

Domjan, M., & Purdy, J. E. (1995). Animal research in psychology. *American Psychologist, 50,* 496–503.

Donnellan, M. B., Trzesniewski, K. H., Robins, R. W., Moffitt, T. E., & Caspi, A. (2005). Exploring the link between self-esteem and externalizing behaviors: Low self-esteem is related to antisocial behavior, conduct disorder, and delinquency. *Psychological Science, 16,* 328–335.

D'Onofrio, B. M., Turkheimer, E. N, Emery, R., Slutske, W., Heath, A., Madden, P. A. F., et al. (2006). A genetically informed study of the processes underlying the association between parental marital instability and offspring adjustment. *Developmental Psychology, 42,* 486–499.

Donovan, J. J., & Radosevich, D. R. (1999). A meta-analytic review of the distribution of practice effect: Now you see it, now you don't. *Journal of Applied Psychology, 84,* 795–805.

Dorus, E., Dorus, W., & Rechtschaffen, A. (1971). The incidence of novelty in dreams. *Archives of General Psychiatry, 25,* 364–368.

Dosajh, N. L. (1996). Projective techniques with particular reference to inkblot tests. *Journal of Projective Psychology and Mental Health, 3,* 59–68.

Doty, R. L. (2001). *Handbook of olfaction and gustation.* New York: Marcel Dekker.

Doty, R. L., Deems, D., & Stellar, S. (1988). Olfactory dysfunction in Parkinson's disease: A general deficit unrelated to neurologic signs, disease stage, or disease duration. *Neurology, 38,* 1237–1244.

Doty, R. L., Shaman, P., Applebaum, S. L., Giberson, R., Siksorski, L., & Rosenberg, L. (1984). Smell identification ability: Changes with age. *Science, 226,* 1441–1443.

Doublet, S. (2000). *The stress myth.* Freemans Reach, New South Wales, Australia: Ipsilon Publishing.

Douglas, R. M., Hemilä, H., D'Souza, R., Chalker, E. B., & Treacy, B. (2004). Vitamin C for preventing and treating the common cold. *Cochrane Database System Review, 4,* CD000980.

Dovidio, J., Piliavin, J., Schroeder, D., & Penner, L. (2006). *The social psychology of prosocial behavior.* Mahwah, NJ: Lawrence Erlbaum.

Dowman, J., Patel, A., & Rajput, K. (2005). Electroconvulsive therapy: Attitudes and misconceptions. *The Journal of ECT, 21,* 84–87.

Downey, G., & Coyne, J. C. (1990). Children of depressed parents: An integrative review. *Psychological Bulletin, 108,* 50–76.

Downs, C. A., & Harrison, S. K. (1985). Embarrassing age spots or just plain ugly? Physical attractiveness stereotyping as a instrument of sexism on American television commercials. *Sex Roles, 13,* 9–19.

Driscoll, R., Davis, K. E., & Lipetz, M. E. (1972). Parental interference and romantic love: The Romeo and Juliet effect. *Journal of Personality and Social Structure, 24*, 1–10.

Drory, A. (1986). Graphology and job performance: A validation study. In B. Nevo (Ed.), *Scientific aspects of graphology* (pp. 165–173). Springfield, IL: Charles C. Thomas.

Druckman, D., & Bjork, R. A. (Eds.). (1994). *Learning, remembering, believing: Enhancing human performance.* Washington, DC: National Academy Press.

Druckman, D., & Swets, J. A. (Eds.). (1988). *Enhancing human performance: Issues, theories, and techniques.* Washington, DC: National Academy Press.

DuBreuil, S. C., Garry, M., & Loftus, E. F. (1998). Tales from the crib: Age-regression and the creation of unlikely memories. In S. J. Lynn & K. M. McConkey (Eds.), *Truth in memory* (pp. 137–160). Washington, DC: American Psychological Association.

DuBrin, J. R., & Zastowny, T. R. (1988). Predicting early attrition from psychotherapy: An analysis of a large private practice cohort. *Psychotherapy, 25*, 393–498.

Duenwald, M. (2002, May 7). Religion and health: New research revives and old debate. *New York Times,* D5.

Duff, G. (2003). Selective serotonin reuptake inhibitors: Use in children and adolescents with major depressive disorder. Retrieved April 16, 2006, from http://medicines.mhra.gov /uk/ourwork/monitorsafequalmed /safetymessages/cemssri_101203.pdf.

Duggal S., & Stroufe L. A. (1998). Recovered memory of childhood sexual trauma: A documented case from a longitudinal study. *Journal of Traumatic Stress, 11*, 301–321.

Dunbar, R. (1993). Coevolution of neocortical size, group size, and language in humans. *Behavioral and Brain Sciences, 16*, 681–735.

Dunbar, R. (1996). *Grooming, gossip, and the evolution of language.* London: Faber & Faber.

Dunbar, R. (1998). Theory of mind and the evolution of language. In J. R. Hurford, M. Studdert-Kennedy, & C. Knigh (Eds.), *Approaches to the evolution of language* (pp. 92–110). Cambridge, England: Cambridge University Press.

Dunbar, R. (2003). Psychology. Evolution of the social brain. *Science, 302,* 1160–1161.

Duncan, B. (1976). Differential social perception and attribution of intergroup violence. *Journal of Personality and Social Psychology, 34*, 590–398.

Duncan, C. P. (1976). Recognition of names of eminent psychologists. *Journal of the History of the Behavioral Sciences, 12*, 325–329

Duncan, G. (1996). Income dynamics and health. *International Journal of Health Services, 26*, 419-444.

Duncan, J., Seitz, R. J., Kolodny, J., Bor, D., Herzog, H., Ahmed, A., et al. (2000). A neural basis for general intelligence. *Science, 289*, 457–460.

Duncker, K. (1945). On problem-solving. *Psychological Monographs* (No. 270).

Dunn, R. L., & Schwebel, A. I. (1995). Meta-analytic review of marital therapy outcome research. *Journal of Family Psychology, 9*, 58–68.

Dunning, D., Heath, C., & Suls, J. (2004). Flawed self-assessment: Implications for health, education, and the workplace. *Psychological Science in the Public Interest, 5*, 69–106.

Dunning, D., Johnson, K. L., Ehrlinger, J., & Kruger, J. (2003). Why people fail to recognize their own incompetence. *Current Directions in Psychological Science, 12*, 83–87.

Dunnington, G. W. (1955). *Carl Friedrich Gauss: Titan of science.* New York: Hafner.

Dusky vs. United States (1960), *362*, US 402.

Dusseldorp, E., van Elderen, T., Maes, S., Meulman, J., & Kraaij, V. (1999). A meta-analysis of psychoeducational programs for coronary heart disease patients. *Health Psychology, 18*, 506–519.

Dutton, D. G., & Aron, A. (1974). Some evidence for heightened sexual attraction under conditions of high anxiety. *Journal of Personality and Social Psychology, 30*, 510–517.

Dweck, C. S. (2002). Beliefs that make smart people dumb. In R. Sternberg (Ed.), *Why smart people can be so stupid* (pp. 24–41). New Haven. CT: Yale University Press.

Dweck, C. S. (2006). *Mindset: The new psychology of success.* New York: Random House.

Dykman, B. M., Horowitz, L., Abramson, L. Y., & Usher, M. (1991). Schematic and situational determinants of depressed and nondepressed students' interpretation of feedback. *Journal of Abnormal Psychology, 199*, 45–55.

Dysken, M. W., Kooser, J. A., Haraszti, J. S., & Davis, J. M. (1979). Clinical usefulness of sodium amobarbitol interviewing. *Archives of General Psychiatry, 36*, 789–794.

Eagly, A. H., Ashmore, R. D., Makhijani, M. G., & Longo, L. C. (1991). What is beautiful is good, but. . . : A meta-analytic review of research on the physical attractiveness stereotype. *Psychological Bulletin, 110*, 109–128.

Eagly, A. H., & Carli, L. L. (1981). Sex of researchers and sex-typed communications as determinants of sex differences in influenceability: A meta-analysis of social influence studies. *Psychological Bulletin, 90,* 1–20.

Eagly, A. H., & Crowley, M. (1986). Gender differences in helping behavior: A meta-analytic review of the social psychological literature. *Psychological Bulletin, 100*, 283–308.

Eagly, A. H., & Steffen, V. J. (1986). Gender and aggressive behavior: A meta-analytic review of the social psychological literature. *Psychological Bulletin, 100*, 309–330.

Eagly, A. H., & Wood, W. (1999). The origins of sex differences in human behavior: Evolved dispositions versus social roles. *American Psychologist, 54*, 408–423.

Eagly, A. H., Wood, W., & Johannesen-Schmidt, M. C. (2004). Social role theory of sex differences and similarities: Implications for the partner preferences of women and men. In A. H. Eagly, A. Beall, & R. S. Sternberg (Eds.), *The psychology of gender* (2nd ed., pp. 269–295). New York: Guilford Press.

Earleywine, M. (2005). Cannabis: Attending to subjective effects to improve drug safety. In M. Earleywine (Ed.), *Mind-altering drugs: The science of subjective experience* (pp. 240–257). Washington, DC: American Psychological Association.

Eaton, W. W., Dryman, A., & Weissman, M. M. (1991). Panic and phobia. In L. N. Robins & D. A., Reiger (Eds.), *Psychiatric disorders in America.* New York: Free Press.

Ebbinghaus, H. (1964). Translation of memory: A contribution to experimental psychology (H. A. Ruger & C. E. Bussenius, Trans.). New York: Dover. (Original work published 1885)

Eberhardt, J. L., & Randall, J. L. (1997). The essential notion of race. *Psychological Science, 8*, 198–20.

Edmonston, W. E. (1991). Anesis. In S. J. Lynn & J. W. Rhue (Eds.), *Theories of hypnosis: Current models and perspectives* (pp. 197–240). New York: Guilford.

Edwards, D. A. (1970). Post-neonatal androgenization and adult aggressive behavior in female mice. *Physiology and Behavior, 5*, 465–467.

Edwards, D. M., Franks, P., Friedgood, D., Lobban, G., & Mackay, H. C. G. (1969). *An experiment on obedience.* Unpublished student report, University of the Witwatersrand, Johannesburg, South Africa.

Edwards, K., & Smith, E. E. (1996). A disconfirmation bias in the evaluation of arguments. *Journal of Personality and Social Psychology, 71*, 5–24.

Egan, L. C., Santos, L. R., & Bloom, P. (2007). The origins of cognitive dissonance: Evidence from children and monkeys. *Psychological Science, 18,* 978–983.

Ehrenwald, J. (1974). Out-of-the-body experiences and the denial of death. *Journal of Nervous and Mental Disease, 159*, 227–233.

Ehrlinger, J., Gilovich, T., & Ross, L. (2005). Peering into the bias blind spot: People's assessment of bias in themselves and others. *Personality and Social Psychology Bulletin, 31*, 680–690.

Ehrsson, H. H. (2007). The experimental induction of out-of-body experiences. *Science, 317*, 1048.

Ehrsson, H. H., Spence, C., & Passingham, R. E. (2004). That's my hand! Activity in premotor cortex reflects feeling of ownership of a limb. *Science, 305*, 875–877.

Eibl-Eibesfeldt, I. (1973). The expressive behaviour of the deaf-and-blind-born. In M. von Cranach & I. Vine (Eds.), *Social communication and movement* (pp. 163–194). London: Academic Press.

Eich, E., & Hyman, R. (1991). Subliminal self help. In D. Druckman & R. A. Bjork (Eds.), *In the mind's eye: Enhancing human performance* (pp. 107–119). Washington, DC: National Academy Press.

Eigsti, I. M., Zayas, V., Mischel, W., Shoda, Y., Ayduk, O., Dadlani, M. B., et al. (2006). Predicting cognitive control from preschool to late adolescence and young adulthood. *Psychological Science, 17*, 478–484.

Eimas, P. D., Siqueland, E. R., Jusczyk, P., & Vigorito, J. (1971). Speech perception in infants. *Science, 171*, 303–306.

Eisenberger, N. I., Lieberman, M. D., & Williams, K. D. (2003). Does rejection hurt? An fMRI study of social exclusion. *Science, 302*, 290–292.

Eisenberger, R., & Cameron, J. (1996). Detrimental effects of reward: Reality of or myth? *American Psychologist, 51*, 1153–1166.

Eisler, R. M., & Ragsdale, K. (1992). Masculine gender role and midlife transition in men. In V. B. Van Hasselt & M. Hersen (Eds), *Handbook of social development: A lifespan perspective* (pp. 455–471). New York: Plenum Press.

Eisner, D. A. (2000). *The death of psychotherapy: From Freud to alien abductions.* Westport, CT: Praeger.

Ekman, P. (1994). Strong evidence for universals in facial expressions: A reply to Russell's mistaken critique. *Psychological Bulletin, 115*, 268–287.

Ekman, P. (2001). *Telling lies: Clues to deceit in the marketplace, politics, and marriage.* New York: Norton.

Ekman, P., & Davidson, R. (1993). Voluntary smiling changes regional brain activity. *Psychological Science, 5*, 342–345.

Ekman, P., Davidson, R. J., & Friesen, W. V. (1990). Duchenne's smile: Emotional expression and brain physiology II. *Journal of Personality and Social Psychology, 58*, 342–353.

Ekman, P., & Friesen, W. (1986). A new pancultural facial expression of emotion. *Motivation and Emotion, 10*, 159–168.

Ekman, P., & Friesen, W. V. (1971). Constants across cultures in the face and emotion. *Journal of Personality and Social Psychology, 17*, 124–129.

Ekman, P., & Friesen, W. V. (1975). *Unmasking the face: A guide to recognizing emotions from facial clues.* Englewood Cliffs, NJ: Prentice-Hall.

Ekman, P., Levenson, R. W., & Friesen, W. V. (1983). Autonomic nervous system activity distinguishes between emotions. *Science, 221*, 1208–1210.

Ekman, P., & Oster, H. (1979). Facial expressions of emotion. *Annual Review of Psychology, 20*, 527–554.

Ekman, P., & O'Sullivan, M. (1991). Who can catch a liar? *American Psychologist, 46*, 913–920.

Ekman, P., O'Sullivan, M., & Frank, M. G. (1999). A few can catch a liar. *Psychological Science, 10*, 263–266.

Elfenbein, H. A., & Ambady, N. (2002). On the universality and cultural specificity of emotion recognition: A meta-analysis. *Psychological Bulletin, 128*, 203–235.

Elkin, I. (1994). The NIMH Treatment of Depression Collaborative Research Program: Where we began and where we are now. In A. E. Bergin & S. L. Garfield (Eds.), *Handbook of psychotherapy and behavior change* (4th ed., pp. 114–135). New York: Wiley.

Elkind, D. (1967). Egocentrism in adolescence. *Child Development, 38*, 1025–1034.

Ellenberger, H. F. (1970). *The discovery of the unconscious: The history and evolution of dynamic psychiatry.* New York: Basic Books.

Ellinwood, E. H., & Hamilton, J. G. (1991). Case report of a needle phobia. *Journal of Family Practice, 32*, 420–423.

Elliott, R. (2002). The effectiveness of humanistic therapies: A meta-analysis. In D. J. Cain & J. Seeman (Eds.), *Humanistic psychotherapies: Handbook of research and practice* (pp. 57–81). Washington, DC: American Psychological Association.

Elliott, R., & Greenberg, L. S. (2002). Process-experiential psychotherapy. In D. J. Cain & J. Seeman (Eds.), *Humanistic psychotherapies: Handbook of research and practice* (pp. 279–306). Washington, DC: American Psychological Association.

Ellis, A. (1958). *Sex without guilt.* New York: Lyle Stuart.

Ellis, A. (1962). *Reason and emotion in psychotherapy.* Secaucus, NJ: Citadel Press.

Ellis, A. (1962). *Research and emotion in psychotherapy.* New York: Lyle Stuart.

Ellis, A. (1977). The basic clinical theory of rational-emotive therapy. In A. Ellis & R. Grieger (Eds.), *Handbook of rational-emotive therapy* (pp. 3–34). New York: Springer.

Ellis, A., & Dryden, W. (1997). *The practice of rational-emotive behavior therapy.* New York: Springer Publishing.

Ellis, L., & Ames, M. A. (1987). Neurohormonal functioning and sexual orientation: A theory of homosexuality-heterosexuality. *Psychological Bulletin, 101*, 233–258.

Ellison, C. G., & Levin, S. L. (1998). The religion-health connection: Evidence, theory, and future directions. *Health Education and Behavior, 25*, 700–720.

Ellsworth, C. P., Muir, D. W., & Hains, S. M. (1993). Social competence and person-object differentiation: An analysis of the still-face effect. *Developmental Psychology, 29*, 63–73.

Elman, J. (1993). Incremental learning, or the importance of starting small. *Cognition, 49*, 71–99.

Elms, A. C. (1972). *Social psychology and social relevance.* Boston: Little, Brown.

Elzinga, B. M., van Dyck, R., & Spinhoven, P. (1998). Three controversies about dissociative identity disorder. *Clinical Psychology and Psychotherapy, 5*, 13–23.

Emery, C., & Lilienfeld, S. O. (2004). The validity of child sexual abuse survivor checklists in the popular psychology literature: A Barnum effect? *Professional Psychology: Science and Practice, 35*, 268–274.

Emery, G. (2005). Psychic predictions 2005. *Skeptical Inquirer, 29*(2), 7–8.

Emler, N. (2001). *Self-esteem: The costs and causes of low self-worth.* York, North Yorkshire, England: Joseph Rowntree Foundation.

Emmelkamp, P. M. G., & Kamphuis, J. H. (2005). Aversion relief. In M. Hersen & J. Rosqvist (Eds.), *Encyclopedia of behavior modification and cognitive behavior therapy. Volume I: Adult clinical application* (pp. 39–40). Thousand Oaks, CA: Sage.

Emmelkamp, P. M. G., Bruynzeel, M., Drost, L., & van der Mast, C. A. P. G. (2001). Virtual reality treatment in acrophobia: A comparison with exposure in vivo. *CyberPsychology & Behavior, 4*, 335–339.

Emmelkamp, P. M. G., Krijn, M., Hulsbosch, A. M., de Vries, S., Schuemie, M. J. & Van der Mast, C. A. P. G. (2002). Virtual reality treatment versus exposure in vivo: A comparative evaluation in acrophobia. *Behaviour Research and Therapy, 40*, 509–516.

Emmons, R. A., McCullough, M. E., & Tsang, J. (2003). The assessment of gratitude. In S. Lopez & C. R. Snyder (Eds.), *Handbook of positive psychology assessment* (pp. 327–342). Washington, DC: American Psychological Association.

Emory, E. K., & Toomey, K. A. (1988). Environmental stimulation and human fetal responsiveness in late pregnancy. In W. P. Smotherman & S. R. Robinson (Eds.), *Behavior of the fetus* (pp. 141–161). Caldwell, NJ: Telford Press.

Emrick, C. D. (1987). Alcoholics Anonymous: Affiliation processes and effectiveness as treatment. *Alcoholism: Clinical and Experimental Research, 11*, 416–423.

Engel, A. K., & Singer, W. (2001). Temporal binding and the neural correlates of sensory awareness. *Trends in Cognitive Science, 5*, 6–25.

Engle, R. W. (2002). Working memory capacity as executive attention. *Current Directions in Psychological Science, 11*, 19–23.

Engler, J., & Goleman, D. (1992). *A consumer's guide to psychotherapy.* New York: Simon & Shuster.

Entwisle, D. R. (1972). To dispel fantasies about fantasy-based measures of achievement motivation. *Psychological Bulletin, 77*, 377–391.

Epley, N., Savitsky, K., & Kachelski, R. A. (1999). What every skeptic should know about subliminal persuasion. *Skeptical Inquirer, 23*, 40–45, 58.

Epstein, R. (2007). Giving psychology away: A personal journey. *Perspectives on Psychological Science, 1*, 389–400.

Epstein, R. (2007, February). The truth about online dating. *Scientific American Mind.* Retrieved March 5, 2007, from www.sciam.com /article.cfm?articleID=79C583A1-E7F2-99DF-3BE62D88C9C352E0.

Epstein, S. (1979). The stability of behavior: I. On predicting more of the people more of the time. *Journal of Personality and Social Psychology, 37*, 1097–1126.

Epstein, S. (1990). Cognitive-experiential self-theory. In L. Pervin (Ed.), *Handbook of personality theory and research: Theory and research* (pp. 165–192). New York: Guilford Publications.

Epstein, S., Lipson, A., Holstein, C., & Huh, E. (1992). Irrational reactions to negative outcomes: Evidence for two conceptual systems. *Journal of Personality and Social Psychology, 62*, 328–339.

Erblich, J., Earleywine, M., Erblich, B., & Bovberg, D. H. (2003). Biphasic stimulant and sedative effects of ethanol: Are children of alcoholics really different? *Addictive Behaviors, 28*, 1129–1139.

Erdelyi, M. (1994). Hypnotic hypermnesia: The empty set of hypermnesia. *International Journal of Clinical and Experimental Hypnosis, 42*, 379–390.

Erdelyi, M. H. (2006). The unified theory of repression. *Behavioral and Brain Sciences, 29*, 499–551.

Erickson, E. (1950). *Childhood and society.* New York: Norton.

Ericsson, K. A., Chase, W. G., & Faloon, S. (1980). Acquisition of a memory skill. *Science, 208*, 1181–1182.

Ericsson, K. A., Krampe, R. Th., & Tesch-Römer, C. (1993). The role of deliberate practice in the acquisition of expert performance. *Psychological Review, 100*, 363–406.

Erikson, E. (1963). *Childhood and society* (2nd ed.). New York: W. W. Norton.

Erikson, E. (1968). *Identity: Youth and crisis.* London: Faber & Faber.

Erikson, E. H. (1970). Reflections on the dissent of contemporary youth. *International Journal of Psychoanalysis, 51*, 11–22.

Ernst, C., & Angst, J. (1983). *Birth order.* Berlin, Germany: Springer-Verlag.

Ernst, E. (2002). Heavy metals in traditional Indian remedies. *European Journal of Clinical Pharmacology, 57*, 891–896.

Esch, T., & Stefano, G. B. (2005). The neurobiology of love. *Neuro Endocrinology Letters, 26*, 175–192.

Eslinger, P. J., & Damasio, A. R. (1985). Severe disturbance of higher cognition after bilateral frontal lobe ablation. Patient EVR. *Neurology, 35*, 1731–1741.

Esterling, B. A., Kiecolt-Glaser, J. K., & Glaser, R. (1996). Psychosocial modulation of cytokine-induced natural killer cell activity in older adults. *Psychosomatic Medicine, 58*, 264–272.

Esterson, A. (1993). *Seductive mirage: An exploration of the work of Sigmund Freud.* Chicago: Open Court.

Evans, C. J. (2004). Secrets of the opium poppy revealed. *Neuropharmacology. 47*(Suppl. 1), 293–299.

Evans, M. J. (1989). Potential for genetic manipulation of mammals. *Molecular & Biological Medicine, 6*, 557–565.

Evans, R. B. (1972). Titchener and his lost system. *Journal of the History of the Behavioral Sciences, 8*, 168–180.

Eve, R. A. (2007) Science education and belief in pseudoscience: Good news— But the glass is still two-thirds empty. *Skeptic, 13*(3), 14–15.

Eveleth, P. B., & Tanner, J. M. (1976). *Worldwide variation in human growth.* Cambridge, England: Cambridge University Press.

Eveleth, P. B., & Tanner, J. M. (1990). *Worldwide variation in human growth* (2nd ed.). Cambridge, England: Cambridge University Press.

Eyferth, K. (1961). Leistungen verschidener Gruppen von Besatzungskindern in Hamburg-Wechsler Intelligenztest fur Kinder (HAWIK) [Performance of different groups of occupation children on the Hamburg-Wechsler Intelligence Test for Children]. *Archhiv fur die gesamte Psychologie, 113,* 222–241.

Eysenck, H. J. (1952). The effects of psychotherapy: An evaluation. *Journal of Consulting Psychology, 16,* 319–324.

Eysenck, H. J. (1973). *Eysenck on extraversion.* New York: Wiley.

Eysenck, H. J. (1991). Dimensions of personality: 16, 5, or 3?—Criteria for a taxonomic paradigm. *Personality and Individual Differences, 12,* 773–790.

Eysenck, H. J. (1994). *Test your IQ.* Toronto, Ontario, Canada: Penguin Books.

Eysenck, H. J., & Schoenthaler, S. J. (1997). Raising IQ level by vitamin and mineral supplementation. In R. Sternberg & E. Grigorenko (Eds.), *Intelligence, heredity, and environment* (pp. 363–392). Cambridge, England: Cambridge University Press.

Eysenck, H. J., & Wilson, G. D. (1973). *The experimental study of Freudian theories.* London: Methuen.

Fabbro, F. (1999). *The neurolinguistics of bilingualism. An introduction.* Hove, England: Psychology Press.

Fagen, J. (1971, Spring). The importance of Fritz Perls having been. *Voices, 7,* 16–20.

Fagen, J. F. (1979). Contrast effects in the rat: A developmental study. *Developmental Psychobiology, 12,* 83–92.

Fagg, G. E., & Foster, A. C. (1983). Amino acid neurotransmitters and their pathways in the mammalian central nervous system. *Neuroscience, 9,* 701–719.

Fagot, B., Hagan, R., Leinbach, M., & Kronsberg, S. (1985). Differential reactions to assertive and communicative acts of toddler girls and boys. *Child Development, 56,* 1499–1505.

Fairbairn, R. (1946). Endopsychic structure considered in terms of object relationships. *Psychoanalytic Quarterly, 5,* 54–69.

Fairburn, C. G., Cooper, Z., & Shafran, R. (2003). Cognitive behaviour therapy for eating disorders: A "transdiagnostic" theory and treatment. *Behavior Research and Therapy, 41,* 509–528.

Fancher, R. (1985). *The intelligence men: Makers of the IQ controversy.* New York: W. W. Norton.

Fang, X., & Corso, P. S. (2007). Child maltreatment, youth violence, and intimate partner violence: Developmental relationships. *American Journal of Preventive Medicine, 33,* 281–290.

Fang, X., Singh, S., & AhluWalia, R. (2007). An examination of different explanations for the mere exposure effect. *Journal of Consumer Research, 34,* 97–103.

Farber, B. A., & Lane, J. S. (2002). Effective elements of the therapy relationship: Positive regard and support. In J. Norcross (Ed.), *Psychotherapy relationships that work: Therapists' relational contributions to effective psychotherapy* (pp. 175–194). New York: Oxford.

Farthing, G. W. (1992). *The psychology of consciousness.* Englewood Cliffs, NJ: Prentice Hall.

Farvolden, P., & Woody, E. Z. (2004). Hypnosis, memory and frontal executive functioning. *International Journal of Clinical and Experimental Hypnosis, 52,* 3–26.

Farwell, L. A., & Donchin, E. (1991). The truth will out: Interrogative polygraphy ("lie detection") with event-related brain potentials. *Psychophysiology, 28,* 531–547.

Fazio, R. H. (1995). Attitudes as object-evaluation associations: Determinants, consequences, and correlates of attitude accessibility. In R. E. Petty & J. A. Krosnick (Eds.), *Attitude strength: Antecedents and consequences* (pp. 247–283). Mahwah, NJ: Lawrence Erlbaum.

Fazio, R. H., Jackson, J. R., Dunton, B. C., & Williams, C. J. (1995). Variability in automatic activation as an unobtrusive measure of racial attitudes: A bona fide pipeline? *Journal of Personality and Social Psychology, 69,* 1013–1027.

Fazio, R. H., & Olson, M. A. (2003). Implicit measures in social cognition: Their meaning and use. *Annual Review of Psychology, 54,* 297–327.

Febbraro, G. A. R., Clum, G. A., Roodman, A. A., & Wright, J. H. (1999). The limits of bibliotherapy: A study of the differential effectiveness of self-administered interventions in individuals with panic attacks. *Behavior Therapy, 30,* 209–222.

Fechner, G. T. (1860). *Elemente der Psychophysik.* Leipzig, Germany: Breitkopf und Haertel.

Federal Bureau of Investigation. (2005). *Crime in the United States.* Washington, DC: Author.

Fehr, B. (1996). *Friendship processes.* Thousand Oaks, CA: Sage Publications.

Feinberg, T. E, & Keenan, J. P. (2005). Where in the brain is the self? *Conscious and Cognition, 14,* 661–678.

Feingold, A. (1988). Cognitive gender differences are disappearing. *American Psychologist, 43,* 95–103.

Feingold, A. (1992). Good-looking people are not what we think. *Psychological Bulletin, 111,* 304–341.

Feinman, S. (1978). The blind as "ordinary people." *Journal of Visual Impairment and Blindness, 72,* 231–238.

Feldman, Barrett, L. F., Lindquist, K., Bliss-Moreau, E., Duncan, S., Gendron, M., Mize, J., & Brennan, L. (2007). Of mice and men: Natural kinds of emotion in the mammalian brain? *Perspectives on Psychological Science, 2,* 297-312.

Feldman Barrett, L. (2006). Are emotions natural kinds? *Perspectives on Psychological Science, 1,* 28–58.

Feldman, M. D., Ford, C. V., & Reinhold, T. (1995). *Patient or pretender: Inside the strange world of factitious disorders.* New York: Wiley.

Feldman-Summers, S., Montano, D. E., Kasprzyk, D., & Wagner, B. (1980). Influence attempts when competing views are gender-related: Sex as credibility. *Psychology of Women Quarterly, 5,* 311–320.

Felner, R. D., Ginter, M. A., Boike, M. F., & Cowen, E. L. (1981). Parental death or divorce in childhood: Problems, interventions, and outcomes in a school based mental health project. *Journal of Primary Prevention, 1,* 240–246.

Fenson, L., Dale, P. S., Reznick, J. S., Bates, E., Thal, D. J., & Pethick, S. J. (1994). Variability in early communicative development. *Monographs of the Society for Research in Child Development, 59* (5, Serial No. 173).

Fenton, R. (2007, November 2). Drowsy driving is big killer in U.S. *ABC News.* Retrieved November 8, 2007, from http://abcnews.go.com/Health /wireStory?id=3811426.

Ferguson, D. M., Horwood, L. J., & Beautrais, A. L. (1999). Is sexual orientation related to mental health problems and suicidality in young people? *Archives of General Psychiatry, 56,* 876–880.

Fergusson, D. M., Swain-Campbell, N. R., & Horwood, L. (2002). Deviant peer affiliations, crime, and substance use: A fixed effects regression analysis. *Journal of Abnormal Child Psychology, 30,* 419–430.

Fernandez, E., & McDowell, J. J. (1995). Response-reinforcement relationships in chronic pain syndrome: Applicability of Herrnstein's law. *Behaviour Research and Therapy, 33,* 855–863.

Fernandez, E., & Sheffield, J. (1996). Relative contributions of life events versus daily hassles to the frequency and intensity of headaches. *Headache, 36,* 595–602.

Ferri, M., Amoto, L., & Davoli, M. (2006). Alcoholics Anonymous and other 12-step programmes for alcohol dependence. The Cochrance Review. Art. No: CDOO5032.DOI: 10.1002/14651858. CD005032.pub2.

Ferris, C. F. (1996). The rage of innocents. *The Sciences, 36,* 22–26.

Feske, U., & Chambless, D. L. (1995). Cognitive behavioral versus exposure only treatment for social phobia: A meta-analysis. *Behavior Therapy, 26,* 695–720.

Festinger, L. (1954). A theory of social comparison processes. *Human Relations, 7,* 117–140.

Festinger, L., & Carlsmith, J. M. (1959). Cognitive consequences of forced compliance. *Journal of Abnormal and Social Psychology, 58,* 202–210.

Festinger, L., Pepitone, A., & Newcomb, T. (1952). Some consequences of deindividuation in a group. *Journal of Abnormal and Social Psychology, 47,* 382–389.

Festinger, L., Reicken, H. W., & Schacter, S. (1956). *When prophecy fails.* Minneapolis, MN: University of Minnesota Press.

Festinger, L., Riecken, H. W., & Schachter, S. (1956). *When prophecy fails.* New York: Harper.

Festinger, L., Schachter, S., & Black, K. (1950). *Social pressures in informal groups.* New York: Harper.

Fetto, J. (2003, March 1,). Drug money—Americans spent estimated $20 billion on OTC remedies in 2002, vs. $10 billion in 1990—Brief article. *American Demographics.* FindArticles.com.24 Sep. 2006. http:// www.findarticles.com /p/aritcles/mi_m4021/is_2_25/ai_97818965.

Feynman, R. P. (with R. Leighton). (1985). *Surely you're joking, Mr. Feynman: Adventures of a curious character.* New York: Norton.

Fiatarone, M. A., Marks, E. C., Ryan, N. D., Meredith, C. N., Lipsitz, L. A., & Evans, W. J. (1990). High-intensity strength training in nonagenarians. *Journal of the American Medical Association, 263,* 3029–3034.

Fidelman, U. (1993), Intelligence and the brain's consumption of energy: What is intelligence? *Personality and Individual Differences, 14,* 283–286.

Field, T. (2003). Stimulation of preterm infants. *Pediatrics in Review, 24,* 4–10.

Fields, R. D. (2007, February/March). Sex and the secret nerve. *Scientific American Mind,* 21–27.

Fillmore, K. M., Kerr, W. C., Stockwell, T., Chikritzhs, T., & Bostrom, A. (2006). Moderate alcohol use and reduced mortality risk: Systematic error in prospective studies. *Addiction Research and Theory, 14,* 101–132.

Finch, J. F., & Cialdini, R. B. (1989). Another indirect tactic of (self-)image management: Boosting. *Personality and Social Psychology Bulletin, 15,* 222–232.

Fine, C. (2006). *A mind of its own: How your brain distorts and deceives.* New York: W. W. Norton.

Finkenauer, C., Luminet, O. L., Gisle, L., El-Ahmadi, A., vanderLinden, M., & Philippot, P. (1998). Flashbulb memories and the underlying mechanisms of their formation: Toward an emotional-integrative model. *Memory & Cognition, 26,* 516–531.

Finlay-Jones, R. A., & Brown, G. W. (1981). Types of stressful life event and the onset of anxiety and depressive disorder. *Psychological Medicine, 11,* 803–815.

Finn, S. E., & Kamphuis, J. H. (1995). What a clinician needs to know about base rates. In J. N. Butcher (Ed.), *Clinical personality assessment: Practical approaches* (pp. 224–235). New York: Oxford University Press.

Finzi, E., & Wasserman, E. (2006). Treatment of depression with botulinum toxin A: A case series. *Dermatologic Surgery, 32,* 645–650.

Fiorito, G., & Scotto, P. (1993). Observational learning in *Octopus vulgaris. Science, 256,* 545–546.

First, M. B., Spitzer, R. L., Gibbon, M., & Williams, J. B. W. (1996). *Structured clinical interview for DSM-IV Axis I disorders—Patient Edition (SCID-I/P, Version 2.0).* New York: Biometrics Research Department, New York State Psychiatric Institute.

Firth, C. D. (1992). *The cognitive neuropsychology of schizophrenia.* Hillsdale, NJ: Erlbaum.

Fischer, K. W. (1978). The question of decalage between object permanence and person permanence. *Developmental Psychology, 14,* 1–10.

Fischer, P., Greitemeyer, T., Pollozek, F., & Frey, D. (2006). The unresponsive bystander: Are bystanders more responsive in dangerous emergencies? *European Journal of Social Psychology, 36,* 267–278.

Fischoff, B. (1975). Hindsight does not equal foresight: The effect of outcome knowledge on judgment under uncertainty. *Journal of Experimental Psychology: Human Perception and Performance, 1,* 288–299.

Fisher, S., & Greenberg, R. (1996). *Freud scientifically appraised.* New York: Wiley.

Fiske, S. T. (2002). What we know about bias and intergroup conflict, problem of the century. *Current Directions in Psychological Science, 11,* 123–128.

Fiske, S. T., & Taylor, S. E. (1991). *Social cognition* (2nd ed.). New York: McGraw Hill.

Fitts, S. N., Gibson, P., Redding, C. A., & Deiter, P. J. (1989). Body dysmorphic disorder: Implications for its validity as a DSM-III-R clinical syndrome. *Psychological Reports, 64,* 655–658.

Fivush, R. (1988). The functions of event memory: Some comments on Nelson and Barsalou. In U. Neisser & E. Winograd (Eds.), *Remembering reconsidered: Ecological and traditional approaches to the study of memory* (pp. 277–282). New York: Cambridge University Press.

Fivush, R., & Hudson, J. A. (Eds.). (1990). *Knowing and remembering in young children.* New York: Cambridge University Press.

Fixsen, D. L., Phillips, E. L., Phillips, E. A., & Wolf, M. M. (1976). The teaching-family model of group home treatment. In W. E. Craighead, A. Kazdin, & M. J. Mahoney (Eds.), *Behavior modification.* Boston: Houghton Mifflin.

Flavell, J., Friedrichs, A., & Hoyt, J. (1970). Developmental changes in memorization processes. *Cognitive Psychology, 1,* 324–340.

Flavell, J. H. (1992). Cognitive development: Past, present and future. *Developmental Psychology, 28,* 998–1005.

Flavell, J. H., Beach, D. H., & Chinsky, J. M. (1966). Spontaneous verbal rehearsal in a memory test as a function of age. *Child Development, 37,* 283–299.

Flynn, C. P. (1982). Meanings and implications of NDEr transformations: Some preliminary findings and implications. *Anabiosis: The Journal of Near-Death, 2,* 3–15.

Flynn, J. R. (1981). The mean IQ of Americans: Massive gains 1932 to 1978. *Psychological Bulletin, 95,* 29–51.

Flynn, J. R. (1987). Massive IQ gains in 14 nations: What IQ tests really measure. *Psychological Bulletin, 101,* 171–191.

Flynn, J. R. (1998). IQ gains over time: Toward finding the causes. In U. Neisser (Ed.), *The rising curve* (pp. 25–66). Washington, DC: American Psychological Association.

Foa, E. B., & Kozak, M. J. (1986). Emotional processing of fear: Exposure to corrective information. *Psychological Bulletin, 99,* 20–35.

Foa, E. B., & Rothbaum, B. O. (1998). *Treating the trauma of rape: Cognitive behavioral therapy for PTSD.* New York: Guilford Press.

Foa, E., & Kozak, M. J. (1986). Emotional processing of fear: Exposure to corrective information. *Psychological Bulletin, 99,* 20–35.

Foer, J. (2007). Remember this. *National Geographic, 212,* 32–57.

Fonagy, P., Steele, H., & Steele, M. (1991). Maternal representations of attachment during pregnancy predict the organization of infant-mother attachment at one year of age. *Child Development, 62,* 891–905.

Food and Drug Administration. (2004a). Labeling change request letter for antidepressant medications. Retrieved April 22, 2006, from http://www.fda.gov/cder/drug/antidepressants/SSRIlabelChange.htm.

Ford, C. S., & Beach, F. (1951). *Patterns of sexual behavior.* New York: Harper and Row.

Ford, D. E., & Kamerow, D. B. (1989). Epidemiologic study of sleep disturbances and psychiatric disorders. An opportunity for prevention. *Journal of the American Medical Association, 263,* 1479–1484.

Ford, M., & Widiger, T. (1989). Sex bias in the diagnosis of histrionic and antisocial personality disorders. *Journal of Consulting and Clinical Psychology, 57,* 301–305.

Fordyce, W. E. (1976). *Behavioral methods for chronic pain and illness.* St. Louis, MO: C. V. Mosby.

Forer, B. R. (1949). The fallacy of personal validation. *Journal of Abnormal and Social Psychology, 44,* 118–123.

Forshaw, M. (2002). *Essential health psychology.* New York: Oxford University Press.

Forsyth, J. P., & Eifert, G. (1996). "Cleaning-up cognition" in triple-response fear assessment through individualized functional behavior analysis. *Journal of Behavior Therapy and Experimental Psychiatry, 27,* 87–98.

Fortenberry, D. J., Temkit, M., Wanzhu, T., Graham, C. A., Katz, B. P., & Orr, D. P. (2005). Daily mood, partner support, sexual interest, and sexual activity among adolescent women. *Health Psychology, 24,* 252–257.

Foster, S., & Gurman, A. (1985). Family therapies. In S. Lynn & J. P. Garske (Eds.), *Contemporary psychotherapies: Models and methods* (pp. 377–418). Columbus, OH: Charles E. Merrill Publishing.

Foulkes, D. (1962). Dream reports from different stages of sleep. *Journal of Abnormal and Social Psychology, 65,* 14–25.

Foulkes, D. (1982). *Children's dreams.* New York: Wiley.

Foulkes, D. (1985). *Dreaming: A cognitive-psychological analysis.* New York: L. Erlbaum Associates.

Foulkes, D. (1999). *Children's dreaming and the development of consciousness.* Cambridge, MA: Harvard University Press.

Foulkes, D., & Rechtschaffen, A. (1964). Presleep determinants of dream content: Effects of two films. *Perceptual and Motor Skills, 19,* 983–1005.

Fowler, C. A., & Dekle, D. J. (1991). Listening with eye and hand: Cross-modal contributions to speech perception. *Journal of Experimental Psychology: Human Perception & Performance, 17,* 816–828.

Fowler, K. A., Lilienfeld, S. O., & Patrick, C. P. (2007, April). *Detecting psychopathic traits from thin slices of behavior.* Poster presented at the Society for the Scientific Study of Psychopathy Conference, St. Petersburg Beach, Florida.

Fowler, K. A., O'Donohue, W. T., & Lilienfeld, S. O. (2007). Personality disorders in perspective. In W. T. O'Donohue, K. A. Fowler, & S. O. Lilienfeld (Eds.), *Personality disorders: Toward the DSM-V* (pp. 1–19). Los Angeles, CA: Sage.

Fowles, D. C. (1980). The three arousal model: Implications of Gray's two-factor learning theory for heart rate, electrodermal activity, and psychopathy. *Psychophysiology, 17,* 87–104.

Fox, M. J. (2002). *Lucky man: A memoir.* New York: Hyperion.

Francis, C. K., Oberman, A., & Saunders, E. (1994). Who's at risk and why. (Cardiovascular disease). Racial and ethnic differences in CVD. *Patient Care, 28,* 28–39.

Frank, J. D. (1961). *Persuasion and healing: A comparative study of psychotherapy* (2nd ed.). Baltimore: Johns Hopkins University Press.

Frank, J. D., & Frank, J. B. (1991). *Persuasion and healing: A comparative study of psychotherapy* (3rd ed.). Baltimore: Johns Hopkins University Press.

Frank, L. K. (1948). *Projective methods.* Springfield, IL: Charles C. Thomas.

Frankl, V. E. (1965). *The doctor and the soul: From psychotherapy to logotherapy.* New York: Alfred Knopf.

Franklin, M. E., & Foa, E. B. (2002). Cognitive behavioral treatment of obsessive-compulsive disorder. In P. Nathan & J. Gorman (Eds.), *A guide to treatments that work* (2nd ed., pp. 367–386). Oxford, England: Oxford University Press.

Franz, V. H., Bulthoff, H. H., & Fahle, M. (2003). Grasp effects of the Ebbinghaus illusion: Obstacle avoidance isn't the explanation. *Experimental Brain Research, 149,* 470–477.

Frayser, S. G. (1989). Sexual and reproductive relationships: Cross-cultural evidence and biosocial implications. *Medical Anthropology, 11,* 385–407.

Frederick, S., & Lowenstein, G. (1999). Hedonic adaptation. In D. Kahneman, E. Diener, & N. Schwarz (Eds.), *Well-being: The foundations of hedonic psychology* (pp. 302–329). New York: Russell Sage Foundation.

Frederickson, R. (1992). *Repressed memories.* New York: Fireside/Parkside.

Fredrickson, B. L. (2001). The role of positive emotions in positive psychology: The broaden-and-build theory of positive emotions. *American Psychologist, 56,* 218–226.

Fredrickson, B. L. (2003). The value of positive emotions. *American Scientist, 91,* 330–335.

Freedman, C. G., & Freedman, N. C. (1969). Behavioral differences between Chinese-American and European-American newborns. *Nature, 224,* 122.

Freedman, D. G. (1964). Smiling in blind infants and the issue of innate versus acquired. *Journal of Child Psychology and Psychiatry, 5,* 171–184.

Freedman, D. G. (1978). Ethnic differences in babies. *Human Nature, 2,* 36–43.

Freedman, D. G., & DeBoer, M. (1979). Biological and cultural differences in early child development: A review. *Annual Review of Anthropology, 8*, 579–600.

Freedman, J. L. (2002). *Media violence and its effects on aggression: Assessing the scientific evidence.* Toronto, Ontario, Canada: University of Toronto Press.

Freedman, J. L., & Fraser, S. C. (1966). Compliance without pressure: The foot-in-the door technique. *Journal of Personality and Social Psychology, 4*, 195–203.

Freiheit, S. R., Vye, D., Swan, R., & Cady, M. (2004). Cognitive-behavioral therapy for anxiety: Is dissemination working? *The Behavior Therapist, 27*, 25–32.

Freire, R., & Cheng, H. W. (2004). Experience-dependent changes in the hippocampus of domestic chicks: A model for spatial memory. *European Journal of Neuroscience, 20*, 1065–1068.

French, C. C. (1992). Population stereotypes and belief in the paranormal: Is there a relationship? *Australian Psychologist, 27*, 57–58.

Freud, A. (1937). *The ego and the mechanisms of defense.* London: Hogarth Press and Institute of Psycho-Analysis.

Freud, A. (1962). *The ego and the mechanisms of defense.* New York: McKay.

Freud, S. (1897). Freud in a letter to Fleiss, 1897. (1953). In E. Jones, *The life and works of Sigmund Freud* (Vol. 1). New York: Basic Books.

Freud, S. (1900). *The interpretation of dreams* (J. Crick, Trans.). London: Oxford University Press.

Freud, S. (1900). *The interpretation of dreams.* New York: Macmillan.

Freud, S. (1901). *The psychopathology of everyday life* (Vol. VI). London: Hogarth.

Freud, S. (1917/1953). "Mourning and Melancholia" in *The Standard Edition of the Complete Psychological Works of Sigmund Freud* (Vol. 14, pp. 239–258). (James Strachey, Trans. and ed.). London: Hogarth Press.

Freud, S. (1923). *The ego and the id. Standard Edition, 19*, 3–66.

Freud, S. (1932). *New introductory lectures in psychoanalysis.* New York: W. W. Norton.

Freud, S. (1933). *New introductory lectures on psychoanalysis.* New York: Carleton House.

Freud, S. (1935). *A general introduction to psychoanalysis.* New York: Washington Square Press.

Freund, K., Watson, R., & Rienzo, D. (1989). Heterosexuality, homosexuality, and erotic age preference. *The Journal of Sex Research, 26*, 107–117.

Frey, M. C., & Detterman, D. K. (2004). Scholastic assessment or g? The relationship between the SAT and general cognitive ability. *Psychological Science, 15*, 373–398.

Frick, P. J., & Marsee, M. A. (2006). Psychopathy and developmental pathways to antisocial behavior in youth. In C. J. Patrick (Ed.), *Handbook of psychopathy* (pp. 353–374). New York: Guilford Press.

Friedlander, M. L. (1984). Psychotherapy talk as social control. *Psychotherapy, 21*, 335–341.

Friedman, J. M. (1996). *The effects of drugs on the fetus and nursing infant: A handbook for healthcare professionals.* Baltimore: Johns Hopkins University Press.

Friedman, M., Powell, L. H., Thoreson, C. E., Ulmer, D., Price, V., Gill, J. J., et al. (1987). Effect of discontinuance of Type A behavioral counseling on Type A behavior and cardiac recurrence rate of post myocardial infarction patients. *American Heart Journal, 114*, 483–490.

Friedman, M., & Rosenman, R. H. (1959). Association of a specific overt behavior pattern with increases in blood cholesterol, blood clotting time, incidence of arcus senilis and clinical coronary artery disease. *Journal of the American Medical Association, 169*, 1286–1296.

Friedman, M., & Rosenman, R. H. (1974). *Type A behavior and your heart.* New York: Alfred A. Knopf.

Friedman, M. A., & Wishman, M. A. (1998). Sociotropy, autonomy, and bulimic symptomatology. *International Journal of Eating Disorders, 23*, 439–442.

Friedman, R. A. (2006). Mental illness and violence: How strong is the link? *New England Journal of Medicine, 355*, 2064–2066.

Friedman, R. S., & Arndt, J. (2005). Reexploring the connection between terror management theory and dissonance theory. *Personality and Social Psychology Bulletin, 31*, 1217–1225.

Friesen, W. V. (1972). *Cultural differences in facial expressions in a social situation: An experimental test of the concept of display rules.* Unpublished doctoral dissertation, University of California, San Francisco.

Frieze, I. H., Peterson, J. E., Johnson, P. B., Ruble, D. N., & Zellman, G. (1978). *Women and sex roles: A social psychological perspective.* New York: W. W. Norton.

Frijda, N. H. (1986). *The emotions.* Cambridge, England: Cambridge University.

Frishberg, N. (1975). Arbitrariness and iconicity: Historical change in American Sign Language. *Language, 51*, 696–719.

Frisina, P. G., Borod, J. C., & Lepore, S. J. (2004). A meta-analysis of the effects of written disclosure on the health outcomes of clinical populations. *The Journal of Nervous and Mental Disease, 192*, 629–634.

Fritsch, G. T., & Hitzig, E. (1870). Über die elektrische Erregbarkeit des Grosshirns. *Archivfur Anatomie, Physiologie und Wissenschaftliche Medizin*, 330–332.

Frohman, E. M., & Martin, J. B. (1987). Genetic markers in Huntington's disease. *Western Journal of Medicine, 147*, 486.

Fromm, E. (1941). *Escape from freedom.* New York: Avon Books.

Fromm, E., & Nash, M. R. (1997). *Hypnosis and psychoanalysis. Mental Health Library Series, No. 5.* Guilford, CT: International Universities Press.

Fromm-Reichmann, F. (1948). Notes on the development of treatment of schizophrenics by psychoanalysis and psychotherapy. *Psychiatry, 11*, 263–273.

Frontera, W. R., Meredith, C. N., O'Reilly, K. P., Knuttgen, H. H., & Evans, W. J. (1988). Strength conditioning in older men: Skeletal muscle hypertrophy and improved function. *Journal of Applied Physiology, 64*, 1038–1044.

Fu, K. M., Johnston, T. A., Shah, A. S., Arnold, L., Smiley, J., Hackett, T. A., et al. (2003). Auditory cortical neurons respond to somatosensory stimulation. *Journal of Neuroscience, 23*, 7510–7515.

Fuchs, A. H., & Milar, K. S. (2004). Psychology as a science. In D. K. Freedheim (Ed.), *Handbook of psychology: History of psychology* (Vol. 1, pp. 1–26). New York: Wiley.

Fuhriman, A., & Burlingame, G. M. (1994). Group psychotherapy: Research and practice. In A. Fuhriman & G. M. Burlingame (Eds.), *Handbook of group psychotherapy: An empirical and clinical synthesis* (pp. 3–40). New York: John Wiley & Sons.

Fukuda, H., & Takahashi, J. (2005). Embryonic stem cells as a cell source for treating Parkinson's disease. *Expert Opinion on Biological Therapy, 5*, 1273–1280.

Fukuda, K., Ogilvie, R., Chilcott, L., Venditteli, A., & Takeuchi, T. (1998). High prevalence of sleep paralysis in Canadian and Japanese college students. *Dreaming, 8*, 59–66.

Fuller, R. K., & Roth, H. P. (1979). Disulfiram for the treatment of alcoholism. An evaluation in 128 men. *Annals of Internal Medicine, 90*, 901–904.

Fulton, J. T. (2000). *Processes in biological vision.* Corona Del Mar, CA. Published August 2000, revised February 2005. Available on the Internet at http://www.4colorvision.com.

Fulton, M. M., & Allen, E. R. (2005). Polypharmacy in the elderly: A literature review. *Journal of the American Academy of Nurse Practitioners, 17*, 123–132.

Funder, D. C. (1991). Global traits: A neo-Allportian approach to personality. *Psychological Science, 2*, 31–39.

Furmark, T., Tillfors, M., Marteinsdottir, I., Fischer, H., Pissiota, A., Langstrom, B., et al. (2002). Common changes in cerebral blood flow in patients with social phobia treated with citalopram or cognitive-behavioral therapy. *Archives of General Psychiatry, 59*, 425–433.

Fuster, J. M. (2000). Executive frontal functions. *Experimental Brain Research, 133*, 66–70.

Gabbard, G. O. (2000). *Psychodynamic psychiatry in clinical practice.* Washington, DC: American Psychiatric Press.

Gage, F. H. (2002). Neurogenesis in the adult brain. *Journal of Neuroscience, 22*, 612–613.

Galambos, S. J., & Hakuta, K. (1988). Subject-specific and task-specific characteristics of metalinguistic awareness in bilingual children. *Applied Psycholinguistics, 9*, 141–162.

Galanter, M. (1980). Psychological induction into the large group: Findings from a modern religious sect. *American Journal of Psychiatry, 137*, 1574–1579.

Gallo, E. (1994). Synchronicity and the archetypes: The imprecision of C. G. Jung's language and concepts. *Skeptical Inquirer, 18*, 376–403.

Gallo, L. C., & Matthews, K. A. (2003). Understanding the association between socioeconomic status and physical health: Do negative emotions play a role? *Psychological Bulletin, 129*, 10–51.

Gallup, G. G., Jr. (1979). Self-awareness in primates. *American Scientist, 67*, 417–421.

Gallup, G. G., Jr., & Suarez, S. D. (1985). Alternatives to the use of animals in psychological research. *American Psychologist, 40*, 1104–1111.

Galton, F. (1869). *Hereditary genius: An inquiry into its laws and consequences.* London: Macmillan.

Galton, F. (1876). The history of twin, as a criterion of the relative powers of nature and nurture. *Journal of the Anthropological Institute of Great Britain and Ireland, 5*, 391–406.

Galton, F. (1880). Statistics of mental imagery. *Mind, 5*, 301–318.

Galvez, R., & Greenough, W. T. (2005). Sequence of abnormal dendritic spine development in primary somatosensory cortex of a mouse model of the fragile X mental retardation syndrome. *American Journal of Medical Genetics A, 135*, 155–160.

Gambrill, E. D. (1992). Self-help books: Pseudoscience in the guise of science? *Skeptical Inquirer 16*(4), 389–399.

Gamer, M., Rill, H.-G., Vossel, G., & Gödert, H. W. (2006). Psychophysiological and vocal measures in the detection of guilty knowledge. *International Journal of Psychophysiology, 60,* 76–87.

Ganaway, G. (1989). Historical truth versus narrative truth: Clarifying the role of exogenous trauma in the etiology of multiple personality disorder and its variants. *Dissociation, 2,* 205–220.

Gangestad, S., & Scheyd, G. J. (2005). The evolution of human physical attractiveness. *Annual Review of Anthropology, 34,* 523–548.

Garb, H. (1998). *Studying the clinician: Judgment, research, and psychological assessment.* Washington, DC: American Psychological Association.

Garb, H. N. (1984). The incremental validity of information used in personality assessment. *Clinical Psychology Review, 4,* 641–655.

Garb, H. N. (1998). Improving psychological assessment. In Garb, H. N. (Ed.), *Studying the clinician: Judgement research and psychological assessment* (pp. 231–248). Washington, DC: American Psychological Association.

Garb, H. N., Wood, J. M., Lilienfeld, S. O., & Nezworski, T. (2005). Roots of the Rorschach controversy. *Clinical Psychology Review, 25,* 97–118.

Garcia, J., & Koelling, R. A. (1966). The relation of cue to consequence in avoidance learning. *Psychonomic Science, 4,* 123–124.

Garcia, S. M., Weaver, K., Moskowitz, G. B., & Darley, J. M. (2002). Crowded minds: The implicit bystander effect. *Journal of Personality and Social Psychology, 83,* 843–853.

Gardner, C. D., Kiazand, A., Alhassan, S., Kim, S., Stafford, R. S., Balise, R., et al. (2007). Comparison of the Atkins, Zone, Ornish, and LEARN diets for change in weight and related risk factors among overweight premenopausal women. *Journal of the American Medical Association, 297,* 969–977.

Gardner, H. (1983). *Frames of mind: The theory of multiple intelligences.* New York: Basic Books.

Gardner, H. (1999). *Intelligence reframed: Multiple intelligences for the 21st century.* New York: Basic Books.

Gardner, M. (1957). *Fads and fallacies in the name of science.* New York: Dover.

Gardner, M. (1958). *Fads and fallacies in the name of science.* New York: Dover.

Gardner, W. L., Gabriel, S., & Diekman, A. B. (2000). Interpersonal processes. In J. T. Cacioppo, L. G. Tassinary, & G. G. Berntson (Eds.), *Handbook of psychophysiology* (2nd ed., pp. 643–664). New York: Cambridge University Press.

Garfield, S. L. (1978). Research on client variables. In S. Garfield & A. Bergin (Eds.), *Handbook of psychotherapy and behavior change.* New York: John Wiley & Sons.

Garfield, S. L., & Kurtz, R. (1976). Clinical psychologists in the 1970s. *American Psychologist, 31,* 1–9.

Garmezy, N., Masten, A. S., & Tellegen, A. (1984). The study of stress and competence in children: A building block for developmental psychopathology. *Child Development, 55,* 97–111.

Garmezy, N., Masten, A. S., & Tellegen, A. (1984). The study of stress and competence in children: A building block for developmental psychopathology. *Child Development, 55,* 97–111.

Garner, D. M. (1997). Psychoeducational principles in the treatment of eating disorders. In D. M. Garner & P. E. Garfinkel (Eds.), *Handbook for treatment of eating disorders* (pp. 145–177). New York: Guilford Press.

Garner, D. M., & Fairburn, C. G. (1988). Relationship between anorexia nervosa and bulimia nervosa: Diagnostic implications. In P. E. Garfinkel & D.M. Garner, (Eds.), *Diagnostic issues in anorexia nervosa and bulimia nervosa* (pp. 56–79). New York: Brunner/Mazel.

Garner, D. M., Garfinkel, P. E., Schwartz, D., & Thompson, M. (1980). Cultural expectations of thinness in women. *Psychological Reports, 47,* 483–491.

Garske, J. P., & Anderson, T. (2003). Toward a science of psychotherapy research. In S. Lilienfeld, S. J. Lynn, & J. Lohr (Eds.), *Science and pseudoscience in clinical psychology* (pp. 145–175). New York: Guilford.

Garske, J. P., & Lynn, S. J. (1985). *Toward a general scheme for psychotherapy: Effectiveness, common factors, and integration* (pp. 497–516). Columbus, OH: Charles E. Merrill.

Gasperini, M., Scherillo, P., Manfredonia, M. G., Franchini, L., & Smeraldi, E. (1993). A study of relapse in subjects with mood disorder on lithium treatment. *European Neuropsychopharmacology, 3,* 103–110.

Gatchel, R. J. (2001). Biofeedback and self-regulation of physiological activity: A major adjunctive treatment modality in health psychology. In A. Baum, T. A. Revenson, & J. E. Singer (Eds.), *Handbook of health psychology* (pp. 95–103). Mahwah, NJ: Lawrence Erlbaum.

Gatchel, R. J., & Baum, A. (1983). *An introduction to health psychology.* Reading, MA: Addison-Wesley.

Gatchel, R. J., & Oortd, M. S. (2003). *Clinical psychology and primary health care.* Washington, DC: American Psychological Association.

Gathercole, V. C. M. (2002a). Command of the mass/count distinction in bilingual and monolingual children: An English morphosyntactic distinction. In D. K. Oller & R. E. Eilers (Eds.), *Language and literacy in bilingual children* (pp. 175–206). Clevedon, England: Multilingual Matters.

Gathercole, V. C. M. (2002b). Grammatical gender in bilingual and monolingual children: A Spanish morphosyntactic distinction. In D. K. Oller & R. E. Eilers (Eds.), *Language and literacy in bilingual children* (pp. 207–219), Clevedon, England: Multilingual Matters.

Gaudiano, B. A., & Epstein-Lubow, G. (in press). Controversies about antidepressants and the promotion of evidence-based treatment alternatives for depression. *The Scientific Review of Mental Health Practices.*

Gawronski, B., LeBel, E. P., & Peters, K. R. (2007). What do implicit measures tell us? Scrutinizing the validity of three common assumptions. *Perspectives on Psychological Science, 2,* 181–193.

Gazzaniga, M. S. (1973). *Fundamentals of psychology: An introduction.* Oxford, England: Academic Press.

Gazzaniga, M. S. (2000). Cerebral specialization and interhemispheric communication: Does the corpus callosum enable the human condition? *Brain, 123,* 1293–1326.

Gazzaniga, M. S. (2002). The split brain revisited. *Scientific American, 279,* 27–31.

Gazzaniga, M. S., Ivry, R., & Mangun, G. R. (2002). *Fundamentals of cognitive neuroscience* (2nd ed.). New York: W. W. Norton.

Geary, D. C. (1996). Sexual selection and sex differences in mathematical abilities. *Behavioral and Brain Sciences, 19,* 229–284.

Geen, R. G. (2001). *Human aggression* (2nd ed.). New York: Taylor & Francis.

Geier, A. B., Rozin, P., & Doros, G. (2006). Unit bias: A new heuristic that helps explain the effect of portion size on food intake. *Psychological Science, 17,* 521–525.

Geiser, S., & Studley, R. (2002). UC and the SAT: Predictive validity and differential impact of the SAT I and SAT II at the University of California. *Educational Assessment, 8,* 1–26.

Gellatly, A. R. (1987). Acquisition of a concept of logical necessity. *Human Development, 30,* 32–47.

Gelman, R., & Gallistel, C. (1978). *The child's understanding of number.* Cambridge, MA: Harvard University Press.

Gelman, S. A. (2003). *The essential child: Origins of essentialism in everyday thought.* New York: Oxford University Press.

Genesee, F. (1985). Second language learning through immersion: A review of U.S. programs. *Review of Educational Research, 55,* 541–561.

Gentile, D. A., & Anderson, C. A. (2003). Violent video games: The newest media violence hazard. In D. A. Gentile (Ed.), *Media violence and children* (pp. 131–152). Westport, CT: Praeger Publishing.

George, M. S., Sackheim, H., Rush, A. J., Marangell, L. B., Nahas, Z., Husain, M. M., et al. (2000). Vagus nerve stimulation: A new tool for treatment-resistant depression. *Biological Psychiatry, 47,* 287–295.

Georgiadis, J. R., Kortekaas, R., Kuipers, R., Nieuwenburg, A., Pruim, J., Reinders, A. A., et al. (2006). Regional cerebral blood flow changes associated with clitorally induced orgasm in healthy women. *European Journal of Neuroscience, 24,* 3305–3316.

Gerard S., Smith B. H., & Simpson J. A. (2003). A randomized controlled trial of spiritual healing in restricted neck movement. *Journal of Alternative & Complementary Medicine, 9,* 467–477.

Gergen, K. J. (1973). Social psychology as history. *Journal of Personality and Social Psychology, 26,* 309–320.

German, T. P., & Barrett, H. C. (2005). Functional fixedness in a technologically sparse culture. *Psychological Science, 16,* 1–5.

Gernbacher, M. A., Dawson, M., & Goldsmith, H. H. (2005). Three reasons not to believe in an autism epidemic. *Current Directions in Psychological Science, 14,* 55–58.

Geschwind, N. (1983). Interictal behavior changes in epilepsy. *Epilepsia, 24*(Suppl. 1), S23–S30.

Gewirtz, J. C., & Davis, M. (2000). Using Pavlovian "higher-order" conditioning paradigms to investigate the neural substrates of emotional learning and memory. *Learning and Memory, 7,* 257–266.

Gibb, B. E., & Alloy, L. B. (2006). A prospective test of the hopelessness theory of depression in children. *Journal of Clinical Child and Adolescent Psychology, 35,* 264–274.

Gibb, B. E., & Coles, M. E. (2005). Cognitive vulnerability-stress models of psychopathology: A developmental perspective. In B. L. Hankin & J. R. Z. Abela (Eds.), *Development of psychopathology: A vulnerability-stress perspective* (pp. 104–135). Thousand Oaks, CA: Sage.

Gibb, C., & Randall, P. E. (1988). Metalinguistic abilities and learning to read. *Educational Research, 30,* 135–141.

Gibbs, J. C. (2006). Should Kohlberg's cognitive developmental approach to morality be replaced with a more pragmatic approach? Comment on Krebs and Denton (2005). *Psychological Review, 113,* 666–671.

Gibson, E. J., & Walk, R. D. (1960). The "visual cliff." *Scientific American, 202,* 64–71.

Gick, M. L., & Holyoak, K. J. (1983). Schema induction and analogical transfer. *Cognitive Psychology, 14,* 1–38.

Gigerenzer, G. (2001). The adaptive toolbox. In G. Gigerenzer & R. Selten (Eds.), *Bounded rationality: The adaptive toolbox* (pp. 37–50). Cambridge, MA: MIT Press.

Gigerenzer, G. (2004). Dread risk, September 11, and fatal traffic accidents. *Psychological Science, 15,* 286–287.

Gigerenzer, G. (2007). *Gut feelings: The intelligence of the unconscious.* New York: Viking Press.

Gigerenzer, G., & Goldstein, D. G. (1996). Reasoning the fast and frugal way: Models of bounded rationality. *Psychological Review, 103,* 650–669.

Gignac, G. E., Stough, C., & Loukomitis, S. (2004). Openness, intelligence, and self-report intelligence, *Intelligence, 32,* 133–143.

Gilbert, D. (2006). *Stumbling on happiness.* New York: Knopf.

Gilbert, D. T., Pinel, E. C., Wilson, T. D., Blumberg, S. J., & Wheatley, T. (1998). Immune neglect: A source of durability bias in affective forecasting. *Journal of Personality and Social Psychology, 75,* 617–638.

Gilbertson, T. A., Fontenot D. T., Liu, L., Zhang, H., & Monroe, W. T. (1997). Fatty acid modulation of K+ channels in taste receptor cells: Gustatory cues for dietary fat. *American Journal of Physiology, 272*(4 Pt. 1), C1203–C1210.

Giles, J. (2002). Electroconvulsive therapy and the fear of deviance. *Journal for the Theory of Social Behaviour, 32,* 61–87.

Giles, J. (2007). Degrees in homeopathy slated as unscientific. *Nature, 446,* 352–352.

Gill, M. (1954). Psychoanalysis and exploratory psychotherapy. *Journal of the American Psychoanalytic Association, 2,* 771–797.

Gillham, N. W. (2001). *A life of Sir Francis Galton: From African exploration to the birth of eugenics.* New York: Oxford University Press.

Gilligan, C. (1982). *In a different voice: Psychological theory and women's development.* Cambridge, MA: Harvard University Press.

Gilovich, T. (1991). *How we know what isn't so: The fallibility of human reason in everyday life.* New York: Free Press.

Gilovich, T., Griffin, D., & Kahneman, D. (Eds.). (2002). *Heuristics and biases: The psychology of intuitive judgment.* New York: Cambridge University Press.

Gilovich, T., Vallone, R., & Tversky, A. (1985). The hot hand in basketball: On the misperception of random sequences. *Cognitive Psychology, 17,* 295–314.

Gladwell, M. (2005). *Blink: The power of thinking without thinking.* Boston: Little, Brown, & Company.

Gladwell, M. (2007, November 12). Dangerous minds: Criminal profiling made easy. *New Yorker.* Retrieved November 9, 2007, from http://www.newyorker.com/reporting/2007/11/12/071112fa_fact_gladwell.

Gizewski, E. R., Gasser, T., de Greiff, A., Boehm, A., & Forsting, M. (2003). Cross-modal plasticity for sensory and motor activation patterns in blind subjects. *Neuroimage, 19,* 968–975.

Gladwell, M. (2005). *Blink: The power of thinking without thinking.* New York: Little, Brown.

Glanzer, M., & Cunitz, A. R. (1966). Two storage mechanisms in free recall. *Journal of Verbal Learning & Verbal Behavior, 5,* 351–360.

Glazer, W. M., Morgenstern, H., & Douchette, J. (1994). Race and tardive dyskinesia among outpatients at a CMHC. *Hospital and Community Psychiatry, 45,* 38–42.

Gleaves, D. H. (1996). The sociocognitive model of dissociative identity disorder: A reexamination of the evidence. *Psychological Bulletin, 120,* 42–59.

Gleaves, D. H., May, M. C., & Cardena, E. (2001). An examination of the diagnostic validity of dissociative identity disorder. *Clinical Psychology Review, 21,* 577–608.

Gleitman, H. (1971). Forgetting of long term memories in animals. In W. K. Honig & P. H. R. James (Eds.), *Animal memory* (pp. 1–44). London: Academic Press.

Glickman, S. E., Frank, L. G., Davidson, J. M., Smith, E. R., & Siiteri, P. K. (1987). Androstenedione may organize or activate sex-reversed traits in female spotted hyenas. *Proceedings of the National Academy of Sciences, 84,* 3444–3447.

Glynn, S., & Mueser, K. T. (1992). Social learning. In R. P. Lieberman (Ed.), *Handbook of psychiatric rehabilitation* (pp. 127–152). New York: Macmillan.

Gobel, S. M., & Rushworth, M. F. (2004). Cognitive neuroscience: Acting on numbers. *Current Biology, 14,* R517–519.

Godden, D. R., & Baddeley, A. D. (1975). Context dependency in two natural environments: On land and underwater. *British Journal of Psychology, 91,* 99–104.

Goertzel, T. (1994). Belief in conspiracy theories. *Political Psychology, 15,* 733–744.

Goethals, G. R., & Reckman, R. F. (1973). The perception of consistency in attitudes. *Journal of Experimental Social Psychology, 9,* 491–501.

Goffman, E. (1959) The presentation of self in everyday life. London: Penguin.

Gold, J. M., Murray, R. F., Bennett, P. J., & Sekuler, A. B. (2000). Deriving behavioural receptive fields for visually completed contours. *Current Biology, 10,* 663–666.

Gold, P. E., Cahill, L., & Wenk, G. L. (2002). Gingko biloba: A cognitive enhancer? *Psychological Science in the Public Interest, 3,* 2–11.

Gold, S. N., & Heffner, C. L. (1998). Sexual addiction: Many conceptions, minimal data. *Clinical Psychology Review, 18,* 367–381.

Goldapple, K., Segal, Z., Garson, C., Lau, M., Bieling, P., Kennedy, S., & Mayberg, H. (2004). Modulation of cortical-limbic pathways in major depression: Treatment-specific effects of cognitive behavior therapy. *Archives of General Psychiatry, 61,* 34-41.

Goldberg, L. (1986). Some informal explorations and ruminations about graphology. In B. Nevo (Ed.), *Scientific aspects of graphology* (pp. 281–293). Springfield, IL: Charles C. Thomas.

Goldberg, L. R. (1969). The search for configural relationships in personality assessment: The diagnosis of psychosis vs. neurosis from the MMPI. *Multivariate Behavioral Research, 4,* 523–536.

Goldberg, L. R. (1993). The structure of phenotypic personality traits. *American Psychologist, 48,* 26–34.

Golden, N., & Sacker, I. M. (1984). An overview of the etiology, diagnosis, and management of anorexia nervosa. *Clinical Pediatrics, 23,* 209–214.

Goldfield, B. A., & Reznick, J. S. (1990). Early lexical acquisition: Rate, content, and the vocabulary spurt. *Journal of Child Language, 23,* 241–246.

Goldfried, M. R., & Davison, G. C. (1976). *Clinical behavior therapy.* New York: Holt, Rinehart, & Winston.

Goldfried, M. R., Raue, P. J., & Castonguay, L. G. (1998). The therapeutic focus in significant sessions of master therapists: A comparison of cognitive-behavioral and psychodynamic-interpersonal interventions. *Journal of Consulting and Clinical Psychology, 66,* 803–810.

Goldin, C., & Rouse, C. (2000). Orchestrating impartiality. *American Economic Review, 90,* 715–741.

Goldin-Meadow, S. (2000). Beyond words: The importance of gesture to researchers and learners. *Child Development, 71,* 231–239.

Goldin-Meadow, S., & Mylander, C. (1998). Spontaneous sign systems created by deaf children in two cultures. *Nature, 391,* 279–281.

Goldin-Meadow, S., & Sandhofer, C. M. (1999). Gestures convey substantive information about a child's thoughts to ordinary listeners. *Developmental Science, 2,* 67–74.

Goldman, M. S., Darkes, J., & Del Boca, F. K. (1999). Expectancy mediation of biopsychosocial risk for alcohol use and alcoholism. In I. Kirsch (Ed.), *How expectancies shape experience* (pp. 232–262). Washington, DC: American Psychological Association.

Goldman-Rakic, P. S. (1996). Regional and cellular fractionation of working memory. *Proceedings of the National Academy of Sciences U.S.A., 93,* 13473–13480.

Goldreich, D., & Kanics, I. M. (2003). Tactile acuity is enhanced in blindness. *Journal of Neuroscience, 23,* 3439–3445.

Goldstein, A. J., & Chambless, D. L. (1978). A reanalysis of agoraphobia. *Behaviour Research and Therapy, 9,* 47–59.

Goldstein, D. G., & Gigerenzer, G. (1999). The recognition heuristic: How ignorance makes us smart. In G. Gigerenzer, P. M. Todd, & the ABC Research Group (Eds.), *Simple heuristics that make us smart* (pp. 37–58). London: Oxford University Press.

Goldston, D. B., Daniel, S. S., Reboussin, B., Reboussin, D., Frazier, P. H., & Harris, A. (2001). Cognitive risk factors and suicide attempts among formerly hospitalized adolescents: A prospective naturalistic study. *Journal of the American Academy of Child and Adolescent Psychiatry, 40,* 155–162.

Goleman, D. (1995). *Emotional Intelligence.* New York: Bantam Books.

Golin, S., Terrell, T. & Johnson, B. (1977). Depression and the illusion of control. *Journal of Abnormal Psychology, 86,* 440–442.

Golombok, S. (2000). *Parenting: What really counts?* London: Routledge.

Gonzaga, G. C., Turner, R. A., Keltner, D., Campos, B., & Altemus, M. (2006). Romantic love and sexual desire in close relationships, *Emotion, 6,* 163–179.

Good, W., Jan, J. E., & Luis, D. (1994). Cortical visual Impairment in children. *Survey of Ophthalmology, 38,* 351–364.

Goodall, J. (1990). *Through a window.* Boston: Houghton Mifflin.

Goodall, J., & van Lawick, H. (1971). *In the shadow of man.* Boston: Houghton-Mifflin.

Goode, E. (2000, January 18). Among the inept, researchers discover, ignorance is bliss. *New York Times.* Retrieved August 1, 2006, from http://query.nytimes.com/gst/fullpage.html?res=9E03EFD61E3AF93BA25752C0A9669C8B63.

Goodman, J. A., Krahn, L. E., Smith, G. G., Rummans, T. A., & Pileggi, T. S. (1999). Patient satisfaction with electroconvulsive therapy. *Mayo Clinic Proceedings, 74,* 967–971.

Goodwin D. W., Powell, B., Brenner, D., Hoine, H., & Sterne J. (1969). Alcohol and recall: State dependent effects in man. *Science, 163,* 1358–1360.

Goodwin, D. K. (2005). *Team of rivals: The political genius of Abraham Lincoln.* New York: Simon & Schuster.

Goodwin, D. W. (1995). Alcohol amnesia. *Addiction, 90,* 315–317.

Goodwin F. K., & Jamison K. R. (1990), *Manic-depressive illness.* New York: Oxford University Press.

Gorassini, D., & Olson, J. (1995). Does self-perception change explain the foot-in-the door effect? *Journal of Personality and Social Psychology, 69,* 91–105.

Gorassini, D. R., & Spanos, N. P. (1986). A social-cognitive skills approach to the successful modification of hypnotic susceptibility. *Journal of Personality and Social Psychology, 50,* 1004–1012.

Gordon, H. (2002). The suicide bomber: Is it a psychiatric phenomenon? *Psychiatric Bulletin, 26,* 285–287.

Gordon, P. (2004). Numerical cognition without words: Evidence from amazonia. *Science, 306,* 496–499.

Gorenstein, E. E. (1984). Debating mental illness: Implications for science, medicine, and social policy. *American Psychologist, 39,* 50–56.

Gorn, G. J. (1982). The effects of music in advertising on choice behavior: A classical conditioning approach. *Journal of Marketing, 46,* 94–101.

Gorsuch, R. L. (1988). Psychology of religion. *Annual Review of Psychology, 39,* 201–221.

Gortmaker, S. L., Must, A., Perrin, J. M., Sobol, A. M., & Dietz, W. H. (1993). Social and economic consequences of overweight in adolescence and young adulthood. *New England Journal of Medicine, 329,* 1009–1012.

Gortner, E. T., Gollan, J. K., Dobson, K. S., & Jacobson, N. S. (1998). Cognitive-behavioral treatment for depression: Relapse prevention. *Journal of Consulting and Clinical Psychology, 66,* 377–384.

Gosling, S. D. (2001). From mice to men: What can we learn about personality from animal research? *Psychological Bulletin, 127,* 45–86.

Gosling, S. D., Ko, S. J., Mannarelli, T., & Morris, M. E. (2002). A room with a cue. Personality judgments based on offices and bedrooms. *Journal of Personality & Social Psychology, 82,* 379–398.

Gotlib, I., & Robinson, L. A. (1982). Responses to depressed individuals: Discrepancies between self-report and observer-rated behavior. *Journal of Abnormal Psychology, 91,* 231–240.

Gotlib, I. H., & Hammen, C. L. (1992). *Psychological aspects of depression: Toward a cognitive-interpersonal integration.* New York: Wiley.

Gottdiener, J. S., Green, H. A., Henry, W. L., Borer, J. S., & Ebert, M. H. (1978). Effects of self-induced starvation on cardiac size and function in anorexia nervosa. *Circulation, 58,* 425–433.

Gottesman, I. I. (1991). *Schizophrenia genesis: The origins of madness.* New York: W. H. Freeman.

Gottesman, I. I. & Shields, J. (1972). *Schizophrenia and genetics: A twin study vantage point.* New York: Academic Press.

Gottesmann, C. (2002). The neurochemistry of waking and sleeping mental activity: The disinhibition-dopamine hypothesis. *Psychiatry and Clinical Neuroscience, 56,* 345–354.

Gottfredson, L. S. (1997). Why g matters: The complexity of everyday life. *Intelligence, 24,* 79–132.

Gottfredson, L. S. (2003). On Sternberg's "Reply to Gottfredson." *Intelligence, 31,* 415–424.

Gottfredson, L. S. (2004). Intelligence: Is it the epidemiologists' elusive "fundamental cause" of social class inequalities in health? *Journal of Personality and Social Psychology, 86,* 174–199.

Gottheil, E., & Weinstein, S. O. (1983). Cocaine: An emerging problem. In S. Akhtar (Ed.), *New psychiatric syndromes; DSM III and beyond.* New York: Jason Aronson.

Gottman, J. M., & Levenson, R. W. (1999). What predicts change in marital interaction over time? A study of alternative models. *Family Processes, 38,* 143–158.

Gough, H. G. (1957). *California Psychological Inventory manual.* Palo Alto, CA: Consulting Psychologists Press.

Gould, S.J. (1997). Nonoverlapping magisteria. *Natural History, 106,* 16-22.

Gould, E., & Gross, C. G. (2002). Neurogenesis in adult mammals: Some progress and problems. *Journal of Neuroscience, 22,* 619–623.

Gould, R. (1978). *Transformations: Growth and change in adult life.* New York: Simon and Schuster.

Gould, R. A., & Clum, G. A. (1993). A meta-analysis of self-help treatment approaches. *Clinical Psychology Review, 13,* 169–186.

Gould, S. J. (1980). *The panda's thumb.* New York: W. W. Norton.

Gould, S. J. (1981) *The mismeasure of man.* New York: W. W. Norton.

Gould, S. J. (1997). Nonoverlapping magisteria. *Natural History, 106,* 16–22.

Gould, S. J., & Vrba, E. S. (1982). Exaptation—A missing term in the science of form. *Paleobiology, 8,* 4–15.

Goulding, P. (1992). *Classical music: The 50 greatest composers and their 1000 greatest works.* New York: Ballantine.

Gouldner, A. W. (1960). The norm of reciprocity: A preliminary statement. *American Sociological Review, 25,* 161–178.

Gove, W. R., Hughes, M., & Style, C. B. (1983). Does marriage have positive effects on the psychological well-being of the individual? *Journal of Health and Social Behavior, 24,* 122–131.

Graber, J. A., Petersen, A. C., & Brooks-Gunn, J. (1996). Pubertal processes: Methods, measures, and models. In J. A. Graber, J. Brooks-Gunn, & A. C. Petersen (Eds.), *Transitions through adolescence: Interpersonal domains and context* (pp. 23–53). Hillsdale, NJ: Erlbaum.

Grace, A. A. (1992). The depolarization block hypothesis of neuroleptic action: Implications for the etiology and treatment of schizophrenia. *Journal of Neural Transmission, 36*(Suppl.), 91–131.

Graf, P. (1990). Life-span changes in implicit and explicit memory. *Bulletin of the Psychonomic Society, 28,* 353–358.

Graf, R. G. (1973). Speed reading: Remember the tortoise. *Psychology Today, 7,* 112–113.

Graham, J. R. (2006). *MMPI-2: Assessing personality and psychopathology* (3rd ed.). New York: Oxford University Press.

Graham, S. J., Scaife, J. C., Langley, R. W., Bradshaw, C. M., Szabadi, E., Xi, L., et al. (2005). Effects of lorazepam on fear-potentiated startle responses in man. *Journal of Psychopharmacology, 19,* 249–258.

Granello, D. H., & Beamish, P. M. (1998). Reconceptualizing codependency in women: A sense of connectedness, not pathology. *Journal of Mental Health Counseling, 20,* 344–358.

Granqvist, P., Fredrikson, M., Unge, P., Hagenfeldt, A., Valind, S., Larhammar, D., et al. (2005). Sensed presence and mystical experiences are predicted by suggestibility, not by the application of transcranial weak complex magnetic fields. *Neuroscience Letters, 379,* 1–6.

Grawe, K., Donati, R., & Bernauer, F. (1998). *Psychotherapy in transition.* Seattle, WA: Hogrefe & Huber.

Gray, C. R., & Gummerman, K. (1975). The enigmatic eidetic image: A critical examination of methods, data, and theories. *Psychological Bulletin, 82,* 383–407.

Gray, J. (1981). A critique of Eysenck's theory of personality. In H. J. Eysenck (Ed.), *A model for personality* (pp. 246–276). New York: Springer.

Gray, J. A. (1982). *The neuropsychology of anxiety: An enquiry into the functions of the septo-hippocampal system.* Oxford, England: Oxford University Press.

Gray, J. A., & McNaughton, N. (2000). *The neuropsychology of anxiety: An inquiry into the functions of the septo-hippocampal system.* Oxford, England: Oxford University Press.

Gray, W. D. (1991). *Thinking critically about New Age ideas.* Belmont, CA: Wadsworth.

Graybiel, A. M., Aosaki, T., Flaherty, A. W., & Kimura, M. (1994). The basal ganglia and adaptive motor control. *Science, 265,* 1826–1831.

Greeley, A. M. (1975). *The sociology of the paranormal: A reconnaissance* (Sage Research Papers in the Social Sciences, Vol. 3, Series No. 90-023). Beverly Hills, CA: Sage.

Greeley, A. M. (1987). Mysticism goes mainstream. *American Health, 6,* 47–49.

Greeley, J., & Oei, T. (1999). Alcohol and tension reduction: 1987–1997. In K. E Leonard & H. T. Blane (Eds.), *Psychological theories of drinking and alcoholism* (2nd ed., pp.14–53). New York: Guilford.

Green, C. D. (1992). Is unified positivism the answer to psychology's disunity? *American Psychologist, 48,* 1057–1058.

Green, D. M., & Swets, J. A. (1966). *Signal detection theory and psychophysics.* New York: Wiley.

Green, J. P. (2000). Treating women who smoke: The benefits of using hypnosis. In L. Hornyak & J. P. Green (Eds.), *Healing from within: The use of hypnosis in women's health care* (pp. 91–118). Washington, DC: American Psychological Association.

Green, J. P., & Lynn, S. J. (2005). Hypnosis vs. relaxation: Accuracy and confidence in dating international news events. *Applied Cognitive Psychology, 19,* 679–691.

Green, J. P., Page, R. A., Rasekhy, B. A., Johnson, L. K., & Bernhardt, S. E. (2006). Cultural views and attitudes about hypnosis: A survey of college students across four countries. *International Journal of Clinical and Experimental Hypnosis, 54,* 263–280.

Green, R. (1987). *The "sissy boy syndrome" and the development of homosexuality.* New Haven, CT: Yale University Press.

Greenberg, D. J., Hillman, D., & Grice, D. (1973). Infant and stranger variables related to stranger anxiety in the first year of life. *Development Psychology, 9,* 207–212.

Greenberg, J., & Jonas, E. (2003). Psychological motives and political orientation: The left, the right, and the rigid: Comment on Jost et al. (2003). *Psychological Bulletin, 129,* 376–382.

Greenberg, L. (1993). Emotional change processes in psychotherapy. In M. Lewis & J. Haviland (Eds.), *Handbook of Emotion* (pp. 499–510). New York: Guilford Press.

Greenberg, L. R. (2002). *Emotion-focused therapy: Coaching clients to work through their feelings.* Washington, DC: American Psychological Association.

Greenberg, L. S., Elliot, R., & Lietaer, G. (1994). Research on humanistic and experiential psychotherapies. In A. E. Bergin & L. S. Garfield (Eds.), *Handbook of psychotherapy and behavior change* (4th ed., pp. 509–539). New York: Wiley.

Greenberg, L. S., Rice, L. N., & Elliott, R. (1993). *Facilitating emotional change: The moment-by-moment process.* New York: Guilford Press.

Greenberg, L. S., & Watson, J. C. (1998). Experiential therapy of depression: Differential effects of client-centered relationship conditions and process experiential interventions. *Psychotherapy Research, 8,* 210–224.

Greene, R.L. (2000). *The MMPI-2: An interpretive manual* (2nd ed.). Boston: Allyn & Bacon.

Greenfield, P. (1998). The cultural evolution of IQ. In U. Neisser (Ed.), *The rising curve: Long-term gains in IQ and related measures* (pp. 81–122). Washington, DC: American Psychological Association.

Greenfield, P. M., & Savage-Rumbaugh, E. S. (1991). Imitation, grammatical development, and the invention of proto- grammar by an ape. In N. A. Krasnegor, D. M. Rumbaugh, R. L. Schiefelbusch, & M. Studdert-Kennedy (Eds.), *Biological and behavioral determinants of language development* (pp. 235–258). Hillsdale, NJ: Lawrence Erlbaum.

Greenglass, E. (2002). Proactive coping. In E. Frydenberg (Ed.), *Beyond coping: Meeting goals, vision, and challenges* (pp. 37–62). London: Oxford University Press.

Greenough, W. T. (1997). We can't just focus on the first three years. *American Psychological Association Monitor on Psychology, 28,* 19.

Greenspan, S., Loughlin, G., & Black, R. S. (2001). Credulity and gullibility in people with developmental disabilities: A framework for future research. In L. M. Glidden (Ed.), *International review of research in mental retardation, Vol. 24* (pp. 101–135). New York: Academic Press.

Greenspan, S., & Switzky, H. N. (Eds.). (2003). *What is mental retardation? Ideas for the new century.* Washington, DC: American Association on Mental Retardation.

Greenwald, A. G., & Gillmore, G. M. (1997). Grading leniency is a removable contaminant of student ratings. *American Psychologist, 52,* 1209–1217.

Greenwald, A. G., McGhee, D. E., & Schwartz, J. L. K. (1998). Measuring individual differences in implicit cognition: The implicit association test. *Journal of Personality and Social Psychology, 74,* 1464–1480.

Greenwald, A. G., & Nosek, B. A. (2001). Health of the Implicit Association Test at age 3. *Zeitschrift für Experimentelle Psychologie, 48,* 85–93.

Greenwald, A. G., Pratkanis, A. R., Leippe, M. R., & Baumgardner, M. H. (1986). Under what conditions does theory obstruct research progress? *Psychological Review, 93,* 216–229.

Greenwald, A. G., Spangenberg, E. R., Pratkanis, A. R., & Eskenazi, J. (1991). Double-blind tests of subliminal self-help audio tapes. *Psychological Science, 2,* 119–122.

Gregory, R. J., Canning S. S., Lee, T. W., & Wise, J. (2004). Cognitive bibliotherapy for depression: A meta-analysis. *Professional Psychology: Research and Practice, 35,* 275–280.

Gresham, L. G., & Shimp, T. A. (1985). Attitude toward the advertisement and bran attitudes: A classical conditioning perspective. *Journal of Advertising, 14,* 10–17, 49.

Greyson, B. (2000). Near-death experiences. In E. Cardena, S. J. Lynn, & S. Krippner (Eds.), *Varieties of anomalous experiences* (pp. 315–352). Washington, DC: American Psychological Association.

Griffiths, P. E. (1997). *What emotions really are: The problem of psychological categories.* Chicago: Chicago University Press.

Griffiths, R. R., Richards, W. A., McCann, U. & Jesse, R. (2006). Psilocybin can occasion mystical-type experiences having substantial and sustained personal meaning and spiritual significance. *Psychopharmacology, 187,* 268–283.

Grill, H. J., & Kaplan, J. M. (2002). The neuroanatomical axis for control of energy balance. *Frontiers in Neuroendocrinology, 21,* 2–40.

Grill, H. J., Schwartz, M. W., Kaplan, J. M., Foxhall, J. S., Breininger, J., & Baskin, D. G. (2002). Evidence that the caudal brainstem is a target for the inhibitory effect of leptin on food intake. *Endocrinology, 143,* 239–246.

Grinker, R. R., & Werble, B. (1977). *The borderline patient.* New York: Aronson.

Grisso, T. (2003). *Evaluating competencies: Forensic assessments and instruments* (2nd ed). New York: Kluwer.

Grissom, R. J. (1996). The magical number, 7±2 meta-meta-analysis of the probability of superior outcome in comparisons involving therapy, placebo, and control. *Journal of Consulting and Clinical Psychology, 64,* 973–982.

Gritz, E. R. (1980). Smoking behavior and tobacco abuse. In N. K. Mello (Ed.), *Advances in substance abuse, Vol. 1* (pp. 91–158). Greenwich, CT: JAI Press.

Grob, G. N. (1997). Deinstitutionalization: The illusion of policy. *Journal of Policy History, 9*(1), 48–73.

Gross, J. J., & Muñoz, R. F. (1995). Emotional regulation and mental health. *Clinical Psychology: Science & Practice, 2,* 151–164.

Gross, P. R. (2004). Race: No such thing. *New Criterion, 22.* Retrieved October 20, 2007, from www.newcriterion.com /archive/22/april04/race.htm.

Grossman, H. J. (Ed.). (1983). *Classification in mental retardation* (Rev. ed.). Washington, DC: American Association on Mental Deficiency.

Grove, W. M., & Tellegen, A. (1991). Problems in the classification of personality disorders. *Journal of Personality Disorders, 5,* 31–41.

Grunbaum, A. (1984). *The foundations of psychoanalysis: A philosophical critique.* Berkeley, CA: University of California Press.

Gruneber, M. M., and Sykes, R. N. (1991). Individual differences and attitudes to the keyword method of foreign language learning. *Language Learning Journal, 4,* 60–62.

Gruneberg, M. M., and Pascoe, K. (1996). The effectiveness of the keyword method for receptive and productive foreign vocabulary learning in the elderly. *Contemporary Educational Psychology, 21,* 102–109.

Gu, Q. (2002). Neuromodulatory transmitter systems in the cortex and their role in cortical plasticity. *Neuroscience, 111,* 815–835.

Guan, J., & Wade, M. G. (2000). The effect of aging on adaptive eye-hand coordination. *Journal of Gerontology: Psychological Sciences, 55B,* 151–162.

Gueguen, N., & Pascual, A. (2005). Foot-in-the-door and door-in-the-face: A comparative meta-analytic study. *Psychological Reports, 96,* 122–128.

Guéguen N., Pascual A., & Dagot L. (2002). The low-ball technique: An application in a field setting, *Psychological Reports, 91,* 81–84.

Guenther, R. K. (1998). *Human cognition.* Upper Saddle River, NJ: Prentice Hall.

Guilford, J. P. (1954). *Psychometric methods* (2nd ed.). New York: McGraw-Hill.

Guilford, J. P. (1967). *The nature of human intelligence.* New York: McGraw-Hill.

Gula, R. J. (2006). *Nonsense: A handbook of logical fallacies.* Mount Jackson, VA: Axios Press.

Gulya, M., Galluccio, L., Wilk, A., & Rovee-Collier, C. (2001). Infants' long-term memory for a serial list: Recognition and reactivation. *Developmental Psychobiology, 38,* 174–185.

Gupta, S. (2007, May 24). Herbal remedies' potential dangers. Time Inc. Retrieved from http://www.time.com/time/magazine/article/0,9171,1625175,00.html.

Gussow, W. (1963). A preliminary report of kayak-angst among the Eskimo of West Greenland: A study in sensory deprivation. *International Journal of Social Psychiatry, 9,* 18–26.

Gustafsson, J.-E. (1988). Hierarchical models of individual differences in cognitive abilities. In R. J. Sternberg (Ed.), *Advances in the psychology of human intelligence, Vol. 4* (pp. 35–71). Hillsdale, NJ: Erlbaum.

Haaga, D. A., Dyck, M. J., & Ernst, D. (1991). Empirical status of cognitive theory of depression. *Psychological Bulletin, 110,* 215–236.

Haber, R. N. (1979). Twenty years of haunting eidetic imagery: Where's the ghost? *Behavioral and Brain Sciences, 2,* 583–629.

Hafer, C. L., & Begue, L. (2005). Experimental research on just-world theory: Problems, developments, and future challenges. *Psychological Bulletin, 131,* 128–167.

Hagen, M. (2001). Damaged goods? What, if anything, does science tell us about the long-term effects of childhood sexual abuse? *Skeptical Inquirer, 24*(1), 54–59.

Hahlweg, K., & Markman, H. J. (1988). Effectiveness of behavioral marital therapy: Empirical status of behavioral techniques in preventing and alleviating marital distress. *Journal of Consulting and Clinical Psychology, 56,* 440–447.

Haier R. J., Siegel, B. V., MacLachlan, A., Soderling, E., Lottenberg, S., & Buchsbaum, M. S. (1992). Regional glucose metabolic changes after learning a complex visuospatial/motor task: A positron emission tomographic study. *Brain Research, 570,* 134–143.

Haimerl, C. J., & Valentine, E. (2001). The effect of contemplative practice on interpersonal, and transpersonal dimensions of the self-concept. *Journal of Transpersonal Psychology, 33,* 37–52.

Halberstadt, J., & Rhodes, G. (2003). It's not just the average face that's attractive: The attractiveness of averageness of computer-manipulated birds, fish, and automobiles. *Psychonomic Bulletin and Review, 10,* 149–156.

Haldeman, D. (1994). The practice and ethics of sexual orientation conversion therapy. *Journal of Consulting and Clinical Psychology, 62,* 221–227.

Haley, J. (1976). *Problem-solving therapy.* San Francisco: Jossey-Bass.

Hall, C. S. (1984). A ubiquitous sex difference in dreams, revisited. *Journal of Personality and Social Psychology, 46,* 1109–1117.

Hall, C., & Domhoff, G. W. (1963). Aggression in dreams. *International Journal of Social Psychiatry, 9,* 259-267.

Hall, C., & Nordby, V. J. (1972). *The individual and his dreams.* Winnipeg, Manitoba, Canada: New American Library.

Hall, C., & Van de Castle, R. (1966). *Content analysis of dreams.* New York: Appleton Century-Crofts.

Hall, E. T. (1966). *The hidden dimension*. New York: Anchor Books.

Hall, E. T. (1976). *Beyond culture*. New York: Doubleday.

Hall, J. A. (1978). Gender effects in decoding nonverbal cues. *Psychological Bulletin, 85*, 845–857.

Hall, J. A. Y., and Kimura, D. (1994). Dermatoglyphic asymmetry and sexual orientation in men. *Behavioral Neuroscience, 108*, 1203–1206.

Hall, J. R., & Benning, S. D. (2006). The "successful" psychopath: Adaptive and subclinical manifestations of psychopathy in the general population. In C. J. Patrick (Ed.), *Handbook of psychopathy* (pp. 459–478). New York: Guilford Press.

Hall, T. (1970). *Carl Friedrich Gauss: A biography*. Cambridge, MA: MIT Press.

Halpern, D. F. (1981). The determinants of illusory-contour perception. *Perception, 10*, 199–213.

Halpern, D. F. (1992). *Sex differences in cognitive abilities* (2nd ed.). Hillsdale, NJ: Erlbaum.

Halpern, D. F., Benbow, C. P., Geary, D. C., Gur, R. C., Hyde, J. S., & Gernsbacher, M. A. (2007). The science of sex differences in science and mathematics. *Psychological Science in the Public Interest, 8*, 1–51,

Halweg, K., Goldstein, M. J., Neuchterlein, K. H., Magana, A. B., Mintz, J., Doane, J. A., et al. (1989). Expressed emotion and patient-relative interaction in families of recent onset schizophrenics. *Journal of Consulting and Clinical Psychology, 57*, 11–18.

Hamann, A., & Matthaei, S. (1996). Regulation of energy balance by leptin. *Experimental Clinical Endocrinology Diabetes, 104*, 293–300.

Hamilton, D. L., & Rose, T. L. (1980). Illusory correlation and the maintenance of stereotypic beliefs. *Journal of Personality and Social Psychology, 39*, 832–845.

Hamilton, R. J. (1998). Substance withdrawal. In L. R. Goldfrank et al., *Goldfrank's Toxicologic Emergencies* (6th ed., pp. 1127–1143). New York: McGraw-Hill Professional Publishing.

Hamilton, S., Rothbart, M., & Dawes, R. M. (1986). Sex bias, diagnosis, and DSM III. *Sex Roles, 15*, 279–284.

Hammen, C. (1991). Generation of stress in the course of unipolar depression. *Journal of Abnormal Psychology, 100*, 555–561.

Hampson, E., Rovet, J. F., & Altman, D. (1998). Spatial reasoning in children with congenital adrenal hyperplasia due to 21-hydroxylase deficiency. *Developmental Neuropsychology, 14*, 299–320.

Haney, C., Banks, W. C., & Zimbardo, P. G. (1973). Interpersonal dynamics in a simulated prison. *International Journal of Criminology & Penology, 1*, 69–97.

Hansen, E. S., Hasselbalch, S., Law, J., & Bolwig, T. G. (2002). The caudate nucleus in obsessive-compulsive disorder. Reduced metabolism following treatment with paroxetine: A PET study. *International Journal of Neuropsychopharmacology, 5*, 1–10.

Hansen, T., Olkkonen, M., Walter, S., & Gegenfurtner, K. R. (2006). Memory modulates colour appearance. *Nature Neuroscience, 9*, 1367–1368.

Hansford, B., & Hattie, J. (1982). The relationship between self and achievement performance measures. *Review of Educational Research, 52*, 123–142.

Hanson, D. R., & Gottesman, I. I. (2005). Theories of schizophrenia: A genetic-inflammatory-vascular synthesis. *Biomed Central Medical Genetics, 6*, Published online 2005 February 11. Doi: 10.1186/1471-2350-6-7.

Haraldson, E., & Houtkooper, J. (1995). Meta-analysis of 10 experiments on perceptual defensiveness and ESP. *Journal of Parapsychology, 59*, 251–271.

Harding, C. M., Zubin, J., & Strauss, J. S. (1992). Chronicity in schizophrenia: Revisited. *British Journal of Psychiatry Supplement, 18*, 27–37.

Hardy, K. R. (1957). Determinants of conformity and attitude change. *Journal of Abnormal and Social Psychology, 4*, 289–294.

Hardy, C., & Latane, B. (1986). Social loafing on a cheering task. *Social Science, 71*, 165–172.

Hare, E. H. (1962). Masturbatory insanity: The history of an idea. *Journal of Mental Science, 108*, 2–25.

Hare, R. D. (1978). Electrodermal and cardiovascular correlates of psychopathy. In R. D. Hare, & D. Schalling (Eds.), *Psychopathic behavior: Approaches to research* (pp. 107–144). Chichester, England: John Wiley & Sons.

Hare, R. D. (1993). *Without conscience: The disturbing world of the psychopaths among us*. New York: Simon & Schuster.

Hare, R. D. (2003). *The Hare Psychopathy Checklist—Revised*. Toronto, Ontario, Canada: Multi-Health Systems.

Harford, T., & Muthen, B. O. (2001). The dimensionality of alcohol abuse and dependence: A multivariate analysis of DSM-IV symptoms in the National Longitudinal Survey of Youth. *Journal of Studies in Alcohol, 62*, 150–157.

Hariri, A. R., Mattay, V. S., Tessitore, A., Kolachana, B., Fera, F., Goldman, D., et al. (2002). Serotonin transporter genetic variation and the response of the human amygdala. *Science, 297*, 400–403.

Harkins, E. B. (1978). Effects of empty nest transition on self-report of psychological and physical well-being. *Journal of Marriage and the Family, 40*, 549–556.

Harkins, S. G., Latane, B., & Williams, K. D. (1980). Social loafing: Allocating effort or taking it easy? *Journal of Experimental Social Psychology, 16*, 457–465.

Harkness, A. R. (2007). Personality traits are essential for a complete clinical science. In S. O. Lilienfeld and W. O'Donohue (Eds.), *The great ideas of clinical science: 17 concepts that every mental health professional should understand* (pp. 263–290). New York: Routledge.

Harkness, A. R., & Lilienfeld, S. O. (1997). Individual differences science for treatment planning: Personality traits. *Psychological Assessment, 9*, 349–360.

Harkness, A. R., Tellegen, A., & Waller, N. G. (1995). Differential convergence of self-report and informant data for multi-dimensional personality questionnaire traits: Implications for the construct of negative emotionality. *Journal of Personality Assessment, 64*, 185–204.

Harkness, K. L., & Luther, J. (2001). Clinical risk factors for the generation of life events in major depression. *Journal of Abnormal Psychology, 110*, 564–572.

Harlow, H. F. (1958). The nature of love. *American Psychologist, 13*, 673–685.

Harlow, J. M. (1848). Passage of an iron rod through the head. *Boston Medical and Surgical Journal, 39*, 389–393. (Republished in *Journal of Neuropsychiatry and Clinical Neuroscience, 1991, 11*, 281–283.)

Harmon-Jones, E., & Allen, J. J. B. (2001). The role of affect in the mere exposure effect: Evidence from psychophysiological and individual differences approaches. *Personality and Social Psychology Bulletin, 27*, 889–898.

Harmon-Jones, E., & Judson, M. (1999). *Cognitive dissonance: Progress on a pivotal theory in social psychology*. Washington, DC: Braun Brumfield.

Harris, J. L., & Qualls, C. D. (2000). The association of elaborative or maintenance rehearsal with age, reading comprehension, and verbal working memory performance. *Aphasiology, 14*, 515–526.

Harris, J. R. (1995). Where is the child's environment? A group socialization theory of development. *Psychological Review, 102*, 458–489.

Harris, J. R. (1998). *The nurture assumption: Why children turn out the way they do*. New York: Free Press.

Harris, J. R. (2002). *The nurture assumption: Why children turn out the way they do*. New York: Free Press.

Harris, J. R. (2006). *No two alike: Human nature and human individuality*. New York: W. W. Norton.

Harris, M. (1976). History and significance of the emic/etic distinction. *Annual Review of Anthropology, 5*, 329–350.

Hart, B., & Risley, T. R. (1995). *Meaningful differences in the everyday experience of young American children*. Baltimore: Paul H. Brookes.

Hartmann, E., Russ, D., Oldfield, M., Falke, R., & Skoff, B. (1980). Dream content: Effects of L-dopa. *Sleep Research, 9*, 153.

Hartmann, H. (1939). *Ego psychology and the problem of adaptation*. New York: International Universities Press.

Hartmann, H. (1950). Comment on the psychoanalytic theory of the ego. *The Psychoanalytic Study of the Child, 5*, 74–96.

Hartschorne, H., & May, M. A. (1928). *Studies in the nature of character: Vol. 1. Studies in deceit*. New York: Macmillan.

Harvey, J. H., & Weary, G. (1984). Current issues in attribution theory and research. *Annual Review of Psychology, 35*, 427–460.

Harvey, P. D., Koren, D., Reichenberg, A., & Bowie, C. R. (2006). Negative symptoms and cognitive deficits: What is the nature of their relationship? *Schizophrenia Bulletin, 32*, 250–258.

Harvey, P. D., Reichenberg, A., & Bowie, C. R. (2006). Cognition and aging in psychopathology: Focus on schizophrenia and depression (pp. 389–409). In S. Nolen-Hoeksema, T. D. Cannon, & T. Widiger (Eds.), *Annual Review of Clinical Psychology* (Vol. 2). Palo Alto, CA: Annual Reviews.

Hasegawa, H., & Jamieson, G. A. (2002). Conceptual issues in hypnosis research: Explanations, definitions and the state/non-state debate. *Contemporary Hypnosis, 19*, 103–117.

Hasler, G., Buysse, D. J., Klaghofer, R., Gamma, A., Ajdacic, V., Eich, D., et al. (2004). The association between short sleep duration and obesity in young adults: A 13-year prospective study. *Sleep, 27*, 661–666.

Hatfield, E., Aronson, V., Abrahams, D., & Rottman, L. (1966). The importance of physical attractiveness in dating behavior. *Journal of Personality and Social Psychology, 4*, 508–516.

Hatfield, E., & Rapson, R. (1996). *Love and sex: Cross-cultural perspectives*. Boston: Allyn & Bacon.

Hatfield, E., & Walster, G. W. (1978). *A new look at love*. Reading, MA: Addison-Wesley.

Hathaway, S. R., & McKinley, J. C. (1940). A multiphasic personality schedule (Minnesota): I. Construction of the schedule. *Journal of Psychology, 14*, 73–84.

Hauri, P. J. (1998). Insomnia. *Clinical Chest Medicine, 19*, 157–168.

Hauser, M. D., & Fitch, W. T. (2003). What are the uniquely human components of the language faculty? In M. H. Christiansen & S. Kirby (Eds.),

Language evolution. Studies in the evolution of language (pp. 158–181). London: Oxford University Press.

Hauser, M. D. (2002). Nature vs. nurture redux. *Science, 298,* 1554–1555.

Hauser, R. M. (1998). Trends in black-white test score differences: I. Uses and misuses of NAEP/SAT data. In U. Neisser (Ed.), *The rising curve: Long-term gains in IQ and related measures* (pp. 219–249). Washington, DC: American Psychological Association.

Haxby, D. G. (1995). Treatment of nicotine dependence. *American Journal of Health-System Pharmacy, 52,* 265–281.

Hayduk, L. (1983). Personal space: Where we now stand. *Psychological Bulletin, 94,* 293–335.

Hayes, B. (2006). Gauss' day of reckoning. *American Scientist, 94,* 200–205.

Hayes, R., & Dennerstein, L. (2005). The impact of aging on sexual function and sexual dysfunction in women: A review of population-based studies. *Journal of Sex Research, 2,* 317–330.

Hayes, S. C., Strosahl, K., & Wilson, K. G. (1999). *Acceptance and commitment therapy.* New York: Guilford Press.

Hayward, L. R. C. (1960). The subjective meaning of stress. *British Journal of Psychology, 33,* 185–194.

Hazelrigg, M. D., Cooper, H. M., & Borduin, C. M. (1987). Evaluating the effectiveness of family therapies: An integrative review and analysis. *Psychological Bulletin, 101,* 428–442.

Healy, A. F., & McNamara, D. S. (1996). Verbal learning and memory: Does the modal model still work? *Annual Review of Psychology, 47,* 143–172.

Hearne, K. M. T. (1978). *Lucid dreams: An electrophysiological and psychological study.* Unpublished doctoral dissertation, University of Liverpool, Liverpool, England.

Heath, T. P., Melichar, J. K., Nutt, D. J., & Donaldson, L. F. (2006). Human taste thresholds are modulated by serotonin and noradrenaline. *Journal of Neuroscience, 26,* 12664–12671.

Heaton, J. A., & Wilson, N. L. (1995). *Tuning in trouble: Talk TV's destructive impact on mental health.* San Francisco: Jossey-Bass.

Hebb, D. O. (1949). *The organization of behavior.* New York: John Wiley.

Hebebrand, J., Wulftange, H., Goerg, T., Ziegler, A., Hinney, N., Barth, H., et al. (2000). Epidemic obesity: Are genetic factors involved via increased rates of assortative mating? *International Journal of Obesity, 24,* 345–353.

Hedges, L. V., & Nowell, A. (1995). Sex differences in mental test scores, variability, and numbers of high-scoring individuals. *Science, 269,* 41–45.

Hedley, A., Ogden, C., Johnson, C. L., Carroll, M. D., Curtin, L. R., & Flegal, K. M. (2004). Prevalence of overweight and obesity among US children, adolescents, and adults, 1999–2002. *Journal of the American Medical Association, 291,* 2847–2850.

Heidbreder, E. (1933). *Seven psychologies.* New York: Appleton-Century-Crofts.

Heider, F. (1958). *The psychology of interpersonal relations.* New York: Wiley.

Heilbrun, K., & Kramer, G. (2001). Advances in risk assessment and implications for forensic practice: A five year update (1995–2000). *Journal of Forensic Psychology Practice, 1,* 55–63.

Heimberg, R. G., & Juster, H. R. (1995). Cognitive-behavioral treatments: Literature review. In R. G. Heimberg, M. R. Liebowitz, D. A. Hope, & F. R. Schneier (Eds.), *Social phobia. Diagnosis, assessment, and treatment.* New York: Guilford Press.

Heims, H. C., Critchley, H. D., Dolan, R., Mathias, C. J., & Cipolotti, L. (2004). Social and motivational functioning is not critically dependent on feedback of autonomic responses: Neuropsychological evidence from patients with pure autonomic failure. *Neuropsychologia, 42,* 1979–1988.

Heindel, J. J. (2003). Endocrine disruptors and the obesity epidemic. *Toxicological Sciences, 76,* 247–249.

Heine, S. J., Lehman, D. R., Markus, H. R., & Kitayama, S. (1999). Is there a universal need for positive self-regard? *Psychological Review, 106,* 766–794.

Heini, A. F., & Weinsier, R. L. (1997). Divergent trends in obesity and fat intake patterns: The American paradox. *American Journal of Medicine, 102,* 259–264.

Heinrichs, C., Munson, P., Counts, D., Cutler, G., Jr., & Baron, J. (1995). Patterns of human growth. *Science, 268,* 442–447.

Heller, S. (1999). *The complete idiot's guide to conquering fear and anxiety.* New York: Alpha.

Helliwell, J. F., & Putnam, R. D. (2004). The social context of well-being. *Philosophical Transactions of the Royal Society (London) Series B, 359,* 1435–1446.

Helmes, E., & Reddon, J. R. (1993). A perspective on developments in assessing psychopathology: A critical review of the MMPI and MMPI-2. *Psychological Bulletin, 113,* 453–471.

Helmholtz, H. von. (1850). Über die Theorie der zusammengesetzten Farben. *Archiv für Anatomie, Physiologie und wissenschaftliche Medizin,* 461–482.

Helson, H. (1948). Adaptation-level as a basis for a quantitative theory of frames of reference. *Psychological Review, 55,* 297–313.

Helson, R., & Srivastava, S. (2002). Creativity and wisdom: Similarities, differences, and how they develop. *Personality and Social Psychology Bulletin, 28,* 1430–1440.

Hempel, A., Hempel, E., Schonknecht, P. L., Stippich, C., & Schroder, J. (2003). Impairment in basal limbic function in schizophrenia during affect recognition. *Psychiatry Research, 122,* 115–124.

Hendersen, R. W. (1985). Fearful memories: The motivational significance of forgetting. In F. R. Brush & J. B. Overmier (Eds.), *Affect, conditioning, and cognition: Essays on the determinants of behavior* (pp. 43–53). Hillsdale, NJ: Erlbaum.

Henderson, J. M., & Hollingworth, A. (1999). The role of fixation position in detecting scene changes across saccades. *Psychological Science, 10,* 438–443.

Henig, R. M. (2006, February 5). Looking for the lie. *New York Times Magazine,* 46–53, 76, 83.

Henriques, G. (2004). Psychology defined. *Journal of Clinical Psychology, 60,* 1207–1221.

Henriques, G., Wenzel, A., Brown, G. K., & Beck, A. T. (2005). Suicide attempters' reaction to survival as a risk factor for eventual suicide. *American Journal of Psychiatry, 162,* 2180–2182.

Henriques, J. B., & Davidson, R. J. (2000). Decreased responsiveness to reward in depression. *Cognition and Emotion, 14,* 711–724.

Henshaw, J. M. (2006). *Does measurement measure up? How numbers reveal and conceal the truth.* Baltimore: Johns Hopkins University Press.

Herbert, J. D., Sharp, I. R., & Gaudiano, B. A. (2002). Separating fact from fiction in the etiology and treatment of autism: A scientific review of the evidence. *Scientific Review of Mental Health Practice, 1,* 25–45.

Herbert, M. R. (2005). Large brains in autism: The challenge of pervasive abnormality. *Neuroscientist, 11,* 417–440.

Herculano-Houzel, S. (2002). Do you know your brain? A survey on public neuroscience literacy at the closing of the decade of the brain. *Neuroscientist, 8,* 98–110.

Hergenhahn, B. R. (2000). *An introduction to the history of psychology* (4th ed.). Pacific Grove, CA: Wadsworth.

Herman, C. P., & Mack, D. (1975). Restrained and unrestrained eating. *Journal of Personality, 43,* 647–660.

Herman, C. P., & Polivy, J. (1975). Anxiety, restraint and eating behavior. *Journal of Abnormal Psychology, 84,* 666–672.

Herman, C. P., & Polivy, J. (1980). Restrained eating. In A. J. Stunkard (Ed.), *Obesity* (pp. 208–225). Philadelphia: W. B. Saunders.

Hermanussen, M. (1998). The analysis of short-term growth. *Hormone Research, 49,* 53–64.

Hermanussen, M., & Geiger-Benoit, K. (1995). No evidence for saltation in human growth. *Annals of Human Biology, 22,* 341–345.

Hermanussen, M., Geiger-Benoit, K., Burmeister, J., & Sippell, W. G. (1988). Knemometry in childhood: Accuracy and standardization of a new technique of lower leg length measurement. *Annals of Human Biology, 15,* 1–16.

Herrell, R., Goldberg, J., True, W. R., Ramakrishnan, V., Lyons, M., Eisen, S., et al. (1999). Sexual orientation and suicidality. *Archives of General Psychiatry, 56,* 657–661.

Herrmann, C.S., & Friederici, A.D. (2001). Object processing in the infant brain. *Science, 292,* 163.

Herrmann, N. (1996). *The whole brain business book.* New York: McGraw-Hill.

Herrnstein, R. J. (1966). Superstition: A corollary of the principles of operant conditioning. In W. K. Honig (Ed.), Operant behavior: Areas of research and application (pp. 33–51). New York: Appleton-Century-Crofts.

Herrnstein, R. J., & Murray, C. (1994). *The bell curve: Intelligence and class structure in American life.* New York: Free Press.

Herskowitz, J. (1987). *The popcorn diet plus.* New Delhi, India: Pharos Books.

Hertwig, R., Pacur, T., & Kurzenhauser, S. (2005). Judgments of risk frequencies: Tests of possible cognitive mechanisms. *Journal of Experimental Psychology: Learning, Memory, and Cognition, 31,* 621–642.

Hess, R. A. (2003). Estrogen in the adult male reproductive tract: A review. *Reproductive and Biological Endocrinology, 9,* 1–52.

Hesse, E. (1999). The adult attachment interview: Historical and current perspectives. In J. Cassidy & P. Shaver (Eds.), *Handbook of attachment: Theory, research, and clinical applications* (pp. 395–433). New York: Guilford Press.

Hetherington, A. W., & Ranson, S. W. (1940). Hypothalamic lesions and adiposity in the rat. *Anatomical Record, 78,* 149–158.

Hetherington, E. M., Cox, M., & Cox, R. (1985). Long-term effects of divorce and remarriage on the adjustment of children. *Journal of the American Academy of Child Psychiatry, 24,* 518–530.

Hetherington, E. M., & Stanley-Hagan, M. (1995). Parenting in divorced and remarried families. In M. Bornstein (Ed.), *Handbook on parenting. Volume 3: Status and social conditions of parenting* (pp. 233–254). Mahwah, NJ: Lawrence Erlbaum.

Hick, W. E. (1952). On the rate of gain of information. *Quarterly Journal of Experimental Psychology, 4,* 11–26.

Higgins, J. E., & Endler, N. (1995). Coping, life stress, and psychological and somatic distress. *European Journal of Personality, 9,* 253–270.

Highstein, S. M., Fay, R. R., & Popper A. N. (2004). *The vestibular system.* Berlin, Germany: Springer-Verlag.

Higuchi, S., Matsushita, S., Murayama, M., Takagai, S., & Hayashida, M. (1995). Alcohol and aldehyde dehydrogenase polymorphisms and the risk for alcoholism. *American Journal of Psychiatry, 152,* 1219–1221.

Hilgard, E. R. (1977). *Divided consciousness: Multiple controls in human thought and action.* New York: Wiley.

Hilgard, E. R. (1986). *Divided consciousness: Multiple controls in human thought and action* (expanded ed.). New York: Wiley.

Hilgard, E. R. (1994). Neodissociation theory. In S. J. Lynn & J. W. Rhue (Eds.), *Dissociation: Clinical, theoretical and research perspectives* (pp. 32–51). New York: Guilford Press.

Hilgetag, C. C., Burns, G. A., O'Neill, M. A., Scannell, J. W., & Young, M. P. (2000). Anatomical connectivity defines the organization of clusters of cortical areas in the macaque monkey and the cat. *Philosophical Transactions of the Royal Society London Biological Sciences, 355,* 91–110.

Hill, C., Rubin, Z., & Peplau, L. A. (1976). Breakups before marriage: The end of 103 affairs. *Journal of Social Issues, 32,* 147–168.

Hill, E. L., & Frith, U. (2003). Understanding autism: Insights from mind and brain. In U. Frith & E. Hill (Eds.), *Autism: Mind and brain* (pp. 1–19). New York: Oxford University Press.

Hill, E. L., & Frith, U. (2003). Understanding autism: Insights from mind and brain. *Philosophical Transactions of the Royal Society B: Biological Sciences, 358,* 281–289.

Hiller, J. (2005). Gender differences in sexual motivation. *Journal of Men's Health and Gender, 2,* 339–345.

Himes, S. M., & Thompson, J. K. (2007). Fat stigmatization in television shows and movies: A content analysis. *Obesity, 15,* 712–718.

Hines, T. (1987). Left brain/right brain mythology and implications for management and training. *The Academy of Management Review, 12,* 600–606.

Hines, T. (2003). *Pseudoscience and the paranormal: A critical examination of the evidence* (2nd ed.). Buffalo, NY: Prometheus.

Hingson, R., Heeren, T., & Winter, M. R. (2006). Drinking onset and alcohol dependence: Age at onset, duration, and severity. *Archives of Pediatrics and Adolescent Medicine, 160,* 739–746.

Hinsz, V. B. (1989). Facial resemblance in engaged and married couples. *Journal of Social and Personal Relationships, 6,* 223–229.

Hirsh-Pasek, K., & Golinkoff. R. (1996). *The origins of grammar.* Cambridge, MA: MIT Press.

Hoagland, R. C. (1987). The monuments of Mars: A city on the edge of forever. Berkeley, CA: North Atlantic Books.

Hobson, J., Pace-Schott, E., & Stickgold, R. (2000). Dreaming and the brain: Towards a cognitive neuroscience of conscious states. *Behavioral and Brain Sciences, 23,* 793–842.

Hobson, J. A. (2002). *Dreaming: An introduction to the science of sleep.* New York: Oxford University Press.

Hobson, J. A., & McCarley, R. M. (1977). The brain as a dream state generator: An activation-synthesis hypothesis. *American Journal of Psychiatry, 134,* 1335–1348.

Hock, R. R. (2002). *Forty studies that changed psychology: Explorations into the history of psychological research* (4th ed.). Upper Saddle River, NJ: Prentice Hall.

Hodson, G., & Costello, K. (2007). Interpersonal disgust, ideological orientations, and dehumanization as predictors of intergroup attitudes. *Psychological Science, 18,* 691–698.

Hoekstra, R. E., Ferrara, T. B., Couser, R. J., Payne, N. R., & Connett, J. E. (2004). Survival and long-term neurodevelopmental outcome of extremely premature infants born at 23–26 weeks' gestation age at a tertiary center. *Pediatrics, 113,* e1–e6.

Hoffman, M. B., & Morse, S. J. (2006, July 30). The insanity defense goes back on trial. Retrieved October 22, 2007, from http://www.nytimes.com/2006/07/30/opinion/30hoffman.html?_r=1&oref=slogin.

Hoffrage, U. (2004). Overconfidence. In R. F. Pohl (Ed.), *Cognitive illusions: Fallacies and biases in thinking, judgment, and memory* (pp. 235–254). Hove, England: Psychology Press.

Hogensen, G. B. (2001). The Baldwin effect: A neglected influence on C. G. Jung's evolutionary thinking. *Journal of Analytical Psychology, 46,* 591–611.

Hohmann, G. W. (1966). Some effects of spinal cord lesions on experienced emotional feelings. *Psychophysiology, 3,* 143–156.

Hokanson, J. E., & Butler, A. C. (1992). Cluster analysis of depressed college students' social behaviors. *Journal of Personality and Social Psychology, 62,* 273–280.

Holahan, C., & Moos, R. H. (1991). Life stressors, personal and social resources and depression: A four-year structural model. *Journal of Abnormal Psychology, 100,* 31–38.

Holahan, M. R., Rekart, J. L., Sandoval, J., & Routtenberg, A. (2006). Spatial learning induces presynaptic structural remodeling in the hippocampal mossy fiber system of two rat strains. *Hippocampus, 16,* 560–570.

Holden, J. E., Jeong, Y., & Forrest, J. M. (2005). The endogenous opioid system and clinical pain management. *AACN Clinical Issues, 16,* 291–301.

Hollander, E., Neville, D., Frenkel, M., Josephson, S., & Liebowitz, M. (1992). Body dysmorphic disorder. *Psychosomatics, 33,* 156–165.

Hollon, S. D., Haman, K. L., & Brown, L. L. (2002). Cognitive-behavioral treatment of depression. In I. H. Gotlib & C. L. Hammen (Eds.), *Handbook of depression* (pp. 383–403). New York: Guilford.

Hollon, S. D., Thase, M. E., & Markowitz, J. C. (2002). Treatment and prevention of depression. *Psychological Science in the Public Interest, 3,* 2002.

Holloway, R. L. (1983). Cerebral brain endocast pattern of Australopithecus afarensis hominid. *Nature, 303,* 420–422.

Holmes, C., Wurtz, P., Waln, R., Dungan, D., & Joseph, C. (1984). Relationship between the Luscher Color Test and the MMPI. *Journal of Clinical Psychology, 40,* 126–128.

Holmes, D. S. (1974). Investigation of repression: Differential recall of material experimentally or naturally associated with ego threat. *Psychological Bulletin, 81,* 632–653.

Holmes, D. S. (1978). Projection as a defense mechanism. *Psychological Bulletin, 85,* 677–688.

Holmes, D. S. (1987). The influence of meditation versus rest on physiological arousal. In M. West (Ed.), *The psychology of meditation* (pp. 81–103). Oxford, England: Clarendon Press.

Holmes, D. S. (1990). The evidence for repression: An examination of sixty years of research. In J. L. Singer (Ed.), *Repression and dissociation* (pp. 85–102). Chicago: University of Chicago Press.

Holmes, T. H., & Masuda, M. (1974). Life change and illness susceptibility. In B. S. Dohrenwend & P. P. Dohrenwend (Eds.), *Stressful life events: Their nature and effects* (pp. 45–72). New York: Wiley.

Holmes, T. H., & Rahe, R. H. (1967). The Social Readjustment Scale. *Journal of Psychosomatic Research, 11,* 213–218.

Holzman, P. S., Solomon, C. M., Levin, S., & Waternaux, C. S. (1984). Pursuit eye movement dysfunctions in schizophrenic patients and their relatives. *Archives of General Psychiatry, 45,* 1140–1141.

Homa, D. (1983). An assessment of two extraordinary speed-readers. *Bulletin of the Psychonomic Society, 21,* 123–126.

Homant, R. J., & Kennedy, D. B. (1998). Psychological aspects of crime scene profiling. *Criminal Justice and Behavior, 25,* 319–343.

Honda, H., Shimizu, Y., & Rutter, M. (2005). No effect of MMR withdrawal on the incidence of autism: A total population study. *Journal of Child Psychology and Psychiatry, 46,* 572–579.

Honts, C. R., Raskin, D. C., & Kircher, J. C. (1994). Mental and physical countermeasures reduce the accuracy of polygraph tests. *Journal of Applied Psychology, 79,* 252–259.

Hook, E. B., & Lindsjo, A. (1978). Down syndrome in live births by single year maternal age interval in a Swedish study: Comparison with results from a New York State study. *American Journal of Human Genetics, 30,* 19–27.

Hooker, C. I., Germine, L. T., Knight, R. T., & D'Esposito, M. (2006). Amygdala response to facial expressions reflects emotional learning. *Journal of Neuroscience, 26,* 8915–8922.

Hopkins, B., & Westra, T. (1988). Maternal handling and motor development: An intracultural study. *Genetic, Social, and General Psychology Monographs, 114,* 377–408.

Hoppa, H., & Hallstrom, T. (1981). Weight gain in adulthood in relation to socioeconomic factors, mental illness, and personality traits: A prospective study of middle-aged men. *Journal of Psychosomatic Research, 25,* 83–89.

Horgan, J. (1999). *The undiscovered mind: How the human brain defies replication, medication, and explanation.* New York: Free Press.

Horn, J. L. (1994). The theory of fluid and crystallized intelligence. In R. J. Sternberg (Ed.), *The encyclopedia of intelligence* (pp. 443–451). New York: Macmillan.

Horn, J. L., & Hofer, S. M. (1992). Major abilities and development in the adult period. In R. J. Sternberg & C. A. Berg (Eds.), *Intellectual development* (pp. 44–99). New York: Cambridge University Press.

Horney, K. (1939). *New ways in psychoanalysis.* New York: Norton.

Horney, K. (1945). *Our inner conflicts: A constructive theory of neurosis.* New York: Summit Books.

Horvath, A. O., & Bedi, R. P. (2002). The alliance. In J. C. Norcross (Ed.), *Psychotherapy relationships that work: Therapist contributions and responsiveness to patients* (pp. 37–69). New York: Oxford University Press.

Hosoda, H., Kojima, M., & Kangawa, K. (2002). Ghrelin and the regulation of food intake and energy balance. *Molecular Interventions, 2,* 494–503.

Houle, T. T., Dhingra, L. K., Remble, T. A., Rokicki, L. A., & Penzien, D. B. (2006). Not tonight, I have a headache? *Headache: The Journal of Head and Face Pain, 46,* 983–990.

Hounsfield, G. N. (1973). Computerized transverse axial scanning (tomography). 1. Description of system. *British Journal of Radiology, 46,* 1016–1022.

House, J. S., Robbins, C., & Metzner, H. L. (1982). The association of social relationships and activities with mortality: Prospective evidence from the Tecumseh Community Health Study. *American Journal of Epidemiology, 116,* 123–140.

Howe, M., & Courage, M. (1993). On resolving the enigma of infantile amnesia. *Psychological Bulletin, 113,* 305–326.

Howes, O. D., & Salkovskis, P. M. (1998). Health anxiety in medical students. *Lancet, 351,* 1332.

Hróbjartsson, A., & Götzsche, P. C. (2001). Is the placebo powerless? An analysis of clinical trials comparing placebo with no treatment. *New England Journal of Medicine, 344,* 1594–1602.

Hu, X.-Z., Lipsky, R. H., Zhu, G., Akhtar, L. A., Taubman, J., Greenberg, B. D., et al. (2006). Serotonin transporter promoter gain-of-function genotypes are linked to obsessive-compulsive disorder. *American Journal of Human Genetics, 78,* 815–826.

Hubel, D. H, & Wiesel, T. N. (1962). Receptive fields, binocular interaction and functional architecture in the cat's visual cortex. *Journal of Physiology, 160,* 106–154.

Hubel, D. H., & Wiesel, T. N. (1963). Shape and arrangement of columns in cat's striate cortex. *Journal of Physiology, 165,* 559–568.

Hudson, L. (1967). *Contrary imaginations: A psychological study of the English schoolboy.* Harmondsworth, England: Penguin.

Huff, D. (1954). *How to lie with statistics.* New York: W. W. Norton.

Hughes, L. B., Beasley, T. M., Patel, H., Tiwari, H. K., Morgan, S. L., Baggott, J. E., et al. (2006). Racial or ethnic differences in allele frequencies of single-nucleotide polymorphisms in the methylenetetrahydrofolate reductase gene and their influence on response to methotrexate in rheumatoid arthritis. *Annals of Rheumatic Diseases, 65,* 213–218.

Huitema, B. E., & Stein, C. R. (1993). Validity of the GRE without restriction of range. *Psychological Reports, 72,* 123–127.

Hulbert, A. (2003). *Raising America: Experts, parents, and a century of advice about children.* New York: Knopf.

Hull, C. L. (1943). *Principles of behavior.* New York: Appleton-Century-Crofts.

Hull, J. G., & Bond, C. F. (1986). Social and behavioral consequences of alcohol consumption and expectancy: A meta-analysis. *Psychological Bulletin, 99,* 347–360.

Hunsley, J., & Bailey, J. M. (1999). The clinical utility of the Rorschach: Unfulfilled promises and an uncertain future. *Psychological Assessment, 11,* 266–277.

Hunsley, J., & DiGuilio, G. (2002). Dodo bird, Phoenix, or urban legend? *Scientific Review of Mental Health Practice, 1,* 11–22.

Hunsley, J., Lee, C. M., & Wood, J. (2003). Controversial and questionable assessment techniques. In S. O. Lilienfeld, J. M. Lohr, & S. J. Lynn (Eds.), *Science and pseudoscience in contemporary clinical psychology* (pp. 39–76). New York: Guilford.

Hunt, E., & Carlson, J. (2007). Considerations relating to the study of group differences in intelligence. *Perspectives on Psychological Science, 2,* 194–213.

Hunt, H., Ruzycki-Hunt, K., Pariak, D., & Belicki, K. (1993). The relationship between dream bizarreness and imagination: Artifact or essence? *Dreaming, 3,* 179–199.

Hunt, M. (1993). *The story of psychology.* New York: Doubleday.

Hunt, M. (1997). *How science takes stock: The story of meta-analysis.* New York: Russell Sage Foundation.

Hunt, M. (1999). *The new know-nothings: The political foes of the scientific study of human nature.* New Brunswick, NJ: Transaction Publishers.

Hunter, E. (1951). *Brainwashing in Red China.* New York: Vanguard.

Hunter, J. E., & Hunter, R. F. (1984). Validity and utility of alternative predictors of job performance. *Psychological Bulletin, 96,* 72–98.

Hunter, J., Schmidt, F., & Hunter, R. (1979). Differential validity of employment tests by race: A comprehensive review and analysis. *Psychological Bulletin, 85,* 721–735.

Hunter, R. A., & Macalpine, I. (1963). *Three hundred years of psychiatry: 1535–1860.* London: Oxford University Press.

Huntjens, R., Peters, M., Woertman, L., Bovenschen, L., Martin, R., & Postma, A. (2006). Inter-identity amnesia in dissociative identity disorder: A simulated memory impairment? *Psychological Medicine, 36,* 857–863.

Hura, S. L., & Echols, C. H. (1996). The role of stress and articulatory difficulty in children's earliest productions. *Developmental Psychology, 32,* 165–176.

Hurwitz, E. L., Aker, A. H., Adams, H. L., Meeker, W. C., & Shekelle, P. G. (1996). Manipulation and mobilization of the cervical spine. A systematic review of the literature. *Spine, 21,* 1746–1759.

Huston, T. L., Ruggiero, M., Conner, R., & Geis, G. (1981). Bystander intervention into crime: A study based on naturally-occurring episodes. *Social Psychology Quarterly, 44,* 14–23.

Hutcheson, D. M., Everitt, B. J., Robbins, T. W., & Dickinson, A. (2001). The role of withdrawal in heroin addiction: Enhances reward or promotes avoidance? *Nature Neuroscience, 4,* 943–947.

Hutchins, S. S. (1999). *The psychosocial reality, variability, and the compositionality of English phonesthemes.* Unpublished doctoral dissertation, Emory University, Atlanta, GA.

Hyde, J. S. (1995). Women and maternity leave: Empirical data and public policy. *Psychology of Women Quarterly, 19,* 299–313.

Hyde, J. S. (2005). The gender similarities hypothesis. *American Psychologist, 60,* 581–592.

Hyde, J. S., Fennema, E., & Lamon, S. J. (1990). Gender differences in mathematics performance: A meta-analysis. *Psychological Bulletin, 107,* 139–155.

Hyman, I. E., Husband, T. H., & Billings, F. J. (1995). False memories of childhood experiences. *Applied Cognitive Psychology 9,* 181–197.

Hyman, R. (1977). Cold reading: How to convince strangers that you know all about them. *The Zetetic, 1*(2), 18–37.

Hyman, R. (1989). *The elusive quarry: A scientific appraisal of psychical research.* Buffalo, NY: Prometheus Books.

Hyman, R. (1996). *The evidence for psychic functioning: Claims vs. reality.* Skeptical Inquirer, 20, 24–26.

Hyman, R. (2002). When and why are smart people stupid? In R. Sternberg (Ed.), *Why smart people can be so stupid* (pp. 1–23). New Haven, CT: Yale University Press.

Hyman, R. (2003, January/February). How not to test mediums: Critiquing the afterlife experiments. *Skeptical Inquirer, 27*(1), 20–30.

Iacono, W. G. (1985). Psychophysiologic markers of psychopathology: A review. *Canadian Psychology, 26,* 96–112.

Iacono, W. G. (2001). Forensic 'lie detection': Procedures without scientific basis. *Journal of Forensic Psychology Practice, 1,* 75–86.

Iacono, W. G., & Lykken, D. T. (1997). The validity of the lie detector: Two surveys of scientific opinion. *Journal of Applied Psychology, 82,* 426–433.

Iacono, W. G., & Patrick, C. J. (2006). Polygraph ("lie detector") testing: Current status and emerging trends. In I. B. Weiner & A. Hess (Eds.), *Handbook of forensic psychology* (3rd ed., pp. 552–588). New York: Wiley.

Ideno, J., Mizukami, H., Kakehashi, A., Saito, Y., Okada, T., Urabe, M., et al. (2007). Prevention of diabetic retinopathy by intraocular soluble flt-1 gene transfer in a spontaneously diabetic rat model. *International Journal of Molecular Medicine, 19,* 75–79.

Ikemi, Y., & Nakagawa, S. (1962). A psychosomatic study of contagious dermatitis. *Kyushu Journal of Medical Science, 13,* 335–350.

Ilardi, S. S., & Craighead, W. E. (1994). The role of nonspecific factors in cognitive therapy for depression. *Clinical Psychology: Science and Practice, 9,* 138–156.

Ilardi, S. S., & Feldman, D. (2001). The cognitive neuroscience paradigm: A unifying meta-theoretical framework for the science and practice of clinical psychology. *Journal of Clinical Psychology, 57,* 1067–1088.

Ilardi, S. S., Rand, K., & Karwoski, L. (2007). The cognitive neuroscience perspective allows us to understand abnormal behavior at multiple levels of complexity. In S. O. Lilienfeld & W. O. O'Donohue (Eds.), *The great ideas of clinical science: 17 Principles that all mental health professionals should understand* (pp. 291–309). New York: Routledge.

Illes, J., Francis, W. S., Desmond, J. E., Gabrieli, J. D. E., Glover, G. H., Poldrack, R., et al. (1999). Convergent cortical representation of semantic processing in bilinguals. *Brain and Language, 70,* 347–363.

Ingram, R. (2003). Origins of cognitive vulnerability to depression. *Cognitive Therapy and Research, 27,* 77–88.

Ingram, R. E., Scott, W., & Siegle, G. (1998). Depression: Social and cognitive aspects. In T. Millon, P. H. Blaney, & R. D. Davis (Eds.), *Oxford textbook of psychopathology* (pp. 203–226). New York: Oxford Press.

Intons-Peterson, M. J., & Fournier, J. (1986). External and internal memory aids: When and how often do we use them? *Journal of Experimental Psychology: General, 115,* 267–280.

Ioannidis, J. P. A. (2005). Contradicted and initially stronger effects in highly cited clinical research. *Journal of the American Medical Association, 294,* 218–228.

Irle, E. (1985). Combined lesions of septum, amygdala, hippocampus, anterior thalamus, mammillary bodies and cingulate and subicular cortex fail to impair the acquisition of complex learning tasks. *Experimental Brain Research, 58,* 346–361.

Irle, E., & Markowitsch, H. J. (1990). Functional recovery after limbic lesions in monkeys. *Brain Research Bulletin, 25,* 79–92.

Irvin, J. E., Bowers, C. A., Dunn, M. E., & Wang, M. C. (1999). Efficacy of relapse prevention: A meta-analytic review. *Journal of Consulting and Clinical Psychology, 67,* 563–570.

Irwin, H. J. (1985). Parapsychological phenomena and the absorption domain. *Journal of the American Society for Psychical Research, 79,* 1–11.

Isen, A., Clark, M., & Schwartz, M. (1976). Duration of the effect of good mood on helping: Footprints in the sand of time. *Journal of Personality & Social Psychology, 34,* 385–393.

Isen, A. M., Rosenzweig, A. S., & Young, M. J. (1991). The influence of positive affect on clinical problem solving. *Medical Decision Making, 11,* 221–227.

Isenberg, D. J. (1986). Group polarization: A critical review and meta-analysis. *Journal of Personality and Social Psychology, 50,* 1141–1151.

Ivey, A. E., Ivey, M. B., & Simek-Morgan, L. (1993). *Counseling and psychotherapy: A multi-cultural perspective* (3rd ed.). Boston: Allyn & Bacon.

Ivie, R., & Ray, K. N. (2005). *Women in physics and astronomy, 2005.* College Park, MD: American Institute of Physics.

Izard, C. (1994). Innate and universal facial expressions: Evidence from developmental and cross-country research. *Psychological Bulletin, 115,* 288–299.

Izard, C. E. (1971). *The face of emotion.* New York: Appleton-Century-Crofts.

Jackson, D. N. (1971). The dynamics of structured personality tests: 1971. *Psychological Review, 78,* 229–248.

Jackson, D. N., & Rushton, J. P. (2006). Males have greater g: Sex differences in general mental ability from 100,000 17- to 18-year olds on the Scholastic Assessment Test. *Intelligence, 34,* 479–486.

Jackson, J. M., & Padgett, V. R. (1982). With a little help from my friend: Social loafing and the Lennon-McCartney songs. *Personality and Social Psychology Bulletin, 8,* 672–677.

Jackson, K. M., & Sher, K. J. (2003). Alcohol use disorders and psychological distress: A prospective state-trait analysis. *Journal of Abnormal Psychology, 112,* 599–613.

Jackson, P. B., & Finney, M. (2002). Negative life events and psychological distress among young adults. *Social Psychology Quarterly, 65,* 186–201.

Jackson, R. D., LaCroix, A. Z., & Gass, M., Wallace, R. B., Robbins, J., Lewis, C.E., et al. (2006). Calcium plus vitamin D supplementation and risk of fractures. *New England Journal of Medicine, 354,* 669–683.

Jacobi, J. (1973). *The psychology of C. G. Jung.* New Haven, CT: Yale University Press.

Jacobs, D. M. (1992). *Secret life: First-hand accounts of UFO abductees.* New York: Simon & Schuster.

Jacobs, G. D., Heilbronner, R. L., & Stanley, J. M. (1984). The effects of short term flotation REST on relaxation: A controlled study. *Health Psychology, 3,* 99–112.

Jacobs, G. D., Pace-Schott, E. F., Stickgold, R., & Otto, M. W. (2004). Cognitive behavior therapy and pharmacotherapy for insomnia: A randomized controlled trial and direct comparison. *Archives of Internal Medicine, 164,* 1888–1896.

Jacobson, E. (1938). *Progressive relaxation.* Chicago: University of Chicago Press.

Jacobson, J., Mulick, J., & Schwartz, A. (1995). A history of facilitated communication. *American Psychologist, 50,* 750–765.

Jacobson, N. S., Dobson, K. S., Truax, P. A., Addis, M. E., Koerner, K., Gollan, J. K., et al. (1996). A component analysis of cognitive-behavioral treatment for depression. *Journal of Consulting and Clinical Psychology, 64,* 295–304.

Jacobson, S. W., Chiodo, L. M., & Jacobson, J. L. (1999). Breastfeeding effects on intelligence quotient in 4- and 11-year-old children. *Pediatrics, 103,* e71.

Jacoby, L. L., Kelley, C., Brown, J., & Jasechko, J. (1989). Becoming famous overnight: Limits on the ability to avoid unconscious influences of the past. *Journal of Personality & Social Psychology, 56,* 326–338.

Jacoby, L. L., & Rhodes, M. G. (2006). False remembering the aged. *Current Directions in Psychological Science, 15,* 49–53.

Jaffe, E. (2004). What was I thinking? Kahneman explains how intuition leads us astray. *Association for Psychological Science Observer, 17,* 5.

Jaffe, J. H. (1970). Drug addiction and drug abuse. In L. S. Goodan, & A. Gilman (Eds.), *The pharmacological basis of therapeutics* (4th ed.). New York: Macmillan.

James, W. (1890). *The principles of psychology.* Cambridge, MA: Harvard University Press.

Jameson, K. A., Highnote, S., & Wasserman, L. (2001). Richer color experience in observers with multiple photopigment opsin genes. *Psychonomic Bulletin and Review, 8,* 244–261.

Jamieson, G. A., & Sheehan, P. W. (2004). An empirical test of Woody and Bowers's dissociated-control theory of hypnosis. *International Journal of Clinical and Experimental Hypnosis, 52,* 232–249.

Jamison, K. R. (1989). Mood disorders and patterns of creativity in British writers and artists. *Psychiatry, 52,* 125–134.

Jamison, K. R. (1993). *Touched with fire: Manic-depressive illness and the artistic temperament.* New York: Free Press.

Janevic, M. R., & Connell, C. M. (2001). Racial, ethnic, and cultural differences in the dementia caregiving experience. *The Gerontologist, 41,* 334–347.

Janis, I. L. (1972). *Victims of groupthink.* Boston: Houghton Mifflin.

Janos, P. M., & Robinson, N. M. (1985). Psychosocial development in intellectually gifted children. In F. D. Horowitz & M. O'Brien (Eds.), *The gifted and talented: Developmental perspectives* (pp. 149–195). Washington, DC: American Psychological Association.

Jansen, K. L. R. (1991). Transcendental explanations and the near-death experience. *Lancet, 337,* 207–243.

Javornisky, G. (1979). Task content and sex differences in conformity. *Journal of Psychology, 108,* 213–220.

Jay, K., & Young, A. (1979). *Out of the closets: Voices of gay liberation.* New York: BJ Publishing Group.

Jefferson, T., Herbst, J. H., & McCrae, R. R. (1998). Associations between birth order and personality traits: Evidence from self-reports and observer ratings. *Journal of Research in Personality, 32,* 498–509.

Jenike, M. A., Baer, L., Ballantine, T., Martuza, R. L., Tynes, S., Giriunas, I., et al. (1991). Cingulotomy for refractory obsessive compulsive disorder. A long term follow-up of 33 patients. *Archives of General Psychiatry, 48,* 548–555.

Jenny, C., Roesler, T. A., & Poyer, K. L. (1994). Are children at risk for sexual abuse by homosexuals? *Pediatrics, 94,* 41–44.

Jensen, A. R. (1969). How much can we boost I.Q. and scholastic achievement? *Harvard Educational Review, 33,* 1–123.

Jensen, A. R. (1973). *Educability and group differences.* London: Methuen.

Jensen, A. R. (1977). Cumulative deficit of blacks in the rural south. *Developmental Psychology, 13,* 184–191.

Jensen, A. R. (1980). *Bias in mental testing.* New York: Free Press.

Jensen, A. R. (1993). Test validity: g versus "tacit knowledge." *Current Directions in Psychological Science, 2,* 9–10.

Jensen, A. R. (1993). Why is reaction time correlated with psychometric g? *Current Directions in Psychological Science, 2,* 53–56.

Jensen, A. R. (1998). *The g factor: The science of mental ability.* Westport, CT: Praeger.

Jensen, A. R. (2006). *Clocking the mind: Mental chronometry and individual differences.* Oxford, England: Elsevier.

Jensen, A. R., & McGurk, F. C. (1987). Black-White bias in "cultural" and "noncultural" test items. *Personality and Individual Differences, 8,* 295–301.

Jensen, P. S., Garcia, J. A., Glied, S., Crow, M., Foster, M., Schlander, M., et al. (2005). Cost-effectiveness of ADHD treatments: Findings from the multimodal treatment study of children with ADHD. *American Journal of Psychiatry, 162,* 1628–1636.

Jensvold, M. F., & Turner, S. M. (1988). The woman who hadn't been out of her house in 25 years. In J. A. Talbott & A. Z. A. Manevitz (Eds.), *Psychiatric house calls* (pp. 161–167). Washington, DC: American Psychiatric Association Press.

Jerison, H. J. (1983). The evolution of the mammalian brain as an information processing system. In J. F. Eisenberg and D. G. Kleiman (Eds.), Advances in the study of mammalian behavior. *America Society of Mammalogists Special Publication, 7,* 632–661.

Jick, H., Kayue, J. A., & Jick, S. S. (2004). Antidepressants and the risk of suicidal behaviors. *Journal of the American Medical Association, 292,* 338–343.

Joensson, E. G., Noethen, M. M., Gustavsson, J. P., Neidt, N., Forslund, K., Mattila-Evendon, et al. (1998). Lack of association between dopamine D4 receptor gene and personality traits. *Psychological Medicine, 28,* 985–989.

Jog, M. S., Kubota, Y., Connolly, C. I., Hillegaart, V., & Graybiel, A. M. (1999). Building neural representations of habits. *Science, 286,* 1745–1749.

Johanson, A., Risberg, J., Tucker, D. M., & Gustafson, L. (2006). Changes in frontal lobe activity with cognitive therapy for spider phobia. *Applied Neuropsychology, 13,* 34–41.

Johanson, C. E. Balster, R. L., & Bonese, K. (1976). Self-administration of psychomotor stimulant drugs: The effects of unlimited access. *Pharmacology, Biochemistry, and Behavior, 4,* 45–51.

John, O. P., & Robins, R. W. (1994). Accuracy and bias in self-perception: Individual differences in self-enhancement and the role of narcissism. *Journal of Personality and Social Psychology, 66,* 206–219.

Johnson, C. L., Tobin, D. L., & Steinberg, S. L. (1989). Etiological, developmental and treatment considerations for bulimia. Special issue: The bulimic college student: Evaluation, treatment and prevention. *Journal of College Student Psychotherapy, 3,* 57–73.

Johnson, F., & Wardle, J. (2005). Dietary restraint, body dissatisfaction, and psychological distress: A prospective analysis. *Journal of Abnormal Psychology, 114,* 119–125.

Johnson, G. B. (1966). Penis envy? Or pencil-needing? *Psychological Reports, 19,* 758.

Johnson, J. G., & Miller, S. M. (2005). Attributional, life-event, and affective predictors of onset of depression, anxiety, and negative attributional style. *Cognitive Therapy and Research, 14,* 417–430.

Johnson, J. S., & Newport, E. L. (1989). Critical period effects in second language learning: The influence of maturational state on the acquisition of English as a second language. *Cognitive Psychology, 21,* 60–99.

Johnson, M. H. (1992). Imprinting and the development of face recognition: From chick to man. *Current Directions in Psychological Science, 1,* 52–55.

Johnson, M. H. (1998). The neural basis of cognitive development. In W. Damon (Ed.), *Handbook of child psychology: Vol. 2: Cognition, perception, and language* (pp. 1–49). Hoboken, NJ: Wiley.

Johnson, M. K. (2001). The psychology of false memories. In N. J. Smeltzer & P. B. Baltes (Eds.), *International encyclopedia of social and behavioral sciences, Vol. 8* (pp. 5254–5259). Amsterdam, NY: Elsevier Science.

Johnson, M. K., Hashtroudi, S., & Lindsay, D. S. (1993). Source monitoring. *Psychological Bulletin, 114,* 3–28.

Johnson, M. K., & Raye, C. L. (1981). Reality monitoring. *Psychological Review, 88,* 67–85.

Johnson, P. (2005). Obesity: Epidemic or myth? *Skeptical Inquirer, 29,* 25-29.

Johnson, R. D., & Downing, L. L. (1979). Deindividuation and valence of cues: Effects on prosocial and anti-social behavior. *Journal of Personality and Social Psychology, 37,* 1532–1538.

Johnson, S., & Noonan, P. (1972). Effects of acceptance and reciprocation of self-disclosure on the development of trust. *Journal of Counseling Psychology, 19,* 411–4516.

Johnson, S. L., Sandrow, D., Meyer, B., Winters, R., Miller, I., Solomon D., et al. (2000). Increases in manic symptoms after life events involving goal attainment. *Journal of Abnormal Psychology, 109,* 721–727.

Johnston, L. D., O'Malley, P. M., & Bachman, J. G. (2002). *Monitoring the future national results on adolescent drug use: Overview of key findings, 2001.* Bethesda, MD: National Institute on Drug Abuse (DHHS/PHS).

Johnston, L. D., O'Malley, P. M., & Bachman, J. G. (2003). *Monitoring the future national results on adolescent drug use: Overview of key findings, 2002.* Bethesda, MD: National institute on Drug Abuse (DHHS/PHS).

Joiner, T. E., & Coyne, J. C. (1999). *The interactional nature of depression: Advances in interpersonal approaches.* Washington, DC: American Psychological Association.

Joiner, T. E., Heatherton, T. F., Rudd, M. D., & Schmidt, N. B. (1997). Perfectionism, perceived weight status, and bulimic symptoms: Two studies testing a diathesis stress model. *Journal of Abnormal Psychology, 106,* 145–153.

Jones, A. (1969). Stimulus-seeking behavior. In J. Zubek (Ed.), *Sensory deprivation: Fifteen years of research* (pp. 167–206). New York: Appleton-Century-Crofts.

Jones, B. E. (2003). Arousal systems. *Frontiers in Bioscience, 8,* 438–451.

Jones, E. E., & Harris, V. A. (1967). The attribution of attitudes. *Journal of Experimental Social Psychology, 3,* 1–24.

Jones, E. E., & Nisbett, R. E. (1972). The actor and the observer: Divergent perceptions of the causes of the behavior. In E. E. Jones, D. E. Kanouse, H. H. Kelley, R. E. Nisbett, S. Valins & B. Weiner (Eds.), *Attribution: Perceiving the causes of behavior* (pp. 79–94). Morristown, NJ: General Learning Press.

Jones, F., & Bright, J. (2001). *Stress: Myth, theory, and research.* Harlow, England: Prentice Hall.

Jones, J. C., & Barlow, D. H. (1990). The etiology of posttraumatic stress disorder. *Clinical Psychology Review, 10,* 299–328.

Jones, J. H. (1993). *Bad blood: The Tuskegee Syphilis Experiment* (2nd ed.). New York: Free Press.

Jones, L. L., Oudega, M., Bunge, M. B., & Tuszynski, M. H. (2001). Neurotrophic factors, cellular bridges and gene therapy for spinal cord injury. *Journal of Physiology, 15,* 83–89.

Jones, R. T. (1971). Tetrahydrocannabinol and the marijuana-induced social "high," or the effects of the mind on marijuana. In A. J. Singer (Vol. Ed.), *Annals of the New York Academy of Sciences, Vol. 191. Marijuana: Chemistry, pharmacology, and patterns of social use* (pp. 155–165). New York: New York Academy of Sciences.

Jordan, H. A. (1969). Voluntary intragastric feeding: Oral and gastric contributions to food intake and hunger in man. *Journal of Comparative and Physiological Psychology, 68,* 498–506.

Jorm, A. F., Korten, A. E., Jacomb, P. A., Chrisensen, H., Rodgers, B., & Pollitt, P. (1997). "Mental Health Literacy": A survey of the public's ability to recognize mental disorders and their beliefs about the effectiveness of treatment. *Medical Journal of Australia, 166,* 182.

Joseph, R. (1988). Dual mental functioning in a split-brain patient. *Journal of Clinical Psychology, 44,* 770–779.

Jost, J. T., Glaser, J., Sulloway, F., & Kruglanski, A. W. (2003). Political conservatism as motivated social cognition. *Psychological Bulletin, 129,* 339–375.

Jouvet, M. (1962). Recherches sur les structures nerveuses et les mechanismes responsables des different-es phases du sommeil physiologique. *Archives italiannes de Biologie, 100,* 125–206.

Juan, S. (2006). *The odd brain: Mysteries of our weird and wonderful brains explained.* Kansas City: Andrews McMeel Publishing.

Julien, R. M. (2004). *A primer of drug action* (10th ed.). San Francisco: W. H. Freeman.

Jung, C. G. (1936). *Archetypes and the collective unconscious.* Princeton, NJ: Princeton University Press.

Jung, C. G. (1950). On mandalas. In *The collected works of C. G. Jung* (Vol. 9ii). Princeton, NJ: Princeton University Press.

Jung, C. G. (1958). Flying saucers: A modern myth of things seen in the skies. In *The collected works of C. G. Jung* (Vol. 14). Princeton, NJ: Princeton University Press.

Jung, C. G. (1964). Approaching the unconscious. In C. G. Jung & M.-L. von Franz (Eds.), *Man and his symbols* (pp. 18–103). New York: Doubleday.

Jus, A., Jus, K., Gautier, J., Villenueve, A., Pires, P., Lachance, R., et al. (1973). Dream reports after reserpine in chronic lobotomized schizophrenic patients. *Vie médicale au Canada français, 2,* 843–848.

Kabat-Zinn, J. (2003). Mindfulness-based interventions in context: Past, present, and future. *Clinical Psychology: Science & Practice, 10,* 144–156.

Kagan, J. (1974). Discrepancy, temperament and infant distress. In M. Lewis & L. Rosenblum (Eds.), *The origins of fear* (pp. 229–248). New York: Wiley.

Kagan, J. (1976). Emergent themes in human development. *American Scientist, 64,* 186–196.

Kagan, J. (1994). *Three seductive ideas.* Cambridge, MA: Harvard University Press.

Kagan, J. (1998). Biology and the child. W. Damon & N. Eisenberg (Eds.), *Handbook of child psychology, Vol. 3: Social, emotional, and personality development* (5th ed., pp. 177–235). Hoboken, NJ: John Wiley.

Kagan, J., Reznick, J. S., & Snidman, N. (1988). Biological bases of childhood shyness. *Science, 240,* 167–171.

Kagan, J., Snidman, N., Arcus, D., & Reznick, J. S. (1994). *Galen's prophecy: Temperament in human nature.* New York: Basic Books.

Kageyama, T. (1999). Loudness in listening to music with portable headphone stereos. *Perceptual and Motor Skills, 88,* 423.

Kahill, S. (1984). Human figure drawing in adults: An update of the empirical evidence, 1967–1982. *Canadian Psychology, 25,* 395–410.

Kahneman, D. (2003). Maps of bounded rationality: Psychology for behavioral economics. *American Economic Review, 93,* 1449–1475.

Kahneman, D., Krueger, A., Schkade, D., Schwarz, N., & Stone, A. (2006). Would you be happier if you were richer? A focusing illusion. *Science, 312,* 1908–1910.

Kahneman, D., Slovic, P., & Tversky, A. (Eds.). (1982). *Judgment under uncertainty: Heuristics and biases.* New York: Cambridge University Press.

Kaiser, J., & Lutzenberger, W. (2005). Human gamma-band activity: A window to cognitive processing. *Neuroreport, 16,* 207–211.

Kaliouby, E., Teeters, A. E., & Picard, R. W. (2006). *An exploratory social-emotional prosthetic for autism spectrum disorders.* International Workshop on Wearable and Implantable Body Sensor Networks, p. 3, April 3–5, 2006, MIT Media Lab, Cambridge, MA.

Kamrin, M. A. (1988). *Toxicology: A primer on toxicology principles and applications.* Boca Raton, FL: Lewis Publishers.

Kandel, D., Yamaguchi, K., & Chen, K. (1992). Stages of progression in drug involvement from adolescence to adulthood: Further evidence of the Gateway theory. *Journal of Studies of Alcohol, 53,* 447–457.

Kandel, E. R. (2001). The molecular biology of memory storage: A dialogue between genes and synapses. *Science, 294,* 1030–1038.

Kanders, B. S., & Blackburn, G. L. (1992). Reducing primary risk factors by therapeutic weight loss. In T. A. Wadden & T. B. VanItallie (Eds.), *Treatment of the seriously obese patient* (pp. 213–230). New York: Guilford Press.

Kane, B. S., Shinohara, K., Neuhaus, J., Hudes, E. S., Goldberg, H., & Avins, A. L. (2006). Saw palmetto for benign prostatic hyperplasia. *New England Journal of Medicine, 354,* 557–566.

Kane, M. J., Hambrick, D. Z., & Conway, A. R. A. (2005). Working memory capacity and fluid intelligence are strongly related constructs: Comment on Ackerman, Beier, and Boyle (2004). *Psychological Bulletin, 131,* 66–71.

Kanner, A. D., Coyne, J. C., Schaefer, C., & Lazarus, R. S. (1981). Comparison of two modes of stress measurement: Daily hassles and uplifts versus major life events. *Journal of Behavioral Medicine, 4,* 1–39.

Kanzler, H. R., & Rosenthal, R. N. (2003). Dual diagnosis: Alcoholism and co-morbid psychiatric disorders. *American Journal of Addiction, 12*(Suppl. 1), 21–40.

Kaplan, H. S. (1977). Hypoactive sexual desire. *Journal of Sex and Marital Therapy, 3,* 3–9.

Kaplan, R. M. (1982). Nader's raid on the testing industry: Is it in the best interests of the consumer? *American Psychologist, 37,* 15–23.

Kaplan, R. M., & Saccuzzo, D. P. (2005). *Psychological testing: Principles, applications, and issues.* Belmont, CA: Thomson Wadsworth.

Kaptchuk, T. J., Statson, W. B., Davis, R. B., Legedza, A. R. T., Schnyer, R. N., Kerr, C. E., et al. (2006). Sham device versus inert pill: A randomized controlled trial comparing two placebo treatments for arm pain due to repetitive strain injury. *British Medical Journal, 18,* 391–397.

Karasek, R., & Theorell, T. (1990). *Health work: Stress, productivity and the reconstruction of life.* New York: Basic Books.

Karau, S. J., & Williams, K. D. (1993). Social loafing: A meta-analytic review and theoretical integration. *Journal of Personality and Social Psychology, 65,* 681–706.

Karlen, S. J., & Krubitzer, L. (2006). The evolution of the neocortex in mammals: Intrinsic and extrinsic contributions to the cortical phenotype. *Novartis Found Symposium 270,* 159–169.

Karlin, R. A., & Orne, M. T. (1996). Commentary on *Borawick v. Shay:* Hypnosis, social influence, incestuous child abuse, and satanic ritual abuse: The iatrogenic creation of horrific memories for the remote past. *Cultic Studies Journal, 13*(1), 42–94.

Karon, B. P. (1994). *Effective psychoanalytic therapy of schizophrenia and other severe disorders* (APA Videotape Series). Washington, DC: American Psychological Association.

Karon, B. P. (2000). A clinical interpretation of the Thematic Apperception Test, Rorschach, and other clinical data: A reexamination of the statistical versus clinical prediction. *Professional Psychology: Research and Practice, 31,* 230–233.

Kassin, S. (2004). *Psychology* (4th ed.). Upper Saddle River, NJ: Prentice Hall.

Kassin, S. M., Ellsworth, P. C., & Smith, V. L. (1989). The "general acceptance" of psychological research on eyewitness testimony: A survey of the experts. *American Psychologist, 44,* 1089–1098.

Kassin, S. M., & Gudjonsson, G. H. (2004). The psychology of confession: A review of the literature and issues. *Psychological Science in the Public Interest, 5,* 33–67.

Kassin, S. M., Tubb, V. A., Hosch, H. M., & Memon, A. (2001). On the "general acceptance" of eyewitness testimony research. *American Psychologist, 56,* 405–416.

Katz, D. A., & McHorney, C. A. (1998). Clinical correlates of insomnia in patients with chronic illness. *Archives of Internal Medicine, 158,* 1099–1107.

Katz, D. A., & McHorney, C. A. (2002). The relationship between insomnia and health-related quality of life in patients with chronic illness. *Journal of Family Practice, 51,* 229–235.

Katz, J. (1988). *Seductions of crime: Moral and sensual attractions in doing evil.* New York: Basic Books.

Katzev, R., & Brownstein, R. (1989). The influence of enlightenment on compliance. *Journal of Social Psychology, 129,* 335–347.

Katzman, D. K. (2005). Medical complications in adolescents with anorexia nervosa: A review of the literature. *International Journal of Eating Disorders, 37*(Suppl.), S52–S59.

Kayser, C., Petkov, C. I., Augath, M., & Logothetis, N. K. (2007). Functional imaging reveals visual modulation of specific fields in auditory cortex. *Journal of Neuroscience, 27,* 1824–1835.

Kazdin, A. E. (1978). The application of operant techniques in treatment, rehabilitation, and education. In S. L. Garfield & A. E. Bergin (Eds.), *Handbook of psychotherapy and behavior change* (2nd ed.). New York: John Wiley & Sons.

Kazdin, A. E. (2005). Treatment outcomes, common factors, and continued neglect of mechanisms of change. *Clinical Psychology: Science and Practice, 12,* 184–188.

Kazdin, A. E., & Hersen, M. (1980). The current status of behavior therapy. *Behavior Modification, 4,* 283–302.

Kazdin, A. E., Marciano, P. L., & Whitley, M. K. (2005). The therapeutic alliance in cognitive-behavioral treatment of children referred for oppositional, aggressive, and antisocial behavior. *Journal of Consulting and Clinical Psychology, 73,* 725–730.

Kazdin, A. E., & Wilcoxin, L. A. (1976). Systematic desensitization and nonspecific treatment effects: A methodological evaluation. *Psychological Bulletin, 83,* 729–758.

Keane, T. M., Zimering, R. T., & Cadell, J. M. (1985). A behavioral formulation of posttraumatic stress disorder in Vietnam veterans. *The Behavior Therapist, 8,* 9–12.

Keefe, R. S., Silverman, J. M., Mohs, R. C., Siever, L. J., Harvery, P. D., Friedman, L., et al. (1997). Eye tracking, attention, and schizotypal symptoms in nonpsychotic relatives of patients with schizophrenia. *Archives of General Psychiatry, 54,* 169–176.

Keefe, R., & Harvey, P. D. (1994). *Understanding schizophrenia: A guide to the new research on causes and treatment.* New York: Free Press.

Keel, P. K., & Klump, K. L. (2003). Are eating disorders culture-bound syndromes? Implications for conceptualizing their etiology. *Psychological Bulletin, 129,* 747–769.

Keen, S. (1986). *Faces of the enemy: Reflections of the hostile imagination.* San Francisco: Harper & Row.

Keinan, G., & Almagor, M. (1989). A reevaluation of the relationships between psychotherapeutic orientation and perceived personality characteristics. *Psychotherapy, 26,* 218–226.

Keith, S. J., Gunderson, J. G., Reifman, A., Buchsbaum, S., & Mosher, L. R. (1976). Special report: Schizophrenia, 1976. *Schizophrenia Bulletin, 2,* 510–565.

Keith, S. W., Redden, D. T., Katzmarzyk, P. T., Boggiano, M. M., Hanlon, E. C., Benca, R. M., et al. (2005). Putative contributors to the secular increase in obesity: exploring the roads less traveled. *International Journal of Obesity, 30,* 1585–1594.

Kelemen, D. (1999). The scope of teleological thinking in preschool children. *Cognition, 70,* 241–272.

Kellehear, A. (1993). Culture, biology, and the near-death experience: A reappraisal. *Journal of Nervous and Mental Disease, 181,* 148–156.

Keller, H. (1910). Before the soul dawn. *The world I live in* (pp. 113–14). New York: Century.

Kellner, R. (1985). Functional somatic symptoms and hypochondriasis. *Archives of General Psychiatry, 42,* 821–833.

Kelly, T. H., Cherek, D. R., Steinberg, J. L., & Robinson, D. (1988). Effects of provocation and alcohol on human aggressive behavior. *Drug and Alcohol Dependence, 21,* 105–112.

Kendall, T., Pilling, S., & Whittington, C. J. (2005). Are the SSRIs and atypical antidepressants safe and effective for children and adolescents? *Current Opinion in Psychiatry, 18,* 21–25.

Kendeigh, S. C. (1941). Territorial and mating behavior of the house wren. *Illinois Biographical Monographs, 18*(3) (Serial No. 120).

Kendell, R. E. (1975). The concept of disease and its implications for psychiatry. *British Journal of Psychiatry, 127,* 305–315.

Kendler, K. S. (2005). Toward a philosophical structure for psychiatry. *American Journal of Psychiatry, 162,* 433–440.

Kendler, K. S., & Diehl, S. R. (1993). The genetics of schizophrenia: A current, genetic-epidemiologic perspective. *Schizophrenia Bulletin, 19,* 261–285.

Kendler, K. S., Gardner, C. O., & Prescott, C. A. (2003). Personality and the experience of environmental adversity. *Psychological Medicine, 33,* 1193–1202.

Kendler, K. S., & Karkowski-Shuman, L. (1997). Stressful life events and genetic liability to major depression: Genetic control of exposure to the environment? *Psychological Medicine, 27,* 539–547.

Kendler, K. S., Neale, M. C., Kessler, R. C., Heath, A. C., & Eaves, L. J. (1993). A test of the equal-environment assumption in twin studies of psychiatric illness. *Behavior Genetics, 23,* 21–27.

Kendler, K. S., Neale, M. C., Kessler, R. C., Heath, A. C., & Eaves, L. J. (1993). Reliability of diagnosis and heritability. *Archives of General Psychiatry, 50,* 863–870.

Kendler, K. S., Thornton, L. M., & Gardner, C. O. (2000). Stressful life events and previous episodes in the etiology of major depression in women: An evaluation of the "kindling" hypothesis. *American Journal of Psychiatry, 157,* 1243–1251.

Kendler, K. S., Thornton, L. M., & Gardner, C. O. (2001). Genetic risk, number of previous depressive episodes, and stressful life events in predicting onset of major depression. *American Journal of Psychiatry, 158,* 582–586.

Kennedy, J. (2006). How the blind draw. *Scientific American Special Issue: Secrets of the Senses, 16*(3), 44–51.

Kennedy, S., Kiecolt-Glaser, J. K., & Glaser, R. (1990). Social support, stress, and the immune system. In B. R. Sarason, I. G. Sarason, & G. R. Pierce (Eds.), *Social support: An interactional view* (pp. 253–266). New York: Wiley.

Kennedy, S. H., Konarski, J. Z., Segal, Z. V., Lau, M. A., Bieling, P. J., McIntyre, R. S., et al. (2007). Differences in brain glucose metabolism between responders to CBT and Venlafaxine in a 16-week randomized controlled trial. *American Journal of Psychiatry, 164,* 778–788.

Kenrick, D. T., & Funder, D. C. (1988). Profiting from controversy: Lessons from the person-situation debate. *American Psychologist, 43,* 23–34.

Kenrick, D. T., Neuberg, S. L., & Cialdini, R. B. (2005). *Social psychology: Unraveling the mystery* (3rd ed.). Boston: Allyn & Bacon.

Kenrick, D. T., Neuberg, S. L., & Cialdini, R. B. (2005). *Social psychology: Unraveling the mystery* (3rd ed). Boston: Allyn & Bacon.

Kenrick, N. E. (1997). *Dispelling misconceptions of psychotherapy: A videotaped guide for incoming clients.* Unpublished doctoral dissertation: California School of Professional Psychology, Berkeley, CA.

Kent, R. D., & Miolo, G. (1995). Phonetic abilities in the first year of life. In P. Flether & B. MacWhinney (Eds.), *The handbook of child language* (pp. 303–334). San Diego, CA: Academic Press.

Keppel, G., & Underwood, B. J. (1962). Proactive inhibition in short-term retention of single items. *Journal of Verbal Learning and Verbal Behavior, 1,* 153–161.

Kernberg, O. (1975). *Borderline conditions and pathological narcissism.* New York: Jason Aronson.

Kernberg, O. F. (1967). Borderline personality organization. *Journal of American Psychoanalytical Association, 15,* 641–685.

Kessler, R., Price, R., & Wortman, C. (1985). Social factors in psychopathology: Stress, social support and coping processes. *Annual Review of Psychology, 36,* 351–372.

Kessler, R., Sonnega, A., Bromet, E., Hughes, M., & Nelson, C. (1995). Post-traumatic stress disorder in the National Comorbidity Survey. *Archives of General Psychiatry, 52,* 1048–1060.

Kessler, R. C., Berglund, P., Demler, O., Jin, R., Koretz, D., Merikangas, K. R., et al. (2003). The epidemiology of major depressive disorder: Results from the National Comorbidity Survey Replication (NCS-R). *Journal of the American Medical Association, 289,* 3095–3105.

Kessler, R. C., Berglund, P., Demler, O., Jin, R., & Walters, E. E. (2005). Lifetime prevalence and age-of-onset distributions of DSM-IV disorders in the National Comorbidity Survey Replication. *Archives of General Psychiatry, 62,* 593–602.

Kessler, R. C., McGonagale, K. A., Zhao, S., Nelson, C. B., Hughes, M., Eshleman, S., et al. (1994). Lifetime and 12-month prevalence of DSM-III-R psychiatric disorders in the United States: Results from the National Comorbidity Survey. *Archives of General Psychiatry, 51,* 8–19.

Kessler, R. C., Soukup, J., Davis, R. B., Foster, D. F., Wilkey, S. A., van Rompay, M. I., et al. (2001). The use of complementary and alternative therapies to treat anxiety and depression in the United States. *American Journal of Psychiatry, 158,* 289–294.

Keuzenkamp, S., Bos, D., Duyvendak, J. W., & Hekma, G. (2006). *Acceptance of homosexuality in the Netherlands. Ministry of Health, Welfare, and Sport.* The Hague, Netherlands: Social and Cultural Planning Bureau.

Kevles, D. J. (1985). *In the name of eugenics: Genetics and the uses of human heredity.* New York: Knopf.

Key, W. B. (1973). *Subliminal seduction.* Englewood Cliffs, NJ: Signet.

Keyes, C. L. M., & Haidt, J. (Eds.). (2003). *Flourishing: Positive psychology and the life well lived.* Washington, DC: American Psychological Association.

Keys, A., Brozek, J., Henschel, A., Mickelsen, O., & Taylor, H. L. (1950). *The biology of human starvation* (2 vols.). Minneapolis, MN: University of Minnesota Press.

Khuchua, Z., Wozniak, D. F., Bardgett, M. E., Yue, Z., McDonald, M., Boero, J., et al. (2003). Deletion of the N-terminus of murine map2 by gene targeting disrupts hippocampal ca1 neuron architecture and alters contextual memory. *Neuroscience, 119,* 101–111.

Kiecolt-Glaser, J. K., Marucha, P. T., Malarkey, W. B., Mercado, A., M., & Glaser, R. (1995). Slowing of wound healing by psychological stress. *Lancet, 346,* 1194–1196.

Kiecolt-Glaser, J. K., McGuire, L., Robles, T. F., & Glaser, R. (2002). Psychoneuroimmunology: Psychological influences on immune function and health. *Journal of Consulting and Clinical Psychology, 70,* 537–547.

Kiesler, C. A., & Kiesler, S. B. (1969). *Conformity.* Menlo Park. CA: Addison-Wesley.

Kihlstrom, J. F. (1987). The cognitive unconscious. *Science, 237,* 1445–1452.

Kihlstrom, J. F. (1992). Hypnosis: A sesquicentennial essay. *International Journal of Clinical and Experimental Hypnosis, 40,* 301–314.

Kihlstrom, J. F. (1997). *Philosophical Transactions of the Royal Society: Biological Sciences* as part of a special issue, L. R. Squire & D. L. Schacter (Eds.), *Biological and Psychological Perspectives on Memory and Memory Disorders, 372,* 1727–1732.

Kihlstrom, J. F. (1998). Dissociations and dissociation theory in hypnosis: Comment on Kirsch & Lynn (1998). *Psychological Bulletin, 123,* 186–191.

Kihlstrom, J. F. (2003). The fox, the hedgehog, and hypnosis. *International Journal of Clinical & Experimental Hypnosis, 51,* 166–189.

Kihlstrom, J. F. (2005). Dissociative disorders. In S. Nolen-Hoeksema, T. D. Cannon, & T. Widiger (Eds.), *Annual Review of Clinical Psychology, 1,* 227–254.

Kilham, W., & Mann, L. (1974). Level of destructive obedience as a function of transmitter and executant roles in the Milgram obedience paradigm. *Journal of Personality and Social Psychology, 29,* 696–702.

Kilmartin, C. (2006). Depression in men: Communication, diagnosis and therapy. *The Journal of Men's Health & Gender, 2,* 95–99.

Kim, H., & Marcus, H. R. (1999). Deviance or uniqueness, harmony or conformity? A cultural analysis. *Journal of Personality and Social Psychology, 77,* 785–800.

Kim, J. H. S., Relkin, N. R., Lee, K. M., & Hirsch, J. (1997). Distinct cortical areas associated with native and second languages. *Nature, 388,* 171–174.

Kimble, G. A. (1989). Psychology from the standpoint of a generalist. *American Psychologist, 44,* 491–499.

Kimble, G. A., Wertheimer, M., & White, C. L. (Eds.). (1991). *Portraits of pioneers in psychology.* Hillsdale, NJ: Erlbaum.

Kimura, D. (1999). *Sex and cognition.* Cambridge, MA: MIT Press.

King, A. C., Houle, T., deWit, H., Holdstock, L., & Schuster, A. (2002). Biphasic alcohol response differs in heavy versus light drinkers. *Alcoholism: Clinical and Experimental Research, 26,* 827–835.

King, D., Grizeau, R., Bendel, R., & Delarond, S.R. (1998). Smoking behavior among French and American women. *Preventive Medicine, 27,* 520–529.

King, J. E., & Figueredo, A. J. (1997). The five-factor model plus dominance in chimpanzee personality. *Journal of Research in Personality, 31,* 257–271.

Kinney, J., & Leaton, G. (1995). *Loosening the grip: A handbook of drug information* (5th ed.). St. Louis, MO: C. V. Mosby.

Kinney, J., & Leaton, G. (1995). *Loosening the grip: A handbook of alcohol information* (5th ed.). St. Louis, MO: Mosby.

Kinsey, A. C., Pomeroy, W. B., & Martin, C. E. (1948). *Sexual behavior in the human male.* Philadelphia: W. B. Saunders.

Kinsey, A. C., Pomeroy, W. B., Martin, C. E., & Gebhard, P. H. (1953). *Sexual behavior in the human female.* Philadelphia: W. B. Saunders.

Kippes, C., & Garrison, C. B. (2006). Are we in the midst of an autism epidemic? A review of prevalence data. *Missouri Medicine, 103*(1), 65–68.

Kircher, J. C., Horowitz, S. W., & Raskin, D. C. (1988). Meta-analysis of mock crime studies of the control question polygraph technique. *Law and Human Behavior, 12,* 79–90.

Kirk, J. M., Doty, P., & deWit, H. (1998). Effects of expectancies on subjective responses to oral delta-9-tetrahydrocannabinol. *Pharmacology, Biochemistry, and Behavior, 59,* 287–293.

Kirk, S. A., & Kutchins, H. (1992). *The selling of DSM: The rhetoric of science in psychiatry.* Hawthorne, NY: Aldine de Gruyter.

Kirmayer, L. J., & Young, A. (1999). Culture and context in the evolutionary concept of mental disorder. *Journal of Abnormal Psychology, 108,* 446–452.

Kirsch, I. (1990). *Changing expectations: A key to effective psychotherapy.* Pacific Grove, CA: Brooks/Cole.

Kirsch, I. (1991). The social learning theory of hypnosis. In S. J. Lynn & J. Rhue (Eds.), *Theories of hypnosis: Current models and perspectives* (pp. 439–466). New York: Guilford Press.

Kirsch, I. (1994) Clinical hypnosis as a nondeceptive placebo: Empirically derived techniques. *American Journal of Clinical Hypnosis, 37,* 95–106.

Kirsch, I. (1999). *How expectancies shape experience.* Washington, DC: American Psychological Association.

Kirsch, I. (2003). Hidden administration as ethical alternatives to the balanced placebo design. *Prevention & Treatment, 6,* Article 5. Available from http://journals.apa.org/prevention/volume6/pre0060005c.html.

Kirsch, I., & Council, J. R. (1992). Situational and personality correlates of suggestibility. In E. Fromm & M. Nash (Eds.), *Contemporary hypnosis research* (pp. 267–292). New York: Guilford.

Kirsch, I., Council, J. R., & Mobayed, C. (1987). Imagery and response expectancy as determinants of hypnotic behavior. *British Journal of Experimental and Clinical Hypnosis, 4,* 25–31.

Kirsch, I., & Lynn, S. J. (1995). The altered state of hypnosis: Changes in the theoretical landscape. *American Psychologist, 50,* 846–858.

Kirsch, I., & Lynn, S. J. (1998). Dissociation theories of hypnosis. *Psychological Bulletin, 123,* 100–115.

Kirsch, I., & Lynn, S. J. (1999). Automaticity in clinical psychology. *American Psychologist, 54,* 504–515.

Kirsch, I., Lynn, S. J., Vigorito, M., & Miller, R. R. (2004). The role of cognition in classical and operant conditioning. *Journal of Clinical Psychology, 60,* 369–392.

Kirsch, I., Montgomery, G., & Sapirstein, G. (1995). Hypnosis as an adjunct to cognitive behavioral psychotherapy: A meta-analysis. *Journal of Consulting and Clinical Psychology, 63,* 214–220.

Kirsch, I., Moore, T., Scoboria, A., & Nicholls, S. (2002). The emperor's new drugs: An analysis of antidepressant medication data submitted to the U.S. Food and Drug Administration. *Prevention & Treatment, 5,* Article 23, Retrieved from: http://journals.apa.org/prevention/volume25/pre0050023a.

Kirsch, I., & Sapirstein, G. (1998). Listening to Prozac but hearing placebo: A meta-analysis of antidepressant medication. *Prevention & Treatment, 1,* art. 0002a. Retrieved February 15, 2003, from http://journals.apa.org/prevention/volume1/pre0010002a.html.

Kirsch, I., & Scoboria, A. (2001). Apples, oranges, and placebos: Heterogeneity in a meta-analysis of placebo effects. *Advances in Mind-Body Medicine, 17,* 307–309.

Kirsch, I., Silva, C. E., Carone, J. E., Johnston, J. D., & Simon, B. (1989). The surreptitious observation design: An experimental paradigm for distinguishing artifact from essence in hypnosis. *Journal of Abnormal Psychology, 98,* 132–136.

Kirschen, M. P., Jaworska, A., & Illes, J. (2006). Subjects' expectations in neuroimaging research. *Journal of Magnetic Resonance Imaging, 23,* 205–209.

Kirschner, P. A., Sweller, J., & Clark, R. E. (2006). Why minimal guidance during instruction does not work: An analysis of the failure of constructivist, discovery, problem-based, experiential, and inquiry-based teaching. *Educational Psychologist, 41,* 75–86.

Kish, S. J. (2002). How strong is the evidence that brain serotonin neurons are damaged in human users of ecstacy? *Pharmacology, Biochemistry, and Behavior, 71,* 845–855.

Kisker, G. W. (1964). *The disorganized personality.* New York: McGraw-Hill.

Kistner, J. A., David-Ferdon, C. F., Repper, K. K., & Joiner, T. E. Jr. (2006). Bias and accuracy of children's perceptions of peer acceptance: Prospective associations with depressive symptoms. *Journal of Abnormal Child Psychology, 34,* 349–361.

Klahr, D., & MacWhinney, B. (1998). Information processing. In W. Damon (Ed.), *Handbook of child psychology: Vol. 2: Cognition, perception, and language* (pp. 631–678). Hoboken, NJ: Wiley.

Klahr, D., & Nigam, M. (2004). The equivalence of learning paths in early science instruction: Effects of direct instruction and discovery learning. *Psychological Science, 15,* 661–667.

Klaus, M. H., & Kennell, J. H. (1976). *Maternal-infant bonding.* St. Louis, MO: Mosby.

Klein, D. F. (1998). Listening to meta-analysis but hearing bias. *Prevention & Treatment, 1,* art. 0006c. Retrieved February 15, 2003, from http://journals.apa.org/prevention/volume1/pre0010006c.html.

Klein, D. F. (1998). Listening to meta-analysis but hearing bias. *Prevention & Treatment, 1,* Article 0006c, Retrieved May 12, 2006, from http://journals.apa.org/prevention/volume0001/pre0010006c.html.

Klein, M. (1932). *The psychoanalysis of children.* London: Hogarth Press.

Klein, M. (1948). *Contributions to psychoanalysis.* London: Hogarth Press.

Klein, M. (1949). *The psycho-analysis of children.* London: Hogarth.

Klein, M. H., Kolden, G. G., Michels, J., & Chisholm-Stockard, S. (2002). Effective elements of the therapy relationship: Congruence/genuineness. In J. C. Norcross (Ed.), *Psychotherapy relationships that work: Therapists' relational contributions to effective psychotherapy* (pp. 195–215). London: Oxford University Press.

Klein, P. D. (1997). Multiplying the problems of intelligence by eight: A critique of Gardner's theory. *Canadian Journal of Education, 22,* 377–394.

Klein, S., Burke, L. E., Bray, G. A., Blair, S., Allison, D. B., Pi-Sunyer, X., et al. (2004). AHA scientific statement: Clinical implications of obesity with specific focus on cardiovascular disease. *Circulation, 1110,* 2952–2967.

Kleinknecht, R. A., Dinnel, D. L., Kleinknecht, E. E., Hiruma, N., & Harada, N. (1997). Cultural factors in social anxiety: A comparison of social phobia and Taijin Kyofusho. *Journal of Anxiety Disorders, 11,* 157–177.

Kleinknecht, R. A., Dinnel, D. L., Tanouye-Wilson, S., & Lonner, W. J. (1994). Cultural variation in social anxiety and phobia: A study of Taijin Kyofusho. *The Behavior Therapist, 17*(8), 175–178.

Kleinman, A. (1988). *Rethinking psychiatry: From cultural category to personal experience.* New York: Free Press.

Kleinman, P. H., Wish, E. D., Deren, S., Rainone, G., & Morehouse, E. (1988). Daily marijuana use and problem behaviors among adolescents. *International Journal of Addictions, 23,* 87–107.

Klerman, G. L., & Weissman, M. M. (Eds.). (1993). *New applications of interpersonal psychotherapy.* Washington, DC: American Psychiatric Press.

Klerman, G. L., Weissman, M. M., Rounsaville, B. J., & Chevron, E. S. (1984). *Interpersonal psychotherapy of depression.* New York: Basic Books.

Klimoski, R. (1992). Graphology in personnel selection. In B. L. Beyerstein & D. F. Beyerstein (Eds.), *The write stuff: Evaluations of graphology—The study of handwriting analysis* (pp. 232–268). Buffalo, NY: Prometheus Books.

Klinger (2000). Daydreams. In A.E. Kazdin (Ed.), *Encyclopedia of psychology.* New York: Oxford University Press/American Psychological Association.

Klink, M., & Quan, S. F. (1987). Prevalence of reported sleep disturbances in a general adult population and their relationship to obstructive airways diseases. *Chest, 91,* 540–546.

Kluft, R. P. (1984). Multiple personality in childhood. *Psychiatric Clinics of North America, 7,* 121–134.

Kluger, A. N., & Tikochinsky, J. (2001). The error of accepting the "theoretical" null hypothesis: The rise, fall and resurrection of common sense hypotheses in psychology. *Psychological Bulletin, 127,* 408–423.

Klusmann, D. (2002). Sexual motivation and the duration of partnership. *Archives of Sexual Behavior, 31,* 275–287.

Knight, J. R., Wechsler, H., Kuo, M., Seibring, M., Weitzman, E. R., & Schuckit, M. (2002). Alcohol abuse and dependence among U.S. college students. *Journal of Studies on Alcohol, 63,* 263–270.

Knoth, R., Boyd, K., & Singer, B. (1988). Empirical tests of sexual selection theory: Predictions of sex differences in onset, intensity, and time course of sexual arousal. *Journal of Sex Research, 24,* 73–89.

Knox, D., Zusman, M., & Nieves, W. (1997). College students' homogamous preferences for a date and mate. *College Student Journal, 31,* 445–448.

Knox, J. J., Coppieters, M. W., & Hodges, P. W. (2006). Do you know where your arm is if you think your head has moved? *Experimental Brain Research, 173,* 94–101.

Knutson, B., Wolkowitz, O. M., Cole, S. W., Chan, T., Moore, E. A., Johnson, R. C., et al. (1988). Selective alteration of personality and social behavior by serotonergic intervention. *American Journal of Psychiatry, 155,* 373–379.

Kobasa, S. C., Hiler, R. R. J., & Maddi, S. R. (1979). Who stays healthy under stress? *Journal of Occupational Medicine, 21,* 595–598.

Kobasa, S. C., Maddi, S. R., & Kahn, S. (1982). Hardiness and health: A prospective study. *Journal of Personality and Social Psychology, 42,* 168–177.

Koch, C. (1993). Computational approaches to cognition: The bottom-up view. *Current Opinion in Neurobiology, 3,* 203–208.

Kochanek, K. D., Murphy, S. L., Anderson, R. N., & Scott, C. (2002). *Deaths: Final data for 2002.* National Vital Statistics Reports, Vol. 53, No. 5. Hyattsville, MD: National Center for Health Statistics.

Kochanska, G., Gross, J. N., Lin, M.-H., & Nichols, K. E. (2002). Guilt in young children: Development, determinants, and relations with a broader system of standards. *Child Development, 73,* 461–482.

Kocsis, R. N., Hayes, A. F., & Irwin, H. J. (2002). Investigative experience and accuracy in psychological profiling of a violent crime. *Journal of Interpersonal Violence, 17,* 811–823.

Koenig, H. G., McCullough, M. E., & Larson, D. B. (2001). *Handbook of religion and health.* New York: Oxford University Press.

Koerner, B. I. (2002, November 1). Lie detector roulette. *Mother Jones.* Retrieved from http://www.newamerica.net/publications/articles/2002/lie_detector_roulette.

Kohlberg, L. (1965, March 26). *Relationships between the development of moral judgment and moral conduct.* Paper presented at the Annual Meeting of the Society for Research in Child Development, Minneapolis, MN.

Kohlberg, L. (1976). Moral stages and moralization: The cognitive-developmental approach. In T. Lickona (Ed.), *Moral development and behavior: Theory, research and social issues* (pp. 31–53). New York: Holt, Rinehart and Winston.

Kohlberg, L. (1981). *The philosophy of moral development: Moral stages and the idea of justice.* San Francisco: Harper & Row.

Kohlberg, L., & Turiel, E. (1971). Moral development and moral education. In G. Lesser (Ed.), *Psychology and educational practice.* Chicago: Scott Foresman.

Kohn, A. (1993). *Punished by rewards: The trouble with gold stars, incentive plans, As, praise and other bribes.* Boston: Houghton Mifflin.

Kohut, H. (1971). *The analysis of the self.* New York: International Universities Press.

Koivisto, M., & Revonsuo, A. (2007). How meaning shapes seeing. *Psychological Science, 18,* 845-849.

Kollins, S. H. (2003). Delay discounting is associated with substance use in college students. *Addictive Behaviors, 28,* 1167–1173.

Kollman, D. M., Brown, T. A., Liverant, G. I., & Hofmann, S. G. (2006). A taxometric investigation of the latent structure of social anxiety disorder in outpatients with anxiety and mood disorders. *Depression and Anxiety, 23,* 190–199.

Konner, M. (1990). *Why the reckless survive—And other secrets of human nature.* New York: Viking.

Kopsowa, A. J. (2003). Divorce and suicide risk. *Journal of Epidemiology and Community Health, 57,* 993.

Koriat, A., & Bjork, R. A. (2005). Illusions of competence in monitoring one's knowledge during study. *Journal of Experimental Psychology: Learning, Memory, and Cognition, 31,* 187–194.

Kosfeld, M., Heinrichs, M., Zaks, P., Fischbacher, U., & Fehr, E. (2005). Oxytocin increases trust in humans. *Nature, 435,* 673–676.

Kounios, J., Frymiare, J. L., Bowden, E. M., Fleck, J. I., Subramaniam, K., Parrish, T. B., et al. (2006). The prepared mind: Neural activity prior to problem presentation predicts subsequent solution by sudden insight. *Psychological Science, 17,* 882–890.

Kozorovitskiy, Y., & Gould, E. (2003). Adult neurogenesis: A mechanism for brain repair? *Journal of Clinical & Experimental Neuropsychology, 25,* 721–732.

Krackow, E., Lynn, S. J., & Payne, D. (2005–2006). Death of Princess Diana: The effects of memory enhancement procedures on flashbulb memories. *Imagination, Cognition, and Personality, 25,* 197–220.

Krall, G. T., & Valerie L. (1990). The measurement of stress by voice analysis. *Journal of Social Behavior and Personality, 5/6,* 723–731.

Kramer, P. (2007). *Freud: Inventor of the modern mind.* New York: HarperCollins.

Kramer, P. D. (1993). *Listening to Prozac.* New York: Penguin Books.

Kratzig, G. P., & Arbuthnott, K. D. (2006). Perceptual learning style and learning proficiency: A test of the hypothesis. *Journal of Educational Psychology, 98,* 238–246.

Kraus, S. J. (1995). Attitudes and the prediction of behaviour: A meta-analysis of the empirical literature. *Personality and Social Psychology Bulletin, 21,* 58–75.

Kraut, R. E., & Poe, D. (1980). Behavioral roots of person perception: The deception judgments of customs inspectors and laymen. *Journal of Personality and Social Psychology, 39,* 784–798.

Krauthammer C. (1987, January 12). Casablanca In color? *Time.* Retrieved October 20, 2007, from *http://www.time.com/time/magazine/article /0,9171,963207,00.html.*

Krebs, D. L., & Denton, K. (2005). Toward a more pragmatic approach to morality: A critical evaluation of Kohlberg's model. *Psychological Review, 112,* 629–649.

Kreppner, J. M., O'Connor, T. G., Rutter, M., & English and Romanian Adoptees Study Team. (2001). Is inattention/hyperactivity a deprivation disorder? *Journal of Abnormal Child Psychology, 29,* 513–528.

Kreschel, P. J. (1990). John B. Watson at J. Walter Thompson: The legitimization of 'science' in advertising. *Journal of Advertising, 19,* 49–60.

Kristensen, P., & Bjerkedal, T. (2007). Explaining the relation between birth order and intelligence. *Science, 316,* 1717.

Krubitzer, L., & Kaas, J. (2005). The evolution of the neocortex in mammals: How is phenotypic diversity generated? *Current Opinion in Neurobiology, 15,* 444–453.

Krueger, J. I., & Funder, D. C. (2004). Towards a balanced social psychology: Causes, consequences and cures for the problem-seeking approach to social behavior and cognition. *Behavioral and Brain Sciences* 27, 313–327.

Krueger I. J., & Mueller A. R. (2002). Unskilled, unaware, or both? The better-than-average heuristic and statistical regression predict errors in estimates of own performance. *Journal of Personality and Social Psychology, 82,* 180–188.

Krueger, R., & Piasecki, T., M. (2002). Toward a dimensional and psychometrically-informed approach to conceptualizing psychopathology. *Behaviour Research and Therapy, 40,* 485–499.

Krueger, R. F., Hicks, B. M., & McGue, M. (2001). Altruism and antisocial behavior: Independent tendencies, unique personality correlates, distinct etiologies. *Psychological Science, 12,* 397–402.

Krueger, R. F., Hicks, B. M., & McGue, M. (2001). Altruism and antisocial behavior: Independent tendencies, unique personality correlates, distinct etiologies. *Psychological Science, 12,* 397–402.

Krueger, R. F., Schmutte, P. S., Caspi, A., Moffitt, T. E., Campbell, K, & Silva P. A. (1994). Personality traits are linked to crime among men and women: Evidence from a birth cohort. *Journal of Abnormal Psychology, 103,* 328–338.

Kruger, J., & Dunning, D. (1999). Unskilled and unaware of it: How difficulties in recognizing one's own incompetence lead to inflated self-assessments. *Journal of Personality and Social Psychology, 77,* 1121–1134.

Kruger, J., Epley, N., Parker, J., & Ng, Z. (2005). Egocentrism over email: Can we communicate as well as we think? *Journal of Personality and Social Psychology, 89,* 925–936.

Kruger, J., Savitsky, K., & Gilovich, T. (1999). Superstition and the regression effect. *Skeptical Inquirer, 23,* 24–29.

Kuhn, D. (2007). Jumping to conclusions. *Scientific American Mind, 18*(1), 44–51.

Kuhn, D., & Dean, D. (2005). Is developing scientific thinking all about learning to control variables? *Psychological Science, 16,* 866–870.

Kuhn, D., Garcia-Mila, M., Zohar, A., & Andersen, C. (1995). Strategies of knowledge acquisition. *Monographs of the Society for Research in Child Development, 60,* Serial No. 4.

Kuleshnyk, I. (1984). The Stockholm syndrome: Toward an understanding. *Social Action & the Law, 10,* 37–42.

Kulik, J. A., Bangert-Drowns, R. L., & Kulik, C.-L. C. (1984). Effectiveness of coaching for aptitude tests. *Psychological Bulletin, 95,* 179–188.

Kumari, V. (2006). Do psychotherapies produce neurobiological effects? *Acta Neuropsychiatrica, 18,* 61–70.

Kuncel, N. R., & Hezlett, S. A. (2007). Standardized tests predict graduate students' success. *Science, 315,* 1080–1081.

Kunda, Z. (1999). *Social cognition: Making sense of people.* Cambridge, MA: The MIT Press.

Kunst-Wilson, W. R., & Zajonc, R. B. (1980). Affective discrimination of stimuli that cannot be recognized. *Science, 207,* 557–558.

Kurth, T., Gaziano, J. M., Berger, K., Kase, C. S., Rexrode, K. M., Cook, N. R., et al. (2003). Body mass index and the risk of stroke in men. *Archives of Internal Medicine, 163,* 2557–2662.

Kurtus, R. (2000). I walked on fire and lived to tell about it. Retrieved May 24, 2007, from http://www.school-for-champions.com/excellence/firewalk.htm.

Kurtz, P. (1991). *The transcendental temptation.* Buffalo, NY: Prometheus Books.

Kushner, H. I. (1993). Taking Erikson's identity seriously: Psychoanalyzing the psychohistorian. *Psychohistory Review, 22,* 7–34.

Kushner, M. (1968). The operant control of intractable sneezing. In C. D. Spielberger, R. Fox, & B. Masterson (Eds.), *Contributions to general psychology.* New York: Roland Press.

LaBerge, D., & Samuels, S. J. (1974). Towards a theory of automatic information processing in reading. *Cognitive Psychology, 6,* 293–323.

LaBerge, S. (1980). *Lucid dreaming: An exploratory study of consciousness during sleep.* Unpublished doctoral dissertation, Stanford University, Stanford, CA.

Laberge, S. (2000). Lucid dreaming: Evidence and methodology. *Behavioral and Brain Sciences, 23,* 962–963.

LaBerge, S., Nagel, L., Dement, W., & Zarcone, V. (1981). Lucid dreaming verified by volitional communication during REM sleep. *Perceptual and Motor Skills, 52,* 727–732.

LaBerge, S., & Rheingold, H. (1990). *Exploring the world of lucid dreaming.* New York: Ballantine.

Labott, S. M. (2004). COPD and other respiratory diseases. In P. Camic & S. Knight (Eds.), *Clinical handbook of health psychology* (pp. 59–74). Cambridge, MA: Hogrefe & Huber Publishers.

Lacasse J. R., & Leo, J. (2005). Serotonin and depression: A disconnect between the advertisements and the scientific literature. *PLoS Medicine, 2,* 101–106.

LaChaussee, J. L., Kissileff, H. R., Walsh, B. T., & Hadigan, C. M. (1992). The single item meal as a measure of binge-eating behavior in patients with bulimia nervosa. *Physiology & Behavior, 51,* 593–600.

LaFreniere, P. J., & Sroufe, L. A. (1985). Profiles of peer competence in the preschool: Interrelations among measures, influence of social ecology, and relation to attachment history. *Development Psychology, 21,* 56–69.

LaFreniere, P. L., Strayer, F. F., & Gauthier, R. (1984). The emergence of same-sex affiliative preference among preschool peers: A developmental/ethological perspective. *Child Development, 55,* 1958–1965.

Lagercrantz, H., & Slotkin, T. A. (1986). The "stress" of being born. *Scientific American, 254,* 100–107.

Lalich, J. (2004). *Bounded choice: True believers and charismatic cults.* Berkeley, CA: University of California Press.

Lalumière, M. L., Blanchard, R., & Zucker, K. L. (2000). Sexual orientation and handedness in men and women: A meta-analysis. *Psychological Bulletin, 126,* 575–592.

Lamal, P. A. (1979). College students' common beliefs about psychology. *Teaching of Psychology, 6,* 155–158.

Lamb, H. R., & Bachrach, L. L. (2001). Some perspectives on deinstitutionalization. *Psychiatric Services, 52,* 1039–1045.

Lamb, M. E. (1975). Fathers: The forgotten contributors to child development. *Human Development, 18,* 245–266.

Lamb, M. E., Thompson, R. A., Gardner, W. P., Charnov, E. L., & Estes, D. (1984). Security of infantile attachment as assessed in the "strange situation": Its study and biological interpretation. *Behavioral and Brain Sciences, 7,* 127–171.

Lambert, M. J. (2003). *Bergin and Garfield's handbook of psychotherapy and behavior change.* New York: John Wiley.

Lambert, M. J., & Ogles, B. M. (2004). The efficacy and effectiveness of psychotherapy. In M. J. Lambert (Ed.), *Bergin and Garfield's handbook of psychotherapy and behavior change* (5th ed., pp. 139–193). New York: Wiley.

Lampl, M., Veldhuis, J. D., & Johnson, M. L. (1992). Saltation and stasis—A model of human growth. *Science, 258,* 801–803.

Landers, D. M. (1998). Exercise and mental health. *Exercise Science, 7,* 131–146.

Landrum, E. (2001, Fall). I'm getting my bachelor's degree in psychology: What can I do with it? *Eye on Psi Chi, 6*(1), 22–24.

Lang, A. R., Goeckner, D. J., Adesso, V. J., & Marlatt, G. A. (1975). Effects of alcohol on aggression in male social drinkers. *Journal of Abnormal Psychology, 84,* 509–518.

Lange, C. G. (1885). *Om sindsbevaegelser: et psyko-fysiologisk studie.* Kjbenhavn: Jacob Lunds. Reprinted in C. G. Lange and W. James (Eds.), *The emotions.* I. A. Haupt (Trans.). Baltimore: Williams & Wilkins.

Langer, E. J., & Rodin, J. (1976). The effects of choice and enhanced personal responsibility for the aged: A field experiment in an institutional setting. *Journal of Personality and Social Psychology, 34,* 191–198.

Langlois, J., Kalakanis, L., Rubenstein, A., Larson, A., Hallam, M., & Smoot, M. (2000). Maxims or myths of beauty? A meta-analytic and theoretical review. *Psychological Bulletin, 126,* 390–423.

Langlois, J. H., & Downs, A. C. (1980). Mothers, fathers, and peers as socialization agents of sex-typed play behaviors in young children. *Child Development, 51,* 1237–1247.

Langlois, L., & Ruggman, L. (1990). Attractive faces are only average. *Psychological Science, 1,* 115–121.

Lanning, K. V. (1989). *Child sex rings: A behavioral analysis.* Washington, DC: National Center for Missing and Exploited Children.

LaPiere, R. T. (1934). Attitudes vs. action. *Social Forces, 13,* 230–237.

Larimer, M. E., Palmer, R. S., & Marlatt, G. A. (1999). Relapse prevention: An overview of Marlatt's cognitive-behavioural model. *Alcohol Research and Health, 23,* 151–160.

Larsen, K. S., Ashlock, J., Carroll, C., Foote, S., Keller, J., Seese, G., & Watkins, D. (1974). Laboratory aggression where the victim is a small dog. *Social Behavior and Personality, 2,* 174–176.

Larson, R., & Richards, M. (1994). *Divergent realities: The emotional lives of mothers, fathers, and adolescents*. New York: Basic Books.

Larsson, L. G., Grimby, G., & Karlsson, J. (1979). Muscle strength and speed of movement in relation to age and muscle morphology. *Journal of Applied Physiology, 46*, 451–456.

Lashley, K. S. (1929). *Brain mechanisms and intelligence*. Chicago: University of Chicago Press.

Lasky, R. E., Suradal-Lasky, A., & Klein, R. E. (1975). VOT discrimination by four to six and a half month old infants from Spanish environments. *Journal of Experimental Child Psychology, 20*, 215–225.

Latané, B., & Darley, J. M. (1968). Group inhibition of bystander intervention in emergencies. *Journal of Personality and Social Psychology, 10*, 215–221.

Latané, B., & Darley, J. M. (1970). *The unresponsive bystander: Why doesn't he help?* New York: Appleton-Century-Crofts.

Latané, B., & Nida, S. (1981). Ten years of research on group size and helping. *Psychological Bulletin, 89*, 308–324.

Latané, B., & Rodin, J. (1969). A lady in distress: Inhibiting effects of friends and strangers on bystander intervention. *Journal of Experimental Social Psychology, 5*, 189–302.

Latané, B., Williams, K., & Harkins, S. (1979). Many hands make light the work: The causes and consequences of social loafing. *Journal of Personality and Social Psychology, 37*, 822–832.

Laumann, E. O., Gagnon, J. H., Michael, R. T., & Michaels, S. (1994). *The social organization of sexuality: Sexual practices in the United States*. Chicago: University of Chicago Press.

Laumann, E. O., Paik, A., & Rosen, R. (1999). Sexual dysfunction in the United States: Prevalence and predictors. *Journal of the American Medical Association, 281*, 537–544.

Laurin, D., Verreault, R., Lindsay, J., MacPherson, K., & Rockwood, K. (2001). Physical activity and risk of cognitive impairment and dementia in elderly persons. *Archives of Neurology, 58*, 498–504.

Laursen, B., Coy, K. C., & Collins, W. (1998). Reconsidering changes in parent-child conflict across adolescence: A meta-analysis. *Child Development, 69*, 817–832.

Lauterbur, P. (1973). Image formation by induced local interaction; examples employing magnetic resonance. *Nature, 242*, 192.

Lawson, K. A., Wright, M. E., Subar, A., Mouw, T., Schatzkin, A., & Leitzmann, M. F. (2007). Multivitamin use and risk of prostate cancer in the National Institutes of Health–AARP Diet and Health Study. *Journal of the National Cancer Institute, 99*, 754–764.

Lazar, S. W., Bush, G., Gollub, R. L., Fricchione, G. L., Khalsa, G., & Benson, H. (2000). Functional brain mapping of the relaxation response and meditation. *NeuroReport, 7*, 1581–1585.

Lazarus, A. A. (2006). *Brief but comprehensive psychotherapy: The multimodal way*. New York: Springer Publishing.

Lazarus, A. (2003). Multimodal therapy: Technical eclecticism with minimal integration. In J. C. Norcross & M. R. Goldfried (Eds.), *Handbook of psychotherapy integration* (pp. 231–263). New York: Oxford Press.

Lazarus, A. A. (1981). *The practice of multimodal therapy*. New York: McGraw-Hill.

Lazarus, R. (1999). *Stress and emotion: A new synthesis*. New York: Springer Publishing.

Lazarus, R. S. (1984). On the primacy of cognition. *American Psychologist, 39*, 124–129.

Lazarus, R. S. (2003). Does the positive psychology movement have legs? *Psychological Inquiry, 14*, 93–109.

Lazarus, R. S., & Folkman, S. (1984). *Stress, appraisal, and coping*. New York: Springer.

Le Bon, G. (1895). *Psychology of the crowd*. New York: Viking Press.

LeBar K.S. & Phelps E.A. (1998) Arousal mediated memory consolidation: Role of the medial temporal lobe in humans. *Psychological Science, 9*, 490–493.

Lederman, L. M. (1996). A strategy for saving science. *Skeptical Inquirer, 20*, 23–28.

LeDoux, J. (1996). *The emotional brain: The mysterious underpinnings of emotional life*. New York: Simon & Schuster.

LeDoux, J. E. (2000). Emotion circuits in the brain. *Annual Review of Neuroscience, 23*, 155–184.

Lee, K., & Ashton, M. C. (2004). Psychometric properties of the HEXACO personality inventory. *Multivariate Behavioral Research, 39*, 329–358.

Leeper, P. (1988). Having a place to live is vital to good health. *NewsReport, 38*, 5–8.

Lefever, G., Arcona, A., & Antonuccio, D. (2003). ADHD among American schoolchildren: Evidence of overdiagnosis and overuse of medication. *The Scientific Review of Mental Health Practice, 21*, 49–60.

Legerstee, M. (1991). The role of person and object in eliciting early imitation. *Journal of Experimental Child Psychology, 51*, 423–433.

Leggenhager, B., Todi, T., Metzinger, T., & Blanke, O. (2007). Video ergo sum: Manipulating body self-consciousness. *Science, 317*, 1096–1099.

Leggio, M. G., Mandolesi, L., Federico, F., Spirito, F., Ricci, B., Gelfo, F., et al. (2005). Environmental enrichment promotes improved spatial abilities and enhanced dendritic growth in the rat. *Behavioral Brain Research, 163*, 78–90.

Lehman, D. R., Chiu, C.-Y., & Schaller, M. (2004). Psychology and culture. *Annual Review of Psychology, 55*, 689–714.

Leichsenring, F., Rabung, S., & Leibing, E. (2004). The efficacy of short-term psychodynamic psychotherapy in specific psychiatric disorders. *Archives of General Psychiatry, 61*, 1208–1216.

Leichtman, M., & Ceci, S. (1995). The effects of stereotypes and suggestions on preschoolers' reports. *Developmental Psychology, 31*, 568–578.

Leigh, B. C., & Stacy, A. (2004). Alcohol expectancies and drinking in different age groups. *Addiction, 99*, 215–227.

Leitenberg, H. (1976). *Handbook of behavior modification and behavior therapy*. Englewood Cliffs, NJ: Prentice-Hall.

Leitenberg, H., & Henning, K. (1995). Sexual fantasy. *Psychological Bulletin, 117*, 469–496.

Lejoyeux, M., & Ades, J. (1997). Antidepressant discontinuation: A review of the literature. *Journal of Clinical Psychiatry, 58*(Suppl. 7), 11–15.

Leman, K. (1998). *The new birth order book: Why you are the way you are*. Grand Rapids, MI: Baker Book House.

Lenneberg, E. (1967). *Biological foundations of language*. New York: Wiley.

Lenroot, R. K., & Giedd, J. N. (2006). Brain development in children and adolescents: Insights from anatomical magnetic resonance imaging. *Neuroscience and Biobehavioral Reviews, 30*, 718–729.

Lenzenweger, M. F., McLachlan, G., & Rubin, D. B. (2007). Resolving the latent structure of schizophrenia endophenotypes using expectation-maximization–based finite mixture modeling. *Journal of Abnormal Psychology, 116*, 16–29.

Leo, P. (2006, September 13). Here's the skinny on fashion models. *Pittsburgh Post-Gazette*. Retrieved November 17, 2006, from www.post-gazette.com/pg /06256/721288-294 .stm).

Leonard, B. E. (1997). The role of noradrenaline in depression: A review. *Journal of Psychopharmacology, 11*, S39–47.

Lepper, M. R., Greene, D., & Nisbett, R. E. (1973). Undermining children's intrinsic interest with extrinsic rewards: A test of the "overjustification" hypothesis. *Journal of Personality and Social Psychology, 28*, 129–137.

Lerner, M. J. (1980). *The belief in a just world: A fundamental delusion*. New York: Plenum Press.

Leslie, M. (2000). The vexing legacy of Lewis Terman. Retrieved from http://www.stanfordalumni.org/news/magazine/2000/julaug/articles/terman.html.

Lester, D., Kaminsky, S., & McGovern, M. (1993). Sheldon's theory of personality in young children. *Perceptual and Motor Skills, 77*, 1330.

Lester, D., Yang, B., & Lindsay, M. (2004). Suicide bombers: Are psychological profiles possible? *Studies in Conflict & Terrorism, 27*, 283–295.

Lett, J. (1990, Winter). A field guide to critical thinking. *Skeptical Inquirer, 14*, 153–160.

Leuchter, A. F., Cook, I. A., Witte, E. A., Morgan, M., & Abrams, M. (2002). Changes in brain function of depressed subjects during treatment with a placebo. *American Journal of Psychiatry, 159*, 122–129.

Leuner, B., Gould, E., & Shors, T. J. (2006). Is there a link between adult neurogenesis and learning? *Hippocampus, 16*, 216–224.

Levant, R. F. (2004). The empirically validated treatments movement: A practitioner/educator perspective. *Clinical Psychology: Science and Practice, 11*, 219–224.

Levenberg, S. B. (1975). Professional training, psychodiagnostic skill, and kinetic family drawings. *Journal of Personality Assessment, 39*, 389–393.

Levenson, R. (2005, April). Desperately seeking Phil. *APS Observer*. Retrieved from http://www.psychologicalscience.org/observer/getArticle.cfm?id=1749.

Levenstein, S., Ackerman, S., Kiecolt-Glaser, J. K., & Dubois, A. (1999). Stress and peptic ulcer disease. *Journal of the American Medical Association, 281*, 10–11.

Levenstein, S. Kaplan, G. A., & Smith, M. W. (1997). Psychological predictors of peptic ulcer incidence in the Alameda County Study. *Journal of Clinical Gastroenterology, 24*, 140–146.

Lever, J. (1995, August 22). The 1995 Advocate survey of sexuality and relationship: The women. *Advocate*, 212–230.

Levin, B. E., Dunn-Meynell, A. A., & Routh, V. H. (1999). Regulatory, integrative, and comparative physiology. *American Journal of Physiology, 276*, 1223–1231.

Levin, D. T., & Simons, D. J. (1997). Failure to detect changes to attended objects in motion pictures. *Psychonomic Bulletin and Review, 4*, 501–506.

Levin, J. (2001). *God, faith, and health: Exploring the spirituality-healing connection*. New York: John Wiley & Sons.

Levine (1987)

Levine, B. (1979). *Group psychotherapy: Practice and development*. Englewood Cliffs, NJ: Prentice-Hall.

Levine, D. S. (1998). *Explorations in common sense and common nonsense*. http://www.uta.edu/psychology/faculty/levine/EBOOK/index.htm.

Levine, J. R., Young, M. L, & Baroudi. C. (2003). *The Internet for dummies* (9th ed.). New York: Wiley.

Levine, S. C., Vasilyeva, M., Lourenco, S. F., Newcombe, N. S., & Huttenlocher, J. (2005). Research report: Socioeconomic status modifies the sex difference in spatial skill. *Psychological Science, 16,* 841–845.

Levis, D. J. (1995). Decoding traumatic memory: Implosive theory of psychopathology. In W. O. Donohue & L. Kranser (Eds.), *Theories in behavior therapy* (pp. 173–207). Washington, DC: American Psychological Association.

Levitan, L., & LaBerge, S. (1990). Beyond nightmares: Lucid resourcefulness vs. helpless depression. *NightLight, 2,* 1–6.

Levy, D. L., Holzman, P. S., Matthysse, S., & Mendell, N. R. (1993). *Schizophrenia Bulletin, 19,* 461–536.

Levy, F., Hay, D. A., McStephen, M., Wood, C., & Waldman, I. (1997). Attention-deficit hyperactivity disorder: A category or a continuum? Genetic analysis of a large-scale twin study. *Journal of the American Academy of Child and Adolescent Psychiatry, 36,* 737–744.

Lewin, K. (1935). *A dynamic theory of personality.* New York: McGraw-Hill.

Lewin, K. (1947). Frontiers in group dynamics: II. Channels of group life; social planning and action research. *Human Relations, 1,* 143–153.

Lewin, K. (1951). *Field theory in social science: Selected theoretical papers.* D. Cartwright (Ed.), New York: Harper & Row.

Lewin, T. (2006, August 31). Students' path to small colleges can bypass SAT. *New York Times.* Retrieved October 27, 2007, from http://www.nytimes.com /2006/08/31/education/31sat.html?_r=1&n=Top/Reference /Times%20Topics/People/L/Lewin,%20Tamar&oref=slogin.

Lewinsohn, P. M. (1974). A behavioral approach to depression. In R. J. Friedman & M. M. Katz (Eds.), *Psychology of depression: Contemporary theory and research* (pp. 157–158). Oxford, England: John Wiley & Sons.

Lewinshohn, P. M., Hoberman, H. M., & Rosenbaum, M. A. (1988). A prospective study of risk factors for unipolar depression. *Journal of Abnormal Psychology, 97,* 251–264.

Lewinsohn, P. M., & Rosenbaum, M. (1987). Recall of parental behavior by acute depressives, remitted depressives, and nondepressives. *Journal of Personality and Social Psychology, 52,* 611–620.

Lewis, M., & Brooks-Gunn, J. (1979). *Social cognition and the acquisition of self.* New York: Plenum.

Lewis, M., Brooks-Gunn, J. & Jasker, J. J. (1985). Individual differences in visual self-recognition as a function of mother-infant attachment relationship. *Developmental Psychobiology, 21,* 1181–1187.

Lewis, W. A., & Bucher, A. M. (1992). Anger, catharsis, the reformulated frustration-aggression hypothesis, and health consequences. *Psychotherapy, 29,* 385–392.

Lewontin, R. C. (1970). Further remarks on race and the genetics of intelligence. *Bulletin of the Atomic Scientists, 26,* 23–25.

Lewontin, R. C. (1972). The apportionment of human diversity. *Evolutionary Biology, 6,* 381–398.

Li, Y., Liu, J., Liu, F., Guo, G., Anme, T., & Ushijima, H. (2000). Maternal child-rearing behaviors and correlates in rural minority areas of Yunnan, China. *Journal of Developmental & Behavioral Pediatrics, 21,* 114–122.

Libet, B. (1985). Unconscious cerebral initiative and the role of conscious will in voluntary action. *Behavioral and Brain Science, 8,* 529–566.

Lichtenstein, S., Slovic, P., Fischhoff, B., Layman, M., & Combs, B. (1978). Judged frequency of lethal events. *Journal of Experimental Psychology: Human Learning and Memory, 4,* 551–578.

Lick, J. (1975). Expectancy, false galvanic skin response feedback, and systematic desensitization in the modification of phobic behavior. *Journal of Consulting and Clinical Psychology, 43,* 557–557.

Lidz, C. W., Mulvey, E. P., & Gardner, W. (1993). The accuracy of predictions of violence to others. *Journal of the American Medical Association, 269,* 1007–1111.

Lidz, T. (1973). *The origin and treatment of schizophrenic disorders.* New York: Basic Books.

Lie, D. C., Song, H., Colamarino, S. A., Ming, G. L., & Gage, F. H. (2004). Neurogenesis in the adult brain: New strategies for central nervous system diseases. *Annual Review of Pharmacology & Toxicology, 44,* 399–421.

Lieber, C. M. (2003). Alcohol and health: A drink a day won't keep the doctor away. *Cleveland Clinic Journal of Medicine, 70,* 945–953.

Lieberman, J. A., & Koreen, A. R. (1993). Neurochemistry and neuroendocrinology of schizophrenia: A selective review. *Schizophrenia Bulletin, 2,* 371–428.

Lieberman, M. A. (1975). Group methods. In F. H. Kanfer & A. P. Goldstein (Eds.), *Helping people change.* New York: Pergamon Press.

Lieberman, P. (1973). On the evolution of language: A unified view. *Cognition, 2,* 59–94.

Lieberman, P. (1998). *Eve spoke: Human language and human evolution.* New York: Norton.

Lieberman, P., Crelin, E. S., & Klatt, D. H. (1972). Phonetic ability and related anatomy of the newborn and adult human, Neanderthal man, and the chimpanzee. *American Anthropologist, 74,* 287–307.

Liem, E. B., Lin, C. M., Suleman, M. I., Doufas, A. G., Gregg, R. G., Veauthier, J. M., et al. (2004). Anesthetic requirement is increased in redheads. *Anesthesiology, 101,* 279–283.

Lilienfeld, S. O. (1994). Conceptual problems in the assessment of psychopathy. *Clinical Psychology Review, 14,* 17–38.

Lilienfeld, S. O. (1995). *Seeing both sides: Classic controversies in abnormal psychology.* Pacific Grove, CA: Brooks/Cole.

Lilienfeld, S. O. (1996). Anxiety sensitivity is not distinct from trait anxiety. In R. M. Rapee (Ed.), *Current controversies in the anxiety disorders* (pp. 228–244). New York: Guilford.

Lilienfeld, S. O. (1998). Pseudoscience in contemporary clinical psychology: What it is and what we can do about it. *Clinical Psychologist, 51,* 3–9.

Lilienfeld, S. O. (1999). New analyses raise doubts about replicability of ESP findings. *Skeptical Inquirer, 23*(6), 9, 12.

Lilienfeld, S. O. (1999). Projective measures of personality and psychopathology: How well do they work? *Skeptical Inquirer, 23,* 32–39.

Lilienfeld, S. O. (1999, March/April). ABC's *20/20* features segment on "goggle therapy" for depression and anxiety. *Skeptical Inquirer, 23,* 8–9.

Lilienfeld, S. O. (1999, November/December). New analyses raise doubts about replicability of ESP findings. *Skeptical Inquirer, 24,* 9–10.

Lilienfeld, S. O. (2004). Defining psychology: Is it worth the trouble? *Journal of Clinical Psychology, 60,* 1249–1253.

Lilienfeld, S. O. (2007). Psychological treatments that can cause harm. *Perspectives on Psychological Science, 2,* 53–70.

Lilienfeld, S. O., Alliger, G. M., & Mitchell, K. E. (1995). Why integrity testing remains controversial. *American Psychologist, 50,* 457–458.

Lilienfeld, S.O., & Arkowitz, H. (2007). Autism: An epidemic? *Scientific American Mind, 18*(2), 82–83.

Lilienfeld, S. O., & Fowler, K. A. (2006). The self-report assessment of psychopathy: Problems, pitfalls, and promises. In C. J. Patrick (Ed.), *Handbook of psychopathy* (pp. 107–132). New York: Guilford.

Lilienfeld, S. O., Fowler, K., Lohr, J., & Lynn, S. J. (2005). Pseudoscience, non-science, and nonsense in clinical psychology: Dangers and remedies. In N. Cummings, & G. Koocher (Eds.), *Destructive trends in mental health: The well intentioned road to hell* (pp. 187–218). New York: Brunner/Routledge.

Lilienfeld, S. O., & Landfield, K. (in press). Issues in diagnosis. In E. Craighead, D. J. Miklowitz, & L.W. Craighead (Eds.), *Psychopathology: History, diagnosis, and empirical foundations.* New York: Wiley.

Lilienfeld, S. O., & Lynn, S. J. (2003). Dissociative identity disorder: Multiple personality, multiple controversies. In S. O

Lilienfeld, S. O., Lynn, S. J., Kirsch, I., Chaves, J. F., Sarbin, T. R., Ganaway, G. K., et al. (1999). Dissociative identity disorder and the sociocognitive model: Recalling the lessons of the past. *Psychological Bulletin, 125,* 507–523.

Lilienfeld, S. O., Lynn, S. J., & Lohr, J. M. (2003). *Science and pseudoscience in clinical psychology.* New York: Guilford Press.

Lilienfeld, S. O., & Marino, L. (1995). Mental disorder as a Roschian concept: A critique of Wakefield's "harmful dysfunction" analysis. *Journal of Abnormal Psychology, 104,* 411–420.

Lilienfeld, S. O., Ruscio, J. P., & Lynn, S. J. (in press). *Navigating the mindfield: A user's guide to distinguishing science from pseudoscience in mental health.* Amherst, NY: Prometheus Books.

Lilienfeld, S. O., & Waldman, I. D. (2000, November 13). Race and IQ: What the science says. *Emory Report,* 3.

Lilienfeld, S. O., & Waldman, I. D. (2004). Comorbidity and Chairman Mao. *World Psychiatry, 3,* 26–27.

Lilienfeld, S. O., Waldman, I. D., & Israel, A. C. (1994). A critical examination of the use of the term "comorbidity" in psychopathology research. *Clinical Psychology: Science and Practice, 1,* 71–83.

Lilienfeld, S. O., Wood, J. M., & Garb, H. N. (2001). The scientific status of projective techniques. *Psychological Science in the Public Interest, 1,* 27–66.

Lim, S.-L., & Kim, J.-H. (2005). Cognitive processing of emotional information in depression, panic, and somatoform disorder. *Journal of Abnormal Psychology, 114,* 50–61.

Limb, C. J. (2006). Structural and functional neural correlates of music perception. *Anatomical Record, Part A, Discoveries in Molecular, Cellular, and Evolutionary Biology, 288,* 435–446.

Lindeman, M. (1998). Motivation, cognition and pseudoscience. *Scandinavian Journal of Psychology, 39,* 257–265.

Linden, D. E. (2006). How psychotherapy changes the brain—The contribution of functional neuroimaging. *Molecular Psychiatry, 11,* 528–538.

Lindle, R. S., Metter, E. J., Lynch, N. A., Fleg, J. L., Fozard, J. L., Tobin, J., et al. (1997). Age and gender comparisons of muscle strength in 654 women and men aged 20–93 yr. *Journal of Applied Physiology, 83,* 1581–1587.

Lindman, R. (1982). Social and solitary drinking: Effects on consumption and mood in male social drinkers. *Physiology and Behavior, 28,* 1093–1095.

Lindsay, D. S., & Read, J. D. (1994). Psychotherapy and memories of childhood sexual abuse: A cognitive perspective. *Applied Cognitive Psychology, 8*, 281–338.

Lindsay, R. C. L., & Wells, G. L. (1985). Improving eyewitness identifications from lineups: Simultaneous versus sequential lineup presentation. *Journal of Applied Psychology, 70*(3), 556–564.

Linehan, M. M. & Schmidt, H. III (1995). The dialectics of effective treatment of borderline personality disorder. In W.T. O'Donohue & L. Krasner (Eds.), *Theories in behavior therapy* (pp. 553-584). Washington D.C.: American Psychological Association.

Linehan, M. M. (1993). *Cognitive behavioral treatment of borderline personality disorder.* New York: Guilford Press.

Linehan, M. M., Heard, H. L., & Armstrong, H. E. (1993). Naturalistic follow-up of a behavioral treatment for chronically parasuicidal borderline patients. *Archives of General Psychiatry, 50*, 971–974.

Link, B. G., Phelan, J. C., Bresnahan, M., Stueve, A., & Pescosolido, B. A. (1999). Public conceptions of mental illness: Labels, causes, dangerousness and social distance. *American Journal of Public Health, 89*, 1328–1333.

Link, N. F., Sherer, S. E., & Byrne, P. N. (1977). Moral judgment and moral conduct in the psychopath. *Canadian Psychiatric Association Journal, 22*, 341–346.

Linton, H. B., & Langs, R. J. (1964). Subjective reactions to lysergic acid diethylamide (LSD-25) measured by a questionnaire. *Archives of General Psychiatry, 10*, 469–485.

Lipp, H. P., & Wolfer, D. P. (1998). Genetically modified mice and cognition. *Current Opinion in Neurobiology, 8*, 272–280.

Lisman, J., & Raghavachari, S. (2006). A unified model of the presynaptic and postsynaptic changes during LTP at CA1 synapses. *Science STKE, 10*, 11.

Lisman, S. A. (1974). Alcoholic black-out state dependent learning? *Archives of General Psychiatry, 30*, 46–53.

Lissman, T. L., & Boehnlein, J. K. (2001). A critical review of Internet information about depression. *Psychiatric Services, 52*, 1046–1050.

Littauer, H., Sexton, H., & Wynn, R. (2005). Qualities clients wish for in their therapists. *Scandanavian Journal of Caring Science, 19*, 28–31.

Littlewood, R. (2004). Unusual psychiatric syndromes: An introduction. *Psychiatry, 3*, 1–3.

Littman, R. A., & Manning, H. M. (1954). A methodological study of cigarette brand discrimination. *Journal of Applied Psychology, 38*, 185–190.

Littrell, J. (1998). Is the experience of painful emotion therapeutic? *Clinical Psychology Review, 18*, 71–102.

Litz, B. T., Gray, M. J., Bryant, R., & Adler, A. B. (2002). Early intervention for trauma: Current status and future directions. *Clinical Psychology: Science and Practice, 9*, 112–134.

Lock, M. (1998). Menopause: Lessons from anthropology. *Psychosomatic Medicine, 60*, 410–419.

Locke, E. A. (2005). Why emotional intelligence is an invalid concept. *Journal of Organizational Behavior, 26*, 425–431.

Loehlin, J. C. (1992). *Genes and environment in personality development.* Newbury Park, CA: Sage.

Loehlin, J. C. (1997). A test of J. R. Harris's theory of peer influences on personality. *Journal of Personality and Social Psychology, 72*, 1197–1201.

Loehlin, J. C., Lindzey, G., & Spuhler, J. N. (1977). *Race differences in intelligence.* San Francisco: W. H. Freeman.

Loehlin, J. C., Vandenberg, S. G., & Osborne, R. T. (1973). Blood group genes and Negro–White ability differences. *Behavior Genetics, 3*, 263–270.

Loehlin, J. C., Willerman, L., & Horn, J. M. (1988). Human behavior genetics. *Annual Review of Psychology, 39*, 101–133.

Loevinger, J. (1987). *Paradigms of personality.* New York: W. H. Freeman.

Loevinger, J. (1998). *Technical foundations for measuring ego development: The Washington University Sentence Completion Test.* Mahwah, NJ: Erlbaum.

Loewenstein, J., Thompson, L., & Gentner, D. (1999). Analogical encoding facilitates knowledge transfer in negotiation. *Psychonomic Bulletin & Review, 6*, 586–597.

Loewi, O. (1921) Uber humorale Ubertragbarkeit der Herznervenwirkung. I. *Pflugers Archiv, 189*, 239–242.

Loftus, E. F. (1979). *Eyewitness testimony.* Cambridge, MA: Harvard University Press.

Loftus, E. F. (1993). The reality of repressed memories. *American Psychologist, 48*, 518–537.

Loftus, E. F. (1993). The reality of repressed memories. *American Psychologist, 48*, 518–537.

Loftus, E. F. (1997, September). Creating false memories. *Scientific American, 277*, 70–75.

Loftus, E. F., Coan, J. A., & Pickrell, J. E. (1996). Manufacturing false memories using bits of reality. In L. M. Reder (Ed.), *Implicit memory and metacognition* (pp. 195–220). Mahwah, NJ: Lawrence Erlbaum Associates.

Loftus, E. F., & Guyer, M. J. (2002, May/June). Who abused Jane Doe? The hazards of the single case history. *Skeptical Inquirer, 26*, 24–32.

Loftus, E., & Ketcham, K. (1994). *The myth of repressed memory.* New York: St. Martin's Press.

Loftus, E. F., & Loftus, G. R. (1980). On the permanence of stored information in the human brain. *American Psychologist, 35*, 409–420.

Loftus, E. F., & Mazzoni, G. A. L. (1998). Using imagination and personalized suggestion to change people. *Behavior Therapy, 29*, 691–706.

Loftus, E. F., Miller, D. G., & Burns, H. J. (1978). Semantic integration of verbal information into a visual memory. *Human Learning and Memory, 4*, 19–31.

Loftus E. F., & Palmer, J. C. (1974). Reconstruction of automobile destruction: An example of the interaction between language and memory. *Journal of Learning and Verbal Behavior, 13*, 585–589.

Loftus, E. F., & Pickrell, J. E. (1995). The formation of false memories. *Psychiatric Annals, 25*, 720–725.

Logue, M. B., Sher, K. J., & Frensch, P. A. (1992). Purported characteristics of adult children of alcoholics: A possible "Barnum effect." *Professional Psychology: Research and Practice, 23*, 226–232.

Lohr, J. M., DeMalo, C., & McGlynn, F. D. (2003). Specific and nonspecific treatment factors in the experimental analysis of behavioral treatment efficacy. *Behavior Modification, 27*, 322–368.

Lohr, J. M., Hooke, W., Gist, R., & Tolin, D. F. (2003). Novel and controversial treatments for trauma-related disorders. In S. O. Lilienfeld, S. J. Lynn, & J. M. Lohr (Eds.), *Science and pseudoscience in clinical psychology* (pp. 243–272). New York: Guilford.

Lohr, J. M., Olatunji, B. O., Baumeister, R. F., & Bushman, B. J. (in press). The pseudopsychology of anger venting and empirically supported alternatives. *Scientific Review of Mental Health Practice.*

Lohr, J. M., Tolin, D. F., & Lilienfeld, S. O. (1998). Efficacy of eye movement desensitization and reprocessing. *Behavior Therapy, 29*, 123–156.

Lømo, T. (2003). The discovery of long-term potentiation. *Philosophical Transactions of the Royal Society of London Series B: Biological Sciences, 358*, 617–620.

Long, G.T. & Krall, V.L. (1990). The measurement of stress by voice analysis. *Journal of Social Behavior and Personality, 5*, 723-731.

Longley, J., & Pruitt, D. G. (1980). Groupthink: A critique of Janis's theory. In L. Wheeler (Ed.), *Review of personality and social psychology* (Vol. I, pp. 74–93). Beverly Hills, CA: Sage.

Lopez, D. J. (2002). Snaring the Fowler: Mark Twain debunks phrenology. *Skeptical Inquirer, 26*, 33–36.

Lopez, S. R., Nelson Hipke, K., Polo, A. J., Jenkins, J. H., Karno, M., Vaughn, C., et al. (2004). Ethnicity, expressed emotion, attributions, and course of schizophrenia: Family warmth matters. *Journal of Abnormal Psychology, 113*, 428–439.

Loprinzi, C. L., Levitt, R., Barton, E. L., Sloan, J. A., Atherton, P. J., Smith, D. J., et al. (2005). Evaluation of shark cartilage in patients with advanced cancer: A North Central Center Cancer Treatment Group trial. *Cancer, 104*, 176–182.

Lorber, M. F. (2004). Autonomic psychophysiology of aggression, psychopathy, and conduct problems: A meta-analysis. *Psychological Bulletin, 130*, 531–552.

Lorenz, K. (1937). The nature of instinct. In C. H. Schiller (Ed.), *Instinctive behavior: The development of a modern concept.* New York: International Universities Press.

Lorenz, K. (1971). *Studies in animal and human behavior* (Vol. 2). Cambridge, MA: Harvard University Press.

Lortie-Lussier, M., Cote, L., & Vachon, J. (2000). The consistency and continuity hypotheses revisited through the dreams of women at two periods of their lives. *Dreaming, 10*, 67–76.

Lourenco, O., & Machado, A. (1996). In defense of Piaget's theory: A reply to 10 common criticisms. *Psychological Review, 103*, 143–164.

Lowe, M. R. (1993). The effects of dieting on eating behavior: A three-factor model. *Psychological Bulletin, 114*, 100–121.

Lowe, M. R., & Levine, A. S. (2005). Eating motives and the controversy over dieting: Eating less than needed versus less than wanted. *Obesity Research, 13*, 797–806.

Lowe, M. R., Gleaves, D. H., & Murphy-Eberenz, K. P. (1998). On the relation of dieting and bingeing in bulimia-nervosa. *Journal of Abnormal Psychology, 107*, 263–271.

Lubinski, D. (2000). Scientific and social significance of assessing individual differences: Sinking shafts at a few critical points. In S. T. Fiske (Ed.), *Annual Review of Psychology, 51*, 404–444.

Lubinski, D., & Benbow, C. P. (1995). An opportunity for empiricism: Review of Howard Gardner's *Multiple intelligences: The theory in practice.* *Contemporary Psychology, 40*, 935–938.

Lubinski, D., Benbow, C. P., Webb, R. M., & Bleske-Rechek, A. (2006). Tracking exceptional human capital over two decades. *Psychological Science, 17*, 194–199.

Lubinski, D., & Humphreys, L. G. (1992). Some bodily and medical correlates of mathematical giftedness and commensurate levels of socioeconomic status. *Intelligence, 16*, 99–115.

Luborsky, L., Crits-Christoph, P., McLellan, T., Woody, G., Piper, W., Imber, S., et al. (1986). Do therapists vary much in their success? Findings from four outcome studies. *American Journal of Orthopsychiatry, 56*, 501–512.

Luborsky, L., McLellan, A. T., Diguer, L., Woody, G., & Seligman, D. A. (1997). The psychotherapist matters: Comparison of outcomes across twenty-two therapists and seven patient samples. *Clinical Psychology: Science and Practice, 4*, 53–65.

Luborsky, L., Mellon, J., van Ravenswaay, P., Childress, A. R., Colen, K., Hole, A., et al. (1985). A verification of Freud's grandest clinical hypothesis: The transference. *Clinical Psychology Review, 5*, 231–246.

Luchies, C. W., Schiffman, J., Richards, L. G., Thompson, M. R., Bazuin, D., & DeYoung, A. J. (2002). Effects of age, step direction, and reaction condition on the ability to step quickly. *Journals of Gerontology: Series A: Biological Sciences and Medical Sciences, 57A*, M246–M249.

Luchins, A. S. (1946). Classroom experiments on mental set. *American Journal of Psychology, 59*, 295–298.

Luchins, D. J., Weinberger, D. R., & Wyatt, R. J. (1982). Schizophrenia and cerebral asymmetry detected by computed tomography. *American Journal of Psychiatry, 139*, 753–757.

Ludwig, A. M., Brandsma, J. M., Wilbur, C. B., Bendfeldt, F., & Jameson, D. H. (1972). The objective study of a multiple personality: Or, are four heads better than one? *Archives of General Psychiatry, 26*, 298–310.

Luna, B., & Sweeney, J. A. (2004). The emergence of collaborative brain function: fMRI studies of the development of response inhibition. In R. E. Dahl & L. P. Spear (Eds.), *Adolescent brain development: Vulnerabilities and opportunities* (pp. 296–309). New York: New York Academy of Sciences.

Lunberg, I., Frost, J., & Petersen, O. (1988). Effects of extensive program for stimulating phonological awareness in preschool children. *Reading Research Quarterly, 23*, 263–284.

Luo, S., & Klohnen, E. C. (2005). Assortative mating and marital quality in newlyweds: A couple-centered approach. *Journal of Personality and Social Psychology, 88*, 304–325.

Luria, A. (1976). *Cognitive development: Its cultural and social foundations.* (M. Lopez-Morillas & L. Solotaroff, Trans.). Cambridge, MA: Harvard University Press.

Luscher, M., & Scott, I. (1969) *The Luscher Color Test.* New York: Random House.

Lutz, A., Greischar, L. L., Rawlings, N. B., Ricard, M., & Davidson, R. J. (2004). Long-term meditators self-induce high-amplitude gamma synchrony during mental practice. *Proceedings of the National Academy of Sciences U.S.A., 101*, 16369–16373.

Luu, P. & Posner, M. I. (2003). Anterior cingulate cortex regulation of sympathetic activity. *Brain, 126*, 2119–2120.

Lykken, D. T. (1957). A study of anxiety in the sociopathic personality. *Journal of Abnormal and Social Psychology, 55*, 6–10.

Lykken, D. T. (1959). The GSR in the detection of guilt. *Journal of Applied Psychology, 43*, 385–388.

Lykken, D. T. (1960). The validity of the guilty knowledge technique: The effects of faking. *Journal of Applied Psychology, 44*, 258–262.

Lykken, D. T. (1978). The psychopath and lie detector. *Psychophysiology, 15*, 137–142.

Lykken, D. T. (1982). If a man be mad. *The Sciences, 22*, 11–13.

Lykken, D. T. (1993). Predicting violence in the violent society. *Applied and Preventive Psychology, 2*, 13–20.

Lykken, D. T. (1995). *The antisocial personalities.* Mahwah, NJ: Lawrence Erlbaum Associates.

Lykken, D. T. (1998). *A tremor in the blood: Uses and abuses of the lie detector* (2nd ed.). Reading, MA: Perseus.

Lykken, D. T. (2000). *Happiness: The nature and nurture of joy and contentment.* New York: St. Martin's Griffin.

Lykken, D. T. (2000). The causes and costs of crime and a controversial cure. *Journal of Personality, 68*, 559–605.

Lykken, D. T., & Tellegen, A. (1996). Happiness is a stochastic phenomenon. *Psychological Science, 7*, 186–189.

Lynam, D. R., Milich, R., Zimmerman, R., Novak, S. P., Logan, T. K., Martin, C., et al. (1999). Project DARE: No effects at 10-year follow-up. *Journal of Consulting and Clinical Psychology, 67*, 590–593.

Lynn, Neufeld, Green, Rhue, & Sandbert (1996)

Lynn, R. (1996) *Dysgenics: Genetic deterioration in modern populations.* Westport, CT: Praeger.

Lynn, R. (1998). In support of the nutrition theory. In U. Neisser (Ed.), *The rising curve: Long-term gains in IQ and related measures* (pp. 207–218). Washington, DC: American Psychological Association.

Lynn, R. (2006). *Race differences in intelligence: An evolutionary analysis.* Augusta, GA: Washington Summit Books.

Lynn, R., & Irwing, P. (2004). Sex differences on the Progressive Matrices: A meta-analysis. *Intelligence, 32*, 481–498.

Lynn, S. J. (1978). Three theories of self-disclosure exchange. *Journal of Experimental Social Psychology, 14*, 466–479.

Lynn, S. J., & Bates, K. (1985). The reaction of others to enacted depression: The effects of attitude and topic valence. *Journal of Social and Clinical Psychology, 3*, 268–282.

Lynn, S. J., & Frauman, D. (1985). Group psychotherapy. In S. J. Lynn, & J. P. Garske (Eds.), *Contemporary psychotherapies: Models and methods* (pp. 419–458). Columbus, OH: Merrill Press.

Lynn, S. J., & Garske, J. (1985). *Contemporary psychotherapies: Models and methods.* Columbus, OH: Merrill Publishing.

Lynn, S. J., & Kirsch, I. (2006). *Essentials of clinical hypnosis: An evidence-based approach.* Washington, DC: American Psychological Association.

Lynn, S. J., Kirsch, I., & Hallquist, M. (in press). The social-cognitive theory of hypnosis. In M. R. Nash & A. M. Barnier (Eds.), *Oxford handbook of hypnosis.* New York: Oxford Press.

Lynn, S. J., Knox, J., Fassler, O., Lilienfeld, S. O., & Loftus, E. (2004). Trauma, dissociation, and memory. In J. Rosen (Ed.), *Posttraumatic stress disorder: Issues and controversies.* New York: Wiley.

Lynn, S. J., Lock, T., Loftus, E. F., Krackow, E., & Lilienfeld, S. O. (2003). The remembrance of things past: Problematic memory recovery techniques in psychotherapy. In S. O. Lilienfeld, S. J. Lynn, & J. M. Lohr (Eds.), *Science and pseudoscience in clinical psychology* (pp. 205–239). New York: Guilford Press.

Lynn, S. J., Lock, T. J., Myers, B., & Payne, D. G. (1997). Recalling the unrecallable: Should hypnosis be used to recover memories in psychotherapy? *Current Directions in Psychological Science, 6*, 79–83.

Lynn, S. J., Matthews, A., & Barnes, S. (in press). Hypnosis and memory: From Bernheim to the present. In K. Markman, W. Klein, & J. Suhr (Eds.), *Handbook of imagination and mental simulation.* New York: Psychology Press.

Lynn, S. J., Nash, M. R., Rhue, J. W., Frauman, D. C., & Sweeney, C. A. (1984). Nonvolition, expectancies, and hypnotic rapport. *Journal of Abnormal Psychology, 93*, 295–303.

Lynn, S. J., & Pintar, J. (1997). A social narrative model of dissociative identity disorder. *Australian Journal of Clinical and Experimental Hypnosis, 25*, 1–7.

Lynn, S. J., Pintar, J., Sandberg, D., Fite, R. F., Ecklund, K., & Stafford, J. (2003). Towards a social narrative model of revictimization. In L. Koenig, A. O'Leary, L. Doll, & W. Pequenat (Eds.), *From child sexual assault to adult sexual risk: Trauma, revictimization, and intervention.* Washington, DC: American Psychological Association.

Lynn, S. J., & Rhue, J. W. (1988). Fantasy proneness: Hypnosis, developmental antecedents, and psychopathology. *American Psychologist, 43*, 35–44.

Lynn, S. J., & Rhue, J. W. (1991). An integrative model of hypnosis. In S. J. Lynn & J. W. Rhue (Eds.), *Theories of hypnosis: Current models and perspectives* (pp. 397–438). New York: Guilford Press.

Lynn, S. J., Rhue, J. W., & Weekes, J. R. (1990). Hypnotic involuntariness: A social-cognitive analysis. *Psychological Review, 97*, 169–184.

Lynn, S. J., Surya Das, L., Hallquist, M. N., & Williams, J. C. (2006). Mindfulness, acceptance, and hypnosis: Cognitive and clinical perspectives. *International Journal of Clinical and Experimental Hypnosis, 54*, 143–166.

Lynn, S. J., Weekes, J. R., & Milano, M. (1989). Reality versus suggestion: Pseudomemory in hypnotizable and simulating subjects. *Journal of Abnormal Psychology, 98*, 75–79.

Lynskey, M. T., Heath, A. C., Bucholz, K. K., Slutske, W. S., Madden, P. A. F., Nelson, E. C., et al. (2003). Escalation of drug use in early-onset cannabis users vs. co-twin controls. *Journal of the American Medical Association, 289*, 427–433.

Lytton, H., & Romney, D. M. (1991). Parents' differential socialization of boys and girls: A meta-analysis. *Psychological Bulletin, 109*, 267–296.

Lyubomirsky, S., King, L. A., & Diener, E. (2005). The benefits of frequent positive affect: Does happiness lead to success? *Psychological Bulletin, 131*, 803–855.

Lyvers, M., Barling, N., & Harding-Clark, J. (2006). Effect of belief in "psychic healing" on self-reported pain in chronic pain sufferers. *Journal of Psychosomatic Research, 60*, 59–61.

Maas, J., & Toivanen, K. (1978). *Candid Camera* and the behavioral sciences. *Teaching of Psychology, 5*, 226–228

Maccoby, E. E., & Jacklin, C. N. (1974). *Psychology of sex differences.* Stanford, CA: Stanford University Press.

Maccoby, E. E., & Jacklin, C. N. (1980). Sex differences in aggression: A rejoinder. *Child Development, 51*, 964–980.

Maccoby, E. E., & Martin, J. A. (1983). Socialization in the context of the family: Parent–child interaction. In P. H. Mussen (Ed.) & E. M. Hetherington (Vol. Ed.), *Handbook of child psychology: Vol. 4. Socialization, personality, and social development* (4th ed., pp. 1–101). New York: Wiley.

Machover, K. (1949). *Personality projection in the drawing of the human figure.* Springfield, IL: Charles C. Thomas.

Mack, J. E. (2000). *Passport to the cosmos: Human transformation and alien encounters.* New York: Three Rivers Press.

MacKillop, J., Lisman, S. A., Weinstein, A., & Rosenbaum, D. (2003). Controversial treatments for alcoholism. In S. O. Lilienfeld, S. J. Lynn, & J. W. Lohr (Eds.), *Science and pseudoscience in clinical psychology* (pp. 273–306). New York: Guilford.

MacKillop, J., Lynn, S. J., & Meyers, E. (2004). The impact of stage hypnosis on audience members and participants. *International Journal of Clinical and Experimental Hypnosis, 52*, 313–329.

Mackintosh, M. J. (1998). *IQ and human intelligence*. Oxford, England: Oxford University Press.

MacLeod, C. M., (1991). Half a century of research on the Stroop effect: An integrative review. *Psychological Bulletin, 109*, 163–203.

Macmillan, M. (2000). Restoring Phineas Gage: A 150th retrospective. *Journal of the History of Neuroscience, 9*, 46–66.

Macrae, C. N., & Bodenhausen, G. V. (2000). Social cognition: Thinking categorically about others. *Annual Review of Psychology, 51*, 93–120.

Maddi, S. R. (1985). Existential psychotherapy. In S. J. Lynn & J. Garske (Eds.), *Contemporary psychotherapies: Models and methods* (pp. 191–220). Columbus, OH: Charles E. Merrill.

Maddi, S. R. (2002). The story of hardiness: Twenty years of theorizing, research, and practice. *Consulting Psychology Journal, 54*, 173–185.

Maddi, S. R. (2004). On hardiness and other pathways to resilience. *American Psychologist, 60*, 261–262.

Maddi, S. R., & Kobasa, S. C. (1984). *The hardy executive: Health under stress.* Homewood, IL: Dow Jones-Irwin.

Madsen K. M., Hviid, A., Vestergaard, M., Schendel, D., Wohlfart, J., Thorsen, P., et al. (2002). A population-based study of measles, mumps and rubella vaccination and autism. *New England Journal of Medicine, 347*, 1477–1482.

Maes, H. M., Neale, M. C., & Eaves, L. J. (1997). Genetic and environmental factors in relative body weight and human adiposity. *Behavior Genetics, 27*, 325–351.

Magee, W. J., Eaton, W. W., Wittchen, H. U., McGonagle, K. A., & Kessler, R. C. (1996). Agoraphobia, simple phobia, and social phobia in the National Comorbidity Survey. *Archives of General Psychiatry, 53*, 159–168.

Maguire, E. A., Gadian, D. G., Johnsrude, I. S., Good, C. D., Ashburner, J., Frackowiak, R. S., et al. (2000). Navigation-related structural change in the hippocampi of taxi drivers. *Proceedings of the National Academy of Sciences U.S.A., 97*, 4398–4403.

Mahoney, M. J. (1977). Publication prejudices: An experimental study of confirmatory bias in the peer review system. *Cognitive Therapy and Research, 1*, 161–175.

Mahowald, M., & Schenck, C. (2000). Principles and practice of sleep medicine. New York: W. B. Saunders.

Maia, T. V., & McClelland, J. L. (2004). A re-examination of the evidence for the somatic marker hypothesis: What participants know in the Iowa gambling task. *Proceedings of the National Academy of Sciences, 101*, 16075–16080.

Maier, I. C., & Schwab, M. E. (2006). Sprouting, regeneration and circuit formation in the injured spinal cord: factors and activity. *Philosophical Transactions of the Royal Society London B Biological Sciences, 361*, 1611–1634.

Mailick, M. D., Holden, G., & Walther, V. N. (1994). Coping with childhood asthma. *Health and Social Work, 19*, 103–111.

Main, M., & Cassidy, J. (1988). Categories of response to reunion with the parent at age 6: Predictable from infant attachment classifications and stable over a 1-month period. *Developmental Psychology, 24*, 415–426.

Malcom, K. (1989). Patients' perceptions and knowledge of electroconvulsive therapy. *Psychiatric Bulletin, 13*, 161–165.

Malenka, R. C., & Nicoll, R. A. (1999). Long-term potentiation—A decade of progress? *Science, 285*, 1870–1874.

Malina, R. M., & Bouchard, C. (1991). *Growth, maturation, and physical activity.* Champaign, IL: Human Kinetics.

Malinoski, P., Lynn, S. J., & Sivec, H. (1998). The assessment, validity, and determinants of early memory reports: A critical review. In S. J. Lynn & K. McConkey (Eds.), *Truth in memory* (pp. 109–136). New York: Guilford.

Malony, H. N., & Lovekin, A. A. (1985). *Glossolalia: Behavioral science perspectives on speaking in tongues.* New York: Oxford University Press.

Mandiyan, V. S., Coats. J. K., & Shah, N. M. (2005). Deficits in sexual and aggressive behaviors in Cnga2 mutant mice. *Nature Neuroscience, 8*, 1660–1662.

Mandler, G., Nakamura, Y., & Shebo-Van Zandt, B. J. (1987). Nonspecific effects of exposure on stimuli that cannot be recognized. *Journal of Experimental Psychology: Learning, Memory, & Cognition, 13*, 646–648.

Mandler, J. M. (1984). *Stories, scripts, and scenes: Aspects of schema theory.* Hillsdale, NJ: Lawrence Erlbaum.

Mandler, J. M. (2000). Perceptual and conceptual processes in infancy. *Journal of Cognition and Development, 1*, 3–36.

Mann, J. (1969). The use of sodium amobarbital in psychiatry. *Ohio State Medical Journal, 65*, 700–702.

Mann, L. B. (2005, February 22). Oscar nominee: Fact or fiction? *Washington Post*, HE01.

Mann, T., Tomiyama, A.J., Westling, E., Lew, A., Samuels, B., & Chatman, J. (2007). Medicare's search for effective obesity treatments: Diets are not the answer. *American Psychologist, 62*, 220–233.

Manning, R., Levine, M,, & Collins, A. (2007). The Kitty Genovese murder and the social psychology of helping: The parable of the 38 witnesses. *American Psychologist, 62*, 555–562.

Mantell, D. M. (1971). The potential for violence in Germany. *Journal of Social Issues, 27*, 101–112.

Maquet, P., & Franck, G. (1997). REM Sleep and the amygdala. *Molecular Psychiatry, 2*, 195–196.

Maquet, P., Peters, J. M., Aerts, J., Delfiore, G., Degueldre, C., Luxen, A., et al. (1996). Functional neuroanatomy of human rapid-eye-movement sleep and dreaming. *Nature, 383*, 163–166.

Maren, S. (2005). Building and burying fear memories in the brain. *Neuroscientist, 11*, 89–99.

Maren, S. (2005). Synaptic mechanisms of associative memory in the amygdala. *Neuron, 15*, 783–786.

Marian, V., & Neisser, U. (2000). Language-dependent recall of autobiographical memories. *Journal of Experimental Psychology: General, 129*, 361–368.

Maricq, H. R. (1963). Capillary pattern in familial schizophrenics: A study of nailfold capillaries. *Circulation, 27*, 406–413.

Marieb, E.N. (2001). *Human anatomy and physiology* (5th edition). Boston, MA: Cummings.

Marino, L. (2005). Big brains matter in novel environments. *Proceedings of the National Academy of Sciences USA, 102*, 5306–5307.

Marino, L., & Lilienfeld, S. (1998). Dolphin-assisted therapy: Flawed data, flawed conclusions. *Anthrozoos, 11*(4), 194–200.

Marino, L., & Lilienfeld, S. O. (2007). Dolphin assisted therapy: More flawed data and more flawed conclusions. *Anthrozoos, 20*, 239–249.

Marino, L., McShea, D. W., & Uhen, M. D. (2004). Origin and evolution of large brains in toothed whales. *Anatomical Record Part A: Discoveries in Molecular, Cellular, & Evolutionary Biology, 281*, 1247–1255.

Maris, R. I., Berman, A. L., Maltsberger, J. T., & Yufit, R. I. (1992). *Assessment and prediction of suicide.* New York: Guilford Press.

Markman, A. B., & Gentner, D. (1993). Structural alignment during similarity comparisons. *Cognitive Psychology, 25*, 431–467.

Markovsky, B., & Thye, S. (2001). Social influences on paranormal beliefs. *Sociological Perspectives, 41*, 21–44.

Marks, R. P., Swinson, M., Basoglu, K., & Kuch, H. (1993). Alpraxolam and exposure alone and combined in panic disorder with agoraphobia. *British Journal of Psychiatry, 162*, 788–799.

Markus, H., & Kitayama, S. (1991). Culture and the self: Implications for cognition, emotion, and motivation. *Psychological Review, 98*, 224–253.

Marlatt, G. A. (1983). The controlled-drinking controversy: A commentary. *American Psychologist, 10*, 1097–1110.

Marlatt, G. A., & Gordon, J. R. (Eds.). (1985). *Relapse prevention: Maintenance strategies in the treatment of addictive behaviors.* New York: Guilford Press.

Marlatt, G. A. (2002). Buddhist philosophy and the treatment of addictive behavior. *Cognitive and Behavioral Practice, 9*, 44–47.

Marlatt, G. A., & Rosenhow, D. J. (1980). Cognitive processes in alcohol use: Expectancy and balanced placebo design. In N. K. Mello (Ed.), *Advances in substance abuse: Behavioral and biological research* (pp. 159–199). Greenwich, CT: JAI Press.

Marshall, G. D., & Zimbardo, P. G. (1979). Affective consequences of inadequately explained arousal. *Journal of Personality and Social Psychology, 37*, 970–988.

Marshall, J. (1969). *Law and psychology in conflict.* New York: Anchor Books.

Marston, W. M. (1938). *The lie detector test.* New York: Richard R. Smith.

Mart, E. G. (1999). Problems with the diagnosis of factitious disorder by proxy in forensic settings. *American Journal of Forensic Psychology, 17*, 69–82.

Martin, D. (2006, November 20). *The truth about happiness may surprise you.* Retrieved from www.cnn.com/2006/HEALTH/conditions/11/10/happiness.overview/index.html

Martin, N. G., Eaves, L. J., Heath, A. C., Jardine, R., Feingold, L. M., & Eysenck, H. J. (1986). Transmission of social attitudes. *Proceedings of the National Academy of Sciences, 83*, 4364–4368.

Martin, S. D., Martin, E., Rai, S. S., Richardson, M. A., & Royall, R. (2001). Brain blood flow changes in depressed patients treated with interpersonal psychotherapy or venlafaxine hydrochloride: Preliminary findings. *Archives of General Psychiatry, 58*, 641–648.

Martino, S. C., Collins, R. L., Elliott, M. C., Strachman, A., Kanouse, D. E., & Berry, S. H. (2006). Exposure to degrading versus nondegrading music lyrics and sexual behavior among youth. *Pediatrics, 118*, 430–441.

Martinot, M.-L., Bragulat, V., Artiges, E., Dolle, F., Hinnen, F., Jouvent, R., et al. (2001). Decreased presynaptic dopamine function in the left caudate of depressed patients with affective flattening and psychomotor retardation. *American Journal of Psychiatry, 158,* 314–316.

Maruta, T., Colligan, R. C., Malinchoc, M., & Offord, K. P. (2000). Optimists vs pessimists: Survival rate among medical patients over a 30-year period. *Mayo Clinic Proceedings, 75,* 140–143

Mashour, G. A., Walker, E. E., Martuza, R. L. (2005). Psychosurgery: Past, present, and future. *Brain Research Reviews, 48,* 409–419.

Maslach, C. (1979). Negative and emotional biasing of unexplained arousal. *Journal of Personality and Social Psychology, 37,* 953–969.

Maslow, A. (1971). *The farther reaches of human nature.* New York: Viking Press.

Maslow, A. H. (1954). *Motivation and personality.* New York: Harper and Row.

Mason, L. I., Alexander, C. N., Travis, F. T., Marsh, G., Orme-Johnson, D. W., Gackenbach, J., et al. (1997). Electrophysiological correlates of higher states of consciousness during sleep in long-term practitioners of the transcendental meditation program. *Sleep, 20,* 102–110.

Mastekaasa, A. (1994). The subjective well-being of the previously married: The importance of unmarried cohabitation and time since widowhood or divorce. *Social Forces, 73,* 665–692.

Masters, W. H., & Johnson, V. E. (1966). *Human sexual response.* Boston: Little, Brown.

Masters, W. H., & Johnson, V. E. (1979). *Homosexuality in perspective.* Boston: Little, Brown.

Masuzaki, H., Paterson, J., Shinyama, H., Morton, N. M., Mullins, J. J., Secki, J. R., et al. (2001). A transgenic model of visceral obesity and the metabolic syndrome. *Science, 294,* 2166–2170.

Matarazzo, J. D. (1972). *Wechsler's measurement and appraisal of adult intelligence* (5th ed.). Baltimore: Williams & Wilkins.

Matarazzo, J. D. (1980). Behavioral health and behavioral medicine: Frontiers for a new health psychology. *American Psychologist, 35,* 807–817.

Matarazzo, J. D. (1983). The reliability of psychiatric and psychological diagnosis. *Clinical Psychology Review, 3,* 103–145.

Matarazzo, J. D., & Weins, A. N. (1977). Black Intelligence Test of Cultural Homogeneity and Wechsler Adult Intelligence Scale scores of black and white police applicants. *Journal of Applied Psychology, 62,* 57–63.

Mathalon, D. H., Heinks, T., & Ford, J. M. (2004). Selective attention in schizophrenia: Sparing and loss of executive control. *American Journal of Psychiatry, 161,* 872–881.

Mather, M., Canli, T., English, T., Whitfield, S., Wais, P., Ochsner, K., et al. (2004). Amygdala responses to emotionally valenced stimuli in older and younger adults. *Psychological Science, 15,* 259–263.

Mathews, A., Richards, A., & Eysenck, M. W. (1989). Interpretation of homophones related to threat in anxiety states. *Journal of Abnormal Psychology, 98,* 31–34.

Mathews, V., Wang, Y., Kalnin, A. J., Mosier, K. M., Dunn, D. W., & Kronenberger, W. G. (2006). *Short-term effects of violent video game playing: An fMRI study.* Annual Meeting of the Radiological Society of North America, Chicago, IL.

Matsumoto, D., & Ekman, P. (2004). The relationship between expressions, labels, and descriptions of contempt. *Journal of Personality and Social Psychology, 87,* 529–540.

Matsumoto, D., & Willingham, B. (2006). The thrill of victory and the agony of defeat: Spontaneous expressions of medal winners of the 2004 Athens Olympic Games. *Journal of Personality and Social Psychology, 91,* 568–581.

Matsumoto, D., Yoo, S. H., Hirayama, S., & Petrova, G. (2005). Development and validation of a measure of display rule knowledge: The Display Rule Assessment Inventory. *Emotion, 5,* 23–40.

Mattes, R. D. (2005). Fat taste and lipid metabolism in humans. *Physiology & Behavior, 86,* 691–697.

Mattes, R. D., Hollis, J., Hayes, D., & Stunkard, A. J. (2005). Appetite measurement and manipulation misgivings. *Journal of the American Dietetic Association, 105,* 87–97.

Matthews, A., & MacLeod, C. (2005). Cognitive vulnerability to emotional disorders. In S. Nolen-Hoeksema, T. D. Cannon, & T. Widiger (Eds.), *Annual Review of Clinical Psychology* (Vol. 1, pp. 167–196). Palo Alto, CA: Annual Reviews.

Matthews, D. A., Larson, D. B., & Barry, C. P. (1993). *The faith factor: An annotated bibliography of clinical research on spiritual subjects* (Vol. 1). Rockville, MD: National Institute for Mental Healthcare Research.

Matthews, G., Zeidner, M., & Roberts, R. (2002). *Emotional intelligence: Science and myth.* London: MIT Press.

Matthews, K.A., Gump, B.B., Harris, K.F., Haney, T.L., & Barefoot, J.C. (2004). Hostile behaviors predict cardiovascular mortality among men enrolled in the Multiple Risk Factor Intervention Trial. *Circulation, 109,* 66–70.

Matthews, S. C., Camacho, A., Mills, P. J., & Dimsdale, J. E. (2003). The Internet for medical information about cancer: Help or hindrance? *Psychosomatics, 44,* 100–103.

Max, D. T. (2007, January 7). Happiness 101. *New York Times.* Retrieved from http://www.nytimes.com/2007/01/07/magazine/07happiness.t.html?ex=1183608000&en=946a9bb65d8be3b7&ei=5070.

May, R. (1969). *Love and will.* New York: Norton.

May, R. (1983). *The discovery of being.* New York: Norton.

Mayer, J. (1955). Regulation of energy intake and the body weight: The glucostatic theory and the lipostatic hypothesis. *Annals of the New York Academy of Sciences, 63,* 15–43.

Mayer-Gross, W., Slater, E., & Roth, M. (1969). *Clinical psychiatry* (3rd ed.). Baltimore: Williams & Wilkins. Revised and reprinted 1977, Balliere, Tindall, London.

Mayo, E. (1933). *The human problems of an industrial civilization.* New York: Macmillan.

Mazur, A., & Rosa, E. (1977). An empirical test of McClelland's "achieving society" theory. *Social Forces, 55,* 769–774.

Mazure, C. M. (1998). Life stressors as risk factors in depression. *Clinical Psychology: Science and Practice, 5,* 291–313.

Mazzoni, G. A., Loftus, E. F., Seitz, A., & Lynn, S. J. (1999). Creating a new childhood: Changing beliefs and memories through dream interpretation. *Applied Cognitive Psychology, 13,* 125–144.

Mazzoni, G. A. L., Loftus, E. F., & Kirsch, I. (2001). Changing beliefs about implausible autobiographical events: A little plausibility goes a long way. *Journal of Experimental Psychology: Applied, 7,* 31–39.

Mazzoni, G. A. L., Lombardo, P., Malvagia, S., & Loftus, E. F. (1999). Dream interpretation and false beliefs. *Professional Psychology: Research and Practice, 30,* 45–50.

McBride, P. E. (1992). The health consequences of smoking: Cardiovascular diseases. *Medical Clinics of North America, 76,* 333–353.

McCabe, D. P., & Castel, A. D. (in press). Seeing is believing: The effect of brain images on judgments of scientific reasoning. *Cognition.*

McCall Smith, A., & Shapiro, C. M. (1997). Sleep disorders and the criminal law. In C. Shapiro & A. McCall Smith (Eds.), *Forensic aspects of sleep* (pp. 29–64). Chichester, England: John Wiley & Sons.

McCall, R. B., & Carriger, M. S. (1993). A meta-analysis of infant habituation and recognition memory performance as predictors of later IQ. *Child Development, 64,* 57–79.

McCann, J. T., Shindler, K. L., & Hammond, T. R. (2003). The science and pseudoscience of expert testimony. In S. O. Lilienfeld, S. J. Lynn, & J. M. Lohr (Eds.), *Science and pseudoscience in clinical psychology* (pp. 77–108). New York: Guilford.

McCarty, C. A., Lau, A. S., Valeri, S. M., & Weisz, J. R. (2004). Parent-child interactions proxy for behavior. *Journal of Abnormal Child Psychology, 32,* 83–93.

McCarty, D. L. (1980). Investigation of a visual imagery mnemonic device for acquiring face-name associations. *Journal of Experimental Psychology: Human Learning and Memory, 2,* 145–155.

McCarty, R. (2001, April). Negative stereotypes: A personal view. *Monitor on Psychology, 32*(4), 31.

McClearn, G. E., Johansson, B., Berg, S., Pedersen, N. L., Ahern, F., Petrill, et al. (1997). Substantial genetic influence on cognitive abilities in twins 80+ years old. *Science, 276,* 1560–1563.

McClelland, D. C. (1961). *The achieving society.* Princeton, NJ: Van Nostrand.

McClelland, D. C., Atkinson, J. W., Clark, R. A., & Lowell, E. L. (1953). *The achievement motive.* New York: Appleton Century-Crofts.

McClelland, D. C., Atkinson, J. W., Clark, R. A., & Lowell, E. L. (1958). A scoring manual for the achievement motive. In J. W. Atkinson (Ed.), *Motives in fantasy, action, and society* (pp. 179–204). Princeton, NJ: Van Nostrand.

McClelland, J. L. (1995). A connectionist perspective on knowledge and development. In T. J. Simon & G. S. Halford (Eds.), *Developing cognitive competence: New approaches to process modeling* (pp. 157–204). Hillsdale, NJ: Erlbaum.

McClelland, J. L., & Plaut, D. C. (1993). Computational approaches to cognition: Top-down approaches. *Current Opinion in Neurobiology, 3,* 209–216.

McClintock, J. B., & Lawrence, J. M. (1982). Photoresponse and associative learning in Luidia clathrata (Say) (Echinodermata: Asteroidea). *Marine Behavior and Physiology, 9,* 13–21.

McCloskey, M., Wible, C. G., & Cohen, N. J. (1988). Is there a special flashbulb-memory mechanism? *Journal of Experimental Psychology: General, 117,* 171–181.

McClure, E. B. (2000). A meta-analytic review of sex differences in facial expression processing and their development in infants, children, and adolescents. *Psychological Bulletin, 126,* 424–453.

McConkey, K. M. (1986). Opinions about hypnosis and self-hypnosis before and after hypnotic testing. *International Journal of Clinical and Experimental Hypnosis, 34,* 311–319.

McConkey, K. M. (1991). The construction and resolution of experience and behavior in hypnosis. In S. J. Lynn & J. W. Rhue (Eds.), *Theories of hypnosis: Current models and perspectives* (pp. 542–563). New York: Guilford Press.

McConkie, G. W., & Currie, C. B. (1996). Visual stability across saccades while viewing complex pictures. *Journal of Experimental Psychology: Human Perception & Performance, 22,* 563–581.

McCord, J. (2003). Cures that harm: Unanticipated outcomes of crime prevention programs. *The Annals of the American Academy of Political and Social Science, 587,* 16–30.

McCrae, R. R., & Costa, P. T. (1989). Reinterpreting the Myers-Briggs type indicator from the perspective of the Five-Factor Model of Personality. *Journal of Personality, 57,* 17–40.

McCrae, R. R., & Costa, P. T. (1994). The stability of personality: Observation and evaluations. *Current Directions in Psychological Science, 3,* 173–175.

McCrae, R. R., & Costa, P. T. (1995). Trait explanations in personality psychology. *European Journal of Personality, 9,* 231–252.

McCrae, R. R, & Costa, P. T. (1997). Personality trait structure as a human universal. *American Psychologist, 52,* 509–516.

McCrae, R. R., & Terracciano, A. (2006). National character and personality. *Current Directions in Psychological Science, 15,* 156–161.

McCullough, M. E., Tsang, J., & Brion, S. (2003). Personality traits in adolescence as predictors of religiousness in early adulthood: Findings from the Terman longitudinal study. *Personality and Social Psychology Bulletin, 29,* 980–991.

McCutcheon, L. E. (1991). A new test of misconceptions about psychology. *Psychological Reports, 68,* 647–653.

McCutcheon, L. E., & McCutcheon, L. E. (1994). Not guilty by reason of insanity: Getting it right or perpetuating the myths? *Psychological Reports, 74,* 764–766.

McDaniel, M. A. (2005) Big-brained people are smarter: A meta-analysis of the relationship between in vivo brain volume and intelligence. *Intelligence, 33,* 337–346.

McDaniel, M. A., Maier, S. F., & Einstein, G. O. (2002). "Brain-specific" nutrients: A memory cure? *Psychological Science in the Public Interest, 3,* 12–38.

McDaniel, M. A., & Pressley, M. (1989). Keyword and context instruction of new vocabulary meanings: Effects on text comprehension and memory. *Journal of Educational Psychology, 81,* 204–213.

McDaniel, M. A., Whetzel, D. L., Schmidt, F. L., & Maurer, S. D. (1994). The validity of employment interviews: A comprehensive review and meta-analysis. *Journal of Applied Psychology, 79,* 599–616.

McDermott J. F. (2001). Emily Dickinson revisited: A study of periodicity in her work. *American Journal of Psychiatry, 158,* 686–690.

McDonough, L., Choi, S., & Mandler, J. M. (2003). Understanding spatial relations: Flexible infants, lexical adults. *Cognitive Psychology, 46,* 229–259.

McElroy, S. L., Phillips, K. A., Keck, P. E., Jr., Hudson, J. I., & Pope, H. G. (1993). Body dysmorphic disorder: Does it have a psychotic subtype? *Journal of Clinical Psychiatry, 54,* 389–395.

McFall, R. M. (1996). Making psychology incorruptible. *Applied & Preventive Psychology, 5,* 9–15.

McFall, R. M. (2006). Doctoral training in clinical psychology. *Annual Review of Clinical Psychology, 2,* 21–49.

McGilly, K., & Siegler, R. S. (1989). How children choose among serial recall strategies. *Child Development, 60,* 172–182.

McGinn, C. (2002). *Knowledge and reality: Selected essays.* New York: Oxford University Press.

McGrath, J. (1991). Ordering thoughts on thought disorder. *British Journal of Psychiatry, 158,* 307–316.

McGue, M. (1999). The behavioral genetics of alcoholism. *Current Directions in Psychological Science, 8,* 109–115.

McGue, M., & Lykken, D. T. (1992). Genetic influence on risk of divorce. *Psychological Science, 3,* 368–373.

McGuire, P. K., Shah, G. M. S., & Murray, R. M. (1993). Increased blood flow in Broca's area during auditory hallucinations. *Lancet, 342,* 703–706.

McGuire, W. J. (1964). Inducing resistance to persuasion: Some contemporary approaches. In L. Berkowitz (Ed.), *Advances in experimental social psychology* (Vol. 1, pp. 191–229). San Diego, CA: Academic Press.

McGuire, W. J., & Papageorgis, D. (1961). The relative efficacy of various types of prior belief-defense in producing immunity against persuasion. *Journal of Abnormal and Social Psychology, 62,* 327–337.

McGurk, H., & MacDonald, J. (1976). Hearing lips and seeing voices. *Nature, 264,* 746–748.

McHugh, P. R. (1993). Multiple personality disorder. *Harvard Mental Health Newsletter, 10*(3), 4–6.

McKenzie, I. K. (2004). The Stockholm syndrome revisited: Hostages, relationships, prediction, control, and psychological science. *Journal of Police Crisis Negotiations, 4,* 5–21.

McKinney, M., & Jacksonville, M. C. (2005). Brain cholinergic vulnerability: Relevance to behavior and disease. *Biochemical Pharmacology, 70,* 1115–1124.

McLafferty, C. L., Jr. (2006). Examining unproven assumptions of Galton's nature-nurture paradigm. *American Psychologist, 61,* 177–178.

McLaughlin, T. F., & Williams, R. L. (1988). The token economy. In J. C. Witt, S. N. Elliott, & F. M. Gresham (Eds.), *Handbook of behavior therapy in education* (pp. 469–487). New York: Plenum Press.

McLeod, J. D. (1991). Childhood parental loss and adult depression. *Journal of Health and Social Behavior, 32,* 205–220.

McMonagle, T., & Sultana, A. (2000). Token economy for schizophrenia. *Cochrane Database of Systematic Reviews,* Issue 3. Art. No.: CD001473. DOI: 10.1002/14651858.CD001473.

McNally, R. J. (2003). *Remembering trauma.* Cambridge, MA: Belknap Press.

McNally, R. J., Bryant, R. A., & Ehlers, A. (2003). Does early psychological intervention promote recovery from posttraumatic stress? *Psychological Science in the Public Interest, 4,* 45–79.

McNally, R. J., & Clancy, S. A. (2005). Sleep paralysis, sexual abuse, and space alien abduction. *Transcultural Psychiatry, 42,* 113–122.

McNally, R. J., & Lukach, B. M. (1991). Behavioral treatment of zoophilic exhibitionism. *Journal of Behavioral Research and Experimental Psychiatry, 22,* 281–284.

McNally, R. M., & Eke, M. (1996). Anxiety sensitivity, suffocation fear, and breath-holding duration as predictors of response to carbon dioxide challenge. *Journal of Abnormal Psychology, 105,* 146–149.

McNeil, D. E., Arkowitz, H. S., & Pritchard, B. E. (1987). The response of others to face-to-face interaction with depressed patients. *Journal of Abnormal Psychology, 96,* 341–344.

McNiel, D. E., Eisner, J. P., & Binder, R. L. (2000). The relationship between command hallucinations and violence. *Psychiatric Services, 51,* 1288–1292.

McQuiston-Surrett, D., Malpass, R. S., & Tredoux, C. G. (2006). Sequential vs. simultaneous lineups: A review of methods, data, and theory. *Psychology, Public Policy and Law, 12*(2), 137–169.

McRae, C., Cherin, E., Yamazaki, G., Diem, G., Vo, A. H., Russell, D., et al. (2004). Effects of perceived treatment on quality of life and medical outcomes in a double-blind placebo surgery trial. *Archives of General Psychiatry, 61,* 412–420.

Meacham, J. (1990). The loss of wisdom. In R. J. Sternberg (Ed.), *Wisdom: Its nature, origins, and development* (pp. 181–211). New York: Cambridge University Press.

Meador, B. D. , & Rogers, C. R. (1979). Person centered therapy. In J. R. Corsini (Ed.), *Current psychotherapies.* Itasca, IL: F. E. Peacock Publishers.

Meads, C., & Nouwen, A. (2005). Does emotional disclosure have any effects? A systematic review of the literature with meta-analyses. *International Journal of Technology Assessment in Health Care, 21,* 153–164.

Mealanson, K. J., Westersterp-Plantenga, M. S., Saris, W. H., Smith, F. J., & Campfield, L. A. (1999). Blood glucose patterns and appetite in time-blinded humans: Carbohydrate versus fat. *American Journal of Physiology, 277,* 337–345.

Mednick, S. A., Machon, R. A., Huttunen, M. O., & Bonett, D. (1988). Adult schizophrenia following prenatal exposure to an influenza epidemic. *Archives of General Psychiatry, 45,* 189–192.

Medvec, V. H., Madey, S., & Gilovich, T. (1995). When less is more: Counterfactual thinking and satisfaction among Olympic medal winners. *Journal of Personality and Social Psychology, 69,* 603–610.

Meehl, P. E. (1945). The dynamics of "structured" personality tests. *Journal of Clinical Psychology, 1,* 296–303.

Meehl, P. E. (1956). Wanted: A good cookbook. *American Psychologist, 11,* 263–272.

Meehl, P. E. (1962). Schizotaxia, schizotypy, and schizophrenia. *American Psychologist, 17,* 827–838.

Meehl, P. E. (1967). Theory-testing in psychology and physics: A methodological paradox. *Philosophy of Science, 34,* 103–115.

Meehl, P. E. (1972). Reactions, reflections, projections. In J. N. Butcher (Ed.), *Objective personality assessment: Changing perspectives* (pp. 131–189). New York: Academic Press.

Meehl, P. E. (1972). Specific genetic etiology, psychodynamics, and therapeutic nihilism. *International Journal of Mental Health, 1,* 10–27.

Meehl, P. E. (1978). Theoretical risks and tabular asterisks: Sir Karl, Sir Ronald, and the slow progress of soft psychology. *Journal of Consulting and Clinical Psychology, 46,* 806–834.

Meehl, P. E. (1990). Toward an integrated theory of schizotaxia, schizotypy, and schizophrenia. *Journal of Personality Disorders, 4,* 1–99.

Meehl, P. E. (1993). Philosophy of science: Help or hindrance? *Psychological Reports, 72,* 707–733.

Meehl, P. E. (1995). Psychoanalysis is not yet a science: Comment on Shevrin. *Journal of the American Psychoanalytic Association, 43,* 1015–1023.

Meehl, P. E., & Rosen, A. (1955). Antecedent probability and the efficiency of psychometric signs, patterns, or cutting scores. *Psychological Bulletin, 52,* 194–216.

Meeker, W., & Barber, T. (1971). Toward an explanation of stage hypnosis. *Journal of Abnormal Psychology, 77,* 61–70.

Megargee, E. I. (1972). *The California Psychological Inventory handbook*. San Francisco: Jossey-Bass.

Mehl, M. R., Vazire, S., Ramírez-Esparza, N., Slatcher, R. B., & Pennebaker, J. W. (2007). Are women really more talkative than men? *Science, 317*, 82.

Meichenbaum, D. (1985). Cognitive-behavioral therapies. In S. J. Lynn, & J. P. Garske (Eds.), *Contemporary psychotherapies: Models and methods* (pp. 261–286). Columbus, OH: Charles E. Merrill.

Meichenbaum, D. (1994). A clinical handbook/practical therapist manual for assessing and treating adults with post-traumatic stress disorder (PTSD). Clearwater, FL: Institute Press.

Meichenbaum, D. (1996). Stress inoculation training for coping with stressors. *The Clinical Psychologist, 49*, 4–10.

Meichenbaum, D., & Turk, D. C. (1987). *Facilitating treatment adherence: A practitioner's guidebook*. New York: Plenum.

Meissner, C. A., & Brigham, J. C. (2001). Thirty years of investigating the own-race bias in memory for faces: A meta-analytic review. *Psychology, Public Policy, and Law, 7*, 3–35.

Mellinger, D. M., & Lynn, S. J. (2003). *The monster in the cave: How to face your fear and anxiety and live your life*. New York: Berkeley.

Melton, G. B., Petrilla, J., Poythress, N. G., & Slobogin, L. A. (1997). *Psychological evaluations for the courts: A handbook for mental health professionals and lawyers* (2nd ed.). New York: Guilford Press.

Melton, G. J. (1999). *Brainwashing and the cults: The rise and fall of a theory*. Retrieved October 29, 2007, from http://www.cesnur.org/testi/melton.htm.

Melzack, R. (1975). The McGill Pain Questionnaire: Major properties and scoring methods. *Pain, 1*(3), 277–299.

Melzack, R. (1990, February). The tragedy of needless pain. *Scientific American, 262*, 27–33.

Memom, A., Hope, L., & Bull, R. (2003). Exposure duration: Effects on eyewitness accuracy and confidence. *British Journal of Psychology, 94*, 339–354.

Menchola, B. L., Arkowitz, H., & Burke, B. L. (2007). Efficacy of self-administered treatments for depression and anxiety: A meta-analysis. *Professional Psychology: Research and Practice, 38*, 421–429.

Mendel, G. (1866). Versuche über Pflanzen-Hybriden. *Verhandlungen des naturforschenden Vereines in Brünn [Proceedings of the Natural History Society of Brünn], 4*, 1–47.

Mendelowicz, M. V., & Stein, M. B. (2000). Quality of life in individuals with anxiety disorders. *American Journal of Psychiatry, 157*, 669–682.

Menini, A., Picco, C., & Firestein, S. (1995). Quantal-like current fluctuations induced by odorants in olfactory receptor cells. *Nature, 373*, 435–437.

Menninger, K. (1958). *Theory of psychoanalytic technique*. New York: Basic Books.

Mercer, J. (2002). Attachment therapy: A treatment without empirical support. *Scientific Review of Mental Health Practice, 1*, 105–122.

Mercer, J. (2002). Attachment therapy: A treatment without empirical support. *The Scientific Review of Mental Health Practice, 1*, 9–16.

Mercer, J., Sarner, L., & Rosa, L. (2003). *Attachment therapy on trial: The torture and death of Candace Newmaker*. Westport, CT: Praeger.

Merckelbach, H., Devilly, G., & Rassin, E. (2002). Alters in dissociative identity disorder: Metaphors or genuine entities? *Clinical Psychology Review, 22*, 481–497.

Merikle, P. M. (1988). Subliminal auditory tapes: An evaluation. *Psychology and Marketing, 46*, 355–372.

Merleau-Ponty, M. (1962). *Phenomenology of perception*. London: Routledge and Kegan Paul.

Merskey, H. (1992). The manufacture of personalities: The production of multiple personality disorder. *British Journal of Psychiatry, 160*, 327–340.

Merton, R. K. (1942). The normative structure of science. In N. W. Storer (Ed.), *The Sociology of Science* (pp. 267–278). Chicago: University of Chicago Press.

Messick, S. (1992). Multiple intelligence or multilevel intelligence? Selective emphasis on distinctive properties of hierarchy: On Gardner's *Frames of Mind* and Sternberg's *Beyond IQ* in the context of theory and research on the structure of human abilities. *Psychological Inquiry, 3*, 365–384.

Meston, C. M. (1997). Aging and sexuality. *Western Journal of Medicine, 167*, 285–290.

Meston, C. M., & Frohlich, P. F. (2003). Love at first fright: Partner salience moderates roller coaster–induced excitation transfer. *Archives of Sexual Behavior, 32*, 537–544.

Meyer, A. (Ed.). (1981). The Hamburg Short Psychotherapy Comparison Experiment. *Psychotherapy and Psycho-somatics, 35*, 81–207.

Meyer, I. H., Dietrich, J. D., & Schwartz, S. (2007, October 22). Lifetime prevalence of mental disorders and suicide attempts in diverse lesbian, gay, and bisexual populations. *American Journal of Public Health*. [Epub ahead of print]

Meyer, J. P., & Pepper, S. (1977). Need compatibility and marital adjustment in young married couples. *Journal of Personality and Social Psychology, 35*, 331–342.

Meyer, M. (2006). Commentary on "Innate sex differences supported by untypical traffic fatalities." *Chance, 19*(1), 18–19.

Michaels, J. W., Blommel, J. W., Brocato, R. M., Linkous, R. A., & Rowe, J. S. (1982). Social facilitation and inhibition in a natural setting. *Replications in Social Psychology, 2*, 21–24.

Michalski, R. L., & Shackelford, T. K. (2001). Methodology, birth order, intelligence, and personality. *American Psychologist, 56*, 520–521.

Middlemist, R. D., Knowles, E. S., & Matter, C. F. (1976). Personal space invasions in the laboratory: Suggestive evidence for arousal. *Journal of Personality and Social Psychology, 33*, 541–546.

Mieda, M., Willie, J. T., Hara, J., Sinton, C. M., Sakurai, T., & Yanagisawa, M. (2004). Orexin peptides prevent cataplexy and improve wakefulness in an orexin neuron-ablated model of narcolepsy in mice. *Proceedings of the National Academy of Sciences, 10*, 4649–4654.

Milan, M. A., Montgomery, R. W., & Rogers, E. C. (1994). Theoretical orientation revolution in clinical psychology: Fact or fiction? *Professional Psychology: Research and Practice, 25*, 398–402.

Milgram, S. (1963). Behavioral study of obedience. *Journal of Abnormal and Social Psychology, 67*, 371–378.

Milgram, S. (1964). Issues in the study of obedience: A reply to Baumrind. *American Psychologist, 19*, 848–852.

Milgram, S. (1974). *Obedience to authority: An experimental view*. New York: Harper & Row.

Miller, E. R., Pastor-Barriuso, R., Dalal, D., Riemersma, R. A., Appel, L. A., & Guallar, E. (2005). Meta-analysis: High-dosage vitamin E supplementation may increase all-cause mortality. *Annals of Internal Medicine, 142*, 37–46.

Miller, G. A. (1956). The magical number seven, plus or minus two: Some limits on our capacity for processing information. *Psychological Review, 63*, 81–97.

Miller, G. A. (1969). Psychology as a means of promoting human welfare. *American Psychologist, 24*, 1063–1075.

Miller, K. F., Smith, C. M., Zhu, J., & Zhang, H. (1995). Preschool origins of cross-national differences in mathematical competence: The role of number-naming systems. *Psychological Science, 6*, 56–60.

Miller, L. C. (2000). Initial assessment of growth, development, and the effects of institutionalization in internationally adopted children. *Pediatric Annals, 29*, 224–233.

Miller, L. K. (1999). The savant syndrome: Intellectual impairment and exceptional skill, *Psychological Bulletin, 125*, 31–46.

Miller, M. A., & Rahe, R. H. (1997). Life changes scaling for the 1990s. *Journal of Psychosomatic Research, 43*, 279–292.

Miller, N. E. (1978). Biofeedback and visceral learning. *Annual Review of Psychology* (Vol. 29). Palo Alto, CA: Annual Reviews.

Miller, R. H. (2006). The promise of stem cells for neural repair. *Brain Research, 1091*, 258–264.

Miller, S. D. (1989). Optical differences in cases of multiple personality disorder. *Journal of Nervous and Mental Disease, 177*, 480–486.

Miller, S. D., Duncan, B. L., & Hubble, M. A. (2005). Outcome-informed clinical work. In J. C. Norcross & M. R. Goldfried (Eds.), *Handbook of psychotherapy integration* (2nd ed., pp. 84–102). New York: Oxford.

Miller, W. R., & Hester, R. K. (1980). Treating the problem drinker: Modern approaches. In W. R. Miller (Ed.), *The addictive behaviors: Treatment of alcoholism, drug abuse, smoking, and obesity* (pp. 11–141). Oxford, England: Pergamon Press.

Miller, W. R., Brown, J. M., Simpson, T. L., Handmaker, N. S., Bien, T. H., Luckie, L. R., et al. (1995). What works? A methodological analysis of the alcohol treatment outcome literature. In R. K. Hester (Ed.), *Handbook of alcoholism treatment approaches: Effective alternatives* (2nd ed., pp. 12–44). Boston: Allyn & Bacon.

Miller, W. R., & Rollnick, S. (2002). *Motivational interviewing: Preparing people for change*. New York: Guilford Press.

Miller, Z. (1999, August 31). Music fertilizes the mind. *Atlanta Journal Constitution*, A17.

Millon, T. (1975). Reflections on Rosenhan's "On being sane in insane places." *Journal of Abnormal Psychology, 84*, 456–461.

Mills, A., & Lynn, S. J. (2000). Past-life experiences. In E. Cardena, S. J. Lynn, & S. Krippner (Eds.), *The varieties of anomalous experience*. New York: Guilford.

Milner, A. D., & and Goodale, M. A. (1995). *The visual brain in action*. Oxford, England: Oxford University Press.

Milner, B. (1964) Some effects of frontal lobectomy in man. In J. M. Warren & K. Akert (Hrsg.), *The frontal granular cortex and behavior*. New York: McGraw-Hill.

Milner, B. (1965) Visually-guided maze learning in man: Effects of bilateral hippocampal, bilateral frontal and unilateral cerebral lesions. *Neuropsychologia, 3*, 317–338.

Milner, B. (1972). Disorders of learning and memory after temporal lobe lesions in man. *Clinical Neurosurgery, 19*, 421–446.

Milton, J., & Wiseman, R. (1999). Does Psi exist? Lack of replication of an anomalous process of information transfer. *Psychological Bulletin, 125*(4), 387–391.

Mindell, A. (1990). *Working on yourself alone: Inner dreambody work.* New York: Arkana.

Mindus, P., Bergstrom, K., Levander, S. E., Noren, G., Hindmarsh, T., Thoumas, K. A., et al. (1987). Magnetic resonance images related to clinical outcome after psychosurgical intervention in severe anxiety disorder. *Journal of Neurological Neurosurgery and Psychiatry, 50,* 1288–1293.

Mineka, S. (1992). Evolutionary memories, emotional processing, and the emotional disorders. In D. Medin (Ed.), *The psychology of learning and motivation* (Vol. 28, pp. 161–206). San Diego, CA: Academic.

Mineka, S., & Thomas, C. (1999). Mechanisms of change in exposure therapy for anxiety disorders. In T. Dalgleish & M. J. Power (Eds.), *Handbook of cognition and emotion* (pp. 747–764). Chichester, England: Wiley.

Mineka, S., and Cook, M. (1993). Mechanisms involved in the observational conditioning of fear. *Journal of Experimental Psychology: General, 122,* 23–38.

Mingroni, M. A. (2007). Resolving the IQ paradox: Heterosis as a cause of the Flynn effect and other trends. *Psychological Review, 114,* 806–829.

Minow, N. (2005, December 14). Are "educational" baby videos a scam? Research lacking to support claims. *Chicago Tribune.* Retrieved from http://blogfromthepond.blogspot.com/2005/12/are-educational-baby-videos-scam.html.

Minsky, M. (1986). *The society of mind.* New York: Simon and Schuster.

Mintz, I. (1977). A note on the addictive personality: Addiction to placebos. *American Journal of Psychiatry, 134,* 3–27.

Minuchin, S. (1974). *Families and family therapy.* Cambridge, MA: Harvard University Press.

Miranda, F. S. B., Caballero, R. B., Gomez, M. N. G., & Zamorano, M. A. M. (1981). Obediencia a la authoridad [Obedience to authority]. *Psiquis, 2,* 212–221.

Miranda, J., & Green, B. L. (1999). The need for mental health services research focusing on poor young women. *Journal of Mental Health Policy and Economics, 2,* 73–89.

Mischel, W. (1968). *Personality and assessment.* New York: Wiley.

Mischel, W. (1973). Toward a cognitive social learning reconceptualization of personality. *Psychological Review, 80,* 252–283.

Mischel, W. (1981). *Introduction to personality* (3rd ed.). New York: Holt, Rinehart and Winston.

Mischel, W., & Ayduk, O. (2004). Willpower in a cognitive-affective processing system: The dynamics of delay of gratification. In R. F. Baumeister & K. D. Vohs (Eds.), *Handbook of self-regulation: Research, theory, and applications* (pp. 99–129). New York: Guilford.

Mischel, W., Shoda, Y., & Peake, P. K. (1988). The nature of adolescent competencies predicted by preschool delay of gratification. *Journal of Personality and Social Psychology, 54,* 687–696.

Mischel, W., Shoda, Y., & Rodriguez, M. L. (1989). Delay of gratification in children. *Science, 244,* 933–938.

Mishkin, M., Malamut, B., & Bachevalier, J. (1984). Memories and habits: Two neural systems. In G. Lynch, J. McGaugh, & N. Weinberger (Eds.), *Neurobiology of Learning and Memory* (pp. 65–77). New York: Guilford.

Mita, T. H., Dermer, M., & Knight, J. (1977). Reversed facial images and the mere-exposure hypothesis. *Journal of Personality & Social Psychology, 13,* 89–111.

Mitchell, J. P., Macrae, C. N., & Banaji, M. R. (2006). Dissociable medial prefrontal contributions to judgments of similar and dissimilar others. *Neuron, 50,* 655–663.

Mitchell, S. A., & Black, M. J. (1995). *Freud and beyond: A history of modern psychoanalytic thought.* New York: Basic Books.

Mittal, V. A., Tesser, K. D., Trottman, H. D., Esterberg, M., Dhruv, S. H., Simenova, D. I., et al. (2007). Movement abnormalities and the progression of prodromal symptomatology in adolescents at risk for psychotic disorders. *Journal of Abnormal Psychology, 116,* 260–267.

Mix, K. S. (1999). Similarity and numerical equivalence appearances count. *Cognitive Development, 14,* 269–297.

Mix, K. S., Huttenlocher, J., & Levin, S. C. (1996). Do preschool children recognize auditory-visual numerical correspondences? *Child Development, 67,* 1592–1608.

Moffitt, P. F., Kalucy, E. C., Kalucy, R. S., Baum, F. E., & Cooke, R. D. (1991). Sleep difficulties, pain, and other correlates. *Journal of Internal Medicine, 230,* 245–249.

Moffitt, T. E. (1983). The learning theory model of punishment: Implications for delinquency deterrence. *Criminal Justice and Behavior, 10,* 131–158.

Molé, P. (2006). Skepticism in the classroom: A high school science teacher in the trenches. *Skeptic, 12*(3), 62–70.

Monahan, J. (1984). The prediction of violent behavior: Toward a second generation of theory and policy. *American Psychologist, 141,* 10–15.

Monahan, J. (1992). Mental disorder and violent behavior: Perceptions and evidence. *American Psychologist, 47,* 511–521.

Monahan, J. (2000). Violence and mental disorder: Recent research. In M. Crowner & D. Bernay (Eds.), *Understanding and treating aggressive psychiatric patients* (pp. 167–178). Washington, DC: American Psychiatric Press.

Monroe, L. J., Rechtschaffen, A., Foulkes, D., & Jensen, J. (1965). Discriminability of REM and NREM reports. *Journal of Personality and Social Psychology, 2,* 456–460.

Monroe, R. (1955). *Schools of psychoanalytic thought.* New York: Dryden.

Monroe, S. M. (1983). Major and minor events as predictors of psychological distress: Further issues and findings. *Journal of Behavioral Medicine, 6,* 189–205.

Monte, C. F. (1995). *Beneath the mask: An introduction to theories of personality.* Fort Worth, TX: Harcourt Brace College Publishers.

Monteith, M., & Winters, J. (2002). Why we hate. *Psychology Today, 35*(3), 44–52.

Monti, P. M., Abrams, D. B., Kadden, R. M., & Rohsenow, D. J. (1989). *Treating alcohol dependence: A coping skills training guide.* New York: Guilford Press.

Monti, P. M., Gulliver, S. B., & Myers, M. G. (1994). Social skills training for alcoholics: Assessment and treatment. *Alcohol and Alcoholism, 29,* 627–637.

Moody, R. A. (1975). *Life after life.* Covington, GA: Mockingbird Books.

Moody, R. A. (1977). *Reflections on life after life.* St. Simon's Island, GA: Mockingbird Books.

Mook, D. (1983). In defense of external invalidity. *American Psychologist, 38,* 379–387.

Moon, C., Cooper, R. P., & Fifer, W. P. (1993). Two-day-olds prefer their native language. *Infant Behavior & Development, 16,* 495–500.

Moon, Y. (1986). A review of cross-cultural studies on moral judgment development using the Defining Issues Test. *Behavior Science Research, 20,* 147–177.

Mooney, C. (2003, November/December). King of the paranormal. *Skeptical Inquirer, 27,* 35–40.

Moons, W. G., & Mackie, D. M. (2007). Thinking straight while seeing red: The influence of anger on information processing. *Personality and Social Psychology Bulletin, 33,* 706–720.

Moore, B., & Fine, B. (Eds.). (1995). *Psychoanalysis: The major concepts.* New Haven, CT: Yale University Press.

Moore, D. W. (2005, June 16). Three in four Americans believe in paranormal. *Gallup Poll News Service.* Retrieved February 20, 2007, from http://www.gallup.com/poll/content/default.aspx?ci=16915.

Moore, G. E. (1988). *Principia ethica.* Buffalo, NY: Prometheus.

Moore, T. E. (1992). Subliminal perception: Facts and fallacies. *Skeptical Inquirer, 16,* 273–281.

Moore, T. E. (1996). Scientific consensus and expert testimony: Lessons from the Judas Priest trial. *Skeptical Inquirer, 20,* 32–38.

Moore, T.M., Scarpa, A. and Raine, A. (2002). A meta-analysis of serotonin metabolite 5-HIAA and antisocial behavior. *Aggressive Behavior, 28,* 299-316.

Moreland, R. L., & Beach, R. (1992). Exposure effects in the classroom: The development of affinity among students. *Journal of Experimental Social Psychology, 28,* 255–276.

Morelock, M., & Feldman, D. H. (1993). Prodigies and savants: What they have to tell us about giftedness and human cognition. In K. Heller, F. Monks, & H. Passow (Eds.), *International handbook for research on giftedness and talent* (pp. 161–181). Oxford, England: Pergamon Press.

Morgan, C. D., & Murray, H. A. (1935). A method for investigating fantasies. *Archives of Neurology and Psychiatry, 34,* 289–304.

Morier, D., & Podlipentseva, J. (1997, April). *Mortality salience effects on paranormal beliefs and essay ratings.* Paper presented at the 77th Annual Meeting of the Western Psychological Association, Seattle, WA.

Morin, C. M., Hauri, P. J., Espic, C. A., Spielman, A.J., Buyesse, D. J., & Bootzin, R. R. (1999). Nonpharmacologic treatment of chronic insomnia. *Sleep, 22,* 1134–1155.

Morris, J. N., Clayton, D. G., Everitt, M. G., Semmence, A. M., & Burgess, E. H. (1990). Exercise in leisure time: Coronary heart attack and death rates. *British Heart Journal, 63,* 325–334.

Morris, M. W., & Peng, K. (1994). Culture and cause: American and Chinese attributions for social and physical events. *Journal of Personality and Social Psychology, 67,* 949–971.

Morris, R. (1984). Developments of a water-maze procedure for studying spatial learning in the rat. *Journal of Neuroscience Methods, 11,* 47–60.

Morrison, J. (1997). *When psychological problems mask medical disorders: A guide for psychotherapists.* New York: Guilford.

Morrison, T., & Morrison, M. (1995). A meta-analytic assessment of the predictive validity of the quantitative and verbal components of the Graduate Record Examination with grade point average representing the criterion of graduate success. *Educational & Psychological Measurement, 55,* 309–316.

Morse G. (1999). The nocebo effect: Scattered findings suggest that negative thinking can harm patients' health. *Hippocrates, 10*. Retrieved February 5, 2007, from http://www.hippocrates.com/archive/november1999/11departments/11integrative.html.

Mortensen, E. L., Michaelson, K. F., Sanders, S. A., & Reinisch, J. M. (2002). The association between duration of breastfeeding and adult intelligence. *Journal of the American Medical Association, 287*, 2365–2371.

Morton, E. W. (1977). On the occurrence and significance of motivation-structural roles in some bird and mammal sounds. *American Naturalist, 111*, 855–869.

Morton, E. W. (1982). Grading, discreteness, redundancy, and motivation-structural rules. In D. E. Kroodmsa & E. H. Miller (Eds.), *Acoustic communication in birds* (pp. 182–212). New York: Academic Press.

Moscovitch, M., Rosenbaum, R. S., Gilboa, A., Addis, D. R., Westmacott, R., Grady, C., et al. (2005). Functional neuroanatomy of remote episodic, semantic and spatial memory: A unified account based on multiple trace theory. *Journal of Anatomy, 207*, 35–66.

Mosholder, A. D., & Willy, M. (2006). Suicidal adverse events in pediatric randomized, controlled clinical trials of antidepressant drugs are associated with active drug treatment: A meta-analysis. *Journal of Child & Adolescent Psychopharmacology, 16*, 25–32.

Motta, R. W., Little, S. G., & Tobin, M. I. (1993). The use and abuse of human figure drawings. *School Psychology Quarterly, 8*, 162–169.

Mowrer, O. H. (1960/1973). *Learning theory and behavior.* New York: Wiley.

Mrosovsky, N., & Poley, T. L. (1977). Set points for body weight and fat. *Behavioral Biology, 20*, 205–223.

Mrozeck, D. K., & Spiro, A. (2005). Change in life satisfaction during adulthood: Findings from the Veteran Affairs normative aging study. *Journal of Personality and Social Psychology, 88*, 189–192.

Mrozek, D. K., & Kolarz, C.M. (1998). The effect of age on positive and negative affect: A developmental perspective on happiness. *Journal of Personality and Social Psychology, 75*, 1333–1349.

Msefti, R. M., Murphy, R. A., Simpson, J., & Kornbrot, D. E. (2005). Depressive realism and outcome density bias in contingency judgments: The effect of the context and inter-trial interval. *Journal of Experimental Psychology: General, 134*, 10–22.

MTA Cooperative Group. (1999). Moderators and mediators of treatment response for children with attention-deficit/hyperactivity disorder. *Archives of General Psychiatry, 56*, 1088–1096.

Mueser, K. T., & Liberman, R. P. (1995). Behavior therapy in practice. In B. Bongar, & L. E. Beutler (Eds.), *Comprehensive textbook of psychotherapy: Theory and practice* (pp. 84–110). New York: Oxford University Press.

Mueser, K. T., & McGurk, S. R. (2004). Schizophrenia. *Lancet, 363*, 2063–2072.

Mukamal, K. J., Chung, H., Jenny, N. S., Kuller, L. H., Longstreth, W. T., Jr., Mittleman, M. A., et al. (2005). Alcohol use and risk of ischemic stroke among older adults: The cardiovascular health study. *Stroke, 36*, 1830–1834.

Mukamal, K. J., Cinigrave, K. M., Mittleman, M. A., Camargo, C. A., Stampfer, M. J., Willett, W. C., et al. (2003). Roles of drinking pattern and type of alcohol consumed in coronary heart disease in men. *New England Journal of Medicine, 348*, 109–118.

Mulick, J. A., Jacobsen, J. W., & Kobe, F. H. (1993, Spring). Anguished silence and helping hands: Autism and facilitated communication. *Skeptical Inquirer, 17*, 281–287.

Muller, F. J., Snyder, E. Y., & Loring, J. F. (2006). Gene therapy: can neural stem cells deliver? *Nature Reviews Neuroscience, 7*, 75–84.

Müller, J. (1826). *Zur vergleichenden Physiologie des Gesichtssinnes des Menschen und der Tiere.* Leipzig, Germany: C. Knobloch.

Murdock, B. B. (1962). The serial position effect of free recall. *Journal of Experimental Psychology, 64*, 482–488.

Murphy, C. (1999). Loss of olfactory function in dementing disease. *Physiology & Behavior, 66*, 177–182.

Murphy, F. C., Nimmo-Smith, I., & Lawrence, A. D. (2003). Functional neuroanatomy of emotion: A meta-analysis. *Cognitive, Affective, & Behavioral Neuroscience, 3*, 207–233.

Murphy, J. B. (1976). Psychiatric labeling in cross-cultural perspective: Similar kinds of disturbed behavior appear to be labeled abnormal in diverse cultures. *Science, 191*, 1019–1028.

Murray, E. J., & Jacobson, L. I. (1978). Cognition and learning in traditional and behavioral therapy. In S. L. Garfield, & A. E. Bergin (Eds.), *Handbook of psychotherapy and behavior change* (2nd ed.). New York: John Wiley & Sons.

Murray, H. A. (1938). *Explorations in personality.* New York: Oxford University Press.

Murrie, D. C., & Redding, R. E. (2006). Mental disorders and the law. In D. S. Clark (Ed.), *Encyclopedia of law and society: American and global perspectives.* Thousand Oaks, CA: Sage.

Murstein, B. I. (1972). Physical attractiveness and marital choice. *Journal of Personality and Social Psychology, 22*, 8–12.

Murstein, B. I. (1977). The stimulus-value-role (SVR) theory of dyadic relationship. In S. Duck (Ed.), *Theory and practice in interpersonal attraction* (pp. 105–127). New York: Academic Press.

Muscarella, F., & Cunningham, M. R. (1996). The evolutionary significance and social perception of male pattern baldness and facial hair. *Ethology and Sociobiology, 17*, 99–117.

Musella, D. P. (2005, September/October). Gallup poll shows that Americans' belief in the paranormal persists. *Skeptical Inquirer, 29*, 5.

Mutrie, N. (1988). Exercise as a treatment for moderate depression in the UK health service. *Sport, Health, Psychology and Exercise Symposium Proceedings* (pp. 96–105). London: The Sports Council and Health Education Authority.

Myers D. G. (2000). The funds, friends, and faith of happy people. *American Psychologist, 55*(1), 56–67.

Myers, D. (1993). *Social psychology.* New York: McGraw Hill.

Myers, D., & Bishop, G. D. (1970). Discussion effects on racial attitudes. *Science, 169*, 778–789.

Myers, D. G. (1993). *The pursuit of happiness.* London: Aquarian.

Myers, D. G. (2002). *Intuition: Its powers and perils.* New Haven, CT: Yale University Press.

Myers, D. G., & Diener, E. (1996). The pursuit of happiness. *Scientific American*, 70–72.

Myers, D. G., & Kaplan, M. F. (1976). Group-induced polarization in simulated juries. *Personality and Social Psychology Bulletin, 2*, 63–66.

Myers, D. G., & Lamm, H. (1976). The group polarization phenomenon. *Psychological Bulletin, 83*, 602–627.

Myrtek, M. (2001). Meta-analyses of prospective studies on coronary heart disease, type A personality, and hostility. *International Journal of Cardiology, 79*, 245-251.

Nachev, P., & Husain, M. (2006). Disorders of visual attention and the posterior parietal cortex. *Cortex, 42*, 766–773.

Nagel, B. J., Schweinsburg, A. D., Phan, V., & Tapert, S. F. (2005). Reduced hippocampal volume among adolescents with alcohol use disorders without psychiatric comorbidity. *Psychiatry Research: Neuroimaging, 139*, 181–190.

Nahemow, L., & Lawton, M. P. (1975). Similarity and propinquity in friendship formation. *Journal of Personality and Social Psychology, 32*, 205–213.

Nairn, A. (1980). *The reign of ETS: The corporation that makes up minds.* Washington, DC: Ralph Nader.

Naito, E. (2004). Sensing limb movements in the motor cortex: How humans sense limb movement. *Neuroscientist, 10*, 73–82.

Namy, L. L., & Waxman, S. R. (2000). Naming and exclaiming: Infants' sensitivity to naming contexts. *Journal of Cognition and Development, 1*, 405–428.

Nash, M. R. (1987). What, if anything, is regressed about hypnotic age regression? A review of the empirical literature. *Psychological Bulletin, 102*, 42–52.

Nash, M. R. (1991). Hypnosis as a special case of psychological regression. In S. J. Lynn & J. W. Rhue (Eds.), *Theories of hypnosis: Current models and perspectives* (pp. 171–194). New York: Guilford Press.

Nash, M. R. (1997). Why scientific hypnosis needs psychoanalysis (or something like it). *International Journal of Clinical and Experimental Hypnosis, 45*, 291–300.

Nash, M. R., & Barnier, A. (Eds.). (in press). *The Oxford handbook of hypnosis.* New York: Oxford Press.

Nass, C., Brave, S., & Takayama, L. (2006). Socializing consistency: From technical homogeneity to human epitome. In P. Zhang & D. Galletta (Eds.), *Human-computer interaction in management information systems: Foundations* (pp. 373-391). Armonk, NY: M. E. Sharpe

National Cancer Institute. (2000, December 12). *Fact sheet: Questions and answers about smoking cessation.* Retrieved November 2005 from http://www.cancer.gov/cancertopics/factsheet/tobacco/cessation.

National Center for Complementary and Alternative Medicine. (2002). *What is complementary and alternative medicine?* (publication no. D156). Gaithersburg, MD: NCCAM.

National Center for Health Statistics. (2005). *Health, United States, 2005.* Atlanta, GA: Centers for Disease Control.

National Center for Health Statistics. (2005). *Life expectancy at birth, 65 and 85 years of age, United States, selected years 1900–2004.* Retrieved from http://209.217.72.34/aging/TableViewer/tableView.aspx?ReportId=438.

National Heart, Lung, and Blood Institute. (1998). *Behavioral research in cardiovascular, lung, and blood health and disease.* Washington, DC: U.S. Department of Health and Human Services.

National Institute of Mental Health. (2004). Suicide facts and statistics, U.S., 2001. U.S. Department of Health and Human Services. www.nimh.nih.gov/tools/helpusing.cfm, posted 4/09/2004.

National Institute on Alcohol Abuse and Alcoholism (1998, July). Alcohol and sleep, no. 41. http://pubs.niaaa.nih.gov/publications/aa41.htm.

National Opinion Research Center. (2003). *General social surveys, 1972–2002: Cumulative codebook.* Chicago: Author.

National Research Council. (1998). Preventing reading difficulties in young children. In C. E. Snow, M. S. Burns, & P. Griffin (Eds.), Washington, DC: National Academies Press.

Navarro, A. M. (1993). Effectiveness of psychotherapy with Latinos in the United States: A revised meta-analysis. *Interamerican Journal of Psychology, 27,* 131–146.

Neath, I., & Surprenant, A. M. (2003). *Human memory* (2nd ed.). Pacific Grove, CA: Wadsworth.

Needham, A., & Baillargeon, R. (1993). Intuitions about support in 4.5-month-old infants. *Cognition, 47,* 121–148.

Neely, J. (1976) Semantic priming and retrieval from lexical memory: Evidence for facilitory and inhibitory processes. *Memory and Cognition, 4,* 648–654.

Neher, A. (1990). *The psychology of transcendence.* New York: Dover.

Neimeyer, R. (2000). Searching for the meaning of meaning: Grief therapy and the process of reconstruction. *Death Studies, 24,* 541–558.

Neisser, U. (1967). *Cognitive psychology.* New York: Appleton-Century-Crofts.

Neisser, U. (1982). Snapshots or benchmarks? In U. Neisser (Ed.), *Memory observed: Remembering in natural contexts* (pp. 9–31). San Francisco: Freeman.

Neisser, U. (1998). *The rising curve: Long-term gains in IQ and related measures.* Washington, DC: American Psychological Association.

Neisser, U., Boodoo, G., Bouchard, T. J., Jr., Boykin, A. W., Brody, N., Ceci, S. J., et al. (1996). Intelligence: Knowns and unknowns. *American Psychologist, 51,* 77–101.

Neisser, U., & Harsch, N. (1992). Phantom flashbulbs: False recollections of hearing the news about *Challenger.* In E. Winograd & U. Neisser (Eds.), *Affect and accuracy in recall: Studies of flashbulb memories* (pp. 9–31). Cambridge, England: Cambridge University.

Neisser, U., & Hyman, I. (Eds.). (1999). *Memory observed: Remembering in natural contexts.* New York: Worth Publishers.

Neisser, U., & Hyman, I. E., Jr. (Eds.). (2000). *Memory observed: Remembering in natural contexts* (2nd ed.). New York: Worth.

Neisser, U., Wonograd, E., Bergman, E. T., Schreiber, C. A., Palmer, S. E., & Weldon, M. S. (1996). Remembering the earthquake: Direct experience vs. hearing the news. *Memory, 4,* 337–357.

Nelson, K. (1977). The syntagmatic-paradigmatic shift revisited: A review of research and theory. *Psychological Bulletin, 84,* 93–116.

Nelson, R. E., & Craighead, W. E. (1977), Selective recall of positive and negative feedback, self-control behaviors, and depression. *Journal of Abnormal Psychology, 86,* 379–388.

Nelson, R., & Hayes, S. C. (1986). The nature of behavioral assessment. In R. O. Nelson & S. C. Hayes (Eds.), *Conceptual foundations of behavioral assessment* (pp. 3–41). New York: Guilford.

Nelson, T. O. (1985). Ebbinghaus's contribution to the measurement of retention: Savings during relearning. *Journal of Experimental Psychology: Human Learning and Memory, 11,* 472–479.

Nemeroff, C. B., Kalali, A., Keller, M. B., Charney, D. S., Lenderts, S. E., Cascade, E. F., et al. (2007). Impact of publicity concerning pediatric suicidality data on physician practice patterns in the United States. *Archives of General Psychiatry, 64,* 397.

Nettle, D. (2005). *Happiness: The science behind your smile.* Oxford, England: Oxford University Press.

Neuchterlein, K. H., & Dawson, M. E. (1984). Information processing and attentional functioning in the developmental course of schizophrenia disorders. *Schizophrenia Bulletin, 10,* 160–203.

Neville, R. (1978). Psychosurgery. In W. Reich (Ed.), *Encyclopedia of bioethics* (Vol. 3). New York: Free Press.

Newberg, A., Alavi, A., Baime, M., Pourdehnad, M., Santanna, J., & d'Aquili, E. (2001). The measurement of regional cerebral blood flow during the complex cognitive task of meditation: A preliminary psychiatry research study. *Neuroimaging, 106,* 113–122.

Newcomb, M. D., & Bentler, P. M. (1988). Impact of adolescent drug use and social support on problems of young adults: A longitudinal analysis. *Journal of Abnormal Psychology, 97,* 64–75.

Newcomb, T. M. (1961). *The acquaintance process.* New York: Holt, Rinehart and Winston.

Newell, A., & Simon, H. A. (1972). *Human problem solving.* Englewood Cliffs, NJ: Prentice

Newman, A. J., Bavelier, D., Corina, D., Jezzard, P., & Neville, H. J. (2002). A critical period for right hemisphere recruitment in American Sign Language processing. *Nature Neuroscience, 5,* 76–80.

Newman, J. P., & Kosson, D. S. (1986). Passive avoidance learning in psychopathic and nonpsychopathic offenders. *Journal of Abnormal Psychology, 95,* 252–256.

Newport, E. L. (1990). Maturational constraints on language learning. *Cognitive Science, 14,* 11–28.

Newport, E. L., Bavelier, D., & Neville, H. J. (2001). Critical thinking about critical periods: Perspectives on a critical period for language acquisition. In E. Dupoux (Ed.), *Language, brain and cognitive development: Essays in honor of Jacques Mehler.* Cambridge, MA: MIT Press.

Newport, E. L., & Meier, R. (1985). The acquisition of American Sign Language. In D. Slobin (Ed.), *The cross-linguistic study of language acquisition, Vol. 1* (pp. 881–938). Hillsdale, NJ: Erlbaum.

Newport, F., & Strausberg, M. (2001). *Americans' belief in psychic and paranormal phenomena is up over last decade.* Gallup News Service, 8 June. Retrieved October 23, 2007, from www.gallup.com/poll/releases/pr010608.asp.

Newsweek. (1978, December 18). The ten faces of Billy. *Newsweek,* p. 106.

Ngandu, T., von Strauss, E., Helkala, E.-L., Winbland, B., Nissinen, A., Tuomilehto, J., et al. (2007). Education and dementia: What lies behind the association? *Neurology, 69,* 1442–1450.

Niaura, R., Todaro, J. F., Stroud, L., Spiro, A., Ward, K. D., & Weiss, S. (2002). Hostility, the metabolic syndrome, and incident coronary heart disease. *Health Psychology, 21,* 588–593.

Nickell, J. (1993). *Looking for a miracle: Weeping icons, relics, stigmata, visions and healing cures.* New York: Prometheus Books.

Nickel, J. (2000, May/June). Aura photography: A candid shot. *Skeptical Inquirer, 24,* 15–17.

Nickerson, R. S. (1998). Confirmation bias: A ubiquitous phenomenon in many guises. *Review of General Psychology, 2,* 175–220.

Nickerson, R. S., & Adams, J. J. (1979). Long-term memory for a common object. *Cognitive Psychology, 11,* 287–307.

Nicol, S. E., & Gottesman, I. I. (1983). Clues to the genetics and neurobiology of schizophrenia. *American Scientist, 71,* 398–404.

NIDA. (2002). *Research report: Marijuana abuse.* National Institute on Drug Abuse. NIH Publication No. 05-3859, Printed June 2005. Rockville, MD: National Clearinghouse on Alcohol and Drug Information.

Niedenthal, P. M. (2007). Embodying emotion. *Science, 316,* 1002–1005.

Nielsen, T. A. (1999). Mentation during sleep: The NREM/REM distinction. In R. Lydic & H. A. Baghdoyan (Eds.), *Handbook of behavioral state control: Molecular and cellular mechanisms.* Boca Raton, FL: CRC Press.

Nigg, J. T., & Goldsmith, H. H. (1994). Genetics of personality disorders: Perspectives from personality and psychopathology research. *Psychological Bulletin, 115,* 346–380.

Nigro, G., & Neisser, N. (1983). Point of view in personal memories. *Cognitive Psychology, 15,* 467–482.

Nisbett, R. E. (1968). Birth order and participation in dangerous sports. *Journal of Personality and Social Psychology, 8,* 351–353.

Nisbett, R. E. (1968). Determinants of food intake in human obesity. *Science, 159,* 1254–1255.

Nisbett, R. E. (1972). Hunger, obesity, and the ventromedial hypothalamus. *Psychological Review, 79,* 433–453.

Nisbett, R. E. (1995). Race, IQ and scientism. In S. Fraser (Ed.), *The bell curve wars* (pp. 36–57). New York: HarperCollins.

Nisbett, R. E. (2003). *The geography of thought: How Asians and Westerners think differently . . . and why.* New York: Free Press.

Nisbett, R. E., & Cohen, D. (1996). *Culture of honor: The psychology of violence in the South.* Boulder, CO: Westview.

Nisbett, R. E., Peng, K., Choi, I., & Norenzayan, A. (2001). Culture and systems of thought: Holistic vs. analytic cognition. *Psychological Review, 108,* 291–310.

Nisbett, R. E., & Ross, L. D. (1980). Human inference: Strategies and shortcomings of social judgment. Englewood Cliffs, NJ: Prentice-Hall.

Nisbett, R. E., & Wilson, T. D. (1977). Telling more than we can know: Verbal reports on mental processes. *Psychological Review, 84,* 231–259.

Nisbett, R. E., & Wilson, T. D.. (1977). The halo effect: Evidence for the unconscious alteration of judgments. *Journal of Personality and Social Psychology, 35,* 450–456.

Noel, J. G., Wann, D. L., & Branscombe, N. R. (1995). Peripheral ingroup membership status and public negativity toward outgroups. *Journal of Personality and Social Psychology, 68,* 127–137.

Noelle-Neumann, E. (1970). Wanted: Rules for wording structured questionnaires. *Public Opinion Quarterly, 34,* 191–201.

Nofzinger, E. A., Mintun, M. A., Wiseman, M. B., Kupfer, D. J., & Moore, R. Y. (1997). Forebrain activation in REM sleep: An FDG PET study. *Brain Research, 770,* 192–201.

Nolen-Hoeksema, S. (1987). Sex differences in unipolar depression: Evidence and theory. *Psychological Bulletin, 101,* 259–282.

Nolen-Hoeksema, S. (2000). The role of rumination in depressive disorders and mixed anxiety/depressive symptoms. *Journal of Abnormal Psychology, 109,* 504–511.

Nolen-Hoeksema, S. (2002). Gender differences in depression. In I. H. Gotlib & C. L. Hammen (Eds.), *Handbook of depression* (pp. 492–509). New York: Guilford.

Nolen-Hoeksema, S. (2003). *Women who think too much: How to break free of overthinking and reclaim your life.* New York: Holt.

Nolen-Hoeksema, S., & Girgus, J. S. (1994). The emergence of gender differences in depression during adolescence. *Psychological Bulletin, 115,* 424–443.

Nolen-Hoeksema, S., Girgus, J. S., & Seligman, M. E. P. (1992). Predictors and consequences of childhood depressive symptoms: A 5-year longitudinal study. *Journal of Abnormal Psychology, 101,* 405–422.

Norcross, J., & Beutler, L. (1997). Determining the relationship of choice in brief therapy. In J. N. Butcher (Ed.), *Personality assessment in managed health care* (pp. 42–60). New York: Oxford University Press.

Norcross, J. C. (2005). A primer on psychotherapy integration. In J. C. Norcross & M. R. Goldfried (Eds.), *Handbook of psychotherapy integration* (2nd ed., pp. 3–23). New York: Oxford.

Norcross, J. C., Garofalo, A., & Koocher, G. (2006). Discredited psychological treatments and tests: A Delphi poll. *Professional Psychology: Research and Practice, 137,* 515–522.

Norcross, J. C., & Goldfried, M. R. (2005). *Handbook of psychotherapy integration* (2nd ed.). New York: Oxford University Press.

Norcross, J. C., Karpiak, C. P., & Santoro, S. O. (2005). Clinical psychologists across the years: The Division of Clinical Psychology from 1960 to 2003. *Journal of Clinical Psychology, 61,* 1467–1483.

Norcross, J. C., Ratzin, A. C., & Payne, D. (1989). Ringing in the new year: The change processes and reported outcomes of resolutions. *Addictive Behaviors, 14,* 205–212.

Norcross, J. C., Strausser, D. J., & Missar, C. D. (1988). The process and outcomes of psychotherapists' personal treatment experiences. *Psychotherapy, 25,* 36–43.

Norcross, J. C., & Vangarelli, D. J. (1989). The resolution solution: Longitudinal examination of New Year's change attempts. *Journal of Substance Abuse, 1,* 127–134.

Norem, J. K. (2001). *The positive power of negative thinking.* New York: Basic Books.

Norem, J. K., & Cantor, N. (1986). Defensive pessimism: "Harnessing" anxiety as motivation. *Journal of Personality and Social Psychology, 52,* 1208–1217.

Norem, J. K., & Chang, E. C. (2002). The positive psychology of negative thinking. *Journal of Clinical Psychology, 37,* 1204–1238.

Norman, D. (1998). *The design of everyday things.* London: MIT Press.

North, A. C., Linley, P. A., & Hargreaves, D. J. (2000). Social loafing in a co-operative classroom task. *Educational Psychology, 20,* 389–392.

Novaco, R. W. (1994). Clinical problems of anger and its assessment and regulation through a stress coping skills approach. In W. O'Donohue & L. Krasner (Eds.), *Handbook of skills training* (pp. 320–338). New York: Pergamon Press.

Nowicki, S., & Duke, M. (2002). *Will I ever fit in?* New York: Free Press.

Noyes, R. (1980). Attitude change following near-death experience. *Psychiatry, 43,* 234–242.

Noyes, R., & Kletti, R. (1976). Depersonalization in the face of life-threatening danger: An interpretation. *Omega, 7,* 103–114.

Nuttin, J. M. (1985). Narcissism beyond Gestalt and awareness: The name letter effect. *European Journal of Social Psychology, 15,* 353–361.

O'Brien, T. (1990). *The things they carried.* New York: Broadway.

Ocampo-Garces, A., Molina, E., Rodrigues, A., & Vivaldi, E. A. (2000). Homeostasis of REM sleep after total and selective sleep deprivation in the rat. *Journal of Neurophysiology, 84,* 2699–2702.

OCD-UK (2005). What is obsessive-compulsive disorder? Retrieved March 17, 2007, from http://www.ocduk.org/1/ocd.htm.

O'Connor, P., & Brown, G. (1984). Supportive relationships: Fact or fancy? *Journal of Personal and Social Relationships, 1,* 159–175.

O'Connor, T. G., Deater-Deckard, K., Fulker, D., Rutter, M., & Plomin, R. (1998). Genotype-environment correlations in late childhood and early adolescence: Antisocial behavioral problems and coercive parenting. *Developmental Psychology, 34,* 970–981.

O'Connor, T., Rutter, M., & English Romanian Adoptees Study Team. (2000). Attachment disorder behaviour following early severe deprivation: Extension and longitudinal follow up. *Journal of the American Academy of Child and Adolescent Psychiatry, 39,* 703–711.

O'Donohue, W. T., Lilienfeld, S. O., & Fowler, K. A. (2007). Science is an essential safeguard against human error. In S. O. Lilienfeld & W. T. O'Donohue (Eds.), *The great ideas of clinical science: 17 principles that every mental health professional should understand* (pp. 3–27). New York: Routledge.

Office of Applied Studies. (2004). *Results from the 2003 National Survey on Drug Use and Health: National findings* (DHHS Publication No. SMA 04-3964, NSDUH Series H-25). Rockville, MD: Substance Abuse and Mental Health Services Administration.

Office of Technology Assessment. (1990). *The use of integrity tests for pre-employment screening.* Washington, DC: U.S. Congress Office of Technology Assessment.

Ogawa, S., Lee, T. M., Kay, A. R., & Tank, D. W. (1990). Brain magnetic resonance imaging with contrast dependent on blood oxygenation. *Proceedings of the National Academy of Sciences, U.S.A., 87,* 9868–9872.

Ogden, C., Carroll, M., Curtin, L., McDowell, M., Tabak, C., & Flegal, K. (2006). Prevalence of overweight and obesity in the Unites States, 1999–2004. *Journal of the American Medical Association, 295,* 1549–1555.

Ogilvie, R., Hunt, H., Kushniruk, A., & Newman, J. (1983). Lucid dreams and the arousal continuum. *Sleep Research, 12,* 182.

Ogrodniczuk, J. S., & Piper, W. E. (1999). Use of transference interpretations in dynamically oriented individual psychotherapy for patients with personality disorders. *Journal of Personality Disorders, 13,* 297–311.

Ohayon, M., Priest, R., Caulet, M., & Guilleminault, C. (1996). Hypnagogic and hypnopompic hallucinations: Pathological phenomena? *British Journal of Psychiatry, 169,* 459–467.

O'Keefe, D. J., & Figge, M. (1997). A guilt-based explanation of the door-in-the-face influence strategy. *Human Communication Research, 24,* 64–81.

O'Keefe, D. J., & Hale, S. L. (2001). An odds-ratio-based meta-analysis of research on the door-in-the-face influence strategy. *Communication Reports, 14,* 31–38.

O'Keefe, J. (1976). Place units in the hippocampus of the freely moving rat. *Experimental Neurology, 51,* 78–109.

Oldfield, K. (1998). The GRE as fringe science. *Skeptic, 6*(1), 68–72.

Olds, J. (1958). Satiation effects in self-stimulation of the brain. *Journal of Comparative and Physiological Psychology, 51,* 675–678.

O'Leary, K. D. (1980). Pills or skills for hyperactive children. *Journal of Applied Behavior Analysis, 13,* 191–204.

Olfson, M., Marcus, S., Sackheim, H. A., Thompson, J., & Pincus, H. A. (1998). Use of ECT for the inpatient treatment of recurrent major depression. *American Journal of Psychiatry, 155,* 22–29.

Oliver, M. B., & Hyde, J. S. (1993). Gender differences in sexuality: A meta-analysis. *Psychological Bulletin, 114,* 29–51.

Olkin, R., & Taliaferro, G. (2005). Evidence-based practices have ignored people with disabilities. In J. C. Norcross, L. E. Beutler, & R. F. Levant (Eds.), *Evidence-based practices in mental health* (pp. 353–358). Washington, DC: American Psychological Association.

Olsson, A., Ebert, J. P., Banaji, M. R., & Phelps, E. A. (2005). The role of social groups in the persistence of learned fear. *Science, 309,* 785–787.

Olweus, D. (1993). *Bullying at school: What we know and what we can do.* Oxford, England: Blackwell.

Ondeck, D. M. (2003). Impact of culture on pain. *Home Health Care Management Practice, 15,* 255–257.

Ones, D. S., Viswesvaran, C., & Dilchert, S. (2005). Personality at work: Raising awareness and correcting misconceptions. *Human Performance, 18,* 389–404.

Ones, D. S., Viswesvaran, C., & Schmidt, F. L. (1993). Comprehensive meta-analysis of integrity test validities. *Journal of Applied Psychology, 78,* 679–703.

Oppenheim K. (2006). Jesse Sullivan powers robotic arms with his mind. CNN.com, March 23; http://www.cnn.com/2006/US/03/22/btsc .oppenheim.bionic/.

Oppenheim, R. W. (1991). Cell death during development of the nervous system. *Annual Review of Neuroscience, 14,* 453–501.

Orlanksy, M. D., & Bonvillian, J. D. (1984). The role of iconicity in early sign language acquisition. *Journal of Speech and Hearing Disorders, 49,* 287–292.

Orlinsky, D. E., Grawe, K., & Parks, B. K. (1994). Process and outcome in psychotherapy—Noch einmal. In A. E. Bergin & S. L. Garfield (Eds.), *Handbook of psychotherapy and behavior change* (4th ed., pp. 270–376). New York: Wiley.

Orlinksy, D. E., & Howard, K. I. (1986). Process and outcome in psychotherapy. In S. L. Garfield & A. E. Bergin (Eds.), *Handbook of psychotherapy and behavior change* (3rd ed., pp. 311–384). New York: Wiley.

Orne, M. T. (1959). The nature of hypnosis: Artifact and essence. *Journal of Abnormal Psychology, 58,* 277–299.

Orne, M. T. (1962). On the social psychology of the psychological experiment: With particular reference to demand characteristics and their implications. *American Psychologist, 17,* 776–783.

Orne, M. T. (1965). Undesirable effects of hypnosis: The determinants and management. *International Journal of Clinical and Experimental Hypnosis, 13,* 226–237.

Orne, M. T. (1979). On the simulating subject as a quasi-control group in hypnosis research: What, why and how? In E. Fromm & R. Shor (Eds.), *Hypnosis: Developments in research and new perspectives* (2nd ed., pp. 519–565). Chicago: Aldine.

Ornstein, R. E. (1997). *The right mind: Making sense of the hemispheres.* Orlando, FL: Harcourt Brace.

Ortony, A., Clore, G. L., & Collins, A. (1988). *The cognitive structure of emotions.* New York: Cambridge University Press.

Ortony, A., & Turner, T. J. (1990). What's basic about basic emotions? *Psychological Review, 97,* 315–331.

Osborn, A. F. (1957). Applied imagination: Principles and procedures of creative problem solving (Rev. ed.). New York: Charles Scribner's Sons.

Ost, L.-G., Sterner, U., & Lindahlt, I.-L. (1984). Physiological responses in blood phobics. *Behaviour Research and Therapy, 22,* 109–117.

Ott, R. (1995). The natural wrongs about animal rights and animal liberation. *Journal of the American Veterinary Medical Association, 207,* 1023–1030.

Otto, M. W., Smits, J. A. J., & Reese, H. E. (2005). Combined psychotherapy and pharmacotherapy for mood and anxiety disorders in adults: Review and analysis. *Clinical Psychology: Science & Practice, 12,* 72–86.

Overmier, J. B., & Murison, R. (1997). Animal models reveal the "psych" in the psychosomatics of peptic ulcer. *Current Directions in Psychological Research, 6,* 180–184.

Overmier, J. B., & Seligman, M. E. P. (1967). Effects of inescapable shock upon subsequent escape and avoidance responding. *Journal of Comparative and Physiological Psychology, 63,* 28–33.

Overskeid, G. (2007). Looking for Skinner and finding Freud. *American Psychologist, 65,* 590–595.

Oyserman, D., Coon, H. M., & Kemmelmeier, M. (2002). Rethinking individualism and collectivism: Evaluation of theoretical assumptions and meta-analyses. *Psychological Bulletin, 128,* 3–72.

Ozer, E., Best, S., & Lipsey, T., & Weiss, D. L. (2003). Predictors of posttraumatic stress disorder symptoms in adults: A meta-analysis. *Psychological Bulletin, 129,* 52–73.

Paffenbarger, R. S., Hyde, R. T., Wing, A. L., & Hsich, C. C. (1986). Physical activity, all-cause mortality, and longevity of college alumni. *New England Journal of Medicine, 314,* 605–613.

Pagel, J. F. (2003). Non-dreamers. *Sleep Medicine, 4,* 235–241.

Pahnke, W. (1970). Drugs and mysticism. In B. Aaronson & H. Osmond (Eds.), *Psychedelics: The uses and implications of hallucinogenic drugs* (pp. 145–165). Garden City, NY: Anchor Books.

Paivio, A. (1969). Mental imagery in associative learning and memory. *Psychological Review, 76,* 341–363.

Palmer, L. K. (1995). Effects of a walking program on attributional style, depression, and self-esteem in women. *Perceptual and Motor Skills, 81,* 891–898.

Palmisano, S., Allison, R. S., & Howard, I. P. (2006). Illusory scene distortion occurs during perceived self-rotation in roll. *Vision Research, 46,* 4048–4058.

Panagiotakos, D. B., Pitsavos, C., Chrysohoou, C., Stefanadis, C., & Toutouzas, P. K. (2002). *Risk Stratification of Coronary Heart Disease, In Greece: Final Results from CARDIO2000 Epidemiological Study. Preventive Medicine, 35,* 548–556.

Panksepp, J. (2005). Beyond a joke: From animal laughter to human joy? *Science, 208,* 62–63.

Panksepp, J. (2007). Neurologizing the psychology of affects: How appraisal-based constructivism and basic emotion theory can coexist. *Perspectives in Psychological Science, 2,* 281–296.

Panksepp, J., & Panksepp, J. B. (2000). The seven sins of evolutionary psychology. *Evolution and Cognition, 6,* 108–131.

Paquette, V., Lévesque, J., Mensour, B., Leroux, J.-M., Beaudoin, G., Bourgouin, P., et al. (2003). Change the mind and you change the brain: Effects of cognitive-behavioral therapy on the neural correlates of spider phobia. *NeuroImage, 18,* 401–409.

Paris, J. (1999). Borderline personality disorder. In T. Millon, P. H. Blaney, & R. D. Davis (Eds.), *Oxford textbook of psychopathology* (pp. 628–653). New York: Oxford University Press.

Paris, J. (2000). *Myths of childhood.* New York: Brunner/Mazel.

Park, B., & Rothbart, M. (1982). Perception of out-group homogeneity and levels of social categorization: Memory for the subordinate attributes of in-group and out-group members. *Journal of Personality and Social Psychology, 42,* 1051–1068.

Park, D. C., Smith, A. D., & Cavanaugh, J. C. (1990). Metamemories of memory researchers. *Memory and Cognition, 18,* 321–327.

Park, M. A. (1982). Palmistry: Science or hand jive? *Skeptical Inquirer, 5,* 198–208.

Park, N., Peterson, C., & Seligman, M. E. P. (2004). Strengths of character and well-being. *Journal of Social and Clinical Psychology, 23,* 603–619.

Park, R. (2000). *Voodoo science: The road from foolishness to fraud.* New York: Oxford University Press.

Parke, R. (1996). *Fatherhood.* Cambridge, MA: Harvard University Press.

Parker, E. S., Cahill, L., & McGaugh, J. L. (2006). A case of unusual autobiographical remembering. *Neurocase, 12,* 35–49.

Parker, G. (1982). Re-searching the schizoprenogenic mother. *Journal of Nervous and Mental Disease, 170,* 452–462.

Parloff, M. B. (1976, February 21). Shopping for the right therapy. *Saturday Review,* 14–16.

Parnell, T. F., & Day, D. O. (Eds.). (1997). *Munchausen by proxy syndrome: Misunderstood child abuse.* London: Sage Publications.

Parra, E. J., Marcini, A., Akey, J., Martinson, J., Batzer, M. A., Cooper, R., et al. (1998). Estimating African American admixture proportions by use of population-specific alleles. *American Journal of Human Genetics, 63,* 1839–1851.

Pascalis, O., de Schonen, S., Morton, J., deRurelle, C., & Fabre-Grenet, M. (1995). Mother's face recognition by neonates: A replication and an extension. *Infant Behavior and Development, 8,* 79–85.

Pascual-Leone, J. (1989). An organismic process model of Witkin's field dependence-independence. In T. Globerson and T. Zelniker (Eds.), *Cognitive style and cognitive development* (pp. 36–70). Norwood, NJ: Ablex.

Pasewark, R. A., & Pantle, M. L. (1979). Insanity plea: Legislator's view. *American Journal of Psychiatry, 136,* 222–223.

Passini, F. T., & Norman, W. T. (1966). A universal conception of personality structure? *Journal of Personality and Social Psychology, 4,* 44–49.

Pate, R. R., Pratt, M., Blair, S. N., Haskell, W. L., Macera, C. A., Bouchard, C., et al. (1995). Physical activity and public health: A recommendation from the Centers for Disease Control and the American College of Sports Medicine. *Journal of the American Medical Association, 273,* 402–407.

Patel, G. A., & Sathian, K. (2000). Visual search: Bottom-up or top-down? *Frontiers in Bioscience, 5,* D169–193.

Patrick, C. J. (Ed.). (2006). *Handbook of psychopathy.* New York: Guilford Press.

Patrick, C. J., & Iacono, W. G. (1989). Psychopathy, threat, and polygraph test accuracy. *Journal of Applied Psychology, 74,* 347–355.

Patrick, C. J., & Iacono, W. G. (1991). Validity of the control question polygraph test: The problem of sampling bias. *Journal of Applied Psychology, 76,* 229–238.

Patterson, C. J. (1992). Children of lesbian and gay parents. *Child Development, 63,* 1025–1042.

Patterson, C. J., & Chan, R. W. (1996). Gay fathers and their children. In R. P. Cabaj and T. S. Stein (Eds.), *Textbook of homosexuality and mental health* (pp. 371–393). Washington, DC: American Psychiatric Press.

Paul, A. M. (2004). *The cult of personality: How personality tests are leading us to miseducate our children, mismanage our companies, and misunderstand ourselves.* New York: Free Press.

Paul, G. L., & Lentz, R. J. (1977). *Psychosocial treatment of chronic mental patients.* Cambridge, MA: Harvard University Press.

Paul, G., & Lentz, R. J. (1977). *Psychosocial treatment of chronic mental patients: Milieu versus social-learning programs.* Cambridge, MA: Harvard University Press.

Paulhus, D. L. (1991). Measurement and control of response bias. In J. P. Robinson & P. R. Shaver (Eds.), *Measures of personality and social psychological attitudes* (pp. 17–59). San Diego, CA: Academic Press.

Paulus, P. B., Larey, T. S., & Ortega, A. H. (1995). Performance and perceptions of brainstormers in an organizational setting. *Basic and Applied Social Psychology, 17,* 249–265

Paulus, T. M. (2004). Collaboration or cooperation? Small group interactions in a synchronous educational environment. In T. S. Roberts (Ed.), *Computer-supported collaborative learning in higher education* (pp. 100–124). Hershey, PA: Idea Group.

Pavlov, I. P. (1927). *Conditioned reflexes.* Oxford, England: Oxford University Press.

Paykel, E. S. (2003). Life events and affective disorders. *Acta Psychiatrica Scandinavia Supplement, 108,* 61–66.

Peacock, E. J., & Wong, P. T. (1990). The Stress Appraisal Measure (SAM): A multidimensional approach to cognitive appraisal. *Stress Medicine, 6,* 227–236.

Pearlin, L. I., & Lieberman, M. A. (1979). Social sources of emotional distress. In J. Simmons (Ed.), *Research in community and mental health* (pp. 217–248). Greenwich, CT: JAI Press.

Pearson, B. Z., & Fernàndez, S. C. (1994). Patterns of interaction in the lexical growth in two languages of bilingual infants and toddlers. *Language Learning, 44,* 617–653.

Pearson, B. Z., Fernàndez, S. C., & Oller, D. K. (1993). Lexical development in bilingual infants and toddlers: Comparison to monolingual norms. *Language Learning, 43,* 93–120.

Pearson, H. (2006). Mouse data hint at human pheromones. *Nature, 442,* 495.

Pechman, C., & Stewart, D. W. (1989). Advertising repetition: A critical review of wear-in and wear-out. In J. H. Leigh and C. R. Martin Jr. (Eds.), *Current issues and research in advertising 1988* (pp. 285–289). Ann Arbor, MI: University of Michigan.

Pederson Mussell, M., Crosby, R. D., Crow, S. J., Knopke, A.J., Peterson, C. B., Wonderlich, S. A., et al. (2000). Utilization of empirically supported psychotherapy treatments for individuals with eating disorders: A survey of psychologists. *International Journal of Eating Disorders, 27,* 230–237.

Pedersen, N. L., Plomin, R., McClearn, G. E., & Friberg, L. (1988). Neuroticism, extraversion, and related traits in adult twins reared apart and reared together. *Journal of Personality and Social Psychology, 55,* 950–957.

Pederson, N. L., Plomin, R., Nesselroade, J. R., & McClearn, G. E. (1992). A quantitative genetic analysis of cognitive abilities during the second half of the life span. *Psychological Science, 3,* 346–352.

Pelham, B. W., Carvallo, M., & Jones, J. T. (2005). Implicit egotism. *Current Directions in Psychological Science, 14,* 106–110.

Pelham, B. W., Mirenberg, M. C., & Jones, J. T. (2002). Why Susie sells seashells by the seashore: Implicit egotism and major life decisions. *Journal of Personality and Social Psychology, 82,* 469–487.

Pelkonnen, M., & Marttunen, M. (2003). Child and adolescent suicide: Epidemiology, risk factors, and approaches to prevention. *Psychiatric Drugs, 5,* 243–265.

Penfield, W. (1958). *The excitable cortex in conscious man.* Liverpool, England: Liverpool University Press.

Penfield, W., & Perot, P. (1963). The brain's record of auditory and visual experience. A final summary and discussion. *Brain, 86,* 595–696.

Pennebaker, J. W. (1997). Writing about emotional experiences as a therapeutic process. *Psychological Science, 8,* 162–166.

Penner, L. A., Dovidio, J. F., Schroeder, D. A., & Piliavin, J. A. (2005). Prosocial behavior: Multilevel perspectives. *Annual Review of Psychology, 56,* 365–392.

Pepperberg, I. M. (1999). *The Alex studies: Cognitive and communicative abilities of grey parrots.* Cambridge, MA: Harvard University Press.

Perkins, D. N. (1981). *The mind's best work.* Cambridge, MA: Harvard University Press.

Perlmutter, M. (1983). Learning and memory through adulthood. In M. W. Riley, B. B. Hess, & K. Bond (Eds.), *Aging in society: Selected reviews of recent research.* Hillsdale, NJ: Erlbaum.

Perls, F. S. (1971). *Gestalt therapy verbatim.* New York: Bantam Books.

Perry, J. C. (1992). Problems and considerations in the valid assessment of personality disorders. *American Journal of Psychiatry, 149,* 1645–1653.

Perry, M., Church, R., & Goldin-Meadow, S. (1988). Transitional knowledge in the acquisition of concepts. *Cognitive Development, 3,* 359–400.

Perry, W. G., Jr. (1970). *Forms of intellectual and ethical development in the college years.* Oxford, England: Holt, Rinehart & Winston.

Persinger, M. A. (1987). *Neuropsychological bases of God beliefs.* New York: Praeger.

Persinger, M. A. (1993). Vectorial cerebral hemisphericity as differential sources for the sensed presence, mystical experiences, and religious conversions. *Perceptual and Motor Skills, 76,* 915–930.

Persinger, M. A. (1994). Near-death experiences: Determining the neuroanatomical pathways by experiential patterns and simulation in experimental settings. In L. Besette (Ed.), *Healing: Beyond suffering or death* (pp. 277–286). Chabanel, Quebec, Canada: MNH.

Persinger, M. A. (2002). The sensed presence within experimental settings: Implications for the male and female concept of self. *Journal of Psychology, 137,* 5–16.

Pessah, M. A., & Roffwarg, H. P. (1972). Spontaneous middle ear muscle activity in man: A rapid eye movement sleep phenomenon. *Science, 178,* 773–776.

Peters, D. P., & Ceci, S. J. (1982) Peer-review practices of psychology journals: The fate of published articles, submitted again. *Behavioral and Brain Sciences, 5,* 187–195.

Peterson, C. (2000). The future of optimism. *American Psychologist, 55,* 44–55.

Peterson, C., & Seligman, M. E. P. (2003). Character strengths before and after September 11. *Psychological Science, 14,* 381–384.

Peterson, C., & Seligman, M. E. P. (2004). *Character strengths and virtues: A handbook and classification.* New York: Oxford University Press.

Peterson, L. R., & Peterson, M. J. (1959). Short-term retention of individual verbal items. *Journal of Experimental Psychology, 58,* 193–198.

Peterson, R. A. (2001). On the use of college students in social science research: Insights from a second-order meta-analysis. *Journal of Consumer Research, 28,* 450–461.

Petitto, L. A., & Marentette, P. F. (1991). Babbling in the manual mode: Evidence for the ontogeny of language. *Science, 251,* 1493–1496.

Petitto, L. A., Zatorre, R. J., Gauna, K., Nikelski, E. J., Dostie, D., & Evans, A. C. (2000). Speech-like cerebral activity in profoundly deaf people processing sign language: Implications for the neural basis of human language. *Proceedings of the National Academy of Sciences, 97,* 13961–13966.

Petry, N. M., Tennen, H., & Affleck, G. (2000). Stalking the elusive client variable in psychotherapy research. In C. R. Snyder, & R. Ingram (Eds.), *Handbook of psychological change* (pp. 88–108). New York: John Wiley & Sons.

Pettigrew, T. F. (1958). Personality and sociocultural factors in intergroup attitudes: A cross-national comparison. *Journal of Conflict Resolution, 2,* 29–42.

Pettigrew, T. F. (1979). The ultimate attribution error: Extending Allport's cognitive analysis of prejudice. *Personality and Social Psychology Bulletin, 5,* 461–476.

Pettigrew, T. F. (1998). Intergroup contact theory. *Annual Review of Psychology, 49,* 65–85.

Pettinati, H. M., Tamburello, T. A., Ruetsch, C. R., & Kaplan, F. N. (1994). Patient attitudes toward electroconvulsive therapy. *Psychopharmacological Bulletin, 30,* 471–475.

Petty, R. E., & Caccioppo, J. T. (1986). *Communication and persuasion: Central and peripheral routes to attitude change.* New York: Springer Verlag.

Pew Research Center. (2006, February 13). Are we happy yet? Retrieved from http://pewresearch.org/pubs/301/are-we-happy-yet.

Pezdek, K., Blandon-Gitlin, I., & Moore, C. (2003). Children's face recognition memory: More evidence for the cross-race effect. *Journal of Applied Psychology, 88,* 760–763.

Pezdek, K., Finger, K., & Hodge, D. (1997). Planting false childhood memories: The role of event plausibility. *Psychological Science, 8,* 437–441.

Phares, J. (1979). *Clinical psychology.* Homewood, IL: Dorsey Press.

Phares, V., & Compas, B. E. (1992). The role of fathers in child and adolescent psychopathology: Make room for daddy. *Psychological Bulletin, 111,* 387–412.

Phelps, E. A. (2004). Human emotion and memory: Interactions of the amygdala and hippocampal complex. *Current Opinion in Neurobiology, 14,* 198–202.

Phil, R. O. (1999). Substance abuse: Etiological considerations. In T. Millon, P. Blaney, & R. D. Davis (Eds.), *Oxford handbook of psychopathology* (pp. 249–276). New York: Oxford University Press.

Phillips, D. P., & Wills, J. S. (1987). A drop in suicides around major national holidays. *Suicide and Life Threatening Behavior, 17,* 1–12.

Phillips, K., & Fulker, D. W. (1989). Quantitative genetic analysis of longitudinal trends in adoption designs with application to IQ in the Colorado Adoption Project. *Behavior Genetics, 19,* 621–658.

Phillips, K. A., McElroy, S. L., Keck, P. E., Pope, H. G., & Hudson, J. I. (1993). Body dysmorphic disorder: 30 Cases of imagined ugliness. *American Journal of Psychiatry, 150,* 302–308.

Phillips, M. L., Young, A. W., Senior, C., Brammer, M., Andrew, A. J., Calder, J., et al. (1997). A specific neural substrate for perceiving facial expressions of disgust. *Nature, 389,* 495–498.

Phillips, M. R., Wolf, A. S., & Coons, D. J. (1988). Psychiatry and the criminal justice system: Testing the myths. *American Journal of Psychiatry, 145,* 605–610.

Phillips, W. T., Kiernan, M., & King, A. C. (2001). The effects of physical activity on physical and psychological health. In A. Baum, T. A. Revenson, & J. E. Singer (Eds.), *Handbook of health psychology* (pp. 627–660). Mahwah, NJ: Lawrence Erlbaum.

Piaget, J. (1932). *The moral judgment of the child.* London: Kegan Paul.

Piatelli-Palmarini, M. (1994). *Inevitable illusions: How mistakes of reason rule our minds.* New York: John Wiley & Sons.

Piccione, C., Hilgard, E. R., & Zimbardo, P. G. (1989). On the degree of stability of measured hypnotizability over a 25-year period. *Journal of Personality and Social Psychology, 56,* 289–295.

Pigott, T. A., Myers, K. R., & Williams, D. A. (1996). Obsessive-compulsive disorder: A neuropsychiatric perspective. In: R. M. Rapee (Ed.), *Current controversies in the anxiety disorders* (pp. 134–160). New York: Guilford.

Piliavin, I. M., Rodin, J., & Piliavin, J. A. (1969). Good samaritanism: An underground phenomenon? *Journal of Personality and Social Psychology, 13,* 289–299.

Pillemer, D. B. (1984). Flashbulb memories of the assassination attempt on President Reagan. *Cognition, 16,* 63–80.

Pinker, S. (1994). *How the mind works.* New York: Norton.

Pinker, S. (1997). *How the mind works.* New York: W. W. Norton.

Pinker, S. (2002). *The blank slate: The modern denial of human nature.* New York: Penguin.

Pinker, S. (2005, February 14). The science of difference: Sex ed. *The New Republic, 232,* 15–17.

Pinsk, M. A., DeSimone, K., Moore, T., Gross, C. G., & Kastner, S. (2005). Representations of faces and body parts in macaque temporal cortex: A functional MRI study. *Proceedings of the National Academy of Sciences, U.S.A., 102,* 6996–7001.

Pinto, A. C. (1992). Medidas de categorizacao: Frequencia de producao e de tipicidade. *Jornal de Psicologia, 10,* 10–15.

Piper, A. (1993). "Truth serum" and "recovered memories" of sexual abuse: A review of the evidence. *Journal of Psychiatry & Law, 21*(4), 447–471.

Piper, A. (1997). *Hoax and reality: The bizarre world of multiple personality disorder.* Northvale, NJ: Jason Aronson.

Pirke, K. M., & Ploog, D. (1987). Biology of human starvation. In P. J. V. Beumont, G. D. Burrows, & R. C. Casper (Eds.), *Handbook of eating disorders: Part 1: Anorexia and bulimia nervosa* (pp. 79–102). New York: Elsevier.

Piske, T., MacKay, I. R. A., & Flege, J. E. (2001). Factors affecting degree of foreign accent in an L2: A review. *Journal of Phonetics, 29,* 191–215.

Pitman, R. K., Sanders, K. M., Zusman, R. M., Healy, A. R., Cheema, F., Lasko, N. B., et al. (2002). Pilot study of secondary prevention of posttraumatic stress disorder with propranolol. *Biological Psychiatry, 51,* 189–192.

Pittas, A. G., Hariharan, R., Stark, P. C., Hajduk, C. L., Greenberg, A. S., & Roberts, S. B. (2005). Interstitial glucose level is a significant predictor of energy intake in free-living women with healthy body weight. *Journal of Nutrition, 135,* 1070–1074.

Platt, J. R. (1964). Strong inference. *Science, 146,* 347–353.

Plomin, R., Corley, R., DeFries, J. C., & Fulker, D. W. (1990). Individual differences in television viewing in early childhood: Nature as well as nurture. *Psychological Science, 1,* 371–377.

Plomin, R., & Crabbe, J. (2000). DNA. *Psychological Bulletin, 126,* 806–828.

Plomin, R., & Daniels, D. (1987). Why are children in the same family so different from one another? *Behavioral and Brain Sciences, 10,* 1–16.

Plomin, R., DeFries, J. C., & Loehlin, J. C. (1977). Genotype-environment interaction and correlation in the analysis of human behavior. *Psychological Bulletin, 84,* 309–322.

Plomin, R., DeFries, J. C., McClearn, G. E., & Rutter, M. (1997). *Behavioral genetics* (3rd ed.). New York: W. H. Freeman.

Plomin, R., DeFries, J. C., & Roberts, M. K. (1977). Assortative mating by unwed biological parents of adopted children. *Science, 196,* 449–450.

Plomin, R., Fulker, D. W., Corley, R., & DeFries, J. C. (1997). Nature, nurture, and cognitive development from 1 to 16 years: A parent-offspring adoption study. *Psychological Science, 8,* 442–447.

Plomin, R., & Kovas, Y. (2005). Generalist genes and learning disabilities. *Psychological Bulletin, 131,* 592–617.

Plomin, R., & McClearn, G. E. (Eds.), *Nature, nurture and psychology.* Washington, DC: American Psychological Association.

Plunkett, K., Karmiloff-Smith, A., Bates, E., Elman, J. L., & Johnson, M. H. (1997). Connectionism and developmental psychology. *Journal of Child Psychology and Psychiatry, 38,* 53–80.

Plutchik, R. (2000). *Emotions in the practice of psychotherapy: Clinical implications of affect theories.* Washington, DC: American Psychological Association.

Plutchik, R. (2003). *Emotions and life: Perspectives from psychology, biology, and evolution.* Washington, DC: American Psychological Association.

Plutchik, R., & Kellerman, H. (Eds.). (1986). *Emotion: Theory, research, and experience: Biological foundations of emotion.* New York: Academic Press.

Pohorecky, L. (1977). Biphasic action of ethanol. *Biobehavioral Review, 1,* 231–240.

Poizner, H., Klima, E. S., & Bellugi, U. (1987). *What the hands reveal about the brain.* Cambridge, MA: MIT Press.

Polivy, J., & Hermann, C. P. (2002). If you first don't succeed. False hopes of self-change. *American Psychologist, 57,* 677–689.

Polivy, J., Schueneman, A. L., & Carlson, K. (1976). Alcohol and tension reduction: Cognitive and physiological effects. *Journal of Abnormal Psychology, 85,* 595–600.

Pollard, K. S., Salama, S. R., King, B., Kern, A. D., Dreszer, T., Katzman, S., et al. (2006, October 13). Forces shaping the fastest evolving regions in the human genome. *PLoS Genetics, 2*(10), e168.

Pollitt, E., Gorman, K. S., Engle, P. L., Martorell, R., & Rivera, J. (1993). Early supplementary feeding and cognition: Effects over two decades. *Monographs of the Society for Research in Child Development, 58* (7, Serial No. 235).

Polusny, M. A., & Follerre, V. M. (1996). Remembering childhood sexual abuse: A national survey of psychologists' clinical practices, beliefs, and personal experiences. *Professional Psychology: Research and Practice, 27,* 41–52.

Pontón, M. O., & Gorsuch, R. L. (1988). Prejudice and religion revisited: A cross-cultural investigation with a Venezuelan sample. *Journal for the Scientific Study of Religion, 27,* 260–271.

Poole, D. A., Lindsay, D. S., Memon, A., & Bull, R. (1995). Psychotherapists' opinions, practices, and experiences with recovery of memories of incestuous abuse. *Journal of Consulting and Clinical Psychology, 68,* 426–437.

Pope, H. G., & Hudson, J. I. (1992). Is childhood sexual abuse a risk factor for bulimia nervosa? *American Journal of Psychiatry, 149,* 455–463.

Pope, H. G., Jr., Poliakoff, M. B., Parker, M. P., Boynes, M., & Hudson, J. I. (2007). Is dissociative amnesia a culture-bound syndrome? Findings from a survey of historical literature. *Psychological Medicine, 37,* 225–233.

Popper, K. R. (1959). *The logic of scientific discovery.* New York: Basic Books.

Popper, K. R. (1965). *The logic of scientific discovery.* New York: Harper.

Porte, H., & Hobson, J. A. (1986). Bizarreness in REM and NREM reports. *Sleep Research, 15,* 81.

Porter, S., & Peace, K. A. (2007). The scars of memory: A prospective longitudinal investigation of the consistency of traumatic and positive emotional memories in adulthood. *Psychological Science, 18,* 435–441.

Porter, S., Yuille, J. C., & Lehman, D. R. (1999). The nature of real, implanted, and fabricated memories for emotional childhood events: Implications for the recovered memory debate. *Law and Human Behavior, 23,* 517–538.

Posner, G. P., & Sampson, W. (1999, Fall/Winter). Chinese acupuncture for heart surgery anesthesia. *The Scientific Review of Alternative Medicine, 3*(2), 15–19.

Posner, M. I., & Levitin, D. J. (2002). Imaging the future. In D. J. Levitin. (Ed.), *Foundations of cognitive psychology: Core readings* (pp. 841–854). Cambridge, MA: MIT Press.

Posner, M. I., & Snyder, C. R. R. (1975). Facilitation and inhibition in the processing of signals. In P. M. A. Rabbitt & S. Dornic (Eds.), *Attention and performance* (pp. 669–682). New York: Academic Press.

Posthuma, D., & de Geus, E. J. C. (2006). Progress in the molecular-genetic study of intelligence. *Current Directions in Psychological Science, 15,* 151–155.

Postmes, T., & Spears, R. (1998). Deindividuation and antinormative behavior: A meta-analysis. *Psychological Bulletin, 123,* 238–259.

Potts, R. G. (2004). Spirituality, religion, and the experience of illness. In P. Camic & S. Knight (Eds.), *Clinical handbook of health psychology: A practical guide to effective interventions* (pp. 297–314). Cambridge, MA: Hogrefe & Huber.

Powers, D. E. (1993). Coaching for the SAT: A summary of the summaries and an update. *Educational Measurement: Issues and Practice, 12,* 24–39.

Powers, D. E., & Rock, D. A. (1999). Effects of coaching on SAT I: Reasoning test scores. *Journal of Educational Measurement, 36,* 93–118.

Pratkanis, A. R. (1992). The cargo-cult science of subliminal persuasion. *Skeptical Inquirer, 16,* 260–272.

Pratkanis, A. R. (1995, July/August). How to sell a pseudoscience. *Skeptical Inquirer, 19,* 19–25.

Premack, D., & Woodruff, G. (1978). Does the chimpanzee have a theory of mind? *Behavioral and Brain Sciences, 1,* 515–526.

Presley, S. (1997). *Why people believe in ESP for the wrong reasons.* Retrieved October 15, 2006, from http://www.rit.org/essays/think/esp.html.

Price, R. H., & Bouffard, D. L. (1974). Behavioral appropriateness and situational constraint as dimensions of social behavior. *Journal of Personality and Social Psychology, 30,* 579–586.

Priel, B., & de Schonen, S. (1986). Self-recognition: A study of a population without mirrors. *Journal of Experimental Child Psychology, 41,* 237–250.

Prince, C. G., & Berthouze, L. (2004). Third International Workshop on Epigenetic Robotics (EpiRob03). *Interaction Studies: Social Behaviour and Communication in Biological and Artificial Systems, 5,* 155–159.

Prince, M. J., Harwood, R. H., Blizard, R. A., Thomas, A., & Mann, A. H. (1997). Social support deficits, loneliness and life events as risk factors for depression in old age. The Gospel Oak Project VI. *Psychological Medicine, 27,* 323–332.

Prinz, J. J. (2004). *Gut reactions: A perceptual theory of emotion.* New York: Oxford University Press.

Prochaska, J. O., & DeClemente, C. C. (1982). Transtheoretical therapy: Toward a more integrative model of change. *Psychotherapy: Theory, Research, and Practice, 20,* 161–173.

Prochaska, J. O., & DiClemente, C. C. (1984). *The transtheoretical approach: Crossing the traditional boundaries of therapy.* Homewood, IL: Dow Jones-Irwin.

Prochaska, J. O., & Norcross, J. C. (2002). Stages of change. In J. C. Norcross (Ed.), *Psychotherapy relationships that work.* New York: Oxford University Press.

Prochaska, J. O., & Norcross, J. C. (2007). *Systems of psychotherapy: A transtheoretical approach* (6th ed.). Pacific Grove, CA: Brooks/Cole.

Project MATCH Research Group. (1997). Matching alcoholism treatments to client heterogeneity: Project MATCH posttreatment drinking outcomes. *Journal of Studies on Alcohol, 58,* 7–29.

Pronin, E., Gilovich, T., & Ross, L. (2004). Objectivity in the eye of the beholder: Divergent perceptions of bias in self versus others. *Psychological Review, 3,* 781–799.

Pronk, N. P., & Wing, R. R. (1994). Physical activity and long-term maintenance of weight loss. *Obesity Research, 2,* 587–599.

Pronko, N. H. (1963). *Abnormal psychology.* Baltimore: Williams & Wilkins.

Proske, U. (2006). Kinesthesia: The role of muscle receptors. *Muscle Nerve, 34,* 545–558.

Provine, R. R. (1996). Laughter. *American Scientist, 84,* 38–45.

Provine, R. R. (2000). *Laughter: A scientific investigation.* New York: Viking.

Pukay-Martin, N. D., Cristiani, R. S., Saveanu, R., & Bornstein, R. A. (2003). The relationship between stressful life events and cognitive function in HIV-infected men. *Journal of Neuropsychiatry: Clinical Neurosciences, 15,* 436–441.

Purcell, K. (1963). Distinctions between subgroups of asthmatic children: Children's perceptions of events associated with asthma. *Pediatrics, 31,* 486–494.

Purves, D., Lotto, R. B., & Nundy, S. (2002). Why we see what we do. *American Scientist, 90,* 236.

Pyszczynski, T., Solomon, S., & Greenberg, J. (2003). *In the wake of 9/11: The psychology of terror.* Washington, DC: American Psychological Association.

Quart, E. (2006, July/August). Extreme parenting. *Salon.com.* Retrieved from http://www.theatlantic.com/doc/prem/200607/parenting.

Quick, D. C. (1999, March/April). Joint pain and weather. *Skeptical Inquirer, 23,* 49–51.

Quick, J. C., Quick, J. D., Nelson, D. L., & Hurrell, J. J. (1997). *Preventive stress management in organizations.* Washington, DC: American Psychological Association.

Quinn, P. C., & Eimas, P. D. (1996). Perceptual cues that permit categorical differentiation of animal species by infants. *Journal of Experimental Child Psychology, 63,* 189–211.

Quinn, P. J., O'Callaghan, M. J., Williams, G. M., Najman, J. M., Andersen, M. J., & Bor, W. (2001). The effect of breastfeeding on child development at 5 years: A cohort study. *Journal of Paediatrics and Child Health, 37,* 465–469.

Quiroga, R. Q., Reddy, G., Kreiman, G., Koch, C., & Fried, I. (2005). Invariant visual representation by single neurons in the human brain. *Nature, 435,* 1102–1107.

Quiroga, R. Q., Reddy, L., Kreiman, G., Koch, C., & Fried, I. (2005). Invariant visual representation by single neurons in the human brain. *Nature, 435,* 1102–1107.

Rabinowitz, J., & Renert, N. (1997). Clinicians' predictions of length of psychotherapy. *Psychiatric Services, 48,* 97–99.

Rachid, F., & Bertschy, G. (2006). Safety and efficacy of repetitive transcranial magnetic stimulation in the treatment of depression: A critical appraisal of the last 10 years. *Neurophysiologie Clinique, 36,* 157–183.

Rachman, S. (1977). The conditioning theory of fear-acquisition: A critical examination. *Behaviour Research and Therapy, 15,* 375–387.

Rachman, S. (1994). Psychological treatment of panic: Mechanisms. In B. E. Wolfe & J. D. Maser (Eds.), *Treatment of panic disorder: A consensus development conference* (pp. 133–148). Washington, DC: American Psychiatric Press.

Rachman, S., & Hodgson, R. J. (1968). Experimentally induced "sexual fetishism": Replication and development. *Psychological Record, 18,* 25–27.

Rafnsson, F. D., Jonsson, F. H., & Windle, M. (2006). Coping strategies, stressful life events, problem behaviors, and depressed affect. *Anxiety, Stress, & Coping, 19,* 241–257.

Raimy, V. C. (Ed.). (1950). *Training in clinical psychology (Boulder Conference).* New York: Prentice-Hall.

Rainville, P., Bechara, A., Naqvi, N., & Damasio, A. R. (2006). Basic emotions are associated with distinct patterns of cardiorespiratory activity. *International Journal of Psychophysiology, 61,* 5–18.

Rakison, D. H. (2005). The perceptual to conceptual shift in infancy and early childhood: A surface or deep distinction? In L. Gershkoff-Stowe, & D. H. Rakison (Eds.), *Building object categories in developmental time* (pp. 131–158). Mahwah, NJ: Erlbaum.

Ramachandran, V. S., & Hubbard, E. M. (2001). Synaesthesia: A window into perception, thought and language. *Journal of Consciousness Studies, 8,* 33–34.

Ramachandran, V. S., & Rogers-Ramachandran, D. C. (1996). Synaesthesia in phantom limbs induced with mirrors. *Proceedings of the Royal Society of London, 263,* 377–386.

Randi, J. (1982). *Flim-flam!* Amherst, NY: Prometheus Books.

Range, L. M., Menyhert, A., Walsh, M. L., Hardin, K. N., Ellis, J. B., & Craddick, R. (1991). Letters of recommendation: Perspectives, recommendations, and ethics. *Professional Psychology: Research and Practice, 22,* 389–392.

Rankin, J. L. (2005). *Parenting experts: Their advice, the research, and getting it right.* Westport, CT: Praeger.

Rasmussen, K., Sampson, S. M., & Rummans, T. A. (2002). Electroconvulsive therapy and newer modalities for the treatment of medication-refractory mental illness. *Mayo Clinic Proceedings, 77,* 552–556.

Rassin, E., Merckelbach, H., & Spaan, V. (2001). When dreams become a royal road to confusion: Realistic dreams, dissociation, and fantasy proneness. *Journal of Nervous and Mental Disease, 189,* 478–481.

Raudenbush, S. W. (1984). Magnitude of teacher expectancy effects on pupil IQ as a function of the credibility of expectancy induction: A synthesis of findings from 18 experiments. *Journal of Educational Psychology, 76,* 85–97.

Raulin, M.R., & Lilienfeld, S.O. (in press). Research paradigms in the study of psychopathology. In T. Millon, P. Blaney, and R. Davis (eds.), *Oxford textbook of psychopathology.* New York: Oxford University Press.

Raulin, M. L., & Lilienfeld, S. O. (1999). Research strategies for studying psychopathology. In T. Millon, P. H. Blaney, & R. D. Davis (Eds.), *The Oxford textbook of psychopathology* (pp. 49–78). New York: Oxford University Press.

Rauscher, F. H., Shaw, G. L., & Ky, K. N. (1993). Music and spatial task performance. *Nature, 365,* 611.

Raven, J., Raven, J. C., & Court, J. H. (1998). *Manual for Raven's Advanced Progressive Matrices.* Oxford, England: Oxford Psychologists Press.

Ray, O. S., & Ksir, C. (1998). *Drugs, society, and human behavior* (8th ed). St. Louis, MO: Mosby.

Rayner, K., Foorman, B. R., Perfetti, C. A., Pesetsky, D., & Seidenberg, M. S. (2002). How should reading be taught? *Scientific American, 286,* 84.

Raz, S., & Raz, N. (1990). Structural brain abnormalities in the major psychoses: A quantitative review of the evidence from computerized imaging. *Psychological Bulletin, 108,* 93–108.

Razoumnikova, O. (2000). Functional organization of different brain areas during convergent and divergent thinking: An EEG investigation. *Cognitive Brain Research, 10,* 11–18.

Reasoner, R. (2000). *Self-esteem and youth: What research has to say about it.* Port Ludlow, WA: International Council for Self-Esteem.

Rechtschaffen, A. (1998). Current perspectives on the function of sleep. *Perspectives inBiology and Medicine, 41*(3), 359–390.

Rechtschaffen, A., Verdone, P., & Wheaton, J. (1963). Reports of mental activity during sleep. *Canadian Psychiatry, 8,* 409–414.

Redding, R. E. (1998). How common-sense psychology can inform law and psycholegal research. *University of Chicago Law School Roundtable, 5,* 107–142.

Redfern, M. S., Muller, M. L., Jennings, J. R., & Furman, J. M. (2002). Attentional dynamics in postural control during perturbations in young and older adults. *Journals of Gerontology: Series A: Biological Sciences and Medical Sciences, 57A,* B298–B303.

Redlinger, W. E., & Park, T. Z. (1980). Language mixing in young bilinguals. *Journal of Child Language, 3,* 449–455.

Reed, E. W., & Reed, S. C. (1965). *Mental retardation: A family study.* Philadelphia: W. B. Saunders.

Regan, P. C., & Berscheid, E. (1997). *Lust: What we know about human sexual desire.* Thousand Oaks, CA: Sage.

Rehberg, R. A., & Rosenthal, E. R. (1978). *Class and merit in the American high school.* New York: Longman.

Reich, W. (1949). *Character analysis.* New York: Orgone Institute Press.

Reichenbach, H. (1938). *Experience and prediction.* Chicago: University of Illinois Press.

Reichenbach, S., Sterchi, R., Scherer, M., Trelle, S., Bürgi, E., Bürgi, U., et al. (2007). Meta-analysis: Chondroitin for osteoarthritis of the knee or hip. *Annals of Internal Medicine, 146,* 580–590.

Reicher, S. D., & Haslam, S. A. (2006). Rethinking the social psychology of tyranny: The BBC Prison Study. *British Journal of Social Psychology, 45,* 1–40.

Reid, B. (2002, April 30). The nocebo effect: Placebo's evil twin. *Washington Post,* HF01.

Reiner, W. G., & Gearhart, J. P. (2004). Discordant sexual identity in some genetic males with cloacal exstrophy assigned to female sex at birth. *New England Journal of Medicine, 350,* 333–341.

Reinsel, R., Wollman, M., & Antrobus, J. (1986). Effects of environmental context and cortical activation on thought. *Journal of Mind and Behavior, 7,* 250–276.

Reis, F. L., Masson, S., deOliveira, A. R., & Brandao, M. L. (2004). Dopaminergic mechanisms in the conditioned and unconditioned fear as assessed by the two-way avoidance and light switch-off tests. *Pharmacology, Biochemistry and Behavior, 79,* 359–365.

Reisenzein, R. (1983). The Schachter theory of emotion: Two decades later. *Psychological Bulletin, 94,* 239–264.

Reiss, D., & Marino, L. (2001). Mirror self-recognition in the bottlenose dolphin: A case of cognitive convergence. *Proceedings of the National Academy of Sciences, 98,* 5937–5942.

Reiss, S., & McNally, R. J. (1985). The expectancy model of fear. In S. Reiss & R. R. Bootzin (Eds.), *Theoretical issues in behavior therapy* (pp. 107–121). New York: Academic Press.

Reivich, M., Kuhl, D., Wolf, A., Greenberg, J., Phelps, M., Ido, T., et al. (1979). The [18F]fluorodeoxyglucose method for the measurement of local cerebral glucose utilization in man. *Circulation Research, 44,* 127–137.

Remefedi, G., French, S., Story, M., Resnick, M. D., & Blum, R. (1998). The relationship between suicide risk and sexual orientation: Results of a population-based study. *American Journal of Public Health, 88,* 57–60.

Renken, B., Egeland, B., Marvinney, D., Mangeldorf, S., & Sroufe, L. A. (1989). Early childhood antecedents of aggression and passive-withdrawal in early elementary school. *Journal of Personality, 57,* 257–281.

Rensink, R. A., O'Regan, J. K., & Clark, J. (1997). To see or not to see: The need for attention to perceive changes in scenes. *Psychological Science, 8,* 368–373.

Repetti, R., Taylor, S., and Seeman, T. (2002). Risky families: Family social environments and the mental and physical health of offspring. *Psychological Bulletin 128,* 330–366.

Resnick, S. M., Pham, D. L., Kraut, M. A., Zonderman, A. B., & Davatzikos, C. (2003). Longitudinal magnetic resonance imaging studies of older adults: A shrinking brain. *Journal of Neuroscience, 23,* 3295–3301.

Restak, R. 1984. *The Brain.* New York: Bantam Books.

Revelle, W., Humphreys, M. S., Simon, L., & Gilliland, K. (1980). The interactive effect of personality, time of day, and caffeine: A test of the arousal model. *Journal of Experimental Psychology: General, 109,* 1–31.

Revonsuo, A. (2000). The reinterpretation of dreams: An evolutionary hypothesis of the function of dreaming. *Behavioral and Brain Sciences, 23,* 877–901.

Reyna, V. F., & Farley, F. (2006). Risk and rationality in adolescent decision making: Implications for theory, practice, and policy. *Psychological Science in the Public Interest, 7*(1), 1–44.

Reynolds, D. (2003, April 25). Panel recommends counseling for sterilization survivors. *Inclusion Daily Express.* Retrieved from http://www.inclusiondaily.com/news/institutions/nc/eugenics.htm#042503.

Rhine, J. B. (1938). Experiments bearing on the precognition hypothesis: I. Preshuffling card calling. *Journal of Parapsychology, 2,* 38–54.

Rhodes, G., Halberstadt, J., & Brajkovich, G. (2001). Generalization of mere exposure effects to averaged composite faces. *Social Cognition, 19,* 57–70.

Rhule, D. M. (2005). Take care to do no harm: Harmful interventions for youth problem behavior. *Professional Psychology: Research and Practice, 36,* 618–625.

Ribar, R. J., Oakes, L. M., & Spalding, T. L. (2004). Infants can rapidly form new categorical representations. *Psychonomic Bulletin & Review, 11,* 536–541.

Ricciardelli, L. A. (1992). Bilingualism and cognitive development in relation to threshold theory. *Journal of Psycholinguistic Research, 21,* 301–316.

Rice, B. (1982). The Hawthorne defect: Persistence of a flawed theory. *Psychology Today, 16*(2), 71–74.

Richards, J. M., Butler, E. A., & Gross, J. J. (2003). Emotion regulation in romantic relationships: The cognitive consequences of concealing feelings. *Journal of Social and Personal Relationships, 20,* 599–620.

Richardson, R., Riccio, C., & Axiotis, R. (1986). Alleviation of infantile amnesia in rats by internal and external contextual cues. *Developmental Psychobiology, 19,* 453–462.

Rickels, K., Hesbacher, P. T., Weise, C. C., Gray, B., & Feldman, H. S. (1970). Pills and improvement: A study of placebo response in psychoneurotic outpatients. *Psychopharmacologia, 16*(4), 318–328.

Ridgway, S. H. (2002). Asymmetry and symmetry in brain waves from dolphin left and right hemispheres: Some observations after anesthesia, during quiescent hanging behavior, and during visual obstruction. *Brain, Behavior, and Evolution, 60,* 265–274.

Ridley, M. (2003). *Nature via nurture: Genes, experience, and what makes us human.* New York: HarperCollins.

Rieber, R. W. (1999). Hypnosis, false memory, and multiple personality: A trinity of affinity. *History of Psychiatry, 10,* 3–11.

Riesenhuber, M., & Poggio, T. (1999). Hierarchical models of object recognition in cortex. *Nature Neuroscience, 2,* 1019–1025.

Rime, B., Bouvy, B., Leborgne, B., & Rouillon, F. (1978). Psychopathy and nonverbal behavior in interpersonal situations. *Journal of Abnormal Psychology, 87,* 636–643.

Rimland, B. (2004). Association between thimerosol-containing vaccine and autism. *Journal of the American Medical Association, 291,* 180.

Rimm, D., & Cunningham, M. (1985). The behavior therapies. In S. J. Lynn & J. P. Garske (Eds.), *Contemporary psychotherapies: Models and methods.* Columbus, OH: Merrill.

Rimm, D., & Masters, J. C. (1979). *Behavior therapy: Techniques and empirical findings* (2nd ed.). New York: Academic Press.

Rind, B., Tromovitch, P., & Bauserman, R. (1998). A meta-analytic examination of assumed properties of child sexual abuse using college samples. *Psychological Bulletin, 124,* 22–53.

Rind, B., Tromovitch, P., & Bauserman, R. (1998). A metal-analytic examination of assumed properties of child sexual abuse using college samples. *Psychological Bulletin, 124,* 22–53.

Ring, K. (1984). *Healing toward omega: In search of the meaning of the near-death experience.* New York: Morrow.

Ringwalt, C. L., & Greene, J. M. (1993, March). *Results of school districts' drug prevention coordinators survey.* Paper presented at the Alcohol, Tobacco, and Other Drugs Conference on Evaluating School-Linked Prevention Strategies, San Diego, CA.

Ris, M. D., Dietrich, K. N., Succop, P. A., Berger, O. G., & Bornschein, R. L. (2004). Early exposure to lead and neuropsychological outcome in adolescence. *Journal of the International Neuropsychological Society, 10,* 261–270.

Risen, J., & Gilovich, T. (2007). Informal logical fallacies. In R. J. Sternberg, H. L. Roediger, & D. F. Halpern (Eds.), *Critical thinking in psychology* (pp. 110–130). New York: Cambridge University Press.

Roberts, B. W., & DelVecchio, W. F. (2000). The rank-order consistency of personality traits from childhood to old age: Review of longitudinal studies. *Psychological Bulletin, 126,* 3–25.

Roberts, B. W., Walton, K., & Viechtbauer, W. (2006). Patterns of mean-level change in personality traits across the life course: A meta-analysis of longitudinal studies. *Psychological Bulletin, 132,* 1–25.

Roberts, C. J., & Lowe, C. R. (1975). Where have all the conceptions gone? *Lancet, i,* 498–501.

Roberts, L. A., Large, C. H., Higgins, M. J., Stone, T. W., O'Shaughnessy, C. T., & Morris, B. J. (1998). Increased expression of dendritic mRNA following the induction of long-term potentiation. *Molecular Brain Research, 56,* 38–44.

Roberts, R. E., Strawbridge, W. J., Deleger, S., & Kaplan, G. A. (2002). Are the fat more jolly? *Annals of Behavioral Medicine, 24,* 169–180.

Roberts, W. M., Howard, J., & Hudspeth, A. J. (1988). Hair cells: Transduction, tuning, and transmission in the inner ear. *Annual Review of Cell Biology, 4,* 63–92.

Robins, E., & Guze, S. B. (1970). Establishment of diagnostic validity in psychiatric illness: Its application to schizophrenia. *American Journal of Psychiatry, 126,* 983–987.

Robins, L., & Rieger, D. (1991). *Psychiatric disorders in America: The epidemiologic catchment area study.* New York: Free Press.

Robins, L. N. (1975). Narcotic use in southeast Asia and afterward: An interview study of 898 Vietnam returnees. *Archives of General Psychiatry, 32,* 955–961.

Robins, L. N., Helzer, J. E., & Davis, D. H. (1975). Narcotic use in Southeast Asia and afterward: An interview study of 898 Vietnam returnees. *Archives of General Psychiatry, 32,* 955–961.

Robinson, D. G., Woerner, M. G., McMeniman, M., Mendelowitz, A., & Bilder, R. M. (2004). Systematic and functional recovery from a first episode of schizophrenia or schizoaffective disorder. *American Journal of Psychiatry, 161,* 473–479.

Robinson, D. S. (2007). The role of dopamine and norepinephrine in depression. *Primary Psychiatry, 14,* 21–23.

Robinson, P. (2006, February 9). *Wired for speech: How voice activates and advances the human-computer relationship.* Times Higher Educational Supplement. Retrieved October 26, 2007, from http://www.cl.cam.ac.uk/~pr10/publications/thes06.pdf.

Rochat, P. (2002). Ego function of early imitation. In A. N. Meltzoff & W. Prinz (Eds.), *The imitative mind: Development, evolution, and brain bases* (pp. 85–97). New York: Cambridge.

Rock, A. (2004). *The mind at night: The new science of how and why we dream.* New York: Basic Books.

Rodgers, J., Cleveland, H., van der Oord, E., & Rowe, D. (2000). Resolving the debate over birth order, family size, and intelligence. *American Psychologist, 55,* 599–612.

Roediger, H. L., & Crowder, R. G. (1976). A serial position effect in recall of United States presidents. *Bulletin of the Psychonomic Society, 8,* 275–278.

Roediger, H. L., & McDermott, K. B. (1995). Creating false memories: Remembering words not presented in lists. *Journal of Experimental Psychology: Learning, Memory, and Cognition, 21,* 803–814.

Roediger, H. L., & McDermott, K. B. (1999). False alarms and false memories. *Psychological Review, 106,* 406–410.

Roelfs, K., Hoogduin, K. A., Keijsers, G. P., Naring, G. W., Moene, F. C., & Sandijck, P. (2002). Hypnotic susceptibility in patients with conversion disorder. *Journal of Abnormal Psychology, 11,* 390–395.

Roelfsema, P. R. (2006). Cortical algorithms for perceptual grouping. *Annual Review of Neuroscience, 29,* 203–227.

Roethlisberger, F. J., & Dickson, W. J. (1939). *Management and the worker.* Cambridge, MA: Harvard University Press.

Rogers, C. R. (1942). *Counseling and psychotherapy.* New York: Houghton Mifflin.

Rogers, C. R. (1947). Some observations on the organization of personality. *American Psychologist, 2,* 358–368.

Rogers, C. R. (1957). The necessary and sufficient conditions of therapeutic personality change. *Journal of Consulting Psychology, 21,* 95–103.

Rogers, C. R. (1961). *On becoming a person.* Boston: Houghton Mifflin.

Rogers, C. R., & Dymond, R. (1954). *Psychotherapy and personality change.* Chicago: University of Chicago Press.

Rogers, M., & Smith, K. H. (1993). Public perceptions of subliminal advertising. *Journal of Advertising Research, 33,* 10–18.

Rogers, R. (Ed.). (1997). *Clinical assessment of malingering and deception* (2nd ed.). New York: Guilford Press.

Rogers, R. W., & Prentice-Dunn, S. (1981). Deindividuation and anger-mediated interracial aggression: Unmasking regressive racism. *Journal of Personality and Social Psychology, 41*, 63–73.

Rogoff, B. (1998). Cognition as a collaborative process. In D. Kuhn & R. S. Seigler (Eds.), *Handbook of child psychology, Vol. 2: Cognition, perception, & language* (5th ed., pp. 679–744). New York: Wiley.

Rogoff, B., & Chavajay, P. (1995). What's become of research on the cultural basis of cognitive development? *American Psychologist, 50*, 859–877.

Rolls, E. T. (2004). The functions of the orbitofrontal cortex. *Brain & Cognition, 55*, 11–29.

Romanczyk, R. G., Arnstein, L., Soorya, L. V., & Gillis, J. (2003). The myriad of controversial treatments for autism: A critical evaluation of efficacy. In S. O. Lilienfeld, S. J. Lynn, & J. M. Lohr (Eds.), *Science and pseudoscience in clinical psychology* (pp. 363–395). New York: Guilford.

Roney, J. R., Hanson, K. N., Durante, K. M., & Maestripieri, D. (2006). Reading men's faces: Women's mate attractiveness judgments track men's testosterone and interest in infants. *Proceedings of the Royal Society of London B, 273*, 2169–2175.

Ropeik, D., & Gray, G. (2003). *Risk: A practical guide for deciding what's really safe and what's really dangerous in the world around you.* Boston: Houghton Mifflin.

Rosch, E. (1973). Natural categories. *Cognitive Psychology, 4*, 328–350.

Rose, R. J., & Ditto, W. B. (1983). A developmental-genetic analysis of common fears from early adolescence to early adulthood. *Child Development, 54*, 361–368.

Rosen, G. M. (1993). Self-help or hype? Comments on psychology's failure to advance self-care. *Professional Psychology: Research and Practice, 24*, 340–345.

Rosen, G. M. (2006). DSM's cautionary guideline to rule out malingering can protect the PTSD data base. *Journal of Anxiety Disorders, 20*, 530–535.

Rosen, G. M. (Ed.). (2004). *Posttraumatic stress disorder: Issues and controversies.* Chichester, England: Wiley.

Rosen, G. M., Glasgow, R. E., & Moore, T. (2003). Self-help therapy: The science and business of giving psychology away. In S. O. Lilienfeld, S. J. Lynn & J. M. Lohr (Eds.), *Science and pseudoscience in clinical psychology* (pp. 399–424). New York: Guilford.

Rosen, G. M., Glasgow, R. E., & Moore, T. E. (2003). Self-help therapy: The science and business of giving psychology away. In S. O. Lilienfeld, S. J. Lynn, & J. M. Lohr (Eds.), *Science and Pseudoscience in Clinical Psychology* (pp. 399-424). New York: Guilford Press.

Rosen, J. C. (1995). The nature of body dysmorphic disorder and treatment with cognitive behavior therapy. *Cognitive and Behavioral Practice, 2*, 143–166.

Rosenberg, H. (1993). Prediction of controlled drinking by alcoholics and problem drinkers. *Psychological Bulletin, 113*, 129–139.

Rosenberg, K. M., & Daly, H. B. (1993). *Foundations of behavioral research: A basic question approach.* Fort Worth, TX: Harcourt Brace Jovanovich College.

Rosenberg, P. (1973). The effects of mood altering drugs: Pleasures and pitfalls. In R. F. Hardy & J. G. Cull (Eds.), *Drug dependence and rehabilitation approaches.* Springfield, IL: Charles C. Thomas.

Rosenberg, S. D., Rosenberg, H. J., & Farrell, M. P. (1999). The midlife crisis revisited. *Journal of Personality and Social Psychology, 77*, 415–427.

Rosenblum, D., & Lewis, M. (1999). The relations among body image, physical attractiveness, and body mass in adolescence. *Child Development, 70*, 50–64.

Rosenfarb, I. S., Bellack, A. S., & Aziz, N. (2006). Family interactions and the course of schizophrenia in African-American and white patients. *Journal of Abnormal Psychology, 115*, 112–120.

Rosenfeld, J. P. (2005). "Brain fingerprinting": A critical analysis. *Scientific Review of Mental Health Practice, 4*(1), 20–37.

Rosenhan, D. (1973). On being sane in insane places. *Science, 179*, 250–258.

Rosenhan, D. L., & Seligman, M. E. P. (1989). *Abnormal psychology.* New York: W. W. Norton.

Rosenman, R. H., Brand, R. J., Jenkins, C. D., Friedman, M., Straus, R., & Wurm, M. (1975). Coronary heart disease in the Western Collaborative Group Study: Final follow-up experience of $8\frac{1}{2}$ years. *Journal of the American Medical Association, 233*, 872–877.

Rosenman, R. H., Friedman, M., Straus, R., Wurm, M., Kositchek, R., Hahn, W., et al. (1964). A predictive study of coronary heart disease: The Western Collaborative Group Study. *Journal of the American Medical Association, 189*, 15–22.

Rosensweig, S. (1936). Some implicit common factors in diverse methods in psychotherapy. *American Journal of Orthopsychiatry, 6*, 412–415.

Rosenthal, D. (1963). *The Genain Quadruplets.* New York: Basic Books.

Rosenthal, R. (1979). The "file drawer problem" and tolerance for null results. *Psychological Bulletin, 86*, 638–641.

Rosenthal, R. (1994) Interpersonal expectancy effects: A 30-year perspective. *Current Directions in Psychological Science, 3*, 176–179.

Rosenthal, R. (2003). Covert communication in laboratories, classroom, and the truly real world. *Current Directions in Psychological Science, 12*, 151–154.

Rosenthal, R., & DiMatteo, M. R. (2001). Meta-analysis: Recent developments in quantitative methods for literature reviews. *Annual Review of Psychology, 52*, 59–82.

Rosenthal, R., & Fode, K. L. (1963). Psychology of the scientist: V. Three experiments in experimenter bias. *Psychological Reports, 12*, 491–511.

Rosenthal, R., & Jacobson, L. (1966). Teachers' expectancies: Determinants of pupils' IQ gains. *Psychological Reports, 1*, 115–118.

Rosenthal, R., & Jacobson, L. (1968). *Pygmalion in the classroom.* New York: Holt, Rinehart and Winston.

Rosnow, R. L. (1980). Psychology of rumor reconsidered. *Psychological Bulletin, 87*, 578–591.Ross, L. (1977). The intuitive psychologist and his shortcomings: Distortions in the attribution process. In L. Berkowitz (Ed.), *Advances in experimental social psychology* (Vol. 10, pp. 174–221). New York: Academic Press.

Rosnow, R. L. (2002). The nature and role of demand characteristics in scientific inquiry. *Prevention and Treatment, 5*(1). Retrieved March 10, 2005, from http://content.apa.org/journals/pre/5/1/37.

Ross, C. A., & Pam, A. (1994). *Pseudoscience in biological psychiatry: Blaming the body.* New York: Wiley.

Ross, H., & Plug, C. (2002). *The mystery of the moon illusion.* Oxford, England: Oxford University Press.

Ross, L., Amabile, T. M., & Steinmetz, J. L. (1977). Social roles, social control and biases in social perception. *Journal of Personality and Social Psychology, 35*, 485–494.

Ross, L., Lepper, M. R., & Hubbard, M. (1975). Perseverance in self-perception and social perception: Biased attributional processes in the debriefing paradigm. *Journal of Personality and Social Psychology, 32*, 880–892.

Ross, L., & Nisbett, L. E. (1991). *The person and the situation: Essential contributions of social psychology.* New York: McGraw Hill.

Ross, L., & Ward, A. (1996). Naive realism: Implications for social conflict and misunderstanding. In T. Brown, E. Reed, & E. Turiel (Eds.), *Values and knowledge* (pp. 103–135). Hillsdale, NJ: Lawrence Erlbaum Associates.

Ross, M. (1989). Relation of implicit theories to the construction of personal histories. *Psychological Review, 96*, 341–357.

Rossman, B., Minuchin, S., & Lieberman, R. (1975). Family lunch session: An introduction to family therapy in anorexia nervosa. *American Journal of Orthopsychiatry, 45*, 846–853.

Rotenberg, K. J., & Mann, L. (1986). The development of the norm of the reciprocity of self-disclosure and its function in children's attraction to peers. *Child Development, 57*, 1349–1357.

Roth, S., & Cohen, L. J. (1986). Approach, avoidance, and coping with stress. *American Psychology, 41*, 813–819.

Rothbaum, B. O., Anderson, P., Zimand, E., Hodges, L., Lang, D., & Wilson, J. (2006). Virtual reality exposure therapy and standard (in vivo) exposure therapy in the treatment of fear of flying. *Behavior Therapy, 37*, 80–90.

Rothbaum, B. O., Hodges, L., Ready, D., Graap, K., & Alarcon, R. D. (2001). Virtual reality exposure therapy for Vietnam veterans with posttraumatic stress disorder. *Journal of Clinical Psychiatry, 62*, 617–622.

Rothbaum, R., Weisz, J., Pott, M., Miyake, K., & Morelli, G. (2000). Attachment and culture: Security in Japan and the U.S. *American Psychologist, 55*, 1093–1104.

Rothschild, R., & Quitkin, F. M. (1992). Review of the use of pattern analysis to differentiate true drug and placebo responses. *Psychotherapy and Psychosomatics, 58*, 170–177.

Rotter, J. B. (1966). Generalized expectancies for internal versus external control of reinforcement. *Psychological Monographs* (1, Whole No. 609).

Rotton, J., & Kelly, I. W. (1985). Much ado about the full moon: A meta-analysis of lunar-lunacy research. *Psychological Bulletin, 97*, 286–306.

Rovee-Collier, C. (1993). The capacity for long-term memory in infancy. *Current Directions in Psychological Science, 2*, 130–135.

Rowan, J. (1998). Maslow amended. *Journal of Humanistic Psychology, 38*, 81–93.

Rowe, D. C. (1994). *The limits of family influence: Genes, experience, and behavior.* New York: Guilford Press.

Rowland, I. (2001). *The full facts on cold reading* (2nd ed.). London, England: Author.

Rowling, J. K., (1998). *Harry Potter and the Sorcerer's Stone.* New York: Arthur A. Levine Books.

Roy, A. (1992). Suicide in schizophrenia. *International Review of Psychiatry, 4,* 205–209.

Roy, M., McNeale, M. C., Pedersen, N. L., Mathe, A. A., & Kendler, K. S. (1995). A twin study of generalized anxiety disorder and major depression. *Psychological Medicine, 25,* 1037–1049.

Roy, M. M., & Christenfeld, N. J. S. (2004). Do dogs resemble their owners? *Psychological Science, 15,* 361–363.

Roy-Byrne P. P. (2005). The GABA-benzodiazepine receptor complex: Structure, function, and role in anxiety. *Journal of Clinical Psychiatry, 66*(Suppl. 2), 14–20.

Royce, J., Darlington, R., & Murray, H. (1983). Pooled analyses: Findings across studies. In The Consortium for Longitudinal Studies (Ed.), *As the twig is bent: Lasting effects of preschool programs* (pp. 411–459). Hillsdale, NJ: Erlbaum.

Rozin, P., & Fallon, A. (1987). A perspective on disgust. *Psychological Review, 94,* 23–41.

Rozin, P., Millman, L., & Nemeroff, C. (1986). Operation of the laws of sympathetic magic in disgust and other domains. *Journal of Personality and Social Psychology, 50,* 703–712.

Rozin, P., & Stoess, C. (1993). Is there a general tendency to become addicted? *Addictive Behaviors, 18,* 81–87.

Ruben, J., Schwiemann, J., Deuchert, M., Meyer, R., Krause, T., Curio, G., et al. (2001). Somatotopic organization of human secondary somatosensory cortex. *Cerebral Cortex, 11,* 463–473.

Rubenzer, S. J., Faschingbauer, T. R., & Ones, D. S. (2000, August). *Assessing the U.S. presidents using the Revised NEO Personality Inventory.* Paper presented at the Annual Convention of the American Psychological Association, Washington, DC.

Rubin, M. L., & Walls, G. L. (1969). *Fundamentals of visual science* (p. 546). Springfield, IL: Thomas.

Rubin, V., & Comitas, L. (1975). *Ganja in Jamaica: A medical anthropological study of chronic marihuana use.* The Hague, Netherlands: Mouton.

Rudebeck, P. H., Buckley, M. J., Walton, M. E., & Rushworth, M. F. (2006). A role for the macaque anterior cingulate gyrus in social valuation. *Science, 313,* 1310–1312.

Rudolph, K. D., Hammen, C., Burge, D., Lindberg, N., Herzberg, D., & Daley, S. E. (2000). Toward an interpersonal life-stress model of depression: The developmental context of stress generation. *Development and Psychopathology, 12,* 215–234.

Ruff, R. M., & Parker, S. B. (1993). Gender- and age-specific changes in motor speed and eye-hand coordination in adults: Normative values for the Finger Tapping and Grooved Pegboard tests. *Perceptual and Motor Skills, 76,* 1219–1230.

Rumelhart, D. E. (1980). Schemata: The building blocks of cognition. In R. J. Spiro, B. Bruce, & W. F. Brewer (Eds.), *Theoretical issues in reading and comprehension.* Hillsdale, NJ: Erlbaum.

Rumelhart, D. E., & McClelland, J. L. (1986). *Parallel distributed processing* (Vol. 1). Cambridge, MA: MIT Press.

Rupp, H. (2003). *Sex segregation in rhesus monkeys* (Macaca mulatta). Unpublished Master's thesis, Emory University, Atlanta, Georgia.

Ruscio, J. (2000). Risky business: Vividness, availability, and the media paradox. *Skeptical Inquirer, 24,* 22–26.

Ruscio, J. (2003). Diagnoses and the behaviors they denote: A critical evaluation of the labeling theory of mental illness. *Scientific Review of Mental Health Practice, 3,* 5–22.

Ruscio, J. (2005). Exploring controversies in the art and science of polygraph testing. *Skeptical Inquirer, 29*(1), 34–39.

Rush, A. J., Marangell, L. B., Sackeim, H. A., George, M. S., Brannan, S. K., Davis, S. M., et al. (2005). Vagus nerve stimulation for treatment-resistant depression: A randomized, controlled acute phase trial. *Biological Psychiatry, 58,* 347–354.

Rushton, J. P. (1995). *Race, evolution, and behavior: An evolutionary perspective.* New Brunswick, NJ: Transaction Publishers.

Rushton, J. P. (1999). Secular gains in IQ note related to the g factor and inbreeding depression—Unlike Black-White differences: A reply to Flynn. *Personality and Individual Differences, 26,* 381–389.

Rushton, J. P., & Bogaert, A. F. (1987). Race differences in sexual behavior: Testing an evolutionary hypothesis. *Journal of Research in Personality, 21,* 529–551.

Rushton, J. P., & Campbell, A. C. (1977). Modelling, vicarious reinforcement, and extraversion on blood donating in adults: Immediate and long term effects. *European Journal of Social Psychology, 7,* 297–306.

Rushton, J. P., Brainerd, C. J., & Presley, M. (1983). Behavioral development and construct validity: The principle of aggregation. *Psychological Bulletin, 94,* 18–38.

Rushton, J. P., Russell, R. J. H., & Wells, P. A. (1985). Personality and genetic similarity theory. *Journal of Social and Biological Structures, 8,* 174–197.

Russell, J. A. (1994). Is there universal recognition of emotion from facial expression? A review of cross-cultural studies. *Psychological Bulletin, 115,* 102–141.

Rust, S. (2006, April 3). Autism epidemic doubted. *Milwaukee Sentinel.* Retrieved April 16, 2006, from http://www.jsonline.com/story/index.aspx?id=412874.

Rutter, M. (1972). *Maternal deprivation reassessed.* Oxford, England: Penguin.

Rutter, M. (1995). Maternal deprivation. In M. H.Bornstein (Ed.), *Handbook of parenting, Vol. 4: Applied and practical parenting* (pp. 3–31). Hillsdale, NJ: Erlbaum.

Rutter, M. (2000). Genetic studies of autism: From the 1970s into the millennium. *Journal of Abnormal Child Psychology, 28,* 3–14.

Ryan, R. (1976). *Blaming the victim.* New York: Vintage Books.

Ryan, R. M. (1985). Thematic Apperception Test. In D. J. Keyser & R. C. Swetland (Eds.), *Test critiques* (Vol. 2, pp. 799–814). Kansas City, MO: Test Corporation of America.

Ryback, R. S. (1971). The continuum and specificity of the effects of alcohol on memory. *Quarterly Journal of Studies on Alcohol, 32,* 995–1016.

Saba, G., Schurhoff, F., & Leboyer, M. (2006). Therapeutic and neurophysiologic aspects of transcranial magnetic stimulation in schizophrenia. *Neurophysiologie Clinique, 36,* 185–194.

Sabbagh, C. (2005). An integrative etic–emic approach to portraying the halutziut system of societal equity. *Journal of Cross-Cultural Psychology, 36,* 147–166.

Sabom, M. (1982). *Recollections of death: A medical investigation.* New York: Harper & Row.

Sacco, W. P., & Dunn, V. K. (1990). Effect of actor depression on observer attributions: Existence and impact of negative attributions toward the depressed. *Journal of Personality and Social Psychology, 59,* 517–524.

Sackeim, H. A., Prudic, J., Fuller, R., Keilp, J., Lavori, P. W., & Olfson, M. (2007). The cognitive effects of electroconvulsive therapy in community settings. *Neuropsychopharmacology, 32,* 244–254.

Sackett, P. R., & Decker, P. J. (1979). Detection of deception in the employment context: A review and critical analysis. *Personnel Psychology, 32,* 487–506.

Sackett, P. R., Hardison, C. M., & Cullen, M. J. (2004). On interpreting stereotype threat as accounting for Black-White differences on cognitive tests. *American Psychologist, 59,* 7–13.

Sackett, P. R., & Wanek, J. E. E. (1996). New developments in the use of measures of honesty, integrity, conscientiousness, dependability, trustworthiness, and reliability for personnel selection. *Personnel Psychology, 49,* 787–829.

Sackheim, H. (1988). The efficacy of electroconvulsive therapy. *Annals of the New York Academy of Sciences, 462,* 70–75.

Sacks, O. (1985). *The man who mistook his wife for a hat: And other clinical tales.* New York: Touchstone.

Sadato, N. (2005). How the blind "see" Braille: Lessons from functional magnetic resonance imaging. *Neuroscientist, 11,* 577–582.

Sadler, P., & Woody, E. (in press). Does the more vivid imagery of high hypnotizables depend on greater cognitive effort? A test of dissociation and social-cognitive theories of hypnosis. *International Journal of Clinical and Experimental Hypnosis.*

Safer, D. J. (2000). Are stimulants overprescribed for youths with ADHD? *Annals of Clinical Psychiatry, 12,* 55–62.

Sagan, C. (1993). *Broca's brain: Reflections on the romance of science.* New York: Ballantine Books.

Sagan, C. (1995). *The demon-haunted world: Science as a candle in the dark.* New York: Random House.

Sageman, M. (2004). *Understanding terror networks.* Philadelphia: University of Pennsylvania Press.

Saha, S., Chant, D., Welham, J., & McGrath, J. (2005). *PLoS Medicine, 2,* e141doi:10.1371/journal.pmed.0020141.

Sahu, A. (2003). Leptin signaling in the hypothalamus: Emphasis on energy homeostasis and leptin resistance. *Front Neuroendocrinology, 24,* 225–233.

Saint-Cyr, J. A., Taylor, A. E., & Lang, A. E. (1988). Procedural learning and neostriatal dysfunction in man. *Brain, 111,* 941–959.

Salber, E. J., Freeman, H. E., & Abelin, T. (1968). Needed research on smoking: Lessons from the Newton study. In E. F. Borgatta & R. R. Evans (Eds.), *Smoking, health and behavior.* Chicago: Aldine.

Salekin, R. T. (2002). Psychopathy and therapeutic pessimism: Clinical lore or clinical reality? *Clinical Psychology Review, 22,* 79–112.

Saletan, W. (2004, May 12). The Stanford Prison Experiment doesn't explain Abu Ghraib. *Slate.* Retrieved December 2, 2004, from http://slate.msn.com/id/2100419/.

Salgado, J. F., Anderson, N., Mocsoso, S., Bertua, C., deFruyt, F., & Rolland, J. P. (2003). A meta-analytic study of general mental ability validity for different occupations in the European community. *Journal of Applied Psychology, 88,* 1068–1081.

Salovey, P., & Mayer, J. D. (1990). Emotional intelligence. *Imagination, Cognition, and Personality, 9,* 185–211.

Salter, D., McMillan, D., Richards, M., Talbot, T., Hodges, J., Bentovim, A., et al. (2003). Development of sexually abusive behavior in sexually victimized males: A longitudinal study. *Lancet, 361,* 471.

Salthouse, T. A. (1996). The processing-speed theory of adult age differences in cognition. *Psychological Review, 103,* 403–428.

Salthouse, T. A. (2004). Localizing age-related individual differences in a hierarchical structure. *Intelligence, 32,* 541–561.

Saltzman, S. (1982). Obsessions and agoraphobia. In D. Chambless & A. Goldstein (Eds.), *Agoraphobia: Multiple perspectives on theory and treatment.* New York: Wiley.

Samuelson, L. K., & Smith, L. B. (1998). Memory and attention make smart word learning: An alternative account of Akhtar, Carpenter, and Tomasello. *Child Development, 69,* 94–104.

Sanchez-Andres, J. V., Olds, J. L., & Alkon, D. L. (1993). Gated informational transfer within the mammalian hippocampus: A new hypothesis. *Behavioral Brain Research, 54,* 111–106.

Sanders, C. E., Lubinski, D., & Benbow, C. P. (1995). Does the Defining Issues Test measure psychological phenomena distinct from verbal ability? An examination of Lykken's query. *Journal of Personality and Social Psychology, 69,* 498–504.

Sanderson, W. C., & Barlow, D. H. (1990). A description of patients diagnosed with DSM-III-R generalized anxiety disorder. *Journal of Nervous and Mental Disease, 178,* 588–591.

Santa Maria, M. P., Baumeister, A. A., & Gouvier, W. D. (1999). Public knowledge and misconceptions about electroconvulsive therapy: A demographically stratified investigation. *International Journal of Rehabilitation and Health, 4,* 111–116.

Santor, D. A., & Kusumakar, V. (2001). Open trial of interpersonal therapy in adolescents with moderate to severe major depression: Effectiveness of novice IPT therapists. *Journal of the American Academy of Child and Adolescent Psychiatry, 40,* 236–240.

Saper, R. B. , Kales, S. N., Paquin, J., Burns, M. J., Eisenberg, D. M., Davis, R. B., et al. (2004). Heavy metal content of Ayurvedic herbal medicine products. *Journal of the American Medical Association, 292,* 2868–2873.

Sapir, E. (1929). The status of linguistics as a science. *Language,* 5, 209.

Sappington, A. A. (1990). Recent psychological approaches to the free will versus determinism issue. *Psychological Bulletin, 108,* 19–29.

Sar, V., Koyuncu, A., Ozturk, E, Yargic, L., Kundakci, T., Yazici, A., et al. (2007). Dissociative disorders in the psychiatric emergency ward. *General Hospital Psychiatry, 29,* 45–50.

Sarafino, E. P. (2006). *Health psychology: Biopsychosocial interactions* (5th ed.). Hoboken, NJ: John Wiley & Sons.

Sarbin, T. R. (1950). Contributions to role-taking theory: I. Hypnotic behavior. *Psychological Review, 57,* 225–270.

Sarbin, T. R., & Coe, W. C. (1972). *Hypnosis: A social psychological analysis of influence communication.* New York: Holt, Rinehart & Winston.

Sarbin, T. R., & Coe, W. C. (1979). Hypnosis and psychopathology: Replacing old myths with fresh metaphors. *Journal of Abnormal Psychology, 88,* 506–526.

Sarbin, T. R., & Slagle, R. W. (1979). Hypnosis and psychophysiological outcomes. In E. Fromm & R. E. Shor (Eds.), *Developments in research and new perspectives* (pp. 273–303). New York: Aldine

Sarich, V., & Miele, F. (2004). *Race: The reality of human differences.* Boulder, CO: Westview Press.

Sarter, M., & Bruno, J. P. (2000). Cortical cholinergic inputs mediating arousal, attentional processing and dreaming: Differential afferent regulation of the basal forebrain by telencephalic and brainstem afferents. *Neuroscience, 95,* 933–952.

Sarwer, D. B., & Wadden, T. A. (1999). The treatment of obesity: What's new, what's recommended. *Journal of Women's Health and Gender-Based Medicine, 8,* 483–493.

Satel, S. L. (1999). *Drug treatment: The case for coercion.* Washington, DC: American Enterprise Institute Press.

Satir, V. (1964). *Conjoint family therapy.* New York: Science and Behavior Books.

Saufley, W. H., Otaka, S. R., & Bavaresco, J. L. (1985). Context effects: Classroom tests and context independence. *Memory & Cognition, 13,* 522–528.

Savage-Rumbaugh, E. S. (1986). *Ape language: From conditioned response to symbol.* New York: Columbia University Press.

Savic, I., Berglund, H., & Lindstrom, P. (2005). Brain response to putative pheromones in homosexual men. *Proceedings of the National Academy of Sciences, U.S.A., 17,* 7356–7361.

Savitz, J., Solms, M., Pietersen, E., Ramesar, R., & Flor-Henry, P. (2004). Dissociative identity disorder associated with mania and change in handedness. *Cognitive and Behavioral Neurology, 17,* 233–237.

Saxe, L. (1991). Lying: Thoughts of an applied social psychologist. *American Psychologist, 46,* 409–415.

Saxe, L., & Ben-Shakhar, G. (1999). Admissibility of polygraph tests: The application of scientific standards post-Daubert. *Psychology, Public Policy and Law, 5,* 203–223.

Sayette, M. A. (1999). Does drinking reduce stress? *Alcohol Research and Health, 23,* 250–255.

Scalafani, A., & Kluge, L. (1974). Food motivation and body weight levels in hypothalamic hyperphagic rats. *Physiological Psychology, 86,* 28–46.

Scarr, S. (1985). An author's frame of mind [Review of *Frames of mind: The theory of multiple intelligences*]. *New Ideas in Psychology, 3,* 95–100.

Scarr, S., & McCartney, K. (1983). How people make their own environments: A theory of genotype-environment effects. *Child Development, 54,* 424–435.

Scarr, S., Pakstis, A. J., Katz, S. H., & Barker, W. B. (1977). Absence of a relationship between degree of White ancestry and intellectual skills within a Black population. *Human Genetics, 39,* 69–86.

Scarr, S., Webber, P. L., Weinberg, R. A., & Wittig, M. A. (1981). Personality resemblance among adolescents and their parents in biologically related and adoptive families. *Journal of Personality and Social Psychology, 40,* 885–898.

Scarr, S., & Weinberg, R. A. (1976). IQ test performance of Black children adopted by White families. *American Psychologist, 31,* 726–739.

Schachter, S. (1968). Obesity and eating. *Science, 161,* 751–761.

Schachter, S. (1971). Some extraordinary facts about obese humans and rats. *American Psychologist, 26,* 129–144.

Schachter, S., & Gross, L. (1968). Manipulated time and eating behavior. *Journal of Personality and Social Psychology, 10,* 98–106.

Schachter, S., & Singer, J. E. (1962). Cognitive, social and physiological determinants of emotional state. *Psychological Review, 69,* 379–399.

Schacter, D. (1996). *Searching for memory: The brain, the mind, and the past.* New York: Basic Books.

Schacter, D. L. (2001). *The seven sins of memory.* Boston: Houghton-Mifflin.

Schacter, D. L., & Moscovitch, M. (1984). Infants, amnesics, and dissociable memory systems. In M. Moscovitch (Ed.), *Infant memory* (pp. 173–216). New York: Plenum.

Schacter, S. (1959). *The psychology of affiliation: Experimental studies of the sources of gregariousness.* Stanford, CA: Stanford University Press.

Schacter, S.L. (1996). *Searching for memory: The brain, the mind, and the past.* New York: Basic Books.

Schadler, M., & Thissen, D. M. (1981). The development of automatic word recognition and reading skill. *Memory & Cognition, 9,* 132–141.

Schaefer, C., Coyne, J. C., & Lazarus R. S. (1981). The health-related functions of social support. *Journal of Behavioral Medicine, 4,* 381–406.

Schaie, K. W. (1996). *Intellectual development in adulthood: The Seattle longitudinal study.* New York: Cambridge University Press.

Schaler, J. (2004). *Addiction is a choice.* La Salle, IL: Open Court Books.

Schallhorn, S. C., Amesbury, E. C., & Tanzer, D. J. (2006). Avoidance, recognition, and management of LASIK complications. *American Journal of Ophthalmology, 141,* 733–739.

Schank, R. C., & Abelson, R. (1977). *Scripts, plans, goals, and understanding.* Hillsdale, NJ: Erlbaum.

Schatzberg, A. F. (1998). Noradrenergic versus serotonergic antidepressants: Predictors of treatment response. *Journal of Clinical Psychiatry, 59*(Suppl. 14), 15–18.

Scheck, B., Neufeld, P., & Dwyer, J. (2000). *Actual innocence.* New York: Random House.

Scheerenberger, R. C. (1983). *A history of mental retardation.* Baltimore: P. H. Brooks Publishing.

Scheff, S. W., Price, D. A., Schmitt, F. A., DeKosky, S. T., & Mufson, E. J. (2007). Synaptic alterations in CA1 in mild Alzheimer disease and mild cognitive impairment. *Neurology, 68,* 1501–1508.

Scheff, T. J. (1984). *Being mentally ill: A sociological theory.* New York: Aldine.

Scheier, M. F., & Carver, C. S. (1992). Effects of optimism on psychological and physical well-being: Theoretical overview and empirical update. *Cognitive Therapy and Research, 16,* 201–228.

Schellenberg, G. D. (2006). Early Alzheimer's disease genetics. *Journal of Alzheimer's Disease, 9,* 367–372.

Schenck, C. H. (2006). Paradox lost: Midnight in the battleground of sleep and dreams. Violent moving nightmares page. Retrieved January 3, 2006, from: http://www.parasomnias-rbd.com/.

Scher, C. D., Ingram, R. E., & Segal, Z. V. (2005). Cognitive reactivity and vulnerability: Empirical evaluation of construct activation and cognitive diatheses in unipolar depression. *Clinical Psychology Review, 25,* 487–510.

Scherer, K. R. (1988). Criteria for emotion-antecedent appraisal: A review. In V. Hamilton, G. H. Bower, & N. H. Frijda (Eds.), *Cognitive perspectives on emotion and motivation* (pp. 89–126). Dordrecht: Nijhoff.

Schick, T., & Vaughn, L. (2004). *How to think about weird things: Critical thinking for a new age.* Boston: McGraw Hill.

Schienle, A., Stark, R., Walter, B., Blecker, C., Ott, U., Kirsch, P., et al. (2002). The insula is not specifically involved in disgust processing: An fMRI study. *Neuroreport, 13,* 2023–2026.

Schiff, M., Duyme, M., Dumaret, A., & Tomkiewicz, S. (1982). How much can we boost scholastic achievement and IQ scores? A direct answer from a French adoption study. *Cognition, 12,* 165–196.

Schiffman, S. S., & Graham, B. G. (2000). Taste and smell perception affect appetite and immunity in the elderly. *European Journal of Clinical Nutrition, 54*(Suppl. 3), S54–S63.

Schkade, D. A., & Kahneman, D. (1998). Does living in California make people happy? A focusing illusion in judgments of life satisfaction. *Psychological Science, 9,* 340–346.

Schlegel, A., & Barry, H., III. (1991). *Adolescence: An anthropological inquiry.* New York: Free Press.

Schmahmann, J. D. (2004). Disorders of the cerebellum: Ataxia, dysmetria of thought, and the cerebellar cognitive affective syndrome. *Journal of Neuropsychiatry & Clinical Neurosciences, 16,* 367–378.

Schmidt, F. L., & Hunter, J. E. (1993). Tacit knowledge, practical intelligence, general mental ability and job knowledge. *Current Directions in Psychological Science, 2,* 8–9.

Schmidt, J. P., & Hancey, R. (1979). Social class and psychiatric treatment: Application of a decision-making model to use patterns in a cost-free clinic. *Journal of Consulting and Clinical Psychology, 47,* 771–772.

Schmidt, N. B., Lerew, D. R., & Jackson, R. J. (1997). The role of anxiety sensitivity in the pathogenesis of panic: Prospective evaluation of spontaneous panic attacks during acute stress. *Journal of Abnormal Psychology, 105,* 353–359.

Schmidt, P. J., Murphy, J. H., Haq, N., Rubinow, D. R., & Danaceau, M. A. (2004). Stressful life events, personal losses, and perimenopause-related depression. *Archives of Women's Mental Health, 7,* 19–26.

Schmolk, H., Buffalo, E. A., & Squire, L. R. (2000). Memory distortions develop over time. Recollections of the O. J. Simpson trial verdict after 15 and 32 months. *Psychological Science, 11,* 39–45.

Schnall, P. L., Pieper, C., Schwartz, J. E., Karasek, R. A., Schlussel, Y., Devereux, R. B., et al. (1990). The relationship between "job strain," workplace diastolic blood pressure, and left ventricular mass index: Results of a case-control study. *Journal of the American Medical Association, 263,* 1929–1935.

Schneider, D. (2006). Smart as we can get? *American Scientist, 94,* 311–312.

Schneider, K., Bugental, J. F. T., & Pierson, J. F. (Eds.). (2001). *The handbook of humanistic psychology.* Thousand Oaks, CA: Sage.

Schneider, W., & Bjorklund, D. F. (1998). Memory. In W. Damon, R. S. Siegler, & D. Kuhn (Eds.), *Handbook of child psychology, Vol. 2.,* (pp. 467–521). New York: Wiley.

Schneidman, E. S., Farberow, N. L., & Litman, R. E. (1970). The psychology of suicide. New York: Science House.

Schoenbaum, M. (1997). Do smokers understand the mortality effects of smoking? Evidence from the health and retirement survey. *American Journal of Public Health, 87,* 755–759.

Schoenborn, C. A., Adams, P. F., Barnes, P. M., Vickerie, J. L., & Schiller, J. S. (2004). Health behaviors of adults: United States, 1999–2001. National Center for Health Statistics. *Vital Health Statistics, 10,* 219.

Schoeneman, T. J. (1984). The mentally ill witch in textbooks of abnormal psychology: Current status and implications of a fallacy. *Professional Psychology, 15,* 299–314.

Schoenwolf, G. (1997). *The dictionary of dream interpretation, including a glossary of dream symbols.* Northvale, NJ: Jason Aronson.

Schofield, W. (1964). *Psychotherapy: The purchase of friendship.* Englewood Cliffs, NJ: Prentice-Hall.

Schofield, W., & Balian, L. (1959). A comparative study of the personal histories of schizophrenics and non-psychiatric patients. *Journal of Abnormal and Social Psychology, 59,* 216–225.

Schonfield, D. (1967). Memory loss with age: Acquisition and retrieval. *Psychological Reports, 20,* 223–226.

Schonfield, D., & Robertson, B. A. (1966). Memory storage and aging. *Canadian Journal of Psychology, 20,* 228–236.

Schooler, C. (1998). Environmental complexity and the Flynn effect. In U. Neisser (Ed.), *The rising curve: Long-term gains in IQ and related measures* (pp. 67–79). Washington, DC: American Psychological Association.

Schooler, J. W. (1997). Reflections on a memory discovery. *Child Maltreatment, 2,* 126–133.

Schothorst, P. F., & van Engeland, H. (1996). Long term behavioral sequelae of prematurity. *Journal of the American Academy of Child and Adolescent Psychiatry, 35,* 175–183.

Schreiber, F. R. (1973). *Sybil.* New York: Warner.

Schreirer, H. A., & Libow, J. A. (1995). *Hurting for love: Munchausen by proxy syndrome.* New York: Guilford Press.

Schretlen, D. J. (1997). Dissimulation on the Rorschach and other projective measures. In R. Rogers (Ed.), *Clinical assessment of malingering and deception* (2nd ed., pp. 208–222). New York: Guilford.

Schuckit, M. A. (1988). Reactions to alcohol in sons of alcoholics and controls. Alcoholism: *Clinical and Experimental Research, 12,* 465–470.

Schuckit, M. A. (1994). A clinical model of genetic influences in alcohol dependence. *Journal of Studies of Alcohol, 55,* 5–17.

Schuckit, M. A. (1998). Biological, psychological, and environmental predictors of the alcoholism risk: A longitudinal study. *Journal of Studies on Alcohol, 59,* 485–494.

Schulz, M. S., Cowan, C. P., & Cowan, P. A. (2006). Promoting healthy beginnings: A randomized controlled trial of preventive intervention to preserve marital quality during the transition to parenthood. *Journal of Consulting and Clinical Psychology, 74,* 20–31.

Schuman, H., Steeh, C., Bobo, L., & Krysan, M. (1997). *Racial attitudes in America: Trends and interpretations* (Rev. ed.). Cambridge, MA: Harvard University Press.

Schwartz, B. L. (1999). Sparkling at the end of the tongue: The etiology of the tip-of-the-tongue phenomenology. *Psychonomic Bulletin & Review, 6*(3), 379–393.

Schwartz, C. E., Wright, C. I., Shin, L. M., Kagan, J., & Rauch, S. L. (2003). Inhibited and uninhibited infants "grown up": Adult amygdalar response to novelty. *Science, 300,* 1952–1953.

Schwartz, G. F. (2005). The biology of eating behavior in obesity. *Obesity Research, 12,* 102–106.

Schwartz, J. M., & Bayette, B. (1996). *Brain lock: Free yourself from obsessive-compulsive behavior: A four-step self-treatment method to change your brain chemistry.* New York: HarperCollins.

Schwartz, J. M., Stoessel, P. M., Baxter, L. R., Martin, K. M., & Phelps, M. E. (1996). Systematic changes in cerebral glucose metabolic rate after successful behavior modification treatment of obsessive-compulsive disorder. *Archives of General Psychiatry, 53,* 109–113.

Schwartz, M. B., Vartanian, L. R., Nosek, B. A., & Brownell, K. D. (2006). The influence of one's own body weight on implicit and explicit anti-fat bias. *Obesity, 14,* 440–447.

Schwartz, M. F., & Masters, W. H. (1984). The Masters and Johnson treatment program for dissatisfied homosexual men. *American Journal of Psychiatry, 141,* 173–181.

Schwartz, N. W., Woods, S. C., Porte, D., Seeley, R. J., & Baskin, D. G. (2000). Central nervous system control of food intake. *Nature, 404,* 661–671.

Schwarz, E. D., Kowalski, J. M., & McNally, R. J. (1993). Malignant memories: Posttraumatic changes in memory in adults after a school shooting. *Journal of Traumatic Stress, 4,* 545–553.

Schwarz, N. (1999). Self-reports: How the questions shape the answers. *American Psychologist, 54,* 93–105.

Schwarzer, R., & Taubert, S. (2002). Tenacious goal pursuits and striving toward personal growth: Proactive coping. In E. Fydenberg (Ed.), *Beyond coping: Meeting goals, visions and challenges* (pp. 19–35). London: Oxford University Press.

Schweder, R., Mahapatra, M., & Miller, J. (1987). Culture and moral development. In J. Kagan & S. Lamb (Eds.), *The emergence of morality in young children* (pp. 1–83). Chicago: University of Chicago Press.

Science Daily. (2007, February 27). Science literacy: How do Americans stack up. Retrieved February 28, 2007, from http://www.sciencedaily.com /releases/2007/02/070218134322.htm.

Scoboria, A., Mazzoni, G., Kirsch, I., & Milling, L.S. (2002). Immediate and persistent effect of misleading questions and hypnosis on memory reports. *Journal of Experimental Psychology: Applied, 8,* 26–32.

Scolville, W. B., & Milner, B. (1957). Loss of recent memory after bilateral hippocampal lesions. *Journal of Neurology, Neurosurgery, and Psychiatry, 20,* 11–21.

Scott, D., Lambie, I., Henwood, D., & Lamb, R. (2003). Profiling stranger rapists: It's not so elementary, Doctor Watson. *American Journal of Forensic Psychology, 21,* 31–49.

Scovern, A. W., & Kilmann, P. R. (1980). Status of electroconvulsive therapy: Review of the outcome literature. *Psychological Bulletin, 87,* 260–295.

Scull, A., Mackenzie, C., & Hervey, N. (1996). *Masters of Bedlam: The transformation of the mad-doctoring trade.* Princeton, NJ: Princeton University Press.

Searleman, A. (2003, February). Is there such a thing as a photographic memory? And if so, can it be learned? *Scientific American Online:* www.sciam.com /askexpert_question.cfm?articleID=0001148.

Sears, D. O. (1986). College sophomores in the laboratory: Influences of a narrow data base on social-psychology's view of human nature. *Journal of Personality and Social Psychology, 51,* 515–530.

Sears, D. O., & Henry, P. J. (2003). The origins of symbolic racism. *Journal of Personality and Social Psychology, 85,* 259–275.

Sebrechts, M. M., Marsh, R. L., & Seamon, J. G. (1989). Secondary memory and very rapid forgetting. *Memory & Cognition, 17,* 693–700.

Sechrest, L. (1963). Incremental validity: A recommendation. *Educational and Psychological Measurement, 12,* 153–158.

Segal, M. W. (1974). Alphabet and attraction: An unobtrusive measure of the effect of propinquity in a field setting. *Journal of Personality and Social Psychology, 30,* 654–657.

Segal, N. (1999). *Twins and what they tell us about human behavior.* New York: Dutton.

Segal, Z. V., Williams, S., & Teasdale, J. (2002). *Mindfulness-based cognitive therapy for depression: A new approach to preventing relapse.* New York: Guilford.

Segall, M. H., Campbell, D. T., & Herskovits, M. J. (1966). The influence of culture on visual perception. Indianapolis, IN: Bobbs-Merrill.

Segerstrom, S. C. (2005). Optimism and immunity: Do positive thoughts always lead to positive effects? *Brain, Behavior, and Immunity, 19,* 195–200.

Segerstrom, S. C., Taylor, S. E., Kemeny, M. E., & Fahey, J. L. (1998). Optimism is associated with mood, coping, and immune change in response to stress. *Journal of Personality and Social Psychology, 74,* 1646–1655.

Segrin, C. (2000). Social skill deficits associated with depression. *Clinical Psychology Review, 20,* 379–403.

Seidman, L. J., Pantelis, C., Keshavan, M., Faraone, S., Goldstein, J., Horton, N. J., et al. (2003). A review and new report of medial temporal lobe dysfunction as a vulnerability indicator for schizophrenia: A magnetic resonance imaging morphometric family study of the parahippocampal gyrus. *Schizophrenia Bulletin, 29,* 803–830.

Seitz, A. R., & Watanabe, T. (2003). Psychophysics: Is subliminal learning really passive? *Nature, 422,* 36.

Sekuler, R., Sekuler, A. B., & Lau, R. (1997). Sound alters visual motion perception. *Nature, 385,* 308.

Selden, S. (1999). *Inheriting shame: The story of eugenics and racism in America.* New York: Teachers College Press.

Seligman, M. (1990). *Learned optimism.* New York: Knopf.

Seligman, M. E. P. (1971). Phobias and preparedness. *Behavior Therapy, 2,* 307–320.

Seligman, M. E. P. (1975). *Helplessness: On depression, development, and death.* San Francisco: Freeman.

Seligman, M. E. P. (1998). *Learned optimism* (2nd ed.). New York: Pocket Books.

Seligman, M. E. P., & Csikszentmihalyi, M. (2000). Positive psychology: An introduction. *American Psychologist, 55,* 5–14.

Seligman, M. E. P., & Maier, S. F. (1967). Failure to escape traumatic shock. Journal of Experimental *Psychology, 74,* 1–9.

Seligman, M. E. P., & Pawelski, J. O. (2003). Positive psychology: FAQs. *Psychological Inquiry, 14,* 159–163.

Seligman, M. P. (1995). The effectiveness of psychotherapy: The *Consumer Reports* survey. *American Psychologist, 50,* 965–974.

Selye, H. (1956). *The stress of life.* New York: McGraw Hill.

Senghas, A., & Coppola, M. (2001). Children creating language: How Nicaraguan sign language acquired a spatial grammar. *Psychological Science, 12,* 323–328.

Serbin, L. A., & O'Leary, K.D. (1975). How nursery schools teach girls to shut up. *Psychology Today, 9*(7), 56–58.

Serman, N., Johnson, J. G., Geller, P. A., Kanost, R. E., & Zacharapoulou, H. (2002). Personality disorders associated with substance use among American and Greek adolescents. *Adolescence, 37,* 841–854.

Serpell, R. (1979). How specific are perceptual skills? *British Journal of Psychology, 70,* 365–380.

Sevdalis, N., & Harvey, N. (2007). Biased forecasting of postdecisional affect. *Psychological Science, 18,* 678–681.

Seyfarth, R. M., & Cheney, D. L. (1997). Behavioral mechanisms underlying vocal communication in nonhuman primates. *Animal Learning & Behavior, 25,* 249–267.

Shade, E. D., Ulrich, C. M., Wener, M. H., Wood, B., Yasui, Y., Lacroix, K., et al. (2004). Frequent intentional weight loss is associated with lower natural killer cell cytotoxicity in postmenopausal women: Possible long-term immune effects. *Journal of the American Dietetic Association, 104,* 903–912.

Shadish, W. R., & Baldwin, S. A. (2005). Effects of behavioral marital therapy: A meta-analysis of randomized controlled trials. *Journal of Consulting and Clinical Psychology, 73,* 6–14.

Shadish, W. R., Cook, T. D., & Campbell, D. T. (2002). *Experimental and quasi-experimental designs for generalized causal inference.* Boston, MA: Houghton Mifflin.

Shaffer, H. J. (2000). Addictive personality. In A. E. Kazdin (Ed.), *Encyclopedia of psychology* (Vol. 1, pp. 35–36). Washington, DC: American Psychological Association and Oxford University Press.

Shakow, D. (1962). Segmental set: A theory of the formal psychological deficit in schizophrenia. *Archives of General Psychiatry, 6,* 1–17.

Shamsuzzaman, A. S., Gersh, B. J., & Somers, V. K. (2003). Obstructive sleep apnea: Implications for cardiac and vascular disease. *Journal of the American Medical Association, 290,* 1906–1914.

Shanab, M. E., & Yahya, K. A. (1977). A behavioral study of obedience in children. *Journal of Personality and Social Psychology, 35,* 530–536.

Shannon, C. E. (1948). A mathematical theory of communication. *Bell System Technical Journal, 27,* 379–423, 623–656.

Shapiro, A. F., Gottman, J. M., & Carrere, S. (2000). The baby and the marriage: Identifying factors that buffer against decline in marital satisfaction after the first baby arrives. *Journal of Family Psychology, 14,* 59–70.

Shapiro, D. A., & Shapiro, D. (1982). Meta-analysis of comparative therapy outcome studies: A replication and refinement. *Psychological Bulletin, 92,* 581–604.

Shapiro, D. H. (1992). Adverse effects of meditation: A preliminary investigation of long-term meditators. *International Journal of Psychosomatics, 39,* 62–67.

Shapiro, F. (1989). Eye movement desensitization: A new treatment for post-traumatic stress disorder. *Journal of Behavior Therapy and Experimental Psychiatry, 20,* 211–217.

Shapiro, F. (1995). *Eye movement desensitization and reprocessing: Basic principles, protocols, and procedures.* New York: Guilford Press.

Shapiro, F., & Forrest, M. S. (1997). *EMDR: The breakthrough therapy for overcoming anxiety, stress, and trauma.* New York: Basic Books.

Shapiro, S. L., Schwartz, G. E. R., & Bonner, G. (1998). The effects of mindfulness-based stress reduction on medical and pre-medical students. *Journal of Behavioral Medicine, 21,* 581–599.

Shapiro, S. L., & Walsh, R. (2003). An analysis of recent meditation research and suggestions for future directions. *The Humanistic Psychologist, 31,* 86–113.

Sharm, B. P. (1972). Cannabis and its users in Nepal. *British Journal of Psychology, 127,* 550–555.

Sharma, P., & Chaturvedi, S. K. (1995). Conversion disorder revisited. *Acta Psychiatrica Scandinavica, 92,* 301–304.

Shaw, P., Greenstein, D., Lerch, J., Clasen, L., Lenroot, R., Gogtay, N., et al. (2006). Intellectual ability and cortical development in children and adolescents. *Nature, 440,* 676–679.

Shea, S. C. (1998). *Psychiatric interviewing: The art of understanding* (2nd ed). Philadelphia: W. B. Saunders.

Shedler, J., & Block, J. (1990). Adolescent drug use and psychological health: A longitudinal inquiry. *American Psychologist, 45,* 612–630.

Sheehan, P. W. (1991). Hypnosis, context, and commitment. In S. J. Lynn & J. W. Rhue (Eds.), *Theories of hypnosis: Current models and perspectives* (pp. 520–541). New York: Guilford Press.

Sheldon, K. M., & Lyubomirsky, S. (2006a). How to increase and sustain positive emotion: The effects of expressing gratitude and visualizing best possible selves. *The Journal of Positive Psychology, 1,* 73–82.

Sheldon, W. (1971). The New York study of physical constitution and psychotic pattern. *Journal of the History of the Behavioral Sciences, 7,* 115–126.

Shenk, J. W. (2005). *Lincoln's melancholy: How depression challenged a president and fueled his greatness.* Boston: Houghton Mifflin.

Shepperd, J. A., & Koch, E. J. (2005). Pitfalls in teaching judgment heuristics. *Teaching of Psychology, 32,* 43–46.

Sher, K. J., Grekin, E. R., & Williams, N. A. (2005). The development of alcohol use disorders. In S. Nolen-Hoeksema, T. D. Cannon, & T. Widiger (Eds.), *Annual Review of Clinical Psychology, 1,* 493–524.

Sher, K. J., Wood, M. D., Richardson, A. E., & Jackson, K. M. (2005). Subjective effects of alcohol 1: Effects of the drink and drinking context. In M. Earleywine (Ed.), *Mind-altering drugs: The science of subjective experience* (pp. 86–134). Washington, DC: American Psychological Association.

Sherif, M. (1936). *The psychology of social norms.* New York: Harper.

Sherif, M., Harvey, O. J., White, B. J., Hood, W. R., & Sherif, C. W. (1961). *The Robbers Cave experiment: Intergroup conflict and cooperation.* Middletown, CT: Wesleyan University Press.

Sherif, M., & Sherif, C. W. (1969). *Social psychology.* New York: Harper & Row.

Sherman, R. A., Sherman, C. J., & Parker, L. (1984). Chronic phantom and stump pain among American veterans: Results of a survey. *Pain, 18,* 83–95.

Shermer, M. (1997). *Why people believe weird things: Pseudoscience, superstition, and other confusions of our time.* New York: W. H. Freeman.

Shermer, M. (2002). *Why people believe weird things: Pseudoscience, superstition, and other confusions of our time* (2nd ed.). New York: W. H. Freeman.

Shermer, M. (2004, June). Death by theory. *Scientific American, 290,* 48.

Sherrington, C. S. (1906). *The integrative action of the nervous system.* New York: Charles Scribner's Sons.

Shimamura, A. P. (1992). Organic amnesia. In L. Squire (Ed.), *Encyclopedia of learning and memory* (pp. 30–35). New York: Macmillan.

Shimamura, A. P., Berry, J. M., Mangels, J. A., Rusting, C. L., & Jurica, P. J. (1995). Memory and cognitive abilities in university professors: Evidence for successful aging. *Psychological Science, 6,* 271–277.

Shin, S.-M., Chow, C., Camacho-Gonsalves, T., Levy, R. J., Allen, E., & Leff, S. H. (2005). A meta-analytic review of racial-ethnic matching for African American and Caucasian American clients and clinicians. *Journal of Counseling Psychology, 52,* 45–56.

Shlien, J., & Levant, R. (1984). Introduction. In Levant, R., & Shlien, J. (Eds.), *Client-centered therapy and the person-centered approach: New directions in theory, research and practice* (pp. 1–16). New York: Praeger.

Shomstein, S., & Yantis, S. (2006). Parietal cortex mediates voluntary control of spatial and nonspatial auditory attention. *Journal of Neuroscience, 26,* 435–439.

Shors, T. J., & Matzel, L. D. (1999). Long-term potentiation: What's learning got to do with it? *Behavioral and Brain Sciences, 20,* 597–655.

Showalter, E. (1997). *Hystories: Hysterical epidemics and modern culture.* New York: Columbia University Press.

Shrout, P. E., Link, B. G., Dohrenwend, B. P., Skodol, A. E., Stueve, A., & Mirotznik, J. (1989). Characterizing life events as risk factors for depression: The role of fateful loss events. *Journal of Abnormal Psychology, 98,* 460–467.

Shweder, R. A., Mahapatra, M., & Miller, J. G. (1990). Culture and moral development. In J. W. Stigler, R. A. Shweder, & G. S. Herdt (Eds.), *Cultural psychology: Essays on comparative human development* (pp. 130–204). New York: Cambridge University Press.

Sieff, E. M., Dawes, R. M., & Loewenstein, G. (1999). Anticipated versus actual reaction to HIV test results. *American Journal of Psychology, 112,* 297–311.

Siegel, J. (2005). Clues to the function of mammalian sleep. *Nature, 437,* 1264–1271.

Siegelbaum, S. A., Camardo, J. S., & Kandel, E. R. (1982, September 30). Serotonin and cyclic AMP close single K+ channels in Aplysia sensory neurons. *Nature, 299,* 413–417.

Siegler, R. S. (1992). The other Alfred Binet. *Developmental Psychology, 28,* 179–190.

Siegler, R. S. (1995). Children's thinking: How does change occur? In F. E. Weinert & W. Schneider (Eds.), *Memory performance and competencies: Issues in growth and development* (pp. 405–430). Hillsdale, NJ: Erlbaum.

Siever, L. J., & Davis, K. L. (2004). The pathophysiology of schizophrenia disorders: Perspectives from the spectrum. *American Journal of Psychiatry, 161,* 398–413.

Sigman, M., & Whaley, S. E. (1998). The role of nutrition in the development of intelligence. In U. Neisser (Ed.), *The rising curve: Long-term gains in IQ and related measures* (pp. 155–182). Washington, DC: American Psychological Association.

Sigurdsson, T., Doyere, V., Cain, C. K., & LeDoux, J. E. (2007). Long-term potentiation in the amygdala: A cellular mechanism of fear learning and memory. *Neuropharmacology, 52,* 215–227.

Silveira, J. M., & Seeman, M. V. (1995). Shared psychotic disorder: A critical review of the literature. *Canadian Journal of Psychiatry, 40,* 389–395.

Silventoinen, K. (2003). Determinants of variation in adult body height. *Journal of Biosocial Science, 35,* 263–285.

Silventoinen, K., Sammalisto, S., Perola, M., Boomsma, D. I., Cornes, B. K., Davis, C., et al. (2003). Heritability of adult body height: A comparative study of twin cohorts in eight countries. *Twin Research, 6,* 399–408.

Silver, E., Circincione, C., & Steadman, H. J. (1994). Demythologizing inaccurate perceptions of the insanity defense. *Law and Human Behavior, 18,* 63–70.

Silverman, S. (1987, July). Medical "miracles": Still mysterious despite claims of believers. *Psicientific American,* pp. 5–7. *Newsletter of the Sacramento Skeptics Society,* Sacramento, CA.

Simeon, D., Gross, S., Guralnik, O., Stein, D. J., Schmeidler, J., & Hollander, E. (1997). Feeling unreal: 30 Cases of DSM-III-R depersonalization. *American Journal of Psychiatry, 154,* 1107–1113.

Simon, G., von Kopff, M., Saunders, K., Miglioretti, D. L., Crane, K., Van Belle, K., et al. (2006). Association between obesity and psychiatric disorders in the U.S. population. *Archives of General Psychiatry, 63,* 824–830.

Simon, M. J., & Salzberg, H. C. (1985). The effect of manipulated expectancies on posthypnotic amnesia. *International Journal of Clinical and Experimental Hypnosis, 33,* 40–51.

Simon, R. I. (2006). Imminent suicide: The illusion of short-term prediction. *Suicide and Life-Threatening Behavior, 36,* 296–301.

Simon-Moffat, A. (2002). New fossils and a glimpse of evolution. *Science, 25,* 613–615.

Simons, R. C., & Hughes, C. C. (1986). *The culture-bound syndromes: Folk illnesses of psychiatric and anthropological interest.* Boston: D. Reidel Publishing.

Simons, D. J., & Chabris, C. F. (1999). Gorillas in our midst: Sustained inattentional blindness for dynamic events. *Perception, 28,* 1059–1074.

Simonton, D. K. (1997). Creative productivity: A predictive and explanatory model of career trajectories and landmarks. *Psychological Review, 104,* 66–89.

Simonton, D. K. (1999). *Origins of genius.* New York: Cambridge Press.

Simonton, D. K. (2006). Presidential IQ, openness, intellectual brilliance and leadership: Estimates and correlations for 42 U.S. chief executives. *Political Psychology, 27,* 511–526.

Simpson, G. M., & Kline, N. S. (1976). Tardive dyskinesias: Manifestations, etiology, and treatment. In M. D. Yahr (Ed.), *The basal ganglia* (pp. 167–183). New York: Raven Press.

Singer, M. (1979, January). Coming out of the cults. *Psychology Today,* 72–82.

Singer, M. T., & Lalich, J. (1996). *Crazy therapies.* Baltimore: Jossey-Bass.

Singer, M. T., & Nievod, A. (2003). New age therapies. In S. Lilienfeld, S. J. Lynn, & J. Lohr (Eds.), *Science and pseudoscience in clinical psychology* (pp. 176–204). New York: Guilford.

Singh, D. (1993). Adaptive significance of female physical attractiveness: Role of waist-to-hip ratio. *Journal of Personality and Social Psychology, 65,* 293–307.

Singh, D. (1995). Female judgment of male attractiveness and desirability for relationships: Role of waist-to-hip ratio and financial status. *Journal of Personality and Social Psychology, 69,* 1089–1101.

Sinkavich, F. J. (1995). Performance and metamemory: Do students know what they don't know? *Instructional Psychology, 22,* 77–87.

Skeem, J. L., Monahan, J., & Mulvey, E. P. (2002). Psychopathy, treatment involvement, and subsequent violence among civil psychiatric patients. *Law and Human Behavior, 26,* 577–603.

Skinner, B. F. (1938). *The behavior of organisms: An experimental analysis.* New York: Appleton-Century-Crofts.

Skinner, B. F. (1948). Superstition in the pigeon. *Journal of Experimental Psychology, 38,* 168–172.

Skinner, B. F. (1953). *Science and human behavior.* New York: Macmillan.

Skinner, B. F. (1971). *Beyond freedom and dignity.* New York: Knopf.

Skinner, B. F. (1974). *About behaviorism.* New York: Vintage Books.

Skinner, B. F. (1990). Can psychology be a science of mind? *American Psychologist, 4,* 1206–1210.

Skinner, E., Edge, K., Altman, J., & Sherwood, H. (2003). Searching for the structure of coping: A review and critique of category systems for classifying ways of coping. *Psychological Bulletin, 129,* 216–219.

Slade, T., & Andrews, G. (2005). Latent structure of depression in a community sample: A taxometric analysis. *Psychological Medicine, 35,* 489–497.

Slater, A. (1997). Can measures of infant habituation predict later intellectual ability? *Archives of Diseases of the Child, 77,* 474–476.

Slater, L. (2004). *Opening Skinner's box: Great psychological experiments of the 20th century.* New York: W. W. Norton.

Slavin, R. E., & Cooper, R. (1999). Improving intergroup relations: Lessons learned from cooperative learning programs. *Journal of Social Issues, 55,* 647–663.

Slegel, D. E., Benson, K. L., Zarcone, V. P., & Schubert, E. D. (1991). Middle-ear muscle activity and its association with motor activity in the extremities and head in sleep. *Lancet, 337,* 597–599.

Sloan, R. P., Bagiella, E., & Powell, T. (1999). Religion, spirituality, and medicine. *Lancet, 353,* 644–647.

Sloane, R. B., Staples, F., Cristol, A., Yorkston, N., & Whipple, K. (1975). *Psychotherapy versus behavior therapy.* Cambridge, MA: Harvard University Press.

Slovic, P., & Peters, E. (2006). Risk perception and affect. *Current Directions in Psychological Science, 15,* 322–325.

Slutske, W. S., Heath, A. C., Dinwiddie, S. H., Madden, P. A., & Bucholz, K. K. (1998). Common genetic risk factors for conduct disorder and alcohol dependence. *Journal of Abnormal Psychology, 107,* 363–374.

Smith, D., & Dumont, F. (1995). A cautionary study: Unwarranted interpretations of the Draw-A-Person Test. *Professional Psychology: Research and Practice, 26,* 298–303.

Smith, D. B. (2007). *Muses, madmen, and prophets: Rethinking the history, science, and meaning of auditory hallucination.* New York: Penguin Press.

Smith, D. M., Langa, K. M., Kabeto, M. U., & Ubel, P. A. (2005). Health, wealth, and happiness: Financial resources buffer subjective well-being after the onset of a disability *Psychological Science, 16,* 663–666.

Smith, E. E., Shoben, E. J., & Rips, L. J. (1974). Structure and process in semantic memory: A featural model for semantic decision. *Psychological Review, 81,* 214–241.

Smith, G. P. (1996). The direct and indirect controls of meal size. *Neuroscience Biobehavioral Review, 20,* 40–46.

Smith, G. T., Spillane, N. S., & Annus, A. M. (2006). Implications of an emerging integration of universal and culturally-specific psychologies. *Perspectives on Psychological Science, 1,* 211–233.

Smith, J. D., & Dumont, F. (2002). Confidence in psychodiagnosis: What makes us so sure? *Clinical Psychology and Psychotherapy, 9,* 292–298.

Smith, L., Fagan, J. F., & Ulvund, S. E. (2002). The relation of recognition memory in infancy and parental socioeconomic status to later intellectual competence. *Intelligence, 30,* 247–259.

Smith, M. (1980). *Michelle remembers.* New York: St. Martins Press.

Smith, M., & Hall, C. S. (1964). An investigation of regression in a long dream series. *Journal of Gerontology, 19,* 66–71.

Smith, M. L. (1980). Teacher expectations. *Evaluation in Education, 4,* 53–55.

Smith, M. L., & Glass, G. V. (1977). Meta-analysis of psychotherapy outcome studies. *American Psychologist, 32,* 752–760.

Smith, M. T., & Haythornthwaite, J. A. (2004). How do sleep disturbance and chronic pain inter-relate? Insights from the longitudinal and cognitive-behavioral clinical trials literature. *Sleep Medicine Review, 8,* 119–132.

Smith, P. K., & Daglish, L. (1977). Sex differences in parent and infant behavior in the home. *Child Development, 48,* 1250–1254.

Smith, R. A. (2001). *Challenging your preconceptions: Thinking critically about psychology.* Pacific Grove, CA: Wadsworth.

Smith, S. L., Gerhardt, K. J., Griffiths, S. K., Huang, X., & Abrams, R. M. (2003). Intelligibility of sentences recorded from the uterus of a pregnant ewe and from the fetal inner ear. *Audiology & Neuro-otology, 8,* 347–353.

Smith, S. M. (1979). Remembering in and out of context. *Journal of Experimental Psychology: Human Learning and Memory, 5,* 460–471.

Smith, S. M., Brown, H. O., Toman, J. E., & Goodman, L. S. (1947). The lack of cerebral effects of d-tubercurarine. *Anesthesiology, 8,* 1–14.

Smith, S. M., Lindsay, R. C. L., & Pryke, S. (2000). Postdictors of eyewitness errors: Can false identification be diagnosed? *Journal of Applied Psychology, 85,* 542–550.

Smith, S. M., Lindsay, R. C. L., Pryke, S., & Dysart, J. E. (2001). Postdictors of eyewitness errors: Can false identifications be diagnosed in the cross race situation? *Psychology, Public Policy, and Law, 7,* 153–169.

Smith, S. S. (2005). NCHS Dataline. *Public Health Reports, 120,* 353–354.

Smith, T. W., & Gallo, L. C. (2001). Personality traits as risk factors for physical illness. In A. Baum, T. A. Revenson, & J. Singer (Eds.), *Handbook of health psychology* (pp. 139–173). Mahwah, NJ: Erlbaum.

Smith, T. W., Snyder, C. R., & Perkins, S. C. (1983). Psychiatric consultation in somatization disorder: A randomized, controlled trial. *New England Journal of Medicine, 314,* 1407–1413.

Smithies, O. (1993). Animal models of human genetic diseases. *Trends in Genetics, 9,* 112–116.

Smythe, I. H. (2007). The secret behind "The Secret": What is attracting millions to the "Law of Attraction"? *Skeptic, 13*(2), 8–11.

Snarey, J. (1982). *The social and moral development of kibbutz founders and Sabras: A cross-sectional and longitudinal cross-cultural study.* Thesis presented to the faculty of the Graduate School of Education, Harvard University, Cambridge, MA.

Snelson, J. S. (1993). The ideological immune system: Resistance to new ideas in science. *Skeptic, 1*(4), 44–55.

Sniezck (1999)

Snowden, D. (2003). Narrative patterns: The perils and possibilities of using story in organizations. In E. Prusak & L. Prusak (Eds.), *Narrative patterns in creating value with knowledge.* Oxford, England: Oxford University Press.

Snyder, C. R., Shenkel, R. J., & Lowery, C. R. (1977). Acceptance of personality interpretations: The "Barnum effect" and beyond. *Journal of Consulting and Clinical Psychology, 45,* 104–114.

Snyder, M. (1974). Self monitoring of expressive behavior. *Journal of Personality and Social Psychology, 30,* 526–537.

Snyder, M., & Gangestad, S. (1986). On the nature of self-monitoring: Matters of assessment, matters of validity. *Journal of Personality and Social Psychology, 51*(1), 125–139.

Snyder, M., & Swann, W. B. (1978). Hypothesis-testing processes in social interaction. *Journal of Personality and Social Psychology, 36,* 1202–1212.

Snyder, S. H. (1975). *Madness and the brain.* New York: McGraw-Hill.

Snyder, T. J., & Gackenbach, J. (1988). Individual differences associated with lucid dreaming. In J. Gackenbach & S. Laberge (Eds.), *Conscious mind, sleeping brain: Perspectives on lucid dreaming* (pp. 221–260). New York: Plenum.

So, K., & Orme-Johnson, D. (2001). Three randomized experiments on the longitudinal effects of the transcendental meditation technique on cognition. *Intelligence, 29,* 419–440.

Soar, K., Parrott, A. C., & Fox, H. C. (2004). Persistent neuropsychological problems after 7 years of abstinence from recreational ecstasy (MDMA): A case study. *Psychological Reports, 95,* 192–196.

Sobell, M. B., & Sobell, L. C. (1973). Alcoholics treated by individualized behavior therapy: One year treatment outcome. *Behaviour Research and Therapy, 11,* 599–618.

Sobell, M. B., & Sobell, L. C. (1976). Second year treatment outcome of alcoholics treated by individualized behavior therapy: Results. *Behaviour Research and Therapy, 14,* 195–215.

Solms, M. (1997). *The neuropsychology of dreams: A clinico-anatomical study.* Mahwah, NJ: Lawrence Erlbaum Associates.

Solms, M. (2000). Dreaming and REM sleep are controlled by different brain mechanisms. *Behavioral and Brain Sciences, 23,* 843–850.

Solms, M., & Turnbull, O. (2002). The brain and the inner world. New York: Other Press.

Solomon, P. R., Adams, F., Silver, A., Zimmer, J., & DeVeaux, R. (2002). Ginkgo for memory enhancement: A randomized controlled trial. *Journal of the American Medical Association, 288,* 835–840.

Solomon, R. (2002). *That takes ovaries!: Bold females and their brazen acts.* New York: Three Rivers Press.

Solomon, S., Greenberg, J., & Pyszczynski, T. (2000). Pride and prejudice: Fear of death and social behavior. *Current Directions in Psychological Science, 6,* 200–204.

Solomon, S. S., & King, J. G. (1995). Influence of color on fire vehicle accidents. *Journal of Safety Research, 26,* 41–48.

Sommers, C. H., & Satel, S. (2005). *One nation under therapy: How the helping culture is eroding self-reliance.* New York: St. Martin's Press.

Sommers-Flanagan, J., & Sommers-Flanagan, R. (1995). Intake interviewing with suicidal patients: A systematic approach. *Professional Psychology: Research and Practice, 26,* 41–47.

Soper, B., Milford, G., & Rosenthal, G. (1995). Belief when evidence does not support theory. *Psychology & Marketing, 12,* 415–422.

Sorace, A. (2007). The more, the merrier: Facts and beliefs about the bilingual mind. In S. Della Sala (Ed.), *Tall tales about the mind and the brain: Separating fact from fiction* (pp. 193–203). Oxford, England: Oxford University Press

Sorensen, T. I., Price, R. A., Stunkard, A. J., & Schulsinger, F. (1989). Genetics of obesity in adult adoptees and their biological siblings. *British Medical Journal, 298,* 87–90.

Sorkhabi, N. (2005). Applicability of Baumrind's parent typology to collective cultures: Analysis of cultural explanations of parent socialization effects. *International Journal of Behavioral Development, 29,* 552–563.

Spalt, L. (1980). Hysteria and antisocial personality: A single disorder? (1980). *Journal of Nervous and Mental Disease, 168,* 456–464.

Spangler, W. D. (1992). Validity of questionnaire and TAT measures of need for achievement: Two meta-analyses. *Psychological Bulletin, 112,* 140–154.

Spanos, N. P. (1986). Hypnotic behavior: A social-psychological interpretation of amnesia, analgesia, and "trance logic." *The Behavioral and Brain Sciences, 9,* 499–502.

Spanos, N. P. (1991). A sociocognitive approach to hypnosis. In S. J. Lynn & J. W. Rhue (Eds.), *Theories of hypnosis: Current models and perspectives* (pp. 324–361). New York: Guilford Press.

Spanos, N. P. (1994). Multiple identity enactments and multiple personality disorder: A sociocognitive perspective. *Psychological Bulletin, 116,* 143–165.

Spanos, N. P. (1996). *Multiple identities and false memories: A sociocognitive perspective.* Washington, DC: American Psychological Association.

Spanos, N. P., Burgess, C. A., Roncon, V., Wallace-Capretta, S., & Cross, W. (1993). Surreptitiously observed hypnotic responding in simulators and skill-trained and untrained high hypnotizables. *Journal of Personality and Social Psychology, 65,* 391–398.

Spanos, N. P., Cobb, P. C., & Gorassini, D. (1985). Failing to resist hypnotic test suggestions: A strategy for self-presenting as deeply hypnotized. *Psychiatry, 48,* 282–292.

Spanos, N. P., & Hewitt, E. C. (1980). The hidden observer in hypnotic analgesia: Discovery or experimental creation? *Journal of Personality and Social Psychology, 39,* 1201–1214.

Spanos, N. P., Menary, E., Gabora, M. J., DuBreuil, S. C., & Dewhirst, B. (1991). Secondary identity enactments during hypnotic past-life regression: A sociocognitive perspective. *Journal of Personality and Social Psychology, 61,* 308–320.

Spanos, N. P., Radtke, H. L., & Bertrand, L. D. (1984). Hypnotic amnesia as strategic enactment: Breaching amnesia in highly susceptible subjects. *Journal of Personality and Social Psychology, 47,* 1155–1169.

Spearman, C. (1927). *The abilities of man.* New York: Macmillan.

Spehr, M., Gisselmann, G., Poplawski, A., Riffel, J. A., Wetzel, C. H., Zimmer, R. K., et al. (2003). Identification of a testicular odorant receptor mediating human sperm chemotaxis. *Science, 299,* 2054–2058.

Spelke, E. S. (1994). Initial knowledge: Six suggestions. *Cognition, 50,* 431–445.

Spelke, E. S. (2005). Sex differences in intrinsic aptitude for mathematics and science: A critical review. *American Psychologist, 60,* 950–958.

Spencer, N. A., McClintock, M. K., Sellergren, S. A., Bullivant, S., Jacob, S., & Mennella, J. A. (2004). Social chemosignals from breastfeeding women increase sexual motivation. *Hormones and Behavior, 46,* 362–370.

Sperling, G. (1960). The information available in brief visual presentations. *Psychological Monographs: General and Applied, 74*(11, Whole No. 498), 1–29.

Sperry, R. W. (1974). Lateral specialization in the surgically separated hemispheres. In F. Schmitt & F. Worden (Eds.), *Neurosciences third study program* (pp. 5–19). Cambridge. MA: MIT Press.

Spiegler, M. (1983). *Contemporary behavior therapy.* Palo Alto, CA: Mayfield.

Spiegler, M. D., & Guevremont, D. C. (2003). *Contemporary behavior therapy* (4th ed). Belmont, CA: Wadsworth/Thompson Learning.

Spitzer, R. (2003). Can some gay men and lesbians change their sexual orientation? 200 participants reporting a change from homosexual to heterosexual orientation. *Archives of Sexual Behavior, 32,* 403–417.

Spitzer, R. L. (1975). On pseudoscience, science, logic in remission, and psychiatric diagnosis: A critique of Rosenhan's "On being sane in insane places." *Journal of Abnormal Psychology, 84,* 442–452.

Spoormacher, V., & Van den Bout, J. (2006). Lucid dreaming treatment for nightmares: A pilot study. *Psychotherapy and Psychosomatics, 75,* 389–394.

Spotts, J. F., & Shontz, F. C. (1983). Drug-induced ego states. 1. The *International Journal of the Addictions, 18,* 119–151.

Spotts, J. V., & Shontz, F. C. (1976). *The lifestyles of nine American cocaine users: Trips to the land of cockaiqne.* [Alcohol, Drug Abuse , and Mental Health Administration, NIDA Issue No. 16]. Washington, DC: Department of Health, Education, and Welfare, PHS; U. S. Government Printing Office.

Sprecher, S. (1998). Insider's perspectives on reasons for attraction to a close other. *Social Psychology Quarterly, 61,* 287–300.

Sprecher, S., Barbee, A., & Schwartz, P. (1995). "Was it good for you, too?": Gender differences in first sexual experiences. *Journal of Sex Research, 32,* 3–15.

Squire, L. R. (1987). *Memory and brain.* New York: Oxford University Press.

Sroufe, L. A. (1983). Infant-caregiver attachment and patterns of adaptation in preschool: The roots of maladaptation and competence. In M. Perlmutter (Ed.), *Minnesota Symposium on Child Psychology* (Vol. 16, pp. 41–81). Hillsdale, NJ: Erlbaum.

Seligman, D. (1994). *A question of intelligence.* New York: Citadel Press.

Staats, A. W. (1991). Unified positivism and unification psychology: Fad or new field? *American Psychologist, 46,* 899–912.

Stampfl, T. G., & Levis, D. J. (1967). Essentials of implosive therapy: A learning theory-based psychodynamic behavioral therapy. *Journal of Abnormal Psychology, 72,* 496–503.

Standing, L. (1973). Learning 10,000 pictures. *Quarterly Journal of Experimental Psychology, 25,* 207–222.

Standing, L., Conezio, J., & Haber, R. N. (1970). Perception and memory for pictures: Single-trial learning of 2500 visual stimuli. *Psychonomic Science, 19,* 73–74.

Stangor, C., & McMillan, D. (1992). Memory for expectancy-congruent and expectancy-incongruent information: A review of the social and social developmental literatures. *Psychological Bulletin, 111,* 42–61.

Stanovich, K. (2004). *How to think straight about psychology* (5th ed.). New York: HarperCollins.

Stanovich, K. (2006). *How to think straight about psychology* (8th ed.). Boston: Allyn & Bacon.

Stanovich, K. E., & West, R. F. (1989). Exposure to print and orthographic processing. *Reading Research Quarterly, 24,* 402–433.

Stanovich, K. E., & West, R. F. (2000). Individual differences in reasoning: Implications for the rationality debate? *Behavioral and Brain Sciences, 23,* 645–665.

Stanovich, K., & West, R. F. (2002). Individual differences in reasoning: Implications for the rationality debate? In T. Gilovich, D. Griffin, & D. Kahneman (Eds.), *Heuristics and biases: The psychology of intuitive thought* (pp. 421–440). New York: Cambridge University Press.

Stathopoulou, G., Powers, M. B., Berry, A. C., Smits, J. A. J., & Otto, M. W. (2006). Exercise interventions for mental health: A quantitative and qualitative review. *Clinical Psychology: Science and Practice, 13,* 179–193.

Steadman, H. J., Mulvey, E. P., Monahan, J., Robbins, P. C., Appelbaum, P., Grisso, T., et al. (1 998). Violence by people discharged from acute psychiatric inpatient facilities and by others in the same neighborhoods. *Archives of General Psychiatry, 55,* 1–9.

Steblay, N. M. (1992). A meta-analytic review of the weapon focus effect. *Law and Human Behavior, 16,* 413–424.

Steblay, N. M., & Bothwell, R. K. (1994). Evidence for hypnotically refreshed testimony: The view from the laboratory. *Law and Human Behavior, 18,* 635–651.

Steblay, N. M., Deisert, J., Fulero, S., & Lindsay, R. C. L. (2001). Eyewitness accuracy rates in sequential and simultaneous lineup presentations: A meta-analytic comparison. *Law and Human Behavior, 25,* 459–474.

Steblay, N., Dysart, J. E., Fulero, S., & Lindsay, R. C. L. (2003). Eyewitness accuracy rates in police showup and lineup presentations: A meta-analytic comparison. *Law and Human Behavior, 27,* 523–540.

Steele, C. M. (1997). A threat in the air: How stereotypes shape the intellectual identities and performance of women and African-Americans. *American Psychologist, 52,* 613–629.

Steele, C. M., & Aronson, J. (1995). Stereotype threat and the intellectual test performance of African-Americans. *Journal of Personality and Social Psychology, 69,* 797–811.

Steele, K. M., Bass, K. E., & Crook, M. D. (1999). The mystery of the Mozart effect: Failure to replicate. *Psychological Science, 10,* 366–369.

Steele, M., Weiss, M., Swanson, J., Wang, J., Prinzo, R., & Binder, C. (2006). A randomized, controlled effectiveness trial of OROS-methylphenidate compared to usual care with immediate release methylphenidate in ADHD. *Canadian Journal of Clinical Pharmacology, 14,* 50–62.

Stein, M. B., Jang, K. L., & Livesley, W. J. (1999). Heritability of anxiety sensitivity: A twin study. *American Journal of Psychiatry, 156,* 246–251.

Steinberg, L. (2001). We know some things: Adolescent-parent relationships in retrospect and prospect. *Journal of Research in Adolescence, 11,* 1–20.

Steinhardt. L. (1998). Sand, water, and universal form in sandplay and art therapy. *Art Therapy, 15,* 252–260.

Steinmark, W. W., & Borkovec, T. D. (1974). Active and placebo treatment effects on moderate insomnia under counterdemand and positive demand instruction. *Journal of Abnormal Psychology, 83,* 157–163.

Stephan, W. G. (1978). School desegregation: An evaluation of predictions made in *Brown v. Board of Education. Psychological Bulletin, 85,* 217–238.

Stepp, L. S. (2007, April 24). For Virginia Tech survivors, memories will be powerful. Washingtonpost.com.. Retrieved June 18, 2007, from www.washingtonpost.com/wp-dyn/content/article/2007/04/20/AR2007042001790_pf.html.

Stern, A. (1938). Psychoanalytic investigation of and therapy in the borderline group of neuroses. *Psychoanalytical Quarterly, 7,* 467–489.

Stern, E. R, & Mangels, J. A. (2006). An electrophysiological investigation of preparatory attentional control in a spatial Stroop task. *Journal of Cognitive Neuroscience, 18,* 1004–1017.

Stern, J. M., Ray, W. J., & Davis, C. M. (1980). *Psychophysiological recording.* New York: Oxford University Press.

Stern, S. L., Dhanda, R., & Hazuda, H. P. (2001). Hopelessness predicts mortality in older Mexican and European Americans. *Psychosomatic Medicine, 63,* 344–351.

Stern, W. (1912). *The psychological methods of intelligence testing* (G. Whipple, Trans.). Baltimore: Warwick and York.

Sternberg, R. (2003). A duplex theory of hate: Development and application to terrorism, massacres, and genocide. *Review of General Psychology, 7,* 299–328.

Sternberg, R. G. (Ed.). (2004). *The psychology of hate.* Washington, DC: American Psychological Association.

Sternberg, R. J. (1983). Components of human intelligence. *Cognition, 15,* 1–48.

Sternberg, R. J. (1986). A triangular theory of love. *Psychological Review, 93,* 119–135.

Sternberg, R. J. (1988). *The triarchic mind: A new theory of human intelligence.* New York: Penguin Books.

Sternberg, R. J. (1988). Triangulating love. In R. J. Sternberg & M. L. Barnes (Eds.), *The psychology of love* (pp. 119–138). London: Yale University Press.

Sternberg, R. J. (2002). Smart people are not stupid, but they sure can be foolish: The imbalance theory of foolishness. In R. J. Sternberg (Ed.), *Why smart people can be so stupid.* New Haven, CT: Yale University Press.

Sternberg, R. J. (2003). Intelligence. In I. B. Weiner & D. K. Freedheim (Eds.), *Comprehensive handbook of psychology, Vol. 1* (pp. 135–156). New York: Wiley.

Sternberg, R. J., Conway, B. E., Ketron, J. L., & Bernstein, M. (1981). People's conceptions of intelligence. *Journal of Personality and Social Psychology, 41,* 37–55.

Sternberg, R. J., & Detterman, D. K. (Eds.). (1986). *What is intelligence? Contemporary viewpoints on its nature and definition.* Norwood, NJ: Ablex.

Sternberg, R. J., Grigorenko, E. L., & Kidd, K. K. (2005). Intelligence, race, and genetics. *American Psychologist, 60,* 46–59.

Sternberg, R. J., & Lubart, T. I. (1992). Buy low and sell high: An investment approach to creativity. *Current Directions in Psychological Science, 1,* 1–5.

Sternberg, R. J., & Wagner, R. K. (1993). *Thinking Styles Inventory.* Unpublished instrument.

Sternberg, R. J., Wagner, R. K., Williams, W. M., & Horvath, J. A. (1995). Testing common sense. *American Psychologist, 50,* 912–927.

Sternberg, R. J., & Williams, W. M. (1997). Does the Graduate Record Examination predict meaningful success in the graduate training of psychologists? A case study. *American Psychologist, 52,* 630–641.

Stevens, S. E., Hynan, M. T., & Allen, M. (2000). A meta-analysis of common factor and specific treatment effects across the outcome domains of the phase model of psychotherapy. *Clinical Psychology: Science and Practice, 7,* 273–290.

Stevenson, I. (1960). The evidence for survival from claimed memories of former incarnations. Part I: Review of the data. *Journal of the American Society for Psychical Research, 54,* 51–71.

Stevenson, I. (1974). *Twenty cases suggestive of reincarnation* (2nd rev. ed.), Charlottesville, VA: University Press of Virginia.

Stewart, J. R. (1977). Cattle mutilations: An episode of collective delusion, *The Zetetic, 1*(2), 55–66.

Stewart, T. L., LaDuke, J. R., Bracht, C., Sweet, B. A. M., & Gamarel, K. E. (2003). Do the "eyes" have it? A program evaluation of Jane Elliott's "Blue-Eyes/Brown-Eyes" diversity training exercise. *Journal of Applied Social Psychology, 33,* 1898–1921.

Stice, E., Cameron, R., Killen, J. D., Hayward, C., & Taylor, C. B. (1999). Naturalistic weight reduction efforts prospectively predict growth in relative weight and onset of obesity among female adolescents. *Journal of Consulting and Clinical Psychology, 67,* 967–974.

Stice, E., Presnell, K., Shaw, H., & Rhode, P. (2005). Psychological and behavioral risk factors for obesity onset in adolescent girls: A prospective study. *Journal of Consulting and Clinical Psychology, 73,* 195–202.

Stickgold, R., James, L., & Hobson, J. A. (2002). Visual discrimination learning requires sleep after training. *Nature Neuroscience, 3,* 1235–1236.

Stierlin, H. (1972). *Conflict and reconciliation: A study in human relations and schizophrenia* (2nd ed.). New York: Science House.

Stoerig, P., & Cowey, A. (1997). Blindsight in man and monkey. *Brain, 120,* 535–559.

Stokoe, W. C., Casterline, D. C., & Croneberg, C. G. (1976). *A dictionary of American Sign Language on linguistic principles.* Silver Spring, MD: Linstok.

Stone, A., Webb, R., & Mahootian, S. (1991). The generality of gesture-speech mismatch as an index of transitional knowledge: Evidence from a control-of-variables task. *Cognitive Development, 6,* 301–313.

Stone, A. A. (1982). The insanity defense on trial. *Hospital and Community Psychiatry, 33,* 636–640.

Storch, E., Bagner, D., Geffken, G., & Baumeister, A. (2004). Association between overt and relational aggression and psychosocial adjustment in undergraduate college students. *Violence and Victims, 19,* 689–700.

Strack, F., Martin, L., & Stepper, S. (1988). Inhibiting and facilitating conditions of the human smile: A nonobtrusive test of the facial feedback hypothesis. *Journal of Personality and Social Psychology, 54,* 768–777.

Strauch, I., & Meier, B. (1996). *In search of dreams: Results of experimental dream research.* Albany, NY: SUNY Press.

Strayer, D. L., Drews, F. A., & Johnston, W. A. (2003). Cell phone-induced failures of visual attention during simulated driving. *Journal of Experimental Psychology: Applied, 9,* 23–32.

Strentz, T., & Auerbach, S. M. (1988). Adjustment to the stress of simulated captivity: Effects of emotion-focused versus problem-focused preparation on hostages differing in locus of control. *Journal of Personality and Social Psychology, 55,* 652–660.

Striano, T., Tomasello, M., & Rochat, P. (2001). Social and object support for early symbolic play. *Developmental Science, 4,* 442–455.

Stricker, G., & Gold, J. (2003). Integrative approaches to psychotherapy. In A. S. Gurman & S. B. Messer (Eds.), *Essential psychotherapies* (2nd ed., pp. 317–349). New York: Guilford.

Strickland, T. L., Stein, R., Lin, K. M., Risby, E., & Fong, R. (1997). The pharmacologic treatment of anxiety and depression in African Americans: Considerations for the general practitioner. *Archives of Family Medicine, 6,* 371–375.

Stroebe, W. (2000). *Social psychology and health* (2nd ed.). Buckingham, England: Open University Press.

Strohl, K. P., & Redline, S. (1996). Recognition of obstructive sleep apnea. *American Journal of Respiratory and Critical Care Medicine, 154,* 279–289.

Stromeyer, C. F., & Psotka, J. (1970). The detailed texture of eidetic imagery. *Nature, 225,* 346–349.

Strong, M., & Prinz, P. (1997). A study of the relationship between American Sign Language and English literacy. *Journal of Deaf Studies and Deaf Education, 2,* 37–46.

Stroop, J. R. (1935). Studies of interference in serial verbal reactions. *Journal of Experimental Psychology, 18,* 643–662.

Strupp, H. H., & Hadley, S. W. (1979). Specific vs. nonspecific factors in psychotherapy. *Archives of General Psychiatry, 36,* 1125–1136.

Strupp, H. H., Fox, R. E., & Lessler, K. (1969). *Patients view their therapy.* Baltimore: Johns Hopkins University Press.

Strupp, H. H., Hadley, S. W., & Gomez-Schwartz, B. (1978). *Psychotherapy for better or worse: An analysis of the problem of negative effects.* New York: Jason Aronson.

Stuart, E. W., Shimp, T. A., & Engle, R. W. (1987). Classical conditioning of consumer attitudes: Four experiments in an advertising context. *Journal of Consumer Research, 14,* 334–349.

Stuart, R. B. (1967). Behavioral control of overeating. *Behavior Research and Therapy, 5,* 357–365.

Stuart, R. B. (2004). Twelve practical suggestions for achieving multicultural competence. *Professional Psychology: Research and Practice, 35,* 3–9.

Stuart, R. B., & Heiby, E. M. (in press). To prescribe or not prescribe: Eleven exploratory questions. *The Scientific Review of Mental Health Practice.*

Stunkard, A. (1975). Satiety is a conditioned reflex. *Journal of Psychosomatic Medicine, 37,* 383–387.

Stunkard, A. J., Foch, T. T., & Hrubec, Z. (1986). A twin study of human obesity. *Journal of the American Medical Association, 256,* 51–54.

Stunkard, A. J., Harris, J. R., Pedersen, N. L., & McClearn, G. E. (1990). The body-mass index of twins who have been reared apart. *New England Journal of Medicine, 322,* 1483–1487.

Stunkard, A. J., Sorensen, T. I., Hanis, C., Teasdale, T. W., Chakraborty, R., Schull, W. J., et al. (1986). An adoption study of human obesity. *New England Journal of Medicine, 314,* 193–198.

Substance Abuse and Mental Health Services Administration. (2001). *Summary of findings from the 2000 National Household Survey on Drug Abuse* (NHSDA Series: H-13, DHHS Publication No. SMA 01-3549). Rockville, MD.

Sue, S. (1993, November). *Measurement, testing, and ethnic bias: Can solutions be found?* Keynote Address at the Ninth Buros-Nebraska Symposium on Measurement and Testing, Lincoln, NE, September.

Sue, S., & Lam. A. G. (2002). Cultural and demographic diversity. In J. C. Norcross (Ed.), *Psychotherapy relationships that work* (pp. 401–421). New York: Oxford University Press.

Sue, S., & Zane, N. (2006). Ethnic minority populations have been neglected by evidence-based practices. In J. C. Norcross, L. E. Beutler, & R. F. Levant (Eds.), *Evidence-based practices in mental health* (pp. 329–337). Washington, DC: American Psychological Association.

Sue, S. W. (1998). In search of cultural competence in psychotherapy and counseling. *American Psychologist, 53,* 440–448.

Sue, S. W., & Sue, D. (2003). *Counseling the culturally diverse: Theory and practice* (4th ed.). New York: Wiley.

Sullivan, H. S. (1954). *The psychiatric interview.* New York: W. W. Norton.

Sullivan, M. L., Rouse, D., Bishop, S., & Johnston, S. (1997). Thought suppression, catastrophizing, and pain. *Cognitive Therapy and Research, 21,* 555–568.

Sullivan, P. F. (1995). Mortality of anorexia nervosa. *American Journal of Psychiatry, 152,* 1073–1074.

Sullivan, P. F., Fifield, W. J., Kennedy, M. A., Mulder, R. T., Sellman, J. D., & Joyce, P. R. (1998). No association between novelty seeking and the type 4 dopamine receptor gene (DRD4) in two New Zealand samples. *American Journal of Psychiatry, 155,* 98–101.

Sulloway, F. J. (1990). *Born to rebel: Birth order, family dynamics, and creative lives.* New York: Pantheon.

Sulloway, F. J. (1991). Reassessing Freud's case histories: The social construction of psychoanalysis. *Isis, 82,* 245–275.

Sulloway, F. J. (1996). *Born to rebel: Birth order, family dynamics and creative lives.* New York: Pantheon Books.

Sullum, J. (2003). *Saying yes: In defense of drug use.* New York: Teacher/Putnam.

Sultan, S., Andronikof, A., Reveillere, C., & Lemmel, G. (2006). A Rorschach stability study in a nonpatient adult sample. *Journal of Personality Assessment, 87,* 330–348.

Sunar, D. (2002). The psychology of morality. In W. J. Lonner, D. L. Dinnel, S. A. Hayes, & D. N. Sattler (Eds.), *Online readings in psychology and culture* (Unit 2, Chap. 11) (http://www.wwu.edu/~culture), Center for Cross-Cultural Research, Western Washington University, Bellingham, WA.

Sundet, J. M., Barlaug, D. G., & Torjussen, T. M. (2004). The end of the Flynn effect? A study of secular trends in mean intelligence test scores of Norwegian conscripts during half a century. *Intelligence, 32,* 349–362.

Susser, E. S., & Lin, S. P. (1992). Schizophrenia after prenatal exposure to the Dutch Hunger Winter of 1944–1945. *Archives of General Psychiatry, 49,* 983–988.

Sutherland, S. (1992). *Irrationality: Why we don't think straight!* New Brunswick, NJ: Rutgers University Press.

Swaiman, K. F., & Ashwal, S. (1999). *Pediatric neurology: Principles and practice* (3rd ed.). St. Louis, MO: Mosby.

Swann, W. B., Jr., & Pelham, B. W. (2002). Who wants out when the going gets good? Psychological investment and preference for self-verifying college roommates. *Journal of Self and Identity, 1,* 219–233.

Swartz, M., Blazer, D., George, L., & Winfield, I. (1990). Estimating the prevalence of borderline personality disorder in the community. *Journal of Personality Disorders, 4,* 257–272.

Swenson, C. (1968). Empirical evaluations of human figure drawings: 1957–1966. *Psychological Bulletin, 70,* 20–44.

Swim, J. K. (1994). Perceived versus meta-analytic effect sizes: An assessment of the accuracy of gender stereotypes. *Journal of Personality and Social Psychology, 66,* 21–36.

Symons, D. (1979). *The evolution of human sexuality.* New York: Oxford University Press.

Szasz, T. (1978). Should psychiatric patients ever be hospitalized involuntarily? Under any circumstances—No. In J. P. Brady & H. K. H. Brodie (Eds.), *Controversy in psychiatry* (pp. 965–977). Philadelphia: W. B. Saunders.

Szasz, T. (1991). *Insanity.* Chichester, England: Wiley.

Szasz, T. S. (1960). The myth of mental illness. *American Psychologist, 15,* 113–118.

Szasz, T. S. (2006). *Mental illness as a brain disease: A brief history lesson.* Cybercenter for Liberty and Responsibility. Retrieved December 22, 2006, from www.szasz.com/freeman13.html.

Taiminen, T., & Jääskeläinen, S. K. (2001). Intense and recurrent déjà vu experiences related to amantadine and phenylpropanolamine in a healthy male. *Journal of Clinical Neuroscience, 8,* 460–462.

Tajfel, H. (1982). *Social identity and intergroup relations.* Cambridge, England: Cambridge University Press.

Tajfelt, H., Billig, M., Bundy, R., & Flament, C. L. (1971). Social categorization and intergroup behavior. *European Journal of Social Psychology, 1,* 149–177.

Talbott, S. (2002). *The cortisol connection diet: The breakthrough program to control stress and lose weight.* Alameda, CA: Hunter House.

Talmi, D., Grady, C. L., Goshen-Gottstein, Y., & Moscovitch, M. (2005). Neuroimaging the serial position curve: An fMRI test of the single-process vs. dual process (STM-LTM) model. *Psychological Science, 16,* 716–723.

Tanaka, T. (1966). A study of conditioned response in hydra. *Annals of Animal Psychology, 16,* 37–41.

Tang, Y., Nyengaard, J. R., De Groot, D. M., & Gundersen, H. J. (2001). Total regional and global number of synapses in the human brain neocortex. *Synapse, 41,* 258–273.

Tanner, J. M. (1990). *Fetus into man: Physical growth from conception to maturity* (Rev. ed.). Boston: Harvard University Press.

Tanner, J. M. (1998). Sequence, tempo, and individual variation in growth and development of boys and girls aged twelve to sixteen. R. E. Muuss & H. D. Porton (Eds.), *Adolescent behavior and society: A book of readings* (5th ed., pp. 34–46). New York: McGraw-Hill.

Tanner, L. (2006, August 6). Sexual lyrics prompt teens to have sex. *Associated Press.* Retrieved August 6, 2006, from http://www.sfgate.com/cgibin /article.cgi?f=/n/a/2006/08/06/national/a215010D94.DTL.

Tart, C. T. (1968). A psychophysiological study of out-of-the-body experiences in a selected subject. *International Journal of Parapsychology, 9,* 251–258.

Tasker, F., & Golombok, S. (1995). Adults raised as children in lesbian families. *American Journal of Orthopsychiatry, 65,* 203–215.

Tassinary, L. G., & Hansen, K. A. (1998). A critical test of the waist-to-hip ratio hypothesis of female physical attractiveness. *Psychological Science, 9,* 150–155.

Taubes, G. (2007, September 16). Do we really know what makes us healthy? *New York Times Magazine,* Retrieved September 23, 2007, from http:// www.nytimes.com.

Tautz, J., Rohrseitz, K., & Sandeman, D. C. (1996). One-strided waggle dance in bees. *Nature, 382,* 32.

Tavris, C. (1989). *Anger: The misunderstood emotion.* New York: Touchstone.

Tavris, C., & Aronson, E. (2007). *Mistakes were made (but not by me): How we justify foolish beliefs, bad decisions, and hurtful acts.* New York: Harcourt.

Taylor, A. K., & Kowalski, P. (2004). Naive psychological science: The prevalence, strength, and sources of misconceptions. *Psychological Record, 54,* 15–25.

Taylor, H. (2003). The religious and other beliefs of Americans 2003. The Harris Poll #11, February 26, 2003. Rochester, NY: Harris Interactive Inc.

Taylor, J., & Lang, A. R. (2006). Psychopathy and substance use disorders. In C. J. Patrick (Ed.), *Handbook of psychopathy* (pp. 495 511). New York: Guilford Press.

Taylor, R. (1975, May/June). Electroconvulsive treatment (ECT): The control of therapeutic power. *Exchange,* 32–37.

Taylor, S. E., & Brown, J. D. (1988). Illusion and well-being—A social psychological perspective on mental health. *Psychological Bulletin, 103,* 193–210.

Taylor, S. E., & Brown, J. D. (1994). Positive illusions and well-being revisited: Separating fact from fiction. *Psychological Bulletin, 116,* 21–27.

Taylor, S. E., Klein, L. C., Lewis, B. P., Gruenewald, T. L., Gurung, R. A. R., & Updegraff, J. A. (2000). Biobehavioral responses to stress in females: Tend-and-befriend, not fight-or-flight. *Psychological Review, 107,* 411–429.

Taylor, S. P. (1993). Experimental investigation of alcohol-induced aggression in humans. *Alcohol Health and Research World, 17,* 108–112.

Taylor-Clarke, M., Kennett, S., & Haggard, P. (2002). Vision modulates somatosensory cortical processing. *Current Biology, 12,* 233–236.

Teasdale, J. D. (1985). Psychological treatments for depression: How do they work? *Behaviour Research and Therapy, 23,* 157–165.

Teasdale, J. D., Segal, Z. V., & Williams, J. M. G. (2003). Mindfulness training and problem formulation. *Clinical Psychology: Science and Practice, 10,* 157–160.

Tedeschi, J. T., Schlenker, B. R., & Bonoma, T. V. (1971). Cognitive dissonance: Private ratiocination or public spectacle? *American Psychologist, 26,* 680–695.

Teitelbaum, P., & Epstein, A. N. (1962). The lateral hypothalamic syndrome: Recovery of feeding and drinking after lateral hypothalamic lesions. *Psychological Review, 69,* 74–90.

Tellegen, A. (1982). *Brief manual for the Multidimensional Personality Questionnaire.* Unpublished manuscript, University of Minnesota. (Original work created 1978)

Tellegen, A. (1985). Structures of mood and personality and their relevance to assessing anxiety, with an emphasis on self-report. In A. H. Tuma & J. D. Maser (Eds.), *Anxiety and the anxiety disorders* (pp. 681–706). Hillsdale, NJ: Lawrence Erlbaum.

Tellegen, A. (1991). Personality traits: Issues of definition, evidence, and assessment. In D. Cicchetti & W. M. Grove (Eds.), *Thinking clearly about psychology: Essays in honor of Paul Everett Meehl* (pp. 10–35). Minneapolis, MN: University of Minnesota Press.

Tellegen, A., & Atkinson, G. (1974). Openness to absorbing and self-altering experiences ("absorption"), a trait related to hypnotic susceptibility. *Journal of Abnormal Psychology, 83,* 268–277.

Tellegen, A., Lykken, D. T., Bouchard, T. J., Wilcox, K. J., Segal, N. L., & Rich, S. (1988). Personality similarity in twins reared apart and together. *Journal of Personality and Social Psychology, 54,* 1031–1039.

Teplin, L. A., McClelland, G. M., Abram, K. M., & Weiner, D. (2005). Crime victimization in adults with severe mental illness: Comparison with the national crime victimization survey. *Archives of General Psychiatry, 62,* 911–921.

Terman, L. M., & Oden, M. H. (1959). *Genetic studies of genius: Vol. 5. The gifted group at mid-life.* Stanford, CA: Stanford University Press.

Terr, L. (1988). Chowchilla revisited: The effects of psychic trauma four years after a school-bus kidnapping. *American Journal of Psychiatry, 140,* 1543–1550.

Tesser, A., & Leone, C. (1977). Cognitive schemas and thought as determinants of attitude change. *Journal of Experimental Social Psychology, 13,* 340–356.

Tetlock, P. E. (2005). *Expert political judgment: How good is it? How can we know?* Princeton, NJ: Princeton University Press.

Tett, R. P., Jackson, D. N., & Rothstein, M. (1991). Personality measures as predictors of job performance: A meta-analytic review. *Personnel Psychology, 44,* 703–742.

Teyber, E., & McClure, E. T. (2000). Therapist variables. In C. R. Snyder & R. E. Ingram (Eds.), *Handbook of psychological change* (pp. 62–87). New York: John C. Wiley & Sons.

Thase, M. E. (2000). Psychopharmacology in conjunction with psychotherapy. In C. R. Snyder & R. E. Ingram (Eds.), *Handbook of psychological change* (pp. 474–498). New York: John Wiley & Sons.

Thelen, E. (1995). Time-scale dynamics and the development of an embodied cognition. In R. F. Port & T. van Gelder (Eds.), *Mind as motion: Explorations in the dynamics of cognition* (pp. 69–100). Cambridge, MA: MIT Press.

Thelen, E., & Fisher, D. M. (1982). Newborn stepping: An explanation for a "disappearing" reflect. *Developmental Psychology, 18,* 760–775.

Thelen, E., & Smith, L. B. (1994). *A dynamic systems approach to the development of cognition and action.* Cambridge, MA: MIT Press.

Thelen, E., & Ulrich, B. D. (1991). Hidden skills: A dynamic systems analysis of treadmill stepping during the first year. *Monographs of the Society for Research in Child Development, 56,* Serial No. 223.

Theorell, T., & Rahe, R. H. (1975). Life change events, ballistocardiography, and coronary death. *Journal of Human Stress, 1,* 18–24.

theory of development. *Psychological Review, 102,* 458–489.

Tholey, P. (1988). A model for lucidity training as a means of self-healing and psychological growth. In J. Gackenbach & S. LaBerge (Eds.), *Conscious mind, sleeping brain* (pp. 263–287). New York: Plenum.

Thomas, A., & Chess, S. (1977). *Temperament and development.* New York: Brunner/Mazel.

Thomas, M. (2004). Was Einstein learning disabled? Anatomy of a myth. *Skeptic, 10*(4), 40–47.

Thomas, P. (1997). *The dialectics of schizophrenia.* Bristol, England: Free Association Books.

Thompson, D. L., & Ahrens, M. J. (2004). *The grapefruit solution: Lower your cholesterol, lose weight, and achieve optimal health with nature's wonderful fruit.* [Brochure]. Linx Corporation.

Thompson, J. K., & Heinberg, L. J. (1999). Thes media's influence on body image disturbance and eating disorders: We've reviled them, now can we rehabilitate them? *Journal of Social Issues, 55,* 339–353.

Thompson, J. K., Heinberg, L. J., Altabe, M. N., & Tantleff-Dunn, S. (2004). *Exacting beauty: Theory, assessment, and treatment of body image disturbance.* Washington, DC: American Psychological Association.

Thompson, J. K., Herbozo, S. M., Himes, S. M., & Yamamiya, Y. (2005) Weight-related teasing in adults. In K. D. Brownell, L., Rudd, R. M. Puhl, & M. B. Schwartz (Eds.), *Weight bias: Nature, consequences and remedies* (pp. 137–149). New York: Guilford Press.

Thompson, P. (1980). Margaret Thatcher: A new illusion. *Perception, 9,* 483–484.

Thompson, R. A. (1998). Early sociopersonality development. In W. Damon (Series Ed.) & N. Eisenberg (Vol. Ed.), *Handbook of child psychology: Vol. 3. Social, emotional, and personality development* (5th ed., pp. 25–104). New York: Wiley.

Thompson, R., Emmorey, K., & Gollan, T. (2005). Tip-of-the-fingers experiences by ASL signers: Insights into the organization of a sign-based lexicon. *Psychological Science, 16,* 856–860.

Thompson, W. F., Schellenberg, E. G., & Husain, G. (2001). Arousal, mood, and the Mozart effect. *Psychological Science, 12,* 248–251.

Thorn, B., Rich, M. A., & Boothby, J. L. (1999). Pain beliefs and coping attempts: Conceptual model building. *Pain Forum, 8,* 169–171.

Thorndike, E. L. (1898). *Animal intelligence: An experimental study of the associative processes in animals.* New York: Macmillan.

Thorndike, E. L. (1903). *Educational psychology.* New York: Lemcke & Buechner.

Thorndike, E. L. (1911). *Animal intelligence: Experimental studies.* New York: Macmillan.

Thorpe, K., Greenwood, R., Eivers, A., & Rutter, M. (2001). Prevalence and developmental course of 'secret language'. *International Journal of Language & Communication Disorders, 36,* 43–62.

Thurman, D., Alverson, C., Dunn, K., Guerrero, J., & Sniezek, J. (1999). Traumatic brain injury in the United States: A public health perspective. *Journal of Head Trauma Rehabilitation, 14,* 602–615.

Thurstone, L. L. (1938). *Primary mental abilities.* Chicago: University of Chicago Press.

Tiggemann, M., & Pickering, A. S. (1996). Role of television in adolescent women's body dissatisfaction and drive for thinness. *International Journal of Eating Disorders, 20,* 199–203.

Tincoff, R., & Jusczyk, P. W. (1999). Some beginnings of word comprehension in 6-month-olds. *Psychological Science, 10,* 172–175.

Tloczynski, J., & Tantriella, M. (1998). A comparison of the effects of Zen breath meditation or relaxation on college adjustment. *Psychologia: An International Journal of Psychology in the Orient, 41,* 32–43.

Todorovic, A., & Haskell-Luevano, C. (2005). A review of melanocortin receptor small molecule ligands. *Peptides, 26,* 2026–2036.

Tolman, E. C. (1948). Cognitive maps in rats and men. *Psychological Review, 55,* 189–208.

Tolman, E. C., & Honzik, C. H. (1930). Introduction and removal of reward, and maze performance in rats. *University of California Publications in Psychology, 4,* 257–275.

Tolnay, S. E., & Beck, E. M. (1995). *A festival of violence: An analysis of southern lynchings, 1882–1930.* Urbana, IL: University of Illinois Press.

Tomasello, M. (1999). *The cultural origins of human cognition.* Cambridge, MA: Harvard University Press.

Tomasello, M., Strosberg, R., & Akhtar, N. (1996). Eighteen-month-old children learn words in non-ostensive contexts. *Journal of Child Language, 23,* 157–176.

Tomkins, S. S. (1962). *Affect, imagery, consciousness: Vol. 1: The positive affects.* New York: Springer.

Tomkins, S. S., & McCarter, R. (1964). What and where are the primary affects? Some evidence for a theory. *Perceptual and Motor Skills, 18,* 119–158.

Tooth, J. C., & Newton, M. P. (1961). Leucotomy in England and Wales 1942–1954. Reports on public health and medical subjects No. 104. London, Her Majesty's Stationary Office.

Torgersen, S. (1983). Genetic factor in anxiety disorders. *Archives of General Psychiatry, 40,* 1085–1089.

Torgersen, S., Lygren, S., Oien, P. A., Skre, I., Onstad, S., Edvardsen, J., et al. (2000). A twin study of personality disorders. *Comprehensive Psychiatry, 41,* 416–425.

Torrey, E. F. (1997). *Out of the shadows: Confronting America's mental illness crisis.* New York: John Wiley.

Torrey, E. G., Miller, J., Rawlings, R., & Yolken, R. H. (1997). Seasonality of births in schizophrenia and bipolar disorder: A review of the literature. *Schizophrenia Research, 28,* 1–38.

Tracy, J. L., & Robins, R. W. (2007). Emerging insights into the nature and function of pride. *Current Directions in Psychological Science, 16,* 147–150.

Travis, F. (2001). Autonomic and EEG patterns distinguish transcending from other experiences during transcendental meditation practice. *International Journal of Psychophysiology, 42,* 1–9.

Treffert, D. A., & Christensen, D. D. (2005, December). Inside the mind of a savant. *Scientific American, 293,* 108–113.

Treisman, A. (1960). Contextual cues in selective listening. *Quarterly Journal of Experimental Psychology, 12,* 242–248.

Trenkwalder, C., Walters, A. S., & Hening, W. (1996). Periodic limb movements and restless legs syndrome. *Neurologic Clinics, 14,* 629–650.

Triandis, H. C. (1989). The self and social behavior in differing cultural contexts. *Psychological Review, 96,* 506–520.

Triandis, H. C., & Suh, E. M. (2002). Cultural influences on personality. *Annual Review of Psychology, 53,* 133–160.

Triplett, N. (1897). The dynamogenic factors in pacemaking and competition. *American Journal of Psychology, 9,* 507–533.

Trivers, R. (2000). The elements of a scientific theory of self-deception. *Annals of the New York Academy of Sciences, 907,* 114–131.

Tronick, E., Thomas, R., & Daltabuit, M. (1994). The Quechua manta pouch: A caretaking practice for buffering the Peruvian infant against the multiple stressors of high altitude. *Child Development, 65,* 1005–1013.

Troxel, W. M., Matthews, K. A., Bromberger, J. T., & Sutton-Tyrell, K. (2003). Chronic stress burden, discrimination, and subclinical carotid artery disease in African American and Caucasian women. *Health Psychology, 22,* 300–309.

Trull, T. J., & Durett, C. A. (2005). Categorical and dimensional models of personality disorder. *Annual Review of Clinical Psychology, 1,* 355–380.

Truzzi, M. (1978). On the extraordinary: An attempt at clarification. *Zetetic Scholar, 1,* 11–22.

Tschirgi, J. E. (1980). Sensible reasoning: A hypothesis about hypotheses. *Child Development, 51,* 1–10.

Tsien, J. Z. (2000). Linking Hebb's coincidence-detection to memory formation. *Current Opinions in Neurobiology, 10,* 266–273.

Tucker, J. A., Vucinich, R., & Sobell, M. (1982). Alcohol's effects on human emotions. *International Journal of the Addictions, 17,* 155–180.

Tulving, E. (1972). Episodic and semantic memory. In E. Tulving & W. Donaldson (Eds.), *Organization of memory* (pp. 378–402). New York: Academic Press.

Tulving, E. (1982). Synergistic ecphory in recall and recognition. *Canadian Journal of Psychology, 36,* 130–147.

Tulving, E., & Thomson, D. M. (1973). Encoding specificity and retrieval processes in episodic memory. *Psychological Review, 80,* 352–373.

Turk, D. C. (1996). Psychological aspects of pain and disability. *Journal of Musculoskeletal Pain, 4,* 145–154.

Turk, D. J., Heatherton, T. F., Kelley, W. M., Funnell, M. G., Gazzaniga, M. S., & Macrae, C. N. (2002). Mike or me? Self-recognition in a split-brain patient. *Nature Neuroscience, 5,* 841–842.

Turkeltaub, P. E., Gareau, L., Flowers, D. L., Zeffiro, T. A., & Eden, G. F. (2003). Development of neural mechanisms for reading. *Nature Neuroscience, 6*(7), 767–773.

Turkheimer, E. (2000). Three laws of behavior genetics and what they mean. *Current Directions in Psychological Science, 9,* 160–163.

Turkheimer, E., Haley, A., Waldron, M., D'Onofrio, B., & Gottesman, I. I. (2003). Socioeconomic status modifies heritability of IQ in young children. *Psychological Science, 14,* 623–628.

Turner, R., Bauer, R., Woelkart, K., Hulsey, T., & Gangemi, J. D. (2005). An evaluation of *Echinacea angustifolia* in experimental rhinovirus infections. *New England Journal of Medicine, 353,* 341–348.

Turner, R. J., Wheaton, B., & Lloyd, D. A. (1995). The epidemiology of stress. *American Sociological Review, 60,* 104–125.

Turner, S. M., Beidel, D. C., & Wolff, P. L. (1996). Is behavioral inhibition related to the anxiety disorders? *Clinical Psychology Review, 16,* 57–172.

Tversky, A., & Kahneman, D. (1974). Judgment under uncertainty: Heuristics and biases. *Science, 185,* 1124–1131.

Twenge, J. M., Catanese, K. R., & Baumeister, R. F. (2002). Social exclusion causes self-defeating behavior. *Journal of Personality and Social Psychology, 83,* 606–615.

Tyas, S. L. (2001). Alcohol use and the risk of developing Alzheimer's disease. *Alcohol Research and Health, 25,* 299–306.

Tyson, G. A. (1987). *Introduction to psychology.* Johannesburg, South Africa: Westro Educational Books.

UK ECT Review Group. (2003, March 8). Efficacy and safety of electroconvulsive therapy in depressive disorders: A systematic review and meta-analysis. *Lancet, 361,* 799–808.

U.S. Census Bureau (2000). *Married-couple and unmarried-partner households: 2000.* Retrieved from http://www.census.gov/prod/2003pubs/censr-5.pdf.

U.S. Census Bureau (2005). America's Families and Living Arrangements: 2005. Retrieved from http://www.census.gov/population/www/socdemo/hh-fam/cps2005.html.

U.S. Department of Health and Human Services. (1996). *Physical activity and health: Report of the surgeon general.* Washington, DC: U.S Department of Health and Human Services, Centers for Disease Control and Prevention, National Center for Chronic Disease Prevention and Health Promotion.

U.S. Department of Health, Education, and Welfare. (1990). *Smoking and health: A report of the surgeon general* (DHEW Publication No. PHS79-50066). Washington, DC: Author.

U.S. Surgeon General. (2001). *Mental health: Culture, race, and ethnicity—A supplement to mental health: A report of the Surgeon General.* Rockville, MD: U.S. Department of Health and Human Services.

Uddin, L. Q., Rayman, J., & Zaidel, E. (2005). Split-brain reveals separate but equal self-recognition in the two cerebral hemispheres. *Consciousness & Cognition, 14,* 633–640.

Ullman, L., & Krasner, L. (1975). *A psychological approach to abnormal behavior.* Englewood Cliffs, NJ: Prentice-Hall.

Ullman, S. E., Filipas, H. H., Townsend, S. M., & Starzynski, L. L. (2005). Trauma exposure, posttraumatic stress disorder and problem drinking in sexual assault survivors. *Journal of Studies of Alcohol, 66,* 610–619.

Ulrich, R. E. (1991). Animal rights, animal wrongs and the question of balance. *Psychological Science, 2,* 197–201.

Underwood, A. (2007, June 12). It's called "sexsomnia." *Newsweek,* p. 53.

Underwood, B. J. (1957) Interference and forgetting. *Psychological Review, 64,* 49–60.

Uttal, W. R. (2001). *The new phrenology: The limits of localizing cognitive processes in the brain.* Cambridge, MA: Bradford Books/MIT Press.

Uttal, W. R. (2003). *Psychomythics: Sources of artifacts and misconceptions in scientific psychology.* Mahwah, NJ: Lawrence Erlbaum.

Vaillant, G. E. (1977). *Adaptation to life.* Boston: Little, Brown and Company.

Vaillant, G. E. (1983). *The natural history of alcoholism.* Cambridge, MA: Harvard University Press.

Vaillant, G. E., & Milofsky, E. (1980). Natural history of male psychological health: IX. Empirical evidence for Erikson's model of the life cycle. *American Journal of Psychiatry, 137,* 1348–1359.

Vaitl, D., Birbaumer, N., Gruzelier, Gamieson, G. A., Kotchoubey, B., Kubler, A., et al. (2005). Psychobiology of altered states of consciousness. *Psychological Bulletin, 131,* 98–127.

Valenstein, E. (1986). *Great and desperate cures: The rise and decline of psychosurgery and other radical treatments for mental illness.* New York: Basic Books.

Valenstein, E. S. (1973). *Brain control.* New York: John Wiley & Sons.

Valentine, T., Darling, S., & Donnelly, M. (2004). Why are average faces attractive? The effect of view and averageness on the attractiveness of female faces. *Psychonomic Bulletin & Review, 11,* 482–487.

Valiant, G. E., & Milofsky, E. S. (1982). Natural history of male alcoholism IV. Paths to recovery. *Archives of General Psychiatry, 39,* 127–133.

Vallee, B. L. (1988, June). Alcohol in the Western world: A history. *Scientific American, 278,* 80–85.

Van de Castle, R. (1994). *Our dreaming mind.* New York: Ballantine Books.

Van den Heuvel, O. A., van de Wetering, B., Veltman, D. J., & Pauls, D. L. (2000). Genetic studies of panic disorder: A review. *Journal of Clinical Psychiatry, 61,* 756–766.

van der Kolk, B., Britz, R., Burr, W., Sherry, S., & Hartmann, E. (1984). Nightmares and trauma: A comparison of nightmares after combat with life-long nightmares in veterans. *American Journal of Psychiatry, 141,* 187–190.

Van Eeden, F. (1913). A study of dreams. *Proceedings of the Society for Psychical Research, 26,* 431–461.

van Hecke, M. L. (2007). *Blind spots: Why smart people do dumb things.* Amherst, NY: Prometheus Books.

van Ijzendoorn, M. H., & De Wolff, M. S. (1997). In search of the absent father: Meta-analyses on infant-father attachment. *Child Development, 68,* 604–609.

van Ijzendoorn, M. H., & Sagi, A. (1999). Cross-cultural patterns of attachment: Universal and cultural dimensions. In J. Cassidy & P. R. Shaver (Eds.), *Handbook of attachment: Theory, research, and clinical applications* (pp. 713–734). New York: Guilford.

Van Litalie, T. B. (1990). The glucostatic theory 1953–1988: Roots and branches. *International Journal of Obesity, 14,* 1–10.

Van Lommel, P., van Wees, R., Meyers, V., & Elfferich, I. (2001). Near-death experiences in survivors of cardiac arrest: A prospective study in the Netherlands. *Lancet, 358,* 2039–2045.

van Rillaer, J. (1991). Strategies of dissimulation in the pseudosciences. *New Ideas in Psychology, 9,* 235–244. Vaughan, E. D. (1977). Misconceptions about psychology among introductory psychology students. *Teaching of Psychology, 4,* 138–141.

Van Rooy, D. L., & Viswesvaran, C. (2004). Emotional intelligence: A meta-analytic investigation of predictive validity and nomological net. *Journal of Vocational Behavior, 65,* 71–95.

Vane, J. R. (1981). The Thematic Apperception Test: A review. *Clinical Psychology Review, 1,* 319–336.

Vanger, P. (1987). An assessment of social skill deficiencies in depression. *Comprehensive Psychiatry, 28,* 508–512.

Vanman, E. J., Paul, B. Y., Ito, T. A., & Miller, N. (1997). The modern face of prejudice and structural features that moderate the effect of cooperation on affect. *Journal of Personality and Social Psychology, 73,* 941–959.

Vanman, E. J., Saltz, J. L., Nathan, L. R., & Warren, J. A. (2004). Racial discrimination by low-prejudiced Whites: Facial movements as implicit measures of attitudes related to behavior. *Psychological Science, 15,* 711–714.

Vartanian, L. R. (2000). Revisiting the imaginary audience and personal fable constructs of adolescent egocentrism: A conceptual review. *Adolescence, 35,* 639–661.

Verdon, C. M., Saba, G., & Januel, D. (2004). Transcranial magnetic stimulation in cognition and neuropsychology. *Encephale, 30,* 363–368.

Verdoux, H. (2004). Perinatal risk factors for schizophrenia: How specific are they? *Current Psychiatry Reports, 6,* 162–167.

Vermetten, E., & Bremner, J. D. (2003). Olfaction as a traumatic reminder in posttraumatic stress disorder: Case reports and review. *Journal of Clinical Psychiatry, 64,* 202–207.

Vernon, P. A. (1987). *Speed of information processing and intelligence.* Norwood, NJ: Ablex.

Vernon, P. E. (1971). *The structure of human abilities.* London: Methuen.

Vetere, A. (2001). Structural family therapy. *Child Psychology and Psychiatry Review, 6,* 133–139.

Victor, M., & Ropper, A. H. (2005). *Adams & Victor's principles of neurology* (8th ed.). New York: McGraw Hill.

Vila, G., Nollet-Clemencon, C., deBlic, J., Mouren-Simeoni, M.-C., & Scheinmann, P. (2000). Prevalence of DSM-IV anxiety and affective disorders in a pediatric population of asthmatic children and adolescents. *Journal of Affective Disorders, 58,* 223–231.

Vita, A., Dieci, G., Giobbio, A., Caputo, L., Ghrinighelli, M., & Comazzi, M., et al. (1995). Language and thought disorder in schizophrenia: Brain morphological correlates. *Schizophrenia Research, 15,* 243–251.

Vincent, P. (1971). Factors influencing patient noncompliance: A theoretical approach. *Nursing Research, 20,* 509–516.

Vitale, J. E., & Newman, J. P. (2001). Using the Psychopathy Checklist-Revised with female samples: Reliability, validity, and implications for clinical utility. *Clinical Psychology: Science and Practice, 8,* 117–132.

Vitello, P. (2006, June 12). A ringtone meant to fall on deaf ears. *New York Times.* Retrieved from http://www.nytimes.com/2006/06/12/technology /12ring.html?_r=1&emc=eta1&oref=slogi.

Vittengl, J. R., & Holt, C. S. (2000). Getting acquainted: The relationship of self-disclosure and social attraction to positive affect. *Journal of Social and Personal Relationships, 17,* 53–66.

Voevodsky, J. (1974). Evaluation of a deceleration warning light for reducing rear-end automobile collisions. *Journal of Applied Psychology, 59,* 270–273.

Vohs, K. D., Catanese, K. R., & Baumeister, R. F. (2004). Sex in "his" versus "her" relationships. In J. H. Harvey, A. Wenzel, & S. Sprecher (Eds.), *The handbook of sexuality in close relationships* (pp. 455–474). Mahwah, NJ: Lawrence Erlbaum Associates.

Volgmaier, M. M., Seidman, L. J., Niznikiewicz, M. A., Dickey, C. C., Shenton, M. E., & McCarley, R. W. (2000). Verbal and nonverbal neuropsychological test performance in subjects with schizotypal personality disorder. *American Journal of Psychiatry, 157,* 787–797.

Volkow, N. D., Wang, G. J., Fowler, J. S., & Ding, Y. (2005). Imaging the effects of methylphenidate on brain dopamine: New model on its therapeutic actions for attention-deficit/hyperactivity disorder. *Biological Psychiatry, 57,* 1410–1415.

von Frisch, K. (1967). *The dance language and orientation of bees.* London: Oxford University Press.

Voncken, M. J., Bogels, S. M., & deVries, K. (2003). Interpretation and judgmental biases in social phobias. *Behavior Research and Therapy, 41,* 1481–1488.

Voyer, D., Voyer, S., & Bryden, M. P. (1995). Magnitude of sex differences in spatial abilities: A meta-analysis and consideration of critical variables. *Psychological Bulletin, 117,* 250–270.

Vrught, A., & Kerkstra, A. (1984). Sex differences in nonverbal communication. *Semiotica, 50,* 141.

Vyse, S. A. (1997). *Believing in magic: The psychology of superstition.* New York: Oxford University Press.

Vyse, S. A. (2000). *Believing in magic: The psychology of superstition.* New York: Oxford University Press.

Wachtel, P. L. (1977). *Psychoanalysis and behavior therapy: Toward an integration.* New York: Basic Books.

Wachtel, P. L. (1997). *Psychoanalysis, behavior therapy, and the relational world.* Washington, DC: American Psychological Association.

Wadden, T. A., & Stunkard, A. J. (1993). Psychosocial consequence of obesity and dieting: Research and clinical findings. In A. J. Stunkard & T. A. Wadden (Eds.), *Obesity: Theory and therapy* (pp. 163–177). New York: Raven.

Wade, K. A., Garry, M., Read, J. D., & Lindsay D. S. (2002). A picture is worth a thousand lies: Using false photographs to create false childhood memories. *Psychonomic Bulletin & Review, 9,* 597–603.

Wager, T. D., Rilling, J. K., Smith, E. E., Sokolik, A., Casey, K. L., Davidson, R. J., et al. (2004). Placebo-induced changes in fMRI in anticipation and experience of pain. *Science, 303,* 1162–1167.

Wagner, M. W., & Monnet, M. (1979). Attitudes of college professors toward extra-sensory perception. *Zetetic Scholar, 5,* 7–16.

Wagner, R. K., & Sternberg, R. J. (1986). Tacit knowledge and intelligence in the everyday world. In R. J. Sternberg & R. K. Wagner (Eds.), *Practical intelligence: Nature and origins of competence in the everyday world* (pp. 51–83). Cambridge, England: Cambridge University Press.

Wagstaff, G. (1998). The semantics and physiology of hypnosis as an altered state: Towards a definition of hypnosis. *Contemporary Hypnosis, 15,* 149–165.

Wahl, O. (1997). *Consumer experience with stigma: Results of a national survey.* Alexandria, VA: NAMI.

Wahl, O. F. (1997). *Media madness: Public images of the mentally ill.* New Brunswick, NJ: Rutgers University Press.

Waid, W. M., & Orne, M. T. (1982). Reduced electrodermal response to conflict, failure to inhibit dominant behaviors, and delinquency proneness. *Journal of Personality and Social Psychology, 43,* 769–774.

Wakefield, A. J., Murch, S., Anthony, A., Linnell, J., Casson, D. M., Casson, M., et al. (1998). Ileal lymphoid nodular hyperplasia, non-specific colitis, and regressive developmental disorder in children. *Lancet, 351,* 637–641.

Wakefield, J. C. (1992). The concept of mental disorder: On the boundary between biological facts and social values. *American Psychologist, 47,* 373–388.

Wakefield, J. C. (2006). Is behaviorism becoming a pseudo-science? Power versus scientific rationality in the eclipse of token economies by biological psychiatry in the treatment of schizophrenia. *Behavior and Social Issues, 15,* 202–221.

Walach, H., & Kirsch, I. (2003). Herbal treatments and antidepressant medication: Similar data, divergent conclusions. In S. O. Lilienfeld, S. J. Lynn, & J. M. Lohr (Eds.), *Science and pseudoscience in clinical psychology* (pp. 306–330). New York: Guilford.

Waldman, I. D. (2005). Statistical approaches to complex phenotypes: Evaluating neuropsychological endophenotypes for attention-deficit/hyperactivity disorder. *Biological Psychiatry, 57,* 1347–1356.

Waldman, I. D., & Gizer, I. R. (2006). The genetics of attention deficit hyperactivity disorder. *Clinical Psychology Review, 26,* 396–432.

Waldman, I. D., Lilienfeld, S. O., & Lahey, B. B. (1995). Toward construct validity in the childhood disruptive behavior disorders: Classification and diagnosis in DSM-IV and beyond. In T. H. Ollendick & R. J. Prinz (Eds.), *Advances in clinical child psychology* (Vol. 17, pp. 323–363). New York: Plenum Press.

Walker, E. Kestler, L. Bollini, A., & Hochman, K. (2004). Schizophrenia: Etiology and course. *Annual Review of Psychology, 55,* 401–430.

Walker, E., & Lewine, R. J. (1990). Prediction of adult-onset schizophrenia from childhood home movies of the patients. *American Journal of Psychiatry, 147,* 1052–1056.

Walker, E. F., Baum, K., & Diforio, D. (1998). Developmental changes in the behavioral expression of vulnerability for schizophrenia. In M. Lenzenweger & B. Dworkin (Eds.), *Experimental psychopathology and pathogenesis of schizophrenia* (pp. 469–492). Washington, DC: American Psychological Association.

Walker, E. F., & DiForio, D. (1997). Schizophrenia: A neural-diathesis stress model. *Psychological Review, 104,* 1–19.

Walker, M. P., Brakefield, A., Morgan, J., Hobson, J. A., & Stickgold, R. (2002). Practice, with sleep, makes perfect. *Neuron, 35,* 205–211.

Walker-Andrews, A. S., & Dickson, L. R. (1997). Infants' understanding of affect. In S. Hala (Ed.), *The development of social cognition. Studies in developmental psychology* (pp. 161–186). Hove, England: Psychology Press/Erlbaum (UK) Taylor & Francis.

Wall, P. (2000). *Pain.* New York: Columbia University Press.

Wallace, R. K. (1986). *The Maharishi technology of the unified field: The neurophysiology of enlightenment.* Fairfield, IA: MIU Neuroscience Press.

Wallach, H., & Kirsch, I. (2003). Herbal treatments and antidepressant medication: Similar data, divergent conclusions. In S. O. Lilienfeld, S. J. Lynn, & J. M. Lohr (Eds.), *Science and pseudoscience in clinical psychology* (pp. 306–332). New York: Guilford.

Wallechinsky, D., Wallace, D., & Wallace, H. (1977). *The book of lists.* New York: Bantam Books.

Waller, N. G., Kojetin, B. A., Bouchard, T. J., Lykken, D. T., & Tellegen, A. (1990). Genetic and environmental influences on religious interests, attitudes, and values: A study of twins reared apart and together. *Psychological Science, 1,* 1–5.

Wallerstein, J. S. (1989, January 22). Children after divorce: Wounds that don't heal. *New York Times Magazine,* pp. 19, 42.

Walonick, D. S. (1994). *Do researchers influence survey results with their question wording choices?* Retrieved May 5, 2006, from http://www.statpac.com/research-papers/researcher-bias.doc.

Walsh, B. T. (1993). Binge eating in bulimia nervosa. In C. G. Fairburn & G. T. Wilson (Eds.), *Binge eating: Nature, assessment, and treatment* (pp. 37–49). New York: Guilford.

Walsh, B. T., Hadigan, C. M., Kissileff, H. R., & LaChaussee, J. L. (1992). Bulimia nervosa: A syndrome of feast and famine. In G. H. Anderson & S. H. Kennedy (Eds.), *The biology of feast and famine.* New York: Academic Press.

Walsh, D. C., Hingson, R. W., Merrigan, D. M., Levenson, S. M., Cupples, L. A., Heeren, T., et al. (1991). A randomized trial of treatment options for alcohol abusing workers. *New England Journal of Medicine, 325,* 775–782.

Walsh, F. (1999). Families in later life: Challenges and opportunities. In B. Carter & M. McGoldrick (Eds.), *The expanded family life cycle: Individual, family and social perspectives* (3rd ed., pp. 307–326). Boston: Allyn & Bacon.

Walster, E., Berscheid, E., & Walster, G. W. (1973). New directions in equity theory and research. *Journal of Personality and Social Psychology, 25,* 151–176.

Walters, G. D., & Greene, R. L. (1988). Differentiating between schizophrenia and manic inpatients by means of the MMPI. *Journal of Personality Assessment, 52,* 91–95.

Walton, D. E. (1978). An exploratory study: Personality factors and theoretical orientations of therapists. *Psychotherapy: Theory, Research, and Practice, 15,* 390–395.

Wampold, B. E. (2001). *The great psychotherapy debate: Models, methods, and findings.* Mahwah, NJ: Lawrence Erlbaum Associates.

Wampold, B. E., Minami, T., Baskin, T. W., & Tierney, S. C. (2002). A meta-(re)analysis of the effects of cognitive therapy versus "other therapies" for depression. *Journal of Affective Disorders, 68,* 159–165.

Wampold, B. E., Monding, W., Moody, M., Stich, I., Benson, K., & Ahn, H. (1997). A meta-analysis of outcome studies comparing bona fide psychotherapies: Empirically "all must have prizes." *Psychological Bulletin, 122,* 203–215.

Wark, D. M. (2006). Alert hypnosis: A review and case report. *American Journal of Clinical Hypnosis, 48,* 291–300.

Warwick, H. M. C., & Salkovskis, P. M. (1990). Hypochondriasis. *Behaviour Research and Therapy, 21,* 105–117.

Waschbusch, D. A., & Hill, G. P. (2003). Empirically supported, promising, and unsupported treatments for children with attention-deficit/hyperactivity disorder. In S. O. Lilienfeld, S. J. Lynn, & J. M. Lohr (Eds.), *Science and pseudoscience in clinical psychology* (pp. 333–362). New York: Guilford.

Wason, P. C. (1966). Reasoning. In B. M. Foss (Ed.), *New horizons in psychology* (pp. 135–151). Harmondsworth, England: Penguin.

Watanabe, S., Sakamoto, J., & Wakita, M. (1995). Pigeons' discrimination of paintings by Monet and Picasso. *Journal of the Experimental Analysis of Behavior, 63,* 65–174.

Watkins, C. E., Campbell, V. L., Neiberding, R., & Hallmark, R. (1995). Contemporary practice of psychological assessment by clinical psychologists. *Professional Psychology: Science and Practice, 26,* 54–60.

Watson, D., & Clark, L. A. (1984). Negative affectivity: The disposition to experience negative emotional states. *Psychological Bulletin, 96,* 465–490.

Watson, J. B. (1913). Psychology as the behaviorist views it. *Psychological Review, 20,* 158–177.

Watson, J. B., & Rayner, R. (1920). Conditioned emotional reactions. *Journal of Experimental Psychology, 3,* 1–14.

Watson, J. C., Gordon, L. B., Stermac, L., Steckley, P., & Kalogerakos, F. (2003). Comparing the effectiveness of both process-experiential with cognitive-behavioral psychotherapy in the treatment of depression. *Journal of Consulting and Clinical Psychology, 71,* 773–781.

Watson, R. I. (1973). Investigation into deindividuation using a cross-cultural survey technique. *Journal of Personality and Social Psychology, 25,* 342–345.

Watzlawick, P., Beavin, J., & Jackson, D. D. (1967). *Pragmatics of human communication: A study of interactional patterns, pathologies, and paradoxes.* New York: W. W. Norton.

Watzlawick, P., Weakland, J. H., & Fisch, R. (1974). *Change: Principles of problem formation and problem resolution.* New York: Norton.

Waugh, N. C., & Norman, D. A. (1965). Primary memory. *Psychological Review, 72,* 89–104.

Waxman, S. R., & Namy, L. L. (1997). Challenging the notion of a thematic preference in young children. *Developmental Psychology, 33,* 555–567.

Wayment, H. A., & Peplau, L. A. (1995). Social support and well-being among lesbian and heterosexual women: A structural modeling approach. *Personality and Social Psychology Bulletin, 21,* 1189–1199.

Wearing, D. (2005). *Forever today.* New York: Doubleday.

Wechsler D. (1997). Wechsler Memory Scale III. San Antonio, TX: The Psychological Corporation.

Wechsler, D. (1939). *The measurement of adult intelligence.* Baltimore: Williams & Wilkins.

Weed, N. C., Ben-Porath, Y. S., & Butcher, J. N. (1990). Failure of Weiner and Harmon MMPI subtle scales as personality descriptors and as validity indicators. *Psychological Assessment, 2,* 281–285.

Wegner, D. (2005). The illusion of conscious will. *Behavioral and Brain Sciences, 27,* 649–692.

Wegner, D. M. (1989). *White bears and other unwanted thoughts: Suppression, obsession, and the psychology of mental control.* London: Guilford Press.

Wegner, D. M. (1997). When the antidote is the poison: Ironic mental control processes. *Psychological Science, 8,* 148–150.

Wegner, D. M. (2002). *The illusion of conscious will.* Cambridge, MA: MIT Press.

Wegner, D. M. (2003). The mind's self-portrait. *Annals of the New York Academy of Sciences, 1001,* 1–14.

Wegner, D. M. (2004). Precis of the illusion of conscious will. *Behavioral and Brain Sciences, 27,* 649–692.

Wegner, D. M., Fuller, V. A., & Sparrow, B. (2003). Clever Hands: Uncontrolled intelligence in facilitated communication. *Journal of Personality and Social Psychology, 85,* 5–19.

Wei, M., Kampert, J. B., Barlow, C. E., Nichaman, M. Z., Gibbons, L. W., Paffenbarger, R. S., et al. (1999). Relationship between low cardiorespiratory fitness and mortality in normal weight, overweight, and obese men. *Journal of the American Medical Association, 282,* 1547–1553.

Weil, A. (1972). *The natural mind.* New York: Houghton Mifflin.

Weil, A. (2000). *Spontaneous healing: How to discover and embrace your body's natural ability to maintain and heal itself.* New York: Ballantine Books.

Weinberg, R. A., Scarr, S., & Waldman, I. D. (1992). The Minnesota Transracial Adoption Study: A follow-up of IQ test performance at adolescence. *Intelligence, 16,* 117–135.

Weinberger, J., & Hardaway, R. (1990). Separating science from myth in subliminal psychodynamic activation. *Clinical Psychology Review, 10,* 727-756.

Weinberger, D. R. (1987). Implications of normal brain development for the pathogenesis of schizophrenia. *Archives of General Psychiatry, 44,* 660–669.

Weinberger, D. R., Elvevag, B., & Giedd, J. N., (2005). *The adolescent brain: A work in progress, The National Campaign to Prevent Teen Pregnancy*. Retrieved from http://www.teenpregnancy.org/resources/reading/pdf/BRAIN.pdf.

Weinberger, N. M. (2004). Music and the brain. *Scientific American, 291*(5), 88–95.

Weiner, I. B. (1997). Current status of the Rorschach Inkblot Method. *Journal of Personality Assessment, 68*, 5–19.

Weinert, F. (1989). The impact of schooling on cognitive development: One hypothetical assumption, some empirical results, and many theoretical implications. *EARLI News, 8*, 3–7.

Weisberg, R. W. (1994). Genius and madness? A quasi-experimental test of the hypothesis that manic-depression increases creativity. *Psychological Science, 5*, 361–367.

Weisberg, D. S., Keil, F. C., Goodstein, J., Rawson, E., & Gray, J. R. (in press). The seductive allure of neuroscience explanations. *Journal of Cognitive Neuroscience*.

Weiskrantz, L. (1986). *Blindsight: A case study and its implications*. Oxford, England: Oxford University Press.

Weisner, W., & Cronshaw, S. (1988). A meta-analytic investigation of interview format and degree of structure on the validity of the employment interview. *Journal of Occupational Psychology, 61*, 275–290.

Weiss, B. L. (1988). *Many lives, many masters*. New York: Simon & Schuster.

Weiss, L. H., & Schwarz, J. C. (1996). The relationship between parenting types and older adolescents' personality, academic achievement, adjustment, and substance use. *Child Development, 67*, 2101–2114.

Weissman, M. M., Klerman, G. L., Paykel, E. S., Prusoff, B. A., & Hanson, B. (1974). Treatment effects on the social adjustment of depressed outpatients. *Archives of General Psychiatry, 30*, 771–778.

Weissman, M. M., Markowitz, J. C., & Klerman, G. L. (2000). *Comprehensive guide to interpersonal psychotherapy*. New York: Basic Books.

Weisz, J. R., Donenberg, G. R., Han, S. S., & Weiss, B. (1995). Bridging the gap between laboratory and clinic in child and adolescent psychotherapy. *Journal of Consulting and Clinical Psychotherapy, 63*, 542–549.

Weisz, J. R., Weiss, B., Han, S. S., Granger, D. A., & Morton, T. (1995). Effects of psychotherapy with children and adolescents revisited: A meta-analysis of treatment outcome studies. *Psychological Bulletin, 117*, 450–468.

Weisz, C., & Wood, L. F. (2005). Social identity support and friendship outcomes. *Journal of Social and Personal Relationships, 22*, 416–432.

Weitzenhoffer, A. M., & Hilgard, E. (1962). *Stanford Hypnotic Susceptibility Scale: Form C*. Palo Alto, CA: Consulting Psychologists Press.

Welford, A. (1977). Mental workload as a function of demand, capacity, strategy and skill: Synthesis report. *Travail Humain, 40*, 283–304.

Wellman, H. M., Cross, D., & Watson, J. (2001). Meta-analysis of theory-of-mind development: The truth about false belief. *Child Development, 72*, 655–684.

Wellman, H. M., & Gelman, S. A. (1998). Knowledge acquisition in foundational domains. In W. Damon (Ed.), *Handbook of child psychology: Vol. 2: Cognition, perception, and language* (pp. 523–573). Hoboken, NJ: Wiley.

Wells, G. L., & Bradford, A. L. (1998). "Good, you identified the suspect": Feedback to eyewitnesses distorts their reports of the witnessing experience. *Journal of Applied Psychology, 83*, 360–376.

Wells, G. L., & Olson, E. (2003). Eyewitness identification. *Annual Review of Psychology, 54*, 277–295.

Wells, G. L., Memon, A., & Penrod, S. D. (2006). Eyewitness evidence: Improving its probative value. *Psychological Science in the Public Interest, 7*(2), 45–75.

Wells, G. L., & Loftus, E. F. (Eds.). (1984). *Eyewitness testimony: Psychological perspectives*. New York: Cambridge University Press.

Wenk, G. L. (2006). Neuropathologic changes in Alzheimer's disease: Potential targets for treatment. *Journal of Clinical Psychiatry, 67*(Suppl. 3), 3–7.

Werch, C. E., & Owen, D. (2002). Iatrogenic effects of alcohol and drug prevention programs. *Journal of Studies on Alcohol, 63*, 581–590.

Werker, J. F., Gilbert, J. H. V., Humphrey, K., & Tees, R. C. (1981). Developmental aspects of cross-language speech perception. *Child Development, 52*, 349–355.

Werker, J. F., & Tees, R. C. (1984). Cross-language speech perception: Evidence for perceptual reorganization during the first year of life. *Infant Behavior and Development, 7*, 49–63.

Werth, J. L. (2001). U.S. involuntary mental health commitment statutes: Requirements for persons perceived to be a potential harm to self. *Suicide and Life-Threatening Behavior, 31*, 348–357.

Westen, D. (1991). Clinical assessment of object relations using the TAT. *Journal of Personality Assessment, 56*, 56–74.

Westen, D. (1998). The scientific legacy of Sigmund Freud: Toward a psychodynamically informed psychological science. *Psychological Bulletin, 124*, 333–371.

Westen, D., Feit, A., & Zittel, C. (1999). Methodological issues in research using projective methods. In P. C. Kendall & J. N. Butcher (Eds.), *Handbook of research methods in clinical psychology* (2nd ed., pp. 224–240). New York: Wiley.

Westen, D., Kilts, C., Blagov, P., Harenski, K., & Hamann, S. (2006). The neural basis of motivated reasoning: An fMRI study of emotional constraints on political judgment during the U.S. presidential election of 2004. *Journal of Cognitive Neuroscience, 18*, 1947–1958.

Westen, D., Novotny, C. M., & Thompson-Brenner, H. (2004). The empirical status of empirically supported psychotherapies: Assumptions, findings, and reporting in controlled clinical trials. *Psychological Bulletin, 130*, 631–663.

Westerman, M. A., Foote, J. P., & Winton, A. (1995). Change in coordination across phases of psychotherapy and outcome: Two mechanisms for the role played by patients' contribution to the alliance. *Journal of Consulting and Clinical Psychology, 63*, 672–675.

Weston, K. (1991). *Families we choose: Lesbians, gays, kinship*. New York: Columbia University Press.

Westphal, M., & Bonanno, G. A. (2004). Emotional self-regulation. In M. Beauregard (Ed.), *Consciousness, emotional self-regulation, and the brain* (pp. 1–34). Philadelphia: Benjamins.

Wetzler, S. E., & Sweeney, J. A. (1986). Childhood amnesia: An empirical demonstration. In D. C. Rubin (Ed.), *Autobiographical memory* (pp. 191–201). New York: Cambridge University Press.

Whaley, A. L., & Davis, K. E. (2007). Cultural competence and evidence-based practice in mental health services: A complementary perspective. *American Psychologist, 62*, 563–574.

Whinnery, J. E. (1997). Psychophysiologic correlates of unconsciousness and near-death experiences. *Journal of Near-Death Studies, 15*, 231–258.

White, A. (2006). *A global projection of subjective well-being: The first published map of world happiness*. Retrieved October 30, 2007, from http://news.bbc.co.uk/2/shared/bsp/hi/pdfs/28_07_06_happiness_map.pdf.

White, A. M., & Swartzwelder, H. (2005). Age-related effects of alcohol on memory and memory-related brain function in adolescents and adults. In M. Galanter (Ed.), *Recent developments in alcoholism: Vol. 17. Alcohol problems in adolescents and young adults* (pp. 161–176). New York: Kluwer Academic/Plenum Publishers.

Whiting, B. B., & Edwards, C. P. (1988). *Children of different worlds: The formation of social behavior*. Cambridge, MA: Harvard University Press.

Whitley, B. E., & Lee, S. E. (2000). The relationship of authoritarianism and related constructs to attitudes towards homosexuality. *Journal of Applied Social Psychology, 30*, 144–170.

Whorf, B. L. (1956). *Language, thought, and reality: Selected writings of Benjamin Lee Whorf* (J. B. Carroll, Ed.). Cambridge, MA: MIT Press.

Wickelgren, W. A. (1965). Acoustic similarity and retroactive interference in shortterm memory. *Journal of Verbal Learning and Verbal Behavior, 4*, 53–61.

Wicker, A.W. (1969). Attitudes versus actions: The relationship of verbal and overt behavioral responses to attitude objects. *Journal of Social Issues, 25*, 41–78.

Wicker, B., Keysers, C., Plailly, J., Royet, J. P., Gallese, V., & Rizzolatti, G. (2003). Both of us disgusted in my insula: The common neural basis of seeing and feeling disgust. *Neuron, 40*, 655–664.

Widerman, M. W., & Allgeier, E. R. (1996). Expectations and attributions regarding extramarital sex among young married individuals. *Journal of Psychology and Human Sexuality, 8*, 21–35.

Widiger, T. A., & Clark, L. A. (2000). Toward DSM-V and the classification of psychopathology. *Psychological Bulletin, 126*, 946–963.

Widmer, E. D., Treas, J., & Newcomb, R. (1998). Attitudes toward nonmarital sex in 24 countries. *Journal of Sex Research, 35*, 349–357.

Widom, C. S. (1977). A methodology for studying noninstitutionalized psychopaths. *Journal of Consulting and Clinical Psychology, 45*, 674–683.

Widyanto, L., & Griffiths, M. (2005). "Internet addiction": A critical review. *International Journal of Mental Health and Addiction, 4*, 31–51.

Wigal, T., Greenhill, L., Chuang, S., McGough, J., Vitiello, B., Skrobala, A., et al. (2006). Safety and tolerability of methylphenidate in preschool children with ADHD. *Journal of the American Academy of Adolescent Psychiatry, 45*, 1294.

Wilcox, A. J., Baird, D. D., Dunson, D. B., McConnaughey, D. R., Kesner, J. S., & Weinberg, C. R. (2004). On the frequency of intercourse around ovulation: Evidence for biological influences. *Human Reproduction, 19*, 539–543.

Wilkins, W. (1971). Desensitization: Social and cognitive factors underlying the effectiveness of Wolpe's procedure. *Psychological Bulletin, 76*, 311–317.

Willems, P. J. (2000). Genetic causes of hearing loss. *New England Journal of Medicine, 342*, 1101–1109.

Willerman L. (1979). *The psychology of individual and group differences*. San Francisco: Freedman.

Willerman, R., Schultz, J. N., Rutledge, J. N., & Bigler, D. D. (1991). In vivo brain size and intelligence, *Intelligence, 15*, 223–228.

Williams, D., & Skoric, M. (2005). Internet fantasy violence: A test of aggression in an online game. *Communication Monographs, 72*, 217–233.

Williams, R. L. (1972). *The BITCH test (Black Intelligence Test of Cultural Homogeneity)*. St. Louis, MO: Washington University.

Williams, W. M., & Ceci, S. J. (1997, September/October). "How'm I doing?" *Change, 29*(5), 13–23.

Williams, W. M., & Ceci, S. J. (1998). *Escaping the advice trap*. Kansas City, MO: Andrews McMeel.

Williamson, D. A., Womble, L. G., Smeets, M. A. M., Netemeyer, R. G., Thaw, J. M., Kutlesic, V., et al. (2002). Latent structure of eating disorder symptoms: A factor analytic and taxometric investigation. *American Journal of Psychiatry, 159*, 412–418.

Willingham, D. T. (2002). *Allocating student study time: "Massed" versus "distributed" practice*. Retrieved May 22, 2006, from www.aft.org/american_educator/summer2002/askcognitivescientist.html.

Willingham, D. T. (2004). Reframing the mind: Howard Gardner became a hero among educators simply by redefining talents as "intelligences." *Education Next, 4*, 18–24.

Willingham, D. T. (2007, Summer). Why is critical thinking so hard to teach? *American Educator, 31*(2), 8–19.

Wills, T. A., Fegan, M. F. (2001). Social networks and social support. In A. S. Baum, T. A. Revenson, J. E. Singer (Ed.), *Handbook of Health Psychology* (pp. 209-234). Mahwah, NJ: Lawrence Erlbaum Associates.

Wilson, E. O. (1998). *Consilience: The unity of knowledge*. New York: Vintage Books.

Wilson, G. T., & Lawson, D. M. (1978, June). Expectancies, alcohol, and sexual arousal in women. *Journal of Abnormal Psychology, 87*, 358–367.

Wilson, G. T., & O'Leary, K. D. (1980). *Principles of behavior therapy*. Englewood Cliffs, NJ: Prentice-Hall.

Wilson, J. Q. (1995). *The moral sense*. New York: Free Press.

Wilson, J. Q., & Herrnstein, R. J. (1985). *Crime and human nature: The definitive study of the causes of crime*. New York: Simon & Schuster.

Wilson, N. (2003). Commercializing mental health issues: Entertainment, advertising, and psychological advice. In S. O. Lilienfeld, S. J. Lynn, & J. M. Lohr (Eds.), *Science and pseudoscience in clinical psychology* (pp. 425–459). New York: Guilford.

Wilson, N. L. (2003). The epidemic of advice-giving: Radio and talk show psychologists. In S. O. Lilienfeld, J. M. Lohr, & S. J. Lynn (Eds.), *Science and pseudoscience in contemporary clinical psychology* (pp. 425–460). New York: Guilford Press.

Wilson, S. C., & Barber, T. X. (1981). Vivid fantasy and hallucinatory abilities in the life histories of excellent hypnotic subjects ("somnambules"): Preliminary report with female subjects. In E. Kunger (Ed.), *Imagery: Concepts, results, and applications* (pp. 133–149). New York: Plenum Press.

Wilson, S. C., & Barber, T. X. (1983). The fantasy-prone personality: Implications for understanding imagery, hypnosis, and parapsychological phenomena. In A. A. Sheikh (Ed.), *Imagery: Current theory, research, and application* (pp. 340–387). New York: Wiley.

Wilson, S., Scherr, P.A., Schneider, J.A., Tang, Y. & Bennett, D.A. (2007). Relation of cognitive activity to risk of developing Alzheimer disease *Neurology, 69*, 1911 - 1920.

Wilson, T. D. (2002). *Strangers to ourselves: Discovering the adaptive unconscious*. Cambridge, MA: Harvard University Press.

Wimmer, H., & Perner, J. (1983). Beliefs about beliefs: Representation and constraining function of wrong beliefs in young children's understanding of deception. *Cognition, 13*, 103–128.

Windle, M., & Davies, P. T. (1999). Depression and heavy alcohol use among adolescents: Concurrent and prospective relations. *Developmental Psychopathology, 11*, 823–844.

Winemiller, M. H., Billow, R. G., Laskowski, E. R., & Harmsen, W. S. (2003). Effect of magnetic vs. sham-magnetic insoles on plantar heel pain. *Journal of the American Medical Association, 290*, 1474–1478.

Winer, G. A., Cottrell, J. E., Gregg, V., Fournier, J. S., & Bica, L. A. (2002). Fundamentally misunderstanding visual perception. Adults' belief in visual emissions. *American Psychologist, 57*, 417–424.

Wing, L., & Potter, D. (2002). The epidemiology of autistic spectrum disorders: Is the prevalence rising? *Mental Retardation and Developmental Disabilities Research Review*s, 8, 151–161.

Wing, R. R., & Hill, J. O. (2001). Successful weight loss maintenance. *Annual Review of Nutrition, 21*, 323–341.

Wing, R. R., & Jeffrey, R. W. (1999). Benefit of recruiting participants with friends and increasing social support for weight loss and maintenance. *Journal of Consulting and Clinical Psychology, 67*, 132–138.

Wing, R. R., & Polley, B. A. (2001). Obesity. In A. Baum, T. A. Revenson, & J. E. Singer (Eds.), *Handbook of health psychology* (pp. 263–279). Mahwah, NJ: Lawrence Erlbaum.

Winner, E. (1999). Uncommon talents: Gifted children, prodigies, and savants. *Scientific American Presents: Exploring Intelligence, 9*, 32–37.

Winnicott, D. (1958). *Collected papers—Through pediatrics to psychoanalysis*. New York: Basic Books.

Winnicott, D. W. (1953). Transitional objects and transitional phenomena. *International Journal of Psychoanalysis, 34*, 89–97.

Winnicott, D. W. (1958). *Collected papers. Through pediatrics to psychoanalysis*. London: Tavistock Publications.

Winograd, E., & Killinger, W. A., Jr. (1983). Relating age at encoding in early childhood to adult recall: Development of flashbulb memories. *Journal of Experimental Psychology: General, 112*, 413–422.

Winograd, E., Peluso, J. P., & Glover, T. A. (1998). Individual differences in susceptibility to memory illusions. *Applied Cognitive Psychology, 12*, S5–S27.

Winter, A. (2005). The making of "truth serum." *Bulletin of the History of Medicine, 79*, 500–533.

Winton, W. M. (1987). Do introductory textbooks present the Yerkes-Dodson law correctly? *American Psychologist, 42*, 202–203.

Wise, R. A. (1996). Neurobiology of addiction. *Current Opinions in Neurobiology, 6*, 243–251.

Wiseman, C. V., Gray, J. J., Moismann, J. E., & Ahrens, A. H. (1990). Cultural expectations in thinness in women: An update. *International Journal of Eating Disorders, 11*, 85–89.

Wissler, C. (1901). *The correlation of mental and physical tests*. New York: Columbia University.

Witelson, S. F., Kigar, D. L., & Harvey, T. (1999). The exceptional brain of Albert Einstein. *Lancet, 353*, 2149–2153.

Witt, M., & Wozniak, W. (2006). Structure and function of the vomeronasal organ. *Advances in Otorhinolaryngology, 63*, 70–83.

Wittchen, H. U. (2002). Generalized anxiety disorder: Prevalence, burden, and cost to society. *Depression and Anxiety, 16*, 162–171.

Wittmann, A. D., Frahm, J., & Hänicke, W. (1999). Magnetresonanz-tomografie des gehirns von Carl Friedrich Gauss. *Mitt Gauss-Ges, 36*, 9–19.

Witty, P. A., & Jenkins, M. D. (1934). The educational achievements of a group of gifted Negro children. *Journal of Educational Psychology, 25*, 585–597.

Woehrer, C. E. (1982). The influence of ethnic families on intergenerational relationships and later life transitions. In F. M. Berardo (Ed.), *The Annals of the American Academy of Political and Social Science* (pp. 65–78). Beverly Hills, CA: Sage.

Wojciszke, B. (2002). From the first sight to the last breath: A six-stage model of love. *Polish Psychological Bulletin, 33*, 15–25.

Wolfe, V. A., & Pruitt, S. D. (2003). Insomnia and sleep disorders. In L. M. Cohen, D. E. McChargue, & F. L. Collins (Eds.), *The health psychology handbook* (pp. 425–440). Thousand Oaks, CA: Sage.

Wolford, G., Miller, M. B., & Gazzaniga, M. (2001). The left hemisphere's role in hypothesis formation. *Journal of Neuroscience, 20*(RC 64), 1–4.

Wolfsdorf, B. A., Freeman, J., D'Eramo, K., & Spirito, A. (2003). Mood states: Depression, anger, and anxiety. In A. Spirito & J. Overholser (Eds.), *Evaluating and treating adolescent suicide attempters: From research to practice* (pp. 53–88). New York: Academic Press.

Wollen, K. A., Weber, A., & Lowry, D. H. (1972). Bizarreness versus interaction of mental images as determinants of learning. *Cognitive Psychology, 3*, 518–523.

Woloshin, S., Schwartz, L. M., & Welch, H. G. (2002). Risk charts: Putting cancer in context. *Journal of the National Cancer Institute, 94*, 799–804.

Wolpe, J. (1958). *Psychotherapy by reciprocal inhibition*. Palo Alto, CA: Stanford University Press.

Wolpert, L. (1993). *The unnatural nature of science*. Cambridge, MA: Harvard University Press.

Wood J. M., & Bootzin R. R. (1990). The prevalence of nightmares and their independence from anxiety. *Journal of Abnormal Psychology, 99*, 64–68.

Wood, J. M., Garb, H. N., & Nezworski, M. T. (2006, August). *Psychometrics: Better measurement makes better clinicians*. Paper presented at the annual conference of the American Psychological Association. New Orleans, Louisiana.

Wood, J. M., & Lilienfeld, S. O. (1999). The Rorschach Inkblot Test: A case of overstatement? *Assessment, 6*, 341–351.

Wood, J. M., Lilienfeld, S. O., Garb, H. N., & Nezworski, M. T. (2000). The Rorschach test in clinical diagnosis: A critical review, with a backward look at Garfield (1947). *Journal of Clinical Psychology, 56*, 395–430.

Wood, J. M., Nezworski, M. T., & Stejskal, W. J. (1996). The comprehensive system for the Rorschach: A critical examination. *Psychological Science, 7*, 3–10.

Wood, J. M., Nezworski, M. T., Lilienfeld, S. O., & Garb, H. N. (2003). *What's wrong with the Rorschach? Science confronts the controversial inkblot test*. San Francisco: Jossey-Bass.

Wood, W. (2000). Attitude change: Persuasion and social influence. *Annual Review of Psychology, 51*, 539–570.

Wood, W., Wong, F. Y., & Chachere, J. G. (1991). Effects of media violence on viewers' aggression in unconstrained social interaction. *Psychological Bulletin, 109*, 371–383.

Woods, S. C., Seeley, R. J., Porte, D., & Schwartz, N. W. (1998). Signals that regulate food intake and energy homeostasis. *Science, 280*, 1378–1383.

Woody, E., & Farvolden, P. (1998). Dissociation in hypnosis and frontal executive function. *American Journal of Clinical Hypnosis, 40*, 206–216.

Woody, E. Z., & Bowers, K. S. (1994). A frontal assault on dissociated control. In S. J. Lynn & J. W. Rhue (Eds.), *Dissociation: Clinical and theoretical perspectives* (pp. 52–79). New York: Guilford.

Woolf, N. J. (1991). Cholinergic systems in mammalian brain and spinal cord. *Progress in Neurobiology, 37*, 475–524.

Woolf, N. J. (1998). A structural basis for memory storage in mammals. *Progress in Neurobiology, 55*, 59–77.

Woolf, N. J. (2006). Microtubules in the cerebral cortex: Role in memory and consciousness. In J. A. Tuszynski (Ed.), *The emerging physics of consciousness* (pp. 49–94). Berlin, Germany: Springer-Verlag.

Word, C. O., Zanna, M., & Cooper, J. (1974). The nonverbal mediation of self-fulfilling prophecies in interracial interaction. *Journal of Experimental Social Psychology, 10*, 109–120.

World Health Organization (WHO). (2004). *Global status report on alcohol 2004.* Geneva, Switzerland: WHO, Department of Mental Health and Substance Abuse.

Wulff, D. M. (2000). Mystical experiences. In E. Cardeña, S. J. Lynn, & S. Krippner (Eds.), *Varieties of anomalous experience: Examining the scientific evidence.* (pp. 397–440). Washington, DC: American Psychological Association.

Wynn, K. (1992). Addition and subtraction by human infants. *Nature, 358*, 749–750.

Wysocki, C. J., & Preti, G. (2004). Facts, fallacies, fears, and frustrations with human pheromones. *Anatomical Record. A: Discoveries in Molecular, Cellular, & Evolutionary Biology, 281*, 1201–1211.

Yalom, I. (1980). *Existential psychotherapy.* New York: Basic Books.

Yalom, I. (1985). *The theory and practice of group psychotherapy.* New York: Basic Books.

Yamaguchi, S., & Ninomiya, K. (2000). Umami and food palatability. *Journal of Nutrition, 130*(4S Suppl.), 921S–926S.

Yamey, G., & Shaw, P. (2002). Is extreme racism a mental illness? No. *Western Journal of Medicine, 176*, 5.

Yang, S., & Sternberg, R. J. (1997). Taiwanese Chinese people's conceptions of intelligence. *Intelligence, 25*, 21–36.

Yang, Y. C., Nweby, T. J., & Bill, R. L. (2005). Using Socratic questions to promote critical thinking skills through asynchronous discussion forums in distance learning environments. *The American Journal of Distance Education, 19*, 163–181.

Yapko, M. D. (1994). *Suggestions of abuse: True and false memories of childhood sexual trauma.* New York: Simon and Schuster.

Yartz, A. R., & Hawk, L. W., Jr. (2001). Psychophysiological assessment of anxiety: Tales from the heart. In M. M. Antony, S. M. Orsillo, & L. Roemer (Eds.), *Practitioner's guide to empirically-based measures of anxiety* (pp. 25–30). New York: Kluwer Academic/Plenum.

Yehuda, R., Resnick, H., Kahana, B., & Giller, E. L. (1993). Long-lasting hormonal alterations to extreme stress in humans: Normative or maladaptive? *Psychosomatic Medicine, 55*, 287–297.

Yerkes, R. M., & Dodson, J. D. (1908). The relation of strength of stimulus to rapidity of habit-formation. *Journal of Comparative Neurology and Psychology, 18*, 459–482.

Young, J., & Cooper, L. M. (1972). Hypnotic recall amnesia as a function of manipulated expectancy. *Proceedings of the 80th Annual Convention of the American Psychological Association, 7*, 857–858.

Young, L., & Nestle, M. (2002). The contribution of expanding portion sizes to the US obesity epidemic. *American Journal of Public Health, 92*, 246–249.

Young, M., Denny, G., Young, T., & Luquis, R. (2000). Sexual satisfaction among married women. *American Journal of Health Studies, 16*, 73–84.

Young, R. M., Oei, T. P. S., & Knight, R. G. (1990). The tension reduction hypothesis revisited: An alcohol expectancy perspective. *British Journal of Addiction, 85*, 31–40.

Young, S. M., & Pinsky, D. (2006). Narcissism and celebrity. *Journal of Research in Personality, 40*, 463–471.

Young, T. (1802). On the theory of light and colours. *Philosophical Transactions of the Royal Society of London, 92*, 12–48.

Young, W. C., Goy, R. W., & Phoenix C. H. (1964). Hormones and sexual behavior. *Science, 143*, 212–218.

Youngren, M. A., & Lewinsohn, P. M. (1980). The functional relationship between depressed and problematic interpersonal behavior. *Journal of Abnormal Psychology, 89*, 333–341.

Yusuf, S., Hawken, S., Ounpuu, S., Dans, T., Avezum, A., Lanas, F., et al. (2004). Effect of potentially modifiable risk factors associated with myocardial infarction in 52 countries (the INTERHEART study): Case-control study. *Lancet, 364*, 937–952.

Zabrucky, K., & Ratner, H. H. (1986). Children's comprehension monitoring and recall of inconsistent stories. *Child Development, 57*, 1401–1418.

Zadra, A. (1996). Recurrent dreams: Their relation to life events. In D. Barrett (Ed.), *Trauma and dreams* (pp. 231–247). Cambridge, MA: Harvard University Press.

Zaidel, D. W. (1994). A view of the world from a split brain perspective. In E. M. R. Critchley (Ed.), *The neurological boundaries of reality* (pp. 161–174). London: Farrand Press.

Zajonc, R. (1975). Birth order and intelligence: Dumber by the dozen. *Psychology Today, 8*(8), 37–43.

Zajonc, R. B. (1965). Social facilitation. *Science, 149*, 169–274.

Zajonc, R. B. (1968). Attitudinal effects of mere exposure. *Journal of Personality and Social Psychology Monographs, 9*, 1–27.

Zajonc, R. B. (1984). On the primacy of affect. *American Psychologist, 39*, 117–123.

Zajonc, R. B. (2001). Mere exposure: A gateway to the subliminal. *Current Directions in Psychological Science, 10*, 225–228.

Zajonc, R. B., Adelmann, P. K., Murphy, S. T., & Niedenthal, P. M. (1987). Convergence in the physical appearance of spouses. *Motivation and Emotion, 11*, 335–346.

Zajonc, R. B., Heingartner, A., & Herman, E. M. (1969). Social enhancement and impairment of performance in the cockroach. *Journal of Personality and Social Psychology, 13*, 83–92.

Zajonc, R. B., Murphy, S. T., & Inglehart, M. (1989). Feeling and facial efference: Implications for the vascular theory of emotion. *Psychological Review, 96*, 395–416.

Zakay, D., & Lobel, T. E. (1983). Perceptual deprivation, extraversion-introversion and the autokinetic phenomenon. *Personality and Individual Differences, 4*, 355–358.

Zautra, A. J. (2003). *Emotions, stress, and health.* New York: Oxford University Press

Zborowski, M. J., & Garske, J. P. (1993). Interpersonal deviance and consequent social impact in hypothetically schizophrenia-prone men. *Journal of Abnormal Psychology, 102*, 482–489.

Zeinah, M. M., Engel, S. A., Thompson, P. M., & Bookheimer, S. Y. (2003). Dynamics of the hippocampus during encoding and retrieval of face-name pairs. *Science, 299*, 577–580.

Zernike, K. (2000). Girls a distant 2nd in geography gap among U.S. pupils. *New York Times.* Retrieved September 12, 2006, from http://query.nytimes.com/gst/fullpage.html?res=9C02E4D6143CF932A05756C0A9669C8B63&n=Top/Reference/Times%20Topics/People/Z/Zernike,%20Kate.

Zhang, A. Y., & Snowden, L. R. (1999). Ethnic characteristics of mental disorders in five U.S. communities. *Cultural Diversity and Ethnic Minority Psychology, 5*, 134–136.

Zillman, D. (1988). Cognition-excitation interdependencies in aggressive behavior. *Aggressive Behavior, 14*, 51–64.

Zillmann, D., Katcher, A. H., & Milavsky, B. (1972). Excitation transfer from physical exercise to subsequent aggressive behavior. *Journal of Experimental Social Psychology, 8*, 247–259.

Zimbardo, P. G. (1997, May). What messages are behind today's cults? *American Psychological Association Monitor, 28*(5), 14.

Zimbardo, P. G. (2004). Does psychology make a significant difference in our lives? *American Psychologist, 59*, 339–351.

Zimbardo, P. G. (2004, May 9). Power turns good soldiers into "bad apples." *Boston Globe.* Retrieved May 15, 2005, from http://www.boston.com/news/globe/editorial_opinion/oped/articles/2004/05/09/power_turns_good_soldiers_into_bad_apples/.

Zimbardo, P. G. (2007). *The Lucifer effect: How good people turn evil.* New York: Random House.

Zimbardo, P. G., Weisenberg, M., Firestone, I., & Levy, M. (1965). Communicator effectiveness in producing public conformity and private attitude change. *Journal of Personality, 33*, 233–255.

Zimmer, H., Mecklinger, A., & Lindenberger, U. (2006). *Binding in human memory.* Oxford, England: Oxford University Press.

Zimmerman, M. (1994). Diagnosing personality disorders: A review of issues and research methods. *Archives of General Psychiatry, 51*, 225–245.

Zinbarg, R. (1993). Information processing and classical conditioning: Implications for exposure therapy and the integration of cognitive therapy and behavior therapy. *Journal of Behavior Therapy and Experimental Psychiatry, 24*, 129–139.

Zinbarg, R. E., & Barlow, D. H. (1996). The structure of anxiety and the anxiety disorders: A hierarchical model. *Journal of Abnormal Psychology, 105*, 81–193.

Zink, C. F., Pagnoni, G., Martin-Skurski, M. E., Chappelow, J. C., & Berns, G. S. (2004). Human striatal responses to monetary reward depend on saliency. *Neuron, 42*, 509–517.

Zion, I. B., Tessler, R., Cohen, L., Lerer, E., Raz, Y., Bachner-Melman, R., et al. (2006). Polymorphisms in the dopamine D4 receptor gene (DRD4) contribute to individual differences in human sexual behavior: Desire, arousal and sexual function. *Journal for Molecular Psychiatry, 11*, 782–786.

Zivotofsky, A. Z., Edelman, S., Green, T., Fostick, L., & Strous, R. D. (2007). Hemisphere asymmetry in schizophrenia as revealed through line bisection, line trisection, and letter cancellation. *Brain Research, 1142*, 70–79.

Zubin, J., & Spring, B. (1977). Vulnerability: A new view of schizophrenia. *Journal of Abnormal Psychology, 86*, 103–126.

Zuckerman, M. (1979). *Sensation seeking: Beyond the optimal level of arousal.* Hillsdale, NJ: Erlbaum.

Zuckerman, M. (1989). Personality in the third dimension: A psychobiological approach. *Personality and Individual Differences, 10*, 391–418.

Zuckerman, M. (1994). *Behavioral expressions and biosocial bases of sensation seeking.* New York: Cambridge University Press.

Zuckerman, M., DePaulo, B. M., & Rosenthal, R. (1981). Verbal and nonverbal communication of deception. In L. Berkowitz (Ed.), *Advances in experimental and social psychology* (Vol. 14, pp. 1–59). New York: Academic Press.

Zuckerman, M., & Hopkins, J. (1966). Hallucinations or dreams: A study of arousal levels and reported visual sensations during sensory deprivation. *Perceptual and Motor Skills, 22*, 447–459.

Zuger, B. (1988). Is early effeminate behavior in boys early homosexuality. *Comprehensive Psychiatry, 29*, 509–519.

Zullow, H. M., Oettingen, G., Peterson, C., & Seligman, M. E. P. (1988). Pessimistic explanatory style in the historical record. *American Psychologist, 43*, 673–682.

Zuroff, D. C., Mongrain, M., & Santor, D. A. (2004). Investing in the personality vulnerability research program: Current dividends and future growth: Rejoinder to Coyne, Thompson, and Whiffen. *Psychological Bulletin, 130*, 518–522.

Name Index

Subject Index

Note: Boldface terms and page numbers are key terms; page numbers followed by f indicate figures; those followed by t indicate tables.

A

Absentmindedness, 311
Absolute refractory period, 126–127, 126f
Absolute threshold, 153–154, 154f
Absolute value, of correlation, 73
Abstinence violation effect, 692
Abstract thinking, 356
  intelligence as, 356–357
Abu Ghraib, 543–544
Acalculia, 111
Accelerated learning, 266
Acceptance and commitment therapy, 690
Accommodation, 409
Acetylcholine, 114, 127t, 128
  in memory, 290
  in REM sleep, 206
**Acquired immunodeficiency syndrome (AIDS),
  505**
Acquisition, 236, 236f
Action potential, 124f, **126**–127, 126f
Activation-synthesis theory, 205–206, 206f
Acupuncture, 525–526
Acute stress disorder, 502, 502t
Ad hoc categories, 344, 592
Adaptation
  characteristic, 606
  dark, 165–166
  in natural selection, 138. *See also* Evolution
  sensory, 153
Adaptive conservatism, 565
Adderall, 700t
Addiction, 663–664. *See also* Alcohol use/abuse;
    Drug abuse
  higher-order conditioning in, 238
Additive color mixing, 163, 163f
Adjustive value, 221
Adler, Alfred, 594
Adolescence, 430–434. *See also* Children
  antidepressant use in, suicide risk for, 702
  brain maturation in, 143
  cognitive development in, 432–433
  identity formation in, 433–434, 434f
  impulsivity in, 432
  physical development in, 431–432, 431f
  puberty in, 431–432, 431f
  role experimentation in, 433
Adoption studies, 141
  of intelligence, 376
  of personality, 582
Adrenal glands, 122–123, 122f
  in stress response, 500, 500f
Adrenaline, 122
Ad hoc immunizing hypothesis, 45
Adult children of alcoholics, 615
Adult development, 435–439. *See also* Marriage
  careers in, 435
  diverse paths in, 435
  in early adulthood, 435–436
  love and commitment in, 435–436
  in midlife, 436–437

  in older years, 437–438
  parenthood in, 436
Advertising. *See also* Persuasion
  classical conditioning in, 238–239
  mere exposure effect and, 454–455
  subliminal messages in, 28, 156–157
Affect heuristic, 355
Affective forecasting, 466
African Americans. *See* Cultural factors;
    Race/ethnicity
Age
  biological, 437
  chronological, 437
  concepts of, 437–438
  functional, 438
  maternal, birth defects and, 438, 438f
  psychological, 437
  social, 438
Age regression
  hypnotic, 215–216, 274, 302–303
  mental, 364
Age-related changes
  in agility and coordination, 438–439
  in body proportions, 405, 405f
  in brain, 144
  in cognitive function, 358, 364, 439
  in happiness, 464–465
  in hearing, 176
  in intelligence, 358, 364, 439
  in memory, 299–303, 439
  in physical condition, 438, 438f
  in sexual activity, 478
  in smell, 183
  in taste, 183
  in vision, 165
Aggression, 556–558. *See also* Violence
  arousal and, 556
  cultural aspects of, 558
  gender differences in, 557–558
  genetic factors in, 402
  identification with aggressor in, 590, 5889t
  media violence and, 258–259, 258f, 556
  monoamine oxidase and, 402
  observational learning of, 257–259
  personality traits and, 557
  physical punishment and, 246–247
  relational, 557–558
  self-esteem and, 467
  situational factors in, 556–557
  social rejection and, 557–558
  substance abuse and, 556–557
Agnosia, visual, 175
Agonist drugs, 128
Agoraphobia, 640–641
Agreeableness, as Big Five trait, 604–605
Aha reaction, 243, 243f
Air travel, fear of, 499–501
Alarm calls, 329
Alarm reaction, in stress response, 499–500
Alcohol hallucinosis, 221

Alcohol use/abuse, 218–221, 663–665
  adult children of alcoholics and, 615
  aggression and, 556–557
  Alcoholics Anonymous and, 691–692
  in Asian Americans, 219, 665
  aversion therapy for, 687
  blood alcohol concentration in, 219, 219f
  controlled drinking vs. abstinence in, 692
  delirium tremens in, 220–221
  dependence in, 663–664
  effects of, 219, 219f
  genetic factors in, 665
  higher-order conditioning in, 238
  historical perspective on, 218–219
  learning and expectancies in, 665
  moderation vs. abstention in, 517
  myths about, 220t
  personality factors in, 664–665
  placebo effect in, 220
  sociocultural aspects of, 664
  symptoms of, 664t
  tension reduction hypothesis for, 665
  tolerance in, 220
  withdrawal in, 220–221
Alcoholics Anonymous, 691–692
Alien abductions, 37–39, 106, 215
**Alternative and complementary therapies, 505,
  523**–527
  acupuncture, 525–526
  body-based, 525
  chiropractic, 525
  energy-based, 525–526
  herbal/nutritional remedies, 290, 524–525
  homeopathy, 526
  memory-boosting, 290
  reasons for using, 524t, 526–527
  regulation of, 525
  safety and effectiveness of, 526–527
Altruism, 555
Alzheimer's disease, 114
  neurofibrillary tangles in, 144, 144f, 300, 300f
  senile plaques in, 144, 144f, 300, 300f
American Psychological Association (APA), 9–10
  ethical guidelines of, 92
American Psychological Society (APS), 9–10
American Sign Language, 330–331
Americans with Disabilities Act (ADA), 372
Ames room, 172, 172f
Amnesia, 298–299. *See also* Memory; Memory loss
  anterograde, 26, 298
  case studies of, 298–299
  dissociative, 652
  generalized, 298–299
  infantile (childhood), 302–303, 589
  myths about, 298–299
  posthypnotic, 215
  retrograde, 298
  spontaneous, 215
Amok, 629
Amphetamine, 222, 700t

Credits

TEXT AND ART

Prologue

Figure P.1, p. 2: From *Great Ideas of Clinical Science: 17 Principles That Every Mental Health Professional Should Understand* by Ilardi, Rand, and Karwoski. Copyright 2007 by Taylor & Francis Group LLC—Books. Reproduced with permission of Taylor & Francis Group LLC—Books in the format Textbook via Copyright Clearance Center.

Cartoon, p. 18: © The New Yorker Collection 2003 Michael Shaw from cartoonbank.com. All Rights Reserved.

Figure P.5, p. 19: Copyright © 2007 by the American Psychological Association. Reproduced with permission.

Figure P.6, p. 20: Figure 1 from Libet, B. (1985). Unconscious cerebral initiative and the role of conscious will in voluntary action. *Behavioral and Brain Sciences* 8: 529–566. Reprinted with the permission of Cambridge University Press.

Chapter 1

Figure 1.1, p. 26: From *Mind Sights*, by Roger Shepard. Copyright © 1990 by Roger Shepard. Used by permission of Henry Holt and Company.

Cartoon, p. 34: © ScienceCartoonsPlus.com.

Cartoon, p. 43: © Bil Keane, Inc. King Features Syndicate.

Cartoon, p. 43: © ScienceCartoonsPlus.com.

Table 1.3, p. 45: Used by permission of the Skeptical Inquirer www.csicop.org.

Cartoon, p. 47: © Nick Kim, nearingzero.net.

Cartoon, p. 48: © ScienceCartoonsPlus.com.

Table 1.4, p. 54: Reprinted with the permission of The Free Press, a Division of Simon & Schuster Adult Publishing Group, from *How We Know It Isn't So: The Fallibility of Human Reason in Everyday Life* by Thomas Gilovich. Copyright © 1991 by Thomas Gilovich. All rights reserved.

Chapter 2

Figure 2.6, p. 78: Used with permission from Jon Mueller.

Cartoon, p. 81: © ScienceCartoonsPlus.com.

Cartoon, p. 82: © ScienceCartoonsPlus.com.

Figure 2.7, p. 90: From Anderson, C.A., Lindsay, J.J., & Bushman, B.J. (1999). Research in the psychological laboratory: Truth or triviality? *Current Directions in Psychological Science, 8*, 3–9. Reprinted with permission from Blackwell Publishing.

Cartoon, p. 94: © ScienceCartoonsPlus.com.

Cartoon, p. 96: Reprinted with permission from www.CartoonStock.com.

Cartoon, p. 99: © ScienceCartoonsPlus.com.

Chapter 3

Figure 3.1, p. 109: © Dorling Kindersley.

Figure 3.2, p. 109: © Dorling Kindersley.

Figure 3.5, p. 112: Adapted from Figure 12.9, p. 438, from *Human Anatomy & Physiology, 7th ed.* by Elaine N. Marieb and Katja Hoehn. Copyright © 2007 by Pearson Education, Inc. Reprinted by permission.

Figure 3.11, p. 116: Adapted from Figure 12.5, p. 434, from *Human Anatomy & Physiology, 7th ed.* by Elaine N. Marieb and Katja Hoehn. Copyright © 2007 by Pearson Education, Inc. Reprinted by permission.

Figure 3.14, p. 119: Left image © Dorling Kindersley; right image from *Biological Psychology* w/CD + INFOTRAC 9th edition by KALAT. 2007. Reprinted with permission of Wadsworth, a division of Thomson Learning: www.thomsonrights.com. Fax 800-730-2215.

Figure 3.17, p. 123: From Sternberg, R.J. (2004) *Psychology*, 4th ed. Belmont, CA: Wadsworth (p. 100). Adapted with permission from the author.

Figure 3.18, p. 124: Combustion © Dorling Kindersley.

Figure 3.22, p. 126: From Sternberg, R.J. (2004) *Psychology*, 4th ed. Belmont, CA: Wadsworth (pp. 72–73). Adapted with permission from the author.

Table 3.2, p. 127: From Carlson, Neil R., C. Donald Heth, et al. *Science of Behavior, The 6/e.* Published by Allyn & Bacon, Boston, MA. Copyright © 2007 by Pearson Education. Adapted by permission of the publisher.

Cartoon, p. 136: © ScienceCartoonsPlus.com.

Figure 3.28, p. 142: Adapted from Figure 12.3, p. 432, from *Human Anatomy & Physiology, 7th ed.* by Elaine N. Marieb and Katja Hoehn. Copyright © 2007 by Pearson Education, Inc. Reprinted by permission.

Figure 3.29, p. 143: Adapted from *Behavioral Brain Research, 163*, Maria Giuseppa Leggio et al., Environmental enrichment promotes improved spatial abilities and enhanced dendritic growth in the rat, 78–90, Copyright 2005, with permission from Elsevier.

Chapter 4

Figure 4.1, p. 152: From *An Anatomy of Thought* by Ian Glynn. Published by Oxford University Press, 1999.

Cartoon, p. 153: © ScienceCartoonsPlus.com.

Figure 4.5, p. 157: Original drawing by W. E. Hill, 1915.

Figure 4.7, p. 158: Reprinted with permission from Edward H. Adelson.

Figure 4.8, p. 158: Reprinted with permission from Dr. Dale Purves.

Figure 4.13, p. 164: © Dorling Kindersley.

Figure 4.15, p. 165: Reprinted with permission from St. Luke's Cataract & Laser Institute of Tarpon Spring, FL.

Figure 4.19, p. 168: Figure 1C from Herrmann & Friederici, SCIENCE 292: 163 (2001). Reprinted with permission from AAAS.

Figure 4.21, p. 169: From coolopticalillusions.com. Reprinted with permission.

Figure 4.24, p. 173: Reprinted with permission from Imprint Academic.

Figure 4.29, p. 178: Mira Shade © Dorling Kindersley.

Unnumbered Figure, p. 183: Reprinted from *Neuron*, Vol. 20, Bruno Wicker, Christian Keysers, Jane Plailly, Jean-Pierre Royet, Vittorio Gallese and Giacomo Rizzolatti, "Both of Us Disgusted in My Insula: The Common Neural Basis of Seeing and Feeling Disgust," 655–664, Copyright 2003, with permission from Elsevier.

Chapter 5

Cartoon, p. 209: Reprinted with permission from www.CartoonStock.com.

Table 5.2, p. 209: Copyright © 2000 by the American Psychological Association. Reproduced with permission.

Cartoon, p. 210: © Chris Slane. Reprinted with permission.

Chapter 6

Cartoon, p. 245: © The New Yorker Collection 1993 Tom Cheney from www.cartoonbank.com. All Rights Reserved.

Cartoon, p. 257: © Hilary B. Price. King Features Syndicate.

Figure 6.11, p. 258: Copyright © 2003 by the American Psychological Association. Reproduced with permission.

Figure 6.12, p. 261: Copyright © 1963 by the American Psychological Association. Reproduced with permission.

Chapter 7

Figure 7.2, p. 277: Adapted from *Cognitive Psychology*, 11, R.S. Nickerson and J.J. Adams, Long-term memory for a common object, 287–307, 1979, with permission from Elsevier.

Figure 7.3, p. 278: Figure taken from "Human Memory: A Proposed System and Its Control Processes." This article was published in *The Psychology of Learning and Motivation: Advances in Research and Theory*, Vol. 2, edited by K. W. Spence and J. T. Spence, pp. 89–195, New York: Academic Press. Copyright Elsevier (1968). Reprinted by permission.

Figure 7.8, p. 284: Copyright © 1984 by the American Psychological Association. Reproduced with permission.

Figure 7.13, p. 291: Adapted from Bransford, J. D., & Johnson, M. K. Figure taken from "Contextual Prerequisites for Understanding: Some Investigations of Comprehension and Recall." This article was published in *Journal of Verbal Learning and Verbal Behavior*, Vol. 11, pp. 89–195. Copyright Elsevier (1972). Reprinted by permission.

Figure 7.14, p. 292: From Bartlett, F. C. (1932). *Remembering: A study in experimental and social psychology*, page 65. Cambridge, England: Cambridge University Press. Reprinted with the permission of Cambridge University Press.

Figure 7.19, p. 298: Reprinted by permission of Macmillan Publishers Ltd: *Nature*, Quiroga et al. (2005), Invariant visual representation by single neurons in the human brain. *Nature*, 435, 1102–1107, copyright 2005.

Unnumbered Figure, p. 299: Copyright ©1997 Society for Neuroscience.

Figure 7.21, p. 299: Adapted from *Biological Psychology* w/CD + INFOTRAC 9th edition by KALAT. 2007. Reprinted with permission of Wadsworth, a division of Thomson Learning: www.thomsonrights.com. Fax 800-730-2215.

Cartoon, p. 300: © ScienceCartoonsPlus.com

Figure 7.22, p. 300: The medical illustration is provided courtesy of Alzheimer's Disease Research, a program of the American Health Assistance Foundation: http://www.ahaf.org.

Chapter 8

Cartoon, p. 320: © The New Yorker Collection 1987 Michael Maslin from cartoonbank.com. All Rights Reserved.

Cartoon, p. 322: © 1997 Thaves. Reprinted with permission.

Figure 8.3, p. 325: From Fenson, Dale, Reznick, et al. 1994. Variability in early communicative development. Monographs of the Society for Research in Child Development, 59 (5, Serial No. 173). Reprinted with permission from Blackwell Publishers.

Figure 8.9, p. 331: Adapted from http://lifeprint.com/asl101/pages-signs/ with permission from William Vicars.

Figure 8.10, p. 333: Reprinted from *Cognitive Psychology, 21,* Johnson & Newport, Decline in language performance with age, 60–99, Figure 1, Copyright 1989, with permission from Elsevier.

Figure 8.15, p. 343: From *Mind Sights,* by Roger Shepard. Copyright © 1990 by Roger Shepard. Used by permission of Henry Holt and Company.

Table 8.6, p. 346: From *Cognitive Psychology, 15* , M.L. Gick & K. J. Holyoak, Schema induction and analogical transfer, 1–38, Copyright 1983, with permission from Elsevier.

Lyrics, p. 347: "Doin' What Comes Natur'lly" by Irving Berlin © Copyright 1946 by Irving Berlin © Copyright Renewed. International Copyright Secured. All Rights Reserved. Reprinted by Permission.

Chapter 9

Figure 9.2, p. 357: Smith, G., G. (2001). "Interaction evokes reflection: Learning Efficiency in Spatial Visualization," selected as one of the 25 best ED-MEDIA 2001 papers by the editors of The Interactive Multimedia Electronic Journal of Computer-Enhanced Learning and published in a multimedia version in IMEJ http://imej.wfu.edu/articles/2001/2/05 /index.asp. Reprinted with permission.

Figure 9.5, p. 360: Adapted from Wagner, R. K., & Sternberg, R. J. (Eds.) (1986). *Practical intelligence: Nature and origins of competence in the everyday world,* pp. 60–61. Cambridge: Cambridge University Press. Reprinted with the permission of Cambridge University Press.

Figure 9.8, p. 365: Reprinted with permission of the Pickler Memorial Library and the Dolan DNA Learning Center.

Figure 9.9, p. 366: *Wechsler Adult Intelligence Scale–Third Edition (WAIS-III).* Copyright © 1977 by Harcourt Assessment, Inc. Reproduced with permission. All rights reserved.

Figure 9.10, p. 367: *Raven's Progressive Matrices (Advanced).* Copyright © 1976, 1947, 1943 by Harcourt Assessment, Inc. Reproduced with permission. All rights reserved.

Table 9.2, p. 371: Reprinted from Simonton, D.K., 2006, "Presidential IQ, openness, intellectual brilliance and leadership: Estimates and correlations for 42 U.S. chief executives." *Political Psychology, 27,* 511–526.

Unnumbered Figure, p. 371: From http://www.nytimes.com/2005/10/25/health/policy/25cons.html, "And Now, A Warning About Drug Labels" by Deborah Franklin.

Figure 9.13, p. 373: Hauser, Robert M. 2002. "Meritocracy, cognitive ability, and the sources of occupational success." CDE Working Paper 98-07 (rev). Center for Demography and Ecology, The University of Wisconsin-Madison, Madison, Wisconsin. Reprinted with permission from Robert M. Hauser.

Cartoon, p. 373: © Kevin Menzie. Reprinted with permission.

Figure 9.14, p. 379: Copyright © 1984 by the American Psychological Association. Reproduced with permission.

Figure 9.15, p. 380: Used with permission from the American Institute of Physics.

Figure 9.17, p. 381: From Transformational studies of the internal representation of 3-dimensional objects by J. Metzler & R. N. Shepard. In R. L. Solso, ed., *Theories of cognitive psychology: The Loyola Symposium.* Potomac, MD. Published by Lawrence Erlbaum Associates, 1974.

Figure 9.21, p. 385: Reprinted with permission from Robert L. Williams, Ph.D.

Figure 9.22, p. 389: From Weisberg, R. W. (1994). Genius and madness? A quasi-experimental test of the hypothesis that manic-depression increases productivity. *Psychological Science, 5,* 361–367. Reprinted with permission from Blackwell Publishers.

Chapter 10

Figure 10.1, p. 402: From Caspi, A., McClay, J., Moffitt, T.E., Mill, J., Martin, J., Craig, I.W., Taylor, A., & Poulton, R. (2002). "The Role of Genotype in the Cycle of Violence in Maltreated Children." SCIENCE, 297, 851–854, Figure 1. Reprinted with permission from AAAS.

Figure 10.2, p. 403: Adapted from Figure 28.4, p. 118, from *Human Anatomy & Physiology, 7th Ed.* by Elaine N. Marieb and Katja Hoehn. Copyright © 2007 by Pearson Education, Inc. Reprinted by permission.

Figure 10.6, p. 407: Adapted from Konczak, J. & Dichgans, J. (1997). The development toward stereotypic arm kinematics during reaching in the first 3 years of life. *Exp Brain Res, 117,* 346–354, with kind permission of Springer Science and Business Media.

Figure 10.8, p. 410: Reprinted with permission from *Human Development, 7e,* by Diane E. Papalia et al. © 1998 by The McGraw-Hill Companies, Inc.

Figure 10.10, p. 413: Reprinted from *Cognition, 20,* R. Baillargeon, E.S. Spelke, & S. Wasserman, Object Permanence in Five-month-old infants, 191–208, 1985, with permission from Elsevier.

Figure 10.13, p. 416: Reprinted from *Cognitive Development,14,* K. S. Mix, Similarity and numerical equivalence appearances count, 269–297, 1999, with permission from Elsevier.

Figure 10.14, p. 418: From Waters, E, Matas, L, and Sroufe, L.A. (1975). Infants' reactions to an approaching stranger: Description, validation, and functional significance of wariness. *Child Development, 46,* 348–356. Reprinted with permission from Blackwell Publishing.

Figure 10.15, p. 420: Copyright 1978 from *Patterns of Attachment* by M.D. S. Ainsworth et al. Reproduced by permission of Lawrence Erlbaum Associates, Inc., a division of Taylor & Francis Group.

Figure 10.18, p. 434: From Good, Thomas L. & Jere Brophy *Contemporary Educational Psychology, 5/e.* Published by Allyn & Bacon, Boston, MA. Copyright © 1995 by Pearson Education. Adapted by permission of the publisher.

Chapter 11

Figure 11.1, p. 449: From Aronoff, J., Barclay, AM, & Stevenson, LA., The recognition of threatening facial stimuli, *Journal of Personality and Social Psychology,* 1988, April 54 (4), 647–655.

Figure 11.2, p. 451: Adapted from Dr. Silvia Helena Cardoso, http://www.cerebromente.org.br/n05/mente/tub6.gif

Figure 11.3, p. 454: Pairs of polygons used in the mere exposure research of Robert Zajonc from *Laboratory Manual - Cognitive Science in Context Laboratory - Spring 2006* (Nick Epley: Cornell University), http://www.csic.cornell.edu. Reprinted by permission Nicholas Epley.

Figure 11.4, p. 456: Microsoft product screen shots reprinted with permission from Microsoft Corporation.

Cartoon, p. 457: Sidney Harris, www.CartoonStock.com. Used by permission.

Figure 11.5, p. 457: Adapted from "The Social-Cue Reader" by Jennifer Schuessler from *The New York Times* Magazine, December 10, 2006. © 2006 The New York Times. Reprinted by permission.

Cartoon, p. 458: Sidney Harris, www.CartoonStock.com. Used by permission.

Table 11.1, p. 463: "VIA Classification," www.viastrengths.org. Copyright © Values In Action Institute (VIA Institute on Character) 2003. Reprinted by permission.

Figure 11.8, p. 463: Measure Your Happiness: Take the Satisfaction with Life Scale from http://www.psych.uiuc.edu/~ediener/SWLS.htm. Ed Diener, Robert A. Emmons, Randy J. Larsen and Sharon Griffin as noted in the 1985 article in *the Journal of Personality Assessment.*

Figure 11.9, p. 464: "The Value of Positive Emotions," by Barbara L. Fredrickson, *American Scientist,* July-August 2003 (91). Used by permission.

Figure 11.10, p. 464: "Power of positive thinking extends, it seems, to aging" by Mary Duenwald, *The New York Times,* November 19, 2002. Copyright © 2002 The New York Times. Used by permission.

Figure 11.11, p. 464: From Diener, E., & Seligman, M. E. P. (2004), "Beyond money: Toward an economy of well-being," *Psychological Science in the Public Interest,* Vol 5, No. 1, p. 3. Used by permission of Blackwell Publishing.

Figure 11.12, p. 467: From Pew Research Center Report, "Are we happy yet?" February 13, 2006, http://pewresearch.org/pubs/301/are-we-happy-yet. Reprinted by permission.

Table 11.2, p. 468: From Denollet, J. "DS14: Standard assessment of negative affectivity, social inhibition, and Type D personality" in *Psychosomatic Medicine,* 2005; 67, 89-97. Used by permission of Lippincott Williams & Wilkins, www.lww.com <http://www.lww.com/>

Figure 11.14, p. 470: From the web component of *Psychology: A ConnecText 4E* by Pettijohn. Copyright © 1998 by The McGraw-Hill Companies. Reproduced by permission of McGraw-Hill Contemporary Learning Series.

Figure 11.18, p. 477: From Rathus, Spencer A., Jeffrey S. Nevis, et al. *Human Sexuality In A World of Diversity, 7E.* Published by Allyn and Bacon, Boston, MA. Copyright © 2008 by Pearson Education. Reprinted by permission of the publisher.

Chapter 12

Figure 12.1, p. 497: Reprinted from "The Social Readjustment Scale" by T.H. Holmes, & R.H. Rahe, *Journal of Psychosomatic Research,* Vol. 11, Issue 2, August 1967, p. 214, with permission from Elsevier. http://www.sciencedirect .com/science/journal/00223999

Figure 12.2, p. 499: Image from http://www.users.bigpond.com/fmcdonald/triphasic2001_files/image002.jpg. – Selye's General Adaptation Syndrome
Cartoon, p. 507: Randy Glasbergen, www.glasbergen.com. Used by permission.
Table 12.2, p. 508: From Denollet, J. "DS14: Standard assessment of negative affectivity, social inhibition, and Type D personality" in *Psychosomatic Medicine*, 2005; 67, 89–97. Used by permission of Lippincott Williams & Wilkins, www.lww.com
Cartoon, p. 512: Randy Glasbergen, www.glasbergen.com. Used by permission.
Cartoon, p. 516: Randy Glasbergen, www.glasbergen.com. Used by permission.
Cartoon, p. 526: Cartoon by Nick D. Kim, nearingzero.net. Used by permission.

Chapter 13

Figure 13.1, p. 537: Reprinted from *Journal of Experimental Social Psychology*, 3, E.E. Jones & V.A. Harris, The attribution of attitudes, 1–24, 1967, with permission from Elsevier.
Figure 13.2, p. 538: Reprinted with permission from William K. Hartmann.
Figure 13.4, p. 540: From Opinions and Social Pressure by S. E. Asch. Published in *Scientific American*, 193, 31–35, 1955.
Figure 13.5, p. 542: Reprinted with permission from Philip Zimbardo, Ph.D., Professor Emeritus, Stanford University.
Cartoon, p. 544: © The New Yorker Collection 1979 Henry Martin from cartoonbank.com. All Rights Reserved.
Figure 13.8, p. 557: Adapted from http://www-personal.umich.edu/~tnienber/poster/crime.html by Troy Nienberg.
Figure 13.9, p. 560: Copyright © 2002 by the American Psychological Association. Reproduced with permission.

Chapter 14

Table 14.1, p. 581: Copyright © 1988 by the American Psychological Association. Reproduced with permission.
Table 14.2, p. 582: Copyright © 1981 by the American Psychological Association. Reproduced with permission.
Cartoon, p. 586: Reprinted with permission from www.CartoonStock.com. © ScienceCartoonsPlus.com.
Cartoon, p. 595: © ScienceCartoonsPlus.com.
Table 14.6, p. 599: Reprinted with permission of Psychtests.com.
Figure 14.6, p. 611: Reprinted with permission from University of Minnesota Press.
Figure 14.8, p. 613: Reprinted by permission of the publishers from Henry A. Murray, THEMATIC APPERCEPTION TEST, Card 12 F, Cambridge, Mass: Harvard University Press, Copyright ©1943 by the President and Fellows of Harvard College, Copyright © 1971 by Henry A. Murray.
Figure 14.9, p. 614: Reprinted with permission from The British Academy of Graphology.

Chapter 15

Figure 15.1, p. 627: From *Out of the Shadows: Confronting America's Mental Illness Crisis* by E. Fuller Torrey, M.D. Reprinted with permission of John Wiley & Sons, Inc.
Cartoon, p. 628: Clay Bennett / © 1999 The Christian Science Monitor (www.csmonitor.com). All rights reserved. Used by permission.
Table 15.1, p. 628: Source: Hall, Timothy McCajor. "Culture-bound syndromes in China," http://homepage.mac.com/mccajor/cbs.html, 12 Feb 1998, revised 4 Nov 2006.
Figure 15.2, p. 629: From "Cultural representations of thinness in women, redux: *Playboy* magazine's depiction of beauty from 1979 to 1999" by Mia Foley Sypeck, et al. from Body Image, Vol. 3, Issue 3, September, 2006. Copyright Elsevier, 2006. Reprinted by permission.
Table 15.3, p. 634: Reprinted with permission from the *Diagnostic and Statistical Manual of Mental Disorders, Fourth Edition*, Text Revision (Copyright 2000). American Psychiatric Publishing.
Table 15.4, p. 634: Reprinted with permission from the *Diagnostic and Statistical Manual of Mental Disorders, Fourth Edition*, Text Revision (Copyright 2000). American Psychiatric Publishing.
Table 15.6, p. 639: From "Lifetime Prevalence and Age-of-Onset Distributions of DSM-IV Disorders in the National Comorbidity Survey Replication" by Kessler, et al. *Archive General Psychiatry* Vol. 62, June 2005, p. 596. Copyright © 2005 American Medical Association. Reprinted by permission.
Figure 15.4, p. 651: From "Lethal Beauty" by Edward Guthmann, *San Francisco Chronicle*, October 30, 2005.
Cartoon, p. 653: (www.CartoonStock.com) Dan Rosandich, www.CartoonStock.com. Used by permission.
Figure 15.5, p. 659: From Fundamentals of *Neuropsychopharmacology* by Robert S. Feldman. Reprinted by permission of Sinauer Associates.
Table 15.13, p. 664: Reprinted with permission from the *Diagnostic and Statistical Manual of Mental Disorders, Fourth Edition*, Text Revision (Copyright 2000). American Psychiatric Publishing.

Chapter 16

Cartoon, p. 672 (Comic book cover): Copyright © William M. Gaines, Agent, Inc. Used by permission.
Cartoon, p. 672 ("Lassie, get help!"): © The New Yorker Collection 1989 Danny Shanahan from cartoonbank.com. All Rights Reserved.
Table 16.3, p. 681: "Simulated conversation between client and computer, Eliza" by Joseph Weizenbaum as appeared in *Communications of the ACM*, Vol. 9, No. 1, January 1966: 36. Used by permission of Joseph Weizenbaum.
Table 16.4, p. 684: From Rimm, D., & Masters, J. C. (1979). *Behavior therapy; Techniques and Empirical Findings, 2E.*
Song Lyrics, p. 687: Adapted from "Love Me, Love Me, Only Me!" by Albert Ellis. Reprinted with permission of Albert Ellis Institute.
Table 16.5, p. 688: Ellis, A., 1977, *Handbook of Rational-Emotive Therapy*, Springer.
Figure 16.3, p. 694: E. M. Sellers, M.D., Ph.D. (1988). Defining rational prescribing of psychactive drugs. *British Journal of Addiction*, 83, 21–34. Used by permission of Blackwell Publishing.
Table 16.8, p. 696: From "Psychotherapy on trial" by Hal Arkowit and Scott O. Lilienfield, *Scientific American*, April/May 2006. Copyright © 2006 by Scientific American, Inc. All rights reserved. Used by permission.

PHOTO CREDITS

Prologue

p. 1: © Blue Line Pictures/Getty Images; p. 3, Top: Deepak Buddhiraja/India Picture/Corbis; p. 3, Middle: Frederic Lucano/Getty Images; p. 3, Bottom: Mike Powell/Getty Images; p. 4, Top: Picture Partners/Alamy; p. 4, Middle: Ken Kaminesky/Take 2 Productions/Corbis; p. 4, Bottom: Henry Westheim Photography/Alamy; p. 5, Top: Bettmann/Corbis; p. 5, Middle & Bottom: Courtesy of Hannah Faye Chua; p. 6: Archives of the History of American Psychology; p. 8, Top: Rainer Holz/zefa/Corbis; p. 8, Bottom: Mary Evans Picture Library/The Image Works; p. 9: Wisconsin Historical Society, WHS Image ID# PH_2808; p. 10: Michael Newman/PhotoEdit Inc.; p. 11, Top: Photo Researchers, Inc.; p. 11, Bottom: Archives of the History of American Psychology; p. 12, Top: M Nader/Getty Images; p. 12, Middle: Bob Daemmrich/The Image Works; p. 12, Bottom: Colin Young-Wolff/PhotoEdit; p. 13, Top: Gerrit Greve/Corbis; p. 13, Bottom: Freud Museum Photo Library; p. 14, #1: Courtesy of Dr. Elizabeth F. Loftus; p. 14, #2: Courtesy of Leslie J. Yonce; p. 14, #3: AP Images/Joe Cavaretta, File; p. 14, #4: Rose Hartman/Time Life Pictures/Getty Images; p. 14, Bottom: Blue Shadows/Alamy; p. 15, Top: Fat Chance Productions/Corbis; p. 15, Bottom: Photo of Kenneth & Mamie Clark used with Permission of the University Archives, Columbia University in the city of New York; p. 16: Surgi Stock/Taxi/Getty Images; p. 17, Top: Tom Lindfors Photography; p. 17, Bottom: Phil Walter/Getty Images; p. 18, Cole: AP Images/Alik Keplicz; p. 18, Gore: AP Images/Angela Rowlings; p. 18, Stewart: Paul Hawthorne/Getty Images; p. 18, Jarreau: AP Images/Robert E. Klein; p. 20: Nina Leen/Time Life Pictures/Getty Images

Chapter 1

p. 22: © Photothèque R. Magritte-ADAGP/Art Resource, NY; p. 24: AP Images/Oscar Sosa; p. 25: AP Images/Stuart Ramson; p. 26: Courtesy of Professor Tania Lombrozo; p. 27: Dion Ogust/The Image Works; p. 29: Reproduced by permission, The John Rylands University Library of Manchester, and provided through the courtesy of Roger J. Wood, Faculty of Life Sciences, University of Manchester; p. 31: C.J. GUNTHER/AFP/Getty Images; p. 32: David Young-Wolff/PhotoEdit Inc.; p. 33: David Young-Wolff/PhotoEdit Inc.; p. 35: Ron Chapple Stock/Corbis; p. 36: © The Royal Society; p. 37: Mary Evans Picture Library/The Image Works; p. 39: Danny Feld/© NBC/Courtesy: Everett Collection; pp. 40 and 59, Top: Topham/The Image Works; p. 40, Bottom: Tim Fitzharris/Minden Pictures/Getty Images; p. 41: Design Pics Inc./Alamy; p. 46: David Young-Wolff/PhotoEdit Inc.; p. 47, Bottom: Photo Courtesy of Annie Pickert. Journals: Psychological Bulletin & Psychological Review, published by American Psychological Association; Psychological Science published by Blackwell Publishing; p. 48: AP Images/Wilfredo Lee; p. 49, Top: Mario Perez/© ABC/Courtesy: Everett Collection; pp. 49, Bottom and 61: Hulton Archive/Getty Images; p. 50: Robert McGouey/Alamy; p. 51, Top: AP Images/Nashville Tennesean, Bill Steber, File; p. 51, Middle: Roger Ressmeyer/NASA/Corbis; p. 51, Bottom: Topham/The Image Works; p. 52: Stewart Cohen/Getty Images; pp. 53 and 61, both: Corbis; p. 55, Top: Tore Bergsaker/Sygma/Corbis; p. 55, Bottom: Jamie Grill/Iconia/Getty Images; p. 57, Top: Purestock/Getty Images Royalty Free; p. 57, Middle: AP Images/HO; p. 57, Bottom: AP Images/John Bazemore

p. 344, Top: Bob Krist/Corbis; p. 344, Bottom: David Grossman/The Image Works; pp. 345 and 351: Richard Price/Taxi/Getty Images

Chapter 9

p. 352: Erich Lessing/Art Resource, NY; p. 354: PhotoSpin, Inc./Alamy; p. 355, Top: Courtesy of Carol Dweck; p. 355, Bottom: SSPL/The Image Works; p. 356, Top: AP Images/Sony-Jeopardy; p. 356, Bottom: Kazuyoshi Nomachi/Corbis; p. 358, Top: Bettmann/Corbis; p. 358, Middle: Contographer Æ/Corbis; p. 358, Bottom: Elsa/Getty Images; p. 360: AP Images/Charles Dharapak; p. 361: Topham/The Image Works; p. 362: Courtesy of Dr. Sandra Witelson; p. 364: Sara D. Davis/Chicago Tribune/MCT/Newscom; p. 366: Stockdisc Classic/Alamy; p. 369: Nathaniel S.Butler/NBAE via Getty Images; p. 370: Courtesy of Dr. Petra Hauf, CRC in Culture and Human Development, St. Francis Xavier University Department of Psychology; p. 372: Grabowsky U./SV-Bilderdienst/The Image Works; p. 374: Miramax/Courtesy Everett Collection; p. 375, Top: Brad Wilson/Stone/Getty Images; p. 375, Bottom: MP Imagery/ Alamy; p. 376: Josef Polleross/The Image Works; pp. 377, Top and 393: Jason Lindsey/Alamy; p. 377, Bottom: Nancy Sheehan Photography; p. 382: Ian Shaw/Alamy; p. 385: Courtesy of Frank C. Worrell; p. 386: Malcolm Case-Green/Alamy; p. 387: Nick Adams/Getty Images; pp. 388 and 395: Richard A. Cooke/Corbis; p. 389: Lebrecht Music Collection; p. 390: Bettmann/Corbis; p. 391, Top: Bettmann/Corbis; p. 391, Bottom: Courtesy of Unity Church of North Easton Restoration Project (www.historicunitychurch.com)

Chapter 10

p. 396: Provided by Al Seckel/IllusionWorks; p. 398: Monte S. Buchsbaum, M.D., Mount Sinai School of Medicine, New York, N.Y.; p. 399, Top: Private Collection/The Bridgeman Art Library; p. 399, Bottom: Peter Beavis/Taxi/Getty Images; pp. 400 and 440: Bureau L.A. Collection/Corbis; p. 401, Top: Corbis Premium RF/Alamy; p. 401, Middle: AP Images; p. 401, Bottom: Reuters/Corbis; p. 403, Top: RBM Online/epa/Corbis; p. 403, Middle: Petit Format/Photo Researchers, Inc.; p. 403, Bottom: Ace Stock Limited /Alamy; p. 405: David H. Wells/Corbis; p. 406: Elizabeth Crews/The Image Works; pp. 407 and 440: Keren Su/Corbis; p. 408, Top: Bill Anderson/Photo Researchers, Inc.; p. 408, Bottom: Novosti/Sovfoto/Eastfoto; p. 409, Both: Laura Dwight/PhotoEdit Inc. ; p. 411: James Shaffer/PhotoEdit, Inc; p. 414, Top Left: Stuart Gregory/Digital Vision/Getty Images Royalty Free; p. 414, Top Right: A. Ramey/PhotoEdit Inc.; p. 414, Bottom: Courtesy of David H. Rakison; p. 415: Courtesy of Lorraine E. Bahrick, Professor, Director, Infant Development Research Center, Florida International University Department of Psychology; p. 416, Top: Courtesy of Peter Gordon; p. 416, Bottom: Spencer Grant/PhotoEdit, Inc.; p. 419, Top: Nina Leen/Time Life Pictures/Getty Images; p. 419, Bottom: AP Images/Amy Sancetta; pp. 420 and 442: Nina Leen//Time Life Pictures/Getty Images; p. 422: Kayoco/zefa/Corbis; p. 423, Top: Courtesy of Annie Pickert; p. 423, Bottom: Kenzaburo Fukuhara/Corbis; p. 424: Jeff Greenberg/ The Image Works; p. 426: Courtesy of Annie Pickert; p. 427: Eric Miller/St. Paul Pioneer Press/Newscom; p. 428: Polka Dot Images /Jupiter Images Royalty Free; p. 429: Courtesy of Melissa Hines; p. 430: Mira/Alamy; p. 431: Paul Barker/AFP/Getty Images; p. 432: Mary Kate Denny/PhotoEdit, Inc; p. 433: Davis Turner/CNP/Corbis; p. 435, Top Left: Rachel Epstein/The Image Works; p. 435, Top Right: Tony Freeman/PhotoEdit, Inc.; pp. 435, Bottom and 443: Ariel Skelley/Blend Images/Getty Images Royalty Free; p. 436: David Young-Wolff/PhotoEdit, Inc.; p. 437, Top: Peter Hvizdak/The Image Works; p. 437, Bottom: Courtesy of Nancy Law & Laura Namy; p. 438: JUPITERIMAGES/Thinkstock/Alamy; p. 439, Top: Robert Michael/Corbis; p. 439, Bottom and 443 Bottom: Malie Rich-Griffith/Infocuspictures.com/Alamy

Chapter 11

p. 444: "La Vie en Rose" by Sandro Del Prete; pp. 446, Top and 489: Topham /The Image Works; p. 446, Bottom: Reprinted by permission of Harvard Business School Press. From *Toxic Emotions at Work* by Peter J. Frost. Boston, MA 2003. Cover. Copyright © 2003 by the Harvard Business School Publishing Corporation; all rights reserved; p. 447, Top: NMPFT/SSPL/The Image Works; p. 447, Bottom: Issei Kato/Reuters/Corbis; p. 448: PAUL EKMAN GROUP, LLC.; p. 449, Top: PhotosIndia/Getty Images Royalty Free; p. 449, Bottom: Richard Lord/The Image Works; p. 450, Top: Tim Davis/Corbis; p. 450, Bottom: AP Images/Gurinder Osan; p. 453: AM Corporation/Alamy; p. 455: VStock LLC/Index Open; p. 460, Top: Courtesy Everett Collection; pp. 460, Bottom and 488: Robert E Daemmrich/Stone/Getty Images; p. 461: AP Images/Denis Paquin; pp. 462 and 489: David Shaw/Alamy; p. 465, Top: Tom & Dee Ann McCarthy/Corbis; p. 465, Bottom: Greg Hinsdale/Corbis; p. 466, Top: Michael J. Doolittle/The Image Works; p. 466, Bottom: Tim Wimborne /Reuters/Corbis; p. 467, Top: Kay Nietfeld /epa/Corbis; p. 467, Bottom: Gary Caskey/Reuters/Corbis; p. 469: Bill Greenblatt/UPI/Newscom; p. 473: PHOTOTAKE Inc./Alamy; p. 474: AP Images/ Shakh Aivazov; p. 475: Rita Maas/StockFood Creative/Getty Images; p. 476, Top: Bill Aron/PhotoEdit Inc.;

p. 476, Bottom: Spots Illustration/Jupiterimages Royalty Free; p. 478, Top: Larry Mulvehill/The Image Works; pp. 478, Bottom and 490: (c) Fox Searchlight/courtesy Everett Collection; p. 479: AP Images/Zack Seckler; p. 480: AP Images/Hermann J. Knippertz; p. 482, Top and Bottom: Reuters TV/ Reuters/Corbis; p. 484, Left: © Lisa O'Connor/ZUMA/Corbis; pp. 484 Right and 491: © Lisa O'Connor/ ZUMA/Corbis; p. 485, Top: Courtesy of Judy Langlois; p. 485, Bottom: The Print Collector/Alamy; p. 486, Top: Jane Burton/Photo Researchers, Inc.; p. 486, Bottom: Sion Touhig/Getty Images; p. 487: JLP/Jose L. Pelaez/Corbis

Chapter 12

p. 492: Al Seckel/IllusionWorks; p. 494: Matt McDermott/CORBIS SYGMA; p. 495: Steven Puetzer/NonStock/Jupiter Images; p. 496, Top: Viviane Moos/Corbis; pp. 496 and 528, Middle: Mario Tama/Getty Images; p. 496, Bottom: Kristy-Anne Glubish/Design Pics/Corbis; p. 498: CoverSpot/Alamy; p. 499, Top: AP Images; p. 499, Bottom: Yoshikazu Tsuno /AFP/Getty Images; pp. 501 and 528, Top: Randy Faris/Corbis; p. 501, Bottom: Joshua Lott/ Bloomberg News/Landov; p. 502: Ali Abbas/epa/Corbis; p. 503: Bill Beatty/ Visuals Unlimited; p. 504: David Parker/Photo Researchers, Inc.; p. 505, Top: Courtesy of Baylor College of Medicine; p. 505, Collage, Top Left: John Birdsall/The Image Works; p. 505, Collage, Top Center: LLC, Vstock/Index Open; p. 505, Collage, Top Right: John Birdsall/The Image Works; p. 505, Collage, Middle Left: Gavin Hellier/JAI/Corbis; p. 505, Collage, Middle Center: Dennis MacDonald/PhotoEdit Inc.; p. 505, Collage, Middle Right: Jed Share and Kaoru/Corbis; p. 505, Collage, Bottom Left: Design Pics, Inc./Index Open; p. 505, Collage, Bottom Center: Bill Aron/PhotoEdit Inc.; p. 505, Collage, Bottom Right: Stockbyte/Alamy; p. 505, Bottom Left: Evan Agostini/ ImageDirect/Getty Images; p. 505, Bottom Right: Bill Olive/Getty Images; p. 506: Bill Aron/PhotoEdit Inc.; p. 507: Courtesy of the following: Author is the National Heart, Lung, and Blood Institute. Place of publication is Bethesda, Maryland. Publishers are US Department of Health and Human Services, Public Health Service, National Institutes of Health, National Heart Lung and Blood Institute; pp. 508 and 529: Noel Hendrickson/Digital Vision/Getty Images Royalty Free; p. 510: Veronika Burmeister/Visuals Unlimited; pp. 511 and 530: Zoriah/The Image Works; p. 512: Bill Aron/PhotoEdit Inc.; p. 513, Top: Colin Young-Wolff/PhotoEdit Inc.; p. 514: Emely/zefa/Corbis; p. 515: Journal-Courier/Steve Warmowski/The Image Works; p. 516, Top: Dana White/PhotoEdit Inc.; p. 516, Middle: Bill Aron/PhotoEdit Inc.; p. 517, Top: Charles Thatcher/Stone/Getty Images; p. 517, Bottom: Topham/The Image Works; p. 518: Karen Kasmauski/Corbis; p. 519: Push Pictures/Corbis; pp. 520, Top and 531: Stockbyte/Alamy; p. 520, Bottom: Peter Hvizdak/The Image Works; p. 522: Rod Rolle/Getty Images; p. 523: Tony Freeman/PhotoEdit Inc.; p. 525, Top: Guy Cali/Corbis; p. 525, Bottom: VStock/Alamy; p. 527, Top: David J. Green/Alamy; p. 527, Bottom: Topham/The Image Works

Chapter 13

p. 532: Art © Vik Muniz/Licensed by VAGA, New York, NY; p. 535, Top: Sourcebooks; p. 535, Middle: Fortean/Topham/The Image Works; p. 535, Bottom: The Kobal Collection/20th Century Fox/Dreamworks; p. 536: Lynne Fernandes/The Image Works; p. 538: Joe McBride/Stone/Getty Images; p. 540: Dr. Solomon Asch; p. 543, Box, Top Left & Bottom Left: PG Zimbardo, Inc.; p. 543, Box, Top Right: AP Images; p. 543, Box, Bottom Right: Courtesy Wikipedia.com/Zuma Press; p. 543, Right: Courtesy of PG Zimbardo, Inc.; p. 544: AP Images/Daniel Luna; p. 545, Top: NASA/Getty Images; p. 545, Bottom: AP Images/Ahn Young-joon; p. 546, Top: Fred Prouser/Reuters/ Corbis; p. 546, Bottom: Paramount/The Kobal Collection/Ken Regan; p. 547, Left: AP Images/Joe Holloway Jr., Files; p. 547, Right: AP Images/File; p. 548, Top: Archives of the History of American Psychology; p. 548, Remaining Three and 573, Bottom: Stanley Milgram, with the permission of Alexandra Milgram; p. 549: Stanley Milgram, with the permission of Alexandra Milgram; p. 550: William Philpott/Reuters/Corbis; pp. 551 and 573: Photograph by Frans de Waal; p. 552, Top: The New York Times Photo Archives; p. 552, Middle: AP Images; p. 552, Bottom: AP Images/Detroit Free Press, Steven R. Nickerson; pp. 553 and 573: Justin Guariglia/National Geographic/Getty Images; p. 554, Top: Chrissie Cowan/Syracuse Newspapers/The Image Works; p. 554, Middle: David Young-Wolff/PhotoEdit; p. 554, Bottom: Keystone/Getty Images; p. 555: Keith Brofsky/Digital Vision/Getty Images Royalty Free; p. 556: Stock4B/Getty Images; p. 557: BananaStock/Jupiterimages Royalty Free; p. 558, Left: Mark Mainz/Getty Images; p. 558, Right: AP Images/The Daily Nonpareil/Ben DeVries; p. 559: Bob Daemmrich/PhotoEdit Inc.; p. 560: Peter Kramer/Getty Images; p. 563: AP Images/Kevork Djansezian; p. 564: Barry Austin Photography/Photodisc/Getty Images Royalty Free; p. 565: Mike Kepka/San Francisco Chronicle/Corbis; p. 568: Top & Bottom Right: Index Open; Bottom Left: PhotoDisc/Getty Images; p. 570: Bob Daemmrich

Chapter 14

p. 576: Gala Contemplating the Mediterranean Sea Which at Twenty Meters Becomes the Portrait of Abraham Lincoln-Homage to Rothko (Second version). 1976. Oil on canvas: 75.5 x 99.25 inches. © Salvador Dalí. Fundación Gala-Salvador Dalí, (Artist Rights Society), 2006. Collection of the Salvador Dalí Museum, Inc., St. Petersburg, FL, 2006.; p. 578: Julia Eisenberg/Lichtfilm GmbH; p. 579: Rose Prouser/Reuters/Corbis; p. 580: Barry Sweet/epa/Corbis; p. 581: Thomas Wanstall/The Image Works; pp. 583 and 618, Top: © P Deliss/Godong/Corbis; p. 584: Library of Congress # LOT 11831-A; p. 585: Imagno/Austrian Archives/Getty Images; p. 588: Spencer Grant/PhotoEdit Inc.; p. 590: Tom Smart/Deseret News/Getty Images; p. 591: Universal/The Kobal Collection; pp. 593 and 618: Mary Evans/Sigmund Freud Copyrights/The Image Works; p. 594: AP Images; pp. 595 and 619: Ian Woodcock/Illustration Works/Getty Images; p. 596, Top: Bettmann/Corbis; p. 596, Bottom: Malcolm Case-Green/Alamy; p. 597: Ursula Klawitter/zefa/Corbis; pp. 598 and 619: Spencer Grant/PhotoEdit Inc.; p. 600: Jennifer Tzar; p. 601, Top: Carl Rogers Memorial Library; p. 601, Bottom Left and 620: © Hulton-Deutsch Collection/Corbis; p. 601, Bottom Right and 620: © JP Laffont/Sygma/Corbis; p. 602: Sally and Richard Greenhill/Alamy; p. 605, Top: David Young-Wolff/PhotoEdit Inc.; p. 605, Bottom: Bettmann/Corbis; p. 606, Top: C. Devan/zefa/Corbis; p. 606, Bottom Left: David R. Frazier/The Image Works; p. 606, Bottom Right: Bill Stormont/Corbis; p. 607, Top: Ausloeser/zefa/Corbis; p. 607, Bottom: Marco Cristofori/Corbis; p. 612, Top: Amamanta Family Anatomically Correct Dolls, www.amamantafamily.com; p. 612, Bottom: Hulton Archive/Getty Images; p. 615: Mark Harwood/Alamy; p. 616, Top: The Kobal Collection/CBS-TV; p. 616, Bottom: Tony Freeman/PhotoEdit Inc.

Chapter 15

p. 622: Old Age, Adolescence and Infancy (The Three Ages). 1940. Salvador Dali (1904-1989 Spanish). Oil on canvas. Salvador Dali Museum, St. Petersburg, Florida, USA/SuperStock, Inc.; p. 625: ColorBlind Images/Blend Images/Corbis; p. 626, Top: Bettmann/Corbis; p. 626, Bottom: Corbis; p. 627: North Wind Picture Archives/Alamy; p. 628, Top: Colin Young-Wolff/PhotoEdit Inc.; p. 628, Bottom: Aladin Abdel Naby/Reuters; p. 630: Ed Quinn/Corbis; p. 631, Top: AP Images/Tony Dejak; p. 631, Bottom: David Young-Wolff/PhotoEdit Inc.; p. 632: Janine Wiedel Photolibrary/Alamy, p. 633: American Psychiatric Association; p. 635, Top: Rolf Nobel/VISUM/The Image Works; p. 635, Bottom: John Lund/Tiffany Schoepp/Blend Images/Getty Images; pp. 637 and 666: AP Images/Steve Ueckert, Pool; p. 638: Bettmann/Corbis; p. 639: JUPITERIMAGES/BananaStock/Alamy; p. 640, Top: Andrew Cowin; Travel Ink/Corbis; p. 640, Bottom: George Bryce/Animals Animals; p. 641, Top and 667: Tom Grill/Corbis; p. 641, Bottom: Photographer's Mate First Class Alan D. Monyelle/US Navy/Reuters/Corbis; p. 643, Top: Time Life Pictures; Getty Images; p. 643, Bottom: Miramax/Courtesy Everett Collection; p. 644: Rosanne Olson/Digital Vision/Getty Images Royalty Free; p. 647: Rob Melnychuk/Digital Vision/Getty Images Royalty Free; p. 649: Steven Puetzer/Photographer's Choice/Getty Images; pp. 652 and 668: AP Images/The Denver Post, Karl Gehring; p. 654, Top: Mitchell Gerber/Corbis; pp. 654, Middle and 668 Bottom: Phillip Dvorak/Imags.com; p. 654, Bottom, both: Wellcome Library, London; p. 656: Courtesy of Laurentian University Neuroscience Research Group; p. 657: Grunnitus Studio/Photo Researchers, Inc.; p. 658: Courtesy NIH—Dr. Daniel Weinberger, Clinical Brain Disorders Branch; p. 660: Kateland Photo; p. 661: Stockbyte/Getty Images Royaly Free; p. 662: Paramount/Courtesy Everett Collection; pp. 663 and 669: AP Images/Florida Department of Corrections; p. 664: VCL/Taxi/Getty Images

Chapter 16

p. 670: De Denker van Escher geobserveed door de therapeut van Magritte 60x50 cm, 1997. Used with permission of the artist, Jos De mey. Provided courtesy of Impossible World.; p. 673: Formcourt (Form Advertising)/Alamy; pp. 675 and 706: HBO/Courtesy Everett Collection; p. 678, Top and 706, Bottom: The Gallery Collection/Corbis; p. 678, Bottom: Richard Hutchings/PhotoEdit, Inc.; p. 680, Top: Peter Vinton, Jr.; p. 680, Bottom: Bill Aron/PhotoEdit Inc.; p. 682: Gabe Palacio/Getty Images Entertainment; p. 683: Amanda Rohde/iStockphoto; pp. 684 and 707: Rainer Jensen/dpa/Corbis; p. 685: Tony Hutchings/Photographer's Choice/Getty Images; p. 688: ©Michael Fenichel; p. 691, Top: Manchan/Digital Vision/Getty Images Royalty Free; pp. 691, Bottom and 708: Mary Kate Denny/PhotoEdit Inc.; p. 693, Top: Burke/Triolo Productions/Brand X/Corbis Royalty Free; p. 693, Bottom: Mary Evans Picture Library/Alamy; p. 695: Joel Gordon; p. 696: INSADCO Photography/Alamy; p. 697: Robert Pitts /Landov; p. 698: John Foxx/Stockbyte/Getty Images Royalty Free; p. 699: Tom McCarthy/PhotoEdit Inc.; p. 702, Top: Thinkstock/Corbis; p. 702, Bottom: Steve Liss/Time & Life Pictures/Getty Images; p. 703, Top: Marcelo Wain/iStockphoto; pp. 703, Bottom and 709: Will & Deni McIntyre/Photo Reasearchers, Inc.; p. 705, Top: Robert Sciarrino/Star Ledger/Corbis; pp. 705, Middle and 709: Ray Fisher/Time & Life Pictures/Getty Images; p. 705, Bottom: Jim Clare/Nature Picture Library